CASES AND MATERIALS

INTERNET COMMERCE
THE EMERGING LEGAL FRAMEWORK

SECOND EDITION

by

MARGARET JANE RADIN
William Benjamin Scott and Luna M. Scott Professor of Law
Stanford University

JOHN A. ROTHCHILD
Associate Professor of Law
Wayne State University

R. ANTHONY REESE
Thomas W. Gregory Professor of Law
The University of Texas at Austin

GREGORY M. SILVERMAN
Associate Professor of Law
Seattle University

NEW YORK, NEW YORK
FOUNDATION PRESS

© 2002 FOUNDATION PRESS
© 2006 By FOUNDATION PRESS
        395 Hudson Street
        New York, NY 10014
        Phone Toll Free 1–877–888–1330
        Fax (212) 367–6799
        foundation–press.com
Printed in the United States of America

ISBN–13: 978–1–58778–918–2
ISBN–10: 1–58778–918–3

 TEXT IS PRINTED ON 10% POST CONSUMER RECYCLED PAPER

This book is dedicated to

JOHN W. RADIN

ൟ

STUART (1926-2004) AND LORRAINE ROTHCHILD

ൟ

CHRISTOPHER

ൟ

VERONIQUE, CYRIL, AND ALEXANDER, *for their support and patience over the course of this project.*

*

PREFACE TO THE SECOND EDITION

Even though the Internet is a relatively new economic and social phenomenon, it has already become a truism that things move very quickly in Internet time. Our first edition is only a little over three years old, but that handful of years seems to span an era. Certain topics that were prominent in the first edition, such as the proposed Uniform Computer Information Transactions Act (UCITA), seem now to be primarily of historical interest. (UCITA remains important, of course, in the two states in which it was enacted.) Other topics explored in the first edition, such as the way the legal framework for Internet commerce is enmeshed with information law and policy generally, have become more central.

We remain committed to the same underlying general theme that motivated our first edition: lawyers who counsel business clients, or litigate on their behalf, must be conversant with the legal issues that arise from commercial use of the Internet. We are particularly interested in the legal infrastructure or framework that makes online transactions viable, and potentially profitable: the basic contours of property and contract that create a working exchange system, the issues of jurisdiction and dispute resolution that shape the system's functioning, and the limits on these systems imposed by various regulatory regimes from tort law to consumer protection and privacy law to taxation and payment modalities.

Our first edition was subtitled "The Emerging Legal Framework." Although more of the legal framework for Internet commerce has emerged, and some of it has shifted, in the three years since our first edition appeared, we are retaining the subtitle, because the framework is still emerging. For example, as this edition goes to press, it is clear that peer-to-peer (P2P) file sharing is an important phenomenon but not yet clear how it will fit within a legal framework of exchange. It is clear that paying for the use of software is an important economic phenomenon, but there is not yet consensus on how the rules of contract should be updated to deal with these transactions. Courts have recognized that applying the Digital Millennium Copyright Act's provisions on technological protection measures to software embedded in consumer products can have perverse results for competition policy, but the scope of these provisions remains unclear.

In the second edition we have changed the chapter ordering to make teaching from the book easier. The most important change places the chapter on contracts (together with authentication and electronic signatures) after the materials on copyright rather than before. This change is meant to facilitate understanding the debates about "licensing" (versus "sale") of information goods, as well as the debates about when (or if) state contract law should be preempted by federal intellectual property law.

We have retained the glossary of technical terms and the appendices outlining the basic functioning of computer networks and the domain name system. The glossary is also available online at our website, at www.ecommercecasebook.com, as are a number of sample syllabi. We have replaced the bibliography with individual suggestions for further reading after various sections of the text. We hope these ancillary materials help to make the book user-friendly.

We have appreciated the feedback from users of the first edition, and we invite further suggestions. In Internet time, we need all the help we can get.

> MARGARET JANE RADIN
> JOHN A. ROTHCHILD
> R. ANTHONY REESE
> GREGORY M. SILVERMAN

December 2005

ACKNOWLEDGMENTS

We would like to thank our talented and dedicated research assistants for their help in putting this book together: Colin T. Cameron, Alissa Centivany, Debra Krauss, and Jeremy Mulder. Many good ideas for improving the book have come from our students and teaching colleagues. Special thanks to Joan Hartman, whose help was, as always, indispensable.

Excerpts from the following materials are reprinted with the permission of the copyright owners:

Ashbourn, Julian, *Biometrics and PKI*, www.techonline.com/community/related_content/20675.

Banushi, Nikoletta, Can e-mail seal a sales deal? *Shattuck v. Klotzbach*, Boston Globe, Mar. 16, 2002, at E1.

Bell, Tom W., *Fair Use vs. Fared Use: The Impact of Automated Rights Management on Copyright's Fair Use Doctrine*, 76 N.C. L. Rev. 557 (1998).

Benkler, Yochai, *Constitutional Bounds of Database Protection: The Role of Judicial Review in the Creation and Definition of Private Rights in Information*, 15 Berkeley Tech. L.J. 535 (2000).

Burk, Dan L. & Cohen, Julie E., *Fair Use Infrastructure for Rights Management Systems*, 15 Harv. J.L. & Tech. 41 (2001).

Burk, Dan L., *The Trouble with Trespass*, 4 J. Small & Emerging Bus. L. 27, 33 (2000).

Consumers Union, *Uniform Electronic Transactions Act: Consumer Nightmare or Opportunity?* (Aug. 23, 1999).

Creative Commons, *Some Rights Reserved: Building a Layer of Reasonable Copyright*, creativecommons.org/about/history.

Creative Commons, *Choosing a License*, creativecommons.org/about/licenses/index_html.

Creative Commons, *"Commons deed" for an Attribution–NonCommercial license*, creativecommons.org/licenses/by-nc/2.5/.

Creative Commons, *"Legal code" for an Attribution–NonCommercial License*, creativecommons.org/licenses/by-nc/2.5/legalcode.

Dreyfuss, Rochelle Cooper, *Are Business Method Patents Bad For Business?*, 16 Santa Clara Computer & High Tech. L.J. 263 (2000).

European Consumer Centre Network, *Realities of the European Online Marketplace*, 6, 10 (2003).

Free Software Foundation, *What is Copyleft?* Copyright © 1996, 1997, 1998, 1999, 2000, 2001, 2002, 2003, 2004, 2005 Free Software Foundation, Inc., 51 Franklin St - Fifth Floor, Boston, MA 02110-1301 USA. Verbatim copying and distribution of this entire article are permitted worldwide, without royalty, in any medium, provided this notice, and the copyright notice, are preserved.

Friedman, David D. & Macintosh, Kerry L., *The Cash of the Twenty-First Century*, 17 Santa Clara Computer & High Tech. L.J. 273 (2001).

Goldsmith, Jack L., *Against Cyberanarchy*, 65 U. Chi. L. Rev. 1199 (1998).

Grusd, Jared Earl, *Internet Business Methods: What Role Does and Should Patent Law Play?*, 4 Va. J.L. & Tech. 9, 28–29 (1999).

Hayes, David L., *Advanced Copyright Issues on the Internet*, 7 Tex. Int. Prop. L.J. 1 (1998).

Helfer, Laurence R. and Dinwoodie, Graeme B., *Designing Non-National Systems: The Case of the Uniform Domain Name Dispute Resolution Policy*, 43 Wm. & Mary L. Rev. 141 (2001). © 2001 by the William and Mary Law Review. All rights reserved.

ICANN, *Registrar Accreditation Agreement*, May 17, 2001. © 2001 by the Internet Corporation for Assigned Names and Numbers. All rights reserved.

Johnson, David R. & Post, David, *Law and Borders—The Rise of Law in Cyberspace*, 48 Stan. L. Rev. 1367 (1996).

Kuttner, Kenneth N., & McAndrews, Kenneth N., *Personal On-Line Payments*, Econ. Pol'y Rev., Dec. 1, 2001, at 35. Reprinted by permission of the Federal Reserve Bank of New York.

Lemley, Mark A., *Beyond Preemption: The Law and Policy of Intellectual Property Licensing*, 87 Calif. L. Rev. 111 (1999). © 1999 by California Law Review and Mark A. Lemley. All rights reserved. Reprinted by permission of the Regents of the University of California.

Lemley, Mark A., *The Modern Lanham Act and the Death of Common Sense*, 108 Yale L.J. 1687 (1999). Reprinted by permission of The Yale Law Journal Company and William S. Hein Company.

Lessig, Lawrence, *Code and Other Laws of Cyberspace 6* (1999). Reprinted by permission of The Perseus Books Group.

Lessig, Lawrence, *The Problem with Patents*, The Industry Standard, Apr. 23, 1999.

Litman, Jessica, *Information Privacy/Information Property*, 52 Stan. L. Rev. 1283 (2000).

Litman, Jessica, *The Exclusive Right to Read*, 13 Cardozo Arts & Ent. L.J. 29 (1994).

Long, Tony, *It's Just the 'internet' Now*, Wired News (Aug. 16, 2004).

Mann, Ronald J., *Regulating Internet Payment* Intermediaries, 82 Tex. L. Rev. 681 (2004).

McCarthy, J. Thomas, *McCarthy on Trademarks and Unfair Competition* (2002). © 2002 by West Group, all rights reserved.

Merrill, Charles R., *Proof of Who, What and When in Electronic Commerce Under the Digital Signature Guidelines*, 542 PLI/Pat 185 (1998). The author practices Information Technology law as a partner of McCarter & English, LLP, headquartered in Newark, New Jersey.

Middlebrook, Stephen T. & John Muller, *Thoughts on Bots: The Emerging Law of Electronic Agents*, 56 Bus. Law. 341 (2000). © 2000 by the American Bar Association. Reprinted by permission.

Multistate Tax Commission, *Computer Company's Provision of In-State Repair Services Creates Nexus*, NB 95–1 (1995).

National Conference of Commissioners on Uniform State Laws, *Uniform Electronic Transactions Act* (1999). © 1999 by National Conference of Commissioners on Uniform State Laws.

National Conference of Commissioners on Uniform State Laws, *Uniform Money Services Act* (2001). © 2001 by National Conference of Commissioners on Uniform State Laws.

National Notary Association, *A Position on Digital Signatures and Notarization*. Published by the National Notary Association, 9350 De Soto Avenue, Chatsworth, California 91311-4926.

Nimmer, David, *A Riff on Fair Use in the Digital Millennium Copyright Act*, 148 U. Pa. L. Rev. 673 (2000). Reprinted by permission of David Nimmer, Visiting Professor, UCLA School of Law.

Oakes, Chris, *Patently Absurd*, Wired News (Mar. 3, 2000).

OECD, *Clarification on the Application of the Permanent Establishment Definition in E-Commerce: Changes to the Commentary on the Model Tax Convention on Article 5* (2000). © 2000 OECD.

OECD Technical Advisory Group on Treaty Characterisation of Electronic Commerce Payments, *Tax Treaty Characterization Issues Arising from E-Commerce* (Feb. 1, 2001). © 2001 OECD.

Pontius, Kevin L., *Prior User Rights In Business Methods* (2000).

Radin, Margaret Jane, *Distributed Denial of Service Attacks: Who Pays?*, 6 No. 9 Cyberspace Law. 2 (2001) (Part I) and 6 No. 10 Cyberspace Law. 2 (2002) (Part II).

Radin, Margaret Jane, *Incomplete Commodification in the Computerized World*, in The Commodification of Information (Niva Elkin–Koren & Neil Weinstock Netanel eds., 2002).

Radin, Margaret Jane, *Online Standardization and the Integration of Text and Machine*, 70 Fordham L. Rev. 1125 (2002).

Radin, Margaret Jane, *Humans, Computers, and Binding Commitment*, 75 Indiana L.J. 1125 (2000).

Raskind, Leo J., *The State Street Bank Decision: The Bad Business of Unlimited Patent Protection for Methods of Doing Business*, 10 Fordham I.P., Media & Ent. L.J. 61 (1999).

Ratliff, Evan, *Patent Upending*, Wired, June 2000.

Reese, R. Anthony, *Copyright and Internet Music Transmissions: Existing Law, Major Controversies, Possible Solutions*, 55 U. Miami L. Rev. 237 (2001).

Reese, R. Anthony, *The Public Display Right: The Copyright Act's Neglected Solution to the Controversy over RAM "Copies"*, 2001 U. Ill. L. Rev. 83 (2001).

Reidenberg, Joel R. & Gamet–Pol, Françoise, *The Fundamental Role of Privacy and Confidence in the Network*, 30 Wake Forest L. Rev. 105 (1995).

Samuelson, Pamela, *Mapping the Digital Public Domain*, 66 Law & Contemp. Probs. 147 (2003).

Schreft, Stacey L., *Clicking with Dollars: How Consumers Can Pay for Purchases from E-tailers*, Econ. Rev., First Quarter 2002, at 37.

Shirky, Clay, *The Case Against Micropayments* (2000).

Smedinghoff, Thomas J., *The Legal Requirements for Creating Secure and Enforceable Electronic Transactions* (2004).

Stefik, Mark and Silverman, Alex, *The Bit and the Pendulum: Balancing the Interests of Stakeholders in Digital Publishing*, 16 No. 1 Computer Lawyer 1 (1999). © 1999 by Aspen Publishers, Inc.

Thornburg , Elizabeth G., *Going Private: Technology, Due Process, and Internet Dispute Resolution*, 34 U.C. Davis L. Rev. 151 (2000). © 2000 by Elizabeth G. Thornburg. Journal issue © 2000 by the Regents of the University of California. Reprinted with Permission.

TRUSTe, *TRUSTe Program Requirements*.

VeriSign Service Agreement, Version Number 6.2. © 2002 by Verisign, Inc. All rights reserved.

*

SUMMARY OF CONTENTS

TABLE OF CONTENTS

CHAPTER FOUR
CONSUMER PROTECTION ONLINE 290

CHAPTER FIVE
JUDICIAL JURISDICTION OVER DISPUTES IN INTERNET COMMERCE 326

CHAPTER SEVEN

CHAPTER EIGHT
CONTROLLING INFORMATION ASSETS: DATABASES 667

CHAPTER NINE
TECHNOLOGICAL PROTECTION OF DIGITAL GOODS 700

*

TABLE OF AUTHORITIES

Principal cases are in bold type. Non-principal cases are in roman type. References are to Pages.

CASES

ARTICLES AND BOOKS

STATUTES, LEGISLATIVE MATERIALS, MODEL LAWS, REGULATIONS

EUROPEAN UNION AND OTHER INTERNATIONAL MATERIALS

TREATIES

REPORTS

MISCELLANEOUS

*

CASES AND MATERIALS

INTERNET COMMERCE
THE EMERGING LEGAL FRAMEWORK

SECOND EDITION

*

CHAPTER ONE
REGULATORY PARADIGMS FOR ELECTRONIC COMMERCE

Governments regulate many aspects of our lives. Regulation of commercial activity is particularly pervasive: state and federal governments set standards for product safety, require disclosure of information concerning products offered for sale, prohibit deceptive marketing practices, regulate banks and securities offerings, enforce contracts, prohibit pornography, and limit gambling.

The advent of the Internet as a medium for conducting commercial transactions raises questions about the role of governments in regulating online activity. Some have argued for a regime of radical laissez-faire with respect to online activity, excluding the government entirely from this realm of human interaction. Others view the Internet as nothing more than a new medium of communication, and argue that the government's authority and obligation to regulate a particular activity cannot depend on the mode of communication that is used in connection with that activity. The borderless nature of the Internet, which makes international communication no slower or more expensive than local communication, and the difficulties involved in limiting certain types of online communication to a particular subgroup of the online audience, create additional dilemmas when the government does seek to regulate online activity.

The materials in this chapter focus on the differences between the Internet and other modes of human interaction, and address the question of the proper role of governments in regulating online activity.

I. SETTING THE STAGE: THE LEGITIMACY AND POSSIBILITY OF GOVERNMENT REGULATION OF ONLINE ACTIVITY

Theorists of online regulation have established a lively dialogue on the propriety of government regulation of online activity. Consider the following perspectives:

A. RADICAL SEPARATISM

John Perry Barlow, *A Declaration of the Independence of Cyberspace* (1996)
www.eff.org/~barlow/Declaration-Final.html

Governments of the Industrial World, you weary giants of flesh and steel, I come from Cyberspace, the new home of Mind. On behalf of the future, I ask you of the past to leave us alone. You are not welcome among us. You have no sovereignty where we gather.

We have no elected government, nor are we likely to have one, so I address you with no greater authority than that with which liberty itself always speaks. I declare the global social space we are building to be naturally independent of the tyrannies you seek to impose on us. You have no moral right to rule us nor do you possess any methods of enforcement we have true reason to fear.

Governments derive their just powers from the consent of the governed. You have neither solicited nor received ours. We did not invite you. You do not know us, nor do you know our world. Cyberspace does not lie within your borders. Do not think that you can build it, as though it were a public construction project. You cannot. It is an act of nature and it grows itself through our collective actions.

You have not engaged in our great and gathering conversation, nor did you create the wealth of our marketplaces. You do not know our culture, our ethics, or the unwritten codes that already provide our society more order than could be obtained by any of your impositions.

You claim there are problems among us that you need to solve. You use this claim as an excuse to invade our precincts. Many of these problems don't exist. Where there are real conflicts, where there are wrongs, we will identify them and address them by our means. We are forming our own Social Contract. This governance will arise according to the conditions of our world, not yours. Our world is different.

Cyberspace consists of transactions, relationships, and thought itself, arrayed like a standing wave in the web of our communications. Ours is a world that is both everywhere and nowhere, but it is not where bodies live.

We are creating a world that all may enter without privilege or prejudice accorded by race, economic power, military force, or station of birth.

We are creating a world where anyone, anywhere may express his or her beliefs, no matter how singular, without fear of being coerced into silence or conformity.

Your legal concepts of property, expression, identity, movement, and context do not apply to us. They are all based on matter, and there is no matter here.

Our identities have no bodies, so, unlike you, we cannot obtain order by physical coercion. We believe that from ethics, enlightened self-interest, and the commonweal, our governance will emerge. Our identities may be distributed across many of your jurisdictions. The only law that all our constituent cultures would generally recognize is the Golden Rule. We hope we will be able to build our particular solutions on that basis. But we cannot accept the solutions you are attempting to impose.

. . .

In China, Germany, France, Russia, Singapore, Italy and the United States, you are trying to ward off the virus of liberty by erecting guard posts at the frontiers of Cyberspace. These may keep out the contagion for a small time, but they will not work in a world that will soon be blanketed in bit-bearing media.

Your increasingly obsolete information industries would perpetuate themselves by proposing laws, in America and elsewhere, that claim to own speech itself throughout the world. These laws would declare ideas to be another industrial product, no more noble than pig iron. In our world, whatever the human mind may create can be reproduced and distributed infinitely at no cost. The global conveyance of thought no longer requires your factories to accomplish.

These increasingly hostile and colonial measures place us in the same position as those previous lovers of freedom and self-determination who had to reject the authorities of distant, uninformed powers. We must declare our virtual selves immune to your sovereignty, even as we continue to consent to your rule over our bodies. We will spread ourselves across the Planet so that no one can arrest our thoughts.

We will create a civilization of the Mind in Cyberspace. May it be more humane and fair than the world your governments have made before.

David R. Johnson & David Post, *Law and Borders—The Rise of Law in Cyberspace*
48 STAN. L. REV. 1367 (1996).

INTRODUCTION

Global computer-based communications cut across territorial borders, creating a new realm of human activity and undermining the feasibility—and legitimacy—of laws based on geographic boundaries. While these electronic communications play havoc with geographic boundaries, a new boundary, made up of the screens and passwords that separate the virtual world from the "real world" of atoms, emerges. This new boundary defines a distinct Cyberspace that needs and can create its own law and legal institutions. Territorially based law-makers and law-enforcers find this new environment deeply threatening. But established territorial authorities may yet learn to defer to the self-regulatory efforts of Cyberspace participants who care most deeply about this new digital trade in ideas, information, and services. Separated from doctrine tied to territorial jurisdictions, new rules will emerge to govern a wide range of new phenomena that have no clear parallel in the nonvirtual world. These new rules will play the role of law by defining legal personhood and property, resolving disputes, and crystallizing a collective conversation about online participants' core values.

I. BREAKING DOWN TERRITORIAL BORDERS

A. *Territorial Borders in the "Real World"*

We take for granted a world in which geographical borders—lines separating physical spaces—are of primary importance in determining legal rights and responsibilities. Territorial borders, generally speaking, delineate areas within which different sets of legal rules apply. There has until now been a general correspondence between borders drawn in physical space (between nation states or other political entities) and borders in "law space." For example, if we were to superimpose a "law map" (delineating areas where different rules apply to particular behaviors) onto a political map of the world, the two maps would overlap to a significant degree, with clusters of homogeneous applicable law and legal institutions fitting within existing physical borders.

. . .

2. *When Geographic Boundaries for Law Make Sense.*

Physical borders are not, of course, simply arbitrary creations. Although they may be based on historical accident, geographic borders for law make sense in the real world. Their logical relationship to the development and enforcement of legal rules is based on a number of related considerations.

Power. Control over physical space, and the people and things located in that space, is a defining attribute of sovereignty and statehood. Law-making requires some mechanism for law enforcement, which in turn depends on the ability to exercise physical control over, and impose coercive sanctions on, law-violators. For example, the U.S. government does not impose its trademark law on a Brazilian business operating in Brazil, at least in part because imposing sanctions on the Brazilian business would require assertion of physical control over business owners. Such an assertion of control would conflict with the Brazilian government's recognized monopoly on the use of force over its citizens.

Effects. The correspondence between physical boundaries and "law space" boundaries also reflects a deeply rooted relationship between physical proximity and the effects of any particular behavior. That is, Brazilian trademark law governs the use of marks in Brazil because that use has a more direct impact on persons and assets within Brazil than anywhere else. For example, a large sign over "Jones' Restaurant" in Rio de Janeiro is unlikely to have an impact on the operation of "Jones' Restaurant" in Oslo, Norway, for we may assume that there is no substantial overlap between the customers, or competitors, of these two entities. Protection of the former's trademark does not—and probably should not—affect the protection afforded the latter's.

Legitimacy. We generally accept the notion that the persons within a geographically defined border are the ultimate source of law-making authority for activities within that border. The "consent of the governed" implies that those subject to a set of laws must have a role in their formulation. By virtue of the preceding considerations, those people subject to a sovereign's laws, and most deeply affected by those laws, are the individuals who are located in particular physical spaces. Similarly, allocation of responsibility among levels of government proceeds on the assumption that, for many legal problems, physical proximity between the responsible authority and those most directly affected by the law will improve the quality of decision making, and that it is easier to determine the will of those individuals in physical proximity to one another.

Notice. Physical boundaries are also appropriate for the delineation of "law space" in the physical world because they can give notice that the rules change when the boundaries are crossed. Proper boundaries have signposts that provide warning that we will be required, after crossing, to abide by different rules, and physical boundaries—lines on the geographical map—are generally well-equipped to serve this signpost function.

B. *The Absence of Territorial Borders in Cyberspace*

Cyberspace radically undermines the relationship between legally significant (online) phenomena and physical location. The rise of the global computer network is destroying the link between geographical location and: (1) the *power* of local governments to assert control over online behavior; (2) the *effects* of online behavior on individuals or things; (3) the *legitimacy* of a local sovereign's efforts to regulate global phenomena; and (4) the ability of physical location to give *notice* of which sets of rules apply. The Net thus radically subverts the system of rule-making based on borders between physical spaces, at least with respect to the claim that Cyberspace should naturally be governed by territorially defined rules.

Cyberspace has no territorially based boundaries, because the cost and speed of message transmission on the Net is almost entirely independent of physical location. Messages can be transmitted from one physical location to any other location without degradation, decay, or substantial delay, and without any physical cues or barriers that might otherwise keep certain geographically remote places and people separate from one another. The Net enables transactions between people who do not know, and in many cases cannot know, each other's physical location. Location remains vitally important, but only location within a *virtual* space consisting of the "addresses" of the machines between which messages and information are routed. The system is indifferent to the *physical* location of those machines, and there is no necessary connection between an Internet address and a physical jurisdiction. Although the domain name initially assigned to a given machine may be associated with an Internet Protocol address that corresponds to that machine's physical location (for example, a ".uk" domain name extension), the machine may be physically moved without affecting its domain name. Alternatively, the owner of the domain name might request that the name become associated with an entirely different machine, in a different physical location. Thus, a server with a ".uk" domain name need not be located in the United Kingdom, a server with a ".com" domain name may be anywhere, and users, generally speaking, are not even aware of the location of the server that stores the content that they read.

The power to control activity in Cyberspace has only the most tenuous connections to physical location. Nonetheless, many governments' first response to electronic communications crossing their territorial borders is to try to stop or regulate that flow of information. Rather than permitting self-regulation by participants in online transactions, many governments establish trade barriers, attempt to tax border-crossing cargo, and respond especially sympathetically to claims that information coming into the jurisdiction might prove harmful to local residents. . . .

But efforts to control the flow of electronic information across physical borders—to map local regulation and physical boundaries onto Cyberspace—are likely to prove futile, at least in countries that hope to participate in global commerce. Individual electrons can easily, and without any realistic prospect of detection, "enter" any sovereign's territory. The volume of electronic communications crossing territorial boundaries is just too great in relation to the resources available to government authorities. United States Customs officials have generally given up. They assert jurisdiction only over the physical goods that cross the geographic borders they guard and claim no right to force declarations of the value of materials transmitted by modem. Banking and securities regulators seem likely to lose their battle to impose local regulations on a global financial marketplace. And state attorneys general face serious challenges in seeking to intercept the electrons that transmit the kinds of consumer fraud that, if conducted physically within the local jurisdiction, would be easier to shut down.

Faced with their inability to control the flow of electrons across physical borders, some authorities strive to inject their boundaries into the new electronic medium through filtering mechanisms and the establishment of electronic barriers. Others have been quick to assert the right to regulate all online trade insofar as it might adversely affect local citizens. The Attorney General of Minnesota, for example, has asserted the right to regulate gambling that occurs on a foreign web page that a local resident accessed and "brought into" the state. The New Jersey securities regulatory agency has similarly asserted the right to shut down any offending Web page accessible from within the state.

But such protective schemes will likely fail as well. First, the determined seeker of prohibited communications can simply reconfigure his connection so as to appear to reside in a location outside the particular locality, state, or country. Because the Net is engineered to work on the basis of "logical," not geographical, locations, any attempt to defeat the independence of messages from physical locations would be as futile as an effort to tie an atom and a bit together. And, moreover, assertions of law-making authority over Net activities on the ground that those activities constitute "entry into" the physical jurisdiction can just as easily be made by any territorially-based authority. If Minnesota law applies to gambling operations conducted on the World Wide Web because such operations foreseeably affect Minnesota residents, so, too, must the law of any physical jurisdiction from which those operations can be accessed. By asserting a right to regulate whatever its citizens may access on the Net, these local authorities are laying the predicate for an argument that Singapore or Iraq or any other sovereign can regulate the activities of U.S. companies operating in Cyberspace from a location physically within the United States. All such Web-based activity, in this view, must be subject simultaneously to the laws of all territorial sovereigns.

Nor are the effects of online activities tied to geographically proximate locations. Information available on the World Wide Web is available simultaneously to anyone with a connection to the global network. The notion that the effects of an activity taking place on that website radiate from a physical location over a geographic map in concentric circles of decreasing intensity, however sensible that may be in the nonvirtual world, is incoherent when applied to Cyberspace. A website physically located in Brazil, to continue with that example, has no more of an effect on individuals in Brazil than does a website physically located in Belgium or Belize that is accessible in Brazil. Usenet discussion groups, to take another example, consist of continuously changing collections of messages that are routed from one network to another, with no centralized location at all. They exist, in effect, everywhere, nowhere in particular, and only on the Net.

Territorial regulation of online activities serves neither the legitimacy nor the notice justifications. There is no geographically localized set of constituents with a stronger and more legitimate claim to regulate it than any other local group. The strongest claim to control comes from the participants themselves, and they could be anywhere. And in Cyberspace, physical borders no longer function as signposts informing individuals of the obligations assumed by entering into a new, legally significant, place. Individuals are unaware of the existence of those borders as they move through virtual space.

The rise of an electronic medium that disregards geographical boundaries throws the law into disarray by creating entirely new phenomena that need to become the subject of clear legal rules but that cannot be governed, satisfactorily, by any current territorially based sovereign. For example, although privacy on the Net may be a familiar concept, analogous to privacy doctrine for mail systems, telephone calls, and print publications, electronic communications create serious questions regarding the nature and adequacy of geographically based privacy protections. Communications that create vast new transactional records may pass through or even simultaneously exist in many different territorial jurisdictions. What substantive law should we apply to protect this new, vulnerable body of transactional data? May a French policeman lawfully access the records of communications traveling across the Net from the United States to Japan? Similarly, whether it is permissible for a commercial entity to publish a record of all of any given individual's postings to Usenet newsgroups, or whether it is permissible to implement an interactive Web page application that inspects a user's "bookmarks" to determine which other pages that user has visited, are questions not readily addressed by existing legal regimes—both because the phenomena are novel and because any given local territorial sovereign cannot readily control the relevant, globally dispersed, actors and actions.

Because events on the Net occur everywhere but nowhere in particular, are engaged in by online personae who are both "real" (possessing reputations, able to perform services, and deploy intellectual assets) and "intangible" (not necessarily or traceably tied to any particular person in the physical sense), and concern "things" (messages, databases, standing relationships) that are not necessarily separated from one another by any physical boundaries, no physical jurisdiction has a more compelling claim than any other to subject these events exclusively to its laws.

. . .

B. The Internet as Evolutionary, Not Revolutionary

Jack L. Goldsmith, *Against Cyberanarchy*
65 U. Chi. L. Rev. 1199 (1998).

. . .

II. "Real-Space" Jurisdictional Conflict Management

The skeptics [who argue that governments cannot regulate online activity] are in the grip of a nineteenth century territorialist conception of how "real space" is regulated and how "real-space" conflicts of law are resolved. This conception was repudiated in the middle of [the twentieth] century. The skeptics' first mistake, therefore, is to measure the feasibility and legitimacy of national regulation of cyberspace against a repudiated yardstick. This Section offers a more accurate picture of real-space jurisdictional conflict management as a prelude to analysis of the skeptics' claims.

. . .

. . . Today, the Constitution permits a state to apply its law if it has a "significant contact or significant aggregation of contacts, creating state interests, such that choice of its law is neither arbitrary nor fundamentally unfair." In practice, this standard is notoriously easy to satisfy. It prohibits the application of local law only when the forum state has no interest in the case because the substance of the lawsuit has no relationship to the state. Customary international law limits on a nation's regulation of extraterritorial events are less clear because there are few international decisions on point, and because state practice does not reveal a settled custom. Nonetheless, it seems clear that customary international law, like the United States Constitution, permits a nation to apply its law to extraterritorial behavior with substantial local effects. In addition, both the Constitution and international law permit a nation or state to regulate the extraterritorial conduct of a citizen or domiciliary. In short, in modern times a transaction can legitimately be regulated by the jurisdiction where the transaction occurs, the jurisdictions where significant effects of the transaction are felt, and the jurisdictions where the parties burdened by the regulation are from.

This expansion of the permissible bases for the application of local law has revolutionized conflict of laws in the second half of [the twentieth] century. Any number of choice-of-law regimes are now consistent with constitutional and international law. The earlier belief in a unique governing law for all transnational activities has given way to the view that more than one jurisdiction can legitimately apply its law to the same transnational activity. The uniformity promised by the traditional approach has thus been replaced by the reality of overlapping jurisdictional authority. This means that the application of one jurisdiction's law often comes at the expense of the nonapplication of the conflicting laws of other interested jurisdictions. Because choice-of-law rules often differ from jurisdiction to jurisdiction, and because a forum applies its own choice-of-law rules, the choice of forum is now often critical to the selection of governing law. In this milieu, *ex ante* notice of a specific governing law is no longer a realistic goal in many transnational situations. Not surprisingly, the Constitution and international law impose very weak notice requirements on the application of local law to extraterritorial activity.

This modern world of jurisdictional conflict poses obvious difficulties for participants in transnational transactions. . . . [C]onflicts of law can arise when parties to a transnational transaction do not specify the governing default law, or when the transaction implicates a mandatory law that conflicts with the otherwise-applicable law. Absent a governing international law, transnational activity in these contexts will usually be governed by the law of a single jurisdiction. And absent international choice-of-law rules, the forum's choice-of-law rules will determine the governing law. In regulatory contexts, the forum will invariably apply local law. But regardless of which substantive law the forum applies, the application of that law will frequently create spillover effects on activities in other countries and on the ability of other interested nations to apply their own law. In our increasingly integrated world, these spillover effects are likely to extend to many countries.

Consider, for example, the Supreme Court's decision in *Hartford Fire Insurance Co. v. California*.[50] The Court held that the concerted refusal by London reinsurers to sell certain types of reinsurance to insurers in the United States violated the Sherman Act. The reinsurers' acts in England were legal under English law. But the Court determined that the reinsurers were nonetheless subject to U.S. regulation because their actions "produced substantial effect[s]" in the United States. U.S. law thus regulated the activities of English companies in England at the expense of the nonapplication of English law. Similarly, had an English court applied English law to adjudge the reinsurers' acts to be legal, it would have produced spillover effects on consumers in the United States, and would have come at the expense of the nonapplication of U.S. law. No matter which law governed the reinsurers' acts, the application of that law would have produced spillover effects on the English reinsurers' activities in other jurisdictions, and on the activities of persons in other jurisdictions adversely affected by the reinsurers' acts.

A similar phenomenon occurs in many domestic and international conflicts contexts. For example, the European Commission recently imposed strict conditions on a merger (already approved by the Federal Trade Commission) between two American companies with no manufacturing facilities in Europe. Minnesota applied its pro-plaintiff stacking rules for automobile insurance coverage to an accident in Wisconsin among Wisconsin residents. A United States federal grand jury ordered the local branch of a foreign bank, a nonparty, to disclose bank records in the Bahamas in possible violation of Bahamian law. California applied its workmen's compensation law to benefit an employee of a California corporation who suffered a tort while working in Alaska—even though Alaska purported to make its worker's compensation scheme exclusive, and even though the employment contract specified that Alaska law governed. New York applied its tort law to a car accident in Canada. California taxed a British corporation based on the California portion of its world profits.

In these situations and countless others, one jurisdiction regulates extraterritorial conduct in a way that invariably affects individual behavior and regulatory efforts in other jurisdictions. These spillover effects constitute the central problem of modern conflict of laws. The problem is pervasive. It is also inevitable, because the price of eliminating these spillovers—abolishing national or subnational lawmaking entities, or eliminating transnational activity—is prohibitively high. Most of the dizzying array of modern choice-of-law methodologies are devoted to minimizing these spillovers while at the same time preserving the sovereign prerogative to regulate effects within national borders. International harmonization

---

[50] 509 U.S. 764 (1993).

efforts seek to achieve similar aims, often at the expense of national prerogatives.

There is widespread debate about which approach, or combination of approaches, is preferable. Resolution of this debate is less important for present purposes than two uncontested assumptions that underlie it. The first assumption is that in the absence of consensual international solutions, prevailing concepts of territorial sovereignty permit a nation to regulate the local effects of extraterritorial conduct even if this regulation produces spillover effects in other jurisdictions. The second assumption is that such spillover effects are a commonplace consequence of the unilateral application of any particular law to transnational activity in our increasingly interconnected world. It is against this background that the skeptics' descriptive and normative claims must be assessed.

. . .

III. IS CYBERSPACE REGULATION FEASIBLE?

This Section argues that the skeptics' claims about the infeasibility of national regulation of cyberspace rest on an underappreciation of the realities of modern conflict of laws, and of the legal and technological tools available to resolve multijurisdictional cyberspace conflicts. From the perspective of jurisdiction and choice of law, regulation of cyberspace transactions is no less feasible than regulation of other transnational transactions.

. . .

[As explained above, private legal ordering] has the potential to resolve many, but not all, of the challenges posed by multijurisdictional cyberspace activity. Cyberspace activities for which *ex ante* consent to a governing legal regime is either infeasible or unenforceable are not amenable to private ordering. Such activities remain subject to the skeptics' concerns about multiple or extraterritorial national regulation. . . . The skeptics' concerns are further attenuated, however, by limitations on every nation's ability to enforce its laws. A nation can purport to regulate activity that takes place anywhere. The Island of Tobago can *enact* a law that purports to bind the rights of the whole world. But the effective scope of this law depends on Tobago's ability to *enforce* it. And in general a nation can only enforce its laws against: (i) persons with a presence or assets in the nation's territory; (ii) persons over whom the nation can obtain personal jurisdiction and enforce a default judgment against abroad; or (iii) persons whom the nation can successfully extradite.

A defendant's physical presence or assets within the territory remains the primary basis for a nation or state to enforce its laws. The large majority of persons who transact in cyberspace have no presence or assets in the jurisdictions that wish to regulate their information flows in cyberspace. Such regulations are thus likely to apply primarily to Internet service providers and Internet users with a physical presence in the regulating jurisdiction. Cyberspace users in other territorial jurisdictions will indirectly feel the effect of the regulations to the extent that they are dependent on service or content providers with a presence in the regulating jurisdiction. But for almost all users, there will be no threat of extraterritorial legal liability because of a lack of presence in the regulating jurisdictions.

A nation or state can also enforce its laws over an entity with no local presence or assets if it can obtain personal jurisdiction over the entity and enforce a local default judgment against that entity abroad. The domestic interstate context presents a much greater threat in this regard than does the international context. This is because the Full Faith and Credit Clause requires a state to enforce the default judgment of a sister state that had personal jurisdiction over the defendant. This threat is attenuated, however, by constitutional limits on a state's assertion of personal jurisdiction. The Due Process Clauses prohibit a state from asserting personal jurisdiction over an entity with no local presence unless the entity has purposefully directed its activities to the forum state and the assertion of jurisdiction is reasonable.

Application of this standard to cyberspace activities presents special difficulties. Under standard assumptions about cyberspace architecture, persons can upload or transmit information knowing that it could reach any and all jurisdictions, but not knowing which particular jurisdiction it might reach. Can every state where these transmissions appear assert specific personal jurisdiction over the agent of the information under the purposeful availment and reasonableness tests? . . . [T]here is relatively little reason at present, and even less reason in the near future, to believe that the mere introduction of information into cyberspace will *by itself* suffice for personal jurisdiction over the agent of the transmission in every state where the information appears. Most courts have required something more than mere placement of information on a web page in one state as a basis for personal jurisdiction in another state where the web page is accessed.[1] For a variety of reasons, these decisions have limited specific personal jurisdiction to cases in which there are independent indicia that the out-of-state defendant knowingly and purposefully directed the effects of out-of-state conduct to a particular state where the acts were deemed illegal.

. . .

[Concerns] about the extraterritorial enforcement of local default judgments . . . are less pronounced in the international context. In contrast to the domestic interstate context, customary international law imposes few enforceable controls on a country's assertion of personal jurisdiction, and there are few treaties on the subject. However, also in contrast to domestic law, there is no full faith and credit obligation to enforce foreign judgments in the international sphere. If one country exercises personal jurisdiction on an exorbitant basis, the resulting judgment is unlikely to be enforced in another country. In addition, local public policy exceptions to the enforcement of foreign judgments are relatively commonplace in the international sphere, especially when the foreign judgment flies in the face of the enforcing state's regulatory regime. For these reasons, there is little concern that a foreign default judgment will be enforceable against cyberspace users who live outside the regulating jurisdiction.

---

[1] [The rules that courts have developed to address assertions of personal jurisdiction based on a defendant's online conduct are discussed in Chapter 5, *infra.*—Eds.]

The final way that a nation can enforce its regulations against persons outside its jurisdiction is by seeking extradition. . . . International extradition is governed largely by treaty. A pervasive feature of modern extradition treaties is the principle of double criminality. This principle requires that the charged offense be criminal in both the requesting and the requested jurisdictions. This principle, and its animating rationale, make it unlikely that there will be international cooperation in the enforcement of exorbitant unilateral criminal regulations of cyberspace events.

This review of transnational enforcement jurisdiction makes clear that the skeptics exaggerate the threat of multiple regulation of cyberspace information flows. This threat must be measured by a regulation's enforceable scope, not by its putative scope. And the enforceable scope is relatively narrow. It extends only to individual users or system operators with presence or assets in the enforcement jurisdiction, or (in the U.S.) to entities that take extra steps to target cyberspace information flows to states where such information flows are illegal. Such regulatory exposure is a significant concern for cyberspace participants. But it is precisely how regulatory exposure operates in "real space." And it is far less significant than the skeptics' hyperbolic claim that *all* users of the Web will be simultaneously subject to *all* national regulations.

. . .

John Rothchild, *Protecting the Digital Consumer: The Limits of Cyberspace Utopianism*
74 IND. L.J. 893 (1999).

. . .

The cyberspace utopians [who deny that governments have legitimate authority over online activity] reach their anti-regulatory conclusions through arguments that are flawed in several respects. First, they mischaracterize the salient aspects of online communications. Second, they exaggerate the difficulties that the special characteristics of online communications pose for extension of the existing regulatory regime to online commercial transactions, ignoring the fact that many of those characteristics apply also to other communications media. Third, they make no effort to adapt the existing regulatory regime to the requirements of the new medium. Fourth, they make unsupportable assumptions about the ability of users of online communications to control deceptive marketing practices.

1. The Special Characteristics of Online Communications Do Not Undermine the Legitimacy of Territorially Based Jurisdiction

The key flaw in the normative component of the utopians' argument is that the harmful effects of deceptive marketing practices accomplished through use of the Internet are felt not solely in the realm of cyberspace, but also and unavoidably by a flesh-and-blood resident of a real-world geographic area subject to the territorial jurisdiction of a sovereign. If a sovereign has the right and responsibility to protect its citizens from fraudulent solicitations delivered by postal mail, telephone, radio, television, or print media, it has an equal right and responsibility to protect them from fraud delivered via the Internet. . . .

The person responsible for online deceptive marketing practices is likewise a resident of a geographic territory subject to the jurisdiction of a territorial sovereign. Physical presence within the territorial jurisdiction of a sovereign has since ancient times stood as the paradigm basis for assertion of jurisdiction in personam. No reason appears why a wrongdoer should be able to nullify this basis of jurisdiction merely by choosing to communicate through the online medium, rather than through other means of communication at a distance.

a. Online Communications, Though Universally Accessible, Have Locally Differentiated Impact

The contention that "[t]he effects of cyberspace transactions are felt *everywhere*, simultaneously and equally in all corners of the global network,"[268] is factually incorrect. It is true that certain types of online communications, such as websites and newsgroup postings, are simultaneously and equally *accessible* from any geographic location with the necessary online access. However, the *effects* resulting from that access may vary greatly from place to place. Most pertinently to the present context, a solicitation to enter into a fraudulent transaction has a very different effect in a jurisdiction where a resident actually enters into the proposed transaction than in other jurisdictions where residents read the solicitation but do not act upon it. In both jurisdictions there is some resulting pollution of the commercial dialogue, by virtue of the misinformation that is conveyed to consumers, but only in the former jurisdiction does any consumer suffer direct financial injury. Therefore, it is hardly "indeterminate" to speak of online conduct that " 'has or is intended to have substantial effect within [a State's] territory' " — one standard formulation of the principle governing whether a state has jurisdiction to prescribe rules applicable to a person located outside its territorial scope. . . .

b. Cost and Speed Advantages of Online Communications Create Only Practical Issues

The fact that "the cost and speed of message transmission on the Net is almost entirely independent of physical location"[271] creates practical problems for law enforcement authorities, but does not radically undermine the territorial basis of jurisdiction. The cost of first-class postage within the United States is typically the same regardless of the geographic separation of the sender and recipient, and it may take only a few days longer for a letter to cross the country than it does to cross a state or a city. The cost of overnight mail delivery within the United States, and the length of time required for delivery, are the same or nearly the same no matter where the sender and recipient are located. The cost of an interstate telephone call within the United States varies little with the distance between the two

---

[268] *See* [David G. Post, *Governing Cyberspace*, 43 WAYNE L. REV. 155,] 162 [1996].

[271] David R. Johnson & David Post, [*Law and Borders — The Rise of Law in Cyberspace*, 48 STAN. L. REV. 1367,] 1370 [(1996)].

speakers. Yet we do not consider that the use of direct mail or telemarketing as a medium for conveying commercial communications radically undermines the geographic basis for jurisdiction within the United States; we do not declare "telespace" or "mailspace" to be a "place" unconnected with any territorial jurisdiction. Instead, the legal systems of the various jurisdictions within the United States have developed a more-or-less elaborate jurisprudence for determining under what circumstances a seller located in one state may be brought within the jurisdiction of a court located in another state.

. . .

c. Virtual Addressing Does Not Undermine Territorial Sovereignty

The fact that "there is no necessary connection between an Internet address and a physical jurisdiction" likewise gives rise to practical difficulties, but does not call into question the territorial basis for jurisdiction. This fact may make it difficult for injured parties and enforcement authorities to identify the perpetrator of prohibited conduct, but is without any deeper significance. It is equally true that there is no necessary connection between a toll-free telephone number—the only "address" that a purchaser may ever have for a vendor that operates via telemarketing—and the physical location of the vendor communicating through that telephone number. Mail forwarding services likewise divorce a seller's address from his physical location. Yet assertion of jurisdiction by territorially based sovereigns is not thought on that account to be illegitimate.

d. Physical Location of Online Interlocutors Is Not Unknowable

The assertion that the Internet allows transactions between people "who do not and *cannot* know the physical location of the other party" is not quite correct. The statement refers to the fact, as discussed above, that an online address—ether an e-mail address, the URL of a website, or a pseudonym used in a chat session—does not itself reveal the physical location of the person who communicates using that address. In many of the most common types of interactions that occur online, it is true that neither party knows the physical location of the other. For example, the owner of a website may not know the location of those who access the site; those who access a website may not know the location of the owner of the site; those who read newsgroup postings may not know the location of the message posters; and recipients of unsolicited commercial e-mail messages may not know the location of the sender. However, it is not true that online communicators *cannot* know the location of their interlocutors. Most obviously, there is nothing to prevent a website, e-mail message, or newsgroup posting from stating the physical address of the person communicating through it.

In the more particular case of online commerce, the vendor most typically *can and does* know the location of his customers. This is because most of the online commerce that takes place at present involves shipping a physical good (flowers, computers, books, compact disks, etc.) to a geographic address. In many cases, even sellers of digital goods that are transmitted via the network likewise *can and do* know the location of their customers. This is so when there is an ongoing commercial relationship between the two parties which involves sending invoices or other physical items to the customer's geographic location. There are, it is true, commercial transactions involving digital goods in which the nature of the transaction does not *require* either party to know the location of the other—for example, the transmission of information via the network on a one-time basis, with payment by credit card or digital cash. However, even in those cases there are steps that a seller can take—some more reliable, but more cumbersome, than others—to ascertain the physical location of the buyer. For example, the seller may require the buyer to provide a telephone number or fax number, which indicates the buyer's physical location; may perform a pre-sale verification of location through postal mail; or may access motor vehicle or voter registration records. In the future, digital certificates indicating the holder's address may become available.

It is of course an everyday occurrence to communicate by telephone or postal mail without being aware of the location of one's interlocutor. . . . The ability of wrongdoers to conceal their location when using these traditional means of communication is viewed by law enforcement officials as an impediment to law enforcement that must be handled with due regard for privacy interests; it has never been considered a factor that divests territorially based sovereigns of their authority to enforce the law. Likewise, the fact that it is possible to communicate via the Internet without revealing one's physical location does not undermine the geographic basis of jurisdiction over online transactions.

. . .

2. The Argument from Futility Refutes Only One, Particularly Poor, Enforcement
   Approach

Attempting to police borders within cyberspace is said to be futile because of the large number of border crossing points. "Physical roads and ports linking sovereign territories are few in number, and geographic boundaries can be fenced and policed. In contrast, the number of starting points for an electronic 'trip' out of a given country is staggering, consisting of every telephone capable of connecting outside the territory." Furthermore, the volume of online communications is so great that "a customs house on an electronic border would cause a massive traffic jam." The same is true, however, of communications by telephone and postal mail. Since both voice and data are transmitted along the same copper and fiber optic pathways, it is as infeasible to bottle up telephone conversations as it is to contain online communications. The routes by which postal mail moves from sender to recipient are likewise "staggering" in number. The volume of postal mail is so great that each item can be subjected to no more than a perfunctory customs clearance procedure, and the idea of screening all telephone calls for content is so ridiculous that it has probably never been seriously proposed.

The basic flaw in the argument from futility is that it assumes the wrong enforcement paradigm—namely, preventing prohibited communications from reaching residents of a particular territorial jurisdiction. Although governments have attempted to apply this paradigm—notably Germany, in its efforts to prevent its citizens from gaining access to pornography and hate speech, and Singapore, which requires local Internet service providers to filter out "prohibited material" —

this is not the only approach available to a territorial sovereign that wishes to protect its citizens from deceptive commercial communications. The better approach is the one that is currently applied to communications at a distance. No restrictions are placed on a seller's ability to communicate with potential buyers. However, if a seller proposes or procures a commercial transaction through deceptive marketing methods, in violation of the law of the jurisdiction where a buyer is located, the seller may be subject to enforcement action by the government of that jurisdiction.

. . .

4. Deceptive Marketing Practices Are Not Likely To Be Adequately Controlled by Market Forces Alone

The cyberspace utopians argue that market forces are sufficient to prevent and redress consumer injury from deceptive marketing practices, and that government intervention is therefore unnecessary. This view fails to take account of the fact that the problem of fraud—whether perpetrated online or via some other means of communication—is highly resistant to control by market forces. . . .

It is easy to see why online deceptive marketing practices are unlikely to be controlled by market forces alone. The main lines of defense that the market erects—consumer sovereignty, industry self-regulation, and contract—are overmatched by online swindlers. By conveying misinformation to consumers, swindlers intend to interfere with the workings of consumer sovereignty, and they often succeed. While the market has evolved several mechanisms for improving the flow of information to online consumers—certification systems have been put into practice; ratings systems allow consumers to filter out certain categories of websites; non-governmental organizations provide consumers with information about online scams—these are simply online versions of mechanisms that pre-existed the Internet. Although they can certainly help in alleviating the problem of fraud in online commercial transactions, they are not likely to be significantly more effective than their offline analogues.

Vendors have also put into effect various types of online self-regulation: trade associations have promulgated industry codes of conduct, which may be implemented through a "hallmark" program; operators of online malls offer redress to consumers who are victimized by certain types of fraud at their sites, and screen the businesses that they allow to set up shop; one large Internet service provider "has decided not to provide website hosting or Internet access services to entities engaged in Internet-based gambling or other wagered activities which are determined to be illegal"; the online industry is engaged in a coordinated effort to develop software tools enabling parents to filter the online material to which their children are exposed. Yet these initiatives too are likely to fall short of what is required to control online deceptive marketing practices, for the simple reason that self-regulation "only binds the 'good guys.' Companies that do not have a reputation at stake have no ethical or business incentive to abide by self-regulatory principles. . . ." Legitimate marketers recognize that a reputation for honesty is a prerequisite to long-term business success. The market provides them with a strong incentive to keep their customers happy. But perpetrators of fraud have no such interest. They do not need or expect to profit from repeat business or referrals from satisfied customers, and do not expect to remain long in the market. They have no incentive to follow voluntary codes of conduct. Once a fraudulent operation becomes known in the marketplace as such, its perpetrator simply pulls up stakes and moves on to the next scam.

. . .

The cyberspace utopians' penchant for viewing cyberspace as a "place" that is separate from the sphere of ordinary discourse leads them to frame the question, wrongly, as: "Should the government regulate cyberspace?" Cyberspace is not a place, but rather an obfuscatory reference to a means by which people may communicate with each other. The right question is therefore, "What is the appropriate role of government in regulating commercial transactions that are carried out through the use of online communication technologies?"

. . .

Tony Long, *It's Just the 'internet' Now*
WIRED NEWS (Aug. 16, 2004)
www.wired.com/news/culture/0,1284,64596,00.html

Effective with this sentence, Wired News will no longer capitalize the "I" in internet.

At the same time, Web becomes web and Net becomes net.

Why? The simple answer is because there is no earthly reason to capitalize any of these words. Actually, there never was.

True believers are fond of capitalizing words, whether they be marketers or political junkies or, in this case, techies. If It's Capitalized, It Must Be Important. In German, where all nouns are capitalized, it makes sense. It makes no sense in English. . . .

Still, the decision wasn't made lightly. Style changes are rarely capricious, since change plays havoc with the editor's sacred cow, consistency.

But in the case of internet, web and net, a change in our house style was necessary to put into perspective what the internet is: another medium for delivering and receiving information. That it transformed human communication is beyond dispute.

But no more so than moveable type did in its day. Or the radio. Or television.

This should not be interpreted as some kind of symbolic demotion. Think of it more as a stylistic reality check. . . . [B]y lowercasing internet, web and net, Wired News is simply giving the medium its proper due.

EXTENSIONS

Exit. One version of the efficacy argument posits that an Internet user who is dissatisfied with the set of rules to which he is subject may, at negligible cost, relocate to a more congenial jurisdiction. On the network, the argument runs, physical proximity is irrelevant: a user can make full use of the Internet without regard to his physical location or the identity of the provider through which he gains access to the network.

So, for example, if the United States enacts a law banning online gambling, the owner of a gambling website can move the site to servers located in Antigua or some other jurisdiction where such operations are permissible, without making a change in the site's URL. A German proprietor of a site featuring Nazi hate speech, which is illegal under German law, can move the site to servers in the United States where it is protected by the First Amendment, and can continue to operate the site from her location in Germany. Data havens may be expected to arise—jurisdictions that place few or no restrictions on the flow of bits in and out of servers located within their borders. The ultimate expression of this tendency is illustrated by Sealand, a country consisting of an abandoned antiaircraft platform located off the cost of England, whose sole economic activity consists of hosting web servers. The company that provides the web hosting services, HavenCo Ltd., permits all content except for child pornography and spam. *See* Gareth Rubin, *The World's Most Bizarre Fantasy Island*, Express (UK), Sept. 11, 2004 ("[R]etired Army major Roy Bates mounted a one-man raid [of the platform, and] unilaterally declared it the Principality of Sealand, a sovereign state. He was the new Prince, his wife Joan the Princess and [son] Michael the 14-year-old heir apparent."); Havenco, www.havenco.com.

The network's facilitation of decentralized siting of business assets may also tend to increase the attractiveness of tax havens. An online business can locate its servers in a traditional tax haven, such as Bermuda or the Cayman Islands, while its owners and managers remain in their home (high-tax) countries, operating the business remotely via the network. This approach may not work well for U.S. citizens, since the United States taxes its citizens on their worldwide income. But there is as yet little precedent in the area.

If exit is truly costless, one result might be market-style competition among the promulgators of "rule sets," which will gain and lose subjects as network users vote with their feet. *See* David G. Post, *Anarchy, State, and the Internet: An Essay on Law-Making in Cyberspace*, 1995 J. Online L. art. 3. What are the limitations on an Internet user's ability to "exit" a rule set that displeases him? Are the costs of exit really negligible?

QUESTIONS FOR DISCUSSION

Grounds for objection. The excerpts from Barlow and Johnson & Post discuss four grounds on which objection to government regulation of online activity might be based: *legitimacy* ("Governments derive their just powers from the consent of the governed. You have neither solicited nor received ours."); *efficacy* ("Law-making requires some mechanism for law enforcement, which in turn depends on the ability to exercise physical control over, and impose coercive sanctions on, law-violators."); *jurisdictional cacophony* ("[T]hese local authorities are laying the predicate for an argument that Singapore or Iraq or any other sovereign can regulate the activities of U.S. companies operating in Cyberspace from a location physically within the United States."); and *superfluity* ("You claim there are problems among us that you need to solve. . . . Where there are real conflicts, where there are wrongs, we will identify them and address them by our means."). How do the responses from Goldsmith and Rothchild address these objections? Are the responses persuasive? Is there a defensible distinction between one's capacity as a citizen of a territorially defined sovereign, and one's capacity as (to use the utopian formulation) a citizen of cyberspace?

FURTHER READING

- Niva Elkin-Koren & Eli M. Salzberger, Law, Economics and Cyberspace

(2004) (arguing that various features of the digital networked environment undermine traditional economic analysis)

- Dan Hunter, *Cyberspace as Place and the Tragedy of the Digital Anticommons*, 91 CAL. L. REV. 439 (2003) (discussing the role of the "place" metaphor in theorizing about regulating the Internet)

- Justin Hughes, *The Internet and the Persistence of Law*, 44 B.C. L. REV. 359 (2003) (discussing several mechanisms that may bring about international convergence of laws affecting the Internet)

- Mark A. Lemley, *Place and Cyberspace*, 91 CAL. L. REV. 521 (2003) (discussing the influence the cyberspace-as-place metaphor has exerted on courts)

II. A PLURALIST APPROACH TO REGULATION OF ONLINE CONDUCT

In the world at large, a variety of constraints combine to regulate human behavior to an extent that makes society possible. No single constraint is alone adequate, and different types of constraints are appropriate in different situations. Parents, teachers, and religious authorities inculcate values that govern us internally. Individuals enter into contracts, and usually adhere to them; if a dispute arises, they may call upon an arbitrator or judge to determine their obligations, and may rely upon the coercive power of the state to enforce their rights. Governments promulgate rules of conduct that are likewise enforced through coercive sanctions. Neighbors generally settle their disputes peacefully without external intervention. The avenues for having an effect on others are limited by physics, geography, and technology.

The same variety of constraints must govern activity that takes place using online means of communication: a unitary approach, relying on a single method of constraining behavior, is unlikely to succeed. The task is rather to construct a toolbox of regulatory approaches that are applicable to online activity, and to select the proper tool for each job.

Consider the following regulatory devices. In what online situations would you expect their use to be particularly appropriate? Particularly inappropriate? What combination of government actions and market forces might encourage the implementation of each mechanism?

A. TRANSNATIONAL CYBERSPACE LAW

Several commentators have suggested that online commercial activity should be regulated by a transnational law of cyberspace. What is envisioned is a set of rules that is independent of all national legal systems, and applies only to online commercial transactions. Precedent for such a set of rules exists in the form of the law merchant, or *lex mercatoria*, which developed in the middle ages to govern disputes between merchants who interacted at trade fairs and in other venues away from their homes. According to the standard account, the *lex mercatoria* had several special characteristics: "1) it was transnational; 2) its principal source was mercantile customs; 3) it was administered not by professional judges but by merchants themselves; 4) its procedure was speedy and informal; and 5) it stressed equity, in the medieval sense of fairness, as an overriding principle." Harold J. Berman & Colin Kaufman, *The Law of International Commercial Transactions* (Lex Mercatoria), 19 HARV. INT'L L.J. 221, 225 (1978). In the eighteenth and nineteenth centuries the medieval law merchant lost its transnational character as it was absorbed into national legal systems.

Some scholars argue that since the middle of the twentieth century a "new *lex mercatoria*" has been developing, through arbitration of international commercial disputes and through codification efforts by the International Institute for the Unification of Private Law (UNIDROIT), www.unidroit.org, and the United Nations Commission on International Trade Law (UNCITRAL), www.uncitral.org. However, the character, and even the existence, of both old and new *lex mercatoria* has been widely disputed. *See* Keith Highet, *The Enigma of the Lex Mercatoria*, 63 TUL. L. REV. 613 (1989) (characterizing the "new *lex mercatoria*" as devoid of any substantive content beyond principles of common sense); Emily Kadens, *Order Within Law, Variety Within Custom: The Character of the Medieval Merchant Law*, 5 CHI. J. INT'L L. 39, 40 (2004) (describing the traditional understanding of the old *lex mercatoria* "at least partly inaccurate in almost every respect. The law merchant was not a systematic law; it was not standardized across Europe; it was not synonymous with commercial law; it was not merely a creation of merchants without vital input from governments and princes.").

Proponents of a transnational law of cyberspace see an analogy between online commercial transactions and the medieval trade fairs that gave rise to the old *lex mercatoria*:

> Many people interact frequently over networks, but not always with the same people each time so that advance contractual relations are not always practical. Commercial transactions will more and more take place in cyberspace, and more and more those transactions will cross national boundaries and implicate different bodies of law. Speedy resolution of disputes will be as desirable as it was in the Middle Ages! The means of an informal court system are in place in the form of on-line discussion groups and electronic mail. A "Law Cyberspace" co-existing with existing laws would be an eminently practical and efficient way of handling commerce in the networked world.

I. Trotter Hardy, *The Proper Legal Regime for "Cyberspace,"* 55 U. PITT. L. REV. 993, 1021 (1994).

Whatever the prospects of a wide-ranging transnational law governing Internet commerce, such a body of law has in fact developed with respect to one narrow category of disputes: those involving claims of bad-faith registration of domain names, in violation of trademark rights. The Internet Corporation for Assigned Names and Numbers ("ICANN"), a transnational entity that is responsible for certain aspects of Internet governance, has promulgated a set of (substantive and procedural) rules for resolution of such disputes using quasi-arbitral forums, called the Uniform Domain Name Dispute Resolution Policy ("UDRP"). *See* ICANN, www.icann.org/udrp/udrp.htm. ICANN and the UDRP are addressed more fully *infra*, in Chapter 3, Part IV.

B. REGULATION BY TRANSACTIONAL INTERMEDIARIES

Any entity that is an indispensable participant in online transactions can regulate conduct through contractual or technological restrictions. Rules of this sort can serve the same function as positive law. Consider the possible regulatory roles of several types of intermediaries:

1. *Internet service providers.* ISPs commonly state, in their Terms of Service, rules to which a subscriber must agree as a condition to using the ISP's services. For example, most

ISPs prohibit their subscribers from sending unsolicited commercial e-mail. Other restrictions commonly found in Terms of Service include prohibitions of material infringing intellectual property rights, and material that is defamatory, fraudulent, threatening, or graphically sexual. Some commentators envision a broader regulatory role for ISPs, proposing that a system of contracts between Internet users and the ISPs through which they gain online access, supplemented by contracts among ISPs, could yield pervasive regulation of online conduct. *See* Robert L. Dunne, *Deterring Unauthorized Access to Computers: Controlling Behavior in Cyberspace Through a Contract Law Paradigm*, 35 JURIMETRICS J. 1, 12-14 (1994).

In addition to regulating by contract, ISPs might regulate by implementing new technology. For example, in 2005 the Federal Trade Commission and its counterparts in other countries sent letters to 3,000 ISPs around the world, asking them to implement technology aimed at preventing spammers from hijacking consumers' computers and using them to send spam. *See* Federal Trade Commission, *Operation Spam Zombies*, www.ftc.gov/bcp/conline/edcams/spam/zombie/index.htm.

2. *Payment intermediaries.* Credit card issuers and online payment systems (such as PayPal) can have a dramatic effect on the availability of particular goods and services online. If the most widely used payment intermediaries make their services unavailable for certain transactions, then few such transactions will take place. The restrictions may be stated in contracts between the payment intermediary and online merchants who want to be able to use the intermediary to accept payment from purchasers. Enforcement is simple: a non-complying merchant will not get paid, and may lose the right to accept payments via the offended intermediary.

Credit card associations and banks that issue credit cards have become an important regulator of online gambling. About half of the states forbid their residents from placing bets via the Internet, but many gamblers ignore those prohibitions. What they cannot ignore, however, is the progressive disappearance of convenient methods of funding their online gambling accounts. Starting in the late 1990s, some credit card issuers began instituting policies prohibiting use of their cards for online gambling. The issuers' withdrawal from this line of business is usually not due to any moral objection to gambling, but rather reflects a business judgment. In many instances, gamblers who lose big money either dispute the charges on their credit-card bill, or refuse to pay, generating headaches and losses for the card issuers. At least one gambler even sued her credit card issuer for allowing her to gamble. Dedicated gamblers can work around these policies by funding their accounts in advance via check or wire transfer, but the inconvenience of these methods deters many potential gamblers.

The trend of payment intermediaries withdrawing from online gambling transactions has been helped along through action by law enforcement authorities. Citibank, the largest issuer of credit cards in the United States, continued to process these transactions until, in 2002, it reached an agreement with the Attorney General of the State of New York to ban use of its cards for online gambling. Other issuing banks then fell in line. PayPal, the largest online payment service, reached a similar settlement after being sued by New York, and eBay, when it acquired PayPal, extended this policy nationally.

Payment intermediaries have also begun to have an impact on adult-oriented websites. In late 2002 Visa announced that adult sites would be among those considered "high risk" merchants. As a result, Visa will assess issuers a $500 registration fee, and a $250 annual renewal fee, for each such site to which the issuer pays charges. Visa says that these fees are necessary because adult sites generate disproportionate quantities of fraud and charge-backs, and are therefore more expensive to deal with. In 2003, PayPal implemented a policy banning payments for sexually explicit goods.

Credit card associations also regulate the practices of online merchants relating to data security. Several of the largest associations (including Visa, MasterCard, American Express, and Discover) have adopted a code of practice to which merchants accepting their cards must adhere. The code includes a dozen security measures that merchants must implement, including: installing a firewall, changing vendor-supplied default passwords, using encryption, restricting internal access to stored data, and testing security systems. Merchants that do not comply may be assessed fines, or may lose the right to accept credit cards. *See Payment Card Industry Data Security Standard* (2005), sdp.mastercardintl.com/pdf/pcd_manual.pdf.

In 2005, the major credit card companies and PayPal began disallowing the use of their cards for online sales of cigarettes to individuals across state lines, after state and federal regulators advised them that nearly all such sales are illegal. Some states have laws prohibiting such interstate sales, while other states are concerned about the loss of tax revenues that may result when a consumer in a high-tax state purchases cigarettes from a seller in a low-tax state.

3. *Online auction operators.* Auction sites place limitations on the types of goods that may be sold using their services. eBay, the largest online auction site, posts a lengthy list of items that may not be listed for sale, consisting largely of items that are illegal to sell, such as bootleg recordings, counterfeit currency, human body parts, and cable television descramblers. Yahoo!'s auction site, in addition to prohibiting illegal items, bans "[a]ny item that promotes, glorifies, or is directly associated with groups or individuals known principally for hateful or violent positions or acts, such as Nazis or the Ku Klux Klan." Yahoo!, *Yahoo!Auctions Guidelines*, auctions.shopping.yahoo.com/html/guidelines.html. Yahoo!'s decision to ban these items, which are legal under U.S. law, likely was influenced by a French court's effort to curtail trafficking in such items through application of French law. *See* Part III(A), *infra.*

4. *Search engines.* Search engines have begun to give the cold shoulder to online gambling. In April 2004 both Google and Yahoo! announced they would no longer run advertisements for online gambling. (However, a search using appropriate terms will still yield gambling establishments among the search results.) The U.S. Justice Department had made known its view that carrying advertising for online gambling that is illegal in the United States might constitute an aiding-and-abetting offense, and had initiated a grand jury investigation of media outlets that carry such advertising. Several big media companies, including Clear Channel Communications and Discovery Networks, also have dropped advertisements for online gambling.

5. *Operators of the domain name system.* Those who want to maintain a persistent presence on the World Wide Web must register a domain name. The system for allocating domain names is highly centralized. Ultimate responsibility lies with the Internet Corporation for Assigned Names and Numbers ("ICANN"), which authorizes domain name registrars to assign domain names to registrants. ICANN contractually obligates domain name registrars to agree to implement a mechanism for resolving trademark-based disputes about the rightful ownership of a domain name, called the Uniform Domain Name Dispute Resolution

Policy ("UDRP"), and the registrars contractually obligate domain name registrants to abide by the UDRP. The UDRP is examined in Chapter 3, Part IV, *infra*.

6. *Package delivery companies*. In 2005, DHL agreed under pressure from state and federal regulators to stop delivering cigarettes to individual purchasers. At this writing regulators are in talks with other delivery companies in an effort to extend the ban.

QUESTIONS FOR DISCUSSION

1. *Accountability*. Should we be concerned about the degree of unaccountable regulatory authority that is exercised by private transactional intermediaries? Is the market an adequate substitute for democratic accountability?

2. *Scope for regulation by intermediaries*. In what areas is regulation by private transactional intermediaries most likely to be effective? How should we expect private regulatory regimes to differ from those resulting from political processes?

3. *Appropriateness of contractual ordering*. Is the use of contracts as a governance device more problematic in connection with online transactions than in any other application? Consider the argument that contracts are *less* problematic in the online context, because the online medium reduces transaction costs and enables true bargaining over contract terms.

FURTHER READING

- Margaret Jane Radin & R. Polk Wagner, *The Myth Of Private Ordering: Rediscovering Legal Realism in Cyberspace*, 73 CHI.-KENT L. REV. 1295, 1310-13 (1998) (critiquing the use of contracts to govern online conduct)

C. SELF-REGULATION VIA NORMS

Certain social groups, such as the cattle ranchers in California that Robert C. Ellickson studied in *Order Without Law* (1991), settle disputes by reference to internally generated norms of behavior, which do not necessarily correspond with, and may even be contrary to, legal rules. Some commentators believe that participants in online transactions should settle their differences in the same way, by reference to "netiquette." Consider, however, the following objections to this approach: (1) Norms typically develop in small, close-knit, homogeneous communities whose membership remains static over time. The community of Internet participants, by contrast, is large, individualistic, heterogeneous, and dynamic. (2) There is no reason to expect that norms developed within the online community will adequately control negative externalities affecting offline interests. (3) Enforcement of online norms is problematic: the defects of vigilantism are well-known, courts may have difficulty discerning applicable norms, and code-based enforcement may not reflect the will of the governed. *See* Mark A. Lemley, *The Law and Economics of Internet Norms*, 73 CHI.-KENT L. REV. 1257 (1998).

FURTHER READING

- Neil Weinstock Netanel, *Cyberspace Self-Governance: A Skeptical View from Liberal Democratic Theory*, 88 CAL. L. REV. 395 (2000) (arguing that self-ordering by participants in online transactions would result in a poorer implementation of the ideals of liberal democracy than our existing representative democracy)

D. COORDINATED PRIVATE ACTIONS VIA ANTI-SPAM BLACKLISTS

One approach to combating spam is the publication of a blacklist of Internet addresses that are associated with the sending of spam. The blacklist is made available to ISPs that operate mail servers, which implement the list by refusing to deliver e-mail to or receive e-mail from addresses served by mail hosts that are on the list. The first and best known of these lists is the Mail Abuse Prevention System Realtime Blackhole List, known for short as the MAPS RBL. The MAPS RBL, consisting of a list of IP addresses that is continually updated, was created in 1997 by Internet pioneer and anti-spam activist Paul Vixie. (In 2005 the MAPS RBL was acquired by Trend Micro Inc., which operates the service under its own brand name.) The IP addresses that are placed on the list are those of operators that are thought to send spam, to operate "open relays" (mail servers configured so that third parties can commandeer them to send spam), or to provide supporting services to senders of spam. Other blacklists maintained by MAPS include online hosting providers that are thought to host websites that engage in spamming, and websites that are set up by known spammers. The goal of those who produce these lists is to provide blacklisted ISPs and website operators with a powerful incentive to get themselves off the list, which they can accomplish by conforming to rules established by the blacklist provider. *See* MAPS, www.mail-abuse.com.

The creators of these blacklists do not themselves block the delivery of any e-mail. They simply make the lists available—either for free, or for a fee—and each operator of a mail server decides individually whether to block mail based on the list.

Consider the following objections to anti-spam blacklists: (1) The blacklist provider applies a contestable definition of what constitutes spam: for example, it may treat commercial e-mail as unsolicited unless the sender has implemented a double opt-in procedure, even though some believe that a single opt-in is sufficient; (2) Placement of an ISP on a blacklist results in blocking mail from all subscribers of the ISP, most of whom are not spammers; (3) The operators of these lists have unaccountable power to block the delivery of e-mail, which may result in significant economic and reputational harm; this unaccountable power is subject to abuse. *See* Sabra-Anne Kelin, Note, *State Regulation of Unsolicited Commercial E-Mail*, 16 BERKELEY TECH. L.J. 435, 442-43 (2001).

For consideration of legal approaches to combating unsolicited commercial e-mail, see Chapter 12, Part I, *infra.*

FURTHER READING

- *Media3 Technologies, LLC v. Mail Abuse Prevention System, LLC*, 2001 WL 92389 (D.Mass.2001) (denying preliminary injunction to web-hosting company that MAPS branded "spam-friendly" and placed on the RBL, finding that plaintiff had not established likelihood of success on defamation, tortious interference with business relations, or unfair trade practices claims), excerpted *infra* in Chapter 12, Part I(F)

- A. Michael Froomkin, *Habermas@Discourse.net: Toward a Critical Theory of Cyberspace*, 116 HARV. L. REV. 749, 832-34 (2003) (critiquing the use of anti-spam blacklists)

- Lawrence Lessig, *The Spam Wars*, THE INDUSTRY STANDARD, Dec. 31, 1998, www.lessig.org/content/standard/0,1902,3006,00.html (same)

QUESTIONS FOR DISCUSSION

Evaluation of control by concerted private action. Is MAPS providing a service to the community by drawing attention to ISPs that are contributing to the problem of bulk unsolicited commercial e-mail that is clogging the network, thereby enabling other ISPs to implement their voluntary decisions to avoid doing business with those who engage in such harmful practices? Is MAPS operating an illegal secondary boycott that unfairly penalizes subscribers of the blacklisted ISPs, and tortiously interferes with the ISPs' contractual relations? Has MAPS unjustifiably arrogated to itself the right to create rules establishing acceptable conduct by ISPs? Has it done any more than propose a set of rules that has come to be accepted by a substantial portion of the market?

E. REGULATION VIA CODE

Several commentators, including most prominently Lawrence Lessig, have drawn attention to the role of what Lessig terms "code" or "architecture" in regulating online behavior. Lessig identifies four types of constraints on behavior: laws, norms, the market, and code. The first three of these need little explanation. Laws are rules of conduct that are enforced through the coercive power of the state. Norms are rules that arise more or less spontaneously within a certain community, and are enforced primarily through peer pressure. The market constrains through the mechanisms of price and availability: you can buy only what the market offers to sell, and your economic resources limit what things you can acquire.

"Code" is a constraint that derives from physical facts about the world. The impossibility of traveling faster than light constrains our ability to visit other galaxies. A lock constrains a prospective burglar's ability to break and enter. Closer to the present context, technological facts exert a regulatory force. Liquid crystal displays enable mobile computing, which was infeasible when the available technology consisted of cathode ray tube displays. The existence of telephone caller ID limits our ability to communicate anonymously. Code can also consist of what computer programmers mean by the term: software instructions that control the operation of computing hardware. The availability of strong encryption constrains the ability of others to intercept our communications. The feature set of a software application regulates our ability to make use of it in a manner not intended by the developer.

Some types of code-based regulation are immutable—we can't overcome the constraint of the light-speed limit. But the code that is of greatest interest to regulation of online conduct is, like the Internet itself, socially constructed. That is, the code that regulates online behavior is whatever we decide to make it. "We can build, or architect, or code cyberspace to protect values that we believe are fundamental, or we can build, or architect, or code cyberspace to allow those values to disappear. . . . Code is never found; it is only ever made, and only ever made by us." LAWRENCE LESSIG, CODE AND OTHER LAWS OF CYBERSPACE 6 (1999).

The Internet was originally conceived as a tool for communication among academic researchers. In fulfilling that mission, uninhibited communication was important but regulability was not. The network was therefore designed with features that promoted communicational freedom, at the expense of regulability. These design features made it difficult for businesses to identify, recognize, and associate characteristics with online interlocutors. Certain features of the offline world make it feasible to gather information of this sort. Natural features, such as the uniqueness of fingerprints, and constructed features, such as the requirement that cars carry license plates, help to identify and keep track of people. The basic design of the network lacks those features or their online equivalents. "This minimalism in design is intentional. It reflects both a political decision about disabling control and a technological decision about the optimal network design. The designers were not interested in advancing social control; they were concerned with network efficiency." *Id.* at 33.

But, according to Lessig, "the invisible hand of cyberspace is building an architecture that is quite the opposite of what it was at cyberspace's birth. The invisible hand, through commerce, is constructing an architecture that perfects control—an architecture that makes possible highly efficient regulation." *Id.* at 6. The beginnings of an effort to create trackable identities on the network may be seen in the spread of passwords and cookie files. An online service can use passwords to discriminate between those who are entitled to access and those who are not. Cookies allow website visitors to be assigned a persistent identity, with which the visitor's attributes may be associated. But for e-commerce really to succeed, argues Lessig, "the Net will need a far more general architecture of trust—an architecture that makes possible secure and private transactions." *Id.* at 40. The elements of this architecture include "(1) authentication, to ensure the identity of the person you are dealing with; (2) authorization, to ensure that the person is sanctioned for a particular function; (3) privacy, to ensure that others cannot see what exchanges there are; (4) integrity, to ensure that the transmission is not altered en route; and (5) nonrepudiation, to ensure that the sender of a message cannot deny that he sent it." *Id.* These features may be implemented through digital certificates, supported by encryption and a public key infrastructure. (For a discussion of digital certificates, see Chapter 10, Part I(E), *infra.*)

Lessig believes that commercial imperatives are likely to foster the spread of such an architecture, with or without government intervention, through the establishment of incentives that make Internet users *want* to use digital certificates. The government, if it chose, could add impetus to this process—not by directly regulating individuals, but by creating incentives for individuals and regulating intermediaries. *Id.* at 50. For example, the government could require websites to deny access to visitors who lack the proper credentials, could impose a tax on e-commerce but exempt buyers who hold a certificate showing their state of residence, or could provide online services for free to those presenting a certificate. *Id.* at 50–51.

Lessig argues that the development of an infrastructure that meets the needs of e-commerce will have the side effect of making it easier for governments to regulate the Internet: "an ID-enabled world facilitates regulation." *Id.* at 54. He offers the example of online gambling. At present, it is difficult for any one state to prevent its citizens from gambling online. If the state takes legal action against a gambling operation located in the state, the operation can easily relocate to another jurisdiction without impinging on the ability of residents of the state to access its services—an incident of the fact that addressing on the Internet is logical rather than geographical. Lessig asks us to imagine a world where each Internet user possessed a digital certificate that contained pertinent information about him, including the country and state of his residence. That would enable gambling websites to discriminate among prospective customers, denying access to those whose certificate indicated they were from a state or country that prohibited gambling by its citizens. The legal system of each country where a server hosting an online gambling site was located would require hosting services within its jurisdiction to give effect to the gambling laws of other jurisdictions, so that wherever a gambling site was hosted, it would be required by local law to honor the laws of other jurisdictions.

Decisions about what code to implement are made through several mechanisms. A commercial venture or an independent standard-setting body can propose a protocol, which becomes generally adopted either because it works better than the alternatives or because network effects create powerful incentives to adopt it. A software product may gain widespread acceptance in the market and drive out alternatives. In addition, Lessig points out, a government may regulate "indirectly," by decreeing that code should be constructed to accomplish a desired regulatory effect. He offers some examples: (1) the Communications Assistance for Law Enforcement Act of 1994 requires that the digitally switched telephone network be designed to make it easy for the government to intercept telephone calls using wiretaps; (2) the Audio Home Recording Act of 1992 requires digital audio tape recorders to be equipped with a chip that limits a user's ability to make high-quality copies of copies; (3) the Digital Millennium Copyright Act of 1998 makes it a crime to create and sell software that defeats copyright management protection devices. *Id.* at 44–49.

QUESTIONS FOR DISCUSSION

1. *Private indirect control.* Should we be concerned that regulation by code, as an indirect form of regulation, is less visible than direct regulation, and therefore less subject to control by political constraints? Should we be more or less concerned about non-governmental creators of code, who are presumptively motivated by the desire for profit rather than by public interest considerations?

2. *Regulability.* Do you agree with Professor Lessig that e-commerce is likely to push the Internet in the direction of regulability? What forms might that take, beyond the widespread use of digital certificates?

FURTHER READING

- Joel R. Reidenberg, *Lex Informatica: The Formulation of Information Policy Rules Through Technology*, 76 TEX. L. REV. 553 (1998) (discussing the role of technology in regulating online behavior)

F. AN EXPERIMENT IN HYBRID GOVERNANCE: ICANN

Resources made available on the Internet are useful only to the extent they can be identified, located, and retrieved. To this end, each resource has some sort of identifier associated with it, which allows the resource to be summoned. Domain names are at the core of the system that allows identifiers to be associated with Internet resources. All website addresses, and all e-mail addresses, are built upon domain names. To access a page on the website maintained by the New York Times, one uses an identifier that has the form "www.nytimes.com/page_id." To send an e-mail message to an employee of the New York Times, one uses an identifier of the form "name@nytimes.com." In both cases, the domain name is "nytimes.com."

Intense controversies have arisen with respect to domain names. These controversies are explored in Chapter 3, *infra*. Trademark owners have complained about the assignment to others of domain names incorporating their trademark. Non-commercial users, and small businesses, have decried efforts by trademark holders to maintain absolute control over domain names that resemble their trademarks. Some have argued for broad expansion of the number of top-level domains—the suffix of a domain name, like .com, .org, or .us, that is used to organize the domain name space—to make more domain name combinations available. Others have argued for a go-slow approach to expansion of the domain name space.

Governance of the mechanisms by which domain names are managed, known as the domain name system ("DNS"), has passed through several hands during the brief history of the Internet. In the 1970s and 1980s, before the Internet gained any commercial significance, the predecessor of the DNS was controlled by several academic and non-profit institutions, under contracts with agencies of the U.S. government. In 1993, the National Science Foundation ("NSF") contracted with Network Solutions, Inc. ("NSI"), a private for-profit corporation, to manage the DNS. The contract gave NSI the exclusive right to register domain names in the .com, .org, and .net global top-level domains ("gTLDs"). Beginning in 1995, NSF allowed NSI to charge registrants for its domain registration services.

Most of the policymaking relating to the DNS remained under the control of the U.S. government—including the all-important decision whether to add new gTLDs—but NSI of necessity began to take on certain governance functions. Perhaps the most important of these was its creation of a frequently amended policy for handling trademark disputes involving domain name registrations. The need for such a policy became clear as lawsuits alleging cybersquatting began to proliferate, and NSI was sometimes named as a defendant in actions for trademark infringement. *See, e.g., Lockheed Martin Corp. v. Network Solutions, Inc.*, 194 F.3d 980 (9th Cir.1999).

Under NSI's policy, a trademark owner could initiate a challenge to a person's right to register (and thereby gain control of) a domain name by submitting evidence that the registration of the domain name violated the trademark owner's rights. The challenger could meet this requirement with evidence that the domain name was identical to a trademark it owned that was registered under either federal or foreign law. Upon receipt of such evidence, NSI would offer the registrant an opportunity to show that it too owned a trademark on the domain name. If the registrant could not produce such a registration, NSI would put the domain name on "hold," preventing the registrant from using it, pending resolution of the dispute.

NSI's domain name dispute policy engendered great dissatisfaction among domain name registrants, in part due to the phenomenon of "reverse domain name hijacking"— abuse of the policy by trademark owners that asserted spurious claims of infringement with the goal of preventing registrants from using domain names that they coveted.

In 1997, responding to pressure from commercial interests and foreign governments, the Clinton administration began consultations aimed at privatizing governance of the DNS. In June 1998, the U.S. Department of Commerce ("DOC") issued a policy statement, known as the DNS White Paper, that called for the creation of "a new, not-for-profit corporation formed by private sector Internet stakeholders to administer policy for the Internet name and address system." The White Paper set out several characteristics that the new corporation would have to possess before DOC would devolve DNS governance functions upon it.

Among other things, the corporation would have to be incorporated and headquartered in the United States; be governed by a board of directors, with international membership, designed to represent various specified constituencies; operate "on the basis of a sound and transparent decision-making process, which protects against capture by a self-interested faction"; and rely on the advice of internal councils dedicated to specific subject areas. The White Paper also specified several policies that it "anticipated" the new corporation would implement, including requiring information identifying domain name registrants to be publicly available (for the benefit of trademark holders that might wish to challenge a registration), and setting up and requiring registrants to abide by a dispute resolution system that would resolve claims of "cyberpiracy or cybersquatting." DOC pledged to enter into an agreement with the new corporation under which the latter would take over certain responsibilities for management of the DNS then under the control of government contractors. *See* Management of Internet Names and Addresses, 63 Fed. Reg. 31,741 (June 10, 1998).

In October 1998, Jon Postel, an Internet pioneer who had been involved in administration of the DNS and its predecessors since the 1970s, formed a corporation—the Internet Corporation for Assigned Names and Numbers ("ICANN")—that was designed to qualify as the new corporation described in the White Paper. DOC requested certain changes to ICANN's articles of incorporation and bylaws, to which ICANN acceded. The transfer of DNS responsibilities to ICANN was accomplished through a complex set of memoranda of understanding and contracts among DOC, ICANN, and NSI that were entered in 1998 and 1999. Those agreements gave ICANN a significant breadth of policy-making authority, but kept it on a short leash, as the agreements carried an expiration date, and DOC retained authority over perhaps the most contentious DNS-related issue, creation of new global top-level domains.

ICANN's first substantial exercise of policy-making authority was its creation of the Uniform Domain Name Dispute Resolution Policy ("UDRP"), replacing NSI's widely criticized dispute policy. The UDRP grew out of a study and recommendation from the World Intellectual Property Organization, an agency of the United Nations that represents the interests of intellectual property rights holders, upon the proposal of the United States. (The UDRP is discussed in more detail in Chapter 3, Part IV, *infra*.) Other ICANN actions that have had a significant impact on Internet users, trademark holders, and others include authorizing a set of new gTLDs, including .biz, .coop, and .info (while refusing to authorize others), and accrediting and regulating domain-name registrars and registries.

What is the source of ICANN's authority over the DNS? This is a difficult question. The best short answer may be that it is a combination of (1) DOC's recognition of ICANN, as reflected in certain agreements among DOC, ICANN, and NSI; (2) the U.S. government's control over most of the servers that house the authoritative root of the DNS; and (3) the network effects of adhering to a single authoritative root. (For background on the technical operation of the DNS and the role of authoritative root servers, see Appendix B.) But ICANN's authority has not gone unchallenged. Several companies have tried to set up alternative domain name roots, not sanctioned or under the control of ICANN. Internet users that take their domain name resolution services from an alternative root can reach addresses under all of the ICANN-sanctioned domains, including gTLDs like .com and country code TLDs like .us, as well as those under domains not sanctioned by ICANN, like .shop, .golf, and .law. For contrasting views on the desirability of alternative roots, see New.net, *A Proposal to Introduce Market–Based Principles into Domain Name Governance* (2001), new.net/NewnetPaper.pdf; ICANN, *Keeping the Internet a Reliable Global Public Re-*

source: Response to New.net "Policy Paper" (2001), www.icann.org/icp/icp-3-background/response-to-new.net-09jul01.htm.

QUESTIONS FOR DISCUSSION

1. *Who should manage the infrastructure of the Internet?* What entity should have control of the domain name system? Should the United States, in view of its central role in creating the Internet, be accorded some preeminent role in its management, or should the Internet be treated as a truly transnational resource? Does the fact that ICANN is incorporated in the United States give the United States an unfair advantage in controlling the DNS? What types of institutional structures are available for management of transnational resources? Can useful parallels be drawn from the systems that have evolved for managing international waters? space? Antarctica? global warming?

2. *Controversy over .xxx.* Proposals for establishment of .xxx as a gTLD dedicated to adult entertainment content have been floated since the late 1990s. In June 2005, ICANN announced that it had tentatively approved the creation of this domain. In August 2005, ICANN received a letter from an official of the U.S. Department of Commerce, advising that DOC had received thousands of letters from individuals opposed to the .xxx domain, and requesting that ICANN delay its final approval of the domain. ICANN complied, and at this writing has not announced any further action in connection with the proposed domain. Was DOC's intervention in ICANN's decisional processes appropriate? Was ICANN's response appropriate? Should ICANN be equally responsive to concerns expressed by government officials from other countries?

FURTHER READING

- A. Michael Froomkin, *Wrong Turn in Cyberspace: Using ICANN to Route Around the APA and the Constitution*, 50 DUKE L.J. 17 (2000) (arguing that DOC's delegation of authority to ICANN is illegal, in violation of the Administrative Procedures Act)
- Jonathan Weinberg, *ICANN and the Problem of Legitimacy*, 50 DUKE L.J. 187 (2000) (discussing the issue of ICANN's legitimacy in broader terms)

G. FEDERALISM AND INTERNATIONALISM IN THE REGULATION OF INTERNET COMMERCE

Most observers recognize that governments have a role to play in making and enforcing laws applying to certain aspects of Internet commerce. Several different institutions may generate such laws.

First, there are state legislatures, which have traditionally produced the bulk of legislation applying to commercial activities. State legislatures may do their work both individually and through the uniform law process. An example of individual state legislative action dealing with Internet commerce is the enactment of laws regulating unsolicited commercial e-mail. About 38 states have enacted such laws, no two of which are identical, though most of them follow a few standard approaches. The uniform law process is initiated by the National Conference of Commissioners on Uniform State Laws ("NCCUSL"), an organization consisting of more than 300 commissioners, appointed by the states, who draft model legislation which is then proposed for enactment by state legislatures. Examples of legislation applying to Internet commerce that has been developed through this process include the Uniform Electronic Transactions Act ("UETA"), which has been adopted by about 46 states and the District of Columbia, and the highly controversial Uniform Computer Information Transactions Act ("UCITA"), which has been adopted by two states and "banned" by several others. (On UETA, *see* Chapter 10, Part I(E), *infra*.)

Second, Congress may enact federal laws regulating Internet commerce. One example of such legislation is the Electronic Signatures in Global and National Commerce Act ("ESIGN"), 15 U.S.C. §§ 7001–06, which regulates electronic contracting and is similar to UETA. Another is the Children's Online Privacy Protection Act ("COPPA"), 15 U.S.C. §§ 6501–05, which regulates the collection of personal information from children. (On ESIGN, *see* Chapter 10, part I(E), *infra*; on COPPA, *see* Chapter 6, Part VI, *infra*.) Within the European Union, the analogue to federal legislation is the body of directives and regulations promulgated by the European Commission. An example of such legislation is the Directive on Electronic Commerce, discussed in Chapter 13, Part I, *infra*.

Third, international institutions may create rules that are implemented by national governments. Examples include the Model Law on Electronic Commerce, promulgated by the United Nations Commission on International Trade Law (discussed in Chapter 10, Part I, *infra*); the Guidelines for Consumer Protection in the Context of Electronic Commerce, promulgated by the Organisation for Economic Co-operation and Development; and two treaties negotiated under the auspices of the World Intellectual Property Organization, which resulted in enactment of the anticircumvention provisions of the Digital Millennium Copyright Act, 17 U.S.C. §§ 1201–05 (discussed in Chapter 9, Part II, *infra*).

What are the advantages and disadvantages of each of these sources of legal rules governing the Internet? An argument frequently made in favor of federal legislation is that Internet commerce, being inherently national in scope, requires a uniform body of regulation, since it is costly and inefficient for vendors to attempt to comply with a tangle of 50 inconsistent state laws. This was one of the stated rationales for Congress's 2003 enactment of the Controlling the Assault of Non-Solicited Pornography and Marketing Act of 2003, the "CAN-SPAM" Act, which preempts portions of the state spam statutes mentioned above. (The CAN-SPAM Act is discussed in Chapter 12, Part I(E), *infra*.) Consider these possible responses: (1) NCCUSL's uniform law process has worked well in the case of UETA, and is capable of generating additional laws regulating e-commerce. (2) In this new and rapidly evolving form of commerce, a state-by-state approach is preferable, since it allows for experimentation with competing approaches. (3) Commercial activity has traditionally been regulated primarily by the states. Businesses that market nationally have managed to cope with this scheme. (4) The state legislative processes are less subject to regulatory capture than is Congress.

A potential obstacle to state regulation of the Internet is that it may be found inconsistent with the U.S. Constitution's Commerce Clause, and thus invalidated. *See* Part III(C), *infra*.

Creating legal rules through international processes may be thought ill-suited to the regulation of Internet commerce because these processes typically move very slowly.

FURTHER READING

- Bruce H. Kobayashi & Larry E. Ribstein, *Uniformity, Choice of Law and Software Sales*, 8 GEO. MASON L. REV. 261 (1999) (arguing in favor of non-uniform approaches)

So much for theories as to how online activity *might* be regulated. What the following chapters reveal is how, a decade after the removal of the National Science Foundation's Acceptable Use Policy in 1995, which marked the start of Internet commerce, online commercial activity *actually is* regulated. As we will see, regulation of online activity is a complex interweaving of elements:

- New positive law, enacted wholly or partly in response to the new legal issues that Internet commerce raises. These include enactments both by Congress (the Anticybersquatting Consumer Protection Act, the Computer Fraud and Abuse Act, Controlling the Assault of Non-Solicited Pornography and Marketing Act, the Communications Decency Act, the Digital Millennium Copyright Act, and the Electronic Transactions in Global and National Commerce Act) and by state legislatures (state enactments of the Uniform Electronic Transactions Act, state spam laws, and harmonization of state laws via the Streamlined Sales Tax Project).

- The pre-existing body of law, applied to online activities (the Uniform Commercial Code and other state contracting laws, the laws of defamation and trespass to chattels, the Federal Trade Commission Act and state consumer protection laws, the copyright, trademark, and patent laws, and the constitutional and state laws of personal jurisdiction).

- Transnational law (the Uniform Domain Name Dispute Resolution Policy).

- Contracts (Terms of Service promulgated by Internet service providers and website operators).

- Self-regulation (website privacy policies, industry codes of conduct).

III. REGULATORY REACH IN A BORDERLESS WORLD: THE PROBLEM OF CONTROLLING ACTIVITY BASED OUTSIDE THE JURISDICTION

The Internet gives increased salience to the issue of the extraterritorial reach of domestic law—that is, the ability of a sovereign to apply its laws to activity originating from outside its territorial jurisdiction. The distance-erasing characteristics of online communications give rise to several scenarios in which conduct originating in one country may have substantial effects in another. Consider, for example: (1) A website that offers to sell goods that are legal in the country where the website is hosted or where the seller is located, but illegal in other countries. The goods might be offered either for physical delivery, such as unapproved pharmaceuticals or Nazi memorabilia, or electronically, such as obscenity or online gambling. (2) A website that posts speech that is legal in the host country but illegal in others. Sexually explicit material, defamation, information on making bombs, or hate speech might have the status of protected speech in some countries but not in others. (3) A website that posts material that is illegal both in the country where it originates and in the country where it is received.

A. JUDICIAL TREATMENT OF EXTRATERRITORIAL ASSERTIONS OF REGULATORY AUTHORITY

1. Extraterritorial application of anti-hate-speech laws. Yahoo! Inc., a U.S. corporation, operates a website that (among many other things) provides a forum in which individuals may auction goods to a worldwide online audience. Yahoo! never possesses or takes title to the goods being sold, but earns a commission each time a sale is completed under its auspices. Two French anti-racism groups filed a lawsuit against Yahoo! in a French court, alleging violation of a French law that makes it illegal to traffic in Nazi memorabilia. The items that gave rise to the lawsuit were offered for sale via Yahoo!'s original, English-language site, aimed primarily at the U.S. market, and hosted at yahoo.com. Yahoo! also maintained a French-language auction site, at yahoo.fr, which did not allow the sale of items that, like Nazi memorabilia, were illegal under French law.

Yahoo! argued that it was technically infeasible to prevent citizens of France from accessing the auction site or particular items offered for sale, while still offering the items to citizens of other countries (such as the United States) where the sales were perfectly legal. Yahoo! also objected that the French court had no jurisdiction over it, since its services were directed at persons located in the United States, its servers were located in the United States, and an order requiring Yahoo! to prevent access to Nazi items would violate the First Amendment and therefore be unenforceable in U.S. courts.

In May 2000, the French court ordered Yahoo! to "take all necessary measures to prevent and render impossible any access via Yahoo.com to the Nazi artifact auction service and to any other site or service that may be construed as constituting a justification of Nazism or a denial of Nazi crimes." But the court stayed the effect of its order, and appointed an international panel of experts to report on the feasibility of preventing persons located in France from accessing auctions of Nazi items.

The panel of experts reported back to the court that while it was technically infeasible to identify with 100% accuracy the geographic location of website visitors, it was possible to identify about 70% of the French visitors based on the IP address of the visitor's computer. Thus, the experts concluded, it is technologically feasible for Yahoo! to block access by 70% of French Internet users through IP address identification. And in fact, contrary to Yahoo!'s protestations of technical infeasibility, Yahoo! had already implemented a system for determining the geographic location of site visitors, as demonstrated by the fact that a visitor accessing yahoo.com from a computer located in France was greeted with banner advertisements in the French language.

Based on the experts' report, in November 2000 the court directed Yahoo! to comply with its May 2000 order within three months, or be subject to a daily fine of about $13,000. *See Association "Union des Etudiants Juifs de France" v. Yahoo! Inc.* (Trib. gr. inst. Nov. 20, 2000), www.legalis.net/cgi-iddn/french/affiche-jnet.cgi?droite=decisions/responsabilite/ord_tgi-paris_201100.htm, unofficial translation at www.gigalaw.com/library/france-yahoo-2000-11-20-lapres.html.

In January 2001, Yahoo! announced that it was banning from its auctions items that might incite racism, including items associated with Naziism and the Ku Klux Klan. Its Auction Guidelines were modified to prohibit:

> Any item that promotes, glorifies, or is directly associated with groups or in-

dividuals known principally for hateful or violent positions or acts, such as Nazis or the Ku Klux Klan. Official government-issue stamps and coins are not prohibited under this policy. Expressive media, such as books and films, may be subject to more permissive standards as determined by Yahoo! in its sole discretion.

Yahoo!, *Yahoo!Auctions Guidelines*, <u>auctions.shopping.yahoo.com/html/guidelines.html</u>. Those guidelines also ban a range of other items, including "[a]ny item that is harmful to minors, obscene, or otherwise objectionable," guns and other weapons, cigarettes, illegal drugs, drug paraphernalia, prescription drugs and medical devices, items that infringe trademark or copyright, counterfeit items, body parts, explosives, fake or non-fake government-issued IDs, gambling items, used underwear, and "[a]ny other item that violates any applicable federal, state or local law or regulation or which Yahoo! determines, in it sole discretion, is inappropriate for sale through the services provided by Yahoo!". *Id.*

Yahoo! stated that the new policy was not in response to the French court order, but rather due to complaints from users and from anti-racism organizations. The ban on Nazi items does not fully comply with the French court's order, since it does not cover books, movies, music, or government-issued coins and stamps, and does not extend to Yahoo!'s non-commercial communication forums.

2. Extraterritorial application of defamation laws. In *Dow Jones & Company Inc v Gutnick,* [2002] HCA 56 (Austl.), the High Court of Australia approved the trial court's assertion of jurisdiction over Dow Jones & Co., a U.S. corporation, based on the company's publication on the Internet of an allegedly defamatory article. The article appeared in *Barron's Online*, the online version of Dow Jones's print publication *Barron's*. Joseph Gutnick, a resident of the Australian state of Victoria, brought a defamation action against Dow Jones in a Victoria court. Dow Jones maintained that the court should decline jurisdiction under the doctrine of forum non conveniens, which under Victoria law would be applicable if the Victoria court was a "clearly inappropriate forum." Dow Jones argued that *Barron's Online* was published in New Jersey, the location of the servers hosting it. From this it would follow that the substantive law to be applied in deciding the case is New Jersey law, which would make the Victoria court a clearly inappropriate forum. Thus the decision hinged on where the article was deemed to be published.

The court held, contrary to Dow Jones's contention, that publication of a defamatory statement is "a bilateral act—in which the publisher makes it available and a third party has it available for his or her comprehension." Therefore, the article was published, with respect to Gutnick's cause of action, not when Dow Jones placed it on its web server, but only when subscribers in Victoria accessed it. For similar reasons, the court held that the defamation occurred in Victoria, and that Victoria law governed: "It is where that person downloads the material that the damage to reputation may be done. Ordinarily then, that will be the place where the tort of defamation is committed." Since jurisdiction in Victoria was proper, and Victoria law would be applied, the Victoria court was not a "clearly inappropriate forum," and there was no basis for declining jurisdiction.

The court responded to publishers' fears that its holding would expose them to unlimited risk of lawsuits worldwide with the observations: (1) a plaintiff can win damages only in a location where he has a reputation, which limits the choice of forum; (2) a judgment for damages is enforceable only in locations where the defendant has reachable assets; and (3) publishers can easily determine in advance which law will apply in defamation cases: "the spectre which Dow Jones sought to conjure up in the present appeal, of a publisher forced to consider every article it publishes on the World Wide Web against the defamation laws of every country from Afghanistan to Zimbabwe is seen to be unreal when it is recalled that in all except the most unusual of cases, identifying the person about whom material is to be published will readily identify the defamation law to which that person may resort."

Several courts have followed the *Gutnick* decision, asserting jurisdiction over defendants located outside the forum country in cases alleging defamation arising from online publications. *See Lewis v. King*, [2004] EWCA Civ 1329 (Q.B.) (U.K.) ("[I]t makes little sense to distinguish between one jurisdiction and another in order to decide which the defendant has 'targeted,' when in truth he has 'targeted' every jurisdiction where his text may be downloaded"); *Richardson v. Schwartzenegger*, [2004] EWHC 2422 (Q.B.) (U.K.) ("[I]t is well settled now that an internet publication takes place in any jurisdiction where the relevant words are read or downloaded"); *Bangoura v. Washington Post*, 235 D.L.R. (4th) 564 (Ont.Super.Ct.2004) (Can.) ("Defamation is to be located at the place where the damage to reputation occurs.").

B. TREATY LIMITATIONS ON REGULATION OF ACTIVITY ORIGINATING IN ANOTHER COUNTRY

The multilateral treaties administered by the World Trade Organization may constitute a significant new limitation on extraterritorial assertions of regulatory authority. The principal treaties are the General Agreement on Tariffs and Trade ("GATT"), the General Agreement on Trade in Services ("GATS"), www.wto.org/english/docs_e/legal_e/26-gats_01_e.htm, and the Agreement on Trade-Related Aspects of Intellectual Property Rights ("TRIPS"). In agreeing to these treaties, the 148 WTO member countries, which include the United States and nearly all of the world's other major trading countries, have accepted limitations on their regulatory authority in the name of promoting international trade.

In June 2003, the government of Antigua and Barbuda challenged U.S. efforts to prevent U.S. citizens from engaging in online gambling, arguing that these efforts violated the GATS. The island nation is home to dozens of online gambling enterprises, which are legal under Antiguan law, and the United States is their biggest market. The U.S. anti-gambling laws have on several occasions been enforced against Antigua-based online gambling. *See United States v. Cohen*, 260 F.3d 68 (2d Cir.2001) (U.S. citizen operating bookmaking operation based in Antigua convicted under 18 U.S.C. § 1084); *People ex rel. Vacco v. World Interactive Gaming Corp.*, 714 N.Y.S.2d 844 (N.Y.Sup.Ct.1999) (U.S. corporation based in New York violated state and federal laws through actions of its wholly owned Antiguan subsidiary).

In April 2005, the WTO's Appellate Body[2] found, on narrow grounds, that the United States was in violation of its obligations under the GATS, on account of a trio of federal laws (the Wire Act, 18 U.S.C. § 1084; the Travel Act, 18 U.S.C. § 1952; and the Illegal Gambling Business Act, 18 U.S.C. § 1995) that make it illegal to supply gambling and betting services remotely. The Appellate Body held that these laws were in principle permissible under a provision of the GATS allowing laws limiting trade if they are "measures . . .

---

[2] Disputes brought before the WTO are heard initially by a panel consisting of three experts from different countries who are appointed to hear a particular case. The Appellate Body is a seven-member standing tribunal that hears appeals from panel decisions. More information on the WTO is available at www.wto.org.

necessary to protect public morals or to maintain public order." However, the United States failed to make the required additional showing that these laws did not constitute "arbitrary" or "unjustifiable" discrimination, in light of another provision of federal law (the Interstate Horseracing Act, 15 U.S.C. §§ 3002, 3004) that allows off-track betting to be offered by domestic but not by foreign suppliers. *See United States—Measures Affecting the Cross-Border Supply of Gambling and Betting Services*, AB-2005-1 (2005), www.wto.org/english/tratop_e/dispu_e/285abr_e.pdf. According to the U.S. Trade Representative, the United States will respond to the ruling by clarifying the scope of the Interstate Horseracing Act, rather than by repealing the ban on online gambling.

EXTENSIONS

1. *Individual liability.* In addition to suing Yahoo! Inc., French anti-racism groups also sought to have Yahoo!'s former chief executive Timothy Koogle held *criminally* liable for allowing the auction of Nazi items, under a French law making it illegal to justify or condone war crimes. In April 2005 a French appeals court affirmed the trial court's dismissal of the prosecution, ruling that prosecutors had failed to demonstrate that the offering of Nazi memorabilia amounted to presentation of war crimes in a favorable light, the prerequisite for a criminal violation.

2. *Enforceability of foreign judgments in U.S. courts.* In *Yahoo! Inc. v. La Ligue Contre le Racisme et l'Antisemitisme*, 379 F.3d 1120 (9th Cir.2004), *reh'g en banc granted*, 399 F.3d 1010 (9th Cir.2005), the court rejected on jurisdictional grounds Yahoo!'s attempt to obtain a declaratory judgment stating that the French order was not enforceable in the United States because inconsistent with the First Amendment. (This case is discussed in Chapter 5, Part II(B), *infra*.)

3. *Businesses' response to extraterritorial assertions of regulatory authority.* In 2003, a committee of the American Bar Association and the International Chamber of Commerce performed a survey of 277 business enterprises in 45 countries to assess the impact upon them of the risk that their Internet-based commercial activities will expose them to regulatory jurisdiction of other countries. Among the tentative findings of the survey: (1) North American companies are more concerned than their Asian and European counterparts about the risk of being subject to a foreign jurisdiction; (2) more than half of media companies surveyed (compared to only 36% of all respondents) said they had modified their conduct to mitigate that risk; (3) companies seeking to avoid doing business in higher-risk jurisdictions generally identify the user's location though user registration or self-identification, and rarely through use of passwords, credit card matching, cookies, or geolocation technologies. *See* GLOBAL INTERNET JURISDICTION: THE ABA/ICC SURVEY (2004), www.abanet.org/buslaw/newsletter/0023/materials/js.pdf.

QUESTIONS FOR DISCUSSION

1. *Approaches to controlling offensive foreign content.* Consider some other approaches that national governments might take to prevent offensive foreign content from reaching its citizens via the Internet: (1) establishing a national filtering system; (2) requiring domestic ISPs to implement filtering; (3) making it illegal for its residents to receive the content; (4) establishing uniform global restrictions that all countries will enforce against content providers located within their jurisdiction. What are the pros and cons of each approach, from the standpoints of efficacy and enforceability?

2. *Extraterritorial reach of U.S. constitutional principles.* Suppose a French court held a U.S. citizen liable for defamation, based on speech she uttered while physically located in

France, under standards inconsistent with the First Amendment. A U.S. court might refuse to enforce that order, as in *Matusevitch v. Telnikoff*, 877 F.Supp. 1 (D.D.C.1995), *aff'd*, 159 F.3d 636 (D.C.Cir.1998) (Table). Is such a decision unsupportable, as an extraterritorial application of the U.S. Constitution?

C. Commerce Clause Limitations on State Power to Regulate Online Activities

Statement of Minnesota Attorney General on Internet Jurisdiction (1995)
[formerly posted on the Minnesota Attorney General's website]

WARNING TO ALL INTERNET USERS AND PROVIDERS

THIS MEMORANDUM SETS FORTH THE ENFORCEMENT POSITION OF THE MINNESOTA ATTORNEY GENERAL'S OFFICE WITH RESPECT TO CERTAIN ILLEGAL ACTIVITIES ON THE INTERNET.

PERSONS OUTSIDE OF MINNESOTA WHO TRANSMIT INFORMATION VIA THE INTERNET KNOWING THAT INFORMATION WILL BE DISSEMINATED IN MINNESOTA ARE SUBJECT TO JURISDICTION IN MINNESOTA COURTS FOR VIOLATIONS OF STATE CRIMINAL AND CIVIL LAWS.

. . .

American Libraries Association v. Pataki
969 F.Supp. 160 (S.D.N.Y.1997).

■ PRESKA, DISTRICT JUDGE.

The Internet may well be the premier technological innovation of the present age. Judges and legislators faced with adapting existing legal standards to the novel environment of cyberspace struggle with terms and concepts that the average American five-year-old tosses about with breezy familiarity. Not surprisingly, much of the legal analysis of Internet-related issues has focused on seeking a familiar analogy for the unfamiliar. . . . I find, as described more fully below, that the Internet is analogous to a highway or railroad. This determination means that the phrase "information superhighway" is more than a mere buzzword; it has legal significance, because the similarity between the Internet and more traditional instruments of interstate commerce leads to analysis under the Commerce Clause.

BACKGROUND

The plaintiffs in the present case filed this action challenging New York Penal Law § 235.21(3) (the "Act" or the "New York Act"), seeking declaratory and injunctive relief. Plaintiffs contend that the Act is unconstitutional both because it unduly burdens free speech in violation of the First Amendment and because it unduly burdens interstate commerce in violation of the Commerce Clause. Plaintiffs moved for a preliminary injunction enjoining enforcement of the Act; defendants opposed the motion. . . . For the reasons that follow, the motion for a preliminary injunction is granted.

I. Parties to the Action

Plaintiffs in the present action represent a spectrum of individuals and organizations who use the Internet to communicate, disseminate, display, and access a broad range of communications. All of the plaintiffs communicate online both within and outside the State of New York, and each plaintiff's communications are accessible from within and outside New York. . . .

II. The Challenged Statute

The Act in question amended N.Y. Penal Law § 235.21 by adding a new subdivision. The amendment makes it a crime for an individual:

> Knowing the character and content of the communication which, in whole or in part, depicts actual or simulated nudity, sexual conduct or sado-masochistic abuse, and which is harmful to minors, [to] intentionally use[] any computer communication system allowing the input, output, examination or transfer, of computer data or computer programs from one computer to another, to initiate or engage in such communication with a person who is a minor.

Violation of the Act is a Class E felony, punishable by one to four years of incarceration. The Act applies to both commercial and non-commercial disseminations of material.

. . .

III. The Internet

The Internet is a decentralized, global communications medium linking people, institutions, corporations, and governments all across the world. [The court describes the various modes of communication via the Internet, including e-mail, mailing lists, USENET newsgroups, chat rooms, and the Web.]

. . .

Regardless of the aspect of the Internet they are using, Internet users have no way to determine the characteristics of their audience that are salient under the New York Act—age and geographic location. In fact, in online communications through newsgroups, mailing lists, chat rooms, and the Web, the user has no way to determine with certainty that any particular person has accessed the user's speech. . . . As the poet said, "I shot an arrow into the air; it fell to the earth I know not where."

. . . In the present case, as discussed more fully below, the Internet fits easily within the parameters of interests traditionally protected by the Commerce Clause. The New York Act represents an unconstitutional intrusion into interstate commerce; plaintiffs are therefore entitled to the preliminary injunction that they seek.

DISCUSSION

. . .

II. Federalism and the Internet: The Commerce Clause

The borderless world of the Internet raises profound questions concerning the relationship among the several states and the relationship of the federal government to each state, questions that go to the heart of "our federalism." . . . The Act at issue in the present case is only one of many efforts by state legislators to control the chaotic environment of the Internet. For example, the Georgia legislature has enacted a recent law prohibiting Internet users from "falsely identifying" themselves online. Ga. Stat. [16–9–93.1].[3] Similar legislation is pending in California. . . . Texas and Florida have concluded that law firm web pages (apparently including those of out of state firms) are subject to the rules of professional conduct applicable to attorney advertising. . . . Further, states have adopted widely varying approaches in the application of general laws to communications taking place over the Internet. Minnesota has aggressively pursued out-of-state advertisers and service providers who reach Minnesotans via the Internet; Illinois has also been assertive in using existing laws to reach out-of-state actors whose connection to Illinois occurs only by virtue of an Internet communication. Florida has taken the opposite route, declining to venture into online law enforcement until various legal issues (including, perhaps, the one discussed in the present opinion) have been determined.

The unique nature of the Internet highlights the likelihood that a single actor might be subject to haphazard, uncoordinated, and even outright inconsistent regulation by states that the actor never intended to reach and possibly was unaware were being accessed. Typically, states' jurisdictional limits are related to geography; geography, however, is a virtually meaningless construct on the Internet. The menace of inconsistent state regulation invites analysis under the Commerce Clause of the Constitution, because that clause represented the framers' reaction to overreaching by the individual states that might jeopardize the growth of the nation—and in particular, the national infrastructure of communications and trade—as a whole. See *Quill Corp. v. North Dakota,* 504 U.S. 298 (1992) ("Under the Articles of Confederation, state taxes and duties hindered and suppressed interstate commerce; the Framers intended the Commerce Clause as a cure for these structural ills."); see also The Federalist Nos. 7, 11 (A. Hamilton).

The Commerce Clause is more than an affirmative grant of power to Congress. . . . In what commentators have come to term its negative or "dormant" aspect, the Commerce Clause restricts the individual states' interference with the flow of interstate commerce in two ways. The Clause prohibits discrimination aimed directly at interstate commerce, *see, e.g., Philadelphia v. New Jersey,* 437 U.S. 617 (1978), and bars state regulations that, although facially nondiscriminatory, unduly burden interstate commerce, *see, e.g., Kassel v. Consolidated Freightways Corp. of Del.,* 450 U.S. 662 (1981). Moreover, courts have long held that state regulation of those aspects of commerce that by their unique nature demand cohesive national treatment is offensive to the Commerce Clause. *See, e.g., Wabash, St. L. & P. Ry. Co. v. Illinois,* 118 U.S. 557 (1887) (holding railroad rates exempt from state regulation).

Thus, as will be discussed in more detail below, the New York Act is concerned

---

[3] [In *ACLU v. Miller,* 977 F.Supp. 1228 (N.D.Ga.1997), the District Court enjoined enforcement of this statute, finding that plaintiffs were likely to prevail on their claim that the statute violates the First Amendment.—Eds.]

with interstate commerce and contravenes the Commerce Clause for three reasons. First, the Act represents an unconstitutional projection of New York law into conduct that occurs wholly outside New York. Second, the Act is invalid because although protecting children from indecent material is a legitimate and indisputably worthy subject of state legislation, the burdens on interstate commerce resulting from the Act clearly exceed any local benefit derived from it. Finally, the Internet is one of those areas of commerce that must be marked off as a national preserve to protect users from inconsistent legislation that, taken to its most extreme, could paralyze development of the Internet altogether. Thus, the Commerce Clause ordains that only Congress can legislate in this area, subject, of course, to whatever limitations other provisions of the Constitution (such as the First Amendment) may require.

A. The Act Concerns Interstate Commerce

At oral argument, the defendants advanced the theory that the Act is aimed solely at intrastate conduct. This argument is unsupportable in light of the text of the statute itself, its legislative history, and the reality of Internet communications. . . .

. . .

The conclusion that the Act must apply to interstate as well as intrastate communications receives perhaps its strongest support from the nature of the Internet itself. The Internet is wholly insensitive to geographic distinctions. In almost every case, users of the Internet neither know nor care about the physical location of the Internet resources they access. . . .

Moreover, no aspect of the Internet can feasibly be closed off to users from another state. An internet user who posts a Web page cannot prevent New Yorkers or Oklahomans or Iowans from accessing that page and will not even know from what state visitors to that site hail. Nor can a participant in a chat room prevent other participants from a particular state from joining the conversation. . . .

E-mail, because it is a one-to-one messaging system, stands on a slightly different footing than the other aspects of the Internet. Even in the context of e-mail, however, a message from one New Yorker to another New Yorker may well pass through a number of states en route. . . .

. . .

The New York Act, therefore, cannot effectively be limited to purely intrastate communications over the Internet because no such communications exist. No user could reliably restrict her communications only to New York recipients. Moreover, no user could avoid liability under the New York Act simply by directing his or her communications elsewhere, given that there is no feasible way to preclude New Yorkers from accessing a website, receiving a mail exploder message or a newsgroup posting, or participating in a chat room. Similarly, a user has no way to ensure that an e-mail does not pass through New York even if the ultimate recipient is not located there, or that a message never leaves New York even if both sender and recipient are located there.

. . .

. . . The next question that requires an answer as a threshold matter is whether the types of communication involved constitute "commerce" within the meaning of the Clause. . . . The non-profit nature of certain entities that use the Internet or of certain transactions that take place over the Internet does not take the Internet outside the Commerce Clause. . . . The Supreme Court has expressly held that the dormant commerce clause is applicable to activities undertaken without a profit motive. . . .

. . .

The courts have long recognized that railroads, trucks, and highways are themselves "instruments of commerce," because they serve as conduits for the transport of products and services. *See Kassel v. Consolidated Freightways Corp.,* 450 U.S. 662 (1981); *Southern Pacific Co. v. Arizona,* 325 U.S. 761, 780 (1945). The Internet is more than a means of communication; it also serves as a conduit for transporting digitized goods, including software, data, music, graphics, and videos which can be downloaded from the provider's site to the Internet user's computer. . . .

The inescapable conclusion is that the Internet represents an instrument of interstate commerce, albeit an innovative one; the novelty of the technology should not obscure the fact that regulation of the Internet impels traditional Commerce Clause considerations. The New York Act is therefore closely concerned with interstate commerce, and scrutiny of the Act under the Commerce Clause is entirely appropriate. As discussed in the following sections, the Act cannot survive such scrutiny, because it places an undue burden on interstate traffic, whether that traffic be in goods, services, or ideas.

B. New York Has Overreached by Enacting a Law That Seeks To Regulate Conduct Occurring Outside its Borders

The interdiction against direct interference with interstate commerce by state legislative overreaching is apparent in a number of the Supreme Court's decisions. . . .

. . . In *Edgar v. MITE,* 457 U.S. 624 (1982), the Court examined the constitutionality of an Illinois anti-takeover statute that required a tender offeror to notify the Secretary of State and the target company of its intent to make a tender offer and the terms of the offer 20 days before the offer became effective. During the twenty-day period, the offeror was barred from communicating its offer to the shareholders, but the target company was free to disseminate information to its shareholders concerning the impending offer. . . . The Court concluded "the Illinois statute is a direct restraint on interstate commerce and has a sweeping extraterritorial effect," because the statute would prevent a tender offeror from communicating its offer to shareholders both within and outside Illinois. Acceptance of the offer by any of the shareholders would result in interstate transactions; the Illinois statute effectively stifled such transactions during the waiting period and thereby disrupted prospective interstate commerce. Under the Commerce Clause, the projection of these extraterritorial "practical effect[s]," regardless of the legislators' intentions, " 'exceeded the inherent limits of the State's power.' " *Id.* at 642–43 (quoting *Shaffer v. Heitner,* 433 U.S. 186 (1977)).

In the present case, a number of witnesses testified to the chill that they felt as a result of the enactment of the New York statute; these witnesses refrained from engaging in particular types of interstate commerce. . . .

. . .

The "extraterritoriality" analysis of the *Edgar* opinion commanded only a plurality of the Court. Later majority holdings, however, expressly adopted the underlying principles on which Justice White relied in *Edgar. See Healy v. The Beer Institute,* 491 U.S. 324 (1989); *Brown–Forman Distillers Corp. v. New York State Liquor Authority,* 476 U.S. 573 (1986). . . .

. . .

The nature of the Internet makes it impossible to restrict the effects of the New York Act to conduct occurring within New York. . . . New York has deliberately imposed its legislation on the Internet and, by doing so, projected its law into other states whose citizens use the Net. This encroachment upon the authority which the Constitution specifically confers upon the federal government and upon the sovereignty of New York's sister states is per se violative of the Commerce Clause.

C. The Burdens the Act Imposes on Interstate Commerce Exceed Any Local Benefit

Even if the Act were not a per se violation of the Commerce Clause by virtue of its extraterritorial effects, the Act would nonetheless be an invalid indirect regulation of interstate commerce, because the burdens it imposes on interstate commerce are excessive in relation to the local benefits it confers. The Supreme Court set forth the balancing test applicable to indirect regulations of interstate commerce in *Pike v. Bruce Church,* 397 U.S. 137 (1970). *Pike* requires a two-fold inquiry. The first level of examination is directed at the legitimacy of the state's interest. The next, and more difficult, determination weighs the burden on interstate commerce in light of the local benefit derived from the statute.

In the present case, I accept that the protection of children against pedophilia is a quintessentially legitimate state objective—a proposition with which I believe even the plaintiffs have expressed no quarrel. . . . Even with the fullest recognition that the protection of children from sexual exploitation is an indisputably valid state goal, however, the present statute cannot survive even the lesser scrutiny to which indirect regulations of interstate commerce are subject under the Constitution. . . .

The local benefits likely to result from the New York Act are not overwhelming. The Act can have no effect on communications originating outside the United States. . . . Further, in the present case, New York's prosecution of parties from out of state who have allegedly violated the Act, but whose only contact with New York occurs via the Internet, is beset with practical difficulties, even if New York is able to exercise criminal jurisdiction over such parties. The prospect of New York bounty hunters dragging pedophiles from the other 49 states into New York is not consistent with traditional concepts of comity.

Moreover, the State has espoused an interpretation of the Act that, if accepted, would further undermine its effectiveness. According to defendant, the Act reaches only pictorial messages that are harmful to minors and has no impact on purely textual communications. . . .

The Act is, of course, not the only law in New York's statute books designed to protect children against sexual exploitation. The State is able to protect children through vigorous enforcement of the existing laws criminalizing obscenity and child pornography. *See United States v. Thomas*, 74 F.3d 701, 704–05 (6th Cir.1995). Moreover, plaintiffs do not challenge the sections of the statute that criminalize the sale of obscene materials to children, over the Internet or otherwise, and prohibit adults from luring children into sexual contact by communicating with them via the Internet. See N.Y. Penal Law § 235.21(1); N.Y. Penal Law § 235.22(2). The local benefit to be derived from the challenged section of the statute is therefore confined to that narrow class of cases that does not fit within the parameters of any other law. The efficacy of the statute is further limited, as discussed above, to those cases which New York is realistically able to prosecute.

. . .

Balanced against the limited local benefits resulting from the Act is an extreme burden on interstate commerce. The New York Act casts its net worldwide; moreover, the chilling effect that it produces is bound to exceed the actual cases that are likely to be prosecuted, as Internet users will steer clear of the Act by significant margin. At oral argument, the State asserted that only a small percentage of Internet communications are "harmful to minors" and would fall within the proscriptions of the statute; therefore, the State argued, the burden on interstate commerce is small. On the record before me, I conclude that the range of Internet communications potentially affected by the Act is far broader than the State suggests. I note that in the past, various communities within the United States have found works including *I Know Why the Caged Bird Sings* by Maya Angelou, *Funhouse* by Dean Koontz, *The Adventures of Huckleberry Finn* by Mark Twain, and *The Color Purple* by Alice Walker to be indecent. Even assuming, arguendo, that the Act applies only to pictures, a number of Internet users take advantage of the medium's capabilities to communicate images to one another and, again, I find that the range of images that might subject the communicator to prosecution (or reasonably cause a communicator to fear prosecution) is far broader than defendants assert. For example, many libraries, museums and academic institutions post art on the Internet that some might conclude was "harmful to minors." Famous nude works by Botticelli, Manet, Matisse, Cezanne and others can be found on the Internet. In this regard, I point out that a famous painting by Manet which shows a nude woman having lunch with two fully clothed men was the subject of considerable protest when it first was unveiled in Paris, as many observers believed that it was "scandalous." Lesser known artists who post work over the Internet may face an even greater risk of prosecution, because the mantle of respectability that has descended on Manet is not associated with their as yet obscure names. . . .

. . .

The severe burden on interstate commerce resulting from the New York statute is not justifiable in light of the attenuated local benefits arising from it. The alternative analysis of the Act as an indirect regulation on interstate commerce therefore also mandates the issuance of the preliminary injunction sought by plaintiffs.

D. The Act Unconstitutionally Subjects Interstate Use of the Internet to Inconsistent Regulations

Finally, a third mode of Commerce Clause analysis further confirms that the plaintiffs are likely to succeed on the merits of their claim that the New York Act is unconstitutional. The courts have long recognized that certain types of commerce demand consistent treatment and are therefore susceptible to regulation only on a national level. The Internet represents one of those areas; effective regulation will require national, and more likely global, cooperation. Regulation by any single state can only result in chaos, because at least some states will likely enact laws subjecting Internet users to conflicting obligations. Without the limitations imposed by the Commerce Clause, these inconsistent regulatory schemes could paralyze the development of the Internet altogether.

In numerous cases, the Supreme Court has acknowledged the need for coordination in the regulation of certain areas of commerce. . . . The Court in [*Wabash, St. L. & P. Ry. Co. v. Illinois*, 118 U.S. 557, 574–75 (1886)] struck the Illinois statute at issue, which purported to establish interstate railway rates, stating "that this species of regulation is one which must be, if established at all, of a general and national character, and cannot be safely and wisely remitted to local rules and regulations, we think is clear from what has already been said." *Id.* at 577.

. . .

In *Bibb v. Navajo Freight Lines, Inc.*, 359 U.S. 520 (1959), the Court examined an Illinois statute that required the use of contour mudguards on trucks in Illinois. The Court took note of the fact that straight or conventional mudguards were permissible in most other states and actually required in Arkansas. *Id.* 359 U.S. at 526. Recognizing the need for coordinated legislation, the Court stated that "the conflict between the Arkansas regulation and the Illinois regulation . . . suggests that this regulation of mudguards is not one of those matters 'admitting of diversity of treatment, according to the special requirements of local conditions.' " *Id.* at 528 (quoting *Sproles v. Binford*, 286 U.S. 374, 390 (1932)). The Court struck the Illinois law as imposing an undue burden on interstate commerce, in part because Illinois was insisting upon "a design out of line with the requirements of almost all the other states." *Id.*

The Internet, like the rail and highway traffic at issue in the cited cases, requires a cohesive national scheme of regulation so that users are reasonably able to determine their obligations. Regulation on a local level, by contrast, will leave users lost in a welter of inconsistent laws, imposed by different states with different priorities. New York is not the only state to enact a law purporting to regulate the content of communications on the Internet. Already Oklahoma and Georgia have enacted laws designed to protect minors from indecent communications over the Internet; as might be expected, the states have selected different methods to accomplish their aims. Georgia has made it a crime to communicate anonymously over the Internet, while Oklahoma, like New York, has prohibited the online transmission of material deemed harmful to minors. *See* Ga. Code Ann. § 16–19–93.1 (1996); Okla. Stat. tit. 21, § 1040.76 (1996).

Moreover, the regulation of communications that may be "harmful to minors" taking place over the Internet poses particular difficulties. . . . Courts have long recognized . . . that there is no single "prevailing community standard" in the United States. Thus, even were all 50 states to enact laws that were verbatim copies of the New York Act, Internet users would still be subject to discordant responsibilities.

As discussed at length above, an Internet user cannot foreclose access to her work from certain states or send differing versions of her communication to different jurisdictions. In this sense, the Internet user is in a worse position than the truck driver or train engineer who can steer around Illinois or Arizona, or change the mudguard or train configuration at the state line; the Internet user has no ability to bypass any particular state. The user must thus comply with the regulation imposed by the state with the most stringent standard or forego Internet communication of the message that might or might not subject her to prosecution. . . .

Further development of the Internet requires that users be able to predict the results of their Internet use with some degree of assurance. Haphazard and uncoordinated state regulation can only frustrate the growth of cyberspace. The need for uniformity in this unique sphere of commerce requires that New York's law be stricken as a violation of the Commerce Clause.

. . .

State v. Heckel
24 P.3d 404 (Wash.2001) (en banc).

■ OWENS, J.—The State of Washington filed suit against Oregon resident Jason Heckel, alleging that his transmissions of electronic mail (e-mail) to Washington residents violated Washington's commercial electronic mail act, chapter 19.190 RCW (the Act). On cross-motions for summary judgment, the trial court dismissed the State's suit against Heckel, concluding that the Act violated the dormant Commerce Clause of the United States Constitution. This court granted the State's request for direct review. We hold that the Act does not unduly burden interstate commerce. We reverse the trial court's dismissal of the State's suit, vacate the order on attorney fees, and remand this matter for trial.

FACTS

As early as February 1996, defendant Jason Heckel, an Oregon resident doing business as Natural Instincts, began sending unsolicited commercial e-mail (UCE), or "spam," over the Internet.[1] In 1997, Heckel developed a 46-page on-line booklet

---

[1] " 'Commercial electronic mail message' means an electronic mail message sent for the purpose of promoting real property, goods, or services for sale or lease." RCW

entitled "How to Profit from the Internet." The booklet described how to set up an on-line promotional business, acquire free e-mail accounts, and obtain software for sending bulk e-mail. From June 1998, Heckel marketed the booklet by sending between 100,000 and 1,000,000 UCE messages per week. To acquire the large volume of e-mail addresses, Heckel used the Extractor Pro software program, which harvests e-mail addresses from various on-line sources and enables a spammer to direct a bulk-mail message to those addresses by entering a simple command. . . . The order form included the Salem, Oregon, mailing address for Natural Instincts. Charging $39.95 for the booklet, Heckel made 30 to 50 sales per month.

In June 1998, the Consumer Protection Division of the Washington State Attorney General's Office received complaints from Washington recipients of Heckel's UCE messages. The complaints alleged that Heckel's messages contained misleading subject lines and false transmission paths. Responding to the June complaints, David Hill, an inspector from the Consumer Protection Division, sent Heckel a letter advising him of the existence of the Act. The Act provides that anyone sending a commercial e-mail message from a computer located in Washington or to an e-mail address held by a Washington resident may not use a third-party's domain name without permission, misrepresent or disguise in any other way the message's point of origin or transmission path, or use a misleading subject line.[6] RCW 19.190.030 makes a violation of the Act a per se violation of the Consumer Protection Act, chapter 19.86 RCW (CPA).

. . .

On October 22, 1998, the State filed suit against Heckel, stating three causes of action. First, the State alleged that Heckel had violated RCW 19.190.020(1)(b) and, in turn, the CPA, by using false or misleading information in the subject line of his UCE messages. Heckel used one of two subject lines to introduce his solicitations: "Did I get the right e-mail address?" and "For your review—HANDS OFF!" In the State's view, the first subject line falsely suggested that an acquaintance of the recipient was trying to make contact, while the second subject line invited the misperception that the message contained classified information for the particular recipient's review.

19.190.010(2). . . .

[6] "(1) No person may initiate the transmission, conspire with another to initiate the transmission, or assist the transmission, of a commercial electronic mail message from a computer located in Washington or to an electronic mail address that the sender knows, or has reason to know, is held by a Washington resident that:

"(a) Uses a third party's internet domain name without permission of the third party, or otherwise misrepresents or obscures any information in identifying the point of origin or the transmission path of a commercial electronic mail message; or

"(b) Contains false or misleading information in the subject line.

"(2) For purposes of this section, a person knows that the intended recipient of a commercial electronic mail message is a Washington resident if that information is available, upon request, from the registrant of the Internet domain name contained in the recipient's electronic mail address." RCW 19.190.020.

As its second cause of action, the State alleged that Heckel had violated RCW 19.190.020(1)(a), and thus the CPA, by misrepresenting information defining the transmission paths of his UCE messages. Heckel routed his spam through at least a dozen different domain names without receiving permission to do so from the registered owners of those names. For example, of the 20 complaints the Attorney General's Office received concerning Heckel's spam, 9 of the messages showed "13.com" as the initial ISP to transmit his spam. The 13.com domain name, however, was registered as early as November 1995 to another individual, from whom Heckel had not sought or received permission to use the registered name. In fact, because the owner of 13.com had not yet even activated that domain name, no messages could have been sent or received through 13.com.

Additionally, the State alleged that Heckel had violated the CPA by failing to provide a valid return e-mail address to which bulk-mail recipients could respond. When Heckel created his spam with the Extractor Pro software, he used at least a dozen different return e-mail addresses with the domain name "juno.com" (Heckel used the Juno accounts in part because they were free). None of the Juno e-mail accounts was readily identifiable as belonging to Heckel; the user names that he registered generally consisted of a name or a name plus a number (*e.g.*, "marlin1374," "cindyt5667," "howardwesley13," "johnjacobson1374," and "sjtowns"). During August and September 1998, Heckel's Juno addresses were canceled within two days of his sending out a bulk e-mail message on the account. According to Heckel, when Juno canceled one e-mail account, he would simply open a new one and send out another bulk mailing. Because Heckel's accounts were canceled so rapidly, recipients who attempted to reply were unsuccessful. . . . The State asserted that Heckel's use of such ephemeral e-mail addresses in his UCE amounted to a deceptive practice in violation of RCW 19.86.020.

The State sought a permanent injunction and, pursuant to RCW 19.86.140 and .080 of the CPA, requested civil penalties, as well as costs and a reasonable attorney fee. In early 2000, the parties cross-moved for summary judgment. On March 10, 2000, the trial court entered an order granting Heckel's motion and denying the State's cross motion. The court found that the Act violated the Commerce Clause (U.S. CONST. art. I, § 8, cl. 3) and was "unduly restrictive and burdensome." . . . Challenging the trial court's finding that the Act violated the Commerce Clause, the State sought this court's direct review. . . .

ISSUE

Does the Act, which prohibits misrepresentation in the subject line or transmission path of any commercial e-mail message sent to Washington residents or from a Washington computer, unconstitutionally burden interstate commerce?

ANALYSIS

. . .

Heckel's Challenge under the Commerce Clause. The Commerce Clause grants Congress the "power . . . [t]o regulate commerce with foreign nations, and among the several states." Implicit in this affirmative grant is the negative or "dormant" Commerce Clause—the principle that the states impermissibly intrude on this federal power when they enact laws that unduly burden interstate commerce. Analysis of a state law under the dormant Commerce Clause generally follows a two-step process. We first determine whether the state law openly discriminates against interstate commerce in favor of intrastate economic interests. If the law is facially neutral, applying impartially to in-state and out-of-state businesses, the analysis moves to the second step, a balancing of the local benefits against the interstate burdens . . . . [*Pike v. Bruce Church, Inc.*, 397 U.S. 137 (1970)].

The Act is not facially discriminatory. The Act applies evenhandedly to in-state and out-of-state spammers: "*No person*" may transmit the proscribed commercial e-mail messages "from a computer located in Washington or to an electronic mail address that the sender knows, or has reason to know, is held by a Washington resident." RCW 19.190.020(1) (emphasis added). Thus, just as the statute applied to Heckel, an Oregon resident, it is enforceable against a Washington business engaging in the same practices.

Because we conclude that the Act's local benefits surpass any alleged burden on interstate commerce, the statute likewise survives the *Pike* balancing test. The Act protects the interests of three groups—ISPs, actual owners of forged domain names, and e-mail users. The problems that spam causes have been discussed in prior cases and legislative hearings. . . .[4] To handle the increased e-mail traffic attributable to deceptive spam, ISPs must invest in more computer equipment. Operational costs likewise increase as ISPs hire more customer service representatives to field spam complaints and more system administrators to detect accounts being used to send spam.

Along with ISPs, the owners of impermissibly used domain names and e-mail addresses suffer economic harm. For example, the registered owner of "local-host.com" alleged that his computer system was shut down for three days by 7,000 responses to a bulk-mail message in which the spammer had forged the e-mail address "nobody@localhost.com" into his spam's header. *Seidl v. Greentree Mortgage Co.*, 30 F. Supp. 2d 1292, 1297–98 (D.Colo.1998) . . . .

Deceptive spam harms individual Internet users as well. When a spammer distorts the point of origin or transmission path of the message, e-mail recipients cannot promptly and effectively respond to the message (and thereby opt out of future mailings); their efforts to respond take time, cause frustration, and compound the problems that ISPs face in delivering and storing the bulk messages. And the use of false or misleading subject lines further hampers an individual's ability to use computer time most efficiently. When spammers use subject lines "such as 'Hi There!,' 'Information Request,' and 'Your Business Records,' " it becomes "virtually impossible" to distinguish spam from legitimate personal or business messages. Individuals who do not have flat-rate plans for Internet access but pay instead by the minute or hour are harmed more directly, but all Internet users (along

---

[4] [The court quotes from *CompuServe Inc. v. Cyber Promotions, Inc.*, 962 F.Supp. 1015 (S.D.Ohio 1997), which is excerpted in Chapter 12, Part I(C)(1), *infra.*—Eds.]

with their ISPs) bear the cost of deceptive spam.

. . .

Under the *Pike* balancing test, "[i]f a legitimate local purpose is found, then the question becomes one of degree." 397 U.S. at 142. In the present case, the trial court questioned whether the Act's requirement of truthfulness (in the subject lines and header information) would redress the costs associated with bulk e-mailings. As legal commentators have observed, however, "the truthfulness requirements (such as the requirement not to misrepresent the message's Internet origin) make spamming unattractive to the many fraudulent spammers, thereby reducing the volume of spam." Jack L. Goldsmith & Alan O. Sykes, *The Internet and the Dormant Commerce Clause*, 110 Yale L.J. 785, 819 (2001). Calling "simply wrong" the trial court's view "that truthful identification in the subject header would do little to relieve the annoyance of spam," the commentators assert that "[t]his identification alone would allow many people to delete the message without opening it (which takes time) and perhaps being offended by the content." *Id*. The Act's truthfulness requirements thus appear to advance the Act's aim of protecting ISPs and consumers from the problems associated with commercial bulk e-mail.

To be weighed against the Act's local benefits, the only burden the Act places on spammers is the requirement of truthfulness, a requirement that does not burden commerce at all but actually "facilitates it by eliminating fraud and deception." *Id*. Spammers must use an accurate, nonmisleading subject line, and they must not manipulate the transmission path to disguise the origin of their commercial messages. While spammers incur no costs in complying with the Act, they do incur costs for noncompliance, because they must take steps to introduce forged information into the header of their message. In finding the Act "unduly burdensome," the trial court apparently focused not on what spammers must do to comply with the Act but on what they must do if they choose to use deceptive subject lines or to falsify elements in the transmission path. To initiate *deceptive* spam without violating the Act, a spammer must weed out Washington residents by contacting the registrant of the domain name contained in the recipient's e-mail address. This focus on the burden of *non*compliance is contrary to the approach in the *Pike* balancing test, where the United States Supreme Court assessed the cost of compliance with a challenged statute. *Pike,* 397 U.S. at 143. Indeed, the trial court could have appropriately considered the filtering requirement a burden only if Washington's statute had banned outright the sending of UCE messages to Washington residents. We therefore conclude that Heckel has failed to prove that "the burden imposed on . . . commerce [by the Act] is *clearly excessive* in relation to the putative local benefits." *Id*. at 142 (emphasis added).

Drawing on two "unsettled and poorly understood" aspects of the dormant Commerce Clause analysis, Heckel contended that the Act (1) created inconsistency among the states and (2) regulated conduct occurring wholly outside of Washington. The inconsistent-regulations test and the extraterritoriality analysis are appropriately regarded as facets of the *Pike* balancing test. The Act survives both inquiries. At present, 17 other states have passed legislation regulating electronic solicitations. The truthfulness requirements of the Act do not conflict with any of the requirements in the other states' statutes, and it is inconceivable that any state would ever pass a law requiring spammers to use misleading subject lines or transmission paths. Some states' statutes do include additional requirements; for example, some statutes require spammers to provide contact information (for opt-out purposes) or to introduce subject lines with such labels as "ADV" or "ADV–ADLT." But because such statutes "merely create additional, but not irreconcilable, obligations," they "are not considered to be 'inconsistent' " for purposes of the dormant Commerce Clause analysis. *Instructional Sys., Inc. v. Computer Curriculum Corp.*, 35 F.3d 813, 826 (3d Cir.1994). The inquiry under the dormant Commerce Clause is not whether the states have enacted different anti-spam statutes but whether those differences create compliance costs that are "clearly excessive in relation to the putative local benefits." *Pike*, 397 U.S. at 142. We do not believe that the differences between the Act and the anti-spam laws of other states impose extraordinary costs on businesses deploying spam.

Nor does the Act violate the extraterritoriality principle in the dormant Commerce Clause analysis. Here, there is no "sweeping extraterritorial effect" that would outweigh the local benefits of the Act. *Edgar v. MITE Corp.*, 457 U.S. 624, 642 (1982). Heckel offers the hypothetical of a Washington resident who downloads and reads the deceptive spam while in Portland or Denver. He contends that the dormant Commerce Clause is offended because the Act would regulate the recipient's conduct while out of state. However, the Act does not burden interstate commerce by regulating when or where recipients may open the proscribed UCE messages. Rather, the Act addresses the conduct of spammers in targeting Washington consumers. Moreover, the hypothetical mistakenly presumes that the Act must be construed to apply to Washington residents when they are out of state, a construction that creates a jurisdictional question not at issue in this case.

In sum, we reject the trial court's conclusion that the Act violates the dormant Commerce Clause. Although the trial court found particularly persuasive *American Libraries Association v. Pataki*, 969 F. Supp. 160 (S.D.N.Y.1997), that decision—the first to apply the dormant Commerce Clause to a state law on Internet use—is distinguishable in a key respect. At issue in *American Libraries* was a New York statute that made it a crime to use a computer to distribute harmful, sexually explicit content to minors. The statute applied not just to initiation of e-mail messages but to all Internet activity, including the creation of websites. Thus, under the New York statute, a website creator in California could inadvertently violate the law simply because the site could be viewed in New York. Concerned with the statute's "chilling effect," *id.* at 179, the court observed that, if an artist "were located in California and wanted to display his work to a prospective purchaser in Oregon, he could not employ his virtual [Internet] studio to do so without risking prosecution under the New York law." 969 F. Supp. at 174. In contrast to the New York statute, which could reach all content posted on the Internet and therefore subject individuals to liability based on unintended access, the Act reaches only those deceptive UCE messages directed to a Washington resident or initiated from a computer located in Washington; in other words, the Act does not impose liability for messages that are merely routed through Washington or that are read by a Washington resident who was not the actual addressee.

. . .

EXTENSIONS

1. *Geolocation technologies.* The *Pataki* court's analysis is based in part on its premise that "[t]he nature of the Internet makes it impossible to restrict the effects of the New York Act to conduct occurring within New York . . . [since an] Internet user . . . lacks the ability to prevent New Yorkers from visiting a particular website or viewing a particular news-group posting or receiving a particular mail exploder." Geolocation technologies, which enable a website operator to ascertain the geographic location of a website visitor based on the IP address of the visitor's computer, undermine that premise at least with respect to websites. These technologies are in wider use now than when *Pataki* was decided. Companies offering geolocation services claim accuracy rates of close to 100 percent in identifying the visitor's country, and 75–80 percent in identifying the visitor's city. *See, e.g.*, Geobytes, www.geobytes.com. It is also possible, but more expensive, for a website operator to allow website access only to those visitors who have established their location by some offline means of communication, such as by telephoning from an ascertainable area code or mailing a form of identification that establishes one's residency.

2. *Judgment against Heckel.* After the *Heckel* court upheld Washington's spam statute, the enforcement action against Jason Heckel returned to the trial court. In October 2002, the court entered a $98,000 judgment against Heckel, which was affirmed on appeal. *State v. Heckel*, 93 P.3d 189 (Wash.App.2004).

3. *Other decisions mixed.* Several other courts have followed *Pataki*'s analysis to invalidate state statutes regulating the dissemination of indecent material to minors via the Internet. *See PSINet, Inc. v. Chapman*, 362 F.3d 227 (4th Cir.2004) (invalidating statute that prohibits making available, for commercial purposes, material that is harmful to juveniles); *American Booksellers Foundation v. Dean*, 342 F.3d 96 (1st Cir.2003) (invalidating statute that prohibits providing indecent material to a minor through "acts occurring outside the presence of the minor"); *ACLU v. Johnson*, 194 F.3d 1149 (10th Cir.1999) (invalidating statute that prohibits using "a computer communications system that allows the input, output, examination or transfer of computer data or computer programs from one computer to another" to send indecent material to a minor); *MaryCLE, LLC v. First Choice Internet, Inc.*, 2004 WL 2895955 (Md.Cir.Ct.2004) (invalidating state statute that regulates unsolicited commercial e-mail), *appeal pending*.

Other courts have upheld state statutes regulating Internet commerce against a Commerce Clause challenge. *See Ford Motor Co. v. Texas Dep't of Transportation*, 264 F.3d 493 (5th Cir.2001) (upholding statute that prohibits an automobile manufacturer from operating a website that offers used cars for sale); *Commonwealth v. Jaynes*, 65 Va. Cir. 355 (Va.Cir.Ct.2004) (upholding statute that regulates unsolicited commercial e-mail); *Ferguson v. Friendfinders, Inc.*, 115 Cal.Rptr.2d 258 (Cal.Ct.App.2002) (upholding statute that regulates unsolicited commercial e-mail); *Hatch v. Superior Court*, 94 Cal.Rptr.2d 453 (Cal.Ct.App.2000) (upholding statute making it illegal to provide indecent material to minors "by electronic mail, the Internet . . . or a commercial online service," and distinguishing *Pataki*).

4. *Interstate shipment of wine.* The Internet has made it much easier for consumers to purchase wine directly from wine producers. Many of these purchases are interstate. However, the growth in sales of wine via the Internet has been hampered by state laws that prohibit or tightly regulate the interstate shipment of alcoholic beverages. With the end of Prohibition in 1933, most states enacted a three-tier system to regulate the distribution of alcohol. Under this system, the manufacturer ships its product to a distributor, which is licensed to do business in the state where it is located; the distributor supplies licensed retailers; and retailers sell to consumers.

Under these three-tier systems a manufacturer of alcoholic beverages, such as a winery, is generally not allowed to sell directly to consumers: it is not permissible to skip the middlemen. Some state laws, however, allow in-state wineries to ship directly to in-state consumers, while forbidding or making it economically infeasible for out-of-state wineries to do so. In *Granholm v. Heald*, 125 S.Ct. 1885 (2005), the Supreme Court invalidated two such state laws as inconsistent with the Dormant Commerce Clause. The Court held that the laws of Michigan and New York are facially discriminatory against out-of-state wineries, and that the states had not advanced any adequate justification for the disparity in treatment. In particular, the Court rejected the states' argument that a ban on direct shipments was necessary to "keep[] alcohol out of the hands of minors. . . . Minors, the States argue, have easy access to credit cards and the Internet and are likely to take advantage of direct wine shipments as a means of obtaining alcohol illegally." The Court found there was "little evidence that the purchase of wine over the Internet by minors is a problem." The Court also held that the Twenty-First Amendment to the U.S. Constitution, which prohibits importation of alcoholic beverages into states in violation of state law, does not overcome the Commerce Clause violation.

Direct-shipment bans generally do not single out Internet commerce for special treatment, but restrict any shipment into a state no matter how the order was placed. However, Minnesota's reciprocity statute explicitly excludes direct-to-consumer sales via the Internet:

> [A] winery licensed in a state which affords Minnesota wineries an equal reciprocal shipping privilege, or a winery located in Minnesota, may ship, for personal use and not for resale, not more than two cases of wine . . . in any calendar year to any resident of Minnesota age 21 or over. . . . No person may . . . accept orders for shipments authorized by this section by use of the Internet.

MINN. STAT. § 340A.417(a), (c).

For discussion of the issues raised by direct-shipment bans from the standpoint of competition policy, see FEDERAL TRADE COMMISSION STAFF, POSSIBLE ANTICOMPETITIVE BARRIERS TO E-COMMERCE: WINE (2003), www.ftc.gov/os/2003/07/winereport2.pdf.

QUESTIONS FOR DISCUSSION

1. *Need for national regulation.* Consider the implications of the *Pataki* court's statement that "[t]he Internet . . . requires a cohesive national scheme of regulation so that users are reasonably able to determine their obligations." Does this mean that states could not enforce (1) consumer protection statutes against deceptive marketing practices transmitted via the Internet? (2) criminal conspiracy laws against conspiracies carried out online? Does it matter whether the state law is applied against a resident of the state, rather than an out-of-stater?

2. *Proposed "Jurisdictional Certainty Over Digital Commerce Act."* In 2001 a bill was introduced in Congress that would prevent states from regulating Internet commerce in digital goods. The bill defined a "digital commercial transaction" as a transaction for a good or service that is delivered or provided entirely by means of the Internet. The bill recited findings that "[s]tate regulation of . . . digital commercial transactions creates significant and harmful burdens on interstate commerce [and] will seriously impede the growth of such transactions, decreasing the viability of electronic commerce as an alternative instrument or channel of commerce." It accordingly preempted state regulation: "No State or political subdivision thereof may enact or enforce any law, rule, regulation, standard, or other provision having the force or effect of law that regulates, or has the effect of regulating, digital commercial transactions." H.R. 2421, 107th Cong. (2001). Do the problems posed by state regulation of digital commerce justify complete preemption of such regulation? Does it make sense in this context to distinguish between online transactions in *digital* goods and services and online transactions in other types of goods and services?

FURTHER READING

- Jack L. Goldsmith & Alan O. Sykes, *The Internet and the Dormant Commerce Clause*, 110 YALE L.J. 785 (2001)

IV. REGULATED INDUSTRIES ONLINE

A broad range of commercial activities have historically been subject to pervasive regulation: consider gambling, medicine, the practice of law, auctions, and telephone service. What happens when these activities move online? Should they be governed by the same regulatory scheme as applies to their offline analogues? The following materials address two types of regulated conduct: online pharmacies, and Internet telephony.

A. ONLINE PHARMACIES

In response to the escalating cost of prescription drugs in the United States, and the availability of the same drugs from Canadian sources at lower prices, several states have begun to encourage their citizens to fill their prescriptions via websites that Canadian pharmacies operate. *See, e.g.,* State of Wisconsin, *Prescription Drug Resource Center*, drugsavings.wi.gov ("Just across the border, citizens in Canada can walk into their corner drugstore and buy the same safe prescriptions we have here, but at a fraction of the price."); State of Minnesota, *Minnesota RxConnect Online*, www.state.mn.us/cgi-bin/portal/mn/jsp/home.do?agency=Rx ("This site . . . provides information about accessing lower-cost prescription medicine from Canada and the United Kingdom.").

The Food and Drug Administration has strongly opposed the practice by U.S. citizens of purchasing pharmaceuticals via foreign websites, on the ground that the safety of these sources cannot be assured. The state initiatives favoring such purchases have spawned a remarkable series of letters from the FDA to state governors, urging them to desist from encouraging their citizens to purchase prescription drugs from Canada:

DEPARTMENT OF HEALTH AND HUMAN SERVICES

Food and Drug Administration
Rockville, MD 20857

February 23, 2004

Via Fax: (312) 814-6183

The Honorable Tim Pawlenty
The Governor of Minnesota
Office of the Governor
130 State Capitol
75 Rev. Dr. Martin Luther King Jr. Blvd.
St. Paul, Minnesota 55155

Dear Governor Pawlenty:

Recently Minnesota launched a state-sponsored website called "Minnesota RXConnect." This website provides information on Canadian websites that illegally sell unapproved pharmaceuticals. We strongly believe that this state endorsement of foreign internet "pharmacies" is unsafe, unsound, and ill-considered. We appreciate the need to find safe ways to make affordable prescription drugs available to all Americans, but we urge you to reconsider your action and work with our help on legal, proven ways to provide greater access to more affordable pharmaceuticals that are assured to be safe and effective.

When you recommend to your citizens that they go outside of our regulatory system and enter into a "buyer beware" gray zone, you assist those who put profits before patient health. Your actions also shine a bright light on a path that can (and, indeed, is) used not only by profiteers masquerading as pharmacists, but by outright criminals who do not pause before actively feeding counterfeit drugs into the marketplace.

Your own taskforce has pointed out widespread, significant problems related to illegally purchasing non-FDA approved pharmaceuticals from foreign Internet pharmacies. Even Canadian pharmacies that participate in the Canadian Internet Pharmacy Association, which claims to "self-regulate" safety, were observed engaging in dangerous practices on a single voluntary, pre-announced "visit" by Minnesota State officials who have no regulatory authority over the foreign businesses. Even on these single, preannounced visits, your state officials noted dozens of safety problems, such as:

- One pharmacy had a technician, not a trained pharmacist, enter prescriptions into the pharmacy computer. This practice precluded a trained pharmacist from having an opportunity to catch any prescribing errors. . . .

- One pharmacy failed to label its products, but instead just shipped the labels unattached in the same shipping container, even when patients received multiple medications in one shipment.

- Drugs requiring refrigeration were being shipped un-refrigerated with no evidence that the products would remain stable.

- One pharmacy had no policy in place for drug recalls. Representatives of the pharmacy allegedly said that the patient could contact the pharmacy about a recall "if they wished".

- Several pharmacies failed to conduct drug utilization reviews, failed to check patient profiles for allergies, and failed to check new prescriptions to verify their accuracy.

- Several pharmacies dispensed grossly improper amounts of medications, e.g., a 250-count bottle of Lanoxin, which is far larger than is consistent with good prescribing for this medicine.

  . . .

- All of the pharmacies generally allowed customers to fax in their own prescriptions. This not only fails to assure the validity of the prescription; it means that patients can get multiple drug orders from a single prescription, including for more risky drugs.

  . . .

Many drugs obtained through at least one of the pharmacies were apparently not even of Canadian origin, and many of the drugs were obtained from a difficult-to-follow path of writing and rewriting prescriptions across multiple Canadian provinces. Also disturbing was the statement from one of the pharmacy presidents who allegedly said, "We won't have any problems getting drugs. We have creative ways to get them." Given the clear evidence of questionable sources of these prescription drugs, do you or anyone know what methods are being used and might be used in the future to obtain these drugs, let alone to assure their safety?

Most importantly, a one-time preannounced "visit" to any Internet pharmacy is no substitute for the comprehensive system for assuring the safety of the prescription drugs used by Americans. Regulatory oversight by both federal and state authorities has been proven time and again to be essential to assure the safety and effectiveness of drugs not only in the State of Minnesota, but nationwide. . . .

We are also concerned that you chose not to make public the serious concerns about the safety of international Internet pharmacy practices noted by every provincial pharmacy board in Canada. When we met with you we noted the potential tort liability that a state could be subject to if a citizen purchases an unapproved, illegal drug on your advice, and suffers an injury as a result. Your failure to warn your citizens that you have found substantial deficiencies in these foreign pharmacies may well increase your vulnerability in this area.

There are very good reasons why Health Canada (our counterpart across the border) continues to state that they cannot and will not guarantee the safety of drugs exported across the border through Internet pharmacies. Your continued support and active promotion of Minnesota ConnectRX is unwise and, most urgently, unsafe. At a minimum, your statement that you cannot assure the safety of drugs purchased from these sites seems like a questionable way to limit your own liability if and when Americans who visit these websites fail to get the quality care they deserve, or worse.

Your actions are especially concerning when there are many other safe, legal, and proven ways that the state could pursue with assistance from the Federal government to lower drug costs for Minnesotans. As we noted when we met with you, we and others in the Federal government are ready to work with you to implement these approaches for the people of Minnesota. These approaches include: promoting access to FDA-approved generic drugs, which are proven safe and effective, account for the majority of prescriptions filled in the U.S., and generally cost less than the generic drugs sold in Canada; disease management programs to help educate patients and practitioners about low cost ways to meet medical needs; and implementation of the new Medicare Drug Discount Program, which will become effective in June and will enable seniors who lack medical coverage to obtain medicines at reduced prices.

. . .

. . . We can do better than simply giving Minnesotans a foreign fax number and wishing them luck.

Sincerely,

/s/

William K. Hubbard
Associate Commissioner for Policy and
Planning

The FDA has sent similar letters to governors and other officials in the District of Columbia, North Carolina, New Hampshire, Wisconsin, and other states. *See* FDA, *Importing Prescription Drugs*, www.fda.gov/oc/opacom/hottopics/importdrugs.

In addition, the FDA has sent a number of warning letters to U.S. companies that assist U.S. citizens in purchasing prescription drugs from Canadian sources. In one such letter, the FDA spells out its legal position:

DEPARTMENT OF HEALTH AND HUMAN SERVICES

Public Health Service
Food and Drug Administration
Rockville, MD 20857

FEB 18, 2004

WARNING LETTER

<u>VIA FEDERAL EXPRESS</u>
<u>& FAX TO 1-304-366-8343</u>
Ms. Carole Becker
President
Discount Prescriptions from Canada, Inc.
709 Benoni Ave.
Fairmont, WV 26554

Dear Ms. Becker:

The Food and Drug Administration (FDA) has learned that you operate a commercial business that helps United States (U.S.) consumers to obtain prescription drugs from Canada. Specifically, you are running an operation that sends U.S. prescriptions, credit card information, and paperwork including "Customer Purchasing Agreements," "New Account Forms," "Medical History Forms," and "Physician Info Forms" to CanAmerica Drugs, Inc. (CanAm), located in Manitoba, Canada. Alternatively, you submit the same information on your customer's behalf to CanAm via its website, www.canamericadrugs.com. CanAm then arranges for a corresponding prescription from a Canadian doctor and then fills the prescription and sends the drugs directly to the U.S. consumer. As discussed in greater detail below, your actions violate the Federal Food, Drug and Cosmetic Act (Act), 21 U.S.C. §§ 301-397. Your actions also present a significant risk to public health, and you mislead the public about the safety of the drugs obtained through CanAm.

Legal Violations

Virtually every shipment of prescription drugs from Canadian pharmacies to U.S. consumers violates the Act. Even if a prescription drug is approved in the U.S., it is a violation of the Act for anyone other than its original manufacturer to import the drug back into the U.S. if that drug was originally manufactured in the United States before it was sent abroad. 21 U.S.C. § 381(d)(1). Moreover, drugs shipped into the U.S. from Canadian pharmacies are generally unapproved (21 U.S.C. § 355), labeled incorrectly (21 U.S.C. § 352), and/or dispensed without a valid prescription (21 U.S.C. § 353(b)(1)). Thus, their shipment into the U.S. from

Canada violates the Act. See, e.g., 21 U.S.C. § 331(a), (d), (t).

Canadian and other foreign versions of FDA-approved drugs are generally considered unapproved in the United States because FDA approvals are manufacturer-specific, product-specific, and include many requirements relating to the product, such as manufacturing location, formulation, source and specifications of active ingredients, processing methods, manufacturing controls, container/closure system, and appearance. 21 C.F.R. § 314.50. Frequently, drugs sold outside of the United States are not manufactured by a firm that has FDA approval for that drug. Moreover, even if the manufacturer has FDA approval, the version produced for foreign markets usually does not meet all of the requirements of the U.S. approval, and thus it is unapproved in this country. 21 U.S.C. § 355.

In order to ensure compliance with the Act when they ship prescription drugs to U.S. consumers, businesses and individuals must ensure, among other things, that the drugs sold: (1) are FDA-approved; (2) if manufactured in the U.S., are imported only by the manufacturer; and (3) comply with the applicable FDA approval in all respects, including manufacturing location, formulation, source and specifications of active ingredients, processing methods, manufacturing controls, container/closure system, and appearance. 21 C.F.R. § 314.50. They must also ensure that each drug meets all U.S. labeling requirements. 21 U.S.C. § 352. The drug must also be dispensed by a pharmacist pursuant to a valid prescription. 21 U.S.C. § 353(b)(1).

It is extremely unlikely that any pharmacy located in Canada could ensure that all of the applicable legal requirements are met. Consequently, almost every time that an individual or business ships a prescription drug from Canada, the individual or business violates the Act. Moreover, individuals and businesses, such as Discount Prescriptions from Canada, Inc. and its responsible personnel, that cause those shipments also violate the Act. 21 U.S.C. § 331 ("The following acts and the causing thereof are hereby prohibited").

You state and CanAm states on the web site www.canamericadrugs.com that a U.S. consumer can legally import as much as a 90-day supply of a prescription drug. This is misleading. FDA's Personal Importation Policy is our statement of enforcement policy and it assists the Agency in exercising its enforcement discretion with respect to imports by individuals of drugs for their personal use. Under certain defined circumstances, as a matter of enforcement discretion, FDA allows consumers to import otherwise illegal drugs. Under this policy, FDA may permit individuals and their physicians to bring into the United States small quantities of drugs sold abroad for a patient's treatment of a serious condition for which effective treatment may not be available domestically. FDA has followed this approach with products that do not present an unreasonable risk and for which there is no known commercialization and promotion to U.S. residents. See FDA Regulatory Procedures Manual, Chapter 9, Subchapter: Coverage of Personal Importations.

However, the Personal Importation Policy is not intended to allow importation of drugs which are commercialized and promoted to U.S. residents by operations such as yours. The Policy is also not intended to apply to foreign versions of U.S.

approved drugs. Finally, while the Personal Importation Policy describes the Agency's enforcement priorities, it does not change the law.

<u>FDA's Public Health Concerns and Your Misleading Statements about Drug Safety</u>

Your store-front operation and the CanAm website mislead U.S. consumers to believe that drugs from Canada are as safe as domestically dispensed prescription drugs. You tell your customers: "the prescription drugs from Canada are identical to the prescription I would get filled at my local pharmacy except that they are packaged differently in blister packaging. That is the only difference from the approved U.S. version." That is a false and misleading statement. Prescription drugs purchased from foreign countries generally are not FDA-approved, do not meet FDA standards, and are not the same as the drugs purchased in the United States. Drugs from foreign countries do not have the same assurance of safety as drugs actually regulated by the FDA. Because drugs from foreign countries have been manufactured, shipped, held and/or repackaged outside of FDA's safety oversight, they could be outdated, contaminated, counterfeit or contain too much or too little of the active ingredient. In addition, foreign dispensers of drugs to Americans may provide patients with incorrect medications, incorrect strengths, medicines that should not be used in people with certain conditions or with other medications, or medications without proper directions for use. These risks are exacerbated by the fact that many of the products that you are soliciting U.S. consumers to buy are indicated for serious medical conditions.

. . .

<u>Action Needed</u>

This letter is not intended to identify all of the ways in which your activities violate United States law. It is your responsibility to ensure that you are in compliance with applicable legal requirements.

Please notify this office in writing within fifteen working days of your receipt of this letter of the specific steps that you will take to assure that your operations are in full compliance with United States law. . . . If you do not promptly correct your violations, FDA may take legal action without further notice. Possible actions include seizure and/or injunction. Further, federal agencies are advised of the issuance of all Warning Letters about drugs so that they may take this information into account when considering the award of contracts.

> Sincerely,
>
> /s/
>
> David J. Horowitz, Esq.
> Director
> Office of Compliance
> Center for Drug Evaluation and Research
> Food and Drug Administration

Why do prescription drugs cost so much less in Canada (and other developed countries) than in the United States? Drug pricing is an extremely complex matter, dependent on many factors including the structure of each nation's health-care system, but for present purposes it is enough to say that drug manufacturers charge more in the U.S. market because they can. Economists refer to this strategy as price discrimination: selling a given item at different prices to different customers. The aim of price discrimination is to maximize the seller's profits by selling the item at a higher price to purchasers who are willing to pay that price, and selling it at a lower price to purchasers who are not willing to pay more. A drug manufacturer that follows this strategy will charge a higher price for a particular product when selling to the U.S. market than when selling to the Canadian market.

To make price discrimination work, the seller must be able to prevent arbitrage, which occurs when a customer buys the item in a low-price market, and resells it for a profit in a high-price market. If there is large-scale arbitrage, the seller cannot maintain differential selling prices, as arbitrageurs undercut the seller in the high-price markets. The Internet has greatly facilitated arbitrage in the market for prescription drugs, enabling Canadian distributors to purchase drugs from the manufacturers at low prices and resell them to customers in the United States at prices that yield them a profit while still undercutting distributors in the United States.

One would therefore expect the drug manufacturers to have a strong interest in preventing sales of their products between low-price and high-price markets. The manufacturers have in fact taken action to protect their interests, refusing to sell their products to Canadian distributors who are known to resell to customers in the United States via Internet commerce. Some online sellers have responded by seeking indirect sources of drugs in Europe. *See* Angela Zimm & John Lauerman, *U.S. Drugmakers Have New Foe: Europe*, MONTREAL GAZETTE, Apr. 2, 2005, at B18.

EXTENSIONS

FDA enforcement action. In *U.S. v. Rx Depot, Inc.*, 290 F.Supp.2d 1238 (N.D. Okla.2003), the FDA sued a Nevada company that helped U.S. residents to obtain prescription drugs from Canada. Company employees, operating out of 85 storefronts throughout the United States, would fax the customer's prescription and credit card information to a cooperating pharmacy located in Canada. A Canadian doctor would rewrite the prescription, and the pharmacy would ship the drugs directly to the customer. The court entered a preliminary injunction, holding that the defendant's actions violated several provisions of the FDA Act. In particular, the court found that the defendant violated 21 U.S.C. § 331(d) by furnishing an unapproved new drug, namely a generic version of an FDA-approved drug, and violated § 381(d)(1) by reimporting from Canada an FDA-approved drug manufactured in the United States. The action was resolved through entry of a consent order.

FURTHER READING

- *Prescription Drugs: The Facts About Canada*, CONSUMER REPORTS, Oct. 2005, at 50 (advising that drugs from Canada are safe, and that brand-name drugs from Canada are often cheaper but generic drugs more expensive than their U.S. counterparts)

- David M. Smith, Note, *Consumer Protection or Veiled Protectionism? An Overview of Recent Challenges to State Restrictions on E-Commerce*, 15 LOY. CONSUMER L. REV. 359 (2003) (discussing state regulation of Internet commerce involving replacement contact lenses, funeral caskets, auctions, and wine sales)

B. INTERNET TELEPHONY

Traditional telephone services use the public switched telephone network ("PSTN"), which is based on a circuit-switching technology that reserves specific communications resources for the duration of a phone call. In the past few years, several services have emerged that allow users to engage in real-time voice communications over the Internet. This new technology is called voice over Internet Protocol ("VoIP"), or Internet telephony. Unlike traditional calls routed over the PSTN, calls made using VoIP travel at least part of their route in the form of packets of information, using the same packet-switching technology that routes all types of data over the Internet. VoIP offers certain efficiency advantages over the PSTN, since the latter requires a dedicated circuit for the duration of the call, even during breaks in the conversation, while the former consumes resources only when conversation is being transmitted.

A subscriber to a VoIP service can communicate with others in three ways: from one computer (which may be a dedicated telephone-like instrument) to another computer; from one phone to another phone; or from a computer to a phone or vice-versa. In a computer-to-computer call, the conversation travels the whole route in the form of data packets. In a phone-to-phone or a phone-to-computer call, the conversation is converted as necessary between the circuit-switched format used on the PSTN, and the packet-switched format used on the Internet. Thus, a portion of the communication path involves one or both users' local exchange carrier ("LEC").

Several types of regulation apply to telephone services. The Federal Communications Commission, acting under authority granted by the Communications Act of 1934, 47 U.S.C. §§ 151–615, regulates various aspects of telecommunications, such as the access charges that long distance companies must pay to LECs for using their facilities to complete calls. In addition, states (through their Public Service Commissions or Public Utilities Commissions) impose their own regulations on telecommunications services, such as required payment of fees to support 911 emergency services.

An unresolved issue is the extent to which state and federal regulation of the PSTN is applicable to VoIP services. The regulation of a communications service depends largely on whether it is classified as a "telecommunications service" or an "information service." If the former, it may be regulated both by the FCC and by state Public Service Commissions. If the latter, it is only subject to a limited form of federal regulation; state regulation is pre-empted.[5] An "information service" is one that gives a user the "capability for generating, acquiring, storing, transforming, processing, retrieving, utilizing, or making available information via telecommunications." 47 U.S.C. § 153(20). A "telecommunications service" is one that transmits information between points "without change in the form or content of the information as sent and received." *Id.* § 153(43), 153(46). A key regulatory issue is whether a VoIP service is an "information service" by virtue of its translation of communications between circuit-switched and packet-switched formats.

The FCC is at this writing engaged in a rulemaking aimed at determining how VoIP should be regulated. *See In re IP-Enabled Services*, F.C.C. 04-28, W.C. Docket No. 04-36

---

[5] *See, e.g., California v. Federal Communications Commission*, 39 F.3d 919, 931–33 (9th Cir.1994), which upholds an FCC decision preempting state regulation of "enhanced services." Since passage of the Telecommunications Act of 1996, "enhanced services" are referred to as "information services."

(2004), hraunfoss.fcc.gov/edocs_public/attachmatch/FCC-04-28A1.pdf. Some of the issues to be resolved include the classification of VoIP services; jurisdictional limits on the FCC's authority; 911 regulations for VoIP services; and the applicability to VoIP of the Communications Assistance for Law Enforcement Act, 47 U.S.C. §§ 1001–21 (which requires telecommunications carriers to ensure their services are capable of surveillance by law enforcement agencies).

In the meantime, the FCC has, through declaratory rulings,[6] stated its present opinion on the regulatory status of certain types of VoIP services. For example, the FCC has determined that a computer-to-computer VoIP service offered by pulver.com, known as Free World Dialup ("FWD"), is an "information service," and not a "telecommunications service," since it is the user's Internet service provider, not FWD, that actually transmits the communication. *See In re Petition for Declaratory Ruling that pulver.com's Free World Dialup is Neither Telecommunications Nor a Telecommunications Service*, F.C.C. 04-27, W.C. Docket No. 03-45, (2004),   hraunfoss.fcc.gov/edocs_public/attachmatch/FCC-04-27A1.pdf. On the other hand, the FCC determined that a phone-to-phone VoIP service offered by AT&T is a telecommunications service, and is therefore subject to interstate access charges. The FCC reasoned that AT&T's service is functionally equivalent to connecting two callers using the PSTN: users "obtain only voice transmission with no net protocol conversion, rather than information services such as access to stored files." *See In re Petition for Declaratory Ruling that AT&T's Phone-to-Phone IP Telephony Services are Exempt from Access Charges*, F.C.C. 04-97, W.C. Docket No. 02-361, at ¶ 12 (2004), hraunfoss.fcc.gov/edocs_public/attachmatch/FCC-04-97A1.pdf. The FCC noted, however, that its determination should be viewed as provisional, pending the outcome of its current rulemaking proceeding.

While the content of federal regulation of VoIP service is yet to be determined, the FCC has held that state regulation is generally preempted by the federal regulatory scheme. In 2003, the Minnesota Public Utilities Commission issued an order applying the state telephone regulations to Vonage's DigitalVoice VoIP service. Among other things, the state regulations required Vonage to obtain a certificate of authority to provide telephone service, file a tariff, and enable 911 emergency service calls. Vonage filed suit in federal court, seeking an injunction against enforcement of the PUC order. The district court held that Vonage's service is an "information service" and therefore, under the federal Communications Act, not subject to regulation. Since the PUC order conflicted with this congressional policy, it was preempted. *Vonage Holdings Corp. v. Minnesota Pub. Utilities Comm'n*, 290 F.Supp.2d 993 (D.Minn.2003). Vonage also petitioned the FCC for a declaratory ruling, and the FCC likewise determined that the PUC order was preempted, though without reaching the question whether VoIP was an "information service." The FCC reasoned that because the interstate and intrastate aspects of Vonage's service are inextricably intertwined, the entire service is exclusively within federal jurisdiction. In its ruling the FCC left undecided whether federal preemption permitted Minnesota to apply to Vonage its "general laws governing entities conducting business within the state, such as laws concerning taxation; fraud; general commercial dealings; and marketing, advertising, and other business practices." *In re Vonage Holdings Corporation Petition for Declaratory Ruling Concerning an Order of the Minnesota Public Utilities Commission*, F.C.C. 04-267, WC Docket No. 03-

---

[6] The FCC may release a "declaratory ruling" to clarify an issue under its jurisdiction. 47 C.F.R. § 1.2; 5 U.S.C. § 554.

211 (2004), hraunfoss.fcc.gov/edocs_public/attachmatch/FCC-04-267A1.pdf.

The FCC filled part of the vacuum created by its preemption of the Minnesota PUC order by issuing its own order requiring VoIP providers to implement systems for routing 911 calls to the emergency services agency. The FCC noted that there have been reports of instances in which VoIP subscribers found themselves in emergency situations with no ability to reach the 911 operator. Considering this an untenable situation, the order requires compliance within 120 days, acknowledging that this is "an aggressively short amount of time" for compliance given the need to develop the requisite technology. *In re E911 Requirements for IP-Enabled Service Providers*, F.C.C. 05-116, WC Docket No. 05-196 (2005), hraunfoss.fcc.gov/edocs_public/attachmatch/FCC-05-116A1.pdf.

CHAPTER TWO
PROTECTING COMMERCIAL IDENTITY ONLINE: TRADEMARKS

In the world of bricks and mortar, it is widely held that the success of a retail establishment is highly dependent on its physical location. In the virtual world of electronic commerce, by contrast, physical location is almost irrelevant. From the standpoint of access by potential customers, it matters very little whether a company's web server is located in New York, Paris, Hong Kong or some remote region of Siberia. On the Web, every store is as close as the nearest network access device—whether it be a desktop computer, a laptop, a personal digital assistant, a television with a set-top box or a Web-enabled cell phone. Only when e-commerce must rely upon the traditional commercial infrastructure of brick-and-mortar companies does location matter. If I buy a television from an e-commerce website, the cost of that television and the time required for its delivery to my home will depend in part on the distance of that company's distribution center from my house. By contrast, for transactions involving information goods such as software, music and other digital products that can be delivered as well as purchased online, the physical location of the company does not matter to the consumer, though it may matter to taxing and regulatory authorities.

If physical location is not an essential predicate to commercial success online, what is? While there is no consensus answer to this question, many observers believe that developing and protecting one's commercial identity is critical. A strong brand seamlessly integrated into the search and navigation technologies with which consumers identify and connect to e-commerce websites is as important online as physical location is offline.

Brand identities serve an efficiency-enhancing role by reducing the costs that consumers incur locating goods and services that meet their needs. A brand identity reduces consumer search costs by conveying important information to consumers, at a very low cost. Within a product category, a strong brand signifies that the item it marks originates from a particular company, has a known level of quality, and enjoys a specific array of product features and characteristics. Such information is important for making informed and rational choices in the marketplace.

Branding is even more important in the online commercial environment than it has been in the world of bricks and mortar. In the offline world, consumers might become physically familiar with a store they frequent, might come to know the employees personally, might even live in the same neighborhood with them. In the online world, branding is the main thing consumers have to go on in deciding whether to trust a company or its product. Moreover, in the offline world, if a product is unsatisfactory, a consumer may have some confidence that it can be exchanged if there is a known physical store the consumer can return to, but trying to fix transactions that have gone wrong becomes more uncertain in the online environment, because electronic presence seems much more shadowy and ephemeral. Brand X website might fail to deliver a satisfactory product, and might be here today and gone tomorrow.

For these reasons, trademark law is one of the most important areas of law for Internet commerce, and the advent of Internet commerce has seen significant developments in trademark law. Perhaps the most significant of these developments is the creation of an entirely new form of intangible asset, the Internet domain name, and the disputes that have arisen over who owns and controls this asset. Among the most significant features of the most popular domain names, giving rise to difficult governance questions, are their uniqueness and international scope—even if many companies around the world have the same corporate name, there is only one dot-com for that name. We will take up the issues surrounding domain names in Chapter 3.

Meanwhile, in this chapter we explore how established trademark law applies to online businesses and their efforts to protect their brands, in two different ways. Traditional trademark law is based on the danger of confusing consumers about the source and quality of the product they are buying. Contemporary trademark protection has, in the case of powerful, well-established, "famous" brands, provided additional protection in the form of actions for trademark dilution. Dilution does not turn on consumer confusion, so it establishes much broader exclusion rights for those brands that can make use of it.

In this chapter we also explore the limits of trademark protection; that is, the balance between the exclusion rights afforded to the brand owner and the needs of competitors or the general public to use the words or images that constitute or are similar to the trademark. For example, generic words for a product cannot be trademarks because competitors need to use the word to describe their own products. "Computer" cannot be the trademark for a computer product. In fact, if a trademark becomes so popular that it becomes a generic word for the product—"aspirin" is one example—trademark protection ceases. In addition to economic issues of the scope that must be afforded to competitors, free speech issues also arise. For example, can a company use trademark law to quash a parody site like chasemanhattansucks.com?

I. INTRODUCTION: TRADEMARK BASICS

A trademark is "a word, name, symbol, device, or other designation . . . that is distinctive of a person's goods or services and that is used in a manner that identifies those goods or services and distinguishes them from the goods or services of others." RESTATEMENT (THIRD) OF UNFAIR COMPETITION § 9 (1995). In addition to words and names, such designations may include, *inter alia*, numbers, letters, slogans, pictures, characters, sounds, graphic designs, and product and packaging features.

Trademarks are protectible under both state and federal law. While trademarks were originally a creature of the common law, and common-law trademarks still exist, Congress and state legislatures have enacted statutes providing for their registration and protection. At common law and under these statutes, the trademark owner has, subject to certain limitations, the exclusive right to use the protected mark in commerce.

> The purpose underlying any trade-mark statute is twofold. One is to protect the public so that it may be confident that, in purchasing a product bearing a particular trade-mark which it favorably knows, it will get the product which it asks for and wants to get. Secondly, where the owner of a trade-mark has spent energy, time, and money in presenting to the public the product, he is protected in his investment from its misappropriation by pirates and cheats.

Id. § 9 (Reporter's Notes, cmt. c) (quoting S. REP. NO. 79–1333, at 3 (1946)).

To qualify for protection, a word, name or other designation must (1) be distinctive, (2) be used in commerce, (3) be affixed or otherwise associated with goods and services, and (4) signify the source or origin of those goods and services with which it is associated.

As to the first criterion, distinctiveness, marks may be either inherently distinctive, or may acquire distinctiveness through their use in commerce. Courts refer to inherently distinctive marks as *arbitrary, fanciful* or *suggestive*. EXXON is a fanciful mark, while APPLE, when applied to computers, is an arbitrary mark. The use of fanciful or arbitrary marks in connection with the goods and services with which they are associated has no meaning or significance other than as a trademark. Suggestive marks, in contrast, suggest some attribute or characteristic of the goods and services with which they are associated. For example, THE MONEY STORE suggests that the company with which it is associated provides money lending services. Similarly, EVERREADY when applied to batteries suggests that the batteries will have a long life.

Other marks, while not inherently distinctive, may acquire distinctiveness through their use in commerce. Courts call these marks *descriptive*. Descriptive marks are so called because they purport to describe some attribute or characteristic of the goods and services with which they are associated. For example, TENDER VITTLES applied to cat food suggests that the product has a certain desirable consistency. A descriptive mark that acquires distinctiveness is said to have "secondary meaning," and it is only the "secondary meaning" that is protected, not the term's primary meaning in ordinary language:

> There are but a limited number of words and images suitable for use in describing a product, and sellers own neither the English language nor common depictions of goods. . . . If descriptive words and pictures could be appropriated without evidence of a secondary meaning, sellers could snatch for themselves the riches of the language and make it more difficult for new entrants to identify their own products; consumers would be worse off.

Scandia Down Corp. v. Euroquilt, Inc., 772 F.2d 1423, 1430 (7th Cir.1985).

A word, name, symbol or other designation that is generic is not protectible as a trademark. For example, APPLE, when applied to apples, is not protectible, and neither is SHREDDED WHEAT when applied to small edible "pillows" of shredded wheat. While a generic term can never become a trademark, a protectible trademark may lose its protection if it becomes generic. This process is sometimes called "genericide." THERMOS, ASPIRIN and DRY ICE are examples of marks that lost their protection in this fashion. The potential loss of trademark protection through genericide explains why employees of 3M and Xerox always say, respectively, "clear cellophane tape" instead of "scotch tape" and "photocopies" instead of "xeroxes." Since the use of a generic term is not protected under the law of trademark, if a term is or becomes generic, anyone can use it.

Generally, the owner of a protectible mark is the person or entity that first adopts and uses that mark in commerce. For this reason, the trademark owner is sometimes called the senior user of the mark. Anyone who subsequently uses the same or a confusingly similar mark is referred to as a junior user. Senior users have priority of use, and therefore priority of right, over junior users. Since the effective date of the Trademark Revision Act of 1988, one can establish priority of use for inherently distinctive marks that one has not yet used in commerce by filing an intent-to-use application to obtain a federal trademark registration. *See* Lanham Act § 1(b), 15 U.S.C. § 1051(b). Under this application process, the registrant must actually adopt and use the mark in commerce within six months, a period which the U.S. Patent and Trademark Office ("PTO") may extend for six month periods, up to three years. *See id.* § 1051(d).

The senior user of a protectible mark may significantly increase its level of protection by registering that trademark on the Principal Register of the PTO. There are two application procedures through which one can request registration of a trademark: a use-based application pursuant to 15 U.S.C. § 1051(a) (under which the applicant must specify the date it first used the mark and the date it first used the mark in commerce, and the goods in connection with which the mark is used), and an intent-to-use application pursuant to 15 U.S.C. § 1051(b) (under which the applicant must specify the goods in connection with which the applicant has a bona fide intention to use the mark). Both types of applicants must specify the class of goods and services in connection with which the mark will be used, and must provide an actual specimen of such good.

PTO Trademark Examining Attorneys review applications to determine whether they satisfy statutory requirements and whether they are subject to any of the statutory bars set forth in 15 U.S.C. § 1052(a)–(e). These provisions of the Lanham Act prohibit the registration of marks that comprise or consist of, *inter alia*, (a) immoral, deceptive or scandalous matter, (b) the flag or coat of arms or other insignia of the United States, or any state, municipality, or foreign country, (c) the name, portrait or signature of a living person without that person's consent, (d) a word, name or other designation that is confusingly similar to another mark already registered, or (e) matter that applied to the applicant's goods is merely descriptive, deceptively misdescriptive, primarily geographically descriptive (unless it is a mark indicating regional origin such as "Made in America"), primarily geographically deceptively misdescriptive, primarily a surname, or primarily functional. If the Examining Attorney determines that the application is barred under one of these provisions, he or she will then determine whether the claimed mark has acquired secondary meaning and may nevertheless be registered under exceptions to the statutory bar set forth in 15 U.S.C. § 1052(f). If the application satisfies statutory requirements for registration, it is published in the Official Gazette of the PTO.[1] Upon publication, anyone who believes that he or she would be damaged by the registration may file an opposition. If all opposition proceedings are resolved in the applicant's favor, then a certificate of registration will be issued. Adverse determinations by the Examining Attorney may be appealed to the Trademark Trial and Appeals Board and then to the Court of Appeals for the Federal Circuit.

Federal registration of a trademark on the Principal Register confers substantial benefits on the trademark owner. The trademark owner may bring actions for trademark infringement in federal court, *id.* § 1121(a), and may recover damages, *id.* § 1117(a)–(c). In any legal proceeding, the trademark owner's registration is "prima facie evidence of the validity of the registered mark and of the registration of the mark, of the registrant's ownership of the mark, and of the registrant's exclusive right to use the registered mark in commerce on or in connection with the goods or services specified in the registration subject to any conditions or limitations stated therein." *Id.* § 1115(a). Moreover, under the incontestability provision of the Lanham Act, after five years the registration becomes conclusive evidence of those matters. *Id.* § 1115(c). Finally, the defenses that a junior user can raise against a trademark owner with a federal registration are significantly reduced. *Id.* § 1115(b).

---

[1] Sometimes a claimed mark will comprise both registrable and unregistrable matter. In such cases, the applicant may be required to disclaim any federal trademark rights in the unregistrable matter before the Examining Attorney will approve the application for publication in the Official Gazette. 15 U.S.C. § 1056.

Descriptive marks that have not yet acquired secondary meaning may not be registered on the Principal Register but may be placed on the Supplemental Register. Once they acquire secondary meaning they may then be registered on the Principal Register. While not conferring as many benefits as the Principal Register, registration on the Supplemental Register nonetheless provides some advantages. For example, it allows the trademark owner to bring an action for infringement in federal court, prevents the registration of other marks that may cause confusion, permits registration abroad based on the United States registration, gives notice of use to all those who perform trademark searches, and permits the trademark owner to use the ® symbol. *See generally id.* §§ 1091–96.

Trademarks that are deemed "famous" are also entitled, under federal law and the law of many states, to protection against dilution. The Federal Trademark Dilution Act of 1995 defines "dilution" as "the lessening of the capacity of a famous mark to identify and distinguish goods or services, regardless of the presence or absence of (1) competition between the owner of the famous mark and other parties, or (2) likelihood of confusion, mistake, or deception." *Id.* § 1127. Trademark dilution can occur even when there is no infringement— that is, there is no likelihood of confusion between the diluting mark and the trademark being diluted.

Registration of a trademark with the PTO or use in commerce in the United States confers protection against infringing use only in the United States. Because there is no international registration regime, a trademark owner that wants to protect its mark must register the mark in every country where it does business. Many countries allow registration of a mark before the owner has made any use of it. This has resulted in situations where trademark owners in one country had to buy rights to marks in other countries they wanted to enter from registrants who anticipated them.

From the foregoing discussion of trademark law, we may discern a tripartite framework in which to consider the possible commercial exploitation of trademarks and other symbols, words and names. If a term is generic, then one may freely use it. No one may claim an exclusive right to use a generic term, word or symbol. If, however, a term is distinctive— inherently or because it has acquired secondary meaning—and has been used as a trademark, then one may not use in commerce or otherwise commercially exploit that mark or any other possible mark that is confusingly similar to it. Finally, if a mark has become famous from its use as a trademark, then one may not use in commerce or otherwise commercially exploit any other mark that would dilute the famous mark even if there is no likelihood of confusion between the famous mark and the possible diluting mark. The laws barring the commercial use of infringing and diluting marks are not absolute and some uses are permitted as exceptions to these rules. These exceptions are characterized as affirmative defenses that may be raised in actions for trademark infringement and trademark dilution.

The organization of the present chapter conforms to the structure of this general framework. In Part II of this chapter, we consider traditional trademark infringement. In Part III, we focus on trademark dilution. Finally, in Part IV we consider various defenses that have been raised in actions for trademark infringement and dilution online.

II. Traditional Trademark Infringement: The Requirement of Consumer Confusion

A. Infringement Resulting from Traditional Confusion

As Oliver Wendell Holmes noted in 1890, the law of trademarks was created "to prevent one man from palming off his goods as another's, from getting another's business or injuring his reputation by unfair means and, perhaps, from defrauding the public." *Chadwick v. Covell*, 23 N.E. 1068, 1069 (Mass.1890). The law of trademarks may therefore be viewed as a branch of unfair competition law. As the First Circuit has observed, the law of unfair competition comprises a "broad class of business torts of which trademark infringement is one species." *Keebler Co. v. Rovira Biscuit Corp.*, 624 F.2d 366 (1st Cir.1980).

In a typical trademark infringement lawsuit, the senior user of a mark sues a junior user of the same or similar mark, alleging that consumers are likely to confuse the senior user's goods and services with those of the junior user. *See, e.g.,* Lanham Act § 32(1), 15 U.S.C. § 1114(1). "When comparing marks to determine the likelihood of consumer confusion, 'the correct test is whether a consumer who is somewhat familiar with the plaintiff's mark would likely be confused when presented with defendant's mark alone.' " *Clinique Laboratories, Inc. v. Dep Corp.*, 945 F.Supp. 547, 552 (S.D.N.Y.1996). Usually, the alleged consumer confusion concerns the source or origin of the goods or services in question. Equally actionable, however, is consumer confusion about whether there is an affiliation, relation of sponsorship or other connection between the senior and junior users of the mark. *See, e.g.,* Lanham Act § 43(a), 15 U.S.C. § 1125(a).

The following cases highlight the fact that infringing uses of a trademark are possible online as well as off.

Playboy Enterprises, Inc. v. Universal Tel-A-Talk, Inc.
1998 WL 767440 (E.D.Pa.1998).

■ McGlynn, District Judge.

Plaintiff, Playboy Enterprises, Inc. ("PEI") filed this action on October 2, 1996, alleging trademark infringement and related causes of action under the Lanham Act, 15 U.S.C. §§ 1114–1125 and Pennsylvania's anti-dilution law, 54 Pa.C.S.A. § 1124, et seq. at defendant's web site "adult-sex.com/playboy." The Court entered a temporary restraining order and later a consent decree enjoining the defendants use of PEI's trademarks. Thereafter, the complaint was amended to include a counterfeiting claim under 15 U.S.C. § 1116(d). . . .

FINDINGS OF FACT

, 1. Plaintiff Playboy Enterprises, Inc. (PEI), is a Delaware corporation having offices at 730 Fifth Avenue, New York, New York and a principal place of business in Chicago, Illinois.

2. Defendant Universal Tel–A–Talk, Inc. is a Pennsylvania corporation having a principal place of business in Philadelphia, Pennsylvania. Defendant Stanley Huberman is the president and sole shareholder.

3. Defendant Adult Discount Toys is a business entity having a principal place of business in Philadelphia, Pennsylvania and is owned by defendant Stanley Huberman.

. . .

5. Since 1953, PEI has published *Playboy* magazine. *Playboy* magazine is read by approximately 10 million readers each month and is published worldwide in 16 international editions.

6. *Playboy* magazine is known for its display of erotic and provocative pictorials of PEI models and adult entertainment material.

7. PEI and its licensees have sold a wide variety of merchandise; such as, wearing apparel, cosmetics, sunglasses, watches and other personal accessories under the trademark PLAYBOY, in interstate commerce, including the Commonwealth of Pennsylvania.

8. PEI is the owner of a number of U.S. trademark registrations for the mark PLAYBOY. . . .

9. Over the years, PEI has sold merchandise bearing the PLAYBOY trademark. Through its licenses, products bearing the PLAYBOY trademark are sold throughout the United States and in more than 50 countries around the world. PEI and its licensees have and continue to spend considerable time and money promoting the PLAYBOY trademark. As a result of PEI's longstanding use of the PLAYBOY trademark, the PLAYBOY trademark has become well known and has developed a secondary meaning, such that the public has come to associate it with PEI.

10. In addition to the PLAYBOY trademark, PEI also utilizes a Rabbit Head Design trademark (hereafter the "RABBIT HEAD DESIGN") in connection with *Playboy* magazine and a wide variety of goods sold by PEI and/or its licensees. Since 1954, PEI has used the RABBIT HEAD DESIGN mark in connection with *Playboy* magazine. The RABBIT HEAD DESIGN mark traditionally appears in the masthead of *Playboy* magazine. PEI has also used the RABBIT HEAD DESIGN in connection with a wide variety of merchandise and services.

11. PEI also owns a number of U.S. trademark registrations for the RABBIT HEAD DESIGN mark . . . .

12. In addition to the PLAYBOY trademarks and RABBIT HEAD DESIGN, the mark "BUNNY" has been registered by PEI with the United States Patent and Trademark Office.

. . .

14. Over the years, PEI has sold merchandise bearing the RABBIT HEAD DESIGN mark. Through its licensees, products bearing the RABBIT HEAD DESIGN mark are sold throughout the United States and in more than 50 countries around the world. Products bearing the RABBIT HEAD DESIGN mark are available

worldwide by mail order catalog and through PLAYBOY specialty boutiques, department stores, art galleries and museum shops. PEI and its licensees have spent considerable time and money promoting products bearing the RABBIT HEAD DESIGN mark nationwide and throughout the world. As a result of PEI's long-standing use of the RABBIT HEAD DESIGN mark, the RABBIT HEAD DESIGN mark has become famous and has developed significant goodwill and secondary meaning, such that the public has come to associate it exclusively with PEI.

15. As a result of PEI's use and promotion of the RABBIT HEAD DESIGN mark, the mark BUNNY has also become associated with PEI in connection with adult entertainment services. Indeed, the RABBIT HEAD DESIGN trademark is commonly referred to by the public as the "Playboy Bunny."

16. The Internet is an international computer "super-network" of over 15,000 computer networks which is used by 30 million or more individuals, corporations, organization and educational institutions worldwide. Users of the Internet can access each others computers, can communicate directly with each other (by means of electronic mail or "e-mail"), and can access various types of data and information. Each Internet user has an address, consisting of one or more address components, which address is otherwise commonly referred to within the Internet as a "domain" or "domain name."

17. Domain names serve as an address for sending and receiving e-mail and for posting information or providing other services. On the Internet, a domain name serves as the primary identifier of the source of information, products or services. It is common practice for companies to form Internet domain names by combining their trade name or one of their famous trademarks as a prefix and their business category as a suffix. The suffix ".com" (usually pronounced "dot com") identifies a service provider as commercial in nature.

18. The domain name is one component of the "Uniform Resource Locator" ("URL"). The URL may also include root directories and subdirectories which serve as a guide to the contents of a website.

19. In August, 1994, PEI launched www.playboy.com on the Internet on the World Wide Web. The website currently receives approximately six million "hits" a day. The trademark www.playboy.com offers access to some of PEI's copyrighted images and other contents from *Playboy* magazine and other PEI publications. www.playboy.com has also been registered with the U.S. Patent and Trademark Office.

20. PEI also operates cyber.playboy.com, a subscription and pay per visit website (the "PLAYBOY CYBER CLUB") which allows members access to individual PLAYMATE home pages, video clips from PLAYMATE home pages, video clips from PLAYBOY home video and PLAYBOY TV and contents of *Playboy* magazine.

21. Both www.playboy.com and cyber.playboy.com are used by PEI to promote subscriptions to its monthly *Playboy* magazine, to display erotic pictorials of PEI models, and to advertise and sell PEI's merchandise and other services under PEI's trademarks. PEI's websites prominently feature the PEI trademarks PLAYBOY and RABBIT HEAD DESIGN, as well as photographs, articles of interest, PEI merchan-

dise, videos and subscription information for *Playboy* magazine. PEI's Website contains electronic versions of *Playboy* magazine in that it displays the contents of *Playboy* magazine on-line. An Internet user is able to view the contents of *Playboy* magazine by visiting www.playboy.com or the PLAYBOY CYBER CLUB.

22. Defendant Universal Tel–A–Talk, Inc. created and is maintaining several Internet World Wide Web sites which may be accessed throughout the United States, including the Commonwealth of Pennsylvania.

23. On or about October 2, 1996, PEI learned that Universal–Tel–A–Talk, Inc. was using PEI's registered trademarks PLAYBOY and BUNNY in conjunction with their website to advertise on-line a collection of photographs, which both plaintiff and defendant describe as "hard core." However, neither side has defined that term, at least on this record, except as a modifier of the term sexually explicit photographs.

24. Defendant Universal Tel–A–Talk, Inc.'s website advertises and offers a subscription service called "Playboy's Private Collection" (located at www.adult-sex.com) (hereafter "Defendant's website") for a charge of $3.95 per month, which features hard core photographs. The PLAYBOY trademark is prominently featured in defendants' website. Defendants also used the term "Bunny" on the navigational bar of the introductory page of the defendants' website. The navigational bar serves as a table of contents and appears on the bottom of the introductory screens and web pages. When a user clicks onto one of six "Bunny" segments of the navigational bar on the introductory page, the user becomes connected to another level of hard core on-line services offered by Defendants.

25. A subscriber to defendants' "Playboy's Private Collection" service is greeted by a "home page" which is the equivalent of the cover and table of contents page of a magazine in that it displays the name of the site and a menu of information that is available for review. A subscriber to defendants' Playboy subscription service, upon assessing the URL "adult-sex.com/playboy/members" is welcomed by defendants' home page which reads: "Welcome to PLAYBOYS PRIVATE COLLECTION." Defendants' website www.adult-sex.com is an on-line collection of "hard core" photographs sold under the PLAYBOY and BUNNY trademarks and portrayed as an extension of PEI's *Playboy* magazine. Defendants' unlawful use of the PLAYBOY trademark also appears at least twice on every printed web page. "Playboys Private Collection" appears on the upper left-hand corner and the URL "adult-sex.com/playboy/members/pictures" appears at the upper right-hand corner.

26. Subscribers can "click" onto a portion of the home page which reads: "Let me see the pictures in Playboys Private Collection" and obtain a lengthy list of hard core photographs on a variety of topics which may be viewed on screen, downloaded to disk or printed.

27. Defendants also provided an electronic mail address which utilizes the PLAYBOY trademark in the text of defendants' website. The home page of defendants' service invites subscribers to "Send E-mail to Playboy@adult-sex.com."

28. Defendant has also "linked" their adult-sex website to PEI's website at "Playboy.com." A "link" is a connection of one website to another.

29. Defendants are not now and never have been authorized by PEI to use the PLAYBOY trademark or the BUNNY trademark in connection with any business or service.

. . .

DISCUSSION

. . .

PEI has alleged infringement of the PLAYBOY trademark under § 32 of the Lanham Act (Count I), § 43(a) of the Lanham Act (Count II) and the common law of the Commonwealth of Pennsylvania (Count IV). The test for infringement is the same for each count, namely, whether the alleged infringement creates a likelihood of confusion. *See Scott Paper Co. v. Scott's Liquid Gold*, 589 F.2d 1225 (3d Cir.1978).

In order to succeed on the merits, a plaintiff must establish that: "(1) the marks are valid and legally protectible; (2) the marks are owned by the plaintiff; and (3) the defendants' use of the marks to identify goods or services is likely to create confusion concerning the origin of the goods and services." *Opticians Ass'n v. Independent Opticians*, 920 F.2d 187, 192 (3d Cir.1990).

The trademark PLAYBOY has attained incontestable status pursuant to 15 U.S.C. § 1065. PEI's ownership of incontestable U.S. Registrations for the PLAYBOY trademark constitutes prima facie evidence of PEI's ownership of the PLAYBOY trademark and the validity of the mark. *Optician's Ass'n v. Independent Opticians*, 920 F.2d at 194.

In determining whether a likelihood of confusion exists, the court may take into account

(1) the degree of similarity between the owner's mark and the alleged infringing mark; (2) the strength of owner's mark; (3) the price of the goods and other factors indicative of the care and attention expected of consumers when making a purchase; (4) the length of time the defendant has used the mark without evidence of actual confusion arising; (5) the intent of the defendant in adopting the mark; (6) the evidence of actual confusion; (7) whether the goods, though not competing, are marketed through the same channels of trade and advertised through [sic] the same media; (8) the extent to which the targets of the parties' sales efforts are the same; (9) the relationship of the goods in the minds of the public because of the similarity of function; (10) other facts suggesting that the consuming public might expect the prior owner to manufacture a product in the defendant's market. *Scott Paper Co. v. Scott's Liquid Gold, supra* at 1229.

Defendants' use of the words "Playboy" and "Bunny" in their website and in the identifying directories of defendants' URL's are identical to PEI's duly registered trademarks PLAYBOY and BUNNY. PEI's registered trademarks have previously been adjudicated as very strong. *See, Playboy Enterprise, Inc. v. Chuckleberry Pub., Inc.*, 687 F.2d 563 (2d Cir.1982). Suggestive marks are entitled to protection without proof of secondary meaning. *See e.g., Dominion Bankshares Corp. v. Devon*

Holding Co., Inc., 690 F.Supp. 338, 345 (E.D.Pa.1988); *American Diabetes Assn. v. National Diabetes Ass'n,* 533 F.Supp. 16, 214 U.S.P.Q. 231, 233 (E.D.Pa.1981).

Even if secondary meaning were required, PEI has established that the PLAYBOY trademark and the RABBIT HEAD DESIGN trademark for adult entertainment goods and services have become famous, and have acquired significant secondary meaning, such that the public has come to associate these trademarks with PEI.

Defendants intentionally adopted PLAYBOY and BUNNY trademarks in an effort to capitalize on PEI's established reputation in the PLAYBOY and RABBIT HEAD DESIGN marks. This is evidenced by defendant's establishment of a "link" between their website and PEI's actual PLAYBOY website at "Playboy.com" and their appropriation of the words "playboy" and "Bunny" to advertise their own on-line service.

Evidence of actual confusion is not required. It has long been recognized that because evidence of confusion is notoriously difficult to obtain, it is not necessary to find a likelihood of confusion. *See, e.g., Coach Leatherware Co. v. Ann Taylor, Inc.,* 933 F.2d 162 (2d Cir.1991); *Lois Sportswear U.S.A., Inc. v. Levi Strauss & Co.,* 631 F.Supp. 735, 743 (S.D.N.Y.), *aff'd,* 799 F.2d 867 (2d Cir.1986); *Brockum Co. v. Blaylock,* 729 F.Supp. 438, 445 (E.D.Pa.1990) (lack of evidence of actual confusion is not a bar to injunctive relief). PEI and defendant market their services through the same channel of trade: the Internet. The consuming public is likely to believe the PEI is connected with defendants' hard core. . . .

. . .

"Trademark policies are designed to '(1) to protect consumers from being misled as to the enterprise, or enterprises, from which the goods or services emanate or with which they are associated; (2) to prevent an impairment of the value of the enterprise which owns the trademark; and (3) to achieve these ends in a manner consistent with the objectives of free competition.' " *Intel Corp. v. Terabyte International, Inc.,* 6 F.3d 614, 618 (9th Cir.1993) (quoting Anti–Poly, Inc. v. General Mills Fun Group, 611 F.2d 296, 300–01 (9th Cir.1979)).

. . .

Accordingly, the Court arrives at the following

CONCLUSIONS OF LAW

. . .

2. Defendants have infringed on Plaintiff's PLAYBOY trademark. . . .

Albert v. Spencer
1998 WL 483462 (S.D.N.Y.1998).

■ JOHN S. MARTIN, JR., DISTRICT JUDGE.

Plaintiff and defendant both use the title AISLE SAY for theater reviews. Plaintiff whose reviews currently appear regularly in "Singles Almanac," a magazine distributed to approximately 40,000 people in the greater New York area, has used the title AISLE SAY for nineteen years. Defendant has published theater reviews on an Internet web site using the title AISLE SAY since 1995.

The Court is faced with the situation of two good faith users of the same trade name who operate in distinct markets. Plaintiff has never registered AISLE SAY. While the Court accepts plaintiff's testimony that she introduced herself to defendant in 1992 and mentioned AISLE SAY to him, the Court also credits the testimony of defendant that he has no recollection of this event and was not aware of the plaintiff's use of the name at the time he established his website. To avoid confusion, defendant has added a disclaimer to his web page stating that it is not connected to the plaintiff's column. Plaintiff did, however, introduce the testimony of two theater professionals who had been confused by the fact that two reviewers were using the name AISLE SAY.

DISCUSSION

As in all such cases, the parties have placed emphasis on the eight factors set forth by the Second Circuit in *Polaroid Corp. v. Polarad Elecs. Corp.*, 287 F.2d 492, 495 (2d Cir.1961). The factors are: (1) the strength of the plaintiff's mark; (2) the similarity between the two marks; (3) the proximity of the products in the marketplace; (4) the likelihood that the prior user will bridge the gap between the two products; (5) evidence of actual confusion; (6) defendant's bad faith; (7) the quality of the defendant's product; and (8) the sophistication of the relevant consumer group. *Id.*

A review of the *Polaroid* factors does not provide a clear guide to the proper outcome of this dispute:

1. Strength of the mark. A mark's strength is defined as its tendency to identify goods as emanating from a particular source. This is assessed according to two factors: first, the degree to which the mark is inherently distinctive; and second, the degree to which it is distinctive in the marketplace. The inherent distinctiveness of a mark is gauged according to whether it is generic, descriptive, suggestive or fanciful.

Plaintiff argues that AISLE SAY is a strong mark because it is fanciful, and defendant argues that it is weak because plaintiff's column is known to a relatively small number of persons. While the Court would consider the mark as more suggestive than fanciful, the mark is original enough that plaintiff would have the right to register it and enforce it against a bad faith user. Defendant is correct, however, that plaintiff's use of the mark is not widely known. Still, this factor favors plaintiff.

2. Similarity of the marks. There is no question that the marks are for practical purposes identical, and this factor favors plaintiff.

3. The competitive proximity of the products. If one considers the product simply as theater reviews, plaintiff and defendant's products are in direct competition. However, it is more appropriate to ask whether plaintiff's reviews compete with defendant's reviews for readers. The answer to that question is no, because plaintiff's reviews appear in print in a specific magazine while defendant publishes his reviews only at his website. Thus, this factor favors defendant.

4. The likelihood that plaintiff will bridge the gap. Plaintiff does not contend that she has any plans to distribute her reviews on the Internet. Thus, this factor favors defendant.

5. Actual confusion. While there was evidence showing some confusion involving two theater professionals, there was no evidence that either the magazine readers of plaintiff's reviews or the Internet visitors to the defendant's website were confused. Thus, this factor appears neutral at best.

6. The defendant's good faith. The Court is persuaded that defendant acted in complete good faith in adopting the name AISLE SAY for his website, and this factor strongly favors defendant.

7. The quality of the defendant's product. While the evidence indicates that the defendant's reviews are highly regarded, this is a subjective matter and one can understand why someone like plaintiff, who takes great pride in her work, would be concerned that someone else's reviews would be attributed to her. Thus, this factor favors plaintiff.

8. The sophistication of the buyers. To the extent that this factor focuses on the likelihood that the purchaser will be so familiar with the relevant market that he or she will not be confused as to the source of the review, it favors plaintiff, since a sophisticated playgoer may still be unsophisticated concerning the difference between reviews on the Internet and reviews in a magazine.

While four of the eight factors favor plaintiff and only three favor defendant, most of the factors favoring plaintiff tilt only slightly in her favor. Moreover, the eight factor test is not exclusive, and is not to be applied mechanically by totting up the number of factors weighing in each party's favor. . . .

"The essence of . . . unfair competition claims, under both federal and New York law 'is that the use of the infringing term creates the likelihood of consumer confusion . . . The essential inquiry is whether an appreciable number of ordinary prudent prospective [customers] are likely to be confused or misled.' " *Marshak v. Green*, 505 F.Supp. 1054, 1058 (S.D.N.Y.1981). . . .

Here, a balancing of the relevant factors suggests that defendant should not be prohibited from using a name that he adopted in good faith, because there is no danger that an appreciable number of consumers will be misled as to the source of the review they are reading.

Given the fact that there is no real competition between plaintiff's and defendant's reviews and that defendant has added a disclaimer to his website, it is unlikely that plaintiff will suffer any real economic disadvantage or damage to her reputation if defendant is permitted to continue to use AISLE SAY to identify his website. To enjoin defendant from using the name AISLE SAY would cause him far greater harm.

CONCLUSION

For the foregoing reasons, the complaint is dismissed.

Niton Corp. v. Radiation Monitoring Devices, Inc.
27 F.Supp.2d 102 (D.Mass.1998).

■ ROBERT E. KEETON, DISTRICT JUDGE.

Two innovative enterprises of modest size are coexisting almost side-by-side without friction. They are not in direct competition. Each, however, has possibilities for success and expansion. The success of both will, some months or years away, bring them to competing with each other and with larger entities whose operations may, by then, be international or global in scope.

Enter upon this tranquil scene the Internet and its inducements to each of the two modest enterprises to obtain web sites. They do so, and soon begin to worry about each other. As they learn more, one comes into a United States district court with a complaint and prayer for preliminary injunction against the other. They accept a suggestion from the judge that the request for injunctive relief be tried along with all other claims and defenses on an expedited discovery and trial schedule.

One soon learns, by chance, that the other's web sites and means of attracting Internet users to them are deceptive and immediately harmful. Forthwith, the matter is back before the district court with a renewed request for immediate intervention.

This is a classic illustration of a new kind of litigation for which nothing in past experience comes even close to preparing trial judges and the advocates appearing before them. But the case must be decided, and quickly, unless mediation within or outside court sponsorship produces an even quicker solution.

In the matter before me, I conclude that court intervention is appropriate but not in a classic form of preliminary injunction. For the reasons summarized here, my order is more provisional and tentative in nature and is entitled Preliminary Injunction Subject to Modification.

. . .

Plaintiff Niton Corporation is in the business of manufacturing and selling x-ray fluorescence ("XRF") instruments and software designed to detect the presence or absence of lead in paint. Defendant Radiation Monitoring Devices ("RMD") is in the business of manufacturing XRF instruments that detect lead in paint. One of these products is called the LPA–1. Niton's product employs the "L–Shell" and "K-shell" methods while RMD's product employs only the "K–Shell" method. By the time this civil action is commenced, Niton and RMD are aiming to sell to the same potential entities, in many instances, one or more of their respective products. Niton contends, and RMD denies, that the two companies are the only companies in the American market for XRF instruments and software.

In its complaint, Niton alleges that RMD uses false and misleading statements in RMD's advertising, marketing and promotion of its own product in Massachusetts and interstate commerce. Niton asserts that these statements "misrepresent the true nature, characteristics, capabilities, and qualities of RMD's product" and, as a result, reflect on Niton's products. Niton further contends that these misleading statements are contained on RMD's World Wide Web page on the Internet. . . .

. . .

Furthermore, Niton maintains that RMD has made false, misleading, and deceptive statements to third parties about Niton's products. . . .

. . .

In response, RMD has filed in this civil action a counterclaim against Niton for using false and misleading statements in its advertising, marketing and promotion of Niton products.

As stated above, the two companies were involved in this litigation when Niton learned, by chance, that RMD's web sites and the means of attracting Internet users to the sites were deceptive and misleading. In an affidavit, a Niton employee in charge of maintaining Niton's Internet web site, Robert Bowley, asserts that, on November 5, 1998, he discovered that the "META" descriptions of RMD's web sites included references to Niton's home page that were unusual. The term "META description" refers to words that identify an Internet site, and the term "META" keywords refers to keywords that are listed by the web page creator when creating the web site. An Internet user then uses a web search engine that searches the "META" keywords and identifies a match or a "hit".

Upon further inspection of the "META" descriptions, Bowley found that several of the web addresses appeared to be for Niton's home page, but were actually for pages of RMD's web sites. Although no links to Niton were visible in the surface text of the RMD web sites, Bowley was able to use Netscape's "View Source" command to look at the source code for the RMD web sites.

Using this feature, Bowley discovered that the "META" descriptions of RMD's web sites were identical to those he had used when creating the Niton web site. Bowley discovered that several keywords, such as "radon", that were relevant to products Niton sold, but not to products sold or marketed by RMD, nevertheless appeared in RMD's web site source code.

After this discovery, Bowley asserts that he performed an Internet web search using the phrase "home page of Niton Corporation" and turned up several "hits". Only three of the "hits" were for pages on Niton's web site. The other five matches referred him to pages on RMD's web sites. According to Bowley, the "META" description of the five RMD pages is "The Home Page of Niton Corporation, makers of the finest lead, radon, and multi-element detectors."

In his affidavit, Bowley states that he repeated the search for "home page of Niton Corporation" using several other web search engines and came up with the same results. Finally, Bowley asserts that he performed a search for "Niton Corporation" and "home page" and came up with hits that described themselves as being the "Home Page of Niton Corporation" but gave the web address of RMD's web site.

I find a likelihood of success of plaintiff in establishing before the finder of fact, at trial, the credibility of Bowley's findings recited here.

For the foregoing reasons, the Clerk is directed to enter forthwith on a separate document a Preliminary Injunction Subject to Modification in the form attached to this Opinion.

Preliminary Injunction Subject to Modification

. . .

On the basis of all the oral and filed submissions, the court finds: (a) that plaintiff has shown a likelihood of success on the merits of its contention that RMD's Internet web sites and means of attracting users of the Internet to examine these web sites have been used by RMD in a way likely to lead users to believe that the employees of RMD are "makers of the finest radon detectors," that RMD is also known as Niton Corporation, that RMD is affiliated with Niton Corporation, that RMD makes for Niton products marketed by Niton, and that RMD web sites are Niton web sites . . . . For the reasons expressed here and orally at the hearings of November 13 and 18, 1998, it is ORDERED:

Defendant Radiation Monitoring Devices, Inc. ("RMD"), its officers, directors, agents, servants, employees, and those persons in active concert or participation with them who receive notice in fact of this Order are hereby enjoined from using RMD's Internet web sites and means of attracting users of the Internet to examine those web sites in a way that is likely to lead users to believe:

(1) that the employees of RMD are "makers of the finest radon detectors," or

(2) that RMD is also known as Niton Corporation, or

(3) that RMD is affiliated with Niton Corporation, or

(4) that RMD makes for Niton any product marketed by Niton, or

(5) that RMD web sites are Niton web sites.

. . .

This Order is subject to modification by this court upon motion of an interested party for good cause shown. RMD may, at any time, apply to this court for a modification of this Order upon a showing of good cause for determining that an alternative form of relief is more appropriate than an injunction. Such a showing of good cause may be made by RMD's showing that it has developed or proposes to develop a modification of its web sites and means of attracting users of the Internet to examine those web sites

(a) that, if practiced, would not be a violation of this order, or

(b) that would be a violation of the terms of this Order, absent modification, but for special reasons shown, an alternative form of remedy allowing RMD to proceed on specified conditions, including compensation or security to Niton against harm, is more appropriate than an injunction.

EXTENSIONS

Metatagging and Search Engines. The most direct way to view a web site in your web browser is to type that site's web address (also known as its Uniform Resource Locator, or "URL") into the text box on the address bar of a web browser. The principal reason why so many businesses desire to use their trademark as a domain name is because it provides a highly intuitive, direct link to their company website. But not all websites have such obvious addresses, and we often find ourselves at a loss as we try to guess the URL that points to the web site we are trying to locate.

After a few unsuccessful guesses, most people enlist the aid of Internet search engines and directories. A *search engine* or *directory* is a searchable index of resources available on the Internet. A large majority of these resources are web pages, but one can also locate postings to USENET newsgroups, documents on FTP servers, and even the content of some databases. The user interface for this searchable index is usually a simple text box on a web page with a button labeled "search." The user types one or more search terms into the text box and presses the button to initiate a search. These terms, called *keywords*, are then passed off to the software that searches the index for Internet resources that contain those terms. It is not unusual for hundreds and even thousands of matches to be discovered. The web addresses of these resources are then arranged in a descending order of relevance according to relevance criteria adopted by the particular search engine or directory and returned to the user as a list of hyperlinks on a series of web pages. Often these hyperlinks are accompanied by additional information about the website. Reviewing these results pages, the user can often identify the website or other resource that she is attempting to locate and with a click of the mouse proceed directly to it.

The central difference between a search engine and a directory is that a search engine is compiled by an autonomous software agent called a *spider*. A spider moves through the Internet by following links from one website to another, searching for and retrieving various Internet resources. The manner in which a particular spider conducts its search and the decision criteria by which it decides which resources to retrieve are both determined by the programming logic and algorithms composing that spider. Well-known search engines include Altavista, Excite, Google, HotBot, Lycos and Northern Light. A directory, by contrast, is an index that is compiled by human beings. Because directories are compiled by humans, they tend to have fewer, but higher quality, links. The most widely used directories as of this writing are Yahoo!, LookSmart, Open Directory Project (ODP), NBCi and Ask Jeeves. Recognizing that their strengths are complementary, search engines and directories have begun to partner with one another, forming so-called hybrid search engines. For example, Google now provides search results for Yahoo! and is powered in part by the Open Directory Project.

The relevance ranking that a web page receives from a search engine is determined by an algorithm built into that search engine's software. As a result, if a website operator understands how a search engine's relevancy algorithm works, the operator can design and optimize the website to receive a higher ranking on the results pages that search engine returns to its users. Many search engines employ relevancy algorithms that take account of the presence of search terms (1) in certain "tagged" locations within the HTML code that comprises the web page, (2) in the text of the web page, and (3) in the URL of the web page.

Web site designers can try to increase their relevancy score under the first criterion by including as many likely keywords as possible within the HTML tags—even when the keywords have little or nothing to do with the content of the web page. This strategy, often referred to as "metatagging," has become so ubiquitous that many search engines now discount the presence of keywords within these tags.

The IBM corporate website provides a good example of how metatags are used:

```
<meta name="DESCRIPTION" content="The IBM corporate
home page, entry point to information about IBM prod-
ucts and services"/>

<meta name="'KEYWORDS" content="ibm, international
business machines, internet, e-business, ebusiness,
personal computer, personal system, e-commerce, ecom-
merce, pc, workstation, mainframe, unix, technical
support, homepage, home page"/>
```

www.ibm.com (page source code).

To enhance the relevance ranking of a web page under the second criterion, some website operators repeat likely keywords over and over again on a web page. To prevent this repetitive text from being seen by visitors to this website, site operators set the color of this text to the color of the background. Thus, while the repeated keywords remain invisible to humans viewing the web page through a browser, they are nonetheless visible to a search engine's spider. Keywords repeated in this fashion are sometimes referred to as buried code or invisible or hidden text.

The third strategy for enhancing the relevance ranking of a website—obtaining a domain name that contains a likely keyword, or using the keyword as part of the directory structure of the website—can be seen in *Playboy v. Universal Tel–A–Talk, supra* ("www.adult-sex.com/playboy"). (Domain names are considered in Chapter 3, *infra*).

Recognizing the value that website operators place on a high relevance ranking, some search engines and directories have attempted to sell higher rankings directly. For a price, some search engines will guarantee a premium relevance ranking for searches containing certain keywords. Others allow companies to bid on keywords, giving the highest relevance ranking to the highest bidder. In a related practice, some search engines and directories sell premium placements for banner ads on the results pages of searches involving certain keywords. For example, let us say a search engine user types in the keyword "washing machine." If Maytag has purchased a premium placement for its banner ad on results pages generated from a search using the keyword "washing machine," then the results pages returned to the user would prominently display Maytag's banner ad.

Metatagging raises several trademark issues, including: Is it trademark infringement or dilution to embed another's trademark in HTML tags on your web page? What about repeating another's trademark as buried code or invisible text on your web page? Is it unlawful for a search engine or directory to sell premium placements for banner ads keyed to another's trademark? How about the sale of an enhanced relevancy ranking for searches keyed to another's trademark?

In *Horphag Research Ltd. v. Pellegrini*, 337 F.3d 1036 (9th Cir.2003), the court held that defendant's use of plaintiff's trademark in the metatags of his website infringed plaintiff's trademark. Plaintiff owned the trademark PYCNOGENOL for a pharmaceutical product. Defendant sold pharmaceuticals, including plaintiff's product, via a website, and used "Pycnogenol" in the metatags of his site. The court held that this use of the mark was prima facie infringing. It rejected defendant's defense of nominative fair use, on the ground that defendant's conduct failed to meet the requirement that "the user must do nothing that would, in conjunction with the mark, suggest sponsorship or endorsement by the trademark holder"; here, the court held, defendant's "references to Pycnogenol spawn confusion as to sponsorship and attempt to appropriate the cachet of the trademark Pycnogenol to his product." *Compare J.K. Harris & Co, LLC v. Kassel*, 253 F.Supp.2d 1120 (N.D.Cal.2003) (holding defendant entitled to defense of nominative fair use, where defendant made extensive references on its website to plaintiff, a competitor, "by a) 'creating keyword density' using Plaintiff's trade name and permutations thereof; b) creating 'header Tags' and 'underline Tags' around sentences that use Plaintiff's trade name; c) using Plaintiff's trade name as a 'keyword' in numerous areas of the web site; d) using various 'hot links' to web sites with information about Plaintiff.").

What sort of confusion might result from use of another's trademark in this manner? Consider the doctrine of initial interest confusion, addressed in the next section.

B. INFRINGEMENT RESULTING FROM INITIAL INTEREST CONFUSION

Brookfield Communications, Inc. v. West Coast Entertainment Corp.
174 F.3d 1036 (9th Cir.1999).

■ O'SCANNLAIN, CIRCUIT JUDGE:

We must venture into cyberspace to determine whether federal trademark and unfair competition laws prohibit a video rental store chain from using an entertainment-industry information provider's trademark in the domain name of its web site and in its web site's metatags.

I

Brookfield Communications, Inc. ("Brookfield") appeals the district court's denial of its motion for a preliminary injunction prohibiting West Coast Entertainment Corporation ("West Coast") from using in commerce terms confusingly similar to Brookfield's trademark, "MovieBuff." Brookfield gathers and sells information about the entertainment industry. Founded in 1987 for the purpose of creating and marketing software and services for professionals in the entertainment industry, Brookfield initially offered software applications featuring information such as recent film submissions, industry credits, professional contacts, and future projects. These offerings targeted major Hollywood film studios, independent production companies, agents, actors, directors, and producers.

Brookfield expanded into the broader consumer market with computer software featuring a searchable database containing entertainment-industry related information marketed under the "MovieBuff" mark around December 1993. Brookfield's "MovieBuff" software now targets smaller companies and individual consumers who are not interested in purchasing Brookfield's professional level alternative, The Studio System, and includes comprehensive, searchable, entertainment-industry databases and related software applications containing information such as movie credits, box office receipts, films in development, film release schedules, entertainment news, and listings of executives, agents, actors, and directors. This "MovieBuff" software comes in three versions—(1) the MovieBuff Pro Bundle, (2) the MovieBuff Pro, and (3) MovieBuff—and is sold through various retail stores, such as Borders, Virgin Megastores, Nobody Beats the Wiz, The Writer's Computer Store, Book City, and Samuel French Bookstores.

Sometime in 1996, Brookfield attempted to register the World Wide Web ("the Web") domain name "moviebuff.com" with Network Solutions, Inc. ("Network Solutions"), but was informed that the requested domain name had already been registered by West Coast. Brookfield subsequently registered "brookfield-

comm.com" in May 1996 and "moviebuffonline.com" in September 1996. Sometime in 1996 or 1997, Brookfield began using its web sites to sell its "MovieBuff"
computer software and to offer an Internet-based searchable database marketed
under the "MovieBuff" mark. Brookfield sells its "MovieBuff" computer software
through its "brookfieldcomm.com" and "moviebuffonline.com" web sites and offers subscribers online access to the MovieBuff database itself at its "inholly-
wood.com" web site.

On August 19, 1997, Brookfield applied to the Patent and Trademark Office
(PTO) for federal registration of "MovieBuff" as a mark to designate both goods
and services. Its trademark application describes its product as "computer software providing data and information in the field of the motion picture and television industries." Its service mark application describes its service as "providing
multiple-user access to an on-line network database offering data and information
in the field of the motion picture and television industries." Both federal trademark
registrations issued on September 29, 1998. Brookfield had previously obtained a
California state trademark registration for the mark "MovieBuff" covering "computer software" in 1994.

In October 1998, Brookfield learned that West Coast—one of the nation's largest
video rental store chains with over 500 stores—intended to launch a web site at
"moviebuff.com" containing, inter alia, a searchable entertainment database similar to "MovieBuff." West Coast had registered "moviebuff.com" with Network
Solutions on February 6, 1996 and claims that it chose the domain name because
the term "Movie Buff" is part of its service mark, "The Movie Buff's Movie Store,"
on which a federal registration issued in 1991 covering "retail store services featuring video cassettes and video game cartridges" and "rental of video cassettes and
video game cartridges." West Coast notes further that, since at least 1988, it has
also used various phrases including the term "Movie Buff" to promote goods and
services available at its video stores in Massachusetts, including "The Movie Buff's
Gift Guide"; "The Movie Buff's Gift Store"; "Calling All Movie Buffs!"; "Good
News Movie Buffs!"; "Movie Buffs, Show Your Stuff!"; "the Perfect Stocking
Stuffer for the Movie Buff!"; "A Movie Buff's Top Ten"; "The Movie Buff Discovery Program"; "Movie Buff Picks"; "Movie Buff Series"; "Movie Buff Selection
Program"; and "Movie Buff Film Series."

On November 10, Brookfield delivered to West Coast a cease-and-desist letter
alleging that West Coast's planned use of the "moviebuff.com" would violate
Brookfield's trademark rights; as a "courtesy" Brookfield attached a copy of a
complaint that it threatened to file if West Coast did not desist.

The next day, West Coast issued a press release announcing the imminent
launch of its web site full of "movie reviews, Hollywood news and gossip, provocative commentary, and coverage of the independent film scene and films in
production." The press release declared that the site would feature "an extensive
database, which aids consumers in making educated decisions about the rental and
purchase of" movies and would also allow customers to purchase movies, accessories, and other entertainment-related merchandise on the web site.

Brookfield fired back immediately with a visit to the United States District Court for the Central District of California, and this lawsuit was born. In its first amended complaint filed on November 18, 1998, Brookfield alleged principally that West Coast's proposed offering of online services at "moviebuff.com" would constitute trademark infringement and unfair competition in violation of §§ 32 and 43(a) of the Lanham Act, 15 U.S.C. §§ 1114, 1125(a). Soon thereafter, Brookfield applied *ex parte* for a temporary restraining order ("TRO") enjoining West Coast "[f]rom using . . . in any manner . . . the mark MOVIEBUFF, or any other term or terms likely to cause confusion therewith, including *moviebuff.com*, as West Coast's domain name, . . . as the name of West Coast's website service, in buried code or metatags on their home page or web pages, or in connection with the retrieval of data or information on other goods or services."

. . .

V

. . .

B

[The court concluded that West Coast's use of the domain name *moviebuff.com* infringes the trademark of Brookfield.] Because Brookfield requested that we also preliminarily enjoin West Coast from using marks confusingly similar to "Movie-Buff" in metatags and buried code, we must also decide whether West Coast can, consistently with the trademark and unfair competition laws, use "MovieBuff" or "moviebuff.com" in its HTML code.

At first glance, our resolution of the infringement issues in the domain name context would appear to dictate a similar conclusion of likelihood of confusion with respect to West Coast's use of "moviebuff.com" in its metatags. Indeed, all eight likelihood of confusion factors outlined [above]—with the possible exception of purchaser care, which we discuss below—apply here as they did in our analysis of domain names; we are, after all, dealing with the same marks, the same products and services, the same consumers, etc. Disposing of the issue so readily, however, would ignore the fact that the likelihood of confusion in the domain name context resulted largely from the associational confusion between West Coast's domain name "moviebuff.com" and Brookfield's trademark "MovieBuff." The question in the metatags context is quite different. Here, we must determine whether West Coast can use "MovieBuff" or "moviebuff.com" in the metatags of its web site at "westcoastvideo.com" or at any other domain address *other than* "moviebuff.com" (which we have determined that West Coast may not use).

Although entering "MovieBuff" into a search engine is likely to bring up a list including "westcoastvideo.com" if West Coast has included that term in its metatags, the resulting confusion is not as great as where West Coast uses the "moviebuff.com" domain name. First, when the user inputs "MovieBuff" into an Internet search engine, the list produced by the search engine is likely to include both West Coast's and Brookfield's web sites. Thus, in scanning such list, the Web user will often be able to find the particular web site he is seeking. Moreover, even if the Web user chooses the web site belonging to West Coast, he will see that the domain name of the web site he selected is "westcoastvideo.com." Since there is no confusion resulting from the domain address, and since West Coast's initial web page prominently displays its own name, it is difficult to say that a consumer is likely to be confused about whose site he has reached or to think that Brookfield somehow sponsors West Coast's web site.

Nevertheless, West Coast's use of "moviebuff.com" in metatags will still result in what is known as initial interest confusion. Web surfers looking for Brookfield's "MovieBuff" products who are taken by a search engine to "westcoastvideo.com" will find a database similar enough to "MovieBuff" such that a sizeable number of consumers who were originally looking for Brookfield's product will simply decide to utilize West Coast's offerings instead. Although there is no source confusion in the sense that consumers know they are patronizing West Coast rather than Brookfield, there is nevertheless initial interest confusion in the sense that, by using "moviebuff.com" or "MovieBuff" to divert people looking for "MovieBuff" to its web site, West Coast improperly benefits from the goodwill that Brookfield developed in its mark. Recently in *Dr. Seuss,* we explicitly recognized that the use of another's trademark in a manner calculated "to capture initial consumer attention, even though no actual sale is finally completed as a result of the confusion, may be still an infringement." *Dr. Seuss,* 109 F.3d at 1405 (citing *Mobil Oil Corp. v. Pegasus Petroleum Corp.,* 818 F.2d 254, 257–58 (2d Cir.1987)).

The *Dr. Seuss* court, in recognizing that the diversion of consumers' initial interest is a form of confusion against which the Lanham Act protects, relied upon *Mobil Oil.* In that case, Mobil Oil Corporation ("Mobil") asserted a federal trademark infringement claim against Pegasus Petroleum, alleging that Pegasus Petroleum's use of "Pegasus" was likely to cause confusion with Mobil's trademark, a flying horse symbol in the form of the Greek mythological Pegasus. Mobil established that "potential purchasers would be misled into an initial interest in Pegasus Petroleum" because they thought that Pegasus Petroleum was associated with Mobil. *Id.* at 260. But these potential customers would generally learn that Pegasus Petroleum was unrelated to Mobil well before any actual sale was consummated. *See id.* Nevertheless, the Second Circuit held that "[s]uch initial confusion works a sufficient trademark injury." *Id.*

Mobil Oil relied upon its earlier opinion in *Grotrian, Helfferich, Schulz, Th. Steinweg Nachf. v.* Steinway & Sons, 523 F.2d 1331, 1341–42 (2d Cir.1975). Analyzing the plaintiff's claim that the defendant, through its use of the "Grotrian–Steinweg" mark, attracted people really interested in plaintiff's "Steinway" pianos, the Second Circuit explained:

> We decline to hold, however, that actual or potential confusion at the time of purchase necessarily must be demonstrated to establish trademark infringement under the circumstances of this case.

> The issue here is not the possibility that a purchaser would buy a Grotrian-Steinweg thinking it was actually a Steinway or that Grotrian had some connection with Steinway and Sons. The harm to Steinway, rather, is the likelihood that a consumer, hearing the "Grotrian-Steinweg" name and thinking it had some connection with "Steinway,"

would consider it on that basis. The "Grotrian–Steinweg" name therefore would attract potential customers based on the reputation built up by Steinway in this country for many years.

Grotrian, 523 F.2d at 1342.

Both *Dr. Seuss* and the Second Circuit hold that initial interest confusion is actionable under the Lanham Act, which holdings are bolstered by the decisions of many other courts which have similarly recognized that the federal trademark and unfair competition laws do protect against this form of consumer confusion. *See Green Prods.,* 992 F.Supp. 1070, 1076 (N.D.Iowa 1997) ("In essence, ICBP is capitalizing on the strong similarity between Green Products' trademark and ICBP's domain name to lure customers onto its web page."). [Eight other citations omitted.] *But see Astra Pharm. Prods., Inc. v. Beckman Instruments, Inc.,* 718 F.2d 1201, 1206–08 (1st Cir.1983) (suggesting that only confusion that affects "the ultimate decision of a purchaser whether to buy a particular product" is actionable); *Teletech Customer Care Mgmt. (Cal.), Inc. v. Tele–Tech Co.,* 977 F.Supp. 1407, 1410, 1414 (C.D.Cal.1997) (finding likelihood of initial interest confusion but concluding that such "brief confusion is not cognizable under the trademark laws").

Using another's trademark in one's metatags is much like posting a sign with another's trademark in front of one's store. Suppose West Coast's competitor (let's call it "Blockbuster") puts up a billboard on a highway reading—"West Coast Video: 2 miles ahead at Exit 7"—where West Coast is really located at Exit 8 but Blockbuster is located at Exit 7. Customers looking for West Coast's store will pull off at Exit 7 and drive around looking for it. Unable to locate West Coast, but seeing the Blockbuster store right by the highway entrance, they may simply rent there. Even consumers who prefer West Coast may find it not worth the trouble to continue searching for West Coast since there is a Blockbuster right there. Customers are not confused in the narrow sense: they are fully aware that they are purchasing from Blockbuster and they have no reason to believe that Blockbuster is related to, or in any way sponsored by, West Coast. Nevertheless, the fact that there is only initial consumer confusion does not alter the fact that Blockbuster would be misappropriating West Coast's acquired goodwill. *See Blockbuster Entertainment Group, Div. of Viacom, Inc. v. Laylco, Inc.,* 869 F.Supp. 505, 513 (E.D.Mich. 1994) (finding trademark infringement where the defendant, a video rental store, attracted customers' initial interest by using a sign confusingly [similar] to its competitor's even though confusion would end long before the point of sale or rental); *see also Dr. Seuss,* 109 F.3d at 1405; *Mobil Oil,* 818 F.2d at 260; *Green Prods.,* 992 F.Supp. at 1076.

The few courts to consider whether the use of another's trademark in one's metatags constitutes trademark infringement have ruled in the affirmative. For example, in a case in which Playboy Enterprises, Inc. ("Playboy") sued AsiaFocus International, Inc. ("AsiaFocus") for trademark infringement resulting from Asia-Focus's use of the federally registered trademarks "Playboy" and "Playmate" in its HTML code, a district court granted judgment in Playboy's favor, reasoning that AsiaFocus intentionally misled viewers into believing that its web site was connected with, or sponsored by, Playboy. *See Playboy Enters. v. Asiafocus Int'l, Inc.,* No.

CIV.A. 97–734–A, 1998 WL 724000, at *3, *6–*7 (E.D.Va. Apr.10, 1998).

In a similar case also involving Playboy, a district court in California concluded that Playboy had established a likelihood of success on the merits of its claim that defendants' repeated use of "Playboy" within "machine readable code in Defendants' Internet Web pages, so that the PLAYBOY trademark [was] accessible to individuals or Internet search engines which attempt[ed] to access Plaintiff under Plaintiff's PLAYBOY registered trademark" constituted trademark infringement. *See Playboy Enters. v. Calvin Designer Label,* 985 F.Supp. 1220, 1221 (N.D.Cal.1997). The court accordingly enjoined the defendants from using Playboy's marks in buried code or metatags. *See id.* at 1221–22.

In a metatags case with an interesting twist, a district court in Massachusetts also enjoined the use of metatags in a manner that resulted in initial interest confusion. *See Niton,* 27 F.Supp.2d at 102–05. In that case, the defendant Radiation Monitoring Devices ("RMD") did not simply use Niton Corporation's ("Niton") trademark in its metatags. Instead, RMD's web site directly copied Niton's web site's metatags and HTML code. As a result, whenever a search performed on an Internet search engine listed Niton's web site, it also listed RMD's site. Although the opinion did not speak in terms of initial consumer confusion, the court made clear that its issuance of preliminary injunctive relief was based on the fact that RMD was purposefully diverting people looking for Niton to its web site. *See id.* at 104–05.

Consistently with *Dr. Seuss,* the Second Circuit, and the cases which have addressed trademark infringement through metatags use, we conclude that the Lanham Act bars West Coast from including in its metatags any term confusingly similar with Brookfield's mark. West Coast argues that our holding conflicts with *Holiday Inns,* in which the Sixth Circuit held that there was no trademark infringement where an alleged infringer merely took advantage of a situation in which confusion was likely to exist and did not affirmatively act to create consumer confusion. *See Holiday Inns, Inc. v. 800 Reservation, Inc.* 86 F.3d 619, 622 (6th Cir.1996) (holding that the use of "1–800–405–4329"—which is equivalent to "1–800–H[zero]LIDAY"—did not infringe Holiday Inn's trademark, "1–800–HOLIDAY"). Unlike the defendant in *Holiday Inns,* however, West Coast was not a passive figure; instead, it acted affirmatively in placing Brookfield's trademark in the metatags of its web site, thereby *creating* the initial interest confusion. Accordingly, our conclusion comports with *Holiday Inns.* . . .

. . . .

VI

[The court concludes that "[p]reliminary injunctive relief is appropriate here to prevent irreparable injury to Brookfield's interests in its trademark 'MovieBuff' and to promote the public interest in protecting trademarks generally as well."]

. . .

Playboy Enterprises, Inc. v. Netscape Communications Corp.
354 F.3d 1020 (9th Cir.2004).

■ T.G. NELSON, CIRCUIT JUDGE.

Playboy Enterprises International, Inc. (PEI) appeals from the district court's grant of summary judgment in favor of Netscape Communications Corporation and Excite, Inc. PEI sued defendants for trademark infringement and dilution. . . . Because we conclude that genuine issues of material fact preclude summary judgment on both the trademark infringement and dilution claims, we reverse and remand.

I. Facts

This case involves a practice called "keying" that defendants use on their Internet search engines. Keying allows advertisers to target individuals with certain interests by linking advertisements to pre-identified terms. To take an innocuous example, a person who searches for a term related to gardening may be a likely customer for a company selling seeds. Thus, a seed company might pay to have its advertisement displayed when searchers enter terms related to gardening. After paying a fee to defendants, that company could have its advertisements appear on the page listing the search results for gardening-related terms: the ad would be "keyed" to gardening-related terms. Advertisements appearing on search result pages are called "banner ads" because they run along the top or side of a page much like a banner.[1]

Defendants have various lists of terms to which they key advertisers' banner ads. Those lists include the one at issue in this case, a list containing terms related to sex and adult-oriented entertainment. Among the over-400 terms in this list are two for which PEI holds trademarks: "playboy" and "playmate." Defendants *require* adult-oriented companies to link their ads to this set of words. Thus, when a user types in "playboy," "playmate," or one of the other listed terms, those companies' banner ads appear on the search results page.[3]

PEI introduced evidence that the adult-oriented banner ads displayed on defendants' search results pages are often graphic in nature and are confusingly labeled or not labeled at all. In addition, the parties do not dispute that buttons on the banner ads say "click here." When a searcher complies, the search results page disappears, and the searcher finds him- or herself at the advertiser's website. PEI presented uncontroverted evidence that defendants monitor "click rates," the ratio between the number of times searchers click on banner ads and the number of times the ads are shown. Defendants use click rate statistics to convince advertisers

---

[1] Not all banner ads are keyed. Some advertisers buy space for their banner ads but only pay to have their ads displayed randomly. Such ads cost less because they are un-targeted and are therefore considered less effective.

[3] The search results page lists websites relevant to the search terms pursuant to the search engine's computer program. A user can click on any item in the list to link to the website of the organization listed. Defendants' search results pages for the terms "playboy" and "playmate" include links to PEI's websites.

to renew their keyword contracts. The higher the click rate, the more successful they deem a banner ad.

PEI sued defendants, asserting that they were using PEI's marks in a manner that infringed upon and diluted them. The district court denied PEI's request for a preliminary injunction, and this court affirmed in an unpublished disposition. On remand, the parties filed cross-motions for summary judgment. The district court granted summary judgment in favor of defendants. We reverse.

II. Standard of Review

We review the district court's grant of summary judgment de novo. Viewing the evidence in the light most favorable to PEI, and drawing all reasonable inferences in PEI's favor, we must determine whether there are any genuine issues of material fact and whether the district court correctly applied the relevant substantive law. . . .

III. Discussion

A. Trademark Infringement

With regard to PEI's trademark infringement claim, the parties disagree on three points. First, the parties dispute whether a direct or a contributory theory of liability applies to defendants' actions. We conclude that defendants are potentially liable under one theory and that we need not decide which one. Second, the parties disagree regarding whether PEI has successfully shown that a genuine issue of material fact exists regarding the likelihood of consumer confusion resulting from defendants' use of PEI's marks. We conclude that a genuine issue of material fact does exist. Finally, the parties dispute whether any affirmative defenses apply. We conclude that no defenses apply. We will address each dispute in turn.

1. Theory of liability.

Whether the defendants are directly or merely contributorily liable proves to be a tricky question. However, we need not decide that question here. We conclude that defendants are either directly or contributorily liable. Under either theory, PEI's case may proceed. Thus, we need not decide this issue.

2. PEI's case for trademark infringement.

The "core element of trademark infringement," the likelihood of confusion, lies at the center of this case.[10] No dispute exists regarding the other requirements set forth by the statute: PEI clearly holds the marks in question and defendants used the marks in commerce without PEI's permission.

PEI's strongest argument for a likelihood of confusion is for a certain kind of confusion: initial interest confusion.[13] Initial interest confusion is customer confu-

---

[10] *Brookfield Communications, Inc. v. West Coast Entm't Corp.*, 174 F.3d 1036, 1053 (9th Cir.1999). . . .

[13] Indeed, we find insufficient evidence to defeat summary judgment on any other theory.

sion that creates initial interest in a competitor's product.[14] Although dispelled before an actual sale occurs, initial interest confusion impermissibly capitalizes on the goodwill associated with a mark and is therefore actionable trademark infringement.

PEI asserts that, by keying adult-oriented advertisements to PEI's trademarks, defendants actively create initial interest confusion in the following manner. Because banner advertisements appear immediately after users type in PEI's marks, PEI asserts that users are likely to be confused regarding the sponsorship of unlabeled banner advertisements.[16] In addition, many of the advertisements instruct users to "click here." Because of their confusion, users may follow the instruction, believing they will be connected to a PEI cite. Even if they realize "immediately upon accessing" the competitor's site that they have reached a site "wholly unrelated to" PEI's, the damage has been done: Through initial consumer confusion, the competitor "will still have gained a customer by appropriating the goodwill that [PEI] has developed in its [ ] mark."[17]

PEI's theory strongly resembles the theory adopted by this court in *Brookfield Communications, Inc. v. West Coast Entertainment Corporation.* . . .

In this case, PEI claims that defendants, in conjunction with advertisers, have misappropriated the goodwill of PEI's marks by leading Internet users to competitors' websites just as West Coast video misappropriated the goodwill of Brookfield's mark. Some consumers, initially seeking PEI's sites, may initially believe that unlabeled banner advertisements are links to PEI's sites or to sites affiliated with PEI. Once they follow the instructions to "click here," and they access the site, they may well realize that they are not at a PEI-sponsored site. However, they may be perfectly happy to remain on the competitor's site, just as the *Brookfield* court surmised that some searchers initially seeking Brookfield's site would happily remain on West Coast's site. The Internet user will have reached the site because of defendants' use of PEI's mark. Such use is actionable.

Although analogies to *Brookfield* suggest that PEI will be able to show a likelihood of confusion sufficient to defeat summary judgment, we must test PEI's theory using this circuit's well-established eight-factor test for the likelihood of confusion to be certain. Accordingly, we turn to that test now.

The Ninth Circuit employs an eight-factor test, originally set forth in *AMF Inc. v. Sleekcraft Boats*[24] to determine the likelihood of confusion. [In applying the *Sleekcraft* factors, the court gave considerable weight to evidence of actual confusion, namely an expert study demonstrating that a statistically significant number of consumers searching for the terms "playboy" or "playmate" would believe that banner ads containing adult content on result pages were sponsored by PEI. The

---

[14] *Brookfield*, 174 F.3d at 1062–63.

[16] Note that if a banner advertisement clearly identified its source or, even better, overtly compared PEI products to the sponsor's own, no confusion would occur under PEI's theory.

[17] *Brookfield*, 174 F.3d at 1057.

[24] 599 F.2d 341, 348–49 (9th Cir.1979).

court additionally found some evidence of defendants' intent to confuse, in their failure to label the banner ads or to remove the terms "playboy" and "playmate" from their list of keywords.]

■ BERZON, CIRCUIT JUDGE, Concurring.

I concur in Judge Nelson's careful opinion in this case, as it is fully consistent with the applicable precedents. I write separately, however, to express concern that one of those precedents was wrongly decided and may one day, if not now, need to be reconsidered *en banc.*

I am struck by how analytically similar keyed advertisements are to the meta-tags found infringing in *Brookfield Communications v. West Coast Entertainment Corp.,* 174 F.3d 1036 (9th Cir.1999). In *Brookfield,* the court held that the defendant could not use the trademarked term "moviebuff" as one of its metatags. Metatags are part of the HTML code of a web page, and therefore are invisible to internet users. Search engines use these metatags to pull out websites applicable to search terms. . . .

Specifically, *Brookfield* held that the use of the trademarked terms in metatags violated the Lanham Act because it caused "initial interest confusion." *Brookfield,* 174 F.3d at 1062–66. The court explained that even though "there is no source confusion in the sense that consumers know [who] they are patronizing, . . . there is nevertheless initial interest confusion in the sense that, by using 'moviebuff.com' or 'MovieBuff' to divert people looking for 'MovieBuff' to its website, [the defendant] improperly benefits from the goodwill that [the plaintiff] developed in its mark." *Id.* at 1062.

As applied to this case, *Brookfield* might suggest that there could be a Lanham Act violation *even if* the banner advertisements were clearly labeled, either by the advertiser or by the search engine. I do not believe that to be so. So read, the metatag holding in *Brookfield* would expand the reach of initial interest confusion from situations in which a party is initially confused to situations in which a party is never confused. I do not think it is reasonable to find initial interest confusion when a consumer is never confused as to source or affiliation, but instead knows, or should know, from the outset that a product or web link is not related to that of the trademark holder because the list produced by the search engine so informs him.

There is a big difference between hijacking a customer to another website by making the customer think he or she is visiting the trademark holder's website (even if only briefly), which is what may be happening in this case when the banner advertisements are not labeled, and just distracting a potential customer with another *choice,* when it is clear that it is a choice. True, when the search engine list generated by the search for the trademark ensconced in a metatag comes up, an internet user might *choose* to visit westcoastvideo.com, the defendant's website in *Brookfield,* instead of the plaintiff's moviebuff.com website, but such choices do not constitute trademark infringement off the internet, and I cannot understand why they should on the internet.

For example, consider the following scenario: I walk into Macy's and ask for the

Calvin Klein section and am directed upstairs to the second floor. Once I get to the second floor, on my way to the Calvin Klein section, I notice a more prominently displayed line of Charter Club clothes, Macy's own brand, designed to appeal to the same people attracted by the style of Calvin Klein's latest line of clothes. Let's say I get diverted from my goal of reaching the Calvin Klein section, the Charter Club stuff looks good enough to me, and I purchase some Charter Club shirts instead. Has Charter Club or Macy's infringed Calvin Klein's trademark, simply by having another product more prominently displayed before one reaches the Klein line? Certainly not. . . .

Similarly, suppose a customer walks into a bookstore and asks for Playboy magazine and is then directed to the adult magazine section, where he or she sees Penthouse or Hustler up front on the rack while Playboy is buried in back. One would not say that Penthouse or Hustler had violated Playboy's trademark. This conclusion holds true even if Hustler paid the store owner to put its magazines in front of Playboy's.

One can test these analogies with an on-line example: If I went to Macy's website and did a search for a Calvin Klein shirt, would Macy's violate Calvin Klein's trademark if it responded (as does Amazon.com, for example) with the requested shirt and pictures of other shirts I might like to consider as well? I very much doubt it.

Accordingly, I simply cannot understand the broad principle set forth in *Brookfield*. Even the main analogy given in *Brookfield* belies its conclusion. The Court gives an example of Blockbuster misdirecting customers from a competing video store, West Coast Video, by putting up a highway billboard sign giving directions to Blockbuster but telling customers that a West Coast Video store is located there. *Brookfield*, 174 F.3d at 1064. Even though customers who arrive at the Blockbuster realize that it is not West Coast Video, they were initially misled and confused. *Id.*

But there was no similar misdirection in *Brookfield*, nor would there be similar misdirection in this case were the banner ads labeled or otherwise identified. The *Brookfield* defendant's website was described by the court as being accurately listed as westcoastvideo.com in the applicable search results. Consumers were free to choose the official moviebuff.com website and were not hijacked or misdirected elsewhere. I note that the billboard analogy has been widely criticized as inapplicable to the internet situation, given both the fact that customers were not misdirected and the minimal inconvenience in directing one's web browser back to the original list of search results. . . .

The degree to which this questionable aspect of *Brookfield* affects this case is not clear to me. Our opinion limits the present holding to situations in which the banner advertisements are not labeled or identified. Whether, on remand, the case will remain so limited is questionable. PEI may seek to reach labeled advertisements as well.

There will be time enough to address the continuing vitality of *Brookfield* should the labeled advertisement issue arise later. I wanted to flag the issue, however, as another case based on the metatag aspect of *Brookfield* was decided recently, *Hor-*

phag Research Ltd. v. Pellegrini, 337 F.3d 1036 (9th Cir.2003),[1] so the issue is a recurring one. Should the question arise again, in this case or some other, this court needs to consider whether we want to continue to apply an insupportable rule.

Government Employees Insurance Company v. Google, Inc.
330 F.Supp.2d 700 (E.D.Va.2004).

■ LEONIE M. BRINKEMA, DISTRICT JUDGE.

Before the Court are Motions to Dismiss filed by defendants Google, Inc. ("Google") and Overture Services, Inc. ("Overture"), in which the two defendants move, pursuant to Fed. R. Civ. P. 12(b)(6), to dismiss plaintiff's First Amended Complaint for failure to state a claim. . . . For the reasons discussed below, the motions will be granted in part and denied in part.

I. Background

Plaintiff Government Employees Insurance Company ("GEICO") brings an eight-count complaint against defendants Google and Overture based on defendants' use of GEICO trademarks in selling advertising on defendants' Internet search engines. The first five claims in the complaint allege, respectively, trademark infringement, contributory trademark infringement, vicarious trademark infringement, false representation, and dilution under the Lanham Act, 15 U.S.C. § 1051 *et seq*. Claim 6 alleges common law unfair competition . . . under Virginia state law.

As alleged by plaintiff, Google and Overture operate Internet search engines, which are used by consumers to search the World Wide Web for, among other things, Websites offering products and services. The search engines work by comparing search terms entered by the Internet user with databases of Websites maintained by the search engine, generating a results page that lists the Websites matching the search term. A search term may be any term that the user believes may assist her in retrieving the information sought, from a proper name such as Anton Dvorak, a generic term such as "squirrel," or a trademark such as plaintiff's "GEICO" mark. Both Google and Overture also sell advertising linked to search terms, so that when a consumer enters a particular search term, the results page displays not only a list of Websites generated by the search engine program using neutral and objective criteria, but also links to Websites of paid advertisers (listed as "Sponsored Links"). As the holder of trademark rights to marks incorporating the term "GEICO,"[2] plaintiff alleges that defendants' practice of selling advertising linked to the trademarks directly violates the Lanham Act, contributes to third parties violating the Act, and also constitutes various state law torts.

Defendants move to dismiss, arguing that the practices alleged by GEICO in the complaint do not violate the Lanham Act as a matter of law, and that the state law

---

[1] [*Horphag Research v. Pellegrini* is discussed in Part II(A), *supra*. — Eds.]

[2] The complaint alleges that plaintiff has obtained federal trademark registration for "GEICO" and "GEICO DIRECT."

claims are inadequately pled.

II. Analysis

. . .

A. Lanham Act claims

A plaintiff alleging causes of action for trademark infringement and unfair competition must show 1) that it possesses a mark; 2) that the defendant used the mark; 3) that the defendant's use of the mark occurred "in commerce"; 4) that the defendant used the mark "in connection with the sale, offering for sale, distribution, or advertising" of goods and services; and 5) that the defendant used the mark in a manner likely to confuse customers. 15 U.S.C. §§ 1114, 1125(a); *People for the Ethical Treatment of Animals v. Doughney*, 263 F.3d 359, 364 (4th Cir.2001) (internal quotations omitted).[3]

1. Trademark use

Defendants argue that the facts alleged by plaintiff do not establish the third and fourth prongs of a Lanham Act cause of action. Specifically, defendants argue that the complaint fails to alleges facts supporting a claim that defendants use the marks "in commerce" and "in connection with the sale, offering for sale, distribution, or advertising of goods and services" (hereinafter "trademark use"), because the complaint does not allege that defendants used plaintiff's trademarks in a way that identifies the user as the source of a product or indicates the endorsement of the mark owner. Defendants further argue that because they only use the trademarks in their internal computer algorithms to determine which advertisements to show, this use of the trademarks never appears to the user. Therefore, the user cannot be confused as to the origin of goods.

Defendants support their argument as to the legal meaning of trademark use with cases that have found the use of trademarks by software companies to generate pop-up Internet advertisements not to constitute "trademark use" of those marks under the Lanham Act. Those cases are based on a finding that the marks were not used by the company making the pop-up software to identify the source of its goods or services. See *U-Haul Int'l, Inc. v. WhenU.com. Inc.*, 279 F.Supp. 2d 723, 727 (E.D.Va. 2003); *Wells Fargo & Co. v. WhenU.com. Inc.*, 293 F.Supp. 2d 734, 762 (E.D.Mich. 2003). In *U-Haul*, the court held that WhenU, the pop-up software company, did not place the U-Haul trademarks in commerce, it merely used them for a "pure machine-linking function." Defendants also rely upon *Interactive Products Corp. v. a2z Mobile Office Solutions*, 326 F.3d 687, 695 (6th Cir.2003), which held that the use of a trademark within a longer Web address did not constitute a trademark use under the infringement test, distinguishing such a use from use of a trademark in the domain name itself. In *Interactive*, the trademark at issue was "LapTraveler," and the allegedly infringing address was

---

[3] The elements of trademark infringement and unfair competition under the Lanham Act are identical to the elements of unfair competition under Virginia state law. Accordingly, our discussion of the Lanham Act claims applies equally to Claim 6, plaintiff's claim of common law unfair competition.

"a2zsolutions.com/desks/floor/laptraveler/dkfl-lt.htm." The court held that such use of the trademark was a purely technical use, rather than a "trademark use." However, if the trademark had been used in the heart of the domain name, for example as "www.laptraveler.com," the use would be a "trademark use," and could be infringing.

Plaintiff focuses on cases which have reached the opposite conclusion. In *1-800 Contacts. Inc. v. WhenU.com*, 309 F.Supp. 2d 467 (S.D.N.Y.2003), on facts identical to those found in the *U-Haul* and *Wells Fargo* cases, the court found that WhenU was making "trademark use" of the plaintiff's trademark in two ways—by using plaintiff's mark in the advertising of competitor's websites, and by including plaintiff's mark in the directory of terms that triggers pop-up advertisements. Similarly, on facts nearly identical to the facts pled by GEICO, the Ninth Circuit held that the use of plaintiff's trademarks as advertising keywords by the Netscape and Excite search engines potentially created the likelihood of confusion, and the court found no dispute that the defendants used the marks in commerce. *Playboy Enterprises, Inc. v. Netscape Comm. Corp.*, 354 F.3d 1020, 1024 (9th Cir.2004). In the Fourth Circuit's *PETA* decision, it specifically rejected the argument that the defendant's use of the PETA trademark in a domain name was not in connection with goods and services: "[the defendant] need only have prevented users from obtaining or using PETA's goods or services, or need only have connected the website to other's goods or services." 263 F.3d at 365. Similarly, courts have found that the use of trademarks in "metatags," which are invisible text within websites that are used by search engines for indexing, constitute a use in commerce under the Lanham Act. See *Bihari v. Gross.* 119 F.Supp.2d 309 (S.D.N.Y.2000) . . . .

Of the two lines of cases cited by the parties, the Court finds that plaintiff's authorities are better reasoned. Under those cases, as well as an unstrained reading of the complaint, the Court finds that plaintiff has pled sufficient facts which, taken as true for purposes of this motion, allege "trademark use." Contrary to defendants' argument, the complaint is addressed to more than the defendants' use of the trademarks in their internal computer coding. The complaint clearly alleges that defendants use plaintiff's trademarks to sell advertising, and then link that advertising to results of searches. Those links appear to the user as "sponsored links." Thus, a fair reading of the complaint reveals that plaintiff alleges that defendants have unlawfully used its trademarks by allowing advertisers to bid on the trademarks and pay defendants to be linked to the trademarks.

Under the analysis in *PETA* defendants' offer of plaintiff's trademarks for use in advertising could falsely identify a business relationship or licensing agreement between defendants and the trademark holder. In other words, when defendants sell the rights to link advertising to plaintiff's trademarks, defendants are using the trademarks in commerce in a way that may imply that defendants have permission from the trademark holder to do so. This is a critical distinction from the *U-Haul* case, because in that case the only "trademark use" alleged was the use of the trademark in the pop-up software—the internal computer coding. WhenU allowed advertisers to bid on broad categories of terms that included the trademarks, but did not market the protected marks themselves as keywords to which advertisers could directly purchase rights.

Plaintiff further alleges that under theories of contributory and vicarious liability, defendants are liable when the advertisers themselves make "trademark use" of the GEICO marks by incorporating them into the advertisements, which are likely to deceive customers into believing that the advertisers provide accurate information about GEICO products or are somehow related to GEICO. Plaintiff also alleges that defendants exercise significant control over the content of advertisements that appear on their search results pages, and accordingly defendants are liable for Lanham Act violations by the advertisers. Accepting as true the facts alleged by plaintiff regarding the inclusion of the marks in advertisements and defendants' overall control of their advertising program, we find that plaintiffs have alleged facts sufficient to support their claims that advertisers make a "trademark use" of GEICO's marks, and that defendants may be liable for such "trademark use."

Accordingly, we find that plaintiff has sufficiently alleged that defendants used plaintiff's protected marks in commerce. This decision does not necessarily mean that defendants' use of plaintiff's trademarks violates either the Lanham Act or Virginia common law of unfair competition. That decision cannot be reached until discovery has been completed. "Where keyword placement of advertising is being sold, the portals and search engines are taking advantage of the drawing power and goodwill of these famous marks. The question is whether this activity is fair competition or whether it is a form of unfair free riding on the fame of well-known marks." J. Thomas McCarthy, McCarthy on Trademarks & Unfair Competition § 25:70.1 (2004). Whether defendants' uses are legitimate fair uses of the trademarks in competition, and whether they create a likelihood of confusion, are fact-specific issues not properly resolved through a motion to dismiss. . . .

[The court also rejected Google's and Overture's challenges to GEICO's claims of secondary liability for trademark infringement by those defendants' advertisers, primarily by holding that GEICO had sufficiently alleged trademark use of its marks by the advertisers. The court, however, granted the defendants' motion to dismiss state law claims of tortious interference with prospective economic advantage and statutory business conspiracy.]

Bihari v. Gross
119 F.Supp.2d 309 (S.D.N.Y.2000).

■ SCHEINDLIN, DISTRICT JUDGE.

Plaintiffs Marianne Bihari and Bihari Interiors, Inc. (collectively "Bihari") move to preliminarily enjoin defendants Craig Gross and Yolanda Truglio (collectively "Gross") from using the names "Bihari" or "Bihari Interiors" in the domain names or metatags of any of their websites ("the Gross websites"), claiming that such use violates the Anticybersquatting Consumer Protection Act ("ACPA"), 15 U.S.C. § 1125(d)(1), and infringes on Bihari's common-law service mark in violation of § 43(a) of the Lanham Act, 15 U.S.C. § 1125(a)(1)(A). . . . Neither party has requested an evidentiary hearing. For the reasons set forth below, Bihari's motion for preliminary injunctive relief is denied.

I. Introduction

[The court presents a brief description of the Internet, domain names and meta-tags.]

II. Background

A. *The Failed Contract*

Marianne Bihari is an interior designer who has been providing interior design services in New York City, New Jersey, Connecticut, California, Florida and Italy since 1984. Since 1989, she has been continuously doing business as Bihari Interiors or Marianne Bihari d/b/a Bihari Interiors. The Bihari Interiors name is well known, particularly in the New York City high-end residential interior design market. Bihari does not engage in paid advertising to promote her services; rather, she relies on referrals from clients and other design-industry professionals.

Craig Gross is a former client of Bihari Interiors. Yolanda Truglio is Gross's girl-friend. On February 12, 1998, Gross, on behalf of 530 East 76th Street, Inc., retained Bihari Interiors to provide interior and architectural design services for his condo-minium apartment on East 76th Street ("the Contract"). For various reasons not relevant to this action, the relationship between Bihari and Gross soured, and the Contract was never completed.

On June 14, 1999, Gross filed suit against Marianne Bihari and Bihari Interiors in New York State Supreme Court alleging fraud and breach of contract ("the State Suit"). On August 12, 1999, Gross submitted an amended verified complaint in the State Suit. On April 3, 2000, the state court dismissed two of the fraud claims, but granted Gross a right to replead one of those claims. Gross has since filed a second amended complaint which is currently pending in New York State Supreme Court . . . .

B. *The Alleged Harassment*

Approximately two months after Gross first filed the complaint in the State Suit, on August 10, 1999, Bihari, Gross and Truglio engaged in settlement negotia-tions, which were ultimately unsuccessful. Four days later, Gross registered the domain names "bihari.com" and "bihariinteriors.com". On August 16, 1999, Bihari received an anonymous facsimile alerting her to the website. The following day, Bihari accessed the website "www.bihariinteriors.com". Disturbed by the unau-thorized use of her name and her business name in the domain name, as well as the disparaging statements on the website, Bihari contacted her attorney. On Au-gust 31, 1999, Bihari's attorney sent a letter to Gross demanding that he terminate the website. *See* Amended Complaint Rather than complying with Bihari's de-mand, Gross delivered to Bihari's residence pens bearing the words "www.bihariinteriors.com". In addition, Bihari alleges that subsequent to the de-livery of the pens, Bihari received frequent "hang-up telephone calls" which lasted until approximately November 22, 1999. Bihari filed a criminal complaint for ag-gravated harassment against Gross and Truglio on October 3, 1999, but the District

Attorney's office declined to prosecute.

Bihari was the subject of a criminal complaint several months later. Before the contract relationship between Gross and Bihari deteriorated, Bihari Interiors sold Gross three sofas purchased from a vendor. Bihari Interiors made the initial payments for the sofas. By the terms of the Contract, if Bihari Interiors failed to pay in full by a certain date, the vendor would be free to resell the sofas. After the payment deadline expired, Gross paid the vendor the balance due on the sofas, thereby avoiding payment of Bihari Interiors' commission. The sofas, however, were not delivered to Gross, but to Bihari, who took possession of them pending resolution of the State Suit. Bihari alleges that Gross then filed a criminal complaint against her for theft of the sofas. On December 20, 1999, Bihari was arrested, held for approximately six hours, and "charged with criminal possession of stolen property in the fifth degree, a misdemeanor offense." On January 24, 2000, Bihari was informed that the District Attorney's office had declined to prosecute her case.

C. *The Websites*

On March 7, 2000, Bihari served Gross with the instant Complaint and motion for injunctive relief. Gross then offered to take down the "bihariinteriors.com" website pending a preliminary injunction hearing. He has since relinquished the domain names "bihari.com" and "bihariinteriors.com" and is taking all necessary steps to return those domain names to Network Solutions, Inc., the provider of domain name registrations.

On March 7, 2000, the day that Bihari served Gross with the Complaint, Bihari also learned of another website created by Gross, "designcam.com", by using an Internet search engine and searching for the words "Bihari Interiors". Bihari discovered that the "designscam.com" website contained the same content as the "bihariinteriors.com" website. Then, on March 11, 2000, Gross registered a fourth website, "manhattaninteriordesign.com", containing the identical material as "designscam.com".

All of the Gross websites use "Bihari Interiors" as metatags embedded within the websites' HTML code. The description metatags of the Gross websites state "This site deals with the problems experienced when hiring a new [sic] York City (Manhattan) designer. It discusses Marianne Bihari [,] fraud and deceit and interior decorating."

D. *The Website Content*

Each of the Gross websites is critical of Bihari and her interior design services. An Internet user accessing any of the websites first sees a large caption reading "The Real Story Behind Marianne Bihari & Bihari Interiors." Directly beneath this title are three photographic reproductions of scenic New York. Beneath the photographs is a counter indicating how many visitors the website has had. As of June 26, 2000, the counter indicated that 9,774 people have visited the website since August 15, 1999. Also appearing on the first page of the websites are various hyperlinks including "Tips on Picking a Designer," "New York City Information," "Who's Who in Interior Design," "Kabalarians Philosophy," "A Humorous Look," "Tell A Friend," "Send E-Mail," "Sign or Read the Guest Book," and "Participate in the Bihari Poll."

A long block of text appears beneath these hyperlinks and it states:

> Welcome to the first website designed to protect people from the alleged ill intentions of Marianne Bihari & Bihari Interiors. Keep in mind that this site reflects only the view points and experiences of one Manhattan couple that allegedly fell prey to Marianne Bihari & Bihari Interiors. There possibly may be others that have experienced similar alleged fraud and deceit from Marianne Bihari & Bihari Interiors. Please feel free to e-mail us if you think you were victimized by Marianne Bihari & Bihari Interiors. Our goal is to protect you from experiencing the overwhelming grief and aggravation in dealing with someone that allegedly only has intentions to defraud. If you think you need advice before entering into a contract with Marianne Bihari & Bihari Interiors—Please Click Here.

Below this text a viewer finds additional hyperlinks to "The Initial Meeting," "The Contract," "The Scam," and "The Law Suit" [sic]. Viewers who connect with these links do not immediately receive the information, but are told that if they send an e-mail, they will receive a copy of the requested information.

In addition to these comments, the Gross websites contain a "guestbook" where visitors leave messages for other visitors to the websites. Some of the guestbook entries indicate that potential clients declined to retain Bihari's services because of the Gross websites. Other messages simply comment or inquire about the Gross websites' design. Many other entries disparage Bihari and Bihari Interiors. Bihari alleges that many of the guestbook entries were written by Gross and Truglio, and do not reflect true dissatisfaction with Bihari or Bihari Interiors.

The "designscam.com" and "manhattaninteriordesign.com" websites also contain a box which presents in blinking green letters the following incomplete statement quoted from Bihari's March 3, 2000 Affidavit: "I was arrested and charged with criminal possession of stolen property in the Fifth Degree." Gross neither includes the rest of the sentence—which reveals that the arrest was for a misdemeanor offense—nor informs the reader that the District Attorney's Office declined to prosecute the case.

In June 2000, Gross launched amended versions of the "designcam.com" and "manhattaninteriordesign.com" websites. The new websites are substantially identical to the former version, with two exceptions. Gross deleted the statement, "Our goal is to protect you from experiencing the overwhelming grief and aggravation in dealing with someone that allegedly only has intentions to defraud." *Second,* he added two hyperlinks—from the words "alleged fraud" and "lawsuit"—to a copy of the First Amended Complaint in the State Suit.

E. *Motive and Intent*

The parties dispute defendants' motive and intent in creating the websites. Bihari alleges that Gross's motive was to harass Bihari and to pressure her into settling the State Suit. Gross counters that he created the websites because he was disturbed by Bihari's "deceitful practices," and was "dedicated to assisting consumers who are in the process of choosing a designer in New York City, as well as informing others of my experiences with Bihari." While there is no direct proof that Gross's motive is to pressure Bihari to settle the State Suit, there is proof that Gross intends to harm Bihari's business. Gross's specific intent, as memorialized in his own words on his websites, is to warn potential customers of Bihari's "alleged ill intentions" and to "protect" them from experiencing "the overwhelming grief and aggravation" he has experienced in dealing with Bihari. Undeniably, Gross's intent is to cause Bihari commercial harm. . . .

IV. Discussion

. . .

A claim of trademark infringement under § 43(a) of the Lanham Act requires the plaintiff to show (1) that she has a valid mark that is entitled to protection under the Lanham Act, and (2) that use of that mark by another "is likely to cause confusion . . . as to the affiliation, connection, or association of such person with another person, or as to the origin, sponsorship, or approval of [the defendant's] goods, services, or commercial activities by another person." 15 U.S.C. § 1125(a)(1)(A); *Estee Lauder Inc. v. The Gap, Inc.*, 108 F.3d 1503, 1508–09 (2d Cir.1997). As discussed more fully below, Bihari has failed to demonstrate a likelihood of success on the merits of this claim because Gross's use of the "Bihari Interiors" mark in the metatags is not likely to cause confusion and is protected as a fair use.

. . .

d. Initial Interest Confusion

Even if actual confusion is unlikely, Plaintiffs argue that there is a likelihood of "initial interest confusion." Accepting, arguendo, the concept of initial interest confusion in an Internet case,[14] Bihari has failed to prove a likelihood of initial interest confusion.

An infringement action may be based on a claim that the alleged infringement creates initial consumer interest, even if no actual sale is completed as a result of the confusion. In the cyberspace context, the concern is that potential customers of one website will be diverted and distracted to a competing website. The harm is that the potential customer believes that the competing website is associated with the website the customer was originally searching for and will not resume searching for the original website.

The Ninth Circuit recently provided a useful metaphor for explaining the harm of initial interest confusion in cyberspace:

---

[14] Although the Second Circuit has not explicitly applied this doctrine in an Internet case, the Ninth Circuit has. *See Brookfield Communications*, 174 F.3d at 1062–63 (relying on *Mobil Oil Corp. v. Pegasus Petroleum Corp.*, 818 F.2d 254, 257–58 (2d Cir.1987)). In addition, at least two courts in the Second Circuit have analyzed a trademark case involving metatags by applying the initial interest confusion doctrine. *See New York State Society of Certified Public Accountants*, 79 F.Supp.2d at 341; *OBH, Inc. v. Spotlight Magazine, Inc.*, 86 F.Supp.2d 176, 190 (W.D.N.Y.2000); *but see BigStar Entertainment, Inc. v. Next Big Star, Inc.*, 105 F.Supp.2d 185, 207–210 (S.D.N.Y.2000) (refusing to apply initial interest confusion doctrine).

> Using another's trademark in one's metatags is much like posting a sign with another's trademark in front of one's store. Suppose West Coast's, [the defendant], competitor (let's call it "Blockbuster") puts up a billboard on a highway reading—"West Coast Video: 2 miles ahead at Exit 7"—where West Coast is really located at Exit 8 but Blockbuster is located at Exit 7. Customers looking for West Coast's store will pull off at Exit 7 and drive around looking for it. Unable to locate West Coast, but seeing the Blockbuster store right by the highway entrance, they may simply rent there. Even consumers who prefer West Coast may find it not worth the trouble to continue searching for West Coast since there is a Blockbuster right there.

Brookfield Communications, 174 F.3d at 1064.[15]

The highway analogy pinpoints what is missing in this case. Inserting "Bihari Interiors" in the metatags is not akin to a misleading "billboard," which diverts drivers to a competing store and "misappropriat[es] [plaintiff's] acquired goodwill." *Id.* ("[T]he fact that there is only initial consumer confusion does not alter the fact that [the defendant] would be misappropriating [the plaintiff's] good will."). Far from diverting "people looking for information on Bihari Interiors," as plaintiffs allege, the Gross websites provide users with information about Bihari Interiors. Furthermore, the Gross websites cannot divert Internet users away from Bihari's website because Bihari does not have a competing website. *See BigStar Entertainment,* 105 F.Supp.2d at 209–10 (stating that initial interest confusion does not arise where parties are not in close competitive proximity).

Furthermore, users are unlikely to experience initial interest confusion when searching the Internet for information about Bihari Interiors. In support of their motion, Plaintiffs' counsel provided a typical search result when "Bihari Interiors" is entered into the search field. The search revealed twelve websites, eight of which appear to be the Gross websites. Of those eight, five bear the heading "Manhattan Interior Design Scam—Bihari Interiors." Each website with that heading contains the following description underneath the title: "This site deals with the problems experienced when hiring a New York City (Manhattan) designer. It discusses Marianne Bihari[,] fraud and deceit and. . . ." An Internet user who reads this text, and then sees the domain name of "designscam.com" or "manhattaninteriordesign.com", is unlikely to believe that these websites belong to Bihari Interiors or Bihari. . . .

The few decisions holding that use of another entity's trademark in metatags constitutes trademark infringement involved very different circumstances. *Niton Corp. v. Radiation Monitoring Devices, Inc.,* 27 F.Supp.2d 102 (D.Mass.1998), for example, provides a good example of the use of metatags to divert a competitor's customers. *First,* Radiation Monitoring Devices ("RMD") and Niton Corporation

---

[15] Use of the highway billboard metaphor is not the best analogy to a metatag on the Internet. The harm caused by a misleading billboard on the highway is difficult to correct. In contrast, on the information superhighway, resuming one's search for the correct website is relatively simple. With one click of the mouse and a few seconds delay, a viewer can return to the search engine's results and resume searching for the original website.

("Niton") were direct competitors. *Second*, RMD did not simply use Niton's trademark in its metatag. Rather, RMD directly copied Niton's metatags and HTML code. As a result, an Internet search using the phrase "home page of Niton Corporation" revealed three matches for Niton's website and five for RMD's website. *See id.* at 104. RMD obviously was taking advantage of Niton's good will to divert customers to the RMD website.

Similarly, in *Playboy Enters., Inc. v. Asiafocus Int'l, Inc.*, No. Civ. A. 97–734–A, 1998 WL 724000, at *3, **6–7 (E.D.Va. Apr.10, 1998), the court enjoined use of the marks "Playboy" and "Playmate" in the domain name and metatags of defendant's website. The defendant provided adult nude photos on web pages located at "asian-playmates.com" and "playmates-asian.com". The "Playboy" and "Playmate" trademarks were embedded in the metatags such that a search for Playboy Enterprises Inc.'s ("Playboy") website would produce a list that included "asian-playmates.com". *See also Playboy Enters., Inc. v. Calvin Designer Label*, 985 F.Supp. 1220, 1221 (N.D.Cal.1997) (preliminarily enjoining defendant's website, "www.playboyxxx.com" and repeated use of the "Playboy" trademark in defendant's metatags). Defendants in these cases were clearly attempting to divert potential customers from Playboy's website to their own.

Even *Brookfield Communications*, where initial interest confusion was first applied to metatags, presents convincing proof of diversion. Brookfield sought to protect its trademark in its "MovieBuff" software, which provides entertainment-industry information. Brookfield had created a website offering an Internet-based searchable database under the "Moviebuff" mark. The defendant, West Coast, a video rental store chain, registered a site at "moviebuff.com" which also contained a searchable entertainment database. The court held that defendant's use of the "moviebuff.com" domain name constituted trademark infringement. The court also enjoined West Coast from using any term confusingly similar to "moviebuff" in the metatags based on the initial interest confusion caused by the use of Brookfield's mark, which would redound to West Coast's financial benefit.

In each of these cases, the defendant was using the plaintiff's mark to trick Internet users into visiting defendant's website, believing either that they were visiting plaintiff's website or that the defendant's website was sponsored by the plaintiff. [In contrast to those cases,] Gross's use of the "Bihari Interiors" mark in the metatags is not a bad-faith attempt to trick users into visiting his websites, but rather a means of cataloging those sites.

. . .

V. Conclusion

For the foregoing reasons, Bihari's motion for a preliminary injunction is denied in its entirety. . . .

EXTENSIONS

---

1. *More initial interest confusion.* In *Promatek Industries, Ltd. v. Equitrac Corporation*, 300 F.3d 808 (7th Cir.2002), the court followed the approach of *Brookfield Communications* to hold that a company may not use in the metatags of its website the trademark of a competitor, even where the company services products made by the competitor and identified by the trademark. The court held that Promatek was likely to succeed in establishing that initial interest confusion would likely result from Equitrac's use in its metatags of the term "Copitrak"—despite the fact that Equitrac actually does provide maintenance and service on Copitrak equipment. Does this decision imply that Equitrac could not use the term "Copitrak" in visible text on its website, such as "We service Copitrak equipment."? Note that search engines rely primarily on the visible text in selecting sites for their search results.

2. *Keyword Advertising and Trademark Use: Further Developments.* The question that the *GEICO* decision addressed—whether a search engine's use of a trademarked term as an advertising keyword constitutes a "use" of the term within the scope of the trademark owner's rights under the Lanham Act—was also considered in *Google, Inc. v. American Blind & Wallpaper Factory, Inc.*, 2005 WL 832398 (N.D.Cal.2005). Declining to dismiss the trademark owner's complaint against Google for failure to state a claim, the court refused to hold that Google did not *use* the mark in a way prohibited under the Lanham Act, relying in part on the analysis in *Playboy v. Netscape Communications*, *supra*: "In light of the very liberal standard applicable to Rule 12(b)(6) motions, the Ninth Circuit's expansive holding in *Playboy*, and the obvious commercial importance of this case to the parties and others similarly situated, the Court concludes that resolution of the novel legal questions presented by this case should await the development of a full factual record." *Id.*

3. *Keyword Advertising and Likelihood of Confusion.* GEICO's claims against Google went to trial in December 2004, and during the trial Judge Brinkema orally granted in part a Google motion for judgment as a matter of law, ruling that GEICO had failed to show any likelihood that a Google user would be confused by sponsored links displayed in response to the user's search on GEICO's trademarked term, if the sponsored link itself did not contain the trademarked term. Judge Brinkema also ruled that GEICO had shown that sponsored links containing the term "GEICO" were likely to confuse consumers, but did not determine whether Google itself (as opposed to the advertisers who used "GEICO" in their sponsored links) was liable for infringement.

QUESTIONS FOR DISCUSSION

1. *Initial interest confusion and metatags.* In *Bihari v. Gross*, the court rejects plaintiffs' argument that the defendant's websites cause initial interest confusion and are, therefore, infringing. One reason for the court's conclusion is that the plaintiff had no website. Would the result have changed if the plaintiff did have a website? Five of the eight websites operated by the defendant appear to have included a "description" metatag which contained the statement that "This site deals with the problems experienced when hiring a New York City (Manhattan) Designer. It discusses Marianne Bihari fraud and deceit . . . ." Assuming that this description was presented on the results page containing links to defendant's websites, would this strengthen or weaken plaintiffs' argument for finding initial interest confusion?

2. *Contributory initial interest confusion.* In *Playboy Enterprises v. Netscape*, the court expressed uncertainty as to whether Netscape's infringement, if ultimately proved, would be direct or contributory: "Whether the defendants are directly or merely contributorily liable proves to be a tricky question. However, we need not decide that question here. We conclude that defendants are either directly or contributorily liable." The court thus extended the scope of *Brookfield* by recognizing, for the first time, the theory of *contributory* initial interest confusion. The decision breaks ground on two fronts, applying both the theory of initial interest confusion and that of contributory infringement to novel factual situations.

Do you agree with Judge Berzon's criticism of *Brookfield*? If her view were adopted, would there be any sort of online conduct to which the doctrine of initial interest confusion could apply?

C. CONTEXTUAL POP-UP ADVERTISING

Online advertising using contextual pop-up ads has recently gained prominence, and has spawned a series of lawsuits. The most widely distributed versions of such adware are programs distributed by WhenU.com, Inc. and by Claria Corp. (formerly Gator Corp.). As of mid-2004, each company claimed that its software was installed on tens of millions of consumers' computers, and that it served ads on behalf of hundreds of advertisers. The software, once installed on a user's computer, analyzes the user's online activity and serves ads targeted to that activity.

These pop-up ads have caused considerable dismay among businesses whose websites are obscured in whole or in part by advertisements for their competitors. For example, a consumer who is viewing U-Haul's site, and therefore presumptively interested in renting a truck or trailer, may suddenly be presented with an ad for Ryder, U-Haul's competitor.

A number of businesses were sufficiently dismayed that they brought an action against WhenU.com, alleging that presentation of the pop-up ads constituted trademark infringement and copyright infringement. Two district courts granted WhenU.com summary judgment on the trademark claims against it, on the ground that there was no use in commerce of the plaintiffs' trademarks, a prerequisite for a Lanham Act claim. *U-Haul International, Inc. v. WhenU.com, Inc.*, 279 F.Supp.2d 723, 725–26 (E.D.Va.2003); *Wells Fargo & Co. v. WhenU.com, Inc.*, 293 F.Supp.2d 734 (E.D.Mich.2003). However, in *1-800 Contacts, Inc. v. WhenU.com, Inc.*, 309 F.Supp.2d 467 (S.D.N.Y.2003), the court granted a preliminary injunction, holding plaintiff was likely to succeed in proving that the pop-up ads were actionable as trademark infringement, a decision that the following Second Circuit opinion reviews:

1-800 Contacts, Inc. v. WhenU.Com, Inc.
2005 WL 1524515 (2d Cir.2005).

■ JOHN M. WALKER, JR., CHIEF JUDGE.

Defendant-appellant WhenU.com, Inc. ("WhenU") is an internet marketing company that uses a proprietary software called "SaveNow" to monitor a computer user's internet activity in order to provide the computer user ("C-user") with advertising, in the form of "pop-up ads," that is relevant to that activity. Plaintiff-appellee 1-800 Contacts, Inc. ("1-800") is a distributor that sells contact lenses and related products by mail, telephone, and internet website. At the time 1-800 filed this action . . ., it owned a registered trademark in the service mark "WE DELIVER. YOU SAVE." and had filed applications with the United States Patent and Trademark Office on July 8, 1999, to register the service mark "1-800CONTACTS",[2] and on October 2, 2000, to register the service mark of "1-800CONTACTS" in a specific color-blocked design logo.

---

[2] 1-800 obtained registration for this service mark on January 21, 2003.

1-800 filed a complaint alleging, inter alia,[4] that WhenU was infringing 1-800's trademarks, in violation of the Lanham Act, 15 U.S.C. §§ 1114(1), 1125(a)(1), by causing pop-up ads of 1-800's competitors to appear on a C-user's desktop when the C-user has accessed 1-800's website. [T]he district court granted 1-800's motion for a preliminary injunction as it related to 1-800's trademark claims . . . *1-800 Contacts, Inc. v. WhenU.com*, 309 F.Supp.2d 467 (S.D.N.Y.2003) ("1-800-Contacts"). WhenU has filed this interlocutory appeal.

We hold that, as a matter of law, WhenU does not "use" 1-800's trademarks within the meaning of the Lanham Act, 15 U.S.C. § 1127, when it (1) includes 1-800's website address, which is almost identical to 1-800's trademark, in an unpublished directory of terms that trigger delivery of WhenU's contextually relevant advertising to C-users; or (2) causes separate, branded pop-up ads to appear on a C-user's computer screen either above, below, or along the bottom edge of the 1-800 website window. . . .

BACKGROUND

I. The Internet and Windows

By way of introduction to this case we incorporate the district court's helpful tutorial on the . . . Microsoft Windows operating environment as it pertains to this litigation: . . .

> [M]any [C-users] access the Internet with computers that use the Microsoft Windows operating system ("Windows"). Windows allows a [C-user] to work in numerous software applications simultaneously. In Windows, the background screen is called the "desktop." When a software program is launched, a "window" appears on the desktop, within which the functions of that program are displayed and operate. A [C-user] may open multiple windows simultaneously, allowing the [C-user] to launch and use more than one software application at the same time. Individual windows may be moved around the desktop, and because the computer screen is two-dimensional, one window may obscure another window, thus appearing to be "in front of" another window.

[*1-800 Contacts*, 309 F.Supp.2d] at 475 (internal citations omitted). Some programs on a C-user's computer, such as a calendar or e-mail application, may cause windows to open on the C-user's desktop independently of any contemporaneous action by the C-user. See *Wells Fargo & Co. v. WhenU.com, Inc.*, 293 F.Supp.2d 734 (E.D.Mich.2003) . . . .

---

[4] In addition to the trademark claims, 1-800 asserts claims for (1) unfair competition, false designation of origin, trademark dilution, and cybersquatting, in violation of § 43 of the Lanham Act, 15 U.S.C. § 1125; (2) copyright infringement and contributory copyright infringement, in violation of the Federal Copyright Act, 17 U.S.C. §§ 101, et seq.; and (3) state law claims for trademark dilution and injury to business reputation, in violation of N.Y. Gen. Bus. L. § 360-l; and (4) common law claims for unfair competition and tortious interference with prospective economic advantage.

Several claims name Vision Direct, Inc., one of the 1-800 competitors whose advertisements were featured in WhenU's pop-up ads, as either defendant or co-defendant with WhenU.

II. The Challenged Conduct

The specific conduct at issue in this case has been described in detail by the district court, see *1-800 Contacts*, 309 F.Supp.2d at 476–78, as well as other courts that have addressed similar claims against WhenU, see *Wells Fargo*, 293 F.Supp.2d at 738–40, 743–46; *U-Haul Int'l, Inc. v. WhenU.com, Inc.*, 279 F.Supp.2d 723, 725–26 (E.D.Va.2003). Accordingly, we recite only those facts relevant to this appeal.

WhenU provides a proprietary software called "SaveNow" without charge to individual C-users, usually as part of a bundle of software that the C-user voluntarily downloads from the internet. "Once installed, the SaveNow software requires no action by the [C-user] to activate its operations; instead, the SaveNow software responds to a [C-user]'s 'in-the-moment' activities by generating pop-up advertisement windows" that are relevant to those specific activities. *1-800 Contacts*, 309 F.Supp.2d at 477. To deliver contextually relevant advertising to C-users, the SaveNow software employs an internal directory comprising "approximately 32,000 [website addresses] and [address] fragments, 29,000 search terms and 1,200 keyword algorithms," *Wells Fargo*, 293 F.Supp.2d at 743 ¶ 58, that correlate with particular consumer interests to screen the words a C-user types into a web browser or search engine or that appear within the internet sites a C-user visits.

When the SaveNow software recognizes a term, it randomly selects an advertisement from the corresponding product or service category to deliver to the C-user's computer screen at roughly the same time the website or search result sought by the C-user appears. As the district court explained,

> The SaveNow software generates at least three kinds of ads—an ad may be a small 'pop-up' . . . [that appears] in the bottom right-hand corner of a [C-user]'s screen; it may be a 'pop-under' advertisement that appears behind the webpage the [C-user] initially visited; or it may be a 'panoramic' ad[] that stretches across the bottom of the [C-user]'s computer screen.

1-800 Contacts, 309 F.Supp.2d at 478. Each type of ad appears in a window that is separate from the particular website or search-results page the C-user has accessed. In addition, a label stating "A WhenU Offer—click ? for info." appears in the window frame surrounding the ad, together with a button on the top right of the window frame marked "?" that, when clicked by the C-user, displays a new window containing information about WhenU and its ads,[7] as well as instructions for uninstalling the resident SaveNow software.

---

[7] Specifically, C-users are informed that

"this offer is brought to you by WhenU.com, through the SaveNow service. SaveNow alerts you to offers and services at the moment when they are most relevant to you. SaveNow does not collect any personal information or browsing history from its users. Your privacy is 100 percent protected. The offers shown to you by SaveNow are not affiliated with the site you are visiting. For more about SaveNow, click here or e-mail information at WhenU.com. At WhenU, we are committed to putting you in control of your Internet experience."

1-800 Contacts, 309 F. Supp. 2d at 478 n. 22.

Usually there is a "few-second" delay between the moment a user accesses a website, and the point at which a SaveNow pop-up advertisement appears on the [C-user]'s screen.

If a SaveNow user who has accessed the 1-800 Contacts website and has received a WhenU.com pop-up advertisement does not want to view the advertisement or the advertiser's website, the user can click on the visible portion of the [1-800] window . . ., [which will move] the 1-800 Contacts website . . . to the front of the screen display, with the pop-up ad moving behind the website window. Or, . . . the [C-user] can close the pop-up website by clicking on its "X," or close, button. If the user clicks on the pop-up ad, the main browser window (containing the 1-800 Contacts website) will be navigated to the website of the advertiser that was featured inside the pop-up advertisement.

Id. at 476–77 (internal citations omitted).

In its complaint, 1-800 alleges that WhenU's conduct infringes 1-800's trademarks, in violation of Sections 32(1) and 43(a) of the Lanham Act, 15 U.S.C. §§ 1114(1), 1125(a), by delivering advertisements of 1-800's competitors (e.g., Vision Direct, Inc.) to C-users who have intentionally accessed 1-800's website. Although somewhat difficult to discern from the complaint, the allegations that pertain specifically to 1-800's trademark claims appear to be as follows: (1) WhenU's pop-up ads appear "on," "over," or "on top of" the 1-800 website without 1-800's authorization, and change its appearance; (2) as a result, the ads impermissibly "appear to be an integral and fully authorized part of [1-800's] website"; (3) in addition, WhenU's unauthorized pop-up ads "interfere with and disrupt the carefully designed display of content" on the website, thereby altering and hindering a C-user's access to 1-800's website; (4) WhenU is thereby "free-riding" and "trad[ing] upon the goodwill and substantial customer recognition associated with the 1-800 Contacts marks"; and (5) WhenU is using 1-800's trademarks in a manner that creates a likelihood of confusion.

. . .

DISCUSSION

WhenU challenges the district court's finding that WhenU "uses" 1-800's trademarks within the meaning of the Lanham Act, 15 U.S.C. § 1127. In the alternative, WhenU argues that the district court erred in finding that WhenU's pop-up ads create a likelihood of both source confusion and "initial interest confusion," as to whether WhenU is "somehow associated with [1-800] or that [1-800] has consented to [WhenU's] use of the pop-up ad[s]." Because we agree with WhenU that it does not "use" 1-800's trademarks, we need not and do not address the issue of likelihood of confusion.

I. Legal Standards

. . .

B. Lanham Act

In order to prevail on a trademark infringement claim for registered trademarks, pursuant to 15 U.S.C. § 1114, or unregistered trademarks, pursuant to 15

U.S.C. § 1125(a)(1), a plaintiff must establish that (1) it has a valid mark that is entitled to protection under the Lanham Act; and that (2) the defendant used the mark, (3) in commerce, (4) "in connection with the sale . . . or advertising of goods or services," 15 U.S.C. § 1114(1)(a), (5) without the plaintiff's consent. In addition, the plaintiff must show that defendant's use of that mark "is likely to cause confusion . . . as to the affiliation, connection, or association of [defendant] with [plaintiff], or as to the origin, sponsorship, or approval of [the defendant's] goods, services, or commercial activities by [plaintiff]." 15 U.S.C. § 1125(a)(1)(A).

The only issue before us on appeal is . . . whether the district court erred in finding that 1-800 had demonstrated a likelihood of success on its trademark claims. . . . [T]he district court erred as a matter of law in finding that WhenU "uses" 1-800's trademark. Because 1-800 cannot establish an essential element of its trademark claims, not only must the preliminary injunction be vacated, but 1-800's trademark infringement claims must be dismissed as well.

II. "Use" Under the Lanham Act

The Lanham Act defines "use in commerce," in relevant part, as follows:

> . . . For purposes of this Chapter, a mark shall be deemed to be in use in commerce —
>
> (1) on goods when —
>
> (A) it is placed in any manner on the goods or their containers or the displays associated therewith or on the tags or labels affixed thereto, or if the nature of the goods makes such placement impracticable, then on documents associated with the goods or their sale, and
>
> (B) the goods are sold or transported in commerce, and
>
> (2) on services when it is used or displayed in the sale or advertising of services and the services are rendered in commerce . . .

15 U.S.C. § 1127.

> In issuing the preliminary injunction, the district court held that WhenU
>
> use[s] [1-800]'s mark in two ways. First, in causing pop-up advertisements for Defendant Vision Direct to appear when SaveNow users have specifically attempted to access [1-800]'s website — on which Plaintiff's trademark appears — [WhenU is] displaying Plaintiff's mark "in the . . . advertising of" Defendant Vision Direct's services . . . [and, t]hus, . . . [is] "using" Plaintiff's marks that appear on Plaintiff's website.
>
> Second, Defendant WhenU.com includes Plaintiff's [website address], <www.1800contacts. com>, [which incorporates 1-800's trademark,] in the proprietary WhenU.com directory of terms that triggers pop-up advertisements on SaveNow users' computers. In so doing, Defendant WhenU.com "uses" Plaintiff's mark . . . to advertise and publicize companies that are in direct competition with Plaintiff.

1-800 Contacts, 309 F.Supp.2d at 489.

Prior to the district court's decision, two other courts had addressed the issue of "use" as it applies to WhenU's specific activities and reached the opposite conclusion. In *Wells Fargo & Co. v. WhenU.com, Inc.,* 293 F.Supp.2d 734 (E.D.Mich.2003), the district court denied Wells Fargo's motion for a preliminary injunction after finding that WhenU's inclusion of plaintiff Wells Fargo's trademarked website address in WhenU's proprietary directory of keywords was not "use" for purposes of the Lanham Act, and that WhenU did not alter or interfere with Wells Fargo's website in any manner. The district court in *U-Haul International, Inc. v. WhenU.com, Inc.,* 279 F.Supp.2d 723 (E.D.Va.2003), employing a very similar analysis, granted summary judgment in favor of WhenU after concluding that WhenU's inclusion of U-Haul's trademarked website address in the SaveNow directory was not actionable because it was for a "pure machine-linking function" that was not "use" under the Lanham Act. *Id. at 728* (internal quotation marks omitted).

In the case before us, the district court's consideration of these two comprehensive decisions on the precise issue at hand was confined to a footnote in which it cited the cases, summarized their holdings in parentheticals, and concluded, without discussion, that it "disagree[d] with, and [was] not bound by these findings." *1-800 Contacts,* 309 F.Supp.2d at 490 n.43. Unlike the district court, we find the thorough analyses set forth in both *U-Haul* and *Wells Fargo* to be persuasive and compelling.

A. The SaveNow Directory

The district court held that WhenU's inclusion of 1-800's website address in the SaveNow directory constitutes a prohibited "use" of 1-800's trademark. We disagree.

At the outset, we note that WhenU does not "use" 1-800's trademark in the manner ordinarily at issue in an infringement claim: it does not "place" 1-800 trademarks on any goods or services in order to pass them off as emanating from or authorized by 1-800. The fact is that WhenU does not reproduce or display 1-800's trademarks at all, nor does it cause the trademarks to be displayed to a C-user. Rather, WhenU reproduces 1-800's website address, <www.1800contacts.com>, which is similar, but not identical, to 1-800's 1-800CONTACTS trademark.

The district court found that the differences between 1-800's trademarks and the website address utilized by WhenU were insignificant because they were limited to the addition of the "www." and ".com" and the omission of the hyphen and a space. We conclude that, to the contrary, the differences between the marks are quite significant because they transform 1-800's trademark—which is entitled to protection under the Lanham Act—into a word combination that functions more or less like a public key to 1-800's website.

Moreover, it is plain that WhenU is using 1-800's website address precisely because it is a website address, rather than because it bears any resemblance to 1-800's trademark, because the only place WhenU reproduces the address is in the SaveNow directory. Although the directory resides in the C-user's computer, it is inaccessible to both the C-user and the general public. See *id.* at 476 (noting that directory is scrambled to preclude access). Thus, the appearance of 1-800's website address in the directory does not create a possibility of visual confusion with 1-

800's mark. More important, a WhenU pop-up ad cannot be triggered by a C-user's input of the 1-800 trademark or the appearance of that trademark on a webpage accessed by the C-user. Rather, in order for WhenU to capitalize on the fame and recognition of 1-800's trademark—the improper motivation both 1-800 and the district court ascribe to WhenU—it would have needed to put the actual trademark on the list.[11]

In contrast to some of its competitors, moreover, WhenU does not disclose the proprietary contents of the SaveNow directory to its advertising clients nor does it permit these clients to request or purchase specified keywords to add to the directory. See *GEICO v. Google, Inc.*, 330 F.Supp.2d 700, 703–04 (E.D.Va.2004) (distinguishing WhenU's conduct from defendants' practice of selling "keywords" to its advertising clients) . . . ; see also *U-Haul*, 273 F.Supp.2d at 728 (discussing other practices).[12]

A company's internal utilization of a trademark in a way that does not communicate it to the public is analogous to a individual's private thoughts about a trademark. Such conduct simply does not violate the Lanham Act, which is concerned with the use of trademarks in connection with the sale of goods or services in a manner likely to lead to consumer confusion as to the source of such goods or services. See 15 U.S.C. § 1127 . . . .

Accordingly, we conclude that WhenU's inclusion of the 1-800 website address in its SaveNow directory does not infringe on 1-800's trademark.

B. The Pop-up Advertisements

The primary issue to be resolved by this appeal is whether the placement of pop-up ads on a C-user's screen contemporaneously with either the 1-800 website or a list of search results obtained by the C-user's input of the 1-800 website address constitutes "use" under the Lanham Act, 15 U.S.C. §§ 1114(1), 1125(a). The district court reasoned that WhenU, by "causing pop-up advertisements for Defendant Vision Direct to appear when SaveNow users have specifically attempted to access [1-800]'s website, . . . [is] displaying [1-800]'s mark in the . . . advertising of . . . Vision Direct's services." *1-800 Contacts*, 309 F.Supp.2d at 489.

The fatal flaw with this holding is that WhenU's pop-up ads do not display the 1-800 trademark. The district court's holding, however, appears to have been based on the court's acceptance of 1-800's claim that WhenU's pop-up ads appear "on" and affect 1-800's website. See, *e.g., id.* at 479 (stating that WhenU has "no relation-

---

[11] This observation, however, is not intended to suggest that inclusion of a trademark in the directory would necessarily be an infringing "use." We express no view on this distinct issue.

[12] We think it noteworthy that prior to filing its lawsuit against WhenU, 1-800 entered into agreements with WhenU competitors Gator and Yahoo! to have its own pop-up and banner ads delivered to C-users in response to the C-users' input of particular website addresses and keywords that were specified by 1-800. Included in the list 1-800 provided to Gator, for instance, were the website addresses for several of 1-800's competitors, including defendant-appellee Vision Direct, Coastal Contacts, and Lens Express.

ship with the companies *on* whose websites the pop-up advertisements appear") (emphasis omitted) (emphasis added). As we explained above, the WhenU pop-up ads appear in a separate window that is prominently branded with the WhenU mark; they have absolutely no tangible effect on the appearance or functionality of the 1-800 website.

More important, the appearance of WhenU's pop-up ad is not contingent upon or related to 1-800's trademark, the trademark's appearance on 1-800's website, or the mark's similarity to 1-800's website address. Rather, the contemporaneous display of the ads and trademarks is the result of the happenstance that 1-800 chose to use a mark similar to its trademark as the address to its web page and to place its trademark on its website. The pop-up ad, which is triggered by the C-user's input of 1-800's website address, would appear even if 1-800's trademarks were not displayed on its website. A pop-up ad could also appear if the C-user typed the 1-800 website address, not as an address, but as a search term in the browser's search engine, and then accessed 1-800's website by using the hyperlink that appeared in the list of search results.

In addition, 1-800's website address is not the only term in the SaveNow directory that could trigger a Vision Direct ad to "pop up" on 1-800's website. For example, an ad could be triggered if a C-user searched for "contacts" or "eye care," both terms contained in the directory, and then clicked on the listed hyperlink to 1-800's website.

Exemplifying the conceptual difficulty that inheres in this issue, the district court's decision suggests that the crux of WhenU's wrongdoing—and the primary basis for the district court's finding of "use"—is WhenU's alleged effort to capitalize on a C-user's specific attempt to access the 1-800 website. As the court explained it,

> WhenU.com is doing far more than merely "displaying" Plaintiff's mark. WhenU's advertisements are delivered to a SaveNow user when the user directly accesses Plaintiff's website—thus allowing Defendant Vision Direct to profit from the goodwill and reputation in Plaintiff's website that led the user to access Plaintiff's website in the first place.

1-800 Contacts, 309 F.Supp.2d at 490. Absent improper use of 1-800's trademark, however, such conduct does not violate the Lanham Act. See *TrafFix Devices, Inc. v. Mktg. Displays, Inc.*, 532 U.S. 23, 29 (2001); *Kellogg Co. v. Nat'l Biscuit Co.*, 305 U.S. 111, 122 (1938) (holding that Kellogg's sharing in the goodwill of the unprotected "Shredded Wheat" market was "not unfair"); see also William P. Kratzke, Normative Economic Analysis of Trademark Law, 21 Memphis St. U. L. Rev. 199, 223 (1991) (criticizing importation into trademark law of "unjust enrichment" and "free riding" theories based on a trademark holder's goodwill). Indeed, it is routine for vendors to seek specific "product placement" in retail stores precisely to capitalize on their competitors' name recognition. For example, a drug store typically places its own store-brand generic products next to the trademarked products they emulate in order to induce a customer who has specifically sought out the trademarked product to consider the store's less-expensive alternative. WhenU employs this same marketing strategy by informing C-users who have sought out a specific trademarked product about available coupons, discounts, or alternative products that may be of interest to them.

1-800 disputes this analogy by arguing that unlike a drugstore, only the 1-800 website is displayed when the pop-up ad appears. This response, however, ignores the fact that a C-user who has installed the SaveNow software receives WhenU pop-up ads in a myriad of contexts, the vast majority of which are unlikely to have anything to do with 1-800 or the C-user's input of the 1-800 website address.[14]

The cases relied on by 1-800 do not alter our analysis. As explained in detail by the court in *U-Haul*, they are all readily distinguishable because WhenU's conduct does not involve any of the activities those courts found to constitute "use." *U-Haul*, 279 F.Supp. at 728–29. Significantly, WhenU's activities do not alter or affect 1-800's website in any way. Nor do they divert or misdirect C-users away from 1-800's website, or alter in any way the results a C-user will obtain when searching with the 1-800 trademark or website address. *Id.* at 728-29. Compare *Playboy Enters., Inc. v. Netscape Communications Corp.*, 354 F.3d 1020, 1024 (9th Cir.2004) (holding that infringement could be based on defendant's insertion of unidentified banner ads on C-user's search-results page); *Brookfield Communs., Inc. v. West Coast Entertainment Corp.*, 174 F.3d 1036 (9th Cir.1999) (holding that defendant's use of trademarks in "metatags," invisible text within websites that search engines use for ranking results, constituted a "use in commerce" under the Lanham Act); see generally *Bihari v. Gross*, 119 F.Supp.2d 309 (S.D.N.Y.2000) (discussing Brookfield and similar cases).[15]

In addition, unlike several other internet advertising companies, WhenU does not "sell" keyword trademarks to its customers or otherwise manipulate which category-related advertisement will pop up in response to any particular terms on the internal directory. See, *e.g.*, *GEICO*, 330 F.Supp.2d at 703-04 (finding that Google's sale to advertisers of right to use specific trademarks as "keywords" to trigger their ads constituted "use in commerce"). In other words, WhenU does not link trademarks to any particular competitor's ads, and a customer cannot pay to have its pop-up ad appear on any specific website or in connection with any particular trademark. Instead, the SaveNow directory terms trigger categorical associations (e.g., www.1800Contacts.com might trigger the category of "eye care"), at which point, the software will randomly select one of the pop-up ads contained in the eye-care category to send to the C-user's desktop.

Perhaps because ultimately 1-800 is unable to explain precisely how WhenU "uses" its trademark, it resorts to bootstrapping a finding of "use" by alleging

---

[14] Indeed, although we do not address the district court's finding of a likelihood of confusion, we note that 1-800's claim that C-users will likely be confused into thinking that 1-800 has sponsored its competitor's pop-up ads is fairly incredulous given that C-users who have downloaded the SaveNow software receive numerous WhenU pop-up ads—each displaying the WhenU brand—in varying contexts and for a broad range of products.

[15] We note that in distinguishing cases such as *Brookfield*, *Playboy* and *Bihari*, we do not necessarily endorse their holdings. See *Playboy*, 354 F.3d at 1034–36 (Berzon, C.J., concurring, noting disagreement with holding in *Brookfield*).

other elements of a trademark claim. For example, 1-800 invariably refers to WhenU's pop-up ads as "unauthorized" in an effort, it would seem, to establish by sheer force of repetition the element of unauthorized use of a trademark. Not surprisingly, 1-800 cites no legal authority for the proposition that advertisements, software applications, or any other visual image that can appear on a C-user's computer screen must be authorized by the owner of any website that will appear contemporaneously with that image. The fact is that WhenU does not need 1-800's authorization to display a separate window containing an ad any more than Corel would need authorization from Microsoft to display its WordPerfect word-processor in a window contemporaneously with a Word word-processing window. Moreover, contrary to 1-800's repeated admonitions, WhenU's pop-up ads are authorized — if unwittingly — by the C-user who has downloaded the SaveNow software.

1-800 also argues that WhenU's conduct is "use" because it is likely to confuse C-users as to the source of the ad. It buttresses this claim with a survey it submitted to the district court that purportedly demonstrates, inter alia, that (1) a majority of C-users believe that pop-up ads that appear on websites are sponsored by those websites, and (2) numerous C-users are unaware that they have downloaded the SaveNow software. 1-800 also relies on several cases in which the court seemingly based a finding of trademark "use" on the confusion such "use" was likely to cause. See, e.g., *Bihari*, 119 F.Supp.2d at 318 (holding that defendant's use of trademarks in metatags constituted a "use in commerce" under the Lanham Act in part because the hyperlinks "effectively act[ed] as a conduit, steering potential customers away from Bihari Interiors and toward its competitors"); *GEICO*, 330 F.Supp. 2d at 703–04 (finding that Google's sale to advertisers of right to have specific trademarks trigger their ads was "use in commerce" because it created likelihood of confusion that Google had the trademark holder's authority to do so). Again, this rationale puts the cart before the horse. Not only are "use," "in commerce," and "likelihood of confusion" three distinct elements of a trademark infringement claim, but "use" must be decided as a threshold matter because, while any number of activities may be "in commerce" or create a likelihood of confusion, no such activity is actionable under the Lanham Act absent the "use" of a trademark. 15 U.S.C. § 1114; see *People for the Ethical Treatment of Animals v. Doughney*, 263 F.3d 359, 364 (4th Cir.2001). Because 1-800 has failed to establish such "use," its trademark infringement claims fail.

. . .

CONCLUSION

For the foregoing reasons, we reverse the district court's entry of a preliminary injunction and remand with instructions to (1) dismiss with prejudice 1-800's trademark infringement claims against WhenU, and (2) proceed with 1-800's remaining claims.

EXTENSIONS

1. *Additional keyword advertising litigation.* In May 2003, a multidistrict litigation panel centralized a group of nine actions filed by and against Gator Corp. in the U.S. District Court for the Northern District of Georgia. *In re Gator Corp. Software Trademark & Copyright Litigation*, 259 F.Supp.2d 1378 (J.P.M.L.2003). Website operators are also seeking to swat the pop-ups by suing, in addition to the companies that deploy the ads, the advertisers on whose behalf they are deployed. For example, in May 2004 L.L. Bean sued Nordstrom, JC Penney, Atkins Nutritionals, and Gevalia Kaffee, whose ads popped up over L.L. Bean's website. Claria responded by suing L.L. Bean.

2. *Legislative approaches.* In March 2004, the Utah legislature enacted a law aimed in part at eliminating pop-up ads. Spyware Control Act, UTAH CODE ANN. § 13–39–101 to –401. The Act prohibits deployment of "a context based triggering mechanism to display an advertisement that partially or wholly covers or obscures paid advertising or other content on an Internet website in a way that interferes with a user's ability to view the Internet website." § 13–39–201(1)(c). "Context based triggering mechanism" is defined as

> a software based trigger or program residing on a consumer's computer that displays an advertisement according to:
>
> > (a) the current Internet website accessed by a user; or
> >
> > (b) the contents or characteristics of the current Internet website accessed by a user.

§ 13–39–102(1).

This provision appears to prohibit entirely the advertising model WhenU and Claria employ. Press reports indicate that 1-800 Contacts, Inc., a Utah company and plaintiff in *1-800 Contacts v. WhenU.com, supra,* lobbied for passage of the Act. WhenU.com filed an action challenging the Act, alleging that it violates the Dormant Commerce Clause, the First Amendment, and other constitutional and statutory provisions. In June 2004, a Utah state court issued a preliminary injunction against enforcement of the Act, finding WhenU.com likely to succeed on its Commerce Clause claim. *WhenU.com Inc. v. Utah*, No. 040907578 (Utah Dist.Ct.2004).

III. TRADEMARK DILUTION

Trademark infringement protects a trademark owner from another using his or her mark in connection with competing goods and services. It does not, however, prohibit another from using that mark in connection with noncompeting goods and services. So long as the trademark is used in connection with goods and services that do not compete with the goods and services of the trademark owner, the trademark has not been infringed. A cause of action for *trademark dilution* may, however, be available to certain trademark owners to prevent use by others even absent infringement.

Trademark dilution was federalized by the Federal Trademark Dilution Act of 1995, 15 U.S.C. § 1125(c). (Previously, dilution had been available in some states under common law or by statute.) In its federal incarnation, dilution is defined as "the lessening of the capacity of a famous mark to identify and distinguish goods or services." *Id.* § 1127. Significantly, the use of another's trademark on noncompeting goods or services may dilute that trademark even if that use does not involve consumer confusion, mistake or deception. *Id.* Equally significant, however, is the limitation of this cause of action to *famous* trademarks. As we note below, attempts to define fame for the purposes of federal trademark dilution have occasioned a split in the circuits.

Historically, courts have recognized only two forms of trademark dilution: *blurring* and *tarnishment.* Thus, for example, Section 25 of the *Restatement (Third) of Unfair Competition* states:

> An actor is subject to liability under an antidilution statute if the actor uses [the trademark of another] in a manner that is likely to associate the other's mark with the goods, services, or business of the actor and:
>
> > (a) the other's mark is highly distinctive and the association of the mark with the actor's goods, services, or business is likely to cause a reduction in that distinctiveness; or
> >
> > (b) the association of the other's mark with the actor's goods, services, or business, or the nature of the actor's use, is likely to disparage the other's goods, services, or business or tarnish the images associated with the other's mark.

RESTATEMENT (THIRD) OF UNFAIR COMPETITION § 25(1) (1995). The *Restatement* distinguishes between blurring and tarnishment in paragraphs (a) and (b) respectively. In dilution by blurring,

> the assumption is that the relevant public sees the junior user's use, and intuitively knows, because of the context of the junior user's use, that there is no connection between the owners of the respective marks. However, even with those who perceive distinct sources and affiliation, the ability of the senior user's mark to serve as a unique identifier of the plaintiff's goods or services is weakened because the relevant public now also associates that designation with a new and different source. Hence, the unique and distinctive link between the plaintiff's mark and its goods or services is "blurred."

4 J. THOMAS MCCARTHY, MCCARTHY ON TRADEMARKS AND UNFAIR COMPETITION § 24:70 (4th ed.2002). In dilution by tarnishment, "[t]he selling power of a trademark . . . [is] undermined by a use of the mark with goods or services such as illicit drugs or pornography that 'tarnish' the mark's image through inherently negative or unsavory associations, or with goods or services that produce a negative response when linked in the minds of prospective purchasers with the goods or services of the [senior] user, such as the use on insecticide of a trademark similar to one previously used by [the senior user] on food products." RESTATEMENT (THIRD) OF UNFAIR COMPETITION § 25(1), cmt. c (1995). While both blurring and tarnishment require that the diluted trademark become associated with the goods or services of another, blurring occurs when this association is likely to reduce the distinctive quality of that mark, whereas tarnishment is found when this association is likely to tarnish that mark's image.

Some proponents of the Federal Trademark Dilution Act heralded it as, among other things, a means of combating "cybersquatting"—the practice of registering another's trademark as a domain name with the intent of selling it for a profit, usually to the trademark owner. In the remainder of this Part, we consider domain name disputes involving claims of dilution. In reading the following materials, consider when dilution can appropriately be found absent blurring or tarnishment. (Cybersquatting is considered in more detail in Chapter 3, Part II, *infra.*)

Federal Trademark Dilution Act
15 U.S.C. §§ 1125(c) & 1127 (§§ 43(c) & 45 of the Lanham Act).

§ 1125. False designations of origin, false descriptions, and dilution forbidden

(c) Remedies for dilution of famous marks.

(1) The owner of a famous mark shall be entitled, subject to the principles of equity and upon such terms as the court deems reasonable, to an injunction against another person's commercial use in commerce of a mark or trade name, if such use begins after the mark has become famous and causes dilution of the distinctive quality of the mark, and to obtain such other relief as is provided in this subsection. In determining whether a mark is distinctive and famous, a court may consider factors such as, but not limited to—

(A) the degree of inherent or acquired distinctiveness of the mark;

(B) the duration and extent of use of the mark in connection with the goods or services with which the mark is used;

(C) the duration and extent of advertising and publicity of the mark;

(D) the geographical extent of the trading area in which the mark is used;

(E) the channels of trade for the goods or services with which the mark is used;

(F) the degree of recognition of the mark in the trading areas and channels of trade used by the mark's owner and the person against whom the injunction is sought;

(G) the nature and extent of use of the same or similar marks by third parties; and

(H) whether the mark was registered under the Act of March 3, 1881, or: the Act of February 20, 1905, or on the principal register.

(2) In an action brought under this subsection, the owner of the famous mark shall be entitled only to injunctive relief as set forth in § 1116 of this title unless the person against whom the injunction is sought willfully intended to trade on the owner's reputation or to cause dilution of the famous mark. If such willful intent is proven, the owner of the famous mark shall also be entitled to the remedies set forth in §§ 1117(a) and 1118 of this title, subject to the discretion of the court and the principles of equity.

(3) The ownership by a person of a valid registration under the Act of March 3, 1881, or the Act of February 20, 1905, or on the principal register shall be a complete bar to an action against that person, with respect to that mark, that is brought by another person under the common law or a statute of a State and that seeks to prevent dilution of the distinctiveness of a mark, label, or form of advertisement.

(4) The following shall not be actionable under this section:

(A) Fair use of a famous mark by another person in comparative commercial advertising or promotion to identify the competing goods or services of the owner of the famous mark.

(B) Noncommercial use of a mark.

(C) All forms of news reporting and news commentary.

§ 1127. Construction and definitions; intent of chapter

The term "dilution" means the lessening of the capacity of a famous mark to identify and distinguish goods or services, regardless of the presence or absence of —

(1) competition between the owner of the famous mark and other parties, or

(2) likelihood of confusion, mistake, or deception.

Toys "R" Us, Inc. v. Feinberg
26 F.Supp.2d 639 (S.D.N.Y.1998), *vacated & remanded*, 201 F.3d 432 (2d Cir.1999).

■ SCHWARTZ, DISTRICT JUDGE.

. . .

Plaintiff Geoffrey, Inc. is a wholly owned subsidiary of Toys "R" Us, Inc. Geoffrey owns the rights to the Toys "R" Us and related trademarks, licensing their use to Toys "R" Us and its various subsidiaries. Plaintiffs have been making use of the Toys "R" Us mark for over 35 years. The range of products sold in Toys "R" Us stores has grown and now includes, in addition to toys, over 11,000 different items such as clothing, lamps, telephones, stereos, calculators, computers, audio and visual tapes, pools, and sporting goods. The Toys "R" Us mark is prominently featured in national and regional advertising, and throughout Toys "R" Us stores. Since 1983, Toys "R" Us has owned and operated a chain of retail children's clothing stores under the mark Kids "R" Us. There are 698 Toys "R" Us stores in the United States, and 443 in foreign countries, with annual sales over $11 billion. As a result of over $100 million in advertising annually, and an intensive effort to maintain high quality goods and services, Toys "R" Us has become one of the most famous and widely known marks in the world.

Toys "R" Us has also worked diligently to maintain its reputation as a family oriented store with a wholesome image. Toys "R" Us has sought to project the image of a store where children are the first concern, and was one of the first stores to refuse to carry or sell toy guns — a fact widely publicized.

Plaintiff Geoffrey, Inc., in addition to the Toys "R" Us mark which it licenses to its co-plaintiff, owns a number of federal trademark registrations containing the phrase " 'R' Us." For example, Geoffrey has registered Babies "R" Us, Bikes "R" Us, Books "R" Us, Computers "R" Us, Dolls "R" Us, Games "R" Us, Mathematics "R" Us, Movies "R" Us, Parties "R" Us, Portraits "R" Us, Shoes "R" Us, and Sports "R" Us. Plaintiffs also own common law rights over various other "R" Us marks, such as Treats "R" Us, Gifts "R" Us, and 1–800–Toys–R–Us, by virtue of the exclusive use of those marks.

Finally, Geoffrey also owns various internet domain names including tru.com, toysrus.com, kidsrus.com, boysrus.com, dollsrus.com, galsrus.com, girlsrus.com, babiesrus.com, computersrus.com, guysrus.com, mathematicsrus.com, movies-rus.com, opportunitiesrus.com, partiesrus.com, poolsrus.com, portraitsrus.com, racersrus.com, supervaluesrus.com, treatsrus.com, tykesrus.com, sportsrus.com, giftsrus.com, and toysrusregistry.com. Toys "R" Us operates an internet website located at www.toysrus.com.

Plaintiffs make use of various of these marks and others through ownership or licensing, resulting in the extensive use of the "R" Us family of marks, under the control and supervision of plaintiffs.

Defendant Richard Feinberg is the sole proprietor of codefendant We Are Guns, a firearms store doing business at 15 Farm Lane, Norton, Massachusetts. Feinberg runs his business predominantly in Massachusetts, but also sells products on the internet and has, "on occasion, shipped products to New York firearms dealers." Feinberg's business had been previously known as "Guns Are Us." The business's name was changed to "Guns are We" and then to "We Are Guns" in response to objections by plaintiffs. Feinberg maintains a website located at www.gunsareus.com and has registered the domain name "gunsareus.com" with InterNIC.

Plaintiffs brought this suit seeking damages and an injunction prohibiting defendants from operating the website at gunsareus.com and from reverting back to either of the trade names "Guns are Us" or "Guns Are We." . . .

The Court finds no issue of material fact as to whether defendants' use of the internet domain name gunsareus.com can serve as the basis for a dilution claim under . . . § 43(c) of the Lanham Act, 15 U.S.C. § 1125(c), . . . There are two types of dilution claims, (1) blurring, and (2) tarnishment. As a matter of law, plaintiff has failed to present a prima facie case under either theory.

The owner of a famous mark is entitled to an injunction "against another person's commercial use in commerce of a mark or trade name, if such use begins after the mark has become famous and causes dilution of the distinctive quality of the mark." *See Toys "R" Us, Inc. v. Akkaoui*, 1996 WL 772709 (N.D.Cal., Oct. 29, 1996) (barring the use by defendants of the name "Adults 'R Us"), *citing* 15 U.S.C. § 1125(c)(1). Dilution does not depend on a showing of either likelihood of confusion between the marks, or competition between the owner of the mark and other parties. *See* 15 U.S.C. § 1127.

First, plaintiffs have failed to establish the existence of a triable issue of fact as to whether maintaining a website with the domain name "gunsareus.com" will blur, or lessen the capacity of plaintiffs' marks to identify and distinguish their goods or services. While it is conceivable that the proliferation of trade names ending in " 'R" Us," unassociated with plaintiffs, might cause such blurring, this case is nowhere near such a situation. This case involves a website that merely uses the letters "gunsareus" as its internet domain name. Defendants neither make use of the single letter "R" nor do they space or color the letters and words in a manner remotely related to plaintiffs. The name "gunsareus" appears in all lower case letters with no spaces in between the letters. The Court finds that the use of such an internet domain name, without naming the website itself "Guns 'R' Us" or "Guns Are Us," will not, as a matter of law, blur the distinctiveness of plaintiffs' "R" Us family of marks.

Second, the Court also finds an absence of a triable issue of fact as to whether defendants have diluted plaintiffs' mark by tarnishment. Dilution by tarnishment occurs when "a famous mark is improperly associated with an inferior or offensive product or service." *See Ringling Bros.*, 937 F.Supp. at 209 (*citing Hormel Foods Corp. v. Jim Henson Prods., Inc.*, 73 F.3d 497, 506 (2d Cir.1996)). Courts have found such negative connotations in situations where a mark was used in the context of drugs, nudity, and sex. *See e.g., Dallas Cowboys Cheerleaders, Inc. v. Pussycat Cinema, Ltd.*, 467 F.Supp. 366 (S.D.N.Y.1979) (pornography); *Coca–Cola Co. v. Gemini Rising, Inc.*, 346 F.Supp. 1183 (E.D.N.Y.1972) (cocaine); *Eastman Kodak Co. v. Rakow*, 739 F.Supp. 116, 118 (W.D.N.Y.1989) (crude comedy routine).

The Court, however, finds it unlikely that defendants' website will be associated with plaintiffs' stores and products at all. As stated earlier, the differing product areas, absence of the single letter "R" in the name, and peculiarities of an internet domain name make any association with plaintiffs' products extremely unlikely. In addition, defendant does not sell to the general public outside of Massachusetts. Its internet site is used almost exclusively to sell to firearms dealers.

In sum, the parties have demonstrated an absence of any material issues of fact, requiring judgment to be issued as a matter of law. Defendants' decision to cease using the trade names "Guns Are Us" and "Guns Are We" eliminates the need or basis for the Court to decide whether those trade names infringe on or dilute plaintiffs marks. Defendants' website, entitled Guns Are We, but with the domain name gunsareus.com, does not violate any of plaintiffs' rights under federal or state trademark and unfair competition law.

CONCLUSION

For the reasons set forth above, plaintiffs' motion for summary judgment is denied in its entirety, and summary judgment is granted in favor of defendants.

Avery Dennison Corp. v. Sumpton
189 F.3d 868 (9th Cir.1999).

■ TROTT, CIRCUIT JUDGE:

Jerry Sumpton and Freeview Listings Ltd. (together, "Appellants") appeal an injunction in favor of Avery Dennison Corp., entered after summary judgment for Avery Dennison on its claims of trademark dilution under the Federal Trademark Dilution Act of 1995, 15 U.S.C. § 1125(c) (Supp. II 1996) (amending the Lanham Trademark Act of 1946, 15 U.S.C. §§ 1051–1127 (1994)), and the California dilution statute, Cal. Bus. & Prof. Code § 14330 (West 1987). The district court published an opinion, 999 F.Supp. 1337 (C.D.Cal.1998), holding that Appellants' maintenance of domain name registrations for <avery.net> and <dennison.net> diluted two of Avery Dennison's separate trademarks, "Avery" and "Dennison." (Note that when referencing Internet addresses, domain-name combinations, e-mail addresses, and other Internet-related character strings, we use the caret symbols ("< >"), in order to avoid possible confusion.) The district court then entered an injunction ordering Appellants to transfer the domain-name registrations to Avery Dennison in exchange for $300 each.

We have jurisdiction under 28 U.S.C. § 1291 (1994). Because Avery Dennison failed to create a genuine issue of fact on required elements of the dilution cause of action, we reverse and remand with instructions to enter summary judgment for Appellants and to consider Appellants' request for attorneys' fees in light of this decision.

I. Background

We are the third panel of this court in just over a year faced with the challenging task of applying centuries-old trademark law to the newest medium of communication—the Internet. (*See Brookfield Communications, Inc. v. West Coast Enter. Corp.*, 174 F.3d 1036 (9th Cir.1999), and *Panavision Int'l, L.P. v. Toeppen*, 141 F.3d 1316 (9th Cir.1998).) Although we attempt to set out the background facts as clearly as possible, the interested reader may wish to review some of the following sources for a more complete understanding of the Internet: *Brookfield*, 174 F.3d at 1044–45; *Intermatic, Inc. v. Toeppen*, 947 F.Supp. 1227, 1230–32 (N.D.Ill.1996); and Marshall Leaffer, *Domain Names, Globalization and Internet Commerce*, 6 Ind. J. Global Legal Stud. 139, 139–46 (1998).

Two communicative functions of the Internet are relevant to this appeal: the capacity to support web sites and the corollary capacity to support electronic mail ("e-mail"). A web site, which is simply an interactive presentation of data which a user accesses by dialing into the host computer, can be created by any user who reserves an Internet location—called an Internet protocol address—and does the necessary programming. Because an Internet protocol address is a string of integer numbers separated by periods, for example, <129.137.84.101>, for ease of recall and use a user relies on a "domain-name combination" to reach a given web site. The registrar of Internet domain names, Network Solutions, Inc. ("NSI"),[1] maintains a database of registrations and translates entered domain-name combinations into Internet protocol addresses. When accessing a web site, a user enters the character string <http://www.>, followed by the reserved domain-name combination. The domain-name combination must include a top-level domain ("TLD"), which can be <.com>, <.net>, <.org>, <.gov> or <.edu>, among others, although some, like <.gov> and <.edu>, are reserved for specific purposes. The combination also includes a second-level domain ("SLD"), which can be any word not already reserved in combination with the TLD. Once a domain-name combination is reserved, it cannot be used by anybody else, unless the first registrant voluntarily or

---

[1] At the time of publication of this opinion, NSI is no longer the exclusive registrar of domain names. A new competitive scheme is being implemented by the Commerce Department, and one competitor, "register.com," is currently in operation. . . .

otherwise relinquishes its registration.

A web site can be programmed for multiple purposes. Some merchants maintain a form of "electronic catalog" on the Internet, permitting Internet users to review products and services for sale. A web site can also be programmed for e-mail, where the provider licenses e-mail addresses in the format <alias@SLD.TLD>, with <alias> selected by the e-mail user. A person or company maintaining a web site makes money in a few different ways. A site that aids in marketing goods and services is an asset to a merchant. E-mail providers make money from licensing fees paid by e-mail users. Money is also made from advertising and links to other web sites.

II. Facts

Sumpton is the president of Freeview, an Internet e-mail provider doing business as "Mailbank." Mailbank offers "vanity" e-mail addresses to users for an initial fee of $19.95 and $4.95 per year thereafter, and has registered thousands of domain-name combinations for this purpose. Most SLDs that Mailbank has registered are common surnames, although some represent hobbies, careers, pets, sports interests, favorite music, and the like. One category of SLDs is titled "Rude" and includes lewd SLDs, and another category, titled "Business," includes some common trademark SLDs. Mailbank's TLDs consist mainly of <.net> and <.org>, but some registered domain name combinations, including most in the "Business" and "Rude" categories, use the TLD <.com>. Mailbank's surname archives include the domain-name combinations <avery.net> and <dennison.net>.

Avery Dennison sells office products and industrial fasteners under the registered trademarks "Avery" and "Dennison," respectively. "Avery" has been in continuous use since the 1930s and registered since 1963, and "Dennison" has been in continuous use since the late 1800s and registered since 1908. Avery Dennison spends more than $5 million per year advertising its products, including those marketed under the separate "Avery" and "Dennison" trademarks, and the company boasts in the neighborhood of $3 billion in sales of all of its trademarks annually. No evidence indicates what percentage of these dollar figures apply to the "Avery" or "Dennison" trademarks. Avery Dennison maintains a commercial presence on the Internet, marketing its products at <avery.com> and <averydennison.com>, and maintaining registrations for several other domain-name combinations, all using the TLD <.com>.

Avery Dennison sued Appellants, alleging trademark dilution under the Federal Trademark Dilution Act and California Business and Professional Code § 14330. Avery Dennison also sued NSI, alleging contributory dilution and contributory infringement. The district court granted summary judgment to NSI on Avery Dennison's claims. The district court then concluded as a matter of law that the disputed trademarks were famous and denied summary judgment to Appellants and granted summary judgment to Avery Dennison on its dilution claims, entering an injunction requiring Appellants to transfer the registrations to Avery Dennison. 999 F.Supp. at 1342.

III. Trademark Law

Trademark protection is "the law's recognition of the psychological function of symbols." *Mishawaka Rubber & Woolen Mfg. Co. v. S.S. Kresge Co.*, 316 U.S. 203 (1942). Two goals of trademark law are reflected in the federal scheme. On the one hand, the law seeks to protect consumers who have formed particular associations with a mark. On the other hand, trademark law seeks to protect the investment in a mark made by the owner.

Until recently, federal law provided protection only against infringement of a registered trademark, or the unregistered trademark analog, unfair competition. *See* §§ 32 and 43(a) of the Lanham Trademark Act of 1946, as amended, 15 U.S.C. §§ 1114, 1125(a) (1994). These causes of action require a plaintiff to prove that the defendant is using a mark confusingly similar to a valid, protectable trademark of the plaintiff's. *Brookfield*, 174 F.3d at 1046.

Many states, however, have long recognized another cause of action designed to protect trademarks: trademark dilution. Lori Krafte–Jacobs, Comment, Judicial Interpretation of the Federal Trademark Dilution Act of 1995, 66 U. Cin. L.Rev. 659, 660–62 (1998) (discussing the evolution of the dilution doctrine). With the 1995 enactment of the Federal Trademark Dilution Act, dilution became a federal-law concern. Unlike infringement and unfair competition laws, in a dilution case competition between the parties and a likelihood of confusion are not required to present a claim for relief. *See* 15 U.S.C. § 1127 (Supp. II 1996) (definition of "dilution"); Leslie F. Brown, *Note, Avery Dennison Corp. v. Sumpton*, 14 Berkeley Tech. L.J. 247, 249 (1999). Rather, injunctive relief is available under the Federal Trademark Dilution Act if a plaintiff can establish that (1) its mark is famous; (2) the defendant is making commercial use of the mark in commerce; (3) the defendant's use began after the plaintiff's mark became famous; and (4) the defendant's use presents a likelihood of dilution of the distinctive value of the mark. *Panavision Int'l, L.P. v. Toeppen*, 141 F.3d 1316, 1324 (9th Cir.1998) (interpreting 15 U.S.C. § 1125(c)(1)).

California's dilution cause of action is substantially similar, providing relief if the plaintiff can demonstrate a "[l]ikelihood of injury to business reputation or of dilution of the distinctive quality of a mark . . ., notwithstanding the absence of competition between the parties or the absence of confusion as to the source of goods or services." Cal. Bus. & Prof. Code § 14330. We have interpreted § 14330, like the Federal Trademark Dilution Act, to protect only famous marks. *Fruit of the Loom, Inc. v. Girouard*, 994 F.2d 1359, 1362–63 (9th Cir.1993); *see* 3 J. Thomas McCarthy, *Trademarks and Unfair Competition* § 24:108 (Supp.1998).

. . .

V. Dilution Protection

We now turn to the dilution causes of action at issue in this case, brought under the Federal Trademark Dilution Act and California Business and Professional Code § 14330.

In *Panavision*, we held that both the Federal Trademark Dilution Act and § 14330 were implicated when the defendant registered domain-name combinations using famous trademarks and sought to sell the registrations to the trademark owners. 141 F.3d at 1318, 1327. Three differences made *Panavision* easier than the instant case. First, the defendant did not mount a challenge on the famousness prong of the dilution tests. *Panavision,* 141 F.3d at 1324. Second, the *Panavision* defendant did not challenge the factual assertion that he sought to profit by arbitrage with famous trademarks. *Id.* at 1324–25. Third, the diluting registrations in *Panavision* both involved the TLD <.com>. In the instant case, by contrast, Appellants contest Avery Dennison's claim of famousness, Appellants contend that the nature of their business makes the trademark status of "Avery" and "Dennison" irrelevant, and the complained-of registrations involve the TLD <. net>.

A. *Famousness*

The district court considered evidence submitted by Avery Dennison regarding marketing efforts and consumer association with its marks and concluded as a matter of law that "Avery" and "Dennison" were famous marks entitled to dilution protection. 999 F.Supp. at 1339. We hold that Avery Dennison failed to create a genuine issue of fact on the famousness element of both dilution statutes.[4]

Dilution is a cause of action invented and reserved for a select class of marks — those marks with such powerful consumer associations that even non-competing uses can impinge on their value. *See generally* Frank L. Schechter, *The Rational Basis for Trademark Protection,* 40 Harv. L.Rev. 813 (1927) (proposing a cause of action for dilution); Krafte–Jacobs, *supra,* at 689–91. Dilution causes of action, much more so than infringement and unfair competition laws, tread very close to granting "rights in gross" in a trademark. *See* 3 McCarthy, *supra,* § 24:108. In the infringement and unfair competition scenario, where the less famous a trademark, the less the chance that consumers will be confused as to origin, *see AMF Inc. v. Sleekcraft Boats,* 599 F.2d 341, 349 (9th Cir.1979), a carefully-crafted balance exists between protecting a trademark and permitting non-infringing uses. In the dilution context, likelihood of confusion is irrelevant. *See* 15 U.S.C. § 1127; Cal. Bus. and Prof.Code § 14330; *Panavision,* 141 F.3d at 1326. If dilution protection were accorded to trademarks based only on a showing of inherent or acquired distinctiveness, we would upset the balance in favor of over-protecting trademarks, at the expense of potential non-infringing uses. *See Fruit of the Loom,* 994 F.2d at 1363 ("[The plaintiff] would sweep clean the many business uses of this quotidian word.").

We view the famousness prong of both dilution analyses as reinstating the balance — by carefully limiting the class of trademarks eligible for dilution protection, Congress and state legislatures granted the most potent form of trademark protection in a manner designed to minimize undue impact on other uses. *See San Francisco Arts & Athletics, Inc. v. United States Olympic Comm.,* 483 U.S. 522, 564 n. 25 (1987) (Brennan, J., dissenting) (citing 2 J. McCarthy, *Trademarks & Unfair Competition* § 24:16, at 229 (2d ed.1984)) (discussing limits on the dilution doctrine that help prevent overprotection of trademarks).

---

[4] Although the famousness of "Avery" and "Dennison" is disputed, no dispute exists on the third element of dilution under *Panavision:* Appellants' use must begin after the marks became famous. Any fame that Avery Dennison's marks have acquired existed before November, 1996, when Appellants' use began.

Therefore, to meet the "famousness" element of protection under the dilution statutes, " 'a mark [must] be truly prominent and renowned.' " *I.P. Lund Trading ApS v. Kohler Co.,* 163 F.3d 27, 46 (1st Cir.1998) (quoting 3 McCarthy, *supra,* § 24.91). In a 1987 report, which recommended an amendment to the Lanham Act to provide a federal dilution cause of action, the Trademark Review Commission of the United States Trademark Association emphasized the narrow reach of a dilution cause of action: "We believe that a limited category of trademarks, those which are truly famous and registered,[5] are deserving of national protection from dilution." Trademark Review Commission, *Report & Recommendations,* 77 Trademark Rep. 375, 455 (Sept.-Oct.1987).

The Federal Trademark Dilution Act lists eight non-exclusive considerations for the famousness inquiry, 15 U.S.C. § 1125(c)(1)(A)–(H), which are equally relevant to a famousness determination under Business and Professional Code § 14330, *see Panavision,* 141 F.3d at 1324 ("Panavision's state law dilution claim is subject to the same analysis as its federal claim.").

. . .

We note the overlap between the statutory famousness considerations and the factors relevant to establishing acquired distinctiveness, which is attained "when the purchasing public associates the [mark] with a single producer or source rather than just the product itself." *First Brands Corp. v. Fred Meyer, Inc.,* 809 F.2d 1378, 1383 (9th Cir.1987). Proof of acquired distinctiveness is a difficult empirical inquiry which a factfinder must undertake, *Taco Cabana Int'l, Inc. v. Two Pesos, Inc.,* 932 F.2d 1113, 1119–20 & n. 7 (5th Cir.1991), *aff'd,* 505 U.S. 763 (1992), considering factors including:

> [1] whether actual purchasers . . . associate the [mark] with [the plaintiff];
>
> [2] the degree and manner of [the plaintiff's] advertising;
>
> [3] the length and manner of [the plaintiff's] use of the [mark]; and
>
> [4] whether [the plaintiff's] use of the [mark] has been exclusive.

Clamp Mfg. Co. v. Enco Mfg. Co., 870 F.2d 512, 517 (9th Cir.1989). Furthermore, registration on the principal register creates a presumption of distinctiveness—in the case of a surname trademark, acquired distinctiveness. 15 U.S.C. § 1057(b) (1994); *Americana Trading Inc. v. Russ Berrie & Co.,* 966 F.2d 1284, 1287 (9th Cir.1992) ("[R]egistration carries a presumption of secondary meaning.").

However, the Federal Trademark Dilution Act and Business and Professional Code § 14330 apply "only to those marks which are both truly distinctive *and* famous, and therefore most likely to be adversely affected by dilution." S. Rep. No.

---

[5] The Trademark Review Commission's recommended amendment is very similar to the language of the eventually-enacted Federal Trademark Dilution Act. The main difference relevant to the famousness inquiry is that the Commission's recommendation only permitted a cause of action to the owner of a registered mark, while the owner of any protectable mark or trade name can bring a cause of action under the enacted version of the Federal Trademark Dilution Act.

100–515, at 42 (emphasis added). The Trademark Review Commission stated that "a higher standard must be employed to gauge the fame of a trademark eligible for this extraordinary remedy." 77 Trademark Rep. at 461. Thus, "[t]o be capable of being diluted, a mark must have a degree of distinctiveness and 'strength' beyond that needed to serve as a trademark." 3 McCarthy, *supra,* § 24:109; *see also* Krafte–Jacobs, *supra,* at 690 ("If all marks are distinctive, and a showing of distinctiveness meets the element of fame, what marks would be outside the protection of the FTDA? [T]he FTDA does not indicate that any particular degree of distinctiveness should end the inquiry." (interpreting the Federal Trademark Dilution Act)). We have previously held likewise under California Business and Professional Code § 14330. *Accuride Int'l, Inc. v. Accuride Corp.,* 871 F.2d 1531, 1539 (9th Cir.1989) (requiring more than mere distinctiveness).

Applying the famousness factors from the Federal Trademark Dilution Act to the facts of the case at bench, we conclude that Avery Dennison likely establishes acquired distinctiveness in the "Avery" and "Dennison" trademarks, but goes no further. Because the Federal Trademark Dilution Act requires a showing greater than distinctiveness to meet the threshold element of fame, as a matter of law Avery Dennison has failed to fulfill this burden.

1. *Distinctiveness*

We begin with the first factor in the statutory list: "inherent or acquired distinctiveness." § 1125(c)(1)(A). No dispute exists that "Avery" and "Dennison" are common surnames—according to evidence presented by Appellants, respectively the 775th and 1768th most common in the United States. A long-standing principle of trademark law is the right of a person to use his or her own name in connection with a business. *See Howe Scale Co. v. Wyckoff, Seamans & Benedict,* 198 U.S. 118, 140 (1905). This principle was incorporated into the Lanham Act, which states that a mark that is "primarily merely a surname" is not protectable unless it acquires secondary meaning. 15 U.S.C. § 1052(e)(4), (f) (1994); *Abraham Zion Corp. v. Lebow,* 761 F.2d 93, 104 (2d Cir.1985); *see L.E. Waterman Co. v. Modern Pen Co.,* 235 U.S. 88, 94 (1914) (pre-Lanham Act case stating that protection from confusion is available to the holder of a surname trademark that has acquired public recognition); *Horlick's Malted Milk Corp. v. Horluck's, Inc.,* 59 F.2d 13, 15 (9th Cir.1932) (pre-Lanham Act case limiting the defendant's right to use his surname as a trademark where the name had acquired public recognition from the efforts of a competitor). Avery Dennison cannot claim that "Avery" and "Dennison" are inherently distinctive, but must demonstrate acquired distinctiveness through secondary meaning.

The drafters of the Federal Trademark Dilution Act continued the concern for surnames when adding protection against trademark dilution to the federal scheme. On early consideration of the Act, the report from the Senate Judiciary Committee emphasized: "[T]he committee intended to give special protection to an individual's ability to use his or her own name in good faith." S. Rep. No. 100–515, at 43 (1988). The Federal Trademark Dilution Act imports, at a minimum, the threshold secondary-meaning requirement for registration of a surname trademark.

Avery Dennison maintains registrations of both "Avery" and "Dennison" on the principal register, prima facie evidence that these marks have achieved the secondary meaning required for protection from infringement and unfair competition. *See Americana Trading*, 966 F.2d at 1287. We reject Appellants' argument that the distinctiveness required for famousness under the Federal Trademark Dilution Act is inherent, not merely acquired distinctiveness. *See* 15 U.S.C. § 1125(c)(1)(A) (referring to "inherent or acquired distinctiveness"). However, because famousness requires a showing greater than mere distinctiveness, the presumptive secondary meaning associated with "Avery" and "Dennison" fails to persuade us that the famousness prong is met in this case.

2. *Overlapping Channels of Trade*

We next consider the fifth and sixth factors of the statutory inquiry: the channels of trade for the plaintiff's goods and the degree of recognition of the mark in the trading areas and channels of trade used by plaintiff and defendant. § 1125(c)(1)(E), (F). The drafters of the Federal Trademark Dilution Act broke from the Trademark Review Commission's recommendation that only marks "which have become famous throughout a substantial part of the United States" could qualify for protection. *Report & Recommendation*, 77 Trademark Rep. at 456. Instead, fame in a localized trading area may meet the threshold element under the Act if plaintiff's trading area includes the trading area of the defendant. S.Rep. No. 100–515, at 43; *Washington Speakers Bureau, Inc. v. Leading Auths., Inc.*, 33 F.Supp.2d 488, 503–04 (E.D.Va.1999) (*citing I.P. Lund*, 163 F.3d at 46; *Teletech Customer Care Mgt., Inc. v. Tele–Tech Co.*, 977 F.Supp. 1407, 1413 (C.D.Cal.1997)). The rule is likewise for specialized market segments: specialized fame can be adequate only if the "diluting uses are directed narrowly at the same market segment." *Washington Speakers*, 33 F.Supp.2d at 503. No evidence on the record supports Avery Dennison's position on these two prongs of the famousness inquiry.

In *Teletech*, fame in a narrow market segment was present when the plaintiff showed "that the Teletech Companies may be the largest provider of primarily inbound integrated telephone and Internet customer care nationwide." 977 F.Supp. at 1409. The defendant was "a contractor providing engineering and installation services to the telecommunications industry," and maintained the domain-name combination, <teletech.com>. *Id.* at 1409–10. The court held that the showing on the threshold element under the Federal Trademark Dilution Act was adequate to qualify for a preliminary injunction. *Id.* at 1413. In *Washington Speakers*, both the plaintiff and defendant were in the business of scheduling speaking engagements for well-known lecturers. 33 F.Supp.2d at 490, 503 and n. 31 (citing cases). In the instant case, by contrast, Appellants' sought-after customer base is Internet users who desire vanity e-mail addresses, and Avery Dennison's customer base includes purchasers of office products and industrial fasteners. No evidence demonstrates that Avery Dennison possesses any degree of recognition among Internet users or that Appellants direct their e-mail services at Avery Dennison's customer base.

3. *Use of the Marks by Third Parties*

The seventh factor, "the nature and extent of use of the same . . . marks by third parties," § 1125(c)(1)(G), undercuts the district court's conclusion as well. All relevant evidence on the record tends to establish that both "Avery" and "Dennison" are commonly used as trademarks, both on and off of the Internet, by parties other than Avery Dennison. This evidence is relevant because, when "a mark is in widespread use, it may not be famous for the goods or services of one business." *Report & Recommendation*, 77 Trademark Rep. at 461; *see Accuride*, 871 F.2d at 1539 (affirming the district court's holding that widespread use of elements of a trademark helped to defeat a dilution claim).

The record includes copies of five trademark registrations for "Avery" and "Averys," a computer printout of a list of several businesses with "Avery" in their names who market products on the Internet, and a list of business names including "Avery," which, according to a declaration submitted by NSI, is a representative sample of over 800 such businesses. The record also contains a computer printout of a list of several businesses with "Dennison" in their names which market products on the Internet and a list of business names including "Dennison," a representative sample of over 200 such businesses. Such widespread use of "Avery" and "Dennison" makes it unlikely that either can be considered a famous mark eligible for the dilution cause of action.

4. *Other Famousness Factors*

Avery Dennison argues that evidence of extensive advertising and sales, international operations, and consumer awareness suffices to establish fame. We agree that the remaining four statutory factors in the famousness inquiry likely support Avery Dennison's position. Both "Avery" and "Dennison" have been used as trademarks for large fractions of a century and registered for decades. Avery Dennison expends substantial sums annually advertising each mark, with some presumable degree of success due to Avery Dennison's significant annual volume of sales. In addition, Avery Dennison markets its goods internationally. *See* 15 U.S.C. § 1125(c)(1)(B)–(D), (G). However, we disagree that Avery Dennison's showing establishes fame.

Avery Dennison submitted three market research studies regarding perceptions of the "Avery" and "Avery Dennison" brands. Discussion groups through which one study was conducted were formed "using Avery client lists," and produced the conclusion that the "Avery" name has "positive associations . . . among current customers." Surveyed persons in the other two studies were mostly "users and purchasers of office products" and "[o]ffice supply consumers." The one consumer group that did not necessarily include office supply purchasers for businesses was still required to be "somewhat" or "very" familiar with Avery products in order to be counted.

Avery Dennison's marketing reports are comparable to a survey we discussed in *Anti–Monopoly, Inc. v. General Mills Fun Group, Inc.*, 684 F.2d 1316 (9th Cir.1982), proving only the near tautology that consumers already acquainted with Avery and Avery Dennison products are familiar with Avery Dennison. *See id.* at 1323–24. The marketing reports add nothing to the discussion of whether consumers in general have any brand association with "Avery" and "Avery Dennison," and no evidence of product awareness relates specifically to the "Dennison" trademark. Although proper consumer surveys might be highly relevant to a showing of fame, we reject any reliance on the flawed reports submitted by Avery Dennison.

Finally, Avery Dennison—like any company marketing on the Internet—markets its products worldwide. *See* 15 U.S.C. § 1125(c)(1)(D). By itself, this factor carries no weight; worldwide use of a non-famous mark does not establish fame. Because famousness requires more than mere distinctiveness, and Avery Dennison's showing goes no further than establishing secondary meaning, we hold that Avery Dennison has not met its burden to create a genuine issue of fact that its marks are famous. Avery Dennison's failure to fulfill its burden on this required element of both dilution causes of action mandates summary judgment for Appellants.

5. *Likelihood of Confusion Remains Irrelevant*

We recognize that our discussion of the breadth of fame and overlapping market segments begins to sound like a likelihood of confusion analysis, and we agree with Avery Dennison that likelihood of confusion should not be considered under either the Federal Trademark Dilution Act or Business and Professional Code § 14330. However, as we discuss above, the famousness element of the dilution causes of action serves the same general purpose as the likelihood of confusion element of an infringement or unfair competition analysis—preventing the trademark scheme from granting excessively broad protection at the expense of legitimate uses. *See Fruit of the Loom*, 994 F.2d at 1363 ("Whittling away will not occur unless there is at least some subliminal connection in a buyer's mind between the two parties' uses of their marks."). The close parallels between the two analyses are therefore not surprising; nor do they cause us concern.

B. *Commercial Use*

Addressing the second element of a cause of action under the Federal Trademark Dilution Act, the district court held that Appellants' registration of <avery.net> and <dennison.net> constituted commercial use. 999 F.Supp. at 1339–40. We disagree.

Commercial use under the Federal Trademark Dilution Act requires the defendant to be using the trademark as a trademark, capitalizing on its trademark status. *See Panavision*, 141 F.3d at 1325. Courts have phrased this requirement in various ways. In a classic "cybersquatter" case, one court referenced the defendants "intention to arbitrage" the registration which included the plaintiff's trademark. *Intermatic*, 947 F.Supp. at 1239. Another court, whose decision we affirmed, noted that the defendant "traded on the value of marks as marks." *Panavision Int'l, L.P. v. Toeppen*, 945 F.Supp. 1296, 1303 (C.D.Cal.1996), *aff'd*, 141 F.3d 1316 (9th Cir.1998). In our *Panavision* decision, we considered the defendant's "attempt to sell the trademarks themselves." 141 F.3d at 1325.

All evidence in the record indicates that Appellants register common surnames in domain-name combinations and license e-mail addresses using those surnames, with the consequent intent to capitalize on the surname status of "Avery" and "Dennison." Appellants do not use trademarks qua trademarks as required by the caselaw to establish commercial use. Rather, Appellants use words that happen to be trademarks for their non-trademark value. The district court erred in holding that Appellants' use of <avery.net> and <dennison.net> constituted commercial use under the Federal Trademark Dilution Act, and this essential element of the dilution causes of action likewise mandates summary judgment for Appellants.

C. *Dilution*

The district court then considered the dilution requirement under both statutes, holding that Appellants' use of <avery.net> and <dennison.net> caused dilution, or a likelihood of dilution, of "Avery" and "Dennison." 999 F.Supp. at 1340–41. We hold that genuine issues of fact on this element of the causes of action should have precluded summary judgment for Avery Dennison.

Two theories of dilution are implicated in this case. First, Avery Dennison argues that Appellants' conduct is the cybersquatting dilution that we recognized in *Panavision. See* 141 F.3d at 1326–27. Second, Avery Dennison argues that Appellants' conduct in housing the <avery.net> and <dennison.net> domain names in the same database as various lewd SLDs causes tarnishment of the "Avery" and "Dennison" marks.

1. *Cybersquatting*

Cybersquatting dilution is the diminishment of " 'the capacity of the [plaintiff's] marks to identify and distinguish the [plaintiff's] goods and services on the Internet.' " *Panavision,* 141 F.3d at 1326 (quoting the *Panavision* district court, 945 F.Supp. at 1304). We recognized that this can occur if potential customers cannot find a web page at <trademark.com.> *Id.* at 1327; *see also Brookfield,* 174 F.3d at 1045 ("The Web surfer who assumes that 'X.com' will always correspond to the web site of company X or trademark X will, however, sometimes be misled."). Dilution occurs because " '[p]rospective users of plaintiff's services . . . may fail to continue to search for plaintiff's own home page, due to anger, frustration or the belief that plaintiff's home page does not exist.' " *Panavision,* 141 F.3d at 1327 (quoting *Jews for Jesus v. Brodsky,* 993 F.Supp. 282, 306–07 (D.N.J.1998)).

In the instant case, Appellants registered the TLD <.net>, rather than <.com>, with the SLDs <avery> and <dennison>. As we recognized in *Panavision,* <.net> applies to networks and <.com> applies to commercial entities. 141 F.3d at 1318. Evidence on the record supports this distinction, and courts applying the dilution cause of action to domain-name registrations have universally considered <trademark.com> registrations. *See* Brown, *Note, supra,* at 251–54 (discussing cases); *id.* at 262–63 (addressing the <.com> versus <.net> distinction). Although evidence on the record also demonstrates that the <.com> and <.net> distinction is illusory, a factfinder could infer that dilution does not occur with a <trademark.net> registration. This genuine issue of fact on the question of cybersquatting dilution should have prevented summary judgment for Avery Dennison.

2. *Tarnishment*

Tarnishment occurs when a defendant's use of a mark similar to a plaintiff's presents a danger that consumers will form unfavorable associations with the mark. *See Hasbro, Inc. v. Internet Ent. Group, Ltd.,* 40 U.S.P.Q.2d 1479, 1480, 1996 WL 84853 (W.D.Wash.1996) (<candyland.com> as a domain-name combination for a sexually explicit web site diluted plaintiff's trademark, "Candyland," for a children's game); 3 McCarthy, *supra,* § 24:104. The district court did not reach Avery Dennison's claims regarding tarnishment.

Avery Dennison offers, as an alternative ground for affirming the district court, the fact that Appellants house <avery.net> and <dennison.net> at the same web site as lewd domain-name registrations. However, the evidence likewise indicates that to move from <avery.net> or <dennison.net> to a lewd SLD requires "linking" through the Mailbank home page, which might remove any association with the "Avery" and "Dennison" trademarks that the Internet user might have had. *See Fruit of the Loom,* 994 F.2d at 1363 (requiring some connection between the two parties' uses of their marks). Whether Appellants' use of the registrations presents a danger of tarnishment is an issue of fact that could not be decided on summary judgment. . . .

VII. Conclusion

We reverse the district court's summary judgment in favor of Avery Dennison and remand with instructions to enter summary judgment for Sumpton and Freeview.

REVERSED and REMANDED.

EXTENSIONS

1. *Cybersquatters or entrepreneurs?* In *Avery Dennison v. Sumpton,* the district court held that "Avery" and "Dennison" were famous marks, and that defendants had made commercial use of them. These holdings were reversed on appeal. The district court went on to address the equities of the parties' claims to the two domain names. The court expressed great skepticism concerning defendants' explanation of their business model:

> Defendants allege that they have invested approximately $1,200,000 in their business. They allege that they are providing internet services to their licensees that the licensees could not offer for themselves, i.e., the ability to allow multiple uses of the same surnames as domain names, and the ability to spread the cost of maintaining the domain name registrations among all of the users.

> Defendants also point out that their use of the ".net" designation does not deny plaintiff access to the internet through use of its trademarks as domain names. Plaintiff has registered names corresponding to its trademarks under the ".com" designation, which is the designation specified for commercial use. According to the defendants, the internet registration system contemplates that the ".net" designation will be reserved for use by Internet service providers, and that it will not be used for marketing of commercial products. Defendants argue that their own use of the ".net" designation is within the contemplation of the internet registration system.

> Plaintiffs contend that none of defendants' arguments is apt. They contend that the internet registration system simply does not authorize "cybersquatting." They contend that it does not authorize the registration of *any* domain names that are commonly used by others to identify themselves, not for the purpose of use by the registrant as domain names, but rather for sale or license to others.

The court agrees. This is not a case involving a dispute over a domain name between persons or entities that have previously used the name to identify themselves or their products. Defendants' claimed "service" depends on their first having preempted 12,000 domain names, so that others who customarily use a name to identify themselves can use a domain name for that purpose only with the permission of the defendants. Moreover, anyone who desires to use any of those 12,000 names for any purpose, other than as an e-mail address, is entirely precluded from doing so. In light of the fact that many of the most popular on-line services provide e-mail addresses without charge, limiting domain name registrations to this purpose is almost certainly not the highest and best use. Finally, the ".net" designation has not been preserved according to the original intent, and many registrants, including trademark holders, have registered domain names with ".net" designations that are not internet providers.

The court is extremely dubious that licensing domain names for use as e-mail addresses is defendants' true business. As previously noted, this limitation is voluntary. It would be extremely difficult to enforce if defendants' right to the exclusive use of these domain names was ever held to exist. Thereafter, it would appear that the laws of economics would require the defendants to sell or license each of their 12,000 names to the highest bidder for whatever use the buyer or licensee wished to make of them.

Avery Dennison v. Sumpton, 999 F.Supp. 1337, 1341–42 (C.D.Cal.1998), *rev'd*, 189 F.3d 868 (9th Cir.1999).

Do you agree that defendants' purported business model is a sham? Was the district court too facile in condemning defendants as cybersquatters? Consider the district court's explanation: "Defendants are 'cybersquatters,' as that term has come to be commonly understood. They have registered over 12,000 internet domain names not for their own use, but rather to prevent others from using those names without defendants' consent." Is cybersquatting, as thus understood, more worthy of condemnation than the action of any other entrepreneur who gains control of a resource that is in limited supply (real estate, stock in a corporation, chromium) and makes it available to others for a price?

2. *Fame.* While it is unsurprising that "Toys 'R' Us" is viewed as a "famous" trademark, you might find it odd that the court in *Teletech Customer Care Management v. Tele–Tech,* 977 F.Supp. 1407 (C.D.Cal.1997), found "TeleTech" to be a famous mark. If "TeleTech" is a famous mark, one might conclude that the legal threshold for fame under 15 U.S.C. § 1125(c) is very low, but the Ninth Circuit in *Avery Dennison v. Sumpton, supra,* applied a rather more rigorous standard. The Seventh Circuit wrestled with this question in *Syndicate Sales, Inc. v. Hampshire Paper Corp.,* 192 F.3d 633 (7th Cir.1999):

At an initial glance, there appears to be a wide variation of authority on this issue. Some cases apparently hold that fame in a niche market is insufficient for a federal dilution claim, while some hold that such fame is sufficient. However, a closer look indicates that the different lines of authority are addressing two different contexts. Cases holding that niche-market fame is insufficient generally address the context in which the plaintiff and defendant are using the mark in separate markets. On the other hand, cases stating that niche-market renown is a factor indicating fame address a context like the one here, in which the plaintiff and defendant are using the mark in the same or related markets. *See Teletech Customer Care Management, Inc. v. Tele–Tech Co.,* 977 F.Supp. 1407, 1413 (C.D.Cal.1997). The validity of this distinction is supported by the Restatement and a commentator:

A mark that is highly distinctive only to a select class or group of purchasers

> may be protected from diluting uses directed at that particular class or group. For example, a mark may be highly distinctive among purchasers of a specific type of product. In such circumstances, protection against a dilution of the mark's distinctiveness is ordinarily appropriate only against uses specifically directed at that particular class of purchasers; uses of the mark in broader markets, although they may produce an incidental diluting effect in the protected market, are not normally actionable.

Restatement (Third) of Unfair Competition § 25 cmt. e (1995); *see also* 4 J. Thomas McCarthy, *McCarthy on Trademarks and Unfair Competition* § 24:112, at 24–204 to 24–205 (1999).

Moreover, one of the factors in § 1125(c) for determining the existence of fame indicates that fame may be constricted to a particular market. That factor is "the degree of recognition of the mark in the trading areas and channels of trade used by the marks' owner and the person against whom the injunction is sought." 15 U.S.C. § 1125(c)(1)(F). We acknowledge, of course, that the narrowness of the market in which a plaintiff's mark has fame is a factor that must be considered in the balance. . . . However, when the defendant allegedly uses a mark in the same market as the plaintiff, the narrowness of that market is less important. We therefore hold that the district court erred in concluding that the trade dress was not famous based solely on the niche-market status of the baskets.

Syndicate Sales, Inc. v. Hampshire Paper Corp., 192 F.3d at 640–41. Do you find the Seventh Circuit's explanation of the *TeleTech* holding convincing? Apparently the Second Circuit did not. In *TCPIP Holding Company, Inc. v. Haar Communications, Inc.,* 244 F.3d 88 (2d Cir.2001), the Second Circuit notes that

> the benefits of the [Federal Trademark] Dilution Act are available to owners of a "famous" mark. The Act does not tell *how* famous a mark must be. Nor does it provide any direct guidance as to how courts should answer the question. The word "famous" is susceptible to many widely different understandings. If a hypothetical Grendel's Coffee Shop in Smalltown, U.S.A. has for years been the favorite hangout of Smalltown high school students, Grendel's may well be famous among the students and graduates of Smalltown High. Or another mark for a catalogue selling rare plant specimens may be famous among 100,000 collectors scattered throughout the country. Are those then "famous" marks within the meaning of the statute? The argument might be made that if the plaintiff's mark is "famous" in any sense coming within a dictionary definition, it qualifies for the statute's protection. . . .

> It seems most unlikely that Congress intended to confer on marks that have enjoyed only brief fame in a small part of the country, or among a small segment of the population, the power to enjoin all other users throughout the nation in all realms of commerce. The examples of eligible "famous marks" given in the House Report—Dupont, Buick, and Kodak, *see* H.R.Rep. No. 104–374, at 3 (1995), *reprinted in* 1995 U.S.C.C.A.N. 1029, 1030—are marks that for the major part of the century have been household words throughout the United States. They are representative of the best known marks in commerce. Once again, we recognize that examples in a legislative report cannot be taken as defining the limits of a statute's coverage. Putting together the extraordinary power the Act confers on a "famous" mark and the improbability that Congress intended to grant such outright exclusivity to marks that are famous in only a small area or segment of the nation, with the hints to be gleaned from the House Report, we

think Congress envisioned that marks would qualify as "famous" only if they carried a substantial degree of fame.

TCPIP Holding Company, Inc. v. Haar Communications, Inc., 244 F.3d at 98–99. Is it possible to reconcile the Second and Seventh Circuit discussions of congressional intent? If not, which do you find more convincing?

3. *Actual harm v. likelihood of harm.* A split in the circuits has developed over the issue whether a claim for trademark dilution under the Federal Trademark Dilution Act requires proof of actual harm or merely a showing that harm is likely. In *Ringling Bros—Barnum & Bailey Combined Shows, Inc. v. Utah Div. of Travel Development,* 170 F.3d 449 (4th Cir.1999), the Fourth Circuit required a showing of actual harm. By contrast, in *Nabisco, Inc. v. PF Brands, Inc.,* 191 F.3d 208 (2d Cir.1999), the court held that likelihood of future harm is sufficient to support an injunction.

The Supreme Court answered this question in *Moseley v. V Secret Catalogue, Inc.,* 537 U.S. 418 (2003). In *Moseley,* the petitioner contended that the FTDA required proof of actual harm, rather than mere likelihood of harm. The court agreed and stated:

> The relevant text of the FTDA . . . provides that "the owner of a famous mark" is entitled to injunctive relief against another person's commercial use of a mark or trade name if that use "*causes dilution* of the distinctive quality" of the famous mark. 15 U.S.C. § 1125(c)(1) (emphasis added). This text unambiguously requires a showing of actual dilution, rather than a likelihood of dilution. . . .

> Of course, that does not mean that the consequences of dilution, such as an actual loss of sales or profits, must also be proved. To the extent that language in the Fourth Circuit's opinion in the *Ringling Bros.* case suggests otherwise, see 170 F.3d, at 460–465, we disagree. We do agree, however, with that court's conclusion that, at least where the marks at issue are not identical, the mere fact that consumers mentally associate the junior user's mark with a famous mark is not sufficient to establish actionable dilution. As the facts of that case demonstrate, such mental association will not necessarily reduce the capacity of the famous mark to identify the goods of its owner, the statutory requirement for dilution under the FTDA. For even though Utah drivers may be reminded of the circus when they see a license plate referring to the "greatest *snow* on earth," it by no means follows that they will associate "the greatest show on earth" with skiing or snow sports, or associate it less strongly or exclusively with the circus. "Blurring" is not a necessary consequence of mental association. (Nor, for that matter, is "tarnishing.").

Id. at 432–34. Does this holding discourage or preclude the use of injunctions by potential plaintiffs when conduct that is likely to dilute their mark comes to their attention?

4. *A split in the circuits over descriptive trademarks.* Does a trademark have to be inherently distinctive to qualify for protection under the Federal Trademark Dilution Act? In the cases discussed above, none of the marks was descriptive (i.e., none of them had acquired distinctiveness; all were inherently distinctive). Does this mean that descriptive marks that have acquired secondary meaning are not protected under 15 U.S.C. § 1125(c)? That is exactly the conclusion reached by the Second Circuit in *TCPIP Holding Company, Inc. v. Haar Communications, Inc.,* 244 F.3d 88 (2d Cir.2001):

> In order to qualify for the Act's protection, the mark must be famous. By definition, every mark that is famous, in the sense intended by the Act, has a high degree of acquired distinctiveness. Thus, no mark can qualify for the Act's protection without acquired distinctiveness. If that acquired distinctiveness satisfies not

only the fame requirement, but also the distinctiveness requirement, then there will never be a case when a court needs to consider whether the mark has inherent distinctiveness. The statute's invitation to courts to consider the mark's degree of inherent distinctiveness would serve no function.

We therefore understand Clause (A) of § 1125(c)(1) to invite two inquiries: (1) Has the plaintiff's mark achieved a sufficient degree of consumer recognition ("acquired distinctiveness") to satisfy the Act's requirement of fame? (2) Does the mark possess a sufficient degree of "inherent distinctiveness" to satisfy the Act's requirement of "distinctive quality." The latter requirement cannot be satisfied by the mere fact that the public has come to associate the mark with the source. Thus, weak, non-distinctive, descriptive marks do not qualify for the Act's protection, even if famous.

TCPIP Holding Company, Inc. v. Haar Communications, Inc., 244 F.3d at 98. In *Times Mirror Magazines, Inc. v. Las Vegas Sports News, L.L.C.*, 212 F.3d 157 (3d Cir.2000), the Third Circuit reached the opposite conclusion: that a descriptive trademark that had acquired secondary meaning was indeed covered by the Federal Trademark Dilution Act. Rejecting the idea that 15 U.S.C. § 1125(c) involves a test for distinctiveness separate and apart from its test for fame, the Third Circuit noted that

> [t]o be a "mark" eligible in the first place for protection under [§ 1125(c)(1)], basic trademark principles dictate that a designation has to be "distinctive" either inherently or through acquisition of secondary meaning.

4 McCarthy on Trademarks and Unfair Competition § 24:91 (footnotes omitted).

McCarthy explains the legislative history behind § 1125(c)(1)'s "distinctive and famous" language:

> The 1987 Trademark Review Commission Report, the genesis of the language contained in the 1996 federal Act, said that the dual mention of both "distinctive and famous" in the introduction to the list of factors was inserted to emphasize the policy goal that to be protected, a mark had to be truly prominent and renowned. The double-barreled language "distinctive and famous" reflected the goal that protection should be confined to marks "which are both distinctive, as established by federal registration at a minimum, and famous, as established by separate evidence." The Commission inserted the term "distinctive" as hyperbole to emphasize the requirement that the mark be registered, for without inherent or acquired distinctiveness, the designation would not have been a mark that should have federally registered in the first place. The Trademark Review Commission Report reveals that the Commission saw distinctiveness and fame as two sides of the same evidentiary coin which requires widespread and extensive customer recognition of the plaintiff's mark. However, when in the 1995 House amendment, the requirement of federal registration was dropped from the Bill, Congress neglected to also drop the mention of "distinctive" introducing the list of factors. Thus, the word "distinctive" was left floating in the statute, unmoored to either any statutory requirement or underlying policy goal.

Id. (footnotes omitted).

Accordingly, we are not persuaded that a mark be subject to separate tests for fame and distinctiveness. . . . Having decided that Times Mirror has proved that its mark had gained secondary meaning and a high degree of distinctiveness in the market, there is no necessity for proving an additional test of distinctiveness.

Times Mirror Magazines, Inc. v. Las Vegas Sports News, L.L.C., 212 F.3d at 167–68. Is there a conflict here between the language of the federal statute and the statute's legislative history? Is the statutory language sufficiently unclear so that the Third Circuit's primary reliance on the legislative history is warranted? Which approach makes the most sense to you?

QUESTIONS FOR DISCUSSION

Trademark combinatorics and domain permutations. The court in *Toys "R" Us v. Feinberg* notes that "Geoffrey also owns various internet domain names including tru.com, toysrus.com, kidsrus.com, boysrus.com, dollsrus.com, galsrus.com, girlsrus.com, babiesrus.com, computersrus.com, guysrus.com, mathematicsrus.com, moviesrus.com, opportunitiesrus.com, partiesrus.com, poolsrus.com, portraitsrus.com, racersrus.com, supervaluesrus.com, treatsrus.com, tykesrus.com, sportsrus.com, giftsrus.com, and toysrusregistry.com." Would the registration or use of these domain names by somebody other than Geoffrey constitute trademark infringement?

IV. TRADEMARK DEFENSES ONLINE

A. TRADITIONAL FAIR USE

Brookfield Communications, Inc. v. West Coast Entertainment Corp.
174 F.3d 1036 (9th Cir.1999).

■ O'SCANNLAIN, CIRCUIT JUDGE:

[The statement of facts and the Lanham Act claims are excerpted in Part II(B), *supra.*]

. . .

Contrary to West Coast's contentions, we are not in any way restricting West Coast's right to use terms in a manner which would constitute fair use under the Lanham Act. *See New Kids on the Block v. News America Pub., Inc.,* 971 F.2d 302, 306–09 (9th Cir.1992); *see also August Storck K.G. v. Nabisco, Inc.,* 59 F.3d 616, 617–18 (7th Cir.1995). It is well established that the Lanham Act does not prevent one from using a competitor's mark truthfully to identify the competitor's goods, *see, e.g., Smith v. Chanel, Inc.,* 402 F.2d 562, 563 (9th Cir.1968) (stating that a copyist may use the originator's mark to identify the product that it has copied), or in comparative advertisements, *see New Kids on the Block,* 971 F.2d at 306–09. This fair use doctrine applies in cyberspace as it does in the real world. *See Radio Channel Networks, Inc. v. Broadcast.Com, Inc.,* No. 98 Civ. 4799, 1999 WL 124455, at *5-*6 (S.D.N.Y. Mar.8, 1999); *Bally Total Fitness Holding Corp. v. Faber,* 29 F.Supp.2d 1161 (C.D.Cal.1998); *Playboy Enterprises, Inc. v. Terri Welles,* 7 F.Supp.2d 1098, 1103–04 (S.D.Cal.1998).

In *Welles,* the case most on point, Playboy sought to enjoin former Playmate of the Year Terri Welles ("Welles") from using "Playmate" or "Playboy" on her website featuring photographs of herself. *See* 7 F.Supp.2d at 1100. Welles's website advertised the fact that she was a former Playmate of the Year, but minimized the use of Playboy's marks; it also contained numerous disclaimers stating that her site was neither endorsed by nor affiliated with Playboy. The district court found that

Welles was using "Playboy" and "Playmate" not as trademarks, but rather as descriptive terms fairly and accurately describing her web page, and that her use of "Playboy" and "Playmate" in her website's metatags was a permissible, good faith attempt to index the content of her website. It accordingly concluded that her use was permissible under the trademark laws. *See id.* at 1103–04.[2]

We agree that West Coast can legitimately use an appropriate descriptive term in its metatags. But "MovieBuff" is not such a descriptive term. Even though it differs from "Movie Buff" by only a single space, that difference is pivotal. The term "Movie Buff" is a descriptive term, which is routinely used in the English language to describe a movie devotee. "MovieBuff" is not. The term "MovieBuff" is not in the dictionary. *See Merriam-Webster's Collegiate Dictionary* 762 (10th ed.1998); *American Heritage College Dictionary* 893 (3d ed.1997); *Webster's New World College Dictionary* 889 (3d ed.1997); *Webster's Third New Int'l Dictionary* 1480 (unabridged 1993). Nor has that term been used in any published federal or state court opinion. In light of the fact that it is not a word in the English language, when the term "MovieBuff" *is* employed, it is used to refer to Brookfield's products and services, rather than to mean "motion picture enthusiast." The proper term for the "motion picture enthusiast" is "Movie Buff," which West Coast certainly *can* use. It cannot, however, omit the space.

Moreover, West Coast is not absolutely barred from using the term "Movie-Buff." As we explained above, that term can be legitimately used to describe Brookfield's product. For example, its web page might well include an advertisement banner such as "Why pay for MovieBuff when you can get the same thing here for FREE?" which clearly employs "MovieBuff" to refer to Brookfield's products. West Coast, however, presently uses Brookfield's trademark not to reference Brookfield's products, but instead to describe its own product (in the case of the domain name) and to attract people to its website in the case of the metatags. That is not fair use.

. . .

Bihari v. Gross
119 F.Supp.2d 309 (S.D.N.Y.2000).

■ SCHEINDLIN, DISTRICT JUDGE.

[The statement of facts and the Lanham Act claims are excerpted in Part II(B), *supra.*]

. . .

e. The Fair Use Doctrine

Even if the Gross websites cause consumer confusion, use of the "Bihari Interi-

---

[2] [The district court subsequently entered summary judgment in favor of Welles, and the court of appeals affirmed in substantial part. *See Playboy Enterprises, Inc. v. Welles*, 78 F.Supp.2d 1066 (S.D.Cal.1999), *aff'd in part, rev'd in part, & remanded*, 279 F.3d 796 (9th Cir.2002). The appellate decision is excerpted in Part IV(B), *infra.*—Eds.]

ors" mark in the metatags is protected as a fair use. The Lanham Act codified a common law fair use defense in 15 U.S.C. § 1115(b)(4). The fair use doctrine applies to the Internet as readily as to the print media. *See Radio Channel Networks, Inc. v. Broadcast.Com, Inc.*, 98 Civ. 4799, 1999 WL 124455, at **5–6 (S.D.N.Y. Mar.8, 1999) (permitting defendant's fair use of the term "The Radio Channel" on its website, which transmits broadcasts over the Internet, even though plaintiff had registered the service mark "The Radio Channel").

"Fair use is established when the challenged term is a use, otherwise than as a mark, . . . of a term or device which is descriptive of and used fairly and in good faith only to describe the goods or services of such party. . . ." 15 U.S.C. § 1115(b)(4). In other words, "fair use permits others to use a protected mark to describe aspects of their own goods." *Car–Freshner Corp. v. S.C. Johnson & Son, Inc.*, 70 F.3d 267, 270 (2d Cir.1995). It is not necessary that the plaintiff's mark be classified as "descriptive" to benefit from the fair use defense. Instead, the central considerations are whether the defendant has used the mark (1) in its descriptive sense, and (2) in good faith. *See id.*

(i) Use of the Term in its Descriptive Sense

The requirement that a trademark be used in its descriptive sense is met where the mark is used in an index or catalog, or to describe the defendant's connection to the business claiming trademark protection. *See Nihon Keizai Shimbun, Inc. v. Comline Bus. Data, Inc.*, 166 F.3d 65, 73–74 (2d Cir.1999) (permitting fair use defense where defendant, a company that gathers news articles and sells "abstracts" summarizing the articles, routinely used the plaintiff's mark in the reference line of its abstracts to identify the source of the article abstracted by the defendant); Restatement (Third) of Unfair Competition § 28 cmt. a (1995) (fair use defense protects a subsequent user's use of a personal name designation "if the name is used solely to indicate truthfully the named person's connection with the goods, services, or business."). Applying this general rule to the metatag context, Professor McCarthy states: "[T]he fair use defense applies . . . if another's trademark is used in a meta tag solely to describe the defendant or defendant's goods or services. . . ." 4 J. Thomas McCarthy, *McCarthy on Trademarks and Unfair Competition* ("McCarthy"), § 25:69 at 25–137 (4th ed.1999). This position finds support in recent cases. In *Playboy Enters., Inc. v. Welles*, 7 F.Supp.2d 1098 (S.D.Cal.1998), Playboy sought to enjoin Terri Welles, a former "Playmate of the Month" and "Playmate of the Year", from utilizing the trademarked terms "Playboy" and "Playmate" in the metatags of Welles' website. The court denied the injunction, holding that use of the trademarked terms in the metatags is a fair use. . . . *See also Brookfield Communications*, 174 F.3d at 1066 (stating that West Coast can use Brookfield's trademark on its website to "legitimately . . . describe Brookfield's product. For example, [West Coast can] . . . include an advertisement banner such as 'Why pay for MovieBuff when you can get the same thing here for FREE?' ").

Here, Gross has included "Bihari Interiors" in the metatags of his websites because the websites provide information about Bihari Interiors and Marianne Bihari. Gross has not used the terms "Bihari Interiors" and "Bihari" in the metatags as a mark, but rather, to fairly identify the content of his websites. In short, Gross uses the "Bihari Interiors" mark in its descriptive sense only.

Moreover, use of the "Bihari Interiors" mark in the metatags of his websites is the only way Gross can get his message to the public. *See Bally Total Fitness*, 29 F.Supp.2d at 1165 ("Prohibiting [the defendant] from using Bally's name in the machine readable code would effectively isolate him from all but the most savvy of Internet users."). A broad rule prohibiting use of "Bihari Interiors" in the metatags of websites not sponsored by Bihari would effectively foreclose all discourse and comment about Bihari Interiors, including fair comment. Courts must be particularly cautious of overextending the reach of the Lanham Act and intruding on First Amendment values. *Cf. Rogers v. Grimaldi*, 875 F.2d 994, 998 (2d Cir.1989) (holding that movie titles using a celebrity's name will not be actionable under the Lanham Act unless the title has no artistic relevance to the underlying work or if the title misleads as to the source or the content of the work); 4 *McCarthy*, § 27:91 at 27–140 ("Whether through the use of statutory interpretation or concern for free speech, traditional protections for commentators and critics on business and commercial affairs must not be jettisoned. It is important to create critical breathing space for legitimate comment and criticism about products and services."). The Second Circuit's warning in a recent Internet case to proceed cautiously when dealing with the frontier of expressive speech on the Internet is particularly instructive:

> In considering whether domain names constitute expressive speech, we observe that the lightning speed development of the Internet poses challenges for the common-law adjudicative process—a process which, ideally while grounded in the past, governs the present and offers direction for the future based on understandings of current circumstances. Mindful of the often unforeseeable impact of rapid technological change, we are wary of making legal pronouncements based on highly fluid circumstances, which almost certainly will give way to tomorrow's new realities.

Name.Space, Inc. v. Network Solutions, Inc., 202 F.3d 573 (2d Cir.2000) (stating that top level domain names may, one day, constitute expressive speech).

(ii) Gross's Good Faith

To benefit from the defense of fair use, Gross must have acted in good faith. The inquiry into a defendant's good faith focuses on whether "the defendant adopted its mark with the intention of capitalizing on plaintiff's reputation and goodwill and any confusion between his and the senior user's product." *Lang v. Retirement Living Pub. Co., Inc.*, 949 F.2d 576, 583 (2d Cir.1991).

Bihari argues, in a conclusory fashion, that Gross did not adopt the "Bihari Interiors" mark in good faith. Rather, Gross intended to divert individuals searching for information about Bihari Interiors to his websites. This argument is not persuasive. Metatags serve as a cataloging system for a search engine. Gross has the right to catalog the contents of his websites. Furthermore, the fact that Gross knew of the prior use of the "Bihari Interiors" mark does not in itself prove a lack of good faith. "[P]rior knowledge of [plaintiff's] trade name does not give rise to a necessary inference of bad faith, because adoption of a trademark with actual knowledge of another's prior registration . . . may be consistent with good faith." *Lang*, 949 F.2d at 583–84; Restatement (Third) of Unfair Competition § 28 cmt. d ("Knowledge of a prior trademark use of the term does not in itself prove a lack of good faith.").

In addition, the domain names of the Gross websites and the disclaimer prove that Gross is using "Bihari Interiors" in good faith. The domain names of his websites in no way confuse Internet users into believing that his site is actually that of Bihari Interiors. *See, e.g., Planned Parenthood*, 1997 WL 133313, at **8–10 (defendant's anti-abortion website violates the Lanham Act because, among other reasons, it was registered at "www.plannedparenthood.com", and the site greeted users with "Welcome to the PLANNED PARENTHOOD HOME PAGE"). Moreover, the Gross websites include a disclaimer: "Keep in mind that this site reflects only the view points and experiences of one Manhattan couple. . . ." Although a disclaimer cannot insulate Gross from liability, it indicates good faith use of the service marks and weighs in Gross's favor. *See Consumers Union of United States, Inc. v. General Signal Corp.*, 724 F.2d 1044, 1053 (2d Cir.1983) ("Disclaimers are a favored way of alleviating consumer confusion as to source or sponsorship"). Even if the Gross websites are mean-spirited and vindictive, bad faith cannot be imputed as well to Gross's use of the "Bihari Interiors" mark in the metatags. *See Nihon Keizai Shimbun*, 166 F.3d at 74 (holding that use of plaintiff's mark is in good faith even though "other aspects of defendants' behavior may have evidenced bad faith."). . . .

QUESTIONS FOR DISCUSSION

1. *Fair use and metatags*. In *Bihari v. Gross*, Gross was successful in his fair use defense, while in *Brookfield Communications v. West Coast Entertainment*, West Coast was not. Why was one successful and the other not? Do both courts understand the fair use defense in the same way? If West Coast Entertainment had had a discussion and critique of the plaintiff's MovieBuff database on its website, would the Ninth Circuit have permitted West Coast to succeed on its fair use defense? Does it matter that the word "MovieBuff" is not a descriptive term that can be found in a dictionary? For a case where a defendant that used an affiliate's trademark as a keyword in a metatag succeeded in its fair use defense, *see Trans Union LLC v. Credit Research, Inc.*, 142 F.Supp.2d 1029 (N.D.Ill.2001).

2. *Fair use and dilution*. Is the fair use defense effective against claims of trademark dilution under 15 U.S.C. § 1125(c)? *See id.* § 1125(c)(4). Does this provision resolve the question? What if the mark is being used to identify the defendant's goods and services? What if the mark is being used to identify the defendant rather than the defendant's goods and services?

B. NOMINATIVE USE

Playboy Enterprises, Inc. v. Welles
279 F.3d 796 (9th Cir.2002).

■ T.G. NELSON, CIRCUIT JUDGE.

Playboy Enterprises, Inc. (PEI), appeals the district court's grant of summary judgment as to its claims of trademark infringement [and trademark dilution] . . . against Terri Welles [and] Terri Welles, Inc. . . . We have jurisdiction pursuant to 28

U.S.C. § 1291, and we affirm in part and reverse in part. . . .

I. Background

Terri Welles was on the cover of Playboy in 1981 and was chosen to be the Playboy Playmate of the Year for 1981. Her use of the title "Playboy Playmate of the Year 1981," and her use of other trademarked terms on her website are at issue in this suit. During the relevant time period, Welles' website offered information about and free photos of Welles, advertised photos for sale, advertised memberships in her photo club, and promoted her services as a spokesperson. A biographical section described Welles' selection as Playmate of the Year in 1981 and her years modeling for PEI. After the lawsuit began, Welles included discussions of the suit and criticism of PEI on her website and included a note disclaiming any association with PEI.[1]

PEI complains of four different uses of its trademarked terms on Welles' website: (1) the terms "Playboy" and "Playmate" in the metatags of the website; (2) the phrase "Playmate of the Year 1981" on the masthead of the website; (3) the phrases "Playboy Playmate of the Year 1981" and "Playmate of the Year 1981" on various banner ads, which may be transferred to other websites; and (4) the repeated use of the abbreviation "PMOY '81" as the watermark on the pages of the website.[3] PEI claimed that these uses of its marks constituted trademark infringement, dilution, false designation of origin, and unfair competition. The district court granted defendants' motion for summary judgment. PEI appeals the grant of summary judgment on its infringement and dilution claims. We affirm in part and reverse in part.

. . .

III. Discussion

A. Trademark Infringement

Except for the use of PEI's protected terms in the wallpaper of Welles' website, we conclude that Welles' uses of PEI's trademarks are permissible, nominative uses. They imply no current sponsorship or endorsement by PEI. Instead, they serve to identify Welles as a past PEI "Playmate of the Year."

We articulated the test for a permissible, nominative use in *New Kids On The Block v. New America Publishing, Inc.*[8] The band, New Kids On The Block, claimed trademark infringement arising from the use of their trademarked name by several newspapers. The newspapers had conducted polls asking which member of the band New Kids On The Block was the best and most popular. The papers' use of

---

[1] The disclaimer reads as follows: "This site is neither endorsed, nor sponsored, nor affiliated with Playboy Enterprises, Inc. PLAYBOY® PLAYMATE OF THE YEAR® AND PLAYMATE OF THE MONTH® ARE REGISTERED trademarks of Playboy Enterprises, Inc."

[3] PEI claims that "PMOY" is an unregistered trademark of PEI, standing for "Playmate of the Year."

[8] 971 F.2d 302 (9th Cir.1992).

the trademarked term did not fall within the traditional fair use doctrine. Unlike a traditional fair use scenario, the defendant newspaper was using the trademarked term to describe not its own product, but the plaintiff's. Thus, the factors used to evaluate fair use were inapplicable. The use was nonetheless permissible, we concluded, based on its nominative nature.

We adopted the following test for nominative use:

> First, the product or service in question must be one not readily identifiable without use of the trademark; second, only so much of the mark or marks may be used as is reasonably necessary to identify the product or service; and third, the user must do nothing that would, in conjunction with the mark, suggest sponsorship or endorsement by the trademark holder.

We noted in *New Kids* that a nominative use may also be a commercial one.

In cases in which the defendant raises a nominative use defense, the above three-factor test should be applied instead of the test for likelihood of confusion set forth in [*AMF Inc. v. Sleekcraft Boats*, 599 F.2d 341 (9th Cir.1979)]. The three-factor test better evaluates the likelihood of confusion in nominative use cases. When a defendant uses a trademark nominally, the trademark will be identical to the plaintiff's mark, at least in terms of the words in question. Thus, application of the *Sleekcraft* test, which focuses on the similarity of the mark used by the plaintiff and the defendant, would lead to the incorrect conclusion that virtually all nominative uses are confusing. The three-factor test—with its requirements that the defendant use marks only when no descriptive substitute exists, use no more of the mark than necessary, and do nothing to suggest sponsorship or endorsement by the mark holder—better addresses concerns regarding the likelihood of confusion in nominative use cases.

We group the uses of PEI's trademarked terms into three for the purpose of applying the test for nominative use. First, we analyze Welles' use of the terms in headlines and banner advertisements. We conclude that those uses are clearly nominative. Second, we analyze the use of the terms in the metatags for Welles' website, which we conclude are nominative as well. Finally, we analyze the terms as used in the wall-paper of the website. We conclude that this use is not nominative and remand for a determination of whether it infringes on a PEI trademark.

1. Headlines and banner advertisements.

To satisfy the first part of the test for nominative use, "the product or service in question must be one not readily identifiable without use of the trademark[.]" This situation arises "when a trademark also describes a person, a place or an attribute of a product" and there is no descriptive substitute for the trademark. In such a circumstance, allowing the trademark holder exclusive rights would allow the language to "be depleted in much the same way as if generic words were protectable." In *New Kids*, we gave the example of the trademarked term, "Chicago Bulls." We explained that "one might refer to the 'two-time world champions' or 'the professional basketball team from Chicago,' but it's far simpler (and more likely to be understood) to refer to the Chicago Bulls." Moreover, such a use of the trademark would "not imply sponsorship or endorsement of the product because the mark is used only to describe the thing, rather than to identify its source." Thus, we concluded, such uses must be excepted from trademark infringement law.

The district court properly identified Welles' situation as one which must also be excepted. No descriptive substitute exists for PEI's trademarks in this context. The court explained:

> [T]here is no other way that Ms. Welles can identify or describe herself and her services without venturing into absurd descriptive phrases. To describe herself as the "nude model selected by Mr. Hefner's magazine as its number-one prototypical woman for the year 1981" would be impractical as well as ineffectual in identifying Terri Welles to the public.

We agree. Just as the newspapers in *New Kids* could only identify the band clearly by using its trademarked name, so can Welles only identify herself clearly by using PEI's trademarked title.

The second part of the nominative use test requires that "only so much of the mark or marks may be used as is reasonably necessary to identify the product or service[.]" *New Kids* provided the following examples to explain this element: "[A] soft drink competitor would be entitled to compare its product to Coca–Cola or Coke, but would not be entitled to use Coca–Cola's distinctive lettering." Similarly, in a past case, an auto shop was allowed to use the trademarked term "Volkswagen" on a sign describing the cars it repaired, in part because the shop "did not use Volkswagen's distinctive lettering style or color scheme, nor did he display the encircled 'VW' emblem." Welles' banner advertisements and headlines satisfy this element because they use only the trademarked words, not the font or symbols associated with the trademarks.

The third element requires that the user do "nothing that would, in conjunction with the mark, suggest sponsorship or endorsement by the trademark holder." As to this element, we conclude that aside from the wallpaper, which we address separately, Welles does nothing in conjunction with her use of the marks to suggest sponsorship or endorsement by PEI. The marks are clearly used to describe the title she received from PEI in 1981, a title that helps describe who she is. It would be unreasonable to assume that the Chicago Bulls sponsored a website of Michael Jordan's simply because his name appeared with the appellation "former Chicago Bull." Similarly, in this case, it would be unreasonable to assume that PEI currently sponsors or endorses someone who describes herself as a "Playboy Playmate of the Year in 1981." The designation of the year, in our case, serves the same function as the "former" in our example. It shows that any sponsorship or endorsement occurred in the past.[25]

In addition to doing nothing in conjunction with her use of the marks to suggest sponsorship or endorsement by PEI, Welles affirmatively disavows any sponsorship or endorsement. Her site contains a clear statement disclaiming any con-

---

[25] We express no opinion regarding whether an individual's use of a current title would suggest sponsorship or endorsement.

nection to PEI. Moreover, the text of the site describes her ongoing legal battles with the company.[26]

For the foregoing reasons, we conclude that Welles' use of PEI's marks in her headlines and banner advertisements is a nominative use excepted from the law of trademark infringement.

2. Metatags.

Welles includes the terms "playboy" and "playmate" in her metatags. Metatags describe the contents of a website using keywords. Some search engines search metatags to identify websites relevant to a search. Thus, when an internet searcher enters "playboy" or "playmate" into a search engine that uses metatags, the results will include Welles' site.[28] Because Welles' metatags do not repeat the terms extensively, her site will not be at the top of the list of search results. Applying the three-factor test for nominative use, we conclude that the use of the trademarked terms in Welles' metatags is nominative.

As we discussed above with regard to the headlines and banner advertisements, Welles has no practical way of describing herself without using trademarked terms. In the context of metatags, we conclude that she has no practical way of identifying the content of her website without referring to PEI's trademarks.

A large portion of Welles' website discusses her association with Playboy over the years. Thus, the trademarked terms accurately describe the contents of Welles' website, in addition to describing Welles. Forcing Welles and others to use absurd turns of phrase in their metatags, such as those necessary to identify Welles, would be particularly damaging in the internet search context. Searchers would have a much more difficult time locating relevant websites if they could do so only by correctly guessing the long phrases necessary to substitute for trademarks. We can hardly expect someone searching for Welles' site to imagine the same phrase proposed by the district court to describe Welles without referring to Playboy—"the nude model selected by Mr. Hefner's organization. . . ." Yet if someone could not remember her name, that is what they would have to do. Similarly, someone searching for critiques of Playboy on the internet would have a difficult time if internet sites could not list the object of their critique in their metatags.

There is simply no descriptive substitute for the trademarks used in Welles' metatags. Precluding their use would have the unwanted effect of hindering the free flow of information on the internet, something which is certainly not a goal of trademark law. Accordingly, the use of trademarked terms in the metatags meets the first part of the test for nominative use.

---

[26] By noting Welles' affirmative actions, we do not mean to imply that affirmative actions of this type are necessary to establish nominative use. *New Kids* sets forth no such requirement, and we do not impose one here.

[28] We note that search engines that use their own summaries of websites, or that search the entire text of sites, are also likely to identify Welles' site as relevant to a search for "playboy" or "playmate," given the content of the site.

We conclude that the metatags satisfy the second and third elements of the test as well. The metatags use only so much of the marks as reasonably necessary[30] and nothing is done in conjunction with them to suggest sponsorship or endorsement by the trademark holder. We note that our decision might differ if the metatags listed the trademarked term so repeatedly that Welles' site would regularly appear above PEI's in searches for one of the trademarked terms.

3. Wallpaper/watermark.

The background, or wallpaper, of Welles' site consists of the repeated abbreviation "PMOY '81," which stands for "Playmate of the Year 1981." Welles' name or likeness does not appear before or after "PMOY '81." The pattern created by the repeated abbreviation appears as the background of the various pages of the website. Accepting, for the purposes of this appeal, that the abbreviation "PMOY" is indeed entitled to protection, we conclude that the repeated, stylized use of this abbreviation fails the nominative use test.

The repeated depiction of "PMOY '81" is not necessary to describe Welles. "Playboy Playmate of the Year 1981" is quite adequate. Moreover, the term does not even appear to describe Welles—her name or likeness do not appear before or after each "PMOY '81." Because the use of the abbreviation fails the first prong of the nominative use test, we need not apply the next two prongs of the test.

Because the defense of nominative use fails here, and we have already determined that the doctrine of fair use does not apply, we remand to the district court. The court must determine whether trademark law protects the abbreviation "PMOY," as used in the wallpaper.

B. Trademark Dilution

The district court granted summary judgment to Welles as to PEI's claim of trademark dilution. We affirm on the ground that all of Welles' uses of PEI's marks, with the exception of the use in the wallpaper which we address separately, are proper, nominative uses. We hold that nominative uses, by definition, do not dilute the trademarks.

Federal law provides protection against trademark dilution:

> The owner of a famous mark shall be entitled, subject to the principles of equity and upon such terms as the court deems reasonable, to an injunction against another person's commercial use in commerce of a mark or trade name, if such use begins after the mark has become famous and causes dilution of the distinctive quality of the mark. . . .

Dilution, which was not defined by the statute, has been described by the courts as "the gradual 'whittling away' of a trademark's value." . . .

Dilution works its harm not by causing confusion in consumers' minds regard-

---

[30] It is hard to imagine how a metatag could use more of a mark than the words contained in it, but we recently learned that some search engines are now using pictures. Searching for symbols, such as the Playboy bunny, cannot be far behind. That problem does not arise in this case, however, and we need not address it.

ing the source of a good or service, but by creating an association in consumers' minds between a mark and a different good or service. . . .

Uses that do not create an improper association between a mark and a new product but merely identify the trademark holder's products should be excepted from the reach of the anti-dilution statute. Such uses cause no harm. The anti-dilution statute recognizes this principle and specifically excepts users of a trademark who compare their product in "commercial advertising or promotion to identify the competing goods or services of the owner of the famous mark."[40]

For the same reason uses in comparative advertising are excepted from anti-dilution law, we conclude that nominative uses are also excepted. A nominative use, by definition, refers to the trademark holder's product. It does not create an improper association in consumers' minds between a new product and the trademark holder's mark.

When Welles refers to her title, she is in effect referring to a product of PEI's. She does not dilute the title by truthfully identifying herself as its one-time recipient any more than Michael Jordan would dilute the name "Chicago Bulls" by referring to himself as a former member of that team, or the two-time winner of an Academy Award would dilute the award by referring to him or herself as a "two-time Academy Award winner." Awards are not diminished or diluted by the fact that they have been awarded in the past. Similarly, they are not diminished or diluted when past recipients truthfully identify themselves as such. It is in the nature of honors and awards to be identified with the people who receive them. Of course, the conferrer of such honors and awards is free to limit the honoree's use of the title or references to the award by contract. So long as a use is nominative, however, trademark law is unavailing.

The one exception to the above analysis in this case is Welles' use of the abbreviation "PMOY" on her wallpaper. Because we determined that this use is not nominative, it is not excepted from the anti-dilution provisions. Thus, we reverse as to this issue and remand for further proceedings. We note that if the district court determines that "PMOY" is not entitled to trademark protection, PEI's claim for dilution must fail. The trademarked term, "Playmate of the Year" is not identical or nearly identical to the term "PMOY." Therefore, use of the term "PMOY" cannot, as a matter of law, dilute the trademark "Playmate of the Year."

. . .

QUESTIONS FOR DISCUSSION

1. *Traditional fair use vs. nominative use.* Is Welles's use of the trademarks belonging to Playboy Enterprises protected under the traditional fair use defense as well as the nominative use defense? In *Brookfield Communications*, the court appears to suggest that the traditional fair use test privileges Welles's use of these marks when it writes:

> The district court found that Welles was using "Playboy" and "Playmate" not as trademarks, but rather as descriptive terms fairly and accurately describing her

---

[40] 15 U.S.C. § 1125(c)(4)(A).

web page, and that her use of "Playboy" and "Playmate" in her website's meta-tags was a permissible, good faith attempt to index the content of her website. It accordingly concluded that her use was permissible under the trademark laws.

Is the court in *Brookfield Communications* correct that the marks were being used to describe Welles's website? How else might one view their use?

2. *Reference, necessity and repetition.* The first prong of the nominative use test is that "the product or service in question must be one not readily identifiable without use of the trademark." The Ninth Circuit points out that "[t]he background, or wallpaper, of Welles' site consists of the repeated abbreviation 'PMOY '81,' which stands for 'Playmate of the Year 1981.' " It then concludes that the use of "PMOY '81" as wallpaper fails the first prong of the nominative use test because "[t]he repeated depiction of 'PMOY '81' is not necessary to describe Welles. 'Playboy Playmate of the Year 1981' is quite adequate." Does the court mean that the abbreviation is not necessary because one can use the unabbreviated phrase? Is the court perhaps actually objecting to the repeated use of the abbreviation rather than to the abbreviation itself?

C. FIRST AMENDMENT

Planned Parenthood Federation of America, Inc. v. Bucci
42 U.S.P.Q.2d 1430 (S.D.N.Y.1997).

■ KIMBA M. WOOD, DISTRICT JUDGE.

Plaintiff Planned Parenthood Federation of America, Inc. ("Planned Parenthood") has moved to preliminarily enjoin defendant Richard Bucci ("Bucci"), doing business as Catholic Radio, from using the domain name "plannedparenthood.com," and from identifying his web site on the Internet under the name "www.plannedparenthood.com." The Court held a hearing on February 20, 1997 and February 21, 1997, and now issues the preliminary injunction sought by Planned Parenthood.

I. Undisputed Facts

The parties do not dispute the following facts. Plaintiff Planned Parenthood, founded in 1922, is a non-profit, reproductive health care organization that has used its present name since 1942. Plaintiff registered the stylized service mark "Planned Parenthood" on the Principal Register of the United States Patent and Trademark Office on June 28, 1955, and registered the block service mark "Planned Parenthood" on the Principal Register of the United States Patent and Trademark Office on September 9, 1975. Plaintiff's 146 separately incorporated affiliates, in 48 states and the District of Columbia, are licensed to use the mark "Planned Parenthood." Plaintiff expends a considerable sum of money in promoting and advertising its services. The mark "Planned Parenthood" is strong and incontestable.

Plaintiff operates a web site at "www.ppfa.org," using the domain name "ppfa.org." Plaintiff's home page offers Internet users resources regarding sexual and reproductive health, contraception and family planning, pregnancy, sexually transmitted diseases, and abortion, as well as providing links to other relevant web sites. In addition, plaintiff's home page offers Internet users suggestions on how to get involved with plaintiff's mission and solicits contributions.

Defendant Bucci is the host of "Catholic Radio," a daily radio program broadcast on the WVOA radio station in Syracuse, New York. Bucci is an active participant in the anti-abortion movement. Bucci operates web sites at "www.catholicradio.com" and at "lambsofchrist.com." On August 28, 1996, Bucci registered the domain name "plannedparenthood.com" with Network Solutions, Inc. ("NSI"), a corporation that administers the assignment of domain names on the Internet. After registering the domain name, Bucci set up a web site and home page on the Internet at the address "www.plannedparenthood.com."

Internet users who type in the address "www.plannedparenthood.com," or who use a search engine such as Yahoo! or Lycos to find web sites containing the term "planned parenthood," can reach Bucci's web site and home page. Once a user accesses Bucci's home page, she sees on the computer screen the words "Welcome to the PLANNED PARENTHOOD HOME PAGE!" These words appear on the screen first, because the text of a home page downloads from top to bottom. Tr. 2/20/97 at 47. Once the whole home page has loaded, the user sees a scanned image of the cover of a book entitled *The Cost of Abortion*, by Lawrence Roberge ("Roberge"), under which appear several links: "Foreword," "Afterword," "About the Author," "Book Review," and "Biography."

After clicking on a link, the user accesses text related to that link. By clicking on "Foreword" or "Afterword," the Internet user simply accesses the foreword or afterword of the book *The Cost of Abortion*. That text eventually reveals that *The Cost of Abortion* is an anti-abortion book. The text entitled "About the Author" contains the curriculum vitae of author Roberge. It also notes that "Mr. Roberge is available for interview and speaking engagements," and provides his telephone number. The "Book Review" link brings the Internet user to a selection of quotations by various people endorsing *The Cost of Abortion*. Those quotations include exhortations to read the book and obtain the book. "Biography" offers more information about Roberge's background.

II. Disputed Facts

The parties dispute defendant's motive in choosing plaintiff's mark as his domain name. Plaintiff alleges that defendant used plaintiff's mark with the "specific intent to damage Planned Parenthood's reputation and to confuse unwitting users of the Internet." Pl. Rep. Mem. at 2. Discussing the difference between the domain name at issue here and defendant's other web sites, defendant's counsel states that "[t]he WWWPLANNNEDPARENTHOOD.COM [sic] website . . . enables Defendant's message to reach a broader audience." Def. Mem. in Opp. at 3. Defendant's counsel made the following statement to the Court regarding defendant's use of plaintiff's mark to designate his web site:

> My belief is that it was intended to reach people who would be sympathetic to the proabortion position. . . . [I]t is an effort to get the . . . political and social message to people we might not have been otherwise able to reach. I think it's analogous to putting an advertisement in the New York Times rather than The National Review. You are more likely to get people who are sympathetic to the proabortion position, and that's who you want to reach. I believe that is exactly what Mr. Bucci did when he

selected Planned Parenthood.

Defendant did not dispute that his counsel was correct in that statement. Defendant's counsel also admitted that Bucci was trying to reach Internet users who thought, in accessing his web site, that they would be getting information from plaintiff.

. . .

2. The First Amendment Exception

Defendant also argues that his use of the "planned parenthood" mark is protected by the First Amendment. As defendant argues, trademark infringement law does not curtail or prohibit the exercise of the First Amendment right to free speech. I note that plaintiff has not sought, in any way, to restrain defendant from speech that criticizes Planned Parenthood or its mission, or that discusses defendant's beliefs regarding reproduction, family, and religion. The sole purpose of the Court's inquiry has been to determine whether the use of the "planned parenthood" mark as defendant's domain name and home page address constitutes an infringement of plaintiff's trademark. Defendant's use of another entity's mark is entitled to First Amendment protection when his use of that mark is part of a communicative message, not when it is used to identify the source of a product. *Yankee Publishing. Inc. v. News America Publishing, Inc.*, 809 F.Supp. 267, 275 (S.D.N.Y.1992). By using the mark as a domain name and home page address and by welcoming Internet users to the home page with the message "Welcome to the Planned Parenthood Home Page!" defendant identifies the web site and home page as being the product, or forum, of plaintiff. I therefore determine that, because defendant's use of the term "planned parenthood" is not part of a communicative message, his infringement on plaintiff's mark is not protected by the First Amendment.

Defendant argues that his use of the "Planned Parenthood" name for his web site is entitled to First Amendment protection, relying primarily on the holding of *Yankee Publishing*, 809 F.Supp. at 275. In that case, Judge Leval noted that the First Amendment can protect unauthorized use of a trademark when such use is part of an expression of a communicative message: "the Second Circuit has construed the Lanham Act narrowly when the unauthorized use of the trademark is for the purpose of a communicative message, rather than identification of product origin." *Id.* Defendant argues that his use of the "Planned Parenthood" name for his web site is a communicative message.

However, *Yankee Publishing* carefully draws a distinction between communicative messages and product labels or identifications:

> When another's trademark . . . is used without permission for the purpose of source identification, the trademark law generally prevails over the First Amendment. Free speech rights do not extend to labelling or advertising products in a manner that conflicts with the trademark rights of others.

Id. at 276. Defendant offers no argument in his papers as to why the Court should determine that defendant's use of "plannedparenthood.com" is a communicative message rather than a source identifier. His use of "plannedparenthood.com" as a domain name to identify his web site is on its face more analogous to source identification than to a communicative message; in essence, the name identifies the web site, which contains defendant's home page. The statement that greets Internet users who access defendant's web site, "Welcome to the Planned Parenthood Home Page," is also more analogous to an identifier than to a communication. For those reasons, defendant's use of the trademarked term "planned parenthood" is not part of a communicative message, but rather, serves to identify a product or item, defendant's web site and home page, as originating from Planned Parenthood.

Defendant's use of plaintiff's mark is not protected as a title under *Rogers v. Grimaldi*, 875 F.2d 994, 998 (2d Cir.1989). There, the Court of Appeals determined that the title of the film "Ginger and Fred" was not a misleading infringement, despite the fact that the film was not about Ginger Rogers and Fred Astaire, because of the artistic implications of a title. The Court of Appeals noted that "[f]ilmmakers and authors frequently rely on word-play, ambiguity, irony, and allusion in titling their works." *Id.* The Court of Appeals found that the use of a title such as the one at issue in *Rogers* was acceptable "unless the title has no artistic relevance to the underlying work"; even when the title has artistic relevance, it may not be used to "explicitly mislead[ ] [the consumer] as to the source or content of the work." *Id.* Here, even treating defendant's domain name and home page address as titles, rather than as source identifiers, I find that the title "plannedparenthood.com" has no artistic implications, and that the title is being used to attract some consumers by misleading them as to the web site's source or content. Given defendant's testimony indicating that he knew, and intended, that his use of the domain name "plannedparenthood.com" would cause some "pro-abortion" Internet users to access his web site, he cannot demonstrate that his use of "planned parenthood" is entitled to First Amendment protection.

. . .

Bally Total Fitness Holding Corp. v. Faber
29 F.Supp.2d 1161 (C.D.Cal.1998).

■ PREGERSON, DISTRICT JUDGE.

Andrew S. Faber's motion for summary judgment came before the Court for oral argument on November 23, 1998. After reviewing and considering the materials submitted by the parties and hearing oral argument, the Court GRANTS Faber's motion for summary judgment.

BACKGROUND

Bally Total Fitness Holding Corp. ("Bally") brings this action for trademark infringement, unfair competition, and dilution against Andrew S. Faber ("Faber") in connection with Bally's federally registered trademarks and service marks in the terms "Bally," "Bally's Total Fitness," and "Bally Total Fitness," including the name and distinctive styles of these marks. Bally is suing Faber based on his use of Bally's marks in a website he designed.

Faber calls his site "Bally sucks." The website is dedicated to complaints about Bally's health club business. When the website is accessed, the viewer is presented with Bally's mark with the word "sucks" printed across it. Immediately under this, the website states "Bally Total Fitness Complaints! Un-Authorized."

Faber has several websites in addition to the "Bally sucks" site. The domain in which Faber has placed his websites is "www.compupix.com." Faber's other websites within "www.compupix.com" include the "Bally sucks" site (URL address "www.compupix.com/ballysucks"); "Images of Men," a website displaying and selling photographs of nude males (URL address "www.compupix.com/index.html"); a website containing information regarding the gay community (URL address "www.compupix.com/gay"); a website containing photographs of flowers and landscapes (URL address "www.compupix.com/fl/index.html"); and a website advertising "Drew Faber Web Site Services" (URL address "www.compupix.com/biz.htm").

On April 22, 1998, Bally applied for a temporary restraining order directing Faber to withdraw his website from the Internet. Bally represents that when its application for a TRO was initially filed, the "Bally sucks" site contained a direct link to Faber's "Images of Men" site. In his opposition to the application for a TRO, Faber indicated that this link had been removed. The Court denied Bally's application on April 30, 1998.

Bally brought a motion for summary judgment on its claims of trademark infringement, trademark dilution, and unfair competition which the Court denied on October 20, 1998. In that order, the Court ordered Faber to bring a motion for summary judgment. This motion is now before the Court.

DISCUSSION

. . .

B. *Trademark Infringement*

. . .

2. *Likelihood of confusion*

[The court addresses the eight-factor test for likelihood of confusion set forth in *AMF Inc. v. Sleekcraft Boats*, 599 F.2d 341 (9th Cir.1979), including:]

g. *Defendant's intent in selecting the mark*

Here, Faber purposely chose to use Bally's mark to build a "web site that is 'dedicated to complaint, issues, problems, beefs, grievances, grumblings, accusations, and gripes with Bally Total Fitness health clubs.' " Faber, however, is exercising his right to publish critical commentary about Bally. He cannot do this without making reference to Bally.[4] In this regard, Professor McCarthy states:

---

[4] Bally concedes that Faber has some right to use Bally's name as part of his consumer commentary. However, Bally argues that Faber uses more than is necessary when making his commentary and that he has alternative means of communication. Specifically, Bally argues that Faber could use the name "Bally" or "Bally Total Fitness" in block lettering without using Bally's stylized "B" mark or distinctive script. This argument, however,

The main remedy of the trademark owner is not an injunction to suppress the message, but a rebuttal to the message. As Justice Brandeis long ago stated, "If there be time to expose through discussion the falsehood and fallacies, to avert the evil by the process of education, the remedy to be applied is more speech, not enforced silence."

5 McCarthy, § 31:148 at 31–216.

Applying Bally's argument would extend trademark protection to eclipse First Amendment rights. The courts, however, have rejected this approach by holding that trademark rights may be limited by First Amendment concerns. *See L.L. Bean, Inc. v. Drake Publishers, Inc.,* 811 F.2d 26 (1st Cir.1987).

. . .

C. *Trademark Dilution*

. . .

[T]he courts have held that trademark owners may not quash unauthorized use of the mark by a person expressing a point of view. *See L.L. Bean,* 811 F.2d at 29, *citing Lucasfilm Ltd. v. High Frontier,* 622 F.Supp. 931, 933–35 (D.D.C.1985). This is so even if the opinion may come in the form of a commercial setting. *See Id.* at 33 (discussing Maine's anti-dilution statute). In *L.L. Bean,* the First Circuit held that a sexually-oriented parody of L.L. Bean's catalog in a commercial adult-oriented magazine was non-commercial use of the trademark. *See Id.* The court stated:

> If the anti-dilution statute were construed as permitting a trademark owner to enjoin the use of his mark in a noncommercial context found to be negative or offensive, then a corporation could shield itself from criticism by forbidding the use of its name in commentaries critical of its conduct. The legitimate aim of the anti-dilution statute is to prohibit the unauthorized use of another's trademark in order to market incompatible products or services. The Constitution does not, however, permit the range of the anti-dilution statute to encompass the unauthorized use of a trademark in a noncommercial setting such as an editorial or artistic context.

Id.

Here, Bally wants to protect its valuable marks and ensure that they are not tarnished or otherwise diluted. This is an understandable goal. However, for the reasons set forth above, Faber's "Bally sucks" site is not a commercial use.

Even if Faber's use of Bally's mark is a commercial use, Bally also cannot show tarnishment. Bally cites several cases such as the "Enjoy Cocaine" and "Mutant of Omaha" cases for the proposition that this site and its relationship to other sites tarnishes their mark. *See Mutual of Omaha Ins. Co. v. Novak,* 648 F.Supp. 905

---

would create an artificial distinction that does not exist under trademark law. Trademarks are defined broadly to include both names and stylized renditions of those names or other symbols. 15 U.S.C. §§ 1051, 1127 (1997). Furthermore, the purpose of a trademark is to identify the source of goods. *Id.* § 1127. An individual who wishes to engage in consumer commentary must have the full range of marks that the trademark owner has to identify the trademark owner as the object of the criticism. (*See infra* Part I–C.)

(D.Neb.1986) (discussing both infringement and disparagement), *aff'd* 836 F.2d 397 (8th Cir.1987) (addressing infringement, but not disparagement); *Coca–Cola v. Gemini Rising, Inc.*, 346 F.Supp. 1183 (E.D.N.Y.1972).

There are, however, two flaws with Bally's argument. First, none of the cases that Bally cites involve consumer commentary. In *Coca–Cola,* the court enjoined the defendant's publication of a poster stating "Enjoy Cocaine" in the same script as Coca–Cola's trademark. *See Coca–Cola,* 346 F.Supp. at 1192. Likewise, in *Mutual of Omaha,* the court prohibited the use of the words "Mutual of Omaha," with a picture of an emaciated human head resembling the Mutual of Omaha's logo on a variety of products as a means of protesting the arms race. *See Mutual of Omaha,* 836 F.2d at 398. Here, however, Faber is using Bally's mark in the context of a consumer commentary to say that Bally engages in business practices which Faber finds distasteful or unsatisfactory. This is speech protected by the First Amendment. *See L.L. Bean,* 811 F.2d at 29; McCarthy, § 24:105 at 24–191. As such, Faber can use Bally's mark to identify the source of the goods or services of which he is complaining. This use is necessary to maintain broad opportunities for expression. *See Restatement (Third) of Unfair Competition* § 25(2), cmt. i (1995) (stating "extension of the antidilution statutes to protect against damaging nontrademark uses raises substantial free speech issues and duplicates other potential remedies better suited to balance the relevant interests").

. . .

Name.Space, Inc. v. Network Solutions, Inc.
202 F.3d 573 (2d Cir.2000).

■ KATZMANN, CIRCUIT JUDGE:

[Plaintiff Name.Space, Inc. set up an alternative system of domain names, including 530 new global top-level domains ("gTLDs") that were not included within the official domain name system. Some of the new domain names, such as ".forpresident," ".formayor," and ".microsoft.free.zone," had arguably expressive content, contrasting in that respect with the existing three-letter gTLDs, such as .com, .net, and .org. Name.Space asked Network Solutions, Inc. ("NSI"), then the sole domain-name registrar, to include references to the new gTLDs in the zone files of the root servers that it maintained, which would make the new gTLDs available to virtually all Internet users, but NSI refused. Name.Space filed an action against NSI, charging it with antitrust violations. NSI then sought authorization from the National Science Foundation, the federal agency that then supervised the domain name system, to comply with Name.Space's request, but NSF declined, whereupon Name.Space added NSF as a defendant. In one count of the complaint, Name.Space alleged that by refusing to incorporate the new gTLDs into the domain name system, NSF had infringed its rights under the First Amendment. In the following excerpt the court discusses the First Amendment claim.]

. . .

II. First Amendment

Name.Space challenges the district court's holding that it "has not met the burden of demonstrating that the three letter top level domain portion of an Internet domain name is expressive speech." *PGMedia*, 51 F.Supp.2d at 407 *(citing Clark v. Community for Creative Non-Violence, 468 U.S. 288, 293 n. 5 (1984)).* Although we affirm the district court's dismissal of Name.Space's First Amendment claims, we do so for different reasons. "We may, of course, affirm on any basis for which there is a record sufficient to permit conclusions of law, including grounds upon which the district court did not rely." *Cromwell Assocs. v. Oliver Cromwell Owners, Inc.,* 941 F.2d 107, 111 (2d Cir.1991) (citations omitted).

In considering whether domain names constitute expressive speech, we observe that the lightning speed development of the Internet poses challenges for the common-law adjudicative process—a process which, ideally while grounded in the past, governs the present and offers direction for the future based on understandings of current circumstances. Mindful of the often unforeseeable impact of rapid technological change, we are wary of making legal pronouncements based on highly fluid circumstances, which almost certainly will give way to tomorrow's new realities. *Cf. Columbia Broad. Sys., Inc. v. Democratic Nat'l Comm.,* 412 U.S. 94, 102 (1973) ("The problems of regulation are rendered more difficult because the broadcast industry is dynamic in terms of technological change; solutions adequate a decade ago are not necessarily so now, and those acceptable today may well be outmoded 10 years hence."). "A law that changes every day is worse than no law at all." LON L. FULLER, THE MORALITY OF LAW 37, 79–81 (rev. ed.1969).

The district court adopted an analogy between Internet alphanumeric addresses and telephone numbers, and held that domain names are akin to source identifiers rather than to communicative messages. *See PGMedia,* 51 F.Supp.2d at 407–08. We disagree. It is certainly true that while "[i]t is possible to find some kernel of expression in almost every activity a person undertakes[,] . . . such a kernel is not sufficient to bring the activity within the protection of the First Amendment." *City of Dallas v. Stanglin,* 490 U.S. 19, 25 (1989). Further, the district court is not alone in suggesting that an analogy between Internet domain names and telephone number mnemonics (for example, 1–800–FLOWERS) may be appropriate. *See, e.g., Panavision Int'l, L.P. v. Toeppen,* 141 F.3d 1316, 1325 (9th Cir.1998) (comparing domain name to 1–800–HOLIDAY); *PGMedia,* 51 F.Supp.2d at 407–08 (citing cases). However, the nature of domain names is not susceptible to such a uniform, monolithic characterization. As the Supreme Court has stated in an analogous and related context, "aware as we are of the changes taking place in the law, the technology, and the industrial structure related to telecommunications, . . . we believe it unwise and unnecessary definitively to pick one analogy or one specific set of words now."[12] *Denver Area Educ. Telecomms. Consortium, Inc. v. Federal Communications Comm'n,* 518 U.S. 727, 742 (1996) (Breyer, J., plurality) (citations omitted). The existing gTLDs are not protected speech, but only because the current DNS and

---

[12] Therefore, different analogies, including analogies to book and movie titles, street addresses, and telephone numbers may be appropriate in different circumstances.

Amendment No. 11 limit them to three-letter afterthoughts such as .com and .net, which are lacking in expressive content. The district court did not address the possibility that longer and more contentful gTLDs like ".jones_for_president" and ".smith_for_senate" may constitute protected speech, such as political speech or parody. *See, e.g., Cliffs Notes, Inc. v. Bantam Doubleday Dell Publ'g Group, Inc.*, 886 F.2d 490, 493 (2d Cir.1989) (noting that title of book "Spy Notes" is parody constituting protected speech); *Rogers v. Grimaldi*, 875 F.2d 994, 998 (2d Cir.1989) (holding that title of movie "Ginger and Fred" contained "expressive element" implicating First Amendment).

The Internet in general, and the DNS in particular, is marked by extraordinary plasticity. The DNS has already undergone considerable change in the Internet's brief history to date, and may undergo even more radical changes in the near future under the auspices of ICANN and DNSO. There is nothing inherent in the architecture of the Internet that prevents new gTLDs from constituting expressive speech. How broad the permissible bandwidth of expression is in this context depends on the future direction of the DNS. Therefore, "we should be shy about saying the final word today about what will be accepted as reasonable tomorrow," particularly "when we know too little to risk the finality of precision." *Denver Area*, 518 U.S. at 777–78 (Souter, J., concurring).

Further, the functionality of domain names does not automatically place them beyond the reach of the First Amendment. Although domain names do have a functional purpose, whether the mix of functionality and expression is "sufficiently imbued with the elements of communication" depends on the domain name in question, the intentions of the registrant, the contents of the website, and the technical protocols that govern the DNS. *Spence v. Washington*, 418 U.S. 405, 409–10 (1974) ("[T]he context in which a symbol is used for purposes of expression is important, for the context may give meaning to the symbol." (citation omitted)). Functionality and expression are therefore not mutually exclusive: for example, automobile license plates have a functional purpose, but that function can be served as well by vanity plates, which in a small way can also be expressive. Similarly, domain names may be employed for a variety of communicative purposes with both functional and expressive elements, ranging from the truly mundane street address or telephone number-like identification of the specific business that is operating the website, to commercial speech and even core political speech squarely implicating First Amendment concerns.

In short, while we hold that the existing gTLDs do not constitute protected speech under the First Amendment, we do not preclude the possibility that certain domain names and new gTLDs, could indeed amount to protected speech. The time may come when new gTLDs could be used for "an expressive purpose such as commentary, parody, news reporting or criticism," comprising communicative messages by the author and/or operator of the website in order to influence the public's decision to visit that website, or even to disseminate a particular point of view. *United We Stand Am., Inc. v. United We Stand Am. N. Y., Inc.*, 128 F.3d 86, 93 (2d Cir.1997) (citation omitted).

We do not view *Planned Parenthood Federation of America v. Bucci* as holding to the contrary. *See* No. 97 Civ. 0629, 1997 WL 133313, at *10–11 (S.D.N.Y. Mar. 24, 1997), *aff'd*, 152 F.3d 920 (2d Cir.1998) (unpublished table decision). In *Bucci*, a trademark infringement case, the court held that the defendant's particular use of the domain name "plannedparenthood.com" was as a "source identifier" rather than a "communicative message," while leaving open the possibility that a domain name could constitute such a message under other circumstances. *See id.* In reaching this conclusion, the *Bucci* court conducted precisely the kind of particularistic, context-sensitive analysis that is appropriate here, including analyses of the domain name itself, the way the domain name is being used, the motivations of the author of the website in question, the contents of the website, and so on. *See id.* Domain names and gTLDs *per se* are neither automatically entitled to nor excluded from the protections of the First Amendment, and the appropriate inquiry is one that fully addresses particular circumstances presented with respect to each domain name.

Taubman Co. v. Webfeats
319 F.3d 770 (6th Cir.2003).

■ SUHRHEINRICH, CIRCUIT JUDGE.

   . . .

[Plaintiff Taubman, which owned a trademark on "The Shops at Willow Bend," brought an infringement action against defendant Mishkoff for registering and operating an informational website at "shopsatwillowbend.com" and for setting up several complaint sites, including "taubmansucks.com" and "shopsatwillowbendsucks.com." The court discussed the relationship between the Lanham Act and the First Amendment.]

Mishkoff proposes that, regardless of whether his use of Taubman's marks violates the Lanham Act, any injunction prohibiting his use violates the Constitution as a prior restraint on his First Amendment right of Free Speech. Since Mishkoff has raised Free Speech concerns, we will first explain the interrelation between the First Amendment and the Lanham Act. First, this Court has held that the Lanham Act is constitutional. *Semco, Inc. v. Amcast, Inc.*, 52 F.3d 108, 111–12 (6th Cir.1995) (stating that reach of Lanham Act is limited so as to be constitutional); *see also Seven-Up v. Coca-Cola Co.*, 86 F.3d 1379, 1383 n. 6 (5th Cir.1996). The Lanham Act is constitutional because it only regulates commercial speech, which is entitled to reduced protections under the First Amendment. *Central Hudson Gas & Elec. Corp. v. Public Serv. Comm'n of New York*, 447 U.S. 557, 563 (1980) (stating that regulation of commercial speech is subject only to intermediate scrutiny). Thus, we must first determine if Mishkoff's use is commercial and therefore within the jurisdiction of the Lanham Act, worthy of lesser First Amendment protections.

If Mishkoff's use is commercial, then, and only then, do we analyze his use for a likelihood of confusion. If Mishkoff's use is also confusing, then it is misleading commercial speech, and outside the First Amendment. *See* 134 Cong. Rec. 31, 851 (Oct. 19, 1988) (statement of Rep. Kastenmeier) (stating that § 43 of the Lanham Act only affects misleading commercial speech); *cf. Va. Bd. of Pharmacy v. Va. Citizens*

Consumer Council, Inc., 425 U.S. 748, 771 & n. 24 (1976) (stating that misleading commercial speech is not protected by the First Amendment); *Bonito Boats, Inc. v. Thunder Craft Boats, Inc.*, 489 U.S. 141, 157 (1989) (stating that a trademark owner has at best a quasi-property right in his mark, and can only prevent its use so as to maintain a confusion-free purchasing public) (quoting *Crescent Tool Co. v. Kilborn & Bishop Co.*, 247 F. 299, 301 (2d Cir.1917) (L. Hand, J.)).

Hence, as per the language of the Lanham Act, any expression embodying the use of a mark not "in connection with the sale . . . or advertising of any goods or services," and not likely to cause confusion, is outside the jurisdiction of the Lanham Act and necessarily protected by the First Amendment. Accordingly, we need not analyze Mishkoff's constitutional defenses independent of our Lanham Act analysis. . .

. . .

We find that Mishkoff's use of Taubman's mark in the domain name "taubmansucks.com" is purely an exhibition of Free Speech, and the Lanham Act is not invoked. And although economic damage might be an intended effect of Mishkoff's expression, the First Amendment protects critical commentary when there is no confusion as to source, even when it involves the criticism of a business. Such use is not subject to scrutiny under the Lanham Act. In fact, Taubman concedes that Mishkoff is "free to shout 'Taubman Sucks!' from the rooftops. . . ." . . . Essentially, this is what he has done in his domain name. The rooftops of our past have evolved into the internet domain names of our present. We find that the domain name is a type of public expression, no different in scope than a billboard or a pulpit, and Mishkoff has a First Amendment right to express his opinion about Taubman, and as long as his speech is not commercially misleading, the Lanham Act cannot be summoned to prevent it.

QUESTIONS FOR DISCUSSION

1. *Communication vs. source identification. Planned Parenthood v. Bucci* sets out the rule that a defendant's "use of another entity's mark is entitled to First Amendment protection when his use of that mark is part of a communicative message, not when it is used to identify the source of a product." It held that the defendant's use of "plannedparenthood.com" was not expressive. If the defendant had instead registered "plannedparenthoodsucks.com," would the case have come out the other way?

2. *Trademark as part of a URL.* In *Bally v. Faber*, the defendant used plaintiff's trademark not as part of the domain name, which is compupix.com, but rather as a subdirectory under that domain, www.compupix.com/ballysucks. Does the trademark serve as a source identifier when used in this role? Does the court recognize any distinction between use of the trademark in the URL, and use of it in the text of the website? Recognizing that the plaintiff was entitled to identify Bally as the target of its criticism, was it entitled to do so by including its trademark in the URL?

CHAPTER THREE
PROTECTING COMMERCIAL IDENTITY ONLINE: DOMAIN NAMES

In the offline world, as long as I know the physical location of a store, I can find my way to it even if I have forgotten its name. On the web, however, a company's name or online brand often *is* the way to its website. For example, I reach the website of Amazon.com by typing "www.amazon.com" into the address bar of my web browser. The text string "www.amazon.com" is called a *uniform resource locator*, or "URL". Typically a company's URL includes the company name or a reference to a product or brand for which the company is known. A company's domain name becomes, in effect, its brand identity on the Web.[1]

If I want to locate the website of a particular company or a brand, but do not know the site's URL, I can try several expedients. I might start by guessing that the URL will be the company's name, followed by a .com, and preceded by a www. This will frequently work. If that fails, I can enter the company or brand name into a search engine such as Google, HotBot, Yahoo! or MSN Search. After completing my search, the search engine returns a list of hyperlinks. If the search engine is well designed, the URL I am seeking should be among the first group of hyperlinks that is returned.

When this system works as expected, my search costs are very low: typing in a URL is quick and easy, and using a search engine is only slightly more involved. But suppose a well-known company or brand name is registered as a domain name by a person who has no affiliation with the company or brand. In that case, my search costs may be significantly increased. Typing in "www.company_name.com" will not yield the desired website, but may instead lead to the site of a competitor; to a website offering to sell the domain name; or to a site with content completely unrelated to the company, such as one offering sexually explicit images. I may fare better typing the company name into a search engine, but depending on the search algorithm employed the link I am looking for may lie somewhere beyond the first page of returned links, and my patience may run out before reaching it. The situation is complicated by the fact that in the world of bricks and mortar many different companies may share the same or similar trademarks under certain circumstances, whereas there is only one dot-com domain name for each word that might be a trademark. If I type www.apple.com into my browser, I could be looking for Apple Bank or Apple Records, but the site belongs to Apple Computer.

When somebody other than a trademark owner obtains a domain name consisting of or incorporating a trademark, several types of costs may arise: (1) increased search costs for consumers; (2) consumer confusion, as may occur if a consumer reaches the website of a

---

[1] A domain name consists of two parts separated by a period: a second-level domain ("SLD") and a top-level domain name ("TLD"). The SLD occurs to the left of the TLD. Thus, in the domain name "amazon.com," "amazon" is the SLD and "com" is the TLD. The name associated with the company or its products is typically used as the SLD. TLDs are not unique to a particular company but are used to organize SLDs into groups for the purpose of administering the Internet address system—called the domain name system—much as house numbers are grouped by street, city and state for the purpose of the postal address system.

competitor rather than that of the company he is seeking; (3) efficiency losses due to the diminished capacity of trademarks to identify companies and products; and (4) harm to companies identified by trademarks, who may lose potential customers.

The practice of obtaining domain names containing words identical or similar to trademarks owned by somebody else commenced soon after the Internet became a commercialized venue. Some people, recognizing the value of a domain name containing a certain word before the owner of a corresponding trademark did, obtained domain names by the dozen, the hundred, and in some cases even by the thousand. This entailed a modest investment—usually $35–50 a year per domain name—which these people hoped to recoup many-fold by selling the domain names to the owners of the corresponding trademarks. In some quarters (particularly among owners of well-established trademarks), it was assumed that domain names corresponding to a trademark ought "naturally" to belong to the trademark owner (or one of the owners, in case the word corresponded to more than one trademark, as in Apple Computer, Apple Bank, and Apple Records). Those who obtained such domain names hoping to sell them to trademark owners were branded as "cybersquatters" or "cyberpirates," and harshly criticized as unethically and illegally seeking to capitalize on goodwill in a trademark that was built up by somebody else. In fact, Congress responded to this practice by enacting a statute designed specifically to end it—the Anticybersquatting Consumer Protection Act ("ACPA"), Pub. L. No. 106–113 (1999), which is addressed in detail in Part II, *infra*. In other quarters (particularly among academics seeking to preserve a robust public domain), the practice has been viewed more benignly: simply a case of one group of entrepreneurs reacting more quickly to a market opportunity than others.

As mentioned earlier, difficulties arise when different companies have the same or similar words in their trademarks and thus feel that they have legitimate claims to the same web address. Just as every house has a unique street address, every website must be built on a unique domain name. Given the obvious advantages of having a Web address built around a company's name, it often happens that two companies with similar names desire the same domain name. The oldest feminist bookstore in the United States is the Amazon Bookstore in Minneapolis, Minnesota. Once it recognized the growing importance of the Web as a distribution channel, it wanted a website with the address "www.amazon.com." The Amazon Bookstore believed its claim to this Web address was superior to that of the Internet company of similar name. After all, the Amazon Bookstore is the older and more established business—a fact of some significance under the law of trademark. While this dispute was ultimately settled out of court, other disputes over web addresses have not ended so amicably. In fact, another judgmental term, "reverse domain name hijacking," has been applied to some second-comers who try to wrest a domain name from a company with a similar trademark that got there first.

Difficulties also arise when individuals have an interest in making noncommercial uses of names and symbols that are either identical or confusingly similar to somebody's trademark. For example, consider a person whose nickname is very similar to some company's trade name. One might expect that such an individual should be able to use his or her nickname as a domain name, provided it is not already claimed by another. As a noncommercial use, it should fall outside the strictures of trademark law. Yet many trademark owners have argued that the use of any domain name on the Internet is necessarily a commercial use and some courts have been receptive to these arguments.

In response to perceived abuses by both trademark owners and cybersquatters, a new body of law has developed to provide needed regulation and dispute resolution. In this chapter, we focus on these legal issues and developments.

I. TRADITIONAL TRADEMARK LAW AND DOMAIN NAMES

As Internet-based e-commerce began to gather steam, it wasn't long before enterprising individuals and companies recognized the value of a well-chosen domain name. Soon the domain name gold rush was on, as individuals and corporations staked their claim to control various domain names. As a group, corporate trademark owners were relatively late to the party, and often found that their trademark or brand name had already been claimed as a domain name by another. While some companies simply purchased the right to use their trademark as a domain name from the person who previously obtained it, other companies refused to negotiate, arguing that the use of their trademarks as domain names was a form of trademark infringement or dilution. Trademark owners filed lawsuits, and the courts had to come to grips with the relationship between the domain name system and the law of trademarks, balancing the interest of the public to make noncommercial use of these new and evolving digital technologies with the interests of trademark owners in preserving the commercial value of their brands. In this section, we explore how the courts have grappled with this issue and evaluate the balance that they have struck.

A. TRADEMARK INFRINGEMENT

Lockheed Martin Corp. v. Network Solutions, Inc.
985 F.Supp. 949 (C.D.Cal.1997), *aff'd*, 194 F.3d 980 (9th Cir.1999).

■ PREGERSON, DISTRICT JUDGE.

The motion by defendant Network Solutions, Inc. ("NSI") for summary judgment came before the Court on October 6, 1997. After reviewing and considering the materials submitted by the parties and hearing oral argument, the Court grants the motion in its entirety.

I. Background

The issue presented by this litigation is whether NSI violated federal trademark law by accepting registrations of Internet domain names that are identical or similar to Lockheed Martin Corporation's ("Lockheed") SKUNK WORKS service mark. Lockheed asserts that NSI directly infringed and diluted its mark by accepting the registrations. Lockheed also asserts that NSI is liable as a contributory infringer because NSI did not comply with Lockheed's demands to cancel the registrations.

As to direct infringement, the Court concludes that NSI has not used Lockheed's service mark in connection with the sale, offering for sale, distribution or advertising of goods or services, and therefore cannot be liable for infringement under 15 U.S.C. § 1114(1)(a) or for unfair competition under 15 U.S.C. § 1125(a).

As to dilution, the Court finds that NSI has not made a commercial use of domain names as trademarks, and therefore cannot satisfy the commercial use element of dilution under 15 U.S.C. § 1125(c).

As to contributory infringement, there are two potential bases for liability. First, a defendant is liable if it intentionally induced others to infringe a mark. Second, a defendant is liable if it continued to supply a product to others when the defendant knew or had reason to know that the party receiving the product used it to infringe a mark.

Lockheed has not presented evidence that NSI induced others to infringe Lockheed's service mark. Therefore, NSI is not liable under the first basis.

As to the knowledge basis, the Court concludes that NSI's limited role as a registrar of domain names coupled with the inherent uncertainty in defining the scope of intellectual property rights in a trademark militates against finding that NSI knew or had reason to know of potentially infringing uses by others. Furthermore, contributory infringement doctrine does not impose upon NSI an affirmative duty to seek out potentially infringing uses of domain names by registrants.

A. The Parties

For over 50 years, plaintiff Lockheed and its predecessors have operated "Skunk Works," an aerospace development and production facility. Lockheed owns the federally registered "SKUNK WORKS" service mark.

Defendant NSI is a publicly traded corporation with its principal place of business in Herndon, Virginia. Under a contract with the National Science Foundation, NSI is the exclusive registrar of most Internet domain names.

B. The Internet

. . .

1. The Domain Name System

Web sites, like other information resources on the Internet, are currently addressed using the Internet "domain name system." A numbering system called the "Internet Protocol" gives each individual computer or network a unique numerical address on the Internet. The "Internet Protocol number," also known as an "IP number," consists of four groups of digits separated by periods, such as "192.215.247.50." For the convenience of users, individual resources on the Internet are also given names. Specialized computers known as "domain name servers" maintain tables linking domain names to IP numbers.

Domain names are arranged so that reading from right to left, each part of the name points to a more localized area of the Internet. For example, in the domain name "cacd.uscourts.gov," "gov" is the top-level domain, reserved for all networks associated with the federal government. The "uscourts" part specifies a second-level domain, a set of the networks used by the federal courts. The "cacd" part specifies a sub-network or computer used by the United States District Court for the Central District of California.

If a user knows or can deduce the domain name associated with a web site, the user can directly access the web site by typing the domain name into a Web browser, without having to conduct a time-consuming search. Because most businesses with a presence on the Internet use the ".com" top-level domain, Internet users intuitively try to find businesses by typing in the corporate or trade name as the second-level domain name, as in "acme.com." Second-level domain names, the name just to the left of ".com," must be exclusive. Therefore, although two companies can have non-exclusive trademark rights in a name, only one company can have a second-level domain name that corresponds to its trademark. For example, Juno Lighting, a maker of lamps, sought to establish a web site with the address "juno.com," a domain name already in use by Juno Online Services, which uses the domain name as part of e-mail addresses for hundreds of thousands of e-mail customers. *See Juno Online Servs., L.P. v. Juno Lighting, Inc.*, 979 F.Supp. 684 (N.D.Ill.1997). In short, the exclusive quality of second-level domain names has set trademark owners against each other in the struggle to establish a commercial presence on the Internet, and has set businesses against domain name holders who seek to continue the traditional use of the Internet as a non-commercial medium of communication.

2. NSI's Role in the Domain Naming System

Under a contract with the National Science Foundation, NSI manages domain name registrations for the ".com," ".net," ".org," ".edu," and ".gov" top-level domains. The contract authorizes NSI to charge $100 for an initial two-year registration and $50 annually starting the third year. NSI registers approximately 100,000 Internet domain names per month. Registration applications are made via e-mail and in more than 90% of registrations no human intervention takes place. On average, a new registration occurs approximately once every 20 seconds.

NSI performs two functions in the domain name system. First, it screens domain name applications against its registry to prevent repeated registrations of the same name. Second, it maintains a directory linking domain names with the IP numbers of domain name servers. The domain name servers, which are outside of NSI's control, connect domain names with Internet resources such as web sites and e-mail systems.

NSI does not make an independent determination of an applicant's right to use a domain name. Nor does NSI assign domain names; users may choose any available second-level domain name. In 1995, NSI responded to the problem of conflicting claims to domain names by instituting a domain name dispute policy. Under the current policy, in effect since September 9, 1996,[2] NSI requires applicants to represent and warrant that their use of a particular domain name does not interfere with the intellectual property rights of third parties. Under the policy, if a trademark holder presents NSI with a United States Patent and Trademark Office registration of a trademark identical to a currently registered domain name, NSI will require the domain name holder to prove that it has a pre-existing right to use the name. If the domain name holder fails to do so, NSI will cancel the registration. NSI's policy has been criticized as favoring trademark owners over domain name

---

[2] [NSI's domain name dispute policy was superseded in 1999 by the Uniform Domain Name Dispute Resolution Policy, instituted by the Internet Corporation for Assigned Names and Numbers. *See* Part IV, *infra*; *see also* Chapter 1, Part II(F), *supra*, and Chapter 14, Part II(C)(1), *infra*—Eds.]

holders, and favoring owners of federally registered marks over owners of non-registered marks, because owners of federally registered marks can invoke NSI's policy to effectively enjoin the use of identical domain name's without having to make any showing of infringement or dilution. 2 Jerome Gilson & Jeffrey M. Samuels, Trademark Protection and Practice, §§ 5.11[4][B], at 5–239, 5.11[5], at 5–243 (1997) (noting that NSI's policy is tilted in favor of trademark owners, who can deprive registrants of domain names without meeting the likelihood of confusion test for infringement or showing that the domain name dilutes the mark); Gayle Weiswasser, Domain Names, the Internet, and Trademarks: Infringement in Cyberspace, 13 Santa Clara Computer & High Tech. L. J. 137, 172–73 (1997).

If a trademark holder and domain name registrant take their dispute to court, NSI will deposit the domain name in the registry of the court. This process maintains the status quo; the domain name remains active while in the registry of the court.

C. Factual Background

Most of the underlying facts of this case are not in dispute. The dispute at summary judgment is over the interpretation of the law and the application of the law to the facts. The Court finds that there is no genuine issue as to the following facts:

1. Lockheed owns the federally registered SKUNK WORKS service mark for "engineering, technical consulting, and advisory services with respect to designing, building, equipping, and testing commercial and military aircraft and related equipment."

. . .

6. On May 7, 1996, Lockheed sent NSI a letter advising NSI that Lockheed owned the SKUNK WORKS mark and requesting that NSI cease registering domain names that referred to or included the names "skunk works" or "skunkworks" or otherwise infringed Lockheed's mark. Lockheed also requested that NSI provide Lockheed with a list of registered domain names that contain the words "skunk works" or any variation thereof. Lockheed's letter did not include a certified copy of its trademark registration.

7. On June 18, 1996, Lockheed sent NSI a second letter, informing NSI that the registrant of "skunkworks.com" had agreed to stop using the domain name, and that the registrant of "skunkworks.net" was being sued in federal district court. The letter did not refer to the lawsuit by docket number or caption, nor did it include a copy of the complaint or other pleading.

. . .

9. On September 18, 1996, NSI's Internet business manager, David Graves, wrote to Lockheed's counsel in response to the May 7 and June 18 letters. NSI informed Lockheed that NSI could not provide a list of all domain names that included "skunk works" or any variation thereof, but that Lockheed could use the public "Whois" database of domain name registrations to find this information. NSI further informed Lockheed that upon receipt of a file-stamped copy of the

complaint in the "skunkworks.net" case, NSI would immediately deposit the domain name in the registry of the court, maintaining the status quo until the court ordered otherwise.

[Paragraphs 2–5, 8, 10 and 11 describe specific individuals and the domain names that they registered with NSI. The domain names included skunkworks.com, skunkwrks.com, skunkwerks.com, skunkworx.com, and the-skunkworks.com.]

D. Procedural Background

Lockheed filed this action on October 22, 1996, alleging infringement, unfair competition, dilution and contributory infringement under the Lanham Act, and seeking injunctive and declaratory relief. NSI answered the complaint and counterclaimed for declaratory relief.

On March 19, 1997, this Court denied NSI's motion to dismiss for failure to join the domain name registrants as indispensable parties under Federal Rule of Civil Procedure 19(b). *Lockheed Martin Corp. v. Network Solutions, Inc.*, 43 U.S.P.Q.2d 1056 (C.D.Cal.1997).

On September 29, 1997, this Court denied Lockheed's motion to file a first amended complaint adding a cause of action for "contributory dilution." The Court denied the motion on the bases of futility, undue delay and prejudice.

NSI's present motion seeks summary judgment on all of Lockheed's claims.

II. Discussion

This Court has subject matter jurisdiction over Lanham Act claims pursuant to 28 U.S.C. §§ 1331 and 1338(a). NSI has consented to personal jurisdiction by appearing in this action. Fed.R.Civ.P. 12(h)(1).

. . .

B. Trademark Infringement Under Lanham Act § 32, 15 U.S.C. § 1114(1)

Section 32 of the Lanham Act prohibits any person from using another's mark without permission "in connection with the sale, offering for sale, distribution or advertising of any goods or services on or in connection with which such use is likely to cause confusion, or to cause mistake, or to deceive. . . ." 15 U.S.C. § 1114(1). To be liable under § 32, a person must use the mark on competing or related goods in a way that creates a likelihood of confusion. *AMF Inc. v. Sleekcraft Boats*, 599 F.2d 341, 348 (9th Cir.1979). Before considering the likelihood of confusion, however, the Court must determine whether NSI, by accepting registrations, has used the SKUNK WORKS mark in connection with the sale, distribution or advertising of goods or services. *See Planned Parenthood Fed'n of America, Inc. v. Bucci*, 42 U.S.P.Q.2d 1430, 1434 (S.D.N.Y.1997).

Domain names present a special problem under the Lanham Act because they are used for both a non-trademark technical purpose, to designate a set of computers on the Internet, and for trademark purposes, to identify an Internet user who offers goods or services on the Internet. *See* 2 Gilson, *supra*, §§ 5.11[3], at 5–235, 5.11[5], at 5–243–44 (distinguishing the technical use of domain names from the trademark use to identify goods or services). When a domain name is used only to indicate an address on the Internet, the domain name is not functioning as a trademark.[3] *See Walt–West Enters., Inc. v. Gannett Co., Inc.,* 695 F.2d 1050, 1059–60 (7th Cir.1982) (radio station frequency used in "utilitarian sense of calling the listener's attention to a location on the FM dial" is not protectable under trademark law). Like trade names, domain names can function as trademarks, and therefore can be used to infringe trademark rights. Domain names, like trade names, do not act as trademarks when they are used merely to identify a business entity; in order to infringe they must be used to identify the source of goods or services. *Cf. In re Unclaimed Salvage & Freight Co.,* 192 U.S.P.Q. 165, 168 (T.T.A.B.1976) (affirming refusal of registration of trade name as trademark where specimen demonstrated use only to identify applicant as a business); U.S. Dept. of Commerce, Patent and Trademark Office, Trademark Manual of Examining Procedure § 1202.02, at 1202–4 (2d ed. May 1993) (directing examiners to refuse registration of material that functions only to identify a business).

NSI's acceptance of domain name registrations is connected only with the names' technical function on the Internet to designate a set of computers. By accepting registrations of domain names containing the words "skunk works," NSI is not using the SKUNK WORKS mark in connection with the sale, distribution or advertising of goods and services. NSI merely uses domain names to designate host computers on the Internet. This is the type of purely "nominative" function that is not prohibited by trademark law. *See New Kids on the Block v. New America Pub., Inc.,* 971 F.2d 302, 307 (9th Cir.1992) (noting that laws against infringement do not apply to "non-trademark use of a mark"); *Lucasfilm, Ltd. v. High Frontier,* 622 F.Supp. 931, 933 (D.D.C.1985) (holding that property rights in a trademark do not extend to the use of the trademark to express ideas unconnected with the sale or offer for sale of goods or services).

This is not to say that a domain name can never be used to infringe a trademark. However, something more than the registration of the name is required before the use of a domain name is infringing. In *Planned Parenthood Fed'n of America. Inc. v. Bucci,* for example, the defendant registered the domain name "plannedparenthood.com" and used it as the address of a web site promoting his book on abortion. 42 U.S.P.Q.2d 1430, 1432 (S.D.N.Y.1997). The defendant admitted that he used the domain name hoping that people looking for the Planned Parenthood's site would find his site. *Id.* at 1433. The defendant argued that registration without more is not a commercial use of a mark. *Id.* at 1436–37. The court, however, found that the defendant did "more than merely register a domain name; he has created a home page that uses plaintiff's mark as its address, conveying the impression to Internet users that plaintiff is the sponsor of defendant's web site." *Id.* at 1437. The infringing use in *Planned Parenthood* was not registration of the plaintiff's mark with NSI, but rather the use of the plaintiff's trademark "as a domain name to identify his web site" in a manner that confused Internet users as to the source or sponsorship of the products offered there. *Id.* at 1440; *cf. Teletech Customer Care*

---

[3] [*See* § II.A of the PTO's Examination Guide No. 2–99, excerpted in Part VI, *infra*–Eds.]

Management (California), Inc. v. Tele–Tech Co., 977 F.Supp. 1407 (C.D.Cal.1997) (finding that the plaintiff was not likely to prevail on the merits of an infringement claim because the plaintiff demonstrated only that customers were likely to be confused as to location of web site, not as to source of goods or services).

The cases dealing with vanity telephone numbers are consistent with the conclusion that registration of a domain name, without more, does not constitute use of the name as a trademark. A toll-free telephone number with an easy-to-remember letter equivalent is a valuable business asset. As with domain names, courts have held that the promotion of a confusingly similar telephone number may be enjoined as trademark infringement and unfair competition. *Dial–A–Mattress Franchise Corp. v. Page,* 880 F.2d 675, 678 (2d Cir.1989); *American Airlines, Inc. v. A 1–800–A–M–E–R–I–C–A–N Corp.,* 622 F.Supp. 673 (N.D.Ill.1985). The infringing act, however, is not the mere possession and use of the telephone number. If it were, trademark holders would be able to eliminate every toll-free number whose letter equivalent happens to correspond to a trademark. In *Holiday Inns, Inc., v. 800 Reservation, Inc.,* 86 F.3d 619 (6th Cir.1996), the district court held that the defendant's use of 1–800 H[zero]LIDAY infringed the plaintiff's trademark in the telephone number 1–800–HOLIDAY. *Id.* at 620. The court of appeals reversed, holding that Holiday Inns's trademark rights in its vanity telephone number did not allow it to control use by others of confusingly similar telephone numbers. Although the defendant's toll-free number was often misdialed by customers seeking 1–800–HOLIDAY, the defendant never promoted the number in connection with the HOLIDAY trademark; but only promoted it as 1–800–405–4329. *Id.* at 623. Because the defendant had used the number only as a telephone number, and not as a trademark, the court of appeals held that the defendant had not infringed the plaintiff's trademark. *Id.* at 625–26.

Domain names and vanity telephone numbers both have dual functions. Domain names, like telephone numbers, allow one machine to connect to another machine. Domain names, like telephone numbers, are also valuable to trademark holders when they make it easier for customers to find the trademark holder. Where the holder of a vanity telephone number promotes it in a way that causes a likelihood of confusion, the holder has engaged in an infringing use. *American Airlines,* 622 F.Supp. at 682 (mere use of telephone number is not infringing, but misleading use of trademarked term in yellow pages advertisement is infringing). But, where, as with NSI, the pure machine-linking function is the only use at issue, there is no trademark use and there can be no infringement.

In the ordinary trademark infringement case, where there is no question that the defendant used the mark, the analysis proceeds directly to the issue of whether there is a likelihood of confusion. Here, however, because NSI has not used Lockheed's service mark in connection with goods or services, the Court need not apply the test for likelihood of confusion. NSI, therefore, is entitled to judgment as a matter of law on the § 32 claim.

1. Printer and Publisher Liability Under 15 U.S.C. § 1114(2)(A), (B)

Lockheed asserts that NSI has infringed its service mark as a "printer" of the mark under 15 U.S.C. § 1114(2)(A). This assertion misapprehends NSI's function as a domain name registrar. To the extent that registrants of SKUNK WORKS-type domain names infringed the mark, they did so by using it on web sites or other Internet resources in a way that created a likelihood of confusion as to source or sponsorship. NSI is not an Internet service provider. It does not provide host computers for web sites or other Internet resources. NSI's role is restricted to publishing a list of domain names, their holders, and the IP numbers of the domain name servers that perform the directory functions associated with the domain names.

NSI's role is fundamentally dissimilar from that of telephone directory publishers whose conduct has been found enjoinable under § 1114(2)(A). *See Century 21 Real Estate Corp. of Northern Illinois v. R.M. Post Inc.*, 8 U.S.P.Q.2d 1614, 1617 (N.D.Ill.1988) (denying motion to dismiss where yellow pages' publishers were alleged to have printed infringing trademark in listing of former licensee who no longer had right to use trademark). There, the telephone directory printers supplied the material that directly caused the likelihood of confusion. In the domain name context, the domain name registration itself does not infringe the trademark. Infringement occurs when the domain name is used in certain ways. For example, a domain name may infringe trademark rights when it is used in connection with a web site that advertises services in competition with those of the trademark owner. *See, e.g., Cardservice International, Inc. v. McGee*, 950 F.Supp. 737, 738 (E.D.Va.1997); *Comp Examiner Agency, Inc. v. Juris, Inc.*, 1996 WL 376600 (C.D.Cal.1996). Where domain names are used to infringe, the infringement does not result from NSI's publication of the domain name list, but from the registrant's use of the name on a web site or other Internet form of communication in connection with goods or services. NSI is not a "printer or publisher" of web sites, or any other form of Internet "publication." As discussed below in the section on contributory infringement, NSI's involvement with the use of domain names does not extend beyond registration. NSI's liability cannot be premised on an argument that it prints or publishes the list of domain names, because the list is not the instrument or forum for infringement. NSI's liability, if it exists at all, would stem from registrants' use of domain names in connection with other services not provided by NSI. This type of liability is properly analyzed under contributory liability doctrine, not as printer and publisher liability under § 1114(2)(A).

C. Unfair Competition Under Lanham Act § 43(a), 15 U.S.C. § 1125(a)

Lockheed has followed the common practice of alleging unfair competition under § 43(a) of the Lanham Act along with trademark infringement under § 32. Both causes of action depend on a demonstration of a likelihood of confusion. 1 J. Thomas McCarthy, *McCarthy on Trademarks and Unfair Competition* § 2:8 (1997). Federal unfair competition requires use of the mark in connection with goods or services. 15 U.S.C. § 1125(a)(1). As discussed above, NSI's acceptance of registrations for domain names resembling SKUNK WORKS is not a use of the mark in connection with goods or services.

A recent district court decision illustrates the application of federal unfair competition law to the domain name context. *Juno Online Servs., L.P. v. Juno Lighting, Inc.*, 979 F.Supp. 684 (N.D.Ill. Sept.29, 1997). During a dispute over the domain name "juno.com," Juno Lighting registered the domain name "juno-online.com" in the hopes of persuading Juno Online Services to switch its e-mail service to that domain name. Juno Online sued Juno Lighting for federal unfair competition. The district court dismissed the unfair competition claim because Juno Online alleged only that Juno Lighting registered the name with NSI, and did not allege further use of the name to create a web site or to advertise its services. *Id.* at 690–92. The court held that registration of a trademark as a domain name does not constitute use of the trademark on the Internet in connection with goods or services, and therefore was not prohibited by § 43(a). *Id.* This reasoning applies more strongly to NSI, which has not registered domain names resembling SKUNK WORKS for its own use, but has merely accepted domain name registrations from others.

[The court next considered Lockheed's trademark dilution claim and concluded that "NSI's acceptance of domain name registrations is not a 'commercial use' within the meaning of the Federal Trademark Dilution Act."]

[The court also dismissed Lockheed's contributory infringement claim, finding that Lockheed lacked the requisite knowledge of the infringing activity. The Court of Appeals affirmed the ruling on contributory infringement, holding that a registrar's registration of a domain name does not constitute the supply of an infringing "product," as would be necessary for the registrar to be found a contributory infringer.]

III. Conclusion

. . .

Because summary judgment on the above claims is based on Lockheed's lack of a legal right to control the domain name registration process, there is no case or controversy between these parties. Therefore, the Court grants NSI's motion for summary judgment as to Lockheed's declaratory judgment cause of action.

If the Internet were a technically ideal system for commercial exploitation, then every trademark owner would be able to have a domain name identical to its trademark. But the parts of the Internet that perform the critical addressing functions still operate on the 1960s and 1970s technologies that were adequate when the Internet's function was to facilitate academic and military research. Commerce has entered the Internet only recently. In response, the Internet's existing addressing systems will have to evolve to accommodate conflicts among holders of intellectual property rights, and conflicts between commercial and non-commercial users of the Internet. "In the long run, the most appropriate technology to access web sites and e-mail will be directories that point to the desired Internet address. Directory technology of the necessary scale and complexity is not yet available, but when it is developed it will relieve much of the pressure on domain names." *Domain Name System, Hearings Before the Subcommittee on Basic Research of the House Science Committee,* 105th Cong., 1997 WL 14151463 (September 30, 1997) (testimony of Barbara A. Dooley, Executive Director, Commercial Internet Exchange Association). No doubt trademark owners would like to make the Internet safe for their intellectual property rights by reordering the allocation of existing domain names so that each trademark owner automatically owned the domain name corresponding to the owner's mark. Creating an exact match between Internet addresses and trademarks will require overcoming the problem of concurrent uses of the same trademark in different classes of goods and geographical areas. Various solutions to this problem are being discussed, such as a graphically-based Internet directory that would allow the presentation of trademarks in conjunction with distinguishing logos, new top-level domains for each class of goods, or a new top-level domain for trademarks only. The solution to the current difficulties faced by trademark owners on the Internet lies in this sort of technical innovation, not in attempts to assert trademark rights over legitimate non-trademark uses of this important new means of communication.

Green Products Co. v. Independence Corn By–Products Co.
992 F.Supp. 1070 (N.D.Iowa 1997).

■ MELLOY, CHIEF JUDGE.

The sole issue before the Court is whether to compel Independence Corn By-Products Co. (ICBP) to convey the domain name "greenproducts.com" to the plaintiff, Green Products Co. (Green Products), for its use during the pendency of this litigation.

Green Products claims that ICBP violated § 43(a) of the Lanham Trademark Act, 15 U.S.C. § 1125(a), as well as state laws, when ICBP registered the domain name "greenproducts.com" as one of its own domain names on the internet. Green Products moved for a preliminary injunction: (1) to enjoin ICBP from using the domain name "greenproducts.com", (2) to enjoin ICBP from using the expressions "green products" and "green pet products" as the whole or part of a trademark, trade name, or domain name, and (3) to compel ICBP to convey the ownership of the domain name "greenproducts.com" to Green Products.

In response, ICBP agreed to the first and second parts of Green Products' request, but it resisted the third part. During the pendency of the litigation, ICBP has consented (1) not to use the domain name "greenproducts.com", and (2) not to use the expressions "green products" and "green pet products" as the whole or part of any trademark, trade name, or domain name, but ICBP will continue to use those names "in ways that do not constitute trademark infringement, such as comparative advertising." In order to analyze the merits of Green Products' motion to compel ICBP to transfer ownership of the domain name "greenproducts.com" during the pendency of the litigation, the Court will begin with a brief background of relevant language and information.

Background

[The court begins with a description of the Internet and domain names.]

In the case before this Court, Green Products and ICBP are direct competitors in the corncob by-products industry. On May 30, 1997, ICBP registered two domain names, "icbp.com" and "bestcob.com", with the goal of eventually designing a website that users could find through either domain name. On June 9, 1997, ICBP registered seven other domain names–five of which are formed by using the trade names of ICBP's competitors: e.g., "greenproducts.com." On July 16, 1997, Green Products tried to register "greenproducts.com" and "freshnest.com" (a sister company's name), but was told that ICBP had already registered those two domain names. Green Products then filed a complaint and a motion for a preliminary injunction against ICBP.

Discussion

A. Preliminary Injunction Standards

To decide whether to grant the motion for a preliminary injunction, the Court must consider: (1) the probability that Green Products will succeed on the merits; (2) the threat of irreparable harm to Green Products; (3) the state of the balance between this harm and the injury that granting the injunction will inflict on other parties; and (4) the public interest. *See Dataphase Sys., Inc. v. CL Sys., Inc.,* 640 F.2d 109, 113 (8th Cir.1981) (en banc). When weighing these factors, "no single factor is itself dispositive; in each case all factors must be considered to determine on balance whether they weigh towards granting the injunction." *Calvin Klein Cosmetics Corp. v. Lenox Labs., Inc.,* 815 F.2d 500, 503 (8th Cir.1987).

. . .

B. Analysis of Dataphase Factors

1. Probability that Green Products will succeed on the merits

. . .

An essential element to a trademark infringement action is that the plaintiff must prove that a defendant's use of a particular name " 'creates a likelihood of confusion, deception, or mistake among an appreciable number of ordinary buyers as to the source or association' between the two names." *Maritz, Inc. v. Cybergold, Inc.,* 947 F.Supp. 1338, 1339 (E.D.Mo.1996) (quoting *Duluth News–Tribune v. Mesabi Publ'g Co.,* 84 F.3d 1093, 1096 (8th Cir.1996)). Factors relevant to determine the likelihood of confusion or deception are:

(1) the strength of the trademark;

(2) the similarity between the plaintiff's and defendant's marks;

(3) the competitive proximity of the parties' products;

(4) the alleged infringer's intent to confuse the public;

(5) evidence of any actual confusion; and

(6) the degree of care reasonably expected of the plaintiff's potential customers.

Maritz, 947 F.Supp. at 1340, *citing Anheuser–Busch, Inc. v. Balducci Publications,* 28 F.3d 769, 774 (8th Cir.1994). The Court will next examine each of these factors in turn, although not all of the factors are applicable in this case.

In order to determine whether the trademark is entitled to protection, the Court examines the first factor–strength of the trademark–and classifies the plaintiffs mark as either (1) arbitrary or fanciful, (2) suggestive, (3) descriptive, or (4) generic.

An arbitrary or fanciful mark is the strongest type of mark and is afforded the highest level of protection. At the other end, a generic term is used by the general public to identify a category of goods, so it does not receive trademark protection. Suggestive and descriptive marks fall somewhere in between. A suggestive mark is one that requires some measure of imagination to reach a conclusion about the nature of the product. In contrast, a descriptive mark "immediately conveys the nature or function of the product and is entitled to protection only if it has become distinctive by acquiring a secondary meaning." Here, the Court finds that Green Products' trademark—the name "Green Products' "—is at least suggestive. The name "Green Products" requires at least some imagination to connect it with corncob by-products.

The next factor requires the Court to consider the similarity between the plaintiffs and defendant's marks. ICBP concedes that its domain name "greenproducts.com" is "undisputedly similar to the mark Green Products Co." However, ICBP also argues that its use of the mark must be viewed in the context of the marketplace, and that the "domain name only has meaning as an Internet address linking to ICBP's future web site and the web site will take every precaution to ensure there is no consumer confusion."

In essence, ICBP's argument is that the Court should only compare the similarity of domain names and websites linked to those domain names–not the similarity of ICBP's domain name and Green Products' trademark–because ICBP is not "selling a product on store shelves using the mark 'greenproducts.com'."

The Court finds ICBP's argument clever, but ultimately unpersuasive. ICBP's argument is analogous to saying that ICBP has the right to hang a sign in front of its store that reads, "Green Products." When customers enter the store expecting to be able to see (and possibly, to buy) products made by Green Products, ICBP then announces, "Actually, this store isn't owned by Green Products; it's owned by ICBP. We don't sell anything made by Green Products, but as long as you're here, we'll tell you how our products are better than Green Products." In essence, ICBP is capitalizing on the strong similarity between Green Products' trademark and ICBP's domain name to lure customers onto its web page.

Turning to the third factor, the competitive proximity of the parties' products, ICBP concedes that ICBP and Green Products are both competitors in the corncob byproducts industry. Despite being direct competitors, ICBP argues that this Court should not focus on their similar corn by-products, but on domain names and their respective websites: "the relevant 'products' for the likelihood of confusion analysis are not corncob products because ICBP does not sell any corncob products with the mark 'greenproducts.com' on a label or package design." Instead, ICBP suggests, the Court should analyze whether a website located at "greenproducts.com" is proximate to a website located at "green-products.com" or "greenproductsco.com." ICBP believes that these domain names are not proximate, because anyone who knows Green Products' domain name can use that name to go directly to Green Products' website and "will likely never even see ICBP's web site." ICBP does, however, concede that the websites are "proximate in the sense that a person guessing at Green Product Co.'s domain name might access ICBP's website if it first tries 'greenproducts.com'. . . ."

ICBP's argument basically boils down to the idea that the Court should view the domain names as mere addresses which–along with the websites attached to each name–are products in and of themselves. The Court disagrees. There is a close competitive proximity between the products that the two companies sell, and there is also a close competitive proximity between the domain name "greenproducts.com" and the trademark "Green Products". The domain name "greenproducts.com" identifies the internet site to those who reach it, "much like a person's name identifies a particular person, or, more relevant to trademark disputes, a company's name identifies a specific company." *Cardservice,* 950 F.Supp. 737. Because customers who do not know what a company's domain name is will often guess that the domain name is the same as the company's name, a "domain name mirroring a corporate name may be a valuable corporate asset, as it facilitates communication with a customer base." *MTV Networks,* 867 F.Supp. at 203–204 n. 2.

Alternatively, even if this Court were persuaded that it should only compare the alphanumeric domain names (and not the products that each company sells, nor the similarity between ICBP's domain name and Green Products' trademark), this Court would still find a close proximity between the domain name "greenproducts.com" and any of the alternative domain names that ICBP suggests, such as "green-products.com", "greenproductsco.com", or "greenproducts-co.com." Under either analysis, there is a close competitive proximity, and that close competitive proximity further increases the opportunity of consumer confusion.

Fourth, this Court examines whether ICBP intended to cause consumer confusion by creating an ICBP website accessed through the domain name "greenproducts.com." ICBP maintains that it had no intent to "pass off" its products as those of Green Products, and that its only intent was to distinguish ICBP's products from those of Green Products through comparative advertising. ICBP believes that there will be no consumer confusion because internet users will immediately know that the website belongs to ICBP once the actual web page appears on the screen (after users have typed the domain name "greenproducts.com"). To support this argument, ICBP distinguishes its planned website from that in *Planned Parenthood Fed. of Am., Inc. v. Bucci,* 42 U.S.P.Q.2d 1430 (S.D.N.Y.1997), where an anti-abortion activist who registered the domain name "plannedparenthood.com" to lure pro-abortion internet users onto his website designed a web page that deceptively announced that it was "Planned Parenthood's" site–instead of clearly announcing that the Planned Parenthood Federation of America had nothing to do with it.

While it is true that the *Planned Parenthood* court discussed how the graphics and design of the web page misled users into believing that the Planned Parenthood Federation was operating an anti-abortion web page, *see* 42 U.S.P.Q.2d at 1432, ICBP overlooks the fact that the *Planned Parenthood* court also found that a disclaimer would not have cured the confusion caused by the domain name:

> Due to the nature of Internet use, defendant's appropriation of plaintiffs mark as a domain name and home page address cannot adequately be remedied by a disclaimer. Defendant's domain name and home page address are external labels that, on their face, cause confusion among

> Internet users and may cause Internet users who seek plaintiffs website to expend time and energy accessing defendant's website. Therefore, I determine that a disclaimer on defendant's home page would not be sufficient to dispel the confusion induced by his home page address and domain name.

Planned Parenthood, 42 U.S.P.Q.2d at 1441.

Because ICBP's website has not been designed yet, this Court will make no finding as to whether ICBP's web page is likely to cause consumer confusion between the products of ICBP and those of Green Products. However, based on the briefs, affidavits, and evidence presented at the hearing, this Court finds that the use of plaintiff's trademark as defendant's own domain name is likely to cause consumer confusion as to who owns the site. Just as customers entering a store that advertises "Green Products" as its store name would be initially confused to find, upon entering the store, that ICBP actually owned it, so will customers typing the domain name "greenproducts.com" be initially confused to find that ICBP owns the website.

The Court acknowledges that such an interpretation of "consumer confusion" is somewhat different than that typically used to find consumer confusion in trademark infringement cases. Typically, the courts examine whether a company intended to confuse consumers into thinking that its own products were made by a competitor company. *See, e.g., SquirtCo v. Seven-Up Co.,* 628 F.2d 1086, 1091 (8th Cir.1980) ("Intent on the part of the alleged infringer to pass off its goods as the product of another raises an inference of likelihood of confusion, but intent is not an element of a claim for trademark infringement.").

Here, ICBP did not intend to sell its corn by-products by passing them off as having been made by Green Products. However, ICBP did intend to pass off its domain name as though it belonged to Green Products. As a result of the confusion in thinking that Green Products' website could be found through the "greenproducts.com" domain name, ICBP could deceptively lure potential customers onto its own turf, where customers would be told how ICBP is better than Green Products. This Court finds that such a deceptive use of a competitor's trademark as a way to lure customers away from the competitor is a kind of consumer confusion.

Moreover, even if such an interpretation of "consumer confusion" is not the relevant mode of inquiry, this Court also finds that ICBP's ownership of the domain name "greenproducts.com"—even without an adjoining website—could cause consumer confusion about the corporate status of Green Products. Currently, if internet users browsing the web type the domain name "greenproducts.com", they are told that "[n]o documents match the query." After reading this message, users might randomly input other domain names, guessing that Green Products is registered under some variation of its trademark. Other users might try to find out who owns the domain name "greenproducts.com" by using various functions on the web where people can type specific domain names and find out who owns them.[4] Users who do this will learn that ICBP owns the "greenproducts.com" website,

---

[4] [Here the court is referring to a "whois" search—Eds.]

and they will also learn the address and phone number of ICBP. Potential custom-ers who see this information may be confused into thinking that ICBP has taken over Green Products, or that Green Products has merged into ICBP. As a result, customers may decide to buy from ICBP, believing that Green Products no longer exists or that ICBP now owns it. The consumer confusion thereby caused by ICBP's ownership of the domain name "greenproducts.com" during the pendency of liti-gation would cause Green Products to lose customers.

The fifth factor is incidents of actual confusion. Green Products concedes that because the website is not yet operational, there have been no incidents of actual confusion, so the Court need not examine this factor further.

The last factor is the degree of care reasonably expected of Green Products' po-tential customers. To determine this, the Court looks at the "ordinary purchaser, buying under the normally prevalent conditions of the market and giving the at-tention such purchasers usually give in buying that class of goods." *General Mills, Inc. v. Kellogg Co.,* 824 F.2d 622, 627 (8th Cir.1987). . . . Based on all the evidence be-fore it at this point in the proceedings . . . this Court finds that ordinary internet users do not undergo a highly sophisticated analysis when searching for domain names [and that] . . . an ordinary internet user trying to find Green Products' web-site would likely guess that Green Products' domain name was the same as its trademark, and thus type "greenproducts.com". . . .

Based on this overall balancing, this Court finds a substantial probability that Green Products will prevail on the merits.

2. Irreparable harm to Green Products

The Court next analyzes the degree of harm, if any, that Green Products would suffer if not granted a preliminary injunction. The Eighth Circuit has held that a district court can presume irreparable injury from a finding of probable success on the merits of a § 43(a) Lanham Trademark Act case. *Sports Design,* 871 F.Supp. at 1165, *citing Sanborn Mfg.,* 997 F.2d at 489. While this Court could thus presume ir-reparable injury based on its finding of probable success on the merits, it will also examine the specific circumstances of this case in order to decide whether allowing ICBP to retain ownership of the domain name "greenproducts.com" during the pendency of litigation would cause irreparable harm to Green Products.

Although ICBP has consented to putting the domain name "greenpro-ducts.com" on hold until the final merits are determined, Green Products is con-cerned that even though ICBP would not have an actual website that could be viewed by typing the domain name "greenproducts.com", customers could use other functions on the web to discover that ICBP owns that domain name. As a result, potential or actual customers might mistakenly conclude that ICBP has pur-chased the Green Products corporation, or that Green Products has merged with ICBP. This confusion could result in Green Products losing both customers and revenue during the pendency of the litigation, and it would be impossible to calcu-late how much money or how many customers were lost.

For these reasons, in addition to the fact that the Court believes that Green Products is likely to succeed on the merits, the Court finds that it would cause

Green Products irreparable harm if ICBP were allowed to retain ownership of the domain name "greenproducts.com" during the pendency of the litigation.

3. Balance between this harm and the injury that granting the injunction will inflict on other parties

ICBP has not finalized what its web page will look like, has not advertised that it owns a web page that can be viewed by typing the domain name "greenproducts.com", and has not listed "greenproducts.com" as one of its domain names in the Thomas Register. If ICBP is compelled to relinquish ownership of the domain name "greenproducts.com" to Green Products during the pendency of the litigation, ICBP would still be able to launch its own website via its registered domain names "icbp.com" or "bestcob.com". Furthermore, the act of transferring ownership of "greenproducts.com" would not hinder ICBP's ability to launch a website that compares its products to those of Green Products: ICBP could still design and implement a website that compares the products of ICBP to those of Green Products, and internet users could access this website through ICBP's other registered domain names.

While these factors weigh in support of compelling ICBP to transfer ownership of the domain name, there are also certain factors that weigh against the transfer. For example, if ICBP were to prevail at trial, Green Products would have to transfer the "greenproducts.com" domain name back to ICBP. This could cause some initial confusion, and possibly hostility, from customers who might have become accustomed to accessing Green Products' website through the "greenproducts.com" domain name. In addition, because Green Products would like to advertise its domain name "greenproducts.com" in the Thomas Register, and because final changes to the printed version of the Thomas Register must be made by November 1, 1997, neither Green Products nor ICBP will be able to change the 1998 edition of the printed Thomas Register if ICBP prevails at trial. As a result, ICBP worries that it "would risk incurring the anger of these customers if that domain name was suddenly switched...."

After weighing the potential harm that ICBP would experience by not being able to use its competitor's trademark as its own domain name, against the harm Green Products would experience by not being able to use its own trademark as its domain name, this Court finds that the harm to Green Products is more extensive and severe than the harm to ICBP. Although ICBP would experience some harm by transferring ownership of the domain name during the pendency of litigation, the transfer is not irreversible; if ICBP ultimately prevails on the merits, the Court will transfer ownership of the domain name back to ICBP. Additionally, even though some customers who may have become accustomed to finding Green Products' web page through the "greenproducts.com" domain name may be initially upset when they find that the domain name "greenproducts.com" has become the domain name for ICBP's web page (if ICBP prevails at trial), any harm that ICBP may experience because of Green Products' temporary ownership of the domain name could be tempered by a carefully designed web page or by hyperlinks to Green Products' web page. Moreover, given ICBP's goal of distinguishing its products from those of Green Products, the opportunity for ICBP to establish a comparative advertising website located through the "greenproducts.com" domain name could be even more advantageous to ICBP if Green Products has already attracted customers to the "greenproducts.com" domain name.

For all of the above reasons, and especially considering the fact that the transfer of ownership is not irreversible because the Court will order the domain name transferred back to ICBP if ICBP prevails in litigation, the Court finds that the harm to Green Products is more extensive and severe than the harm to ICBP.

. . .

Cardservice International, Inc. v. McGee
950 F.Supp. 737 (E.D.Va.1997), aff'd mem., 129 F.3d 1258 (4th Cir.1997).

■ CLARKE, DISTRICT JUDGE.

This matter comes before this Court for the hearing of evidence in the bench trial of whether Plaintiff Cardservice International, Inc., is entitled to a permanent injunction pursuant to 15 U.S.C. § 1116 against Defendants Webster R. McGee and WRM & Associates banning the use by the Defendants of words similar to Plaintiff's trademark "Cardservice". . . .

I.

This action was brought by Cardservice International seeking injunctive relief and damages for alleged infringements of its trademark "Cardservice" by the Defendants. Cardservice International provides credit and debit card processing and processes "billions of dollars in transactions annually." Cardservice International registered the trademark "Cardservice International" with the United States Patent and Trademark Office as Reg. No. 1,864,924 effective Nov. 29, 1994. No claim was made to the exclusive right to the word "international."

McGee, through his sole proprietorship WRM & Associates has also provided credit and debit card services. Cardservice International claims that in 1994, McGee applied to become a representative of Cardservice International. McGee claims that he was only associated with an agent of Cardservice International, but never sought to become associated with Cardservice International itself. In March of 1995 and without the permission of Cardservice International, McGee registered the internet domain name "cardservice.com" with Network Solutions, Inc., the company responsible for regulating use of domain names on the internet. In advertisements located at the internet site "cardservice.com", McGee advertised merchant card services through a company held out to be "EMS–Card Service on the Caprock".

In May and August 1995, Cardservice International contacted McGee by letter demanding that McGee "cease and desist all Cardservice related activity." Subsequent discussions between Cardservice International and McGee focused on McGee's use of "cardservice.com". When McGee refused to surrender the domain name, Cardservice International retained counsel, who called McGee's attention to Cardservice International's trademark and again demanded that McGee cease and desist use of the term "Cardservice" and any variation of it on the internet.

McGee refused to relinquish "cardservice.com" or to cease use of "Card Service" on the internet. McGee claimed that the name of his business inserts a space between "card" and "service" and that he is therefore not in violation of the trademark laws. He further claimed that "cardservice.com" was one word because the internet does not allow spaces in domain names. When Cardservice International expanded its services onto the internet, it was forced to use the domain name "cardsvc.com".

Cardservice International then filed this action in September 1996. Cardservice International filed counts alleging violations of § 32 of the Lanham Act, 15 U.S.C. § 1114, for trademark infringement; § 43(a) of the Lanham Act, 42 U.S.C. § 1125(a), for unfair competition; and common law unfair competition, misappropriation, and unjust enrichment. McGee answered these allegations and filed counterclaims seeking declaratory relief that he was the proper owner of the domain name "cardservice.com.", that Cardservice International had interfered with Defendants' business relationships by attempting to have the domain name "cardservice.com" transferred from McGee to Cardservice International, and that Cardservice International had engaged in trademark misuse and wire fraud. . . .

On January 13, 1997, the Court also proceeded with the bench trial on the merits of Cardservice International's claim in which Cardservice International sought attorneys fees and a permanent injunction. McGee indicated his desire to end the litigation and stated that he would not contest Cardservice International's evidence.

II.

The Court ruled from the Bench that Cardservice International is entitled to a permanent injunction against McGee and WRM & Associates requiring the Defendants to cease use of any variation of the registered mark "Cardservice" and to relinquish any interest in the domain name "cardservice.com". Federal Rule of Civil Procedure 65(d) requires this Court to state the reasons for the grant of the permanent injunction.

First, the Court addresses a preliminary issue. McGee has argued that because he registered the domain name "cardservice.com" with Network Solutions, he is entitled to the domain name. McGee cites Network Solutions' policy of granting domain names on a first-come-first-served basis. Such a policy cannot trump federal law. Holders of valid trademarks under federal law are not subject to company policy, nor can the rights of those trademark holders be changed without congressional actions. If trademark laws apply to domain names, anyone who obtains a domain name under Network Solutions' "first-come-first-served" policy must do so subject to whatever liability is provided for by federal law.

. . .

. . . The Fourth Circuit has stated that in order to prevail in actions under [Sections 32 and 43 of the Lanham Act, 15 U.S.C. §§ 1114(1) and 1125(a)], "a complainant must demonstrate that it has a valid, protectable trademark and that the defendant's use of a colorable imitation of the trademark is likely to cause confusion among consumers." *Lone Star Steakhouse & Saloon v. Alpha of Virginia,* 43 F.3d 922 (4th Cir.1995).

It is undisputed that Cardservice International owns a valid, protectable trademark. Until McGee informed the Court that he would not contest Cardservice International's evidence, he primarily argued that his use of "cardservice.com" and "Card Service on the Caprock" would not cause confusion on the internet. The Court disagrees and finds that there is a likelihood of confusion between Cardservice International's registered mark and McGee's use of "cardservice.com" and "Card Service" on the internet.

The factors relevant to a determination of whether there is a likelihood of confusion are as follows:

a)   the strength or distinctiveness of the mark;

b)   the similarity of the two marks;

c)   the similarity of the goods/services the marks identify;

d)   the similarity of the facilities the two parties use in their businesses;

e)   the similarity of the advertising used by the two parties;

f)   the defendant's intent;

g)   actual confusion.

Pizzeria Uno Corp. v. Temple, 747 F.2d 1522, 1527 (4th Cir.1984). Not all of these factors are relevant to any given set of facts, nor must all factors be in the registrant's favor for a finding of confusion. *Id.*

In this case, several of the *Pizzeria Uno* factors favor a finding that McGee's use of "cardservice.com" and "Card Service" is likely to cause confusion. It is clear that McGee's use of "cardservice.com" and "Card Service on the Caprock" are strikingly similar to Cardservice International's registered mark. Although McGee's use of the term "Card Service" does not exactly duplicate "Cardservice", minor differences between the registered mark and the unauthorized use of the mark do not preclude liability under the Lanham Act when the unauthorized use is likely to cause confusion. *See Lone Star Steakhouse, supra* (finding use of "Lone Star Grill" to be an infringement of registered mark "Lone Star Steakhouse and Saloon"). The use of the term "cardservice" in Defendants' domain name exactly duplicates the registered mark "Cardservice".

Further, both parties are using the internet as the facility to provide their services. Because of the nature of the internet and domain names in particular, this factor becomes even more important in cases of trademark infringement over the internet. Domain names present a unique circumstance when determining the likelihood of confusion caused by possible trademark violations. Traditionally, trademark disputes involved two or more parties using the same or similar mark. *Intermatic Inc. v. Toeppen,* 947 F.Supp. 1227, 1233–34 (N.D.Ill.1996) (Williams, Mag.). With regard to domain names, however, only one party can hold any particular domain name. *Id.* Who has access to that domain name is made even more important by the fact that there is nothing on the internet equivalent to a phone book or directory assistance. A customer who is unsure about a company's domain name will often guess that the domain name is also the company's name. For this reason, "a domain name mirroring a corporate name may be a valuable corporate asset, as it facilitates communication with a customer base." *MTV Networks, Inc. v. Curry,* 867 F.Supp. 202, 203–04 n. 2 (S.D.N.Y.1994). Thus, a domain name is more than a mere internet address. It also identifies the internet site to those who reach it, much like a person's name identifies a particular person, or, more relevant to trademark disputes, a company's name identifies a specific company.

Because of McGee's use of "cardservice.com", Cardservice International has no access to an internet domain name containing its registered mark, and must use a different domain name. Cardservice International's customers who wish to take advantage of its internet services but do not know its domain name are likely to assume that "cardservice.com" belongs to Cardservice International. These customers would instead reach McGee and see a home page for "Card Service". They would find that McGee's internet site offers advertisements for and provides access to the same services as Cardservice International—credit and debit card processing. Many would assume that they have reached Cardservice International or, even if they realize that is not who they have reached, take advantage of McGee's services because they do not otherwise know how to reach Cardservice International. Such confusion is not only likely, but, according to McGee, has actually occurred at least four or five times since he began using "cardservice.com". Transcript of Preliminary Injunction Hearing at 366.

Such a result is exactly what the trademark laws were designed to protect against. Cardservice International has obtained a trademark to ensure that the name "cardservice" will be associated by consumers only with Cardservice International. Regardless of the fact that McGee's business is small compared to Cardservice International's, confusion will result among consumers who are seeking Cardservice International by searching for its trademark as a domain name on the internet. The fact that Cardservice International has been awarded a trademark means that it should not be forced to compete with others who would also use the words "cardservice". The terms of the Lanham Act do not limit themselves in any way which would preclude application of federal trademark law to the internet. Unauthorized use of a domain name which includes a protected trademark to engage in commercial activity over the internet constitutes use "in commerce", 15 U.S.C. § 1114(1), of a registered mark. Such use is in direct conflict with federal trademark law. *See ActMedia, Inc. v. Active Media Int'l,* 1996 WL 466527 (N.D.Ill. July 17, 1996) (finding defendant's use of domain name "actmedia.com" precluded plaintiff from reserving the domain name incorporating its registered mark and therefore violated 15 U.S.C. § 1125); *see also Panavision Int'l v. Toeppen,* 945 F.Supp. 1296 (C.D.Cal.1996) (finding defendant's reservation of domain name "panavision.com" which incorporated registered mark of plaintiff to be in violation of the Federal Trademark Dilution Act of 1995, 15 U.S.C. § 1125(c)).

Accordingly, the Court finds that McGee's use of "cardservice.com" and "Card Service on the Caprock" constitutes trademark infringement in violation of the

Lanham Act and that Cardservice International is entitled to a permanent injunction against such use pursuant to 15 U.S.C. § 1116. The Court emphasizes that its finding against McGee is based on evidence which McGee ultimately chose not to contest at trial.

. . .

EXTENSIONS

Directories. Directories are the electronic file folders found on most personal computers. One can point to a directory on a host computer connected to the Internet by appending to the fully qualified domain name of that host a forward slash "/" followed by the name of the particular directory. Thus, when I type

www.whitehouse.gov/press releases/

into the address bar of my web browser, I am served the default web page contained in the "press release" directory that resides on the host computer designated by the URL www.whitehouse.gov. With respect to trademark infringement, this raises the question whether the use of another's trademark as a directory name can constitute infringement. If so, how would you defend such a lawsuit? What is the difference between using another's trademark as a domain name and as a directory name? Is the use of another's trademark as a directory name fair use? *See, e.g., Patmont Motor Werks, Inc. v. Gateway Marine, Inc.,* 1997 WL 811770 n. 6 (N.D.Cal.1997). (For material on trademark fair use, *see* Chapter 2, Part IV(A), *supra.*)

In *Interactive Products Corp. v. A2Z Mobile Office Solutions*, Inc., 326 F.3d 687 (6th Cir.2003), plaintiff brought a trademark infringement action based on defendant's use of plaintiff's trademark LAP TRAVELER in the post-domain-name portion of the URL of a page on its website. The URL was "a2zsolutions.com/desks/floor/laptraveler/dkfl-lt.htm." The court affirmed the district court's grant of summary judgment to the defendant, explaining: "Because post-domain paths do not typically signify source, it is unlikely that the presence of another's trademark in a post-domain path of a URL would ever violate trademark law."

QUESTIONS FOR DISCUSSION

1. *Is registration "commercial use"?* In *Lockheed Martin Corp. v. Network Solutions, Inc.,* the court holds that mere registration of a domain name is not use "in connection with any goods or services" or "commercial use," and therefore cannot constitute trademark infringement or dilution. To the same effect is *Bird v. Parsons*, 289 F.3d 865 (6th Cir.2002). In *Green Products Co. v. Independence Corn By-Products Co.,* in contrast, the court finds commercial use even though the defendant has done no more than register a domain name that is similar to a trademark owned by Green Products. The *Green Products* court reasons that the act of registering a domain name creates a public record showing that the registrant owns that domain name. By conducting a "whois" search, members of the public will see this record and erroneously infer that the registrant has acquired that company and that the goods and services of this company now originate from and are affiliated with this registrant—thereby establishing a connection to goods and services as well as consumer confusion over their origin and affiliation. Which view do you find more convincing?

2. *Initial interest confusion and disclaimers.* Offline, initial interest confusion is sometimes condemned as a form of "bait and switch." In holding that a bar named "The Velvet Elvis" infringed trademarks held by the Elvis Presley estate, a court noted: "[O]nce in the door, the confusion has succeeded because some patrons may stay, despite realizing that the bar has no relationship with" the Elvis Presley estate. *Elvis Presley Enters. v. Capece*, 141 F.3d 188, 204 (5th Cir.1998). Does initial interest confusion have the same consequence and significance online as it does in the world of bricks and mortar? Would the presence of disclaimers on the website affect your answer? The court in *Green Products* quotes the court in *Planned Parenthood Fed. Of Am., Inc. v. Bucci*, 42 U.S.P.Q.2d 1430 (S.D.N.Y. 1997), for the proposition that disclaimers on a website will not cure confusion caused by that website's domain name. Therein the court argued that "Defendant's domain name and home page address . . . may cause Internet users who seek plaintiff's web site to expend time and energy accessing defendant's web site. Therefore, I determine that a disclaimer on defendant's home page would not be sufficient to dispel the confusion induced by his home page address and domain name." *Id.* at 1441. Do you agree with this analysis?

3. *Registration to block another's use.* Under the reasoning of the *Lockheed* court, could a company register a competitor's trademark as a domain name in order to prevent that competitor from using it as a domain name so long as the registrant did not actually use it on the Internet? *See Juno Online Services, L.P. v. Juno Lighting, Inc.,* 979 F.Supp. 684 (N.D.Ill.1997), discussed in Part II(C) of the *Lockheed Martin* opinion.

4. *E-mail addresses vs. websites.* When courts discuss the use of a domain name on the Internet, their examples involve a "fully qualified" domain name that points to a website. Is it possible to infringe another's trademark with a domain name if one only uses that domain name as part of an e-mail address? *See America Online, Inc. v. IMS,* 24 F.Supp.2d 548 (E.D.Va.1998).

COMPARATIVE NOTE

Similar approach in U.K. The courts in the United Kingdom have embraced the reasoning of the *Green Products* case and held that mere registration of a domain name can constitute trademark infringement. *See British Telecommunications plc v. One in a Million Ltd.*, [1998] 4 All E.R. 476 (C.A.):

> It is accepted that the name Marks & Spencer denotes Marks & Spencer plc and nobody else. Thus anybody seeing or hearing the name realises that what is being referred to is the business of Marks & Spencer plc. It follows that registration by the appellants of a domain name including the name Marks & Spencer makes a false representation that they are associated or connected with Marks & Spencer plc. This can be demonstrated by considering the reaction of a person who taps into his computer the domain name marksandspencer.co.uk and presses a button to execute a "whois" search. He will be told that the registrant is One In A Million Limited. A substantial number of persons will conclude that One In A Million Limited must be connected or associated with Marks & Spencer plc. That amounts to a false representation which constitutes passing off.

B. TRADEMARK DILUTION

Panavision International, L.P. v. Toeppen
141 F.3d 1316 (9th Cir.1998).

■ DAVID R. THOMPSON, CIRCUIT JUDGE:

This case presents two novel issues. We are asked to apply existing rules of personal jurisdiction to conduct that occurred, in part, in "cyberspace." In addition, we are asked to interpret the Federal Trademark Dilution Act as it applies to the

Internet.

Panavision accuses Dennis Toeppen of being a "cyber pirate" who steals valuable trademarks and establishes domain names on the Internet using these trademarks to sell the domain names to the rightful trademark owners.

The district court found that under the "effects doctrine," Toeppen was subject to personal jurisdiction in California. *Panavision International, L.P. v. Toeppen,* 938 F.Supp. 616, 620 (C.D.Cal.1996). The district court then granted summary judgment in favor of Panavision, concluding that Toeppen's conduct violated the Federal Trademark Dilution Act of 1995, 15 U.S.C. § 1125(c), and the California Anti-dilution statute, California Business & Professions Code § 14330. *Panavision International, L.P. v. Toeppen,* 945 F.Supp. 1296, 1306 (C.D.Cal.1996).

Toeppen appeals. He argues that the district court erred in exercising personal jurisdiction over him because any contact he had with California was insignificant, emanating solely from his registration of domain names on the Internet, which he did in Illinois. Toeppen further argues that the district court erred in granting summary judgment because his use of Panavision's trademarks on the Internet was not a commercial use and did not dilute those marks.

We have jurisdiction under 28 U.S.C. § 1291 and we affirm.

I.

BACKGROUND

[The court begins with a description of the Internet and domain names.]

Panavision holds registered trademarks to the names "Panavision" and "Panaflex" in connection with motion picture camera equipment. Panavision promotes its trademarks through motion picture and television credits and other media advertising.

In December 1995, Panavision attempted to register a website on the Internet with the domain name Panavision.com. It could not do that, however, because Toeppen had already established a website using Panavision's trademark as his domain name. Toeppen's web page for this site displayed photographs of the City of Pana, Illinois.

On December 20, 1995, Panavision's counsel sent a letter from California to Toeppen in Illinois informing him that Panavision held a trademark in the name Panavision and telling him to stop using that trademark and the domain name Panavision.com. Toeppen responded by mail to Panavision in California, stating he had the right to use the name Panavision.com on the Internet as his domain name. Toeppen stated:

> If your attorney has advised you otherwise, he is trying to screw you. He wants to blaze new trails in the legal frontier at your expense. Why do you want to fund your attorney's purchase of a new boat (or whatever) when you can facilitate the acquisition of "PanaVision.com" cheaply and simply instead?

Toeppen then offered to "settle the matter" if Panavision would pay him

$13,000 in exchange for the domain name. Additionally, Toeppen stated that if Panavision agreed to his offer, he would not "acquire any other Internet addresses which are alleged by Panavision Corporation to be its property."

After Panavision refused Toeppen's demand, he registered Panavision's other trademark with NSI as the domain name Panaflex.com. Toeppen's web page for Panaflex.com simply displays the word "Hello."

Toeppen has registered domain names for various other companies including Delta Airlines, Neiman Marcus, Eddie Bauer, Lufthansa, and over 100 other marks. Toeppen has attempted to "sell" domain names for other trademarks such as intermatic.com to Intermatic, Inc. for $10,000 and americanstandard.com to American Standard, Inc. for $15,000.

. . .

II.

DISCUSSION

A. Personal Jurisdiction

[The court considers the issue of personal jurisdiction and concludes that the lower court properly exercised personal jurisdiction over Toeppen.]

B. Trademark Dilution Claims

The Federal Trademark Dilution Act provides:

> The owner of a famous mark shall be entitled . . . to an injunction against another person's commercial use in commerce of a mark or trade name, if such use begins after the mark has become famous and causes dilution of the distinctive quality of the mark. . . .

15 U.S.C. § 1125(c).

The California Anti-dilution statute is similar. *See* Cal. Bus. & Prof.Code § 14330. It prohibits dilution of "the distinctive quality" of a mark regardless of competition or the likelihood of confusion. The protection extends only to strong and well recognized marks. Panavision's state law dilution claim is subject to the same analysis as its federal claim.

In order to prove a violation of the Federal Trademark Dilution Act, a plaintiff must show that (1) the mark is famous; (2) the defendant is making a commercial use of the mark in commerce; (3) the defendant's use began after the mark became famous; and (4) the defendant's use of the mark dilutes the quality of the mark by diminishing the capacity of the mark to identify and distinguish goods and services. 15 U.S.C. § 1125(c).

Toeppen does not challenge the district court's determination that Panavision's trademark is famous, that his alleged use began after the mark became famous, or that the use was in commerce. Toeppen challenges the district court's determination that he made "commercial use" of the mark and that this use caused "dilution" in the quality of the mark.

1. Commercial Use

Toeppen argues that his use of Panavision's trademarks simply as his domain names cannot constitute a commercial use under the Act. Case law supports this argument. *See Panavision International, L.P. v. Toeppen,* 945 F.Supp. 1296, 1303 (C.D.Cal.1996) ("Registration of a trade[mark] as a domain name, without more, is not a commercial use of the trademark and therefore is not within the prohibitions of the Act."); *Academy of Motion Picture Arts & Sciences v. Network Solutions, Inc.,* 989 F.Supp. 1276, 1997 WL 810472 (C.D.Cal. Dec.22, 1997) (the mere registration of a domain name does not constitute a commercial use); *Lockheed Martin Corp. v. Network Solutions, Inc.,* 985 F.Supp. 949 (C.D.Cal.1997) (NSI's acceptance of a domain name for registration is not a commercial use within the meaning of the Trademark Dilution Act).

Developing this argument, Toeppen contends that a domain name is simply an address used to locate a web page. He asserts that entering a domain name on a computer allows a user to access a web page, but a domain name is not associated with information on a web page. If a user were to type Panavision.com as a domain name, the computer screen would display Toeppen's web page with aerial views of Pana, Illinois. The screen would not provide any information about "Panavision," other than a "location window" which displays the domain name. Toeppen argues that a user who types in Panavision.com, but who sees no reference to the plaintiff Panavision on Toeppen's web page, is not likely to conclude the web page is related in any way to the plaintiff, Panavision.

Toeppen's argument misstates his use of the Panavision mark. His use is not as benign as he suggests. Toeppen's "business" is to register trademarks as domain names and then sell them to the rightful trademark owners. He "act[s] as a 'spoiler,' preventing Panavision and others from doing business on the Internet under their trademarked names unless they pay his fee." *Panavision,* 938 F.Supp. at 621. This is a commercial use. *See Intermatic Inc. v. Toeppen,* 947 F.Supp. 1227, 1230 (N.D.Ill.1996) (stating that "[o]ne of Toeppen's business objectives is to profit by the resale or licensing of these domain names, presumably to the entities who conduct business under these names.").

As the district court found, Toeppen traded on the value of Panavision's marks. So long as he held the Internet registrations, he curtailed Panavision's exploitation of the value of its trademarks on the Internet, a value which Toeppen then used when he attempted to sell the Panavision.com domain name to Panavision.

In a nearly identical case involving Toeppen and Intermatic Inc., a federal district court in Illinois held that Toeppen's conduct violated the Federal Trademark Dilution Act. *Intermatic,* 947 F.Supp. at 1241. There, Intermatic sued Toeppen for registering its trademark on the Internet as Toeppen's domain name, intermatic.com. It was "conceded that one of Toeppen's intended uses for registering the Intermatic mark was to eventually sell it back to Intermatic or to some other party." *Id.* at 1239. The court found that "Toeppen's intention to arbitrage the 'intermatic.com' domain name constitute[d] a commercial use." *Id. See also Teletech Customer Care Management, Inc. v. Tele-Tech Co.,* 977 F.Supp. 1407 (C.D.Cal.1997) (granting a preliminary injunction under the Trademark Dilution Act for use of a trademark as a domain name).

Toeppen's reliance on *Holiday Inns, Inc. v. 800 Reservation, Inc.*, 86 F.3d 619 (6th Cir.1996), 519 U.S. 1093 (1997) is misplaced. In *Holiday Inns*, the Sixth Circuit held that a company's use of the most commonly *misdialed* number for Holiday Inns' 1–800 reservation number was not trademark infringement.

Holiday Inns is distinguishable. There, the defendant did not use Holiday Inns' trademark. Rather, the defendant selected the most commonly misdialed telephone number for Holiday Inns and attempted to capitalize on consumer confusion.

A telephone number, moreover, is distinguishable from a domain name because a domain name is associated with a word or phrase. A domain name is similar to a "vanity number" that identifies its source. Using Holiday Inns as an example, when a customer dials the vanity number "1–800–Holiday," she expects to contact Holiday Inns because the number is associated with that company's trademark. A user would have the same expectation typing the domain name HolidayInns.com. The user would expect to retrieve Holiday Inns' web page.

Toeppen made a commercial use of Panavision's trademarks. It does not matter that he did not attach the marks to a product. Toeppen's commercial use was his attempt to sell the trademarks themselves.[5] Under the Federal Trademark Dilution Act and the California Anti-dilution statute, this was sufficient commercial use.

2. Dilution

"Dilution" is defined as "the lessening of the capacity of a famous mark to identify and distinguish goods or services, regardless of the presence or absence of (1) competition between the owner of the famous mark and other parties, or (2) likelihood of confusion, mistake or deception." 15 U.S.C. § 1127.

Trademark dilution on the Internet was a matter of Congressional concern. Senator Patrick Leahy (D–Vt.) stated:

> [I]t is my hope that this anti-dilution statute can help stem the use of deceptive Internet addresses taken by those who are choosing marks that are associated with the products and reputations of others.

141 Cong. Rec. § 19312–01 (daily ed. Dec. 29, 1995) (statement of Sen. Leahy). *See*

---

[5] *See Boston Pro. Hockey Assoc., Inc. v. Dallas Cap & Emblem Mfg., Inc.*, 510 F.2d 1004 (1975), which involved the sale of National Hockey League logos. The defendant was selling the logos themselves, unattached to a product (such as a hat or sweatshirt). The court stated: "The difficulty with this case stems from the fact that a reproduction of the trademark itself is being sold, unattached to any other goods or services." *Id.* at 1010. The court concluded that trademark law should protect the trademark itself. "Although our decision here may slightly tilt the trademark laws from the purpose of protecting the public to the protection of the business interests of plaintiffs, we think that the two become . . . intermeshed. . . ." *Id.* at 1011. "Whereas traditional trademark law sought primarily to protect consumers, dilution laws place more emphasis on protecting the investment of the trademark owners." *Panavision*, 945 F.Supp. at 1301.

also Teletech Customer Care Management, Inc. v. Tele-Tech Co., Inc., 977 F.Supp. 1407, 1413 (C.D.Cal.1997).

To find dilution, a court need not rely on the traditional definitions such as "blurring" and "tarnishment." Indeed, in concluding that Toeppen's use of Panavision's trademarks diluted the marks, the district court noted that Toeppen's conduct varied from the two standard dilution theories of blurring and tarnishment. *Panavision,* 945 F.Supp. at 1304. The court found that Toeppen's conduct diminished "the capacity of the Panavision marks to identify and distinguish Panavision's goods and services on the Internet." *Id. See also Intermatic,* 947 F.Supp. at 1240 (Toeppen's registration of the domain name, "lessens the capacity of Intermatic to identify and distinguish its goods and services by means of the Internet.").

This view is also supported by *Teletech.* There, TeleTech Customer Care Management Inc., ("TCCM"), sought a preliminary injunction against Tele-Tech Company for use of TCCM's registered service mark, "TeleTech," as an Internet domain name. *Teletech,* 977 F.Supp. at 1410. The district court issued an injunction, finding that TCCM had demonstrated a likelihood of success on the merits on its trademark dilution claim. *Id.* at 1412. The court found that TCCM had invested great resources in promoting its servicemark and Teletech's registration of the domain name teletech.com on the Internet would most likely dilute TCCM's mark. *Id.* at 1413.

Toeppen argues he is not diluting the capacity of the Panavision marks to identify goods or services. He contends that even though Panavision cannot use Panavision.com and Panaflex.com as its domain name addresses, it can still promote its goods and services on the Internet simply by using some other "address" and then creating its own web page using its trademarks.

We reject Toeppen's premise that a domain name is nothing more than an address. A significant purpose of a domain name is to identify the entity that owns the website. "A customer who is unsure about a company's domain name will often guess that the domain name is also the company's name." *Cardservice Int'l v. McGee,* 950 F.Supp. 737, 741 (E.D.Va.1997). "[A] domain name mirroring a corporate name may be a valuable corporate asset, as it facilitates communication with a customer base." *MTV Networks, Inc. v. Curry,* 867 F.Supp. 202, 203–204 n. 2 (S.D.N.Y.1994).

Using a company's name or trademark as a domain name is also the easiest way to locate that company's website. Use of a "search engine" can turn up hundreds of websites, and there is nothing equivalent to a phone book or directory assistance for the Internet. *See Cardservice,* 950 F.Supp. at 741.

Moreover, potential customers of Panavision will be discouraged if they cannot find its web page by typing in "Panavision.com," but instead are forced to wade through hundreds of websites. This dilutes the value of Panavision's trademark. We echo the words of Judge Lechner, quoting Judge Wood: "Prospective users of plaintiff's services who mistakenly access defendant's website may fail to continue to search for plaintiff's own home page, due to anger, frustration or the belief that plaintiff's home page does not exist." *Jews for Jesus v. Brodsky,* 993 F.Supp. 282, 306–

07 (D.N.J.1998) (Lechner, J., quoting Wood, J. in *Planned Parenthood v. Bucci*, 1997 WL 133313 at *4); *see also Teletech*, 977 F.Supp. at 1410 (finding that use of a search engine can generate as many as 800 to 1000 matches and it is "likely to deter web browsers from searching for Plaintiff's particular web site").

Toeppen's use of Panavision.com also puts Panavision's name and reputation at his mercy. *See Intermatic*, 947 F.Supp. at 1240 ("If Toeppen were allowed to use 'intermatic.com,' Intermatic's name and reputation would be at Toeppen's mercy and could be associated with an unimaginable amount of messages on Toeppen's web page.").

We conclude that Toeppen's registration of Panavision's trademarks as his domain names on the Internet diluted those marks within the meaning of the Federal Trademark Dilution Act, 15 U.S.C. § 1125(c), and the California Anti-dilution statute, Cal.Bus. & Prof.Code § 14330.

. . .

Ty Inc. v. Perryman
306 F.3d 509 (7th Cir.2002).

■ POSNER, CIRCUIT JUDGE.

Ty Inc., the manufacturer of Beanie Babies, the well-known beanbag stuffed animals, brought this suit for trademark infringement against Ruth Perryman. Perryman sells second-hand beanbag stuffed animals, primarily but not exclusively Ty's Beanie Babies, over the Internet. Her Internet address ("domain name"), a particular focus of Ty's concern, is bargainbeanies.com. She has a like-named Web site (http://www.bargainbeanies.com) where she advertises her wares. Ty's suit is based on the federal antidilution statute, 15 U.S.C. § 1125(c), which protects "famous" marks from commercial uses that cause "dilution of the distinctive quality of the mark." See *Nabisco, Inc. v. PF Brands, Inc.*, 191 F.3d 208, 214–16 (2d Cir.1999). The district court granted summary judgment in favor of Ty and entered an injunction that forbids the defendant to use "BEANIE or BEANIES or any colorable imitation thereof (whether alone or in connection with other terms) within any business name, Internet domain name, or trademark, or in connection with any non-Ty products." Perryman's appeal argues primarily that "beanies" has become a generic term for beanbag stuffed animals and therefore cannot be appropriated as a trademark at all, and that in any event the injunction (which has remained in effect during the appeal) is overbroad.

The fundamental purpose of a trademark is to reduce consumer search costs by providing a concise and unequivocal identifier of the particular source of particular goods. The consumer who knows at a glance whose brand he is being asked to buy knows whom to hold responsible if the brand disappoints and whose product to buy in the future if the brand pleases. This in turn gives producers an incentive to maintain high and uniform quality, since otherwise the investment in their trademark may be lost as customers turn away in disappointment from the brand. A successful brand, however, creates an incentive in unsuccessful competitors to pass off their inferior brand as the successful brand by adopting a confusingly similar trademark, in effect appropriating the goodwill created by the producer of the successful brand. The traditional and still central concern of trademark law is to provide remedies against this practice.

Confusion is not a factor here, however . . . . Perryman is not a competing producer of beanbag stuffed animals, and her Web site clearly disclaims any affiliation with Ty. But that does not get her off the hook. The reason is that state and now federal law also provides a remedy against the "dilution" of a trademark, though as noted at the outset of this opinion the federal statute is limited to the subset of "famous" trademarks and to dilutions of them caused by commercial uses that take place in interstate or foreign commerce. "Beanie Babies," and "Beanies" as the shortened form, are famous trademarks in the ordinary sense of the term: "everybody has heard of them"; they are "truly prominent and renowned," in the words of Professor McCarthy, 4 *McCarthy on Trademarks and Unfair Competition* § 24:109, p. 24–234 (2001), as distinguished from having a merely local celebrity. *TCPIP Holding Co. v. Haar Communications Inc.*, 244 F.3d 88, 98–99 (2d Cir.2001). And while both this court and the Third Circuit have held, in opposition to the Second Circuit's *TCPIP* decision, that "fame," though it cannot be local, may be limited to "niche" markets, *Syndicate Sales, Inc. v. Hampshire Paper Corp.*, 192 F.3d 633, 640–41 (7th Cir.1999); *Times Mirror Magazines, Inc. v. Las Vegas Sports News, L.L.C.*, 212 F.3d 157, 164 (3d Cir.2000), this is not a conflict to worry over here; Ty's trademarks are household words. And Perryman's use of these words was commercial in nature and took place in interstate commerce, and doubtless, given the reach of the aptly named World Wide Web, in foreign commerce as well.

But what is "dilution"? There are (at least) three possibilities relevant to this case, each defined by a different underlying concern. First, there is concern that consumer search costs will rise if a trademark becomes associated with a variety of unrelated products. Suppose an upscale restaurant calls itself "Tiffany." There is little danger that the consuming public will think it's dealing with a branch of the Tiffany jewelry store if it patronizes this restaurant. But when consumers next see the name "Tiffany" they may think about both the restaurant and the jewelry store, and if so the efficacy of the name as an identifier of the store will be diminished. Consumers will have to think harder — incur as it were a higher imagination cost-- to recognize the name as the name of the store. *Exxon Corp. v. Exxene Corp.*, 696 F.2d 544, 549–50 (7th Cir.1982); cf. *Mead Data Central, Inc. v. Toyota Motor Sales, U.S.A., Inc.*, 875 F.2d 1026, 1031 (2d Cir.1989) ("The [legislative] history [of New York's antidilution statute] disclosed a need for legislation to prevent such 'hypothetical anomalies' as 'Dupont shoes, Buick aspirin tablets, Schlitz varnish, Kodak pianos, Bulova gowns' "); 4 *McCarthy on Trademarks and Unfair Competition, supra*, § 24:68, pp. 24–120 to 24–121. So "blurring" is one form of dilution.

Now suppose that the "restaurant" that adopts the name "Tiffany" is actually a striptease joint. Again, and indeed even more certainly than in the previous case, consumers will not think the striptease joint under common ownership with the jewelry store. But because of the inveterate tendency of the human mind to proceed by association, every time they think of the word "Tiffany" their image of the fancy jewelry store will be tarnished by the association of the word with the strip joint. *Hormel Foods Corp. v. Jim Henson Productions, Inc.*, 73 F.3d 497, 507 (2d Cir.1996); 4 *McCarthy on Trademarks and Unfair Competition, supra*, § 24:95, pp. 24–195, 24–198. So "tarnishment" is a second form of dilution. Analytically it is a subset of blurring, since it reduces the distinctness of the trademark as a signifier of the trademarked product or service.

Third, and most far-reaching in its implications for the scope of the concept of dilution, there is a possible concern with situations in which, though there is neither blurring nor tarnishment, someone is still taking a free ride on the investment of the trademark owner in the trademark. Suppose the "Tiffany" restaurant in our first hypothetical example is located in Kuala Lumpur and though the people who patronize it (it is upscale) have heard of the Tiffany jewelry store, none of them is ever going to buy anything there, so that the efficacy of the trademark as an identifier will not be impaired. If appropriation of Tiffany's aura is nevertheless forbidden by an expansive concept of dilution, the benefits of the jewelry store's investment in creating a famous name will be, as economists say, "internalized" — that is, Tiffany will realize the full benefits of the investment rather than sharing those benefits with others — and as a result the amount of investing in creating a prestigious name will rise.

This rationale for antidilution law has not yet been articulated in or even implied by the case law, although a few cases suggest that the concept of dilution is not exhausted by blurring and tarnishment, see *Panavision Int'l, L.P. v. Toeppen*, 141 F.3d 1316, 1326 (9th Cir.1998); *Intermatic, Inc. v. Toeppen*, 947 F.Supp. 1227, 1238–39 (N.D.Ill.1996); *Rhee Bros., Inc. v. Han Ah Reum Corp.*, 178 F.Supp.2d 525, 530 (D.Md.2001), and the common law doctrine of "misappropriation" might conceivably be invoked in support of the rationale that we have sketched. See Rochelle Cooper Dreyfuss & Roberta Rosenthal Kwall, *Intellectual Property: Cases and Materials on Trademark, Copyright and Patent Law* 137–38 (1996). The validity of the rationale may be doubted, however. The number of prestigious names is so vast (and, as important, would be even if there were no antidilution laws) that it is unlikely that the owner of a prestigious trademark could obtain substantial license fees if commercial use of the mark without his consent were forbidden despite the absence of consumer confusion, blurring, or tarnishment. Competition would drive the fee to zero since, if the name is being used in an unrelated market, virtually every prestigious name will be a substitute for every other in that market.

None of the rationales we have canvassed supports Ty's position in this case. Perryman is not producing a product, or a service, such as dining at a restaurant, that is distinct from any specific product; rather, she is selling the very product to which the trademark sought to be defended against her "infringement" is attached. You can't sell a branded product without using its brand name, that is, its trademark. Supposing that Perryman sold *only* Beanie Babies (a potentially relevant qualification, as we'll see), we would find it impossible to understand how she could be thought to be blurring, tarnishing, or otherwise free riding to any significant extent on Ty's investment in its mark. To say she was would amount to saying that if a used car dealer truthfully advertised that it sold Toyotas, or if a muffler manufacturer truthfully advertised that it specialized in making mufflers for installation in Toyotas, Toyota would have a claim of trademark infringement. Of course there can be no aftermarket without an original market, and in that sense sellers in a trademarked good's aftermarket are free riding on the trademark. But in that attenuated sense of free riding, almost everyone in business is free riding.

Ty's argument is especially strained because of its marketing strategy. As we explained in an earlier case brought by Ty, *Ty, Inc. v. GMA Accessories, Inc.*, 132 F.3d 1167, 1173 (7th Cir.1997), Ty deliberately produces a quantity of each Beanie Baby that fails to clear the market at the very low price that it charges for Beanie Babies. The main goal is to stampede children into nagging their parents to buy the new Baby lest they be the only kid on the block who doesn't have it. A byproduct (or perhaps additional goal) is the creation of a secondary market, like the secondary market in works of art, in which prices on scarce Beanie Babies are bid up to a market-clearing level. Perryman is a middleman in this secondary market, the market, as we said, that came into existence as the result, either intended or foreseen, of a deliberate marketing strategy. That market is unlikely to operate efficiently if sellers who specialize in serving it cannot use "Beanies" to identify their business. Perryman's principal merchandise is Beanie Babies, so that to forbid it to use "Beanies" in its business name and advertising (Web or otherwise) is like forbidding a used car dealer who specializes in selling Chevrolets to mention the name in his advertising.

It is true that Web search engines do not stop with the Web address; if Perryman's Web address were www.perryman.com but her Web page mentioned Beanies, a search for the word "Beanies" would lead to her Web page. Yet we know from the events that led up to the passage in 1999 of the Anticybersquatting Consumer Protection Act, 15 U.S.C. § 1125(d), that many firms value having a domain name or Web address that signals their product. (The "cybersquatters" were individuals or firms that would register domain names for the purpose of selling them to companies that wanted a domain name that would be the name of their company or of their principal product.) After all, many consumers search by typing the name of a company in the Web address space (browser) on their home page rather than by use of a search engine. We do not think that by virtue of trademark law producers own their aftermarkets and can impede sellers in the aftermarket from marketing the trademarked product. In this respect the case parallels our most recent decision dealing with Ty's intellectual property, in which we found that Ty was attempting to control the market in collectors' guides to Beanie Babies by an overly expansive interpretation of its copyrights. *Ty, Inc. v. Publications Int'l Ltd.*, 292 F.3d 512 (7th Cir.2002).

We surmise that what Ty is seeking in this case is an extension of antidilution law to forbid commercial uses that accelerate the transition from trademarks (brand names) to generic names (product names). Words such as "thermos," "yo-yo," "escalator," "cellophane," and "brassiere" started life as trademarks, but eventually lost their significance as source identifiers and became the popular names of the product rather than the name of the trademark owner's brand, and when that happened continued enforcement of the trademark would simply have undermined competition with the brand by making it difficult for competitors to indicate that they were selling the same product—by rendering them in effect speechless. Ty is doubtless cognizant of a similar and quite real danger to "Beanie Babies" and "Beanies." . . .

Although there is a social cost when a mark becomes generic—the trademark owner has to invest in a new trademark to identify his brand—there is also a social benefit, namely an addition to ordinary language. A nontrivial number of words in common use began life as trademarks. . . . An interpretation of antidilution law as arming trademark owners to enjoin uses of their mark that, while not confusing, threaten to render the mark generic may therefore not be in the public interest. Moreover, the vistas of litigation that such a theory of dilution opens up are staggering. Ty's counsel at argument refused to disclaim a right to sue the publishers of dictionaries should they include an entry for "beanie," lower-cased and defined as a beanbag stuffed animal, thus accelerating the transition from trademark to generic term. He should have disclaimed such a right. See *Illinois High School Ass'n v. GTE Vantage Inc.*, 99 F.3d 244, 246 (7th Cir.1996); 2 *McCarthy on Trademarks and Unfair Competition, supra,* § 12:28, pp. 12–79 to 12–81.

. . .

. . . [G]iven Perryman's status as a seller in the secondary market created as a result of Ty's marketing strategy, we cannot imagine a state of facts consistent with the extensive record compiled in the summary judgment proceeding that could possibly justify an injunction against Perryman's representing in her business name and Internet and Web addresses that she is doing what she has a perfect right to do, namely sell Beanie Babies. . . .

VACATED AND REMANDED WITH INSTRUCTIONS.

Bosley Medical Institute, Inc. v. Kremer
403 F.3d 672 (9th Cir.2005).

■ SILVERMAN, CIRCUIT JUDGE.

Defendant Michael Kremer was dissatisfied with the hair restoration services provided to him by the Bosley Medical Institute, Inc. In a bald-faced effort to get even, Kremer started a website at www.BosleyMedical.com, which, to put it mildly, was uncomplimentary of the Bosley Medical Institute. The problem is that "Bosley Medical" is the registered trademark of the Bosley Medical Institute, Inc., which brought suit against Kremer for trademark infringement and like claims. Kremer argues that noncommercial use of the mark is not actionable as infringement under the Lanham Act. Bosley responds that Kremer is splitting hairs.

Like the district court, we agree with Kremer. We hold today that the noncommercial use of a trademark as the domain name of a website—the subject of which is consumer commentary about the products and services represented by the mark—does not constitute infringement under the Lanham Act.

. . .

I. Background

Bosley Medical provides surgical hair transplantation, restoration, and replacement services to the public. Bosley Medical owns the registered trademark "BOSLEY MEDICAL,"[1] has used the mark "BOSLEY MEDICAL" since 1992, and registered the mark with the United States Patent and Trademark Office in January 2001. Bosley has spent millions of dollars on advertising and promotion throughout the United States and the rest of the world.

Michael Kremer is a dissatisfied former patient of Bosley. Unhappy with the results of a hair replacement procedure performed by a Bosley physician in Seattle, Washington, he filed a medical malpractice lawsuit against Bosley Medical in 1994. That suit was eventually dismissed.

In January 2000, Kremer purchased the domain name www.BosleyMedical.com, the subject of this appeal, as well as the domain name www.BosleyMedicalViolations.com, which is not challenged by Bosley. Five days after registering the domain name, Kremer went to Bosley Medical's office in Beverly Hills, California and delivered a two-page letter to Dr. Bosley, Founder and President of Bosley Medical. The first page read:

> Let me know if you want to discuss this. Once it is spread over the internet it will have a snowball effect and be too late to stop. M. Kremer [phone number]. P.S. I always follow through on my promises.

The second page was entitled "Courses of action against BMG" and listed eleven items. The first item stated: "1. Net web sites disclosing true operating nature of BMG. Letter 3/14/96 from LAC D.A. Negative testimonials from former clients. Links. Provide BMG competitors with this information." The letter contains no mention of domain names or any other reference to the Internet.

Kremer began to use www.BosleyMedical.com in 2001. His site summarizes the Los Angeles County District Attorney's 1996 investigative findings about Bosley, and allows visitors to view the entire document. It also contains other information that is highly critical of Bosley. Kremer earns no revenue from the website and no goods or services are sold on the website. There are no links to any of Bosley's competitors' websites. BosleyMedical.com does link to Kremer's sister site, BosleyMedicalViolations.com, which links to a newsgroup entitled alt.baldspot, which in turn contains advertisements for companies that compete with Bosley. BosleyMedical.com also contained a link to the Public Citizen website. Public Citizen . . . represents Kremer in this case.

Bosley brought this suit alleging trademark infringement, dilution, unfair competition, various state law claims, and a libel claim . . . . Bosley sought to take discovery aimed at the trademark and libel claims. The magistrate judge granted limited discovery on the libel claims. Following discovery, Bosley dismissed the libel claims . . . . [The parties cross-moved for partial summary judgment on Bosley's trademark claims.]

---

[1] Bosley also owns the following trademarks: BOSLEY, BOSLEY HEALTHY HAIR, BOSLEY HEALTHY HAIR FORMULA, and BOSLEY HEALTHY HAIR COMPLEX.

Ruling that Kremer's use of "Bosley Medical" in the domain name was non-commercial and unlikely to cause confusion, the district court entered summary judgment for Kremer on the federal claims . . . . Bosley now appeals.

. . .

III. Analysis

A. Trademark Infringement and Dilution Claims

The Trademark Act of 1946 ("Lanham Act") prohibits uses of trademarks, trade names, and trade dress that are likely to cause confusion about the source of a product or service. See 15 U.S.C. §§ 1114, 1125(a). In 1996, Congress amended § 43 of the Lanham Act to provide a remedy for the dilution of a famous mark. See 15 U.S.C. § 1125(c).

Infringement claims are subject to a commercial use requirement. The infringement section of the Lanham Act, 15 U.S.C. § 1114, states that any person who "uses in commerce any reproduction, counterfeit, copy, or colorable imitation of a registered mark in connection with the sale, offering for sale, distribution, or advertising of any goods or services on or in connection with which such use is likely to cause confusion, or to cause mistake, or to deceive . . ." can be held liable for such use. 15 U.S.C. § 1114(1)(a).

In 1996, Congress expanded the scope of federal trademark law when it enacted the Federal Trademark Dilution Act ("FTDA"). The FTDA allows the "owner of a famous mark" to obtain "an injunction against another person's *commercial use in commerce* of a mark or trade name . . . ." 15 U.S.C. § 1125(c)(1) (emphasis added). While the meaning of the term "commercial use in commerce" is not entirely clear, we have interpreted the language to be roughly analogous to the "in connection with" sale of goods and services requirement of the infringement statute. See *Mattel, Inc. v. MCA Records, Inc.*, 296 F.3d 894, 903 (9th Cir.2002) ("Although this statutory language is ungainly, its meaning seems clear: It refers to a use of a famous and distinctive mark to sell goods other than those produced or authorized by the mark's owner.") . . . .

The inclusion of these requirements in the Lanham Act serves the Act's purpose: "to secure to the owner of the mark the goodwill of his business and to protect the ability of consumers to distinguish among competing producers." *Two Pesos, Inc. v. Taco Cabana, Inc.*, 505 U.S. 763, 774 (1992) (internal quotation marks and citations omitted). In other words, the Act is designed to protect consumers who have formed particular associations with a mark from buying a competing product using the same or substantially similar mark and to allow the mark holder to distinguish his product from that of his rivals. . . .

The Supreme Court has made it clear that trademark infringement law prevents only unauthorized uses of a trademark in connection with a commercial transaction in which the trademark is being used to confuse potential consumers. . . . As the Second Circuit held, "the Lanham Act seeks to prevent consumer confusion that enables a seller to pass off his goods as the goods of another . . . . Trademark infringement protects only against mistaken *purchasing decisions* and not against confusion generally." *Lang v. Ret. Living Publ'g Co., Inc.*, 949 F.2d 576, 582–83 (2d

Cir.1991) (internal quotation marks and citation omitted) (emphasis added).

As a matter of First Amendment law, commercial speech may be regulated in ways that would be impermissible if the same regulation were applied to non-commercial expressions. *Florida Bar v. Went For It, Inc.*, 515 U.S. 618, 623 (1995). "The First Amendment may offer little protection for a competitor who labels its commercial good with a confusingly similar mark, but trademark rights do not entitle the owner to quash an unauthorized use of the mark by another who is communicating ideas or expressing points of view." *Mattel,* 296 F.3d at 900 (internal quotation marks and citations omitted).

The district court ruled that Kremer's use of Bosley's mark was noncommercial. To reach that conclusion, the court focused on the "use in commerce" language rather than the "use in connection with the sale of goods" clause. This approach is erroneous. "Use in commerce" is simply a jurisdictional predicate to any law passed by Congress under the Commerce Clause. See *Steele v. Bulova Watch Co.,* 344 U.S. 280, 283 (1952) . . . . 15 U.S.C. § 1127 states that "unless the contrary is plainly apparent from the context . . . the word 'commerce' means all commerce which may lawfully be regulated by Congress." Therefore, the district court should have determined instead whether Kremer's use was "in connection with a sale of goods or services" rather than a "use in commerce." However, we can affirm the district court's grant of summary judgment on any ground supported by the record. The question before us, then, boils down to whether Kremer's use of Bosley Medical as his domain name was "in connection with a sale of goods or services." If it was not, then Kremer's use was "noncommercial" and did not violate the Lanham Act.

Bosley argues that it has met the commercial use requirement in three ways. First, it argues that a mark used in an otherwise noncommercial website or as a domain name for an otherwise noncommercial website is nonetheless used in connection with goods and services where a user can click on a link available on that website to reach a commercial site. *Nissan Motor Co. v. Nissan Computer Corp.,* 378 F.3d 1002 (9th Cir.2004). However, Bosley's reliance on *Nissan* is unfounded.

In *Nissan*, Nissan Motor Company sued Nissan Computer Corporation for using the Internet websites www.Nissan.com and www.Nissan.net. *Id.* at 1006. In *Nissan*, however, commercial use was undisputed, as the core function of the defendant's website was to advertise his computer business. Additionally, the defendant in *Nissan*, like the defendant in *Taubman Co. v. Webfeats,* 319 F.3d 770 (6th Cir.2003), placed links to other commercial businesses directly on their website. Kremer's website contains no commercial links, but rather contains links to a discussion group, which in turn contains advertising. This roundabout path to the advertising of others is too attenuated to render Kremer's site commercial. At no time did Kremer's BosleyMedical.com site offer for sale any product or service or contain paid advertisements from any other commercial entity. See *TMI, Inc. v. Maxwell,* [368 F.3d 433 (5th Cir.2004)] (holding that the commercial use requirement is not satisfied where defendant's site had no outside links).

Bosley also points out that Kremer's site contained a link to Public Citizen, the public interest group representing Kremer throughout this litigation. We hold that

Kremer's identification of his lawyers and his provision of a link to same did not transform his noncommercial site into a commercial one.

Bosley's second argument that Kremer's website satisfies the "in connection with the sale of goods or services" requirement of the Lanham Act is that Kremer created his website to enable an extortion scheme in an attempt to profit from registering BosleyMedical.com. In *Panavision International, L.P. v. Toeppen*, 141 F.3d 1316 (9th Cir.1998), this court held that a defendant's "commercial use was his attempt to sell the trademarks themselves." *Id.* at 1325. Similarly, in *Intermatic Inc. v. Toeppen*, 947 F.Supp. 1227 (N.D.Ill.1996), the court found that "Toeppen's intention to arbitrage the 'intermatic.com' domain name constituted a commercial use." *Id.* at 1239 . . . .

However, in this case, there is no evidence that Kremer was trying to sell the domain name itself. The letter delivered by Kremer to Bosley's headquarters is a threat to expose negative information about Bosley on the Internet, but it makes no reference whatsoever to ransoming Bosley's trademark or to Kremer's use of the mark as a domain name.

. . .

Bosley's third and final argument that it satisfied the commercial use requirement of the Lanham Act is that Kremer's use of Bosley's trademark was in connection with Bosley's goods and services. In other words, Kremer used the mark "in connection with goods and services" because he prevented users from obtaining the plaintiff's goods and services. See *People for the Ethical Treatment of Animals v. Doughney*, 263 F.3d 359 (4th Cir.2001) ("*PETA*"). In *PETA*, defendants created a site that promoted ideas antithetical to those of the PETA group. The Fourth Circuit held that the defendant's parody site, though not having a commercial purpose and not selling any goods or services, violated the Lanham Act because it "prevented users from obtaining or using PETA's goods or services." *Id.* at 365.

However, in *PETA*, the defendant's website "provided links to more than 30 commercial operations offering goods and services." *Id.* at 366. To the extent that the *PETA* court held that the Lanham Act's commercial use requirement is satisfied because the defendant's use of the plaintiff's mark as the domain name may deter customers from reaching the plaintiff's site itself, we respectfully disagree with that rationale. While it is true that www.BosleyMedical.com is not sponsored by Bosley Medical, it is just as true that it is *about* Bosley Medical. The *PETA* approach would place most critical, otherwise protected consumer commentary under the restrictions of the Lanham Act. Other courts have also rejected this theory as over-expansive. See *L.L. Bean, Inc. v. Drake Publishers, Inc.*, 811 F.2d 26, 33 (1st Cir.1987); see also *Ford Motor Co. v. 2600 Enters.*, 177 F.Supp.2d 661, 664 (E.D.Mich.2001).

The *PETA* court's reading of the Lanham Act would encompass almost all uses of a registered trademark, even when the mark is merely being used to identify the object of consumer criticism.[2] This broad view of the Lanham Act is supported by

---

[2] In fact, such a holding would suggest that any time a non-holder of a trademark uses the mark as his domain name, he would violate the Lanham Act. However, when Congress amended the Lanham Act to add the Anticybersquatting Consumer Protection Act, it lim-

neither the text of the statute nor the history of trademark laws in this country. "Trademark laws are intended to protect" consumers from purchasing the products of an infringer "under the mistaken assumption that they are buying a product produced or sponsored by [the trademark holder]." *Beneficial Corp. v. Beneficial Capital Corp.*, 529 F.Supp. 445, 450 (S.D.N.Y.1982). Limiting the Lanham Act to cases where a defendant is trying to profit from a plaintiff's trademark is consistent with the Supreme Court's view that "[a trademark's] function is simply to designate the goods as the product of a particular trader and to protect his good will against the sale of another's product as his." *United Drug Co. v. Theodore Rectanus Co.*, 248 U.S. 90, 97 (1918) . . . .

The Second Circuit held in *United We Stand America, Inc. v. United We Stand, America New York, Inc.*, 128 F.3d 86, 90 (2d Cir.1997), that the "use in connection with the sale of goods and services" requirement of the Lanham Act does not require any actual *sale* of goods and services. Thus, the appropriate inquiry is whether Kremer offers *competing* services to the public. Kremer is not Bosley's competitor; he is their critic. His use of the Bosley mark is not in connection with a sale of goods or services—it is in connection with the expression of his opinion *about* Bosley's goods and services.

The dangers that the Lanham Act was designed to address are simply not at issue in this case. The Lanham Act, expressly enacted to be applied in commercial contexts, does not prohibit all unauthorized uses of a trademark. Kremer's use of the Bosley Medical mark simply cannot mislead consumers into buying a competing product—no customer will mistakenly purchase a hair replacement service from Kremer under the belief that the service is being offered by Bosley. Neither is Kremer capitalizing on the good will Bosley has created in its mark. Any harm to Bosley arises not from a competitor's sale of a similar product under Bosley's mark, but from Kremer's criticism of their services. Bosley cannot use the Lanham Act either as a shield from Kremer's criticism, or as a sword to shut Kremer up.[3]

. . .

We affirm the district court's entry of summary judgment in favor of Kremer with respect to the infringement and dilution claims. . . .

Mark A. Lemley, *The Modern Lanham Act and the Death of Common Sense*
108 YALE L.J. 1687 (1999).

. . .

II. The Expanding Boundaries of Trademark Rights

Courts seem to be replacing the traditional rationale for trademark law with a conception of trademarks as property rights, in which trademark "owners" are

---

ited violations only to situations where a person registers the site with a bad faith intent to profit. To find a Lanham Act violation without finding commercial use may contradict Congress' intent.

[3] Because we hold that Kremer's use of Bosley's mark was noncommercial, we do not reach the issue of initial interest confusion which was addressed in *Interstellar Starship Services, Ltd. v. Epix, Inc.*, 304 F.3d 936 (9th Cir.2002).

given strong rights over the marks without much regard for the social costs of such rights. There appear to be three basic parts to this trend. First, we sometimes seem to be making trademark law for the extreme case, but we then apply that law to a large number of run-of-the-mill trademarks. Second, courts increasingly treat brands as things owned in their own right, rather than as advertising connected with a particular product. Finally, courts have not been sufficiently sensitive to legitimate free speech concerns in cases where trademark owners seek to restrict noncompetitive uses of the trademark.

A. Making Law for the Extreme Case

In a number of recent instances, trademark law has been expanded quite significantly by means of new legal rules that make sense in a limited number of cases, but that then enter widespread use where they make less sense. The tendency is perhaps a natural one. If Congress creates a new statute that protects some but not all trademark owners, every trademark owner will want his or her mark to be included in the new group and will seek to receive the added protections of the new rule. If courts are not careful to restrain the new doctrine, it will soon take on a life of its own. I call this the problem of "doctrinal creep."

1. Dilution

The most obvious example of doctrinal creep in trademark law is dilution. Dilution laws are directed against the possibility that the unique nature of a mark will be destroyed by companies who trade on the renown of the mark by selling unrelated goods, such as Kodak pianos or Buick aspirin. But because consumers need not be confused for dilution to occur, dilution laws represent a fundamental shift in the nature of trademark protection.

Dilution laws are largely a product of the last fifty years. Approximately half of the states now have dilution statutes. But most recent attention has been focused on the federal dilution statute, which was added in 1995. The federal statute, like most state dilution statutes, protects only "famous" marks. The statute offers a nonexclusive list of eight factors for courts to consider in determining whether a mark is "distinctive and famous." The clear intention seems to have been to restrict dilution doctrine to a relatively small class of nationally known trademarks whose fame is sufficiently great that the risk of blurring by multiple noncompeting uses is significant. But courts applying the state and federal dilution statutes have been quite willing to conclude that a local favorite, or a rather obscure company, is "famous" within the meaning of the Act. Thus, marks such as Intermatic, Gazette, Dennison, Nailtiques, TeleTech, Wedgewood (for new homes, not china), Papal Visit 1999, and Wawa have been declared famous. Worse, many courts seem willing to find dilution without even inquiring into the fame of the mark. Dilution doctrine has also been expanded to encompass not only noncompeting but also nonidentical marks, to protect famous trade dress and product configurations, to attack longstanding uses of descriptive marks to describe products, to aid trademark owners in ordinary cases against competitive marks by dispensing with the need to demonstrate consumer confusion, and even to create a cause of action against consumers (or the press) who do not use marks properly. While the federal law is still relatively new, and so prediction is difficult, we may be moving toward a world in which "famous" marks protected even in the absence of consumer confusion are the rule rather than the exception. The result, as one commentator has noted, is to grant a "trademark in gross"—one unconnected to a particular product—to a wide variety of owners. . . .

3. Cybersquatters and Domain Names

Courts have also stretched trademark doctrine to accommodate the extreme case involving Internet domain names and "cybersquatters." Cybersquatters like Dennis Toeppen acted early to lock up a number of Internet domain names that reflect trademarks or corporate names, for a variety of possible purposes. Courts that have considered suits by trademark owners against cybersquatters have uniformly held that obtaining someone else's trademark as a domain name is either trademark infringement or dilution. In many cases, this is clearly the right result. If I register my competitor's name on the Internet, so that potential customers who enter that name will arrive at my site instead, I am clearly creating confusion in an attempt to profit commercially. In other cases, though, courts have had to stretch the "commercial use in commerce" requirement to the vanishing point in order to "catch" cybersquatters. Thus, courts have held that owning a domain name that you do not use is "use in commerce" if you hope to sell the domain name to the trademark owner. And several courts have even held that noncommercial use of a domain name is "commercial use in commerce," reasoning that *any* use on the Internet is automatically a use in commerce. This is in striking contrast to the meaning of the term in ordinary trademark cases.

Toeppen and Bucci are not particularly sympathetic defendants, and trademark or some other law *should* provide a cause of action against those who capture a domain name that clearly ought to belong to someone else in order to extort money from trademark owners. Still, there is something troubling about the erosion of the commercial use and use in commerce requirements. We may find that extending trademark protection to cover noncommercial uses of a mark, however compelling the instant case, sets a dangerous precedent for the law. Indeed, we need not look too far. The cybersquatter precedents are already being used by trademark owners to take domain names away from arguably legitimate users, such as people who want to register their last names as Internet domains and those who build a "gripe site" to complain about a specific product or company.

4. What's Going on Here?

. . .

. . . I think the modern dilution . . . cases take a good idea and stretch it too far. . . . [M]ost trademarks are not sufficiently well-known that their use on unrelated products would create even an association in the minds of consumers. Rather, these legal doctrines are being used to serve other purposes, ones that trademark theory does not support.[91] The explosion in product configuration cases in the last twenty years has a lot more to do with acquiring or extending de facto patent and copyright protection through a back door than with protecting consumers from confusion. And the insistence by seemingly every trademark owner that its marks must be thought famous is motivated less by genuine concerns about blurring than by a desire to "keep up with the Cokes" and get the benefit of the same property protection that truly famous marks now receive. One can understand why trademark owners want these things, of course, but we must look to the public interest, not private interests, to decide whether trademark owners should get them.[93]

. . .

III. Restoring Common Sense to Trademark Law

If I am right that trademark owners are obtaining property rights that trademark theory cannot justify, what should be done? For the most part, I believe the courts can handle this problem, if they are vigilant in relating the protection plaintiffs seek to the principles of trademark theory and rejecting claims that are not well-founded on trademark principles. We do not need new legal rules here; what we need is the principled and vigorous application of the old rules. Courts should ask, as [Professor Ralph] Brown does, exactly what new incentives do we need trademark law to create? How are consumers hurt by the conduct at issue? And what are the interests of society at large? Brown's answer to these questions still rings true today: "[T]he only interests in trade symbols worth protecting are those against loss of sales or loss of reputation."[142]

Courts should of course protect trademarks against uses that are likely to cause confusion, and against true cases of dilution. And they should be willing to recognize that trademarks can come in many forms, including product configuration, sounds, and colors. But they should resist the inevitable attempts by trademark owners to expand these categories without limit. In particular, they should recognize that the Lanham Act is not a general anti-copying statute—and indeed that not all copying of a competitor's product is bad.

Eradicating the property rationale for trademarks, and restoring common sense to the Lanham Act, will be hard work. The forces arrayed in favor of propertization

---

[91] Kratzke argues that dilution doctrine is misguided because it ignores consumer injury. William P. Kratzke, Normative Economic Analysis of Trademark Law, 21 Memphis St. U. L. Rev. 199, 285 (1991). He has a point: Dilution statutes do not commonly require proof of consumer confusion or an appropriate substitute. Properly conceived, however, I think dilution law is protecting consumers against a real harm: the loss of the informational value of a famous trademark through crowding.

[93] . . . For a delightful exposition of this critical fact, which seems to have gotten lost in the debate over trademark law, see Jessica Litman, *Breakfast with Batman: The Public Interest in the Advertising Age*, 108 Yale L.J. 1717, 1725, who notes: "There has been inexorable pressure to recognize as an axiom the principle that if something appears to have substantial value to someone, the law must and should protect it as property."

[142] Ralph S. Brown, Jr., *Advertising and the Public Interest: Legal Protection of Trade Symbols*, 57 Yale L.J. 1165, 1201 (1948), *reprinted in* 108 Yale L.J. 1619, 1621 (1999). . . .

are powerful indeed. And it is true, as Brown points out, that "the restraining influence of the courts is largely passive."[144] But the courts do have some tools available for this project. The federal dilution statute vests great discretion in the courts
in deciding whether a mark is famous. To date, courts have not imposed significant limitations on parties seeking to designate their marks as famous, but they
certainly could (and should) do so. . . . Taking the likelihood of confusion requirement, the fair use doctrine, and the doctrine of non-trademark use seriously will
also help prevent unwarranted expansion of trademark rights in ways unforeseen
by the drafters of the Lanham Act. Finally, the First Amendment stands (or should
stand) as a bulwark against the increasingly common effort to use trademark law
to suppress speech.

. . .

QUESTIONS FOR DISCUSSION

1. *Toeppen as a reseller.* The Internet Corporation for Assigned Names and Numbers
("ICANN") controls the market for registrars through the process of accreditation. (For a
description of ICANN and its function, *see* Chapter 1, Part II(F), *supra.*) Accredited registrars, however, are permitted to provide their services through unaccredited resellers so long
as the accredited registrar is listed in the TLD registry as the registrar of record. Why
shouldn't we construe Toeppen as such a reseller, albeit one with a limited stock of premium domain names? Looked at in this way, isn't Toeppen's business—like NSI's—
"connected only with the names' technical function on the Internet"?

2. *Commercial use.* In *Bird v. Parsons*, 289 F.3d 865 (6th Cir.2002), the court held that
neither a domain name registrar nor a third-party reseller of domain names makes commercial use of domain names. If Toeppen's use is commercial, why isn't use by a domain name
registrar or reseller?

3. *Surnames.* Is the registration of surnames as second-level domain names and the subsequent licensing of those domain names as e-mail addresses to people with the same surname a commercial use within the meaning of the Federal Trademark Dilution Act? *See
Avery Dennison Corporation v. Sumpton*, 189 F.3d 868 (9th Cir.1999), excerpted in Chapter 2, Part III, *supra.*

4. *Confusing trademarks with property?* The law of trademarks was developed to protect a company's good will, thereby creating an incentive for companies to invest in promoting and improving their products for the benefit of the public. It was a tort-like doctrine
springing from the tort of unfair competition. Do you agree with Professor Lemley that
trademark law as it is being applied to domain names has lost touch with its original purpose? Does the current development of trademark dilution doctrine online serve the public
interest or is it a windfall to large corporate interests? How could laws designed to protect
against unfair competitive practices be construed as conferring property rights?

5. *Sale of domain names.* Take a look at www.greatdomains.com, "a Verisign Company," where exchange of domain names is flourishing. Examples: On June 24, 2002, Pass-
over.com was listed for $90,000, and DowQuotes.com was listed for $60,000. Are these
proprietors doing anything illegal? If not, should the law be changed to make what they are
doing illegal?

6. *Domain name entrepreneurs in a market economy.* We live in a society that generally

---

[144] *Id.* at 1206.

employs free markets to allocate efficiently the goods and services that our country produces. Entrepreneurial initiative and vision are generally rewarded with wealth and prestige. Is it then a bit odd that the domain name entrepreneurs have been vilified as "cybersquatters"? These entrepreneurs took some risks: they paid registration fees when the future development of Internet commerce was not yet assured. Why didn't our society permit a free market to develop in which each domain name would end up in the hands of the person or company who could put it to its highest and best use, trademark owner or not?

II. THE ANTICYBERSQUATTING CONSUMER PROTECTION ACT

Trademark infringement and dilution remain important as legal theories under which trademark owners assert rights to a domain name registered to someone else. For the trademark owner to prevail on an infringement theory, use in commerce and consumer confusion must be shown, and in some cases, these are hurdles the trademark owner might not be able to clear. For example, one who registers a domain name desired by a trademark owner but does not offer it for sale to the owner or otherwise use it in any way will likely escape liability, even if the domain name is identical or similar to the trademark. While a dilution claim does not require a showing of consumer confusion, such claims are only available to those trademark owners who can convince a court that their marks are "famous." As one scholar has commented:

> In the author's opinion, there is a very poor fit between the actions of a cybersquatter and the federal Anti-dilution Act. The prototypical cybersquatter does not use the reserved domain name as its mark before the public, so there is no traditional dilution by blurring or tarnishment. Thus, the courts have had to create a wholly new category of "dilution" in order to find a legal weapon to combat this new and different form of reprehensible commercial activity. But this legal tool only protects "famous" marks, requiring that the courts expand and devalue the category of "famous" marks in order to combat cybersquatting.

4 J. THOMAS MCCARTHY, MCCARTHY ON TRADEMARKS AND UNFAIR COMPETITION § 25:77 (4th ed.2002).

To address these problems the Congress enacted the Anticybersquatting Consumer Protection Act ("ACPA"), Pub. L. No. 106–113 (1999). While the Act codifies much of the pre–2000 caselaw, it also introduces a number of significant innovations. For example, it makes actionable the bad faith registration of a domain name that is identical or confusingly similar to another's trademark. It limits such liability, however, to domain name registrants, codifying a domain name registrar's freedom from liability established in the *Lockheed Martin* case. *See* 15 U.S.C. §§ 1125(d)(1) and 1114(D)(iii). The Act also creates an *in rem* action against offending domain names—an important new option for trademark owners when federal courts do not have *in personam* jurisdiction over the domain name registrant. *See id.* § 1125(d)(2). Yet another innovation is a provision allowing the trademark owner to elect statutory damages in lieu of actual damages. *See id.* §§ 1117(d). These damages can be as large as $100,000 per registered domain name. The Act also creates a cause of action against registrants who register the non-trademarked names of others without their consent with intent to profit by resale. *See id.* § 1129.

In the remainder of this Part, we first consider the overview of the Act provided in the report of the United States Senate that accompanied the legislation. We then look at three cases involving, respectively, an *in personam* action against a domain name registrant, an *in rem* action against a domain name, and an action against a cybersquatter in which statutory damages are elected. While the Act clearly grants immunity to domain name registrars for acts of selling another's trademark as a domain name, it is significantly less clear whether the Act creates a statutory framework that adequately addresses the public's right to make noncommercial uses of words and names that are identical or confusingly similar to another's trademark. It also remains to be seen how the threshold requirement that registration be with "bad faith intent to profit" will be interpreted and applied.

Senate Report 106–140
The Anticybersquatting Consumer Protection Act (1999).

The practice of cybersquatting harms consumers, electronic commerce, and the goodwill equity of valuable U.S. brand names, upon which consumers increasingly rely to locate the true source of genuine goods and services on the Internet. Online consumers have a difficult time distinguishing a genuine site from a pirate site, given that often the only indications of source and authenticity of the site, or the goods and services made available thereon, are the graphical interface on the site itself and the Internet address at which it resides. As a result, consumers have come to rely heavily on familiar brand names when engaging in online commerce. But if someone is operating a website under another brand owner's trademark, such as a site called "cocacola.com" or "levis.com," consumers bear a significant risk of being deceived and defrauded, or at a minimum, confused. The costs associated with these risks are increasingly burdensome as more people begin selling pharmaceuticals, financial services, and even groceries over the Internet. Regardless of what is being sold, the result of online brand name abuse, as with other forms of trademark violations, is the erosion of consumer confidence in brand name identifiers and in electronic commerce generally.

Cybersquatters target distinctive marks for a variety of reasons. Some register well-known brand names as Internet domain names in order to extract payment from the rightful owners of the marks, who find their trademarks "locked up" and are forced to pay for the right to engage in electronic commerce under their own brand name. For example, . . . the Committee . . . heard testimony that Warner Bros. was reportedly asked to pay $350,000 for the rights to the names "warner-records. com", "warner-bros-records.com", "warner-pictures.com", "warner-bros-pictures", and "warnerpictures.com".

Others register well-known marks as domain names and warehouse those marks with the hope of selling them to the highest bidder, whether it be the trademark owner or someone else. For example, . . . the Committee . . . heard testimony regarding a similarly enterprising cybersquatter whose partial inventory of domain names—the listing of which was limited by the fact that Network Solutions will only display the first 50 records of a given registrant—includes names such as Coca–Cola, Pepsi, Burger King, KFC, McDonalds, Subway, Taco Bell, Wendy's, BMW, Chrysler, Dodge, General Motors, Honda, Hyundai, Jaguar, Mazda, Mercedes, Nissan, Porsche, Rolls–Royce, Saab, Saturn, Toyota, and Volvo, all of which are available to the highest bidder through an online offer sheet.

In addition, cybersquatters often register well-known marks to prey on consumer confusion by misusing the domain name to divert customers from the mark owner's site to the cybersquatter's own site, many of which are pornography sites that derive advertising revenue based on the number of visits, or "hits," the site receives. For example, the Committee was informed of a parent whose child mistakenly typed in the domain name for "dosney.com," expecting to access the family-oriented content of the Walt Disney home page, only to end up staring at a screen of hardcore pornography because a cybersquatter had registered that domain name in anticipation that consumers would make that exact mistake. Other instances of diverting unsuspecting consumers to pornographic websites involve malicious attempts to tarnish a trademark owner's mark or to extort money from the trademark owner, such as the case where a cybersquatter placed pornographic images of celebrities on a site under the name "pentium3.com" and announced that it would sell the domain name to the highest bidder. Others attempt to divert unsuspecting consumers to their sites in order to engage in unfair competition. For example, the business operating under the domain name "disneytransportation.com" greets online consumers at its site with a picture of Mickey Mouse and offers shuttle services in the Orlando area and reservations at Disney hotels, although the company is in no way affiliated with the Walt Disney Company and such fact is not clearly indicated on the site. Similarly, the domain name address "wwwcarpoint.com," without a period following "www", was used by a cybersquatter to offer a competing service to Microsoft's popular Carpoint car buying service.

Finally, and most importantly, cybersquatters target distinctive marks to defraud consumers, including to engage in counterfeiting activities. For example, the Committee heard testimony regarding a cybersquatter who registered the domain names "attphonecard.com" and "attcallingcard.com" and used those names to establish sites purporting to sell calling cards and soliciting personally identifying information, including credit card numbers. . . . Of even greater concern was the example of an online drug store selling pharmaceuticals under the name "propeciasales.com" without any way for online consumers to tell whether what they are buying is a legitimate product, a placebo, or a dangerous counterfeit.

The need for legislation banning cybersquatting

Current law does not expressly prohibit the act of cybersquatting. The World Intellectual Property Organization (WIPO) has identified cybersquatting as a global problem and recognized in its report on the domain name process that, "[f]amous and well-known marks have been the special target of a variety of predatory and parasitical practices on the Internet."[10] . . .

Instances of cybersquatting continue to grow each year because there is no clear deterrent and little incentive for cybersquatters to discontinue their abusive practices. While the Federal Trademark Dilution Act has been useful in pursuing cybersquatters, cybersquatters have become increasingly sophisticated as the case

---

[10] World Intellectual Property Organization, Management of Internet Names and Addresses: Intellectual Property Issues 8 (1999).

law has developed and now take the necessary precautions to insulate themselves from liability. For example, many cybersquatters are now careful to no longer offer the domain name for sale in any manner that could implicate liability under existing trademark dilution case law. And, in cases of warehousing and trafficking in domain names, courts have sometimes declined to provide assistance to trademark holders, leaving them without adequate and effective judicial remedies. This uncertainty as to the trademark law's application to the Internet has produced inconsistent judicial decisions and created extensive monitoring obligations, unnecessary legal costs, and uncertainty for consumers and trademark owners alike.

In cases where a trademark owner can sue, the sheer number of domain name infringements, the costs associated with hundreds of litigation matters, and the difficulty of obtaining damages in standard trademark infringement and dilution actions are significant obstacles for legitimate trademark holders. Frequently, these obstacles lead trademark owners to simply "pay off" cybersquatters, in exchange for the domain name registration, rather than seek to enforce their rights in court.

. . .

Under the bill, as amended, the abusive conduct that is made actionable is appropriately limited just to bad-faith registrations and uses of others' marks by persons who seek to profit unfairly from the goodwill associated therewith. . . .

The Committee intends the prohibited "use" of a domain name to describe the use of a domain name by the domain name registrant, with the bad-faith intent to profit from the goodwill of the mark of another. The concept of "use" does not extend to uses of the domain name made by those other than the domain name registrant, such as the person who includes the domain name as a hypertext link on a web page or as part of a directory of Internet addresses.

In addition, the bill, as amended, balances the property interests of trademark owners with the interests of Internet users who would make fair use of others' marks or otherwise engage in protected speech online. First, the bill sets forth a number of balancing factors that a court may wish to consider in deciding whether the requisite bad-faith intent is present in any given case. . . . [Codified at 15 U.S.C. § 1125(d)(1)(B)(i)(I)–(IX)], [e]ach of these factors reflect indicators that, in practice, commonly suggest bad-faith intent or a lack thereof in cybersquatting cases. . . .

Second, the amended bill underscores the bad-faith requirement by requiring a court to remit statutory damages in any case where a defendant believed, and the court finds that the defendant had reasonable grounds to believe, that the registration or use of the domain name was a fair or otherwise lawful use. In addition, the bill makes clear that the newly created statutory damages shall apply only with respect to bad-faith conduct occurring on or after the date of enactment of the bill.

Definition of "domain name"

The bill, as amended, provides a narrow definition of the term "domain name" in order to tailor the bill's reach narrowly to the problem sought to be addressed. Thus, the term "domain name" describes any alphanumeric designation which is registered with or assigned by any domain name registrar, domain name registry, or other domain name registration authority as part of an electronic address on the Internet. This definition essentially covers the second-level domain names assigned by domain name registration authorities (i.e., the name located immediately to the left of the ".com," ".net", ".edu," and ".org" generic top level domains), but is technology neutral enough to accommodate names other than second-level domains that are actually registered with domain name registration authorities, as may be the case should Internet domain name registrars begin to issue third or fourth level domains. The limited nature of the definition is important in that it excludes such things as screen names, file names, and other identifiers not assigned by a domain name registrar or registry, which have little to do with cybersquatting in practice.

In rem jurisdiction

As amended, the bill provides for in rem jurisdiction, which allows a mark owner to seek the forfeiture, cancellation, or transfer of an infringing domain name by filing an in rem action against the name itself, provided the domain name itself violates substantive Federal trademark law, where the mark owner has satisfied the court that it has exercised due diligence in trying to locate the owner of the domain name but is unable to do so. A significant problem faced by trademark owners in the fight against cybersquatting is the fact that many cybersquatters register domain names under aliases or otherwise provide false information in their registration applications in order to avoid identification and service of process by the mark owner. The bill, as amended, will alleviate this difficulty, while protecting the notions of fair play and substantial justice, by enabling a mark owner to seek an injunction against the infringing property in those cases where, after due diligence, a mark owner is unable to proceed against the domain name registrant because the registrant has provided false contact information and is otherwise not to be found.

Additionally, some have suggested that dissidents and others who are online incognito for legitimate reasons might give false information to protect themselves and have suggested the need to preserve a degree of anonymity on the Internet particularly for this reason. Allowing a trademark owner to proceed against the domain names themselves, provided they are, in fact, infringing or diluting under the Trademark Act, decreases the need for trademark owners to join the hunt to chase down and root out these dissidents or others seeking anonymity on the Net. The approach in the amended bill is a good compromise, which provides meaningful protection to trademark owners while balancing the interests of privacy and anonymity on the Internet.

Encouraging cooperation and fairness in the effort to combat cybersquatting

Like the underlying bill, the substitute amendment encourages domain name registrars and registries to work with trademark owners to prevent cybersquatting by providing a limited exemption from monetary damages for domain name registrars and registries that suspend, cancel, or transfer domain names pursuant to a court order or in the implementation of a reasonable policy prohibiting the registration of infringing domain names. The amended bill goes further, however, in

order to protect the rights of domain name registrants against overreaching trademark owners. Under the amended bill, a trademark owner who knowingly and
materially misrepresents to the domain name registrar or registry that a domain
name is infringing is liable to the domain name registrant for damages, including
costs and attorneys' fees, resulting from the suspension, cancellation, or transfer of
the domain name. In addition, the court may award injunctive relief to the domain
name registrant by ordering the reactivation of the domain name or the transfer of
the domain name back to the domain name registrant. The bill, as amended, also
promotes the continued ease and efficiency users of the current registration system
enjoy by codifying current case law limiting the secondary liability of domain
name registrars and registries for the act of registration of a domain name.[11]

Preservation of first amendment rights and trademark defenses

Finally, the substitute amendment includes an explicit savings clause making
clear that the bill does not affect traditional trademark defenses, such as fair use, or
a person's first amendment rights, and it ensures that any new remedies created by
the bill will apply prospectively only.

In summary, the legislation is a balanced approach to protecting the legitimate
interests of businesses, Internet users, e-commerce, and consumers.

. . .

Sporty's Farm L.L.C. v. Sportsman's Market, Inc.
202 F.3d 489 (2d Cir.2000).

■ CALABRESI, CIRCUIT JUDGE:

This case originally involved the application of the Federal Trademark Dilution
Act ("FTDA") to the Internet. *See* Federal Trademark Dilution Act of 1995, Pub.L.
No. 104–98, 109 Stat. 985 (codified at 15 U.S.C. §§ 1125, 1127 (Supp.1996)). While
the case was pending on appeal, however, the Anticybersquatting Consumer Protection Act ("ACPA"), Pub.L. No. 106–113 (1999), *see* H.R.Rep. No. 106–479 (Nov.
18, 1999), was passed and signed into law. That new law applies to this case.

BACKGROUND

I

. . .

Over the last few years, the commercial side of the Internet has grown rapidly.
Web pages are now used by companies to provide information about their products in a much more detailed fashion than can be done through a standard adver-

---

[11] *See Panavision Int'l v. Toeppen*, 141 F.3d 1316, 1319 (9th Cir.1998) (holding that NSI is
not responsible for making "a determination about registrant's right to use a domain
name."); *Lockheed Martin Corporation v. Networks Solutions, Inc.*, 985 F.Supp. 949 (C.D.Ca.1997)
(holding registrar not liable); *Academy of Motion Picture Arts and Science v. Network Solutions,
Inc.*, 989 F.Supp. 1276, (C.D.Ca.1997) (holding that holder of registered trademarks could not
obtain a preliminary injunction against domain name registrar).

tisement. Moreover, many consumers and businesses now order goods and ser-vices directly from company web pages. Given that Internet sales are paperless and have lower transaction costs than other types of retail sales, the commercial potential of this technology is vast.

For consumers to buy things or gather information on the Internet, they need an easy way to find particular companies or brand names. The most common method of locating an unknown domain name is simply to type in the company name or logo with the suffix .com. If this proves unsuccessful, then Internet users turn to a device called a search engine. A search engine will find all web pages on the Internet with a particular word or phrase. Given the current state of search en-gine technology, that search will often produce a list of hundreds of websites through which the user must sort in order to find what he or she is looking for. As a result, companies strongly prefer that their domain name be comprised of the company or brand trademark and the suffix .com. *See* H.R.Rep. No. 106–412, at 5 (1999).

Until recently, domain names with the .com top level domain could only be ob-tained from Network Solutions, Inc. ("NSI"). Now other registrars may also assign them. But all these registrars grant such names primarily on a first-come, first-served basis upon payment of a small registration fee. They do not generally inquire into whether a given domain name request matches a trademark held by someone other than the person requesting the name. *See id.*

Due to the lack of any regulatory control over domain name registration, an Internet phenomenon known as "cybersquatting" has become increasingly com-mon in recent years. *See, e.g.,* Panavision Int'l, L.P. v. Toeppen, 141 F.3d 1316 (9th Cir.1998). Cybersquatting involves the registration as domain names of well-known trademarks by non-trademark holders who then try to sell the names back to the trademark owners. Since domain name registrars do not check to see whether a domain name request is related to existing trademarks, it has been sim-ple and inexpensive for any person to register as domain names the marks of es-tablished companies. This prevents use of the domain name by the mark owners, who not infrequently have been willing to pay "ransom" in order to get "their names" back. *See* H.R.Rep. No. 106–412, at 5–7; S.Rep. No. 106–140, at 4–7 (1999).

II

Sportsman's is a mail order catalog company that is quite well-known among pilots and aviation enthusiasts for selling products tailored to their needs. In recent years, Sportsman's has expanded its catalog business well beyond the aviation market into that for tools and home accessories. The company annually distributes approximately 18 million catalogs nationwide, and has yearly revenues of about $50 million. Aviation sales account for about 60% of Sportsman's revenue, while non-aviation sales comprise the remaining 40%.

In the 1960s, Sportsman's began using the logo "*sporty*" to identify its catalogs and products. In 1985, Sportsman's registered the trademark *sporty's* with the United States Patent and Trademark Office. Since then, Sportsman's has complied with all statutory requirements to preserve its interest in the *sporty's* mark. *Sporty's* appears on the cover of all Sportsman's catalogs; Sportsman's international toll free number is 1–800–4*sportys;* and one of Sportsman's domestic toll free phone numbers is 1–800–*Sportys.* Sportsman's spends about $10 million per year advertising its *sporty's* logo.

Omega is a mail order catalog company that sells mainly scientific process measurement and control instruments. In late 1994 or early 1995, the owners of Omega, Arthur and Betty Hollander, decided to enter the aviation catalog business and, for that purpose, formed a wholly-owned subsidiary called Pilot's Depot, LLC ("Pilot's Depot"). Shortly thereafter, Omega registered the domain name sportys.com with NSI. Arthur Hollander was a pilot who received Sportsman's catalogs and thus was aware of the *sporty's* trademark.

In January 1996, nine months after registering sportys.com, Omega formed another wholly-owned subsidiary called Sporty's Farm and sold it the rights to sportys.com for $16,200. Sporty's Farm grows and sells Christmas trees, and soon began advertising its Christmas trees on a sportys.com web page. When asked how the name Sporty's Farm was selected for Omega's Christmas tree subsidiary, Ralph S. Michael, the CEO of Omega and manager of Sporty's Farm, explained, as summarized by the district court, that

> in his own mind and among his family, he always thought of and referred to the Pennsylvania land where Sporty's Farm now operates as *Spotty's farm.* The origin of the name . . . derived from a childhood memory he had of his uncle's farm in upstate New York. As a youngster, Michael owned a dog named Spotty. Because the dog strayed, his uncle took him to his upstate farm. Michael thereafter referred to the farm as Spotty's farm. The name Sporty's Farm was . . . a subsequent derivation.

(emphasis added). There is, however, no evidence in the record that Hollander was considering starting a Christmas tree business when he registered sportys.com or that Hollander was ever acquainted with Michael's dog Spotty.

In March 1996, Sportsman's discovered that Omega had registered sportys.com as a domain name. Thereafter, and before Sportsman's could take any action, Sporty's Farm brought this declaratory action seeking the right to continue its use of sportys.com. Sportsman's counterclaimed and also sued Omega as a third-party defendant for, *inter alia,* (1) trademark infringement, (2) trademark dilution pursuant to the FTDA, and (3) unfair competition under state law. Both sides sought injunctive relief to force the other to relinquish its claims to sportys.com. While this litigation was ongoing, Sportsman's used "sportys-catalogs.com" as its primary domain name.

After a bench trial, the court rejected Sportsman's trademark infringement claim and all related claims that are based on a "likelihood of [consumer] confusion" since "the parties operate wholly unrelated businesses [and t]herefore, confusion in the marketplace is not likely to develop." *Id.* at 282–83. But on Sportsman's trademark dilution action, where a likelihood of confusion was not necessary, the district court found for Sportsman's. . . . The court also held, however, that Sportsman's could only get injunctive relief and was not entitled to "punitive damages . . . profits, and attorney's fees and costs" pursuant to the FTDA since

Sporty Farm and Omega's conduct did not constitute willful dilution under the FTDA. *Id.* at 292–93.

Finally, the district court ruled that, although Sporty's Farm had violated the FTDA, its conduct did not constitute a violation of CUTPA [the Connecticut Unfair Trade Practices Act]. . . .

The district court then issued an injunction forcing Sporty's Farm to relinquish all rights to sportys.com. And Sportsman's subsequently acquired the domain name. Both Sporty's Farm and Sportsman's appeal. Specifically, Sporty's Farm appeals the judgment insofar as the district court granted an injunction in favor of Sportsman's for the use of the domain name. Sportsman's, on the other hand, in addition to urging this court to affirm the district court's injunction, cross-appeals, quite correctly as a procedural matter, the district court's denial of damages under both the FTDA and CUPTA. . . .

III

As we noted above, while this appeal was pending, Congress passed the ACPA. That law was passed "to protect consumers and American businesses, to promote the growth of online commerce, and to provide clarity in the law for trademark owners by prohibiting the bad-faith and abusive registration of distinctive marks as Internet domain names with the intent to profit from the goodwill associated with such marks–a practice commonly referred to as 'cybersquatting'." S.Rep. No. 106–140, at 4. In particular, Congress viewed the legal remedies available for victims of cybersquatting before the passage of the ACPA as "expensive and uncertain." H.R.Rep. No. 106–412, at 6. . . . In short, the ACPA was passed to remedy the perceived shortcomings of applying the FTDA in cybersquatting cases such as this one.

The new act accordingly amends the Trademark Act of 1946, creating a specific federal remedy for cybersquatting. New 15 U.S.C. § 1125(d)(1)(A) reads:

A person shall be liable in a civil action by the owner of a mark, including a personal name which is protected as a mark under this section, if, without regard to the goods or services of the parties, that person–

> (i)   has a bad faith intent to profit from that mark, including a personal name which is protected as a mark under this section; and
>
> (ii)   registers, traffics in, or uses a domain name that–
>
> > (I)   in the case of a mark that is distinctive at the time of registration of the domain name, is identical or confusingly similar to that mark;
> >
> > (II)   in the case of a famous mark that is famous at the time of registration of the domain name, is identical or confusingly similar to or dilutive of that mark; . . .

The Act further provides that "a court may order the forfeiture or cancellation of the domain name or the transfer of the domain name to the owner of the mark," 15 U.S.C. § 1125(d)(1)(C), if the domain name was "registered before, on, or after the date of the enactment of this Act," Pub.L. No. 106–113, § 3010. It also provides that damages can be awarded for violations of the Act, but that they are not "available with respect to the registration, trafficking, or use of a domain name that occurs before the date of the enactment of this Act." *Id.*

DISCUSSION

This case has three distinct features that are worth noting before we proceed further. First, our opinion appears to be the first interpretation of the ACPA at the appellate level. Second, we are asked to undertake the interpretation of this new statute even though the district court made its ruling based on the FTDA. Third, the case before us presents a factual situation that, as far as we can tell, is rare if not unique: A Competitor X of Company Y has registered Y's trademark as a domain name and then transferred that name to Subsidiary Z, which operates a business wholly unrelated to Y. These unusual features counsel that we decide no more than is absolutely necessary to resolve the case before us.

A. Application of the ACPA to this Case

The first issue before us is whether the ACPA governs this case. The district court based its holding on the FTDA since the ACPA had not been passed when it made its decision. Because the ACPA became law while this case was pending before us, we must decide how its passage affects this case. As a general rule, we apply the law that exists at the time of the appeal. *See, e.g., Hamm v. City of Rock Hill*, 379 U.S. 306, 312–13 (1964) (" '[I]f subsequent to the judgment and before the decision of the appellate court, a law intervenes and positively changes the rule which governs, the law must be obeyed, or its obligation denied.' " (quoting *United States v. Schooner Peggy*, 5 U.S. (1 Cranch) 103, 110 (1801))).

But even if a new law controls, the question remains whether in such circumstances it is more appropriate for the appellate court to apply it directly or, instead, to remand to the district court to enable that court to consider the effect of the new law. We therefore asked for additional briefing from the parties regarding the applicability of the ACPA to the case before us. After receiving those briefs and fully considering the arguments there made, we think it is clear that the new law was adopted specifically to provide courts with a preferable alternative to stretching federal dilution law when dealing with cybersquatting cases. Indeed, the new law constitutes a particularly good fit with this case. Moreover, the findings of the district court, together with the rest of the record, enable us to apply the new law to the case before us without difficulty. Accordingly, we will do so and forego a remand.

B. "Distinctive" or "Famous"

Under the new Act, we must first determine whether *sporty's* is a distinctive or famous mark and thus entitled to the ACPA's protection. *See* 15 U.S.C. § 1125(d)(1)(A)(ii)(I), (II). The district court concluded that *sporty's* is both distinctive and famous. We agree that *sporty's* is a "distinctive" mark. As a result, and without casting any doubt on the district court's holding in this respect, we need not, and hence do not, decide whether *sporty's* is also a "famous" mark.

Distinctiveness refers to inherent qualities of a mark and is a completely different concept from fame. A mark may be distinctive before it has been used—when its fame is nonexistent. By the same token, even a famous mark may be so ordinary, or descriptive as to be notable for its lack of distinctiveness. *See Nabisco, Inc. v. PF Brands, Inc.*, 191 F.3d 208, 215–26 (2d Cir.1999). We have no doubt that *sporty's*, as used in connection with Sportsman's catalogue of merchandise and advertising, is inherently distinctive. Furthermore, Sportsman's filed an affidavit under 15 U.S.C. § 1065 that rendered its registration of the *sporty's* mark incontestable, which entitles Sportsman's "to a presumption that its registered trademark is inherently distinctive." *Equine Technologies, Inc. v. Equitechnology, Inc.*, 68 F.3d 542, 545 (1st Cir.1995). We therefore conclude that, for the purposes of § 1125(d)(1)(A)(ii)(I), the *sporty's* mark is distinctive.

C. "Identical and Confusingly Similar"

The next question is whether domain name sportys.com is "identical or confusingly similar to" the *sporty's* mark.[11] 15 U.S.C. § 1125(d)(1)(A)(ii)(I). . . . [A]postrophes cannot be used in domain names. . . . As a result, the secondary domain name in this case (sportys) is indistinguishable from the Sportsman's trademark (*sporty's*). *Cf. Brookfield Communications, Inc. v. West Coast Entertainment Corp.*, 174 F.3d 1036, 1055 (9th Cir.1999) (observing that the differences between the mark "MovieBuff" and the domain name "moviebuff.com" are "inconsequential in light of the fact that Web addresses are not caps-sensitive and that the '.com' top-level domain signifies the site's commercial nature"). We therefore conclude that, although the domain name sportys.com is not precisely identical to the *sporty's* mark, it is certainly "confusingly similar" to the protected mark under § 1125(d)(1)(A)(ii)(I). *Cf. Wella Corp. v. Wella Graphics, Inc.*, 874 F.Supp. 54, 56 (E.D.N.Y.1994) (finding the new mark "Wello" confusingly similar to the trademark "Wella").

D. "Bad Faith Intent to Profit"

We next turn to the issue of whether Sporty's Farm acted with a "bad faith intent to profit" from the mark *sporty's* when it registered the domain name sportys.com. 15 U.S.C. § 1125(d)(1)(A)(i). The statute lists nine factors to assist courts in determining when a defendant has acted with a bad faith intent to profit from the use of a mark. But we are not limited to considering just the listed factors when making our determination of whether the statutory criterion has been met. The factors are, instead, expressly described as indicia that "may" be considered along with other facts. *Id.* § 1125(d)(1)(B)(i).

We hold that there is more than enough evidence in the record below of "bad faith intent to profit" on the part of Sporty's Farm (as that term is defined in the statute), so that "no reasonable factfinder could return a verdict against" Sportsman's. *Norville v. Staten Island Univ. Hosp.*, 196 F.3d 89, 95 (2d Cir.1999). First, it is clear that neither Sporty's Farm nor Omega had any intellectual property rights in

---

[11] We note that "confusingly similar" is a different standard from the "likelihood of confusion" standard for trademark infringement adopted by this court in *Polaroid Corp. v. Polarad Electronics Corp.*, 287 F.2d 492 (2d Cir.1961). *See Wella Corp. v. Wella Graphics, Inc.*, 37 F.3d 46, 48 (2d Cir.1994).

sportys.com at the time Omega registered the domain name. *See id.* § 1125(d)(1)(B)(i)(I). Sporty's Farm was not formed until nine months after the domain name was registered, and it did not begin operations or obtain the domain name from Omega until after this lawsuit was filed. Second, the domain name does not consist of the legal name of the party that registered it, Omega. *See id.* § 1125(d)(1)(B)(i)(II). Moreover, although the domain name does include part of the name of Sporty's Farm, that entity did not exist at the time the domain name was registered.

The third factor, the prior use of the domain name in connection with the bona fide offering of any goods or services, also cuts against Sporty's Farm since it did not use the site until after this litigation began, undermining its claim that the offering of Christmas trees on the site was in good faith. *See id.* § 1125(d)(1)(B)(i)(III). Further weighing in favor of a conclusion that Sporty's Farm had the requisite statutory bad faith intent, as a matter of law, are the following: (1) Sporty's Farm does not claim that its use of the domain name was "noncommercial" or a "fair use of the mark," *see id.* § 1125(d)(1)(B)(i)(IV), (2) Omega sold the mark to Sporty's Farm under suspicious circumstances, *see Sporty's Farm v. Sportsman's Market*, No. 96CV0756 (D.Conn. Mar. 13, 1998) (describing the circumstances of the transfer of sportys.com); 15 U.S.C. § 1125(d)(1)(B)(i)(VI), and, (3) as we discussed above, the *sporty's* mark is undoubtedly distinctive, *see id.* § 1125(d)(1)(B)(i)(IX).

The most important grounds for our holding that Sporty's Farm acted with a bad faith intent, however, are the unique circumstances of this case, which do not fit neatly into the specific factors enumerated by Congress but may nevertheless be considered under the statute. We know from the record and from the district court's findings that Omega planned to enter into direct competition with Sportsman's in the pilot and aviation consumer market. As recipients of Sportsman's catalogs, Omega's owners, the Hollanders, were fully aware that *sporty's* was a very strong mark for consumers of those products. It cannot be doubted, as the court found below, that Omega registered sportys.com for the primary purpose of keeping Sportsman's from using that domain name. Several months later, and after this lawsuit was filed, Omega created another company in an unrelated business that received the name Sporty's Farm so that it could (1) use the sportys.com domain name in some commercial fashion, (2) keep the name away from Sportsman's, and (3) protect itself in the event that Sportsman's brought an infringement claim alleging that a "likelihood of confusion" had been created by Omega's version of cybersquatting. Finally, the explanation given for Sporty's Farm's desire to use the domain name, based on the existence of the dog Spotty, is more amusing than credible. Given these facts and the district court's grant of an equitable injunction under the FTDA, there is ample and overwhelming evidence that, as a matter of law, Sporty's Farm's acted with a "bad faith intent to profit" from the domain name sportys.com as those terms are used in the ACPA.[13] *See Luciano v. Olsten Corp.*, 110 F.3d 210, 214 (2d Cir.1997) (stating that, as a matter of law, judgment

---

[13] We expressly note that "bad faith intent to profit" are terms of art in the ACPA and hence should not necessarily be equated with "bad faith" in other contexts.

may be granted where "the evidence in favor of the movant is so overwhelming that 'reasonable and fair minded [persons] could not arrive at a verdict against [it].'" (quoting *Cruz v. Local Union No. 3*, 34 F.3d 1148, 1154 (2d Cir.1994) (alteration in original))).

E. Remedy

Based on the foregoing, we hold that under § 1125(d)(1)(A), Sporty's Farm violated Sportsman's statutory rights by its use of the sportys.com domain name.[14] The question that remains is what remedy is Sportsman's entitled to. The Act permits a court to "order the forfeiture or cancellation of the domain name or the transfer of the domain name to the owner of the mark," § 1125(d)(1)(C) for any "domain name [ ] registered before, on, or after the date of the enactment of [the] Act," Pub.L. No. 106–113, § 3010. That is precisely what the district court did here, albeit under the pre-existing law, when it directed a) Omega and Sporty's Farm to release their interest in sportys.com and to transfer the name to Sportsman's, and b) permanently enjoined those entities from taking any action to prevent and/or hinder Sportsman's from obtaining the domain name. That relief remains appropriate under the ACPA. We therefore affirm the district court's grant of injunctive relief.

We must also determine, however, if Sportsman's is entitled to damages either under the ACPA or pre-existing law. Under the ACPA, damages are unavailable to Sportsman's since sportys.com was registered and used by Sporty's Farm prior to the passage of the new law. *See id.* (stating that damages can be awarded for violations of the Act but that they are not "available with respect to the registration, trafficking, or use of a domain name that occurs before the date of the enactment of this Act.").

But Sportsman's might, nonetheless, be eligible for damages under the FTDA since there is nothing in the ACPA that precludes, in cybersquatting cases, the award of damages under any pre-existing law. *See* 15 U.S.C. § 1125(d)(3) (providing that any remedies created by the new act are "in addition to any other civil action or remedy otherwise applicable"). Under the FTDA, "[t]he owner of the famous mark shall be entitled only to injunctive relief unless the person against whom the injunction is sought *willfully* intended to trade on the owner's reputation or to cause dilution of the famous mark." *Id.* § 1125(c)(2) (emphasis added). Accordingly, where willful intent to dilute is demonstrated, the owner of the famous mark is—subject to the principles of equity—entitled to recover (1) damages (2) the dilutor's profits, and (3) costs. *See id.; see also id.* § 1117(a) (specifying remedies).

We conclude, however, that damages are not available to Sportsman's under the FTDA. The district court found that Sporty's Farm did not act willfully. We

---

[14] The statute provides that a party "shall be *liable* in a civil action by the owner of a mark" if it meets the statutory requirements. 15 U.S.C. § 1125(d)(1)(A) (emphasis added). Although the statute uses the term "liable," it does not follow that damages will be assessed. As we discuss below, damages can be awarded for violations of the Act but they are not "available with respect to the registration, trafficking, or use of a domain name that occurs [,as in this case,] before the date of the enactment of this Act." Pub.L. No. 106–113, § 3010.

review such findings of "willfulness" by a district court for clear error. *See Bambu Sales, Inc. v. Ozak Trading Inc.*, 58 F.3d 849, 854 (2d Cir.1995). Thus, even assuming the *sporty's* mark to be famous, we cannot say that the district court clearly erred when it found that Sporty's Farm's actions were not willful. To be sure, that question is a very close one, for the facts make clear that, as a Sportsman's customer, Arthur Hollander (Omega's owner) was aware of the significance of the *sporty's* logo. And the idea of creating a Christmas tree business named Sporty's Farm, allegedly in honor of Spotty the dog, and of giving that business the sportys.com domain name seems to have occurred to Omega only several months after it had registered the name. Nevertheless, given the uncertain state of the law at the time that Sporty's Farm and Omega acted, we cannot say that the district court clearly erred in finding that their behavior did not amount to willful dilution. It follows that Sportsman's is not entitled to damages under the FTDA.

Sportsman's also argues that it is entitled to damages under state law. Because neither the FTDA nor the ACPA preempts state remedies such as CUTPA, damages under Connecticut law are not barred, and hence may be available to Sportsman's. *See* H.R.Rep. No. 104–374, at 4 (1995), *reprinted in* 1996 U.S.C.C.A.N. 1029, 1031; 15 U.S.C. § 1125(d)(3). [The court concludes that damages are not available.]

In sum, then, we hold that the injunction issued by the district court was proper under the new anticybersquatting law, but that damages are not available to Sportsman's under the ACPA, the FTDA, or CUTPA.

F. Retroactivity

Sporty Farm's also contends that even if its actions would today violate the FTDA or the ACPA, any injunction requiring it to relinquish use of sportys.com is impermissibly retroactive. We find Sporty's Farm's position to be meritless. . . .

CONCLUSION

The judgment of the district court is AFFIRMED in all particulars.

Alitalia-Linee Aeree Italiane, S.p.A. v. Casinoalitalia.Com
128 F.Supp.2d 340 (E.D.Va.2001).

■ Ellis, District Judge.

In this trademark dispute, the plaintiff, an Italian airline, has sued both the foreign registrant of an allegedly infringing domain name *in personam* and the domain name itself *in rem*. At issue on plaintiff's summary judgment motion is whether, consistent with the Anticybersquatting Consumer Protection Act ("ACPA" or the "Act"), a mark owner may maintain *in personam* claims against a domain name registrant concurrently with an *in rem* claim against the domain name. Also presented is the related question whether the Virginia long-arm statute constitutionally reaches the foreign registrant.

I.

Plaintiff Alitalia–Linee Aeree Italiane S.p.A. ("Alitalia") is Italy's national airline and is in the business of providing air cargo service and passenger transportation between Italy and the United States, among other foreign countries. Alitalia is the owner of a United States Trademark Registration issued on March 21, 1995, for the mark "Alitalia." Alitalia's founders coined the term "Alitalia," which has been used by the airline since 1957, by combining the words "Ali," which in Italian means "wings," and "d'Italia," which means "Italian"; the term "Alitalia," therefore, literally means "Italian wings."

Since Alitalia began operation in 1957, the airline has made continuous and widespread use of the mark "Alitalia" through extensive advertising and other means by which the carrier promotes and sells its services. In this regard, Alitalia spends approximately $60 million per year in advertising and promoting the "Alitalia" logo and mark. In addition, Alitalia maintains a website for its airline business at <www.alitalia.it> and has registered the Internet domain names <www.alitalia.com> and <www.alitalia.net>. A search of the Internet for the word "alitalia," however, returns not only Alitalia's website, but also an Internet site using the domain name <casinoalitalia.com>, which has no affiliation or connection whatever to Alitalia.

Defendant Technologia JPR, Inc., ("JPR") has registered the domain name <casinoalitalia.com> with registrar Network Solutions, Inc., ("NSI"). JPR is an entity established under the laws of the Dominican Republic, and JPR's NSI registration information lists JPR's place of business (including administrative, technical, and billing contacts) as located in Santo Domingo, Dominican Republic. JPR conducts its business entirely outside of the United States, and the company has no offices or other physical presence in the United States; it neither owns nor leases property in the United States and has no employees in the United States. Alitalia claims that JPR registered the domain name on or about October 13, 1999, although it appears from NSI's registration information that JPR registered the domain name with NSI in August 1998.

It is evident from a visit to <casinoalitalia.com> that the website exists for the purpose of conducting the business of online casino gambling. A visitor to the website can play one or more online casino games—e.g., blackjack, poker, keno, slots, craps, and roulette—by opening an account with <casinoalitalia.com> and purchasing casino "credits" that may be used to play individual games. Players can then win credits that can be redeemed for U.S. currency. In this regard, the website appears to be an attempt to simulate the experience of gambling at a conventional "brick and mortar" casino.

A visit to the website also reveals that the term "Alitalia" appears on the first page. Given this, Alitalia, which has not given JPR permission to use the mark "Alitalia" or any variation thereof for any purpose, claims that the domain name <casinoalitalia.com> and JPR's unauthorized use of the term "alitalia" create a false impression that Alitalia promotes the business of online gambling and/or any other enterprise pursued by defendants. Indeed, Alitalia claims that the word "casino" means "brothel," so that a literal translation of "casinoalitalia" is "alitalia's brothel." Thus, argues Alitalia, the site appears in the minds of consumers familiar with the Italian language to offer the services of a brothel associated or affiliated with Alitalia. In this regard, plaintiff contends, the website <casinoalitalia.com>

irreparably harms, tarnishes, and dilutes the goodwill, reputation, and image of the Alitalia mark.

In March of this year, Alitalia brought a four-count complaint stating claims for (i) trademark infringement, under 15 U.S.C. § 1114 *et seq.*, against JPR (Count I); (ii) violation of the Lanham Act, 15 U.S.C. §§ 1125(a), (c), against JPR (Count II); (iii) common law unfair competition against JPR (Count III); and (iv) violation of the ACPA against JPR and <casinoalitalia.com> (Count IV). Alitalia has moved for summary judgment on all four counts. In doing so, Alitalia argues, remarkably, that the ACPA entitles it to proceed concurrently both *in rem* and *in personam*. Whether this is so presents a threshold question that must be resolved before proceeding to resolve the remaining questions of personal jurisdiction and summary judgment. JPR has entered a limited appearance for the purpose of challenging personal jurisdiction.[4]

II.

The ACPA creates two avenues by which claimants may seek a remedy for "cyberpiracy." The first, found in § 1 of the ACPA, is a remedy for owners of a mark *in personam* against a person who, with "a bad faith intent to profit from that mark[,] . . . registers, traffics in, or uses a domain name" that:

> (I) in the case of a mark that is distinctive at the time of registration of the domain name, is identical or confusingly similar to that mark;

> (II) in the case of a famous mark that is famous at the time of registration of the domain name, is identical or confusingly similar to or dilutive of that mark; or

> (III) is a trademark, work, or name protected by reason of § 706 of Title 18 or § 220506 of Title 36.

15 U.S.C. § 1125(d)(1)(A). A plaintiff proceeding under § 1 has available a full panoply of legal and equitable remedies. Specifically, such a plaintiff may seek compensatory damages, including disgorgement of defendant's profits, or elect to recover, "instead of actual damages and profits, an award of statutory damages in the amount of not less than $1,000 and not more than $100,000 per domain name, as the court considers just." 15 U.S.C. § 1117(a) and (d).[5] In addition, a § 1 plaintiff may seek injunctive relief, including "the forfeiture or cancellation of the domain name or the transfer of the domain name to the owner of the mark." 15 U.S.C. § 1125(d)(1)(C); *see Sporty's Farm LLC v. Sportsman's Market, Inc.*, 202 F.3d 489, 500 (2d Cir.2000).

---

[4] *See Caesars World, Inc. v. Caesars–Palace.Com*, 112 F.Supp.2d 505, 509 (E.D.Va.2000) (noting that "*in personam* jurisdiction cannot be based merely on an appearance in an *in rem* action"); *Harrods Ltd. v. Sixty Internet Domain Names*, 110 F.Supp.2d 420, 421–23 (E.D.Va.2000) (holding that "no personal jurisdiction over the owner of the res is acquired by bringing . . . [an *in rem*] action" under the ACPA, and a plaintiff "cannot pursue any cause of action with the potential to impose personal liability" simply by virtue of filing an ACPA *in rem* action).

[5] The damages awarded may be "for any sum above the amount found as actual damages, not exceeding three times such amount." 15 U.S.C. § 1117(a).

A mark owner's second avenue of relief is appropriately found in § 2 of the ACPA, which provides that, where a domain name infringes a federally registered trademark or violates any right of the mark's owner under the Lanham Act, "[t]he owner . . . may file an *in rem* civil action against a domain name in the judicial district in which the domain name registrar, domain name registry, or other domain name authority that registered or assigned the domain name is located." 15 U.S.C. § 1125(d)(2)(A). But importantly, a mark owner may file an *in rem* cause of action only where the court finds that the owner of the mark either (i) "is not able to obtain *in personam* jurisdiction over a person who would have been a defendant in a civil action under [Section 1]" ("Option I") or (ii) "through due diligence was not able to find a person who would have been a defendant in a civil action under [Section 1]" ("Option II").[6] *Id.* § 1125(d)(2)(A)(i)–(ii).

Thus, the ACPA limits a court's *in rem* jurisdiction over a domain name on a finding that Option I or II exists.[7] And further, as a precondition to using Option II, a mark owner is required to exercise due diligence in attempting to find a suitable defendant. *See id.* § 1125(d). This attempt must include (i) "a notice of the alleged violation and intent to proceed [*in rem*] to the registrant of the domain name at the postal and e-mail address provided by the registrant to the registrar," and (ii) "publish[ed] notice of the [*in rem*] action as the court may direct promptly after filing." *Id.* § 1125(d)(2)(A)(ii)(II). Only if the owner complies with these requirements *and* nonetheless fails to find a suitable defendant who may be sued *in personam* may the owner maintain an *in rem* action against the domain name. And significantly, the relief afforded in an ACPA *in rem* action is limited to "a court order for the forfeiture or cancellation of the domain name or the transfer of the domain name to the owner of a mark." *Id.* § 1125(d)(2)(D)(i).

These provisions, given their plain meaning, compel the conclusion that the ACPA provides mark owners with two mutually exclusive avenues for relief against putative infringers. A mark owner may proceed either *in personam* against an infringer or, in certain circumstances where this cannot be done, the owner may proceed *in rem* against the domain name; a mark owner may not proceed against

---

[6] For purposes of brevity, the term "suitable defendant" herein refers to Section 2's requirement that suit be brought against "a person who would have been a defendant in a civil action under [§ 1]" — i.e., a person who "registers, traffics in, or uses a domain name" in a way that violates the ACPA. 15 U.S.C. § 1125(d).

[7] The ACPA strangely provides that the owner of a mark may "file" an *in rem* action if the court makes a finding that the requirements of either Option I or Option II are met. 15 U.S.C. § 1125(d)(2)(A). This language suggests, nonsensically, that such a finding must precede the filing of the suit. It is evident, however, that a court cannot make such a finding *before* the *in rem* action is "filed," which ordinarily means the formality of filing a complaint with the Office of the Clerk and paying applicable filing fees. This is so because such a finding must occur within the confines of a controversy between real parties. . . . Thus, § 1125(d)(2)(A) must be interpreted to mean that a mark owner may *maintain* an *in rem* action against a domain name only if the court finds, after suit is filed, that the requirements of either Option I or Option II are met. *Cf. Caesars World*, 112 F.Supp.2d at 505 ("[T]o force plaintiff to prove its case before filing would stand the Act on its head.").

both at the same time.[9] This follows from the fact that the ACPA's plain language limits the use of *in rem* jurisdiction to two situations, labeled here as Options I and II, where there is no *in personam* jurisdiction over the domain name registrant. Option I allows a mark owner to proceed *in rem* only where the identity and location of the registrant or user of an infringing domain name are known, but *in personam* jurisdiction cannot be obtained over this entity. Option II deals with those situations where the registrant or user of the offending domain name cannot be found and thus simply adds that this jurisdiction may be resorted to only where an infringer cannot be identified or found. In other words, the ACPA provides for *in rem* jurisdiction against a domain name only in those circumstances where *in personam* jurisdiction is not available.[10]

Further confirmation for the conclusion that *in personam* and *in rem* jurisdictions under the ACPA are mutually exclusive is found in the different remedies available under each jurisdictional grant. Where there exists *in personam* jurisdiction over a putative infringer, a mark owner has available a full panoply of remedies, including damages and injunctive relief. *See* 15 U.S.C. § 1117(a), (d). Yet, the remedy available in the event a mark owner must proceed *in rem* is far more limited; it is restricted to the forfeiture or cancellation of the domain name or the domain name's transfer to the mark owner. *See id.* § 1125(d)(2)(D)(i).[11] Significantly, this *in rem* remedy is included in the broader set of remedies available to a plaintiff proceeding *in personam* against a putative infringer. *See id.* § 1125(d)(1)(C). In other words, where *in personam* jurisdiction exists, there is no need to proceed *in rem*, for

---

[9] Alitalia's argument to the contrary mistakenly relies on § 4 of the ACPA, which provides that "[t]he *in rem* jurisdiction established under [§ 2] shall be in addition to any other jurisdiction that otherwise exists, whether *in rem* or *in personam*." 15 U.S.C. § 1125(d)(4). . . . The better reading of § 4—one that harmonizes all of the ACPA's provisions and gives effect to the Act's animating purpose—is that the Section serves to facilitate § 2 Option II *in rem* relief by allowing a mark owner to maintain an *in rem* cause of action upon a showing that the owner through due diligence was not able to find a suitable defendant, but *in personam* jurisdiction over a suitable defendant might "otherwise exist" were such a defendant identified and found. Thus, for example, § 4 would prevent a previously unidentified suitable defendant from attacking collaterally an *in rem* proceeding by making a showing that *in personam* jurisdiction in fact existed, notwithstanding the mark owner's inability to find the defendant through due diligence. . . .

[10] This result is consistent with the settled principle that *in rem* jurisdiction is an alternative basis for jurisdiction where *in personam* jurisdiction is not available. *See generally* 4 Charles A. Wright and Arthur R. Miller, Federal Practice and Procedure § 1070 (2d ed. 1987) . . . .

[11] This limitation is consistent with the extraordinary nature of *in rem* relief, which adjudicates the rights of interested parties in the res *in absentia* and therefore may raise serious due process concerns in certain circumstances. See, e.g., *Shaffer v. Heitner*, 433 U.S. 186, 206–09 (1977) (observing that "if a direct assertion of personal jurisdiction over the defendant would violate the Constitution, it would seem that an indirect assertion of that jurisdiction should be equally impermissible" and holding that the exercise of *in rem* jurisdiction must comply with the due process requirements elucidated in *International Shoe Co. v. Washington*, 326 U.S. 310 (1945)) . . . .

the broader *in personam* remedies include the limited *in rem* remedy. It follows from this difference in available remedies that the *in rem* and *in personam* jurisdictional grants are exclusive and may not be simultaneously invoked or pursued by a mark owner. Indeed, to conclude otherwise would attribute a nonsensical purpose to the ACPA—namely, to provide duplicative and superfluous jurisdictional grants and remedies.

Yet another factor pointing to the exclusivity of *in rem* and *in personam* jurisdiction under the ACPA is the statutory requirement in Option I that the mark owner, as a condition to proceeding *in rem,* must bear the burden of demonstrating the absence of *in personam* jurisdiction over a suitable defendant. Unless the ACPA's *in rem* and *in personam* jurisdictional grants are mutually exclusive, a mark owner pursuing both simultaneously would then be in the odd, if not absurd, position of proving at once the presence and absence of *in personam* jurisdiction over the putative infringer. A mark owner simply cannot simultaneously establish both (i) that *in personam* jurisdiction over a suitable defendant cannot be obtained *and* (ii) that *in personam* jurisdiction over a putative infringer can be obtained.[13]

A hypothetical scenario helps illustrate the ACPA's operation in this regard. When a mark owner becomes aware of an infringing use, the owner's first step, typically, is to ascertain the infringer's identity and location by reference to information available from the infringing website or the pertinent domain name registrant. With this information in hand, the owner must then proceed to determine whether the circumstances of Option I or II exist. In this regard, if the owner determines that the putative infringer resides, does business, or is otherwise present in any judicial district in the United States,[14] then the inquiry is ended, and the owner, in these circumstances, must proceed *in personam* against the infringer and is precluded by the ACPA from proceeding *in rem* against the offending domain name. But Congress recognized that in many circumstances mark owners may obtain some identifying information concerning an infringer, but nonetheless may be unable to locate that entity or obtain jurisdiction over the infringer. Often these

---

[13] In this regard, a mark owner may not simultaneously file an *in rem* cause of action and an *in personam* claim in the hope that one claim will survive the court's jurisdictional inquiry. Rather, a mark owner must choose prior to filing whether to proceed *in rem* against the domain name or *in personam* against a putative infringer. Of course, if a mark owner's first choice falters, the alternative may then be pursued by refiling or seeking to amend the complaint.

[14] The ACPA does not explicitly answer the question whether a mark owner must disprove the existence of *in personam* jurisdiction over a suitable defendant in any judicial district in the United States or only in the forum where the domain name registrar is located. Although this question need not be answered here, . . . the likely answer is that the mark owner must show the absence of *in personam* jurisdiction in any judicial district in the United States. *See, e.g., Heathmount A.E. Corp. v. Technodome.Com.,* 106 F.Supp.2d 860, 867 (E.D.Va. 2000) ("There are two situations in which [Option I] comes into play: first, where the registrant of the domain name is not subject to personal jurisdiction *in any U.S. court* and, second, where a domain name registrant has transferred ownership of the domain name to another individual who is not subject to personal jurisdiction.") (emphasis added). . . .

situations occur where the putative infringer is located in a foreign country and/or provided the domain name registrar with inaccurate or false identifying information. To accommodate these possibilities, Congress included § 2 of the ACPA, so that in these circumstances, an owner could still seek a remedy—albeit a more limited one—by proceeding *in rem* against the domain name itself. But, before allowing a mark owner to proceed in this extraordinary fashion, Congress required the owner to exercise due diligence in the search for the infringer. *See* 15 U.S.C. § 1125(d)(2)(A)(ii)(II).

Because the ACPA's *in rem* and *in personam* jurisdictional grants are mutually exclusive, Alitalia may not invoke and pursue both simultaneously. Either there is *in personam* jurisdiction over JPR, in which event the *in rem* count must be dismissed and JPR then afforded an opportunity to appear and contest Alitalia's summary judgment arguments, or there is no *in personam* jurisdiction over JPR,[17] in which event Alitalia may proceed only *in rem* against the domain name <casinoalitalia.com> and Alitalia will be entitled to summary judgment if the record discloses no triable issue of fact. Thus, the next step in the analysis is to address whether JPR is subject to jurisdiction in Virginia pursuant to the Commonwealth's long-arm statute. *See* Va.Code § 8.01–328.1. [In the remainder of the opinion the court concludes that JPR is subject to *in personam* jurisdiction in Virginia, and therefore Alitalia cannot maintain its ACPA *in rem* cause of action against *casinoalitalia.com*.]

Electronics Boutique Holdings Corp. v. Zuccarini
56 U.S.P.Q.2d 1705 (E.D.Pa.2000).

■ SCHILLER, J.

Presently before the court is plaintiff Electronics Boutique Holding Corporation's action for Internet cybersquatting against defendant John Zuccarini. A hearing on the merits consolidated with a hearing on damages was held on October 10, 2000. For the reasons set forth below, I find in favor of plaintiff Electronics Boutique Holdings Corporation.

I. Procedural background

On August 10, 2000, plaintiff Electronics Boutique Holding Corporation ("EB") filed a complaint against defendant John Zuccarini ("Mr. Zuccarini"), individually and trading as Cupcake Patrol and/or Cupcake Party, alleging violations of the Anticybersquatting Consumer Protection Act of 1999, 15 U.S.C. § 1125(d) ("ACPA"), violations of § 43(a) of the Lanham Act, 15 U.S.C. § 1125(a), dilution,

---

[17] In this regard, Alitalia bears the burden of disproving jurisdiction by a preponderance of the evidence. *See Heathmount*, 106 F.Supp.2d at 862–63 (holding that "[u]nder § 1125(d)(2), a plaintiff must 'disprove' the presence of personal jurisdiction in order to proceed in rem," and "bear[s] the burden to demonstrate some indicia of due diligence in trying to establish personal jurisdiction over an individual who has been identified as a potential defendant but is not subject to jurisdiction.").

common law service mark infringement and unfair competition.

Also on August 10, 2000, I granted EB's motion for a temporary restraining order, enjoining the use of domain names "www.electronicboutique.com," "www.eletronicsboutique.com," "www.electronicbotique.com," "www.ebwold.com," "www.ebworl.com." (collectively "domain misspellings") or any other domain name or mark identical to or confusingly similar to EB's registered service marks until August 20, 2000, and directing Mr. Zuccarini to deactivate the domain misspellings and present the Court with evidence of the deactivations within three days of the Court's Order. Additionally, I scheduled a hearing on EB's motion for a preliminary injunction to take place on August 15, 2000.

On August 15, 2000, upon representations by EB that its attempts to effect service upon Mr. Zuccarini at his home, which is also his workplace, were unsuccessful, I granted EB's motion for alternative service, extension of the temporary restraining order, and continuance of the hearing on EB's motion for a preliminary injunction. I authorized EB to effect service through the United States Marshals' service. The hearing on EB's motion for preliminary injunction was continued until August 29, 2000.

Mr. Zuccarini failed to appear, through counsel or otherwise, for the August 29 hearing. On that date, I granted EB's motion for preliminary injunction based on its ACPA claims, finding that Mr. Zuccarini had actual notice of this matter and that the requirements for the issuance of a preliminary injunction had been satisfied. I scheduled a hearing on the merits of EB's ACPA claims for October 10, 2000.

Mr. Zuccarini failed to obtain counsel and refused to appear himself for the October 10, 2000, hearing.

II. Findings of Fact

At the October 10, 2000, hearing I found as follows: EB, a specialty retailer in video games and personal computer software, operates more than 600 retail stores, primarily in shopping malls, and also sells its products via the Internet. EB has registered several service marks on the principal register of the United States Patent and Trademark Office for goods and services of electric and computer products, including "EB" and "Electronics Boutique." EB has applications for several other service marks on the principal register of the United States Patent and Trademark Office for goods and services of electric and computer products, including "ebworld.com." EB has continuously used its service marks in its business since 1977. They have appeared in print, trade literature, advertising, and on the Internet.

EB's online store can be accessed via the Internet at "www.ebworld.com" and "www.electronicsboutique.com." EB registered its "EBWorld" domain name on December 19, 1996 and its "Electronics Boutique" domain name on December 30, 1997. EB has invested heavily in promoting its website to online customers. EB has expended a considerable amount of resources towards making its website consumer friendly. An easy-to-use website is critical to EB's ability to generate revenue directly through Internet customers and indirectly as support for EB's "brick and mortar" stores. Over the last eight months, online purchases have yielded an average of more than 1.1 million in sales per month and EB has logged more than

2.6 million online visitors.

On May 23, 2000, Mr. Zuccarini registered the domain names "www.electronicboutique.com," and "www.electronicbotique.com." One week later, Mr. Zuccarini registered the domain names "www.ebwold.com" and "www.ebworl.com." When a potential or existing online customer, attempting to access EB's website, mistakenly types one of Mr. Zuccarini's domain misspellings, he is "mousetrapped"[8] in a barrage of advertising windows, featuring a variety of products, including credit cards, internet answering machines, games, and music. The Internet user cannot exit the Internet without clicking on the succession of advertisements that appears. Simply clicking on the "X" in the top right-hand corner of the screen, a common way to close a web browser window, will not allow a user to exit. Mr. Zuccarini is paid between 10 and 25 cents by the advertisers for every click. Sometimes, after wading through as many as 15 windows, the Internet user could gain access to EB's website.

III. Conclusions of law

A. EB's request for a permanent injunction

. . .

[The court concludes that EB is entitled to a permanent injunction on its ACPA claim.]

. . .

B. EB's request for statutory damages

Pursuant to 15 U.S.C. § 1117(d), a plaintiff seeking recovery under the ACPA may elect to recover statutory damages in lieu of actual damages and profits. A court may award statutory damages in an amount between $1,000 and $100,000 per infringing domain name based on the court's determination of what is just. *See* 15 U.S.C. § 1117(d). EB has elected to recover statutory damages in this matter. The recovery of "statutory damages in cybersquatting cases, both [ ] deter[s] wrongful conduct and [ ] provide[s] adequate remedies for trademark owners who seek to enforce their rights in court." S.REP. No. 106–140 (1999).

I emphasize that the actual damages suffered by EB as a result of lost customers and goodwill is incalculable. In proceedings before this Court, Mr. Zuccarini admitted that he yields between $800,000 and $1,000,000 annually from the thousands of domain names that he has registered. *See Shields v. Zuccarini*, 2000 WL 1053884, at *1 (E.D.Pa. July 18, 2000). Advertisers pay Mr. Zuccarini between 10 and 25 cents each time an Internet user clicks on one of their ads posted on Mr. Zuccarini's websites. Many of the domain names registered by Mr. Zuccarini are misspellings of famous names and infringe on the marks of others. . . .

---

[8] The term "mousetrapped" was used by Judge Dalzell, United States District Judge for the Eastern District of Pennsylvania, to describe the situation an Internet user encounters upon accessing one of Mr. Zuccarini's domain names in a matter in which Mr. Zuccarini was sued by a different plaintiff for similar conduct. *See Shields v. Zuccarini*, 89 F.Supp.2d 634, 635 (E.D.Pa.2000).

In addition, Mr. Zuccarini has victimized a wide variety of people and entities. This Court has permanently enjoined Mr. Zuccarini from using domain names that are "substantially similar" to the marks of another plaintiff, finding Mr. Zuccarini's "conduct utterly parasitic and in complete bad faith." *Shields v. Zuccarini*, 2000 WL 1056400, at *1 (E.D.Pa. June 5, 2000). Other cases alleging similar conduct have been brought against Mr. Zuccarini by Radio Shack, Office Depot, Nintendo, Hewlett–Packard, the Dave Matthews Band, *The Wall Street Journal, Encyclopedia Britannica*, the distributor of Guinness beers and Spiegel's catalog in various federal courts and arbitration fora. Demands regarding similar conduct have been made on Mr. Zuccarini by the Sports Authority, Calvin Klein, and Yahoo!. Mr. Zuccarini's conduct even interferes with the ability of the public to access health information by preying on hospitals and prescription drugs. Pl. Exh. 5, Zuccarini Dep. at 70, 73, *Shields v. Zuccarini*, No. 00–494, (E.D.Pa.) (admitting the registration of domain names containing misspellings of the Mayo Clinic and the weight loss drug Xenical).

I also note that Mr. Zuccarini's conduct is not easily deterred. *See Shields*, 2000 WL 1053884, at *1 (E.D.Pa. July 18, 2000) (observing that Mr. Zuccarini failed to get the "crystalline message" of the Court in its March 22 Opinion and June 5 Order). Strikingly, Mr. Zuccarini registered the domain misspellings at issue in this matter after this Court preliminarily enjoined him from using misspellings of another individual's mark. *See Shields*, 89 F.Supp.2d at 642–43.

Furthermore, since this Court permanently enjoined Mr. Zuccarini from using other domain misspellings, assessed statutory damages in the amount of $10,000 per infringing domain name against him, and required him to bear the plaintiff's costs and attorneys' fees, Mr. Zuccarini has unexplainedly registered hundreds of domain names which are misspellings of famous people's names, famous brands, company names, television shows, and movies, victimizing, among others, the Survivor television show, Play Station and Carmageddon video game products, singers Kylie Minogue, Gwen Stefani and J.C. Chasez, *The National Enquirer*, and cartoon characters the Power Puff Girls. Mr. Zuccarini boldly thumbs his nose at the rulings of this court and the laws of our country. Therefore, I find that justice in this case requires that damages be assessed against Mr. Zuccarini in the amount of $100,000 per infringing domain name, for a total of $500,000.

C. Attorneys' fees and costs

EB has requested that it be awarded attorneys' fees and the costs of this litigation. The ACPA authorizes this Court to award "reasonable attorney fees to the prevailing party" in "exceptional cases." 15 U.S.C. § 1117(a). In determining whether a case is "exceptional" under § 1117(a), the Third Circuit has required "a finding of culpable conduct on the part of the losing party, such as bad faith fraud, or knowing infringement." *Ferrero U.S.A., Inc. v. Ozak Trading, Inc.*, 952 F.2d 44, 47 (3d Cir.1991). As described above, Mr. Zuccarini acted in complete bad faith by knowingly and intentionally trading on the goodwill and reputation of EB in an attempt to mislead the public. Therefore, I find that EB is entitled to attorney's fees.

. . .

I will award EB the full amount of its $30,653.34 request.

. . .

EXTENSIONS

1. *Typosquatting.* In *Electronics Boutique Holdings Corp. v. Zuccarini*, the defendant engaged in what has become known as typosquatting. A typosquatter identifies common spelling, typing and keyboarding errors that people make when entering a well-known URL into the address bar of a web browser. The typosquatter then registers these variations on the domain name in order to increase traffic to his or her own website or sell the variations to the owner of the domain name from which the variations were derived.

Typosquatting has an analogy in the brick-and-mortar world. In *Holiday Inns, Inc. v. 800 Reservation, Inc.*, 86 F.3d 619 (6th Cir.1996), the court had to determine whether it was a violation of Sections 32 or 43(a) of the Lanham Act, 15 U.S.C. §§ 1114 and 1125(a), for the defendant to use a telephone number that it had derived as a common dialing error from a competitor's vanity number:

> Holiday Inns, Inc., filed this Lanham Act suit against the defendants, alleging unfair competition and infringement of its trademark telephone number, 1-800-HOLIDAY, known as a "vanity number." The defendants, Call Management Systems, Inc. (a consulting firm that obtains and services 1-800 telephone numbers for businesses), 800 Reservations, Inc. (an agency that makes reservations for a number of hotel chains, including Holiday Inns), and Earthwinds Travel, Inc. (a travel agency) had secured the use and were engaged in using a telephone number that potential Holiday Inns customers frequently dial by mistake when they unintentionally substitute the number zero for the letter "O." That number, 1-800-405-4329, corresponds to the alphanumeric 1–800–H[zero]LIDAY, known in the trade as a "complementary number." It is referred to in this opinion as "the 405 number" to distinguish it from the Holiday Inns numeric, 1-800-465-4329. The district court, although noting that the defendants were violating only the "spirit" and not the "letter" of the Lanham Act, nevertheless granted Holiday Inns partial summary judgment and permanently enjoined 800 Reservations and Call Management from using the 405 number. . . . For the reasons stated below, we conclude that the defendants' use of the 405 number did not violate the Lanham Act . . .

> The plain language of § 32 of the Lanham Act forbids only the "*use* in commerce [of] any reproduction, counterfeit, copy, or colorable imitation of a registered mark . . . which . . . is likely *to cause* confusion." 15 U.S.C. § 1114 (emphasis added). Additionally, § 43(a) of the Act provides a cause of action only against "[a] person who . . . *uses* in commerce any word, term, name, symbol, or device . . . or any false designation of origin, false or misleading description of fact, or false or misleading representation of fact. . . ." 15 U.S.C. § 1125(a) (emphasis added). The defendants in this case never *used* Holiday Inns's trademark nor any facsimile of Holiday Inns's marks.

> Moreover, the defendants did not *create* any confusion; the confusion already existed among the misdialing public. . . .

Should the Sixth Circuit's reasoning apply to typosquatting, and if so did the court in *Electronics Boutique* reach the wrong outcome? Does it matter that in *Electronics Boutique* the court was applying the ACPA, rather than the trademark infringement provisions of the Lanham Act? Is the court's comment in *Sporty's Farm L.L.C. v. Sportsman's Market, supra,* at n.26, "that 'confusingly similar' [under the ACPA] is a different standard from the 'likelihood of confusion' standard for trademark infringement" relevant to your answer?

2. *A pure heart and empty head defense?* The ACPA, 15 U.S.C. § 1125(d)(1)(B)(ii), states that "[b]ad faith intent described under subparagraph (A) shall not be found in any case in which the court determines that the person believed and had reasonable grounds to believe that the use of the domain name was a fair use or otherwise lawful." One commentator has remarked:

> This might be dubbed the "pure heart and empty head defense" because it might appear to reward the cybersquatter who intended no harm and mistakenly thought that his or her conduct was lawful. This defense has the potential to reward both ignorance of the law and unawareness of the fact that cybersquatting violates widely accepted standards of fair competition. Therefore, a court should, in the author's view, make use of this "reasonable belief" defense very sparingly and only in the most unusual cases. . . . Otherwise, every cybersquatter [will] solemnly aver that it [is] entitled to this defense because it believed that its conduct was lawful.

4 J. THOMAS MCCARTHY, MCCARTHY ON TRADEMARKS AND UNFAIR COMPETITION § 25:78 (4th ed.2002). Is there any way that a court might avoid this absolute ignorance-of-the-law defense and thus avoid the perverse incentives and consequences that concern Professor McCarthy? Does a cybersquatter have any duty to inquire? Should a person who is willfully blind or who deliberately fails to inquire, knowing what the answer is likely to be, avoid liability? *See, e.g., Louis Vuitton S.A. v. Lee,* 875 F.2d 584 (7th Cir.1989) (for purposes of civil damages under 15 U.S.C. § 1117(b), it is sufficient that a retailer "failed to inquire further because he was afraid of what the inquiry would yield"). On the other hand, does the statute invite courts to infer bad faith from the mere fact that the court feels that the particular conduct was unfair competition? Is this standard too loose to protect people who might have competing claims that are arguably legitimate, even if distasteful to the trademark owner?

3. *Liability of registrars and registries.* The ACPA limits to certain narrow circumstances the liability of a domain name registrar or registry based on its "refusing to register, removing from registration, transferring, temporarily disabling, or permanently canceling a domain name." 15 U.S.C. § 1114(2)(D)(ii). A registrar or registry is subject to damages liability only in cases involving bad faith. *Id.* § 1114(2)(D)(iii). It is subject to injunctive relief only if it fails to tender control of the domain name to the court, modifies the status of the domain name except pursuant to court order, or otherwise fails to comply with a court order. *Id.* § 1114(2)(D)(i)(II).

In *Hawes v. Network Solutions, Inc.,* 337 F.3d 377 (4th Cir.2003), plaintiff Hawes sought relief against a registrar that transferred control of the disputed domain name to a French court, before which was pending L'Oreal's trademark action against Hawes. The court dismissed the claim:

> The statutory provision upon which Count I rests exposes a registrar to liability under the Lanham Act—by providing an exception to a registrar's general exemption from liability under the Act—when the registrar, without court permission, transfers a domain name "during the pendency of [an] action." 15 U.S.C. § 1114(2)(D)(i)(II)(bb). Hawes did allege that Network Solutions tendered control over the domain name to the French court after L'Oreal commenced an action in France against Hawes for infringing L'Oreal's French trademarks, but the pendency of a foreign action is irrelevant to the question of whether a registrar is exposed to liability under the Lanham Act. . . . In this case, there was no anticybersquatting action or reverse anticybersquatting action under the ACPA pending in any court at the time Network Solutions transferred the domain name

<lorealcomplaints.com>. Because there was no action adjudicating Lanham Act liability, there could be no allegation that Network Solutions was not cooperating with a court in a domain name dispute involving domain name hijacking or reverse domain name hijacking, and thus there could be no basis to consider an exception from the limitation of liability.

Might a registrar that wrongfully transfers a domain name be liable on a theory of conversion? *See Kremen v. Cohen*, 337 F.3d 1024 (9th Cir.2003), holding that plaintiff stated a claim for conversion under California law against a registrar that transferred ownership of sex.com in response to a forged authorization letter. To reach this result, the court had to find that a domain name constitutes property:

> Property is a broad concept that includes "every intangible benefit and prerogative susceptible of possession or disposition." . . . We apply a three-part test to determine whether a property right exists: "First, there must be an interest capable of precise definition; second, it must be capable of exclusive possession or control; and third, the putative owner must have established a legitimate claim to exclusivity." . . . Domain names satisfy each criterion. Like a share of corporate stock or a plot of land, a domain name is a well-defined interest. Someone who registers a domain name decides where on the Internet those who invoke that particular name—whether by typing it into their web browsers, by following a hyperlink, or by other means—are sent. Ownership is exclusive in that the registrant alone makes that decision. Moreover, like other forms of property, domain names are valued, bought and sold, often for millions of dollars . . . .

> Finally, registrants have a legitimate claim to exclusivity. Registering a domain name is like staking a claim to a plot of land at the title office. It informs others that the domain name is the registrant's and no one else's. Many registrants also invest substantial time and money to develop and promote websites that depend on their domain names. Ensuring that they reap the benefits of their investments reduces uncertainty and thus encourages investment in the first place, promoting the growth of the Internet overall. . . .

Do you agree that a domain name is property? Does the ACPA's provision for in rem actions against domain names assume that they are property? *Compare Lockheed Martin Corp. v. Network Solutions, Inc.*, 194 F.3d 980 (9th Cir.1999) (domain name registrar is not liable for contributory trademark infringement, since registration of a domain name is provision of a service, not supply of a "product"); *Wornow v. Register.Com, Inc.*, 778 N.Y.S.2d 25 (Sup.Ct.App.Div.2004) ("We are in accord with authorities holding that a domain name that is not trademarked or patented is not personal property, but rather a contract right . . . .").

4. Lockheed Martin v. NSI *reprise.* Soon after the passage of the ACPA, Lockheed Martin decided to take another bite at the apple and brought suit against Network Solutions under the ACPA. Lockheed argued that defendant violated the Act by "registering, maintaining, or trafficking in ten specific domain names that allegedly infringe its LOCKHEED MARTIN and SKUNK WORKS marks." *Lockheed Martin Corp. v. Network Solutions, Inc.*, 141 F.Supp.2d 648, 654 (N.D.Tex.2001). The court held, that the word "registers" in 15 U.S.C. § 1125(d)(1)(A) "obviously refers to a person who presents a domain name for registration, not to the registrar." *Id.* The court also noted that liability for using a domain name within the meaning of 15 U.S.C. § 1125(d)(1)(A) is limited by § 1125(d)(1)(D) to "the domain name registrant or that registrant's authorized licensee." With respect to bad-faith intent, the court wrote that "[a]lthough the list [of factors under § 1125(d)(1)(B)(i)(I)–(IX) for determining bad-faith intent] is not exclusive, none of the conditions and conduct listed would be applicable to a person functioning solely as a registrar or registry of domain names." *Id.* On the basis of this analysis, the court granted summary judgment for NSI.

5. *Minimum contacts and in rem jurisdiction.* In one of the first *in rem* actions brought under the ACPA, *Caesars World, Inc. v. Caesars-Palace.Com,* 112 F.Supp.2d 502 (E.D.Va.2000), the defendant challenged the constitutionality of 15 U.S.C. § 1125(d)(2) under the Due Process Clause of the United States Constitution. In this case, the court noted:

> The question before this court, therefore, is whether *in rem* jurisdiction over defendants who are not subject to the personal jurisdiction of this court, or any other, meets the due process standards under the Constitution.

> In this regard, defendant Casares.com argues that under *Shaffer v. Heitner,* 433 U.S. 186 (1977), *in rem* jurisdiction is only constitutional in those circumstances where the res provides minimum contacts sufficient for *in personam* jurisdiction. The court rejects this argument, and concludes that under *Shaffer,* there must be minimum contacts to support personal jurisdiction only in those *in rem* proceedings where the underlying cause of action is unrelated to the property which is located in the forum state. Here the property, that is, the domain name, is not only related to the cause of action but is its entire subject matter. Accordingly, it is unnecessary for minimum contacts to meet personal jurisdiction standards.

> To the extent that minimum contacts are required for *in rem* jurisdiction under *Shaffer,* moreover, the fact of domain name registration with Network Solutions, Inc., in Virginia supplies that. Given the limited relief afforded by the Act, namely "the forfeiture or cancellation of the domain name or the transfer of the domain name to the owner of the mark," no due process violation occurs here as to defendants personally. 15 U.S.C. § 1125(d)(2)(D). The court considers the enactment of the Anticybersquatting Consumer Protection Act a classic case of the distinction between *in rem* jurisdiction and *in personam* jurisdiction and a proper and constitutional use of *in rem* jurisdiction.

Caesars World, Inc. v. Caesars-Palace.Com, 112 F.Supp.2d at 504.

Several more recent cases have upheld the constitutionality of the ACPA's in rem jurisdictional provision, as applied to foreign defendants over which in personam jurisdiction cannot be obtained. *See, e.g., Porsche Cars North America, Inc. v. Porsche.net,* 302 F.3d 248, 259–60 (4th Cir.2002); *Harrods Ltd. v. Sixty Internet Domain Names,* 302 F.3d 214 (4th Cir.2002). For an argument that such an application of the in rem jurisdictional provision violates due process, see Catherine T. Struve & R. Polk Wagner, *Realspace Sovereigns in Cyberspace: Problems with the Anticybersquatting Consumer Protection Act,* 17 BERKELEY TECH. L.J. 989, 998–1018 (2002).

6. *General appearance.* If the owner of an offending domain name makes a general appearance to defend that domain name in an *in rem* action brought under 15 U.S.C. § 1125(d)(2), does that owner become subject to the *in personam* jurisdiction of the court? *See Caesars World, Inc. v. Caesars-Palace.Com,* 112 F.Supp.2d 505 (E.D.Va.2000) ("We have recently addressed that issue and determined that *in personam* jurisdiction cannot be based merely on an appearance in an *in rem* action.").

7. *Notice.* Often in an *in rem* action where the owner of the *res* is not known or cannot be found, notice of the action is effected by publication in newspapers for a certain period of time. Under 15 U.S.C. § 1125(d)(2)(B), notice and service of process is accomplished by

> (aa) sending a notice of the alleged violation and intent to proceed under this paragraph to the registrant of the domain name at the postal and e-mail ad-

dress provided by the registrant to the registrar; and

     (bb) publishing notice of the action as the court may direct promptly after filing the action.

15 U.S.C. § 1125(d)(2)(A)(ii)(II)(aa) and (bb). If a plaintiff can confirm that the registrant received actual notice once the plaintiff sent a letter to the registrant's postal and e-mail address, may the court waive the requirement of publication under 15 U.S.C. § 1125(d)(2)(B) and (A)(ii)(II)(bb)? *See Banco Inverlat, S.A. v. www.inverlat.com,* 112 F.Supp.2d 521 (E.D.Va.2000).

    8. *Waiting period under the ACPA.* Before filing an *in rem* action under the ACPA, the trademark owner must proceed in a manner that will permit the court to find that the owner

     (I) is not able to obtain in personam jurisdiction over a person who would have been a defendant in a civil action under paragraph (1); or

     (II) through due diligence was not able to find a person who would have been a defendant in a civil action under paragraph (1).

15 U.S.C. § 1125(d)(2)(A)(ii). Section 1125(d)(2)(A)(ii)(II)(aa) requires that due diligence include "sending a notice of the alleged violation and intent to proceed under this paragraph to the registrant of the domain name at the postal and e-mail address provided by the registrant to the registrar." These provisions raise the question of how long a trademark owner must wait after sending the required notice before filing an *in rem* action in federal court. The ACPA is silent on this question. In *Lucent Technologies, Inc. v. Lucentsucks.com*, 95 F.Supp.2d 528 (E.D.Va.2000), the plaintiff waited only 8 days. The owner of the domain name moved to dismiss on the ground that the plaintiff had failed to exercise due diligence. In resolving this issue the court wrote:

> Where Congress has specified a waiting period by statute in situations analogous to the ACPA *in rem* provision, ten days is the shortest amount of time specified. Perhaps the statutory provision most analogous to the provision at issue is Rule C of the Federal Rules of Civil Procedure, which allows an *in rem* action "to enforce any maritime lien" or whenever a federal statute provides for "a maritime action in rem or a proceeding analogous thereto." Fed.R.Civ.P. C(1). The rule permits the claimant of property that is subject to an *in rem* action 10 days after the rem has been seized to file a claim and 20 days after that to serve an answer. Fed.R.Civ.P. C(6). In the standard *in personam* action, Rule 12 of the Federal Rules of Civil Procedure allows 20 days after service of process to file an answer. Fed.R.Civ.P. 12(a)(1)(A).

> Neither Rule C nor Rule 12 are directly on point. In our case, we are considering what notice is required before an *in rem* action is instituted, and how long a plaintiff must wait to file an *in rem* action after sending notice by mail and e-mail, which may or may not reach the addressee. In contrast, Rule C specifies the waiting period *after* an *in rem* action is instituted, and Rule 12 specifies a waiting period after service of process is complete, that is, after actual notice has occurred. Nevertheless, taken together, these rules strongly suggest that Congress would not consider eight days to be a sufficient waiting period after mailing notice of a potential *in rem* action to a person who may be affected by that action.

Lucent Technologies, Inc. v. Lucentsucks.com, 95 F.Supp.2d at 533–34. Based on the discussion in *Lucent Technologies*, what is a reasonable waiting period?

    9. *Bad-faith intent and in rem actions under the ACPA.* The ACPA envisions two situations in which an *in rem* action would be appropriate. The first, described in 15 U.S.C. § 1125(d)(2)(A)(ii)(I), is a situation in which the trademark owner knows the identity of the offending domain name registrant but the federal courts cannot obtain *in personam* jurisdiction over her. The second, described in *id.* § 1125(d)(2)(A)(ii)(II), is a situation in which the identity of the offending domain name registrant is unknown. In *BroadBridge Media, L.L.C. v. Hypercd.com,* 106 F.Supp.2d 505 (S.D.N.Y.2000), a case of the first kind in which the offending domain name registrant was known, but the court could not exercise *in personam* jurisdiction over that registrant, the trademark owner questioned whether proof of the registrant's bad faith intent was necessary in an *in rem* action under the ACPA. The court said that it understood plaintiff's argument that it need not show bad faith, but concluded that

> bad faith intent to profit is a necessary element. . . . Congress clearly intended to use the bad faith element of the statute as a way to narrow the breadth of the statute. "The bill is carefully and narrowly tailored, however, to extend only to cases where the plaintiff can demonstrate the defendant . . . *used* the offending domain name with bad-faith intent to profit from the goodwill of a mark belonging to someone else. Thus, the bill does not extend to innocent domain name registrations by . . . someone who is aware of the trademark status of the name but registers a domain name containing the mark for any reason other than with bad faith intent to profit from the goodwill associated with that mark." H.R. Conf. Rep. 106–412 (emphasis added); *see also Northern Light Technology, Inc. v. Northern Lights Club,* 97 F.Supp.2d 96 (D.Mass.2000). Reflecting this intent, Congress limited the in rem action against a domain name to those situations where the court finds the owner is unable "to obtain in personam jurisdiction over a the person *who would have been a defendant under paragraph (1)."* 15 U.S.C. § 1125(d)(2)(A)(i)(I) (emphasis added). To be brought in as a defendant under paragraph (1) requires, in addition to other elements, a bad faith intent to profit.

Query how one would demonstrate bad faith where the registrant is unknown. Commenting on this problem, one commentator has noted that sometimes

> an in rem procedure is needed precisely because the domain name holder cannot be located. The holder usually cannot be located precisely because little or nothing is known about that person. In that event, it may be very difficult for the plaintiff to have any evidence of bad faith. Even negative evidence may be unavailable, such as the lack of the domain name registrant's IP rights in the name. It is improbable that the trademark owner can find evidence of bad faith of a domain name owner who cannot be personally served because he or she gave a fictitious name, a non-existent address and inaccurate contact information. In such a case, the courts should interpret the "bad faith" requirement with considerable leniency and flexibility, or else the usefulness of the in rem procedure will be curtailed.

4 J. THOMAS MCCARTHY, MCCARTHY ON TRADEMARKS AND UNFAIR COMPETITION § 25:79 (4TH ED.2002).

The statute provides for notice to the registrant by publication rather than by actual notice; does this lenient standard establishing who may be a defendant in an *in rem* action conflict with a narrow legal rule concluding that such defendants may not be liable absent specific proof of their bad faith?

10. *Personal names.* Section 2(b) of the ACPA, codified as 15 U.S.C. § 1129, provides protection against the registration of non-trademarked personal names by cybersquatters. It reads:

(1) In general

(A) Civil liability. Any person who registers a domain name that consists of the name of another living person, or a name substantially and confusingly similar thereto, without that person's consent, with the specific intent to profit from such name by selling the domain name for financial gain to that person or any third party, shall be liable in a civil action by such person.

(B) Exception. A person who in good faith registers a domain name consisting of the name of another living person, or a name substantially and confusingly similar thereto, shall not be liable under this paragraph if such name is used in, affiliated with, or related to a work of authorship protected under title 17 [the Copyright Act] including a work made for hire as defined in § 101 of title 17, and if the person registering the domain name is the copyright owner or licensee of the work, the person intends to sell the domain name in conjunction with the lawful exploitation of the work, and such registration is not prohibited by a contract between the registrant and the named person. The exception under this subparagraph shall apply only to a civil action brought under paragraph (1) and shall in no manner limit the protections afforded under the Trademark Act of 1946 (15 U.S.C. §§ 1051 et seq.) or other provision of Federal or State law.

(2) Remedies. In any civil action brought under paragraph (1), a court may award injunctive relief, including the forfeiture or cancellation of the domain name or the transfer of the domain name to the plaintiff. The court may also, in its discretion, award costs and attorneys fees to the prevailing party.

. . .

Is the protection afforded non-trademarked personal names as broad as the protection granted trademarks under 15 U.S.C. § 1125(d)? Is the intent requirement under § 1129(1)(A) the same as the intent requirement under § 1125(d)(1)(A)(i)? Are all names covered? In particular, would nicknames, stage names, and pen names be covered under § 1129(1)(A)? Are the remedies available under § 1129(C) the same as those available for violations under § 1125(d)(1)? Can you describe a scenario that would fall within the exception described in § 1129(1)(B)?

11. *The ACPA and metatags.* In *Bihari v. Gross,* 119 F.Supp.2d 309 (S.D.N.Y.2000), the court held that the ACPA does not apply to the use of another's trademark as a keyword in metatags. This result is consistent with Senate Rep. 106–140, which states that the ACPA is inapplicable to "such things as screen names, file names, and other identifiers not assigned by a domain name registrar or registry, which have little to do with cybersquatting in practice."

12. *The ACPA and commercial use.* In the *Bosley Medical* opinion, *supra,* the Ninth Circuit considered whether Kremer might have violated the ACPA even though the court had concluded that he had not used Bosley Medical's trademark commercially:

The district court dismissed Bosley's ACPA claim for the same reasons that it dismissed the infringement and dilution claims—namely, because Kremer did not make commercial use of Bosley's mark. However, the ACPA does not contain a commercial use requirement, and we therefore reverse.

Kremer argues that the "noncommercial use" proviso that appears in the dilution portion of § 1125 applies to cybersquatting claims with equal force. Admittedly, the language in § 1125 is confusing. 15 U.S.C. § 1125(c)(4) reads: "The following shall not be actionable under this section: . . . (B) Non-commercial use of a mark." 15 U.S.C. § 1125(c)(4)(B). Kremer asserts that by using the word "section," rather than the more precise term "subsection," Congress meant for the proviso to apply to all of § 1125, as opposed to subsection (c).

This argument fails for two reasons. The noncommercial use exception, which appears in a different part of the Lanham Act, is in direct conflict with the language of the ACPA. The ACPA makes it clear that "use" is only one possible way to violate the Act ("registers, traffics in, or uses"). Allowing a cybersquatter to register the domain name with a bad faith intent to profit but get around the law by making noncommercial use of the mark would run counter to the purpose of the Act. "The use of a domain name in connection with a site that makes a noncommercial or fair use of the mark does not necessarily mean that the domain name registrant lacked bad faith." *Coca-Cola Co. v. Purdy,* 382 F.3d 774, 778 (8th Cir.2004) (internal quotation marks and citation omitted); see also H.R. Rep. No. 106–412 at 11 (1999) ("This factor is not intended to create a loophole that otherwise might swallow the bill, however, by allowing a domain name registrant to evade application of the Act by merely putting up a noninfringing site under an infringing domain name."). "It is a well-established canon of statutory construction that a court should go beyond the literal language of a statute if reliance on that language would defeat the plain purpose of the statute." *Bob Jones Univ. v. United States,* 461 U.S. 574, 586 (1983).

Additionally, one of the nine factors listed in the statute that courts must consider is the registrant's "bona fide non-commercial or fair use of the mark in a site accessible under the domain name." 15 U.S.C. § 1125(d)(1)(B)(i)(IV). This factor would be meaningless if the statute exempted all non-commercial uses of a trademark within a domain name. We try to avoid, where possible, an interpretation of a statute "that renders any part of it superfluous and does not give effect to all of the words used by Congress." *Nevada v. Watkins,* 939 F.2d 710, 715 (9th Cir.1991) (internal quotation marks and citation omitted).

Finally, other courts that have construed the ACPA have not required commercial use. [See *DaimlerChrysler v. The Net, Inc.,* 388 F.3d. 201, 204 (6th Cir.2004).] See also *Ford Motor Co. v. Catalanotte,* 342 F.3d 543, 546 (6th Cir.2003); *E. & J. Gallo Winery v. Spider Webs Ltd.,* 129 F.Supp.2d 1033, 1047–48 (S.D.Tex.2001), aff'd, 286 F.3d 270 (5th Cir.2002) ("As reflected by the language of the ACPA and the case law interpreting it, there is no requirement . . . that the 'use' be a commercial use to run afoul of the ACPA.").

The district court erred in applying the commercial use requirement to Bosley's ACPA claim. Rather, the court should confine its inquiry to the elements of the ACPA claim listed in the statute, particularly to whether Kremer had a bad faith intent to profit from his use of Bosley's mark in his site's domain name. Bosley has met the first prong of the ACPA (that the domain name is identical to the mark) because Kremer used an unmodified version of Bosley's mark as his domain name.

. . . We remand the ACPA claim for further proceedings.

QUESTIONS FOR DISCUSSION

1. *Partial bad faith.* Much human behavior is the result of mixed motives. While one motive for a particular action may be good and legitimate, another may be less laudable. A central element for liability under the ACPA is that the person have "a bad faith intent to profit from the mark." 15 U.S.C. § 1125(d)(1)(A)(i). How should the courts decide a case in which a person acts partly in good faith? In such a case the domain name registrant may have a good-faith legitimate claim to the domain name, but still realize that it might have value to another. Just this situation was presented in *Virtual Works, Inc. v. Volkswagen of America, Inc.*, 238 F.3d 264 (4th Cir.2001). In this case, the court noted that "Virtual Works chose *vw.net* over other domain names not just because 'vw' reflected the company's own initials, but also because it foresaw the ability to profit from the natural association of *vw.net* with the VW mark." 238 F.3d at 269–70.

2. *Dilution by linking.* Imagine that an individual registers a domain name in violation of the ACPA. If I use that domain name to create a hyperlink to that person's website, am I also liable for using a domain name that is identical or confusingly similar to or dilutive of another's trademark under 15 U.S.C. § 1125(d)(1)(A)? What if I am aware that the domain name was unlawfully registered? What about individuals who operate a search engine or other directory service on the Internet: are they liable if they index a website under such a domain name?

GlobalSantaFe Corp. v. GlobalSantaFe.com
250 F.Supp.2d 610 (E.D.Va.2003).

■ ELLIS, DISTRICT JUDGE.

GlobalSantaFe Corporation ("GlobalSantaFe"), the plaintiff in this *in rem* suit under the Anticybersquatting Consumer Protection Act ("ACPA"), 15 U.S.C. § 1125(d)(2), successfully demonstrated that the domain name <globalsantafe.com> infringes its trademark and accordingly obtained a Judgment Order directing Hangang Systems, Inc. ("Hangang"), the registrar of the infringing domain name, to transfer the name to GlobalSantaFe. Yet, because a Korean court enjoined Hangang from transferring the domain name, GlobalSantaFe now seeks a further amendment of the Judgment Order directing the ".com" registry, VeriSign Global Registry Services ("VeriSign"), to cancel the domain name. Thus, the question presented here is whether the ".com" registry in the United States may be ordered to cancel a domain name that has already been found to be registered in violation of the ACPA, where, as here, the foreign registrant has obtained an injunction from a foreign court barring the foreign registrar from transferring the domain name.

I.

The facts are straightforward. Prior to their merger, Global Marine Inc. ("Global Marine") and Santa Fe International Corporation ("Santa Fe") were both involved in the business of contract drilling and related services. . . . Since 1958, Global Marine had conducted business under its GLOBAL MARINE mark and in 1969 Global Marine was issued a federal trademark for the mark. While Santa Fe's mark was not registered, the company had used its SANTA FE mark in conducting and promoting its services since 1946, and customers and others came to associate the mark with Santa Fe's services.

On September 3, 2001, Global Marine and Santa Fe publicly announced their agreement to merge into an entity to be known as GlobalSantaFe Corporation. Less than one day later, Jongsun Park registered the domain name <globalsantafe.com> with the Korean registrar Hangang. The domain name was subsequently transferred to Fanmore Corporation, a Korean entity, with Jong Ha Park ("Park") listed as the administrative, billing and technical contact. The website currently linked to the domain name is simply a placeholder site marked "under construction."

On October 5, 2001, just over one month after the announcement and Jongsun Park's registration of the <globalsantafe.com> domain name, Global Marine and Santa Fe filed this ACPA *in rem* action against the domain name. Service was perfected as required under the ACPA by sending notice of the alleged violation and the pending *in rem* action to the postal and email addresses of the listed registrant and by publishing notice of the action in two Korean newspapers. *See* 15 U.S.C. § 1125(d)(2)(A)(ii)(aa) & (bb). In the meantime, on November 20, 2001, the merger of the two companies became effective, resulting in the publicly traded GlobalSantaFe company with a market value of approximately $6 billion. On November 15, 2001, GlobalSantaFe applied for a federal trademark registration for the GLOBAL-SANTAFE mark under four separate categories, and those applications are pending. On December 20, 2001 the registrar, Hangang, deposited the registrar certificate for the domain name with the Clerk of this Court, and by doing so "tender[ed] to the Court complete control and authority over the registration" for <globalsantafe.com>, as required by the ACPA, 15 U.S.C. § 1125(d)(2)(D)(i)(I). The registrant failed to appear, either in person or through pleadings, to defend its right to use the domain name.

In response to the registrant's apparent default, the matter was referred to a magistrate judge for proposed findings of fact and recommendations pursuant to 28 U.S.C. § 636(b)(1)(B). The magistrate judge's Report and Recommendation concluded that the registration of the domain name violated the ACPA and that the registrant acted in bad faith,[7] and recommended that the domain name be transferred to GlobalSantaFe. Following consideration of the Report and on the basis of an independent review of the entire record, this Court adopted the Report's findings of fact and recommendations as its own, entered judgment by default in favor of GlobalSantaFe, and ordered VeriSign to transfer the domain name <globalsantafe.com> to GlobalSantaFe. Shortly after this Judgment Order entered, GlobalSantaFe sought an amendment to add Hangang, the registrar, as the entity ordered to transfer the domain name. On April 1, 2002, an Amended Judgment Order was entered, directing both Hangang and Verisign to "take all appropriate steps to transfer the domain name" to GlobalSantaFe.

On April 9, 2002, Park filed an application for an injunction in the District Court of Seoul, Korea, requesting that court to issue an injunction prohibiting Hangang from transferring the domain name as ordered by this Court. The District Court of Seoul provisionally granted this injunction by order dated September 17, 2002, finding that this Court likely lacked jurisdiction over the matter. In light of these proceedings and the Korean court's order, it appears that Hangang has refused to transfer the domain name as directed by Order of this Court. GlobalSantaFe, therefore, now seeks by motion a second amended judgment, which not only directs Hangang and VeriSign to transfer the domain name, but additionally directs

---

[7] The Fourth Circuit has subsequently held that a plaintiff may prevail in an *in rem* trademark infringement action without alleging and proving bad faith. *See Harrods Ltd. v. Sixty Internet Domain Names*, 302 F.3d 214, 228 (4th Cir.2002).

VeriSign, the registry, to cancel the infringing domain name pursuant to the ACPA until the domain name is transferred to GlobalSantaFe.

II.

Under the ACPA, suits may be brought *in rem* against a domain name provided certain jurisdictional requirements are met. In addition to meeting these jurisdictional requirements, GlobalSantaFe must also show (i) that it is entitled to relief under the ACPA, (ii) that cancellation is an available remedy under the ACPA, (iii) that the particular method of cancellation requested by GlobalSantaFe is effective and appropriate, and (iv) that concerns of international comity do not preclude such a remedy in the face of the Korean court's injunction. Jurisdiction and entitlement to relief were settled by the Amended Judgment Order, as reviewed briefly below. Also discussed briefly below is the availability of a cancellation remedy under the ACPA. The questions concerning the mechanisms by which cancellation of a domain name may be accomplished and the issues of international comity merit more extensive consideration.

A. Jurisdictional Requirements under the ACPA

In rem ACPA suits must meet several jurisdictional requirements. First, the ACPA allows a trademark owner to file an *in rem* action only in specific jurisdictions, namely "in the judicial district in which the domain name registrar, domain name registry, or other domain name authority that registered or assigned the domain name is located." 15 U.S.C. § 1125(d)(2)(A). This statutory requirement is satisfied here because the domain name registry in this case, VeriSign, is located within this district in Dulles, Virginia.

Second, *in rem* actions under the ACPA are appropriate only if there is no personal jurisdiction over the registrant in any district. *See* ACPA, § 1125(d)(2)(A)(ii)(I). This requirement is also plainly met, as there is no evidence that Park or Fanmore have conducted or transacted business in any district in the United States, nor is there any evidence that their actions constitute sufficient minimum contacts to support personal jurisdiction in the United States. . . . While it is true that the infringing domain name is included in the VeriSign registry, this is not enough to establish minimum contacts; indeed, even if the registrar were also located in this district, the resultant contacts would still be too minimal to support jurisdiction. *See America Online, Inc., et al. v. Huang,* 106 F.Supp.2d 848, 856–58 (E.D.Va.2000) (holding that registration of a domain name in this district with Network Solutions, Inc., which at the time performed both the registrar and the registry functions, did not constitute sufficient minimum contacts to support suit in this district.). Nor does the nature of the website operating at <globalsantafe.com> provide a jurisdictional nexus; it is a passive, placeholder site, consisting largely of the notice that the site is "under construction," and therefore is not itself a basis for jurisdiction over the registrant. . . . . Thus, there is no personal jurisdiction over Park or Fanmore in this district or, it appears, in any district in this country.

Third, GlobalSantaFe has properly perfected service, as required by the ACPA, by sending notice to the registrant's listed email and postal addresses and by publishing notice in Korean newspapers as directed by Order dated October 23, 2002. *See* 15 U.S.C § 1125(d)(2)(A)(ii)(aa) & (bb).

Finally, the Fourth Circuit has recently affirmed that *in rem* jurisdiction, as authorized by the ACPA, is not a violation of the Due Process Clause of the Constitution, where, as here, "the property itself is the source of the underlying controversy between the plaintiff and defendant," and jurisdiction is assigned "based on the location of the property." *See Porsche Cars North Amer., Inc. v. Porsche.net et al.*, 302 F.3d 248, 260 (4th Cir.2002) . . . .

B. Substantive Violation of the ACPA

The substantive merits of GlobalSantaFe's ACPA claim are manifest. As the magistrate judge concluded, and as is immediately apparent on its face, the domain name <globalsantafe.com> is confusingly similar to the marks of Global Marine and Santa Fe, and identical to the mark of the merged entity GlobalSantaFe. . . . With regard to Park and Fanmore's rights to the GLOBALSANTAFE mark, if any, the record shows that the original registrant clearly registered the <globalsantafe.com> domain name after, and in response to, GlobalSantaFe's use of the GLOBALSANTAFE mark in its merger announcement. Furthermore, there is no indication of any prior use of the GLOBALSANTAFE mark, legitimate or otherwise, by the original registrant, Fanmore, or Park. In sum, the magistrate judge properly concluded that the registration of the <globalsantafe.com> domain name, within one day of the merger announcement, is a clear violation of GlobalSantaFe's trademark rights. . . . Thus, the registration of <globalsantafe.com> was in clear violation of the ACPA, and GlobalSantaFe is accordingly entitled to transfer or cancellation of the domain name under § 1125(d)(2)(D)(i).

C. Availability of Cancellation under the ACPA

The Amended Judgment Order issued on April 1, 2002 directs both VeriSign and Hangang to take all steps necessary to transfer the domain name to plaintiffs within 10 days of receipt of the order. Yet Hangang, the registrar, has not complied with the Order, presumably because it is subject to a Korean court order arising from a case filed by Park shortly after the April 1 Order. It is understandable that the registrar would obey the order of a domestic court despite an order of this court. Notably, while Hangang was named as the defendant in the Korean proceeding, it has not been formally joined as a party in this matter. Further, there is no evidence in the record that Hangang operates in the United States or has sufficient minimum contacts with the United States to satisfy the due process requirements for personal jurisdiction; thus it does not appear on this record that Hangang could be hailed [sic] into this Court or any other court in the United States for the purpose of enforcing this Court's order.

. . .

The ACPA plainly authorizes cancellation as one of the remedies for domain name infringement in *in rem* suits. Thus, the ACPA provides that "[t]he remedies in an *in rem* action under this paragraph shall be limited to a court order for the forfeiture or *cancellation* of the domain name or the transfer of the domain name to the owner of the mark." *See* 15 U.S.C. § 1125(d)(2)(D)(i) (emphasis added). Significantly, the statute does not further describe what transfer or cancellation of a domain name entails. Therefore, an order to transfer or cancel a domain name must give these remedies their natural meaning and effect, in light of the structure and operation of the domain name system. Similarly, the statute does not provide any guidance as to which remedy is more appropriate in a given situation. Thus, because it is unmistakably clear that both transfer and cancellation are proper remedies under the statute, the appropriateness of either remedy in a given situation will depend on the remedy or remedies requested by the aggrieved party and the appropriateness of those remedies given the specific facts of the case.

D. The Mechanics of Domain Name Transfer and Cancellation

Given the clear authorization of cancellation as a remedy under the ACPA, a significant practical question is presented here, namely, how is cancellation of a domain name to be effectuated? It is important to explore the answers to this question to ensure that any order issued properly accommodates the practical realities of the problem.

There are at least three principle [sic] means to achieve cancellation of a domain name. First, the current registrar of the domain name can cancel a domain name by directing the registry to delete the registration information from the Registry Database. Second, the registry for the pertinent top-level domain can disable the domain name in that top-level domain by placing it on "hold" status and rendering it inactive. Third, the pertinent registry can cancel a domain name by acting unilaterally to delete the registration information without the pertinent registrar's cooperation. The technical and practical implications of each of these cancellation means merit exploration. As a predicate to this, it is necessary to review the general structure of the domain name system, including the contracts governing the roles of the registrars and the registry with regard to transfer and cancellation of a domain name.

. . . Each computer connected to the Internet has a unique identity, established by its unique Internet Protocol address ("IP address"). An IP address consists of four numbers between 0 and 255, separated by periods. IP addresses are used to route all transmissions through the Internet. Yet, IP addresses are difficult for individual users of the Internet to remember, a problem which led to development of the domain name system ("DNS"). The DNS allows an individual user to identify a computer using an easier-to-remember alphanumeric "domain name," such as "www.globalsantafe.com," rather than the numerical IP address. The DNS "resolves" the domain name by identifying the particular IP address associated with each domain name.

Significantly, the DNS is not a single master file in one location containing all the registered domain names and the corresponding IP addresses, but rather a hierarchical and distributed system, with each "name server" providing information for its "zone." Under this hierarchical system, the domain name "space" is divided into top-level domains ("TLDs"), such as ".com" and ".net." Each TLD name server provides the information necessary to direct domain name queries to the second-level domain (SLD) name server responsible for the domain name in question. Thus, VeriSign, as the registry for all domain names ending in ".com," is responsible for directing domain name queries regarding the "globalsantafe.com" second level domain to the appropriate SLD name server. This SLD name server, in turn, matches the domain name, e.g. "www.globalsantafe.com," with its specific numeric IP address. In other words, the ".com" TLD zone file maintained by VeriSign contains a list of all second level domains within the ".com" zone linked to the IP addresses of the SLD name servers for those second level domains, while the "globalsantafe.com" SLD name server maintains the file which matches all domain names in the "globalsantafe.com" SLD zone to the IP addresses of the individual host computers.

Registering, transferring, or deleting a domain name typically involves interaction between the registrar and the registry.[23] The relationship between the registry and the registrars is governed by several contracts, including the Registry-Registrar Agreement, the Registrar Accreditation Agreement, and the .com Registration Agreement.[24] These contracts allocate the responsibilities of a registry and related registrars and establish the processes for domain name registration. The registrars handle the retail side of domain name registration, selling domain names to individual domain name registrants. The registry, in turns [sic], performs a central but more limited function, namely maintaining and operating the unified Registry Database, which contains all domain names registered by all registrants and registrars in a given top level domain, as well as the associated TLD zone file used to resolve domain name queries in that domain. Thus, for each domain name in the ".com" TLD, VeriSign, the ".com" registry, is responsible for maintaining and propagating the following information: (i) the domain name, (ii) the IP addresses of the primary and secondary name server for that domain name, (iii) the name of the registrar for the domain name, and (iv) the expiration date for the registration. *See* Registrar Accreditation Agreement § 3.2. Hangang, in turn, as one of many ".com" registrars, maintains the same information for each domain name it sells to a registrant, and in addition, maintains records containing the name and address of the registrant as well as information regarding a technical and administrative contact for each domain name.[25] *See id.* § 3.3.

---

[23] There is only one registry that maintains the central database for all domain names in a given TLD. By contrast, there are numerous registrars authorized to register domain names in a given TLD for an individual registrant. . . .

[24] VeriSign operates as the exclusive registry for ".com" domain names pursuant to a contract with the U.S. Department of Commerce and the Internet Corporation for Assigned Names and Numbers ("ICANN"), and also enters into standard contracts with the various ".com" registrars. These contracts can be found on the ICANN website, at http://www.icann.org/tlds/agreements/verisign/com-index.htm (May 25, 2001) (.com Registration Agreement and Registry-Registrar Agreement); http://www.icann.org/registrars/ra-agreement-17may01.htm (May 17, 2001) (Registrar Accreditation Agreement).

[25] Thus, while VeriSign's Registry Database provides information as to which *registrar* registered a given domain name, it does not include information identifying who the individual *registrant* for a domain name is, or where the registrant is located. Only the registrar maintains that information.

Interaction between registrars and the registry is highly structured and automated. Registrar-registry communications occur over a secure electronic connection. The registry's role is almost entirely passive, namely to process the registrar's orders while checking to ensure that there are no conflicts within the central Registry Database such as duplicate domain name registrations. Registrars initiate virtually all changes to the Registry Database, by issuing automated commands to the registry, such as ADD, CHECK, RENEW, DEL (delete), MOD (modify), and TRANSFER. See .com Registry Agreement App. C.

There are contractual restrictions in VeriSign's authorizing contracts which generally bar VeriSign from changing the information in the Registry Database on its own initiative. First, VeriSign's authorizing contract specifies that it can only register domain names in response to requests from registrars, and that it cannot act as a registrar with respect to the registry's TLD. . . . Second, the standard form Registry-Registrar Agreement grants VeriSign only a limited license to use the registration data submitted by the registrar "for propagation of and the provision of authorized access to the TLD zone files."[29] Thus, as contemplated in the agreements, transfer or cancellation of a domain name normally requires the approval or initiative of the current registrar.

With this general background regarding the domain name system and the registrar-registry relationship, the three principle [sic] means of cancelling a domain name can be meaningfully explored.

Under normal procedures, a domain name is canceled by the issuance of a delete command by the domain name's current registrar. The current registrar uses the DEL command to instruct the registry to delete all information regarding the domain name from the Registry Database and the TLD zone file. . . . The removal of this information completely and effectively cancels the domain name. This is so, because any attempt to use the domain name will fail, owing to the removal of the pertinent information from the registry's TLD zone file. Importantly, because the registration information has been deleted from the Registry Database, the individual domain name will once again be available for registration to any registrant on a first-come, first-served basis.[32] This method of cancellation also has the virtue of using the established channels for registrar-registry communication to effectuate complete cancellation of the domain name. Yet, this approach requires cooperation by the current registrar, and thus may not be effective in situations where, as here, the registrar has declined to cooperate and is beyond the jurisdiction of United States courts.[33]

---

[29] *See* Registry-Registrar Agreement § 2.5.

[32] Transfer of a domain name, unlike cancellation, does not open up the domain name to registration on a first-come, first-served basis, but rather reassigns the domain name to the acquiring registrar and registrant. . . .

[33] The usual process for transfer likewise requires cooperation by the current registrar. Transfers are normally commenced by a TRANSFER request issued to the registry by the transferee's registrar; yet, the registry must notify the current registrar of the transfer request and may not process the transfer request absent approval by the current registrar. . . .

The second means of cancellation does not require the approval or initiative of the current registrar. Although VeriSign is not contractually authorized to delete a domain name registration on its own initiative, the registry may nonetheless unilaterally disable a domain name. VeriSign can render a domain name "inactive" by placing the domain name in REGISTRY-HOLD status. When a domain name is placed on REGISTRY-HOLD status, the domain name is removed from the TLD zone file but the information in the Registry Database is otherwise unchanged. The practical effect of this type of cancellation is twofold. On the one hand, the removal of the domain name from the TLD zone file renders it functionally useless, as attempts to locate the domain name and an associated IP address in the DNS will fail. On the other hand, the domain name remains registered to the current, infringing registrant and cannot be registered by the trademark holder or anyone else. Thus, the infringing domain name is rendered "inactive" but remains registered. In other words, if the domain name <globalsantafe.com> were disabled in this manner, individual users who attempted to access the domain name on the Internet would receive an error message indicating that the domain name could not be found, yet GlobalSantaFe could not register the domain name for its own use because it would still be registered by Park and Fanmore.

This disabling approach offers less than a complete cancellation remedy, yet it has a significant advantage over cancellation pursuant to a registrar's command; namely that VeriSign is contractually authorized to take this action unilaterally without the cooperation of the current registrar. Thus, this disabling approach may be preferable in circumstances where, as here, a recalcitrant registrar is beyond a court's jurisdiction. Unfortunately, where the current registrant is simply holding the domain name rather than putting it to any practical use, as is true here, disabling the domain name will have minimal practical effect—the trademark holder will still not be able to use the domain name, and the cybersquatter can continue squatting on the domain name as long as he keeps the registration active.[36]

A third means of cancellation involves a court order directing VeriSign to act unilaterally to cancel the domain name by deleting the registration information in the Registry Database and removing the domain name from the TLD zone file, without regard to the current registrar's lack of cooperation and the normal contractual procedures for cancellation. As discussed in the *Cable News Network* case, VeriSign's maintenance and control of the central Registry Database and the vital .com TLD zone file "effectively enables Verisign to transfer control of any '.com' domain name.' " *Cable News Network, L.P. v. CNNews.com*, 177 F.Supp.2d 506, 514 n.16 (E.D.Va.2001); *aff'd in relevant part, vacated in part* 56 Fed.Appx. 599 (4th Cir.2003). Similarly, it is apparent that VeriSign's physical control of these files enables VeriSign to cancel any ".com" domain name by deleting the relevant information in the Registry Database and the TLD zone file.[37] It may be that taking such

---

[36] Disabling a domain name would have greater practical effect in situations where the infringing domain name is used to direct traffic to a website that itself further infringes on the trademark holder's rights through dilution or direct infringement. In these situations, disabling the domain name will help to stem the flow of traffic to the infringing website.

[37] In this regard, unilateral transfer pursuant to a court order is more complex than uni-

a step would require a change in VeriSign's procedures and programming to allow the registry to delete the information without approval by the current registrar. Yet, nothing in the record indicates cancelling a domain name without the current registrar's consent is beyond VeriSign's physical or technical capabilities.

With regard to unilateral cancellation or transfer, it should be noted that VeriSign has indicated that it would oppose an order directing VeriSign unilaterally to transfer or cancel a domain name on grounds that such an order would require VeriSign to violate its contracts with the registrar and with ICANN and to interfere with the registrar-registrant contract. Yet, it is not clear that VeriSign would, in fact, be acting in violation of its authorizing contract, as transferring or canceling a domain name pursuant to a direct court order does not constitute "acting as a registrar" in contravention of the authorizing contract from ICANN. Furthermore, Hangang is in breach of its duties under the Registry-Registrar agreement and the Registrar Certificate it submitted owing to its failure to transfer the domain name pursuant to the April 1 Order. Thus, it is not clear to what extent VeriSign is still bound by the terms of the limited license granted by Hangang, particularly when Hangang has already tendered to the Court "complete control and authority over the registration" of <globalsantafe.com>. . . . Finally, VeriSign's contractual agreements with ICANN and Hangang cannot serve to limit the trademark rights and remedies granted to GlobalSantaFe by federal law under the Lanham Act and the ACPA. While the ACPA expressly authorizes a "court order for the . . . cancellation of the domain name," it does not require that such orders be directed only at the current registrar, nor does it shield the registry from cancellation orders. 15 U.S.C. § 1125(d)(2)(D)(i). Thus, VeriSign's contracts with ICANN and with the registrar should not be read to limit GlobalSantaFe's federal trademark rights and remedies. Simply put, the interest in vindicating congressionally provided trademark rights trumps contract. In any event, for the reasons that follow, it is not necessary to reach the question of unilateral transfer or deletion of a domain name by the registry in this case.

In sum, all three means of cancellation may be appropriate means of carrying out the cancellation remedy granted by the ACPA. To be sure, it is normally appropriate to direct a cancellation order primarily at the current domain name registrar and to direct that cancellation proceed through the usual channels. However, in situations, where, as here, such an order has proven ineffective at achieving cancellation, it becomes necessary to direct the registry to act unilaterally to carry out the cancellation remedy authorized under the ACPA. In this regard, a court is not limited merely to the disabling procedure envisioned by VeriSign's contractual agreements, but may also order the registry to delete completely a domain name registration pursuant to the court's order, just as the registry would in response to a registrar's request. Indeed, in order to vindicate the purposes of the ACPA, disabling alone in many cases may not be sufficient, for it does not oust the cyber-

---

lateral cancellation because it involves not merely the deletion of information within VeriSign's control, but also the substitution of new registrar and local name server information for the domain name, and hence the cooperation of the *acquiring* registrar.

squatter from his perch, but rather allows the cybersquatter to remain in possession of the name in violation of the trademark holder's rights.

In this regard, the physical location of the ".com" registry within this district is quite significant, for it is the location of the registry here which establishes the situs of the power to transfer or cancel the domain name within this district, pursuant to the ACPA, even if the registrar has not submitted a registrar certificate granting the court authority over the disputed domain name. . . . Significantly, if the infringing domain name were registered in a top-level domain whose registry was outside the United States, jurisdiction in the United States might be avoided entirely, provided the registrar is also foreign and the individual registrant lacks sufficient contacts with the forum to meet the due process requirements for personal jurisdiction. In other words, there is a significant gap in the ACPA's trademark enforcement regime for domain names registered under top-level domain names, such as the foreign country code domain names, whose registry is located outside the United States.

The current ability to assert jurisdiction over a large number of domain names in this district pursuant to the ACPA hinges on two factors, (i) the location of VeriSign within this district and (ii) the current popularity of the ".com" and ".net" top-level domain names, particularly for commercial Internet operations. Either factor may change in the future. Indeed, a recent law review article concerning the ACPA argues that an aggressive assertion of United States jurisdiction and control over the domain name system based on its essentially arbitrary physical geography may have the unintended consequence of causing a segmentation of the domain name system as other countries seek to assert their own control over the Internet by establishing competing and conflicting systems physically located outside the United States.[39] Even absent such segmentation, desire to avoid United States jurisdiction may cause foreign registrants to choose to use domain names within their respective country code top-level domains, whose registries are located in and operated by the foreign countries, rather than the currently popular "generic" domain names such as ".com" and ".net." The result may be an increasing number of domain names registered out of the reach of United States jurisdiction, but accessible to United States users through the universal domain name system, which in turn will pose a serious challenge to the enforcement of United States trademark rights on the Internet.

In any event, in this case, the narrow issue presented is whether the circumstances justify a second amendment of the judgment order to include an order directing VeriSign to cancel the domain name by disabling it. Given the nature of the specific relief requested by GlobalSantaFe, it is unnecessary to consider whether complete cancellation of the domain name by VeriSign is appropriate here. As discussed *supra*, cancellation of the infringing domain name is clearly authorized as a remedy under the ACPA, and disabling the domain name through removal of the

---

[39] *See* Catherine T. Struve and R. Polk Wagner, Realspace Sovereigns in Cyberspace: Problems with the Anticybersquatting Consumer Protection Act, 17 Berkeley Tech. L J. 989, 1019–1041 (2002).

pertinent information from the TLD zone file is the least intrusive practical means of achieving cancellation without the cooperation of the registrar. Thus, the amended judgment order requested by GlobalSantaFe in this matter is legally valid and practically appropriate.

D. International Comity

The remaining question in this motion for further amendment in aid of execution of judgment is whether concerns of international comity dictate deference to the injunction issued by the Korean court. In this regard, neither the general law regarding abstention in favor of a foreign court's adjudication of *in rem* actions, nor the specific concerns raised by the facts of this case counsel against the requested cancellation remedy.

The law regarding competing jurisdiction in *in rem* actions is clear: "[A]ccording to longstanding precedent and practice, the first court seized of jurisdiction over property, or asserting jurisdiction in a case requiring control over property, may exercise that jurisdiction to the exclusion of any other court." *See Sec. and Exch. Comm'n v. Banner Fund Int'l*, 211 F.3d 602, 611 (D.C.Cir.2000); *Al-Abood v. El-Shamari*, 217 F.3d 225, 231 (4th Cir.2000) (recognizing the first-in-time rule for determining jurisdiction in *in rem* actions, but finding it inapplicable in that case). This doctrine, known as the *Princess Lida* doctrine, applies only to *in rem* or *quasi in rem* cases, and requires federal courts to decline jurisdiction over a particular property or *res* over which another court has already asserted jurisdiction. *See Al-Abood*, 217 F.3d at 231; *Princess Lida of Thurn & Taxis v. Thompson*, 305 U.S. 456, 465–66 (1939). Although originally developed in the context of federalism, the first-in-time rule has since been applied to federal cases with parallel proceedings underway in another country. *See Banner Fund*, 211 F.3d at 611; *Dailey v. Nat'l Hockey League*, 987 F.2d 172, 175–76 (3d Cir.1993).

With regard to the first-in-time rule, the facts clearly establish that this Court was the first to assert jurisdiction over the domain name. Park's application for an injunction was filed with the District Court of Seoul on April 9, 2002, six months after GlobalSantaFe's filing of the *in rem* action in this Court. *See Banner Fund*, 211 F.3d at 612 (using the filing of the action as the relevant date for the first-in-time analysis). In fact, Park's initiation of proceedings in the foreign court also followed (i) Hangang's deposit of the registrar's certificate with this Court, on December 20, 2001, and (ii) both the original Judgment Order entered on March 25, 2002 and the Amended Judgment Order entered on April 1, 2002. Clearly, then, this Court is not obligated under the rule in *Princess Lida* to cede jurisdiction over the domain name in light of the subsequent order issued by the Korean court.

. . . Here, acquiescence to the order of a foreign court is particularly inappropriate, since the foreign proceeding did not commence until the matter had been fully adjudicated here. Moreover, the Korean proceeding was obviously begun with the intent of blocking the Judgment Order, which was already announced. Thus, in this case there is no basis for ceding jurisdiction to the Korean court, or granting deference to its order blocking the transfer of the domain name.

Although the *Princess Lida* first-in-time rule supports this Court's jurisdiction in this matter and counsels against deference to the Korean court ruling, the international aspect of this case and the existence of conflicting court orders compiles [sic] consideration of the important question of comity among nations. *See Banner Fund,* 211 F.3d at 612 (holding that the international proceeding did not deprive the district court of jurisdiction, but did "raise a concern with comity among nations"). First, "[c]omity ordinarily requires that courts of a separate sovereign not interfere with concurrent proceedings based on the same transitory claim, at least until a judgment is reached in one action." *Id.* (citing *Laker Airways, Ltd. v. Sabena, Belgian World Airlines,* 731 F.2d 909, 937 (D.C.Cir.1984)). This factor does not counsel against amending the Judgment Order in this case to include cancellation, for the Korean and American proceedings are not concurrent. Indeed, in this case, judgment had already issued before the Korean proceeding was commenced. Park initiated the Korean court proceedings specifically to block the already-issued final judgment in this case. Second, "a domestic forum is not compelled to acquiesce in pre or postjudgment conduct by litigants which frustrates the significant policies of the domestic forum." *Id.* (citing *Laker Airways,* 731 F.2d at 915). In this regard, "in determining whether to apply comity to the Order of a foreign court of competent jurisdiction we must consider our own laws and the public policy, as well as the rights of our residents under the laws of the United States." *In re Enercons Virginia, Inc.,* 812 F.2d 1469, 1473 (4th Cir.1987). Registrants Park and Fanmore violated GlobalSantaFe's trademark rights under United States law by registering the domain name <globalsantafe.com>. Clearly, there is significant interest in this forum in protecting and vindicating GlobalSantaFe's trademark rights against this violation, as well as in ensuring that the ".com" registry, located within this district, is not used in furtherance of the violation. In sum, there is clearly no basis for abstention on comity grounds where, as here (i) the proceedings are not concurrent, the Korean proceeding having been commenced in an effort to block enforcement of the already issued judgment in this case, (ii) the foreign court proceeding is intended to frustrate the enforcement of the Judgment of this Court, and (iii) that Judgment supports significant public policies under United States law. Thus, comity concerns do not bar the amendment of the Judgment Order to grant GlobalSantaFe the additional remedy of cancellation to which it is entitled under the ACPA.

III.

Accordingly, by accompanying orders, GlobalSantaFe's motion in aid of execution of judgment is granted, and a Second Amended Judgment Order is entered, which additionally orders VeriSign to disable the <globalsantafe.com> domain name until it is transferred as ordered to GlobalSantaFe. Specifically, VeriSign is directed not to delete entirely the pertinent domain name registration information in the Registry Database, but rather to disable the domain name by eliminating the currently associated domain name server IP numbers from the TLD zone file.

. . .

QUESTIONS FOR DISCUSSION

1. *The role of U.S.-based registries in regulating domain names.* The location in the United States of VeriSign, the registry for the .com top-level domain, as well as registries of other popular top-level domains, means that U.S. courts have a degree of control over the disposition of domain names that courts in other countries do not enjoy. How would you expect a U.S.-based registry to react to an order from a court in Canada, Antigua, or China, directing it to cancel or transfer the registration of a domain name held by a U.S. citizen? What options would other countries have if U.S. courts began exercising their authority over U.S.-based registries in a manner perceived as overreaching?

2. *Transfer of domain name as remedy.* In *America Online, Inc. v. AOL.org*, 259 F.Supp.2d 449 (E.D.Va.2003), the court was faced with a situation in which a Chinese registrar failed to comply with the court's order to transfer the domain name to the plaintiff, and instead allowed the registrant to transfer the domain name to a South Korean registrar. The court held that the ACPA authorizes a court to direct a registry to transfer the registration of a domain name to the prevailing plaintiff—a remedy going beyond those which the *GlobalSantaFe* court considered. The court rejected an argument that such an order would be unfair to the foreign registrant, observing: "By choosing to register a domain name in the popular '.org' top-level domain, these foreign registrants deliberately chose to use a top-level domain controlled by a United States registry. They chose, in effect, to play Internet ball in American cyberspace." The court went on to note that foreign registrants can easily avoid the jurisdiction of a U.S. court simply by registering their domain name in a top-level domain whose registry is located in some other country, such as by choosing a country-code top-level domain, like .cn (China) or .kr (South Korea). Is this a persuasive response to the fairness issue?

III. TRADEMARK ISSUES ARISING FROM GRIPE SITES

Taubman Co. v. Webfeats
319 F.3d 770 (6th Cir.2003).

■ SUHRHEINRICH, CIRCUIT JUDGE.

. . .

I. Facts

Mishkoff is a resident of Carrollton, Texas, and a web designer by trade. Upon hearing the news that Taubman, a Delaware corporation with its principal place of business in Michigan, was building a shopping mall called "The Shops at Willow Bend," in Plano, Texas, Mishkoff registered the domain name, "shopsatwillowbend.com," and created an internet website with that address. Mishkoff had no connection to the mall except for the fact that it was being built near his home.

Mishkoff's website featured information about the mall, with a map and links to individual websites of the tenant stores. The site also contained a prominent disclaimer, indicating that Mishkoff's site was unofficial, and a link to Taubman's official site for the mall, found at the addresses "theshopsatwillowbend.com," and "shopwillowbend.com."

Mishkoff describes his site as a "fan site," with no commercial purpose. The site did, however, contain a link to the website of a company run by Mishkoff's girl-friend, Donna Hartley, where she sold custom-made shirts under the name "shirt-biz.com;" and to Mishkoff's site for his web design business, "Webfeats."

When Taubman discovered that Mishkoff had created this site, it demanded he remove it from the internet. Taubman claimed that Mishkoff's use of the domain name "shopsatwillowbend.com" infringed on its registered mark, "The Shops at Willow Bend." Taubman filed a complaint on August 7, 2001, claiming, *inter alia,* trademark infringement under the Lanham Act, 15 U.S.C. § 1114, asking for a preliminary injunction, and demanding surrender of Mishkoff's domain name.

Mishkoff responsively registered five more domain names: 1) taubman-sucks.com; 2) shopsatwillowbendsucks.com; 3) theshopsatwillowbendsucks.com; 4) willowbendmallsucks.com; and 5) willowbendsucks.com. All five of these web names link to the same site, which is a running editorial on Mishkoff's battle with Taubman and its lawyers, and exhaustively documents his proceedings in both the district court and this Court, both through visual scans of filed motions, as well as a first person narrative from Mishkoff. In internet parlance, a web name with a "sucks.com" moniker attached to it is known as a "complaint name," and the process of registering and using such names is known as "cybergriping." . . .

On October 11, 2001, the district court granted Taubman's motion for a preliminary injunction, enjoining Mishkoff from using the first host name, "shopsatwillowbend.com." On October 15, 2001, Taubman filed a motion to amend the preliminary injunction to include the five "complaint names" used by Mishkoff. On December 7, 2001, the district court allowed the amendment and enjoined Mishkoff from using the complaint names.

. . .

III. Analysis

Mishkoff claims the injunctions preventing his use of the domain name "shopsatwillowbend.com" and the five "complaint names" are inappropriate because Taubman has not demonstrated a likelihood of success on the merits and because the orders represent a prior restraint on his First Amendment right to speak.

. . .

B. Propriety of the Injunctions

1. Likelihood of Success on the Merits

The likelihood of success of Taubman's claim rests with the language of the Lanham Act, 15 U.S.C. § 1114(1), which imposes liability for infringement of trademarks on:

Any person who shall, without the consent of the registrant

a) use in commerce any reproduction, counterfeit, copy, or colorable imitation of a registered mark in connection with the sale, offering for sale, distribution, or advertising of any goods or services on or in connection with which such use is likely to cause confusion, or to cause mistake, or to deceive . . . .

. . . .

a. November 9 Injunction—The "shopsatwillowbend" Website

In regard to the first website, "shopsatwillowbend.com," Mishkoff argues that his use is completely non-commercial and not confusing, and therefore speech entitled to the full protections of the First Amendment. Taubman offers three arguments that Mishkoff is using its name commercially to sell or advertise goods or services. First, Mishkoff had a link to a site owned by Hartley's blouse company, "shirtbiz.com." Second, he had a link to his own site for his web design company, Webfeats. Third, Mishkoff had accepted a $1000 offer to relinquish the name to Taubman.

Although Mishkoff claims his intention in creating his website was non- commercial, the proper inquiry is not one of intent. *Daddy's Junky Music Stores, Inc. v. Big Daddy's Family Music Center*, 109 F.3d 275, 287 (6th Cir.1997). In that sense, the Lanham Act is a strict liability statute. *See Hard Rock Café Licensing Corp. v. Concession Servs., Inc.*, 955 F.2d 1143, 1152 n. 6 (7th Cir.1992). If consumers are confused by an infringing mark, the offender's motives are largely irrelevant. *Wynn Oil Co. v. Thomas*, 839 F.2d 1183, 1188 (6th Cir.1988) (citing *Lois Sportswear, U.S.A., Inc. v. Levi Strauss & Co.*, 799 F.2d 867, 875 (2d Cir.1986)). We believe the advertisements on Mishkoff's site, though extremely minimal, constituted his use of Taubman's mark "in connection with the advertising" of the goods sold by the advertisers. This is precisely what the Lanham Act prohibits.

However, Mishkoff had at least removed the shirtbiz.com link prior to the injunction. A preliminary injunction is proper only to prevent an on-going violation. *See, e.g. Hecht Co. v. Bowles*, 321 U.S. 321, 329–30 (1944) (recounting the historical role of courts of equity and stating that purpose of injunctive relief is "to deter, not to punish"). As long as Mishkoff has no commercial links on either of his websites, including links to shirtbiz.com, Webfeats, or any other business, we find no use "in connection with the advertising" of goods and services to enjoin, and the Lanham Act cannot be properly invoked.[3]

Taubman's assertion that its offer to buy the domain name "shopsatwillowbend.com" from Mishkoff qualifies Mishkoff's use of the mark as "in connection with the sale of goods" is meritless. Although other courts have held that a so-called cybersquatter, who registers domain names with the intent to sell the name to the trademark holder, uses the mark "in connection with the sale of goods," they have also limited their holdings to such instances where the defendant had made a habit and a business of such practices. *See, e.g., E & J Gallo Winery v. Spider Webs Ltd.*, 286 F.3d 270, 270 (5th Cir.2002) (noting that defendant had made a business practice of selling domain names on eBay for no less than $10,000); *Panavision Int'l, L.P. v. Toeppen*, 141 F.3d 1316 (9th Cir.1998).

---

[3] Mishkoff sent a letter to Taubman's attorneys on August 10, 2001, referencing the removal of the shirtbiz.com link, and declaring that Mishkoff "will not place any advertising of any kind on the site in the future." It is unclear whether Mishkoff also removed the Webfeats link at this time. To be clear, we also find the Webfeats link to be "use in connection with the advertising of goods and services" which likewise must remain removed to avoid a finding of commerciality.

. . . In contrast, not only has Mishkoff not made a practice of registering and selling domain names, but he did not even initiate the bargaining process here. Although Taubman's counsel intimated at oral argument that Mishkoff had in fact initiated the negotiation process, correspondence in the record supports the opposite conclusion, and shows that Taubman first offered Mishkoff $1000 to relinquish the site on August 16, 2001, and Mishkoff initially accepted it under threat of litigation. Hence, this case is distinguishable from *Panavision*. There is no evidence that Mishkoff's initial motive in selecting Taubman's mark was to re-sell the name. Therefore, we hold his use of the name "shopsatwillowbend.com" is not "in connection with the sale of goods."

Even if Mishkoff's use is commercial speech, i.e., "in connection with the sale . . . or advertising of any goods or services," and within the jurisdiction of the Lanham Act, there is a violation only if his use also creates a likelihood of confusion among customers. 15 U.S.C. § 1114(1). Moreover, the only important question is whether there is a likelihood of confusion *between the parties' goods or services. Bird v. Parsons*, 289 F.3d 865, 877 (6th Cir.2002). Under Lanham Act jurisprudence, it is irrelevant whether customers would be confused as to the origin of the websites, unless there is confusion as to the origin of the respective products. *See also Daddy's Junky Music Stores*, 109 F.3d at 280.

Since its inception, Mishkoff had always maintained a disclaimer on the website, indicating that his was not the official website. In *Holiday Inns, Inc. v. 800 Reservation, Inc.*, 86 F.3d 619 (6th Cir.1996), we found the existence of a disclaimer very informative, and held that there was no likelihood of confusion, partly on that basis.

. . .

We find the analysis here indistinguishable from the disclaimer analysis in *Holiday Inns*. Mishkoff has placed a conspicuous disclaimer informing customers that they had not reached Taubman's official mall site. Furthermore, Mishkoff placed a hyperlink to Taubman's site within the disclaimer. We find this measure goes beyond even what was done by the defendant in *Holiday Inns*. There, a customer who reached the defendant's hotline in error had to hang up and redial the correct Holiday Inns number. *Id.* Here, a misplaced customer simply has to click his mouse to be redirected to Taubman's site. Moreover, like *Holiday Inns*, the customers who stumble upon Mishkoff's site would otherwise have reached a dead address. They would have received an error message upon typing "shopsatwillowbend.com," simply stating that the name was not a proper domain name, with no message relating how to arrive at the official site. Hence, Mishkoff's website and its disclaimer actually serve to re-direct lost customers to Taubman's site that might otherwise be lost. Accordingly, we find no likelihood that a customer would be confused as to the source of Taubman's and Mishkoff's respective goods.

b. December 7 Injunction—The "sucks" Site

In regard to Mishkoff's "complaint site," Taubman claims that Mishkoff's use is necessarily "in connection with the sale of goods" because his intent behind the use of the names "taubmansucks.com," *et al.*, is to harm Taubman economically.

In *Planned Parenthood Fed'n of Amer., Inc. v. Bucci,* 1997 WL 133313 (S.D.N.Y. March 24, 1997), *aff'd,* 1998 WL 336163 (2d Cir. Feb. 9, 1998), the defendant usurped the domain name "plannedparenthood.com" and created a website displaying anti-abortion pictures and pro-life messages in clear contradiction of the plaintiff's stated mission. *Id.* at *1. The court there found that, although not selling or advertising any goods, the defendant's use of Planned Parenthood's mark was commercial because he had used plaintiff's mark and attempted to cause economic harm. *Id.* at *4. (noting that Lanham Act is applicable because "defendant's action in appropriating plaintiff's mark has a connection to *plaintiff's* distribution of its services").

Following *Planned Parenthood,* Taubman argues that all cybergriping sites are per se commercial and "in connection with the sale of goods." However, *Planned Parenthood,* as an unpublished district court opinion, is not binding on this Court, and is nonetheless distinguishable. Even if Mishkoff's use is commercial, it must still lead to a likelihood of confusion to be violative of the Lanham Act. 15 U.S.C. § 1114(1). In *Planned Parenthood,* the defendant used the plaintiff's trade name as a domain name, without the qualifying moniker "sucks," or any other such addendum to indicate that the plaintiff was not the proprietor of the website. In contrast, "taubmansucks.com" removes any confusion as to source. We find no possibility of confusion and no Lanham Act violation.

. . .

IV. Conclusion

For the foregoing reasons, we REVERSE the decision of the district court and dissolve both preliminary injunctions preventing Mishkoff from using the domain name, "shopsatwillowbend.com," and the five "complaint names" listed above.

TMI, Inc. v. Maxwell
368 F.3d 433 (5th Cir.2004).

■ PRADO, CIRCUIT JUDGE.

Following a bench trial, the district court determined that Appellant Joseph Maxwell's website that complained about Appellee TMI, Inc. violated the anti-dilution provision of the Lanham Act, 15 U.S.C. § 1125(c); the Anti-Cybersquatting Consumer Protection Act ("ACPA"), 15 U.S.C. § 1125(d); and the Texas Anti-Dilution Statute, Tex. Bus. & Com. Code § 16.29. Concluding that Maxwell's site, as a non-commercial gripe site, violates none of these statutes, we reverse and render judgment in favor of Maxwell.

Appellant Joseph Maxwell intended to buy a house from Appellee TMI, Inc., a company that builds houses under the name TrendMaker Homes. Unhappy with what he viewed as the salesperson's misrepresentations about the availability of a certain model, Maxwell decided to create a website to tell his story. To this end, Maxwell registered an internet domain name — www.trendmakerhome.com — that resembled TMI's TrendMaker Homes mark. (TMI had already been using the domain name www.trendmakerhomes.com.) Maxwell registered his domain name for a year; after the year passed, Maxwell removed the site and let the registration expire.

During its existence, the site contained Maxwell's story of his dispute with TMI, along with a disclaimer at the top of the home page indicating that it was not TMI's site. It also contained what Maxwell called the Treasure Chest. Maxwell envisioned the Treasure Chest as a place for readers to share and obtain information about contractors and tradespeople who had done good work. During the year of the site's existence, the Treasure Chest only contained one name, that of a man who had performed some work for Maxwell. The site did not contain any paid advertisements.

The parties agree that some e-mail intended for TMI was sent to Maxwell's site. They also agree that Maxwell forwarded each of these messages to TMI.

Shortly after Maxwell's registration expired, TMI sent Maxwell a letter demanding that he take down the site and relinquish the www.trendmakerhome.com domain name. In response, Maxwell attempted to re-register the domain name. His attempt was unsuccessful, however, because TMI had acquired the domain name once Maxwell's registration expired. Instead, Maxwell registered the domain name www.trendmakerhome.info. This lawsuit followed. Because of the suit, Maxwell has never posted any content on the trendmakerhome.info site.

. . .

Commercial Use Requirement

We first address whether the two relevant sections of the Lanham Act — the anti-dilution provision and ACPA — require commercial use for liability.[2] The district court concluded that ACPA requires commercial use, but did not address commercial use in the context of the anti-dilution provision. TMI argues that the anti-dilution provision applies even in the absence of commercial use.

In making this argument, TMI does not address the anti-dilution provision's language, which conditions liability on commercial use . . . . We conclude that, under the statute's language, Maxwell's use must be commercial to fall under the anti-dilution provision.

On the other hand, ACPA's language does not contain such a specific commercial-use requirement. Under ACPA, the owner of a mark can recover against a person who, acting with "a bad faith intent to profit from that mark . . . registers, traffics in, or uses a domain name that . . . is identical or confusingly similar to that mark." 15 U.S.C. § 1125(d). ACPA thus bases liability on a bad faith intent to profit. ACPA lists nine non-exclusive factors for courts to consider when determining whether a defendant had a bad faith intent to profit. One of those factors is "the

---

[2] This Court has previously determined that § 43(a) of the Lanham Act, 15 U.S.C. § 1125(a)(1), which addresses false and misleading descriptions, only applies to commercial speech. *See Procter & Gamble Co. v. Amway Corp.*, 242 F.3d 539, 547 (5th Cir.2001).

person's bona fide noncommercial or fair use of the mark in a site accessible under the domain name." 15 U.S.C. § 1125(d)(1)(B)(i)(IV).

This Court has addressed ACPA and commercial use in *E. & J. Gallo Winery v. Spider Webs Ltd.*, 286 F.3d 270, 276 n. 3 (5th Cir.2002). . . . Because Spider Web's use was so clearly commercial, the Court noted that it did not need to decide whether ACPA also requires use in commerce. *Id.* at 276 n. 3. The Sixth Circuit, too, recently determined that it did not need to consider arguments about whether ACPA covers non-commercial use, "as the statute directs a reviewing court to consider only a defendant's 'bad faith intent to profit' from the use of a mark held by another party." *Lucas Nursery & Landscaping, Inc. v. Grosse*, 359 F.3d 806, 809 (6th Cir.2004). Like the *Lucas Nursery* court, we, too, do not need to decide this question in this case.

. . .

Bad faith intent to profit

ACPA lists nine non-exclusive factors for courts to consider when determining whether a defendant had a bad faith intent to profit from use of the mark. [15 U.S.C. § 1125(d)(1)(B)(i).]

Much of the district court's analysis of bad faith intent to profit focuses on Maxwell's behavior during the settlement negotiations and, particularly, his backing out of the settlement. Although the district court listed the nine relevant factors, in the Memorandum and Order it did not explain how those factors apply to this case.

Maxwell's behavior differs from other registrations made with bad faith intent to profit. For example, in *Gallo*, and other cases, the defendant essentially held hostage a domain name that resembled a mark with the intention of selling it back to the mark's owner. So, too, is Maxwell's use different from that of the defendant in *Virtual Works, Inc. v. Volkswagen of America, Inc.*, 238 F.3d 264 (4th Cir.2001), where Virtual Works registered the domain name "VW.net" for its own website, but also hoping to sell the name to Volkswagen, whose VW mark the domain name resembled.

In contrast to these instances of bad faith intent to profit, the Sixth Circuit recently affirmed a trial court's finding that a disgruntled customer who posted a website similar to Maxwell's did not have a bad faith intent to profit. *Lucas Nursery & Landscaping, Inc. v. Grosse*, 359 F.3d at 811. In *Lucas Nursery*, a former customer of Lucas Nursery registered the domain name "lucasnursery.com" and used the site to post her complaints about the nursery's work. *Id.* at 808. The nursery sued her under ACPA. *Id.* After addressing the purposes behind ACPA, the *Lucas Nursery* court concluded that the former customer did not have the kind of intent to profit that the act was designed to prohibit. *Id.* at 808–11.

As in *Lucas Nursery*, here "[t]he paradigmatic harm that the ACPA was enacted to eradicate—the practice of cybersquatters registering several hundred domain names in an effort to sell them to the legitimate owners of the mark—is simply not present." *Id.* at 810. Also here, as in *Lucas Nursery*, the site's purpose as a method to inform potential customers about a negative experience with the company is key. As the Sixth Circuit noted:

> Perhaps most important to our conclusion are, [defendant's] actions, which seem to have been undertaken in the spirit of informing fellow consumers about the practices of a landscaping company that she believed had performed inferior work on her yard. One of the ACPA's main objectives is the protection of consumers from slick internet peddlers who trade on the names and reputations of established brands. The practice of informing fellow consumers of one's experience with a particular service provider is surely not inconsistent with this ideal.

Id. at 811.

In short, after analyzing the statutory factors and ACPA's purpose, we are convinced that TMI failed to establish that Maxwell had a bad faith intent to profit from TMI's mark and that the district court's conclusion to the contrary was clearly erroneous. Although factors I, II, III and IX seem to fall in favor of TMI because Maxwell had no pre-existing use of the TrendMaker name and Maxwell did not dispute that the mark was distinctive and famous, importantly, factors IV, V, VI, VII, and VIII favor Maxwell. Under factor IV, Maxwell made bona fide noncommercial use of the mark in his site, and for purposes of factor V, TMI made no showing that Maxwell intended to divert customers from its own site. Turning to factor VI, Maxwell never offered to sell the domain name, and certainly never had a pattern of selling domain names to mark owners. Maxwell did not behave improperly when providing contact information, as addressed in factor VII. Factor VIII concerns the registration of multiple domain names; Maxwell's registration of his second site related to TrendMaker Homes does not argue in favor of finding bad faith intent to profit. Maxwell registered the second domain name for the same purposes as the first one and only after his registration of the first name expired. Finally, like the *Lucas Nursery* court, we particularly note that Maxwell's conduct is not the kind of harm that ACPA was designed to prevent.

. . .

Conclusion

For these reasons, we reverse the judgment of the district court and render judgment in favor of Maxwell.

EXTENSIONS

"Sucks" sites and the UDRP. Numerous disputes involving "sucks" sites have been resolved by panels applying the Uniform Domain Name Dispute Resolution Policy ("UDRP"), which is discussed in Part IV, *infra.* As one panel explains:

> There is a split among the UDRP decisions regarding whether a "-sucks" domain name is confusingly similar to the trademark to which it is appended. The majority of the decisions have found confusing similarity. In a minority of decisions, and in some dissenting opinions, Panelists have deemed a "-sucks" addition to a well-known trademark to be an obvious indication that the domain name is not affiliated with that trademark owner. This Panel, however, concurs with the notion that every case must be assessed on its own merits, . . . and there-

fore does not accept the *per se* rule, resulting in an automatic finding of no confusing similarity. . . .

A reading of UDRP precedent reveals that Panels have routinely found confusing similarity when a domain name incorporates Complainant's well-known mark and merely adds a generic or slang term. Many Panels have specifically found that the addition of the slang word "sucks" does not mitigate confusing similarity from the perspective of a person searching on the Internet. . . .

The panel also made a point of distinguishing between legitimate protest sites and "cybersquatter" sites. In the case before it, the domain names wachoviasucks.com, wachovia-sucks.com, and wachoviabanksucks.com led Internet users not to protest sites but rather to competing financial services. The panel found that the registrant had no legitimate interest in using the domain names for this purpose. *Wachovia Corporation v. Alton Flanders*, Case No. D2003–0596 (WIPO 2003).

QUESTIONS FOR DISCUSSION

The rules applying to gripe sites. Based on these two cases, what steps must the operator of a gripe site take (and not take) to avoid liability for trademark infringement, dilution, or cybersquatting? Is it enough to post a prominent disclaimer? Use "sucks" as part of the domain name? Avoid any arguably commercial use of the site? Given the statement in *Taubman v. Webfeats* that for infringement liability the only cognizable confusion is that between the origin of the respective products, can a pure gripe site ever constitute trademark infringement? Given the analysis in *TMI v. Maxwell* of the ACPA's requirement of bad-faith intent to profit, can a pure gripe site ever be actionable under the ACPA?

IV. ICANN's UNIFORM DOMAIN NAME DISPUTE RESOLUTION POLICY

To avoid becoming embroiled in disputes between trademark owners and domain name registrants—which often take the form of costly court proceedings—domain name registrars have adopted dispute resolution policies and procedures. The first domain name registrar to adopt a dispute resolution policy was Network Solutions, Inc. ("NSI"), until recently the sole registrar for the .com, .net and .org top-level domains.[5] Under this policy, NSI would suspend the use of any disputed domain name if the complaining party could prove that it had a trademark registration in any country in the world for a mark identical to the disputed domain name. Thus, a complaining party could register a mark in Tunisia, a country in which marks are granted by registration only, and render someone else's domain name inoperative. Once a domain name was put "on hold," it was no longer available for use by anyone and its status could only be altered by order of a court of competent jurisdiction stating which party was entitled to use the disputed domain name. The NSI policy satisfied no one. Domain name registrants complained that NSI improperly suspended use of a domain name before a court had an opportunity to determine whether use of that domain name infringed a trademark of the complaining party. Owners of registered trademarks complained that the NSI policy did not prevent the use of domain names that were confusingly

---

[5] NSI adopted its first dispute resolution policy in 1995. This policy was followed by a series of revisions of which the last was NSI Policy Revision 03, effective February 25, 1998. Beginning in 1999, the successor regime under ICANN was put in place.

similar, but not identical, to their trademarks. Finally, owners of unregistered, common law or state trademarks complained that the NSI policy did not recognize their trademark rights at all. General dissatisfaction with the NSI policy in large measure fueled the process that led to the creation of ICANN and the requirement that all ICANN-accredited domain name registrars adopt its Uniform Domain Name Dispute Resolution Policy ("UDRP").[6]

Like the predecessor NSI policy, the UDRP is intended to prevent ICANN as well as its approved registrars from becoming embroiled in disputes surrounding domain names. As Section 6 of the UDRP states unequivocally, a domain name registrar "will not participate in any way in any dispute between you and any party . . . regarding the registration and use of your domain name." That same section also provides that the domain name registrant "shall not name [the domain name registrar] as a party or otherwise include [it] in any such proceeding." To reduce the need for resort to the courts, the UDRP sets up a streamlined alternative dispute resolution process. Through this process, a trademark owner can challenge a domain name registrant's right to use a disputed domain name before an ICANN-approved administrative panel.

Under the rules of procedure governing UDRP proceedings,[7] the administrative panel must render a written decision concerning this challenge within approximately forty-five days of the commencement of the proceeding. Consistent with the streamlined character of the process, a panel's decision is usually based upon a single submission by each of the parties and neither party is given the opportunity for discovery. If the complaining party is successful and no other litigation is pending, then ten business days after receiving the decision, the domain name registrar will either cancel or transfer the disputed domain name registration in accordance with the panel's decision. If, however, the domain name registrant brings an action in a court of competent jurisdiction before the end of this ten-day period, then the domain name registrar will continue the status quo until a final judgment is obtained. *See* UDRP §§ 3, 4(i) and (k), and 8.

While the UDRP has been the target of considerable criticism, it is nonetheless considered a significant advance over the NSI policy for at least four reasons. First, under the UDRP the use of disputed domain names is no longer suspended. A domain name registrant may continue to use his or her domain name while the complaining party's rights in the domain name are being determined before an ICANN-approved arbitration panel or a court of competent jurisdiction. *See* UDRP § 7. Second, the UDRP permits trademark owners to challenge the use of domain names that are confusingly similar to their trademarks. It is worth noting that while the UDRP expands the grounds upon which a trademark owner may challenge the use of a domain name, unlike the Anticybersquatting Consumer Protection Act, the UDRP does not permit a trademark owner to challenge the use of a domain name because it is dilutive of his or her famous trademark. *Compare* UDRP § 4(a)(i) *with* 15 U.S.C. § 1125(d)(1)(A)(ii)(II). Third, the UDRP applies not only to nationally registered trademarks but also to state and common law trademarks. Fourth, and most significantly, proceedings under the UDRP are limited to domain name disputes in which the disputed domain name "has been registered and is being used in bad faith." UDRP § 4(a)(iii). The

---

[6] *See* Uniform Domain Name Dispute Resolution Policy (adopted Oct. 24, 1999), www.icann.org/dndr/udrp/policy.htm. For further discussion of ICANN, *see* Chapter 1, Part II(F), *supra*.

[7] *See* Rules for Uniform Domain Name Dispute Resolution Policy (adopted Oct. 24, 1999), www.icann.org/udrp/udrp-rules–24oct99.htm.

UDRP is specifically targeted at cybersquatting. It does not apply if the domain name registrant has registered the disputed domain name in good faith. Examples of good faith registration would include those made in connection with a bona fide offering of goods or services, registration of a name by which the domain name registrant has been commonly known, as well as the registration of another's trademark so long as the domain name registrant is making a legitimate noncommercial or fair use of that mark. *See* UDRP § 4(c).

In the remainder of this Part, we focus on the general structure of the dispute resolution process created by the UDRP and how the UDRP has been interpreted by both administrative panelists and the federal courts. In particular, the first excerpt looks at whether the UDRP implements a dispute resolution framework that is conducive to the impartial resolution of disputes between trademark owners and domain name registrants and to the development of a consistent domain name jurisprudence. Next is a decision by an administrative panel that considers, among other things, the status of foreign trademarks rights under the UDRP. Finally, we consider one federal district court's view of the significance of an administrative panel's decision under the UDRP for related federal litigation involving the disputed domain name.

Laurence R. Helfer & Graeme B. Dinwoodie, *Designing Non-National Systems: The Case of the Uniform Domain Name Dispute Resolution Policy*
43 Wm. & Mary L. Rev. 141 (2001).

. . .

In practice as well as in construction, the UDRP has proven to be a remarkable development in the history of international dispute settlement. Even had trademark owners filed only a handful of complaints with panels and even had those complaints concerned only core domain-name abuses, the system would be worthy of serious scrutiny. But precisely the opposite trend has occurred.

In the first twenty-one months of the UDRP's existence, panels operating under the auspices of ICANN-approved dispute settlement providers have been inundated with cases. As of September 2001, filed complaints numbered over 4300. UDRP panels have issued over 3500 published decisions, with more than three-quarters of these decisions ordering domain names transferred to the complaining trademark owners. Although domain name registrants have achieved a few sporadic (but important) victories during the last few months, beginning in the earliest days of the UDRP panels interpreted the Policy and Rules expansively in ways that generally favored intellectual property owners over domain name registrants. These rulings occurred notwithstanding the clear intent of the UDRP drafters to limit the panels' authority to core cases of domain-name abuse, and at a time when both ICANN and WIPO were considering their own expansion of the UDRP to new gTLDs and existing country code domain names (ccTLDs) as well as to names and identifiers not covered by the present Policy. . . .

[T]he UDRP is composed of elements found in judicial, arbitral, and ministerial decision-making systems. . . . Within any single judicial, arbitral, or ministerial decision-making system, a variety of checking mechanisms constrain the power of decision makers. As a working typology, we divide these mechanisms into three distinct categories, which we refer to as creational, external, and internal checking functions. These checking mechanisms serve several important objectives. They bolster the legitimacy of decision-making outcomes and the accountability of decision makers, they confine decision making within the bounds of a system's institutional capacity, they correct errors, and they ensure consistent outcomes in factually and legally comparable cases.

When elements from different decision-making systems are combined, however, the checking mechanisms that operate in any one system cannot automatically be imported into the new hybrid system. In the case of the UDRP, checking devices found in one or another of the adjudicatory, arbitral, and ministerial models are insufficient in themselves to constrain UDRP panel decision making; oftentimes, they are simply inappropriate. Moreover, ambiguities and contradictions as to the source and content of the UDRP's checking functions send conflicting messages to panels and create incentives for them to act in ways the UDRP's drafters did not intend. . . .

The success of arbitration—its speed, its decision making tailored more closely to parties' intent than to default principles of law, and its finality ensured by less intrusive external review by courts—is premised upon two important characteristics not present here. First, the parties in arbitration have consented to these reduced forms of external checks, and second, the decision of the arbitrator affects only the parties and has limited if any value in articulating broader norms or rules. Neither the parties (by virtue of their consent) nor society (because the arbitration affects only the disputants) can therefore object to the truncated external checking mechanisms that are found in the arbitral model.

By contrast, parties to non-national UDRP proceedings are strangers and have not, other than formally, consented to the arbitral procedures thereunder, and the process by which the UDRP was created cannot serve as a genuine proxy for their consent. And if UDRP decision making is to effect the creation of norms, as we (and the proponents of the UDRP) intend and as the publication of decisions makes inevitable, then some of the control features found in a traditional adjudicatory model must be incorporated.

This does not mean that we should simply adopt an adjudicatory template, however. Courts remain predominantly national in nature, and court proceedings remain slow and expensive. So the wholesale adoption of the adjudicatory model is not attractive as a solution to a non-national problem. Instead, only selective incorporation of some of the checking features of that model is advisable.

Adoption of adjudicatory features, of course, will slow down the decision-making process, and thus, one might wish to reinject speed. Here, the ministerial model has a role to play. Ministerial decision making has the advantage of speed but it is restricted to cases where the application of the relevant rules is routinized. Much of the non-national decision making that occurs in the UDRP is not so routine. Consequently, although we might wish to incorporate aspects of the ministerial model, we cannot rely wholly on it as an antecedent because the functions it delegates to decision makers assume a far less discretionary form of decision making than we contemplate here. It would appear then that the non-national model could benefit from some—but not all—aspects of this pre-existing model. . . .

[M]uch of the UDRP was built in part upon an arbitral model of decision making. The resolution of disputes between private parties pursuant to what are nominally contractual obligations; the use of lawyers, academics, and retired judges as decision makers; the creation of multiple, independent dispute settlement centers; and the role of the parties in choosing the panel all reflect arbitral antecedents. . . .

When viewed in the aggregate, the most important constraints on arbitral decision makers are ex ante creational checks rather than ex post external or internal checks. The parties' ultimate control over an arbitrator's power flows from their virtually unfettered right to choose the substantive and procedural rules according to which the arbitral panel will decide their dispute. For this reason, negotiating the terms of the agreement to arbitrate is perhaps the most effective means of preserving accountability, preventing errors and controlling excesses of arbitral power. . . .

Consider the implications of this balance of arbitral checking functions for the UDRP. By imposing uniform, mandatory dispute settlement rules upon all domain-name registrants, ICANN eliminated the ability of registrants to opt out of UDRP dispute settlement proceedings or to tailor the system to their needs. When an individual registers a domain name with any registrar of names in the three unrestricted generic top level domains anywhere in the world, she confronts a non-negotiable contract of adhesion. She cannot specify the subject matter of the disputes upon which the panel is empowered to rule or the procedures that it will follow, and she has (consistent with the inapt analogy to arbitral models) only limited control (via her selection of registrar, and hence the courts of mutual jurisdiction from which to seek redress) over the mechanisms by which panel excesses or errors may be challenged or reviewed.

In effect, all of the key substantive and procedural terms of the UDRP "arbitration" agreement are prenegotiated by ICANN, which merely heightens the importance of the content of the UDRP's two foundational documents and the legitimacy of the process by which they were drafted. If these foundational documents fairly balance the substantive interests of trademark owners and domain-name registrants and if they contain equivalent procedural rights for both parties, then using ICANN as a proxy for individualized negotiation of a dispute settlement agreement may well be an acceptable and efficient alternative. If, by contrast, these foundational documents are substantively or procedurally skewed, or if the process by which they were created is open to challenge on legitimacy and accountability grounds, then the arbitral "bargain" struck by ICANN is itself called into question and a decisive check on the authority of UDRP panels has been cast into doubt. . . .

These concerns over the UDRP's creational checking functions are further exacerbated by the fact that external checks are even more attenuated in the UDRP context than they are for international arbitration, both with respect to institutional controls and controls by national courts. Consider first the external checks imposed by the four dispute settlement providers and ICANN itself. Under many systems of institutional arbitration . . . arbitral centers retain the authority to enforce each panelist's obligation to be both independent and impartial, first by requiring panelists to disclose any circumstances giving rise to doubts over those two attributes, and second by entertaining challenges from the parties to a particular panelist.

The system of neutrality enforcement contemplated under the UDRP is substantially more attenuated. Although the UDRP Rules do impose a duty on all panelists to be impartial and independent, the means by which that duty is enforced differ according to dispute settlement provider and thus vary from case to case. One provider gives no specific provision for party challenges; another allows challenges only within a fixed period of time after the initial appointment of a panelist; whereas a third (and perhaps a fourth) permits challenges at any time during the proceedings if doubts about a particular panelist arise. In addition, the grounds upon which challenges will be recognized vary widely. The fact that ICANN permits dispute settlement providers to adopt different standards of review of a panelist's independence and impartiality suggests that providers may compete with one another over the substantive and procedural bases for panelist challenges. Whether such competition is likely to lead to more or less stringent panelist review is uncertain, however, and turns in part on the decision-making incentives created by the UDRP's panel selection rules, an issue we address [below].

The absence of meaningful external controls by national courts over UDRP proceedings is even more striking. As an initial matter, however, the claim that external checking functions are more limited for the UDRP than for international arbitration seems contrary to the plain terms of the Policy. After all, the drafters expressly designed the UDRP as a soft-law system that supplements but does not supplant national court adjudication of domain name disputes. If de novo review by a national court is possible, then it would seem that the UDRP's external checking functions are far stronger than the extremely limited national court checking mechanisms at work in arbitration. Several features of the UDRP significantly undermine this argument, however, particularly with respect to external checking functions affecting domain name registrants. These features suggest that the UDRP may be soft law in theory, but much harder law in practice.

Consider first the filing of a complaint by a respondent in a court of so-called "mutual jurisdiction" to challenge a UDRP panel decision ordering her domain name to be canceled or transferred (described somewhat loosely as an "appeal" in the preparatory documents). The extremely short ten-day window within which respondents must file such a proceeding is likely to exert a significant deterrent effect on national court review. Initiating litigation is often a time-consuming and complex process, particularly for individuals and businesses with limited financial resources who may be forced to find an attorney to litigate in a foreign jurisdiction. Of course, nothing precludes a respondent from filing national court proceedings after the ten-day window has expired. The registrant's incentives to do so once a domain name has been canceled or transferred will be substantially diminished, however, particularly when the removal of the domain name disrupts her established or planned business operations. From a cost-benefit perspective, it may be preferable to transfer operations to a different domain name or even to abandon a start-up enterprise altogether. Empirical evidence on this point is anecdotal, but the most comprehensive database of national court challenges to UDRP rulings lists only twenty-five cases in federal district court and one foreign case out of the more than 3500 UDRP panel decisions to date.

Second, it is unclear whether respondents who do muster the resources to appeal panel decisions in fact possess a cause of action against a trademark owner under national laws seeking retention of the domain name. . . . [T]he Anti-Cybersquatting Consumer Protection Act . . . permits domain-name registrants whose domain name has been canceled or transferred pursuant to the UDRP (or a similar policy) to file a civil action in U.S. federal court against the prevailing party in order to establish that the registration and use of the domain name was lawful under the Lanham Act. If the domain-name registrant is successful, the court may "grant injunctive relief to the domain name registrant, including the reactivation of the domain name or transfer of the domain name to the domain name registrant." To our knowledge, no other national law provides such a cause of action.

Third, respondents who frame their claims not as an appeal of the merits of a UDRP ruling but rather as a challenge to excesses of panel power are equally unlikely to prevail. In traditional international arbitral proceedings, nation-states have enacted detailed statutory regimes to allow losing parties to challenge awards, albeit on very limited grounds. But it is doubtful that hybrid UDRP decisions qualify as arbitral awards under these statutes, particularly given the de novo national court review contemplated by the Policy. Courts in the United States, at least, have indicated that they would not be bound by panel findings, which suggests a clear intent not to treat panel decisions as arbitral awards. For this reason, it is doubtful that national courts possess any grant of power to review UDRP panel abuses as such.

. . .

Uncertainty over the location of national court review and the substantive law to be applied raises a fourth doubt regarding national courts' ability to provide adequate external checks on UDRP panel abuses. Initially, one would expect that, as a result of the mutual jurisdiction provision in the UDRP, courts in jurisdictions where registrars are based might develop an expertise and interest in reviewing UDRP panel decisions. . . . But the mutual jurisdiction provision is unlikely over time to centralize such expertise. Even assuming that trademark owners will select the domicile of the registrar as the court of mutual jurisdiction rather than the domicile of the domain-name registrant, the geographic location of registrars is slowly diversifying under ICANN's competitive registration policy. . . .

Finally, the attenuation of national courts' external checking function is manifested by the automatic nature of UDRP enforcement. Unlike international arbitrations subject to the New York Convention, there is no requirement that prevailing UDRP complainants institute separate national court proceedings to enforce their awards—a crucial check on arbitral power. Instead, enforcement of UDRP awards in favor of trademark owners are automatic unless the respondent takes steps to appeal. This shift of the burden of enforcement removes any opportunity for a "second look" at the arbitral award, thereby destabilizing one of the features that makes the strong presumption favoring enforcement of arbitral awards acceptable in the first place.

For the foregoing reasons, national courts are unlikely to exercise significant de facto external checks on abuses of authority by UDRP panels, notwithstanding the de jure power that they are given under the terms of the Policy. This leaves internal checking functions as the principal method by which arbitral-type excesses are to be checked. Yet UDRP panels have only weak incentives to limit their own authority.

[P]anelists and institutions operating in international arbitration cases compete for business of both complaining and responding parties. They thus have an incentive to stay within the boundaries of the arbitral agreement and to issue awards that encourage repeat business from both parties. In the UDRP, by contrast, competition incentives are skewed in favor of complainant intellectual property owners. It is complainants, not respondents, who choose the dispute settlement provider and who pay panel fees in all single-panelist cases. In principle, respondents may convert a single-member panel to a three-person panel after receiving the complaint. In practice, the large number of cases in which respondents fail to appear and the added cost of choosing a three-person panel for those who do significantly diminish the impact of respondents' choice on the incentives of providers and decision makers.

Confirming fears expressed by some participants during the ICANN review-and-comment process, evidence suggests that dispute settlement providers are acting on the "irresistible incentive to . . . develop a reputation for deciding cases in favor of complainants." Providers now publish statistics on their win/loss records and other information about their decisions, information which serves as indirect advertising to trademark owners intent on choosing the most complainant-friendly provider. There is also anecdotal evidence that providers have adopted more overt methods to attract complainants by boasting of the tough stance their panelists have taken in UDRP disputes. These features have already created a public perception that some dispute settlement providers are more complainant friendly than others, a fact that the case statistics support (although the cause-and-effect dynamic is still unclear).

In addition, consider the identity of the individuals who serve as UDRP panelists. Most are practicing intellectual property attorneys, while a somewhat lower number are retired judges and legal academics. It is at least an open question whether decision makers from the private sector can sufficiently distance themselves from the milieu in which they practice to self-limit their own powers and develop balanced norms for the trademark-domain name interface. This is particularly true if panelists are permitted to trade on their UDRP expertise by representing trademark owners in future domain-name disputes.

Taken together, these skewed internal checking functions are likely to place significant pressure on UDRP decision makers to rule in favor of complaining trademark owners. If, however, the disputes subject to the UDRP were both unambiguous and narrow, then the Policy itself might exert an adequate constraining force to prevent panelists from acting on these pressures. As we explain below, however, the UDRP provides panelists with discretionary decision-making authority, making it unlikely that the text of the Policy will exert such a constraining effect. . . .

[T]he first three subsections of paragraph 4 of the Policy . . . set forth the elements that a complainant must prove to justify a transfer or cancellation of a domain name. Paragraphs 4(b) and 4(c) list the circumstances demonstrating, on the one hand, a respondent's "registration and use" of a domain name in bad faith, and on the other, her "rights or legitimate interests" in the domain name sufficient to defeat a complaint. If the UDRP were designed as a system of constrained judicial decision making, these enumerated circumstances would be dispositive of all claims and all defenses. Under such a system panels would admittedly still have interpretative discretion to decide in each dispute whether the facts presented fell within the parameters of the enumerated rules and to resolve ambiguities contained within the rules themselves. However, the exclusive nature of the categories would exert considerable constraining force, preventing panels from expanding the Policy very far beyond the heartland of cases circumscribed by the text.

The UDRP's drafters, however, did not limit panelists' discretion to these enumerated grounds. Instead, they labeled these exemplars as "circumstances" which existed only "in particular but without limitation" to other situations of bad faith, on the one hand, or rights and legitimate expectations, on the other. Such an obvious and open-ended invitation to lawmaking sends a clear message to panels that they can exercise independent authority in determining which sorts of unenumerated circumstances justify a ruling in favor of complainants or respondents. Without constraints on these open-ended clauses, panels are left with little to guide the exercise of their discretionary lawmaking powers. Not surprisingly, this omission has produced a schism between panels that strictly construe the UDRP and those that interpret the Policy more expansively to curb a broader range of conduct by domain-name registrants.[8] . . .

ICANN's conflicting signals to UDRP panels concerning their adjudicatory powers also affects their adoption of internal checking mechanisms. On a basic level, the requirement that all decisions be published and reasoned exerts a con-

---

[8] [In a portion of the article not reproduced here, the authors document their claim that some panels have interpreted the UDRP more expansively to curb a broader range of conduct by domain-name registrants, noting the following: "Several panels have extended the UDRP to cases involving legitimate disputes over domain name ownership or to bad faith registration without corresponding bad faith use, categories of cases that the drafters expressly excluded from the Policy. More striking still is a line of cases permitting surname and geographic name owners to bring successful complaints against domain name registrants (either by ignoring the elements required to prove a claim or by very expansive interpretation of the notion of common law trademark rights). Not only did these rulings ignore the drafters' desire to limit the UDRP to trademark controversies, they also were issued at a time when WIPO was studying whether to recommend an expansion of the Policy to encompass these precise intellectual property rights."—Eds.]

straining effect on gross errors and excesses of authority. Panelists know that the decisions they author will be available to all potentially affected parties, including not only the litigants, but future litigants, other panelists, and ICANN. They thus have a significant interest in ensuring that their rulings meet at least minimal levels of competence and persuasiveness, particularly if they hope to receive future UDRP assignments.

Beyond this bare minimum level of competence, however, there are few structural incentives for panels to produce carefully reasoned decisions. Well-reasoned decisions require at least a modicum of deliberation, a quality that the time and cost-sensitive UDRP does not favor. Consider the following: Panels normally must issue a decision within less than forty-five days after a complaint is filed. Panelists are private adjudicators with other responsibilities outside of the UDRP competing for their time. Also, the modest compensation panelists receive for their services pales in comparison to the fees they can receive as practicing attorneys or deciding other arbitral matters. Each of these pressures are likely to limit the attention that panelists can devote to drafting reasoned opinions. . . .

The UDRP's hybrid decision-making structure poses a more fundamental challenge to developing a consistent domain name jurisprudence. The arbitral model upon which much of the UDRP was founded places limited weight on past awards as sources of authority. It also focuses more on resolving disputes between the parties than on articulating governing legal norms or creating a jurisprudence to guide future conduct by nonparties. . . . [The authors conclude that] it is questionable whether the UDRP as presently constituted can achieve jurisprudential coherence.

Madonna Ciccone, p/k/a Madonna v. Dan Parisi and "Madonna.com"
Case No. D2000–0847 (WIPO Oct. 12, 2000).

1. The Parties

The Complainant is Madonna Ciccone, an individual professionally known as Madonna.

The Respondent is "Madonna.com," the registrant for the disputed domain name, located in New York, New York, U.S.A. or Dan Parisi, the listed contact for the domain name.

2. The Domain Name(s) and Registrar(s)

The disputed domain name is *madonna.com*.

The registrar is Network Solutions, Inc., 505 Huntmar Park Drive, Herndon, Virginia 20170, U.S.A.

3. Procedural History

This action was brought in accordance with the ICANN Uniform Domain Name Dispute Resolution Policy, dated October 24, 1999 ("the Policy") and the ICANN Rules for Uniform Domain Name Dispute Resolution Policy, dated October 24, 1999 ("the Rules").

The Complaint was received by the WIPO Arbitration and Mediation Center on July 21, 2000 (e-mail) and on July 24, 2000 (hardcopy). The Response was received on August 23, 2000 (e-mail) and on August 28, 2000 (hardcopy). Both parties are represented by Counsel. There have been no further submissions on the merits.

Respondent elected to have the case decided by a three-member panel. David E. Sorkin was appointed as the Respondent's nominee. James W. Dabney was selected as the Complainant's nominee. Mark V.B. Partridge was appointed as presiding panelist.

It appears that all requirements of the Policy and the Rules have been satisfied by the parties, WIPO and the Panelists.

4. Factual Background

Complainant is the well-known entertainer Madonna. She is the owner of U.S. Trademark Registrations for the mark MADONNA for entertainment services and related goods (Reg. No. 1,473,554 and 1,463,601). She has used her name and mark MADONNA professionally for entertainment services since 1979. Complainant's music and other entertainment endeavors have often been controversial for featuring explicit sexual content. In addition, nude photographs of Madonna have appeared in Penthouse magazine, and Complainant has published a coffee-table book entitled "Sex" featuring sexually explicit photographs and text.

Respondent is in the business of developing web sites. On or about May 29, 1998, Respondent, through its business Whitehouse.com, Inc., purchased the registration for the disputed domain name from Pro Domains for $20,000. On June 4, 1998, Respondent registered MADONNA as a trademark in Tunisia. On or about June 8, 1998, Respondent began operating an "adult entertainment portal web site." The web site featured sexually explicit photographs and text, and contained a notice stating "Madonna.com is not affiliated or endorsed by the Catholic Church, Madonna College, Madonna Hospital or Madonna the singer." By March 4, 1999, it appears that Respondent removed the explicit sexual content from the web site. By May 31, 1999, it appears that the site merely contained the above notice, the disputed domain name and the statement "Coming soon Madonna Gaming and Sportsbook."

On June 9, 1999, Complainant, through her attorneys, objected to Respondent's use of the Madonna.com domain name. On June 14, 1999, Respondent through its counsel stated: "As I assume you also know, Mr. Parisi's website [sic] was effectively shut down before you sent your letter, and is now shut down altogether. He is in the process of donating his registration for the domain name."

The word "Madonna," which has the current dictionary definition as the Virgin Mary or an artistic depiction of the Virgin Mary, is used by others as a trademark, trade name and personal name. After Respondent's receipt of Complainant's objection, it appears that Respondent had communication with Madonna Rehabilitation Hospital regarding the transfer of the domain name to the Hospital. It further appears that Respondent has not identified all of its communications on this matter.

Nevertheless, the transfer had not taken place at the time this proceeding was commenced.

By his own admission, Respondent has registered a large number of other domain names, including names that matched the trademarks of others. Other domain names registered by Respondent include <wallstreetjournal.com> and <edgaronline.com>. See Response, Exhibit A, 30, 35.

5. Parties' Contentions

A. Complainant

Complaint contends that the disputed domain name is identical to the registered and common law trademark MADONNA in which she owns rights. She further contends that Respondent has no legitimate interest or rights in the domain name. Finally, Complainant contends that Respondent obtained and used the disputed domain name with the intent to attract Internet users to a pornographic web site for commercial gain based on confusion with Complainant's name and mark.

B. Respondent

Respondent does not dispute that the disputed domain name is identical or confusingly similar to Complainant's trademark. Respondent, however, claims that Complainant cannot show a lack of legitimate interest in the domain name because Respondent (a) made demonstrable preparation to use the domain name for a bona fide business purpose; (b) holds a bona fide trademark in the word MADONNA; and (c) has attempted to make bona fide noncommercial use of the name by donating it to the Madonna Rehabilitation Hospital.

Respondent also contends that it has not registered and used the domain name in bad faith because (a) there is no evidence that its primary motivation was to sell the disputed domain name; (b) the domain name was not registered with an intent to prevent Complainant from using her mark as a domain name; (c) respondent is not engaged in a pattern of registering domain names to prevent others from doing so; (d) the use of a disclaimer on the web site precludes a finding that Respondent intentional[ly] seeks to attract users for commercial gain based on confusion with Complainant's mark; and (e) the use of a generic term to attract business is not bad faith as a matter of law. Finally, Respondent claims that Complainant cannot legitimately claim tarnishment because she has already associated herself with sexually explicit creative work.

6. Discussion and Findings

A. The Evidentiary Standard For Decision

Paragraph 4(a) of the Policy directs that the complainant must prove each of the following:

> (i) that the domain name registered by the respondent is identical or confusingly similar to a trademark or service mark in which the complainant has rights; and,

> (ii) that the respondent has no legitimate interests in respect of the domain name; and,

(iii) that the domain name has been registered and used in bad faith.

A threshold question in proceedings under the Policy is to identify the proper standard for reaching a decision on each of these issues. The limited submissions allowed under the Policy makes these proceedings somewhat akin to a summary judgment motion under the United States Federal Rules of Civil Procedure. On a summary judgment motion, the movant has the burden of showing that there are no disputes of material facts. All doubts are to be resolved in favor of the non-moving party. If there are material disputes of fact, the motion must be denied and the case will advance to a hearing before a trier of fact, either judge or jury.

Although the nature of the record is similar to that found on a summary judgment motion, our role is different than that of the Court on a summary judgment motion. Paragraph 15 of the Rules states that the "Panel shall decide a complaint on the basis of the statements and documents submitted and in accordance with the Policy . . ." Paragraph 10 of the Rules provides that the "Panel shall determine the admissibility, relevance, materiality and weight of the evidence." Paragraph 4 of the Policy makes repeated reference to the Panel's role in making findings of fact based on the evidence.

Based on the Policy and the Rules, we disagree with the view that disputes over material facts should not be decided in these proceedings. Rather, it is clear to us that our role is to make findings of fact as best we can based on the evidence presented provided the matters at issue are within the scope of the Policy. There may be circumstances due to the inherent limitations of the dispute resolution process or for other reasons where it would be appropriate for a panel to decline to decide a factual dispute. However, the mere existence of a genuine dispute of material fact should not preclude a panel from weighing the evidence before it and reaching a decision.

Since these proceedings are civil, rather than criminal, in nature, we believe the appropriate standard for fact finding is the civil standard of a preponderance of the evidence (and not the higher standard of "clear and convincing evidence" or "evidence beyond a reasonable doubt"). Under the "preponderance of the evidence" standard a fact is proved for the purpose of reaching a decision when it appears more likely than not to be true based on the evidence. We recognize that other standards may be employed in other jurisdictions. However, the standard of proof employed in the United States seems appropriate for these proceedings generally, and in particular for this proceeding which involves citizens of the United States, actions occurring in the United States and a domain name registered in the United States.

In this case, there are factual disputes over Respondent's intent in obtaining and using the disputed domain name. For the reasons just stated, these disputes do not preclude a decision. Instead, we reach a decision based on the preponderance of the evidence submitted by the parties on the basic issues under the Policy.

B. Similarity of the Disputed Domain Name and Complainant's Mark

As noted above, Respondent does not dispute that its domain name is identical or confusingly similar to a trademark in which the Complainant has rights. Accordingly, we find that Complainant has satisfied the requirements of Paragraph 4(c)(i) of the Policy.

C. Lack of Rights or Legitimate Interests In Domain Name

Complainant has presented evidence tending to show that Respondent lacks any rights or legitimate interest in the domain name. Respondent's claim of rights or legitimate interests is not persuasive.

First, Respondent contends that its use of the domain name for an adult entertainment web site involved prior use of the domain name in connection with a bona fide offering of goods or services. The record supports Respondent's claim that it used the domain name in connection with commercial services prior to notice of the dispute. However, Respondent has failed to provide a reasonable explanation for the selection of Madonna as a domain name. Although the word "Madonna" has an ordinary dictionary meaning not associated with Complainant, nothing in the record supports a conclusion that Respondent adopted and used the term "Madonna" in good faith based on its ordinary dictionary meaning. We find instead that name was selected and used by Respondent with the intent to attract for commercial gain Internet users to Respondent's web site by trading on the fame of Complainant's mark. We see no other plausible explanation for Respondent's conduct and conclude that use which intentionally trades on the fame of another can not constitute a "bona fide" offering of goods or services. To conclude otherwise would mean that a Respondent could rely on intentional infringement to demonstrate a legitimate interest, an interpretation that is obviously contrary to the intent of the Policy.

Second, Respondent contends that it has rights in the domain name because it registered MADONNA as a trademark in Tunisia prior to notice of this dispute. Certainly, it is possible for a Respondent to rely on a valid trademark registration to show prior rights under the Policy. However, it would be a mistake to conclude that mere registration of a trademark creates a legitimate interest under the Policy. If an American-based Respondent could establish "rights" vis a vis an American Complainant through the expedient of securing a trademark registration in Tunisia, then the ICANN procedure would be rendered virtually useless. To establish cognizable rights, the overall circumstances should demonstrate that the registration was obtained in good faith for the purpose of making bona fide use of the mark in the jurisdiction where the mark is registered, and not obtained merely to circumvent the application of the Policy.

Here, Respondent admits that the Tunisia registration was obtained merely to protect his interests in the domain name. Respondent is not located in Tunisia and the registration was not obtained for the purpose of making bona fide use of the mark in commerce in Tunisia. A Tunisian trademark registration is issued upon application without any substantive examination. Although recognized by certain treaties, registration in Tunisia does not prevent a finding of infringement in jurisdictions outside Tunisia. Under the circumstances, some might view Respondent's Tunisian registration itself as evidence of bad faith because it appears to be a pretense to justify an abusive domain name registration. We find at a minimum that it does not evidence a legitimate interest in the disputed name under the circumstances of this case.

Third, Respondent claims that its offer to transfer the domain name to the Madonna Hospital in Lincoln, Nebraska, is a legitimate noncommercial use under Paragraph 4(c)(iii) of the Policy. We disagree. The record is incomplete on these negotiations. Respondent has failed to disclose the specifics of its proposed arrangement with Madonna Hospital. Complainant asserts that the terms of the transfer include a condition that Madonna Hospital not transfer the domain name registration to Complainant. It also appears that the negotiations started after Complainant objected to Respondent's registration and use of the domain name. These circumstances do not demonstrate a legitimate interest or right in the domain name, and instead suggest that Respondent lacks any real interest in the domain name apart from its association with Complainant. Further, we do not believe these circumstances satisfy the provisions of Paragraph 4(c)(iii), which applies to situations where the Respondent is actually making noncommercial or fair use of the domain name. That certainly was not the situation at the time this dispute arose and is not the situation now.

Respondent cites examples of other parties besides Complainant who also have rights in the mark MADONNA, but that does not aid its cause. The fact that others could demonstrate a legitimate right or interest in the domain name does nothing to demonstrate that Respondent has such right or interest.

Based on the record before us, we find that Complainant has satisfied the requirements of Paragraph 4(a)(ii) of the Policy.

D. Bad Faith Registration and Use

Under Paragraph 4(b)(iv) of the Policy, evidence of bad faith registration and use of a domain name includes the following circumstances:

> (iv) by using the domain name, you have intentionally attempted to attract, for commercial gain, Internet users to your web site or other on-line location, by creating a likelihood of confusion with the complainant's mark as to the source, sponsorship, affiliation, or endorsement of your web site or location or of a product or service on your web site or location.

The pleadings in this case are consistent with Respondent's having adopted <madonna.com> for the specific purpose of trading off the name and reputation of the Complainant, and Respondent has offered no alternative explanation for his adoption of the name despite his otherwise detailed and complete submissions. Respondent has not explained why <madonna.com> was worth $20,000 to him or why that name was thought to be valuable as an attraction for a sexually explicit web site. Respondent notes that the complainant, identifying herself as Madonna, has appeared in Penthouse and has published a "Sex" book. The statement that "madonna" is a word in the English language, by itself, is no more of a defense than would be the similar statement made in reference to the word "coke". Respondent has not even attempted to tie in his web site to any dictionary definition of madonna. The only plausible explanation for Respondent's actions appears to be an intentional effort to trade upon the fame of Complainant's name and mark for commercial gain. That purpose is a violation of the Policy, as well as U.S. Trademark Law.

Respondent's use of a disclaimer on its web site is insufficient to avoid a finding of bad faith. First, the disclaimer may be ignored or misunderstood by Internet users. Second, a disclaimer does nothing to dispel initial interest confusion that is inevitable from Respondent's actions. Such confusion is a basis for finding a violation of Complainant's rights. *See Brookfield Communications Inc. v. West Coast Entertainment Corp.*, 174 F.3d 1036 (9th Cir.1999).

The Policy requires a showing of bad faith registration and use. Here, although Respondent was not the original registrant, the record shows he acquired the registration in bad faith. The result is the equivalent of registration and is sufficient to fall within the Policy. Indeed, Paragraph 4(b)(i) of the Policy treats acquisition as the same as registration for the purposes of supporting a finding of bad faith registration. We therefore conclude that bad faith acquisition satisfies the requirement of bad faith registration under the Policy.

Respondent's reliance on a previous ICANN decision involving the domain name <sting.com> is misplaced. *See Gordon Sumner p/k/a/ Sting v. Michael Urvan*, Case No. 2000-0596 (WIPO July 24, 2000). In the Sting decision there was evidence that the Respondent had made bona fide use of the name Sting prior to obtaining the domain name registration and there was no indication that he was seeking to trade on the good will of the well-known singer. Here, there is no similar evidence of prior use by Respondent and the evidence demonstrates a deliberate intent to trade on the good will of complainant. Where no plausible explanation has been provided for adopting a domain name that corresponds to the name of a famous entertainer, other Panels have found a violation of the Policy. *See Julia Fiona Roberts v. Russell Boyd*, Case No. D2000–0210 (WIPO May 29, 2000); *Helen Folsade Adu p/k/a Sade v. Quantum Computer Services Inc.*, Case No. D2000–0794 (WIPO September 26, 2000).

There is also evidence in the record which tends to support Complainant's claim that Respondent's registration of the domain name prevents Complainant from reflecting her mark in the corresponding .com domain name and that Respondent has engaged in a pattern of such conduct. It is admitted that Respondent registers a large number of domain names and that some happen to correspond to the names or marks of others. We find, however, that the record is inconclusive on this basis for finding bad faith and do not rely on this evidence for our conclusion.

Respondent asserts that we should reject Complainant's claims because she has been disingenuous in claiming that her reputation could be tarnished by Respondent's actions. Respondent suggests that her reputation cannot be tarnished because she has already associated herself with sexually explicit creative work. That argument misses the point. Even though Complainant has produced sexually explicit content of her own, Respondent's actions may nevertheless tarnish her reputation because they resulted in association with sexually explicit content which Complainant did not control and which may be contrary to her creative intent and standards of quality. In any event, we do not rely on tarnishment as a basis for our decision.

Because the evidence shows a deliberate attempt by Respondent to trade on Complainant's fame for commercial purposes, we find that Complainant has satisfied the requirements of Paragraph 4(a)(iii) of the Policy.

7. Decision

Under Paragraph 4(i) of the Policy, we find in favor of the Complainant. The disputed domain name is identical or confusingly similar to a trademark in which Complainant has rights; Respondent lacks rights or legitimate interests in the domain name; and the domain name has been registered and used in bad faith. Therefore, we decide that the disputed domain name <madonna.com> should be transferred to the Complainant.

Weber–Stephen Products Co. v. Armitage Hardware and Building Supply, Inc.
54 U.S.P.Q.2d 1766 (N.D.Ill.2000).

■ ASPEN, CHIEF J.

Defendant Armitage Hardware (Armitage) owns a number of internet domain names that plaintiff Weber–Stephen Products Company (Weber) alleges intentionally and in bad faith use Weber's registered trademarks and service marks in a deceptive, confusing, and misleading manner. Weber initiated an administrative proceeding before the World Intellectual Property Organization (WIPO), pursuant to the Uniform Domain Name Dispute Resolution Policy of the Internet Corporation for Assigned Names and Numbers (ICANN Policy), requesting that the administrative panel issue a decision transferring Armitage's domain names to Weber or canceling Armitage's domain names. The following day, Weber also filed suit in this Court, alleging "cyberpiracy" as well as other claims, such as trademark infringement. Weber told this Court that it had commenced an ICANN proceeding to resolve the issue of whether Armitage was using its domain names in bad faith, which is the only issue that the ICANN administrative panel has power to decide under the Policy. Weber also said that because it expected a decision from the panel within 45 to 50 days from the filing of its ICANN complaint (the Policy provides for expedited review), it would not be seeking injunctive relief in this Court with respect to Armitage's registration of the Weber domain names unless the panel declines to cancel and/or to transfer the domain names to Weber.

We understand that the panel is scheduled to issue a decision as soon as May 5, 2000. Before us now is Armitage's motion to declare the administrative proceeding non-binding and to stay this case in favor of the administrative action, or alternatively—should we find the other proceeding to be binding—to stay it while we consider whether Armitage's participation in that proceeding can be compelled. Armitage's concern is that if the panel's arbitration decision is binding on this Court, Armitage will suffer irreparable harm because our review of the panel's decision will necessarily be circumscribed pursuant to the deference accorded arbitrators' decisions under the Federal Arbitration Act.

The ICANN is a new, quasi-governmental internet-regulating body, and its Policy (approved on October 24, 1999) provides for a "mandatory administrative proceeding" in disputes between domain name owners and trademark owners and purportedly applies to every domain name registrant who registers its domain names through an ICANN-accredited registrar. Armitage contends that it did not agree to the administrative proceeding and thus cannot be compelled to participate in it. However, Armitage will participate if we declare that the proceeding is non-binding, that we owe no deference to the proceeding, and that WIPO, ICANN, and Network Solutions, Inc. (Armitage's ICANN-accredited registrar) cannot take any action adverse to Armitage until this matter is resolved in this Court.

No federal court has yet considered the legal effect of a WIPO proceeding. However, the ICANN Policy and its accompanying rules do contemplate the possibility of parallel proceedings in federal court. First, the Policy provides that ICANN will cancel or transfer domain name registrations upon "our receipt of an order from a court . . . of competent jurisdiction, requiring such action; *and/or . . .* our receipt of a decision of an Administrative Panel requiring such action in any administrative proceeding . . . conducted under this Policy." ICANN Policy at ¶ 3. Also, the procedural rules governing the Policy provide that if legal proceedings are initiated prior to or during an administrative proceeding with regard to a domain name dispute that is the subject of the administrative complaint, the panel has the discretion to decide whether to suspend or terminate the administrative proceeding or whether to proceed and make a decision. Uniform Domain Name Dispute Resolution Rules, at ¶ 18. And the language of the Policy suggests that the administrative panels' decisions are not intended to be binding on federal courts. For example, under the heading "Availability of Court Proceedings," the ICANN Policy provides:

> The mandatory administrative proceeding requirements set forth in Paragraph 4 shall not prevent either you or the complainant from submitting the dispute to a court of competent jurisdiction for independent resolution before such mandatory administrative proceeding is commenced or after such proceeding is concluded. If an Administrative Panel decides that your domain name registration should be canceled or transferred, we will wait ten (10) business days . . . before implementing that decision. We will then implement the decision unless we have received from you during that ten (10) business day period official documentation (such as a copy of a complaint, file-stamped by the clerk of the court) that you have commenced a lawsuit against the complainant in a jurisdiction to which the complainant has submitted . . . If we receive such documentation within the ten (10) business day period, we will not implement the Administrative Panel's decision, and we will take no further action, until we receive (i) evidence satisfactory to us of a resolution between the parties; (ii) evidence satisfactory to us that your lawsuit has been dismissed or withdrawn; or (iii) a copy of an order from such court dismissing your lawsuit or ordering that you do not have the right to continue to use your domain name.

ICANN Policy at ¶ 4(k).[3] Furthermore, Armitage's counsel sent an e-mail inquiry to <domain.disputes@wipo.int>, and the response from the WIPO Arbitration and Mediation Center said that the administrative panel's determination would be binding on the registrar of the domain name, but that "[t]his decision is not binding upon a court, and a court may give appropriate weight to the Administrative Panel's decision." Albeit a vague and rather unhelpful interpretation, Weber does not take issue with this WIPO statement.

We conclude that this Court is not bound by the outcome of the ICANN administrative proceedings. But at this time we decline to determine the precise standard by which we would review the panel's decision, and what degree of deference (if any) we would give that decision. Neither the ICANN Policy nor its governing rules dictate to courts what weight should be given to a panel's decision, and the WIPO e-mail message stating that "a court may give appropriate weight to the Administrative Panel's decision" confirms the breadth of our discretion.

Because both parties to this case have adequate avenues of recourse should they be unhappy with the administrative panel's imminent decision, we find no need to stay the pending ICANN administrative action. Instead, we hereby stay this case pending the outcome of those proceedings. It is so ordered.

Barcelona.com, Inc. v. Excelentisimo Ayuntamiento de Barcelona
330 F.3d 617 (4th Cir.2003).

■ NIEMEYER, CIRCUIT JUDGE.

[A citizen of Spain created a Delaware corporation, Barcelona.com, Inc. ("Bcom"), to own the domain name barcelona.com, and to operate it as an information site for tourists to Barcelona, Spain. The City Council of Barcelona brought a UDRP proceeding against the domain name, claiming a Spanish trademark registration on various terms incorporating the word "Barcelona." After the UDRP Panel ruled in favor of the City Council, Bcom commenced an action under § 1114(2)(D)(v) against the City Council in federal district court in Virginia. In the following excerpt, the court discusses the relationship between a UDRP decision and an action under the ACPA involving the same domain name.]

[D]omain names are issued pursuant to contractual arrangements under which the registrant agrees to a dispute resolution process, the UDRP, which is designed to resolve a large number of disputes involving domain names, but this process is not intended to interfere with or modify any "independent resolution" by a court of competent jurisdiction. Moreover, the UDRP makes no effort at unifying the law of trademarks among the nations served by the Internet. Rather, it forms part of a

---

[3] The Policy continues: "All other disputes between you and any party other than us regarding your domain name registration that are not brought pursuant to the mandatory administrative proceeding provisions . . . shall be resolved between you and such other party through any court, arbitration or other proceeding that may be available." ICANN Policy at ¶ 5.

contractual policy developed by ICANN for use by registrars in administering the issuance and transfer of domain names. Indeed, it explicitly anticipates that judicial proceedings will continue under various nations' laws applicable to the parties.

The ACPA recognizes the UDRP only insofar as it constitutes a part of a policy followed by registrars in administering domain names, and the UDRP is relevant to actions brought under the ACPA in two contexts. First, the ACPA limits the liability of a registrar in respect to registering, transferring, disabling, or cancelling a domain name if it is done in the "implementation of *a reasonable policy*" (including the UDRP) that prohibits registration of a domain name "identical to, confusingly similar to, or dilutive of another's mark." 15 U.S.C. § 1114(2)(D)(ii)(II) (emphasis added). Second, the ACPA authorizes a suit by a domain name registrant whose domain name has been suspended, disabled or transferred *under that reasonable policy* (including the UDRP) to seek a declaration that the registrant's registration and use of the domain name involves no violation of the Lanham Act as well as an injunction returning the domain name.

Thus, while a decision by an ICANN-recognized panel might be a condition of, indeed the reason for, bringing an action under 15 U.S.C. § 1114(2)(D)(v), its recognition *vel non* is not jurisdictional. Jurisdiction to hear trademark matters is conferred on federal courts by 28 U.S.C. §§ 1331 and 1338, and a claim brought under the ACPA, which amended the Lanham Act, is a trademark matter over which federal courts have subject matter jurisdiction.

Moreover, any decision made by a panel under the UDRP is no more than an agreed-upon administration that is *not* given any deference under the ACPA. To the contrary, because a UDRP decision is susceptible of being grounded on principles foreign or hostile to American law, the ACPA authorizes reversing a panel decision if such a result is called for by application of the Lanham Act.

In sum, we conclude that we have jurisdiction over this dispute brought under the ACPA and the Lanham Act. Moreover, we give the decision of the WIPO panelist no deference in deciding this action under § 1114(2)(D)(v). *See Dluhos v. Strasberg,* 321 F.3d 365, 373–74 (3d Cir.2003) (holding that 15 U.S.C. § 1114(2)(D)(v) requires the federal court to approach the issues raised in an action brought under that provision *de novo* rather than to apply the deferential review appropriate to actions governed by the Federal Arbitration Act); *Sallen v. Corinthians Licenciamentos LTDA,* 273 F.3d 14, 28 (1st Cir.2001) (explaining that "a federal court's interpretation of the ACPA supplants a WIPO panel's interpretation of the UDRP"). Thus, for our purposes, the WIPO panelist's decision is relevant only to serve as the reason for Bcom, Inc.'s bringing an action under § 1114(2)(D)(v) to reverse the WIPO panelist's decision.

EXTENSIONS

---

1. *Foreign trademark rights.* In *Madonna v. Parisi* the domain name registrant had registered the disputed domain name in Tunisia. Under Tunisian law, the registrant had legitimate trademark rights in the name. Paragraph 4(a)(ii) of the UDRP states that the complainant must show that the domain name registrant has "no rights or legitimate interests in respect of the domain name." The Panel dismissed the domain name registrant's trademark rights under Tunisian law as a source of such rights, stating:

> If an American-based Respondent could establish "rights" vis a vis an American Complainant through the expedient of securing a trademark registration in Tunisia, then the ICANN procedure would be rendered virtually useless. To establish cognizable rights, the overall circumstances should demonstrate that the registration was obtained in good faith for the purpose of making bona fide use of the mark in the jurisdiction where the mark is registered, and not obtained merely to circumvent the application of the Policy.

The Panel thus seems to concede that the UDRP, read literally, might compel a result in favor of the registrant. To avoid this result, the Panel concludes that any "rights" in the mark must be "cognizable," and to be "cognizable," they must have been acquired in good faith and used in the jurisdiction conferring those rights. How far does a UDRP panel's authority to interpret its own grant of authority extend? A UDRP panel is not a court and its power to arbitrate a dispute rests ultimately on the domain name registrant's consent to the arbitration clause contained in the domain name registration agreement. Once the domain name registrant had demonstrated trademark rights under Tunisian law, should the Panel have suggested the parties proceed to a court of law to adjudicate their respective rights in the disputed domain name?

2. *Licensing rights.* Paragraph 4(a)(i) of the UDRP requires that the complainant prove that the disputed "domain name is identical or confusingly similar to a trademark or service mark in which the complainant has rights." What kind of rights must a complainant have under the UDRP? In *NBA Properties, Inc. v. Adirondack Software Corp.*, Case No. D2000–1211 (WIPO Dec. 8, 2000), the complainant was the exclusive licensee of the trademark owner. The disputed domain name was knicks.com. The trademark "Knicks" is owned by Madison Square Garden, L.P., the owner and operator of the New York Knicks basketball team. This trademark had been exclusively licensed to the complainant, the exclusive licensing and merchandising agent for the National Basketball Association and its member teams, including the New York Knicks. The domain name registrant had registered the disputed domain name without the consent of the trademark owner or the complainant. Notwithstanding the complainant's status as the exclusive licensee of the trademark, the Panel held that the "Complainant has not shown that it has rights in the KNICKS trademark relied upon." More specifically, the Panel stated:

> The record fails to make clear what *rights in the trademark* Complainant claims to have. The rights of a licensee are contract rights with respect to, not *in*, the licensed marks. So it is also in the case of a licensing and merchandising agent.

> There may well be circumstances in which the contract rights possessed by an exclusive licensee vest in him substantially all the powers of an owner of the licensed property. However, such circumstances have not been shown to exist here.

> The Policy [i.e., the UDRP] is believed by the Panel to envision a transfer of a disputed domain name to a complainant/trademark owner as a route to unification of control over the uses of the domain name and the trademark. However, Complainant's request for an order transferring the disputed name to Complainant in this case would place ownership of the domain name in an entity other than the trademark owner without consent from the trademark owner.

Should rights in a trademark under an exclusive licensing agreement be considered "rights in a trademark" for the purposes of the UDRP? If you were negotiating or drafting a trademark licensing agreement on behalf of the licensee, how would you attempt to ensure that your client could initiate a proceeding under the UDRP?

3. *Use in bad faith.* Earlier, we saw that the Anticybersquatting Consumer Protection Act imposed liability on a domain name registrant who "registers, traffics in, *or* uses a domain name" with bad-faith intent to profit from it. 15 U.S.C. § 1125(d)(1)(A)(ii) (emphasis added). By contrast, the ICANN UDRP permits a registrar to "cancel, transfer or otherwise make changes to domain name registrations" if the disputed "domain name has been registered *and* is being used in bad faith." UDRP ¶ 4(a)(iii) (emphasis added). Consider a domain name registrant who registers another's trademark as a domain name in bad faith but who never uses it as part of an e-mail address or fully qualified domain name. Clearly, the trademark owner could bring an action under the ACPA. Could the owner also initiate proceedings under the UDRP? In *Telstra Corp. Ltd. v. Nuclear Marshmallows*, Case No. D2000-0003 (WIPO Feb. 18, 2000), the Panel had to decide just such a case. Turning to consider Paragraph 4(a)(iii), the Panel observed:

> It is less clear cut whether the Complainant has proved the third element in paragraph 4(a) of the Uniform Policy, namely that the domain name "has been registered and is being used in bad faith" by Respondent. The Administrative Panel notes two things about this provision. First, the provision contains the conjunction "and" rather than "or". Secondly, the provision refers to both the past tense ("has been registered") and the present tense ("is being used").

> The significance of the use of the conjunction "and" is that paragraph 4(a)(iii) requires the Complainant to prove use in bad faith as well as registration in bad faith. That is to say, bad faith registration alone is an insufficient ground for obtaining a remedy under the Uniform Policy. . . . [T]he Second Staff Report on Implementation Documents for the Uniform Dispute Resolution Policy submitted to the ICANN Board at its meeting on October 24, 1999 . . . at paragraph 4.5, contains the following relevant statement and recommendation:

>> Several comments (submitted by INTA and various trademark owners) advocated various expansions to the scope of the definition of abusive registration. For example:

>> a. These comments suggested that the definition should be expanded to include cases of either registration or use in bad faith, rather than both registration and use in bad faith. These comments point out that cybersquatters often register names in bulk, but do not use them, yet without use the streamlined dispute-resolution procedure is not available. While that argument appears to have merit on initial impression, it would involve a change in the policy adopted by the Board. The WIPO report, the DNSO recommendation, and the registrars-group recommendation all required both registration and use in bad faith before the streamlined procedure would be invoked. Staff recommends that this requirement not be changed without study and recommendation by the DNSO.

> From the fact that the ICANN Board accepted the approach recommended in the Second Staff Report, and thus adopted the Uniform Policy in the form originally proposed, it is clear that ICANN intended that bad faith registration alone not give rise to a remedy under the Uniform Policy. For a remedy to be available, the Complainant must prove both that the domain was registered in bad faith and that it is being used in bad faith.

> This interpretation is confirmed, and clarified, by the use of both the past and present tenses in paragraph 4(a)(iii). . . . [T]he requirement in paragraph 4(a)(iii) that the domain name "has been registered and is being used in bad faith" will be satisfied only if the Complainant proves that the registration was undertaken in bad faith *and* that the circumstances of the case are such that Respondent is con-

tinuing to act in bad faith.

Has the Complainant proved that the domain name "has been registered in bad faith" by the Respondent? [The Panel finds that it has.]

Has the Complainant proved the additional requirement that the domain name "is being used in bad faith" by the Respondent? The [disputed] domain name . . . does not resolve to a website or other on-line presence. There is no evidence that a website or other on-line presence is in the process of being established which will use the domain name. There is no evidence of advertising, promotion or display to the public of the domain name. Finally, there is no evidence that the Respondent has offered to sell, rent or otherwise transfer the domain name to the Complainant, a competitor of the Complainant, or any other person. In short, there is no positive action being undertaken by the Respondent in relation to the domain name.

This fact does not, however, resolve the question. . . . [T]he relevant issue is not whether the Respondent is undertaking a positive action in bad faith in relation to the domain name, but instead whether, in all the circumstances of the case, it can be said that the Respondent is acting in bad faith. The distinction between undertaking a positive action in bad faith and acting in bad faith may seem a rather fine distinction, but it is an important one. The significance of the distinction is that the concept of a domain name "being used in bad faith" is not limited to positive action; inaction is within the concept. That is to say, it is possible, in certain circumstances, for inactivity by the Respondent to amount to the domain name being used in bad faith.

This understanding of paragraph 4(a)(iii) is supported by the actual provisions of the Uniform Policy. Paragraph 4(b) of the Uniform Policy identifies, without limitation, circumstances that "shall be evidence of the registration and use of a domain name in bad faith", for the purposes of paragraph 4(a)(iii). Only one of these circumstances (paragraph 4(b)(iv)), by necessity, involves a positive action post-registration undertaken in relation to the domain name (using the name to attract custom to a website or other on-line location). The other three circumstances contemplate either a positive action or inaction in relation to the domain name. That is to say, the circumstances identified in paragraphs 4(b)(i), (ii) and (iii) can be found in a situation involving a passive holding of the domain name registration. Of course, these three paragraphs require additional facts (an intention to sell, rent or transfer the registration, for paragraph 4(b)(i); a pattern of conduct preventing a trade mark owner's use of the registration, for paragraph 4(b)(ii); the primary purpose of disrupting the business of a competitor, for paragraph 4(b)(iii)). Nevertheless, the point is that paragraph 4(b) recognises that inaction (eg. passive holding) in relation to a domain name registration can, in certain circumstances, constitute a domain name being used in bad faith. Furthermore, it must be recalled that the circumstances identified in paragraph 4(b) are "without limitation"—that is, paragraph 4(b) expressly recognises that *other* circumstances can be evidence that a domain name was registered and is being used in bad faith.

The question that then arises is what circumstances of inaction (passive holding) other than those identified in paragraphs 4(b)(i), (ii) and (iii) can constitute a domain name being used in bad faith? This question cannot be answered in the abstract; the question can only be answered in respect of the particular facts of a specific case. That is to say, in considering whether the passive holding of a domain name, following a bad faith registration of it, satisfies the requirements of paragraph 4(a)(iii), the Administrative Panel must give close attention to all the circumstances of the Respondent's behaviour. A remedy can be obtained under the Uniform Policy only if those circumstances show that the Respondent's passive holding amounts to acting in bad faith

Based on the rationale of this decision, under what circumstances might passive holding not constitute bad-faith use?

4. *Country-code TLDs.* In addition to the .com, .net and .org gTLD domains, as well as the more recently activated .aero, .biz, .coop, .info, .museum, and .name domains, a number of ccTLD registries have adopted the UDRP. As a result the UDRP also applies to the .ag, .as, .bs, .cy, .gt, .na, .nu, .tt, .tv, .ve and .ws TLDs.

5. *Challenging an adverse UDRP decision in federal court.* The Anticybersquatting Consumer Protection Act expressly grants a domain name registrant the right to file a civil action if a registrar pursuant to a reasonable policy—such as the UDRP—suspends, disables or transfers his or her domain name. Section 32(2)(D)(v) of the Lanham Act, 15 U.S.C. § 1114(2)(D)(v), states:

> A domain name registrant whose domain name has been suspended, disabled, or transferred under a policy described under clause (ii)(II) may, upon notice to the mark owner, file a civil action to establish that the registration or use of the domain name by such registrant is not unlawful under this chapter. The court may grant injunctive relief to the domain name registrant, including the reactivation of the domain name or transfer of the domain name to the domain name registrant.

Does this provision create a right to appeal an adverse UDRP decision in federal court? What law does a federal court apply in such an action? Why do you think this provision was included in the Anticybersquatting Consumer Protection Act? Does it merely codify a contract remedy that was already available to a domain name registrant? Is it required by 15 U.S.C. § 1114(2)(D)(i)? Does it create a quasi-intellectual property right in domain names under federal law? One commentator has stated that this provision "creates a distinct federal claim for ownership of a domain name." 4 J. THOMAS MCCARTHY, MCCARTHY ON TRADEMARKS AND UNFAIR COMPETITION § 25:74.2 (4th ed. 2002). Do you agree?

Barcelona.com, Inc. v. Excelentisimo Ayuntamiento de Barcelona, excerpted *supra*, illustrates the interaction between Section 1114(2)(D)(v) and foreign law. The District Court held that the City Council had superior rights to the domain name, based on its Spanish trademarks, but the Court of Appeals reversed. The court held that the lower court had erred by applying Spanish law. It explained that Section 1114(2)(D)(v) requires the registrant to show that its use of the domain name "is not unlawful under this chapter," that is, under the Lanham Act, making Spanish law irrelevant. Applying the Lanham Act, the court found, Bcom wins: a purely geographical term such as "Barcelona" is not protectible as a trademark without a showing of secondary meaning, of which there was no evidence.

Is this an appropriate outcome? If not, how might it be avoided? Should UDRP decisions not be trumped by determinations under national laws? Does the ACPA overreach by requiring the application of U.S. law to a trademark controversy in which the real parties are a Spanish city and a Spanish citizen? How did the District Court obtain jurisdiction over the City Council? Could the City Council have protected its interests by filing an action in a Spanish court?

6. *Reverse domain name hijacking and abuse of process.* Reverse domain name hijacking is defined in the UDRP Rules as "using the Policy in bad faith to attempt to deprive a registered domain-name holder of a domain name." *See* Rules for Uniform Domain Name Dispute Resolution Policy ¶ 1 (Definitions) (Oct. 24, 1999), www.icann.org/dndr/udrp/

uniform-rules.htm. Pursuant to Paragraph 15(e) of the Rules:

> If after considering the submissions the Panel finds that the complaint was brought in bad faith, for example in an attempt at Reverse Domain Name Hijacking or was brought primarily to harass the domain-name holder, the Panel *shall* declare in its decision that the complaint was brought in bad faith and constitutes an abuse of the administrative proceeding.

(emphasis added). Although the panel is required to make this declaration, neither the UDRP nor the Rules provides any penalty for initiating a UDRP proceeding in bad faith. In ICANN's Second Staff Report on Implementation Documents for the Uniform Dispute Resolution Policy (Oct. 24, 1999), www.icann.org/udrp/udrp-second-staff-report-24oct99.htm, penalties were rejected as "outside ICANN's scope." Regarding reverse domain name hijacking the Report observed in Section 4.10:

> The final point of substantive guidance in the Board's Santiago resolutions is that the policy should define and minimize reverse domain-name hijacking. The definition of "reverse domain name hijacking" is included in paragraph 1 of the rules. The implementation documents contain several measures to minimize that practice. First, paragraph 15(e) of the rules provides that an administrative panel finding that a complaint was brought in bad faith shall note that fact in its decision. A second measure to minimize reverse domain-name hijacking is the enhanced notice requirement for the initial complaint in paragraph 2(a) of the rules. The clarification that the complainant bears the burden of proof (paragraph 4(a) of the policy statement) and the lengthening of the time for a domain-name holder to seek court review of an adverse decision (paragraph 4(k) of the policy statement) should also minimize reverse domain-name hijacking. Some commentators representing non-commercial interests stated that more punitive measures should be provided to discourage reverse domain-name hijacking. Staff believes such punishment is outside ICANN's scope.

What does the ICANN staff mean by "outside ICANN's scope"? What is ICANN's role in a UDRP proceeding?

For domain name registrants in the United States, ICANN's failure to provide any remedy to the victims of those who use the UDRP process to reverse hijack domain names was rectified by the Anticybersquatting Consumer Protection Act. Section 32(2)(D)(iv) of the Lanham Act, 15 U.S.C. § 1114(2)(D)(iv), states:

> If a registrar, registry, or other registration authority takes an action described under clause (ii) based on a knowing and material misrepresentation by any other person that a domain name is identical to, confusingly similar to, or dilutive of a mark, the person making the knowing and material misrepresentation *shall be liable for any damages, including costs and attorney's fees,* incurred by the domain name registrant as a result of such action. The court may also grant injunctive relief to the domain name registrant, including the reactivation of the domain name or the transfer of the domain name to the domain name registrant.

(emphasis added). Does this provision create an action for malicious prosecution or abuse of process with respect to a UDRP proceeding? Would this remedy be available to domain name registrants who are not United States citizens and who live in foreign countries? Would it matter whether such a registrant registered the domain name with a U.S.-based domain name registrar?

V. REGISTERING DOMAIN NAMES WITH A DOMAIN NAME REGISTRAR

A domain name can be the focus of two wholly separate and unrelated kinds of registration procedures: a domain name registration and a trademark registration. The former is required, the latter optional. When we speak simply of domain name registration we generally intend to refer to the process of creating a new second-level domain (SLD) under an established top-level domain (TLD) such as .com, .net or .org. In this process, a person or firm—the registrant—contacts a domain name registrar and requests the use of a particular name as a domain name in the DNS. The registrar then contacts the registry for that top-level domain and asks whether the desired name is still available. If no one has previously registered it, then the registrar may process the request and register the desired name to the registrant. In this Part, we consider domain name registrations. In the next Part, we consider the circumstances under which a domain name may be registered as a trademark.

Successfully registering a domain name with an accredited domain name registrar confers no legal rights to use that domain name on the registrant beyond those created by the registration agreement itself. When a registrar registers a domain name, it no more immunizes the registrant from the legal claims of others than a state immunizes a company when it grants its application for incorporation under a name that infringes the trademark or trade name of another. *See* 1 & 4 J. THOMAS MCCARTHY, MCCARTHY ON TRADEMARKS AND UNFAIR COMPETITION §§ 9:8 & 25:73.3 (4th ed.2002): "[R]egistration of a mark or name with NSI does not itself confer any federal trademark rights on the registrant."

Although registration of a domain name does not confer on the registrant any special rights to use that domain name, one might still wonder whether the *fact* of registration would count as a use in commerce for the purpose of establishing priority under the federal trademark laws. The Ninth Circuit Court of Appeals in *Brookfield Communications, Inc. v. West Coast Entertainment Corp.*, 174 F.3d 1036 (9th Cir.1999), excerpted in Chapter 2, Part II(B), *supra*, answered this question in the negative. Brookfield's lawsuit against West Coast was precipitated by West Coast's use of the domain name "moviebuff.com" for its website. The case turned in part on who had first used the term "moviebuff" for Internet products and services. West Coast argued that it had priority because it had registered this domain name with Network Solutions before the filing date of Brookfield's application for a federal trademark registration. Rejecting this argument the court wrote:

> To resolve whether West Coast's use of "moviebuff.com" constitutes trademark infringement or unfair competition, we must first determine whether Brookfield has a valid, protectable trademark interest in the "MovieBuff" mark. Brookfield's registration of the mark on the Principal Register in the Patent and Trademark Office constitutes prima facie evidence of the validity of the registered mark and of Brookfield's exclusive right to use the mark on the goods and services specified in the registration. *See* 15 U.S.C. §§ 1057(b); 1115(a). Nevertheless, West Coast can rebut this presumption by showing that it used the mark in commerce first, since a fundamental tenet of trademark law is that ownership of an inherently distinctive mark such as "MovieBuff" is governed by priority of use. . . .
>
> Brookfield first used "MovieBuff" on its Internet-based products and services in August 1997, so West Coast can prevail only if it establishes first use

earlier than that. In the literal sense of the word, West Coast "used" the term "moviebuff.com" when it registered that domain address in February 1996. Registration with Network Solutions, however, does not in itself constitute "use" for purposes of acquiring trademark priority. The Lanham Act grants trademark protection only to marks that are used to identify and to distinguish goods or services in commerce—which typically occurs when a mark is used in conjunction with the actual sale of goods or services. The purpose of a trademark is to help consumers identify the source, but a mark cannot serve a source-identifying function if the public has never seen the mark and thus is not meritorious of trademark protection until it is used in public in a manner that creates an association among consumers between the mark and the mark's owner.

Id. at 1046-51.

While it does not confer any rights other than those created by the registration contract itself, registration of a domain name in the commercial gTLDs .aero, .biz, .com, .coop, .info, .museum, .name, .net and .org (and some of the ccTLDs) does impose two significant requirements on all registrants. First, all registrants must agree to be bound by the ICANN Uniform Domain Name Dispute Resolution Policy (discussed in Part IV, *supra*). Second, all registrants must agree to give the public access to their registration data. These requirements are imposed indirectly on registrants through ICANN's accreditation of registrars. ICANN's control of the root file not only permits it to appoint the registry of each top-level domain, but it also permits ICANN to dictate which companies may act as registrars for these domains. The process through which ICANN exercises this control is called *registrar accreditation.* All registrations in the commercial gTLDs must go through an ICANN-accredited registrar.

To become an accredited registrar, a registrar must enter into a standard Registrar Accreditation Agreement with ICANN. Through this agreement, ICANN obligates all accredited registrars to require domain name registrants to agree (1) to be bound by ICANN's Uniform Domain Name Dispute Resolution Policy and (2) to have personal and technical information collected as part of the registration process made available to the public. The impact with respect to these two issues of the Registrar Accreditation Agreement on an accredited registrar's registration agreement with a domain name registrant can be seen by comparing the following excerpts.

ICANN, Registrar Accreditation Agreement (May 17, 2001).
www.icann.org

This REGISTRAR ACCREDITATION AGREEMENT ("Agreement") is by and between the Internet Corporation for Assigned Names and Numbers, a California non-profit, public benefit corporation, and [Registrar Name], a [Organization type and jurisdiction] ("Registrar"), and shall be deemed made on _____, at Los Angeles, California, USA.

. . .

3. REGISTRAR OBLIGATIONS.

. . .

3.3   *Public Access to Data on Registered Names.* During the Term of this Agreement:

3.3.1 At its expense, Registrar shall provide an interactive web page and a port 43 Whois service providing free public query-based access to up-to-date (i.e., updated at least daily) data concerning all active Registered Names sponsored by Registrar for each TLD in which it is accredited. The data accessible shall consist of elements that are designated from time to time according to an ICANN adopted specification or policy. Until ICANN otherwise specifies by means of an ICANN adopted specification or policy, this data shall consist of the following elements as contained in Registrar's database:

3.3.1.1   The name of the Registered Name;

3.3.1.2   The names of the primary nameserver and secondary nameserver(s) for the Registered Name;

3.3.1.3   The identity of Registrar (which may be provided through Registrar's website);

3.3.1.4   The original creation date of the registration;

3.3.1.5   The expiration date of the registration;

3.3.1.6   The name and postal address of the Registered Name Holder;

3.3.1.7   The name, postal address, e-mail address, voice telephone number, and (where available) fax number of the technical contact for the Registered Name; and

3.3.1.8   The name, postal address, e-mail address, voice telephone number, and (where available) fax number of the administrative contact for the Registered Name.

. . .

3.3.4 Registrar shall abide by any ICANN specification or policy established as a Consensus Policy according to § 4 that requires registrars to cooperatively implement a distributed capability that provides query-based Whois search functionality across all registrars. . . .

3.7   *Business Dealings, Including with Registered Name Holders.*

. . .

3.7.7 Registrar shall require all Registered Name Holders to enter into an electronic or paper registration agreement with Registrar including at least the following provisions:

3.7.7.1   The Registered Name Holder shall provide to Registrar accurate and reliable contact details and promptly correct and update them during the term of the Registered Name registration, including: the full name, postal address, e-mail address, voice telephone number, and fax number if available of the Registered Name Holder; name of authorized person for contact purposes in the case of a Registered Name Holder that is an organization, association, or corporation; and the data elements listed in Subsections 3.3.1.2, 3.3.1.7 and 3.3.1.8.

3.7.7.2   A Registered Name Holder's willful provision of inaccurate or unreliable information, its willful failure promptly to update information provided to Registrar, or its failure to respond for over fifteen calendar days to inquiries by Registrar concerning the accuracy of contact details associated with the Registered Name Holder's registration shall constitute a material breach of the Registered Name Holder-registrar contract and be a basis for cancellation of the Registered Name registration.

3.7.7.3   Any Registered Name Holder that intends to license use of a domain name to a third party is nonetheless the Registered Name Holder of record and is responsible for providing its own full contact information and for providing and updating accurate technical and administrative contact information adequate to facilitate timely resolution of any problems that arise in connection with the Registered Name. A Registered Name Holder licensing use of a Registered Name according to this provision shall accept liability for harm caused by wrongful use of the Registered Name, unless it promptly discloses the identity of the licensee to a party providing the Registered Name Holder reasonable evidence of actionable harm.

. . .

3.7.7.9   The Registered Name Holder shall represent that, to the best of the Registered Name Holder's knowledge and belief, neither the registration of the Registered Name nor the manner in which it is directly or indirectly used infringes the legal rights of any third party.

3.7.7.10 For the adjudication of disputes concerning or arising from use of the Registered Name, the Registered Name Holder shall submit, without prejudice to other potentially applicable jurisdictions, to the jurisdiction of the courts (1) of the Registered Name Holder's domicile and (2) where Registrar is located.

3.7.7.11 The Registered Name Holder shall agree that its registration of the Registered Name shall be subject to suspension, cancellation, or transfer pursuant to any ICANN adopted specification or policy, or pursuant to any registrar or registry procedure not inconsistent with an ICANN adopted specification or policy, (1) to correct mistakes by Registrar or the Registry Operator in registering the name or (2) for the resolution of disputes concerning the Registered Name. . . .

VeriSign Service Agreement
Version Number 6.2.

. . .

ADDITIONAL TERMS APPLICABLE TO REGISTRANTS OF DOMAIN NAMES

. . .

4. VeriSign's Disclosure of Certain Information. Subject to the requirements of our privacy statement, in order for us to comply [with] the current rules and policies for the domain name system, you hereby grant to VeriSign the right to disclose

to third parties through an interactive publicly accessible registration database the following mandatory information that you are required to provide when registering or reserving a domain name: (i) the domain name(s) registered by you; (ii) your name and postal address; (iii) the name(s), postal address(es), e-mail address(es), voice telephone number and where available the fax number(s) of the technical and administrative contacts for your domain name(s); (iv) the Internet protocol numbers of the primary nameserver and secondary nameserver(s) for such domain name(s); (v) the corresponding names of those nameservers; (vi) the original creation date of the registration; and (vii) the expiration date of the registration. We, as are all accredited domain name registrars, are also required to make this information available in bulk form to third parties who agree not to use it to (a) allow, enable or otherwise support the transmission of mass unsolicited, commercial advertising or solicitations via telephone, facsimile, or e-mail (spam) or (b) enable high volume, automated, electronic processes that apply to our systems to register domain names.

5. Domain Name Dispute Policy. If you registered a domain name through us, you agree to be bound by our current domain name dispute policy that is incorporated herein and made a part of this Agreement by reference. The current version of the domain name dispute policy may be found at our website: www.netsol.com/en_US/legal/dispute-policy.jhtml.

6. Domain Name Dispute Policy Modifications. You agree that we, in our sole discretion, may modify our dispute policy. We will post any such revised policy on our website at least thirty (30) calendar days before it becomes effective. You agree that, by maintaining the reservation or registration of your domain name after modifications to the dispute policy become effective, you have agreed to these modifications. You acknowledge that if you do not agree to any such modification, you may terminate this Agreement. We will not refund any fees paid by you if you terminate your Agreement with us.

7. You agree that, if your use of our domain name registration services is challenged by a third party, you will be subject to the provisions specified in our dispute policy in effect at the time of the dispute. For any dispute with, or challenge by, a third party concerning or arising from your use of a domain name registered with us or your use of our domain name registration services, you agree to submit to subject matter jurisdiction, personal jurisdiction and venue of the United States District Court for the Eastern District of Virginia, Alexandria Division and the courts of your domicile. . . .

. . .

EXTENSIONS

1. *"Whois" lookups.* The contact and technical information that a domain name registrant is required to supply in the registration process is made publicly available through what is call a *whois look-up.* The information available includes the name, address and other contact information of the registrant, and the IP addresses of the domain's primary and secondary name servers. *Whois* is the name of the database that a registrar uses to make registration data available to the public. It is called a whois database because it answers the question "*who is* the registrant of this domain name?"

2. *Country code top level domains.* Each country designates the registry for its own ccTLD. Contact information for the registries and registrars of the various ccTLDs can be found at www.iana.org/cctld/cctld-whois.htm. Some ccTLDs may have a commercial value unrelated to the country for which it is the top-level domain. For example, any website having some connection to television might want to register its domain name in the .tv domain—the top-level domain for Tuvalu, a small island nation in the South Pacific. Similarly, any holder of a federally registered trademark who wants to use it as a domain name but also want to "show" that it is a federally registered trademark might consider registering it as a domain name in the .tm domain—the top-level domain for Turkmenistan.

3. *Interpleader actions.* To avoid becoming embroiled in a dispute between a domain name registrant and trademark owner, registrars have filed interpleader actions in which they deposit the contested domain name with the court. Is this procedure always available to a registrar? Are there some circumstances in which an interpleader action is not appropriate? *See Network Solutions, Inc. v. Clue Computing, Inc.*, 946 F.Supp. 858 (D.Colo.1996).

QUESTIONS FOR DISCUSSION

Competition among registrars. Beginning in 1999, ICANN introduced competition among registrars for the commercial gTLDs. A registrant can now choose from among a multitude of registrars on the basis of the fee they charge and other services they provide. Fees vary significantly among registrars; some provide free registration services in connection with other services that they offer, such as web hosting. Initial and renewal registration terms must be offered in one-year increments and no registrar may offer a term longer than ten years. Why is the market allowed to determine the fee and term of a domain name registration but not the dispute resolution policy to which the registrant is subject?

VI. Registering Domain Names as Trademarks

In addition to registering a domain name for use in establishing a website or e-mail address, one may also register a domain name as a trademark under the Lanham Act of 1946, 15 U.S.C. §§ 1051–1127. In this section, we consider some of the issues that arise in connection with registering a domain name as a trademark.

Not all domain names can be registered as federal trademarks. To qualify for registration, a domain name must be within registrable subject matter. The next excerpt explores how the rules regarding registrable subject matter apply to domain names. We conclude this Part with a Federal Circuit decision that may require the PTO to modify its policy with respect to generic domain names.

U.S. Patent and Trademark Office, Examination Guide No. 2–99, Marks Composed, in Whole or in Part, of Domain Names (Sept. 29, 1999)
www.uspto.gov/web/offices/tac/notices/guide299.htm

   . . .

Applications for registration of marks consisting of domain names are subject to the same requirements as all other applications for federal trademark registration. This Examination Guide identifies and discusses some of the issues that commonly arise in the examination of domain name mark applications.

II. Use as a Mark

A. Use Applications

A mark composed of a domain name is registrable as a trademark or service mark only if it functions as a source identifier. The mark as depicted on the specimens must be presented in a manner that will be perceived by potential purchasers as indicating source and not as merely an informational indication of the domain name address used to access a website. *See In re Eilberg*, 49 USPQ2d 1955 (TTAB 1998).[9]

In *Eilberg*, the Trademark Trial and Appeal Board (Board) held that a term that only serves to identify the applicant's domain name or the location on the Internet where the applicant's website appears, and does not separately identify applicant's services, does not function as a service mark. The applicant's proposed mark was WWW.EILBERG.COM, and the specimens showed that the mark was used on letterhead and business cards in the following manner:

WILLIAM H. EILBERG
ATTORNEY AT LAW
820 HOMESTEAD ROAD, P.O. BOX 7
JENKINTOWN, PENNSYLVANIA 19046
215-885-4600
FAX: 215-885-4603
EMAIL WHE@EILBERG.COM

PATENTS, TRADEMARKS
AND COPYRIGHTS   WWW.EILBERG.COM

The Board affirmed the examining attorney's refusal of registration on the ground that the matter presented for registration did not function as a mark, stating that:

> [T]he asserted mark, as displayed on applicant's letterhead, does not function as a service mark identifying and distinguishing applicant's legal services and, as presented, is not capable of doing so. As shown, the asserted mark identifies applicant's Internet domain name, by use of which one can access applicant's website. In other words, the asserted mark WWW.EILBERG.COM merely indicates the location on the Internet where applicant's website appears. It does not separately identify applicant's legal services as such. *Cf. In re The Signal Companies, Inc.*, 228 USPQ 956 (TTAB 1986).

> This is not to say that, if used appropriately, the asserted mark or portions thereof may not be trademarks or [service marks]. For example, if applicant's law firm name were, say, EILBERG.COM and were presented prominently on applicant's letterheads and business cards as the name under which applicant was rendering its legal services, then that

---

[9] ["TTAB" stands for Trademark Trial and Appeal Board. The TTAB is a unit of the PTO that resolves registration disputes, including appeals from decisions of trademark examiners refusing to register a mark.—Eds.]

mark may well be registrable.

Id. at 1956.

The examining attorney must review the specimens in order to determine how the proposed mark is actually used. It is the perception of the ordinary customer that determines whether the asserted mark functions as a mark, not the applicant's intent, hope or expectation that it do so. *See In re Standard Oil Co.*, 275 F.2d 945, 125 USPQ 227 (C.C.P.A. 1960).

If the proposed mark is used in a way that would be perceived as nothing more than an address at which the applicant can be contacted, registration must be refused. Examples of a domain name used only as an Internet address include a domain name used in close proximity to language referring to the domain name as an address, or a domain name displayed merely as part of the information on how to contact the applicant.

> Example: The mark is WWW.XYZ.COM for on-line ordering services in the field of clothing. Specimens of use consisting of an advertisement that states "visit us on the web at www.xyz.com" do not show service mark use of the proposed mark.

> Example: The mark is XYZ.COM for financial consulting services. Specimens of use consisting of a business card that refers to the service and lists a phone number, fax number, and the domain name sought to be registered do not show service mark use of the proposed mark.

. . .

B. Advertising One's Own Products or Services on the Internet is not a Service

Advertising one's own products or services is not a service. *See In re Reichhold Chemicals, Inc.*, 167 USPQ 376 (TTAB 1970); TMEP[10] § 1301.01(a)(ii). Therefore, businesses that create a website for the sole purpose of advertising their own products or services cannot register a domain name used to identify that activity. In examination, the issue usually arises when the applicant describes the activity as a registrable service, e.g., "providing information about [a particular field]," but the specimens of use make it clear that the website merely advertises the applicant's own products or services. In this situation, the examining attorney must refuse registration because the mark is used to identify an activity that does not constitute a "service" within the meaning of the Trademark Act. Trademark Act §§ 1, 2, 3 and 45, 15 U.S.C. §§ 1051, 1052, 1053 and 1127.

. . .

D. Marks Comprised Solely of TLDs for Domain Name Registry Services

If a mark is composed solely of a TLD for "domain name registry services" (e.g., the services currently provided by Network Solutions, Inc. of registering .com domain names), registration should be refused under Trademark Act §§ 1, 2, 3 and 45, 15 U.S.C. §§ 1051, 1052, 1053 and 1127, on the ground that the TLD would not

---

[10] ["TMEP" stands for Trademark Manual of Examining Procedure, which consists of the PTO's guidelines for trademark examiners.—Eds.]

be perceived as a mark. The examining attorney should include evidence from the NEXIS® database, the Internet, or other sources to show that the proposed mark is currently used as a TLD or is under consideration as a new TLD.

If the TLD merely describes the subject or user of the domain space, registration should be refused under Trademark Act § 2(e)(1), 15 U.S.C. § 2(e)(1), on the ground that the TLD is merely descriptive of the registry services.

E. Intent-to-Use Applications

A refusal of registration on the ground that the matter presented for registration does not function as a mark relates to the manner in which the asserted mark is used. Therefore, generally, in an intent-to-use application, a mark that includes a domain name will not be refused on this ground until the applicant has submitted specimens of use with either an amendment to allege use under Trademark Act § 1(c), or a statement of use under Trademark Act § 1(d), 15 U.S.C. § 1051(c) or (d). However, the examining attorney should include an advisory note in the first Office Action that registration may be refused if the proposed mark, as used on the specimens, identifies only an Internet address. This is done strictly as a courtesy. If information regarding this possible ground for refusal is not provided to the applicant prior to the filing of the allegation of use, the Office is in no way precluded from refusing registration on this basis.

III. Surnames

If a mark is composed of a surname and a TLD, the examining attorney must refuse registration because the mark is primarily merely a surname under Trademark Act § 2(e)(4), 15 U.S.C. § 1052(e)(4). A TLD has no trademark significance. If the primary significance of a term is that of a surname, adding a TLD to the surname does not alter the primary significance of the mark as a surname. . . .

IV. Descriptiveness

If a proposed mark is composed of a merely descriptive term(s) combined with a TLD, the examining attorney should refuse registration under Trademark Act § 2(e)(1), 15 U.S.C. § 1052(e)(1), on the ground that the mark is merely descriptive. This applies to trademarks, service marks, collective marks and certification marks.

> *Example*: The mark is SOFT.COM for facial tissues. The examining attorney must refuse registration under § 2(e)(1).

> *Example*: The mark is NATIONAL BOOK OUTLET.COM for retail book store services. The examining attorney must refuse registration under § 2(e)(1).

The TLD will be perceived as part of an Internet address, and does not add source identifying significance to the composite mark. *Cf. In re Page*, 51 USPQ2d 1660 (TTAB 1999) (addition of a telephone prefix such as "800" or "888" to a descriptive term is insufficient, by itself, to render the mark inherently distinctive); *In re Patent & Trademark Services Inc.*, 49 USPQ2d 1537 (TTAB 1998) (PATENT & TRADEMARK SERVICES INC. is merely descriptive of legal services in the field of intellectual property; the term "Inc." merely indicates the type of entity that performs the services and has no significance as a mark); *In re The Paint Products Co.*, 8

USPQ2d 1863 (TTAB 1988) (PAINT PRODUCTS CO. is no more registrable as a trademark for goods emanating from a company that sells paint products than it would be as a service mark for retail paint store services offered by such a company); *In re E.I. Kane, Inc.*, 221 USPQ 1203 (TTAB 1984) (OFFICE MOVERS, INC. incapable of functioning as a mark for moving services; addition of the term "Inc." does not add any trademark significance to matter sought to be registered). *See also* TMEP § 1209.01(b)(12) regarding marks comprising in part "1–800," "888," or other telephone numbers.

V. Generic Refusals

If a mark is composed of a generic term(s) for applicant's goods or services and a TLD, the examining attorney must refuse registration on the ground that the mark is generic and the TLD has no trademark significance. *See* TMEP § 1209.01(b)(12) regarding marks comprised in part of "1–800" or other telephone numbers. Marks comprised of generic terms combined with TLDs are not eligible for registration on the Supplemental Register, or on the Principal Register under Trademark Act § 2(f), 15 U.S.C. § 1052(f). This applies to trademarks, service marks, collective marks and certification marks.

> *Example*: TURKEY.COM for frozen turkeys is unregistrable on either the Principal or Supplemental Register.

> *Example*: BANK.COM for banking services is unregistrable on either the Principal or Supplemental Register.

The examining attorney generally should not issue a refusal in an application for registration on the Principal Register on the ground that a mark is a generic name for the goods or services unless the applicant asserts that the mark has acquired distinctiveness under § 2(f) of the Trademark Act, 15 U.S.C. § 1052(f). Absent such a claim, the examining attorney should issue a refusal on the ground that the mark is merely descriptive of the goods or services under § 2(e)(1), and provide an advisory statement that the matter sought to be registered appears to be a generic name for the goods or services. TMEP § 1209.02.

VI. Marks Containing Geographical Matter

The examining attorney should examine marks containing geographic matter in the same manner that any mark containing geographic matter is examined. *See generally* TMEP §§ 1210.05 and 1210.06. Depending on the manner in which it is used on or in connection with the goods or services, a proposed domain name mark containing a geographic term may be primarily geographically descriptive under § 2(e)(2) of the Trademark Act, 15 U.S.C. § 1052(e)(2), or primarily geographically deceptively misdescriptive under § 2(e)(3) of the Trademark Act, 15 U.S.C. § 1052(e)(3), and/or merely descriptive or deceptively misdescriptive under § 2(e)(1) of the Trademark Act, 15 U.S.C. § 1052(e)(1).

Geographic matter may be merely descriptive of services provided on the Internet

When a geographic term is used as a mark for services that are provided on the Internet, sometimes the geographic term describes the subject of the service rather than the geographic origin of the service. Usually this occurs when the mark is composed of a geographic term that describes the subject matter of information services (e.g., NEW ORLEANS.COM for "providing vacation planning information about New Orleans, Louisiana by means of the global computer network"). In these cases, the examining attorney should refuse registration under Trademark Act § 2(e)(1) because the mark is merely descriptive of the services.

. . .

IX. Likelihood of Confusion

In analyzing whether a domain name mark is likely to cause confusion with another pending or registered mark, the examining attorney must consider the marks as a whole, but generally should accord little weight to the TLD portion of the mark. *See* TMEP § 1207.01(b) *et seq.*

. . .

In re Dial-A-Mattress Operating Corp.
240 F.3d 1341 (Fed.Cir.2001).

■ MAYER, CHIEF JUDGE.

. . .

Background

Dial–A–Mattress sells mattresses and related bedding through retail stores and a telephone "shop-at-home" service. In 1996, it filed an intent-to-use application to register "1–888–M–A–T–R–E–S–S" as a service mark for "telephone shop-at-home retail services in the field of mattresses." . . .

After several office actions, the examiner rejected the "1–888–M–A–T–R–E–S–S" application because the mark is generic for the relevant services and therefore unregisterable. The examiner found that even if it is not generic, it is "merely descriptive" and Dial–A–Mattress presented insufficient evidence of acquired distinctiveness to permit registration of the mark under § 2(f) of the Trademark Act.

Dial–A–Mattress appealed the rejection to the Trademark Trial and Appeal Board, which affirmed. . . .

Discussion

. . .

The determination of whether a mark is generic is made according to a two-part inquiry: "First, what is the genus of the goods or services at issue? Second, is the term sought to be registered . . . understood by the relevant public primarily to refer to that genus of goods or services?" *H. Marvin Ginn Corp.*, 782 F.2d at 990. Placement of a term on the fanciful-suggestive-descriptive-generic continuum is a question of fact. *In re Merrill Lynch, Pierce, Fenner & Smith, Inc.*, 828 F.2d at 1569–70. The Director of the United States Patent and Trademark Office (Director) bears the burden of proving a term generic. *In re The Am. Fertility Soc'y*, 188 F.3d 1341, 1345 (Fed.Cir.1999). Any competent source suffices to show the relevant purchasing public's understanding of a contested term, including purchaser testimony, consumer surveys, dictionary definitions, trade journals, newspapers and other publications.

Where a term is a "compound word" (such as "Screenwipe"), the Director may satisfy his burden of proving it generic by producing evidence that each of the constituent words is generic, and that "the separate words joined to form a compound have a meaning identical to the meaning common usage would ascribe to those words as a compound." *In re Gould Paper Corp.*, 834 F.2d 1017, 1018 (Fed.Cir. 1987). . . . The *In re Gould* test is applicable only to "compound terms formed by the union of words" where the public understands the individual terms to be generic for a genus of goods or services, and the joining of the individual terms into one compound word lends "no additional meaning to the term." *Id.* at 1348–49.

Here, there is no dispute that the genus is telephone shop-at-home services for retail mattresses. Nor does Dial–A–Mattress contest the following evidence and legal conclusions offered by the Director: (1) the area code designation (888) in the proposed mark by itself is devoid of source-indicating significance; (2) "matress" is the legal "equivalent" of the word "mattress"; and (3) the word "mattress" standing alone is generic for retail services in the field of mattresses.

Instead, Dial–A–Mattress contends that the board erred in holding this quantum of evidence sufficient to demonstrate that the term "1–888–M–A–T–R–E–S–S" is generic. . . .

> . . .

We conclude that the board applied the wrong test in holding that the Director meets his burden of proving an alphanumeric telephone number generic merely by showing that it is composed of a non-source-indicating area code and a generic term. "The commercial impression of a trademark is derived from it as a whole, not from its elements separated and considered in detail. For this reason, it should be considered in its entirety. . . ." *Estate of P.D. Beckwith, Inc. v. Comm'r of Patents*, 252 U.S. 538, 545–46 (1920). The Director must produce evidence of the meaning the relevant purchasing public accords the proposed mnemonic mark "as a whole." *In re The Am. Fertility Soc'y*, 188 F.3d at 1348; *see also H. Marvin Ginn Corp.*, 782 F.2d at 990–91. *In re Gould* does not apply here because "1–888–M–A–T–R–E–S–S" a mnemonic formed by the union of a series of numbers and a word bears closer conceptual resemblance to a phrase than a compound word. *See In re The Am. Fertility Soc'y*, 188 F.3d at 1348–49 (explicitly limiting the holding of *In re Gould* to "compound terms formed by the union of words"). It is devoid of source-indicating significance, but "(888)" is not a word and is not itself a generic term for selling by telephone.

Analyzing the "1–888–M–A–T–R–E–S–S" mark as a whole, substantial evidence does not support the conclusion that the mark is generic. There is no record evidence that the relevant public refers to the class of shop-at-home telephone mattress retailers as "1–888–M–A–T–R–E–S–S." *See H. Marvin Ginn Corp.*, 782 F.2d at 991. "Telephone shop-at-home mattresses" or "mattresses by phone" would be more apt generic descriptions. Like the title "Fire Chief" for a magazine in the field of fire fighting, a phone number is not literally a genus or class name, but is at most descriptive of the class. *Id.* Moreover, like the term "cash management account," "1–888–M–A–T–R–E–S–S" does not "immediately and unequivocally" describe the service at issue. *See In re Merrill Lynch, Pierce, Fenner & Smith, Inc.,* 828 F.2d at 1571.

Finally, given that telephone numbers consist of only seven numbers and typically can be used by only one entity at a time, a competitor of a business that has obtained a telephone number corresponding to a "mattress" mnemonic for all practical purposes is already precluded from using and promoting the number. A rule precluding registerability merely shifts the race from the Trademark Office to the telephone company. . . .

[In the remainder of the opinion the court finds that 1–888–MATTRES is descriptive and that Dial–A–Mattress presented sufficient evidence of acquired distinctiveness to permit registration of the mark under § 2(f) of the Trademark Act.]

QUESTIONS FOR DISCUSSION

1. *Web address as service mark.* As the above PTO *Examination Guide* makes clear, a website that merely advertises and sells the goods and services of the site owner would not constitute a separate service supporting a service mark registration under the Lanham Act. To qualify as an information service, a website must provide some additional value beyond the promotion and sale of the site owner's goods and services. Must the site owner charge for this additional value that the site provides before it will qualify as an information service sufficient to support a federal service mark registration? *See Capital Speakers, Inc. v. Capital Speakers Club,* 41 U.S.P.Q.2d 1030 (T.T.A.B.1996).

2. *Generic term + .com.* Is a domain name comprising a generic term and the top-level domain name .com registrable as a trademark? In *In re Dial-A-Mattress Operating Corporation,* the court concluded that the *In re Gould* test did not apply to "1–888–M–A–T–R–E–S–S" because it was more like a phrase than a compound word. Do you think that the court would have reached the same conclusion if it had been considering a domain name? Recall that a domain name replaces a number, namely an IP address. Central to the court's reasoning was the fact that the proposed mnemonic mark was composed of a number and a word. How would you describe the composition of a domain name? Is .com an English word? Is .com a generic term for selling over the Internet? Are all websites with a domain name in the .com domain engaged in selling goods or services? Or is .com simply an "area code" for the domain name system?

In Part V of *Examination Guide No. 2–99,* excerpted above, the U.S. Patent and Trademark Office states that "[i]f a mark is composed of a generic term(s) for applicant's goods or services and a TLD, the examining attorney must refuse registration on the ground that the mark is generic and the TLD has no trademark significance." Is this policy consistent with *In re Dial-A-Mattress Operating Corporation?*

3. *A race to register.* The court in *In re Dial-A-Mattress Operating Corporation* also notes that since

> telephone numbers consist of only seven numbers and typically can be used by only one entity at a time, a competitor of a business that has obtained a telephone number corresponding to a "mattress" mnemonic for all practical purposes is already precluded from using and promoting the number. A rule precluding registerability merely shifts the race from the Trademark Office to the telephone company.

Does this same line of reasoning apply to domain names? Once one company registers a particular domain name, aren't all other companies for all practical purposes precluded from using and promoting that same domain name? Does a rule precluding registrability of a domain name formed from a generic term and a top-level domain name merely shift the race from the Trademark Office to a domain name registrar?

CHAPTER FOUR
CONSUMER PROTECTION ONLINE

When consumers spend their money to purchase goods and services, they must inevitably rely to some degree upon information from the seller. Sellers sometimes provide information about their offerings that is false or misleading, and sometimes fail to carry out their contractual undertakings, with the result that consumers do not receive what they were led to expect when they entered into the transaction. The law of consumer protection is the government's response to the fact that sellers sometimes engage in such deceptive marketing practices.

This chapter addresses the incidence of deceptive marketing practices, and the role of consumer protection, in business-to-consumer ("B2C") electronic commerce. E-commerce is a form of distance selling, bearing a family resemblance to the better-established techniques of telemarketing, catalog sales, and direct mail marketing. With each of these marketing methods, the buyer and seller never meet face to face—in contrast to sales occurring at brick-and-mortar retail establishments or at the purchaser's home or office. Distance selling methods offer consumers significant benefits, including efficiency gains from eliminating the time and expense involved in traveling to a retail establishment, a broader selection of goods, and potentially lower prices. Digital networks also offer consumers new techniques for defining their preferences and identifying the optimal providers of what they seek.

But distance selling via digital networks holds potential perils as well, presenting unscrupulous sellers with enhanced opportunities to engage in deceptive marketing practices and avoid getting caught. When consumers buy goods at a distance, they lose the ability to examine the goods before purchasing. A faraway seller will find it easier to be nonresponsive to dissatisfied customers than will a seller in the customer's own community. A buyer who purchases long distance may not even know where the seller is physically located.

In recognition of these dangers, legislatures have enacted special regulatory regimes applying to distance selling, including the Telemarketing and Consumer Fraud and Abuse Prevention Act, 15 U.S.C. §§ 6101–08, implemented by the Telemarketing Sales Rule, 16 C.F.R. Part 310; the Telephone Disclosure and Dispute Resolution Act, 15 U.S.C. §§ 5701, 5711–14, 5721–24, implemented by the Trade Regulation Rule Pursuant to the Telephone Disclosure and Dispute Resolution Act of 1992, 16 C.F.R. Part 308; and, in the European Union, Directive 97/7/EC of the European Parliament and of the Council of 20 May 1997 on the protection of consumers in respect of distance contracts, 1997 O.J. (L 144) 19, europa.eu.int/comm/consumers/policy/developments/dist_sell/dist01_en.pdf. *See* John Rothchild, *Making the Market Work: Enhancing Consumer Sovereignty Through the Telemarketing Sales Rule and the Distance Selling Directive*, 21 J. CONSUMER POL'Y 279 (1998).

The discussion in this chapter will focus on several themes: How does Internet commerce differ from other forms of distance selling? What is the proper role of the government in controlling online deceptive marketing practices? How can consumer protection be promoted through code-based solutions?

I. Background: Overview of Consumer Protection Regulation

A. Consumer Protection in a Market Economy

A market economy is characterized by the existence of a sphere of activity within which sellers and buyers are allowed considerable leeway to structure the terms of their commercial interactions. Market participants arrive through negotiation at a bargain that each views as advantageous: for example, the local department store would prefer to have one fewer washing machine in its inventory and a little more money in its cash registers, while a householder would rather have a new washing machine and a little less money. A deal is struck. The consumer agrees to pay the store $500, and the store agrees to supply a certain model of washing machine. The money and machine change hands. The welfare of each participant in the exchange is enhanced, as the buyer receives a labor-saving device that he values more highly than the money he expended and the store (and ultimately the store's owners, its stockholders) gains a profit on the sale.

The transaction also has some ancillary effects. The store's competitors, which did not make the sale, receive an incremental incentive to offer better prices or service so as to gain future sales and profits. The consumer's decision to buy that particular washing machine causes economic resources to flow toward production of that model rather than others. The purchasing decisions of many consumers in aggregate insure that resources are used to produce the goods that they want, and not the ones that they do not want, since anyone who persists in making the latter will sooner or later go out of business.

Deceptive marketing practices interfere with this happy scenario at several junctures. First, if the goods are not as advertised, the transaction may decrease the purchaser's welfare. A purchaser might prefer a new washing machine to $500 if it performed as advertised, but might prefer to keep her money and her old washing machine if the new machine did not live up to its billing. At a minimum, mischaracterization of goods prevents consumers from maximizing their welfare within their budget constraints. Second, the transaction harms the seller's competitors, which might have won the sale and the accompanying profits if the seller had not misrepresented the washing machine's characteristics. Third, the deception skews the allocation of productive resources away from the welfare-maximizing allocation, by encouraging manufacturers to make more washing machines of the type that was sold only through misrepresentations of its characteristics.

Consumer protection thus has a dual function: it reduces the amount of harm suffered by consumers through being deceived into entering non-welfare-maximizing transactions, and it makes the market work better by promoting competition.

B. The Legal Framework for Consumer Protection

The legal framework for controlling misleading advertising and fraudulent trade practices consists of several elements. At the federal level, the statute with the broadest subject-matter coverage is the Federal Trade Commission Act, 15 U.S.C. § 41 et seq., which prohibits "unfair or deceptive acts or practices in or affecting commerce." The FTC Act is enforced by the Federal Trade Commission, which has authority to issue administrative complaints and orders, and to bring injunctive actions in federal district court. The FTC has also promulgated and enforces a host of trade regulation rules, under authority conferred by the FTC Act, and other regulations under the authority of specific acts of Congress. Those rules and regulations appear at 16 C.F.R. Parts 300 et seq. The FTC also has enforcement authority under a variety of other statutes, most prominently those governing consumer credit, such as the Truth in Lending Act, 15 U.S.C. §§ 1601–1667f, the Fair Credit Billing Act, 15 U.S.C. §§ 1666–1666j, and the Fair Credit Reporting Act, 15 U.S.C. §§ 1681–1681(u).

Other federal agencies have authority to protect consumers within a more circumscribed subject matter. The Food and Drug Administration works to insure the safety of food, drugs, and cosmetics. The Securities and Exchange Commission regulates the securities markets, and the Commodity Futures Trading Commission oversees the commodities markets. The Consumer Product Safety Commission is charged with reducing the risks associated with consumer products.

Complementing the federal regulatory framework are trade regulation and consumer protection statutes at the state level. These statutes, which are sometimes referred to as "little FTC Acts," prohibit a wide range of deceptive trade practices. In addition to general prohibitions against unfair and deceptive practices, many of these statutes include more detailed treatments of specific subject matters, such as pyramid sales, lotteries, prize promotions, failure to have sufficient goods to meet reasonably expectable demand, and creating confusion about the source or sponsorship of goods. These statutes are enforced by the state attorney general or other state enforcement officials. Unlike the FTC Act, some of these statutes also give a private right of action to injured consumers and competitors.

Within the European Union, the regulatory framework for consumer protection consists of the national laws of each member state, as amplified by Directives that the European Commission promulgates.[1] The most significant Directives from the standpoint of consumer protection are the Directive on Misleading Advertising,[2] which establishes the basic rules against deceptive marketing practices, and the Directive on Distance Selling,[3] which applies to sales made at a distance via means such as direct mail, print advertising, catalogues, telephone, and e-mail, and features a pre-sale disclosure requirement, a seven-day right of withdrawal, a requirement that goods be shipped within thirty days, and other provisions. Of direct pertinence to Internet commerce, the Directive on Electronic Commerce[4]

---

[1] An EC Directive is a set of legal rules on a particular subject, established through a lawmaking process at the EU community level, that EU member states are required by treaty to implement through enactment of national laws.

[2] Council Directive 84/450/EEC of 10 September 1984 relating to the approximation of the laws, regulations and administrative provisions of the Member States concerning misleading advertising, 1984 O.J. (L 250) 17, *amended by* Directive 97/55/EC of European Parliament and of the Council of 6 October 1997 amending Directive 84/450/EEC concerning misleading advertising so as to include comparative advertising, 1997 O.J. (L 290) 18, europa.eu.int/eur-lex/en/consleg/pdf/1984/en_1984L0450_do_001.pdf.

[3] Directive 97/7/EC of the European Parliament and of the Council of 20 May 1997 on the protection of consumers in respect of distance contracts, 1997 O.J. (L 144) 19, europa.eu.int/comm/consumers/policy/developments/dist_sell/dist01_en.pdf.

[4] Directive 2000/31/EC of the European Parliament and of the Council of 8 June 2000 on certain legal aspects of information society services, in particular electronic commerce, in the Internal Market, 2000 O.J. (L 178) 1, europa.eu.int/ISPO/ecommerce/legal/documents/2000_31ec/2000_31ec_en.pdf.

requires that online advertising communications, including unsolicited commercial e-mail, be clearly identifiable as such, and calls upon member states to encourage the settlement of disputes through alternative dispute resolution mechanisms.

In 1999, the Organisation for Economic Co-operation and Development released a set of guidelines intended to assist governments in designing consumer protection regulation for e-commerce, and to assist trade associations in devising self-regulatory schemes. Guidelines for Consumer Protection in the Context of Electronic Commerce (1999), www.oecd.org/dataoecd/18/13/34023235.pdf.

II. The Extent of Fraudulent Practices Online

A. Fraud-Facilitating Features of the Online Environment

The Internet presents unscrupulous marketers with plenty of opportunity to engage in consumer fraud, and they are taking advantage of that opportunity. Several features of the online environment facilitate fraudulent conduct, and make it more difficult for law enforcement agencies to control such conduct. First, the low cost of setting up and conducting business on the Internet invites new entrepreneurial ventures in large numbers—many of which consist of no more than an individual armed with a computer, a connection to the Internet, and a desire for gain. Some percentage of these entrepreneurs will put profit before all else and use fraudulent techniques to separate consumers from their money. A proliferation of small operators, each obtaining small amounts of money from a few victims, creates severe difficulties for law enforcement agencies charged with controlling deceptive marketing practices. The small size of each operation makes it uneconomic to bring the traditional machinery of law enforcement to bear, yet the amount lost to fraud may be very large in the aggregate.

Second, it is cheaper and easier to simulate a respectable business on the Web than it is using other media. A professional-looking website can be created at a fraction of the cost required to create a storefront or office that conveys an aura of respectability. When making their purchasing decisions in a world of imperfect information, consumers must rely on clues of this sort, which economists refer to as "signaling." Their experience in the brick-and-mortar world—that a respectable-looking edifice betokens a trustworthy business—may lead them astray in the online world.

Third, the fact that the marginal cost of online communications approaches zero makes it profitable to engage in deceptive marketing techniques that would be unprofitable using other communications media. Imagine yourself in the position of an entrepreneur who is assessing the viability of a money-making scheme that consists of using deceptive communications to entice consumers to pay money for a product that is worthless, or that she has no intention of delivering. The endeavor will be profitable only if the vendor's revenues exceed her costs. In an operation of this sort, a major component of the vendor's costs will be those associated with marketing her product—traditionally by direct mail, telemarketing, or advertising in the print or broadcast media. The high cost of marketing through these traditional media serves to limit such ventures, since only attractive propositions, and those marketed through the use of sophisticated targeting methods, will yield a high enough response rate to result in a profit. For example, a direct mail piece consisting of a flyer that proclaims

> MAKE $10,000 A MONTH WORKING FROM HOME, PART TIME. NO
> EXPERIENCE REQUIRED. SATISFACTION GUARANTEED. SEND $5
> FOR INSTRUCTIONS.

would almost certainly be a money-loser, since the cost of sending such a letter is roughly one dollar, and the response rate will be considerably less than 20 percent, the breakeven point neglecting all other costs.

The advent of online marketing techniques radically alters the economics of the situation. If marketing costs are low enough, it becomes possible to make money using remarkably unattractive propositions delivered through unsophisticated marketing techniques. Bulk unsolicited commercial e-mail, better known as "spam," is one such technique. CD-ROMs containing 10 million e-mail addresses can be purchased for less than $100, and the marginal cost of sending e-mail messages is extremely small. According to one estimate, a single communication costs a spammer about one-thirtieth of a cent. At that cost, a marketer sending the above solicitation letter would break even with a response rate of .006 percent (1 million solicitations yielding 60 responses), and anything beyond that would be pure profit. In fact, a spammer can make a profit even with a response rate of zero: clicking the "unsubscribe" link in a spam message may result in the spammer receiving a commission for referring you to a third-party website.

This same economic calculus has brought about a resurgence in the popularity of chain letters and other pyramid schemes. Chain letters soliciting money have circulated in this country since at least the 1930s.[5] A chain letter instructs the recipient that he will receive a great deal of money if he (1) sends a certain sum of money to each of several people whose names and addresses are listed, (2) crosses off one of the names and replaces it with his own, and (3) forwards a copy of the revised letter to several friends. These letters are illegal, because it is mathematically certain that all participants except those in the first few levels of the pyramid will lose money. Because it is easy and costless to forward these letters via e-mail, they circulate in much larger numbers than those sent by postal mail, which require paper, envelopes, and postage.

Fourth, the distributed nature of online communications reduces the power of responsible speech intermediaries, by circumventing their function of filtering out misleading and fraudulent marketing practices. For example, the television networks have highly evolved codes of acceptable advertising practices. Proposed advertising must be submitted in advance for review. If a network finds an ad to be in poor taste, misleading, or otherwise in violation of its code, it will not run the ad. Other media outlets, such as print publications, are discriminating to lesser and varying degrees, but still filter out some of the worst advertising. Online advertisers, by contrast, typically are subject only to the online service providers' Acceptable Use Policies, which are both lenient and rarely enforced. Note, however, that the online medium may *increase* the ability of payment intermediaries, such as credit card systems, to mediate disputes, since all transactions are at a distance and there are at present no widely adopted non-intermediated digital payment systems.

Fifth, the typically wide geographic distribution of the victims of online fraud helps the

---

[5] The popularity of the Send-a-Dime chain letter craze peaked in 1935. *See* N.Y. TIMES (May 28, 1935) (cited in Daniel W. VanArsdale, *Chain Letter Evolution* (1998), www.silcom.com/~barnowl/chain-letter/evolution.html.

wrongdoer to avoid law enforcement agencies. Marketing communications that are distributed via the Web or e-mail have national and international reach. A deceptive marketer located in one state may have a few victims in each of numerous other states or localities, and a careful deceptive marketer will avoid having any victims in his home state. A law enforcement agency in the jurisdiction where a victim is located lacks the resources to investigate a fraud that is committed by a marketer located hundreds or thousands of miles away, and that affects only a few of its constituents. A law enforcement agency in the marketer's home state also lacks the incentive to pursue the marketer, since there are no victims in that home jurisdiction.

Complaint intake services convey some idea of the types of fraud that are most prevalent on the Internet. The National Fraud Information Center, a project of the non-profit National Consumers League, collects complaints from consumers who have been defrauded in Internet commerce and forwards the complaints to law enforcement authorities. During 2004, the majority of the complaints it received—51 percent—concerned online auctions. The next most commonly reported frauds, in order, were those involving general merchandise, Nigerian money offers, phishing scams, misinformation concerning adult services, fake checks, and lotteries. *See* National Fraud Information Center, *Internet Scams—Fraud Trends 2004*, www.fraud.org/2004-internet%20scams.pdf.

The technology of online communications has made possible novel variations on the theme of consumer fraud. A couple of cases are illustrative. In *FTC v. Audiotex Connection, Inc.*, No. CV–97–0726 (E.D.N.Y.1997) (consent order), the defendants operated several websites, including www.beavisbutthead.com, www.sexygirls.com, and www.1adult.com, featuring adult-oriented images. The websites stated that visitors could view these images for free if they first downloaded a viewer program called "david.exe." But david.exe was no mere viewer program. Once downloaded and executed, it stealthily turned off the computer's speakers, disconnected the computer from its Internet connection, and dialed out to a phone number in Moldova through which it reconnected to the Internet. Charges for this international call accrued at more than $2 per minute. And the call remained connected even after the user shut down the browser, until the user turned off the computer. Thousands of users consequently incurred long-distance charges totaling hundreds of thousands of dollars. The defendants received a portion of the charges that victims paid to the foreign phone company.

Another new form of consumer deception is called "mousetrapping." The perpetrator configures a series of domain names in such a way that a site visitor who tries to leave one website is treated to a series of new browser windows that open automatically to display advertising sites, and efforts to depart those websites lead to more of the same. In *FTC v. Zuccarini*, 2002–1 Trade Cas. ¶ 73,690 (E.D.Pa.2002), the Commission charged that the defendant had registered thousands of domain names consisting of typographical variations on the URLs of popular sites, such as harrypottor.com mimicking harrypotter.com. Upon accidentally landing on such a website by mistyping the desired URL, the hapless visitor confronts a cascade of dozens of new browser windows featuring advertisements many of which are sexually explicit. Clicking on the browser's "Close" or "X" button only launches additional windows. The court issued a permanent injunction against this practice, including an order for payment of $1.8 million towards consumer redress. *See also FTC v. Pereira*, No. 99–1367–A (E.D.Va.2001) (consent order) (mousetrapping accomplished through altered versions of 25 million web pages).

A new type of entity capable of engaging in consumer fraud is the domain name registrar. In *FTC v. Network Solutions, Inc.*, No. 03–1907 (D.D.C.2003) (consent order), the FTC charged that Network Solutions, Inc. ("NSI") had engaged in deceptive marketing practices aimed at tricking domain name registrants into transferring their registrations to NSI. According to the FTC, NSI sent notices falsely stating that the recipient's registration was about to expire, and failing to disclose that "renewal" of the registration would result in switching the registration to NSI. And in *FTC v. 1268957 Ontario*, No. 01–CV–0423–JEC (N.D.Ga.2002) (consent order), the FTC alleged that a Canadian domain name registrar had tricked domain name holders into registering additional domain names by falsely advising them that a third party was attempting to register a similar name. The registrar faxed domain holders notices stating "URGENT NOTICE OF IDENTICAL DOMAIN NAME APPLICATION BY A THIRD PARTY," and offered to register the name for the recipient for a fee of $70. The defendants settled with the FTC, agreeing to pay $375,000 into a consumer redress fund.

An incident involving spoofing of a website illustrates a type of fraud that is possible in the offline world, but much easier online. A would-be scammer, apparently located in South Ural, Russia, created a replica of the PayPal.com website. PayPal is an online payment system. The perpetrator sent e-mails to intended victims, falsely informing them that a sum of money had been transferred to their PayPal account, and inviting them to check their balance by logging on to PayPal.com. The e-mail contained a link to a bogus login page at PayPaI.com—the "l" in PayPal replaced by an "I." With many on-screen fonts, the capital "I" looks just like a lower-case "l." The victim's login information was sent to the perpetrator, which might have allowed him to access the victim's account and help himself to the victim's funds.

The nature of the online medium makes spoofing much easier than in other contexts. The coding that creates a web page may be freely downloaded, and then uploaded to a different URL. Successfully duplicating a storefront or a mail-order catalogue is a much more difficult and expensive operation, and therefore less likely to occur.

Website spoofing has become more sophisticated and much more widespread, as it has been transformed into "phishing." According to the Anti-Phishing Working Group, an industry association, reported phishing attacks rose from 176 in January 2004 to 6,957 in October 2004 and 15,050 in June 2005. Over 90 percent of phishing attacks were targeted at the financial services sector, including companies such as Citibank, eBay, PayPal, U.S. Bank, and Barclay's. *See Anti-Phishing Working Group*, www.antiphishing.org.

Here is an example of such an attack:

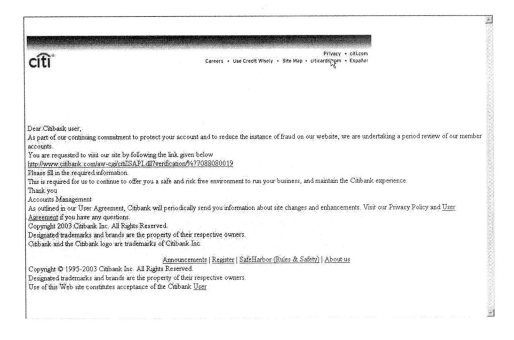

Dear Citibank user,

As part of our continuing commitment to protect your account and to reduce the instance of fraud on our website, we are undertaking a period review of our member accounts.

You are requested to visit our site by following the link given below

http://www.citibank.com/aw-cgi/citiISAPI.dll?verification/%77088080019

Please fill in the required information.

This is required for us to continue to offer you a safe and risk free environment to run your business, and maintain the Citibank experience.

Thank you

Accounts Management

As outlined in our User Agreement, Citibank will periodically send you information about site changes and enhancements. Visit our Privacy Policy and User Agreement if you have any questions.

Copyright 2003 Citibank Inc. All Rights Reserved.

Designated trademarks and brands are the property of their respective owners.

Citibank and the Citibank logo are trademarks of Citibank Inc.

Announcements | Register | SafeHarbor (Rules & Safety) | About us

Copyright © 1995-2003 Citibank Inc. All Rights Reserved.

Designated trademarks and brands are the property of their respective owners.

Use of this Web site constitutes acceptance of the Citibank User

---

• sign on • open account • contact us • search • privacy • citi.com

PRODUCTS & SERVICES   PLANNING & TOOLS   INVESTING & MARKETS   HELP DESK

MY citi

Update your ATM/Debit Card on your Citibank account :

Use this secure form to update your ATM/Debit Card information on your Citibank account. The transmitted ATM/Debit Card information is protected by the industry standard encrypted SSL connection.

ATM/Debit Card (CIN): [   ]

Expiration Date: [Month ▼] [Year ▼]

Pin Number: [   ]

Email Address: [   ]

Your User ID: [   ]

Your Password: [   ]

[Submit]

Welcome to the place where you can do it all!

To get started using My Citi, just sign on with your User ID and Password. Then you can take advan

Award Winning Services

The #1 Online Bank 1

Free Online Bill Payment

The easiest way to pay virtually anyone, anytime!

Your Home Page

The one place to manage your Citi accounts

learn more >
take a tour

get started >
register for free

Sign on with an
ATM/Debit Card number
and PIN

1Citibank was ranked the #1 overall online bank by Gomez™, the Internet Quality Measurement firm, in its Internet Banker Scorecard™ for Q4 2003. Gomez, the Gomez logo and Gomez Internet Banker Scorecard are trademarks of Gomez, Inc.

about us | careers | locations | site map

My Citi gives you access to accounts and services provided by Citibank and its affiliates.
Citibank, N.A., Citibank, F.S.B., Citibank (West), FSB. Member FDIC.

LENDER

citi
Citi.com

A member of citigroup

Citigroup Privacy Promise
Terms & Conditions
Copyright © 2003 Citicorp

The first screenshot shows the e-mail that is sent to initiate the phishing expedition. The second shows the website, a spoof of Citibank's site, that is reached upon clicking on the link in the e-mail. The victim enters his user ID and password, and wakes up the next morning with a zero balance in his account.

Phishing scams may violate several laws. *See FTC v. _____*, No. 03–5275 (C.D.Cal.2003) (consent order) (name of defendant, a minor, redacted in original) (alleging violations of the FTC Act and the Gramm–Leach–Bliley Act). In 2005, Virginia enacted the first state law directed specifically at phishing scams. The law makes it a felony "to use a computer to obtain, access, or record, through the use of material artifice, trickery or deception," any of several categories of personally identifying information. VA. CODE § 18.2–152.5:1.

EXTENSIONS

New payment mechanisms. Novel aspects of the online medium can create new vulnerabilities. Consider the ramifications of the introduction of new payment mechanisms. (These mechanisms are considered in Chapter 15, *infra.*) Consumers who are accustomed to the protections they receive when they make a purchase using a credit card may be surprised to find that those protections are absent when they use online payment mechanisms. If a purchaser makes a purchase using a credit card, and the seller does not carry out its end of the bargain, the purchaser may dispute the charge by initiating a chargeback. Under the Fair Credit Billing Act, 15 U.S.C. §§ 1666–1666j, this sets in motion a process in which the credit card issuer attempts to mediate the dispute between seller and buyer. If the parties are unable to reach a mutually agreeable resolution, the issuer may require the merchant to absorb the loss.

This dispute resolution scheme, which was mandated by federal law and has been extended more broadly on a voluntary basis by the major credit card companies, is not available when payments are made via other mechanisms, such as cash, check, money order, or debit card. As some consumers have learned to their surprise and dismay, chargebacks are not necessarily available for purchases made using online payment mechanisms. The most popular alternative payment mechanisms for making online purchases is PayPal. To use PayPal, a customer funds an account with a deposit from a credit card, personal check, or transfer from another PayPal user. Once an account is funded, the holder can direct that a payment be made to an online seller. Funds are transferred immediately, which benefits both buyer and seller by eliminating the delay in shipment of goods that would result if the seller waited for the buyer's check to clear.

When the PayPal account is funded using a credit card, the availability of chargebacks has varied depending on which credit card is used: Visa and MasterCard permitted chargebacks, but American Express and Discover did not. In 2003, American Express and Discover entered Assurances of Discontinuance with the New York Attorney General, in which they agreed to extend their normal billing-dispute procedure to complaints from consumers who funded their PayPal account with a charge on their credit card.

If the seller fails to deliver, the buyer may also have recourse under PayPal's Buyer Complaint policy. An earlier version of PayPal's User Agreement (in effect at least from 2000–02) stated that PayPal "does not ensure the quality, safety, or legality of the merchandise received, nor that the seller will even ship the merchandise." The June 2005 version of the Agreement offers more protections:

> PayPal's Buyer Complaint Policy provides a method for buyers to issue formal complaints regarding goods paid for through PayPal but never received, and re-

garding goods purchased on eBay and paid for through PayPal that the buyer receives but that are significantly not as described by the seller. The availability of this system as a back-up to direct communication between the buyer and the seller, and as a way to encourage such communication, helps maintain a safe trading community. . . . Buyer complaints must be filed within 45 days of the payment. Even if the buyer's claim is justified, the buyer will receive a recovery only if there are funds in the seller's account. RECOVERY OF YOUR CLAIM IS NOT GUARANTEED.

The Buyer Complaint Policy only applies to payments for tangible, physical goods which can be shipped, and excludes all other payments, including but not limited to payments for intangibles, for services or for licenses and other access to digital content. . . . Before filing a claim, you should contact the seller and attempt to resolve the dispute. If you are unable to resolve the dispute in this manner, you can file a claim in PayPal's Resolution Center. . . . PayPal will contact the seller and investigate your claim. If the claim involves non-delivery of goods, the seller must present appropriate proof of shipment to the buyer's specified address. If the claim is granted, PayPal will seek to collect from the seller by debiting the seller's PayPal account. . . .

PayPal, *Buyer Complaint Policy*, www.paypal.com/cgi-bin/webscr?cmd=p/gen/ua/policy_buyer_complaint-outside.

QUESTIONS FOR DISCUSSION

Extension of chargebacks. Do you think federal law should extend chargeback-like rights to new online payment mechanisms, regardless of the method by which they are funded? If so, should similar protections be extended to debit cards? Checks? Should we expect that market forces will impel the purveyors of new payment mechanisms to extend chargeback-like protections voluntarily, as a way of competing for customers?

COMPARATIVE NOTE

Cross-border electronic commerce—the European experience. In 2002–03, the European Consumer Centre's Network conducted a study of cross-border e-commerce shopping within the European Union, making a series of test purchases and analyzing the results. One of the study's findings is that there is very little cross-border business-to-consumer e-commerce:

> The first major obstacle for the researchers was to actually find webtraders that offered crossborder sales. We knew that most e-commerce companies operate mainly in their domestic market, however it still came as a bit of a surprise to learn that it's only a very small minority of the EU based webtraders that offered their products and services to the whole of the internal market. . . . The webtraders that did not sell to foreign consumers could be divided into two categories. The first relates to those that limited their market by language and the second to those that explicitly informed the consumer that they did not deliver abroad or to certain specified countries. . . . The Internet and e-commerce is often described or even defined as a global and border-less shopping mall, however according to our study it seems to be a domestic or regional marketplace.

Substantively, the study found that consumers who do engage in such e-commerce may encounter a variety of difficulties:

> A total of 114 orders were made in the shopping exercise, with all orders be-

ing cross-border and within the EU. However, only 75 of those orders resulted in a delivery. That means that 34% of the orders were not delivered. Of even more concern was the fact that 8% of the ordered products were not delivered even if they had been paid for.

Payment was often instantly withdrawn from the researcher's credit card when he/she places an order. That happened in 24% of the cases where credit cards were used. This payment policy causes problems, especially when many of the paid goods are not delivered.

We returned 57 of the 75 products we received. In 18 of those cases we did not receive any refund. That means that 31.5% of the returned goods were not refunded. Only 37% of all returns resulted in a reimbursement including the delivery fee.

According to the Distance Selling Directive, the consumer has the right to withdraw from the contract without reason within a specific number of days. Nevertheless, 24% of the webtraders that we returned the products to asked for a reason. The question could very well be optional, however it was often presented in such a way that the consumer might believe that an acceptable reason was a demand for the reimbursement.

EUROPEAN CONSUMER CENTRE NETWORK, REALITIES OF THE EUROPEAN ONLINE MARKETPLACE 6, 10 (2003), www.konsumenteuropa.se/Documents/Engelska/EEC_e-commerce_report.pdf. A follow-up study, based on an analysis of consumer complaints, found a similar pattern of problems. EUROPEAN CONSUMER CENTRE NETWORK, THE EUROPEAN ONLINE MARKETPLACE: CONSUMER COMPLAINTS 2004 (2005), www.ecic.ie/publications/reports/ecc_reports/eur_online_marketplace_2004.pdf.

B. REGULATORY AGENCY RESPONSES

Law enforcement agencies have been active in enforcing the laws prohibiting deceptive marketing practices in the online context. Some representative cases that the FTC has brought include:

Pyramid schemes. In *FTC v. Mall Ventures, Inc.*, No. CV04–0463 (C.D.Cal.2004) (consent order), the FTC charged defendants with operating a pyramid investment scheme in the guise of an Internet shopping mall. Defendants claimed that investors could make $1,000 per month if they were just "1% successful," rising to $117,000 per month after five years. Over 50,000 consumers invested in the scheme, paying more than $34 million, and few recouped their investment. Other cases against pyramid schemes include *FTC v. NexGen3000.com, Inc.*, No. CIV–03–120 (D.Ariz.2005) (consent order) (online shopping mall) and *FTC v. Fortuna Alliance, L.L.C.*, No. C96–799M (W.D.Wash.1997) (consent order) (pyramid scheme with payments purported based on a mathematical formula called the Fibonacci Series).

Failure to deliver goods. In *FTC v. Hare*, No. 98–8194 (M.D.Fla.1998) (consent order), the defendant offered goods for sale via an online auction. The FTC alleged that defendant received money from winning bidders, but failed to ship the goods they had ordered. After settling with the FTC, the defendant pled guilty to a charge of criminal wire fraud based on the same conduct.

Deceptive health claims. In *FTC v. Liverite Products,* No. SA 01–778 (C.D.Cal.2001) (consent order), the defendants agreed to settle charges that they made numerous unsubstantiated claims about the efficacy of their "Liverite" dietary supplement products to treat or prevent a wide range of liver diseases, such as cirrhosis and hepatitis. The products included Liverite, the Ultimate Liver Aid; Liverite 3 in 1 for Men; Liverite 3 in 1 for Women; and Liverite Sports. These products consisted chiefly of beef liver extract. They were sold via several websites, as well as in retail stores and by telephone.

Credit repair schemes. In "Operation New ID/Bad Idea," conducted in 1999, the FTC, together with more than a dozen federal, state, and local law enforcement agencies, brought 59 cases against defendants who claimed they could help consumers clean up their credit histories. The assistance that defendants provided consisted of advising consumers to set up a new identity by obtaining a new taxpayer identification number. This method, unfortunately, is quite illegal.

The Securities and Exchange Commission has also been active in enforcing the securities laws in the online context. The most common types of online securities fraud are the offering of phony or overvalued investments, and stock price manipulation.

Investment fraud. In *SEC v. Grabarnick*, No. 02–Civ.–20875 (S.D.Fla.2004), the SEC charged defendants with promoting investments in unregistered partnership units through bulk e-mail messages and website postings. Interested investors who responded to the online solicitations were contacted by telemarketers, who sold the units by making false claims about the profitability of the investments. More than 580 investors spent over $10 million for worthless investments. *See also SEC v. Briden*, No. 99–CV–11009 (D.Mass.2003) (consent order) (fraudulent offering of "prime bank" securities over the Internet).

Stock price manipulation. The Internet is a cheap and easy way of spreading misinformation about a stock for the purpose of manipulating its price. This is frequently employed in a "pump-and-dump" scheme: the perpetrator pumps up the stock price by spreading baseless positive information about it, and then dumps his own holdings at the inflated price. The price then drops back to its pre-manipulation level. In *SEC v. Invest Better 2001*, 2005 WL 2385452 (S.D.N.Y.2005), the SEC charged defendants with manipulating the prices of fifteen publicly traded companies by posting over 6,000 messages on Internet message boards. Defendants bought and sold millions of shares of stock, profiting from price movements resulting from their postings. The court imposed a civil penalty against defendants.

For additional information about SEC enforcement against online securities violations, see Securities and Exchange Commission, *Internet-Related Litigation Announcements*, www.sec.gov/divisions/enforce/internetenforce/litreleases.shtml.

FURTHER READING

- Joseph J. Cella III & John Reed Stark, SEC Enforcement and the Internet: Meeting the Challenge of the Next Millennium, 52 BUS. LAW. 815 (1997)

C. NEW LAW ENFORCEMENT TOOLS

If the technology of Internet communications facilitates fraudulent conduct, and makes possible entirely new types of fraud, it also gives law enforcement officials new tools with which to fight fraud. First, centralized searching technology makes it easier to monitor and detect online scams. It is a simple matter to search the entire Web for particular keywords indicating likely scams. Fraudulent unsolicited commercial e-mail is frequently forwarded to central repositories, allowing it to be archived and searched. Perusing a newsgroup archive can turn up consumers who have been victimized by a scam, and who can provide evidence against the perpetrators. By contrast, it is not feasible to monitor the unthinkably large number of offline means of transmitting fraudulent schemes—print and broadcast media, direct mail, and telemarketing all put together.

Second, consumer protection agencies can use the Internet as a means of disseminating information that helps consumers protect themselves against online fraud. One innovative approach involves the use of "teaser" websites, which are designed to draw consumers' attention and to deliver an educational message. The home page of a teaser site proposes an offer that seems too good to be true, such as a get-rich-quick scheme, diet program, or discount vacation plan. As the user clicks through to subsequent pages, he may view even more outrageous claims or testimonials, and is invited to become a participant by sending money. The final page reveals that the site was constructed by a government agency for the purpose of demonstrating to consumers how easy it is to fall for scams, and directs the user to sources of further information about how to avoid becoming a victim. Examples of teaser sites can be found at *McWhortle,* www.mcwhortle.com; *The Ultimate Prosperity Page,* www.wemarket4u.net/prosperity/index.html; and *EZ Travels,* www.wemarket4u.net/eztrvlagent/index.html.

The Internet also presents consumers with additional avenues for protecting themselves. Searching newsgroup archives can provide information about other consumers' experiences with a vendor or a product. Sites like *Complaints.com,* www.complaints.com, and *Rip-Off Report,* www.ripoffreport.com, accept consumer complaints and post them for all to see. Ratings sites such as *Epinions.com,* www.epinions.com, collect consumer experiences and product reviews. The site at www.consumer.gov provides links to the full range of consumer information available from the government. Online bookstores offer book reviews just when they are needed. Online resources can even assist consumers in defining their own preferences.

FURTHER READING

- Mark S. Nadel, *The Consumer Product Selection Process in an Internet Age: Obstacles to Maximum Effectiveness and Policy Options,* 14 HARV. J.L. & TECH. 183 (2000) (identifying and discussing obstacles to consumers' use of Internet resources to aid them in making informed marketplace choices)

III. ONLINE ADVERTISING ISSUES

As a general matter, legal rules that regulate the content of advertising are equally applicable regardless of the medium through which an advertisement is communicated. But it is not always clear what those rules mean when applied to the online context. Rules that were written before the dawn of the digital age frequently contain language that is clear enough when applied to traditional communications media, but that raises issues of interpretation when applied to online communications. Features of online technologies that have no obvious offline analogue, such as metatags and sponsored search engine results, likewise require careful application of rules written at a time when such technologies were yet unimagined.

A. INFORMATION DISCLOSURES IN ADVERTISING

Advertising can mislead both through what it says, and through what it fails to say. If an advertisement makes a claim that, standing alone, is ambiguous or is otherwise likely to mislead a potential purchaser, then the advertiser may be required to disclose qualifying information to insure that consumers will not be misled.

A Federal Trade Commission staff report discusses how the laws against misleading advertising apply to online advertising. The report sets out the general rules governing the use of advertising disclosures, and then applies these principles to website advertising.

FEDERAL TRADE COMMISSION, DOT COM DISCLOSURES (2000)
www.ftc.gov/bcp/conline/pubs/buspubs/dotcom/index.pdf

. . .

A. Background on Disclosures

Advertisers must identify all express and implied claims that the ad conveys to consumers. When identifying claims, advertisers should not focus only on individual phrases or statements, but should consider the ad as a whole, including the text, product name and depictions. If an ad makes express or implied claims that are likely to be misleading without certain qualifying information, the information must be disclosed. Advertisers must determine which claims might need qualification and what information should be provided in a disclosure. If qualifying information is necessary to prevent an ad from being misleading, advertisers must present the information clearly and conspicuously.

A disclosure only qualifies or limits a claim, to avoid a misleading impression. It cannot cure a false claim. If a disclosure provides information that contradicts a claim, the disclosure will not be sufficient to prevent the ad from being deceptive. In that situation, the claim itself must be modified.

Many [Federal Trade] Commission rules and guides spell out the information that must be disclosed in connection with certain claims. In many cases, these disclosures prevent a claim from being misleading or deceptive. Other rules and guides require disclosures to ensure that consumers receive material information about the terms of a transaction, or to further public policy goals. These disclosures also must be clear and conspicuous.

B. The Clear and Conspicuous Requirement

Disclosures that are required to prevent deception—or to provide consumers material information about a transaction—must be presented "clearly and conspicuously." Whether a disclosure meets this standard is measured by its performance—that is, how consumers actually perceive and understand the disclosure within the context of the entire ad. The key is the *overall net impression* of the ad—that is, whether the claims consumers take from the ad are truthful and substantiated.

In reviewing their online ads, advertisers should adopt the perspective of a reasonable consumer. They also should assume that consumers don't read an entire

Web site, just as they don't read every word on a printed page. In addition, it is important for advertisers to draw attention to the disclosure. Making the disclosure available somewhere in the ad so that consumers who are looking for the information *might* find it doesn't meet the clear and conspicuous standard.

Even though consumers have control over what and how much information they view on Web sites, they may not be looking for—or expecting to find— disclosures. Advertisers are responsible for ensuring that their messages are truthful and not deceptive. Accordingly, disclosures must be communicated effectively so that consumers are likely to notice and understand them.

C. What are Clear and Conspicuous Disclosures?

There is no set formula for a clear and conspicuous disclosure. In all media, the best way to disclose information depends on what information must be provided and the nature of the advertisement. Some disclosures are quite short, while others are more detailed. Some ads use only text, while others use graphics, video and audio. Advertisers have the flexibility to be creative in designing their ads, so long as necessary disclosures are communicated effectively and the overall message conveyed to consumers is not misleading.

To evaluate whether a particular disclosure is clear and conspicuous, consider:

- the **placement** of the disclosure in an advertisement and its **proximity** to the claim it is qualifying,

- the **prominence** of the disclosure,

- whether items in other parts of the advertisement **distract attention** from the disclosure,

- whether the advertisement is so lengthy that the disclosure needs to be **repeated**,

- whether disclosures in audio messages are presented in an adequate **volume** and **cadence** and visual disclosures appear for a sufficient **duration**, and

- whether the language of the disclosure is **understandable** to the intended audience.

. . .

1. Proximity and Placement

A disclosure is more effective if it is placed near the claim it qualifies or other relevant information. Proximity increases the likelihood that consumers will see the disclosure and relate it to the relevant claim or product. For print ads, an advertiser might measure proximity in terms of whether the disclosure is placed adjacent to the claim, or whether it is separated from the claim by text or graphics. The same approach can be used for Internet ads. Websites, however, are interactive and have a certain depth—with multiple pages linked together and pop-up screens, for example—that may affect how proximity is evaluated.

a. Evaluating Proximity in the Context of a Web Page

Some disclosures must be made when an ad contains a certain claim (often referred to as a "triggering claim"). On a Web page, the disclosure is more likely to be effective if consumers view the claim and disclosure together on the same screen. Even if a disclosure is not tied to a particular word or phrase, it is more likely that consumers will notice it if it is placed next to the information, product, or service to which it relates.

In some circumstances, it may be difficult to ensure that a disclosure appears on the "same screen" as a claim or product information. Some disclosures are long and difficult to place next to the claims they qualify. In addition, computers and other information "appliances" have varying screen sizes that display Web sites differently. In these situations, consumers may need to scroll to view a disclosure. If scrolling is necessary, advertisers should ask whether consumers are likely to do it. If consumers don't scroll, they may miss important qualifying information and be misled.

In these circumstances, advertisers are advised to:

Use text or visual cues to encourage consumers to scroll. Text prompts can indicate that more information is available. An explicit instruction like "see below for important information on diamond weights" will alert consumers to scroll and look for the information. The text prompt should be tied to the disclosure that it refers to. General or vague statements, such as "see below for details," provide no indication about the subject matter or importance of the information that consumers will find and are not adequate cues.

The visual design of the page also could help alert consumers to the availability of more information. For example, text that clearly continues below the screen, whether spread over an entire page or in a column, would indicate that the reader needs to scroll for additional information. Advertisers should consider how the Web page is displayed by the default Web browser setting for which the ad is designed, as well as for different display options.

A scroll bar on the side of a computer screen is not a sufficiently effective visual cue. Although the scroll bar may indicate to some consumers that they have not reached the end of a page, many consumers may not look at the scroll bar. In fact, some consumers access the Internet with devices that don't display a scroll bar.

Avoid Web page formats that discourage scrolling. The design of some pages might indicate that there is no more information on the page and no need to continue scrolling. If the text ends before the bottom of the screen or readers see several inches of blank space, chances are they will stop scrolling and miss the disclosure. In addition, if there is a lot of unrelated information—either words or graphics—separating a claim and a disclosure, even a consumer who is prompted to scroll might miss the disclosure or not relate it to a distant claim they've already read.

b. Hyperlinking to a Disclosure

With hyperlinks, additional information, including disclosures, might be placed on a Web page entirely separate from the relevant claim. Disclosures that are an integral part of a claim or inseparable from it, however, should be placed on the same page and immediately next to the claim. In these situations, the claim and the disclosure should be read at the same time, without referring the consumer somewhere else to obtain the disclosure. This is particularly true for cost information or certain health and safety disclosures. For example, if the total cost of a product is advertised on one page, but there are significant additional fees that the consumer would not expect to be charged, the existence of those additional fees should be disclosed on the same page and immediately adjacent to the total cost claim. In other situations, it may not even be necessary to use a hyperlink to convey disclosures. Often, disclosures consist of a word or phrase that may be easily incorporated into the text, along with the claim. This placement increases the likelihood that consumers will see the disclosure and relate it to the relevant claim.

Under some conditions, however, a disclosure accessible by a hyperlink may be sufficiently proximate to the relevant claim. Hyperlinked disclosures may be particularly useful if the disclosure is lengthy or if it needs to be repeated (because of multiple triggers, for example). The key considerations for effective hyperlinks are:

- the labeling or description of the hyperlink,

- the consistency in the use of hyperlink styles,

- its placement and prominence on the Web page, and

- the handling of the disclosure on the click-through page.

Choosing the right label for the hyperlink. A hyperlink that leads to a disclosure should be labeled clearly and conspicuously. The hyperlink's label—the text or graphic assigned to it—affects whether consumers actually click on it and see and read the disclosure.

- **Make it obvious.** Consumers should be able to tell that they can click on a hyperlink to get more information.

- **Label the link to convey the importance, nature and relevance of the information it leads to.** The hyperlink should give consumers a *reason* to click on it. That is, the label should make clear that the link is related to a particular advertising claim or product and indicate the nature of the information to be found by clicking on it. The hyperlink label should use clear, understandable text. Although the label itself does not need to contain the complete disclosure, it may be useful to incorporate part of the disclosure to indicate the type and importance of the information the link leads to.

- **Don't be coy.** Some text links may provide no indication about why a claim is qualified or the nature of the disclosure. In most cases, simply hyperlinking a single word or phrase in the text of an ad may not be effective. Although some consumers may understand that there is additional information available, they may have different ideas about the nature of the information and its significance. The same may be true of hyperlinks that simply say "disclaimer," "more information," "details," or "terms and conditions."

- **Don't be subtle.** Asterisks or other symbols by themselves may not be effective. Typically, they provide no clues about why the claim is qualified or the nature of the disclosure. In fact, consumers may view an asterisk or another symbol as just another graphic on the page. Even if a Web site explains that a particular symbol is a hyperlink to important information, consumers might miss the explanation, depending on where they enter the site and how they navigate through it.

Using hyperlink styles consistently allows consumers to know when a link is available. Although the text or graphics used to signal a hyperlink may differ among Web sites, treating hyperlinks inconsistently within a single site can increase the chances that consumers will *not* notice — or click on — a disclosure hyperlink. For example, if hyperlinks usually are underlined in a site, chances are consumers wouldn't recognize italicized text as being a link, and could miss the disclosure.

Placing the link near relevant information and making it noticeable. The hyperlink should be proximate to the claim that triggers the disclosure so that consumers can notice it easily and relate it to the claim. Typically, this means that the hyperlink is adjacent to the triggering term or other relevant information. Consumers may miss disclosure hyperlinks that are separated from the relevant claim by text, graphics, blank space, or intervening hyperlinks. Format, color or other graphics treatment also can help to ensure that consumers notice the link. (See below for more information on prominence.)

Getting to the disclosure on the click-through page should be easy. The click-through page — that is, the page the hyperlink leads to — must contain the complete disclosure. The disclosure must be displayed prominently. Distracting visual factors, extraneous information, and many "click-away" opportunities to link elsewhere before viewing the disclosure can obscure an otherwise adequate disclaimer.

- **Get consumers to the message quickly.** The hyperlink should take consumers directly to the disclosure. They shouldn't have to search a click-through page or go to other pages for the information. In addition, the disclosure should be easy to understand.

- **Assessing the effectiveness of a hyperlink disclosure is important.** Tools are available to allow advertisers to evaluate the effectiveness of disclosures through hyperlinks. For example, advertisers can monitor click-through rates — how often consumers click on a hyperlink and view the click-through page — for accurate data on the efficacy of the hyperlink. Advertisers also can evaluate the amount of time visitors spend on a certain page, which may indicate whether consumers are reading the disclosure.

- **Don't ignore your data.** If hyperlinks are not followed, another method of conveying the required information would be necessary.

c. Using High Tech Methods For Proximity and Placement

Disclosures may be displayed on Web sites in many ways. For example, a disclosure may be placed in a frame that remains constant even as the consumer scrolls down the page or navigates through another part of the site. A disclosure also might be displayed in a window that pops-up or on interstitial pages that appear while another Web page is loading. New techniques for displaying information are being unveiled all the time. But there are special considerations for evaluating whether a technique is appropriate for providing required disclosures.

- **Don't ignore technological limitations.** A scrolling marquee—information that scrolls through a box on a Web site—may display differently depending on the type of browser a consumer uses. Similarly, some browsers or information appliances may not support or display frames properly, so a disclosure placed in one portion of the frame may not be viewable. Certain Internet tools may overcome this limitation by determining if a consumer's Web browser can view frames and if not, serving a page that is formatted differently. Without such tools, advertisers should be concerned about whether a required disclosure will appear; if it won't, they should choose different ways to communicate the disclosure.

- **Recognize and respond to characteristics of each technique.** Some consumers may miss information presented in a pop-up window or on an interstitial page if the window or page disappears and they are unable or unaware of how to access it. Others may inadvertently minimize a pop-up screen by clicking on the main page and may not know how to make the pop-up screen reappear. There may be ways to get around these drawbacks, such as requiring the consumer to take some affirmative action to proceed past the pop-up or interstitial (for example, by clicking on a "continue" button).

- **Research can help.** Research may be useful to help advertisers determine whether a particular technique is an effective method of communicating information to consumers. For example, research may show that consumers don't actually read information in pop-up windows because they immediately close the pop-up on the page they want to view. It also may indicate whether consumers relate information in a pop-up window or on an interstitial page to a claim or product they haven't encountered yet. Advertisers should consider this information in determining effective methods of presenting required disclosures.

d. Displaying Disclosures Prior to Purchase

Disclosures must be effectively communicated to consumers before they make a purchase or incur a financial obligation. Disclosures are more likely to be effective if they are provided in the context of the ad, when the consumer is considering the purchase. Where advertising and selling are combined on a Web site, disclosures should be provided before the consumer makes the decision to buy, say, before clicking on an "order now" button or a link that says "add to shopping cart."

- **Don't focus only on the order page.** Some disclosures must be made in connection with a particular claim or product. Consumers may not relate a disclosure on the order page to information they viewed many pages earlier. It also is possible that after surfing a company's Web site, some consumers may decide to purchase the product from the company's "bricks and mortar" store. Those consumers would miss any disclosures placed only on the ordering page.

e. Evaluating Proximity With Banner Ads

Most banner ads displayed today are teasers. Because of their small size, they generally do not provide complete information about a product or service. Instead, consumers must click through to the Web site to get more information and learn the terms of an offer. In some instances, a banner may contain a claim that requires qualification.

- **Disclose required information in the banner itself or clearly and conspicuously on the Web site it links to.** In some cases, a required disclosure can be incorporated into a banner ad easily. Because of the space constraints of banner ads, other disclosures may be too detailed to be disclosed effectively in the banner. In some instances, these disclosures may be communicated effectively to consumers if they are made clearly and conspicuously on the Web site the banner links to and while consumers are deciding whether to buy a product or service. In determining whether the disclosure should be placed in the banner itself or on the Web site the banner links to, advertisers should consider how important the information is to prevent deception, how much information needs to be disclosed, the burden of disclosing it in the banner ad, how much information the consumer may absorb from the ad, and how effective the disclosure would be if it was made on the Web site.

- **Use creativity to incorporate or flag required information.** Scrolling text or rotating panels in a banner can present an abbreviated version of a required disclosure that indicates that there is additional important information and a more complete disclosure available on the click-through page. With lengthier disclosures, the banner can direct consumers to the Web site for more information. The full disclosure then must be clearly and conspicuously displayed on the Web site.

- **Provide any required disclosures in interactive banners.** Some banner ads allow consumers to interact within the banner, so that they may conduct a transaction without clicking through to a Web site. If consumers can get complete information about a product or make a purchase within an interactive banner, all required disclosures should be included in the banner.

2. Prominence

It's the advertiser's responsibility to draw attention to the required disclosures.

- **Display disclosures prominently so they are noticeable to consumers.**

The size, color, and graphics of the disclosure affect its prominence.

- **Size Matters.** Disclosures that are at least as large as the advertising copy are more likely to be effective.

- **Color Counts.** A disclosure in a color that contrasts with the background emphasizes the text of the disclosure and makes it more noticeable. Information in a color that blends in with the background of the ad is likely to be missed.

- **Graphics Help.** Although using graphics to display a disclosure is not required, they may make the disclosure more prominent.

- **Evaluate the size, color, and graphics of the disclosure in relation to other parts of the Web site.** The size of a disclosure should be compared to the type size of the claim and other text on the page. If a claim uses a particular color or graphic treatment, the disclosure can be formatted the same way to help ensure that consumers who view the claim are able to view the disclosure as well. In addition, the graphic treatment of the disclosure may be evaluated in relation to how graphics are used to convey other items in the ad.

- **Don't bury it.** The prominence of the disclosure also may be affected by other factors. A disclosure that is buried in a long paragraph of unrelated text would not be effective. The unrelated text detracts from the message and makes it unlikely that a consumer would notice the disclosure or recognize its importance. Even though the unrelated information may be useful, advertisers must ensure that the disclosure is communicated effectively.

3. Distracting Factors in Ads

The clear and conspicuous analysis does not focus only on the disclosure itself. It also is important to consider the entire ad. Elements like graphics, sound, text or even hyperlinks that lead to other pages or sites, may result in consumers not noticing, reading or listening to the disclosure.

- **Don't let other parts of an ad get in the way.** On television, moving visuals behind a text message make the text hard to read and may distract consumers' attention from the message. Using graphics online raises similar concerns: flashing images or animated graphics may reduce the prominence of a disclosure. Graphics on a Web page *alone* may not undermine the effectiveness of a disclosure. It is important, however, to consider all the elements in the ad, not just the text of the disclosure.

4. Repetition

It may be necessary to disclose important information more than once in an advertisement to convey a non-deceptive message. Repeating a disclosure makes it more likely that a consumer will notice and understand it. Still, the disclosure need not be repeated so often that consumers would ignore it and that it would clutter the ad.

- **Repeat disclosures on lengthy Web sites, as needed.** Consumers can access and navigate Web sites differently. Many consumers may access a site through its homepage, but others might enter in the middle, perhaps by linking to that page from a search engine or another Web site. Consumers also might not click-on every page of the site and may not choose to scroll to the bottom of each page. And many may not read every word on every page of a Web site. As a result, advertisers should question whether consumers who see only a portion of their ad are likely to miss a necessary disclosure and be misled.

- **Repeat disclosures with repeated claims, as needed.** If claims requiring some qualification are repeated throughout an ad, it may be necessary to repeat the disclosure too. In some situations, a disclosure is tied so closely to a claim that it must always accompany the claim to prevent deception. Depending on the disclosure, a clearly-labeled hyperlink could be repeated on various pages so that the full disclosure would be placed on only one page of the site.

5. Multimedia Messages

Internet ads may contain audio messages, video clips and other animated segments with claims that require qualification. As with radio and television ads, the disclosure should accompany the claim. In evaluating whether disclosures in these multimedia portions of online ads are clear and conspicuous, advertisers should evaluate all of the factors discussed in this paper and these special considerations:

- **For audio claims, use audio disclosures.** The disclosure should be in a volume and cadence sufficient for a reasonable consumer to hear and understand it. The volume of the disclosure can be evaluated in relation to the rest of the message, and in particular, the claim. Of course, consumers who do not have speakers, appropriate software, or appliances with audio capabilities will not hear the claim or the disclosure. Because some consumers may miss the audio portion of an ad, disclosures triggered by a claim or other information in an ad's text should not be placed solely in an audio clip.

- **Display visual disclosures for a sufficient duration.** Visual disclosures presented in video clips or other dynamic portions of online ads should appear for a duration sufficient for consumers to notice, read and understand them. As with brief video superscripts in television ads, fleeting disclosures on Web sites are not likely to be effective.

. . .

EXTENSIONS

Deceptive use of a domain name. In 1997, an Australian company called Internic Software, Inc. offered domain name registration services through its website located at www.internic.com. At the time, a U.S. company named Network Solutions, Inc. had the sole authority to register domain names in the most popular top-level domains. Network Solutions offered its registration services through a website at www.internic.net. The term

"InterNIC," a commonly used abbreviation for Internet Network Information Center, designated a cooperative agreement among several government and private entities that was responsible for overseeing the domain name system. Registration of a domain name through Network Solutions cost $100 for two years. A consumer who used the services of Internic Software was charged $250 for a two-year registration; the company merely forwarded the registration information to Network Solutions, which performed the registration.

At the request of Network Solutions, staff of the Federal Trade Commission sent it a letter opining that the practices of Internic Software were deceptive and in violation of the FTC Act. (Ironically, Internic Software had obtained the registration of its own domain name, internic.com, from Network Solutions itself.) The letter stated that the disclaimer on the Internic Software website—"Internic Software is not affiliated with, or part of Network Solutions, Inc., or its InterNIC operation which can be found at www.internic.net"—was inadequate to cure the false impression created by the company's name and domain name.

The FTC referred the matter to its Australian counterpart, the Australian Competition and Consumer Commission, which brought a court action against Internic Software. The ACCC settled the matter, obtaining the company's agreement to stop using the name "Internic" and to refund $161,000 to the 12,000 customers who had paid it for domain registrations.

QUESTIONS FOR DISCUSSION

1. *Self-monitoring.* Online advertisers have the technological capability of monitoring the effectiveness of certain types of website disclosures that goes far beyond what is possible with other advertising media. Web servers may easily be configured to keep a record of each page that a site visitor accesses. If disclosure information is made available via a link from the page containing the advertising claims, the server logs will reveal how often a visitor clicks on the link and views the disclosure page. By contrast, there is no practical way of ascertaining whether the reader of a print advertisement views disclosure information that appears in fine print at the bottom of the ad. Should advertisers be required to analyze their server logs for this purpose? In a law enforcement action predicated on inadequate disclosure, should an analysis of server logs be admissible as evidence that the disclosure did not effectively convey information to site visitors?

2. *Display variables.* Websites may be viewed through a wide variety of Internet access devices, ranging in display size from a television set several feet on a side down to a tiny screen on a mobile telephone, with widely varying screen resolutions, and with various versions of website browser software. Each combination of screen size, resolution, and browser software may display the information presented by a website differently. For example, some site visitors will see the entirety of an advertisement and the accompanying disclosure on a single screen, while other visitors will need to scroll down to see all of the page. Given this variety of display variables at the site visitor's end, and the inability of a website advertiser to control how the information it provides will be received, how feasible is it for a website advertiser to observe the niceties of the FTC's rules on advertising disclosures?

3. *Is more always better?* Online technology allows a seller advertising its products via a website to add almost limitless quantities of additional information about those products at minimal cost—unlike the case with print, broadcast, and most other advertising media. Is there such a thing as providing consumers with *too much* information?

B. APPLICABILITY OF RULES WITH TERMS LIKE "WRITTEN," "WRITING," "PRINTED" OR "DIRECT MAIL"

The FTC has promulgated and enforces a variety of rules applying to advertising. Nearly all of these were drafted before commercial activity via the Internet became widespread. The drafters of these rules naturally chose their language in the expectation that they would apply to advertising disseminated through the existing communications media, mainly print (including periodicals and direct mail), broadcast (radio and television) and, more recently, telephone (telemarketing).

How do these rules apply to advertising appearing on websites, on electronic bulletin boards, and in e-mail? As the FTC explains in *Dot Com Disclosures, supra,* "Many rules and guides address claims about products or services or advertising in general and are not limited to any particular medium used to disseminate those claims or advertising. Therefore, the plain language of many rules and guides applies to claims made on the Internet."

Some rules are by their own terms limited to marketing conducted through a particular medium of communication. For example, the Telemarketing Sales Rule, which prohibits deceptive and abusive methods of "telemarketing," applies only to telephone solicitations. The scope of the rule is limited by its definition of "telemarketing" as "a . . . program . . . which is conducted to induce the purchase of goods or services by use of one or more telephones." 16 C.F.R. § 310.2(u).

Interestingly, the version of the Telemarketing Sales Rule that the FTC originally proposed in 1995 contained a much broader definition of "telemarketing," one that would have included online solicitations. "Telemarketing" was there defined as "a . . . program . . . which is conducted to induce payment for goods or services by use of one or more telephones (including the use of a facsimile machine, computer modem, or any other telephonic medium)." 60 Fed. Reg. 8,329 (Feb. 14, 1995). After receiving comments on the proposed rule from the public, the FTC published a revised proposed rule, which differed substantially from the initial version. Among many other changes, the revised proposed rule dropped the language from the definition of "telemarketing" that would have swept online solicitations within its scope. The FTC explained why it had dropped coverage of online solicitations: "After considering many comments that objected to the Rule's coverage of on-line services, the Commission acknowledges that it does not have the necessary information available to it to support coverage of on-line services under the Rule." 60 Fed. Reg. 30,411 (June 8, 1995).

Still other rules have been amended to take account of technological change. Consider the Mail or Telephone Order Merchandise Rule, 16 C.F.R. Part 435. When originally promulgated in 1975, the Mail Order Rule, as it was then known, applied only to merchandise ordered by mail. It required sellers of goods that are ordered by mail to ship the goods within the time the seller specified, or within 30 days if no shipping date is specified. If the seller could not ship within the applicable period, the seller had to notify the customer of the delay, and either obtain the customer's consent to delayed shipment, or cancel the order and make a prompt refund.

In its 1993 rule review proceeding, the FTC recognized that times had changed. Due in part to technological innovations in the provision of telephone services and payment mechanisms, ordering by telephone had become as common as ordering by mail. The Commission accordingly decided to amend the Rule so that it applies to merchandise ordered both by mail and by telephone. It accomplished this by making the Rule applicable to "mail or telephone order sales," defining that term to mean "sales in which the buyer has ordered merchandise from the seller by mail or telephone, regardless of the method of payment or the method used to solicit the order." 16 C.F.R. § 435.2(a).

The Commission also added a definition of "telephone": "any direct or indirect use of the telephone to order merchandise, regardless of whether the telephone is activated by, or the language used is that of human beings, machines, or both." *Id.* § 435.2(b). The Commission intended by this rather curious locution to "reach orders placed by facsimile machines or computers with telephone modems." 58 Fed. Reg. 49,097 (Sept. 21, 1993). While the phrase sounds rather quaint to modern ears, the Commission deserves credit for being significantly ahead of its time. The Commission proposed this definition of telephone in a Notice of Proposed Rulemaking published in 1989—at a time when the Internet was the preserve of academics, and commercial activity was prohibited. Online commerce was at that time very limited, and was conducted mostly over proprietary networks, such as CompuServe and Prodigy, and via dial-up electronic bulletin board systems.

The Rule's definition of telephone is showing its age. Users typically access the Internet without any use of a telephone. With a standard dialup account, data travels from computer memory, through a modem, into a wire that is plugged into a telephone jack, across telephone lines and fiber-optic cable, and through similar steps to the memory of the recipient computer. Although data travels through infrastructure that also carries telephone calls, there is no use of a telephone at either end. When Internet access is supplied by a cable carrying television signals or a wireless link, the resemblance to a telephone becomes even more tenuous.

EXTENSIONS

Electronic transmission is not "mail." In *Opay v. Experian Information Solutions, Inc.*, 681 N.W.2d 394 (Minn.Ct.App.2004), the court held that a state law capping the price of credit reports received "by mail" does not apply to those received via an electronic transmission. The court reasoned that the term "mail" clearly did not apply to electronic transmissions when the statute was enacted in 1992, and the legislature's failure to amend the statute in the face of technological change indicates an intent to retain the original meaning.

C. BLURRING OF ADVERTISING AND EDITORIAL CONTENT

Modern marketing science has devised promotional methods that increasingly blur the distinction between advertising and editorial content. The marketer's arsenal includes (a) "infomercials," program-length television features that have the look of a television program but are actually just lengthy advertisements; (b) "advertorials," print advertisements that are designed to look like editorials; and (c) "product placement," which involves marketers paying money to producers to have their products appear in television or movie scenes, as part of the script or background.

The online medium makes possible some new variations on this theme, through manipulation of search engine results. Search engines are indispensable for locating information on the Internet. The user enters a word or phrase, clicks on "Search," and the search engine returns a result, typically consisting of an ordered list of links to material on the Web. This list of links is usually lengthy, consisting of several or many screens of text, and those near the top of the list are more likely to be followed than those near the bottom. Operators of commercial websites usually perceive an interest in having their site turn up high on the list of results of certain searches.

Some website owners seek to improve their rankings in search engine results by placing selected search terms in metatags and other invisible website text, and by purchasing keywords from search engines. (These practices are discussed more fully in Chapter II, Part A, *supra*.) This is perfectly appropriate if the text that is used corresponds to the website owner's trademarks, or a truthful description of the types of goods the site offers. But metatags can also be used in a deceptive manner. This may occur when the marketer of a product seeks to draw visitors to its website by using metatags suggesting characteristics that the product does not in fact possess. In *FTC v. Lane Labs—USA, Inc.*, No. 00–CV–3174 (D.N.J.2000) (consent order), the FTC charged the defendants with deceptive trade practices based, in part, on terms that defendants used in metatags on a website promoting their products. Those products contained shark cartilage, and defendants promoted them as a cure for cancer. The metatags included the terms "cancer treatment," "prostate cancer," "chemotherapy," "cancer patients," "cancer survivors," and "non-toxic cancer therapy." The FTC alleged that claims that shark cartilage cured cancer were unsubstantiated, and that it was therefore deceptive to make such claims. According to the complaint: "Defendants' use of these metatag references increases the likelihood that consumers who research the topics of cancer and skin cancer and effective cancer and skin cancer treatments on the Internet will find information about BeneFin, SkinAnswer and other Lane Labs products." The district court entered a stipulated judgment, which prohibits the defendants from making false claims about its products and requires them to pay $1 million for consumer redress and to finance a clinical study of the efficacy of shark cartilage as a cancer cure.

Website operators can also affect their rankings in search engine results through sponsorship payments. Most major search engines provide "sponsored results" in addition to their normal listings. To participate in the sponsored result listings, an advertiser agrees to pay a certain amount of money in connection with a particular search term. When a user enters a search using a sponsored search term, the search results list the sponsoring advertisers websites in order based on the amount each advertiser has agreed to pay, with the highest-paying advertiser listed first. The advertiser pays the agreed amount each time a user clicks on a link in the sponsored results listing that brings the user to the advertiser's website. The payment amounts, which are determined through a bidding process, range from one cent up to several dollars per click-through. All other search results, consisting of websites that did not pay to sponsor the search term, generally appear in a separate listing.

In June 2002, staff of the Federal Trade Commission sent letters to a number of search engine operators concerning their listings of sponsored search engine results. The FTC letter cited a survey by Consumers Union, which "found that 60% of Internet users had no idea that certain search engines were paid fees to list some sites more prominently than others in their search results." In light of this survey evidence, the letter deemed it important for search engines to disclose clearly that certain of their results were paid placements, in order to prevent consumers from being deceived. *See* Letter from Heather Hippsley to Search Engine Operators (June 27, 2002), www.ftc.gov/os/closings/staff/commercialalertattatch.htm. The United Kingdom's Advertising Standards Authority has expressed a similar position. *See Britain Cracks Down on Paid Search* (June 16, 2004), news.com.com/2100-1024_3-5235529.html.

QUESTIONS FOR DISCUSSION

1. *Metatag abuse.* What is the vice of using irrelevant terms in metatags, from the consumer protection perspective? Is a consumer misled when a search returns websites that are not relevant to her search terms? In a case like *Lane Labs*, suppose that the metatags falsely suggested product characteristics but the visible text on the site was completely truthful: would this be deceptive? Is the problem better conceptualized as bait-and-switch, rather than as deceptive advertising? *See* Ira S. Nathenson, *Internet Infoglut and Invisible Ink: Spamdexing Search Engines with Meta Tags*, 12 HARV. J.L. & TECH. 43, 93–98 (1998).

2. *Sponsored search engine disclosure.* What sort of disclosure is required to prevent paid search engine results from being deceptive? Segregation of the sponsored links in a separate section of the page? Labeling them as "Sponsored Listings"? "Featured Listings"? Should they be labeled "Advertisement," as advertisements in print publications sometimes are if they resemble editorial content?

D. ONLINE SWEEPSTAKES

The use of sweepstakes is a common marketing technique, and one that is gaining popularity in the online environment. A sweepstakes is a contest that is conducted, usually by a business, to attract the attention of prospective customers. The company invites individuals to participate by submitting an entry, selects winners using some chance-based mechanism, and awards prizes to the winners.

A properly structured sweepstakes is legal, but care must be taken to insure that it does not amount to a lottery, which (if operated by a private party) is illegal in all fifty states. A lottery is a contest that includes the elements of consideration, prize, and chance. "Prize" and "chance" are the elements that sweepstakes and lotteries have in common: each type of contest awards some sort of prize, and selects the winners through a chance-based mechanism. What distinguishes a legal sweepstakes from an illegal lottery is therefore the element of "consideration," which refers to the requirements for a participant to enter. States laws vary considerably in what is deemed to be "consideration" for purposes of constituting an illegal lottery. In some states, there is consideration only if an entrant is required to part with something of value to him. In other states, there is consideration as long as the entrant expends enough effort to support formation of a contract. The two approaches are well canvassed in *Blackburn v. Ippolito*, 156 So.2d 550 (Fla.Dist.Ct.App.1963).

QUESTIONS FOR DISCUSSION

Consideration. A web-based company runs a sweepstakes. The entry form is available at the company's website. The form requires entrants to supply their name, address, telephone number, and e-mail address. If the contest has a rule requiring entrants to agree to receive marketing materials from the sweepstakes operator, is this a "consideration" requirement that makes the contest an illegal lottery? What if the rules require the entrant to take a tour of the operator's website and view its product offerings? What if an entrant must fill out a form disclosing demographic information, or her personal preferences?

IV. Consumer Issues Relating to Electronic Signature Statutes

Electronic signature statutes seek to promote electronic commerce by allowing parties to enter into contracts and conduct other transactions without the use of paper documentation. A general discussion of these statutes appears in Chapter 10, Part I(E), *infra.* Here we will address the impact of these laws on consumer protection.

The shift to paperless transactions may raise special issues in the consumer context. According to one consumer advocate, electronic signature laws such as UETA are founded on the premises that electronic documents (including e-mail) are as reliable as paper documents, that electronic signatures offer the same protections as handwritten signatures, and that it is reasonable to defer to the parties' decision to use electronic communications. But these premises may not hold in the case of consumer transactions:

> The first premise will be true in only some consumer situations. An electronic record may be just as good as a written record for an inexpensive transaction that is completed in a short time. On the other hand, a consumer entering into a five-year car loan or a 30-year mortgage needs the note and contract in a form which he or she can keep. Home computers are replaced every few years, and previously downloaded contracts are unlikely to be copied over to a new system. Change-of-terms notices for a service provider operating only on the Internet probably can be delivered by e-mail, but a notice that your car is being recalled for a safety problem should arrive in the mail.

> The first premise also assumes that e-mail arrives at least as reliably as regular mail, which is contrary to the experience of many consumers. Consumers currently may change e-mail addresses more frequently than they move. Those with e-mail addresses seem to check them either far more frequently or far less frequently than their daily check of the regular mail. In addition, an Internet e-mail provider may go out of business, leaving a consumer with no choice but to obtain a new e-mail address.

> As to the second premise, an electronic signature does not always fully serve the purposes of a written signature. Where there is a risk of forgery, a written signature may provide additional safeguards because it may be harder to forge than a purported electronic signature. An electronic click made at home may not serve the purpose of emphasizing the seriousness or the particular risks of a transaction as well as a written signature.

> The third premise of UETA is reflected in the broad deference it gives to the autonomy of contracting parties. It defers to the agreement without distinguishing between negotiated agreements and standard form contracts or contracts of adhesion. This approach could give wide latitude to drafters of standard form contracts to define and impose the conditions of electronic communication.

> For example, UETA adopts the principle that each party should be able to determine when it will receive information electronically, and when it wishes to insist on receiving a paper communication. This sounds good in theory, but in practice it allows one-sided contracts. UETA also allows an on-line seller to insist on sending all information to the consumer electronically. The seller, however, can require that the consumer communicate any complaints, refund requests, billing disputes or other communications to the same company only by

regular mail.

Consumers Union, *Uniform Electronic Transactions Act: Consumer Nightmare or Opportunity?* (Aug. 23, 1999), www.consumersunion.org/finance/899nclcwc.htm.

Congress, in enacting the Electronic Signatures in Global and National Commerce Act ("ESIGN"), was highly cognizant of the impact the legislation would have on consumer protections. Consumer issues surfaced constantly during the congressional debates that led up to passage of ESIGN, and were the source of the most contentious disagreements over the shape of the legislation. Like other electronic signature legislation, ESIGN establishes a general rule of non-discrimination against electronic signatures, contracts, and documents. But ESIGN includes important derogations from this general principle in the case of laws and rules that require sellers to provide written notices and disclosures to consumers. The following addresses the most important of these consumer protections: a prescribed procedure for obtaining consumer consent to electronic disclosures, preservation of timing, proximity, and other similar aspects of disclosure requirements, and exclusion of certain important types of consumer notifications.

A. CONSUMER CONSENT TO ELECTRONIC DISCLOSURES

Electronic Signatures in Global and National Commerce Act, § 101
15 U.S.C. § 7001.

SEC. 101. GENERAL RULE OF VALIDITY

(a) **In General.**--Notwithstanding any statute, regulation, or other rule of law (other than this title and title II), with respect to any transaction in or affecting interstate or foreign commerce—

(1) a signature, contract, or other record relating to such transaction may not be denied legal effect, validity, or enforceability solely because it is in electronic form; and

(2) a contract relating to such transaction may not be denied legal effect, validity, or enforceability solely because an electronic signature or electronic record was used in its formation.

. . .

(c) **Consumer Disclosures.** —

(1) **Consent to Electronic Records.** — Notwithstanding subsection (a), if a statute, regulation, or other rule of law requires that information relating to a transaction or transactions in or affecting interstate or foreign commerce be provided or made available to a consumer in writing, the use of an electronic record to provide or make available (whichever is required) such information satisfies the requirement that such information be in writing if—

(A) the consumer has affirmatively consented to such use and has not withdrawn such consent;

(B) the consumer, prior to consenting, is provided with a clear and conspicuous statement—

(i) informing the consumer of (I) any right or option of the consumer to have the record provided or made available on paper or in nonelectronic form, and (II) the right of the consumer to withdraw the consent to have the record provided or made available in an electronic form and of any conditions, consequences (which may include termination of the parties' relationship), or fees in the event of such withdrawal;

(ii) informing the consumer of whether the consent applies (I) only to the particular transaction which gave rise to the obligation to provide the record, or (II) to identified categories of records that may be provided or made available during the course of the parties' relationship;

(iii) describing the procedures the consumer must use to withdraw consent as provided in clause (i) and to update information needed to contact the consumer electronically; and

(iv) informing the consumer (I) how, after the consent, the consumer may, upon request, obtain a paper copy of an electronic record, and (II) whether any fee will be charged for such copy;

(C) the consumer—

(i) prior to consenting, is provided with a statement of the hardware and software requirements for access to and retention of the electronic records; and

(ii) consents electronically, or confirms his or her consent electronically, in a manner that reasonably demonstrates that the consumer can access information in the electronic form that will be used to provide the information that is the subject of the consent; and

(D) after the consent of a consumer in accordance with subparagraph (A), if a change in the hardware or software requirements needed to access or retain electronic records creates a material risk that the consumer will not be able to access or retain a subsequent electronic record that was the subject of the consent, the person providing the electronic record—

(i) provides the consumer with a statement of (I) the revised hardware and software requirements for access to and retention of the electronic records, and (II) the right to withdraw consent without the imposition of any fees for such withdrawal and without the imposition of any condition or consequence that was not disclosed under subparagraph (B)(i); and

(ii) again complies with subparagraph (C).

(2) Other Rights. —

(A) Preservation of Consumer Protections. — Nothing in this title affects the content or timing of any disclosure or other record required to be provided or made available to any consumer under any statute, regulation, or other rule of law.

(B) Verification or Acknowledgment.--If a law that was enacted prior to this Act expressly requires a record to be provided or made available by a specified method that requires verification or acknowledgment of receipt, the record may be provided or made available electronically only if the method used provides verification or acknowledgment of receipt (whichever is required).

(3) Effect of Failure to Obtain Electronic Consent or Confirmation of Consent.--The legal effectiveness, validity, or enforceability of any contract executed by a consumer shall not be denied solely because of the failure to obtain electronic consent or confirmation of consent by that consumer in accordance with paragraph (1)(C)(ii).

. . .

(6) Oral Communications.--An oral communication or a recording of an oral communication shall not qualify as an electronic record for purposes of this subsection except as otherwise provided under applicable law.

. . .

(e) Accuracy and Ability to Retain Contracts and Other Records.--Notwithstanding subsection (a), if a statute, regulation, or other rule of law requires that a contract or other record relating to a transaction in or affecting interstate or foreign commerce be in writing, the legal effect, validity, or enforceability of an electronic record of such contract or other record may be denied if such electronic record is not in a form that is capable of being retained and accurately reproduced for later reference by all parties or persons who are entitled to retain the contract or other record.

(f) Proximity.--Nothing in this title affects the proximity required by any statute, regulation, or other rule of law with respect to any warning, notice, disclosure, or other record required to be posted, displayed, or publicly affixed.

. . .

One of the fundamental principles of ESIGN's validation of electronic signatures and documents is that no party (other than a government agency) is *required* to use or accept them. ESIGN § 101(b)(2). As a general matter, ESIGN does not involve itself with the question of how parties may demonstrate their willingness to make use of electronic signatures and documents. But ESIGN derogates from this approach in the case of certain consumer disclosures. If a state or federal statute or rule requires a seller to furnish information to a consumer "in writing," ESIGN prescribes a special protocol that the seller must follow to obtain the consumer's consent to receive the information in electronic form. This procedure is designed to insure that a consumer's waiver of her right to receive the disclosure on paper is informed and intentional, and that the electronic disclosure will be a reasonable substitute for the written one. Before seeking the consumer's consent, the seller must provide the consumer with "a clear and conspicuous statement" containing several categories of information. The notice must:

- Inform the consumer of any option to receive the disclosure in written form, and of her right to withdraw her consent, and the consequences thereof;

- Inform the consumer whether the consent applies only to the instant transaction, or to a series of future transactions as well;

- Describe the procedures the consumer must follow to withdraw consent, and to update her contact information;

- Inform the consumer how to obtain a paper copy of the disclosure even after consenting, and whether any fee will be charged for the paper copy; and

- Provide the consumer with a statement of the hardware and software needed to access and retain the electronic records.

§ 101(c)(1)(B) and (C).

Once the consumer receives all of this information, she must "affirmatively consent[]" to receiving electronic disclosures. Furthermore, "affirmative consent" is rigorously defined. The consumer must "consent[] electronically, or confirm[] his or her consent electronically, in a manner that reasonably demonstrates that the consumer can access information in the electronic form that will be used to provide the information that is the subject of the consent." ESIGN § 101(c)(1)(C)(ii). So if the seller intends to provide the disclosure information in the form of, say, a Corel WordPerfect Version 8 document, the consumer must consent through some action that demonstrates she can access such documents.

The seller's obligations do not end here. If, after obtaining the consumer's consent, the seller changes the manner in which it provides the disclosures, such that the consumer needs new computer hardware or software to access or retain the disclosures, the seller must notify the seller of the new hardware or software requirements, give the consumer a cost-free means of withdrawing her consent, and once again obtain the consumer's consent in a manner that demonstrates she can access the disclosure in its new format. ESIGN § 101(c)(1)(D).

UETA, like ESIGN, also provides that electronic records are valid only between parties who have consented to use of them. (*See* Chapter 10, Part I(E), *supra*.) Unlike ESIGN, however, UETA contains no heightened consent procedure applying to consumer disclosures. The general consent provision, applicable to all transactions, states: "This [Act] applies only to transactions between parties each of which has agreed to conduct transactions by electronic means. Whether the parties agree to conduct a transaction by electronic means is determined from the context and surrounding circumstances, including the parties' conduct." UETA § 5(b). The Comment to this provision elaborates:

> Subsection (b) provides that the Act applies to transactions in which the parties have agreed to conduct the transaction electronically. In this context it is essential that the parties' actions and words be broadly construed in determining whether the requisite agreement exists. Accordingly, the Act expressly provides that the party's agreement is to be found from all circumstances, including the parties' conduct. The critical element is the intent of a party to conduct a transaction electronically.

UETA § 5, cmt. 4.

QUESTIONS FOR DISCUSSION

---

1. *UETA and consent.* Is the UETA standard for assessing consent insufficiently protective in the context of consumer disclosures? Do you agree with the following assessment:

E-Sign's requirement that consumer consent be given or confirmed electronically is of crucial importance. Paper consent to future electronic transactions creates a risk that consumers will be offered boilerplate paper agreements to receive future electronic notices that they may or may not be able to open and read. The federal requirement that consent be given or confirmed electronically eliminates this risk, at least for notices legally required to be in writing.

In contrast, UETA merely requires agreement but does not specify how that agreement is to be proven. Instead, UETA states that agreement can be determined from the context and circumstances. UETA undercuts its own basic premise of agreement by permitting the agreement to conduct transactions electronically to be found from the context, including conduct.

Gail Hillebrand & Margot Saunders, *E-Sign and UETA: What Should States Do Now?*, 5 NO. 10 CYBERSPACE LAW. 2, 5 NO. 11 CYBERSPACE LAW. 8 (Parts I & II) (2001). Do you think, to the contrary, that the consent procedure in ESIGN § 101(c) is unduly burdensome on both sellers and consumers, a paternalistic interference with freedom of contract? For an evaluation of the consumer consent provisions, see FEDERAL TRADE COMMISSION & DEPARTMENT OF COMMERCE, ELECTRONIC SIGNATURES IN GLOBAL AND NATIONAL COMMERCE ACT: THE CONSUMER CONSENT PROVISION IN § 101(c)(1)(C)(ii) (2001), www.ftc.gov/os/2001/06/esign7.htm.

2. *UETA preempts ESIGN.* Note that ESIGN contains a "reverse preemption" provision: Section 101 is superseded by state law, if that state law happens to be an enactment of the 1999 version of UETA, or some equivalent alternative scheme. ESIGN § 102(a). This reverse preemption would extend to ESIGN § 101(c), the consumer-consent provision. Why would the drafters of ESIGN have crafted a detailed and highly protective consumer consent provision, only to allow it to be superseded by a far less protective provision of state law?

B. PRESERVATION OF EXISTING CONSUMER PROTECTIONS

ESIGN exhibits additional solicitude to consumer interests by preserving certain features of laws and rules designed to protect consumers from deceptive marketing practices. Three provisions in particular have this function:

1. *Content or timing requirements.* "Nothing in this title affects the content or timing of any disclosure or other record required to be provided or made available to any consumer under any statute, regulation, or other rule of law." ESIGN § 101(c)(2)(A). One example of a "timing" requirement is the FTC's Cooling-Off Rule, which requires a door-to-door seller to furnish the buyer with a notice of his right to cancel the transaction "at the time the buyer signs the door-to-door sales contract"—that is, during the face-to-face meeting between buyer and seller. Rule Concerning Cooling-Off Period for Sales Made at Homes or at Certain Other Locations, 16 C.F.R. § 429.1(b). The ESIGN "content or timing" provision means that a seller cannot comply with the Rule by sending the notice to the buyer's e-mail address at some time after the transaction is completed, even if the buyer so consents.

2. *Verification or acknowledgment requirements.* "If a law that was enacted prior to this Act expressly requires a record to be provided or made available by a specified method that requires verification or acknowledgment of receipt, the record may be provided or made available electronically only if the method used provides verification or acknowledgment of receipt (whichever is required)." ESIGN § 101(c)(2)(B). This would apply in the case of a law requiring that a party provide information to a consumer through the use of certified

mail, return receipt requested, which generates an acknowledgment of receipt.

3. *Proximity requirements.* "Nothing in this title affects the proximity required by any statute, regulation, or other rule of law with respect to any warning, notice, disclosure, or other record required to be posted, displayed, or publicly affixed." ESIGN § 101(f). The two most important types of proximity requirements in consumer disclosure rules are (1) a requirement that a disclosure be physically attached to or printed on an item, and (2) a requirement that a qualifying statement be in close proximity to the advertising claim to which it applies.

Some examples of "physically attached" requirements include (1) the FTC's Hobby Protection Rule, requiring an imitation political item to be "plainly and permanently marked with the calendar year in which such item was manufactured," and an imitation numismatic item to be "plainly and permanently marked 'COPY' "; *see* Rules and Regulations Under the Hobby Protection Act, 16 C.F.R. §§ 304.5, 304.6; (2) the Care Labeling Rule, requiring manufacturers and importers to "attach care labels so that they can be seen or easily found when the product is offered for sale"; if the label cannot be seen through the package, "the care information must also appear on the outside of the package or on a hang tag fastened to the product"; *see* Care Labeling of Textile Wearing Apparel and Certain Piece Goods as Amended, 16 C.F.R. § 423.6; and (3) the Packaging and Labeling Rules, requiring a label to be "affixed to or appearing upon any consumer commodity or affixed to or appearing upon a package containing any consumer commodity"; *see* Regulations Under Section 4 of the Fair Packaging and Labeling Act, 16 C.F.R. § 500.2(e).

Examples of "close proximity" requirements appear in (1) the Textile Rules, requiring disclosure of the generic name of a textile fiber "in immediate proximity and conjunction with" use of a fiber trademark; see Rules and Regulations Under the Textile Fiber Products Identification Act, 16 C.F.R. § 303.41(b); and (2) the Appliance Labeling Rule, requiring disclosure of energy efficiency information "on each page [of a catalogue] that lists" appliances subject to the Rule; Rule Concerning Disclosures Regarding Energy Consumption and Water Use of Certain Home Appliances and Other Products Required Under the Energy Policy and Conservation Act, 16 C.F.R. § 305.14(a).

ESIGN's preservation-of-proximity-requirements provision makes it clear that ESIGN does not negate regulatory requirements such as these—for example, by allowing a seller to make an advertising claim in a print advertisement, and refer the reader to a website address for disclosures that qualify the claim.

QUESTIONS FOR DISCUSSION

ESIGN and the Cooling Off Rule. Under ESIGN, may a seller comply with the Cooling-Off Rule by e-mailing the required notice to the buyer's e-mail address, at the time of the transaction, using a handheld wireless Internet access device? By sitting down with the consumer at her own home computer, and showing her how to access the notice on the seller's website? What would be an example of a "content" provision that is preserved by ESIGN § 101(c)(2)(A)?

C. EXCEPTIONS FOR CERTAIN NOTIFICATIONS

The general rule of ESIGN, validating communication of information using electronic signatures, does not apply to certain kinds of notices that are considered especially critical to the welfare of consumers. These are notices of "(A) the cancellation or termination of utility services (including water, heat, and power); (B) default, acceleration, repossession, foreclosure, or eviction, or the right to cure, under a credit agreement secured by, or a rental agreement for, a primary residence of an individual; (C) the cancellation or termination of health insurance or benefits or life insurance benefits (excluding annuities); or (D) recall of a product, or material failure of a product, that risks endangering health or safety." ESIGN § 103(b)(2). (ESIGN Section 103 is set out fully in Chapter 10, Part I(E)(2), *supra*.).

Note that UETA contains no exceptions applying to notices of these types. Therefore, UETA validates electronic versions of these notices as long as the general consent rule of UETA Section 5 is satisfied.

UETA specifically exempts transactions governed by laws relating to wills, codicils, and testamentary trusts, as well as (optionally with the enacting state) certain provisions of the Uniform Commercial Code and UCITA. It also contains a fill-in-the-blank provision, inviting the enacting state to exempt "other laws, if any." UETA § 3(b)(4). That is, a state that enacts UETA may specify that certain additional state laws will be unaffected by UETA's validation of electronic signatures and documents, with the result that signature and writing requirements in those statutes will continue to require the use of paper documents signed by hand. This has the effect of blunting UETA's impact on signature and writing requirements in existing state laws. California, the first state to enact UETA, filled in that blank with a long list of regulatory provisions, many of which are designed to protect consumers. As a result, these statutes continued to require that disclosures to consumers be made using paper documents. *See* CAL. CIV. CODE § 1633.3(c). Partly in reaction to this move by California, ESIGN's reverse preemption provision does not extend to state laws that a state exempts from its enactment of UETA, to the extent those laws are inconsistent with ESIGN. *See* ESIGN § 102(a)(1). Therefore, California's attempt to limit the scope of its version of UETA is nullified by ESIGN, to the extent it is deemed inconsistent with ESIGN.

QUESTIONS FOR DISCUSSION

1. *Exemption of consumer notices.* ESIGN's exclusion of certain types of important consumer notices seems to reflect an assumption that electronic notices are less reliable than their paper counterparts. If so, what is the justification for validating the use of electronic notifications in other circumstances, which can involve large sums of money or be otherwise as significant to consumers as the exempted notices? If we believe that the consumer-consent procedure specified in ESIGN § 101(c) is adequate to prevent consumers from inadvertently waiving important rights, why wouldn't we reach the same conclusion with respect to notices of the exempted type?

Unlike ESIGN, UETA does not exempt these kinds of consumer notices from electronic delivery. Does this aspect of UETA, or any other state law explicitly allowing notices of this type to be furnished electronically, survive ESIGN's exemption of such notices?

2. *Enforceability.* ESIGN § 101(c)(3) states: "The legal effectiveness, validity, or enforceability of any contract executed by a consumer shall not be denied solely because of the failure to obtain electronic consent or confirmation of consent by that consumer in accordance with [§ 101(c)(1)(C)(ii)]"—the provision that requires consent to be tendered in a manner that demonstrates that the consumer can access electronic records of the sort the seller intends to use for the disclosures. If a contract procured in violation of this provision is nevertheless enforceable, what incentive does a seller have to comply with the provision?

Does Section 101(c)(3) contain a negative pregnant, implying that a contract *may* be held unenforceable if the seller fails to comply with some provision of Section 101(c) *other* than Section 101(c)(1)(C)(ii)?

3. *Pre-transaction disclosures.* The consumer-consent provision of ESIGN § 101(c) applies to any law or rule that "requires that information relating to a transaction or transactions in or affecting interstate or foreign commerce be provided or made available to a consumer in writing." The term "transaction" is defined as:

> an action or set of actions relating to the conduct of business, consumer, or commercial affairs between two or more persons, including any of the following types of conduct—
>
> (A) the sale, lease, exchange, licensing, or other disposition of (i) personal property, including goods and intangibles, (ii) services, and (iii) any combination thereof; and
>
> (B) the sale, lease, exchange, or other disposition of any interest in real property, or any combination thereof.

ESIGN § 106(13). Does the consumer-consent provision apply to an advertisement, with respect to consumers who view the advertisement but who do not engage with the seller in any exchange of money for goods or services?

COMPARATIVE NOTE

It is quite common for U.S.-based websites to post Terms of Service stating that the terms are subject to change, with or without notice to users. For example, MSN.com's Terms of Use state:

> Microsoft reserves the right to change the terms, conditions, and notices under which it offers the MSN Web Sites, including any charges associated with the use of the MSN Web Sites. You are responsible for regularly reviewing these terms, conditions and notices, and any additional terms posted on any MSN Web Site. Your continued use of the MSN Web Sites after the effective date of such changes constitutes your acceptance of and agreement to such changes.

MSN Website Terms of Use and Notices, privacy.msn.com/tou.

Such subject-to-change provisions may be illegal under European Union law. In *AOL Bertelsmann Online France v. UFC Que Choisir* (Cour de Cassation 2004) (Fr.), a French court held that 31 clauses in America Online's subscriber agreement were inconsistent with French law, including provisions giving AOL the right to modify the agreement on thirty days' notice, limiting AOL's liability, and allowing AOL to terminate the agreement at its pleasure. The French law is a transposition of the EU Directive on Unfair Commercial Practices,[6] which prohibits a range of business-to-consumer commercial practices that are deemed to be "unfair."

---

[6] Directive 2005/29/EC of the European Parliament and of the Council of 11 May 2005 concerning unfair business-to-consumer commercial practices in the internal market, 2005 O.J. (L 149) 22, http://europa.eu.int/eur-lex/lex/LexUriServ/site/en/oj/2005/l_149/l_14920050611en00220039.pdf.

CHAPTER FIVE

JUDICIAL JURISDICTION OVER DISPUTES IN INTERNET COMMERCE

For a court to adjudicate a case it must have *subject-matter jurisdiction* over the matter in controversy and *personal jurisdiction* over the parties before it. This chapter concerns the application of these doctrines to cases that arise from online transactions, focusing primarily on personal jurisdiction, which has been most salient for courts attempting to adjudicate Internet commerce disputes.

Several aspects of online communications have created difficulties for courts that are called upon to apply the rules of personal jurisdiction. First, because websites, newsgroups, and Internet mailing lists are accessible with equal ease from any location where there is Internet access, courts must navigate between the equally unpalatable options of holding that online activity subjects a defendant to jurisdiction in every state (and indeed every country), or that online activity is not a basis for jurisdiction at all. Second, it is often difficult to determine where an online activity should be deemed to take place. Since jurisdictional issues depend crucially on the location of the acts that give rise to a dispute, difficulty in locating actions causes difficulty in resolving jurisdictional issues.

As you read through these materials, keep the following questions in mind: (1) Are existing jurisdictional doctrines adequate to handle the issues presented when online contacts are urged as the basis for jurisdiction? Should the courts develop a new law of jurisdiction for "cyberspace"? (2) What factors should lead to a finding that a defendant, by operating a website that may be accessed everywhere, has purposely directed its activity at a particular state? (3) Should there be different standards for evaluating contacts depending on the cause of action involved? For example, should a website that defames be treated differently from one that deceptively describes products offered for sale by the site owner? (4) To what extent are the issues presented by online communications analogous to those presented by telephone, mail, and other means of communicating at a distance? To what extent are they different?

I. BACKGROUND: PERSONAL JURISDICTION

Personal jurisdiction, also sometimes referred to a jurisdiction *in personam*, jurisdiction over the person, or jurisdiction to adjudicate, refers to the power of a court to exercise authority over a particular defendant that a plaintiff seeks to bring before it. The rules establishing the circumstances under which a court may assert jurisdiction over a defendant in a civil case derive from several sources, including Rule 4 of the Federal Rules of Civil Procedure, the Due Process Clauses of the Fourteenth and Fifth Amendments to the U.S. Constitution, state statutes conferring authority on state courts to exercise jurisdiction over persons located outside of the state (known as "long-arm statutes"), and substantive law giving rise to federal causes of action. The issue that is most commonly presented is whether a court may assert jurisdiction over a defendant who is not located within the state in which the court sits.

When an action is brought in state court, the court's authority to assert jurisdiction over a defendant located outside the state's borders is determined by the state's long-arm statute and by the Due Process Clause of the Fourteenth Amendment. The same is true for most actions brought in federal court, whether the cause of action is created by state law (and the court's diversity jurisdiction is invoked) or by federal law (based on the court's federal question jurisdiction).[1] This is due to Rule 4(k)(1)(A) of the Federal Rules of Civil Procedure, which provides that service of process, a prerequisite for assertion of jurisdiction, may be effectuated only as provided by the law of the state in which the court is located.

Where the Fourteenth Amendment's Due Process Clause is applicable, the court may assert jurisdiction only if the defendant has certain "minimum contacts" with the state in which the court sits. *International Shoe Co. v. Washington*, 326 U.S. 310, 316 (1945). Courts distinguish between "general jurisdiction" and "specific jurisdiction." If the defendant's contacts with the forum state are sufficiently "continuous and systematic," the court may conclude that it has general jurisdiction over the defendant. In that case, the court may assert jurisdiction over the defendant on any cause of action, regardless of whether it arises from the defendant's forum contacts. *Helicopteros Nacionales de Colombia, S.A. v. Hall*, 466 U.S. 408 (1984).

For specific jurisdiction, the defendant's contacts with the forum state need not be so strong, but the cause of action must arise from the forum contacts. The test for specific jurisdiction consists of three components: (1) there must be "some act by which the defendant purposely avails itself of the privilege of conducting activities within the forum State," *Hanson v. Denckla*, 357 U.S. 235, 263 (1958); (2) the cause of action must " 'arise out of or relate to' " the defendant's contacts with the forum state, *Burger King Corp. v. Rudzewicz*, 471 U.S. 462, 472 (1985) (quoting *Helicopteros Nacionales, supra*, 466 U.S. at 414); and (3) assertion of jurisdiction must be reasonable, comporting with " 'fair play and substantial justice,' " *Burger King, supra*, at 476 (quoting *International Shoe, supra*, 326 U.S. at 320).

State long-arm statutes are of two general types. The first type sets forth the specific circumstances under which a court of that state may assert jurisdiction over defendants who are not residents of the state. The statutes with which we will be concerned typically authorize jurisdiction over defendants who (1) transact business in the state, (2) cause tortious injury within the state by some act or omission either within or outside the state, or (3) solicit business within the state. Long-arm statutes of the second type provide, or have been construed to mean, that jurisdiction is authorized to the full extent allowed by the Due Process Clause.

Thus, when the court is in a state whose long-arm statute is not coextensive with the due process requirement, resolution of the jurisdictional issue requires a two-stage inquiry: first, whether assertion of jurisdiction is consistent with the state long-arm statute, and second,

---

[1] Some federal statutes that create a cause of action authorize service of process wherever the defendant may be found. *E.g.*, 15 U.S.C. § 22; 15 U.S.C. § 53(b). In a federal question case arising from such a statute, the long-arm statute drops out of the picture, since Rule 4(k)(1)(D) provides for jurisdiction "when authorized by a statute of the United States." Under these circumstances, the only territorial limitation on service of process is that imposed by the Due Process Clause of the Fifth Amendment, which requires that the defendant have certain contacts with the United States. Furthermore, Rule 4(k)(2) allows jurisdiction in a federal question case to be based on national contacts, if the defendant is not subject to the jurisdiction of the courts of any state.

These grounds for jurisdiction are rarely applicable in cases where jurisdiction is based on online conduct, and will not be discussed further.

whether assertion of jurisdiction is consistent with the Due Process Clause. In a state where the long-arm statute goes to the limits of due process, the first stage of the inquiry drops out, and the only issue is whether assertion of jurisdiction is consistent with due process. In the materials that follow, we first explore (in Part II) the due process requirement, and then address (in Part III) state long-arm statutes that are not coextensive with due process. We then consider choice of law (Part IV), and related matters (Part V).

II. THE DUE PROCESS REQUIREMENT APPLIED TO ONLINE ACTIVITIES

A. OPERATION OF WEBSITES

The central difficulty presented when a court's jurisdiction over the defendant is premised on defendant's operation of a website is that due process requires that the defendant purposely direct its actions at a particular state, while a website is accessible by residents of *all* states on an equal basis. The challenge for the courts has been to identify those features of websites that demonstrate that the site owner intentionally directed its activity at one or more particular states.

1. The Three-Category Approach to Websites: *Zippo*

Zippo Manufacturing. Co. v. Zippo Dot Com, Inc.
952 F.Supp. 1119 (W.D.Pa.1997).

■ McLAUGHLIN, DISTRICT JUDGE.

This is an Internet domain name dispute. At this stage of the controversy, we must decide the Constitutionally permissible reach of Pennsylvania's Long Arm Statute, 42 Pa.C.S.A. § 5322, through cyberspace. Plaintiff Zippo Manufacturing Corporation ("Manufacturing") has filed a five count complaint against Zippo Dot Com, Inc. ("Dot Com") alleging trademark dilution, infringement, and false designation under the Federal Trademark Act, 15 U.S.C. § 1051–1127. In addition, the Complaint alleges causes of action based on state law trademark dilution under 54 Pa.C.S.A. § 1124, and seeks equitable accounting and imposition of a constructive trust. Dot Com has moved to dismiss for lack of personal jurisdiction and improper venue pursuant to Fed.R.Civ.P. 12(b)(2) and (3) or, in the alternative, to transfer the case pursuant to 28 U.S.C. § 1406(a). For the reasons set forth below, Defendant's motion is denied.

I. BACKGROUND

The facts relevant to this motion are as follows. Manufacturing is a Pennsylvania corporation with its principal place of business in Bradford, Pennsylvania. Manufacturing makes, among other things, well known "Zippo" tobacco lighters. Dot Com is a California corporation with its principal place of business in Sunnyvale, California. Dot Com operates an Internet Web site and an Internet news service and has obtained the exclusive right to use the domain names "zippo.com", "zippo.net" and "zipponews.com" on the Internet.

Dot Com's Web site contains information about the company, advertisements and an application for its Internet news service. The news service itself consists of three levels of membership — public/free, "Original" and "Super." Each successive level offers access to a greater number of Internet newsgroups. A customer who wants to subscribe to either the "Original" or "Super" level of service, fills out an on-line application that asks for a variety of information including the person's name and address. Payment is made by credit card over the Internet or the telephone. The application is then processed and the subscriber is assigned a password which permits the subscriber to view and/or download Internet newsgroup messages that are stored on the Defendant's server in California.

Dot Com's contacts with Pennsylvania have occurred almost exclusively over the Internet. Dot Com's offices, employees and Internet servers are located in California. Dot Com maintains no offices, employees or agents in Pennsylvania. Dot Com's advertising for its service to Pennsylvania residents involves posting information about its service on its Web page, which is accessible to Pennsylvania residents via the Internet. Defendant has approximately 140,000 paying subscribers worldwide. Approximately two percent (3,000) of those subscribers are Pennsylvania residents. These subscribers have contracted to receive Dot Com's service by visiting its Web site and filling out the application. Additionally, Dot Com has entered into agreements with seven Internet access providers in Pennsylvania to permit their subscribers to access Dot Com's news service. Two of these providers are located in the Western District of Pennsylvania.

The basis of the trademark claims is Dot Com's use of the word "Zippo" in the domain names it holds, in numerous locations in its Web site and in the heading of Internet newsgroup messages that have been posted by Dot Com subscribers. When an Internet user views or downloads a newsgroup message posted by a Dot Com subscriber, the word "Zippo" appears in the "Message–Id" and "Organization" sections of the heading. The news message itself, containing text and/or pictures, follows. Manufacturing points out that some of the messages contain adult oriented, sexually explicit subject matter.

. . .

III. DISCUSSION

A. Personal Jurisdiction

1. The Traditional Framework

Our authority to exercise personal jurisdiction in this case is conferred by state law. Fed.R.Civ.P. 4(e) . . . . The extent to which we may exercise that authority is governed by the Due Process Clause of the Fourteenth Amendment to the Federal Constitution. *Kulko v. Superior Court of California*, 436 U.S. 84, 91 (1978).

Pennsylvania's long arm jurisdiction statute is codified at 42 Pa.C.S.A. § 5322(a). The portion of the statute authorizing us to exercise jurisdiction here permits the exercise of jurisdiction over non-resident defendants upon:

(2) Contracting to supply services or things in this Commonwealth.

42 Pa.C.S.A. § 5322(a). It is undisputed that Dot Com contracted to supply Internet

news services to approximately 3,000 Pennsylvania residents and also entered into agreements with seven Internet access providers in Pennsylvania. Moreover, even if Dot Com's conduct did not satisfy a specific provision of the statute, we would nevertheless be authorized to exercise jurisdiction to the "fullest extent allowed under the Constitution of the United States." 42 Pa.C.S.A. § 5322(b).

. . .

2. The Internet and Jurisdiction

In *Hanson v. Denckla*, the Supreme Court noted that "[a]s technological progress has increased the flow of commerce between States, the need for jurisdiction has undergone a similar increase." *Hanson v. Denckla*, 357 U.S. 235, 250–51 (1958). Twenty seven years later, the Court observed that jurisdiction could not be avoided "merely because the defendant did not *physically* enter the forum state." *Burger King*, 471 U.S. at 476. The Court observed that:

> [I]t is an inescapable fact of modern commercial life that a substantial amount of commercial business is transacted solely by mail and wire communications across state lines, thus obviating the need for physical presence within a State in which business is conducted.

Id.

Enter the Internet, a global " 'super-network' of over 15,000 computer networks used by over 30 million individuals, corporations, organizations, and educational institutions worldwide." *Panavision Intern., L.P. v. Toeppen*, 938 F.Supp. 616 (C.D.Cal.1996) (citing *American Civil Liberties Union v. Reno*, 929 F.Supp. 824, 830–48 (E.D.Pa.1996)). "In recent years, businesses have begun to use the Internet to provide information and products to consumers and other businesses." *Id.* The Internet makes it possible to conduct business throughout the world entirely from a desktop. With this global revolution looming on the horizon, the development of the law concerning the permissible scope of personal jurisdiction based on Internet use is in its infant stages. The cases are scant. Nevertheless, our review of the available cases and materials reveals that the likelihood that personal jurisdiction can be constitutionally exercised is directly proportionate to the nature and quality of commercial activity that an entity conducts over the Internet. This sliding scale is consistent with well developed personal jurisdiction principles. At one end of the spectrum are situations where a defendant clearly does business over the Internet. If the defendant enters into contracts with residents of a foreign jurisdiction that involve the knowing and repeated transmission of computer files over the Internet, personal jurisdiction is proper. *E.g. CompuServe, Inc. v. Patterson*, 89 F.3d 1257 (6th Cir.1996). At the opposite end are situations where a defendant has simply posted information on an Internet Web site which is accessible to users in foreign jurisdictions. A passive Web site that does little more than make information available to those who are interested in it is not grounds for the exercise [of] personal jurisdiction. *E.g. Bensusan Restaurant Corp. v. King*, 937 F.Supp. 295 (S.D.N.Y.1996). The middle ground is occupied by interactive Web sites where a user can exchange information with the host computer. In these cases, the exercise of jurisdiction is determined by examining the level of interactivity and commercial nature of the exchange of information that occurs on the Web site. *E.g. Maritz, Inc. v. Cybergold,*

Inc., 947 F.Supp. 1328 (E.D.Mo.1996).

Traditionally, when an entity intentionally reaches beyond its boundaries to conduct business with foreign residents, the exercise of specific jurisdiction is proper. *Burger King*, 471 U.S. at 475. Different results should not be reached simply because business is conducted over the Internet. In *CompuServe, Inc. v. Patterson*, 89 F.3d 1257 (6th Cir.1996), the Sixth Circuit addressed the significance of doing business over the Internet. In that case, Patterson, a Texas resident, entered into a contract to distribute shareware through CompuServe's Internet server located in Ohio. *CompuServe*, 89 F.3d at 1260. From Texas, Patterson electronically uploaded thirty-two master software files to CompuServe's server in Ohio via the Internet. *Id.* at 1261. One of Patterson's software products was designed to help people navigate the Internet. *Id.* When CompuServe later began to market a product that Patterson believed to be similar to his own, he threatened to sue. *Id.* CompuServe brought an action in the Southern District of Ohio, seeking a declaratory judgment. *Id.* The District Court granted Patterson's motion to dismiss for lack of personal jurisdiction and CompuServe appealed. *Id.* The Sixth Circuit reversed, reasoning that Patterson had purposefully directed his business activities toward Ohio by knowingly entering into a contract with an Ohio resident and then "deliberately and repeatedly" transmitted files to Ohio. *Id.* at 1264–66.

In *Maritz, Inc. v. Cybergold, Inc.*, 947 F.Supp. 1328 (E.D.Mo.1996), the defendant had put up a Web site as a promotion for its upcoming Internet service. The service consisted of assigning users an electronic mailbox and then forwarding advertisements for products and services that matched the users' interests to those electronic mailboxes. *Maritz*, 947 F.Supp. at 1330. The defendant planned to charge advertisers and provide users with incentives to view the advertisements. *Id.* Although the service was not yet operational, users were encouraged to add their address to a mailing list to receive updates about the service. *Id.* The court rejected the defendant's contention that it operated a "passive Web site." *Id.* at 1333–34. The court reasoned that the defendant's conduct amounted to "active solicitations" and "promotional activities" designed to "develop a mailing list of Internet users" and that the defendant "indiscriminately responded to every user" who accessed the site. *Id.* at 1333–34.

Inset Systems, Inc. v. Instruction Set, 937 F.Supp. 161 (D.Conn.1996) represents the outer limits of the exercise of personal jurisdiction based on the Internet. In *Inset Systems*, a Connecticut corporation sued a Massachusetts corporation in the District of Connecticut for trademark infringement based on the use of an Internet domain name. *Inset Systems*, 937 F.Supp. at 162. The defendant's contacts with Connecticut consisted of posting a Web site that was accessible to approximately 10,000 Connecticut residents and maintaining a toll free number. *Id.* at 165. The court exercised personal jurisdiction, reasoning that advertising on the Internet constituted the purposeful doing of business in Connecticut because "unlike television and radio advertising, the advertisement is available continuously to any Internet user." *Id.* at 165.

Bensusan Restaurant Corp. v. King, 937 F.Supp. 295 (S.D.N.Y.1996) reached a different conclusion based on a similar Web site. In *Bensusan*, the operator of a New

York jazz club sued the operator of a Missouri jazz club for trademark infringement. *Bensusan*, 937 F.Supp. at 297. The Internet Web site at issue contained general information about the defendant's club, a calendar of events and ticket information. *Id.* However, the site was not interactive. *Id.* If a user wanted to go to the club, she would have to call or visit a ticket outlet and then pick up tickets at the club on the night of the show. *Id.* The court refused to exercise jurisdiction based on the Web site alone, reasoning that it did not rise to the level of purposeful availment of that jurisdiction's laws. The court distinguished the case from *CompuServe, supra,* where the user had " 'reached out' from Texas to Ohio and 'originated and maintained' contacts with Ohio." *Id.* at 301.[2]

Pres–Kap, Inc. v. System One, Direct Access, Inc., 636 So.2d 1351 (Fla.App.1994), *review denied,* 645 So.2d 455 (Fla.1994) is not inconsistent with the above cases. In *Pres–Kap,* a majority of a three-judge intermediate state appeals court refused to exercise jurisdiction over a consumer of an on-line airline ticketing service. *Pres–Kap* involved a suit on a contract dispute in a Florida court by a Delaware corporation against its New York customer. *Pres–Kap,* 636 So.2d at 1351–52. The defendant had leased computer equipment which it used to access an airline ticketing computer located in Florida. *Id.* The contract was solicited, negotiated, executed and serviced in New York. *Id.* at 1352. The defendant's only contact with Florida consisted of logging onto the computer located in Florida and mailing payments for the leased equipment to Florida. *Id.* at 1353. *Pres–Kap* is distinguishable from the above cases and the case at bar because it addressed the exercise of jurisdiction over a consumer of on-line services as opposed to a seller. When a consumer logs onto a server in a foreign jurisdiction he is engaging in a fundamentally different type of contact than an entity that is using the Internet to sell or market products or services to residents of foreign jurisdictions. The *Pres–Kap* court specifically expressed concern over the implications of subjecting users of "on-line" services with contracts with out-of-state networks to suit in foreign jurisdictions. *Id.* at 1353.

3. Application to this Case

First, we note that this is not an Internet advertising case in the line of *Inset Systems* and *Bensusan, supra.* Dot Com has not just posted information on a Web site that is accessible to Pennsylvania residents who are connected to the Internet. This is not even an interactivity case in the line of *Maritz, supra.* Dot Com has done more than create an interactive Web site through which it exchanges information with Pennsylvania residents in hopes of using that information for commercial gain later. We are not being asked to determine whether Dot Com's Web site alone constitutes the purposeful availment of doing business in Pennsylvania. This is a "doing business over the Internet" case in the line of *CompuServe, supra.* We are being asked to determine whether Dot Com's conducting of electronic commerce with Pennsylvania residents constitutes the purposeful availment of doing business in Pennsylvania. We conclude that it does. Dot Com has contracted with approximately 3,000 individuals and seven Internet access providers in Pennsylvania. The

---

[2] [On appeal, the district court's decision in *Bensusan* was affirmed on state-law grounds. The decision of the court of appeals is excerpted in Part III(B)(1), *infra.*—Eds.]

intended object of these transactions has been the downloading of the electronic messages that form the basis of this suit in Pennsylvania.

We find Dot Com's efforts to characterize its conduct as falling short of purposeful availment of doing business in Pennsylvania wholly unpersuasive. At oral argument, Defendant repeatedly characterized its actions as merely "operating a Web site" or "advertising." Dot Com also cites to a number of cases from this Circuit which, it claims, stand for the proposition that merely advertising in a forum, without more, is not a sufficient minimal contact. This argument is misplaced. Dot Com has done more than advertise on the Internet in Pennsylvania. Defendant has sold passwords to approximately 3,000 subscribers in Pennsylvania and entered into seven contracts with Internet access providers to furnish its services to their customers in Pennsylvania.

Dot Com also contends that its contacts with Pennsylvania residents are "fortuitous" within the meaning of *World–Wide Volkswagen*, 444 U.S. 286 (1980). Defendant argues that it has not "actively" solicited business in Pennsylvania and that any business it conducts with Pennsylvania residents has resulted from contacts that were initiated by Pennsylvanians who visited the Defendant's Web site. The fact that Dot Com's services have been consumed in Pennsylvania is not "fortuitous" within the meaning of *World–Wide Volkswagen*. In *World–Wide Volkswagen*, a couple that had purchased a vehicle in New York, while they were New York residents, were injured while driving that vehicle through Oklahoma and brought suit in an Oklahoma state court. *World–Wide Volkswagen*, 444 U.S. at 288. The manufacturer did not sell its vehicles in Oklahoma and had not made an effort to establish business relationships in Oklahoma. *Id.* at 295. The Supreme Court characterized the manufacturer's ties with Oklahoma as fortuitous because they resulted entirely out the fact that the plaintiffs had driven their car into that state. *Id.*

Here, Dot Com argues that its contacts with Pennsylvania residents are fortuitous because Pennsylvanians happened to find its Web site or heard about its news service elsewhere and decided to subscribe. This argument misconstrues the concept of fortuitous contacts embodied in *World–Wide Volkswagen*. Dot Com's contacts with Pennsylvania would be fortuitous within the meaning of *World–Wide Volkswagen* if it had no Pennsylvania subscribers and an Ohio subscriber forwarded a copy of a file he obtained from Dot Com to a friend in Pennsylvania or an Ohio subscriber brought his computer along on a trip to Pennsylvania and used it to access Dot Com's service. That is not the situation here. Dot Com repeatedly and consciously chose to process Pennsylvania residents' applications and to assign them passwords. Dot Com knew that the result of these contracts would be the transmission of electronic messages into Pennsylvania. The transmission of these files was entirely within its control. Dot Com cannot maintain that these contracts are "fortuitous" or "coincidental" within the meaning of *World–Wide Volkswagen*. When a defendant makes a conscious choice to conduct business with the residents of a forum state, "it has clear notice that it is subject to suit there." *World–Wide Volkswagen*, 444 U.S. at 297. Dot Com was under no obligation to sell its services to Pennsylvania residents. It freely chose to do so, presumably in order to profit from those transactions. If a corporation determines that the risk of being subject to personal jurisdiction in a particular forum is too great, it can choose to sever its connection to the state. *Id.* If Dot Com had not wanted to be amenable to jurisdiction in Pennsylvania, the solution would have been simple—it could have chosen not to sell its services to Pennsylvania residents.

Next, Dot Com argues that its forum-related activities are not numerous or significant enough to create a "substantial connection" with Pennsylvania. Defendant points to the fact that only two percent of its subscribers are Pennsylvania residents. However, the Supreme Court has made clear that even a single contact can be sufficient. *McGee*, 355 U.S. at 223. The test has always focused on the "nature and quality" of the contacts with the forum and not the quantity of those contacts. *International Shoe*, 326 U.S. at 320. The Sixth Circuit also rejected a similar argument in *CompuServe* when it wrote that the contacts were "deliberate and repeated even if they yielded little revenue." *CompuServe*, 89 F.3d at 1265.

. . .

IV. CONCLUSION

We conclude that this Court may appropriately exercise personal jurisdiction over the Defendant and that venue is proper in this judicial district.

EXTENSIONS

Bensusan. One of the cases the court relied upon in formulating its three-category analysis is the district court opinion in *Bensusan Restaurant Corp. v. King*, 937 F.Supp. 295 (S.D.N.Y.1996), *aff'd*, 126 F.3d 25 (2d Cir.1997). (The appellate decision is excerpted in Part III(B), *infra*.) After finding that the relevant provisions of the long-arm statute were not satisfied, the district court went on, in what might be considered dictum, to inquire whether assertion of jurisdiction would be consistent with due process. It stated:

> Creating a site, like placing a product into the stream of commerce, may be felt nationwide—or even worldwide—but, without more, it is not an act purposefully directed toward the forum state. See Asahi Metal Indus. Co. v. Superior Court, 480 U.S. 102, 112 (1987) (plurality opinion). There are no allegations that King actively sought to encourage New Yorkers to access his site, or that he conducted any business—let alone a continuous and systematic part of its business—in New York. There is in fact no suggestion that King has any presence of any kind in New York other than the Web site that can be accessed worldwide. Bensusan's argument that King should have foreseen that users could access the site in New York and be confused as to the relationship of the two Blue Note clubs is insufficient to satisfy due process.

Id. at 301. Distinguishing *CompuServe, Inc. v. Patterson*, 89 F.3d 1257 (6th Cir.1996), excerpted in Part II(C), *infra*, the court concluded that this case "contains no allegations that King in any way directed any contact to, or had any contact with, New York or intended to avail itself of any of New York's benefits." *Id.*

QUESTIONS FOR DISCUSSION

The Zippo categorization. In *Zippo*, the court made an effort to synthesize existing decisions on the circumstances under which operation of a website can give rise to jurisdiction. It found that those decisions have arranged websites on a "spectrum," consisting of two polar situations separated by a broad middle ground: (1) "situations where a defendant clearly does business over the Internet," by "enter[ing] into contracts with residents of a foreign jurisdiction that involve the knowing and repeated transmission of computer files over the Internet," in which case "personal jurisdiction is proper"; (2) "situations where a defendant has simply posted [a] passive website that does little more than make information available to those who are interested in it," which "is not grounds for the exercise [of] personal jurisdiction"; and (3) "interactive Web sites where a user can exchange information with the host computer," in which case "the exercise of jurisdiction is determined by examining the level of interactivity and commercial nature of the exchange of information that occurs on the Web site." Numerous subsequent decisions have adopted this approach.

How helpful is this categorization? (1) Is the "level of interactivity" that a website presents an indication of purposeful activity directed at the forum state? What would be the result of applying such a rule to telephone calls, which are as "interactive" as any website? (2) What about the "commercial nature" of the interactivity? Should a non-profit entity that commits an online tort be less susceptible to extraterritorial jurisdiction than a commercial entity that engages in the same activities? What about someone who engages in defamation for spiteful, but not commercial, purposes?

Consider this evaluation: (1) The rule applying to "passive" websites is an application of existing law holding that advertising in a nationally circulated publication does not alone support jurisdiction in every state where the publication is distributed. (2) The rule applying to websites that enable contracts with forum residents is an application of existing law holding that contracts with forum residents, regardless of the means of communication through which they are entered, may be sufficient to support jurisdiction. (3) The rule applicable to the middle category of "interactive" websites focuses inappropriately on the level and commercial nature of the site's interactivity, which are poor proxies for whether the defendant has "purposely avail[ed] itself of the privilege of conducting activities within the forum State." *Hanson v. Denckla*, 357 U.S. 235, 263 (1958). Consider also the following criticism of the interactivity criterion:

> [T]he distinction drawn by the Zippo court between actively managed, telephone-like use of the Internet and less active but "interactive" websites is not entirely clear to this court. Further, the proper means to measure the site's "level of interactivity" as a guide to personal jurisdiction remains unexplained. Finally, this court observes that the need for a special Internet-focused test for "minimum contacts" has yet to be established.

Winfield Collection, Ltd. v. McCauley, 105 F.Supp.2d 746, 750 (E.D.Mich.2000).

For another (rare) judicial criticism of the *Zippo* approach, see *Hy Cite Corp. v. Badbusinessbureau.com*, 297 F.Supp.2d 1154 (W.D.Wisc.2004).

2. Passive Websites and the Requirement of "Something More"

Cybersell, Inc. v. Cybersell, Inc.
130 F.3d 414 (9th Cir.1997).

■ RYMER, CIRCUIT JUDGE.

We are asked to hold that the allegedly infringing use of a service mark in a home page on the World Wide Web suffices for personal jurisdiction in the state where the holder of the mark has its principal place of business. Cybersell, Inc., an Arizona corporation that advertises for commercial services over the Internet, claims that Cybersell, Inc., a Florida corporation that offers web page construction services over the Internet, infringed its federally registered mark and should be amenable to suit in Arizona because cyberspace is without borders and a web site which advertises a product or service is necessarily intended for use on a world wide basis. The district court disagreed, and so do we. Instead, applying our normal "minimum contacts" analysis, we conclude that it would not comport with "traditional notions of fair play and substantial justice," *Core–Vent Corp. v. Nobel Indus. AB*, 11 F.3d 1482, 1485 (9th Cir.1993) (quoting *International Shoe Co. v. Washington*, 326 U.S. 310, 316 (1945)), for Arizona to exercise personal jurisdiction over an allegedly infringing Florida web site advertiser who has no contacts with Arizona other than maintaining a home page that is accessible to Arizonans, and everyone else, over the Internet. We therefore affirm.

I

Cybersell, Inc. is an Arizona corporation, which we will refer to as Cybersell AZ. It was incorporated in May 1994 to provide Internet and web advertising and marketing services, including consulting. The principals of Cybersell AZ are Laurence Canter and Martha Siegel, known among web users for first "spamming" the Internet. Mainstream print media carried the story of Canter and Siegel and their various efforts to commercialize the web.

On August 8, 1994, Cybersell AZ filed an application to register the name "Cybersell" as a service mark. The application was approved and the grant was published on October 30, 1995. Cybersell AZ operated a web site using the mark from August 1994 through February 1995. The site was then taken down for reconstruction.

Meanwhile, in the summer of 1995, Matt Certo and his father, Dr. Samuel C. Certo, both Florida residents, formed Cybersell, Inc., a Florida corporation (Cybersell FL), with its principal place of business in Orlando. Matt was a business school student at Rollins College, where his father was a professor; Matt was particularly interested in the Internet, and their company was to provide business consulting services for strategic management and marketing on the web. At the time the Certos chose the name "Cybersell" for their venture, Cybersell AZ had no home page on the web nor had the PTO granted their application for the service mark.

As part of their marketing effort, the Certos created a web page at http://www.cybsell.com/cybsell/index.htm. The home page has a logo at the top with "CyberSell" over a depiction of the planet earth, with the caption underneath "Professional Services for the World Wide Web" and a local (area code 407) phone number. It proclaims in large letters "Welcome to CyberSell!" A hypertext link allows the browser to introduce himself, and invites a company not on the web—but interested in getting on the web—to "Email us to find out how!"

Canter found the Cybersell FL web page and sent an e-mail on November 27, 1995 notifying Dr. Certo that "Cybersell" is a service mark of Cybersell AZ. Trying to disassociate themselves from Canter and Siegel, the Certos changed the name of Cybersell FL to WebHorizons, Inc. on December 27 (later it was changed again to

WebSolvers, Inc.) and by January 4, 1996, they had replaced the CyberSell logo at the top of their web page with WebHorizons, Inc. The WebHorizons page still said "Welcome to CyberSell!"

Cybersell AZ filed the complaint in this action January 9, 1996 in the District of Arizona, alleging trademark infringement, unfair competition, fraud, and RICO violations. On the same day Cybersell FL filed suit for declaratory relief with regard to use of the name "Cybersell" in the United States District Court for the Middle District of Florida, but that action was transferred to the District of Arizona and consolidated with the Cybersell AZ action. Cybersell FL moved to dismiss for lack of personal jurisdiction. The district court denied Cybersell AZ's request for a preliminary injunction, then granted Cybersell FL's motion to dismiss for lack of personal jurisdiction. Cybersell AZ timely appealed.

II

The general principles that apply to the exercise of personal jurisdiction are well known. As there is no federal statute governing personal jurisdiction in this case, the law of Arizona applies. Under Rule 4.2(a) of the Arizona Rules of Civil Procedure, an Arizona court

> may exercise personal jurisdiction over parties, whether found within or outside the state, to the maximum extent permitted by the Constitution of this state and the Constitution of the United States.

The Arizona Supreme Court has stated that under Rule 4.2(a), "Arizona will exert personal jurisdiction over a nonresident litigant to the maximum extent allowed by the federal constitution." . . . Thus, Cybersell FL may be subject to personal jurisdiction in Arizona so long as doing so comports with due process.

A court may assert either specific or general jurisdiction over a defendant. . . . Cybersell AZ concedes that general jurisdiction over Cybersell FL doesn't exist in Arizona, so the only issue in this case is whether specific jurisdiction is available.

We use a three-part test to determine whether a district court may exercise specific jurisdiction over a nonresident defendant:

> (1) The nonresident defendant must do some act or consummate some transaction with the forum or perform some act by which he purposefully avails himself of the privilege of conducting activities in the forum, thereby invoking the benefits and protections[;] (2)[t]he claim must be one which arises out of or results from the defendant's forum-related activities[; and] (3)[e]xercise of jurisdiction must be reasonable.

Ballard v. Savage, 65 F.3d 1495, 1498 (9th Cir.1995) (citations omitted).

Cybersell AZ argues that the test is met because trademark infringement occurs when the passing off of the mark occurs, which in this case, it submits, happened when the name "Cybersell" was used on the Internet in connection with advertising. Cybersell FL, on the other hand, contends that a party should not be subject to nationwide, or perhaps worldwide, jurisdiction simply for using the Internet.

A

Since the jurisdictional facts are not in dispute, we turn to the first requirement, which is the most critical. As the Supreme Court emphasized in *Hanson v. Denckla*, "it is essential in each case that there be some act by which the defendant purposefully avails itself of the privilege of conducting activities within the forum State, thus invoking the benefits and protections of its laws." 357 U.S. 235, 253 (1958). We recently explained in *Ballard* that

> the "purposeful availment" requirement is satisfied if the defendant has taken deliberate action within the forum state or if he has created continuing obligations to forum residents. "It is not required that a defendant be physically present within, or have physical contacts with, the forum, provided that his efforts 'are purposefully directed' toward forum residents."

Ballard, 65 F.3d at 1498 (citations omitted).

We have not yet considered when personal jurisdiction may be exercised in the context of cyberspace, but the Second and Sixth Circuits have had occasion to decide whether personal jurisdiction was properly exercised over defendants involved in transmissions over the Internet, *see CompuServe, Inc. v. Patterson*, 89 F.3d 1257 (6th Cir.1996); *Bensusan Restaurant Corp. v. King*, 937 F.Supp. 295 (S.D.N.Y. 1996), *aff'd*, 126 F.3d 25 (2d Cir.1997), as have a number of district courts.

. . .

"Interactive" web sites present somewhat different issues. Unlike passive sites such as the defendant's in *Bensusan*, users can exchange information with the host computer when the site is interactive. Courts that have addressed interactive sites have looked to the "level of interactivity and commercial nature of the exchange of information that occurs on the Web site" to determine if sufficient contacts exist to warrant the exercise of jurisdiction. *See, e.g., Zippo Mfg. Co. v. Zippo Dot Com, Inc.*, 952 F.Supp. 1119, 1124 (W.D.Pa.1997) (finding purposeful availment based on Dot Com's interactive web site and contracts with 3000 individuals and seven Internet access providers in Pennsylvania allowing them to download the electronic messages that form the basis of the suit); *Maritz, Inc. v. Cybergold, Inc.*, 947 F.Supp. 1328, 1332–33 (E.D.Mo.) (browsers were encouraged to add their address to a mailing list that basically subscribed the user to the service), *reconsideration denied*, 947 F.Supp. 1338 (1996).

Cybersell AZ points to several district court decisions which it contends have held that the mere advertisement or solicitation for sale of goods and services on the Internet gives rise to specific jurisdiction in the plaintiff's forum. However, so far as we are aware, no court has ever held that an Internet advertisement alone is sufficient to subject the advertiser to jurisdiction in the plaintiff's home state. *See, e.g., Smith v. Hobby Lobby Stores*, 968 F.Supp. 1356 (W.D.Ark.1997) (no jurisdiction over Hong Kong defendant who advertised in trade journal posted on the Internet without sale of goods or services in Arkansas). Rather, in each, there has been "something more" to indicate that the defendant purposefully (albeit electronically) directed his activity in a substantial way to the forum state.

Inset Systems, Inc. v. Instruction Set, Inc., 937 F.Supp. 161 (D.Conn.1996), is the case most favorable to Cybersell AZ's position. Inset developed and marketed computer software throughout the world; Instruction Set, Inc. (ISI) provided computer technology and support. Inset owned the federal trademark "INSET"; but ISI obtained "INSET.COM" as its Internet domain address for advertising its goods and services. ISI also used the telephone number "1-800-US-INSET." Inset learned of ISI's domain address when it tried to get the same address, and filed suit for trademark infringement in Connecticut. The court reasoned that ISI had purposefully availed itself of doing business in Connecticut because it directed its advertising activities via the Internet and its toll-free number toward the state of Connecticut (and all states); Internet sites and toll-free numbers are designed to communicate with people and their businesses in every state; an Internet advertisement could reach as many as 10,000 Internet users within Connecticut alone; and once posted on the Internet, an advertisement is continuously available to any Internet user.

Cybersell AZ further points to the court's statement in *EDIAS Software International, L.L.C. v. BASIS International Ltd.*, 947 F.Supp. 413 (D.Ariz.1996), that a defendant "should not be permitted to take advantage of modern technology through an Internet Web page and forum and simultaneously escape traditional notions of jurisdiction." *Id.* at 420. In that case, EDIAS (an Arizona company) alleged that BASIS (a New Mexico company) sent advertising and defamatory statements over the Internet through e-mail, its web page, and forums. However, the court did not rest its minimum contacts analysis on use of the Internet alone; in addition to the Internet, BASIS had a contract with EDIAS, it made sales to EDIAS and other Arizona customers, and its employees had visited Arizona during the course of the business relationship with EDIAS.

Some courts have also given weight to the number of "hits" received by a web page from residents in the forum state, and to other evidence that Internet activity was directed at, or bore fruit in, the forum state. See, e.g., *Heroes, Inc. v. Heroes Found.*, 958 F.Supp. 1 (D.D.C.1996) (web page that solicited contributions and provided toll-free telephone number along with the defendant's use on the web page of the allegedly infringing trademark and logo, along with other contacts, provided sustained contact with the District), *amended by* No. Civ.A. 96–1260(TAF) (1997); *Pres–Kap, Inc. v. System One, Direct Access, Inc.*, 636 So.2d 1351 (Fla.Dist.Ct.App.1994) (declining jurisdiction where defendant consumer subscribed to plaintiff's travel reservation system but was solicited and serviced instate by the supplier's local representative).

In sum, the common thread, well stated by the district court in *Zippo*, is that "the likelihood that personal jurisdiction can be constitutionally exercised is directly proportionate to the nature and quality of commercial activity that an entity conducts over the Internet." *Zippo*, 952 F.Supp. at 1124.

B

Here, Cybersell FL has conducted no commercial activity over the Internet in Arizona. All that it did was post an essentially passive home page on the web, using the name "CyberSell," which Cybersell AZ was in the process of registering as a federal service mark. While there is no question that anyone, anywhere could access that home page and thereby learn about the services offered, we cannot see how from that fact alone it can be inferred that Cybersell FL deliberately directed its merchandising efforts toward Arizona residents.

Cybersell FL did nothing to encourage people in Arizona to access its site, and there is no evidence that any part of its business (let alone a continuous part of its business) was sought or achieved in Arizona. To the contrary, it appears to be an operation where business was primarily generated by the personal contacts of one of its founders. While those contacts are not entirely local, they aren't in Arizona either. No Arizonan except for Cybersell AZ "hit" Cybersell FL's web site. There is no evidence that any Arizona resident signed up for Cybersell FL's web construction services. It entered into no contracts in Arizona, made no sales in Arizona, received no telephone calls from Arizona, earned no income from Arizona, and sent no messages over the Internet to Arizona. The only message it received over the Internet from Arizona was from Cybersell AZ. Cybersell FL did not have an "800" number, let alone a toll-free number that also used the "Cybersell" name. The interactivity of its web page is limited to receiving the browser's name and address and an indication of interest—signing up for the service is not an option, nor did anyone from Arizona do so. No money changed hands on the Internet from (or through) Arizona. In short, Cybersell FL has done no act and has consummated no transaction, nor has it performed any act by which it purposefully availed itself of the privilege of conducting activities, in Arizona, thereby invoking the benefits and protections of Arizona law.

We therefore hold that Cybersell FL's contacts are insufficient to establish "purposeful availment." Cybersell AZ has thus failed to satisfy the first prong of our three-part test for specific jurisdiction. We decline to go further solely on the footing that Cybersell AZ has alleged trademark infringement over the Internet by Cybersell FL's use of the registered name "Cybersell" on an essentially passive web page advertisement. Otherwise, every complaint arising out of alleged trademark infringement on the Internet would automatically result in personal jurisdiction wherever the plaintiff's principal place of business is located. That would not comport with traditional notions of what qualifies as purposeful activity invoking the benefits and protections of the forum state. *See Peterson v. Kennedy*, 771 F.2d 1244, 1262 (9th Cir.1985) (series of phone calls and letters to California physician regarding plaintiff's injuries insufficient to satisfy first prong of test).

. . .

EXTENSIONS

1. *Passive websites.* In cases involving websites that are nothing more than online advertisements, most courts have had little difficulty concluding that the website could not support jurisdiction. *See, e.g., Jennings v. AC Hydraulic A/S*, 383 F.3d 546 (7th Cir.2004); *Soma Medical Int'l v. Standard Chartered Bank*, 196 F.3d 1292 (10th Cir.1999). Some early cases found jurisdiction based on the operation of websites that would now be considered passive. *E.g., Maritz, Inc. v. Cybergold, Inc.*, 947 F.Supp. 1328 (E.D.Mo.1996) (finding jurisdiction based on the fact that defendant's website was accessed 131 times by residents of the forum state); *Hasbro Inc. v. Clue Computing Inc.*, 994 F.Supp. 34 (D.Mass.

1997) (jurisdiction based on the facts that defendant stated on its website that it had done work for a company located in the forum state, the website contained a link allowing a visitor to send an e-mail message to the site owner, and defendant failed to take any measures to avoid contacts in the forum state); *Inset Systems, Inc. v. Instruction Set, Inc.*, 937 F.Supp. 161 (D.Conn.1996) (jurisdiction based on defendant's operation of a website that displayed its toll-free telephone number).

2. *Reformulation of the* Zippo *criterion.* In *ALS Scan, Inc. v. Digital Service Consultants, Inc.*, 293 F.3d 707, 714 (4th Cir.2002), the Fourth Circuit, stating that it was "adopting and adapting the *Zippo* model," held:

> [W]e conclude that a State may, consistent with due process, exercise judicial power over a person outside of the State when that person (1) directs electronic activity into the State, (2) with the manifested intent of engaging in business or other interactions within the State, and (3) that activity creates, in a person within the State, a potential cause of action cognizable in the State's courts. Under this standard, a person who simply places information on the Internet does not subject himself to jurisdiction in each State into which the electronic signal is transmitted and received.

The Third Circuit, citing *ALS Scan v. Digital Service Consultants* with approval, has similarly emphasized "the requirement that the defendant intentionally interact with the forum state via the web site in order to show purposeful availment." *Toys "R" Us, Inc. v. Step Two, S.A.*, 318 F.3d 446, 452 (3d Cir.2003). Consider whether this formulation deviates substantively from the *Zippo* court's statement of the standard.

3. *Targeting the forum state.* The *Cybersell* court, endorsing the three-category approach set forth in *Zippo*, held that mere operation of a website is insufficient to support personal jurisdiction: "something more" is required "to indicate that the defendant purposefully (albeit electronically) directed his activity in a substantial way to the forum state." What should count as a "something more" that is sufficient to support jurisdiction over the owner of a website? One gloss on this requirement is that the defendant must "deliberately direct" its website advertising at the residents of the forum state. *Fernandez v. McDaniel Controls, Inc.*, 999 F.Supp. 1365, 1368 (D.Haw.1998). Some courts, however, have found deliberate targeting of the forum state under circumstances that suggest no more than a willingness to do business with anyone, anywhere. *See System Designs, Inc. v. New Custom-Ware Co.*, 248 F.Supp.2d 1093 (D.Utah 2003) (defendant is deemed to have targeted Utah because its website lists its clients including "AT & T, Sprint, and Dell—all companies with substantial connections to Utah"); *Enterprise Rent-A-Car Co. v. U-Haul Int'l, Inc.*, 327 F.Supp.2d 1032 (E.D.Mo.2004) (rental vehicle website that provides information and rentals to customers wherever located is deemed "specifically directed to [forum] residents"). *Non*-targeting of a particular state may be easier to establish. In *JB Oxford Holdings, Inc. v. Net Trade, Inc.*, 76 F.Supp.2d 1363 (S.D.Fla.1999), the defendant operated an online stock brokerage. It accepted account applications only from residents of the states in which it was registered to do business, which did not include Florida, the forum state. The court found that defendant had engaged in "purposeful avoidance of the privilege of conducting business in the forum state," and held that the site did not satisfy the due process requirements for jurisdiction.

QUESTIONS FOR DISCUSSION

What constitutes "deliberate direction"? Is "deliberate direction" a workable criterion? Consider whether the following constitute deliberate direction of advertising at a particular state: (a) What if the website contains a list of shipping costs to each of the 50 states? Does this constitute purposeful availment of each state? (b) What if the site notes that a particular

product that it offers may be of special interest to residents of Illinois, or to New England-
ers, or to Westerners? (c) What if the site contains a map showing driving instructions from
each of the states neighboring its brick-and-mortar location? What if it includes a link to a
mapping site that will generate driving directions to its location from anywhere in the country? *Cf. Millennium Enterprises, Inc. v. Millennium Music, LP*, 33 F. Supp. 2d 907
(D.Or.1999) (inclusion of local map of defendant's location does not demonstrate intent to
target residents of forum state 3,000 miles away).

3. The Interactivity Criterion

The middle category in *Zippo*'s taxonomy of website jurisdictional contacts is occupied
by those sites deemed to be interactive. Most courts have been unwilling to find that interactivity of a website alone constitutes "purposeful availment" of the forum state. Cases in
which interactive features of a website were found insufficient to support jurisdiction include: *Carefirst of Maryland, Inc. v. Carefirst Pregnancy Centers, Inc.*, 334 F.3d 390 (4th
Cir.2003) ("semi-interactive" website that solicits donations); *Revell v. Lidov*, 317 F.3d 467
(5th Cir.2002) (website hosting a bulletin board that allows users to post messages); *Ameripay, LLC v. Ameripay Payroll, Ltd.*, 334 F.Supp.2d 629 (D.N.J.2004) (website that "allows
software download, remote software installation, and payroll account monitoring"); *American Information Corp. v. American Infometrics, Inc.*, 139 F.Supp.2d 696 (D.Md. 2001)
(website allowing prospective employees to submit their resumes via the website); *People
Solutions, Inc. v. People Solutions, Inc.*, 2000 WL 1030619 (N.D.Tex.2000) (website containing "interactive pages that allow customers to test Defendant's products, download
product demos, obtain product brochures and information, and order products online"); *JB
Oxford Holdings, Inc. v. Net Trade, Inc.*, 76 F.Supp.2d 1363 (S.D.Fla.1999) (website allowing visitors to apply for a securities trading account online); *Agar Corp. v. Multi–Fluid,
Inc.*, 45 U.S.P.Q.2d 1444 (S.D.Tex.1997) (website featuring links allowing visitors to provide feedback and register).

Courts that have found an interactive website to satisfy due process requirements for jurisdiction usually have involved actual or potential transactions with forum residents. *See
Snowney v. Harrah's Entertainment, Inc.*, 112 P.3d 28 (Cal.2005) ("Defendants' Web site,
which quotes room rates to visitors and permits visitors to make reservations at their hotels,
is interactive and, at a minimum, falls within the middle ground of the *Zippo* sliding
scale."); *I & JC Corp. v. Helen of Troy L.P.*, 164 S.W.3d 877 (Tex.Ct.Apps.2005) (defendant's website "is interactive [since] individuals may order off the website"); *Enterprise
Rent-A-Car Co. v. U-Haul Int'l, Inc.*, 327 F.Supp.2d 1032 (E.D.Mo.2004) (rental vehicle
website that allows customers to reserve vehicles).

EXTENSIONS

Actual vs. potential interaction. Should a website be found to support jurisdiction, based
on the interactivity criterion, simply because it exhibits the *potential* for interaction with
residents of the forum state, or must there be *actual* interaction with forum residents? In
Millennium Enterprises, Inc. v. Millennium Music, LP, 33 F.Supp.2d 907 (D.Or.1999), the
plaintiff, which operated music stores in Oregon under the name "Music Millennium,"
claimed that defendant infringed its trademark in that name by operating in South Carolina
under the name "Millennium Music." Defendant's website allowed visitors to purchase
compact disks, join a discount club, and request franchising information, but no residents of
Oregon had made any purchases via the website or engaged in any online communication

with the defendant. The court rejected the view that potential interactivity is sufficient to satisfy due process: it held that there must in addition be some "deliberate action" within the forum state, consisting of either transactions with residents of the forum state or other conduct purposefully directed at them. The court stated: "Until transactions with Oregon residents are consummated through defendants' Web site, defendants cannot reasonably anticipate that they will be brought before this court . . . ."

On the other hand, in *Rainy Day Books, Inc. v. Rainy Day Books & Café, L.L.C.*, 186 F.Supp.2d 1158, 1165 (D.Kan.2002), the court held that actual transactions were not required. The only evidence of sales to residents of the forum jurisdiction consisted of sales to "family and acquaintances" of plaintiff, initiated at plaintiff's behest. The court held that evidence of actual book sales to forum residents was unnecessary: such evidence "merely supports Plaintiff's contention that Defendant's website is a commercial website accessible by Kansas residents." *See also Audi AG v. D'Amato*, 341 F.Supp.2d 734 (E.D.Mich.2004) (actual sales unnecessary for jurisdiction as long as website offers goods for sale).

QUESTIONS FOR DISCUSSION

1. *Evaluation of due process caselaw.* Zippo and its progeny, of which we shall see more later in this chapter, take a *sui generis* approach to the question whether a defendant's operation of a website can constitute the "minimum contacts" with the forum state that due process requires, resulting in a body of doctrine applying solely to websites. Consider the alternative of treating websites as a technologically more sophisticated version of older communications media, such as nationally circulated periodicals and toll-free telephone numbers, and incrementally updating the caselaw applying to those media. Would this result in a more coherent jurisprudence of website-based jurisdiction? *See* Richard S. Zembek, Comment, *Jurisdiction and the Internet: Fundamental Fairness in the Networked World of Cyberspace*, 6 ALB. L.J. SCI. & TECH. 339 (1996). Should the answer turn on whether websites are all very much like each other and very different from other media of communication?

2. *Communication by other online means.* Should the dissemination of a statement via e-mail, an electronic bulletin board system ("BBS"), Internet mailing list, chat room, or newsgroup carry the same weight, for purposes of evaluating jurisdictional contacts, as placing the same statement on a website? Consider the variations among these modes of online communication according to the following criteria:

- *Persistence.* A website persists for as long as the site owner chooses (unless it is shut down by the access provider for violation of the Terms of Service or some other reason). A message posted on a BBS persists as long as the manager of the forum chooses, which may be anywhere from of a few hours to indefinitely. Newsgroup postings may be archived by third-party systems forever. An e-mail message persists for as long as the recipient chooses. Chat sessions may be ephemeral, or they may persist if archived on the users' computers.

- *Mediation.* Websites, e-mail, newsgroups, and chat sessions are unmediated: no intermediary decides whether a communication will be allowed to occur. BBSs and mailing lists may or may not be mediated.

- *Accessibility.* Websites and newsgroups are accessible by anyone with Internet access. E-mail messages are normally available only to the intended recipient. Chat sessions may be limited to the interlocutors one selects, or may be open to the public. BBSs are often proprietary, with membership criteria determined by the board's manager. Mailing lists may be either open or closed.

- *Geographic determinacy.* One who communicates via a website, newsgroup,

BBS, or (usually) a mailing list or chat session normally does not know the geographic location of those who receive the communication. Methods of limiting access to the communication based on the location of the visitor exist, but they do not always work and in most contexts are infeasible. One may direct an e-mail to a person known to reside in a particular place, but one cannot know where the recipient will be located at the time she reads the message.

FURTHER READING

- Michael A. Geist, *Is There a There There? Toward Greater Certainty for Internet Jurisdiction*, 16 BERKELEY TECH. L.J. 1345 (2001) (arguing in favor of a "targeting" approach to jurisdiction)

B. THE "EFFECTS" OF ONLINE ACTIVITIES

In *Calder v. Jones*, 465 U.S. 783 (1984), the Supreme Court held that the "minimum contacts" due process requirement may be satisfied on the basis of the "effects" that out-of-state conduct has in the forum state. In that case, the Court held that a California court could assert jurisdiction over a Florida publisher that published an article defaming the plaintiff, in view of the fact that plaintiff resided in California. The Court reasoned that the defendants had engaged in "intentional, and allegedly tortious, actions [that were] expressly aimed at California," and that "they knew that the brunt of the injury would be felt" by the plaintiff in California. *Id.* at 789–90. The Ninth Circuit summarized the effects test as follows:

> personal jurisdiction can be predicated on (1) intentional actions (2) expressly aimed at the forum state (3) causing harm, the brunt of which is suffered—and which the defendant knows is likely to be suffered—in the forum state.

Core–Vent Corp. v. Nobel Industries AB, 11 F.3d 1482, 1486 (9th Cir.1993).

Plaintiffs have frequently urged courts to find jurisdiction based on the effects test in cases where the claims are predicated on infringement of intellectual property rights or defamation, and the alleged violations occur through use of a website or some other online means of communication. The courts have shown varying degrees of willingness to apply the effects test in the online context.

Panavision International, L.P. v. Toeppen
141 F.3d 1316 (9th Cir.1998).

■ DAVID R. THOMPSON, CIRCUIT JUDGE:

. . . We are asked to apply existing rules of personal jurisdiction to conduct that occurred, in part, in "cyberspace." . . .

. . .

Toeppen appeals. He argues that the district court erred in exercising personal jurisdiction over him because any contact he had with California was insignificant, emanating solely from his registration of domain names on the Internet, which he did in Illinois. . . .

We have jurisdiction under 28 U.S.C. § 1291 and we affirm. The district court's exercise of jurisdiction was proper and comported with the requirements of due process. Toeppen did considerably more than simply register Panavision's trademarks as his domain names on the Internet. He registered those names as part of a scheme to obtain money from Panavision. Pursuant to that scheme, he demanded $13,000 from Panavision to release the domain names to it. His acts were aimed at Panavision in California, and caused it to suffer injury there.

. . .

I

BACKGROUND

[The facts of this case are set forth in Chapter 3, Part I(B), *supra*.]

. . .

II

DISCUSSION

A. Personal Jurisdiction

. . . California's long-arm statute permits a court to exercise personal jurisdiction over a defendant to the extent permitted by the Due Process Clause of the Constitution. . . .

. . .

2. Specific Jurisdiction

We apply a three-part test to determine if a district court may exercise specific jurisdiction:

> (1) The nonresident defendant must do some act or consummate some transaction with the forum or perform some act by which he purposefully avails himself of the privilege of conducting activities in the forum, thereby invoking the benefits and protections of its laws; (2) the claim must be one which arises out of or results from the defendant's forum-related activities; and (3) exercise of jurisdiction must be reasonable.

Omeluk v. Langsten Slip & Batbyggeri A/S, 52 F.3d 267, 270 (9th Cir.1995) (quotation omitted).

The first of these requirements is purposeful availment.

a. Purposeful Availment

The purposeful availment requirement ensures that a nonresident defendant will not be haled into court based upon "random, fortuitous or attenuated" contacts with the forum state. *Burger King Corp. v. Rudzewicz*, 471 U.S. 462, 475 (1985). This requirement is satisfied if the defendant "has taken deliberate action" toward the forum state. *Ballard v. Savage*, 65 F.3d 1495, 1498 (9th Cir.1995). It is not required that a defendant be physically present or have physical contacts with the forum, so long as his efforts are "purposefully directed" toward forum residents. *Id.*

i. Application to the Internet

Applying principles of personal jurisdiction to conduct in cyberspace is relatively new. "With this global revolution looming on the horizon, the development of the law concerning the permissible scope of personal jurisdiction based on Internet use is in its infant stages. The cases are scant." *Zippo Mfg. Co. v. Zippo Dot Com, Inc.*, 952 F.Supp. 1119, 1123 (W.D.Pa.1997). We have, however, recently addressed the personal availment aspect of personal jurisdiction in a case involving the Internet. *See Cybersell, Inc. v. Cybersell, Inc.*, 130 F.3d 414 (9th Cir.1997).

. . . We held the Arizona court could not exercise personal jurisdiction over Cybersell FL, because it had no contacts with Arizona other than maintaining a web page accessible to anyone over the Internet. *Id.* at 419–420.

. . .

In the present case, the district court's decision to exercise personal jurisdiction over Toeppen rested on its determination that the purposeful availment requirement was satisfied by the "effects doctrine." That doctrine was not applicable in our *Cybersell* case. There, we said: "Likewise unpersuasive is Cybersell AZ's reliance on *Panavision International v. Toeppen*, 938 F.Supp. 616 (C.D.Cal.1996), [the district court's published opinion in this case,] where the court found the 'purposeful availment' prong satisfied by the effects felt in California, the home state of Panavision, from Toeppen's alleged out-of-state scheme to register domain names using the trademarks of California companies, including Panavision, for the purpose of extorting fees from them. Again, there is nothing analogous about Cybersell FL's conduct." *Cybersell*, 130 F.3d at 420 n.6.

Our reference in *Cybersell* to "the effects felt in California" was a reference to the effects doctrine.

ii. The Effects Doctrine

In tort cases, jurisdiction may attach if the defendant's conduct is aimed at or has an effect in the forum state. . . . *[S]ee Calder v. Jones*, 465 U.S. 783 (1984) (establishing an "effects test" for intentional action aimed at the forum state). Under *Calder*, personal jurisdiction can be based upon: "(1) intentional actions (2) expressly aimed at the forum state (3) causing harm, the brunt of which is suffered—and which the defendant knows is likely to be suffered—in the forum state." *Core–Vent Corp. v. Nobel Industries AB*, 11 F.3d 1482, 1486 (9th Cir.1993).

As the district court correctly stated, the present case is akin to a tort case. *Panavision*, 938 F.Supp. at 621 . . . . Toeppen purposefully registered Panavision's trademarks as his domain names on the Internet to force Panavision to pay him money. *Panavision*, 938 F.Supp. at 621. The brunt of the harm to Panavision was felt in California. Toeppen knew Panavision would likely suffer harm there because, although at all relevant times Panavision was a Delaware limited partnership, its principal place of business was in California, and the heart of the theatrical motion picture and television industry is located there. *Id.* at 621–622.

The harm to Panavision is similar to the harm to the Indianapolis Colts football team in *Indianapolis Colts, Inc. v. Metropolitan Baltimore Football Club Ltd. Partnership*,

34 F.3d 410 (7th Cir.1994). There, the Indianapolis Colts brought a trademark infringement action in the district court in Indiana against the Canadian Football League's new team, the "Baltimore CFL Colts." *Id.* at 411. The Seventh Circuit held that the Baltimore CFL Colts team was subject to personal jurisdiction in Indiana even though its only activity directed toward Indiana was the broadcast of its games on nationwide cable television. *Id.* Because the Indianapolis Colts used their trademarks in Indiana, any infringement of those marks would create an injury which would be felt mainly in Indiana, and this, coupled with the defendant's "entry" into the state by the television broadcasts, was sufficient for the exercise of personal jurisdiction. *Id.*

Toeppen argues he has not directed any activity toward Panavision in California, much less "entered" the state. He contends that all he did was register Panavision's trademarks on the Internet and post websites using those marks; if this activity injured Panavision, the injury occurred in cyberspace.[2]

We agree that simply registering someone else's trademark as a domain name and posting a website on the Internet is not sufficient to subject a party domiciled in one state to jurisdiction in another. *Cybersell*, 130 F.3d at 418. As we said in *Cybersell*, there must be "something more" to demonstrate that the defendant directed his activity toward the forum state. *Id.* Here, that has been shown. Toeppen engaged in a scheme to register Panavision's trademarks as his domain names for the purpose of extorting money from Panavision. His conduct, as he knew it likely would, had the effect of injuring Panavision in California where Panavision has its principal place of business and where the movie and television industry is centered. Under the "effects test," the purposeful availment requirement necessary for specific, personal jurisdiction is satisfied.

. . .

III

CONCLUSION

Toeppen engaged in a scheme to register Panavision's trademarks as his domain names on the Internet and then to extort money from Panavision by trading on the value of those names. Toeppen's actions were aimed at Panavision in California and the brunt of the harm was felt in California. The district court properly exercised personal jurisdiction over Toeppen.

. . .

---

[2] In a subset of this argument, Toeppen contends that a large organization such as Panavision does not suffer injury in one location. *See Cybersell*, 130 F.3d at 420 (A corporation "does not suffer harm in a particular geographic location in the same sense that an individual does."). However, in *Core–Vent*, we stated that *Calder v. Jones*, 465 U.S. 783 (1984), does not preclude a determination that a corporation suffers the brunt of harm in its principal place of business. *Core–Vent*, 11 F.3d at 1487. Panavision was previously a limited partnership and is now a corporation. Under either form of business organization, however, the brunt of the harm suffered by Panavision was in the state where it maintained its principal place of business, California.

[The portion of the court's opinion affirming the district court's summary judgment for Panavision on its trademark dilution claim is reproduced in Chapter 3, Part I(B), *supra*.]

Revell v. Lidov
317 F.3d 467 (5th Cir.2002).

■ PATRICK E. HIGGINBOTHAM, CIRCUIT JUDGE:

Oliver "Buck" Revell sued Hart G.W. Lidov and Columbia University for defamation arising out of Lidov's authorship of an article that he posted on an internet bulletin board hosted by Columbia. The district court dismissed Revell's claims for lack of personal jurisdiction over both Lidov and Columbia. We affirm.

I

Hart G.W. Lidov, an Assistant Professor of Pathology and Neurology at the Harvard Medical School and Children's Hospital, wrote a lengthy article on the subject of the terrorist bombing of Pan Am Flight 103, which exploded over Lockerbie, Scotland in 1988. The article alleges that a broad politically motivated conspiracy among senior members of the Reagan Administration lay behind their willful failure to stop the bombing despite clear advance warnings. Further, Lidov charged that the government proceeded to cover up its receipt of advance warning and repeatedly misled the public about the facts. Specifically, the article singles out Oliver "Buck" Revell, then Associate Deputy Director of the FBI, for severe criticism, accusing him of complicity in the conspiracy and cover-up. The article further charges that Revell, knowing about the imminent terrorist attack, made certain his son, previously booked on Pan Am 103, took a different flight. At the time he wrote the article, Lidov had never been to Texas, except possibly to change planes, or conducted business there, and was apparently unaware that Revell then resided in Texas.

Lidov has also never been a student or faculty member of Columbia University, but he posted his article on a website maintained by its School of Journalism. In a bulletin board section of the website, users could post their own works and read the works of others. As a result, the article could be viewed by members of the public over the internet.

Revell, a resident of Texas, sued the Board of Trustees of Columbia University, whose principal offices are in New York City, and Lidov, who is a Massachusetts resident, in the Northern District of Texas. Revell claimed damage to his professional reputation in Texas and emotional distress arising out of the alleged defamation of the defendants, and sought several million dollars in damages. Both defendants moved to dismiss for lack of personal jurisdiction under Federal Rule of Civil Procedure 12(b)(2). The district court granted the defendants' motions, and Revell now appeals.

II

A

Our question is whether the district court could properly exercise personal jurisdiction over Hart Lidov and Columbia University, an issue of law we review *de novo*. . . .

. . . Because Texas's long-arm statute reaches to the constitutional limits, we ask . . . if exercising personal jurisdiction over Lidov and Columbia would offend due process.

The Due Process Clause of the Fourteenth Amendment permits a court to exercise personal jurisdiction over a foreign defendant when (1) "that defendant has purposefully availed himself of the benefits and protections of the forum state by establishing 'minimum contacts' with the forum state; and (2) the exercise of jurisdiction over that defendant does not offend 'traditional notions of fair play and substantial justice.' " . . .

. . .

C

Turning to the issue of specific jurisdiction, the question is whether Revell has made out his *prima facie* case with respect to the defendants' contacts with Texas. . .

Revell urges that, given the uniqueness of defamation claims and their inherent ability to inflict injury in far-flung jurisdictions, we should abandon the imagery of *Zippo*. It is a bold but ultimately unpersuasive argument. Defamation has its unique features, but shares relevant characteristics with various business torts. Nor is the *Zippo* scale, as has been suggested, in tension with the "effects" test of *Calder v. Jones* for intentional torts,[30] which we address in Part II.D.

For specific jurisdiction we look only to the contact out of which the cause of action arises—in this case the maintenance of the internet bulletin board. Since this defamation action does not arise out of the solicitation of subscriptions or applications by Columbia, those portions of the website need not be considered.

The district court concluded that the bulletin board was "*Zippo*-passive" and therefore could not create specific jurisdiction. . . . But in this case, any user of the internet can post material to the bulletin board. This means that individuals *send* information to be posted, and *receive* information that others have posted. In *Mink [v. AAAA Dev. LLC*, 190 F.3d 333 (5th Cir.1999)] and *Zippo*, a visitor was limited to expressing an interest in a commercial product. Here the visitor may participate in an open forum hosted by the website. Columbia's bulletin board is thus interactive, and we must evaluate the extent of this interactivity as well as Revell's arguments with respect to *Calder*.

---

[30] We need not decide today whether or not a "*Zippo*-passive" site could still give rise to personal jurisdiction under *Calder*, and reserve this difficult question for another time.

D

. . .

2

Revell urges that, measured by the "effects" test of *Calder,* he has presented his *prima facie* case for the defendants' minimum contacts with Texas. At the outset we emphasize that the "effects" test is but one facet of the ordinary minimum contacts analysis, to be considered as part of the full range of the defendant's contacts with the forum.

We find several distinctions between this case and *Calder*—insurmountable hurdles to the exercise of personal jurisdiction by Texas courts. First, the article written by Lidov about Revell contains no reference to Texas, nor does it refer to the Texas activities of Revell, and it was not directed at Texas readers as distinguished from readers in other states. Texas was not the focal point of the article or the harm suffered, unlike *Calder,* in which the article contained descriptions of the California activities of the plaintiff, drew upon California sources, and found its largest audience in California. This conclusion fits well with our decisions in other intentional tort cases where the plaintiff relied upon *Calder.* In those cases we stated that the plaintiff's residence in the forum, and suffering of harm there, will not alone support jurisdiction under *Calder.* We also find instructive the defamation decisions of the Sixth, Third, and Fourth Circuits in *Reynolds v. International Amateur Athletic Federation,*[42] *Remick v. Manfredy,*[43] and *Young v. New Haven Advocate,*[44] respectively.

. . .

In *Remick* the plaintiff, a Pennsylvania lawyer, sued several individuals for defamation arising out of two letters sent to the plaintiff in Pennsylvania containing oblique charges of incompetence and accusations that the plaintiff was engaged in extortion of the defendants. The letters concerned the termination of the plaintiff's representation of one of the defendants, a professional boxer. One of the two letters was read by individuals other than the plaintiff when it was faxed to the plaintiff's Philadelphia office. The court held, however, that since there was nothing in the letter to indicate that it was targeted at Pennsylvania residents other than the plaintiff, personal jurisdiction could not be obtained under *Calder.* Furthermore, the court noted that allegations that the charges in the letter had been distributed throughout the "boxing community" were insufficient, because there was no assertion that Pennsylvania had a "unique relationship with the boxing industry, as distinguished from the relationship in *Calder* between California and the motion picture industry, with which the *Calder* plaintiff was associated."[53]

Similarly, in *Young v. New Haven Advocate,* two newspapers in Connecticut

---

[42] 23 F.3d 1110 (6th Cir.1994).

[43] 238 F.3d 248 (3d Cir.2001).

[44] 315 F.3d 256, 258 (4th Cir.2002).

[53] [*Remick,* 238 F.3d at 259.]

posted on the internet articles about the housing of Connecticut prisoners in Virginia that allegedly defamed a Virginia prison warden. The Fourth Circuit held that Virginia could not exercise personal jurisdiction over the Connecticut defendants because "they did not manifest an intent to aim their websites or the posted articles at a Virginia audience."[55] Following its decision in *ALS Scan, Inc. v. Digital Service Consultants*,[56] it reasoned that "application of *Calder* in the Internet context requires proof that the out-of-state defendant's Internet activity is expressly directed at or directed to the forum state."[57] It observed that more than simply making the news article accessible to Virginians by defendants' posting of the article on their internet sites was needed for assertion of jurisdiction: "The newspapers must, through the Internet postings, manifest an intent to *target* and *focus* on Virginia readers."[58]

As with *Remick* and *Young*, the post to the bulletin board here was presumably directed at the entire world, or perhaps just concerned U.S. citizens. But certainly it was not directed specifically at Texas, which has no especial relationship to the Pan Am 103 incident. Furthermore, here there is nothing to compare to the targeting of California readers represented by approximately 600,000 copies of the *Enquirer* the *Calder* defendants knew would be distributed in California, the *Enquirer*'s largest market.

3

As these cases aptly demonstrate, one cannot purposefully avail oneself of "some forum someplace"; rather, as the Supreme Court has stated, due process requires that "the defendant's conduct and connection with the forum State are such that he should reasonably anticipate being haled into court there."[60] Lidov's affidavit, uncontroverted by the record, states that he did not even know that Revell was a resident of Texas when he posted his article. Knowledge of the particular forum in which a potential plaintiff will bear the brunt of the harm forms an essential part of the *Calder* test. The defendant must be chargeable with knowledge of the forum at which his conduct is directed in order to reasonably anticipate being haled into court in that forum, as *Calder* itself and numerous cases from other circuits applying *Calder* confirm. Demanding knowledge of a particular forum to which conduct is directed, in defamation cases, is not altogether distinct from the requirement that the forum be the focal point of the tortious activity because satisfaction of the latter will ofttimes provide sufficient evidence of the former.

Lidov must have known that the harm of the article would hit home wherever Revell resided. But that is the case with virtually any defamation. A more direct aim is required than we have here. In short, this was not about Texas. If the article had a geographic focus it was Washington, D.C.

---

[55] [315 F.3d 256, 258 (4th Cir.2002).]

[56] 293 F.3d 707 (4th Cir.2002).

[57] *Young*, 315 F.3d at 262 (citing *ALS*, 293 F.3d at 714).

[58] *Id*.

[60] *Burger King Corp. v. Rudzewicz*, 471 U.S. 462, 474 (1985).

III

Our ultimate inquiry is rooted in the limits imposed on states by the Due Process Clause of the Fourteenth Amendment. It is fairness judged by the reasonableness of Texas exercising its power over residents of Massachusetts and New York. This inquiry into fairness captures the reasonableness of hauling a defendant from his home state before the court of a sister state; in the main a pragmatic account of reasonable expectations—if you are going to pick a fight in Texas, it is reasonable to expect that it be settled there. It is not fairness calibrated by the likelihood of success on the merits or relative fault. Rather, we look to the geographic focus of the article, not the bite of the defamation, the blackness of the calumny, or who provoked the fight.

. . .

IV

In sum, Revell has failed to make out a *prima facie* case of personal jurisdiction . . . . Considering both the "effects" test of *Calder* and the low-level of interactivity of the internet bulletin board, we find the contacts with Texas insufficient to establish the jurisdiction of its courts, and hence the federal district court in Texas, over . . . Lidov. . . .

EXTENSIONS

1. *Scope of the effects test: the requirement of wrongful conduct. Panavision*, quoting *Core–Vent*, characterizes the effects test as requiring "intentional actions" knowingly directed at the plaintiff. Is it a further requirement that those actions be wrongful? In *Bancroft & Masters, Inc. v. Augusta National Inc.*, 223 F.3d 1082 (9th Cir.2000), the plaintiff, a California computer company named Bancroft & Masters, sought a declaratory judgment that its registration and use of masters.com did not infringe defendant's trademark "Masters." The defendant, which sponsored golfing's annual Masters Tournament, had sent a letter to the domain name registrar, Network Solutions, Inc., challenging plaintiff's registration of masters.com, and invoking NSI's dispute-resolution policy. The district court held that it did not have jurisdiction based on the effects test. After noting that *Panavision* involved a purposeful scheme to extort money, it distinguished *Panavision* on the ground that "[n]o such intentional scheme or tortious conduct is alleged in this action." The court of appeals reversed. It explained that the effects test is satisfied "when the defendant is alleged to have engaged in wrongful conduct targeted at a plaintiff whom the defendant knows to be a resident of the forum state." It continued:

> Applying these concepts to the instant case, we conclude that B & M has demonstrated purposeful availment by ANI under the *Calder* effects test. ANI acted intentionally when it sent its letter to NSI. The letter was expressly aimed at California because it individually targeted B & M, a California corporation doing business almost exclusively in California. Finally, the effects of the letter were primarily felt, as ANI knew they would be, in California. [ANI] was well aware that B & M currently held the masters.com website and that it was B & M that would be affected if the NSI dispute resolution procedures were triggered. This is sufficient to satisfy *Calder* and thereby demonstrate the purposeful availment necessary for an exercise of specific jurisdiction.

Did the court correctly apply the effects test in this case? What was the wrongful conduct on which jurisdiction was based? Two of the three judges on the panel concurred with this observation:

> The "effects test" has normally been restricted to tortious conduct in which the "aimer" in state Y was seeking to injure wrongfully the target in state X. I concur in the opinion only on the assumption that Augusta National, through its letter to NSI, engaged in tortious conduct, i.e., that they intended to effect a conversion of the masters.com domain name.

> I am skeptical of Bancroft & Masters's selection of masters.com as its domain name. I suspect that Augusta National's initial reaction was similar. Therefore, I do not find it implausible that Augusta National, through its letter to NSI, merely intended to protect its trademark from dilution and infringement. . . . Jurisdiction in California would be ripe for challenge if following the development of trial it should appear that Augusta National acted reasonably and in good faith to protect its trademark against an infringer.

The concurrence seems to suggest that a final determination on jurisdiction should be made once the case has gone to trial. Does this adequately protect the defendant's due process rights? How else might the defendant's motion to dismiss have been handled?

In *Yahoo! Inc. v. La Ligue Contre le Racisme et l'Antisemitisme*, 379 F.3d 1120 (9th Cir.2004), *reh'g en banc granted*, 399 F.3d 1010 (9th Cir.2005), the majority reaffirmed its statement in *Bancroft & Masters* that defendant's conduct must be "wrongful" to satisfy the requirements of the effects test, but held that plaintiff had not established the requisite wrongful conduct. The defendants, LICRA and UEJF, had sued Yahoo! in a French court, and obtained an order requiring Yahoo! to prevent citizens of France from accessing those portions of its websites containing Nazi-related materials. (The proceedings in the French court are discussed in Chapter I, Part III(A), *supra*.) Yahoo! then brought an action against LICRA and UEJF in the federal district court for the Northern District of California, where Yahoo!'s headquarters was located, seeking a declaratory judgment stating that the French order was not enforceable in the United States because inconsistent with the First Amendment. LICRA and UEJF moved to dismiss, arguing that the court did not have jurisdiction over them. The Court of Appeals, in a split decision reversing the District Court, held that it lacked jurisdiction over the French defendants. The court explained that the effects test would be satisfied only if the French entities' actions in connection with the litigation "qualify as wrongful conduct targeted at Yahoo!." The conduct by LICRA and UEJF that Yahoo! asserted supported jurisdiction under the effects test consisted of three actions: (1) before initiating the French litigation, "LICRA sent a cease-and-desist letter to Yahoo! in Santa Clara, California, demanding that Yahoo! prohibit the display of the Nazi materials because the practice was illegal in France"; (2) LICRA and UEJF filed the action against Yahoo! in the French court, seeking an order requiring "that Yahoo! perform certain acts on its server and remove certain Nazi items from its website in California"; and (3) LICRA and UEJF served process on Yahoo! in California, using the mechanisms specified in the Hague Service Convention. The majority found nothing wrongful in this conduct:

> France is within its rights as a sovereign nation to enact hate speech laws against the distribution of Nazi propaganda in response to its terrible experience with Nazi forces during World War II. Similarly, LICRA and UEJF are within their rights to bring suit in France against Yahoo! for violation of French speech law. The only adverse consequence experienced by Yahoo! as a result of the acts with which we are concerned is that Yahoo! must wait for LICRA and UEJF to come to the United States to enforce the French judgment before it is able to raise its First Amendment claim. However, it was not wrongful for the French organizations to place Yahoo! in this position.

The dissenting judge disagreed with the majority's statement of the legal standard. According to the dissent, a defendant's conduct need not be "wrongful" to constitute "express aiming": "[A]lthough wrongful conduct will satisfy the Supreme Court's constitutional standard for the exercise of in personam jurisdiction, it is not necessarily required in all cases; indeed, I believe that the Supreme Court's 'express aiming' test may be met by a defendant's intentional targeting of his actions at the plaintiff in the forum state." The dissenting judge would have held that the French defendants' conduct, albeit not wrongful, was expressly aimed at Yahoo! in California, and therefore supported jurisdiction under the effects test.

What explains the difference between the result here and that in *Bancroft & Masters, Inc. v. Augusta National, Inc.*? Given the majority's rationale, could Yahoo! have satisfied the requirements of the effects test through artful pleading? Should the international aspect of the case affect the jurisdictional analysis?

2. *Scope of the effects test: where does a corporation feel harm?* One element of the effects test is that the injury that defendant causes must result in harm to plaintiff *in the forum state*. Some courts have questioned whether a corporation feels harm in any particular location. Thus, in *Cybersell, Inc. v. Cybersell, Inc.*, 130 F.3d 414 (9th Cir.1997), excerpted in Part II(A)(2), *supra*, the court found the effects test inapplicable, stating: "Nor does the 'effects' test apply with the same force to [the defendant corporation] as it would to an individual, because a corporation 'does not suffer harm in a particular geographic location in the same sense that an individual does.' " *Id.* at 420 (quoting *Core–Vent Corp. v. Nobel Industries AB*, 11 F.3d 1482, 1486 (9th Cir.1993)). *See also Hy Cite Corp. v. Badbusinessbureau.com*, 297 F.Supp.2d 1154 (W.D.Wisc.2004) ("Even if a corporation has its principal place of business in the forum state, it does not follow necessarily that it makes more sales in that state than any other or that harm to its reputation will be felt more strongly in that state.").

But other courts have held that a corporation suffers harm in the place where it is headquartered or has its principal place of business. Thus, in *Panavision, supra*, 141 F.3d at 1322 n.2, the court stated: "Panavision was previously a limited partnership and is now a corporation. Under either form of business organization, however, the brunt of the harm suffered by Panavision was in the state where it maintained its principal place of business, California." *See also Audi AG v. D'Amato*, 341 F.Supp.2d 734 (E.D.Mich.2004) (corporation feels harm at its corporate headquarters). The same result has been reached for harm consisting of trademark infringement. *See Enterprise Rent-A-Car Company v. U-Haul Intern., Inc.*, 327 F.Supp.2d 1032 (E.D.Mo.2004) ("trademark infringement is a tort, and the economic effects of infringement are felt where the trademark owner has its principal place of business").

Still other courts have treated an individual with a national reputation like a corporation, holding that the individual does not experience harm where he is located. In *Barrett v. Catacombs Press*, 44 F.Supp.2d 717 (E.D.Pa.1999), the plaintiff operated a website called Quackwatch, which posted extensive information concerning health frauds and quackery and was nationally known. The court found that defendant's allegedly defamatory statements did not cause the "brunt" of the harm to be experienced in Pennsylvania, where plaintiff lived and worked: "While we agree that Pennsylvania residents are among the recipients or viewers of such defamatory statements, they are but a fraction of other worldwide Internet users who have received or viewed such statements." *See also Bailey v. Turbine Design, Inc.*, 86 F.Supp.2d 790 (W.D.Tenn.2000).

3. *Scope of the effects test: defendant's knowledge of plaintiff's location.* The effects test is satisfied only if the defendant knows that the plaintiff is located in the forum state. Some courts have applied this criterion more stringently than others. In *Panavision, supra*, the court seemed willing to infer that Toeppen knew Panavision was located in California from the fact that "the heart of the theatrical motion picture and television industry is located there." *See also System Designs, Inc. v. New CustomWare Co.*, 248 F.Supp.2d 1093 (D.Utah 2003) (suggesting that a defendant charged with trademark infringement should be deemed to know the location of the trademark owner based on the relevant entry in the national trademark registry).

4. *Foreseeability vs. "expressly aimed."* Several decisions have emphasized that jurisdiction exists under the effects test only if the defendant "expressly aimed" its conduct at the plaintiff in the forum state, and that mere foreseeability that the defendant's conduct would have such an effect is not sufficient. *See Revell v. Lidov*, excerpted above, and *Young v. New Haven Advocate*, 315 F.3d 256 (4th Cir.2002), discussed in the *Revell v. Lidov* excerpt. *Cf. Wagner v. Mishkin*, 660 N.W.2d 593 (N.D.2003) (allegedly defamatory material posted on a website *was* expressly aimed at North Dakota, where the website's URL was www.undnews.com (the "und" referring to University of North Dakota) and the postings addressed UND issues).

In *Pavlovich v. Superior Court*, 58 P.3d 2 (Cal.2002), the California Supreme Court was sharply divided over whether a California court had jurisdiction under the effects test over an out-of-state defendant based on his website posting of the source code of DeCSS, software that circumvents the anti-copying technology used on DVDs. The four-justice majority held that mere foreseeability that posting the code would adversely affect components of the entertainment industry located in California does not satisfy the requirements of the effects test, since this conduct was not expressly aimed at California. A three-justice dissent disagreed. *See also Metro-Goldwyn-Mayer Studios Inc. v. Grokster, Ltd.*, 243 F.Supp.2d 1073, 1089 (C.D.Cal.2003) (finding the effects test satisfied by the defendant's conduct in making allegedly infringing peer-to-peer file-sharing software available for download, since the software was allegedly used to share music and video files in violation of the owners' copyrights, and defendant "reasonably should be aware that many, if not most, music and video copyrights are owned by California-based companies.").

QUESTIONS FOR DISCUSSION

1. *"Something more."* Consider the court's statement: "We agree that simply registering someone else's trademark as a domain name and posting a website on the Internet is not sufficient to subject a party domiciled in one state to jurisdiction in another. . . . As we said in *Cybersell*, there must be 'something more' to demonstrate that the defendant directed his activity toward the forum state." What was the "something more" that the court found dispositive? Requesting payment in exchange for relinquishing the domain name? Is *Panavision* consistent with *Cybersell*?

2. *Improper motivation.* Is the defendant's motivation in registering the domain names relevant to the effects test analysis? To what extent does the decision turn on the court's view that Toeppen's conduct and motivation were reprehensible? Consider the following criticism of *Panavision*:

> *Panavision* appears to be one of those cases where "hard cases make bad law." . . . Except perhaps in the clearest case of a cybersquatter or where intent is undisputed, this court believes it would be a serious mistake for personal jurisdiction to turn on the issue of the defendant's intent, which itself is a major merits issue. [The district court's decision in] *Panavision* thus is distinguishable, and to the extent it is not distinguishable, the Court declines to follow it.

Hearst Corp. v. Goldberger, 1997 WL 97097, *19 (S.D.N.Y.1997). Is the criticism valid? What would be the rationale for factoring intent into the analysis "in the clearest case of a cybersquatter or where intent is undisputed"?

Several cases have distinguished *Panavision* on the ground that unlike Toeppen the defendant was not tainted by impure motives. *See K.C.P.L., Inc. v. Nash*, 49 U.S.P.Q.2d 1584 (S.D.N.Y.1998) ("the facts alleged do not show [defendant] to be a 'cyber pirate' "); *No Mayo–San Francisco v. Memminger*, 1998 WL 544974 (N.D.Cal.1998) (distinguishing *Panavision*, since defendant was no "cyber pirate").

3. *Trademark registration alone as basis for jurisdiction.* The *Panavision* court took the position that "simply registering someone else's trademark as a domain name and posting a website on the Internet is not sufficient to subject a party domiciled in one state to jurisdiction in another." In *Ford Motor Co. v. Great Domains, Inc.*, 141 F.Supp.2d 763, 775 n.2 (E.D.Mich.2001), the court expressed a contrary view:

> Simply registering a domain name that incorporates a trademark can be a violation of the Lanham Act, if done with "bad faith intent to profit from that mark." 15 U.S.C. § 1125(d)(1). Thus, registering a domain name that incorporates a trademark for which only the mark owner could have a legitimate use could be sufficient under *Calder* to support the assertion of personal jurisdiction in the mark owner's place of residence.

Which court got it right? Does the 1999 passage of the Anticybersquatting Consumer Protection Act, 15 U.S.C. § 1125(d)(1), *see* Chapter 3, Part II, *supra*, affect the jurisdictional analysis?

4. *A merger of* Zippo *and* Calder? Reconsider the Fourth Circuit's reformulation of the *Zippo* test in *ALS Scan, Inc. v. Digital Service Consultants, Inc.*, 293 F.3d 707 (4th Cir.2002), discussed in Part II(A)(2), *supra*. The court observes that its reformulation of *Zippo* "is not dissimilar to that applied by the Supreme Court in *Calder v. Jones*." What differences, if any, remain between the *Zippo* test as so reformulated and the effects test?

C. ENTERING INTO COMMERCIAL TRANSACTIONS VIA ONLINE COMMUNICATIONS

The fact that the defendant has entered into contracts or had other commercial dealings with residents of the forum state may supply the "minimum contacts" necessary for assertion of jurisdiction to comport with the requirements of due process. This rule is the basis for the "jurisdiction exists" category of the taxonomy of websites described in *Zippo Mfg. Co. v. Zippo Dot Com, Inc.*, 952 F.Supp. 1119, 1124 (W.D.Pa.1997), excerpted in Part II(A)(1), *supra*: "If the defendant enters into contracts with residents of a foreign jurisdiction that involve the knowing and repeated transmission of computer files over the Internet, personal jurisdiction is proper." The high-water mark for application of the rule came in *McGee v. International Life Insurance Co.*, 355 U.S. 220 (1957), where the Supreme Court upheld jurisdiction by a California court over an insurance company defendant with its principal place of business in Texas, on the basis of a single contract of insurance that the company had with a resident of California. The Court found that the contract had the requisite "substantial connection with" California, since "[t]he contract was delivered in California, the premiums were mailed from there and the insured was a resident of that State when he died." *Id.* at 223. Commenting on the trend, during the preceding 80 years, "toward expanding the permissible scope of state jurisdiction over foreign corporations and other nonresidents," the Court observed:

> In part this is attributable to the fundamental transformation of our national economy over the years. Today many commercial transactions touch two or more States and may involve parties separated by the full continent. With this

increasing nationalization of commerce has come a great increase in the amount of business conducted by mail across state lines. At the same time modern transportation and communications have made it much less burdensome for a party sued to defend himself in a State where he engages in economic activity.

Id. at 222–23. That was in 1957. During the intervening 50 years, the advent of communication via low-cost long-distance telephone service, telecopier, and e-mail, improvements in modes of transportation, and increased nationalization and globalization of commerce have accelerated the trend that the Court noted. Still, the Court continues to reject the view that "an individual's contract with an out-of-state party *alone* can automatically establish sufficient minimum contacts in the other party's home forum." *Burger King Corp. v. Rudzewicz,* 471 U.S. 462, 478 (1985). It has instead

emphasized the need for a "highly realistic" approach that recognizes that a "contract" is "ordinarily but an intermediate step serving to tie up prior business negotiations with future consequences which themselves are the real object of the business transaction." . . . It is these factors—prior negotiations and contemplated future consequences, along with the terms of the contract and the parties' actual course of dealing—that must be evaluated in determining whether the defendant purposefully established minimum contacts within the forum.

Id. at 479.

CompuServe, Inc. v. Patterson
89 F.3d 1257 (6th Cir. 1996).

■ BAILEY BROWN, CIRCUIT JUDGE.

In a case that requires us to consider the scope of the federal courts' jurisdictional powers in a new context, a computer network giant, CompuServe, appeals the dismissal, for lack of personal jurisdiction, of its complaint in which it sought a declaratory judgment that it had not infringed on the defendants' common law copyrights or otherwise engaged in unfair competition. The district court held that the electronic links between the defendant Patterson, who is a Texan, and Ohio, where CompuServe is headquartered, were "too tenuous to support the exercise of personal jurisdiction." The district court also denied CompuServe's motion for reconsideration. Because we believe that CompuServe made a prima facie showing that the defendant's contacts with Ohio were sufficient to support the exercise of personal jurisdiction, we REVERSE the district court's dismissal and REMAND this case for further proceedings consistent with this opinion.

I. BACKGROUND

CompuServe is a computer information service headquartered in Columbus, Ohio. It contracts with individual subscribers, such as the defendant, to provide, *inter alia,* access to computing and information services via the Internet, and it is the second largest such provider currently operating on the so-called "information super highway." A CompuServe subscriber may use the service to gain electronic access to more than 1700 information services.

CompuServe also operates as an electronic conduit to provide its subscribers computer software products, which may originate either from CompuServe itself or from other parties. Computer software generated and distributed in this manner is, according to CompuServe, often referred to as "shareware." Shareware makes money only through the voluntary compliance of an "end user," that is, another CompuServe subscriber who may or may not pay the creator's suggested licensing fee if she uses the software beyond a specified trial period. The "end user" pays that fee directly to CompuServe in Ohio, and CompuServe takes a 15% fee for its trouble before remitting the balance to the shareware's creator.

Defendant, Richard Patterson, is an attorney and a resident of Houston, Texas who claims never to have visited Ohio. Patterson also does business as FlashPoint Development. He subscribed to CompuServe, and he also placed items of "shareware" on the CompuServe system for others to use and purchase. When he became a shareware "provider," Patterson entered into a "Shareware Registration Agreement" ("SRA") with CompuServe. Under the SRA, CompuServe provides its subscribers with access to the software, or shareware, that Patterson creates. The SRA purports to create an independent contractor relationship between Patterson and CompuServe, whereby Patterson may place software of his creation on CompuServe's system. The SRA does not mention Patterson's software by name; in fact, it leaves the content and identification of that software to Patterson.

The SRA incorporates by reference two other documents: the CompuServe Service Agreement ("Service Agreement") and the Rules of Operation, both of which are published on the CompuServe Information Service. Both the SRA and the Service Agreement expressly provide that they are entered into in Ohio, and the Service Agreement further provides that it is to "be governed by and construed in accordance with" Ohio law. These documents appear to be standardized and entirely the product of CompuServe. It bears noting, however, that the SRA asks a new shareware "provider" like Patterson to type "AGREE" at various points in the document, "[i]n recognition of your on line agreement to all the above terms and conditions." Thus, Patterson's assent to the SRA was first manifested at his own computer in Texas, then transmitted to the CompuServe computer system in Ohio.

From 1991 through 1994, Patterson electronically transmitted 32 master software files to CompuServe. These files were stored in CompuServe's system in Ohio, and they were displayed in different services for CompuServe subscribers, who could "download" them into their own computers and, if they chose to do so, pay for them. Patterson also advertised his software on the CompuServe system, and he indicated a price term in at least one of his advertisements. CompuServe asserts that Patterson marketed his software exclusively on its system. Patterson, for his part, stated that he has sold less than $650 worth of his software to only 12 Ohio residents via CompuServe.

Patterson's software product was, apparently, a program designed to help people navigate their way around the larger Internet network. CompuServe began to market a similar product, however, with markings and names that Patterson took to be too similar to his own. Thus, in December of 1993, Patterson notified CompuServe (appropriately via an electronic mail or "E-mail" message) that the terms "WinNAV," "Windows Navigator," and "FlashPoint Windows Navigator" were common law trademarks which he and his company owned. Patterson stated that

CompuServe's marketing of its product infringed these trademarks, and otherwise constituted deceptive trade practices. CompuServe changed the name of its program, but Patterson continued to complain. CompuServe asserts that, if Patterson's allegations of trademark infringement are correct, they threaten CompuServe's software sales revenue with a loss of approximately $10.8 million.

After Patterson demanded at least $100,000 to settle his potential claims, CompuServe filed this declaratory judgment action in the federal district court for the Southern District of Ohio, relying on the court's diversity subject matter jurisdiction. CompuServe sought, among other things, a declaration that it had not infringed any common law trademarks of Patterson or FlashPoint Development, and that it was not otherwise guilty of unfair or deceptive trade practices. Patterson responded pro se with a consolidated motion to dismiss on several grounds, including lack of personal jurisdiction. Patterson also submitted a supporting affidavit, in which he denied many jurisdictional facts, including his having ever visited Ohio. CompuServe then filed a memorandum in opposition to Patterson's consolidated motion, along with several supporting exhibits.

The district court, considering only these pleadings and papers, granted Patterson's motion to dismiss for lack of personal jurisdiction in a thorough and thoughtful opinion. . . .

II. ANALYSIS

. . .

B. Personal Jurisdiction.

This case presents a novel question of first impression: Did CompuServe make a prima facie showing that Patterson's contacts with Ohio, which have been almost entirely electronic in nature, are sufficient, under the Due Process Clause, to support the district court's exercise of personal jurisdiction over him?

The Supreme Court has noted, on more than one occasion, the confluence of the "increasing nationalization of commerce" and "modern transportation and communication," and the resulting relaxation of the limits that the Due Process Clause imposes on courts' jurisdiction. *E.g., World–Wide Volkswagen Corp. v. Woodson,* 444 U.S. 286, 293 (1980) (quoting *McGee v. International Life Ins. Co.,* 355 U.S. 220, 223 (1957)). Simply stated, there is less perceived need today for the federal constitution to protect defendants from "inconvenient litigation," because all but the most remote forums are easily accessible for the pursuit of both business and litigation. *Id.* The Court has also, however, reminded us that the due process rights of a defendant should be the courts' primary concern where personal jurisdiction is at issue. *Insurance Corp. v. Compagnie des Bauxites de Guinee,* 456 U.S. 694, 702 n.10 (1982).

The Internet represents perhaps the latest and greatest manifestation of these historical, globe-shrinking trends. It enables anyone with the right equipment and knowledge—that is, people like Patterson—to operate an international business cheaply, and from a desktop. That business operator, however, remains entitled to the protection of the Due Process Clause, which mandates that potential defendants be able "to structure their primary conduct with some minimum assurance as to where the conduct will and will not render them liable to suit." *World–Wide Volkswagen*, 444 U.S. at 297. Thus, this case presents a situation where we must reconsider the scope of our jurisdictional reach.

. . .

The Ohio long-arm statute allows an Ohio court to exercise personal jurisdiction over nonresidents of Ohio on claims arising from, inter alia, the nonresident's transacting any business in Ohio. Ohio Rev. Code Ann. § 2307.382(A) (Anderson 1995). It is settled Ohio law, moreover, that the "transacting business" clause of that statute was meant to extend to the federal constitutional limits of due process, and that as a result Ohio personal jurisdiction cases require an examination of those limits. . . .

Further, personal jurisdiction may be either general or specific in nature, depending on the nature of the contacts in a given case. . . . In the instant case, because CompuServe bases its action on Patterson's act of sending his computer software to Ohio for sale on its service, CompuServe seeks to establish such specific personal jurisdiction over Patterson. *Id.*

As always in this context, the crucial federal constitutional inquiry is whether, given the facts of the case, the nonresident defendant has sufficient contacts with the forum state that the district court's exercise of jurisdiction would comport with "traditional notions of fair play and substantial justice." *International Shoe Co. v. Washington*, 326 U.S. 310, 316 (1945) (quoting *Milliken v. Meyer*, 311 U.S. 457, 463 (1940)) . . . . This court has repeatedly employed three criteria to make this determination:

> First, the defendant must purposefully avail himself of the privilege of acting in the forum state or causing a consequence in the forum state. Second, the cause of action must arise from the defendant's activities there. Finally, the acts of the defendant or consequences caused by the defendant must have a substantial enough connection with the forum to make the exercise of jurisdiction over the defendant reasonable.

[*Reynolds v. Int'l Amateur Athletic Fed'n*, 23 F.3d 1110, 1116 (6th Cir.1994).]

We conclude that Patterson has knowingly made an effort—and, in fact, purposefully contracted—to market a product in other states, with Ohio-based CompuServe operating, in effect, as his distribution center. Thus, it is reasonable to subject Patterson to suit in Ohio, the state which is home to the computer network service he chose to employ.

To support this conclusion, we will address each of the above three criteria seriatim, bearing in mind that (1) CompuServe need only make a prima facie case of personal jurisdiction, and (2) we cannot weigh Patterson's affidavit in the analysis, given that the district court addressed his motion to dismiss without holding an evidentiary hearing. . . .

1. The "purposeful availment" requirement.

. . .

There is no question that Patterson himself took actions that created a connection with Ohio in the instant case. He subscribed to CompuServe, and then he entered into the Shareware Registration Agreement when he loaded his software onto the CompuServe system for others to use and, perhaps, purchase. Once Patterson had done those two things, he was on notice that he had made contracts, to be governed by Ohio law, with an Ohio-based company. Then, he repeatedly sent his computer software, via electronic links, to the CompuServe system in Ohio, and he advertised that software on the CompuServe system. Moreover, he initiated the events that led to the filing of this suit by making demands of CompuServe via electronic and regular mail messages.

The real question is whether these connections with Ohio are "substantial" enough that Patterson should reasonably have anticipated being haled into an Ohio court. The district court did not think so. It looked to "cases involving interstate business negotiations and relationships" and held that the relationship between CompuServe and Patterson, because it was marked by a "minimal course of dealing," was insufficient to satisfy the purposeful availment test. *Compare Reynolds*, 23 F.3d at 1118–21 (holding that the contacts between an England-based association and an Ohio plaintiff in a contract case were "superficial" where, although mail and telephone communications had taken place, the parties had engaged in no prior negotiations and expected no future consequences) *and Health Communications, Inc. v. Mariner Corp.*, 860 F.2d 460, 463–65 (D.C.Cir.1988) (finding no jurisdiction over a nonresident purchaser who had bought services from a corporation in the forum state) *with [Burger King Corp. v. Rudzewicz, 471 U.S. 462, 479-82 (1985)]* (finding significant the defendant's reaching beyond Michigan to negotiate with a Florida corporation for the purchase of a long-term franchise). The district court deemed this case closer to *Reynolds* and *Health Communications* than to *Burger King Corp.*, and thus it found no purposeful availment on the part of Patterson.

We disagree. The contract cases upon which the district court relied are both distinguishable in important ways. Patterson, unlike the nonresident defendant in Reynolds, entered into a written contract with CompuServe which provided for the application of Ohio law, and he then purposefully perpetuated the relationship with CompuServe via repeated communications with its system in Ohio. And, unlike the nonresident defendant in Health Communications, Patterson was far more than a purchaser of services; he was a third-party provider of software who used CompuServe, which is located in Columbus, to market his wares in Ohio and elsewhere.

In fact, it is Patterson's relationship with CompuServe as a software provider and marketer that is crucial to this case. The district court's analysis misses the mark because it disregards the most salient facts of that relationship: that Patterson chose to transmit his software from Texas to CompuServe's system in Ohio, that myriad others gained access to Patterson's software via that system, and that Patterson advertised and sold his product through that system. Though all this happened with a distinct paucity of tangible, physical evidence, there can be no doubt that Patterson purposefully transacted business in Ohio. *See Plus System, Inc. v. New England Network, Inc.*, 804 F.Supp. 111, 118–19 (D.Colo.1992) (finding personal jurisdiction over a nonresident computer network defendant because, *inter alia*, that defendant benefitted from the intangible computer services provided by the plaintiff's own computer network system); *cf. United States v. Thomas*, 74 F.3d 701, 706–07 (6th Cir.1996) (upholding a conviction under federal obscenity laws where the defendants transmitted computer-generated images across state lines, despite the defendants' argument that the images were intangible).

Moreover, this was a relationship intended to be ongoing in nature; it was not a "one-shot affair." . . . . Patterson sent software to CompuServe repeatedly for some three years, and the record indicates that he intended to continue marketing his software on CompuServe. . . . Patterson deliberately set in motion an ongoing marketing relationship with CompuServe, and he should have reasonably foreseen that doing so would have consequences in Ohio.

Admittedly, merely entering into a contract with CompuServe would not, without more, establish that Patterson had minimum contacts with Ohio. *Burger King Corp.*, 471 U.S. at 478. By the same token, Patterson's injection of his software product into the stream of commerce, without more, would be at best a dubious ground for jurisdiction. *Compare Asahi Metal Indus. Co. v. Superior Court*, 480 U.S. 102 (1987) (O'Connor, J.) (plurality op.) ("The placement of a product into the stream of commerce, without more, is not an act of the defendant purposefully directed toward the forum State.") *with id.* at 117 (Brennan, J., concurring in part) (rejecting the plurality's position on the stream of commerce theory). Because Patterson deliberately did both of those things, however, and because of the other factors that we discuss herein, we believe that ample contacts exist to support the assertion of jurisdiction in this case, and certainly an assertion of jurisdiction by the state where the computer network service in question is headquartered.

. . . Patterson frequently contacted Ohio to sell his computer software over CompuServe's Ohio-based system. Patterson repeatedly sent his "goods" to CompuServe in Ohio for their ultimate sale. CompuServe, in effect, acted as Patterson's distributor, albeit electronically and not physically.

Further, we must reject the district court's reliance on the *de minimis* amount of software sales which Patterson claims he enjoyed in Ohio. As this court recently stated, "It is the '*quality*' of [the] contacts," and not their number or status, that determines whether they amount to purposeful availment. *Reynolds*, 23 F.3d at 1119 (emphasis added) (quoting *LAK, Inc. v. Deer Creek Enters.*, 885 F.2d 1293, 1301 (6th Cir.1989). Patterson's contacts with CompuServe here were deliberate and repeated, even if they yielded little revenue from Ohio itself.

Moreover, we should not focus solely on the sales that Patterson made in Ohio, because that ignores the sales Patterson may have made through CompuServe to others elsewhere. Patterson sought to make those sales from Texas by way of CompuServe's system in Ohio, and the sales then involved the passage of funds through Ohio to Patterson in Texas. . . .

We also find instructive the Supreme Court case of *McGee v. International Life Insurance Co.*, 355 U.S. 220 (1957), which held that due process did not prohibit California from asserting jurisdiction over a Texas insurance company based upon its issuance of a single insurance contract in California and the receipt of premium payments mailed from California. The *McGee* Court reasoned that (1) the company had consciously sought the contract with the California insured, and (2) "the suit was based on a contract which had substantial connection with that State." *Id.* at 223.

Similarly, in the instant case, Patterson consciously reached out from Texas to Ohio to subscribe to CompuServe, and to use its service to market his computer software on the Internet. He entered into a contract which expressly stated that it would be governed by and construed in light of Ohio law. . . . As the *Burger King Corp.* Court noted, the purposeful direction of one's activities toward a state has always been significant in personal jurisdiction cases, particularly where individuals purposefully derive benefits from interstate activities. *Burger King Corp.*, 471 U.S. at 472–73. Moreover, the Court continued, it could be unfair to allow individuals who purposefully engage in interstate activities for profit to escape having to account in other states for the proximate consequences of those activities. *Id.* (citing *Kulko v. Superior Court*, 436 U.S. 84, 96 (1978)).

Finally, we note this court's own finding of purposeful availment based (in part) on analogous litigation threats in *American Greetings Corp. v. Cohn*, 839 F.2d 1164, 1170 (6th Cir.1988). The *American Greetings Corp.* case involved an Ohio corporation's suit, in Ohio, against a California shareholder who had threatened to file a lawsuit to invalidate an amendment to the company's articles of incorporation. *Id.* at 1165. . . . This court [found] purposeful availment because of the defendant's letters and telephone calls to Ohio, in which he had threatened suit and had sought money to release his claim. Thus, this court stated, the defendant himself had "originated and maintained the required contacts with Ohio." *Id.* at 1170.

In the instant case, the record demonstrates that Patterson not only purposefully availed himself of CompuServe's Ohio-based services to market his software, but that he also "originated and maintained" contacts with Ohio when he believed that CompuServe's competing product unlawfully infringed on his own software. Patterson repeatedly sent both electronic and regular mail messages to CompuServe about his claim, and he posted a message on one of CompuServe's electronic forums, which outlined his case against CompuServe for anyone who wished to read it. Moreover, the record shows that Patterson demanded at least $100,000 to settle the matter.

Thus, we believe that the facts which CompuServe has alleged, viewed in the light most favorable to CompuServe, support a finding that Patterson purposefully availed himself of the privilege of doing business in Ohio. He knowingly reached out to CompuServe's Ohio home, and he benefitted from CompuServe's handling of his software and the fees that it generated.

. . .

Finally, because of the unique nature of this case, we deem it important to note what we do not hold. We need not and do not hold that Patterson would be subject to suit in any state where his software was purchased or used; that is not the case before us. *See World–Wide Volkswagen*, 444 U.S. at 296 (rejecting the idea that a seller of chattels could "appoint the chattel his agent for service of process"). We also do not have before us an attempt by another party from a third state to sue Patterson in Ohio for, say, a "computer virus" caused by his software, and thus we need not address whether personal jurisdiction could be found on those facts. Finally, we need not and do not hold that CompuServe may, as the district court posited, sue any regular subscriber to its service for nonpayment in Ohio, even if the subscriber is a native Alaskan who has never left home. Each of those cases may well arise someday, but they are not before us now.

III. CONCLUSION

Because we believe that Patterson had sufficient contacts with Ohio to support the exercise of personal jurisdiction over him, we REVERSE the district court's dismissal and REMAND this case for further proceedings consistent with this opinion.

EXTENSIONS

1. *Entering into contracts as grounds for jurisdiction.* In most cases where the defendant entered into contracts with residents of the forum state through Internet communications, and the claims arose from those contracts, the court has held the due process requisites for personal jurisdiction to be satisfied. Contracts supporting jurisdiction may be for the sale of goods, *e.g. Washington v. www.DirtCheapCig.com, Inc.*, 260 F.Supp.2d 1048 (W.D.Wash.2003) (jurisdiction based on defendant's sales of cigarettes to forum residents via its website), or provision of services, *e.g. Alitalia–Linee Aeree Italiane S.p.A. v. Casinoalitalia.Com*, 128 F.Supp.2d 340 (E.D.Va.2001) (jurisdiction based on fact that five residents of forum state gambled via defendant's online casino). Domain name registrars are no exception to the rule that entering into contracts with forum residents can support jurisdiction. In *Bird v. Parsons*, 289 F.3d 865 (6th Cir.2002), the court held that plaintiff had made out a prima facie case of jurisdiction over a domain name registrar, based on plaintiff's allegation that the registrar had registered domain names for 4,666 residents of the forum state.

Some court have held that a defendant's sales to residents of the forum state were insufficient to support jurisdiction, where the defendant offered the items via an online auction. In *Winfield Collection, Ltd. v. McCauley*, 105 F.Supp.2d 746 (E.D.Mich.2000), plaintiff alleged that defendant infringed his copyrights on home-craft patterns by selling crafts she made using the patterns via eBay. Defendant made two sales to forum residents. The court reasoned that "the function of an auction is to permit the highest bidder to purchase the property offered for sale, and the choice of that highest bidder is therefore beyond the control of the seller." Since defendant did not choose to sell to forum residents—forum residents instead chose to buy from defendant—the sales did not demonstrate purposeful availment of the forum state. To the same effect is *Metcalf v. Lawson*, 802 A.2d 1221 (N.H.2002). Does offering goods for sale to the highest bidder via an auction site differ, in terms of purposeful targeting of the purchasers, from offering goods for sale at a fixed price?

2. *Manufactured contracts.* The existence of contracts with forum state residents is such a strong ground for jurisdiction that plaintiffs will go out of their way to manufacture a contract if none exists. In *Millennium Enterprises, Inc. v. Millennium Music, LP*, 33 F.Supp.2d 907 (D.Or.1999), the defendant was a South Carolina corporation that sold music CDs at retail stores in its home state and via its website. The plaintiff was an Oregon seller of music CDs, and brought suit in its home state, arguing for jurisdiction premised on defendant's

sale of a lone CD to an Oregon resident. The court's opinion relates that the purchase was made by an employee of an acquaintance of plaintiff's counsel, and therefore was presumably instigated by plaintiff's counsel. The court expressed dismay at plaintiff's counsel's "lack of candor," and disregarded the sale as a basis for jurisdiction. A similar attempt to manufacture jurisdiction by orchestrating a sale into the forum state is rejected in *Toys "R" Us, Inc. v. Step Two, S.A.*, 318 F.3d 446 (3d Cir.2003). But in *Rainy Day Books, Inc. v. Rainy Day Books & Café, L.L.C.*, 186 F.Supp.2d 1158 (D.Kan.2002), the court was untroubled by the fact that the plaintiff manufactured contacts with the forum state by inducing family and friends to make purchases via the defendant's website: "Plaintiff's activities in obtaining evidence that a Kansas resident could purchase books from Defendant's website do not constitute the manufacture of the contacts necessary for the Court to exercise personal jurisdiction. Proof of an actual book sale to a Kansas resident from Defendant's website merely supports Plaintiff's contention that Defendant's website is a commercial website accessible by Kansas residents."

3. *Is a single sale sufficient?* In *Ty, Inc. v. Baby Me, Inc.*, 64 U.S.P.Q.2d 1442 (N.D.Ill.2001), the court held that a two-person operation located in Hawaii was subject to jurisdiction in Illinois based on one sale, consisting of three Baby Me plush toys, via its website to a purchaser located in Illinois. But in *Carefirst of Maryland, Inc. v. Carefirst Pregnancy Centers, Inc.*, 334 F.3d 390 (4th Cir.2003), the court refused to base jurisdiction on defendant's single contract with a web hosting provider located in the forum state, characterizing the contact as "de minimis."

Is a single *purchase* from a seller located in the forum state sufficient to support jurisdiction over the purchaser? *See Machulsky v. Hall*, 210 F.Supp.2d 531 (D.N.J.2002) (holding a single purchase insufficient).

QUESTIONS FOR DISCUSSION

1. *Multiple factors.* In *CompuServe v. Patterson* the court did not base its decision on the existence of a contract alone, since "merely entering into a contract with CompuServe would not, without more, establish that Patterson had minimum contacts with Ohio." It found that jurisdiction was justified based on a combination of factors: Patterson (1) subscribed to CompuServe, (2) entered into the Shareware Registration Agreement, which stated that disputes would be governed by Ohio law, (3) repeatedly sent his software to CompuServe via online means, (4) advertised and made his software available for download on CompuServe's system, (5) received revenues from sales of the software via CompuServe, less a 15 percent fee, (6) threatened to sue CompuServe for trademark infringement and demanded $100,000 to settle his claims, and (7) made actual sales of his software through this arrangement, to people living in Ohio and elsewhere. Which, if any, of these factors was essential to the court's decision? How much guidance does the decision offer in resolving future cases?

2. *Location of CompuServe's servers.* Several of the factors that the court relied upon involve Patterson's use of CompuServe's proprietary online system, including the storage of his software on CompuServe's computers so that it could be downloaded by subscribers. Would it make any difference if CompuServe's computers were located not in Ohio, but in Indiana? In Tajikistan? Some courts have found the location of computer servers that enable online communications relevant to the jurisdictional analysis. *See* Part II(E), *infra*.

3. *Contract with plaintiff whose location is unknown.* Does defendant's entering into a contract with plaintiff support jurisdiction in the plaintiff's home forum even if the defendant is unaware of the plaintiff's location? This is a frequent scenario in Internet transactions, although courts rarely address the issue. If the contract involves purchase of a digital good or service that may be delivered electronically via the network, and may be paid for by credit card or an online payment mechanism, the seller need never learn the location of the buyer. Such digital items include subscriptions to e-zines, databases that are accessed online, provision of Internet access, online gambling, software that is downloaded, music in MP3 format, and digitized photographs. In such circumstances, can a seller be found to have purposely directed her conduct at the state where the buyer is located? Does a person enter into a contract with an unlocated party at peril of being subjected to jurisdiction wherever that party happens to reside?

D. DISTRIBUTION OF PUBLICATIONS ONLINE

Under the generally applicable law of personal jurisdiction, distribution of publications in the forum state can support an assertion of jurisdiction. In *Keeton v. Hustler Magazine, Inc.*, 465 U.S. 770 (1984), the Court held that defendant's sale of 10,000 to 15,000 copies of its magazine in the forum state each month "is sufficient to support an assertion of jurisdiction in a libel action based on the contents of the magazine." *Id.* at 773–74. The Court explained: "Such regular monthly sales of thousands of magazines cannot by any stretch of the imagination be characterized as random, isolated, or fortuitous." *Id.* at 774.

What are the applicable criteria when the basis for jurisdiction is the defendant's distribution of electronic publications in the forum state? One approach is illustrated in *Scherr v. Abrahams*, 1998 WL 299678 (N.D.Ill.1998). The plaintiff brought an action alleging various business interference torts, based on defendant's distribution of a humor and satire publication called the Annals of Improbable Research. The hard-copy version of the publication had fewer than 60 subscribers in the forum state, as well as a smaller number of newsstand sales. The court quoted *Keeton v. Hustler, supra,* for the proposition that jurisdiction is proper " 'whenever a substantial number of copies are regularly sold and distributed' " in the forum state. Comparing the 60 to 120 (hard) copies that defendant circulated in the forum state with the 10,000 to 15,000 circulated in *Keeton* (and the 600,000 circulated in *Calder v. Jones*, 465 U.S. 783 (1984)), the court concluded that defendant's circulation was "insubstantial" and therefore did not support jurisdiction.

The court then went on to consider the *online* circulation of the magazine as an independent basis for jurisdiction. According to the court, the defendant stated that the online version of the magazine was sent, free of charge, to about 20,000 people who had placed their e-mail addresses on a mailing list, and the mailing list was accessed via the defendant's website. Perceiving the involvement of a website, the court shifted from the *Keeton* criterion of "substantiality" of the circulation in the forum state to the *Zippo* criterion of the "level of interactivity and commercial nature of the exchange of information that occurs on the Web site." It rejected defendant's characterization of the site as "passive," since the fact that visitors to the site were able to subscribe to the mailing list meant that the site was "one in which the user can exchange information with the host computer." But it found that the level of interactivity presented by the website was "rather low: the only exchange is the listing of a person's e-mail address for an electronic copy of the" magazine; and it found that the commercial nature of the exchange of information was low, since "[n]o money is exchanged," and the only commercial content of the magazine was advertisements for the hard-copy version of the magazine and other products that defendant offered for sale. The court therefore concluded that the online circulation of the magazine did not support jurisdiction.

Naxos Resources (U.S.A.) Ltd. v. Southam Inc., 1996 WL 662451 (C.D.Cal.1996), arose in a different factual context. The plaintiff claimed that it had been defamed in an article that defendants published, and premised jurisdiction on the fact that the article was made available via an online information provider. The court found that the "article was disseminated on LEXIS, which is available in California [the forum state] . . . . Thus, defendants did knowingly disseminate the allegedly tortious material in California, and thus 'purposefully availed' themselves of the privileges of conducting activities there." The court concluded, however, that it did not have jurisdiction over the defendants, since plaintiff's claim did not "arise from" the forum-related activities. The decision seems to indicate that one who provides written material to an online information provider has thereby met the "purposeful availment" element of the due process jurisdictional test in any place where the material may be downloaded.

In *Toys "R" Us, Inc. v. Step Two, S.A.*, 318 F.3d 446 (3d Cir.2003), the court held that sending an electronic newsletter to residents of the forum state does not support jurisdiction unless it demonstrates purposeful availment of the forum. This suggests that the operator of a website who allows visitors to subscribe to an electronic publication by submitting an e-mail address does not thereby become subject to jurisdiction wherever those subscribers may be located.

QUESTIONS FOR DISCUSSION

1. *Applying* Zippo. Is the *Zippo* analysis appropriate on the facts of *Scherr v. Abrahams*? Was jurisdiction premised on the circulation of the magazine, or on defendant's use of its website as a means of obtaining subscribers to the magazine? If defendant had advertised the availability of the online magazine through a medium other than its website, how would the jurisdictional issue be analyzed? If the website had offered additional opportunities for users to "exchange information with the host computer," so that the level of interactivity was rather high, should the jurisdictional analysis have come out differently?

2. Keeton *analysis.* How would the *Keeton* analysis apply to the situation in *Naxos Resources v. Southam*? Is it sufficient that the defendant knows that by virtue of its availability on LEXIS the article *may* have a substantial circulation in California? Would the plaintiff be required to introduce evidence of how many California residents actually accessed the publication via LEXIS? Does it make a difference that the article is made available in the forum state not directly by the defendant, but by a third-party distributor? Is providing a publication to an online service like LEXIS comparable to injecting a manufactured item into the stream of commerce? Consider the applicability of *World–Wide Volkswagen Corp. v. Woodson*, 444 U.S. 286, 297–98 (1980) ("The forum State does not exceed its powers under the Due Process Clause if it asserts personal jurisdiction over a corporation that delivers its products into the stream of commerce with the expectation that they will be purchased by consumers in the forum State."). Consider also the contending opinions in *Asahi Metal Industry Co., Ltd. v. Superior Court*, 480 U.S. 102, 112 (1987) ("The placement of a product into the stream of commerce, without more, is not an act of the defendant purposefully directed toward the forum State.") (opinion of O'Connor, J.); *id.* at 117 (agreeing with the view of "most courts and commentators" that "jurisdiction premised on the placement of a product into the stream of commerce is consistent with the Due Process Clause [without any need for] a showing of additional conduct") (opinion of Brennan, J.).

E. USE OF COMPUTER EQUIPMENT LOCATED IN THE FORUM STATE

Communication via computer networks almost inevitably involves the accessing of computer equipment that is located at some distance from the person initiating the communication. This may come about in several ways: (1) When you access a website, you cause the computer hosting the website to transmit packets of information to your own computer. (2) Information that is transmitted via the network, whether consisting of the contents of a Web page, an e-mail message, or any other data, generally is relayed through one or more intermediary computers on its way from sender to recipient. (3) Accessing information located in a remote database causes activity by the computer on which the database is stored. (4) Accessing the Internet via a dial-up connection results in activity by the service provider's computers. (5) Posting a message to, or receiving a message from, a computer bulletin board system causes activity on the part of the computer on which the BBS is hosted. (6) Communication via a proprietary online service may result in activity by the service's remotely located computers.

May a person's use of a computer network that results in activity on the part of a remote piece of computer equipment constitute contacts with the state in which that equipment is located, sufficient to satisfy the due process requirements for assertion of personal jurisdiction?

1. Location of a Web Server, or Location of the Server's Owner

Several courts have considered whether a court may assert jurisdiction based on the defendant's use of a service provider located in the forum state to host its website. The cases do not always clearly distinguish between the location of the computer equipment on which the files constituting a website are stored, and the location of the company (state of incorporation? principal place of business?) that owns the equipment.

In *Jewish Defense Organization, Inc. v. Superior Court*, 85 Cal.Rptr.2d 611 (Cal.Ct.App.1999), plaintiff brought an action for defamation in a California court. Defendants' only relevant contacts with California consisted of contracting with Internet service providers, "located in California," to host a website which they maintained from their residence in New York. The court concluded "that defendants' conduct of contracting, via computer, with Internet service providers, which may be California corporations or which may maintain offices or databases in California, is insufficient to constitute 'purposeful availment.'" But in *3DO Co. v. Poptop Software Inc.*, 49 U.S.P.Q.2d 1469, 1472 (N.D.Cal.1998), the court found it relevant that "Defendants use a San Francisco-based company as a server to operate a website that distributes allegedly infringing copies of [software]."

In *Carefirst of Maryland, Inc. v. Carefirst Pregnancy Centers, Inc.*, 334 F.3d 390 (4th Cir.2003), the court held that use of a web-hosting provider headquartered in the forum state is not a sufficient ground for asserting jurisdiction: "It is unreasonable to expect that, merely by utilizing servers owned by a Maryland-based company, [defendant] should have foreseen that it could be haled into a Maryland court and held to account for the contents of its website." The court observed that the hosting provider's servers were not located in

Maryland, but in Massachusetts.

2. Location of a Computer Holding a Database

In *Pres-Kap, Inc. v. System One, Direct Access, Inc.*, 636 So.2d 1351 (Fla.Dist.Ct.App. 1994), plaintiff sued a New York corporation for breach of contract. Under the contract in question, plaintiff provided defendant with computer terminals and access to a computer database that was held on a computer located in Florida. Defendant's only connections with Florida were that it made rental payments under the contract to plaintiff's Florida billing office, and it accessed data from plaintiff's computer located in Florida. The court held that these contacts do not amount to sufficient contacts with Florida to support jurisdiction. It explained:

> Indeed, a contrary decision would, we think, have far-reaching implications for business and professional people who use "on-line" computer services for which payments are made to out-of-state companies where the database is located. Across the nation, in every state, customers of "on-line" computer information networks have contractual arrangements with out-of-state supplier companies, putting such customers in a situation similar, if not identical, to the defendant in the instant case. Lawyers, journalists, teachers, physicians, courts, universities, and business people throughout the country daily conduct various types of computer-assisted research over telephone lines linked to supplier databases located in other states.[2] Based on the trial court's decision below, users of such "on-line" services could be haled into court in the state in which supplier's billing office and database happen to be located, even if such users, as here, are solicited, engaged, and serviced entirely instate by the supplier's local representatives. Such a result, in our view, is wildly beyond the reasonable expectations of such computer-information users, and, accordingly, the result offends traditional notions of fair play and substantial justice.

F. COMBINING OFFLINE AND ONLINE CONTACTS

A number of cases have held that the due process standard may be satisfied by a combination of online activities and other contacts with the forum state. In some of these cases, the court suggests that it would not have been able to assert jurisdiction but for the defendant's online activities. For example, in *CompuServe, Inc. v. Patterson*, 89 F.3d 1257, 1265 (6th Cir.1996), excerpted in Part II(C), *supra*, the court noted that neither Patterson's contract with CompuServe, nor his placing software into the stream of commerce by making it available online, would by itself have been sufficient to support jurisdiction, but the two actions in combination (together with other contacts) satisfied the due process requirement. In *Neogen Corp. v. Neo Gen Screening, Inc.*, 282 F.3d 883 (6th Cir.2002), the court found it "a close question" whether defendant's website alone supported jurisdiction, but held that jurisdiction was clearly established by a combination of the website with defendant's other forum contacts.

In *Toys "R" Us, Inc. v. Step Two, S.A.*, 318 F.3d 446, 456 (3d Cir.2003), the court held that the district court erred by not allowing jurisdictional discovery concerning non-Internet

---

[2] For example, Westlaw is based in St. Paul, Minnesota, and all bills are generated and paid in St. Paul. . . . Lexis is based in Dayton, Ohio, and all bills for use of the Lexis System are generated in and paid in Dayton. . . .

contacts with the forum state. The district court had focused exclusively on the defendant's website as the source of contacts with the forum state, finding other contacts irrelevant. The appellate court explained: "The court's unwavering focus on the web site precluded consideration of other Internet and non-Internet contacts—indicated in various parts of the record—which, if explored, might provide the 'something more' needed to bring [defendant] within our jurisdiction."

As Internet commerce becomes more widespread, it may be that this mixed mode of jurisdictional analysis will become the dominant one.

G. JURISDICTION OVER A FOREIGN DEFENDANT BASED ON AGGREGATION OF NATIONAL CONTACTS—RULE 4(K)(2)

As we have seen, a court's assertion of jurisdiction over a defendant that is not a resident of the forum state satisfies the requirements of due process if the defendant has the requisite minimum contacts with the forum state. For defendants located outside the United States, another basis for acquiring jurisdiction is available. Rule 4(k)(2) of the Federal Rules of Civil Procedure provides:

> (k) Territorial Limits of Effective Service.
>
> . . .
>
> (2) If the exercise of jurisdiction is consistent with the Constitution and laws of the United States, serving a summons or filing a waiver of service is also effective, with respect to claims arising under federal law, to establish personal jurisdiction over the person of any defendant who is not subject to the jurisdiction of the courts of general jurisdiction of any state.

Under this provision, a federal court may, with respect to a federal claim, assert jurisdiction over a foreign defendant that lacks sufficient contacts with any one state to satisfy due process requirements if the defendant's contacts with the United States *as a whole* amount to "minimum contacts."

In *Graduate Management Admission Council v. Raju*, 241 F.Supp.2d 589 (E.D.Va.2003), the court, after determining that the foreign defendant lacked "minimum contacts" with Virginia, turned to Rule 4(k)(2). To determine whether the defendant, Raju, had sufficient contacts with the United States, the court applied the Fourth Circuit's reformulation of the *Zippo* test,[3] substituting "United States" where that formulation refers to the forum state. Thus, jurisdiction would be proper if Raju "'directed his electronic activity' into the United States, with the intent of engaging in business 'within the United States,' as required by the first and second elements of the *ALS* test." *Id.* at 597–98. The electronic activity in question consisted of a website, through which Raju offered practice questions for the Graduate Management Admission Test, allegedly infringing plaintiff's copyrights and trademark. The court evaluated Raju's conduct as follows:

> The record clearly indicates that Raju directed his activity at the United States market and specifically targeted United States customers. The intended market for business conducted through a website can be determined by considering the apparent focus of the website as a whole. *See Young v. New Haven Ad-*

---

[3] That reformulation is presented in *ALS Scan, Inc. v. Digital Service Consultants, Inc.*, 293 F.3d 707 (4th Cir.2002), discussed in Part II(A)(2), *supra*.

vocate, 315 F.3d 256, 263–64 (4th Cir.2002) (Examining the "general thrust and content" of the newspapers' websites, including the local focus of the stories, local advertisements and classifieds, local weather and traffic information, and links to local institutions, in determining that "the overall content of both websites is decidedly local."). The relevant question is whether the website is "designed to attract or serve a [United States] audience." *Id.*

There is ample evidence that Raju targeted the United States market. First, and most significantly, the GMATplus site provides specific ordering information for United States customers. The ordering information page directs customers who "live in the United States or Canada" to contact Western Union or MoneyGram, and provides the toll free numbers for use by those customers. Other customers are directed simply to "contact [their] local MoneyGram office" or use a hyperlink to MoneyGram to find the nearest local office. No other countries apart from the United States and Canada are mentioned by name on the ordering information page. Thus, ordering information for customers in the United States (and Canada) is provided first and with more specificity than for customers from other countries. Second, the ordering information page informs customers that materials will "reach most parts of the world (including the US) within 3–5 working days." Third, the prices for the products are listed in dollars, presumably United States dollars. . . . Finally, Raju confirmed his apparent intent to serve United States customers by shipping his materials to the two Virginia residents mentioned in the record.

In sum, it is quite clear upon review of the GMATplus website and the record as a whole that while Raju may have aimed his website at the entire, worldwide market of GMAT test takers, he specifically directed his electronic activity at the United States market and did in fact ship materials in the United States.

Id. at 598. *See also Quokka Sports, Inc. v. Cup Int'l Ltd.*, 99 F.Supp.2d 1105 (N.D.Cal.1999) (sufficient contacts with the United States where (1) defendants "purposefully went to the United States registrar, NSI, to get a '.com' " domain name, rather than staying at home and registering a .nz domain; (2) the website featured banner advertisements from ten U.S. companies; some of the ads, when clicked, displayed a page designed for U.S. consumers; (3) defendants quoted advertising rates to prospective advertisers in U.S. dollars; (4) the website offered to sell travel packages that were priced in U.S. dollars; and (5) the website offered books for sale, in affiliation with Amazon.com, a U.S. company).

III. APPLICATION OF STATE LONG-ARM STATUTES TO WEBSITES

As noted above, in Part I, some state long-arm statutes are interpreted to allow jurisdiction on any basis consistent with due process, while other statutes are more restrictive than due process requires. Statutes in the latter category may prescribe a variety of grounds for jurisdiction. The types of provisions that are most likely to be called into play when jurisdiction is based on a website are those which provide for jurisdiction on claims arising from (1) transaction of business within the state, (2) causing tortious injury within the state, by conduct either within or outside the state, and (3) soliciting business within the state.

A. TRANSACTION OF BUSINESS WITHIN THE STATE

Under what circumstances does operation of a website, by someone located outside the forum state, constitute transaction of business within the forum state?

It is clear that merely operating a website that is accessible in the forum state does not constitute transaction of business in the state. In *Patriot Systems, Inc. v. C–Cubed Corp.*, 21 F.Supp.2d 1318 (D.Utah 1998), the court arrived at this conclusion through application of the *Zippo* analysis. It found that defendant's website was a "passive" one, and therefore did not amount to transaction of business in the state. The reliance on *Zippo*, although out of context here since *Zippo* concerned the requirements for due process, leads to a reasonable result. In *Hearst Corp. v. Goldberger*, 1997 WL 97097 (S.D.N.Y.1997), the court analogized the defendant's website to "an advertisement in a national magazine," and held that such advertisements are not sufficient to provide personal jurisdiction under the New York long-arm provision based on transaction of business in the state. And in *Knight-McConnell v. Cummins*, 2005 WL 1398590 (S.D.N.Y.2005), the court held that posting of allegedly defamatory material on a website does not constitute transaction of business in the state where the plaintiff is located.

Conversely, it should be clear that making sales to residents of the forum state via defendant's website *does* constitute transaction of business in the state. Thus, in *Novak v. Overture Services, Inc.*, 309 F.Supp.2d 446 (E.D.N.Y.2004), the court held that defendant transacted business in New York by virtue of a website that featured a product catalogue, and through which the defendant derived $6,000 per year in sales to forum residents. But in *Alternate Energy Corp. v. Redstone*, 328 F.Supp.2d 1379 (S.D.Fla.2004), the court held that defendant's sale of access to a subscribers-only section of a website did not constitute the transaction of business in the forum state, where only an "unknown, relatively small number" of forum residents were subscribers. Can this holding be understood as application of a de minimis exception?

Suppose the defendant offers to sell plaintiff a domain name that consists of or contains plaintiff's trademark. Does this amount to transaction of business in the state where plaintiff resides? In *PurCo Fleet Services, Inc. v. Towers*, 38 F.Supp.2d 1320 (D.Utah 1999), an individual set up a Utah corporation, plaintiff PurCo Fleet Services, Inc., in competition with his former employer, defendant Fleet Financial Corporation, a Florida corporation. Defendant, for the avowed purpose of "injur[ing] PurCo," registered the domain name "purco.com," and set it up to redirect visitors to defendant's own website. Defendant offered "to bargain away whatever rights it has in the domain name 'purco.com' and variations thereof in exchange for part of a cash settlement from PurCo involving this and other pending litigation." The court found this case similar to *Panavision Int'l, L.P. v. Toeppen*, 141 F.3d 1316 (9th Cir.1998), excerpted in Part II(C), *supra*, since, as in *Panavision*, plaintiff alleged that defendants registered purco.com "to extort money" from plaintiff. The court held that by offering to sell the domain name to plaintiff, and by responding to an inquiry from an employee of plaintiff who reached defendant through the purco.com domain, defendant used its website to transact business in Utah.

Compare *PurCo* with *K.C.P.L., Inc. v. Nash*, 49 U.S.P.Q.2d 1584 (S.D.N.Y.1998). Plaintiff, a corporation located in New York, was the owner of a trademark on "Reaction," and defendant had registered the domain "reaction.com". Defendant had set up a website at that domain, but had not yet posted any content on it, and the URL merely pointed to a generic "Under Construction" web page. Defendant claimed to be developing a business that would be operated through a website at reaction.com. When plaintiff learned that defendant had registered reaction.com, it offered to purchase the domain name. Defendant asked $8,000 for the rights, but plaintiff rejected his offer, and sent defendant a cease-and-desist letter instead. Plaintiff later offered $1,500 for the domain, which defendant rejected. Plaintiff then filed suit alleging trademark infringement and related claims. The court held that defendant's offer to sell the domain name to plaintiff did not constitute transaction of business in New York. Its reasoning appears to be based on defendant's intent in registering the domain name. Thus, the court rejected plaintiff's characterization of defendant "as a 'cyber pirate' [and] its labeling of his conduct as 'extortion,' " viewing defendant instead as an honest businessman who was having a hard time getting his startup off the ground. The court also declined to rely on *Panavision v. Toeppen, supra*, since "the facts alleged do not show [defendant] to be a 'cyber pirate' " like the defendant in *Panavision*. To the same effect is *Radio Computing Services, Inc. v. Roland Computing Services*, 2003 WL 1107443 (S.D.N.Y.2003).

EXTENSIONS

1. *Transmitting music files.* Does transmitting music files to the forum state via the Internet constitute transaction of business in the forum state? In *Freeplay Music, Inc. v. Cox Radio, Inc.*, 2005 WL 1500896 (S.D.N.Y.2005), the court held that an out-of-state defendant does not transact business in New York by streaming music via its website. Compare *Arista Records, Inc. v. Sakfield Holding Co. S.L.*, 314 F.Supp.2d 27 (D.D.C.2004), holding that the downloading of a music file from defendant's website does constitute transaction of business in the place where the person downloading the file is located.

2. *Registering a domain name.* Does a party transact business in a state merely by registering a domain name with a domain name registrar located in that state? In *America Online, Inc. v. Huang*, 106 F.Supp.2d 848, 855 (E.D.Va.2000), the court observed that "the act of registering a domain name over the Internet, the payment of the small, annual maintenance fee, and [the registrar's] registration, seem so modest in scope and nature that it is difficult to view it as 'transacting business' in the registrar's state of residence."

3. *E-mail communications.* Can engaging in e-mail communications with forum residents constitute transaction of business in the forum? In *Media3 Technologies, LLC v. Mail Abuse Prevention System, LLC*, 2001 WL 92389 (D.Mass.2001), the court found transaction of business by virtue of "at least six email and telephone communications" between plaintiff and defendant.

B. Causing Tortious Injury Within the State, by Conduct Either Within or Outside the State

Most long-arm statutes provide for jurisdiction over a defendant who has caused tortious injury within the state. These provisions come in two varieties: those which require conduct within the state, and those which allow jurisdiction to be based on conduct occurring outside the state. The latter usually specify some additional conduct tying the defendant more closely to the forum state.

1. Tortious Conduct in the State

Bensusan Restaurant Corp. v. King
126 F.3d 25 (2d Cir.1997).

■ VAN GRAAFEILAND, CIRCUIT JUDGE:

Bensusan Restaurant Corporation, located in New York City, appeals from a judgment of the United States District Court for the Southern District of New York (Stein, J.) dismissing its complaint against Richard B. King, a Missouri resident, pursuant to Fed.R.Civ.P. 12(b)(2) for lack of personal jurisdiction. We affirm.

Columbia, Missouri is a small to medium size city far distant both physically and substantively from Manhattan. It is principally a white-collar community, hosting among other institutions Stephens College, Columbia College and the University of Missouri. It would appear to be an ideal location for a small cabaret featuring live entertainment, and King, a Columbia resident, undoubtedly found this to be so. Since 1980, he has operated such a club under the name "The Blue Note" at 17 North Ninth Street in Columbia.

Plaintiff alleges in its complaint that it is "the creator of an enormously successful jazz club in New York City called 'The Blue Note,' " which name "was registered as a federal trademark for cabaret services on May 14, 1985." Around 1993, a Bensusan representative wrote to King demanding that he cease and desist from calling his club The Blue Note. King's attorney informed the writer that Bensusan had no legal right to make the demand.

Nothing further was heard from Bensusan until April 1996, when King, at the suggestion of a local web site design company, ThoughtPort Authority, Inc., permitted that company to create a web site or cyberspot on the internet for King's cabaret. This work was done in Missouri. Bensusan then brought the instant action in the Southern District of New York, alleging violations of §§ 32(1) and 43(a) of the Lanham Act, 15 U.S.C. §§ 1114(1) and 1125(a), and § 3(c) of the Federal Trademark Dilution Act of 1995, 15 U.S.C. § 1125(c), as well as common law unfair competition.

In addition to seeking trebled compensatory damages, punitive damages, costs and attorney's fees, Bensusan requests that King be enjoined from:

> using the mark "The Blue Note", or any other indicia of the Blue Note in any manner likely to cause confusion, or to cause mistake, or to deceive, or from otherwise representing to the public in any way that [King's club] is in any way sponsored, endorsed, approved, or authorized by, or affiliated or connected with, Plaintiff or its CABARET, by means of using any name, trademark, or service mark of Plaintiff or any other names whatsoever, including but not limited to removal of Defendant's web site . . . .

The web site describes King's establishment as "Mid–Missouri's finest live entertainment venue, . . . [l]ocated in beautiful Columbia, Missouri," and it contains monthly calendars of future events and the Missouri telephone number of King's box office. Initially, it contained the following text:

> The Blue Note's CyberSpot should not be confused with one of the world's finest jazz club Blue Note, located in the heart of New York's Greenwich Village. If you should ever find yourself in the big apple give them a visit.

This text was followed by a hyperlink that could be used to connect a reader's computer to a web site maintained by Bensusan. When Bensusan objected to the above-quoted language, King reworded the disclaimer and removed the hyperlink, substituting the following disclaimer that continues in use:

> The Blue Note, Columbia, Missouri should not be confused in any way, shape, or form with Blue Note Records or the jazz club, Blue Note, located in New York. The CyberSpot is created to provide information for Columbia, Missouri area individuals only, any other assumptions are purely coincidental.

The district court dismissed the complaint in a scholarly opinion that was published in 937 F.Supp. 295 (1996). Although we realize that attempting to apply established trademark law in the fast-developing world of the internet is somewhat like trying to board a moving bus, we believe that well-established doctrines of personal jurisdiction law support the result reached by the district court.

. . .

The New York law dealing with personal jurisdiction based upon tortious acts of a non-domiciliary who does not transact business in New York is contained in sub-paragraphs (a)(2) and (a)(3) of CPLR § 302, and Bensusan claims jurisdiction with some degree of inconsistency under both sub-paragraphs. Because King does not transact business in New York State, Bensusan makes no claim under § 302(a)(1). The legislative intent behind the enactment of sub-paragraphs (a)(2) and (a)(3) best can be gleaned by reviewing their disparate backgrounds. Sub-paragraph (a)(2), enacted in 1962, provides in pertinent part that a New York court may exercise personal jurisdiction over a non-domiciliary who "in person or though an agent" commits a tortious act within the state. The New York Court of Appeals has construed this provision in several cases. In *Feathers v. McLucas*, 209 N.E.2d 68 (N.Y. 1965), the Court held that the language "commits a tortious act *within* the state," as contained in sub-paragraph (a)(2), is "plain and precise" and confers personal jurisdiction over non-residents *"when they commit acts within the state."* *Id.* at 77 (internal quotation marks omitted). *Feathers* adopted the view that CPLR § 302(a)(2) reaches only tortious acts performed by a defendant who was physically present in New York when he performed the wrongful act. The official Practice Commentary to CPLR § 302 explains that "if a New Jersey domiciliary were to lob a bazooka shell across the Hudson River at Grant's tomb, *Feathers* would appear to bar the New York courts from asserting personal jurisdiction over the New Jersey domiciliary in an action by an injured New York plaintiff." C302:17. The comment goes on to conclude that:

> As construed by the *Feathers* decision, jurisdiction cannot be asserted over a nonresident under this provision unless the nonresident commits an act in this state. This is tantamount to a requirement that the defendant or his agent be physically present in New York. . . . In short, the

failure to perform a duty in New York is not a tortious act in this state, under the cases, unless the defendant or his agent enters the state.

. . .

[W]e recognize that the interpretation of sub-paragraph (a)(2) in the line of cases above cited has not been adopted by every district judge in the Second Circuit. However, the judges who differ are in the minority. In the absence of some indication by the New York Court of Appeals that its decision[] in *Feathers* . . . no longer represent[s] the law of New York, we believe it would be impolitic for this Court to hold otherwise. Applying these principles, we conclude that Bensusan has failed to allege that King or his agents committed a tortious act in New York as required for exercise of personal jurisdiction under CPLR § 302(a)(2). The acts giving rise to Bensusan's lawsuit—including the authorization and creation of King's web site, the use of the words "Blue Note" and the Blue Note logo on the site, and the creation of a hyperlink to Bensusan's web site—were performed by persons physically present in Missouri and not in New York. Even if Bensusan suffered injury in New York, that does not establish a tortious act in the state of New York within the meaning of § 302(a)(2). . . .

Bensusan's claims under sub-paragraph (a)(3) can be quickly disposed of. Sub-paragraph (a)(2) left a substantial gap in New York's possible exercise of jurisdiction over non-residents because it did not cover the tort of a non-resident that took place outside of New York but caused injury inside the state. Accordingly, in 1966 the New York Legislature enacted sub-paragraph (a)(3), which provides in pertinent part that New York courts may exercise jurisdiction over a non-domiciliary who commits a tortious act without the state, causing injury to person or property within the state. However, once again the Legislature limited its exercise of jurisdictional largess. Insofar as is pertinent herein it restricted the exercise of jurisdiction under sub-paragraph (a)(3) to persons who expect or should reasonably expect the tortious act to have consequences in the state and in addition derive substantial revenue from interstate commerce. To satisfy the latter requirement, Bensusan relies on the arguments that King participated in interstate commerce by hiring bands of national stature and received revenue from customers—students of the University of Missouri—who, while residing in Missouri, were domiciliaries of other states. These alleged facts were not sufficient to establish that substantial revenues were derived from interstate commerce, a requirement that "is intended to exclude non-domiciliaries whose business operations are of a local character." . . . King's "Blue Note" cafe was unquestionably a local operation.

For all the reasons above stated, we affirm the judgment of the district court.

EXTENSIONS

1. *An unusually restrictive provision.* New York's Civil Practice Law and Rules § 302(a)(2), which allows jurisdiction over one who "commits a tortious act within the state," is unusual in that it has been interpreted to require the defendant's physical presence within the state. Given that interpretation, the court of appeals had little difficulty disposing of this ground of jurisdiction, since there was no claim that the defendant committed any act while physically present in New York. To the same effect is *K.C.P.L., Inc. v. Nash*, 49 U.S.P.Q.2d 1584 (S.D.N.Y.1998) (website does not satisfy requirement of physical presence in New York).

The district court arrived at the same result through a more circuitous route. It expansively characterized the issue as "whether the creation of a Web site, which exists either in Missouri or in cyberspace—i.e., anywhere the Internet exists—with a telephone number to order the allegedly infringing product, is an offer to sell the product in New York." *Bensusan Restaurant Corp. v. King*, 937 F.Supp. 295, 299 (S.D.N.Y.1996), *aff'd*, 126 F.3d 25 (2d Cir.1997). After noting the steps that a New York resident would have to take in order to purchase tickets to defendant's club in Missouri, the court concluded that any trademark infringement "would have occurred in Missouri, not New York." *Id.*

2. *Other long-arm statutes.* Other states' long-arm provisions allowing jurisdiction based on commission of a tort within the state have not been interpreted so restrictively as New York's, giving rise to issues concerning where a tort committed through online communication is deemed to be located.

a. In *Digital Equipment Corp. v. AltaVista Technology, Inc.*, 960 F.Supp. 456 (D.Mass.1997), the court drew an analogy between trademark infringement that occurs on a website and infringement that arrives in the state via other means of communication. After citing cases holding that misrepresentations made to forum residents via telex, telephone, and mail meet the long-arm statute's requirement of tortious conduct "in" the state, the court said: "Using the Internet under the circumstances of this case is as much knowingly 'sending' into Massachusetts the allegedly infringing and therefore tortious uses of Digital's trademark as is a telex, mail, or telephonic transmission." *Id.* at 466. Likewise, in *Maritz, Inc. v. Cybergold, Inc.*, 947 F.Supp. 1328 (E.D.Mo.1996), the infringing material on defendant's website was found to be a tortious act "in" the forum state, since it was an extraterritorial act that had an effect (namely, injury of the plaintiff) in the state.

b. In *Playboy Enterprises, Inc. v. AsiaFocus Int'l Inc.*, 1998 WL 724000 (E.D.Va.1998), the court held that "each act of access to the defendants' Internet sites by a Virginia computer user completed a 'tortious injury by an act . . . in this Commonwealth,' " quoting the applicable provision of the Virginia long-arm statute. In the court's view, the infringement was located in the state where a computer user made use of the infringing product by means of online access. Similarly, in *E-Data Corp. v. Micropatent Corp.*, 989 F.Supp. 173 (D.Conn.1997), the court assumed that the location of the tortious conduct (patent infringement) would be in the state where a computer user made use of the infringing product by means of online access.

If a long-arm provision requiring a tortious act "in" the state is interpreted to be met by a defendant's operation of a website while outside the state, does this render meaningless the more restrictive provisions allowing jurisdiction based on tortious injury arising from an act outside the state?

2. Tortious Conduct Outside the State, Plus Additional Connection to the Forum

Statutes allowing jurisdiction based on conduct that occurs outside the state and causes tortious injury within the state generally require some additional connection between the defendant and the state. The most common such additional requirements are (1) that the defendant "regularly does or solicits business in the state," and (2) that the defendant engages in some other "persistent course of conduct in the state."

Thus, in *Bird v. Parsons*, 289 F.3d 865 (6th Cir.2002), the court held it had jurisdiction over an out-of-state domain name registrar that allegedly infringed the plaintiff's trademark rights. It found that the injury resulting from trademark infringement is tortious and "occurs both in places where the plaintiff does business and in the state where its primary office is located," and therefore the alleged infringement satisfied the requirement of in-state harm. The fact that the defendant had registered domain names for thousands of forum residents demonstrated that it regularly conducted business in the state. Similarly, in *Venture Tape Corp. v. McGills Glass Warehouse*, 292 F.Supp.2d 230 (D.Mass.2003), where the plaintiff alleged trademark infringement based on the defendant's use of its marks in invisible HTML code on its website, the court found the requisite harm within the forum state since "in trademark infringement cases, the injury is said to have occurred where the trademark owner is located." Compare *Freeplay Music, Inc. v. Cox Radio, Inc.*, 2005 WL 1500896 (S.D.N.Y.2005), which held that injury resulting from copyright infringement is located where the infringing use occurs, and therefore allegedly infringing streaming of music via a website does not cause harm in the forum state.

A few early decisions held that the mere operation of a website constitutes regular solicitation of business, or a persistent course of conduct, in any state from which the site may be accessed. In *TELCO Communications v. An Apple A Day*, 977 F.Supp. 404 (E.D.Va. 1997), the court held that by issuing allegedly defamatory press releases via the Internet[4] the defendant met the "regularly soliciting business" provision of the long-arm statute: "Because they conducted their advertising and soliciting over the Internet, which could be accessed by a Virginia resident 24 hours a day, the Defendants did so regularly for purposes of the long-arm statute." *Id.* at 407. The court in *Digital Equipment Corp. v. AltaVista Technology, Inc.*, 960 F.Supp. 456, 467 (D.Mass.1997), reached the same result, likewise noting that defendant's website was "generally accessible twenty-four hours a day and seven days a week to all Massachusetts residents who can access the Web."

But in *Auto Channel, Inc. v. Speedvision Network, LLC*, 995 F.Supp. 761, 765 (W.D. Ky.1997), the court held that a passive website did not satisfy the "solicitation of business" requirement: "[T]he mere fact that Internet users in Kentucky can view advertisements in web pages provided by [defendants] falls far short of demonstrating that Defendants advertise in Kentucky."

C. REGULARLY SOLICITING BUSINESS IN THE STATE

As discussed above, solicitation of business may supply the "plus" factor required by provisions that base jurisdiction on a tortious act committed outside the state. But some long-arm statutes make the regular (or repeated) solicitation of business in the forum state an independent ground for jurisdiction.

An early application of such a provision to website contacts occurred in *Inset Systems, Inc. v. Instruction Set, Inc.*, 937 F.Supp. 161 (D.Conn.1996), a trademark infringement case in which jurisdiction was premised on defendant's operation of a website using the allegedly infringing mark. The court found that the website constituted repeated solicitation of

---

[4] The court's opinion is not clear on this point, but it appears that the press releases were posted on a third party's website.

business in Connecticut, reasoning that the defendant

> has been continuously advertising over the Internet, which includes at least 10,000 access sites in Connecticut. Further, unlike hard-copy advertisements . . . , which are often quickly disposed of and reach a limited number of potential consumers, Internet advertisements are in electronic printed form so that they can be accessed again and again by many more potential consumers.

Id. at 164. The court made no reference to whether Connecticut residents actually did access the site, or whether the site offered any interactive features. The same is true in *Black & Decker (U.S.) Inc. v. Pro–Tech Power Inc.*, 26 F.Supp.2d 834 (E.D.Va.1998), which arrived at the same conclusion.

In other cases—two of them in the same district court that decided *Inset*, though before different judges—the lack of actual access by forum residents was found to be dispositive. The court in *E-Data Corp. v. Micropatent Corp.*, 989 F.Supp. 173 (D.Conn.1997), while noting *Inset*'s finding that there were at least 10,000 Internet users in Connecticut, held that "plaintiff's mere presumption that one of these 10,000 users must have visited [defendant's] Web site and viewed these solicitations is insufficient to meet plaintiff's burden" to show that defendant engaged in repeated solicitation of business. In *MacMullen v. Villa Roma Country Club*, 1998 WL 867271 (Conn.Super.Ct.1998), the court held that defendant's website did not satisfy the "solicitation of business" requirement, since "[t]here is no factual showing that any Connecticut resident actually accessed the defendant's website." And in *American Homecare Federation, Inc. v. Paragon Scientific Corp.*, 27 F.Supp.2d 109, 114 (D.Conn.1998), the court held that a website advertisement of an essay-writing contest is not "repeated solicitation of business," where "no essays were received from Connecticut and no inquiries regarding the contest were received from this State."

QUESTIONS FOR DISCUSSION

Does availability = solicitation? The *Inset* court noted the persistent availability of websites as a factor in its analysis. Should this be relevant to a determination whether the site constitutes *repeated* solicitation? Is there a new solicitation each time a visitor accesses the site? If so, is there a new solicitation each time a reader opens up a magazine and reads an advertisement? Compare the "single publication rule" applicable to defamation actions, which states that "[a]ny one edition of a book or newspaper, or any one radio or television broadcast, exhibition of a motion picture or similar aggregate communication is a single publication," giving rise to a single cause of action. RESTATEMENT (SECOND) OF TORTS § 577A(3) (1965). The rule likewise applies to "any similar aggregate communication that reaches a large number of persons at the same time." *Id.* cmt. c. The purpose of the rule is to "protect[] defendants and the courts from the numerous suits that might be brought for the same words if each person reached by such a large-scale communication could serve as the foundation for a new action." *Id.* Is the rationale of this rule applicable to websites?

D. LOCATION OF COMPUTER EQUIPMENT AS A FACTOR UNDER LONG-ARM STATUTES

Some courts have found that the location of the computer servers that are used in posting a message on a BBS is determinative in applying state long-arm provisions. (As discussed in Part II(E), *supra*, some courts have also considered the location of computer equipment relevant to the due process analysis.) In *Krantz v. Air Line Pilots Ass'n, Int'l*,

427 S.E.2d 326 (Va.1993), the defendant posted, on a proprietary BBS operated by a labor union, a statement that allegedly tortiously interfered with plaintiff's employment. The BBS was operated by the union "from its offices in Herndon, Virginia." Other union members accessed the BBS and read the message, resulting in harm to plaintiff. The court found that, by virtue of the fact that the BBS was "a Virginia facility," defendant's posting of the message supported jurisdiction under a provision of the state's long-arm statute allowing jurisdiction over a defendant who causes "tortious injury by an act or omission in this Commonwealth." Other courts have followed *Krantz* in giving great weight to the location of the computers hosting a BBS or newsgroup. *See Bochan v. La Fontaine*, 68 F.Supp.2d 692 (E.D.Va.1999) (jurisdiction in Virginia based on posting a USENET message: "because the postings were accomplished through defendant's AOL account, they were transmitted first to AOL's USENET server hardware, located in Loudon County, Virginia"); *TELCO Communications v. An Apple A Day*, 977 F.Supp. 404 (E.D.Va.1997) (jurisdiction in Virginia based on electronic distribution of press releases through various outlets, including America Online, which is headquartered in Virginia); *Mitchell v. McGowan*, 1998 U.S. Dist. LEXIS 18587 (E.D.Va.1998) (no jurisdiction in Virginia based on posting a message on a newsgroup, since "the computer bulletin board . . . is based in Texas").

In 1999, the Virginia legislature added a provision to the state long-arm statute that is aimed at extending jurisdiction to cover situations in which a remote user accesses computers located in Virginia. The provision states: "Using a computer or computer network located in the Commonwealth shall constitute an act in the Commonwealth." VA. CODE § 8.01–328.1(B). This statement of what shall be deemed "an act in the Commonwealth" becomes operative when combined with other provisions of the long-arm statute, such as those granting jurisdiction over a claim arising from a person's "[t]ransacting any business in this Commonwealth," "[c]ontracting to supply services or things in this Commonwealth," or "[c]ausing tortious injury by an act or omission in this Commonwealth." *Id.* § 8.01–328.1(A)(1)–(3). A person is deemed to "use" a computer "when he attempts to cause or causes a computer or computer network to perform or to stop performing computer operations." *Id.* § 18.2–152.2. In *Verizon Online Services, Inc. v. Ralsky*, 203 F.Supp.2d 601 (E.D.Va. 2002), the court applied this provision to find that sending bulk unsolicited commercial e-mail to subscribers of Verizon's Internet access services constitutes an "act" in Virginia, since Verizon's e-mail servers are located in that state. Accordingly, jurisdiction over the defendant could be predicated on the long-arm statute's provision based on "[c]ausing tortious injury by an act or omission in this Commonwealth."

EXTENSIONS

Remote USENET servers. The court in *Bochan v. La Fontaine* notes that after being stored on AOL's USENET server, the allegedly defamatory messages were "transmitted to other USENET servers around the world." Is there a rationale for holding that the involvement of AOL's server justifies jurisdiction in Virginia, without concluding that the involvement of other USENET servers that propagated the message likewise justify jurisdiction wherever they may be located?

Other courts have been troubled by the notion that the automatic functioning of a USENET server should be treated as the legal equivalent of volitional conduct. For example, one court rejected a plaintiff's argument that an Internet service provider that operates a USENET server is directly liable for copyright infringement based on material that a subscriber posts to a newsgroup. It explained: "Plaintiff's theory would create many separate acts of infringement and, carried to its natural extreme, would lead to unreasonable liability .... [P]laintiff's theory further implicates a Usenet server that carries ... messages to other servers regardless of whether that server acts without any human intervention beyond the initial setting up of the system. It would also result in liability for every single Usenet server in the worldwide link of computers transmitting [messages] to every other computer. ... There is no need to construe the [Copyright] Act to make all of these parties infringers." *Religious Technology Center v. Netcom On-Line Communication Services, Inc.*, 907 F.Supp.1361, 1369–70 (N.D.Cal.1995). (This case is excerpted in Chapter 7, Part V(A), *infra*.) Should similar considerations govern in the context of personal jurisdiction?

QUESTIONS FOR DISCUSSION

1. *Virginia's updated long-arm statute.* Does the amendment of the Virginia statute, declaring that accessing an in-state computer is "an act in the Commonwealth," succeed in overcoming the perplexities that result when attempting to ascertain the location of events that are accomplished through online communications? If a person in State A transacts business with a person in State B by sending an e-mail message that is routed through a server located in Virginia, is this "use" of the server that gives rise to jurisdiction over the person in State A? What if the person in State A defames a person in State B by posting a message in a newsgroup that is hosted on a server located in Virginia? Some of the computers that constitute America Online are located in Virginia. Under this statute, does jurisdiction arise in Virginia every time two AOL members, located anywhere in the world, transact business using their AOL accounts? *See Verizon Online Services, Inc. v. Ralsky*, 203 F.Supp.2d 601 (E.D.Va.2002) (the "using a computer" amendment supports jurisdiction over a spammer who sent millions of messages to plaintiff's subscribers, since the messages were routed through mail servers located in Virginia).

2. *Relocation of servers.* In *Bochan v. La Fontaine*, should the geographic location of America Online's USENET server be determinative of the jurisdictional analysis? What if AOL happened to locate its USENET server outside Virginia? What if it had several servers, some in Virginia and some elsewhere, and USENET postings were routed randomly to one server or the other? What if the postings in question were to an AOL bulletin board rather than to USENET, and the BBS server was located outside Virginia? Should it matter whether defendants had knowledge of the location of the server?

3. *E-mail servers.* Assume that any time an AOL user sends e-mail, it is routed through the company's main servers in Virginia. On the reasoning employed in *Bochan v. La Fontaine*, would the Virginia courts have jurisdiction over any lawsuit arising from e-mail messages sent between AOL users located in, say, Tennessee and California?

4. *Relevance of location.* Should the location of the computer servers that are used in transmitting or storing newsgroup or BBS messages be determinative in the jurisdictional inquiry? Should this even be a relevant factor? If the location of such computer equipment is deemed relevant, shouldn't the same be true for the location of the ISP through which a user obtains access to the Internet? The location of the server on which a website is hosted? The location of a proxy server that caches frequently accessed data? How about the location of the name servers that are queried each time a user accesses a website? Is it coherent to speak of the "location" of a newsgroup?

IV. CHOICE OF LAW

The transborder nature of online communications can create difficulties in determining which jurisdiction's law governs a particular dispute. Sometimes the parties to the dispute will have agreed contractually on the governing law. Often these contracts will be enforceable, especially in commercial agreements, though sometimes a court will prefer its own jurisdiction's policies over those of a foreign jurisdiction. In the absence of such an agreement, the court must apply the forum jurisdiction's choice-of-law rules.

John Rothchild, *Protecting the Digital Consumer: The Limits of Cyberspace Utopianism*
74 IND. L.J. 893 (1999).

... A court with jurisdiction to adjudicate a particular controversy will not necessarily apply the law of the state in which it is located. If the parties are located in the forum jurisdiction, and all of the operative facts occurred there, a court will apply the *lex fori*. However, where the controversy has "a significant relationship to more than one state," the court must resort to choice-of-law principles in order to determine which jurisdiction's laws it will apply to resolve the controversy.

Choice-of-law issues are notoriously difficult to resolve even in relatively simple contexts. The complexities of transnational commercial activities conducted via the Internet may give rise to particularly thorny choice-of-law questions. Due to the nature of online communications, an online transaction may routinely involve several jurisdictions. For example, a person in State *A* may make a communication through a Web site hosted on a computer located in State *B*, that is received by a person in State *C* who obtains access to the Internet through a server located in State *D* (which is owned and operated by a company headquartered in State *E*), and that results in a transaction involving the shipment of physical goods or downloading of digital goods from a source located in State *F*.

Among states of the United States, the two most popular approaches to resolving choice-of-law issues are *lex loci delicti* and "most significant relationship." Under the rule of *lex loci delicti*, the applicable law is the law of the place "where the last event necessary to make an actor liable for an alleged tort takes place." ... The "most significant relationship" approach involves a balancing test that is dependent on a number of factors. One standard exposition of the test that applies where the cause of action is based on fraud or misrepresentation takes cognizance of six factors: (1) the place where the plaintiff acted in reliance upon the defendant's representations, (2) the place where the plaintiff received the representations, (3) the place where the defendant made the representations, (4) the residence and nationality of the parties, (5) the place where a tangible thing which is the subject of the transaction was situated, and (6) the place where the plaintiff was to render performance under the fraudulently induced contract.[102]

Where the cause of action arises from contract, and the parties have not effectively selected the governing substantive law, the relevant criteria in a choice-of-law analysis are (1) the place of contracting, (2) the place of negotiation of the contract, (3) the place of performance, (4) the location of the subject matter of

---

[102] [*See* RESTATEMENT (SECOND) OF CONFLICT OF LAWS § 148(2).]

the contract, and (5) the location of the parties.[104]

The special characteristics of online communications create difficulties in the application of these criteria. For example, does a person "make" or "receive" an online communication (a) where the maker of the communication is located at the time he transmits it, (b) where the computer through which the maker of the communication connects to the network is located, (c) where the computer through which the recipient of the communication connects to the network is located, (d) where the computer from which the purchaser downloads his e-mail is located, or (e) where the recipient of the communication is located at the time he receives it? When performance consists of the delivery of a digital good, does performance occur at the sending end or the receiving end? Is the result different if the seller transmits the good by making it available for download from the seller's Web site? What is the situs of contracting or negotiation of a contract that is arrived at through online communications?

The novel issues raised by choice-of-law analysis of online transactions will thus center around what is deemed to be the *location* of various persons and events. As is the case with jurisdiction, the location of online events and the persons who bring them about can be difficult to assess.

. . .

Jack L. Goldsmith, *Against Cyberanarchy*
65 U. CHI. L. REV. 1199 (1998).

. . .

[T]ransnational transactions in cyberspace, like transnational transactions mediated by telephone and mail, will continue to give rise to disputes that present challenging choice-of-law issues. For example: "Whose substantive legal rules apply to a defamatory message that is written by someone in Mexico, read by someone in Israel by means of an Internet server located in the United States, injuring the reputation of a Norwegian?" . . . .

It would be silly to try to formulate a general theory of how such issues should be resolved. One lesson of this century's many failures in top-down choice-of-law theorizing is that choice-of-law rules are most effective when they are grounded in and sensitive to the concrete details of particular legal contexts. This does not mean that standards are better than rules in this context. It simply means that in designing choice-of-law rules or standards, it is better to begin at the micro rather than macro level, and to examine recurrent fact patterns and implicated interests in discrete legal contexts rather than devise a general context-transcendent theory of conflicts.

With these caveats in mind, I want to explain in very general terms why the residual choice-of-law problems implicated by cyberspace are not significantly dif-

---

[104] [*See id.* § 188(2).]

ferent from those that are non-cyberspace conflicts. Cyberspace presents two related choice-of-law problems. The first is the problem of complexity. This is the problem of how to choose a single governing law for cyberspace activity that has multijurisdictional contacts. The second problem concerns situs. This is the problem of how to choose a governing law when the locus of activity cannot easily be pinpointed in geographical space. Both problems raise similar concerns. The choice of any dispositive geographical contact or any particular law in these cases will often seem arbitrary because several jurisdictions have a legitimate claim to apply their law. Whatever law is chosen, seemingly genuine regulatory interests of the nations whose laws are not applied may be impaired.

The problems of complexity and situs are genuine. They are not, however, unique to cyberspace. Identical problems arise all the time in real space. In fact, they inhere in every true conflict of laws. Consider the problem of complexity. The hypotheticals concerning copyright infringements and multistate libels in cyberspace are no more complex than the same issues in real space. They also are no more complex or challenging than similar issues presented by increasingly prevalent real-space events such as airplane crashes, mass torts, multistate insurance coverage, or multinational commercial transactions, all of which form the bread and butter of modern conflict of laws. Indeed, they are no more complex than a simple products liability suit arising from a two-car accident among residents of the same state, which can implicate the laws of several states, including the place of the accident, the states where the car and tire manufacturers are headquartered, the states where the car and tires were manufactured, and the state where the car was purchased.

Resolution of choice-of-law problems in these contexts is challenging. But the skeptics overstate the challenge. Not every geographical contact is of equal significance. For example, in the copyright hypothetical above, the laws of the source country and the end-use countries have a much greater claim to governing the copyright action than the laws of the country of the person who built the server and the country of the server whose hyperlink pointed to the server that contained the infringing material. The limits on enforcement jurisdiction may further minimize the scope of the conflict. In addition, even in extraordinarily complex cases where numerous laws potentially apply, these laws will often involve similar legal standards, thus limiting the actual choice of law to two or perhaps three options. Finally, these complex transactions need not be governed by a single law. Applying different laws to different aspects of a complex transaction is a perfectly legitimate choice-of-law technique.

The application of a single law to complex multijurisdictional conflicts will sometimes seem arbitrary and will invariably produce spillover effects. But as explained above, the arbitrariness of the chosen law, and the spillovers produced by application of this law, inhere in all conflict situations in which two or more nations, on the basis of territorial or domiciliary contacts, have a legitimate claim to apply their law. When in particular contexts the arbitrariness and spillovers become too severe, a uniform international solution remains possible. Short of such harmonization, the choice-of-law issues implicated by cyberspace transactions are no more complex than the issues raised by functionally identical multijurisdictional transactions that occur in real space all the time.

Like the problem of complexity, the situs problem is a pervasive and familiar feature of real-space jurisdictional conflicts. A classic difficulty is the situs of intangibles like a debt or a bank deposit. More generally, the situs problem arises whenever legally significant activity touches on two or more states. For example, when adultery committed in one state alienates the affections of a spouse in another, the situs of the tort is not self-evident. It depends on what contact the forum's choice-of-law rule deems dispositive. Similar locus difficulties arise when the tort takes place over many states, such as when poison is administered in one state, takes effect in another, and kills in a third. The situs problem even arises when a bodily injury occurs in one state based on negligence committed in another, for there is no logical reason why the place of injury should be viewed as the place of the tort any more than should the place of negligence. In all of these situations, the importance of any particular geographical contact is never self-evident; it is a legal rather than a factual consideration that is built into the forum's choice-of-law rules. As the geographical contacts of a transaction proliferate, the choice of any one contact as dispositive runs the risk of appearing arbitrary. But again, this problem pervades real-space conflicts of law and is not unique to cyberspace conflicts.

. . . [S]everal factors diminish the skeptics' concerns about the infeasibility of applying traditional choice-of-law tools to cyberspace. For example, the skeptics are wrong to the extent that they believe that cyberspace transactions must be resolved on the basis of geographical choice-of-law criteria that are sometimes difficult to apply to cyberspace, such as where events occur or where people are located at the time of the transaction. But these are not the only choice-of-law criteria, and certainly not the best in contexts where the geographical locus of events is so unclear. Domicile (and its cognates, such as citizenship, principal place of business, habitual residence, and so on) are also valid choice-of-law criteria that have particular relevance to problems, like those in cyberspace, that involve the regulation of intangibles or of multinational transactions. The skeptics are further mistaken to the extent that their arguments assume that all choice-of-law problems must be resolved by multilateral choice-of-law methodologies. A multilateral methodology asks which of several possible laws governs a transaction, and selects one of these laws on the basis of specified criteria. Multilateral methods accentuate the situs and complexity problems. But the regulatory issues that are most relevant to the cyberspace governance debate almost always involve unilateral choice-of-law methods that alleviate these problems. A unilateral method considers only whether the dispute at issue has close enough connections to the forum to justify the application of local law. If so, local law applies; if not, the case is dismissed and the potential applicability of foreign law is not considered. For example, a jurisdiction typically does not apply foreign criminal law. If a Tennessee court has personal jurisdiction over someone from across the Virginia border who shot and killed an in-stater, the court does not consider whether Tennessee or Virginia law applies. It considers only whether Tennessee law applies. If so, the case proceeds; if not, it is dismissed.

Unilateral choice-of-law methods make the complexity and situs problems less significant. They do not require a determination of which of a number of possible laws apply. Nor do they require a court to identify where certain events occurred. What matters is simply whether the activity has local effects that are significant enough to implicate local law. By failing to recognize that courts can and will use unilateral rather than multilateral choice-of-law methods to resolve cyberspace conflicts, the skeptics again exaggerate the challenge of cyberspace regulation.

. . .

V. RELATED MATTERS

A. SUBJECT-MATTER JURISDICTION

A court has subject-matter jurisdiction over a case if the substance of the case brings it within the court's adjudicatory authority. The involvement of online communications in the activities giving rise to a lawsuit rarely creates new issues with respect to subject-matter jurisdiction. The subject-matter jurisdiction of federal district courts is established by statute (subject to certain constitutional limitations, such as the justiciability requirements). Most generally, the district courts have jurisdiction over cases in which the parties are citizens of different states, or citizens of a state and a foreign country, and cases that arise under federal law. *See* 28 U.S.C. § 1332 (diversity jurisdiction); 28 U.S.C. § 1331 (federal question jurisdiction). Questions of citizenship, and of whether a cause of action arises under federal law, are rarely affected by whether the communication relating to the cause of action takes place online or offline. The subject-matter jurisdiction of state courts is likewise generally unaffected by the involvement of online communications.

One situation in which online communications may raise novel issues is where subject-matter jurisdiction depends upon the existence of interstate commerce. The most general constitutional basis for exercise of federal legislative authority is the Commerce Clause, which authorizes Congress "To regulate Commerce with foreign Nations, and among the several States, and with the Indian Tribes." U.S.CONST. art. I, § 8, cl. 3. Many federal statutes apply by their terms only to interstate activities—e.g., 15 U.S.C. § 1125(a) & (c) (trademark infringement and dilution require use of a mark "in commerce"); 15 U.S.C. § 1263 (prohibiting "[t]he introduction or delivery for introduction into interstate commerce of any misbranded hazardous substance or banned hazardous substance"); 16 U.S.C. § 824 (regulating "the transmission of electric energy in interstate commerce"). Federal statutes that do not contain an explicit commerce limitation, but are premised on the Commerce Clause, likewise may be applied consistently with the Constitution only if the case involves interstate commerce.

Several federal statutes regulate certain types of *communications* that occur in interstate commerce. For example, the Wire Fraud statute makes it illegal to "transmit[] . . . by means of wire . . . communication in interstate or foreign commerce" any communication for the purpose of executing any scheme to obtain money by fraud. 18 U.S.C. § 1343. Similarly, the federal threats statute makes it illegal to "transmit[] in interstate or foreign commerce any communication containing any threat to kidnap any person or any threat to injure the person of another." 18 U.S.C. § 875(c). Normally these statutes are applicable in situations where a person in one state engages in a communication with a person in another state, thereby satisfying the interstate commerce requirement. But what if the two people who are communicating are located in a single state, and they communicate via an online medium that routes the communication through another state? Is the communication in interstate commerce?

The court gave an affirmative answer to this question in *United States v. Kammersell*, 7 F.Supp.2d 1196 (D.Utah 1998), *aff'd*, 196 F.3d 1137 (10th Cir.1999), which involved a defendant who was charged with making a threat in violation of 18 U.S.C. § 875(c). Defendant had sent a threatening communication from his location in Utah to the target, also located in Utah. The communication, an America Online "insta-message," was routed through AOL's server in Virginia. The court found that this communication was in interstate commerce, on a plain reading of the statute. " 'Transmits . . . in interstate commerce' is not ambiguous. . . . Its plain meaning encompasses the conduct in this case. . . . The fact that the recipient of the threat was located in the same state is of no consequence." 7 F.Supp.2d at 1199–1200, 1202.

In concluding that the location of the two communicators is irrelevant, the court relied on (a) *United States v. Whiffen*, 121 F.3d 18 (1st Cir.1997), finding that a call from a New Hampshire location to another New Hampshire phone number, which was automatically transferred so that the caller was speaking with a person located in Florida, was in interstate commerce; (b) *United States v. Alkhabaz*, 104 F.3d 1492 (6th Cir.1997), which found it indisputable that e-mail transmissions between a person located in Ontario and a person located in Michigan are in interstate or foreign commerce; and (c) *United States v. Kelner*, 534 F.2d 1020 (2d Cir.1976), which found the interstate commerce requirement satisfied by a threat transmitted via a television broadcast that was received outside the state where the broadcaster was located, though the target of the threat was located in the same state as the broadcaster.

QUESTIONS FOR DISCUSSION

1. *Communication in interstate commerce.* Do you agree with the court in *U.S. v. Kammersell* that the term "interstate commerce" unambiguously includes a communication between two people located in the same state, if it is routed through another state? Do the three cases the court relies on support this conclusion? Could the term be fairly read as encompassing only communications between people located in different states? If America Online happened to have a server located in Utah, through which the message was routed, the court would presumably have concluded that the communication was not in interstate commerce. Is it sensible for subject-matter jurisdiction to turn on such a fortuity?

2. *Other scenarios.* How would the *Kammersell* court's reasoning apply in a situation where a person accesses a website whose owner is located in the same state, but the server hosting the website is located in another state? What if the web server and both communicators are located in a single state, but some of the packets constituting the communication are routed through a server located in another state? What if a person sends a threat via Federal Express to a recipient located in the same state, but the airplane carrying the letter touches down in Memphis, where Federal Express has its hub? *See* Katherine C. Sheehan, *Predicting the Future: Personal Jurisdiction for the Twenty-First Century*, 66 U. CIN. L. REV. 385, 419 (1998) (noting that at one time "most Federal Express packages, regardless of origin or destination, were routed through Memphis, Tennessee").

FURTHER READING

For an analysis of *Kammersell* as an example of a case whose outcome depends on whether we view the Internet from an internal or an external perspective, see Orin S. Kerr, *The Problem of Perspective in Internet Law*, 91 GEO. L.J. 357, 373-74 (2003).

B. GENERAL JURISDICTION

May operation of a website constitute sufficient contacts with a state to support general jurisdiction? As discussed in Part I, *supra*, a defendant's contacts with a state will support general jurisdiction over his activities—that is, jurisdiction over any claims brought against the defendant, regardless of whether they arise from the forum contacts—if they are "continuous and systematic." This criterion presents a much higher hurdle than that which the plaintiff must clear to establish specific jurisdiction.

Unsurprisingly, courts have ruled that in circumstances where other types of forum contacts are inadequate, the presence of online contacts may supply the additional connection with the forum state needed to support a finding that the court has general jurisdiction over the defendant. Thus, in *Coremetrics, Inc. v. Atomic Park.com, LLC*, 370 F.Supp.2d 1013 (N.D.Cal.2005), the court enumerated a variety of types of contact between the defendant and the forum state, some involving online communications and some not; noted that none of these contacts individually constituted "continuous and systematic" dealings with the forum; but held that in combination they "are sufficiently substantial, continuous, and systematic so as to support a finding of general jurisdiction."

A few courts have held that operation of a website alone can confer general jurisdiction. In *Gammino v. SBC Communications, Inc.*, 2005 WL 724130 (E.D.Pa.2005), the court held that it could assert general jurisdiction over defendant SBC, a large regional telecommunications company. The requisite connection to the forum state consisted of the fact that "Pennsylvania residents can enter the SBC website seeking residential and business telecommunication products and services," and that SBC "can and does provide services and products to Pennsylvania residents." The court concluded "that this evidences that SBC's internet contacts are for the purposeful availment of conducting business with Pennsylvania residents. Such purposeful availment consequently subjects SBC to the general personal jurisdiction of this court." In *Arista Records, Inc. v. Sakfield Holding Co. S.L.*, 314 F.Supp.2d 27 (D.D.C.2004), the court asserted general jurisdiction over a Spanish company based on the company's operation of a website that allowed users to download files containing plaintiff's copyrighted music. The court held that "defendant maintained continuous and systematic contacts with the District of Columbia by entering into hundreds of contractual relationships with District residents through the [defendant's] website and enabling the transfer of music files into the District, pursuant to those arrangements." Have these courts properly applied the "continuous and systematic" criterion? *Cf. ALS Scan, Inc. v. Digital Service Consultants, Inc.*, 293 F.3d 707 (4th Cir.2002) ("We are not prepared at this time to recognize that a State may obtain general jurisdiction over out-of-state persons who regularly and systematically transmit electronic signals into the State via the Internet based solely on those transmissions.")

Other courts have held that online contacts alone do not support general jurisdiction. Courts have declined to find general jurisdiction based on a passive website, *Mid City Bowling Lanes & Sports Palace, Inc. v. Ivercrest, Inc.*, 35 F.Supp.2d 507 (E.D.La.1999); an interactive website, *ESAB Group, Inc. v. Centricut*, LLC, 34 F.Supp.2d 323 (D.S.C.1999); a website that does not allow the transaction of business, *ALS Scan, Inc. v. Digital Service Consultants, Inc.*, 293 F.3d 707 (4th Cir.2002); a website that allows visitors to make hotel reservations online, *Rodriguez v. Circus Circus Casinos, Inc.*, 2001 WL 21244 (S.D.N.Y.2001); hosting a website on a server located in the forum state, *Jewish Defense Organization, Inc. v. Superior Court*, 85 Cal.Rptr.2d 611 (Cal.Ct.App.1999); online publication of an allegedly defamatory article, *Naxos Resources (U.S.A.) Ltd. v. Southam Inc.*, 1996 WL 662451 (C.D.Cal.1996); and posting messages on a proprietary bulletin board system, *California Software Inc. v. Reliability Research, Inc.*, 631 F.Supp. 1356 (C.D.Cal.1986). Still other courts have held that entering into contracts with residents of the forum state via a website does not support general jurisdiction. *See Bird v. Parsons*, 289 F.3d 865 (6th Cir.2002) (no general jurisdiction over domain name registrar, based on registration of domain names for 4,666 forum residents); *Robbins v. Yutopian Enterprises, Inc.*, 202 F.Supp.2d 426 (D.Md.2002) (no general jurisdiction over merchant, based on its entering into 46 transactions with residents of the forum state through its website and toll-free telephone number).

Courts have not been consistent in the standard they use for assessing the availability of general jurisdiction in cases involving Internet communications. Some courts apply the generally applicable standard, inquiring whether the defendant's contacts with the forum state are "continuous and systematic," finding no need to devise a special test for Internet-related cases. *E.g., Bird v. Parsons*, 289 F.3d 865 (6th Cir.2002) (noting that the "continuous and systematic" criterion "is directly applicable to the present case"). Other courts have applied the *Zippo* three-category analysis. For example, in *Mieczkowski v. Masco Corp.*, 997 F.Supp.782 (E.D.Tex.1998), the defendant furniture seller's contacts with the forum state included selling $5.7 million of products to forum residents over a six-year period, sending direct mailings to forum residents twice a year, purchasing 0.2 percent of its furniture from a company located in the forum state, and maintaining a website. The court analyzed the significance of the website through application of the *Zippo* three-category approach: it classified the site as an interactive one, and looked to the *Zippo* factors of the "level of interactivity and commercial nature of the exchange of information." The court added: "It should be noted that the majority of courts that have addressed this issue have done so in the context of specific jurisdiction analysis. However, the Court sees no reason why the analysis should not be applied equally to cases involving a general jurisdiction analysis." *Id.* at 786 n.3. Can it be correct to use a single criterion, namely that proposed in *Zippo*, both to determine whether a website meets the requirements for specific jurisdiction and to determine whether it meets the more stringent requirements for general jurisdiction? In *Revell v. Lidov*, 317 F.3d 467, 471 (5th Cir.2002), the Fifth Circuit acknowledged that its adoption of the *Zippo* test as the gauge of general jurisdiction in an earlier case had been mistaken: "While we deployed this sliding scale in *Mink v. AAAA Development LLC* [, 190 F.3d 333 (5th Cir.1999)], it is not well adapted to the general jurisdiction inquiry, because even repeated contacts with forum residents by a foreign defendant may not constitute the requisite substantial, continuous and systematic contacts required for a finding of general jurisdiction . . . ."

CHAPTER SIX
PRIVACY ONLINE

In this chapter we explore the law and policy of protecting information privacy in a networked world. One widely cited work defines "information privacy" as "the claim of individuals, groups, or institutions to determine for themselves when, how, and to what extent information about them is communicated to others." ALAN F. WESTIN, PRIVACY AND FREEDOM 7 (1967). The commercialization of the Internet, which is awash with personal information of all types and which allows this information to be collected, manipulated, and transmitted cheaply and easily, predictably has raised a multitude of novel information privacy issues.

Some of the key issues we will address in this chapter are: Will the market take care of online privacy, or is legislation needed? Do the economic benefits of a less-restrictive online privacy policy justify the resulting privacy intrusions? Should privacy in the online world be treated differently from privacy in the offline world?

I. BACKGROUND: PRIVACY PROTECTION IN THE ONLINE COMMERCIAL ENVIRONMENT

A. LEGAL PROTECTION OF INFORMATION PRIVACY IN THE UNITED STATES

Perhaps the most salient characteristic of legal protection of information privacy in the United States is its ad hoc nature. Some types of information transfers are heavily regulated, while other types, seemingly no less significant to individual privacy interests, are unregulated and left to the mercies of the marketplace. There is no grand scheme that rationalizes the patchwork of legal protections applying to personal information, but only a series of historical accidents and political outcomes that explain them.

For example, the Video Privacy Protection Act of 1988, 18 U.S.C. § 2710, limits disclosure of records of videotape rentals.[1] Information about an individual's book purchases, however, is unregulated.

The General Education Provisions Act was amended in 2002 by adding a provision requiring school boards to provide parents with annual notifications of "[a]ctivities involving the collection, disclosure, or use of personal information collected from students for the purpose of marketing or for selling that information." 20 U.S.C. § 1232h(c)(2)(C)(i). Parents must be offered an opportunity "to opt the student out of participation" in such activities. *Id.* § 1232h(c)(2)(A)(ii). The requirement, which applies to both online and offline collections of information, was inspired in part by unhappiness about arrangements under which technology companies would provide schools with free computers or Internet access

---

[1] This statute was enacted in response to outrage over the disclosure of the video rental records of Judge Robert Bork during the Senate's consideration of his nomination to be a Justice of the Supreme Court. The disclosure of Judge Bork's video viewing habits revealed nothing racier than James Bond movies.

in exchange for the right to monitor students' activities online.

Regulations issued by the Department of Health and Human Services pursuant to statutory authority contained in Section 264(c)(1) of the Health Insurance Portability and Accountability Act of 1996, *reprinted at* 42 U.S.C. § 1320d–2 note, limit disclosure of individually identifiable health information by health care providers, health plans, and health care clearinghouses, without the consent of the individual, except in defined circumstances. 45 C.F.R. pts. 160 & 164.

Several federal laws protect the privacy of financial information. These include the Fair Credit Reporting Act of 1970 ("FCRA"), 15 U.S.C. §§ 1681–81u, which regulates the disclosure of information from a consumer's credit report; the Fair and Accurate Credit Transactions Act of 2003, amending the FCRA by adding provisions aimed at preventing identity theft; the Fair Debt Collection Practices Act of 1977, 15 U.S.C. §§ 1692–92o, which prevents debt collectors from disclosing information about a consumer's debt to third parties; the Right to Financial Privacy Act of 1978, 12 U.S.C. §§ 3401–22, which regulates the federal government's access to financial information held by a financial institution; and the Gramm–Leach–Bliley Act of 1999, 15 U.S.C. §§ 6801–10, which requires financial institutions to provide consumers with notice and an opportunity to opt out before disclosing certain types of personal financial information to nonaffiliated third parties.

Other laws protect the privacy of information transmitted via telecommunications systems. The Electronic Communications Privacy Act of 1986, 18 U.S.C. §§ 2510–22, 2701–11, prohibits unauthorized interception of electronic communications, including e-mail, and unauthorized access of stored electronic communications. The Telecommunications Act of 1996 includes a provision that protects transactional information concerning telephone calls, including amount of usage and the destination of calls. 47 U.S.C. § 222. The Cable Communications Policy Act of 1984 requires cable operators to disclose to their customers what types of personally identifiable information ("PII") they collect, and how they use and disclose such information; limits the permissible purposes for collection of PII from subscribers; limits disclosures of subscribers' PII; gives subscribers the right to access and correct PII concerning them that a cable operator holds; and requires cable operators to destroy PII that is no longer needed for its original purpose. 47 U.S.C. § 551.

The Family Education Rights and Privacy Act of 1974, 20 U.S.C. § 1232g, regulates handling of student records by educational institutions that receive federal funds. The statute limits disclosure of student records absent parental consent, and gives parents a right to access their children's records and correct inaccuracies.

Many states have adopted some version of the common-law torts for invasion of privacy. These are set out in the *Restatement* as the torts of "unreasonable intrusion upon the seclusion of another," "appropriation of the other's name or likeness," "unreasonable publicity given to the other's private life," and "publicity that unreasonably places the other in a false light before the public." Restatement (Second) of Torts § 652A (1965). Several courts have held that certain types of collection and disclosure of personal information that commonly occur in the context of Internet commerce do not state a cause of action under these torts. *See Dwyer v. American Express Co.*, 652 N.E.2d 1351 (Ill.App.Ct.1995) (no cause of action against credit card company that provides marketers with cardholder's identity in a categorization by spending habits); *Shibley v. Time, Inc.*, 341 N.E.2d 337 (Ohio Ct.App.1975) (no cause of action against magazine publishers that sell their subscription lists to marketers).

In *Remsburg v. Docusearch Inc.*, 816 A.2d 1001 (N.H.2003), the New Hampshire Supreme Court considered the availability of several causes of action in a situation involving disclosure of personal information to a stalker. The defendant was an Internet-based information service, which provided the stalker with his victim's Social Security number, employment address, and home address. The stalker went to the victim's workplace and murdered her, and the victim's estate sued. The court held that the facts stated no cause of action for appropriation of name or likeness, or for intrusion upon seclusion based on disclosure of the victim's work address. However, it held that "a person whose [Social Security number] is obtained by an investigator from a credit reporting agency without the person's knowledge or permission may have a cause of action for intrusion upon seclusion for damages caused by the sale of the SSN, but must prove that the intrusion was such that it would have been offensive to a person of ordinary sensibilities." It also held that release of personal information could support a negligence claim: "The threats posed by stalking and identity theft lead us to conclude that the risk of criminal misconduct is sufficiently foreseeable so that an investigator has a duty to exercise reasonable care in disclosing a third person's personal information to a client." (In March 2004, the parties settled the action with a payment of $85,000 to the plaintiff.)

Other constitutional and statutory provisions affect the *government*'s handling of personal information. The Fourth Amendment to the Constitution limits the government's ability to search for and seize information in which a person holds a reasonable expectation of privacy. The Privacy Act of 1974, 5 U.S.C. § 552a, places some (not very stringent) limitations on the government's use and disclosure of personal information that it holds, and gives individuals a right to access information pertaining to them and to challenge inaccuracies. The Driver's Privacy Protection Act of 1974, 18 U.S.C. § 2721–25, places limitations (also not very stringent) on disclosure of personal information by a state department of motor vehicles.[2]

The only federal statute that specifically addresses the collection of information online is the Children's Online Privacy Protection Act ("COPPA"), 15 U.S.C. §§ 6501–05, which regulates collection of personal information from children, as well as disclosure and use of such information. COPPA is discussed in Part VI, *infra*.

Several state laws regulate online privacy. California's Online Privacy Protection Act of 2003, CAL. BUS. & PROF. CODE §§ 22575–78, requires website operators to post and obey a privacy policy. Several states have enacted legislation requiring the disclosure of online security breaches. These laws are discussed in Part IV(C), *infra*.

To the extent that online transfers of personal information are within the scope of laws designed for the offline world, they are likewise subject to this ad hoc set of legal and marketplace controls. As we shall see, many types of online collection of information have no easy offline analogue, and in the absence of new legal rules are regulated only by the marketplace.

---

[2] This statute was enacted partly in response to the murder of actress Rebecca Schaeffer, whose killer reportedly obtained her address from records made publicly available for a two-dollar fee by the California Department of Motor Vehicles.

B. WHAT'S NEW ABOUT THE ONLINE ENVIRONMENT?

Is there anything about online communications that gives rise to fundamentally new issues relating to information privacy? Digitization of transactional information, and the use of automatic data processing, were occurring long before the Internet became widely available as a medium for commercial transactions. For decades, digitized data on consumer buying habits and credit usage have been collected in databases and used to target marketing and to make decisions on extension of credit. As long ago as 1967, Alan Westin noted that "general information gathering and the dossier have been radically accelerated by the advent of the electronic digital computer, with its capacity to store more records and manipulate them more effectively and rapidly than was ever possible before." ALAN F. WESTIN, PRIVACY AND FREEDOM 160 (1967). Moreover, vast quantities of transactional information in digitized, personally identifiable form are collected in offline transactions, through widespread use of credit and debit cards, in pay-per-call telephone billing, in sales conducted at a distance through catalogs and telemarketing, and by means of merchant affinity cards.

Yet use of the Internet for business-to-consumer transactions has introduced some novelties that may have an important bearing on information privacy issues. First, widespread use of computers and open-standard networks has made the process of collecting, storing, correlating, transferring, accessing, and otherwise manipulating data much faster and cheaper. The low cost of collecting personal information means that more of it is collected. The low cost of manipulating data means that more value can be mined from it, which raises the incentives both to collect and to disclose it. The information gathered in this way may be used to create personal profiles, allowing customized advertising messages to be targeted at particular individuals.

Second, the online medium allows pre-transactional data to be captured. When you are browsing at a website, it is a simple matter for the site owner to capture your clickstream information. This includes the identity of every page you have viewed, and any text you enter into web pages, such as search strings. For example, if you research a particular medical problem, the subject of your research can be recorded. If you read an online magazine, the publisher can know which articles you read, and how long you spent on each. If you browse at an online bookstore, the store can get an idea of your reading interests. If you browse at a travel site, the site owner learns something about the travel destinations that interest you. The nature of the online medium makes it economically feasible to store and manipulate such data. By contrast, in offline shopping it is infeasible and uneconomic for merchants to follow you around as you shop, take notes on what items you look at, and record this information in digital form.[3]

Third, anonymous payment mechanisms are not widely available online. In offline shopping you can pay with cash if you want to leave no record of a purchase. When you make a purchase online, your use of a payment mechanism—usually a credit card, or an online payment service such as PayPal—generates data that connect you to the purchase.

Fourth, most items that you purchase online must be shipped to you, requiring you to

---

[3] This may be changing. Some retailers are placing surveillance cameras and microphones in their stores to gather information on customers' shopping habits. *See* Stephanie Simon, *Shopping with Big Brother*, L.A. TIMES, May 1, 2002, at A1.

disclose your home address to the merchant. This is also true of other distance selling techniques such as catalogue sales, direct mail, and telemarketing, but not of purchasing in brick-and-mortar stores.

Fifth, in online transactions the seller is able to capture data surreptitiously. Through the use of cookies, web bugs, and other technologies of surveillance, discussed in Part III, *infra*, a website operator can gather personally identifiable information about an Internet user who thinks he is browsing anonymously. By contrast, in a telephone conversation the seller gathers only the information that the consumer chooses to provide—with the possible exception of his telephone number, which can be surreptitiously collected using caller ID. When shopping in person, it is possible for the seller to collect information through spying techniques, but this is unlikely to be feasible or cost effective.

Sixth, the Internet makes it easier to gather personal information from children without a parent's authorization. In offline shopping settings a child is more likely to be accompanied by an adult, or at least to be recognized as a child.

FEDERAL TRADE COMMISSION, PRIVACY ONLINE: FAIR INFORMATION PRACTICES IN THE ELECTRONIC MARKETPLACE (2000) (Statement of Commissioner Leary)
www.ftc.gov/reports/privacy2000/learystmt.pdf

[In this report, the Federal Trade Commission recommends "that Congress enact legislation that, in conjunction with continuing self-regulatory programs, will ensure adequate protection of consumer privacy online."]

STATEMENT OF COMMISSIONER THOMAS B. LEARY CONCURRING IN PART AND DISSENTING IN PART

. . .

Recognition of the privacy concerns specific to e-commerce should not obscure the fact that in significant respects online privacy concerns are identical to those raised by offline commerce. The same technology that facilitates the efficient compilation and dissemination of personal information by online companies also allows offline companies to amass, analyze and transfer vast amounts of consumers' personal information. Offline companies collect and compile information about consumers' purchases from grocery stores, pharmacies, retailers, and mail order companies, in particular.

It is also not possible to distinguish offline and online privacy concerns on the basis of the nature of the information collected. With the exception of online profiling, it is the same information. The Report's recommendation would require Amazon.com to comply with the fair information practice principles but not the local bookstore which can compile and disseminate the same information about the reading habits of its customers. The consumer polls, upon which the Report places such significant reliance, demonstrate that consumer concerns about the disclosure of personal information are not dependent on how the data has been collected.

Moreover, it is impractical to maintain such a distinction. Businesses are likely to have a strong incentive to consolidate personal information collected, regardless of the mode of collection, in order to provide potential customers with the most personalized message possible. Already, companies are seeking to merge data collected offline with data collected online. In light of this reality, the majority's recommendation would result in perverse and arbitrary enforcement. Enforcement actions would depend on the source of and method used to collect a particular piece of consumer data rather than on whether there was a clear-cut violation of a company's announced privacy policy or mandated standards.

Finally, the Report's focus only on online privacy issues could ultimately have a detrimental impact on the growth of online commerce, directly contrary to the Report's objectives. It is clear from the Advisory Committee's Report on Access and Security and from limited portions of the Commission's own Report that implementation of the fair information practices will be complex and may create significant compliance costs. Online companies will be placed at a competitive disadvantage relative to their offline counterparts that are not forced to provide consumers with the substantive rights of notice, choice, access and security. Traditional brick and mortar companies that have an online presence or are considering entry into the electronic marketplace will be forced to assess how the cost of regulation will affect their participation in that sector.

A better approach would be to establish a level playing field for online and offline competitors and to address consumers' privacy concerns through clear and conspicuous privacy disclosures. Any privacy concerns that are unique to a particular medium or that involve particular categories of information (however collected) can continue to be addressed through separate legislation.

. . .

Joel R. Reidenberg & Françoise Gamet–Pol, *The Fundamental Role of Privacy and Confidence in the Network*
30 WAKE FOREST L. REV. 105 (1995).

. . .

In the 1960s and early 1970s, computing and telecommunications were generally controlled by the federal government and large corporations. The emergence of personal computers and networking in the mid–1980s, however, contributed to a shift in power to the commercial sector. Smaller private-sector organizations gained access to sophisticated information-processing capabilities through inexpensive equipment. Individuals and small, private organizations obtained access to vast information resources through services such as Prodigy, Compuserve, and America Online. In essence, the Internet and private networks gave globalized access to information to both individuals and small organizations. Globalized access to information and real-time interactivity multiply the options available to users of information, both individuals and businesses. Interactive communications produce numerous transaction records, thereby multiplying choices regarding the use of information as well.

At the beginning of the 1990s, information processing was decentralizing even within large corporations as networks replaced mainframe computers. Today, in the mid–1990s, the decentralization of information processing has made omnipresent surveillance possible by organizations and even individuals. This decentralization enables any network participant to centralize data, for although bits of information are scattered throughout the network, they are accessible from any place on the network. This, however, is not the extent of decentralization's effects. Sophisticated information providers and intelligent networks already enable combinations of audiovisual images and sounds with other interactive services. Further, decentralization of information processing in the United States dramatically broadened the role of private-sector data processing and shifted power from the federal government to private-sector organizations. These private organizations now have exclusive control over the decisions regarding the collection and use of personal information.

. . .

QUESTIONS FOR DISCUSSION

1. *Separating online and offline privacy.* Are the privacy issues presented by the online medium sufficiently different from offline privacy issues to merit independent legislative treatment? Is it feasible to disentangle the two realms and apply different rules to each? Would application of different rules to the two realms result in harmful distortion of business or consumer economic incentives?

2. *Argument for piecemeal approach.* The concept of privacy is very broad. The interest of individuals in keeping others from knowing of their reading habits may differ from their interest in keeping their medical conditions confidential, and these may differ from their interest in keeping their sexual conduct secret, and all of these may differ from their interest in keeping quiet their past brushes with the law. Even if the piecemeal approach to privacy protection in the United States has come about without serious thought to privacy as a whole, might it nevertheless turn out to be a better approach than the unitary scheme applied in the European Union?

C. TENSIONS WITHIN THE IDEA OF PRIVACY

It is undeniable that privacy serves a number of valuable functions. Most generally, the ability to control what other people can learn about you provides a sphere of free action that is a basic human necessity. The right to keep your identity information secret can help to protect you from stalkers, abusive ex-spouses, and others whose company you wish to avoid, and makes identity theft less likely.[4] Anonymity enables people to blow the whistle on wrongdoing without fear of retribution.

---

[4] "Identity theft" refers to the wrongful use of a person's identifying information to obtain goods and services fraudulently. An identity thief who learns the victim's name, date of birth, and Social Security number might open a credit card account in the victim's name, go on a spending spree, and then ignore the bills. Since the card is in the victim's name, the card issuer will believe the charges to have been incurred by the victim, and will seek to hold the victim accountable. Although in theory the victim should not suffer due to the actions of the identity thief, in practice it can take months or years, and enormous efforts, before the victim clears her name and regains her credit standing. The Federal Trade Commission maintains a website about identity theft at www.consumer.gov/idtheft.

Like nearly all other interests that the law recognizes, however, the interest in privacy is not absolute: there are also competing societal interests that may be harmed by the protection of privacy. One way to address these competing interests is to ask "how do we balance the need to use information (by government, commerce, and individuals) with the natural desire of individuals to decide what information about themselves will be exposed to others?" INFORMATION INFRASTRUCTURE TASK FORCE, INFORMATION POLICY COMMITTEE, OPTIONS FOR PROMOTING PRIVACY ON THE NATIONAL INFORMATION INFRASTRUCTURE 7 (1997). These competing interests may be organized under the headings of *accountability*, *free circulation of ideas*, and *efficiency*.

Accountability. Privacy, when it takes the form of anonymity, enables speakers to avoid being held accountable for the consequences of their speech. Although the First Amendment broadly protects the right to free expression, limits the government's authority to impose sanctions on a person based on his speech, and even guarantees anonymity in certain circumstances,[5] there are recognized exceptions to these rights. For example, the First Amendment does not prevent the government from imposing liability based on defamation, unauthorized disclosure of trade secrets, false advertising, threats of violence, blackmail, obscenity, advocacy of imminent lawless action, and other speech acts. Anonymity interferes with the law's ability to protect the interests represented by these derogations from an absolute right of freedom of expression. Laws, norms, and self-regulatory practices that protect privacy must take these same competing interests into account.

Privacy as invisibility—a person's ability to control who may learn her whereabouts or how she may be contacted—may also interfere with legitimate societal interests. Invisibility makes it harder for single parents to track down deadbeat spouses, for litigants to locate witnesses, and for law enforcement authorities to collar criminal suspects.

Free circulation of ideas. The First Amendment's Free Speech Clause serves several interests, among them encouraging the free flow of information within what is frequently referred to as the "marketplace of ideas." The Supreme Court has held that this interest is weighty enough to overcome substantial opposing interests, in view of our "profound national commitment to the principle that debate on public issues should be uninhibited, robust, and wide-open, and that it may well include vehement, caustic, and sometimes unpleasantly sharp attacks on government and public officials."[6] Protection of privacy, when it takes the form of limiting disclosure of information that is considered personal, interferes with this goal. Thus, publication of personal information that touches on matters of public concern, and that is true and was legally obtained, is almost always protected.[7] But, when the First Amendment right to free association—the right to nondisclosure of the identity of those with whom one chooses to associate—is opposed to society's interest in the free flow of information, free association may sometimes prevail. Thus, compelled disclosure of membership lists has been held to violate the First Amendment.[8] In addition, in the context

---

[5] *See McIntyre v. Ohio Elections Commission*, 514 U.S. 334 (1995).

[6] *New York Times Co. v. Sullivan*, 376 U.S. 254, 270 (1964).

[7] *See Florida Star v. B.J.F.*, 491 U.S. 524 (1989) (First Amendment trumps state law forbidding publication of the name of a victim of a sexual offense); *Landmark Communications, Inc. v. Virginia*, 435 U.S. 829 (1978) (First Amendment overcomes law prohibiting publication of names of judges who are under investigation for misconduct).

[8] *See N.A.A.C.P. v. Alabama*, 357 U.S. 449 (1958) (preventing compelled production of NAACP's membership list).

of reproductive rights the Supreme Court has recognized a constitutionally protected privacy interest "in avoiding disclosure of personal matters."[9]

Limiting disclosure of personal information can interfere with the ability of researchers and investigative journalists to do their work. Protected private information may be newsworthy itself, or may lead to other newsworthy information.

Efficiency. Privacy is also sometimes opposed to the societal interest in facilitating efficient commercial transactions. Data collected from commercial transactions involving individual consumers are used to create profiles of prospective customers that enable marketers to target promotional solicitations to consumers who the marketers consider more likely to find them of interest. This results in a higher return rate, and therefore reduces the cost of marketing. Giving individuals a right to prevent the use of their transactional data for these purposes interferes with the creation of lists that permit such targeting. In addition to making marketing more expensive, it may also be contrary to the individual's own interests in minimizing the quantity of junk mail and telemarketing that she receives, since a lower return rate might mean that more solicitations must be sent out. Limiting businesses' use of transactional information can make it harder for new entrants to compete:

> Because trade in consumer information serves an important economic function, regulatory obstacles to collecting this information can have hidden economic costs. . . . The mandatory opt-in rule would favor larger and older companies at the expense of newer, smaller ones. Established companies could afford more costly lists more easily than could small companies. And established companies would also have less need for lists, since they would have been in business long enough to collect information on their own. *The brunt of an opt-in law would thus be borne by small, new businesses or nonprofits struggling to establish a customer base.* . . . Under mandatory opt-in, firms that could afford to send direct mail would no longer be able to target it effectively. That would lead to fewer, more expensive options for those who shop at home—the elderly, the disabled, rural residents, and anyone without a car—because their mobility is restricted. In a world without readily available, cheap marketing lists, it is doubtful that another company like Lands' End would ever be born. Mandatory opt-in could preclude, not only the development of new businesses, but the development of whole new business models and product lines designed to serve groups of customers that could never before be identified. Had mandatory opt-in rules been in place a hundred years ago, for example, consumer credit reporting might never have developed.

Solveig Singleton, *Privacy as Censorship: A Skeptical View of Proposals to Regulate Privacy in the Private Sector*, CATO POLICY ANALYSIS NO. 295 (1998), www.cato.org/pubs/pas/pa-295.pdf.

Privacy of medical records can interfere with the provision of emergency medical services. If consent is required before medical personnel may access the records of a person in need of emergency treatment, and the person is in a condition that makes it impossible for her to grant that consent, provision of medical services may be delayed or based on incomplete information.

The ability to conceal information that reflects badly on yourself, in the name of privacy, can interfere with the ability of others to make rational decisions concerning you; as

---

[9] *Whalen v. Roe*, 429 U.S. 589, 599 (1977).

for example if the fact of your criminal record is unavailable to a potential employer, business associate, or spouse, or if your poor credit history is unavailable to a prospective lender.

QUESTIONS FOR DISCUSSION

Balancing competing values. Evaluate the following argument: Expressing the problem of privacy protection as one of "balancing" competing values is a formulation that leads to no stable solution. We are better off thinking of it as an optimization problem, which we can approach either from a utilitarian or a moral rights perspective. From a utilitarian perspective, we should extend the right of privacy as far as it will yield benefits exceeding its costs. From a moral rights perspective, we should sometimes protect privacy for its own sake, regardless of the costs entailed.

FURTHER READING

- ALAN F. WESTIN, PRIVACY AND FREEDOM 32–39 (1967) (offering an extended discussion of the functions of individual privacy, under the rubrics of "personal autonomy, emotional release, self-evaluation, and limited and protected communication")

- ANITA L. ALLEN, UNEASY ACCESS: PRIVACY FOR WOMEN IN A FREE SOCIETY (1988) (presenting a philosophical perspective on the functions of individual privacy)

- Eugene Volokh, *Freedom of Speech and Information Privacy: The Troubling Implications of a Right to Stop People from Speaking About You*, 52 STAN. L. REV. 1049 (2000) (criticizing, from a First Amendment perspective, proposals to protect information privacy through legal restrictions on the disclosure of information)

II. FAIR INFORMATION PRACTICE PRINCIPLES

One widely followed approach to information privacy issues is to gauge the sufficiency of privacy protections by reference to a set of principles defining fair information practices. Statements of these principles have had an important impact on policy discussions concerning information privacy on the Internet.

FEDERAL TRADE COMMISSION, PRIVACY ONLINE: A REPORT TO CONGRESS (1998)
www.ftc.gov/reports/privacy3/priv-23a.pdf

. . .

III. Fair Information Practice Principles

A. Fair Information Practice Principles Generally

Over the past quarter century, government agencies in the United States, Canada, and Europe have studied the manner in which entities collect and use personal information—their "information practices"—and the safeguards required to assure those practices are fair and provide adequate privacy protection.[27] The re-

---

[27] Fair information practice principles were first articulated in a comprehensive manner in the United States Department of Health, Education and Welfare's seminal 1973 report entitled *Records, Computers and the Rights of Citizens* (1973) [hereinafter "HEW Report"]. In

sult has been a series of reports, guidelines, and model codes that represent widely-accepted principles concerning fair information practices.

Common to all of these documents [hereinafter referred to as "fair information practice codes"] are five core principles of privacy protection: (1) Notice/Awareness; (2) Choice/Consent; (3) Access/Participation; (4) Integrity/Security; and (5) Enforcement/Redress.

1. Notice/Awareness

The most fundamental principle is notice. Consumers should be given notice of an entity's information practices before any personal information is collected from them. Without notice, a consumer cannot make an informed decision as to whether and to what extent to disclose personal information. Moreover, three of the other principles discussed below—choice/consent, access/participation, and enforcement/redress—are only meaningful when a consumer has notice of an entity's policies, and his or her rights with respect thereto.

While the scope and content of notice will depend on the entity's substantive information practices, notice of some or all of the following have been recognized as essential to ensuring that consumers are properly informed before divulging personal information:

- identification of the entity collecting the data;

- identification of the uses to which the data will be put;

- identification of any potential recipients of the data;

- the nature of the data collected and the means by which it is collected if not obvious (passively, by means of electronic monitoring, or actively, by asking the consumer to provide the information);

- whether the provision of the requested data is voluntary or required, and the consequences of a refusal to provide the requested information; and

- the steps taken by the data collector to ensure the confidentiality, integrity and quality of the data.

Some information practice codes state that the notice should also identify any available consumer rights, including: any choice respecting the use of the data;

---

the twenty-five years that have elapsed since the HEW Report, a canon of fair information practice principles has been developed by a variety of governmental and inter-governmental agencies. In addition to the HEW Report, the major reports setting forth the core fair information practice principles are: The Privacy Protection Study Commission, *Personal Privacy in an Information Society* (1977) . . . ; Organization for Economic Cooperation and Development, *OECD Guidelines on the Protection of Privacy and Transborder Flows of Personal Data* (1980) . . . ; Information Infrastructure Task Force, Information Policy Committee, Privacy Working Group, *Privacy and the National Information Infrastructure: Principles for Providing and Using Personal Information* (1995) . . . ; U.S. Dept. of Commerce, *Privacy and the NII: Safeguarding Telecommunications-Related Personal Information* (1995) . . . ; *The European Union Directive on the Protection of Personal Data* (1995) . . . ; and the Canadian Standards Association, *Model Code for the Protection of Personal Information: A National Standard of Canada* (1996) . . . .

whether the consumer has been given a right of access to the data; the ability of the consumer to contest inaccuracies; the availability of redress for violations of the practice code; and how such rights can be exercised.

In the Internet context, notice can be accomplished easily by the posting of an information practice disclosure describing an entity's information practices on a company's site on the Web. To be effective, such a disclosure should be clear and conspicuous, posted in a prominent location, and readily accessible from both the site's home page and any Web page where information is collected from the consumer. It should also be unavoidable and understandable so that it gives consumers meaningful and effective notice of what will happen to the personal information they are asked to divulge.

2. Choice/Consent

The second widely-accepted core principle of fair information practice is consumer choice or consent. At its simplest, choice means giving consumers options as to how any personal information collected from them may be used. Specifically, choice relates to secondary uses of information—*i.e.*, uses beyond those necessary to complete the contemplated transaction. Such secondary uses can be internal, such as placing the consumer on the collecting company's mailing list in order to market additional products or promotions, or external, such as the transfer of information to third parties.

Traditionally, two types of choice/consent regimes have been considered: opt-in or opt-out. Opt-in regimes require affirmative steps by the consumer to allow the collection and/or use of information; opt-out regimes require affirmative steps to prevent the collection and/or use of such information. The distinction lies in the default rule when no affirmative steps are taken by the consumer. Choice can also involve more than a binary yes/no option. Entities can, and do, allow consumers to tailor the nature of the information they reveal and the uses to which it will be put. Thus, for example, consumers can be provided separate choices as to whether they wish to be on a company's general internal mailing list or a marketing list sold to third parties. In order to be effective, any choice regime should provide a simple and easily-accessible way for consumers to exercise their choice.

In the online environment, choice easily can be exercised by simply clicking a box on the computer screen that indicates a user's decision with respect to the use and/or dissemination of the information being collected. The online environment also presents new possibilities to move beyond the opt-in/opt-out paradigm. For example, consumers could be required to specify their preferences regarding information use before entering a Web site, thus effectively eliminating any need for default rules.

3. Access/Participation

Access is the third core principle. It refers to an individual's ability both to access data about him or herself—*i.e.*, to view the data in an entity's files—and to contest that data's accuracy and completeness. Both are essential to ensuring that data are accurate and complete. To be meaningful, access must encompass timely and inexpensive access to data, a simple means for contesting inaccurate or incomplete data, a mechanism by which the data collector can verify the information, and the means by which corrections and/or consumer objections can be added to the data file and sent to all data recipients.

4. Integrity/Security

The fourth widely accepted principle is that data be accurate and secure. To assure data integrity, collectors must take reasonable steps, such as using only reputable sources of data and cross-referencing data against multiple sources, providing consumer access to data, and destroying untimely data or converting it to anonymous form.

Security involves both managerial and technical measures to protect against loss and the unauthorized access, destruction, use, or disclosure of the data. Managerial measures include internal organizational measures that limit access to data and ensure that those individuals with access do not utilize the data for unauthorized purposes. Technical security measures to prevent unauthorized access include encryption in the transmission and storage of data; limits on access through use of passwords; and the storage of data on secure servers or computers that are inaccessible by modem.

5. Enforcement/Redress

It is generally agreed that the core principles of privacy protection can only be effective if there is a mechanism in place to enforce them. Absent an enforcement and redress mechanism, a fair information practice code is merely suggestive rather than prescriptive, and does not ensure compliance with core fair information practice principles. Among the alternative enforcement approaches are industry self-regulation; legislation that would create private remedies for consumers; and/or regulatory schemes enforceable through civil and criminal sanctions.

a. Self-Regulation

To be effective, self-regulatory regimes should include both mechanisms to ensure compliance (enforcement) and appropriate means of recourse by injured parties (redress). Mechanisms to ensure compliance include making acceptance of and compliance with a code of fair information practices a condition of membership in an industry association; external audits to verify compliance; and certification of entities that have adopted and comply with the code at issue. A self-regulatory regime with many of these principles has recently been adopted by the individual reference services industry.

Appropriate means of individual redress include, at a minimum, institutional mechanisms to ensure that consumers have a simple and effective way to have their concerns addressed. Thus, a self-regulatory system should provide a means to investigate complaints from individual consumers and ensure that consumers are aware of how to access such a system.

If the self-regulatory code has been breached, consumers should have a remedy for the violation. Such a remedy can include both the righting of the wrong (*e.g.*, correction of any misinformation, cessation of unfair practices) and compensation for any harm suffered by the consumer. Monetary sanctions would serve both to compensate the victim of unfair practices and as an incentive for industry compliance. Industry codes can provide for alternative dispute resolution mechanisms to provide appropriate compensation.

b. Private Remedies

A statutory scheme could create private rights of action for consumers harmed by an entity's unfair information practices. Several of the major information practice codes, including the seminal 1973 HEW Report, call for implementing legislation. The creation of private remedies would help create strong incentives for entities to adopt and implement fair information practices and ensure compensation for individuals harmed by misuse of their personal information. Important questions would need to be addressed in such legislation, *e.g.*, the definition of unfair information practices; the availability of compensatory, liquidated and/or punitive damages; and the elements of any such cause of action.

c. Government Enforcement

Finally, government enforcement of fair information practices, by means of civil or criminal penalties, is a third means of enforcement. Fair information practice codes have called for some government enforcement, leaving open the question of the scope and extent of such powers. Whether enforcement is civil or criminal likely will depend on the nature of the data at issue and the violation committed.

. . .

___

EXTENSIONS

1. *A widely recognized formulation.* This formulation of the fair information practice principles underpins several industry self-regulatory efforts aimed at online privacy. See, for example, the principles implemented by the TRUSTe privacy seal program, discussed in Part V(B), *infra*, the guidelines adopted by the Online Privacy Alliance, discussed in Part V(A), *infra*, and the content of website privacy notices created by the Direct Marketing Association's privacy policy generator, discussed in Part V(A), *infra*.

2. *Choice: Opt-in vs. opt-out.* The question whether the exercise of choice should be through an opt-in or an opt-out mechanism has provoked heated debate. Since few Internet users exercise any choice they are offered, the default option is the one that is "selected" in the vast majority of cases. Marketers therefore strongly prefer opt-out. Privacy advocates are critical of opt-out, on the ground that it does not represent the exercise of informed consent on the part of the user.

In a case brought by a company protesting FCC privacy regulations, the Tenth Circuit held that an FCC regulation requiring opt-in consent to the use and disclosure of customer information by telecommunications carriers is an unconstitutional regulation of speech, in violation of the First Amendment. *See U.S. West, Inc. v. Federal Communications Commission*, 182 F.3d 1224 (10th Cir.1999). The regulation in question was an interpretation of certain elements of a consumer privacy provision enacted as part of the Telecommunication Act of 1996. The privacy provision established that a telecommunications carrier could use its customers' personal information for certain marketing purposes only "with the approval of the customer." Under the challenged regulation, this approval had to be obtained through an opt-in method. The carriers preferred to obtain the required approval through an opt-out approach, under which a customer's approval would be inferred from her failure to express disapproval. Since the speech in question consisted of marketing messages, the court analyzed the regulation under the standards that apply to commercial speech. The court held that the government had failed adequately to establish that the carriers' use of customers' personal information for marketing purposes results in any real harm to the customers' privacy interests. The court also held that the FCC had failed to establish that the opt-in requirement was "narrowly tailored" to achieve its objective, given the availability of the less-restrictive opt-out approach: "[T]he FCC record does not adequately show that an opt-out strategy would not sufficiently protect customer privacy. The respondents merely speculate that there are a substantial number of individuals who feel strongly about their privacy, yet would not bother to opt-out if given notice and the opportunity to do so. Such speculation hardly reflects the careful calculation of costs and benefits that our commercial speech jurisprudence requires." *Id.* at 1239.

3. *Access.* The question of appropriate access has been a thorny issue for U.S. policy-makers. A blue-ribbon advisory committee assembled by the FTC was able to do little more than agree to disagree on such issues as what access consists of, what information should be subject to access, how to implement access when information is shared among various third parties, and who should bear the cost of access. *See* FINAL REPORT OF THE FEDERAL TRADE COMMISSION ADVISORY COMMITTEE ON ONLINE ACCESS AND SECURITY (2000), www.ftc.gov/acoas/papers/finalreport.htm. The European Commission's Data Protection Directive includes an access right that is in some respects equivocal, but does give the data subject a right to "communication to him in an intelligible form of the data undergoing processing and of any available information as to their source," and also "as appropriate the rectification, erasure or blocking of data the processing of which does not comply with the provisions of this Directive, in particular because of the incomplete or inaccurate nature of the data." Directive 95/46/EC of the European Parliament and of the Council of 24 October 1995 on the protection of individuals with regard to the processing of personal data and on the free movement of such data, art. 12, 1995 O.J. (L 281) 31, at 42, europa.eu.int/comm/justice_home/fsj/privacy/law/index_en.htm, discussed in Part V(D), *infra.*

4. *Security.* There have been a number of publicized incidents in which personal information maintained by an e-commerce website was inadvertently disclosed to third parties, usually as result of a software defect, human error, or intrusion by hackers. Is the custodian of personal information liable for such unintentional disclosures?

The FTC has brought several actions charging that online sellers represented that personal customer information was maintained securely, when in fact it was vulnerable to unauthorized access by third parties. The FTC's theory is that the release of the information demonstrated the falsity of the company's representation in its privacy policy that its technology maintained the confidentiality and security of users' personal information. *In re Petco Animal Supplies, Inc.,* FTC Docket No. C–4143 (2005) (consent order); *In re MTS, Inc.,* FTC Docket No. C–4110 (2004) (consent order); *In re Guess?, Inc.,* FTC Docket No. C–4091 (2003) (consent order); *In re Microsoft Corp.,* FTC Docket No. C–4069 (2002) (consent order); *In re Eli Lilly and Co.,* FTC Docket No. C–4047 (2002) (consent order).

State laws are also potentially applicable to privacy-policy violations. In April 2004 the New York Attorney General settled with Barnes & Noble.com charges that an exposure of customer data via its website was inconsistent with its posted privacy policy, and therefore violated the New York deceptive business practices law.

QUESTIONS FOR DISCUSSION

1. *Substantive content of notice.* Should the "Notice" principle extend to the *content* of a website's privacy practices, or only to whether those practices are disclosed in a clear and conspicuous manner? Consider the following hypothetical privacy notice:

> We collect and retain all of the personally identifiable information we can extract from your online activities, including all of your clickstream activity. Using a cookie, we associate this information with your online identity. We also make every effort to link this information to your real-world identity, and are usually successful. We will use the information we have gathered to target you with customized marketing materials to whatever extent we find profitable. We will also avail ourselves of every opportunity to sell, rent, share, or trade your personal information with any other commercial entity if by doing so we can turn a buck.

Is this privacy statement objectionable from the standpoint of the fair information practice principles?

2. *Comprehensibility of notice.* Website privacy notices tend to be long, rambling, full of legalese, diluted with extraneous material, and generally incomprehensible to most people. One analysis of the privacy policies posted at some of the most heavily trafficked sites on the Web found that they were all written at a college reading level or higher, while most people in the United States read at a tenth-grade level or below. One of these policies was eight pages long, containing 3,405 words and 167 sentences. *See* Will Rodger, *Privacy Isn't Public Knowledge*, USA TODAY, Jun. 7, 2000, at 3D. How easily comprehensible must a privacy notice be for it to be considered adequate notice? Is the subject of online privacy so complex that it is impossible for a website to disclose its practices in a brief and understandable manner? In 2005, several websites, including IBM.com and MSN.com, implemented short-form privacy notices, consisting of about one screenful of summary information with links to a more detailed statement of the privacy policy. Is this sort of notice significantly more usable than the standard long form?

3. *Regulation of notices?* Various provisions of consumer protection law require sellers to give notices to consumers, and regulate the content and presentation of those notices. Should privacy notices be similarly regulated? Compare Chapter 4, Part III(A), *supra*.

III. ONLINE TECHNOLOGIES OF SURVEILLANCE AND THEIR IMPLICATIONS FOR DATA PRIVACY

When accessing the Internet from your personal computer it is natural to assume that, unless you choose to identify yourself, your activities are anonymous. That is an illusion. Network technology has spawned mechanisms that allow a website operator to learn the identity and track the online activities of those who visit the website, and enable senders of e-mail to receive notification when the recipient opens the message. Cookies brand an Internet user's computer with a unique identifying number that facilitates tracking, and web bugs allow web pages and e-mail messages to "call home" and report the information they have gathered. This surveillance is carried out in a manner that is invisible to most Internet users, and that may be difficult to prevent. Privacy advocates view this surveillance as one of the most serious and intrusive threats to the privacy interests of Internet users.

A. COOKIES

When you use your computer to access a website, your computer transmits certain information to the website, including the URL of the web page you are seeking to access (which tells the website what data you want it to send to you), the IP address of your computer (which tells the website where to send the data so that you can receive it), the URL of the web page you were viewing immediately before accessing the site, and certain configuration information about your computer. This information is usually not sufficient to allow the website operator to recognize you, the next time you access the site, as someone who has previously visited the site.[10] Nor does it generally allow the website operator to ascertain your real-world identity.

Cookies were designed to overcome this identity gap. A cookie is a text file, containing a unique identification code, that a website's server causes to be placed on a user's computer when the user accesses the site.[11] The next time the user visits the website, the server reads the cookie it left behind on the user's computer, and is able to recognize the user—or at least the user's computer—as one who has previously visited the site. Cookies can also contain additional information, such as a password or user preferences, that can be read by the originating server.

This rather simple capability has profound implications for the privacy of website visitors. Each time you access a website, you transmit clickstream information to the site, consisting at a minimum of the URL of each page you visit at the site. Once a site has assigned your computer a unique identification code, it can collect all of the clickstream data created by visits using your computer and associate those data with your identification code. Thus, a website can create a dossier of information that is associated with your computer, and can use this information to personalize its interaction with you.

For example, if you visit an online bookseller, and perform a search for books on military history, the website may add to your dossier the fact that you have exhibited an interest in that subject. The next time you visit that site, it may display a selection of new releases relating to military history. If on some later visit to that website you purchase a book, the website will be able to associate all the information in your dossier not only with the unique identifier of the cookie, but also with your real-world identity, since in placing your order you will have conveyed your name, address, and other personally identifying information.

The website operator can now use all of the information it has collected about you to tailor special offers it conveys to you by direct mail and telemarketing, as well as via e-mail. Your dossier becomes a more valuable commodity, which can be rented to a broader range of other sellers. Your activities in visiting that website, past and future, are no longer anonymous.

---

[10] With the dial-up connections that most people use to access the Internet from their home computers, the IP address is usually "dynamic": it may change each time the computer dials in and makes a new connection to the Internet. Since this identifier is not persistent, it does not allow a website operator to identify a visitor. Some types of broadband connections, such as digital subscriber line and cable, may use "static" IP addresses: the address of the computer is always the same, giving the computer a persistent identity. The same is true of most connections to the Internet through a local area network.

[11] Cookies come in different flavors. "Session" cookies are maintained in your computer's memory while your computer is connected to the Internet, and disappear as soon as you close your browser. "Persistent" cookies are written to a file on the hard drive of your computer—usually either into a file named something like "cookies.txt," or into a file directory named "cookies." It is only persistent cookies that allow a website to recognize your computer in subsequent visits to the site.

B. GLOBALLY UNIQUE HARDWARE IDENTIFIERS

As described above, installing cookies is a way of branding a computer with a persistent, globally unique identifier that allows the computer to be identified from across the network. A cookie is software—it is a data file that is written to a computer's hard drive. Another type of persistent globally unique identifier ("GUID") is one that is embedded in the computer's hardware. Like a cookie, hardware GUIDs can be read remotely from across the network.

One common type of hardware GUID is the identifier that is inscribed on Ethernet cards. An Ethernet card is a device installed in a personal computer that allows it to interconnect with other computers through a local area network ("LAN"). The protocol that is used for routing communications within a LAN requires each of the computers belonging to the LAN to have a unique address. This address is derived from the unique serial number of each computer's Ethernet card.

Within the context of a LAN, the existence of a unique identifier on the Ethernet card raises no privacy concerns, since nobody who uses a computer on the LAN expects that his communications across the LAN will be anonymous. But in early 1999, a privacy researcher named Richard M. Smith announced his discovery of a peculiar feature of the online registration program for Microsoft's Windows 98 operating system. If the computer whose copy of Windows 98 was being registered contained an Ethernet card, the registration program would extract the card's unique identification number, place it on the computer's hard drive as a cookie, and transmit the number to Microsoft. When a user of the computer created a document using certain Microsoft application programs, including Word 98 and Excel 98, this GUID would be inserted into the document in a manner that made it invisible to the average user but easily available to those in the know. This gave Microsoft the ability to identify the author of any such document, by looking up the document's GUID in the GUID database created by the Windows 98 registration process. It would also give anybody with access to a computer the ability to identify documents as having originated from that computer, and would make it possible to prove that two particular documents originated from the same computer.

Microsoft received a good deal of criticism after this practice was revealed, and it sought to make amends by announcing it would stop collecting GUIDs in the registration process, delete the GUID database it had assembled from Windows 98 registrations, and make available a program to delete the GUID from an individual computer's Windows registry. It also pledged to remove from its Office 2000 suite of applications the ability to insert GUIDs in documents.

C. WEB BUGS

A web page, as it resides on a server, consists of a text file that includes both the text that your browser displays as the content of the page and instructions coded in HTML that tell the browser how to format that content. If the web page incorporates a graphic image, the image will not itself be found in the HTML code. Instead, the code contains an instruction that tells your browser to fetch the image from a particular location on the server hosting the website, or on any other server connected to the Internet, and to place it on the web page it is displaying to you.

The HTML protocol allows your browser to append a string of text to the fetch request it sends to the server, and the server is able to read this text. A web bug is an instruction that pretends to be fetching an image to display on your web page, but in fact has the sole purpose of transmitting information from *your* computer to the server computer.[12] The image it fetches generally consists of a single pixel that is the same color as the pixel of the web page over which it is placed, and that therefore has no visible effect on the site visitor's computer. Web bugs are sometimes euphemistically referred to as "clear GIFs," "1 x 1 GIFs," or "web beacons."

A web bug can transmit several types of information to the server at which it is pointed, including the visiting computer's IP address, the URL of the page on which the bug is placed, the time the page containing the bug was displayed, and the identification code contained in any cookie that was placed by that server. What makes a web bug so much more powerful than a cookie alone its ability to transmit information *to a server other than the one that holds the web page the visitor is viewing*. Suppose, for example, that the sporting goods website you are visiting displays a banner advertisement from an online bookseller. The code making up the web page of the sporting goods site you are viewing contains an instruction telling your browser to fetch the image constituting the banner ad from a server maintained by the bookseller. The instruction causes your browser to transmit to the bookseller's server the URL of the page you are visiting—let us say, one featuring a tennis racquet. The bookseller's server is then able to place on the web page you are about to view a banner ad that it thinks will interest you, such as one featuring a book on the history of racquet sports. The bookseller's server is also able to place a cookie on your computer, so that it can begin to assemble a dossier on you. Note that this transmission of information to the bookseller occurs even though you have not clicked on its banner ad or taken any other action expressing an interest in the bookseller.

Now imagine that some company managed to place web bugs on thousands of websites, including the most popular sites on the Web. This company would be in a position to assemble quite a detailed profile of your online activities. Every time you viewed a page at any one of those websites, that fact would be transmitted to the company and added to your dossier. If you ever divulged your real-world identity at any of those websites, the company would be able to associate your identity with all of the data it had assembled about you. If the company were able to link this dossier with other collections of information about your offline activities, quite a lot of information about you would be available in one easily sortable, searchable, transmissible digital package, and various commercial entities might find such a package highly valuable.

As discussed below, this is the method that network advertising servers use to gather information that may be used in targeting online advertising.

D. E-MAIL AND DOCUMENT BUGS

E-mail messages that display graphics and styled text are constructed out of the same HTML code that constitutes web pages, and are equally capable of harboring web bugs. Such a bug might consist of an instruction to fetch an invisible graphic from the e-mail-sender's server, and while doing so to transmit information back to the server. For example,

---

[12] An instruction that is placed in the code of a web page for the bona fide purpose of fetching a graphic image may have a dual character, functioning also as a means of conveying information back to the server.

when you open the message the web bug can "call home" and report the time and date you opened it. The sender thereby learns that you do in fact read your e-mail, and through sending a series of messages may discern the time of day you typically check your e-mail. A job applicant could use this technique to determine whether companies to which he e-mailed his resume opened it.

A more advanced type of bug, which works only in e-mail readers with JavaScript enabled, can transmit back to the original sender any comments you add to the e-mail when you forward it to somebody else. This technique, which is known as "e-mail wiretapping," would allow the original sender to eavesdrop on an entire e-mail conversation between two people who converse by using the "Reply" button to send messages back and forth.

Bugs can also be inserted into documents produced by word processing, spreadsheet, presentation, and other software applications. These documents can include code that fetches a graphical image from a remote server, via the Internet. If the instruction is coded to retrieve an invisible 1 x 1 pixel dummy graphic, it can be used just like any other web bug. This sort of instruction will routinely transfer to the server the host name and IP address of the computer holding the document, and has the ability to set and read cookies. The bug would report back to the document's creator each time it is accessed on a computer with a live Internet connection. The document creator could therefore be alerted whenever the document was forwarded to and opened by somebody else. If it was a confidential document, and the bug reported that it had been opened on a computer with a host name other than the one for which it was intended, the creator would know it had been leaked and might be able to determine from the host name the organization that received it. If the document was copyrighted, the creator could determine whether it has been distributed in violation of the copyright.

E. SPYWARE AND ADWARE

Spyware has emerged as among the most salient threats to online privacy. The terminology is in flux, and definitional issues abound, but "spyware" generally refers to software that resides on a user's computer and surreptitiously gathers information concerning usage of the computer. The software either transmits the gathered information to some remote location, for either innocent or nefarious purposes, or uses it to select and display on the user's computer a targeted advertisement. Software with the latter purpose is also referred to as "adware." The most widespread variants of adware at present are programs distributed by WhenU.com and Claria Corp. (Trademark issues arising from adware are discussed in Chapter 2, Part II(C), *supra.*)

The phenomenon of spyware first came to light with the revelation by privacy researcher Richard M. Smith that two popular types of multimedia software were surreptitiously gathering information from users' computers. In 1999, Smith discovered that Real-Jukebox, free downloadable software that organizes and plays music files, was transmitting to RealNetworks, the maker of the software, information on users' listening habits, including the number of songs stored on the user's hard drive, the file formats in which they are stored, and the user's preferred music genre. All of this information was combined with a GUID assigned to each user, allowing dossiers to be compiled. This collection of information occurred without notice to users, either in the RealNetworks website privacy policy or in the RealJukebox license agreement. In response to the outcry over this revelation, Real-Networks modified its software to prevent this sort of information collection, rewrote its privacy policy, created an outside board to advise it on privacy issues, and joined the Online Privacy Alliance. In 2002, Smith found that Windows Media Player for Windows XP was engaged in a similar undisclosed collection of information. *See* Richard M. Smith, *Privacy*, www.computerbytesman.com/privacy/index.htm.

Spyware is often installed on a user's computer without notice, or with notice that many regard as inadequate. The spyware often arrives by piggybacking on some vector software that the user innocently downloads; the accompanying license agreement may disclose that the spyware will also be installed, but few users read the disclosure and fewer understand its implications. In the case of "drive-by downloads," the spyware is downloaded and installed with no notice whatsoever. The more insidious versions can be difficult or impossible for the average user to detect or remove.

In 2004, the Utah legislature enacted the first state law regulating spyware and adware. Spyware Control Act, UTAH CODE ANN. §§ 13–39–101 to –401. The Act restricts the use of two types of software. First, it prohibits the installation on another person's computer of "spyware," a term that the statute defines in a complex set of provisions. Simplifying a bit, a program is prohibited as spyware if it monitors usage of the computer on which it is installed, and either reports the usage information to a remote computer or displays advertisements on the user's computer in response to that usage, *but only if* the software fails to obtain the user's consent after making prescribed disclosures. *Id.* § 13–39–102(4). (There is also a provision that excludes cookies and diagnostic software from the definition of "spyware." *Id.* § 13–39–102(5).) Second, the Act prohibits use of software that delivers contextual pop-up advertisements—a prohibition that appears to be aimed at the type of adware distributed by WhenU.com and Claria. In a constitutional challenge filed by WhenU.com, a Utah state court issued a preliminary injunction against enforcement of the Act, finding plaintiff likely to succeed on its claim that the Act violates the Dormant Commerce Clause. *WhenU.com Inc. v. Utah*, Civil No. 040907578 (Utah Dist.Ct.2004). The Utah legislature subsequently amended the statute in an effort to remove the constitutional objection.

In 2004 California also enacted a law regulating spyware. The law prohibits a variety of deceptive practices, such as causing software to be installed on a computer if the software changes the computer's browser settings, collecting personally identifiable information from the computer, installing software that prevents itself from being uninstalled, or using the computer to relay spam. CAL. BUS. & PROF. CODE § 22947–22947.6. The law does not, however, require that the user be given notice that software is being downloaded to and installed on her computer. For that reason, the statute has been harshly criticized by some privacy advocates. Industry members that have an interest in online marketing, including Claria Corp., have applauded the statute.

During 2005, several additional states enacted spyware legislation. At this writing there are several bills pending in Congress that address spyware. *See* Internet Spyware (I-SPY) Prevention Act of 2005, H.R. 744, 109th Cong. (2005); Securely Protect Yourself Against Cyber Trespass Act ("Spy Act"), H.R. 29, 109th Cong. (2005).

EXTENSIONS

Application of consumer protection laws. Distribution of adware and spyware may violate consumer protection laws, if adequate disclosures are omitted. One case challenging adware as a consumer protection violation involved free software, called "SpyBlast," that was promoted as "Personal Computer Security and Protection Software from unauthorized users." In fact, the software caused adware to be installed on the user's computer, which analyzed the user's web surfing and delivered pop-up advertisements. The Federal Trade Commission charged the company that distributed the software with deceptive practices, for failure adequately to disclose the nature of the software. The company consented to entry of an order requiring it to disclose the software's adware function. *In re Advertising.com, Inc.*, FTC Docket No. C–4147 (2005) (consent order).

QUESTIONS FOR DISCUSSION

GUIDs. Is the proliferation of software- and hardware-based GUIDs something to be feared and fought? Is it an inevitable and largely beneficent consequence of the growing importance of network communications in all facets of life and the consequent necessity to privilege security and easy identification over privacy and anonymity?

COMPARATIVE NOTE

Opt-in for cookies? In 2001, the European Commission considered adding to a Directive a provision requiring a website to ask a site visitor's permission before placing a cookie on the visitor's hard drive. How would such a provision affect the conduct of online advertising and marketing? Would consumers be better or worse off with such a provision? In answering these questions, consider the fact that the major browsers can be configured to notify the user of all cookies being sent, and give the user an opportunity to refuse to receive them. To what extent do you think users are availing themselves of this opportunity?

FURTHER READING

- CENTER FOR DEMOCRACY AND TECHNOLOGY, GHOSTS IN OUR MACHINES: BACKGROUND AND POLICY PROPOSALS ON THE "SPYWARE" PROBLEM (2003) (providing a taxonomy of types of spyware, discussing legislative proposals, and recommending a multifaceted response), www.cdt.org/privacy/031100spyware.pdf

- Much useful material was generated in the Federal Trade Commission's April 2004 workshop titled "Monitoring Software on Your PC: Spyware, Adware, and Other Software," www.ftc.gov/bcp/workshops/spyware/index.htm.

IV. PRIVACY ISSUES

A. ONLINE PROFILING

Commercial websites frequently feature banner advertisements, which are rectangular panels appearing on website pages that contain promotional material and are usually hyperlinked to the website of the company placing the ad. As with print and broadcast media, these advertisements may be placed through a contractual arrangement between the website owner and the advertiser, according to which the advertiser pays the website owner to insert its ad into the code making up the website.

Advertisements can also be placed on websites through a third-party intermediary known as a network advertising server. The ad server contracts with advertisers who want their banner ads placed on websites, and contracts with website owners for the right to place ads on their sites. When a user pulls up a web page on a site that belongs to an ad server's network, the ad server determines what banner advertisement to display on the page based on the information that the server has obtained about the user (more accurately, about whoever uses that computer to browse the Web). The collection of information generated when Internet users browse the Web, and association of that information with a particular web-browsing computer or individual, is known as online profiling.

FEDERAL TRADE COMMISSION, ONLINE PROFILING: A REPORT TO CONGRESS (2000)
www.ftc.gov/os/2000/06/onlineprofilingreportjune2000.pdf

. . .

II. WHAT IS ONLINE PROFILING?

A. Overview

Over the past few years, online advertising has grown exponentially in tandem with the World Wide Web. Online advertising revenues in the U.S. grew from $301 million in 1996 to $4.62 billion in 1999, and were projected to reach $11.5 billion by 2003. A large portion of that online advertising is in the form of "banner ads" displayed on Web pages—small graphic advertisements that appear in boxes above or to the side of the primary site content. Currently, tens of billions of banner ads are delivered to consumers each month as they surf the World Wide Web. Often, these ads are not selected and delivered by the Web site visited by a consumer, but by a network advertising company that manages and provides advertising for numerous unrelated Web sites. DoubleClick, Engage, and 24/7 Media, three of the largest Internet advertising networks, all estimate that over half of all online consumers have seen an ad that they delivered.

In general, these network advertising companies do not merely supply banner ads; they also gather data about the consumers who view their ads. This is accomplished primarily by the use of "cookies" and "Web bugs" which track the individual's actions on the Web. Among the types of information that can be collected by network advertisers are: information on the Web sites and pages within those sites visited by consumers; the time and duration of the visits; query terms entered into search engines; purchases; "click-through" responses to advertisements; and the Web page a consumer came from before landing on the site monitored by the particular ad network (the referring page). All of this information is gathered even if the consumer never clicks on a single ad.

The information gathered by network advertisers is often, but not always, anonymous, *i.e.*, the profiles are frequently linked to the identification number of the advertising network's cookie on the consumer's computer rather than the name of a specific person. This data is generally referred to as non-personally identifiable information ("non-PII"). In some circumstances, however, the profiles derived from tracking consumers' activities on the Web are linked or merged with personally identifiable information ("PII"). This generally occurs in one of two ways when consumers identify themselves to a Web site on which the network advertiser places banner ads.[15] First, the Web site to whom personal information is pro-

---

[15] A previously anonymous profile can also be linked to personally identifiable information in other ways. For example, a network advertising company could operate its own Web

vided may, in turn, provide that information to the network advertiser. Second, depending upon how the personal information is retrieved and processed by the Web site, the personally identifying information may be incorporated into a URL string that is automatically transmitted to the network advertiser through its cookie.

Once collected, consumer data can be analyzed and combined with demographic and "psychographic"[18] data from third-party sources, data on the consumer's offline purchases, or information collected directly from consumers through surveys and registration forms. This enhanced data allows the advertising networks to make a variety of inferences about each consumer's interests and preferences. The result is a detailed profile that attempts to predict the individual consumer's tastes, needs, and purchasing habits and enables the advertising companies' computers to make split-second decisions about how to deliver ads directly targeted to the consumer's specific interests.

The profiles created by the advertising networks can be extremely detailed. A cookie placed by a network advertising company can track a consumer on any Web site served by that company, thereby allowing data collection across disparate and unrelated sites on the Web. Also, because the cookies used by ad networks are generally persistent, their tracking occurs over an extended period of time, resuming each time the individual logs on to the Internet. When this "clickstream" information is combined with third-party data, these profiles can include hundreds of distinct data fields.

Although network advertisers and their profiling activities are nearly ubiquitous, they are most often invisible to consumers. All that consumers see are the Web sites they visit; banner ads appear as a seamless, integral part of the Web page on which they appear and cookies are placed without any notice to consumers. Unless the Web sites visited by consumers provide notice of the ad network's presence and data collection, consumers may be totally unaware that their activities online are being monitored.

B. An Illustration of How Network Profiling Works

Online consumer Joe Smith goes to a Web site that sells sporting goods. He clicks on the page for golf bags. While there, he sees a banner ad, which he ignores as it does not interest him. The ad was placed by USAad Network. He then goes to a travel site and enters a search on "Hawaii." USAad Network also serves ads on this site, and Joe sees an ad for rental cars there. Joe then visits an online bookstore and browses through books about the

---

site at which consumers are asked to provide personal information. When consumers do so, their personal information could be linked to the identification number of the cookie placed on their computer by that company, thereby making all of the data collected through that cookie personally identifiable.

[18] Psychographic data links objective demographic characteristics like age and gender with more abstract characteristics related to ideas, opinions and interests. Data mining specialists analyze demographic, media, survey, purchasing and psychographic data to determine the exact groups that are most likely to buy specific products and services. . . . Psychographic profiling is also referred to in the industry as "behavioral profiling."

world's best golf courses. USAad Network serves ads there, as well. A week later, Joe visits his favorite online news site, and notices an ad for golf vacation packages in Hawaii. Delighted, he clicks on the ad, which was served by the USAad Network. Later, Joe begins to wonder whether it was a coincidence that this particular ad appeared and, if not, how it happened.

At Joe's first stop on the Web, the sporting goods site, his browser will automatically send certain information to the site that the site needs in order to communicate with Joe's computer: his browser type and operating system; the language(s) accepted by the browser; and the computer's Internet address. The server hosting the sporting goods site answers by transmitting the HTTP header and HTML source code for the site's home page, which allows Joe's computer to display the page.

Embedded in the HTML code that Joe's browser receives from the sporting goods site is an invisible link to the USAad Network site which delivers ads in the banner space on the sporting goods Web site. Joe's browser is automatically triggered to send an HTTP request to USAad which reveals the following information: his browser type and operating system; the language(s) accepted by the browser; the address of the referring Web page (in this case, the home page of the sporting goods site); and the identification number and information stored in any USAad cookies already on Joe's computer. Based on this information, USAad will place an ad in the pre-set banner space on the sporting goods site's home page. The ad will appear as an integral part of the page. If an USAad cookie is not already present on Joe's computer, USAad will place a cookie with a unique identifier on Joe's hard drive. Unless he has set his browser to notify him before accepting cookies, Joe has no way to know that a cookie is being placed on his computer. When Joe clicks on the page for golf bags, the URL address of that page, which discloses its content, is also transmitted to USAad by its cookie.

When Joe leaves the sporting goods site and goes to the travel site, also serviced by USAad, a similar process occurs. The HTML source code for the travel site will contain an invisible link to USAad that requests delivery of an ad as part of the travel site's page. Because the request reveals that the referring site is travel related, USAad sends an advertisement for rental cars. USAad will also know the identification number of its cookie on Joe's machine. As Joe moves around the travel site, USAad checks his cookie and modifies the profile associated with it, adding elements based on Joe's activities. When Joe enters a search for "Hawaii," his search term is transmitted to USAad through the URL used by the travel site to locate the information Joe wants and the search term is associated with the other data collected by the cookie on Joe's machine. USAad will also record what advertisements it has shown Joe and whether he has clicked on them.

This process is repeated when Joe goes to the online bookstore. Because USAad serves banner ads on this site as well, it will recognize Joe by his cookie identification number. USAad can track what books Joe looks at, even though he does not buy anything. The fact that Joe browsed for books about golf courses around the world is added to his profile.

Based on Joe's activities, USAad infers that Joe is a golfer, that he is interested in traveling to Hawaii someday, and that he might be interested in a golf vacation. Thus, a week later, when Joe goes to his favorite online news site, also served by USAad, the cookie on his computer is recognized and he is presented with an ad for golf vacation packages in Hawaii. The ad grabs his attention and appeals to his interests, so he clicks on it.

. . .

DoubleClick, Inc., a leading network advertising server, raised the hackles of privacy advocates when it announced, in June 1999, that it was merging with Abacus Direct Corp., a direct marketing research firm that held in its databases information about catalogue purchases of around 90 million U.S. households. Thereafter, in a revision to its website privacy notice, DoubleClick announced, in language indecipherable to the great majority of Internet users, that it intended to link information acquired from websites within its network with data in the Abacus databases. This would allow it to associate previously anonymous click-stream data with the real-world identities of Internet users, and to combine information about consumers' offline purchases with data about their online activities.

In March 2000, facing a barrage of criticism from privacy advocates and a round of bad publicity, DoubleClick reversed course and announced that it would not go forward with the planned information merger "until there is agreement between government and industry on privacy standards." Statement From Kevin O'Connor, CEO of DoubleClick (Mar. 2, 2000), www.doubleclick.net.

EXTENSIONS

1. *Benefits of network advertising.* Network advertising servers describe the benefits of the services they provide as follows:

> Effective Internet advertising is fundamental to the accessibility and dynamism of this revolutionary medium. Advertising underwrites the rich variety of online content choices available to consumers at no cost or at a far lower cost than would otherwise be possible. By delivering customized advertising, network advertisers offer substantial benefits for consumers and the advertiser. In addition, many small and emerging Web companies depend on network advertisers to compete against more well-established companies and their Web sites. Effective Internet advertising thus helps to maintain the low barriers to entry that have played a crucial role in the robust competition and innovation that have fueled this medium.

Network Advertising Initiative: Self-Regulatory Principles for Online Preference Marketing by Network Advertisers, at 2, www.networkadvertising.org/images/NAI_Principles.pdf.

2. *Opting out of online profiling.* The major network advertising servers allow individual Internet users to opt out of their tracking systems. *See, e.g.,* DoubleClick, *Privacy*, www.doubleclick.com/us/about_doubleclick/privacy/. How likely is it that users will avail themselves of this option? Would it be preferable from the standpoint of fair information practices if the website that is harboring the web bug—the site that the user is actually visiting—provided the disclosure? In its Privacy Policy, Yahoo! discloses that it allows network advertisers to collect information about visitors to its website. It advises visitors: "If you would like an ad network to not set or use cookies on your computer, you must visit each ad network's web site individually and opt out (if they offer this capability)." Yahoo!, *Third*

Party and Affiliate Cookies on Yahoo!, privacy.yahoo.com/privacy/us/adservers/details.html. It continues with a list of links to a number of network advertisers' websites—34 of them at this writing.

3. *Network advertisers' self-regulatory plan.* In response to the FTC's study of the privacy implications of online profiling, the network advertising industry developed and proposed a self-regulatory program designed to implement the fair information practice principles. *See Network Advertising Initiative: Self-Regulatory Principles for Online Preference Marketing by Network Advertisers,* www.networkadvertising.org/images/NAI_Principles.pdf. Consider whether this approach offers Internet users substantial privacy benefits. For a critical appraisal of the Network Advertising Initiative, see Electronic Privacy Information Center, *Network Advertising Initiative: Principles Not Privacy* (2000), www.epic.org/privacy/internet/NAI_analysis.html.

In late 2002, the companies forming the Network Advertising Initiative issued a set of self-regulatory guidelines applying to the use of web bugs. The guidelines require disclosure of the use of these devices in the privacy policy of a site that uses them, and in e-mail messages that harbor them. Site visitors and e-mail recipients must be afforded choice as to whether their personally identifiable information collected via a web bug is transferred to a third party, but the choice may be implemented through an opt-out system. *See Web Beacons—Guidelines for Notice and Choice* (2002), www.networkadvertising.org/Web_Beacons_11-1-04.pdf.

4. *Application of anti-surveillance laws to ad servers.* Network advertising servers create profiles of Internet users by tapping into the clickstream information that users exchange with the websites they visit. For this to happen, the websites with which the advertising server has contractual arrangements must modify the code that constitutes their web pages by inserting statements that direct clickstream information to the ad server. In collecting this information, does the ad server violate (i) the Electronic Communication Privacy Act ("ECPA"), 18 U.S.C. § 2511 (also known as the Wiretap Act), which makes it unlawful to "intentionally intercept[] . . . any . . . electronic communication"? (ii) another provision of ECPA, 18 U.S.C. § 2701 (also known as the Stored Communications Act), which prescribes penalties for anyone who "(1) intentionally accesses without authorization a facility through which an electronic communication service is provided; or (2) intentionally exceeds an authorization to access that facility; and thereby obtains, alters, or prevents authorized access to a wire or electronic communication while it is in electronic storage in such system."? *See Chance v. Avenue A, Inc.*, 165 F.Supp.2d 1153 (W.D.Wash.2001) (dismissing claims under §§ 2511 and 2701, finding that website's consent to hosting of ad server's code negates violation); *In re DoubleClick Inc. Privacy Litigation*, 154 F.Supp.2d 497 (S.D.N.Y.2001) (same).

Does accessing cookies violate the Computer Fraud and Abuse Act, 18 U.S.C. § 1030(a)(2)(C), which makes it unlawful to "intentionally access[] a computer without authorization . . . and thereby obtain[] . . . information"? It seems doubtful that the $5,000 "damage or loss" threshold could be met. *See Chance v. Avenue A, Inc., supra*; *In re DoubleClick Inc. Privacy Litigation, supra.*

Does the website that hosts the code that allows DoubleClick to collect clickstream information violate these provisions? *See In re Intuit Privacy Litigation*, 138 F.Supp.2d 1272 (C.D.Cal.2001) (dismissing claims under §§ 2511 and 1030, but permitting plaintiffs to pursue claims under § 2701).

5. *Application of consumer protection laws.* In August 2002, the Attorneys General of ten states, citing their respective state consumer protection laws as a basis, entered a settlement agreement with DoubleClick Inc. Under the terms of the agreement, DoubleClick will (1) require each website that allows DoubleClick to collect clickstream data from site visitors to disclose DoubleClick's practices in the website's privacy policy; (2) retain in a segregated form any data it collects on behalf of a single website; and (3) post on its own website a privacy policy describing its practices with respect to user data that it collects, and allow users to opt in to receive notifications via e-mail of any changes DoubleClick makes to its privacy policy. *See In re DoubleClick, Inc.*, news.findlaw.com/hdocs/docs/cyberlaw/agsdclick82602agr.pdf.

6. *Microsoft's "Passport" system.* In late 1999, Microsoft launched an online information management system called Passport; in 2002, Microsoft entered into a settlement agreement with the Federal Trade Commission, settling charges that it had made false and deceptive statements about the privacy aspects of Passport. A user of Passport enters personal information into the system, such as her name, address, age, occupation, e-mail address, hobbies and interests, and a personal statement. The information is used to create a profile of the user, and is in some circumstances made accessible to e-commerce websites. The FTC's complaint alleges that Microsoft (1) falsely represented that the privacy of Passport users was protected through effective security technology, (2) falsely represented that using Passport makes online purchases safer and more secure, (3) collected personally identifiable information beyond that which was described in the Passport privacy policy, and (4) falsely represented that its Kids Passport service allows parents to control the information that their children can supply to websites. In the settlement Microsoft agreed to end these practices. *See In re Microsoft Corp.*, FTC Docket No. C–4069 (2002) (consent order).

QUESTIONS FOR DISCUSSION

1. *Balancing interests.* How would you balance the privacy interests of Internet users against the asserted benefits of information collection by network advertisers? Are Internet users entitled to meaningful notice about the practices of network advertising servers, and true, opt-in choice about whether to allow their clickstream data to be collected for purposes of online profiling? Would you favor a rule requiring opt-in consent to online profiling if the result would be a reduction in the quantity of freely available (advertiser-supported) information on the Internet?

2. *Gmail and privacy.* In March 2004 Google launched a testing period for Gmail, its new webmail service. Gmail is a free service, and offers its subscribers an enormous 1,000 megabytes of message storage space (several hundred times as much as its competitors offered at the time), as well as proprietary methods of organizing and storing messages. The price of admission: Google scans the text of incoming and outgoing messages, and serves advertisements based on analysis of the text. If, for example, the e-mail text suggests that you are planning a vacation, you might receive advertisements from airlines or travel agencies. No sooner was Gmail announced than privacy objections were raised on several fronts. Privacy advocates urge that Gmail's scanning of message text violates wiretap laws; a bill regulating the service was introduced in the California legislature; and German officials stated that Gmail would likely violate German privacy laws. Do you agree that the Gmail service raises privacy concerns? Can a Gmail subscriber validly consent to the scanning of *incoming* messages? Is scanning message content for the purpose of targeting advertisements any more of a privacy problem than scanning to filter out spam or pornography?

FURTHER READING

- Michael R. Siebecker, *Cookies and the Common Law: Are Internet Advertisers Trespassing on Our Computers?*, 76 S. CAL. L. REV. 893 (2003) (arguing that a website that writes a cookie on a user's hard drive has committed actionable trespass to chattels)

- Matthew A. Goldberg, Comment, *The Googling of Online Privacy: Gmail, Search-Engine Histories and the New Frontier of Protecting Private Information on the Web*, 9 LEWIS & CLARK L. REV. 249 (2005) (arguing that Google's unauthorized disclosure to third parties of information gleaned from Gmail messages violates the Stored Communications Act)

B. ONLINE PRIVACY POLICIES: USES AND ABUSES

1. Failure to Honor Privacy Policy

Many websites post privacy policies that advise visitors about how personal data submitted to the website will be used. But these policies are not always honored. Existing laws that forbid deceptive marketing practices can be applied when a website makes representations in its privacy policy concerning its handling of site visitors' personal information, and then fails to honor its promises.

One such law is the Federal Trade Commission Act, which forbids "unfair or deceptive acts or practices in or affecting commerce." 15 U.S.C. § 45(a)(1). In *In re GeoCities*, FTC Docket No. C–3850 (1999), the FTC charged that GeoCities, a provider of free website hosting services, violated the Act by its failure to observe its privacy policy. In its privacy notice, GeoCities stated: "We will not share this information with anyone without your permission." The FTC alleged that, contrary to this statement, GeoCities provided its customers' personal identifying information to third-party marketers. GeoCities consented to entry of an order that prohibited future misrepresentations and required it to post a website privacy policy containing specified categories of information.

What if the disclosure of information is inadvertent? The FTC has brought several actions charging that online sellers represented that personal customer information was maintained securely, when in fact it was vulnerable to unauthorized access by third parties. The FTC's theory is that the release of the information demonstrated the falsity of the company's representation in its privacy policy that its technology maintained the confidentiality and security of users' personal information. *See In re Petco Animal Supplies, Inc.*, FTC Docket No. C-4143 (2005) (consent order); *In re MTS, Inc.*, FTC Docket No. C-4110 (2004) (consent order); *In re Guess?, Inc.*, FTC Docket No. C-4091 (2003) (consent order); *In re Microsoft Corp.*, FTC Docket No. C-4069 (2002) (consent order); *In re Eli Lilly and Co.*, FTC Docket No. C-4047 (2002) (consent order).

State laws are also potentially applicable to privacy-policy violations. In April 2004 the New York Attorney General settled with Barnes & Noble.com charges that an exposure of customer data via its website was inconsistent with its posted privacy policy, and therefore violated the New York deceptive business practices law.

2. Privacy Promises in Bankruptcy

Suppose the owner of a website that has operated under a policy of never disclosing its customers' personal data files for bankruptcy. Does the company's customer list, with its associated transactional data, become an asset of the bankruptcy estate, subject to sale for the benefit of the company's creditors?

The issue arose in the case of Toysmart.com, an online toy retailer. Toysmart's privacy policy stated: "Personal information voluntarily submitted by visitors to our site, such as name, address, billing information and shopping preferences, is never shared with a third party." The policy also stated: "When you register with toysmart.com, you can rest assured that your information will never be shared with a third party." The company announced that it was going out of business, and offered to sell its assets, including its customer lists, to the highest bidder. Toysmart's creditors subsequently filed a petition against it for involuntary bankruptcy.

The FTC filed a lawsuit against Toysmart to prevent the sale of the customer information, alleging that to do so in the face of its privacy promise would be a deceptive practice in violation of the FTC Act. The FTC reached a settlement with Toysmart, under which the customer information could only be sold as part of a package including the entire website, and only to a purchaser that agreed to abide by the terms of Toysmart's privacy notice. But the Attorneys General of 38 states objected to the settlement as being insufficiently protective of consumers, reasoning that when a company says it will "never" disclose personal information, it should be held to its word. The controversy was ultimately resolved when Walt Disney Co., the majority owner of Toysmart, agreed to pay $50,000 for the customer information and immediately to destroy that information.

EXTENSIONS

1. *Confusion about whose privacy policy applies.* In *In re Vision I Properties, LLC*, FTC Docket No. C-4135 (2005) (consent order), the FTC charged the respondent with unfair trade practices in connection with its online shopping-cart software. The software was implemented by various merchant sites, to perform the usual e-commerce checkout functions. While some merchant sites posted privacy policies stating that they would not disclose customer information, the respondent made use of the customer information it captured from sites using its software by renting the information to third-party marketers. The FTC alleged that the respondent failed adequately to inform the merchant sites of its own uses of the customer information, and failed to inform customers that the merchants' privacy policies did not apply to its own uses.

2. *Privacy as contractual obligation.* Does an undertaking in a website privacy policy give rise to an enforceable contract? That is, if a website operator discloses a user's personal information in contravention of the website privacy policy, can the user sue the website operator for breach of contract? Courts have thus far not been receptive to such claims. In *In re Jetblue Airways Corp. Privacy Litigation*, 379 F.Supp.2d 299 (E.D.N.Y.2005), plaintiff airline passengers sued JetBlue over its disclosure of personal information contained in their passenger records to a government contractor, which used the data to devise ways of increasing airline security. One of plaintiffs' theories was that JetBlue breached its contract with them, by disclosing the information in violation of its website privacy policy. The court dismissed the contract claim. It found that plaintiffs had adequately alleged that a "contract was formed at the moment they made flight reservations in reliance on express promises contained in JetBlue's privacy policy." However, the court held that plaintiffs had failed adequately to allege that they had suffered damages as a result of the disclosure, which is an element of a contract claim under New York law. The court held that loss of privacy is not cognizable as economic loss flowing from the alleged breach. It explained that, although plaintiffs may have had an expectation that JetBlue would adhere to its privacy promise, the alleged violation of that promise caused them no economic loss. *See also In re Northwest Airlines Privacy Litigation*, 2004 WL 1278459 (D.Minn.2004) ("absent an allegation that Plaintiffs actually read the privacy policy . . . Plaintiffs have failed to allege an essential element of a contract claim").

QUESTIONS FOR DISCUSSION

1. *What constitutes disclosure?* It is not always easy to determine whether a particular event constitutes disclosure of information to another party. Suppose Company A operates a website that provides free information about medical problems, with a privacy policy that states: "We will never sell, share, rent, trade, or otherwise disclose your personal information to anyone, ever." Is there a violation of the privacy policy if (1) Company A is sold, as a going concern, to Company B, which is also a provider of free medical information? (2) Company A is sold, as a going concern, to Company C, which is a pharmaceutical marketing company? (3) Company A acquires Company D, a pharmaceutical marketing company, as a subsidiary, and transfers the information to Company's D's marketing department? (4) Company A expands its business by beginning to sell pharmaceuticals, and uses its customer data for marketing? (5) Company A's stockholders sell a majority of the company's stock to new stockholders? (6) Company A goes out of business, and sells its database of personal information together with the rights to its trademark?

2. *Online vs. offline.* Toysmart got into trouble because its website operated under a highly protective privacy policy. If Toysmart had been a brick-and-mortar toy store that went bankrupt, it would most likely not have stated any privacy policy, and there would be not have been any objection to sale of its customer information. Does it make sense for the two situations to be treated differently? Did the FTC and the states overreact to the proposed sale of Toysmart's customer information?

3. *The lesson of* Toysmart. In view of Toysmart's difficulties, how would you advise a commercial website to structure its privacy policy? How likely is it that prospective customers would refuse to patronize a website because its privacy policy allowed customer information to be transferred without limitation in case of merger, acquisition, restructuring, or bankruptcy? Will prospective creditors be less willing to lend to an e-commerce business if its privacy policy makes customer information unavailable as an asset to satisfy debts?

3. Modification of a Website Privacy Policy

In the aftermath of the Toysmart controversy, Amazon.com implemented a change in its privacy policy. In September 2000 it sent e-mail messages to its 23 million customers announcing the change. The e-mails (with some non-substantive variations) read:

> Dear Customer,
>
> We're sorry for this intrusion. We know that you've asked not to receive certain types of e-mail from Amazon.com. From that request, it's clear that privacy issues are important to you. As we've recently updated our privacy policy, we did think it very important to contact you by e-mail to inform you of these changes.
>
> To read the revised Privacy Notice, visit: www.amazon.com/privacy-notice
>
> And again—please accept our apologies for sending you this e-mail. Thanks for shopping with us.
>
> Sincerely,
>
> Amazon.com

Amazon.com's privacy notice had previously stated:

> Amazon.com does not sell, trade or rent your personal information to others. We may choose to do so in the future with trustworthy third parties, but you can tell us not to by sending a blank e-mail message to *never@amazon.com.*

The revised policy said:

> **Business Transfers:** As we continue to develop our business, we might sell or buy stores or assets. In such transactions, customer information generally is one of the transferred business assets. Also, in the unlikely event that Amazon.com, Inc., or substantially all of its assets are acquired, customer information will of course be one of the transferred assets.

The revised policy also eliminated the option to direct Amazon.com not to disclose personal information to third parties.

As a result of this modification, the Electronic Privacy Information Center, a privacy advocacy group, severed its relationship with Amazon.com, through which Amazon.com was a favored distributor of EPIC's publications. In a letter to its subscribers, EPIC explained: "Recently Amazon announced that it could no longer guarantee that it would not disclose customer information to third parties. Because of this decision, and in the absence of legal or technical means to assure privacy for Amazon customers, we have decided that we can no longer continue our relationship with Amazon." Letter from Marc Rotenberg (Sept. 13, 2000), www.epic.org/privacy/internet/amazon/letter.html.

Yahoo! generated controversy when, in early 2002, it notified tens of millions of its registered users that it was both modifying its privacy policy and opting its users into receiving marketing messages. The modified policy gave notice that Yahoo! may convey marketing messages not only by e-mail, but also by telephone and postal mail. Yahoo! also added 13 new categories of marketing messages that it would begin sending to users, with a selection button next to each that indicated the user wished to receive those messages. To opt out, a user would have to click on "No" 13 times.

In *In re Gateway Learning Corp.*, FTC Docket No. C–4120 (2004) (consent order), the FTC charged an online seller of "Hooked on Phonics" educational materials with violations of the FTC Act by an attempted retroactive downgrading of its website privacy policy. The policy initially stated unequivocally that Gateway company "do[es] not sell, rent or loan any personally identifiable information regarding our consumers with any third party unless we receive a customer's explicit consent." Gateway later posted a revised policy, stating that it might provide customer information "to reputable companies whose products or services you may find of interest," and then did in fact disclose to third-party marketers customer information that it had acquired under the initial privacy policy. Gateway consented to an order prohibiting it from applying a revised privacy policy retroactively, absent opt-in consent from the affected consumers.

EXTENSIONS

Retroactive application of a modified privacy policy. If a website changes its privacy policy, which policy applies to information collected before the change is announced? As part of a settlement of a class-action lawsuit against it alleging privacy violations, Double-Click, Inc. agreed, for a period of two years, that "[a]n Internet user's online data . . . collected by DoubleClick under one version of DoubleClick's privacy policy will not be used in a manner materially inconsistent with that privacy policy, unless DoubleClick has that Internet user's permission to do otherwise." *In re DoubleClick Privacy Litigation*, No. 00-CIV-0641 (S.D.N.Y. settlement approved May 21, 2002).

C. STATE-LAW REQUIREMENT TO POST A PRIVACY POLICY

California's Online Privacy Protection Act of 2003, CAL. BUS. & PROF. CODE §§ 22575–78, which became effective on July 1, 2004, is the first state law that requires website operators to post and obey a privacy policy. The requirements of the Act apply to commercial websites and proprietary online services that collect personally identifiable information ("PII") "from individual consumers who use or visit the commercial Web site or online service and who reside in California." Those sites and services are required to post a privacy policy that conveys four pieces of information: (1) the types of PII that the site collects, and the types of third parties to which it discloses that PII; (2) a description of any option the site offers consumers to access and request changes to the PII collected about them; (3) a description of any process by which the site operator notifies visitors of changes to the privacy policy; and (4) the policy's effective date. *Id.* § 22575(a), (b).

The privacy policy must either appear on the website's home page, or must be accessible via a link on the home page that is made conspicuous in a prescribed manner or that otherwise is "so displayed that a reasonable person would notice it." *Id.* § 22577(b). PII is defined broadly to include name, address, telephone number, e-mail address, and "[a]ny other identifier that permits the physical or online contacting of a specific individual." *Id.* § 22577(a). The Act does not define what constitutes a "commercial" website, which can be expected to give rise to the usual uncertainty in borderline cases.

A violation of the Act consists of either failing to post a policy, or failing to comply with it. *Id.* § 22576. An unusual element of the enforcement scheme is that a website operator is liable for failure to post a policy only if it has been notified of noncompliance with the Act, and fails to post a policy within thirty days. *Id.* § 22575(a).

Consider the reach of the Act: Are there any commercial websites that it does not purport to regulate? Is this reach consistent with the Dormant Commerce Clause? Do you think the Act will have a significant impact on website operators who are located in California? Outside California? Is this an area that calls for federal, rather than state-by-state, regulation?

Also in 2003, the California legislature determined that the disclosures of information-sharing practices conveyed in website privacy policy notices failed to provide Californians with the information they needed to make rational choices about whether to share their personal information with a given business. To remedy this situation, the legislature enacted a law requiring businesses (regardless of their location) to disclose to their California customers, upon the customer's request, a list of the categories of personal information concerning the customer that the business has disclosed to a third party for the third party's direct marketing purposes. The disclosure must also identify the third parties that received the personal information. "Direct marketing" is defined to exclude solicitation for charitable contributions or political fundraising, and businesses with fewer than twenty employees are exempted from the disclosure requirement. The law went into effect on January 1, 2005. CAL. CIV. CODE § 1798.83. The rights that the law grants are non-waivable, and injured customers have a private right of action for damages, civil penalties, and attorney's fees. *Id.* § 1798.84.

The effect of the law is significantly diminished by inclusion of a provision allowing an alternative mode of compliance. If a business states in its privacy policy that it will not disclose personal information to third-party marketers unless the customer opts in to that disclosure, *or that it will only disclose personal information if the customer fails to opt out*, the business may comply with the law merely by providing the customer with a cost-free method of exercising the right to prevent disclosure. *Id.* § 1798.93(c)(2). Thus, the law seems to amount to nothing more than a requirement to provide customers with a weak version of the fair information practice principle of choice.

FURTHER READING

- STATE OF CALIFORNIA DEP'T OF CONSUMER AFFAIRS, CALIFORNIA INFORMATION-SHARING DISCLOSURES AND PRIVACY POLICY STATEMENTS (2004) (offering guidance on complying with California laws requiring notice of disclosures to third-party marketers and posting of website privacy policies), www.privacy.ca.gov/recommendations/infosharingdisclos.pdf

D. SECURITY BREACHES

In 2002, partly in response to an intrusion into a state payroll database that allowed access to personal information on 265,000 state government employees, California enacted a law requiring the operator of a database to disclose to all affected individuals any breach of a database that results in unauthorized access to personal information about those individuals. *See* CAL. CIV. CODE § 1798.82. The number and magnitude of reported security breaches skyrocketed in 2005. *See* Privacy Rights Clearinghouse, *A Chronology of Data Breaches Since the ChoicePoint Incident*, www.privacyrights.org/ar/ChronDataBreaches.htm (listing more than fifty security breaches from February to August 2005). In 2005, a number of other states followed California's lead, enacting their own laws requiring disclosure of security breaches.

The Federal Trade Commission has taken the position that a business's carelessness in handling its customers' financial data may constitute a violation of the FTC Act. In *In re BJ's Wholesale Club, Inc.*, FTC Docket No. C–4148 (2005) (consent order), the FTC alleged that BJ's had failed to employ reasonable measures to safeguard its customers' credit card information. In particular, the complaint alleged, BJ's

> (1) did not encrypt the information while in transit or when stored on the in-store computer networks; (2) stored the information in files that could be accessed anonymously—that is, using a commonly known default user id and password; (3) did not use readily available security measures to limit access to its computer networks through wireless access points on the networks; (4) failed to employ sufficient measures to detect unauthorized access or conduct security investigations; and (5) created unnecessary risks to the information by storing it for up to 30 days when it no longer had a business need to keep the information, and in violation of bank rules.

As a result of these security shortfall, hackers accessed BJ's systems through wireless access points, and used the credit card information to make millions of dollars of fraudulent purchases. The FTC alleged that this constituted an "unfair act or practice" in violation of the FTC Act.[13] BJ's settled the case, consenting to entry of an order requiring it to imple-

---

[13] An act is "unfair" if it "causes or is likely to cause substantial injury to consumers which is not reasonably avoidable by consumers themselves and not outweighed by countervailing benefits to consumers or to competition." 15 U.S.C. § 45(n).

ment a comprehensive information security program.

In March 2005, FTC Chairman Deborah Platt Majoras recommended to Congress that it enact laws requiring data brokers to maintain stronger controls over personal information so as to prevent security breaches and identity theft. At this writing several bills that would require disclosure of security breaches are pending in Congress. *See, e.g.*, H.R. 3374, Consumer Notification and Financial Data Protection Act of 2005, 109th Cong. (2005).

FURTHER READING

- CALIFORNIA OFFICE OF PRIVACY PROTECTION, RECOMMENDED PRACTICES ON NOTIFICATION OF SECURITY BREACH INVOLVING PERSONAL INFORMATION (2003) (guide to compliance with California's security breach law), www.privacy.ca.gov/recommendations/secbreach.pdf

E. PIERCING THE VEIL OF ONLINE ANONYMITY

Many Internet users engage in online speech under a pseudonym, on the assumption that the speech cannot be associated with their real-world identity. This assumption has frequently turned out to be unwarranted. If a user furnishes her true identity when acquiring online access from an Internet service provider, when registering a domain name, or when registering at a website that offers a bulletin board or other forum for public communication, then the institution holding that identity information frequently has the capability of associating an online pseudonym, such as an e-mail address, user name, or screen name, with the speaker's real-world identity.

In a number of cases, companies have brought defamation actions against individuals who have posted anonymous comments online that are critical of the company. After initiating the lawsuit, the company issues a subpoena to an ISP, bulletin board host, or other entity that knows the online speaker's real-world identity, seeking disclosure of that identifying information. If the entity complies with the subpoena, the company learns the identity of its critic, and can proceed with the lawsuit, or pursue various other avenues of retaliation. Revelation of the critic's identity can have severe consequences if she happens to be an employee of the company, or involved in some business relationship with it. In some of these cases, the company has dropped the defamation lawsuit after learning the identity of its critic. Privacy advocates have branded this a misuse of the judicial system, claiming that the lawsuits were frivolous and were filed for the sole purpose of unmasking the critic.

In many of these cases, the subpoena recipient complies with the subpoena by divulging the speaker's identity, without giving the speaker prior notice or an opportunity to contest the subpoena. In a few cases, however, the propriety of such discovery has been challenged.

Columbia Insurance Co. v. Seescandy.com
185 F.R.D. 573 (N.D.Cal.1999).

■ JENSEN, DISTRICT JUDGE.

On February 22, 1999, plaintiff Columbia Insurance Company filed a motion for a temporary restraining order and an order to show cause why a preliminary injunction should not issue. . . . The Court hereby denies the motion without prejudice to refiling and orders plaintiff to submit a brief with the Court within 14 days addressing the issue of whether the Court should authorize discovery to establish defendant's identity sufficiently such that he may be served in compliance with the Federal Rules of Civil Procedure.

I. BACKGROUND

A. *Factual-Background and Procedural History*

On February 22, 1999, plaintiff Columbia Insurance Company ("Columbia") filed this action seeking injunctive relief, damages, and an accounting of profits. Columbia is the assignee of various trademarks related to the operation of See's Candy Shops, Inc. ("See's"). See's is the predecessor in interest to the trademarks at issue in this case and holds a license from Columbia to use the marks.

The domain names "seescandy.com" and "seecandys.com" have been registered with Network Solutions, Inc. ("NSI") by someone other than plaintiff.

. . .

As of September 24, 1998, the seescandy domain name was registered to seescandy.com. The address was given only as "CA, 90706," which is for Bellflower, California. The administrative and billing contacts were listed as Salu Kalu, who could be contacted by e-mail at hostmaster@fluctuate.com. The telephone number given, 408–555–1212, is the local number for information in the San Jose area. The fluctuate.com domain, as of February 21, 1999 is registered to a Ravi Kumar of Artesia, California.

On December 22, 1998, the record was changed to show the owner as R, L of Artesia, California; however, the zip code given, 90706 is for Cerritos, California. The phone number was again given as the number for information, but the area code had been changed from 408 to 714. The contact e-mail address had been changed to RL@fluctuate.com. In addition, the domain was now shown as being hosted by websp.com.

On February 13, 1999, the record was modified again to list the address as P.O. Box 1300, Artesia, California, with the zip code changed from 90706 to 90702, which is an actual zip code for Artesia, California. The telephone number was also changed to (562) 807-0297.

As of January 22, 1999, the domain name seecandys.com was registered to Sees Candys and had the contact listed as Robby Kumar. The address was given as Tustin, California 92782; the e-mail address as dns@fluctuate.com; and the telephone number as (310) 860–0229.

On February 25, 1999, both the seescandy.com and seescandys.com domains were changed from the web host of websp.com to simplenet.net. Simplenet.net is a San Diego, California company.

Plaintiff has sued defendants for (1) infringement of federally registered service and trademarks, in particular "SEE'S," "SEE'S CANDIES," and "FAMOUS OLD TIME"; (2) federal unfair competition; (3) federal trademark dilution; [and similar state causes of action]. . . .

. . .

II. DISCUSSION

The Court will not grant a temporary restraining order against defendants at this time because such a ruling would be futile. Plaintiff has not been able to collect the information necessary to serve the complaint on defendants. As a result any temporary restraining order issued could only be in effect for a limited time and would be unlikely to have any effect on defendant whom plaintiff has not yet located. Once the order expired plaintiff would be unable to obtain a preliminary injunction because such relief cannot be imposed *ex parte*.

Service of process can pose a special dilemma for plaintiffs in cases like this in which the tortious activity occurred entirely on-line. The dilemma arises because the defendant may have used a fictitious name and address in the commission of the tortious acts. Traditionally, the default requirement in federal court is that the plaintiff must be able to identify the defendant sufficiently that a summons can be served on the defendant. *See* Fed.R.Civ.P. 4. This requires that the plaintiff be able to ascertain the defendant's name and address.

As a general rule, discovery proceedings take place only after the defendant has been served; however, in rare cases, courts have made exceptions, permitting limited discovery to ensue after filing of the complaint to permit the plaintiff to learn the identifying facts necessary to permit service on the defendant. *See e.g., Gillespie v. Civiletti*, 629 F.2d 637, 642 (9th Cir.1980) (finding the district court abused its discretion in dismissing the case with respect to the John Doe defendants without requiring the named defendants to answer interrogatories seeking the names and addresses of the supervisors in charge of the relevant facilities during the relevant time period); *Estate of Rosenberg by Rosenberg v. Crandell*, 56 F.3d 35, 37 (8th Cir.1995) (permitting a suit naming fictitious parties as defendants to go forward because the allegations in the complaint were "specific enough to permit the identity of the party to be ascertained after reasonable discovery") . . . .

In the Ninth Circuit such exceptions to the general rule have been generally disfavored. *See Gillespie*, 629 F.2d at 642. However, a district court does have jurisdiction to determine the facts relevant to whether or not it has in personam jurisdiction in a given case. *See Wells Fargo & Co. v. Wells Fargo Express Co.*, 556 F.2d 406, 430 n.24 (9th Cir.1977). A district court's decision to grant discovery to determine jurisdictional facts is a matter of discretion. *See id.*

With the rise of the Internet has come the ability to commit certain tortious acts, such as defamation, copyright infringement, and trademark infringement, entirely on-line. The tortfeasor can act pseudonymously or anonymously and may give fictitious or incomplete identifying information. Parties who have been injured by these acts are likely to find themselves chasing the tortfeasor from Internet Service Provider (ISP) to ISP, with little or no hope of actually discovering the identity of the tortfeasor.

In such cases the traditional reluctance for permitting filings against John Doe defendants or fictitious names and the traditional enforcement of strict compliance with service requirements should be tempered by the need to provide injured parties with a forum in which they may seek redress for grievances. However, this need must be balanced against the legitimate and valuable right to participate in online forums anonymously or pseudonymously. People are permitted to interact pseudonymously and anonymously with each other so long as those acts are not in violation of the law. This ability to speak one's mind without the burden of the other party knowing all the facts about one's identity can foster open communication and robust debate. Furthermore, it permits persons to obtain information relevant to a sensitive or intimate condition without fear of embarrassment. People who have committed no wrong should be able to participate online without fear that someone who wishes to harass or embarrass them can file a frivolous lawsuit and thereby gain the power of the court's order to discover their identity.

Thus some limiting princip[les] should apply to the determination of whether discovery to uncover the identity of a defendant is warranted. The following safeguards will ensure that this unusual procedure will only be employed in cases where the plaintiff has in good faith exhausted traditional avenues for identifying a civil defendant pre-service, and will prevent use of this method to harass or intimidate.

First, the plaintiff should identify the missing party with sufficient specificity such that the Court can determine that defendant is a real person or entity who could be sued in federal court. . . . This requirement is necessary to ensure that federal requirements of jurisdiction and justiciability can be satisfied. . . .

Plaintiff's papers establish that the listed defendants who remain in the case after March 4, 1999 appear to be aliases for a person known as Ravi or Robby Kumar of Artesia, California ("the Kumar defendants"). Most of the addresses listed by aliases associated with the Kumar defendants show a California domicile, which indicates that the Court likely has jurisdiction over defendants. Plaintiffs are suing the following aliases, all of which are alleged to be owners or operators of the domain names seescandy.com and seescandys.com: Seescandy.com, Sees Candys, hostmaster dns, fluctuate, foolio, x2, ticker talk, RL, and Salu Kalu. Salu Kalu was listed as the contact for seescandy.com in September of 1998. RL is a person who was listed as the contact person for seescandy.com as of January 16, 1999. Hostmaster DNS is the name of the contact person listed for seescandy.com as of February 8, 1999. It is important to note that Hostmaster DNS is a common generic term used to describe the system operator in charge of running a domain name server. It is thus highly problematic as an identifier of a defendant. However, Hostmaster's e-mail address is dns@foolio.com, which ties this alias to the Kumar defendants. Fluctuate is the second level domain of fluctuate.com, which is listed in the WHOIS as registered to tickertalk, for whom the contact is Robby Kumar. Fluctuate.com is the domain that provides all the mailboxes for the e-mail addresses listed as contacts for the seescandy.com and seescandys.com domains. X2 is the listed registrant of the domain name x2.org, for whom the contact is listed as Ticker Talk with the E-mail address of dns@foolio.com. Foolio is the listed registrant for foolio.com, for whom the contact is Salu Kalu, and which is the domain hosting the E-mail address of the contact, Ticker Talk, for the x2.org domain. Most convincing of all, See's has been in contact by e-mail with a person who goes by the name "Ravi." In his e-mail message, Ravi has indicated a desire to sell the subject domain names to See's and has provided See's with evidence that consumers have been actually confused by these websites, for which Ravi claims to hold registration rights. The Court finds that there appears to be only one person behind all these registrations, a Ravi or Robby Kumar, who may also be known as Salu Kalu. The Court finds that plaintiff has made a satisfactory showing that there is an actual person behind these acts who would be amenable to suit in federal court.

Second, the party should identify all previous steps taken to locate the elusive defendant. This element is aimed at ensuring that plaintiffs make a good faith effort to comply with the requirements of service of process and specifically identifying defendants. . . . Plaintiff's counsel has certified that the following efforts were made to contact defendants: (1) calls were made to the two non-directory information services telephone numbers. One was a non-working number and nobody answered the other one. Simultaneous with the filing of the motion for a temporary restraining order and preliminary injunction plaintiff served its complaint, brief, and all accompanying papers to the official addresses provided to NSI, only one of which was a complete mailing address. Plaintiff also served these documents, sans exhibits, by electronic mail to the e-mail addresses associated with the domains registered by Ravi Kumar, Robby Kumar, RL, Salu Kalu, and Hostmaster DNS. Although such service is not sufficient to comply with the Federal Rules of Civil Procedure, the Court finds that such acts do show that plaintiff has made a good faith effort to specifically identify defendant and to serve notice on defendant.

Third, plaintiff should establish to the Court's satisfaction that plaintiff's suit against defendant could withstand a motion to dismiss. . . . A conclusory pleading will never be sufficient to satisfy this element. Pre-service discovery is akin to the process used during criminal investigations to obtain warrants. The requirement that the government show probable cause is, in part, a protection against the misuse of *ex parte* procedures to invade the privacy of one who has done no wrong. A similar requirement is necessary here to prevent abuse of this extraordinary application of the discovery process and to ensure that plaintiff has standing to pursue an action against defendant. . . . Thus, plaintiff must make some showing that an act giving rise to civil liability actually occurred and that the discovery is aimed at revealing specific identifying features of the person or entity who committed that act.

Plaintiff has demonstrated that [its] trademark infringement claim could survive a motion to dismiss and therefore [has] satisfied this element. The test for infringement of a federally registered trademark (Count I) and for false designation of origin (Count II) under the Lanham Act is whether the alleged infringing act creates a likelihood of confusion. . . . [P]laintiff can show actual confusion, courtesy of the 31 e-mails provided by defendant. . . . Defendant Ravi has informed plaintiff by e-mail that people have requested catalogs and have tried to order candy from the websites located at seescandy.com and seescandys.com.

. . . [Plaintiff's] showing is sufficient to demonstrate that the Kumar defendants have committed an unlawful act for which a federal cause of action can subsist.

Lastly, the plaintiff should file a request for discovery with the Court, along with a statement of reasons justifying the specific discovery requested as well as identification of a limited number of persons or entities on whom discovery process might be served and for which there is a reasonable likelihood that the discovery process will lead to identifying information about defendant that would make service of process possible. *See Gillespie*, 629 F.2d at 642 (stating that discovery should not be permitted if it is not likely to uncover the identity of the defendant). As ordered below, plaintiff has 14 days to make a filing with the Court with respect to the process the Court should consider ordering.

II. CONCLUSION AND ORDER

Plaintiff shall have 14 days from the date of this order to submit a brief with the Court setting forth specifically the forms of discovery process, the justification for such process, and the persons or entities on whom they are to be served that plaintiff expects will achieve the end of providing the missing identifying information necessary for service of process. If plaintiff does not yet have sufficient information to satisfy the Court that such process should be ordered, plaintiff may so indicate and later reapply for such discovery once the facts necessary to make the required showing have been uncovered.

EXTENSIONS

1. *Other standards for entitlement to pre-service discovery.* Different courts have devised different standards to resolve the issue presented in *Columbia Insurance Co. v. Seescandy.com*, namely how to balance an anonymous online speaker's interest in remaining anonymous against the interest of others in redress for injury caused by unlawful speech. Here are several of them, arranged roughly in order of increasing burden on the plaintiff:

a. *Good faith.* In *In re Subpoena Duces Tecum to America Online, Inc.*, 2000 WL 1210372 (Va.Cir.Ct.2000), *rev'd on other grounds sub nom. America Online, Inc. v. Anonymous Publicly Traded Co.*, 542 S.E.2d 377 (Va.2001), the court held that it would approve a subpoena aimed at discovering the identity of an anonymous online speaker only if it is satisfied "that the party requesting the subpoena has a legitimate, good faith basis to contend that it may be the victim of conduct actionable in the jurisdiction where suit was filed [and that] the subpoenaed identity information is centrally needed to advance that claim." *See also Doe v. 2TheMart.com Inc.*, 140 F.Supp.2d 1088 (W.D.Wash.2001) (requiring good faith in the issuance of the subpoena, rather than in the filing of the action).

b. *Prima facie case.* In *Dendrite Int'l, Inc. v. Doe*, 775 A.2d 756 (N.J.Super.Ct.App.Div.2001), the court, citing *Columbia Insurance v. Seescandy.com* with approval, set forth a four-factor test:

[T]he trial court should first require the plaintiff to undertake efforts to notify the anonymous posters that they are the subject of a subpoena or application for an order of disclosure . . . . [Second,] [t]he court shall also require the plaintiff to identify and set forth the exact statements purportedly made by each anonymous poster that plaintiff alleges constitutes actionable speech. [Third,] [t]he complaint and all information provided to the court should be carefully reviewed to determine whether plaintiff has set forth a prima facie cause of action against the fictitiously-named anonymous defendants. . . . Finally, assuming the court concludes that the plaintiff has presented a prima facie cause of action, the court must balance the defendant's First Amendment right of anonymous free speech against the strength of the prima facie case presented and the necessity for the disclosure of the anonymous defendant's identity to allow the plaintiff to properly proceed.

Id. at 760–71. The first and second of these requirements do not present constitute significant obstacles to the plaintiff, but the third one does. Consider whether the fourth, "balancing" criterion is appropriate: is not the purpose of the first three requirements to balance the competing interests? What criteria is a court to apply in striking this balance? *See also Sony Music Entertainment Inc. v. Does 1-40*, 326 F.Supp.2d 556 (S.D.N.Y.2004) (considering also the strength of the defendant's expectation of privacy).

c. *Withstand summary judgment.* In *Doe v. Cahill*, 2005 WL 2455266 (Del. 2005), the court, after considering and rejecting several other standards, adopted the following: "before a defamation plaintiff can obtain the identity of an anonymous defendant through the compulsory discovery process he must support his defamation claim with facts sufficient to defeat a summary judgment motion." This means the plaintiff "must introduce evidence creating a genuine issue of material fact for all elements of a defamation claim" (with the exception of the element of actual malice in a suit by a public figure, since that evidence is likely to be unavailable until the defendant's identity is known).

2. *Cable operators as ISPs.* If the anonymous speaker's ISP happens to operate a cable television system, the ISP may be subject to the restrictions of the Cable Communications Policy Act of 1984, 47 U.S.C. § 551, which prohibits a cable operator from disclosing personally identifiable information about its subscribers except under specified circumstances. Absent the subscriber's consent, a court order will generally be required before the cable operator may disclose the subscriber's identity. *See Fitch v. Doe*, 869 A.2d 722 (Me.2005) (applying 47 U.S.C. § 551(c)(2)(B)).

3. *State regulation of subpoenas.* Several states have enacted or are considering laws regulating the issuance of subpoenas aimed at discovering the identity of anonymous online speakers. The Virginia law includes the following provisions:

- Thirty days prior to the subpoena's return date, the party seeking the information must file with the court a copy of the subpoena, with supporting material showing:
  - the speaker may have made illegal communications or engaged in other actionable conduct;
  - other reasonable efforts to identify the speaker were unsuccessful;
  - the identity of the speaker is central to the case; and
  - the recipient of the subpoena is likely to have responsive information.
- The recipient of the subpoena must attempt to notify the speaker that the subpoena was received, giving the speaker sufficient time to contest the subpoena.
- The party seeking the information must serve on the recipient a prescribed notice, explaining the recipient's responsibilities under the law.

VA. CODE ANN. § 8.01–407.1.

How does this statutory approach compare with the rules set forth in *Columbia Insurance Co. v. Seescandy.com*?

4. *Notice to anonymous defendants.* In *Doe v. Cahill, supra*, the court added a notification requirement:

[T]o the extent reasonably practicable under the circumstances, the plaintiff must undertake efforts to notify the anonymous poster that he is the subject of a subpoena or application for order of disclosure. The plaintiff must also withhold action to afford the anonymous defendant a reasonable opportunity to file and serve opposition to the discovery request. Moreover, when a case arises in the internet context, the plaintiff must post a message notifying the anonymous defendant of the plaintiff's discovery request on the same message board where the allegedly defamatory statement was originally posted.

Is posting the required notice on the message board where the alleged defamation appeared a method calculated to reach the defendant? Note that notification of the subscriber is required by statute if the identity information is sought from a cable operator. 47 U.S.C. § 551(c)(2). The Virginia statute, *supra*, also calls for such notice.

5. *John Doe fights back.* In *Doe a/k/a Aquacool_2000 v. Yahoo! Inc.,* No. CV–00–04993 (C.D.Cal. filed May 11, 2000), the plaintiff was an individual who had posted comments on a Yahoo! message board that were critical of his former employer, a company named AnswerThink Consulting Group, Inc. The comments were posted pseudonymously, attributed to "Aquacool_2000." AnswerThink filed a defamation action against Aquacool_2000 and several other unnamed defendants, and served a subpoena on Yahoo! seeking the disclosure of their identities. Yahoo! complied with the subpoena, disclosing Aquacool_2000's real-world identity, without notifying him or seeking his consent. Upon learning Aquacool_2000's identity, AnswerThink fired him and took other punitive action against him.

Aquacool_2000 then filed an action against Yahoo!, alleging that the disclosure of his identity violated his free speech rights under the U.S. and California Constitutions, and that it constituted unfair competition and false advertising under California law. He also alleged that Yahoo! was in breach of contract, and had committed negligent misrepresentation, by failing to abide by its website privacy policy. The policy stated: "We will notify you at the time of data collection or transfer if your data will be shared with a third party and you will always have the option of not permitting the transfer." It also stated that Yahoo! would disclose a member's personal information "when we believe in good faith that the law requires it."

Yahoo! later modified its Privacy Policy so that it states: "We respond to subpoenas, court orders or legal process," and does not promise any notification before doing so.

QUESTIONS FOR DISCUSSION

1. *Balancing interests.* In *Columbia Insurance v. Seescandy.com,* was there any danger that allowing discovery of the defendant's identity would chill the online speech of defendant or others similarly situated? Of the standards discussed in Extensions, Note 1, *supra,* which do you think most appropriately balances the interests of tort victims in obtaining redress and the interests of anonymous online speakers in remaining anonymous?

2. *Identity of third-party witnesses.* Should the standard for evaluating whether to enforce a subpoena seeking the identity of an anonymous third-party witness be different from the standard applying to discovering the identity of a defendant? *See Doe v. 2TheMart.com Inc.,* 140 F.Supp.2d 1088 (W.D.Wash.2001) (holding that a more stringent standard should apply).

FURTHER READING

- Lyrissa Barnett Lidsky, *Silencing John Doe: Defamation & Discourse In Cyberspace,*

49 DUKE L.J. 855 (2000) (arguing that anonymous online speech presents special difficulties which courts should address by applying a modified version of the opinion defense)

V. MODELS FOR PROTECTING ONLINE PRIVACY

Nearly everybody agrees that Internet users have legitimate privacy interests. There is
much less agreement about the proper approach to protecting those interests, in view of the
competing interests with which privacy protection can interfere. Several different models of
online privacy protection have been implemented or proposed. Most observers agree that
none of these approaches is by itself sufficient, and advocate some combination. To understand their strengths and weaknesses, it will be useful to consider the approaches individually.

A. MODEL I: INDUSTRY SELF-REGULATION VIA CODES OF CONDUCT

The champions of self-regulation have been more vocal on the subject of privacy than
on any other subject relating to online communications. Large segments of the business
community, as well as some agencies of government, have forcefully argued that government regulation of online privacy should be the approach of last resort, and that all interested parties will be better off if regulators leave protection of privacy to the market. The
Clinton Administration's 1997 policy paper on electronic commerce endorsed a combination of self-regulation and technological tools as the preferred means to implement privacy
protections online. *See* WILLIAM J. CLINTON & ALBERT GORE, JR., A FRAMEWORK FOR
GLOBAL ELECTRONIC COMMERCE (1997), www.ta.doc.gov/digeconomy/framewrk.htm.

Following a pattern exhibited in many other industries, the online industry's efforts at
self-regulation to protect online privacy were driven by the perceived threat of government
regulation. An early wake-up call, not widely heeded, was congressional reaction to the
problem of children's access to sexually explicit material online. Congress attempted to
stamp out this problem with the 1996 Communications Decency Act. The U.S. Supreme
Court invalidated provisions of the Act that restricted the posting of "indecent" or "patently
offensive" material, finding them unconstitutional in violation of the First Amendment. *See
Reno v. American Civil Liberties Union*, 521 U.S. 844 (1997).

The Federal Trade Commission's explorations of the issue of online privacy in a series
of workshops and reports, and a string of well-publicized privacy scares, hit closer to home,
giving impetus to both industry self-regulation and calls for government regulation. In June
1996, the FTC held a public workshop to learn about online privacy. Sensing that the government might be gearing up to regulate in this arena, two trade associations, the Interactive
Services Association and the Direct Marketing Association, announced at the workshop
their release of self-regulatory guidelines on protecting privacy online, marketing to children, and use of unsolicited commercial e-mail and newsgroup postings. In July 1996,
TRUSTe launched its privacy seal program. *See* Part V(B), *infra*.

In September 1996, privacy advocates drew attention to a service called P–Trak that
LexisNexis offered. When originally introduced, P–Trak allowed subscribers to enter an
individual's name and address, and to retrieve personal information including the individ-

ual's Social Security number. In response to expressions of outrage that publicity about P–Trak raised, LexisNexis modified the service so that it did not return Social Security numbers, but still allowed a subscriber to enter a Social Security number and retrieve the holder's name, address, two prior addresses, telephone number, and birth month and year. This did not answer the objections, since the information P–Trak provided could still be used in aid of stalking, identity theft, and other unsavory practices. Publicity surrounding this service prompted members of Congress to request that the FTC conduct a study of the issue. The FTC's announcement that it would conduct the requested study spurred several companies in the business of furnishing personal information about individuals, known as "look-up services," to form an association, called the Individual Reference Services Group ("IRSG"), for the purpose of developing a self-regulatory scheme that would respond to the perceived abuses that gave rise to the study. Among other things, the IRSG principles placed limitations on the disclosure of non-public personal information by look-up services, depending on the sensitivity of the information requested and the identity of the requester; required the services to protect against misuse of non-public information; and granted individuals access to non-public information concerning them. In a 1997 report, the FTC praised IRSG's effort as "more comprehensive and far-reaching than any other voluntary, industry-wide program in the information sector," but noted certain shortcomings in the principles and exhorted the industry to do more. *See* FEDERAL TRADE COMMISSION, INDIVIDUAL REFERENCE SERVICES: A REPORT TO CONGRESS (1997), www.ftc.gov/bcp/privacy/wkshp97/irsdoc1.htm. The IRSG dissolved itself in late 2001, explaining that there was no further need for the self-regulatory program given Congress's enactment of the Gramm–Leach–Bliley Act of 1999, 15 U.S.C. §§ 6801–10. The Act and its implementing regulations govern the disclosure by a financial institution of a consumer's personal financial information, and the redisclosure and reuse of such information. Compliance with the regulations implementing the Act was required starting July 1, 2001.

In March 1998, the FTC conducted a survey of 1,402 commercial websites to assess the extent to which they collected personal identifying information ("PII") from users, and to determine whether sites that collected PII gave users notice of their information-handling policies. In June 1998, the FTC issued a report detailing the results of the survey, as well as its assessment of self-regulatory guidelines that online industry had produced. It found that more than 85% of commercial websites collected PII, but only 14% of them provided any notice of their information practices. It also found that 89% of sites directed to children collected PII from children, but very few of those made any effort to obtain parental consent. Based on the results of its survey, the FTC recommended that Congress enact legislation regulating online collection and use of information from children, but deferred any recommendation on a regulatory response to collection of PII from adults. *See* FEDERAL TRADE COMMISSION, PRIVACY ONLINE: A REPORT TO CONGRESS (1998), www.ftc.gov/reports/privacy3/priv-23a.pdf.

Congress responded by enacting the Children's Online Privacy Protection Act, 15 U.S.C. §§ 6501–05, discussed in Part VI, *infra*. In congressional testimony discussing the report in July 1998, the FTC opined that "unless industry can demonstrate that it has developed and implemented broad-based and effective self-regulatory programs by the end of this year, additional governmental authority in this area would be appropriate and necessary." Prepared Statement of the Federal Trade Commission on "Consumer Privacy on the World Wide Web," Before the Subcommittee on Telecommunications, Trade and Consumer Protection of the House Committee on Commerce, United States House of Representatives (July 21, 1998), www.ftc.gov/os/1998/07/privac98.htm.

The online industry responded with the formation of an industry group, called the Online Privacy Alliance, with a membership including some of the biggest and best-known companies with online business activities. In June 1998, just three weeks after publication of the FTC's report, the OPA released a set of guidelines for online privacy designed to demonstrate that the industry was able to police itself, and that government regulation was not required. OPA's 50 members pledged to abide by these guidelines, which require companies engaged in online activities to adopt and implement a privacy policy that addresses the fair information practices principles of notice, choice, data security, and data quality and access. Online Privacy Alliance, *Guidelines for Online Privacy Policies* (June 22, 1998), www.privacyalliance.org/resources/ppguidelines.shtml. The Guidelines were to be enforced through a third-party seal program. Online Privacy Alliance, *Effective Enforcement Of Self Regulation* (July 21, 1998), www.privacyalliance.org/resources/enforcement.shtml.

In a July 1999 report to Congress on the status of self-regulation, the FTC praised the industry for the progress it had made in the prior year, and expressed the view that legislative action was not warranted, but concluded that the industry needed to do much more to protect the privacy of Internet users. The report cited two website surveys conducted in 1999 finding that a majority of websites posted at least some sort of privacy disclosure, but few (10% in one study, 22% in the other) of them addressed all four of the substantive fair information practice principles (notice, choice, access, and security). FEDERAL TRADE COMMISSION, SELF-REGULATION AND PRIVACY ONLINE: A REPORT TO CONGRESS (1999), www.ftc.gov/os/1999/07/privacy99.pdf.

Evaluations of the efficacy of self-regulation then began to turn less favorable. A February 2000 report on the privacy practices of the most popular consumer-oriented health care websites found that "on a number of sites personally identified information is collected through the use of cookies and banner advertisements by third parties without the host sites disclosing this practice. There are also instances where personally identified data is transferred to third parties in direct violation of stated privacy policies." CALIFORNIA HEALTH-CARE FOUNDATION, PRIVACY: REPORT ON THE PRIVACY POLICIES AND PRACTICES OF HEALTH WEB SITES 4 (2000), www.chcf.org/topics/view.cfm?itemID=12497. In a March 2000 cover article, *Business Week* magazine strongly endorsed federal legislation to protect online privacy. It labeled the existing state of self-regulation a "sham": Privacy policies "are usually buried at the bottom of the page, and seem to be drafted by life-forms on a distant planet"; when websites offer privacy options, they are too hard to find; few sites offer users access to the information that has been collected about them; and there is little enforcement of privacy rules. *See It's Time for Rules in Wonderland*, BUS. WK., Mar. 20, 2000, at 82.

Then in May 2000, the FTC released a report finding that self-regulation had failed, and recommending that Congress enact online privacy legislation. The report described the results of yet another survey of website privacy practices and policies. As in the 1999 studies, the FTC found that a majority of the sites (88% of a random sample and 100% of the 100 most popular sites) displayed at least one privacy disclosure. However, only a minority (20% of the former and 42% of the latter) implemented, even in part, all four of the fair information practice principles. The FTC also found that privacy seal programs had not achieved widespread adoption: 8% of the random sites, and 45% of the most popular sites, displayed a privacy seal. Based on these findings, the FTC concluded that self-regulation alone was insufficient, and stated: "While there will continue to be a major role for industry self-regulation in the future, the Commission recommends that Congress enact legislation that, in conjunction with continuing self-regulatory programs, will ensure adequate protection of consumer privacy online." FEDERAL TRADE COMMISSION, PRIVACY ONLINE: FAIR INFORMATION PRACTICES IN THE ELECTRONIC MARKETPLACE ii-iii (2000), www.ftc.gov/reports/privacy2000/privacy2000.pdf.

Following issuance of this report, a number of bills addressing online privacy issues in a variety of ways were introduced in Congress, but none proceeded to enactment. In the meantime, President George W. Bush replaced the Chairman of the FTC with an appointee favoring a market-based approach to privacy protection. In October 2001, the FTC Chairman announced that the agency no longer supported federal legislation to protect online privacy, having concluded there was a need "to develop better information about how such legislation would work and the costs and benefits it would generate." Timothy J. Muris, *Protecting Consumers' Privacy: 2002 and Beyond* (Oct. 4, 2001), www.ftc.gov/speeches/muris/privisp1002.htm.

QUESTIONS FOR DISCUSSION

1. *Privacy policy generators.* In an effort at self-regulation, several organizations created privacy-policy generators: web-based tools that allow a website operator to create an individualized website privacy policy based on a template or component parts. Take a look at the privacy-policy generators located at Direct Marketing Association, *Create Your Own Privacy Policies*, www.the-dma.org/privacy/privacypolicygenerator.shtml; and Organisation for Economic Co-operation and Development, *Developing a Privacy Policy and Statement*, www.oecd.org/document/1/0,2340,en_2649_34255_28863233_1_1_1_1,00.html. Try using one of these tools to create a privacy statement. Do you think that your statement, if posted on a website at the other end of a link on the website's homepage labeled "Privacy," is something that website visitors would find useful? How could you modify it to make it more useful?

2. *Enforcement of voluntary codes.* What mechanisms does a trade association have available to enforce compliance with a code of conduct? How effective are those mechanisms likely to be?

FURTHER READING

- ELECTRONIC PRIVACY INFORMATION CENTER, PRIVACY SELF-REGULATION: A DECADE OF DISAPPOINTMENT (2005) (finding that industry self-regulation of privacy online has been unsuccessful, and calling on the FTC and Congress to adopt a more interventionist approach), www.epic.org/reports/decadedisappoint.html

B. MODEL II: THIRD-PARTY CERTIFICATION VIA PRIVACY SEALS

It is difficult or impossible for consumers to make an unaided rational assessment of the quality and characteristics of many goods that are offered in the marketplace. Which of the hundreds of cordless telephones offered for sale has the best sound? Which will last the longest? Which refrigerator is the most energy efficient? Which produce contains the least pesticide residues? If a consumer were to attempt to get answers to these questions through her own research, she would give up long before reaching her goal, finding that it would cost more effort than the item is worth.

The same holds for the experience of visiting a website, which may be regarded as a "product." One of the characteristics of this product is the website's privacy policy. Internet users may wish to "shop" for websites to visit based on a number of criteria, including what the site will do with the visitor's personal information. But how is a potential visitor to assess this characteristic? The privacy policies that websites post are frequently extremely long, complex, and difficult to understand, and most people will consider it not worth their time to decipher the verbiage. Even if someone did take the trouble to get her lawyer's opinion on a website's privacy policy, there is no simple way to determine whether the site actually adheres to its policy.

The market for goods has produced several mechanisms designed to remedy this type of information shortfall. Third-party evaluators, such as Consumer Reports, perform tests on competing products and report their results. Other third-party evaluators, such as Underwriters Laboratories, certify that a product meets certain minimum quality standards and license the use of their trademarked seal in connection with the product to so indicate. A well-known brand may serve the same purpose: to protect the brand, a manufacturer or reseller may spend whatever it takes to make sure that purchasers are satisfied. Or a manufacturer may offer a warranty on its products, or a money-back guarantee, to assure potential purchasers that even if the product is in some way defective they will be protected.

Responding to the need to furnish website visitors with information about the privacy characteristics of websites, the market has developed third-party seal systems. The best-known privacy seals are those issued by TRUSTe, a nonprofit entity that was founded by the Electronic Frontier Foundation and the CommerceNet Consortium, and the Council of Better Business Bureaus, which operates the familiar network of BBB's. TRUSTe's seal, which it refers to as a "trustmark," looks like this:

A TRUSTe licensee is also required to display another mark:

This mark is hyperlinked to TRUSTe's site, www.truste.org, so that when clicked it returns a notice indicating that the site displaying it is indeed a licensee—or an indication that the trustmark is a counterfeit.

To qualify for a TRUSTe seal, a website must comply with a set of requirements that TRUSTe has promulgated. As TRUSTe explains:

ALL TRUSTe®-licensed sites must provide:

User controls, including:

- An email unsubscribe function

- An opt-out function limiting the sharing of personally identifiable information (PII) with outside parties

- Access management permitting users to update stored PII or have it changed by the Licensee

<u>Security measures</u>, ensuring:

- Secured Socket Layers (SSLs), or other comparable technology, that encrypts pages collecting sensitive information such as credit card numbers

A <u>complaint resolution process</u>, providing:

- Comprehensive contact information for appropriate Web site employees
- A link to the TRUSTe Watchdog site for third-party dispute resolution

A <u>privacy statement</u>, including the following disclosures:

- What PII is collected and how it will be used
- Identity of the party collecting PII
- Whether PII is shared with third parties
- The use of any tracking technology
- Whether PII is supplemented with information from other sources
- Choice options available to consumers
- How consumers can access PII they have provided
- That there are security measures in place
- Procedures for filing and addressing consumer complaints

In addition, the privacy statement must:

- Be linked from the home page and from every page where PII is collected
- Bear the TRUSTe "Click to Verify" link so consumers know whether the company is a TRUSTe licensee or not

TRUSTe, *TRUSTe Program Requirements*, <u>www.truste.org/requirements.php</u>.

TRUSTe monitors the websites displaying its trustmark for ongoing compliance with the program requirements. TRUSTe's monitoring consists of (1) an automated scan of each website, twice yearly, designed to detect violations of the site's privacy policy; (2) "seeding" a site's e-mail list with dummy addresses, to see if the site honors its user's e-mail preferences; and (3) encouraging consumers to submit a complaint if they believe a website has violated its privacy policy. TRUSTe, *TRUSTe Oversight*, <u>www.truste.org/about/compliance_monitoring.php</u>.

The Better Business Bureau's privacy seal program has similar elements. *See* BBBOnLine, *BBBOnLine Privacy Seal*, <u>www.bbbonline.com/privacy</u>.

One limitation of TRUSTe's seal program was illustrated by its response to a complaint against the privacy practices of Microsoft, a TRUSTe licensee and one of its Premier Corporate Sponsors. As discussed in Part III(B), *supra*, in 1999 it was discovered that the globally unique identifier contained within a computer's Ethernet card was being transmitted to

Microsoft during the Windows 98 registration process, and was being electronically stamped onto documents created with Microsoft Office 98 application programs. A privacy advocate, Jason Catlett, lodged a complaint against Microsoft with TRUSTe. After investigating the complaint, TRUSTe determined that Microsoft had not violated its TRUSTe license agreement. TRUSTe explained that its certification applied only to the Microsoft.com website, and the website privacy policy did in fact disclose that Microsoft would capture the Ethernet identifier during the registration process. Thus, although both Microsoft and TRUSTe acknowledged that a "privacy breach" had occurred, none of TRUSTe's rules was violated. *See* TRUSTe, *Watchdog #1723—Microsoft Statement of Finding*, www.truste.org/consumers/watchdog_advisories/0399_microsoft.php.

QUESTIONS FOR DISCUSSION

Message conveyed to site visitors. Internet users who have not taken the trouble to study the details of TRUSTe's privacy seal program are likely to assume that the presence of a TRUSTe trustmark on a website indicates that the site's information practices are in some way protective of privacy interests. Is this assumption warranted? If a site visitor views the trustmark as a proxy for a protective privacy policy, she may dispense with reading the policy statement itself. How does this impact the goal of transmitting to site visitors the information they need to make an informed decision whether to trust their personal information to a website?

C. Model III: Empowerment of Individuals Through Technological Tools

Another market-based approach to protecting online privacy is to make available to Internet users technological tools that they can use to protect themselves. Several different types of privacy-protection tools are available.

E-mail encryption. It has frequently been observed that unencrypted e-mail messages are as vulnerable to prying eyes as is a message on a postcard sent through postal mail. An ordinary e-mail message can be intercepted and read while it is in transit from sender to recipient, or while it resides on an intermediary server or on the sender's or the recipient's computer. Encrypting an e-mail message makes it unreadable except by the intended recipient. Most e-mail encryption systems are based on an asymmetric-key protocol, called OpenPGP, that is derived from Pretty Good Privacy ("PGP"). PGP was created by Phil Zimmermann, who released the first version of it in 1991. PGP-based systems are available in both freeware and commercial versions.

Anonymous surfing. When you use a browser to view a website, information is transmitted from your computer to the server hosting the website, passing through intermediary servers along the way. You can prevent this flow of information from being traced to your computer by using a service that sits as an intermediary between your computer and the web server. Normally, when you want to access a page on a website your computer sends a request to the website's server and receives a response from it. When you use an intermediary service, the request from your browser is routed to the intermediary, rather than to the site you wish to access. The intermediary service then sends a request to the website, without transmitting any information relating to you. The intermediary receives the requested web page, and then relays it to you. There is no direct connection between your computer and the website server, so the website operator is unable to gather any information about you, and is unable to place a cookie on your computer. Some intermediary services also encrypt the traffic between your computer and the intermediary, to prevent unauthorized access of that data flow.

Banner ad and popup blockers. Blockers prevent banner advertisements from displaying on a web page, and prevent popup advertising windows from opening. Some web browsers have popup blocking capability built in.

Cookie managers. A cookie manager allows the user to control the placement of cookies on his hard drive. The cookie manager may be configured to allow the placement of cookies from specified websites, but deny access to others. It also allows the user to view the cookies present on his computer and to edit or delete them selectively. Web browsers have long included rudimentary cookie-control options, but freestanding programs offer more options.

File encryption. Encryption software encodes the files stored on the user's hard drive, so that an intruder is unable to read them.

Anonymous remailers. An anonymous remailer is a service that acts as an intermediary between the sender and recipient of electronic messages, such as message board postings. The remailer receives the message, strips off the information identifying the sender, and relays the message to its destination. Sophisticated remailer systems send a message through a series of remailers, so that none of the intermediaries is able to associate the sender's identity with the recipient's.

Hard drive erasers. Unknown to most users, a computer's hard drive retains several sorts of information with privacy implications. The browser's cache stores web pages that the user has recently accessed, and the browser's history file records the URLs of sites that the user has visited. Some browsers store search strings, passwords, and other information typed into web-based forms, for use by the autocompletion feature. Hard drives are often littered with "temporary" files that have become permanent. Deleting files does not completely remove them from the hard drive: an attempt to delete a file may do no more than move it to a different location of the hard drive, into a "recycle bin," and deleted files can often be retrieved using special recovery software. A hard drive eraser program can be set automatically to delete these traces of online activity, removing files in a way that makes it impossible to recover them.

Firewalls. A firewall acts as a gateway between your computer and the Internet, blocking undesired incoming traffic and preventing unauthorized access of your computer. This can help to prevent viruses from entering your computer, and prevents hackers from reading files on your computer remotely.

Spam filters. The purpose of a spam filter is to analyze incoming e-mail messages, determine which of them are likely to consist of unsolicited commercial e-mail, and either block those messages or divert them to a special folder. Spam filters do not work perfectly: they inevitably fail to recognize some messages as spam, and identify as spam some messages that the user actually wants to receive.

Spyware detectors. Anti-spyware programs search a user's hard drive and identify code that appears to be spyware. The user is then given the option to delete the detected spyware.

Platform for Privacy Preferences ("P3P"). P3P is a framework developed by the World

Wide Web Consortium[14] that allows automated interaction between a web server and a client browser concerning the privacy practices of the website and the privacy preferences of the user. When a user accesses a P3P-compliant website, the server automatically communicates the website's privacy policy to the user's browser. The browser is configured with the user's privacy preferences. For example, if the user is unwilling to have his personal information shared with any third party, he can indicate that preference in his browser settings. When he accesses a website, his browser compares the site's policies with his own preferences. If the site meets his privacy requirements, the browser accesses the website. If not, the browser may alert him of the mismatch, and allow him to decide whether to bypass the site. A description and technical specification of the current version of P3P is available at W3C, *The Platform for Privacy Preferences 1.1 Specification* (July 1, 2005), www.w3.org/TR/2005/WD-P3P11-20050701.

Critics of P3P note that website operators will have little incentive to take the trouble to implement P3P. Given the complexity of configuring a browser with one's privacy preferences, most users will leave their browsers in their default configurations, which will likely not be highly protective of privacy, since that would result in denying access to a large number of popular websites. Even users who want strong privacy protection will probably leave their browsers configured to a low level of protection, since otherwise there will be few sites they can visit. As a result, P3P will not create any meaningful incentives for websites to implement fair information practices. Internet users will get only the illusion, but not the reality, of sovereignty in the marketplace for privacy. Furthermore, no mechanism currently exists for enforcement of privacy promises embedded in P3P code. For a critique of P3P, see Electronic Privacy Information Center, *Pretty Poor Privacy: An Assessment of P3P and Internet Privacy* (2000), www.epic.org/reports/prettypoorprivacy.html. For a review of the development of P3P, highlighting the role of privacy advocates in its development, see Lorrie Faith Cranor, *The Role of Privacy Advocates and Data Protection Authorities in the Design and Deployment of the Platform for Privacy Preferences*, doi.acm.org/10.1145/543482.543506.

EXTENSIONS

Users poorly informed. While some privacy-protection tools (such as spyware detectors) are widely adopted, most are not. One reason for consumers' lack of interest in privacy-protection tools is that they have little information about the collection of their personal information that occurs online, and the uses that may be made of that information. A survey conducted in early 2003 found that "the overwhelming majority of U.S. adults who use the internet at home have no clue about data flows—the invisible, cutting edge techniques whereby online organizations extract, manipulate, append, profile and share information about them. Even if they have a sense that sites track them and collect individual bits of their data, they simply don't fathom how those bits can be used. [In addition,] 57% of U.S. adults who use the internet at home believe incorrectly that when a website has a privacy policy, it will not share their personal information with other websites or companies." ANNENBERG PUBLIC POLICY CENTER OF THE UNIVERSITY OF PENNSYLVANIA,

---

[14] The World Wide Web Consortium, usually referred to as W3C, is an international consortium of member organizations that develops standards and guidelines for operation of the Web. It publishes its work in the form of Recommendations that Internet users may choose to adopt. The founding (and current) director of W3C is Tim Berners-Lee, who is generally credited with having invented the Web. *See* www.w3c.org.

AMERICANS AND ONLINE PRIVACY: THE SYSTEM IS BROKEN 3 (2003), www.annenbergpublicpolicycenter.org/04_info_society/2003_online_privacy_version_09.pdf. *See also* PEW INTERNET & AMERICAN LIFE PROJECT, TRUST AND PRIVACY ONLINE: WHY AMERICANS WANT TO REWRITE THE RULES (2000) (finding that 56 percent of Web users do not know what a cookie is), www.pewinternet.org/pdfs/PIP_Trust_Privacy_Report.pdf.

QUESTIONS FOR DISCUSSION

1. *Costs of self-empowerment.* The use of privacy-protection technologies entails significant costs for Internet users. A user must invest a substantial amount of time and effort to research the various tools, select the one she thinks will best suit her purposes, install it, and learn how to use it. Adding a new piece of software to one's computer always carries the risk that it will be buggy or incompatible with other software on the system, costing more time and effort. Some of these tools significantly degrade a user's experience in accessing the Web, by slowing down communications or by adding additional procedures that must be followed when accessing a new website. Some of them are free, but others carry a purchase price or subscription fee. How much burden is it appropriate for Internet users to shoulder to protect themselves from invasions of their privacy?

2. *Does individual empowerment obviate regulation?* Should the availability of tools like these lead legislators and regulators to the conclusion that government intervention to protect privacy online is unnecessary? How would you distinguish this argument from the following one? "Door locks, window bars, burglar alarms, and private guard services are widely available. Heavy-handed government intervention in the form of criminalization of burglary is therefore unnecessary. We should instead devote more resources to educating householders to make use of these tools and protect themselves."

3. *Will tools emerge without law?* Lawrence Lessig argues that technology enabling automated negotiations over privacy between a website and a prospective site visitor, like P3P, will not emerge unless the law mandates it, since "[t]he power of commerce is not behind any such change." LAWRENCE LESSIG, CODE AND OTHER LAWS OF CYBERSPACE 163 (1999). Do you agree? Are the imperatives of commerce necessarily opposed to implementation of fair information practices?

4. *Bringing privacy protection tools to the masses.* What would it take for privacy protecting tools to be widely adopted by individual users? One commentator suggests that "a massive educational effort would be needed and a universal system would need to be developed that would be compatible with most Internet sites, relatively easy for consumers to use, and difficult for data seekers to evade," and that "it would require government intervention to require privacy technology as a standard installation or default preference in most computers." James P. Nehf, *Recognizing the Societal Value in Information Privacy*, 78 WASH. L. REV. 1, 60-61 (2003). Do you agree?

FURTHER READING

- The Electronic Privacy Information Center maintains a listing of privacy-protection technologies. *EPIC Online Guide to Practical Privacy Tools*, www.epic.org/privacy/tools.html.

D. MODEL IV: PLENARY REGULATION—THE EC DIRECTIVE

The European approach to information privacy is very different from the U.S. approach. Beginning in the 1970s, many European countries enacted "data protection" laws that were broad in scope and were backed up by data protection commissions and commissioners.

These laws varied widely in their substantive provisions as well as in the associated enforcement schemes. In order to promote a more uniform legal treatment of personal data, and as part of its ongoing effort to remove barriers to trade among countries within the European Union, in 1995 (effective 1998) the European Commission promulgated a Directive addressing data protection. *See* Directive 95/46/EC of the European Parliament and of the Council of 24 October 1995 on the protection of individuals with regard to the processing of personal data and on the free movement of such data, 1995 O.J. (L 281) 31, europa.eu.int/comm/justice_home/fsj/privacy/law/index_en.htm.

Consistent with the European model of regulation, the Directive is broad in scope and detailed in its prescriptions. As you read the following material, consider whether such an approach would be suited to the U.S. context.

1. Provisions of the Directive

The Directive places limitations on the "processing" of "personal data." "Personal data" means "any information relating to an identified or identifiable natural person"; that person is referred to as the "data subject." Art. 2(a). "Processing" of personal data is broadly defined as any operation that is performed on personal data, including "collection, recording, organization, storage, adaptation or alteration, retrieval, consultation, use, disclosure by transmission, dissemination or otherwise making available, alignment or combination, blocking, erasure or destruction." Art. 2(b). There are exceptions for certain important functions that governments perform, as well as for processing "by a natural person in the course of a purely personal or household activity." Art. 3(2).

The Directive applies to processing of personal data "wholly or partly by automatic means," and to non-automatic processing "of personal data which form part of a filing system." Art. 3(1). A "filing system" is "any structured set of personal data which are accessible according to specific criteria." Art. 2(c). Thus, any manipulation of personal data through the use of computers is covered by the Directive. Manipulation of noncomputerized personal data is covered if the records are maintained in an organized format that makes it possible to retrieve records with particular characteristics. This would seem to include most business records: sending a copy of a document stored in one's file drawer that contains personal information would likely be within the scope of the Directive.

The Directive places several types of limitations on the processing of personal data by a "data controller," which is defined as any person with a role in determining "the purposes and means of the processing of personal data." Art. 2(d). First, there are limitations on what data may be collected and how it must be maintained. Personal data may only be collected for specified purposes, and may not be processed "in a way incompatible with those purposes." The quantity of data collected must not be "excessive" in relation to those purposes. Data must be accurate and kept up to date. And data may be retained in a form that makes them identifiable to a data subject only for as long as necessary to accomplish the purposes for collection. Art. 6(1)(b)–(e).

Second, there is a general consent requirement: processing of personal data is allowed only if "the data subject has unambiguously given his consent." Art. 7(a). The requisite consent is strictly defined, as a "freely given specific and informed indication of his wishes by which the data subject signifies his agreement to personal data relating to him being processed." Art. 2(h). This consent requirement is, however, subject to a number of exceptions, including where processing is necessary (1) to the performance of a contract to which the data subject is a party, (2) for compliance with a legal obligation, (3) to protect the data subject's vital interests, (4) to further the public interest, or (5) to the achievement of the data controller's legitimate interests that are not outweighed by the data subject's fundamental rights and freedoms. Art. 7(b)–(f). The data subject also has a specifically enumerated right to object to the use of data concerning him for the purposes of direct marketing. Art. 14(b).

Third, there is a general prohibition against the processing of certain types of sensitive personal information, namely that "revealing racial or ethnic origin, political opinions, religious or philosophical beliefs, [and] trade-union membership." The prohibition also extends to *any* data, whether personal or not, "concerning health or sex life." Art. 8(1). The exceptions from this prohibition include (1) where the data subject has given explicit consent, (2) where processing is necessary to satisfy the requirements of employment laws, (3) where processing is necessary to protect vital interests, and the data subject is incapable of giving consent, (4) certain uses by non-profit entities, (5) where the data are made public by the data subject or must be revealed in connection with legal claims, and (6) use in connection with provision of medical services. Art. 8(2)–(3). The Directive also gives every person a limited right "not to be subject to a decision which produces legal effects concerning him or significantly affects him and which is based solely on automated processing of data intended to evaluate certain personal aspects relating to him, such as his performance at work, creditworthiness, reliability, conduct, etc." Art. 15(1).

Fourth, the data controller must furnish certain information to the data subject. Information that is required to be disclosed includes the identity of the data controller, the purposes for processing the data, and whatever additional information is required "to guarantee fair processing in respect of the data subject." Arts. 10 & 11.

Fifth, data subjects have the right to obtain from the data controller, "at reasonable intervals and without excessive delay or expense," (1) confirmation whether data concerning the subject are being processed, and if so information regarding the purposes of the processing, the categories of information processed, and the identity of the recipients of the information, (2) the data that are being processed and their source, and (3) "the logic involved in any automatic processing" of data that results in the making of decisions that significantly affect the data subject. Art. 12(a). The data subject may also demand that the controller correct inaccurate data, and if practicable advise third parties to which the data were disclosed of the correction. Art. 12(b) & (c).

Sixth, data controllers must assure the confidentiality and security of the data they process. Arts. 16 & 17.

Seventh, a data controller must notify the national supervisory authority, which the Directive requires each EU member state to set up, before commencing any automatic processing of data. Art. 18. The notification must include the name and address of the controller, the purposes of the processing, the categories of data subjects and categories of data relating to them that are involved in the processing, the categories of recipients to which the data may be disclosed, whether any data will be transferred to non-EU countries, and a description of security measures. The supervisory authority must then examine any operations involved in the proposed processing that are among those the member state has determined are "likely to present specific risks to the rights and freedoms of data subjects." Art. 20(1). The supervisory authority must also maintain a publicly accessible register of the data processing operations of which it is notified. Art. 21.

Eighth, the Directive places limitations on a controller's transfer of personal data to a country outside the European Union. Transfers of personal data to a "third country" are allowed only if "the third country in question ensures an adequate level of protection" to the data. Art. 25(1). The determination of adequacy is contextual, depending on "all the circumstances surrounding a data transfer operation," such as "the nature of the data, the purpose and duration of the proposed processing operation or operations, the country of origin and country of final destination, the rules of law, both general and sectoral, in force in the third country in question and the professional rules and security measures which are complied with in that country." Art. 25(2). Data may be transferred to a third country even absent "adequate" protection if (1) the data subject consents "unambiguously," (2) the transfer is necessary for the performance of a contract between the data subject and the controller, (3) the transfer is necessary for the performance of a contract between the controller and a third party that is for the benefit of the data subject, (4) the transfer is needed on public interest grounds or in connection with a legal claim, (5) the transfer is needed to protect the "vital interests" of the data subject, or (6) the data are publicly available. Art. 26(1). A lack of adequate protection in the third country may also be overcome if the controller puts in place "adequate safeguards" for the protection of privacy, such as through contractual arrangements with the data recipient. Art. 26(2).

The Directive's effects are profound and wide-ranging. Most commercial transactions involving individual purchasers generate transactional information that includes personal data. Businesses have a strong incentive to retain these data in a personally identifiable form, since that endows them with substantial value: the information may be used to solicit additional purchases, and may be sold or rented to other businesses for their own marketing purposes. Practically any operation that is performed on such data will fall within the scope of the Directive. Personal data are also generated in educational settings, in the provision of medical services, through charitable activities, and in other noncommercial undertakings. Most of these data are stored in a digital format and are processed by computers: this processing by "automatic means" brings it within the scope of the Directive. Even data maintained in the form of paper documents are likely to be subject to the Directive as belonging to a "filing system."

Of greatest relevance to the United States is the Article 25 limitation on transfers of personal data to "third countries," of which the United States is one. Enormous quantities of personal data are routinely transferred from European Union countries to the United States (and other "third countries"), and are therefore potentially affected by the Directive. For example:

- The Directive could apply to e-mail messages that are sent from within the EU to some country outside the EU. If a message contains personal information that relates only to the sender, then the sender's act of sending it would certainly constitute unambiguous consent in satisfaction of Art. 26(1)(a). But if the message relates to someone other than the sender, there will not necessarily be consent or satisfaction of any of the other Art. 26 exemptions. The same logic applies to paper documents that are sent via postal mail or facsimile transmission, as long as the documents form part of a "filing system."

- The Directive applies to websites that collect personal information, which is true of nearly all commercially oriented websites. If the site is operated from within the EU, there is no question of the Directive's applicability. If the site is operated from outside the EU, the question becomes trickier. It is unclear whether an EU member state can assert jurisdiction over a website that is operated by a company located in the United States, and that resides on a server located in the United States, on the ground that the site is collecting data from individuals located within that member state.

- The use of online surveillance devices, such as cookies and web bugs, would seem to fall within the Directive's scope. Placing a cookie on the hard drive of a site visitor's computer may allow a website to identify the visitor, and to accumulate personal data about the visitor's browsing habits. If the website uses a third-party advertising server, such as DoubleClick, a visit to the site may result in the transfer of personal data to the ad server. Using web bugs, a site operator or e-mail sender can collect personal data about when the recipient accesses a web page or e-mail message. If the visitor that is located in an EU country, and the website operator, ad server, or e-mail sender is in some other country, Article 25 limitations apply.

- Corporations that operate in more than one country routinely make intra-company transfers of personal information that are also cross-border transfers. This would be true of personal data that reside on a corporate intranet, and that are accessible by employees in different countries. The company may maintain transactional information in a distributed fashion on computers located both within and outside the EU, and may need to combine the data on its "third country" computers. With client-server system architectures, a server located within the EU may routinely transfer personal data to clients outside the EU, and vice versa. Information about a company's employees is especially likely to fall within the scope of the Directive, and to undergo transfers that will be transborder if the company's operations are multinational. The same will be true for many other corporate-wide functions, such as auditing and accounting, use of consultants, and handling of customer service.

If the European Commission determines that a particular country does not provide "adequate" protection to personal data, various effects might ensue. A company that has operations both within the EU and in the inadequately protective third country might have an incentive to move certain data processing operations from the third country to an EU country. For example, it might move its human resources office to Europe, or engage European accountants and auditors, to avoid the need to transfer personal information involved in those functions to the third country. Or the company might respond by decentralizing its operations, erecting a "firewall" between its European operations and its activities in the third country. If the European operations are a small part of its business, the company might sell off those operations; if the third-country operations are small, it might jettison that part of its business instead. A company headquartered in the third country might find it infeasible to hire employees located in European Union countries.

On the other hand, the effects of the Directive on businesses located in countries with inadequate protections might be moderated by the exemptions provided by Art. 26. In particular, the provision allowing transborder transfers upon consent of the data subject might, if expansively interpreted, overcome the most serious of the limitations imposed by Art. 25.

2. The U.S.–EU Safe Harbor Principles

The European Commission's adoption of the Directive sparked a flurry of negotiations between the United States (led by the Department of Commerce) and the EC, aimed at averting the possibility that trans-Atlantic flows of personal data would be halted by a finding that the United States does not provide adequate protections satisfying Article 25. The result of these negotiations was the EU's approval of a set of "safe harbor" principles to which U.S. companies could subscribe and thereby be deemed to ensure an adequate level of protection.

Safe Harbor Privacy Principles (2000)
www.export.gov/safeharbor

The European Union's comprehensive privacy legislation, the Directive on Data Protection (the Directive), became effective on October 25, 1998. It requires that transfers of personal data take place only to non-EU countries that provide an "adequate" level of privacy protection. While the United States and the European Union share the goal of enhancing privacy protection for their citizens, the United States takes a different approach to privacy from that taken by the European Union. The United States uses a sectoral approach that relies on a mix of legislation, regulation, and self regulation. Given those differences, many U.S. organizations have expressed uncertainty about the impact of the EU-required "adequacy standard" on personal data transfers from the European Union to the United States.

To diminish this uncertainty and provide a more predictable framework for such data transfers, the Department of Commerce is issuing this document and Frequently Asked Questions ("the Principles") under its statutory authority to foster, promote, and develop international commerce. . . .

Decisions by organizations to qualify for the safe harbor are entirely voluntary. . . . Organizations that decide to adhere to the Principles must comply with the Principles in order to obtain and retain the benefits of the safe harbor and publicly declare that they do so. . . .

. . .

"Personal data" and "personal information" are data about an identified or identifiable individual that are within the scope of the Directive, received by a U.S. organization from the European Union, and recorded in any form.

NOTICE: An organization must inform individuals about the purposes for which it collects and uses information about them, how to contact the organization with any inquiries or complaints, the types of third parties to which it discloses the information, and the choices and means the organization offers individuals for limiting its use and disclosure. This notice must be provided in clear and conspicuous language when individuals are first asked to provide personal information to the organization or as soon thereafter as is practicable, but in any event before the organization uses such information for a purpose other than that for which it was originally collected or processed by the transferring organization or discloses it for the first time to a third party.[1]

CHOICE: An organization must offer individuals the opportunity to choose (opt out) whether their personal information is (a) to be disclosed to a third party or (b) to be used for a purpose that is incompatible with the purpose(s) for which it was originally collected or subsequently authorized by the individual. Individuals must be provided with clear and conspicuous, readily available, and affordable mechanisms to exercise choice.

For sensitive information (i.e. personal information specifying medical or health conditions, racial or ethnic origin, political opinions, religious or philosophical beliefs, trade union membership or information specifying the sex life of the individual), they must be given affirmative or explicit (opt in) choice if the information is to be disclosed to a third party or used for a purpose other than those for which it was originally collected or subsequently authorized by the individual through the exercise of opt in choice. In any case, an organization should treat as sensitive any information received from a third party where the third party treats and identifies it as sensitive.

ONWARD TRANSFER: To disclose information to a third party, organizations must apply the Notice and Choice Principles. Where an organization wishes to transfer information to a third party that is acting as an agent, as described in the [footnote], it may do so if it first either ascertains that the third party subscribes to the Principles or is subject to the Directive or another adequacy finding or enters into a written agreement with such third party requiring that the third party provide at least the same level of privacy protection as is required by the relevant Principles. If the organization complies with these requirements, it shall not be held responsible (unless the organization agrees otherwise) when a third party to which it transfers such information processes it in a way contrary to any restrictions or representations, unless the organization knew or should have known the third party would process it in such a contrary way and the organization has not taken reasonable steps to prevent or stop such processing.

SECURITY: Organizations creating, maintaining, using or disseminating personal information must take reasonable precautions to protect it from loss, misuse and unauthorized access, disclosure, alteration and destruction.

DATA INTEGRITY: Consistent with the Principles, personal information must be relevant for the purposes for which it is to be used. An organization may not process personal information in a way that is incompatible with the purposes for which it has been collected or subsequently authorized by the individual. To the extent necessary for those purposes, an organization should take reasonable steps to ensure that data is reliable for its intended use, accurate, complete, and current.

ACCESS: Individuals must have access to personal information about them that

---

[1] It is not necessary to provide notice or choice when disclosure is made to a third party that is acting as an agent to perform task(s) on behalf of and under the instructions of the organization. The Onward Transfer Principle, on the other hand, does apply to such disclosures.

an organization holds and be able to correct, amend, or delete that information where it is inaccurate, except where the burden or expense of providing access would be disproportionate to the risks to the individual's privacy in the case in question, or where the rights of persons other than the individual would be violated.

ENFORCEMENT: Effective privacy protection must include mechanisms for assuring compliance with the Principles, recourse for individuals to whom the data relate affected by non-compliance with the Principles, and consequences for the organization when the Principles are not followed. At a minimum, such mechanisms must include (a) readily available and affordable independent recourse mechanisms by which each individual's complaints and disputes are investigated and resolved by reference to the Principles and damages awarded where the applicable law or private sector initiatives so provide; (b) follow up procedures for verifying that the attestations and assertions businesses make about their privacy practices are true and that privacy practices have been implemented as presented; and (c) obligations to remedy problems arising out of failure to comply with the Principles by organizations announcing their adherence to them and consequences for such organizations. Sanctions must be sufficiently rigorous to ensure compliance by organizations.

To get the benefit of the safe harbor, a company must annually certify to the Department of Commerce that it will adhere to the principles, and must so state in its own privacy policy. The company must also be subject to an enforcement mechanism, which may be implemented either through self-regulation or by participation in a third-party oversight program.

Self-regulation is permissible only if the company is subject to the enforcement authority of the Federal Trade Commission, under 15 U.S.C. § 45, or (in the case of air carriers) the Department of Transportation ("DOT"), under 49 U.S.C. § 41712. These statutes allow the respective agencies to take enforcement action against a company that engages in deceptive conduct by representing it will abide by the principles but failing to do so.

TRUSTe offers a third-party EU safe-harbor privacy program, which consists of verification that a company's privacy policy and practices are compliant with the safe-harbor principles, together with a dispute-resolution procedure. Companies that participate in TRUSTe's program are entitled to display TRUSTe's EU Safe Harbor privacy seal. *See* TRUSTe, *Expand Your Privacy Practices*, www.truste.org/businesses/ eu_safe_harbor_seal.php.

The Department of Commerce maintains a list of companies that have certified their adherence to the safe-harbor principles. *See* Dep't of Commerce, *Safe Harbor List*, web.ita.doc.gov/safeharbor/shlist.nsf/webPages/safe+harbor+list.

3. Approved Contractual Terms

In addition to the safe-harbor principles, the EC has approved two different types of contractual clauses that will make up for a third country's failure to have laws establishing an adequate level of protection for privacy. If the clauses are included in a contract governing the transfer of data from a person in the EU to a person in a third country, then the data may be transferred consistently with Article 26(2). *See* Commission Decision 2004/915/EC of 27 December 2004 amending Decision 2001/497/EC as regards the introduction of an alternative set of standard contractual clauses for the transfer of personal data to third countries, 2004 O.J (L 385) 74, europa.eu.int/eur-lex/lex/LexUriServ/site/en/oj/2004/l_385/l_38520041229en00740084.pdf; Commission Decision 2001/497/EC of 15 June 2001 on standard contractual clauses for the transfer of personal data to third countries, under Directive 95/46/EC, 2001 O.J. (L 181) 19, europa.eu.int/eur-lex/pri/en/oj/dat/2001/l_181/l_18120010704en00190031.pdf.

EXTENSIONS

1. *Effectiveness of the Directive.* It may be questioned whether the Data Protection Directive, as implemented by national laws in each of the EU countries, with its detailed and enforceable regulatory scheme, will provide Internet users with stronger privacy protections than the U.S. system, which is based primarily on self-regulation and marketplace enforcement mechanisms. A study conducted in early 2000 found that websites based in the EU did not provide better notice or more robust choice than websites based in the U.S., and that the best of the lot were the most-trafficked U.S.-based cites. *See* CONSUMERS INTERNATIONAL, PRIVACY@NET: AN INTERNATIONAL COMPARATIVE STUDY OF CONSUMER PRIVACY ON THE INTERNET (2001), www.consumersinternational.org.

2. *Interpretation of the Directive.* In late 2003 the European Court of Justice issued its first interpretation of the Directive as applied to the Internet context. A Swedish individual named Bodil Lindqvist created a website containing personal information about parishioners in her church. She did this not for any commercial purpose, but to facilitate communication among the parishioners. She was prosecuted for violation of Swedish law implementing the Directive, and was convicted and fined. The appellate court referred to the ECJ several questions concerning interpretation of the Directive. The ECJ generally gave an extremely broad reading of the Directive, holding that placing the information on the website entailed processing of personal data by automatic means under Article 3(1), bringing the activity within the scope of the Directive; and that Lindqvist was not entitled to the exception in Article 3(2) for processing of data "by a natural person in the course of a purely personal or household activity." However, the ECJ held that posting personal data on a website does not constitute transfer to a "third country" under Article 25. *Bodil Lindqvist*, Case C-101/01 (E.C.J. 2003).

3. *EC's evaluation of the Safe Harbor Principles.* In 2004, staff of the European Commission evaluated the implementation of the Safe Harbor Principles during the first three years of their operation. The staff report noted some deficiencies in compliance with the Principles, and requested that the Department of Commerce and the Federal Trade Commission be more proactive in bringing about compliance. *See* The implementation of Commission Decision 520/2000/EC on the adequate protection of personal data provided by the Safe Harbour Privacy Principles and related Frequently Asked Questions issued by the US Department of Commerce, SEC (2004) 1323 (Commission Staff Working Document), europa.eu.int/comm/justice_home/fsj/privacy/docs/adequacy/sec-2004-1323_en.pdf.

4. *Transfer of airline passenger data.* In the wake of the September 11, 2001 terrorist attacks, Congress passed a law requiring airlines operating flights to or from the United States to provide U.S. Customs and Border Protection[15] with access to the passenger data con-

---

[15] In March 2003, the U.S. Customs Service and several other agencies were combined to form a new agency, called U.S. Customs and Border Protection, within the Department of Homeland Security.

tained in the airlines' reservation systems, known as Passenger Name Records ("PNR"). European Commission officials objected that this requirement was not consistent with the Data Protection Directive. Negotiations ensued, resulting in an agreement under which the United States undertook to protect the privacy of the PNR information through adoption of a set of policies and procedures, and the EC determined that Customs and Border Protection provided "an adequate level of protection for PNR data transferred from the Community concerning flights to or from the United States," thereby allowing the transfer of passenger data. *See* Commission Decision 2004/535/EC of 14 May 2004 on the adequate protection of personal data contained in the Passenger Name Record of air passengers transferred to the United States' Bureau of Customs and Border Protection, 2004 O.J. (L 235) 11, <u>europa.eu.int/smartapi/cgi/sga_doc?smartapi!celexapi!prod!CELEXnumdoc&lg=EN&numdoc=32004D0535&model=guichett</u>.

QUESTIONS FOR DISCUSSION

1. *Virtual exit.* Can a European website owner evade the Directive by moving the site "offshore"—that is, operating it from servers located outside the EU?

2. *Unambiguous consent.* Article 26(1)(a) of the Directive allows transfer of personal information outside of the EU, even where the recipient country does not offer "adequate" safeguards, as long as "the data subject has given his consent unambiguously to the proposed transfer." Does this contemplate prior consent, or would consent obtained after the transfer suffice? Does the language suggest that consent must be of the opt-in variety, or would opt-out suffice? Could consent be implied from the data subject's status as employee of the data controller? For consent to be valid, would the data subject have to be informed that the transfer would be to a country that lacks adequate privacy protections? What would be the practical implications of these various interpretations?

3. *Onward transfer.* How does the Directive apply to personal data once it is in the hands of an authorized recipient? Does it matter whether the recipient is located in a European Union country, in a third country with adequate protections, or in a third country without adequate protections?

4. *Comparison of safe harbor with U.S. principles and practice.* How do the safe-harbor principles differ from the FTC's articulation of the fair information practice principles? In what ways do they go beyond existing U.S. law and self-regulatory practice?

COMPARATIVE NOTE

Third country adequacy determinations. The European Commission has determined that several "third countries" provide "an adequate level of protection" to personal data, and therefore are not subject to the Article 25 limitations on transfer of data to countries outside the EU. As of this writing, adequacy determination have been made with respect to Switzerland, Canada, Argentina, the Bailiwick of Guernsey, and the Isle of Man. *See Commission decisions on the adequacy of the protection of personal data in third countries,* europa.eu.int/comm/justice_home/fsj/privacy/thridcountries/index_en.htm.

FURTHER READING

- PETER P. SWIRE & ROBERT E. LITAN, NONE OF YOUR BUSINESS: WORLD DATA FLOWS, ELECTRONIC COMMERCE, AND THE EUROPEAN PRIVACY DIRECTIVE (1998) (including detailed treatment of the Directive, and especially of the Art. 25 limitation on transmission of personal data outside the EU)

- Tracey DiLascio, Note, *How Safe Is the Safe Harbor? U.S. and E.U. Data Privacy Law and the Enforcement of the FTC's Safe Harbor Program*, 22 B.U. INT'L L.J. 399 (2004) (critically examining FTC's enforcement against privacy violations)

E. MODEL V: COMMODIFICATION OF PRIVACY?

Kenneth C. Laudon, *Extensions to the Theory of Markets and Privacy: Mechanics of Pricing Information,* **in U.S. DEP'T OF COMMERCE, PRIVACY AND SELF-REGULATION IN THE INFORMATION AGE (1997)** www.ntia.doc.gov/reports/privacy/privacy_rpt.htm

. . .

The theory of markets and privacy begins with the understanding that the current crisis in the privacy of personal information is a result of market failure and not "technological progress" alone. The market failure has occurred because of a poor social choice in the allocation of property rights. Under current law, the ownership right to personal information is given to the collector of that information, and not to the individual to whom the information refers. Individuals have no property rights in their own personal information. As a result, they cannot participate in the flourishing market for personal information, i.e., they receive no compensation for the uses of their personal information. As a further consequence, the price of personal information is so low that information-intense industries become inefficient in its use. The price is low because the price of personal information does not reflect the true social costs of coping with personal information. The market is dominated by privacy-invading institutions. And as a further result, there is a disturbing growth in privacy invasion, an excessive and abusive disregard for the interests of many in keeping elements of their life private, or at least under their control.

. . .

An earlier paper attempted to lay the legal and economic foundation for a true marketplace for personal information. In this marketplace, individuals would retain the ownership in their personal information and have the right, but not the obligation, to sell this information either to institutional users directly, or more likely, to information intermediaries who would aggregate the information into useful tranches (e.g. blocks of one thousand individuals with known demographic characteristics) and sell these information baskets on a National Information Exchange.

Individual ownership of personal information can be anchored within British and American common law. The common law tort of appropriation protects the right of celebrities to own their images, likenesses, voices, and other elements of their persona. To appropriate personal images of celebrities for commercial purposes without consent or payment is recognized by the courts as an appropriation. Likewise, it is conceivable that courts and juries could be convinced to protect the personal "data images" of ordinary citizens. These data images have somewhat less resolution than a photographic image, but they are increasingly and profoundly descriptive and predictive of human behavior. As computers extend their powers, these data images will approach photographic resolutions.

The economic foundation for individual ownership of personal information can be found in the theory of markets (and related theories of governance) and the theory of externalities. Markets are likely the most efficient mechanisms for allocating scarce resources. Governments should intervene in markets only if markets fail. Markets do fail under conditions of monopoly, asymmetries in power and information, and in the case of public goods, e.g., clean air. Governments should either seek to restore markets or regulate the activity. In the case of personal information, the market has failed because of asymmetries in power and information brought about by poor social choice in the allocation of property rights to information. The price of personal information is far too low, and therefore its abuse in the form of privacy invasion is far too cost beneficial to those institutions that dominate the market. The function of government here should be to restore the power of one class of participants in the market, namely individuals, by vesting ownership of personal information in the individual. A second function of government is to ensure the orderly functioning of a personal information marketplace.

The failure of the marketplace results in significant negative externalities for individuals. These externalities are experienced as excessive indirect and direct costs involved in "coping" with information. Coping costs include tangible costs like excessively large mail handling facilities (public and private), and loss of attention, as well as intangible costs like loss of serenity, privacy, and solitude. These negative externalities must be balanced against the positive externalities of nearly unlimited exploitation of personal information which results in enormous amounts of marketing information being delivered to consumers (whether they want it or not). However, it can no longer be argued that these positive externalities fully compensate individuals or society for the negative costs of unlimited exploitation of personal information.

. . .

Jessica Litman, *Information Privacy/Information Property*
52 STAN. L. REV. 1283 (2000).

. . .

Imagine the commercial world wide web in a world that treats personal data as alienable personal property. If personal data are alienable, then by ordering that free computer, downloading that free MP3 recording of a hit song, downloading and installing that software, you will surely have consummated the transfer. We could make a rule that the terms of such a transfer must be disclosed as part of the inevitable click-through license, and just as surely, they would be, and everyone would click "I accept" without even reading them. Indeed, arguably, for any website for which access requires clicking an "I accept" box, the fact that you, for instance, read the *New York Times* on the Web at a considerable savings over the newsstand rate will support the claim of transfer.

It's no better out here in meatspace. Imagine that a person, and let's for the sake of convenience and brevity call her "I," has initial ownership of information about herself, that is, me. I sign up for a check cashing card at the supermarket, or a shopper's club discount card, and, in return for the convenience of paying by check or a steady stream of small discounts on products I may or may not buy, I waive, forfeit, or assign any ownership rights I might have in whatever information resides in an ongoing record of my purchases.

The store, meanwhile, has its own proprietary interest in the compiled purchasing records of each and all of its customers, and will rely on that interest to sell facts about me to whomever. Whomever, of course, has a property interest in those facts because it paid for them, and will be able to combine them with facts about other people and more facts about me from other sources. Whomever may use that collection of data to make up a list of people who are ripe for Discover Card® solicitations, or who might be interested in a mail order catalog for folks suffering from depression, or who, based on recent medical and pharmaceutical purchases, might be eager to purchase some no-questions-asked life insurance.

What makes the whole situation worse is that privacy is one of those things that many people don't believe they really need until they find themselves with something to keep secret. If easy assignment is the rule, they may no longer have the power to preserve their secrecy; even if they could, the exceptional nature of their asserting a privacy claim will tip off those from whom this is a secret that there is an interesting secret there. So, if someone who is deemed to have waived any property rights in the information supplied to businesses in return for product discounts should suddenly find himself diagnosed with hemorrhoids, or herpes, or HIV, he may have no practical way to recapture his secrecy.

Now, imagine the world we have made. We each owned our own personal data initially, but we've assigned them for value to some business, which has sold them to some other business, which combines them with other data to generate a profile of each of us, and sells or rents that profile out. Nor is it unrealistic to imagine those businesses asserting their property interest in their collections of data: There is a lot of that going around. In October [1999], the *New York Times* reported that the NIH Recombinant DNA Advisory Committee had been stymied in its efforts to require more complete disclosure of the safety problems encountered in gene therapy by pharmaceutical companies' insistence that that information is proprietary.

The market in personal data is the problem. Market solutions based on a property rights model won't cure it; they'll only legitimize it.

. . .

Margaret Jane Radin, *Incomplete Commodification in the Computerized World*, in THE COMMODIFICATION OF INFORMATION (Niva Elkin–Koren & Neil Weinstock Netanel eds., 2002).

. . .

. . . It makes a big difference whether privacy is thought of as a human right, attaching to persons by virtue of their personhood, or as a property right, something that can be owned and controlled by persons. The difference has to do with the rhetorical significance of alienability. Human rights are presumptively market-inalienable, whereas property rights are presumptively market-alienable.

Consider the situation if some particular type of privacy, for example data regarding a person's information buying habits, is conceived of and treated as a human right. Then to gain access to and use the private data, in ways other than sanctioned by society, violates a human right. We could think of such violation as a tort, if we have in mind torts against personal integrity rather than against business interests. If a defendant wanted to argue that the data subject had waived or transferred the right, probably by means of a contract, such an argument would face an uphill battle. As a human right, at least presumptively the right would be non-waivable and non-transferable. Human rights are rooted in a noncommodified understanding of personhood and the attributes and context necessary to constitute and maintain personhood. Because the rhetoric of human rights tends to assume inalienability, whoever wants to argue for alienability has a substantial burden. It is not the case, of course, that such rights are never in practice held to have been waived. Rather, because the rhetoric leans toward inalienability, such holdings at least require some argumentative footwork. (Of course, too, if such footwork comes to be routinely performed, then the concept of inalienable human rights will be undermined.)

The situation is reversed if data privacy is conceived of and treated as a property right of the data subject. In that case, to gain access to and use the private data, in ways other than those sanctioned by society, is a violation of a property right. We could think of this violation as a tort, if we have in mind torts against property or business interests—like theft of trade secrets—rather than against personal integrity. In this case, a defendant who wanted to argue that the subject's privacy rights had been transferred or waived would have a much easier time. In the PPFK [private-property-plus-free-contract] system, transferability (alienability) of property rights is presumed. The market system depends both upon private property and free contract; neither can function without the other to support a market. They are tightly connected rhetorically as well as in the actual world of exchange. Some thinkers believe that alienability is inherent in the concept of private property. At minimum, once something is conceived of as private property, arguing for market-inalienability is an uphill battle.

The difference in the presumptive starting points of these two rhetorical perspectives may say a lot about the difference between the EU and the U.S. when it comes to privacy. The data marketers in the U.S. argue that data they have collected (by the sweat of their corporate brows) belongs to them, not to the subjects.

Thus, some consumer advocates in the U.S. believe that legislation declaring that the property right belongs to the data subject will provide protection for privacy. According to the EU view, which treats privacy more like a noncommodified human right and less like a commodified property right, this would be inadequate to protect data subjects.

Indeed, defeating the property claims of the data marketers and vesting the property right in the data subject instead would be a Pyrrhic victory. In either case the issue of waiver and transferability—market alienability—is paramount. It appears that online commerce will be governed more and more by contracts between providers and users, and less by a priori (default) entitlement structures. . . . [W]aivers or transfers can turn out to be ubiquitous, in which case it will not much matter where the rights started out. . . .

. . .

As the debate proceeds about how to conceive of and protect digital data, at least we should realize that we have had these arguments before, in the offline world, about such things as whether consumers can waive product liability, or whether form leases can have tenants waive implied warranty of habitability and live in a cheaper but unsafe and unhealthy dwelling. On the one side, PPFK rhetoric argues that users have the right to waive or transfer whatever rights they have, for a consideration; on the other side, human rights rhetoric argues that users cannot waive rights that are important to personal integrity and self-constitution, at least unless we are very sure that they are doing so in possession of full understanding of the consequences. Debate will be advanced if we work on what sort of an incomplete commodification is appropriate for various aspects of privacy; that is, which aspects of the individual's interests in various kinds of data privacy are more appropriately conceived of as human (personal) rights and which are more appropriately conceived of as property (economic) rights.

. . .

EXTENSIONS

1. *Privacy as property in the courts.* Some courts have held that individuals generally have no enforceable property right in their personal information. *See, e.g., U.S. News & World Report, Inc. v. Avrahami*, 1996 WL 1065557 (Va.Cir.Ct.1996), *reh'g denied, Avrahami v. U.S. News & World Report, Inc.*, No. 961837 (Va.1996) (holding that an individual has no property right in his name, so commercial exchange of names on a mailing list does not violate state statute or common law).

2. *Additional critique.* Consider this additional critique of the propertization approach:

In the United States, information privacy has historically been defined as an individual concern rather than a general societal value or a public interest problem. . . . Enforcement largely depends on individuals recognizing an injury and seeking redress when the legal norms are breached. . . . In contrast, when a problem is viewed as a general societal concern, and a resolution in the public interest is sought, enforcement of the legal norm is primarily through government agency oversight and regulation. . . . [I]n the modern digital world, information privacy should be viewed as a societal value justifying a resolution in the public interest, much like environmental policy and other societal concerns, with less emphasis on individual self-policing and market-based mechanisms.

James P. Nehf, *Recognizing the Societal Value in Information Privacy*, 78 WASH. L. REV. 1, 5-7 (2003).

FURTHER READING

- Paul M. Schwartz, *Property, Privacy, and Personal Data*, 117 HARV. L. REV. 2055, 2087-90 (2004) (arguing that privacy is a public good, constitutive of civil society and a prerequisite to democratic self-governance, so that propertizing property is no more sensible than propertizing freedom of speech)

VI. CHILDREN'S PRIVACY: CHILDREN'S ONLINE PRIVACY PROTECTION ACT

A. ANTECEDENTS

Since the earliest policy discussions of online privacy, marketing to children has been recognized as presenting special privacy issues. The FTC first publicly broached the issue of children's privacy online in a 1996 public workshop, attended by a variety of industry and consumer representatives. While a wide range of views was presented, the FTC noted: "A consensus seemed to emerge among Workshop participants that: (1) children are a special audience; (2) information collection from children raises special concerns; (3) there is a need for some degree of notice to parents of Web sites' information practices; and (4) parents need to have some level of control over the collection of their children's information." FEDERAL TRADE COMMISSION, STAFF REPORT: PUBLIC WORKSHOP ON CONSUMER PRIVACY ON THE GLOBAL INFORMATION INFRASTRUCTURE (1996), pt. IV, www.ftc.gov/reports/privacy/privacy1.htm. There was no consensus, however, on whether government intervention was required to protect children's privacy online, or whether the market could be entrusted with that assignment. At one extreme, the Direct Marketing Association and Interactive Services Association proposed a set of guidelines that would put virtually no crimp in marketers' collection of personal information from children. At the other, the Center for Media Education and the Consumer Federation of America asked the FTC to adopt guidelines that would require parental consent before collecting personal information from children under 16, preceded by full and effective disclosure of the collector's information practices. *See id.* app. C.

The first self-regulatory effort to address children's online privacy came in 1997, when the Council of Better Business Bureaus' Children's Advertising Review Unit ("CARU") amended its *Self Regulatory Guidelines for Children's Advertising* by adding a section addressing online marketing.[16] This section called upon online sellers to provide notice of the intended uses of the personally identifiable information they collect from children, and to

---

[16] The Council of Better Business Bureaus, an industry group that operates the well-known system of BBBs, created CARU in 1974 "to promote responsible children's advertising" through an alliance with the advertising trade associations. Children's Advertising Review Unit, *About the Children's Advertising Review Unit*, www.caru.org/about. For an assessment of the effectiveness of CARU's Guidelines, see Angela J. Campbell, *Self-Regulation and the Media*, 51 FED. COMM. L.J. 711, 735–44 (1999).

make "reasonable efforts" to obtain parental consent to the collection of that information. The term "reasonable efforts" was defined as requiring different procedures "depending on the type and sensitivity of the information collected."

At about the same time, staff of the FTC addressed whether a particular website's collection of information from children was deceptive, in violation of the FTC Act. In May 1996 the Center for Media Education, a nonprofit organization concerned with children's media issues, petitioned the FTC to investigate a website called "KidsCom," at www.kidscom.com. The site, which was directed at children aged 4 to 15, induced children to provide personally identifiable information and product preference information with the promise that by doing so they would earn "KidsKash points" that could be redeemed for prizes at the "Loot Locker." The site did not disclose that "[i]nformation collected from some of these surveys was provided to private companies on an aggregate, anonymous basis." The FTC staff held that this practice likely was deceptive and unfair, in violation of the FTC Act: "It is a deceptive practice to represent that a Web site is collecting personally identifiable information from a child for a particular purpose (e.g., to earn points to redeem a premium), when the information will also be used for another purpose which parents would find material [i.e., marketing purposes], in the absence of a clear and prominent disclosure to that effect." Letter from Jodie Bernstein, Director, Bureau of Consumer Protection, FTC to Kathryn C. Montgomery, President, Center for Media Education (July 15, 1997), www.ftc.gov/os/1997/07/cenmed.pdf. Despite its finding of a likely violation, the FTC staff declined to bring an enforcement action, noting that the practices in question had been corrected, and that KidsCom had not released any personally identifiable information for commercial marketing purposes.

In a June 1998 report to Congress, the FTC recommended that Congress enact legislation to deal with children's online privacy issues. The report detailed the results of a survey of website privacy policies that FTC staff had conducted. Among the sites surveyed were 212 sites directed to children. Although 89 percent of these sites collected personal information from children, only 23 percent instructed children to ask their parents for permission before submitting personal information, and only 1 percent required prior parental consent. The report concluded: "The results reveal a very low level of compliance with the basic parental control principles contained in the [KidsCom] staff opinion letter and the CARU guidelines more than seven months after these documents were released." FEDERAL TRADE COMMISSION, PRIVACY ONLINE: A REPORT TO CONGRESS 38 (1998), www.ftc.gov/reports/ privacy3. In light of the failure of the market to provide appropriate protections to children's online privacy, and finding that its existing authority under the FTC Act was likely not broad enough to allow it to require such protections, the FTC recommended that Congress enact legislation requiring notice and parental consent before collecting personal identifying information from children online.

B. COPPA AND THE FTC'S IMPLEMENTING RULE

Congress responded by enacting the Children's Online Privacy Protection Act, 15 U.S.C. §§ 6501–05, which prescribes standards for the collection of personal information from children online and directs the Federal Trade Commission to promulgate a regulation implementing those standards. The FTC's Children's Online Privacy Protection Rule, 16 C.F.R. Part 312, imposes requirements on operators of websites that are "directed to children" under the age of 13, and on operators of websites who have "actual knowledge" that they are collecting "personal information" from children. *Id.* § 312.3. Only those websites that are "operated for commercial purposes" are covered. *Id.* § 312.2. "Personal information" is defined as "individually identifiable information about an individual collected online," including name, physical address, e-mail address, telephone number, social security number, and a persistent identifier (such as one contained in a cookie file or in hardware) that is associated with individually identifiable information. It also includes any information, such as age, personal interests, or transactional records, that is associated with a personal identifier. *Id.*

The Rule imposes several obligations on covered website operators. First, the operator must include on the home page of the website, and on any other page where personal information is collected from children, a link to a notice setting out the operator's information practices. The notice must disclose (1) identity and contact information for all operators that collect personal information from children through the site, (2) the types of personal information collected, (3) how the operator may use that information, (4) whether information is disclosed to third parties, (5) the fact that the operator may collect no more information from children than necessary for the stated purpose of the collection, and (6) a parent's right to access and delete a child's personal information. *Id.* § 312.4(b).

Second, the website operator is required to make reasonable efforts to obtain "verifiable parental consent" before collecting information from children. *Id.* § 312.5(a). The reasonableness of a method for obtaining consent will depend on the available technology. The Rule offers several examples of what might constitute acceptable methods of obtaining consent: a parent's signature on a consent form returned by postal mail or facsimile, a parent's use of a credit card, a telephone call from a parent to "trained personnel," a digital certificate, or an e-mail containing a password. Consent to purely internal uses of a child's information, not involving disclosure to third parties, may also be obtained by less secure means, such as through an e-mail to a parent followed up with a confirmation. *Id.* § 312.5(b)(2). In seeking a parent's consent, the site operator must provide the parent with notice of the site's information practices. *Id.* § 312.4(c).

Third, the operator is required to give the parent of a child from whom personal information has been collected an opportunity to review that information, to direct the operator to delete it, and to withdraw consent to any future collection of information. *Id.* § 312.6.

Fourth, the operator may not condition a child's participation in any online activity on the child's disclosure of more personal information than is needed for purposes of her participation in the activity. *Id.* § 312.7.

Fifth, the operator must maintain reasonable procedures to protect the confidentiality, security, and integrity of personal information it has collected from children. *Id.* § 312.8.

The Rule also provides for a safe harbor in the form of compliance with approved self-regulatory guidelines. The guidelines must implement requirements that are "substantially similar" to those contained in the Rule, and that offer "the same or greater protections for children." There must also be a mechanism for assessment of compliance with the guidelines, and effective incentives for compliance. *Id.* § 312.10(b). The FTC has approved several safe-harbor programs, including ones operated by the Council of Better Business Bureaus' Children's Advertising Review Unit, and TRUSTe.

The FTC enforces the Rule through its existing enforcement mechanisms, which enable it to seek injunctions and civil penalties against website operators that do not comply with the Rule.

EXTENSIONS

"Directed to children." The Rule states that in determining whether a website is "directed to children," the FTC "will consider [the site's] subject matter, visual or audio content, age of models, language or other characteristics of the website or online service, as well as whether advertising promoting or appearing on the website or online service is directed to children. The Commission will also consider competent and reliable empirical evidence regarding audience composition; evidence regarding the intended audience; and whether a site uses animated characters and/or child-oriented activities and incentives." 16 C.F.R. § 312.2. How should the FTC classify a website that appeals to a range of visitors, say from 10 to 16? Should it depend on the percentage of visitors who state they are under 13?

According to an FTC staff opinion letter, a website that offers to sell products of interest to children under 13 is not ipso facto a website that is "directed to children" for purposes of COPPA. A group of privacy advocacy organizations filed a complaint with the FTC, requesting a determination that Amazon.com was in violation of COPPA by virtue of the "Toy Store" portion of its website. The staff letter found that the site was not "directed to children," since (1) the website states that only adults, and not children, may purchase toys, (2) the vocabulary used on the site is directed to adults, and (3) the site does not offer activities of interest to children, such as games, puzzles, or contests. Letter from Mary K. Engle, Associate Director, Division of Advertising Practices, Federal Trade Commission, to Marc Rotenberg, Executive Director, Electronic Privacy Information Center (Nov. 24, 2004), www.epic.org/privacy/amazon/ftc_amazon.pdf.

QUESTIONS FOR DISCUSSION

1. *Screening for children.* The simplest mechanism by which a website can screen for visitors who are under 13 is to ask them their age. Would you expect there to be many in the under-13 crowd who are savvy enough and interested enough to lie about their age? Does this make age-screening by self-identification useless? Can you think of any better mechanism for ascertaining whether a visitor is under 13?

2. *"Verifiable parental consent."* Are the mechanisms for obtaining parental consent that the FTC endorses unduly burdensome on website operators? On parents? Websites that have implemented parental consent mechanism to comply with COPPA have found it to be an expensive proposition. Compliance may also require disabling certain features of a site, such as interactive capabilities that result in third-party disclosure of personal information. Some sites have found it impracticable to comply, and have opted instead to limit their services to users who (say they) are 13 or over. Parents may also not be too happy about being asked to disclose their credit card number before their child may get access to a website, viewing this as an invasion of their own privacy.

CHAPTER SEVEN
CONTROLLING DIGITAL GOODS: COPYRIGHT

Businesses involved in e-commerce may confront copyright issues in several different contexts. First, almost all businesses, whether online or offline, and whether selling hard goods or information goods, will market their products using literature, catalogue copy, images, and other materials that they wish to prevent others from copying. Second, some businesses, both online and offline, have information goods (software, movies, music, books, or other "content") as their stock in trade; these businesses want to prevent competitors and "pirates" from appropriating their products. Third, some businesses, native to the online environment, depend upon transmitting, aggregating, or repackaging digitized content, some of which is subject to copyrights owned by others. New copyright issues arise in all three of these contexts, due to the digitized format in which information goods and other materials are maintained on the network.

One of the great strengths of the Internet as a platform for commerce is the ease and efficiency with which information can be distributed in the global marketplace. If a company wishes to announce a new product to the world, it need only post the announcement on the company's website, or on electronic mailing lists or bulletin boards whose membership might have an interest in the product. In addition, the company can e-mail an announcement to those who have expressed an interest in learning of such a product, or discuss it in chat rooms and live online fora dedicated to a topic to which the product is relevant. The Internet may also be used to distribute customer service information quickly and inexpensively.

But the very ease and efficiency with which the Internet permits information to be copied and distributed is regarded by some as a great danger. To content producers—such as movie studios, book publishers, software producers, artists, composers, music publishers, and record companies—the Internet poses a threat that some perceive as of the greatest magnitude. Once an information product is reduced to a digital file, such as a movie on a DVD or a song on a CD, perfect copies of it can be distributed world-wide in unlimited numbers at virtually no cost—perfect because one of the characteristics of digital information products is that every copy perfectly duplicates the original. Accordingly, if a company loses control of its information assets on the Internet, the market value of those assets may drop to near zero—the marginal cost of copying and distributing them.

In part for this reason, traditional content companies have been slow to embrace the Internet as anything other than a marketing channel. While the Internet could also provide these companies with a low-cost, 24/7 distribution channel for delivering their digital goods and services, many content companies consider the risk to their principal assets simply too great.

In an analogue world, the risk to a company's information assets was lower. It has been possible for decades, for example, to make copies of printed materials through xerography, and copies of recorded music on audio cassettes. But those technologies posed only a limited threat to content industries due to economic and technological constraints. It is usually cheaper to purchase an authorized copy of a book than to buy (or make) a pirated version reproduced through xerography, and the quality of the original is higher.[1] Copying via

---

[1] For certain types of printed works, however, such as sheet music, a photocopy may be signifi-

audiocassette usually costs less than buying an authorized version, but the quality degrades quickly with successive generations of copying further removed from the original. With the emergence of digital technologies, the economics and quality factors began to incline more favorably toward unauthorized copying and distribution. Floppy disks containing software or data, and CDs containing music, can be copied cheaply and easily, and with no loss in quality, even after multiple generations of copies. The need physically to distribute the media bearing the content, however, acts as a constraint on unauthorized distribution: special efforts must be made to conceal the factories needed to engage in large-scale piracy, and large shipments of physical media are susceptible to discovery and confiscation. Large-scale copying and distribution via the Internet largely eliminates these constraints.

Content companies have been reluctant to make their material available online for another reason as well: the law governing rights in information goods, the law of copyright, is less well settled online than offline. In many ways, the law of copyright applies online just as one would expect. Images and text posted on a web page are governed by copyright in the same way that images and text in a mail-order catalog are. Similarly, digital music files online generally receive the same protection as music recorded on an audio CD. What causes uncertainty online is not these established applications of copyright law, but rather the novel uses of digital goods in a purely digital environment.

For example, the use of any kind of digital information on a computer, and any transmission of information from one computer to another, involves temporary storage of that information. Is the unauthorized storage of such information a violation of the copyright owner's exclusive right to make copies? Is transmitting a digital file a violation of the copyright owner's exclusive distribution right? Does the appearance of an image in a web browser implicate the copyright owner's right to publicly display that work? If the transmission of a file over the Internet requires its conversion from one file format to another, is that a violation of the copyright owner's exclusive right to prepare derivative works? Also unresolved are issues concerning how the copyright laws apply to the many new and emerging business models that use, manipulate, repurpose, and repackage digital goods in ways unanticipated by the drafters of the copyright laws.

In the last few years, Congress has enacted significant amendments to federal copyright law aimed at addressing some of the unique issues raised by the Internet. Courts have also done their part, extending traditional copyright doctrine into the digital domain. Nonetheless, much uncertainty remains.

In light of these legal uncertainties and the greater threat of unauthorized copying online, some companies have embraced self-help technologies in an effort to reduce the business risks involved in making digitized content available on the Internet. Chief among these self-help measures has been the use of encryption-based software programs—sometimes called "digital rights management" systems or simply "trusted systems"—that control access to and copying of information goods. In recognition of the importance of these systems to the development of Internet commerce, two recent international treaties require signatory states to enact legislation making circumventing such systems unlawful. We address trusted systems and the laws supporting their use in Chapter 9, *infra*.

---

cantly cheaper than an authorized version.

I. A BRIEF OVERVIEW OF THE LAW OF COPYRIGHT

Copyright is a set of statutory rights that writers, artists, composers, musicians, and other authors acquire in connection with their original creations. These rights constitute a legal monopoly, allowing authors (or the transferees of their rights) to prevent others for a limited time from making certain uses of the protected works, and to condition the use of those works on whatever terms they see fit.

Federal copyright law derives from Article 1, Section 8, Clause 8 of the United States Constitution, which confers on the federal government the power "[t]o promote the Progress of Science and useful Arts, by securing for limited Times to Authors . . . the exclusive Right to their . . . Writings . . . ." Exercising this power, Congress enacted the first copyright law in 1790, and has amended it many times since. The current copyright law, codified in Title 17 of the U.S. Code, was adopted in 1976, and has been much amended since then.

The goal of copyright is to encourage the creation and distribution of original works of authorship, by enabling authors to exploit the economic value of their creations. Works of authorship have the special property that, once disclosed to the public, they may be reproduced by others in such a way that little of their value translates into income to the author. For example, if it were cost-free to make a perfect copy of a book, and if the law did not proscribe such copying, then it is likely the publisher would be able to sell only one copy of each book at cover price, making it economically infeasible to publish. If authors are unable to convert the fruits of their labor into income, they will cease to create, or at least create less. Because society as a whole benefits from the creation of literary, artistic, musical, and other works of authorship, the law grants authors the right to prevent others from making use of their works without paying for that privilege.

The Copyright Act of 1976 accomplishes this by granting authors a set of "exclusive rights" with respect to the works they create. These are the rights (1) to reproduce the work, (2) to prepare derivative works based on the work, (3) to distribute copies of the work to the public, (4) to perform the work publicly, (5) to display the work publicly, and (6) in the case of sound recordings, to perform the copyrighted work publicly by means of a digital audio transmission. 17 U.S.C. § 106. A person who exercises any of these rights without the permission of the copyright holder is said to "infringe" the copyright, and is liable for damages and subject to injunctive relief.

The works of authorship that copyright protects span the range of human imagination, including literary works, computer programs, musical compositions, dramatic works, pantomimes and choreographic works, drawings, paintings, photographs, motion pictures and other audiovisual works (including computer games), sound recordings, and architectural works. *See id.* § 102(a). Works are entitled to protection only if they are original: the author must have created the work independently rather than copying it from another, and the work must involve some minimal quantum of creativity. Only the author's *expression* is protectible; the ideas, concepts, principles, and facts communicated by that expression are not within the protection of copyright. *See id.* § 102(b).

Copyright protection exists from the moment a work of authorship is fixed in some tangible medium of expression, such as by writing a text or musical composition on paper, recording a performance on audiotape or videotape, making a drawing or painting, or saving a file to a hard drive. The observance of formalities, such as placing a © symbol on each copy of the work or timely registering it with the Copyright Office, is not a prerequisite to copyright protection, but may yield significant advantages to the copyright holder in an infringement action. Under current law, protection generally lasts until 70 years after the death of the author. In the case of "works made for hire," which are works produced by an employee within the scope of his employment (as well as certain works produced by independent contractors), copyright lasts for 95 years from publication, but no more than 120 years from creation.

Copyright seeks to maintain an appropriate balance between the interests of authors in benefiting from the economic value of their works, and the interests of the public, and of subsequent authors, in having access to the works that copyright is designed to encourage. To this end, the Copyright Act imposes certain limitations on copyright holders' exercise of their exclusive rights. The most important of these limitations is known as "fair use," which allows free use of copyrighted works in circumstances where the user or the public derives significant benefit and the copyright owner suffers only minor harm. *See id.* § 107. The copyright statute also contains a variety of narrow exemptions for libraries, nonprofit and educational users, limited uses on business premises, noncommercial copying of musical recordings, and other circumstances. *See, e.g., id.* §§ 108, 110, & 1008. In addition, the Copyright Act grants compulsory licenses for certain uses, giving anyone the right to make use of a copyrighted work upon payment of a royalty rate determined by law. *See, e.g., id.* §§ 114 & 115.

Because the socially optimal balance between authorial rights and public access changes over time as new forms of expression emerge and new uses for copyrighted works develop, the law of copyright has been regularly amended to accommodate new and emerging technologies and forms of commerce. Historically, for example, the development and commercialization of photography, telegraphy, radio, motion pictures, broadcast and cable television, xerography, audio and video recording equipment, and the computer have all led to amendments to federal copyright law.

II. Copyright in the Internet Commerce Environment

A. Subject Matter and Standards for Protection

§ 102. Subject matter of copyright: In general[2]

(a) Copyright protection subsists, in accordance with this title, in original works of authorship fixed in any tangible medium of expression, now known or later developed, from which they can be perceived, reproduced, or otherwise communicated, either directly or with the aid of a machine or device. Works of authorship include the following categories:

(1) literary works;

(2) musical works, including any accompanying words;

(3) dramatic works, including any accompanying music;

---

[2] Statutory excerpts in this Chapter are from the Copyright Act, 17 U.S.C. §§ 101 et seq., unless otherwise indicated.

(4) pantomimes and choreographic works;

(5) pictorial, graphic, and sculptural works;

(6) motion pictures and other audiovisual works;

(7) sound recordings; and

(8) architectural works.

. . .

§ 101. Definitions

. . .

A work is "fixed" in a tangible medium of expression when its embodiment in a copy or phonorecord, by or under the authority of the author, is sufficiently permanent or stable to permit it to be perceived, reproduced, or otherwise communicated for a period of more than transitory duration. A work consisting of sounds, images, or both, that are being transmitted, is "fixed" for purposes of this title if a fixation of the work is being made simultaneously with its transmission.

. . .

"Copies" are material objects, other than phonorecords, in which a work is fixed by any method now known or later developed, and from which the work can be perceived, reproduced, or otherwise communicated, either directly or with the aid of a machine or device. . . .

"Phonorecords" are material objects in which sounds, other than those accompanying a motion picture or other audiovisual work, are fixed by any method now known or later developed, and from which the sounds can be perceived, reproduced, or otherwise communicated, either directly or with the aid of a machine or device. . . .

H.R. Rep. No. 1476
Copyright Act of 1976 (94th Cong., 2d Sess.) (1976).

SECTION 102. GENERAL SUBJECT MATTER OF COPYRIGHT

. . .

Fixation in tangible form

As a basic condition of copyright protection, the bill perpetuates the existing requirement that a work be fixed in a "tangible medium of expression," and adds that this medium may be one "now known or later developed," and that the fixation is sufficient if the work "can be perceived, reproduced, or otherwise communicated, either directly or with the aid of a machine or device." This broad language is intended to avoid the artificial and largely unjustifiable distinctions, . . . under which statutory copyrightability in certain cases has been made to depend upon the form or medium in which the work is fixed. Under the bill it makes no difference what the form, manner, or medium of fixation may be—whether it is in words, numbers, notes, sounds, pictures, or any other graphic or symbolic indicia, whether embodied in a physical object in written, printed, photographic, sculptural, punched, magnetic, or any other stable form, and whether it is capable of perception directly or by means of any machine or device "now known or later developed."

. . .

The bill seeks to resolve, through the definition of "fixation" in section 101, the status of live broadcasts—sports, news coverage, live performances of music, etc.— that are reaching the public in unfixed form but that are simultaneously being recorded. When a football game is being covered by four television cameras, with a director guiding the activities of the four cameramen and choosing which of their electronic images are sent out to the public and in what order, there is little doubt that what the cameramen and the director are doing constitutes "authorship." The further question to be considered is whether there has been a fixation. If the images and sounds to be broadcast are first recorded (on a video tape, film, etc.) and then transmitted, the recorded work would be considered a "motion picture" subject to statutory protection against unauthorized reproduction or retransmission of the broadcast. If the program content is transmitted live to the public while being recorded at the same time, the case would be treated the same; the copyright owner would not be forced to rely on common law rather than statutory rights in proceeding against an infringing user of the live broadcast.

Thus, assuming it is copyrightable—as a "motion picture" or "sound recording," for example—the content of a live transmission should be accorded statutory protection if it is being recorded simultaneously with its transmission. On the other hand, the definition of "fixation" would exclude from the concept purely evanescent or transient reproductions such as those projected briefly on a screen, shown electronically on a television or other cathode ray tube, or captured momentarily in the "memory" of a computer.

Under the first sentence of the definition of "fixed" in section 101, a work would be considered "fixed in a tangible medium of expression," if there has been an authorized embodiment in a copy or phonorecord and if that embodiment "is sufficiently permanent or stable" to permit the work "to be perceived, reproduced, or otherwise communicated for a period of more than transitory duration." The second sentence makes clear that, in the case of "a work consisting of sounds, images, or both, that are being transmitted," the work is regarded as "fixed" if a fixation is being made at the same time as the transmission.

Under this definition "copies" and "phonorecords" together will comprise all of the material objects in which copyrightable works are capable of being fixed. The definitions of these terms in section 101, together with their usage in section 102 and throughout the bill, reflect a fundamental distinction between the "original work" which is the product of "authorship" and the multitude of material objects in which it can be embodied. Thus, in the sense of the bill, a "book" is not a work of authorship, but is a particular kind of "copy." Instead, the author may write a "literary work," which in turn can be embodied in a wide range of "copies" and "phonorecords," including books, periodicals, computer punch cards, microfilm, tape recordings, and so forth. It is possible to have an "original work of authorship" without having a "copy" or "phonorecord" embodying it, and it is also possible to have a "copy" or "phonorecord" embodying something that does not qualify as an "original work of authorship." The two essential elements—original work and tangible object—must merge through fixation in order to produce subject matter copyrightable under the statute.

. . .

INFORMATION INFRASTRUCTURE TASK FORCE, WORKING GROUP ON INTELLECTUAL PROPERTY RIGHTS, INTELLECTUAL PROPERTY AND THE NATIONAL INFORMATION INFRASTRUCTURE (1995)
www.uspto.gov/web/offices/com/doc/ipnii/ipnii.pdf

. . .

The form of the fixation and the manner, method or medium used are virtually unlimited. . . .

In digital form, a work is generally recorded (fixed) as a sequence of binary digits (zeros and ones) using media specific encoding. This fits within the House Report's list of permissible manners of fixation. Virtually all works also will be fixed in acceptable material objects—i.e., copies or phonorecords. For instance, floppy disks, compact discs (CDs), CD-ROMs, optical disks, compact discs–interactive (CD-Is), digital tape, and other digital storage devices are all stable forms in which works may be fixed and from which works may be perceived, reproduced or communicated by means of a machine or device.[61]

The question of whether interactive works are fixed (given the user's ability to constantly alter the sequence of the "action") has been resolved by the courts in the context of video games and should not present a new issue in the context of the NII. Such works are generally considered sufficiently fixed to qualify for protection.[62] The sufficiency of the fixation of works transmitted via the NII, however, where no copy or phonorecord has been made prior to the transmission, may not be so clear.

. . .

EXTENSIONS

1. *Originality.* In addition to being fixed, a work of authorship must be "original" in order to qualify for federal copyright protection. The Supreme Court explained this requirement in *Feist Publications, Inc. v. Rural Telephone Serv.*, 499 U.S 340 (1991):

> Original, as the term is used in copyright, means only that the work was independently created by the author (as opposed to copied from other works), and

---

[61] *See, e.g., Stern Electronics, Inc. v. Kaufman*, 669 F.2d 852, 855 (2d Cir.1982) (putting work in "memory devices" of a computer "satisf[ies] the statutory requirement of a 'copy' in which the work is 'fixed' ").

[62] *See, e.g., Atari Games Corp. v. Oman*, 888 F.2d 878 (D.C. Cir.1989).

that it possesses at least some minimal degree of creativity. To be sure, the requisite level of creativity is extremely low; even a slight amount will suffice. The vast majority of works make the grade quite easily, as they posses some creative spark, "no matter how crude, humble, or obvious" it might be. [1 M. Nimmer & D. Nimmer, Copyright] § 1.08[C][1]. Originality does not signify novelty; a work may be original even though it closely resembles other works so long as the similarity is fortuitous, not the result of copying.

2. *Unfixed works.* Although unfixed works are not protected by federal copyright law, they may be protected under state law.

QUESTIONS FOR DISCUSSION

---

1. *Uniform Resource Locators.* Is the URL for a Web page copyrightable? (*See Ticketmaster Corp. v. Tickets.com, Inc.*, 2003 Copr.L.Dec. ¶ 28,607 (C.D.Cal.2003), excerpted in Part III(C), *infra.*)

2. *Fixation on the Web.* Today, many web pages are created "on the fly" using technologies such as Active Server Pages ("ASP"). These technologies are used when the information that must be displayed on a web page changes frequently, such as an e-commerce site's available inventory, sports scores, stock quotations, or the identity of the viewer. Typically, once the page is requested, an ASP application will assemble that web page by first acquiring the needed information from a database or cookie and then inserting it into appropriate HTML code. The web server will then send the newly created page to the web browser that requested it. The web page created by the ASP application may only exist momentarily in the random access memory of the server before it is sent to the requesting browser. In such a case, is the web page copyrightable subject matter? Does it meet the fixation requirement? Upon what additional facts might your answer depend?

B. Exclusive Rights

1. Generally

§ 106. Exclusive rights in copyrighted works.

Subject to sections 107 through 121, the owner of a copyright under this title has the exclusive rights to do and to authorize any of the following:

(1) to reproduce the copyrighted work in copies or phonorecords;

(2) to prepare derivative works based upon the copyrighted work;

(3) to distribute copies or phonorecords of the copyrighted work to the public by sale or other transfer of ownership, or by rental, lease, or lending;

(4) in the case of literary, musical, dramatic, and choreographic works, pantomimes, and motion pictures and other audiovisual works, to perform the copyrighted work publicly;

(5) in the case of literary, musical, dramatic, and choreographic works, pantomimes, and pictorial, graphic, or sculptural works, including the individual images of a motion picture or other audiovisual work, to display the copyrighted work publicly; and

(6) in the case of sound recordings, to perform the copyrighted work

publicly by means of a digital audio transmission.

H.R. Rep. No. 1476
Copyright Act of 1976 (94th Cong., 2d Sess.) (1976).

. . .

SECTION 106. EXCLUSIVE RIGHTS IN COPYRIGHTED WORKS

General scope of copyright

The five fundamental rights that the bill gives to copyright owners—the exclusive rights of reproduction, adaptation, publication, performance, and display—are stated generally in section 106. These exclusive rights, which comprise the so-called "bundle of rights" that is a copyright, are cumulative and may overlap in some cases. Each of the five enumerated rights may be subdivided indefinitely and . . . each subdivision of an exclusive right may be owned and enforced separately.

The approach of the bill is to set forth the copyright owner's exclusive rights in broad terms in section 106, and then to provide various limitations, qualifications, or exemptions in the 12 sections that follow. Thus, everything in section 106 is made "subject to sections 107 through [121]," and must be read in conjunction with those provisions.

. . .

Rights of reproduction, adaptation, and publication

The first three clauses of section 106 . . . extend to every kind of copyrighted work. The exclusive rights encompassed by these clauses, though closely related, are independent; they can generally be characterized as rights of copying, recording, adaptation, and publishing. A single act of infringement may violate all of these rights at once, as where a publisher reproduces, adapts, and sells copies of a person's copyrighted work as part of a publishing venture. Infringement takes place when any one of the rights is violated: where, for example, a printer reproduces copies without selling them or a retailer sells copies without having anything to do with their reproduction. The references to "copies or phonorecords," although in the plural, are intended here and throughout the bill to include the singular (1 U.S.C. § 1).

Reproduction.—Read together with the relevant definitions in section 101, the right "to reproduce the copyrighted work in copies or phonorecords" means the right to produce a material object in which the work is duplicated, transcribed, imitated, or simulated in a fixed form from which it can be "perceived, reproduced, or otherwise communicated, either directly or with the aid of a machine or device." As under the present law, a copyrighted work would be infringed by reproducing it in whole or in any substantial part, and by duplicating it exactly or by imitation or simulation. Wide departures or variations from the copyrighted works would still be an infringement as long as the author's "expression" rather than merely the author's "ideas" are taken. . . .

"Reproduction" under clause (1) of section 106 is to be distinguished from "display" under clause (5). For a work to be "reproduced," its fixation in tangible form must be "sufficiently permanent or stable to permit it to be perceived, reproduced, or otherwise communicated for a period of more than transitory duration." Thus, the showing of images on a screen or tube would not be a violation of clause (1), although it might come within the scope of clause (5).

. . .

2. The Reproduction Right

MAI Systems Corp. v. Peak Computer, Inc.
991 F.2d 511 (9th Cir.1993).

■ BRUNETTI, CIRCUIT JUDGE:

Peak Computer, Inc. and two of its employees appeal the district court's order issuing a preliminary injunction pending trial as well as the district court's order issuing a permanent injunction following the grant of partial summary judgment.

I. FACTS

MAI Systems Corp., until recently, manufactured computers and designed software to run those computers. The company continues to service its computers and the software necessary to operate the computers. MAI software includes operating system software, which is necessary to run any other program on the computer.

Peak Computer, Inc. is a company organized in 1990 that maintains computer systems for its clients. Peak maintains MAI computers for more than one hundred clients in Southern California. This accounts for between fifty and seventy percent of Peak's business.

Peak's service of MAI computers includes routine maintenance and emergency repairs. Malfunctions often are related to the failure of circuit boards inside the computers, and it may be necessary for a Peak technician to operate the computer and its operating system software in order to service the machine.

In August, 1991, Eric Francis left his job as customer service manager at MAI and joined Peak. Three other MAI employees joined Peak a short time later. Some businesses that had been using MAI to service their computers switched to Peak after learning of Francis's move.

II. PROCEDURAL HISTORY

On March 17, 1992, MAI filed suit in the district court against Peak, Peak's president Vincent Chiechi, and Francis. The complaint includes counts alleging copyright infringement, misappropriation of trade secrets, trademark infringement, false advertising, and unfair competition.

MAI asked the district court for a temporary restraining order and preliminary injunction pending the outcome of the suit. The district court issued a temporary restraining order on March 18, 1992 and converted it to a preliminary injunction on March 26, 1992. On April 15, 1992, the district court issued a written version of the preliminary injunction along with findings of fact and conclusions of law. [The Ninth Circuit stayed the preliminary injunction in part in June, 1992.]

. . .

[The district court eventually granted partial summary judgment for MAI and entered a permanent injunction on the issues of copyright infringement and mis-appropriation of trade secrets, which the Ninth Circuit then stayed the permanent injunction in part pending this appeal.]

III. STANDARD OF REVIEW

. . .

A grant of summary judgment is reviewed de novo. . . .

. . .

IV. COPYRIGHT INFRINGEMENT

The district court granted summary judgment in favor of MAI on its claims of copyright infringement and issued a permanent injunction against Peak on these claims. The alleged copyright violations include: (1) Peak's running of MAI software licensed to Peak customers; (2) Peak's use of unlicensed software at its head-quarters; and, (3) Peak's loaning of MAI computers and software to its customers. Each of these alleged violations must be considered separately.

A. Peak's running of MAI software licensed to Peak customers

To prevail on a claim of copyright infringement, a plaintiff must prove owner-ship of a copyright and a " 'copying' of protectable expression" beyond the scope of a license. . . .

MAI software licenses allow MAI customers to use the software for their own internal information processing. This allowed use necessarily includes the loading of the software into the computer's random access memory ("RAM") by a MAI customer. However, MAI software licenses do not allow for the use or copying of MAI software by third parties such as Peak. Therefore, any "copying" done by Peak is "beyond the scope" of the license.

It is not disputed that MAI owns the copyright to the software at issue here, however, Peak vigorously disputes the district court's conclusion that a "copying" occurred under the Copyright Act.

The Copyright Act defines "copies" as:

> material objects, other than phonorecords, in which a work is fixed by any method now known or later developed, and from which the work can be perceived, reproduced, or otherwise communicated, either di-rectly or with the aid of a machine or device.

17 U.S.C. § 101.

The Copyright Act then explains:

> A work is "fixed" in a tangible medium of expression when its embodi-ment in a copy or phonorecord, by or under the authority of the author, is sufficiently permanent or stable to permit it to be perceived, repro-

duced, or otherwise communicated for a period of more than transitory duration.

17 U.S.C. § 101.

The district court's grant of summary judgment on MAI's claims of copyright infringement reflects its conclusion that a "copying" for purposes of copyright law occurs when a computer program is transferred from a permanent storage device to a computer's RAM. This conclusion is consistent with its finding, in granting the preliminary injunction, that: "the loading of copyrighted computer software from a storage medium (hard disk, floppy disk, or read only memory) into the memory of a central processing unit ("CPU") causes a copy to be made. In the absence of ownership of the copyright or express permission by license, such acts constitute copyright infringement." We find that this conclusion is supported by the record and by the law.

Peak concedes that in maintaining its customer's computers, it uses MAI operating software "to the extent that the repair and maintenance process necessarily involves turning on the computer to make sure it is functional and thereby running the operating system." It is also uncontroverted that when the computer is turned on the operating system is loaded into the computer's RAM. As part of diagnosing a computer problem at the customer site, the Peak technician runs the computer's operating system software, allowing the technician to view the systems error log, which is part of the operating system, thereby enabling the technician to diagnose the problem.

Peak argues that this loading of copyrighted software does not constitute a copyright violation because the "copy" created in RAM is not "fixed." However, by showing that Peak loads the software into the RAM and is then able to view the system error log and diagnose the problem with the computer, MAI has adequately shown that the representation created in the RAM is "sufficiently permanent or stable to permit it to be perceived, reproduced, or otherwise communicated for a period of more than transitory duration."

After reviewing the record, we find no specific facts (and Peak points to none) which indicate that the copy created in the RAM is not fixed. While Peak argues this issue in its pleadings, mere argument does not establish a genuine issue of material fact to defeat summary judgment. A party opposing a properly supported motion for summary judgment may not rest upon the mere allegations or denials in pleadings, but "must set forth specific facts showing that there is a genuine issue for trial." Fed. R. Civ. Pro. 56(e).

The law also supports the conclusion that Peak's loading of copyrighted software into RAM creates a "copy" of that software in violation of the Copyright Act. In *Apple Computer, Inc. v. Formula Int'l, Inc.*, 594 F.Supp. 617, 621 (C.D.Cal.1984), the district court held that the copying of copyrighted software onto silicon chips and subsequent sale of those chips is not protected by § 117 of the Copyright Act. Section 117 allows "the 'owner'[5] of a copy of a computer program to make or author-

---

[5] Since MAI licensed its software, the Peak customers do not qualify as "owners" of the

ize the making of another copy" without infringing copyright law, if it "is an essential step in the utilization of the computer program" or if the new copy is "for archival purposes only." 17 U.S.C. § 117 (Supp. 1988). One of the grounds for finding that § 117 did not apply was the court's conclusion that the permanent copying of the software onto the silicon chips was not an "essential step" in the utilization of the software because the software could be used through RAM without making a permanent copy. The court stated:

> RAM can be simply defined as a computer component in which data and computer programs can be temporarily recorded. Thus, the purchaser of [software] desiring to utilize all of the programs on the diskette could arrange to copy [the software] into RAM. This would only be a temporary fixation. It is a property of RAM that when the computer is turned off, the copy of the program recorded in RAM is lost.

Apple Computer at 622.

While we recognize that this language is not dispositive, it supports the view that the copy made in RAM is "fixed" and qualifies as a copy under the Copyright Act.

We have found no case which specifically holds that the copying of software into RAM creates a "copy" under the Copyright Act. However, it is generally accepted that the loading of software into a computer constitutes the creation of a copy under the Copyright Act. See e.g. *Vault Corp. v. Quaid Software Ltd.*, 847 F.2d 255, 260 (5th Cir.1988) ("the act of loading a program from a medium of storage into a computer's memory creates a copy of the program"); 2 *Nimmer on Copyright*, § 8.08 at 8-105 (1983) ("Inputting a computer program entails the preparation of a copy."); *Final Report of the National Commission on the New Technological Uses of Copyrighted Works*, at 13 (1978) ("the placement of a work into a computer is the preparation of a copy"). We recognize that these authorities are somewhat troubling since they do not specify that a copy is created regardless of whether the software is loaded into the RAM, the hard disk or the read only memory ("ROM"). However, since we find that the copy created in the RAM can be "perceived, reproduced, or otherwise communicated," we hold that the loading of software into the RAM creates a copy under the Copyright Act. 17 U.S.C. § 101. We affirm the district court's grant of summary judgment as well as the permanent injunction as it relates to this issue.

[The court also affirmed the permanent injunction with respect to copyright infringement as it related to Peak's use of unlicensed MAI software at Peak's headquarters and to Peak's loaning of MAI computers and software to Peak's customers.]

. . .

The district court's grant of summary judgment is AFFIRMED in part and REVERSED in part. This case is REMANDED for proceedings consistent with this opinion.

---

software and are not eligible for protection under § 117.

INFORMATION INFRASTRUCTURE TASK FORCE, WORKING GROUP ON INTELLECTUAL PROPERTY RIGHTS, INTELLECTUAL PROPERTY AND THE NATIONAL INFORMATION INFRASTRUCTURE (1995)
www.uspto.gov/web/offices/com/doc/ipnii/ipnii.pdf

. . .

a. THE RIGHT TO REPRODUCE THE WORK

The fundamental right to reproduce copyrighted works in copies and phonorecords will be implicated in innumerable NII[3] transactions. Indeed, because of the nature of computer-to-computer communications, it will be implicated in most NII transactions. For example, when a computer user accesses a document resident on another computer, the image on the user's screen exists—under contemporary technology—only by virtue of the copy that is *reproduced* in the user's computer memory. It has long been clear under U.S. law that the placement of copyrighted material into a computer's memory is a reproduction of that material (because the work in memory then may be, in the law's terms, "perceived, reproduced, or . . . communicated . . . with the aid of a machine or device").[202]

The 1976 Copyright Act, its legislative history, the *CONTU Final Report*, and repeated holdings by courts make it clear that in each of the instances set out below, one or more copies is made.[203]

- When a work is placed into a computer, whether on a disk, diskette, ROM, or other storage device or in RAM for more than a very brief period, a copy is made.[204]

- When a printed work is "scanned" into a digital file, a copy—the digital

---

[3] [The Report uses the abbreviation "NII" to refer to the "National Information Infrastructure," its general term for the digital network environment.—Eds.]

[202] In 1978, the *CONTU Final Report* noted, "[T]he application of principles already embodied in the language of the [current] copyright law achieves the desired substantive legal protection for copyrighted works which exist in machine-readable form. The introduction of a work into a computer memory would, consistent with the [current] law, be a reproduction of the work, one of the exclusive rights of the copyright proprietor." *CONTU Final Report* at 40. *See also MAI Systems Corp. v. Peak Computer, Inc.*, 991 F.2d 511, 519 (9th Cir.1993), *cert. denied*, 114 S. Ct. 671 (1994); *Vault Corp. v. Quaid Software Ltd.*, 847 F.2d 255, 260 (5th Cir.1988); *Advanced Computer Services v. MAI Systems Corp.*, 845 F.Supp. 356 (E.D. Va. 1994); *Triad Systems Corp. v. Southeastern Express Co.*, 1994 U.S. Dist. LEXIS 5390 (N.D. Cal. March 18, 1994); 2 NIMMER ON COPYRIGHT § 8.08[A] (1994).

[203] That copying has occurred does not necessarily mean that infringement has occurred. When copying is (1) authorized by the copyright owner, (2) exempt from liability as a fair use, (3) otherwise exempt under the provisions of Sections 108–119 or Chapter 10 of the Copyright Act, or (4) of such a small amount as to be *de minimis*, then there is no infringement liability.

[204] *See, e.g., MAI Systems Corp. v. Peak Computer, Inc.*, 991 F.2d 511, 519 (9th Cir.1993). (While this court's determination with respect to fair use may be open to question, its holding that booting a PC involves copying the operating system seems quite unexceptional.)

file itself — is made.

- When other works — including photographs, motion pictures, or sound recordings — are digitized, copies are made.

- Whenever a digitized file is "uploaded" from a user's computer to a bulletin board system (bbs) or other server, a copy is made.

- Whenever a digitized file is "downloaded" from a bbs or other server, a copy is made.

- When a file is transferred from one computer network user to another, multiple copies generally are made.[205]

- Under current technology, when an end-user's computer is employed as a "dumb" terminal to access a file resident on another computer such as a bbs or Internet host, a copy of at least the portion viewed is made in the user's computer. Without such copying into the RAM or buffer of the user's computer, no screen display would be possible.

TROTTER HARDY, PROJECT LOOKING FORWARD: SKETCHING THE FUTURE OF COPYRIGHT IN A NETWORKED WORLD (1998).
www.copyright.gov/reports/thardy.pdf

4.3 RAM Copies

. . .

There is much ferment in both technology and copyright circles about the copyright significance of the temporary appearance of digital information in computer memory. Computers have more than one kind of "memory," so it is useful to keep them straight. Most of the time, the concern centers on a computer's "internal" or "random-access memory." Abbreviated "RAM," this internal memory is an essential part of the operation of computers. It is where the brain of the computer — the processor — stores the instructions and data it operates on.[105] These days most RAM memory in desktop and other computers lies in one or more computer "chips," which look like small black or gray squares stuck on a printed circuit board. These squares contain quite a number of transistors, resistors, and the like that are microscopically tiny (and covered up in any event by the black or gray

---

[205] For example, if an author transfers a file (such as a manuscript) to a publisher with an Internet account, copies will typically, at a minimum, be made (a) in the author's Internet server, (b) in the publisher's Internet server, (c) in the publisher's local area network server, and (d) in the editor's microcomputer. It has been suggested that such "copying" of files in intermediate servers is only of transitory duration and consequently not covered by the reproduction right. However, it is clear that if the "copy" exists for more than a period of transitory duration, the reproduction right is implicated. Whether such reproduction is an infringement would be a separate determination.

[105] Technically most computers cannot "operate" on data in this RAM; they must pull it into various parts, called "registers," of the processor itself to do any actual manipulation. But the distinctions do not matter for purposes of this Report.

outer shell). They have no moving parts, and like the processor chip itself, are therefore "solid state" devices.

Most computers also have another storage memory in the form of "disk" storage. The "disk" may be a floppy disk, or a hard disk. This form of storage is also sometimes referred to as computer "memory," but this Report will refer to it as "disk storage" to distinguish it from RAM storage. . . . Commonly today, [disks] work on the principle of a tape recorder: the disk surface is coated with a magnetic material that can selectively be exposed to a magnetic field and thus altered. A specially designed "head" moves over the surface of the disk as it rotates and either "magnetizes" small spots on the disk ("writes") or recognized previously-magnetized spots on ("reads") the disk. Other disk storage technologies involve optical techniques: marking a disk with physical "pits" or tiny spots of dye, for example.

The "RAM copy" issue deals with the other type of computer memory, the solid state or "internal" memory of computers. It is in this memory that a computer must make "copies" of some sort in order to function. This might happen when a computer is looking at a piece of e-mail to determine whether the recipient has an account on that computer, or whether the e-mail must be directed onward to another computer. It might take only a few thousandths of a single second to make that determination, after which the computer is "through" with that piece of (possibly) copyrighted information.

A computer RAM "copy" must also be made in other circumstances, particularly whenever a computer program is run. A program is a set of instructions. If it resides on a disk, it cannot at that point be "run." First, the instructions must be brought into the computer's RAM memory. That is a form of copying (and has been so held; see the next paragraph). In fact, though this discussion seldom comes up in the caselaw, even the copy in RAM is not enough to enable the computer to run the program. For that to happen, the computer must move each of the instructions, often only one or two instructions at a time, into the "CPU," or "central processing unit." It is there that the instructions are actually "obeyed" by the computer. So it is possible to look at the running of a program as necessitating more than one form of "copying" inside the computer.

Debates go on over the issue whether copyright law should define the term "copy" in such a way that brief instantiations of copyrightable works in computer memory are "copies." The argument that it should not is based on the observation that a reliance on "copying" for copyright purposes arose when "copies" were very tangible, long lasting objects: books, 35mm film reels, audio tape cassettes, etc. These objects are produced deliberately, typically under the direct control of a single entity, such as a record company or a book publisher. Imposing liability for copying in a world of this sort of tangible objects seems to make intuitive sense and be relatively straightforward.

On the other hand, as with caching, a RAM copy is not inherently short-lived. With most personal computers today, the RAM memory is erased when the power is turned off. If the power is not turned off, the memory persists. Other kinds of

RAM memory use different technology and retain their data even when the power is turned off. As with caching, then, RAM copies come in a wide variety of types, durations, and purposes. A number of cases, most notably *MAI v. Peak*,[108] have either held or implied that the first step, bringing the instructions from a disk of some kind into RAM memory, constitutes the making of a "copy" of the program for copyright purposes. That is, the process results in the creation of a copy that if not expressly or impliedly authorized or a fair use, is a potentially infringing violation of the copyright owner's rights.

. . .

Digital information, at least for the foreseeable future, means information that is under the control of computers. With present technology, a digital computer cannot "run" without some sort of "copying" of information and data into the computer's internal RAM memory. Therefore any access to or use of digital information means access to or use of information that is under the control of a computer, and therefore means that some computer program must be executed. If a computer program is executed, a RAM copy is created. In this manner, "access to and use of information" and "copyright" can be tied together . . . .

EXTENSIONS

1. *RAM Storage as "reproduction" and control over digital information.* The view that nearly all temporary storage in RAM constitutes the making of a "copy" or "phonorecord" covered by the Section 106(1) reproduction right has been controversial in large part due to the point made in the immediately preceding paragraph: accessing any digitally stored information, at least using current technology, requires storage in RAM or something like it. This has led some to argue that treating RAM storage as "reproduction" may give copyright owners too much control over the use of their works:

> [T]echnological miracles . . . , however, have served up some unanticipated windfalls for the copyright owner. The most crucial example is the evolution of the reproduction right into something more encompassing than envisioned in any copyright revision until now. United States copyright law has always given copyright owners some form of exclusive reproduction right. It has never before now given them an exclusive *reading* right, and it is hard to make a plausible argument that Congress would have enacted a law giving copyright owners control of reading. A handful of recent interpretations of the statute, however, insist that one reproduces a work every time one reads it into a computer's random access memory. For all works encoded in digital form, any act of reading or viewing the work would require the use of a computer, and would, under this interpretation, involve an actionable reproduction. . . .

> If a bargain between the public and the authors and producers of copyrighted

---

[108] MAI Sys. Corp. v. Peak Computer, Inc., 991 F.2d 511, 518-19 (9th Cir.1993), *cert. dismissed*, 510 U.S. 1033 (1994). *See also* DSC Communications Corp. v. DGI Technologies, Inc., 81 F.3d 597, 600 (5th Cir.1996); Triad Sys. v. Southeastern Express Co., 64 F.3d 1330, 1335 (9th Cir.1995), *cert. denied*, 516 U.S. 1145 (1996); Religious Tech. Center v. Netcom On-line Comm., 907 F.Supp. 1361, 1368 (N.D. Cal. 1995); In re Independent Servs. Orgs. Litigation, 910 F.Supp. 1537, 1541 (D. Kan. 1995); Advanced Computer Servs. of Mich., Inc. v. MAI Sys. Corp., 845 F.Supp. 356, 362-64 (E.D.Va. 1994). . . .

works were negotiated (at arms length) and drafted up today, it might include a reproduction right, but it surely wouldn't include a "reading" right. It might include a performance right but not a "listening" right; it might have a display right, but it wouldn't have a "viewing" right. From the public's vantage point, the fact that copyright owners are now in a position to claim exclusive "reading," "listening," and "viewing" rights is an accident of drafting: when Congress awarded authors an exclusive reproduction right, it did not mean what it may mean today.

Jessica Litman, *The Exclusive Right to Read*, 13 CARDOZO ARTS & ENT. L.J. 29, 40, 43 (1994). Professor Raymond Nimmer has similarly observed

The idea that reading a digital text entails a potential copyright violation shifts policy. That shift, even if desirable, should occur because of an express policy choice rather than because new technology technically triggers concepts originally designed for a world of photocopy machines, recorders, and the like.

RAYMOND NIMMER, INFORMATION LAW, ¶ 4.08[1], at 4–30.

2. *RAM Storage as "reproduction" and control over Internet transmissions.* Treating temporary storage in RAM as within the Section 106(1) reproduction right also raises significant questions about potential for widespread liability on the part of entities that process the transmission of material over the Internet. David Hayes has detailed the "ubiquitous nature" of RAM "copies" in transmissions over the Internet:

Under current technology, information is transmitted through the Internet using a technique known broadly as packet switching. Specifically, data to be transmitted through the network is broken up into smaller units or packets of information, which are in effect labeled as to their proper order. The packets are then sent through the network as discrete units, often through multiple different paths and often at different times. As the packets are released and forwarded through the network, each "router" computer makes a temporary (ephemeral) copy of each packet and transmits it to the next router according to the best path available at that instant until it arrives at its destination. . . . The packets, which frequently do not arrive in sequential order, are then "reassembled" at the receiving end into proper order to reconstruct the data that was sent. Thus, only certain subsets (packets) of the data being transmitted are passing through the RAM of a node computer at any given time, although a complete copy of the transmitted data may be created and/or stored at the ultimate destination computer, either in the destination computer's RAM, on its hard disk, or in portions of both.

David L. Hayes, *Advanced Copyright Issues on the Internet*, 7 TEX. INT. PROP. L. J. 1, 5 (1998). And Mark Lemley has detailed the minimum number of such "copies" that even a simple transmission over the Internet will create:

If one accepts the argument that RAM copies are actionable under § 106(1), the number of copies made in even the most routine Net transactions increases dramatically. Obviously, each act of uploading or downloading makes a RAM copy in the recipient's computer, but that is only the beginning. When a picture is downloaded from a Website, the modem at each end will buffer each byte, as will the router, the receiving computer, the Web browser, the video decompression chip, and the video display board. Those seven copies will be made on each such transaction.

Mark A. Lemley, *Dealing with Overlapping Copyrights on the Internet*, 22 U. DAYTON L. REV. 547, 554-55 (1997).

QUESTIONS FOR DISCUSSION

1. *Evanescent reproductions.* Can the *MAI* view of RAM storage, and the IITF's endorsement of it, be reconciled with the statement in the 1976 Act's legislative history that "the definition of 'fixation' would exclude from the concept purely evanescent or transient reproductions such as those projected briefly on a screen, shown electronically on a television or other cathode ray tube, or captured momentarily in the 'memory' of a computer"?

2. *Implications of RAM storage as "reproduction."* Treating RAM storage as reproduction means that every time an Internet user views or listens to any material on a Web page or in a newsgroup posting or e-mail message, a "copy" or "phonorecord" is made. If the copy is not authorized, by the copyright owner or some provision of copyright law, then copyright infringement occurs. Does the Copyright Act authorize any such viewing or listening? If or when it doesn't, who, if anyone, needs to be concerned as a practical matter about the acts of infringement that technically occur when the end user accesses the copyrighted work?

3. *Computer maintenance.* In 1998, the Copyright Act was amended in order essentially to change the result of the *MAI* decision with respect to computer maintenance. The statue allows "the owner or lessee of a machine to make or authorize the making of a copy of a computer program if such copy is made solely by virtue of the activation of a machine that lawfully contains an authorized copy of the computer program, for purposes only of maintenance or repair of that machine," under certain conditions. 17 U.S.C. § 117(c), (d). Does the enactment of this specific exemption for copies made by turning on a computer indicate that Congress accepted the more general view that storage in RAM generally *is* the making of a "copy"?

4. *Disk cache.* In many instances, when works of authorship in digital form are viewed over a network they are stored in a disk cache that often retains the material for a longer period of time than RAM storage typically does. Does this mean that, even if temporary RAM storage were not considered to be a "reproduction," most acts of accessing works of authorship online would potentially constitute copyright infringement?

3. The Derivative Work Right

H.R. Rep. No. 1476
Copyright Act of 1976 (94th Cong., 2d Sess.) (1976).

. . .

SECTION 106. EXCLUSIVE RIGHTS IN COPYRIGHTED WORKS

. . .

Preparation of derivative works.--The exclusive right to prepare derivative works, specified separately in clause (2) of section 106, overlaps the exclusive right of reproduction to some extent. It is broader than that right, however, in the sense that reproduction requires fixation in copies or phonorecords, whereas the preparation of a derivative work, such as a ballet, pantomime, or improvised performance, may be an infringement even though nothing is ever fixed in tangible form.

To be an infringement the "derivative work" must be "based upon the copyrighted work," and the definition in section 101 refers to "a translation, musical arrangement, dramatization, fictionalization, motion picture version, sound recording, art reproduction, abridgment, condensation, or any other form in which a work may be recast, transformed, or adapted." Thus, to constitute a violation of section 106(2), the infringing work must incorporate a portion of the copyrighted work in some form; for example, a detailed commentary on a work or a programmatic musical composition inspired by a novel would not normally constitute infringements under this clause.

. . .

Lewis Galoob Toys, Inc. v. Nintendo Of America, Inc.
964 F.2d 965 (9th Cir.1992).

■ FARRIS, CIRCUIT JUDGE:

Nintendo of America appeals the district court's judgment following a bench trial (1) declaring that Lewis Galoob Toys' Game Genie does not violate any Nintendo copyrights and dissolving a temporary injunction and (2) denying Nintendo's request for a permanent injunction enjoining Galoob from marketing the Game Genie. . . . We affirm.

FACTS

The Nintendo Entertainment System is a home video game system marketed by Nintendo. To use the system, the player inserts a cartridge containing a video game that Nintendo produces or licenses others to produce. By pressing buttons and manipulating a control pad, the player controls one of the game's characters and progresses through the game. The games are protected as audiovisual works under 17 U.S.C. § 102(a)(6).

The Game Genie is a device manufactured by Galoob that allows the player to alter up to three features of a Nintendo game. For example, the Game Genie can increase the number of lives of the player's character, increase the speed at which the character moves, and allow the character to float above obstacles. The player controls the changes made by the Game Genie by entering codes provided by the Game Genie Programming Manual and Code Book. The player also can experiment with variations of these codes.

The Game Genie functions by blocking the value for a single data byte sent by the game cartridge to the central processing unit in the Nintendo Entertainment System and replacing it with a new value. If that value controls the character's strength, for example, then the character can be made invincible by increasing the value sufficiently. The Game Genie is inserted between a game cartridge and the Nintendo Entertainment System. The Game Genie does not alter the data that is stored in the game cartridge. Its effects are temporary.

DISCUSSION

1. *Derivative work*

The Copyright Act of 1976 confers upon copyright holders the exclusive right to prepare and authorize others to prepare derivative works based on their copyrighted works. *See* 17 U.S.C. § 106(2). Nintendo argues that the district court erred in concluding that the audiovisual displays created by the Game Genie are not derivative works. . . .

A derivative work must incorporate a protected work in some concrete or permanent "form." The Copyright Act defines a derivative work as follows:

> A "derivative work" is a work based upon one or more preexisting works, such as a translation, musical arrangement, dramatization, fictionalization, motion picture version, sound recording, art reproduction, abridgment, condensation, *or any other form in which a work may be recast, transformed, or adapted.* A work consisting of editorial revisions, annotations, elaborations, or other modifications which, as a whole, represent an original work of authorship, is a "derivative work."

17 U.S.C. § 101 (emphasis added). The examples of derivative works provided by the Act all physically incorporate the underlying work or works. The Act's legislative history similarly indicates that "the infringing work must incorporate a portion of the copyrighted work in some form." 1976 U.S. Code Cong. & Admin. News 5659, 5675. *See also Mirage Editions, Inc. v. Albuquerque A.R.T. Co.,* 856 F.2d 1341, 1343-44 (9th Cir.1988) (discussing same).

Our analysis is not controlled by the Copyright Act's definition of "fixed." The Act defines copies as "material objects, other than phonorecords, in which a work is *fixed* by any method." 17 U.S.C. § 101 (emphasis added). The Act's definition of "derivative work," in contrast, lacks any such reference to fixation. *See id.* Further, we have held in a copyright infringement action that "[i]t makes no difference that the derivation may not satisfy certain requirements for statutory copyright registration itself." *Lone Ranger Television v. Program Radio Corp.,* 740 F.2d 718, 722 (9th Cir.1984). *See also* Paul Goldstein, *Derivative Rights and Derivative Works in Copyright,* 30 J. Copyright Soc'y U.S.A. 209, 231 n.75 (1983) ("the Act does not require that the derivative work be protectable for its preparation to infringe"). . . . A derivative work must be fixed to be *protected* under the Act, *see* 17 U.S.C. § 102(a), but not to *infringe.*

The argument that a derivative work must be fixed because "[a] 'derivative work' is a work," 17 U.S.C. § 101, and "[a] work is 'created' when it is fixed in a copy or phonorecord for the first time," *id.,* relies on a misapplication of the Copyright Act's definition of "created":

> A work is 'created' when it is fixed in a copy or phonorecord for the first time; where a work is prepared over a period of time, the portion of it that has been fixed at any particular time constitutes the work as of that time, and where the work has been prepared in different versions, each version constitutes a separate work.

Id. The definition clarifies the *time* at which a work is *created.* If the provision were a definition of "work," it would not use that term in such a casual manner. The Act does not contain a definition of "work." Rather, it contains specific definitions: "audiovisual works," "literary works," and "pictorial, graphic and sculptural works," for example. The definition of "derivative work" does not require fixation.

The district court's finding that no independent work is created is supported by the record. The Game Genie merely enhances the audiovisual displays (or underlying data bytes) that originate in Nintendo game cartridges. The altered displays do not incorporate a portion of a copyrighted work in some concrete or permanent *form*. Nintendo argues that the Game Genie's displays are as fixed in the hardware and software used to create them as Nintendo's original displays. Nintendo's argument ignores the fact that the Game Genie cannot produce an audiovisual display; the underlying display must be produced by a Nintendo Entertainment System and game cartridge. Even if we were to rely on the Copyright Act's definition of "fixed," we would similarly conclude that the resulting display is not "embodied," *see* 17 U.S.C. § 101, in the Game Genie. It cannot be a derivative work.

Mirage Editions is illustrative. Albuquerque A.R.T. transferred artworks from a commemorative book to individual ceramic tiles. *See Mirage Editions*, 856 F.2d at 1342. We held that "[b]y borrowing and mounting the preexisting, copyrighted individual art images without the consent of the copyright proprietors . . . [Albuquerque A.R.T.] has prepared a derivative work and infringed the subject copyrights." *Id.* at 1343. The ceramic tiles *physically* incorporated the copyrighted works in a form that could be sold. Perhaps more importantly, sales of the tiles supplanted purchasers' demand for the underlying works. Our holding in *Mirage Editions* would have been much different if Albuquerque A.R.T. had distributed lenses that merely enabled users to view several artworks simultaneously.

Nintendo asserted at oral argument that the existence of a $150 million market for the Game Genie indicates that its audiovisual display must be fixed. We understand Nintendo's argument; consumers clearly would not purchase the Game Genie if its display was not "sufficiently permanent or stable to permit it to be perceived . . . for a period of more than transitory duration." 17 U.S.C. § 101. But, Nintendo's reliance on the Copyright Act's definition of "fixed" is misplaced. Nintendo's argument also proves too much; the existence of a market does not, and cannot, determine conclusively whether a work is an infringing derivative work. For example, although there is a market for kaleidoscopes, it does not necessarily follow that kaleidoscopes create unlawful derivative works when pointed at protected artwork. The same can be said of countless other products that enhance, but do not replace, copyrighted works.

Nintendo also argues that our analysis should focus exclusively on the audiovisual displays created by the Game Genie, *i.e.*, that we should compare the altered displays to Nintendo's original displays. Nintendo emphasizes that " '[a]udiovisual works' are works that consist of a series of related images . . . *regardless of the nature of the material objects . . . in which the works are embodied*." 17 U.S.C. § 101 (emphasis added). The Copyright Act's definition of "audiovisual works" is inapposite; the *only* question before us is whether the audiovisual displays created by the Game Genie are "derivative works." The Act does not similarly provide that a work can be a derivative work regardless of the nature of the material objects in which the work is embodied. A derivative work must incorporate a protected work in some concrete or permanent form. We cannot ignore the actual source of the Game Genie's display.

Nintendo relies heavily on *Midway Mfg. Co. v. Artic Int'l, Inc.*, 704 F.2d 1009 (7th Cir.1983). *Midway* can be distinguished. The defendant in *Midway*, Artic International, marketed a computer chip that could be inserted in Galaxian video games to speed up the rate of play. The Seventh Circuit held that the speeded-up version of Galaxian was a derivative work. *Id.* at 1013-14. Artic's chip substantially copied and *replaced* the chip that was originally distributed by Midway. Purchasers of Artic's chip also benefited economically by offering the altered game for use by the general public. The Game Genie does not physically incorporate a portion of a copyrighted work, nor does it supplant demand for a component of that work. The court in *Midway* acknowledged that the Copyright Act's definition of "derivative work" "must be stretched to accommodate speeded-up video games." *Id.* at 1014. Stretching that definition further would chill innovation and fail to protect "society's competing interest in the free flow of ideas, information, and commerce." *Sony Corp. of America v. Universal Studios, Inc.,* 464 U.S. 417, 429 (1984).

In holding that the audiovisual displays created by the Game Genie are not derivative works, we recognize that technology often advances by improvement rather than replacement. *See* Christian H. Nadan, Note, *A Proposal to Recognize Component Works: How a Teddy Bears on the Competing Ends of Copyright Law*, 78 CAL. L. REV. 1633, 1635 (1990). Some time ago, for example, computer companies began marketing spell-checkers that operate within existing word processors by signaling the writer when a word is misspelled. These applications, as well as countless others, could not be produced and marketed if courts were to conclude that the word processor and spell-checker combination is a derivative work based on the word processor alone. The Game Genie is useless by itself, it can only enhance, and cannot duplicate or recast, a Nintendo game's output. It does not contain or produce a Nintendo game's output in some concrete or permanent form, nor does it supplant demand for Nintendo game cartridges. Such innovations rarely will constitute infringing derivative works under the Copyright Act.

[The court also affirmed the district court's conclusion "that Game Genie users are making a fair use of Nintendo's displays."]

AFFIRMED.

[Judge Rymer concurred in the judgment for the reasons stated by the district court.]

Micro Star v. FormGen Inc.
154 F.3d 1107 (9th Cir.1998).

■ KOZINSKI, CIRCUIT JUDGE.

Duke Nukem routinely vanquishes Octabrain and the Protozoid Slimer. But what about the dreaded Micro Star?

I

FormGen Inc., GT Interactive Software Corp. and Apogee Software, Ltd. (collectively FormGen) made, distributed and own the rights to Duke Nukem 3D (D/N-3D), an immensely popular (and very cool) computer game. D/N-3D is played from the first-person perspective; the player assumes the personality and point of view of the title character, who is seen on the screen only as a pair of hands and an occasional boot, much as one might see oneself in real life without the aid of a mirror. Players explore a futuristic city infested with evil aliens and other hazards. The goal is to zap them before they zap you, while searching for the hidden passage to the next level. The basic game comes with twenty-nine levels, each with a different combination of scenery, aliens, and other challenges. The game also includes a "Build Editor," a utility that enables players to create their own levels. With FormGen's encouragement, players frequently post levels they have created on the Internet where others can download them. Micro Star, a computer software distributor, did just that: It downloaded 300 user-created levels and stamped them onto a CD, which it then sold commercially as Nuke It (N/I). N/I is packaged in a box decorated with numerous "screen shots," pictures of what the new levels look like when played.

Micro Star filed suit in district court, seeking a declaratory judgment that N/I did not infringe on any of FormGen's copyrights. FormGen counterclaimed, seeking a preliminary injunction barring further production and distribution of N/I. Relying on *Lewis Galoob Toys, Inc. v. Nintendo of Am., Inc.,* 964 F.2d 965 (9th Cir.1992), the district court held that N/I was not a derivative work and therefore did not infringe FormGen's copyright. The district court did, however, grant a preliminary injunction as to the screen shots, finding that N/I's packaging violated FormGen's copyright by reproducing pictures of D/N-3D characters without a license. The court rejected Micro Star's fair use claims. Both sides appeal their losses.

. . .

III

To succeed on the merits of its claim that N/I infringes FormGen's copyright, FormGen must show (1) ownership of the copyright to D/N-3D, and (2) copying of protected expression by Micro Star. FormGen's copyright registration creates a presumption of ownership, and we are satisfied that FormGen has established its ownership of the copyright. We therefore focus on the latter issue.

FormGen alleges that its copyright is infringed by Micro Star's unauthorized commercial exploitation of user-created game levels. In order to understand FormGen's claims, one must first understand the way D/N-3D works. The game consists of three separate components: the game engine, the source art library and the MAP files.[2] The game engine is the heart of the computer program; in some sense, it *is* the program. It tells the computer when to read data, save and load games, play sounds and project images onto the screen. In order to create the audiovisual display for a particular level, the game engine invokes the MAP file that corresponds to that level. Each MAP file contains a series of instructions that tell the game engine (and, through it, the computer) what to put where. For instance, the MAP file might say scuba gear goes at the bottom of the screen. The

---

[2] So-called because the files all end with the extension ".MAP". Also, no doubt, because they contain the layout for the various levels.

game engine then goes to the source art library, finds the image of the scuba gear, and puts it in just the right place on the screen.[3] The MAP file describes the level in painstaking detail, but it does not actually contain any of the copyrighted art itself; everything that appears on the screen actually comes from the art library. Think of the game's audiovisual display as a paint-by-numbers kit. The MAP file might tell you to put blue paint in section number 565, but it doesn't contain any blue paint itself; the blue paint comes from your palette, which is the low-tech analog of the art library, while you play the role of the game engine. When the player selects one of the N/I levels, the game engine references the N/I MAP files, but still uses the D/N-3D art library to generate the images that make up that level.

FormGen points out that a copyright holder enjoys the exclusive right to prepare derivative works based on D/N-3D. *See* 17 U.S.C. § 106(2) (1994). According to FormGen, the audiovisual displays generated when D/N-3D is run in conjunction with the N/I CD MAP files are derivative works that infringe this exclusivity. Is FormGen right? The answer is not obvious.

The Copyright Act defines a derivative work as

> a work based upon one or more preexisting works, such as a translation, musical arrangement, dramatization, fictionalization, motion picture version, sound recording, art reproduction, abridgment, condensation, or any other form in which a work may be recast, transformed, or adapted. A work consisting of editorial revisions, annotations, elaborations, or other modifications which, as a whole, represent an original work of authorship, is a "derivative work."

Id. § 101. The statutory language is hopelessly overbroad, however, for "[e]very book in literature, science and art, borrows and must necessarily borrow, and use much which was well known and used before." *Emerson v. Davies,* 8 F.Cas. 615, 619 (C.C.D.Mass.1845) (No. 4436). . . . To narrow the statute to a manageable level, we have developed certain criteria a work must satisfy in order to qualify as a derivative work. One of these is that a derivative work must exist in a "concrete or permanent form," *Galoob,* 964 F.2d at 967, and must substantially incorporate protected material from the preexisting work. Micro Star argues that N/I is not a derivative work because the audiovisual displays generated when D/N-3D is run with N/I's MAP files are not incorporated in any concrete or permanent form, and the MAP files do not copy any of D/N-3D's protected expression. It is mistaken on both counts.

The requirement that a derivative work must assume a concrete or permanent form was recognized without much discussion in *Galoob.* There, we noted that all

---

[3] Actually, this is all a bit metaphorical. Computer programs don't actually go anywhere or fetch anything. Rather, the game engine receives the player's instruction as to which game level to select and instructs the processor to access the MAP file corresponding to that level. The MAP file, in turn, consists of a series of instructions indicating which art images go where. When the MAP file calls for a particular art image, the game engine tells the processor to access the art library for instructions on how each pixel on the screen must be colored in order to paint that image.

the Copyright Act's examples of derivative works took some definite, physical form and concluded that this was a requirement of the Act. *See Galoob,* 964 F.2d at 967-68. Obviously, N/I's MAP files themselves exist in a concrete or permanent form; they are burned onto a CD-ROM. But what about the audiovisual displays generated when D/N-3D runs the N/I MAP files—i.e., the actual game level as displayed on the screen? Micro Star argues that, because the audiovisual displays in *Galoob* didn't meet the "concrete or permanent form" requirement, neither do N/I's.

In *Galoob,* we considered audiovisual displays created using a device called the Game Genie, which was sold for use with the Nintendo Entertainment System. The Game Genie allowed players to alter individual features of a game, such as a character's strength or speed, by selectively "blocking the value for a single data byte sent by the game cartridge to the [Nintendo console] and replacing it with a new value." *Galoob,* 964 F.2d at 967. Players chose which data value to replace by entering a code; over a billion different codes were possible. The Game Genie was dumb; it functioned only as a window into the computer program, allowing players to temporarily modify individual aspects of the game.

Nintendo sued, claiming that when the Game Genie modified the game system's audiovisual display, it created an infringing derivative work. We rejected this claim because "[a] derivative work must incorporate a protected work in some concrete or permanent form." *Galoob,* 964 F.2d at 967. The audiovisual displays generated by combining the Nintendo System with the Game Genie were not incorporated in any permanent form; when the game was over, they were gone. Of course, they could be reconstructed, but only if the next player chose to reenter the same codes.[4]

Micro Star argues that the MAP files on N/I are a more advanced version of the Game Genie, replacing old values (the MAP files in the original game) with new values (N/I's MAP files). But, whereas the audiovisual displays created by Game Genie were never recorded in any permanent form, the audiovisual displays generated by D/N-3D from the N/I MAP files are in the MAP files themselves. In *Galoob,* the audiovisual display was defined by the original game cartridge, not by the Game Genie; no one could possibly say that the data values inserted by the Game Genie described the audiovisual display. In the present case the audiovisual display that appears on the computer monitor when a N/I level is played is described—in exact detail—by a N/I MAP file.

---

[4] A low-tech example might aid understanding. Imagine a product called the Pink Screener, which consists of a big piece of pink cellophane stretched over a frame. When put in front of a television, it makes everything on the screen look pinker. Someone who manages to record the programs with this pink cast (maybe by filming the screen) would have created an infringing derivative work. But the audiovisual display observed by a person watching television through the Pink Screener is not a derivative work because it does not incorporate the modified image in any permanent or concrete form. The Game Genie might be described as a fancy Pink Screener for video games, changing a value of the game as perceived by the current player, but never incorporating the new audiovisual display into a permanent or concrete form.

This raises the interesting question whether an exact, down to the last detail, description of an audiovisual display (and—by definition—we know that MAP files do describe audiovisual displays down to the last detail) counts as a permanent or concrete form for purposes of *Galoob*. We see no reason it shouldn't. What, after all, does sheet music do but describe in precise detail the way a copyrighted melody sounds? See 1 William F. Patry, *Copyright Law and Practice* 168 (1994) ("[A] musical composition may be embodied in sheet music . . . ."). To be copyrighted, pantomimes and dances may be "described in sufficient detail to enable the work to be performed from that description." *Id.* at 243. Similarly, the N/I MAP files describe the audiovisual display that is to be generated when the player chooses to play D/N-3D using the N/I levels. Because the audiovisual displays assume a concrete or permanent form in the MAP files, *Galoob* stands as no bar to finding that they are derivative works.

In addition, "[a] work will be considered a derivative work only if it would be considered an infringing work if the material which it has derived from a preexisting work had been taken without the consent of a copyright proprietor of such preexisting work." *Mirage Editions v. Albuquerque A.R.T. Co.*, 856 F.2d 1341, 1343 (*quoting* 1 *Nimmer on Copyright* § 3.01 (1986)). "To prove infringement, [FormGen] must show that [D/N-3D's and N/I's audiovisual displays] are substantially similar in both ideas and expression." *Litchfield v. Spielberg*, 736 F.2d 1352, 1356 (9th Cir.1984) (emphasis omitted). Similarity of ideas may be shown by comparing the objective details of the works: plot, theme, dialogue, mood, setting, characters, etc. *See id.* Similarity of expression focuses on the response of the ordinary reasonable person, and considers the total concept and feel of the works. *See id.* at 1356-57. FormGen will doubtless succeed in making these showings since the audiovisual displays generated when the player chooses the N/I levels come entirely out of D/N-3D's source art library.

Micro Star further argues that the MAP files are not derivative works because they do not, in fact, incorporate any of D/N-3D's protected expression. In particular, Micro Star makes much of the fact that the N/I MAP files reference the source art library, but do not actually contain any art files themselves. Therefore, it claims, nothing of D/N-3D's is reproduced in the MAP files. In making this argument, Micro Star misconstrues the protected work. The work that Micro Star infringes is the D/N-3D story itself—a beefy commando type named Duke who wanders around post-Apocalypse Los Angeles, shooting Pig Cops with a gun, lobbing hand grenades, searching for medkits and steroids, using a jetpack to leap over obstacles, blowing up gas tanks, avoiding radioactive slime. A copyright owner holds the right to create sequels, and the stories told in the N/I MAP files are surely sequels, telling new (though somewhat repetitive) tales of Duke's fabulous adventures. A book about Duke Nukem would infringe for the same reason, even if it contained no pictures.[5]

---

[5] We note that the N/I MAP files can only be used with D/N-3D. If another game could use the MAP files to tell the story of a mousy fellow who travels through a beige maze, killing vicious saltshakers with paperclips, then the MAP files would not incorporate the pro-

[The court then concluded that N/I was "not protected by fair use." It also ruled that any license granted by FormGen in connection with user-created game levels only allowed those levels to be "offered [to others] solely for free," and not to be sold commercially as Micro Star had done. The court also rejected Micro Star's claims that FormGen had abandoned or misused its copyrights.]

IV

Because FormGen will likely succeed at trial in proving that Micro Star has infringed its copyright, we reverse the district court's order denying a preliminary injunction and remand for entry of such an injunction. Of course, we affirm the grant of the preliminary injunction barring Micro Star from selling N/I in boxes covered with screen shots of the game.

AFFIRMED in part, REVERSED in part, and REMANDED.

QUESTIONS FOR DISCUSSION

1. *Derivative work/reproduction overlap.* Why does the House Report state that the derivative work right "overlaps" the reproduction right? Is this overlap of any practical importance?

2. *"Fixed."* Can you reconcile the *Galoob* court's conclusion that a derivative work can infringe even if it is not "fixed" (as that term is defined in the Copyright Act) with its conclusion that a derivative work "must incorporate a protected work in some concrete or permanent form"? Can you reconcile that latter conclusion with the statement in the House Report that "the preparation of a derivative work, such as a ballet, pantomime, or improvised performance, may be an infringement even though nothing is ever fixed in tangible form"?

3. *"Ideas."* Why does the *Micro Star* court say that the infringement plaintiff must show that the defendant's work is substantially similar in *ideas* to the plaintiff's, when Section 102(b) of the 1976 Act provides that "[i]n no case does copyright protection for an original work of authorship extend to any idea . . . regardless of the form in which it is described, explained, illustrated, or embodied in such work"?

4. *"Concrete or permanent."* To the extent that Micro Star's MAP files met the Ninth Circuit's "concrete or permanent form" requirement, might the Game Genie Programming Manual and Code Book provided by Galoob have met that requirement?

5. *Source art library infringement.* If Micro Star had, as the court suggested in footnote 5, created MAP files that the *Duke Nukem 3D* game engine and source art library could have used to play a game with entirely different settings, characters, and plots, would Micro Star not have been liable for creating an infringing derivative work of FormGen's source art library?

EXTENSIONS

1. *Translation.* Several Web sites now offer allow users to view a Web page in a language other than that in which it was originally posted. AltaVista's Babelfish will translate among 12 different languages, and Google will translate among eight. A user need simply enter a Web site's URL and specify the "from" and "to" languages, and the service will show the user a page with the text in the target language (and usually with all of the

tected expression of D/N-3D because they would not be telling a D/N-3D story.

page's graphic elements unaltered). *See* babelfish.altavista.com/ and www.google.com/language_tools. What are the copyright consequences when a user enters a URL at one of these services and the service transmits to the user the page with the translated text?

While those who post Web pages might welcome translation services as a way of expanding their audience, they might also object for various reasons. One might have to do with the quality of the translation. These services must obviously rely on machine translation in order to translate Web pages on demand, rather than attempting to translate in advance every possible permutation in advance. Machine translation is still relatively crude, as one journalist has noted, producing in one instance "It is having a defective day of hats" when the phrase "She is having a bad hair day" was translated from English to Italian and back again. Tina Kelly, *Even Helpful Translation Software Sometimes Weaves a Tangled Web*, N.Y. TIMES, Apr. 30, 1998, www.nytimes.com/library/tech/98/04/circuits/articles/30tran.html.

For businesses, cultural missteps engendered by machine translation may raise more significant issues. Online machine translation services generally do not affect a page's graphics, which may not communicate effectively to viewers from non-English-speaking cultures. For example, a website's home page is called a "welcome" page in French, making an English-language website's use of a small graphic picture of a house potentially confusing to French speakers who view the website using translation software. *Id.*

> And the thumbs-up sign used occasionally in American marketing? In Iran, that signifies a different raised finger, said [Wei-Tai] Kwok, whose company [DAE Interactive Marketing], based in San Francisco, helps businesses build culturally appropriate Web sites.

Id. Businesses have long needed to pay attention to cultural differences when creating marketing materials in different languages, but a company may have much less control when a potential customer takes the initiative to use an online machine translation service to render the company's English-language materials into another language.

In other instances, those who post material on the Web might object to services that translate Web page text not into ordinary language but into "dialects" such as "Redneck," "Jive," "Cockney," "Elmer Fudd," "Swedish Chef," "Moron," "Pig Latin," and "Hacker" (The Dialectizer, rinkworks.com/dialect/); the language of Pikachu (The Pikachizer, pikachize.eye-of-newt.com/); or the way in which rap musician Snoop Dog might render it (The Shizzolator, www.asksnoop.com/). In the case of the Dialectizer, Bank of America requested that the service exclude its sites, apparently concerned about the potential for some customers to be offended. Julia Lipman, *The big price of having a little fun on the Web*, DIGITALMASS, May 24, 2000, www.anu.edu.au/mail-archives/link/link0005/0872.html. Do these types of sites raise different issues than Babelfish or Google's translation services?

2. *Pop-up advertisements.* "Pop-up" advertising software, often bundled together with free software available for download, can trigger advertisements to pop up on a user's screen based on the user's online activity. In some instances, a user's typing a particular Web address or search term will trigger a pop-up ad that the software deems related to that address or search term, and sometimes the ad that pops up is for a competitor of the Web site that the user is viewing. Several Web site owners have sued over this practice, alleging violations of both copyright and trademark law.

Three district courts have rejected claims by the owners of various Web sites that the disseminator of the pop-up software and advertisements has cause infringement of the right to prepare derivative works of the Web sites. *U-Haul Int'l, Inc. v. WhenU.com, Inc.*, 279 F.Supp.2d 723 (E.D.Va.2003); *Wells Fargo & Co. v. WhenU.com, Inc.*, 293 F.Supp.2d 734 (E.D.Mich.2003); *1-800 Contacts, Inc. v. When U.com, Inc.*, 309 F.Supp.2d 467

(S.D.N.Y.2003).

The *Wells Fargo* court resolved the copyright issues as follows:

> Plaintiffs claim that WhenU violates their exclusive right to prepare "derivative works." To prevail on this claim, plaintiffs would have to show that WhenU has incorporated the plaintiffs' websites into a new work. 17 U.S.C. § 101 (defining derivative work as "[a] work based on one or more preexisting works" that is "recast, transformed or adopted").
>
> Plaintiffs have not made the necessary showing as to WhenU because WhenU merely provides a software product to computer users. The SaveNow software does not access plaintiffs' websites; therefore, it does not incorporate them into a new work. Accordingly, plaintiffs' claim that the defendant violates their right to create derivative works can only be understood as a contributory copyright theory.
>
> Moreover, SaveNow users do not infringe plaintiffs' right to prepare derivative works because consumers who cause the display of WhenU advertisements or coupons on their screens do not alter plaintiffs' websites. Plaintiffs' websites reside on separate servers. The WhenU Window has no physical relationship to plaintiffs' websites, and does not modify the content displayed in any other open window.
>
> Even if the presence of an overlapping window could be said to change the appearance of the underlying window on a computer screen, the mere alteration of the manner in which an individual consumer's computer displays the content sent by plaintiffs' websites does not create a "derivative work." *Lewis Galoob Toys v. Nintendo of Am.*, 780 F.Supp. 1283, 1291 (N.D. Cal. 1991) (indicating that "the consumer may experiment with the product and create new variations of play, for personal enjoyment, without creating a derivative work"), *aff'd*, 964 F.2d 965 (9th Cir.1992).
>
> *New York Times Co., Inc. v. Tasini*, 533 U.S. 483, (2001), does not hold to the contrary. Unlike the publisher in *Tasini*, WhenU is not copying or making additions to or deletions from plaintiffs' actual copyrighted works. Contrary to plaintiffs' claim, WhenU has not added anything to plaintiffs' web pages. If one were able to look at the HTML code of plaintiffs' sites, one would not see any changes as a result of WhenU's advertisements. In this respect, the effect of WhenU's advertisements on plaintiffs' sites is more akin to the affect of a video game accessory in *Lewis Galoob Toys.*
>
> In *Lewis Galoob Toys*, . . . Nintendo argued that the attachment of the Game Genie to its copyrighted works created a derivative work.
>
> The district court rejected Nintendo's argument, finding that a consumer utilizing the Game Genie for noncommercial, private enjoyment "neither generates a fixed transferable copy of the work, nor exhibits or performs the work for commercial gain." *Id.* at 1291. The court explained,
>
>> [I]inherent in the concept of a "derivative work" is the ability for that work to exist on its own, fixed and transferable from the original work . . . once the Game Genie and its attached game cartridge are disconnected from the NES, or the power is turned off, those changes disappear and the video game reverts to its original form.
>
> *Id.* WhenU's conduct affects plaintiffs' sites in a comparable manner. It only temporarily changes the way the sites are viewed by consumers. As soon as the advertisements are "disconnected"—that is closed or minimized—plaintiffs'

sites revert to their original form. If anything, WhenU's advertisements modify their sites far less that the Game Genie altered users' NES video game experience.

The Court also finds irrelevant a series of cases cited by plaintiffs in which copyrighted material was not merely altered, but also publicly re-transmitted in the altered form. . . . In marked contrast, plaintiffs here do not allege any general or public re-transmission of the alleged derivative work by computer users.

Plaintiffs base their allegations of copyright violation on the assertion that, because WhenU ads modify the pixels on a computer user's on-screen display, this modification creates a "derivative work." The Court finds this argument unpersuasive in light of plaintiffs' expert's admission that pixels form part of the hardware of a computer and are owned and controlled by the computer user who chooses what to display on the screen. Plaintiffs do not have any property interest in the content of a user's pixels, much less a copyright interest.

Further, in order for a work to qualify as a derivative work, it must be independently copyrightable. *Woods v. Bourne Co.,* 60 F.3d 978, 990 (2d Cir.1995). To be independently copyrightable, it must be "fixed" - that is, it must be "sufficiently permanent or stable to permit it to be . . . reproduced." See 17 U.S.C. §§ 101, 102 . . . *See also Lewis Galoob Toys v. Nintendo of Am.,* 964 F.2d 965, 967 (noting that "[a] derivative work must incorporate a protected work in some concrete or permanent 'form' "); *Micro Star v. FormGen, Inc.,* 154 F.3d 1107, 1111 n.4 (9th Cir.1998) (noting, by way of example, that covering a television screen with pink cellophane, while modifying the appearance of the copyrighted programs, would not create a derivative work "because it does not incorporate the modified image in any permanent or concrete form").

The pixels on a computer screen are updated every 1/70th of a second. The alteration of pixels is therefore far too transitory an occurrence to form a basis for a copyright violation. The appearance of a WhenU advertisement on a consumer's computer screen at the same time as one of the plaintiffs' web pages is also a transitory occurrence that might never be duplicated exactly on that or another person's computer screen. *U-Haul,* 279 F.Supp.2d at 731. Accordingly, the WhenU advertisement does not create a work that is sufficiently permanent to be independently copyrightable, and hence does not create a derivative work. Since SaveNow users do not infringe the plaintiffs' right to prepare derivative works, WhenU is not liable for contributory infringement.

293 F.Supp.2d. 734.

The *1-800 Contacts* court provided a similar rationale, focusing on the potentially very transitory nature of the changed appearance of the user's screen when an advertisement pops up in front of a window on the user's screen showing a plaintiff's Web site. "Applying the "fixation" requirement here, Plaintiff has failed to show that its website, and Defendants' pop-up advertisements are "sufficiently permanent or stable to permit it to be perceived, reproduced or otherwise communicated for a period of more than transitory duration." 17 U.S.C. § 101. Indeed, Defendants' pop-up ad windows may be moved, obscured, or "closed" entirely—thus completely disappearing from perception, with a single click of a mouse." 309 F.Supp.2d 467.

In addition, the court rejected the argument that the changed appearance of the user's screen when an advertisement pops up constituted a derivative work:

[F]or Plaintiff to prevail, it must show that Defendants have "recast, transformed, or adapted" the 1-800 Contacts website. None of these three actions seems to describe what is done to Plaintiff's website by Defendants' pop-up ads, since Plaintiff's website remains "intact" on the computer screen. Defendants' pop-up ads may "obscure" or "cover" a portion of Plaintiff's website—but they do not "change" the website, and accordingly do not "recast, transform or adapt" the website. *Lee v. A.R.T. Company,* 125 F.3d 580, 582 (7th Cir.1997) (mounting plaintiff's art works on ceramic tiles did not create "derivative work," and therefore did not infringe plaintiff's copyright). Moreover, if obscuring a browser window containing a copyrighted website with another computer window produces a "derivative work," then any action by a computer user that produced a computer window or visual graphic that altered the screen appearance of Plaintiff's website, however slight, would require Plaintiff's permission. A definition of "derivative work" that sweeps within the scope of the copyright law a multi-tasking Internet shopper whose word-processing program obscures the screen display of Plaintiff's website is indeed "jarring," and not supported by the definition set forth at 17 U.S.C. § 101. *See id.*

309 F.Supp.2d 467. Are the views of these courts with respect to fixation correct interpretations of what is required for the preparation of a derivative work to infringe, in light of the House Report? Are the conclusions that there was not sufficient fixation in the case of pop-up ads consistent with the view seen in previous cases that temporary storage in RAM constitutes the making of a "copy"?

3. *Filtering and derivative works.* Before allowing a web page to be displayed in a browser, filtering software may be used to screen the page and determine whether it contains a particular type of content. Web filtering technologies may employ a variety of approaches to ascertain the content of a web page. Such filtering software might screen a web page for particular keywords, attempt to interpret the images contained on the page, or identify the HTML tags used to format the page. Once targeted content is identified, the filtering software can either prevent the browser from displaying the web page, block the entire site, or excise the targeted content and permit the remainder of the page to be displayed. If the offending content is excised, how would you characterize the resulting web page for the purpose of copyright? Who, if anyone, owns the copyright in the cleansed web page? Does creation of the cleansed web page infringe any of the exclusive rights held by the copyright owner of the original web page?

4. The Distribution and Public Display Rights

§ 101. Definitions

. . .

To "display" a work means to show a copy of it, either directly or by means of a film, slide, television image, or any other device or process, or, in the case of a motion picture or any other audiovisual work, to show individual images nonsequentially.

. . .

To perform or display a work "publicly" means—

(1) to perform or display it at a place open to the public or at any place where a substantial number of persons outside of a normal circle of a family and its social acquaintances is gathered; or

(2) to transmit or otherwise communicate a performance or display of

the work to a place specified by clause (1) or to the public, by means of any device or process, whether the members of the public capable of receiving the performance or display receive it in the same place or in separate places and at the same time or different times.

. . .

To "transmit" a performance or display is to communicate it by any device or process whereby images or sounds are received beyond the place from which they are sent.

H.R. Rep. No. 1476
Copyright Act of 1976 (94th Cong., 2d Sess.) (1976).

. . .

SECTION 106. EXCLUSIVE RIGHTS IN COPYRIGHTED WORKS . . .

Public distribution.-- Clause (3) of section 106 establishes the exclusive right of publications: The right "to distribute copies or phonorecords of the copyrighted work to the public by sale or other transfer of ownership, or by rental, lease, or lending." Under this provision the copyright owner would have the right to control the first public distribution of an authorized copy or phonorecord of his work, whether by sale, gift, loan, or some rental or lease arrangement. Likewise, any unauthorized public distribution of copies or phonorecords that were unlawfully made would be an infringement. As section 109 makes clear, however, the copyright owner's rights under section 106(3) cease with respect to a particular copy or phonorecord once he has parted with ownership of it.

Rights of public performance and display
   . . .

Right of public display.—Clause (5) of section 106 represents the first explicit statutory recognition in American copyright law of an exclusive right to show a copyrighted work, or an image of it, to the public. . . . The bill would give the owners of copyright in "literary, musical, dramatic, and choreographic works, pantomimes, and pictorial, graphic, or sculptural works," including the individual images of a motion picture or other audiovisual work, the exclusive right "to display the copyrighted work publicly."

Definitions

Under the definitions of "perform," "display," "publicly," and "transmit" in section 101, the concepts of public performance and public display cover not only the initial rendition or showing, but also any further act by which that rendition or showing is transmitted or communicated to the public. . . . Although any act by which the initial performance or display is transmitted, repeated, or made to recur would itself be a "performance" or "display" under the bill, it would not be actionable as an infringement unless it were done "publicly," as defined in section 101. Certain other performances and displays, in addition to those that are "private," are exempted or given qualified copyright control under sections 107 through 118.

. . .

R. Anthony Reese, *The Public Display Right: The Copyright Act's Neglected Solution to the Controversy over RAM "Copies"*
2001 U. ILL. L. REV. 83.

. . .

II. THE DISPLAY RIGHT AS A RIGHT TO TRANSMIT . . .

The 1976 Act grants the public display right to owners of copyright in most categories of copyrightable works, including, importantly, literary works and works of visual art.[3] What does the public display right protect? A careful reading of three related provisions of the 1976 Act—the definitions of "display" and of "publicly" display, and the principal limitation on the display right—shows that, despite very broad language in the definitions, the public display right primarily encompasses transmissions of displays to the public—such as television broadcasts or Internet transmissions.

1. Definition of "Display"

The definition of "display" explains the basic scope of the right: "To 'display' a work means to show a copy of it, either directly or by means of a film, slide, television image, or any other device or process." Understanding this definition properly requires knowing the meaning of "copy," a term of art in copyright law. The statute defines "copies" as "material objects . . . in which a work is fixed . . . and from which the work can be perceived, reproduced, or otherwise communicated, either directly or with the aid of a machine or device."[6] Examples of "direct" displays of copies would thus include placing a printed copy of a book on a bookshelf, posting a printed copy of a New Yorker cartoon or article on a refrigerator door,[7] or hanging an original painting on a wall. Examples of "indirect" displays would include using a slide projector to project onto a screen a slide of a New Yorker cartoon, using an opaque projector to project onto a screen a printed New Yorker article or cartoon, or making visible on a computer monitor an image of that article or cartoon stored on a CD-ROM.[10]

---

[3] . . . The most significant categories of works to which the display right does not extend are sound recordings and architectural works. . . .

[6] . . . Because "[t]he term 'copies' includes the material object . . . in which the work is first fixed," what is colloquially called an "original" is, for copyright purposes, a "copy." [17 U.S.C. § 101 ("copies").] . . .

[7] See Ringgold v. Black Entm't Television, Inc., 126 F.3d 70, 74 & n.2 (2d Cir.1997) (discussing Pierre N. Leval, Nimmer Lecture: Fair Use Rescued, 44 UCLA L. REV. 1449, 1457 (1997)).

[10] See 1976 HOUSE REPORT, . . . at 64. The Report noted:

In addition to the direct showings of a copy of a work, 'display' would include the projection of an image on a screen or other surface by any method, . . . and the showing of an image on a cathode ray tube, or similar viewing apparatus connected with any sort of information storage and retrieval system.

Id.

2. Definition of "Publicly"

Although the Act defines "display" in very broad terms that encompass a great many activities, the copyright owner's exclusive right is not a right to make all displays but only a right "to display the copyrighted work publicly." The definition of "publicly" displaying a work sets out two ways in which a display can be public and introduces the concept of transmission into the public display right.

First, one displays a work publicly by displaying a copy in a public or semipublic place.[13] Thus, if a New Yorker cartoon is hung not on a refrigerator in a private home but on the wall of an art museum open to anyone willing to pay the admission fee, then the cartoon has been displayed publicly.

Second, a display can be public if it is transmitted: it is a public display of a work "to transmit or otherwise communicate a . . . display of the work" if the transmission is either (a) to a public or semipublic place or (b) "to the public."[15] The term "the public" is never defined in the Copyright Act, but the definition of "publicly" display states that a transmission is a public display "whether the members of the public capable of receiving the . . . display receive it in the same place or in separate places and at the same time or at different times." Read together with the definition of "transmit" — "to communicate [a display] by any device or process whereby images . . . are received beyond the place from which they are sent" — this provision sweeps all types of visual transmissions into the category of public display, as the drafters of the statute explained:

> [T]he concept[] of . . . public display include[s] not only . . . displays that occur initially in a public place, but also acts that transmit or otherwise communicate a . . . display of the work to the public by means of any device or process. The definition of "transmit" . . . is broad enough to include all conceivable forms and combinations of wired or wireless communications media, including but by no means limited to radio and television broadcasting as we know them. Each and every method by which the images . . . comprising a . . . display are picked up and conveyed is a "transmission," and if the transmission reaches the public in [any] form, the case comes within the scope of [the public display right].
>
> . . .
>
> [T]he display of a visual image of a copyrighted work would be an infringement if the image were transmitted by any method (by closed or open circuit television, for example, or by a computer system) from one place to members of the public located elsewhere.[18]

---

[13] "Publicly" displaying a work is defined to include displaying it either "at a place open to the public or at any place where a substantial number of persons outside of a normal circle of a family and its social acquaintances is gathered." *Id.* § 101 ("publicly," clause (1)). The second category of place described in clause (1) is usually referred to as a "semipublic place."

[15] 17 U.S.C. § 101 ("publicly," clause (2)); *see* 1976 HOUSE REPORT . . . at 63 ("[T]he concept[] of . . . public display cover[s] not only the initial . . . showing, but also any further act by which that . . . showing is transmitted or communicated to the public.").

[18] 1976 HOUSE REPORT . . . at 64, 80 (emphasis added).

So, for example, broadcasting over television (or transmitting over a cable television system) an image of a New Yorker cartoon would constitute a public display of the cartoon. Similarly, transmitting the text of a law review article between computers via a telephone line (or other wired or wireless connection) so that multiple recipients can each read the text on their computer screens—even if they do so in different places and at different times—would be a public display of the article.[19] Thus, the definition of "publicly" brings transmissions of images and text squarely within the public display right.

3. Exemption for Most Nontransmitted Public Displays

. . . The most important limitation on the public display right effectively restricts the scope of the right to transmissions to the public. Section 109(c) provides that:

> Notwithstanding the [exclusive right of public display], the owner of a particular copy lawfully made under this title, or any person authorized by such owner, is entitled, without the authority of the copyright owner, to display that copy publicly, either directly or by the projection of no more than one image at a time, to viewers present at the place where the copy is located.[21]

The committee report accompanying the 1976 Act explains this provision in detail:

> . . . Section 109[(c)] adopts the general principle that the lawful owner of a copy of a work should be able to put his copy on public display without the consent of the copyright owner. . . .
>
> The exclusive right of public display granted by section 106(5) would not apply where the owner of a copy wishes to show it directly to the public, as in a gallery or display case, or indirectly, as through an opaque projector. Where the copy itself is intended for projection, as in the case of a photographic slide, negative, or transparency, the public projection of a single image would be permitted as long as the viewers are "present at the place where the copy is located."

Section 109(c) thus allows most "in-person," as opposed to transmitted, public displays of a copyrighted work. . . . That exemption . . . also effectively limits the public display right to displays that are made by transmission.

. . .

The emergence of computer networks has vastly increased the number of transmitted displays that take place. A web page that provides access to, for exam-

---

[19] The 1976 HOUSE REPORT explains that a display is "public" if "the potential recipients of the transmission represent a limited segment of the public, such as the occupants of hotel rooms or the subscribers of a cable television service." 1976 HOUSE REPORT . . . at 65. A single transmission of a text to a single recipient might not, however, be a "public" display.

[21] *Id.* § 109(c). The House Report explains that "[t]he concept of 'the place where the copy is located' is generally intended to refer to a situation in which the viewers are present in the same physical surroundings as the copy, even though they cannot see the copy directly." 1976 HOUSE REPORT. . . at 80.

ple, a New Yorker cartoon transmits a display of a copy of that cartoon to everyone who accesses that web page. The copy that is displayed is a computer file containing information in digital format that can be interpreted by a computer program (such as a web browser) to make the image visible on a computer screen. That file is generally stored on the hard drive of the website's computer (or "server"). When a user accesses the cartoon on the website, the information in that file is transmitted to the user's computer, which can interpret the information in order to make the cartoon visible on the user's screen. The website has thus transmitted a display of its copy of the cartoon to the end user. As computer networks—not only the Internet, but proprietary computer networks such as Lexis and Westlaw—have become more common, millions of transmitted displays now occur on a daily basis.

. . .

Playboy Enterprises, Inc. v. Frena
839 F.Supp. 1552 (M.D.Fla.1993).

■ SCHLESINGER, DISTRICT JUDGE.

This cause is before the Court on Plaintiff's First Motion for Partial Summary Judgment (Copyright Infringement) as to Defendant Frena. In its motion, Plaintiff requests that the Court grant partial summary judgment that Defendant Frena infringed Plaintiff's copyrights and specifically that the 170 image files in question infringed Plaintiff's copyrights in 50 of Plaintiff's copyrighted magazines.

Defendant George Frena operates a subscription computer bulletin board service, Techs Warehouse BBS ("BBS"), that distributed unauthorized copies of Plaintiff Playboy Enterprises, Inc.'s ("PEI") copyrighted photographs. BBS is accessible via telephone modem to customers. For a fee, or to those who purchase certain products from Defendant Frena, anyone with an appropriately equipped computer can log onto BBS. Once logged on subscribers may browse though different BBS directories to look at the pictures and customers may also download the high quality computerized copies of the photographs and then store the copied image from Frena's computer onto their home computer.[1] Many of the images found on BBS include adult subject matter. One hundred and seventy of the images that were available on BBS were copies of photographs taken from PEI's copyrighted materials.

Defendant Frena admits that these materials were displayed on his BBS, that he never obtained authorization or consent from PEI, and that each of the accused computer graphic files on BBS is substantially similar to copyrighted PEI photographs. Defendant Frena also admits that each of the files in question has been downloaded by one of his customers.

Subscribers can upload material onto the bulletin board so that any other sub-

---

[1] The process of transferring the image from the bulletin board to one's personal computer is known as downloading.

scriber, by accessing their computer, can see that material.[3] Defendant Frena states in his Affidavit . . . that he never uploaded any of PEI's photographs onto BBS and that subscribers to BBS uploaded the photographs. Defendant Frena states that as soon as he was served with a summons and made aware of this matter, he removed the photographs from BBS and has since that time monitored BBS to prevent additional photographs of PEI from being uploaded.

Summary judgment is appropriate "if . . . there is no genuine issue as to any material fact and . . . the moving party is entitled to judgment as a matter of law." Fed. R. Civ. P. 56(c). . . .

. . .

I. COPYRIGHT INFRINGEMENT

The Copyright Act of 1976 gives copyright owners control over most, if not all, activities of conceivable commercial value. The statute provides that

> the owner of a copyright . . . has the exclusive rights to do and to authorize any of the following: (1) to reproduce the copyrighted work in copies . . . : (2) to prepare derivative works based upon the copyrighted work; (3) to distribute copies . . . of the copyrighted work to the public . . . and (5) in the case of . . . pictorial . . . works . . . to display the copyrighted work publicly.

17 U.S.C. § 106. Engaging in or authorizing any of these categories without the copyright owner's permission violates the exclusive rights of the copyright owner and constitutes infringement of the copyright. *See* 17 U.S.C. § 501(a).

To establish copyright infringement, PEI must show ownership of the copyright and "copying" by Defendant Frena.

[The court concluded there was no dispute that PEI owned copyrights on the photographs in question.]

Next, PEI must demonstrate copying by Defendant Frena. Since direct evidence of copying is rarely available in a copyright infringement action, copying may be inferentially proven by showing that Defendant Frena had access to the allegedly infringed work, that the allegedly infringing work is substantially similar to the copyrighted work, and that one of the rights statutorily guaranteed to copyright owners is implicated by Frena's actions.

[Finding no dispute over access or substantial similarity, the court proceeded] to determine whether Defendant Frena violated one of the rights statutorily guaranteed to copyright owners under 17 U.S.C. § 106. *See* 17 U.S.C. § 501(a).

Public distribution of a copyrighted work is a right reserved to the copyright owner, and usurpation of that right constitutes infringement. PEI's right under 17 U.S.C. § 106(3) to distribute copies to the public has been implicated by Defendant Frena. Section 106(3) grants the copyright owner "the exclusive right to sell, give away, rent or lend any material embodiment of his work." 2 MELVILLE B. NIMMER,

---

[3] The process of transferring the image from one's personal computer to the bulletin board is known as uploading.

Nimmer on Copyright § 8.11[A], at 8-124.1 (1993). There is no dispute that Defendant Frena supplied a product containing unauthorized copies of a copyrighted work. It does not matter that Defendant Frena claims he did not make the copies itself [sic].

Furthermore, the "display" rights of PEI have been infringed upon by Defendant Frena. *See* 17 U.S.C. § 106(5). The concept of display is broad. *See* 17 U.S.C. § 101. It covers "the projection of an image on a screen or other surface by any method, the transmission of an image by electronic or other means, and the showing of an image on a cathode ray tube, or similar viewing apparatus connected with any sort of information storage and retrieval system." H.R. Rep. No. 1476, 94th Cong., 2d Sess. 64 (Sept. 3, 1976). The display right precludes unauthorized transmission of the display from one place to another, for example, by a computer system. *See* [*id*].

"Display" covers any showing of a "copy" of the work, "either directly or by means of a film, slide, television image or any other device or process." 17 U.S.C. § 101. However, in order for there to be copyright infringement, the display must be public. A "public display" is a display "at a place open to the public or . . . where a substantial number of persons outside of a normal circle of [a] family and its social acquaintances is gathered." A place is "open to the public" in this sense even if access is limited to paying customers. 2 MELVILLE B. NIMMER, Nimmer on Copyright § 8.14[C], at 8-169 n.36 (1993); *see Columbia Pictures Indus., Inc. v. Redd Horne Inc.*, 749 F.2d 154 (3d Cir.1984).

Defendant's display of PEI's copyrighted photographs to subscribers was a public display. Though limited to subscribers, the audience consisted of "a substantial number of persons outside of a normal circle of [a] family and its social acquaintances."

[The court also concluded that Frena's activities did not qualify as fair use, in large part because they were commercial in nature and would likely have an adverse effect on the value of PEI's copyrighted works.]

There is irrefutable evidence of direct copyright infringement in this case. It does not matter that Defendant Frena may have been unaware of the copyright infringement. Intent to infringe is not needed to find copyright infringement. Intent or knowledge is not an element of infringement, and thus even an innocent infringer is liable for infringement; rather, innocence is significant to a trial court when it fixes statutory damages, which is a remedy equitable in nature.

Frena argues that his commercial use was so insignificant as to justify holding for him under the principle of *de minimis non curat lex*. The Court disagrees. The detrimental market effects coupled with the commercial-use presumption negates the fair use defense. Defendant Frena infringed Plaintiff's copyrights; specifically, the 170 image files in question infringed Plaintiff's copyrights in 50 of Plaintiff's copyrighted magazines. The Court finds that the undisputed facts mandate partial summary judgment that Defendant Frena's unauthorized display and distribution of PEI's copyrighted material is copyright infringement under 17 U.S.C. § 501.

. . .

Plaintiff's First Motion for Partial Summary Judgment (Copyright Infringement) as to Defendant Frena is GRANTED. . .

QUESTIONS FOR DISCUSSION

1. *Downloading vs. photocopying.* In *Playboy v. Frena*, how does Frena's act of making the material available for download differ from the act of a library in keeping original magazines on its shelves and allowing members of the public to make copies using an on-premises photocopy machine?

2. *"Distribution."* Was the *Frena* court correct that a "distribution" of a "copy" had occurred in that case? Consider the IITF's discussion of the *Frena* court's finding that the conduct involved there "implicated" the distribution right :

> Whether the litigants in *Playboy* put the issue properly in dispute or not, the right to distribute copies of a work has traditionally covered the right to convey a possessory interest in a tangible copy of the work. Indeed, the first sale doctrine implements the common law's abhorrence of restraints on alienation of property by providing that the distribution right does not generally prevent owners of lawfully made copies from alienating them in a manner of their own choosing. It is clear that a Frena subscriber, at the end of a transaction, possessed a copy of a Playboy photograph, but it is perhaps less clear whether, under the current law, Frena "distributed" that photograph and whether Frena or the subscriber "reproduced" it (and, if the latter, whether current law clearly would have made Frena contributorily liable for the unauthorized reproduction).

INFORMATION INFRASTRUCTURE TASK FORCE, WORKING GROUP ON INTELLECTUAL PROPERTY RIGHTS, INTELLECTUAL PROPERTY AND THE NATIONAL INFORMATION INFRASTRUCTURE 69 (1995), www.uspto.gov/web/offices/com/doc/ipnii/ipnii.pdf.

Even if no "distribution" had occurred within the literal terms of the Copyright Act, should the courts interpret the concept of distribution beyond those literal terms? Was doing so necessary in order to hold Frena liable for infringement? Will it generally be necessary to impose copyright liability on defendants?

5. The Public Performance Right

The copyright owner's exclusive right to publicly perform certain types of works is considered in detail in connection with digital music in Part IV of this Chapter, *infra*. Note, however, that the public performance right extends to "literary, musical, dramatic, and choreographic works, pantomimes, and motion pictures and other audiovisual works." 17 U.S.C. § 106(4). The 1976 Act explains that to "perform" a work "means to recite, render, play, dance, or act it, either directly or by means of any device or process or, in the case of a motion picture or other audiovisual work, to show its images in any sequence or to make the sounds accompanying it audible." 17 U.S.C. § 101 ("perform"). The definition of when a work is performed "publicly" is the same as the definition, discussed in the preceding section, of when a work is displayed "publicly"—that is, a performance is public if it occurs in a public or semi-public place, or if it is transmitted either to such a place or "to the public." 17 U.S.C. § 101 ("publicly").

C. LIMITATIONS ON EXCLUSIVE RIGHTS

1. Fair Use

§ 107. Limitations on exclusive rights: Fair use

Notwithstanding the provisions of sections 106 and 106A, the fair use of a copyrighted work, including such use by reproduction in copies or phonorecords or by any other means specified by that section, for purposes such as criticism, comment, news reporting, teaching (including multiple copies for classroom use), scholarship, or research, is not an infringement of copyright. In determining whether the use made of a work in any particular case is a fair use the factors to be considered shall include —

(1) the purpose and character of the use, including whether such use is of a commercial nature or is for nonprofit educational purposes;

(2) the nature of the copyrighted work;

(3) the amount and substantiality of the portion used in relation to the copyrighted work as a whole; and

(4) the effect of the use upon the potential market for or value of the copyrighted work.

The fact that a work is unpublished shall not itself bar a finding of fair use if such finding is made upon consideration of all the above factors.

Los Angeles Times v. Free Republic
54 U.S.P.Q.2d 1453 (C.D.Cal.2000).

■ MORROW, J.

Plaintiffs Los Angeles Times and The Washington Post Company publish newspapers in print and online versions. Defendant Free Republic is a "bulletin board" website whose members use the site to post news articles to which they add remarks or commentary. Other visitors to the site then read the articles and add their comments. For the most part, Free Republic members post the entire text of articles in which they are interested: among these are verbatim copies of articles from the Los Angeles Times and Washington Post websites. Plaintiffs' complaint alleges that the unauthorized copying and posting of the articles on the Free Republic site constitutes copyright infringement.

Defendants have now moved for summary judgment. They assert that the copying of news articles onto their website is protected by the fair use doctrine. Plaintiffs have filed a cross-motion for partial summary judgment, arguing that defendants may not invoke fair use as a defense. . . .

. . .

Defendants also allege that the First Amendment protects the posting of plaintiffs' news articles to their website. They contend that, absent wholesale copying,

Free Republic visitors will be unable to express their criticism and comments. There are other methods in which the visitors' rights of free expression can be protected, however, and the court cannot conclude that enforcing plaintiffs' rights under the copyright law impermissibly restricts defendants' right to free speech.

I. FACTUAL BACKGROUND

A. The Parties

Plaintiffs publish the Los Angeles Times and The Washington Post in print and online at "http://www.latimes.com" and "http://www.washingtonpost.com." Their respective websites contain the current edition of the newspaper, which can be viewed free of charge, and archived articles that users must pay to view. The Times charges $1.50 to view an archived article, while the Post charges from $1.50 to $2.95 depending on the time of day. In addition to income generated in this fashion, the websites also produce advertising and licensing revenue for the papers. Because advertising is sold "CPM" (cost per thousand), the revenue generated from this source depends on the volume of traffic the sites experience during a given period. The parties dispute the extent to which being able to access archived articles at a different site for free affects plaintiffs' ability to advertise, license, and sell the archived articles.

Defendant Jim Robinson is the owner and operator of defendants Electronic Orchard and Free Republic. Although no longer actively engaged in business, Electronic Orchard is a for profit limited liability company that offers "Internet programming and design services." Free Republic is a limited liability corporation that operates freerepublic.com. The website, which has been operational since 1996, allows registered visitors to "post" news articles and comments concerning them on the site. Registered members may then post additional comments. Free Republic has approximately 20,000 registered participants. The website receives as many as 100,000 hits per day, and between 25 and 50 million page views each month.

Plaintiffs contend that "perfect copies" of news articles appearing in their publications and on their websites are posted to the Free Republic site. Defendants maintain that the posted articles are merely "purported copies" of the original, and assert that one can verify that a posting is an exact copy only by visiting plaintiffs' websites. Defendants nonetheless apparently concede that *some* of the postings are verbatim copies of original articles.

. . .

The parties dispute whether Free Republic is a for-profit or not-for-profit entity.

. . .

The parties also dispute whether the posting of plaintiffs' news articles to the Free Republic site causes an increase or decrease in traffic at the Times and Post websites, whether it diminishes the available market for sale of plaintiffs' news articles, and whether it has a negative impact on plaintiffs' ability to license the works. Defendants assert that plaintiffs' websites actually gain viewers because people go to them after visiting the Free Republic site. Plaintiffs maintain they lose traffic when Internet users read an article posted on freerepublic.com rather than visiting the Times or Post websites. They further assert that their ability to sell copies of the archived articles and their ability to license the works is diminished by having copies made freely available on the Free Republic site.

II. DISCUSSION

A. Legal Standard Governing Motions For Summary Judgment

A motion for summary judgment must be granted when ". . . there is no genuine issue as to any material fact and . . . the moving party is entitled to a judgment as a matter of law." Fed.R.Civ.P. 56(c). . . .

. . .

Fair use is a mixed question of law and fact. *Harper & Row, Publishers, Inc. v. Nation Enter.*, 471 U.S. 539, 560, (1985). It is nonetheless proper to decide the issue at the summary judgment stage if the historical facts are undisputed and the only question is the proper legal conclusion to be drawn from those facts. . . .

. . .

. . . Because the parties address the availability of a *defense* to copyright infringement, their motions assume for present purposes that such a claim can be proved. The court expresses no opinion as to whether this is so, given that the "copying" of news articles at issue in this case is to a large extent copying by third-party users of the Free Republic site. The court also makes no determination as to whether plaintiffs have in any manner consented to the copying of their articles.

C. The Fair Use Defense

The fair use defense is a limitation on the exclusive right of a copyright owner "to reproduce the copyrighted work in copies." 17 U.S.C. § 106(1). It is codified at 17 U.S.C. § 107 . . .

. . .

Because fair use is an affirmative defense to a claim of infringement, defendants carry the burden of proof on the issue. . . .

1. The Purpose And Character Of The Use

The first factor listed in § 107 is "the purpose and character of the use, including whether such use is of a commercial nature or is for nonprofit educational purposes." This factor assesses whether "the new work 'merely supersedes the objects' of the original creation, or instead adds something new, with a further purpose or different character, altering the first with new expression, meaning, or message; it asks, in other words, whether and to what extent the new work is 'transformative.'" *Campbell v. Acuff-Rose Music, Inc.*, 510 U.S. 569, 579 (1994) . . . "[T]he more transformative the new work, the less will be the significance of other factors, like commercialism, that may weigh against a finding of fair use."

Inquiry concerning the character and purpose of a challenged use should be guided by the examples provided in the statute—i.e., whether the use was for purposes of "criticism, comment, news reporting, teaching . . ., scholarship, or research." The list, however, is not intended to be exhaustive or to single out any particular use as presumptively fair. *Harper & Row, supra, 471 U.S. at 561.* Indeed, the fact that a use falls within one of these categories "is simply one factor in [the] fair use analysis." *Id.* Similarly, while the statute draws a distinction between non-profit and commercial use, not every commercial use of a copyrighted work is presumptively unfair. *Campbell, supra, 510 U.S. at 579.*

a. The Purpose Of Free Republic's Use And The Extent To Which Its Work Is Transformative

There is no dispute that at least some of the items posted on the Free Republic website are exact copies of plaintiffs' articles. While defendants assert there is "no evidence" that *all* of the Times and Post articles that have been posted are verbatim copies, the evidence they have presented reveals that, generally, exact copies of whole or substantial portions of articles are posted.

There is little transformative about copying the entirety or large portions of a work verbatim. As the Supreme Court said in *Campbell, supra:*

"[W]hether a 'substantial portion of the infringing work was copied verbatim' from the copyrighted work is a relevant question, . . . for it may reveal a dearth of transformative character or purpose under the first factor, or a greater likelihood of market harm under the fourth; a work composed primarily of an original, particularly its heart, with little added or changed, is more likely to be a merely superseding use, fulfilling demand for the original." *Campbell, supra,* 510 U.S. at 587–88.

Defendants proffer two reasons why their full text copying of plaintiffs' articles is nonetheless transformative. First, they assert that the copies of the articles found on the Free Republic site do not in reality substitute for the originals found on plaintiffs' web pages. Second, they contend they copy no more than necessary to fulfill their purpose of criticizing the manner in which the media covers current events and politics. Each of these contentions will be examined in turn.

Defendants' first argument—that the copies of plaintiffs' articles found on the Free Republic site do not substitute for those on plaintiffs' sites—focuses on readers' ability to access and review specific articles in which they are interested. Defendants contend that using the Free Republic site to read current articles would be impractical since there is a delay between the time information is posted to the site and the time it is indexed by third-party search engines. Additionally, they assert that the imprecision of search language makes it difficult to locate archived articles at the site. These arguments overlook the fact that the Free Republic site has its own search engine that apparently has immediate search capability.

Even were this not true, the articles posted on the Free Republic site ultimately serve the same purpose as "that [for which] one would normally seek to obtain the original—to have it available . . . for ready reference if and when [website visitors adding comments] need[] to look at it." *American Geophysical Union v. Texaco, Inc.,* 60 F.3d 913, 918 (2d Cir.1995) (the court held that the first fair use factor weighed against a defendant that encouraged its employees to make unauthorized photocopies of articles in scientific and medical journals and keep them in their offices for ready reference).

Defendants' web page acknowledges this. It states, *inter alia*, that the Free Republic site is a place where visitors "can often find breaking news and up to the minute updates." Indeed, it is clear from the content of the representative pages submitted by defendants that visitors can read copies of plaintiffs' current and archived articles at the Free Republic site. For those who visit the site regularly, therefore, the articles posted there serve as substitutes for the originals found on plaintiffs' websites or in their newspapers.

Defendants next argue that their use of plaintiffs' works is transformative because registered Free Republic users add comments and criticism concerning the articles following a posting. Copying portions of a copyrighted work for the purpose of criticism or commentary is often considered fair use. The fact that criticism is involved, however, does end the inquiry. Rather, it must be considered in combination with other circumstances to determine if the first factor favors defendants. . . .

Since the first posting of an article to the Free Republic site often contains little or no commentary, it does not significantly transform plaintiffs' work. In [*Religious Technology Center v. Netcom On-Line Communication Services, Inc.*, 923 F.Supp. 1231, 1243 (N.D. Cal. 1995)], defendant posted verbatim copies of works copyrighted by the Church of Scientology to an Internet website "with little or no added comment or criticism." The court found that the works were only "minimally transformative" because "unlike the typical critic, [defendant] add[ed] little new expression to the Church's works." The court specifically rejected defendant's argument that his copying was fair use because subsequent visitors added further comments. It concluded that while the copying of "works that were previously posted by their authors on the basis of an implied license or fair use argument" might be justified, such a defense would not be available "where the first posting made an unauthorized copy of a copyrighted work."

Similarly, in *Religious Technology Center v. Lerma*, [1996 U.S. Dist. LEXIS 15454, (E.D.Va. 1996)], defendant downloaded or scanned into his computer portions of works copyrighted by the Church of Scientology. He then posted segments of the works on the Internet. Defendant argued that his use was transformative, because he was a "dedicated researcher delving into the theory and scholarship of Scientology," and was "providing materials which 'add new value to public knowledge and understanding, thereby advancing the goals of copyright as set forth in the Constitution.' " The court rejected this argument, noting that it did "not justify the wholesale copying and republication of copyrighted material," and concluding that "[t]he degree of copying by [defendant] combined with the absence of commentary on most of his Internet postings, is inconsistent with the scholarship exception."

Additionally, even where copying serves the "criticism, comment and news reporting" purposes highlighted in § 107, its extent cannot exceed what is necessary to the purpose. . . . Thus, an individualized assessment of the purpose for which defendants are copying the works and a comparison of that purpose to the amount copied is required.

Here, it seems clear that the primary purpose of the postings to the Free Republic site is to facilitate discussion, criticism and comment by registered visitors. Defendants contend that copying all or parts of articles verbatim is necessary to facilitate this purpose. They argue that full text posting is required because links expire after a week or two, and because unsophisticated Internet users will have difficulty accessing a linked site. Defendants' assertion that links expire after a period of time is presumably a reference to the fact that articles are available on plaintiffs' websites free of charge only for a certain number of days. Thereafter, there is a charge for viewing and/or printing them. That this is so does not make linking plaintiffs' websites to the Free Republic site "impractical." It merely requires that Free Republic visitors pay a fee for viewing plaintiffs' articles just as other members of the public do. Similarly, defendants' suggestion that articles are posted to the Free Republic site long after they are published is not supported by the representative postings they have submitted. These reflect that the vast majority of comments are posted the same day the articles appear or within one to three days afterwards. Finally, defendants' assertion that unsophisticated Internet users would be confused by links is unpersuasive. Linking is familiar to most Internet users, even those who are new to the web.

As evidence that verbatim copying is in fact not necessary to defendants' purpose, plaintiffs cite the fact that defendants provided a hypertext link to *Jewish World Review*'s website at its request, and requested that registered Free Republic visitors no longer copy the publication's articles verbatim. That defendants accommodated *Jewish World Review* belies their current contention that only verbatim posting of articles will serve the criticism and comment purposes of the Free Republic site. Indeed, they acknowledge that honoring *Jewish World Review*'s request "did not significantly detract from the purpose of the *freerepublic.com* website."

The fact that linking the text of an article as it appears on plaintiffs' websites to the Free Republic site, or summarizing the article's text, is not as easy or convenient for Free Republic users as full text posting does not render the practice a fair use. Rather, the focus of the inquiry must be whether verbatim copying is necessary to defendants' critical purpose.

Defendants have not met their burden of demonstrating that verbatim copying of all or a substantial portion of plaintiffs' articles is necessary to achieve their critical purpose. They argue that the purpose of full text posting is to enable Free Republic users to criticize the manner in which the media covers current events. The statement of purpose found on the website, however, is somewhat different. There, defendants state that visitors to the Free Republic site "are encouraged to comment on the news of the day . . . and . . . to contribute whatever information they may have to help others better understand a particular story." In fact, a review of the representative articles submitted by defendants reveals that visitors' commentary focuses much more on the news of the day than it does on the manner in which the media reports that news. This is significant, since the extent of copying that might be necessary to comment on the nature of the media's coverage of a news event is arguably greater than the amount needed to facilitate comment on the event itself. Commentary on news events requires only recitation of the underlying facts, not verbatim repetition of another's creative expression of those facts in a news article. So too, the fact that a particular media outlet published a given story, or approached that story from a particular angle can be communicated to a large degree without posting a full text copy of the report.[49] For this reason, the court concludes that verbatim posting of plaintiffs' articles is "more than is necessary" to further defendants' critical purpose.

For all these reasons, the court concludes that defendants' use of plaintiffs' articles is minimally, if at all, transformative.

b. Commercial Nature Of The Free Republic Website

In addition to examining defendants' purpose in copying plaintiffs' articles, the first fair use factor also directs that the court evaluate the "character" of the use. The mere fact that a use is commercial does not "give rise to a presumption of unfairness." *Sony Computer Entertainment, Inc. v. Connectix Corp.* , 203 F.3d 596, 606 (9th Cir.2000). Rather, a defendant's commercial purpose is only "a separate factor that tends to weigh against a finding of fair use." *Campbell, supra,* 510 U.S. at 585. Thus, a court evaluating the first fair use factor "must weigh the extent of any transformation . . . against the significance of other factors, including commercialism, that militate against fair use." *Sony Computer,* 203 F.3d at 607.

The parties vigorously dispute whether defendants' operation of the Free Republic website is a profit or non-profit venture as those terms are used in § 107. Their disagreement focuses on the corporate status of Free Republic, and on the extent to which defendants' operation of the website generates revenue, donations, and commissions.

. . .

Nonetheless, defendants' operation possesses many characteristics of a non-profit entity. It does not market or sell a product, and does not generate revenue in the traditional sense. "The commercial nature of a use is a matter of degree, not an absolute. . . ." *Maxtone-Graham v. Burtchaell,* 803 F.2d 1253, 1262 (2d Cir.1986). Here, while the Free Republic operation has commercial aspects, its overall character is more properly viewed as non-commercial.

Additionally, the Free Republic site provides a public service by fostering debate and discussion regarding the issues of the day. This too is a factor that should be taken into account in assessing the character of defendants' use of plaintiffs' copyrighted material.

Section 107(1) does not mandate "a clear-cut choice between two polar characterizations, 'commercial' and 'non-profit.' " *Maxtone-Graham, supra, 803 F.2d at 1262.* Here, choosing one of these two extremes does not properly reflect the nature of the Free Republic site, or defendants' activities in operating it. Rather, attempting the "sensitive balancing of interests" required for application of the fair use

---

[49] Indeed, a few Free Republic visitors summarize the content of news articles rather than post verbatim copies of the text with little apparent impact on the quantity and quality of the commentary their postings attract.

doctrine, the court finds that the operation of the Free Republic site is only minimally commercial.

The relevant inquiry, however, "is not whether the sole motive of the use is monetary gain but whether the user stands to profit from exploitation of the copyrighted material without paying the customary price." *Harper & Row, supra,* 471 U.S. at 562. Here, defendants and registered third-party visitors to the Free Republic site copy and post plaintiffs' news articles, which are then available to others visiting the site free of charge. Since the general purpose of the site is to provide a forum where individuals can discuss current events and media coverage of them, posting copies of plaintiffs' articles assists in attracting viewers to the site.

. . .

. . . Defendants do not generate revenue or profits from posting plaintiffs' articles on the Free Republic website. At most, they derive indirect economic benefit by enhancing the website's cachet, increasing registrations, and hence increasing donations and other forms of support. Coupled with the fact that Free Republic has many of the attributes of a non-profit organization, this indirect benefit argues against a finding that the use is strictly commercial. Rather, it is more appropriate to conclude that, while defendants do not necessarily "exploit" the articles for commercial gain, their posting to the Free Republic site allows defendants and other visitors to avoid paying the "customary price" charged for the works. See *Harper & Row, supra,* 471 U.S. at 562.

c. Conclusion Regarding First Fair Use Factor

Following *Campbell,* it is clear that the court must balance and weigh the various elements of the first fair use factor in deciding whether it favors plaintiffs or defendants. In the process, it must bear in mind that "the concept of a 'transformative use' is central to a proper analysis under the first factor." *American Geophysical, supra,* 60 F.3d at 923. For this reason, "[t]he more critical inquiry under the first factor and in fair use analysis generally is . . . whether and to what extent the new work is transformative," not whether the use is commercial. *Castle Rock [Entertainment, Inc. v. Carol Publishing Group, Inc.,* 150 F.3d 132, 142 (2d. Cir.1998)].

Here, the court has found that defendants' copying of plaintiffs' articles is minimally, if at all, transformative. The comments of the individual who posts an article generally add little by way of comment or criticism to its substance. The extent of the copying is more than is necessary to foster the critical purpose it is designed to serve. Because the copying is verbatim, encompasses large numbers of articles, and occurs on an almost daily basis, the evidence supports a finding that defendants (and visitors to the Free Republic page) engage in extensive, systematic copying of plaintiffs' works.

Weighed against the essentially non-transformative nature of defendants' use is the fact that they do not directly derive revenue or profit from the posting of plaintiffs' articles, and the fact that their operation of the Free Republic website has many characteristics of a non-profit venture. So too, their use of plaintiffs' articles appears to be intended more for public benefit than for private commercial gain.

Since the "central purpose" of the inquiry on the first fair use factor is to determine "whether the new work merely 'supersede[s]' the objects' of the original creation, . . . or instead adds something new" (*Campbell, supra*, 510 U.S. at 579), the court finds that the non-transformative character of the copying in this case tips the scale in plaintiffs' favor, and outweighs the non-profit/public benefit nature of the purpose for which the copying is performed. This is particularly true since the posting of plaintiffs' articles to the Free Republic site amounts to "systematic . . . multiplying [of] the available number of copies" of the articles, "thereby serving the same purpose" for which licenses are sold or archive charges imposed. The first fair use factor thus favors plaintiffs.

2. The Nature Of The Copyrighted Work

The second factor identified in § 107 recognizes "that some works are closer to the core of intended copyright protection than others, with the consequence that fair use is more difficult to establish when the former works are copied." *Campbell, supra*, 510 U.S. at 586. Thus, "the more creative a work, the more protection it should be accorded from copying; correlatively, the more informational or functional the plaintiff's work, the broader should be the scope of the fair use defense." NIMMER, [*Nimmer on Copyright*], § 13.05[A][2][a]. Newspaper articles to a large extent gather and report facts. Nonetheless, a news reporter must determine which facts are significant and recount them in an interesting and appealing manner.

A number of cases that have analyzed alleged copying of news articles or videotapes of news events have concluded that the second fair use factor weighs in the defendant's favor. . . .

While plaintiffs' news articles certainly contain expressive elements, they are predominantly factual. Consequently, defendants' fair use claim is stronger than it would be had the works been purely fictional. The court conclude[s] that the second factor weighs in favor of a finding a fair use of the news articles by defendants in this case.

3. The Amount And Substantiality Of The Portion Used In Relation To The Copyrighted Work As A Whole

Defendants concede that they have copied and posted entire articles published in plaintiffs' newspapers . . .

The fact that exact copies of plaintiffs' article are posted to the Free Republic site weighs strongly against a finding of fair use in this case. . . .

. . .

4. The Effect Of The Use On The Potential Market For Or Value Of The Copyrighted Work

The fourth factor examines "the effect of the use upon the potential market for or value of the copyrighted work." It requires evaluating not only the extent of market harm caused by the alleged infringer's use, but also " 'whether unrestricted and widespread conduct of the sort engaged in by the defendant . . . would result in a substantially adverse impact on the potential market' for the original." *Campbell, supra*. In this regard, it is significant if widespread use of the type in which the defendant is engaged would "diminish[] potential sales, interfer[e] with market-ability, or usurp[] the market" for the original. *Sega, supra,* 977 F.2d at 1523 (noting that if copying had this effect, "all other considerations might be irrelevant"). Markets for derivative works, i.e., those markets 'that creators of original works would in general develop or license others to develop,' must be considered in addition to the market for the original. *Campbell, supra,* 510 U.S. at 590, 592.

In assessing the fourth factor, courts frequently contrast a use that "suppresses" or "destroys" the market for the original or derivative works with one that "usurps" or "substitutes" for those markets. "[A] work that merely supplants or supersedes another is likely to cause a substantially adverse impact on the potential market of the original, [while] a transformative work is less likely to do so." *Sony Computer, supra,* 203 F.3d at 607.

Applying these principles to the present case, the undisputed evidence shows that the Free Republic website has approximately 20,000 registered users, receives as many as 100,000 hits per day, and attracts between 25 and 50 million page views each month. The evidence also shows that visitors to the site are able to read full text copies of articles from plaintiffs' newspapers and archives without purchasing the papers, visiting plaintiffs' websites or paying the fee plaintiffs charge for retrieving an article from their archives. While defendants argue that the Free Republic site is a "poor substitute" for locating plaintiffs' articles on their websites, the court has found that for those individuals who visit the site, the articles posted to freerepublic.com do substitute for the original works. Given the number of registered visitors, hits and page views Free Republic attracts, the court cannot accept defendants' assertion that the site has only a *de minimis* effect on plaintiffs' ability to control the market for the copyrighted works.[56]

Moreover, this kind of *de minimis* argument has been rejected by the courts. . . .

. . . This is precisely defendants' argument here—that the Free Republic site is small in comparison to the sites operated by plaintiffs, is not known to the general public, and thus could not divert a substantial amount of business from plaintiffs. As the copyright holders, however, plaintiffs have the "right to control" access to the articles, and defendants' activities affect a market plaintiffs currently seek to exploit.

Plaintiffs assert they have lost and will lose revenue because visitors to the Free

---

[56] In his declaration, Richard Stout opines that the detrimental impact of the Free Republic site on plaintiffs' websites is "trivial." He bases this conclusion on the fact that the volume of traffic visiting the Free Republic site is "trivial" in comparison with the number of visitors to plaintiffs' sites, and that only a small percentage of the articles that appear on the Free Republic site are from plaintiffs' publications. Thus, he concludes that the "general public" wishing to read articles from plaintiffs' publications has "no reason to believe" that the Free Republic site is a better place to view plaintiff's articles than the papers' own websites. This overlooks the fact that those who visit the Free Republic site can read plaintiffs' articles without visiting their websites. As to those individuals, the articles posted to the Free Republic site clearly substitute for the originals, and make a visit to plaintiffs' websites unnecessary.

Republic site can read plaintiffs' archived news articles without paying the fee they would be charged for accessing the articles at plaintiffs' sites. Similarly, plaintiffs contend that defendants' use affects their ability to generate licensing revenue, since the fact that the articles are available for free viewing on Free Republic's web page diminishes their value to licensees. Finally, plaintiffs argue that defendants' copying reduces the number of people visiting their sites, and thus causes them to lose advertising revenue calculated on the number of hits they receive.

Defendants respond that plaintiffs have not adduced evidence of lost revenue resulting from operation of the Free Republic site. This, however, is not determinative. In [*Los Angeles News Service v. Reuters Television International, Inc.*, 149 F.3d 987, 994 (9th Cir.1998)], defendants copied plaintiffs' news footage without permission. Plaintiffs could not prove that they had lost sales of the footage or that they had suffered any actual adverse market effect. The court noted that allowing a customer to buy the footage from defendants rather than plaintiffs lessened the market for plaintiffs' footage, and concluded that "such actions if permitted would result in a substantially adverse impact on the potential market for the original works." . . .

Here, plaintiffs have shown that they are attempting to exploit the market for viewing their articles online, for selling copies of archived articles, and for licensing others to display or sell the articles. Defendants' use "substitutes" for the originals, and has the potential of lessening the frequency with which individuals visit plaintiffs' websites, of diminishing the market for the sale of archived articles, and decreasing the interest in licensing the articles. . . .

Defendants counter that there is no evidence that people who view the articles on the Free Republic site would ever have visited plaintiffs' websites. It is not necessary, however, to show with certainty that future harm will result. See [*Sony Corporation of America v. Universal City Studios, Inc.*, 464 U.S. 417, 451 (1984)]. Rather, "[w]hat is necessary is a showing by a preponderance of the evidence that some meaningful likelihood of future harm exists." *Id.* That likelihood is present when articles that would otherwise be available only at sites controlled or licensed by plaintiffs are available at a different site as well. The [l]ikelihood only increases when one considers the impact on the market if defendants' practice of full text copying were to become widespread.

Defendants also contend that plaintiffs actually benefit from having their articles posted verbatim on the Free Republic site. While they argue that plaintiffs' sites receive "literally tens of thousands, if not hundreds of thousands of hits per month" as a result of referrals from the Free Republic site, this overstates their expert's quantification of the number of referral hits. In his declaration[,] Richard Stout states that the Los Angeles Times' website receives approximately 20,000 hits per month from users who visit the Free Republic site before accessing the Times' site. Stout estimates that these referral hits generate approximately $1,000 in revenue for the paper each month. Defendants argue that this information regarding referral hits demonstrates that plaintiffs' advertising revenue is not diminished because of a reduction in the number of hits to their sites. Stout's declaration, however, does not address how many hits are *diverted* from plaintiffs' websites as a consequence of the posting of articles to the Free Republic site, and this is the pertinent inquiry in terms of potential market harm.

Defendants assert the evidence regarding referral hits demonstrates that Free Republic is creating a demand for plaintiffs' works. Even if this is the case, it does not mandate a conclusion that the fourth fair use factor favors defendants. Courts have routinely rejected the argument that a use is fair because it increases demand for the plaintiff's copyrighted work.

In short, plaintiffs have demonstrated that they are attempting to exploit the market for viewing their articles online, for selling copies of archived articles, and for licensing others to display or sell the articles. They have demonstrated that the availability of verbatim copies of the articles at the Free Republic site has the potential to interfere with these markets, particularly if it becomes a widespread practice. . . . Defendants, who bear the burden of proof on fair use, have not rebutted this showing by proving "an absence of 'usurpation' harm to" plaintiffs. *Infinity Broadcasting [Corp. v. Kirkwood*, 150 F.3d 104, 111 (2d Cir.1998)]. Accordingly, the fourth factor weighs against a finding of fair use in this case.

5. Balancing The Fair Use Factors

In sum, three of the four fair use factors weigh in plaintiffs' favor. Moreover, the factor that favors defendants—the nature of the copyrighted work—does not provide strong support for a fair use finding, since defendants copied both the factual *and* the expressive elements of plaintiffs' news articles. Conversely, the amount and substantiality of the copying and the lack of any significant transformation of the articles weigh heavily in favor of plaintiffs on this issue. The court thus finds that defendants may not assert a fair use defense to plaintiffs' copyright infringement claim. . . .

D. First Amendment Defense

Defendants assert, as a separate defense, the fact that the First Amendment protects their posting of copies of plaintiffs' news articles to the Free Republic website. Defendants contend that visitors to the Free Republic site will be unable to express their views concerning the manner in which the media covers current events since the omissions and biases in the articles will be difficult to communicate to readers without the full text of the article available.

In *Harper & Row, supra,* Nation magazine reprinted, without authorization, 300 words from the memoirs of President Gerald Ford. The Court noted that factual information concerning current events contained in news articles is not protected by copyright. It stated, however, that "copyright assures those who write and publish factual narratives . . . that they may at least enjoy the right to market the original expression contained therein as just compensation for their investment." It stressed that copyright fosters free expression because it "supplies the economic incentive to create and disseminate ideas" by "establishing a marketable right to the use of one's expression." It noted that copyright also promotes the countervailing First Amendment right to refrain from speech by protecting the owner of a copyrighted work from being forced to publish it. For all these reasons, the Court concluded that "that copyright's idea/expression dichotomy 'strike[s] a definitional balance between the First Amendment and the Copyright Act by permitting free communication of facts while still protecting an author's expression.' " Accordingly, it rejected defendant's First Amendment argument that material could be copied because it was "newsworthy," and "limited its inquiry to 'the traditional equities of fair use,' unexpanded by any free speech concerns." NIMMER, supra, § 1.10[B][2] (quoting *Harper & Row, supra,* 471 U.S. at 560). Courts have generally interpreted this discussion in *Harper & Row* to mean that First Amendment considerations are subsumed within the fair use [a]nalysis.

Nimmer argues that if the "copying of the expression is essential effectively to convey the idea expressed," then the First Amendment protects the copying regardless of copyright. As [one court] noted, "[n]o court has adopted Nimmer's proposal." . . .

Even assuming this is true, defendants have failed to show that copying plaintiffs' news articles verbatim is essential to communication of the opinions and criticisms visitors to the website express. As discussed above in connection with analysis of defendants' fair use defense, visitors' comments more often concern the underlying news event than they do the manner in which that event was covered by the media. And, even where media coverage is the subject of the critique, the gist of the comments (which concern the fact that a particular media outlet published a story or approached the story from a particular angle) can generally be communicated without full text copying of the article. The availability of alternatives—such as linking and summarizing—further undercuts any claim that First Amendment rights are implicated. While defendants and other users of the Free Republic site may find these options less ideal than copying plaintiffs' articles verbatim, this does not demonstrate that a First Amendment violation will occur if full text posting is prohibited.

III. CONCLUSION

For the foregoing reasons, plaintiffs' motion for summary adjudication with respect to fair use is granted, and defendants' motion is denied.

2. The First Sale Doctrine

§ 109. Limitations on exclusive rights: Effect of transfer of particular copy or phonorecord

Notwithstanding the provisions of section 106(3), the owner of a particular copy or phonorecord lawfully made under this title, or any person authorized by such owner, is entitled, without the authority of the copyright owner, to sell or otherwise dispose of the possession of that copy or phonorecord. . . .

DMCA SECTION 104 REPORT: A REPORT OF THE REGISTER OF COPYRIGHTS PURSUANT TO § 104 OF THE DIGITAL MILLENNIUM COPYRIGHT ACT (2001)
www.copyright.gov/reports/studies/dmca/sec-104-report-vol-1.pdf

. . .

Our mandate was to evaluate "the effects of the amendments made by [title I of the DMCA] and the development of electronic commerce and associated technology on the operation of sections 109 and 117 of title 17, United States Code; and the relationship between existing and emergent technology and the operation of sections 109 and 117. . . ."

. . .

The common-law roots of the first sale doctrine allowed the owner of a particular copy of a work to dispose of that copy. This judicial doctrine was grounded in the common-law principle that restraints on the alienation of tangible property are to be avoided in the absence of clear congressional intent to abrogate this principle. This doctrine appears in section 109 of the Copyright Act of 1976. . . .

. . .

II. VIEWS OF THE PUBLIC

. . .

The greatest area of contention in the [public's] comments [submitted during the preparation of the report] was the question of whether to expand the first sale doctrine to permit digital transmission of lawfully made copies of works. Although some proponents argued that such transmissions are already permitted by the current language of section 109, most thought that clarification of this conclusion by Congress would be advisable since the absence of express statutory language could lead to uncertainty.

The proponents of revising section 109 argued that the transmission of a work that was subsequently deleted from the sender's computer is the digital equivalent of giving, lending, or selling a book. Allowing consumers to transfer the copy of the work efficiently by means of online transmission would foster the principles of the first sale doctrine. These principles have promoted economic growth and creativity in the analog world and should be extended to the digital environment. Proponents of this argument sought amendment to section 109 to allow a person to forward a work over the Internet and then delete that work from his computer.

Others opposed such an amendment for a number of reasons. Opponents pointed out that the first sale doctrine is a limitation on the distribution right of copyright owners and has never implicated the reproduction right which is, in their view, a "cornerstone" of copyright protection. In addition, the impact of the doctrine on copyright owners was also limited in the off-line world by a number of factors, including geography and the gradual degradation of books and analog works. The absence of such limitations would have an adverse effect on the market for digital works. Opponents also believed that proposals that depend on the user deleting his copy would be unverifiable, leading to virtually undetectable cheating. Given the expanding market for digital works without a digital first sale doctrine, opponents questioned the consumer demand for such a change in the law.

. . .

III. EVALUATION AND RECOMMENDATIONS

. . .

A. The Effect Of Title I of the DMCA on the Operation of Sections 109 and 117

The arguments raised concerning the adverse effects of . . . technological protection measure[s such as encryption] on the operation of section 109 are flawed. The first sale doctrine is primarily a limitation on copyright owner's distribution right. Section 109 does not guarantee the existence of secondary markets for works. There are many factors which could affect the resale market for works, none of which could be said to interfere with the operation of section 109. The need for a particular device on which to view the work is not a novel concept and does not constitute an effect on section 109. VHS videocassettes for example, must be played on VHS VCRs.

A plausible argument can be made that section 1201 [which prohibits the circumvention of technological measures such as encryption used in connection with copyrighted works] may have a negative effect on the operation of the first sale doctrine in the context of works tethered to a particular device. In the case of tethered works, even if the work is on removable media, the content cannot be accessed on any device other than the one on which it was originally made. This process effectively prevents disposition of the work. However, the practice of tethering a copy of a work to a particular hardware device does not appear to be widespread at this time, at least outside the context of electronic books. Given the relative infancy of digital rights management, it is premature to consider any legislative change at this time. Should this practice become widespread, it could have serious consequences for the operation of the first sale doctrine, although the ultimate effect on consumers is unclear.

. . .

B. THE EFFECT OF ELECTRONIC COMMERCE AND TECHNOLOGICAL CHANGE ON SECTIONS 109 AND 117

There is no dispute that section 109 applies to works in digital form. Physical copies of works in a digital format, such as CDs or DVDs, are subject to section 109 in the same way as physical copies in analog form. Similarly, a lawfully made tangible copy of a digitally downloaded work, such as a work downloaded to a floppy disk, Zip™ disk, or CD-RW, is clearly subject to section 109. The question we address here is whether the transmission of a work to another person falls within—or should fall within—the scope of section 109.

1. *The First Sale Doctrine in the Digital World*

a. Evaluation of Arguments Concerning First Sale

The first sale doctrine is primarily a limitation on the copyright owner's exclusive right of distribution. It does not limit the exclusive right of reproduction. While disposition of a work downloaded to a floppy disk would only implicate the distribution right, the transmission of a work from one person to another over the Internet results in a reproduction on the recipient's computer, even if the sender subsequently deletes the original copy of the work. This activity therefore entails an exercise of an exclusive right that is not covered by section 109.

Proponents of expansion of the scope of section 109 to include the transmission and deletion of a digital file argue that this activity is essentially identical to the transfer of a physical copy and that the similarities outweigh the differences. While it is true that there are similarities, we find the analogy to the physical world to be flawed and unconvincing.

Physical copies degrade with time and use; digital information does not. Works in digital format can be reproduced flawlessly, and disseminated to nearly any point on the globe instantly and at negligible cost. Digital transmissions can adversely effect the market for the original to a much greater degree than transfers of physical copies. Additionally, unless a "forward-and-delete" technology is employed to automatically delete the sender's copy, the deletion of a work requires an additional affirmative act on the part of the sender subsequent to the transmission. This act is difficult to prove or disprove, as is a person's claim to have transmitted only a single copy, thereby raising complex evidentiary concerns. There were conflicting views on whether effective forward and delete technologies exist today. Even if they do, it is not clear that the market will bear the cost of an expensive technological measure.

The underlying policy of the first sale doctrine as adopted by the courts was to give effect to the common law rule against restraints on the alienation of tangible property. The tangible nature of a copy is a defining element of the first sale doctrine and critical to its rationale. The digital transmission of a work does not implicate the alienability of a physical artifact. When a work is transmitted, the sender is exercising control over the intangible work through its reproduction rather than common law dominion over an item of tangible personal property. Unlike the physical distribution of digital works on a tangible medium, such as a floppy disk, the transmission of works interferes with the copyright owner's control over the intangible work and the exclusive right of reproduction. The benefits to further expansion simply do not outweigh the likelihood of increased harm.

Digital communications technology enables authors and publishers to develop new business models, with a more flexible array of products that can be tailored and priced to meet the needs of different consumers. We are concerned that these proposals for a digital first sale doctrine endeavor to fit the exploitation of works online into a distribution model—the sale of copies—that was developed within the confines of pre-digital technology. If the sale model is to continue as the dominant method of distribution, it should be the choice of the market, not due to legislative fiat.

We also examined how other countries are addressing the applicability of the first sale—or exhaustion—doctrine to digital transmissions. We found that other countries are addressing digital transmissions under the communication to the public right and are not applying the principle of exhaustion, or any other analog thereof, to digital transmissions.

b. Recommendation Concerning the Digital First Sale Doctrine

We recommend no change to section 109 at this time. Although speculative concerns have been raised, there was no convincing evidence of present-day problems. In order to recommend a change in the law, there should be a demonstrated need for the change that outweighs the negative aspects of the proposal. The Copyright Office does not believe that this is the case with the proposal to expand the scope of section 109 to include digital transmissions. The time may come when Congress may wish to address these concerns should they materialize.

The fact that we do not recommend adopting a "digital first sale" provision at this time does not mean that the issues raised by libraries are not potentially valid concerns. Similarly, our conclusion that certain issues are beyond the scope of the present study does not reflect our judgment on the merits of those issues.

The library community has raised concerns about how the current marketing of works in digital form affects libraries with regard to five specifically enumerated categories: interlibrary loans, off-site accessibility, archiving/preservation, availability of works, and use of donated copies. Most of these issues arise from terms and conditions of use, and costs of license agreements. One arises because, when the library has only online access to the work, it lacks a physical copy of the copyrighted work that can be transferred. These issues arise from existing business models and are therefore subject to market forces. We are in the early stages of electronic commerce. We hope and expect that the marketplace will respond to the various concerns of customers in the library community. However, these issues may require further consideration at some point in the future. Libraries serve a vital function in society, and we will continue to work with the library and publishing communities on ways to ensure the continuation of library functions that are critical to our national interest.

. . .

EXTENSIONS

Exceptions from the first-sale right for record and software rental. In the early 1980s, record rental stores began to proliferate. These stores would rent you an LP record for a dollar or two, allowing you to keep it for a few days. As was clear to all, nearly everyone who patronized these establishments was making a copy of the record on audio cassette tape, and adding the tape to their collection. At the instance of music copyright holders, Congress enacted the Record Rental Amendment of 1984, Pub. L. No. 98–450, 98 Stat. 1727 (1984), which amended the Copyright Act's codification of the first-sale right, 17 U.S.C. § 109. The amendment limits the first-sale right, so that it no longer permits the rental, lease, or lending of phonorecords (that is, records, tapes, and other physical objects containing sound recordings) for commercial purposes. In 1990, Congress similarly limited the applicability of the first-sale right to computer programs, by enacting a parallel amendment of Section 109. *See* Computer Software Rental Amendments Act of 1990, Pub. L. No. 101–650, 104 Stat. 5089, 5134 (1990).

These two congressional actions exemplify a clash between an owner's right to dispose of his chattels as he sees fit, which is recognized in the common law's strong distaste for restraints on alienation, and a copyright holder's statutory right to control distribution of his works. The boundary between these two rights is fluid, and shifts with technological and societal developments. Can you think of any aspects of online technology, or the societal changes it has spawned, that call for a rethinking of where this boundary should be drawn?

QUESTIONS FOR DISCUSSION

1. *"Copies" and the first-sale right.* 17 U.S.C. § 109(a) provides that "the owner of a particular copy . . . is entitled . . . to sell or otherwise dispose of the possession of that copy." A purchaser of a CD-ROM containing software does not thereby gain ownership of the copyright in the software, but only the right to use it in ways that do not conflict with the rights of the copyright owner. Does the purchaser gain ownership of the CD-ROM disk itself? If so, does the first-sale doctrine apply, allowing the purchaser to dispose of the CD-ROM as she chooses? *See* Melville B. Nimmer & David Nimmer, Nimmer on Copyright § 8.12[B][1]. What if she purchases the software by downloading it from a website onto her computer's hard drive? Does the first-sale doctrine allow her to e-mail the software to somebody else, if she deletes it from her own computer's hard drive? Does it allow her to sell the computer without first deleting the software? Suppose she downloads the software directly to a floppy diskette. Does the first-sale doctrine allow her to give the diskette to somebody else?

2. *Common law underpinnings of the first-sale right.* The Report identifies the common law's disfavor of restraints on alienation of tangible personal property as underlying copyright law's first-sale doctrine. The Report notes that digital transmissions involve intangible rather than tangible property, suggesting that restraints on retransmission of digital files, even of the "forward and delete" variety, do not implicate the principles underlying the first-sale doctrine. Of course, expectations about the proper scope of control over tangible personal property evolved over time. Technology that enables transmissions of digital files embodying works of authorship, though, has only been widely available for a relatively short time. How are popular attitudes about the appropriate control that the owner of digital file should exercise likely to evolve, and how should copyright law adapt to reflect those attitudes?

3. *Secondary markets.* The Copyright Office Report focused on the question of how the first-sale doctrine should apply to digital transmissions of a work of authorship itself. Internet commerce, though, is also affecting the operation of the first-sale doctrine in the market for traditional tangible copies of copyrighted works. Used copies of literary works, sound recordings, and motion pictures can now be located and purchased more easily and quickly than before through online markets such as Amazon Marketplace or eBay. One 2005 study found that "online sales of general-interest used books are growing at a rate of more than 30 percent a year, while sales of used books at stores are almost flat," though only about 3 percent of the money that Americans spend on general-interest books went to buy used books. Edward Wyatt, *Internet Grows as Factor in Used-Book Business*, N.Y. Times, Sept. 29, 2005. (The used *textbook* market, though, is much larger.) Publishers and authors have complained in particular about the availability of used copies of books on Amazon very quickly after the books are first published. *Id.* Should the first-sale doctrine be changed in any way because it is now easier to find and buy used books online than it was before the Internet?

III. Copyright and Common Internet Activities

A. Linking and Framing

David L. Hayes, *Advanced Copyright Issues on the Internet*
7 Tex. Int. Prop. L. J. 1 (1998).

. . .

The practice of "linking" is another activity that is ubiquitous on the World Wide Web. A "link" is an embedded electronic address that "points" to another Web location. Links may be of at least two different types. The first type, which will be referred to as an "out link," merely provides a vehicle by which a person browsing a Web page can go to another site by clicking on the link. The out link stores the electronic address of the destination site, and clicking on the link sends that address to the browser, which in turn moves the user to the new destination site.

A second type of link, which will be referred to as an "in-line link," is a pointer to a document, image, audio clip or the like somewhere on the Web contained in another's Web page which, in effect, pulls in the image, text or audio clip from the other Web page into the current document for display. In other words, a user looking at A's Web page will see on that page image, text, or an audio clip that actually was "pulled in" from site owner B's Web page. When material from an in-line link is displayed within the "frame" or window border of a page of the linking website, this type of linking is often referred to as "framing."[487] The linking site is sometimes referred to as a "para-site," with obvious pejorative connotations.

Both out links and in-line links raise a number of potential copyright issues. An out link that points to a site containing infringing material may, for example, cause further infringing reproductions, public performances, public distributions, public displays, digital performances of sound recordings, and/or importations to occur when the user reaches that site and the infringing material is downloaded, imported and/or performed or displayed to the linking user. Even if material on the destination site is not infringing of its own right, the reproductions, distributions, and displays that occur as a result of the out link may not be authorized, since the out link may have been established (as is generally the case) without the explicit permission of the owner of material on the destination site. Under the WIPO treaties, the result of clicking on the out link may be to generate an unauthorized access and transmission of the destination material. Or the out link itself may be considered to be an unauthorized "making available to the public" of the material on the destination site — the owner of the destination site may wish to retain complete control of how and when information on its site is presented to the public.

It is unclear whether an out link might also be considered the creation of an unauthorized derivative work. Viewed in one way, an out link could be considered nothing more than a reference to another work, much like a citation in a law review article, that should not be considered a derivative work. One could argue that the material on the linked site is neither altered by the link nor "incorporated" into the linking site, but is seen in its original form when the user arrives there as a result of the link.

Viewed a different way, one could treat a site as a virtual collective work comprised of all material available to be viewed by the user in the course of browsing through the site. Links cause an "incorporation" — at least in a virtual sense — of the linked material into this collective work, thereby in some sense creating a derivative work. If the linked site material enhances the value of the linking site, the

---

[487] "Frame" technology is a page presentation capability available in both the Netscape Navigator and the Microsoft Internet Explorer browsers that enables the display of multiple, independently scrollable panels on a single screen. Frames may contain many types of elements, including text, hypertext, graphics, scrollable regions, and other frames.

linked site owner might argue that the linking site is "based upon" the linked site and therefore constitutes a derivative work.

The fair use or implied license doctrine may apply to many out links, because it is no doubt the case that many site owners will want their material disseminated as widely as possible, and references in to the site through links from other sites will be considered desirable. However, in some instances the linked site owner may argue that out links cause harm, and such harm should defeat a fair use or implied license defense. For example, nonconsensual links may result in burdensome amounts of traffic on the linked site from users the linked site is not targeting. The owner of the linked site could argue that such unwanted traffic prevents the owner from distributing copyrighted material on its site to its desired audience, thereby harming the potential market for its material. Alternatively, if the linking site is undesirable for some reason in the eyes of the linked site, the linked site might allege the linking diminishes the commercial value of its copyrighted material at the linked site. This might be the case, for example, if a site distributing pornographic material were to link to a religious site distributing religious material.

In addition to the issues of direct infringement discussed above, if a linked site contains infringing material, the link may give rise to contributory infringement on the part of the linking site, particularly if the linking site is promoting the copying, transmission, public display or public performance of material at the linked site.

. . .

In-line links may provide an even more direct basis for legal liability than out links. An in-line link causes a reproduction of the linked material to be "pulled in" to the linking site, and therefore may cause an infringement of the right of reproduction, display, or performance, or may constitute the creation of an unauthorized derivative work, just as if material had been clipped from a printed source and placed in one's own material. . . .

Although beyond the scope of this paper, both out links and in-line links may raise issues of trademark infringement as well as copyright infringement. . . .

To date, there have been a number of cases challenging linking on copyright grounds.

1. The *Shetland Times* Case

A recent case out of Scotland illustrates one type of harm that a linked site owner perceived to result from links to its site. In *Shetland Times Ltd. v. Wills*,[490] the plaintiff, Shetland Times (Times), maintained a website containing copies of articles that appeared in the printed version of its newspaper. Users visiting the site were initially presented with a "front page" containing headlines. Clicking on a headline linked the user to the full text of the article. The Times planned to sell advertising space on the front page.

The defendant, The Shetland News (News), also maintained a website. News took verbatim the headlines from Times' site and placed them on News' Web page

---

[490] Shetland Times Ltd. v. Willis, 1997 Sess. Cas. 316 (Sess. 1996).

to allow users at News' site to link directly to the full text of Times' articles, without having to first view Times' front page. This bypassing of Times' front page obviously caused harm to Times' ability to sell advertising on the front page, since those readers of Times' articles who arrived at the articles through links from News' site would never see the ads. Times sued News in the Scotland Court of Sessions, alleging that News' copying of Times' headlines constituted copyright infringement.

The court issued an "interim interdict" (a temporary order) pending a full hearing, ruling that the headlines could be considered copyrightable literary works. The court rejected the defendant's argument that the headlines were not the product of sufficient skill or effort, finding that because many of the headlines consisted of eight or so words that imparted information, copying of the headlines might at least in some instances constitute copyright infringement.

The parties subsequently settled their dispute by agreeing that News would be permitted to link to stories on Times' website by means of headlines only in the following manner. Each link to any individual story would be acknowledged by the legend *A Shetland Times Story* appearing underneath each headline and of the same or similar size as the headline, adjacent to any such headline or headlines there would appear a button showing legibly the Times masthead logo and the legend and the button would each be hypertext links to the Times online headline page.[501]

. . . Although it is unclear how such a case would be decided under United States . . . law, the case is a good illustration of the copyright issues that may arise out of the act of linking.

. . .

3. The *Ticketmaster* Case

In April 1997, Ticketmaster Corporation brought an action in federal district court against Microsoft Corporation[533] based on links from Microsoft's "Seattle Sidewalk" website to Ticketmaster's website. In February 1998, Ticketmaster filed a Second Amended Complaint,[535] which asserts claims for copyright and trademark infringement, as well as for unfair competition based on various common law and state law theories.

Ticketmaster maintains a website (www.ticketmaster.com) through which it sells and markets tickets to various entertainment events. The "Seattle Sidewalk" site, one of a number of city guides maintained by Microsoft on The Microsoft Network, offers a guide to entertainment and restaurants available in the Seattle area. Microsoft placed links on the Seattle Sidewalk to the Ticketmaster site so that

---

[501] *Publisher's Statement: Internet Dispute Settled* (last modified Nov. 17, 1997) <www.shetland-times.co.uk/st/daily/dispute.htm>.

[533] Ticketmaster Corp. v. Microsoft Corp., No. 97-3055 DDP (C.D. Cal. filed Apr. 28, 1997). . . .

[535] Second Amended Complaint, Ticketmaster Corp. v. Microsoft Corp., No. 97-3055 RAP (C.D. Cal. filed Feb. 12, 1998).

users of the Seattle Sidewalk could purchase tickets to events of interest online through Ticketmaster. Negotiations between Microsoft and Ticketmaster for an agreement allowing Microsoft to profit from linkage to and association with Ticketmaster's website failed, and Microsoft established the links—which in several instances bypassed the home page of the Ticketmaster site—without permission from Ticketmaster.

. . .

Ticketmaster also asserted claims of copyright infringement, based on the allegations that (i) in creating links to the Ticketmaster site, Microsoft repeatedly viewed and thus copied onto its own computers the copyrighted contents of Ticketmaster's website, and (ii) in the operation of the links, Microsoft was reproducing, publicly distributing and displaying without permission Ticketmaster's copyrighted website material.

In Microsoft's answer to Ticketmaster's complaint,[549] Microsoft alleged that Ticketmaster could not complain about Microsoft's link to Ticketmaster's home page because Ticketmaster knew when it set up its website that owners of other Web pages would create such links. Microsoft noted that when an event requires tickets, Microsoft routinely provides information about how to obtain them, including prices, telephone numbers, and, where appropriate, hypertext links to relevant Web pages. Microsoft alleged that such information is freely available to the public and is not proprietary to Ticketmaster. Microsoft asserted numerous defenses, including (i) that Ticketmaster, when it chose to set up Web pages, assumed the risk that others would use its name and URLs, (ii) that Ticketmaster is estopped from complaining about Microsoft's link because Ticketmaster encourages users to seek out its website and refer others to the site, and (iii) that Microsoft's presentation of information about Ticketmaster on its Seattle Sidewalk site is commercial speech protected by the First Amendment.

Although Microsoft removed some or all of its links to the Ticketmaster site after the complaint was filed, the lawsuit remains unresolved.

4. The *Futuredontics* Case

In September 1997, Futuredontics, Inc., owner of a website relating to its dental referral service, filed a complaint against a defendant that was framing material from Futuredontics' website in the defendant's website.[556] The frame displaying Futuredontics' website material included the defendant's logo, information on the defendant, and links to the defendant's other web pages. Futuredontics claimed that such framing constituted the creation of an infringing derivative work. The defendant moved to dismiss the complaint for failure to state a claim, arguing that its frame should be viewed as merely a "lens" which enabled Internet users to

---

[549] Microsoft's Answer to First Amended Complaint, Affirmative Defenses and Counterclaims, Ticketmaster Corp. v. Microsoft Corp., No. 97-3055 DDP (C.D. Cal. answer filed May 28, 1997). . . .

[556] Futuredontics, Inc. v. Applied Anagramatics, Inc., 45 U.S.P.Q.2d (BNA) 2005, 2008 (C.D. Cal. 1998).

view the information that Futuredontics itself placed on the Internet. The court denied the defendant's motion, ruling that existing authority did not resolve the legal issue, and Futuredontics' complaint therefore sufficiently alleged a copyright infringement claim. Interestingly, however, the court had previously denied Futuredontics' motion for a preliminary injunction, ruling that Futuredontics had failed to establish a probability of success.

TROTTER HARDY, PROJECT LOOKING FORWARD: SKETCHING THE FUTURE OF COPYRIGHT IN A NETWORKED WORLD (1998).
www.copyright.gov/reports/thardy.pdf

. . .

In-line linking and framing

Everyone familiar with the WWW understands that an enormous advantage of the Web is that most documents and sites contain "links" to other documents and sites. That is the whole point of the WWW: it would not be a "web" or be "worldwide" if it did not contain links to other information.

Fewer people presently understand that "links" come in several flavors. The ones just referred to are perhaps the most commonly thought of; they might be described as "links out" to other information. Another type of link is referred to as an "in-line link," which in contrast to the first type might be thought of as "links in" to other information.

An in-line link is a pointer to a document somewhere on the WWW that causes that document to appear to be located on the "receiving" site. Let us say that Web page owner *A* puts up a document on *A's* web site. Part of that document contains a link to a picture located on, say Web site *B*. Many such links are used to direct a user "out" to another image or bit of text. Typically, such a link will be represented in text form by the use of a blue type font, often underlined as well. A user understands that "clicking" on the blue text will cause a jump to some other document, and perhaps some other computer.

But the in-line link, in contrast, in effect *pulls* the other image or bit of text into the current document for display. In other words, the user looking at site owner *A's* Web page will see on that page an image that actually was "pulled in" from site owner *B's* Web page, even though it appears to be a part of *A's* page. For all practical purposes, it *is* a part of *A's* web page, at least as far as the viewing user is concerned.

This has already happened once in a way that raised—but did not resolve—the copyright issue. An individual at the Princeton University for a while kept an in-line link to the "Dilbert" cartoon of the day. The cartoon appears on copyright owner United Media's site, but to browsers of the individual's site, the cartoon appeared to be residing "there." Reportedly, United Media sent the individual a "cease and desist" letter, after which he ceased and desisted the in-line linking.

When the first draft of this Report was written in the fall of 1996, this section ended with these words: "Certainly this [in-line linking] is an issue that will be revisited in the future. Because it involves technology that is already working today, one can expect the issue to arise fairly soon." By February, 1997, a law suit involving "in-line linking" had in fact been filed.

A site on the WWW known as "TotalNews" provides links to a variety of other news sites on the Web, including CNN, CBS, NPR, and others. The linking mechanism was initially implemented in such a way that the news organizations' Web pages appeared to be "on" the TotalNews page. This particular variant of in-line linking is popularly known as "framing," as it involves a border from one site — the frame — surrounding or edging the content from another site.

Here is a screen capture of the TotalNews home page, taken on March 9, 1997.

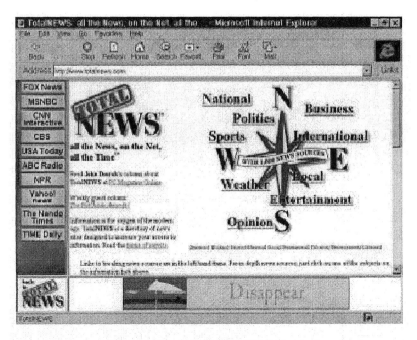

Figure 10: Screen capture of TotalNews home page,
from <http://www.totalnews.com> on March 9, 1997.

Though it may not be apparent, the screen image consists of several different parts. The overall screen shows a Web browser and its menus and button icons along the top. Within the browser's window appear several images from the TotalNews site. These images are divided into several "frames" or segments. One of these frames appears along the left side of the page and contains a series of buttons with the names of various news organizations: FOX News, MSNBC, and so on. To the right of this narrow frame is a wider one that contains the TotalNews logo and a compass rose. At the time of the litigation, when a user clicked on one of the buttons in the left side frame, that frame remained in place, but the content of the larger frame with the compass rose was replaced with content from the selected news site.

This next screen capture shows what happened, for example, when a user clicked on the "CNN Interactive" button.

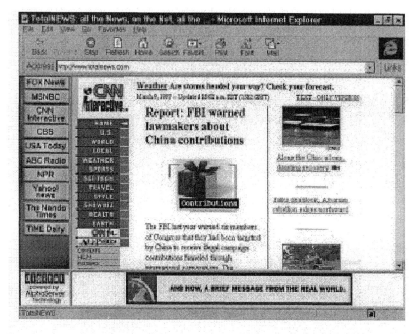

Figure 11: Screen capture showing what appears after clicking on the "CNN Interactive" button in the left frame of the TotalNews home page, from <http://www.totalnews.com> on March 9, 1997.

Notice that the frame or border on the left and bottom of the screen remained the same, and the small address window showing a URL continued to display the TotalNews Internet address.

On February 20, 1997, some the news organizations[188] listed in the left frame filed suit against TotalNews, alleging a number of causes of action including misappropriation, trademark dilution, trademark infringement, false designation of origin, tortious interference with contract, and copyright infringement.[189]

---

[188] The Washington Post, Cable News Network, Times Mirror, Dow Jones and Reuters New Media.

[189] Paragraph 30 of the complaint states:

At the heart of Defendants' wrongful conduct is a practice known as "framing" that causes Plaintiffs' websites to appear not in the form that Plaintiffs intended, but in an altered form designed by Defendants for their own economic advantage. The totalnews.com website consists of lists of numerous "name-brand" news sources, including the famous trademarks exclusively associated with Plaintiffs in the public mind. When a user of totalnews.com "clicks" on one of those famous

The complaint was not specific in its allegation of copyright infringement as to which rights are involved. Presumably the issues would include whether the TotalNews site was copying or publicly displaying or publicly performing or creating a derivative work of the works at issue.

In June, 1997, the case was settled;[190] we do not, therefore, have any judicial resolution of the issues involved. As of early 1998, the TotalNews site was no longer consistently framing other sites.

. . .

Regardless of these particular instances of framing, the technology is widely used on the Internet. Technology also exists for Web site owners to prevent other sites from framing them,[191] but not everyone is aware of either the technology or the likelihood of framing. The issue therefore remains open as a legal matter. The general issue here is one of a "new use" of existing copyrighted works. . . .

EXTENSIONS

Ticketmaster v. Microsoft. In January 1999, Ticketmaster and Microsoft settled the dispute discussed above. The parties agreed not to reveal the terms of the settlement, but Ticketmaster did say that "Microsoft had agreed to no longer link Sidewalk to pages deep within the Ticketmaster site, where visitors might not even realize they were using Ticketmaster's services." Instead, Sidewalk would link visitors to Ticketmaster's home page. Bob Tedeschi, *Ticketmaster and Microsoft Settle Suit on Internet Linking*, N.Y. TIMES, Feb. 15, 1999. For further background on the Ticketmaster case, see Seth Schiesel, *Choosing Sides In Ticketmaster vs. Microsoft*, N.Y. TIMES, May 5, 1997, www.nytimes.com/library/cyber/digicom/050597digicom.html.

---

trademarks with the computer mouse, the user accesses a Plaintiff's corresponding website. (In Internet parlance, the trademarks here function as "hyperlinks": areas on the screen that, when clicked on, take the user directly to another website.) Plaintiff's site, however, does not then fill the screen as it would had the user accessed Plaintiff's site either directly or by means of a hyperlink from a website that does not "frame" linked sites. Nor does Plaintiff's URL appear at the top of the screen as it normally would. Instead, part of Plaintiff's site is inserted in a window designed by Defendants to occupy only a portion of the screen. Masking part of Plaintiff's site is the totalnews.com "frame," including, inter alia, the "TotalNEWS" logo, totalnews.com URL, and advertisements that others have purchased from Defendants.

The Washington Post Company v. Total News, Inc., (S.D.N.Y. February 20, 1997) 97 Civ. 1190 (PKL).

[190] *See* STIPULATION AND ORDER OF SETTLEMENT AND DISMISSAL, 97 Civ. 1190 (PKL) (S.D.N.Y. June 6, 1997) . . . .

[191] The technical community is aware of the matter: *see* Arnoud Engelfriet, *Frames FAQ: Avoiding getting 'framed': Is there a way to prevent getting framed.?* <www.htmlhelp.com/design/frames/faq/framed.html>, as of February 28, 1998. . . .

QUESTIONS FOR DISCUSSION

1. Shetland Times *case under U.S. law.* What would the likely outcome of the *Shetland Times* dispute have been if it had been decided under U.S. law?

2. *Contractual prohibitions.* Some Web sites have posted terms and conditions for the use of the site that prohibit framing or in-line linking without permission, such as the following:

> No Framing. Without the prior written permission of Scientific American, you may not frame or establish inline links to any of the content of our website, nor may you incorporate into another website or other product or service any intellectual property of Scientific American or any of its licensors. Requests for permission to frame, or to establish inline links to, our content may be sent to the Permissions Department, either by email, or at the address above.

Scientific American Visitor Agreement, www.sciam.com/page.cfm?section=visitoragreement. To what extent are such prohibitions likely to be effective?

FURTHER READING

- For more details on the in-line linking of the Dilbert cartoon mentioned in the Hardy report, see the Dilbert Hack Page Archives, www.cs.rice.edu/~dwallach/dilbert/.

- For the views of one of the founders of the Web on linking, see Tim Berners-Lee, *Links and Law*, www.w3.org/DesignIssues/LinkLaw, and *Links and Law: Myths*, www.w3.org/DesignIssues/LinkMyths.html. Links to much background information about linking and framing are available at Stefan Bechtold's Link Controversy Page, www.jura.uni-tuebingen.de/~s-bes1/lcp.html.

B. SEARCH ENGINES

Kelly v. Arriba Soft Corp.
336 F.3d 811 (9th Cir.2003).

■ T.G. NELSON, CIRCUIT JUDGE.

. . .

This case involves the application of copyright law to the vast world of the internet and internet search engines. The plaintiff, Leslie Kelly, is a professional photographer who has copyrighted many of his images of the American West. Some of these images are located on Kelly's web site or other web sites with which Kelly has a license agreement. The defendant, Arriba Soft Corp.,[1] operates an internet search engine that displays its results in the form of small pictures rather than the more usual form of text. Arriba obtained its database of pictures by copying images from other web sites. By clicking on one of these small pictures, called "thumbnails," the user can then view a large version of that same picture within the context of the Arriba web page.

---

[1] Arriba Soft has changed its name since the start of this litigation. It is now known as "Ditto.com."

When Kelly discovered that his photographs were part of Arriba's search engine database, he brought a claim against Arriba for copyright infringement. The district court found that Kelly had established a prima facie case of copyright infringement based on Arriba's unauthorized reproduction and display of Kelly's works, but that this reproduction and display constituted a non-infringing "fair use" under Section 107 of the Copyright Act. Kelly appeals that decision, and we affirm in part and reverse in part. The creation and use of the thumbnails in the search engine is a fair use. However, the district court should not have decided whether the display of the larger image is a violation of Kelly's exclusive right to publicly display his works. Thus, we remand for further proceedings consistent with this opinion.

I.

The search engine at issue in this case is unconventional in that it displays the results of a user's query as "thumbnail" images. When a user wants to search the internet for information on a certain topic, he or she types a search term into a search engine, which then produces a list of web sites that contain information relating to the search term. Normally, the list of results is in text format. The Arriba search engine, however, produces its list of results as small pictures.

To provide this service, Arriba developed a computer program that "crawls" the web looking for images to index. This crawler downloads full-sized copies of the images onto Arriba's server. The program then uses these copies to generate smaller, lower-resolution thumbnails of the images. Once the thumbnails are created, the program deletes the full-sized originals from the server. Although a user could copy these thumbnails to his computer or disk, he cannot increase the resolution of the thumbnail; any enlargement would result in a loss of clarity of the image.

The second component of the Arriba program occurs when the user double-clicks on the thumbnail. From January 1999 to June 1999, clicking on the thumbnail produced the "Images Attributes" page. This page used in-line linking to display the original full-sized image, surrounded by text describing the size of the image, a link to the original web site, the Arriba banner, and Arriba advertising.

In-line linking allows one to import a graphic from a source website and incorporate it in one's own website, creating the appearance that the in-lined graphic is a seamless part of the second web page. The in-line link instructs the user's browser to retrieve the linked-to image from the source website and display it on the user's screen, but does so without leaving the linking document. Thus, the linking party can incorporate the linked image into its own content. As a result, although the image in Arriba's Images Attributes page came directly from the originating web site and was not copied onto Arriba's server, the user would not realize that the image actually resided on another web site.

From July 1999 until sometime after August 2000, the results page contained thumbnails accompanied by two links: "Source" and "Details." The "Details" link produced a screen similar to the Images Attributes page but with a thumbnail rather than the full-sized image. Alternatively, by clicking on the "Source" link or the thumbnail from the results page, the site produced two new windows on top of the Arriba page. The window in the forefront contained solely the full-sized image. This window partially obscured another window, which displayed a reduced-size version of the image's originating web page. Part of the Arriba web page was visible underneath both of these new windows.[4]

In January 1999, Arriba's crawler visited web sites that contained Kelly's photographs. The crawler copied thirty-five of Kelly's images to the Arriba database. Kelly had never given permission to Arriba to copy his images and objected when he found out that Arriba was using them. Arriba deleted the thumbnails of images that came from Kelly's own web sites and placed those sites on a list of sites that it would not crawl in the future. Several months later, Arriba received Kelly's complaint of copyright infringement, which identified other images of his that came from third-party web sites. Arriba subsequently deleted those thumbnails and placed those third-party sites on a list of sites that it would not crawl in the future.

The district court granted summary judgment in favor of Arriba. Kelly's motion for partial summary judgment asserted that Arriba's use of the thumbnail images violated his display, reproduction, and distribution rights. Arriba cross-moved for summary judgment. For the purposes of the motion, Arriba conceded that Kelly established a prima facie case of infringement. However, it limited its concession to the violation of the display and reproduction rights *as to the thumbnail images*. Arriba then argued that its use of the thumbnail images was a fair use.

The district court did not limit its decision to the thumbnail images alone. The court granted summary judgment to Arriba, finding that its use of both the thumbnail images and the full-size images was fair. In doing so, the court broadened the scope of Kelly's original motion to include a claim for infringement of the full-size images. The court also broadened the scope of Arriba's concession to cover the prima facie case for both the thumbnail images and the full-size images. The court determined that two of the fair use factors weighed heavily in Arriba's favor. Specifically, the court found that the character and purpose of Arriba's use was significantly transformative and the use did not harm the market for or value of Kelly's works. Kelly now appeals this decision.

II.

We review a grant of summary judgment *de novo*. We also review the court's finding of fair use, which is a mixed question of law and fact, by this same standard. "In doing so, we must balance the nonexclusive factors set out in 17 U.S.C. § 107."

The district court's decision in this case involves two distinct actions by Arriba that warrant analysis. The first action consists of the reproduction of Kelly's images to create the thumbnails and the use of those thumbnails in Arriba's search engine. The second action involves the display of Kelly's larger images when the user clicks on the thumbnails. We conclude that, as to the first action, the district court

---

[4] Currently, when a user clicks on the thumbnail, a window of the home page of the image appears on top of the Arriba page. There is no window just containing the image.

correctly found that Arriba's use was fair. However, as to the second action, we conclude that the district court should not have reached the issue because neither party moved for summary judgment as to the full-size images and Arriba's response to Kelly's summary judgment motion did not concede the prima facie case for infringement as to those images.

A.

An owner of a copyright has the exclusive right to reproduce, distribute, and publicly display copies of the work. To establish a claim of copyright infringement by reproduction, the plaintiff must show ownership of the copyright and copying by the defendant. As to the thumbnails, Arriba conceded that Kelly established a prima facie case of infringement of Kelly's reproduction rights.

A claim of copyright infringement is subject to certain statutory exceptions, including the fair use exception. This exception "permits courts to avoid rigid application of the copyright statute when, on occasion, it would stifle the very creativity which that law is designed to foster."[11] The statute sets out four factors to consider in determining whether the use in a particular case is a fair use.[12] We must balance these factors in light of the objectives of copyright law, rather than view them as definitive or determinative tests. We now turn to the four fair use factors.

1. Purpose and character of the use.

The Supreme Court has rejected the proposition that a commercial use of the copyrighted material ends the inquiry under this factor.[14] Instead,

> [t]he central purpose of this investigation is to see . . . whether the new work merely supersede[s] the objects of the original creation, or instead adds something new, with a further purpose or different character, altering the first with new expression, meaning, or message; it asks, in other words, whether and to what extent the new work is transformative.[15]

The more transformative the new work, the less important the other factors, including commercialism, become.

There is no dispute that Arriba operates its web site for commercial purposes and that Kelly's images were part of Arriba's search engine database. As the district court found, while such use of Kelly's images was commercial, it was more incidental and less exploitative in nature than more traditional types of commercial use.[17] Arriba was neither using Kelly's images to directly promote its web site nor

---

[11] *Dr. Seuss Enters., L.P. v. Penguin Books USA, Inc.,* 109 F.3d 1394, 1399 (9th Cir.1997) (internal quotation marks omitted).

[12] The four factors are: (1) the purpose and character of the use, including whether such use is of a commercial nature or is for nonprofit educational purposes; (2) the nature of the copyrighted work; (3) the amount and substantiality of the portion used in relation to the copyrighted work as a whole; and (4) the effect of the use upon the potential market for or value of the copyrighted work. 17 U.S.C. § 107.

[14] *Campbell v. Acuff-Rose Music, Inc.,* 510 U.S. 569, 579 (1994).

[15] *Id.* . . .

[17] *See, e.g., A & M Records, Inc. v. Napster, Inc.,* 239 F.3d 1004, 1015 (9th Cir.2001)

trying to profit by selling Kelly's images. Instead, Kelly's images were among thousands of images in Arriba's search engine database. Because the use of Kelly's images was not highly exploitative, the commercial nature of the use weighs only slightly against a finding of fair use.

The second part of the inquiry as to this factor involves the transformative nature of the use. We must determine if Arriba's use of the images merely superseded the object of the originals or instead added a further purpose or different character. We find that Arriba's use of Kelly's images for its thumbnails was transformative.

Although Arriba made exact replications of Kelly's images, the thumbnails were much smaller, lower-resolution images that served an entirely different function than Kelly's original images. Kelly's images are artistic works intended to inform and to engage the viewer in an aesthetic experience. His images are used to portray scenes from the American West in an aesthetic manner. Arriba's use of Kelly's images in the thumbnails is unrelated to any aesthetic purpose. Arriba's search engine functions as a tool to help index and improve access to images on the internet and their related web sites. In fact, users are unlikely to enlarge the thumbnails and use them for artistic purposes because the thumbnails are of much lower-resolution than the originals; any enlargement results in a significant loss of clarity of the image, making them inappropriate as display material.

Kelly asserts that because Arriba reproduced his exact images and added nothing to them, Arriba's use cannot be transformative. Courts have been reluctant to find fair use when an original work is merely retransmitted in a different medium.[19] Those cases are inapposite, however, because the resulting use of the copyrighted work in those cases was the same as the original use. For instance, reproducing music CDs in computer MP3 format does not change the fact that both formats are used for entertainment purposes. Likewise, reproducing news footage into a different format does not change the ultimate purpose of informing the public about current affairs.

Even in *Infinity Broadcast Corp. v. Kirkwood*, where the retransmission of radio broadcasts over telephone lines was for the purpose of allowing advertisers and radio stations to check on the broadcast of commercials or on-air talent, there was nothing preventing listeners from subscribing to the service for entertainment purposes. Even though the intended purpose of the retransmission may have been different from the purpose of the original transmission, the result was that people

---

("[C]ommercial use is demonstrated by a showing that repeated and exploitative unauthorized copies of copyrighted works were made to save the expense of purchasing authorized copies.").

[19] *See Infinity Broad. Corp. v. Kirkwood,* 150 F.3d 104, 108 (2d Cir.1998) (concluding that retransmission of radio broadcast over telephone lines is not transformative); *UMG Recordings, Inc. v. MP3.com, Inc.,* 92 F.Supp.2d 349, 351 (S.D.N.Y. 2000) (finding that reproduction of audio CD into computer MP3 format does not transform the work); *Los Angeles News Serv.,* 149 F.3d at 993 (finding that reproducing news footage with-out editing the footage "was not very transformative").

could use both types of transmissions for the same purpose.

This case involves more than merely a retransmission of Kelly's images in a different medium. Arriba's use of the images serves a different function than Kelly's use—improving access to information on the internet versus artistic expression. Furthermore, it would be unlikely that anyone would use Arriba's thumbnails for illustrative or aesthetic purposes because enlarging them sacrifices their clarity. Because Arriba's use is not superseding Kelly's use but, rather, has created a different purpose for the images, Arriba's use is transformative.

Comparing this case to two recent cases in the Ninth and First Circuits reemphasizes the functionality distinction. In *Worldwide Church of God v. Philadelphia Church of God, Inc.*,[21] we held that copying a religious book to create a new book for use by a different church was not transformative. The second church's use of the book was merely to make use of the same book for another church audience. The court noted that "where the use is for the same intrinsic purpose as [the copyright holder's] . . . such use seriously weakens a claimed fair use."[23]

On the other hand, in *Núñez v. Caribbean International News Corp.*,[24] the First Circuit found that copying a photograph that was intended to be used in a modeling portfolio and using it instead in a news article was a transformative use. By putting a copy of the photograph in the newspaper, the work was transformed into news, creating a new meaning or purpose for the work. The use of Kelly's images in Arriba's search engine is more analogous to the situation in *Núñez* because Arriba has created a new purpose for the images and is not simply superseding Kelly's purpose.

The Copyright Act was intended to promote creativity, thereby benefiting the artist and the public alike. To preserve the potential future use of artistic works for purposes of teaching, research, criticism, and news reporting, Congress created the fair use exception. Arriba's use of Kelly's images promotes the goals of the Copyright Act and the fair use exception. The thumbnails do not stifle artistic creativity because they are not used for illustrative or artistic purposes and there-fore do not supplant the need for the originals. In addition, they benefit the public by enhancing information-gathering techniques on the internet.

In *Sony Computer Entertainment America, Inc. v. Bleem*,[27] we held that when Bleem copied "screen shots" from Sony computer games and used them in its own advertising, it was a fair use. In finding that the first factor weighed in favor of Bleem, we noted that "comparative advertising redounds greatly to the purchasing public's benefit with very little corresponding loss to the integrity of Sony's copyrighted material."[29] Similarly, this first factor weighs in favor of Arriba due to the public benefit of the search engine and the minimal loss of integrity to Kelly's im-

---

[21] 227 F.3d 1110 (9th Cir.2000).

[23] *Id.*

[24] 235 F.3d 18 (1st Cir.2000).

[27] 214 F.3d 1022 (9th Cir.2000).

[29] *Id.* at 1027.

ages.

2. Nature of the copyrighted work.

"Works that are creative in nature are closer to the core of intended copyright protection than are more fact-based works."[30] Photographs that are meant to be viewed by the public for informative and aesthetic purposes, such as Kelly's, are generally creative in nature. The fact that a work is published or unpublished also is a critical element of its nature. Published works are more likely to qualify as fair use because the first appearance of the artist's expression has already occurred. Kelly's images appeared on the internet before Arriba used them in its search image. When considering both of these elements, we find that this factor weighs only slightly in favor of Kelly.

3. Amount and substantiality of portion used.

"While wholesale copying does not preclude fair use per se, copying an entire work militates against a finding of fair use."[33] However, the extent of permissible copying varies with the purpose and character of the use. If the secondary user only copies as much as is necessary for his or her intended use, then this factor will not weigh against him or her.

This factor neither weighs for nor against either party because, although Arriba did copy each of Kelly's images as a whole, it was reasonable to do so in light of Arriba's use of the images. It was necessary for Arriba to copy the entire image to allow users to recognize the image and decide whether to pursue more information about the image or the originating web site. If Arriba only copied part of the image, it would be more difficult to identify it, thereby reducing the usefulness of the visual search engine.

4. Effect of the use upon the potential market for or value of the copyrighted work.

This last factor requires courts to consider "not only the extent of market harm caused by the particular actions of the alleged infringer, but also 'whether unrestricted and widespread conduct of the sort engaged in by the defendant . . . would result in a substantially adverse impact on the potential market for the original."[35] A transformative work is less likely to have an adverse impact on the market of the original than a work that merely supersedes the copyrighted work.

Kelly's images are related to several potential markets. One purpose of the photographs is to attract internet users to his web site, where he sells advertising space as well as books and travel packages. In addition, Kelly could sell or license his photographs to other web sites or to a stock photo database, which then could offer the images to its customers.

Arriba's use of Kelly's images in its thumbnails does not harm the market for Kelly's images or the value of his images. By showing the thumbnails on its results

---

[30] *A & M Records,* 239 F.3d at 1016 (citing *Campbell,* 510 U.S. at 586).

[33] *Worldwide Church of God,* 227 F.3d at 1118.

[35] *Campbell,* 510 U.S. at 590 (quoting 3 M. Nimmer & D. Nimmer, *Nimmer on Copyright* § 13.05[A][4] (1993)) (ellipses in original).

page when users entered terms related to Kelly's images, the search engine would guide users to Kelly's web site rather than away from it. Even if users were more interested in the image itself rather than the information on the web page, they would still have to go to Kelly's site to see the full-sized image. The thumbnails would not be a substitute for the full-sized images because the thumbnails lose their clarity when enlarged. If a user wanted to view or download a quality image, he or she would have to visit Kelly's web site.[37] This would hold true whether the thumbnails are solely in Arriba's database or are more widespread and found in other search engine databases.

Arriba's use of Kelly's images also would not harm Kelly's ability to sell or license his full-sized images. Arriba does not sell or license its thumbnails to other parties. Anyone who downloaded the thumbnails would not be successful selling full-sized images enlarged from the thumbnails because of the low resolution of the thumbnails. There would be no way to view, create, or sell a clear, full-sized image without going to Kelly's web sites. Therefore, Arriba's creation and use of the thumbnails does not harm the market for or value of Kelly's images. This factor weighs in favor of Arriba.

Having considered the four fair use factors and found that two weigh in favor of Arriba, one is neutral, and one weighs slightly in favor of Kelly, we conclude that Arriba's use of Kelly's images as thumbnails in its search engine is a fair use.

B.

As mentioned above, the district court granted summary judgment to Arriba as to the full-size images as well. However, because the court broadened the scope of both the parties' motions for partial summary judgment and Arriba's concession on the prima facie case, we must reverse this portion of the court's opinion.

With limited exceptions that do not apply here, a district court may not grant summary judgment on a claim when the party has not requested it. The parties did not move for summary judgment as to copyright infringement of the full-size images. Further, Arriba had no opportunity to contest the prima facie case for infringement as to the full-size images. Accordingly, we reverse this portion of the district court's opinion and remand for further proceedings.

CONCLUSION

We hold that Arriba's reproduction of Kelly's images for use as thumbnails in Arriba's search engine is a fair use under the Copyright Act. However, we hold that the district court should not have reached whether Arriba's display of Kelly's full-sized images is a fair use because the parties never moved for summary judg-

---

[37] We do not suggest that the inferior display quality of a reproduction is in any way dispositive or will always assist an alleged infringer in demonstrating fair use. In this case, however, it is extremely unlikely that users would download thumbnails for display purposes, as the quality full-size versions are easily accessible from Kelly's web sites.

In addition, we note that in the unique context of photographic images, the quality of the reproduction may matter more than in other fields of creative endeavor. The appearance of photographic images accounts for virtually their entire aesthetic value

ment on this claim and Arriba never conceded the prima facie case as to the full-size images. The district court's opinion is affirmed as to the thumbnails and reversed as to the display of the full-sized images. We remand for further proceedings consistent with this opinion.

AFFIRMED in part, REVERSED in part, and REMANDED.

EXTENSIONS

Search engines and the public display right. In February 2002, the Ninth Circuit issued its first opinion in this case, reported at 280 F.3d 934, in which it did address the claim of infringement as to the full-size images. The court ruled that Arriba's activities constituted unauthorized public display of Kelly's photos and did not qualify as fair use. Here are excerpts from the court's analysis of the public display issue (but not the fair use question) in its original opinion, which pursuant to a petition for rehearing from Arriba was withdrawn and replaced by the 2003 opinion above:

> The second part of our analysis concerns Arriba's inline linking to and framing of Kelly's full-sized images. This use of Kelly's images does not entail copying them but, rather, importing them directly from Kelly's web site. Therefore, it cannot be copyright infringement based on the reproduction of copyrighted works as in the previous discussion. Instead, this use of Kelly's images infringes upon Kelly's exclusive right to "display the copyrighted work publicly."

> *1. Public display right.*

> In order for Kelly to prevail, Arriba must have displayed Kelly's work without his permission and made that display available to the public. The Copyright Act defines "display" as showing a copy of a work. . . . By inline linking and framing Kelly's images, Arriba is showing Kelly's original works without his permission.

> The legislative history goes on to state that " 'display' would include the projection of an image on a screen or other surface by any method, the transmission of an image by electronic or other means, and the showing of an image on a cathode ray tube, or similar viewing apparatus connected with any sort of information storage and retrieval system."[40] This language indicates that showing Kelly's images on a computer screen would constitute a display.

> The Act's definition of the term "publicly" encompasses a transmission of a display of a work to the public "by means of any device or process, whether the members of the public capable of receiving the performance or display receive it in the same place or in separate places and at the same time or at different times." A display is public even if there is no proof that any of the potential recipients was operating his receiving apparatus at the time of the transmission. By making Kelly's images available on its web site, Arriba is allowing public access to those images. The ability to view those images is unrestricted to anyone with a computer and internet access.

> The legislative history emphasizes the broad nature of the display right, stating that "[e]ach and every method by which the images or sounds comprising a performance or display are picked up and conveyed is a 'transmission,' and if the transmission reaches the public in [any] form, the case comes within the

---

[40] [H.R. REP. No. 94-1476, at 64 (1976).]

scope of [the public performance and display rights] of section 106."[43] Looking strictly at the language of the Act and its legislative history, it appears that when Arriba imports Kelly's images into its own web page, Arriba is infringing upon Kelly's public display right. The limited case law in this area supports this conclusion.

[The court noted that "[n]o cases have addressed the issue of whether inline linking or framing violates a copyright owner's public display rights," but it discussed other cases that it found relevant to the question.]

Although Arriba does not download Kelly's images to its own server but, rather, imports them directly from other web sites, . . . [b]y allowing the public to view Kelly's copyrighted works while visiting Arriba's web site, Arriba created a public display of Kelly's works. . . .

[Previous cases also] highlighted the fact that the defendants took an active role in creating the display of the copyrighted images. The reason for this emphasis is that several other cases held that operators of bulletin board systems and internet access providers were not liable for copyright infringement.[54] These cases distinguished direct infringement from contributory infringement and held that where the defendants did not take any affirmative action that resulted in copying copyrighted works, but only maintained a system that acted as a passive conduit for third parties' copies, they were not liable for direct infringement. . . .

. . . Arriba is directly liable for infringement. Arriba actively participated in displaying Kelly's images by trolling the web, finding Kelly's images, and then having its program inline link and frame those images within its own web site. Without this program, users would not have been able to view Kelly's images within the context of Arriba's site. Arriba acted as more than a passive conduit of the images by establishing a direct link to the copyrighted images. Therefore, Arriba is liable for publicly displaying Kelly's copyrighted images without his permission.

To the extent that a public display occurred when one of Kelly's photographs was transmitted to an Arriba user as part of an Arriba page, who was making that transmission? Is it clear that the display of Kelly's images is attributable to Arriba Soft? As the court indicates, the files constituting the full-sized images never resided on or even passed through Arriba Soft's computer servers. Arriba Soft's website contained only links pointing to the URLs of the images where they resided on Kelly's site. When a user clicked on such a link, the user's browser sent a request to Kelly's computer, which Kelly's server interpreted as: "Please send me the image file that you are storing at the address www.goldrush1849.com/images/coloma.jpg." Kelly's server was configured so that it automatically granted such requests, by transmitting the requested image to the user, whose browser then displayed it graphically. (It is easy to configure a server otherwise. For example, many servers are configured so that certain pages are served *only* to requesters who are linking from a page within the site.) Thus the user's browser and Kelly's server communicated directly with each other; Arriba Soft was not an intermediary.

This is the same sequence of events that occurs whenever a user clicks on a link, and is

---

[43] [H.R. Rep. No. 94-1476, at 64 (1976).]

[54] *See e.g. Religious Tech. Ctr. v. Netcom On-Line Communication Servs., Inc.,* 907 F.Supp. 1361, 1372-73 (N.D.Cal.1995*)* (holding that operator of a computer bulletin board system that forwarded messages from subscribers to other subscribers was not liable for displaying copyrighted works because it took no role in controlling the content of the information but only acted as passive conduit of the information) . . . .

served a page, image, or other resource from the linked-to site. If Arriba Soft is responsible for the display that occurs when a user clicks a link on its site that points to an image file on another site, it would seem to follow that every other website owner is equally responsible for displaying material residing on other sites simply by virtue of pointing a link at that material. If the material is copyrighted, and the copyright owner does not authorize the display, then the owner of the website containing the link would seem to be engaging in an infringing display every time a user clicks on the link. Can this be a proper application of the Copyright Act? The previous paragraph above contains a URL pointing to an image on Kelly's website; does this constitute an infringing display by the author or publisher of this book? Would it make any difference if this were an electronic book, so that the URL were a working hyperlink? Compare *Ticketmaster Corp. v. Tickets.Com, Inc.*, 54 U.S.P.Q.2d 1344 (C.D.Cal.2000), *superseded and withdrawn*, 2000 Copr.L.Dec. ¶ 28,146 (C.D.Cal.2000), discussed in Note 2 of the Extensions following the next principal excerpt.

QUESTIONS FOR DISCUSSION

Google News. Visit the Google News page at news.google.com/nwshp?hl=en. What claims might copyright owners have against Google based on its activities at this page? What defenses might Google have? In March 2005, Agence France-Presse (AFP), the French news agency, sued Google, claiming that the Google News page infringed on AFP's copyrights. (A copy of the complaint is available at law.marquette.edu/goldman/afpgooglecomplaint.pdf.)

C. DATA EXTRACTION AND AGGREGATION

Ticketmaster Corp. v. Tickets.Com, Inc.
2003 Copr.L.Dec. ¶ 28,607 (C.D.Cal.2003).

■ HARRY L. HUPP, SENIOR DISTRICT JUDGE.

This motion by defendant Tickets.com, Inc. (hereafter TX) for summary judgment on plaintiffs Ticketmaster Corporation and Ticket Online–CitySearch, Inc. (hereafter collectively TM), intellectual property issues is denied as to the contract claim of TM and granted as to the copyright and trespass to chattels claims, which are dismissed by this minute order.

At this point in the case, both parties have narrowed their claims. TM, the original plaintiff, has narrowed its intellectual property claims to a contract theory, a copyright theory, and a trespass to chattels theory. The court finds triable issues of fact on the contract theory and finds no triable issues of fact and grants summary judgment on the copyright and trespass to chattels claims.

Many of the factual items are not contested, although the legal result of applying the law to the uncontested facts is heavily contested. Among the uncontested facts are the following: Both TM and TX are in the business of selling tickets to all kinds of "events" (sports, concerts, plays, etc.) to the public. They are in heavy competition with one another, but operate in distinctive ways. TM is the largest company in the industry. It sells tickets by the four methods of ticket selling — venue box office, retail outlets, by telephone, and over the internet. Telephone and internet sales require the customer to establish credit with the ticket seller (usually by credit card). Internet sales have been the fastest growing segment of the industry. TX at the time of the events considered in this motion was primarily (but not exclusively) an internet seller. Both TM and TX maintain a web page reachable by anyone with an internet connection. Each of their web pages has many subsidiary (or interior) web pages which describe one event each and provide such basic information as to location, date, time, description of the event, and ticket prices. The TM interior web pages each have a separate electronic address or Uniform Resource Locator ("URL") which, if possessed by the internet user, allows the user to reach the web page for any particular event by by-passing the "home" web page and proceeding past the index to reach the interior web page for the event in question. The TM interior web pages provide telephone numbers for customers or allow the customer to order tickets to the event by interactive computer use. A charge is made for the TM service.

TM principally does business by exclusive contracts with the event providers or their producers, and its web pages only list the events for which TM is the exclusive ticket seller. TX also sells tickets to a number of events for which it is the ticket seller. At one point, its web pages attempted to list all events for which tickets were available whether or not TX sold the tickets. Its interior web pages also listed the event, the date, time, ticket prices, and provided for internet purchase if TX could sell the tickets. When TX could not sell the tickets, it listed ticket brokers who sold at premium prices. In early 2000, TX discontinued this practice of listing events with tickets sold by other ticket brokers. Until early 2000, in situations where TM was the only source of tickets, TX provided a "deep link" by which the customer would be transferred to the interior web page of TM's web site, where the customer could purchase the ticket from TM. This process of "deep linking" is the subject of TM's complaint in this action, of which there is now left the contract, copyright, and trespass theories.

Starting in 1998 and continuing to July 2001, when it stopped the practice, TX employed an electronic program called a "spider" or "crawler" to review the internal web pages (available to the public) of TM. The "spider" "crawled" through the internal web pages to TM and electronically extracted the electronic information from which the web page is shown on the user's computer. The spider temporarily loaded this electronic information into the Random Access Memory ("RAM") of TX's computers for a period of from 10-15 seconds. TX then extracted the factual information (event, date, time, tickets prices, and URL) and discarded the rest (which consisted of TM identification, logos, ads, and other information which TX did not intend to use; much of this discarded material was protected by copyright). The factual information was then organized in the TX format to be displayed on the TX internal web page. The TX internal web page carried no TM identification and had only the factual information about the event on it which was taken from TM's interior web page but rearranged in TX format plus any information or advertisement added by TX. From March 1998, to early 2000, the TX user was provided the deep linking option described above to go directly from the TX web site to the relevant TM interior web page. This option stopped (or was stopped by TM) in early 2000. For an unknown period afterward, the TX customer was given the option of linking to the TM home page, from which the customer

could work his way to the interior web page in which he was interested. (The record does not reveal whether this practice still exists or whether TM objects to it.)
Thus, the intellectual property issues in this case appear to be limited to events
which occurred between November 1998, when spidering started, and July 2001,
when it stopped. The "deep linking" aspect of the case is relevant only from
March 1998, to early 2000, when it stopped.

The contract aspect of the case derives from a notice placed on the home page
of the TM web site which states that anyone going beyond that point into the interior web pages of the web site accepts certain conditions, which include, relevant
to this case, that all information obtained from the website is for the personal use of
the user and may not be used for commercial purposes. [The court ruled that the
evidence raised a genuine issue of fact as to whether an enforceable contract had
been formed by TX using TM's Web site with knowledge of TM's asserted conditions, so that TX was not entitled to summary judgment on TM's contract claim.
However, the court rejected TM's claim that TX's activities constituted trespass to
chattels.]

The copyright issues are more difficult. They divide into three issues. The first
is whether the momentary resting in the TX computers of all of the electronic signals which are used to form the video representation to the viewer of the interior
web pages of the TX computer constitutes actionable copyright infringement. The
second is whether the URLs, which were copied and used by TX, contain copyrightable material. The third is whether TX's deep-linking caused the unauthorized
public display of TM event pages. In examining these questions, we must keep in
mind a prime theorem of copyright law — facts, as such, are not subject to copyright
protection. What is subject to copyright protection is the manner or mode of expression of those facts. Thus, addresses and telephone numbers contained in a directory do not have copyright protection despite the fact that time, money, and
effort went into compiling the information. Similarly, in this case, the existence of
the event, its date and time, and its ticket prices, are not subject to copyright. Anyone is free to print (or show on the internet) such information. Thus, if TX had sat
down a secretary at the computer screen with instructions manually to go through
TM's web sites and pick out and write down purely factual information about the
events, and then feed it into the TX web pages (using the TX distinctive format
only), no one could complain. The objection is that the same thing was done with
an electronic program. However, the difference is that the spider picks up all of the
electronic symbols which, if it had been put on a monitor with the right software,
would duplicate the TM web page. However, this is not the way it was done. The
spider picks up the electronic symbols and loads them momentarily (for 10 to 15
seconds) into the RAM of the TX computers, where a program picks up the factual
data (not protected), places same into the TX format for its web pages, and immediately discards the balance, which may consist of TM logos, TM advertisements,
TM format for presentation of the material, and other material which is copyrightable. Thus, the actual copying (if it can be called that) is momentary while the non-
protected material, all open to the public, is extracted. Is this momentary resting of
the electronic symbols from which a TM web page could be (but is not) con-

structed fair use where the purpose is to obtain nonprotected facts? The court thinks the answer is "yes". There is not much law in point. However, there are two Ninth Circuit cases which shed light on the problem. They are *Sony Computer Entm't, Inc. v. Connectix Corp.* (9Cir'00) 203 F3d 596 and *Sega Enters. v. Accolade, Inc.* (9Cir'92) 977 F2d 1510. In each of these cases, the alleged infringer attempted to get at non-protected source code by reverse engineering of the plaintiff's copyrighted software. In doing so, the necessary method was to copy the software and work backwards to derive the unprotected source code. The copied software was then destroyed. In each case, this was held to be fair use since it was necessary to temporarily copy the software to obtain the non-protected material. There may be a difference with this case, however; at least TM claims so. It asserts in its points and authorities that taking the temporary copy in this case was not the only way to obtain the unprotected information, and that TX was able to, and in actuality did purchase such information from certain third-parties. Both *Sony* and *Sega* stated that the fair use was justified because reverse engineering (including taking a temporary copy) was the only way the unprotected information could be obtained. Although this court recognizes that the holdings of *Sony* and *Sega* were limited to the specific context of "disassembling" copyrighted object code in order to access unprotected elements contained in the source code, this court believes that the "fair use" doctrine can be applied to the current facts.

Taking the temporary copy of the electronic information for the limited purpose of extracting unprotected public facts leads to the conclusion that the temporary use of the electronic signals was "fair use" and not actionable. In determining whether a challenged use of copyrighted material is fair, a court must keep in mind the public policy underlying the Copyright Act: to secure a fair return for an author's creative labor and to stimulate artistic creativity for the general good. This court sees no public policy that would be served by restricting TX from using spiders to temporarily download TM's event pages in order to acquire the unprotected, publicly available factual event information. The rest of the event page information (which consisted of TM identification, logos, ads, and other information) was discarded and not used by TX and is not exposed to the public by TX. In temporarily downloading TM's event pages to its RAM through the use of spiders, TX was not exploiting TM'S creative labors in any way: its spiders gathered copyrightable and non-copyrightable information alike but then immediately discarded the copyrighted material. It is unlikely that the spiders could have been programmed to take only the factual information from the TM web pages without initially downloading the entire page.

Consideration of the fair use factors listed in 17 USC § 106 supports this result. First, TX operates its site for commercial purposes, and this fact tends to weigh against a finding of fair use. *Campbell v. Acuff-Rose Music* ('94), 510 U.S. 569 at 585. TX's use of the data gathered from TM's event pages was only slightly transformative. As for the second factor, the nature of the copyrighted work, the copying that occurred when spiders download the event page, access the source code for each page, and extract the factual data embedded in the code, is analogous to the process of copying that the Sony court condoned (however, the Court recognizes that the fair use holding from that decision does not fit perfectly onto the facts at hand). Third, because TX's final product—the TX web site—did not contain any infringing material, the "amount and substantiality of the portion used" is of little weight. *Connectix* (9Cir'00) 203F3d at 606. The fourth factor (the effect on the market value of the copyrighted work) is, of course nil, and weighs towards finding fair use. TM's arguments and evidence regarding loss of advertising revenue . . . are not persuasive.

The second copyright problem is whether the URLs (Uniform Resource Locator) are subject to copyright protection. The URLs are copied by TX and, while TX was deep hyper-linking to TM interior web pages, were used by TX to allow the deep-linking (by providing the electronic address of the particular relevant TM interior web page). This electronic address is kept in TX's computer (not provided to the customer) but was used to connect the customer to the TM interior web page when the customer pushed the button to be transferred to the web page of the broker who sells the tickets. In fact, anyone who uses the TM interior web page—TM customer or not—uses the URL to get there, although sometimes through another computer which also has the URL. TM contends that, although the URLs are strictly functional, they are entitled to copyright protection because there are several ways to write the URL, and, thus, original authorship is used. The court disagrees. A URL is simply an address, open to the public, like the street address of a building, which, if known, can enable the user to reach the building. There is nothing sufficiently original to make the URL a copyrightable item, especially the way it is used. There appear to be no cases holding the URLs to be subject to copyright. On principle, they should not be.

The third copyright problem is whether TX's deep linking caused the unauthorized public display of TM event pages in violation of TM's exclusive rights of reproduction and display under 17 U.S.C. § 106. The Ninth Circuit in *Kelly v. Arriba Soft Corp.* (9Cir'02) 280 F3d 934, recognized that inline linking and framing of full-sized images of plaintiff's copyrighted photographs within the defendant's web site violated the plaintiff's public display rights. In that case, defendant's web site contained links to plaintiff's photographs (which were on plaintiff's publicly available website). Users were able to view plaintiff's photographs within the context of defendant's site: Plaintiff's images were "framed" by the defendant's window, and were thus surrounded by defendant web page's text and advertising. In one short paragraph in a declaration offered on the preliminary injunction motion, TM alleges that when a user was deep-linked from the TX site to a TM event page, a smaller window was opened. The smaller window was described as containing a page from the TM web site which was "framed" by the larger window. At the time of the preliminary injunction motion, TX stated that whether "framing" occurs or not depends on the settings on the user's computer, over which TX has no control. Thus, framing occurred on some occasions but not on others. However, TX says that it "did not try to disguise a sale by use of frames occurring on the Tickets.com website." TX further states that when users were linked to TM web pages, the TM event pages were clearly identified as belonging to TM.

However, even if the TM interior web site page was "framed" within the TX web page, this case is distinguishable from *Kelly*. In *Kelly*, the defendant's site would display a variety of "thumbnail" images as a result of the user's search. By clicking on the desired thumbnail image, a user could view the "Images Attributes" page, which displayed the original full-size image, a description of its dimensions, a link to the originating web site, and defendant's banner and advertising. The full-size image was not technically located on defendant's web site, but was taken directly from the originating web site. However, only the image itself, and not any other part of the originating web site, was displayed on the "Images Attributes" page. The Ninth Circuit determined that by importing plaintiff's images into its own web page, and by showing them in the context of its own site, defendant infringed upon plaintiff's exclusive public display right.

In this case, a user on the TX site was taken directly to the originating TM site, containing all the elements of that particular TM event page. Each TM event page clearly identified itself as belonging to TM. Moreover, the link on the TX site to the TM event page contained the following notice: *"Buy this ticket from another online ticketing company. Click here to buy tickets.* These tickets are sold by another ticketing company. Although we can't sell them to you, the link above will take you directly to the other company's web site where you can purchase them." (2d Am. Compl. Ex. I) (emphasis in original) Even if the TM site may have been displayed as a smaller window that was literally "framed" by the larger TX window, it is not clear that, as matter of law, the linking to TX event pages would constitute a showing or public display in violation of 17 U.S.C. § 106(5). Accordingly, summary judgment is granted on the copyright claims of TM and it is eliminated from this action.

EXTENSIONS

1. *Copyright and facts.* On the lack of copyright protection in factual information, *see* the *Feist* case, excerpted in Chapter 8, Part I, *infra*.

2. *Linking revisited.* In an earlier decision in the *Tickets.com* litigation, the judge addressed the basic question of whether Tickets.com's linking to Ticketmaster raised copyright issues:

> [H]yperlinking does not itself involve a violation of the Copyright Act . . . since no copying is involved, the customer is automatically transferred to the particular genuine web page of the original author. There is no deception in what is happening. This is analogous to using a library's card index to get reference to particular items, albeit faster and more efficiently.

Ticketmaster Corp v. Tickets.com, Inc., 54 U.S.P.Q.2d 1344 (C.D.Cal.2000).

3. *Similar decision.* At least one other district court has taken a similar view that extracting factual data from a copyrighted Web site constitutes fair use. *Nautical Solutions Marketing, Inc. v. Boats.com*, 2004 Copr.L.Dec. ¶ 28,815 (M.D.Fla.2004).

QUESTIONS FOR DISCUSSION

Machine versus human extraction. Is the *Tickets.com* court correct to say that no one could complain if a human Tickets.com employee viewed each of Ticketmaster's Web pages on a computer screen and wrote down (or entered into a computer file) the unprotected factual information? Would Ticketmaster have any copyright claim against such activity? Would Tickets.com's fair use defense be any different in that context?

IV. DIGITAL MUSIC

A. FUNDAMENTALS OF DIGITAL MUSIC COPYRIGHT

R. Anthony Reese, *Copyright and Internet Music Transmissions: Existing Law, Major Controversies, Possible Solutions*
55 U. MIAMI L. REV. 237 (2001).

. . .

I. COPYRIGHT LAW RELEVANT TO INTERNET MUSIC TRANSMISSIONS

A. *Musical Works and Sound Recordings: Two Separate Copyrights*

Every musical recording involves two separate copyrightable works: a "musical work" and a "sound recording." A musical work is the sequence of notes, and often words, that a songwriter or composer creates. For example, when Cole Porter sat down at a piano and wrote the lyrics and music to the song "Ev'ry Time We Say Goodbye," he created a musical work protectible by copyright law. That work can be recorded in many ways, including in printed sheet music that a musician can use to play or sing the song. A sound recording, in contrast, is a fixation of sounds, including a fixation of a performance of someone playing and singing a musical work. For instance, when Ella Fitzgerald and her accompanists went into a studio in the 1950s and performed Cole Porter's song "Ev'ry Time We Say Goodbye," the recording of that performance resulted in a sound recording. When Annie Lennox recorded the same song in the 1990s, her recorded performance was another sound recording of Porter's musical work. Transmitting recorded musical performances over the Internet involves transmitting both the sound recording and the musical work embodied in the recording.[10] U.S. copyright law grants different rights and limitations to musical works and sound recordings, increasing the complexity of the copyright implications of such transmissions, particularly when the copyright rights in those works are owned or administered by different parties.

B. *The Copyright Owners' Relevant Rights: Reproduction and Public Performance*

1. THE REPRODUCTION RIGHT

Copyright law grants copyright owners the right to control certain uses of their works, including the exclusive rights to reproduce and to publicly perform copyrighted works. These are the rights most relevant to Internet music transmissions. The right to reproduce a copyrighted work is the oldest right of the copyright owner and applies to both musical works and sound recordings. Copyright owners of musical works and sound recordings have the exclusive right to reproduce their works in "phonorecords," which are "material objects in which sounds . . . are

---

[10] Transmitting live musical performances would generally involve only the copyright in the musical work, since a live, unfixed performance is not protected by copyright, which extends only to fixed works. Unauthorized transmission of a live performance, however, may violate 17 U.S.C. § 1101(a)(2) (1998).

fixed . . . and from which the sounds can be perceived, reproduced, or otherwise communicated, either directly or with the aid of a machine or device."[13] A phonorecord can be a vinyl LP, a cassette tape, a compact disc, or a hard drive or floppy diskette containing an MP3 file. These are all tangible objects in which sounds are fixed and from which, given the proper hardware (and, in some cases, software), those sounds can be made audible. The reproduction right generally encompasses making any phonorecord of a copyrighted work.

Any single phonorecord of music is a phonorecord of both the sound recording fixed in the phonorecord and any musical work performed in that sound recording. For example, a compact disc of Ella Fitzgerald's album *The Cole Porter Songbook* constitutes a phonorecord of Cole Porter's musical work "Ev'ry Time We Say Goodbye" and a phonorecord of Ella Fitzgerald's sound recording of that musical work. Someone who makes a tape of that compact disc therefore produces a new phonorecord, the tape, of both the musical work and the sound recording. The same is true of someone who "rips" an MP3 version of the song from a compact disc, or who downloads such a version from a Web site and stores the MP3 file on a hard drive or other storage medium.

2. LIMITATIONS ON THE REPRODUCTION RIGHT IN MUSICAL WORKS: THE COMPULSORY MECHANICAL LICENSE AND DIGITAL PHONORECORD DELIVERIES

The "compulsory mechanical license" limits the copyright owner's exclusive right to make phonorecords of most musical works.[15] Once the owner allows someone to make and sell phonorecords of a musical work, anyone else can make his or her own phonorecords of that work. This requires compliance with certain procedural requirements and paying a fee established by the Copyright Office.[16] This license essentially allows the making of so-called "cover" recordings, where a performer records a song that another performer previously recorded. As long as the compulsory license requirements are complied with, one can go into a recording studio and record, for example, a performance of the song "Yesterday" as it was written by John Lennon and Paul McCartney and sell compact discs of the recording without the permission of the copyright owner of that musical work. In fact, most performers who make cover recordings do not actually get a compulsory license from the Copyright Office. Instead, they usually obtain a license from the Harry Fox Agency, which acts as licensing agent for the U.S. copyright owners (usually music publishing companies) of most musical works.

The compulsory mechanical license grants reproduction and distribution rights only for musical works, not sound recordings. The license would not allow one to record and sell compact discs of the Beatles' original recording of "Yesterday" (in-

---

[13] *Id.* § 101 ("phonorecords"). Musical work copyright owners also have the exclusive right to reproduce their works in copies, such as sheet music. *See id.* ("copies").

[15] 17 U.S.C. § 115 (1998). The compulsory license extends to "nondramatic" musical works. *Id.*

[16] The current rate is usually 7.55 cents for each phonorecord. For the full schedule of rates, *see* 37 C.F.R. §§ 255.2, 255.3 (1999). For an album containing several copyrighted musical works, the royalty would be payable for each phonorecord of each work.

stead of recording and selling compact discs of one's own performance of the song). Every compact disc made would be a phonorecord of both the Lennon and McCartney musical work "Yesterday" and of the Beatles' sound recording of "Yesterday." The compulsory license confers only a reproduction privilege in the *musical work*. In order to make the compact discs, one would need permission from the copyright owner of the Beatles' sound recording, who would be free to refuse permission or to charge any price for that permission.[19] The compulsory mechanical license therefore primarily assists recording artists and record companies who want to make and sell their own recordings of songs by other songwriters.

In 1995, Congress amended the compulsory mechanical license to allow reproducing and distributing musical works by means of "digital phonorecord delivery" (hereinafter "DPD"). A DPD is a digital transmission of a sound recording that results in a "specifically identifiable reproduction by or for any transmission recipient of a phonorecord."[20] For example, if one connects to a Web site such as MP3.com or Emusic.com and downloads an MP3 file of the song "Yesterday," the Web site digitally transmits a sound recording of a performance of "Yesterday." At the end of the transmission that MP3 file is stored on that individual's hard drive—a phonorecord. Thus, the Web site has made a digital phonorecord delivery. If the site has obtained a compulsory mechanical license for the composition "Yesterday" and pays the specified royalty rate, then its transmission will not infringe the composition's copyright. The royalty rate, currently identical to the rate for making and selling a physical compact disc or cassette, is set every two years by a two-step process that encourages voluntary, industry-wide negotiations to establish rates to be adopted by the Copyright Office. If negotiations fail, any interested party can petition the Copyright Office to hold an arbitration proceeding to set the fees. The compulsory license only confers the right to make DPDs of the musical work, not any particular sound recording. If a little-known band tries to drum up interest in its music by allowing people to download its cover version of "Yesterday" from its Web site, the band itself will likely own the copyright in the sound recording of its performance. Therefore, the band will have the right to digitally deliver phonorecords of the sound recording, in addition to the right to digitally deliver phonorecords of the Lennon and McCartney musical work given by the compulsory mechanical license. If a Web site allows users to download the Beatles' recording of "Yesterday," then the Web site will need the permission of the owner of the copyright in that sound recording.

3. THE PUBLIC PERFORMANCE RIGHT: MUSICAL WORKS

The second exclusive right relevant to Internet music transmissions is the right to publicly perform a copyrighted work. The Copyright Act defines "performing" a work very broadly. One performs Cole Porter's song, "Ev'ry Time We Say Good-

---

[19] Indeed, the compulsory mechanical license for the musical work is not available for making phonorecords of another party's sound recording unless the licensee has authorization for reproduction from the owner of the rights in the sound recording. 17 U.S.C. § 115(a)(1) (1998).

[20] Id. § 115(d).

bye," if one sings the lyrics to the song, plays the song on a piano, plays a compact disc of the song on a stereo, or plays an MP3 file of the song on a personal computer or a portable playback device. Although all of those activities "perform" the musical work, they infringe the copyright only if done "publicly." A performance can be public in two ways. First, one "publicly" performs a work by performing it in a public or semi-public place, such as by singing "Ev'ry Time We Say Goodbye" in a nightclub. Second, and more important for music on the Internet, transmitting a performance is a public performance if the transmission is "to the public, by means of any device or process, whether the members of the public capable of receiving the performance . . . receive it in the same place or in separate places and at the same time or at different times."[23] A radio station that broadcasts a performance of "Ev'ry Time We Say Goodbye" publicly performs the musical work by transmitting a performance to the public. Similarly, a Web site that transmits the recording to users in streaming audio publicly performs the musical work by transmitting a performance to the public. This is true even if each listener is located alone in her own home and only one listener hears the song at any given time. Even if the Web site limits its transmissions to subscribing users who pay a monthly fee, its transmissions will be "to the public."

No general compulsory license exists for the public performance right in musical works; to publicly perform such a work requires the permission of the copyright owner. Because public performances of musical works are fleeting and occur in widely dispersed locations, enforcement of the public performance right has challenged copyright owners. In response, copyright owners created collective rights societies to administer and enforce the public performance right. The principal societies in the United States are the American Society of Composers, Authors and Publishers ("ASCAP"), Broadcast Music, Inc. ("BMI"), and SESAC, Inc. (formerly the Society of European State Authors and Composers). The societies are made up of copyright owners (usually songwriters and music publishers) who grant the society the nonexclusive right to license public performances of their musical works. The societies, in turn, grant blanket licenses to entities that engage in public performances, such as radio and television stations, nightclubs and concert halls, restaurants and retail establishments. In return for a license fee (generally calculated as a percentage of the licensee's revenue), the licensee obtains the right to perform publicly any work in the society's repertoire, and the ASCAP, BMI, and SESAC repertoires collectively include virtually all copyrighted American music.

4. SOUND RECORDINGS: THE DIGITAL TRANSMISSION PERFORMANCE RIGHT

Congress granted the exclusive public performance right to copyright owners of musical works, but not to copyright owners of sound recordings.[26] As a result, a nightclub or radio station that plays a compact disc of Annie Lennox singing "Ev'ry Time We Say Goodbye" publicly performs both Cole Porter's musical work

---

[23] *Id.* § 101 ("publicly"). The Copyright Act defines "transmit" quite broadly: "To 'transmit' a performance . . . is to communicate it by any device or process whereby . . . sounds are received beyond the place from which they are sent." *Id.*

[26] 17 U.S.C. § 106(4) (1995).

and Annie Lennox's sound recording but needs permission only from the copyright owner of Porter's music and lyrics and not from the copyright owner of Lennox's sound recording.

In 1995, Congress granted sound recording copyright owners a limited public performance right: the right to perform their sound recordings publicly "by means of a digital audio transmission."[27] A Web site that streams a recording of Annie Lennox singing "Ev'ry Time We Say Goodbye" to listeners over the Internet publicly performs the sound recording by means of a digital audio transmission. That activity would be covered by the digital transmission performance right.

Congress also enacted significant limitations on the digital transmission performance right. The scope of the copyright owner's right varies with the type of digital transmission. There are four basic types. The first is a transmission made by an "interactive service" that either transmits a particular sound recording requested by the recipient or transmits a program specially created for the recipient. Several kinds of transmissions are interactive. The archetypal interactive service is the much-prophesied "celestial jukebox," an on-demand service that allows a recipient (who pays a monthly subscription fee or a per-use charge) to connect to a repository of sound recordings and select a particular recording that is immediately transmitted to the recipient's speakers. [Such a service would be] offering an interactive service, because the subscriber will receive, on request, the transmission of a particular sound recording that she selected. Transmissions by an interactive service are subject to the sound recording copyright owner's digital transmission performance right, so the transmitter needs the permission of the copyright owner prior to making transmissions of the subject recording. The sound recording copyright owner is entitled to charge any price for such permission or to deny permission entirely.[30]

Noninteractive service transmissions basically fall into three categories. First, there are nonsubscription broadcast transmissions.[31] Such transmissions are entirely exempt from a copyright owner's digital transmission performance right, so obtaining permission from the sound recording copyright owner is not necessary.[32] Permission for the public performance of any musical work would be required, though.[33] Many radio stations, in addition to broadcasting over the radio airwaves,

---

[27] 17 U.S.C. § 106(6) (1995). Essentially, a digital audio transmission is a transmission in any non-analog format that embodies a sound recording. 17 U.S.C. § 114(j)(5) (1994 & Supp. IV 1998).

[30] In fact, 17 U.S.C. §§ 114(d)(3) and 114(h) (1994 & Supp. IV 1998) impose some limits on the ability of sound recording copyright owners to grant exclusive licenses to interactive services and require, in certain circumstances, that owners who license the digital transmission right to affiliates make licenses available to similar services on no-less-favorable terms.

[31] These are "transmission[s] made by a terrestrial broadcast station licensed as such" by the FCC. 17 U.S.C. § 114(j)(3).

[32] *Id.* § 114(d)(1)(A). Certain other types of transmissions are also exempt. *Id.* §§ 114(d)(1)(B), (C).

[33] *Id.* § 114(d)(4)(B)(i).

now have Web sites where they simultaneously transmit identical programming in streaming audio format. For example, public radio station KUT in Austin, Texas, has a Web site (www.kut.org) that allows users to hear in real time the programming that KUT is broadcasting over the airwaves to central Texas. . . . In response to a petition by the Recording Industry Association of America ("RIAA"), the trade association for the major recording labels, the Copyright Office [in 2000] amended its regulations to provide that an Internet simulcast by a licensed AM or FM broadcaster is not within the "nonsubscription broadcast transmission" exemption from the digital transmission performance right.[35] . . .

Second, certain noninteractive transmissions other than broadcast transmissions, although not exempt from the digital transmission performance right, are eligible for a compulsory license of the digital transmission performance right.[37] For example, a hypothetical Web site, WebJazz, that runs a jazz "Web radio station" and streams jazz music to those who visit the site, just as a radio station would broadcast jazz music over the airwaves, would be eligible for such a license.[38] The transmissions are not interactive because WebJazz's programmers, not the site's listeners, select which songs are played. A noninteractive transmitter like WebJazz must adhere to a long list of detailed conditions to qualify for the compulsory license.[39] Those conditions seek to limit the license to those transmissions thought least likely to substitute for the sale of records. Therefore, the conditions attempt to prevent listeners from getting advance notice of which songs are to be transmitted so that they could record them or listen to them "on demand." Some conditions concern the programming that is transmitted. For example, WebJazz cannot transmit, during any three-hour period, more than three different tracks from any one compact disc or more than four different tracks by the same recording artist.[41] Other conditions govern the technology and interfaces used for the

---

[35] *See* Public Performance of Sound Recordings: Definition of a Service, 65 Fed. Reg. 77,292 (Dec. 11, 2000). The regulation makes clear that the compulsory license for Web transmissions of sound recordings, discussed in the next paragraph, is available to over-the-air broadcasters for their Internet simulcasts if they meet the statute's detailed conditions for the license.

[37] 17 U.S.C. § 114(d)(2).

[38] Both subscription and nonsubscription transmissions are eligible for the license, so the site might support itself either by limiting access to subscribers or by transmitting advertising to its listeners. *See id.* §§ 114(j)(9), (14). If the transmission is nonsubscription, it must, in order to qualify for the statutory license, be part of a service whose "primary purpose" is to provide audio or entertainment programming to the public and not to sell or promote particular products or services. *Id.* § 114(j)(6).

[39] The conditions are set forth in *id.* §§ 114(d)(2)(A), (C).

[41] 17 U.S.C. §§ 114(d)(2)(C)(i) and 114(j)(13) [defining "sound recording performance complement"]. Other programming-related conditions include a ban on advance publication of program schedules or specific titles to be played, § 114(d)(2)(C)(ii), minimum time limits for the program of which a transmission of a sound recording is a part, § 114(d)(2)(C)(iii), a requirement to transmit recordings from lawfully made phonorecords and not from bootleg recordings, § 114(d)(2)(C)(vii), and a bar on transmitting visual images along with the audio transmission in a way likely to confuse recipients as to the endorsement or affiliation of the

transmission.[42] If WebJazz meets all the conditions, then it can obtain a compulsory license to transmit any sound recording by complying with Copyright Office procedures and paying the license fee. As with the compulsory mechanical license for DPDs, the license fee is to be determined every two years by voluntary negotiations among the parties to establish an industry-wide consensus on rates that would then be adopted by the Copyright Office. Failing that, rates would be set by an arbitration proceeding in the Copyright Office.[43] . . . The compulsory license, like the broadcast exemption, applies only to the digital transmission performance right in sound recordings and not to the public performance right in musical works. A transmitter that qualifies for the compulsory license will therefore still need to obtain musical work performance licenses, usually from ASCAP, BMI, and SESAC.

Third, noninteractive transmissions that are not broadcast transmissions and that do not meet the conditions for the compulsory license are fully subject to the digital transmission performance right. Persons making such transmissions must generally obtain the permission of the copyright owner. If WebJazz wanted to program "all Ella Fitzgerald, all the time," it would not be able to comply with the limit of four tracks by one artist in three hours. Thus, it would not qualify for the compulsory license. WebJazz would therefore need permission for its digital transmission of each sound recording from the copyright owners. . . .

Table 1 summarizes the relevant reproduction and performance rights of copyright owners of musical works and sound recordings, and the limitations on those rights.

---

recording artist or copyright owner, § 114(d)(2)(C)(iv).

[42] For example, the transmitter must identify, in text displayed to the recipient during the performance, the title of the recording, the title of the record from which it comes, and the name of the recording artist. 17 U.S.C. § 114(d)(2)(C)(ix). Other conditions of this type include not causing the receiving equipment to change channel, § 114(d)(2)(A)(ii), transmitting any identifying information encoded in the sound recording by the copyright owner, § 114(d)(2)(A)(iii), accommodating and not interfering with technical measures used by copyright owners to identify or protect their works, § 114(d)(2)(C)(viii), not taking any affirmative steps to cause the making of a phonorecord by the recipient of the transmission and setting the transmission equipment to limit such recording if possible, § 114(d)(2)(C)(vi), and cooperating to prevent the scanning of transmissions in order to select a particular recording to be transmitted, § 114(d)(2)(C)(v).

[43] 17 U.S.C. § 114(f)(2).

TABLE 1

	Reproduction Right	Public Performance Right
Musical Work	• General Exclusive Right of Copyright Owner • Compulsory Mechanical License available for Digital Phonorecord Deliveries	• General Exclusive Right of Copyright Owner • Blanket License available through ASCAP, BMI, and SESAC
Sound Recording	• General Exclusive Right of Copyright Owner • No compulsory license available	• No general exclusive right in copyright owner • Limited right to public performance by means of digital audio transmission (see Table 2)

Table 2 summarizes the basic structure of the limitations on the digital transmission performance right.

TABLE 2

Type of Transmission		Public Performance Right by means of Digital Audio Transmission
Noninteractive Transmission	Nonsubscription "Broadcast" Transmissions	Exempt from exclusive right
	• Compliant Subscription Transmissions • Compliant Eligible Nonsubscription Transmissions	Compulsory License available
	All Other Noninteractive Transmissions	Exclusive Right of Copyright Owner
Transmission By Interactive Service		Exclusive Right of Copyright Owner

EXTENSIONS

1. *Compulsory licenses.* Earlier in the chapter, we saw that several defenses may serve to limit the exclusive rights conferred on the owner of a copyright under 17 U.S.C. § 106. The statutory, or "compulsory," license is another device that limits the scope of these exclusive rights. To promote a particular socially beneficial use of a copyrighted work by persons other than the owner of the copyright, Congress may grant a license to use such a work to anyone whose use satisfies the conditions set forth in the statute creating the license and who pays the prescribed royalty.

By creating a compulsory licensing scheme for particular socially beneficial uses of copyrighted works, Congress obviates the need for licensees to negotiate directly with copyright owners. Statutory licenses, like the privilege of fair use, thereby reduce transaction costs that might otherwise prevent such socially beneficial uses. As a tool for implementing public policy, a compulsory license has certain advantages over the fair use defense. First, a compulsory license allows Congress precisely to target the particular kinds of uses that it desires to promote. The statute granting the license can include detailed conditions that must be satisfied before a person may enjoy the benefit of this license. Second, by creating a compulsory license Congress can require the licensee to pay a royalty to the copyright owner, balancing the interests of the public and copyright owners.

Finally, a compulsory license provides the user of another's work with greater certainty that the use is noninfringing. While broad in scope, the doctrine of fair use is uncertain in application: the four factors a court must weigh when determining whether a particular defendant is entitled to this defense are very general and require a nuanced analysis of the alleged infringing activity. As a result, until the matter is fully litigated, a person cannot be certain whether use of another's work is noninfringing. Such uncertainty may chill socially beneficial uses of copyrighted works.

Compulsory licenses are a derogation from the sweeping "exclusive rights" that the Copyright Act grants to copyright owners, and apply only to a few specific categories of activity, such as those discussed in the preceding excerpt.

2. *Licensing terms and royalty rates.* Under 17 U.S.C. § 114(f), the Librarian of Congress is charged with establishing the rates and terms for statutory licenses for certain non-exempt transmissions of digital audio music. In June 2002, the Librarian established royalty rates under which a webcaster must pay $0.0007 each time it streams a song to a recipient (i.e., seven cents each time it streams 100 songs). *See* Determination of Reasonable Rates and Terms for the Digital Performance of Sound Recordings and Ephemeral Recordings, 67 Fed. Reg. 45,239 (July 8, 2002). Webcasters say they cannot afford to pay these rates, and will be driven out of business. The recording industry contends that the rates have been set so low they are effectively being forced to subsidize online broadcasters. *See* Jon Healey, *Net Radio, Labels At Odds Over Royalties*, L.A. TIMES, June 24, 2002, at Part 3, p.1. Should the royalty rate be set at a level that makes webcasting viable under current business models? In June 2003, the royalty rate paid by Webcasters was increased to $0.000762.

Should the Copyright Office's construction of Section 114's substantive provisions be reviewable by a court, and if so, what standard of review should the reviewing court employ? In *Bonneville International Corp. v. Peters*, 347 F.3d 485 (3d Cir.2003), the court held that the Copyright Office had correctly interpreted Section 114(d)(1)(A) when it determined that a radio station's simultaneous streaming of its broadcast via the Internet did not qualify for that subsection's exemption from the public performance right. However, the court left unresolved the degree of deference a court owes to the Copyright Office when reviewing such a rulemaking determination.

The terms and conditions set by the Copyright Office in July 2002 for the Webcasting statutory license under Section 114 were upheld by the D.C. Circuit, applying an "exceptionally deferential" standard of review. *Beethoven.com LLC v. Librarian of Congress*, 394 F.3d 939 (D.C.Cir.2005). *See also Recording Industry Association of America v. Librarian of Congress*, 176 F.3d 528 (D.C.Cir.1999) (upholding rates in initial proceeding for statutory licenses for subscription transmissions).

3. *The Small Webcaster Settlement Act of 2002.* Unable to afford the royalty rates paid by traditional broadcasters and concerned about their lack of participation in the arbitration royalty panel proceedings under Title 17, small webcasters asked Congress to encourage copyright holders to establish a royalty rate based on a percentage of revenue. In response, Congress passed the Small Webcaster Settlement Act of 2002 ("SWSA"), Pub. L. No. 107–321, 116 Stat. 2780, which amends the Section 112 and Section 114 statutory licenses of the Copyright Act as they relate to small webcasters and noncommercial webcasters. Although SWSA sets up an alternative rate structure for small and nonprofit webcasters, such as college radio stations and individuals who want to stream music over the Internet, it does not require any specific rates; these must be negotiated between groups representing the interests of music copyright holders and those representing the small and noncommercial webcasters.

Pursuant to SWSA, SoundExchange, the agent designated by the Librarian of Congress for collecting royalty payments under the Section 112 and Section 114 statutory licenses, negotiated an initial agreement with Voice of Webcasters, a coalition of small commercial webcasters. This agreement calls for royalties to be paid through 2002 at a rate of 8 percent of the small webcaster's gross revenue, or 5 percent of expenses, whichever is greater. Royalty rates increase in subsequent years. The agreement runs through December 31, 2004. *See* Notification of Agreement Under the Small Webcaster Settlement Act of 2002, 67 Fed. Reg. 78,510 (Dec. 24, 2002).

4. *Interactive services.* The use of the Internet to deliver music makes it technologically possible for webcasters to offer personalized programming for individual listeners. Each listener can create a channel that provides music and other programming customized in real-time to that listener's present mood and unique tastes. As a result, personalized webcasts and interactive Internet music delivery generally have caused traditional broadcasters and record companies much anxiety, fearing diversion of their customers. Reacting to the concerns of these industries, Congress limited the exemption under Section 114(d)(1) and the statutory license under Section 114(d)(2) to noninteractive services. Thus, interactive services are fully subject to the digital performance right in sound recordings. Section 114(j)(7) defines an interactive service as

> one that enables a member of the public to receive a transmission of a program specially created for the recipient, or on request, a transmission of a particular sound recording, whether or not as part of a program, which is selected by or on behalf of the recipient. The ability of individuals to request that particular sound recordings be performed for reception by the public at large, or in the case of a subscription service, by all subscribers of the service, does not make a service interactive, if the programming on each channel of the service does not substantially consist of sound recordings that are performed within 1 hour of the request or at a time designated by either the transmitting entity or the individual making such request. If an entity offers both interactive and noninteractive services (either concurrently or at different times), the noninteractive component shall not be treated as part of an interactive service.

17 U.S.C. § 114(j)(7). A music service that falls within the scope of this definition must negotiate licenses for the music it offers, company-by-company and recording-by-recording. To be successful and at the same time avoid these additional costs, Internet music services need to qualify for the statutory license under Section 114(d)(2) while offering value-added services and features that distinguish their music service from traditional broadcasters.

Consider one Internet music service that appears to be pushing the limits of the Section 114(d)(2) statutory license. The service allows a listener to create a "station" or "channel" with a playlist of up to twenty-five of the listener's favorite recording artists. The station then plays music by these artists and others who have a similar musical style. Listeners can use a radio timeline to select music from particular time periods, a tempo tuner to select "faster" or "slower" music depending on the listener's mood, as well as a feature to skip to the next song. In your opinion, should such a service be considered a noninteractive service that falls within the scope of the Section 114(d)(2) statutory license, or is it an interactive service?

QUESTIONS FOR DISCUSSION

1. *Scope of the Section 114 statutory license.* Section 114 creates a compulsory license allowing "[t]he performance of a sound recording publicly" through certain types of digital transmissions. 17 U.S.C. § 114(d)(2). This provision also places limitations on the scope of this license:

> Nothing in this section annuls or limits in any way—
>
> (i) the exclusive right to publicly perform a musical work, including by means of a digital audio transmission, under section 106(4);
>
> (ii) the exclusive rights in a sound recording or the musical work embodied therein under sections 106(1), 106(2) and 106(3); . . .

17 U.S.C. § 114(d)(4)(B)(i) and (ii).

Review the exclusive rights of a copyright owner set forth in 17 U.S.C. § 106(1)–(6), and bear in mind that a sound recording (the Annie Lennox recording, in Professor Reese's example) and a musical work (the Cole Porter composition) are two different copyrighted works, which receive different types of protection under Section 106. To which type of work does the Section 114 compulsory license apply? To which of the copyright holder's exclusive rights does it apply? To which rights does it not apply?

2. *Public performances of sound recordings.* Why does the Copyright Act not grant sound recording copyright owners the exclusive right over public performances of their work generally? (Sound recordings first obtained federal copyright protection in the 1970s. Who would have been most opposed to a public performance right at that time?) With respect to the sound recording copyright owner's limited right public performance by digital audio transmission, why are interactive transmissions entirely within the control of the copyright owner, and not subject to any specific exemption or statutory license?

B. PUBLIC PERFORMANCE: STREAMING TRANSMISSIONS

R. Anthony Reese, *Copyright and Internet Music Transmissions: Existing Law, Major Controversies, Possible Solutions*
55 U. MIAMI L. REV. 237 (2001).

. . .

A. Streaming Transmissions

The provisions of U.S. copyright law outlined in Part I govern the two major types of music transmissions available over the Internet today: streaming and downloading musical files. A digital music file can be streamed to a user. Over the World Wide Web, for example, a user might connect to the Web site of the Red Hot Organization and find a streaming audio file of Annie Lennox's recording of "Ev'ry Time We Say Goodbye" from the album *Red, Hot + Blue.* The user might then request that the Web site transmit that file. As the site transmits the information in the file, the user's computer makes the recording audible through the computer's speakers. During the transmission, the user's computer temporarily stores or "buffers" segments of the recording before making them audible, in order to allow (usually) uninterrupted playback of the recording even if network congestion slows the transmission. As the recording is played, however, the part of the file that is played is removed from the buffer and replaced with subsequent portions of the recording. At the end of the transmission, the user has heard the entire recording. Generally, no copy of the recording remains stored on the computer. If the user wishes to hear the streamed recording again, she must again connect to the Red Hot Web site and request that it transmit the file again.

Such streaming transmissions may fit a wide variety of Internet music business models. A user might hear streaming transmissions from the Web site of a particular musician or record label that wishes to promote particular recordings, from a Web "radio station" that transmits a variety of music in the same way that over-the-air radio stations do, or from a "music locker" service that stores particular songs selected (and possibly purchased) by the user to provide the user access to those songs from any Internet-connected computer.

A streaming transmission over the Internet clearly constitutes a digital transmission performance of the sound recording transmitted and of any musical work embodied in that sound recording. Such a transmission will infringe the public performance rights unless the person making it has permission or is otherwise excused. For example, WebJazz may want to transmit Annie Lennox's recording of "Ev'ry Time We Say Goodbye" in streaming audio as part of its Webcast. With respect to Annie Lennox's sound recording, WebJazz will either be exempt from the digital transmission right entirely (if it makes a nonsubscription broadcast transmission), be entitled to transmit the stream under the a compulsory license (if the transmission is noninteractive and meets all the license conditions), or be required to obtain permission from the copyright owner (if the stream is available to listeners on demand). The transmitter will need to obtain permission to perform Cole Porter's musical work publicly. ASCAP, BMI, and SESAC each provide blanket licenses for such transmissions of the works in their respective repertoires.

The major copyright question with respect to streaming audio transmissions is whether every such transmission constitutes not only a public performance of the works transmitted but also a reproduction of those works. The reproduction and performance rights are independent of one another. The statutory language and legislative history contemplate that a single transmission could involve the exercise of both reproduction and public performance rights. Such a transmission occurs where the recipient can both hear the song received and store a copy of it.

The more significant aspect of the question is whether *every* streaming audio transmission reproduces both the musical work and the sound recording transmitted, even if the recipient does not retain any copy of the music at the end of the transmission, as is the case with an ordinary streaming transmission. This possibility arises largely because of the temporary storage in random-access memory (hereinafter "RAM") that occurs in essentially every computer. As a streaming audio transmission is received, the digits that represent the sounds to be played back by the recipient's streaming audio software will temporarily be stored in the RAM of the recipient's computer, until they are processed by the software, played back, and replaced in RAM by subsequently transmitted digits.[49] In cases not involving

---

[49] Reproduction may also occur because the streaming software may temporarily store (or cache) the received data on the hard drive of the recipient's computer, where it may remain until it is written over by other data. There is little doubt that such storage technically

streaming transmissions, at least two federal appellate courts have held that storing a copyrightable work in RAM constitutes reproduction of the work in violation of the copyright owner's exclusive reproduction right.[50] Many have criticized these decisions as inconsistent with the statutory language and the legislative history of the Copyright Act. Some lower courts and government officials have, however, adopted this view, suggesting that courts may rule that temporary RAM storage that occurs automatically in the course of every streaming audio transmission constitutes a reproduction of the copyrighted works transmitted.

The legislative history of the compulsory DPD license indicates that at least some RAM storage as part of a streaming transmission will constitute the reproduction of a phonorecord. For purposes of license rates, the statute distinguishes between ordinary DPDs and "incidental" DPDs.[55] The legislative history provides the following example to explain the distinction:

> [I]f a transmission system was designed to allow transmission recipients to hear sound recordings substantially at the time of transmission, but the sound recording was transmitted in a high-speed burst of data and stored in a computer memory for prompt playback (such storage being technically the making of a phonorecord), and the transmission recipient could not retain the phonorecord for playback on subsequent occasions (or for any other purpose), delivering the phonorecord to the transmission recipient would be incidental to the transmission.[56]

Thus, at least streaming transmissions where the entire transmitted sound recording is stored at one time in the RAM of the recipient's computer for playback would appear to involve the making of a DPD. It is not clear, however, whether the temporary RAM storage of small portions of a sound recording involved in the buffering typically done by streaming software today would constitute a DPD. . . .

. . .

The practical implications of treating the RAM storage that occurs during streaming audio transmissions as a phonorecord are extremely significant. Every streaming audio transmission would need to be authorized not only as a public performance of both the sound recording transmitted and the musical work embodied in that sound recording, but also as a reproduction of each of those works.

EXTENSIONS

1. *Musical work public performance licenses.* For more information on licensing on Internet transmissions by the musical copyright performing rights societies, see their relevant Web pages at www.ascap.com/weblicense/, www.bmi.com/licensing/webcaster/, and www.sesac.com/licensing/internetLicensing.asp.

---

constitutes the reproduction of the stored work in a phonorecord.

[50] Stenograph L.L.C. v. Bossard Assocs., 144 F.3d 96 (D.C. Cir.1998); MAI Systems Corp. v. Peak Computer, Inc., 991 F.2d 511 (9th Cir.1993).

[55] 17 U.S.C. § 115(c)(3)(C), (D).

[56] S. Rep. No. 104–128 at 39.

2. *Streaming, temporary storage, and reproduction.* In August 2001, the Copyright Office issued a study that addressed, among other issues, the question of whether temporary storage that occurs during a streaming audio transmission constitutes actionable reproduction. While the Copyright Office staunchly defended the general proposition that temporary storage in RAM constituted reproduction within the copyright owner's control, it was sympathetic to the problems that view posed for music transmitters:

> There was compelling evidence presented . . . on the uncertainty surrounding temporary buffer copies made in RAM in the course of rendering a digital musical stream. Specifically, webcasters asserted that the unknown legal status of buffer copies exposes webcasters to demands for additional royalty payments from the owner of the sound recording, as well as potential infringement liability.

> The buffer copies identified by the webcasting industry exist for only a short period of time and consist of small portions of the work. Webcasters argue that these reproductions are incidental to the licensed performance of the work and should not be subject to an additional license for a reproduction that is only a means to an authorized end. Buffer copies implicate the reproduction right, thus potentially resulting in liability. There is, therefore, a legitimate concern on the part of webcasters and other streaming music services as to their potential liability.

> We believe that there is a strong case that the making of a buffer copy in the course of streaming is a fair use. Fair use is a defense that may limit any of the copyright owner's exclusive rights, including the reproduction right implicated in temporary copies. In order to assess whether a particular use of the works at issue is a fair use, section 107 requires the consideration and balancing of four mandatory, but nonexclusive, factors on a case-by-case basis. . . .

> . . . [F]air use is also an "equitable rule of reason." In the case of temporary buffer copies, we believe that the equities unquestionably favor the user. The sole purpose for making the buffer copies is to permit an activity that is licensed by the copyright owner and for which the copyright owner receives a performance royalty. In essence, copyright owners appear to be seeking to be paid twice for the same activity. Additionally, it is technologically necessary to make buffer copies in order to carry out a digital performance of music over the Internet. Finally, the buffer copies exist for too short a period of time to be exploited in any way other than as a narrowly tailored means to enable the authorized performance of the work. On balance, therefore, the equities weigh heavily in favor of fair use. . . .

> Representatives of the webcasting industry expressed concern that the case-by-case fair use defense is too uncertain a basis for making rational business decisions. We agree. . . .

> We recommend that Congress enact legislation amending the Copyright Act to preclude any liability arising from the assertion of a copyright owner's reproduction right with respect to temporary buffer copies that are incidental to a licensed digital transmission of a public performance of a sound recording and any underlying musical work.

> The economic value of licensed streaming is in the public performances of the musical work and the sound recording, both of which are paid for. The buffer copies have no independent economic significance. They are made solely to enable the performance of these works. The uncertainty of the present law potentially allows those who administer the reproduction right in musical works to

prevent webcasting from taking place—to the detriment of other copyright owners, webcasters and consumers alike—or to extract an additional payment that is not justified by the economic value of the copies at issue. Congressional action is desirable to remove the uncertainty and to allow the activity that Congress sought to encourage through the adoption of the section 114 webcasting compulsory license to take place.

Although we believe that the fair use defense probably does apply to temporary buffer copies, this approach is fraught with uncertain application in the courts. This uncertainty, coupled with the apparent willingness of some copyright owners to assert claims based on the making of buffer copies, argues for statutory change. We believe that the narrowly tailored scope of our recommendation will minimize, if not eliminate, concerns expressed by copyright owners about potential unanticipated consequences.

DMCA SECTION 104 REPORT: A REPORT OF THE REGISTER OF COPYRIGHTS PURSUANT TO § 104 OF THE DIGITAL MILLENNIUM COPYRIGHT ACT xxiii–xxvii (2001).

C. DIGITAL REPRODUCTION OF MUSIC

1. Generally

UMG Recordings, Inc. v. MP3.Com, Inc.
92 F.Supp.2d 349 (S.D.N.Y. 2000).

■ RAKOFF, DISTRICT JUDGE.

The complex marvels of cyberspatial communication may create difficult legal issues; but not in this case. Defendant's infringement of plaintiffs' copyrights is clear. Accordingly, on April 28, 2000, the Court granted [plaintiffs'] motion for partial summary judgment holding defendant liable for copyright infringement. This opinion will state the reasons why.

The pertinent facts, either undisputed or, where disputed, taken most favorably to defendant, are as follows:

The technology known as "MP3" permits rapid and efficient conversion of compact disc recordings ("CDs") to computer files easily accessed over the Internet. Utilizing this technology, defendant MP3.com, on or around January 12, 2000, launched its "My.MP3.com" service, which is advertised as permitting subscribers to store, customize, and listen to the recordings contained on their CDs from any place where they have an Internet connection. To make good on this offer, defendant purchased tens of thousands of popular CDs in which plaintiffs held the copyrights, and, without authorization, copied their recordings onto its computer servers so as to be able to replay the recordings for its subscribers.

Specifically, in order to first access such a recording, a subscriber to MP3.com must either "prove" that he already owns the CD version of the recording by inserting his copy of the commercial CD into his computer CD-ROM drive for a few seconds (the "Beam-it Service") or must purchase the CD from one of defendant's cooperating online retailers (the "instant Listening Service"). Thereafter, however, the subscriber can access via the Internet from a computer anywhere in the world the copy of plaintiffs' recording made by defendant. Thus, although defendant seeks to portray its service as the "functional equivalent" of storing its subscribers' CDs, in actuality defendant is re-playing for the subscribers converted versions of the recordings it copied, without authorization, from plaintiffs' copyrighted CDs. On its face, this makes out a presumptive case of infringement under the Copyright Act of 1976 ("Copyright Act") . . . .[1]

Defendant argues, however, that such copying is protected by the affirmative defense of "fair use." *See* 17 U.S.C. § 107. In analyzing such a defense, the Copyright Act specifies four factors that must be considered: "(1) the purpose and character of the use, including whether such use is of a commercial nature or is for nonprofit educational purposes; (2) the nature of the copyrighted work; (3) the amount and substantiality of the portion used in relation to the copyrighted work as a whole; and (4) the effect of the use upon the potential market for or value of the copyrighted work." *Id.* Other relevant factors may also be considered, since fair use is an "equitable rule of reason" to be applied in light of the overall purposes of the Copyright Act. *Sony Corporation of America v. Universal City Studios, Inc.*, 464 U.S. 417, 448, 454 (1984).

Regarding the first factor — "the purpose and character of the use" — defendant does not dispute that its purpose is commercial, for while subscribers to My.MP3.com are not currently charged a fee, defendant seeks to attract a sufficiently large subscription base to draw advertising and otherwise make a profit. Consideration of the first factor, however, also involves inquiring into whether the new use essentially repeats the old or whether, instead, it "transforms" it by infusing it with new meaning, new understandings, or the like. *See, e.g., Campbell v. Acuff-Rose Music, Inc.*, 510 U.S. 569, 579 (1994); see also Pierre N. Leval, "Toward a Fair Use Standard," 103 *Harv. L. Rev.* 1105, 1111 (1990). Here, although defendant recites that My.MP3.com provides a transformative "space shift" by which subscribers can enjoy the sound recordings contained on their CDs without lugging around the physical discs themselves, this is simply another way of saying that the unauthorized copies are being retransmitted in another medium — an insufficient basis for any legitimate claim of transformation.

Here, defendant adds no new "new aesthetics, new insights and understandings" to the original music recordings it copies, *see Castle Rock [Entertainment, Inc. v. Carol Publishing Group, Inc.]*, 150 F.3d [132,] 142 [(2d. Cir.1998)] (internal quotation marks omitted), but simply repackages those recordings to facilitate their transmis-

---

[1] Defendant's only challenge to plaintiffs' *prima face* case of infringement is the suggestion, buried in a footnote in its opposition papers, that its music computer files are not in fact "reproductions" of plaintiffs' copyrighted works within the meaning of the Copyright Act. *See, e.g.,* 17 U.S.C. § 114(b). Specifically, defendant claims that the simulated sounds on MP3-based music files are not physically identical to the sounds on the original CD recordings. Defendant concedes, however, that the human ear cannot detect a difference between the two. Moreover, defendant admits that a goal of its copying is to create a music file that is sonically as identical to the original CD as possible. In such circumstances, some slight, humanly undetectable difference between the original and the copy does not qualify for exclusion from the coverage of the Act.

sion through another medium. While such services may be innovative, they are not transformative.

Regarding the second factor—"the nature of the copyrighted work"—the creative recordings here being copied are "close[] to the core of intended copyright protection," *Campbell,* 510 U.S. at 586, and, conversely, far removed from the more factual or descriptive work more amenable to "fair use," *see Nihon Keizai Shimbun, Inc. v. Comline Business Data, Inc.,* 166 F.3d 65, 72–73 (2d Cir.1999).

Regarding the third factor—"the amount and substantiality of the portion [of the copyrighted work] used [by the copier] in relation to the copyrighted work as a whole"—it is undisputed that defendant copies, and replays, the entirety of the copyrighted works here in issue, thus again negating any claim of fair use. *See Infinity Broadcast,* 150 F.3d at 109 ("[T]he more of a copyrighted work that is taken, the less likely the use is to be fair . . . ."); *see generally* Leval, *supra,* at 1122 ("[T]he larger the volume . . . of what is taken, the greater the affront to the interests of the copyright owner, and the less likely that a taking will qualify as a fair use").

Regarding the fourth factor—"the effect of the use upon the potential market for or value of the copyrighted work"—defendant's activities on their face invade plaintiffs' statutory right to license their copyrighted sound recordings to others for reproduction. *See* 17 U.S.C. § 106. Defendant, however, argues that, so far as the derivative market here involve[d] is concerned, plaintiffs have not shown that such licensing is "traditional, reasonable, or likely to be developed." *American Geophysical,* 60 F.3d at 930 & n. 17. Moreover, defendant argues, its activities can only enhance plaintiffs' sales, since subscribers cannot gain access to particular recordings made available by MP3.com unless they have already "purchased" (actually or purportedly), or agreed to purchase, their own CD copies of those recordings.

Such arguments . . . are unpersuasive. Any allegedly positive impact of defendant's activities on plaintiffs' prior market in no way frees defendant to usurp a further market that directly derives from reproduction of the plaintiffs' copyrighted works. This would be so even if the copyrightholder had not yet entered the new market in issue, for a copyrightholder's "exclusive" rights, derived from the Constitution and the Copyright Act, include the right, within broad limits, to curb the development of such a derivative market by refusing to license a copyrighted work or by doing so only on terms the copyright owner finds acceptable. Here, moreover, plaintiffs have adduced substantial evidence that they have in fact taken steps to enter that market by entering into various licensing agreements.

Finally, regarding defendant's purported reliance on other factors, *see Campbell,* 510 U.S. at 577, this essentially reduces to the claim that My.MP3.com provides a useful service to consumers that, in its absence, will be served by "pirates." Copyright, however, is not designed to afford consumer protection or convenience but, rather, to protect the copyrightholders' property interests. Moreover, as a practical matter, plaintiffs have indicated no objection in principle to licensing their recordings to companies like MP3.com; they simply want to make sure they get the remuneration the law reserves for them as holders of copyrights on creative works. Stripped to its essence, defendant's "consumer protection" argument amounts to nothing more than a bald claim that defendant should be able to misappropriate plaintiffs' property simply because there is a consumer demand for it. This hardly appeals to the conscience of equity.

In sum, on any view, defendant's "fair use" defense is indefensible and must be denied as a matter of law. Defendant's other affirmative defenses, such as copyright misuse, abandonment, unclean hands, and estoppel, are essentially frivolous and may be disposed of briefly. While defendant contends, under the rubric of copyright misuse, that plaintiffs are misusing their "dominant market position to selectively prosecute only certain online music technology companies," the admissible evidence of records shows only that plaintiffs have reasonably exercised their right to determine which infringers to pursue, and in which order to pursue them. The abandonment defense must also fall since defendant has failed to adduce any competent evidence of an overt act indicating that plaintiffs, who filed suit against MP3.com shortly after MP3.com launched its infringing My.MP3.com service, intentionally abandoned their copyrights. Similarly, defendant's estoppel defense must be rejected because defendant has failed to provide any competent evidence that it relied on any action by plaintiffs with respect to defendant's My.MP3.com service. Finally, the Court must reject defendant's unclean hands defense given defendant's failure to come forth with any admissible evidence showing bad faith or misconduct on the part of plaintiffs.

The Court has also considered defendant's other points and arguments and finds them sufficiently without merit as not to warrant any further comment.

Accordingly, the Court, for the foregoing reasons, has determined that plaintiffs are entitled to partial summary judgment holding defendant to have infringed plaintiffs' copyrights.

EXTENSIONS

MP3 settlements. MP3 eventually reached settlements with the five major U.S. record labels. *See* Jim Hu, *MP3.com pays $53.4 million to end copyright suit*, CNET NEWS.COM, Nov. 15, 2000, news.cnet.com/news/0-1005-200-3581102.html. Owners of copyrights in musical works also sued MP3.com over the MyMP3 service. *See MP3.com Under Fire Again*, WIRED NEWS, Mar. 22, 2000, www.wired.com/news/business/0,1367,35107,00.html. A settlement agreement was also reached in that suit. *See MP3.com's 30(Mil)-for-1 Deal*, WIRED NEWS, Oct. 18, 2000, www.wired.com/news/politics/0,1283,39523,00.html.

QUESTIONS FOR DISCUSSION

MyMP3's wrongful conduct. What precisely did MP3.com do wrong? Was it the copying of "tens of thousands of popular CDs" to the company's servers so that its customers would not have to individually upload each CD using the Beam-it Service (and so that MP3.com would not have to store a separate copy of each CD bought by each individual user through the Instant Listening Service)? Was it transmitting music identified in a user's MyMP3.com account from the company's servers to the user's computer? Both?

R. Anthony Reese, *Copyright and Internet Music Transmissions: Existing Law, Major Controversies, Possible Solutions*
55 U. MIAMI L. REV. 237 (2001).

. . .

B. Download Transmissions

The other major type of Internet music transmission, aside from streaming audio, is the downloading of a file of recorded music. Over the World Wide Web, for example, a user might connect to the Red Hot Organization's Web site and find an MP3 file of Annie Lennox's recording of "Ev'ry Time We Say Goodbye." The user can direct the Web site to transmit the music file to her, and the user's computer will store the received file, typically on the computer's hard drive. At the end of the transmission, the user has her own copy of the file on her computer hard drive, and she can listen to the recording embodied in that file whenever she wants, without any need to be connected to the Web site that originally transmitted it. With appropriate equipment, the user can copy the file onto a compact disc or onto the storage device of a portable, Walkman-like player that will allow her to listen to the recording away from her computer.

Download transmissions may be provided by various types of Internet entities. A user might download a music file from the Web site of a recording artist or record label which provides downloads for promotional purposes. The user might also download a file from a Web site specializing in downloadable music by many artists . . . Or, instead of downloading from a Web site, the user might download a music file directly from the hard drive of another user's computer using file-sharing software such as Napster or Gnutella.

A user who downloads an MP3 file of Annie Lennox's recording of "Ev'ry Time We Say Goodbye" reproduces in a phonorecord—the new file on the user's hard drive—both Lennox's sound recording and Cole Porter's musical work. To make that phonorecord without infringing those copyrights will generally require permission from both copyright owners. Permission to reproduce Annie Lennox's sound recording can only be obtained from the owner of the copyright in that sound recording—usually the record label that originally issued the recording. Once the sound recording copyright owner has authorized the reproduction, permission to make a phonorecord of Cole Porter's musical work by means of a digital phonorecord delivery can be obtained in the form of the compulsory mechanical license or a mechanical license from the Harry Fox Agency. Some question may exist as to who exactly is committing the act of reproduction.[72] Under any view,

---

[72] One possibility would be to view the downloading end user as the party who is making the new phonorecord. The user, after all, has instructed her computer to connect to the computer where the digital musical file is stored, to request that the file be transmitted to her computer, and to store the transmitted file as it is received. Another possibility would be to view the party that transmits the file to the end user as making the reproduction: the transmission of the data from the transmitter's computer to the receiving computer's hard drive results in the new copy of the file. A third possibility would be to view both the transmitter and the downloading user as acting jointly to reproduce the file; therefore, they would be jointly liable for any infringement involved.

however, the party transmitting the file probably faces liability for copyright infringement, either direct or contributory, if the transmission is not authorized.[73] As a result, no matter who is seen, as a technical matter, to be making the new phonorecord on the download recipient's hard drive, the entity transmitting the file likely will need reproduction licenses.

The major copyright question regarding download transmissions is the flip side of the question about streaming transmissions as reproductions: do download transmissions constitute not only a reproduction of the transmitted music but also a public performance by digital transmission, such that the transmitter will need permission from the owners of the public performance rights as well? Again, the statutory language contemplates that a transmission resulting in a DPD—a download—might also be a public performance of the works delivered[74] and makes clear that the compulsory DPD license does not grant the licensee any public performance rights.[75] The statutory framework, however, does not answer the question of whether any particular download transmission is a public performance.

It is easy to conceive of a download transmission that clearly would be a public performance of the works transmitted. For example, a Web site could transmit a music file to a user so that the user's computer, as it receives the transmitted information, both stores that information on the user's hard drive and makes the transmitted recording audible through the computer's speakers. Such a transmission would be both a reproduction of the sound recording and the musical work embodied in the file (by means of a digital phonorecord delivery) and a public performance of those works (by means of a digital audio transmission to the public). Thus, the transmitter would need permission to reproduce and to publicly perform both works.

Currently, however, typical download transmissions do not allow the end user to hear the song as the digital musical file is being received. Instead, the recipient's computer stores the received file, and the recipient can then, at her leisure, choose to play back the file in order to hear the recording.[76] Although widely perceived as extremely generous to copyright owners in its interpretation of copyright law in the Internet context, the Clinton Administration's White Paper addressing intellectual property rights and computer networks nevertheless took the position that such a transmission, "without the capability of simultaneous 'rendering' " of the work, "rather clearly" did not constitute a public performance. ASCAP and BMI have asserted, however, that every transmission of a musical work to the public,

---

[73] If the transmitter is considered to be the party making the new phonorecord, then the transmitter will be directly liable. If the end user is considered to be the party making the reproduction, then the transmitter will likely face liability for contributory infringement. . . .

[74] 17 U.S.C. § 115(d) (Supp. IV 1998).

[75] *Id.* § 115(c)(3)(K)(i) (Supp. IV 1998).

[76] When the user plays back the recording, she will be performing the sound recording and the musical work it embodies, but unless she plays the song in a public or semi-public place, her performance will not infringe because it is a not a public performance.

whether or not the transmission allows the user to hear the work in the course of the transmission, is a public performance for which permission of the copyright owner is needed—generally in the form of an ASCAP or BMI blanket license.

Neither the language of the Copyright Act, nor its legislative history, appears to resolve this question conclusively, and policy arguments exist on both sides of the matter. But answering the question of whether a download transmission constitutes a public performance may not, at the moment, be of particular urgency because the answer may make little practical difference in the business operations of most transmitters.

For performances of musical works, the practical impact turns on whether Web sites that provide download transmissions also provide streaming transmissions. For example, many download sites offer users the chance to listen to a song—or an excerpt of a song—before deciding whether to download it. Some of these sites might not hold performance licenses in the belief that the fair use doctrine excuses their public performances. Their reliance on the fair use doctrine, though, is probably misplaced because the streaming of any large-scale selection—even of thirty-second excerpts from songs—would not likely qualify as fair use. To comply with copyright law, sites that offer such streaming transmissions are likely to need a performance license. If most download sites also engage in some streaming transmissions, those sites—regardless of any download transmissions—will be publicly performing musical works and will already need licenses from the relevant performing rights societies.

Performance licenses are readily available to operators of these sites because the repertoires of ASCAP, BMI, and SESAC cover the vast majority of copyrighted music, these societies grant blanket licenses that allow the performance of any work in their respective repertoire for the same fee, and at least ASCAP and BMI must, under the antitrust consent decrees that govern their operations, grant licenses to any user willing to pay a reasonable license fee.[80] Thus, applying the performance right to downloads does not raise issues regarding the availability of a performance license but rather raises issues regarding the cost of such a license.

Because ASCAP, BMI, and SESAC grant blanket performance licenses that cover both streaming and download transmissions of all compositions in their repertories, a Web site that already needs performance licenses for its streaming transmissions will not incur any significant additional transaction costs in securing performance licenses for its download transmissions. The cost of the licenses also should not depend on whether a license is needed only for streaming transmissions or for both streaming and download transmissions. Whatever total price the licensor and the licensee are willing to agree to for the performance license can be spread over either the licensee's total transmissions (streams and downloads) or

---

[80] *See* United States v. Broad. Music, Inc., 1996–1 Trade Cas. (CCH) ¶ 71,378, at 76,891 (S.D.N.Y. Nov. 18, 1994); United States v. The Am. Soc'y of Composers, Authors & Publishers, 1950–51 Trade Cas. (CCH) ¶ 62,595, at 63, 754 (S.D.N.Y. Mar. 14, 1950). The amount of the reasonable license fee is subject to determination by the District Court, Southern District of New York. *Id.*

over a subset of those transmissions (streams only). For example, if all transmissions were to be considered performances and if the parties agreed on a rate of one cent per transmission, then a site that makes a thousand transmissions (both streaming and download) would incur a license fee of ten dollars. If, however, only streaming transmissions are required to be licensed, and if only one half of the licensee's transmissions are streams, then a price of two cents per transmission yields the same total price of ten dollars for one thousand total transmissions.

Thus, with respect to musical works, whether considering downloads to be performances has any practical impact on transmitters depends on whether sites that provide downloads also engage in streaming transmissions and therefore already require performance licenses. If they do engage in streaming, the impact would seem to be minimal; if they do not, then the impact is potentially greater . . . .[85]

Of course, the public performance question affects sound recording copyrights as well. If a download transmission is a public performance of the musical work, then it is also a digital transmission performance of the sound recording. Here again, under current conditions, characterizing a download to be a performance seems unlikely to have a significant economic impact on download Web sites. Because the download results in a reproduction of the sound recording that is transmitted, the transmitter will already need a reproduction license for the transmission. The compulsory DPD license covers only musical works, so the transmitter will have to obtain permission to transmit the sound recording directly from the copyright owner of that work. Where reproduction and digital transmission performance rights in sound recordings are owned by the same entity, as is currently the case for most sound recordings, the copyright owner—with whom the download transmitter will already have to negotiate—will be able to grant the transmitter permission to make the download under both the reproduction and performance rights. No additional transaction costs will be incurred in locating the relevant copyright owner and negotiating permission to perform. Moreover, permission is likely to be equally available (or equally unavailable) whether a download is just a reproduction or is both a reproduction and a performance be-

---

[85] Requiring performance licenses would not have a significant impact on all music Web sites, however. For example, if those who run such sites make available their *own* recordings of their *own* compositions, then no third-party licenses will be required whatsoever. The same holds true if a third-party site makes such works available at the request of a performer because the performer will herself be able to license the reproduction and performance rights in both the sound recording and the musical work. Transmitting recordings of other people's musical works, on the other hand, will require a mechanical DPD license at a typical cost of 7.55 cents per work per transmission, and if the site transmits recordings of those works by performers other than the site owner, then a reproduction license for the sound recording (at whatever price the copyright owner charges) will also be necessary. A Web site that can afford to pay for the necessary reproduction licenses may be able to pay the cost of a performance license. Requiring a performance license for download transmissions therefore may not necessarily make download transmissions by such sites so costly that they will not be made, but instead may raise the cost of the transmission to the end user, change the allocation of revenue from the transmission between the transmitter and the copyright owner, or both.

cause no compulsory reproduction license is available for sound recordings. And in the absence of divided ownership and any compulsory license, the price the download transmitter would pay for a reproduction and performance license for a download transmission should not be any greater than the price for a reproduction license alone for the same transmission. If the parties can agree on a price for the license, it will make little difference to either party whether that entire price is designated as the cost for a reproduction license or whether a portion is designated as the cost for a reproduction license and the remainder is designated as the cost for a performance license. It appears that ownership of the reproduction and digital transmission performance rights is not currently divided. Therefore, a transmitter generally will be able to obtain both rights from a single party.

In summary, unless a significant number of download-only sites would need performance licenses which they could not afford, the question of whether a download transmission is a public performance perhaps can await resolution until it becomes clear that answering the question will make a difference. . . .

EXTENSIONS

The Copyright Office's view. In the same report discussed in the preceding section, in which the Copyright Office took the view that a transmitter of streaming audio should not be liable for the temporary storage that occurs during its transmission, the Copyright Office also considered the "flip side" question raised in the preceding excerpt about whether every download transmission is also a public performance:

> Given our recommendations concerning temporary copies that are incidental to digital performances of sound recordings and musical works, fairness requires that we acknowledge the symmetrical difficulty that is faced in the online music industry: digital performances that are incidental to digital music downloads. Just as webcasters appear to be facing demands for royalty payments for incidental exercise of the reproduction right in the course of licensed public performances, it appears that companies that sell licensed digital downloads of music are facing demands for public performance royalties for a technical "performance" of the underlying musical work that allegedly occurs in the course of transmitting it from the vendor's server to the consumer's computer.

> Although we recognize that it is an unsettled point of law that is subject to debate, we do not endorse the proposition that a digital download constitutes a public performance even when no contemporaneous performance takes place. If a court were to find that such a download can be considered a public performance within the language of the Copyright Act, we believe the that arguments concerning fair use and the making of buffer copies are applicable to this performance issue as well. It is our view that no liability should result from a technical "performance" that takes place in the course of a download.

DMCA SECTION 104 REPORT: A REPORT OF THE REGISTER OF COPYRIGHTS PURSUANT TO § 104 OF THE DIGITAL MILLENNIUM COPYRIGHT ACT xxvii–xxviii (2001).

A&M Records, Inc. v. Napster, Inc.
239 F.3d 1004 (9th Cir.2001).

■ Beezer, Circuit Judge:

[In this opinion, the Ninth Circuit reviewed a preliminary injunction granted to musical work and sound recording copyright owners against Napster, which offered software and other services for a peer-to-peer ("p2p") file sharing network. The following excerpt describes Napster's technology and the p2p network, and reviews the district courts conclusion that Napster's users engaged in copyright infringement, for which Napster might be held liable.]

I

. . .

Napster facilitates the transmission of MP3 files between and among its users. Through a process commonly called "peer-to-peer" file sharing, Napster allows its users to: (1) make MP3 music files stored on individual computer hard drives available for copying by other Napster users; (2) search for MP3 music files stored on other users' computers; and (3) transfer exact copies of the contents of other users' MP3 files from one computer to another via the Internet. These functions are made possible by Napster's MusicShare software, available free of charge from Napster's Internet site, and Napster's network servers and server-side software. . . .

A. Accessing the System

In order to copy MP3 files through the Napster system, a user must first access Napster's Internet site and download the MusicShare software to his individual computer. Once the software is installed, the user can access the Napster system. A first-time user is required to register with the Napster system by creating a "user name" and password.

B. Listing Available Files

If a registered user wants to list available files stored in his computer's hard drive on Napster for others to access, he must first create a "user library" directory on his computer's hard drive. The user then saves his MP3 files in the library directory, using self-designated file names. He next must log into the Napster system using his user name and password. His MusicShare software then searches his user library and verifies that the available files are properly formatted. If in the correct MP3 format, the names of the MP3 files will be uploaded from the user's computer to the Napster servers. The content of the MP3 files remains stored in the user's computer.

Once uploaded to the Napster servers, the user's MP3 file names are stored in a server-side "library" under the user's name and become part of a "collective directory" of files available for transfer during the time the user is logged onto the Napster system. The collective directory is fluid; it tracks users who are connected in real time, displaying only file names that are immediately accessible.

C. Searching For Available Files

. . .

Software located on the Napster servers maintains a "search index" of Napster's collective directory. To search the files available from Napster users currently connected to the network servers, the individual user accesses a form in the Music-Share software stored in his computer and enters either the name of a song or an artist as the object of the search. The form is then transmitted to a Napster server and automatically compared to the MP3 file names listed in the server's search index. Napster's server compiles a list of all MP3 file names pulled from the search index which include the same search terms entered on the search form and transmits the list to the searching user. The Napster server does not search the contents of any MP3 file; rather, the search is limited to "a text search of the file names indexed in a particular cluster. Those file names may contain typographical errors or otherwise inaccurate descriptions of the content of the files since they are designated by other users." *Napster*, 114 F.Supp.2d at 906.

. . .

D. Transferring Copies of an MP3 file

To transfer a copy of the contents of a requested MP3 file, the Napster server software obtains the Internet address of the requesting user and the Internet address of the "host user" (the user with the available files). The Napster servers then communicate the host user's Internet address to the requesting user. The requesting user's computer uses this information to establish a connection with the host user and downloads a copy of the contents of the MP3 file from one computer to the other over the Internet, "peer-to-peer." . . .

. . .

III

Plaintiffs claim Napster users are engaged in the wholesale reproduction and distribution of copyrighted works, all constituting direct infringement.[2] The district court agreed. We note that the district court's conclusion that plaintiffs have presented a prima facie case of direct infringement by Napster users is not presently appealed by Napster. . . .

A. Infringement

Plaintiffs must satisfy two requirements to present a prima facie case of direct infringement: (1) they must show ownership of the allegedly infringed material and (2) they must demonstrate that the alleged infringers violate at least one exclusive right granted to copyright holders under 17 U.S.C. § 106. *See* 17 U.S.C. § 501(a) (infringement occurs when alleged infringer engages in activity listed in § 106); *see also Baxter v. MCA, Inc.*, 812 F.2d 421, 423 (9th Cir.1987); *see, e.g., S.O.S., Inc. v. Pay-*

---

[2] Secondary liability for copyright infringement does not exist in the absence of direct infringement by a third party. *Religious Tech. Ctr. v. Netcom On-Line Communication Servs., Inc.*, 907 F.Supp. 1361, 1371 (N.D. Cal.1995) ("[T]here can be no contributory infringement by a defendant without direct infringement by another."). It follows that Napster does not facilitate infringement of the copyright laws in the absence of direct infringement by its users.

day, Inc., 886 F.2d 1081, 1085 n.3 (9th Cir.1989) ("The word 'copying' is shorthand for the infringing of any of the copyright owner's five exclusive rights . . . ."). Plaintiffs have sufficiently demonstrated ownership. The record supports the district court's determination that "as much as eighty-seven percent of the files available on Napster may be copyrighted and more than seventy percent may be owned or administered by plaintiffs." *Napster,* 114 F.Supp.2d at 911.

The district court further determined that plaintiffs' exclusive rights under § 106 were violated: "here the evidence establishes that a majority of Napster users use the service to download and upload copyrighted music. . . . And by doing that, it constitutes—the uses constitute direct infringement of plaintiffs' musical compositions, recordings." *A&M Records, Inc. v. Napster, Inc.,* 2000 WL 1009483, at *1 (N. D. Cal. July 26, 2000) (transcript of proceedings). The district court also noted that "it is pretty much acknowledged . . . by Napster that this is infringement." *Id.* We agree that plaintiffs have shown that Napster users infringe at least two of the copyright holders' exclusive rights: the rights of reproduction, § 106(1); and distribution, § 106(3). Napster users who upload file names to the search index for others to copy violate plaintiffs' distribution rights. Napster users who download files containing copyrighted music violate plaintiffs' reproduction rights.

. . .

B. Fair Use

Napster contends that its users do not directly infringe plaintiffs' copyrights because the users are engaged in fair use of the material. Napster identifies three specific alleged fair uses: sampling, where users make temporary copies of a work before purchasing; space-shifting, where users access a sound recording through the Napster system that they already own in audio CD format; and permissive distribution of recordings by both new and established artists.

The district court considered factors listed in 17 U.S.C. § 107, which guide a court's fair use determination. These factors are: (1) the purpose and character of the use; (2) the nature of the copyrighted work; (3) the "amount and substantiality of the portion used" in relation to the work as a whole; and (4) the effect of the use upon the potential market for the work or the value of the work. The district court first conducted a general analysis of Napster system uses under § 107, and then applied its reasoning to the alleged fair uses identified by Napster. The district court concluded that Napster users are not fair users. We agree. We first address the court's overall fair use analysis.

1. Purpose and Character of the Use

This factor focuses on whether the new work merely replaces the object of the original creation or instead adds a further purpose or different character. In other words, this factor asks "whether and to what extent the new work is 'transformative.' " *See Campbell v. Acuff-Rose Music, Inc.,* 510 U.S. 569, 579 (1994).

The district court first concluded that downloading MP3 files does not transform the copyrighted work. *Napster,* 114 F.Supp.2d at 912. This conclusion is supportable. Courts have been reluctant to find fair use when an original work is merely retransmitted in a different medium. *See, e.g., Infinity Broadcast Corp. v. Kirkwood*, 150 F.3d 104, 108 (2d Cir.1994) (concluding that retransmission of radio broadcast over telephone lines is not transformative); *UMG Recordings, Inc. v. MP3. com, Inc.*, 92 F.Supp.2d 349, 351 (S.D.N.Y.) . . . .

This "purpose and character "element also requires the district court to determine whether the allegedly infringing use is commercial or noncommercial. *See Campbell*, 510 U.S. at 584-85. A commercial use weighs against a finding of fair use but is not conclusive on the issue. *Id.* The district court determined that Napster users engage in commercial use of the copyrighted materials largely because (1) "a host user sending a file cannot be said to engage in a personal use when distributing that file to an anonymous requester" and (2) "Napster users get for free something they would ordinarily have to buy." *Napster*, 114 F.Supp.2d at 912. The district court's findings are not clearly erroneous.

Direct economic benefit is not required to demonstrate a commercial use. Rather, repeated and exploitative copying of copyrighted works, even if the copies are not offered for sale, may constitute a commercial use. *See Worldwide Church of God v. Philadelphia Church of God*, 227 F.3d 1110, 1118 (9th Cir.2000) (stating that church that copied religious text for its members "unquestionably profit[ed]" from the unauthorized "distribution and use of [the text] without having to account to the copyright holder"); *American Geophysical Union v. Texaco, Inc.*, 60 F.3d 913, 922 (2d Cir.1994) (finding that researchers at for-profit laboratory gained indirect economic advantage by photocopying copyrighted scholarly articles). In the record before us, commercial use is demonstrated by a showing that repeated and exploitative unauthorized copies of copyrighted works were made to save the expense of purchasing authorized copies. Plaintiffs made such a showing before the district court

We also note that the definition of a financially motivated transaction for the purposes of criminal copyright actions includes trading infringing copies of a work for other items, "including the receipt of other copyrighted works." *See* No Electronic Theft Act ("NET Act"), Pub.L. No. 105-147, [17] U.S.C. § 101 (defining "Financial Gain").

2. The Nature of the Use

Works that are creative in nature are "closer to the core of intended copyright protection" than are more fact-based works. *See Campbell*, 510 U.S. at 586. The district court determined that plaintiffs' "copyrighted musical compositions and sound recordings are creative in nature . . . which cuts against a finding of fair use under the second factor." *Napster*, 114 F.Supp.2d at 913. We find no error in the district court's conclusion.

3. The Portion Used

"While 'wholesale copying does not preclude fair use per se,' copying an entire work 'militates against a finding of fair use.' " *Worldwide Church*, 227 F.3d at 1118 (quoting *Hustler Magazine, Inc. v. Moral Majority, Inc.*, 796 F.2d 1148, 1155 (9th Cir.1986)). The district court determined that Napster users engage in "wholesale copying" of copyrighted work because file transfer necessarily "involves copying the entirety of the copyrighted work." *Napster*, 114 F.Supp.2d at 913. We agree. We note, however, that under certain circumstances, a court will conclude that a use is fair even when the protected work is copied in its entirety. *See, e.g., Sony Corp. v. Universal City Studios, Inc.*, 464 U.S. 417, 449-50 (1984) (acknowledging that fair use of time-shifting necessarily involved making a full copy of a protected work).

4. Effect of Use on Market

"Fair use, when properly applied, is limited to copying by others which does not materially impair the marketability of the work which is copied." *Harper & Row Publishers, Inc. v. Nation Enters.*, 471 U.S. 539, 566-67 (1985). "[T]he importance of this [fourth] factor will vary, not only with the amount of harm, but also with the relative strength of the showing on the other factors." *Campbell*, 510 U.S. at 591 n. 21. The proof required to demonstrate present or future market harm varies with the purpose and character of the use:

> A challenge to a noncommercial use of a copy-righted work requires proof either that the particular use is harmful, or that if it should become widespread, it would adversely affect the potential market for the copy-righted work. . . . *If the intended use is for commercial gain, that likelihood [of market harm] may be presumed. But if it is for a noncommercial purpose, the likelihood must be demonstrated.*

Sony, 464 U.S. at 451 (emphases added).

Addressing this factor, the district court concluded that Napster harms the market in "at least" two ways: it reduces audio CD sales among college students and it "raises barriers to plaintiffs' entry into the market for the digital download-ing of music." *Napster*, 114 F.Supp.2d at 913. The district court relied on evidence plaintiffs submitted to show that Napster use harms the market for their copy-righted musical compositions and sound recordings. In a separate memorandum and order regarding the parties' objections to the expert reports, the district court examined each report, finding some more appropriate and probative than others. *A & M Records, Inc. v. Napster, Inc.*, [114 F.Supp.2d 896 (N.D. Cal. 2000)]. . . .

[The plaintiffs' evidence included reports by three experts: Dr. E. Deborah Jay; Michael Fine, Chief Executive Officer of Soundscan; and Dr. David J. Teece. Jay surveyed a random sample of college and university students on their reasons for using Napster and the impact Napster had on their music purchases. The trial court, recognizing that the Jay Report surveyed only one segment of Napster users, found "evidence of lost sales attributable to college use to be probative of irrepara-ble harm." Fine found that online file sharing had resulted in a loss of "album" sales within college markets, and while the trial court expressed some concerns regarding Fine's methodology and findings, it refused to exclude the report as evi-dence of harm. Teece studied whether plaintiffs had suffered or were likely to suf-fer harm in their existing and planned businesses due to Napster use.

Napster offered a report by Dr. Peter S. Fader that concluded that Napster *bene-fited* the music industry because MP3 music file-sharing stimulated more audio CD sales than it displaced. The district court found problems in the Fader's administra-tion of his survey and the lack of objective data in his report and decided the report's generality rendered it "of dubious reliability and value," and so did not rely on Fader's report in its fair use findings.]

The district court cited both the Jay and Fine Reports in support of its finding that Napster use harms the market for plaintiffs' copyrighted musical compositions and sound recordings by reducing CD sales among college students. The district court cited the Teece Report to show the harm Napster use caused in raising barriers to plaintiffs' entry into the market for digital downloading of music. The district court's careful consideration of defendant's objections to these reports and decision to rely on the reports for specific issues demonstrates a proper exercise of discretion in addition to a correct application of the fair use doctrine. Defendant has failed to show any basis for disturbing the district court's findings.

We, therefore, conclude that the district court made sound findings related to Napster's deleterious effect on the present and future digital download market. Moreover, lack of harm to an established market cannot deprive the copyright holder of the right to develop alternative markets for the works. *See L.A. Times v. Free Republic*, 54 U.S.P.Q.2d 1453, 1469-71 (C.D. Cal. 2000) (stating that online market for plaintiff newspapers' articles was harmed because plaintiffs demonstrated that "[defendants] are attempting to exploit the market for viewing their articles online"); *see also UMG Recordings*, 92 F.Supp.2d at 352 ("Any allegedly positive impact of defendant's activities on plaintiffs' prior market in no way frees defendant to usurp a further market that directly derives from reproduction of the plaintiffs' copyrighted works."). Here, similar to *L.A. Times* and *UMG Recordings*, the record supports the district court's finding that the "record company plaintiffs have already expended considerable funds and effort to commence Internet sales and licensing for digital downloads." 114 F.Supp.2d at 915. Having digital downloads available for free on the Napster system necessarily harms the copyright holders' attempts to charge for the same downloads.

Judge Patel did not abuse her discretion in reaching the above fair use conclusions, nor were the findings of fact with respect to fair use considerations clearly erroneous. We next address Napster's identified uses of sampling and space-shifting.

5. Identified Uses

Napster maintains that its identified uses of sampling and space-shifting were wrongly excluded as fair uses by the district court.

a. Sampling

Napster contends that its users download MP3 files to "sample" the music in order to decide whether to purchase the recording. Napster argues that the district court: (1) erred in concluding that sampling is a commercial use because it conflated a noncommercial use with a personal use; (2) erred in determining that sampling adversely affects the market for plaintiffs' copyrighted music, a requirement if the use is non-commercial; and (3) erroneously concluded that sampling is not a fair use because it determined that samplers may also engage in other infringing activity.

The district court determined that sampling remains a commercial use even if some users eventually purchase the music. We find no error in the district court's determination. Plaintiffs have established that they are likely to succeed in proving that even authorized temporary downloading of individual songs for sampling purposes is commercial in nature. *See Napster,* 114 F.Supp.2d at 913. The record supports a finding that free promotional downloads are highly regulated by the record company plaintiffs and that the companies collect royalties for song samples available on retail Internet sites. *Id.* Evidence relied on by the district court demonstrates that the free downloads provided by the record companies consist of thirty-to-sixty second samples or are full songs programmed to "time out," that is, exist only for a short time on the downloader's computer. *Id.* at 913-14. In comparison, Napster users download a full, free and permanent copy of the recording. *Id.* at 914-15. The determination by the district court as to the commercial purpose and character of sampling is not clearly erroneous.

The district court further found that both the market for audio CDs and market for online distribution are adversely affected by Napster's service. As stated in our discussion of the district court's general fair use analysis: the court did not abuse its discretion when it found that, overall, Napster has an adverse impact on the audio CD and digital download markets. Contrary to Napster's assertion that the district court failed to specifically address the market impact of sampling, the district court determined that "[e]ven if the type of sampling supposedly done on Napster were a non-commercial use, plaintiffs have demonstrated a substantial likelihood that it would adversely affect the potential market for their copyrighted works if it became widespread." *Napster,* 114 F.Supp.2d at 914. The record supports the district court's preliminary determinations that: (1) the more music that sampling users download, the less likely they are to eventually purchase the recordings on audio CD; and (2) even if the audio CD market is not harmed, Napster has adverse effects on the developing digital download market.

Napster further argues that the district court erred in rejecting its evidence that the users' downloading of "samples" increases or tends to increase audio CD sales. The district court, however, correctly noted that "any potential enhancement of plaintiffs' sales . . . would not tip the fair use analysis conclusively in favor of defendant." *Id.* at 914. We agree that increased sales of copyrighted material attributable to unauthorized use should not deprive the copyright holder of the right to license the material. *See Campbell,* 510 U.S. at 591 n. 21 ("Even favorable evidence, without more, is no guarantee of fairness. Judge Leval gives the example of the film producer's appropriation of a composer's previously unknown song that turns the song into a commercial success; the boon to the song does not make the film's simple copying fair."); *see also L.A. Times,* 54 U.S.P.Q.2d at 1471-72. Nor does positive impact in one market, here the audio CD market, deprive the copyright holder of the right to develop identified alternative markets, here the digital download market. *See* [54 U.S.P.Q.2d] at 1469-71.

We find no error in the district court's factual findings or abuse of discretion in the court's conclusion that plaintiffs will likely prevail in establishing that sampling does not constitute a fair use.

b. Space-Shifting

Napster also maintains that space-shifting is a fair use. Space-shifting occurs when a Napster user downloads MP3 music files in order to listen to music he already owns on audio CD. Napster asserts that we have already held that space-shifting of musical compositions and sound recordings is a fair use. *See Recording Indus. Ass'n of Am. v. Diamond Multimedia Sys., Inc.,* 180 F.3d 1072, 1079 (9th Cir.1999) ("Rio [a portable MP3 player] merely makes copies in order to render portable, or 'space-shift, 'those files that already reside on a user's hard drive. . . . Such copying is a paradigmatic noncommercial personal use."). *See also generally Sony,* 464 U.S. at 423 (holding that "time-shifting," where a video tape recorder owner records a television show for later viewing, is a fair use).

We conclude that the district court did not err when it refused to apply the "shifting" analyses of *Sony* and *Diamond*. Both *Diamond* and *Sony* are inapposite because the methods of shifting in these cases did not also simultaneously involve distribution of the copyrighted material to the general public; the time or space-shifting of copyrighted material exposed the material only to the original user. In *Diamond*, for example, the copyrighted music was transferred from the user's computer hard drive to the user's portable MP3 player. So too *Sony*, where "the majority of VCR purchasers . . . did not distribute taped television broadcasts, but merely enjoyed them at home." *Napster,* 114 F.Supp.2d at 913. Conversely, it is obvious that once a user lists a copy of music he already owns on the Napster system in order to access the music from another location, the song becomes "available to millions of other individuals," not just the original CD owner. *See UMG Recordings,* 92 F.Supp.2d at 351-52 (finding spaceshifting of MP3 files not a fair use even when previous ownership is demonstrated before a download is allowed).

c. Other Uses

Permissive reproduction by either independent or established artists is the final fair use claim made by Napster. The district court noted that plaintiffs did not seek to enjoin this and any other noninfringing use of the Napster system, including: chat rooms, message boards and Napster's New Artist Program. Plaintiffs do not challenge these uses on appeal.

We find no error in the district court's determination that plaintiffs will likely succeed in establishing that Napster users do not have a fair use defense. . . .

. . .

2. The Audio Home Recording Act

The Audio Home Recording Act of 1992 ("AHRA"), Pub. L. No. 102–563, 106 Stat. 4248 (1992), was enacted in response to the release into the consumer marketplace of digital audio tape ("DAT") recorders. A DAT recorder may be used by consumers to make copies of audio recordings in digital format. Like music recorded on a CD, music recorded on DAT can be copied repeatedly, through multiple generations, with no loss of fidelity to the original. Holders of copyrights in musical works and recordings feared that availability of DAT recorders would lead to widespread copying of recorded music, cutting into sales of tapes and CDs. Manufacturers of DAT recorders entered into negotiations involving record companies, music publishers, musicians, and other participants in the music industry, arriving at a settlement that Congress ratified by enacting the AHRA.

The central feature of the AHRA is a simple quid pro quo. First, the music industry receives a technological solution to the problem of unauthorized copying of music recordings. All DAT recorders and similar devices, which in the statute are called "digital audio recording devices" ("DARDs"), must be outfitted with a Serial Copy Management System. 17 U.S.C. § 1002(a). This technology allows an original recording to be copied any number of times, but prevents the copying of a copy. Second, the music industry receives a stream of royalty payments deriving from sales of DARDs and the media (e.g., digital audio tapes) upon which these devices record. Manufacturers and importers of these devices pay a royalty of two percent of the sales price, and manufacturers and importers of recording media pay three percent of the sales price, into a fund that is distributed to music copyright holders and to recording artists. 17 U.S.C. § 1003–06.

In return, the manufacturers of the recording devices are free to market them, without the threat of being sued as contributory infringers. This is accomplished by Section 1008 of the AHRA.

Recording Indus. Ass'n Of Am. v. Diamond Multimedia Systems Inc.
180 F.3d 1072 (9th Cir.1999).

■ O'SCANNLAIN, CIRCUIT JUDGE

In this case involving the intersection of computer technology, the Internet, and music listening, we must decide whether the Rio portable music player is a digital audio recording device subject to the restrictions of the Audio Home Recording Act of 1992.

I

This appeal arises from the efforts of the Recording Industry Association of America and the Alliance of Artists and Recording Companies (collectively, "RIAA") to enjoin the manufacture and distribution by Diamond Multimedia Systems ("Diamond") of the Rio portable music player. The Rio is a small device (roughly the size of an audio cassette) with headphones that allows a user to download MP3 audio files from a computer and to listen to them elsewhere. The dispute over the Rio's design and function is difficult to comprehend without an understanding of the revolutionary new method of music distribution made possible by digital recording and the Internet; thus, we will explain in some detail the brave new world of Internet music distribution.

A

The introduction of digital audio recording to the consumer electronics market in the 1980's is at the root of this litigation. Before then, a person wishing to copy an original music recording—e.g., wishing to make a cassette tape of a record or compact disc—was limited to analog, rather than digital, recording technology. With analog recording, each successive generation of copies suffers from an increasingly pronounced degradation in sound quality. For example, when an analog cassette copy of a record or compact disc is itself copied by analog technology, the resulting "second-generation" copy of the original will most likely suffer from the hiss and lack of clarity characteristic of older recordings. With digital recording, by contrast, there is almost no degradation in sound quality, no matter how many generations of copies are made. Digital copying thus allows thousands of perfect or near perfect copies (and copies of copies) to be made from a single original recording. Music "pirates" use digital recording technology to make and to distribute near perfect copies of commercially prepared recordings for which they have not licensed the copyrights.

Until recently, the Internet was of little use for the distribution of music because the average music computer file was simply too big: the digital information on a single compact disc of music required hundreds of computer floppy discs to store, and downloading even a single song from the Internet took hours. However, various compression algorithms (which make an audio file "smaller" by limiting the audio bandwidth) now allow digital audio files to be transferred more quickly and stored more efficiently. MPEG-1 Audio Layer 3 (commonly known as "MP3") is the most popular digital audio compression algorithm in use on the Internet, and the compression it provides makes an audio file "smaller" by a factor of twelve to one without significantly reducing sound quality. MP3's popularity is due in large part to the fact that it is a standard, non-proprietary compression algorithm freely available for use by anyone, unlike various proprietary (and copyright-secure) competitor algorithms. Coupled with the use of cable modems, compression algorithms like MP3 may soon allow an hour of music to be downloaded from the Internet to a personal computer in just a few minutes.

These technological advances have occurred, at least in part, to the traditional music industry's disadvantage. By most accounts, the predominant use of MP3 is the trafficking in illicit audio recordings, presumably because MP3 files do not contain codes identifying whether the compressed audio material is copyright protected. Various pirate websites offer free downloads of copyrighted material, and a single pirate site on the Internet may contain thousands of pirated audio computer files.

RIAA represents the roughly half-dozen major record companies (and the artists on their labels) that control approximately ninety percent of the distribution of recorded music in the United States. RIAA asserts that Internet distribution of serial digital copies of pirated copyrighted material will discourage the purchase of legitimate recordings, and predicts that losses to digital Internet piracy will soon surpass the $300 million that is allegedly lost annually to other more traditional forms of piracy.[1] RIAA fights a well-nigh constant battle against Internet piracy,

---

[1] Whether or not piracy causes such financial harm is a subject of dispute. Critics of the industry's piracy loss figures have noted that a willingness to download illicit files for free does not necessarily correlate to lost sales, for the simple reason that persons willing to accept an item for free often will not purchase the same item, even if no longer freely available. *See* Lewis Kurlantzick & Jacqueline E. Pennino, *The Audio Home Recording Act of 1992 and the Formation of Copyright Policy*, 45 J. Copyright Soc'y U.S.A. 497, 506 (1998). Critics further note that the price of commercially available recordings already reflects the existence of copying

monitoring the Internet daily, and routinely shutting down pirate websites by sending cease-and-desist letters and bringing lawsuits. There are conflicting views on RIAA's success—RIAA asserts that it can barely keep up with the pirate traffic, while others assert that few, if any, pirate sites remain in operation in the United States and illicit files are difficult to find and download from anywhere online.

In contrast to piracy, the Internet also supports a burgeoning traffic in legitimate audio computer files. Independent and wholly Internet record labels routinely sell and provide free samples of their artists' work online, while many unsigned artists distribute their own material from their own websites. Some free samples are provided for marketing purposes or for simple exposure, while others are teasers intended to entice listeners to purchase either mail order recordings or recordings available for direct download (along with album cover art, lyrics, and artist biographies). Diamond cites a 1998 "Music Industry and the Internet" report by Jupiter Communications which predicts that online sales for pre-recorded music will exceed $1.4 billion by 2002 in the United States alone.

Prior to the invention of devices like the Rio, MP3 users had little option other than to listen to their downloaded digital audio files through headphones or speakers at their computers, playing them from their hard drives. The Rio renders these files portable. More precisely, once an audio file has been downloaded onto a computer hard drive from the Internet or some other source (such as a compact disc player or digital audio tape machine), separate computer software provided with the Rio (called "Rio Manager") allows the user further to download the file to the Rio itself via a parallel port cable that plugs the Rio into the computer. The Rio device is incapable of effecting such a transfer, and is incapable of receiving audio files from anything other than a personal computer equipped with Rio Manager.

Generally, the Rio can store approximately one hour of music, or sixteen hours of spoken material (e.g., downloaded newscasts or books on tape). With the addition of flash memory cards, the Rio can store an additional half-hour or hour of music. The Rio's sole output is an analog audio signal sent to the user via headphones. The Rio cannot make duplicates of any digital audio file it stores, nor can it transfer or upload such a file to a computer, to another device, or to the Internet. However, a flash memory card to which a digital audio file has been downloaded can be removed from one Rio and played back in another.

B

RIAA brought suit to enjoin the manufacture and distribution of the Rio, alleging that the Rio does not meet the requirements for digital audio recording devices under the Audio Home Recording Act of 1992, 17 U.S.C. § 1001 *et seq.* (the "Act"), because it does not employ a Serial Copyright Management System ("SCMS") that sends, receives, and acts upon information about the generation and copyright

---

and the benefits and harms such copying causes; thus, they contend, the current price of recordings offsets, at least in part, the losses incurred by the industry from home taping and piracy. *See id.* at 509-10.

status of the files that it plays. *See id.* § 1002(a)(2).[2] RIAA also sought payment of the royalties owed by Diamond as the manufacturer and distributor of a digital audio recording device. *See id.* § 1003.

The district court denied RIAA's motion for a preliminary injunction, holding that RIAA's likelihood of success on the merits was mixed and the balance of hardships did not tip in RIAA's favor. *See generally Recording Indus. Ass'n of America, Inc. v. Diamond Multimedia Sys., Inc.,* 29 F.Supp.2d 624 (C.D. Cal. 1998) ("*RIAA I*"). RIAA brought this appeal.

II

The initial question presented is whether the Rio falls within the ambit of the Act. The Act does not broadly prohibit digital serial copying of copyright protected audio recordings. Instead, the Act places restrictions only upon a specific type of recording device. Most relevant here, the Act provides that "[n]o person shall import, manufacture, or distribute any *digital audio recording device* . . . that does not conform to the Serial Copy Management System ["SCMS"] [or] a system that has the same functional characteristics." 17 U.S.C. § 1002(a)(1), (2) (emphasis added). The Act further provides that "[n]o person shall import into and distribute, or manufacture and distribute, any *digital audio recording device* . . . unless such person records the notice specified by this section and subsequently deposits the statements of account and applicable royalty payments." *Id.* § 1003(a) (emphasis added). Thus, to fall within the SCMS and royalty requirements in question, the Rio must be a "digital audio recording device," which the Act defines through a set of nested definitions.

The Act defines a "digital audio recording device" as:

> any machine or device of a type commonly distributed to individuals for use by individuals, whether or not included with or as part of some other machine or device, the digital recording function of which is designed or marketed for the primary purpose of, and that is capable of, making a digital audio copied recording for private use . . . .

Id. § 1001(3) (emphasis added).

A "digital audio copied recording" is defined as:

> a reproduction in a digital recording format of a *digital musical recording,* whether that reproduction is made directly from another digital musical recording or indirectly from a transmission.

Id. § 1001(1) (emphasis added).

A "digital musical recording" is defined as:

> *a material object —*
>
> > (i) in which are fixed, in a digital recording format, *only sounds, and material, statements, or instructions incidental to those fixed sounds, if*

---

[2] At the time the preliminary injunction was sought and denied, the Rio did not incorporate SCMS; Diamond asserts that it has now incorporated such a system into the Rio Manager software, though not into the Rio itself.

any, and

> (ii) from which the sounds and material can be perceived, repro-
> duced, or otherwise communicated, either directly or with the aid of
> a machine or device.

Id. § 1001(5)(A) (emphasis added).

In sum, to be a digital audio recording device, the Rio must be able to reproduce, either "directly" or "from a transmission," a "digital music recording."

III

We first consider whether the Rio is able directly to reproduce a digital music
recording — which is a specific type of material object in which only sounds are
fixed (or material and instructions incidental to those sounds).

A

The typical computer hard drive from which a Rio directly records is, of course,
a material object. However, hard drives ordinarily contain much more than "only
sounds, and material, statements, or instructions incidental to those fixed sounds."
Indeed, almost all hard drives contain numerous programs (e.g., for word processing, scheduling appointments, etc.) and databases that are not incidental to any
sound files that may be stored on the hard drive. Thus, the Rio appears not to
make copies from digital music recordings, and thus would not be a digital audio
recording device under the Act's basic definition unless it makes copies from
transmissions.

Moreover, the Act expressly provides that the term "digital musical recording"
does not include:

> *a material object —*
>
> (i) in which the fixed sounds consist entirely of spoken word re-
> cordings, or
>
> (ii) *in which one or more computer programs are fixed*, except that a
> digital recording may contain statements or instructions constituting
> the fixed sounds and incidental material, and statements or instruc-
> tions to be used directly or indirectly in order to bring about the per-
> ception, reproduction, or communication of the fixed sounds and in-
> cidental material.

Id. § 1001(5)(B) (emphasis added). As noted previously, a hard drive is a material
object in which one or more programs are fixed; thus, a hard drive is excluded
from the definition of digital music recordings. This provides confirmation that the
Rio does not record "directly" from "digital music recordings," and therefore
could not be a digital audio recording device unless it makes copies "from transmissions."

B

The district court rejected the exclusion of computer hard drives from the definition of digital music recordings under the statute's plain language (after noting
its "superficial appeal") because it concluded that such exclusion "is ultimately
unsupported by the legislative history, and contrary to the spirit and purpose of

the [Act]." *RIAA I*, 29 F.Supp.2d at 629. We need not resort to the legislative history because the statutory language is clear. *See City of Auburn v. United States*, 154 F.3d 1025, 1030 (9th Cir.1998) ("[W]here statutory command is straightforward, 'there is no reason to resort to legislative history.' " (quoting *United States v. Gonzales*, 520 U.S. 1, 6 (1997))). Nevertheless, we will address the legislative history here, because it is consistent with the statute's plain meaning and because the parties have briefed it so extensively.[4]

1

The Senate Report states that "if the material object contains computer programs or data bases that are not incidental to the fixed sounds, then the material object would not qualify" under the basic definition of a digital musical recording. S. Rep. 102-294 (1992), *reprinted at* 1992 WL 133198, at * 118-19. The Senate Report further states that the definition "is intended to cover those objects commonly understood to embody sound recordings and their underlying works." *Id.* at *97. A footnote makes explicit that this definition only extends to the material objects in which songs are normally fixed: "[t]hat is recorded compact discs, digital audio tapes, audio cassettes, long-playing albums, digital compact cassettes, and mini-discs." *Id.* at n. 36. There are simply no grounds in either the plain language of the definition or in the legislative history for interpreting the term "digital musical recording" to include songs fixed on computer hard drives.

RIAA contends that the legislative history reveals that the Rio does not fall within the specific exemption from the digital musical recording definition of "a material object in which one or more computer programs are fixed." 17 U.S.C. § 1001(5)(B)(ii). The House Report describes the exemption as "revisions reflecting exemptions for talking books and *computer programs*." H.R. Rep. 102-873(I) (1992), *reprinted at* 1992 WL 232935, at *35 (emphasis added); *see also id.* at *44 ("In addition to containing *an express exclusion of computer programs* in the definition of 'digital musical recording'. . . .") (emphasis added). We first note that limiting the exemption to computer programs is contrary to the plain meaning of the exemption. As Diamond points out, a computer program is not a material object, but rather, a literary work, *see, e.g., Apple Computer, Inc. v. Franklin Computer Corp.*, 714 F.2d 1240, 1249 (3d Cir.1983) ("[A] computer program . . . is a 'literary work.' "), that can be fixed in a variety of material objects, *see* 17 U.S.C. § 101 (" 'Literary works' are works . . . expressed in words, numbers, or other verbal or numerical symbols or indicia, *regardless of the nature of the material objects, such as books . . . tapes, disks, or cards, in which they are embodied.*") (emphasis added). Thus, the plain language of the exemption at issue does not exclude the copying of programs from coverage by the Act, but instead, excludes copying from various types of material objects. Those objects include hard drives, which indirectly achieve the desired result of

---

[4] There is no precedent (other than the district court's order) to guide the panel's interpretation of the Act. The Act has only been discussed once in a published opinion by another federal court, and there, only to explain why it had no effect on the Copyright Act provisions at issue in that case. *See ABKCO Music, Inc. v. Stellar Records, Inc.*, 96 F.3d 60, 65-66 (2d Cir.1996).

excluding copying of programs. But by its plain language, the exemption is not limited to the copying of programs, and instead extends to any copying from a computer hard drive.

Moreover, RIAA's assertion that computer hard drives do not fall within the exemption is irrelevant because, regardless of that portion of the legislative history which addresses the *exemption* from the definition of digital music recording, *see id.* § 1001(5)(B)(ii), the Rio does not reproduce files from something that falls within the plain language of the basic *definition* of a digital music recording, *see id.* § 1001(5)(A).

2

The district court concluded that the exemption of hard drives from the definition of digital music recording, and the exemption of computers generally from the Act's ambit, "would effectively eviscerate the [Act]" because "[a]ny recording device could evade [ ] regulation simply by passing the music through a computer and ensuring that the MP3 file resided momentarily on the hard drive." *RIAA I,* 29 F.Supp.2d at 630. While this may be true, the Act seems to have been expressly designed to create this loophole.

a

Under the plain meaning of the Act's definition of digital audio recording devices, computers (and their hard drives) are not digital audio recording devices because their "primary purpose" is not to make digital audio copied recordings. *See* 17 U.S.C. § 1001(3). Unlike digital audio tape machines, for example, whose primary purpose is to make digital audio copied recordings, the primary purpose of a computer is to run various programs and to record the data necessary to run those programs and perform various tasks. The legislative history is consistent with this interpretation of the Act's provisions, stating that "the typical personal computer would not fall within the definition of 'digital audio recording device,' " S. Rep. 102-294, at *122, because a personal computer's "recording function is designed and marketed primarily for the recording of data and computer programs," *id.* at *121. Another portion of the Senate Report states that "[i]f the 'primary purpose' of the recording function is to make objects other than digital audio copied recordings, then the machine or device is not a 'digital audio recording device,' *even if the machine or device is technically capable of making such recordings." Id.* (emphasis added). The legislative history thus expressly recognizes that computers (and other devices) have recording functions capable of recording digital musical recordings, and thus implicate the home taping and piracy concerns to which the Act is responsive. Nonetheless, the legislative history is consistent with the Act's plain language—computers are *not* digital audio recording devices.[6]

---

[6] Indeed, Diamond asserted at oral argument (and supports the assertion with the affidavit of a direct participant in the negotiations and compromises that resulted in the final language of the Act) that the exclusion of computers from the Act's scope was part of a carefully negotiated compromise between the various industries with interests at stake, and without which, the computer industry would have vigorously opposed passage of the Act.

b

In turn, because computers are not digital audio recording devices, they are not required to comply with the SCMS requirement and thus need not send, receive, or act upon information regarding copyright and generation status. *See* 17 U.S.C. § 1002(a)(2). And, as the district court found, MP3 files generally do not even carry the codes providing information regarding copyright and generation status. *See RIAA I*, 29 F.Supp.2d at 632. Thus, the Act seems designed to allow files to be "laundered" by passage through a computer, because even a device with SCMS would be able to download MP3 files lacking SCMS codes from a computer hard drive, for the simple reason that there would be no codes to prevent the copying.

Again, the legislative history is consistent with the Act's plain meaning. As the Technical Reference Document that describes the SCMS system explains, "[d]igital audio signals . . . that have no information concerning copyright and/or generation status *shall be recorded* by the [digital audio recording] device so that the digital copy is copyright asserted and original generation status." *Technical Reference Document for the Audio Home Recording Act of 1992*, II-A, Par. 10, *reprinted in* H.R. Rep. 102-780(I), 32, 43 (1992) (emphasis added). Thus, the incorporation of SCMS into the Rio would allow the Rio to copy MP3 files lacking SCMS codes so long as it marked the copied files as "original generation status." And such a marking would allow another SCMS device to make unlimited further copies of such "original generation status" files, *see, e.g.*, H.R. Rep. 102-873(I), at *47 ("Under SCMS . . . consumers will be able to make an unlimited number of copies from a digital musical recording."), despite the fact that the Rio does not permit such further copies to be made because it simply cannot download or transmit the files that it stores to any other device. Thus, the Rio without SCMS inherently allows *less* copying than SCMS permits.

c

In fact, the Rio's operation is entirely consistent with the Act's main purpose — the facilitation of personal use. As the Senate Report explains, "[t]he purpose of [the Act] is to ensure the right of consumers to make analog or digital audio recordings of copyrighted music for their *private, noncommercial use*." S. Rep. 102-294, at *86 (emphasis added). The Act does so through its home taping exemption, *see* 17 U.S.C. § 1008, which "protects all noncommercial copying by consumers of digital and analog musical recordings," H.R. Rep. 102-873(I), at *59. The Rio merely makes copies in order to render portable, or "space-shift," those files that already reside on a user's hard drive. *Cf. Sony Corp. of America v. Universal City Studios*, 464 U.S. 417, 455 (1984) (holding that "time-shifting" of copyrighted television shows with VCR's constitutes fair use under the Copyright Act, and thus is not an infringement). Such copying is paradigmatic noncommercial personal use entirely consistent with the purposes of the Act.

IV

Even though it cannot directly reproduce a digital music recording, the Rio would nevertheless be a digital audio recording device if it could reproduce a digital music recording "from a transmission." 17 U.S.C. § 1001(1).

. . .

[After examining the statutory language and legislative history, the court concluded that] a device falls within the Act's provisions if it can indirectly copy a digital music recording by making a copy from a transmission of that recording. Because the Rio cannot make copies from transmissions, but instead, can only make copies from a computer hard drive, it is not a digital audio recording device.[7]

V

For the foregoing reasons, the Rio is not a digital audio recording device subject to the restrictions of the Audio Home Recording Act of 1992. The district court properly denied the motion for a preliminary injunction against the Rio's manufacture and distribution. Having so determined, we need not consider whether the balance of hardships or the possibility of irreparable harm supports injunctive relief.

AFFIRMED.

EXTENSIONS

The AHRA and p2p file sharing. The Ninth Circuit in the *Napster* case, excerpted above, also considered Napster's claim that it was not liable for copyright infringement under the AHRA's limit on infringement suits:

> Napster alleges that two statutes insulate it from liability. First, Napster asserts that its users engage in actions protected by § 1008 of the Audio Home Recording Act of 1992, 17 U.S.C. § 1008. . . .
>
> The statute states in part:
>
> *No action may be brought under this title alleging infringement of copyright* based on the manufacture, importation, or distribution of a digital audio recording device, a digital audio recording medium, an analog recording device, or an analog recording medium, or *based on the noncommercial use by a consumer of such a device or medium* for making digital musical recordings or analog musical recordings.
>
> 17 U.S.C. § 1008 (emphases added). Napster contends that MP3 file exchange is the type of "noncommercial use" protected from infringement actions by the statute. Napster asserts it cannot be secondarily liable for users' nonactionable exchange of copyrighted musical recordings.
>
> The district court rejected Napster's argument, stating that the Audio Home Recording Act is "irrelevant" to the action because: (1) plaintiffs did not bring claims under the Audio Home Recording Act; and (2) the Audio Home Re-

---

[7] We further note that any transmission reproduced indirectly must pass through a computer, as an MP3 file, to reach the Rio. As we explained in part III.B.2, *supra*, computers are exempted from the requirement of reading and transmitting SCMS codes, and MP3 files do not incorporate such codes. Thus, requiring the Rio to implement SCMS because it can indirectly reproduce a transmission of a digital music recording would be, as the district court concluded, "an exercise in futility." *RIAA I*, 29 F.Supp.2d at 632. SCMS would not alter the Rio's ability to reproduce such transmissions, just as it would not alter the Rio's ability to reproduce digital music recordings uploaded to a computer hard drive.

cording Act does not cover the downloading of MP3 files. *Napster,* 114 F.Supp.2d at 916 n. 19.

We agree with the district court that the Audio Home Recording Act does not cover the downloading of MP3 files to computer hard drives. First, "[u]nder the plain meaning of the Act's definition of digital audio recording devices, computers (and their hard drives) are not digital audio recording devices because their 'primary purpose' is not to make digital audio copied recordings." *Recording Indus. Ass'n of Am. v. Diamond Multimedia Sys., Inc.,* 180 F.3d 1072, 1078 (9th Cir.1999). Second, notwithstanding Napster's claim that computers are "digital audio recording devices," computers do not make "digital music recordings" as defined by the Audio Home Recording Act. *Id.* at 1077 (citing S. Rep. 102-294) ("There are simply no grounds in either the plain language of the definition or in the legislative history for interpreting the term 'digital musical recording' to include songs fixed on computer hard drives.").

239 F.3d 1004, 1024–25 (9th Cir.2001).

QUESTIONS FOR DISCUSSION

1. *RIAA decision implications.* Should consumers of digital music and portable digital music players such as the Rio or the iPod be happy or unhappy with the decision in *RIAA v. Diamond Multimedia*?

2. *Insulation for burning?* If a computer user downloads an MP3 file from the Internet, and burns it directly onto a CD-R disk using her computer's CD-RW drive, is she insulated from infringement liability under the AHRA, 17 U.S.C. § 1008? Consult the definitions of "digital audio recording device" and "digital audio recording medium" in 17 U.S.C. § 1001.

V. SECONDARY LIABILITY

Since at least the beginning of the twentieth century, copyright law has evolved doctrines that impose liability for copyright infringement not only on those who themselves actually commit infringing acts of reproduction, distribution, adaptation, public performance, or public display, but also on certain third parties. The principal secondary liability doctrines are contributory infringement and vicarious liability.

The classic statement of the test for contributory infringement, which holds a defendant liable for her actions that contributed to someone else's act of direct infringement, is in *Gershwin Publishing Corp. v. Columbia Artists Management, Inc.,* 443 F.2d 1159, 1162 (2d Cir.1971): "One who, with knowledge of the infringing activity, induces, causes or materially contributes to the infringing conduct of another, may be held liable as a 'contributory' infringer."

The doctrine of vicarious liability holds a defendant vicariously liable for someone else's act of direct infringement based on the relationship between the defendant and the infringer. The doctrine grew out of classic tort law principles of *respondeat superior,* which in certain circumstances impose liability on an employer for torts committed by her employees. Vicarious liability in copyright law, though, has expanded far beyond the employment relationship, and the classic statement of the modern test comes again from the *Gershwin* case: "[E]ven in the absence of an employer-employee relationship one may be vicariously liable if he has the right and ability to supervise the infringing activity and also has a direct financial interest in such activities." *Id.*

The materials in this part consider the extent to which copyright law imposes, or should impose, liability on entities that provide a variety of online services (entities usually referred to as Internet service providers ("ISPs") or online service providers ("OSPs")) for infringement committed by the users of those services.

A. INTERNET SERVICE PROVIDER LIABILITY GENERALLY

Religious Technology Center v. Netcom On-Line Communication Services, Inc.
907 F.Supp. 1361 (N.D.Cal.1995).

■ WHYTE, DISTRICT JUDGE.

This case concerns an issue of first impression regarding intellectual property rights in cyberspace. Specifically, this order addresses whether the operator of a computer bulletin board service ("BBS"), and the large Internet access provider that allows that BBS to reach the Internet, should be liable for copyright infringement committed by a subscriber of the BBS.

Plaintiffs Religious Technology Center ("RTC") and Bridge Publications, Inc. ("BPI") hold copyrights in the unpublished and published works of L. Ron Hubbard, the late founder of the Church of Scientology ("the Church"). Defendant Dennis Erlich ("Erlich")[3] is a former minister of Scientology turned vocal critic of the Church, whose pulpit is now the Usenet newsgroup[4] alt.religion.scientology ("a.r.s."), an on-line forum for discussion and criticism of Scientology. Plaintiffs maintain that Erlich infringed their copyrights when he posted portions of their works on a.r.s. Erlich gained his access to the Internet through defendant Thomas

---

[3] Issues of Erlich's liability were addressed in this court's order of September 22, 1995. That order concludes in part that a preliminary injunction against Erlich is warranted because plaintiffs have shown a likelihood of success on their copyright infringement claims against him. Plaintiffs likely own valid copyrights in Hubbard's published and unpublished works and Erlich's near-verbatim copying of substantial portions of plaintiffs' works was not likely a fair use. To the extent that Netcom and Klemesrud argue that plaintiffs' copyrights are invalid and that Netcom and Klemesrud are not liable because Erlich had a valid fair use defense, the court previously rejected these arguments and will not reconsider them here.

[4] The Usenet has been described as

a worldwide community of electronic BBSs that is closely associated with the Internet and with the Internet community. ¶ The messages in Usenet are organized into thousands of topical groups, or "Newsgroups" . . . . ¶ As a Usenet user, you read and contribute ("post") to your local Usenet site. Each Usenet site distributes its users' postings to other Usenet sites based on various implicit and explicit configuration settings, and in turn receives postings from other sites. Usenet traffic typically consists of as much as 30 to 50 Mbytes of messages per day. ¶ Usenet is read and contributed to on a daily basis by a total population of millions of people . . . . ¶ There is no specific network that is the Usenet. Usenet traffic flows over a wide range of networks, including the Internet and dial-up phone links.

[Daniel] Dern, [THE INTERNET GUIDE FOR NEW USERS] 196-97 [(1994)].

Klemesrud's ("Klemesrud's") BBS "support.com." Klemesrud is the operator of the BBS, which is run out of his home and has approximately 500 paying users. Klemesrud's BBS is not directly linked to the Internet, but gains its connection through the facilities of defendant Netcom On-Line Communications, Inc. ("Netcom"), one of the largest providers of Internet access in the United States.

After failing to convince Erlich to stop his postings, plaintiffs contacted defendants Klemesrud and Netcom. Klemesrud responded to plaintiffs' demands that Erlich be kept off his system by asking plaintiffs to prove that they owned the copyrights to the works posted by Erlich. However, plaintiffs refused Klemesrud's request as unreasonable. Netcom similarly refused plaintiffs' request that Erlich not be allowed to gain access to the Internet through its system. Netcom contended that it would be impossible to prescreen Erlich's postings and that to kick Erlich off the Internet meant kicking off the hundreds of users of Klemesrud's BBS. Consequently, plaintiffs named Klemesrud and Netcom in their suit against Erlich, although only on the copyright infringement claims.[5]

On June 23, 1995, this court heard the parties' arguments on eight motions, three of which relate to Netcom and Klemesrud and are discussed in this order: (1) Netcom's motion for summary judgment; (2) Klemesrud's motion for judgment on the pleadings; and (3) plaintiffs' motion for a preliminary injunction against Netcom and Klemesrud. For the reasons set forth below, the court grants in part and denies in part Netcom's motion for summary judgment and Klemesrud's motion for judgment on the pleadings and denies plaintiffs' motion for a preliminary injunction.

I. NETCOM'S MOTION FOR SUMMARY JUDGMENT OF NONINFRINGEMENT

A. Summary Judgment Standards

. . . Summary judgment is proper when ". . . there is no genuine issue as to any material fact and . . . the moving party is entitled to judgment as a matter of law." Fed. R. Civ. P. 56(c). . . .

B. Copyright Infringement

. . . The court has already determined that plaintiffs have established that they own the copyrights to all of the Exhibit A and B works, except item 4 of Exhibit A. The court also found plaintiffs likely to succeed on their claim that defendant Erlich copied the Exhibit A and B works and was not entitled to a fair use defense. Plaintiffs argue that, although Netcom was not itself the source of any of the infringing materials on its system, it nonetheless should be liable for infringement, either directly, contributorily, or vicariously. Netcom disputes these theories of infringement and further argues that it is entitled to its own fair use defense.

---

[5] The First Amended Complaint ("FAC") contains three claims: (1) copyright infringement of BPI's published literary works against all defendants; (2) copyright infringement of RTC's unpublished confidential works against all defendants; and (3) misappropriation of RTC's trade secrets against defendant Erlich only.

1. Direct Infringement

Infringement consists of the unauthorized exercise of one of the exclusive rights of the copyright holder delineated in section 106. 17 U.S.C. § 501. Direct infringement does not require intent or any particular state of mind,[10] although willfulness is relevant to the award of statutory damages. 17 U.S.C. § 504(c).

Many of the facts pertaining to this motion are undisputed. The court will address the relevant facts to determine whether a theory of direct infringement can be supported based on Netcom's alleged reproduction of plaintiffs' works. The court will look at one controlling Ninth Circuit decision addressing copying in the context of computers and two district court opinions addressing the liability of BBS operators for the infringing activities of subscribers. The court will additionally examine whether Netcom is liable for infringing plaintiffs' exclusive rights to publicly distribute and display their works.

a. *Undisputed Facts*

The parties do not dispute the basic processes that occur when Erlich posts his allegedly infringing messages to a.r.s. Erlich connects to Klemesrud's BBS using a telephone and a modem. Erlich then transmits his messages to Klemesrud's computer, where they are automatically briefly stored. According to a prearranged pattern established by Netcom's software, Erlich's initial act of posting a message to the Usenet results in the automatic copying of Erlich's message from Klemesrud's computer onto Netcom's computer and onto other computers on the Usenet. In order to ease transmission and for the convenience of Usenet users, Usenet servers maintain postings from newsgroups for a short period of time—eleven days for Netcom's system and three days for Klemesrud's system. Once on Netcom's computers, messages are available to Netcom's customers and Usenet neighbors, who may then download the messages to their own computers. Netcom's local server makes available its postings to a group of Usenet servers, which do the same for other servers until all Usenet sites worldwide have obtained access to the postings, which takes a matter of hours.

Unlike some other large on-line service providers, such as CompuServe, America Online, and Prodigy, Netcom does not create or control the content of the information available to its subscribers. It also does not monitor messages as they are posted. It has, however, suspended the accounts of subscribers who violated its terms and conditions, such as where they had commercial software in their posted files. Netcom admits that, although not currently configured to do this, it may be

---

[10] The strict liability for copyright infringement is in contrast to another area of liability affecting online service providers: defamation. Recent decisions have held that where a BBS exercised little control over the content of the material on its service, it was more like a "distributor" than a "republisher" and was thus only liable for defamation on its system where it knew or should have known of the defamatory statements. *Cubby, Inc. v. CompuServe, Inc.,* 776 F.Supp. 135 (S.D.N.Y. 1991). By contrast, a New York state court judge found that Prodigy was a publisher because it held itself out to be controlling the content of its services and because it used software to automatically prescreen messages that were offensive or in bad taste. *Stratton Oakmont, Inc. v. Prodigy Services Co.,* [1995 N.Y. Misc. LEXIS 229].

possible to reprogram its system to screen postings containing particular words or coming from particular individuals. Netcom, however, took no action after it was told by plaintiffs that Erlich had posted messages through Netcom's system that violated plaintiffs' copyrights, instead claiming that it could not shut out Erlich without shutting out all of the users of Klemesrud's BBS.

b. *Creation of Fixed Copies*

The Ninth Circuit addressed the question of what constitutes infringement in the context of storage of digital information in a computer's random access memory ("RAM"). *MAI Systems Corp. v. Peak Computer, Inc.,* 991 F.2d 511, 518 (9th Cir.1993). In *MAI,* the Ninth Circuit upheld a finding of copyright infringement where a repair person, who was not authorized to use the computer owner's licensed operating system software, turned on the computer, thus loading the operating system into RAM for long enough to check an "error log." . . .

In the present case, there is no question after *MAI* that "copies" were created, as Erlich's act of sending a message to a.r.s. caused reproductions of portions of plaintiffs' works on both Klemesrud's and Netcom's storage devices. Even though the messages remained on their systems for at most eleven days, they were sufficiently "fixed" to constitute recognizable copies under the Copyright Act. *See* Information Infrastructure Task Force, *Intellectual Property and the National Information Infrastructure: The Report of the Working Group on Intellectual Property Rights* 66 (1995) ("IITF Report").

c. *Is Netcom Directly Liable for Making the Copies?*

Accepting that copies were made, Netcom argues that Erlich, and not Netcom, is directly liable for the copying. *MAI* did not address the question raised in this case: whether possessors of computers are liable for incidental copies automatically made on their computers using their software as part of a process initiated by a third party. Netcom correctly distinguishes *MAI* on the ground that Netcom did not take any affirmative action that directly resulted in copying plaintiffs' works other than by installing and maintaining a system whereby software automatically forwards messages received from subscribers onto the Usenet, and temporarily stores copies on its system. Netcom's actions, to the extent that they created a copy of plaintiffs' works, are necessary to having a working system for transmitting Usenet postings to and from the Internet. Unlike the defendants in *MAI,* neither Netcom nor Klemesrud initiated the copying. The defendants in *MAI* turned on their customers' computers thereby creating temporary copies of the operating system, whereas Netcom's and Klemesrud's systems can operate without any human intervention. Thus, unlike *MAI,* the mere fact that Netcom's system incidentally makes temporary copies of plaintiffs' works does not mean Netcom has caused the copying. The court believes that Netcom's act of designing or implementing a system that automatically and uniformly creates temporary copies of all data sent through it is not unlike that of the owner of a copying machine who lets the public make copies with it.[12] Although some of the people using the machine

---

[12] Netcom compares itself to a common carrier that merely acts as a passive conduit for information. In a sense, a Usenet server that forwards all messages acts like a common car-

may directly infringe copyrights, courts analyze the machine owner's liability under the rubric of contributory infringement, not direct infringement. *See* [Niva] Elkin-Koren, [*Copyright Law and Social Dialogue on the Information Superhighway: The Case Against Copyright Liability of Bulletin Board Operators*, 13 CARDOZO ARTS & ENT. L. J. 346,] 363 [(1990)] (arguing that "contributory infringement is more appropriate for dealing with BBS liability, first, because it focuses attention on the BBS-users relationship and the way imposing liability on BBS operators may shape this relationship, and second because it better addresses the complexity of the relationship between BBS operators and subscribers"). Plaintiffs' theory would create many separate acts of infringement and, carried to its natural extreme, would lead to unreasonable liability. It is not difficult to conclude that Erlich infringes by copying a protected work onto his computer and by posting a message to a newsgroup. However, plaintiffs' theory further implicates a Usenet server that carries Erlich's message to other servers regardless of whether that server acts without any human intervention beyond the initial setting up of the system. It would also result in liability for every single Usenet server in the worldwide link of computers transmitting Erlich's message to every other computer. These parties, who are liable under plaintiffs' theory, do no more than operate or implement a system that is essential if Usenet messages are to be widely distributed. There is no need to construct the

---

rier, passively retransmitting every message that gets sent through it. Netcom would seem no more liable than the phone company for carrying an infringing facsimile transmission or storing an infringing audio recording on its voice mail. As Netcom's counsel argued, holding such a server liable would be like holding the owner of the highway, or at least the operator of a toll booth, liable for the criminal activities that occur on its roads. Since other similar carriers of information are not liable for infringement, there is some basis for exempting Internet access providers from liability for infringement by their users. The IITF Report concluded that "[i]f an entity provided only the wires and conduit—such as the telephone company, it would have a good argument for an exemption if it was truly in the same position as a common carrier and could not control who or what was on its system." IITF Report at 122. Here, perhaps, the analogy is not completely appropriate as Netcom does more than just "provide the wire and conduits." Further, Internet providers are not natural monopolies that are bound to carry all the traffic that one wishes to pass through them, as with the usual common carrier. Section 111 of the Copyright Act codifies the exemption for passive carriers who are otherwise liable for a secondary transmission. However, the carrier must not have any direct or indirect control over the content or selection of the primary transmission. In any event, common carriers are granted statutory exemptions for liability that might otherwise exist. Here, Netcom does not fall under this statutory exemption, and thus faces the usual strict liability scheme that exists for copyright. Whether a new exemption should be carved out for online service providers is to be resolved by Congress, not the courts. *Compare* Comment, "Online Service Providers and Copyright Law: The Need for Change," 1 SYRACUSE J. LEGIS. & POL'Y 197, 202 (1995) (citing recommendations of online service providers for amending the Copyright Act to create liability only where a "provider 'has actual knowledge that a work that is being or has been transmitted onto, or stored on, its system is infringing,' and has the 'ability and authority' to stop the transmission, and has, after a reasonable amount of time, allowed the infringing activity to continue' ") *with* IITF Report at 122 (recommending that Congress not exempt service providers from strict liability for direct infringements).

Act to make all of these parties infringers. Although copyright is a strict liability statute, there should still be some element of volition or causation which is lacking where a defendant's system is merely used to create a copy by a third party.

Plaintiffs point out that the infringing copies resided for eleven days on Netcom's computer and were sent out from it onto the "Information Superhighway." However, under plaintiffs theory, any storage of a copy that occurs in the process of sending a message to the Usenet is an infringement. While it is possible that less "damage" would have been done if Netcom had heeded plaintiffs' warnings and acted to prevent Erlich's message from being forwarded,[13] this is not relevant to its *direct* liability for copying. The same argument is true of Klemesrud and any Usenet server. Whether a defendant makes a direct copy that constitutes infringement cannot depend on whether it received a warning to delete the message. This distinction may be relevant to contributory infringement, however, where knowledge is an element.

The court will now consider two district court opinions that have addressed the liability of BBS operators for infringing files uploaded by subscribers.

d. *Playboy Case*

Playboy Enterprises, Inc. v. Frena involved a suit against the operator of a small BBS whose system contained files of erotic pictures. 839 F.Supp. 1552, 1554 (M.D. Fla. 1993). A subscriber of the defendant's BBS had uploaded files containing digitized pictures copied from the plaintiff's copyrighted magazine, which files remained on the BBS for other subscribers to download. The court did not conclude, as plaintiffs suggest in this case, that the BBS is itself liable for the unauthorized *reproduction* of plaintiffs' work; instead, the court concluded that the BBS operator was liable for violating the plaintiff's right to publicly *distribute and display* copies of its work.

In support of their argument that Netcom is directly liable for copying plaintiffs' works, plaintiffs cite to the court's conclusion that "[t]here is no dispute that [the BBS operator] supplied a product containing unauthorized copies of a copyrighted work. It does not matter that [the BBS operator] claims he did not make the copies [him]self." *Id.* at 1556. It is clear from the context of this discussion that the *Playboy* court was looking only at the exclusive right to distribute copies to the public, where liability exists regardless of whether the defendant makes copies. Here, however, plaintiffs do not argue that Netcom is liable for its public distribution of copies. Instead, they claim that Netcom is liable because its computers in fact made copies. Therefore, the above-quoted language has no bearing on the issue of direct liability for unauthorized reproductions. Notwithstanding *Playboy*'s holding that a BBS operator may be directly liable for *distributing or displaying* to the public copies of protected works, this court holds that the storage on a defen-

---

[13] The court notes however, that stopping the distribution of information once it is on the Internet is not easy. The decentralized network was designed so that if one link in the chain be closed off, the information will be dynamically rerouted through another link. This was meant to allow the system to be used for communication after a catastrophic event that shuts down part of it.

dant's system of infringing copies and retransmission to other servers is not a direct infringement by the BBS operator of the exclusive right to *reproduce* the work where such copies are uploaded by an infringing user. *Playboy* does not hold otherwise.[16]

e. *Sega Case*

A court in this district addressed the issue of whether a BBS operator is liable for copyright infringement where it solicited subscribers to upload files containing copyrighted materials to the BBS that were available for others to download. *Sega Enterprises Ltd. v. MAPHIA*, 857 F.Supp. 679, 683 (N.D. Cal. 1994). The defendant's "MAPHIA" BBS contained copies of plaintiff Sega's video game programs that were uploaded by users. The defendant solicited the uploading of such programs and received consideration for the right to download files. Access was given for a fee or to those purchasing the defendant's hardware device that allowed Sega video game cartridges to be copied. The court granted a preliminary injunction against the defendant, finding that plaintiffs had shown a prima facie case of direct and contributory infringement. The court found that copies were made by unknown users of the BBS when files were uploaded and downloaded. Further, the court found that the defendant's knowledge of the infringing activities, encouragement, direction and provision of the facilities through his operation of the BBS constituted contributory infringement, even though the defendant did not know exactly when files were uploaded or downloaded.

This court is not convinced that *Sega* provides support for a finding of direct infringement where copies are made on a defendant's BBS by users who upload files. Although there is some language in *Sega* regarding *direct* infringement, it is entirely conclusory:

> Sega has established a *prima facie* case of direct copyright infringement under 17 U.S.C. § 501. Sega has established that unauthorized copies of its games are *made* when such games are uploaded to the MAPHIA bulletin board, here with the knowledge of Defendant Scherman. These games are thereby placed on the storage media of the electronic bulletin board by unknown users.

Id. at 686 (emphasis added). The court's reference to the "knowledge of Defendant" indicates that the court was focusing on contributory infringement, as knowledge is not an element of direct infringement. Perhaps, *Sega's* references to direct infringement and that "copies . . . are made" are to the direct liability of the "unknown users," as there can be no contributory infringement by a defendant without direct infringement by another. Thus, the court finds that neither *Playboy* nor *Sega* requires finding Netcom liable for direct infringement of plaintiffs' exclusive right to reproduce their works.[17]

---

[16] The court further notes that *Playboy* has been much criticized. *See, e.g.*, L. Rose, NETLAW 91-92 (1995). The finding of direct infringement was perhaps influenced by the fact that there was some evidence that defendants in fact knew of the infringing nature of the works, which were digitized photographs labeled "Playboy" and "Playmate."

[17] To the extent that *Sega* holds that BBS operators are directly liable for copyright in-

f. *Public Distribution and Display?*

Plaintiffs allege that Netcom is directly liable for making *copies* of their works. They also allege that Netcom violated their exclusive rights to publicly display copies of their works. There are no allegations that Netcom violated plaintiffs' exclusive right to publicly distribute their works. However, in their discussion of direct infringement, plaintiffs insist that Netcom is liable for "maintain[ing] copies of [Erlich's] messages on its server for eleven days for access by its subscribers and 'USENET neighbors'" and they compare this case to the *Playboy* case, which discussed the right of public distribution. Plaintiffs also argued this theory of infringement at oral argument. Because this could be an attempt to argue that Netcom has infringed plaintiffs' rights of public distribution and display, the court will address these arguments.

Playboy concluded that the defendant infringed the plaintiff's exclusive rights to publicly distribute and display copies of its works. 839 F.Supp. at 1556-57. The court is not entirely convinced that the mere possession of a digital copy on a BBS that is accessible to some members of the public constitutes direct infringement by the BBS operator. Such a holding suffers from the same problem of causation as the reproduction argument. Only the subscriber should be liable for causing the distribution of plaintiffs' work, as the contributing actions of the BBS provider are automatic and indiscriminate. Erlich could have posted his messages through countless access providers and the outcome would be the same: anyone with access to Usenet newsgroups would be able to read his messages. There is no logical reason to draw a line around Netcom and Klemesrud and say that they are uniquely responsible for distributing Erlich's messages. Netcom is not even the first link in the chain of distribution—Erlich had no direct relationship with Netcom but dealt solely with Klemesrud's BBS, which used Netcom to gain its Internet access. Every Usenet server has a role in the distribution, so plaintiffs' argument would create unreasonable liability. Where the BBS merely stores and passes along all messages sent by its subscribers and others, the BBS should not be seen as causing these works to be publicly distributed or displayed.

Even accepting the *Playboy* court's holding, the case is factually distinguishable. Unlike the BBS in that case, Netcom does not maintain an archive of files for its users. Thus, it cannot be said to be "suppl[ying] a product." In contrast to some of its larger competitors, Netcom does not create or control the content of the information available to its subscribers; it merely provides *access* to the Internet, whose content is controlled by no single entity. Although the Internet consists of many different computers networked together, some of which may contain infringing files, it does not make sense to hold the operator of each computer liable as an infringer merely because his or her computer is linked to a computer with an infring-

---

fringement when users upload infringing works to their systems, this court respectfully disagrees with the court's holding for the reasons discussed above. Further, such a holding was dicta, as there was evidence that the defendant knew of the infringing uploads by users and, in fact, actively encouraged such activity, thus supporting the contributory infringement theory.

ing file. It would be especially inappropriate to hold liable a service that acts more like a conduit, in other words, one that does not itself keep an archive of files for more than a short duration. Finding such a service liable would involve an unreasonably broad construction of public distribution and display rights. No purpose would be served by holding liable those who have no ability to control the information to which their subscribers have access, even though they might be in some sense helping to achieve the Internet's automatic "public distribution" and the users' "public" display of files.

g. Conclusion

The court is not persuaded by plaintiffs' argument that Netcom is directly liable for the copies that are made and stored on its computer. Where the infringing subscriber is clearly directly liable for the same act, it does not make sense to adopt a rule that could lead to the liability of countless parties whose role in the infringement is nothing more than setting up and operating a system that is necessary for the functioning of the Internet. Such a result is unnecessary as there is already a party directly liable for causing the copies to be made. Plaintiffs occasionally claim that they only seek to hold liable a party that refuses to delete infringing files after they have been warned. However, such liability cannot be based on a theory of direct infringement, where knowledge is irrelevant. The court does not find workable a theory of infringement that would hold the entire Internet liable for activities that cannot reasonably be deterred. Billions of bits of data flow through the Internet and are necessarily stored on servers throughout the network and it is thus practically impossible to screen out infringing bits from noninfringing bits. Because the court cannot see any meaningful distinction (without regard to knowledge) between what Netcom did and what every other Usenet server does, the court finds that Netcom cannot be held liable for direct infringement. *Cf.* IITF Report at 69 (noting uncertainty regarding whether BBS operator should be directly liable for reproduction or distribution of files uploaded by a subscriber).[19]

2. Contributory Infringement

Netcom is not free from liability just because it did not directly infringe plaintiffs' works; it may still be liable as a contributory infringer. . . . Liability for participation in the infringement will be established where the defendant, "with knowledge of the infringing activity, induces, causes or materially contributes to the infringing conduct of another." *Gershwin Publishing Corp. v. Columbia Artists Management, Inc.,* 443 F.2d 1159, 1162 (2d Cir.1971). . . .

---

[19] Despite that uncertainty, the IITF Report recommends a strict liability paradigm for BBS operators. *See* IITF Report at 122-24. It recommends that Congress not exempt on-line service providers from strict liability because this would prematurely deprive the system of an incentive to get providers to reduce the damage to copyright holders by reducing the chances that users will infringe by educating them, requiring indemnification, purchasing insurance, and, where efficient, developing technological solutions to screening out infringement. Denying strict liability in many cases would leave copyright owners without an adequate remedy since direct infringers may act anonymously or pseudonymously or may not have the resources to pay a judgment. *Id.*

a. *Knowledge of Infringing Activity*

Plaintiffs insist that Netcom knew that Erlich was infringing their copyrights at least after receiving notice from plaintiffs' counsel indicating that Erlich had posted copies of their works onto a.r.s. through Netcom's system. Despite this knowledge, Netcom continued to allow Erlich to post messages to a.r.s. and left the allegedly infringing messages on its system so that Netcom's subscribers and other Usenet servers could access them. Netcom argues that it did not possess the necessary type of knowledge because (1) it did not know of Erlich's planned infringing activities when it agreed to lease its facilities to Klemesrud, (2) it did not know that Erlich would infringe prior to any of his postings, (3) it is unable to screen out infringing postings before they are made, and (4) its knowledge of the infringing nature of Erlich's postings was too equivocal given the difficulty in assessing whether the registrations were valid and whether Erlich's use was fair. The court will address these arguments in turn.

Netcom cites cases holding that there is no contributory infringement by the lessors of premises that are later used for infringement unless the lessor had knowledge of the intended use at the time of the signing of the lease. *See, e.g., Deutsch v. Arnold,* 98 F.2d 686, 688 (2d Cir.1938).[20] The contribution to the infringement by the defendant in *Deutsch* was merely to lease use of the premises to the infringer. Here, Netcom not only leases space but also serves as an access provider, which includes the storage and transmission of information necessary to facilitate Erlich's postings to a.r.s. Unlike a landlord, Netcom retains some control over the use of its system. Thus, the relevant time frame for knowledge is not when Netcom entered into an agreement with Klemesrud. It should be when Netcom provided its services to allow Erlich to infringe plaintiffs' copyrights. It is undisputed that Netcom did not know that Erlich was infringing before it received notice from plaintiffs. Netcom points out that the alleged instances of infringement occurring on Netcom's system all happened prior to December 29, 1994, the date on which Netcom first received notice of plaintiffs' infringement claim against Erlich. Thus, there is no question of fact as to whether Netcom knew or should have known of Erlich's infringing activities that occurred more than 11 days before receipt of the December 28, 1994 letter.

However, the evidence reveals a question of fact as to whether Netcom knew or should have known that Erlich had infringed plaintiffs' copyrights following receipt of plaintiffs' letter. Because Netcom was arguably participating in Erlich's public distribution of plaintiffs' works, there is a genuine issue as to whether Netcom knew of any infringement by Erlich before it was too late to do anything about it. If plaintiffs can prove the knowledge element, Netcom will be liable for contributory infringement since its failure to simply cancel Erlich's infringing message and thereby stop an infringing copy from being distributed worldwide consti-

---

[20] Adopting such a rule would relieve a BBS of liability for failing to take steps to remove infringing works from its system even after being handed a court's order finding infringement. This would be undesirable and is inconsistent with Netcom's counsel's admission that Netcom would have an obligation to act in such circumstances.

tutes substantial participation in Erlich's public distribution of the message.

Netcom argues that its knowledge after receiving notice of Erlich's alleged infringing activities was too equivocal given the difficulty in assessing whether registrations are valid and whether use is fair. Although a mere unsupported allegation of infringement by a copyright owner may not automatically put a defendant on notice of infringing activity, Netcom's position that liability must be unequivocal is unsupportable. While perhaps the typical infringing activities of BBSs will involve copying software, where BBS operators are better equipped to judge infringement, the fact that this involves written works should not distinguish it. Where works contain copyright notices within them, as here, it is difficult to argue that a defendant did not know that the works were copyrighted. To require proof of valid registrations would be impractical and would perhaps take too long to verify, making it impossible for a copyright holder to protect his or her works in some cases, as works are automatically deleted less than two weeks after they are posted. The court is more persuaded by the argument that it is beyond the ability of a BBS operator to quickly and fairly determine when a use is not infringement where there is at least a colorable claim of fair use. Where a BBS operator cannot reasonably verify a claim of infringement, either because of a possible fair use defense, the lack of copyright notices on the copies, or the copyright holder's failure to provide the necessary documentation to show that there is a likely infringement, the operator's lack of knowledge will be found reasonable and there will be no liability for contributory infringement for allowing the continued distribution of the works on its system.

Since Netcom was given notice of an infringement claim before Erlich had completed his infringing activity, there may be a question of fact as to whether Netcom knew or should have known that such activities were infringing. Given the context of a dispute between a former minister and a church he is criticizing, Netcom may be able to show that its lack of knowledge that Erlich was infringing was reasonable. However, Netcom admits that it did not even look at the postings once given notice and that had it looked at the copyright notice and statements regarding authorship it would have triggered an investigation into whether there was infringement. These facts are sufficient to raise a question as to Netcom's knowledge once it received a letter from plaintiffs on December 29, 1994.

b. *Substantial Participation*

Where a defendant has knowledge of the primary infringer's infringing activities, it will be liable if it "induces, causes or materially contributes to the infringing conduct of" the primary infringer. *Gershwin Publishing*, 443 F.2d at 1162. Such participation must be substantial.

Providing a service that allows for the automatic distribution of all Usenet postings, infringing and noninfringing, goes well beyond renting a premises to an infringer. It is more akin to the radio stations that were found liable for rebroadcasting an infringing broadcast. *See, e.g., Select Theatres Corp. v. Ronzoni Macaroni Corp,* 59 U.S.P.Q. 288, 291 (S.D.N.Y. 1943). Netcom allows Erlich's infringing messages to remain on its system and be further distributed to other Usenet servers worldwide.

It does not completely relinquish control over how its system is used, unlike a landlord. Thus, it is fair, assuming Netcom is able to take simple measures to prevent further damage to plaintiffs' copyrighted works, to hold Netcom liable for contributory infringement where Netcom has knowledge of Erlich's infringing postings yet continues to aid in the accomplishment of Erlich's purpose of publicly distributing the postings. Accordingly, plaintiffs do raise a genuine issue of material fact as to their theory of contributory infringement as to the postings made after Netcom was on notice of plaintiffs' infringement claim.

3. Vicarious Liability

Even if plaintiffs cannot prove that Netcom is contributorily liable for its participation in the infringing activity, it may still seek to prove vicarious infringement based on Netcom's relationship to Erlich. A defendant is liable for vicarious liability for the actions of a primary infringer where the defendant (1) has the right and ability to control the infringer's acts and (2) receives a direct financial benefit from the infringement. Unlike contributory infringement, knowledge is not an element of vicarious liability.

a. *Right and Ability To Control*

The first element of vicarious liability will be met if plaintiffs can show that Netcom has the right and ability to supervise the conduct of its subscribers. Netcom argues that it does not have the right to control its users' postings before they occur. Plaintiffs dispute this and argue that Netcom's terms and conditions, to which its subscribers[22] must agree, specify that Netcom reserves the right to take remedial action against subscribers. Plaintiffs argue that under "netiquette," the informal rules and customs that have developed on the Internet, violation of copyrights by a user is unacceptable and the access provider has a duty take measures to prevent this; where the immediate service provider fails, the next service provider up the transmission stream must act. Further evidence of Netcom's right to restrict infringing activity is its prohibition of copyright infringement and its requirement that its subscribers indemnify it for any damage to third parties. Plaintiffs have thus raised a question of fact as to Netcom's right to control Erlich's use of its services.

Netcom argues that it could not possibly screen messages before they are posted given the speed and volume of the data that goes through its system. Netcom further argues that it has never exercised control over the content of its users' postings. Plaintiffs' expert opines otherwise, stating that with an easy software modification Netcom could identify postings that contain particular words or come from particular individuals.[23] Plaintiffs further dispute Netcom's claim that it

---

[22] In this case, Netcom is even further removed from Erlich's activities. Erlich was in a contractual relationship only with Klemesrud. Netcom thus dealt directly only with Klemesrud. However, it is not crucial that Erlich does not obtain access directly through Netcom. The issue is Netcom's right and ability to control the use of its system, which it can do indirectly by controlling Klemesrud's use.

[23] However, plaintiffs submit no evidence indicating Netcom, or anyone, could design software that could determine whether a posting is infringing.

could not limit Erlich's access to Usenet without kicking off all 500 subscribers of Klemesrud's BBS. As evidence that Netcom has in fact exercised its ability to police its users' conduct, plaintiffs cite evidence that Netcom has acted to suspend subscribers' accounts on over one thousand occasions. Further evidence shows that Netcom can delete specific postings. Whether such sanctions occurred before or after the abusive conduct is not material to whether Netcom can exercise control. The court thus finds that plaintiffs have raised a genuine issue of fact as to whether Netcom has the right and ability to exercise control over the activities of its subscribers, and of Erlich in particular.

b. *Direct Financial Benefit*

Plaintiffs must further prove that Netcom receives a direct financial benefit from the infringing activities of its users. For example, a landlord who has the right and ability to supervise the tenant's activities is vicariously liable for the infringements of the tenant where the rental amount is proportional to the proceeds of the tenant's sales. *Shapiro, Bernstein,* 316 F.2d at 306. However, where a defendant rents space or services on a fixed rental fee that does not depend on the nature of the activity of the lessee, courts usually find no vicarious liability because there is no direct financial benefit from the infringement. . . .

Plaintiffs argue that courts will find a financial benefit despite fixed fees. In *Polygram International Publishing, Inc. v. Nevada/TIG, Inc.,* 855 F.Supp. 1314, 1330–33 (D.Mass.1994), the court found a trade show organizer vicariously liable for the infringing performance of an exhibitor because, although the infringement did not affect the fixed rental fee received by the organizers, the organizers benefited from the performances, which helped make the show a financial success. . . . Plaintiffs cite two other cases where, despite fixed fees, defendants received financial benefits from allowing groups to perform infringing works over the radio without having to get an ASCAP license, which minimized the defendants' expenses. Plaintiffs' cases are factually distinguishable. Plaintiffs cannot provide any evidence of a direct financial benefit received by Netcom from Erlich's infringing postings. Unlike *Shapiro, Bernstein,* Netcom receives a fixed fee. There is no evidence that infringement by Erlich, or any other user of Netcom's services, in any way enhances the value of Netcom's services to subscribers or attracts new subscribers. Plaintiffs argue, however, that Netcom somehow derives a benefit from its purported "policy of refusing to take enforcement actions against its subscribers and others who transmit infringing messages over its computer networks." Plaintiffs point to Netcom's advertisements that, compared to competitors like CompuServe and America Online, Netcom provides easy, regulation-free Internet access. Plaintiffs assert that Netcom's policy attracts copyright infringers to its system, resulting in a direct financial benefit. The court is not convinced that such an argument, if true, would constitute a direct financial benefit to Netcom from *Erlich's* infringing activities. Further, plaintiffs' argument is not supported by probative evidence. The only "evidence" plaintiffs cite for their supposition is the declaration of their counsel, Elliot Abelson, who states that

> [o]n April 7, 1995, in a conversation regarding Netcom's position related to this case, Randolf Rice, attorney for Netcom, informed me that Net-

com's executives are happy about the publicity it is receiving in the press as a result of this case. Mr. Rice also told me that Netcom was concerned that it would lose business if it took action against Erlich or Klemesrud in connection with Erlich's infringements.

Netcom objects to this declaration as hearsay and as inadmissible evidence of statements made in compromise negotiations. Whether or not this declaration is admissible, it does not support plaintiffs' argument that Netcom either has a policy of not enforcing violations of copyright laws by its subscribers or, assuming such a policy exists, that Netcom's policy directly financially benefits Netcom, such as by attracting new subscribers. Because plaintiffs have failed to raise a question of fact on this vital element, their claim of vicarious liability fails.

4. First Amendment Argument

Netcom argues that plaintiffs' theory of liability contravenes the first amendment, as it would chill the use of the Internet because every access provider or user would be subject to liability when a user posts an infringing work to a Usenet newsgroup. While the court agrees that an overbroad *injunction* might implicate the First Amendment,[24] imposing *liability* for infringement where it is otherwise appropriate does not necessarily raise a First Amendment issue. The copyright concepts of the idea/expression dichotomy and the fair use defense balance the important First Amendment rights with the constitutional authority for "promot[ing] the progress of science and useful arts," U.S. CONST. art. I, § 8, cl. 8. Netcom argues that liability here would force Usenet servers to perform the impossible—screening all the information that comes through their systems. However, the court is not convinced that Usenet servers are directly liable for causing a copy to be made, and absent evidence of knowledge and participation or control and direct profit, they will not be contributorily or vicariously liable. If Usenet servers were responsible for screening all messages coming through their systems, this could have a serious chilling effect on what some say may turn out to be the best public forum for free speech yet devised.[25] Finally, Netcom admits that its First Amend-

---

[24] For example, plaintiffs' demand that the court order Netcom to terminate Klemesrud's BBS's access to the Internet, thus depriving all 500 of his subscribers, would be overbroad, as it would unnecessarily keep hundreds of users, against whom there are no allegations of copyright infringement, from accessing a means of speech. The overbroadness is even more evident if, as plaintiffs contend, there is a way to restrict only Erlich's access to a.r.s.

[25] Netcom additionally argues that plaintiffs' theory of liability would have a chilling effect on users, who would be liable for merely browsing infringing works. Browsing technically causes an infringing copy of the digital information to be made in the screen memory. *MAI* holds that such a copy is fixed even when information is temporarily placed in RAM, such as the screen RAM. The temporary copying involved in browsing is only necessary because humans cannot otherwise perceive digital information. It is the functional equivalent of reading, which does not implicate the copyright laws and may be done by anyone in a library without the permission of the copyright owner. However, it can be argued that the effects of digital browsing are different because millions can browse a single copy of a work in cyberspace, while only one can read a library's copy at a time.

Absent a commercial or profit-depriving use, digital browsing is probably a fair use; there could hardly be a market for licensing the temporary copying of digital works onto

ment argument is merely a consideration in the fair use argument, which the court will now address.

5. Fair Use Defense

Assuming plaintiffs can prove a violation of one of the exclusive rights guaranteed in section 106, there is no infringement if the defendant's use is fair under section [107]. The proper focus here is on whether Netcom's actions qualify as fair use, not on whether Erlich himself engaged in fair use; the court has already found that Erlich was not likely entitled to his own fair use defense, as his postings contained large portions of plaintiffs' published and unpublished works quoted verbatim with little added commentary.

[The court analyzed the fair use claim under the four statutory factors. With respect to the purpose and character of the defendant's use, the court found that because "Netcom's use of copyrighted materials served a completely different function than that of the plaintiffs, this factor weighs in Netcom's favor, . . . notwithstanding the otherwise commercial nature of Netcom's use." As to the nature of the works used, the court ruled that "because Netcom's use of the works was merely to facilitate their posting to the Usenet, which is an entirely different purpose than plaintiffs' use (or, for that matter, Erlich's use), the precise nature of those works is not important to the fair use determination." With respect to the amount and substantiality of the portion used, the court noted that under the *Sony* decision, "the mere fact that all of a work is copied is not determinative of the fair use question, where such total copying is essential given the purpose of the copying." The court ruled that "Netcom copied no more of plaintiffs' works than necessary to function as a Usenet server. . . . Netcom had no practical alternative way to carry out its socially useful purpose; a Usenet server must copy all files, since the prescreening of postings for potential copyright infringement is not feasible. . . . Accordingly, this factor should not defeat an otherwise valid defense." Finally, as to the effect on the market of or value for the work, the court found that the evidence raised a genuine issue as to the possibility that the postings made available over the Internet by Netcom could hurt the market for plaintiffs' works. In sum, the court said, "Although plaintiffs may ultimately lose on their infringement claims if, among other things, they cannot prove that posting their copyrighted works will harm the market for these works, . . . fair use presents a factual question on which plaintiffs have at least raised a genuine issue of fact. Accordingly, the

---

computer screens to allow browsing. Unless such a use is commercial, such as where someone reads a copyrighted work online and therefore decides not to purchase a copy from the copyright owner, fair use is likely. Until reading a work online becomes as easy and convenient as reading a paperback, copyright owners do not have much to fear from digital browsing and there will not likely be much market effect.

Additionally, unless a user has reason to know, such as from the title of a message, that the message contains copyrighted materials, the browser will be protected by the innocent infringer doctrine, which allows the court to award no damages in appropriate circumstances. In any event, users should hardly worry about a finding of direct infringement; it seems highly unlikely from a practical matter that a copyright owner could prove such infringement or would want to sue such an individual.

court does not find that Netcom's use was fair as a matter of law."]

C. Conclusion

The court finds that plaintiffs have raised a genuine issue of fact regarding whether Netcom should have known that Erlich was infringing their copyrights after receiving a letter from plaintiffs, whether Netcom substantially participated in the infringement, and whether Netcom has a valid fair use defense. Accordingly, Netcom is not entitled to summary judgment on plaintiffs' claim of contributory copyright infringement. However, plaintiffs' claims of direct and vicarious infringement fail.

[The court found that the plaintiffs had not shown a likelihood of success on the merits of their copyright claims nor irreparable harm absent an injunction against Netcom. The only viable theory of infringement, the court held, was contributory infringement, and the court saw little evidence that Netcom knew or should have known that Erlich was engaged in copyright infringement of plaintiffs' works and was not entitled to a fair use defense, especially as they did not receive notice of the alleged infringement until after all but one of the postings were completed. Further, their participation in the infringement was not substantial. Accordingly, the court held that plaintiffs were not entitled to a preliminary injunction.]

EXTENSIONS

1. *Direct infringement: unreasonable and unnecessary liability?* The *Netcom* court, in holding that Netcom is not directly liable for copying, distributing, or publicly displaying materials by virtue of maintaining them on its server, reasons that the alternative "would lead to unreasonable liability." What are the relative costs and benefits of imposing liability on Netcom? Who would be the least cost avoider of the harm resulting from infringement? Was the court's imposition of liability in *Frena* unreasonable? The *Netcom* court also states that imposing liability on Netcom is "unnecessary as there is already a party directly liable for causing the copies to be made." Is this the usual rule in tort actions?

In *CoStar Group Inc. v. LoopNet, Inc.*, 373 F.3d 544 (4th Cir.2004), the court strongly endorsed the principle expressed in Netcom: "Agreeing with the analysis in *Netcom,* we hold that the automatic copying, storage, and transmission of copyrighted materials, when instigated by others, does not render an ISP strictly liable for copyright infringement under §§ 501 and 106 of the Copyright Act."

2. *Liability under the* Netcom *standard.* In *Playboy Enterprises, Inc. v. Russ Hardenburgh, Inc.,* 982 F.Supp. 503 (N.D.Ohio 1997), the court adopted the *Netcom* approach to direct infringement but, contrary to *Netcom,* found the defendants liable under that standard. Plaintiff, Playboy Enterprises, Inc., sued a computer bulletin board system and its owner, alleging they engaged in copyright infringement by making PEI's copyrighted images available for download from the BBS. Subscribers uploaded files to the BBS, which offered them an incentive to do so: "Subscribers were given a 'credit' for each megabyte of electronic data that they uploaded onto the system. For each credit, the subscriber was entitled to download 1.5 extra megabytes of electronic information, in addition to the megabytes available under the normal terms of subscription." Once uploaded, the files were reviewed by a BBS employee, to make sure they were "not pornographic, and not blatantly protected by copyright." *Id.* at 506. Once approved, they were made available for download by other subscribers. The court expressed agreement with the principle, which it attributed to *Netcom,* "that a finding of direct copyright infringement requires some element of direct action or participation." It found the requisite "direct action or participation" in the factors that (1) defendants encouraged subscribers to upload material to the BBS, and (2) defendants employed a screening procedure before making uploaded files available for download. These two factors "transform Defendants from passive providers of a space in which infringing activities happened to occur to active participants in the process of copyright infringement." *Id.* at 512–13.

Do the two factors that the court relies upon warrant treating defendants differently from "passive providers" of a forum for infringement? Does the court's reliance on the second (screening) factor provide BBS operators with a perverse incentive to avoid screening uploads for possible copyright infringement?

In *CoStar Group Inc. v. LoopNet, Inc.*, 373 F.3d 544 (4th Cir.2004), the court held that LoopNet, the operator of a website on which individuals may post photographs, is not directly liable under the *Netcom* principle by virtue of the fact that its employees perform a cursory review of the photographs before allowing them to be posted: "Although LoopNet engages in volitional conduct to block photographs measured by two grossly defined criteria, this conduct, which takes only seconds, does not amount to 'copying,' nor does it add volition to LoopNet's involvement in storing the copy." One judge dissented, believing that this constituted volitional copying under *Netcom*.

3. *Contributory infringement: knowledge of infringement.* In *RTC v. Netcom*, the court holds that Netcom may be contributorily liable for the infringement, based on application of traditional copyright principles, if it had knowledge of the infringing activity and substantially contributed to the infringement. What will constitute the requisite knowledge? The court offers several bits of guidance on this point. First, it says that "[w]here works contain copyright notices within them, as here, it is difficult to argue that a defendant did not know that the works were copyrighted." Does presence of a copyright notice necessarily imply that the posting is infringing? The court continues: "Where a BBS operator cannot reasonably verify a claim of infringement, either because of a possible fair use defense [or] the lack of copyright notices on the copies, the operator's lack of knowledge will be found reasonable and there will be no liability for contributory infringement for allowing the continued distribution of the works on its system." Isn't there always "a possible fair use defense"?

4. *Vicarious liability of corporate officers and employees.* In *Playboy Enterprises, Inc. v. Webbworld, Inc.*, 991 F.Supp. 543 (N.D.Tex.1997), *aff'd mem.*, 168 F.3d 486 (5th Cir.1999), the court held that defendant Webbworld, Inc. directly infringed the copyrights of plaintiff Playboy Enterprises, Inc. by posting Playboy's pictures on its website. The court then addressed the liability of the three individuals who acted as the corporation's principals, one of whom was the corporation's president and sole shareholder. In doing so, it applied the test for vicarious copyright liability: "To show vicarious liability, a plaintiff must prove that a defendant (1) has a direct financial interest in the infringing activity, and (2) has the right and ability to supervise the activity which causes the infringement." *Id.* at 553. The court concluded that all three of the individuals had a direct financial interest in the infringement, as they split the profits from the website's operations. It found that two of the three additionally had the requisite ability to supervise, and therefore held them, but not the third individual, liable as vicarious infringers. Did the court apply the correct test for liability of the individuals? Should it instead, or additionally, have determined whether they were liable as *direct* infringers, either because they themselves performed the actions constituting infringement, or through "piercing the corporate veil"?

5. *Vicarious liability of venture capitalists?* Venture capital firms collect money from investors and invest the money in start-up firms they think are likely to succeed. Of course, the venture capitalists (VCs) only make money if their start-ups succeed and their investors make money, rendering them willing to invest in other ventures sponsored by the VC firm.

Thus, in order to keep control of a start-up's business model and operations during the crucial launch period, VCs often condition funding of a start-up on placement of a member of their firm as interim CEO of the company. For example, at the time the record companies launched their lawsuit against Napster for copyright infringement, its CEO was a member of a VC firm. If Napster is contributorily liable for its users' infringements, is the VC firm vicariously liable?

In 2003, several record companies and music publishers brought an action against media conglomerate Bertelsmann AG, seeking $17 billion in damages based on Bertelsmann's provision of $90 million of funding to Napster as the file-trading company was attempting to transition to a legitimate service. Another group of music-industry plaintiffs sued a venture capital firm that contributed $13 million in funding to Napster.

6. *Vicarious Liability: quantifying financial benefit.* How much of a defendant's income must result from the infringing content to impose vicarious liability? According to the Ninth Circuit, a defendant in an action for vicarious copyright infringement need not derive a "substantial" financial benefit or attribute a specific portion of income to the infringing material. *Ellison v. Robertson*, 357 F.3d 1072, 1078–79 (9th Cir.2004). The court rejected a "quantification" approach to determining whether the financial benefit prong of vicarious liability is met. Rather, it held, "[t]he essential aspect of the 'direct financial benefit' inquiry is whether there is a causal relationship between the infringing activity and any financial benefit a defendant reaps, regardless of *how substantial* the benefit is in proportion to a defendant's overall profits." For a company the size of AOL, the financial contribution of any individual service would seem relatively small compared to AOL's overall income, the court noted, but any earnings attributable to infringing activity would be relevant to the inquiry of vicarious liability.

Nonetheless, the court found that the plaintiff had failed to offer enough evidence for a reasonable juror to conclude that AOL received a direct financial benefit from the infringing activity. While the infringing content may have served as an added benefit that subscribers valued, the evidence did not demonstrate that the activity at issue actually served as a draw for customers and thereby provided a direct financial benefit to AOL. "The record lacks evidence that AOL attracted or retained subscriptions because of the infringement or lost subscriptions because of AOL's eventual obstruction of the infringement. Accordingly, no jury could reasonably conclude that AOL received a direct financial benefit from providing access to the infringing material. Therefore, Ellison's claim of vicarious copyright infringement fails."

QUESTIONS FOR DISCUSSION

Liability for processing credit card payments. Many websites offer content only to customers who pay for that content, and in many instances the customers pay using a credit card. If a website offers credit-card customers copyrighted works without authorization, are the banks and credit-card entities that process the customers' payments to the website liable for the website's infringement? *See Perfect 10, Inc. v. Visa International Service Assn.*, 2004 WL 1773349 (N.D.Cal.2004); *Perfect 10, Inc. v. Visa International Service Assn.*, 2004 WL 3217732 (N.D.Cal.2004).

B. INTERNET SERVICE PROVIDER SAFE HARBORS

In 1998, as Title II of the Digital Millennium Copyright Act (DMCA), Congress amended the 1976 Copyright Act to address specifically the question of the liability of Internet service providers for copyright infringement committed by their customers. The approach adopted was to provide a series of "safe harbors" from liability.

Congress explained the intent behind the safe harbors, codified in Section 512, as follows:

> As to direct infringement, liability is ruled out for passive, automatic acts engaged in through a technological process initiated by another. Thus, the bill essentially codifies the result in the leading and most thoughtful judicial decision to date: *Religious Technology Center v. Netcom On-Line Communication Services, Inc.,* 907 F.Supp. 1361 (N.D.Cal.1995). In doing so, it overrules those aspects of *Playboy Enterprises, Inc. v. Frena,* 839 F.Supp. 1552 (M.D.Fla.1993), insofar as that case suggests that such acts by service providers could constitute direct infringement, and provides certainty that *Netcom* and its progeny, so far only a few district court cases, will be the law of the land.

> As to secondary liability, the bill changes existing law in two primary respects: (1) no monetary relief can be assessed for the passive, automatic acts identified in *Religious Technology Center v. Netcom On-Line Communication Services, Inc.;* and (2) the current criteria for finding contributory infringement or vicarious liability are made clearer and somewhat more difficult to satisfy.

H.R. Rep. No. 105–551, pt. 1, at 11 (1998) (discussing an earlier version of the provision ultimately adopted).

Any entity that comes within the definition of "service provider" in 17 U.S.C. § 512(k) and meets certain threshold eligibility requirements, *see* 17 U.S.C. § 512(*i*), can claim the benefit of the safe harbors. Each safe harbor protects a service provider from liability for copyright infringement based on certain defined activities: transitory digital network communications (§ 512(a)); system caching (§ 512(b)); storage of material on a network at the direction of a user (§ 512(c)); and providing of information location tools (§ 512(d). If the service provider is engaged in an activity covered by one of the safe harbors and meets the specific conditions set forth in the relevant section, then Section 512 shields the provider entirely from monetary liability for copyright infringement based on that activity, and restricts the availability of injunctive relief. *See* 17 U.S.C. § 512(j). If a service provider is not able to claim the benefit of a safe harbor, then its liability for a claim of infringement by a copyright owner is determined by ordinary copyright doctrines.

For an overview of the Section 512 safe harbors, see the Copyright Office's summary of the DMCA at www.copyright.gov/legislation/dmca.pdf. The following sections consider the basic requirements for eligibility for all of the safe harbors and the specific conditions of the safe harbors for transitory digital network communications, for storage of a user's material, and for information location tools.

1. Eligibility for the Safe Harbors

Ellison v. Robertson
357 F.3d 1072 (9th Cir.2004).

■ Pregerson, Circuit Judge

[Robertson allegedly scanned literary works by the science-fiction author Harlan Ellison to create digital files, which Robertson uploaded to the Usenet newsgroup "alt.binaries.e-book." When a message is posted to a Usenet newsgroup, the server to which it is posted temporarily stores the message and automatically transmits the message to connected Usenet servers with which the original server has peer agreements. The Usenet servers that receive the message from peer servers then similarly temporarily store the message and transmit it to their peer servers. The result is that a posted message is quickly transmitted throughout the world. AOL maintains Usenet newsgroup servers so that its members can post and receive Usenet messages. AOL's servers received from its Usenet peer servers Robertson's messages containing Ellison's works, stored those messages, and transmitted them to its Usenet peers and its users who participated in the newsgroup. Ellison sued Robertson, AOL, and others for copyright infringement. In March, 2002, the court granted AOL partial summary judgment. Ellison appealed, and his appeal raised, among other issues, AOL's eligibility for the Section 512 safe harbors under Section 512(i)'s repeat infringer provisions.]

[The appeals court noted the following facts about Ellison's interaction with AOL regarding the alleged infringement:] Ellison learned of the infringing activity and contacted legal counsel. On April 17, 2000, in compliance with the notification procedures the DMCA requires, Ellison's counsel sent an e-mail message to agents of . . . AOL to notify the service providers of the infringing activity. Ellison . . . received nothing from AOL, which claims never to have received the e-mail. . . .

    . . .

AOL changed its contact e-mail address from "copyright@aol.com" to "aol-copyright@aol.com" in the fall of 1999, but waited until April 2000 to register the change with the U.S. Copyright Office. Moreover, AOL failed to configure the old e-mail address so that it would either forward messages to the new address or return new messages to their senders. In the meantime, complaints such as Ellison's went unheeded, and complainants were not notified that their messages had not been delivered. . . .

    . . .

IV. AOL and the Safe Harbors from Liability Under the DMCA

A. Threshold Eligibility Under § 512(i) for OCILLA's Safe Harbors

To be eligible for any of the four safe harbor limitations of liability, a service provider must meet the conditions for eligibility set forth in OCILLA. 17 U.S.C. § 512(i). The safe harbor limitations of liability only apply to a service provider that:

> (A) has adopted and reasonably implemented, and informs subscribers and account holders of the service provider's system or network of, a policy that provides for the termination in appropriate circumstances of subscribers and account holders of the service provider's system or network who are repeat infringers; and

> (B) accommodates and does not interfere with standard technical measures.[11]

---

[11] "Standard technical measures" refers to technical measures that copyright owners use to identify or to protect copyrighted works and: (1) have been developed pursuant to a broad consensus of copyright owners and service providers in an open, fair, voluntary, multi-industry standards process; (2) are available to any person on reasonable and nondis-

17 U.S.C. § 512(i)(1). If a service provider does not meet these threshold require-ments, it is not entitled to invoke OCILLA's safe harbor limitations on liability. 17 U.S.C. § 512(i)(1).

We hold that the district court erred in concluding on summary judgment that AOL satisfied the requirements of § 512(i). There is at least a triable issue of mate-rial fact regarding AOL's eligibility for the safe harbor limitations of liability in this case. Section 512(i)(1)(A) requires service providers to: (1) adopt a policy that pro-vides for the termination of service access for repeat copyright infringers in appro-priate circumstances; (2) implement that policy in a reasonable manner; and (3) inform its subscribers of the policy. It is difficult to conclude as a matter of law, as the district court did, that AOL had "reasonably implemented" a policy against repeat infringers. There is ample evidence in the record that suggests that AOL did not have an effective notification procedure in place at the time the alleged infring-ing activities were taking place. Although AOL did notify the Copyright Office of its correct e-mail address before Ellison's attorney attempted to contact AOL and did post its correct e-mail address on the AOL website with a brief summary of its policy as to repeat infringers, AOL also: (1) changed the e-mail address to which infringement notifications were supposed to have been sent; and (2) failed to pro-vide for forwarding of messages sent to the old address or notification that the e-mail address was inactive. *See Ellison,* 189 F.Supp.2d at 1057-58. AOL should have closed the old e-mail account or forwarded the e-mails sent to the old account to the new one. Instead, AOL allowed notices of potential copyright infringement to fall into a vacuum and to go unheeded; that fact is sufficient for a reasonable jury to conclude that AOL had not reasonably implemented its policy against repeat infringers. . . .

. . .

. . . [B]ecause we conclude that the district court failed to discern triable issues of fact concerning AOL's threshold eligibility under § 512(i) for the DMCA's safe harbor limitations of liability, we reverse the district court's judgment on this mat-ter. . . .

EXTENSIONS

1. *Definition of "service provider."* Section 512's limits on liability apply only to a "service provider" as defined in 17 U.S.C. § 512(k). That section contains two definitions. For the transitory digital network communications safe harbor of Section 512(a), a "service provider" is "an entity offering the transmission, routing, or providing of connections for digital online communications, between or among points specified by a user, of material of the user's choosing, without modification to the content of the material as sent or received." For the remaining safe harbors, the term "means a provider of online services or network access, or the operator of facilities therefor, and includes an entity" that qualifies under the former definition.

Courts have construed these definitions broadly. For example, the Seventh Circuit ruled

criminatory terms; and (3) do not impose substantial costs on service providers or substan-tial burdens on their systems or networks. 17 U.S.C. § 512(i)(2).

that the operator of a peer-to-peer file trading network qualified:

> We turn now to Aimster's defenses under the Online Copyright Infringement Liability Limitation Act, Title II of the Digital Millennium Copyright Act (DMCA), 17 U.S.C. § 512. . . . The DMCA is an attempt to deal with special problems created by the so-called digital revolution. One of these is the vulnerability of Internet service providers such as AOL to liability for copyright infringement as a result of file swapping among their subscribers. Although the Act was not passed with Napster-type services in mind, the definition of Internet service provider is broad ("a provider of online services or network access, or the operator of facilities therefor," 17 U.S.C. § 512(k)(1)(B)), and, as the district judge ruled, Aimster fits it.

In re Aimster Copyright Litigation, 334 F.3d 643, 655 (7th Cir.2003). For similarly broad constructions, often over copyright owner arguments to the contrary, *see Hendrickson v. eBay Inc.*, 165 F.Supp.2d 1082 (C.D.Cal.2001) (holding that online auction site eBay met definition of provider, and that its employees were shielded by the safe harbor as well); *CoStar Group Inc. v. LoopNet, Inc.*, 164 F.Supp.2d 688 (D.Md.2001) (Web page hosting service qualifies as service provider, as definition is not limited to providers of Internet "infrastructure"), *aff'd on other grounds*, 373 F.3d 544 (4th Cir.2004); *Ellison v. Robertson*, 189 F.Supp.2d 1051 (C.D.Cal.2002), *aff'd and rev'd in part*, 357 F.3d 1072 (9th Cir.2004); and *Perfect 10, Inc. v. Cybernet Ventures, Inc.*, 213 F.Supp.2d 1146 (C.D.Cal.2002) (holding that company providing age-verification services to adult-oriented Web sites met definition of "service provider").

2. *Requirement to terminate repeat infringers.* In addition to the Ninth Circuit's opinion in *Ellison* and the district court's opinion in *Perfect 10*, several other decisions have involved Section 512's threshold eligibility requirement of a policy on repeat infringers.

The *Aimster* case involved the operator of a peer-to-peer file-trading network that operated over AOL's instant messaging (AIM) system. One feature of the Aimster system was encryption, as the court explained: "All communications back and forth [over Aimster's peer-to-peer network] are encrypted by the sender by means of encryption software furnished by Aimster as part of the software package downloadable at no charge from the Web site, and are decrypted by the recipient using the same Aimster-furnished software package." When music copyright owners sued Aimster to hold it responsible for infringement committed by users of its network, the court held that Aimster did not meet the eligibility requirement of § 512(*i*):

> The common element of [the] safe harbors is that the service provider must do what it can reasonably be asked to do to prevent the use of its service by "repeat infringers." 17 U.S.C. § 512(i)(1)(A). Far from doing anything to discourage repeat infringers of the plaintiffs' copyrights, Aimster invited them to do so, showed them how they could do so with ease using its system [by providing computerized tutorials instructing users of its software on how to use it for swapping computer files], and by teaching its users how to encrypt their unlawful distribution of copyrighted materials disabled itself from doing anything to prevent infringement.

In re Aimster Copyright Litigation, 334 F.3d 643, 655 (7th Cir.2003), *aff'g* 252 F.Supp.2d 634, 658-59 (N.D.Ill.2002) (describing policy and encryption issues in detail).

Perfect 10 v. CCBill, LLC, 340 F.Supp.2d 1077 (C.D.Cal.2004), involved copyright infringement allegations by the copyright owner of many adult images against companies that provided credit-card payment processing services, age verification services, and internet connectivity service to adult-oriented Web sites that the plaintiff alleged had infringed its copyrights. Several defendants moved for summary judgment based on Section 512's safe harbors, and the court considered whether each had met the eligibility requirements of Section 512(*i*). After noting the *Ellison* court's interpretation of that section, the court articulated its test for compliance as follows:

> The courts have not defined what reasonable implementation of a repeat infringer policy entails. Since the purpose of the DMCA is to relieve internet service providers of the duty of patrolling the Internet for copyright infringements that are not immediately apparent or of which they have no actual knowledge, the DMCA requires that copyright owners inform internet service providers of infringements on the client websites of the internet service providers. *See* § 512(c)(1)(A) and § 512(c)(3). General or vague allegations of copyright infringements are not sufficient to place internet service providers on "notice" of potential copyright infringements. The DMCA provides requirements for proper notification of possible copyright infringements in § 512(c)(3)(A). The purpose behind the notice requirement under the DMCA is to provide the internet service provider with adequate information to find and examine the allegedly infringing material expeditiously. *Hendrickson v. Amazon.com. Inc.*, 298 F.Supp.2d 914, 917 (C.D Cal.2003). "Under the DMCA, a notification from a copyright owner that fails to comply substantially with § 512(c)(3) 'shall not be considered . . . in determining whether a service provider has actual knowledge or is aware of the facts or circumstances from which infringing activity is apparent.' " *Hendrickson v. Amazon.com, Inc.*, 298 F.Supp.2d 914, 917-18 (C.D.Cal.2003). In order for a notification to be "DMCA-compliant," it should substantially fulfill the requirements of § 512(c)(3)(A). *ALS Scan. Inc. v. RemarQ Communities, Inc.*, 239 F.3d 619, 625 (4th Cir.2001). Absolute compliance is not required. *Id.*
>
> Therefore, an internet service provider who receives repeat notifications that substantially comply with the requirements of § 512(c)(3)(A) about one of its clients but does not terminate its relationship with the client, has not reasonably implemented a repeat infringer policy.

340 F.Supp.2d at 1087. For each moving defendant, the court proceeded to evaluate its eligibility under Section 512(*i*) essentially by looking only at whether the plaintiff had produced evidence that the plaintiff had provided DMCA-compliant notifications of claimed infringement under Section 512(c) and that the defendant had not responded to those notifications.

The court also found that one defendant's policy of terminating its service to any Webmaster after receiving three notifications about sites directed by that Webmaster was a reasonable Section 512(*i*) policy, given that the policy must apply to "repeat" infringers and "[i]n order for an infringer to be a 'repeat' infringer, he or she must infringe at least twice."

For additional decisions discussing the requirement for a "repeat infringer" policy, *see A & M Records, Inc. v. Napster, Inc.*, 54 U.S.P.Q.2d 1746 (N.D.Cal.2000); *CoStar Group Inc. v. LoopNet, Inc.*, 164 F.Supp.2d 688 (D.Md.2001), *aff'd on other grounds*, 373 F.3d 544 (4th Cir.2004); *Ellison v. Robertson*, 189 F.Supp.2d 1051 (C.D.Cal.2002), *aff'd and rev'd in part*, 357 F.3d 1072 (9th Cir.2004); *Perfect 10 v. Cybernet Ventures. Inc.*, 213 F.Supp.2d 1146, 1181 (C.D.Cal.2002).

2. Safe Harbor for Network Communications

§ 512. Limitations on liability relating to material online

(a) **Transitory Digital Network Communications.** — A service provider shall not be liable for monetary relief, or, except as provided in subsection (j), for injunctive or other equitable relief, for infringement of copyright by reason of the provider's transmitting, routing, or providing connections for, material through a system or network controlled or operated by or for the service provider, or by reason of the intermediate and transient storage of that material in the course of such transmitting, routing, or providing connections, if —

(1) the transmission of the material was initiated by or at the direction of a person other than the service provider;

(2) the transmission, routing, provision of connections, or storage is carried out through an automatic technical process without selection of the material by the service provider;

(3) the service provider does not select the recipients of the material except as an automatic response to the request of another person;

(4) no copy of the material made by the service provider in the course of such intermediate or transient storage is maintained on the system or network in a manner ordinarily accessible to anyone other than anticipated recipients, and no such copy is maintained on the system or network in a manner ordinarily accessible to such anticipated recipients for a longer period than is reasonably necessary for the transmission, routing, or provision of connections; and

(5) the material is transmitted through the system or network without modification of its content. . . .

Ellison v. Robertson

189 F.Supp.2d 1051 (C.D.Cal.2002), *aff'd in part, rev'd in part,* 357 F.3d 1072 (9th Cir.2004).

■ COOPER, DISTRICT JUDGE.

[The facts of the dispute between Ellison and AOL are summarized in the excerpt from the Ninth Circuit's opinion in the case above. The following excerpt is the district court's discussion of the applicability of the safe harbors to AOL's activity.]

2. Section 512's limitations on liability (a) through (d)

Section 512(n) explicitly provides that each of the four limitation-on-liability safe harbors found in subsections (a) through (d) "describe separate and distinct functions for purposes of applying this section." [17.U.S.C. § 512(n).] As a result, "[w]hether a service provider qualifies for the limitation of liability in any one of the subsections shall be based solely on the criteria in that subsection, and shall not affect a determination of whether the service provider qualifies for the limitations on liability under any other such subsection." *Id.* The DMCA's legislative history provides the following instructional example:

Section 512's limitations on liability are based on functions, and each limitation is intended to describe a separate and distinct function. Consider, for example, a service provider that provides a hyperlink to a site containing infringing material which it then caches on its system in order to facilitate access to it by its users. This service provider is engaging in at least three functions that may be subject to the limitation on liability: transitory digital network communications under subsection (a), system caching under subsection (b), and information locating tools under subsection (d).

H.R. Rep. 105-551(II), at p. 65 (July 22, 1998). In this example, if the service provider met the threshold requirements of subsection (i), "then for its acts of system caching it is eligible for that limitation on liability with corresponding narrow injunctive relief. But if the same company is committing an infringement by using information locating tools to link its users to infringing material, then its fulfillment of the requirements to claim the system caching liability limitation does not affect whether it qualifies for the liability limitation for information location tools." 3 NIMMER ON COPYRIGHT § 12B.06[A], at 12B-53, 54.

Although AOL performs many Internet-service-provider-related functions, Plaintiff's claims against AOL are based solely on its storage of USENET messages on its servers and provision of access to those USENET messages to AOL users and others accessing the AOL system from outside.

AOL claims that it is eligible under both subsections (a) and (c) for a limitation on liability regarding Plaintiff's claims against it.

3. *Subsection (a)'s limitation on liability*

AOL contends that it meets all the criteria for the limitation-on-liability safe harbor found in subsection (a) . . . .

. . .

Subsection (a) does not require ISPs to remove or block access to infringing materials upon receiving notification of infringement, as is the case with subsections (c) and (d).

On the other hand, the term "service provider" is defined more restrictively for subsection (a) than it is throughout the rest of section 512. *See* 17 U.S.C. § 512(k). "As used in subsection (a), the term 'service provider' means an entity offering the transmission, routing, or providing of connections for digital online communication, between or among points specified by a user, of material of the user's choosing, without modification to the content of the material as sent or received."[16] *Id.* In effect, this definition merely restates a number of the requirements that are already set forth in subsection (a). Therefore, Plaintiff's contention that AOL does not meet the restrictive definition of a "service provider" as subsection (k) defines that term for subsection (a) does not need to be addressed separately from Plaintiff's arguments that AOL cannot satisfy the requirements of subsection (a). The Court addresses each of those requirements in turn.

Plaintiff argues that AOL's USENET servers do not engage in "intermediate

---

[16] By contrast, for the purposes of the rest of section 512, the term 'service provider' is defined more broadly as "a provider of online services or network access, or the operator of facilities therefor." 17 U.S.C. § 512(k)(2).

and transient storage" of USENET messages such as the one posted by Robertson. Instead, AOL stores USENET messages containing binary files on its servers for up to fourteen days."[17] AOL, however, claims that the USENET message copies are "intermediate." AOL's role is as an intermediary between the original USENET user who posts a message, such as Robertson, and the recipient USENET users who later choose to view the message.

By itself, the term "intermediate and transient storage" is rather ambiguous. And it is unclear from reading the DMCA whether AOL's storage of USENET messages containing binary files on its servers for fourteen days in order to make those messages accessible to AOL users constitutes "intermediate and transient storage." Certain functions such as the provision of e-mail service or Internet connectivity clearly fall under the purview of subsection (a); other functions such as hosting a web site or chatroom fall under the scope of subsection (c). The question presented by this case is which subsection applies to the function performed by AOL when it stores USENET messages in order to provide USENET access to users. Faced with the ambiguous language in the statute itself, the Court looks to the DMCA's legislative history for guidance in interpretation. The only real guidance is provided in the House Judiciary Committee Report. *See* H.R. Rep. 105-551 (May 22, 1998).

The Court is mindful that reliance on the Report issued by the House Judiciary Committee, "the body that traditionally vets copyright legislation,"[18] is somewhat problematic. The Report's section-by-section analysis was based on an early version of the DMCA which differs in a number of ways from the final version that was eventually enacted by Congress. And the Court recognizes that "even if the language of a given feature [in the earlier version of the bill] does ultimately follow through to the Digital Millennium Copyright Act, the meaning may be different in the context of a law containing vastly more provisions than the [earlier version]." 3 NIMMER ON COPYRIGHT § 12B.01[C], at 12B-19. Nonetheless, the Court believes that the analysis in the House Judiciary Committee Report provides the clearest guidance concerning Congress' intent.

At the time the first House Report was issued, the Committee was considering a version of the bill that differs in many ways from the final version that was eventually enacted into law as the DMCA. However, the previous version's language regarding "the intermediate storage and transmission of material" is very similar to the "intermediate and transient storage of that material" language that is found in the final version of the DMCA. Moreover, the portion of subsection (a) in the previous version, having to do with maintaining material on the system, is also

---

[17] Plaintiff has presented evidence suggesting that despite AOL's 14-day storage protocol, certain USENET messages containing binary files might have resided on AOL's servers for up to thirty-one days, but he makes no claim that such was the case with the messages containing infringing copies of his works (nor with any other infringing messages in the alt.binaries.e-book newsgroup). When deciding whether AOL qualifies for subsection (a)'s limitations on liability, the Court considers only the allegedly infringing postings.

[18] 3 NIMMER ON COPYRIGHT § 12B.01[C], at 12B-18.

extremely similar to the corresponding language found in the enacted version of the DMCA at 512(a)(4).[19] Although other aspects of the bill changed substantially before the final version was enacted into law, the language dealing with the "intermediate storage" did not. Accordingly, the section-by-section analysis found in the First House Report is relevant to interpreting whether AOL's storage of USENET messages in order to provide USENET access to AOL users constitutes (1) "intermediate and transient storage" of (2) copies that are not "maintained on the system or network . . . for a longer period than is reasonably necessary for the transmission, routing, or provision of connections." 17 U.S.C. § 512(a), (a)(4).

The First House Report answers both of those questions with a resounding yes:

> The exempted storage and transmissions are those carried out through an automatic technological process that is indiscriminate — i.e., the provider takes no part in the selection of the particular material transmitted — where the copies are retained no longer than necessary for the purpose of carrying out the transmission. This conduct would ordinarily include forwarding of customers' Usenet postings to other Internet sites in accordance with configuration settings that apply to all such postings . . .

> This exemption codifies the result of *Religious Technology Center v. Netcom On-Line Communications Services, Inc.*, 907 F.Supp. 1361 (N.D. Cal. 1995) ("Netcom"), with respect to liability of providers for direct copyright infringement.[20] See *id.* at 1368-70. In Netcom the court held that a provider

---

[19] The version considered by the House Judiciary Committee, at 512(a)(C) states that "(C) no copy of the material thereby made by the provider is maintained on the provider's system or network in a manner ordinarily accessible to anyone other than the recipients anticipated by the person who initiated the transmission, and no such copy is maintained on the system or network in a manner ordinarily accessible to such recipients for a longer period than is reasonably necessary for the transmission."

The final version of the DMCA provides, at subsection 512(a)(4), that "(4) no copy of the material made by the service provider in the course of such intermediate and transient storage is maintained on the system or network in a manner ordinarily accessible to anyone other than anticipated recipients, and no such copy is maintained on the system or network in a manner ordinarily accessible to such anticipated recipients for a longer period than is reasonably necessary for the transmission, routing, or provision of connections."

[20] Any argument that this codification of *Netcom*'s facts regarding intermediate storage was only meant to apply to direct infringement, and not to vicarious or contributory infringement, is forestalled by subsection (2) of the version of the bill then under consideration by the Judiciary Committee. For subsection (2) makes it clear that the same limitations on liability that apply under subsection (1) for direct infringement also apply to "contributory infringement or vicarious liability, based solely on conduct described in paragraph (1)." *See* H.R. Rep. 105-551(I), at p. 8. In effect, subsection (2) provided that regardless of a plaintiff's theory of infringement — direct, contributory, or vicarious — it was the underlying conduct of the ISP, i.e. the function it was performing, that is central to determining whether the ISP qualifies for a limitation on liability. The section-by-section analysis said this of subsection (2): "Paragraph 512(a)(2) exempts a provider from any type of monetary relief under theories of contributory infringement or vicarious liability for the same activities for which providers are exempt from liability for direct infringement under paragraph 512(a)(1). This provision extends the *Netcom* holding with respect to direct infringement to remove monetary

is not liable for direct infringement where it takes no 'affirmative action that [directly results] in copying . . . works other than by installing and maintaining a system whereby software automatically forwards messages received from subscribers . . . and temporarily stores copies on its system. *By referring to temporary storage of copies, Netcom recognizes implicitly that intermediate copies may be retained without liability for only a limited period of time. The requirement in 512(a)(1) that "no copy be maintained on the system or network . . . for a longer period than reasonably necessary for the transmission" is drawn from the facts of the Netcom case, and is intended to codify this implicit limitation in the Netcom holding.*

H.R. Rep. 105-551(I), at p. 24. (emphasis added).

In *Netcom*, infringing USENET postings were stored on Netcom's servers for up to *eleven days*, during which those postings were accessible to Netcom users. *See Netcom*, 907 F.Supp. at 1368. In AOL's case, messages containing binary files, such as the message posted by Robertson, were stored on AOL's servers for up to *fourteen days*. While "intermediate copies may be retained without liability for only a limited period of time," the three-day difference between AOL's USENET storage and that of Netcom is insufficient to distinguish the two cases.

Accordingly, the Court finds that AOL's storage of Robertson's posts on its USENET servers constitutes "intermediate and transient storage" that was not "maintained on the system or network . . . for a longer period than is reasonably necessary for the transmission, routing, or provision of connections."

While this issue presented the central disagreement regarding AOL's qualifications for subsection(a)'s limitation-on-liability safe harbor, the parties also dispute whether AOL satisfies other requirements set forth in subsection (a).

(1) the transmission of the material was initiated by or at the direction of a person other than the service provider

It is clear that the transmission of Robertson's newsgroup message was not initiated by or at the direction of AOL. In fact, Plaintiff does not appear to even dispute this conclusion.

(2) the transmission, routing, provision of connections, or storage is carried out through an automatic technical process without selection of the material by the service provider

Plaintiff claims that AOL selects the material that is transmitted, routed, and stored in its USENET groups. Namely, AOL decides which newsgroups its subscribers may access through its newsgroup service.

AOL did not select the individual postings on the alt.binaries.e-book newsgroup, let alone the handful of infringing Robertson posts. 512(a)(2) is concerned with "selection of the material," meaning the allegedly infringing material, not material generally. By focusing on AOL's decision to not carry every single news-

---

exposure for such limited activities for claims arising under doctrines of secondary liability. Taken together, paragraphs (1) and (2) mean that providers will never be liable for any monetary damages for this type of transmission of material at the request of third parties or for intermediate storage of such material in the course of the transmission." H. R. Rep. 105-551(I), at p. 25.

group conceivably available, Plaintiff is attempting to slip from the specific to the general, despite the fact that subsection (a) is concerned with the specific material giving rise to the Plaintiff's claims against AOL.

Even if Plaintiff were right, and AOL's treatment of USENET messages in general was the relevant inquiry, AOL's failure to carry every newsgroup available would not disqualify it from subsection (a)(2). Although this would present a closer call, the Court thinks that an ISP would need to take a greater editorial role than merely choosing not to carry certain newsgroups. Although the legislative history states that "subsection (a)(2) means the editorial function of determining what material to send, or the specific sources of material to place on-line," H.R. Rep. 105-551(II) (July 22, 1998), the better interpretation of (a)(2) is that the ISP would have to choose specific postings, or perhaps block messages sent by users expressing opinions with which the ISP disagrees. If an ISP forfeits its ability to qualify for subsection (a)'s safe harbor by deciding not to carry every USENET newsgroup or web site possible, then the DMCA would have the odd effect of punishing ISPs that choose not to carry, for example, newsgroups devoted to child pornography and prostitution, or web sites devoted to ritual torture.[21] Given the concern Congress has shown in other bills for children's access to obscene materials on-line, it would be absurd to conclude that Congress intended such a result with regard to the DMCA.

(3) the service provider does not select the recipients of the material except as an automatic response to the request of another person

Plaintiff argues that AOL selects the recipients of the material because it chooses to engage in USENET peering agreements with some entities but not with others. First, as with (a)(2), Plaintiff's argument fails because section 512(a) is concerned with AOL's selection of the recipients of the material in question in this lawsuit, i.e. Robertson's infringing posts. It is clear that AOL did not select certain recipients for that material. Rather, it was accessible to any AOL user through AOL's USENET newsgroup server. Second, and also analogous to (a)(2), the better interpretation is that AOL would have to direct material to certain recipients (e.g. all AOL members whose names start with "G") but not others. If AOL were to lose its ability to qualify for subsection(a)'s safe harbor because it has peer agreements with some entities but not with others, then the DMCA would appear to place an affirmative obligation on AOL to enter into peering arrangements with every conceivable peering entity in the world. This could not have been Congress' intent.

(5) the material is transmitted through the system without modification of its content

Plaintiff does not seriously contest that AOL does not modify the content of newsgroup messages stored on its servers and transmitted through its system. Moreover, Plaintiff has presented no evidence that AOL in any way modified the content of Robertson's infringing posts.

The Court hereby finds that AOL qualifies for the limitation-on-liability pro-

---

[21] ISPs would also be punished for making the economic decision not to provide access to newsgroups and other sites for which there was no user demand.

vided under subsection 512(a).[22]

. . .

EXTENSIONS

Ninth Circuit decision. On appeal, the Ninth Circuit affirmed this portion of the district court's decision:

> Whether AOL functioned as a conduit service provider in this case presents pure questions of law: was the fourteen day period during which AOL stored and retained the infringing material "transient" and "intermediate" within the meaning of § 512(a)?; was "no . . . copy . . . maintained on the system or network . . . for a longer period than is reasonably necessary for the transmission, routing, or provision of connections?" The district court appropriately answered these questions in the affirmative. In doing so, the court relied upon on the legislative history indicating that Congress intended the relevant language of § 512(a) to codify the result of *Netcom,* 907 F.Supp. at 1361 (provider that stored Usenet messages for 11 days not liable for direct infringement merely for "installing and maintaining a system whereby software automatically forwards messages received from subscribers onto the Usenet, and temporarily stores copies on its system"), and to extend it to claims for secondary liability. We affirm the district court's ruling that AOL is eligible for the safe harbor limitation of liability of § 512(a).[12]

Ellison v. Robertson, 357 F.3d 1072, 1081 (9th Cir.2004).

A & M Records, Inc. v. Napster, Inc.
54 U.S.P.Q.2d 1746 (N.D.Cal.2000).

■ PATEL, J.

[The basic facts or the operation of the Napster peer-to-peer file trading service are discussed in the excerpt from the Ninth Circuit's opinion regarding infringement by Napster users, *supra.* The following excerpt is from a decision of the district court regarding whether Napster was shielded from copyright infringement liability by the Section 512 safe harbors.]

Section 512 of the DMCA addresses the liability of online service and Internet access providers for copyright infringements occurring online. Subsection 512(a) exempts qualifying service providers from monetary liability for direct, vicarious, and contributory infringement and limits injunctive relief to the degree specified in subparagraph 512(j)(1)(B). Interpretation of subsection 512(a), or indeed any of the section 512 safe harbors, appears to be an issue of first impression. . . .

. . .

---

[22] Accordingly, we need not reach the arguments presented by the parties regarding AOL's satisfaction of the requirements of subsection 512(c).

[12] Because a jury has not found AOL liable for copyright infringement and eligible under § 512(i) for the safe harbor limitations of liability, we do not address (nor did the district court) whether AOL could successfully assert the safe harbor under § 512(c).

II. *Subsection 512(a)*

Plaintiffs' principal argument against application of the 512(a) safe harbor is that Napster does not perform the passive conduit function eligible for protection under this subsection. As defendant correctly notes, the words "conduit" or "passive conduit" appear nowhere in 512(a), but are found only in the legislative history and summaries of the DMCA. The court must look first to the plain language of the statute, "construing the provisions of the entire law, including its object and policy, to ascertain the intent of Congress." *United States v. Hockings*, 129 F.3d 1069, 1071 (9th Cir.1997). If the statute is unclear, however, the court may rely on the legislative history. *See Hockings*, 129 F.3d at 1071. The language of subsection 512(a) makes the safe harbor applicable, as a threshold matter, to service providers "transmitting, routing or providing connections for, material *through a system or network* controlled or operated by or for the service provider. . . ." 17 U.S.C. § 512(a) (emphasis added). According to plaintiffs, the use of the word "conduit" in the legislative history explains the meaning of "through a system."

Napster has expressly denied that the transmission of MP3 files ever passes through its servers. Indeed, Kessler declared that "files reside on the computers of Napster users, and are transmitted directly between those computers." MP3 files are transmitted "from the Host user's hard drive and Napster browser, *through the Internet* to the recipient's Napster browser and hard drive." Def. Reply Br. at 3 (emphasis added). The internet cannot be considered "a system or network controlled or operated by or for the service provider," however. 17 U.S.C. § 512(a). To get around this problem, Napster avers (and plaintiffs seem willing to concede) that "Napster's servers and Napster's MusicShare browsers on its users' computers are all part of Napster's overall system." Defendant narrowly defines its system to include the browsers on users' computers. In contrast, plaintiffs argue that either (1) the system does not include the browsers, or (2) it includes not only the browsers, but also the users' computers themselves.

Even assuming that the system includes the browser on each user's computer, the MP3 files are not transmitted "through" the system within the meaning of subsection 512(a). Napster emphasizes the passivity of its role—stating that "[a]ll files transfer directly from the computer of one Napster user *through the Internet* to the computer of the requesting user." Def. Br. at 5 (emphasis added). It admits that the transmission bypasses the Napster server. This means that, even if each user's Napster browser is part of the system, the transmission goes *from* one part of the system *to* another, or *between* parts of the system, but not "through" the system. The court finds that subsection 512(a) does not protect the transmission of MP3 files.

The prefatory language of subsection 512(a) is disjunctive, however. The subsection applies to "infringement of copyright by reason of the provider's transmitting, routing, *or* providing connections through a system or network controlled or operated by or for the service provider." 17 U.S.C. § 512(a) (emphasis added). The court's finding that transmission does not occur "through" the system or network does not foreclose the possibility that subsection 512(a) applies to "routing" or "providing connections." Rather, each of these functions must be analyzed independently.

Napster contends that providing connections between users' addresses "constitutes the value of the system to the users and the public." This connection cannot be established without the provision of the host's address to the Napster browser software installed on the requesting user's computer. The central Napster server delivers the host's address. While plaintiffs contend that the infringing material is not *transmitted* through the Napster system, they provide no evidence to rebut the assertion that Napster supplies the requesting user's computer with information necessary to facilitate a connection with the host.

Nevertheless, the court finds that Napster does not provide connections "through" its system. Although the Napster server conveys address information to establish a connection between the requesting and host users, the connection itself occurs through the Internet. The legislative history of section 512 demonstrates that Congress intended the 512(a) safe harbor to apply only to activities "in which a service provider plays the role of a 'conduit' for the communications of others." H.R. Rep. No. 105-551(II), 105th Cong., 2d Sess. (1998), 1998 WL 414916, at *130. Drawing inferences in the light most favorable to the non-moving party, this court cannot say that Napster serves as a conduit for the connection itself, as opposed to the address information that makes the connection possible. Napster enables or facilitates the initiation of connections, but these connections do not pass through the system within the meaning of subsection 512(a).

Neither party has adequately briefed the meaning of "routing" in subsection 512(a), nor does the legislative history shed light on this issue. Defendant tries to make "routing" and "providing connections" appear synonymous—stating, for example, that "the central Napster server *routes* the transmission by providing the Host's address to the Napster browser that is installed on and in use by User1's computer." However, the court doubts that Congress would have used the terms "routing" and "providing connections" disjunctively if they had the same meaning.[7] It is clear from both parties' submissions that the route of the allegedly infringing material goes through the Internet from the host to the requesting user, not through the Napster server. *See, e.g.,* Def. Br. at 13 ("Indeed, the content of the MP3 files are routed without even passing through Napster's Servers."). The court holds that routing does not occur through the Napster system.

Because Napster does not transmit, route, or provide connections through its system, it has failed to demonstrate that it qualifies for the 512(a) safe harbor, The court thus declines to grant summary adjudication in its favor.

---

[7] Napster sometimes appears to recognize a distinction between the two terms. For example, it states that "the system provides remote users with connection to each other and allows them to transmit and route the information as they choose."

EXTENSIONS

1. *Aimster.* The district court decision in the *Aimster* peer-to-peer litigation took the same approach as the *Napster* decision above regarding the applicability of Section 512(a) to the operator of a peer-to-peer network and determined that Aimster's operations did not come within the scope of the safe harbor. In that case, though, the district court advanced an additional reason why Aimster would not qualify for the safe harbor:

> [Section] 512(a)(5) requires that material be "transmitted through the system or network *without modification of its content.*" However, by Defendants' own admission, Aimster *does* modify the content: "Aimster encrypts all the information that is transferred between users." This modification further belies the notion of Aimster as a mere conduit.

In re Aimster Copyright Litigation, 252 F.Supp.2d 634, 660, n.19 (N.D.Ill.2002), *aff'd*, 334 F.3d 643 (7th Cir.2003).

2. *Payment processing and the safe harbor.* In *Perfect 10 v. CCBill, LLC*, 340 F.Supp.2d 1077 (C.D.Cal.2004), the district court ruled that companies that that provided payment processing services for allegedly infringing adult-oriented Websites qualified for Section 512(a)'s safe harbor because the processing companies were "providing connections for material through a system or network controlled or operated by" the processing companies. The court similarly concluded that a company that that provided age-verification services for allegedly infringing adult-oriented Websites was providing "a connection to the material on its clients' websites through a system which it operates in order to provide its clients with adult verification services," and therefore fell within the scope of Section 512(a) for those services.

3. Safe Harbor for Storing Material at User's Direction

§ 512. Limitations on liability relating to material online

. . .

(c) Information Residing on Systems or Networks at Direction of Users. —

(1) In general. — A service provider shall not be liable for monetary relief, or, except as provided in subsection (j), for injunctive or other equitable relief, for infringement of copyright by reason of the storage at the direction of a user of material that resides on a system or network controlled or operated by or for the service provider, if the service provider —

(A)(i) does not have actual knowledge that the material or an activity using the material on the system or network is infringing;

(ii) in the absence of such actual knowledge, is not aware of facts or circumstances from which infringing activity is apparent; or

(iii) upon obtaining such knowledge or awareness, acts expeditiously to remove, or disable access to, the material;

(B) does not receive a financial benefit directly attributable to the infringing activity, in a case in which the service provider has the right and ability to control such activity; and

(C) upon notification of claimed infringement as described in paragraph (3), responds expeditiously to remove, or disable access to, the material that is claimed to be infringing or to be the subject of infringing activity.

(2) Designated agent. — The limitations on liability established in this subsection apply to a service provider only if the service provider has designated an agent to receive notifications of claimed infringement described in paragraph (3) . . . .

(3) Elements of notification. —

(A) To be effective under this subsection, a notification of claimed infringement must be a written communication provided to the designated agent of a service provider that includes substantially the following:

(i) A physical or electronic signature of a person authorized to act on behalf of the owner of an exclusive right that is allegedly infringed.

(ii) Identification of the copyrighted work claimed to have been infringed, or, if multiple copyrighted works at a single online site are covered by a single notification, a representative list of such works at that site.

(iii) Identification of the material that is claimed to be infringing or to be the subject of infringing activity and that is to be removed or access to which is to be disabled, and information reasonably sufficient to permit the service provider to locate the material.

(iv) Information reasonably sufficient to permit the service provider to contact the complaining party, such as an address, telephone number, and, if available, an electronic mail address at which the complaining party may be contacted.

(v) A statement that the complaining party has a good faith belief that use of the material in the manner complained of is not authorized by the copyright owner, its agent, or the law.

(vi) A statement that the information in the notification is accurate, and under penalty of perjury, that the complaining party is authorized to act on behalf of the owner of an exclusive right that is allegedly infringed.

(B)(i) Subject to clause (ii), a notification from a copyright owner or from a person authorized to act on behalf of the copyright owner that fails to comply substantially with the provisions of subparagraph (A) shall not be considered under paragraph (1)(A) in determining whether a service provider has actual knowledge or is aware of facts or circumstances from which infringing activity is apparent.

(ii) In a case in which the notification that is provided to the service provider's designated agent fails to comply substantially with all the provisions of subparagraph (A) but substantially complies with clauses (ii), (iii), and (iv) of subparagraph (A), clause (i) of this subparagraph applies only if the service provider promptly attempts to contact the person making the notification or takes other reasonable steps to assist in the receipt of notification that substantially complies with all the provisions of subparagraph (A).

ALS Scan, Inc. v. RemarQ Communities, Inc.
239 F.3d 619 (4th Cir.2001).

■ Niemeyer, Circuit Judge:

We are presented with an issue of first impression—whether an Internet service provider enjoys a safe harbor from copyright infringement liability as provided by Title II of the Digital Millennium Copyright Act ("DMCA") when it is put on notice of infringement activity on its system by an imperfect notice. Because we conclude that the service provider was provided with a notice of infringing activity that substantially complied with the Act, it may not rely on a claim of defective notice to maintain the immunity defense provided by the safe harbor. Accordingly, we reverse the ruling of the district court that found the notice fatally defective, and affirm its remaining rulings.

I

ALS Scan, Inc., a Maryland corporation, is engaged in the business of creating and marketing "adult" photographs. It displays these pictures on the Internet to paying subscribers and also sells them through the media of CD ROMs and videotapes. ALS Scan is holder of the copyrights for all of these photographs.

RemarQ Communities, Inc., a Delaware corporation, is an online Internet service provider that provides access to its subscribing members. It has approximately 24,000 subscribers to its newsgroup base and provides access to over 30,000 newsgroups which cover thousands of subjects. These newsgroups, organized by topic, enable subscribers to participate in discussions on virtually any topic, such as fine arts, politics, religion, social issues, sports, and entertainment. For example, RemarQ provides access to a newsgroup entitled "Baltimore Orioles," in which users share observations or materials about the Orioles. It claims that users post over one million articles a day in these newsgroups, which RemarQ removes after about 8-10 days to accommodate its limited server capacity. In providing access to newsgroups, RemarQ does not monitor, regulate, or censor the content of articles posted in the newsgroup by subscribing members. It does, however, have the ability to filter information contained in the newsgroups and to screen its members from logging onto certain newsgroups, such as those containing pornographic material.

Two of the newsgroups to which RemarQ provides its subscribers access contain ALS Scan's name in the titles. These newsgroups—"alt.als" and "alt.binaries.pictures.erotica.als"—contain hundreds of postings that infringe ALS Scan's copyrights. These postings are placed in these newsgroups by RemarQ's subscribers.

Upon discovering that RemarQ databases contained material that infringed

ALS Scan's copyrights, ALS Scan sent a letter, dated August 2, 1999, to RemarQ, stating:

> Both of these newsgroups were created for the sole purpose of violating our Federally filed Copyrights and Tradename. These newsgroups contain virtually all Federally Copyrighted images. . . . Your servers provide access to these illegally posted images and enable the illegal transmission of these images across state lines.

> This is a cease and desist letter. You are hereby ordered to cease carrying these newsgroups within twenty-four (24) hours upon receipt of this correspondence . . . .

> Our ALS Scan models can be identified at http://www.alsscan.com/modlinf2.html[.] Our copyright information can be reviewed at http://www.alsscan.com/copyrite.html[.]

RemarQ responded by refusing to comply with ALS Scan's demand but advising ALS Scan that RemarQ would eliminate individual infringing items from these newsgroups if ALS Scan identified them "with sufficient specificity." ALS Scan answered that RemarQ had included over 10,000 copyrighted images belonging to ALS Scan in its newsgroups over the period of several months and that

> these newsgroups have apparently been created by individuals for the express sole purpose of illegally posting, transferring and disseminating photographs that have been copyrighted by my client through both its websites and its CD-ROMs. The newsgroups, on their face from reviewing messages posted thereon, serve no other purpose.

When correspondence between the parties progressed no further to resolution of the dispute, ALS Scan commenced this action, alleging violations of the Copyright Act and Title II of the DMCA, as well as unfair competition. . . .

In response, RemarQ filed a motion to dismiss the complaint . . . , stating that RemarQ was prepared to remove articles posted in its newsgroups if the allegedly infringing articles were specifically identified. It contended that because it is a provider of access to newsgroups, ALS Scan's failure to comply with the DMCA notice requirements provided it with a defense to ALS Scan's copyright infringement claim.

The district court ruled on RemarQ's motion, stating, "[RemarQ's] motion to dismiss . . . is granted." In making this ruling, the district court held: (1) that RemarQ could not be held liable for direct copyright infringement merely because it provided access to a newsgroup containing infringing material; and (2) that RemarQ could not be held liable for contributory infringement because ALS Scan failed to comply with the notice requirements set forth in the DMCA, 17 U.S.C. § 512(c)(3)(A). This appeal followed. . . .

III

For its principal argument, ALS Scan contends that it substantially complied with the notification requirements of the DMCA and thereby denied RemarQ the "safe harbor" from copyright infringement liability granted by that Act. *See* 17 U.S.C. § 512(c)(3)(A). It asserts that because its notification was sufficient to put

RemarQ on notice of its infringement activities, RemarQ lost its service-provider immunity from infringement liability. It argues that the district court's application of the DMCA was overly strict and that Congress did not intend to permit Internet providers to avoid copyright infringement liability "merely because a cease and desist notice failed to technically comply with the DMCA."

RemarQ argues in response that it did not have "knowledge of the infringing activity as a matter of law," stating that the DMCA protects it from liability because "ALS Scan failed to identify the infringing works in compliance with the Act, and RemarQ falls within the 'safe harbor' provisions of the Act." It notes that ALS Scan never provided RemarQ or the district court with the identity of the pictures forming the basis of its copyright infringement claim. . . .

Title II of the DMCA, designated the "Online Copyright Infringement [Liability] Limitation Act," defines limitations of liability for copyright infringement to which Internet service providers might otherwise be exposed. . . . Neither party to this case suggests that RemarQ is not an Internet service provider for purposes of the Act.

The liability-limiting provision applicable here, 17 U.S.C. § 512(c), gives Internet service providers a safe harbor from liability for "infringement of copyright by reason of the storage at the direction of a user of material that resides on a system or network controlled or operated by or for the service provider" as long as the service provider can show that: (1) it has neither actual knowledge that its system contains infringing materials nor an awareness of facts or circumstances from which infringement is apparent, or it has expeditiously removed or disabled access to infringing material upon obtaining actual knowledge of infringement; (2) it receives no financial benefit directly attributable to infringing activity; and (3) it responded expeditiously to remove or disable access to material claimed to be infringing after receiving from the copyright holder a notification conforming with requirements of § 512(c)(3). Thus, to qualify for this safe harbor protection, the Internet service provider must demonstrate that it has met all three of the safe harbor requirements, and a showing under the first prong—the lack of actual or constructive knowledge—is prior to and separate from the showings that must be made under the second and third prongs.

. . . [W]e conclude that ALS Scan substantially complied with the third prong, thereby denying RemarQ its safe harbor defense.

In evaluating the third prong, requiring RemarQ to remove materials following "notification," the district court concluded that ALS Scan's notice was defective in failing to comply strictly with two of the six requirements of a notification—(1) that ALS Scan's notice include "a list of [infringing] works" contained on the RemarQ site and (2) that the notice identify the infringing works in sufficient detail to enable RemarQ to locate and disable them. 17 U.S.C. § 512(c)(3)(A)(ii), (iii).[3]

---

[3] Section 512(c)(3)(A)(ii), (iii) provides:

   (3) Elements of notification.—

      (A) To be effective under this subsection, a notification of claimed in-

In support of the district court's conclusion, RemarQ points to the fact that ALS Scan never provided it with a "representative list" of the infringing photographs, as required by § 512(c)(3)(A)(ii), nor did it identify those photographs with sufficient detail to enable RemarQ to locate and disable them, as required by § 512(c)(3)(A)(iii). RemarQ buttresses its contention with the observation that not all materials at the offending sites contained material to which ALS Scan held the copyrights. RemarQ's affidavit states in this regard:

> Some, but not all, of the pictures users have posted on these sites appear to be ALS Scan pictures. It also appears that users have posted other non-ALS Scan's erotic images on these newsgroups. The articles in these newsgroups also contain text messages, many of which discuss the adult images posted on the newsgroups.

ALS Scan responds that the two sites in question—"alt.als" & "alt.binaries.pictures.erotica.als" —were created solely for the purpose of publishing and exchanging ALS Scan's copyrighted images. It points out that the address of the newsgroup is defined by ALS Scan's name. As one of its affidavits states:

> [RemarQ's] subscribers going onto the two offending news groups for the purpose of violating [ALS Scan's] copy rights, are actually aware of the copyrighted status of [ALS Scan's] material because (1) each newsgroup has "als" as part of its title, and (2) each photograph belonging to [ALS Scan] has [ALS Scan's] name and/or the copyright symbol next to it.
>
> Each of these two newsgroups was created by unknown persons for the illegal purpose of trading the copyrighted pictures of [ALS Scan] to one another without the need for paying to either (1) become members of [ALS Scan's] web site(s) or (2) purchasing the CD-ROMs produced by[ALS Scan].

ALS Scan presses the contention that these two sites serve no other purpose than to distribute ALS Scan's copyrighted materials and therefore, by directing RemarQ to these sites, it has directed RemarQ to a representative list of infringing materials.

The DMCA was enacted both to preserve copyright enforcement on the Internet and to provide immunity to service providers from copyright infringement liability for "passive," "automatic" actions in which a service provider's system engages through a technological process initiated by another without the knowl-

---

fringement must be a written communication provided to the designated agent of a service provider that includes substantially the following:

. . .

(ii) Identification of the copyrighted work claimed to have been infringed, or, if multiple copyrighted works at a single online site are covered by a single notification, a representative list of such works at that site.

(iii) Identification of the material that is claimed to be infringing or to be the subject of infringing activity and that is to be removed or access to which is to be disabled, and information reasonably sufficient to permit the service provider to locate the material.

edge of the service provider. H.R. CONF. REP. No. 105-796, at 72 (1998). This immunity, however, is not presumptive, but granted only to "innocent" service providers who can prove they do not have actual or constructive knowledge of the infringement, as defined under any of the three prongs of 17 U.S.C. § 512(c)(1). The DMCA's protection of an innocent service provider disappears at the moment the service provider loses its innocence, i.e., at the moment it becomes aware that a third party is using its system to infringe. At that point, the Act shifts responsibility to the service provider to disable the infringing matter, "preserving the strong incentives for service providers and copyright owners to cooperate to detect and deal with copyright infringements that take place in the digital networked environment." H.R. CONF. REP. No. 105-796, at 72 (1998). In the spirit of achieving a balance between the responsibilities of the service provider and the copyright owner, the DMCA requires that a copyright owner put the service provider on notice in a detailed manner but allows notice by means that comport with the prescribed format only "substantially," rather than perfectly. The Act states: "To be effective under this subsection, a notification of claimed infringement must be a written communication provided to the designated agent of a service provider that includes *substantially* the following . . . ." 17 U.S.C. § 512(c)(3)(A) (emphasis added). In addition to substantial compliance, the notification requirements are relaxed to the extent that, with respect to multiple works, not all must be identified—only a "representative" list. *See id.* § 512(c)(3)(A)(ii). And with respect to location information, the copyright holder must provide information that is "reasonably sufficient" to permit the service provider to "locate" this material. *Id.* § 512(c)(3)(A)(iii). This subsection specifying the requirements of a notification does not seek to burden copyright holders with the responsibility of identifying every infringing work—or even most of them—when multiple copyrights are involved. Instead, the requirements are written so as to reduce the burden of holders of multiple copyrights who face extensive infringement of their works. Thus, when a letter provides notice equivalent to a list of representative works that can be easily identified by the service provider, the notice substantially complies with the notification requirements.

In this case, ALS Scan provided RemarQ with information that (1) identified two sites created for the sole purpose of publishing ALS Scan's copyrighted works, (2) asserted that virtually all the images at the two sites were its copyrighted material, and (3) referred RemarQ to two web addresses where RemarQ could find pictures of ALS Scan's models and obtain ALS Scan's copyright information. In addition, it noted that material at the site could be identified as ALS Scan's material because the material included ALS Scan's "name and/or copyright symbol next to it." We believe that with this information, ALS Scan substantially complied with the notification requirement of providing a representative list of infringing material as well as information reasonably sufficient to enable RemarQ to locate the infringing material. To the extent that ALS Scan's claims about infringing materials prove to be false, RemarQ has remedies for any injury it suffers as a result of removing or disabling noninfringing material. *See* 17 U.S.C. § 512(f), (g).

Accordingly, we reverse the district court's ruling granting summary judgment in favor of RemarQ on the basis of ALS Scan's noncompliance with the notification provisions of 17 U.S.C. § 512(c)(3)(A)(ii) and (iii). Because our ruling only removes the safe harbor defense, we remand for further proceedings on ALS Scan's copyright infringement claims and any other affirmative defenses that RemarQ may have. . . .

Hendrickson v. Amazon.com, Inc.
298 F.Supp.2d 914 (C.D.Cal.2003).

■ TERRY J. HATTER, JR., UNITED STATES DISTRICT JUDGE.

Robert Hendrickson ("Hendrickson") owns the copyright to the movie Manson, which he has not released, or authorized to be released, in a digital video disc ("DVD") format. Thus, all copies of Manson sold in a DVD format infringe upon Hendrickson's copyright. 17 U.S.C. § 106(3).

On January 28, 2002, Hendrickson sent a letter to Amazon.com, Inc. ("Amazon"), notifying it that all copies of Manson on DVD infringe his copyright. On October 21, 2002, Hendrickson noticed that a Manson DVD was recently posted for sale by Demetrious Papaioannou ("Papaioannou") on Amazon's website. Two days later, Hendrickson purchased a copy of the DVD from Papaioannou, using Amazon's website credit services to facilitate the transaction.

Hendrickson, then, filed this action against Amazon and Papaioannou. He asserts claims for direct copyright infringement against Amazon and Papaioannou, as well as a vicarious copyright infringement claim against Amazon. Amazon moved for summary judgment, asserting that . . . it is protected against vicarious infringement by the safe harbor provision of the Digital Millennium Copyright Act ("DMCA"), 17 U.S.C. § 512.

The party moving for summary judgment has the initial burden of establishing that there is "no genuine issue as to any material fact and that [it] is entitled to a judgment as a matter of law." . . .

[B]ecause Hendrickson did buy a Manson DVD from the Amazon website, the Court will assume, for purposes of this motion, that Papaioannou committed direct copyright infringement. By showing that there was direct copyright infringement by an independent third party seller, vicarious liability may be transferred to the party that provided the forum and facilitated the sale. *Fonovisa, Inc. v. Cherry Auction, Inc.*, 76 F.3d 259 (9th Cir.1996).

Because Amazon qualifies as an ISP under the DMCA, it is entitled to the safe harbor affirmative defense against a claim of vicarious copyright infringement if it [meets the conditions of Section 512(c)(1)].

Hendrickson's January 28, 2002, letter to Amazon notified Amazon that all Manson DVDs were unauthorized by the copyright owner and that any sales of such DVDs conducted via the Amazon website would be infringing activity in violation of his exclusive right to distribute pursuant to 17 U.S.C. § 106(3). Amazon asserts that the letter neither substantially complied with the identification requirements of the DMCA, nor was it consistent with the intent of the DMCA, which is to facilitate robust development of the internet. The DMCA places the burden on the copyright owner to monitor the internet for potentially infringing sales. "[A] service provider need not monitor its service or affirmatively seek facts indicating infringing activity . . . ." H.R. REP. No. 551(II), 105th Congress, 2nd Session 1998, at 53. To allow a plaintiff to shift its burden to the service provider would be contrary to the balance crafted by Congress. "The goal of § 512 (c)(3)(A)(iii) is to provide the service provider with adequate information to find and examine the allegedly infringing material expeditiously." H.R REP. at 55.

This Court previously granted summary judgment in favor of Hendrickson, in a previous action, by deciding that his January, 2002, letter substantially complied with the requirements as to eight named defendants. To determine the adequacy of Hendrickson's notice, this Court considered the analysis by Judge Kelleher, in *Hendrickson v. eBay, Inc.*, 165 F.Supp.2d. 1082 (C.D. Cal. 2001) ("eBay"), in which that court recognized that:

> There may be instances where a copyright holder need not provide [the ISP] with specific item numbers to satisfy the identification requirement. For example, if a movie studio advised [the ISP] that all listings offering to sell a new movie that has not yet been released in . . . DVD format are unlawful, [the ISP] could easily search its website using the title . . . and identify the offensive listings."

eBay, 165 F.Supp.2d at 1090.

However, because the DMCA is relatively new, the question as to how long an adequate notice should remain viable is still unanswered. "The Committee [did] not intend [to] suggest that a provider must . . . monitor its service . . . ." H.R. REP. at 61. The Committee, also, implied that both the copyright owner and the ISP should cooperate with each other to detect and deal with copyright infringement that take place in the digital networked environment. H.R. REP. at 44. Thus, it was not the intention of Congress that a copyright owner could write one blanket notice to all service providers alerting them of infringing material, thus, relieving him of any further responsibility and, thereby, placing the onus forever on the ISP. However, it is, also, against the spirit of the DMCA if the entire responsibility lies with the copyright owner to forever police websites in search of possible infringers.

In evaluating the balance crafted by Congress, courts traditionally employ a strong presumption that the plain language of a statute expresses congressional intent. The Ninth Circuit has consistently refused to defer to interpretations that conflict with plain statutory language. . . . The actual language of the DMCA is present tense. The service provider must have knowledge that the actual material "is infringing". Alternatively, it must be aware that infringing activity "is apparent". "The term activity is intended to mean activity *using* the material *on the system or network*. The Committee intends such activity to refer to wrongful activity that *is occurring on the site* . . . ." H.R. REP. at 53 (emphasis added). Because the language of the statute is present tense, it clearly indicates that Congress intended for the notice to make the service provider aware of the infringing activity that is occurring at the time it receives the notice.

In interpreting a similar section of the DMCA, Congress states "Online editors and catalogers would not be required to make discriminating judgments about potential copyright infringements." H.R. REP. at 58. Although, the interpretation is referring to the reason for requiring the copyright owner to offer adequate notice, this interpretation must be read in conjunction with the plain language of the statute in addition to the intent of Congress that service providers not have to monitor their websites indefinitely.

Moreover, the purpose behind the notice is to provide the ISP with adequate information to find and examine the allegedly infringing material expeditiously. H.R. REP. at 55. If the infringing material is on the website at the time the ISP receives the notice, then the information, that all Manson DVD's are infringing, can be adequate to find the infringing material expeditiously. However, if at the time the notice is received, the infringing material is not posted, the notice does not enable the service provider to locate infringing material that is not there, let alone do it expeditiously.

Recognizing that Congress tried to craft a balance between the responsibilities of the copyright owner and the ISP, there is a limit to the viability of an otherwise adequate notice. Hedrickson's January, 2002, letter, claiming all Manson DVDs violate his copyright, although adequate for the listings then on Amazon, cannot be deemed adequate notice for subsequent listings and sales, especially, as here, when the infringing item was posted for sale nine months after the date of the notice.

Under the DMCA, a notification from a copyright owner that fails to comply substantially with § 512(c)(3) "shall not be considered under [the first prong of the safe harbor test] in determining whether a service provider has actual knowledge or is aware of the facts or circumstances from which infringing activity is apparent." 17 U.S.C. § 512(c)(3)(B)(i) & (ii). Thus, the first prong is satisfied.

To satisfy the second prong of the test, Amazon must show that it "does not receive a financial benefit directly attributable to the infringing activity, in a case in which the service provider has the right and ability to control such activity." 17 U.S.C. § 512(c)(1)(B). Amazon does receive a financial benefit from its third party sellers, so its only defense is to prove that it does not have the right and ability to control such activity.

Here, the infringing activity is the sale of the unauthorized work, not the posting of the listing. 17 U.S.C. § 106(3). There is no evidence to suggest that Amazon had the ability to know that an infringing sale by a third party seller would occur. Amazon's evidence established that it never possessed the DVD, and never had the opportunity to inspect the item. Amazon merely provided the forum for an independent third party seller to list and sell his merchandise. Amazon was not actively involved in the listing, bidding, sale or delivery of the DVD. The fact that Amazon generated automatic email responses when the DVD was listed and again when it was sold, does not mean that Amazon was actively involved in the sale. Once a third party seller decides to list an item, the responsibility is on the seller to consummate the sale. While Amazon does provide transaction processing for credit card purchases, that additional service does not give Amazon control over the sale. In sum, Amazon's evidence shows that it did not have control of the sale of DVD.

As discussed above, Amazon could not respond to the notice of claimed infringement and remove, or disable access to, the material since the notice was no longer viable. Thus, the third prong of the save harbor provision is not applicable.

Thus, Amazon has proven that it qualifies for the safe harbor affirmative defense of the DMCA. Consequently, to avoid summary judgment, the burden shifts to Hendrickson to introduce evidence which creates a triable issue of fact. Hendrickson has offered no such evidence. Thus, summary judgment in favor of Amazon is appropriate.

4. Safe Harbor for Information Location Tools

The final safe harbor we will consider, Section 512(d), shields Internet service providers from liability for infringement "by reason of the provider referring or linking users to an online location containing infringing material or infringing activity." Before turning to the safe harbor, consider the following case on the general potential for copyright liability for linking to infringing material.

Intellectual Reserve, Inc. v. Utah Lighthouse Ministry, Inc.
75 F.Supp.2d 1290 (D.Utah 1999).

■ CAMPBELL, DISTRICT JUDGE.

This matter is before the court on plaintiff's motion for preliminary injunction. Plaintiff claims that unless a preliminary injunction issues, defendants will directly infringe and contribute to the infringement of its copyright in the *Church Handbook of Instructions* ("Handbook"). Defendants do not oppose a preliminary injunction, but argue that the scope of the injunction should be restricted to only prohibit direct infringement of plaintiff's copyright.[4] Having fully considered the arguments of counsel, the submissions of the parties and applicable legal authorities, the court grants plaintiff's motion for a preliminary injunction. However, the scope of the preliminary injunction is limited.

Discussion

. . .

I. Likelihood of Plaintiff Prevailing on the Merits

First, the court considers whether there is a substantial likelihood that plaintiff will eventually prevail on the merits. Plaintiff alleges that the defendants infringed its copyright directly by posting substantial portions of its copyrighted material on defendants' website, and also contributed to infringement of its copyright by inducing, causing or materially contributing to the infringing conduct of another. To determine the proper scope of the preliminary injunction, the court considers the

---

[4] [Plaintiff is the owner of copyrights in the Handbook and other materials used by the Church of Jesus Christ of Latter-day Saints (the Mormon Church). Defendant is an organization that is critical of the Mormon Church.—Eds.]

likelihood that plaintiff will prevail on either or both of its claims.

. . .

B. Contributory Infringement

According to plaintiff, after the defendants were ordered to remove the Handbook from their website, the defendants began infringing plaintiff's copyright by inducing, causing, or materially contributing to the infringing conduct of others. It is undisputed that defendants placed a notice on their website that the Handbook was online, and gave three website addresses of websites containing the material defendants were ordered to remove from their website. Defendants also posted e-mails on their website that encouraged browsing those websites, printing copies of the Handbook and sending the Handbook to others.

. . .

Liability for contributory infringement is imposed when "one who, with knowledge of the infringing activity, induces, causes or materially contributes to the infringing conduct of another." *Gershwin Publ'g Corp. v. Columbia Artists Mgt., Inc.,* 443 F.2d 1159, 1162 (2d Cir.1971). Thus, to prevail on its claim of contributory infringement, plaintiff must first be able to establish that the conduct defendants allegedly aided or encouraged could amount to infringement. *See Subafilms, Ltd. v. MGM-Pathe Comms. Co.,* 24 F.3d 1088, 1092 (9th Cir.1994). Defendants argue that they have not contributed to copyright infringement by those who posted the Handbook on websites nor by those who browsed the websites on their computers.

> 1. *Can the Defendants Be Liable Under a Theory of Contributory Infringement for the Actions of Those Who Posted the Handbook on the Three Websites?*

[The court determined that "plaintiff at trial is likely to establish that those who have posted the material on the three websites are directly infringing plaintiff's copyright" but that "the evidence now before the court indicates that there is no direct relationship between the defendants and the people who operate the three websites" so that "plaintiff has not shown that defendants [induced, caused, or materially] contributed to the infringing action of those who operate the infringing websites."]

> 2. *Can the Defendants Be Liable Under a Theory of Contributory Infringement for the Actions of Those Who Browse the Three Infringing Websites?*

Defendants make two arguments in support of their position that the activities of those who browse the three websites do not make them liable under a theory of contributory infringement. First, defendants contend that those who browse the infringing websites are not themselves infringing plaintiff's copyright; and second, even if those who browse the websites are infringers, defendants have not materially contributed to the infringing conduct.

> a. Do those who browse the websites infringe plaintiff's copyright?

The first question, then, is whether those who browse any of the three infringing websites are infringing plaintiff's copyright. Central to this inquiry is whether the persons browsing are merely viewing the Handbook (which is not a copyright infringement), or whether they are making a copy of the Handbook (which is a copyright infringement). *See* 17 U.S.C. § 106.

"Copy" is defined in the Copyright Act as: "material objects . . . in which a work is fixed by any method now known or later developed, and from which the work can be perceived, reproduced, or otherwise communicated, either directly or with the aid of a machine or device." 17 U.S.C. § 101. "A work is 'fixed' . . . when its . . . [sic] sufficiently permanent or stable to permit it to be perceived, reproduced, or otherwise communicated for a period of more than transitory duration." *Id.*

When a person browses a website, and by so doing displays the Handbook, a copy of the Handbook is made in the computer's random access memory (RAM), to permit viewing of the material. And in making a copy, even a temporary one, the person who browsed infringes the copyright.[5] *See MAI Systems Corp. v. Peak Computer, Inc.,* 991 F.2d 511, 518 (9th Cir.1993) (holding that when material is transferred to a computer's RAM, copying has occurred; in the absence of ownership of the copyright or express permission by license, such an act constitutes copyright infringement); *Marobie–FL., Inc. v. National Ass'n of Fire and Equip. Distrib.,* 983 F.Supp. 1167, 1179 (N.D.Ill.1997) (noting that liability for copyright infringement is with the persons who cause the display or distribution of the infringing material onto their computer); *see also* Nimmer on Copyright ⏑ 8.08(A)(1) (stating that the infringing act of copying may occur from "loading the copyrighted material . . . into the computer's random access memory (RAM)"). Additionally, a person making a printout or re-posting a copy of the Handbook on another website would infringe plaintiff's copyright.

> b.   Did the defendants induce, cause or materially contribute to the infringement?

The court now considers whether the defendants' actions contributed to the infringement of plaintiff's copyright by those who browse the three websites.

The following evidence establishes that defendants have actively encouraged the infringement of plaintiff's copyright.[6] After being ordered to remove the Handbook from their website, defendants posted on their website: "Church Handbook of Instructions is back online!" and listed the three website addresses. Defen-

---

[5] Although this seems harsh, the Copyright Act has provided a safeguard for innocent infringers. Where the infringer "was not aware and had no reason to believe that his or her acts constituted an infringement of copyright, the court in its discretion may reduce the award of statutory damages. . . ." 17 U.S.C. § 504(c)(2).

[6] Plaintiff at this point has been unable to specifically identify persons who have infringed its copyright because they were induced or assisted by defendants' conduct, however, there is a substantial likelihood that plaintiff will be able to do so after conducting discovery. There is evidence that at least one of the websites has seen a great increase in "hits" recently. Also, plaintiff does not have to establish that the defendants' actions are the sole cause of another's infringement; rather plaintiff may prevail by establishing that defendants' conduct induces or materially contributes to the infringing conduct of another.

dants also posted e-mail suggesting that the lawsuit against defendants would be affected by people logging onto one of the websites and downloading the complete handbook. One of the e-mails posted by the defendants mentioned sending a copy of the copyrighted material to the media. In response to an e-mail stating that the sender had unsuccessfully tried to browse a website that contained the Handbook, defendants gave further instruction on how to browse the material. At least one of the three websites encourages the copying and posting of copies of the allegedly infringing material on other websites. *See* Ex. 4 [to Plaintiff's Reply Brief] ("Please mirror these files. . . . It will be a LOT quicker for you to download the compressed version . . . Needless to say, we need a LOT of mirror sites, as absolutely soon as possible.").

Based on the above, the court finds that the first element necessary for injunctive relief is satisfied.

[In the remainder of the opinion, the court finds the other elements necessary for injunctive relief also satisfied and issues a preliminary injunction.]

. . .

§ 512. Limitations on liability relating to material online

. . .

(d) Information Location Tools. — A service provider shall not be liable for monetary relief, or, except as provided in subsection (j), for injunctive or other equitable relief, for infringement of copyright by reason of the provider referring or linking users to an online location containing infringing material or infringing activity, by using information location tools, including a directory, index, reference, pointer, or hypertext link, if the service provider—

(1)(A) does not have actual knowledge that the material or activity is infringing;

(B) in the absence of such actual knowledge, is not aware of facts or circumstances from which infringing activity is apparent; or

(C) upon obtaining such knowledge or awareness, acts expeditiously to remove, or disable access to, the material;

(2) does not receive a financial benefit directly attributable to the infringing activity, in a case in which the service provider has the right and ability to control such activity; and

(3) upon notification of claimed infringement as described in subsection (c)(3), responds expeditiously to remove, or disable access to, the material that is claimed to be infringing or to be the subject of infringing activity, except that, for purposes of this paragraph, the information described in subsection (c)(3)(A)(iii) shall be identification of the reference or link, to material or activity claimed to be infringing, that is to be removed or access to which is to be disabled, and information reasonably sufficient to permit the service provider to locate that reference or link.

Perfect 10, Inc., v. CCBill, LLC
340 F.Supp.2d 1077 (C.D.Cal.2004).

■ BAIRD, DISTRICT JUDGE.

[This case involved copyright infringement allegations by the copyright owner of many adult images against companies that provided credit-card payment processing services, age verification services, and internet connectivity service to adult-oriented Web sites that the plaintiff alleged had infringed its copyrights. One defendant, Internet Key, claimed protection of the Section 512(d) safe harbor. The court described Internet Key's activities as follows:]

Internet Key is an age verification system for adult content websites. Starting in 1997, Internet Key has provided adult verification services, including providing links, to third-party adult content websites. Currently, Internet Key verifies age and provides a link to approximately 30,000 third-party adult content websites that participate in the SexKey system ("Affiliated Websites"). The Affiliated Websites are not owned by Internet Key although some are owned by employees of WCD Enterprises, another company that Freeman owns. A user (consumer) cannot access an Affiliated Website without proving he or she is of legal age. Internet Key provides each Affiliated Website with a site ID and an HTML code to place on their site. When a new user clicks onto an Affiliated Website, a link that tracks the site ID automatically directs to sexkey.com for age verification. The user is directed to Internet Key's registration page, which contains Internet Key's User Agreement. The User Agreement sets forth terms and conditions that a user must certify and agree in order to subscribe to a SexKey membership. Once the user agrees to all the terms of the User Agreement by checking on a box that the user agrees, the user is provided a user password to access all of the Affiliated Websites in the SexKey system. Internet Key does not store the content of the Affiliated Websites on its computer system. It only stores information related to the Affiliated Websites' URLs, site descriptions and webmaster information. . . . Internet Key also acts as a search engine (similar to Yahoo or Google) for free adult content on the Internet. . .

Perfect 10 contends that Internet Key does not fall within the safe harbor provided by § 512(d) because Internet Key (1) does not use an information location; tool, (2) has actual knowledge of infringements, (2) is aware of facts or circumstances from which infringing activity is apparent.

Perfect 10 argues that Internet Key does not use an information location tool as defined in § 512(d) because Internet Key is not like Yahoo! or Google which provide links to millions of websites with whom it has no relationship. Perfect 10 reasons that because Internet Key merely links to a relatively small universe of websites with whom it has in place contractual relationships and established review procedures, it is not entitled to protection under § 512(d). Section 512(d) does not state that the safe harbor is limited to internet service providers that provide links to millions of websites. Nor does § 512(d) state that the use of an information location tool is limited to internet service providers that do not have contractual relationships with their affiliate websites. Therefore, these arguments are without merit.

Section 512(d) refers to service providers who refer or link users to an online location containing infringing material or infringing activity, by using information location tools, including a directory, index, reference, pointer, or hypertext link. § 512(d). Internet Key's sexkey.com website provides that function and is therefore covered by § 512(d).

Pursuant to § 512(d), the internet service provider must also (1) not be aware of facts or circumstances from which infringing activity is apparent and (2) not receive a financial benefit directly attributable to the infringing activity, in a case in which the service provider has the right and ability to control such activity. Perfect 10 argues that Internet Key fails both of these requirements. Perfect 10 argues that Internet Key should have known there were copyright infringements on its clients' websites because of the disclaimers on some of those websites. The disclaimers generally claim that the copyrighted images are in the public domain or that the webmaster is posting the images for newsworthy purposes. These disclaimers are not sufficient to raise a red flag of copyright infringement. Therefore, Perfect 10 has not demonstrated that Internet Key was aware of facts or circumstances from which infringing was apparent.

The second requirement is that the internet service provider not receive a direct financial benefit directly attributable to the infringing activity when it has the right and ability to control such activity. A right and ability to control infringing activity, "as the concept is used in the DMCA, cannot simply mean the ability of a service provider to remove or block access to materials posted on its website or stored in its system." *CoStar Group, Inc. v. LoopNet, Inc.*, 164 F.Supp.2d 688, 704 (D.Md.2001). Internet Key's right and ability to control infringing activity is limited to disconnecting the webmasters' access to Internet Key's service. That type of control is not sufficient, under the DMCA, to demonstrate a "right and ability to control" the infringing activity. As recognized in *Perfect 10 v. Cybernet Ventures. Inc.*, 213 F.Supp.2d 1146, 1181 (C.D.Cal.2002), "closing the safe harbor based on the mere ability to exclude users from the system is inconsistent with the statutory scheme." Since Internet Key does not have a right and ability to control the infringing activity, the Court need not address whether Internet Key receives a direct financial benefit from the infringing conduct.

VI. SECONDARY LIABILITY AND CONTROL OVER TECHNOLOGY

A. SECONDARY LIABILITY FOR TECHNOLOGY PROVIDERS GENERALLY

Sony Corporation Of America v. Universal City Studios, Inc.
464 U.S. 417 (1984).

■ JUSTICE STEVENS delivered the opinion of the Court.

Petitioners manufacture and sell home video tape recorders. Respondents own the copyrights on some of the television programs that are broadcast on the public airwaves. Some members of the general public use video tape recorders sold by petitioners to record some of these broadcasts, as well as a large number of other broadcasts. The question presented is whether the sale of petitioners' copying equipment to the general public violates any of the rights conferred upon respondents by the Copyright Act.

Respondents commenced this copyright infringement action against petitioners in the United States District Court for the Central District of California in 1976. Respondents alleged that some individuals had used Betamax video tape recorders (VTR's) to record some of respondents' copyrighted works which had been exhibited on commercially sponsored television and contended that these individuals had thereby infringed respondents' copyrights. Respondents further maintained that petitioners were liable for the copyright infringement allegedly committed by Betamax consumers because of petitioners' marketing of the Betamax VTR's. Respondents sought no relief against any Betamax consumer. Instead, they sought money damages and an equitable accounting of profits from petitioners, as well as an injunction against the manufacture and marketing of Betamax VTR's.

After a lengthy trial, the District Court denied respondents all the relief they sought and entered judgment for petitioners. The United States Court of Appeals for the Ninth Circuit reversed the District Court's judgment on respondents' copyright claim, holding petitioners liable for contributory infringement and ordering the District Court to fashion appropriate relief.

An explanation of our rejection of respondents' unprecedented attempt to impose copyright liability upon the distributors of copying equipment requires a quite detailed recitation of the findings of the District Court. In summary, those findings reveal that the average member of the public uses a VTR principally to record a program he cannot view as it is being televised and then to watch it once at a later time. This practice, known as "time-shifting," enlarges the television viewing audience. For that reason, a significant amount of television programming may be used in this manner without objection from the owners of the copyrights on the programs. For the same reason, even the two respondents in this case, who do assert objections to time-shifting in this litigation, were unable to prove that the practice has impaired the commercial value of their copyrights or has created any likelihood of future harm. Given these findings, there is no basis in the Copyright Act upon which respondents can hold petitioners liable for distributing VTR's to the general public. The Court of Appeals' holding that respondents are entitled to enjoin the distribution of VTR's, to collect royalties on the sale of such equipment, or to obtain other relief, if affirmed, would enlarge the scope of respondents' statutory monopolies to encompass control over an article of commerce that is not the subject of copyright protection. Such an expansion of the copyright privilege is beyond the limits of the grants authorized by Congress.

I

The two respondents in this action, Universal City Studios, Inc., and Walt Disney Productions, produce and hold the copyrights on a substantial number of motion pictures and other audiovisual works. . . .

Petitioner Sony manufactures millions of Betamax video tape recorders and markets these devices through numerous retail establishments, some of which are also petitioners in this action.[2] . . .

Several capabilities of the machine are noteworthy. The separate tuner in the Betamax enables it to record a broadcast off one station while the television set is tuned to another channel, permitting the viewer, for example, to watch two simultaneous news broadcasts by watching one "live" and recording the other for later viewing. Tapes may be reused, and programs that have been recorded may be erased either before or after viewing. A timer in the Betamax can be used to activate and deactivate the equipment at predetermined times, enabling an intended viewer to record programs that are transmitted when he or she is not at home. Thus a person may watch a program at home in the evening even though it was broadcast while the viewer was at work during the afternoon. The Betamax is also equipped with a pause button and a fast-forward control. The pause button, when depressed, deactivates the recorder until it is released, thus enabling a viewer to omit a commercial advertisement from the recording, provided, of course, that the viewer is present when the program is recorded. The fast-forward control enables the viewer of a previously recorded program to run the tape rapidly when a segment he or she does not desire to see is being played back on the television screen.

The respondents and Sony both conducted surveys of the way the Betamax machine was used by several hundred owners during a sample period in 1978. Although there were some differences in the surveys, they both showed that the primary use of the machine for most owners was "time-shifting"—the practice of recording a program to view it once at a later time, and thereafter erasing it. Time-shifting enables viewers to see programs they otherwise would miss because they are not at home, are occupied with other tasks, or are viewing a program on another station at the time of a broadcast that they desire to watch. Both surveys also showed, however, that a substantial number of interviewees had accumulated libraries of tapes. Sony's survey indicated that over 80% of the interviewees watched at least as much regular television as they had before owning a Betamax.[4] Respondents offered no evidence of decreased television viewing by Betamax owners.

Sony introduced considerable evidence describing television programs that could be copied without objection from any copyright holder, with special empha-

---

[2] . . . An individual VTR user, William Griffiths, was named as a defendant in the District Court, but respondents sought no relief against him. Griffiths is not a petitioner.

[4] The District Court summarized some of the findings in these surveys as follows:

"According to plaintiffs' survey, 75.4% of the VTR owners use their machines to record for time-shifting purposes half or most of the time. Defendants' survey showed that 96% of the Betamax owners had used the machine to record programs they otherwise would have missed.

"When plaintiffs asked interviewees how many cassettes were in their library, 55.8% said there were 10 or fewer. In defendants' survey, of the total programs viewed by interviewees in the past month, 70.4% had been viewed only that one time and for 57.9%, there were no plans for further viewing."

sis on sports, religious, and educational programming. For example, their survey indicated that 7.3% of all Betamax use is to record sports events, and representatives of professional baseball, football, basketball, and hockey testified that they had no objection to the recording of their televised events for home use.

Respondents offered opinion evidence concerning the future impact of the unrestricted sale of VTR's on the commercial value of their copyrights. The District Court found, however, that they had failed to prove any likelihood of future harm from the use of VTR's for time-shifting.

The District Court's Decision

The lengthy trial of the case in the District Court concerned the private, home use of VTR's for recording programs broadcast on the public airwaves without charge to the viewer. No issue concerning the transfer of tapes to other persons, the use of home-recorded tapes for public performances, or the copying of programs transmitted on pay or cable television systems was raised.

The District Court concluded that noncommercial home use recording of material broadcast over the public airwaves was a fair use of copyrighted works and did not constitute copyright infringement. It emphasized the fact that the material was broadcast free to the public at large, the noncommercial character of the use, and the private character of the activity conducted entirely within the home. Moreover, the court found that the purpose of this use served the public interest in increasing access to television programming, an interest that "is consistent with the First Amendment policy of providing the fullest possible access to information through the public airwaves."[8] Even when an entire copyrighted work was recorded, the District Court regarded the copying as fair use "because there is no accompanying reduction in the market for 'plaintiff's original work.'"

As an independent ground of decision, the District Court also concluded that Sony could not be held liable as a contributory infringer even if the home use of a VTR was considered an infringing use. The District Court noted that Sony had no direct involvement with any Betamax purchasers who recorded copyrighted works off the air. Sony's advertising was silent on the subject of possible copyright infringement, but its instruction booklet contained the following statement:

> "Television programs, films, videotapes and other materials may be copyrighted. Unauthorized recording of such material may be contrary to the provisions of the United States copyright laws."

The District Court assumed that Sony had constructive knowledge of the probability that the Betamax machine would be used to record copyrighted programs, but found that Sony merely sold a "product capable of a variety of uses, some of them allegedly infringing." It reasoned:

> "Selling a staple article of commerce—e. g., a typewriter, a recorder, a

---

[8] The court also found that this "access is not just a matter of convenience, as plaintiffs have suggested. Access has been limited not simply by inconvenience but by the basic need to work. Access to the better program has also been limited by the competitive practice of counterprogramming."

camera, a photocopying machine—technically contributes to any infringing use subsequently made thereof, but this kind of 'contribution,' if deemed sufficient as a basis for liability, would expand the theory beyond precedent and arguably beyond judicial management.

. . .

"... Commerce would indeed be hampered if manufacturers of staple items were held liable as contributory infringers whenever they 'constructively' knew that some purchasers on some occasions would use their product for a purpose which a court later deemed, as a matter of first impression, to be an infringement."

Finally, the District Court discussed the respondents' prayer for injunctive relief, noting that they had asked for an injunction either preventing the future sale of Betamax machines, or requiring that the machines be rendered incapable of recording copyrighted works off the air. The court stated that it had "found no case in which the manufacturers, distributors, retailers and advertisers of the instrument enabling the infringement were sued by the copyright holders," and that the request for relief in this case "is unique."

It concluded that an injunction was wholly inappropriate because any possible harm to respondents was outweighed by the fact that "the Betamax could still legally be used to record noncopyrighted material or material whose owners consented to the copying. An injunction would deprive the public of the ability to use the Betamax for this noninfringing off-the-air recording."

The Court of Appeals' Decision

The Court of Appeals reversed the District Court's judgment on respondents' copyright claim. It did not set aside any of the District Court's findings of fact. Rather, it concluded as a matter of law that the home use of a VTR was not a fair use because it was not a "productive use." It therefore held that it was unnecessary for plaintiffs to prove any harm to the potential market for the copyrighted works, but then observed that it seemed clear that the cumulative effect of mass reproduction made possible by VTR's would tend to diminish the potential market for respondents' works.

On the issue of contributory infringement, the Court of Appeals first rejected the analogy to staple articles of commerce such as tape recorders or photocopying machines. It noted that such machines "may have substantial benefit for some purposes" and do not "even remotely raise copyright problems." VTR's, however, are sold "for the primary purpose of reproducing television programming" and "[virtually] all" such programming is copyrighted material. The Court of Appeals concluded, therefore, that VTR's were not suitable for any substantial noninfringing use even if some copyright owners elect not to enforce their rights.

The Court of Appeals also rejected the District Court's reliance on Sony's lack of knowledge that home use constituted infringement. Assuming that the statutory provisions defining the remedies for infringement applied also to the nonstatutory tort of contributory infringement, the court stated that a defendant's good faith would merely reduce his damages liability but would not excuse the infringing conduct. It held that Sony was chargeable with knowledge of the homeowner's infringing activity because the reproduction of copyrighted materials was either "the most conspicuous use" or "the major use" of the Betamax product.

On the matter of relief, the Court of Appeals concluded that "statutory damages may be appropriate" and that the District Court should reconsider its determination that an injunction would not be an appropriate remedy; and, referring to "the analogous photocopying area," suggested that a continuing royalty pursuant to a judicially created compulsory license may very well be an acceptable resolution of the relief issue.

II

The monopoly privileges that Congress may authorize [under the constitution's Patent and Copyright Clause] are neither unlimited nor primarily designed to provide a special private benefit. Rather, the limited grant is a means by which an important public purpose may be achieved. It is intended to motivate the creative activity of authors and inventors by the provision of a special reward, and to allow the public access to the products of their genius after the limited period of exclusive control has expired.

"The copyright law, like the patent statutes, makes reward to the owner a secondary consideration. In *Fox Film Corp. v. Doyal,* 286 U.S. 123, 127, Chief Justice Hughes spoke as follows respecting the copyright monopoly granted by Congress, 'The sole interest of the United States and the primary object in conferring the monopoly lie in the general benefits derived by the public from the labors of authors.' It is said that reward to the author or artist serves to induce release to the public of the products of his creative genius." *U.S. v. Paramount Pictures, Inc.,* 334 U.S. 131, 158 (1948).

As the text of the Constitution makes plain, it is Congress that has been assigned the task of defining the scope of the limited monopoly that should be granted to authors or to inventors in order to give the public appropriate access to their work product. Because this task involves a difficult balance between the interests of authors and inventors in the control and exploitation of their writings and discoveries on the one hand, and society's competing interest in the free flow of ideas, information, and commerce on the other hand, our patent and copyright statutes have been amended repeatedly.[10]

---

[10] In its Report accompanying the comprehensive revision of the Copyright Act in 1909, the Judiciary Committee of the House of Representatives explained this balance:

"The enactment of copyright legislation by Congress under the terms of the Constitution is not based upon any natural right that the author has in his writings, . . . but upon the ground that the welfare of the public will be served and progress of science and useful arts will be promoted by securing to authors for limited periods the exclusive rights to their writings. . . .

"In enacting a copyright law Congress must consider . . . two questions: First, how much will the legislation stimulate the producer and so benefit the public; and, second, how much will the monopoly granted be detrimental to the public? The granting of such exclusive rights, under the proper terms and conditions, confers a benefit upon the pub-

From its beginning, the law of copyright has developed in response to significant changes in technology. Indeed, it was the invention of a new form of copying equipment—the printing press—that gave rise to the original need for copyright protection. Repeatedly, as new developments have occurred in this country, it has been the Congress that has fashioned the new rules that new technology made necessary. Thus, long before the enactment of the Copyright Act of 1909, it was settled that the protection given to copyrights is wholly statutory. *Wheaton v. Peters,* 8 Pet. 591 (1834). . . .

The judiciary's reluctance to expand the protections afforded by the copyright without explicit legislative guidance is a recurring theme . . . Sound policy, as well as history, supports our consistent deference to Congress when major technological innovations alter the market for copyrighted materials. Congress has the constitutional authority and the institutional ability to accommodate fully the varied permutations of competing interests that are inevitably implicated by such new technology.

In a case like this, in which Congress has not plainly marked our course, we must be circumspect in construing the scope of rights created by a legislative enactment which never contemplated such a calculus of interests. In doing so, we are guided by Justice Stewart's exposition of the correct approach to ambiguities in the law of copyright:

> "The limited scope of the copyright holder's statutory monopoly, like the limited copyright duration required by the Constitution, reflects a balance of competing claims upon the public interest: Creative work is to be encouraged and rewarded, but private motivation must ultimately serve the cause of promoting broad public availability of literature, music, and the other arts. The immediate effect of our copyright law is to secure a fair return for an 'author's' creative labor. But the ultimate aim is, by this incentive, to stimulate artistic creativity for the general public good. 'The sole interest of the United States and the primary object in conferring the monopoly,' this Court has said, 'lie in the general benefits derived by the public from the labors of authors.' *Fox Film Corp. v. Doyal,* 286 U.S. 123. . . . When technological change has rendered its literal terms ambiguous, the Copyright Act must be construed in light of this basic purpose." *Twentieth Century Music Corp. v. Aiken,* 422 U.S. 151 (1975).

Copyright protection "subsists . . . in original works of authorship fixed in any tangible medium of expression." 17 U.S.C. § 102(a). This protection has never accorded the copyright owner complete control over all possible uses of his work.[13] Rather, the Copyright Act grants the copyright holder "exclusive" rights to use and to authorize the use of his work in five qualified ways, including reproduction of the copyrighted work in copies. § 106. All reproductions of the work, however, are

---

lic that outweighs the evils of the temporary monopoly."

[13] . . . While the law has never recognized an author's right to absolute control of his work, the natural tendency of legal rights to express themselves in absolute terms to the exclusion of all else is particularly pronounced in the history of the constitutionally sanctioned monopolies of the copyright and the patent. . . .

not within the exclusive domain of the copyright owner; some are in the public domain. Any individual may reproduce a copyrighted work for a "fair use"; the copyright owner does not possess the exclusive right to such a use. *Compare* § 106 *with* § 107. . . .

The two respondents in this case do not seek relief against the Betamax users who have allegedly infringed their copyrights. Moreover, this is not a class action on behalf of all copyright owners who license their works for television broadcast, and respondents have no right to invoke whatever rights other copyright holders may have to bring infringement actions based on Betamax copying of their works. As was made clear by their own evidence, the copying of the respondents' programs represents a small portion of the total use of VTR's. It is, however, the taping of respondents' own copyrighted programs that provides them with standing to charge Sony with contributory infringement. To prevail, they have the burden of proving that users of the Betamax have infringed their copyrights and that Sony should be held responsible for that infringement.

III

The Copyright Act does not expressly render anyone liable for infringement committed by another. In contrast, the Patent Act expressly brands anyone who "actively induces infringement of a patent" as an infringer, 35 U.S.C. § 271(b), and further imposes liability on certain individuals labeled "contributory" infringers, § 271(c). The absence of such express language in the copyright statute does not preclude the imposition of liability for copyright infringements on certain parties who have not themselves engaged in the infringing activity.[17] For vicarious liability is imposed in virtually all areas of the law, and the concept of contributory infringement is merely a species of the broader problem of identifying the circumstances in which it is just to hold one individual accountable for the actions of another. . . .

. . . [T]he label "contributory infringement" has been applied in a number of lower court copyright cases involving an ongoing relationship between the direct infringer and the contributory infringer at the time the infringing conduct occurred. In such cases, as in other situations in which the imposition of vicarious liability is manifestly just, the "contributory" infringer was in a position to control

---

[17] As the District Court correctly observed, however, "the lines between direct infringement, contributory infringement and vicarious liability are not clearly drawn . . . ." The lack of clarity in this area may, in part, be attributable to the fact that an infringer is not merely one who uses a work without authorization by the copyright owner, but also one who authorizes the use of a copyrighted work without actual authority from the copyright owner.

We note the parties' statements that the questions of Sony's liability under the "doctrines" of "direct infringement" and "vicarious liability" are not nominally before this Court. . . . We also observe, however, that reasoned analysis of respondents' unprecedented contributory infringement claim necessarily entails consideration of arguments and case law which may also be forwarded under the other labels, and indeed the parties to a large extent rely upon such arguments and authority in support of their respective positions on the issue of contributory infringement.

the use of copyrighted works by others and had authorized the use without permission from the copyright owner.[18]   This case, however, plainly does not fall in that category. The only contact between Sony and the users of the Betamax that is disclosed by this record occurred at the moment of sale. The District Court expressly found that "no employee of Sony . . . had either direct involvement with the allegedly infringing activity or direct contact with purchasers of Betamax who recorded copyrighted works off-the-air." And it further found that "there was no evidence that any of the copies made by Griffiths or the other individual witnesses in this suit were influenced or encouraged by [Sony's] advertisements."

If vicarious liability is to be imposed on Sony in this case, it must rest on the fact that it has sold equipment with constructive knowledge of the fact that its customers may use that equipment to make unauthorized copies of copyrighted material. There is no precedent in the law of copyright for the imposition of vicarious liability on such a theory. The closest analogy is provided by the patent law cases to which it is appropriate to refer because of the historic kinship between patent law and copyright law.

In the Patent Act both the concept of infringement and the concept of contributory infringement are expressly defined by statute. The prohibition against contributory infringement is confined to the knowing sale of a component especially

---

[18] The so-called "dance hall cases," . . . are often contrasted with the so-called landlord-tenant cases, in which landlords who leased premises to a direct infringer for a fixed rental and did not participate directly in any infringing activity were found not to be liable for contributory infringement. . . .

In *Shapiro, Bernstein & Co. v. H. L. Green Co.*, 316 F.2d 304 (CA2 1963), the owner of 23 chainstores retained the direct infringer to run its record departments. The relationship was structured as a licensing arrangement, so that the defendant bore none of the business risk of running the department. Instead, it received 10% or 12% of the direct infringer's gross receipts. The Court of Appeals concluded:

"[The dance-hall cases] and this one lie closer on the spectrum to the employer-employee model, than to the landlord-tenant model. . . . [On] the particular facts before us, . . . Green's relationship to its infringing licensee, as well as its strong concern for the financial success of the phonograph record concession, renders it liable for the unauthorized sales of the 'bootleg' records.

". . . [The] imposition of vicarious liability in the case before us cannot be deemed unduly harsh or unfair. Green has the power to police carefully the conduct of its concessionaire . . .; our judgment will simply encourage it to do so, thus placing responsibility where it can and should be effectively exercised."

In *Gershwin Publishing Corp. v. Columbia Artists Management, Inc.*, 443 F.2d 1159 (CA2 1971), the direct infringers retained the contributory infringer to manage their performances. The contributory infringer would contact each direct infringer, obtain the titles of the musical compositions to be performed, print the programs, and then sell the programs to its own local organizations for distribution at the time of the direct infringement. The Court of Appeals emphasized that the contributory infringer had actual knowledge that the artists it was managing were performing copyrighted works, was in a position to police the infringing conduct of the artists, and derived substantial benefit from the actions of the primary infringers. . . .

made for use in connection with a particular patent. There is no suggestion in the statute that one patentee may object to the sale of a product that might be used in connection with other patents. Moreover, the Act expressly provides that the sale of a "staple article or commodity of commerce suitable for substantial noninfringing use" is not contributory infringement. 35 U.S.C. § 271(c).

When a charge of contributory infringement is predicated entirely on the sale of an article of commerce that is used by the purchaser to infringe a patent, the public interest in access to that article of commerce is necessarily implicated. A finding of contributory infringement does not, of course, remove the article from the market altogether; it does, however, give the patentee effective control over the sale of that item. Indeed, a finding of contributory infringement is normally the functional equivalent of holding that the disputed article is within the monopoly granted to the patentee.[21]

For that reason, in contributory infringement cases arising under the patent laws the Court has always recognized the critical importance of not allowing the patentee to extend his monopoly beyond the limits of his specific grant. These cases deny the patentee any right to control the distribution of unpatented articles unless they are "unsuited for any commercial noninfringing use." *Dawson Chemical Co. v. Rohm & Hass Co.*, 448 U.S. 176, 198 (1980). Unless a commodity "has no use except through practice of the patented method," *id.*, at 199, the patentee has no right to claim that its distribution constitutes contributory infringement. "To form the basis for contributory infringement the item must almost be uniquely suited as a component of the patented invention." P. Rosenberg, Patent Law Fundamentals § 17.02[2] (2d ed. 1982). "[A] sale of an article which though adapted to an infringing use is also adapted to other and lawful uses, is not enough to make the seller a contributory infringer. Such a rule would block the wheels of commerce." *Henry v. A. B. Dick Co.*, 224 U.S. 1, 48 (1912), *overruled on other grounds, Motion Picture Patents Co. v. Universal Film Mfg. Co.*, 243 U.S. 502, 517 (1917).

We recognize there are substantial differences between the patent and copyright laws. But in both areas the contributory infringement doctrine is grounded on the recognition that adequate protection of a monopoly may require the courts to look beyond actual duplication of a device or publication to the products or activities that make such duplication possible. The staple article of commerce doctrine must strike a balance between a copyright holder's legitimate demand for effective—not merely symbolic—protection of the statutory monopoly, and the rights of others freely to engage in substantially unrelated areas of commerce. Accordingly, the sale of copying equipment, like the sale of other articles of commerce,

---

[21] It seems extraordinary to suggest that the Copyright Act confers upon all copyright owners collectively, much less the two respondents in this case, the exclusive right to distribute VTR's simply because they may be used to infringe copyrights. That, however, is the logical implication of their claim. The request for an injunction below indicates that respondents seek, in effect, to declare VTR's contraband. Their suggestion in this Court that a continuing royalty pursuant to a judicially created compulsory license would be an acceptable remedy merely indicates that respondents, for their part, would be willing to license their claimed monopoly interest in VTR's to Sony in return for a royalty.

does not constitute contributory infringement if the product is widely used for legitimate, unobjectionable purposes. Indeed, it need merely be capable of substantial noninfringing uses.

IV

The question is thus whether the Betamax is capable of commercially significant noninfringing uses. In order to resolve that question, we need not explore all the different potential uses of the machine and determine whether or not they would constitute infringement. Rather, we need only consider whether on the basis of the facts as found by the District Court a significant number of them would be noninfringing. Moreover, in order to resolve this case we need not give precise content to the question of how much use is commercially significant. For one potential use of the Betamax plainly satisfies this standard, however it is understood: private, non-commercial time-shifting in the home. It does so both (A) because respondents have no right to prevent other copyright holders from authorizing it for their programs, and (B) because the District Court's factual findings reveal that even the unauthorized home time-shifting of respondents' programs is legitimate fair use . . . .

. . .

In summary, the record and findings of the District Court lead us to two conclusions. First, Sony demonstrated a significant likelihood that substantial numbers of copyright holders who license their works for broadcast on free television would not object to having their broadcasts time-shifted by private viewers. And second, respondents failed to demonstrate that time-shifting would cause any likelihood of nonminimal harm to the potential market for, or the value of, their copyrighted works. The Betamax is, therefore, capable of substantial noninfringing uses. Sony's sale of such equipment to the general public does not constitute contributory infringement of respondents' copyrights.

V

"The direction of Art. I is that Congress shall have the power to promote the progress of science and the useful arts. When, as here, the Constitution is permissive, the sign of how far Congress has chosen to go can come only from Congress." *Deepsouth Packing Co. v. Laitram Corp.,* 406 U.S. 518, 530 (1972).

One may search the Copyright Act in vain for any sign that the elected representatives of the millions of people who watch television every day have made it unlawful to copy a program for later viewing at home, or have enacted a flat prohibition against the sale of machines that make such copying possible.

It may well be that Congress will take a fresh look at this new technology, just as it so often has examined other innovations in the past. But it is not our job to apply laws that have not yet been written. Applying the copyright statute, as it now reads, to the facts as they have been developed in this case, the judgment of the Court of Appeals must be reversed.

■ JUSTICE BLACKMUN, with whom JUSTICE MARSHALL, JUSTICE POWELL, and JUSTICE REHNQUIST join, dissenting.

[The following excerpts give the dissent's view on the appropriate standard for evaluating secondary liability in this type of case.]

Sony argues that the manufacturer or seller of a product used to infringe is absolved from liability whenever the product can be put to any substantial noninfringing use. The District Court so held, borrowing the "staple article of commerce" doctrine governing liability for contributory infringement of patents. See 35 U.S.C. § 271.[41] This Court today is much less positive. I do not agree that this technical judge-made doctrine of patent law, based in part on considerations irrelevant to the field of copyright, see generally *Dawson Chemical Co. v. Rohm & Haas Co.*, 448 U.S. 176, 187-199 (1980), should be imported wholesale into copyright law. Despite their common constitutional source, patent and copyright protections have not developed in a parallel fashion, and this Court in copyright cases in the past has borrowed patent concepts only sparingly.

I recognize, however, that many of the concerns underlying the "staple article of commerce" doctrine are present in copyright law as well. As the District Court noted, if liability for contributory infringement were imposed on the manufacturer or seller of every product used to infringe—a typewriter, a camera, a photocopying machine—the "wheels of commerce" would be blocked.

I therefore conclude that if a significant portion of the product's use is noninfringing, the manufacturers and sellers cannot be held contributorily liable for the product's infringing uses. If virtually all of the product's use, however, is to infringe, contributory liability may be imposed; if no one would buy the product for noninfringing purposes alone, it is clear that the manufacturer is purposely profiting from the infringement, and that liability is appropriately imposed. In such a case, the copyright owner's monopoly would not be extended beyond its proper bounds; the manufacturer of such a product contributes to the infringing activities of others and profits directly thereby, while providing no benefit to the public sufficient to justify the infringement.

The Court of Appeals concluded that Sony should be held liable for contributory infringement, reasoning that "[videotape] recorders are manufactured, advertised, and sold for the primary purpose of reproducing television programming,"

---

[41] The "staple article of commerce" doctrine protects those who manufacture products incorporated into or used with patented inventions—for example, the paper and ink used with patented printing machines, *Henry v. A. B. Dick Co.*, 224 U.S. 1 (1912), or the dry ice used with patented refrigeration systems, *Carbice Corp. v. American Patents Corp.*, 283 U.S. 27 (1931). Because a patent holder has the right to control the use of the patented item as well as its manufacture, such protection for the manufacturer of the incorporated product is necessary to prevent patent holders from extending their monopolies by suppressing competition in unpatented components and supplies suitable for use with the patented item. The doctrine of contributory patent infringement has been the subject of attention by the courts and by Congress, and has been codified since 1952, but was never mentioned during the copyright law revision process as having any relevance to contributory copyright infringement.

and "[virtually] all television programming is copyrighted material." While I agree with the first of these propositions,[42] the second, for me, is problematic. The key question is not the amount of television programming that is copyrighted, but rather the amount of VTR usage that is infringing.[43] Moreover, the parties and their amici have argued vigorously about both the amount of television programming that is covered by copyright and the amount for which permission to copy has been given. The proportion of VTR recording that is infringing is ultimately a question of fact, and the District Court specifically declined to make findings on the "percentage of legal versus illegal home-use recording." In light of my view of the law, resolution of this factual question is essential. I therefore would remand the case for further consideration of this by the District Court. . . .

Because of the Court's conclusion concerning the legality of time-shifting, it never addresses the amount of noninfringing use that a manufacturer must show to absolve itself from liability as a contributory infringer. Thus, it is difficult to discuss how the Court's test for contributory infringement would operate in practice under a proper analysis of time-shifting. One aspect of the test as it is formulated by the Court, however, particularly deserves comment. The Court explains that a manufacturer of a product is not liable for contributory infringement as long as the product is "capable of substantial noninfringing uses." Such a definition essentially eviscerates the concept of contributory infringement. Only the most unimaginative manufacturer would be unable to demonstrate that a image-duplicating product is "capable" of substantial noninfringing uses. Surely Congress desired to prevent the sale of products that are used almost exclusively to infringe copyrights; the fact that noninfringing uses exist presumably would have little bearing on that desire. . . .

The Court of Appeals, having found Sony liable, remanded for the District Court to consider the propriety of injunctive or other relief. Because of my conclusion as to the issue of liability, I, too, would not decide here what remedy would be appropriate if liability were found. I concur, however, in the Court of Appeals' suggestion that an award of damages, or continuing royalties, or even some form of limited injunction, may well be an appropriate means of balancing the equities in this case.[51] Although I express no view on the merits of any particular proposal,

---

[42] Although VTR's also may be used to watch prerecorded video cassettes and to make home motion pictures, these uses do not require a tuner such as the Betamax contains. The Studios do not object to Sony's sale of VTR's without tuners. In considering the noninfringing uses of the Betamax, therefore, those uses that would remain possible without the Betamax's built-in tuner should not be taken into account.

[43] Noninfringing uses would include, for example, recording works that are not protected by copyright, recording works that have entered the public domain, recording with permission of the copyright owner, and, of course, any recording that qualifies as fair use. . . .

[51] Other nations have imposed royalties on the manufacturers of products used to infringe copyright. . . . A study produced for the Commission of European Communities has recommended that these requirements "serve as a pattern" for the European community. While these royalty systems ordinarily depend on the existence of authors' collecting socie-

I am certain that, if Sony were found liable in this case, the District Court would be able to fashion appropriate relief. The District Court might conclude, of course, that a continuing royalty or other equitable relief is not feasible. The Studios then would be relegated to statutory damages for proven instances of infringement. But the difficulty of fashioning relief, and the possibility that complete relief may be unavailable, should not affect our interpretation of the statute.

B. Secondary Liability and Peer-to-Peer Networks

Metro-Goldwyn-Mayer Studios Inc. v. Grokster, Ltd.
125 S.Ct. 2764 (2005).

■ Justice Souter delivered the opinion of the Court.

The question is under what circumstances the distributor of a product capable of both lawful and unlawful use is liable for acts of copyright infringement by third parties using the product. We hold that one who distributes a device with the object of promoting its use to infringe copyright, as shown by clear expression or other affirmative steps taken to foster infringement, is liable for the resulting acts of infringement by third parties.

I

A

Respondents, Grokster, Ltd., and StreamCast Networks, Inc., . . . distribute free software products that allow computer users to share electronic files through peer-to-peer networks, so called because users' computers communicate directly with each other, not through central servers. The advantage of peer-to-peer networks over information networks of other types shows up in their substantial and growing popularity. Because they need no central computer server to mediate the exchange of information or files among users, the high-bandwidth communications capacity for a server may be dispensed with, and the need for costly server storage space is eliminated. Since copies of a file (particularly a popular one) are available on many users' computers, file requests and retrievals may be faster than on other types of networks, and since file exchanges do not travel through a server, communications can take place between any computers that remain connected to the network without risk that a glitch in the server will disable the network in its entirety. Given these benefits in security, cost, and efficiency, peer-to-peer networks are employed to store and distribute electronic files by universities, government agencies, corporations, and libraries, among others.[1]

---

ties, such collecting societies are a familiar part of our copyright law. Fashioning relief of this sort, of course, might require bringing other copyright owners into court through certification of a class or otherwise.

[1] Peer-to-peer networks have disadvantages as well. Searches on peer-to-peer networks may not reach and uncover all available files because search requests may not be transmitted to every computer on the network. There may be redundant copies of popular files. The creator of the software has no incentive to minimize storage or bandwidth consumption, the

Other users of peer-to-peer networks include individual recipients of Grokster's and StreamCast's software, and although the networks that they enjoy through using the software can be used to share any type of digital file, they have prominently employed those networks in sharing copyrighted music and video files without authorization. A group of copyright holders (MGM for short, but including motion picture studios, recording companies, songwriters, and music publishers) sued Grokster and StreamCast for their users' copyright infringements, alleging that they knowingly and intentionally distributed their software to enable users to reproduce and distribute the copyrighted works in violation of the Copyright Act, 17 U.S.C. § 101 *et seq.* MGM sought damages and an injunction.

Discovery during the litigation revealed the way the software worked, the business aims of each defendant company, and the predilections of the users. Grokster's eponymous software employs what is known as FastTrack technology, a protocol developed by others and licensed to Grokster. StreamCast distributes a very similar product except that its software, called Morpheus, relies on what is known as Gnutella technology. A user who downloads and installs either software possesses the protocol to send requests for files directly to the computers of others using software compatible with FastTrack or Gnutella. On the FastTrack network opened by the Grokster software, the user's request goes to a computer given an indexing capacity by the software and designated a supernode, or to some other computer with comparable power and capacity to collect temporary indexes of the files available on the computers of users connected to it. The supernode (or indexing computer) searches its own index and may communicate the search request to other supernodes. If the file is found, the supernode discloses its location to the computer requesting it, and the requesting user can download the file directly from the computer located. The copied file is placed in a designated sharing folder on the requesting user's computer, where it is available for other users to download in turn, along with any other file in that folder.

In the Gnutella network made available by Morpheus, the process is mostly the same, except that in some versions of the Gnutella protocol there are no supernodes. In these versions, peer computers using the protocol communicate directly with each other. When a user enters a search request into the Morpheus software, it sends the request to computers connected with it, which in turn pass the request along to other connected peers. The search results are communicated to the requesting computer, and the user can download desired files directly from peers' computers. As this description indicates, Grokster and StreamCast use no servers to intercept the content of the search requests or to mediate the file transfers conducted by users of the software, there being no central point through which the substance of the communications passes in either direction.

Although Grokster and StreamCast do not therefore know when particular files are copied, a few searches using their software would show what is available on the networks the software reaches. MGM commissioned a statistician to conduct a

---

costs of which are borne by every user of the network. Most relevant here, it is more difficult to control the content of files available for retrieval and the behavior of users.

systematic search, and his study showed that nearly 90% of the files available for download on the FastTrack system were copyrighted works.[5] Grokster and StreamCast dispute this figure, raising methodological problems and arguing that free copying even of copyrighted works may be authorized by the rightholders. They also argue that potential noninfringing uses of their software are significant in kind, even if infrequent in practice. Some musical performers, for example, have gained new audiences by distributing their copyrighted works for free across peer-to-peer networks, and some distributors of unprotected content have used peer-to-peer networks to disseminate files, Shakespeare being an example. Indeed, StreamCast has given Morpheus users the opportunity to download the briefs in this very case, though their popularity has not been quantified.

As for quantification, the parties' anecdotal and statistical evidence entered thus far to show the content available on the FastTrack and Gnutella networks does not say much about which files are actually downloaded by users, and no one can say how often the software is used to obtain copies of unprotected material. But MGM's evidence gives reason to think that the vast majority of users' downloads are acts of infringement, and because well over 100 million copies of the software in question are known to have been downloaded, and billions of files are shared across the FastTrack and Gnutella networks each month, the probable scope of copyright infringement is staggering.

Grokster and StreamCast concede the infringement in most downloads, and it is uncontested that they are aware that users employ their software primarily to download copyrighted files, even if the decentralized FastTrack and Gnutella networks fail to reveal which files are being copied, and when. From time to time, moreover, the companies have learned about their users' infringement directly, as from users who have sent e-mail to each company with questions about playing copyrighted movies they had downloaded, to whom the companies have responded with guidance.[6] And MGM notified the companies of 8 million copyrighted files that could be obtained using their software.

Grokster and StreamCast are not, however, merely passive recipients of information about infringing use. The record is replete with evidence that from the moment Grokster and StreamCast began to distribute their free software, each one clearly voiced the objective that recipients use it to download copyrighted works, and each took active steps to encourage infringement.

After the notorious file-sharing service, Napster, was sued by copyright holders for facilitation of copyright infringement, StreamCast gave away a software program of a kind known as OpenNap, designed as compatible with the Napster program and open to Napster users for downloading files from other Napster and OpenNap users' computers. Evidence indicates that "it was always [StreamCast's]

---

[5] By comparison, evidence introduced by the plaintiffs in *A & M Records, Inc. v. Napster, Inc.*, 239 F.3d 1004 (CA9 2001), showed that 87% of files available on the Napster filesharing network were copyrighted . . . .

[6] The Grokster founder contends that in answering these e-mails he often did not read them fully.

intent to use [its OpenNap network] to be able to capture email addresses of [its] initial target market so that [it] could promote [its] StreamCast Morpheus interface to them"; indeed, the OpenNap program was engineered " 'to leverage Napster's 50 million user base.' "

StreamCast monitored both the number of users downloading its OpenNap program and the number of music files they downloaded. It also used the resulting OpenNap network to distribute copies of the Morpheus software and to encourage users to adopt it. Internal company documents indicate that StreamCast hoped to attract large numbers of former Napster users if that company was shut down by court order or otherwise, and that StreamCast planned to be the next Napster. A kit developed by StreamCast to be delivered to advertisers, for example, contained press articles about StreamCast's potential to capture former Napster users, and it introduced itself to some potential advertisers as a company "which is similar to what Napster was." It broadcast banner advertisements to users of other Napster-compatible software, urging them to adopt its OpenNap. An internal e-mail from a company executive stated: " 'We have put this network in place so that when Napster pulls the plug on their free service . . . or if the Court orders them shut down prior to that . . . we will be positioned to capture the flood of their 32 million users that will be actively looking for an alternative.' "

Thus, StreamCast developed promotional materials to market its service as the best Napster alternative. One proposed advertisement read: "Napster Inc. has announced that it will soon begin charging you a fee. That's if the courts don't order it shut down first. What will you do to get around it?" Another proposed ad touted StreamCast's software as the "#1 alternative to Napster" and asked "when the lights went off at Napster . . . where did the users go?" (ellipsis in original).[7] StreamCast even planned to flaunt the illegal uses of its software; when it launched the OpenNap network, the chief technology officer of the company averred that "the goal is to get in trouble with the law and get sued. It's the best way to get in the news."

The evidence that Grokster sought to capture the market of former Napster users is sparser but revealing, for Grokster launched its own OpenNap system called Swaptor and inserted digital codes into its Web site so that computer users using Web search engines to look for "Napster" or "free filesharing" would be directed to the Grokster Web site, where they could download the Grokster software. And Grokster's name is an apparent derivative of Napster.

StreamCast's executives monitored the number of songs by certain commercial artists available on their networks, and an internal communication indicates they aimed to have a larger number of copyrighted songs available on their networks than other file-sharing networks. The point, of course, would be to attract users of a mind to infringe, just as it would be with their promotional materials developed showing copyrighted songs as examples of the kinds of files available through

---

[7] The record makes clear that StreamCast developed these promotional materials but not whether it released them to the public. Even if these advertisements were not released to the public and do not show encouragement to infringe, they illuminate StreamCast's purposes.

Morpheus. Morpheus in fact allowed users to search specifically for "Top 40" songs, which were inevitably copyrighted. Similarly, Grokster sent users a newsletter promoting its ability to provide particular, popular copyrighted materials.

In addition to this evidence of express promotion, marketing, and intent to promote further, the business models employed by Grokster and StreamCast confirm that their principal object was use of their software to download copyrighted works. Grokster and StreamCast receive no revenue from users, who obtain the software itself for nothing. Instead, both companies generate income by selling advertising space, and they stream the advertising to Grokster and Morpheus users while they are employing the programs. As the number of users of each program increases, advertising opportunities become worth more. While there is doubtless some demand for free Shakespeare, the evidence shows that substantive volume is a function of free access to copyrighted work. Users seeking Top 40 songs, for example, or the latest release by Modest Mouse, are certain to be far more numerous than those seeking a free Decameron, and Grokster and StreamCast translated that demand into dollars.

Finally, there is no evidence that either company made an effort to filter copyrighted material from users' downloads or otherwise impede the sharing of copyrighted files. Although Grokster appears to have sent e-mails warning users about infringing content when it received threatening notice from the copyright holders, it never blocked anyone from continuing to use its software to share copyrighted files. StreamCast not only rejected another company's offer of help to monitor infringement, but blocked the Internet Protocol addresses of entities it believed were trying to engage in such monitoring on its networks.

B

After discovery, the parties on each side of the case cross-moved for summary judgment. The District Court limited its consideration to the asserted liability of Grokster and StreamCast for distributing the current versions of their software, leaving aside whether either was liable "for damages arising from past versions of their software, or from other past activities." 259 F.Supp.2d 1029, 1033 (CD Cal. 2003). The District Court held that those who used the Grokster and Morpheus software to download copyrighted media files directly infringed MGM's copyrights, a conclusion not contested on appeal, but the court nonetheless granted summary judgment in favor of Grokster and StreamCast as to any liability arising from distribution of the then current versions of their software. Distributing that software gave rise to no liability in the court's view, because its use did not provide the distributors with actual knowledge of specific acts of infringement.

The Court of Appeals affirmed. 380 F.3d 1154 (CA9 2004). In the court's analysis, a defendant was liable as a contributory infringer when it had knowledge of direct infringement and materially contributed to the infringement. But the court read *Sony Corp. of America v. Universal City Studios, Inc.*, 464 U.S. 417 (1984), as holding that distribution of a commercial product capable of substantial noninfringing uses could not give rise to contributory liability for infringement unless the distributor had actual knowledge of specific instances of infringement and failed to act on that knowledge. The fact that the software was capable of substantial noninfringing uses in the Ninth Circuit's view meant that Grokster and StreamCast were not liable, because they had no such actual knowledge, owing to the decentralized architecture of their software. The court also held that Grokster and StreamCast did not materially contribute to their users' infringement because it was the users themselves who searched for, retrieved, and stored the infringing files, with no involvement by the defendants beyond providing the software in the first place.

The Ninth Circuit also considered whether Grokster and StreamCast could be liable under a theory of vicarious infringement. The court held against liability because the defendants did not monitor or control the use of the software, had no agreed-upon right or current ability to supervise its use, and had no independent duty to police infringement. We granted certiorari.

II

A

MGM and many of the amici fault the Court of Appeals's holding for upsetting a sound balance between the respective values of supporting creative pursuits through copyright protection and promoting innovation in new communication technologies by limiting the incidence of liability for copyright infringement. The more artistic protection is favored, the more technological innovation may be discouraged; the administration of copyright law is an exercise in managing the trade-off. See *Sony, supra,* at 442; see generally Ginsburg, Copyright and Control Over New Technologies of Dissemination, 101 Colum. L. Rev. 1613 (2001); Lichtman & Landes, Indirect Liability for Copyright Infringement: An Economic Perspective, 16 Harv. J. L. & Tech. 395 (2003).

The tension between the two values is the subject of this case, with its claim that digital distribution of copyrighted material threatens copyright holders as never before, because every copy is identical to the original, copying is easy, and many people (especially the young) use file-sharing software to download copyrighted works. This very breadth of the software's use may well draw the public directly into the debate over copyright policy, and the indications are that the ease of copying songs or movies using software like Grokster's and Napster's is fostering disdain for copyright protection, Wu, When Code Isn't Law, 89 Va. L. Rev. 679, 724–726 (2003). As the case has been presented to us, these fears are said to be offset by the different concern that imposing liability, not only on infringers but on distributors of software based on its potential for unlawful use, could limit further development of beneficial technologies. See, *e.g.,* Lemley & Reese, Reducing Digital Copyright Infringement Without Restricting Innovation, 56 Stan. L. Rev. 1345, 1386–1390 (2004); Brief for Innovation Scholars and Economists as *Amici Curiae* 15–20; Brief for Emerging Technology Companies as *Amici Curiae* 19–25; Brief for Intel Corporation as *Amicus Curiae* 20–22.[8]

---

[8] The mutual exclusivity of these values should not be overstated, however. On the one hand technological innovators, including those writing filesharing computer programs, may wish for effective copyright protections for their work. See, *e.g.,* Wu, When Code Isn't Law,

The argument for imposing indirect liability in this case is, however, a powerful one, given the number of infringing downloads that occur every day using StreamCast's and Grokster's software. When a widely shared service or product is used to commit infringement, it may be impossible to enforce rights in the protected work effectively against all direct infringers, the only practical alternative being to go against the distributor of the copying device for secondary liability on a theory of contributory or vicarious infringement.

One infringes contributorily by intentionally inducing or encouraging direct infringement, see *Gershwin Pub. Corp. v. Columbia Artists Management, Inc.*, 443 F.2d 1159, 1162 (CA2 1971), and infringes vicariously by profiting from direct infringement while declining to exercise a right to stop or limit it, *Shapiro, Bernstein & Co. v. H. L. Green Co.*, 316 F.2d 304, 307 (CA2 1963).[9] Although "the Copyright Act does not expressly render anyone liable for infringement committed by another," *Sony Corp. v. Universal City Studios*, 464 U.S., at 434, these doctrines of secondary liability emerged from common law principles and are well established in the law . . . .

B

Despite the currency of these principles of secondary liability, this Court has dealt with secondary copyright infringement in only one recent case, and because MGM has tailored its principal claim to our opinion there, a look at our earlier holding is in order. In *Sony Corp. v. Universal City Studios, supra*, this Court addressed a claim that secondary liability for infringement can arise from the very distribution of a commercial product. There, the product, novel at the time, was what we know today as the videocassette recorder or VCR. Copyright holders sued Sony as the manufacturer, claiming it was contributorily liable for infringement that occurred when VCR owners taped copyrighted programs because it supplied the means used to infringe, and it had constructive knowledge that in-

---

89 Va. L. Rev. 679, 750 (2003). (StreamCast itself was urged by an associate to "get [its] technology written down and [its intellectual property] protected.") On the other hand the widespread distribution of creative works through improved technologies may enable the synthesis of new works or generate audiences for emerging artists. See *Eldred v. Ashcroft*, 537 U.S. 186, 223–226 (2003) (STEVENS, J., dissenting); Van Houweling, Distributive Values in Copyright, 83 Texas L. Rev. 1535, 1539–1540, 1562–1564 (2005); Brief for Sovereign Artists et al. as *Amici Curiae* 11.

[9] We stated in *Sony Corp. of America v. Universal City Studios, Inc.*, 464 U.S. 417 (1984), that " 'the lines between direct infringement, contributory infringement and vicarious liability are not clearly drawn' . . . . Reasoned analysis of [the Sony plaintiffs' contributory infringement claim] necessarily entails consideration of arguments and case law which may also be forwarded under the other labels, and indeed the parties . . . rely upon such arguments and authority in support of their respective positions on the issue of contributory infringement," *id.*, at 435, n. 17 (quoting *Universal City Studios, Inc. v. Sony Corp.*, 480 F.Supp. 429, 457–458 (CD Cal. 1979)). In the present case MGM has argued a vicarious liability theory, which allows imposition of liability when the defendant profits directly from the infringement and has a right and ability to supervise the direct infringer, even if the defendant initially lacks knowledge of the infringement. . . . Because we resolve the case based on an inducement theory, there is no need to analyze separately MGM's vicarious liability theory.

fringement would occur. At the trial on the merits, the evidence showed that the principal use of the VCR was for " 'time-shifting,' " or taping a program for later viewing at a more convenient time, which the Court found to be a fair, not an infringing, use. There was no evidence that Sony had expressed an object of bringing about taping in violation of copyright or had taken active steps to increase its profits from unlawful taping. Although Sony's advertisements urged consumers to buy the VCR to " 'record favorite shows' " or " 'build a library' " of recorded programs, *id.,* at 459 (Blackmun, J., dissenting), neither of these uses was necessarily infringing, *id.,* at 424, 454–455.

On those facts, with no evidence of stated or indicated intent to promote infringing uses, the only conceivable basis for imposing liability was on a theory of contributory infringement arising from its sale of VCRs to consumers with knowledge that some would use them to infringe. *Id.,* at 439. But because the VCR was "capable of commercially significant noninfringing uses," we held the manufacturer could not be faulted solely on the basis of its distribution. *Id.,* at 442.

This analysis reflected patent law's traditional staple article of commerce doctrine, now codified, that distribution of a component of a patented device will not violate the patent if it is suitable for use in other ways. 35 U.S.C. § 271(c); *Aro Mfg. Co. v. Convertible Top Replacement Co.,* 377 U.S. 476, 485 (1964) (noting codification of cases); *id.,* at 486, n. 6 (same). The doctrine was devised to identify instances in which it may be presumed from distribution of an article in commerce that the distributor intended the article to be used to infringe another's patent, and so may justly be held liable for that infringement. "One who makes and sells articles which are only adapted to be used in a patented combination will be presumed to intend the natural consequences of his acts; he will be presumed to intend that they shall be used in the combination of the patent." *New York Scaffolding Co. v. Whitney,* 224 F. 452, 459 (CA8 1915) . . . .

In sum, where an article is "good for nothing else" but infringement, *Canda v. Michigan Malleable Iron Co., supra,* at 489, there is no legitimate public interest in its unlicensed availability, and there is no injustice in presuming or imputing an intent to infringe, see *Henry v. A. B. Dick Co.,* 224 U.S. 1, 48 (1912), overruled on other grounds, *Motion Picture Patents Co. v. Universal Film Mfg. Co.,* 243 U.S. 502 (1917). Conversely, the doctrine absolves the equivocal conduct of selling an item with substantial lawful as well as unlawful uses, and limits liability to instances of more acute fault than the mere understanding that some of one's products will be misused. It leaves breathing room for innovation and a vigorous commerce. See *Sony Corp. v. Universal City Studios, supra,* at 442; *Dawson Chemical Co. v. Rohm & Haas Co.,* 448 U.S. 176, 221 (1980); *Henry v. A. B. Dick Co., supra,* at 48.

The parties and many of the *amici* in this case think the key to resolving it is the *Sony* rule and, in particular, what it means for a product to be "capable of commercially significant noninfringing uses." MGM advances the argument that granting summary judgment to Grokster and StreamCast as to their current activities gave too much weight to the value of innovative technology, and too little to the copyrights infringed by users of their software, given that 90% of works available on one of the networks was shown to be copyrighted. Assuming the remaining 10% to be its noninfringing use, MGM says this should not qualify as "substantial," and the Court should quantify *Sony* to the extent of holding that a product used "principally" for infringement does not qualify. As mentioned before, Grokster and StreamCast reply by citing evidence that their software can be used to reproduce public domain works, and they point to copyright holders who actually encourage copying. Even if infringement is the principal practice with their software today, they argue, the noninfringing uses are significant and will grow.

We agree with MGM that the Court of Appeals misapplied *Sony*, which it read as limiting secondary liability quite beyond the circumstances to which the case applied. *Sony* barred secondary liability based on presuming or imputing intent to cause infringement solely from the design or distribution of a product capable of substantial lawful use, which the distributor knows is in fact used for infringement. The Ninth Circuit has read *Sony's* limitation to mean that whenever a product is capable of substantial lawful use, the producer can never be held contributorily liable for third parties' infringing use of it; it read the rule as being this broad, even when an actual purpose to cause infringing use is shown by evidence independent of design and distribution of the product, unless the distributors had "specific knowledge of infringement at a time at which they contributed to the infringement, and failed to act upon that information." 380 F.3d at 1162 (internal quotation marks and alterations omitted). Because the Circuit found the StreamCast and Grokster software capable of substantial lawful use, it concluded on the basis of its reading of *Sony* that neither company could be held liable, since there was no showing that their software, being without any central server, afforded them knowledge of specific unlawful uses.

This view of *Sony*, however, was error, converting the case from one about liability resting on imputed intent to one about liability on any theory. Because *Sony* did not displace other theories of secondary liability, and because we find below that it was error to grant summary judgment to the companies on MGM's inducement claim, we do not revisit *Sony* further, as MGM requests, to add a more quantified description of the point of balance between protection and commerce when liability rests solely on distribution with knowledge that unlawful use will occur. It is enough to note that the Ninth Circuit's judgment rested on an erroneous understanding of *Sony* and to leave further consideration of the *Sony* rule for a day when that may be required.

C

Sony's rule limits imputing culpable intent as a matter of law from the characteristics or uses of a distributed product. But nothing in *Sony* requires courts to ignore evidence of intent if there is such evidence, and the case was never meant to foreclose rules of fault-based liability derived from the common law.[10] *Sony Corp. v. Universal City Studios*, 464 U.S., at 439 ("If vicarious liability is to be imposed on Sony in this case, it must rest on the fact that it has sold equipment with construc-

---

[10] Nor does the Patent Act's exemption from liability for those who distribute a staple article of commerce, 35 U.S.C. § 271(c), extend to those who induce patent infringement, § 271(b).

tive knowledge" of the potential for infringement). Thus, where evidence goes beyond a product's characteristics or the knowledge that it may be put to infringing uses, and shows statements or actions directed to promoting infringement, *Sony's* staple-article rule will not preclude liability.

The classic case of direct evidence of unlawful purpose occurs when one induces commission of infringement by another, or "entices or persuades another" to infringe, Black's Law Dictionary 790 (8th ed. 2004), as by advertising. Thus at common law a copyright or patent defendant who "not only expected but invoked [infringing use] by advertisement" was liable for infringement "on principles recognized in every part of the law." *Kalem Co. v. Harper Brothers*, 222 U.S., at 62–63 (copyright infringement). . . .

The rule on inducement of infringement as developed in the early cases is no different today.[11] Evidence of "active steps . . . taken to encourage direct infringement," *Oak Industries, Inc. v. Zenith Electronics Corp.*, 697 F.Supp. 988, 992 (ND Ill. 1988), such as advertising an infringing use or instructing how to engage in an infringing use, show an affirmative intent that the product be used to infringe, and a showing that infringement was encouraged overcomes the law's reluctance to find liability when a defendant merely sells a commercial product suitable for some lawful use . . . . Cf. W. Keeton, D. Dobbs, R. Keeton, & D. Owen, Prosser and Keeton on Law of Torts 37 (5th ed. 1984) ("There is a definite tendency to impose greater responsibility upon a defendant whose conduct was intended to do harm, or was morally wrong").

For the same reasons that *Sony* took the staple-article doctrine of patent law as a model for its copyright safe-harbor rule, the inducement rule, too, is a sensible one for copyright. We adopt it here, holding that one who distributes a device with the object of promoting its use to infringe copyright, as shown by clear expression or other affirmative steps taken to foster infringement, is liable for the resulting acts of infringement by third parties. We are, of course, mindful of the need to keep from trenching on regular commerce or discouraging the development of technologies with lawful and unlawful potential. Accordingly, just as *Sony* did not find intentional inducement despite the knowledge of the VCR manufacturer that its device could be used to infringe, 464 U.S., at 439, n. 19, mere knowledge of infringing potential or of actual infringing uses would not be enough here to subject a distributor to liability. Nor would ordinary acts incident to product distribution, such as offering customers technical support or product updates, support liability in themselves. The inducement rule, instead, premises liability on purposeful, culpable expression and conduct, and thus does nothing to compromise legitimate commerce or discourage innovation having a lawful promise.

III

A

The only apparent question about treating MGM's evidence as sufficient to withstand summary judgment under the theory of inducement goes to the need on

---

[11] Inducement has been codified in patent law. Ibid.

MGM's part to adduce evidence that StreamCast and Grokster communicated an inducing message to their software users. The classic instance of inducement is by advertisement or solicitation that broadcasts a message designed to stimulate others to commit violations. MGM claims that such a message is shown here. It is undisputed that StreamCast beamed onto the computer screens of users of Napster-compatible programs ads urging the adoption of its OpenNap program, which was designed, as its name implied, to invite the custom of patrons of Napster, then under attack in the courts for facilitating massive infringement. Those who accepted StreamCast's OpenNap program were offered software to perform the same services, which a factfinder could conclude would readily have been understood in the Napster market as the ability to download copyrighted music files. Grokster distributed an electronic newsletter containing links to articles promoting its software's ability to access popular copyrighted music. And anyone whose Napster or free file-sharing searches turned up a link to Grokster would have understood Grokster to be offering the same file-sharing ability as Napster, and to the same people who probably used Napster for infringing downloads; that would also have been the understanding of anyone offered Grokster's suggestively named Swaptor software, its version of OpenNap. And both companies communicated a clear message by responding affirmatively to requests for help in locating and playing copyrighted materials.

In StreamCast's case, of course, the evidence just described was supplemented by other unequivocal indications of unlawful purpose in the internal communications and advertising designs aimed at Napster users ("When the lights went off at Napster . . . where did the users go?" (ellipsis in original)). Whether the messages were communicated is not to the point on this record. The function of the message in the theory of inducement is to prove by a defendant's own statements that his unlawful purpose disqualifies him from claiming protection (and incidentally to point to actual violators likely to be found among those who hear or read the message). Proving that a message was sent out, then, is the preeminent but not exclusive way of showing that active steps were taken with the purpose of bringing about infringing acts, and of showing that infringing acts took place by using the device distributed. Here, the summary judgment record is replete with other evidence that Grokster and StreamCast, unlike the manufacturer and distributor in *Sony*, acted with a purpose to cause copyright violations by use of software suitable for illegal use.

Three features of this evidence of intent are particularly notable. First, each company showed itself to be aiming to satisfy a known source of demand for copyright infringement, the market comprising former Napster users. StreamCast's internal documents made constant reference to Napster, it initially distributed its Morpheus software through an OpenNap program compatible with Napster, it advertised its OpenNap program to Napster users, and its Morpheus software functions as Napster did except that it could be used to distribute more kinds of files, including copyrighted movies and software programs. Grokster's name is apparently derived from Napster, it too initially offered an OpenNap program, its software's function is likewise comparable to Napster's, and it attempted to divert queries for Napster onto its own Web site. Grokster and StreamCast's efforts to supply services to former Napster users, deprived of a mechanism to copy and distribute what were overwhelmingly infringing files, indicate a principal, if not exclusive, intent on the part of each to bring about infringement.

Second, this evidence of unlawful objective is given added significance by MGM's showing that neither company attempted to develop filtering tools or other mechanisms to diminish the infringing activity using their software. While the Ninth Circuit treated the defendants' failure to develop such tools as irrelevant because they lacked an independent duty to monitor their users' activity, we think this evidence underscores Grokster's and StreamCast's intentional facilitation of their users' infringement.[12]

Third, there is a further complement to the direct evidence of unlawful objective. It is useful to recall that StreamCast and Grokster make money by selling advertising space, by directing ads to the screens of computers employing their software. As the record shows, the more the software is used, the more ads are sent out and the greater the advertising revenue becomes. Since the extent of the software's use determines the gain to the distributors, the commercial sense of their enterprise turns on high-volume use, which the record shows is infringing.[13] This evidence alone would not justify an inference of unlawful intent, but viewed in the context of the entire record its import is clear.

The unlawful objective is unmistakable.

B

In addition to intent to bring about infringement and distribution of a device suitable for infringing use, the inducement theory of course requires evidence of actual infringement by recipients of the device, the software in this case. As the account of the facts indicates, there is evidence of infringement on a gigantic scale, and there is no serious issue of the adequacy of MGM's showing on this point in order to survive the companies' summary judgment requests. Although an exact

---

[12] Of course, in the absence of other evidence of intent, a court would be unable to find contributory infringement liability merely based on a failure to take affirmative steps to prevent infringement, if the device otherwise was capable of substantial noninfringing uses. Such a holding would tread too close to the *Sony* safe harbor.

[13] Grokster and StreamCast contend that any theory of liability based on their conduct is not properly before this Court because the rulings in the trial and appellate courts dealt only with the present versions of their software, not "past acts . . . that allegedly encouraged infringement or assisted . . . known acts of infringement." This contention misapprehends the basis for their potential liability. It is not only that encouraging a particular consumer to infringe a copyright can give rise to secondary liability for the infringement that results. Inducement liability goes beyond that, and the distribution of a product can itself give rise to liability where evidence shows that the distributor intended and encouraged the product to be used to infringe. In such a case, the culpable act is not merely the encouragement of infringement but also the distribution of the tool intended for infringing use. See *Kalem Co. v. Harper Brothers*, 222 U.S. 55, 62–63 (1911); *Cable/Home Communication Corp. v. Network Productions, Inc.*, 902 F.2d 829, 846 (CA11 1990); *A & M Records, Inc. v. Abdallah*, 948 F.Supp. 1449, 1456 (CD Cal. 1996).

calculation of infringing use, as a basis for a claim of damages, is subject to dispute, there is no question that the summary judgment evidence is at least adequate to entitle MGM to go forward with claims for damages and equitable relief.

*   *   *

In sum, this case is significantly different from *Sony* and reliance on that case to rule in favor of StreamCast and Grokster was error. *Sony* dealt with a claim of liability based solely on distributing a product with alternative lawful and unlawful uses, with knowledge that some users would follow the unlawful course. The case struck a balance between the interests of protection and innovation by holding that the product's capability of substantial lawful employment should bar the imputation of fault and consequent secondary liability for the unlawful acts of others.

MGM's evidence in this case most obviously addresses a different basis of liability for distributing a product open to alternative uses. Here, evidence of the distributors' words and deeds going beyond distribution as such shows a purpose to cause and profit from third-party acts of copyright infringement. If liability for inducing infringement is ultimately found, it will not be on the basis of presuming or imputing fault, but from inferring a patently illegal objective from statements and actions showing what that objective was.

There is substantial evidence in MGM's favor on all elements of inducement, and summary judgment in favor of Grokster and StreamCast was error. On remand, reconsideration of MGM's motion for summary judgment will be in order.

The judgment of the Court of Appeals is vacated, and the case is remanded for further proceedings consistent with this opinion.

■ JUSTICE GINSBURG, with whom THE CHIEF JUSTICE and JUSTICE KENNEDY join, concurring.

I concur in the Court's decision, which vacates in full the judgment of the Court of Appeals for the Ninth Circuit, and write separately to clarify why I conclude that the Court of Appeals misperceived, and hence misapplied, our holding in *Sony Corp. of America v. Universal City Studios, Inc.,* 464 U.S. 417 (1984). There is here at least a "genuine issue as to [a] material fact," Fed. Rule Civ. Proc. 56(c), on the liability of Grokster or StreamCast, not only for actively inducing copyright infringement, but also or alternatively, based on the distribution of their software products, for contributory copyright infringement. On neither score was summary judgment for Grokster and StreamCast warranted.

At bottom, however labeled, the question in this case is whether Grokster and StreamCast are liable for the direct infringing acts of others. Liability under our jurisprudence may be predicated on actively encouraging (or inducing) infringement through specific acts (as the Court's opinion develops) or on distributing a product distributees use to infringe copyrights, if the product is not capable of "substantial" or "commercially significant" noninfringing uses. *Sony,* 464 U.S., at 442 . . . While the two categories overlap, they capture different culpable behavior. Long coexisting, both are now codified in patent law. Compare 35 U.S.C. § 271(b) (active inducement liability), with § 271(c) (contributory liability for distribution of a product not "suitable for substantial noninfringing use").

In *Sony*, the Court considered Sony's liability for selling the Betamax video cassette recorder. It did so enlightened by a full trial record. Drawing an analogy to the staple article of commerce doctrine from patent law, the *Sony* Court observed that the "sale of an article . . . adapted to [a patent] infringing use" does not suffice "to make the seller a contributory infringer" if the article "is also adapted to other and lawful uses." *Id.*, at 441 . . . .

"The staple article of commerce doctrine" applied to copyright, the Court stated, "must strike a balance between a copyright holder's legitimate demand for effective — not merely symbolic — protection of the statutory monopoly, and the rights of others freely to engage in substantially unrelated areas of commerce." *Sony*, 464 U.S., at 442. "Accordingly," the Court held, "the sale of copying equipment, like the sale of other articles of commerce, does not constitute contributory infringement if the product is widely used for legitimate, unobjectionable purposes. Indeed, it need merely be capable of substantial noninfringing uses." *Ibid.* Thus, to resolve the *Sony* case, the Court explained, it had to determine "whether the Betamax is capable of commercially significant noninfringing uses." *Ibid.*

To answer that question, the Court considered whether "a significant number of [potential uses of the Betamax were] noninfringing." *Ibid.* The Court homed in on one potential use — private, noncommercial time-shifting of television programs in the home (*i.e.*, recording a broadcast TV program for later personal viewing). Time-shifting was noninfringing, the Court concluded, because in some cases trial testimony showed it was authorized by the copyright holder, and in others it qualified as legitimate fair use. Most purchasers used the Betamax principally to engage in time-shifting, a use that "plainly satisfied" the Court's standard. Thus, there was no need in Sony to "give precise content to the question of how much [actual or potential] use is commercially significant." *Ibid.*[1] Further development was left for later days and cases.

---

[1] JUSTICE BREYER finds in *Sony* a "clear" rule permitting contributory liability for copyright infringement based on distribution of a product only when the product "will be used almost exclusively to infringe copyrights." But cf. *Sony*, 464 U.S., at 442 (recognizing "copyright holder's legitimate demand for effective — not merely symbolic — protection"). *Sony*, as I read it, contains no clear, near-exclusivity test. Nor have Courts of Appeals unanimously recognized JUSTICE BREYER's clear rule. Compare *A&M Records, Inc. v. Napster, Inc.*, 239 F.3d 1004, 1021 (CA9 2001) ("Evidence of actual knowledge of specific acts of infringement is required to hold a computer system operator liable for contributory copyright infringement."), with *In re Aimster Copyright Litigation*, 334 F.3d 643, 649–650 (CA7 2003) ("When a supplier is offering a product or service that has noninfringing as well as infringing uses, some estimate of the respective magnitudes of these uses is necessary for a finding of contributory infringement. . . . But the balancing of costs and benefits is necessary only in a case in which substantial noninfringing uses, present or prospective, are demonstrated."). . . . All Members of the Court agree, moreover, that "the Court of Appeals misapplied *Sony*," at least to the extent it read that decision to limit "secondary liability" to a hardly-ever category, "quite beyond the circumstances to which the case applied."

The Ninth Circuit went astray, I will endeavor to explain, when that court granted summary judgment to Grokster and StreamCast on the charge of contributory liability based on distribution of their software products. Relying on its earlier opinion in *A&M Records, Inc. v. Napster, Inc.*, 239 F.3d 1004 (CA9 2001), the Court of Appeals held that "if substantial noninfringing use was shown, the copyright owner would be required to show that the defendant had reasonable knowledge of specific infringing files." 380 F.3d 1154, 1161 (CA9 2004). "A careful examination of the record," the court concluded, "indicates that there is no genuine issue of material fact as to noninfringing use." *Ibid.* The appeals court pointed to the band Wilco, which made one of its albums available for free downloading, to other recording artists who may have authorized free distribution of their music through the Internet, and to public domain literary works and films available through Grokster's and StreamCast's software. Although it acknowledged MGM's assertion that "the vast majority of the software use is for copyright infringement," the court concluded that Grokster's and StreamCast's proffered evidence met *Sony's* requirement that "a product need only be capable of substantial noninfringing uses." 380 F.3d at 1162.[2]

This case differs markedly from *Sony*. Cf. Peters, Brace Memorial Lecture: Copyright Enters the Public Domain, 51 J. Copyright Soc. 701, 724 (2004) ("The *Grokster* panel's reading of *Sony* is the broadest that any court has given it. . . ."). Here, there has been no finding of any fair use and little beyond anecdotal evidence of noninfringing uses. In finding the Grokster and StreamCast software products capable of substantial noninfringing uses, the District Court and the Court of Appeals appear to have relied largely on declarations submitted by the defendants. These declarations include assertions (some of them hearsay) that a number of copyright owners authorize distribution of their works on the Internet and that some public domain material is available through peer-to-peer networks including those accessed through Grokster's and StreamCast's software. 380 F.3d at 1161; 259 F.Supp.2d 1029, 1035–1036 (CD Cal. 2003).

The District Court declared it "undisputed that there are substantial noninfringing uses for Defendants' software," thus obviating the need for further proceedings. 259 F.Supp.2d, at 1035. This conclusion appears to rest almost entirely on the collection of declarations submitted by Grokster and StreamCast. Review of these declarations reveals mostly anecdotal evidence, sometimes obtained second-hand, of authorized copyrighted works or public domain works available online and shared through peer-to-peer networks, and general statements about the benefits of peer-to-peer technology. . . . These declarations do not support summary judgment in the face of evidence, proffered by MGM, of overwhelming use of Grokster's and StreamCast's software for infringement.[3]

---

[2] Grokster and StreamCast, in the Court of Appeals' view, would be entitled to summary judgment unless MGM could show that that the software companies had knowledge of specific acts of infringement and failed to act on that knowledge—a standard the court held MGM could not meet. 380 F.3d at 1162–1163.

[3] JUSTICE BREYER finds support for summary judgment in this motley collection of decla-

Even if the absolute number of noninfringing files copied using the Grokster and StreamCast software is large, it does not follow that the products are therefore put to substantial noninfringing uses and are thus immune from liability. The number of noninfringing copies may be reflective of, and dwarfed by, the huge total volume of files shared. Further, the District Court and the Court of Appeals did not sharply distinguish between uses of Grokster's and StreamCast's software products (which this case is about) and uses of peer-to-peer technology generally (which this case is not about).

In sum, when the record in this case was developed, there was evidence that Grokster's and StreamCast's products were, and had been for some time, overwhelmingly used to infringe, and that this infringement was the overwhelming source of revenue from the products. Fairly appraised, the evidence was insufficient to demonstrate, beyond genuine debate, a reasonable prospect that substantial or commercially significant noninfringing uses were likely to develop over time. On this record, the District Court should not have ruled dispositively on the contributory infringement charge by granting summary judgment to Grokster and StreamCast.[4]

If, on remand, the case is not resolved on summary judgment in favor of MGM based on Grokster and StreamCast actively inducing infringement, the Court of Appeals, I would emphasize, should reconsider, on a fuller record, its interpretation of *Sony's* product distribution holding.

■ JUSTICE BREYER, with whom JUSTICE STEVENS and JUSTICE O'CONNOR join, concurring.

I agree with the Court that the distributor of a dual-use technology may be liable for the infringing activities of third parties where he or she actively seeks to

---

rations and in a survey conducted by an expert retained by MGM. That survey identified 75% of the files available through Grokster as copyrighted works owned or controlled by the plaintiffs, and 15% of the files as works likely copyrighted. As to the remaining 10% of the files, "there was not enough information to form reasonable conclusions either as to what those files even consisted of, and/or whether they were infringing or non-infringing." Even assuming, as JUSTICE BREYER does, that the *Sony* Court would have absolved Sony of contributory liability solely on the basis of the use of the Betamax for authorized time-shifting, summary judgment is not inevitably appropriate here. *Sony* stressed that the plaintiffs there owned "well below 10%" of copyrighted television programming, 464 U.S., at 443, and found, based on trial testimony from representatives of the four major sports leagues and other individuals authorized to consent to home-recording of their copyrighted broadcasts, that a similar percentage of program copying was authorized, *id.*, at 424. Here, the plaintiffs allegedly control copyrights for 70% or 75% of the material exchanged through the Grokster and StreamCast software, 380 F.3d at 1158, and the District Court does not appear to have relied on comparable testimony about authorized copying from copyright holders.

[4] The District Court's conclusion that "plaintiffs do not dispute that Defendants' software is being used, and could be used, for substantial noninfringing purposes," 259 F.Supp.2d 1029, 1036 (CD Cal. 2003); accord 380 F.3d at 1161, is, to say the least, dubious. In the courts below and in this Court, MGM has continuously disputed any such conclusion.

advance the infringement. I further agree that, in light of our holding today, we need not now "revisit" *Sony Corp. of America v. Universal City Studios, Inc.,* 464 U.S. 417 (1984). Other Members of the Court, however, take up the *Sony* question: whether Grokster's product is "capable of 'substantial' or 'commercially significant' noninfringing uses." (GINSBURG, J., concurring) (quoting *Sony,* at 442). And they answer that question by stating that the Court of Appeals was wrong when it granted summary judgment on the issue in Grokster's favor. I write to explain why I disagree with them on this matter.

I

The Court's opinion in *Sony* and the record evidence (as described and analyzed in the many briefs before us) together convince me that the Court of Appeals' conclusion has adequate legal support.

A

I begin with *Sony's* standard. In *Sony,* the Court considered the potential copyright liability of a company that did not itself illegally copy protected material, but rather sold a machine—a Video Cassette Recorder (VCR)—that could be used to do so. A buyer could use that machine for noninfringing purposes, such as recording for later viewing (sometimes called " 'time-shifting,' " *Sony,* 464 U.S., at 421) uncopyrighted television programs or copyrighted programs with a copyright holder's permission. The buyer could use the machine for infringing purposes as well, such as building libraries of taped copyrighted programs. Or, the buyer might use the machine to record copyrighted programs under circumstances in which the legal status of the act of recording was uncertain (*i.e.,* where the copying may, or may not, have constituted a "fair use," *id.,* at 425–426). Sony knew many customers would use its VCRs to engage in unauthorized copying and " 'library-building.' " *Id.,* at 458–459 (Blackmun, J., dissenting). But that fact, said the Court, was insufficient to make Sony itself an infringer. And the Court ultimately held that Sony was not liable for its customers' acts of infringement.

In reaching this conclusion, the Court recognized the need for the law, in fixing secondary copyright liability, to "strike a balance between a copyright holder's legitimate demand for effective—not merely symbolic—protection of the statutory monopoly, and the rights of others freely to engage in substantially unrelated areas of commerce." *Id.,* at 442. It pointed to patent law's "staple article of commerce" doctrine, under which a distributor of a product is not liable for patent infringement by its customers unless that product is "unsuited for any commercial noninfringing use." *Dawson Chemical Co. v. Rohm & Haas Co.,* 448 U.S. 176, 198 (1980). The Court wrote that the sale of copying equipment, "like the sale of other articles of commerce, does not constitute contributory infringement if the product is widely used for legitimate, unobjectionable purposes. *Indeed, it need merely be capable of substantial noninfringing uses."* *Sony,* 464 U.S., at 442 (emphasis added). The Court ultimately characterized the legal "question" in the particular case as "whether [Sony's VCR] is *capable of commercially significant noninfringing uses"* (while declining to give "precise content" to these terms). *Ibid.* (emphasis added).

It then applied this standard. The Court had before it a survey (commissioned by the District Court and then prepared by the respondents) showing that roughly 9% of all VCR recordings were of the type—namely, religious, educational, and sports programming—owned by producers and distributors testifying on Sony's behalf who did not object to time-shifting. [See] *Sony, supra,* at 424 (7.3% of all Sony VCR use is to record sports programs; representatives of the sports leagues do not object). A much higher percentage of VCR users had at one point taped an authorized program, in addition to taping *un*authorized programs. And the plaintiffs—not a large class of content providers as in this case—owned only a small percentage of the total available unauthorized programming. But of all the taping actually done by Sony's customers, only around 9% was of the sort the Court referred to as authorized.

The Court found that the magnitude of authorized programming was "significant," and it also noted the "significant potential for future authorized copying." 464 U.S., at 444. The Court supported this conclusion by referencing the trial testimony of professional sports league officials and a religious broadcasting representative. It also discussed (1) a Los Angeles educational station affiliated with the Public Broadcasting Service that made many of its programs available for home taping, and (2) Mr. Rogers' Neighborhood, a widely watched children's program. On the basis of this testimony and other similar evidence, the Court determined that producers of this kind had authorized duplication of their copyrighted programs "in significant enough numbers to create a *substantial* market for a noninfringing use of the" VCR. *Id.,* at 447, n.28 (emphasis added).

The Court, in using the key word "substantial," indicated that these circumstances alone constituted a sufficient basis for rejecting the imposition of secondary liability. See *id.,* at 456 ("Sony demonstrated a significant likelihood that *substantial* numbers of copyright holders" would not object to time-shifting (emphasis added)). Nonetheless, the Court buttressed its conclusion by finding separately that, in any event, unauthorized time-shifting often constituted not infringement, but "fair use." *Id.,* at 447–456.

B

When measured against *Sony's* underlying evidence and analysis, the evidence now before us shows that Grokster passes *Sony's* test—that is, whether the company's product is capable of substantial or commercially significant noninfringing uses. For one thing, petitioners' (hereinafter MGM) own expert declared that 75% of current files available on Grokster are infringing and 15% are "likely infringing." That leaves some number of files near 10% that apparently are noninfringing, a figure very similar to the 9% or so of authorized time-shifting uses of the VCR that the Court faced in *Sony.*

As in *Sony,* witnesses here explained the nature of the noninfringing files on Grokster's network without detailed quantification. Those files include:

—Authorized copies of music by artists such as Wilco, Janis Ian, Pearl Jam, Dave Matthews, John Mayer, and others. . . .

—Free electronic books and other works from various online publishers, including Project Gutenberg. . . .

—Public domain and authorized software, such as WinZip 8.1. . . .

—Licensed music videos and television and movie segments distributed via digital video packaging with the permission of the copyright holder. . . .

The nature of these and other lawfully swapped files is such that it is reasonable to infer quantities of current lawful use roughly approximate to those at issue in *Sony*. At least, MGM has offered no evidence sufficient to survive summary judgment that could plausibly demonstrate a significant quantitative difference. To be sure, in quantitative terms these uses account for only a small percentage of the total number of uses of Grokster's product. But the same was true in *Sony*, which characterized the relatively limited authorized copying market as "substantial." (The Court made clear as well in *Sony* that the amount of material then presently available for lawful copying—if not actually copied—was significant, see 464 U.S., at 444, and the same is certainly true in this case.)

Importantly, *Sony* also used the word "capable," asking whether the product is "capable of" substantial noninfringing uses. Its language and analysis suggest that a figure like 10%, if fixed for all time, might well prove insufficient, but that such a figure serves as an adequate foundation where there is a reasonable prospect of expanded legitimate uses over time. See *ibid.* (noting a "significant potential for future authorized copying"). And its language also indicates the appropriateness of looking to potential future uses of the product to determine its "capability."

Here the record reveals a significant future market for noninfringing uses of Grokster-type peer-to-peer software. Such software permits the exchange of any sort of digital file—whether that file does, or does not, contain copyrighted material. As more and more uncopyrighted information is stored in swappable form, it seems a likely inference that lawful peer-to-peer sharing will become increasingly prevalent. . . .

And that is just what is happening. Such legitimate noninfringing uses are coming to include the swapping of: *research information* (the initial purpose of many peer-to-peer networks); *public domain films* (e.g., those owned by the Prelinger Archive); *historical recordings and digital educational materials* (e.g., those stored on the Internet Archive); *digital photos* (OurPictures, for example, is starting a P2P photoswapping service); *"shareware" and "freeware"* (e.g., Linux and certain Windows software); *secure licensed music and movie files* (Intent MediaWorks, for example, protects licensed content sent across P2P networks); *news broadcasts past and present* (the BBC Creative Archive lets users "rip, mix and share the BBC"); *user-created audio and video files* (including "podcasts" that may be distributed through P2P software); *and all manner of free "open content" works collected by Creative Commons* (one can search for Creative Commons material on StreamCast). See . . . Merges, A New Dynamism in the Public Domain, 71 U. Chi. L. Rev. 183 (2004). I can find nothing in the record that suggests that this course of events will not continue to flow naturally as a consequence of the character of the software taken together with the foreseeable development of the Internet and of information technology. . . .

There may be other now-unforeseen noninfringing uses that develop for peer-to-peer software, just as the home-video rental industry (unmentioned in *Sony*) developed for the VCR. But the foreseeable development of such uses, when taken together with an estimated 10% noninfringing material, is sufficient to meet *Sony's* standard. And while Sony considered the record following a trial, there are no facts asserted by MGM in its summary judgment filings that lead me to believe the outcome after a trial here could be any different. The lower courts reached the same conclusion.

Of course, Grokster itself may not want to develop these other noninfringing uses. But *Sony's* standard seeks to protect not the Groksters of this world (which in any event may well be liable under today's holding), but the development of technology more generally. And Grokster's desires in this respect are beside the point.

II

The real question here, I believe, is not whether the record evidence satisfies *Sony*. As I have interpreted the standard set forth in that case, it does. And of the Courts of Appeals that have considered the matter, only one has proposed interpreting *Sony* more strictly than I would do—in a case where the product might have failed under any standard. *In re Aimster Copyright Litigation*, 334 F.3d 643, 653 (CA7 2003) (defendant "failed to show that its service is *ever* used for any purpose other than to infringe" copyrights (emphasis added)) . . .

Instead, the real question is whether we should modify the *Sony* standard, as MGM requests, or interpret *Sony* more strictly, as I believe JUSTICE GINSBURG's approach would do in practice . . .

As I have said, *Sony* itself sought to "strike a balance between a copyright holder's legitimate demand for effective—not merely symbolic—protection of the statutory monopoly, and the rights of others freely to engage in substantially unrelated areas of commerce." *Id.,* at 442. Thus, to determine whether modification, or a strict interpretation, of *Sony* is needed, I would ask whether MGM has shown that *Sony* incorrectly balanced copyright and new-technology interests. In particular: (1) Has *Sony* (as I interpret it) worked to protect new technology? (2) If so, would modification or strict interpretation significantly weaken that protection? (3) If so, would new or necessary copyright-related benefits outweigh any such weakening?

A

The first question is the easiest to answer. *Sony's* rule, as I interpret it, has provided entrepreneurs with needed assurance that they will be shielded from copyright liability as they bring valuable new technologies to market.

Sony's rule is clear. That clarity allows those who develop new products that are capable of substantial noninfringing uses to know, *ex ante,* that distribution of their product will not yield massive monetary liability. At the same time, it helps deter them from distributing products that have no other real function than—or that are specifically intended for—copyright infringement, deterrence that the Court's holding today reinforces (by adding a weapon to the copyright holder's legal arsenal).

Sony's rule is strongly technology protecting. The rule deliberately makes it difficult for courts to find secondary liability where new technology is at issue. It establishes that the law will not impose copyright liability upon the distributors of dual-use technologies (who do not themselves engage in unauthorized copying) unless the product in question will be used almost exclusively to infringe copyrights (or unless they actively induce infringements as we today describe). *Sony* thereby recognizes that the copyright laws are not intended to discourage or to control the emergence of new technologies, including (perhaps especially) those that help disseminate information and ideas more broadly or more efficiently. Thus *Sony's* rule shelters VCRs, typewriters, tape recorders, photocopiers, computers, cassette players, compact disc burners, digital video recorders, MP3 players, Internet search engines, and peer-to-peer software. But *Sony's* rule does not shelter descramblers, even if one could theoretically use a descrambler in a noninfringing way . . . .

Sony's rule is forward looking. It does not confine its scope to a static snapshot of a product's current uses (thereby threatening technologies that have undeveloped future markets). Rather, as the VCR example makes clear, a product's market can evolve dramatically over time. And *Sony*—by referring to a capacity for substantial noninfringing uses—recognizes that fact. *Sony's* word "capable" refers to a plausible, not simply a theoretical, likelihood that such uses will come to pass, and that fact anchors *Sony* in practical reality. Cf. *Aimster, supra,* at 651.

Sony's rule is mindful of the limitations facing judges where matters of technology are concerned. Judges have no specialized technical ability to answer questions about present or future technological feasibility or commercial viability where technology professionals, engineers, and venture capitalists themselves may radically disagree and where answers may differ depending upon whether one focuses upon the time of product development or the time of distribution. Consider, for example, the question whether devices can be added to Grokster's software that will filter out infringing files. MGM tells us this is easy enough to do, as do several *amici* that produce and sell the filtering technology. Grokster says it is not at all easy to do, and not an efficient solution in any event, and several apparently disinterested computer science professors agree. Which account should a judge credit? *Sony* says that the judge will not necessarily have to decide.

Given the nature of the *Sony* rule, it is not surprising that in the last 20 years, there have been relatively few contributory infringement suits—based on a product distribution theory—brought against technology providers (a small handful of federal appellate court cases and perhaps fewer than two dozen District Court cases in the last 20 years). I have found nothing in the briefs or the record that shows that *Sony* has failed to achieve its innovation-protecting objective.

B

The second, more difficult, question is whether a modified *Sony* rule (or a strict interpretation) would significantly weaken the law's ability to protect new technology. Justice Ginsburg's approach would require defendants to produce considerably more concrete evidence—more than was presented here—to earn *Sony's* shelter. That heavier evidentiary demand, and especially the more dramatic (case-by-case balancing) modifications that MGM and the Government seek, would, I believe, undercut the protection that *Sony* now offers.

To require defendants to provide, for example, detailed evidence — say business plans, profitability estimates, projected technological modifications, and so forth — would doubtless make life easier for copyrightholder plaintiffs. But it would simultaneously increase the legal uncertainty that surrounds the creation or development of a new technology capable of being put to infringing uses. Inventors and entrepreneurs (in the garage, the dorm room, the corporate lab, or the boardroom) would have to fear (and in many cases endure) costly and extensive trials when they create, produce, or distribute the sort of information technology that can be used for copyright infringement. They would often be left guessing as to how a court, upon later review of the product and its uses, would decide when necessarily rough estimates amounted to sufficient evidence. They would have no way to predict how courts would weigh the respective values of infringing and noninfringing uses; determine the efficiency and advisability of technological changes; or assess a product's potential future markets. The price of a wrong guess — even if it involves a good-faith effort to assess technical and commercial viability — could be large statutory damages (not less than $750 and up to $30,000 per infringed work). 17 U.S.C. § 504(c)(1). The additional risk and uncertainty would mean a consequent additional chill of technological development.

C

The third question — whether a positive copyright impact would outweigh any technology-related loss — I find the most difficult of the three. I do not doubt that a more intrusive *Sony* test would generally provide greater revenue security for copyright holders. But it is harder to conclude that the gains on the copyright swings would exceed the losses on the technology roundabouts.

For one thing, the law disfavors equating the two different kinds of gain and loss; rather, it leans in favor of protecting technology. As *Sony* itself makes clear, the producer of a technology which permits unlawful copying does not himself engage in unlawful copying — a fact that makes the attachment of copyright liability to the creation, production, or distribution of the technology an exceptional thing. See 464 U.S., at 431 (courts "must be circumspect" in construing the copyright laws to preclude distribution of new technologies). Moreover, *Sony* has been the law for some time. And that fact imposes a serious burden upon copyright holders like MGM to show a need for change in the current rules of the game, including a more strict interpretation of the test. See, *e.g.,* Brief for Motion Picture Studio Petitioners 31 (*Sony* should not protect products when the "primary or principal" use is infringing).

In any event, the evidence now available does not, in my view, make out a sufficiently strong case for change. To say this is not to doubt the basic need to protect copyrighted material from infringement. The Constitution itself stresses the vital role that copyright plays in advancing the "useful Arts." Art. I, § 8, cl. 8. No one disputes that "reward to the author or artist serves to induce release to the public of the products of his creative genius." *United States v. Paramount Pictures, Inc.,* 334 U.S. 131, 158 (1948). And deliberate unlawful copying is no less an unlawful taking of property than garden-variety theft. See, *e.g.*, 18 U.S.C. § 2319 (criminal copyright infringement); § 1961(1)(B) (copyright infringement can be a predicate act under the Racketeer Influenced and Corrupt Organizations Act); § 1956(c)(7)(D) (money laundering includes the receipt of proceeds from copyright infringement). But these highly general principles cannot by themselves tell us how to balance the interests at issue in *Sony* or whether *Sony's* standard needs modification. And at certain key points, information is lacking.

Will an unmodified *Sony* lead to a significant diminution in the amount or quality of creative work produced? Since copyright's basic objective is creation and its revenue objectives but a means to that end, this is the underlying copyright question. . . . And its answer is far from clear.

Unauthorized copying likely diminishes industry revenue, though it is not clear by how much. [Justice Breyer cited several studies on the question.] The extent to which related production has actually and resultingly declined remains uncertain, though there is good reason to believe that the decline, if any, is not substantial. [Justice Breyer cited a report finding that "nearly 70% of musicians believe that file sharing is a minor threat or no threat at all to creative industries," and] Benkler, Sharing Nicely: On Shareable Goods and the Emergence of Sharing as a Modality of Economic Production, 114 Yale L. J. 273, 351–352 (2004) ("Much of the actual flow of revenue to artists—from performances and other sources—is stable even assuming a complete displacement of the CD market by peer-to-peer distribution . . . . It would be silly to think that music, a cultural form without which no human society has existed, will cease to be in our world [because of illegal file swapping]").

More importantly, copyright holders at least potentially have other tools available to reduce piracy and to abate whatever threat it poses to creative production. As today's opinion makes clear, a copyright holder may proceed against a technology provider where a provable specific intent to infringe (of the kind the Court describes) is present. Services like Grokster may well be liable under an inducement theory.

In addition, a copyright holder has always had the legal authority to bring a traditional infringement suit against one who wrongfully copies. Indeed, since September 2003, the Recording Industry Association of America (RIAA) has filed "thousands of suits against people for sharing copyrighted material." Walker, New Movement Hits Universities: Get Legal Music, Washington Post, Mar. 17, 2005, p. E1. These suits have provided copyright holders with damages; have served as a teaching tool, making clear that much file sharing, if done without permission, is unlawful; and apparently have had a real and significant deterrent effect. [Justice Breyer cited several reports of declining use of peer-to-peer networks after the RIAA suits began, as well as an article referring to the continuing "tide of rampant copyright infringement."]

Further, copyright holders may develop new technological devices that will help curb unlawful infringement. Some new technology, called "digital 'watermarking'" and "digital fingerprinting," can encode within the file information about the author and the copyright scope and date, which "fingerprints" can help to expose infringers. . . . Other technology can, through encryption, potentially restrict users' ability to make a digital copy. . . .

At the same time, advances in technology have discouraged unlawful copying by making *lawful* copying (*e.g.,* downloading music with the copyright holder's permission) cheaper and easier to achieve. Several services now sell music for less than $1 per song. (Walmart.com, for example, charges $0.88 each). Consequently, many consumers initially attracted to the convenience and flexibility of services like Grokster are now migrating to lawful paid services (services with copying permission) where they can enjoy at little cost even greater convenience and flexibility without engaging in unlawful swapping. . . .

Thus, lawful music downloading services—those that charge the customer for downloading music and pay royalties to the copyright holder—have continued to grow and to produce substantial revenue. . . . And more advanced types of *non-music-oriented* P2P networks have also started to develop, drawing in part on the lessons of Grokster.

Finally, as *Sony* recognized, the legislative option remains available. Courts are less well suited than Congress to the task of "accommodating fully the varied permutations of competing interests that are inevitably implicated by such new technology." *Sony,* 464 U.S., at 431; see, *e.g.,* Audio Home Recording Act of 1992, 106 Stat. 4237 (adding 17 U.S.C., ch. 10); Protecting Innovation and Art While Preventing Piracy: Hearing Before the Senate Comm. on the Judiciary, 108th Cong., 2d Sess. (July 22, 2004).

I do not know whether these developments and similar alternatives will prove sufficient, but I am reasonably certain that, given their existence, a strong demonstrated need for modifying *Sony* (or for interpreting *Sony's* standard more strictly) has not yet been shown. That fact, along with the added risks that modification (or strict interpretation) would impose upon technological innovation, leads me to the conclusion that we should maintain *Sony,* reading its standard as I have read it. As so read, it requires affirmance of the Ninth Circuit's determination of the relevant aspects of the *Sony* question.

*   *   *

For these reasons, I disagree with JUSTICE GNSBURG, but I agree with the Court and join its opinion.

CHAPTER EIGHT
CONTROLLING INFORMATION ASSETS: DATABASES

Databases are a core technology of Internet commerce. An online retailer could not function if its customers could not search an online database of its inventory. A business-to-business exchange could not function if it did not provide its members with access to a database comprising the suppliers and manufacturers of different categories of goods and services. Without databases, no company conducting business on the Internet could keep track of such critical information as the identity of its customers, the sales and other transactions into which it enters, the settlement of accounts, and the shipment and delivery of its goods and services.

Many online businesses depend on their control of information maintained in databases. For example, Westlaw and Lexis each charge fees to access their comprehensive databases of legal materials. Many companies offer free access to online databases of information in order to sell space on their websites to advertisers. Still other companies compile timely and extensive databases of commercially valuable information such as stock quotes or sports scores and sell or license them to others for use on their websites. Advertisers depend on databases of names and addresses and other marketing information. (Such databases can become problematic from the standpoint of consumer privacy; see Chapter 6, *supra*.)

Most commercial databases are compilations of facts. Facts, however, are not protected under the law of copyright. While the selection and arrangement of facts in a database *may* qualify for protection under copyright law—provided the selection and arrangement are sufficiently original—the factual contents of these databases remain unprotected. Thus, in many circumstances, a person may use the factual contents of another's database without infringing the owner's copyright. Database owners seeking alternative legal protection through state courts and legislatures may be disappointed in their attempts, because of federal copyright law's preemption of state laws, such as the law of misappropriation or unfair competition, that otherwise might provide protection. This state of affairs has led some to call for federal *sui generis* protection for databases along the lines of the European Union's Directive on the Legal Protection of Databases.

Before proceeding to these legal matters, however, it is necessary to have some background on why federal copyright law generally does not protect databases.

I. DATABASES AND THE LAW OF COPYRIGHT

Until the Supreme Court's decision in *Feist Publications v. Rural Telephone Service Co.*, 499 U.S. 340 (1991), there was some confusion over whether factual databases were protected under the law of copyright. Historically, many courts and scholars believed that compilations of facts were protected under the "sweat of the brow" doctrine, which holds that one can acquire a copyright in a compilation of facts by dint of the effort one expends to compile it. The intuitive appeal of this doctrine is nicely set forth by Justice Story, who noted that, although all maps of the same region feature the same selection and arrangement, another person "has no right, without any such surveys and labors, to sit down and copy the whole of the map already produced by the skill and labors of the first party, and thus to rob him of all the fruit of his industry, skill, and expenditures." *Gray v. Russell*, 10 F. Cas. 1035, 1038 (C.C.D.Mass.1839). As Justice Story summarized his point in a later case, "[a] man has a right to the copy-right of a map of a state or country, which he has surveyed or caused to be compiled from existing materials, at his own expense, or skill, or labor, or money." *Emerson v. Davies*, 8 F.Cas. 615, 619 (C.C.D.Mass.1845). If return to one's labor ("sweat of the brow") is grounds for granting an intellectual property right, the lack of creativity and originality in the cartographer's selection and arrangement appears irrelevant.

In 1879, however, the Supreme Court held that "originality" is an absolute prerequisite for copyright protection. In the *Trade-Mark Cases*, 100 U.S. 82 (1879), the Court determined that the federal trademark law was not a valid exercise of Congress's power under the Constitution's Copyright Clause,[1] since trademarks do not necessarily embody the requisite originality. The Court explained that "while the word *writings* [in the Copyright Clause] may be liberally construed, as it has been, to include original designs for engravings, prints, & c., it is only such as are *original*, and are founded in the creative powers of the mind." *Id.* at 94. In *Bleistein v. Donaldson Lithographing Co.*, 188 U.S. 239, 250 (1903), the Court made clear that the quantum of originality required for copyright protection is very low: "a very modest grade of art" will suffice.

When the Supreme Court embraced the originality doctrine, it did not at the same time expressly reject the "sweat of the brow" doctrine. For much of the last century, the lower courts found compilations of facts, such as law reports and directories, protectible either because they embodied the requisite degree of originality, or because substantial labor was expended in compiling them. *See, e.g. Hutchinson Tel. Co. v. Fronteer Directory Co. of Minnesota*, 770 F.2d 128 (8th Cir.1985) (originality); *Schroeder v. William Morrow & Co.*, 566 F.2d 3 (7th Cir.1977) ("sweat of the brow"); *Adventures in Good Eating, Inc. v. Best Places to Eat, Inc.*, 131 F.2d 809 (7th Cir.1942) ("sweat of the brow"); *Jeweler's Circular Publishing Co. v. Keystone Publishing Co.*, 281 F. 83 (2d Cir.1922) ("sweat of the brow"); *West Pub. Co. v. Edward Thompson Co.*, 169 F. 833 (C.C.E.D.N.Y. 1909) ("sweat of the brow"); *Edward Thompson Co. v. American Law Book Co.*, 122 F. 922 (2d Cir.1903) (originality).

With passage of the 1976 Copyright Act, Congress expressly imposed the originality doctrine on compilations protected under the Act: it defined a compilation as "a work formed by the collection and assembling of preexisting materials or of data that are selected, coordinated, or arranged in such a way that the resulting work as a whole constitutes an *original* work of authorship." 17 U.S.C. § 101 (emphasis added).

The significance of this change in the definition of a compilation was not immediately clear. Some courts continued to apply the "sweat of the brow" doctrine, *see, e.g., Illinois Bell Tel. Co. v. Haines & Co.*, 683 F.Supp. 1204 (N.D.Ill.1988), *aff'd*, 905 F.2d 1081 (7th Cir.1990), *vacated and remanded*, 499 U.S. 944 (1991), while others viewed the doctrine as superseded by the new statutory language of originality, *see, e.g., Financial Info., Inc. v. Moody's Investors Serv., Inc.*, 808 F.2d 204 (2d Cir.1986), and *Worth v. Selchow & Righter*

---

[1] "The Congress shall have Power . . . [t]o promote the Progress of Science and useful Arts, by securing for limited Times to Authors and Inventors the exclusive Right to their respective Writings and Discoveries." U.S. CONST., art. I, § 8, cl. 8.

Co., 827 F.2d 569 (9th Cir.1987). Some courts found factual compilations such as telephone directories sufficiently original to meet this standard. *See Hutchinson Tel. Co. v. Fronteer Directory Co. of Minnesota*, 770 F.2d 128 (8th Cir.1985) ("white pages" directory copyrightable); *Southern Bell Tel. and Tel. Co. v. Associated Tel. Directory Publishers*, 756 F.2d 801 (11th Cir.1985) ("yellow pages" directory copyrightable).

Such was the state of the caselaw when, in the following case, the Supreme Court established the standards that a factual compilation must meet to qualify for copyright protection.

Feist Publications, Inc. v. Rural Telephone Service Co.
499 U.S. 340 (1991).

■ JUSTICE O'CONNOR delivered the opinion of the Court.

This case requires us to clarify the extent of copyright protection available to telephone directory white pages.

I

Rural Telephone Service Company, Inc., is a certified public utility that provides telephone service to several communities in northwest Kansas. It is subject to a state regulation that requires all telephone companies operating in Kansas to issue annually an updated telephone directory. Accordingly, as a condition of its monopoly franchise, Rural publishes a typical telephone directory, consisting of white pages and yellow pages. The white pages list in alphabetical order the names of Rural's subscribers, together with their towns and telephone numbers. The yellow pages list Rural's business subscribers alphabetically by category and feature classified advertisements of various sizes. Rural distributes its directory free of charge to its subscribers, but earns revenue by selling yellow pages advertisements.

Feist Publications, Inc., is a publishing company that specializes in area-wide telephone directories. Unlike a typical directory, which covers only a particular calling area, Feist's area-wide directories cover a much larger geographical range, reducing the need to call directory assistance or consult multiple directories. The Feist directory that is the subject of this litigation covers 11 different telephone service areas in 15 counties and contains 46,878 white pages listings—compared to Rural's approximately 7,700 listings. Like Rural's directory, Feist's is distributed free of charge and includes both white pages and yellow pages. Feist and Rural compete vigorously for yellow pages advertising.

As the sole provider of telephone service in its service area, Rural obtains subscriber information quite easily. Persons desiring telephone service must apply to Rural and provide their names and addresses; Rural then assigns them a telephone number. Feist is not a telephone company, let alone one with monopoly status, and therefore lacks independent access to any subscriber information. To obtain white pages listings for its area-wide directory, Feist approached each of the 11 telephone companies operating in northwest Kansas and offered to pay for the right to use its white pages listings.

Of the 11 telephone companies, only Rural refused to license its listings to Feist.

Rural's refusal created a problem for Feist, as omitting these listings would have left a gaping hole in its area-wide directory, rendering it less attractive to potential yellow pages advertisers. In a decision subsequent to that which we review here, the District Court determined that this was precisely the reason Rural refused to license its listings. The refusal was motivated by an unlawful purpose "to extend its monopoly in telephone service to a monopoly in yellow pages advertising." *Rural Telephone Service Co. v. Feist Publications, Inc.*, 737 F.Supp. 610, 622 (D.Kan. 1990).

Unable to license Rural's white pages listings, Feist used them without Rural's consent. Feist began by removing several thousand listings that fell outside the geographic range of its area-wide directory, then hired personnel to investigate the 4,935 that remained. These employees verified the data reported by Rural and sought to obtain additional information. As a result, a typical Feist listing includes the individual's street address; most of Rural's listings do not. Notwithstanding these additions, however, 1,309 of the 46,878 listings in Feist's 1983 directory were identical to listings in Rural's 1982–1983 white pages. Four of these were fictitious listings that Rural had inserted into its directory to detect copying.

Rural sued for copyright infringement in the District Court for the District of Kansas taking the position that Feist, in compiling its own directory, could not use the information contained in Rural's white pages. Rural asserted that Feist's employees were obliged to travel door-to-door or conduct a telephone survey to discover the same information for themselves. Feist responded that such efforts were economically impractical and, in any event, unnecessary because the information copied was beyond the scope of copyright protection. The District Court granted summary judgment to Rural, explaining that "[c]ourts have consistently held that telephone directories are copyrightable" and citing a string of lower court decisions. 663 F.Supp. 214, 218 (1987). In an unpublished opinion, the Court of Appeals for the Tenth Circuit affirmed "for substantially the reasons given by the district court." App. to Pet. for Cert. 4a, judgt. order reported at 916 F.2d 718 (1990). We granted certiorari, 498 U.S. 808 (1990), to determine whether the copyright in Rural's directory protects the names, towns, and telephone numbers copied by Feist.

II

A

This case concerns the interaction of two well-established propositions. The first is that facts are not copyrightable; the other, that compilations of facts generally are. Each of these propositions possesses an impeccable pedigree. That there can be no valid copyright in facts is universally understood. The most fundamental axiom of copyright law is that "[n]o author may copyright his ideas or the facts he narrates." *Harper & Row, Publishers, Inc. v. Nation Enterprises*, 471 U.S. 539, 556 (1985). Rural wisely concedes this point, noting in its brief that "[f]acts and discoveries, of course, are not themselves subject to copyright protection." Brief for Respondent 24. At the same time, however, it is beyond dispute that compilations of facts are within the subject matter of copyright. Compilations were expressly mentioned in the Copyright Act of 1909, and again in the Copyright Act of 1976.

There is an undeniable tension between these two propositions. Many compilations consist of nothing but raw data—*i.e.*, wholly factual information not accompanied by any original written expression. On what basis may one claim a copyright in such a work? Common sense tells us that 100 uncopyrightable facts do not magically change their status when gathered together in one place. Yet copyright law seems to contemplate that compilations that consist exclusively of facts are potentially within its scope.

The key to resolving the tension lies in understanding why facts are not copyrightable. The *sine qua non* of copyright is originality. To qualify for copyright protection, a work must be original to the author. . . . Original, as the term is used in copyright, means only that the work was independently created by the author (as opposed to copied from other works), and that it possesses at least some minimal degree of creativity. 1 M. Nimmer & D. Nimmer, Copyright §§ 2.01[A], [B] (1990) (hereinafter Nimmer). To be sure, the requisite level of creativity is extremely low; even a slight amount will suffice. The vast majority of works make the grade quite easily, as they possess some creative spark, "no matter how crude, humble or obvious" it might be. *Id.*, § 1.08[C][1]. Originality does not signify novelty; a work may be original even though it closely resembles other works so long as the similarity is fortuitous, not the result of copying. To illustrate, assume that two poets, each ignorant of the other, compose identical poems. Neither work is novel, yet both are original and, hence, copyrightable. . . .

Originality is a constitutional requirement. The source of Congress' power to enact copyright laws is Article I, § 8, cl. 8, of the Constitution, which authorizes Congress to "secur[e] for limited Times to Authors . . . the exclusive Right to their respective Writings." In two decisions from the late 19th century — *The Trade–Mark Cases*, 100 U.S. 82 (1879); and *Burrow-Giles Lithographic Co. v. Sarony*, 111 U.S. 53 (1884) — this Court defined the crucial terms "authors" and "writings." In so doing, the Court made it unmistakably clear that these terms presuppose a degree of originality.

. . .

The originality requirement articulated in *The Trade–Mark Cases* and *Burrow–Giles* remains the touchstone of copyright protection today. . . .

It is this bedrock principle of copyright that mandates the law's seemingly disparate treatment of facts and factual compilations. "No one may claim originality as to facts." [Nimmer] § 2.11[A], p. 2–157. This is because facts do not owe their origin to an act of authorship. The distinction is one between creation and discovery: The first person to find and report a particular fact has not created the fact; he or she has merely discovered its existence. To borrow from *Burrow–Giles*, one who discovers a fact is not its "maker" or "originator." 111 U.S., at 58. "The discoverer merely finds and records." Nimmer § 2.03[E]. Census takers, for example, do not "create" the population figures that emerge from their efforts; in a sense, they copy these figures from the world around them. Denicola, Copyright in Collections of Facts: A Theory for the Protection of Nonfiction Literary Works, 81 Colum.L.Rev. 516, 525 (1981) (hereinafter Denicola). Census data therefore do not trigger copyright because these data are not "original" in the constitutional sense. Nimmer § 2.03[E]. The same is true of all facts—scientific, historical, biographical, and news of the day. "[T]hey may not be copyrighted and are part of the public domain available to every person." [*Miller v. Universal City Studios, Inc.*, 650 F.2d 1365, 1369 (CA5 1981).]

Factual compilations, on the other hand, may possess the requisite originality. The compilation author typically chooses which facts to include, in what order to place them, and how to arrange the collected data so that they may be used effectively by readers. These choices as to selection and arrangement, so long as they are made independently by the compiler and entail a minimal degree of creativity, are sufficiently original that Congress may protect such compilations through the copyright laws. Nimmer §§ 2.11[D], 3.03; Denicola 523, n.38. Thus, even a directory that contains absolutely no protectible written expression, only facts, meets the constitutional minimum for copyright protection if it features an original selection or arrangement. . . .

This protection is subject to an important limitation. The mere fact that a work is copyrighted does not mean that every element of the work may be protected. Originality remains the *sine qua non* of copyright; accordingly, copyright protection may extend only to those components of a work that are original to the author. [Patterson & Joyce, Monopolizing the Law: The Scope of Copyright Protection for Law Reports and Statutory Compilations, 36 UCLA L.Rev. 719, 800–02 (1989) (hereinafter Patterson & Joyce).] Ginsburg, Creation and Commercial Value: Copyright Protection of Works of Information, 90 Colum.L.Rev. 1865, 1868, and n. 12 (1990) (hereinafter Ginsburg). Thus, if the compilation author clothes facts with an original collocation of words, he or she may be able to claim a copyright in this written expression. Others may copy the underlying facts from the publication, but not the precise words used to present them. In *Harper & Row*, for example, we explained that President Ford could not prevent others from copying bare historical facts from his autobiography, see 471 U.S., at 556–557, but that he could prevent others from copying his "subjective descriptions and portraits of public figures." *Id.*, at 563. Where the compilation author adds no written expression but rather lets the facts speak for themselves, the expressive element is more elusive. The only conceivable expression is the manner in which the compiler has selected and arranged the facts. Thus, if the selection and arrangement are original, these elements of the work are eligible for copyright protection. See Patry, Copyright in Compilations of Facts (or Why the "White Pages" Are Not Copyrightable), 12 Com. & Law 37, 64 (Dec. 1990) (hereinafter Patry). No matter how original the format, however, the facts themselves do not become original through association. See Patterson & Joyce 776.

This inevitably means that the copyright in a factual compilation is thin. Notwithstanding a valid copyright, a subsequent compiler remains free to use the facts contained in another's publication to aid in preparing a competing work, so long as the competing work does not feature the same selection and arrangement. As one commentator explains it: "[N]o matter how much original authorship the work displays, the facts and ideas it exposes are free for the taking. . . . [T]he very same facts and ideas may be divorced from the context imposed by the author, and re-stated or reshuffled by second comers, even if the author was the first to discover the facts or to propose the ideas." Ginsburg 1868.

It may seem unfair that much of the fruit of the compiler's labor may be used by others without compensation. As Justice Brennan has correctly observed, how-ever, this is not "some unforeseen byproduct of a statutory scheme." *Harper & Row,* 471 U.S., at 589 (dissenting opinion). It is, rather, "the essence of copyright," *ibid.,* and a constitutional requirement. The primary objective of copyright is not to re-ward the labor of authors, but "[t]o promote the Progress of Science and useful Arts." Art. I, § 8, cl. 8. . . . To this end, copyright assures authors the right to their original expression, but encourages others to build freely upon the ideas and in-formation conveyed by a work. *Harper & Row, supra,* 471 U.S., at 556–557. This principle, known as the idea/expression or fact/expression dichotomy, applies to all works of authorship. As applied to a factual compilation, assuming the absence of original written expression, only the compiler's selection and arrangement may be protected; the raw facts may be copied at will. This result is neither unfair nor unfortunate. It is the means by which copyright advances the progress of science and art.

. . .

This, then, resolves the doctrinal tension: Copyright treats facts and factual compilations in a wholly consistent manner. Facts, whether alone or as part of a compilation, are not original and therefore may not be copyrighted. A factual compilation is eligible for copyright if it features an original selection or arrange-ment of facts, but the copyright is limited to the particular selection or arrange-ment. In no event may copyright extend to the facts themselves.

B

As we have explained, originality is a constitutionally mandated prerequisite for copyright protection. The Court's decisions announcing this rule predate the Copyright Act of 1909, but ambiguous language in the 1909 Act caused some lower courts temporarily to lose sight of this requirement.

. . .

Most courts construed the 1909 Act correctly, notwithstanding the less-than-perfect statutory language. They understood from this Court's decisions that there could be no copyright without originality. . . .

. . .

But some courts misunderstood the statute. . . .

Making matters worse, these courts developed a new theory to justify the pro-tection of factual compilations. Known alternatively as "sweat of the brow" or "in-dustrious collection," the underlying notion was that copyright was a reward for the hard work that went into compiling facts. The classic formulation of the doc-trine appeared in *Jeweler's Circular Publishing Co.,* 281 F., at 88:

"The right to copyright a book upon which one has expended labor in its preparation does not depend upon whether the materials which he has collected consist or not of matters which are publici juris, or whether such materials show literary skill *or originality*, either in thought or in language, or anything more than industrious collection. The man who goes through the streets of a town and puts down the names of each of the inhabitants, with their occupations and their street number, acquires material of which he is the author." (emphasis added).

The "sweat of the brow" doctrine had numerous flaws, the most glaring being that it extended copyright protection in a compilation beyond selection and arrangement—the compiler's original contributions—to the facts themselves. Under the doctrine, the only defense to infringement was independent creation. A subsequent compiler was "not entitled to take one word of information previously published," but rather had to "independently wor[k] out the matter for himself, so as to arrive at the same result from the same common sources of information." *Id.*, at 88–89 (internal quotation marks omitted). "Sweat of the brow" courts thereby eschewed the most fundamental axiom of copyright law — that no one may copyright facts or ideas. *See Miller v. Universal City Studios, Inc.*, 650 F.2d, at 1372 (criticizing "sweat of the brow" courts because "ensur[ing] that later writers obtain the facts independently . . . is precisely the scope of protection given . . . copyrighted matter, and the law is clear that facts are not entitled to such protection").

. . .

Without a doubt, the "sweat of the brow" doctrine flouted basic copyright principles. Throughout history, copyright law has "recognize[d] a greater need to disseminate factual works than works of fiction or fantasy." *Harper & Row*, 471 U.S., at 563. Accord, Gorman, Fact or Fancy: The Implications for Copyright, 29 J. Copyright Soc. 560, 563 (1982). But "sweat of the brow" courts took a contrary view; they handed out proprietary interests in facts and declared that authors are absolutely precluded from saving time and effort by relying upon the facts contained in prior works. In truth, "[i]t is just such wasted effort that the proscription against the copyright of ideas and facts . . . [is] designed to prevent." *Rosemont Enterprises, Inc. v. Random House, Inc.*, 366 F.2d 303, 310 (C.A.2 1966). "Protection for the fruits of such research . . . may in certain circumstances be available under a theory of unfair competition. But to accord copyright protection on this basis alone distorts basic copyright principles in that it creates a monopoly in public domain materials without the necessary justification of protecting and encouraging the creation of 'writings' by 'authors.' " Nimmer § 3.04, p. 3–23 (footnote omitted).

C

"Sweat of the brow" decisions did not escape the attention of the Copyright Office. When Congress decided to overhaul the copyright statute and asked the Copyright Office to study existing problems, . . . the Copyright Office promptly recommended that Congress clear up the confusion in the lower courts as to the basic standards of copyrightability. . . .

Congress took the Register's advice. In enacting the Copyright Act of 1976, Congress dropped the reference to "all the writings of an author" and replaced it with the phrase "original works of authorship." 17 U.S.C. § 102(a). In making explicit the originality requirement, Congress announced that it was merely clarifying existing law: "The two fundamental criteria of copyright protection [are] originality and fixation in tangible form. . . . The phrase 'original works of authorship,' which is purposely left undefined, is intended to incorporate without change *the standard of originality established by the courts under the present [1909] copyright statute.*" H.R.Rep. No. 94–1476, p. 51 (1976) (emphasis added) (hereinafter H.R.Rep.); S.Rep. No. 94–473, p. 50 (1975), U.S.Code Cong. & Admin.News 1976, pp. 5659, 5664 (emphasis added) (hereinafter S.Rep.). . . .

To ensure that the mistakes of the "sweat of the brow" courts would not be repeated, Congress took additional measures. . . .

First, to make clear that compilations were not copyrightable *per se,* Congress provided a definition of the term "compilation." Second, to make clear that the copyright in a compilation did not extend to the facts themselves, Congress enacted § 103.

The definition of "compilation" is found in § 101 of the 1976 Act. It defines a "compilation" in the copyright sense as "a work formed by the collection and assembling of preexisting materials or of data *that* are selected, coordinated, or arranged *in such a way that* the resulting work as a whole constitutes an original work of authorship" (emphasis added).

The purpose of the statutory definition is to emphasize that collections of facts are not copyrightable *per se.* It conveys this message through its tripartite structure, as emphasized above by the italics. The statute identifies three distinct elements and requires each to be met for a work to qualify as a copyrightable compilation: (1) the collection and assembly of pre-existing material, facts, or data; (2) the selection, coordination, or arrangement of those materials; and (3) the creation, by virtue of the particular selection, coordination, or arrangement, of an "original" work of authorship. . . .

 . . .

The key to the statutory definition is the second requirement. It instructs courts that, in determining whether a fact-based work is an original work of authorship, they should focus on the manner in which the collected facts have been selected, coordinated, and arranged. This is a straightforward application of the originality requirement. Facts are never original, so the compilation author can claim originality, if at all, only in the way the facts are presented. To that end, the statute dictates that the principal focus should be on whether the selection, coordination, and arrangement are sufficiently original to merit protection.

Not every selection, coordination, or arrangement will pass muster. This is plain from the statute. It states that, to merit protection, the facts must be selected, coordinated, or arranged "in such a way" as to render the work as a whole original. This implies that some "ways" will trigger copyright, but that others will not. . . . Otherwise, the phrase "in such a way" is meaningless and Congress should have defined "compilation" simply as "a work formed by the collection and assembly of preexisting materials or data that are selected, coordinated, or arranged." . . .

As discussed earlier, however, the originality requirement is not particularly stringent. A compiler may settle upon a selection or arrangement that others have used; novelty is not required. Originality requires only that the author make the selection or arrangement independently (*i.e.*, without copying that selection or arrangement from another work), and that it display some minimal level of creativity. Presumably, the vast majority of compilations will pass this test, but not all will. There remains a narrow category of works in which the creative spark is utterly lacking or so trivial as to be virtually nonexistent. . . . Such works are incapable of sustaining a valid copyright. . . .

Even if a work qualifies as a copyrightable compilation, it receives only limited protection. This is the point of § 103 of the Act. Section 103 explains that "[t]he subject matter of copyright . . . includes compilations," § 103(a), but that copyright protects only the author's original contributions—not the facts or information conveyed:

> "The copyright in a compilation . . . extends only to the material contributed by the author of such work, as distinguished from the preexisting material employed in the work, and does not imply any exclusive right in the preexisting material." § 103(b).

As § 103 makes clear, copyright is not a tool by which a compilation author may keep others from using the facts or data he or she has collected. "The most important point here is one that is commonly misunderstood today: copyright . . . has no effect one way or the other on the copyright or public domain status of the preexisting material." H.R.Rep., at 57; S.Rep., at 55, U.S.Code Cong. & Admin. News 1976, p. 5670. The 1909 Act did not require, as "sweat of the brow" courts mistakenly assumed, that each subsequent compiler must start from scratch and is precluded from relying on research undertaken by another. See, *e.g., Jeweler's Circular Publishing Co.,* 281 F., at 88–89. Rather, the facts contained in existing works may be freely copied because copyright protects only the elements that owe their origin to the compiler—the selection, coordination, and arrangement of facts.

In summary, the 1976 revisions to the Copyright Act leave no doubt that originality, not "sweat of the brow," is the touchstone of copyright protection in directories and other fact-based works. . . .

III

There is no doubt that Feist took from the white pages of Rural's directory a substantial amount of factual information. At a minimum, Feist copied the names, towns, and telephone numbers of 1,309 of Rural's subscribers. Not all copying, however, is copyright infringement. To establish infringement, two elements must be proven: (1) ownership of a valid copyright, and (2) copying of constituent elements of the work that are original. . . . The first element is not at issue here; Feist appears to concede that Rural's directory, considered as a whole, is subject to a valid copyright because it contains some foreword text, as well as original material in its yellow pages advertisements. . . .

The question is whether Rural has proved the second element. In other words, did Feist, by taking 1,309 names, towns, and telephone numbers from Rural's white pages, copy anything that was "original" to Rural? Certainly, the raw data does not satisfy the originality requirement. Rural may have been the first to discover and report the names, towns, and telephone numbers of its subscribers, but this data does not " 'ow[e] its origin' " to Rural. *Burrow–Giles*, 111 U.S., at 58. Rather, these bits of information are uncopyrightable facts; they existed before Rural reported them and would have continued to exist if Rural had never published a telephone directory. The originality requirement "rule[s] out protecting . . . names, addresses, and telephone numbers of which the plaintiff by no stretch of the imagination could be called the author." Patterson & Joyce 776.

Rural essentially concedes the point by referring to the names, towns, and telephone numbers as "preexisting material." Section 103(b) states explicitly that the copyright in a compilation does not extend to "the preexisting material employed in the work."

The question that remains is whether Rural selected, coordinated, or arranged these uncopyrightable facts in an original way. As mentioned, originality is not a stringent standard; it does not require that facts be presented in an innovative or surprising way. It is equally true, however, that the selection and arrangement of facts cannot be so mechanical or routine as to require no creativity whatsoever. The standard of originality is low, but it does exist. . . . As this Court has explained, the Constitution mandates some minimal degree of creativity, see *The Trade–Mark Cases*, 100 U.S., at 94; and an author who claims infringement must prove "the existence of . . . intellectual production, of thought, and conception." *Burrow–Giles, supra*, 111 U.S., at 59–60.

The selection, coordination, and arrangement of Rural's white pages do not satisfy the minimum constitutional standards for copyright protection. As mentioned at the outset, Rural's white pages are entirely typical. Persons desiring telephone service in Rural's service area fill out an application and Rural issues them a telephone number. In preparing its white pages, Rural simply takes the data provided by its subscribers and lists it alphabetically by surname. The end product is a garden-variety white pages directory, devoid of even the slightest trace of creativity.

Rural's selection of listings could not be more obvious: It publishes the most basic information—name, town, and telephone number—about each person who applies to it for telephone service. This is "selection" of a sort, but it lacks the modicum of creativity necessary to transform mere selection into copyrightable expression. Rural expended sufficient effort to make the white pages directory useful, but insufficient creativity to make it original.

We note in passing that the selection featured in Rural's white pages may also fail the originality requirement for another reason. Feist points out that Rural did not truly "select" to publish the names and telephone numbers of its subscribers; rather, it was required to do so by the Kansas Corporation Commission as part of its monopoly franchise. . . . Accordingly, one could plausibly conclude that this selection was dictated by state law, not by Rural.

Nor can Rural claim originality in its coordination and arrangement of facts. The white pages do nothing more than list Rural's subscribers in alphabetical order. This arrangement may, technically speaking, owe its origin to Rural; no one disputes that Rural undertook the task of alphabetizing the names itself. But there is nothing remotely creative about arranging names alphabetically in a white pages directory. It is an age-old practice, firmly rooted in tradition and so commonplace that it has come to be expected as a matter of course. . . . It is not only unoriginal, it is practically inevitable. This time-honored tradition does not possess the minimal creative spark required by the Copyright Act and the Constitution.

We conclude that the names, towns, and telephone numbers copied by Feist were not original to Rural and therefore were not protected by the copyright in Rural's combined white and yellow pages directory. As a constitutional matter, copyright protects only those constituent elements of a work that possess more than a *de minimis* quantum of creativity. Rural's white pages, limited to basic subscriber information and arranged alphabetically, fall short of the mark. As a statutory matter, 17 U.S.C. § 101 does not afford protection from copying to a collection of facts that are selected, coordinated, and arranged in a way that utterly lacks originality. Given that some works must fail, we cannot imagine a more likely candidate. Indeed, were we to hold that Rural's white pages pass muster, it is hard to believe that any collection of facts could fail.

. . .

QUESTIONS FOR DISCUSSION

1. *The protection of commercial databases after* Feist. In *Feist*, the Supreme Court held that a factual database or compilation satisfies the Copyright Act's originality requirement if "the author make[s] the selection or arrangement independently (*i.e.*, without copying that selection or arrangement from another work)" and if the selection and arrangement "display some minimal level of creativity." 499 U.S. at 358. The Court adds that "the vast majority of compilations will pass this test, but not all will." *Id.* at 359. In your opinion, will independently compiled electronic databases normally "pass the test," or will they fall into that "narrow category of works in which the creative spark is utterly lacking or so trivial as to be virtually nonexistent"? *Id.*

2. *Perverse incentives?* Imagine a website that provides access to a comprehensive database of all the hospitals in the United States. A user keys in her zip code, and the database returns a list of hospitals in her area, including each hospital's address and telephone number. How would the rule announced in *Feist* apply to such a national database of hospitals? *See Warren Pub., Inc. v. Microdos Data Corp.*, 115 F.3d 1509 (11th Cir.1997). Would it make a difference to your answer if the database of hospitals only listed those hospitals that had an acupuncture therapist on staff? *See Key Publications, Inc. v. Chinatown Today Publishing Enterprises Inc.*, 945 F.2d 509 (2d Cir.1991). What if the database listed all the hospitals in the United States but indicated for each one whether it had an acupuncture therapist on staff?

3. *Impact on consumers.* Is the "originality" requirement for copyrightability of collections of facts pro-consumer, in that it fosters competition among businesses that use or offer facts by preventing businesses from exercising monopoly control over facts? Is it anti-consumer, in that it reduces the incentives of businesses to compile databases of value to consumers?

4. *Interface vs. database.* In *Feist*, the Supreme Court focused on a telephone "white pages" directory, in a hard-copy book format. In book form, information is presented to the reader in the same arrangement in which it is stored. In the case of an electronic database, however, there is no necessary correspondence between the arrangement of data on a hard drive and the arrangement of returned data on a user's computer monitor. Furthermore, the arrangement of data on a hard drive may change each time the database is saved anew. Under the rule announced in *Feist*, how does one gauge the originality in the arrangement of data in an electronic database?

5. *"Thin" copyright.* Even if an electronic database's selection and arrangement of facts is sufficiently original to qualify for copyright protection, the protection afforded is extremely limited. As the Court notes, "the copyright in a factual compilation is thin. Notwithstanding a valid copyright, a subsequent compiler remains free to use the facts contained in another's publication to aid in preparing a competing work, so long as the competing work does not feature the same selection and arrangement." *Feist*, 499 U.S. at 349. In light of the "thin" protection afforded to factual databases, what is the appropriate standard for determining copyright infringement? Compare *Kregos v. Associated Press*, 937 F.2d 700, 709–10 (2d Cir.1991) and *Harper House, Inc. v. Thomas Nelson, Inc.*, 889 F.2d 197, 205 (9th Cir.1989) with *Bellsouth Advertising & Publishing Corp. v. Donnelley Information Publishing, Inc.*, 999 F.2d 1436, 1445 (11th Cir.1993) (en banc).

6. *Overruling* Feist. Can Congress overrule *Feist* by amending the Copyright Act to provide for protection of factual databases?

II. PROTECTION FOR DATABASES UNDER STATE LAW AND THE PROBLEM OF FEDERAL COPYRIGHT PREEMPTION

In *Feist*, the Supreme Court suggested that protection for uncopyrightable databases " 'may in certain circumstances be available under a theory of [state-law] unfair competition.' " 499 U.S. at 374-75 (quoting MELVILLE B. NIMMER & DAVID NIMMER, NIMMER ON COPYRIGHT § 3.04 (1990)). While the owner of a database or compilation of facts who seeks to exclude others from using those facts might seek relief under state law, the circumstances under which a state law cause of action might offer a remedy are significantly limited by federal copyright preemption of state law.

There are two forms of preemption associated with copyright law: first, the general preemption under the supremacy clause of the Constitution afforded in favor of federal law; second, preemption deriving from a specific provision in the Copyright Act, Section 301. Constitutional preemption invalidates a state law that "stands as an obstacle to the accomplishment and execution of the full purposes and objectives of Congress." *Hines v. Davidowitz*, 312 U.S. 52, 67 (1941).

Section 301(a) of the Copyright Act preempts

> all legal or equitable rights that are equivalent to any of the exclusive rights within the general scope of copyright as specified by section 106 in works of authorship that are fixed in a tangible medium of expression and come within the subject matter of copyright as specified by sections 102 and 103.

17 U.S.C. § 301(a). Under this provision, a state cause of action is preempted, and thereby rendered invalid, if two conditions are met. First, the material that the state law purports to protect must be "within the subject matter of copyright." That is, it must be a literary work, musical work, compilation, or one of the other types of works that are capable of receiving copyright protection, as set forth in Sections 102 and 103 of the Copyright Act. A database, as long as it is "fixed in a tangible medium of expression," will meet this subject-matter

requirement, even if (like the telephone white pages at issue in *Feist v. Rural Telephone Service Co.*) it lacks the requisite originality to be copyrightable.

Second, the rights that the state law protects must be "equivalent to" any of the exclusive rights granted by Section 106 of the Copyright Act, namely the rights of reproduction, adaptation, distribution, public performance, and public display. It is often unclear whether a state law satisfies this criterion. As explained in *Computer Associates International v. Altai, Inc.,* 982 F.2d 693, 716–17 (2d Cir.1992), Section 301

> preempts only those state-law rights that "may be abridged by an act which, in and of itself, would infringe one of the exclusive rights" provided by federal copyright law. *See Harper & Row, Publishers, Inc. v. Nation Enters.,* 723 F.2d 195, 200 (2d Cir.1983), *rev'd on other grounds,* 471 U.S. 539 (1985). If an "extra element" is "required instead of or in addition to the acts of reproduction, performance, distribution or display, in order to constitute a state-created cause of action, then the right does not lie 'within the general scope of copyright,' and there is no preemption." 1 Nimmer [on Copyright] § 1.01[B], at 1–14–15; *see also Harper & Row, Publishers, Inc.,* 723 F.2d at 200 (where state law right "is predicated upon an act incorporating elements beyond mere reproduction or the like, the [federal and state] rights are not equivalent" and there is no preemption).
>
> A state law claim is not preempted if the "extra element" changes the "nature of the action so that it is *qualitatively* different from a copyright infringement claim." *Mayer v. Josiah Wedgwood & Sons, Ltd.,* 601 F.Supp. 1523, 1535 (S.D.N.Y.1985). To determine whether a claim meets this standard, we must determine "what plaintiff seeks to protect, the theories in which the matter is thought to be protected and the rights sought to be enforced." 1 Roger M. Milgrim, *Milgrim on Trade Secrets* § 2.06A[3], at 2–150 (1992) . . . . An action will not be saved from preemption by elements such as awareness or intent, which alter "the action's scope but not its nature. . . ." *Mayer,* 601 F.Supp. at 1535.
>
> Following this "extra element" test, we have held that unfair competition and misappropriation claims grounded solely in the copying of a plaintiff's protected expression are preempted by section 301. . . . We also have held to be preempted a tortious interference with contract claim grounded in the impairment of a plaintiff's right under the Copyright Act to publish derivative works. . . .
>
> However, many state law rights that can arise in connection with instances of copyright infringement satisfy the extra element test, and thus are not preempted by section 301. These include unfair competition claims based upon breaches of confidential relationships, breaches of fiduciary duties and trade secrets.

Several types of state laws might offer database owners the protection against unauthorized use that the Copyright Act fails to provide. Among the likely candidates are state laws against misappropriation of intangible property, laws protecting trade secrets, and laws enforcing contractual restraints on the use of a database. Most recently, the common law action of trespass to chattels and computer fraud statutes have been applied to protect databases used in e-commerce.

Misappropriation. The state-law tort of misappropriation is a branch of unfair competition law, which seeks to promote the competitive process by imposing liability for forms of competition that undermine it. The competitive markets can be undermined in many ways. A company may engage in deceptive practices in order to deprive consumers of the information they need to make informed and rational choices in the marketplace, thereby undermining its efficient operation. A company may infringe the trademark of another business in order to create customer confusion over the origin of one's goods, thereby appropriating the other company's good will. A company may appropriate information from another company, thereby gaining an unfair competitive advantage. The tort of misappropriation is intended to combat this last type of harm.

A state law against misappropriation may survive preemption if it is drawn sufficiently narrowly. In *International News Service v. Associated Press*, 248 U.S. 215 (1918), the Supreme Court recognized a federal common law cause of action for misappropriation of "hot news." The hot news in question consisted of uncopyrighted news items, which were written and disseminated by a news-gathering organization, and were copied and disseminated by a competing news-gathering organization. No issue of preemption was presented in that case. But in *National Basketball Association v. Motorola, Inc.*, 105 F.3d 841 (2d Cir.1997), the court addressed the question whether Section 301 preempts a state-law cause of action for misappropriation of hot news. The NBA sought to prevent defendants from operating a service that delivered scores and other data about professional basketball games in progress to handheld pagers carried by subscribers. Defendants acquired the information from television and radio broadcasts of the games, transmitting it to subscribers with a time lag of two to three minutes. The court held that New York's misappropriation law, which protects property rights from "any form of commercial immorality," was preempted. It explained that a state misappropriation law that seeks to protect "hot news" survives preemption only if it satisfies the following conditions:

> (i) a plaintiff generates or gathers information at a cost; (ii) the information is time-sensitive; (iii) a defendant's use of the information constitutes free-riding on the plaintiff's efforts; (iv) the defendant is in direct competition with a product or service offered by the plaintiffs; and (v) the ability of other parties to free-ride on the efforts of the plaintiff or others would so reduce the incentive to produce the product or service that its existence or quality would be substantially threatened.

105 F.3d at 845. Misappropriation laws that meet these conditions, and therefore survive preemption, will offer a rather limited range of protection to database owners.

Trade Secrets. Trade secret laws are likely to survive preemption. These laws make unauthorized disclosure of trade secrets actionable if the information holder makes a reasonable effort to keep the information secret, and the defendant either acquires it by improper means or breaches a duty of confidentiality. These requirements constitute an "extra element" in the state cause of action, beyond those which are sufficient to constitute an infringement of a copyright owner's exclusive rights. *See Architectronics, Inc. v. Control Systems, Inc.*, 935 F.Supp. 425, 441 (S.D.N.Y.1996). Consequently, such a law does not meet Section 301's "equivalent rights" criterion, and it is not preempted. Like non-preempted misappropriation laws, trade secret laws will protect only a narrow category of databases, excluding, for example, all those to which subscribers are provided access.

Breach of Contract. Another state law cause of action that has been used to protect interests in databases and other compilations of fact is breach of contract. Most providers of compilations of information in digital form, whether through online access or on a tangible medium such as a CD-ROM, require a prospective user to agree to various terms and conditions of use before providing access. Online, the terms and conditions may be presented to the user in a scrollable window, with the user manifesting assent by clicking an on-screen button labeled "I accept"; or they may be presented on an interior page of the website, indicated only by a link labeled "Terms" at the bottom of the home page. If the information product is supplied on CD-ROM, the terms and conditions might be presented on the user's computer screen the first time the product is run, or might be on a sheet of paper enclosed within the CD-ROM's packaging. (Whether such presentations of terms can give rise to binding contractual obligation is addressed in Chapter 10, Part I(A), *infra*.)

These clickwrap or shrinkwrap agreements, provided they are enforceable, could give information providers and database owners a significant level of control over their information assets. To the extent that such sets of terms are standardized and widespread within a market, the terms form a substitute for the background intellectual property rights that would prevail without them. The question arises, therefore, whether such terms are preempted by federal copyright law.

State laws enforcing contractual restraints on the use of information contained in a database can be expected generally to survive preemption. In *ProCD, Inc. v. Zeidenberg*, 86 F.3d 1447, 1454 (7th Cir.1996), the court held that a shrinkwrap license limiting the purchaser's use of telephone directory information contained on a CD-ROM was enforceable under state contract law. The court reasoned:

> Rights "equivalent to any of the exclusive rights within the general scope of copyright" are rights established *by law*—rights that restrict the options of persons who are strangers to the author. Copyright law forbids duplication, public performance, and so on, unless the person wishing to copy or perform the work gets permission; silence means a ban on copying. A copyright is a right against the world. Contracts, by contrast, generally affect only their parties; strangers may do as they please, so contracts do not create "exclusive rights."

In *Bowers v. Baystate Technologies*, 320 F.3d 1317 (Fed.Cir.2003), the Federal Circuit adopted the approach set out in *ProCD v. Zeidenberg*, holding that the Copyright Act does not preempt a provision in a shrinkwrap agreement that prohibits reverse engineering of a computer program. The result is striking, since reverse engineering has been held to be fair use, and thus not within the copyright owner's authority to control by exercise of the copyright. As the dissenting judge expressed it: "The case before us is different from *ProCD*. The Copyright Act does not confer a right to pay the same amount for commercial and personal use. It does, however, confer a right to fair use, 17 U.S.C. § 107, which we have held encompasses reverse engineering." *Id.* at 1338 (Dyk, J., concurring in part and dissenting in part). The determination that reverse engineering is fair use reflects a policy judgment balancing the copyright owner's interest in protecting his creations, against the public's interest in the free flow of ideas and robust competition. Under *Bowers*, a copyright owner may upset this balance by insertion of a non-negotiable term in a shrinkwrap agreement.

The reasoning and result in *ProCD v. Zeidenberg* have drawn a good deal of criticism.

> A few courts and commentators have taken the position that federal preemption simply shouldn't apply to contract terms—or at least that it shouldn't apply in the same way—because contracts are different than state statutes. . . . Judge Easterbrook's decision in *ProCD v. Zeidenberg* seems to accept this view, and some courts have taken this logic so far as to conclude that contracts simply can't be preempted by copyright law.

> There are a number of problems with the "contracts are different" idea. First, the reference to "equivalence" seems to direct the analysis only at copyright field preemption under section 301, and thus to ignore both copyright conflicts pre-

emption and any form of patent preemption. Even if contract and copyright are not equivalent, it simply does not follow that federal law places no limits on the enforceability of contracts. Courts that take this position should also be troubled by the significant number of cases that do apply intellectual property rules to preempt contracts.

Second, the viability of the distinction between private contracts and public legislation is diminishing day by day. One of the main changes Article 2B[2] would make in current law would be to render enforceable contract "terms" to which the parties did not agree in the classic sense, and indeed of which one party may be entirely unaware. . . . In other words, Article 2B promises to usher in an era of "private legislation," in which parties who are in a position to write contracts can jointly impose uniform terms that no one can escape. . . .

Third, even truly "private" contracts affect third parties who haven't agreed to the contract terms.

Mark A. Lemley, *Beyond Preemption: The Law and Policy of Intellectual Property Licensing*, 87 CALIF. L. REV. 111, 147–49 (1999). See also David Nimmer, Elliot Brown & Gary N. Frischling, *The Metamorphosis of Contract into Expand*, 87 CALIF. L. REV. 17, 48 (1999) ("[W]hen a breach of contract cause of action—particularly one that does not result from the bargained-for agreement of both parties to its putative execution—is used as a subterfuge to control nothing other than the reproduction, adaptation, public distribution, etc., of works within the subject matter of copyright, then it too should be deemed preempted.").

For a discussion of the availability of state misappropriation and contract claims to protect databases, see Jane C. Ginsburg, *Copyright, Common Law, and Sui Generis Protection of Databases in the United States and Abroad*, 66 U. CIN. L. REV. 151 (1997).

Trespass to Chattels. Databases and compilations of fact, although themselves intangible, must reside on some tangible medium. In the case of online databases, the tangible medium is the computer system on which the database is stored, and which makes access to it possible. A computer system is tangible personal property. In part because of the limited protection factual databases receive under the law of copyright, database owners have attempted to combat unauthorized access to their online databases by bringing lawsuits predicated upon state law causes of action designed to protect against unwanted interferences with personal property. The theory is that if one can bar unauthorized access to the computer system on which one's database resides, one can bar access to the database.

In several cases, database owners have successfully invoked the common law action of trespass to chattels to prevent unauthorized access to their information. *See eBay, Inc. v. Bidder's Edge, Inc.*, 100 F.Supp.2d 1058 (N.D.Cal.2000) (entering preliminary injunction against operator of website that accessed online auction sites and aggregated information collected from them); *Register.com, Inc. v. Verio, Inc.*, 126 F.Supp.2d 238 (S.D.N.Y.2000) (entering preliminary injunction against company that collected domain-registration information from database maintained by registrar). (These cases are excerpted and discussed in Chapter 12, Part II, *infra*.)

---

[2] [Article 2B, a proposed addition to the Uniform Commercial Code, was ultimately promulgated by the National Conference of Commissioners on Uniform State Laws as a freestanding model state law, called the Uniform Computer Information Transactions Act. *See* Chapter10, Part I(B), *supra*.—Eds.]

Under the *Restatement* version of the trespass to chattels cause of action, "[a] trespass to a chattel may be committed by intentionally (a) dispossessing another of the chattel, or (b) using or intermeddling with a chattel in the possession of another." RESTATEMENT (SECOND) OF TORTS § 217 (1965). Based on the "extra element" criterion, at least one court has held that trespass to chattels survives preemption under Section 301. *See eBay. v. Bidder's Edge, supra,* at 1072 ("The right to exclude others from using physical personal property is not equivalent to any rights protected by copyright and therefore constitutes an extra element that makes trespass qualitatively different from a copyright infringement claim.").

Computer Fraud. The federal Computer Fraud and Abuse Act, 18 U.S.C. § 1030, prohibits a range of conduct that is often referred to under the rubric of "hacking." Database owners, characterizing unauthorized access to their information as a form of hacking, have invoked several provisions of the Act to bar such access. The Act makes it illegal to "intentionally access[]" a computer "without authorization," if the access results in at least $5,000 of damage. 18 U.S.C. § 1030(a)(5)(A)(iii). It also provides an action against one who "knowingly and with intent to defraud, accesses a . . . computer without authorization, or exceeds authorized access, and by means of such conduct furthers the intended fraud and obtains anything of value," again if the result is damages of at least $5,000. 18 U.S.C. § 1030(a)(4). Courts have applied these provisions in cases involving unauthorized access to data. *See Register.com, Inc. v. Verio, Inc., supra; EF Cultural Travel BV v. Explorica, Inc.,* 274 F.3d 577 (1st Cir.2001) (affirming entry of preliminary injunction against company that acquired price data from a competitor's website and used it to undercut the competitors prices).

Since this cause of action clearly requires elements beyond those required for copyright infringement, it is likely to survive preemption when applied to protect databases.

QUESTIONS FOR DISCUSSION

1. *Preemption and copyright management systems.* A copyright management system is a technological means of enforcing the terms and conditions of a license automatically, making recourse to the courts unnecessary. Would the widespread use of copyright management systems make the preemption doctrine irrelevant? (Copyright management systems are discussed in Chapter 9, *infra.*)

2. *Future of state-law causes of action.* As we will see in the next Part, database owners have sought legislation that would grant them control over use by others of the information in their databases. Given the availability of the various state-law causes of action described above, is such legislation necessary? If such legislation is enacted, will the state-law causes of action become superfluous?

III. *SUI GENERIS* PROTECTION FOR DATABASES

In light of the limited protection provided to databases and compilations of fact under the law of copyright, and the federal preemption of state-law causes of action that might otherwise remedy this situation, many information providers and trade organizations with an interest in procuring greater legal protection for factual databases have advocated the passage of legislation that creates a *sui generis* right in databases: a legally protected interest in databases independent of federal copyright law as well as state common and statutory law. Two basic models have been proposed for such legislation: the intellectual property model and the unfair competition model.

Under the intellectual property model, the legislation would create a new exclusive property right in databases. Like a copyright or patent, an exclusive right in databases under the intellectual property model would be granted for a limited period of time, alienable by contract and subject to various statutory exceptions, defenses and compulsory licenses.

Under the unfair competition model, the legislation would prohibit particular methods of competition that undermine competitive markets for databases. Like the Lanham Act or the general doctrine of misappropriation, legislation under the unfair competition model would impose liability for conduct that unfairly appropriates commercial value of a database created by another.

Confronting a similar perceived need to strengthen the legal protection of databases and ensure Europe a strong competitive position in the emerging global information marketplace, the European Union embraced the intellectual property model for database protection and adopted a Directive according legal protection to databases. *See* Directive 96/9/EC of the European Parliament and of the Council of the European Union of 11 March, 1996, on the legal protection of databases, 1996 O.J. (L 77) 20, europa.eu.int/ISPO/infosoc/legreg/docs/969ec.html. Under this Directive, all European Union member states were required to enact conforming database protection legislation by January 1, 1998. The details of this Directive are covered in a report published by the United States Copyright Office, excerpted below.

In the United States, the choice between the intellectual property model and the unfair competition model of database protection was presented as a choice between two bills proposed in Congress: the Collections of Information Antipiracy Act and the Consumer and Investor Access to Information Act of 1999. Although these two bills were not enacted, they are worth studying as paradigms of data protection legislation that is likely to be introduced in a future Congress.

The Collections of Information Antipiracy Act, H.R. 354, 106th Cong. (1999) ("H.R. 354"), embraces the intellectual property model and confers on the owner of a database an exclusive right in a "collection of information" enforceable in federal district court without regard to the amount in controversy. Its central provision is Section 1402, which states:

> (a) MAKING AVAILABLE OR EXTRACTING TO MAKE AVAILABLE—Any person who makes available to others, or extracts to make available to others, all or a substantial part of a collection of information gathered, organized, or maintained by another person through the investment of substantial monetary or other resources, so as to cause material harm to the primary market or a related market of that other person, or a successor in interest of that other person, for a product or service that incorporates that collection of information and is offered or intended to be offered in commerce by that other person, or a successor in interest of that person, shall be liable to that person or successor in interest for the remedies set forth in section 1406.

> (b) OTHER ACTS OF EXTRACTION—Any person who extracts all or a substantial part of a collection of information gathered, organized, or maintained by another person through the investment of substantial monetary or other resources, so as to cause material harm to the primary market of that other person, or a successor in interest of that other person, for a product or service that incorporates that collection of information and is offered or intended to be offered in commerce by that other person, or a successor in interest of that person, shall be

liable to that person or successor in interest for the remedies set forth in section 1406.

H.R. 354, 106th Cong. § 1402 (1999). The terms "collection of information" and "information" are defined as follows:

(1) COLLECTION OF INFORMATION—The term "collection of information" means information that has been collected and has been organized for the purpose of bringing discrete items of information together in one place or through one source so that persons may access them. The term does not include an individual work which, taken as a whole, is a work of narrative literary prose, but may include a collection of such works.

(2) INFORMATION—The term "information" means facts, data, works of authorship, or any other intangible material capable of being collected and organized in a systematic way.

Id. § 1401. Section 1406 provides for injunctions, impoundment, monetary damages that can be trebled in the discretion of the court, reasonable attorney's fees and costs. Section 1403 carves out various exceptions to Section 1402, including reasonable uses understood in a manner analogous to fair use under the law of copyright. Nothing in the Act is intended to "restrict the rights of parties freely to enter into licenses or any other contracts with respect to making available or extracting collections of information," nor to "affect rights, limitations, or remedies concerning copyright, or any other rights or obligations relating to information, including laws with respect to patent, trademark, design rights, antitrust, trade secrets, privacy, access to public documents, and the law of contract." *Id.* § 1405. Government collections of information are excluded, as are computer programs and "collections of information gathered, organized, or maintained to address, route, forward, transmit, or store digital online communications, register addresses to be used in digital online communications, or provide or receive access to connections for digital online communications." *Id.* § 1401.

The Consumer and Investor Access to Information Act of 1999, H.R. 1858, 106th Cong. (1999) ("H.R. 1858"), embraces the unfair competition law model of database protection and prohibits the unauthorized sale or distribution of another's database. Its central provision is Section 102, which states:

PROHIBITION AGAINST DISTRIBUTION OF DUPLICATES. It is unlawful for any person, by any means or instrumentality of interstate or foreign commerce or communications, to sell or distribute to the public a database that—

(1) is a duplicate of another database that was collected and organized by another person; and

(2) is sold or distributed in commerce in competition with that other database.

H.R. 1858, 106th Cong. § 102 (1999). The terms "database" and "duplicate" are defined in Section 101 as follows:

(1) DATABASE.—The term "database" means a collection of discrete items of information that have been collected and organized in a single place, or in such a way as to be accessible through a single source, through the investment of substantial monetary or other resources, for the purpose of providing access to those discrete items of information by users of the database. However, a discrete section of a database that contains multiple discrete items of information may

also be treated as a database.

(2) DUPLICATE OF A DATABASE.—A database is "a duplicate" of any other database if the database is substantially the same as such other database, and was made by extracting information from such other database.

Id. § 101. Unlike H.R. 354, H.R. 1858 does not confer any rights on the owner of a database, nor does it provide a private right of action in federal district court. Instead, H.R. 1858 provides that the "Federal Trade Commission shall have jurisdiction, under section 5 of the Federal Trade Commission Act (15 U.S.C. 45), to prevent violations of section 102 of this title." *Id.* § 107(a). Section 107(b) of the Act also grants the FTC rulemaking authority, and subsection (c) states that "[a]ny violation of any rule prescribed under subsection (b) shall be treated as a violation of a rule respecting unfair or deceptive acts or practices under section 5 of the Federal Trade Commission Act (15 U.S.C. 45)."

Notwithstanding Section 102, the Act permits the sale and distribution of information contained in another's database for the purpose of law enforcement and intelligence activities, and for certain news reporting, scientific, educational, or research uses. *Id.* § 103. The Act also places limits on the liability of service providers, and denies relief to one who "has misused the protection afforded" by the Act. *Id.* § 106.

Like H.R. 354, nothing in H.R. 1858 is intended to "restrict the rights of parties freely to enter into licenses or any other contracts with respect to making available or extracting collections of information," nor to "affect rights, limitations, or remedies concerning copyright, or any other rights or obligations relating to information, including laws with respect to patent, trademark, design rights, antitrust, trade secrets, privacy, access to public documents, and the law of contract." *Id.* § 105. Also like H.R. 354, government databases are excluded. Unlike H.R. 354, however, H.R. 1858 does not prohibit sale or distribution to the public of individual items from a protected database. *Id.* § 104.

The two bills appear to offer a choice between two different models for legal protection of databases, but they both would change the balance between what information is property and what is in the public domain. Both approaches remove factual material from the public domain, a topic that Professor Pamela Samuelson addresses in the second excerpt below. Furthermore, database protection schemes may raise constitutional issues. In the third excerpt below, Professor Yochai Benkler considers the constitutional constraints imposed by the U.S. Constitution's Intellectual Property Clause and the First Amendment.

U.S. Copyright Office, Report on Legal Protection for Databases (1997).
www.copyright.gov/reports/db4.pdf

. . .

B. European Database Directive

1. Background

Pursuant to the action plan set out in its 1991 "Follow-up to the Green Paper,"[122] the European Commission proposed in 1992 to harmonize the national laws within the European Union regarding the protection of databases. The Com-

---

[122] Doc. COM (90) 584 final, 17 Jan. 1991. The "Green Paper" referred to is the 1988 "Green Paper on Copyright and the Challenge of Technology," Doc. COM (88) 172 final, 7 June 1988.

mission proposal was adopted in a modified form as a directive to the member states on March 11, 1996.[123] The directive is required to be implemented by the member states by January 1, 1998.

A number of factors appear to have led the European Union (EU) to harmonize the law regarding database protection. The rapid expansion of the Internet raised the EU's awareness of "the exponential growth, in the Community and worldwide, in the amount of information generated and processed annually in all sectors of commerce and industry," and the important role of databases "in the development of an information market within the community."[125] The EU also expressed concern about the "very great imbalance in the level of investment in the database sector both as between the Member States and between the Community and the world's largest database-producing third countries."[126] In addition, the *Feist* decision in the U.S. Supreme Court galvanized concern regarding the adequacy of copyright protection for databases within the EU.

The directive covers compilations of data in any form, and thus includes hard copy compilations as well as electronic databases.[128] The Commission's original proposal was limited to electronic databases, but in the course of deliberations this approach was found unworkable, because it would subject the identical material to differing legal standards based solely on the medium employed. As one of the participants is reported to have stated, "making use of a scanner should not be decisive in granting legal protection." In addition, technologies such as scanning and optical character recognition render even hard-copy databases vulnerable to unauthorized copying and commercial reuse in both hard-copy and electronic form. Moreover, the TRIPs Agreement makes no such distinction.

As adopted, the directive establishes a dual system for protection of databases. One component is copyright protection for the "structure" of the database. The other is a *sui generis* ("of its own kind" — i.e., not falling within existing categories

---

[123] Directive 96/9/EC of the European Parliament and of the Council of the European Union of 11 March 1996 on the legal protection of databases, 1996 O.J. (L 77/20) [hereinafter *Database Directive*].

[125] Database Directive, recitals (10), (9).

[126] *Id.* recital (11).

[128] Database Directive, art. 1(1), recital (14). The term "database" is defined in the directive as "a collection of independent works, data or other materials arranged in a systematic or methodical way and individually accessible by electronic or other means." Art. 1(2). Explicitly excluded from protection under the directive are "computer programs used in the making or operation of databases accessible by electronic means." Art. 1(3). Recital (17) expands on the definition:

[T]he term "database" should be understood to include literary, artistic, musical or other collections of works or collections of other material such as texts, sound, images, numbers, facts, and data; . . . it should cover collections of independent works, data or other materials which are systematically or methodically arranged and can be individually accessed; . . . this means that a recording or an audiovisual, cinematographic, literary or musical work as such does not fall within the scope of this Directive.

of legal protection) intellectual property right in the contents of the database.

2. *Copyright Protection*

The copyright portion of the directive, Chapter II, applies only to the structure or schema of a database, without prejudice to any existing protection under copyright for the database contents.[133] It seeks to harmonize the scope of copyright protection for databases throughout the European Union. It does so in two major respects: First, it sets a uniform standard of originality. Second, it establishes a uniform list of "restricted acts" (i.e., exclusive rights) and exceptions to restricted acts.

Prior to the directive, copyright protection for databases in the member states could be divided into two general groups. In the U.K., Ireland and the Netherlands, the threshold for protection was quite low. In particular, Anglo–Irish common law incorporated a "sweat of the brow" doctrine that developed from the same line of eighteenth and nineteenth century English cases that were cited in early U.S. compilation cases. In the remaining European countries, however, copyright imposed a fairly high threshold of originality to qualify for protection. This is in keeping with the "author's right" approach that prevails throughout most of Continental Europe, which defines originality as an expression of the author's individual personality.

The standard established by the directive requires the database to, "by reason of the selection or arrangement of [its] contents, constitute the author's own intellectual creation."[137] This language was incorporated verbatim from the EU's 1991 directive on the protection of computer programs.[138] It was originally adopted to override the very high standard of originality mandated by the German Supreme Court in the "Inkasso Programm" case and other decisions. At the same time, by requiring an "intellectual creation," the database directive imposes a higher standard of originality than that required under current law in the U.K., Ireland and the Netherlands. The directive thus charts a middle course on the level of originality required. Although the directive's standard of originality has not been tested in practice, the formulation appears to be quite similar to the criteria for protection under U.S. law, as set out in the definition of "compilation" in the Copyright Act and interpreted by the Supreme Court in *Feist*.

The "restricted acts" (exclusive rights of the copyright owner) under the directive are reproduction (temporary or permanent), adaptation, distribution, and communication, display or performance to the public.[141] Authorization is not required for a lawful user to engage in any restricted act "which is necessary for the purposes of access to the contents of the database and normal use of the con-

---

[133] *Id.* art. 3(2).

[137] Database Directive, art. 3(1).

[138] Council Directive 91/250/EEC of 14 May 1991 on the Legal Protection of Computer Programs, 1991 O.J. (L 122/42) [hereinafter *Software Directive*].

[141] Database Directive, art. 5. The directive only covers economic rights under copyright; moral rights are beyond the scope of the directive. *Id.* recital (28).

tents."[142] Any contractual provision to the contrary is "null and void."[143]

In addition to this mandatory exemption, the directive permits member states to provide for limitations on the restricted acts in the following cases:

> (a) in the case of reproduction for private purposes of a non-electronic database;
>
> (b) where there is use for the sole purpose of illustration for teaching or scientific research, as long as the source is indicated and to the extent justified by the non-commercial purpose to be achieved;
>
> (c) where there is use for the purposes of public security o[r] for the purposes of an administrative or judicial procedure;
>
> (d) where other exceptions to copyright which are traditionally authorized under national law are involved, without prejudice to points (a), (b) and (c).[144]

Such exceptions are subject to an overall economic harm limitation, ensuring that they cannot "unreasonably prejudice[] the rightholder's legitimate interests or conflict[] with normal exploitation of the database."[145]

3. Sui Generis Protection

As a supplement to copyright, Chapter III of the directive establishes a *sui generis* form of protection for the contents of databases. The stated justification for this protection is that "in the absence of a harmonized system of unfair-competition legislation or of case-law, other measures are required in addition [to copyright] to prevent the unauthorized extraction and/or re-utilization of the contents of a database," the making of which "requires the investment of considerable human, technical and financial resources while such databases can be copied

---

[142] Database Directive, art. 6(1). *Cf.* Software Directive, art. 5(1).

[143] Database Directive, art. 15.

[144] *Id.* art. 6(2). It has been suggested that article 6(2) "narrow[s] the educational and scientific communities' ability to invoke 'fair use' with respect to copyrightable databases under prior law." Jerome H. Reichman & Pamela Samuelson, *Intellectual Property Rights in Data?*, 50 VAND. L. REV. 51, 79 (1997). This view is based on an interpretation of points (a) through (c) as limitations on the scope of any exception permitted under point (d). *Id.* at 77, n.113. Others view point (d) as allowing "other exceptions to copyright which are traditionally permitted by the Member State concerned to continue." Jens–L. Gaster, *The New EU Directive Concerning the Legal Protection of Data Bases*, in FOURTH ANNUAL CONFERENCE ON INTERNATIONAL INTELLECTUAL PROPERTY LAW & POLICY, 35, 40 (Fordham Univ. School of Law, Apr. 11, 1996).

[145] Database Directive, art. 6(3). This language is patterned after virtually identical language in the Berne Convention, art. 9(2) and TRIPs, art. 13 (which has been relied on by the United States to permit the doctrine of fair use under copyright law). *See also* WIPO Copyright Treaty, art. 10, and accompanying Agreed Statement (noting the understanding that similar treaty language would "permit Contracting Parties to carry forward and appropriately extend into the digital environment limitations and exceptions in their national laws which have been considered acceptable under the Berne Convention.")

or accessed at a fraction of the cost needed to design them independently."[146]

Some of the EU member states originally advocated leaving the protection of the contents of databases to unfair competition law, and the initial Commission proposal described the *sui generis* right as a "right to prevent unfair extraction from a database" for commercial purposes.[147] By mid–1993, however, "an increasing majority of interested parties" were reportedly favoring the creation of a property right along the lines ultimately adopted. The rationale, at least in part, was the perceived difficulty in harmonizing unfair competition law throughout the European Union. In addition, the Commission has noted that "unfair competition rules only come into play once an act has taken place. They do not provide an economic right with clear scope which can be freely transferred."[149]

In some respects the *sui generis* right is similar to the "catalogue rule" existing in the Nordic countries, which provided a model for the Commission. That rule establishes a "related right" for factual compilations, in addition to copyright protection. The catalogue rule provides to the producer of a catalogue, table, or similar matter "in which a large number of information items have been compiled" a right against unauthorized reproduction.[150] Originality is not a requirement for protection, and the term of protection for such "catalogues" is fairly short: 10 years from publication or 15 years from creation, whichever expires sooner.

The essential features of the database directive's *sui generis* right are:

a. Protection for "substantial investment". The *sui generis* right is available for "the maker of a database which shows that there has been qualitatively and/or quantitatively a substantial investment in either the obtaining, verification or presentation of the contents . . ."[151] "Substantial investment" is not defined in the directive. However, the recitals leading up to its provisions indicate that "such investment may consist in the deployment of financial resources and/or the expending of time, effort and energy."[152]

b. Protects against acts of extraction and re-utilization. The rights accorded under the directive are the rights to "prevent extraction and/or re-utilization of the whole or of a substantial part . . . of the contents of that database."[153] "Extraction" is defined as "the permanent or temporary transfer of all or a substantial part of the

---

[146] Database Directive, recitals (6) and (7).

[147] Proposal for a Council Directive on the Legal Protection of Databases, COM(92)24 final, art. 2 [hereinafter *1992 Proposal*].

[149] Submission from the European Community and its Member States to the World Intellectual Property Organization on "An International Treaty on the Protection of Databases," p. 2 (July 1997).

[150] Swedish Copyright Act, art. 49. *See also* Norwegian Copyright Act, art. 43; Danish Copyright Act, art. 71; Finnish Copyright Act, art. 49.

[151] Database Directive, art. 7(1).

[152] *Id.* recital (40).

[153] *Id.* art. 7(1).

contents of a database to another medium by any means or in any form."[154] "Re-utilization" is defined as "any form of making available to the public all or a substantial part of the contents of a database by the distribution of copies, by renting, by on-line or other forms of transmission."[155]

c. "Insubstantial parts" excluded from protection. The maker of a database "may not prevent a lawful user of the database from extracting and/or re-utilizing insubstantial parts of its contents . . . for any purposes whatsoever."[156] Any contractual provision to the contrary is "null and void."[157] The directive does not attempt to define "insubstantial parts," but does state that substantiality is to be "evaluated qualitatively and/or quantitatively."[158]

d. Exceptions for certain uses. The directive permits member states to adopt exceptions from the *sui generis* right for lawful users in three specific categories: (a) extraction for private purposes of the contents of a non-electronic database; (b) "extraction for the purposes of illustration for teaching or scientific research, as long as the source is indicated and to the extent justified by the non-commercial purpose to be achieved"; and (c) "extraction and/or re-utilization for the purposes of public security or an administrative or judicial procedure."[159] These exceptions are similar to those permitted under copyright, but without the additional reference to "other exceptions to copyright which are traditionally authorized under national laws." Nevertheless, the recitals indicate that existing exemptions to any existing similar *sui generis* rights are grandfathered under the directive.[160]

The exceptions must be read in conjunction with provisions in the directive on "obligations of lawful users," prohibiting lawful users of databases that have been made available to the public from "performing acts which conflict with normal exploitation of the database or unreasonably prejudice the legitimate interests of the maker of the database," or "caus[ing] prejudice to the holder of a copyright or related right in respect of the works or subject matter contained in the database."[161]

e. Fifteen year term of protection. The term of protection for the *sui generis* right is fifteen years.[162] This was an increase from the ten-year term that was originally proposed in 1992.[163] Any qualitatively or quantitatively "substantial change," in-

---

[154] *Id.* art. 7(2)(a).

[155] *Id.* art. 7(2)(b).

[156] *Id.* art. 8(1).

[157] *Id.* art. 15.

[158] *Id.* art. 8(1).

[159] *Id.* art. 9. While not stated explicitly in the text of the provision on exceptions, Recital (50) adds the gloss that the purpose of "such operations . . . must not be commercial."

[160] *Id.* recital 52.

[161] *Id.* arts. 8(2), 8(3) (again patterned after Berne Convention, art. 9(2) and TRIPs, art. 13). Recital (50) indicates that articles 8(2) and 8(3) function as a limitation on the exceptions in article 9.

[162] *Id.* art. 10(1).

[163] 1992 Proposal, art. 9(3).

cluding one resulting from an accumulation of small changes, "which would result in the database being considered to be a substantial new investment," qualifies the resulting database for its own fifteen-year term of protection.[164]

f. Available to non-EU nationals only on the basis of reciprocity. The *sui generis* right is available only to database makers who are EU nationals or habitual residents.[165] For purposes of the directive, this would include business entities that have a business presence in the EU (defined as a central administration or principal place of business in the EU, or a registered office in the EU plus a genuine, ongoing operational link with the economy of a member state).[166] The EU can conclude agreements to extend the right to databases made in third countries.[167] Although the provisions of the directive themselves are silent as to the basis for such agreements, the recitals make clear that protection will be offered only on the basis of reciprocity—i.e., where the third country offers "comparable protection" to EU databases.[168]

The original proposal for the directive also included a compulsory license, requiring database vendors who are the sole source of any given information to license that information to competitors on "fair and non-discriminatory terms."[169] This provision proved controversial. It was dropped after the European Court of Justice imposed a similar licensing requirement under existing principles of EU competition law in the "Magill case."[170] At the same time, apparently as part of an overall compromise, changes were made in the scope of the right and the exceptions, as well as the provision on rights of lawful users.

The recitals acknowledge the important role of competition policy in the database area.[172] In addition, the directive establishes a procedure for review every three years to determine, among other things, "whether the application of [the *sui generis*] right has led to abuse of a dominant position or other interference with free competition which would justify appropriate measures being taken, including the establishment of non-voluntary licensing arrangements."[173]

. . .

---

[164] Database Directive, art. 10(3). It is unclear whether the new term of protection would apply to the entire database or only the "substantial new investment."

[165] Database Directive, art. 11(1).

[166] *Id.* art. 11(2).

[167] *Id.* art. 11(3).

[168] *Id.* recital (56).

[169] 1992 Proposal, art. 8(1).

[170] Cases C–241/91 P and C–242/91 P, Radio Telefis Eireann v. Commission of the European Communities, E.C.J. (Apr. 6, 1995) (upholding an order by the Commission requiring television broadcasters to license self-generated programming information to competing publishers of program guides on a non-discriminatory basis).

[172] Database Directive, recital (47) . . . .

[173] *Id.*, art. 16 (3).

Pamela Samuelson, *Mapping the Digital Public Domain*
66 LAW & CONTEMP. PROBS. 147 (2003).

. . .

. . . Several times in the past five years, the U.S. Congress has considered legislation to protect the contents of databases akin to that adopted by the European Union in 1996. The EU regime grants those who have invested substantial resources in making a database fifteen years of exclusive rights to control the extraction and reuse of all or substantial parts of the contents of that database. Database rights are renewable upon further expenditures of resources, and substantiality is to be judged in both qualitative as well as quantitative terms. The most recent EU-style database bill introduced into the U.S. Congress was the [Collections of Information Anti–Piracy Act ("CIAA"), H.R. 354].

Although its sponsors characterize CIAA as a regulation of unfair competition, opponents characterize it as an intellectual property regime that is unconstitutional, bad public policy, or both. CIAA differs from the EU Directive in requiring proof of harm to actual or potential markets and in its "reasonable use" limit on the liability of scientific and educational users for extractions and uses of data in protected compilations, as well as in several outright exemptions (e.g., for news reporting, verification, and genealogical information). However, by conferring rights on compilers to control the use or extraction of all or a substantial part of a collection of information that is the product of substantial investment, CIAA would substantially contract the digital public domain—and not just as to items of information, but also as to public domain works (e.g., Shakespeare's plays) which fall within the meaning of "data" under the legislation. The main reason that CIAA has not been enacted is that organizations of scientists and a coalition of Internet-based firms (including prominently Yahoo!) recognized the serious threats that CIAA posed to the digital public domain and mobilized against this legislation. In the aftermath of the September 11 attacks on the World Trade Center and the Pentagon, Congress has other more urgent matters to consider, but like the Terminator, CIAA will almost certainly be back.

Although CIAA and the EU database law pose substantial threats to the digital public domain, more narrowly crafted legislation to protect data compilations against market failures would not. H.R. 1858 is the alternative bill to CIAA considered during the last Congressional session. It forbids duplicating another firm's database and then engaging in direct competition with it. While this bill would, of course, affect the public domain, it does so in a much narrower and more targeted way than CIAA. Assuming there was persuasive evidence that market failures were occurring or imminent in the database industry because firms were competitively duplicating existing databases, this limitation on the reuse of public domain information would be justifiable. This approach is consistent with the Supreme Court's ruling in *International News Service v. Associated Press* which held that INS had engaged in unfair competition with AP when its reporters took news from early editions of AP newspapers and published it verbatim in INS papers directly competing with AP papers. The Supreme Court's *Feist* decision may have said that "raw facts can be copied at will," but the Court qualified this statement with a reference to its *INS v. AP* decision.

. . .

Yochai Benkler, *Constitutional Bounds of Database Protection: The Role of Judicial Review in the Creation and Definition of Private Rights in Information*
15 Berkeley Tech. L.J. 535 (2000).

. . .

[A] law that assigns to some people rights to prevent others from accessing certain information, or communicating in certain ways, must comply with two constitutional constraints.

First, if the nature of the right is an exclusive right intended to create market incentives for its owners, or protect those owners' investments, by permitting them to exclude others from making valuable uses of the information, then Congress may act only within the confines of the Intellectual Property Clause. It may only give such rights in original works. It cannot create such rights as would enclose or burden access to information or knowledge already available to the public, and it cannot give exclusive rights to control ideas or facts. Furthermore, Congress may only enact rights under other clauses of Article I, Section 8, in particular the Commerce Clause, if these rights are different in kind from the rights that it is empowered, within constitutional bounds, to create under the Intellectual Property Clause. Creating a general right, good against the world, in "the news of the day," for example, is beyond the power of Congress.

Second, private rights to control the use of information, whether created within the confines of the Intellectual Property Clause or properly created outside of that framework, are regulations on speech. As such, they are subject to independent and cumulative review under the First Amendment. . . .

IV. CONSTITUTIONALITY OF THE DATABASE PROTECTION BILLS UNDER THE INTELLECTUAL PROPERTY CLAUSE

If the House of Representatives had purposefully tried to create a test case of the constitutional bounds imposed on it by the Intellectual Property Clause, its members could not have done better than to propose the two main opposing database protection bills reported to the House on September 30, 1999. House Bill 354, reported from the Committee on the Judiciary by Representative Coble, creates a property right in raw information in all but name. As reported, House Bill 354 prohibits extraction of information from a database, both for reuse and dissemination and simply for use, and gives database owners the right to track and prevent uses of information extracted from their database into downstream products—whether or not they compete with the database. . . . House Bill 1858, reported from the Committee on Commerce by Representative Bliley, on the other hand, assiduously shies away from property, and attempts to remain within the confines of unfair competition. It addresses competitors only, not users—either consumers or downstream creative users. It prohibits duplication, defined narrowly as slavish copying of the contents of the database without adding value, for sale of this data in competition with the source database. And it vests enforcement in the Federal Trade Commission. As one reviews the background and components of each proposed law, it becomes clear how House Bill 354 fails both the threshold test imposed by the Intellectual Property Clause and the backstop constraint imposed by the First Amendment, while House Bill 1858 survives at least the former, and probably the latter. . . .

. . .

. . . [T]he Intellectual Property Clause requires that intellectual property-like rights in information be enacted, if at all, only within the confines of that clause. In *Feist*, the Supreme Court stated that that clause did not permit recognition of property rights in the information contents of a collection. In regulating information markets under the general commerce power, Congress may only enact regulations that are different in kind from intellectual property rights, like trademark protection. House Bill 354 is functionally an intellectual property right in the information contents of databases, cannot be passed under the Commerce Clause, and is unconstitutional under the Supreme Court's interpretation of the Intellectual Property Clause throughout this century, and more specifically in *Feist*. House Bill 1858, on the other hand, is a law that regulates one particularly ruinous form of competition, and can therefore properly be passed under the Commerce Clause.

V. CONSTITUTIONALITY OF THE DATABASE PROTECTION BILLS UNDER THE FIRST AMENDMENT

. . .

Both database protection bills are regulations on information use and exchange. Both are thus regulations of speech, in the sense that they are subject to First Amendment scrutiny. For the most part, they are both content-neutral, and should be treated as functionally equivalent to structural media regulations—i.e., laws that regulate information production and exchange with the intent of improving information flows, but do so by regulating how people can and cannot, produce, use, and exchange information. These laws are subject to an intermediate level of scrutiny, most plainly stated in [*Turner Broad. Sys., Inc. v. FCC*, 512 U.S. 622 (1994)]. They must be shown to be aimed at an important government interest, to be capable of actually serving that goal, and not to serve that goal in a manner that is much more restrictive of speech than necessary.

House Bill 354 fails this level of intermediate scrutiny both because there is no basis to believe that the important government interest claimed by its drafters really exists, and because even if there were such basis, it regulates speech much more broadly than necessary to attain its stated goal. No serious evidence was presented to Congress or identified by the committee that the database industry in fact needs any new protection. Evidence identified in the Committee Report for House Bill 1858 specifically refutes the claim that there is a need for something like a property right in raw information in databases—whether it is called a sui generis property right or a robust unfair competition rule. The database industry, and in particular its commercial component, have grown robustly both before and after *Feist*. Short of generalized statements of the possibility of "piracy" there was no evidence to suggest that widespread consumer or competitor practices undercut the ability of commercial database producers to support their continued investment in the production, maintenance, and distribution of databases.

Moreover, despite this lack of evidence, House Bill 354 sweeps much more broadly than necessary given those justifications offered–if not supported–by the Committee Report on the bill. Its general prohibition on extraction, its broad definitions of primary and related markets, the sweep of productive uses it captures for the benefit of existing database owners at the expense of future database producers and their consumers, and the property-like protection (in terms of the economic function of the rights created) it provides for the information contained in databases simply cover too many ways in which people want to and can use information in databases. It prohibits or burdens with uncertainty too many valuable uses of information, both commercial and noncommercial, both amateur and professional, which do not complete with, and certainly do not undercut, commercial database producers. In the absence of serious evidence that the database industry is broken, it imposes this heavy burden for a highly speculative gain.

House Bill 1858 is similarly thin on evidence that there is a real need for a new right. Authors of the Committee Report on that bill do little to support that claim, other than begrudgingly admit that database providers sought some protection, and this seems to have been the minimal protection that would do to ameliorate the pressure whose primary product is House Bill 354. Even with respect to its second section, which creates something like a fifteen minute property right in real-time market information, most of the testimony that supported the bill came from online brokers who sought greater access to the information, while those who testified to a market need for such a right in fact supported the much broader rights created in House Bill 354. Nonetheless, the narrowness of the prohibitions created in House Bill 1858, on both its parts and its placing of enforcement responsibility with the Federal Trade Commission, thereby limiting the risk of anticompetitive abuses of the prohibition by database owners, suggest that the harm that would be imposed by this bill, if passed, would be relatively minimal.

EXTENSIONS

1. *Vague scope.* The EU Directive requires member states to enact legislation creating a sui generis right in "a database which shows that there has been qualitatively and/or quantitatively a *substantial investment* in either the obtaining, verification or presentation of the contents." Directive 96/9/EC of the European Parliament and of the Council of the European Union of 11 March, 1996, on the legal protection of databases, 1996 O.J. (L 77) 20, art. 7(1) (emphasis added). H.R. 1858 applies to "items of information that have been collected and organized in a single place, or in such a way as to be accessible through a single source, through the *investment of substantial monetary or other resources*." H.R. 1858, 106th Cong. § 101 (1999) (emphasis added). Similarly, H.R. 1858 defines a duplication of a database as one that is "*substantially the same* as such other database," *id.* § 101 (emphasis added), and H.R. 354 applies to "[a]ny person who extracts all or a *substantial part* of a collection of information." H.R. 354, 106th Cong. § 1402 (1999) (emphasis added). The EU

Database Directive prohibits the "extraction and/or re-utilization of the whole or of a substantial part . . . of the contents of [a] database," while at the same time requiring that "a lawful user of the database [not be prevented] from extracting and/or re-utilizing insubstantial parts of its contents." Directive Arts. 7(1) & 8(1).

Is vague language of this kind likely to strengthen or weaken the incentive to create large commercial databases? Is it likely to encourage or deter the theft of database contents? Is such language unavoidable or a legislative compromise?

2. *The proposed WIPO Database Treaty.* On August 30, 1996, the same day that the World Intellectual Property Organization ("WIPO") released proposal drafts for two treaties that would ultimately be adopted in substantially different form as the WIPO Copyright Treaty and the WIPO Performances and Phonograms Treaty, WIPO also released a third: the Basic Proposal for the Substantive Provisions of the Treaty on Intellectual Property in Respect of Databases. Unlike the other two proposals, this one was not adopted. Nonetheless, it has focused debate and discussion on whether and how to harmonize the international legal protection of databases.

Article 1 of this draft states that "Contracting Parties shall protect any database that represents a substantial investment in the collection, assembly, verification, organization or presentation of the contents of the database." Article 2 states that the term " 'database' means a collection of independent works, data or other materials arranged in a systematic or methodical way and capable of being individually accessed by electronic or other means." Article 3 states that "[t]he maker of a database eligible for protection under this Treaty shall have the right to authorize or prohibit the extraction or utilization of its contents." Article 4 states that "[t]he rights provided under this Treaty shall be owned by the maker of the database" and that they "shall be freely transferable." Article 5 allows that "Contracting Parties may, in their national legislation, provide exceptions to or limitations of the rights provided in this Treaty in certain special cases that do not conflict with the normal exploitation of the database and do not unreasonably prejudice the legitimate interests of the rightholder." Article 6 requires that "[e]ach Contracting Party shall protect according to the terms of this Treaty makers of databases who are nationals of a Contracting Party." Finally, Article 14 and the Annex to the Treaty require that Contracting Parties put in place some form of enforcement procedure the permits the rights in databases to be enforced against acts of infringement.

Based on the foregoing summary of its central provisions, what model of database protection does the proposed WIPO treaty embrace: the intellectual property model or the unfair competition model? Treaties often require implementing legislation. For example, the WIPO Copyright Treaty and the WIPO Performances and Phonograms Treaty were both implemented in the United States by Title I of the Digital Millennium Copyright Act. Given that the proposed WIPO treaty on database protection imposes an obligation on Contracting Parties to enact appropriate implementing legislation, could the United States have entered into this treaty? Or would the U.S. Constitution preclude it? Recall Professor Benkler's arguments, above.

QUESTIONS FOR DISCUSSION

1. *Defining "database."* How the term "database" or "collection of information" is defined in any database protection legislation will greatly affect the nature and scope of the protection provided. Under the statutory definitions presented in H.R. 354 and H.R. 1858, consider whether the following works would be protected:

(a) websites

(b) the bits fixed on the hard drive of a computer

(c) movies on videotape or DVD, and videogame cartridges

(d) a West Reporter

(e) routing tables found on a Internet router

(f) a library

(g) a tax return

(h) a restaurant check

(i) an online discussion group among scientists

(j) a Powerpoint presentation

(k) a scientific paper presenting research results

(l) a scientific journal

(m) an issue of a law review

(n) an L.L.Bean catalog

(o) a distributed database such as the domain name system

(p) your brain

How would you draft a definition for the term "database" or "collection of information"? Try it and apply your definition to the examples listed above.

2. *Clicks vs. bricks.* Should the United States consider adopting database protection legislation that distinguishes between online and offline electronic databases? What about legislation that distinguishes between digital databases and nondigital ones, such as traditional paper-based library card catalogues?

CHAPTER NINE
TECHNOLOGICAL PROTECTION OF DIGITAL GOODS

Created by a college freshman at Northeastern University in 1999, Napster used an innovative file-sharing technology to enable Internet users to download music at no cost via peer-to-peer file sharing. Napster made it easy for users to trade music encoded in the MP3 format, which compresses recordings into small and portable files without any noticeable sacrifice in sound quality. As Napster's popularity increased—at one point it claimed sixty million users—the recording industry filed multiple lawsuits, accusing Napster of encouraging the illegal copying and distribution of copyrighted music, in violation of the copyright laws. At the same time, recording artists, most notably the heavy metal group Metallica, began criticizing Napster for the large-scale distribution of copyrighted music. The company eventually shut down in response to federal court orders.[1]

Yet even after the courts' declarations that users who exchanged copyrighted music via Napster were violating the copyright laws, file sharing continued, hardly abated, through a variety of other file-trading services that sprang up to fill the void created by Napster's demise. The online sharing of digital versions of copyrighted movies has also become widespread: in some cases, pirated versions of movies are available for download from the Internet before they open on the big screen. The unauthorized uploading and downloading of copyrighted software remains a major irritant to software developers, notwithstanding years of aggressive anti-piracy efforts by industry representatives.

The Napster experience, and the persistent unauthorized trade in other information products despite copyright owners' sustained efforts to banish it from the network, suggests two propositions: first, that individuals, and in some cases businesses, are unlikely voluntarily to conform their behavior to what the courts have declared is the mandate of the copyright laws (at least under current market conditions); and second, that efforts by copyright owners to vindicate their rights by taking legal action against infringers are unlikely to reduce unauthorized reproduction and distribution to a level that copyright owners consider acceptable.

What then are copyright owners to do? One approach is to try to control unauthorized access to information products through the use of trusted systems.

A trusted system, also known as a digital rights management system ("DRMS"), is a technological device—usually implemented through computer code—that controls access to or use of an accompanying information product. Such systems prevent a person from making any use of an information product beyond that which the copyright owner has authorized. A trusted system acts as a self-enforcement mechanism, cutting off access to the information product if the user does something not allowed by the license, such as attempting to send a copy to someone else. Developers of trusted systems envision that these programs will be able to structure the entire package of rights the content owner wishes to allow the user, and that they will be able to "negotiate" with the user's computer to arrive at an "agreement" about the package of rights and its price. To encourage the use of trusted

---

[1] For the legal history of these lawsuits, see Chapter 7, Part V, *supra*.

systems, the Digital Millennium Copyright Act of 1998 added provisions to the Copyright Act making it unlawful both to circumvent the access controls employed by trusted systems, and to manufacture, import, or offer to the public products that are designed to circumvent controls on access and use.

The use of trusted systems has generated a good deal of controversy. Some argue that trusted systems will result in more digital products being available to more people at lower costs than ever before. Others maintain that permitting the use of trusted systems upsets the delicate balance between ownership rights and public access created by the law of copyright, shifting the balance in favor of copyright owners at the expense of the public, by allowing owners to prevent uses that the copyright law permits—for example, use of material that is not copyrightable or whose copyright has expired, or use of copyrighted material that is within fair use. Still others argue that the use of such systems permits industry to make unacceptable incursions into the domain of personal privacy, by tracking, recording, and ultimately commercializing users' personal preferences as reflected in their online use of information goods, such as music, electronic books, movies, and games.

In this chapter, we explore the use of trusted systems from several perspectives. In Part I, we look at the technology itself and the ways it can be used. In Part II, we examine the protections for trusted systems added by the Digital Millennium Copyright Act. In Part III, we look at some of the policy debates that the use of trusted systems has occasioned.

I. INTRODUCTION TO TRUSTED SYSTEMS

Mark Stefik & Alex Silverman, *The Bit and the Pendulum: Balancing the Interests of Stakeholders in Digital Publishing*
16 No. 1 COMPUTER LAW. 1 (1999).

Personal computers and computer networks have the potential to become an ideal basis for digital publishing. But the potential for digital publishing remains just that—a potential. The market for digital works remains nascent, because the medium has failed so far to balance the interests of important stakeholders. Computers and the digital medium are sometimes seen as the root of this problem. In this article we explore how computers designed as trusted systems could bring things more into balance.

By digital publishing, we mean the on-line sale and distribution of digital works. A digital work can be anything in digital form: an article, a book, a program, or any multimedia combination involving programming, music, text, and video. The advantages of the digital media include nearly instant distribution, low production costs, and the convenience of 24-hour automated shopping.

When personal computers and desktop publishing first appeared in the early 1980s, many publishers saw digital publishing as too risky. Although numerous factors influenced publishers' judgments in particular cases, the dominant and recurring factor was the fear of widespread unauthorized copying. Realistically concerned about loss of control over their intellectual assets, many publishers avoided the digital medium. From the publishers' perspective, the pendulum representing the balance of power between creators and consumers had swung too far towards consumers.

In the late 1990s, trusted systems began to appear from several vendors, including Folio, IBM, Intertrust, Xerox, and Wave Systems. Trusted systems vary in their hardware and software security arrangements, but in general, they automatically enforce terms and conditions under which digital works can be used. For example, rights can expire after a period of time. Different people can pay different fees for using a work, depending on digital licenses for membership in such groups as affiliated book clubs. Trusted systems differentiate between different uses such as making a digital copy, rendering a work on a screen, printing a work on a color printer, or extracting a portion of a work for inclusion in a new work. When asked to perform an operation not licensed by a work's specific terms and conditions, a trusted system refuses to carry it out. So dramatically do trusted systems alter the balance of power between publishers and consumers, some observers have suggested that the pendulum has now swung too far towards publishers.

. . .

Copyright and Trusted Systems

Beginning in the 1990s, it was realized that computers could become part of the solution to the copyright problem that they were said to cause. The key was the development of trusted systems technology.

There are two main ideas behind trusted systems: that the terms and conditions governing the authorized use of a digital work can be expressed in a computer-interpretable language, and that computers and software can be designed to enforce those terms and conditions. An example of a rights language is Xerox's DPRL (Digital Property Rights Language).

Digital rights cluster into several categories. Transport rights include rights to copy, transfer, or loan a work. Render rights include playing and printing. Derivative work rights govern extracting portions of a work, controlled editing of changes to it, and embedding of the portion in other works. Other rights govern the making and restoring of backup copies. With trusted systems, a publisher can assign rights to a digital work. Each right can specify fees that must be paid to exercise the right. Each right can specify access conditions that govern who can exercise the right.

Trusted systems enforce the terms and conditions. They also exchange copies of the work only with systems that can prove themselves trusted via challenge-response protocols. In exchanging digital works, trusted systems form a closed network of computers that exclude non-trusted systems and collectively support use of digital works under established rules of commerce. When digital works are sent between trusted systems, the works are encrypted. When digital works are rendered—by printing them on paper, displaying them on monitors, or playing them on speakers—the rendering process can embed machine-readable watermark data in the signal to make it easier to trace the source of any external copying of the works.

In general, the higher the security of a trusted system, the higher its cost.

High-security trusted systems can detect any physical tampering, set off alarms, and erase secret key information inside. Intermediate security trusted systems have more modest physical, encryption, and programmatic defenses. Using challenge-response protocols, trusted systems have the capability to recognize other trusted systems and to determine their security levels. For any particular work, publishers can specify the security level required by a trusted system that can receive it. An expensive industry report might require an expensive and secure corporate trusted system with advanced security measures. A digital newspaper for wide distribution and subsidized by advertisements might require only modest security measures for home computers.

Trusted Systems and the Balance of Interests

There are many stakeholders in digital publishing. Beyond the government itself, U.S. copyright law focuses on two parties or categories of people: rights holders (that is, the authors and publishers who hold the copyrights) and the public. However, trusted systems delegate enforcement and control to computers. One of the effects of this delegation is that it introduces third parties to the arrangement, including distributors, trusted system vendors, financial clearing houses, and multiple governments. This complicates the balance of interests, in that it introduces more parties whose interests need to be considered.

The use of trusted systems to enforce terms and conditions provides a much finer grain of control than copyright law, and moves the legal basis of protection in the direction of contracts and licenses. The finer grain of control includes distinctions between different kinds of usage rights such as copying, loaning, printing, displaying, backup, and so on. It also includes provisions for identifying specific users, specific kinds of devices for rendering, and fees for uses. Further, trusted systems provide a finer grain of control in that it becomes possible for rights holders to monitor and negotiate over transactions in copyrighted works in situations where, in the past, such monitoring and negotiation would have been impractical, if not impossible.

Copyright Law

. . .

Without trusted systems, effective enforcement of copyright in the digital medium can be nearly impossible. Like a proverbial sieve with thousands of little holes, it is too hard and expensive to find all the little infringement leaks of isolated individuals making copies. Furthermore, living with the leaks has its own deep risks. By publishing without copyright enforcement in a community that routinely makes unauthorized copies, rights holders risk that, over time, such copying could become established as common practice or even sanctioned by courts as fair use.

In sum, the move toward digital media poses challenges for copyright law and creates uncertainty for rights holders, especially for would-be publishers in the new media. The uncertainty tends to hamper the adoption of the new media and to discourage publishers from publishing in it. The impracticalities of enforcing copyright on untrusted, networked systems, the gray areas of legal interpretation for digital works, the lack of fine-grained control in copyright law, and the risk of an emerging legal claim of fair use for digital copying all motivate would-be authors and publishers in the digital medium to find means other than copyright law for protecting their interests.

Contract Law and Digital Contracts

In a representative scenario of digital publication on a trusted system, an author begins by creating a digital work. When the work is ready, the author finds a publisher (possibly himself) to develop the work further and to sell it. The publisher develops a set of terms and conditions for use of the work. Using a rights management language like DPRL, the publisher specifies the time period over which the rights apply. He determines what rights to include, for example, whether printing is allowed, whether the work can be loaned out for free, whether there is a special discount for members of a particular book club. He may assign different fees for different rights. For example, he may decide either to disallow creation of derivative works or to encourage creation of such works as a source of further revenue. He may mandate that the reader of the digital work must have proof in the form of a proper digital certificate that he is over 18. In DPRL, each right specification statement includes a type of right, a time specification governing when the right is valid, an access specification governing any special licenses required to exercise the right, and a fee specification governing billing. Using a trusted system, these rights are associated with the digital work, either by bundling them together in an encrypted file or by assigning the work a unique digital identifier and by registering the work and its rights in an on-line database.

Why would a publisher or a consumer want to have a specific and detailed agreement about use? The alternative, based on copyright as used for most printed works, is to have a single fee to purchase a work and then general legal standards about how works can be used. In the previous section we considered motivations for publishers to use specialized terms and conditions for their digital works. Specialized rules also have potential economic advantages for consumers. In the established software market, a software license is typically purchased for a fixed fee. This means that a user who expects to make little use of a software product must pay the same fee as someone who would use it for many hours a day. In some markets, this situation is bad for both publishers and consumers because many low-usage consumers will decide not to purchase the software at all. Trusted systems offer the possibility of differential pricing and "metered use" in which the amount that someone pays to use software depends on how much they use it. One way to look at metered use is that it allows "renting" software, where the rental terms can be flexible enough to provide for decreasing costs or caps with increased volume of use.

Another example of mutual economic advantages concerns the first sale doctrine. When consumers buy a paper book, they receive and own the copy of the book. When they are done with the book, they are free to give it to a friend or to sell the book to someone else. The first sale doctrine from copyright law guarantees these rights. In the DPRL language, the analogous usage right is called a transfer right. When one trusted system transfers a digital work to a second trusted system, the copy on the first trusted system is deleted or deactivated so that it can no longer be used. Analogous to handing a book to a friend, a transfer operation preserves the number of usable copies of the work. Analogous to the first sale doctrine, the terms and conditions on a digital work could allow it to be transferred at no charge.

A free transfer right is exactly what a consumer might want if he or she were buying the digital work for a friend, or intended to share the work serially with others. On the other hand, from a publisher's perspective, a free transfer right is a threat to future sales. If each person who reads a copy of a digital work needs to buy their own copy, the publisher would sell more copies. A publisher could offer two different combinations of rights with a work. In one combination, the consumer pays the "standard" amount for a work, and can transfer the work without a fee just as with the first sale doctrine. In another combination, the consumer gets a discount for a non-transferable work or must pay a fee to transfer it. This discounted purchase might be preferred by a consumer who buys the work for his personal use and who does not anticipate giving it away. Arguably, the first sale doctrine is grounded in experience with paper-based works and the copies were treated as physical objects, independent of their creative content. Like tools or food, such physical objects could be resold at the owner's convenience. Enforcement of a law to prevent resale or giving of books would be difficult in any case, so the first sale doctrine makes sense for paper-based works. For digital works and trusted systems, these considerations are less relevant. The publisher and the consumer are free to enter into an agreement that each sees as economically advantageous.

In many ways, a set of terms and conditions in DPRL is much like a contract or license agreement for using a digital work. For convenience here, we will call such a set of terms and conditions a digital contract. However, it should be remembered that a digital contract differs from an ordinary contract in crucial ways. Notably, in an ordinary contract between people, compliance is not automatic and is the responsibility of the agreeing parties. There may be provisions for monitoring and checking compliance with the terms and conditions, but the responsibility for acting in accordance with the terms falls on the parties, and enforcement of the contract is ultimately the province of the courts. In contrast, with trusted systems, a substantial part of the enforcement of a digital contract is carried out by the trusted systems themselves. In the short term, at least, the consumer does not have an option to disregard a digital contract, for example, to make infringing copies of a digital work. A trusted system will refuse to exercise a right that is not sanctioned by the digital contract. Over the longer term, it may be possible for consumers or consumer advocacy groups to negotiate with publishers to obtain different terms and conditions in the digital contracts, but even then, the new digital contracts will be subject to automatic enforcement by trusted systems.

. . .

Courts provide checks and balances in contract law by deciding what contracts to enforce and how to interpret the terms and conditions of those contracts. With properly designed trusted systems, many of these checks and balances can be made available automatically. Consider a digital publishing scenario again. The author has finished the work and the publisher assigns terms and conditions. Just as there can be conventional (so-called "boilerplate") language used in putting together an agreement, there can be digital boilerplate in the form of templates and default conditions in setting up a digital contract. Suppose that the publisher has included some very unusual terms and conditions in the agreement. When the consumer's trusted system is in communication with the publisher's trusted system, it can first retrieve the terms and conditions of the digital contract. It shows these to the consumer. Before the consumer accepts receipt of the digital work, a program can check for and highlight unusual conditions in the digital contract. Because rights management languages like DPRL are simple and formal languages with limited complexity, simple grammar and predetermined meanings, this checking is straightforward for a computer. In particular, the contract checker can look for unusual or high fees on certain rights, unrealistic expiration dates, or any other requirement that is outside of the usual practice. (As a somewhat bizarre example, consider a digital work that the consumer can copy for free but, surprisingly and inconveniently, costs $10 to delete.) The consumer is given an opportunity to agree to the terms and accept delivery or to refuse the terms and not take delivery of the work. If the consumer agrees, his trusted system can digitally sign a form marking his agreement to the contract. This signing can be digitally notarized by a third party (a "digital notary") known to both parties.

The sequence of events in this example illustrates several checks and balances in the process. Both the publisher and the consumer can use computational aids to check the normalcy and appropriateness of the contract. More than being a labor-saving or time-saving procedure, this approach also helps to compensate for the somewhat less tangible nature of information inside computers. It gives increased confidence to both parties that the terms and conditions used by the trusted systems will be reasonable.

It is helpful to think of a digital contract as encompassing several distinct legal contracts. There is the contract for access to the copyrighted work itself. Further, there is a contract for the service of delivering digital data to the consumer, irrespective of whether that data is or can be copyrighted. For example, if the publisher provides an uncopyrightable database or telephone white pages directory to the consumer via a trusted system, the publisher can fairly charge for this service, even though the consumer could, in principle, get the uncopyrightable data elsewhere or put together the database himself. Similarly, the digital publisher could charge the consumer for a copy of the complete works of Shakespeare even though that is in the public domain, just as print publishers can charge for printed copies of Shakespeare's works. Put another way, like the print publisher, the digital publisher has made life more convenient for the consumer, and the consumer pays the publisher for this convenience. What the publisher of an uncopyrightable or public domain work cannot do is to prevent another publisher from offering consumers the same or a comparable work, as would be the case if the work were copyrighted. Finally, there is a third contract implicit in the digital contract, namely, the service agreement by which the consumer is entitled to access the network of trusted systems in the first place. This agreement may be arranged between the consumer and the publisher, or between the consumer and one or more network service providers who may or may not be affiliated with the publisher.

The idea that a digital contract includes multiple legal contracts provides a coherent rationale for why digital contracts ought to be enforceable, even as to uncopyrightable works. For example, suppose that a publisher provides a public domain work, such as the complete works of Shakespeare, to the consumer via a trusted system. However, the digital contract for this work prohibits the consumer from copying or further transferring the contents of the work, at least not in digital form. The consumer is unhappy about this. He knows that the work is not protected by copyright and, when the bill arrives from the publisher, he refuses to pay, or else sues to get his money back. In court, the consumer argues that for the publisher to charge for what is no longer protected by copyright is in violation of the policy of copyright to establish limited-term monopolies for authors. Therefore, says the consumer, the digital contract should be preempted by the Copyright Act and should be held unenforceable. (The consumer might also argue that, because the publisher accepts the consumer's money while providing in return only a public domain work that ought to be available for free, the agreement fails for lack of consideration). The publisher responds that what is being sold here isn't the work, but rather the service of delivering the work. The publisher says, in effect, "Consumer, by dealing with me, you save time and energy and money over other delivery mechanisms such as conventional bookstores. But if I, as vendor, want to continue successfully to provide this service to others, then I am entitled to collect revenue at every transaction, not just the first one. Therefore, I can legitimately prevent you by this digital contract from transferring the copy of the work I just sold you." We think that the publisher has the better argument here. The consumer can pay the publisher for the right to print out the contents of the book, and can then copy the contents, for example, by hand or by scanning with an untrusted optical scanner. Also, other publishers can produce similar books containing identical texts, and a not-for-profit library could make these texts available for free. In short, the publisher has not overstepped the bounds of copyright.

Another point of possible concern with a digital contract is the extent to which a user is realistically in a position to negotiate the terms of the contract. In court cases concerning the viability of shrinkwrap licenses, one of the legal arguments used to challenge the validity of the license is that a publisher has an advantaged position of power and leaves the user with only a "take it or leave it" proposition. In this situation, many consumers do not bother to read the shrinkwrap license. In the case of trusted systems, it may be important that a consumer agent could be called upon to highlight terms and conditions likely to be unacceptable. In principle, one of the options when such terms are found is for the trusted systems to open a channel for negotiation and possible change of the terms. It is worth noting, however, that one of the main advantages of digital publishing is the possibility of fully automated systems providing 24–hour shopping convenience. In that setting, one might not expect to negotiate the terms of purchase for a mass-market digital work any more than one would expect to negotiate the price of buying a best-seller paperback at a convenience store in the middle of the night. The consumer would simply have to either accept the terms as they stand, or postpone her purchase until such time as a human agent became available to negotiate the terms.

. . .

QUESTIONS FOR DISCUSSION

1. *Implementation of trusted systems.* Digital rights management systems along the lines described in this article have been implemented in several contexts. The Serial Copy Management System, discussed in Chapter 7, Part IV(C)(2), *supra*, has been required for digital audio tape machines since 1992. More recently, some music CDs have been released with coding designed to prevent them from being copied using a CD–RW drive, or even being played on a computer. Motion pictures on DVD are protected by an encryption system called the Content Scramble System, which is designed to prevent unauthorized copying. As discussed in *Universal City Studios, Inc. v. Reimerdes*, excerpted in Part II, *infra*, CSS was cracked and circumvented by a 15-year-old Norwegian computer hobbyist, giving rise to several lawsuits and creating a cause célèbre for both proponents and opponents of trusted systems. Movie DVDs also contain regional coding, which prevents a DVD purchased in one region of the world from playing on a DVD player sold in a different region of the world. Electronic books are released with DRMS technology provided by several manufacturers, including Palm, Microsoft, and Adobe. What are the obstacles to the further implementation of systems such as these?

2. *Limiting users' rights.* The rights that one has with respect to a digital product (a music CD, a movie on DVD, software, data, a text) one purchases may be limited through several methods. First, the copyright laws limit the purchaser's right to copy, adapt, distribute, perform, and display works to which copyright applies. Second, one's rights may be limited by an accompanying set of terms, usually called a license agreement, that is deemed part of the contract between the parties. Third, one's rights may be limited by a digital rights management system incorporated into the product. In what ways do these three methods of limiting the purchaser's rights differ, from the standpoint of both vendor and purchaser? Consider the extent to which such terms may be negotiated; the ability of the parties to renegotiate disputed terms; the availability of legal defenses to enforcement; the costs of enforcement.

3. *A technological arms race.* Trusted systems, like any other technology, are susceptible to circumvention. A piece of computer code designed to prevent unauthorized access to an informational good may be defeated by another piece of computer code. The latter code may itself be neutralized by a counter-measure that plugs the loophole it exploited, giving rise to a circumvention that exploits some different loophole. This has led to a sort of technological arms race, in which trusted-system creators and hackers take turns outwitting one another. Who do you think is more likely to win this arms race: the lock-makers, or the lock-breakers? Do you agree with amateur cryptographer Edgar Allen Poe: "[I]t may be roundly asserted that human ingenuity cannot concoct a cipher which human ingenuity cannot resolve."?[2]

Suppose that the locks are effective enough to keep out all but a tiny proportion of the population, the hacker aristocracy, who are able to defeat any trusted system in existence. Should copyright owners feel safe? Do you agree with the following analogy, offered by Professor Lessig?: "[F]rom the fact that 'hackers could break any security system,' it no more follows that security systems are irrelevant than it follows from the fact that 'a locksmith can pick any lock' that locks are irrelevant. Locks, like security systems on com-

---

[2] Edgar Allan Poe, *A Few Words on Secret Writing*, GRAHAM'S MAGAZINE, July 1841, at 33, 33.

puters, will be quite effective, even if there are norm-oblivious sorts who can break them." Lawrence Lessig, *Reading the Constitution in Cyberspace*, 45 EMORY L.J. 869, 896 n.80 (1996). In the digital world, is there an argument that any system that is less than 100 percent effective is practically worthless?

4. *iTunes and arms races.* Amid the numerous P2P file sharing programs that allow end users to share copyright-protected material there are emerging pay-per-download services. One such service is Apple's *iTunes Music Store*. This service, which has the endorsement of the major music companies and the RIAA, allows a user to download a song for 99 cents and "share" the music on three Macintosh computers that she designates. The song will not play on any machine not so designated.

A feature of the software that is used to download and manage songs, called *Rendezvous,* allowed users to share the purchased song (via "streaming") over a LAN. Users soon discovered that *any* file could be shared over the network using the *Rendezvous* function. (Why would this be an issue from Apple's standpoint?) In response to this discovery, Apple updated the software to disable this capability. There soon followed independent free software, called *iCommune 401(ok)*, that restored this functionality. This software utilized computer code licensed by Apple, which subsequently revoked the license. *See* iCommune, icommune.sourceforge.net. The author of the software then released a stand-alone version of the program that did not use any proprietary code requiring a license from Apple.

This is an example of the technological arms race discussed in Question 3, *supra.* In light of this example, reconsider the questions posed in that Question.

II. SPECIAL PROTECTION FOR TECHNOLOGICAL MANAGEMENT SYSTEMS: TITLE I OF THE DIGITAL MILLENNIUM COPYRIGHT ACT

Congress responded to the technological arms race described above, weighing in on the side of the trusted-system community, with Title I of the Digital Millennium Copyright Act of 1998 ("DMCA"), 17 U.S.C. §§ 1201–05. The drive for regulation of this kind developed in the mid–1990s when the World International Property Organization ("WIPO") Copyright Treaty and the WIPO Performances and Phonograms Treaty were negotiated. Article 11 of the WIPO Copyright Treaty, titled "Obligations concerning Technological Measures," requires:

> Contracting Parties shall provide adequate legal protection and effective legal remedies against the circumvention of effective technological measures that are used by authors in connection with the exercise of their rights under this Treaty or the Berne Convention and that restrict acts, in respect of their works, which are not authorized by the authors concerned or permitted by law.

WIPO Copyright Treaty, Dec. 20, 1996, art. 11, WIPO Doc. CRNR/DC/94, www.wipo.int/eng/diplconf/distrib/94dc.htm.

In addition, Article 12 of the same treaty, "Obligations concerning Rights Management Information," states:

> (1) Contracting Parties shall provide adequate and effective legal remedies against any person knowingly performing any of the following acts knowing, or with respect to civil remedies having reasonable grounds to know, that it will induce, enable, facilitate or conceal an infringement of any right covered by this Treaty or the Berne Convention:
>
> (i) to remove or alter any electronic rights management information without au-

thority;

(ii) to distribute, import for distribution, broadcast or communicate to the public, without authority, works or copies of works knowing that electronic rights management information has been removed or altered without authority.

(2) As used in this Article, "rights management information" means information which identifies the work, the author of the work, the owner of any right in the work, or information about the terms and conditions of use of the work, and any numbers or codes that represent such information, when any of these items of information is attached to a copy of a work or appears in connection with the communication of a work to the public.

Id. art. 12. Nearly identical provisions can also be found in the WIPO Performances and Phonograms Treaty. *See* WIPO Performances and Phonograms Treaty, Dec. 20, 1996, arts. 18 & 19, WIPO Doc. CRNR/DC/95, www.wipo.org/eng/diplconf/distrib/95dc.htm. Enactment of Title I of the DMCA was intended to meet the obligations of the United States under both of these treaties.

A Senate Report on the DMCA describes Title I as follows:

Title I implements the WIPO Copyright Treaty and the WIPO Performances and Phonograms Treaty. These treaties were concluded by the Clinton administration in December 1996. The treaties are best understood as supplements to the Berne Convention for the Protection of Literary and Artistic Works. The Berne Convention is the leading multilateral treaty on copyright and related rights, with 130 countries adhering to it. The United States ratified the Berne Convention in 1989. The two new WIPO treaties were adopted at a diplomatic conference by a consensus of over 150 countries. In general, the Copyright Treaty updates the Berne Convention for digital works and the growth of the Internet and other digital communications networks, and the Performances and Phonograms Treaty supplements the Berne Convention with comprehensive copyright protection for performances and sound recordings (called "phonograms" in international parlance).

The importance of the treaties to the protection of American copyrighted works abroad cannot be overestimated. The treaties, as well as the Berne Convention, are based on the principle of national treatment; that is, that adhering countries are obliged to grant the same protection to foreign works that they grant to domestic works. Even more importantly, the Berne Convention and the treaties set minimum standards of protection. Thus, the promise of the treaties is that, in an increasing[ly] global digital marketplace, U.S. copyright owners will be able to rely upon strong, non-discriminatory copyright protection in most of the countries of the world.

The copyright industries are one of America's largest and fastest growing economic assets. . . . In fact, the copyright industries contribute more to the U.S. economy and employ more workers than any single manufacturing sector, including chemicals, industrial equipment, electronics, food processing, textiles and apparel, and aircraft. More significantly for the WIPO treaties, in 1996 U.S. copyright industries achieved foreign sales and exports of $60.18 billion, for the first time leading all major industry sectors, including agriculture, automobiles and auto parts, and the aircraft industry.

The WIPO treaties contain many important provisions. For example, the Copyright Treaty contains significant provisions such as: . . . (5) an obligation to provide "legal protection and effective legal remedies" against circumventing technological measures, e.g. encryption and password protection, that are used by copyright owners to protect their works from piracy; and (6) an obligation to provide "adequate and effective legal remedies" to preserve the integrity of "rights management information." . . .

The Committee believes that in order to adhere to the WIPO treaties, legislation is necessary in two primary areas–anticircumvention of technological protection measures and protection of the integrity of rights management information, or "copyright management information" (CMI), as it is referred to in the bill. This view is shared by the Clinton administration. In drafting implementing legislation for the WIPO treaties, the Committee has sought to address those two areas, as well as avoid government regulation of the Internet and encourage technological solutions. The Committee is keenly aware that other countries will use U.S. legislation as a model.

S. REP. NO. 105–190, at 9–11 (1998).

A. USING AND TRAFFICKING IN CIRCUMVENTION TECHNOLOGIES

Title I of the DMCA added Chapter 12 to Title 17 of the U.S. Code. The first section of this chapter, Section 1201, deals with using and trafficking in circumvention technologies. Section 1201(a)(1)(A) makes it illegal to "circumvent a technological measure that effectively controls access to a work protected under" the Copyright Act. Section 1201(a)(2) provides:

No person shall manufacture, import, offer to the public, provide, or otherwise traffic in any technology, product, service, device, component, or part thereof, that—

(A) is primarily designed or produced for the purpose of circumventing a technological measure that effectively controls access to a work protected under this title;

(B) has only limited commercially significant purpose or use other than to circumvent a technological measure that effectively controls access to a work protected under this title; or

(C) is marketed by that person or another acting in concert with that person with that person's knowledge for use in circumventing a technological measure that effectively controls access to a work protected under this title.

Section 1201(b)(1) further provides:

No person shall manufacture, import, offer to the public, provide, or otherwise traffic in any technology, product, service, device, component, or part thereof, that—

(A) is primarily designed or produced for the purpose of circumventing protection afforded by a technological measure that effectively protects a right of a copyright owner under this title in a work or a portion thereof;

(B) has only limited commercially significant purpose or use other than to circumvent protection afforded by a technological measure that effectively protects a right of a copyright owner under this title in a work or a portion thereof; or

(C) is marketed by that person or another acting in concert with that person with that person's knowledge for use in circumventing protection afforded by a technological measure that effectively protects a right of a copyright owner under this title in a work or a portion thereof.

Section 1201 thus addresses two types of technological protections of copyrighted works, and two types of forbidden conduct in connection with those protections. The two types of technological protections are those that prevent unauthorized *access* to a work, and those that prevent *use* of a work in a manner that infringes the copyright. The two types of forbidden conduct are the *act of circumventing* a technological protection, and the manufacturing or distribution of a device or software program that disables such a protection, generally referred to as *trafficking*. As a matter of logic, the combination of two technological protections with two types of prohibited conduct could yield four (two times two) prohibitions. In fact, however, Section 1201 only addresses three of those combinations. With respect to the first type of technological protection (preventing unauthorized access), it is illegal both to circumvent it and to traffic in technologies of circumvention. With respect to the second type of technological protection (preventing unauthorized use), it is illegal to traffic in technologies of circumvention, but there is no prohibition against the act of circumvention. The prohibitions of Section 1201 may be represented graphically:

		Type of technological protection	
		Access controls	Use controls
Type of prohibition	Prohibition on circumvention	§ 1201(a)(1)(A)	None
	Prohibition on trafficking	§ 1201(a)(2)	§ 1201(b)(1)

Why does Section 1201 contain no prohibition against the act of circumventing protection of the rights of a copyright owner? The Senate Report explains:

> The prohibition in 1201(a)(1) is necessary because prior to this Act, the conduct of circumvention was never before made unlawful. The device limitation in 1201(a)(2) enforces this new prohibition on conduct. The copyright law has long forbidden copyright infringements, so no new prohibition [on conduct facilitated by the devices prohibited in 1201(b)] was necessary. The device limitation in 1201(b) enforces the longstanding prohibitions on infringements.

S. REP. NO. 105–190, *supra*, at 12.

Thus, according to the Senate Report a prohibition on the act of circumventing a technological measure that prevents infringement of a copyright—which would occupy the upper right-hand box in the above chart—is unnecessary, because it would be redundant with the central provision of the Copyright Act, 17 U.S.C. § 106.

In addition to setting forth the preceding anti-circumvention and anti-trafficking prohibitions, Section 1201 also creates a series of exceptions to them. There are exemptions from the anti-circumvention provisions for nonprofit libraries and educational institutions, law enforcement and intelligence agents, reverse engineering computer programs, encryption research, filtering Web content to determine if it is appropriate for minors, protection of privacy, and testing computer and network security. *See* 17 U.S.C. § 1201(d)–(j). (Some of these exemptions also apply, to a limited extent, to the anti-trafficking provisions.) Moreover, Section 1201(a)(1)(B)–(E) empowers the Librarian of Congress, upon recommendation from the Register of Copyrights, to create additional exceptions to the prohibition against circumventing access controls. Pursuant to this subsection, the Librarian has exempted (through October 27, 2006) additional narrow categories of use: compilations consisting of lists of Internet locations blocked by certain filtering software; software and videogames protected by certain obsolete, damaged, or malfunctioning access controls; and literary works distributed in e-book formats that disable the e-book's read-aloud function. 37 C.F.R. § 201.40. It remains to be seen whether these exceptions can satisfy the concerns of advocates of broader rights for users of protected materials.

Beyond the prohibitions and exceptions created by this section, Section 1201(c)(1) & (2) emphasize that none of the foregoing "shall affect rights, remedies, limitations, or defenses to copyright infringement, including fair use," or "shall enlarge or diminish vicarious or contributory liability for copyright infringement in connection with any technology, product, service, device, component, or part thereof." Moreover, with one exception, Section 1201(c)(3) states that manufacturers of consumer electronics, telecommunications equipment, and computer products are not required to design their products so that they accommodate access and use controls. The one exception is created by Section 1201(k), which requires manufacturers, importers, and distributors of certain devices such as VCRs and camcorders to produce, import and traffic only in devices that employ the copy control technology developed and owned by Macrovision Corporation.[3] By requiring the use of a specific technology, this provision contrasts sharply with the rest of the DMCA, which strives to remain technology-neutral.

To set the stage for examination of the continuing controversies surrounding the DMCA, consider the following portions of its legislative history. While reading it, think about how Congress characterizes the problem the legislation is supposed to solve, and how it conceives of the fit between this statute and pre-existing copyright law. Consider, as well, what role is played by Congress's understanding of existing and foreseeable encryption technology. What interest groups do you think were most influential in crafting this legislation?

Section–By–Section Analysis of H.R. 2281
House Committee on the Judiciary, 105th Congress (Comm. Print 1998).

. . .

Section 1201: Circumvention of Copyright Protection Systems.

Subsection (a) of new Section 1201 applies when a person who is not authorized to have access to a work seeks to gain access by circumventing a technological measure put in place by the copyright owner that effectively controls access to the work.
. . .

[§ 1201(a)(1).] The act of circumventing a technological protection measure put in place by a copyright owner to control access to a copyrighted work is the electronic equivalent of breaking into a locked room in order to obtain a copy of a

---

[3] The reference to Macrovision Corp. occurs not in the statute, but only in the legislative history. *See* H.R. Conf. Rep. No. 105–796, at 67–69 (1998).

book. Subparagraph (A) establishes a general prohibition against gaining unauthorized access to a work by circumventing a technological measure put in place by the copyright owner where such measure effectively controls access to a work protected under Title 17 of the U.S. Code. . . .

. . .

. . . The technological measures — such as encryption, scrambling and electronic envelopes — that this bill protects can be deployed, not only to prevent piracy and other economically harmful unauthorized uses of copyrighted materials, but also to support new ways of disseminating copyrighted materials to users, and to safeguard the availability of legitimate uses of those materials by individuals. These technological measures may make more works more widely available, and the process of obtaining permissions easier.

For example, an access control technology under section 1201(a) would not necessarily prevent access to a work altogether, but could be designed to allow access during a limited time period, such as during a period of library borrowing. Technological measures are also essential to a distribution strategy that allows a consumer to purchase a copy of a single article from an electronic database, rather than having to pay more for a subscription to a journal containing many articles the consumer does not want.

. . .

[§ 1201(a)(2)]. In order to provide meaningful protection and enforcement of the copyright owner's right to control access to his or her copyrighted work, this paragraph supplements the prohibition against the act of circumvention in [§ 1201(a)(1)] with prohibitions on creating and making available certain technologies, products and services used, developed or advertised to defeat technological protections against unauthorized access to a work. . . .

Specifically, [§ 1201(a)(2)] prohibits manufacturing, importing, offering to the public, providing, or otherwise trafficking in certain technologies, products, services, devices, components, or parts that can be used to circumvent a technological protection measure that otherwise effectively controls access to a work protected under Title 17. It is drafted carefully to target "black boxes," and to ensure that legitimate multipurpose devices can continue to be made and sold. For a technology, product, service, device, component, or part thereof to be prohibited under this subsection, one of three conditions must be met. It must:

(1) be primarily designed or produced for the purpose of circumventing;

(2) have only a limited commercially significant purpose or use other than to circumvent; or

(3) be marketed by the person who manufactures it, imports it, offers it to the public, provides it or otherwise traffics in it, or by another person acting in concert with that person, for use in circumventing a technological protection measure that effectively controls access to a work protected under Title 17.

This provision is designed to protect copyright owners, and simultaneously allow the development of technology.

This three-part test, established for determining when the manufacture, distribution or other provision of a product or service constitutes a violation, is the core of the anti-circumvention provisions of this legislation. This test (also spelled out in 1201(b)(1)), as explicated by the Judiciary Committee report, stands on its own. While this legislation is aimed primarily at "black boxes" that have virtually no legitimate uses, trafficking in any product or service that meets one or more of the three points in this test could lead to liability. It is not required to prove that the device in question was "expressly intended to facilitate circumvention." At the same time, the manufacturers of legitimate consumer products such as personal computers, VCR's, and the like have nothing to fear from this legislation because those legitimate devices do not meet the three-part test. The *Sony* test of "capab[ility] of substantial non-infringing uses," while still operative in cases claiming contributory infringement of copyright, is not part of this legislation, however. *Sony Corporation of America v. Universal City Studios, Inc.,* 464 U.S. 417 (1984). The relevant test, spelled out in the plain and unchanged language of the bill, is whether or not a product or service "has only limited commercially significant purpose or use other than to circumvent."

. . .

The Committee on the Judiciary, which possesses primary jurisdiction over this legislation, considered the argument that the lack of a definition of "technological measure" leaves manufacturers in the dark as to the range of protective technologies to which their products must respond. The Committee concluded that any such concern is unfounded. No legitimate manufacturer of consumer electronics devices or computer equipment could reasonably claim to be left in doubt about the course of action to be avoided, simply because the phrase "technological measure" is not itself defined in the bill. The only obligation imposed on manufacturers by this legislation is a purely negative one: to refrain from affirmatively designing a product or a component *primarily* for the purpose of circumventing a protective technology that effectively controls unauthorized access to or uses of a copyrighted work.

Any effort to read into this bill what is not there—a statutory definition of "technological measure"—or to define in terms of particular technologies what constitutes an "effective" measure, could inadvertently deprive legal protection to some of the copy or access control technologies that are or will be in widespread use for the protection of both digital and analog formats. Perhaps more importantly, this approach runs a substantial risk of discouraging innovation in the development of protective technologies. For instance, today the standard form of encryption of digital materials involves scrambling its contents so that they are unintelligible unless processed with a key supplied by the copyright owner or its agent. However, in a field that changes and advances as rapidly as encryption research, it would be short-sighted to write this definition into a statute as the exclusive technological means protected by this bill.

. . .

[§ 1201(b)] applies when a person has obtained authorized access to a copy or a

phonorecord of a work, but the copyright owner has put in place technological measures that effectively protect his or her rights under Title 17 to control or limit the nature of the use of the copyrighted work.

[§ 1201(b)(1)]. Paralleling subsection (a)(2), above, [§ 1201(b)(1)] seeks to provide meaningful protection and enforcement of copyright owners' use of technological measures to protect their rights under Title 17 by prohibiting the act of making or selling the technological means to overcome these protections and facilitate copyright infringement. Paragraph (1) prohibits manufacturing, importing, offering to the public, providing, or otherwise trafficking in certain technologies, products, services, devices, components, or parts thereof that can be used to circumvent a technological measure that effectively protects a right of a copyright owner under Title 17 in a work or portion thereof. Again, for a technology, product, service, device, component, or part thereof to be prohibited under this subsection, one of three conditions must be met. It must:

(1) be primarily designed or produced for the purpose of circumventing;

(2) have only limited commercially significant purpose or use other than to circumvent; or

(3) be marketed by the person who manufactures it, imports it, offers it to the public, provides it, or otherwise traffics in it, or by another person acting in concert with that person, for use in circumventing a technological protection measure that effectively protects the right of a copyright owner under Title 17 in a work or a portion thereof.

Like subsection (a)(2), this provision is designed to protect copyright owners, and simultaneously allow the development of technology.

[§ 1201(b)(2)] defines certain terms used in subsection (b):

(1) "circumvent protection afforded by a technological measure" is defined as "avoiding, bypassing, removing, deactivating, or otherwise impairing a technological measure."

(2) "effectively protects a right of a copyright owner under Title 17"—a technological measure effectively protects a right of a copyright owner under Title 17 "if the measure, in the ordinary course of its operation, prevents, restricts, or otherwise limits the exercise of a right under Title 17 of a copyright owner."

. . .

[§ 1201(c)] provides that section 1201 shall not have any effect on rights, remedies, limitations, or defenses to copyright infringement, including fair use, under Title 17. Paragraph (2) provides that section 1201 shall not alter the existing doctrines of contributory or vicarious liability for copyright infringement in connection with any technology, product, service, device, component or part thereof. Together, these provisions are intended to ensure that none of the provisions in section 1201 affect the existing legal regime established in the Copyright Act and case law interpreting that statute.

. . .

[§ 1201(f)] is intended to allow legitimate software developers to continue engaging in certain activities for the purpose of achieving interoperability to the extent permitted by law prior to the enactment of this chapter. The objective is to ensure that the effect of current case law interpreting the Copyright Act is not changed by enactment of this legislation for certain acts of identification and analysis done in respect of computer programs. *See Sega Enterprises Ltd.* v. *Accolade, Inc.,* 977 F.2d 1510 (9th Cir.1992). The purpose of this subsection is to avoid hindering competition and innovation in the computer and software industry.

[§ 1201(f)(1)] permits the circumvention of access control technologies for the sole purpose of achieving software interoperability. For example, this subsection permits a software developer to circumvent an access control technology applied to a portion or portions of a program in order to perform the necessary steps to identify and analyze the information needed to achieve interoperability. . . . [T]he goal of this section is to ensure that current law is not changed, and not to encourage or permit infringement. Thus, each of the acts undertaken must fall within the scope of fair use or otherwise avoid infringing the copyright of the author of the underlying computer program.

[§ 1201(f)(2)] recognizes that to accomplish the acts permitted under paragraph (1) a person may, in some instances, have to make and use certain tools. In most instances these will be generally available tools that programmers use in developing computer programs, such as compilers, trace analyzers and disassemblers, which do not fall within the prohibition of this section. In certain instances, it is possible that a person may have to develop special tools to achieve the permitted purpose of interoperability. Thus, this provision creates an exception to the prohibition on making circumvention tools contained in sections 1201(a)(2) and (b). These tools can be either software or hardware. Again, this provision is limited by a general ban on acting in a way that constitutes infringing activity.

. . .

[§ 1201(f)(4)] defines "interoperability" as the ability of computer programs to exchange information, and for such programs mutually to use the information which has been exchanged. The seamless exchange of information is a key element of creating an interoperable independently created program. This provision applies to computer programs as such, regardless of their medium of fixation and not to works generally, such as music or audiovisual works, which may be fixed and distributed in digital form. Accordingly, since the goal of interoperability is the touchstone of the exceptions contained in paragraphs (1)–(3), nothing in those paragraphs can be read to authorize the circumvention of any technological protection measure that controls access to any work other than a computer program, or the trafficking in products or services for that purpose.

[§ 1201(g)] is intended to facilitate the purpose of this bill, namely, to improve the ability of copyright owners to prevent the theft of their works, including by applying technological measures. . . .

. . . This subsection provides that generally available encryption testing tools meeting certain specifications will not be made illegal by this Act. If each of these tools has a legitimate and substantial commercial purpose—testing security and effectiveness—it is therefore explicitly excluded from the prohibition in section 1201.

In addition to the exemption contained in this subsection, the testing of specific encryption algorithms would not fall within the scope of 1201, since mathematical formulas as such are not protected by copyright. . . .

. . .

[An] example would be a company, in the course of developing a new cryptographic product, sponsoring a crypto-cracking contest with cash prizes. Contestants would not violate section 1201, since the research acts are specifically authorized.

Significantly, section 1201 does not make illegal cryptographic devices that have substantial legitimate purposes other than to circumvent technological protection measures as applied to a work. For example, many popular word processing and other computer programs include a security feature allowing users to password-protect documents (employing a low-grade form of encryption.) It is not uncommon for users of such products to forget or lose their passwords for such documents, making their own protected works unrecoverable. As a result, many independent programmers have created utilities designed to assist in the recovery of passwords or password-protected works. Several of these utilities are distributed over the Internet as freeware or shareware. Because these utilities have a substantial legitimate use, and because they would be used by persons to gain access to their own works, these devices do not violate section 1201.

. . .

Today, network and website management and security tools increasingly contain components that automatically test a system's security and identify common vulnerabilities. These programs are valuable tools for systems administrators and website operators, to use in the course of their regular testing of their systems' security. Again, because these devices are good products put to a good use, they do not fall within the scope of this statute.

In sum, the prohibition on "devices" as written does not encompass many forms of useful encryption products. Subsection (g) is specifically structured to go further, and allow the development and use of certain additional encryption products used for research purposes.

. . .

Conference Report, Digital Millennium Copyright Act
H.R. Conf. Rep. No. 105–796 (1998).

. . .

Section 1201(j)—Security Testing. . . . It is not the intent of this act to prevent persons utilizing technological measures in respect of computers, computer systems or networks from testing the security value and effectiveness of the technological measures they employ, or from contracting with companies that specialize in such security testing.

Thus, in addition to the exception for good faith encryption research contained in Section 1201(g), the conferees have adopted Section 1201(j) to resolve additional issues related to the effect of the anti-circumvention provision on legitimate information security activities. First, the conferees were concerned that Section 1201(g)'s exclusive focus on encryption-related research does not encompass the entire range of legitimate information security activities. Not every technological means that is used to provide security relies on encryption technology, or does so to the exclusion of other methods. Moreover, an individual who is legitimately testing a security technology may be doing so not to advance the state of encryption research or to develop encryption products, but rather to ascertain the effectiveness of that particular security technology.

The conferees were also concerned that the anti-circumvention provision of Section 1201(a) could be construed to inhibit legitimate forms of security testing. It is not unlawful to test the effectiveness of a security measure before it is implemented to protect the work covered under title 17. Nor is it unlawful for a person who has implemented a security measure to test its effectiveness. In this respect, the scope of permissible security testing under the Act should be the same as permissible testing of a simple door lock: a prospective buyer may test the lock at the store with the store's consent, or may purchase the lock and test it at home in any manner that he or she sees fit—for example, by installing the lock on the front door and seeing if it can be picked. What that person may not do, however, is test the lock once it has been installed on someone else's door, without the consent of the person whose property is protected by the lock.

. . .

Section 1201(j)(4) permits an individual, notwithstanding the prohibition contained in Section 1201(a)(2), to develop, produce, distribute, or employ technological means for the sole purpose of performing acts of good faith security testing under Section 1201(j)(2), provided the technological means do not otherwise violate section 1201(a)(2). It is Congress' intent for this subsection to have application only with respect to good faith security testing. The intent is to ensure that parties engaged in good faith security testing have the tools available to them to complete such acts. The conferees understand that such tools may be coupled with additional tools that serve purposes wholly unrelated to the purposes of this Act. Eligibility for this exemption should not be precluded because these tools are coupled in such a way. The exemption would not be available, however, when such tools are coupled with a product or technology that violates section 1201(a)(2).

Section 1201(k)—Certain Analog Devices and Certain Technological Measures. The conferees included a provision in the final legislation to require that analog video cassette recorders must conform to the two forms of copy control technology that are in wide use in the market today—the automatic gain control copy control technology and the colorstripe copy control technology. Neither are currently required elements of any format of video recorder, and the ability of each technology to work as intended depends on the consistency of design of video recorders or on incorporation of specific response elements in video recorders. Moreover, they do not employ encryption or scrambling of the content being protected.

As a consequence, these analog copy control technologies may be rendered ineffective either by redesign of video recorders or by intervention of "black box" devices or software "hacks". The conferees believe, and specifically intend, that the general circumvention prohibition in Section 1201(b)(2) will prohibit the manufacture and sale of "black box" devices that defeat these technologies. Moreover, the conferees believe and intend that the term "technology" should be read to include the software "hacks" of this type, and that such "hacks" are equally prohibited by the general circumvention provision. Devices have been marketed that claim to "fix" television picture disruptions allegedly caused by these technologies. However, as described in more detail below, there is no justification for the existence of any intervention device to "fix" such problems allegedly caused by these technologies, including "fixes" allegedly related to stabilization or clean up of the picture quality. Such devices should be seen for what they are—circumvention devices prohibited by this legislation.

. . .

EXTENSIONS

1. *Interoperability.* Many products, to be useful, must be designed so as to work in tandem with some other product—they must be designed to be interoperable. Electrical plugs must fit into outlets; software must interoperate with the operating system on which it runs. In designing a plug to fit into an outlet, it is a simple matter to take apart—to disassemble—an outlet and thereby deduce how the plug must be designed to fit it. Doing so may result in destroying the outlet, but runs no risk of legal liability (as long as the disassembler owns the outlet). In designing software to work with an operating system, it is necessary to know something about that system. The act of disassembling an operating system, to see how it works, inevitably involves copying copyrighted computer code, which may infringe rights of the copyright owner. In *Sega Enterprises Ltd. v. Accolade, Inc.*, 977 F.2d 1510 (9th Cir.1992), referenced in the House Committee's Section–By–Section Analysis of H.R. 2281, *supra*, the court considered whether the copyright holder can prevent others from engaging in copying of this sort. The manufacturer of a computer game system, Sega, sued a developer of computer game cassettes, Accolade, alleging that Accolade infringed its copyright by disassembling code contained in the game console, in order to learn how to make its game cassettes interoperate with the console. The court held that the copying involved in disassembling code for this purpose is within fair use, and therefore does not infringe Sega's copyright.

Do the anti-circumvention provisions of Section 1201 threaten to interfere with the ability of competitors to create software products that interoperate as they must in order to function? To what extent do the exemptions contained in Section 1201 allay concerns of this sort?

2. *Encryption research and security testing.* What explains the emphasis on encryption research and security testing in the legislative history? What is your prediction about whether the exemptions in Section 1201 will prove to offer sufficient safe harbors for these activities?

Consider the experience of Princeton University computer science professor Edward Felten. In September 2000, the Secure Digital Music Initiative ("SDMI"), an association of technology companies, issued a public challenge, inviting one and all to attempt to crack the digital watermarking technology that SDMI had selected as a standard for protecting digital music. SDMI offered a $10,000 prize for a successful challenger. Professor Felten and his associates accepted the challenge, and cracked the protection scheme quite readily. Felten wrote a paper about his research on the SDMI watermarks, and planned to present his findings at an academic conference. The Recording Industry Association of American ("RIAA") asked Felten to omit the details of the SDMI watermark technology from his presentation, and sent him a letter stating that revealing his research results "could subject you and you research team to actions under the Digital Millennium Copyright Act."

In the face of this perceived threat, Felten withdrew from the conference. He subsequently filed an action against the RIAA, seeking a declaration that publication of his paper would be lawful. The RIAA and SDMI hastily insisted publicly that they never had any intention of suing Felten, and the court dismissed the case on procedural grounds.

Professor Felten subsequently presented his paper at another conference. The paper, titled "Reading Between the Lines: Lessons from the SDMI Challenge," is available at www.usenix.org/publications/library/proceedings/sec01/craver.pdf. Does presentation or publication of the paper violate Section 1201?

QUESTIONS FOR DISCUSSION

1. *Locked room analogy.* Consider the House Committee Report's declaration that circumventing a technological management system "is the electronic equivalent of breaking into a locked room in order to obtain a copy of a book." Do you agree with this analogy? Consider the differences between "locking up" information and locking up hard goods. To what extent can copyright protection be appropriately conceptualized in terms of traditional physical property? Who would you suppose are the proponents of this analogy?

2. *Section 1201's exemptions.* Copyright law is often described as mediating two conflicting societal interests: the promotion of original works of authorship and public access to those works. Consider the various exemptions to Section 1201's prohibition on circumvention, namely those contained in § 1201(d)–(j). What goals, beyond promoting access to works of authorship, are these exemptions directed at achieving? Does the inclusion of these exemptions ameliorate the extent to which the Section 1201(a)(1)(A) & (a)(2) prohibitions disallow circumvention for purposes that do not infringe copyright–such as fair use of a work, or copying of uncopyrightable facts or ideas?

3. *Software activation.* Various software programs incorporate anti-piracy mechanisms. For example, Windows XP requires an "activation" process designed to attach a particular copy of Windows XP to a particular machine. After activation, a copy of Windows XP cannot subsequently be activated on any other computer. In addition, a user has only 30 days to activate after installing XP. Seven weeks before the official release of Windows XP, programs that circumvented the activation process were already available for download. Some of these programs reset the computer's clock, thus bypassing the thirty-day limitation, while others mimic the activation process itself.

Section 1201 makes it illegal to circumvent copyright protection systems. If you legally purchased Windows XP, yet did not wish to activate the product because you felt the activation process violated your right to privacy, would using a program to circumvent the activation process still be a violation of Section 1201? What if the Windows XP license agreement states that you are licensed to use the software only if you submit to the activation process?

RealNetworks, Inc. v. Streambox, Inc.
2000 WL 127311 (W.D.Wash.2000).

■ PECHMAN, J.

INTRODUCTION

Plaintiff RealNetworks, Inc. ("RealNetworks") filed this action on December 21, 1999. RealNetworks claims that Defendant Streambox has violated provisions of the Digital Millennium Copyright Act ("DMCA"), *17 U.S.C. § 1201 et seq.*, by distributing and marketing products known as the Streambox VCR and the Ripper. . . .

. . .

The Court . . . concludes that a preliminary injunction should be entered to enjoin the manufacture, distribution, and sale of the Streambox VCR . . . .

FINDINGS OF FACT

RealNetworks

1. RealNetworks is a public company based in Seattle, Washington that develops and markets software products designed to enable owners of audio, video, and other multimedia content to send their content to users of personal computers over the Internet.

2. RealNetworks offers products that enable consumers to access audio and video content over the Internet through a process known as "streaming." When an audio or video clip is "streamed" to a consumer, no trace of the clip is left on the consumer's computer, unless the content owner has permitted the consumer to download the file.

3. Streaming is to be contrasted with "downloading," a process by which a complete copy of an audio or video clip is delivered to and stored on a consumer's computer. Once a consumer has downloaded a file, he or she can access the file at will, and can generally redistribute copies of that file to others.

4. In the digital era, the difference between streaming and downloading is of critical importance. A downloaded copy of a digital audio or video file is essentially indistinguishable from the original, and such copies can often be created at the touch of a button. A user who obtains a digital copy may supplant the market for the original by distributing copies of his or her own. To guard against the unauthorized copying and redistribution of their content, many copyright owners do not make their content available for downloading, and instead distribute the content using streaming technology in a manner that does not permit downloading.

5. A large majority of all Internet Web pages that deliver streaming music or video use the RealNetworks' format.

RealNetworks' Products

6. The RealNetworks' products at issue in this action include the "RealProducer," the "RealServer" and the "RealPlayer." These products may be used to-

gether to form a system for distributing, retrieving and playing digital audio and video content via the Internet.

7. Owners of audio or video content may choose to use a RealNetworks product to encode their digital content into RealNetworks' format. Once encoded in that format, the media files are called RealAudio or RealVideo (collectively "RealMedia") files.

8. After a content owner has encoded its content into the RealMedia format, it may decide to use a "RealServer" to send that content to consumers. A RealServer is software program that resides on a content owner's computer that holds RealMedia files and "serves" them to consumers through streaming.

9. The RealServer is not the only available means for distributing RealMedia files. RealMedia files may also be made available on an ordinary web server instead of a RealServer. An end-user can download content from an ordinary web server using nothing more than a freely available Internet browser such as Netscape's Navigator or Microsoft's Internet Explorer.

10. To download streaming content distributed by a RealServer, however, a consumer must employ a "RealPlayer." The RealPlayer is a software program that resides on an end-user's computer and must be used to access and play a streaming RealMedia file that is sent from a RealServer.

RealNetworks' Security Measures

11. RealNetworks' products can be used to enable owners of audio and video content to make their content available for consumers to listen to or view, while at the same time securing the content against unauthorized access or copying.

12. The first of these measures, called the "Secret Handshake" by RealNetworks, ensures that files hosted on a RealServer will only be sent to a RealPlayer. The Secret Handshake is an authentication sequence which only RealServers and RealPlayers know. By design, unless this authentication sequence takes place, the RealServer does not stream the content it holds.

13. By ensuring that RealMedia files hosted on a RealServer are streamed only to RealPlayers, RealNetworks can ensure that a second security measure, which RealNetworks calls the "Copy Switch," is given effect. The Copy Switch is a piece of data in all RealMedia files that contains the content owner's preference regarding whether or not the stream may be copied by end-users. RealPlayers are designed to read this Copy Switch and obey the content owner's wishes. If a content owner turns on the Copy Switch in a particular RealMedia file, when that file is streamed, an end-user can use the RealPlayer to save a copy of that RealMedia file to the user's computer. If a content owner does not turn on the Copy Switch in a RealMedia file, the RealPlayer will not allow an end-user to make a copy of that file. The file will simply "evaporate" as the user listens to or watches it stream.

14. Through the use of the Secret Handshake and the Copy Switch, owners of audio and video content can prevent the unauthorized copying of their content if they so choose.

15. Content owners who choose to use the security measures described above

are likely to be seeking to prevent their works from being copied without their authorization. RealNetworks has proffered declarations from copyright owners that they rely on RealNetworks security measures to protect their copyrighted works on the Internet. Many of these copyright owners further state that if users could circumvent the security measures and make unauthorized copies of the content, they likely would not put their content up on the Internet for end-users.

16. Many copyright owners make content available on their Web site as a means to attract end-users to the Web site; that is, to drive "traffic" to the Web site. The more traffic a Web site generates, the more it can charge for advertisements placed on the Web site. Without RealNetworks' security measures, a copyright owner could lose the traffic its content generates. An end-user could obtain a copy of the content after only one visit and listen to or view it repeatedly without ever returning to the Web site. That end-user could also redistribute the content to others who would then have no occasion to visit the site in the first instance.

17. Copyright owners also use RealNetworks' technology so that end-users can listen to, but not record, music that is on sale, either at a Web site or in retail stores. Other copyright owners enable users to listen to content on a "pay-per-play" basis that requires a payment for each time the end-user wants to hear the content. Without the security measures afforded by RealNetworks, these methods of distribution could not succeed. End-users could make and redistribute digital copies of any content available on the Internet, undermining the market for the copyrighted original.

18. RealNetworks' success as a company is due in significant part to the fact that it has offered copyright owners a successful means of protecting against unauthorized duplication and distribution of their digital works.

. . .

Streambox VCR

23. The Streambox VCR enables end-users to access and download copies of RealMedia files that are streamed over the Internet. While the Streambox VCR also allows users to copy RealMedia files that are made freely available for downloading from ordinary web servers, the only function relevant to this case is the portions of the VCR that allow it to access and copy RealMedia files located on RealServers.

24. In order to gain access to RealMedia content located on a RealServer, the VCR mimics a RealPlayer and circumvents the authentication procedure, or Secret Handshake, that a RealServer requires before it will stream content. In other words, the Streambox VCR is able to convince the RealServer into thinking that the VCR is, in fact, a RealPlayer.

25. Having convinced a RealServer to begin streaming content, the Streambox VCR, like the RealPlayer, acts as a receiver. However, unlike the RealPlayer, the VCR ignores the Copy Switch that tells a RealPlayer whether an end-user is allowed to make a copy of (i.e., download) the RealMedia file as it is being streamed. The VCR thus allows the end-user to download RealMedia files even if the content

owner has used the Copy Switch to prohibit end-users from downloading the files.

26. The only reason for the Streambox VCR to circumvent the Secret Handshake and interact with a RealServer is to allow an end-user to access and make copies of content that a copyright holder has placed on a RealServer in order to secure it against unauthorized copying. In this way, the Streambox VCR acts like a "black box" which descrambles cable or satellite broadcasts so that viewers can watch pay programming for free. Like the cable and satellite companies that scramble their video signals to control access to their programs, RealNetworks has employed technological measures to ensure that only users of the RealPlayer can access RealMedia content placed on a RealServer. RealNetworks has gone one step further than the cable and satellite companies, not only controlling access, but also allowing copyright owners to specify whether or not their works can be copied by end-users, even if access is permitted. The Streambox VCR circumvents both the access control and copy protection measures.

. . .

31. The Streambox VCR poses a threat to RealNetworks' relationships with existing and potential customers who wish to secure their content for transmission over the Internet and must decide whether to purchase and use RealNetworks' technology. If the Streambox VCR remains available, these customers may opt not to utilize RealNetworks' technology, believing that it would not protect their content against unauthorized copying.

. . .

CONCLUSIONS OF LAW

. . .

RealNetworks Has Demonstrated a Reasonable Likelihood of Success on its DMCA Claims With Respect to the Streambox VCR

. . .

Parts of the VCR Are Likely to Violate Sections 1201(a)(2) and 1201(b)

7. Under the DMCA, the Secret Handshake that must take place between a RealServer and a RealPlayer before the RealServer will begin streaming content to an end-user appears to constitute a "technological measure" that "effectively controls access" to copyrighted works. *See* 17 U.S.C. § 1201(a)(3)(B) (measure "effectively controls access" if it "requires the application of information or a process or a treatment, with the authority of the copyright holder, to gain access to the work"). To gain access to a work protected by the Secret Handshake, a user must employ a RealPlayer, which will supply the requisite information to the RealServer in a proprietary authentication sequence.

8. In conjunction with the Secret Handshake, the Copy Switch is a "technological measure" that effectively protects the right of a copyright owner to control the unauthorized copying of its work. *See* 17 U.S.C. § 1201(b)(2)(B) (measure "effectively protects" right of copyright holder if it "prevents, restricts or otherwise limits the exercise of a right of a copyright owner"); 17 U.S.C. § 106(a) (granting copy-

right holder exclusive right to make copies of its work). To access a RealMedia file distributed by a RealServer, a user must use a RealPlayer. The RealPlayer reads the Copy Switch in the file. If the Copy Switch in the file is turned off, the RealPlayer will not permit the user to record a copy as the file is streamed. Thus, the Copy Switch may restrict others from exercising a copyright holder's exclusive right to copy its work.

9. Under the DMCA, a product or part thereof "circumvents" protections afforded a technological measure by "avoiding, bypassing, removing, deactivating or otherwise impairing" the operation of that technological measure. 17 U.S.C. §§ 1201(b)(2)(A), 1201(a)(2)(A). Under that definition, at least a part of the Streambox VCR circumvents the technological measures RealNetworks affords to copyright owners. Where a RealMedia file is stored on a RealServer, the VCR "bypasses" the Secret Handshake to gain access to the file. The VCR then circumvents the Copy Switch, enabling a user to make a copy of a file that the copyright owner has sought to protect.

10. Given the circumvention capabilities of the Streambox VCR, Streambox violates the DMCA if the product or a part thereof: (i) is primarily designed to serve this function; (ii) has only limited commercially significant purposes beyond the circumvention; or (iii) is marketed as a means of circumvention. 17 U.S.C. §§ 1201(a)(2)(A–C), [1201(b)(1)(A–C)]. These three tests are disjunctive. *Id.* A product that meets only one of the three independent bases for liability is still prohibited. Here, the VCR meets at least the first two.

11. The Streambox VCR meets the first test for liability under the DMCA because at least a part of the Streambox VCR is primarily, if not exclusively, designed to circumvent the access control and copy protection measures that RealNetworks affords to copyright owners. 17 U.S.C. §§ 1201(a)(2)(A), [1201(b)(1)(A)].

12. The second basis for liability is met because a portion of the VCR that circumvents the Secret Handshake so as to avoid the Copy Switch has no significant commercial purpose other than to enable users to access and record protected content. 17 U.S.C. § 1201(a)(2)(B), [1201(b)(1)(B)]. There does not appear to be any other commercial value that this capability affords.

13. Streambox's primary defense to Plaintiff's DMCA claims is that the VCR has legitimate uses. In particular, Streambox claims that the VCR allows consumers to make "fair use" copies of RealMedia files, notwithstanding the access control and copy protection measures that a copyright owner may have placed on that file.

14. The portions of the VCR that circumvent the secret handshake and copy switch permit consumers to obtain and redistribute perfect digital copies of audio and video files that copyright owners have made clear they do not want copied. For this reason, Streambox's VCR is not entitled to the same "fair use" protections the Supreme Court afforded to video cassette recorders used for "time-shifting" in *Sony Corp. v. Universal City Studios, Inc.*, 464 U.S. 417 (1984).

15. The *Sony* decision turned in large part on a finding that substantial numbers of copyright holders who broadcast their works either had authorized or would not object to having their works time-shifted by private viewers. *See Sony*, 464 U.S.

at 443, 446. Here, by contrast, copyright owners have specifically chosen to prevent the copying enabled by the Streambox VCR by putting their content on RealServers and leaving the Copy Switch off.

16. Moreover, the *Sony* decision did not involve interpretation of the DMCA. Under the DMCA, product developers do not have the right to distribute products that circumvent technological measures that prevent consumers from gaining unauthorized access to or making unauthorized copies of works protected by the Copyright Act. Instead, Congress specifically prohibited the distribution of the tools by which such circumvention could be accomplished. The portion of the Streambox VCR that circumvents the technological measures that prevent unauthorized access to and duplication of audio and video content therefore runs afoul of the DMCA.

. . .

18. Streambox also argues that the VCR does not violate the DMCA because the Copy Switch that it avoids does not "effectively protect" against the unauthorized copying of copyrighted works as required by [§ 1201(b)(2)(B)]. Streambox claims this "effective" protection is lacking because an enterprising end-user could potentially use other means to record streaming audio content as it is played by the end-user's computer speakers. This argument fails because the Copy Switch, in the ordinary course of its operation when it is on, restricts and limits the ability of people to make perfect digital copies of a copyrighted work. The Copy Switch therefore constitutes a technological measure that effectively protects a copyright owner's rights under section [1201(b)(2)(B)].

19. In addition, the argument ignores the fact that before the Copy Switch is even implicated, the Streambox VCR has already circumvented the Secret Handshake to gain access to a unauthorized RealMedia file. That alone is sufficient for liability under the DMCA. *See* 17 U.S.C. [§ 1201(a)(1)(A)].

20. Streambox's last defense to liability for the VCR rests on § 1201(c)(3) of the DMCA which it cites for the proposition that the VCR is not required to respond to the Copy Switch. Again, this argument fails to address the VCR's circumvention of the Secret Handshake, which is enough, by itself, to create liability under § 1201(a)(2).

21. Moreover, § 1201(c)(3) states that "[n]othing in this section shall require . . . a response to any particular technological measure, so long as . . . the product . . . does not otherwise fall within the prohibitions of subsections (a)(2) or (b)(1)." 17 U.S.C. § 1201(c)(3). As the remainder of the statute and the leading copyright commentator make clear, § 1201(c)(3) does not provide immunity for products that circumvent technological measures in violation of §§ 1201(a)(2) or (b)(1). *See* 17 U.S.C. § 1201(c)(3) (a product need not respond to a particular measure *"so long as such . . . product . . . does not otherwise fall within the prohibitions of subsections (a)(2) or (b)(1))."* (emphasis added); 1 *Nimmer on Copyright* (1999 Supp.), § 12A.05[C]. If the statute meant what Streambox suggests, any manufacturer of circumvention tools could avoid DMCA liability simply by claiming it chose not to respond to the particular protection that its tool circumvents.

22. As set forth above, the Streambox VCR falls within the prohibitions of §§ 1201(a)(2) and 1201(b)(1). Accordingly, § 1201(c)(3) affords Streambox no defense.

. . .

Universal City Studios, Inc. v. Reimerdes
111 F.Supp.2d 294 (S.D.N.Y.2000), *aff'd*, 273 F.3d 429 (2d Cir.2001).

■ LEWIS A. KAPLAN, DISTRICT JUDGE.

Plaintiffs, eight major United States motion picture studios, distribute many of their copyrighted motion pictures for home use on digital versatile disks ("DVDs"), which contain copies of the motion pictures in digital form. They protect those motion pictures from copying by using an encryption system called CSS. CSS-protected motion pictures on DVDs may be viewed only on players and computer drives equipped with licensed technology that permits the devices to decrypt and play—but not to copy—the films.

Late last year, computer hackers devised a computer program called DeCSS that circumvents the CSS protection system and allows CSS-protected motion pictures to be copied and played on devices that lack the licensed decryption technology. Defendants quickly posted DeCSS on their Internet web site, thus making it readily available to much of the world. Plaintiffs promptly brought this action under the Digital Millennium Copyright Act (the "DMCA") to enjoin defendants from posting DeCSS and to prevent them from electronically "linking" their site to others that post DeCSS. Defendants responded with what they termed "electronic civil disobedience"—increasing their efforts to link their web site to a large number of others that continue to make DeCSS available.

Defendants contend that their actions do not violate the DMCA . . . .

Defendants argue first that the DMCA should not be construed to reach their conduct, principally because the DMCA, so applied, could prevent those who wish to gain access to technologically protected copyrighted works in order to make fair—that is, non-infringing—use of them from doing so. They argue that those who would make fair use of technologically protected copyrighted works need means, such as DeCSS, of circumventing access control measures not for piracy, but to make lawful use of those works.

Technological access control measures have the capacity to prevent fair uses of copyrighted works as well as foul. Hence, there is a potential tension between the use of such access control measures and fair use. Defendants are not the first to recognize that possibility. As the DMCA made its way through the legislative process, Congress was preoccupied with precisely this issue. Proponents of strong restrictions on circumvention of access control measures argued that they were essential if copyright holders were to make their works available in digital form because digital works otherwise could be pirated too easily. Opponents contended that strong anti-circumvention measures would extend the copyright monopoly inappropriately and prevent many fair uses of copyrighted material.

Congress struck a balance. The compromise it reached, depending upon future technological and commercial developments, may or may not prove ideal. But the solution it enacted is clear. The potential tension to which defendants point does not absolve them of liability under the statute. There is no serious question that defendants' posting of DeCSS violates the DMCA. . . .

I. The Genesis of the Controversy

As this case involves computers and technology with which many are unfamiliar, it is useful to begin by defining some of the vocabulary.

A. The Vocabulary of this Case

. . .

4. Portable Storage Media

Digital files may be stored on several different kinds of storage media, some of which are readily transportable. Perhaps the most familiar of these are so called floppy disks or "floppies," which now are 3 1/2 inch magnetic disks upon which digital files may be recorded. For present purposes, however, we are concerned principally with two more recent developments, CD-ROMs and digital versatile disks, or DVDs.

A CD-ROM is a five-inch wide optical disk capable of storing approximately 650 MB of data. To read the data on a CD-ROM, a computer must have a CD-ROM drive.

DVDs are five-inch wide disks capable of storing more than 4.7 GB of data. In the application relevant here, they are used to hold full-length motion pictures in digital form. They are the latest technology for private home viewing of recorded motion pictures and result in drastically improved audio and visual clarity and quality of motion pictures shown on televisions or computer screens.

5. The Technology Here at Issue

CSS, or Content Scramble System, is an access control and copy prevention system for DVDs developed by the motion picture companies, including plaintiffs. It is an encryption-based system that requires the use of appropriately configured hardware such as a DVD player or a computer DVD drive to decrypt, unscramble and play back, but not copy, motion pictures on DVDs. The technology necessary to configure DVD players and drives to play CSS-protected DVDs has been licensed to hundreds of manufacturers in the United States and around the world.

DeCSS is a software utility, or computer program, that enables users to break the CSS copy protection system and hence to view DVDs on unlicensed players and make digital copies of DVD movies. The quality of motion pictures decrypted by DeCSS is virtually identical to that of encrypted movies on DVD.

DivX is a compression program available for download over the Internet. It compresses video files in order to minimize required storage space, often to facilitate transfer over The Internet or other networks.

B. Parties

Plaintiffs are eight major motion picture studios. Each is in the business of producing and distributing copyrighted material including motion pictures. Each distributes, either directly or through affiliates, copyrighted motion pictures on DVDs. Plaintiffs produce and distribute a large majority of the motion pictures on DVDs on the market today.

Defendant Eric Corley is viewed as a leader of the computer hacker community and goes by the name Emmanuel Goldstein, after the leader of the underground in George Orwell's classic, *1984*. He and his company, defendant 2600 Enterprises, Inc., together publish a magazine called *2600: The Hacker Quarterly*, which Corley founded in 1984, and which is something of a bible to the hacker community. The name "2600" was derived from the fact that hackers in the 1960's found that the transmission of a 2600 hertz tone over a long distance trunk connection gained access to "operator mode" and allowed the user to explore aspects of the telephone system that were not otherwise accessible. Mr. Corley chose the name because he regarded it as a "mystical thing," commemorating something that he evidently admired. Not surprisingly, *2600: The Hacker Quarterly* has included articles on such topics as how to steal an Internet domain name, access other people's e-mail, intercept cellular phone calls, and break into the computer systems at Costco stores and Federal Express. One issue contains a guide to the federal criminal justice system for readers charged with computer hacking. In addition, defendants operate a web site located at <http://www.2600.com> ("2600.com"), which is managed primarily by Mr. Corley and has been in existence since 1995.[47]

Prior to January 2000, when this action was commenced, defendants posted the source and object code for DeCSS on the 2600.com web site, from which they could be downloaded easily. At that time, 2600.com contained also a list of links to other web sites purporting to post DeCSS.

C. The Development of DVD and CSS

The major motion picture studios typically distribute films in a sequence of so-called windows, each window referring to a separate channel of distribution and thus to a separate source of revenue. The first window generally is theatrical release, distribution, and exhibition. Subsequently, films are distributed to airlines and hotels, then to the home market, then to pay television, cable and, eventually, free television broadcast. The home market is important to plaintiffs, as it represents a significant source of revenue.

Motion pictures first were, and still are, distributed to the home market in the form of video cassette tapes. In the early 1990's, however, the major movie studios began to explore distribution to the home market in digital format, which offered substantially higher audio and visual quality and greater longevity than video cassette tapes. This technology, which in 1995 became what is known today as DVD, brought with it a new problem—increased risk of piracy by virtue of the fact that

---

[47] Interestingly, defendants copyright both their magazine and the material on their web site to prevent others from copying their works.

digital files, unlike the material on video cassettes, can be copied without degradation from generation to generation. In consequence, the movie studios became concerned as the product neared market with the threat of DVD piracy.

Discussions among the studios with the goal of organizing a unified response to the piracy threat began in earnest in late 1995 or early 1996. They eventually came to include representatives of the consumer electronics and computer industries, as well as interested members of the public, and focused on both legislative proposals and technological solutions. In 1996, Matsushita Electric Industrial Co. ("MEI") and Toshiba Corp., presented–and the studios adopted–CSS.

CSS involves encrypting, according to an encryption algorithm, the digital sound and graphics files on a DVD that together constitute a motion picture. A CSS-protected DVD can be decrypted by an appropriate decryption algorithm that employs a series of keys stored on the DVD and the DVD player. In consequence, only players and drives containing the appropriate keys are able to decrypt DVD files and thereby play movies stored on DVDs.

As the motion picture companies did not themselves develop CSS and, in any case, are not in the business of making DVD players and drives, the technology for making compliant devices, i.e., devices with CSS keys, had to be licensed to consumer electronics manufacturers.[60] In order to ensure that the decryption technology did not become generally available and that compliant devices could not be used to copy as well as merely to play CSS-protected movies, the technology is licensed subject to strict security requirements. Moreover, manufacturers may not, consistent with their licenses, make equipment that would supply digital output that could be used in copying protected DVDs. Licenses to manufacture compliant devices are granted on a royalty-free basis subject only to an administrative fee. At the time of trial, licenses had been issued to numerous hardware and software manufacturers, including two companies that plan to release DVD players for computers running the Linux operating system.

With CSS in place, the studios introduced DVDs on the consumer market in early 1997. All or most of the motion pictures released on DVD were, and continue to be, encrypted with CSS technology. Over 4,000 motion pictures now have been released in DVD format in the United States, and movies are being issued on DVD at the rate of over 40 new titles per month in addition to re-releases of classic films. Currently, more than five million households in the United States own DVD players, and players are projected to be in ten percent of United States homes by the end of 2000.

DVDs have proven not only popular, but lucrative for the studios. Revenue from their sale and rental currently accounts for a substantial percentage of the movie studios' revenue from the home video market. Revenue from the home

---

[60] The licensing function initially was performed by MEI and Toshiba. Subsequently, MEI and Toshiba granted a royalty free license to the DVD Copy Control Association ("DVD CCA"), which now handles the licensing function. The motion picture companies themselves license CSS from the DVD CCA.

market, in turn, makes up a large percentage of the studios' total distribution revenue.

D. The Appearance of DeCSS

In late September 1999, Jon Johansen, a Norwegian subject then fifteen years of age, and two individuals he "met" under pseudonyms over the Internet, reverse engineered a licensed DVD player and discovered the CSS encryption algorithm and keys. They used this information to create DeCSS, a program capable of decrypting or "ripping" encrypted DVDs, thereby allowing playback on non-compliant computers as well as the copying of decrypted files to computer hard drives. Mr. Johansen then posted the executable code on his personal Internet web site and informed members of an Internet mailing list that he had done so. Neither Mr. Johansen nor his collaborators obtained a license from the DVD CCA.

Although Mr. Johansen testified at trial that he created DeCSS in order to make a DVD player that would operate on a computer running the Linux operating system, DeCSS is a Windows executable file; that is, it can be executed only on computers running the Windows operating system. Mr. Johansen explained the fact that he created a Windows rather than a Linux program by asserting that Linux, at the time he created DeCSS, did not support the file system used on DVDs. Hence, it was necessary, he said, to decrypt the DVD on a Windows computer in order subsequently to play the decrypted files on a Linux machine. Assuming that to be true, however, the fact remains that Mr. Johansen created DeCSS in the full knowledge that it could be used on computers running Windows rather than Linux. Moreover, he was well aware that the files, once decrypted, could be copied like any other computer files.

In January 1999, Norwegian prosecutors filed charges against Mr. Johansen stemming from the development of DeCSS. The disposition of the Norwegian case does not appear of record.

E. The Distribution of DeCSS

In the months following its initial appearance on Mr. Johansen's web site, DeCSS has become widely available on the Internet, where hundreds of sites now purport to offer the software for download. A few other applications said to decrypt CSS-encrypted DVDs also have appeared on the Internet.

In November 1999, defendants' web site began to offer DeCSS for download. It established also a list of links to several web sites that purportedly "mirrored" or offered DeCSS for download. . . .

F. The Preliminary Injunction and Defendants' Response

The movie studios, through the Internet investigations division of the Motion Picture Association of America ("MPAA"), became aware of the availability of DeCSS on the Internet in October 1999. The industry responded by sending out a number of cease and desist letters to web site operators who posted the software, some of which removed it from their sites. In January 2000, the studios filed this lawsuit against defendant Eric Corley and two others.[91]

After a hearing at which defendants presented no affidavits or evidentiary material, the Court granted plaintiffs' motion for a preliminary injunction barring defendants from posting DeCSS. At the conclusion of the hearing, plaintiffs sought also to enjoin defendants from linking to other sites that posted DeCSS, but the Court declined to entertain the application at that time in view of plaintiffs' failure to raise the issue in their motion papers.

Following the issuance of the preliminary injunction, defendants removed DeCSS from the 2600.com web site. In what they termed an act of "electronic civil disobedience," however, they continued to support links to other web sites purporting to offer DeCSS for download, a list which had grown to nearly five hundred by July 2000. Indeed, they carried a banner saying "Stop the MPAA" and, in a reference to this lawsuit, proclaimed: "We have to face the possibility that we could be forced into submission. For that reason it's especially important that as many of you as possible, all throughout the world, take a stand and mirror these files." Thus, defendants obviously hoped to frustrate plaintiffs' recourse to the judicial system by making effective relief difficult or impossible.

At least some of the links currently on defendants' mirror list lead the user to copies of DeCSS that, when downloaded and executed, successfully decrypt a motion picture on a CSS-encrypted DVD.

G. Effects on Plaintiffs

The effect on plaintiffs of defendants' posting of DeCSS depends upon the ease with which DeCSS decrypts plaintiffs' copyrighted motion pictures, the quality of the resulting product, and the convenience with which decrypted copies may be transferred or transmitted.

As noted, DeCSS was available for download from defendants' web site and remains available from web sites on defendants' mirror list. Downloading is simple and quick—plaintiffs' expert did it in seconds. The program in fact decrypts at least some DVDs. Although the process is computationally intensive, plaintiffs' expert decrypted a store-bought copy of *Sleepless in Seattle* in 20 to 45 minutes. The copy is stored on the hard drive of the computer. The quality of the decrypted film is virtually identical to that of encrypted films on DVD. The decrypted file can be copied like any other.

The decryption of a CSS-protected DVD is only the beginning of the tale, as the decrypted file is very large—approximately 4.3 to 6 GB or more depending on the length of the film—and thus extremely cumbersome to transfer or to store on portable storage media. One solution to this problem, however, is DivX, a compression utility available on the Internet that is promoted as a means of compressing decrypted motion picture files to manageable size.

DivX is capable of compressing decrypted files constituting a feature length

---

[91] The other two defendants entered into consent decrees with plaintiffs. Plaintiffs subsequently amended the complaint to add 2600 Enterprises, Inc. as a defendant.

motion picture to approximately 650 MB at a compression ratio that involves little loss of quality. While the compressed sound and graphic files then must be synchronized, a tedious process that took plaintiffs' expert between 10 and 20 hours, the task is entirely feasible. Indeed, having compared a store-bought DVD with portions of a copy compressed and synchronized with DivX (which often are referred to as "DivX'd" motion pictures), the Court finds that the loss of quality, at least in some cases, is imperceptible or so nearly imperceptible as to be of no importance to ordinary consumers.

The fact that DeCSS-decrypted DVDs can be compressed satisfactorily to 650 MB is very important. A writeable CD-ROM can hold 650 MB. Hence, it is entirely feasible to decrypt a DVD with DeCSS, compress and synchronize it with DivX, and then make as many copies as one wishes by burning the resulting files onto writeable CD-ROMs, which are sold blank for about one dollar apiece. Indeed, even if one wished to use a lower compression ratio to improve quality, a film easily could be compressed to about 1.3 GB and burned onto two CD-ROMs. But the creation of pirated copies of copyrighted movies on writeable CD-ROMs, although significant, is not the principal focus of plaintiffs' concern, which is transmission of pirated copies over the Internet or other networks.

Network transmission of decrypted motion pictures raises somewhat more difficult issues because even 650 MB is a very large file that, depending upon the circumstances, may take a good deal of time to transmit. But there is tremendous variation in transmission times. Many home computers today have modems with a rated capacity of 56 kilobits per second. DSL lines, which increasingly are available to home and business users, offer transfer rates of 7 megabits per second. Cable modems also offer increased bandwidth. Student rooms in many universities are equipped with network connections rated at 10 megabits per second. Large institutions such as universities and major companies often have networks with backbones rated at 100 megabits per second. While effective transmission times generally are much lower than rated maximum capacities in consequence of traffic volume and other considerations, there are many environments in which very high transmission rates may be achieved. Hence, transmission times ranging from three to twenty minutes to six hours or more for a feature length film are readily achievable, depending upon the users' precise circumstances.

At trial, defendants repeated, as if it were a mantra, the refrain that plaintiffs, as they stipulated, have no direct evidence of a specific occasion on which any person decrypted a copyrighted motion picture with DeCSS and transmitted it over the Internet. But that is unpersuasive. Plaintiffs' expert expended very little effort to find someone in an IRC chat room who exchanged a compressed, decrypted copy of *The Matrix*, one of plaintiffs' copyrighted motion pictures, for a copy of *Sleepless in Seattle*. While the simultaneous electronic exchange of the two movies took approximately six hours, the computers required little operator attention during the interim. An MPAA investigator downloaded between five and ten DVD-sourced movies over the Internet after December 1999. At least one web site contains a list of 650 motion pictures, said to have been decrypted and compressed with DivX, that purportedly are available for sale, trade or free download. And although the

Court does not accept the list, which is hearsay, as proof of the truth of the matters asserted therein, it does note that advertisements for decrypted versions of copyrighted movies first appeared on the Internet in substantial numbers in late 1999, following the posting of DeCSS.

The net of all this is reasonably plain. DeCSS is a free, effective and fast means of decrypting plaintiffs' DVDs and copying them to computer hard drives. DivX, which is available over the Internet for nothing, with the investment of some time and effort, permits compression of the decrypted files to sizes that readily fit on a writeable CD-ROM. Copies of such CD-ROMs can be produced very cheaply and distributed as easily as other pirated intellectual property. While not everyone with Internet access now will find it convenient to send or receive DivX'd copies of pirated motion pictures over the Internet, the availability of high speed network connections in many businesses and institutions, and their growing availability in homes, make Internet and other network traffic in pirated copies a growing threat.

These circumstances have two major implications for plaintiffs. First, the availability of DeCSS on the Internet effectively has compromised plaintiffs' system of copyright protection for DVDs, requiring them either to tolerate increased piracy or to expend resources to develop and implement a replacement system unless the availability of DeCSS is terminated. It is analogous to the publication of a bank vault combination in a national newspaper. Even if no one uses the combination to open the vault, its mere publication has the effect of defeating the bank's security system, forcing the bank to reprogram the lock. Development and implementation of a new DVD copy protection system, however, is far more difficult and costly than reprogramming a combination lock and may carry with it the added problem of rendering the existing installed base of compliant DVD players obsolete.

Second, the application of DeCSS to copy and distribute motion pictures on DVD, both on CD-ROMs and via the Internet, threatens to reduce the studios' revenue from the sale and rental of DVDs. It threatens also to impede new, potentially lucrative initiatives for the distribution of motion pictures in digital form, such as video-on-demand via the Internet.

In consequence, plaintiffs already have been gravely injured. As the pressure for and competition to supply more and more users with faster and faster network connections grows, the injury will multiply.

II. The Digital Millennium Copyright Act

A. Background and Structure of the Statute

. . .

The DMCA contains two principal anticircumvention provisions. The first, Section 1201(a)(1), governs "[t]he act of circumventing a technological protection measure put in place by a copyright owner to control access to a copyrighted work," an act described by Congress as "the electronic equivalent of breaking into a locked room in order to obtain a copy of a book."[131] The second, Section

---

[131] H.R.REP. NO. 105–551(I), 105th Cong., 2d Sess. ("JUDICIARY COMM.REP."), at 17 (1998).

1201(a)(2), which is the focus of this case, "supplements the prohibition against the act of circumvention in paragraph (a)(1) with prohibitions on creating and making available certain technologies . . . developed or advertised to defeat technological protections against unauthorized access to a work."[132] As defendants are accused here only of posting and linking to other sites posting DeCSS, and not of using it themselves to bypass plaintiffs' access controls, it is principally the second of the anticircumvention provisions that is at issue in this case.

B. Posting of DeCSS

1. Violation of Anti–Trafficking Provision

Section 1201(a)(2) of the Copyright Act, part of the DMCA, provides that:

No person shall . . . offer to the public, provide or otherwise traffic in any technology . . . that—

> (A) is primarily designed or produced for the purpose of circumventing a technological measure that effectively controls access to a work protected under [the Copyright Act];

> (B) has only limited commercially significant purpose or use other than to circumvent a technological measure that effectively controls access to a work protected under [the Copyright Act]; or

> (C) is marketed by that person or another acting in concert with that person with that person's knowledge for use in circumventing a technological measure that effectively controls access to a work protected under [the Copyright Act].

17 U.S.C. § 1201(a)(2).

In this case, defendants concededly offered and provided and, absent a court order, would continue to offer and provide DeCSS to the public by making it available for download on the 2600.com web site. DeCSS, a computer program, unquestionably is "technology" within the meaning of the statute. "[C]ircumvent a technological measure" is defined to mean descrambling a scrambled work, decrypting an encrypted work, or "otherwise to avoid, bypass, remove, deactivate, or impair a technological measure, without the authority of the copyright owner," so DeCSS clearly is a means of circumventing a technological access control measure. In consequence, if CSS otherwise falls within paragraphs (A), (B) or (C) of Section 1201(a)(2), and if none of the statutory exceptions applies to their actions, defendants have violated and, unless enjoined, will continue to violate the DMCA by posting DeCSS.

a. Section 1201(a)(2)(A)

(1) CSS Effectively Controls Access to Copyrighted Works

During pretrial proceedings and at trial, defendants attacked plaintiffs' Section 1201(a)(2)(A) claim, arguing that CSS, which is based on a 40–bit encryption key, is a weak cipher that does not "effectively control" access to plaintiffs' copyrighted works. They reasoned from this premise that CSS is not protected under this

---

[132] *Id.* at 18.

branch of the statute at all. Their post-trial memorandum appears to have abandoned this argument. In any case, however, the contention is indefensible as a matter of law.

First, the statute expressly provides that "a technological measure 'effectively controls access to a work' if the measure, in the ordinary course of its operation, requires the application of information or a process or a treatment, with the authority of the copyright owner, to gain access to a work." One cannot gain access to a CSS-protected work on a DVD without application of the three keys that are required by the software. One cannot lawfully gain access to the keys except by entering into a license with the DVD CCA under authority granted by the copyright owners or by purchasing a DVD player or drive containing the keys pursuant to such a license. In consequence, under the express terms of the statute, CSS "effectively controls access" to copyrighted DVD movies. It does so, within the meaning of the statute, whether or not it is a strong means of protection.

This view is confirmed by the legislative history, which deals with precisely this point. The House Judiciary Committee section-by-section analysis of the House bill, which in this respect was enacted into law, makes clear that a technological measure "effectively controls access" to a copyrighted work if its *function* is to control access:

> The bill does define the *functions* of the technological measures that are covered—that is, what it means for a technological measure to "effectively control access to a work" . . . and to "effectively protect a right of a copyright owner under this title". . . . The practical, common-sense approach taken by H.R.2281 is that if, in the ordinary course of its operation, a technology actually works in the defined ways to control access to a work . . . then the "effectiveness" test is met, and the prohibitions of the statute are applicable. This test, which focuses on the function performed by the technology, provides a sufficient basis for clear interpretation.[140]

Further, the House Commerce Committee made clear that measures based on encryption or scrambling "effectively control" access to copyrighted works,[141] although it is well known that what may be encrypted or scrambled often may be decrypted or unscrambled. As CSS, in the ordinary course of its operation—that is, when DeCSS or some other decryption program is not employed—"actually works" to prevent access to the protected work, it "effectively controls access" within the contemplation of the statute.

Finally, the interpretation of the phrase "effectively controls access" offered by defendants at trial—viz., that the use of the word "effectively" means that the statute protects only successful or efficacious technological means of controlling ac-

---

[140] HOUSE COMM. ON JUDICIARY, SECTION–BY–SECTION ANALYSIS OF H.R.2281 AS PASSED BY THE UNITED STATES HOUSE OF REPRESENTATIVES ON AUGUST 4, 1998 ("SECTION–BY–SECTION ANALYSIS"), at 10 (Comm.Print 1998) (emphasis in original).

[141] H.R.REP. NO. 105–551(II), 105th Cong., 2d Sess. ("COMMERCE COMM.REP."), at 39 (1998).

cess—would gut the statute if it were adopted. If a technological means of access control is circumvented, it is, in common parlance, ineffective. Yet defendants' construction, if adopted, would limit the application of the statute to access control measures that thwart circumvention, but withhold protection for those measures that can be circumvented. In other words, defendants would have the Court construe the statute to offer protection where none is needed but to withhold protection precisely where protection is essential. The Court declines to do so. Accordingly, the Court holds that CSS effectively controls access to plaintiffs' copyrighted works.

(2) DeCSS Was Designed Primarily to Circumvent CSS

As CSS effectively controls access to plaintiffs' copyrighted works, the only remaining question under Section 1201(a)(2)(A) is whether DeCSS was designed primarily to circumvent CSS. The answer is perfectly obvious. By the admission of both Jon Johansen, the programmer who principally wrote DeCSS, and defendant Corley, DeCSS was created solely for the purpose of decrypting CSS–that is all it does. Hence, absent satisfaction of a statutory exception, defendants clearly violated Section 1201(a)(2)(A) by posting DeCSS to their web site.

b. Section 1201(a)(2)(B)

As the only purpose or use of DeCSS is to circumvent CSS, the foregoing is sufficient to establish a *prima facie* violation of Section 1201(a)(2)(B) as well.

c. The Linux Argument

Perhaps the centerpiece of defendants' statutory position is the contention that DeCSS was not created for the purpose of pirating copyrighted motion pictures. Rather, they argue, it was written to further the development of a DVD player that would run under the Linux operating system, as there allegedly were no Linux compatible players on the market at the time. . . .

. . .

[T]he question whether the development of a Linux DVD player motivated those who wrote DeCSS is immaterial to the question whether the defendants now before the Court violated the anti-trafficking provision of the DMCA. The inescapable facts are that (1) CSS is a technological means that effectively controls access to plaintiffs' copyrighted works, (2) the one and only function of DeCSS is to circumvent CSS, and (3) defendants offered and provided DeCSS by posting it on their web site. Whether defendants did so in order to infringe, or to permit or encourage others to infringe, copyrighted works in violation of other provisions of the Copyright Act simply does not matter for purposes of Section 1201(a)(2). The offering or provision of the program is the prohibited conduct–and it is prohibited irrespective of why the program was written, except to whatever extent motive may be germane to determining whether their conduct falls within one of the statutory exceptions.

2. Statutory Exceptions

Earlier in the litigation, defendants contended that their activities came within several exceptions contained in the DMCA and the Copyright Act and constitute fair use under the Copyright Act. Their post-trial memorandum appears to confine their argument to the reverse engineering exception. In any case, all of their assertions are entirely without merit.

a. Reverse engineering

Defendants claim to fall under Section 1201(f) of the statute, which provides in substance that one may circumvent, or develop and employ technological means to circumvent, access control measures in order to achieve interoperability with another computer program provided that doing so does not infringe another's copyright and, in addition, that one may make information acquired through such efforts "available to others, if the person [in question] . . . provides such information solely for the purpose of enabling interoperability of an independently created computer program with other programs, and to the extent that doing so does not constitute infringement. . . ." They contend that DeCSS is necessary to achieve interoperability between computers running the Linux operating system and DVDs and that this exception therefore is satisfied. This contention fails.

First, Section 1201(f)(3) permits information acquired through reverse engineering to be made available to others only by the person who acquired the information. But these defendants did not do any reverse engineering. They simply took DeCSS off someone else's web site and posted it on their own.

Defendants would be in no stronger position even if they had authored DeCSS. The right to make the information available extends only to dissemination "solely for the purpose" of achieving interoperability as defined in the statute. It does not apply to public dissemination of means of circumvention, as the legislative history confirms. These defendants, however, did not post DeCSS "solely" to achieve interoperability with Linux or anything else.

Finally, it is important to recognize that even the creators of DeCSS cannot credibly maintain that the "sole" purpose of DeCSS was to create a Linux DVD player. DeCSS concededly was developed on and runs under Windows—a far more widely used operating system. The developers of DeCSS therefore knew that DeCSS could be used to decrypt and play DVD movies on Windows as well as Linux machines. They knew also that the decrypted files could be copied like any other unprotected computer file. Moreover, the Court does not credit Mr. Johansen's testimony that he created DeCSS solely for the purpose of building a Linux player. Mr. Johansen is a very talented young man and a member of a well known hacker group who viewed "cracking" CSS as an end it itself and a means of demonstrating his talent and who fully expected that the use of DeCSS would not be confined to Linux machines. Hence, the Court finds that Mr. Johansen and the others who actually did develop DeCSS did not do so solely for the purpose of making a Linux DVD player if, indeed, developing a Linux-based DVD player was among their purposes.

Accordingly, the reverse engineering exception to the DMCA has no application here.

. . .

d. Fair use

Finally, defendants rely on the doctrine of fair use. Stated in its most general terms, the doctrine, now codified in Section 107 of the Copyright Act, limits the exclusive rights of a copyright holder by permitting others to make limited use of portions of the copyrighted work, for appropriate purposes, free of liability for copyright infringement. For example, it is permissible for one other than the copyright owner to reprint or quote a suitable part of a copyrighted book or article in certain circumstances. The doctrine traditionally has facilitated literary and artistic criticism, teaching and scholarship, and other socially useful forms of expression. It has been viewed by courts as a safety valve that accommodates the exclusive rights conferred by copyright with the freedom of expression guaranteed by the First Amendment.

The use of technological means of controlling access to a copyrighted work may affect the ability to make fair uses of the work. Focusing specifically on the facts of this case, the application of CSS to encrypt a copyrighted motion picture requires the use of a compliant DVD player to view or listen to the movie. Perhaps more significantly, it prevents exact copying of either the video or the audio portion of all or any part of the film. This latter point means that certain uses that might qualify as "fair" for purposes of copyright infringement—for example, the preparation by a film studies professor of a single CD-ROM or tape containing two scenes from different movies in order to illustrate a point in a lecture on cinematography, as opposed to showing relevant parts of two different DVDs—would be difficult or impossible absent circumvention of the CSS encryption. Defendants therefore argue that the DMCA cannot properly be construed to make it difficult or impossible to make any fair use of plaintiffs' copyrighted works and that the statute therefore does not reach their activities, which are simply a means to enable users of DeCSS to make such fair uses.

Defendants have focused on a significant point. Access control measures such as CSS do involve some risk of preventing lawful as well as unlawful uses of copyrighted material. Congress, however, clearly faced up to and dealt with this question in enacting the DMCA.

The Court begins its statutory analysis, as it must, with the language of the statute. Section 107 of the Copyright Act provides in critical part that certain uses of copyrighted works that otherwise would be wrongful are "not . . . infringement[s] of copyright." Defendants, however, are not here sued for copyright infringement. They are sued for offering and providing technology designed to circumvent technological measures that control access to copyrighted works and otherwise violating Section 1201(a)(2) of the Act. If Congress had meant the fair use defense to apply to such actions, it would have said so. Indeed, as the legislative history demonstrates, the decision not to make fair use a defense to a claim under Section 1201(a) was quite deliberate.

Congress was well aware during the consideration of the DMCA of the traditional role of the fair use defense in accommodating the exclusive rights of copyright owners with the legitimate interests of noninfringing users of portions of copyrighted works. It recognized the contention, voiced by a range of constituencies concerned with the legislation, that technological controls on access to copyrighted works might erode fair use by preventing access even for uses that would be deemed "fair" if only access might be gained.[162] And it struck a balance among the competing interests.

The first element of the balance was the careful limitation of Section 1201(a)(1)'s prohibition of the act of circumvention to the act itself so as not to "apply to subsequent actions of a person once he or she has obtained authorized access to a copy of a [copyrighted] work. . . ."[163] By doing so, it left "the traditional defenses to copyright infringement, including fair use, . . . fully applicable" provided "the access is authorized."[164]

Second, Congress delayed the effective date of Section 1201(a)(1)'s prohibition of the act of circumvention for two years pending further investigation about how best to reconcile Section 1201(a)(1) with fair use concerns. Following that investigation, which is being carried out in the form of a rule-making by the Register of Copyright, the prohibition will not apply to users of particular classes of copyrighted works who demonstrate that their ability to make noninfringing uses of those classes of works would be affected adversely by Section 1201(a)(1).

Third, it created a series of exceptions to aspects of Section 1201(a) for certain uses that Congress thought "fair," including reverse engineering, security testing, good faith encryption research, and certain uses by nonprofit libraries, archives and educational institutions.

Defendants claim also that the possibility that DeCSS might be used for the purpose of gaining access to copyrighted works in order to make fair use of those works saves them under *Sony Corp. v. Universal City Studios, Inc.*, 464 U.S. 417 (1984). But they are mistaken. *Sony* does not apply to the activities with which defendants here are charged. Even if it did, it would not govern here. *Sony* involved a construction of the Copyright Act that has been overruled by the later enactment of the DMCA to the extent of any inconsistency between *Sony* and the new statute.

Sony was a suit for contributory infringement brought against manufacturers of video cassette recorders on the theory that the manufacturers were contributing to infringing home taping of copyrighted television broadcasts. The Supreme Court held that the manufacturers were not liable in view of the substantial numbers of copyright holders who either had authorized or did not object to such taping by viewers. But *Sony* has no application here.

When *Sony* was decided, the only question was whether the manufacturers could be held liable for infringement by those who purchased equipment from them in circumstances in which there were many noninfringing uses for their equipment. But that is not the question now before this Court. The question here is whether the possibility of noninfringing fair use by someone who gains access to a

---

[162] *See, e.g.*, COMMERCE COMM.REP. 25–26.

[163] JUDICIARY COMM.REP. 18.

[164] *Id.*

protected copyrighted work through a circumvention technology distributed by the defendants saves the defendants from liability under Section 1201. But nothing in Section 1201 so suggests. By prohibiting the provision of circumvention technology, the DMCA fundamentally altered the landscape. A given device or piece of technology might have "a substantial noninfringing use, and hence be immune from attack under Sony's construction of the Copyright Act—but nonetheless still be subject to suppression under Section 1201."[169] Indeed, Congress explicitly noted that Section 1201 does not incorporate Sony.[170]

The policy concerns raised by defendants were considered by Congress. Having considered them, Congress crafted a statute that, so far as the applicability of the fair use defense to Section 1201(a) claims is concerned, is crystal clear. In such circumstances, courts may not undo what Congress so plainly has done by "construing" the words of a statute to accomplish a result that Congress rejected. The fact that Congress elected to leave technologically unsophisticated persons who wish to make fair use of encrypted copyrighted works without the technical means of doing so is a matter for Congress unless Congress' decision contravenes the Constitution . . . . Defendants' statutory fair use argument therefore is entirely without merit.

C. Linking to Sites Offering DeCSS

Plaintiffs seek also to enjoin defendants from "linking" their 2600.com web site to other sites that make DeCSS available to users. Their request obviously stems in no small part from what defendants themselves have termed their act of "electronic civil disobedience"—their attempt to defeat the purpose of the preliminary injunction by (a) offering the practical equivalent of making DeCSS available on their own web site by electronically linking users to other sites still offering DeCSS, and (b) encouraging other sites that had not been enjoined to offer the program. The dispositive question is whether linking to another web site containing DeCSS constitutes "offer[ing DeCSS] to the public" or "provid[ing] or otherwise traf-fic[king]" in it within the meaning of the DMCA.[171] Answering this question requires careful consideration of the nature and types of linking.

Most web pages are written in computer languages, chiefly HTML, which allow the programmer to prescribe the appearance of the web page on the computer screen and, in addition, to instruct the computer to perform an operation if the cursor is placed over a particular point on the screen and the mouse then clicked. Programming a particular point on a screen to transfer the user to another web page when the point, referred to as a hyperlink, is clicked is called linking. Web pages can be designed to link to other web pages on the same site or to web pages maintained by different sites.

---

[169] *RealNetworks, Inc.,* 2000 WL 127311, at *8 . . . .

[170] SECTION–BY–SECTION ANALYSIS 9 ("The *Sony* test of 'capab[ility] of substantial non-infringing uses,' while still operative in cases claiming contributory infringement of copyright, is not part of this legislation. . . .").

[171] 17 U.S.C. § 1201(a)(2).

[T]he links that defendants established on their web site are of several types. Some transfer the user to a web page on an outside site that contains a good deal of information of various types, does not itself contain a link to DeCSS, but that links, either directly or via a series of other pages, to another page on the same site that posts the software. It then is up to the user to follow the link or series of links on the linked-to web site in order to arrive at the page with the DeCSS link and commence the download of the software. Others take the user to a page on an outside web site on which there appears a direct link to the DeCSS software and which may or may not contain text or links other than the DeCSS link. The user has only to click on the DeCSS link to commence the download. Still others may directly transfer the user to a file on the linked-to web site such that the download of DeCSS to the user's computer automatically commences without further user intervention.

The statute makes it unlawful to offer, provide or otherwise traffic in described technology. To "traffic" in something is to engage in dealings in it, conduct that necessarily involves awareness of the nature of the subject of the trafficking. To "provide" something, in the sense used in the statute, is to make it available or furnish it. To "offer" is to present or hold it out for consideration. The phrase "or otherwise traffic in" modifies and gives meaning to the words "offer" and "provide." In consequence, the anti-trafficking provision of the DMCA is implicated where one presents, holds out or makes a circumvention technology or device available, knowing its nature, for the purpose of allowing others to acquire it.

To the extent that defendants have linked to sites that automatically commence the process of downloading DeCSS upon a user being transferred by defendants' hyperlinks, there can be no serious question. Defendants are engaged in the functional equivalent of transferring the DeCSS code to the user themselves.

Substantially the same is true of defendants' hyperlinks to web pages that display nothing more than the DeCSS code or present the user only with the choice of commencing a download of DeCSS and no other content. The only distinction is that the entity extending to the user the option of downloading the program is the transferee site rather than defendants, a distinction without a difference.

Potentially more troublesome might be links to pages that offer a good deal of content other than DeCSS but that offer a hyperlink for downloading, or transferring to a page for downloading, DeCSS. If one assumed, for the purposes of argument, that the *Los Angeles Times* web site somewhere contained the DeCSS code, it would be wrong to say that anyone who linked to the *Los Angeles Times* web site, regardless of purpose or the manner in which the link was described, thereby offered, provided or otherwise trafficked in DeCSS merely because DeCSS happened to be available on a site to which one linked. But that is not this case. Defendants urged others to post DeCSS in an effort to disseminate DeCSS and to inform defendants that they were doing so. Defendants then linked their site to those "mirror" sites, after first checking to ensure that the mirror sites in fact were posting DeCSS or something that looked like it, and proclaimed on their own site that DeCSS could be had by clicking on the hyperlinks on defendants' site. By doing so, they offered, provided or otherwise trafficked in DeCSS, and they continue to do so to this day.

. . .

[The court's discussion of defendants' First Amendment argument is omitted.]

VI. Conclusion

In the final analysis, the dispute between these parties is simply put if not necessarily simply resolved.

Plaintiffs have invested huge sums over the years in producing motion pictures in reliance upon a legal framework that, through the law of copyright, has ensured that they will have the exclusive right to copy and distribute those motion pictures for economic gain. They contend that the advent of new technology should not alter this long established structure.

Defendants, on the other hand, are adherents of a movement that believes that information should be available without charge to anyone clever enough to break into the computer systems or data storage media in which it is located. Less radically, they have raised a legitimate concern about the possible impact on traditional fair use of access control measures in the digital era.

Each side is entitled to its views. In our society, however, clashes of competing interests like this are resolved by Congress. For now, at least, Congress has resolved this clash in the DMCA and in plaintiffs' favor. . . . Accordingly, plaintiffs are entitled to appropriate injunctive and declaratory relief.

In the following decision, the Second Circuit affirmed the decision of the district court that is excerpted above.

Universal City Studios, Inc. v. Corley
273 F.3d 429 (2d Cir.2001).

■ JON O. NEWMAN, CIRCUIT JUDGE.

When the Framers of the First Amendment prohibited Congress from making any law "abridging the freedom of speech," they were not thinking about computers, computer programs, or the Internet. But neither were they thinking about radio, television, or movies. Just as the inventions at the beginning and middle of the 20th century presented new First Amendment issues, so does the cyber revolution at the end of that century. This appeal raises significant First Amendment issues concerning one aspect of computer technology—encryption to protect materials in digital form from unauthorized access. The appeal challenges the constitutionality of the Digital Millennium Copyright Act ("DMCA"), 17 U.S.C. § 1201 *et seq.* (Supp. V 1999) and the validity of an injunction entered to enforce the DMCA.

Defendant–Appellant Eric C. Corley and his company, 2600 Enterprises, Inc., (collectively "Corley," "the Defendants," or "the Appellants") appeal from the amended final judgment of the United States District Court for the Southern District of New York (Lewis A. Kaplan, District Judge), entered August 23, 2000, enjoining them from various actions concerning a decryption program known as "DeCSS." *Universal City Studios, Inc. v. Reimerdes,* 111 F.Supp.2d 346 (S.D.N.Y.2000) (*"Universal II"*). The injunction primarily bars the Appellants from posting DeCSS on their web site and from knowingly linking their web site to any other web site on which DeCSS is posted. *Id.* at 346–47. We affirm.

. . .

Discussion

. . .

II. Constitutional Challenge Based on the Copyright Clause

In a footnote to their brief, the Appellants appear to contend that the DMCA, as construed by the District Court, exceeds the constitutional authority of Congress to grant authors copyrights for a "limited time," *U.S. Const. art. I, § 8, cl. 8,* because it "empower[s] copyright owners to effectively secure perpetual protection by mixing public domain works with copyrighted materials, then locking both up with technological protection measures." Brief for Appellants at 42 n.30. This argument is elaborated in the *amici curiae* brief filed by Prof. Julie E. Cohen on behalf of herself and 45 other intellectual property law professors. *See also* David Nimmer, *A Riff on Fair Use in the Digital Millennium Copyright Act,* 148 U. Pa. L. Rev. 673, 712 (2000). For two reasons, the argument provides no basis for disturbing the judgment of the District Court.

First, we have repeatedly ruled that arguments presented to us only in a footnote are not entitled to appellate consideration. . . . Although an *amicus* brief can be helpful in elaborating issues properly presented by the parties, it is normally not a method for injecting new issues into an appeal, at least in cases where the parties are competently represented by counsel. . . . Second, to whatever extent the argument might have merit at some future time in a case with a properly developed record, the argument is entirely premature and speculative at this time on this record. There is not even a claim, much less evidence, that any Plaintiff has sought to prevent copying of public domain works, or that the injunction prevents the Defendants from copying such works. As Judge Kaplan noted, the possibility that encryption would preclude access to public domain works "does not yet appear to be a problem, although it may emerge as one in the future." *Universal I,* 111 F.Supp.2d at 338 n. 245.

III. Constitutional Challenges Based on the First Amendment

A. Applicable Principles

. . .

[The court finds that computer code can merit First Amendment protection.]

3. The Scope of First Amendment Protection for Computer Code

Having concluded that computer code conveying information is "speech" within the meaning of the First Amendment, we next consider, to a limited extent, the scope of the protection that code enjoys. As the District Court recognized, *Universal I,* 111 F.Supp.2d at 327, the scope of protection for speech generally depends on whether the restriction is imposed because of the content of the speech. Content-based restrictions are permissible only if they serve compelling state interests and do so by the least restrictive means available. *See Sable Communications of California, Inc. v. FCC,* 492 U.S. 115, 126 (1989). A content-neutral restriction is permissible if it serves a substantial governmental interest, the interest is unrelated to the suppression of free expression, and the regulation is narrowly tailored, which "in this context requires . . . that the means chosen do not 'burden substantially more speech than is necessary to further the government's legitimate interests.' " *Turner Broadcasting System, Inc. v. FCC,* 512 U.S. 622, 662 (1994) (*quoting Ward v. Rock Against Racism,* 491 U.S. 781, 799 (1989)).

"[G]overnment regulation of expressive activity is 'content neutral' if it is justified without reference to the content of regulated speech." *Hill v. Colorado,* 530 U.S. 703, 720, (2000). "The government's purpose is the controlling consideration. A regulation that serves purposes unrelated to the content of expression is deemed neutral, even if it has an incidental effect on some speakers or messages but not others." *Ward,* 491 U.S. at 791. . . .

. . .

The Appellants vigorously reject the idea that computer code can be regulated according to any different standard than that applicable to pure speech, *i.e.,* speech that lacks a nonspeech component. Although recognizing that code is a series of instructions to a computer, they argue that code is no different, for First Amendment purposes, than blueprints that instruct an engineer or recipes that instruct a cook. We disagree. Unlike a blueprint or a recipe, which cannot yield any functional result without human comprehension of its content, human decision-making, and human action, computer code can instantly cause a computer to accomplish tasks and instantly render the results of those tasks available throughout the world via the Internet. The only human action required to achieve these results can be as limited and instantaneous as a single click of a mouse. These realities of what code is and what its normal functions are require a First Amendment analysis that treats code as combining nonspeech and speech elements, *i.e.,* functional and expressive elements. *See Red Lion Broadcasting Co. v. FCC,* 395 U.S. 367, 386 (1969) ("[D]ifferences in the characteristics of new media justify differences in the First Amendment standards applied to them." (footnote omitted)).

. . .

The functionality of computer code properly affects the scope of its First Amendment protection.

4. The Scope of First Amendment Protection for Decryption Code

In considering the scope of First Amendment protection for a decryption program like DeCSS, we must recognize that the essential purpose of encryption code is to prevent unauthorized access. Owners of all property rights are entitled to prohibit access to their property by unauthorized persons. Homeowners can install locks on the doors of their houses. Custodians of valuables can place them in safes. Stores can attach to products security devices that will activate alarms if the products are taken away without purchase. These and similar security devices can be circumvented. Burglars can use skeleton keys to open door locks. Thieves can obtain the combinations to safes. Product security devices can be neutralized.

Our case concerns a security device, CSS computer code, that prevents access by unauthorized persons to DVD movies. The CSS code is embedded in the DVD movie. Access to the movie cannot be obtained unless a person has a device, a licensed DVD player, equipped with computer code capable of decrypting the CSS encryption code. In its basic function, CSS is like a lock on a homeowner's door, a combination of a safe, or a security device attached to a store's products.

DeCSS is computer code that can decrypt CSS. In its basic function, it is like a skeleton key that can open a locked door, a combination that can open a safe, or a device that can neutralize the security device attached to a store's products. DeCSS enables anyone to gain access to a DVD movie without using a DVD player.

. . .

At first glance, one might think that Congress has as much authority to regulate the distribution of computer code to decrypt DVD movies as it has to regulate distribution of skeleton keys, combinations to safes, or devices to neutralize store product security devices. However, despite the evident legitimacy of protection against unauthorized access to DVD movies, just like any other property, regulation of decryption code like DeCSS is challenged in this case because DeCSS differs from a skeleton key in one important respect: it not only is capable of performing the function of unlocking the encrypted DVD movie, it also is a form of communication, albeit written in a language not understood by the general public. As a communication, the DeCSS code has a claim to being "speech," and as "speech," it has a claim to being protected by the First Amendment. But just as the realities of what any computer code can accomplish must inform the scope of its constitutional protection, so the capacity of a decryption program like DeCSS to accomplish unauthorized — indeed, unlawful — access to materials in which the Plaintiffs have intellectual property rights must inform and limit the scope of its First Amendment protection. . . .

With all of the foregoing considerations in mind, we next consider the Appellants' First Amendment challenge to the DMCA as applied in the specific prohibitions that have been imposed by the District Court's injunction.

B. First Amendment Challenge

The District Court's injunction applies the DMCA to the Defendants by imposing two types of prohibition, both grounded on the anti-trafficking provisions of the DMCA. The first prohibits posting DeCSS or any other technology for circumventing CSS on any Internet web site. *Universal II*, 111 F.Supp.2d at 346–47, ¶ 1(a), (b). The second prohibits knowingly linking any Internet web site to any other web site containing DeCSS. *Id.* at 347, ¶ 1(c). The validity of the posting and linking prohibitions must be considered separately.

1. Posting

The initial issue is whether the posting prohibition is content-neutral, since, as we have explained, this classification determines the applicable constitutional standard. The Appellants contend that the anti-trafficking provisions of the DMCA and their application by means of the posting prohibition of the injunction are content-based. They argue that the provisions "specifically target . . . scientific expression based on the particular topic addressed by that expression—namely, techniques for circumventing CSS." We disagree. The Appellants' argument fails to recognize that the target of the posting provisions of the injunction—DeCSS—has both a nonspeech and a speech component, and that the DMCA, as applied to the Appellants, and the posting prohibition of the injunction target only the nonspeech component. Neither the DMCA nor the posting prohibition is concerned with whatever capacity DeCSS might have for conveying information to a human being, and that capacity, as previously explained, is what arguably creates a speech component of the decryption code. The DMCA and the posting prohibition are applied to DeCSS solely because of its capacity to instruct a computer to decrypt CSS. That functional capability is not speech within the meaning of the First Amendment. The Government seeks to "justif[y]," *Hill,* 530 U.S. at 720, both the application of the DMCA and the posting prohibition to the Appellants solely on the basis of the functional capability of DeCSS to instruct a computer to decrypt CSS, *i.e.,* "without reference to the content of the regulated speech," *id.* This type of regulation is therefore content-neutral, just as would be a restriction on trafficking in skeleton keys identified because of their capacity to unlock jail cells, even though some of the keys happened to bear a slogan or other legend that qualified as a speech component.

As a content-neutral regulation with an incidental effect on a speech component, the regulation must serve a substantial governmental interest, the interest must be unrelated to the suppression of free expression, and the incidental restriction on speech must not burden substantially more speech than is necessary to further that interest. *Turner Broadcasting,* 512 U.S. at 662. The Government's interest in preventing unauthorized access to encrypted copyrighted material is unquestionably substantial, and the regulation of DeCSS by the posting prohibition plainly serves that interest. Moreover, that interest is unrelated to the suppression of free expression. The injunction regulates the posting of DeCSS, regardless of whether DeCSS code contains any information comprehensible by human beings that would qualify as speech. Whether the incidental regulation on speech burdens substantially more speech than is necessary to further the interest in preventing unauthorized access to copyrighted materials requires some elaboration.

Posting DeCSS on the Appellants' web site makes it instantly available at the click of a mouse to any person in the world with access to the Internet, and such person can then instantly transmit DeCSS to anyone else with Internet access. Although the prohibition on posting prevents the Appellants from conveying to others the speech component of DeCSS, the Appellants have not suggested, much less shown, any technique for barring them from making this instantaneous worldwide distribution of a decryption code that makes a lesser restriction on the code's speech component. It is true that the Government has alternative means of prohibiting unauthorized access to copyrighted materials. For example, it can create criminal and civil liability for those who gain unauthorized access, and thus it can be argued that the restriction on posting DeCSS is not absolutely necessary to preventing unauthorized access to copyrighted materials. But a content-neutral regulation need not employ the least restrictive means of accomplishing the governmental objective. *Id.* It need only avoid burdening "substantially more speech than is necessary to further the government's legitimate interests." *Id.* (internal quotation marks and citation omitted). The prohibition on the Defendants' posting of DeCSS satisfies that standard.[30]

2. Linking

. . .

In applying the DMCA to linking (via hyperlinks), Judge Kaplan recognized, as he had with DeCSS code, that a hyperlink has both a speech and a nonspeech component. It conveys information, the Internet address of the linked web page, and has the functional capacity to bring the content of the linked web page to the user's computer screen (or, as Judge Kaplan put it, to "take one almost instantaneously to the desired destination." *Id.*). As he had ruled with respect to DeCSS code, he ruled that application of the DMCA to the Defendants' linking to web sites containing DeCSS is content-neutral because it is justified without regard to the speech component of the hyperlink. *Id.* The linking prohibition applies whether or not the hyperlink contains any information, comprehensible to a human being, as to the Internet address of the web page being accessed. The linking prohibition is justified solely by the functional capability of the hyperlink.

Applying the *O'Brien/Ward/Turner Broadcasting* requirements for content-neutral regulation, Judge Kaplan then ruled that the DMCA, as applied to the Defendants' linking, served substantial governmental interests and was unrelated to the suppression of free expression. *Id.* We agree. He then carefully considered the "closer call," *id.*, as to whether a linking prohibition would satisfy the narrow tailoring requirement. In an especially carefully considered portion of his opinion, he observed that strict liability for linking to web sites containing DeCSS would risk two impairments of free expression. Web site operators would be inhibited from displaying links to various web pages for fear that a linked page might contain DeCSS, and a prohibition on linking to a web site containing DeCSS would curtail access to whatever other information was contained at the accessed site. *Id.* at 340.

To avoid applying the DMCA in a manner that would "burden substantially more speech than is necessary to further the government's legitimate interests," *Turner Broadcasting,* 512 U.S. at 662 (internal quotation marks and citation omitted), Judge Kaplan adapted the standards of *New York Times Co. v. Sullivan,* 376 U.S. 254, 283 (1964), to fashion a limited prohibition against linking to web sites containing DeCSS. He required clear and convincing evidence

---

[30] We have considered the opinion of a California intermediate appellate court in *DVD Copy Control Ass'n v. Bunner,* 93 Cal.App.4th 648, 113 Cal.Rptr.2d 338 (2001), declining, on First Amendment grounds, to issue a preliminary injunction under state trade secrets law prohibiting a web site operator from posting DeCSS. To the extent that *DVD Copy Control* disagrees with our First Amendment analysis, we decline to follow it.

that those responsible for the link (a) know at the relevant time that the offending material is on the linked-to site, (b) know that it is circumvention technology that may not lawfully be offered, and (c) create or maintain the link for the purpose of disseminating that technology.

Universal I, 111 F.Supp.2d at 341. He then found that the evidence satisfied his three-part test by his required standard of proof. *Id.*

. . .

At oral argument, we asked the Government whether its undoubted power to punish the distribution of obscene materials would permit an injunction prohibiting a newspaper from printing addresses of bookstore locations carrying such materials. In a properly cautious response, the Government stated that the answer would depend on the circumstances of the publication. The Appellants' supplemental papers enthusiastically embraced the arguable analogy between printing bookstore addresses and displaying on a web page links to web sites at which DeCSS may be accessed. Supplemental Brief for Appellants at 14. They confidently asserted that publication of bookstore locations carrying obscene material cannot be enjoined consistent with the First Amendment, and that a prohibition against linking to web sites containing DeCSS is similarly invalid. *Id.*

Like many analogies posited to illuminate legal issues, the bookstore analogy is helpful primarily in identifying characteristics that *distinguish* it from the context of the pending dispute. If a bookstore proprietor is knowingly selling obscene materials, the evil of distributing such materials can be prevented by injunctive relief against the unlawful distribution (and similar distribution by others can be deterred by punishment of the distributor). And if others publish the location of the bookstore, preventive relief against a distributor can be effective before any significant distribution of the prohibited materials has occurred. The digital world, however, creates a very different problem. If obscene materials are posted on one web site and other sites post hyperlinks to the first site, the materials are available for instantaneous worldwide distribution before any preventive measures can be effectively taken.

This reality obliges courts considering First Amendment claims in the context of the pending case to choose between two unattractive alternatives: either tolerate some impairment of communication in order to permit Congress to prohibit decryption that may lawfully be prevented, or tolerate some decryption in order to avoid some impairment of communication. Although the parties dispute the extent of impairment of communication if the injunction is upheld and the extent of decryption if it is vacated, and differ on the availability and effectiveness of techniques for minimizing both consequences, the fundamental choice between impairing some communication and tolerating decryption cannot be entirely avoided.

In facing this choice, we are mindful that it is not for us to resolve the issues of public policy implicated by the choice we have identified. Those issues are for Congress. Our task is to determine whether the legislative solution adopted by Congress, as applied to the Appellants by the District Court's injunction, is consistent with the limitations of the First Amendment, and we are satisfied that it is.

IV. Constitutional Challenge Based on Claimed Restriction of Fair Use

Asserting that fair use "is rooted in and required by both the Copyright Clause and the First Amendment," the Appellants contend that the DMCA, as applied by the District Court, unconstitutionally *"eliminates* fair use" of copyrighted materials, *id.* at 41 (emphasis added). We reject this extravagant claim.

Preliminarily, we note that the Supreme Court has never held that fair use is constitutionally required, although some isolated statements in its opinions might arguably be enlisted for such a requirement. . . .

We need not explore the extent to which fair use might have constitutional protection, grounded on either the First Amendment or the Copyright Clause, because whatever validity a constitutional claim might have as to an application of the DMCA that impairs fair use of copyrighted materials, such matters are far beyond the scope of this lawsuit for several reasons. In the first place, the Appellants do not claim to be making fair use of any copyrighted materials, and nothing in the injunction prohibits them from making such fair use. They are barred from trafficking in a decryption code that enables unauthorized access to copyrighted materials.

Second, as the District Court properly noted, to whatever extent the anti-trafficking provisions of the DMCA might prevent others from copying portions of DVD movies in order to make fair use of them, "the evidence as to the impact of the anti-trafficking provision[s] of the DMCA on prospective fair users is scanty and fails adequately to address the issues." *Universal I,* 111 F.Supp.2d at 338 n. 246.

Third, the Appellants have provided no support for their premise that fair use of DVD movies is constitutionally required to be made by copying the original work in its original format. Their examples of the fair uses that they believe others will be prevented from making all involve copying in a digital format those portions of a DVD movie amenable to fair use, a copying that would enable the fair user to manipulate the digitally copied portions. One example is that of a school child who wishes to copy images from a DVD movie to insert into the student's documentary film. We know of no authority for the proposition that fair use, as protected by the Copyright Act, much less the Constitution, guarantees copying by the optimum method or in the identical format of the original. Although the Appellants insisted at oral argument that they should not be relegated to a "horse and buggy" technique in making fair use of DVD movies, the DMCA does not impose even an arguable limitation on the opportunity to make a variety of traditional fair uses of DVD movies, such as commenting on their content, quoting excerpts from their screenplays, and even recording portions of the video images and sounds on film or tape by pointing a camera, a camcorder, or a microphone at a monitor as it displays the DVD movie. The fact that the resulting copy will not be as perfect or as manipulable as a digital copy obtained by having direct access to the DVD movie in its digital form, provides no basis for a claim of unconstitutional limitation of fair use. A film critic making fair use of a movie by quoting selected lines of dialogue has no constitutionally valid claim that the review (in print or on television) would be technologically superior if the reviewer had not been prevented from using a movie camera in the theater, nor has an art student a valid constitutional claim to fair use of a painting by photographing it in a museum. Fair use has never been held to be a guarantee of access to copyrighted material in order to copy it by the fair user's preferred technique or in the format of the original.

Conclusion

We have considered all the other arguments of the Appellants and conclude that they provide no basis for disturbing the District Court's judgment. Accordingly, the judgment is affirmed.

Chamberlain Group, Inc. v. Skylink Technologies, Inc.
381 F.3d 1178 (Fed.Cir.2004).

■ GAJARSA, CIRCUIT JUDGE.

The Chamberlain Group, Inc. ("Chamberlain") appeals the . . . summary judgment . . . in favor of Skylink Technologies, Inc. ("Skylink"), finding that Skylink is not violating the anti-trafficking provisions of the Digital Millennium Copyright Act ("DMCA"), 17 U.S.C. § 1201 *et seq.*, and dismissing all other claims, including claims of patent infringement. *Chamberlain Group, Inc. v. Skylink Techs., Inc.*, 292 F.Supp.2d 1040 (N.D.Ill.2003) ("*Chamberlain II*"). That same court, in an earlier ruling, denied Chamberlain's motion for summary judgment on its DMCA claims. *Chamberlain Group, Inc. v. Skylink Techs., Inc.*, 292 F.Supp.2d 1023 (N.D.Ill.2003) ("*Chamberlain I*"). Chamberlain does not appeal that denial of its summary judgment motion.

Chamberlain's claims at issue stem from its allegation that the District Court incorrectly construed the DMCA as placing a burden upon Chamberlain to prove that the circumvention of its technological measures enabled unauthorized access to its copyrighted software. But Skylink's accused device enables only uses that copyright law explicitly authorizes, and is therefore presumptively legal. Chamberlain has neither proved nor alleged a connection between Skylink's accused circumvention device and the protections that the copyright laws afford Chamberlain capable of overcoming that presumption. Chamberlain's failure to meet this burden alone compels a legal ruling in Skylink's favor. . . .

BACKGROUND

A. The Applicable Statute

Chamberlain sued Skylink, alleging violations of the patent and copyright laws. . . . The matter on appeal involves only Chamberlain's allegation that Skylink is violating . . . the anti-trafficking provision of § 1201(a)(2). . . .

B. The Dispute

. . . The technology at issue involves Garage Door Openers (GDOs). A GDO typically consists of a hand-held portable transmitter and a garage door opening device mounted in a homeowner's garage. The opening device, in turn, includes both a receiver with associated signal processing software and a motor to open or close the garage door. In order to open or close the garage door, a user must activate the transmitter, which sends a radio frequency (RF) signal to the receiver located on the opening device. Once the opener receives a recognized signal, the signal processing software directs the motor to open or close the garage door.

When a homeowner purchases a GDO system, the manufacturer provides both an opener and a transmitter. Homeowners who desire replacement or spare transmitters can purchase them in the aftermarket. Aftermarket consumers have long been able to purchase "universal transmitters" that they can program to interoperate with their GDO system regardless of make or model. Skylink and Chamberlain are the only significant distributors of universal GDO transmitters.[1] Chamberlain places no explicit restrictions on the types of transmitter that the homeowner may use with its system at the time of purchase. Chamberlain's customers therefore assume that they enjoy all of the rights associated with the use of their GDOs and any software embedded therein that the copyright laws and other laws of commerce provide.

This dispute involves Chamberlain's Security+ line of GDOs and Skylink's Model 39 universal transmitter. Chamberlain's Security+ GDOs incorporate a copyrighted "rolling code" computer program that constantly changes the transmitter signal needed to open the garage door. Skylink's Model 39 transmitter, which does not incorporate rolling code, nevertheless allows users to operate Security+ openers. Chamberlain alleges that Skylink's transmitter renders the Security+ insecure by allowing unauthorized users to circumvent the security inherent in rolling codes. Of greater legal significance, however, Chamberlain contends that because of this property of the Model 39, Skylink is in violation of the anti-trafficking clause of the DMCA's anticircumvention provisions, specifically § 1201(a)(2).

The code in a standard (i.e., non-rolling code) GDO transmitter is unique but fixed. Thus, according to Chamberlain, the typical GDO is vulnerable to attack by burglars who can open the garage door using a "code grabber." According to Chamberlain, code grabbers allow burglars in close proximity to a homeowner operating her garage door to record the signal sent from the transmitter to the opener, and to return later, replay the recorded signal, and open the garage door. Chamberlain concedes, however, that code grabbers are more theoretical than practical burgling devices; none of its witnesses had either firsthand knowledge of a single code grabbing problem or familiarity with data demonstrating the existence of a problem. Nevertheless, Chamberlain claims to have developed its rolling code system specifically to prevent code grabbing.[2]

The essence of the rolling code system is that the transmitted signals are broken into fixed and variable (or "rolling") components. The entire transmitted signal is a

---

[1] Chamberlain's product, the "Clicker," interoperates with both Chamberlain and non-Chamberlain GDOs.

[2] According to Skylink, Chamberlain introduced rolling codes to prevent inadvertent GDO activation by planes passing overhead, not as a security measure.

bit string. The fixed component serves to identify the transmitter. The rolling component cycles through a lengthy cycle of bit strings only some of which are capable of opening the door at any given time, ostensibly so that a burglar replaying a grabbed code is unlikely to send a valid signal—and therefore unlikely to open the garage door.

A user wishing to set up a new transmitter for use with her Security+ GDO must switch the opener to "program mode" and send a signal from the transmitter to the opener. The opener stores both the fixed and rolling components of the transmitted signal. When the user switches the opener back to "operate mode," the system is set and the user may operate the opener with the newly programmed transmitter. In Chamberlain's transmitter, a computer program increases the rolling code by a factor of three each time the user activates the transmitter. When the transmitted signal reaches the receiver, a program in the opener checks to see whether the rolling code received was identical to one of the most recently received 1,024 rolling codes (the "rear window"). If so, it will not activate the motor. If, on the other hand, the rolling code received is among the next 4,096 binary signals (the "forward window"), the receiver will activate the motor.

Not all recognized binary rolling signals are in either the forward or rear windows. If the transmitter sends a single signal outside of either window, the receiver will ignore it. If, however, the transmitter sends two signals outside either window in rapid succession, the opener will again access its programming, this time to determine whether the two signals together comprise a "resynchronization" sequence. If the signals differ by three, the receiver will reset the windows and activate the motor. According to Chamberlain, resynchronization accommodates the possibility that homeowners using the same transmitter for multiple residences may transmit so many signals while out of range of the opener that they exhaust the entire forward window.

Skylink began marketing and selling universal transmitters in 1992. Skylink designed its Model 39, launched in August 2002, to interoperate with common GDOs, including both rolling code and non-rolling code GDOs.[3] Although Chamberlain concedes that the Model 39 transmitter is capable of operating many different GDOs, it nevertheless asserts that Skylink markets the Model 39 transmitter for use in circumventing its copyrighted rolling code computer program. Chamberlain supports this allegation by pointing to the Model 39's setting that operates only Chamberlain's rolling code GDOs.

Skylink's Model 39 does not use rolling code technology. Like Chamberlain's products, however, the Model 39's binary signal contains two components. The first corresponds to the Chamberlain's fixed component identifying the transmitter, and the second simulates the effect of the Chamberlain's rolling code. Like the Chamberlain fixed component, the primary role of the Model 39's identifying component is in programming; a homeowner wishing to use a Model 39 in con-

---

[3] The Model 39 interoperates with at least 15 different brands and dozens of different GDO models, only a few of which include Chamberlain's rolling code. One of the Model 39's settings interoperates only with Chamberlain rolling code GDOs.

junction with a Chamberlain GDO must program the opener to recognize his newly purchased transmitter. When the homeowner actually uses the transmitter, it broadcasts three fixed codes in rapid succession. The first binary signal combines the identifying component with an arbitrary binary sequence. The second binary signal subtracts 1800 from the first signal. The third signal adds three to the second signal. The combination of these three codes transmitted with every press of the Model 39 transmitter button will either cause the Chamberlain GDO to operate in response to the first fixed code or cause the GDO to resynchronize and operate in response to the second and third fixed codes. Chamberlain characterizes this procedure as a circumvention of an important security measure; a code grabber that recorded the Model 39's three codes could later play them back and activate a Chamberlain rolling code GDO without authorization.

These facts frame the dispute now before us on appeal. Though only Chamberlain's DMCA claim is before us, and though the parties dispute whether or not Skylink developed the Model 39 independent of Chamberlain's copyrighted products,[4] it is nevertheless noteworthy that Chamberlain has not alleged either that Skylink infringed its copyright or that Skylink is liable for contributory copyright infringement. What Chamberlain has alleged is that because its opener and transmitter both incorporate computer programs "protected by copyright" and because rolling codes are a "technological measure" that "controls access" to those programs, Skylink is prima facie liable for violating § 1201(a)(2). In the District Court's words, "Chamberlain claims that the rolling code computer program has a protective measure that protects itself. Thus, only one computer program is at work here, but it has two functions: (1) to verify the rolling code; and (2) once the rolling code is verified, to activate the GDO motor, by sending instructions to a microprocessor in the GDO." *Chamberlain I,* 292 F.Supp.2d at 1028.

C. The Summary Judgment Motions

The District Court first considered Chamberlain's motion for summary judgment on its DMCA claim. Chamberlain sued Skylink under 17 U.S.C. § 1201(a)(2), a statutory provision that neither the Seventh Circuit nor any previous District Court in the Seventh Circuit had ever considered. To date, in fact, only the Second Circuit has construed § 1201(a)(2), and that construction focused on First Amendment issues rather than on an application of the statute to case-specific facts. *See Universal City Studios v. Corley,* 273 F.3d 429 (2d Cir.2001) ("Corley"). . . . [T]he District Court denied Chamberlain's motion for summary judgment. . . .

Chamberlain's argument, submitted in both summary judgment motions, rests on its interpretation of the statute's "plain language." Chamberlain contends first, that Skylink "primarily designed or produced [the Model 39] for the purpose of circumventing [Chamberlain's rolling code] technological measure that effectively controls access to [Chamberlain's copyrighted computer programs]," contravening § 1201(a)(2)(A); second, that the Model 39 "has only limited commercially significant purpose or use other than to circumvent [Chamberlain's rolling code] techno-

---

[4] According to Chamberlain, the transmitter program . . . and the computer program in the receiver [are] registered with the United States Copyright Office . . . .

logical measure that effectively controls access to [Chamberlain's copyrighted computer programs]," contravening § 1201(a)(2)(B); and third, that Skylink marketed the Model 39 "for use in circumventing [Chamberlain's rolling code] technological measure that effectively controls access to [Chamberlain's copyrighted computer programs]," contravening § 1201(a)(2)(C).

Skylink submitted several defenses, [including] arguing that . . . (3) consumers use the Model 39 transmitter to activate the Security+ GDOs with Chamberlain's consent . . . . [T]he District Court . . . based its rulings entirely on Skylink's third argument concerning authorization and consent.

Chamberlain submitted two arguments in response to Skylink's assertion that Chamberlain authorized its customers to use the Model 39. First, Chamberlain argued that Skylink bore the burden of proving that its behavior was authorized, and that Skylink's argument was therefore, at best, an affirmative defense rather than a defect in its own pleadings. *Chamberlain II*, 292 F.Supp.2d at 1044. Second, Chamberlain noted that it never gave consumers explicit authorization to program competing universal transmitters into its rolling code openers, at least in part because it never anticipated that any competitor would crack its code. Skylink did not dispute this point, but asserted simply that in the absence of an explicit restriction, consumers must be free to infer that they have purchased the full range of rights that normally accompany consumer products—including those containing copyrighted embedded software.

In assessing the authorization issue, the District Court noted that according to the statute's internal definitions, "circumvent a technological measure" means to "descramble a scrambled work, to decrypt an encrypted work, or otherwise to avoid, bypass, remove, deactivate, or impair a technological measure, *without the authority of the copyright owner*." (17 U.S.C. § 1201(a)(3)(A)) (emphasis added by District Court).

According to undisputed facts, a homeowner who purchases a Chamberlain GDO owns it and has a right to use it to access his or her own garage. At the time of sale, Chamberlain does not place any explicit terms or condition on use to limit the ways that a purchaser may use its products. A homeowner who wishes to use a Model 39 must first program it into the GDO. Skylink characterizes this action as the homeowner's authorization of the Model 39 to interoperate with the GDO. In other words, according to Skylink, Chamberlain GDO consumers who purchase a Skylink transmitter have Chamberlain's implicit permission to purchase and to use any brand of transmitter that will open their GDO. The District Court agreed that Chamberlain's unconditioned sale implied authorization.

Chamberlain also argued that its web page and warranty implied restrictions on the use of competing transmitters. The District Court, however, refused to read an implicit restriction from the mere absence of competing products discussed on Chamberlain's web page, particularly given the longstanding industry practice of marketing universal transmitters. The District Court rejected the alleged implications of Chamberlain's warranties even more strongly, noting that consumers are always free to forego the benefits of a product's warranty and to use consumer products in any way that they choose. . . .

The District Court further noted that under Chamberlain's proposed construction of the DMCA, not only would Skylink be in violation of § 1201(a)(2) (prohibiting trafficking in circumvention devices), but Chamberlain's own customers who used a Model 39 would be in violation of § 1201(a)(1) (prohibiting circumvention). The District Court declined to adopt a construction with such dire implications.

In short, the District Court concluded that because Chamberlain never restricted its customers' use of competing transmitters with its Security+ line, those customers had implicit authorization to use Skylink's Model 39. Because of that implicit authorization, Chamberlain could not possibly meet its burden of proving that Skylink trafficked in a device designed to circumvent a technological measure to gain unauthorized access to Chamberlain's copyrighted computer programs. The District Court therefore granted Skylink's motion for summary judgment on Chamberlain's DMCA claim. Chamberlain timely appealed . . . .

DISCUSSION

A. Jurisdiction

[The court concluded that it had jurisdiction over the appeal because Chamberlain's original complaint, in addition to claims under Section 1201, asserted claims arising under patent law, and the district court had resolved at least one of those claims in its proceedings, making appeal to the Federal Circuit, rather than the Seventh Circuit, proper.]

B. The Parties' Positions

On appeal, the parties have raised a number of issues that we must address both as matters of statutory construction and as they relate to the factual disposition of this case. Chamberlain argues that "Skylink violates the prima facie requirement of anti-trafficking § 1201(a)(2)." According to Chamberlain, "Skylink did not seriously dispute that the operation of its transmitters bypasses Chamberlain's rolling code security measure to gain access to Chamberlain's copyrighted GDO receiver operating software, but instead focuses on an 'authorization' defense." Given that "plain language" interpretation of the statute, Chamberlain also argues that the District Court erred in assigning the plaintiff the burden of proving that access was unauthorized rather than placing the burden on the defendant to prove that the access was authorized. Finally, with the burden thus shifted, Chamberlain argues that Skylink has not met its burden, and that the District Court's grant of summary judgment was therefore in error.

Skylink primarily urges us to adopt both the District Court's construction and its application of its construction to the facts of this case. In particular, Skylink urges us not to place the burden of proving authorization on defendants, arguing that it would be tantamount to reading a new "authority" requirement into the DMCA.[8] To resolve this dispute, we must first construe the relevant portions of the

---

[8] . . . Amicus Consumers Union (CU) urges us to consider the policy implications of Chamberlain's proposed construction to consumers and to aftermarket competitors. According to CU, Chamberlain's proposed construction of the DMCA would enable copyright

DMCA, and then apply the statute, properly construed, to the specific facts at issue.

C. Standard of Review

. . .

Our task is essentially one of statutory construction. It is also a matter of first impression. For us to determine whether or not Skylink was entitled to summary judgment that its Model 39 universal transmitter does not violate the DMCA, we must first determine precisely what § 1201(a)(2) prohibits. . . . [T]here is no binding [Seventh Circuit] precedent governing the substantive issues in this case. The parties have provided numerous citations to persuasive authority from other regional circuits and from District Courts, primarily but not exclusively *Universal City Studios, Inc. v. Reimerdes*, 111 F.Supp.2d 294, 319 (S.D.N.Y.2000) ("Reimerdes"), *aff'd sub nom. Universal City Studios v. Corley*, 273 F.3d 429 (2d Cir.2001) ("Corley"). . . .

D. The Statute and Liability under the DMCA

The essence of the DMCA's anticircumvention provisions is that §§ 1201(a), (b) establish causes of action for liability. They do not establish a new property right. The DMCA's text indicates that circumvention is not infringement, 17 U.S.C. § 1201(c)(1) ("Nothing in this section shall affect rights, remedies, limitations, or defenses to copyright infringement, including fair use, under this title."), and the statute's structure makes the point even clearer. This distinction between property and liability is critical. Whereas copyrights, like patents, are property, liability protection from unauthorized circumvention merely creates a new cause of action under which a defendant may be liable. The distinction between property and liability goes straight to the issue of authorization, the issue upon which the District Court both denied Chamberlain's and granted Skylink's motion for summary judgment.

A plaintiff alleging copyright infringement need prove only "(1) ownership of a valid copyright, and (2) copying of constituent elements of the work that are original." *Feist Pub., Inc. v. Rural Tel. Serv. Co.*, 499 U.S. 340, 361 (1991). "The existence of a license, exclusive or nonexclusive, creates an affirmative defense to a claim of copyright infringement." *I.A.E., Inc. v. Shaver*, 74 F.3d 768, 775 (7th Cir.1996). In other words, under Seventh Circuit copyright law, a plaintiff only needs to show that the defendant has used her property; the burden of proving that the use was authorized falls squarely on the defendant. The DMCA, however, defines circumvention as an activity undertaken "without the authority of the copyright owner." 17 U.S.C. § 1201(a)(3)(A). The plain language of the statute therefore requires a plaintiff alleging circumvention (or trafficking) to prove that the defendant's access

---

owners to engage in a number of practices that would otherwise be considered copyright misuse, an antitrust violation, or a violation of state unfair competition laws. At oral argument, Chamberlain conceded that its proposed construction would, indeed, alter virtually all existing consumer expectations concerning the public's rights to use purchased products containing copyrighted software protected by a technological measure—effectively confirming CU's fears.

was unauthorized—a significant burden where, as here, the copyright laws authorize consumers to use the copy of Chamberlain's software embedded in the GDOs that they purchased. The premise underlying this initial assignment of burden is that the copyright laws authorize members of the public to access a work, but not to copy it. The law therefore places the burden of proof on the party attempting to establish that the circumstances of its case deviate from these normal expectations; defendants must prove authorized copying and plaintiffs must prove unauthorized access.

The distinction between property and liability also addresses an important policy issue that Chamberlain puts into stark focus. According to Chamberlain, the 1998 enactment of the DMCA "renders the pre-DMCA history in the GDO industry irrelevant. By prohibiting the trafficking and use of circumvention technology, the DMCA fundamentally altered the legal landscape. . . . Any analysis of practices within the GDO industry must now be undertaken in light of the DMCA." Chamberlain reiterated and strengthened this assertion at oral argument, claiming that the DMCA overrode all pre-existing consumer expectations about the legitimate uses of products containing copyrighted embedded software. Chamberlain contends that Congress empowered manufacturers to prohibit consumers from using embedded software products in conjunction with competing products when it passed § 1201(a)(1). According to Chamberlain, all such uses of products containing copyrighted software to which a technological measure controlled access are now per se illegal under the DMCA unless the manufacturer provided consumers with explicit authorization. Chamberlain's interpretation of the DMCA would therefore grant manufacturers broad exemptions from both the antitrust laws and the doctrine of copyright misuse.

Such an exemption, however, is only plausible if the anticircumvention provisions established a new property right capable of conflicting with the copyright owner's other legal responsibilities—which as we have already explained, they do not. The anticircumvention provisions convey no additional property rights in and of themselves; they simply provide property owners with new ways to secure their property. Like all property owners taking legitimate steps to protect their property, however, copyright owners relying on the anticircumvention provisions remain bound by all other relevant bodies of law. Contrary to Chamberlain's assertion, the DMCA emphatically did not "fundamentally alter" the legal landscape governing the reasonable expectations of consumers or competitors; did not "fundamentally alter" the ways that courts analyze industry practices; and did not render the pre-DMCA history of the GDO industry irrelevant.

What the DMCA did was introduce new grounds for liability in the context of the unauthorized access of copyrighted material. The statute's plain language requires plaintiffs to prove that those circumventing their technological measures controlling access did so "without the authority of the copyright owner." 17 U.S.C. § 1201(a)(3)(A). Our inquiry ends with that clear language. We note, however, that the statute's structure, legislative history, and context within the Copyright Act all support our construction. They also help to explain why Chamberlain's warranty conditions and website postings cannot render users of Skylink's Model 39 "unauthorized" users for the purposes of establishing trafficking liability under the DMCA.

E. Statutory Structure and Legislative History

The specific statutory provision here at issue is § 1201(a)(2) of the DMCA. . . .

. . .

Because the DMCA is a complex statute creating several new causes of action, each subject to numerous exceptions, we must also ensure that our construction makes sense given the statute's entirety. We must therefore consider briefly the relationship among the liabilities created under §§ 1201(a)(1), (a)(2), and (b). Statutory structure and legislative history both make it clear that § 1201 applies only to circumventions reasonably related to protected rights. Defendants who traffic in devices that circumvent access controls in ways that facilitate infringement may be subject to liability under § 1201(a)(2). Defendants who use such devices may be subject to liability under § 1201(a)(1) whether they infringe or not. Because all defendants who traffic in devices that circumvent rights controls necessarily facilitate infringement, they may be subject to liability under § 1201(b). Defendants who use such devices may be subject to liability for copyright infringement. And finally, defendants whose circumvention devices do not facilitate infringement are not subject to § 1201 liability.

The key to understanding this relationship lies in § 1201(b), which prohibits trafficking in devices that circumvent technological measures tailored narrowly to protect an individual right of the copyright owner while nevertheless allowing access to the protected work. Though § 1201(b) parallels the anti-trafficking ban of § 1201(a)(2), there is no narrowly tailored ban on direct circumvention to parallel § 1201(a)(1). This omission was intentional.

> The prohibition in 1201(a)(1) [was] necessary because prior to [the DMCA], the conduct of circumvention was never before made unlawful. The device limitation in 1201(a)(2) enforces this new prohibition in conduct. The copyright law has long forbidden copyright infringements, so no new prohibition was necessary. The device limitation in 1201(b) enforces the longstanding prohibitions on infringements.

S. Rep. No. 105–90 at 12 (1998).

Prior to the DMCA, a copyright owner would have had no cause of action against anyone who circumvented any sort of technological control, but did not infringe. The DMCA rebalanced these interests to favor the copyright owner; the DMCA created circumvention liability for "digital trespass" under § 1201(a)(1). It also created trafficking liability under § 1201(a)(2) for facilitating such circumvention and under § 1201(b) for facilitating infringement (both subject to the numerous limitations and exceptions outlined throughout the DMCA).[13]

---

[13] For obvious reasons, § 1201(a)(2) trafficking liability cannot exist in the absence of § 1201(a)(1) violations—much as this court has often explained that "indirect [patent] infringement, whether inducement to infringe or contributory infringement, can only arise in the presence of direct infringement, though the direct infringer is typically someone other

The importance of "rebalancing" interests in light of recent technological advances is manifest in the DMCA's legislative history. . . .

The most significant and consistent theme running through the entire legislative history of the anticircumvention and anti-trafficking provisions of the DMCA, §§ 1201(a)(1), (2), is that Congress attempted to balance competing interests, and "endeavored to specify, with as much clarity as possible, how the right against anti-circumvention would be qualified to maintain balance between the interests of content creators and information users." H.R. Rep. No. 105–551, at 26 (1998). The Report of the House Commerce Committee concluded that § 1201 "fully respects and extends into the digital environment the bedrock principle of 'balance' in American intellectual property law for the benefit of both copyright owners and users." *Id.*

The crux of the present dispute over statutory construction therefore stems from a dispute over the precise balance between copyright owners and users that Congress captured in the DMCA's language. . . . We must understand that balance to resolve this dispute.

F. Access and Protection

Congress crafted the new anticircumvention and anti-trafficking provisions here at issue to help bring copyright law into the information age. Advances in digital technology over the past few decades have stripped copyright owners of much of the technological and economic protection to which they had grown accustomed. Whereas large-scale copying and distribution of copyrighted material used to be difficult and expensive, it is now easy and inexpensive. The *Reimerdes* court correctly noted both the economic impact of these advances and their consequent potential impact on innovation. Congress therefore crafted legislation restricting some, but not all, technological measures designed either to access a work protected by copyright, § 1201(a), or to infringe a right of a copyright owner, § 1201(b).

Though as noted, circumvention is not a new form of infringement but rather a new violation prohibiting actions or products that facilitate infringement, it is significant that virtually every clause of § 1201 that mentions "access" links "access" to "protection." The import of that linkage may be less than obvious. Perhaps the best way to appreciate the necessity of this linkage—and the disposition of this case—is to consider three interrelated questions inherent in the DMCA's structure: What does § 1201(a)(2) prohibit above and beyond the prohibitions of § 1201(b)? What is the relationship between the sorts of "access" prohibited under § 1201(a) and the rights "protected" under the Copyright Act? and What is the relationship between anticircumvention liability under § 1201(a)(1) and anti-trafficking liability under § 1201(a)(2)? The relationships among the new liabilities that these three provisions, §§ 1201(a)(1), (a)(2), (b), create circumscribe the DMCA's scope—and therefore allow us to determine whether or not Chamberlain's claim falls within its

---

than the defendant accused of indirect infringement." *Dynacore Holdings Corp. v. U.S. Philips Corp.*, 363 F.3d 1263, 1272 (Fed. Cir.2004).

purview. And the key to disentangling these relationships lies in understanding the linkage between access and protection.

Chamberlain urges us to read the DMCA as if Congress simply created a new protection for copyrighted works without any reference at all either to the protections that copyright owners already possess or to the rights that the Copyright Act grants to the public. Chamberlain has not alleged that Skylink's Model 39 infringes its copyrights, nor has it alleged that the Model 39 contributes to third-party infringement of its copyrights. Chamberlain's allegation is considerably more straightforward: The only way for the Model 39 to interoperate with a Security+ GDO is by "accessing" copyrighted software. Skylink has therefore committed a per se violation of the DMCA. Chamberlain urges us to conclude that no necessary connection exists between access and *copyrights*. Congress could not have intended such a broad reading of the DMCA. . . .

Chamberlain derives its strongest claimed support for its proposed construction from the trial court's opinion in *Reimerdes* . . . . Though Chamberlain is correct in considering some of the *Reimerdes* language supportive, it is the differences between the cases, rather than their similarities, that is most instructive in demonstrating precisely what the DMCA permits and what it prohibits.

The facts here differ greatly from those in *Reimerdes*. There, a group of movie studios sought an injunction under the DMCA to prohibit illegal copying of digital versatile discs (DVDs). The plaintiffs presented evidence that each motion picture DVD includes a content scrambling system (CSS) that permits the film to be played, but not copied, using DVD players that incorporate the plaintiffs' licensed decryption technology. The defendant provided a link on his website that allowed an individual to download DeCSS, a program that allows the user to circumvent the CSS protective system and to view or to copy a motion picture from a DVD, whether or not the user has a DVD player with the licensed technology. The defendant proudly trumpeted his actions as "electronic civil disobedience." *Id.* at 303, 312. The court found that the defendant had violated 17 U.S.C. § 1201(a)(2)(A) because DeCSS had only one purpose: to decrypt CSS.

Chamberlain's proposed construction of the DMCA ignores the significant differences between defendants whose accused products enable copying and those, like Skylink, whose accused products enable only legitimate uses of copyrighted software. Chamberlain's repeated reliance on language targeted at defendants trumpeting their "electronic civil disobedience," *id.* at 303, 312, apparently led it to misconstrue significant portions of the DMCA. Many of Chamberlain's assertions in its brief to this court conflate the property right of copyright with the liability that the anticircumvention provisions impose.

Chamberlain relies upon the DMCA's prohibition of "fair uses . . . as well as foul," *Reimerdes*, 111 F.Supp.2d at 304, to argue that the enactment of the DMCA eliminated all existing consumer expectations about the public's rights to use purchased products because those products might include technological measures controlling access to a copyrighted work. But Chamberlain appears to have overlooked the obvious. The possibility that § 1201 might prohibit some otherwise noninfringing public uses of copyrighted material, *see, e.g. RealNetworks, Inc. v. Streambox, Inc.*, 2000 U.S. Dist. LEXIS 1889 (W.D. Wash., Jan. 18, 2000), arises simply because the Congressional decision to create liability and consequent damages for making, using, or selling a "key" that essentially enables a trespass upon intellectual property need not be identical in scope to the liabilities and compensable damages for infringing that property; it is, instead, a rebalancing of interests that "attempts to deal with special problems created by the so-called digital revolution." *Aimster*, 334 F.3d at 655.

Though *Reimerdes* is not the only case that Chamberlain cites for support, none of its other citations are any more helpful to its cause. [The court distinguished *Lexmark International, Inc. v. Static Control Components, Inc.*, 253 F.Supp.2d 943, 969 (E.D.Ky.2003), *Sony Computer Entertainment America, Inc. v. Gamemasters*, 87 F.Supp.2d 976 (N.D.Cal.1999), and *RealNetworks*, 2000 U.S. Dist. LEXIS 1889, noting that] the access alleged in all three cases was intertwined with a protected right. None of these cases can support a construction as broad as the one that Chamberlain urges us to adopt, even as persuasive authority.

Furthermore, though the severance of access from protection appears plausible taken out of context, it would also introduce a number of irreconcilable problems in statutory construction. The seeming plausibility arises because the statute's structure could be seen to suggest that § 1201(b) strengthens a copyright owner's abilities to protect its recognized rights, while § 1201(a) strengthens a copyright owner's abilities to protect access to its work without regard to the legitimacy (or illegitimacy) of the actions that the accused access enables. Such an interpretation is consistent with the Second Circuit's description: "The focus of subsection 1201(a)(2) is circumvention of technologies designed to *prevent access* to a work, and the focus of subsection 1201(b)(1) is circumvention of technologies designed to *permit access* to a work but *prevent copying* of the work or some other act that infringes a copyright." *Corley*, 273 F.3d at 440–41 (emphasis in original).

It is unlikely, however, that the Second Circuit meant to imply anything as drastic as wresting the concept of "access" from its context within the Copyright Act, as Chamberlain would now have us do. Were § 1201(a) to allow copyright owners to use technological measures to block all access to their copyrighted works, it would effectively create two distinct copyright regimes. In the first regime, the owners of a typical work protected by copyright would possess only the rights enumerated in 17 U.S.C. § 106, subject to the additions, exceptions, and limitations outlined throughout the rest of the Copyright Act—notably but not solely the fair use provisions of § 107.[14] Owners who feel that technology has put those

---

[14] We do not reach the relationship between § 107 fair use and violations of § 1201. The District Court in *Reimerdes* rejected the DeCSS defendants' argument that fair use was a necessary defense to § 1201(a), *Reimerdes*, 111 F.Supp.2d at 317; because any access enables some fair uses, any act of circumvention would embody its own defense. We leave open the question as to when § 107 might serve as an affirmative defense to a prima facie violation of § 1201. For the moment, we note only that though the traditional fair use doctrine of § 107 remains unchanged as a defense to copyright infringement under § 1201(c)(1), circumvention is not infringement.

rights at risk, and who incorporate technological measures to protect those rights from technological encroachment, gain the additional ability to hold traffickers in circumvention devices liable under § 1201(b) for putting their rights back at risk by enabling circumventors who use these devices to infringe.

Under the second regime that Chamberlain's proposed construction implies, the owners of a work protected by both copyright and a technological measure that effectively controls access to that work per § 1201(a) would possess unlimited rights to hold circumventors liable under § 1201(a) merely for accessing that work, even if that access enabled only rights that the Copyright Act grants to the public. This second implied regime would be problematic for a number of reasons. First, as the Supreme Court recently explained, "Congress' exercise of its *Copyright Clause* authority must be rational." *Eldred v. Ashcroft,* 537 U.S. 186, 205 n.10 (2003). In determining whether a particular aspect of the Copyright Act "is a rational exercise of the legislative authority conferred by the Copyright Clause . . . we defer substantially to Congress. It is Congress that has been assigned the task of defining the scope of the limited monopoly that should be granted to authors . . . *in order to give the public appropriate access to their work product." Id.* at 204–05 (citation omitted) (emphasis added). Chamberlain's proposed construction of § 1201(a) implies that in enacting the DMCA, Congress attempted to "give the public appropriate access" to copyrighted works by allowing copyright owners to deny all access to the public. Even under the substantial deference due Congress, such a redefinition borders on the irrational.

That apparent irrationality, however, is not the most significant problem that this second regime implies. Such a regime would be hard to reconcile with the DMCA's statutory prescription that "nothing in this section shall affect rights, remedies, limitations, or defenses to copyright infringement, including fair use, under this title." 17 U.S.C. § 1201(c)(1). A provision that prohibited access without regard to the rest of the Copyright Act would clearly affect rights and limitations, if not remedies and defenses. . . . Chamberlain's proposed construction of § 1201(a) would flatly contradict § 1201(c)(1)—a simultaneously enacted provision of the same statute. We are therefore bound, if we can, to obtain an alternative construction that leads to no such contradiction.

Chamberlain's proposed severance of "access" from "protection" in § 1201(a) creates numerous other problems. Beyond suggesting that Congress enacted by implication a new, highly protective alternative regime for copyrighted works; contradicting other provisions of the same statute including § 1201(c)(1); and ignoring the explicit immunization of interoperability from anticircumvention liability under § 1201(f); the broad policy implications of considering "access" in a vacuum devoid of "protection" are both absurd and disastrous. Under Chamberlain's proposed construction, explicated at oral argument, disabling a burglar alarm to gain "access" to a home containing copyrighted books, music, art, and periodicals would violate the DMCA; anyone who did so would unquestionably have "circumvented a technological measure that effectively controls access to a work protected under [the Copyright Act]." § 1201(a)(1). The appropriate deterrents to this type of behavior lie in tort law and criminal law, not in copyright law. Yet, were we to read the statute's "plain language" as Chamberlain urges, disabling a burglar alarm would be a per se violation of the DMCA.

In a similar vein, Chamberlain's proposed construction would allow any manufacturer of any product to add a single copyrighted sentence or software fragment to its product, wrap the copyrighted material in a trivial "encryption" scheme, and thereby gain the right to restrict consumers' rights to use its products in conjunction with competing products. In other words, Chamberlain's construction of the DMCA would allow virtually any company to attempt to leverage its sales into aftermarket monopolies — a practice that both the antitrust laws and the doctrine of copyright misuse normally prohibit. [The court concluded that the anticircumvention provisions of the DMCA could not be read to limit, expressly or impliedly, the scope of the antitrust laws, so that "plaintiffs alleging DMCA liability to protect their property rights are not exempt from other bodies of law" such as antitrust.]

Finally, the requisite "authorization," on which the District Court granted Skylink summary judgment, points to yet another inconsistency in Chamberlain's proposed construction. The notion of authorization is central to understanding § 1201(a). *See, e.g.,* S. Rep. 105-90 at 28 (1998) ("Subsection (a) applies when a person has not obtained authorized access to a copy or a phonorecord that is protected under the Copyright Act and for which the copyright owner has put in place a technological measure that effectively controls access to his or her work."). Underlying Chamberlain's argument on appeal that it has not granted such authorization lies the necessary assumption that Chamberlain is entitled to prohibit legitimate purchasers of its embedded software from "accessing" the software by using it. Such an entitlement, however, would go far beyond the idea that the DMCA allows copyright owner to prohibit "fair uses . . . as well as foul." *Reimerdes,* 111 F.Supp.2d at 304. Chamberlain's proposed construction would allow copyright owners to prohibit exclusively fair uses even in the absence of any feared foul use. It would therefore allow any copyright owner, through a combination of contractual terms and technological measures, to repeal the fair use doctrine with respect to an individual copyrighted work — or even selected copies of that copyrighted work. Again, this implication contradicts § 1201(c)(1) directly. Copyright law itself authorizes the public to make certain uses of copyrighted materials. Consumers who purchase a product containing a copy of embedded software have the inherent legal right to use that copy of the software. What the law authorizes, Chamberlain cannot revoke.[17]

Chamberlain's proposed severance of "access" from "protection" is entirely inconsistent with the context defined by the total statutory structure of the Copyright Act, other simultaneously enacted provisions of the DMCA, and clear Congressional intent. It "would lead to a result so bizarre that Congress could not have

---

[17] It is not clear whether a consumer who circumvents a technological measure controlling access to a copyrighted work in a manner that enables uses permitted under the Copyright Act but prohibited by contract can be subject to liability under the DMCA. Because Chamberlain did not attempt to limit its customers' use of its product by contract, however, we do not reach this issue.

intended it." *Central Bank*, 511 U.S. at 188. The statutory structure and the legislative history both make it clear that the DMCA granted copyright holders additional legal protections, but neither rescinded the basic bargain granting the public noninfringing and fair uses of copyrighted materials, § 1201(c), nor prohibited various beneficial uses of circumvention technology, such as those exempted under §§ 1201(d),(f),(g),(j).

We therefore reject Chamberlain's proposed construction in its entirety. We conclude that 17 U.S.C. § 1201 prohibits only forms of access that bear a reasonable relationship to the protections that the Copyright Act otherwise affords copyright owners. While such a rule of reason may create some uncertainty and consume some judicial resources, it is the only meaningful reading of the statute. Congress attempted to balance the legitimate interests of copyright owners with those of consumers of copyrighted products. *See* H.R. Rep. No. 105–551, at 26 (1998). The courts must adhere to the language that Congress enacted to determine how it attempted to achieve that balance.

As we have seen, Congress chose to create new causes of action for circumvention and for trafficking in circumvention devices. Congress did not choose to create new property rights. That is the choice that we have identified. . . . Were we to interpret Congress's words in a way that eliminated all balance and granted copyright owners carte blanche authority to preclude all use, Congressional intent would remain unrealized.

Congress chose words consistent with its stated intent to balance two sets of concerns pushing in opposite directions. *See* H.R. Rep. No. 105–551, at 26 (1998). The statute lays out broad categories of liability and broad exemptions from liability. It also instructs the courts explicitly not to construe the anticircumvention provisions in ways that would effectively repeal longstanding principles of copyright law. *See* § 1201(c). The courts must decide where the balance between the rights of copyright owners and those of the broad public tilts subject to a fact-specific rule of reason. Here, Chamberlain can point to no protected property right that Skylink imperils. The DMCA cannot allow Chamberlain to retract the most fundamental right that the Copyright Act grants consumers: the right to use the copy of Chamberlain's embedded software that they purchased.

G. Chamberlain's DMCA Claim

The proper construction of § 1201(a)(2) therefore makes it clear that Chamberlain cannot prevail. A plaintiff alleging a violation of § 1201(a)(2) must prove: (1) ownership of a valid *copyright* on a work, (2) effectively controlled by a *technological measure*, which has been circumvented, (3) that third parties can now *access* (4) *without authorization*, in a manner that (5) infringes or facilitates infringing a right *protected* by the Copyright Act, because of a product that (6) the defendant either (i) *designed or produced* primarily for circumvention; (ii) made available despite only *limited commercial significance* other than circumvention; or (iii) *marketed* for use in circumvention of the controlling technological measure. . . . A plaintiff capable of proving elements (1) through (5) need prove only one of (6)(i), (ii), or (iii) to shift the burden back to the defendant. At that point, the various affirmative defenses enumerated throughout § 1201 become relevant.

The District Court analyzed Chamberlain's allegations in precisely the appropriate manner—a narrow focus on Skylink's behavior, intent, and product within the broader context of longstanding expectations throughout the industry. . . . The District Court granted Skylink's motion for summary judgment because Chamberlain failed to meet its burden on the fourth element, the lack of authorization. . . .

Chamberlain, however, has failed to show not only the requisite lack of authorization, but also the necessary fifth element of its claim, the critical nexus between access and protection. Chamberlain neither alleged copyright infringement *nor explained how the access provided by the Model 39 transmitter facilitates the infringement of any right that the Copyright Act protects.* There can therefore be no reasonable relationship between the access that homeowners gain to Chamberlain's copyrighted software when using Skylink's Model 39 transmitter and the protections that the Copyright Act grants to Chamberlain. The Copyright Act authorized Chamberlain's customers to use the copy of Chamberlain's copyrighted software embedded in the GDOs that they purchased. Chamberlain's customers are therefore immune from § 1201(a)(1) circumvention liability. In the absence of allegations of either copyright infringement or § 1201(a)(1) circumvention, Skylink cannot be liable for § 1201(a)(2) trafficking. The District Court's grant of summary judgment in Skylink's favor was correct. . . .

CONCLUSION

The DMCA does not create a new property right for copyright owners. Nor, for that matter, does it divest the public of the property rights that the Copyright Act has long granted to the public. The anticircumvention and anti-trafficking provisions of the DMCA create new grounds of liability. A copyright owner seeking to impose liability on an accused circumventor must demonstrate a reasonable relationship between the circumvention at issue and a use relating to a property right for which the Copyright Act permits the copyright owner to withhold authorization—as well as notice that authorization was withheld. A copyright owner seeking to impose liability on an accused trafficker must demonstrate that the trafficker's device enables either copyright infringement or a prohibited circumvention. Here, the District Court correctly ruled that Chamberlain pled no connection between unauthorized use of its copyrighted software and Skylink's accused transmitter. This connection is critical to sustaining a cause of action under the DMCA. We therefore affirm the District Court's summary judgment in favor of Skylink.

EXTENSIONS

1. *Anticircumvention and embedded software.* Lexmark is a producer of laser printers and toner cartridges. The cartridges contain computer code, called the Toner Loading Program, embedded in microchips that communicate with the Printer Engine Program, software residing in the printer that controls the cartridge and enables printing. Lexmark holds the copyright to both of these programs. Access to these programs requires the use of an authentication sequence, which prevents unauthorized toner cartridges from being used with the printer. Static Control Components ("SCC") developed the SMARTEK microchip, which can be used to replace the Lexmark microchip when the toner cartridge is remanufactured. The SMARTEK microchip contains a copy of the Lexmark Toner Loading Program and circumvents Lexmark's authentication sequence.

Lexmark filed an action against SCC and sought a preliminary injunction, alleging that SCC was infringing its copyright in the Toner Loading Program and was in violation of Section 1201 by selling a device that circumvented technological measures controlling access to the Toner Loading Program and the Printer Engine Program. In *Lexmark International v. Static Control Components*, 253 F.Supp.2d 943 (E.D.Ky.2003), the district court found that Lexmark was likely to succeed on the merits and granted the injunction, but the appeals court vacated the injunction, ruling that Lexmark had not demonstrated likelihood of success. 387 F.3d 522 (6th Cir.2004).

As to the Section 1201 claim that SCC's chip circumvented a control on "access" to the Printer Engine Program, the court concluded as follows:

> . . . Because Congress did not explain what it means to "gain access to the work," the district court relied on the "ordinary, customary meaning" of "access": "the ability to enter, to obtain, or to make use of" (quoting Merriam-Webster's Collegiate Dictionary 6 (10th ed. 1999)). Based on this definition, the court concluded that "Lexmark's authentication sequence effectively 'controls access' to the Printer Engine Program because it controls the consumer's ability to *make use* of these programs." (emphasis added).
>
> We disagree. It is not Lexmark's authentication sequence that "controls access" to the Printer Engine Program. It is the purchase of a Lexmark printer that allows "access" to the program. Anyone who buys a Lexmark printer may read the literal code of the Printer Engine Program directly from the printer memory, with or without the benefit of the authentication sequence, and the data from the program may be translated into readable source code after which copies may be freely distributed. No security device, in other words, protects access to the Printer Engine Program Code and no security device accordingly must be circumvented to obtain access to that program code.
>
> The authentication sequence, it is true, may well block one form of "access"—the "ability to . . . make use of" the Printer Engine Program by preventing the printer from functioning. But it does not block another relevant form of "access"—the "ability to [] obtain" a copy of the work or to "make use of" the literal elements of the program (its code). Because the statute refers to "controlling access to a work protected under this title," it does not naturally apply when the "work protected under this title" is otherwise accessible. Just as one would not say that a lock on the back door of a house "controls access" to a house whose front door does not contain a lock and just as one would not say that a lock on any door of a house "controls access" to the house after its purchaser receives the key to the lock, it does not make sense to say that this provision of the DMCA applies to otherwise-readily-accessible copyrighted works. Add to this the fact that the DMCA not only requires the technological measure to "control[] access" but also requires the measure to control that access "effectively," 17 U.S.C. § 1201(a)(2), and it seems clear that this provision does not naturally extend to a technological measure that restricts one form of access but leaves another route wide open. *See also id.* § 1201(a)(3) (technological measure must "*require*[] the application of information, or a process or a treatment . . . to gain access to the work") (emphasis added). . . .
>
> Nor are we aware of any cases that have applied this provision of the DMCA to a situation where the access-control measure left the literal code or text of the

computer program or data freely readable. . . .

. . . Lexmark counters that several cases have embraced a "to make use of" definition of "access" in applying the DMCA. While Lexmark is partially correct, these cases (and others as well) ultimately illustrate the liability line that the statute draws and in the end explain why access to the Printer Engine Program is not covered.

In the essential setting where the DMCA applies, the copyright protection operates on two planes: in the literal code governing the work and in the visual or audio manifestation generated by the code's execution. For example, the encoded data on CDs translates into music and on DVDs into motion pictures, while the program commands in software for video games or computers translate into some other visual and audio manifestation. In the cases upon which Lexmark relies, restricting "use" of the work means restricting consumers from making use of the copyrightable expression in the work. *See 321 Studios,* 307 F.Supp.2d at 1095 (movies contained on DVDs protected by an encryption algorithm cannot be watched without a player that contains an access key) . . . . [T]he DMCA applies in these settings when the product manufacturer prevents all access to the copyrightable material and the alleged infringer responds by marketing a device that circumvents the technological measure designed to guard access to the copyrightable material.

The copyrightable expression in the Printer Engine Program, by contrast, operates on only one plane: in the literal elements of the program, its source and object code. Unlike the code underlying video games or DVDs, "using" or executing the Printer Engine Program does not in turn create any protected expression. Instead, the program's output is purely functional: the Printer Engine Program "controls a number of operations" in the Lexmark printer such as "paper feed[,] paper movement[,] [and] motor control." And unlike the code underlying video games or DVDs, no encryption or other technological measure prevents access to the Printer Engine Program. Presumably, it is precisely because the Printer Engine Program is not a conduit to protectable expression that explains why Lexmark (or any other printer company) would not block access to the computer software that makes the printer work. Because Lexmark's authentication sequence does not restrict access to this literal code, the DMCA does not apply.

Lexmark next argues that access-control measures may "effectively control access" to a copyrighted work within the meaning of the DMCA even though the measure may be evaded by an "enterprising end-user." Doubtless, Lexmark is correct that a precondition for DMCA liability is not the creation of an impervious shield to the copyrighted work. . . .

But our reasoning does not turn on the *degree* to which a measure controls access to a work. It turns on the textual requirement that the challenged circumvention device must indeed circumvent *something*, which did not happen with the Printer Engine Program. Because Lexmark has not directed any of its security efforts, through its authentication sequence or otherwise, to ensuring that its copyrighted work (the Printer Engine Program) cannot be read and copied, it cannot lay claim to having put in place a "technological measure that effectively controls access to a work protected under [the copyright statute]." 17 U.S.C. § 1201(a)(2)(B).

Nor can Lexmark tenably claim that this reading of the statute fails to respect Congress's purpose in enacting it, [which involved] concerns about the threat of "massive piracy" of digital works due to "the ease with which [they] can be copied and distributed worldwide virtually instantaneously." S. Rep. No. 105–190, at 8 (1998). . . .

Nowhere in its deliberations over the DMCA did Congress express an interest in creating liability for the circumvention of technological measures designed to prevent consumers from using consumer goods while leaving the copyrightable content of a work unprotected. In fact, Congress added the interoperability provision in part to ensure that the DMCA would not diminish the benefit to consumers of interoperable devices "in the consumer electronics environment." 144 Cong. Rec. E2136 (daily ed. Oct. 13, 1998)(remarks of Rep. Bliley). . . .

As to the Toner Loader Program, the court concluded that SCC's chip did not in fact provide access to the program, and that the program itself might not be protected by copyright, in which case technological measures controlling access to the program would not be protected by § 1201.

Two of the three judges on the appellate panel each wrote concurring opinions, expressing additional views on the interpretation and application of § 1201. The case was remanded for further proceedings on the merits.

2. *Injunctive relief and the Internet.* From the perspective of content producers, the Internet is worrisome due to the ease and efficiency with which digital goods can be copied and distributed. A case in point is the DeCSS computer program that is the focus of the *Reimerdes* decision. In *Reimerdes*, by the time the court issued a preliminary injunction enjoining the defendants from distributing the DeCSS program, it was already available on many websites around the world. Although after the preliminary injunction one could no longer obtain a copy of the program from the defendants' websites, a visit to a search engine would have revealed numerous other sites from which the program could be downloaded. Enjoining distribution of certain digital goods over the Internet once such goods are already available online is arguably an exercise in futility—an argument that the defendants made, by observing that granting "an injunction would be comparable to locking the barn door after the horse is gone." *Reimerdes,* 111 F.Supp.2d at 344. The court admitted that it "has been troubled by that possibility," but concluded that "the countervailing arguments overcome that concern." *Id.*

To begin with, any such conclusion effectively would create all the wrong incentives by allowing defendants to continue violating the DMCA simply because others, many doubtless at defendants' urging, are doing so as well. Were that the law, defendants confronted with the possibility of injunctive relief would be well advised to ensure that others engage in the same unlawful conduct in order to set up the argument that an injunction against the defendants would be futile because everyone else is doing the same thing.

Second, and closely related, is the fact that this Court is sorely "troubled by the notion that any Internet user . . . can destroy valuable intellectual property rights by posting them over the Internet."[273] While equity surely should not act where the controversy has become moot, it ought to look very skeptically at claims that the defendant or others already have done all the harm that might be done before the injunction issues.

The key to reconciling these views is that the focus of injunctive relief is on the defendants before the Court. If a plaintiff seeks to enjoin a defendant from

---

[273] *Religious Technology Center v. Netcom On–Line Communication Services, Inc.,* 923 F.Supp. 1231, 1256 (N.D.Cal.1995).

burning a pasture, it is no answer that there is a wild fire burning in its direction. If the defendant itself threatens the plaintiff with irreparable harm, then equity will enjoin the defendant from carrying out the threat even if other threats abound and even if part of the pasture already is burned.

These defendants would harm plaintiffs every day on which they post DeCSS on their heavily trafficked web site and link to other sites that post it because someone who does not have DeCSS thereby might obtain it. They thus threaten plaintiffs with immediate and irreparable injury. They will not be allowed to continue to do so simply because others may do so as well. . . .

Id. Are you convinced by the court's conclusion that the controversy is not moot? Do you find the court's analogy to a wildfire apposite? Does the Internet, more than any other medium of communication, give rise to cases in which damages are inadequate and an injunction is ineffective? If so, how should the legal system respond?

3. *Criminal penalties under Section 1204.* Section 1204 prescribes criminal penalties for those who violate Section 1201 or 1202 "willfully and for purposes of commercial advantage or private financial gain." For a first offense, the penalties are a fine of up to $500,000, a prison term up to five years, or both. 17 U.S.C. § 1204(a)(1). In July 2001, a Russian computer programmer named Dmitri Sklyarov was arrested by the Federal Bureau of Investigation and charged with violating the anti-circumvention provisions, based on his creation of a program that defeated use controls built into electronic books distributed by Adobe Systems, Inc. The arrest occurred in Las Vegas at the annual Def Con convention, known as a gathering of hackers, where Sklyarov had presented a paper describing the research that led to his creation of the program. The program, as he explained in the paper, had grown out of research about security flaws in e-document security systems that he had done for his Ph.D. dissertation. After three weeks in jail, Sklyarov was released on bail. A grand jury returned a five-count indictment against both Sklyarov and his employer, a Russian software development company called ElcomSoft Co., Ltd., for violations of the anti-trafficking provision, Section 1201(b)(1). Under the indictment, Sklyarov was subject to up to 25 years in prison and a $2,250,000 fine. Sklyarov was not allowed to return to Russia until making a deal with prosecutors, under which he agreed to testify against his employer.

In *United States v. Elcom Ltd.*, 203 F.Supp.2d 1111 (N.D.Cal.2002), the district court rejected arguments that Section 1201 is unconstitutionally vague in violation of the Due Process Clause, that it is vague and overbroad in violation of the First Amendment, and that it is beyond Congress's legislative powers. In December 2002, a jury found ElcomSoft not guilty on all five counts.

QUESTIONS FOR DISCUSSION

1. *How much authority does a copyright owner have?* In a footnote in *Reimerdes*, the court notes that "[d]ecryption or avoidance of an access control measure is not 'circumvention' within the meaning of the statute unless it occurs 'without the authority of the copyright owner.' 17 U.S.C. § 1201(a)(3)(A)." Apparently, defendants' counsel had argued that the defendants' acts did not constitute circumvention within the meaning of § 1201(a)(3)(A). The court sets out defendants' view as follows:

Defendants posit that purchasers of a DVD acquire the right "to perform all acts with it that are not exclusively granted to the copyright holder." Based on this premise, they argue that DeCSS does not circumvent CSS within the meaning of the statute because the Copyright Act does not grant the copyright holder the right to prohibit purchasers from decrypting. As the copyright holder has no statutory right to prohibit decryption, the argument goes, decryption cannot be understood as unlawful circumvention.

Reimerdes, 111 F.Supp.2d at 317 n.137. The court is blunt in its evaluation of this line of reasoning: "The argument is pure sophistry." Should the court have been so quick to dismiss defendants' argument? Does the applicability of the statute turn on the rights of a copyright owner qua copyright owner? If not, does the statute grant rights to a copyright owner which are over and above the rights granted by the Copyright Act? Consider also whether the result is consistent with Section 1201(c)(1), which provides: "Nothing in this section shall affect rights, remedies, limitations, or defenses to copyright infringement, including fair use, under this title."

2. *Is trafficking under Section 1201 a form of secondary liability?* Under the law of copyright, secondary liability for copyright infringement requires proof of direct infringement by another. Is this also the case for liability under Section 1201(b)? Similarly, does liability under Section 1201(a)(2) require proof of a violation of Section 1201(a)(1)? That is, in order to be liable for making or selling tools that will facilitate breaking into a technological protection system to obtain access to information, or disabling technological use restrictions on information, must unauthorized access or copyright infringement by means of those tools actually be shown?

3. *Tunneling and anticircumvention.* A Virtual Private Network ("VPN") is a network that uses the Internet to establish private lines of communication between two machines by a process known as "tunneling." The tunnel is created by encrypting the information traveling between the networked computers. Section 1201 expressly prohibits circumvention of "a technological measure" designed to control access to works protected under Title 17. If a VPN includes copyrighted materials, would use of an unauthorized tunnel to gain access to the copyrighted material on that VPN be a violation of Section 1201? *See Pearl Investments, LLC v. Standard I/O,* 257 F.Supp.2d 326 (D.Me.2003).

4. *Unauthorized use of password as circumvention.* In *I.M.S. Inquiry Management Systems, Ltd. v. Berkshire Information Systems, Inc.,* 307 F.Supp.2d 521 (S.D.N.Y.2004), I.M.S. charged its competitor Berkshire with circumvention in violation of Section 1201, based on Berkshire's accessing and copying copyrighted material that I.M.S. made available only to its subscribers. The material was on a password-protected website, to which Berkshire obtained access by using a password that I.M.S. had issued to a subscriber. After holding that the password protection system qualifies as "a technological measure that effectively controls access to" a copyrighted work, § 1201(a)(1)(A), the court addressed the question whether use of the password without I.M.S.'s authorization constituted circumvention of that measure:

> Circumvention requires either descrambling, decrypting, avoiding, bypassing, removing, deactivating or impairing a technological measure *qua* technological measure. In the instant matter, defendant is not said to have avoided or bypassed the deployed technological measure in the measure's gatekeeping capacity. The Amended Complaint never accuses defendant of accessing the e-Basket system without first entering a plaintiff-generated password.

> More precisely and accurately, what defendant avoided and bypassed was *permission* to engage and move through the technological measure from the measure's author. [But] a cause of action under the DMCA does not accrue upon unauthorized and injurious access *alone;* rather, the DMCA "targets the *circumvention* of digital walls guarding copyrighted material."

Do you agree with the court's reasoning? Would it make a difference if Berkshire had acquired the password by trickery, or theft? Is it possible that obtaining unauthorized access through reverse engineering constitutes circumvention, but accomplishing the same thing by tricking someone into divulging her password does not?

B. Tampering with Copyright Management Information

To fulfill the obligations of the United States under Article 12 of the WIPO Copyright Treaty and Article 19 of the WIPO Performances and Phonograms Treaty, Title I of the Digital Millennium Copyright Act added Section 1202 to Title 17 of the U.S. Code. The addition of Section 1202 actually exceeded the obligations of the United States as a signatory state to the two WIPO treaties. In identical provisions, the two WIPO treaties require that member states enact legislation providing effective legal remedies against persons who "remove or alter any electronic rights management information without authority" as well as against persons who "distribute, import for distribution, broadcast or communicate to the public, without authority, works or copies of works knowing that electronic rights management information has been removed or altered without authority." WIPO Copyright Treaty, Dec. 20, 1996, art. 12, WIPO Doc. CRNR/DC/94, www.wipo.int/eng/diplconf/distrib/94dc.htm; WIPO Performances and Phonograms Treaty, Dec. 20, 1996, art. 19, WIPO Doc. CRNR/DC/95, www.wipo.org/eng/diplconf/distrib/95dc.htm. Section 1202 not only provides effective legal remedies against such conduct, but also prohibits individuals from providing, distributing or importing for distribution, copyright management information that is false. This last prohibition is not required by any international obligation.

Section–By–Section Analysis of H.R. 2281
House Committee on the Judiciary, 105th Congress (Comm. Print. 1998).

. . .

Section 1202: Integrity of Copyright Management Information.

Subsection (a) establishes a general prohibition against knowingly providing, distributing or importing false copyright management information ("CMI"), as defined in subsection (c). There are two prerequisites that must be met for the conduct to be illegal: (1) the person providing, distributing or importing the false CMI must know the CMI is false, and (2) he or she must do so with the intent to induce, enable, facilitate or conceal an infringement of any right under Title 17. The prohibition in this subsection does not apply to the ordinary and customary practices of broadcasters or the inadvertent omission of credits from broadcasts of audiovisual works, since such acts do not involve the provision of false CMI with the requisite knowledge and intent.

Subsection (b) establishes a general prohibition against deliberately removing or altering CMI, and against distributing or importing for distribution altered CMI or distributing, importing for distribution or publicly performing works in which CMI has been removed. Three specific acts are prohibited if they are committed without the authority of the copyright owner or the law, and if they are done knowing, or with respect to civil remedies under section 1203, having reasonable grounds to know, that they will induce, enable, facilitate or conceal a copyright infringement: (1) intentionally removing or altering CMI; (2) distributing or importing for distribution CMI, knowing that it has been altered without the authority of the copyright owner or the law; or (3) distributing, importing for distribution, or publicly performing works, copies of works, or phonorecords, knowing that CMI has been removed or altered without the authority of the copyright owner or the law. As with subsection (a), the prohibition in this subsection does not include the ordinary and customary practices of broadcasters or the inadvertent omission of credits from broadcasts of audiovisual works, since such omissions do not involve the requisite knowledge and intent.

Subsection (c) defines CMI. To fall within the definition, there is a threshold requirement that the information be conveyed in connection with copies or phonorecords, performances or displays of the copyrighted work. The term "conveyed" is used in its broadest sense and is not meant to require any type of transfer, physical or otherwise, of the information. It merely requires that the information be accessible in conjunction with, or appear with, an embodiment of the work itself.

CMI is defined as any of the following: (1) the title of a work or other information that identifies the work; (2) the author's name or other information that identifies the author; (3) the copyright owner's name or other information that identifies the copyright owner; (4) with the exception of public performances of works by radio and television broadcast stations, a performer's name or other information that identifies a performer whose performance is fixed in a non-audiovisual work; (5) with the exception of public performances of works by radio and television broadcast stations, the name of or other identifying information about a writer, performer, or director who is credited in an audiovisual work; (6) terms and conditions for use of a work; and (7) numbers and symbols which refer to, link to, or represent the above information. As noted above, both treaties require that numbers and symbols be included within the definition of CMI. Links, such as embedded pointers and hyperlinks, to the above information are also included. The phrase "links to such information" was included in paragraph (7) because removing or altering a link to the information will have the same adverse effect as removing or altering the information itself. Finally, paragraph (c)(8) of the definition permits the Register of Copyrights to prescribe by regulation other information that, if conveyed in connection with a work, is to be protected as CMI. To protect the privacy of users of copyrighted works, however, the Register of Copyrights may not include within the definition of CMI any information concerning *users* of copyrighted works.

Section 1202 does not mandate the use of CMI, or of any particular type of CMI. It merely protects the integrity of CMI if a party chooses to use it in connection with a copyrighted work, by prohibiting its deliberate deletion or alteration. It also should be noted that the definition of "copyright management information" does not encompass, nor is it intended to encompass, tracking or usage information relating to the identity of users of works. It would be inconsistent with the purpose and construction of this bill and contrary to the protection of privacy to include tracking and usage information within the definition of CMI.

Section 1202 imposes liability for specified acts. It does not address the question of liability for persons who manufacture devices or provide services.

Subsection (d) makes clear that the prohibitions in section 1202 do not prohibit any lawfully authorized investigative, protective or intelligence activity by or at the direction of a federal, state or local law enforcement agency, or of an intelligence agency of the United States.

Subsection (e) recognizes special problems that certain broadcasting entities may have with the transmission of copyright management information. Under this subsection, radio and television broadcasters, cable systems, and persons who provide programming to such broadcasters or systems, who do not intend to induce, enable, facilitate or conceal infringement, are eligible for an exemption from liability for violation of the CMI provisions of subsection (b) in certain, limited circumstances.

. . .

Kelly v. Arriba Soft Corp.

77 F.Supp.2d 1116 (C.D.Cal.1999), *aff'd in part, rev'd in part, and remanded on other grounds*, 280 F.3d 934 (9th Cir.2002).

■ TAYLOR, DISTRICT JUDGE.

[The facts of this case are set forth in Chapter 7, Part III(B), *supra.*]

II. DISCUSSION

These cross motions for summary adjudication present two questions of first impression. . . . [The first, whether the display of copyrighted images by a search engine constitutes fair use, is treated in the excerpt from the opinion of the court of appeals in this case, reproduced in Chapter 7, Part III(B), *supra.*] The second is whether the display of such images without their copyright management information is a violation of the Digital Millennium Copyright Act.

. . .

B. Digital Millennium Copyright Act

. . . Section 1202 of the DMCA governs "integrity of copyright management information." Section 1202(a) prohibits falsification of copyright management information with the intent to aid copyright infringement. Section 1202(b) prohibits, unless authorized, several forms of knowing removal or alteration of copyright management information. Section 1203 creates a federal civil action for violations of these provisions.

Plaintiff argues Defendant violated § 1202(b) by displaying thumbnails of Plaintiff's images without displaying the corresponding copyright management information consisting of standard copyright notices in the surrounding text. Because these notices do not appear in the images themselves, the Ditto crawler did not include them when it indexed the images. As a result, the images appeared in Defendant's index without the copyright management information, and any users retrieving Plaintiff's images while using Defendant's Web site would not see the copyright management information.

Section 1202(b)(1) does not apply to this case. Based on the language and structure of the statute, the Court holds this provision applies only to the removal of copyright management information on a plaintiff's product or original work. Moreover, even if § 1202(b)(1) applied, Plaintiff has not offered any evidence showing Defendant's actions were intentional, rather than merely an unintended side effect of the Ditto crawler's operation.

Here, where the issue is the absence of copyright management information from *copies* of Plaintiff's works, the applicable provision is § 1202(b)(3). To show a violation of that section, Plaintiff must show Defendant makes available to its users the thumbnails and full-size images, which were copies of Plaintiff's work separated from their copyright management information, even though it knows or should know this will lead to infringement of Plaintiff's copyrights. There is no dispute the Ditto crawler removed Plaintiff's images from the context of Plaintiff's Web sites where their copyright management information was located, and converted them to thumbnails in Defendant's index. There is also no dispute the Arriba Vista search engine allowed full-size images to be viewed without their copyright management information.

Defendant's users could obtain a full-sized version of a thumbnailed image by clicking on the thumbnail. A user who did this was given the name of the Web site from which Defendant obtained the image, where any associated copyright management information would be available, and an opportunity to link there. Users were also informed on Defendant's Web site that use restrictions and copyright limitations may apply to images retrieved by Defendant's search engine.[13]

Based on all of this, the Court finds Defendant did not have "reasonable grounds to know" it would cause its users to infringe Plaintiff's copyrights. Defendant warns its users about the possibility of use restrictions on the images in its index, and instructs them to check with the originating Web sites before copying and using those images, even in reduced thumbnail form.

Plaintiff's images are vulnerable to copyright infringement because they are displayed on Web sites. Plaintiff has not shown users of Defendant's site were any more likely to infringe his copyrights, any of these users did infringe, or Defendant should reasonably have expected infringement.

. . . The Court finds there was no violation of DMCA § 1202. Defendant's motion is GRANTED and Plaintiff's motion is DENIED on the DMCA claim.

---

[13] Plaintiff argues Defendant's warnings are insufficient because they do not appear with the thumbnail images on the search result pages produced by the search engine. The Arriba Vista Web site only offered a warning if users clicked on a link to its "Copyright" page. This warning may arguably have been placed in the wrong place to deter some potential copyright infringers. But this does not necessarily mean Defendant "knew" or "should have known" for the purposes of a DMCA violation, especially since Plaintiff offers no evidence of any actual copyright infringement about which Defendant "should have known."

QUESTIONS FOR DISCUSSION

1. *Encouraging the use of CMI.* The House Report excerpted above notes that "Section 1202 does not mandate the use of CMI, or of any particular type of CMI." The Berne Convention precludes formalities as a prerequisite to copyright validity, so that the United States as a signatory would not have been compliant with the treaty had it mandated the use of CMI as a prerequisite to copyright protection. Art. 5(2), Berne Convention for the Protection of Literary and Artistic Works, July 24, 1971, S. TREATY DOC. NO. 99–27 (1986), 828 U.N.T.S. 221, www.wipo.int/treaties/en/ip/berne/trtdocs_wo001.html. Nevertheless, a signatory is not precluded from enacting protection for CMI once owners have chosen to use it. What economic or other policy reasons can you adduce for encouraging the use of CMI by punishing those who alter or remove it?

2. *Safe harbors.* As discussed in Chapter 7, Part V(B)(II), *supra*, 17 U.S.C. § 512(d) offers the operator of a search engine a safe harbor from monetary liability "for infringement of copyright by reason of . . . referring or linking users to an online location containing infringing material or infringing activity." Could the defendant in *Kelly v. Arriba Soft* have successfully defended against the Section 1202 claim based on this provision?

3. *Civil remedies under Section 1203.* Section 1203 sets out the civil remedies available for violations of the anti-circumvention and CMI-protection provisions of Sections 1201 and 1202. In addition to awarding injunctive relief and damages, a court may "order the remedial modification or destruction of any device or product involved in the violation that is in the custody or control of the violator." § 1203(b)(6). This would apparently allow impoundment and destruction of the violator's computer. Is this an inappropriately draconian remedy? Compare 17 U.S.C. § 503(b) (in case of copyright infringement, court may order destruction "of all plates, molds, matrices, masters, tapes, film negatives, or other articles by means of which" infringing materials may be produced).

III. TRUSTED SYSTEMS AND FAIR USE

As we have seen in the preceding materials addressing the DMCA's prohibitions against circumventing technological protection measures and tampering with copyright management information, there is considerable debate among copyright owners, users of copyrighted materials, and commentators about the proper scope of legal protection for trusted systems. A recurring issue has to do with the traditional defense of fair use, and how (or if) it can be carried forward into the era of technological protection. Is the fair use doctrine still viable?

Tom W. Bell, *Fair Use vs. Fared Use: The Impact of Automated Rights Management on Copyright's Fair Use Doctrine*
76 N.C. L. REV. 557 (1998).

. . .

1. Fair Use Is Not Free Use

Despite gross misconceptions to the contrary, fair use never comes for free. One way or another, consumers using conventional media must pay to browse magazines at newsstands, to photocopy and distribute newspaper stories for spontaneous classroom use, to search for quotes and type them into articles, and to otherwise avail themselves of the fair use doctrine. Although such acts do not entail paying licensing fees, they inevitably impose a variety of transaction costs—for personal transport, manipulating paper and ink, searching card catalogs, and so on—that follow from the very nature of conventional media. It makes no difference that consumers pay licensing fees in cash whereas they pay fair use's transaction costs in lost opportunities. Economically speaking, a cost is a cost.

The digital intermedia[3] allow consumers to avoid or reduce such transaction costs. Bits flow directly to homes and offices, copy easily into RAM or magnetic storage, forward instantly to destinations worldwide, and submit easily to electronic searches. Transaction costs remain even here, of course. The burgeoning growth of the Internet and other digital intermedia indicates, however, that consuming bits very often costs less than consuming atoms. The increasing reliance of legal academics on commercial online services, CD-ROMs, and the Internet confirms this observation. Those who decry the advent of fared use thus err when they imply that it must impose a net cost on consumers. To the contrary, fared use offers a considerable likelihood of providing more and better verified, organized, and interlinked information, at less cost, than fair use does now.

2. Fixing Market Failure

Scholars have explained fair use in at least three ways: (1) as a proxy for a copyright owner's implied consent; (2) as part of a bargain between authors and the public, struck on their behalf first by courts and then by Congress; and (3) as a response to a market failure in private attempts to protect authors' expressions from undue copying. . . . The present subsection addresses the third explanation of fair use and argues that, as a response to market failure, the fair use doctrine can and should give way in the face of the effective enforcement of authors' rights through automated rights management.

Lawmakers enacted the Copyright Act to cure an alleged case of market failure: creating a work can cost authors a good deal, whereas copying a work costs free riders very little. Absent special protection from such copying, the argument goes, authors will underproduce and the public will suffer. . . .

Markets, like squeezed balloons, bulge outward where unconstrained. In its attempt to protect authors from the discouraging effects of unfettered copying, copyright law has thus created market failure elsewhere. The costs of avoiding infringement by obtaining permission to use a copyrighted work, and thus avoiding infringement claims, often exceed the benefits of the desired use. Such transaction costs threaten to prevent many socially beneficial uses of copyrighted works from taking place. The doctrine of fair use attempts to cure this particular market failure by excusing as non-infringing a limited (though poorly defined) class of uses of copyrighted works. . . . As Professor Gordon describes it, "courts and Congress have employed fair use to permit uncompensated transfers that are socially desir-

---

[3] This Article uses "digital intermedia" to refer to the Internet, circuit-switched networks, and other interactive channels over which digital information gets distributed and through which automated rights management can function. "Digital intermedia" does not encompass such comparatively non-interactive distribution channels as CDs, CD-ROMs, and digital audio cassettes. [Relocated footnote.—Eds.]

able but not capable of effectuation through the market."[121]

Understanding fair use as a response to market failure does much to explain the vagaries of its development in the case law. . . . [T]he scope of the fair use defense rises and falls with the transaction costs of licensing access to copyrighted works.

Automated rights management radically reduces the transaction costs of licensing access to copyrighted works in digital intermedia. Indeed, as its name suggests, it makes licensing automatic. Insofar as it responds to market failure, therefore, fair use should have a much reduced scope when ARM takes effect. . . .

. . .

3. Maintaining Copyright's Quid Pro Quo

As courts and commentators often have noted, the Constitution demands a public benefit as the price for the limited statutory privileges that copyright creates. In contrast to the view that the fair use doctrine represents a second-best response to pervasive market failure, therefore, some commentators regard the doctrine as an integral part of this constitutional quid pro quo. On this view, fair use provides a public benefit—unbilled access to copyrighted works—to balance the State's grant of a limited monopoly.

Automated rights management at first appears to threaten this bargain. It seems as if ARM restricts the public's access to copyrighted works in digital intermedia without offering a benefit in return. As this subsection's consideration of the issue shows, however, friends of fair use should not assume that ARM will leave the public worse off. To the contrary, it appears likely to provide a net benefit to the public.

By reducing transaction costs throughout the market for copyrighted expressions, ARM benefits the public both directly and indirectly. Having emanated from an intentionally vague statute and developed in various, occasionally contradictory cases, the fair use doctrine necessarily blurs the boundary between valid and invalid copyright claims. High risks of "theft"—here, infringement—increase the insecurity of copyright's protection. Though the resultant uncertainty obviously harms producers and sellers of copyrighted works, it also harms consumers. Academics, artists, commentators, and others desirous of reusing copyrighted works without authorization must borrow at their peril, consult experts on fair use, or, sadly, forego such reuse altogether. ARM's clarifying power directly benefits those who would reuse copyrighted works—and through them their public audiences—by creating harbors safe from the threat of copyright litigation.

Moreover, ARM benefits the public indirectly by increasing the transactional efficiency of the market for expressive works. Like other markets, the market for expressive works does not constitute a zero sum game. And, as Coase observed of markets in general,

---

121 [Wendy J. Gordon, Fair Use As Market Failure: A Structural and Economic Analysis of the Betamax Case and Its Predecessors, 82 Colum. L. Rev. 1600, 1601 (1982) (footnote omitted).]

> [i]t is obviously desirable that rights should be assigned to those who can use them most productively and with incentives that lead them to do so. It is also desirable that, to discover (and maintain) such a distribution of rights, the costs of their transference should be low, through clarity in the law and by making the legal requirements for such transfers less onerous.[137]

ARM, by its systemic improvement of copyright's transactional efficiency, helps us discover and maintain a distribution of rights to expressive works that will increase net social wealth. ARM thus stands to benefit both producers and consumers.

In particular, because it increases the value of expressive works, ARM will put deflationary pressure on the price of accessing them. In general, an asset's current price internalizes the value of its future income stream. Copyrights therefore commonly lose present value because, with the passage of time and their wider distribution, they prove increasingly vulnerable to uncompensated uses. Because it reduces such risks, ARM tends to increase the value of copyrights. But although this windfall might initially accrue to copyright owners, competition among information providers would force access prices downward, toward the marginal costs of obtaining and distributing expressive works. Directly or indirectly, such price pressure would similarly affect the prices that copyright owners can demand. Gains that ARM provides to copyright owners would thus pass on to consumers in the form of reduced access fees.

Because ARM will increase the value of copyrighted works, moreover, it will encourage their greater production and improved distribution. Consumers will thus benefit from better access to information. Access providers will improve the information itself, too, increasing its quantity and making it better organized, verified, interlinked, diverse, up-to-date, and relevant. Although this cornucopia of information may at first come only for a fee, some of it eventually will fall into the public domain. To judge from current implementations of ARM, copyright owners might very well offer limited free access to their wares in an attempt to draw more extensive (and expensive) uses. Entrepreneurs will undoubtedly create other services, at present utterly and inevitably unforeseen, to attract and satisfy consumers of information.

. . .

David Nimmer, *A Riff on Fair Use in the Digital Millennium Copyright Act*
148 U. PA. L. REV. 673 (2000).

. . .

Historically, copyright owners have always had the right to retain their works confidentially. "The owner of the copyright, if he pleases, may refrain from vending or licensing and content himself with simply exercising the right to exclude

---

[137] Ronald H. Coase, The Institutional Structure of Production, in Coase, Essays on Economics and Economists 3, 11 (1994).

others from using his property."[208] In this manner, United States law has accorded de facto recognition to the branch of moral rights called the *droit de divulgation*. Once those same owners consented to initial publication of the work, however, they have historically lost control over its subsequent flow. The first sale doctrine prevented them from barring or demanding a royalty upon subsequent disposition of published copies. The fair use doctrine prevented them from barring or demanding a royalty from such activities as miscellaneous quotations in the context of a review. In this manner, traditional copyright law accorded the public substantial leeway in browsing published works.

The digital revolution places unprecedented stress on those browsing activities. Potentially, it allows copyright owners to control the flow not merely of their unpublished manuscripts, but more importantly, of their published works as well. If copyright owners package their "published" goods in digital envelopes accessible only through passwords, then perhaps they can, indeed, levy a unilateral royalty upon such activities as resales and reviews. At issue here are both factual and legal variables. The former involves a prediction as to the future of technology; the latter demands unprecedented attention to the legal status of such browsing activities as were previously simply beyond practical redress.

Consider the factual angle. Publishers are free to take old works that have fallen into the public domain, to add a bit of original material to them, and to claim a copyright in the newly released whole. Thus, for example, they could collect all cookbooks published in the nineteenth century, write a new introduction to each, and then wrap the product in a digital envelope. The resulting product, considered as a whole, would be subject to copyright protection. Whether that product holds any promise or not, however, depends on how technology develops.

If lending libraries continue to flourish, then anyone with a burning interest in how shrimp was cooked in *fin de siècle* New Orleans could simply check out the relevant volume from her local repository. There is no reason for her to pay to access the digital product–unless she specifically wishes to read the newly composed introductions, as opposed to the underlying books.

On the other hand, if the world develops such that a trip to the library becomes as common as sending messages via the Pony Express, then a different dynamic pertains. If access to works via electronic or photo-optical means becomes the universal norm, and if the only way that the pertinent network allows users to view any instantiation of Louisiana cookbooks of the 1890s is through payment of a fee, then royalties to the publisher of the electronic cookbook would become essentially mandatory. By the same token, if in tomorrow's world only antiquarians maintain phonographs and CD players, the sole effective way to hear an old recording of music might be through the same network service. To the extent that the service charged the same access fee for early 1920s jazz recordings as for new recordings subject to copyright protection, the effective result would be to convert public domain works into royalty-generating items.

---

[208] Fox Film Corp. v. Doyal, 286 U.S. 123, 127 (1932).

In short, depending on how the future unfolds, concern about fair use in the digital environment could range from pointless to vital. The latter scenario requires payment to gain access even to works that nominally lie in the public domain, such as works from centuries past, even if the purpose of the access is for one that the law favors, such as to quote a few sentences for scholarly purposes. Under that scenario, the work itself is effectively placed under lock and key, and the proprietor can charge simply for the initial act of access. Thus arises what one senator calls "the specter of moving our Nation towards a 'pay-per-use' society."[225]

In turn, the legal issue arises of how to conceptualize the browsing activities of users in decades past. Why is it that reviewers could traditionally quote scattered passages from copyrighted works? Is it because they had a right to do so? Could chefs review the techniques of their predecessors as contained in published cookbooks of the past as a matter of right? If so, was the right of constitutional magnitude, safeguarding First Amendment interests of free speech and the advancement of knowledge? Or did the law simply allow those activities, as it would have been economically unproductive to pursue such small scale utilization?

These fundamental questions exert practical consequences. Under the first point of view, any danger to the public's right to browse posed by the digital environment must be negated. In other words, if users have a constitutional right to quote for fair use purposes, then Congress was under an obligation to frame [17 U.S.C.] section 1201 in a manner that preserves that right. Under the second point of view, by contrast, the marketplace can be left to develop—if browsing rights are extinguished in the process, the only lesson to derive is that the economics evidently have changed. Congress, under this viewpoint, need not embody into section 1201 any special solicitude for user rights.

. . .

Let us revert to the public domain cookbook or sound recording that has been combined with a new introduction or other material subject to copyright and brought under a technological protection measure. As of the year 2005, those works could be virtually unavailable through low-tech means yet accessible to those who have paid for the appropriate decryption algorithm or password. In such a world, let us further imagine that Alice hacks her way in, gaining access to the work to avoid paying the license fee associated with taking out an authorized password. Bob does the same but instead to determine if he likes the old jazz song enough to pay the freight for regular access to it. Carol is writing her Ph.D. dissertation on obscure diction and wants to quote archaisms and franglais from the mouths of Creole chefs, which she remembers (from browsing a copy of the book long ago at a second-hand shop) are contained in the cookbook. Finally, Ted is a software virtuoso who boasts that he "can pick any lock." How does their conduct stack up?

Alice is the quintessential violator—hers is the precise conduct against which the basic provision [Section 1201(a)(1)(A)] is aimed. Accordingly, there is no question

---

[225] 144 Cong. Rec. S11887 (daily ed. Oct. 8, 1998) (statement of Sen. Ashcroft).

that her circumvention of a technological measure that effectively controls access to a work protected by a subsisting U.S. copyright places her in violation of the statute. Can she nevertheless take refuge in the fact that the publisher is actually charging for a work in the public domain rather than one protected by copyright? Inasmuch as the publisher has implemented a password scheme that prevents unauthorized access to its works, which themselves are subject to copyright by virtue of the new additions, that argument is unavailing. Although Alice would not run afoul of section 1201 by hacking her way into a domain containing no copyrightable elements, the domain to which she in fact gained unauthorized entry does contain copyrighted elements—notwithstanding that the particular components that she ultimately wished to enjoy lie outside copyright protection. Given that the language of the statute is absolute—"[n]o person shall circumvent a technological measure that effectively controls access to a work protected under this title"[297]—Alice is culpable for the anti-circumvention violation.

What about Bob? Many publishers release shareware, which customers can "try on for size" during a test period. Shareware publishers do not fall within the framework of the anti-circumvention basic provision and its coordinate trafficking offense; instead, they fall under the "additional violations" [Section 1201(b)(1)]. In that context, there is no counterpart basic offense to dovetail with the additional violations, so Bob's conduct would be nonactionable against a shareware publisher. In effect, Bob has elected to treat the subject music as shareware; an honorable listener, he has an unblemished track record of paying for all recordings that he actually adds to his collection.

Ultimately, however, Bob too falls on the wrong side of the tracks laid by section 1201. Although publishers are free to adopt the shareware paradigm, they are not obligated to do so. Bob cannot unilaterally pigeonhole purveyors of works into a category from which they have absented themselves—to make proprietary publishers into shareware publishers. Bob has no right to browse the access-protected works to determine if he wants to buy them. Section 1201 grants such browsing rights only to qualifying libraries and archives, not to individuals such as Bob.

Bob, like Alice, cannot take refuge in the fact that the recordings themselves reside in the public domain, for the language of the statute is such that Bob runs afoul of it. Given that the subject recordings are contained in a file that contains the copyrighted commentary of a renowned musicologist, that the file as a whole is protected by a technological measure that effectively controls access to it, and that Bob hacked his way into that file, all the elements for a section 1201 violation are present—again, notwithstanding that the particular components that Bob ultimately wished to enjoy lie outside copyright protection.

The examples of Alice and Bob seem to bear out the dissenters' initial criticism that "[t]he anti-circumvention language of H.R. 2281, even as amended, bootstraps the limited monopoly into a perpetual right."[304] To be sure, that bootstrapping is

---

[297] 17 U.S.C. § 1201(a)(1)(A).

[304] [Report of the House Comm. on Commerce, H.R. Rep. No. 105–551, pt. 2,] at 85 [(1998)] (Additional Views of Representatives Klug and Boucher). . . .

far from inevitable—it comes to bear only in a world in which the sole effective means of access to the subject cookbook and recording is through the encrypted methodology posited above. Hopefully, that state of affairs would never come to pass—just as one entity was able to obtain a copy of the subject works in order to upload them, so others should be able to do the same. The latter, moreover, can offer those works free of charge. Therefore, it might be that the first publisher's efforts at constructing its own *domaine public payant* will be doomed to failure. The point, however, is that the structure of section 1201, despite protestations to the contrary, does not categorically negate this baleful possibility—unless through the exception for adversely affected users, to which the discussion turns below.

Before reaching those points, however, consider Carol and Ted. Not only is Carol (the Ph.D. candidate) using a public domain work—a circumstance that, as observed in the cases of Alice and Bob, affords only cold comfort—but even such isolated quotation as she is drawing from the work, were it copyrighted, would itself find shelter under the fair use umbrella. Does section 1201 catch even her in its net? It does. For regardless of how lofty her purpose might be, she has violated the elements of the statute. Although, as noted in the discussion of Bob, section 1201 contains no prohibition on disabling technological measures once access to a work has been lawfully gained, as the Commerce Committee dissenters specifically complained, their effort at "legislating an equivalent fair use defense for the new right to control access" was rejected "for reasons not clear to us."[310]

But why does the fair use doctrine itself not come to Carol's rescue? Even though Congress did not add to section 1201 a specific fair use proviso that covers Carol, it at least left the existing provision undisturbed. Given that Carol's activities fall quintessentially within the protection of that defense, why is it inadequate to doom any cause of action against her? The answer lies in how the Copyright Act is structured. On the one hand, the Act forbids copyright infringement subject to a fair use defense. On the other hand, the WIPO Treaties Act adds a wholly separate tort of unauthorized circumvention, to which the fair use defense is inapplicable.

The upshot is that Carol, too, having circumvented a technological measure that effectively controls access to a work protected by U.S. copyright, falls afoul of section 1201. From a traditional copyright standpoint, the purportedly "fair" character of her utilization affords no defense to a charge that she is culpable of a new anti-circumvention violation.

At last reaching Ted (the hacker), to the extent that he advertises his abilities to or performs services for Alice, Bob, or Carol, he would thereby be aiding individuals who themselves fall afoul of section 1201. As such, he would be culpable of a trafficking violation.

. . .

Congress enacted section 1201 based on its perception that "the digital envi-

---

[310] Commerce Rep. (DMCA), *supra* note [304], at 86 (Additional Views of Representatives Klug and Boucher).

ronment poses a unique threat to the rights of copyright owners."[349] Even if that threat is unique, however, it scarcely arises in a vacuum. The tension between property rights and user-access rights does not loom from the approaching digital millennium; it has been a ceaseless part of the millennium now ending.

The lengthy analysis of how section 1201 works in practice leads to the conclusion that its entire edifice of user exemptions is of doubtful puissance. The user safeguards so proudly heralded as securing balance between owner and user interests, on inspection, largely fail to achieve their stated goals. If the courts apply section 1201 as written, the only users whose interests are truly safeguarded are those few who personally possess sufficient expertise to counteract whatever technological measures are placed in their path.

This defect is not a small one. Many legislators characterized the Digital Millennium Copyright Act as "probably one of the most important bills that we have passed this Congress."[354] The fair use issue constitutes "one of the most important provisions of this legislation."[355] Accordingly, it is a source of disappointment to be forced to disagree with the conclusion that Congress "mastered the intricate details of this complex subject and has produced a balanced result."[356]

. . .

In the event that future technology and business models do indeed converge to produce such a pay-per-use world, then the structure of section 1201, notwithstanding pious protests to the contrary, cannot meaningfully serve as the tool to defeat universal pay-per-use and de facto perpetual protection. Instead, courts at that juncture would be called upon to apply section 1201 to that world of the future—whether by upholding it exactly as written, by interpolating into it additional exceptions to give substance to the user exemption that it already contains, or by making the determination that protection for user rights (traditionally protected in the analog world through such devices as fair use and the first sale doctrine) rises to constitutional levels.

. . .

---

[349] Commerce Rep. (DMCA), supra note [304], at 25.

[354] 144 Cong. Rec. H10618 (daily ed. Oct. 12, 1998) (remarks of Rep. Stearns); see also 144 Cong. Rec. S11889 (daily ed. Oct. 8, 1998) (remarks of Sen. Hatch) ("[T]he DMCA is one of the most important bills passed this session. . . .").

[355] 144 Cong. Rec. H7094 (daily ed. Aug. 4, 1998) (remarks of Rep. Bliley); see also 144 Cong. Rec. E2144 (daily ed. Oct. 13, 1998) (remarks of Rep. Tauzin) (asserting that the fair use exception is "the most important contribution that we made to this bill").

[356] 144 Cong. Rec. H7096 (daily ed. Aug. 4, 1998) (remarks of Rep. Boucher).

Dan L. Burk & Julie E. Cohen, *Fair Use Infrastructure for Rights Management Systems*
15 Harv. J.L. & Tech. 41 (2001).

. . .

IV. OPTIONS FOR FAIR USE INFRASTRUCTURE

Currently, the DMCA's anti-circumvention provisions effectively sanction the use of private code to write the public law of fair use out of existence. But the legal regime governing rights management technologies need not be structured in such a fashion. Instead, law could be designed to shift technological development in a direction that balances the incentive structure of copyright protection with copyright's concern for the public domain and for the legitimate fair use privileges of the public. Here, we suggest modifications to the DMCA designed to create incentives for the preservation of fair use in digital media.

Realizing the promise of fair use in a digital rights management environment will require some technical mechanism to allow public access and reuse privileges equivalent to those deemed fair in previous media. In broad brush, there are two ways that such a system might be designed. First, the rights management system itself might be designed to detect and regulate fair use access. Second, a decision-maker external to the rights management system might authorize would-be fair users to override rights management controls. We propose a fair use infrastructure that combines elements of both approaches.

A. Coding for Fair Use

The most direct method of accommodating fair use would be to mandate or prompt the development of rights management systems that directly allow purchasers of a work to make fair use of the content. Optimally, the "breathing space" required for fair uses would be programmed directly into the technical rule set that controls access to the work. The systems might, for example, include provisions allowing users to extract a certain number of bits, or display the work for certain periods of time, or partially perform the work a certain number of times. Depending on the characteristics of the desired use, users would be able to take these actions without having to seek additional permission or pay additional fees.

In reality, an algorithm-based approach to fair use is unlikely to accommodate even the shadow of fair use as formulated in current copyright law. We are not optimistic that system designers will be able to anticipate the range of access privileges that may be appropriate for fair uses to be made of a particular work. Neither are we optimistic that system designers will be able to anticipate the types of uses that would be considered fair by a court. Fair use is irreducibly a situation-specific determination. In some instances, a user may fairly take a work in its entirety—say, for example, where the work is entitled to only thin protection, the use is for a protected purpose such as scholarship, criticism, or software reverse engineering, and/or the use is expected to have no appreciable impact on the market for the work. Indeed, some uses, such as software reverse engineering or automatically searching text, music, or video files for particular words, themes, or images (a process essential for some types of academic research), are impossible if the user cannot gain access to the entire work. In other situations, where three or four of the factors weigh heavily against a particular use, taking much less might exceed fair use.

Building the range of possible uses and outcomes into computer code would require both a bewildering degree of complexity and an impossible level of prescience. There is currently no good algorithm that is capable of producing such an analysis. Relatedly, fair use is a dynamic, equitable doctrine designed to respond to changing conditions of use. Programmed fair use functionality, in contrast, is relatively static. At least for now, there is no feasible way to build rights management code that approximates both the individual results of judicial determinations and the overall dynamism of fair use jurisprudence.

. . .

B. Key Access for Fair Use

The second option for the design of fair use infrastructure involves the introduction of an external decisionmaker into the process for obtaining access to technologically secured works. At present, only human intelligence, reviewing the unique circumstances of a particular use, can determine whether it is likely to be fair. Thus, we might require users to apply for keys to access the encrypted work. This option would allow case-by-case determination of the need for access, building in judgment capabilities that cannot practically be emulated by technical defaults.

One such method might be to place the fair use determination in the rights holder's hands. We cannot, however, recommend a legal rule that would fundamentally shift the decisionmaking authority about whether to proceed with a use from users to owners. As we have described above, fair use frequently condones public access in situations where the collective public interest runs contrary to the rights holder's individual interest. Thus, there may be a strong incentive for the rights holder to deny access just when the public interest most demands access. . . .

In addition, a preauthorization system for fair use is vulnerable to three more general objections. The first and second, closely related, are that a preauthorization requirement would be costly and would chill spontaneous uses. Case by case determination of the fairness of the intended use would require a lengthy and complicated approval process. Even a quick and inexpensive pre-screening procedure, however, will impose some transaction costs and will deter some uses that otherwise would have been made. As noted above, considerable social benefit accrues from this sort of unplanned use. Research and teaching, in particular, are processes that contain an irreducible element of ad hoc adjustment.

The third objection is that application to a third party is likely to compromise the sort of anonymity that users presently enjoy. Anonymity is the current default for fair use access (and indeed for access generally) in traditional media—a copyright holder does not know who has made use of the work, or at what time, or in what manner. Even if the fair use results in publication or dissemination of a subsidiary work, the author need not reveal her name. . . . [W]e are particularly reluctant to recommend that this situation be inverted by requiring revelation to the rights holder of a user's identity and use for every fair use. More generally, there exists a wide range of situations—for example, those involving parodies or other negative critiques—in which the user may prefer to remain anonymous.

. . .

Our proposal hinges upon the concept of key escrow, that is, management of rights management keys by a trusted third party, rather than by the owner of a work. Keys to technologically protected works would be held by the trusted third party, who would release them to users applying for access to make fair use. The trusted third party would be a publicly funded institution that would be statutorily insulated from both direct and indirect copyright infringement liability and subject to regulatory oversight for compliance with its escrow and privacy obligations.

Although, as we have noted, any preauthorization requirement would impinge upon spontaneous uses and thereby threaten the overall flexibility and adaptability of the fair use system, the trusted third party's approval procedure could be designed to minimize this impact. In order to avoid difficult ex ante judgments about particular uses, and to approximate as nearly as possible the cost and incentive structure of traditional fair uses, the third party would not be required, and would not attempt, to make a determination about the bona fides of the access application. Rather, the third party would simply issue keys to applicants via a simple online procedure.

Solving the anonymity problem is far more difficult. The concept of key escrow has been vilified in the past, with good reason, when it constituted the core of a governmental plan that would have systematically undermined the integrity of private communications. But a different sort of privacy interest is at stake here, where the issue is public access to publicly distributed works of authorship, rather than governmental access to private communications. In this instance, the concept of third-party escrow works toward the public interest and could be made to work in favor of preserving privacy, rather than against both goals.

. . .

C. Mixed Fair Use Infrastructure

Each of the two possible mechanisms for preserving fair use in a digital rights management environment has advantages and drawbacks. Automatic fair use functionality does not require human intervention but is unlikely to afford the full spectrum of fair uses allowed by law. The use of a trusted third party intermediary to mediate access, in contrast, potentially allows the full spectrum of uses but is less responsive to anonymity and spontaneity concerns. The optimal result, we suggest, is an infrastructure that combines the two.

The first layer of our proposed fair use infrastructure would involve the design of rights management technologies that incorporate automatic fair use defaults based on customary norms of personal noncommercial use. The legal rule for facilitating this part of the proposal would operate in a fashion similar to current provisions of the Copyright Act designed to encourage copyright registration and deposit, by conditioning copyright enforcement for United States works on implementation of the automatic fair use defaults. To guard against a "race to the bottom" in fair use law, the law would clearly state that the level of copying permitted by the automatic defaults does not define the full extent of permitted fair use.

Those who desire greater fair use access, meanwhile, would turn to the trusted third party intermediary. Under the system, deposit of access keys into key escrow would be facilitated by conditioning anti-circumvention protection for both United States and non-United States works on such deposit. Users who failed to obtain access via the escrow agent would be subject to suit for circumventing technical measures. Those users, however, still might escape liability by successful invocation of a statutory or constitutional defense to circumvention liability. Rights holders that opt not to deposit keys with the escrow agent would be unable to invoke legal protection against circumvention. For such unescrowed works, a "right to hack" would effectively substitute for access via the escrowed keys. . . . [T]he DMCA's ban on the manufacture and distribution of circumvention technologies also would need to be modified to make this defense a realistic possibility. Finally, to preserve the relative anonymity of the key escrow system, the records of applicants and keys issued would need to be guarded by stringent legal protections along the lines described above.

The most likely and appropriate escrow agent would be a publicly funded institution, such as the Library of Congress. . . . [W]e think that a publicly funded institution would be the preferred choice because the public policies underlying fair use require some guarantees of public accountability and institutional longevity.

. . .

. . . The presence of other national laws regarding anti-circumvention highlights the fact that the balance between access and protection must be struck in a global milieu, where the U.S. approach to technical protection is not insular and where our suggestion may find broader application than the American DMCA. Although we have focused on the implementation of a fair use infrastructure within U.S. copyright law, the escrow principles we have outlined here also might find application under the European Union's ("E.U.") new copyright directive, which in some respects reflects greater cognizance of the user access problem than does its American counterpart. Like the DMCA, the E.U. Copyright Directive requires member states to provide legal protection for rights management systems. Unlike its U.S. analogue, however, the E.U. Copyright Directive allows member states to enact legislation requiring that copyright holders provide users with the means to take advantage of exceptions or limitations to the exclusive rights granted under copyright law. These limitations and exceptions, which are enumerated in the directive, specifically include private reproduction, criticism and parody, and news reporting. To prevent user rights from being nullified by technical controls, moreover, the directive creates an incentive for content owners to design technical measures capable of facilitating permitted uses; member states may legislate to compel the provision of means for access only if content owners have not already provided such means voluntarily. The key escrow system that we propose here might be an appropriate means by which member states could ensure user access, or promote voluntary provision of access by copyright owners.

It is worth noting that the E.U. Copyright Directive contemplates nothing so broad, flexible, or indeterminate as the U.S. concept of fair use. Rather, in the European tradition of "fair dealing," the directive lists specific circumstances under which member states may allow a user to make unauthorized use of a copyrighted work. The exceptions and limitations enumerated in the directive are discrete and relatively narrow. Design of a rights management infrastructure that would allow users access commensurate with such exceptions may be less challenging than design of an infrastructure to accommodate U.S.-style fair use. Nonetheless, we expect that it would still be difficult to design an algorithm that could take into account whether, for example, a reproduction is "for private use and for ends that are neither directly nor indirectly commercial," as the directive requires. Thus, the key escrow option discussed here may remain an attractive method of providing user access.

. . .

QUESTIONS FOR DISCUSSION

Assessing the threat. How great a threat to public access and fair use is posed by the use of technological management systems? What factors does Professor Nimmer suggest will determine how serious the threat is? Do you agree with his analysis? Recall that Section 1201 provides that the anti-circumvention provisions do not affect the law of fair use. 17 U.S.C. § 1201(c)(1). Does that mean that these fears are overblown? In considering this question, note that observers have expressed sharply differing views as to what policy best supports fair use. For some, such as Professor Bell, fair use is based primarily on economic efficiency. Under one application of the efficiency criterion, use of copyrighted works is fair where that use would be welfare-maximizing, but the transaction costs of acquiring authorization from the copyright owner through voluntary licensing are too high for the transaction to take place. For others, such as Professors Burk and Cohen, fair use is based on principles of free circulation of information, especially criticism and debate; i.e., fair use is an exception to the exclusive rights of copyright owners that should be retained even absent transaction costs. How much do fears about the future of fair use rest on a non-economic understanding of its purpose? Consider also the argument that if transaction costs are indeed the only basis for the fair use privilege, then there is nothing to fear if the doctrine fades away in the online world of greatly reduced transaction costs. *See* Margaret Jane Radin, *Incomplete Commodification in the Computerized World,* in THE COMMODIFICATION OF INFORMATION (Niva Elkin-Koren & Neil Weinstock Netanel eds., 2002).

CHAPTER TEN
CONTRACTING ONLINE

Businesses are increasingly dealing with each other online, for everyday transactions such as purchasing supplies and for more complex transactions such as engaging in business partnerships. These are often called "B2B" transactions. Businesses are also increasingly dealing with consumers online. These are often called "B2C" transactions. Go to a commercial website of your choice—for example, Disney's at www.disney.com—and scroll down the home page until you come to a small link at the bottom labeled something like "Terms of Use." Click on the link and watch what unfolds. Are these terms contractually binding on you?

Contracting is just as central to online exchange transactions as it is to those that take place offline. In some countries, separate bodies of law govern commercial transactions between businesses and transactions between a business and a consumer. As you will recall from your first-year contracts course, however, American law does not make this distinction, but instead often tends to apply the law differently depending on the nature of the transaction. In this chapter we will follow American law and consider contracting both between businesses and between a business and customers or users.

As contract law accommodates to the digital networked environment, there are a number of issues that are in the process of being sorted out, both by legislative authorities (on the state, national, and international levels) and by the courts. This chapter addresses these issues under the following rubrics:

Contract formation. How will interactions between people and computers create binding commitments? Can binding commitment arise through computer-to-computer interactions? When exactly does the binding commitment come into existence?

These questions call for reconsideration of contract formation. New forms of contracts (or purported contracts) have come into widespread use. We must consider whether binding commitment is created by placing boilerplate terms on an interior website page; whether computers programmed with terms can interact with each other to create binding commitment; and whether terms can be attached to a digital object by a seller or licensor and made binding on the recipient or on all subsequent recipients—that is, everyone in a chain of distribution.

"Writing" and authentication. As you will recall from your first-year contracts course, all U.S. jurisdictions retain a statute of frauds requiring certain types of contracts to be in writing in order to be enforceable. Certain other doctrines (such as the parol evidence rule) look to a written document to ascertain the parameters of the parties' agreement. To what extent will digital communications count as a "writing" for purposes of these legal inquiries? We must consider whether electronic text constitutes "writing" for purposes of statutes that make an agreement enforceable only if it is in writing or doctrines that look to a writing in order to interpret the agreement. As we shall see, in order to facilitate electronic commerce, the meaning of "writing" is being rewritten.

More generally, the problem of authentication has come to the fore. How do we know who made a particular deal? How do we know what the terms are? In the online environment, most transactions are conducted at a distance, and identities and transactional parameters are easily "spoofed." Therefore, concerns about security and authentication are central to the development of electronic commerce, and new forms of identification of parties and guarantees of textual integrity are being developed. We must consider the legal ramifications of these concerns and developments.

Limits on contractual ordering. In the online as in the offline world, certain subjects are off-limits to contract, as are certain kinds of terms; and the circumstances under which a purported contract was arrived at may determine whether it will be deemed enforceable. In the online world, the question of unconscionability arises most often in standardized contracts of adhesion and/or situations of unequal bargaining power. What kinds of contracts, or terms in contracts, will be disallowed? What remedies are available?

In the online world, parties often attempt to select by contract the forum in which disputes will be adjudicated, the governing law under which disputes will be adjudicated, and the type of dispute resolution (whether arbitration or litigation) or remedies available. Although this kind of contractual ordering is prevalent in the offline world, it may be even more important in the online world, because of the distances at which transactions are conducted, and because of the difficulties otherwise attendant upon sorting out whose law governs and what court has jurisdiction. (*See* Chapter 5, *supra.*) But such contracts are not always held valid and enforceable. We will look at some circumstances in which they have been held to be overreaching.

Licensing of intellectual property. The main way that intellectual property owners make money is by licensing their intellectual property to others. Normally these transactions are considered contractual. Many transactions in e-commerce involve a transfer of intellectual property rights. Licenses may be exclusive (in which one transferee receives exclusive rights) or non-exclusive (in which other transferees can be granted the same rights). The major intellectual property regimes contemplate licensing, and we will outline how they do so. We will then consider questions that have arisen in several arenas relevant to e-commerce. For example, to what extent are new digital uses covered by old analogue licenses?

Contracting out of the limits of intellectual property. Intellectual property regimes grant ownership rights that are limited in certain ways. (For example, we saw in Chapter 2 that trademark rights depend upon use in commerce and cannot attach to generic terms. In Chapter 7 we studied the limits of copyright, and in Chapter 11 we will study the limits of patent.) A prevalent practice has developed in e-commerce to try to contract out of those limits and thereby expand the owner's rights, usually by means of browsewrap or clickwrap contracts. We will consider to what extent this expansion of intellectual property rights is or should be legally permissible.

Using contract to enable end-user innovation and creativity. Developments such as open source licensing and the dissemination of Creative Commons licenses enable end-users in the digital networked environment to get more rights than purchasing a copy would normally give under copyright law. We conclude this chapter by taking a look at these phenomena.

I. CONTRACT FORMATION

A. SHRINKWRAP AND ITS ONLINE ANALOGUES

As the *Restatement of Contracts* reminds us, "the formation of a contract requires a bargain in which there is manifestation of mutual assent to the exchange and a consideration." RESTATEMENT (SECOND) OF CONTRACTS § 17 (1979). While there are exceptions to this rule, most contracts require a bargain involving an exchange of promises (a bilateral contract) or a promise for a performance (a unilateral contract).[33] Moreover, the parties to the contract must clearly manifest their assent to the exchange. As Professor Farnsworth notes, "[s]ince it is difficult for a workable system of contract law to take account of assent unless there has been an overt expression of it, courts have required that assent to the formation of a contract be manifested in some way, by words or other conduct, if it is to be effective." E. ALLEN FARNSWORTH, FARNSWORTH ON CONTRACTS § 3.1 (3d ed. 1999).

This requirement is often satisfied in two steps—offer and acceptance. Requiring a manifestation of mutual assent before a contract is formed raises two critical questions: (1) What kind of conduct constitutes a sufficiently overt manifestation of assent to an exchange for the purposes of forming a contract?; and (2) At what point in time is an offeree's acceptance effective and the offeror's power of revocation terminated? These questions are especially challenging when applied to conduct on the Internet. In this and the next section, we consider these questions in regard to electronic contracting.

When determining what kind of online conduct constitutes a sufficiently overt manifestation of assent to an exchange to form a contract, courts have focused on contracts (or purported contracts) in which assent is problematic: shrinkwrap licenses and their online analogues, variously called clickwrap, click-through, and browsewrap licenses.

The term "shrinkwrap license" usually refers to a license agreement, governing a purchaser's use of software or digitized data, that is presented to the purchaser only *after* payment of the purchase price. The term takes its name from the clear plastic wrapping that typically surrounds and seals boxes of software that are offered for sale at retail stores. The license agreement is enclosed within the box, and the shrinkwrap prevents the purchaser from reading its terms until after she pays for the software and is entitled to break the seal.[34] There may or may not be a notice visible on the outside of the box, informing the prospective purchaser that additional terms are enclosed.

A clickwrap agreement is one in which the terms of the agreement are displayed on the computer screen and the computer user is requested to click an on-screen button to indicate

---

[33] The exceptions to this rule include a contract under seal, recognizances, negotiable instruments, negotiable documents and letters of credit. *See* RESTATEMENT (SECOND) OF CONTRACTS, § 6 (1979).

[34] Starting in the early 1990s, license agreements were sometimes printed on the outside of the box, or on a separate card secured under the shrinkwrap, allowing the purchaser to view the terms before purchase. These licenses typically stated that breaking the shrinkwrap would signify the purchaser's assent to the terms. Certain terms, like "Upgrade Version" or "One-Year Toll-Free Support," continue to appear on the outside of the box. This method of presenting terms *pre-purchase*, which is sometimes also referred to as a shrinkwrap license, presents different legal issues from the type of shrinkwrap license in which the terms are presented only after payment.

assent to the displayed terms. A website that displays the terms and says, "Click here to indicate you agree to these terms," is somewhat analogous to a shrinkwrap license that is visible on the outside of the box. The website is programmed so that you won't get to use the site if you don't click the button; analogously, you won't get to use shrinkwrapped software if you don't break the shrinkwrap. But the two situations also differ in an important respect. The existence of the clickwrap agreement is brought unavoidably to the attention of the user: although she need not actually read the terms, the requirement that she click a button labeled "I agree" (or the equivalent) cues her to the fact that she is agreeing to *something*. When the license terms are on the outside of the box, however, it is quite possible for the user to break the seal and use the software without realizing that the vendor has proposed a set of terms.

Some websites disclose the existence of terms governing use of the site with nothing more than a link on the home page labeled "Terms of Use." The website owner intends that this notice will indicate to the user, "By continuing to use this site you agree to a set of terms which you will only see if you choose to click on this link." Some courts and commentators refer to these terms as browsewrap agreements. When a process like this has been held to form a contract, it has usually been required that the user be able to unwind the deal after viewing the terms (i.e., by returning the product for a refund).

If the online contracts now coming before courts are problematic on the issue of sufficient assent to be bound, so too, it must be remembered, are a great many contracts in the offline world. There are quite a few other contracts in the offline world in which the buyer doesn't see many of the terms until after buying the product. We purchase tickets, tour packages, and countless other items (including shrinkwrapped software) over the phone before we see the fine print. Consumer product warranties are often inside the box. In some classes of these contracts, such as the fine-print inserts that come with credit-card bills, new terms are imposed at the seller's will from time to time. In all of these contracts, it appears that the promisor must at least be given the option of declining after the fact to be bound, by unwinding his or her initial acceptance of the product (e.g., ceasing to use the credit card). It does not appear, though, that this option is anything more than theoretically possible. Airlines do not cheerfully refund the purchase price of nonrefundable airline tickets upon the purchaser's refusal to assent to the terms incorporated by reference on the ticket, once having viewed them post-purchase in the airline's business office.

1. Shrinkwrap Agreements

ProCD, Inc. v. Zeidenberg
86 F.3d 1447 (7th Cir.1996).

■ EASTERBROOK, CIRCUIT JUDGE.

Must buyers of computer software obey the terms of shrinkwrap licenses? The district court held not, for two reasons: first, they are not contracts because the licenses are inside the box rather than printed on the outside; second, federal law forbids enforcement even if the licenses are contracts. 908 F.Supp. 640 (W.D.Wis.1996). The parties and numerous amici curiae have briefed many other issues, but these are the only two that matter—and we disagree with the district judge's conclusion on each. Shrinkwrap licenses are enforceable unless their terms are objectionable on grounds applicable to contracts in general (for example, if they violate a rule of positive law, or if they are unconscionable). Because no one argues that the terms of the license at issue here are troublesome, we remand with instructions to enter judgment for the plaintiff.

I

ProCD, the plaintiff, has compiled information from more than 3,000 telephone directories into a computer database. We may assume that this database cannot be copyrighted, although it is more complex, contains more information (nine-digit zip codes and census industrial codes), is organized differently, and therefore is more original than the single alphabetical directory at issue in *Feist Publications, Inc. v. Rural Telephone Service Co.*, 499 U.S. 340 (1991). *See* Paul J. Heald, The Vices of Originality, 1991 Sup.Ct. Rev. 143, 160–68. ProCD sells a version of the database, called SelectPhone™, on CD-ROM discs. (CD-ROM means "compact disc—read only memory." The "shrinkwrap license" gets its name from the fact that retail software packages are covered in plastic or cellophane "shrinkwrap," and some vendors, though not ProCD, have written licenses that become effective as soon as the customer tears the wrapping from the package. Vendors prefer "end user license," but we use the more common term.) A proprietary method of compressing the data serves as effective encryption too. Customers decrypt and use the data with the aid of an application program that ProCD has written. This program, which is copyrighted, searches the database in response to users' criteria (such as "find all people named Tatum in Tennessee, plus all firms with 'Door Systems' in the corporate name"). The resulting lists (or, as ProCD prefers, "listings") can be read and manipulated by other software, such as word processing programs.

The database in SelectPhone™ cost more than $10 million to compile and is expensive to keep current. It is much more valuable to some users than to others. The combination of names, addresses, and SIC codes enables manufacturers to compile lists of potential customers. Manufacturers and retailers pay high prices to specialized information intermediaries for such mailing lists; ProCD offers a potentially cheaper alternative. People with nothing to sell could use the database as a substitute for calling long distance information, or as a way to look up old friends who have moved to unknown towns, or just as an electronic substitute for the local phone book. ProCD decided to engage in price discrimination, selling its database to the general public for personal use at a low price (approximately $150 for the set of five discs) while selling information to the trade for a higher price. It has adopted some intermediate strategies too: access to the SelectPhone™ database is available via the America Online service for the price America Online charges to its clients (approximately $3 per hour), but this service has been tailored to be useful only to the general public.

If ProCD had to recover all of its costs and make a profit by charging a single price—that is, if it could not charge more to commercial users than to the general public—it would have to raise the price substantially over $150. The ensuing reduction in sales would harm consumers who value the information at, say, $200. They get consumer surplus of $50 under the current arrangement but would cease to buy if the price rose substantially. If because of high elasticity of demand in the consumer segment of the market the only way to make a profit turned out to be a price attractive to commercial users alone, then all consumers would lose out—and so would the commercial clients, who would have to pay more for the listings because ProCD could not obtain any contribution toward costs from the consumer market.

To make price discrimination work, however, the seller must be able to control arbitrage. An air carrier sells tickets for less to vacationers than to business travelers, using advance purchase and Saturday-night-stay requirements to distinguish the categories. A producer of movies segments the market by time, releasing first to theaters, then to pay-per-view services, next to the videotape and laserdisc market, and finally to cable and commercial TV. Vendors of computer software have a harder task. Anyone can walk into a retail store and buy a box. Customers do not wear tags saying "commercial user" or "consumer user." Anyway, even a commercial-user-detector at the door would not work, because a consumer could buy the software and resell to a commercial user. That arbitrage would break down the price discrimination and drive up the minimum price at which ProCD would sell to anyone.

Instead of tinkering with the product and letting users sort themselves—for example, furnishing current data at a high price that would be attractive only to commercial customers, and two-year-old data at a low price—ProCD turned to the institution of contract. Every box containing its consumer product declares that the software comes with restrictions stated in an enclosed license. This license, which is encoded on the CD-ROM disks as well as printed in the manual, and which appears on a user's screen every time the software runs, limits use of the application program and listings to non-commercial purposes.

Matthew Zeidenberg bought a consumer package of SelectPhone™ in 1994 from a retail outlet in Madison, Wisconsin, but decided to ignore the license. He formed Silken Mountain Web Services, Inc., to resell the information in the SelectPhone™ database. The corporation makes the database available on the Internet to anyone willing to pay its price—which, needless to say, is less than ProCD charges its commercial customers. Zeidenberg has purchased two additional SelectPhone™ packages, each with an updated version of the database, and made the latest information available over the World Wide Web, for a price, through his corporation. ProCD filed this suit seeking an injunction against further dissemination that exceeds the rights specified in the licenses (identical in each of the three packages Zeidenberg purchased). The district court held the licenses ineffectual because their terms do not appear on the outside of the packages. The court added that the second and third licenses stand no different from the first, even though they are identical, because they *might* have been different, and a purchaser does not agree to—and cannot be bound by—terms that were secret at the time of purchase. 908 F.Supp. at 654.

II

Following the district court, we treat the licenses as ordinary contracts accompanying the sale of products, and therefore as governed by the common law of contracts and the Uniform Commercial Code. Whether there are legal differences between "contracts" and "licenses" (which may matter under the copyright doctrine of first sale) is a subject for another day. *See Microsoft Corp. v. Harmony Computers & Electronics, Inc.,* 846 F.Supp. 208 (E.D.N.Y.1994). Zeidenberg does not argue that Silken Mountain Web Services is free of any restrictions that apply to Zeidenberg himself, because any effort to treat the two parties as distinct would put Silken Mountain behind the eight ball on ProCD's argument that copying the application program onto its hard disk violates the copyright laws. Zeidenberg does argue, and the district court held, that placing the package of software on the shelf is an "offer," which the customer "accepts" by paying the asking price and leaving the store with the goods. *Peeters v. State,* 154 Wis. 111, 142 N.W. 181 (1913). In Wisconsin, as elsewhere, a contract includes only the terms on which the parties have agreed. One cannot agree to hidden terms, the judge concluded. So far, so good—but one of the terms to which Zeidenberg agreed by purchasing the software is that the transaction was subject to a license. Zeidenberg's position therefore must be that the printed terms on the outside of a box are the parties' contract—except for printed terms that refer to or incorporate other terms. But why would Wisconsin fetter the parties' choice in this way? Vendors can put the entire terms of a contract on the outside of a box only by using microscopic type, removing other information that buyers might find more useful (such as what the software does, and on which computers it works), or both. The "Read Me" file included with most software, describing system requirements and potential incompatibilities, may be equivalent to ten pages of type; warranties and license restrictions take still more space. Notice on the outside, terms on the inside, and a right to return the software for a refund if the terms are unacceptable (a right that the license expressly extends), may be a means of doing business valuable to buyers and sellers alike. *See* E. Allan Farnsworth, 1 Farnsworth on Contracts § 4.26 (1990); Restatement (Second) of Contracts § 211 comment a (1981) ("Standardization of agreements serves many of the same functions as standardization of goods and services; both are essential to a system of mass production and distribution. Scarce and costly time and skill can be devoted to a class of transactions rather than the details of individual transactions."). Doubtless a state could forbid the use of standard contracts in the software business, but we do not think that Wisconsin has done so.

Transactions in which the exchange of money precedes the communication of detailed terms are common. Consider the purchase of insurance. The buyer goes to an agent, who explains the essentials (amount of coverage, number of years) and remits the premium to the home office, which sends back a policy. On the district judge's understanding, the terms of the policy are irrelevant because the insured paid before receiving them. Yet the device of payment, often with a "binder" (so that the insurance takes effect immediately even though the home office reserves the right to withdraw coverage later), in advance of the policy, serves buyers' interests by accelerating effectiveness and reducing transactions costs. Or consider the purchase of an airline ticket. The traveler calls the carrier or an agent, is quoted a price, reserves a seat, pays, and gets a ticket, in that order. The ticket contains elaborate terms, which the traveler can reject by canceling the reservation. To use the ticket is to accept the terms, even terms that in retrospect are disadvantageous.

See Carnival Cruise Lines, Inc. v. Shute, 499 U.S. 585 (1991); *see also Vimar Seguros y Reaseguros, S.A. v. M/V Sky Reefer*, 515 U.S. 528 (1995) (bills of lading). Just so with a ticket to a concert. The back of the ticket states that the patron promises not to record the concert; to attend is to agree. A theater that detects a violation will confiscate the tape and escort the violator to the exit. One *could* arrange things so that every concertgoer signs this promise before forking over the money, but that cumbersome way of doing things not only would lengthen queues and raise prices but also would scotch the sale of tickets by phone or electronic data service.

Consumer goods work the same way. Someone who wants to buy a radio set visits a store, pays, and walks out with a box. Inside the box is a leaflet containing some terms, the most important of which usually is the warranty, read for the first time in the comfort of home. By Zeidenberg's lights, the warranty in the box is irrelevant; every consumer gets the standard warranty implied by the UCC in the event the contract is silent; yet so far as we are aware no state disregards warranties furnished with consumer products. Drugs come with a list of ingredients on the outside and an elaborate package insert on the inside. The package insert describes drug interactions, contraindications, and other vital information—but, if Zeidenberg is right, the purchaser need not read the package insert, because it is not part of the contract.

Next consider the software industry itself. Only a minority of sales take place over the counter, where there are boxes to peruse. A customer may place an order by phone in response to a line item in a catalog or a review in a magazine. Much software is ordered over the Internet by purchasers who have never seen a box. Increasingly software arrives by wire. There is no box; there is only a stream of electrons, a collection of information that includes data, an application program, instructions, many limitations ("MegaPixel 3.14159 cannot be used with BytePusher 2.718"), and the terms of sale. The user purchases a serial number, which activates the software's features. On Zeidenberg's arguments, these unboxed sales are unfettered by terms—so the seller has made a broad warranty and must pay consequential damages for any shortfalls in performance, two "promises" that if taken seriously would drive prices through the ceiling or return transactions to the horse-and-buggy age.

According to the district court, the UCC does not countenance the sequence of money now, terms later. (Wisconsin's version of the UCC does not differ from the Official Version in any material respect, so we use the regular numbering system. Wis. Stat. § 402.201 corresponds to UCC § 2–201, and other citations are easy to derive.) One of the court's reasons—that by proposing as part of the draft Article 2B a new UCC § 2–2203 that would explicitly validate standard-form user licenses, the American Law Institute and the National Conference of Commissioners on Uniform Laws have conceded the invalidity of shrinkwrap licenses under current law, *see* 908 F.Supp. at 655–56—depends on a faulty inference. To propose a change in a law's *text* is not necessarily to propose a change in the law's *effect*. New words may be designed to fortify the current rule with a more precise text that curtails uncertainty. To judge by the flux of law review articles discussing shrinkwrap licenses, uncertainty is much in need of reduction—although businesses seem to feel less uncertainty than do scholars, for only three cases (other than ours) touch on the subject, and none directly addresses it. *See Step-Saver Data Systems, Inc. v. Wyse Technology,* 939 F.2d 91 (3d Cir.1991); *Vault Corp. v. Quaid Software Ltd.,* 847 F.2d 255, 268–70 (5th Cir.1988); *Arizona Retail Systems, Inc. v. Software Link, Inc.,* 831 F.Supp. 759 (D.Ariz.1993). As their titles suggest, these are not consumer transactions. *Step-Saver* is a battle-of-the-forms case, in which the parties exchange incompatible forms and a court must decide which prevails. *See Northrop Corp. v. Litronic Industries,* 29 F.3d 1173 (7th Cir.1994) (Illinois law); Douglas G. Baird & Robert Weisberg, *Rules, Standards, and the Battle of the Forms: A Reassessment of* § 2–207, 68 VA. L. REV. 1217, 1227–31 (1982). Our case has only one form; UCC § 2–207 is irrelevant. *Vault* holds that Louisiana's special shrinkwrap-license statute is preempted by federal law, a question to which we return. And *Arizona Retail Systems* did not reach the question, because the court found that the buyer knew the terms of the license before purchasing the software.

What then does the current version of the UCC have to say? We think that the place to start is § 2–204(1): "A contract for sale of goods may be made in any manner sufficient to show agreement, including conduct by both parties which recognizes the existence of such a contract." A vendor, as master of the offer, may invite acceptance by conduct, and may propose limitations on the kind of conduct that constitutes acceptance. A buyer may accept by performing the acts the vendor proposes to treat as acceptance. And that is what happened. ProCD proposed a contract that a buyer would accept by *using* the software after having an opportunity to read the license at leisure. This Zeidenberg did. He had no choice, because the software splashed the license on the screen and would not let him proceed without indicating acceptance. So although the district judge was right to say that a contract can be, and often is, formed simply by paying the price and walking out of the store, the UCC permits contracts to be formed in other ways. ProCD proposed such a different way, and without protest Zeidenberg agreed. Ours is not a case in which a consumer opens a package to find an insert saying "you owe us an extra $10,000" and the seller files suit to collect. Any buyer finding such a demand can prevent formation of the contract by returning the package, as can any consumer who concludes that the terms of the license make the software worth less than the purchase price. Nothing in the UCC requires a seller to maximize the buyer's net gains.

Section 2–606, which defines "acceptance of goods", reinforces this understanding. A buyer accepts goods under § 2–606(1)(b) when, after an opportunity to inspect, he fails to make an effective rejection under § 2–602(1). ProCD extended an opportunity to reject if a buyer should find the license terms unsatisfactory; Zeidenberg inspected the package, tried out the software, learned of the license, and did not reject the goods. We refer to § 2–606 only to show that the opportunity to return goods can be important; acceptance of an offer differs from acceptance of goods after delivery, *see Gillen v. Atalanta Systems, Inc.,* 997 F.2d 280, 284 n.1 (7th Cir.1993); but the UCC consistently permits the parties to structure their relations so that the buyer has a chance to make a final decision after a detailed review.

Some portions of the UCC impose additional requirements on the way parties agree on terms. A disclaimer of the implied warranty of merchantability must be "conspicuous." UCC § 2–316(2), incorporating UCC § 1–201(10). Promises to make firm offers, or to negate oral modifications, must be "separately signed." UCC §§ 2–205, 2–209(2). These special provisos reinforce the impression that, so far as the UCC is concerned, other terms may be as inconspicuous as the forum-selection clause on the back of the cruise ship ticket in *Carnival Lines*. Zeidenberg has not located any Wisconsin case—for that matter, any case in any state—holding that under the UCC the ordinary terms found in shrinkwrap licenses require any special prominence, or otherwise are to be undercut rather than enforced. In the end, the terms of the license are conceptually identical to the contents of the package. Just as no court would dream of saying that SelectPhone™ must contain 3,100 phone books rather than 3,000, or must have data no more than 30 days old, or must sell for $100 rather than $150—although any of these changes would be welcomed by the customer, if all other things were held constant—so, we believe, Wisconsin would not let the buyer pick and choose among terms. Terms of use are no less a part of "the product" than are the size of the database and the speed with which the software compiles listings. Competition among vendors, not judicial revision of a package's contents, is how consumers are protected in a market economy. *Digital Equipment Corp. v. Uniq Digital Technologies, Inc.*, 73 F.3d 756 (7th Cir.1996). ProCD has rivals, which may elect to compete by offering superior software, monthly updates, improved terms of use, lower price, or a better compromise among these elements. As we stressed above, adjusting terms in buyers' favor might help Matthew Zeidenberg today (he already has the software) but would lead to a response, such as a higher price, that might make consumers as a whole worse off.

. . .

Hill v. Gateway 2000, Inc.
105 F.3d 1147 (7th Cir.1997).

■ EASTERBROOK, CIRCUIT JUDGE.

A customer picks up the phone, orders a computer, and gives a credit card number. Presently a box arrives, containing the computer and a list of terms, said to govern unless the customer returns the computer within 30 days. Are these terms effective as the parties' contract, or is the contract term-free because the order-taker did not read any terms over the phone and elicit the customer's assent?

One of the terms in the box containing a Gateway 2000 system was an arbitration clause. Rich and Enza Hill, the customers, kept the computer more than 30 days before complaining about its components and performance. They filed suit in federal court arguing, among other things, that the product's shortcomings make Gateway a racketeer (mail and wire fraud are said to be the predicate offenses), leading to treble damages under RICO for the Hills and a class of all other purchasers. Gateway asked the district court to enforce the arbitration clause; the judge refused, writing that "[t]he present record is insufficient to support a finding of a valid arbitration agreement between the parties or that the plaintiffs were given adequate notice of the arbitration clause." Gateway took an immediate appeal, as is its right. 9 U.S.C. § 16(a)(1)(A).

The Hills say that the arbitration clause did not stand out: they concede noticing the statement of terms but deny reading it closely enough to discover the agreement to arbitrate, and they ask us to conclude that they therefore may go to court. Yet an agreement to arbitrate must be enforced "save upon such grounds as exist at law or in equity for the revocation of any contract." 9 U.S.C. § 2. *Doctor's Associates, Inc. v. Casarotto,* 517 U.S. 681 (1996), holds that this provision of the Federal Arbitration Act is inconsistent with any requirement that an arbitration clause be prominent. A contract need not be read to be effective; people who accept take the risk that the unread terms may in retrospect prove unwelcome. *Carr v. CIGNA Securities, Inc.,* 95 F.3d 544, 547 (7th Cir.1996); *Chicago Pacific Corp. v. Canada Life Assurance Co.,* 850 F.2d 334 (7th Cir.1988). Terms inside Gateway's box stand or fall together. If they constitute the parties' contract because the Hills had an opportunity to return the computer after reading them, then all must be enforced.

ProCD, Inc. v. Zeidenberg, 86 F.3d 1447 (7th Cir.1996), holds that terms inside a box of software bind consumers who use the software after an opportunity to read the terms and to reject them by returning the product. Likewise, *Carnival Cruise Lines, Inc. v. Shute,* 499 U.S. 585 (1991), enforces a forum-selection clause that was included among three pages of terms attached to a cruise ship ticket. *ProCD* and *Carnival Cruise Lines* exemplify the many commercial transactions in which people pay for products with terms to follow; *ProCD* discusses others. 86 F.3d at 1451–52. The district court concluded in *ProCD* that the contract is formed when the consumer pays for the software; as a result, the court held, only terms known to the consumer at that moment are part of the contract, and provisos inside the box do not count. Although this is one way a contract could be formed, it is not the only way: "A vendor, as master of the offer, may invite acceptance by conduct, and may propose limitations on the kind of conduct that constitutes acceptance. A buyer may accept by performing the acts the vendor proposes to treat as acceptance." *Id.* at 1452. Gateway shipped computers with the same sort of accept-or-return offer *ProCD* made to users of its software. *ProCD* relied on the Uniform Commercial Code rather than any peculiarities of Wisconsin law; both Illinois and South Dakota, the two states whose law might govern relations between Gateway and the Hills, have adopted the UCC; neither side has pointed us to any atypical doctrines in those states that might be pertinent; *ProCD* therefore applies to this dispute.

Plaintiffs ask us to limit *ProCD* to software, but where's the sense in that? *ProCD* is about the law of contract, not the law of software. Payment preceding the revelation of full terms is common for air transportation, insurance, and many other endeavors. Practical considerations support allowing vendors to enclose the full legal terms with their products. Cashiers cannot be expected to read legal documents to customers before ringing up sales. If the staff at the other end of the phone for direct-sales operations such as Gateway's had to read the four-page statement of terms before taking the buyer's credit card number, the droning voice would anesthetize rather than enlighten many potential buyers. Others would hang up in a rage over the waste of their time. And oral recitation would not avoid customers' assertions (whether true or feigned) that the clerk did not read term X to them, or that they did not remember or understand it. Writing provides benefits for both sides of commercial transactions. Customers as a group are better off when vendors skip costly and ineffectual steps such as telephonic recitation, and use instead a simple approve-or-return device. Competent adults are bound by such documents, read or unread. For what little it is worth, we add that the box from Gateway was crammed with software. The computer came with an operating system, without which it was useful only as a boat anchor. *See Digital Equipment Corp. v. Uniq Digital Technologies, Inc.*, 73 F.3d 756, 761 (7th Cir.1996). Gateway also included many application programs. So the Hills' effort to limit *ProCD* to software would not avail them factually, even if it were sound legally—which it is not.

For their second sally, the Hills contend that *ProCD* should be limited to executory contracts (to licenses in particular), and therefore does not apply because both parties' performance of this contract was complete when the box arrived at their home. This is legally and factually wrong: legally because the question at hand concerns the *formation* of the contract rather than its *performance*, and factually because both contracts were incompletely performed. *ProCD* did not depend on the fact that the seller characterized the transaction as a license rather than as a contract; we treated it as a contract for the sale of goods and reserved the question whether for other purposes a "license" characterization might be preferable. 86 F.3d at 1450. All debates about characterization to one side, the transaction in *ProCD* was no more executory than the one here: Zeidenberg paid for the software and walked out of the store with a box under his arm, so if arrival of the box with the product ends the time for revelation of contractual terms, then the time ended in *ProCD* before Zeidenberg opened the box. But of course ProCD had not completed performance with delivery of the box, and neither had Gateway. One element of the transaction was the warranty, which obliges sellers to fix defects in their products. The Hills have invoked Gateway's warranty and are not satisfied with its response, so they are not well positioned to say that Gateway's obligations were fulfilled when the motor carrier unloaded the box. What is more, both ProCD and Gateway promised to help customers to use their products. Long-term service and information obligations are common in the computer business, on both hardware and software sides. Gateway offers "lifetime service" and has a round-the-clock telephone hotline to fulfill this promise. Some vendors spend more money helping customers use their products than on developing and manufacturing them. The document in Gateway's box includes promises of future performance that some consumers value highly; these promises bind Gateway just as the arbitration clause binds the Hills.

Next the Hills insist that *ProCD* is irrelevant because Zeidenberg was a "merchant" and they are not. Section 2–207(2) of the UCC, the infamous battle-of-the-forms section, states that "additional terms [following acceptance of an offer] are to be construed as proposals for addition to a contract. Between merchants such terms become part of the contract unless . . .". Plaintiffs tell us that *ProCD* came out as it did only because Zeidenberg was a "merchant" and the terms inside ProCD's box were not excluded by the "unless" clause. This argument pays scant attention to the opinion in *ProCD*, which concluded that, when there is only one form, "sec. 2-207 is irrelevant." 86 F.3d at 1452. The question in *ProCD* was not whether terms were added to a contract after its formation, but how and when the contract was formed—in particular, whether a vendor may propose that a contract of sale be formed, not in the store (or over the phone) with the payment of money or a general "send me the product," but after the customer has had a chance to inspect both the item and the terms. *ProCD* answers "yes," for merchants and consumers alike. Yet again, for what little it is worth we observe that the Hills misunderstand the setting of *ProCD*. A "merchant" under the UCC "means a person who deals in goods of the kind or otherwise by his occupation holds himself out as having knowledge or skill peculiar to the practices or goods involved in the transaction", § 2-104(1). Zeidenberg bought the product at a retail store, an uncommon place for merchants to acquire inventory. His corporation put ProCD's database on the Internet for anyone to browse, which led to the litigation but did not make Zeidenberg a software merchant.

At oral argument the Hills propounded still another distinction: the box containing ProCD's software displayed a notice that additional terms were within, while the box containing Gateway's computer did not. The difference is functional, not legal. Consumers browsing the aisles of a store can look at the box, and if they are unwilling to deal with the prospect of additional terms can leave the box alone, avoiding the transactions costs of returning the package after reviewing its contents. Gateway's box, by contrast, is just a shipping carton; it is not on display anywhere. Its function is to protect the product during transit, and the information on its sides is for the use of handlers

("Fragile!" "This Side Up!" ⚠ ⬆)

rather than would-be purchasers.

Perhaps the Hills would have had a better argument if they were first alerted to the bundling of hardware and legal-ware after opening the box and wanted to return the computer in order to avoid disagreeable terms, but were dissuaded by the expense of shipping. What the remedy would be in such a case—could it exceed the shipping charges?—is an interesting question, but one that need not detain us because the Hills knew before they ordered the computer that the carton would include *some* important terms, and they did not seek to discover these in advance. Gateway's ads state that their products come with limited warranties and lifetime support. How limited was the warranty—30 days, with service contingent on shipping the computer back, or five years, with free onsite service? What sort of support was offered? Shoppers have three principal ways to discover these things. First, they can ask the vendor to send a copy before deciding whether to buy. The Magnuson–Moss Warranty Act requires firms to distribute their warranty terms on request, 15 U.S.C. § 2302(b)(1)(A); the Hills do not contend that Gateway would have refused to enclose the remaining terms too. Concealment would be bad for business, scaring some customers away and leading to excess returns from others. Second, shoppers can consult public sources (computer magazines, the Web sites of vendors) that may contain this information. Third, they may inspect the documents after the product's delivery. Like Zeidenberg, the Hills took the third option. By keeping the computer beyond 30 days, the Hills accepted Gateway's offer, including the arbitration clause.

The Hills' remaining arguments, including a contention that the arbitration clause is unenforceable as part of a scheme to defraud, do not require more than a citation to *Prima Paint Corp. v. Flood & Conklin Mfg. Co.*, 388 U.S. 395 (1967). Whatever may be said pro and con about the cost and efficacy of arbitration (which the Hills disparage) is for Congress and the contracting parties to consider. Claims based on RICO are no less arbitrable than those founded on the contract or the law of torts. *Shearson/American Express, Inc. v. McMahon*, 482 U.S. 220, 238–42 (1987). The decision of the district court is vacated, and this case is remanded with instructions to compel the Hills to submit their dispute to arbitration.

Klocek v. Gateway, Inc.
104 F.Supp.2d 1332 (D.Kan.2000).

■ VRATIL, DISTRICT JUDGE.

William S. Klocek brings suit against Gateway, Inc. and Hewlett–Packard, Inc. on claims arising from purchases of a Gateway computer and a Hewlett–Packard scanner. This matter comes before the Court on the *Motion to Dismiss* which Gateway filed November 22, 1999. . . .

A. Gateway's Motion to Dismiss

Plaintiff brings individual and class action claims against Gateway, alleging that it induced him and other consumers to purchase computers and special support packages by making false promises of technical support. Individually, plaintiff also claims breach of contract and breach of warranty, in that Gateway breached certain warranties that its computer would be compatible with standard peripherals and standard internet services. Gateway asserts that plaintiff must arbitrate his claims under Gateway's Standard Terms and Conditions Agreement ("Standard Terms"). Whenever it sells a computer, Gateway includes a copy of the Standard Terms in the box which contains the computer battery power cables and instruction manuals. At the top of the first page, the Standard Terms include the following notice:

NOTE TO THE CUSTOMER:

This document contains Gateway 2000's Standard Terms and Conditions. By keeping your Gateway 2000 computer system beyond five (5) days after the date of delivery, you accept these Terms and Conditions.

The notice is in emphasized type and is located inside a printed box which sets it apart from other provisions of the document. The Standard Terms are four pages long and contain 16 numbered paragraphs. Paragraph 10 provides the following arbitration clause:

DISPUTE RESOLUTION. Any dispute or controversy arising out of or relating to this Agreement or its interpretation shall be settled exclusively and finally by arbitration. The arbitration shall be conducted in accordance with the Rules of Conciliation and Arbitration of the International Chamber of Commerce. The arbitration shall be conducted in Chicago, Illinois, U.S.A. before a sole arbitrator. Any award rendered in any such arbitration proceeding shall be final and binding on each of the parties, and judgment may be entered thereon in a court of competent jurisdiction.[1]

Gateway urges the Court to dismiss plaintiff's claims under the Federal Arbitration Act ("FAA"), 9 U.S.C. § 1 *et seq.* The FAA ensures that written arbitration agreements in maritime transactions and transactions involving interstate commerce are "valid, irrevocable, and enforceable." 9 U.S.C. § 2.[2] Federal policy favors arbitration agreements and requires that we "rigorously enforce" them. *Shearson/American Exp., Inc. v. McMahon,* 482 U.S. 220, 226 (1987) (quoting *Dean Witter Reynolds, Inc. v. Byrd,* 470 U.S. 213 (1985)); *Moses,* 460 U.S. at 24. "[A]ny doubts concerning the scope of arbitrable issues should be resolved in favor of arbitration." *Moses,* 460 U.S. at 24–25.

FAA Section 3 states:

> If any suit or proceeding be brought in any of the courts of the United States upon any issue referable to arbitration under an agreement in writing for such arbitration, the court in which such suit is pending, upon being satisfied that the issue involved in such suit or proceeding is referable to arbitration under such agreement, shall on application of one of the parties stay the trial of the action until such arbitration has been had in accordance with the terms of the agreement, providing the applicant for the stay is not in default in proceeding with such arbitration.

9 U.S.C. § 3. Although the FAA does not expressly provide for dismissal, the Tenth Circuit has affirmed dismissal where the applicant did not request a stay. *See Armijo v. Prudential Ins. Co. of Am.,* 72 F.3d 793, 797 (10th Cir.1995). Here, neither Gateway nor plaintiff requests a stay. Accordingly, the Court concludes that dismissal is appropriate if plaintiff's claims are arbitrable. . . .

Gateway bears an initial summary-judgment-like burden of establishing that it is entitled to arbitration. *See, e.g., Par–Knit Mills, Inc. v. Stockbridge Fabrics Co.,* 636

---

[1] Gateway states that after it sold plaintiff's computer, it mailed all existing customers in the United States a copy of its quarterly magazine, which contained notice of a change in the arbitration policy set forth in the Standard Terms. The new arbitration policy afforded customers the option of arbitrating before the International Chamber of Commerce ("ICC"), the American Arbitration Association ("AAA"), or the National Arbitration Forum ("NAF") in Chicago, Illinois, or any other location agreed upon by the parties. Plaintiff denies receiving notice of the amended arbitration policy. Neither party explains why—if the arbitration agreement was an enforceable contract—Gateway was entitled to unilaterally amend it by sending a magazine to computer customers.

[2] The FAA does not create independent federal-question jurisdiction; rather, "there must be diversity of citizenship or some other independent basis for federal jurisdiction" before the Court may act. *Moses H. Cone Memorial Hosp. v. Mercury Const. Corp.,* 460 U.S. 1, 25 n. 32 (1983). In this case, plaintiff asserts diversity jurisdiction.

F.2d 51, 54 n.9 (3d Cir.1980) (standard on motion to compel arbitration is same as summary judgment standard) . . . . Thus, Gateway must present evidence sufficient to demonstrate the existence of an enforceable agreement to arbitrate. *See, e.g., Oppenheimer & Co. v. Neidhardt*, 56 F.3d 352, 358 (2d Cir.1995). If Gateway makes such a showing, the burden shifts to plaintiff to submit evidence demonstrating a genuine issue for trial. *Id.* . . . In this case, Gateway fails to present evidence establishing the most basic facts regarding the transaction. The gaping holes in the evidentiary record preclude the Court from determining what state law controls the formation of the contract in this case and, consequently, prevent the Court from agreeing that Gateway's motion is well taken.

Before granting a stay or dismissing a case pending arbitration, the Court must determine that the parties have a written agreement to arbitrate. *See* 9 U.S.C. §§ 3 and 4; *Avedon Engineering, Inc. v. Seatex*, 126 F.3d 1279, 1283 (10th Cir.1997). When deciding whether the parties have agreed to arbitrate, the Court applies ordinary state law principles that govern the formation of contracts. *First Options of Chicago, Inc. v. Kaplan*, 514 U.S. 938, 944 (1995). The existence of an arbitration agreement "is simply a matter of contract between the parties; [arbitration] is a way to resolve those disputes—but only those disputes—that the parties have agreed to submit to arbitration." *Avedon*, 126 F.3d at 1283 (quoting *Kaplan*, 514 U.S. at 943–945). If the parties dispute making an arbitration agreement, a jury trial on the existence of an agreement is warranted if the record reveals genuine issues of material fact regarding the parties' agreement. *See Avedon*, 126 F.3d at 1283.

Before evaluating whether the parties agreed to arbitrate, the Court must determine what state law controls the formation of the contract in this case. *See id.* at 1284. In diversity actions, the Court applies the substantive law, including choice of law rules, that Kansas state courts would apply. *See Moore v. Subaru of Am.*, 891 F.2d 1445, 1448 (10th Cir.1989). Kansas courts apply the doctrine of *lex loci contractus*, which requires that the Court interpret the contract according to the law of the state in which the parties performed the last act necessary to form the contract. *See Missouri Pac. R.R. Co. v. Kansas Gas and Elec. Co.*, 862 F.2d 796, 798 n.1 (10th Cir.1988) (citing *Simms v. Metropolitan Life Ins. Co.*, 9 Kan.App.2d 640, 642–43, 685 P.2d 321 (1984)).

The parties do not address the choice of law issue, and the record is unclear where they performed the last act necessary to complete the contract. Gateway presents affidavit testimony that it shipped a computer to plaintiff on or about August 31, 1997, but it provides no details regarding the transaction. Plaintiff's complaint alleges that plaintiff lives in Missouri and, if Gateway shipped his computer, it presumably shipped it to Missouri. In his response to Gateway's motion, however, plaintiff states that on August 27, 1997 he purchased the computer in person at the Gateway store in Overland Park, Kansas, and took it with him at that time. Depending on which factual version is correct, it appears that the parties may have performed the last act necessary to form the contract in Kansas (with plaintiff purchasing the computer in Kansas), Missouri (with Gateway shipping the computer to plaintiff in Missouri), or some unidentified other states (with Gateway agreeing to ship plaintiff's catalog order and/or Gateway actually shipping the order).[4]

The Court discerns no material difference between the applicable substantive law in Kansas and Missouri and—as to those two states—it perhaps would not need to resolve the choice of law issue at this time. *See Avedon*, 126 F.3d at 1284 (choice of law analysis unnecessary if relevant states have enacted identical controlling statutes); *see also Missouri Pacific*, 862 F.2d at 798 n.1 (applying Kansas law where record did not indicate where final act occurred and parties did not raise issue); *Phillips Petrol. Co. v. Shutts*, 472 U.S. 797, 816 (1985) ("There can be no injury in applying Kansas law if it is not in conflict with that of any other jurisdiction connected to this suit").[5]

The Uniform Commercial Code ("UCC") governs the parties' transaction under both Kansas and Missouri law. *See* K.S.A. § 84-2-102; V.A.M.S. § 400.2-102 (UCC applies to "transactions in goods."); Kansas Comment 1 (main thrust of Article 2 is limited to sales); K.S.A. § 84-2-105(1) V.A.M.S. § 400.2-105(1) ("'Goods' means all things . . . which are movable at the time of identification to the contract for sale . . . ."). Regardless whether plaintiff purchased the computer in person or placed an order and received shipment of the computer, the parties agree that plaintiff paid for and received a computer from Gateway. This conduct clearly demonstrates a contract for the sale of a computer. *See, e.g., Step-Saver Data Sys., Inc. v. Wyse Techn.*, 939 F.2d 91, 98 (3d Cir.1991). Thus the issue is whether the contract of sale includes the Standard Terms as part of the agreement.

State courts in Kansas and Missouri apparently have not decided whether terms received with a product become part of the parties' agreement. Authority from other courts is split. *Compare Step-Saver*, 939 F.2d 91 (printed terms on computer software package not part of agreement); *Arizona Retail Sys., Inc. v. Software Link, Inc.*, 831 F.Supp. 759 (D.Ariz.1993) (license agreement shipped with computer software not part of agreement); *and U.S. Surgical Corp. v. Orris, Inc.*, 5 F.Supp.2d 1201 (D.Kan.1998) (single use restriction on product package not binding agreement); *with Hill v. Gateway 2000, Inc.*, 105 F.3d 1147 (7th Cir.1997) (1997) (arbitration provision shipped with computer binding on buyer); *ProCD, Inc. v. Zeidenberg*, 86 F.3d 1447 (7th Cir.1996) (shrinkwrap license binding on buyer); *and M.A. Mortenson Co., Inc. v. Timberline Software Corp.*, 140 Wash.2d 568, 998 P.2d 305 (2000) (following *Hill* and *ProCD* on license agreement supplied with software).[7] It appears that

[4] While Gateway may have shipped the computer to plaintiff in Missouri, the record contains no evidence regarding how plaintiff communicated his order to Gateway, where Gateway received plaintiff's order or where the shipment originated.

[5] Paragraph 9 of the Standard Terms provides that "[t]his Agreement shall be governed by the laws of the State of South Dakota, without giving effect to the conflict of laws rules thereof." Both Kansas and Missouri recognize choice-of-law provisions, so long as the transaction at issue has a "reasonable relation" to the state whose law is selected. K.S.A. § 84-1-105(1); Mo.Rev.Stat. § 400.1-105(1). At this time, because it must first determine whether the parties ever agreed to the Standard Terms, the Court does not decide whether Kansas or Missouri (or some other unidentified state) would recognize the choice of law provision contained in the Standard Terms.

[7] The *Mortenson* court also found support for its holding in the proposed Uniform Com-

at least in part, the cases turn on whether the court finds that the parties formed their contract *before* or *after* the vendor communicated its terms to the purchaser. *Compare Step-Saver*, 939 F.2d at 98 (parties' conduct in shipping, receiving and paying for product demonstrates existence of contract; box top license constitutes proposal for additional terms under § 2–207 which requires express agreement by purchaser); *Arizona Retail*, 831 F.Supp. at 765 (vendor entered into contract by agreeing to ship goods, or at latest by shipping goods to buyer; license agreement constitutes proposal to modify agreement under § 2–209 which requires express assent by buyer); *and Orris*, 5 F.Supp.2d at 1206 (sales contract concluded when vendor received consumer orders; single-use language on product's label was proposed modification under § 2–209 which requires express assent by purchaser); *with ProCD*, 86 F.3d at 1452 (under § 2–204 vendor, as master of offer, may propose limitations on kind of conduct that constitutes acceptance; § 2–207 does not apply in case with only one form); *Hill*, 105 F.3d at 1148–49 (same); *and Mortenson*, 998 P.2d at 311–314 (where vendor and purchaser utilized license agreement in prior course of dealing, shrinkwrap license agreement constituted issue of contract formation under § 2–204, not contract alteration under § 2–207).

Gateway urges the Court to follow the Seventh Circuit decision in *Hill*. That case involved the shipment of a Gateway computer with terms similar to the Standard Terms in this case, except that Gateway gave the customer 30 days — instead of 5 days — to return the computer. In enforcing the arbitration clause, the Seventh Circuit relied on its decision in *ProCD*, where it enforced a software license which was contained inside a product box. *See Hill*, 105 F.3d at 1148–50. In *ProCD*, the Seventh Circuit noted that the exchange of money frequently precedes the communication of detailed terms in a commercial transaction. *See ProCD*, 86 F.3d at 1451. Citing UCC § 2–204, the court reasoned that by including the license with the software, the vendor proposed a contract that the buyer could accept by using the software after having an opportunity to read the license.[8] *ProCD*, 86 F.3d at 1452. Specifically, the court stated:

> A vendor, as master of the offer, may invite acceptance by conduct, and may propose limitations on the kind of conduct that constitutes acceptance. A buyer may accept by performing the acts the vendor proposes to

---

puter Information Transactions Act ("UCITA") (formerly known as proposed UCC Article 2B) (text located at www.law.upenn.edu/library/ulc/ucita/UCITA_99.htm), which the National Conference of Commissioners on Uniform State Laws approved and recommended for enactment by the states in July 1999. *See Mortenson*, 998 P.2d at 310 n. 6, 313 n. 10. The proposed UCITA, however, would not apply to the Court's analysis in this case. The UCITA applies to computer information transactions, which are defined as agreements "to create, modify, transfer, or license computer information or informational rights in computer information." UCITA, §§ 102(11) and 103. In transactions involving the sale of computers, such as our case, the UCITA applies only to the computer programs and copies, not to the sale of the computer itself. *See* UCITA § 103(c)(2).

[8] Section 2–204 provides: "A contract for sale of goods may be made in any manner sufficient to show agreement, including conduct by both parties which recognizes the existence of such contract." K.S.A. § 84-2-204; V.A.M.S. § 400.2-204.

treat as acceptance.

ProCD, 86 F.3d at 1452. The *Hill* court followed the *ProCD* analysis, noting that "[p]ractical considerations support allowing vendors to enclose the full legal terms with their products." *Hill*, 105 F.3d at 1149.[9]

The Court is not persuaded that Kansas or Missouri courts would follow the Seventh Circuit reasoning in *Hill* and *ProCD*. In each case the Seventh Circuit concluded without support that UCC § 2–207 was irrelevant because the cases involved only one written form. *See ProCD*, 86 F.3d at 1452 (citing no authority); *Hill*, 105 F.3d at 1150 (citing *ProCD*). This conclusion is not supported by the statute or by Kansas or Missouri law. Disputes under § 2–207 often arise in the context of a "battle of forms," *see, e.g., Diatom, Inc. v. Pennwalt Corp.*, 741 F.2d 1569, 1574 (10th Cir.1984), but nothing in its language precludes application in a case which involves only one form. The statute provides:

> Additional terms in acceptance or confirmation.
>
> (1) A definite and seasonable expression of acceptance or a written confirmation which is sent within a reasonable time operates as an acceptance even though it states terms additional to or different from those offered or agreed upon, unless acceptance is expressly made conditional on assent to the additional or different terms.
>
> (2) The additional terms are to be construed as proposals for addition to the contract [if the contract is not between merchants] . . . .

K.S.A. § 84–2–207; V.A.M.S. § 400.2–207. By its terms, § 2–207 applies to an acceptance or written confirmation. It states nothing which requires another form before the provision becomes effective. In fact, the official comment to the section specifically provides that §§ 2–207(1) and (2) apply "where an agreement has been

---

[9] Legal commentators have criticized the reasoning of the Seventh Circuit in this regard. *See, e.g.*, Jean R. Sternlight, *Gateway Widens Doorway to Imposing Unfair Binding Arbitration on Consumers*, FLA. BAR J., Nov. 1997, at 8, 10–12 (outcome in Gateway is questionable on federal statutory, common law and constitutional grounds and as a matter of contract law and is unwise as a matter of policy because it unreasonably shifts to consumers search cost of ascertaining existence of arbitration clause and return cost to avoid such clause); Thomas J. McCarthy et al., *Survey: Uniform Commercial Code*, 53 BUS. LAW. 1461, 1465–66 (Seventh Circuit finding that UCC § 2–207 did not apply is inconsistent with official comment); Batya Goodman, *Honey, I Shrink-Wrapped the Consumer: the Shrinkwrap Agreement as an Adhesion Contract*, 21 CARDOZO L. REV. 319, 344–352 (Seventh Circuit failed to consider principles of adhesion contracts); Jeremy Senderowicz, *Consumer Arbitration and Freedom of Contract: A Proposal to Facilitate Consumers' Informed Consent to Arbitration Clauses in Form Contracts*, 32 COLUM. J.L. & SOC. PROBS. 275, 296–299 (judiciary (in multiple decisions, including *Hill*) has ignored issue of consumer consent to an arbitration clause). Nonetheless, several courts have followed the Seventh Circuit decisions in Hill and ProCD. *See, e.g., M.A. Mortenson Co., Inc. v. Timberline Software Corp.*, 140 Wash.2d 568, 998 P.2d 305 (license agreement supplied with software); *Rinaldi v. Iomega Corp.*, 1999 WL 1442014 (Del.Super. Sept. 3, 1999) (warranty disclaimer included inside computer Zip drive packaging); *Westendorf v. Gateway 2000, Inc.*, 2000 WL 307369 (Del.Ch. March 16, 2000) (arbitration provision shipped with computer); *Brower v. Gateway 2000, Inc.*, 676 N.Y.S.2d 569 (N.Y.App.Div. 1998) (same); *Levy v. Gateway 2000, Inc.*, 1997 WL 823611 (N.Y.Sup. Oct. 31, 1997) (same).

reached orally . . . and is followed by one or both of the parties sending formal memoranda embodying the terms so far agreed and adding terms not discussed." Official Comment 1 of UCC § 2–207. Kansas and Missouri courts have followed this analysis. *See Southwest Engineering Co. v. Martin Tractor Co.,* 205 Kan. 684, 695, 473 P.2d 18, 26 (1970) (stating in dicta that § 2–207 applies where open offer is accepted by expression of acceptance in writing or where oral agreement is later confirmed in writing);[10] *Central Bag Co. v. W. Scott and Co.,* 647 S.W.2d 828, 830 (Mo.App.1983) (§§ 2–207(1) and (2) govern cases where one or both parties send written confirmation after oral contract). Thus, the Court concludes that Kansas and Missouri courts would apply § 2–207 to the facts in this case. *Accord Avedon,* 126 F.3d at 1283 (parties agree that § 2–207 controls whether arbitration clause in sales confirmation is part of contract).

In addition, the Seventh Circuit provided no explanation for its conclusion that "the vendor is the master of the offer." *See ProCD,* 86 F.3d at 1452 (citing nothing in support of proposition); *Hill,* 105 F.3d at 1149 (citing *ProCD*). In typical consumer transactions, the purchaser is the offeror, and the vendor is the offeree. *See Brown Mach., Div. of John Brown, Inc. v. Hercules, Inc.,* 770 S.W.2d 416, 419 (Mo.App.1989) (as general rule orders are considered offers to purchase); *Rich Prods. Corp. v. Kemutec Inc.,* 66 F.Supp.2d 937, 956 (E.D.Wis.1999) (generally price quotation is invitation to make offer and purchase order is offer). While it is possible for the vendor to be the offeror, *see Brown Machine,* 770 S.W.2d at 419 (price quote can amount to offer if it reasonably appears from quote that assent to quote is all that is needed to ripen offer into contract), Gateway provides no factual evidence which would support such a finding in this case. The Court therefore assumes for purposes of the motion to dismiss that plaintiff offered to purchase the computer (either in person or through catalog order) and that Gateway accepted plaintiff's offer (either by completing the sales transaction in person or by agreeing to ship and/or shipping the computer to plaintiff).[11] *Accord Arizona Retail,* 831 F.Supp. at 765 (vendor entered into contract by agreeing to ship goods, or at latest, by shipping goods).

Under § 2–207, the Standard Terms constitute either an expression of acceptance or written confirmation. As an expression of acceptance, the Standard Terms

---

[10] In *Southwest Engineering,* the court was concerned with the existence of an enforceable contract under the UCC statute of frauds and it determined that the parties' notes satisfied the writing requirement. It found that a subsequent letter which contained additional material terms did not become part of the agreement under § 2–207, however, because the parties did not expressly agree to the change in terms. *See Southwest Engineering,* 205 Kan. at 693–94, 473 P.2d at 25. The court further found that § 2–207 did not apply to its analysis because at the time of the letter, the parties had already memorialized the agreement in writing and there was no outstanding offer to accept or oral agreement to confirm. *See Southwest Engineering,* 205 Kan. at 695, 473 P.2d at 26.

[11] UCC § 2–206(b) provides that "an order or other offer to buy goods for prompt or current shipment shall be construed as inviting acceptance either by a prompt promise to ship or by the prompt or current shipment . . ." The official comment states that "[e]ither shipment or a prompt promise to ship is made a proper means of acceptance of an offer looking to current shipment." UCC § 2–206, Official Comment 2.

would constitute a counter-offer only if Gateway expressly made its acceptance conditional on plaintiff's assent to the additional or different terms. K.S.A. § 84-2-207(1); V.A.M.S. § 400.2-207(1). "[T]he conditional nature of the acceptance must be clearly expressed in a manner sufficient to notify the offeror that the offeree is unwilling to proceed with the transaction unless the additional or different terms are included in the contract." *Brown Machine*, 770 S.W.2d at 420.[12] Gateway provides no evidence that at the time of the sales transaction, it informed plaintiff that the transaction was conditioned on plaintiff's acceptance of the Standard Terms. Moreover, the mere fact that Gateway shipped the goods with the terms attached did not communicate to plaintiff any unwillingness to proceed without plaintiff's agreement to the Standard Terms. *See, e.g., Arizona Retail*, 831 F.Supp. at 765 (conditional acceptance analysis rarely appropriate where contract formed by performance but goods arrive with conditions attached); *Leighton Indus., Inc. v. Callier Steel Pipe & Tube, Inc.*, 1991 WL 18413, *6 (N.D.Ill. Feb. 6, 1991) (applying Missouri law) (preprinted forms insufficient to notify offeror of conditional nature of acceptance, particularly where form arrives after delivery of goods).

Because plaintiff is not a merchant, additional or different terms contained in the Standard Terms did not become part of the parties' agreement unless plaintiff expressly agreed to them. *See* K.S.A. § 84-2-207, Kansas Comment 2 (if either party is not a merchant, additional terms are proposals for addition to the contract that do not become part of the contract unless the original offeror expressly agrees).[13] Gateway argues that plaintiff demonstrated acceptance of the arbitration provision by keeping the computer more than five days after the date of delivery. Although the Standard Terms purport to work that result, Gateway has not presented evidence that plaintiff expressly agreed to those Standard Terms. Gateway states only that it enclosed the Standard Terms inside the computer box for plaintiff to read afterwards. It provides no evidence that it informed plaintiff of the five-day review-and-return period as a condition of the sales transaction, or that the parties contemplated additional terms to the agreement.[14] *See Step-Saver*, 939 F.2d at 99 (during negotiations leading to purchase, vendor never mentioned box-top license or obtained buyer's express assent thereto). The Court finds that the act of keeping the computer past five days was not sufficient to demonstrate that plaintiff expressly agreed to the Standard Terms. *Accord Brown Machine*, 770 S.W.2d at 421 (express assent cannot be presumed by silence or mere failure to object). Thus, be-

---

[12] Courts are split on the standard for a conditional acceptance under § 2-207. *See Daitom*, 741 F.2d at 1576 (finding that Pennsylvania would most likely adopt "better" view that offeree must explicitly communicate unwillingness to proceed with transaction unless additional terms in response are accepted by offeror). . . .

[13] The Court's decision would be the same if it considered the Standard Terms as a proposed modification under UCC § 2-209. *See, e.g., Orris*, 5 F.Supp.2d at 1206 (express assent analysis is same under §§ 2-207 and 2-209).

[14] The Court is mindful of the practical considerations which are involved in commercial transactions, but it is not unreasonable for a vendor to clearly communicate to a buyer—at the time of sale—either the complete terms of the sale or the fact that the vendor will propose additional terms as a condition of sale, if that be the case.

cause Gateway has not provided evidence sufficient to support a finding under Kansas or Missouri law that plaintiff agreed to the arbitration provision contained in Gateway's Standard Terms, the Court overrules Gateway's motion to dismiss.

. . .

QUESTIONS FOR DISCUSSION

1. *Compare and contrast.* *ProCD* and *Hill* were both heard in the United States Court of Appeals for the Seventh Circuit and the decision in both cases was written by Judge Easterbrook. The *ProCD* case was decided before the *Hill* case. Does Judge Easterbrook simply apply the same rule in each case or does the latter case extend the former?

2. *"Layered contracting," "rolling contract."* These terms refer to an agreement in which terms are presented only after the buyer has received the product. *ProCD* and *Hill* validate layered contracting. What are the limits on this reasoning? That is, would Judge Easterbrook reject such a contract if there was no opportunity to see the terms after receiving the product? If there was an opportunity to see the terms, but no meaningful opportunity to return the product after seeing them? Are market conditions (whether the market is competitive or monopolized) relevant to Judge Easterbrook's analysis?

Note Judge Easterbrook's response to the draft of UCC Article 2B, which would have explicitly validated shrinkwrap licenses. Under the subsequent title of Uniform Computer Information Transactions Act (UCITA), this model act was enacted in two jurisdictions but failed to become widely enacted. For more on UCITA, see Part I(B), *infra*.

3. *Article 2 amendments.* The 2003 amendment of UCC Section 2–207 carefully avoids taking a position on the applicability of that provision to shrinkwrap licenses. The Official Comment states:

> 5. The section omits any specific treatment of terms attached to the goods, or in or on the container in which the goods are delivered. This article takes no position on whether a court should follow the reasoning in Step–Saver Data Systems, Inc. v. Wyse Technology, 939 F.2d 91 (3d Cir.1991) and Klocek v. Gateway, Inc., 104 F.Supp.2d 1332 (D.Kan.2000) (original 2–207 governs) or the contrary reasoning in Hill v. Gateway 2000, 105 F.3d 1147 (7th Cir.1997) (original 2–207 inapplicable).

UCC § 207 cmt. 5.

The National Conference of Commissioners on Uniform State Laws (NCCUSL) and the American Law Institute (ALI) are the institutional bodies jointly responsible for maintaining and revising the UCC. Why do you think NCCUSL and ALI were unwilling to take a position on this controversy?

4. *Shrinkwrap licenses and distributors.* Suppose a software producer sells several applications bundled together in a single package. The outside of the shrinkwrapped package states that use of the software is conditioned on the user's assent to the End User License Agreement contained in the box. A distributor purchases the software and resells each of the applications individually, which is prohibited by the EULA. The software producer sues the distributor for breach of the EULA. Who wins? *See SoftMan Products Co. v. Adobe Systems Inc.*, 171 F.Supp.2d 1075 (C.D.Cal.2001).

5. *Contract as product.* In *ProCD*, Judge Easterbrook says that "Terms of use are no less a part of 'the product' than are the size of the database and the speed with which the software compiles listings," and in *Hill* he referred to "the bundling of hardware and legalware." What are the implications of this view for the traditional conception of contracts as meeting of the minds? *See* Margaret Jane Radin, *Online Standardization and the Integration of Text and Machine*, 70 FORDHAM L. REV. 1125 (2002), excerpted in Part I(C), *infra*.

2. Clickwrap Agreements

Davidson & Associates, Inc. v. Internet Gateway
334 F.Supp.2d 1164 (E.D.Mo.2004).

■ SHAW, DISTRICT JUDGE.

[Plaintiffs alleged, *inter alia*, that defendants infringed their copyrights and violated the anti-circumvention provisions of the Digital Millennium Copyright Act. Plaintiffs also alleged that defendants breached their EULA and TOU. Defendants counterclaimed for declaratory relief as to noninfringement and also claimed the purported contracts were unenforceable. The Court entered a consent decree and permanent injunction which resolved plaintiffs' copyright and trademark claims and defendants' claim for declaratory judgment. The parties agreed to have the court decide their remaining claims, including the contract claims, based on the parties' summary judgment motions.]

. . .

Blizzard is a California corporation. Vivendi is the parent corporation of Blizzard. The plaintiffs will be collectively referred to as Blizzard. Blizzard creates and sells computer games that are played on personal computers. The particular Blizzard games at issue in this case are entitled "StarCraft," "StarCraft: Brood War," "WarCraft II: Battle.net Edition," "Diablo," and "Diablo II: Lord of Destruction." Blizzard games have sold millions of copies and generated revenue in excess of $480 million since 1998.

The individual defendants are two computer programmers, Ross Combs and Rob Crittenden, and a systems administrator, Jim Jung. The corporate defendant Internet Gateway is an Internet service provider based in St. Peters, Missouri. Jung is the president, co-owner, and day-to-day operator of Internet Gateway.

A. Battle.net Online Gaming Service

In January 1997, Blizzard officially launched Battle.net, a 24-hour online gaming service available to purchasers of its computer games. The Battle.net service currently has nearly 12 million active users who spend more that 2.1 million hours online per day. At any given time, Battle.net servers average about 200,000 concurrent users, with a peak volume of 400,000 concurrent users.

Blizzard has valid copyright registrations covering Battle.net and each of its computer games at issue in this litigation. The only copyright registrations Blizzard has identified in this case concern its Battle.net server program and its individual computer game software. The Battle.net service is a free service that allows owners of certain Blizzard games to play those games, through their personal computers, against each other by linking together over the Internet. Battle.net mode allows users to create and join multi-player games that can be accessed across the Internet, to chat with other potential players, to record wins and losses and save advancements in a password protected individual game account, and to participate with others in tournament play featuring elimination rounds. Players can set up private chat "channels" and private games on the Battle.net service to allow players to determine whom they wish to interact with on the Battle.net service. These Battle.net mode features are accessed from within the games themselves.

In addition to multi-player play over the Internet via Battle.net mode, the games at issue have the capacity for and permit non-Internet multi-player gaming for a limited number of players who connect to each other via a local area computer network ("LAN") such as a home network, via modems connected to telephone lines, or by directly connecting two computers together with cables. The features and functions of Battle.net mode, however, cannot be accessed when players are connected through those means. The parties stipulate that players also have the option of engaging in single player play against the computer.

Like most computer software, Blizzard games can be easily copied and distributed over the Internet. The Battle.net service is designed to prohibit access and use of Battle.net mode by such unauthorized or pirated copies of Blizzard games. Each time a customer logs onto the Battle.net service, a Battle.net server examines the customer's game to check whether the game is using the latest version of the game software. If a Blizzard game does not have the latest software upgrades and fixes, the Battle.net service updates the customer's game before allowing the game to play in Battle.net mode.

B. Technology of the Battle.net Service

Blizzard's games are shipped to customers on CD-ROM disks. Except for the game "Diablo," each authorized version of a Blizzard game comes with a "CD Key," a unique sequence of alphanumeric characters that is printed on a sticker attached to the case in which the CD-ROM was packaged. The user of the game must input the CD Key into his or her computer when installing the game, and it is subsequently stored on the computer for use in logging on to the Battle.net service. The Battle.net service prohibits use of unauthorized or pirated copies of Blizzard games with the Battle.net service.

To log on to the Battle.net service and access Battle.net mode, the game initiates an authentication sequence or "secret handshake" between the game and Battle.net server. First, the game and Battle.net server exchange random numbers (one provided by the game and one provided by the server). The game then takes the random numbers, as well as information from the CD Key, and calculates an encrypted alphanumeric sequence which is sent to the Battle.net server. The game performs this encryption to prevent individuals from stealing the game's CD Key when it is transmitted over the Internet to a Battle.net server. The Battle.net server receives the alphanumeric sequence sent by the game, along with other information sent by the game, and uses this data to determine whether the CD Key information sent by the game is valid. If the CD Key information is valid, the Battle.net server will determine whether the same CD Key is already being used by another game that is currently logged on to that Battle.net server gateway. If the CD Key is both valid and not currently being used by other players on the same Battle.net gateway, the Battle.net server sends a signal to the game that allows the game to enter the Battle.net mode and use the Battle.net gaming services. The Blizzard game waits for this signal before entering Battle.net mode. Battle.net uses an encryption algorithm for this process based on a common encryption algorithm. The standard version of this algorithm was released by the United States government.

C. End User License Agreements ("EULA") and Battle.net Terms of Use ("TOU")

In order to play the Blizzard game contained on a CD-ROM, a user must first install the game onto a computer from the CD-ROM. First, the user inserts the CD-ROM into his or her computer. A menu pops up automatically, and the user chooses to install the game from that menu. Second, the user is presented with the terms of an End User License Agreement ("EULA"). At the end of the EULA, Blizzard includes a button with the text, "I Agree" in it, which the user must click in order to proceed with the installation. The game will not work if the "I Agree" button is not selected. Third, the user is asked to enter a name and the CD Key. Fourth, the user is asked to choose where on his or her computer the program's files should be installed. The files are then installed at the chosen location. Finally, the user is offered the opportunity to register his or her copy of the game with Blizzard via an on-line registration process. After the user has finished registering his copy, or if he or she chooses not to register, the installation process is complete.

Blizzard's Battle.net service has a Terms of Use ("TOU"), which Blizzard presents to users when they first log onto the Battle.net service. First-time users of the Battle.net service are shown the terms of the Battle.net service TOU after a user has installed a Blizzard game and logs onto the Battle.net service for the first time to play with a purchased Blizzard game product. At the end of the TOU, Blizzard includes a button with the text, "Agree" in it, which the user must click before the Battle.net service can be used. The product will not work with the Battle.net service if the "Agree" button is not selected.

For every game at issue in this litigation except for Diablo, the outside packaging of the game states that use of the game is subject to a EULA, and that use of Blizzard's Battle.net service is subject to the Battle.net TOU. The terms of the EULAs and TOU themselves do not appear on the outside packaging. If the user does not agree to the terms of Blizzard's EULAs or Battle.net TOU, he or she may return the game for a full refund of the purchase price within thirty (30) days of the original purchase. The EULA contains the following language:

> YOU SHOULD CAREFULLY READ THE FOLLOWING END USER LICENSE AGREEMENT BEFORE INSTALLING THIS SOFTWARE PROGRAM. BY INSTALLING, COPYING, OR OTHERWISE USING THE SOFTWARE PROGRAM YOU AGREE TO BE BOUND BY THE TERMS OF THIS AGREEMENT. IF YOU DO NOT AGREE TO THE TERMS OF THIS AGREEMENT, PROMPTLY RETURN THE UNUSED SOFTWARE PROGRAM TO THE PLACE OF PURCHASE OR CONTACT BLIZZARD ENTERTAINMENT CUSTOMER SERVICE . . . FOR A FULL REFUND OF THE PURCHASE PRICE WITHIN THIRTY DAYS OF THE ORIGINAL PURCHASE.

The EULA further states "subject to the grant of license hereinabove, you may not, in whole or in part, copy, photocopy, reproduce, translate, reverse engineer, derive source code, modify, disassemble, decompile, create derivative works based on the Program, or remove any proprietary notices or labels on the program without the prior consent, in writing, of Blizzard." The EULA also states that it "shall have been deemed to have been made and executed in the State of California and any dispute arising hereunder shall be resolved in accordance with the law of California."

The Battle.net TOU states: "Blizzard hereby grants, and by using Battle.net you thereby accept, a limited personal non-exclusive license and right to use Battle.net using either a home, work, or portable computer."

> You are entitled to use Battle.net for your own personal use, but you shall not be entitled to (i) sell or grant a security interest in or transfer reproductions of Battle.net to other parties in any way, nor to rent, lease, or license Battle.net to others without the prior written consent of Blizzard; (ii) copy, photocopy, reproduce, translate, reverse engineer, modify, disassemble, or de-compile in whole or in part any Battle.net software; (iii) create derivative works based on Battle.net; (iv) host or provide matchmaking services for any Blizzard software programs or emulate or redirect the communication protocols used by Blizzard as part of Battle.net, through protocol emulation, runneling, modifying, or adding components to the Program, use of a utility program, or any other technique now known or hereafter developed for any purpose, including, but not limited to, network play over the Internet, network play utilizing commercial or non-commercial gaming networks, or as part of content aggregation networks without the prior written consent of Blizzard or exploit Battle.net or any of its parts for any commercial purpose, including but not limited to, use at a location such as a cyber cafe, arcade, or other location where users are charged a fee, whether hourly or otherwise to use Battle.net; (v) use any third-party software to modify Battle.net to change game play, including, but not limited to cheats and/or hacks; (vi) use Blizzard's intellectual property rights contained in Battle.net to create or provide any other means through which Blizzard entertainment software products including, but not limited to, StarCraft, StarCraft: Brood War, Diablo, Diablo II, Warcraft: Orcs & Humans, Warcraft II: Tides of Darkness, Warcraft II: Beyond the Dark Portal, Warcraft II: Battle.net Edition, and Warcraft II may be played by others, including, not limited to, server emulators . . . this agreement shall be governed by and construed with the laws of the State of California, without giving effect to any principles of conflicts of laws.

Defendant Combs installed one Blizzard game, StarCraft, and clicked on the "I Agree" button after the EULA was displayed. Defendant Crittenden installed Blizzard games and clicked on the "I Agree" button after the EULAs were displayed. Defendant Jung installed three Blizzard games, Diablo, Diablo II, and Diablo II: Lord of Destruction, and clicked on the "I Agree" button after the EULAs were displayed. Crittenden and Jung logged onto the Battle.net service and clicked on the "Agree" button after the TOUs were displayed.

D. The bnetd project

The users of the Battle.net service have occasionally experienced difficulties with the service. Blizzard has also received complaints about user profanity and users who cheated to win games by modifying Blizzard's software ("client hacks"). Although Blizzard has taken actions to correct these difficulties with its Battle.net service, including adding additional server capacity, banning cheaters, and providing for private channels and games, defendants were frustrated by the difficulties.

To address their frustrations with Battle.net, the defendants joined a group of non-profit volunteer game hobbyists, programmers, and other individuals called the "bnetd project." Combs, Crittenden, and Jung were lead developers for the bnetd project. Combs led all the developers. The bnetd project was a collaboration focusing on development of the bnetd server, which is a program that attempts to emulate Blizzard's Battle.net service. The bnetd server was created for "hack value"[6] and to address the difficulties that users sometimes experienced with the Battle.net service. In addition, some or all of the defendants developed bnetd, in part, because they believed that Blizzard game players should not be forced to view advertisements displayed via the Battle.net service and that it was morally wrong for Blizzard to require people who want to play Blizzard's games over the Internet to agree to the Battle.net TOU or other restrictions imposed by Blizzard. The bnetd project is a volunteer effort and the project has always offered the bnetd program for free to anyone who wants a copy of it.

The bnetd project was organized and managed over the Internet through a website, available at www.bnetd.org, that was available to the public through equipment provided by defendant Internet Gateway. The bnetd emulator provides a server that would allow gamers unable or not wishing to connect to Battle.net to experience the multi-player features of Blizzard's games, and was designed to allow access to Blizzard games in a multi-player environment without using Battle.net. The bnetd emulator provides matchmaking services for users of Blizzard games who want to play those games in a multi-player environment without using Battle.net. The bnetd project attempted to include all of the user-visible features of the Battle.net service. The bnetd.org website provided online discussion forums and information about the bnetd program, and also provided access to the program's computer code for others to copy and modify.

The bnetd program was intended as a functional alternative to the Battle.net service. To serve this function, bnetd had to be compatible with Blizzard's software. In particular, compatibility required that bnetd speak the same protocol that the Battle.net service speaks. This was necessary for compatibility because the Blizzard games expect servers to speak this protocol, and will therefore be unable to work with any server that does not speak the protocol. By speaking the same protocol, the bnetd program was able to interoperate with Blizzard games. Once game play starts there is no difference between Battle.net and the bnetd emulator from the standpoint of a user who is actually playing the game.

---

[6] The parties do not define "hack value."

Reverse engineering was necessary in order for the defendants to learn Blizzard's protocol language and to ensure that bnetd worked with Blizzard games. It would not have been possible to create a workable bnetd server without reverse engineering Blizzard's software and protocols. Combs used reverse engineering in the process of developing the bnetd server, including a program called "tcpdump" to log communications between Blizzard games and the Battle.net server. Crittenden used reverse engineering in the process of developing the bnetd server, including using a program called "Nextray." Crittenden also used a program called "ripper" to take Blizzard client files which were compiled together in one file and break them into their component parts. Crittenden used the ripper program in order to figure out how Blizzard games displayed ad banners so that people running the bnetd emulator could display ad banners to users in the format that Blizzard uses on the Battle.net service. Combs tried to disassemble a Blizzard game to figure out how to implement a feature that allowed bnetd to protect the password that a user enters when creating an account in Battle.net mode. Crittenden made an unauthorized copy of a Blizzard game in order to test the interoperability of the bnetd server with multiple games.

Blizzard games are designed to connect only to Battle.net servers. To cause a Blizzard game to connect to a bnetd server instead of a Battle.net server, the computer file that contains the Internet address of the Battle.net servers must be modified. Combs participated in the development of a utility program called "BNS" to allow Blizzard games to connect to bnetd servers. The BNS utility is part of the bnetd project. Connecting to a bnetd server without the BNS utility program is more difficult to do and somewhat involved compared to using the BNS utility program. Once the computer files that contains the Internet address of the Battle.net servers has been modified so that the Blizzard game will connect to a bnetd server, the game sends the bnetd server information about its CD Key. It is technically possible for an individual who is using one of the Blizzard games at issue to play his or her game over the Internet via bnetd rather than Battle.net. Blizzard believes that the EULAs and TOUs prohibit this activity.

When the bnetd server receives the CD Key information, unlike Battle.net, it does not determine whether the CD Key is valid or currently in use by another player. The bnetd server computer code always sends the game an "okay" reply regardless of whether the CD Key is valid or currently in use by another player, as the game will otherwise not allow access to Battle.net mode. The bnetd emulator always allows the Blizzard games to access Battle.net mode features even if the user does not have a valid or unique CD Key, because the bnetd emulator does not determine whether the CD Key is valid or currently in use by another player. Blizzard does not disclose the methods it uses to generate CD Keys or to confirm the validity of CD Keys. Therefore, there is no way that defendants could have implemented a check for CD Key validity in the bnetd program. Defendants never advised people to play pirated copies of Blizzard games using the bnetd server.

The bnetd server program is highly configurable, which means that much of the operation of the server is under the control of the administrator running the server. Running a bnetd server allows users to become server administrators and not just players on someone else's server, giving them the ability to allow or deny access to various features of the bnetd server or to modify the computer code of the bnetd server. This allows the administrator of the bnetd server to create a gaming environment with different options than those presented to the user on the Battle.net service. In contrast, the Battle.net service is operated solely by Blizzard.

Combs, Crittenden, and Jung have used a Blizzard game to log into a bnetd server. Crittenden was aware that unauthorized versions of Blizzard games were played on bnetd servers. Jung knew that the bnetd emulator did not require that Blizzard games provide valid CD Keys. Combs suspected that the bnetd server would not know the difference between a real game and a pirated game.

E. Distribution of the bnetd Server Program

Combs and Crittenden sent portions of the bnetd software to Jung to place on the www.bnetd.org website for download, or they put the software on the website themselves. Combs made the bnetd software available on his website located at www.cs.nmsu.edu/~rocombs/sc/. Defendants distributed the BNS utility program, which allowed Blizzard games to connect to bnetd servers. Also, defendants made the source code available as an "open source" application, meaning that others were free to copy the source code and distribute it with or without modifications. Because the bnetd source code was freely available, others developed additional Battle.net emulators based on the bnetd source code. Defendants also distributed binary versions of the bnetd program make it more convenient for users to set up and access the emulator program. Internet Gateway has donated space on its computers for use by the bnetd project. Internet Gateway also hosted a bnetd server that anyone on the Internet could access and use to play Blizzard games in Battle.net mode.

IV. Discussion

. . .

A. Preemption under the Copyright Act

. . . Defendants assert that the Copyright Act preempts the state law of contracts and therefore plaintiffs' state law contract claim is preempted by the Copyright Act.

. . .

In this contract claim, the plaintiffs are alleging that the contract creates a right not existing under copyright law, a right based upon defendants' agreement to the EULA and TOU with Blizzard. The Court agrees that the contractual restriction does create a right not existing under copyright law. The right created is the right to restrict the use of the software through the EULAs and TOU. . . . Therefore, the Court finds that the EULA and TOU are not statutorily preempted by the Copyright Act.[1]

---

[1] [Whether state enforcement of provisions counter to the provisions of the Copyright Act will be preempted is considered in Part III(C), *infra.*—Eds.]

B. Choice of Law Provisions in Contract

. . .

The relevant inquiry is whether the issue involved here is one in which the parties could have resolved by mutual agreement. If so, the Court should honor the parties' choice of law. *See Baxter Int'l Inc. v. Morris*, 976 F.2d 1189, 1195–96 (8th Cir.1992). The Court finds that the parties made an explicit agreement to the choice of law provision. Under Missouri law and the Restatement § 187(1), this Court will give effect to the reasonable expectations of the parties to the Agreement and apply the law of the state chosen by the parties, California. . . .

C. Existence of Contract

. . .

The end user licenses at issue in this case are commonly referred to as "clickwrap" agreements.

> A "clickwrap" agreement appears when a user first installs computer software obtained from an online source or attempts to conduct an Internet transaction involving the agreement and purports to condition further access to the software or transaction on the user's consent to certain conditions there specified; the user consents to these conditions by clicking on a dialog box on the screen, which then proceeds with the remainder of the software installation or Internet transaction.

Kevin W. Grierson, Annotation, *Enforceability of "Clickwrap" or "Shrinkwrap" Agreements Common in Computer Software, Hardware, and Internet Transactions*, 106 A.L.R. 5th 309 n.1 (2003).

The Court finds that the license agreements are enforceable contracts under both California and Missouri law. California courts have enforced end user license agreements, which are valid under California law. *See Adobe Sys. Inc. v. One Stop Micro, Inc.*, 84 F.Supp.2d 1086, 1089–93 (N.D.Cal.2000) (end user license agreement valid under California law); *Hotmail Corp. v. Van$ Money Pie, Inc.*, 1998 WL 388389, at *6 (N.D.Cal.1998) (applying California law, plaintiff likely to prevail on breach of contract claim regarding clickwrap agreement). *Cf. SoftMan Prods. Co. v. Adobe Sys.*, 171 F.Supp.2d 1075, 1087–88 (C.D.Cal.2001) (software reseller was not bound by EULA because it had never assented to the terms and court did not rule on validity of shrinkwrap agreements in general).

Even if Missouri law applied, the license agreement would be enforceable. Missouri has implemented the Uniform Commercial Code. The UCC provides that "a contract for sale of goods may be made in any manner sufficient to show agreement, including conduct by both parties which recognizes the existence of such a contract."[11] MO. REV. STAT. § 400.2–204(1) (2000). "An agreement sufficient to con-

---

[11] The Court assumes, as have several other courts, that the games in question constitute goods under the UCC. *See Specht v. Netscape Communications Corp.*, 306 F.3d 17, 29 n.13 (2nd Cir. 2002) (discusses problems with applying the UCC to licensing of software downloadable from the Internet under California law); *I.Lan Systems, Inc. v. Netscout Serv. Level Corp.*, 183 F.Supp.2d 328, 332 (D.Mass.2002) (court notes UCC does not technically apply to soft-

stitute a contract for sale may be found even though the moment of its making is undetermined." MO. REV. STAT. § 400.2–204(2) (2000). The defendants assert that the licenses are not enforceable because they add additional terms under Mo. Rev. Stat. § 400.2–207, which are to be construed as proposals for additions to the contract. Defendants state that the EULAs and TOU are additional terms which they rejected. Defendants contend that is unfair for them to pay $49.99 for the games and then be unable to install them or access Battle.net without assenting to the EULA and TOU.

The Court finds the EULAs and TOU are enforceable under the UCC. First, the defendants did not purchase the Blizzard software, rather they purchased a license for the software. A sale consists in the passing of title from the seller to the buyer. MO. REV. STAT. § 400.2–106(1) (2000). When defendants purchased the games, they bought a license to use the software, but did not buy the software. Defendants' argument parallels the "first sale doctrine," although defendants do not use this term.

Under the first sale doctrine, "a sale of a lawfully made copy terminates a copyright holder's authority to interfere with subsequent sales or distribution of that particular copy." *Adobe Sys. Inc.*, 84 F.Supp.2d at 1089 (citations omitted). "The first sale doctrine is only triggered by an actual sale. Accordingly, a copyright owner does not forfeit his right of distribution by entering into a licensing agreement." *Id.* . . . The EULAs and TOU in this case explicitly state that title and ownership of the games and Battle.net remain with Blizzard. Defendants do not produce sufficient evidence demonstrating that title and ownership of the games passed to them. Therefore, the Court finds that the first sale doctrine is inapplicable here.

Defendants rely upon *Klocek v. Gateway, Inc.*, 104 F.Supp.2d 1332 (D.Kan.2000), to support their argument that Missouri law would not recognize their assent to the EULAs and TOU as binding contracts. In *Klocek*, the court found that the shrinkwrap agreement was not enforceable under Missouri law. The Court believes that this case is readily distinguishable from *Klocek*. In *Klocek*, the parties disputed whether plaintiff's complaint about repair of his Gateway computer should be submitted to arbitration. The contract was contained in a standard terms and conditions agreement and placed in the box with the Gateway computer. The contract provided that if the customer kept the Gateway computer beyond five (5) days after delivery, the customer accepted the terms and conditions. The court in *Klocek* held that a contract did not exist because "the act of keeping the computer past five days was not sufficient to demonstrate that Klocek expressly agreed to the standard terms." *Id.* at 1341. Additionally, the mere fact that Gateway shipped the goods with the terms attached did not communicate to Klocek any willingness to proceed without Klocek's agreement to the standard terms.

In this case, the defendants do not dispute that (1) the software at issue in this litigation with the exception of Diablo has outside packaging stating it is subject to a EULA and Battle.net is subject to a TOU; (2) the defendants installed the games

---

ware licenses, but assumes that it does under Massachusetts law). . . .

and assented to the EULA; (3) the defendants went to the Battle.net website and assented to the TOU; and (4) the EULA and TOU state it is a license and ownership of software remains with Blizzard. This case is readily distinguishable from *Klocek*, because here the defendants had sufficient notice of the EULAs and TOU. It is true that the terms of the EULAs and TOU were not on the box, but the terms were disclosed before installation of the games and access to Battle.net was granted. The defendants also expressly consented to the terms of the EULA and TOU by clicking "I Agree" and "Agree." *See SoftMan*, 171 F.Supp.2d at 1087 ("Reading a notice on a box is not equivalent to the degree of assent that occurs when the software is loaded onto the computer and the consumer is asked to agree to the terms of the license."). Unlike the plaintiff in *Klocek*, the defendants in this case are not being penalized for inaction, but instead are being held to contract terms to which they assented. Accordingly, the Court finds that the EULA and TOU are enforceable contracts under both Missouri or California law.

　. . .

3. Browsewrap Agreements

Specht v. Netscape Communications Corp.
306 F.3d 17 (2d Cir.2002).

■ SOTOMAYOR, CIRCUIT JUDGE.

This is an appeal from a judgment of the Southern District of New York denying a motion by defendants-appellants Netscape Communications Corporation and its corporate parent, America Online, Inc. (collectively, "defendants" or "Netscape"), to compel arbitration and to stay court proceedings. In order to resolve the central question of arbitrability presented here, we must address issues of contract formation in cyberspace. Principally, we are asked to determine whether plaintiffs-appellees ("plaintiffs"), by acting upon defendants' invitation to download free software made available on defendants' webpage, agreed to be bound by the software's license terms (which included the arbitration clause at issue), even though plaintiffs could not have learned of the existence of those terms unless, prior to executing the download, they had scrolled down the webpage to a screen located below the download button. We agree with the district court that a reasonably prudent Internet user in circumstances such as these would not have known or learned of the existence of the license terms before responding to defendants' invitation to download the free software, and that defendants therefore did not provide reasonable notice of the license terms. In consequence, plaintiffs' bare act of downloading the software did not unambiguously manifest assent to the arbitration provision contained in the license terms.

　. . .

We therefore affirm the district court's denial of defendants' motion to compel arbitration and to stay court proceedings.

Background

I. Facts

In three related putative class actions, plaintiffs alleged that, unknown to them, their use of SmartDownload transmitted to defendants private information about plaintiffs' downloading of files from the Internet, thereby effecting an electronic surveillance of their online activities in violation of two federal statutes, the Electronic Communications Privacy Act, 18 U.S.C. §§ 2510 *et seq.*, and the Computer Fraud and Abuse Act, 18 U.S.C. § 1030.

. . .

In the time period relevant to this litigation, Netscape offered on its website various software programs, including Communicator and SmartDownload, which visitors to the site were invited to obtain free of charge. It is undisputed that five of the six named plaintiffs—Michael Fagan, John Gibson, Mark Gruber, Sean Kelly, and Sherry Weindorf—downloaded Communicator from the Netscape website. These plaintiffs acknowledge that when they proceeded to initiate installation of Communicator, they were automatically shown a scrollable text of that program's license agreement and were not permitted to complete the installation until they had clicked on a "Yes" button to indicate that they accepted all the license terms.[4] If a user attempted to install Communicator without clicking "Yes," the installation would be aborted. All five named user plaintiffs expressly agreed to Communicator's license terms by clicking "Yes." The Communicator license agreement that these plaintiffs saw made no mention of SmartDownload or other plug-in programs, and stated that "[t]hese terms apply to Netscape Communicator and Netscape Navigator" and that "all disputes relating to this Agreement (excepting any dispute relating to intellectual property rights)" are subject to "binding arbitration in Santa Clara County, California."

Although Communicator could be obtained independently of SmartDownload, all the named user plaintiffs, except Fagan, downloaded and installed Communicator in connection with downloading SmartDownload. Each of these plaintiffs allegedly arrived at a Netscape webpage captioned "SmartDownload Communicator" that urged them to "Download With Confidence Using SmartDownload!" At

---

[4] This kind of online software license agreement has come to be known as "clickwrap" (by analogy to "shrinkwrap," used in the licensing of tangible forms of software sold in packages) because it "presents the user with a message on his or her computer screen, requiring that the user manifest his or her assent to the terms of the license agreement by clicking on an icon. The product cannot be obtained or used unless and until the icon is clicked." *Specht*, 150 F.Supp.2d at 593–94 (footnote omitted). Just as breaking the shrinkwrap seal and using the enclosed computer program after encountering notice of the existence of governing license terms has been deemed by some courts to constitute assent to those terms in the context of tangible software, *see, e.g., ProCD, Inc. v. Zeidenberg*, 86 F.3d 1447, 1451 (7th Cir.1996), so clicking on a webpage's clickwrap button after receiving notice of the existence of license terms has been held by some courts to manifest an Internet user's assent to terms governing the use of downloadable intangible software, *see, e.g., Hotmail Corp. v. Van$ Money Pie Inc.*, 47 U.S.P.Q.2d 1020, 1025 (N.D.Cal.1998).

or near the bottom of the screen facing plaintiffs was the prompt "Start Download" and a tinted button labeled "Download." By clicking on the button, plaintiffs initiated the download of SmartDownload. Once that process was complete, SmartDownload, as its first plug-in task, permitted plaintiffs to proceed with downloading and installing Communicator, an operation that was accompanied by the clickwrap display of Communicator's license terms described above.

The signal difference between downloading Communicator and downloading SmartDownload was that no clickwrap presentation accompanied the latter operation. Instead, once plaintiffs Gibson, Gruber, Kelly, and Weindorf had clicked on the "Download" button located at or near the bottom of their screen, and the downloading of SmartDownload was complete, these plaintiffs encountered no further information about the plug-in program or the existence of license terms governing its use. The sole reference to SmartDownload's license terms on the "SmartDownload Communicator" webpage was located in text that would have become visible to plaintiffs only if they had scrolled down to the next screen.

Had plaintiffs scrolled down instead of acting on defendants' invitation to click on the "Download" button, they would have encountered the following invitation: "Please review and agree to the terms of the *Netscape SmartDownload software license agreement* before downloading and using the software." Plaintiffs Gibson, Gruber, Kelly, and Weindorf averred in their affidavits that they never saw this reference to the SmartDownload license agreement when they clicked on the "Download" button. They also testified during depositions that they saw no reference to license terms when they clicked to download SmartDownload, although under questioning by defendants' counsel, some plaintiffs added that they could not "remember" or be "sure" whether the screen shots of the SmartDownload page attached to their affidavits reflected precisely what they had seen on their computer screens when they downloaded SmartDownload.

In sum, plaintiffs Gibson, Gruber, Kelly, and Weindorf allege that the process of obtaining SmartDownload contrasted sharply with that of obtaining Communicator. Having selected SmartDownload, they were required neither to express unambiguous assent to that program's license agreement nor even to view the license terms or become aware of their existence before proceeding with the invited download of the free plug-in program. Moreover, once these plaintiffs had initiated the download, the existence of SmartDownload's license terms was not mentioned while the software was running or at any later point in plaintiffs' experience of the product.

Even for a user who, unlike plaintiffs, did happen to scroll down past the download button, SmartDownload's license terms would not have been immediately displayed in the manner of Communicator's clickwrapped terms. Instead, if such a user had seen the notice of SmartDownload's terms and then clicked on the underlined invitation to review and agree to the terms, a hypertext link would have taken the user to a separate webpage entitled "License & Support Agreements." The first paragraph on this page read, in pertinent part:

The use of each Netscape software product is governed by a license agreement. You must read and agree to the license agreement terms BE-FORE acquiring a product. Please click on the appropriate link below to review the current license agreement for the product of interest to you before acquisition. For products available for download, you must read and agree to the license agreement terms BEFORE you install the software. If you do not agree to the license terms, do not download, install or use the software.

Below this paragraph appeared a list of license agreements, the first of which was "*License Agreement for Netscape* Navigator *and Netscape Communicator Product Family* (Netscape Navigator, Netscape Communicator and Netscape Smart-Download)." If the user clicked on that link, he or she would be taken to yet another webpage that contained the full text of a license agreement that was identical in every respect to the Communicator license agreement except that it stated that its "terms apply to Netscape Communicator, Netscape Navigator, and Netscape SmartDownload." The license agreement granted the user a nonexclusive license to use and reproduce the software, subject to certain terms:

> BY CLICKING THE ACCEPTANCE BUTTON OR INSTALLING OR USING NETSCAPE COMMUNICATOR, NETSCAPE NAVIGATOR, OR NETSCAPE SMARTDOWNLOAD SOFTWARE (THE "PRODUCT"), THE INDIVIDUAL OR ENTITY LICENSING THE PRODUCT ("LICEN-SEE") IS CONSENTING TO BE BOUND BY AND IS BECOMING A PARTY TO THIS AGREEMENT. IF LICENSEE DOES NOT AGREE TO ALL OF THE TERMS OF THIS AGREEMENT, THE BUTTON INDI-CATING NON-ACCEPTANCE MUST BE SELECTED, AND LICENSEE MUST NOT INSTALL OR USE THE SOFTWARE.

Among the license terms was a provision requiring virtually all disputes relating to the agreement to be submitted to arbitration:

> Unless otherwise agreed in writing, all disputes relating to this Agreement (excepting any dispute relating to intellectual property rights) shall be subject to final and binding arbitration in Santa Clara County, California, under the auspices of JAMS/EndDispute, with the losing party paying all costs of arbitration.

. . .

II. Proceedings Below

In the district court, defendants moved to compel arbitration and to stay court proceedings pursuant to the Federal Arbitration Act ("FAA"), 9 U.S.C. § 4, arguing that the disputes reflected in the complaints, like any other dispute relating to the SmartDownload license agreement, are subject to the arbitration clause contained in that agreement. Finding that Netscape's webpage, unlike typical examples of clickwrap, neither adequately alerted users to the existence of SmartDownload's license terms nor required users unambiguously to manifest assent to those terms as a condition of downloading the product, the court held that the user plaintiffs had not entered into the SmartDownload license agreement. *Specht*, 150 F.Supp.2d at 595–96.

. . .

Discussion

I. Standard of Review and Applicable Law

A district court's denial of a motion to compel arbitration is reviewed *de novo*.... The determination of whether parties have contractually bound themselves to arbitrate a dispute—a determination involving interpretation of state law—is a legal conclusion also subject to *de novo* review. ... The findings upon which that conclusion is based, however, are factual and thus may not be overturned unless clearly erroneous....

. . .

The district court properly concluded that in deciding whether parties agreed to arbitrate a certain matter, a court should generally apply state-law principles to the issue of contract formation. *Mehler v. Terminix Int'l Co.*, 205 F.3d 44, 48 (2d Cir.2000); *see also Perry v. Thomas*, 482 U.S. 483, 492 n. 9 (1987) ("[S]tate law, whether of legislative or judicial origin, is applicable [to the determination of whether the parties agreed to arbitrate] *if* that law arose to govern issues concerning the validity, revocability, and enforceability of contracts generally."). Therefore, state law governs the question of whether the parties in the present case entered into an agreement to arbitrate disputes relating to the SmartDownload license agreement. The district court further held that California law governs the question of contract formation here; the parties do not appeal that determination.

. . .

III. Whether the User Plaintiffs Had Reasonable Notice of and Manifested Assent to the SmartDownload License Agreement

Whether governed by the common law or by Article 2 of the Uniform Commercial Code ("UCC"), a transaction, in order to be a contract, requires a manifestation of agreement between the parties. *See Windsor Mills, Inc. v. Collins & Aikman Corp.*, 25 Cal.App.3d 987, 991 (1972) ("[C]onsent to, or acceptance of, the arbitration provision [is] necessary to create an agreement to arbitrate."); *see also* Cal.Com.Code § 2204(1) ("A contract for sale of goods may be made in any manner sufficient to show agreement, including conduct by both parties which recognizes the existence of such a contract.").[13] Mutual manifestation of assent, whether by written or spo-

---

[13] The district court concluded that the SmartDownload transactions here should be governed by "California law as it relates to the sale of goods, including the Uniform Commercial Code in effect in California." *Specht*, 150 F.Supp.2d at 591. It is not obvious, however, that UCC Article 2 ("sales of goods") applies to the licensing of software that is downloadable from the Internet. ... There is no doubt that a sale of tangible goods over the Internet is governed by Article 2 of the UCC. ... Some courts have also applied Article 2, occasionally with misgivings, to sales of off-the-shelf software in tangible, packaged formats. *See, e.g., ProCD*, 86 F.3d at 1450 . . . ; *I.Lan Sys., Inc. v. Nextpoint Networks, Inc.*, 183 F.Supp.2d 328, 332 (D.Mass.2002) . . . .

Downloadable software, however, is scarcely a "tangible" good, and, in part because software may be obtained, copied, or transferred effortlessly at the stroke of a computer key, licensing of such Internet products has assumed a vast importance in recent years. Recogniz-

ken word or by conduct, is the touchstone of contract. . . . [A] consumer's clicking on a download button does not communicate assent to contractual terms if the offer did not make clear to the consumer that clicking on the download button would signify assent to those terms, *see* [*id.* at 992]. California's common law is clear that "an offeree, regardless of apparent manifestation of his consent, is not bound by inconspicuous contractual provisions of which he is unaware, contained in a document whose contractual nature is not obvious." *Id.* . . .

Arbitration agreements are no exception to the requirement of manifestation of assent. . . . Thus, California contract law measures assent by an objective standard that takes into account both what the offeree said, wrote, or did and the transactional context in which the offeree verbalized or acted.

A. The Reasonably Prudent Offeree of Downloadable Software

Defendants argue that plaintiffs must be held to a standard of reasonable prudence and that, because notice of the existence of SmartDownload license terms was on the next scrollable screen, plaintiffs were on "inquiry notice" of those terms.[14] We disagree with the proposition that a reasonably prudent offeree in plaintiffs' position would necessarily have known or learned of the existence of the SmartDownload license agreement prior to acting, so that plaintiffs may be held to have assented to that agreement with constructive notice of its terms. . . . It is true that "[a] party cannot avoid the terms of a contract on the ground that he or she failed to read it before signing." *Marin Storage & Trucking,* [*Inc. v. Benco Contracting & Eng'g, Inc.,* 89 Cal.App.4th 1042, 1049 (2001)]. But courts are quick to add: "An exception to this general rule exists when the writing does not appear to be a contract and the terms are not called to the attention of the recipient. In such a case, no contract is formed with respect to the undisclosed term." *Id.; cf. Cory v. Golden State Bank,* 95 Cal.App.3d 360, 364 (1979) ("[T]he provision in question is effectively hidden from the view of money order purchasers until after the transactions are completed. . . . Under these circumstances, it must be concluded that the Bank's money order purchasers are not chargeable with either actual or constructive notice of the service charge provision, and therefore cannot be deemed to have consented to the provision as part of their transaction with the Bank.").

Most of the cases cited by defendants in support of their inquiry-notice argu-

---

ing that "a body of law based on images of the sale of manufactured goods ill fits licenses and other transactions in computer information," the National Conference of Commissioners on Uniform State Laws has promulgated the Uniform Computer Information Transactions Act ("UCITA"), a code resembling UCC Article 2 in many respects but drafted to reflect emergent practices in the sale and licensing of computer information. . . .

We need not decide today whether UCC Article 2 applies to Internet transactions in downloadable products. The district court's analysis and the parties' arguments on appeal show that, for present purposes, there is no essential difference between UCC Article 2 and the common law of contracts. We therefore apply the common law, with exceptions as noted.

[14] "Inquiry notice" is "actual notice of circumstances sufficient to put a prudent man upon inquiry." . . .

ment are drawn from the world of paper contracting. *See, e.g., Taussig v. Bode & Haslett,* 134 Cal. 260, 66 P. 259 (1901) (where party had opportunity to read leakage disclaimer printed on warehouse receipt, he had duty to do so); *In re First Capital Life Ins. Co.,* 34 Cal.App.4th 1283, 1288 (1995) (purchase of insurance policy after opportunity to read and understand policy terms creates binding agreement); *King v. Larsen Realty, Inc.,* 121 Cal.App.3d 349, 356 (1981) (where realtors' board manual specifying that party was required to arbitrate was "readily available," party was "on notice" that he was agreeing to mandatory arbitration); *Cal. State Auto. Ass'n Inter-Ins. Bureau v. Barrett Garages, Inc.,* 257 Cal.App.2d 71, 76 (1967) (recipient of airport parking claim check was bound by terms printed on claim check, because a "ordinarily prudent" person would have been alerted to the terms); *Larrus v. First Nat'l Bank,* 122 Cal.App.2d 884, 888 (1954) ("clearly printed" statement on bank card stating that depositor agreed to bank's regulations provided sufficient notice to create agreement, where party had opportunity to view statement and to ask for full text of regulations, but did not do so); *see also Hux v. Butler,* 339 F.2d 696, 700 (6th Cir.1964) (constructive notice found where "slightest inquiry" would have disclosed relevant facts to offeree); *Walker v. Carnival Cruise Lines,* 63 F.Supp.2d 1083, 1089 (N.D.Cal.1999) (under California and federal law, "conspicuous notice" directing the attention of parties to existence of contract terms renders terms binding) (quotation marks omitted); *Shacket v. Roger Smith Aircraft Sales, Inc.,* 651 F.Supp. 675, 691 (N.D.Ill.1986) (constructive notice found where "minimal investigation" would have revealed facts to offeree).

As the foregoing cases suggest, receipt of a physical document containing contract terms or notice thereof is frequently deemed, in the world of paper transactions, a sufficient circumstance to place the offeree on inquiry notice of those terms. "Every person who has actual notice of circumstances sufficient to put a prudent man upon inquiry as to a particular fact, has constructive notice of the fact itself in all cases in which, by prosecuting such inquiry, he might have learned such fact." Cal.Civ.Code § 19. These principles apply equally to the emergent world of online product delivery, pop-up screens, hyperlinked pages, clickwrap licensing, scrollable documents, and urgent admonitions to "Download Now!". What plaintiffs saw when they were being invited by defendants to download this fast, free plug-in called SmartDownload was a screen containing praise for the product and, at the very bottom of the screen, a "Download" button. Defendants argue that under the principles set forth in the cases cited above, a "fair and prudent person using ordinary care" would have been on inquiry notice of SmartDownload's license terms. *Shacket,* 651 F.Supp. at 690.

We are not persuaded that a reasonably prudent offeree in these circumstances would have known of the existence of license terms. Plaintiffs were responding to an offer that did not carry an immediately visible notice of the existence of license terms or require unambiguous manifestation of assent to those terms. Thus, plaintiffs' "apparent manifestation of . . . consent" was to terms "contained in a document whose contractual nature [was] not obvious." *Windsor Mills,* 25 Cal.App.3d at 992. Moreover, the fact that, given the position of the scroll bar on their computer screens, plaintiffs may have been aware that an unexplored portion of the Netscape webpage remained below the download button does not mean that they reasonably should have concluded that this portion contained a notice of license terms. . . .

We conclude that in circumstances such as these, where consumers are urged to download free software at the immediate click of a button, a reference to the existence of license terms on a submerged screen is not sufficient to place consumers on inquiry or constructive notice of those terms. The SmartDownload webpage screen was "printed in such a manner that it tended to conceal the fact that it was an express acceptance of [Netscape's] rules and regulations." *Larrus*, 266 P.2d at 147. Internet users may have, as defendants put it, "as much time as they need[ ]" to scroll through multiple screens on a webpage, but there is no reason to assume that viewers will scroll down to subsequent screens simply because screens are there. When products are "free" and users are invited to download them in the absence of reasonably conspicuous notice that they are about to bind themselves to contract terms, the transactional circumstances cannot be fully analogized to those in the paper world of arm's-length bargaining. In the next two sections, we discuss case law and other legal authorities that have addressed the circumstances of computer sales, software licensing, and online transacting. Those authorities tend strongly to support our conclusion that plaintiffs did not manifest assent to SmartDownload's license terms.

B. Shrinkwrap Licensing and Related Practices

Defendants cite certain well-known cases involving shrinkwrap licensing and related commercial practices in support of their contention that plaintiffs became bound by the SmartDownload license terms by virtue of inquiry notice. For example, in *Hill v. Gateway 2000, Inc.*, 105 F.3d 1147 (7th Cir.1997), the Seventh Circuit held that where a purchaser had ordered a computer over the telephone, received the order in a shipped box containing the computer along with printed contract terms, and did not return the computer within the thirty days required by the terms, the purchaser was bound by the contract. *Id.* at 1148–49. In *ProCD, Inc. v. Zeidenberg*, the same court held that where an individual purchased software in a box containing license terms which were displayed on the computer screen every time the user executed the software program, the user had sufficient opportunity to review the terms and to return the software, and so was contractually bound after retaining the product. *ProCD*, 86 F.3d at 1452; *cf.* . . . *Brower v. Gateway 2000, Inc.*, 246 A.D.2d 246, 251 (1st Dep't 1998) (buyer assented to arbitration clause shipped inside box with computer and software by retaining items beyond date specified by license terms); *M.A. Mortenson Co. v. Timberline Software Corp.*, 93 Wash.App. 819 (1999) (buyer manifested assent to software license terms by installing and using software), *aff'd*, 140 Wash.2d 568 (2000); *see also I.Lan Sys.*, 183 F.Supp.2d at 338 (business entity "explicitly accepted the clickwrap license agreement [contained in purchased software] when it clicked on the box stating 'I agree'").

These cases do not help defendants. To the extent that they hold that the purchaser of a computer or tangible software is contractually bound after failing to object to printed license terms provided with the product, *Hill* and *Brower* do not differ markedly from the cases involving traditional paper contracting discussed in the previous section. Insofar as the purchaser in *ProCD* was confronted with conspicuous, mandatory license terms every time he ran the software on his computer, that case actually undermines defendants' contention that downloading in the absence of conspicuous terms is an act that binds plaintiffs to those terms. In *Mortenson*, the full text of license terms was printed on each sealed diskette envelope inside the software box, printed again on the inside cover of the user manual, and notice of the terms appeared on the computer screen every time the purchaser executed the program. *Mortenson*, 970 P.2d at 806. In sum, the foregoing cases are clearly distinguishable from the facts of the present action.

C. Online Transactions

Cases in which courts have found contracts arising from Internet use do not assist defendants, because in those circumstances there was much clearer notice than in the present case that a user's act would manifest assent to contract terms. *See, e.g., Hotmail Corp. v. Van$ Money Pie Inc.*, 47 U.S.P.Q.2d 1020, 1025 (N.D.Cal.1998) (granting preliminary injunction based in part on breach of "Terms of Service" agreement, to which defendants had assented); *America Online, Inc. v. Booker*, 781 So.2d 423, 425 (Fla.Dist.Ct.App.2001) (upholding forum selection clause in "freely negotiated agreement" contained in online terms of service); *Caspi v. Microsoft Network, L.L.C.*, 323 N.J.Super. 118, 732 A.2d 528, 530, 532–33 (N.J.Super.Ct.App.Div. 1999) (upholding forum selection clause where subscribers to online software were required to review license terms in scrollable window and to click "I Agree" or "I Don't Agree"); *Barnett v. Network Solutions, Inc.*, 38 S.W.3d 200, 203–04 (Tex.App. 2001) (upholding forum selection clause in online contract for registering Internet domain names that required users to scroll through terms before accepting or rejecting them); *cf. Pollstar v. Gigmania, Ltd.*, 170 F.Supp.2d 974, 981–82 (E.D.Cal.2000) (expressing concern that notice of license terms had appeared in small, gray text on a gray background on a linked webpage, but concluding that it was too early in the case to order dismissal).[17]

---

[17] . . . . [T]he model code, UCITA, . . . generally recognizes the importance of conspicuous notice and unambiguous manifestation of assent in online sales and licensing of computer information. For example, § 112, which addresses manifestation of assent, provides that a user's opportunity to review online contract terms exists if a "record" (or electronic writing) of the contract terms is "made available in a manner that ought to call it to the attention of a reasonable person and permit review." UCITA, § 112(e)(1) (rev. ed. Aug. 23, 2001). . . .

UCITA § 211 sets forth a number of guidelines for "internet-type" transactions involving the supply of information or software. For example, a licensor should make standard terms "available for review" prior to delivery or obligation to pay (1) by "displaying prominently and in close proximity to a description of the computer information, or to instructions or steps for acquiring it, the standard terms or a reference to an electronic location from which they can be readily obtained," or (2) by "disclosing the availability of the standard terms in a prominent place on the site from which the computer information is offered and promptly furnishing a copy of the standard terms on request before the transfer of the computer information." *Id.* § 211(1)(A–B). . . .

We hasten to point out that UCITA, which has been enacted into law only in Maryland

After reviewing the California common law and other relevant legal authority, we conclude that under the circumstances here, plaintiffs' downloading of Smart-Download did not constitute acceptance of defendants' license terms. Reasonably conspicuous notice of the existence of contract terms and unambiguous manifestation of assent to those terms by consumers are essential if electronic bargaining is to have integrity and credibility. We hold that a reasonably prudent offeree in plaintiffs' position would not have known or learned, prior to acting on the invitation to download, of the reference to SmartDownload's license terms hidden below the "Download" button on the next screen. We affirm the district court's conclusion that the user plaintiffs, including Fagan, are not bound by the arbitration clause contained in those terms.

. . .

CONCLUSION

For the foregoing reasons, we affirm the district court's denial of defendants' motion to compel arbitration and to stay court proceedings.

EXTENSIONS

1. *Reason to know.* In *Klocek,* a case involving a shrinkwrap agreement, as well as in *Specht,* a case involving a browsewrap agreement, the courts voiced concern that the licensors had not given their purported licensees sufficient notice of the licensing terms that the licensors sought to enforce. How important is notice that a product's use is governed by a license to the enforceability of that license? Is it a sufficient condition on enforceability, a necessary condition on enforceability, or neither? In a similar case, one court reasoned:

> The motion to dismiss the second claim (breach of contract) is founded on the "terms and conditions" set forth on the home page of the Ticketmaster site. This provides that anyone going beyond the home page agrees to the terms and conditions set forth, which include that the information is for personal use only, may not be used for commercial purposes, and no deep linking to the site is permitted. In defending this claim, Ticketmaster makes reference to the "shrinkwrap license" cases, where the packing on the outside of the CD stated that opening the package constitutes adherence to the license agreement (restricting republication) contained therein. This has been held to be enforceable. That is not the same as this case because the "shrink-wrap license agreement" is open and obvious and in fact hard to miss. Many websites make you click on "agree" to the terms and conditions before going on, but Ticketmaster does not. Further, the terms and conditions are set forth so that the customer needs to scroll down the home page to find and read them. Many customers instead are likely to proceed to the event page of interest rather than reading the "small print." It cannot be said that merely putting the terms and conditions in this fashion necessarily creates a contract with any one using the web site. The motion is granted with leave to amend in case there are facts showing Tickets' knowledge of them plus

---

and Virginia, does not govern the parties' transactions in the present case, but we nevertheless find that UCITA's provisions offer insight into the evolving online "circumstances" that defendants argue placed plaintiffs on inquiry notice of the existence of the SmartDownload license terms. . . .

facts showing implied agreement to them.

Ticketmaster Corp. v. Tickets.com, Inc., 54 U.S.P.Q.2d 1344 (C.D.Cal.2000).

At a later stage of the proceedings, the *Ticketmaster* court denied the motion of defendant Tickets.com to dismiss Ticketmaster's contract claim. Additional evidence demonstrated that Tickets.com (1) was aware of the statement on the Ticketmaster home page that accessing an interior page of the site indicated acceptance of Ticketmaster's terms and conditions, including its condition that information obtained from the site may not be used for commercial purposes, and (2) nevertheless continued linking to interior pages in disregard of the commercial-use condition. The issue therefore was whether maintaining the links constituted Tickets.com's assent to those conditions. The court observed that it "would prefer a rule that required an unmistakable assent to the conditions easily provided by requiring clicking on an icon which says 'I agree' or the equivalent. Such a rule would provide certainty in trial and make it clear that the user had called to his attention the conditions he or she accepted when using the web site." However, the court concluded that the law was otherwise, it being well established that "no particular form of words is necessary to indicate assent—the offeror may specify that a certain action in connection with his offer is deemed acceptance, and ripens into a contract when the action is taken." *Ticketmaster Corp. v. Tickets.com, Inc.*, 2003 Copr.L.Dec. ¶ 28,607 (C.D.Cal.2003).

The court observed that Ticketmaster had apprised Tickets.com of its no-commercial-use policy by letter, and that Tickets.com had replied with a letter "stating that it did not accept the conditions." Should this statement by Tickets.com be deemed to negate the inference of assent that the court derived from Tickets.com's linking conduct?

In *Register.com, Inc. v. Verio, Inc.*, 356 F.3d 393 (2d Cir.2004), Verio repeatedly queried Register.com's WHOIS database, each time receiving a response containing the requested information together with a statement of terms and conditions that Register.com asserted were applicable to use of the information. The court held that by virtue of these repeated requests, Verio was aware of the terms and had assented to them. As the majority held, "when a benefit is offered subject to stated conditions, and the offeree makes a decision to take the benefit with knowledge of the terms of the offer, the taking constitutes an acceptance of the terms." The draft dissenting opinion[2] demurred to this logic, noting: "Register.com's repeated proposals that terms not authorized by the ICANN Agreement be adopted could reasonably have been repeatedly rejected by Verio. There is no basis to infer that Verio in fact assented . . . ." Which view do you find more persuasive?

2. *Terms and conditions of use.* A large proportion of commercial websites today contain a hyperlink at the bottom of their homepage labeled something like "Terms of Use" (or sometimes just "Terms"). Many websites also have another hyperlink labeled "Privacy Policy." These hyperlinks link to web pages containing an agreement on the terms and conditions for use of the website and the website's privacy policy, respectively. Based upon the cases excerpted above, are such terms and policies binding on the users of the website? Should an agreement setting forth the terms and conditions of use be treated differently from a posted privacy policy? One court, noting that "the usual rule in contract cases is that 'general statements of policy are not contractual,' " held that the privacy policy posted by Northwest Airlines on its website "did not constitute a unilateral contract" that site visitors may enforce. *See In re Northwest Airlines Privacy Litigation*, 2004 WL 1278459 (D.Minn. 2004).

---

[2] The judge who drafted the dissenting opinion died before the decision was issued. The court appended the dissenting opinion as an appendix to the decision.

QUESTIONS FOR DISCUSSION

E-commerce website audits. Assume that the defendant in *Specht v. Netscape* employed a lawyer to draft the license whose enforceability was at issue. Assume further that the lawyer drafted the license and sent it to the client, which then passed it along to the company's information technology department to post on the website. Does this case suggest that proper lawyering requires attention not only to the text of an agreement, but also to its presentation? (Would the license agreements in this case have been held enforceable if they had been presented as clickwrap agreements, requiring the user to click "I Agree" before allowing access to the material on the website?)

B. UCITA

In the late 1990s the National Conference of Commissioners on Uniform State Laws ("NCCUSL"), the organization that developed the Uniform Commercial Code ("UCC") in the 1950s, drafted a model statute embodying a comprehensive, regulatory approach to electronic contracting and the licensing of computer information, much as Article 2 of the UCC takes a comprehensive and regulatory approach to the law of sales. While it was being drafted, the model statute was known as "Proposed Article 2B," and the drafters intended it to be inserted into the UCC after Articles 2 (Sales) and 2A (Leasing). The proposed Article 2B, which would have explicitly validated shrinkwrap licenses and electronic contracting, proved extremely controversial. For example, many state attorneys general opposed it because they felt it undermined their states' law of consumer protection. And many intellectual property scholars felt that it misunderstood the proper role of intellectual property law. As a result, the American Law Institute ("ALI"), the organization responsible for the Restatements of Law as well as jointly responsible, with NCCUSL, for the UCC, refused to approve it for incorporation into the UCC. At that point NCCUSL decided to offer Proposed Article 2B, renamed the Uniform Computer Information Transactions Act ("UCITA"), as a separate, free-standing model act for adoption by the states.

Only two states, Virginia and Maryland, have enacted UCITA. *See* VA. CODE ANN. TITLE 59.1 CH. 43; MD. COMM. CODE ANN. tit. 22. Four others enacted legislation aimed at nullifying its effect within their borders. *See* N.C. GEN. STAT. ANN. § 66–329; W.VA. CODE § 55–8–15; IOWA CODE § 554D.104; VT. STAT. ANN. tit. 9, § 2463a. Faced with continuing opposition from important legal constituencies such as the American Bar Association as well as the ALI and various state consumer protection agencies, in August 2003 NCCUSL announced that it would no longer promote enactment of UCITA by state legislatures. Without NCCUSL's support, it is unlikely that UCITA will be favorably received by any additional state legislatures.

UCITA is nevertheless the law in two states, including Virginia, which is of particular significance because many Internet contracts are governed by Virginia law. Moreover, UCITA's approach to contract formation remains worthy of debate. In this Section we review UCITA's approach to shrinkwrap, clickwrap, and browsewrap contracts. The primary questions presented in the cases discussed above are (1) Under what circumstances is a contract formed when some of the terms are disclosed only after the purchase?, and (2) What are the terms of contracts formed in this manner? UCITA attempts to resolve these questions.

UCITA's rules on contract formation are informed by a few key premises:

First, the formation of a contract, and determination of the terms of a contract, are two separate events. A given action might bring about either one or the other of these events, or both simultaneously.

Second, contracts may be formed, and terms may become contract terms, as a result of various kinds of conduct by the parties, including a failure to act.

Third, contract formation is a process that can take place over an extended period of time. Formation and determination of terms need not occur at a single point in time. Contracts may be formed in a series of layers.

UCITA's basic rule of contract formation is stated in Section 202. A contract may be formed in any manner sufficient to show agreement. § 202(a). In particular, a contract may be formed by interaction of a person with a website or some other electronic agent. This occurs if the person takes some action that he should know the electronic agent will interpret as acceptance. § 206(b). It does not matter if some terms are left open: consistent with the principle that contract formation is a different event from determination of contract terms, the existence of open terms does not defeat contract formation. § 202(b), (c).

Section 202 also directly addresses the situation where terms are provided after the commencement of the transaction. If the parties intend that formation of a contract is to be contingent on their agreement upon some term that is not yet settled, and if the parties are later unable to agree as to that term, then no contract is formed. In that case, the transaction must be unwound: the purchaser gives back or destroys the information product, and the seller gives back the purchaser's money. § 202(e).

If the parties do agree on the post-purchase terms, a contract is formed. But what are its terms? Sections 208 and 209 are relevant here. Some of those terms will have been agreed to in the initial contacts between the parties, leading up to contract formation. In the case of a contract formed as contemplated by § 202(e), where the parties agree that the contract will be formed only if they subsequently agree upon some yet-unadopted term, agreement on that term both forms the contract and makes that term part of the contract. Even after the contract is formed, additional "layers" of terms may be added to it.

These terms become part of the contract through the parties' manifestation of assent to them. According to Section 208(1), if a party manifests assent to a record, then the terms of the record become terms of the contract. (A "record" is information stored in a document, electronic or paper. § 101(a)(55).) This can occur after beginning performance, as long as the parties expected there would be additional terms presented after that point in time; but of course if formation of the contract was intended to be contingent on agreement to such terms, then (as we already know from Section 202(e)) if there is no agreement as to those terms, a contract is not formed. § 208(2).

What, then, constitutes manifestation of assent to a record? This is governed by Section 112, which says that there is a manifestation of assent if three requirements are satisfied.

First, the assenting party must have an opportunity to review what she is assenting to. § 112(a). The party is deemed to have an opportunity to review if two conditions are satisfied. First, the terms must be presented in a manner that ought to call them to the attention of a reasonable person. § 112(e)(1). Second, if the party is presented with the terms only after contract performance begins, she must be accorded a right to return the product if she does not agree with those terms. § 112(e)(3). This is the right of return that Judge Easterbrook assumed to exist in *ProCD v. Zeidenberg, supra*.

A special, safe-harbor rule regarding pre-transaction opportunity to review applies in the case of a transaction via a website. If the terms of a standard-form license are presented before payment or delivery, the purchaser is deemed to have an opportunity to review them as long as the terms, or a reference to them, are displayed "prominently and in close proximity" to the description of the product or to the ordering instructions. In other words, if the terms themselves, or a hyperlink to the terms, or apparently just a URL indicating where the terms can be found, is placed right in view when the purchaser is considering the purchase, then she is deemed to have an opportunity to review them. § 211(1)(A). In addition, it is sufficient if the seller discloses the availability of the terms "in a prominent place on the site," and furnishes a copy promptly upon request. § 211(1)(B). Apparently this means all the seller has to do is state somewhere on the home page of the website that all standard-form terms are available upon request by writing to a specified postal address.

Second, the assenting party must take some action to indicate assent. § 112(a)(2). But that action might consist of inaction. According to the Official Comment: "Assent occurs if a person acts *or fails to act* having reason to know its behavior will be viewed by the other party as indicating assent." § 112, Comment 3(b) (emphasis added). So a failure to return your computer after five days, as occurred in *Hill v. Gateway*, might constitute an indication of assent.

Third, the manifestation of assent has to be attributable to the assenting party. This is determined under general agency law.

Note what manifestation of assent does *not* require. The purchaser need not realize that the terms are available for her to review: it is enough that the terms are made available in a manner that ought to call them to the attention of a reasonable person. She need not actually read the record to which she is assenting. If she does read the terms, she need not understand them. She need not intend to assent to the terms: it is enough if she "intentionally engages in conduct or makes statements with reason to know that the other party or its electronic agent *may* infer from the conduct or statement that the person assents to the record or term." § 112(a)(2) (emphasis added). She need not take any action: in proper circumstances, inaction will suffice.

A significant innovation in UCITA was its introduction of a separate regulatory regime for transactions between a merchant and a consumer (or a consumer-like business purchaser) involving a standard-form contract—called "mass-market transactions." § 102(a)(45). (UCITA's approach to "mass-market" contracting is further discussed in Part I(C), *infra*.) First, manifestation of assent to the terms of such a form can only occur before or during the purchaser's initial use of the product. § 209(a). For example, if the product is a software program, then the terms must be presented to the consumer the first time he runs the program. Second, a term does not become part of the contract if it is "unconscionable," as UCITA defines the word. § 209(a)(1). Third, a term does not become part of the contract if it conflicts with a term on which the parties expressly agreed earlier in the transaction—probably limited to express agreements in writing, since a parol evidence rule comes into play here. § 209(a)(2). Fourth, if the consumer chooses to exercise his right of return, upon disagreeing with the post-purchase terms, the vendor must pay the consumer's reasonable costs of returning the item and of restoring his computer to its condition before installing the product. § 209(b).

In 2002, NCCUSL amended UCITA to try to meet some of the objections to it. New Section 209(a)(4) adds requirements that must be satisfied before a term becomes part of the contract in a mass-market transaction. Under this provision, to become part of the contract a term must be presented to the licensee in a format (paper or electronic) that allows it to be retained. This requirement may be satisfied if the vendor provides the terms "in a copy available at no additional cost on a seasonable request in a record by a licensee that was unable to print or store the license for archival and review purposes."

New Section 209(d) adds a condition to the effectiveness of terms disclosed post-purchase in a mass-market transaction. The original UCITA rule, in Section 209(b), was that in such a transaction the purchaser had to be afforded a right to return the product if she did not accept the terms. But nothing in UCITA's text required the vendor to inform the purchaser of the existence of this right. (There was such a requirement in an Official Comment to Section 112.) The amendment says that the purchaser (which UCITA refers to as the "licensee") must receive notice "that a refund may be obtained from the person to whom the payment was made or other person designated in the notice if the licensee refuses the terms."[3]

EXTENSIONS

ALI software contracting project. After UCITA failed to gain momentum, in part because the ALI failed to endorse it, the ALI began a project that is intended to clarify and set forth approved principles of software contracting. See AMERICAN LAW INSTITUTE, PRINCIPLES OF THE LAW OF SOFTWARE CONTRACTS, PRELIMINARY DRAFT NO. 2 (Aug. 10, 2005). Although at this writing the ALI has not yet released the Principles, the project has been substantially developed and should be of significant use to practitioners and judges when it is released. The Principles are in a form similar to that of the ALI Restatements, with black-letter principles and extensive commentary, notes, and examples. Unlike the broad ("computer information transactions") scope of UCITA, the Principles cover only "the exchange of software for a consideration," not including "digital art or non-literary and non-artistic databases." The Reporters for the project are Professors Robert A. Hillman of Cornell Law School and Maureen O'Rourke of Boston University Law School.

C. STANDARDIZATION

In the past, some courts and commentators have been leery of standard-form contracts, which present the recipient with the choice either of acceding to the proposed terms or foregoing the product or service to which the terms are attached. Yet adhesion contracts (also known as take-it-or-leave-it contracts) have always offered certain advantages. Standardization of contract terms reduces transaction costs, and is practically inevitable with respect to low-value transactions. In addition, a standard-form contract may represent the package of

---

[3] NCCUSL's 2002 amendments to UCITA also deleted Section 816, authorizing a vendor to engage in electronic self-help upon cancellation of a license, a provision that was hugely controversial, and replaced it with Section 815, forbidding the use of electronic self-help.

In April 2004, the Virginia legislature amended Virginia's enactment of UCITA to implement several of NCCUSL's August 2002 amendments. In particular, the Virginia amendment: (1) adopts UCITA's revised treatment of consumer protection laws, and (2) adds a provision making unenforceable a contract provision that "prohibits an end-user licensee from engaging in otherwise lawful public discussion relating to" a computer information product. The Virginia legislature did not, however, adopt NCCUSL's turnaround on the question of electronic self-help, which therefore remains permissible under the law of Virginia.

terms that is most efficient or most valued by customers. In the online environment it is possible that even more contracts will be standardized, especially those which are formed through the interaction of machines. (*See* Part I(D), *infra*.) This section presents some issues raised by standardization in Internet commerce.

Margaret Jane Radin, *Online Standardization and the Integration of Text and Machine*
70 FORDHAM L. REV. 1125 (2002).

. . .

A good technical standard might come about through market emergence. The best product might have won out in a competitive market. Or, we might need some standard for smooth functioning, and be indifferent about which one. On the other hand, an inferior product might have tipped the market and eliminated its competitors; we could be stuck with such a product because no one else can enter unless they can somehow take over the entire market immediately.

The very same reasoning applies to legal standardization. Contracts in an industry might be standard because those are the terms that consumers consistently choose; the standardized contract represents the package of terms that won out in a free market. On the other hand, standardized contracts may reflect collusion or some other market failure such as a "lemons equilibrium" brought about by inadequate consumer information.

Similarly, if a standard arrives by way of promulgation, that in itself also tells us nothing about how it should be evaluated. If a legal standard comes about through legislation, one might think—and courts have tended to think—that the legislative standard is entitled to a presumption that it is socially beneficial, because it was imposed by a collective process or a representative body that takes into account everyone's interests. But we do not have to be thoroughgoing public choice theorists to note the prevalence of industry capture; and to believe that, at least some of the time, interest groups capture the process and get the statute or rule written the way they want it.

This kind of capture happens both in technical and in legal standard-setting. In the technical case, sometimes a company is helpful in getting a standard promulgated, and then it turns out the company had a patent pending, so that everyone who wants to use the standard must license the patent. In the legal case, sometimes interest groups control the drafting process. This is arguably what happened with the anti-circumvention provisions of the Digital Millennium Copyright Act ("DMCA")—captured by the copyright industries—or the pending UCITA— captured by the software industry.

From a policy point of view, then, how a standard is arrived at does not tell us whether it is good or bad, whether it should be welcomed or deplored. In the real world, however, it matters a great deal how standards are arrived at, particularly for legal standards. It is a lot harder to overturn legislation once it is on the books than it is to find a reason to disallow "bottom-up" industry standardization. Not everything about either adhesion contracts or technical standardization, even if unwise, is going to turn out to rise to the level of violation of antitrust laws, federal intellectual property laws, federal consumer protection regulation, or the Constitution; in fact, very little about them will rise to that level. So, it is a very good strategy for industries to capture legislatures or standards-setting bodies, because once they get standards promulgated, it is hard to overturn them.

I believe that there is something deeper going on when it turns out that legal and technical standardization are so closely allied to each other. I believe that the digital revolution is bringing about a seismic shift in our conceptual landscape, which I want to explore here, though only preliminarily. I call this shift the breakdown of the distinction between text and technology, or between expression and functionality, or between words and machine.

The prevalent economic view of contract has broken down the distinction between agreement, formerly thought of as a text, and the product being sold, formerly thought of as a functional object or a collection of functional features. This view of contract actually predates the online environment, but in the online environment it is becoming more powerful. I call this view "contract as product," and contrast it with the view of contract as consent or agreement.

In the "contract as product" view, the contract is part of the product, part of the collection of functional components, and not a separate text about that collection. What does this mean? For example, suppose you buy a cell phone that contains a chip that will wear out within a year, and the phone comes with a set of fine print terms including a clause that says in the event of any dispute arising out of the transaction you must litigate in California under California law. Both the chip and the clause are functionally the same from the economic point of view: if you know that they are there, they will help determine what you are willing to pay for the phone. Notice that in order for the market to function efficiently this view must suppose that at least the marginal consumer must understand what chips and clauses are being purchased. How the product will work, how long it is going to last, what kind of warranties it comes with, what limitations on remedies it comes with—all of these are exactly the same from the economic point of view. The product you are buying is not just the phone, but the phone plus the terms. The contract is not a text about a product, but part of a product.

This contract as product view is suited to adhesion contracts because in such a take-it-or-leave-it transaction there is no dickering over terms and no dickering over the components either. You can buy this product that is going to wear out in a year, over which you will be forced to litigate in California if a dispute arises, or you can walk away and buy something else more to your liking. In order for the market to function efficiently, in this view, one must suppose that other products and/or other terms are available. You don't get to say, "I wish you would remanufacture this so it will not wear out in a year," and you also don't get to say, "I wish you would rewrite the contract so that I can litigate in my home state."

In the offline world, most contracts have been like this for some time, and thus the economic view has suited transactional reality. Nevertheless, lay people have largely continued to conceive of contract as dickered consent between two people.

This lay conception—contract as negotiated text—will, I think, be significantly eroded in the online environment, for two reasons. On the one hand, it is likely that standardized transactions will occupy even more of the transactional universe; and on the other hand, the nature of the transaction is more transparent because the fine print that comes with the functionality being purchased is more accessible to everyone. The contract is merging into the product; the text is merging into the functionality.

The advent of machine-made contracts—the use of programs to create binding commitment—is hastening the breakdown of the distinction between text and machine. Consider business-to-business ("B2B") electronic commerce and the overall transformation of supply-chain management. Manufacturing is becoming ever more automated, and the advent of the machine-made contract completes the picture by automating the supply process. If some computer processor "realizes" that more supplies are needed at a certain part of the assembly process, it can also search certain suppliers and see which can most readily supply what is needed, and it can give the go-ahead for the supplies to be delivered. Computers at each end of the transaction could be programmed with sets of terms; when the buyer computer encounters a seller computer, they could enter into a computerized handshake protocol, and if they determine that they have a set of terms in common they could arrive at a commitment, without a human being having to sign off on it. I think this procedure is going to turn out to be so efficient that it will in fact become the contracting norm in B2B transactions. When (if) this transformation does occur, it will help undermine the distinction between the text and the machine, because computerized contracting will be seen to be integrated with general computerized management of manufacturing processes.

Perhaps the process of integration of text and machine is even clearer in the case of what I call viral contracting. Viral contract—or purported viral contract, because the legal validity of this procedure is not yet determined—occurs when a digital product has digital terms integrated with it, and the product-plus-terms propagates down a chain of distribution, with the intent that the terms be binding on whoever comes into possession of the package. The digital product could be a software program or some other kind of content that someone wishes to propagate. Integrated with such a digital product could be digitally programmed terms that purport to constrain use of the digital product—for example, prohibition of criticism of the program, or prohibition of reverse engineering.[46] The economists'

---

[46] The contractual assurances that earlier coders give to later coders under the General Public License ("GPL") is one example of a widely discussed viral contract currently in use. In theory, the earlier coders' contributions to a software program give these earlier coders property rights under copyright law to exclude later coders from modifying the program—making a derivative work—or from distributing the code. (These property rights depend on the later coders' creations being a "derivative work" of the earlier coders' programs.) Although some prefer to conceive of the GPL as a grant of defeasible property rights, I think it is best viewed as a contractual license that gives the later coders permission to modify and distribute the program if they perform certain affirmative obligations, primarily making their source code available to everyone in a distributional community. Whether the contract

contract-as-product view is here brought to fruition; the digitized product and the digitized terms are literally (not just conceptually) the same in kind and part of a package. Not only does such a package undermine the distinction between text and functionality, it seems difficult to maintain the distinction at all. That is, at this point it seems arbitrary to call one set of programming statements a functional product and another set of programming statements a text.

UCITA explicitly recognizes the prevalence of widespread adhesion contracts in Internet commerce by introducing the notion of a mass-market license, defined as "a standard form used in a mass-market transaction." § 102(44). ("Mass-market transaction" is defined as a transaction involving "a consumer contract," or any other contract if the licensee is substantially in the same position as a consumer. § 102(45).) Section 209 deals with contract formation in the context of a mass-market license, and the Official Comment to that section explicates as follows:

> . . .
>
> 2. **General Rules.** The terms of mass-market contracts can be established in many ways. An oral agreement may suffice as would an agreement to terms in a record. Product descriptions may define the bargain. Parties may agree that terms may be specified later by a party. Three limiting concepts govern where assent to a record is relevant:
>
> > a. **Assent and Agreement.** A party adopts the terms of a mass market license only if it agrees to the record, by manifesting assent or otherwise. A party cannot do so unless it had an opportunity to review the record before it agrees. This means that the record must be available for review and called to the person's attention in a manner such that a reasonable person ought to have noticed it. See Section 112.
> >
> > Adopting terms of a record under this section is pursuant to Section 208, with the limits stated in that section. If the terms of the record are proposed after a party commences performance, the terms are effective only if the party had reason to know that terms would be proposed and assents to the terms when proposed. For mass-market licenses, however, even if reason to know exists at the outset, the terms must be made available no later than the initial use of the information and the person has a statutory right to a return if it refuses the license.
> >
> > b. **Unconscionability and Fundamental Public Policy.** Even if a party agrees to a mass market license, a court may invalidate unconscionable terms or terms against fundamental public policy under rules that apply to all contracts under this Act. . . .
>
> > . . .
>
> 5. **Terms after Initial Agreement.** Mass market licenses may be presented after initial general agreement from the licensee. In some distribution channels this allows a more efficient mode of contracting between end users and remote

---

is valid as between an early coder and a later coder who begins with a version of the program already modified several times since the earlier coder made his contribution has yet to be determined by the courts. [For more on open source licensing and the GPL, see *infra*, Part III(D). — Eds.]

parties; this is especially important where the remote party controls copyright or similar rights in the information. . . .

a. **Timing of Assent.** Agreement to the mass-market record must occur no later than during the initial use of the information. This limits the time during which layered contracting may occur in the mass market and reflects customary practices in software and other industries. . . .

b. **Cost Free Return.** Under subsection (b), if terms are not available for review until after an initial agreement, the party being asked to assent must have a right to reject the terms return the information product. . . .

. . .

EXTENSIONS

1. *Boilerplate in digital works.* In the offline world, the pros and cons of standardized adhesion contracts are extensively debated. *See, e.g.,* Todd. D. Rakoff, *Contracts of Adhesion: An Essay in Reconstruction,* 96 HARV. L. REV. 1173 (1983). The issues surrounding boilerplate are explored from different economic perspectives in *Symposium: "Boilerplate": Foundations of Market Contracts,* 104 MICH. L. REV. __ (forthcoming 2006). To what extent is the use of "boilerplate" online different from its use offline? To what extent are different legal approaches called for? The traditional framework used by courts to determine validated of standardized forms in the office world included Llewellyn's theory of blanket assent, limited by doctrines of reasonable expectations, unconscionability, and void as against public policy. For an argument that the same approach should by and large be suitable in the online world, *see* Robert A. Hillman and Jeffrey J. Rachlinski, *Standard-Form Contracting in The Electronic Age,* 77 N.Y.U. L. REV. 429 (2002).

2. *Approaches to "consent."* Professor Randy Barnett made the following comment in the context of the UCC Article 2 revision process:

> Though the idea of consumers paying for goods before they examine all the terms of the agreement has spooked some academics, their concerns [do not result from] any real impairment of contractual consent. [I] speak here not only as a contracts professor who has written extensively on the importance of contractual consent, but as a frequent consumer of such goods as electronics and software. It is not a bother in the slightest to pay for a good in a store, or online, and then examine the terms in the comfort of my own home provided that I can return the good should I reject the terms. To the contrary, I cannot imagine anything other than an aesthetic objection to this practice. True, consumers who dislike a term in the agreement are put to some inconvenience when they must return a good, as they would in returning any good with which they are not completely satisfied upon inspection, though even they benefit from the lower prices and more specifically tailored terms that result from the practice. But this minor inconvenience in no way warrants a frontal attack on this form of contracting on the grounds of lack of assent. There is certainly assent, though it happens after initial payment. There need no be law against that.

Letter to Lawrence J. Bugge, Esquire, Chairman of the UCC Article 2 Drafting Committee of the National Conference of Commissioners on Uniform State Laws (Mar. 5, 2001). *See also* Randy E. Barnett, *A Consent Theory of Contract,* 86 COLUM. L. REV. 269 (1986). Is this notion of consent an important component of functional standardization? Is it normatively viable?

QUESTIONS FOR DISCUSSION

1. *Impact of mass-market license concept.* As mentioned earlier, *see* Part I(B), *supra*, UCITA was enacted in only two states, and because it is no longer being actively pursued by NCCUSL, is not likely to become the law more generally. Nevertheless, should its conception of mass-market license be broadly adopted?

2. *Standardization or customization?* There are reasons to believe that more and more transactions online will be standardized. Computer-to-computer agreements will have to use standardized sets of terms that they can "agree" on, and if these terms become widely used in this context, they will be used in other contexts as well. Well-drafted sets of terms can be copied and proliferate on the Internet just like other kinds of content. Sets of terms that are validated through widespread use may make globalization of contracting more practical. At the same time, however, customization of terms is technologically feasible in the online environment in ways that it has not been offline. A website could offer you a choice of terms instead of a take-or-leave-it package of fine print. It could disclaim warranties, but offer you a warranty for an extra fee, if you click a box. It could provide for compulsory arbitration, but allow you to purchase the chance to litigate in your home state. And so on. Which scenario do you predict will come to pass? (Or do you think neither scenario will describe the actual state of affairs?) What policy problems do you see associated with these scenarios?

D. AUTOMATED CONTRACTS

A common scenario of Internet commerce involves a human buyer communicating with a computer in order to purchase some goods or services. Consider, for example, a person buying a book from an online book retailer such as Amazon.com or Barnesandnoble.com. The book buyer never communicates with another human being. No human agent of the corporation manifests an intent to sell and ship the book in exchange for payment. The question naturally arises, therefore, whether a person can enter into a contract by negotiating with a computer, that is, by making an offer to or accepting an offer from an electronic agent of a human or corporate principal. What is the legal status of an online order recorded by a machine?

Until recently, the common law and commercial codes presumed that the parties actually negotiating would be individual human beings or legal entities (such as corporations and partnerships) that act through their human agents. Neither legislature nor court had contemplated the rise of electronic commerce and the possibility that a prospective purchaser (or seller) might be negotiating with a machine. Accordingly, the applicability to this situation of rules regarding legal capacity to contract was unclear. Was it possible to form a contract by communicating with a machine? And if so, was it binding or voidable?

The notions of agreement and the manifestation of assent stand at the heart of the law of contract. In this section we explore the transformation of these notions as transactions move online. We first review the tentative recognition of automated contracting in recent statutes. (These statutes are designed primarily to extend the definition of "writing" to cover digital transactions, and will be further considered in Part I(E), *infra*.)

We then present excerpts of two articles considering machine-to-machine contracts, and whether a computer software program can be viewed as the legal agent of its owner or licensee. As we shall see, whether a machine or software program can be the legal agent of a human or corporate principal is controversial and obscure.

1. The Electronic Contracting Statutes: Tentative Recognition of Automated Contracting

The Uniform Electronic Transactions Act ("UETA"), drafted under the auspices of the National Conference of Commissioners on Uniform State Laws ("NCCUSL"), has been widely adopted (46 states as of mid-2004). It was, however, adopted with significant variations among the various states. To encourage greater uniformity in this regard as well as to address the uncertainties regarding electronic contracting that existed in states which had yet to adopt UETA at the time of its enactment, Congress enacted the Electronic Signatures in Global and National Commerce Act ("ESIGN"), Pub. L. No. 106–229, 114 Stat. 464 (2000), whose provisions at the federal level are similar to those of UETA at the state level.

As explained in Part I(E), *infra*, the approach taken by both UETA and ESIGN is non-regulatory and procedural. At bottom, both acts simply state that electronic records and electronic signatures may not be denied legal effect merely because they are in an electronic format. The acts do not determine what renders digitized records and signatures sufficiently reliable to be legally acceptable. State law will still have to determine under what circumstances electronic records and signatures are sufficiently reliable to engender legal effect.

Uniform Electronic Transactions Act, § 2(2), 2(3), 2(5), 2(6)
National Conference of Commissioners on Uniform State Laws (1999).

SECTION 2. DEFINITIONS

In this [Act]:

. . .

(2) "Automated transaction" means a transaction conducted or performed, in whole or in part, by electronic means or electronic records, in which the acts or records of one or both parties are not reviewed by an individual in the ordinary course in forming a contract, performing under an existing contract, or fulfilling an obligation required by the transaction.

(3) "Computer program" means a set of statements or instructions to be used directly or indirectly in an information processing system in order to bring about a certain result.

. . .

(5) "Electronic" means relating to technology having electrical, digital, magnetic, wireless, optical, electromagnetic, or similar capabilities.

(6) "Electronic agent" means a computer program or an electronic or other automated means used independently to initiate an action or respond to electronic records or performances in whole or in part, without review or action by an individual.

. . .

Comment

. . .

2. **"Automated Transaction."** An automated transaction is a transaction performed or conducted by electronic means in which machines are used without human intervention to form contracts and perform obligations under existing contracts. Such broad coverage is necessary because of the diversity of transactions to which this Act may apply.

As with electronic agents, this definition addresses the circumstance where electronic records may result in action or performance by a party although no human review of the electronic records is anticipated. Section 14 provides specific rules to assure that where one or both parties do not review the electronic records, the resulting agreement will be effective.

The critical element in this definition is the lack of a human actor on one or both sides of a transaction. For example, if one orders books from Bookseller.com through Bookseller's website, the transaction would be an automated transaction because Bookseller took and confirmed the order via its machine. Similarly, if Automaker and supplier do business through Electronic Data Interchange, Automaker's computer, upon receiving information within certain pre-programmed parameters, will send an electronic order to supplier's computer. If Supplier's computer confirms the order and processes the shipment because the order falls within pre-programmed parameters in Supplier's computer, this would be a fully automated transaction. If, instead, the Supplier relies on a human employee to review, accept, and process the Buyer's order, then only the Automaker's side of the transaction would be automated. In either case, the entire transaction falls within this definition.

. . .

4. **"Electronic."** The basic nature of most current technologies and the need for a recognized, single term warrants the use of "electronic" as the defined term. The definition is intended to assure that the Act will be applied broadly as new technologies develop. While not all technologies listed are technically "electronic" in nature (e.g., optical fiber technology), the term "electronic" is the most descriptive term available to describe the majority of current technologies. For example, the development of biological and chemical processes for communication and storage of data, while not specifically mentioned in the definition, are included within the technical definition because such processes operate on electromagnetic impulses. However, whether a particular technology may be characterized as technically "electronic," i.e., operates on electromagnetic impulses, should not be determinative of whether records and signatures created, used and stored by means of a particular technology are covered by this Act. This Act is intended to apply to all records and signatures created, used and stored by any medium which permits the information to be retrieved in perceivable form.

5. **"Electronic agent."** This definition establishes that an electronic agent is a machine. As the term "electronic agent" has come to be recognized, it is limited to a tool function. . . .

An electronic agent, such as a computer program or other automated means employed by a person, is a tool of that person. As a general rule, the employer of a tool is responsible for the results obtained by the use of that tool since the tool has no independent volition of its own. However, an electronic agent, by definition, is capable within the parameters of its programming, of initiating, responding or interacting with other parties or their electronic agents once it has been activated by a party, without further attention of that party.

While this Act proceeds on the paradigm that an electronic agent is capable of performing only within the technical strictures of its preset programming, it is conceivable that, within the useful life of this Act, electronic agents may be created with the ability to act autonomously, and not just automatically. That is, through developments in artificial intelligence, a computer may be able to "learn through experience, modify the instructions in their own programs, and even devise new instructions." Allen and Widdison, *Can Computers Make Contracts?* 9 HARV. J.L. & TECH 25 (Winter, 1996). If such developments occur, courts may construe the definition of electronic agent accordingly, in order to recognize such new capabilities.

. . .

Electronic Signatures in Global and National Commerce Act, §§ 101(h) & 106(3)
15 U.S.C. §§ 7001(h) & 7006(3).

SEC. 101. GENERAL RULE OF VALIDITY

. . .

(h) Electronic agents. A contract or other record relating to a transaction in or affecting interstate or foreign commerce may not be denied legal effect, validity, or enforceability solely because its formation, creation, or delivery involved the action of one or more electronic agents so long as the action of any such electronic agent is legally attributable to the person to be bound.

. . .

SEC. 106. DEFINITIONS

. . .

(3) Electronic agent. The term "electronic agent" means a computer program or an electronic or other automated means used independently to initiate an action or respond to electronic records or performances in whole or in part without review or action by an individual at the time of the action or response.

2. Implementing Automated Contracting

Margaret Jane Radin, *Humans, Computers, and Binding Commitment*
75 INDIANA L.J. 1125 (2000).

. . .

By machine-made contract, I am referring to a loose category of transactions that are structured in the first instance by machines, with the humans in the background at some remove. Strictly speaking, it is a machine-implemented transactional structure when I use my personal computer to click on a box on my screen which then registers with a server computer somewhere else. I am dubbing transactional structures (whether or not contractual is a question to be answered) machine-made, however, only if the human pushing the key is not so directly involved. Machine-made contract in this sense falls into two broad categories: computers as electronic "agents," and computers as electronic enforcers.

1. Electronic "Agents"

In this category of machine-made contract, the idea is that two computers (rather than two humans, or one human and one computer) "negotiate" with each other and arrive at "agreement" with each other. Using the term "agency" in the locution "electronic agency" has become common, so I am adopting the usage, but before proceeding I want to register a caveat. The terms should seem peculiar in this context. When a computer does something "for" me that I have allowed it to be programmed to do, it is only an "agent" in a mechanical sense; it carries out the instructions of the program automatically so I will not have to do it manually. The term "agent" means something else when we are considering human "agency." Human "agency" refers to the freedom of autonomous beings. Human "agency" figures prominently in the traditional picture of contract-as-consent: it takes a human "agent" to be able to give voluntary consent. The law of "agency," which developed to cover situations in which one human delegated tasks to another, perhaps partakes of both senses; but no "agent" in a "principal-agent" relationship could be in the mechanized relationship that one who causes a computer to run a program is with that computer's activities. Use of the term "electronic agent" runs together these meanings and may cause us not to see how the issue of consent is being submerged or metamorphosed.

Right now, the computer-to-computer electronic agent scenario is primarily being developed in industrial procurement and general supply-chain management. In the generation following Electronic Data Interchange ("EDI")—a set of protocols developed in the 1980s for information sharing between trading partners—both extranets and the Web are being used to couple the vast power of digital automation with principles of just-in-time manufacture and distribution. In this form of industrial organization, many repetitive tasks are or will be accomplished by machine. Among these tasks are ordering and paying for supplies that are routinely needed at certain points in a process. The ordering, delivery, and payment for such supplies means that there are contractual terms surrounding the transaction—the time of delivery, what to do if the supplies do not arrive in time or are defective, what to do if the payment is late, and all the other transactional parameters that people contract about. All of this can in principle be handled primarily by machine, using computer programs that "negotiate" with each other and enter into "agreements" with each other.

Although automated supply-chain management is in the vanguard of the form of machine-made contract I have (reluctantly) designated electronic agency, in the near future these machine-made contracts may well become very widespread. Electronic agents may shop for us, organize our homes and offices for us, and so on.

2. Electronic Enforcers

In the second category of machine-made contract, known as digital rights management systems or trusted systems, computer programs enforce the terms of a transfer of digital content. The system is "trusted" (more trustworthy than a human) because it is technologically incapable of deviating from the instructions it is given. Those instructions may be, for example, to enforce a thirty-day license by erasing the content from the licensee's machine when the thirty days are up; or to enforce a restriction against copying either by preventing the copy from being made or by erasing the content from the licensee's machine if copying is attempted. Such detailed self-enforcement mechanisms will likely be a significant aspect of the human/computer interface for electronic commerce. They are viewed with alarm by some, but welcomed by others whose vision of anarchic self-ordering in cyberspace includes widespread technological self-enforcement.

. . .

B. Precursors to Machine-Made Contracts

1. The Electronic Agent Scenario

Earlier I described one kind of machine-made contract, an artifact of an automated industrial procurement process in which one firm's machine "negotiates" and "agrees" with another's. At first glance, this situation may look something like the classic "battle of the forms." The "battle" arises where buyer's purchase order, dispatched by one human "agent" for the buyer, has one set of fine-print terms, and seller's invoice, dispatched by a human "agent" for the seller, has another. Always recalling my earlier caveat about the slippage in the meaning of the term "agency," we can see that using electronic agents in the manner envisioned is not quite like the "battle of the forms." In fact, machines can often do better at resolving the battle than humans have done. Suppose machine A, for the seller, runs a program that can accept terms one, two, and three, and machine B, for the buyer, runs a program that can accept terms three, four, and five. Then the machines can "agree" to a term that both parties have approved, namely term three. (Of course, we are now assuming that permitting a computer under one's supervision to run a program that accepts term three counts as "approving" that term; that is a question we will have to investigate later.)

Once we are past the initial simple scenario, the machine-to-machine context leads to difficulties. If machine A accepts terms one, two, and three while machine B accepts terms two, three, and four, the programs would need priority rules for deciding whether to "agree" to two or three. The programs would also have to agree on those priority rules, or at least find a way to have each system of priority rules arrive at the same result. More important, a human "agent" often would want to agree to two only if one is also agreed to. Generally, the individual terms in a set are interdependent; it is the entire set of terms that matters economically. (That is, I might accept a shorter warranty, but only if the price is also lowered.)

Once we realize that it is the entire set of terms that matters, we realize that machine A is likely to be programmed with one or more sets of terms so that it will only do business with machine Bs that are programmed with at least one set of terms in common. This likelihood is one reason to think that standardized sets of terms may become quite prevalent in the digital world. . . .

The capability of machines in resolving some of the battles of the past over terms may put off the point at which human judgment is required. At some point, however, machine capability comes to an end, and we must tackle the difficult job of programming machines to "know" when they must stop and summon a human to exercise human judgment. Consider the situation if sets of terms in the commercial environment are incompletely standardized. Suppose that machine A, programmed with a set of terms M (containing 100 terms including z), encounters machine B programmed with the set of terms M' (containing 99 identical terms but z' instead of z). In that case, since computers are literal-minded, machine A would not accept machine B's terms. But a human might see immediately that the deal should still be made, because the choice between z and z' is unimportant.

It might not solve the problem simply to program machine A to accept terms that are close enough, say ninety-nine percent the same, because the other one percent could always be a doubling of the price or a waiver of intellectual property rights, and machine A will not "know" that unless it can be programmed to "know." Perhaps it could be programmed to deal with all known variants of terms like z that have extant variants. Instead, machine A could perhaps be programmed to alert a human (let out a beep or put a dialogue box on the screen) in the event it encounters set M'. If not, it will probably have to do this at some point, such as when it encounters an unknown variant, unless encounters with unknown terms simply void the deal.

The broader notion of replacing human "agents" with electronic agents will give rise to new problems, or at least new perspectives on old ones. Consider the practice of employing a personal shopper for gifts, or a (human) agent to purchase art for a collection. The human agent can be empowered to make binding purchases for me without my consent to each purchase. It will be more difficult to program a computer to make judgments about what will fit in my collection and what will not, and how it will "know" when it needs to get my approval on a specific item which might be borderline. The kinds of transactional safeguards that will be needed will be different. Fooling a computer is a different sort of operation than defrauding a human. Computers are more easily fooled in many ways. They do not know when you are joking, or when you meant 100 even though you typed 1000. They do not know when a painting is genuine. On the other hand, they are less easily fooled in some other ways—they make fewer errors in mathematics, for example. They are more "trusted" than humans—they do not embezzle, for example. Although the system may crash, a computer—except in science fiction—will not embark on a frolic of its own.

2. Electronic Enforcers

The imposition of terms by a rights management system may resist assimilation to the category of contractual arrangements. Such a system is a faithful "agent" for the purveyor of content, of course, because it makes the content available to the user only on the terms it is programmed to enforce. But a big difference between this arrangement and a contract between the purveyor and a recipient is that contracts can be breached. In many contemporary economic interpretations of contract, the legal system must expect (and welcome) breach when it is efficient under the circumstances. Our system also contemplates breach when the user wants to exercise a citizen's right to test the legality of the terms. When legality is tested, the state (on behalf of the community) passes on the acceptability of the terms, creating a check on what kinds of terms can be implemented. Thus, self-enforcement is not the same as enforcement by a court. The assimilation to contract seems at first glance inapposite; rather, technological management systems look like a species of technological self-help, less like legal enforcement than like sending over a committee of one's friends to intimidate a storekeeper into paying a debt.

On second thought, the buyer's decision to purchase content on the terms enforced by such a system could possibly be construed as contractual. The decision could be understood to mean that the buyer is choosing to use such a system and accepts its consequences. Under the contract-as-product model, the enforcement system is merely a feature of the product, no less than the quality of the content or the length of term for which it is licensed. Yet even under the contract-as-product model, the notion of choice is still present: in order for the buyer to "choose" to purchase the product including the self-enforcement system, the buyer would at least have to know that the enforcement system was in operation and know its possible consequences; other sources of the content without such an enforcement system attached might, depending on the context, also be required for the buyer to be "choosing" to accept such a system. The context to be investigated would include the importance of acquiring the content (for example, is it medical information whose withholding would be life-threatening?) and whether the system is imposed through market power rather than competitive forces. Yet, viewing the transaction from the contract-as-consent model, it looks like a contract in which the buyer cannot purchase the product unless he "agrees" to waive all of his legal enforcement rights in favor of technological self-help at the will of the other party. Even though contracts deviating from the standard picture of autonomous consent are common in the offline world, it is hard to think of any valid contracts in practice in which buyers are held to have entered into such a blanket waiver.

. . .

Stephen T. Middlebrook & John Muller, *Thoughts on Bots: The Emerging Law of Electronic Agents*
56 BUS. LAW. 341 (2000).

. . .

AN INTRODUCTION TO BOTS

Bot is not a rigorously defined term. It is, as you may have guessed, a shortened form of the word robot. Bots are like robots for the Internet, constructed of software, however, rather than hardware. They roam cyberspace accomplishing whatever tasks their masters have set for them. Bot refers to a broad range of software which is frequently divided into narrower, but still imprecisely delineated categories. Consequently, one may read about web crawlers, spiders, worms, shopping bots, aggregators, and myriad other specialized bots. Computer science literature sometimes refers to bots as "autonomous agents" or "intelligent agents." In fact, one commentator has said that "[t]he term bot has become interchangeable with agent." When used in these contexts, the term "agent" is not meant to suggest that the parties involved share the legal relationship of agency but rather connotes the more general idea that the software does what one tells it to do; i.e., it's a bot. The nomenclature is further confused by several recently enacted pieces of legislation which use the term "electronic agent" again to refer to software intermediaries which may or may not legally be agents. In this Article, we will avoid using terms which incorporate the word "agent" to describe bots because they, by their very terms, confuse the fundamental issue of whether a bot should also be deemed to be an "agent" under the law. The legal characterization of a particular bot must be based upon a careful analysis of what the bot does and how it operates and should not be influenced by how software developers or Internet companies choose to label their creations.

In light of the caveats about nomenclature made above, one way to begin to understand what is meant by the term "bot" is to look at some examples. The following types of software are examples of some of the many types of software that are generally considered by the Internet community to be bots:

Web Crawlers. Software which indexes key words on a web page and then moves to each additional web page linked to from the starting page. The web crawler then indexes keywords on each of the newly found web pages and then moves on to every web page linked to from those web pages, ultimately locating and indexing millions of web pages. Bots operating in roughly this fashion are used to create the indexes upon which Internet search engines are built.

Data Mining Bots. Software similar to the bots described above, but whose purpose is not to index each web page found, but rather to gather a certain type of data from each web page. Several corporations are using bots of this type to scan the web for infringing use of copyrighted or trademarked materials. The Securities and Exchange Commission (SEC) has announced its intention to use a bot of this type to search web sites, message boards, and chat rooms for evidence of stock manipulation and fraud.

Online Auction Services. Web sites which enable buyers and sellers to find each other and negotiate a price for a particular piece of merchandise. While still thought of mostly as a consumer-oriented service offering beanie babies, movie memorabilia, and other collector's items, there are a growing number of auction sites designed to foster business-to-business (B2B) transactions.

Online Retailers. Web sites which allow customers to browse an online catalog of products, place orders for selected merchandise, and arrange for delivery. While bookseller Amazon.com is the archetype of the online retailer, there is now a bounty of web sites selling a vast array of merchandise. One can now even order groceries online.

Metasearch Engines. Because they use different bots to index the web, different search engines may provide different search results to the same query. A meta-search engine queries a number of search engines and then presents the combined output to the user.

Person-To-Person Payment Systems. Especially popular with auction enthusiasts, these bots allow individuals to transfer money between each other through various methods, usually including credit cards and electronic funds transfer.

Viruses. While the bots described above are all intended to have a benevolent purpose, there is no reason to believe that a bot, whether as a result of the negligence of poor programming or the malice of wrong doers, cannot have a destructive purpose. Software which surreptitiously spreads itself across the Internet sending out fake email messages and erasing hard disks is as much a bot as its cousins which are indexing the web and enabling e-commerce.

What is it about the software described above that elevates it to the status of bot? Again, there is no definitive answer to this question. Professors Stan Franklin and Art Graesser, however, have compiled a list of attributes which they use to determine when software is behaving like an "autonomous agent."[35] We have adapted their list in order to construct the following table of properties which, when present in a piece of software, suggest that the software operates as a bot:

Property	Description
Reactive	Reacts to changes in the environment
Autonomous	Exercises control over its own actions
Goal-oriented	Seeks purposeful activity
Temporally Continuous	Is a continually running process
Communicative	Communicates with people and other bots
Learning	Changes its behavior based on past experience
Mobile	Transports itself from one machine to another

As a general matter, the bots described above tend to reflect most, if not all, of these properties.

There is no government agency or international standards organization which oversees the bot industry and consequently there are no comprehensive regulations. There are, however, social conventions adhered to by most programmers which dictate how the "well-behaved" bot should act. Of particular interest is a convention that has come to be known as the Standard for Robot Exclusion (SRE). The SRE establishes a voluntary process through which web masters may exclude bots from designated portions of their web sites. Specifically, the SRE sets out how a web site owner, by creating special files on his server or including certain code in his web pages, may dictate which bots may access his web site and what they may

---

[35] Stan Franklin & Art Graesser, *Is it an Agent, or Just a Program? A Taxonomy for Autonomous Agents*, in Third International Workshop on Agent Theories, Architectures, and Languages 4 (1996), www.msci.memphis.edu/franklin/AgentProg.html.

view when they visit. Not all bots, however, are SRE compliant and adherence to the standard is strictly voluntary. Consequently, while there exists a "gentleman's agreement" as to how bots should operate, there are no rules which can be enforced through public or private means. In the absence of any controlling regulatory scheme, parties who believe they have been harmed by bots are attempting to use tort law to protect themselves. . . .

. . .

COMMON LAW PRINCIPLES OF AGENCY GOVERNING BOTS

While the recent enactments of E-SIGN at the federal level and various permutations of UETA at the state level create a framework in which contracts may be created electronically and parties may be bound by the contracts ratified by their electronic agents, these new laws do not tell us much about the relationship between an individual and the bot acting on his or her behalf. Questions of scope of authority, liability for failure to act, or the consequences of the bot committing a tort while acting on the behalf of another receive minimal treatment in the statutes. Given that we would turn to the law of agency in order to understand the relationship between a person and a human servant, it seems prudent to look to the same body of law to inform, although perhaps not to govern absolutely, the relationships between people and their software servants. This conclusion is especially appropriate to the legal analysis surrounding the use of software robots in electronic commerce because the law of agency is, at its heart, a tool by which society fosters economic growth and innovation.

> Although the agency relation may exist without reference to mercantile affairs, as in the case of domestic servants, its primary function in modern life is to make possible the commercial enterprises which could not exist otherwise. The common law has properly been responsive to the needs of commerce, permitting what older systems of law denied, namely a direct relation between the principal and a third person with whom the agent deals, even when the principal is undisclosed.[65]

Agency law should remain responsive to the economic needs of society and thus mold and adapt itself to the new requirements of modern electronic commerce.

A REVIEW OF AGENCY LAW PRINCIPLES

Agency, as defined in the *Restatement (Second) of Agency,* is the legal term for the relationship between two parties wherein one party, with the consent of the other, agrees to act on the behalf of and under the control of the other party. The one for whom the action is to be taken is called "the principal" while the person who is to act is deemed "the agent." Agency is wholly a legal concept which exists when the elements of the relationship are present and which is not dependant upon the parties' desire to enter into, or knowledge of, the agency relationship. While there must be agreement between principal and agent, there need not be a contract and consideration is not a requirement. The agent is said to hold certain powers on be-

---

[65] RESTATEMENT (SECOND) OF AGENCY § 8A cmt. a (1958).

half of the principal. Power in this context is defined as the ability to produce a change in a given legal relation by performing or not performing a given act. In most instances, an agent's power is to modify the legal relations between the principal and a third party, although in certain situations, the agent's power may allow him to modify his own relationship with the principal. A related concept in agency law is that of "authority," which is the power of an agent to bind the principal by acts done in accordance with the principal's manifestations of consent. Thus, an agent who, at the direction of the principal, enters into a contract on behalf of that principal is said to be acting under authority. If the agent were to enter into a contract on behalf of a principal but without the principal's explicit consent, agency law might still find that the agent's actions bind the principal, but the source of the agent's power would derive from something other than authority. Sources of power other than authority include apparent authority, estoppel, and inherent agency power.[73] Under section 26 of the Restatement, authority can be granted through written or oral instructions, and may also be created when the principal's conduct, reasonably interpreted, causes the agent to believe that the principal desires him to act on the principal's behalf.

When an agent acts consistent with his authority, "he has power to affect the legal relations of the principal to the same extent as if the principal had so acted."[75] Consequently, when a third party enters into a contract with a duly authorized agent, the third party may later enforce that contract against the principal. . . .

. . .

AN EXAMPLE OF AGENCY LAW ANALYSIS OF A BOT — PROXY BIDDING ON eBAY

In order to explore the application of agency law to the world of bots and their functions in electronic commerce, we will look at one aspect of a common online commercial transaction involving a bot, namely, proxy bidding on the online auction service eBay.[87] Let's suppose that our bidder has found a large, turn of the century Navajo rug for sale on eBay. The current bid is $500 and, in this price range, bids must be made in increments of $10. Because the rug is finely woven with an intricate pattern and is in excellent condition with minimal moth damage, our bidder is willing to pay up to $750 to acquire it. He enters his maximum bid of $750 along with his user id and password on the bidding screens. eBay processes the bid through its proxy bidding system, which it explains as follows:

> Our bidding system operates as a proxy bid system. This means that a bidder can submit a maximum bid amount and our system will act as a proxy bidder in their absence, executing their bid for them and trying to keep the bid price as low as possible. This way a bidder doesn't have to be at the auction every minute.

---

[73] *Id.* [§ 7]. For an explanation of how power deriving from authority differs from power deriving from apparent authority, estoppel, or inherent agency power, *see id.* § 7 cmt. a.

[75] *Id.* § 12 cmt. a.

[87] <http://www.ebay.com>.

An easier way to think of this would be to think of the bidding system standing in for you as a bidder at a live auction. Let's say you need to be somewhere and can't be present to bid and you ask a friend to go to the auction and bid for you. You tell your friend that you are willing to pay $25 for an item you saw.

The auctioneer starts the bidding at $5 and your friend bids the $5. Then another bidder bids $6 and your friend then bids $7 on your behalf. Then another bidder bids $12 and your friend bids $13 for you. This would keep going until either your friend wins the item for you at or below $25 or the bidding exceeds the $25 you were willing to pay.

At eBay, the proxy bidding system is your friend. This system stands in for you and bids for you against other bidders until either you have won the item at or below the price you set or until another bidder bids higher than the amount you set.

Under the proxy bidding system, eBay accepts our bidder's maximum bid of $750, but initially only bids the $510 necessary to be high bidder. Later that day, another collector of Native American art sees the rug on eBay and bids his maximum of $600 for the item. Following the rules of proxy bidding, eBay raises our bidder's offer to $610 in order to maintain his status as high bidder. The auction closes shortly thereafter and our bidder wins the auction at a final price of $610.

An analysis of the events which leads to our bidder acquiring a wonderful Navajo rug for $610, coupled with eBay's own explanation of the process, inevitably leads to the conclusion that eBay, acting through its automated proxy bidding software, is in a legal sense our bidder's agent.[89] Following eBay's own explanation of the system, it is standing in for the bidder at the auction, bidding on his behalf against other bidders until the point where either he has won the item or the price exceeds the maximum set by our bidder. The relationship between our bidder and eBay clearly falls within the dictates of the Restatement. While eBay does not charge the bidder for its services, placing all the fees upon the seller, consideration is not necessary for an agency relationship to exist. Because agency law binds the principal to the actions of his agent, should our bidder win the auction in which his bids are placed by eBay's proxy bidding system, he would be legally obligated to complete the transaction with the seller.

There is also a clear delegation of authority in compliance with section 17 of the Restatement when our bidder enters his maximum bid amount, user id, and password on the bidding screens and clicks the "place bid" button. Entering this information on the bidding screens and clicking on the appropriate buttons constitutes conduct which eBay can reasonably interpret to mean that our bidder wishes for eBay to act on his behalf. In addition, under the recently enacted ESIGN, our bidder's actions may arguably be viewed as a signed, written authorization to eBay

---

[89] A secondary issue is whether eBay, as the seller's agent, is an "auctioneer" as that term may be defined under state law. An auctioneer, while a type of agent, holds a special relationship with regard to both buyers and sellers and is subject to special rules and regulations. Several State Attorneys General have raised the question of whether eBay constitutes an auctioneer under state law. The issue is not currently resolved. . . .

to bid up to $750 on the rug. Either way, it is clear that our bidder has instructed eBay to act as his agent, setting out the scope of the authority, and that eBay has consented to be his agent. In fact, eBay is acting as the agent of all of the individuals bidding on the rug. Moreover, eBay is also acting as the agent of the seller, making certain items available for sale, limiting bidding to a certain time period, enforcing a reserve minimum selling price, and otherwise acting under the direction of the seller.

If the bidder in our example had searched on eBay for pieces of Native American art to add to his collection, but found nothing that interested him and thus never made a purchase or even placed a bid, eBay would still be acting as his agent. Under the Restatement, a servant need not actually contract for the sale of an item on behalf of the principal to be deemed an agent.[93] Within a principal's authorization of an agent to buy or sell merchandise is the authorization to "find a seller or purchaser from whom or to whom the principal may buy or sell."[94] When our potential bidder entered the terms "navajo rugs" into eBay's search form, he was, for purposes of the Restatement, instructing eBay to find sellers of Navajo rugs from whom he might purchase. By acting on this request and returning a listing of such items currently offered for sale, eBay has become the potential bidder's agent. The scope of the agency at this time is limited to finding items matching the current request, but the authority may be expanded by entering a bid via the online auction service.

. . .

E. FORMALITIES OF CONTRACT FORMATION: WRITING AND SIGNATURE REQUIREMENTS

A great many statutes and regulatory provisions require that certain kinds of contracts be in writing, and signed, and that certain documents and records be in writing. As soon as we began a transition to widespread digitization, it became immediately apparent that the legal categories of written records and signatures had become problematic. Nowadays, many records exist only in digital form, and many deals are entered into by computer.

1. The Problem Posed by Digitization

For some time it was unclear to what extent e-mail deals and digital records could meet legal requirements involving writing and signature. For example, should your name in the signature block ("sig") of your e-mail message constitute binding commitment?

---

[93] RESTATEMENT (SECOND) OF AGENCY § 53(a).

[94] *Id.*

Can e-mail seal a sales deal? *Shattuck v. Klotzbach*
Nikoletta Banushi, Globe Correspondent
BOSTON GLOBE (Mar. 16, 2002), at E1.

Buyers beware, and sellers, too—especially if you communicate with each other by e-mail.

A pretrial decision by a judge in a dispute over a multimillion-dollar home in Marion could end up making real estate deals outlined in e-mail as binding as those put on paper.

The case, *Shattuck v. Klotzbach*, is scheduled to be heard in May in Plymouth Superior Court by Judge Ernest B. Murphy.

The plaintiff, Jonathan P. Shattuck, alleges breach of contract. Last year, he thought he had a deal to buy the house at 5 Main St. in Marion for $1.825 million.

But in September, six months after he began negotiating with Shattuck, defendant David K. Klotzbach backed away from selling his house.

Using e-mail, Shattuck and Klotzbach had settled on the price; the e-mail referred to the purchase and sale agreement that would be prepared.

All the e-mails exchanged by the two parties ended with the "typewritten" names of the senders, according to the judge's decision in which he refused to throw out the case.

That's a crucial point, the judge ruled.

When Shattuck tried to enforce the contract he thought he had, Klotzbach and his lawyers argued that the e-mails were not signed documents, and that there was no binding contract. They sought to have the suit dismissed.

But on Dec. 11, Judge Murphy decided the e-mails, taken together, constituted a legally binding purchase and sale agreement that outlined all the necessary terms of the contract.

Klotzbach had also argued that even if the e-mails bound him, they did not bind the other owner of the house, his wife, Barbara W. Klotzbach, because she had not signed the e-mails.

The judge, though, wrote that "the correspondences suggest that the defendant-wife was aware of the ongoing negotiations concerning the sale of the property. Thus, a reasonable trier of fact could conclude that the defendant-husband's signature on the memorandum acted as a signature of both defendants . . ."

Kevin Clancy, one of the attorneys representing the Klotzbachs, declined to comment.

But Michael J. McGlone, who represents the plaintiff, said Klotzbach and his wife were negotiating to sell to other buyers for $1.96 million—even though they had already agreed to sell to Shattuck for $1.825 million.

And according to the judge's decision not to dismiss the case, the defendant had used e-mail to tell Shattuck this:

"Once we sign the P&S we'd like to close ASAP. You may have your attorney send the P&S and deposit check for 10% of purchase price ($182,500) to my attorney."

The e-mail concluded by saying, "I'm looking forward to closing and seeing you as the owner of '5 Main Street,' the prettiest spot in Marion village."

Said Beth Mitchell, a partner in the Boston law firm Nutter McClennen & Fish who manages its real estate department:

"I think what this case is saying is if you exchange e-mails about the terms of sale — even if you think later you're going to put it all down on paper so you're going to have a more thought-out comprehensive document — you may find you're bound, even though you haven't signed anything.

"I think it's a warning to people that other courts might view this the same way. They better take more care in what they put in their e-mails than what they did before."

Klotzbach may have entered into a binding contract without realizing it, though, said David Drinkwater, president of the Massachusetts Association of Realtors.

"In this case, the seller probably thought what was said in the e-mails wasn't legally binding, but through the court's observation, he intended to make this sale."

"This is the first time in Massachusetts that e-mail communication is sufficient to form a contract," added Philip Lapatin, legal counsel to the Greater Boston Real Estate Board.

"The court just took it one step further in terms of what a signature is."

The decision raises important issues, because people may be using e-mail to communicate at a quicker pace — and increasing the risk of legal complications.

Allowing people to make a legally binding contract with as much ease as the sending of an e-mail may not be in consumers' best interests, some say.

"One of the very unfortunate things about this is that by allowing consumers to casually enter into what might be the most legally important transaction of their life, consumers are not benefited," Lapatin said.

"Even though e-mail is in writing, most people still think of e-mail as an informal form of communicating," he said. "Now the court is saying that it is now a binding document."

"The process of buying and selling is a very personal one," Drinkwater said. "In doing so, they [buyers and sellers] should be seeking the help of someone who does this for a living."

. . .

2. UETA and ESIGN: Legislative Enablement of Electronic Records and Signatures

Authentication is one of the central issues facing contract law in Internet commerce. Forgery is easier in the digital environment than with paper documents, since, in the offline world, there might be witnesses who can vouch for a document's genuineness. When one party seeks to enforce a claimed agreement, and the other party denies any obligation, it becomes necessary to pin down the operative facts about the transaction: whether a bargain was actually entered into, and if so who are the parties and what are the terms. (For example, if one party says the price was $10,000 and the other says the price was $100, we need to be able to know who is telling the truth about the number of zeros.)

The English statute of frauds provided that contracts for the sale of land or for sale of goods over a certain value would be invalid unless in writing, signed, and sealed (bearing the imprint of a seal). The seal requirement gradually fell away, but statutes of frauds still exist, in a variety of contexts. These statutes make a great many contracts unenforceable unless in writing and signed by the party to be charged. What is the fate of the statute of frauds in the digital environment?

Electronic authentication schemes function, among other things, to enable online contracting by granting legal significance to digital signatures in situations where physical signatures otherwise would be required.

In this section we take a look at the central provisions of two electronic contracting statutes, the Uniform Electronic Transactions Act and the Electronic Signatures in Global and National Commerce Act. These acts do not determine what renders digital records and signatures sufficiently reliable to be legally acceptable. Nor do they solve the problem of how to render electronic records and signatures commercially trustworthy. Instead, both acts simply state that electronic records and signatures may not be denied legal effect solely because they are electronic.

a. The Uniform Electronic Transactions Act

Uniform Electronic Transactions Act, §§ 2(4), 2(5), 2(7), 2(8), 2(16), 3, 5 & 7
National Conference of Commissioners on Uniform State Laws (1999).

SECTION 2. DEFINITIONS.

In this [Act]:

. . .

(4) "Contract" means the total legal obligation resulting from the parties' agreement as affected by this [Act] and other applicable law.

(5) "Electronic" means relating to technology having electrical, digital, magnetic, wireless, optical, electromagnetic, or similar capabilities.

. . .

(7) "Electronic record" means a record created, generated, sent, communicated, received, or stored by electronic means.

(8) "Electronic signature" means an electronic sound, symbol, or process at-

tached to or logically associated with a record and executed or adopted by a person with the intent to sign the record.

. . .

(16) "Transaction" means an action or set of actions occurring between two or more persons relating to the conduct of business, commercial, or governmental affairs.

SECTION 3. SCOPE.

(a) Except as otherwise provided in subsection (b), this [Act] applies to electronic records and electronic signatures relating to a transaction.

(b) This [Act] does not apply to a transaction to the extent it is governed by:

(1) a law governing the creation and execution of wills, codicils, or testamentary trusts;

(2) [The Uniform Commercial Code other than Sections 1–107 and 1–206, Article 2, and Article 2A];

(3) [the Uniform Computer Information Transactions Act]; and

(4) [other laws, if any, identified by State].

(c) This [Act] applies to an electronic record or electronic signature otherwise excluded from the application of this [Act] under subsection (b) to the extent it is governed by a law other than those specified in subsection (b).

(d) A transaction subject to this [Act] is also subject to other applicable substantive law.

Comment

1. The scope of this Act is inherently limited by the fact that it only applies to transactions related to business, commercial (including consumer) and governmental matters. . . .

. . .

4. . . . Paragraph [b](2) excludes all of the Uniform Commercial Code other than UCC Sections 1–107 and 1–206, and Articles 2 and 2A. This Act does not apply to the excluded UCC articles, whether in "current" or "revised" form. The Act does apply to UCC Articles 2 and 2A and to UCC Sections 1–107 and 1–206.

5. Articles 3, 4 and 4A of the UCC impact payment systems and have specifically been removed from the coverage of this Act. . . .

. . .

7. This Act does apply, *in toto*, to transactions under unrevised Articles 2 and 2A. There is every reason to validate electronic contracting in these situations. Sale and lease transactions do not implicate broad systems beyond the parties to the underlying transaction, such as are present in check collection and electronic funds transfers. Further sales and leases generally do not have as far reaching effect on the rights of third parties beyond the contracting parties, such as exists in the se-

cured transactions system. Finally, it is in the area of sales, licenses and leases that electronic commerce is occurring to its greatest extent today. To exclude these transactions would largely gut the purpose of this Act.

In the event that Articles 2 and 2A are revised and adopted in the future, UETA will only apply to the extent provided in those Acts.

. . .

SECTION 5. USE OF ELECTRONIC RECORDS AND ELECTRONIC SIGNATURES; VARIATION BY AGREEMENT.

(a) This [Act] does not require a record or signature to be created, generated, sent, communicated, received, stored, or otherwise processed or used by electronic means or in electronic form.

(b) This [Act] applies only to transactions between parties each of which has agreed to conduct transactions by electronic means. Whether the parties agree to conduct a transaction by electronic means is determined from the context and surrounding circumstances, including the parties' conduct.

. . .

SECTION 7. LEGAL RECOGNITION OF ELECTRONIC RECORDS, ELECTRONIC SIGNATURES, AND ELECTRONIC CONTRACTS.

(a) A record or signature may not be denied legal effect or enforceability solely because it is in electronic form.

(b) A contract may not be denied legal effect or enforceability solely because an electronic record was used in its formation.

(c) If a law requires a record to be in writing, an electronic record satisfies the law.

(d) If a law requires a signature, an electronic signature satisfies the law.

Comment

1. This section sets forth the fundamental premise of this Act: namely, that the medium in which a record, signature, or contract is created, presented or retained does not affect its legal significance. . . .

. . .

Uniform Electronic Transactions Act, Prefatory Note
National Conference of Commissioners on Uniform State Laws (1999).

With the advent of electronic means of communication and information transfer, business models and methods for doing business have evolved to take advantage of the speed, efficiencies, and cost benefits of electronic technologies. These developments have occurred in the face of existing legal barriers to the legal efficacy of records and documents which exist solely in electronic media. Whether the legal requirement that information or an agreement or contract must be contained or set forth in a pen and paper writing derives from a statute of frauds affecting the enforceability of an agreement, or from a record retention statute that calls for keeping the paper record of a transaction, such legal requirements raise real barriers to the effective use of electronic media.

. . .

It is important to understand that the purpose of the UETA is to remove barriers to electronic commerce by validating and effectuating electronic records and signatures. It is NOT a general contracting statute—the substantive rules of contracts remain unaffected by UETA. Nor is it a digital signature statute. To the extent that a State has a Digital Signature Law, the UETA is designed to support and compliment that statute.

A. Scope of the Act and Procedural Approach. The scope of this Act provides coverage which sets forth a clear framework for covered transactions, and also avoids unwarranted surprises for unsophisticated parties dealing in this relatively new media. The clarity and certainty of the scope of the Act have been obtained while still providing a solid legal framework that allows for the continued development of innovative technology to facilitate electronic transactions.

Finally, recognition that the paradigm for the Act involves two willing parties conducting a transaction electronically, makes it necessary to expressly provide that some form of acquiescence or intent on the part of a person to conduct transactions electronically is necessary before the Act can be invoked. Accordingly, Section 5 specifically provides that the Act only applies between parties that have agreed to conduct transactions electronically. In this context, the construction of the term agreement must be broad in order to assure that the Act applies whenever the circumstances show the parties intention to transact electronically, regardless of whether the intent rises to the level of a formal agreement.

B. Procedural Approach. Another fundamental premise of the Act is that it be minimalist and procedural. The general efficacy of existing law in an electronic context, so long as biases and barriers to the medium are removed, validates this approach. The Act defers to existing substantive law. . . .

. . .

b. The Electronic Signatures in Global and National Commerce Act

Electronic Signatures in Global and National Commerce Act, §§ 101, 106(13)
15 U.S.C. §§ 7001, 7006(13).

SEC. 101. GENERAL RULE OF VALIDITY

(a) **In general.**—Notwithstanding any statute, regulation, or other rule of law (other than this title and title II), with respect to any transaction in or affecting interstate or foreign commerce—

(1) a signature, contract, or other record relating to such transaction may not

be denied legal effect, validity, or enforceability solely because it is in electronic form; and

(2) a contract relating to such transaction may not be denied legal effect, validity, or enforceability solely because an electronic signature or electronic record was used in its formation.

(b) Preservation of rights and obligations. — This subchapter does not —

(1) limit, alter, or otherwise affect any requirement imposed by a statute, regulation, or rule of law relating to the rights and obligations of persons under such statute, regulation, or rule of law other than a requirement that contracts or other records be written, signed, or in nonelectronic form; or

(2) require any person to agree to use or accept electronic records o electronic signatures, other than a governmental agency with respect to a record other than a contract to which it is a party.

SEC. 106. DEFINITIONS

[ESIGN uses the same definitions as UETA for the terms "electronic," "electronic record," and "electronic signature," set forth *supra*. "Contract" is not defined in ESIGN.]

. . .

(13) Transaction. The term "transaction'" means an action or set of actions relating to the conduct of business, consumer, or commercial affairs between two or more persons, including any of the following types of conduct —

(A) the sale, lease, exchange, licensing, or other disposition of (i) personal property, including goods and intangibles, (ii) services, and (iii) any combination thereof; and

(B) the sale, lease, exchange, or other disposition of any interest in real property, or any combination thereof.

. . .

Senate Report 106–131 to Accompany S. 761
Senate Committee on Commerce, Science, and Transportation (1999).
. . .

PURPOSE OF THE BILL[4]

The purpose of this legislation is to promote electronic commerce by providing a consistent national framework for electronic signatures and transactions.

---

[4] [The Report pertains to the Millennium Digital Commerce Act. This bill was the Senate's version of what ultimately was passed as the Electronic Signatures in Global and National Commerce Act. The final version of the act was agreed to in conference committee.—Eds.]

BACKGROUND AND NEEDS

. . . Presently . . . one of the greatest barriers to the growth of Internet commerce is the lack of consistent, national rules governing the use of electronic signatures. More than forty States have enacted electronic authentication laws, and no two of these laws are the same. This inconsistency deters businesses and consumers from using electronic signature technologies to authorize contracts or transactions.

Fortunately, the National Conference of Commissioners of Uniform State Laws (NCCUSL) is preparing a model State law that adapts existing commercial law to govern electronic commerce. This "Uniform Electronic Transactions Act" (UETA) will create a market-based, technology-neutral legal framework for electronic commerce. It is currently estimated that UETA will be finalized in July of this year.

The impending release of UETA confronts the Congress with a situation similar to that which arose when NCCUSL first released its Uniform Commercial Code (UCC). The release of the UCC began a process that eventually created a predictable regime of commercial law that was adopted by all the States. However, the UCC was not adopted everywhere simultaneously. There was a transition period in which commercial law remained unsettled as States reviewed the UCC, debated its merits, and enacted it into law.

Inevitably, a similar transition period will occur in the case of UETA. This legislation is intended to protect and foster commerce during this transition period by providing a predictable legal regime governing electronic signatures. . . .

. . .

. . .The legislation preempts State law that is inconsistent with UETA, and provides that the electronic records produced in the execution of a digital contract shall not be denied legal effect solely because they are electronic in nature. . . .

This Federal preemption of State law is designed to be an interim measure. It preempts State law until the State enacts uniform standards which are consistent with those contained in this legislation or the UETA. Once States enact the UETA or other legislation governing the use of electronic signatures which is consistent with the UETA, the Federal preemption is lifted. . . .

. . .

Electronic Signatures in Global and National Commerce Act, §§ 102, 103
15 U.S.C. §§ 7002, 7003.

SEC. 102. EXEMPTION TO PREEMPTION.

(a) In General.—A State statute, regulation, or other rule of law may modify, limit, or supersede the provisions of section 101 with respect to State law only if such statute, regulation, or rule of law—

(1) constitutes an enactment or adoption of the Uniform Electronic Transactions Act as approved and recommended for enactment in all the States by the National Conference of Commissioners on Uniform State Laws in 1999, except that any exception to the scope of such Act enacted by a State under section 3(b)(4) of such Act shall be preempted to the extent such exception is inconsistent with this title or title II, or would not be permitted under paragraph (2)(A)(ii) of this subsection; or

(2) (A) specifies the alternative procedures or requirements for the use or acceptance (or both) of electronic records or electronic signatures to establish the legal effect, validity, or enforceability of contracts or other records, if —

    (i) such alternative procedures or requirements are consistent with this title and title II; and

    (ii) such alternative procedures or requirements do not require, or accord greater legal status or effect to, the implementation or application of a specific technology or technical specification for performing the functions of creating, storing, generating, receiving, communicating, or authenticating electronic records or electronic signatures; and

(B) if enacted or adopted after the date of the enactment of this Act, makes specific reference to this Act.

SEC. 103. SPECIFIC EXCEPTIONS.

(a) Excepted Requirements. — The provisions of section 101 shall not apply to a contract or other record to the extent it is governed by —

(1) a statute, regulation, or other rule of law governing the creation and execution of wills, codicils, or testamentary trusts;

(2) a State statute, regulation, or other rule of law governing adoption, divorce, or other matters of family law; or

(3) the Uniform Commercial Code, as in effect in any State, other than sections 1–107 and 1–206 and Articles 2 and 2A.

(b) Additional Exceptions. — The provisions of section 101 shall not apply to —

(1) court orders or notices, or official court documents (including briefs, pleadings, and other writings) required to be executed in connection with court proceedings;

(2) any notice of —

    (A) the cancellation or termination of utility services (including water, heat, and power);

    (B) default, acceleration, repossession, foreclosure, or eviction, or the right to cure, under a credit agreement secured by, or a rental agreement for, a primary residence of an individual;

    (C) the cancellation or termination of health insurance or benefits or life insurance benefits (excluding annuities); or

    (D) recall of a product, or material failure of a product, that risks endangering health or safety; or

(3) any document required to accompany any transportation or handling of hazardous materials, pesticides, or other toxic or dangerous materials.

(c) Review of Exceptions.—

(1) Evaluation required.—The Secretary of Commerce, acting through the Assistant Secretary for Communications and Information, shall review the operation of the exceptions in subsections (a) and (b) to evaluate, over a period of 3 years, whether such exceptions continue to be necessary for the protection of consumers. Within 3 years after the date of enactment of this Act, the Assistant Secretary shall submit a report to the Congress on the results of such evaluation.

(2) Determinations.—If a Federal regulatory agency, with respect to matter within its jurisdiction, determines after notice and an opportunity for public comment, and publishes a finding, that one or more such exceptions are no longer necessary for the protection of consumers and eliminating such exceptions will not increase the material risk of harm to consumers, such agency may extend the application of section 101 to the exceptions identified in such finding.

EXTENSIONS

Adoptions of UETA. How many states have enacted UETA? *See* www.nccusl.org.

QUESTIONS FOR DISCUSSION

1. *Consumer protection.* Note the exemptions for certain consumer transactions in ESIGN. What do you think is the reason for them? *See* www.ftc.gov/os/2001/06/esign7.htm.

2. *Transition.* As we have seen, the legislative history of ESIGN states that it is intended to be transitional until UETA becomes the governing law. In light of the number of jurisdictions that have now enacted UETA, do you think that ESIGN is superseded and obsolete?

3. What Is a Signature? Why Is It Important?

Uniform Electronic Transactions Act, § 2(8)
National Conference of Commissioners on Uniform State Laws (1999).

SECTION 2. DEFINITIONS.

In this [Act]:

. . .

(8) "Electronic signature" means an electronic sound, symbol, or process attached to or logically associated with a record and executed or adopted by a person with the intent to sign the record.

Comment

. . .

7. **"Electronic signature."** The idea of a signature is broad and not specifically defined. Whether any particular record is "signed" is a question of fact. Proof of that fact must be made under other applicable law. This Act simply assures that the signature may be accomplished through electronic means. No specific technology need be used in order to create a valid signature. One's voice on an answering machine may suffice if the requisite intention is present. Similarly, including one's name as part of an electronic mail communication also may suffice, as may the firm name on a facsimile. It also may be shown that the requisite intent was not present and accordingly the symbol, sound or process did not amount to a signature. One may use a digital signature with the requisite intention, or one may use the private key solely as an access device with no intention to sign, or otherwise accomplish a legally binding act. In any case the critical element is the intention to execute or adopt the sound or symbol or process for the purpose of signing the related record.

The definition requires that the signer execute or adopt the sound, symbol, or process with the intent to sign the record. The act of applying a sound, symbol or process to an electronic record could have differing meanings and effects. The consequence of the act and the effect of the act as a signature are determined under other applicable law. However, the essential attribute of a signature involves applying a sound, symbol or process with an intent to do a legally significant act. It is that intention that is understood in the law as a part of the word "sign," without the need for a definition.

This Act establishes, to the greatest extent possible, the equivalency of electronic signatures and manual signatures. Therefore the term "signature" has been used to connote and convey that equivalency. The purpose is to overcome unwarranted biases against electronic methods of signing and authenticating records. The term "authentication," used in other laws, often has a narrower meaning and purpose than an electronic signature as used in this Act. However, an authentication under any of those other laws constitutes an electronic signature under this Act.

   . . .

This definition includes as an electronic signature the standard webpage click through process. . . .

Another important aspect of this definition lies in the necessity that the electronic signature be linked or logically associated with the record. In the paper world, it is assumed that the symbol adopted by a party is attached to or located somewhere in the same paper that is intended to be authenticated, e.g., an allonge[5] firmly attached to a promissory note, or the classic signature at the end of a long contract. These tangible manifestations do not exist in the electronic environment, and accordingly, this definition expressly provides that the symbol must in some way be linked to, or connected with, the electronic record being signed. . . .

A digital signature using public key encryption technology would qualify as an

---

[5] [An "allonge" is "[a] slip of paper sometimes attached to a negotiable instrument for the purpose of receiving further indorsements when the original paper is filled with indorsements." BLACK'S LAW DICTIONARY (7th ed. 1999).—Eds.]

electronic signature, as would the mere inclusion of one's name as a part of an e-mail message—so long as in each case the signer executed or adopted the symbol with the intent to sign.

. . .

Electronic Signatures in Global and National Commerce Act, § 106(5)
15 U.S.C. § 7006(5).

SEC. 106. DEFINITIONS.

. . .

(5) Electronic signature. The term "electronic signature" means an electronic sound, symbol, or process, attached to or logically associated with a contract or other record and executed or adopted by a person with the intent to sign the record.

4. Beyond Legislative Enablement: The Purpose and Requirements of Signatures and Authentication

Thomas J. Smedinghoff, *The Legal Requirements for Creating Secure and Enforceable Electronic Transactions* (2004)
www.bakernet.com/ecommerce/etransactionsarticle.pdf

. . .

3.2   Signature Requirements

Signatures can serve a variety of purposes in a transaction. The primary uses for a signature can be summarized as follows:

- *Expression of Intent*—A signature evidences the signer's intent with respect to the document signed. The nature of the signer's intent will vary with the transaction, and in most cases can be determined only by looking at the context in which the signature was made. A signature may, for example, signify an intent to be bound to the terms of a contract, the approval of a subordinate's request for funding of a project, authorization to a bank to transfer funds, confirmation that the signer has read and reviewed the contents of a memo, an indication that the signer was the author of a document, or merely that the contents of a document have been shown to the signer and that he or she has had an opportunity to review them.

- *Satisfaction of Legal Requirements*—A signature is often used to satisfy a law or regulation that requires the presence of a signature before the document will be considered legally effective. The statute of frauds (which requires contracts for the sale of goods in excess of $500 to be "signed") is, of course, the best example of such a law. In addition, however, thousands of other federal, state, and local statutes and regulations also require certain types of transactions to be documented by a writing and a signature.

- *Security*—Signatures often function as a security device. That is, signatures can be used (1) to authenticate a document (i.e., to identify the signer and indicate that such person is the source of, or has approved, the document), and/or (2) to ensure the integrity of the document (i.e., to ensure that the document has not been altered since it was signed).

Traditionally, under U.S. law, any *symbol* that is made with the *intent* to sign a document can qualify as a legally valid signature. Thus, for example, the definition of "signed" in the Uniform Commercial Code includes "any *symbol*" so long as it is "executed or adopted by a party with present *intention* to authenticate a writing." The primary focus is on the "intention to authenticate" a document, which distinguishes a signature from an autograph. Both E-SIGN and UETA extend this basic approach to the concept of an electronic signature. To be enforceable under U.S. law, they require that an electronic signature possess three elements:

- A sound, symbol, or process,

- Attached to or logically associated with an electronic record, and

- Made with the intent to sign the electronic record.

Electronic signatures that meet these requirements are considered legally enforceable as substitutes for handwritten signatures for most transactions in the U.S. The definition of electronic signature recognizes that there are many different methods by which one can "sign" an electronic record. Although electronic signatures, by their nature, are represented digitally (i.e., as a series of ones and zeroes) they can take many forms, and can be created by many different technologies. Examples of electronic signatures (that qualify under E-SIGN and UETA) include:

- A name typed at the end of an e-mail message by the sender;

- A digitized image of a handwritten signature that is attached to an electronic document (sometimes created via a biometrics-based technology called signature dynamics);

- A secret code, password, or PIN to identify the sender to the recipient (such as that used with ATM cards and credit cards);

- A unique biometrics-based identifier, such as a fingerprint, voice print, or a retinal scan;

- A mouse click (such as on an "I accept" button);

- A sound (e.g., the sound created by pressing "9" on your phone to agree); and

- A "digital signature" (created through the use of public key cryptography).

This is, of course, not an exhaustive list of methods by which one can electronically sign a document. There are other ways of signing an electronic document, and presumably many more will be developed in the future. However, all forms of electronic signature must satisfy the three requirements outlined above.

There is a big difference, however, between an electronic signature that merely satisfies the requirements of E-SIGN and UETA, and a trustworthy electronic signature. As a consequence, parties who desire to engage in electronic transactions may find that merely using a legally compliant electronic signature is not sufficient. As discussed above, clicking a mouse on an "I accept" button or typing a name on an e-mail message both qualify as legally enforceable signatures. But by themselves, they offer no evidence as to "who" clicked the mouse or typed the name that appears on the electronic document. Thus, to say that they are legally enforceable may be somewhat illusory, as a party's ability to authenticate a signature or use it to verify the integrity of a document may be very limited at best. The key is in authenticating the person who applied the symbol or executed the process—i.e., in knowing (and being able to prove) who typed the name or who clicked on the "I accept" button.

For electronic transactions, these security-related signature functions of identity and integrity can be key. When transactions are automated, and conducted over significant distances using easily altered digital technology, the need for a way to ensure the identity of the sender/signer and the integrity of the document becomes pivotal. Thus, while removing the so-called signature "barrier" to electronic transactions may have been an important legislative step, it is also important to recognize that an electronic signature, by itself, may not provide the security that a unique handwritten signature is thought to carry on a paper-based transaction . . . .

3.3   *Record Accessibility Requirements*

Another key requirement for the enforceability of electronic transactions is that the documents that comprise the transaction be communicated in a form that can be retained and accurately reproduced by the receiving party. In the U.S., the Federal E-SIGN legislation provides that the legal effect, validity, or enforceability of an electronic record "may be denied if such electronic record is not in a form that is capable of being retained and accurately reproduced for later reference by all parties or persons who are entitled to retain the contract or other record." Likewise, UETA provides that "if a sender inhibits the ability of a recipient to store or print an electronic record, the electronic record is not enforceable against the recipient."

The European Union Electronic Commerce Directive contains a similar requirement governing contracts with information society services (e.g., for the sale of goods). Under the Directive, contract terms and general conditions "must be made available in a way that allows him to store and reproduce them."

This requirement does not, of course, limit electronic transactions to those parties that possess the technical capability for downloading or printing documents. Rather, the focus is on the form of the document as communicated by the sender, and essentially requires that the sender do nothing to inhibit the ability of the recipient to download, store, or print the applicable record. The fact that the recipient may choose to use a device without such capabilities (for example, a hand-held device without a print capability), should not affect the enforceability of the transaction. On the other hand, such provisions clearly call into question the form of click-wrap agreement typically used on many websites in which the agreement is displayed in a separate window from which it cannot be downloaded or printed.

3.4   Record Retention Requirements

An essential element for the enforceability of all transactions is recordkeeping. In the event of a dispute, it is necessary to produce reliable evidence documenting the terms of the transaction and the agreement to the parties. Similar requirements also exist, for example, to satisfy regulatory requirements (e.g., regulations governing the insurance, securities, and banking industries, etc.), as well as the requirements of government agencies, such as the IRS. For electronic transactions, the issue becomes a question of whether keeping electronic records will satisfy applicable statutes, regulations, or evidentiary rules, and if so, what requirements must be met for acceptable electronic records.

Both E-SIGN and UETA address this issue directly, and impose similar requirements. Essentially, storage of an electronic record will satisfy legal record retention requirements if the stored copy of the electronic record:

- Accurately reflects the information set forth in the record and;

- Remains accessible for later reference.

With respect to evidentiary rules, both E-SIGN and UETA also provide that if a rule of evidence or other rule of law requires a record relating to a transaction to be provided or retained in its original form, this obligation is satisfied by meeting the accuracy and accessibility requirements listed above. These provisions also make clear that records can be kept in electronic-only form. Moreover, it provides a great deal of flexibility to the parties in terms of how they store the records, when and whether they migrate the records to new media, and meeting applicable evidentiary requirements.

. . .

EXTENSIONS

Office of electronic notary. UETA and ESIGN both expressly allow for electronic notarization of records. *See* UETA § 11; ESIGN § 101(g). In response to these legal developments, the National Notary Association (NNA) recently asked, "If electronic notarizations are authorized under the *Uniform Electronic Transactions Act* now being enacted into law in dozens of states, as well as under the new federal *Electronic Signatures in Global and National Commerce Act*, who exactly will perform these electronic notarial acts?" The NNA assumes that "[i]t will largely be Notaries specially commissioned for that purpose" and has "begun formulating parameters and qualifications for the office of Electronic Notary (EN) to be published in detail in a revised *Model Notary Act.*" In a position paper, the NNA expressed its concerns as follows:

> In the states, the allure of e-commerce and new technologies has begun to weaken vital statutory consumer protections against document fraud. In authorizing use of electronic signatures by Notaries, the widely enacted *Uniform Electronic Transactions Act* has spawned implementing laws that ignore the critical role of the trusted impartial witness. Indeed, some states are labeling as "notarization" electronic acts that do not even require a digital signer to appear before a Notary.

The fundamental principles and process of notarization must remain the same regardless of the technology used to make a signature, because, while technology may be perfectible, the basic nature of the human beings who use it is not. Any process—paper-based or electronic—that is called notarization must involve the personal physical appearance of a signer before a commissioned Notary Public.

In the electronic arena, the role of the Notary Public as a trusted impartial witness must not only be retained but strengthened so that execution of contracts and property conveyances will not be compromised by a technology that, despite its complexity, cannot make trustworthy guarantees about a signer's identity, willingness and awareness. The Notary office must be strengthened through well-conceived training, testing and certification programs that stress ethical as well as technical instruction.

Numerous experts share the NNA's view that emerging digital technology heightens rather than diminishes the role of the Notary Public.

In today's society, the Internet permits a risk-free anonymity that has emboldened a new generation of forgers and criminal identity thieves. Identity theft complaints grew from fewer than 40,000 nationwide in 1992 to 750,000 in 1999. "As identity becomes more digital, it becomes possible to reproduce and take on the identity of another (person) much more rapidly," said U.S. Treasury Secretary Laurence Summers. In such an environment, there is more need than ever before for reliable human gatekeepers to prevent the exploitation of technology.

National Notary Association, *A Position on Digital Signatures and Notarization*, www.nationalnotary.org/Digitalsignature.pdf. For more on the role of notaries, see Deborah M. Thaw, *The Notary Office and Its Impact in the 21st Century*, www.nationalnotary.org/news/notaryofficeandimpact.pdf.

QUESTIONS FOR DISCUSSION

1. *Record retention.* As Smedinghoff notes, ESIGN and UETA grant electronic records the legal status of writings not only for the purposes of contract formation and the statute of frauds, but also for purposes of record retention statutes. *See* ESIGN § 101(d); UETA § 12 (1999). Why is regulation of record retention necessary?

2. *Standards for authentication.* As we have noted, electronically typed signatures are more easily forged than pen-and-ink signatures. Do ESIGN and UETA adopt any standards about what level of certainty of authentication of a signature must be achieved in order for it to support binding commitment? About the level of certainty of nonrepudiation or textual integrity that must be achieved? Should states consider adopting such standards over and above the provisions of UETA and ESIGN? (Could they?) Consider this question in light of the excerpt which follows.

5. Elements of Commercial Trustworthiness

Thomas J. Smedinghoff, *The Legal Requirements for Creating Secure and Enforceable Electronic Transactions* (2004)
www.bakernet.com/ecommerce/etransactionsarticle.pdf

. . .

4.   Security – Is the Transaction Trustworthy?[62]

Beyond compliance with the statutory requirements for legal enforceability, the primary concern of parties to an electronic transaction is the pivotal question of "trust." To say that an electronic transaction complies with legal requirements is one thing. To have a sufficient degree of trust in an electronic transaction such that one is willing to ship product, transfer funds, or enter into a binding contractual commitment in real time is something else. The loss of trust can have a significant impact. For example, on August 26, 2002, the Reuters News Agency reported that large South Korean investors had stopped trading stocks online as a result of a disclosure from Daewoo Securities, Korea's fourth largest brokerage, that an unauthorized person had used one of its client accounts to buy almost $22 million of shares. The matter involved the apparently unauthorized purchase of 5 million shares in Delta Information and Communications over a period of 90 seconds. The loss of trust was, of course, immediate. According to the article, one of Korea's biggest institutional investors was quoted as saying "starting today, we started to stop online trading for the time being because of the security risks."

4.1   The Requirements for Trust

Trust, of course, plays a role in virtually all commercial transactions. Regardless of whether the deal is struck in cyberspace or in the more traditional paper-based world, each of the transacting parties must have some level of trust before they will be willing to proceed with the transaction. But trust has different components. Trusting one's business partners has always been important (e.g., Are they reputable and creditworthy? Will they perform as promised?). But in today's e-business environment, companies also need to trust *the transaction itself.* What does trusting the transaction mean? When vital business transactions depend on computer and network availability, the parties need to know that these will work properly and without interruption. When remote communications replace personal contact or a trusted medium such as the mail, the parties need to verify each other's identity. When easily copied and altered electronic records replace signed paper documents, the parties need assurance that these records are authentic and unaltered. And when sensitive data is stored electronically, the parties need assurances that the data is protected and accessible.[64]

---

[62] Portions of this section are adapted from Thomas J. Smedinghoff, Ed., *Online Law*, Chapter 3, by Lorijean G. Oei (1996).

[64] Of course, the requirement for such trust is a relative concept that varies from transaction to transaction, largely depending on how high the stakes are. For example, the level of trust required for an online merchant to ship $200,000 worth of tires is much higher than what is required for an online bookstore to ship a $20 book. The bookstore may not require a

. . .

Ensuring that an electronic transaction is trustworthy, from a legal perspective, requires consideration of four issues: authenticity, integrity, confidentiality, and nonrepudiation.

(a)   Authenticity – Who Sent the Message?

Authenticity is concerned with the *source or origin* of a document or message. Who created or signed the document? Who sent the message? Is it genuine or a forgery?

A party entering into a transaction in reliance on an electronic message must be confident of the source of that message. For example, when a bank receives an electronic payment order from a customer directing that money be paid to a third party, the bank must be able to verify the source of the request and ensure that it is not dealing with an impostor.[67]

Likewise, a party must also be able to establish the authenticity of its electronic transactions should a dispute arise. That party must retain records of all relevant communications pertaining to the transaction and keep those records in such a way that it can show that the records are authentic. For example, if one party to a contract later disputes the nature of its obligations, the other party may need to prove the terms of the contract to a court. A court, however, will first require that the party establish the authenticity of the record that the party retained of that communication before the court will consider it as evidence. A signature *can* be used to authenticate the source of a document. This works very well with handwritten signatures on paper documents, as such signatures can usually be related to a specific person, through handwriting analysis if necessary. But, most legally recognized electronic signatures do not perform this function, or provide such a weak level of authentication that they have little or no evidentiary value for that purpose.[69] For example, while E-SIGN and UETA both recognize that typing one's

---

high level of trust in each transaction, especially where a credit card number is provided and the risk of loss from fraud (e.g., $20) is relatively low. On the other hand, shipping $200,000 worth of product based on electronic message may require a much higher level of trust. Likewise, a bank will require even greater assurances before it will make a multimillion-dollar funds transfer in real time in reliance on an electronic message. At a minimum, the risk of a fraudulent message must be acceptable given the nature and size of the transaction.

[67] See U.C.C. §§ 4A-202, 4A-203 & cmt. (1998). § 4A-202 solves this problem for a bank and its customer who has agreed to transact its banking electronically and to be subject to Article 4A. If the bank verifies the payment order by using a commercially reasonable security procedure, the customer will be bound even if it did not in fact authorize the payment order. § 4A-202(b). If, however, the customer can prove that the person sending the fraudulent payment order did not obtain the information necessary to send such an order from an agent or a source controlled by the customer, the loss is shifted back to the bank. § 4A-203(a)(2). If the bank does not follow the security procedure and the order is fraudulent, the bank generally must cover the loss. § 4A-202(a).

[69] Some forms of electronic signature, such as the cryptographically created digital signature, if properly implemented, can provide strong authentication as to the source of the signature. Certain biometric techniques can also achieve a similar result.

name, clicking a mouse, or almost any other sound or symbol, can constitute a valid electronic signature, it is readily apparent that such signatures, by themselves, do little to authenticate the source of a document. The ultimate question—who typed the name, or who clicked the mouse—often remains unanswered.

Some electronic transaction legislation attempts to address this problem by requiring that an electronic signature contain both information from which the signer can be identified and a level of security designed to ensure that the signature was in fact made by the person identified.[70] However, most electronic transaction legislation (including E-SIGN and UETA) recognizes the validity of electronic signatures that are, in many respects, the legal equivalent of signing a paper contract with an "X". They leave unanswered the question of proving up the identity of the signer.

(b)   Integrity – Has the Document Been Altered?

Integrity is concerned with the accuracy and completeness of the communication. Is the document the recipient received the same as the document that the sender sent? Is it complete? Has the document been altered either in transmission or storage?

The concern regarding integrity flows from the fact that electronic documents are easily altered in a manner that is not detectable. Moreover, because every copy of an electronic document is a perfect reproduction, there is no such thing as an original electronic document. Thus, unlike paper documents, electronic records come with no inherent attributes of integrity.

The recipient of an electronic message must be confident of a communication's integrity before the recipient relies and acts on the message. Integrity is critical to e-commerce when it comes to the negotiation and formation of contracts online, the licensing of digital content, and the making of electronic payments, as well as to proving up these transactions using electronic records at a later date. For example, consider the case of a contractor who wants to solicit bids from subcontractors and submit its proposal to the government online. The contractor must be able to verify that the messages containing the bids upon which it will rely in formulating its proposal have not been altered. Likewise, if the contractor ever needs to prove the amount of a subcontractor's bid, a court will first require that the contractor establish the integrity of the record he retained of that communication before the court will consider it as evidence in the case.

A signature *can* be used to verify the integrity of a document. This works reasonably well with paper documents where a handwritten signature (or initials) placed at the bottom of each page is often a reasonably reliable way of preventing

---

[70] The UNCITRAL Model Law on Electronic Signatures, for example, requires that a signature identify the signer and that it be "as reliable as was appropriate for the purpose" for which the message was generated or communicated. By including these elements in the definition of an electronic signature, this Model Law seeks to require a minimum level of security before such signature will be considered legally enforceable. UNCITRAL Model Law on Electronic Signatures, Article 2(a) and Article 6(1).

undetected alterations. But most legally recognized electronic signatures do not perform this function. Clicking a mouse or typing one's name on an easily altered electronic document is no guarantee of document integrity. Typically, the use of cryptographic algorithms, often coupled with digital signatures, is the only way to detect alteration in an electronic document.

(c)   Confidentiality

Confidentiality is concerned with controlling the disclosure of information. It involves: (1) protecting information so that unauthorized persons cannot have access to it, and/or (2) protecting information so that even if unauthorized access is obtained, the information is unreadable (e.g., by encrypting the information).

Confidentiality may not be an issue in all situations. In some cases, however, it is critical. Maintaining a competitive advantage, or other business reasons, may require that certain information be kept confidential. In addition, statutes and regulations designed to protect the privacy of personally identifiable information typically require that such information be kept confidential, except when used in a manner authorized by law. Likewise, confidentiality may be necessary to protect a property right in information, such as a trade secret right. Information can only qualify as a trade secret if it is not generally known, and reasonable security precautions are taken to maintain secrecy. In addition, confidentiality may be necessary to comply with certain legal obligations, such as an obligation not to disclose the contents of attorney-client communications, or obligations arising as a result of contractual commitments. Confidentiality may also be important for preventing access to and use of information that can cause harm to the owner of the information, such as credit card or bank account numbers, social security numbers.

(d)   Nonrepudiation – Can the Message Be Proved in Court?

Nonrepudiation flows from authenticity and integrity. It is the ability to prove that the originator of a document in an electronic transaction intended to be bound by the terms of the document—i.e., to hold the sender to his communication in the event of a dispute.[75] A person's willingness to rely on a communication, contract, or funds transfer request is typically contingent upon having some level of comfort that he can prevent the sender from denying that he sent the communication (if, in fact, he did send it), or from claiming that the contents of the communication as received are not the same as what the sender sent (if, in fact, they are what was sent). For example, a stockbroker who accepts buy/sell orders over the Internet would not want his client to be able to place an order for a volatile commodity, such as a pork bellies futures contract, and then be able to confirm the order if the market goes up and repudiate the order if the market goes south.

---

[75] *See* Information Security Committee, Electronic Commerce Division, ABA Section of Science & Technology Law, *Digital Signature Guidelines*, August, 1996, available at www.abanet.org/scitech/ec/isc/dsgfree.html. One definition of nonrepudiation is "[s]trong and substantial evidence of the identity of the signer of a message and of message integrity, sufficient to prevent a party from successfully denying the origin, submission or delivery of the message and the integrity of its contents." Id. at § 1.20.

4.2   The Challenge of the Electronic Environment

With paper-based transactions, a party can rely on numerous indicators of trust to ensure the authenticity, integrity, confidentiality, and nonrepudiability of a document. These include using paper (sometimes with letterhead, watermarks, colored backgrounds, or other indicia of reliability) to which the message is affixed and not easily altered, handwritten ink signatures, sealed envelopes for delivery via a trusted third party (such as the U.S. Postal Service), personal contact between the parties, and the like. With the use of electronic documents and electronic communications conducted remotely over the Internet, however, none of these indicators of trust are present. All that can be communicated are bits (0s and 1s) that are in all respects identical and that can be easily copied and modified without detection.

Thus, moving transactions to an electronic environment has two important consequences. First, in many cases it is difficult to know when one can rely on the integrity and authenticity of an electronic message. This, of course, makes difficult those decisions that involve entering into contracts, shipping products, making payments, or otherwise changing one's position in reliance on an electronic message, especially for significant transactions. Second, this lack of reliability can make proving up one's case in court difficult at best. For example, if the defendant denies making the "signature" that is appended to an electronic document, it may be virtually impossible for the plaintiff to prove the authenticity of that electronic signature, absent additional evidence.

If e-commerce is to reach its full potential, however, parties must be able to trust electronic communications for a wide range of transactions, particularly ones where the size of the transaction is substantial or the nature of the transaction is of higher risk. In such cases, a party relying on an electronic communication will need to know, at the time of reliance, whether the message is authentic, whether the integrity of its contents is intact, and, equally important, whether the relying party can establish both of those facts in court if a dispute arises (i.e., nonrepudiation).

4.3   The Law and Trust In Electronic Transactions

Establishing trust in an electronic transaction requires security—specifically, the use of security procedures[77] designed to ensure the authenticity, integrity, confidentiality, and/or nonrepudiation of electronic documents and messages. There are a number of security procedures that can be used to assist in establishing trust for electronic communications. These include:

- Algorithms or codes
- Cryptography and digital signatures
- Identifying words or numbers

---

[77] A security procedure is a procedure employed for the purpose of verifying that an electronic signature, record, or performance is that of a specific person or for detecting changes or errors in the information in an electronic record. UETA § 2(14), and UCC Article 4A § 201.

- Replies and acknowledgments

- Repeat-back acknowledgements

- Using an automated process or system

- Date/time stamping

- Using trusted third parties to retain copies of electronic communications

- Encryption.

Regardless of the security measures employed, it is important to note that, increasingly, the law is recognizing the importance of security procedures in determining the enforceability of an electronic transaction and the allocation of risk in the event of a loss. The first formal recognition of the legal effect of security procedures occurred in 1989 with the approval of Article 4A of the UCC.[80]

Article 4A addresses the electronic transfer of funds by wire.[81] A person who wishes to transfer funds electronically does so by transmitting an electronic message, called a payment order, to his bank. Because that message cannot bear a traditional ink signature, security procedures must be used instead. The UCC recognized this and the reality that a bank receiving a payment order needs something objective on which it can rely in determining whether it may safely act on that order.[82] Article 4A modernized the law by providing that a bank could rely on security procedures as a substitute for the traditional time-tested requirement of a signature to ensure the authenticity and integrity of the message. Thus, under Article 4A, an electronic message purporting to be from a bank's customer that instructs the bank to transfer funds to a payee is considered valid, and the bank is authorized to transfer the funds in accordance with the order if the authenticity and integrity of the order is "verified" pursuant to a "commercially reasonable" security procedure, regardless whether the order was actually authorized by the customer. The bottom line is that Article 4A adopts "security procedures" rather than "signatures" as the basis for verifying electronic transactions and apportioning liability.

Since the advent of UCC Article 4A, the law is starting to recognize that security has a key role to play in electronic transactions. Approaches vary, however, and currently, electronic transactions statutes fall into the falling categories with respect to security:

- *Security not addressed.* Many statutes say nothing at all with regard to the role of security. They merely authorize the use of electronic records and signatures in lieu of paper records and signatures (and in some case provide for other transactional requirements, such as consent), but say nothing about, or give no legal effect to, the use of security procedures. This is the approach taken by ESIGN and UETA.

---

[80] *See* U.C.C. Art. 4A, Funds Transfers (1989). Article 4A has since been adopted in all 50 states.

[81] U.C.C. Art. 4A, Prefatory Note (1990).

[82] U.C.C. § 4A–203 Official Comment.

- *Security as a precondition to enforceability.* Some statutes *require* the use of security, at some level, before the transaction (or some aspect of it) will be legally enforceable. The UNCITRAL Model Law on Electronic Signatures, for example, requires an element of "reliability"—i.e., that electronic signatures be as reliable as appropriate for the circumstances, before the electronic signature will be considered valid. Likewise, the electronic signature must be capable of identifying the signer, another aspect of security. Many of the electronic signature statutes enacted by the various states in the U.S. also took a similar approach (although they are largely preempted by E-SIGN now).[83]

- *Incentives for security—legal presumptions.* A number of statutes provide that almost any form of electronic signature can be enforceable and meet legal signature requirements, while recognizing that some electronic signatures are more trustworthy than others. To encourage the use of those electronic signatures deemed to be more trustworthy, and to provide message recipients with an enhanced level of assurance at the time of reliance regarding the authenticity and integrity of messages using such signatures, these statutes typically provide a legal benefit in the form of an evidentiary presumption regarding the sender's identity and/or the integrity of the document. Thus, these statutes, while not literally requiring security as a precondition to the enforceability of electronic transactions, provide incentives for security by providing a legal benefit (i.e., a presumption) to those who use security to assist them in ensuring that the transaction will be enforceable.

- *Security as a risk allocation device.* Finally, some legislation uses the presence or absence of security as a risk allocation device. UETA, for example, in some cases allocates the risk of loss for errors or mistakes to the party that failed to implement agreed-upon security procedures. Likewise, UCC Article 4A allocates the risk of loss for fraudulent electronic payment orders based on the presence or absence of an agreed-upon security procedure.

A good example of legislation that provides for legal presumptions is the Illinois Electronic Commerce Security Act, which creates a technology-neutral class of trustworthy signatures called "secure electronic signatures."[85] While all electronic

---

[83] Several states enacted electronic signature statutes that adopted security requirements from a decision of the U.S. Comptroller General. *See* U.S. Comptroller General, *Matter of National Institute of Standards and Technology: Use of Electronic Data Interchange Technology to Create Valid Obligations*, 71 Comp. Gen. 109 (1991) (Dec. 13, 1991). Under those statutes an electronic signature is legally effective as a signature only if it is: (1) unique to the person using it; (2) capable of verification; (3) under the sole control of the person using it; and (4) linked to the data in such a manner that if the data is changed, the signature is invalidated. This approach requires attributes of security as a precondition to the validity of the signature itself, something not required for paper-based signatures. . . .

[85] 5 ILL. COMP. STAT. 175/10–110 (1998). This Act also defines a class of secure electronic records. Id. at 175/10–110. See generally, Illinois Commission on Electronic Com-

signatures are enforceable under this Act, an electronic signature that qualifies as a secure electronic signature enjoys a rebuttable presumption that the signature is that of the person to whom it correlates.[86] This approach was followed in the European Union Electronic Signature Directive. Under this Directive, while electronic signatures cannot be denied enforceability solely because they are in electronic form, a more secure form of electronic signatures—referred to as "advance electronic signatures"—are presumed to satisfy legal requirements for signatures, and are presumed admissible as evidence in legal proceedings.[87]

Technology-specific statutes that confer similar legal presumptions on certain cryptographically created "digital signatures" have been enacted in Minnesota, Missouri, Utah, and Washington.[88] To ensure that the digital signature possesses a level of trust sufficient to warrant enhanced legal recognition, these statutes impose a regulatory structure on certification authorities that voluntarily elect to be licensed by the State.[89]

Based on the apparent assumption that all certificates issued by licensed certification authorities are trustworthy, and that a digital signature that is created using the private key corresponding to the public key listed in such a certificate is a trustworthy signature, the legislation has bestowed attributes of trust to messages verifiable by such certificates.[90]

There is, of course, a great deal of debate over whether, or how, the law should address the role of security in electronic transactions. But regardless of the outcome of that public policy debate, there can be no denying that security is an ever-increasing concern for electronic transactions. And even where it is not given special recognition in legislation, it will ultimately become important in the evidentiary process in the event of a dispute. Whether an electronic record is admissible, or the weight that it will be given by the trier of fact, will ultimately depend on the ability of the proponent of the electronic document to establish its authenticity and integrity—factors which hinge upon the sufficiency of the security measures employed under the circumstances.

. . .

---

merce and Crime, Final Report of the Commission on Electronic Commerce and Crime (May 26, 1998) available at www.bakernet.com/ecommerce.

[86] 5 ILL. COMP. STAT. 175/10–120.

[87] Electronic Signature Directive, Article 5(1).

[88] *See* MINN. STAT. ANN. § 325K.20 (West 1998); MO ANN. STAT. § 28.677 (West 1998); UTAH CODE ANN. § 46–3–101 (1998); WASH. REV. CODE § 19/34/900 (West 1998).

[89] *See, e.g.,* MINN. STAT. ANN. § 325K.20; MO ANN. STAT. § 28.677; UTAH CODE ANN. § 46–3–101; WASH. REV. CODE § 19/34/100. The digital signature legislation enacted in Germany, Italy, and Malaysia contains a similar approach.

[90] *See, e.g.,* UTAH CODE ANN. § 406(3). The Utah Digital Signature Act provides that if a digital signature is verified by the public key listed in a valid certificate issued by a licensed certification authority, then a court of the State of Utah "shall presume that": (a) the digital signature is the digital signature of the subscriber listed in that certificate, and (b) the digital signature was affixed by that subscriber with the intention of signing the message. *Id.*

6. Public Key Encryption (A Prevalent Digital Signature Technology)

The most prevalent form of digital signature today is created using encryption and related techniques.

Encryption, for present purposes, is the process of taking a textual message, written in a natural language such as English, and transforming it so that it becomes unreadable except to one who knows how to run the transformation in reverse. The transformation is accomplished through the use of a cryptographic "key." A key may be thought of as a set of rules to follow in transforming the original message into its encrypted form. For example, a very simple cryptographic key might be expressed as: "For each letter in the message, substitute the number representing the place of that letter in the alphabet." Applying this key to the message

"Hello"

would result in transforming it into the encrypted form

"8 5 12 12 15".

The encrypted form is unreadable to one who does not know the key, but anyone who knows the key may easily reverse the transformation and arrive at the original text.

The keys used in public key cryptography work on the same principle, but in a considerably more sophisticated way. Instead of a single key, encryption and decryption are accomplished using a *pair* of keys. Each key consists of a very long number, perhaps several hundred decimal digits in length. The number stands for the set of rules that is used to transform a message into encrypted form, or back again. Each person who wishes to make use of public key cryptography has his own pair of keys, and each pair of keys is unique.

Of each pair of keys, one is designated the *public key* and the other the *private key*. As the names suggest, the owner of a key pair makes his public key generally available to the world—such as by posting it on his Web page, or inserting it at the bottom of outgoing e-mail messages—while keeping the private key strictly to himself.

The two keys making up a key pair are related to each other mathematically so as to yield several useful properties. First, if you encrypt a message with the public key, it can *only* be decrypted using the corresponding private key. This allows you to send a message that can only be read by the intended recipient: you do so by encrypting the message using the recipient's public key. Second, if a message can be decrypted with a particular public key, it can *only* have been encrypted with the corresponding private key. Thus, if you are able to decrypt a message using a particular public key, you have established that it must have been encrypted using the corresponding private key (and, if the private key has been kept private, it must have been encrypted by the owner of that key pair). Third, if the keys are of sufficient length, it is impossible to derive the private key from the public key in any reasonable amount of time, no matter how many computers you have working on the problem. This means that if the owner of a key pair keeps the private key private, there is no way for anybody else to figure out what it is.

The other technique that is used in creating a digital signature is called a *hash function*. Like an encryption key, a hash function is a set of rules that transforms a text message into what looks like gibberish. But a hash function has a different set of properties. First, it transforms any text message, no matter how long, into output of a fixed length. The output is called a *message digest*. For example, a commonly used hash function turns any text message into a message digest consisting of a number with roughly 50 decimal digits. Second, if the text message is altered by even one letter, the hash function produces a different message digest. Third, it is not feasible to run the hash function backwards: starting from the message digest, one cannot reconstruct the original message.

We can now understand how to create a digital signature and use it to sign an electronic text message. This occurs in a series of steps.

First, the sender creates a text message, as an e-mail message, a word processing document, or in some other format.

Second, the sender runs the message through the hash function, transforming it into a message digest.

Third, the sender encrypts the message digest using her private key.

Fourth, the sender sends the original message, together with the encrypted message digest, to the recipient, via e-mail or some other means.

Fifth, the recipient run the message she received through the hash function, transforming it into a message digest.

Sixth, the recipient uses the sender's public key to decrypt the message digest. This establishes that the message must have been encrypted using the sender's private key.

Seventh, the recipient compares the result of Step 5 with the result of Step 6. If they match, then she can be confident that the message she received is exactly the same as the message that the sender sent. If the message had been altered in transit, then it would have generated a message digest different from the one that the sender generated from the original message.

Although this may seem like an onerous and time-consuming process, when implemented properly it is all accomplished automatically and nearly instantaneously by the sender's and recipient's e-mail programs.

So far, we have achieved one of the goals that needs to be met if an electronic signature is to serve the functions of its pen-and-ink predecessor: *data integrity*. Like the indelibility of ink on paper, and the placement of a pen-and-ink signature physically at the end of a message, the application of cryptographic technologies assures that a text has not been tampered with.

What about authentication? Can the recipient of the message be certain that it was sent by the person whose name is attached to it in electronic text? Not yet. So far, nothing in the digital signature process forecloses the possibility that an imposter has publicly posted his own public key, and falsely attributed it to the sender. The message might then have been sent by the imposter, in the name of somebody else. Even if it was actually sent by the person who is identified in the message as the sender, the recipient cannot prove that the sender is lying if the sender seeks to repudiate the message. Thus, we have not yet achieved either authentication or nonrepudiation.

Those goals are achieved by introducing into the system a trusted third party, known as a *certification authority*, or "CA." The CA's role is to attest that a particular public key is associated with a particular individual. The CA ascertains the individual's identity through standard offline means, such as by checking her passport or driver's license while she is physically present, and the individual demonstrates ownership of a key pair. The CA then creates a *digital certificate*. The certificate consists of a text message reading something like: "The public key 467937698316 belongs to Samantha Smith." To prevent tampering with this message, the certificate is signed with the CA's own digital signature: the CA runs the attestation message through a hash function, and encrypts the resulting message digest with its private key.

Digital certificates are maintained in a centralized registry, where they may be accessed by anyone who wants to verify that a particular public key is associated with a particular person or entity. The system by which certificates are created, maintained, accessed, revoked, and otherwise managed is known as the *public key infrastructure*, or "PKI."

With the addition of this infrastructure, the electronic signature can establish both *data integrity* (as described above) and *authentication*. Upon receipt of the message, the recipient consults the digital certificate associated with the public key she used to decrypt the message digest. If the certificate states that the public key belongs to the sender, then the message has been authenticated as issuing from the sender.

The third function of pen-and-ink signatures, *nonrepudiation*, is a bit trickier to achieve. If the indicated sender of a message falsely denies having sent it, can the recipient of the message establish that she is lying? If the procedure described above is followed, the recipient can show that the message was sent by someone in possession of the private key associated with the public key that the CA attests is associated with the sender. But the putative sender might yet maintain (1) that the CA was in error, as she did not own the key pair, or (2) while she owned the key pair, somebody else must have discovered her private key and used it to impersonate her.

The American Bar Association's 1996 *Digital Signature Guidelines: Legal Infrastructure for Certification Authorities and Secure Electronic Commerce* set forth a suggested approach to legal issues arising in connection with digital signatures.

Charles R. Merrill, *Proof of Who, What and When in Electronic Commerce Under the Digital Signature Guidelines*
542 PLI/Pat 185 (1998).

. . .

Hypothetical Example

Bob, a securities broker, has printed out the following document from a file on the hard drive of his PC, which he claims to be a true copy of an e-mail message he received via the Internet.

Alice has an active securities trading account with Bob, in which she maintains a credit balance of securities and cash. Alice has often used Internet e-mail to instruct Bob as to purchases and sales of securities in her account.

> To: Bob@securities-r-us.com
> From: Alice@restaurant.com
> Date: Feb 27, 1997 10:00
>
> Please buy 100 shs of Netscape common stock for my account immediately, at the prevailing market price. /s/ Alice

On Thursday, Feb 27, Bob did buy 100 shares of Netscape common stock for Alice's account. On Friday, Feb 28, the market price of Netscape plummeted, producing a substantial loss on this transaction. Upon receipt of routine written confirmation of purchase of 100 shares for her account, Alice claims, alternatively:

(1) Bob, I never sent any e-mail message! or

(2) Bob, I sent an e-mail message, but it said "sell 100 shs of Netscape"! or

(3) Bob, I sent that e-mail message, but not till Feb 28, after the price fell!

The Challenge of Conducting Secure Electronic Commerce on the Internet

The example illustrates the challenge of conducting secure electronic commerce on the Internet, where, as the famous New Yorker cartoon says, "They can't tell you're a dog." Although the Internet is increasingly attractive as a commercial channel, the dark side is that the Internet is notoriously insecure in its normal configuration as an "open system," where there are no trusted gatekeepers to authenticate identity of users entering the system. Sophisticated hackers are demonstrably able to send messages "spoofing" the identity and e-mail address of others, and to intrude in private communications between others—intercepting, reading, modifying and sending messages along again, without detection. Many believe that if electronic commerce continues to accelerate its volume without substantial improvements in security, commercial losses through such attacks will also grow in volume—motivated not only by mischief but by the "Willie Sutton" syndrome ("Willie, why do you rob banks?" "Because the money's there.")

On August 1, 1996, the Information Security Committee of the American Bar Association Section of Science and Technology published the Digital Signature Guidelines, a four-year collaboration of more than 70 leading technologists and attorneys from all over the world. The Guidelines seek to define a system of public key infrastructure which combines the powerful technological capabilities of an asymmetric cryptosystem with legal principles of commercial law.

. . .

Remember Alice? A Summary of the Legal Issues

Our hypothetical example illustrates a classic case of where a robust system of non-repudiation is needed to block Alice's false denial that she sent the message produced by Bob. If in fact Alice did send that message, a plausible motive could be the intention to remain unfairly flexible at the expense of Bob, by waiting to see the future market price before confirming or denying that she sent the message. Such conduct (if unfair) is recognized and remediable under the equitable principle of "laches" in the Anglo-American legal system.

The problem, of course, and the central dilemma for electronic commerce in an open system, is that in a digital environment based on bits rather than atoms, the jury and the opposing counsel will be deprived of cues or clues which would normally be available for the resolution of disputes in a paper-based and human-contact-based world. Here are the three possible factual theories which face the dispute resolution authority (judge, jury, arbitrator, mediator or the like):

(A) Alice is lying and Bob is truthful. Alice did send the message, and Bob did not falsify it. Alice intended to buy the stock, but after the market dropped, she is repudiating the transaction in order to avoid the loss, committing laches at Bob's expense. (Or she sent "buy" and wants to substitute "sell." Or she sent the message Feb 27 and now claims she sent it Feb 28, after the price dropped.)

(B) Bob is lying and Alice is truthful. Bob has falsified the message and the printout, and Alice never sent it. Bob bought the stock for his own account or for another customer, and after the market dropped, he tried to put the loss on Alice. (Or she did send "buy" and Bob has substituted "sell." Or she did sent the message Feb 28 and Bob has caused his PC to substitute Feb 27.)

(C) Alice and Bob are Both Telling the Truth!! Alice did not send the message, but Bob did receive it on Feb 27. An unknown imposter (for mischievous or other unknown motives) has either:

- Spoofed Alice and sent the message, or

- Intercepted Alice's message and changed "buy" to "sell"

The fact finder could rationally decide (A) or (B) on the basis of the relative credibility of the testimony of Alice or Bob—a process with which the legal system is comfortable and familiar. The most troublesome possibility for a system of jurisprudence is Case (C), where the fact finder decides that both Alice and Bob are truthful, innocent and victimized, yet must then decide which innocent victim should bear the damage caused by an imposter who is usually unknown, judgment-proof, and/or beyond the court's jurisdiction.

Under the facts of the hypothetical example, the e-mail message is "naked" of any cryptographic authentication of any kind. What would happen if the e-mail were digitally signed, and the case were decided in a jurisdiction (e.g., the States of Utah or Washington) where rules similar to the Digital Signature Guidelines are in force?

Deciding the Case under the Digital Signature Guidelines

Step 1. Is there a digital signature on the message? GL 1.11 defines digital signature as the following:

> A transformation of a message using an asymmetric cryptosystem and a hash function such that a person having the initial message and the signer's public key can accurately determine (1) whether the transformation was created using the private key that corresponds to the signer's public key, and (2) whether the initial message has been altered since the transformation was made.

If there is a digital signature on the message, the Guidelines apply, and we proceed to Step 2. This is an "opt-in" system, where the use of digital signatures is entirely optional on the part of users. If the user has not digitally signed the message, the Guidelines do not apply, and existing law does.

Step 2. If a relying party has a message signed with a digital signature and also has a public key available, the crypto software allows the relying party to determine whether the digital signature was created by someone who used the private key corresponding to that public key. The effect is to link the digital signature to that public key. We still know nothing about who signed the document.

Step 3. Do we have a digital certificate issued by a trusted third party certification authority (CA)? . . . Depending upon the rigor of the identification procedures required for the particular class of certificates, the certificate binds the identity of the subscriber to the subscriber's public key, during the typical one-year operational period of the certificate.

Step 4. The next step is to verify the digital signature and message integrity under GL 1.37, which defines that process as:

> In relation to a given digital signature, message and public key, to determine accurately:
>
> > (1) that the digital signature was created during the operational period of a valid certificate by the private key corresponding to the public key listed in the certificate; and
> >
> > (2) the message has not been altered since its digital signature was created.

From Step 2, the software has already told the relying party that the digital signature is linked to the public key available to the relying party. From Step 3, the CA linked the public key of Alice to Alice's identity. Step 4 requires that the digital signature be created during the operational period of a valid certificate (i.e., not before its issue date and not after it has expired or it has been revoked), and if this requirement is satisfied, the digital signature has been "verified". Combining Step 2, Step 3 and Step 4, the digital signature has now been linked with Alice.

Step 5. At this point, the analysis becomes primarily legal, diverging from the yes/no binary approach favored by computer security professionals, into the fuzzy, analog world of the dispute resolution process which determines who wins and loses in a commercial dispute. Guideline 5.6 provides the following rebuttable presumption:

> In resolving a dispute involving a digital signature it is rebuttably presumed that . . .
>
> > (2) a digital signature verified by reference to the public key listed in a valid certificate is the digital signature of the subscriber listed in that certificate,
> >
> > (3) the message associated with a verified digital signature has not been altered from its original form, ...

Under traditional paper-based law, it is often the case that the person relying on a signed document has the burden of proof (both the burden of going forward with evidence and persuading the fact finder with the preponderance of the evidence) that the document was signed by the person to whom it is attributed. Similarly, under Federal Reserve Regulations Reg E and Reg Z governing ATM devices and credit cards, the liability of even a negligent cardholder is generally limited to $50 regardless of how much loss is caused the cardholder's bank. Reflecting the robust security capabilities of asymmetric cryptosystem technology, the Digital Signature Guidelines intentionally reverse that presumption where a digital signature is properly verifiable. If the e-mail message in our hypothetical example was digitally signed and verified by reference to Alice's valid certificate as per the preceding four steps, then Alice is liable to Bob, unless she successfully rebuts the presumption that the e-mail message produced by Bob is signed by Alice and not modified since the time she signed it. There are two major ways Alice may rebut that presumption and avoid liability.

Step 6. The first and most obvious way Alice may rebut the presumption that she signed the message is to carry the burden of proof that the certification authority made a mistake in identifying Alice as the subscriber of the certificate which contains the public key. One factual theory available to Alice is that an imposter spoofed Alice's identity in applying for a certificate in the name of Alice, but bound to the imposter's public key. If Alice succeeds with this theory and the relying party has been damaged by reliance upon the incorrect certificate, then the relying party could seek redress against the CA for damages caused by the CA's error. Under a so-called "closed PKI model" (in contrast with the "open PKI model" which the Guidelines represent) it may be that no one other than the CA itself (or a government or other entity controlling the CA or outsourcing duties to the CA) is entitled to rely upon the CA's certificate.

Step 7. The second way Alice may rebut the presumption that she signed the message is to carry the burden of proof that, although Alice's private key was used to sign the message, the use of Alice's private key was unauthorized by Alice. To do this, Alice would need to overcome the non-repudiation security service provided by the dual-key asymmetric cryptosystem, and carry the burden of proving that she compromised or lost control of her private key, and that the private key was used by another to sign the message, without her authority.

Step 8. Under GL 4.3, Alice has the affirmative duty to safeguard her private key from compromise. If Alice was successful under Step 7 in showing that her private key was used by another to sign the message without her authority, then the inquiry will proceed to the issue of whether Alice's compromise of her private key was negligent. If Alice violated her duty to safeguard her key from compromise, then as between the two innocent parties—Bob the relying party and Alice the subscriber—Alice would bear the loss if reimbursement is not possible against the unauthorized user of Alice's private key. It is not clear under the Guidelines whether Alice would have the burden of proving Alice's due care or whether Bob would have the burden of proving Alice's negligence. Either rule would be a rational approach by a State or other jurisdiction which wished to tilt the playing field more in favor of one of the two parties. The required standard of care is likely to be affected by the extent to which the digital signature software comes to be embedded in smart cards and other hardware devices with the triple compromise protection of (a) tangible token required, (b) secret PIN required, and (c) biometric proof of physical presence.

Step 9. If Alice discovers that her private key has been compromised, she can perhaps cut off her liability to relying parties (at least as to future reliance) by revoking her certificate, so that the certificate becomes listed on a certificate revocation list which cuts off the operational period of the certificate so that no digital signatures created thereafter are verifiable. *See* GL 5.4, regarding reasonable of reliance. An important issue is the extent to which relying parties have constructive notice of certificate revocation lists maintained online and elsewhere CAs, whether or not the relying party has actual notice of the certificate's revocation.

Step 10. Finally, even if Alice for some reason fails to revoke her certificate in time to warn relying parties, under the particular circumstances there may be factual arguments available to her under GL 5.3, regarding unreliable digital signatures, as to why Bob should be required to confirm the transaction with Alice "out-of-band" (e.g., by picking up the telephone) before proceeding to rely.

EXTENSIONS

1. *A natural transition.* A certification authority ("CA") acts as a trusted third party that vouches for parties negotiating online, confirming the identity and other important attributes of persons who are sending and receiving electronic messages and payments over the Internet. Commercial banks fulfill a similar function in the brick-and-mortar economy, especially with respect to international transactions, confirming the identity and vouching for the good reputation of local businesses involved in commercial transactions with parties in other states or countries. Should commercial banks become the certification authorities of the new online economy?

2. *Open vs. closed systems.* The Office of the Comptroller of the Currency explains that

> CA systems may be characterized as primarily open or closed. A fully closed system has contracts defining the rights and obligations of all participants for authenticating messages or transactions. This type of system offers the CA operators less risk exposure because there is little uncertainty regarding obligations. Conversely, a fully open system would not have formal contracts defining the rights and obligations of relying parties in the system. In such a system, the firms that perform the CA activities could be exposed to an uncertain level of risk for each authenticated message or transaction. It is likely during early stages of development that most CA systems will be neither fully open nor fully closed, with contracts defining the rights and responsibilities of at least some, but not all, of the system participants.

OCC Bulletin 99–20, www.occ.treas.gov/ftp/bulletin/99-20.txt.

3. *Technology-specific vs. technology-neutral laws.* A number of states in the United States enacted legislation mandating public key technology and its supporting infrastructure, but some of them updated their legislation to endorse a technology-neutral approach in conjunction with adoption of UETA, and many were preempted by ESIGN. (The extent to which state statutes are preempted by ESIGN is complicated by the fact that ESIGN was meant to encourage enactment of UETA without any changes, but most of the states did make some changes to the official form adopted by NCCUSL, and also because states are permitted to specify alternative procedures for the use of electronic records or signatures provided that such procedures are consistent with ESIGN and technology-neutral. *See* Robert A. Wittie and Jane K. Winn, *Electronic Records and Signatures Under the Federal ESIGN Legislation and the UETA*, 56 BUS. LAW. 293 (2000).) Technology-specific laws pose two principal policy issues. First, such laws are often outdated before the enactment process is finished. Second, the favored technology enjoys something like a government-sanctioned monopoly. Many commentators argue, therefore, that technology-neutral laws— i.e., those that define what must be accomplished, without mandating any particular technology to accomplish it—are preferable. But technology-neutral laws run the risk of being vague and general, and therefore difficult to apply in practice.

4. *PKI and biometric identification.* A PKI-based digital signature is not the only technology that can be used to verify the identity of an individual online. Biometric technologies that can accomplish this function are also being developed. "Biometrics are best defined as measurable physiological and/or behavioural characteristics that can be utilised to verify the identity of an individual. They include fingerprints, retinal and iris scanning, hand geometry, voice patterns, facial recognition and other techniques. They are of interest in any area where it is important to verify the true identity of an individual. Initially, these techniques were employed primarily in specialist high security applications, however we are now seeing their use and proposed use in a much broader range of public facing situations." Julian Ashbourn, *The Biometric White Paper*, www.jsoft.freeuk.com/whitepaper.htm.

While PKI and biometrics may at first appear to be competing methods for verifying the identity of individuals, the two technologies are actually complementary. As Ashbourn observes:

> One of the often repeated concerns lies in the area of key management, and in particular, the likelihood of your private key being misused or perhaps stolen. For example, if the operation of your private key is protected by a PIN, then this may easily be compromised at your workstation by someone who wishes to pretend to be you and makes it his or her business to discover that PIN. Similarly, if the private key is stored on your computer's hard disk, then how easy is it for someone to hack into your computer and copy this file? If someone acquires and is able to use your private key, then your PKI environment is powerless to protect you as this person could intercept messages meant for you and easily decrypt them. Furthermore they could pretend to be you within the context of important transactions, with all the implications that this entails. Key management and key security therefore become paramount within a PKI environment.
>
> Biometrics offer the potential to considerably enhance the PKI model in the same way that they have brought significant benefits to the more conventional user authentication area. Let's take for example the ability to restrict the use of your private key for encryption and decryption. Using a PIN for this provides a certain level of perceived security, although the actual level is rather low. Using a biometric, such as a fingerprint for example, provides a substantially higher level of confidence. The likelihood of someone else using your workstation or mobile computer and successfully using your biometrically protected private key is reduced to almost infinitesimal proportions. . . .

Julian Ashbourn, *Biometrics and PKI*, www.techonline.com/community/related_content/20675.

QUESTIONS FOR DISCUSSION

Certifying risks. Ultimately the CA's guarantee is only as good as its identification of the person who has purchased a certificate. What kind of identification should a CA require in order to issue a certificate? Should a CA be liable to a recipient who relies on a certificate that was in fact issued to an imposter? Should the state license CAs similar to the way it licenses notaries?

In general, what are the risks involved in being a certification authority? Which of these risks are likely to expose a certification authority to legal action? *See* OCC Bulletin 99–20, *supra*; A. Michael Froomkin, *The Essential Role of Trusted Third Parties in Electronic Commerce,* 75 OR. L. REV. 49 (1996) (especially Part III).

COMPARATIVE NOTES

---

1. *European Union Directives.* The European Union has adopted three Directives concerning electronic contracting: (1) the Directive on Electronic Commerce,[36] (2) the Electronic Signature Directive,[37] and (3) the Distance Selling Directive.[38] Although the Electronic Signature Directive does not mandate the use of any particular technology of authentication, the presumptions it sets up strongly favor the use of public key encryption technology.

2. *UNCITRAL.* Much as NCCUSL develops model laws for adoption in the several states of the United States, the United Nations Commission on International Trade Law ("UNCITRAL") develops model laws intended to facilitate international commerce and trade. UNCITRAL has adopted two model laws concerning electronic commerce: (1) UNCITRAL Model Law on Electronic Commerce with Guide to Enactment (1996), with additional article 5*bis* as adopted in 1998, www.uncitral.org/pdf/english/texts/electcom/ml-ec-e.pdf; and (2) UNCITRAL Model Law on Electronic Signatures with Guide to Enactment (2001), www.uncitral.org/pdf/english/texts/electcom/ml-elecsig-e.pdf. UNCITRAL describes the Model Law on Electronic Commerce as follows:

> The Model Law is intended to facilitate the use of modern means of communications and storage of information, with or without the use of such support as the Internet. It is based on the establishment of a functional equivalent for paper-based concepts such as "writing," "signature" and "original." By providing standards by which the legal value of electronic messages can be assessed, the Model Law should play a significant role in enhancing the use of paperless communication. The Model Law also contains rules for electronic commerce in specific areas, such as carriage of goods.

UNCITRAL, www.uncitral.org/uncitral/en/uncitral_texts/electronic_commerce/1996Model.html.

II. LIMITS ON CONTRACTUAL ORDERING

As you will recall from your contracts class, contractual ordering has certain limits. For example, contracts will not be enforced if made by one lacking capacity, or if the contract is illegal, the result of fraud, or made under duress or undue influence. The further limitation expressed in the notion of unconscionability became significant in consumer contracts in the mid-twentieth century, and is included in the Uniform Commercial Code. *See* UCC § 2–302. In the context of online transactions, consumers desiring to escape an onerous clause have most often relied on unconscionability in addition to the defenses to contract formation that we have seen in Part I, *supra*. As we saw in Part I, consumers desiring to mount class action litigation have often found themselves attempting to invalidate a defendant's mandatory arbitration clause, such as Gateway's clause at issue in *Hill v. Gateway* and

---

[36] Directive 2000/31/EC of the European Parliament and of the Council of 8 June 2000 on certain legal aspects of information society services, in particular electronic commerce, in the Internal Market, 2000 O.J. (L 178) 1, europa.eu.int/ISPO/ecommerce/legal/documents/2000_31ec/2000_31ec_en.pdf.

[37] Directive 1999/93/EC of the European Parliament and of the Council of 13 December 1999 on a Community framework for electronic signatures, 2000 O.J. (L 013) 12, europa.eu.int/eur-lex/lex/LexUriServ/LexUriServ.do?uri=CELEX:31999L0093:EN:NOT.

[38] Directive 97/7/EC of the European Parliament and of the Council of 20 May 1997 on the protection of consumers in respect of distance contracts, 1997 O.J. (L 144) 19, europa.eu.int/comm/consumers/policy/developments/dist_sell/dist01_en.pdf.

Klocek v. Gateway. (We will further consider arbitration, and other methods of alternative dispute resolution, in Chapter 14, *infra.*) Another option in plaintiff's arsenal is to argue that the clause is unconscionable.

A. UNCONSCIONABILITY

In re RealNetworks, Inc., Privacy Litigation
2000 WL 631341 (N.D.Ill.2000).

■ KOCORAS, J.

[This case concerns the enforceability of an arbitration provision contained in a clickwrap agreement. RealNetworks makes its RealPlayer and RealJukebox software available at its website for free download. Upon installing the software, the user must agree to a license agreement containing the following clause:

> This License Agreement shall be governed by the laws of the State of Washington, without regard to conflicts of law provisions, and you hereby consent to the exclusive jurisdiction of the state and federal courts sitting in the State of Washington. Any and all unresolved disputes arising under this License Agreement shall be submitted to arbitration in the State of Washington.

[The court continues:]

Defendant cites this clause as binding authority for its assertions that arbitration is required. Intervenor, on the other hand, argues that this clause does not operate to require arbitration for several reasons. First, Intervenor contends that the License Agreement, including the arbitration requirement, does not constitute a "writing." . . . Finally, Intervenor argues that the arbitration provision is unenforceable because it is unconscionable.

. . .

III. Unconscionability

Finally, Intervenor claims that the arbitration agreement is unenforceable because it is both procedurally and substantively unconscionable. Procedural unconscionability involves impropriety during the process of forming a contract, whereas substantive unconscionability pertains to those cases where a clause or term in a contract is allegedly one-sided or overly harsh. *See Public Employees Mutual Ins. Co. v. Hertz Corp.*, 59 Wash.App. 641, 645–46 (1990).

Intervenor argues that the License Agreement is procedurally unconscionable because it failed to provide fair notice of its contents and did not provide a reasonable opportunity to understand its terms before it was enforced. Both of these assertions are incorrect. Intervenor claims that the arbitration provision does not provide fair notice because it is "buried" in the License Agreement. Although burying important terms in a "maze of fine print" may contribute to a contract being found unconscionable, the arbitration provision in the License Agreement is not buried. *But see Public Employees Mutual Ins.*, 59 Wash.App. at 648 (it is not law of Washington that presence of small print in context of standard form agreement necessarily leads to a finding of unconscionability). The License Agreement sets out the arbitration provision in the same size font as the rest of the agreement. *Cf. id.* at 650. Moreover, it is not buried in the middle of the entire agreement or located in a footnote or appendix, but rather comprises the attention-getting final provision of the agreement. Although RealNetworks could have titled the heading containing the arbitration clause, the choice of law provision, and the forum selection clause in a more descriptive manner than "Miscellaneous," RealNetworks' titling it such does not necessarily bury the provision. While RealNetworks did not set off the arbitration provision and purposely draw attention to it, neither did RealNetworks bury the provision in a sea of words. Although burying an arbitration clause could contribute to a finding of unconscionability, the Court is unaware of, and Intervenor has not pointed to, any Washington state caselaw that provides that an arbitration clause is unconscionable if the contract does not draw attention to it.

Moreover, Intervenor claims that the user is not given a reasonable opportunity to understand the arbitration provision because the License Agreement comes in a small pop-up window, which is visually difficult to read, and because it cannot be printed. The Court has already discussed at length the capability of printing the License Agreement, and again rejects Intervenor's contention that the License Agreement cannot be printed. The Court also finds that the size of the pop-up window, although smaller than the desktop, does not make the License Agreement visually difficult to read. The Court finds disingenuous Intervenor's assertion that the License Agreement appears "in very fine print, requiring the user to position himself just inches from the monitor in order to read it." The font size of the License Agreement is no smaller, and possibly larger, than the font size of all the words appearing on the computer's own display. If Intervenor needs to plaster his face against the screen to read the License Agreement, he must then have to do the same to read anything on his computer, in which case, doing so does not seem like an inordinate hardship or an adjustment out of the ordinary for him. In addition, the user has all day to review the License Agreement on the screen. The pop-up window containing the License Agreement does not disappear after a certain time period; so, the user can scroll through it and examine it to his heart's content.

Because the arbitration agreement is not buried in fine print and because a user is given ample opportunity to understand the arbitration provision, the Court does not find that the arbitration agreement is procedurally unconscionable.

In addition, Intervenor asserts that the arbitration provision is substantively unconscionable because it chooses a geographically distant forum, it fails to provide for classwide arbitration, and the costs of arbitration are prohibitive.

The Court rejects Intervenor's claim that choosing Washington state as the arbitration forum renders the arbitration agreement substantively unconscionable. The designation of any state as a forum is bound to be distant to some potential litigants of a corporation that has a nationwide reach. Intervenor would have the Court essentially preclude arbitration agreements from having any forum selection clause in order to prevent the designation of a distant forum to any of these litigants. This Court is not willing to do so. Arbitration provisions containing forum selection clauses have previously been upheld. *See Quist v. Empire Funding Corp.,* 1999 WL 982953, at *3 (N.D.Ill.1999) (enforcing contract of Illinois resident that required arbitration in Texas); *Doctor's Ass'n. Inc. v. Hamilton,* 150 F.3d 157, 163 (2d Cir.1998) (upholding forum selection clause in arbitration clause designating Connecticut as forum). Moreover, some courts have even found that the forum non conveniens doctrine is inapplicable in the context of arbitrations covered under the FAA. *See Al-Salamah Arabian Agencies Co., Ltd. v. Reece,* 673 F.Supp. 748, 751 (M.D.N.C.1987); *Spring Hope Rockwool v. Industrial Clean Air, Inc.,* 504 F.Supp. 1385, 1389 (E.D.N.C.1981). Thus, that Washington is a distant arbitration forum for some does not render the arbitration clause substantively unconscionable.

Intervenor also claims that because litigants cannot pursue classwide arbitration without an arbitration provision providing for it, *see Champ v. Siegel Trading Co.,* 55 F.3d 269, 275 (7th Cir.1995), RealNetworks is effectively preventing potential litigants from seeking classwide arbitration by not expressly providing for classwide arbitration. Further, Intervenor reasons that because consumers in cases such as this have relatively small claims, these consumers' rights to bring a case would essentially be vitiated because the costs of the litigation would be so prohibitive. This Court previously rejected this argument in its prior decision. *See Lieschke,* 2000 WL 198424, at *3. The Seventh Circuit, along with other courts in this district, have considered this issue and upheld arbitration agreements that do not provide for class action and have even upheld arbitration agreements that expressly prohibit class actions. *See Champ,* 55 F.3d at 275–77; *Zawikowski v. Beneficial Nat'l Bank,* 1999 WL 35304, at *2 (N.D.Ill.1999); *see also Lopez v. Plaza Fin. Co.,* 1996 WL 210073, at *3 (N.D.Ill.1996); *cf. Dean Witter Reynolds, Inc. v. Byrd,* 470 U.S. 213, 217 (1985) (the FAA requires district courts to compel arbitration "even where the result would be the possibly inefficient maintenance of separate proceedings in different forums"). Thus, the Court will not find the License Agreement substantively unconscionable because it does not provide for class arbitration.

Further, the Court rejects Intervenor's argument that allegedly prohibitive arbitration costs render the License Agreement unconscionable. The Seventh Circuit has found that the costs of arbitration do not prevent the enforcement of a valid arbitration agreement. *See Hill,* 105 F.3d at 1151 (whatever may be said pro and con about the cost and efficacy of arbitration is for Congress and the contracting parties to consider); *Dorsey v. H.C.P. Sales, Inc.,* 46 F.Supp.2d 804, 807 (N.D.Ill.1999); *see also Koveleskie,* 167 F.3d at 366 (expensive fees do not necessarily preclude arbitration). As such, the potential arbitration costs do not render the arbitration clause substantively unconscionable.

CONCLUSION

For the reasons set forth above, the Court rejects Intervenor's additional arguments in support of Plaintiffs' opposition to arbitration.

Brower v. Gateway 2000, Inc.
676 N.Y.S.2d 569 (N.Y.App.Div.1998).

■ MILONAS, JUSTICE PRESIDING.

Appeal from an order of the Supreme Court (Beatrice Shainswit, J.), entered October 21, 1997 in New York County, which, to the extent appealed from, granted defendants' motion to dismiss the complaint on the ground that there was a valid agreement to arbitrate between the parties.

Appellants are among the many consumers who purchased computers and software products from defendant Gateway 2000 through a direct-sales system, by mail or telephone order. As of July 3, 1995, it was Gateway's practice to include with the materials shipped to the purchaser along with the merchandise a copy of its "Standard Terms and Conditions Agreement" and any relevant warranties for the products in the shipment. The Agreement begins with a "NOTE TO CUSTOMER," which provides, in slightly larger print than the remainder of the document, in a box that spans the width of the page: "This document contains Gateway 2000's Standard Terms and Conditions. By keeping your Gateway 2000 computer system beyond thirty (30) days after the date of delivery, you accept these Terms and Conditions." The document consists of 16 paragraphs, and, as is relevant to this appeal, paragraph 10 of the agreement, entitled "DISPUTE RESOLUTION," reads as follows:

> Any dispute or controversy arising out of or relating to this Agreement or its interpretation shall be settled exclusively and finally by arbitration. The arbitration shall be conducted in accordance with the Rules of Conciliation and Arbitration of the International Chamber of Commerce. The arbitration shall be conducted in Chicago, Illinois, U.S.A. before a sole arbitrator. Any award rendered in any such arbitration proceeding shall be final and binding on each of the parties, and judgment may be entered thereon in a court of competent jurisdiction.

Plaintiffs commenced this action on behalf of themselves and others similarly situated for compensatory and punitive damages, alleging deceptive sales practices in seven causes of action, including breach of warranty, breach of contract, fraud and unfair trade practices. In particular, the allegations focused on Gateway's representations and advertising that promised "service when you need it," including around-the-clock free technical support, free software technical support and certain on-site services. According to plaintiffs, not only were they unable to avail themselves of this offer because it was virtually impossible to get through to a technician, but also Gateway continued to advertise this claim notwithstanding numerous complaints and reports about the problem.

Insofar as is relevant to appellants, who purchased their computers after July 3, 1995, Gateway moved to dismiss the complaint based on the arbitration clause in the Agreement. Appellants argued that the arbitration clause is invalid under UCC 2–207, unconscionable under UCC 2–302 and an unenforceable contract of adhesion. Specifically, they claimed that the provision was obscure; that a customer could not reasonably be expected to appreciate or investigate its meaning and effect; that the International Chamber of Commerce ("ICC") was not a forum commonly used for consumer matters; and that because ICC headquarters were in France, it was particularly difficult to locate the organization and its rules. To illustrate just how inaccessible the forum was, appellants advised the court that the ICC was not registered with the Secretary of State, that efforts to locate and contact the ICC had been unsuccessful and that apparently the only way to attempt to contact the ICC was through the United States Council for International Business, with which the ICC maintained some sort of relationship.

In support of their arguments, appellants submitted a copy of the ICC's Rules of Conciliation and Arbitration and contended that the cost of ICC arbitration was prohibitive, particularly given the amount of the typical consumer claim involved. For example, a claim of less than $50,000 required advance fees of $4,000 (more than the cost of most Gateway products), of which the $2000 registration fee was nonrefundable even if the consumer prevailed at the arbitration. Consumers would also incur travel expenses disproportionate to the damages sought, which appellants' counsel estimated would not exceed $1,000 per customer in this action, as well as bear the cost of Gateway's legal fees if the consumer did not prevail at the arbitration; in this respect, the ICC rules follow the "loser pays" rule used in England. Also, although Chicago was designated as the site of the actual arbitration, all correspondence must be sent to ICC headquarters in France.

The IAS court dismissed the complaint as to appellants based on the arbitration clause in the Agreements delivered with their computers. We agree with the court's decision and reasoning in all respects but for the issue of the unconscionability of the designation of the ICC as the arbitration body.

First, the court properly rejected appellants' argument that the arbitration clause was invalid under UCC 2–207. Appellants claim that when they placed their order they did not bargain for, much less accept, arbitration of any dispute, and therefore the arbitration clause in the agreement that accompanied the merchandise shipment was a "material alteration" of a preexisting oral agreement. Under UCC 2–207(2), such a material alteration constitutes "proposals for addition to the contract" that become part of the contract only upon appellants' express acceptance. However, as the court correctly concluded, the clause was not a "material alteration" of an oral agreement, but, rather, simply one provision of the sole contract that existed between the parties. That contract, the court explained, was formed and acceptance was manifested not when the order was placed but only with the retention of the merchandise beyond the 30 days specified in the Agreement enclosed in the shipment of merchandise. Accordingly, the contract was outside the scope of UCC 2–207.

In reaching its conclusion, the IAS court took note of the litigation in Federal courts on this very issue, and, indeed, on this very arbitration clause. In *Hill v. Gateway 2000, Inc.*, 105 F.3d 1147, plaintiffs in a class action contested the identical Gateway contract in dispute before us, including the enforceability of the arbitration clause. As that court framed the issue, the "[t]erms inside Gateway's box stand or fall together. If they constitute the parties contract because the Hills had an opportunity to return the computer after reading them, then all must be enforced" (*id.*

at 1148). The court then concluded that the contract was not formed with the placement of a telephone order or with the delivery of the goods. Instead, an enforceable contract was formed only with the consumer's decision to retain the merchandise beyond the 30-day period specified in the agreement. Thus, the agreement as a whole, including the arbitration clause, was enforceable.

This conclusion was in keeping with the same court's decision in *ProCD, Inc. v. Zeidenberg*, 86 F.3d 1447 . . . .

. . .

Second, with respect to appellants' claim that the arbitration clause is unenforceable as a contract of adhesion, in that it involved no choice or negotiation on the part of the consumer but was a "take it or leave it" proposition (*see, e.g., Matter of State v. Ford Motor Company*, 74 N.Y.2d 495, 503), we find that this argument, too, was properly rejected by the IAS court. Although the parties clearly do not possess equal bargaining power, this factor alone does not invalidate the contract as one of adhesion. . . .

While returning the goods to avoid the formation of the contract entails affirmative action on the part of the consumer, and even some expense, this may be seen as a trade-off for the convenience and savings for which the consumer presumably opted when he or she chose to make a purchase of such consequence by phone or mail as an alternative to on-site retail shopping. That a consumer does not read the agreement or thereafter claims he or she failed to understand or appreciate some term therein does not invalidate the contract any more than such claim would undo a contract formed under other circumstances. . . . We further note that appellants' claim of adhesion is identical to that made and rejected in *Filias v. Gateway 2000, Inc.*, an unreported case brought to our attention by both parties that interprets the same Gateway agreement (No. 97C 2523 [N.D.Ill., January 15, 1998], *transferred by* 1997 U.S. Dist. LEXIS 7115 [E.D.Mich., Apr. 8, 1997, Zatkoff, J.]).

Finally, we turn to appellants' argument that the IAS court should have declared the contract unenforceable, pursuant to UCC 2–302, on the ground that the arbitration clause is unconscionable due to the unduly burdensome procedure and cost for the individual consumer. The IAS court found that while a class-action lawsuit, such as the one herein, may be a less costly alternative to the arbitration (which is generally less costly than litigation), that does not alter the binding effect of the valid arbitration clause contained in the agreement . . . .

As a general matter, under New York law, unconscionability requires a showing that a contract is "both procedurally and substantively unconscionable when made" (*Gillman v. Chase Manhattan Bank*, 73 N.Y.2d 1, 10). That is, there must be "some showing of 'an absence of meaningful choice on the part of one of the parties together with contract terms which are unreasonably favorable to the other party' [citation omitted]" (*Matter of State of New York v. Avco Financial Service*, 50 N.Y.2d 383, 389). The *Avco* court took pains to note, however, that the purpose of this doctrine is not to redress the inequality between the parties but simply to ensure that the more powerful party cannot "surprise" the other party with some overly oppressive term (*id.*, at 389).

As to the procedural element, a court will look to the contract formation process to determine if in fact one party lacked any meaningful choice in entering into the contract, taking into consideration such factors as the setting of the transaction, the experience and education of the party claiming unconscionability, whether the contract contained "fine print," whether the seller used "high-pressured tactics" and any disparity in the parties' bargaining power (*Gillman v Chase Manhattan Bank, supra*, at 11). None of these factors supports appellants' claim here. Any purchaser has 30 days within which to thoroughly examine the contents of their shipment, including the terms of the Agreement, and seek clarification of any term therein (*e.g., Matter of Ball, supra*, at 161). The Agreement itself, which is entitled in large print "STANDARD TERMS AND CONDITIONS AGREEMENT," consists of only three pages and 16 paragraphs, all of which appear in the same size print. Moreover, despite appellants' claims to the contrary, the arbitration clause is in no way "hidden" or "tucked away" within a complex document of inordinate length, nor is the option of returning the merchandise, to avoid the contract, somehow a "precarious" one. We also reject appellants' insinuation that, by using the word "standard," Gateway deliberately meant to convey to the consumer that the terms were standard within the industry, when the document clearly purports to be no more than Gateway's "standard terms and conditions."

With respect to the substantive element, which entails an examination of the substance of the agreement in order to determine whether the terms unreasonably favor one party . . . , we do not find that the possible inconvenience of the chosen site (Chicago) alone rises to the level of unconscionability. We do find, however, that the excessive cost factor that is necessarily entailed in arbitrating before the ICC is unreasonable and surely serves to deter the individual consumer from invoking the process . . . . Barred from resorting to the courts by the arbitration clause in the first instance, the designation of a financially prohibitive forum effectively bars consumers from this forum as well; consumers are thus left with no forum at all in which to resolve a dispute. In this regard, we note that this particular claim is not mentioned in the *Hill* decision, which upheld the clause as part of an enforceable contract.

While it is true that, under New York law, unconscionability is generally predicated on the presence of both the procedural and substantive elements, the substantive element alone may be sufficient to render the terms of the provision at issue unenforceable . . . . Excessive fees, such as those incurred under the ICC procedure, have been grounds for finding an arbitration provision unenforceable or commercially unreasonable . . . .

In the *Filias* case previously mentioned, the Federal District Court stated that it was "inclined to agree" with the argument that selection of the ICC rendered the clause unconscionable, but concluded that the issue was moot because Gateway had agreed to arbitrate before the American Arbitration Association ("AAA") and sought court appointment of the AAA pursuant to Federal Arbitration Act 9 U.S.C. § 5. The court accordingly granted Gateway's motion to compel arbitration and appointed the AAA in lieu of the ICC. Plaintiffs in that action (who are represented by counsel for appellants before us) contend that costs associated with the AAA process are also excessive, given the amount of the individual consumer's damages, and their motion for reconsideration of the court's decision has not yet been decided. While the AAA rules and costs are not part of the record before us, the parties agree that there is a minimum, nonrefundable filing fee of $500, and appellants claim each consumer could spend in excess of $1,000 to arbitrate in this forum.

Gateway's agreement to the substitution of the AAA is not limited to the *Filias* plaintiffs. Gateway's brief includes the text of a new arbitration agreement that it claims has been extended to all customers, past, present and future (apparently through publication in a quarterly magazine sent to anyone who has ever purchased a Gateway product). The new arbitration agreement provides for the consumer's choice of the AAA or the ICC as the arbitral body and the designation of any location for the arbitration by agreement of the parties, which "shall not be unreasonably withheld." It also provides telephone numbers at which the AAA and the ICC may be reached for information regarding the "organizations and their procedures."

As noted, however, appellants complain that the AAA fees are also excessive and thus in no way have they accepted defendant's offer (*see*, UCC 2–209); because they make the same claim as to the AAA as they did with respect to the ICC, the issue of unconscionability is not rendered moot, as defendant suggests. We cannot determine on this record whether the AAA process and costs would be so "egregiously oppressive" that they, too, would be unconscionable . . . . Thus, we modify the order on appeal to the extent of finding that portion of the arbitration provision requiring arbitration before the ICC to be unconscionable and remand to Supreme Court so that the parties have the opportunity to seek appropriate substitution of an arbitrator pursuant to the Federal Arbitration Act (9 U.S.C. § 1 et seq.), which provides for such court designation of an arbitrator upon application of either party, where, for whatever reason, one is not otherwise designated (9 U.S.C. § 5).

Appellants make the final argument that the arbitration clause does not apply to the cause of action for false advertising (with respect to the promised round-the-clock service) under various sections of the General Business Law on the ground that there is no mention of arbitration in the technical service contract itself. Although they raise this claim for the first time on this appeal, we find the promise of technical support to be within the scope of arbitration as it is clearly a "dispute or controversy arising out or relating to [the] Agreement or its interpretation." Put another way, the service contract does not apply to some separate product that could be retained while the computer products—and the accompanying agreement—could be returned.

. . .

QUESTIONS FOR DISCUSSION

1. *Why litigate?* Why would a disgruntled consumer choose to bring a lawsuit, with its attendant high costs and long delays, rather than allowing the dispute to be decided by an arbitrator?

2. *Effect of high cost of arbitration.* In *In re RealNetworks*, excerpted above, the court cites the Seventh Circuit for the claim that "the costs of arbitration do not prevent the enforcement of a valid arbitration agreement. *See Hill,* 105 F.3d at 1151 (whatever may be said pro and con about the cost and efficacy of arbitration is for Congress and the contracting parties to consider.)." Is it necessary to qualify this statement? Does the court mean that the costs of arbitration are never an adequate basis for declaring an arbitration clause substantively unconscionable? Does the court consider comparing the cost of arbitration with the amount of money at stake in the lawsuit?

3. *Tradeoffs and alternatives.* In *Brower*, the court says that the possible expense involved in returning the computer if the consumer does not like the contract terms accompanying it is acceptable "as a trade-off for the convenience and savings for which the consumer presumably opted when he or she chose to make a purchase of such consequence by phone or mail as an alternative to on-site retail shopping." Is the consumer likely to be aware of the existence of this trade-off at the time she makes the purpose? Does it matter whether she is aware of it?

4. *Procedural criterion.* In *Brower*, the court found that the presentation of the arbitration clause was not procedurally deficient. What standard did it apply in making this determination? Consider the fact that the arbitration clause stated that arbitration would be conducted in Chicago under the rules of the International Chamber of Commerce, but nowhere disclosed that those rules provided that the complainant must pay $4,000 in advance fees, $2,000 of which was nonrefundable even if the complainant prevailed, and that the complainant could be required to pay Gateway's attorney's fees if she lost. Do you agree with the court that Gateway's Standard Terms provided purchasers with the information they required to exercise a "meaningful choice"?

5. *Conscionable options.* If a court finds a provision in a contract to be unconscionable, how should it proceed? Should it invalidate the entire contract? Would this judicial response encourage people not to overreach when they negotiate (or draft adhesion) contracts? Should a court simply delete the provision? How would this affect contracts with unconscionable arbitration clauses? Should a court draft and impose on the parties a conscionable substitute for the provision that the court found unconscionable?

B. THE ENFORCEABILITY OF CHOICE OF LAW AND CHOICE OF FORUM CLAUSES IN ONLINE CONTRACTS

Parties to commercial transactions often seek to establish contractually which court shall have jurisdiction to decide disputes arising from their relationship and which state's law shall govern the contract. (Online jurisdiction is covered in Chapter 5, *supra.*) A contractual clause that specifies which court shall have jurisdiction is known as a forum-selection clause, and one that specifies whose law shall govern is known as a choice of law clause.

While "[f]orum-selection clauses have historically not been favored by American courts," the modern view "is that such clauses are prima facie valid and should be enforced unless enforcement is shown by the resisting party to be 'unreasonable' under the circumstances." *M/S Bremen v. Zapata Off-Shore Co.,* 407 U.S. 1, 9–10 (1972). This rule applies, under federal law, both if the clause was the result of negotiation between two business entities, and if it is contained in a form contract that a business presents to an individual on a take-it-or-leave-it basis. In *Carnival Cruise Lines, Inc. v. Shute,* 499 U.S. 585 (1991), the Supreme Court addressed the enforceability of a forum-selection clause that was among the terms set forth on several pages appended to a cruise-ship ticket. The Court held that the clause was enforceable, despite its not being the product of negotiation, as it was not unreasonable (unconscionable), primarily because the majority thought that the clause would save the defendant money, and those savings would be passed on to the consumer.

Companies that offer goods and services online have an especially strong incentive to define contractually the forum for resolution of disputes, since they may be engaging in transactions with purchasers located in a multiplicity of jurisdictions, and defending lawsuits in scattered locations can be very expensive. Furthermore, since courts typically (though not always) apply the law of the forum in which they sit, suit in foreign jurisdictions subjects sellers to various substantive laws, increasing their costs of complying with applicable law.

Providers of Internet access or other online services frequently include a forum-selection clause in the "Terms of Service" to which subscribers must indicate their assent as part of the process of gaining access to the service. The clause is often one element of a lengthy recitation of conditions that the subscriber may view by scrolling through an on-screen box. The subscriber is often presented with a clickwrap procedure, in which he is asked to indicate assent to the Terms of Service by clicking an on-screen button that says "I Agree." The forum-selection clause may also be presented in other ways, such as through a hyperlink called "Terms and Conditions" or "Legal Notice," or by text that is more or less proximate to the terms of the offer. The extent to which such presentations of terms are in general sufficient for contract formation is explored Part I of this chapter.

Forum-selection clauses very often occur in conjunction with choice-of-law clauses. Most courts that have ruled on the issue have enforced online forum-selection and choice-of-law clauses. Thus, in *Groff v. America Online, Inc.*, 1998 WL 307001 (R.I.Super.Ct. 1998), the plaintiff, an individual in Rhode Island who subscribed to America Online, sued the company in Rhode Island state court, alleging violations of state consumer protection legislation. The process of becoming a member of AOL includes a step in which the applicant must assent to AOL's Terms of Service by clicking an "I Agree" button. The Terms of Service "contains a forum selection clause which expressly provides that Virginia law and Virginia courts are the appropriate law and forum for the litigation between members and AOL." Citing *M/S Bremen v. Zapata Offshore, supra,* the court looked to whether enforcement of the clause would be "unreasonable." It did so by application of a nine-factor test, including such criteria as the place of execution of the contract, public policy of the forum state, location of the parties and witnesses, relative bargaining power of the parties, and "the conduct of the parties." The court concluded that enforcement of the clause would not be unreasonable, and so dismissed the case.

In *Kilgallen v. Network Solutions, Inc.*, 99 F.Supp.2d 125 (D.Mass.2000), the court enforced a forum-selection clause on less supportive facts. Defendant Network Solutions, Inc., at the time the monopoly registrar of domain names in the .com top-level domain, sent plaintiff a notice via e-mail stating that he would soon receive an invoice to pay his annual registration fee. The lengthy notice included a section titled "Domain Name Registration Agreement," paragraph P of which contained a forum-selection clause. A month later, plaintiff received an invoice via e-mail, which stated: "In making payment for the invoice below, Registrant agrees to the terms and conditions of the current Domain Registration Agreement." Plaintiff paid the invoice, but through a series of clerical errors NSI misapplied the payment, and subsequently cancelled the domain name for nonpayment, whereupon another person registered it. Plaintiff sued for breach of contract, and NSI sought to enforce the forum-selection clause. The court enforced the clause, finding that plaintiff had failed to demonstrate that it was unreasonable.

But in *America Online, Inc. v. Superior Court*, 108 Cal.Rptr.2d 699 (Cal.Ct.App.2001), the court declined to enforce AOL's contractual forum-selection and choice-of-law clauses. Plaintiff Mendoza sought to represent a class of former AOL subscribers, who alleged that AOL continued to debit their credit cards for monthly subscription fees even after they cancelled their subscriptions. The complaint alleged several causes of action, including violation of the California Consumers Legal Remedies Act ("CLRA"), CAL. CIV. CODE §§ 1750 *et seq.*, a consumer protection statute that prohibits unfair and deceptive trade practices. AOL filed a motion to stay or dismiss, based on the forum-selection clause contained in its Terms of Service. The clause stated:

> You expressly agree that exclusive jurisdiction for any claim or dispute with AOL or relating in any way to your membership or your use of AOL resides in the courts of Virginia and you further agree and expressly consent to the exercise of personal jurisdiction in the courts of Virginia in connection with any such dispute including any claim involving AOL or its affiliates, subsidiaries, employees, contractors, officers, directors, telecommunications providers and content providers . . . .

The Terms of Service also contained a choice-of-law provision: "The laws of the Commonwealth of Virginia, excluding its conflicts-of-law rules, govern this Agreement and your membership." The trial court denied AOL's motion, and AOL filed a petition for a writ of mandamus.

The appeals court affirmed. It agreed with the trial court that although "[n]ormally, the burden of proof is on the party challenging the enforcement of a contractual forum selection clause," in this case the burden should shift to AOL, in view of the CLRA's non-waiver provision, which states: "Any waiver by a consumer of the provisions of this title is contrary to public policy and shall be unenforceable and void." CAL. CIV. CODE § 1751. The court found: "Where the effect of transfer to a different forum has the potential of stripping California consumers of their legal rights deemed by the Legislature to be non-waivable, the burden must be placed on the party asserting the contractual forum selection clause to prove that the CLRA's anti-waiver provisions are not violated." The court continued:

> AOL correctly posits that California favors contractual forum selection clauses so long as they are entered into freely and voluntarily, and their enforcement would not be unreasonable. . . . This favorable treatment is attributed to our law's devotion to the concept of one's free right to contract, and flows from the important practical effect such contractual rights have on commerce generally. This division has characterized forum selection clauses as "play[ing] an important role in both national and international commerce." . . . We . . . view such clauses as likely to become even more ubiquitous as this state and nation become acculturated to electronic commerce. See [*Carnival Cruise Lines*]. Moreover, there are strong economic arguments in support of these agreements, favoring both merchants and consumers, including reduction in the costs of goods and services and the stimulation of e-commerce.

> But this encomium is not boundless. Our law favors forum selection agreements only so long as they are procured freely and voluntarily, with the place chosen having some logical nexus to one of the parties or the dispute, and so long as California consumers will not find their substantial legal rights signifi-

cantly impaired by their enforcement. Therefore, to be enforceable, the selected jurisdiction must be "suitable," "available," and able to "accomplish substantial justice." (*The Bremen v. Zapata Off-Shore Co.* (1972) 407 U.S. 1, 17 . . .) The trial court determined that the circumstances of contract formation did not reflect Mendoza exercised free will, and that the effect of enforcing the forum selection clause here would violate California public policy by eviscerating important legal rights afforded to this state's consumers. Our task, then, is to review the record to determine if there was a rational basis for the court's findings and the choice it made not to enforce the forum selection clause in AOL's TOS agreement. . . . California courts will refuse to defer to the selected forum if to do so would substantially diminish the rights of California residents in a way that violates our state's public policy. . . .

Id. at 707–08. The court reviewed *Hall v. Superior Court*, 197 Cal.Rptr. 757 (Cal.Ct.App. 1983), which declined to enforce a forum-selection clause naming Nevada as the forum, on the ground that to do so would conflict with the anti-waiver provision of California's Corporate Securities Law of 1968. The court continued:

> The CLRA parallels the Corporate Securities Law of 1968, at issue in *Hall,* insofar as the CRLA is a legislative embodiment of a desire to protect California consumers and furthers a strong public policy of this state. . . . Certainly, the CLRA provides remedial protections *at least* as important as those under the Corporate Securities Law of 1968. Therefore, by parity of reasoning, enforcement of AOL's forum selection clause, which is also accompanied by a choice of law provision favoring Virginia, would necessitate a waiver of the statutory remedies of the CLRA, in violation of that law's anti-waiver provision . . . and California public policy. For this reason alone, we affirm the trial court's ruling.

Id. at 710. The court went on to compare the CLRA with its Virginia counterpart, finding that "Virginia's law provides significantly less consumer protection to its citizens than California law provides for our own." In particular, the Virginia statute did not permit class actions. The court said: "[W]e cannot accept AOL's assertion that the elimination of class actions for consumer remedies if the forum selection clause is enforced is a matter of insubstantial moment. The unavailability of class action relief in this context is sufficient in and by itself to preclude enforcement of the TOS forum selection clause." The court went on to note that

> neither punitive damages, nor enhanced remedies for disabled and senior citizens are recoverable under Virginia's law. More nuanced differences are the reduced recovery under the VCPA for "unintentional" acts, a shorter period of limitations, and Virginia's use of a Lodestar formula alone to calculate attorney fees recovery. . . . Quite apart from the remedial limitations under Virginia law relating to injunctive and class action relief, the cumulative importance of even these less significant differences is substantial. Enforcement of a forum selection clause, which would impair these aggregate rights, would itself violate important California public policy. For this additional reason the trial court was correct in denying AOL's motion to stay or to dismiss.[17]

Id. at 712.

---

[17] Because we affirm on other grounds, we need not decide whether the trial court correctly concluded that the TOS was an unconscionable, adhesion contract . . . or Mendoza's alternative contention that the forum selection clause is unenforceable because it was induced by fraud.

EXTENSIONS

---

1. *Another court invalidates AOL's forum-selection clause.* A Florida court followed *America Online v. Superior Court* in refusing to enforce the same forum-selection clause, where doing so would have deprived plaintiffs of the possibility of bringing a class action. *See America Online, Inc. v. Pasieka*, 870 So.2d 170 (Fla.Dist.Ct.App.2004).

2. *Contract of adhesion.* In *Spera v. America Online, Inc.*, Index No. 06716/97 (N.Y.Sup.Ct.1998), the court enforced a forum-selection clause against a defendant who claimed that AOL had engaged in misleading business practices. Applying New York law, the court rejected plaintiff's arguments that the forum-selection clause was "a contract of adhesion" and that enforcing the clause would be against public policy.

3. *Other limitations on contractual ordering.* As can be seen from the materials in this section, arbitration clauses and forum-selection/choice-of-law clauses are frequently challenged, and often the doctrines invoked are unconscionability or voidness as against public policy. Unconscionability includes the procedural concerns of insufficient notice and inadequate assent, as well as substantive concerns about unfairness or gross disparities in the quid pro quo; public policy is concerned with regimes of contract that interfere with larger social ordering. Is it possible to delineate more precisely which types of individual or social interests should invoke greater judicial scrutiny? As one avenue of thought about the problem, consider stricter scrutiny of attempted contractual waivers of background entitlements in these categories: (1) right of legal enforcement or redress of grievances, (2) human rights (including both individual and cultural rights), and (3) politically weak or vulnerable rights (without a strong constituency to lobby for them). For another avenue of thought, *see* Judith Resnik, *Procedure as Contract*, 80 NOTRE DAME L. REV. 593 (2005).

QUESTIONS FOR DISCUSSION

---

1. *Notice: actual knowledge required?* Should it matter whether the plaintiff actually read the forum-selection clause before clicking "I Agree"? The plaintiff in *Groff v. America Online* claimed in his affidavit: "I never saw, read, negotiated for or knowingly agreed to be bound by the choice of law . . . ." The court was unmoved, reciting the "general rule that a party who signs an instrument manifests his assent to it and cannot later complain that he did not read the instrument or that he did not understand its contents." Is clicking on an "I Agree" button displayed on a computer monitor the equivalent of signing a document, for purposes of indicating that the signing party recognizes the significance of his act? (Reconsider the issues discussed in Part I(E) of this Chapter.) Should the prominence of the forum-selection clause in the sign-up process be a significant factor? The sign-up process that the plaintiff in *Groff* underwent involved numerous screens full of text, taking up 94 pages in hard-copy format. Note that in *Carnival Cruise Lines v. Shute, supra,* the existence of additional contractual terms was signaled to plaintiff by a notice on the face of the ticket that read: **"SUBJECT TO CONDITIONS OF CONTRACT ON LAST PAGES IMPORTANT! PLEASE READ CONTRACT—ON LAST PAGES 1, 2, 3."** 499 U.S. at 587.

2. *Non-waivable provisions.* The holding in *America Online v. Superior Court* turned in part on the California legislature's decision to make consumer rights under the CLRA non-waivable. (The court was also concerned that the plaintiff's class action would be disallowed under Virginia law.) Why would a legislature choose to interfere with consumers' freedom of contract by making consumer rights non-waivable? How might AOL (or any other online seller) respond to such legislation? Contracts in consumer transactions are typically non-negotiable, the stated reason being that the low value of the transaction cannot justify the costs of negotiation. Are there reasons to think that this factor is of less significance online? Do you think that AOL is charging subscribers a competitive market price that takes into account AOL's cost savings from expected enforcement of the forum-selection clause? Is AOL unfairly stuck with charging California subscribers the same price as subscribers in states that are willing to enforce its forum-selection clause?

COMPARATIVE NOTE

The European approach to personal jurisdiction in cross-border disputes is rather different from the U.S. approach. The rules determining which country's courts have jurisdiction over a defendant are set out in a regulation issued by the Council of the European Union, known as the Brussels Regulation. Council Regulation (EC) No 44/2001 of 22 December 2000 on jurisdiction and the recognition and enforcement of judgments in civil and commercial matters, 2001 O.J. (L 12) 1. The Regulation, which became effective on March 1, 2002, is an update of a 1968 treaty among European countries, known as the Brussels Convention. Convention on jurisdiction and the enforcement of judgments in civil and commercial Matters, 1990 O.J. (C 189) 2 (consolidated).

The Regulation establishes the general rule that "[p]ersons domiciled in a Member State shall, whatever their nationality, be sued in the courts of that Member State." Art. 2. But there are a number of derogations from that general rule, allowing a person to be sued in the courts of a country other than the one where he is domiciled. For example, if the action relates to a contract, suit may be brought "in the courts for the place of performance of the obligation in question." Art. 5(1)(a). If the action relates to tort, suit may be brought "in the courts for the place where the harmful event occurred or may occur." Art. 5(3).

There are also special rules for certain consumer contracts, in keeping with the broad distinction between consumer law and commercial law that is followed in European countries. A consumer contract is one that is "concluded by a person, the consumer, for a purpose which can be regarded as being outside his trade or profession." Art. 15(1). Certain types of consumer contracts are *per se* covered by the special rules: these are contracts for the sale of goods on installment credit, and contracts for a loan made to finance the sale of goods. Art. 15(1)(a), (b). Other types of contracts are covered if

> the contract has been concluded with a person who pursues commercial or professional activities in the Member State of the consumer's domicile or, by any means, directs such activities to that Member State or to several States including that Member State, and the contract falls within the scope of such activities.

Art. 15(1)(c).

Two important special rules apply to actions relating to a covered consumer contract. First, the consumer may sue the seller either in the seller's country *or* "in the courts for the place where the consumer is domiciled." Art. 16(1). (But the seller still may sue the consumer only in the consumer's country.) Second, contractual forum-selection clauses are usually unenforceable. A forum-selection agreement is enforceable only if it is "entered into after the dispute has arisen," if it gives the *consumer* a choice of additional courts in which to bring the action, or if it confers jurisdiction on the courts of a country in which both the seller and consumer were "domiciled or habitually resident" at the time the contract was concluded. Art. 17. In other words, a forum-selection clause that deprives a consumer of the right to file suit in the courts of his own country is enforceable *only* if it is entered after the dispute has arisen. This prevents the use of take-it-or-leave-it contracts that deprive consumers of the home-court advantage—a technique that is quite commonly employed by sellers in the United States.

The general definition of consumer contracts in Art. 15(1)(c) was quite controversial. The corresponding provision of the Brussels Convention defined a consumer contract as one as to which "in the State of the consumer's domicile the conclusion of the contract was preceded by a specific invitation addressed to him or by advertising," and "the consumer took in that State the steps necessary for the conclusion of the contract." Brussels Convention, Art. 13(3). One impetus for revision of the Convention was the uncertain application of Art. 13 to consumer contracts concluded online. As the European Commission explained in its proposal for the Regulation:

> The criteria given in Article 13(3) of the Brussels Convention have been re-framed to take account of developments in marketing techniques. . . . The concept of activities pursued in or directed towards a Member State is designed to make clear that [Art. 15(1)(c) of the Regulation] applies to consumer contracts concluded via an interactive website accessible in the State of the consumer's domicile. The fact that a consumer simply had knowledge of a service or possibility of buying goods via a passive website accessible in his country of domicile will not trigger the protective jurisdiction. . . . The removal of the condition in [Art. 13(3)(b) of the Convention] that the consumer must have taken necessary steps for the conclusion of the contract in his home State shall also be seen in the context of contracts concluded via an interactive website. For such contracts the place where the consumer takes these steps may be difficult or impossible to determine, and they may in any event be irrelevant to creating a link between the contract and the consumer's State. The philosophy of new Article 15 is that the cocontractor creates the necessary link when directing his activities towards the consumer's state.

Proposal for a Council Regulation (EC) on jurisdiction and the recognition and enforcement of judgments in civil and commercial matters, COM(1999) 348 final at 16 (July 14, 1999).

Given the special treatment afforded consumer contracts in the European Union, it becomes important to be able to identify which transactions involve consumer contracts. Does the revised wording of the Regulation make it clear under what circumstances a seller's maintenance of a website will subject the seller to the consumer-contract exception, allowing the consumer to sue the seller in the consumer's home country? When is a website "direct[ed] to" a particular country? If it is accessible in that country? If it is written in the national language of the country? If prices are quoted in the currency of that country? Is it clear that this formulation brings more contracts within the consumer-contract exception than the Convention did?

III. LICENSING OF INTELLECTUAL PROPERTY: ISSUES FOR E-COMMERCE

Many transactions in e-commerce involve transfer of intellectual property rights. In general, the main way that intellectual property owners make money is by licensing their intellectual property to others. Normally these transactions are considered contractual. *See, e.g.*, RAYMOND T. NIMMER, LICENSING OF INTELLECTUAL PROPERTY AND OTHER INFORMATION ASSETS 3 (2004) ("A license is a contract.")

In the past, licensing practice has been primarily concerned with transactions between upstream producers of intellectual property. In the online world, however, licenses have proliferated between producers of intellectual property and end users, because such licenses are facilitated by Internet commerce. The mass-market EULA (End User Licensing Agreement) is a significant new development, which raises a number of policy questions.

We will consider the prevalent practice of attempting to use contracts (shrinkwrap, clickwrap, or browsewrap licenses) to expand the owner's rights beyond the set of entitlements granted in federal intellectual property law. We will conclude by looking at open source licensing and Creative Commons licensing, which enable users to receive more rights than they would normally acquire under copyright law by purchasing a copy.

A. LICENSING BASICS AND NEW USES

A license is a contract in which one party grants another the right to enjoy certain intellectual property rights. Normally a license is for less than the full complement of ownership rights, so that the owner retains some rights. (Transfer of the full complement of rights is called an assignment.) Licenses commonly require the licensee to pay a royalty in return for the grant of rights, but also can be royalty-free.

Licenses vary in scope, from a small portion of the licensor's "bundle of sticks" to nearly all of them. Licenses may be for a short or long term. Licenses may be limited in territory or worldwide. Licenses can be exclusive, if only one licensee can exercise the rights (for example, the common kind of license of patent rights to a manufacturer), or non-exclusive, if there is more than one licensee (for example, the common kind of copyright license of a mass-market software product).

Parties that wish to avoid infringing each others' intellectual property rights may cross-license, which means that each is entitled to exercise certain categories of rights belonging to the other. Patent cross-licenses are particularly common in the fields of e-commerce patents and software and computer hardware patents generally, because of the thickets of patents that each party would otherwise need to license, and the uncertainties about patent applicability. (*See* Chapter 11, *infra*.)

Business considerations usually determine licensing terms. Licensing can reduce the investment needed to enter a market, particularly in another country. It can facilitate acquiring specific capabilities while limiting time commitment and the potential liability of the licensor. When entering a license agreement between two intellectual property producers, perhaps the most challenging question for the parties to consider is what the technology or know-how or content is worth. Different questions become important in designing a mass-market EULA, where enforceability and market acceptability are two significant issues.

Parties may normally refuse to license their rights at their discretion, and may structure their licenses at their discretion if they do grant them. Normally licenses are construed under state contract law. Sometimes it is argued that certain provisions should be preempted by federal law. (*See* Part C, *infra*). Sometimes antitrust concerns counsel against licenses that seem anticompetitive. For example, reach-back royalty clauses, in which a licensor receives royalties from innovations produced downstream from its licensee, can raise issues for competition policy. Indeed, sometimes antitrust judgments require parties with market power to grant licenses to competitors or would-be entrants. An important instance of this is the consent decree that governs activities of ASCAP and BMI, the major copyright performing rights royalty-collection organizations. Also, copyright law by statute provides for certain compulsory licenses, meaning that the copyright owner cannot refuse to license.

The following cases involve licensing between producers of intellectual property under circumstances where the scope of the license becomes a central issue, because of a new or different use of the licensed content. They also demonstrate the normal methods that courts use to interpret a license, and the importance of the issue of scope.

Cohen v. Paramount Pictures Corp.
845 F.2d 851 (9th Cir.1988).

■ HUG, CIRCUIT JUDGE.

This case involves a novel issue of copyright law: whether a license conferring the right to exhibit a film "by means of television" includes the right to distribute videocassettes of the film. We hold it does not.

FACTS

Herbert Cohen is the owner of the copyright in a musical composition entitled "Merry-Go-Round" (hereinafter "the composition"). On May 12, 1969, Cohen granted H & J Pictures, Inc., a "synchronization" license, which gave H & J the right to use the composition in a film called "Medium Cool" and to exhibit the film in theatres and on television. Subsequently, H & J assigned to Paramount Pictures all of its rights, title, and interest in the movie "Medium Cool," including all of the rights and interests created by the 1969 license from Cohen to H & J. Sometime later, Paramount furnished a negative of the film to a videocassette manufacturer, who made copies of the film—including a recording of the composition—and supplied these copies to Paramount. Paramount, in turn, sold approximately 2,725 videocassettes of the film, receiving a gross revenue of $69,024.26 from the sales.

On February 20, 1985, Cohen filed suit against Paramount in federal district court alleging copyright infringement. Cohen contended that the license granted to H & J did not confer the right to use the composition in a reproduction of the film in videocassettes distributed for home display. The parties stipulated to the facts and both filed motions for summary judgment. The district court entered judgment in favor of Paramount, and Cohen appeals. We have jurisdiction pursuant to 28 U.S.C. § 1291 (1982).

DISCUSSION

. . . The interpretation of a contract presents a mixed question of law and fact. Where, as here, the district court's decision is based on an analysis of the contract language and the application of contract law, our review is de novo. *Miller v. Safeco Title Ins. Co.*, 758 F.2d 364, 367 (9th Cir.1985).

To resolve this case, we must examine the terms of the license, in order to determine whether the license conveyed the right to use the composition in making and distributing videocassette reproductions of "Medium Cool." The document begins by granting the licensee the "authority . . . to record, in any manner, medium, form or language, the words and music of the musical composition . . . with ['Medium Cool'] . . . to make copies of such recordings and to perform said musical composition everywhere, *all in accordance* with the terms, conditions, and limitations hereinafter set forth . . . ." (Emphasis added.) Paragraph 4 states, "The . . . license herein granted to perform . . . said musical composition is granted for: (a) The exhibition of said motion picture . . . to audiences in motion picture theatres and other places of public entertainment where motion pictures are customarily exhibited . . . (b) The exhibition of said motion picture . . . *by means of television* . . . , including 'pay television', 'subscription television' and 'closed circuit into homes' television. . . ." (Emphasis added.) Finally, paragraph 6 of the license reserves to the grantor "all rights and uses in and to said musical composition, except those herein granted to the Licensee. . . . " Although the language of the license permits the *recording and copying* of the movie with the musical composition in it, in any manner, medium, or form, nothing in the express language of the license authorizes *distribution* of the copies to the public by sale or rental.

One of the separate rights of copyright, as enumerated in section 106 of the Copyright Act, is the right "to distribute copies or phonorecords of the copyrighted work to the public by sale or other transfer of ownership, or by rental, lease, or lending." 17 U.S.C. § 106(3). Thus, the right to distribute copies of the videocassettes by sale or rental remained with the grantor under the reservation of rights provision in paragraph 6, unless in some way it is encompassed within the right to *perform* the work.

The limitation on the right to perform the synchronization with the composition in it is found in paragraph 4 and that paragraph limits the right to perform, or to authorize others to perform, to: 4(a) exhibition of the motion picture to audiences in motion picture theatres and other places of public entertainment where motion pictures are customarily shown, and 4(b) exhibition of the motion picture by means of television, including pay television, subscription television, and "closed circuit into homes" television.

It is obvious that the distribution of videocassettes through sale and rental to the general public for viewing in their homes does not fit within the purpose of category 4(a) above, which is restricted to showing in theatres and other similar public places. Paramount argues that it fits within 4(b), in that the distribution of videocassettes for showing in private homes is the equivalent of "exhibition by means of television." Paragraph 4(b) grants to Paramount the limited right to authorize broadcasters and cable television companies to broadcast the movie over the airwaves or to transmit it by cable, microwave, or some such means from a central location. The words of that paragraph must be tortured to expand the limited right granted by that section to an entirely different means of making that film available to the general public — the distribution of individual videocassettes to the general public for private "performances" in their homes. The general tenor of the section contemplates some sort of broadcasting or centralized distribution, not distribution by sale or rental of individual copies to the general public. Furthermore, the exhibition of the videocassette in the home is not "by means of television." Though videocassettes may be exhibited by using a television monitor, it does not follow that, for copyright purposes, playing videocassettes constitutes "exhibition by television." Exhibition of a film on television differs fundamentally from exhibition by means of a videocassette recorder ("VCR"). Television requires an intermediary network, station, or cable to send the television signals into consumers' homes. The menu of entertainment appearing on television is controlled entirely by the intermediary and, thus, the consumer's selection is limited to what is available on various channels. Moreover, equipped merely with a conventional television set, a consumer has no means of capturing any part of the television display; when the program is over it vanishes, and the consumer is powerless to replay it. Because they originate outside the home, television signals are ephemeral and beyond the viewer's grasp.

Videocassettes, of course, allow viewing of a markedly different nature. Videocassette entertainment is controlled within the home, at the viewer's complete discretion. A consumer may view exactly what he or she wants (assuming availability in the marketplace) at whatever time he or she chooses. The viewer may even "fast forward" the tape so as to quickly pass over parts of the program he or she does not wish to view. By their very essence, then, videocassettes liberate viewers from the constraints otherwise inherent in television, and eliminate the involvement of an intermediary, such as a network.

Television and videocassette display thus have very little in common besides the fact that a conventional monitor of a television set may be used both to receive television signals and to exhibit a videocassette. It is in light of this fact that Paramount argues that VCRs are equivalent to "exhibition by means of television." Yet, even that assertion is flawed. Playing a videocassette on a VCR does not require a standard television set capable of receiving television signals by cable or by broadcast; it is only necessary to have a monitor capable of displaying the material on the magnetized tape.

Perhaps the primary reason why the words "exhibition by means of television" in the license cannot be construed as including the distribution of videocassettes for home viewing is that VCRs for home use were not invented or known in 1969, when the license was executed. The parties both acknowledge this fact and it is noted in the order of the district judge. Thus, in 1969—long before the market for videocassettes burgeoned—Cohen could not have assumed that the public would have free and virtually unlimited access to the film in which the composition was played; instead, he must have assumed that viewer access to the film "Medium Cool" would be largely controlled by theatres and networks. By the same token, the original licensee could not have bargained for, or paid for, the rights associated with videocassette distribution. *See* Comment, *Past Copyright Licenses and the New Video Software Medium*, 29 U.C.L.A. L. REV. 1160, 1184 (1982). The holder of the license should not now "reap the entire windfall" associated with the new medium. *See id.* As noted above, the license reserved to the grantor "all rights and uses in and to said musical composition, except those herein granted to the licensee . . . " This language operates to preclude uses not then known to, or contemplated by, the parties. Thus, by its terms, the contract did not convey the right to reproduce and distribute videocassettes. That right, having not been granted to the licensee, was among those that were reserved.

Moreover, the license must be construed in accordance with the purpose underlying federal copyright law. . . .We would frustrate the purposes of the Act were we to construe this license—with its limiting language—as granting a right in a medium that had not been introduced to the domestic market at the time the parties entered into the agreement.

Paramount directs our attention to two district court cases, which, it contends, compel the opposite result. Both, however, involve licenses that contain language markedly different from the language in the license at hand.

Platinum Record Company, Inc. v. Lucasfilm, Ltd., 566 F.Supp. 226 (D.N.J.1983), involved an agreement executed in 1973 in which plaintiff's predecessor in interest granted Lucasfilm, a film producer, the right to use four popular songs on the soundtrack of the motion picture American Graffiti. The agreement expressly conferred the right to "exhibit, distribute, exploit, market and perform said motion picture, its air, screen and television trailers, perpetually throughout the world *by any means or methods now or hereafter known.*" *Id.* at 227 (emphasis added). Lucasfilm produced American Graffiti under a contract with Universal. *Id.* The film was shown in theatres and on cable, network, and local television. In 1980, a Universal affiliate released the film for sale and rental to the public on videocassettes. *Id.* Plaintiffs brought suit against Universal and its affiliate, alleging that the agreement did not give them the right to distribute the film on videocassettes.

The district court granted summary judgment in favor of the defendants. *Id.* at 226. It reasoned that the language in the agreement conferring the right to exhibit the film "'by any means or methods now or hereafter known'" was "extremely broad and completely unambiguous, and precludes any need in the Agreement for an exhaustive list of specific potential uses of the film . . . It is obvious that the contract in question may 'fairly be read' as including newly developed media, and the absence of any specific mention in the Agreement of videotapes and video cassettes is thus insignificant." *Id.* at 227.

Similarly, the district court in *Rooney v. Columbia Pictures Industries, Inc.*, 538 F.Supp. 211 (S.D.N.Y.1982), *aff'd*, 714 F.2d 117 (2d Cir. 1982), found that the contracts in question, which granted rights to exhibit certain films, also gave defendants the right to sell videocassettes of the films. *Id.* at 228. Like the contract in Platinum, the contracts in Rooney contained sweeping language, granting, for example, the right to exhibit the films "by any present or *future* methods or means," and by "any other means now *known or unknown.*" *Id.* at 223 (emphasis added). The court stated, "The contracts in question gave defendants extremely broad rights in the distribution and exhibition of [the films], plainly intending that such rights would be without limitation unless otherwise specified and further indicating that future technological advances in methods of reproduction, transmission, and exhibition would inure to the benefit of defendants." *Id.* at 228.

In contrast to the contracts in *Platinum* and *Rooney*, the license in this case lacks such broad language. The contracts in those cases expressly conferred the right to exhibit the films by methods yet to be invented. Not only is this language missing in the license at hand, but the license also expressly reserves to the copyright holder all rights not expressly granted. We fail to find the *Rooney* and *Platinum* decisions persuasive.

CONCLUSION

We hold that the license did not give Paramount the right to use the composition in connection with videocassette production and distribution of the film "Medium Cool." The district court's award of summary judgment in favor of Paramount is reversed.

Random House, Inc. v. Rosetta Books LLC
150 F.Supp.2d 613 (S.D.N.Y.2001), *aff'd*, 283 F.3d 490 (2d Cir.2002).

■ SIDNEY H. STEIN, U.S. DISTRICT JUDGE.

In this copyright infringement action, Random House, Inc. seeks to enjoin Rosetta Books LLC and its Chief Executive Officer from selling in digital format eight specific works on the grounds that the authors of the works had previously granted Random House—not Rosetta Books—the right to "print, publish and sell the work[s] in book form." Rosetta Books, on the other hand, claims it is not infringing upon the rights those authors gave Random House because the licensing agreements between the publisher and the author do not include a grant of digital or electronic rights. Relying on the language of the contracts and basic principles of contract interpretation, this Court finds that the right to "print, publish and sell the work[s] in book form" in the contracts at issue does not include the right to publish the works in the format that has come to be known as the "ebook." Accordingly, Random House's motion for a preliminary injunction is denied.

BACKGROUND

In the year 2000 and the beginning of 2001, Rosetta Books contracted with several authors to publish certain of their works—including *The Confessions of Nat Turner* and *Sophie's Choice* by William Styron; *Slaughterhouse-Five, Breakfast of Champions, The Sirens of Titan, Cat's Cradle, and Player Piano* by Kurt Vonnegut; and *Promised Land* by Robert B. Parker—in digital format over the Internet. On February 26, 2001 Rosetta Books launched its ebook business, offering those titles and others for sale in digital format. The next day, Random House filed this complaint accusing Rosetta Books of committing copyright infringement and tortiously interfering with the contracts Random House had with Messrs. Parker, Styron and Vonnegut by selling its ebooks. It simultaneously moved for a preliminary injunction prohibiting Rosetta from infringing plaintiff's copyrights.

A. Ebooks

Ebooks are "digital book[s] that you can read on a computer screen or an electronic device." (www.rosettabooks.com/pages/about_ebooks.html). Ebooks are created by converting digitized text into a format readable by computer software. The text can be viewed on a desktop or laptop computer, personal digital assistant or handheld dedicated ebook reading device. . . .

Included in a Rosetta ebook is a book cover, title page, copyright page and "eforward" all created by Rosetta Books. Although the text of the ebook is exactly the same as the text of the original work, the ebook contains various features that take advantage of its digital format. For example, ebook users can search the work electronically to find specific words and phrases. They can electronically "highlight" and "bookmark" certain text, which can then be automatically indexed and accessed through hyperlinks. They can use hyperlinks in the table of contents to jump to specific chapters.

Users can also type electronic notes which are stored with the related text. These notes can be automatically indexed, sorted and filed. Users can also change the font size and style of the text to accommodate personal preferences; thus, an electronic screen of text may contain more words, fewer words, or the same number of words as a page of the original published book. In addition, users can have displayed the definition of any word in the text. In one version of the software, the word can also be pronounced aloud.

Rosetta's ebooks contain certain security features to prevent users from printing, emailing or otherwise distributing the text. Although it is technologically possible to foil these security features, anyone who does so would be violating the licensing agreement accompanying the software.

B. Random House's licensing agreements

While each agreement between the author and Random House differs in some respects, each uses the phrase "print, publish and sell the work in book form" to convey rights from the author to the publisher.

1. Styron Agreements

Forty years ago, in 1961, William Styron granted Random House the right to publish *The Confessions of Nat Turner*. Besides granting Random House an exclusive license to "print, publish and sell the work in book form," Styron also gave it the right to "license publication of the work by book clubs," "license publication of a reprint edition," "license after book publication the publication of the work, in whole or in part, in anthologies, school books," and other shortened forms, "license without charge publication of the work in Braille, or photographing, recording, and microfilming the work for the physically handicapped," and "publish or permit others to publish or broadcast by radio or television . . . selections from the work, for publicity purposes . . . ."

The publisher agreed in the contract to "publish the work at its own expense and in such style and manner and at such a price as it deems suitable." The contract also contains a non-compete clause that provides, in relevant part, that "the Author agrees that during the term of this agreement he will not, without the written permission of the Publisher, publish or permit to be published any material in book or pamphlet form, based on the material in the work, or which is reasonably likely to injure its sale." Styron's contract with Random House for the right to publish *Sophie's Choice*, executed in 1977, is virtually identical to his 1961 contract to publish *The Confessions of Nat Turner*.

2. Vonnegut Agreements

Kurt Vonnegut's 1967 contract granting Random House's predecessor-in-interest Dell Publishing Co., Inc. the license to publish *Slaughterhouse-Five* and *Breakfast of Champions* follows a similar structure to the Styron agreements. Paragraph # 1 is captioned "grant of rights" and contains those rights the author is granting to the book publisher. . . . One of the rights granted by the author includes the "exclusive right to publish and to license the Work for publication, after book publication . . . in anthologies, selections, digests, abridgements, magazine conden-sations, serialization, newspaper syndication, picture book versions, microfilming, Xerox and other forms of copying, either now in use or hereafter developed."

Vonnegut specifically reserved for himself the "dramatic . . . motion picture (si-lent and sound) . . . radio broadcasting (including mechanical renditions and/or recordings of the text) . . . [and] television" rights. Unlike the Styron agreements, this contract does not contain a non-compete clause.

Vonnegut's 1970 contract granting Dell the license to publish *The Sirens of Titan*, *Cat's Cradle*, and *Player Piano* contains virtually identical grants and reservations of rights as his 1967 contract. However, it does contain a non-compete clause, which provides that "the Author . . . will not publish or permit to be published any edi-tion, adaptation or abridgment of the Work by any party other than Dell without Dell's prior written consent."

3. Parker Agreement

Robert B. Parker's 1982 contract granting Dell the license to publish *Promised Land* is similar to the 1970 Vonnegut contract. Paragraph # 1 contains the "grant of rights," certain of which have been crossed out by the author. . . . Parker also re-served the rights to the "dramatic . . . motion picture (silent and sound) . . . radio broadcasting . . . television . . . mechanical or electronic recordings of the text . . . ." There is also a non-compete clause that provides, in relevant part, that "the Author . . . will not, without the written permission of Dell, publish or permit to be pub-lished any material based on the material in the Work, or which is reasonably likely to injure its sale."

DISCUSSION

A. Preliminary Injunction Standard for Copyright Infringement

Random House seeks a preliminary injunction against Rosetta Book's alleged infringing activity pursuant to 17 U.S.C. § 502(a) of the Copyright Act. In order to obtain a preliminary injunction, Random House must demonstrate "(1) irreparable harm and (2) either (a) a likelihood of success on the merits or (b) sufficiently seri-ous questions about the merits to make them a fair ground for litigation and a bal-ance of hardships tipping decidedly toward the party requesting relief." In addi-tion, if the moving party establishes a prima facie case of copyright infringement, then a presumption of irreparable harm arises.

B. Ownership of a Valid Copyright

Two elements must be proven in order to establish a prima facie case of in-fringement: "(1) ownership of a valid copyright, and (2) copying of constituent elements of the work that are original." *Feist Publications, Inc. v. Rural Tel. Serv. Co.*, 499 U.S. 340, 361 (1991). In this case, only the first element—ownership of a valid copyright—is at issue, since all parties concede that the text of the ebook is identi-cal to the text of the book published by Random House.

It is well settled that although the authors own the copyrights to their works, "the legal or beneficial owner of an exclusive right under a copyright is entitled . . . to institute an action for any infringement of that particular right committed while he or she is the owner of it." 17 U.S.C. § 501(b) . . . . The question for resolution, therefore, is whether Random House is the beneficial owner of the right to publish these works as ebooks.

1. Contract Interpretation of Licensing Agreements — Legal Standards

Random House claims to own the rights in question through its licensing agreements with the authors. Interpretation of an agreement purporting to grant a copyright license is a matter of state contract law. . . .

In New York, a written contract is to be interpreted so as to give effect to the intention of the parties as expressed in the contract's language. . . . The court must consider the entire contract and reconcile all parts, if possible, to avoid an inconsistency. . . .

Determining whether a contract provision is ambiguous is a question of law to be decided by the court. . . . Pursuant to New York law, "contract language is ambiguous if it is capable of more than one meaning when viewed objectively by a reasonably intelligent person who has examined the context of the entire integrated agreement and who is cognizant of the customs, practices, usages and terminology as generally understood in the particular trade or business." *Sayers v. Rochester Tel. Corp. Supplemental Management Pension Plan*, 7 F.3d 1091, 1095 (2d Cir.1993) (internal quotations and citation omitted); *see also Bloom*, 33 F.3d at 522 (citing N.Y. U.C.C. § 2–202, Official Comment 1). "No ambiguity exists when contract language has a 'definite and precise meaning, unattended by danger of misconception in the purport of the [contract] itself, and concerning which there is no reasonable basis for a difference of opinion.' " *Sayers*, 7 F.3d at 1095 (quoting [*Breed v. Insurance Co. of N. Am*, , 46 N.Y.2d 351, 355 (1978))].

If the language of a contract is ambiguous, interpretation of the contract becomes a question of fact for the finder of fact and extrinsic evidence is admissible. . . .

These principles are in accord with the approach the U.S. Court of Appeals for the Second Circuit uses in analyzing contractual language in disputes, such as this one, "about whether licensees may exploit licensed works through new marketing channels made possible by technologies developed after the licensing contract — often called 'new use' problems." *Boosey & Hawkes Music Publishers, Ltd v. Walt Disney Co.*, 145 F.3d 481, 486 (2d Cir.1998). The two leading cases in this Circuit on how to determine whether "new uses" come within prior grants of rights are *Boosey* and *Bartsch v. Metro–Goldwyn–Mayer, Inc.*, 391 F.2d 150 (2d Cir.1968), decided three decades apart.

In *Bartsch*, the author of the play "Maytime" granted Harry Bartsch in 1930 "the motion picture rights [to 'Maytime'] throughout the world," including the right to "copyright, vend, license and exhibit such motion picture photoplays throughout the world; together with the further sole and exclusive rights by mechanical and/or electrical means to record, reproduce and transmit sound, including spoken words. . . ." 391 F.2d at 150. He in turn assigned those rights to Warner Bros. Pictures, which transferred them to MGM. In 1958 MGM licensed its motion picture "Maytime" for viewing on television. Bartsch sued, claiming the right to transmit the play over television had not been given to MGM.

Judge Henry Friendly, for the Second Circuit, wrote in 1968 that "any effort to reconstruct what the parties actually intended nearly forty years ago is doomed to failure." *Id.* at 155. He added that the words of the grant by Bartsch "were well designed to give the assignee [i.e., MGM] the broadest rights with respect to its copyrighted property." *Id.* at 154. The words of the grant were broad enough to cover the new use — i.e. viewing on television — and Judge Friendly interpreted them to do so. This interpretation, he wrote, permitted the licensee to "properly pursue any uses which may reasonably be said to fall within the medium as described in the license." *Id.* at 155. That interpretation also avoided the risk "that a deadlock between the grantor and the grantee might prevent the work's being shown over the new medium at all." *Id.*

In *Boosey*, the plaintiff was the assignee of Igor Stravinsky's copyrights in the musical composition, "The Rite of Spring." In 1939, Stravinsky had licensed Disney's use of "The Rite of Spring" in the motion picture "Fantasia." Fifty-two years later, in 1991, Disney released "Fantasia" in video format and Boosey brought an action seeking, among other relief, a declaration that the grant of rights did not include the right to use the Stravinsky work in video format. In *Boosey*, just as in *Bartsch*, the language of the grant was broad, enabling the licensee "to record in any manner, medium or form, and to license the performance of, the musical composition [for use] in a motion picture." 145 F.3d at 484.

At the Second Circuit, a unanimous panel focused on "neutral principles of contract interpretation rather than solicitude for either party." *Id.* at 487. "What governs," Judge Pierre Leval wrote, "is the language of the contract. If the contract is more reasonably read to convey one meaning, the party benefitted by that reading should be able to rely on it; the party seeking exception or deviation from the meaning reasonably conveyed by the words of the contract should bear the burden of negotiating for language that would express the limitation or deviation. This principle favors neither licensors nor licensees. It follows simply from the words of the contract." *Id.*

2. Application of Legal Standards

Relying on "the language of the license contract and basic principles of interpretation," *Boosey*, 145 F.3d at 487 n.3, as instructed to do so by *Boosey* and *Bartsch*, this Court finds that the most reasonable interpretation of the grant in the contracts at issue to "print, publish and sell the work in book form" does not include the right to publish the work as an ebook. At the outset, the phrase itself distinguishes between the pure content — i.e. "the work" — and the format of display — "in book form." The *Random House Webster's Unabridged Dictionary* defines a "book" as "a written or printed work of fiction or nonfiction, usually on sheets of paper fastened or bound together within covers" and defines "form" as "external appearance of a clearly defined area, as distinguished from color or material; the shape of a thing or person." *Random House Webster's Unabridged Dictionary* (2001), available in searchable form at www.allwords.com.

Manifestly, paragraph # 1 of each contract—entitled either "grant of rights" or "exclusive publication right"—conveys certain rights from the author to the publisher. In that paragraph, separate grant language is used to convey the rights to publish book club editions, reprint editions, abridged forms, and editions in Braille. This language would not be necessary if the phrase "in book form" encompassed all types of books. That paragraph specifies exactly which rights were being granted by the author to the publisher. Indeed, many of the rights set forth in the publisher's form contracts were in fact not granted to the publisher, but rather were reserved by the authors to themselves. For example, each of the authors specifically reserved certain rights for themselves by striking out phrases, sentences, and paragraphs of the publisher's form contract. This evidences an intent by these authors not to grant the publisher the broadest rights in their works.

Random House contends that the phrase "in book form" means to faithfully reproduce the author's text in its complete form as a reading experience and that, since ebooks concededly contain the complete text of the work, Rosetta cannot also possess those rights. While Random House's definition distinguishes "book form" from other formats that require separate contractual language—such as audio books and serialization rights—it does not distinguish other formats specifically mentioned in paragraph # 1 of the contracts, such as book club editions and reprint editions. Because the Court must, if possible, give effect to all contractual language in order to "safeguard against adopting an interpretation that would render any individual provision superfluous," *Sayers*, 7 F.3d at 1095, Random House's definition cannot be adopted.

Random House points specifically to the clause requiring it to "publish the work at its own expense and in such a style and manner and at such a price as [Random House] deems suitable" as support for its position. However, plaintiff takes this clause out of context. It appears in paragraph # 2, captioned "Style, Price and Date of Publication," not paragraph # 1, which includes all the grants of rights. In context, the phrase simply means that Random House has control over the appearance of the formats granted to Random House in the first paragraph; i.e., control over the style of the book.

Random House also cites the non-compete clauses as evidence that the authors granted it broad, exclusive rights in their work. Random House reasons that because the authors could not permit any material that would injure the sale of the work to be published without Random House's consent, the authors must have granted the right to publish ebooks to Random House. This reasoning turns the analysis on its head. First, the grant of rights follows from the grant language alone. *See Boosey*, 145 F.3d at 488. Second, non-compete clauses must be limited in scope in order to be enforceable in New York. *See American Broad. Cos. v. Wolf*, 52 N.Y.2d 394, 403–04 (1981); *Columbia Ribbon & Carbon Mfg. Co., Inc. v. A–1–A Corp.*, 42 N.Y.2d 496, 500 (1977). Third, even if the authors did violate this provision of their Random House agreements by contracting with Rosetta Books—a point on which this Court does not opine—the remedy is a breach of contract action against the authors, not a copyright infringement action against Rosetta Books. . . .

The photocopy clause—giving Random House the right to "Xerox and other forms of copying, either now in use or hereafter developed"—similarly does not bolster Random House's position. Although the clause does appear in the grant language paragraph, taken in context, it clearly refers only to new developments in xerography and other forms of photocopying. Stretching it to include new forms of publishing, such as ebooks, would make the rest of the contract superfluous because there would be no reason for authors to reserve rights to forms of publishing "now in use." This interpretation also comports with the publishing industry's trade usage of the phrase.[6]

Not only does the language of the contract itself lead almost ineluctably to the conclusion that Random House does not own the right to publish the works as ebooks, but also a reasonable person "cognizant of the customs, practices, usages and terminology as generally understood in the particular trade or business," *Sayers*, 7 F.3d at 1095, would conclude that the grant language does not include ebooks. "To print, publish and sell the work in book form" is understood in the publishing industry to be a "limited" grant. *See Field v. True Comics*, 89 F.Supp. 611, 613–14 (S.D.N.Y.1950); *see also* Melville B. Nimmer & David Nimmer, *Nimmer on Copyright*, § 10.14[C] (2001) (citing *Field*).

In *Field v. True Comics*, the court held that "the sole and exclusive right to publish, print and market *in book form*"—especially when the author had specifically reserved rights for himself—was "much more limited" than "the sole and exclusive right to publish, print and market *the book*." 89 F.Supp. at 612 (emphasis added). In fact, the publishing industry generally interprets the phrase "in book form" as granting the publisher "the exclusive right to publish a hardcover trade book in English for distribution in North America." 1 *Lindey on Entertainment, Publishing and the Arts* Form 1.01–1 (2d ed.2000) (using the Random House form contract to explain the meaning of each clause) . . . .

3. Comparison to Prior "New Use" Caselaw

. . . [T]he two leading cases limned above that found that a particular new use was included within the grant language—*Boosey*, 145 F.3d 481 (2d Cir.1998), and *Bartsch*, 391 F.2d 150 (2d Cir.1968)—can be distinguished from this case on four grounds.

First, the language conveying the rights in *Boosey* and *Bartsch* was far broader than here. . . . Second, the "new use" in those cases—i.e. display of a motion picture on television or videocassette—fell squarely within the same medium as the original grant. . . .

In this case, the "new use"—electronic digital signals sent over the Internet—is

---

[6] Similarly, Rosetta's argument that the contractual clause in which the authors reserve motion picture and broadcasting rights for themselves in certain contracts also means that the authors reserved the ebook rights is without merit. Such reservation clauses, unless they expressly cover the new use in question, "contribute[] nothing to the definition of the boundaries of the license." *See Boosey*, 145 F.3d at 488.

a separate medium from the original use—printed words on paper. Random House's own expert concludes that the media are distinct because information stored digitally can be manipulated in ways that analog information cannot. Ebooks take advantage of the digital medium's ability to manipulate data by allowing ebook users to electronically search the text for specific words and phrases, change the font size and style, type notes into the text and electronically organize them, highlight and bookmark, hyperlink to specific parts of the text, and, in the future, to other sites on related topics as well, and access a dictionary that pronounces words in the ebook aloud. The need for a software program to interact with the data in order to make it usable, as well as the need for a piece of hardware to enable the reader to view the text, also distinguishes analog formats from digital formats. . . .

. . .

The third significant difference between the licensee in the motion picture cases cited above and the book publisher in this action is that the licensees in the motion picture cases have actually created a new work based on the material from the licensor. Therefore, the right to display that new work—whether on television or video—is derivative of the right to create that work. In the book publishing context, the publishers, although they participate in the editorial process, display the words written by the author, not themselves.

Fourth, the courts in *Boosey* and *Bartsch* were concerned that any approach to new use problems that "tilts against licensees [here, Random House] gives rise to antiprogressive incentives" insofar as licensees "would be reluctant to explore and utilize innovative technologies." *Boosey*, 145 F.3d at 488, n.4; *see also Bartsch*, 391 F.2d at 155. However, in this action, the policy rationale of encouraging development in new technology is at least as well served by finding that the licensors—i.e., the authors—retain these rights to their works. In the 21st century, it cannot be said that licensees such as book publishers and movie producers are ipso facto more likely to make advances in digital technology than start-up companies.

. . .

C. Balance of Hardships

Because Random House cannot establish a prima facie case of copyright infringement, it is not likely to succeed on the merits and is not entitled to a presumption of irreparable harm. . . .

CONCLUSION

Employing the most important tool in the armamentarium of contract interpretation—the language of the contract itself—this Court has concluded that Random House is not the beneficial owner of the right to publish the eight works at issue as ebooks. This is neither a victory for technophiles nor a defeat for Luddites. It is merely a determination, relying on neutral principles of contract interpretation, that because Random House is not likely to succeed on the merits of its copyright infringement claim and cannot demonstrate irreparable harm, its motion for a preliminary injunction should be denied.

EXTENSIONS

1. Rosetta *on appeal.* In affirming the district court's opinion reproduced *supra*, the Second Circuit's per curiam opinion stated:

> [T]he district court did not abuse its discretion in concluding that appellant had not established the likelihood of its success on the merits. To be sure, there is some appeal to appellant's argument that an "ebook"—a digital book that can be read on a computer screen or electronic device— is simply a "form" of a book, and therefore within the coverage of appellant's licenses. But the law of New York, which determines the scope of Random House's contracts, has arguably adopted a restrictive view of the kinds of "new uses" to which an exclusive license may apply when the contracting parties do not expressly provide for coverage of such future forms. In any case, determining whether the licenses here in issue extend to ebooks depends on fact-finding regarding, inter alia, the "evolving" technical processes and uses of an ebook, and the reasonable expectations of the contracting parties "cognizant of the customs, practices, usages and terminology as generally understood in the . . . trade or business" at the time of contracting. Without the benefit of the full record to be developed over the course of the litigation, we cannot say the district court abused its discretion in the preliminary way it resolved these mixed questions of law and fact.

283 F.3d 490, 491–2 (2d Cir.2002)

2. *Electronic rights to freelance newspaper articles.* In *New York Times Co. v. Tasini,* 533 U.S. 483 (2001), the Supreme Court addressed a question closely related to the issue raised in *Rosetta,* namely whether a newspaper could reuse articles from its print edition in an electronic database. The litigation was commenced by six freelance authors, and concerned articles that they had contributed to three print periodicals (two newspapers and one magazine). "Under agreements with the periodicals' publishers, but without the freelancers' consent, two computer database companies placed copies of the freelancers' articles—along with all other articles from the periodicals in which the freelancers' work appeared—into three databases." *Id.* at 487. (For a discussion of the law applicable to databases and compilations online, *see* Chapter 8, *supra.*)

The two database companies were LEXIS/NEXIS and University Microfilms International ("UMI"). LEXIS/NEXIS placed the articles in its online text-based database known as NEXIS. "Each article appear[ed] as a separate, isolated 'story'—without any visible link to the other stories originally published in the same newspaper or magazine edition." The NEXIS version did "not contain pictures or advertisements," nor did it "reproduce the original print publication's formatting features such as headline size, page placement (e.g., above or below the fold for newspapers), or location of continuation pages." UMI placed the articles in its own text-only database, called the New York Times OnDisc ("NYTO"). In addition, UMI also placed the articles in an image-based database called General Periodicals OnDisc ("GPO"). This database shows "each article exactly as it appeared on printed pages, complete with photographs, captions, advertisements, and other surrounding materials." *Id.* at 490–91.

The plaintiffs alleged that inclusion of their articles in the databases infringed their copyrights. The publishers "maintained that, as copyright owners of collective works, i.e., the original print publications, they had merely exercised 'the privilege' § 201(c) accords them to 'reproduc[e] and distribut[e]' the author's discretely copyrighted contribution." *Id.*

at 508–09. Applying Section 201(c), the Court noted that

> the three Databases present articles to users clear of the context provided either by the original periodical editions or by any revision of those editions. The Databases first prompt users to search the universe of their contents: thousands or millions of files containing individual articles from thousands of collective works (i.e., editions), either in one series (the Times, in NYTO) or in scores of series (the sundry titles in NEXIS and GPO). When the user conducts a search, each article appears as a separate item within the search result. In NEXIS and NYTO, an article appears to a user without the graphics, formatting, or other articles with which the article was initially published. In GPO, the article appears with the other materials published on the same page or pages, but without any material published on other pages of the original periodical. In either circumstance, we cannot see how the Database perceptibly reproduces and distributes the article "as part of" either the original edition or a "revision" of that edition.

Id. at 499–500. The Court likened the databases to an imaginary library:

> For the purpose at hand—determining whether the Authors' copyrights have been infringed—an analogy to an imaginary library may be instructive. Rather than maintaining intact editions of periodicals, the library would contain separate copies of each article. Perhaps these copies would exactly reproduce the periodical pages from which the articles derive (if the model is GPO); perhaps the copies would contain only typescript characters, but still indicate the original periodical's name and date, as well as the article's headline and page number (if the model is NEXIS or NYTO). The library would store the folders containing the articles in a file room, indexed based on diverse criteria, and containing articles from vast numbers of editions. In response to patron requests, an inhumanly speedy librarian would search the room and provide copies of the articles matching patron-specified criteria.

> Viewing this strange library, one could not, consistent with ordinary English usage, characterize the articles "as part of" a "revision" of the editions in which the articles first appeared. In substance, however, the Databases differ from the file room only to the extent they aggregate articles in electronic packages (the LEXIS/NEXIS central discs or UMI CD-ROMs), while the file room stores articles in spatially separate files. The crucial fact is that the Databases, like the hypothetical library, store and retrieve articles separately within a vast domain of diverse texts. Such a storage and retrieval system effectively overrides the Authors' exclusive right to control the individual reproduction and distribution of each Article, 17 U.S.C. §§ 106(1), (3).

In his dissenting opinion, Justice Stevens, joined by Justice Breyer, adopted a different analogy. He wrote:

> A proper analysis of this case benefits from an incremental approach. Accordingly, I begin by discussing an issue the majority largely ignores: whether a collection of articles from a single edition of the New York Times (i.e., the batch of files the Print Publishers periodically send to the Electronic Databases) constitutes a "revision" of an individual edition of the paper. In other words, does a single article within such a collection exist as "part of" a "revision"? Like the majority, I believe that the crucial inquiry is whether the article appears within the "context" of the original collective work. But this question simply raises the further issue of precisely how much "context" is enough.

> The record indicates that what is sent from the New York Times to the Electronic Databases (with the exception of General Periodicals on Disc (GPO)) is

simply a collection of ASCII text files representing the editorial content of the New York Times for a particular day. . . .

I see no compelling reason why a collection of files corresponding to a single edition of the New York Times, standing alone, cannot constitute a "revision" of that day's New York Times. . . .

Once one accepts the premise that a disk containing all the files from the October 31, 2000, New York Times can constitute a "revision," there is no reason to treat any differently the same set of files, stored in a folder on the hard disk of a computer at the New York Times. . . .

If my hypothetical October 31, 2000, floppy disk can be a revision, I do not see why the inclusion of other editions and other periodicals is any more significant than the placement of a single edition of the New York Times in a large public library or in a bookstore. . . .

Id. at 511–12, 517. Justice Stevens then reminded the majority that "[t]he primary purpose of copyright is not to reward the author, but is rather to secure 'the general benefits derived by the public from the labors of authors.' " *Id.* at 519 (quoting MELVILLE B. NIMMER & DAVID NIMMER, NIMMER ON COPYRIGHT § 1.03[A]). He thought that the Court's "decision today unnecessarily subverts this fundamental goal of copyright law in favor of a narrow focus on 'authorial rights.' " He said that while "the desire to protect such rights is certainly a laudable sentiment, copyright law demands that 'private motivation must ultimately serve the cause of promoting *broad public availability* of literature, music, and the other arts.' *Twentieth Century Music Corp. v. Aiken*, 422 U.S. 151, 156 (1975) (emphasis added [by Justice Stevens])." *Id.* at 520.

What is the practical result of *Rosetta* and *Tasini*? Is it just that copyright owners should take care to draft licenses that cover all uses now known or hereafter developed?

B. CHARACTERIZATION OF TRANSACTIONS AS LICENSES TO AVOID COPYRIGHT'S FIRST SALE DOCTRINE

John A. Rothchild, *The Incredible Shrinking First-Sale Rule: Are Software Resale Limits Lawful?*
57 RUTGERS L. REV. 1 (2004).

. . .

The public distribution right entitles the copyright owner to prevent others from distributing copies of the copyrighted work to the public. . . .

Since the public distribution right gives the copyright owner control over distribution of copies of her work, it would seem on its face to restrain one who has purchased a copy from *re*distributing it publicly. For example, the owner of a book would seem to need the copyright owner's permission to resell the book at a garage sale. This is not so, however, because the distribution right is limited by the first-sale doctrine, which allows the owner of a copy to transfer it to somebody else without obtaining the copyright owner's permission.[30] The doctrine takes its name from the fact that it limits the copyright owner's rights to controlling the *first* sale of

---

[30] *See* 17 U.S.C. § 109(a) ("[T]he owner of a particular copy or phonorecord lawfully made . . . is entitled, without the authority of the copyright owner, to sell or otherwise dispose of the possession of that copy or phonorecord.").

a particular copy: the copyright owner has no right to control *subsequent* sales of that copy. Under the first-sale doctrine, the owner of a copy may freely dispose of it either by sale, or by other methods such as donation, lending, lease, or rental. Thus, for example, the copyright owner of a book may not invoke its public distribution right to prevent the owner of a copy of the book from disposing of it by donating it to a library, lending it to a friend, renting it, or selling it.

. . .

A software publisher that wants to control disposition of its products after they reach the hands of end users, thereby controlling the secondary market, can accomplish part of this goal by invoking its exclusive right to distribute its works to the public. That right allows it to prevent anyone in possession of a copy of its software—even assuming the possessor is the lawful "owner" of that copy—from renting, leasing, or lending that copy to anyone else for commercial advantage. But the copyright laws do not grant the software publisher any authority to prevent the owner of a lawfully made software copy from selling it or giving it to someone else, or from lending it to someone else if not for commercial advantage; and these activities constitute the core of the secondary market.

A software publisher could eliminate much of this remaining segment of the secondary market, using the copyright laws, if it were able to prevent an acquirer of its software from gaining ownership of the material object on which the software is distributed. If this could be accomplished, only one narrow aspect of the secondary market would remain outside the software publisher's control: the acquirer's gift, sale, or loan of the software copy in a manner deemed not to be "to the public" for purposes of the public distribution right.

Accomplishing this objective would bring an additional benefit to the software publisher, by rendering section 117(a) of the Copyright Act unavailable. Section 117(a) entitles the "owner of a copy of a computer program" to take two actions with respect to that copy that would otherwise constitute infringement. First, the owner may load the software from that copy onto her computer, or may make and load an adaptation of that software, as required to make use of it. Second, the owner may make a backup copy of it. But these privileges are not available to a person who is not the "owner of a copy" of the program. . . .

Software publishers have employed several strategies aimed at preventing an acquirer of their software from becoming the owner of the material object on which it is distributed, and have achieved a fair measure of success in the courts. First, and most commonly, software publishers assert, in the license agreements accompanying their products, that the software is "licensed" and not sold, or that the publisher "retains title" to copies of the software that it provides to the user. . . .

. . .

It is very common for a license agreement accompanying the transfer of a software product to state that the software is "licensed" to the end user, who is invariably referred to as the "licensee" and never as the "purchaser" of the software. Based upon that characterization of the transaction, the software publisher argues that since the acquirer is only a "licensee" of the software, and not its "owner," the acquirer is not entitled to the rights granted by sections 109(a) and 117(a).[81] . . .

   . . .

Several courts have accepted the software publishers' argument that they do not sell, but only license, their software, and that this disposition of the merchandise makes unavailable the rights granted by sections 109(a) and 117(a) of the Copyright Act. . . . Acceptance of this argument depends upon a curiously persistent confusion between a *computer program* and the *material object* on which it is distributed. The two are quite different. A work of authorship, such as a computer program, is incorporeal. In its pristine state, you can't touch it, see it, hear it, smell it, or taste it. It is like a Platonic Form. On the other hand, the material object in which it is embodied is just that: a material object.

Thus, a literary work, consisting of the words of a book, may be embodied in a material object consisting of ink on paper; a musical work, consisting of the notes of a song, may be embodied in sheet music, or in a recording of a rendition of the song; a pictorial work, consisting of color, line, and shape, may be embodied in paint on canvas. The code of a computer program, consisting as it does of text, is treated under the Copyright Act as a literary work, and may be embodied on a floppy diskette, CD-ROM, hard drive, or some other storage medium.

Although both (1) the copyright in the work of authorship and (2) the material object in which it is fixed are forms of property that are capable of ownership, ownership of one is independent of ownership of the other. Thus, one becomes the owner of a *copyright* either by being the author of the work to which it pertains, or through transfer of copyright ownership. One becomes the owner of a *copy* through the same actions that result in ownership of any other moveable good, typically by purchasing it or otherwise acquiring ownership from the prior owner. But the transfer of ownership of a *copy* of a work does not imply any corresponding transfer of the *copyright* to that work; an artist who sells a painting parts with the canvas but retains the copyright, absent a signed writing assigning the copyright. Likewise, transfer of ownership of the *copyright* to a work does not affect ownership of any particular *copy* embodying that work: an author who assigns the copyright in a literary work to a publisher does not thereby lose ownership of her manuscript embodying the work.

Most crucially for present purposes, *the fact that one is only the licensee, and not the owner, of the copyright is not of any relevance to the question whether one owns the associated copy.* The two ownership interests are entirely independent. It is quite possible, and quite common, for a person to own either the copyright in a work of authorship (in whole or in part), or the material object in which it is fixed, but not both.

Consider the books on your bookshelf. You do not own the copyright to any of the literary works that are embodied in those books (unless, perhaps, you are the

---

[81] *See, e.g.,* Adobe Sys., Inc. v. Stargate Software Inc., 216 F.Supp.2d 1051, 1055 (N.D.Cal.2002) (" 'Adobe does not sell its software. Instead, Adobe distributes its software products under license to a network of distributors . . . .' ") (quoting declaration submitted by Adobe).

author of the work). You may or may not be the owner of any one of the material objects on your shelf: you own the ones that you bought or received as a gift; you do not own the ones that you borrowed from the library. But your ownership of any particular *book* does not depend on whether you own the *copyright* in the corresponding literary work. That is equally true whether you own the copyright or not: if you *are* the author of a literary work, and own the copyright to it, that does not make you the owner of the stack of books embodying that work on display at the bookstore; if you are *not* the copyright owner of the literary work, you may nevertheless be the owner of a particular book embodying it.

The same principles that apply to books apply to music CDs, art posters, movie DVDs, and other information goods in tangible form—including software. Consumers typically own many such material objects, but own few, if any, copyrights to the works embodied in those objects.

Recall that what triggers applicability of the first-sale doctrine of section 109(a), and the prerogatives respecting software under section 117(a), is ownership of the *copy*, not ownership of the *copyright*. It follows that a statement in a software license agreement that the publisher grants the user a license to use the software, but does not transfer ownership of the copyright, does not determine the applicability of either of those provisions.

Some license agreements, however, purport to license not only use of the copyrighted work, but also possession of the material object on which it is distributed. For example, *Vault Corp. v. Quaid Software Ltd.*[96] involves a license agreement that declares: "This copy of the PROLOK Software Protection System and this PROLOK Software Protection Diskette (the 'Licensed Software') are licensed to you, the end-user, for your own internal use." This language explicitly says that both the computer program (i.e., the copyrighted work), and the diskette on which it is distributed (i.e., the material object that embodies the copyrighted work), are licensed, not sold, to the acquirer.

. . .

[A] declaration in a software license agreement purporting to "license" not only use of the computer program, but also possession of the material object on which it is distributed, cannot, on a proper construction of the term "owner" in sections 109(a) and 117(a), prevent the acquirer of the software copy from being entitled to the benefits that those two provisions confer.

To see this, consider what it means to say that one "licenses" a material object. This is nonstandard usage of the term "license." In its standard usage, a license is a grant of permission. Thus, a license in connection with a copyrighted work constitutes permission to use the work in a manner that would otherwise infringe the copyright. Likewise, a license in connection with a patent permits the use of an invention in a way that would otherwise infringe the patent. A marriage license permits one (two, actually) to marry, as a driver's license permits one to drive. In the context of real property, a license is a permission to enter upon land, which

---

[96] [Vault Corp. v. Quaid Software Ltd., 847 F.2d 255, 261 (5th Cir.1988).]

would otherwise be trespass.

The current Copyright Act does not define "license," but uses the term in several contexts to mean permission to use a copyrighted work; the Act never uses the term as a property relation applicable to a copy or phonorecord. Under prior copyright statutes, the term "consent" was used in contexts where "license" is currently used, and likewise denoted permission to use a copyrighted work.

Thus, "license," when used as a verb, means "permit" or "authorize." When used as a noun, it means "permission" or "authorization." It makes perfect sense to say that a copyright owner "licenses" use of a copyrighted work: this means that she permits or authorizes the specified use of the work. What the licensee receives is well described as a license, since it is a permission or authorization to engage in activities that would otherwise infringe the rights of the copyright owner.

But what can it mean to say that one "licenses" (or licenses use of) a material object, such as a CD-ROM or floppy diskette? Based on the foregoing, this is to say that one "permits" or "authorizes" use of it. Such a statement is ambiguous. The law recognizes several types of transactions in which one person "permits" another person to make use of his property. That characterization is equally consistent, for example, with a sale, lease, loan, consignment, pledge, or other bailment of the object. On the other hand, it may be that the "license" of a material object defines a new property relationship—a new "bundle of sticks," to use the conventional metaphor—that fits within none of these categories.

Which of these property relations the term "license" denotes, when applied to a material object, is of crucial importance in assessing the applicability of the first-sale doctrine. If the "license" of a CD-ROM containing software is the equivalent of a sale of the CD-ROM, then the recipient is the owner of the CD-ROM and is entitled to the benefits of sections 109(a) and 117(a) of the Copyright Act. If, on the other hand, such a "license" is the equivalent of a lease or a loan, then the recipient is not entitled to those benefits. If the license constitutes some entirely new species of property relation, then the incidents of that relation must be ascertained before we can determine how the copyright laws apply to it.

. . .

When software is distributed through a standard retail chain of distribution—from the software publisher, through one or more levels of distributors, to a retailer, and finally to the end user—the end user inevitably acquires ownership of the material object on which the software is distributed.

Consider some concrete examples. You walk into a ComputoMart store, select a package containing 50 blank CD-R disks, bring it to the cashier, pay the price indicated, and walk out of the store with your package in hand. Nobody would doubt that you are the "owner" of those disks, free to exercise all of the normal incidents of ownership. . . .

Suppose that while in the same store you pay the indicated price for a copy of Macworld magazine. By the same reasoning you walk out as the owner of the magazine as well. Note that the magazine is a "copy" in the copyright sense: it is a material object in which copyrighted works, consisting of text, pictures, and perhaps other elements, are fixed. The involvement in this transaction of a copyrighted work is irrelevant to the question whether you own the magazine. . . . If somebody grabs the magazine from you, it is theft—even if the grabbing is done by an agent of the copyright owner.

Now suppose that you add an additional item to your shopping cart: a computer game, "The Sims Deluxe Edition," published by Electronic Arts. This item ships on a CD-ROM. Like the Macworld magazine, the CD-ROM is a "copy" in the copyright sense: a material object containing a copyrighted work, namely a computer program. Based on the same logic that applies to the magazine and the blank CD-R, it is clear that you are the owner of the CD-ROM (though not of the copyright in the computer program). If somebody takes the disk from you, you would report it as a theft, and the police, when apprised of the facts, would not refuse to investigate the incident on the ground that you are a mere licensee, and not an owner, of the disk.

In each of these ComputoMart transactions, the context indicates that the transaction is a purchase and sale, and you become the owner of each of the material objects (though of none of the copyrights) once you pay for it.

. . .

Software publishers assert, however, that by virtue of language in the accompanying license agreement, the transaction involving the Sims Deluxe software is different from the other two. While presumably agreeing that you own the blank CD-Rs and the Macworld magazine, they claim you are not the owner of the CD-ROM that holds the software, but only a licensee. They base this claim upon language in the license agreement to the effect that the software is licensed, not sold.

Applying the principles developed above, it is clear that language in the Sims Deluxe license agreement is incapable of bringing about this result. In the ordinary course of distributing its goods through a retail distribution chain, Electronic Arts sold the package containing the software disk to a distributor, which sold it (perhaps via one or more additional levels of distributors) to ComputoMart, which sold it to the end user. In each of those transactions, the ownership of the box, CD-ROM, manuals, and whatever else was in the package was transferred from the seller to the buyer. In the last transaction, ownership was transferred from ComputoMart to the end user. A statement by Electronic Arts in the license agreement can have no effect on the ownership of any of these materials, because *Electronic Arts divested itself of its ownership of the materials in the first transaction.* Once it has ceased to be the owner of the package and its contents, Electronic Arts has no more power to affect their ownership than does any other stranger to the transaction.

. . .

The relationship between a license agreement and the material object it accompanies may be more clearly illustrated by considering the other two items involved in our hypothetical purchase from ComputoMart. Suppose the manufacturer of the blank CD-R disks, Imation Corporation, included in its package of disks, underneath a plastic wrapper that must be broken to get access to the disks, a piece of paper captioned "License Agreement," which states: "The disks contained in this package are licensed, not sold." Surely nobody would believe that such a statement would cause the purchaser of the package not to be the owner of the disks; Imation sold those disks to a distributor, which sold them to ComputoMart, which sold them to the end user. It would be as though General Motors stuck a notice in the glove compartment of a car that it manufactured, stating "This car belongs to General Motors," and then invoked the notice in an action in replevin to recover the car from the person who bought the car from the person who bought the car from the dealer that originally sold it.

But the items in this package, CD-R disks, are precisely the same commodity whose ownership is at issue in the case of the Sims Deluxe program. The only difference is that the latter disk has a copyrighted software program inscribed on it, the rights to which the license agreement may indeed control. But in neither case does the license agreement control the ownership of the disks.

The same holds true of the Macworld magazine. Imagine a declaration on the cover of the magazine stating: "This magazine, and its contents, are licensed, not sold. By opening this magazine you assent to these terms." Nobody would contend that this declaration makes the purchaser of the magazine only a licensee, and not an owner, of the paper and ink constituting the magazine. The purchaser acquired it in a sales transaction from ComputoMart, and the desire of the copyright owner that the purchaser should not gain ownership of the copy of the magazine is irrelevant. Yet the magazine, like the Sims Deluxe CD-ROM, is a material object embodying a copyrighted work.

. . .

EXTENSIONS

Judicial treatment. For some examples of cases that have accepted a software publisher's argument that software distributed with an accompanying license agreement is not subject to the first-sale rule, see *MAI Systems Corp. v. Peak Computer, Inc.*, 991 F.2d 511, 518 n.5 (9th Cir.1993) ("Since MAI licensed its software, the Peak customers do not qualify as 'owners' of the software and are not eligible for protection under § 117."); *DSC Communications Corp. v. Pulse Communications, Inc.*, 170 F.3d 1354, 1361–1362 (Fed.Cir.1999) (license agreement stating that "[a]ll rights, title and interest in the Software are and shall remain with seller, subject, however, to a license to Buyer to use the Software" held to establish that the acquirer is not the owner of its copies of the software); *Microsoft Corp. v. Harmony Computers & Elecs., Inc.*, 846 F.Supp. 208, 213 (E.D.N.Y.1994) ("Plaintiff's counsel declares that Microsoft only licenses and does not sell its Products. . . . Entering a license agreement is not a 'sale' for purposes of the first sale doctrine.").

Courts rejecting such an argument include *Vault Corp. v. Quaid Software Ltd.*, 847 F.2d 255, 268–70 (5th Cir.1988) (holding that the acquirer of a software copy is entitled to the privileges granted by section 117, despite the license agreement's characterization of the transaction as a license); *SoftMan Products Co. v. Adobe Systems Inc.*, 171 F.Supp.2d 1075 (C.D.Cal.2001) (despite characterization as a "license," "the circumstances surrounding the transaction strongly suggest[] that the transaction is in fact a sale rather than a license").

For additional discussion of the first-sale rule, see Chapter 7, Part II(C)(2), *supra*.

Donations to libraries. In light of the preceding excerpt, evaluate the following statement: "Libraries are not able to use CD-ROMs donated to them because the donors are not owners of the CD-ROMs, only licensees, and thus lack the legal authority to transfer the copy of the work they possess." U.S. COPYRIGHT OFFICE, DMCA SECTION 104 REPORT, at 105 (2001).

C. USING LICENSES TO CONTRACT OUT OF THE LIMITS OF INTELLECTUAL PROPERTY

Intellectual property regimes grant ownership rights that are limited in certain ways. (For example, we saw in Chapter 2 that trademark rights depend upon use in commerce and cannot attach to generic terms. In Chapter 7 we studied the limits of copyright, and in Chapter 11 we will study the limits of patent.) A prevalent practice has developed in e-commerce to try to contract out of those limits and thereby expand the owner's rights, usually by means of browsewrap or clickwrap "licenses." In this section we consider to what extent this expansion of intellectual property rights is or should be legally permissible. We begin by taking a look at the kinds of provisions that owners may employ to expand their rights, then look at two significant cases that have validated the practice, at least in certain contexts. These cases raise the important but difficult topic of whether, and under what circumstances, contract, a creature of state law, should be preempted by federal intellectual property law.

Mark A. Lemley, *Beyond Preemption: The Law and Policy of Intellectual Property Licensing*
87 CALIF. L. REV. 111 (1999).

. . .

. . . Intellectual property law is designed to provide creators with a limited set of rights over ideas and inventions in order to serve the instrumental purpose of encouraging more creation. For many good reasons, the law does not grant intellectual property owners boundless control over their creations. First, granting exclusive rights raises the cost of new works to the public, and in some cases means that the public won't get access to the works at all. Second, granting property rights to original creators allows them to prevent subsequent creators from building on their works, which means that a law designed to encourage the creation of first-generation works may actually risk stifling second-generation creative works. Third, the goal of intellectual property is only to provide the "optimal incentive," not the largest incentive possible. Past a certain point, it would be inefficient to withhold works from the public domain in order to provide ever-decreasing "incentives" to their creators. As Larry Lessig has observed, "while we protect real property to protect the owner from harm, we protect intellectual property to provide the owner sufficient incentive to produce such property. 'Sufficient incentive,' however, is something less than 'perfect control.' "

Giving the parties unlimited power under contract law to vary the rules of intellectual property creates considerable tension with this balanced incentive structure. And permitting the parties to alter intellectual property law with a standard-form, unsigned "shrinkwrap license," in which even the fiction of "agreement" is stretched to the vanishing point, exalts the (standard) form of contract law over the substance of intellectual property.

In the following Sections, I describe a few common contractual terms . . . . While many of these common terms are found in contracts drafted by intellectual property owners that interfere with user rights, the reverse is also true—contract provisions drafted by licensees may also interfere with the rights of intellectual property owners. My purpose in the remainder of this Part is only to highlight these areas of potential conflict, and not (yet) to suggest how the conflicts should be resolved. Just because a contractual term creates tension with intellectual property law does not mean that it is necessarily unenforceable. . . .

1. *Patent Law*

Patent law confers broader rights on intellectual property owners than any other intellectual property law. It is therefore the least likely source of problems for the licensor; most of what a licensor wants, patent law already gives her. Nonetheless, patent licensors sometimes do seek to get more than federal patent policy will give them. Two such conflicts are particularly common.

First, licensors generally want licensees to agree not to dispute the validity of the patent being licensed. Licenses up until thirty years ago commonly included provisions by which the licensee agreed that the patent was valid, or at least not to challenge the validity of the patent in court. In *Lear, Inc. v. Adkins*,[45] however, the Supreme Court held that licensees could not give up their rights to challenge the validity of a patent. In that case, the Court expressly rejected on preemption grounds a contract that attempted to "opt out" of the distribution of rights established by patent law.

Second, patentees periodically attempt to extend their control over licensees beyond the scope of the patent itself. They may do this by granting licenses that: (1) extend the term of the patent beyond seventeen years; (2) tie patented to unpatented products in an attempt to capture the market for both; (3) require that the licensee grant back the rights to any improvement patents; or (4) employ other means. Contracts that accomplish such an extension of the patent monopoly have received mixed treatment by the courts. Some clauses, particularly those that extend the length of the patent or copyright term, have been declared unenforceable. Others, particularly grantback clauses, are generally enforceable if they do not run afoul of the antitrust laws. In certain circumstances, courts not only refuse to enforce the license provision; they also punish the patentee for insisting upon it by declaring the entire patent unenforceable. But in any event, it is federal patent policy, not the contract term, that controls the transaction.

Patent contracts can also run afoul of the doctrine of assignor estoppel. Unlike licensee estoppel, which *Lear* prohibits, assignor estoppel prevents the original in-

---

[45] 395 U.S. 653, 670–71 (1969).

ventor and her company from challenging the validity of a patent issued on her own invention, and then assigned to the ultimate patent owner. The Federal Circuit has held that inventors will be estopped from contesting the validity of their own patents as a matter of judicial policy. This policy applies whether or not the inventor sought to reserve the right to challenge the patent when she entered into the assignment agreement.

2. Copyright Law

Copyright law contains a number of compromises between the desires of authors and those of the consuming public. It is therefore not surprising that contracts written by a copyright owner often claim to give the licensor greater rights than are granted by copyright law. Similarly, contracts written by an assignee or licensee sometimes seek to take away rights that the copyright law grants exclusively to authors. Several examples follow.

First, some contracts provide that the licensee may not make *any* copies of the licensed work. If the copyrighted work is a computer program, such a license term conflicts directly with section 117 of the Copyright Act, which gives owners of a copy of a program the right to make both archival copies and copies necessary to run the program. In some cases, the license term may also run afoul of the right to make "fair use" of the copyrighted work. Indeed, it is not very hard to find contractual provisions that claim to preclude any copying by the user, whether or not the copying would be fair use. And one can certainly imagine copyright owners including "no-parody" provisions in their licenses, if courts would enforce them. But fair use is designed precisely to allow nonconsensual uses, and "contracting around" fair use thus presents a conflict with the goals of the doctrine.

Second, many software contracts purport to prohibit reverse engineering of the licensed software. These terms may conflict with a user's apparent right under copyright law to reverse engineer copyrighted works for certain purposes. This is perhaps the most common example in the software industry of a conflict between contractual terms and copyright policy.

Third, software and digital information contract terms often seek to prohibit the licensee from moving a program to an upgraded computer or from altering, upgrading, or "debugging" the program. Such requirements may conflict with at least the spirit, and arguably the letter, of section 117, which gives users the right to copy and adapt the program to the extent necessary to run it on a particular machine. In particular, section 117 was intended to give users the right to upgrade programs themselves, and to transfer software programs to newer hardware or operating systems, even if the transfer requires translation of the code.

Fourth, contract terms commonly prohibit licensees from transferring or assigning their particular copy of a work. Such provisions may conflict with the "first sale" doctrine in copyright law, which gives the owner of a particular copy of a copyrighted work the right to dispose of that copy without the permission of the copyright owner. Whether this is actually a conflict depends on whether the copyright owner "sold" or "licensed" the copy in question; the first sale doctrine does not prevent restrictions on the transfer of licensed items.

Fifth, contractual provisions may seek to prevent the user of a copyrighted work from performing or displaying the program to the public under any circumstances. Such a license provision would conflict with section 110 of the Copyright Act, which expressly immunizes certain performances. Similarly, limitations on certain uses of some types of works may run afoul of other specific exceptions in the Copyright Act, such as the right of libraries to make certain copies, the right of cable and satellite systems to engage in secondary transmission and simultaneous copying subject to compulsory licenses, the rights to make photographic reproductions of some types of copyrighted works without authorization, and the right to play music in jukeboxes subject to an arbitrated compulsory license.

Sixth, copyright owners are granted certain rights that they cannot waive, assign, or license. Most notable here is the right of authors to terminate transfers of rights in the work between thirty-five and forty years after the work was created. This right is effective "notwithstanding any agreement to the contrary." Similarly, the limited moral rights of a visual artist may not be transferred by the author, even if the copyright is assigned; any waivers of the artist's moral rights are strictly limited by statute. Contractual provisions that purport to transfer rights in violation of these provisions present obvious conflicts with the Copyright Act.

Seventh, the Copyright Act specifically defines works "made for hire," and therefore the terms of initial ownership of copyrighted works. It also governs the way in which transfers of copyright ownership may be made, and precludes oral assignment agreements. An agreement that purports to assign a copyright, but that does not comply with the terms of section 204, conflicts with the Copyright Act. Contract law rules that are inconsistent with section 205(d) also set up a conflict, as would contracts that purported to create "works made for hire" but do not fall within the definition of that term in the statute.

Finally, a contract may "shrink the public domain" by withdrawing from public use certain works that are not subject to intellectual property protection. This is what happened in the *ProCD* case,[81] in which the plaintiffs were allowed to protect by shrinkwrap license the very material that the Supreme Court had said could not be protected by copyright.

Whether this is really a "conflict" in any given case is a complex question. Some uncopyrightable materials can be protected under other laws. For example, uncopyrightable information may be patentable, capable of trade secret protection, or protected by common law copyright. The Supreme Court in *Goldstein v. California*[84] observed that the central question is whether the work was denied protection because of a federal determination that it should be unprotected, or whether the federal statute simply did not extend to such a work. Only in the latter case can states "remove" works from the public domain. In cases in which contracts purport to protect information in spite of a federal determination that such information should be unprotected, they will conflict with federal policy.

---

[81] *ProCD, Inc. v. Zeidenberg*, 86 F.3d 1447 (7th Cir.1996).

[84] 412 U.S. 546 (1973).

3. *Trade Secret Law*

Protection for trade secrets is largely provided by state statutes or common law, supplemented by federal law. These legal rules often conflict with the desires of licensors. The most common conflicts involve contractual terms drafted by licensors that prohibit reverse engineering or obviate the need for secrecy. Reverse engineering of a trade secret is explicitly allowed by the Uniform Trade Secrets Act, which means that the Act conflicts with contract law if the contract provides that a licensee may not reverse engineer the licensed product. Similarly, license terms that prevent the licensee from challenging the status of software as a trade secret are in apparent conflict with the legal requirement that a trade secret must in fact be secret to be protectable.

Trade secrets law in most states also places limitations on the enforceability of employee noncompetition agreements and "trailer clauses." At a minimum, states impose an overarching requirement of "reasonableness" on such agreements, viewing them with disfavor and requiring that they be limited in scope and duration and not violative of other public policies. Other states refuse to enforce employee noncompetition agreements at all, or limit their enforcement to long-term rather than at-will employment contracts. Obviously, all of these public-policy limitations are in tension with the contractual terms they restrict.

4. *Trademark Law*

Federal trademark law is designed to prevent consumer confusion in the marketplace by encouraging competitors to use distinctive marks to identify their goods, which allows consumers to distinguish those goods from a competitor's. In order to prevent trademarks from becoming an instrument of consumer confusion, United States trademark law places significant restrictions on a trademark owner's ability to sell or license the mark. These restrictions take two basic forms. First, trademarks cannot be assigned "in gross"—that is, without the goodwill and other assets accompanying the line of business the trademark represents. Second, if a trademark owner licenses the right to produce or sell trademarked goods to another, the owner must supervise the licensee to make sure that the goods produced or sold under the trademark are of comparable quality to existing trademarked products. Failure to comply with these rules can invalidate the trademark altogether.

Correspondingly, garden-variety breach of contract disputes in trademark license cases may have overtones of federal policy. For example, the right to sell goods produced pursuant to a contract in mitigation of breach is an ordinary part of Uniform Commercial Code Article 2. But if the rejected goods contain the licensor's trademark, reselling them can do significant damage to the principles of trademark law, and may be forbidden under federal law. These policy-based contract limitations set up a conflict with the free alienability that is normally a part of state contract law . . . .

ProCD, Inc. v. Zeidenberg
86 F.3d 1447 (7th Cir.1996).

■ EASTERBROOK, CIRCUIT JUDGE.

[The portion of the opinion dealing with contract formation is reproduced in Part I(A) of this Chapter.]

III

The district court held that, even if Wisconsin treats shrinkwrap licenses as contracts, § 301(a) of the Copyright Act, 17 U.S.C. § 301(a), prevents their enforcement. 908 F.Supp. at 656–59. The relevant part of § 301(a) preempts any "legal or equitable rights [under state law] that are equivalent to any of the exclusive rights within the general scope of copyright as specified by section 106 in works of authorship that are fixed in a tangible medium of expression and come within the subject matter of copyright as specified by sections 102 and 103." ProCD's software and data are "fixed in a tangible medium of expression," and the district judge held that they are "within the subject matter of copyright." The latter conclusion is plainly right for the copyrighted application program, and the judge thought that the data likewise are "within the subject matter of copyright" even if, after *Feist*, they are not sufficiently original to be copyrighted. 908 F.Supp. at 656–57. *Baltimore Orioles, Inc. v. Major League Baseball Players Ass'n*, 805 F.2d 663, 676 (7th Cir.1986), supports that conclusion, with which commentators agree. E.g., Paul Goldstein, III *Copyright* § 15.2.3 (2d ed. 1996); Melville B. Nimmer & David Nimmer, *Nimmer on Copyright* § 101[B] (1995); William F. Patry, II *Copyright Law and Practice* 1108–09 (1994). One function of § 301(a) is to prevent states from giving special protection to works of authorship that Congress has decided should be in the public domain, which it can accomplish only if "subject matter of copyright" includes all works of a *type* covered by sections 102 and 103, even if federal law does not afford protection to them. *Cf. Bonito Boats, Inc. v. Thunder Craft Boats, Inc.*, 489 U.S. 141 (1989) (same principle under patent laws).

But are rights created by contract "equivalent to any of the exclusive rights within the general scope of copyright"? Three courts of appeals have answered "no." *National Car Rental Systems, Inc. v. Computer Associates International, Inc.*, 991 F.2d 426, 433 (8th Cir.1993); *Taquino v. Teledyne Monarch Rubber*, 893 F.2d 1488, 1501 (5th Cir.1990); *Acorn Structures, Inc. v. Swantz*, 846 F.2d 923, 926 (4th Cir.1988). The district court disagreed with these decisions, 908 F.Supp. at 658, but we think them sound. Rights "equivalent to any of the exclusive rights within the general scope of copyright" are rights established *by law*—rights that restrict the options of persons who are strangers to the author. Copyright law forbids duplication, public performance, and so on, unless the person wishing to copy or perform the work gets permission; silence means a ban on copying. A copyright is a right against the world. Contracts, by contrast, generally affect only their parties; strangers may do as they please, so contracts do not create "exclusive rights." Someone who found a copy of SelectPhone™ on the street would not be affected by the shrinkwrap license—though the federal copyright laws of their own force would limit the finder's ability to copy or transmit the application program.

Think for a moment about trade secrets. One common trade secret is a customer list. After *Feist,* a simple alphabetical list of a firm's customers, with address and telephone numbers, could not be protected by copyright. Yet *Kewanee Oil Co. v. Bicron Corp.,* 416 U.S. 470 (1974), holds that contracts about trade secrets may be enforced—precisely because they do not affect strangers' ability to discover and use the information independently. If the amendment of § 301(a) in 1976 overruled *Kewanee* and abolished consensual protection of those trade secrets that cannot be copyrighted, no one has noticed—though abolition is a logical consequence of the district court's approach. Think, too, about everyday transactions in intellectual property. A customer visits a video store and rents a copy of *Night of the Lepus.* The customer's contract with the store limits use of the tape to home viewing and re-quires its return in two days. May the customer keep the tape, on the ground that § 301(a) makes the promise unenforceable?

A law student uses the LEXIS database, containing public-domain documents, under a contract limiting the results to educational endeavors; may the student resell his access to this database to a law firm from which LEXIS seeks to collect a much higher hourly rate? Suppose ProCD hires a firm to scour the nation for tele-phone directories, promising to pay $100 for each that ProCD does not already have. The firm locates 100 new directories, which it sends to ProCD with an in-voice for $10,000. ProCD incorporates the directories into its database; does it have to pay the bill? Surely yes; *Aronson v. Quick Point Pencil Co.,* 440 U.S. 257 (1979), holds that promises to pay for intellectual property may be enforced even though federal law (in *Aronson,* the patent law) offers no protection against third-party uses of that property. *See also Kennedy v. Wright,* 851 F.2d 963 (7th Cir.1988). But these illustrations are what our case is about. ProCD offers software and data for two prices: one for personal use, a higher price for commercial use. Zeidenberg wants to use the data without paying the seller's price; if the law student and Quick Point Pencil Co. could not do that, neither can Zeidenberg.

Although Congress possesses power to preempt even the enforcement of con-tracts about intellectual property—or railroads, on which see *Norfolk & Western Ry. v. Train Dispatchers,* 499 U.S. 117 (1991)—courts usually read preemption clauses to leave private contracts unaffected. *American Airlines, Inc. v. Wolens,* 115 S.Ct. 817 (1995), provides a nice illustration. A federal statute preempts any state "law, rule, regulation, standard, or other provision . . . relating to rates, routes, or services of any air carrier." 49 U.S.C. App. § 1305(a)(1). Does such a law preempt the law of contracts—so that, for example, an air carrier need not honor a quoted price (or a contract to reduce the price by the value of frequent flyer miles)? The Court al-lowed that it is possible to read the statute that broadly but thought such an inter-pretation would make little sense. Terms and conditions offered by contract reflect private ordering, essential to the efficient functioning of markets. 115 S. Ct. at 824–25. Although some principles that carry the name of contract law are designed to defeat rather than implement consensual transactions, *id.* at 826 n.8, the rules that respect private choice are not preempted by a clause such as § 1305(a)(1). Section 301(a) plays a role similar to § 1301(a)(1): it prevents states from substituting their own regulatory systems for those of the national government. Just as § 301(a) does not itself interfere with private transactions in intellectual property, so it does not prevent states from respecting those transactions. Like the Supreme Court in *Wolens*, we think it prudent to refrain from adopting a rule that anything with the label "contract" is necessarily outside the preemption clause: the variations and possibilities are too numerous to foresee. *National Car Rental* likewise recognizes the possibility that some applications of the law of contract could interfere with the attainment of national objectives and therefore come within the domain of § 301(a). But general enforcement of shrinkwrap licenses of the kind before us does not create such interference.

Aronson emphasized that enforcement of the contract between Aronson and Quick Point Pencil Company would not withdraw any information from the public domain. That is equally true of the contract between ProCD and Zeidenberg. Everyone remains free to copy and disseminate all 3,000 telephone books that have been incorporated into ProCD's database. Anyone can add SIC codes and zip codes. ProCD's rivals have done so. Enforcement of the shrinkwrap license may even make information more readily available, by reducing the price ProCD charges to consumer buyers. To the extent licenses facilitate distribution of object code while concealing the source code (the point of a clause forbidding disassembly), they serve the same procompetitive functions as does the law of trade secrets. *Rockwell Graphic Systems, Inc. v. DEV Industries, Inc.*, 925 F.2d 174, 180 (7th Cir.1991). Licenses may have other benefits for consumers: many licenses permit users to make extra copies, to use the software on multiple computers, even to incorporate the software into the user's products. But whether a particular license is generous or restrictive, a simple two-party contract is not "equivalent to any of the exclusive rights within the general scope of copyright" and therefore may be enforced.

Bowers v. Baystate Technologies, Inc.
320 F. 3d 1317 (Fed.Cir.2003).

■ RADER, CIRCUIT JUDGE.

    . . .

I.

Harold L. Bowers (Bowers) created a template to improve computer aided design (CAD) software, such as the CADKEY tool of Cadkey, Inc. Mr. Bowers filed a patent application for his template on February 27, 1989. On June 12, 1990, United States Patent No. 4,933,514 ('514 patent) issued from that application.

    . . .

Since the early 1980s, CAD programs have assisted engineers to draft and design on a computer screen. George W. Ford, III, a development engineer and supervisor of quality control at Heinemann Electric, envisioned a way to improve Mr. Bowers' template and CAD software. Specifically, Mr. Ford designed Geodraft, a DOS-based add-on program to operate with CAD. Geodraft allows an engineer to insert technical tolerances for features of the computer-generated design. . . .

In 1989, Mr. Ford offered Mr. Bowers an exclusive license to his Geodraft software. Mr. Bowers accepted that offer and bundled Geodraft and Cadjet together as the Designer's Toolkit. Mr. Bowers sold the Designer's Toolkit with a shrink-wrap license that, *inter alia*, prohibited any reverse engineering.

In 1989, Baystate also developed and marketed other tools for CADKEY. One of those tools, Draft-Pak version 1 and 2, featured a template and [geometric dimensioning and tolerancing] software. In 1988 and 1989, Mr. Bowers offered to establish a formal relationship with Baystate, including bundling his template with Draft-Pak. Baystate rejected that offer, however, telling Mr. Bowers that it believed it had "the in-house capability to develop the type of products you have proposed."

In 1990, Mr. Bowers released Designer's Toolkit. By January 1991, Baystate had obtained copies of that product. Three months later, Baystate introduced the substantially revised Draft-Pak version 3, incorporating many of the features of Designer's Toolkit. Although Draft-Pak version 3 operated in the DOS environment, Baystate later upgraded it to operate with Microsoft Windows TM.

Baystate's introduction of Draft-Pak version 3 induced intense price competition between Mr. Bowers and Baystate. To gain market share over Baystate, Mr. Bowers negotiated with Cadkey, Inc., to provide the Designer's Toolkit free with CADKEY. Mr. Bowers planned to recoup his profits by selling software upgrades to the users that he hoped to lure to his products. Following pressure from Baystate, however, Cadkey, Inc., repudiated its distribution agreement with Mr. Bowers. Eventually, Baystate purchased Cadkey, Inc., and eliminated Mr. Bowers from the CADKEY network—effectively preventing him from developing and marketing the Designer's Toolkit for that program.

On May 16, 1991, Baystate sued Mr. Bowers for declaratory judgment that 1) Baystate's products do not infringe the '514 patent, 2) the '514 patent is invalid, and 3) the '514 patent is unenforceable. Mr. Bowers filed counterclaims for copyright infringement, patent infringement, and breach of contract.

Following trial, the jury found for Mr. Bowers and awarded $1,948,869 for copyright infringement, $3,831,025 for breach of contract, and $232,977 for patent infringement. The district court, however, set aside the copyright damages as duplicative of the contract damages and entered judgment for $5,270,142 (including pre-judgment interest). Baystate filed timely motions for judgment as a matter of law (JMOL), or for a new trial, on all of Mr. Bowers' claims. Baystate appeals the district court's denial of its motions for JMOL or a new trial, while Mr. Bowers appeals the district court's denial of copyright damages. This court has jurisdiction under 28 U.S.C. § 1295(a)(1) (2000).

II.

Baystate raises a number of issues that are not unique to the jurisdiction of this court. On those issues, this court applies the law of the circuit from which the appeal is taken, here the First Circuit. *Glaxo, Inc. v. Novopharm, Ltd.*, 110 F.3d 1562, 1572 (Fed.Cir.1996); *Atari, Inc. v. JS & A Group, Inc.*, 747 F.2d 1422, 1439–40 (Fed.Cir.1984) (*en banc*).

Under the law of the First Circuit, a court of appeals reviews without deference the district court's denial of JMOL. *Larch v. Mansfield Mun. Elec. Dep't*, 272 F.3d 63, 67 (1st Cir.2001). The inquiry is whether the evidence, when viewed from the perspective most favorable to the non-movant, would permit a reasonable jury to find in favor of that party on any permissible claim or theory. *Id.* The First Circuit reviews the district court's denial of a motion for a new trial for manifest abuse of discretion. . . . Further, the First Circuit treats federal preemption as a question of law and reviews it without deference. *United States v. R.I. Insurers' Insolvency Fund*, 80 F.3d 616, 619 (1st Cir.1996) ("[A] federal preemption ruling presents a pure question of law subject to plenary review.").

. . .

A.

Baystate contends that the Copyright Act preempts the prohibition of reverse engineering embodied in Mr. Bowers' shrink-wrap license agreements. Swayed by this argument, the district court considered Mr. Bowers' contract and copyright claims coextensive. The district court instructed the jury that "reverse engineering violates the license agreement only if Baystate's product that resulted from reverse engineering infringes Bowers' copyright because it copies protectable expression." Mr. Bowers lodged a timely objection to this instruction. This court holds that, under First Circuit law, the Copyright Act does not preempt or narrow the scope of Mr. Bowers' contract claim.

Courts respect freedom of contract and do not lightly set aside freely-entered agreements. *Beacon Hill Civic Ass'n v. Ristorante Toscano*, 662 N.E.2d 1015, 1017 (Mass.1996). Nevertheless, at times, federal regulation may preempt private contract. *Cf. Nebbia v. New York*, 291 U.S. 502, 523 (1934) ("Equally fundamental with the private right is [the right] of the public to regulate [the private right] in the common interest."). The Copyright Act provides that "all legal or equitable rights that are equivalent to any of the exclusive rights within the general scope of copyright . . . are governed exclusively by this title." 17 U.S.C. § 301(a) (2000). The First Circuit does not interpret this language to require preemption as long as "a state cause of action requires an extra element, beyond mere copying, preparation of derivative works, performance, distribution or display." *Data Gen. Corp. v. Grumman Sys. Support Corp.*, 36 F.3d 1147, 1164 (1st Cir.1994) (quoting *Gates Rubber Co. v. Bando Chem. Indus.*, 9 F.3d 823, 847 (10th Cir.1993)); *see also Computer Assocs. Int'l v. Altai, Inc.*, 982 F.2d 693, 716 (2d Cir.1992) ("But if an 'extra element' is 'required instead of or in addition to the acts of reproduction, performance, distribution or display, in order to constitute a state-created cause of action, then the right does not lie "within the general scope of copyright," and there is no preemption.' ") (quoting 1 Nimmer on Copyright § 1.01[B] at 1–15). Nevertheless, "not every 'extra element' of a state law claim will establish a qualitative variance between the rights protected by federal copyright law and those protected by state law." *Id.*

In *Data General*, Data General alleged that Grumman misappropriated its trade secret software. 36 F.3d at 1155. Grumman obtained that software from Data General's customers and former employees who were bound by confidentiality agreements to refrain from disclosing the software. *Id.* at 1154–55. In defense, Grumman argued that the Copyright Act preempted Data General's trade secret claim. *Id.* at 1158, 1165. The First Circuit held that the Copyright Act did not preempt the state law trade secret claim. *Id.* at 1165. Beyond mere copying, that state law claim required proof of a trade secret and breach of a duty of confidentiality. *Id.* These additional elements of proof, according to the First Circuit, made the trade secret claim qualitatively different from a copyright claim. *Id.* In contrast, the First Circuit noted that claims might be preempted whose extra elements are illusory, being "mere labels attached to the same odious business conduct." *Id.* at 1165 (quoting *Mayer v. Josiah Wedgwood & Sons, Ltd.*, 601 F.Supp. 1523, 1535 (S.D.N.Y.1985)). For example, the First Circuit observed that "a state law misappropriation claim will not escape preemption . . . simply because a plaintiff must prove that copying was not only unauthorized but also commercially immoral." *Id.*

The First Circuit has not addressed expressly whether the Copyright Act preempts a state law contract claim that restrains copying. This court perceives, however, that *Data General's* rationale would lead to a judgment that the Copyright Act does not preempt the state contract action in this case. Indeed, most courts to examine this issue have found that the Copyright Act does not preempt contractual constraints on copyrighted articles. *See, e.g., ProCD, Inc. v. Zeidenberg*, 86 F.3d 1447 (7th Cir.1996) (holding that a shrink-wrap license was not preempted by federal copyright law); *Wrench LLC v. Taco Bell Corp.*, 256 F.3d 446, 457 (6th Cir.2001) (holding a state law contract claim not preempted by federal copyright law); *Nat'l Car Rental Sys., Inc. v. Computer Assocs. Int'l, Inc.*, 991 F.2d 426, 433 (8th Cir.1993); *Taquino v. Teledyne Monarch Rubber*, 893 F.2d 1488, 1501 (5th Cir.1990); *Acorn Structures v. Swantz*, 846 F.2d 923, 926 (4th Cir.1988); *but see Lipscher v. LRP Publs., Inc.*, 266 F.3d 1305, 1312 (11th Cir.2001).

In *ProCD*, for example, the court found that the mutual assent and consideration required by a contract claim render that claim qualitatively different from copyright infringement. 86 F.3d at 1454. Consistent with *Data General's* reliance on a contract element, the court in *ProCD* reasoned: "A copyright is a right against the world. Contracts, by contrast, generally affect only their parties; strangers may do as they please, so contracts do not create 'exclusive rights.' " *Id.* Indeed, the Supreme Court recently noted "it goes without saying that a contract cannot bind a nonparty." *EEOC v. Waffle House, Inc.*, 534 U.S. 279 (2002). This court believes that the First Circuit would follow the reasoning of *ProCD* and the majority of other courts to consider this issue. This court, therefore, holds that the Copyright Act does not preempt Mr. Bowers' contract claims.

In making this determination, this court has left untouched the conclusions reached in *Atari Games v. Nintendo* regarding reverse engineering as a statutory fair use exception to copyright infringement. *Atari Games Corp. v. Nintendo of Am., Inc.*, 975 F.2d 832 (Fed.Cir.1992). In *Atari*, this court stated that, with respect to 17 U.S.C. § 107 (fair use section of the Copyright Act), "the legislative history of section 107 suggests that courts should adapt the fair use exception to accommodate new technological innovations." *Atari*, 975 F.2d at 843. This court noted "[a] prohibition on all copying whatsoever would stifle the free flow of ideas without serving any legitimate interest of the copyright holder." *Id.* Therefore, this court held "reverse engineering object code to discern the unprotectable ideas in a computer program is a fair use." *Id.* Application of the First Circuit's view distinguishing a state law contract claim having additional elements of proof from a copyright claim does not alter the findings of *Atari*. Likewise, this claim distinction does not conflict with the expressly defined circumstances in which reverse engineering is not copyright infringement under 17 U.S.C. § 1201(f) (section of the Digital Millennium Copyright Act) and 17 U.S.C. § 906 (section directed to mask works).

Moreover, while the Fifth Circuit has held a state law prohibiting all copying of a computer program is preempted by the federal Copyright Act, *Vault Corp. v. Quaid Software, Ltd.*, 847 F.2d 255 (5th Cir.1988), no evidence suggests the First Circuit would extend this concept to include private contractual agreements supported by mutual assent and consideration. The First Circuit recognizes contractual waiver of affirmative defenses and statutory rights. *See United States v. Spector*, 55 F.3d 22, 24–5 (1st Cir.1995) (holding that a contractual waiver of the statute of limitations defense constitutes an "effective waiver of defendant's rights under the statute of limitations" if the agreement were properly executed, and the "waiver is made knowingly and voluntarily."); *Tompkins v. United Healthcare of New England*, 203 F.3d 90, 97 (1st Cir.2000) (stating that "in some circumstances contractual waiver of statutory rights is permissible," citing *Canal Elec. Co. v. Westinghouse Elec. Corp.*, 548 N.E.2d 182, 187 (Mass.1990) ("a contractual waiver of statutory rights is permissible when the statute's purpose is the 'protection of the property rights of individual parties . . . rather than . . . the protection of the general public.' ")). Thus, case law indicates the First Circuit would find that private parties are free to contractually forego the limited ability to reverse engineer a software product under the exemptions of the Copyright Act. Of course, a party bound by such a contract may elect to efficiently breach the agreement in order to ascertain ideas in a computer program unprotected by copyright law. Under such circumstances, the breaching party must weigh the benefits of breach against the arguably de minimus damages arising from merely discerning non-protected code.

. . .

In this case, the contract unambiguously prohibits "reverse engineering." That term means ordinarily "to study or analyze (a device, as a microchip for computers) in order to learn details of design, construction, and operation, perhaps to produce a copy or an improved version." *Random House Unabridged Dictionary* (1993); *see also The Free On-Line Dictionary of Computing* (2001), at http://wombat.doc.ic.ac.uk/foldoc/foldoc.cgi?reverse+engineering (last visited Jul. 17, 2002). Thus, the contract in this case broadly prohibits any "reverse engineering" of the subject matter covered by the shrink-wrap agreement.

The record amply supports the jury's finding of a breach of that agreement. As discussed above, the district court erred in instructing the jury that copyright law limited the scope of Mr. Bowers' contract protection. Notwithstanding that error, this court may affirm the jury's breach of contract verdict if substantial record evidence would permit a reasonable jury to find in favor of Mr. Bowers based on a correct understanding of the law. *Larch v. Mansfield Mun. Elec. Dep't*, 272 F.3d 63, 69 (1st Cir.2001). The shrink-wrap agreements in this case are far broader than the protection afforded by copyright law. Even setting aside copyright violations, the record supports a finding of breach of the agreement between the parties. In view of the breadth of Mr. Bowers' contracts, this court perceives that substantial evidence supports the jury's breach of contract verdict relating to both the DOS and Windows versions of Draft-Pak.

. . .

Baystate does not contest the contract damages amount on appeal. Thus, this court sustains the district court's award of contract damages. Mr. Bowers, however, argues that the district court abused its discretion by dropping copyright damages from the combined damage award. To the contrary, this court perceives no abuse of discretion.

The shrink-wrap license agreement prohibited, *inter alia*, all reverse engineering of Mr. Bowers' software, protection encompassing but more extensive than copyright protection, which prohibits only certain copying. Mr. Bowers' copyright and contract claims both rest on Baystate's copying of Mr. Bowers' software. Following the district court's instructions, the jury considered and awarded damages on each separately. This was entirely appropriate. The law is clear that the jury may award separate damages for each claim, "leaving it to the judge to make appropriate adjustments to avoid double recovery." *Britton v. Maloney*, 196 F.3d 24, 32 (1st Cir.1999) (citing *Spectrum Sports, Inc. v. McQuillan*, 506 U.S. 447, 451 n.3 (1993)); *see also Data Gen. Corp. v. Grumman Sys. Support Corp.*, 825 F.Supp. 340, 346 (D.Mass.1993) ("So long as a plaintiff is not twice compensated for a single injury, a judgment may be comprised of elements drawn from separate . . . remedies."), *aff'd in relevant part*, 36 F.3d 1147 (1st Cir.1994). In this case, the breach of contract damages arose from the same copying and included the same lost sales that form the basis for the copyright damages. The district court, therefore, did not abuse its discretion by omitting from the final damage award the duplicative copyright damages. Because this court affirms the district court's omission of the copyright damages, this court need not reach the merits of Mr. Bowers' copyright infringement claim.

. . .

In sum, this court perceives no basis upon which a reasonable jury could find that Baystate's accused templates infringe claim 1 of the '514 patent. Hence, this court reverses the district court's denial of Baystate's motion for JMOL of non-infringement.

CONCLUSION

Because substantial evidence supports the jury's verdict that Baystate breached its contract with Mr. Bowers, this court affirms that verdict. This court holds also that the district court did not abuse its discretion in omitting as duplicative copyright damages from the damage award. . . .

DYK, CIRCUIT JUDGE, concurring in part and dissenting in part.

I join the majority opinion except insofar as it holds that the contract claim is not preempted by federal law. Based on the petition for rehearing and the opposition, I have concluded that our original decision on the preemption issue, reaffirmed in today's revision of the majority opinion, was not correct. By holding that shrinkwrap licenses that override the fair use defense are not preempted by the Copyright Act, 17 U.S.C. §§ 101 *et seq.*, the majority has rendered a decision in conflict with the only other federal court of appeals decision that has addressed the issue—the Fifth Circuit decision in *Vault Corp. v. Quaid Software Ltd.*, 847 F.2d 255 (5th Cir.1988). The majority's approach permits state law to eviscerate an important federal copyright policy reflected in the fair use defense, and the majority's logic threatens other federal copyright policies as well. I respectfully dissent.

I

Congress has made the Copyright Act the exclusive means for protecting copyright. The Act provides that "all legal or equitable rights that are equivalent to any of the exclusive rights within the general scope of copyright . . . are governed exclusively by this title." 17 U.S.C. § 301(a) (2000). All other laws, including the common law, are preempted. "No person is entitled to any such right or equivalent right in any such work under the common law or statutes of any State." *Id.*

The test for preemption by copyright law, like the test for patent law preemption, should be whether the state law "substantially impedes the public use of the otherwise unprotected" material. *Bonito Boats, Inc. v. Thunder Craft Boats, Inc.*, 489 U.S. 141, 157, 167 (1989) (state law at issue was preempted because it "substantially restricted the public's ability to exploit ideas that the patent system mandates shall be free for all to use."); *Sears, Roebuck & Co. v. Stiffel Co.*, 376 U.S. 225, 231–32 (1964). *See also Eldred v. Ashcroft*, 537 U.S. 186 (2003) (applying patent precedent in copyright case). In the copyright area, the First Circuit has adopted an "equivalent in substance" test to determine whether a state law is preempted by the Copyright Act. *Data Gen. Corp. v. Grumman Sys. Support Corp.* 36 F.3d 1147, 1164–65 (1st Cir.1994). That test seeks to determine whether the state cause of action contains an additional element not present in the copyright right, such as scienter. If the state cause of action contains such an extra element, it is not preempted by the Copyright Act. *Id.* However, "such an action is equivalent in substance to a copyright infringement claim [and thus preempted by the Copyright Act] where the additional element merely concerns *the extent to which* authors and their licensees can prohibit unauthorized copying by third parties." *Id.* at 1165 (emphasis in original).

II

The fair use defense is an important limitation on copyright. Indeed, the Supreme Court has said that "from the infancy of copyright protection, some opportunity for fair use of copyrighted materials has been thought necessary to fulfill copyright's very purpose, 'to promote the Progress of Science and useful Arts. . . .' U.S. Const., Art. I, § 8, cl.8." *Campbell v. Acuff-Rose Music, Inc.*, 510 U.S. 569, 575 (1994). The protective nature of the fair use defense was recently emphasized by the Court in the *Eldred* case, in which the Court noted that "copyright law contains built-in accommodations," including "the 'fair use' defense [which] allows the public to use not only facts an ideas contained in the copyrighted work, but also expression itself in certain circumstances." 537 U.S. 186.

We correctly held in *Atari Games Corp. v. Nintendo of America, Inc.*, 975 F.2d 832, 843 (Fed.Cir.1992), that reverse engineering constitutes a fair use under the Copyright Act.[2] The Ninth and Eleventh Circuits have also ruled that reverse engineering constitutes fair use. *Bateman v. Mnemonics, Inc.*, 79 F.3d 1532, 1539 n.18 (11th Cir.1996); *Sega Enters. Ltd. v. Accolade, Inc.*, 977 F.2d 1510, 1527–28 (9th Cir.1992). No other federal court of appeals has disagreed.

We emphasized in *Atari* that an author cannot achieve protection for an idea simply by embodying it in a computer program. "An author cannot acquire patent-like protection by putting an idea, process, or method of operation in an unintelligible format and asserting copyright infringement against those who try to understand that idea, process, or method of operation." 975 F.2d at 842. Thus, the fair use defense for reverse engineering is necessary so that copyright protection does not "extend to any idea, procedure, process, system, method of operation, concept, principle, or discovery, regardless of the form in which it is described, explained, illustrated, or embodied in such work," as proscribed by the Copyright Act. 17 U.S.C. § 102(b) (2000).

III

A state is not free to eliminate the fair use defense. Enforcement of a total ban on reverse engineering would conflict with the Copyright Act itself by protecting otherwise unprotectable material. If state law provided that a copyright holder could bar fair use of the copyrighted material by placing a black dot on each copy of the work offered for sale, there would be no question but that the state law would be preempted. A state law that allowed a copyright holder to simply label its products so as to eliminate a fair use defense would "substantially impede" the public's right to fair use and allow the copyright holder, through state law, to protect material that the Congress has determined must be free to all under the Copyright Act. *See Bonito Boats*, 489 U.S. at 157.

I nonetheless agree with the majority opinion that a state can permit parties to contract away a fair use defense or to agree not to engage in uses of copyrighted material that are permitted by the copyright law, if the contract is freely negotiated. *See, e.g., Nat'l Car Rental Sys., Inc. v. Computer Assocs. Int'l, Inc.*, 991 F.2d 426 (8th Cir.1993); *Acorn Structures v. Swantz*, 846 F.2d 923, 926 (4th Cir.1988). *See also Taquino v. Teledyne Monarch Rubber*, 893 F.2d 1488 (5th Cir.1990). *But see Wrench LLC v. Taco Bell Corp.*, 256 F.3d 446, 457 (6th Cir.2001) ("If the promise amounts only to a promise to refrain from reproducing, performing, distributing or displaying the work, then the contract claim is preempted."). A freely negotiated agreement represents the "extra element" that prevents preemption of a state law claim that would otherwise be identical to the infringement claim barred by the fair use de-

---

[2] In the patent context, reverse engineering is viewed as an important right of the public. *Bonito Boats*, 489 U.S. at 160.

fense of reverse engineering. *See Data Gen.,* 36 F.3d at 1164–65.

However, state law giving effect to shrinkwrap licenses is no different in substance from a hypothetical black dot law. Like any other contract of adhesion, the only choice offered to the purchaser is to avoid making the purchase in the first place. *See Fuentes v. Shevin,* 407 U.S. 67, 95 (1972). State law thus gives the copyright holder the ability to eliminate the fair use defense in each and every instance at its option. In doing so, as the majority concedes, it authorizes "shrinkwrap agreements . . . [that] are far broader than the protection afforded by copyright law." *Ante.*

IV

There is, moreover, no logical stopping point to the majority's reasoning. The amici rightly question whether under our original opinion the first sale doctrine and a host of other limitations on copyright protection might be eliminated by shrinkwrap licenses in just this fashion. If by printing a few words on the outside of its product a party can eliminate the fair use defense, then it can also, by the same means, restrict a purchaser from asserting the "first sale" defense, embodied in 17 U.S.C. § 109(a), or any other of the protections Congress has afforded the public in the Copyright Act. That means that, under the majority's reasoning, state law could extensively undermine the protections of the Copyright Act.

V

The Fifth Circuit's decision in *Vault* directly supports preemption of the shrinkwrap limitation. The majority states that *Vault* held that "a state law prohibiting all copying of a computer program is preempted by the federal Copyright Act" and then states that "no evidence suggests the First Circuit would extend this concept to include private contractual agreements supported by mutual assent and consideration." *Ante.* But, in fact, the Fifth Circuit held that the specific provision of state law that authorized contracts prohibiting reverse engineering, decompilation, or disassembly of computer programs was preempted by federal law because it conflicted with a portion of the Copyright Act and because it " 'touched upon an area' of federal copyright law." 847 F.2d at 269–70 (quoting *Sears, Roebuck,* 376 U.S. at 229). From a preemption standpoint, there is no distinction between a state law that explicitly validates a contract that restricts reverse engineering (*Vault*) and general common law that permits such a restriction (as here). On the contrary, the preemption clause of the Copyright Act makes clear that it covers "any such right or equivalent right in any such work *under the common law or statutes of any State."* 17 U.S.C. § 301(a) (2000) (emphasis added).

I do not read *ProCD, Inc. v. Zeidenberg,* 86 F.3d 1447 (7th Cir.1996), the only other court of appeals shrinkwrap case, as being to the contrary, even though it contains broad language stating that "a simple two-party contract is not 'equivalent to any of the exclusive rights within the general scope of copyright.' " *Id.* at 1455. In *ProCD,* the Seventh Circuit validated a shrinkwrap license that restricted the use of a CD-ROM to non-commercial purposes, which the defendant had violated by charging users a fee to access the CD-ROM over the Internet. The court held that the restriction to non-commercial use of the program was not equivalent to any rights protected by the Copyright Act. Rather, the "contract reflected private ordering, essential to efficient functioning of markets." *Id.* at 1455. The court saw the licensor as legitimately seeking to distinguish between personal and commercial use. "ProCD offers software and data for two prices: one for personal use, a higher prices for commercial use," the court said. The defendant "wants to use the data without paying the seller's price." *Id.* at 1454. The court also emphasized that the license "would not withdraw any information from the public domain" because all of the information on the CD-ROM was publicly available. *Id.* at 1455.

The case before us is different from *ProCD*. The Copyright Act does not confer a right to pay the same amount for commercial and personal use. It does, however, confer a right to fair use, 17 U.S.C. § 107, which we have held encompasses reverse engineering.

ProCD and the other contract cases are also careful not to create a blanket rule that all contracts will escape preemption. The court in that case emphasized that "we think it prudent to refrain from adopting a rule that anything with the label 'contract' is necessarily outside the preemption clause." 86 F.3d at 1455. It also noted with approval another court's "recogni[tion of] the possibility that some applications of the law of contract could interfere with the attainment of national objectives and therefore come within the domain" of the Copyright Act. *Id.* The Eighth Circuit too cautioned in *National Car Rental* that a contractual restriction could impermissibly "protect rights equivalent to the exclusive copyright rights." 991 F.2d at 432.

I conclude that *Vault* states the correct rule; that state law authorizing shrink-wrap licenses that prohibit reverse engineering is preempted; and that the First Circuit would so hold because the extra element here "merely concerns *the extent to which* authors and their licensees can prohibit unauthorized copying by third parties." *Data Gen.*, 36 F.3d at 1165 (emphasis in original). I respectfully dissent.

EXTENSIONS

1. *Negotiated versus non-negotiated licenses.* In a thoughtful review of the preemption issue, Professor Maureen O'Rourke suggests a nuanced analysis in which negotiated licenses and non-negotiated mass-market licenses should be evaluated differently. Maureen A. O'Rourke, *Drawing the Boundary Between Copyright and Contract: Copyright Preemption of Software License Terms*, 45 DUKE L.J. 479 (1995). She concludes nevertheless that most licenses expanding owners' rights should be upheld, unless doing so would allow the licensor to expand its copyright monopoly beyond the market to which that monopoly was intended to apply. What problems do you foresee courts would encounter in applying this nuanced analysis?

2. *Public policy limitations.* Professor Mark Lemley suggests that other doctrines besides preemption should be brought into play:

> Even if federal law does not preempt enforcement of a specific contract term directly, the law may still restrict enforcement of that term on public policy grounds. Public policy limitations on contractual freedom are fairly common in our society. . . . [O]ne such limitation [is] the contract doctrine of unconscionability. Certain shrinkwrap license terms—such as those featured in a recent Dil-

bert cartoon[180]—may well be held unconscionable. But unconscionability is rarely used, and it is not well-tailored to the needs of intellectual property law. In the intellectual property context, three sets of rules may supplement contract preemption: copyright misuse, federal public policy, and state public policy. Not all of these rules will apply in every case; there will still be plenty of room for contract law to operate. But its operation will not be unfettered by intellectual property policy. . . .

To be sure, not everyone is happy with the idea that public policy overrides contract. Judge Easterbrook has suggested that it should do so only rarely, and advocates of a strong form of private ordering often suggest that "the market" will do a better job of determining public policy than "the law." . . . But in fact, intellectual property is a prime example of an area in which we cannot simply rely on "the agreement of the parties" to choose our public policy. This is true partially because intellectual property licenses are notoriously fallible as indicators of the "intent" of the parties; as we proceed to remove all trace of assent from the notion of contract, the philosophical basis for private ordering disappears as well.

But the problem is more fundamental than this. Intellectual property is a deliberate, government-sponsored departure from the principles of free competition, designed to subsidize creators and therefore to induce more creation. This departure from the competitive model affects third parties who are not participants in the contract. If I agree not to criticize, parody, reverse engineer, improve, adapt, or extend your work, I am not the only one who pays the price for that agreement. All those consumers who would have bought my new product lose value as well, and that value simply isn't accounted for in the deal between the parties. It can't be, because I myself would not be able to capture the full social surplus from those people who would buy my improved product. This potential surplus is accounted for by the constraints and dictates of intellectual property law—it is the very reason intellectual property provides only a limited incentive and not complete control. Those intellectual property rules may not always be pretty, or easy to determine, and they certainly aren't perfect descriptions of an optimal incentive structure. But they are at least an effort to arrive at the right balance of incentives—an effort that would never even be made were we to leave social ordering entirely in the hands of private parties.

Mark A. Lemley, *Beyond Preemption: The Law and Policy of Intellectual Property Licensing*, 87 CALIF. L. REV. 111 (1999).

D. LICENSES THAT EXPAND THE RIGHTS OF USERS

1. Open Source Licensing and Its Significance for E-Commerce

In the early days of computing, programmers shared programs with each other. That is, they shared the source code, which shows how the program was constructed and enables the user to make changes to suit his needs. Nowadays, however, the source code for mass-market software is a closely guarded secret, making it difficult or impossible for others to

---

[180] In the cartoon, Dilbert inadvertently agrees to "spend the rest of my life as a towel boy in Bill Gates' new mansion" when he opens a piece of shrinkwrapped software without reading the entire agreement first (on file with author, pasted to his office door).

understand the code or to modify it. Richard Stallman, a talented and passionate program-mer who was unhappy about this situation, founded the Free Software Foundation ("FSF") in 1982, and became a leader in the free software (or "open source") movement.

As his own contribution to this nascent movement, Stallman wrote and released the source code for a free clone of the UNIX operating system which he called GNU—the ac-ronym stands for the phrase "GNU's Not UNIX," and is pronounced "guh-NEW." To en-sure that GNU source code remained freely available and that users could use, modify, and redistribute it in any way they saw fit, Stallman licensed his program at no charge, rather than dedicating it to the public domain. By using a license, Stallman was able to ensure that any improvements made to the GNU source code would also be made available to others on the same terms that applied to the original program, without restrictions on its use, modifi-cation or redistribution. This license for GNU became known as the GNU General Public License ("GPL"), one of the first "copyleft" or open source licenses. As the FSF explains on its website:

> *Copyleft* is a general method for making a program free software and requir-ing all modified and extended versions of the program to be free software as well.
>
> The simplest way to make a program free is to put it in the public domain, uncopyrighted. This allows people to share the program and their improvements, if they are so minded. But it also allows uncooperative people to convert the program into proprietary software. They can make changes, many or few, and distribute the result as a proprietary product. People who receive the program in that modified form do not have the freedom that the original author gave them; the middleman has stripped it away.
>
> In the GNU project, our aim is to give *all* users the freedom to redistribute and change GNU software. If middlemen could strip off the freedom, we might have many users, but those users would not have freedom. So instead of putting GNU software in the public domain, we "copyleft" it. Copyleft says that anyone who redistributes the software, with or without changes, must pass along the freedom to further copy and change it. Copyleft guarantees that every user has freedom. . . .
>
> To copyleft a program, we first state that it is copyrighted; then we add dis-tribution terms, which are a legal instrument that gives everyone the rights to use, modify, and redistribute the program's code *or any program derived from it* but only if the distribution terms are unchanged. Thus, the code and the free-doms become legally inseparable.
>
> Proprietary software developers use copyright to take away the users' free-dom; we use copyright to guarantee their freedom. That's why we reverse the name, changing "copyright" into "copyleft."

What is Copyleft?, http://www.gnu.org/licenses/licenses.html.

The GNU GPL does not require that free software be given away without charge; it re-quires only that no conditions be placed on a user's right to use, modify and redistribute the program's code or any program derived from it. In Stallman's slogan, "[i]t's free, as in free speech, not free beer." Of course, one may further modify this open source license to re-quire that the program and any programs derived from it be distributed at no cost to users so that it *is* free as in "free beer," and some within the open source movement have done ex-actly this. As with any license of intellectual property, if one does not comply with the conditions imposed by an open source license, then, assuming the conditions are validly imposed, use of the program is without the permission of the licensor and the user may be liable for infringement. Although some open source licenses may permit charging a fee for software and others prohibit it, all open source licenses permit users to use, modify or redistribute the program or any program derived from it without charge and subject only to those conditions imposed by the licensor's original open source license.

Open source programs include operating systems such as GNU and Linux, applications comprising the Internet's programmatic infrastructure such as Sendmail (a program that routes more than eighty percent of the e-mail sent over the Internet) and BIND (a program used to resolve domain names into IP addresses), web server software such as Apache, web browsers such as Netscape's Mozilla, programming languages such as Perl and Python, and a variety of personal desktop applications. Moreover, users of open source software today can be found in both the public and private sectors. According to Mark Webbink, Senior Vice President and General Counsel of Red Hat, Inc., a company that provides, develops and supports the use of open source software in government and industry, users of open source software include the NSA, CIA, Department of Defense (including as the embedded operating system in certain weapons systems), FAA, the White House (web servers), National Science Foundation, Los Alamos National Laboratory, Lawrence Livermore Laboratories, National Center for Supercomputing Applications, United States Postal Service, NOAA, National Institutes for Standards and Technology, Bureau of Public Debt, National Institutes of Health, and Department of the Interior, as well as many large corporations.

In light of the widespread commercial use of open source software, it is perhaps surprising that the legal enforceability of open source licenses such as the GNU GPL has never been tested in the courts. Since each licensee is using material for which copyright is claimed, if the license were declared invalid the licensee might be an infringer; thus, licensees may lack incentive to challenge the license, unless perhaps they can dispute the copyrightability of the work or feel confident that a defense such as fair use would be applicable. The various legal arguments that could be used to attack the enforceability of an open source license include claims that the license lacks consideration, that there was a lack of notice to the licensee, a lack of consent by the licensee, or lack of privity (due to the "viral" nature of certain open source license provisions), that an open source license is an adhesion contract, and that the principal terms of an open source license are unconscionable. Some have also questioned whether an open source license runs afoul of the antitrust or patent laws.

Although the enforceability of a GPL has yet to be challenged in court, currently wending its way through the courts of Utah is a lawsuit—*Caldera Systems, Inc., d/b/a The SCO Group v. International Business Machines Corp.*—in which the plaintiff asserts that Linux, the best known open source software, includes proprietary code developed by AT&T and currently owned by the plaintiff. If true, then users of Linux would have to license this proprietary code to avoid liability for infringement or misappropriation, unless some defense is applicable. The entire open source/free software community is watching this litigation very carefully. For more information on this lawsuit, see *SCO Files Lawsuit Against IBM*, ir.sco.com/ReleaseDetail.cfm?ReleaseID=103273, and Eric Raymond, *OSI Position Paper on the SCO-vs.-IBM Complaint*, www.opensource.org/sco-vs-ibm.html.

For examples and discussion of the various licenses that have been developed by or are related to the free software/open source movement, and for more information on the FSF, visit *Open Source*, www.opensource.org, and *Free Software Foundation*, www.fsf.org.

QUESTIONS FOR DISCUSSION

1. *Losing freedom.* What is the legal basis for Stallman's claim, in the passage quoted above, that putting a program in the public domain could result in an improver ("middleman") being able to "strip away" the freedom that the original developer intended?

2. *Guaranteeing freedom.* In the copyleft paradigm, how exactly is copyright supposed to work to guarantee the users' freedom to modify programs?

3. *Theoretical justification for open source.* One view of open source licensing stresses the ideology of openness; but another view stresses its economic superiority under certain circumstances. For an investigation of the latter perspective, see Yochai Benkler, *Coase's Penguin, or Linux and The Nature of the Firm*, 112 YALE L.J. 369 (2002). To what extent can the open source model be extended beyond software licensing?

4. *Property grants versus servitudes.* Many open source advocates argue passionately that the license is a property grant only, a defeasible interest that ceases to exist if the conditions are not met, and not properly considered contractual. That is because property rights are thought to be more enforceable against transferees of the original license than are contractual obligations, which normally require privity. On the other hand, it has been argued that obligations that run with a digital object are more analogous to servitudes; and, if they turn out to be enforceable, will benefit copyright traditionalists more than open source advocates. For an investigation of these debates, see Molly S. Van Houweling, *Copyright's Servitudes* (forthcoming 2006).

2. Creative Commons

Creative Commons ("CC") is a nonprofit organization founded by Lawrence Lessig and other advocates of "free culture." *See* LAWRENCE LESSIG, FREE CULTURE (2004). Its purpose is to provide a licensing platform in which authors of all kinds of content—films, music, graphic arts, stories, textbooks, etc.—can allow their works to be drawn upon by others and in turn draw upon the works of others, while not giving up their proprietary rights entirely. The implementation of this scheme seeks to automate the process of licensing in order to reduce the transaction costs of acquiring licenses and also to encourage authors to allow their works to be reused in different ways while retaining copyright. In this way, CC hopes to reduce the chilling effect on creativity created by both the substantive default rules of copyright and the transaction costs of seeking out owners and acquiring licenses.

Creative Commons, *"Some Rights Reserved": Building a Layer of Reasonable Copyright*
creativecommons.org/about/history

Too often the debate over creative control tends to the extremes. At one pole is a vision of total control—a world in which every last use of a work is regulated and in which "all rights reserved" (and then some) is the norm. At the other end is a vision of anarchy—a world in which creators enjoy a wide range of freedom but are left vulnerable to exploitation. Balance, compromise, and moderation—once the driving forces of a copyright system that valued innovation and protection equally—have become endangered species.

Creative Commons is working to revive them. We use private rights to create public goods: creative works set free for certain uses. Like the free software and open-source movements, our ends are cooperative and community-minded, but our means are voluntary and libertarian. We work to offer creators a best-of-both-worlds way to protect their works while encouraging certain uses of them—to declare "some rights reserved."

Thus, a single goal unites Creative Commons' current and future projects: to build a layer of reasonable, flexible copyright in the face of increasingly restrictive default rules.

Creative Commons' first project, in December 2002, was the release of a set of copyright licenses free for public use. Taking inspiration in part from the Free Software Foundation's GNU General Public License (GNU GPL), Creative Commons has developed a Web application that helps people dedicate their creative works to the public domain—or retain their copyright while licensing them as free for certain uses, on certain conditions. Unlike the GNU GPL, Creative Commons licenses are not designed for software, but rather for other kinds of creative works: websites, scholarship, music, film, photography, literature, courseware, etc. We hope to build upon and complement the work of others who have created public licenses for a variety of creative works. Our aim is not only to increase the sum of raw source material online, but also to make access to that material cheaper and easier. To this end, we have also developed metadata that can be used to associate creative works with their public domain or license status in a machine-readable way. We hope this will enable people to use our search application and other online applications to find, for example, photographs that are free to use provided that the original photographer is credited, or songs that may be copied, distributed, or sampled with no restrictions whatsoever. We hope that the ease of use fostered by machine-readable licenses will further reduce barriers to creativity.

. . .

Creative Commons, *Choosing a License*
creativecommons.org/about/licenses/index_html

Offering your work under a Creative Commons license does not mean giving up your copyright. It means offering some of your rights to any member of the public but only on certain conditions.

. . .

 Attribution. You let others copy, distribute, display, and perform your copyrighted work—and derivative works based upon it—but only if they give credit the way you request.

Example: Jane publishes her photograph with an Attribution license, because she wants the world to use her pictures provided they give her credit. Bob finds her photograph online and wants to display it on the front page of his website. Bob puts Jane's picture on his site, and clearly indicates Jane's authorship.

Our core licensing suite will also let you mix and match conditions from the list of options below. There are a total of six Creative Commons licenses to choose from our core licensing suite.

Noncommercial. You let others copy, distribute, display, and perform your work—and derivative works based upon it—but for noncommercial purposes only.

Examples: Gus publishes his photograph on his website with a Noncommercial license. Camille prints Gus' photograph. Camille is not allowed to sell the print photograph without Gus's permission.

No Derivative Works. You let others copy, distribute, display, and perform only verbatim copies of your work, not derivative works based upon it.

Example: Sara licenses a recording of her song with a No Derivative Works license. Joe would like to cut Sara's track and mix it with his own to produce an entirely new song. Joe cannot do this without Sara's permission (unless his song amounts to fair use).

Share Alike. You allow others to distribute derivative works only under a license identical to the license that governs your work.

Note: A license cannot feature both the Share Alike and No Derivative Works options. The Share Alike requirement applies only to derivative works.

Example: Gus's online photo is licensed under the Noncommercial and Share Alike terms. Camille is an amateur collage artist, and she takes Gus's photo and puts it into one of her collages. This Share Alike language requires Camille to make her collage available on a Noncommercial plus Share Alike license. It makes her offer her work back to the world on the same terms Gus gave her.

. . .

To facilitate the licensing process, CC provides three formats for each license: a simple summary in plain language, with identifying icons, which CC calls a "commons deed"); a legally precise version ("legal code"); and a machine-readable format ("digital code"). CC has implemented each license in a number of different languages, to facilitate worldwide acceptance. Moreover, the digital code will facilitate implementation of searching for materials that are reusable. For example, Google released Creative Commons-enabled search in November 2005, meaning a user can use Google to search the web for CC-licensed works.

For example, here is CC's "commons deed" for an Attribution-NonCommercial license (from creativecommons.org/licenses/by-nc/2.5/):

You are free:
- to copy, distribute, display, and perform the work
- to make derivative works

Under the following conditions:

Attribution. You must attribute the work in the manner specified by the author or licensor.

Noncommercial. You may not use this work for commercial purposes.

- For any reuse or distribution, you must make clear to others the license terms of this work.
- Any of these conditions can be waived if you get permission from the copyright holder.

Your fair use and other rights are in no way affected by the above.

This is a human-readable summary of the Legal Code (the full license).

Next is CC's "legal code" for the same license (from creativecommons.org/licenses/by-nc/2.5/legalcode):

CREATIVE COMMONS CORPORATION IS NOT A LAW FIRM AND DOES NOT PROVIDE LEGAL SERVICES. DISTRIBUTION OF THIS LICENSE DOES NOT CREATE AN ATTORNEY-CLIENT RELATIONSHIP. CREATIVE COMMONS PROVIDES THIS INFORMATION ON AN "AS-IS" BASIS. CREATIVE COMMONS MAKES NO WARRANTIES REGARDING THE INFORMATION PROVIDED, AND DISCLAIMS LIABILITY FOR DAMAGES RESULTING FROM ITS USE.

License

THE WORK (AS DEFINED BELOW) IS PROVIDED UNDER THE TERMS OF THIS CREATIVE COMMONS PUBLIC LICENSE ("CCPL" OR "LICENSE"). THE WORK IS PROTECTED BY COPYRIGHT AND/OR OTHER APPLICABLE

LAW. ANY USE OF THE WORK OTHER THAN AS AUTHORIZED UNDER THIS LICENSE OR COPYRIGHT LAW IS PROHIBITED.

BY EXERCISING ANY RIGHTS TO THE WORK PROVIDED HERE, YOU ACCEPT AND AGREE TO BE BOUND BY THE TERMS OF THIS LICENSE. THE LICENSOR GRANTS YOU THE RIGHTS CONTAINED HERE IN CONSIDERATION OF YOUR ACCEPTANCE OF SUCH TERMS AND CONDITIONS.

1. Definitions

a. **"Collective Work"** means a work, such as a periodical issue, anthology or encyclopedia, in which the Work in its entirety in unmodified form, along with a number of other contributions, constituting separate and independent works in themselves, are assembled into a collective whole. A work that constitutes a Collective Work will not be considered a Derivative Work (as defined below) for the purposes of this License.

b. **"Derivative Work"** means a work based upon the Work or upon the Work and other pre-existing works, such as a translation, musical arrangement, dramatization, fictionalization, motion picture version, sound recording, art reproduction, abridgment, condensation, or any other form in which the Work may be recast, transformed, or adapted, except that a work that constitutes a Collective Work will not be considered a Derivative Work for the purpose of this License. For the avoidance of doubt, where the Work is a musical composition or sound recording, the synchronization of the Work in timed-relation with a moving image ("synching") will be considered a Derivative Work for the purpose of this License.

c. **"Licensor"** means the individual or entity that offers the Work under the terms of this License.

d. **"Original Author"** means the individual or entity who created the Work.

e. **"Work"** means the copyrightable work of authorship offered under the terms of this License.

f. **"You"** means an individual or entity exercising rights under this License who has not previously violated the terms of this License with respect to the Work, or who has received express permission from the Licensor to exercise rights under this License despite a previous violation.

2. Fair Use Rights. Nothing in this license is intended to reduce, limit, or restrict any rights arising from fair use, first sale or other limitations on the exclusive rights of the copyright owner under copyright law or other applicable laws.

3. License Grant. Subject to the terms and conditions of this License, Licensor hereby grants You a worldwide, royalty-free, non-exclusive, perpetual (for the duration of the applicable copyright) license to exercise the rights in the Work as stated below:

a. to reproduce the Work, to incorporate the Work into one or more Collective Works, and to reproduce the Work as incorporated in the Collective Works;

b. to create and reproduce Derivative Works;

c. to distribute copies or phonorecords of, display publicly, perform publicly, and perform publicly by means of a digital audio transmission the Work including as incorporated in Collective Works;

d. to distribute copies or phonorecords of, display publicly, perform publicly, and perform publicly by means of a digital audio transmission Derivative Works;

The above rights may be exercised in all media and formats whether now known or hereafter devised. The above rights include the right to make such modifications as are technically necessary to exercise the rights in other media and formats. All rights not expressly granted by Licensor are hereby reserved . . . .

4. Restrictions. The license granted in Section 3 above is expressly made subject to and limited by the following restrictions:

a. You may distribute, publicly display, publicly perform, or publicly digitally perform the Work only under the terms of this License, and You must include a copy of, or the Uniform Resource Identifier for, this License with every copy or phonorecord of the Work You distribute, publicly display, publicly perform, or publicly digitally perform. You may not offer or impose any terms on the Work that alter or restrict the terms of this License or the recipients' exercise of the rights granted hereunder. You may not sublicense the Work. You must keep intact all notices that refer to this License and to the disclaimer of warranties. You may not distribute, publicly display, publicly perform, or publicly digitally perform the Work with any technological measures that control access or use of the Work in a manner inconsistent with the terms of this License Agreement. The above applies to the Work as incorporated in a Collective Work, but this does not require the Collective Work apart from the Work itself to be made subject to the terms of this License. If You create a Collective Work, upon notice from any Licensor You must, to the extent practicable, remove from the Collective Work any credit as required by clause 4(c), as requested. If You create a Derivative Work, upon notice from any Licensor You must, to the extent practicable, remove from the Derivative Work any credit as required by clause 4(c), as requested.

b. You may not exercise any of the rights granted to You in Section 3 above in any manner that is primarily intended for or directed toward commercial advantage or private monetary compensation. The exchange of the Work for other copyrighted works by means of digital file-sharing or otherwise shall not be considered to be intended for or directed toward commercial advantage or private monetary compensation, provided there is no payment of any monetary compensation in connection with the exchange of copyrighted works.

c. If you distribute, publicly display, publicly perform, or publicly digitally perform the Work or any Derivative Works or Collective Works, You must keep intact all copyright notices for the Work and provide, reasonable to the medium or means You are utilizing: (i) the name of Original Author (or pseudonym, if applicable) if supplied, and/or (ii) if the Original Author and/or Licensor designate another party or parties (e.g. a sponsor institute, publishing entity, journal) for attribution in Licensor's copyright notice, terms of service or by other reasonable means, the name of such party or parties; the title of the Work if supplied; to the extent reasonably practicable, the Uniform Resource Identifier, if any, that Licensor specifies to be associated with the Work, unless such URI does not refer to the copyright notice or licensing information for the Work; and in the case of a Derivative Work, a credit identifying the use of the Work in the Derivative Work (e.g., "French translation of the Work by Original Author," or "Screenplay based on original Work by Original Author"). Such credit may be implemented in any reasonable manner; provided, however, that in the case of a Derivative Work or Collective Work, at a minimum such credit will appear where any other comparable authorship credit appears and in a manner at least as prominent as such other comparable authorship credit.

. . .

7. Termination

a. This License and the rights granted hereunder will terminate automatically upon any breach by You of the terms of this License. Individuals or entities who have received Derivative Works or Collective Works from You under this License, however, will not have their licenses terminated provided such individuals or entities remain in full compliance with those licenses. Sections 1, 2, 5, 6, 7, and 8 will survive any termination of this License.

b. Subject to the above terms and conditions, the license granted here is perpetual (for the duration of the applicable copyright in the Work). Notwithstanding the above, Licensor reserves the right to release the Work under different license terms or to stop distributing the Work at any time; provided, however that any such election will not serve to withdraw this License (or any other license that has been, or is required to be, granted under the terms of this License), and this License will continue in full force and effect unless terminated as stated above.

. . .

Creative Commons is not a party to this License, and makes no warranty whatsoever in connection with the Work. Creative Commons will not be liable to You or any party on any legal theory for any damages whatsoever, including without limitation any general, special, incidental or consequential damages arising in connection to this license. Notwithstanding the foregoing two (2) sentences, if Creative Commons has expressly identified itself as the Licensor hereunder, it shall have all rights and obligations of Licensor.

Except for the limited purpose of indicating to the public that the Work is licensed under the CCPL, neither party will use the trademark "Creative Commons" or any related trademark or logo of Creative Commons without the prior written consent of Creative Commons. Any permitted use will be in compliance with Creative Commons' then-current trademark usage guidelines, as may be published on its website or otherwise made available upon request from time to time.

Creative Commons may be contacted at http://creativecommons.org/.

EXTENSIONS

Open content in developing areas. Consider the attractiveness of the idea of open content to relatively underdeveloped areas or countries. Gilberto Gil, a very famous singer and musician, is Minister of Culture for Brazil. That country is embracing open source software as an important element in its aspiration to be a significant force in the digital economic and social environment. Brazil's president has instructed government entities and state-run companies to switch gradually to the Linux operating system and other open source systems. Gil believes that open source development can help underdeveloped countries avoid overdependence on more developed countries in the digital arena. Gil has said, "We have no army; we just have our creativity. We are hoping to build a creative economy." *See* Jack Kenny, *Open Revolution*, THE TIMES [LONDON] EDUC. SUPP., Nov. 4, 2005, at 31.

Gil has developed a new digital sampling license under the Creative Commons model. He hopes to get it accepted in schools and elsewhere in society. He hopes that Brazil will be a model for development. His vision is not primarily economic; instead, it is about freedom. Free software is related to the ideal of human freedom, and not to just to being free of charge. His goal is "pushing forward the remodeling of humanity." *Id.*

QUESTIONS FOR DISCUSSION

1. *Pros and cons of "share alike."* The "share alike" feature of the Creative Commons licensing platform is, of course, similar to the feature of the GNU/GPL that attempts to make the obligation to distribute the source code for software improvements run with the distributed software. Reconsider the pros and cons of this arrangement. Some have worried that the "viral" feature of this contractual scheme, if confirmed as legally enforceable, will serve the interests of copyright maximalists much more than the interests of those wishing to strengthen the public domain. *See*, e.g., Niva Elkin-Koren, *What Contracts Can't Do: The Limits of Private Ordering in Facilitating a Creative Commons*, 74 Fordham L. Rev. — (forthcoming 2006):

> [R]eliance on contracts alone is risky. It entails support of strong copyrights and freedom of contract, allowing enforcement against third parties. The legal regime that would validate Creative Commons' licenses would also enforce contracts that restrict access to creative works.

What is your evaluation of this risk?

2. *Transaction costs.* One of the purposes of Creative Commons is to reduce the transaction costs associated with licensing so that more licensing (and hence more cultural remixing) can take place. As we have seen, however, Creative Commons is implementing a fairly large array of different licenses, because of the modular feature which allows licensors to select one of many permutations possible. Will this proliferation of different licenses cause transaction costs of its own? Consider, for example, how a licensee could seek to renegotiate for more rights; how a licensee could determine whether the licensor actually owns the work and is not herself an infringer; whether the licensor can revoke the license and how licensees would obtain that information. What is your assessment of transaction costs as a potential obstacle to widespread implementation of the CC regime?

FURTHER READING

- Robert P. Merges, *A New Dynamism in the Public Domain*, 71 U. Chi. L. Rev. 183 (2005)

CHAPTER ELEVEN
CONTROLLING ONLINE BUSINESS METHODS: PATENT

The application of patent protection to methods for transacting business, electronic and otherwise, is a relatively recent phenomenon, but one that has rapidly become widespread. Be Free, Inc. holds a patent on the ability to target Internet advertising based on user preferences. Priceline.com owns a patent on reverse auctions, a method of selling goods and services through an Internet bidding system whereby a customer commits to buying an item at a specified price if a seller can be found to supply it at that price. DoubleClick, Inc. owns a patent on Web-based banner advertising. And Amazon.com holds a patent on its "One-Click" ordering system, which allows online customers to save time by entering their credit and personal information only once.

Less than a decade ago, many legal experts would have considered patents such as these invalid, because business methods were believed to be specifically excluded from patent protection. In 1998, however, in *State Street Bank and Trust Co. v. Signature Financial Group, Inc.*, 149 F.3d 1368 (Fed.Cir.1998), the Court of Appeals for the Federal Circuit[1] declared that business methods are not categorically outside the subject matter of patent. In other words, an inventive business method, like any other invention, could receive patent protection if the United States Patent and Trademark Office ("PTO") found it to be new, non-obvious, and useful.

State Street Bank prompted a rapid increase in applications for patents on business methods, particularly those involving electronic commerce operations. Some commentators have argued that the Patent Office was unprepared for the flood, and that, as a result, it has failed properly to evaluate patent applications and has issued patents for "inventions" that are obvious and/or non-novel. Others compare the current "flood" with the early years of biotechnology patents, when the patent standards were not yet clear and a solid prior-art database had not yet been established. The PTO and patent applicants may simply be experiencing a similar period of transition. In the meantime, entrepreneurs all over the country are being urged to reexamine their business practices to determine (1) whether those practices might be patentable; and (2) whether those practices have been patented by others.

I. PATENT BASICS

What does it mean to gain patent protection for a business method? A patent is a limited right, granted by the federal government, to prevent others from making, using, selling or offering to sell an invention. In other words, it is a right to exclude competitors for the term of the patent. In the United States, the granting of patents is authorized by Article 1, Section 8, Clause 8 of the Constitution, which gives Congress the power "[t]o promote the Progress

---

[1] The Federal Circuit, a division of the U.S. Court of Appeals, was created in 1982 through a merger of the U.S. Court of Customs and Patent Appeals and the U.S. Court of Claims. The Federal Circuit's jurisdiction is limited to cases involving patents, claims against the United States, and certain other specialized areas of law. Its jurisdiction over such cases is exclusive of the other Circuits.

of Science and useful Arts, by securing for limited Times to . . . Inventors the exclusive Right to their . . . Discoveries." In the absence of some incentive to do otherwise, inventors will choose to keep their inventions secret so as to forestall direct competition. The primary goals of the patent system are to encourage inventors to reveal their secrets to the public, and to encourage investment in the development of new inventions, by granting the inventor a temporary monopoly over the use of her inventions.

Title 35 of the U.S. Code contains the statutory basis for the patent system. Sections 101, 102, 103 and 112 are particularly important. Section 101 defines patentable subject matter as any "new and useful process, machine, manufacture or composition of matter, or any new and useful improvement thereof." 35 U.S.C. § 101. (We will be particularly interested here in the first "new and useful" subject matter identified by Section 101—the process—which is defined as a "process, art or method [including] a new use of a known process, machine, manufacture, composition of matter, or material." *Id.* § 100(b).) In contrast to copyright law, in which the first creator is the owner of the derivative work right, so that subsequent creators must get the first owner's permission for follow-on works, in patent law new and non-obvious improvements to existing technology are patentable by the improver. This means that the owner of the original technology must get the permission of the follow-on innovator in order to practice the state of the art, and vice versa—a situation known as "blocking patents."

Section 102 explains the meaning of "new": that which was not anticipated by printed literature or a patent anywhere in the world more than one year prior to the application and any time prior to the actual "invention" date shown by the applicant; not anticipated by public use in this country more than one year prior to the application date or any time before the invention date; and not commercialized in this country more than one year prior to the application date. *Id.* § 102(a) & (b). Section 102 requires that the patent applicant be the actual inventor or inventors; a patent applied for in the name of the wrong person or from which one or more co-inventors were excluded can be invalidated. Section 103 adds a non-obviousness requirement: an invention that would have been obvious at the time of invention to a person of ordinary skill in the art to which the patent pertains is not patentable. *Id.* § 103(a).[2]

Thus, in order to receive patent protection, any business method, including Internet commerce techniques and software processes, must satisfy the basic threshold requirements for patents generally:

1. *Patentable subject matter.* The types of inventions that may be entitled to patent protection include any process, machine, manufacture, or composition of matter, as well as any improvements on such inventions. *Id.* § 101. Laws of nature, physical phenomena, and abstract ideas (including mathematical algorithms) are not patentable, although a useful process that is otherwise within patentable subject matter does not lose that status merely because it implements one of the foregoing.

2. *Utility.* The process described must be "useful"—it must have a functional purpose and must produce a concrete and tangible result. *Id.* § 101.

3. *Novelty.* The method must be "new": it must be different from what is already known, and must add something new to the prior art. *Id.* §§ 101 & 102.

---

[2] Outside the United States, this requirement usually goes by the name of "inventive step."

4. *Non-obviousness.* The described process must not be obvious (in light of the state of the prior art) to one of ordinary skill in the art at the time of invention. *Id.* § 103.

5. *Legally sufficient disclosure.* As quid pro quo for the privilege of monopoly, the patent must describe the invention in sufficient detail so that one who is skilled in the subject matter can construct it, must describe the best mode of making and using it, and must claim the invention in a clear and distinct manner which can give notice of what is to claimed to competitors and the public. *Id.* § 112.

A patent document consist of several parts: (1) an "abstract," which briefly summarizes the invention; (2) a list of references to the "prior art"—that is, citations to publications, other patents, and other inventions, which may be relevant to establishing whether the invention meets the requirements of novelty and non-obviousness; (3) the "specification," which describes the related art and the advantages of the invention with respect to that art, provides drawings of the invention, explains how to make and use the invention, and outlines the "best mode" of using it; and (4) a set of "claims," which is technically part of the specification, but is normally set out in a separate section of the patent document. The PTO makes a complete set of patent documents available via its website, www.uspto.gov.

The claims delineate exactly what is to be covered by the exclusion right and are the operative part of the patent. Claims usually consist of a preamble, a transitional phrase, and a body that lists the elements of the invention and how they interact. If the application is successful, those claims set the bounds of the property right. Inventions must be "definitely" claimed, that is, the nature and function of the invention must be clear and clearly delimited. *Id.* § 112.

Claims are especially important in questions concerning infringement and validity, when a patent will be evaluated claim by claim. That is, patents may have more than one claim, and some of them have a great many. (Often the broadest claim will be the first one, and narrower claims will be further down the list.) To be liable for patent infringement, it is enough to infringe any one of the patent's claims.

Business method patents allow the owner to prevent others from making, using, selling, or offering to sell a specific operation or set of operations for transacting business. The United States is one of the few countries in which the patentability of business methods is clearly established. In other countries, some business methods have been found patentable, while others have not. Until recently the United States excluded business methods from patentable subject matter—but the exclusion was embedded in common law rather than the Patent Act, and, as we shall see in the *State Street Bank* case, *infra*, it was not robust. Put simply, judges distinguished, at least conceptually, a system for transacting business from a specific apparatus or process for implementing that system. The former was considered to be unpatentable because more akin to an abstract mathematical principle than to a machine or mechanical process. It is possible, too, that judges believed business methods were almost all already known (not novel); if so, the digital era changed that assumption.

EXTENSIONS

Proposed Patent Reform Act. At this writing the Patent Reform Act of 2005, H.R. 2795, 109th Cong. (2005) is pending. If enacted, this would be the most comprehensive patent reform since 1952. Foremost among the reforms would be to shift the United States from the first-to-invent basis for priority to a species of first-to-file system. The United States is alone among developed countries in adhering to a first-to-invent system, so this reform would bring the United States more into harmony with the rest of the world.

II. Background: The (Former) Business Method Exception

Prior to the Federal Circuit's holding in *State Street Bank* (discussed *infra*), most patent attorneys would have advised their clients not to apply for a patent on a pure business practice. The so-called "business method exception" precluded patentability of business practices for most of the twentieth century.

The business method exception made an early appearance in *Hotel Security Checking Co. v. Lorraine Co.*, 160 F. 467 (2d Cir.1908), in which the Second Circuit invalidated a patent that described an accounting system designed to prevent fraud by waiters and cashiers in restaurants and hotels. The system tracked the orders handled by different workers, allowing owners to determine whether money was missing and trace its source: "If there has been no carelessness or dishonesty, the amounts will agree and if there has been, it is easy to discover where the fault lies." *Id.* at 468.

The court held that "there is no patentable novelty either in the physical means employed or in the method described and claimed":

> Section 4886 of the Revised Statutes [the predecessor of 35 U.S.C. § 101] provides, under certain conditions, that "any person who has invented or discovered any new and useful art, machine, manufacture or composition of matter" may obtain a patent therefor. It is manifest that the subject-matter of the claims is not a machine, manufacture or composition of matter. If within the language of the statute at all, it must be as a "new and useful art." One of the definitions given by Webster of the word "art" is as follows: "The employment of means to accomplish some desired end; the adaptation of things in the natural world to the uses of life; the application of knowledge or power to practical purposes." In the sense of the patent law, an art is not a mere abstraction. A system of transacting business disconnected from the means for carrying out the system is not, within the most liberal interpretation of the term, an art. Advice is not patentable. As this court said in *Fowler v. City of New York*, 121 Fed. 747, 58 C.C.A. 113: "No mere abstraction, no idea, however brilliant, can be the subject of a patent irrespective of the means designed to give it effect."

> It cannot be maintained that the physical means described by Hicks,—the sheet and the slips,—apart from the manner of their use, present any new and useful feature. A blank sheet of paper ruled vertically and numbered at the top cannot be the subject of a patent, and, if used in carrying out a method, it can impart no more novelty thereto, than the pen and ink which are also used. In other words, if the "art" described in the specification be old, the claims cannot be upheld because of novelty in the appliances used in carrying it out,—for the reason that there is no novelty.

Id. at 469.

The *Hotel Security* court characterized business methods as abstractions rather than contributions to the progress of the useful arts. Subsequent cases built the court's observation into apparently solid doctrine. In *Berardini v. Tocci*, 200 F. 1021 (2d Cir.1912), a method of transmitting money via a set of coded telegraph messages was found unpatentable on the ground that the method was simply an advisory system for devising code messages, akin to advice on how to improve the practice of painting or baseball. *Conover v. Coe*, 99 F.2d 377 (D.C.Cir.1938), stated the theory plainly, declaring it to be "a rule of universal application that an object is not patentable where its novelty consists wholly . . . in a method or system of doing business." *Id.* at 379.

The exclusion was said to apply even where the business in question was arguably "new," though this was dictum in cases where the court also held the business method to be non-novel. In *Loew's Drive-In Theatres v. Park-In Theatres*, 174 F.2d 547 (1st Cir.1949), the Court of Appeals invalidated a patent for a system of parking cars in the lot of a drive-in movie theater so as to improve patrons' view of the screen. Noting that the arrangement of cars simply adapted an ancient system for arranging seats in a theater, and was therefore neither new nor non-obvious, the Court added that "a system for the transaction of business . . . however novel, useful, or commercially successful is not patentable apart from the means for making the system practically useful." *Id.* at 552.

The business method exception was buttressed by the development of the "mental steps" doctrine. The essence of this doctrine, which still has not been entirely rejected, is that patents embrace only physical effects, rather than the mental steps leading to the effects. *See, e.g., Gottschalk v. Benson*, 409 U.S. 63 (1972); *In re Abrams*, 188 F.2d 165 (C.C.P.A.1951); *In re Shao Wen Yuan*, 188 F.2d 377 (C.C.P.A.1951); *but see In re Musgrave*, 431 F.2d 882 (C.C.P.A.1970). Mental steps were viewed as too abstract to be acceptable subject matter for a patent. Processes that were primarily mental and/or that involved substantial human decisionmaking in their operation were seen as too difficult to describe with the reasonable definiteness required by patent law. Furthermore, human judgment, however well-trained, was seen as a general skill rather than a specific way of achieving a predictable and useful result, and therefore unpatentable. Finally, mental activity—including mental judgments involved in many business practices—was seen as more akin to writing than to machine-building, and therefore appropriately regulated by copyright law.

III. SOFTWARE PATENTS: THE CHANGING LEGAL LANDSCAPE

The business method exception was thus apparently firmly rooted in case law. To understand how this changed, it is helpful to look first to developments in the legal treatment of software. Many business method patent applications involve computer-implemented practices, and, as we will see, it was not coincidental that the demise of the business method exception occurred as a result of litigation over a computer-related invention.

Computer technologies presented serious difficulties for courts evaluating patents, principally because in the 1960s and 70s judges viewed software "inventions" as essentially comprising mathematical formulas—abstract ideas, which are unpatentable, rather than the application of ideas toward a useful end. Thus, for example, the Supreme Court firmly rejected as inherently unpatentable a method for converting binary coded decimal ("BCD") numbers into pure binary numerals that was not limited to any particular art, technology, apparatus, or even a particular end use.

> It is conceded that one may not patent an idea. But in practical effect that would be the result if the formula for converting BCD numerals to pure binary numerals were patented in this case. The mathematical formula involved here

has no substantial practical application except in connection with a digital computer, which means that if the judgment below is affirmed, the patent would wholly pre-empt the mathematical formula and in practical effect would be a patent on the algorithm itself.

Gottschalk v. Benson, 409 U.S. 63, 71–72 (1972).

The Supreme Court softened its position considerably several years later, and laid out a kind of "physical transformation" test for software patentability. The crucial case was *Diamond v. Diehr*, 450 U.S. 175 (1981), in which the Court declared patentable an industrial process that automated a rubber molding procedure by using a computer to calculate repetitively the mathematical equation governing how long to leave the mold closed, and to open the mold automatically when the curing was complete. The Court distinguished this process from an abstract mathematical formula or algorithm by noting that the algorithm in question was used to accomplish *physical transformation* of matter (in this case, uncured rubber).

> [W]hen a claim containing a mathematical formula implements or applies that formula in a structure or process which, when considered as a whole, is performing a function which the patent laws were designed to protect (e.g., transforming or reducing an article to a different state or thing), then the claim satisfies the requirements of § 101.

Id. at 192. In a series of subsequent decisions, the Court of Customs and Patent Appeals developed a counterpart to the physical transformation inquiry established in *Diehr*. *In re Freeman*, 573 F.2d 1237 (C.C.P.A.1978); *In re Walter*, 618 F.2d 758 (C.C.P.A.1980); *In re Abele*, 684 F.2d 902 (C.C.P.A.1982). The test has been summarized as follows: "First, the claim is analyzed to determine whether a mathematical algorithm is directly or indirectly recited. Next, if a mathematical algorithm is found, the claim as a whole is further analyzed to determine whether the algorithm is 'applied in any manner to physical elements or process steps,' and, if it is, it 'passes muster under § 101.' " *In re Pardo*, 684 F.2d 912, 915 (C.C.P.A.1982).

Some members of the Court of Appeals for the Federal Circuit were suspicious of the test, however, and those suspicions were not alleviated by the increasingly attenuated nature of the physicality requirement. In one case, a claim based primarily on an algorithm that reorganized data to produce a picture of the condition of a patient's heart on a hospital monitor was accepted as patentable on the theory that converting electrocardiograph signals into digital signals involved a physical transformation and that the conversion process began with the independent physical activity of a patient's heart function. *Arrhythmia Research Technology Inc. v. Corazonix Corp.*, 958 F.2d 1053 (Fed.Cir.1992). Two years later, a programmed computer was found to be a machine that produced a "useful concrete and tangible result," even though the program in question clearly embodied a mathematical algorithm. *In re Alappat*, 33 F.3d 1526 (Fed.Cir.1994). After *Alappat*, it appeared that a patent applicant need only show practical application of an algorithm to pass as statutory subject matter. In other words, few inventions would be deemed too abstract, by definition, to be excluded from patentability.

Yet the limits of patentability remained unclear. In 1994, a system for calculating auction bids that used simple linear math to group and regroup bids was deemed unpatentable on the theory that bids were not "physical" and, therefore, their reorganization could not involve a physical effect or transformation. *In re Schrader*, 22 F.3d 290 (Fed.Cir.1994).

Schrader brought into sharper relief the potential impact of the computing technology

cases—and the erosion of the mathematical algorithm exception—on the continuing viability of the business method exception. Though the opinion turned on the physical transformation test, *Schrader*'s majority made reference to the business method exception as well,
prompting a prescient dissent from Judge Newman:

> [The business method exception is] an unwarranted encumbrance to the defini-
> tion of statutory subject matter in § 101 . . . that [should] be discarded as er-
> ror-prone, redundant, and obsolete. It merits retirement from the glossary of
> § 101. . . . All of the "doing business" cases could have been decided using the
> clearer concepts of Title 35. Patentability does not turn on whether the claimed
> method does "business" instead of something else, but on whether the method,
> viewed as a whole, meets the requirements of patentability as set forth in §§ 102,
> 103, and 112 of the Patent Act.

In re Schrader, 22 F.3d at 298 (Newman, J., dissenting).

IV. THE DEMISE OF THE BUSINESS METHOD EXCEPTION

Many observers have argued, as Judge Newman suggested in her *In re Schrader* dissent, that the business methods exception, though appropriately removing commonplace or
obvious business practices from the realm of patentability, unfairly penalizes inventors who
devise new methods of conducting business that would otherwise meet the requirements of
patentability.

Though the business methods exception generally acted as a bar to patentability, some
courts declined to invalidate patents that met the novelty and non-obviousness requirements, just because the invention was a "method" related to business procedures. In *Paine,
Webber, Jackson & Curtis v. Merrill Lynch, Pierce, Fenner & Smith*, 564 F.Supp. 1358
(D.Del.1983), the court rejected Paine Webber's argument that Merrill Lynch's patent on a
computer-implemented, data-processing system was "nothing more than familiar business
systems, that is, the financial management of individual brokerage accounts." Instead, the
court found that the patent met the threshold requirements for statutory subject matter under
Section 101.

The court's reasoning carved out a niche allowing some computerized business methods
to be patented, by re-articulating the mechanics of the business methods test:

> the "technological" or "useful" arts inquiry *must* focus on whether the claimed
> subject matter (a method of operating a machine to translate) is statutory [i.e.,
> within patentable subject matter], not on whether the product of the claimed sub-
> ject matter (a translated text) is statutory, not on whether the prior art which the
> claimed subject matter purports to replace (translation by human mind) is statu-
> tory, and *not* on whether the claimed subject matter is presently perceived to be
> an improvement over the prior art, e.g., whether it "enhances" the operation of a
> machine.

Paine, Webber v. Merrill Lynch, 564 F.Supp. at 1369 (quoting *In re Toma*, 575 F.2d 872,
877–78 (C.C.P.A.1978)). Applying this reasoning, the court held that though Merrill
Lynch's financial integration method "would be unpatentable if done by hand, . . . the focus
of analysis should be on the operation of the program on the computer." 564 F.Supp. at
1369. Because the method was implemented through a machine—the computer—the court
held that the patent was within statutory subject matter.

Paine, Webber v. Merrill Lynch demonstrates that long before the official demise of the business methods exception in *State Street Bank*, courts were avoiding the business methods bar by treating computer-implemented business methods like any other computer-implemented invention. *State Street Bank* eliminated the need for this indirect approach to business method patents.

State Street Bank & Trust Co. v. Signature Financial Group, Inc.
149 F.3d 1368 (Fed.Cir.1998).

■ Rich, Circuit Judge.

Signature Financial Group, Inc. (Signature) appeals from the decision of the United States District Court for the District of Massachusetts granting a motion for summary judgment in favor of State Street Bank & Trust Co. (State Street), finding U.S. Patent No. 5,193,056 (the '056 patent) invalid on the ground that the claimed subject matter is not encompassed by 35 U.S.C. § 101 (1994). See *State Street Bank & Trust Co. v. Signature Financial Group, Inc.*, 927 F.Supp. 502 (D.Mass.1996). We reverse and remand because we conclude that the patent claims are directed to statutory subject matter.

BACKGROUND

Signature is the assignee of the '056 patent which is entitled "Data Processing System for Hub and Spoke Financial Services Configuration." The '056 patent issued to Signature on 9 March 1993, naming R. Todd Boes as the inventor. The '056 patent is generally directed to a data processing system (the system) for implementing an investment structure which was developed for use in Signature's business as an administrator and accounting agent for mutual funds. In essence, the system, identified by the proprietary name Hub and Spoke®, facilitates a structure whereby mutual funds (Spokes) pool their assets in an investment portfolio (Hub) organized as a partnership. This investment configuration provides the administrator of a mutual fund with the advantageous combination of economies of scale in administering investments coupled with the tax advantages of a partnership.

State Street and Signature are both in the business of acting as custodians and accounting agents for multi-tiered partnership fund financial services. State Street negotiated with Signature for a license to use its patented data processing system described and claimed in the '056 patent. When negotiations broke down, State Street brought a declaratory judgment action asserting invalidity, unenforceability, and noninfringement in Massachusetts district court, and then filed a motion for partial summary judgment of patent invalidity for failure to claim statutory subject matter under § 101. The motion was granted and this appeal followed.

DISCUSSION

. . .

The following facts pertinent to the statutory subject matter issue are either undisputed or represent the version alleged by the nonmovant. See *Anderson v. Liberty Lobby, Inc.*, 477 U.S. 242, 255 (1986). The patented invention relates generally to a system that allows an administrator to monitor and record the financial information flow and make all calculations necessary for maintaining a partner fund financial services configuration. As previously mentioned, a partner fund financial services configuration essentially allows several mutual funds, or "Spokes," to pool their investment funds into a single portfolio, or "Hub," allowing for consolidation of, inter alia, the costs of administering the fund combined with the tax advantages of a partnership. In particular, this system provides means for a daily allocation of assets for two or more Spokes that are invested in the same Hub. The system determines the percentage share that each Spoke maintains in the Hub, while taking into consideration daily changes both in the value of the Hub's investment securities and in the concomitant amount of each Spoke's assets.

In determining daily changes, the system also allows for the allocation among the Spokes of the Hub's daily income, expenses, and net realized and unrealized gain or loss, calculating each day's total investments based on the concept of a book capital account. This enables the determination of a true asset value of each Spoke and accurate calculation of allocation ratios between or among the Spokes. The system additionally tracks all the relevant data determined on a daily basis for the Hub and each Spoke, so that aggregate year end income, expenses, and capital gain or loss can be determined for accounting and for tax purposes for the Hub and, as a result, for each publicly traded Spoke.

It is essential that these calculations are quickly and accurately performed. In large part this is required because each Spoke sells shares to the public and the price of those shares is substantially based on the Spoke's percentage interest in the portfolio. In some instances, a mutual fund administrator is required to calculate the value of the shares to the nearest penny within as little as an hour and a half after the market closes. Given the complexity of the calculations, a computer or equivalent device is a virtual necessity to perform the task.

. . .

. . . [C]laim 1, properly construed, claims a machine, namely, a data processing system for managing a financial services configuration of a portfolio established as a partnership . . . . A "machine" is proper statutory subject matter under § 101. We note that, for the purposes of a § 101 analysis, it is of little relevance whether claim 1 is directed to a "machine" or a "process," as long as it falls within at least one of the four enumerated categories of patentable subject matter, "machine" and "process" being such categories.

This does not end our analysis, however, because the court concluded that the claimed subject matter fell into one of two alternative judicially-created exceptions to statutory subject matter. The court refers to the first exception as the "mathematical algorithm" exception and the second exception as the "business method" exception. Section 101 reads:

> Whoever invents or discovers any new and useful process, machine, manufacture, or composition of matter, or any new and useful improvement thereof, may obtain a patent therefor, subject to the conditions and requirements of this title.

The plain and unambiguous meaning of § 101 is that any invention falling within one of the four stated categories of statutory subject matter may be patented, provided it meets the other requirements for patentability set forth in Title 35, i.e., those found in §§ 102, 103, and 112, ¶ 2.

The repetitive use of the expansive term "any" in § 101 shows Congress's intent not to place any restrictions on the subject matter for which a patent may be obtained beyond those specifically recited in § 101. Indeed, the Supreme Court has acknowledged that Congress intended § 101 to extend to "anything under the sun that is made by man." *Diamond v. Chakrabarty*, 447 U.S. 303, 309 (1980); *see also Diamond v. Diehr*, 450 U.S. 175, 182 (1981). Thus, it is improper to read limitations into § 101 on the subject matter that may be patented where the legislative history indicates that Congress clearly did not intend such limitations. See *Chakrabarty*, 447 U.S. at 308 ("We have also cautioned that courts 'should not read into the patent laws limitations and conditions which the legislature has not expressed.' " (citations omitted)).

The "Mathematical Algorithm" Exception

The Supreme Court has identified three categories of subject matter that are unpatentable, namely "laws of nature, natural phenomena, and abstract ideas." *Diehr*, 450 U.S. at 185. Of particular relevance to this case, the Court has held that mathematical algorithms are not patentable subject matter to the extent that they are merely abstract ideas. See *Diehr*, 450 U.S. 175, passim; *Parker v. Flook*, 437 U.S. 584 (1978); *Gottschalk v. Benson*, 409 U.S. 63 (1972). In *Diehr*, the Court explained that certain types of mathematical subject matter, standing alone, represent nothing more than abstract ideas until reduced to some type of practical application, i.e., "a useful, concrete and tangible result." *Alappat*, 33 F.3d at 1544.[4]

Unpatentable mathematical algorithms are identifiable by showing they are merely abstract ideas constituting disembodied concepts or truths that are not "useful." From a practical standpoint, this means that to be patentable an algorithm must be applied in a "useful" way. In *Alappat*, we held that data, transformed by a machine through a series of mathematical calculations to produce a smooth waveform display on a rasterizer monitor, constituted a practical application of an abstract idea (a mathematical algorithm, formula, or calculation), because it produced "a useful, concrete and tangible result" — the smooth waveform.

Similarly, in *Arrhythmia Research Technology Inc. v. Corazonix Corp.*, 958 F.2d 1053 (Fed.Cir.1992), we held that the transformation of electrocardiograph signals from a patient's heartbeat by a machine through a series of mathematical calculations constituted a practical application of an abstract idea (a mathematical algorithm, formula, or calculation), because it corresponded to a useful, concrete or tangible thing — the condition of a patient's heart.

---

[4] This has come to be known as the mathematical algorithm exception. This designation has led to some confusion, especially given the *Freeman–Walter–Abele* analysis. By keeping in mind that the mathematical algorithm is unpatentable only to the extent that it represents an abstract idea, this confusion may be ameliorated.

Today, we hold that the transformation of data, representing discrete dollar amounts, by a machine through a series of mathematical calculations into a final share price, constitutes a practical application of a mathematical algorithm, formula, or calculation, because it produces "a useful, concrete and tangible result" — a final share price momentarily fixed for recording and reporting purposes and even accepted and relied upon by regulatory authorities and in subsequent trades.

The district court erred by applying the *Freeman–Walter–Abele* test to determine whether the claimed subject matter was an unpatentable abstract idea. The *Freeman–Walter–Abele* test was designed by the Court of Customs and Patent Appeals, and subsequently adopted by this court, to extract and identify unpatentable mathematical algorithms in the aftermath of *Benson* and *Flook*. See *In re Freeman*, 573 F.2d 1237 (CCPA 1978) as modified by *In re Walter*, 618 F.2d 758 (CCPA 1980). The test has been thus articulated:

> First, the claim is analyzed to determine whether a mathematical algorithm is directly or indirectly recited. Next, if a mathematical algorithm is found, the claim as a whole is further analyzed to determine whether the algorithm is "applied in any manner to physical elements or process steps," and, if it is, it "passes muster under § 101."

In re Pardo, 684 F.2d 912, 915 (CCPA 1982) (citing *In re Abele*, 684 F.2d 902 (CCPA 1982)).

After *Diehr* and *Chakrabarty*, the *Freeman–Walter–Abele* test has little, if any, applicability to determining the presence of statutory subject matter. As we pointed out in *Alappat*, 33 F.3d at 1543, application of the test could be misleading, because a process, machine, manufacture, or composition of matter employing a law of nature, natural phenomenon, or abstract idea is patentable subject matter even though a law of nature, natural phenomenon, or abstract idea would not, by itself, be entitled to such protection. The test determines the presence of, for example, an algorithm. Under *Benson*, this may have been a sufficient indicium of nonstatutory subject matter. However, after *Diehr* and *Alappat*, the mere fact that a claimed invention involves inputting numbers, calculating numbers, outputting numbers, and storing numbers, in and of itself, would not render it nonstatutory subject matter, unless, of course, its operation does not produce a "useful, concrete and tangible result." *Alappat*, 33 F.3d at 1544. After all, as we have repeatedly stated,

> every step-by-step process, be it electronic or chemical or mechanical, involves an algorithm in the broad sense of the term. Since § 101 expressly includes processes as a category of inventions which may be patented and § 100(b) further defines the word "process" as meaning "process, art or method, and includes a new use of a known process, machine, manufacture, composition of matter, or material," it follows that it is no ground for holding a claim is directed to nonstatutory subject matter to say it includes or is directed to an algorithm. This is why the proscription against patenting has been limited to mathematical algorithms. . . .

In re Iwahashi, 888 F.2d 1370, 1374 (Fed.Cir.1989) (emphasis in the original).

The question of whether a claim encompasses statutory subject matter should not focus on *which* of the four categories of subject matter a claim is directed to —

process, machine, manufacture, or composition of matter — but rather on the essential characteristics of the subject matter, in particular, its practical utility. Section 101 specifies that statutory subject matter must also satisfy the other "conditions and requirements" of Title 35, including novelty, nonobviousness, and adequacy of disclosure and notice. See *In re Warmerdam*, 33 F.3d 1354, 1359, (Fed.Cir.1994). For purpose of our analysis, as noted above, claim 1 is directed to a machine programmed with the Hub and Spoke software and admittedly produces a "useful, concrete, and tangible result." *Alappat*, 33 F.3d at 1544. This renders it statutory subject matter, even if the useful result is expressed in numbers, such as price, profit, percentage, cost, or loss.

The Business Method Exception

As an alternative ground for invalidating the '056 patent under § 101, the court relied on the judicially-created, so-called "business method" exception to statutory subject matter. We take this opportunity to lay this ill-conceived exception to rest. Since its inception, the "business method" exception has merely represented the application of some general, but no longer applicable legal principle, perhaps arising out of the "requirement for invention" — which was eliminated by § 103. Since the 1952 Patent Act, business methods have been, and should have been, subject to the same legal requirements for patentability as applied to any other process or method.

The business method exception has never been invoked by this court, or the CCPA, to deem an invention unpatentable. Application of this particular exception has always been preceded by a ruling based on some clearer concept of Title 35 or, more commonly, application of the abstract idea exception based on finding a mathematical algorithm. Illustrative is the CCPA's analysis in *In re Howard*, 394 F.2d 869 (CCPA 1968), wherein the court affirmed the Board of Appeals' rejection of the claims for lack of novelty and found it unnecessary to reach the Board's § 101 ground that a method of doing business is "inherently unpatentable." 394 F.2d at 872.

Similarly, *In re Schrader*, 22 F.3d 290 (Fed.Cir.1994), while making reference to the business method exception, turned on the fact that the claims implicitly recited an abstract idea in the form of a mathematical algorithm and there was no "transformation or conversion of subject matter representative of or constituting physical activity or objects." 22 F.3d at 294 (emphasis omitted).[13]

. . .

Even the case frequently cited as establishing the business method exception to statutory subject matter, *Hotel Security Checking Co. v. Lorraine Co.*, 160 F. 467 (2d Cir.1908), did not rely on the exception to strike the patent. In that case, the patent was found invalid for lack of novelty and "invention," not because it was improper

---

[13] Any historical distinctions between a method of "doing" business and the means of carrying it out blur in the complexity of modern business systems. See *Paine, Webber, Jackson & Curtis v. Merrill Lynch*, 564 F.Supp. 1358 (D.Del.1983) (holding a computerized system of cash management was held to be statutory subject matter).

subject matter for a patent. The court stated "the fundamental principle of the system is as old as the art of bookkeeping, i.e., charging the goods of the employer to the agent who takes them." *Id.* at 469. "If at the time of [the patent] application, there had been no system of bookkeeping of any kind in restaurants, we would be confronted with the question whether a new and useful system of cash registering and account checking is such an art as is patentable under the statute." *Id.* at 472.

This case is no exception. The district court announced the precepts of the business method exception as set forth in several treatises, but noted as its primary reason for finding the patent invalid under the business method exception as follows:

> If Signature's invention were patentable, any financial institution desirous of implementing a multi-tiered funding complex modelled (sic) on a Hub and Spoke configuration would be required to seek Signature's permission before embarking on such a project. *This is so because the '056 Patent is claimed [sic] sufficiently broadly to foreclose virtually any computer-implemented accounting method necessary to manage this type of financial structure.*

927 F.Supp. 502, 516 (emphasis added). Whether the patent's claims are too broad to be patentable is not to be judged under § 101, but rather under §§ 102, 103 and 112. Assuming the above statement to be correct, it has nothing to do with whether what is claimed is statutory subject matter.

In view of this background, it comes as no surprise that in the most recent edition of the Manual of Patent Examining Procedures (MPEP) (1996), a paragraph of § 706.03(a) was deleted. In past editions it read:

> Though seemingly within the category of process or method, a method of doing business can be rejected as not being within the statutory classes. See *Hotel Security Checking Co. v. Lorraine Co.*, 160 F. 467 (2d Cir. 1908) and *In re Wait*, 73 F.2d 982, 22 C.C.P.A. 822 (1934).

MPEP § 706.03(a) (1994). This acknowledgment is buttressed by the U.S. Patent and Trademark 1996 Examination Guidelines for Computer Related Inventions which now read:

> Office personnel have had difficulty in properly treating claims directed to methods of doing business. Claims should not be categorized as methods of doing business. Instead such claims should be treated like any other process claims.

Examination Guidelines, 61 Fed. Reg. 7478, 7479 (1996). We agree that this is precisely the manner in which this type of claim should be treated. Whether the claims are directed to subject matter within § 101 should not turn on whether the claimed subject matter does "business" instead of something else.

CONCLUSION

The appealed decision is reversed and the case is remanded to the district court for further proceedings consistent with this opinion.

QUESTIONS FOR DISCUSSION

1. *Limited to computer-related inventions?* State Street's patent application claimed a computer-related invention, and some commentators have characterized the Federal Circuit opinion as accepting only computer-related business methods as statutory (i.e., patentable) subject matter. Do you agree that the decision should be so interpreted? Or does the decision mean that any business method is potentially patentable?

2. *The mathematical algorithm exception.* The "tangibility" or "physicality" dimensions of the transformation inquiry were largely abandoned in *State Street Bank.* The question whether a claim comprises statutory subject matter, the Federal Circuit insisted, should focus simply on the "practical utility" of the claim, or whether it produced a concrete, tangible and useful result. Numbers were concrete enough to "count" as such a result. What meaning is left for the word "tangible"?

The view that a numerical output can be concrete, tangible and useful was affirmed shortly after *State Street Bank*, in *AT & T v. Excel Communications, Inc.*, 172 F.3d 1352 (Fed.Cir.1999), which concerned a patent on a process for transmitting billing information relating to long-distance telephone calls. The district court had found AT & T's patent to be invalid because, as a mathematical algorithm, it failed to satisfy the statutory subject matter requirements: "The court was of the view that the only physical step in the claims involves data-gathering for the algorithm. Though the court recognized that the claims require the use of switches and computers, it nevertheless concluded that use of such facilities to perform a non-substantive change in the data's format could not serve to convert non-patentable subject matter into patentable subject matter." *Id.* at 1355.

The Federal Circuit reversed, explaining that the statutory subject matter requirements were intended to exclude only "laws of nature, natural phenomena, and abstract ideas," and sharply narrowed the mathematical algorithm exception to "mathematical algorithms in the abstract." *Id.* at 1356. Further, the court interpreted *Diamond v. Diehr* as holding that "even though a mathematical algorithm is not patentable in isolation, a process that applies an equation to a new and useful end 'is at the very least not barred at the threshold by 101.' " *Id.* at 1357 (quoting *Diamond v. Diehr*, 450 U.S. at 188).

In sum, the court explicitly limited the previous "mathematical algorithm exception" to a simple inquiry of patentability: whether "the claimed subject matter as a whole is a disembodied mathematical concept representing nothing more than a 'law of nature' or an 'abstract idea,' or if the mathematical concept has been reduced to some practical application rendering it 'useful.' " *Id.* at 1357.

Applying this criterion, the Federal Circuit found that AT & T's invention fell within the purview of Section 101 statutory requirements, and reversed the holding of the district court:

> Excel argues that method claims containing mathematical algorithms are patentable subject matter only if there is a "physical transformation" or conversion of subject matter from one state into another. The physical transformation language appears in *Diehr, see* 450 U.S. at 184 ("That respondents' claims involve the transformation of an article, in this case raw, uncured synthetic rubber, into a different state or thing cannot be disputed."), and has been echoed by this court in *Schrader*, 22 F.3d at 294, ("Therefore, we do not find in the claim any kind of data transformation.").

The notion of "physical transformation" can be misunderstood. In the first place, it is not an invariable requirement, but merely one example of how a mathematical algorithm may bring about a useful application. As the Supreme Court itself noted, "when [a claimed invention] is performing a function which the patent laws were designed to protect (e.g., transforming or reducing an article to a different state or thing), then the claim satisfies the requirements of § 101."

172 F.3d at 1358–59. Indeed, as a Federal Circuit judge remarked a few months later: "We have come a long way from the days when judges frowned on patents as pernicious monopolies deserving scant regard. Today, patents are the backbone of much of the national economy, and, as this court has recently held, virtually anything is patentable." *Hughes Aircraft v. United States*, 148 F.3d 1384, 1385 (Fed.Cir.1998) (Clevenger, J., dissenting).

A. THE PRIOR-USER DEFENSE

In the wake of the *State Street Bank* decision, entrepreneurs in many fields expressed concern that they might have to pay license fees for the right to continue engaging in long-standing business practices, simply because they had not sought patent protection for those practices and somebody else had. The fact that a user of a practice had invented it independently would not be a defense in a patent infringement suit, unless the defendant were able to show that the patent must be invalidated. Entrepreneurs were concerned that an attempt to invalidate a competitor's patent on the basis of prior invention might not succeed if the patentee could prove that he was in fact first to reduce the method to practice; and where the prior user had been keeping the method secret, an attempt to invalidate the patent based upon prior public use might fail. Responding to these concerns, Congress enacted the First Inventor Defense Act of 1999, Pub. L. No. 106–113, 113 Stat. 1501A–555 (1999), which added Section 273 to Title 35. Section 273 provides:

It shall be a defense to an action for infringement under section 271 of this title with respect to any subject matter that would otherwise infringe one or more claims for a method in the patent being asserted against a person, if such person had, acting in good faith, actually reduced the subject matter to practice at least 1 year before the effective filing date of such patent, and commercially used the subject matter before the effective filing date of such patent.

35 U.S.C. § 273(b)(1).

Although this provision grants prior user rights for "a method," the statute defines "method" as "a method of doing or conducting business." *Id.* § 273(a)(3).

A House Report on the bill noted that it would be "administratively and economically impossible to expect any inventor to apply for a patent on all business methods and processes now deemed patentable." H.R. REP. NO. 106–287, at 45 (1999). The person asserting the defense must prove its applicability by clear and convincing evidence. 35 U.S.C. § 273(b)(4). If the defense is asserted unsuccessfully, and the person asserting it is found not to have had a "reasonable basis" for asserting it, the defendant is liable for the plaintiff's attorney's fees. *Id.* § 273(b)(8).

To understand how the prior-user exception can be expected to work, and to appreciate its limitations, consider the following hypothetical and discussion:

Take the example of Bugs Bunny and Yosemite Sam. Bugs invented a method of systematically marketing carrots (and other roots) via the Rabbitnet (a network of computer networks), and filed for a patent on his "carrot pushing" method on January 15, 1998. Sam, a bitter competitor of Bugs, markets various roots (including carrots) using the same method. When precisely Sam started doing so is clouded in some mystery. The only thing Bugs knows for sure is that whenever he asks Sam to purchase a license on the carrot pushing technology, he is treated to all manner of verbal abuse.

Bugs receives his patent on January 18, 2000 and promptly sues Sam for patent infringement. Sam insists that he was pushing carrots via the Rabbitnet when Bugs was in diapers. How does Sam turn that tough talk into a viable defense?

First, Sam must prove that he was *actually commercially exploiting* the patented method before Bugs filed his application in the Patent Office. Second, Sam must prove that he reduced the patented method to practice . . . at least one year before Bugs' filing date at the Patent Office. The real kicker is that Sam has to prove these things by evidence that meets the high standard of "clear and convincing." This elevated standard is an explicit requirement in the new law. Although Congress created a loophole, they didn't want it to be an easy one to wiggle through.

Can Sam squeeze through this loophole? He has to put on testimony about events that happened over three years ago, and he needs to corroborate that testimony with objective evidence such as paper documents. That corroborating evidence is critical to meeting the clear and convincing standard, and it may not be available after such a long time, assuming that it ever existed in the first place.

The worst case for Bugs is that Sam convinces the judge that he truly was a prior user. This is not the end of the world for Bugs' carrot business. Successfully proving oneself to be a prior user does not invalidate the patent, so Bugs still has his patent. He can still enforce it against other people besides Sam. Although Sam gets a free license to infringe at will, Sam is boxed in and cannot improve on his method in any way that would take advantage of any improvements that Bugs patented. Essentially, Sam's business is frozen in the form it was when Bugs filed his patent application. Even worse for Sam is that he cannot practice his rights at any sites other than the ones he was using on the day Bugs filed his patent application. And, Sam cannot sell his prior user rights; they have no market value in theory.

Suddenly Sam doesn't sound like such a big winner. Sure he gets to stay in business, but the growth of his business is permanently hobbled. And slow growth is death for a Rabbitnet business.

Let's take a look at the downside for Sam if the judge rules against him on his prior user rights defense: Sam has already *admitted* he is an infringer! Bugs doesn't have to prove this element, because Sam shot off his mouth. Unless Sam can scrape up some evidence for another defense (insanity?) he is doomed.

In all seriousness, the practical effect of this new wrinkle in the law is that, in rare cases where an infringer has credible evidence that they can fit through the prior user loophole, it will promote early settlement of the lawsuit. This defense increases risks for both sides, and will motivate them to think twice before going to trial.

Kevin L. Pontius, *Prior User Rights In Business Methods* (2000).

QUESTIONS FOR DISCUSSION

---

1. *Limitation to business methods.* The prior-user defense is limited to business method patents. Is there a convincing reason not to extend the defense to other types of patents? Proponents of the defense have argued that it is particularly necessary in this field, where the PTO has had difficulty sorting out what is patentable and what is not. It is also arguably more difficult for prospective inventors and PTO examiners to search for relevant prior art, because a comprehensive body of prior art does not exist and prior uses may not even be documented. Business methods may be more frequently wholly "internal" to a business's operations than other processes it uses in manufacturing or marketing its products—or so it might be argued. Might a better solution be to go to the root of the problem—the Patent Office—and formulate more rigorous standards for determining patentability? While prior user rights might help resolve some of the unique problems presented by business method patents in the short-run, what effect might they have on the patent system in the long run?

2. *What exactly is a method of doing business?* What criteria should the courts use in determining whether a given method used in commerce is or is not a "method of doing business" for purposes of granting or withholding prior user rights?

3. *Patents vs. trade secrets.* Some prior users may have elected trade secrecy for their business methods because they did not realize, prior to *State Street Bank*, that such processes could be patented. When a developer of an innovative method chooses trade secrecy, it assumes the risk that someone else may obtain a patent on the method, just as it assumes the risk that the secret will leak out and be lost. The coexistence of patent (federal law) and trade secret (state law) rests partly on the fact that trade secrecy is fragile. By giving a defense to prior users of business methods who choose trade secrecy, even after *State Street Bank* made it clear that a patent may be available, has Congress undermined the balance between patent and trade secret law? *See* James R. Barney, *The Prior User Defense: A Reprieve for Trade Secret Owners or a Disaster for the Patent Law?*, 82 J. PAT. & TRADE-MARK OFF. SOC'Y 261 (2000).

B. THE IMPACT OF *STATE STREET BANK* ON THE PATENT AND TRADEMARK OFFICE AND ON THE PATENT SYSTEM AS A WHOLE

Many commentators have argued that the blitz of patent applications on computer-related inventions starting in the 1970s caught the PTO unprepared—without examiners trained in computer science, without the resources to research thoroughly whether the claimed invention was original. Hence, these commentators believe that there are a large number of patents on computer-related inventions whose validity is questionable. Once it became well known that repetitive calculations are better performed by a computer, should an invention that consists of inserting a computer into a process where repetitive calculations are needed count as non-obvious?

Since the early 1990s, the number of patent examiners has increased dramatically, and the PTO reports that the bulk of new examiners are assigned to computer technologies and biotechnologies. Yet the PTO's 2000 Corporate Plan anticipates "continuing recruitment difficulties" due to budget shortfalls and competition from private industry for qualified examiners. Q. Todd Dickinson, *Remarks at the American Bar Association's Summer IPL Conference* (June 23, 2000); USPTO Corporate Plan–FY 2001, Executive Summary at 19.

Responding to criticism of its handling of business method patents, in March 2000 the

PTO implemented a second-look policy: each business method patent is now reviewed by two examiners to help ensure compliance with patent requirements. *See* USPTO, *Business Methods Patent Initiative: An Action Plan*, www.uspto.gov/web/offices/com/sol/actionplan.html.

The PTO's regulations also enable examiners to review business method patents more effectively. For example, examiners may request from the applicant any information reasonably necessary to examine a patent application, including commercial databases that might contain aspects of the invention and information used in the invention process. 37 C.F.R. § 1.105. Similarly, interested third parties may submit prior art for the examiners' benefit. 37 C.F.R. § 1.99. For example, a competitor could mail to the PTO, along with a filing fee, as many as ten patents or publications to be placed in the patent application file. However, a third party could not accompany these submissions with explanations of their relevance to the pending patent. *Id.* The competitor also would have to provide copies of the submitted materials to the applicant, which could help deter patent infringement suits.

The Federal Trade Commission considered the impact of the *State Street Bank* decision in issuing a wide-ranging series of recommendations on the patent review and litigation processes. In a 2003 report, the FTC reviewed the debate over whether business methods should be included as patentable subject matter. The FTC ultimately did not recommend restricting the patentability of business methods but noted the competition concerns raised by broadening the types of practices that may be protected by patents:

> [I]n light of the uncertainty surrounding the benefits and the possible competitive downside from extending patent coverage to new fields, future extensions, and any future reconsideration, by courts or by Congress, of patentable subject matter extensions, require—at a minimum—a conscious policy choice, in addition to a searching and rigorous application of the other patentability criteria. In assessing such future issues, decision makers should ask whether the extension of patentability will "promote the Progress of Science and useful Arts" or instead will hinder competition that can function effectively to spur innovation. Such consideration is consistent with the historical interpretation of Section 101, which typically recognizes that granting patent protection to certain things, such as phenomena of nature and abstract intellectual concepts, would not advance the patent system's Constitutional goals.

FEDERAL TRADE COMMISSION, TO PROMOTE INNOVATION: THE PROPER BALANCE OF COMPETITION AND PATENT LAW AND POLICY 43 (2003), www.ftc.gov/os/2003/10/innovationrpt.pdf.

While the FTC did not make recommendations specific to business method patents, it made a number of suggestions for improving the process for reviewing and granting patents as well as litigating challenges to the validity of patents. For example, the FTC outlined a more rigorous standard to determine whether a patent meets the requirements of nonobviousness, aiming to prevent the patenting of inventions already in the public domain. The FTC highlighted problems with some of the commonly used tests, such as gauging the nonobviousness of an invention by its commercial success or determining whether the prior art would have suggested the invention at issue, and instead offered another analytical framework for evaluating a patent:

> In the context of nonobviousness, "but for" thinking may be useful to better align patent law with competition policy. The concept is simple: to ask whether an invention likely would emerge in roughly the same time frame—that is, with-

out significant delay—"but for" the prospect of a patent. Analogously, one can ask whether disclosure and commercial development of the invention would have occurred as soon "but for" the prospect of a patent. As a theoretical matter, if, even without the prospect of a patent, the invention would emerge (and would be disclosed and commercially developed) without significant delay, then the invention does not warrant a patent.

Id. at 6.

In the area of patent litigation, the FTC suggested lowering the burden of proof for all patent challenges to a "preponderance of the evidence" standard to level the playing field between the patentee and the challenger. While the presumption of a patent's validity is not objectionable,

there is no persuasive reason why the level of that burden should be clear and convincing evidence. As panelists underscored, the PTO's determinations supporting issuance of patents are based only on a preponderance of the evidence. Perhaps even more telling, those determinations are reached under tight time constraints and on an *ex parte* basis allowing minimal opportunity to hear a third party's opposing views. All the failings of *ex parte* examination . . .—limited examiner time, the limited nature of applicants' disclosure obligations, limited access to potentially vital prior art and third-party expertise, the need for examiners to accept applicant's positions on point after point under presumption after presumption—have profound implications given that the burden rests on the PTO to demonstrate that patents should not issue.

Id. at 28.

Some legislators have also attempted to curb what they see as the excesses of the business method patent. In 2001, Representative Howard L. Berman (D–Cal.) proposed the Business Method Patent Improvement Act of 2001, H.R. 1332, 107th Cong. The Act would have required the PTO to publish all business method patent applications after 18 months, distinguishing these from applications for other types of patents, which must be published at 18 months only if the patents have been in filed in one or more non-U.S. jurisdictions. It also would have forced applicants to disclose their prior art searches to the PTO. Most notably, the bill contained a presumption of obviousness for computer-implemented business method inventions:

(d)(1) A business method invention shall be presumed obvious under this section if the only significant difference between the combined teachings of the prior art and the claimed invention is that the claimed invention is appropriate for use with a computer technology, unless—

(A) the application of the computer technology is novel; or

(B) the computer technology is novel and not the subject of another patent or patent application.

The Berman bill generated a variety of responses from legislators, intellectual property associations, and industry leaders. Rep. Rick Boucher (D–Va.), the bill's co-sponsor, criticized the patenting of business methods for protecting obvious practices, citing as an example Priceline's patent for its reverse Internet auction. "It would appear that methods of doing business that are well known and long established in the physical world of bricks and mortar are now being deemed novel and new simply because they are being carried out on the Internet. . . . Under these patents, entire markets are foreclosed to competition and it is difficult to perceive how the continued award of patents along this line advances the greater public good." Subcommittee Hearing on the Business Method Improvement Act of 2001, commdocs.house.gov/committees/judiciary/hju72299.000/hju72299_0f.htm.

Some businesses echoed Rep. Boucher's concerns, emphasizing the pressure placed on companies to build their own arsenal of defensive patents. As a witness noted on behalf of Travelocity.com:

> No prudent business would allow its competitors to patent key business processes without attempting to obtain some patents of their own. And so we, and virtually every other large Internet company, must accept the law as it is and aggressively attempt to obtain patents wherever we can. This has a price for our company and our nation: in addition to the substantial direct legal costs of prosecuting new patent applications, one must consider in such circumstances the enormous time that technical and programming staff devotes to a patent application.

Id.

Other industry leaders criticized the efforts at statutory reform and highlighted the potential problems of treating business method patents differently from other patents, particularly for the United States' compliance with international agreements on intellectual property.

Much of the criticism of the *State Street Bank* decision and business method patents in general has centered on the problem of patent quality and prior art. Patent examiners look closely at relevant publications (including scholarly articles, issued patents, and other printed materials) to see whether an invention is either non-novel or obvious. The ability of patent examiners to conduct such a search may be hampered in the case of business method applications. Rochelle Cooper Dreyfuss summarizes the problem.

> First, because business methods have not been patented in the past, there is very little patent-related prior art readily at hand to the examiner corps. More important, because knowledge about business methods resides mainly in the practices and policies of the firms that use them, even common methods may not be documented in the sorts of materials that examiners can efficiently consult. Unless these difficulties are taken care of—and it is hard to see how the latter can ever be dealt with effectively—invalid patents will inevitably issue.

Rochelle Cooper Dreyfuss, *Are Business Method Patents Bad For Business?*, 16 SANTA CLARA COMPUTER & HIGH TECH. L.J. 263, 269 (2000).

Other commentators concede the point, but note that similar complaints were advanced with respect to biotechnology patent applications in the early 1980s, until the PTO built up a good database of prior art and gained greater evaluative experience. *See, e.g.,* Robert Merges, *As Many as Six Impossible Patents Before Breakfast: Property Rights for Business Concepts and Patent System Reform*, 14 BERKELEY TECH. L.J. 577, 589 (1999). If business method patents are similarly in a transition period, patent quality will soon improve. Are there qualitative differences between biotechnological research and business method development that might undermine this "transition" analogy? Consider the following analysis, also from Dreyfuss:

> One could dismiss the problem of invalid patents as ephemeral—if a patent covers a business method that is really important, it will be challenged and invalidated. But while the potential for successful challenge is certainly real, it is not clear that it is an adequate solution. After all, patents have in terrorem ef-

fects: no one wants to invest in a business that cannot succeed without first winning a lawsuit. Moreover, much can happen during the transition period between allowance and invalidation. For example, many industries experience shake outs. These have the beneficial effect of culling out those firms that are the least competent. But to some extent, business method patents protect businesses from competition. Thus, they can function in a way that preserves inefficiencies in the marketplace.

In some fields, there is another, more enduring, problem[:] . . . lock in. Consider, for example, Amazon.com's patented one-click technology, which has been enforced against BarnesandNoble.com.[3] One click is very nice for shoppers because once they have inputted various bits of shipping and billing information, they can check out quickly on subsequent visits. Accordingly, if Amazon has the exclusive right to one-click, we can expect that many customers will patronize its site. What happens if the patent is eventually invalidated—will there then be effective competition? Probably not because once a book buyer has entered information at Amazon, there is no reason to go elsewhere, particularly now that Amazon has the capacity to further analyze the information and offer its patrons useful suggestions about future purchases. Buyers who rely on such services will not care if the patent is invalidated, and rival sites are permitted to utilize one-click: once locked in to Amazon, shoppers will not likely visit a site that is less informative and requires more work.

Another way to make customers stick is with network effects. An example of a network effect is AOL's instant messenger. A user's ability to exchange e-mail in real time is useful only when the people the user wishes to reach are also on the same system. As a result, the value of the system as a whole depends directly on its size. I do not know whether AOL has protected its system with a patent, but if it has, then instant messenger is a good example of the problem with relying on invalidation. The reason is this: if there were such a patent, it would be extremely significant because it would force everyone interested in instant messenger to sign up with AOL. But once a large (and valuable) network is created, invalidation will not matter at all. True, rivals would appear, but because they would necessarily start small, they would not be able to deliver the same value to their customers. The bottom line is thus a terrible transition problem: patents do not need to be in force for long to exert a substantial effect on competition.

Dreyfuss, *supra*, 16 SANTA CLARA COMPUTER & HIGH TECH. L.J. at 270–272.

Several commentators have argued that even valid business method patents are unnecessary to encourage innovation.

[T]he broad grant of patent protection for methods of doing business is something of a square peg in a sinkhole of uncertain dimensions. Nowhere in the substantial literature on innovation is there a statement that the United States economy suffers from a lack of innovation in methods of doing business. Compared with the business practices of comparable economies we seem to be innovators in distribution and in the service industries. By the casual empiricism of counting the number of graduate business schools, the United States is ahead of other developed economies. This datum, plus the substantial enrollment of foreign students in the graduate schools of business in the United States, permits the

---

[3] [The district court's preliminary injunction enforcing the patent against Barnesandnoble.com was overturned on appeal, and the parties subsequently settled. The case is discussed and excerpted in Part VI, *infra*.—Eds.]

inference that business methods in this country as presently practiced, are considered innovative and attractive, despite the prior absence of patent protection.

There is, moreover, substantial anecdotal evidence that competition alone serves as a sufficient spur to innovation in business methods. The rapid cluster of development in the following businesses casts doubt on the need for the added incentive of patents. Consider the growth of fast food restaurants, self-service gasoline stations, quick oil change facilities, supermarkets for food and office supplies, automatic teller devices and other banking services, electronic fund transfers, supplemental insurance for physician services, and alternatives for long-distance telephone services. To the argument that the economy of the United States would function even better with such patent protection, the model casts doubt. The case for broad patent protection, plausible as a matter of theory, has been qualified by the historical/empirical studies of industries in which there had been broad patent protection.

Moreover, conceding the possibility of free-riding as well as outright piracy of business methods, the absence of patent protection would not leave a total void of legal remedies. There are a variety of federal and state alternative regimes of protection. Copyright, misappropriation, unfair competition, and deceptive practices statutes may serve as alternative means of protection. These regimes may serve to furnish the incentive of protection as well as a means of redress against "dirty tricks" by competitors.

Leo J. Raskind, *The State Street Bank Decision: The Bad Business of Unlimited Patent Protection for Methods of Doing Business*, 10 FORDHAM I.P., MEDIA & ENT. L.J. 61, 92–93 (1999).

Some commentators have hinted that the problems created by trying to apply business method patents to the Internet might be impossible to resolve—and that the Internet would be best served if allowed to develop freely (at least for the time being) without the competitive impediment of patent monopolies. Will the desire to encourage technological development in cyberspace be better served by allowing or not allowing patent protection? Considering the traditional reliance on patents to encourage innovation, could limiting or even eliminating patent protection on the Internet actually lead to *more* innovation? Here is one view.

A patent is a form of regulation. It is a government-granted monopoly—an exclusive right backed by the power of the state. This monopoly is granted by a bureaucrat—a well-meaning, hardworking bureaucrat no doubt, but a bureaucrat nonetheless. This government employee decides whether an idea is novel, useful and nonobvious. If it is, the government guarantees the inventor an exclusive right to the idea for 20 years. Last year, some 150,000 such exclusive rights were granted, up one-third from the year before.

No doubt we are better off with a patent system than without one. Lots of research and invention wouldn't occur without the government's protection. But just because some protection is good, more isn't necessarily better. Especially in cyberspace.

There is growing skepticism among academics about whether such state-imposed monopolies help a rapidly evolving market such as the Internet. What is "novel," "nonobvious" or "useful" is hard enough to know in a relatively stable field. In a transforming market, it's nearly impossible for anyone—let alone an underpaid worker in the U.S. Department of Commerce who spends on average of eight hours evaluating the prior art in a patent and gets paid based on how many he processes—to identify what's "novel." Costly mistakes get made. On average it takes $1.2 million to challenge the validity of a patent, which means it is often cheaper simply to pay the royalties than to establish that the patent isn't deserved.

"Bad patents" thus become the space debris of cyberspace. Nowhere is this clearer than in the context of business-method patents. At a recent conference in Israel, I watched as a lawyer terrified the assembled crowd of Internet startups with stories of the increasing number of business-method patents that now haunt Internet space. Patent No. 5,715,314, for example, gives the holder a monopoly over "network-based sales systems"—we call that e-commerce. Patent No. 5,797,127 forms the basis for Priceline.com and effectively blocks any competitor. Patent No. 4,949,257 covers the purchase of software over a network.

To West Coast coders, it seems bizarre that East Coast coders—the Patent Office—consider these ideas nonobvious. But the real problem is the incentives such a system creates. Awarding patents of that type siphons off resources from technologists to lawyers—from people making real products to people applying for regulatory privilege and protection. An increasingly significant cost of Net startups involves both defensive and offensive lawyering—making sure you don't "steal" someone else's "idea" and quickly claiming as yours every "idea" you can describe in a patent application.

But this is absurd. When the world was given TCP/IP and the collection of protocols it induced, a billion ideas became obvious to anyone who took the time to think. These were not ideas that were discovered because some lone inventor spent years toiling away in his basement, but because TCP/IP was a language with which practically anything could be done. And with very little promise of protection by government, lots was done. The Internet revolution was born long before lawyers arrived on the scene.

Lawrence Lessig, *The Problem with Patents*, THE INDUSTRY STANDARD, Apr. 23, 1999, www.lessig.org/content/standard/0,1902,4296,00.html.

EXTENSIONS

Software patents problematic? Other than the courts' outmoded concerns with the metaphysics of patentable subject matter, which ended with *State Street Bank*, there are at least two reasons why software patents are a troubled area of patent law: (1) the fact that most software developments lose their value in a short time, so that the time it takes to get a patent may exhaust the invention's value; (2) the overlap in protection between patent law and copyright law.

Software became protectible under copyright law in the 1970s when the courts were refusing patent protection. Under copyright law, computer code—both source and object code—is protectible as a literary work. In addition, the structural elements of a computer program, if found to constitute "expression" rather than "ideas," can be copyrighted. It is arguable that patent and copyright were meant to be mutually exclusive, and that this situation is anomalous. Professor Radin argues that this anomaly is symptomatic of a broader breakdown of the distinction between text and machine:

> Computer programs are both text and machine. They are text when considered as code statements, they are machines when considered as devices for accomplishing a task. Copyright law reflects the text perspective (programs are considered literary works); patent law reflects the machine perspective (a programmed computer is a "new machine"). The fact that computer programs are

both copyrightable and patentable is anomalous for intellectual property law. Copyright is supposed to exclude works that are functional; patent is supposed to focus on functionality and exclude texts. Computer programs are the only large area covered both by patent and copyright. This anomaly is obscured to some extent by the fact that copyright and patent regard programs differently: patent focuses on the protocol for accomplishing the task, however the programmer chooses to code it, whereas copyright focuses on the code statements, but also their structure, sequence and organization. The difference between structure, sequence and organization (copyrightable) and useful algorithm, protocol or method (patentable) is, however, conceptually difficult to maintain. This difficulty reflects the fact that computer programs can be understood either as text or machine. Those who write code sometimes genuinely feel that it is their speech and should be protected by the First Amendment. At the same time, it is clear that the primary *raison d'etre* for programs is their technological function, their ability to accomplish a task.

Margaret Jane Radin, *Online Standardization and the Integration of Text and Machine*, 70 FORDHAM L. REV. 1125, 1143–44 (2002).

Had software not been brought within the protection of copyright law, perhaps Congress would have enacted a new form of protection particularly suited to software, perhaps less onerous to apply for and of shorter duration than patents. Commentators argued at the time for such *sui generis* protection, but their arguments did not convince policy makers. *See, e.g.*, Pamela Samuelson, Randall Davis, Mitchell D. Kapor & J.H. Reichman, *A Manifesto Concerning the Legal Protection of Computer Programs*, 94 COLUM. L. REV. 2308 (1994).

QUESTIONS FOR DISCUSSION

---

1. *Availability of prior art.* Is Professor Dreyfuss correct to see little hope of effectively addressing the problem that prior art may reside in the heads of managers rather than the pages of any accessible publication? Would the proliferation of business method patents, perhaps ironically, help resolve the difficulty she identifies?

2. *Improving the system.* Commentators have advanced several proposals aimed at remedying the perceived flaws in the business method patent application examination process. Which of the following strategies would best answer the criticisms advanced above? Would some be harder to implement than others? What reforms would you suggest?

    a. *Reforming the PTO.* Professor Robert Merges has proposed a series of changes in PTO examination procedures to improve patent quality. These include: (1) subcontracting patent examination and search procedures to outside firms that can conduct more comprehensive, efficient searches focusing on specific technologies and/or industries; (2) raising pay and benefits to encourage senior examiners to remain with the office and train new examiners; (3) restructuring the examiner bonus system, which may now encourage examiners to issue more patents and thereby raise their case completion rate, by introducing "error" tracking systems; and (4) revamping the reexamination system to allow more participation by interested third parties and to allow third parties to appeal adverse reexamination decisions. *See* Robert Merges, *As Many as Six Impossible Patents Before Breakfast: Property Rights for Business Concepts and Patent System Reform*, 14 BERKELEY TECH. L.J. 577 (1999). For an argument that putting more resources into the patent-examining process would be inefficient, see Mark A. Lemley, *Rational Ignorance at the Patent Office*, 95 NW. U.L. REV. 1495 (2001).

b. *An opposition procedure.* Many countries allow interested members of the public to file oppositions to a patent during a designated period of time. In 1999 Congress amended the Patent Act to implement such a procedure, called "inter partes reexamination." Optional Inter Partes Reexamination Procedure Act of 1999, Pub. L. No. 106–113, 113 Stat. 1501A–567 (1999), 35 U.S.C. §§ 311–18. Under this procedure, any person may at any time bring to the attention of the PTO prior art that may be relevant to a patent, and may request reexamination of the patent. If the PTO determines that the request raises a substantial new question concerning validity of the patent, it must open a reexamination of the patent. Both the person requesting reexamination and the patentee are entitled to participate in the reexamination. Reexamination may lead to invalidation of the patent. 35 U.S.C. § 311–18. Does this procedure address the concerns about patent quality? The procedure has so far been infrequently invoked. According to the PTO Director, as of October 24, 2000, no one had chosen to take advantage of the new reexamination procedures with respect to a business method patent.

c. *A bounty system.* John R. Thomas argues that the patent system needs bounty hunters. One of the basic assumptions of the patent system is that the validity of patents will be checked by private parties. According to this assumption, a competitor that wishes to use a patented invention, and believes the patent to be invalid, will ignore it; if the patentee seeks to bring an infringement action, she will lose because the competitor will be able to show the invention in question is obvious or non-novel. But this basic assumption may ignore the reality that competitors may decide the costs or risks of litigation are too high. Thomas suggests, therefore, the development of a kind of private bounty system that would reward persons who can show a patent to be invalid. Because the bounty would be paid by the patent applicant, applicants would be encouraged to research potential prior art carefully prior to filing an application. *See* John R. Thomas, *Collusion and Collective Action in the Patent System: A Proposal for Patent Bounties*, 2001 U. ILL. L. REV. 305.

FURTHER READING

- Linda E. Alcorn, *Pursuing Business Methods Patents in the US Patent and Trademark Office*, 20 No. 3 COMPUTER & INTERNET LAW. 27 (2003) (discussing the PTO's handling of business method patents)

- Brian Kahin, *The Expansion of the Patent System: Politics and Political Economy*, FIRST MONDAY, vol. 6, no. 1 (Jan. 2001) (arguing that the problems with the PTO are institutional, and will not be solved by approaches such as those discussed in the text), firstmonday.org/issues/issue6_1/kahin/index.html

C. PATENTS OUTSIDE THE UNITED STATES

In contrast to the expansiveness of the current U.S. approach to patentability of business methods, other countries are taking a more cautious approach. Many nations have been engaged in a drive toward international harmonization of intellectual property law, driven in part by the globalization of commerce, and some have begun to reconsider their limits on patentability in light of U.S. developments. The patent offices of the United States, Japan, and Europe have repeatedly met to discuss software and business method patentability. In June 2000, these three offices reported a "consensus" opinion consisting of two propositions: (1) "A technical aspect is necessary for a computer-implemented business method to be eligible for patenting." and (2) "To merely automate a known human transaction process using well known automation techniques is not patentable." *See Report on Comparative Study Carried Out Under Trilateral Project B3b* (2000), www.european-patent-office.org/tws/b3b_start_page.htm. An Appendix to the report, issued by the President of the European Patent Office, specifies guidelines for evaluating computer-implemented business methods, the key test being whether the invention solves an objective technical problem. *Id.*, app. 6. According to a September 2000 study, at least eight business method patents already have been issued in Japan, with many more expected as the number of applications increases. Economic Research Institute, *Impact of Business Model (Method) Patents: Implications for Corporate Management* (2000). The patentability of business methods outside the United States remains an open question, though it seems the trend toward patentability will continue.

Likewise uncertain is the enforceability of U.S. business method patents against infringers based in other countries. Patent law is territorial. The Patent Act includes as infringements importing an infringing product into the United States, or importing into the United States an unpatented product made abroad by a process patented in the United States. U.S. patent law also makes it an infringement to ship all of the components of a patented invention abroad and manufacture it there. 35 U.S.C. § 271. But in general, those acting outside the territory of the United States are not covered by the U.S. patent law, and may engage in activities which if they occurred in the United States would infringe a patent.

The United States is working with other countries to address these questions. An important international agreement governing patents, to which the United States is a signatory, is the Agreement on Trade-Related Aspects of Intellectual Property Rights ("TRIPS"), www.wto.org/english/tratop_e/trips_e/t_agm0_e.htm. Under Article 1 of TRIPS, signatory countries must treat citizens and foreigners equally under the law; that is, foreigners are free to file applications for U.S. patents on the same terms as U.S. citizens. TRIPS also requires signatory countries to implement certain legal standards for patentability and sets forth a uniform patent term as well. Countries are not required to enforce each other's laws, however, nor are they prevented from excluding some forms of subject matter from protection—apparently including business methods if not sufficiently technological.[4]

QUESTIONS FOR DISCUSSION

Extraterritorial effects. Should a French Web-based company using a business method patented in the United States be liable for patent infringement if the company targets U.S. citizens in its advertising? What if does not target U.S. citizens but its website is nevertheless accessible in the United States? Does it matter if actual goods are shipped to the United States?

---

[4] Article 27(1) of TRIPS provides:

[P]atents shall be available for any inventions, whether products or processes, in all fields of technology, provided that they are new, involve an inventive step and are capable of industrial application. . . . [P]atents shall be available and patent rights enjoyable without discrimination as to the place of invention, the field of technology and whether products are imported or locally produced.

V. EXAMPLES OF E-COMMERCE BUSINESS METHOD PATENTS

The availability of business method patents following *State Street Bank* has had a profound effect on the operation and strategy of e-commerce, as inventors and businesses have flocked to the PTO seeking to patent their methods of doing business. Following are some examples of patents that have issued for Internet-commerce-related business methods. Note that the excerpts include only Claim One of each patent. Claim One is often the shortest and most general in wording—therefore, it often is the *broadest* of the claims of the patent. Because Claim One is often the broadest, it might be deemed by a court or a patent examiner to be invalid, while other narrower claims, more specifically delineating the actual embodiment of the invention developed by the patentee, might be upheld (remember, a patent is evaluated claim by claim).

A. AMAZON.COM'S ONE-CLICK PATENT

Patent Number: 5,960,411

Date of Patent: September 28, 1999

METHOD AND SYSTEM FOR PLACING A PURCHASE ORDER VIA A COMMUNICATIONS NETWORK

. . .

Abstract

A method and system for placing an order to purchase an item via the Internet. The order is placed by a purchaser at a client system and received by a server system. The server system receives purchaser information including identification of the purchaser, payment information, and shipment information from the client system. The server system then assigns a client identifier to the client system and associates the assigned client identifier with the received purchaser information. The server system sends to the client system the assigned client identifier and an HTML document identifying the item and including an order button. The client system receives and stores the assigned client identifier and receives and displays the HTML document. In response to the selection of the order button, the client system sends to the server system a request to purchase the identified item. The server system receives the request and combines the purchaser information associated with the client identifier of the client system to generate an order to purchase the item in accordance with the billing and shipment information whereby the purchaser effects the ordering of the product by selection of the order button.

. . .

BACKGROUND OF THE INVENTION

. . .

The World Wide Web is especially conducive to conducting electronic commerce. Many Web servers have been developed through which vendors can advertise and sell products. The products can include items (e.g., music) that are delivered electronically to the purchaser over the Internet and items (e.g., books) that are delivered through conventional distribution channels (e.g., a common carrier). A server computer system may provide an electronic version of a catalog that lists the items that are available. A user, who is a potential purchaser, may browse through the catalog using a browser and select various items that are to be purchased. When the user has completed selecting the items to be purchased, the server computer system then prompts the user for information to complete the ordering of the items. This purchaser-specific order information may include the purchaser's name, the purchaser's credit card number, and a shipping address for the order. The server computer system then typically confirms the order by sending a confirming Web page to the client computer system and schedules shipment of the items.

Since the purchaser-specific order information contains sensitive information (e.g., a credit card number), both vendors and purchasers want to ensure the security of such information. Security is a concern because information transmitted over the Internet may pass through various intermediate computer systems on its way to its final destination. The information could be intercepted by an unscrupulous person at an intermediate system. To help ensure the security of the sensitive information, various encryption techniques are used when transmitting such information between a client computer system and a server computer system. Even though such encrypted information can be intercepted, because the information is encrypted, it is generally useless to the interceptor. Nevertheless, there is always a possibility that such sensitive information may be successfully decrypted by the interceptor. Therefore, it would be desirable to minimize the sensitive information transmitted when placing an order.

The selection of the various items from the electronic catalogs is generally based on the "shopping cart" model. When the purchaser selects an item from the electronic catalog, the server computer system metaphorically adds that item to a shopping cart. When the purchaser is done selecting items, then all the items in the shopping cart are "checked out" (i.e., ordered) when the purchaser provides billing and shipment information. In some models, when a purchaser selects any one item, then that item is "checked out" by automatically prompting the user for the billing and shipment information. Although the shopping cart model is very flexible and intuitive, it has a downside in that it requires many interactions by the purchaser. For example, the purchaser selects the various items from the electronic catalog, and then indicates that the selection is complete. The purchaser is then presented with an order Web page that prompts the purchaser for the purchaser-specific order information to complete the order. That Web page may be prefilled with information that was provided by the purchaser when placing another order. The information is then validated by the server computer system, and the order is completed. Such an ordering model can be problematic for a couple of reasons. If a purchaser is ordering only one item, then the overhead of confirming the various steps of the ordering process and waiting for, viewing, and updating the purchaser-specific order information can be much more than the overhead of selecting the item itself. This overhead makes the purchase of a single item cumbersome. Also, with such an ordering model, each time an order is placed sensitive information is transmitted over the Internet. Each time the sensitive information is transmitted over the Internet, it is susceptible to being intercepted and decrypted.

. . .

[Claims]

We claim:

1. A method of placing an order for an item comprising:

under control of a client system,

displaying information identifying the item; and

in response to only a single action being performed, sending a request to order the item along with an identifier of a purchaser of the item to a server system;

under control of a single-action ordering component of the server system,

receiving the request;

retrieving additional information previously stored for the purchaser identified by the identifier in the received request; and

generating an order to purchase the requested item for the purchaser identified by the identifier in the received request using the retrieved additional information; and

fulfilling the generated order to complete purchase of the item whereby the item is ordered without using a shopping cart ordering model.

. . .

B. PRICELINE.COM'S PATENT ON REVERSE AUCTIONS

Patent Number: 5,794,207

Date of Patent: August 11, 1998

METHOD AND APPARATUS FOR A CRYPTOGRAPHICALLY ASSISTED COMMERCIAL NETWORK SYSTEM DESIGNED TO FACILITATE BUYER-DRIVEN CONDITIONAL PURCHASE OFFERS

Abstract

The present invention is a method and apparatus for effectuating bilateral buyer-driven commerce. The present invention allows prospective buyers of goods and services to communicate a binding purchase offer globally to potential sellers, for sellers conveniently to search for relevant buyer purchase offers, and for sellers potentially to bind a buyer to a contract based on the buyer's purchase offer. In a preferred embodiment, the apparatus of the present invention includes a controller which receives binding purchase offers from prospective buyers. The controller makes purchase offers available globally to potential sellers. Potential sellers then have the option to accept a purchase offer and thus bind the corresponding buyer to a contract. The method and apparatus of the present invention have applications on the Internet as well as conventional communications systems such as voice telephony.

. . .

SUMMARY OF THE INVENTION

In a preferred embodiment, the present invention provides a method and apparatus for prospective buyers of goods or services to communicate a binding purchase offer globally to potential sellers, for sellers conveniently to search for relevant buyer purchase offers, and for sellers to bind a buyer to a contract based on the buyer's purchase offer. Additionally, the present invention can effectuate performance of the agreement between the buyer and seller by guaranteeing buyer payment for the purchase. The present invention is therefore a highly effective bilateral buyer-driven commerce system which improves the ability of buyers to reach sellers capable of satisfying the buyers' purchasing needs and improves sellers' ability to identify interested buyers.

In one embodiment of this invention, communications between buyers and sellers are conducted using an electronic network and central controller. A buyer who wishes to make a purchase accesses the central controller located at a remote server. The buyer will then create a conditional purchase offer ("CPO") by specifying the subject of the goods he wishes to purchase, a description of the goods he wishes to obtain, and any other conditions the buyer requires. For example, a typical CPO could specify that the buyer wants to purchase a block of four airline tickets from Chicago's O'Hare Airport to Dallas, Tex., the tickets must be from any of the six largest U.S. carriers, the buyer is willing to change planes no more than once so long as the scheduled layover is less than two hours, and the buyer is willing to pay $180 per ticket, plus any applicable taxes.

The buyer then attaches a user identification to the CPO and transmits the CPO to the central controller. Under the present invention, the CPO may be transmitted via numerous means including a world-wide-web interface, electronic mail, voice mail, facsimile, or postal mail. Standard legal provisions and language are then integrated with the CPO to "fill in the gaps" of the buyer's purchase offer. Alternatively, the CPO may be developed while the buyer is on-line with the central controller.

Before communicating the CPO to potential sellers, the central controller authenticates the buyer's identification number against a buyer database. The central controller may require that the buyer provide a credit card number and may also ensure that the buyer has sufficient credit available to cover the purchase price specified in the CPO by contacting the credit card clearinghouse. The central controller then assigns a unique tracking number to the CPO and globally displays the CPO in a manner such that it is available to be viewed by any interested potential sellers. CPOs may be displayed by subject category to make it easier for potential sellers to identify relevant CPOs. Thus, a seller could log onto a website, for example, and see a listing of CPO subject categories. The seller could then choose a particular subject and have the ability to browse CPOs which correspond to that subject category. In one embodiment, the seller may be required to provide qualifications in order to view the CPOs of a given subject category.

If, after reviewing a particular CPO, a potential seller wishes to accept the CPO, the seller communicates his intent to the central controller. The central controller then timestamps the message from the seller and authenticates the identity of the seller and his capacity to deliver the goods sought by the buyer. The system then verifies that the particular CPO is still "active" and capable of being accepted. If a CPO is capable of being accepted only by one seller, it is "completed" when the first qualified seller accepts it. Subsequent sellers will not be able to accept a "completed" CPO. If a seller accepts an active CPO, a unique tracking number is assigned to the seller's acceptance. The acceptance is then stored in a database. The buyer and seller are now parties to a legally binding contract.

. . .

The present invention can also be practiced in off-line embodiments. Instead of using electronic mail or web-based servers, buyers and sellers may communicate with the central controller via telephone, facsimile, postal mail, or another off-line communication tool. For example, buyers may use telephones to create CPOs (with or without the assistance of live agents) and potential sellers may use a telephone to browse and bind CPOs.

. . .

What the present invention accomplishes, which no previous system has done before, is literally to hang buyer money on a "clothesline" for sellers to see. Attached to the money is a note describing what the seller has to agree to do in order to take the money down off the clothesline. There is no uncertainty or waste of time on the part of the seller. He knows that if he can meet the conditions set forth by the buyer, he can immediately close the sale and get paid for it. No hassles. No negotiations.

The invention also allows buyers to reach a large number of remotely located sellers who normally would not be able to afford to find the buyer, but who may be able to provide the buyer with the exact deal the buyer desires. For instance, this might be the case for a car buyer who could precisely define the car and option packages he wanted for a specified price. The present invention allows such a buyer to issue a binding purchase offer which is globally communicated to authorized dealers in the U.S. Any one of those dealers could then decide whether or not to accept the offer. The buyer's advantage is particularly significant when the sellers of products sought by the buyer have no inventory carrying costs, as is the case with insurance sales. Insurance buyers could use the present invention to cast a wide net to reach thousands of potential insurance sellers and potentially find a seller willing to satisfy the buyer's specified purchase conditions.

It is a goal of the present invention to provide a robust system which matches buyers' requirements with sellers capable of satisfying those requirements. The invention provides a global bilateral buyer-driven system for creating binding contracts incorporating various methods of communication, commerce and security for the buyer and the seller. The power of a central controller to field binding offers from buyers, communicate those offers globally in a format which can be efficiently accessed and analyzed by potential sellers, effectuate performance of resulting contracts, resolve disputes arising from those contracts, and maintain billing, collection, authentication, and anonymity makes the present invention an improvement over conventional systems.

[Claims]

What is claimed:

1. A method for using a computer to facilitate a transaction between a buyer and at least one of sellers, comprising:

inputting into the computer a conditional purchase offer which includes an offer price;

inputting into the computer a payment identifier specifying a credit card account, the payment identifier being associated with the conditional purchase offer;

outputting the conditional purchase offer to the plurality of sellers after receiving the payment identifier;

inputting into the computer an acceptance from a seller, the acceptance being responsive to the conditional purchase offer; and

providing a payment to the seller by using the payment identifier.

. . .

C. CYBERGOLD'S PAY-PER-VIEW ADVERTISING PATENT

Patent Number: 5,794,210

Date of Patent: August 11, 1998

ATTENTION BROKERAGE

Abstract

A system provides for the immediate payment to computer and other users for paying attention to an advertisement or other "negatively priced" information distributed over a computer network such as the Internet. Called Attention Brokerage, this is the business of brokering the buying and selling of the "attention" of users. A further invention, Orthogonal Sponsorship, allows advertisers to detach their messages from program content and explicitly target their audience. A special icon or other symbol displayed on a computer screen may represent compensation and allow users to choose whether they will view an ad or other negatively priced information and receive associated compensation. Targeting users may be provided by reference to a data base of digitally stored demographic profiles of potential users. Information can be routed to users based on demographics, and software agents can be used to actively seek out users on a digital network. Private profiles may be maintained for different users and user information may be released to advertisers and other marketers only based on user permission. Users may be compensated for allowing their information to be released. Competing advertisers may "bid" for the attention of users using automatic electronic systems, e.g., "an auction" protocol and these concepts can be generalized to provide an electronic trading house where buyers and sellers can actively find each other and negotiate transactions.

BACKGROUND AND SUMMARY OF THE INVENTION

Historically, advertising has involved a battle of wits between advertiser and consumer. In the mass media, producers of products and services vie with each other to capture the attention of potential consumers, while those same consumers (although generally endorsing the idea of advertising as a way of keeping entertainment and information costs down) strive to evade as many advertising messages as they can. Consumers press the mute button on their TV remotes and "zap" advertisements by flipping between channels, they mentally tune out or "zap" radio commercials, they flip advertising pages of a newspaper or magazine without paying any attention to them, and they subscribe to non-commercial information and entertainment media. Rare indeed is the consumer who actually enjoys being at the receiving end of mass-media advertising.

This state of affairs is not accidental. It is an inevitable result of the environment in which advertising came of age. To make contact with the relatively small percentage of people who might actually want to use a product or service, mass-media advertising has to impact everyone who uses the medium. For example, every reader of the New York Times has to see (though not necessarily read) the display ad for Macy's; every viewer of popular television programs such as "Roseanne" has to sit through (though not necessarily pay attention to) the commercial for Diet Coke.

Although the concept of a consumer's attention as a commodity with intrinsic value has only recently entered public discussion, it has long been implicit in advertising, marketing, and public relations. Since advertisers know that only a small percentage of the audience has a real interest in the product or service being sold, they have learned to rely on entertainment values—constant repetition, snappy jingles, blaring headlines, and sex—to attract the attention of the audience and thereby sell their wares.

In the traditional mass media advertising model, mass media (e.g., television networks, radio stations, newspapers and magazines) develop particular content of interest to certain classes of consumers. The mass media also develops and provides a mechanism to deliver the content to as many potential consumers as possible (e.g., over the air or by cable transmissions, by mass distribution of print media copies, etc.). The mass media may charge audience members for content delivery (e.g., magazine or newspaper subscription fees, cable television subscription fees, or "pay per view" fees), but mass media typically receives most of its revenue from advertisers.

Advertising "sponsorship" in this traditional mass media advertising model has been a mechanism by which economic value is passed indirectly from an advertiser to a consumer. Advertisers "sponsor" content by paying the mass media to deliver their advertisements with the content. Traditionally, advertisers often want their advertisements inextricably embedded within the content itself so the advertisements are more certain to reach the mass media audience. For example, some advertisers have television and radio commentators work advertising "pitches" into their commentary. Other advertisers have televised/photographed race car drivers emblazon their cars with advertising slogans. Still other advertisers have film actors or actresses use the advertiser's products as part of their role playing. Moreover, the now-standard technique of pacing commercial television programming to intersperse advertising at various points within the programming is designed to make it more difficult for viewers to not pay attention to the advertisements.

. . .

The advertising practices described above have a number of drawbacks, both for the advertiser and for society at large. The primary drawback for the advertiser is lack of efficiency. Mass media advertising is inherent both over-inclusive and under-inclusive. For example, the lingerie ads aired during Melrose Place are not delivered to many consumers who are prime candidates for purchasing the product (for example, fashion conscious women who buy a lot of lingerie but don't like Melrose Place and/or don't watch television). In addition, the advertisements are delivered to many consumers (e.g., men who watch Melrose Place) who have no interest in purchasing the products being advertised. From the advertiser's point of view, a lingerie company could advertise more efficiently if it could directly reach women who are explicitly interested in lingerie (or clothes, or fashion).

Society at large is also harmed by this lack of efficiency. As one example, television programming has, to a very large extent, become dictated by factors that will make it appeal to the largest possible audience so it can generate the largest possible advertising revenue. The result is a decrease in the overall diversity of information available and an alarming increase in the homogeneity and "lowest common denominator" appeal of mass media programming. Unlinking sponsorship from the content of the sponsored entertainment or service would benefit the consumer and would also provide broad benefits to society such as greater freedom of speech and making a larger diversity of opinions available to the public.

. . .

The Internet is the first medium that can claim to be both "mass," in the sense that it reaches millions of people all over the globe, and "specialized," in the sense that its technology is capable of targeting information directly to the individual consumer. This is such a fundamental change from all previous information technologies that it has the potential to transform the advertising transaction into an alliance between consumer and advertiser, based on mutual respect and mutual benefits.

The Internet is a system of linked computers that permits fast, low-cost, global communication, entertainment, and information exchange. The Internet may be considered the test-bed for a "Future Net" which will likely encompass the functions now provided by today's Internet, cable and broadcast television, telephone communications (including voice and picture) and other linear and interactive business, telecommunication and entertainment systems. This "Future Net" may be a single network or an amalgamation of two or more independent networks. It is likely that new forms of entertainment and business will emerge, made possible by the Future Net.

Even with the current form of the Information Superhighway (Internet, cable television, video conference, "zines" created by desktop publishing, etc.), competition for the public's time and attention will become increasingly keen. Consumers with hundreds of competing, independent, and widely distributed sources of entertainment and information to choose from will no longer be the passive prisoners of advertising messages that they were in the era of the centralized mass media. So far, however, advertising has been only a marginal—and somewhat unwelcome—presence on the Information Superhighway.

Many consumers of the Information Superhighway view the recent advent of advertising to the wide open spaces of the Internet with deep suspicion and an almost instinctive aversion. But the kind of advertising the skeptics are thinking about—and rejecting—bears little resemblance to the advertising of the future.

The present invention provides a new approach to advertising for the digital age. Advertising in accordance with the present invention is based on the new realities of communication and commerce on the Internet, on-line services, the Future Net, and other computer networks, including networks that distribute information via physical media such as CD-ROM.

The innovations provided by the present invention have the potential to turn what has historically been an uneasy and sometimes hostile stand-off between advertiser and consumer into an alliance based on mutual respect and mutual benefits. The approach provided by the present invention is based on four principles:

attention,

interest,

sponsorship, and

privacy.

Attention

A fundamental premise underlying the present invention is the idea that a consumer's attention is a valuable commodity. The present invention will allow advertisers to pay consumers directly for their time and attention. The notion of direct, immediate payment in this context is new. The rationale for direct payment, from the advertiser's point of view, is that direct payment is a cost-effective way of getting the attention of targeted customers as compared to mass-media advertising.

The present invention provides mechanisms for "attention brokerage"—the business of buying and selling (brokering) the "attention" of consumers. Attention brokerage establishes a market that allows advertisers to compete for the attention of a particular consumer or group of consumers—thereby maximizing efficiency and creating value.

"Negative pricing" is one means by which advertisers could compete for available attention in the system provided in accordance with the present invention. In its simplest form, negative pricing is a "passive" competition: advertisers make fixed offers and viewers select among them. Another innovative idea is "attention bidding," a mechanism by which advertisers actively compete by bidding for a viewer's attention. These bids might be based, in part, on estimates of the viewer's interest and likelihood to buy—estimates derived from access to the viewer's electronic profiles detailing preferences and past consuming behavior. Bids might also be based on other bids, via an "auction" protocol by empowered bidding "agents." The bidding may be explicit or automatic. Viewers may elect to have advertisers bid for their attention or the system may offer bidding without the viewers' knowledge.

Interest

As discussed above, traditional advertising was both under-inclusive and over-inclusive. In contrast, technology provided in accordance with the present invention permits the design of ads that are virtually custom-fitted to consumer preferences, thus ensuring that the ad messages will be welcomed and attentively viewed by the consumer. This ability to finely target (and customize) ads based on the interests of particular individual consumers maximizes efficiency and benefits both the advertisers and the consumers.

For example, when selecting ads for viewing, the consumer would be given the chance to express a preference for certain kinds of ad content. For example, if the consumer is shopping for a computer, he/she might ask to see an advertisement that provides straightforward technical specifications of specific models or configurations. For a movie commercial, one consumer might request a film clip while another asks for a plot summary. Some consumers might enjoy the entertainment value of celebrity-spokesperson ads, while a consumer viewing an ad for food or drink might ask for a list of ingredients or nutrients.

A related innovation, "demographic routing," is a mechanism by which an information package or its agent (or an agent for any goods or service) can be routed directly to interested and willing buyers. Conceptually, this is an addressing mechanism that can be used to route the information to more than one individual, e.g., to all users who are demographically suitable (e.g., "anyone who fits the following profile").

Sponsorship

Since all the ads on the list will be targeted to the consumer's needs, interests, and preferences, it is very likely that she would be inclined to view them even without a cash incentive. However, the system provided by the present invention will offer her one. The present invention provides a "consumer interface button"—for example, the image of a little gold coin ("CyberCoin") next to each title on a list. This use of a consumer interface button—the "CyberCoin"—though reminiscent of the prior art "gems" in video game adventures, is innovative and unique in that it transfers real value.

The "CyberCoin" transaction reflects a radical and innovative change in the meaning of sponsorship. In effect, the advertisers have elected to sponsor the consumer who selects the CyberCoin—that is, they have chosen to pay the consumer directly for her attention rather than using the same funds for mass-market ad campaigns that are far less likely to hit the mark. Thus, the present invention provides a method of separating advertising sponsorship from the editorial content of the medium in which the advertising appears. We call this ability to decouple the advertising content from other content "orthogonal sponsorship."

The technology offered by the present invention breaks (or makes inexplicit) the link between the ad and the content of the sponsored material. Advertisers will not necessarily know what content of entertainment or information they are sponsoring. Instead, advertisers will simply provide ads to the service, explicitly delineate their target audience, and offer some form of compensation for time and attention directly to those viewers willing to "view" ads.

In orthogonal sponsorship, how will advertisers know that they are getting their money's worth? What is to prevent a consumer from clicking the CyberGold button, collecting the credit, and NOT reading the ad? The system provided by the present invention can, as one example, have a built-in system of incentives and checks—a "carrot and stick" approach—to solve this problem. The "carrot" in this example is the consumer's interest in the product or service, which will make him or her unlikely to ignore the ad once it is presented. The "stick" is an element of interactivity designed into the ad that requires the consumer to provide a response or otherwise interact with the ad (thus allowing the service to assure the advertiser that the consumer did indeed watch and pay attention).

The present invention also introduces the concept of "negative pricing of information." In today's marketplace, entertainment and information (sometimes generically referred to as "intellectual property") carries a positive price, or is free. "Negatively priced information" pays the consumer for his or her attention. This is a generalization of direct payment for ad viewing, since the information or content need not be an advertisement in the conventional sense. There is a fine line between certain kinds of information and advertising, particularly when an advertising message can be as straightforward as the technical specs of a new car or computer, and an information message or entertainment can change minds and influence people. Negative pricing could work well for information of this type. For example, it could be used as a means of expressing a political viewpoint, raising the priority of an e-mail message, or getting potential employers to read a resume. Negatively-priced information would find its audience through personal profiles of potential consumers on file in the database.

Privacy

In the system provided by the present invention, the link between the ad and the appropriate viewer is provided by reference to a data base of digitally stored electronic demographic profiles of potential viewers. The viewer profiles are to be private, dynamic, and interactive. The system protects member privacy while at the same time maintaining the personal information files that permit specialized targeting of ads.

Many businesses keep profiles of customer interests and transactions. (For example, some supermarkets keep customer profiles via "savings cards" that allow the market to track each person's purchases and tailor individual promotions.) The system provided by the present invention offers several innovative features and applications for such profiles. Profiles can be private (pseudonymous). That is, they can be used and even marketed while protecting the customer's identity. For example, a merchant may be permitted scan a profile to determine his affinity for the customer, but cannot learn the customer's name or address. Contacts between advertisers and consumers can be brokered by a "profile bank" that protects the consumer's privacy.

The demographic profiles can be constructed through interest questionnaires that the consumer completes when subscribing to the service, and also through electronic tracking of his/her usage of the service (and other habits). Thus, the profiles can be dynamic, evolving with the customer's transaction history. A customer can choose to exclude any transaction (e.g., viewing of certain material or purchasing of certain products) from his profile. Profiles can also be interactive in that a customer may edit his profile at any time to add or delete interest features, and to delete any transaction records. Thus, for example, the customer can delete historical transaction entries evidencing her purchase of an "adult" film if desired. Similarly, the customer can change her profile to express interest in seeing certain types of automobile advertisements, and then, after she has selected and purchased a new car, delete those profile entries.

In addition to the viewer profiles, the system provided by the present invention also may keep the contact information of each member confidential. For example, if an advertiser wants a consumer's name and address, he has to offer to buy it, and the consumer has to agree to the price. Furthermore, the consumer can specify that no advertiser can resell his/her name without permission. An offer to buy a consumer's name and address might look like this: "Please accept $2.00 for your name and address so we can send you more info." If the consumer accepts (e.g., by clicking on the associated "CyberCoin"), her name and address (from her personal data) will be forwarded to the advertiser, and $2 will be transferred from the advertiser to the consumer's account.

Another aspect of the present invention provides a two step technique for the development of an accurate consumer profile. First, a consumer is asked to pro-actively describe him or herself. This forms a "base profile." Then the consumer's actions can be monitored in this example such that a representation of the consumer's actions are "overlaid" upon the self description. This combination of self description combined with monitored actions yields highly accurate and granular consumer profile which can be used to predict consumer interests and behaviors. The system also can generate a base profile from historical data as well as self description.

. . .

[Claims]

What is claimed is:

1. In an arrangement comprising plural computers connected to a digital computer network, said network carrying and routing digital information between

said plural computers, said plural computers including at least one personal computer associated with at least one user, at least one computer associated with at least one attention broker, at least one computer associated with at least one provider of negatively priced information, and at least one computer associated with at least one provider of positively priced information, said network being decentralized in that any pair of said personal and information provider computers may communicate without said communication passing through any of the other said personal and information provider computers, said personal computer having a display device and at least one user input device, the display device being capable of providing a visual display based at least in part on the digital information delivered to the personal computer via said network, said displayed information including at least one visual link associated with one of said information provider computers, said user being able to operate said user input device to select and activate said link in order to erect a network connection to said information provider computer, a method for permitting the provider of negatively priced information to orthogonally sponsor user purchases of positively priced information, the method comprising:

(1) supplying negatively priced information to the personal computer from at least one negatively priced information provider;

(2) providing said user with the opportunity to receive compensation in connection with said negatively priced information by connecting via the network to said attention broker computer;

(3) compensating, via said attention broker computer, the user in connection with the supplied negatively priced information;

(4) presenting the user, via said personal computer display, with a choice of at least one item of positively priced information, and allowing the user to select said item by operating the user input device;

(5) collecting at least one selection from step (4) and communicating, via the network, said selection to at least one computer associated with a positively priced information provider; and

(6) allowing the user to pay for the selected positively priced information at least in part using compensation provided in step (3).

. . .

QUESTIONS FOR DISCUSSION

1. *Broad claims and obviousness.* After reading these sample patents, do you agree with numerous commentators who argue that business method patents have been wrongly granted with broadly sweeping claims that, if ever enforced, would severely injure Internet commerce? What are the implications of allowing broad claims in Internet-related patents, as compared to broad claims in more traditional technologies?

One author has criticized the breadth of the Priceline.com patent claims as follows:

. . . This patent could permit Priceline.com to exclude all other business methods in which buyers propose a price for a product or service, and then sellers bid to supply it. The reach of this patent could extend beyond the airfare context (as it is currently being used) to all industries. Accordingly, it would seem as though the scope of the patent would render it too broad to satisfy the various scope provisions. The issuance of the Priceline.com patent suggests that the USPTO is willing to permit potential patentees to claim extremely broad matter in the Internet context.

The Priceline.com patent also represents a good example of the lenient treatment of the nonobviousness requirement as applied to Internet business methods. Although reverse Dutch Auctions have existed for centuries, the USPTO did not find that it was obvious for Priceline.com to apply the reverse Dutch Auction method to the Internet. The issuance of this patent implies that it would not be obvious for a firm to take any standard business practice and apply it to the Internet. Such a loose interpretation of the nonobviousness doctrine implies that the nonobviousness requirement is no longer being used as a significant bar on commonplace inventions. As such, this interpretation seems to pave the way for the issuance of many Internet business method patents on seemingly regular business methods.

Jared Earl Grusd, *Internet Business Methods: What Role Does and Should Patent Law Play?*, 4 VA. J.L. & TECH. 9, 28–29 (1999).

Do you agree that, pushed to its logical extreme, Claim One of the Priceline patent implies that "any standard business practice" would become patentable when applied to the Internet? If not, can you justify the PTO's determination that the Priceline method satisfies the requirement of non-obviousness?

In October 1999, Priceline.com filed suit against Expedia.com, claiming that Expedia's "Price-Matcher" service, which allowed customers to place bids on airline tickets and hotel rooms, violated Priceline's patent. After a little over a year, the two companies settled the lawsuit in a deal that requires Expedia to pay Priceline royalties for the right to continue to offer its "Price-Matcher" service.

Given the widespread condemnation of the Priceline.com patent, the questionable breadth of the claim, and the issue of possible obviousness, why would Expedia, in which Microsoft at the time held a majority stake, settle the lawsuit rather than seek to have the patent invalidated?

2. *Business method patent factory.* Walker Digital Corp., a creation of Jay Walker, the founder of Priceline.com, is a self-styled laboratory for new business models. The company's business is devising, obtaining, and marketing business method patents of all kinds. According to the company's website, as of late 2005 the company held more than 200 patents. *See* www.walkerdigital.com. The patents range from an automated system for monitoring hospital patients and calling in an expert when needed, to controlling the prices charged by a vending machine. Is Walker Digital's business model the wave of the future? Is it a development that proves our patent system has gone astray in declaring business methods to be propertizable?

3. *Strategic use of Internet commerce patents.* Priceline.com patented its reverse auction business method to solidify its first-mover advantage on the Internet, creating a legal monopoly of its market and blocking out competitors. Arguably, this strategy worked well—it (initially) bolstered investor confidence and enabled Priceline to maintain a strong hold on the reverse-auction market. Most importantly, competitors did not opt to challenge the patent.

As with all patents, Internet business method patents can be used *offensively*, to stop infringing uses by a company's competitors, or *defensively*, as part of settlement or licensing negotiations with a competitor. Competitors frequently enter into agreements to "live and let live" with respect to patent infringement, in order to avoid costly litigation.

The following excerpt addresses some possible defensive and offensive uses of a business's patent portfolio, and the misguided incentive structure that often results. The excerpt suggests that for large businesses, procuring patents is less about promoting progress and innovation than it is about preventing lawsuits:

> In the high-technology age, the patent has become more than a way to protect legitimate intellectual property. It's often the legal equivalent of a Cold War nuclear stockpile: Sue me over your patents and I'll sue you over mine.
>
> "Internet-involved enterprises of all types continue building their own patent portfolios, for both offensive and defensive purposes," said intellectual property attorney Alan Fisch. . . .
>
> As a weapon against competitors, a patent can be a potent offense. "If you have a patent and approach someone else, you can get an injunction [and] cause a lot of harm up front," [Gregory] Aharonian said.
>
> As a result, there's little incentive for companies not to patent everything they can.
>
> "People will throw something into the patent office just to see if they can get something issued," [patent attorney Virginia] Medlen said. "Once it's issued, under law the presumption is that it's valid. And to knock it down the challenger has to produce clear and convincing evidence that the patent is not valid, and that clear and convincing evidence is very difficult to prove."
>
> That's where the defensive counter-patent comes in.
>
> A judge faced with two similar, but competing patents is likely to tell the opponents to settle the issue themselves, rather than try to wade through the subtle differences in court.
>
> "[The counter-patent] is a relatively inexpensive way to present evidence of invalidity," Medlen said. . . .
>
> . . . One industry source said the practice is so common that some big-name companies chock full of communications technology patents have struck agreements not to sue each other. Their other competitors may not be so lucky.

Chris Oakes, *Patently Absurd*, WIRED NEWS (Mar. 3, 2000), www.wired.com/news/politics/0,1283,34695,00.html.

Would it be appropriate to discourage these sorts of settlements and cross-licensing? Though it is debatable whether the current system is truly rewarding and promoting innovation, as it is supposed to, allowing businesses to use patents as defensive bargaining chips might reduce the costs of litigation to both private parties and the courts. *See, e.g.,* Carl Shapiro, *Navigating the Patent Thicket: Cross Licenses, Patent Pools, and Standard Setting, in* INNOVATION POLICY AND THE ECONOMY, VOL. I (Adam B. Jaffe, Josh Lerner, & Scott Stern eds., 2001).

VI. PATENT LITIGATION: AMAZON.COM V. BARNESANDNOBLE.COM

Despite the prevalence of strategic behavior and cross-licensing to settle disputes, some cases do go to trial. To show infringement of an Internet business method patent, a plaintiff must demonstrate that the defendant's conduct matches up exactly to *all* of the elements of one (or more) of the plaintiff's patent claims—that is, that the claim "reads on" the conduct. In addition, a court might find infringement under the "doctrine of equivalents" even if no literal infringement has occurred. The doctrine of equivalents prevents would-be infringers from escaping liability by making trivial changes but copying the essence of the invention. Nonetheless, many business method patents seem to present a fairly easy opportunity to "design around" to avoid infringement.

Amazon.com brought an infringement action against Barnesandnoble.com, alleging that the latter's "Express Lane" checkout system infringed its "One-Click" business method patent, excerpted in Part V(A), *supra*. In the district court, Amazon sought and obtained a preliminary injunction preventing Barnes & Noble from using its "Express Lane" checkout. *See Amazon.com, Inc. v. Barnesandnoble.com, Inc.*, 73 F.Supp.2d 1228 (W.D.Wash.1999).

The district court rejected Barnesandnoble.com's argument that the Amazon.com patent was invalid as obvious and anticipated by the relevant prior art. After analyzing the prior art references, the court found that there were sufficient "differences between each of the prior art references cited by Defendants and the method and system described in the claims of the '411 patent" and that there was no evidence "regarding a teaching, suggestion, or motivation in the prior art that would lead one of ordinary skill in the art of e-commerce to combine the references," *id.* at 1235, which is the kind of evidence needed to establish invalidity on the ground of obviousness.

Further, Amazon.com presented other evidence of non-obviousness that the court found very convincing: "[D]espite their experience with prior art shopping cart models of on-line purchasing, both sides' technical experts acknowledged that they had never conceived of the invention." *Id.* at 1236–37. One expert testified that he found the Amazon.com One-Click technology to be "a huge leap from what was done in the past" and testified that "I've been working in electronic commerce for years now. And I've never thought of the idea of being able to turn a shopping cart or take the idea of clicking on an item and suddenly having the item ship—having the complete process done." *Id.* at 1237. The district court held that the One-Click patent "addressed an unsolved need that had been long-felt (at least in the relatively short period of time that e-commerce has existed), namely streamlining the on-line ordering process to reduce the high percentage of orders that are begun but never completed, i.e., abandoned shopping carts." *Id.* One final objective indicator of non-obviousness cited by the district court was the vast commercial success of the one-click ordering method, as used by both Amazon.com and Barnesandnoble.com. *Id.*

After Barnesandnoble.com lost on its claim of invalidity, there was little evidence to dispute that it had directly copied from Amazon.com. Barnesandnoble.com had consistently promoted its "Express Lane" feature as "One Click Ordering," both internally and to customers. The court found that continuing infringement by Barnesandnoble.com would irreparably harm Amazon.com. The court noted that "customers become loyal to sites with which they become familiar," and allowing Barnesandnoble.com to continue benefiting from the "easy-to-use and easy-to-learn consumer interfaces" Amazon.com had invented would be extremely detrimental to Amazon.com's commercial success. *Id.* at 1238. An important factor weighing in favor of issuing the injunction was the approaching holiday season:

> As many as 10 million new users are expected to make their first on-line purchases during the 1999 holiday season. Millions of these new customers are

likely to be shopping at Amazon.com and Barnesandnoble.com for the first time. Long-term success in e-commerce depends on establishing positive relationships with these new on-line buyers now, to preserve the ability to compete effectively for future sales, which by some estimates will reach $78 billion by the year 2003.

Id. The district court granted Amazon.com's request for a preliminary injunction requiring Barnesandnoble.com to remove the "Express Lane" feature in time for holiday ordering. The injunction, as we will see shortly, was overturned on appeal.

Following the issuance of the preliminary injunction in Amazon.com's favor, Barnesandnoble.com changed its checkout to a two-click scheme. The decision, however, was widely criticized.

An ad-hoc Internet-based opposition emerged to express outrage over Amazon's actions. The one-click concept, they argued, should be unpatentable—it's an utterly obvious use of cookies, which existed long before Amazon's patent application. Richard Stallman, president of the Free Software Foundation and a ringleader of the backlash, launched a boycott against the company, proclaiming that "foolish government policies gave Amazon the opportunity—but an opportunity is not an excuse. Amazon made the choice to obtain this patent, and the choice to use it in court for aggression. The ultimate moral responsibility for Amazon's actions lies with Amazon's executives."

Stallman's boycott didn't get much attention until late February, when Amazon announced yet another business-method patent, this one for its "affiliate program," a revenue-sharing scheme in which other sites refer customers to Amazon's store via Web links. Again, protesters viewed the patent as obvious and absurdly broad. Tim O'Reilly, a prominent publisher of computer books, posted an open letter on his website denouncing Amazon, gathering 10,000 protest signatures in a few days. A cowed Jeff Bezos [Amazon's founder and CEO] responded with an open letter of his own, declining to "give up our patents unilaterally," but expressing concern about the role of patents in the new economy and calling for major patent reform.

Bezos' move turned patents into front-page news. In March, the PTO bowed to the mounting pressure and announced a few quick-fix changes: among them, increased supervision for the patent examiners who oversee business-method patent applications, as well as a promise to hold an open discussion on patent reform with Internet leaders this summer.

Evan Ratliff, *Patent Upending*, WIRED, June 2000, www.wired.com/wired/archive/8.06/patents_pr.html.

QUESTIONS FOR DISCUSSION

1. *District court's analysis.* Do you agree with the district court's analysis of validity and irreparable harm? Do you believe that there was really a "long-felt" need in e-commerce to come up with a more efficient ordering method? If so, how would the existence of such a long-felt need give rise to an inference that Amazon.com's one-click method was non-obvious when invented? Should the commercial success of one-click ordering also be considered as evidence of non-obviousness? Courts routinely consider long-felt need and commercial success in evaluating non-obviousness. But is it possible to distinguish between the commercial success of the one-click method and Amazon.com's business method generally? Were people coming to the site because of the novel method of ordering, or because of the nature of the business?

2. *Responsibility to play nice?* Stallman seems to demand that Amazon.com pursue only patent applications that it truly believes are legitimate. But, if the patent examiner is willing to grant a patent, why would Amazon.com be ethically obligated to refuse it? Can convincing distinctions be drawn between companies that seek business method patents on any possible innovation, and *any* company that attempts to draft its application such that as much as possible is claimed, with as little possible disclosure, when applying for a patent? Where should the responsibility for assuring patent validity lie—with the applicant? the examiner? Congress? the courts?

The district court's ruling on validity was overturned on appeal. While the Federal Circuit agreed that Amazon.com had made a convincing case for infringement, it held that Barnesandnoble.com had raised a substantial question as to the validity of the "One-Click" patent, and remanded the case for further consideration.

Amazon.com, Inc. v. Barnesandnoble.com, Inc.
239 F.3d 1343 (Fed.Cir.2001).

■ CLEVENGER, CIRCUIT JUDGE.

This is a patent infringement suit brought by Amazon.com, Inc. ("Amazon") against barnesandnoble.com, inc., and barnesandnoble.com llc (together, "BN"). Amazon moved for a preliminary injunction to prohibit BN's use of a feature of its website called "Express Lane." BN resisted the preliminary injunction on several grounds, including that its Express Lane feature did not infringe the claims of Amazon's patent, and that substantial questions exist as to the validity of Amazon's patent. The United States District Court for the Western District of Washington rejected BN's contentions. Instead, the district court held that Amazon had presented a case showing a likelihood of infringement by BN, and that BN's challenges to the validity of the patent in suit lacked sufficient merit to avoid awarding extraordinary preliminary injunctive relief to Amazon. The district court granted Amazon's motion, and now BN brings its timely appeal from the order entering the preliminary injunction. We have jurisdiction to review the district court's order under 28 U.S.C. § 1292(c)(1) (1994).

After careful review of the district court's opinion, the record, and the arguments advanced by the parties, we conclude that BN has mounted a substantial challenge to the validity of the patent in suit. Because Amazon is not entitled to preliminary injunctive relief under these circumstances, we vacate the order of the district court that set the preliminary injunction in place and remand the case for further proceedings.

I

This case involves United States Patent No. 5,960,411 ("the '411 patent"), which issued on September 28, 1999, and is assigned to Amazon. On October 21, 1999, Amazon brought suit against BN alleging infringement of the patent and seeking a preliminary injunction.

Amazon's patent is directed to a method and system for "single action" ordering of items in a client/server environment such as the Internet. In the context of the '411 patent, a client/server environment describes the relationship between two computer systems in which a program executing on a client computer system makes a service request from another program executing on a server computer system, which fulfills the request. Typically, the client computer system and the server computer system are located remotely from each other and communicate via a data communication network.

The '411 patent describes a method and system in which a consumer can complete a purchase order for an item via an electronic network using only a "single action," such as the click of a computer mouse button on the client computer system. Amazon developed the patent to cope with what it considered to be frustrations presented by what is known as the "shopping cart model" purchase system for electronic commerce purchasing events. In previous incarnations of the shopping cart model, a purchaser using a client computer system (such as a personal computer executing a web browser program) could select an item from an electronic catalog, typically by clicking on an "Add to Shopping Cart" icon, thereby placing the item in the "virtual" shopping cart. Other items from the catalog could be added to the shopping cart in the same manner. When the shopper completed the selecting process, the electronic commercial event would move to the check-out counter, so to speak. Then, information regarding the purchaser's identity, billing and shipping addresses, and credit payment method would be inserted into the transactional information base by the soon-to-be purchaser. Finally, the purchaser would "click" on a button displayed on the screen or somehow issue a command to execute the completed order, and the server computer system would verify and store the information concerning the transaction.

As is evident from the foregoing, an electronic commerce purchaser using the shopping cart model is required to perform several actions before achieving the ultimate goal of the placed order. The '411 patent sought to reduce the number of actions required from a consumer to effect a placed order. In the words of the written description of the '411 patent:

> The present invention provides a method and system for single-action ordering of items in a client/server environment. The single-action ordering system of the present invention reduces the number of purchaser interactions needed to place an order and reduces the amount of sensitive information that is transmitted between a client system and a server system.

How, one may ask, is the number of purchaser interactions reduced? The answer is that the number of purchaser interactions is reduced because the purchaser has previously visited the seller's website and has previously entered into the database of the seller all of the required billing and shipping information that is needed to effect a sales transaction. Thereafter, when the purchaser visits the seller's website and wishes to purchase a product from that site, the patent specifies that only a single action is necessary to place the order for the item. In the words of the written description, "once the description of an item is displayed, the purchaser need only take a single action to place the order to purchase that item."

II

. . . We set forth below the text of the claims pertinent to our deliberations (*i.e.*, claims 1, 2, 6, 9, and 11), with emphasis added to highlight the disputed claim terms:

[Claim 1 is set forth in Part V(A), *supra*. Claims 2, 6, 9, and 11 are drawn to narrower versions of the one-click method. The court emphasizes the term "single action" as used in each claim.]

The district court interpreted the key "single action" claim limitation, which appears in each of the pertinent claims, to mean:

> The term "single action" is not defined by the patent specification. . . . As a result, the term "single action" as used in the '411 patent appears to refer to one action (such as clicking a mouse button) that a user takes to purchase an item once the following information is displayed to the user: (1) a description of the item; and (2) a description of the single action the user must take to complete a purchase order for that item.

With this interpretation of the key claim limitation in hand, the district court turned to BN's accused ordering system. BN's short-cut ordering system, called "Express Lane," like the system contemplated by the patent, contains previously entered billing and shipping information for the customer. In one implementation, after a person is presented with BN's initial web page (referred to as the "menu page"), the person can click on an icon on the menu page to get to what is called the "product page." BN's product page displays an image and a description of the selected product, and also presents the person with a description of a single action that can be taken to complete a purchase order for the item. If the single action described is taken, for example by a mouse click, the person will have effected a purchase order using BN's Express Lane feature.

BN's Express Lane thus presents a product page that contains the description of the item to be purchased and a "description" of the single action to be taken to effect placement of the order. Because only a single action need be taken to complete the purchase order once the product page is displayed, the district court concluded that Amazon had made a showing of likelihood of success on its allegation of patent infringement.

In response to BN's contention that substantial questions exist as to the validity of the '411 patent, the district court reviewed the prior art references upon which BN's validity challenge rested. The district court concluded that none of the prior art references anticipated the claims of the '411 patent under 35 U.S.C. § 102 (1994) or rendered the claimed invention obvious under 35 U.S.C. § 103 (1994).

III

. . . As the moving party, Amazon is entitled to a preliminary injunction if it can succeed in showing: (1) a reasonable likelihood of success on the merits; (2) irreparable harm if an injunction is not granted; (3) a balance of hardships tipping in its favor; and (4) the injunction's favorable impact on the public interest. . . . Irreparable harm is presumed when a clear showing of patent validity and infringement has been made. . . .

Our case law and logic both require that a movant cannot be granted a preliminary injunction unless it establishes *both* of the first two factors, *i.e.*, likelihood of success on the merits and irreparable harm. . . .

In order to demonstrate a likelihood of success on the merits, Amazon must show that, in light of the presumptions and burdens that will inhere at trial on the merits, (1) Amazon will likely prove that BN infringes the '411 patent, and (2) Amazon's infringement claim will likely withstand BN's challenges to the validity and enforceability of the '411 patent. *Genentech, Inc. v. Novo Nordisk, A/S*, 108 F.3d 1361, 1364 (Fed.Cir.1997). If BN raises a substantial question concerning either infringement or validity, *i.e.*, asserts an infringement or invalidity defense that the patentee cannot prove "lacks substantial merit," the preliminary injunction should not issue. *Id.*

Of course, whether performed at the preliminary injunction stage or at some later stage in the course of a particular case, infringement and validity analyses must be performed on a claim-by-claim basis. . . .

Both infringement and validity are at issue in this appeal. It is well settled that an infringement analysis involves two steps: the claim scope is first determined, and then the properly construed claim is compared with the accused device to determine whether all of the claim limitations are present either literally or by a substantial equivalent. . . .

Only when a claim is properly understood can a determination be made whether the claim "reads on" an accused device or method, or whether the prior art anticipates and/or renders obvious the claimed invention. Because the claims of a patent measure the invention at issue, the claims must be interpreted and given the same meaning for purposes of both validity and infringement analyses. . . .

IV

BN contends on appeal that the district court committed legal errors that undermine the legitimacy of the preliminary injunction. In particular, BN asserts that the district court construed key claim limitations one way for purposes of its infringement analysis, and another way when considering BN's validity challenges. BN asserts that under a consistent claim interpretation, its Express Lane feature either does not infringe the '411 patent, or that if the patent is interpreted so as to support the charge of infringement, then the claims of the patent are subject to a severe validity challenge. When the key claim limitations are properly interpreted, BN thus asserts, it will be clear that Amazon is not likely to succeed on the merits of its infringement claim, or that BN has succeeded in calling the validity of the '411 patent into serious question. In addition, BN asserts that the district court misunderstood the teaching of the prior art references, thereby committing clear error in the factual predicates it established for comprehension of the prior art references.

Amazon understandably aligns itself with the district court, asserting that no error of claim interpretation and no clear error in fact-finding has occurred that would undermine the grant of the preliminary injunction. We thus turn to the legal gist of this appeal.

V

It is clear from the district court's opinion that the meaning it ascribed to the "single action" limitation includes a temporal consideration. The "single action" to be taken to complete the purchase order, according to the district court, only occurs after other events have transpired. These preliminary events required pursuant to the district court's claim interpretation are the presentation of a description of the item to be purchased and the presentation of the single action the user must take to complete the purchase order for the item.

. . .

Our analysis begins with the plain language of the claims themselves. The term "single action" appears in the independent claims of the '411 patent in the following forms: "in response to only a single action being performed" (claims 1 and 9), "single-action ordering component" (claims 1, 6, and 9), "in response to performance of only a single action" (claim 6), "in response to only the indicated single action being performed" (claim 11), and "displaying an indication of a single action that is to be performed to order the identified item" (claim 11).

In claims 1, 6, and 11, the context of the claim makes it clear that the single action is performed after some information about the item is displayed. Claim 1 provides for "displaying information identifying the item," and then immediately recites that "in response to only a single action being performed," a request to purchase the item is sent to a server system. Claim 6 provides for "a display component for displaying information identifying the item," and then immediately recites "the single action ordering component that in response to performance of only a single action" sends a request to purchase the item to a server system. Claim 11 provides for "displaying information identifying the item and displaying an indication of the single action," and then immediately recites that "in response to only the indicated single action being performed" a request to purchase the item is sent to a server system. The context also indicates that the single action is performed, or is capable of being performed, after information about the item is displayed, without any intervening action. Nothing suggests, however, that the single action must be performed after every display or even immediately after the first display of information. Claim 9 does not explicitly provide for displaying information. It merely recites that a request to order an item is "sent in response to only a single action being performed." However, although claim 9 does not recite "displaying," the written description defines the claim 9 language of "single action being performed" to require that information has been displayed.

The ordinary meaning of "single action" as used in the various claims is straightforward, but the phrase alone does not indicate when to start counting actions. Therefore, we must look first to the written description of the '411 patent for further guidance.

The written description supports a construction that after information is "displayed," single-action ordering is an option available to the user, and the counting falls within the scope of the claim when single-action ordering is actually selected by the user. To the extent that the claims are considered ambiguous on this point, the written description defines "single action" to require as much. In the Summary of the Invention, the written description describes an embodiment that "displays information that identifies the item and displays an indication of an action . . . [and] [i]n response to the indicated action being performed" orders the item. Similarly, in the Detailed Description of the Invention, the written description states that "[o]nce the description of an item is displayed, the purchaser need only take a single action." This is consistent for all of the disclosed embodiments.

Therefore, neither the written description nor the plain meaning of the claims require that single action ordering be possible after each and every display of information (or even immediately after the first display of information). The plain language of the claims and the written description require only that single action ordering be possible after some display of information. Indeed, the written description allows for and suggests the possibility that previous displays of information will have occurred before the display immediately preceding an order.

. . .

VI

A

When the correct meaning of the single action limitation is read on the accused BN system, it becomes apparent that the limitations of claim 1 are likely met by the accused system. The evidence on the record concerning the operation of BN's "Express Lane" feature is not in dispute. At the time that the '411 patent was issued, BN offered customers two purchasing options. One was called "Shopping Cart," and the other was called "Express Lane." The Shopping Cart option involved the steps of adding items to a "virtual" shopping cart and then "checking out" to complete the purchase. In contrast, the Express Lane option allowed customers who had registered for the feature to purchase items simply by "clicking" on the "Express Lane" button provided on the "detail page" or "product page" describing and identifying the book or other item to be purchased. The text beneath the Express Lane button invited users to "Buy it now with just 1 click!"

BN's allegedly infringing website thus may be characterized as having "page 1," (the "menu" page) which displays a catalog listing several items but which does not contain an "order" icon, and "page 2," (the "product" or "detail" page) which includes information on one item and also shows an order icon. Someone shopping at this website would look at the catalog on page 1 and perform a first click to go to page 2. Once at page 2, a second click on the ordering icon would cause the order request to be sent. Under the claim construction set forth herein, BN likely infringes claim 1 because on page 2, the item is there displayed (meeting step 1 of the claim) and only a single action thereafter causes the order request to be transmitted (meeting step 2). The method implemented on page 1 of the BN website does not infringe, but the method on page 2 does. This has nothing to do with the state of mind of the purchaser, but simply reflects the ordinary meaning of the words of the claim in the context of the written description and in light of the prosecution history.

. . .

E

After full review of the record before us, we conclude that under a proper claim interpretation, Amazon has made the showing that it is likely to succeed at trial on its infringement case. Given that we conclude that Amazon has demonstrated likely literal infringement of at least the four independent claims in the '411 patent, we need not consider infringement under the doctrine of equivalents. The question remaining, however, is whether the district court correctly determined that BN failed to mount a substantial challenge to the validity of the claims in the '411 patent.

VII

The district court considered, but ultimately rejected, the potentially invalidating impact of several prior art references cited by BN. Because the district court determined that BN likely infringed all of the asserted claims, it did not focus its analysis of the validity issue on any particular claim. Instead, in its validity analysis, the district court appears to have primarily directed its attention to determining whether the references cited by BN implemented the single action limitation.

. . .

In this case, we find that the district court committed clear error by misreading the factual content of the prior art references cited by BN and by failing to recognize that BN had raised a substantial question of invalidity of the asserted claims in view of these prior art references.

Validity challenges during preliminary injunction proceedings can be successful, that is, they may raise substantial questions of invalidity, on evidence that would not suffice to support a judgment of invalidity at trial. *See, e.g., Helifix Ltd. v. Blok–Lok, Ltd.*, 208 F.3d 1339, 1352 (Fed.Cir.2000) (holding that the allegedly anticipatory prior art references sufficiently raised a question of invalidity to deny a preliminary injunction, even though summary judgment of anticipation based on the same references was not supported). The test for invalidity at trial is by evidence that is clear and convincing. *WMS Gaming, Inc. v. Int'l Game Tech.*, 184 F.3d 1339, 1355 (Fed.Cir.1999). To succeed with a summary judgment motion of invalidity, for example, the movant must demonstrate a lack of genuine dispute about material facts and show that the facts not in dispute are clear and convincing in demonstrating invalidity. *Robotic Vision Sys., Inc. v. View Eng'g, Inc.*, 112 F.3d 1163, 1165 (Fed.Cir.1997). In resisting a preliminary injunction, however, one need not make out a case of actual invalidity. Vulnerability is the issue at the preliminary injunction stage, while validity is the issue at trial. The showing of a substantial question as to invalidity thus requires less proof than the clear and convincing showing necessary to establish invalidity itself. That this is so is plain from our cases.

. . .

When the heft of the asserted prior art is assessed in light of the correct legal standards, we conclude that BN has mounted a serious challenge to the validity of Amazon's patent. We hasten to add, however, that this conclusion only undermines the prerequisite for entry of a preliminary injunction. Our decision today on the validity issue in no way resolves the ultimate question of invalidity. That is a matter for resolution at trial. It remains to be learned whether there are other references that may be cited against the patent, and it surely remains to be learned whether any shortcomings in BN's initial preliminary validity challenge will be magnified or dissipated at trial. All we hold, in the meantime, is that BN cast enough doubt on the validity of the '411 patent to avoid a preliminary injunction, and that the validity issue should be resolved finally at trial.

A

One of the references cited by BN was the "CompuServe Trend System." The undisputed evidence indicates that in the mid–1990s, CompuServe offered a service called "Trend" whereby CompuServe subscribers could obtain stock charts for a surcharge of 50 cents per chart. Before the district court, BN argued that this system anticipated claim 11 of the '411 patent. The district court failed to recognize the substantial question of invalidity raised by BN in citing the CompuServe Trend reference, in that this system appears to have used "single action ordering technology" within the scope of the claims in the '411 patent.

First, the district court dismissed the significance of this system partly on the basis that "[t]he CompuServe system was not a world wide web application." This distinction is irrelevant, since none of the claims mention either the Internet or the World Wide Web (with the possible exception of dependent claim 15, which mentions HTML, a program commonly associated with both the Internet and the World Wide Web). Moreover, the '411 patent specification explicitly notes that "[o]ne skilled in the art would appreciate that the single-action ordering techniques can be used in various environments other than the Internet."

More importantly, one of the screen shots in the record . . . indicates that with the CompuServe Trend system, once the "item" to be purchased (*i.e.*, a stock chart) has been displayed (by typing in a valid stock symbol), only a single action (*i.e.*, a single mouse click on the button labeled "Chart ($.50)") is required to obtain immediate electronic delivery (*i.e.*, "fulfillment") of the item. Once the button labeled "Chart ($.50)" was activated by a purchaser, an electronic version of the requested stock chart would be transmitted to the purchaser and displayed on the purchaser's computer screen, and an automatic process to charge the purchaser's account 50 cents for the transaction would be initiated. In terms of the language of claims 2 and 11 in the CompuServe Trend system, the item to be ordered is "displayed" when the screen echoes back the characters of the stock symbol typed in by the purchaser before clicking on the ordering button.

> . . .

. . . Amazon's counsel claimed that the CompuServe Trend system was different from the claims of the '411 patent because it required a user to "log in" at the beginning of each session, and therefore would not send the claimed "identifier" along with a request to purchase each item. However, claim 11 does not require transmission of an identifier along with a request to order an item. This requirement is found only in claims 1, 6, and 9, and their respective dependent claims.

On its face, the CompuServe Trend reference does not mention transmission of the claimed identifier along with a request to purchase each item. Nor does the evidence in the record at this stage indicate that the CompuServe Trend system transmitted such an identifier. BN has therefore not demonstrated that the CompuServe Trend reference anticipates the asserted claims of the '411 patent requiring transmission of such an identifier with the degree of precision necessary to obtain summary judgment on this point. However, as noted above, validity challenges during preliminary injunction proceedings can be successful on evidence that would not suffice to support a judgment of invalidity at trial. *See Helifix*, 208 F.3d at 1352. The record in this case is simply not yet developed to the point where a determination can be made whether the CompuServe Trend system transmits the claimed identifier along with a request to order an item, or whether this limitation is obvious in view of the prior art. . . .

. . .

In view of the above, we conclude that the district court erred in failing to recognize that the CompuServe Trend reference raises a substantial question of invalidity. Whether the CompuServe Trend reference either anticipates and/or renders obvious the claimed invention in view of the knowledge of one of ordinary skill in the relevant art is a matter for decision at trial.

B

In addition to the CompuServe Trend system, other prior art references were cited by BN, but ultimately rejected by the district court. For example, BN's expert, Dr. Lockwood, testified that he developed an on-line ordering system called "Web–Basket" in or around August 1996. The Web–Basket system appears to be an embodiment of a "shopping cart ordering component": it requires users to accumulate items into a virtual shopping basket and to check these items out when they are finished shopping. Because it is an implementation of a shopping cart model, Web Basket requires several confirmation steps for even pre-registered users to complete their purchases.

However, despite the fact that Web–Basket is an embodiment of a shopping cart model, it is undisputed that Web–Basket implemented the Internet Engineering Task Force ("IETF") draft "cookie" specification, and stored a customer identifier in a cookie for use by a web server to retrieve information from a database. In other words, when a user first visited the Web–Basket site, a cookie (*i.e.*, a file stored by the server system on the client system for subsequent use) was used to store an identifier on the user's computer. The first time that a user purchased an item on the Web–Basket site, the information entered by the user necessary to complete the purchase (*e.g.*, name, address) would be stored in a database on the server system indexed by an identifier stored in the cookie on the client system. On subsequent visits, the cookie could be used to retrieve the user identifier, which would serve as the key to retrieve the user's information from the database on the server system.

At the preliminary injunction stage, based on Dr. Lockwood's declaration and testimony during the hearing, BN argued that the Web–Basket reference — combined with the knowledge of one of ordinary skill in the art at the relevant time — renders obvious the claimed invention.

The district court concluded that the Web–Basket system was "inconsistent with the single-action requirements of the '411 patent" because "it requires a multiple-step ordering process from the time that an item to be purchased is displayed." However, as discussed earlier, the undisputed evidence demonstrates that the accused BN Express Lane feature also requires a multiple-step ordering process (*i.e.*, at least two "clicks") *from the time that an item to be purchased is first displayed on the menu page*, yet the district court concluded that BN's Express Lane feature infringed all of the asserted claims of the '411 patent. The district court's failure to recognize the inconsistency in these two conclusions was erroneous.

Moreover, the district court did not address the "cookie" aspects of the Web–Basket reference, and failed to recognize that a reasonable jury could find that the step of storing purchaser data on the server system for subsequent retrieval indexed by an identifier transmitted from the client system was anticipated and/or rendered obvious by the Web–Basket reference.

. . . "[T]he district court apparently based its conclusion of nonobviousness on Dr. Lockwood's "admission" that he personally never thought of combining or modifying the prior art to come up with the claimed "single action" invention. This approach was erroneous as a matter of law. Whatever Dr. Lockwood did or did not *personally* realize at the time based on his actual knowledge is irrelevant. The relevant inquiry is what a hypothetical ordinarily skilled artisan would have gleaned from the cited references at the time that the patent application leading to the '411 patent was filed. *See Kimberly–Clark Corp. v. Johnson & Johnson*, 745 F.2d 1437, 1453 (Fed.Cir.1984) (discussing the origin and significance of the hypothetical ordinarily skilled artisan in detail).

C

BN also presented as a prior art reference an excerpt from a book written by Magdalena Yesil entitled *Creating the Virtual Store* that was copyrighted in 1996. Before the district court, BN argued that this reference anticipated every limitation of claim 11. Before this court, BN also alleges that many other claim limitations are disclosed in the reference, but that there was insufficient time to prepare testimony concerning these limitations, given the district court's accelerated briefing and hearing schedule at the preliminary injunction stage.

In general terms, the reference apparently discusses software to implement a shopping cart ordering model. However, BN focuses on the following passage from Appendix F of the book:

Instant Buy Option

Merchants also can provide shoppers with an Instant Buy button for some or all items, enabling them to skip check out review. This provides added appeal for customers who already know the single item they want to purchase during their shopping excursion.

The district court dismissed the significance of this passage, stating that "[r]ead in context, the few lines relied on by Defendants appear to describe only the elimination of the checkout review step, leaving at least two other required steps to complete a purchase." However, the district court failed to recognize that a reasonable jury could find that this passage provides a motivation to modify shopping cart ordering software to skip unnecessary steps. Thus, we find that this passage, viewed in light of the rest of the reference and the other prior art references cited by BN, raises a substantial question of validity with respect to the asserted claims of the '411 patent.

D

Another reference cited by BN, a print-out from a web page describing the "Oliver's Market" ordering system, generally describes a prior art multi-step shopping cart model. BN argued that this reference anticipates at least claim 9. The reference begins with an intriguing sentence:

A single click on its picture is all it takes to order an item.

Read in context, the quote emphasizes how easy it is to order things on-line. The district court failed to recognize that a reasonable jury could find that this sentence provides a motivation to modify a shopping cart model to implement "single-click" ordering as claimed in the '411 patent. In addition, the district court failed to recognize that other passages from this reference could be construed by a reasonable jury as anticipating and/or rendering obvious the allegedly novel "single action ordering technology" of the '411 patent. For example, the reference states that "[o]ur solution allows one-click ordering anywhere you see a product picture or a price." The reference also describes a system in which a user's identifying information (*e.g.*, username and password) and purchasing information (*e.g.*, name, phone number, payment method, delivery address) is captured and stored in a database "the very first time a user clicks on an item to order," and in which a corresponding cookie is stored on the client system. In this system, the stored information may be retrieved automatically during subsequent visits by reading the cookie. All of these passages further support BN's argument that a substantial question of validity is raised by this prior art reference, either alone or in combination with the other cited references.

E

. . .

The district court also cited certain "secondary considerations" to support its conclusion of nonobviousness. Specifically, the district court cited (1) "copying of the invention" by BN and other e-commerce retailers following Amazon's introduction of its "1–Click®" feature, and (2) "the need to solve the problem of abandoned shopping carts." First, we note that evidence of copying Amazon's "1–Click®" feature is legally irrelevant unless the "1–Click®" feature is shown to be an embodiment of the claims. To the extent Amazon can demonstrate that its "1–

Click®'' feature embodies any asserted claims of the '411 patent under the correct claim interpretation, evidence of copying by BN and others is not sufficient to demonstrate nonobviousness of the claimed invention, in view of the substantial question of validity raised by the prior art references cited by BN and discussed herein.

With respect to the abandoned shopping carts, this problem is not even mentioned in the '411 patent. Moreover, Amazon did not submit any evidence to show either that its commercial success was related to the "1-Click®" ordering feature, or that single-action ordering caused a reduction in the number of abandoned shopping carts. Therefore, we fail to see how this "consideration" supports Amazon's nonobviousness argument.

CONCLUSION

While it appears on the record before us that Amazon has carried its burden with respect to demonstrating the likelihood of success on infringement, it is also true that BN has raised substantial questions as to the validity of the '411 patent. For that reason, we must conclude that the necessary prerequisites for entry of a preliminary injunction are presently lacking. We therefore vacate the preliminary injunction and remand the case for further proceedings.

EXTENSIONS

More patent litigation. Could anyone claim a patent on such a fundamental element of online communication as the hyperlink? British Telecommunications did. In 1977, BT (then the monopoly provider of telephone service in the United Kingdom) applied for a U.S. patent on a method for providing remote users with access to textual information via a telephone network. After a lengthy prosecution history, a patent was granted in 1989. Some years later, BT adopted the view that its patent covered hyperlinks. In 2000, it filed an infringement action against Prodigy Communications Corp., as a test case, with the intention of enforcing the patent against other Internet service providers if successful.

In *British Telecommunications plc v. Prodigy Communications Corp.*, 217 F.Supp.2d 399 (S.D.N.Y.2002), the district court denied BT's claim, granting summary judgment to Prodigy. The key claims of the patent, as the court construed them, described a system that (1) allowed multiple users at remote locations access to data stored on a "central computer"; (2) maintained the data on the central computer in the form of paired "blocks" of information, the first block containing the material to be displayed, and the second block containing addresses of other blocks of information related to the first block; and (3) maintained the "complete address" of each block of information.

The court held that the infringement claim failed on each of these points, since: (1) the Internet does not employ any "central computer" that remote computers may access; in particular, a web server does not constitute such a computer; (2) HTML code is not separated into distinct blocks, but rather intermingles the information to be displayed with the tags conveying formatting and linking information; and (3) a website's URL is not its "complete address," since it must be resolved into an IP address to be functional.

In another case, a holder of patents relating to online sales methods challenged online auction titan eBay. Thomas G. Woolston, an electrical engineer, obtained his patents in 2000 and 2001, based on an application he filed in 1995, and brought an infringement action against eBay. In May 2003, a jury found in Woolston's favor, and awarded a $35 million judgment against eBay. However, the appellate court vacated in part and remanded the case. *See MercExchange, L.L.C. v. eBay, Inc.*, 401 F.3d 1323 (Fed.Cir.2005).

QUESTIONS FOR DISCUSSION

1. *The value of questionable patents.* Litigating a patent all the way through the Federal Circuit to a final determination of validity can take several years, and cost several million dollars. A bit more than half of these litigated patents are upheld. Those who hold questionable, but colorable, patents therefore have quite a bit of room for maneuvering: they can license them cheaply enough so that prospective licensees will not have an incentive to litigate. It is therefore possible to make a good deal of money in licensing questionable patents. Is there reason to think that this sort of behavior will be more common in relation to Internet-commerce patents than with other types of patents?

2. *Patentability of contracts.* Contracts are normally not thought of as patentable, though as texts they are generally copyrightable. Yet contracts perform a function. Can a standardized contract be patented? If it is in digital form? If it is embedded in delivery of a digital product? Is the method of achieving formation of a contract containing the desired terms, through the use of a shrinkwrap license, patentable?

3. *Patent trolls.* Many mainstream patent practitioners believe that firms that acquire patents primarily or solely for the purpose of extracting royalties rather than for the purpose of manufacturing or marketing technology are engaged in unproductive activity, and should be stopped. Firms implementing this business model are often referred to as "trolls" or "bottom feeders."

> It is particularly important that Congress act to prevent abuses of the patent system by so-called "patent trolls," who use the patent system not to develop and make products but to squeeze money out of those who do. While there are no reliable statistics on the extent of the troll problem, there is no question that it is a widespread and extremely serious problem in the semiconductor, computer, and telecommunications industries. Large, innovative companies such as Intel and Cisco never have a week go by without threats of suit from a non-manufacturing patent owner claiming rights in technology that the defendants did not copy from the patent owner—usually they've never even heard of the patent owner—but instead developed independently. While there is a legitimate role for small and individual inventors who patent their technologies and license their ideas to others, increasingly the patent owners are not contributing ideas at all, but popping up years or even decades later and trying to fit an old patent to a different purpose. Trolls do this because the law permits it, and because it gives them a chance to make a lot of money—under current law, far more money than their technology is worth.

Testimony of Mark A. Lemley before the Senate Committee on the Judiciary, *Patent Law Reform: Injunctions and Damages*, 109th Cong. (June 14, 2005), judiciary.senate.gov/testimony.cfm?id=1535&wit_id=4352.

Do you agree that this use of patents is an "abuse" of the system? Or might the "trolls" be firms that are efficient at seeking out infringers and therefore policing the system? If you think that "trolls" are abusing the system, is there reason to think that e-commerce patents are more vulnerable to this kind of abuse than patents in other fields?

CHAPTER TWELVE
ELECTRONIC INTRUSIONS ON INTERCONNECTED COMPUTERS

The interconnection of computers via the Internet makes it possible for one person to engage in conduct using his computer that has unwanted effects on another person's computer. This action at a distance can take several forms. Part I addresses the ubiquitous phenomenon of unsolicited commercial e-mail, commonly referred to as "spam." Part II concerns unauthorized access to websites, and the accompanying unauthorized downloading of information. Part III looks at issues raised by unwanted incoming e-mail that is not commercial in nature. Part IV concerns two sorts of interferences with information flows that raise competition issues: software that redirects information flows from one recipient website to another, and manipulation of search engine rankings.

In response to these intruders, litigants have invoked several legal theories, including computer crime statutes, unfair competition law, and trademark infringement law, and have revived the all-but-forgotten common-law tort of trespass to chattels. The courts have in many instances responded favorably to these legal theories. In addition, both Congress and state legislatures have enacted laws aimed specifically at regulating unsolicited commercial e-mail.

I. UNSOLICITED COMMERCIAL E-MAIL

Electronic mail combines the desirable features of several other modes of communication: it allows asynchronous communications as does postal mail, but travels nearly as fast as a telephone call, and is priced like a face-to-face conversation. Nearly everyone with Internet access is capable of sending and receiving e-mail messages. For these and other reasons, e-mail has become an immensely popular method of both commercial and non-commercial person-to-person communication.

These same features have made e-mail an attractive medium of communication for commercial entities seeking to market their products to a broad audience. Marketers assemble lists of millions of e-mail addresses and, typically without first seeking permission from the holders of those addresses, direct commercial messages to them in large numbers. These messages are known as unsolicited commercial e-mail, unsolicited bulk e-mail, or, more popularly, "spam." If you have an e-mail account, it is extremely likely that you are a recipient of spam.

The advent of spam as a direct marketing tool has elicited a fierce response from consumers and Internet service providers. Opponents of spam argue that the sending of spam unfairly imposes costs on ISPs, recipients of the messages, third-party owners of domain names, and e-mail as a medium of communication. They point out that spam frequently contains deceptive elements, such as false subject lines and routing information, and often promotes objectionable goods and services, such as pornography and fraudulent get-rich-quick schemes. Proponents of spam—who are more likely to refer to it as e-mail marketing or bulk commercial e-mail—defend it as a low-cost marketing tool that can help new market participants mount challenges to existing sellers and introduce new products to the marketplace. In their view, spam is no more objectionable than telemarketing, and market forces should determine whether it continues to be sent.

Spam presents new challenges to courts, legislatures, and the online community. Litigants and courts have responded by exhuming and reviving the ancient common-law action of trespass to chattels, and by applying the more familiar doctrines of trademark and unfair competition. State legislatures have enacted a variety of statutes that regulate spam, and Congress has created a federal regime regulating spam that preempts significant elements of the pre-existing state spam laws. ISPs have applied technological solutions in an attempt to blunt the effects of spam, sometimes giving rise to reprisal lawsuits.

This Part will examine the legal issues that the sending of spam raises, and the various judicial, legislative, and technological responses that it has engendered.

A. THE COSTS OF SPAM

The sending of spam imposes costs primarily on three constituencies: individuals to whom the unsolicited messages are addressed, Internet service providers that process the outgoing and incoming messages, and third-party domain owners whose names are falsely incorporated in the return addresses of spam messages. Spam also harms e-mail as a medium of communication.

Harm to individual users. Spam costs individuals users both time and money. The wasted-time cost borne by consumers in sorting through and deleting unwanted solicitations may be insignificant with respect to any particular message, but becomes substantial in aggregate considering the vast numbers of spam messages that are sent—billions each day, representing 75–80 percent of all e-mail. According to one study, the cost of the time U.S. residents waste deleting spam is more than $21 billion annually. *See* CENTER FOR EXCELLENCE IN SERVICE, 2004 NATIONAL TECHNOLOGY READINESS SURVEY—SUMMARY REPORT (2005), www.rhsmith.umd.edu/ntrs/NTRS_2004.pdf. Large volumes of spam messages may interfere with the ISP's handling of its mail, delaying the delivery of non-spam mail. Users who pay access fees based on the length of time they are connected to the Internet, or who must make a long-distance call to connect with their access provider, incur direct additional costs as a result of spam, since it takes time to download each spam message from the network. Spam also imposes costs on users indirectly, to the extent that ISPs pass spam-related costs along to their subscribers in the form of higher access fees.

Some users also regard spam as an unwarranted intrusion on their privacy. Many spam messages contain material that recipients consider offensive, and that they prefer not to confront in their own homes. Spam messages that contain a hyperlink to a website with adult-oriented material, or that display such material as part of the e-mail itself, are of particular concern to parents of young children. In several related contexts, legislatures have recognized and offered protection to this privacy interest. A statutory provision governing the U.S. Postal Service allows individuals to opt out of receiving postal mail of a salacious nature. 39 U.S.C. § 3008. The Telephone Consumer Protection Act of 1991, 47 U.S.C. § 227, prohibits marketers from delivering prerecorded messages to residential telephones, and prohibits sending unsolicited advertisements to a fax machine. The Telemarketing and Consumer Fraud and Abuse Prevention Act, 15 U.S.C. § 6102(a), directs the Federal Trade Commission to promulgate regulations prohibiting deceptive and abusive practices involving telemarketing. *See* Telemarketing Sales Rule, 16 C.F.R. pt. 310. The courts have upheld these regulations. In *Rowan v. United States Post Office Dep't*, 397 U.S. 728, 736 (1970), upholding the postal statute (39 U.S.C. § 3008) against a First Amendment challenge, the Supreme Court recognized "the very basic right to be free from sights, sounds, and tangible matter we do not want."

A significant proportion of spam harms recipients by presenting them with false and deceptive communications. A review by Federal Trade Commission staff of a random sample of spam determined: (1) 33% of the messages contained false information in the "From" line; (2) 22% contained false information in the "Subject" line; (3) 40% contained indications of falsity in the message text; and (4) 66% had indications of falsity in either the "From" line, the "Subject" line, or the message text. *See* FTC'S DIVISION OF MARKETING PRACTICES, FALSE CLAIMS IN SPAM (2003), www.ftc.gov/reports/spam/030429spamreport.pdf.

Harm to Internet service providers. A consumer might receive several spam messages per day, but ISPs must process through their systems thousands or millions of spam messages every day. The largest ISPs block several *billion* spam messages daily. If spam represents 75 percent of all e-mail, then ISPs must process four times as much e-mail as they would if there were no spam at all. The need to process such a large volume of spam imposes several types of costs upon ISPs. An increase in e-mail volume may require an ISP to upgrade the capacity of its connection to the Internet, or to increase its hard-drive storage capacity, at significant cost. The additional time that users spend online to download spam messages may require the ISP to install additional dial-up lines or bandwidth. Additional staffing is required to handle subscribers' complaints about spam, to install and maintain filtering systems aimed at preventing the delivery of spam, and to respond to system problems that can result when a large influx of spam messages overwhelms an ISP's storage or transmission capacity. Some of these costs are absorbed by the ISP, and the rest are passed on to consumers in the form of higher access fees. The degradation to the performance of an ISP's mail system resulting from large volumes of spam can harm the ISP's reputation.

Harm to third parties. Many recipients of spam find it offensive, and would respond to it with complaints or retaliation if it were easy to locate the sender. Because senders of spam typically send messages in bulk to an enormous number of recipients, responses from offended recipients could overwhelm the sender or its ISP and make it impractical to use spam as a marketing tool. One method spammers have developed to avoid this problem is to falsify the routing information contained in the spam messages, to make it appear that they originated from some other source. When a recipient responds to an e-mail message with a falsified "From" address, the response goes to the domain indicated in that address, rather than to the actual sender of the spam. The result is that innocent owners of domain names, who have nothing to do with the sending of spam, are injured by the large volume of negative responses that are directed to their addresses, which can interfere with their ability to receive e-mail that is really intended for them. These third parties may also suffer reputational harm from the unwarranted association with spam.

Generalized harm to e-mail as a medium of communication. The various harms described above result in a generalized harm to e-mail as a means of communication. Lists of e-mail addresses to which spammers broadcast their messages are typically compiled by software robots that gather addresses from postings in USENET newsgroups and listservs, from websites, and from other online sources. To avoid having their addresses placed on these lists, many users go out of their way to prevent their e-mail addresses from appearing in publicly accessible locations online. They may do so by limiting the public fora in which they will communicate; by identifying postings with obfuscated versions of their e-mail addresses that can be read by humans, but not easily by robots;[1] or by setting up multiple e-mail accounts, reserving some for public postings and others for private use—all of which is socially unproductive activity.

ISPs seeking to filter out spam may misidentify a legitimate mailing to a large group of recipients as spam, causing the messages not to reach the intended recipients. After four major hurricanes hit Florida in 2004, one Florida county established an e-mail-based emergency notification system, which offered to alert subscribers of dangerous weather conditions. But some subscribers failed to receive the messages, because America Online's filtering software tagged them as spam.

Blacklists identifying ISPs that they view as insufficiently diligent in blocking spam may sweep too broadly, with the result that ISPs observing the blacklist refuse mail from innocent holders of domain names that are associated with the blacklisted ISP.

B. BENEFITS OF SPAM

Though they are not often articulated, it is important to recognize that spam has its benefits. Spam is a low-cost means of reaching large numbers of potential customers with marketing messages. The availability of spam therefore may allow a new competitor to enter the market, when it would otherwise not have the resources needed to attract customers. The entry of such a new competitor may result in lower prices, or in the availability of a broader range of goods.

Potential detriments resulting from the regulation of spam may also be viewed, if not as a benefit of spam, at least as a reason for leaving it unregulated. Spam, as commercial speech, is protected by the First Amendment. *See Central Hudson Gas & Electric Corp. v. Public Service Commission*, 447 U.S. 557 (1980). A regulation of spam that is not appropriately limited may violate the First Amendment: the "cure" of government regulation may be worse than the disease. We also may not want ISPs, pursuing their own economic interests, to decide what commercial speech will reach us and what will be filtered out. One could argue that some recipients of spam must be responding to it favorably, or marketers would not continue sending spam. Eliminating spam would deprive those recipients of whatever benefits they perceive in receiving it.

Another possible defense of spam is that it is no worse than other forms of marketing, such as unsolicited commercial postal mail ("junk mail") and telemarketing. Telemarketing, in particular, is arguably considerably more intrusive than spam, since it interrupts whatever we are doing and requires an immediate response. Though these forms of marketing are regulated, as noted above, they are not prohibited.

QUESTIONS FOR DISCUSSION

1. *Spam vs. other kinds of "junk" communications.* Do you think that spam is more or less of a problem than postal "junk mail" and telemarketing? Are consumers more willing to sift through and dispose of unsolicited commercial *postal* mail than they are to deal with

---

[1] For example, if my e-mail address is peter@rabbit.com, I might write it instead as "peter at rabbit dot com"—confusing most of the robots, but few of the human readers.

unsolicited commercial *electronic* mail? Is the burden on e-mail recipients and ISPs any greater than the burden on mailbox holders and the U.S. Postal Service? Are consumers more willing to put up with telemarketing than they are with spam? Are there justifications for regulating spam more stringently than these other marketing methods?

2. *Spam vs. other kinds of Internet marketing.* The Internet is full of advertising, including the banner advertisements that are ubiquitous on the Web, and the practice of interposing a pop-up ad before one can access a web page. Is spam any more problematic than these kinds of advertising?

C. CHALLENGING SPAM IN COURT

The following sections consider several legal theories that have been advanced in litigation as a means of attacking the harms that spam causes.

1. Trespass to Chattels

CompuServe Inc. v. Cyber Promotions, Inc.
962 F.Supp. 1015 (S.D.Ohio 1997).

■ GRAHAM, DISTRICT JUDGE.

This case presents novel issues regarding the commercial use of the Internet, specifically the right of an online computer service to prevent a commercial enterprise from sending unsolicited electronic mail advertising to its subscribers.

Plaintiff CompuServe Incorporated ("CompuServe") is one of the major national commercial online computer services. It operates a computer communication service through a proprietary nationwide computer network. In addition to allowing access to the extensive content available within its own proprietary network, CompuServe also provides its subscribers with a link to the much larger resources of the Internet. This allows its subscribers to send and receive electronic messages, known as "e-mail," by the Internet. Defendants Cyber Promotions, Inc. and its president Sanford Wallace are in the business of sending unsolicited e-mail advertisements on behalf of themselves and their clients to hundreds of thousands of Internet users, many of whom are CompuServe subscribers. . . . This matter is before the Court on the application of CompuServe for a preliminary injunction which would . . . prevent defendants from sending unsolicited advertisements to CompuServe subscribers.

For the reasons which follow, this Court holds that where defendants engaged in a course of conduct of transmitting a substantial volume of electronic data in the form of unsolicited e-mail to plaintiff's proprietary computer equipment, where defendants continued such practice after repeated demands to cease and desist, and where defendants deliberately evaded plaintiff's affirmative efforts to protect its computer equipment from such use, plaintiff has a viable claim for trespass to personal property and is entitled to injunctive relief to protect its property.

I.

. . .

Internet users often pay a fee for Internet access. However, there is no per-message charge to send electronic messages over the Internet and such messages usually reach their destination within minutes. Thus electronic mail provides an opportunity to reach a wide audience quickly and at almost no cost to the sender. It is not surprising therefore that some companies, like defendant Cyber Promotions, Inc., have begun using the Internet to distribute advertisements by sending the same unsolicited commercial message to hundreds of thousands of Internet users at once. Defendants refer to this as "bulk e-mail," while plaintiff refers to it as "junk e-mail." In the vernacular of the Internet, unsolicited e-mail advertising is sometimes referred to pejoratively as "spam."

CompuServe subscribers use CompuServe's domain name "CompuServe.com" together with their own unique alpha-numeric identifier to form a distinctive e-mail mailing address. That address may be used by the subscriber to exchange electronic mail with any one of tens of millions of other Internet users who have electronic mail capability. E-mail sent to CompuServe subscribers is processed and stored on CompuServe's proprietary computer equipment. Thereafter, it becomes accessible to CompuServe's subscribers, who can access CompuServe's equipment and electronically retrieve those messages.

Over the past several months, CompuServe has received many complaints from subscribers threatening to discontinue their subscription unless CompuServe prohibits electronic mass mailers from using its equipment to send unsolicited advertisements. CompuServe asserts that the volume of messages generated by such mass mailings places a significant burden on its equipment which has finite processing and storage capacity. CompuServe receives no payment from the mass mailers for processing their unsolicited advertising. However, CompuServe's subscribers pay for their access to CompuServe's services in increments of time and thus the process of accessing, reviewing and discarding unsolicited e-mail costs them money, which is one of the reasons for their complaints. CompuServe has notified defendants that they are prohibited from using its proprietary computer equipment to process and store unsolicited e-mail and has requested them to cease and desist from sending unsolicited e-mail to its subscribers. Nonetheless, defendants have sent an increasing volume of e-mail solicitations to CompuServe subscribers.

In an effort to shield its equipment from defendants' bulk e-mail, CompuServe has implemented software programs designed to screen out the messages and block their receipt. In response, defendants have modified their equipment and the messages they send in such a fashion as to circumvent CompuServe's screening software. Allegedly, defendants have been able to conceal the true origin of their messages by falsifying the point-of-origin information contained in the header of the electronic messages. Defendants have removed the "sender" information in the header of their messages and replaced it with another address. Also, defendants have developed the capability of configuring their computer servers to conceal their true domain name and appear on the Internet as another computer, further concealing the true origin of the messages. By manipulating this data, defendants have been able to continue sending messages to CompuServe's equipment in spite of CompuServe's protests and protective efforts.

Defendants assert that they possess the right to continue to send these communications to CompuServe subscribers. CompuServe contends that, in doing so, the defendants are trespassing upon its personal property.

. . .

IV.

This Court will now address the . . . aspect of plaintiff's motion in which it seeks to enjoin defendants Cyber Promotions, Inc. and its president Sanford Wallace from sending any unsolicited advertisements to any electronic mail address maintained by CompuServe.

CompuServe predicates this aspect of its motion for a preliminary injunction on the common law theory of trespass to personal property or to chattels, asserting that defendants' continued transmission of electronic messages to its computer equipment constitutes an actionable tort.

Trespass to chattels has evolved from its original common law application, concerning primarily the asportation of another's tangible property, to include the unauthorized use of personal property:

> Its chief importance now, is that there may be recovery . . . for interferences with the possession of chattels which are not sufficiently important to be classed as conversion, and so to compel the defendant to pay the full value of the thing with which he has interfered. Trespass to chattels survives today, in other words, largely as a little brother of conversion.

Prosser & Keeton, *Prosser and Keeton on Torts*, § 14, 85–86 (1984).

The scope of an action for conversion recognized in Ohio may embrace the facts in the instant case. The Supreme Court of Ohio established the definition of conversion under Ohio law in *Baltimore & O. R. Co. v. O'Donnell*, 32 N.E. 476, 478 (1892) by stating that:

> [I]n order to constitute a conversion, it was not necessary that there should have been an actual appropriation of the property by the defendant to its own use and benefit. It might arise from the exercise of a dominion over it in exclusion of the rights of the owner, or withholding it from his possession under a claim inconsistent with his rights. If one take the property of another, for a temporary purpose only, in disregard of the owner's right, it is a conversion. Either a wrongful taking, an assumption of ownership, an illegal use or misuse, or a wrongful detention of chattels will constitute a conversion.

Id. . . . While authority under Ohio law respecting an action for trespass to chattels is extremely meager, it appears to be an actionable tort. . . .

Both plaintiff and defendants cite the Restatement (Second) of Torts to support their respective positions. . . .

The Restatement § 217(b) states that a trespass to chattel may be committed by intentionally using or intermeddling with the chattel in possession of another. Restatement § 217, Comment e defines physical "intermeddling" as follows:

> . . . intentionally bringing about a physical contact with the chattel. The actor may commit a trespass by an act which brings him into an intended physical contact with a chattel in the possession of another[.]

Electronic signals generated and sent by computer have been held to be sufficiently physically tangible to support a trespass cause of action. *Thrifty-Tel, Inc. v. Bezenek*, 46 Cal.App.4th 1559, 1567 (1996); *State v. McGraw*, 480 N.E.2d 552, 554 (Ind.1985) (Indiana Supreme Court recognizing in dicta that a hacker's unauthorized access to a computer was more in the nature of trespass than criminal conversion) and *State v. Riley*, 846 P.2d 1365 (Wash. 1993) (computer hacking as the criminal offense of "computer trespass" under Washington law). It is undisputed that plaintiff has a possessory interest in its computer systems. Further, defendants' contact with plaintiff's computers is clearly intentional. Although electronic messages may travel through the Internet over various routes, the messages are affirmatively directed to their destination.

Defendants, citing Restatement (Second) of Torts § 221, which defines "dispossession," assert that not every interference with the personal property of another is actionable and that physical dispossession or substantial interference with the chattel is required. Defendants then argue that they did not, in this case, physically dispossess plaintiff of its equipment or substantially interfere with it. However, the Restatement (Second) of Torts § 218 defines the circumstances under which a trespass to chattels may be actionable:

> One who commits a trespass to a chattel is subject to liability to the possessor of the chattel if, but only if,
>
> (a) he dispossesses the other of the chattel, or
>
> (b) the chattel is impaired as to its condition, quality, or value, or
>
> (c) the possessor is deprived of the use of the chattel for a substantial time, or
>
> (d) bodily harm is caused to the possessor, or harm is caused to some person or thing in which the possessor has a legally protected interest.

Therefore, an interference resulting in physical dispossession is just one circumstance under which a defendant can be found liable. Defendants suggest that "unless an alleged trespasser actually takes physical custody of the property or physically damages it, courts will not find the 'substantial interference' required to maintain a trespass to chattel claim." . . . It is clear from a reading of Restatement § 218 that an interference or intermeddling that does not fit the § 221 definition of "dispossession" can nonetheless result in defendants' liability for trespass. . . .

A plaintiff can sustain an action for trespass to chattels, as opposed to an action for conversion, without showing a substantial interference with its right to possession of that chattel. *Thrifty-Tel, Inc.*, 46 Cal.App.4th at 1567 (quoting *Zaslow v. Kroenert*, 176 P.2d 1 (Cal. 1946)). Harm to the personal property or diminution of its quality, condition, or value as a result of defendants' use can also be the predicate for liability. Restatement § 218(b).

> An unprivileged use or other intermeddling with a chattel which results in actual impairment of its physical condition, quality or value to the possessor makes the actor liable for the loss thus caused. In the great majority of cases, the actor's intermeddling with the chattel impairs the value of it to the possessor, as distinguished from the mere affront to his dignity as possessor, only by some impairment of the physical condition of the chattel. There may, however, be situations in which the value to the owner of a particular type of chattel may be impaired by dealing with it in a manner that does not affect its physical condition. . . . In such a case, the intermeddling is actionable even though the physical condition of the chattel is not impaired.

The Restatement (Second) of Torts § 218, comment h. In the present case, any value CompuServe realizes from its computer equipment is wholly derived from the extent to which that equipment can serve its subscriber base. Michael Mangino, a software developer for CompuServe who monitors its mail processing computer equipment, states by affidavit that handling the enormous volume of mass mailings that CompuServe receives places a tremendous burden on its equipment. Defendants' more recent practice of evading CompuServe's filters by disguising the origin of their messages commandeers even more computer resources because CompuServe's computers are forced to store undeliverable e-mail messages and labor in vain to return the messages to an address that does not exist. To the extent that defendants' multitudinous electronic mailings demand the disk space and drain the processing power of plaintiff's computer equipment, those resources are not available to serve CompuServe subscribers. Therefore, the value of that equipment to CompuServe is diminished even though it is not physically damaged by defendants' conduct.

Next, plaintiff asserts that it has suffered injury aside from the physical impact of defendants' messages on its equipment. Restatement § 218(d) also indicates that recovery may be had for a trespass that causes harm to something in which the possessor has a legally protected interest. Plaintiff asserts that defendants' messages are largely unwanted by its subscribers, who pay incrementally to access their e-mail, read it, and discard it. Also, the receipt of a bundle of unsolicited messages at once can require the subscriber to sift through, at his expense, all of the messages in order to find the ones he wanted or expected to receive. These inconveniences decrease the utility of CompuServe's e-mail service and are the foremost subject in recent complaints from CompuServe subscribers. Patrick Hole, a customer service manager for plaintiff, states by affidavit that in November 1996 CompuServe received approximately 9,970 e-mail complaints from subscribers about junk e-mail, a figure up from approximately two hundred complaints the previous year. Approximately fifty such complaints per day specifically reference defendants. Defendants contend that CompuServe subscribers are provided with a simple procedure to remove themselves from the mailing list. However, the removal procedure must be performed by the e-mail recipient at his expense, and some CompuServe subscribers complain that the procedure is inadequate and ineffectual.

Many subscribers have terminated their accounts specifically because of the unwanted receipt of bulk e-mail messages. Defendants' intrusions into Compu-Serve's computer systems, insofar as they harm plaintiff's business reputation and goodwill with its customers, are actionable under Restatement § 218(d).

The reason that the tort of trespass to chattels requires some actual damage as a *prima facie* element, whereas damage is assumed where there is a trespass to real property, can be explained as follows:

> The interest of a possessor of a chattel in its inviolability, unlike the simi-lar interest of a possessor of land, is not given legal protection by an ac-tion for nominal damages for harmless intermeddlings with the chattel. In order that an actor who interferes with another's chattel may be liable, his conduct must affect some other and more important interest of the possessor. Therefore, one who intentionally intermeddles with another's chattel is subject to liability only if his intermeddling is harmful to the possessor's materially valuable interest in the physical condition, quality, or value of the chattel, or if the possessor is deprived of the use of the chattel for a substantial time, or some other legally protected interest of the possessor is affected as stated in Clause (c). *Sufficient legal protection of the possessor's interest in the mere inviolability of his chattel is afforded by his privilege to use reasonable force to protect his possession against even harmless interference.*

Restatement (Second) of Torts § 218, Comment e (emphasis added). Plaintiff CompuServe has attempted to exercise this privilege to protect its computer sys-tems. However, defendants' persistent affirmative efforts to evade plaintiff's secu-rity measures have circumvented any protection those self-help measures might have provided. In this case CompuServe has alleged and supported by affidavit that it has suffered several types of injury as a result of defendants' conduct. The foregoing discussion simply underscores that the damage sustained by plaintiff is sufficient to sustain an action for trespass to chattels. However, this Court also notes that the implementation of technological means of self-help, to the extent that reasonable measures are effective, is particularly appropriate in this type of situa-tion and should be exhausted before legal action is proper.

Under Restatement § 252, the owner of personal property can create a privilege in the would-be trespasser by granting consent to use the property. A great portion of the utility of CompuServe's e-mail service is that it allows subscribers to receive messages from individuals and entities located anywhere on the Internet. Cer-tainly, then, there is at least a tacit invitation for anyone on the Internet to utilize plaintiff's computer equipment to send e-mail to its subscribers. . . . However, in or around October 1995, CompuServe employee Jon Schmidt specifically told Mr. Wallace that he was "prohibited from using CompuServe's equipment to send his junk e-mail messages." There is apparently some factual dispute as to this point, but it is clear from the record that Mr. Wallace became aware at about this time that plaintiff did not want to receive messages from Cyber Promotions and that plaintiff was taking steps to block receipt of those messages.

Defendants argue that plaintiff made the business decision to connect to the Internet and that therefore it cannot now successfully maintain an action for trespass to chattels. Their argument is analogous to the argument that because an establishment invites the public to enter its property for business purposes, it cannot later restrict or revoke access to that property, a proposition which is erroneous under Ohio law. *See, e.g., State v. Carriker*, 214 N.E.2d 809 (Ohio App.1964) (the law in Ohio is that a business invitee's privilege to remain on the premises of another may be revoked upon the reasonable notification to leave by the owner or his agents); *Allstate Ins. Co. v. U.S. Associates Realty, Inc.*, 464 N.E.2d 169 (Ohio App.1983) (notice of express restriction or limitation on invitation turns business invitee into trespasser). On or around October 1995, CompuServe notified defendants that it no longer consented to the use of its proprietary computer equipment. Defendants' continued use thereafter was a trespass. Restatement (Second) of Torts §§ 252 and 892A(5); *see also* Restatement (Second) of Torts § 217, Comment f ("The actor may commit a new trespass by continuing an intermeddling which he has already begun, with or without the consent of the person in possession. Such intermeddling may persist after the other's consent, originally given, has been terminated."); Restatement (Second) of Torts § 217, Comment g.

Further, CompuServe expressly limits the consent it grants to Internet users to send e-mail to its proprietary computer systems by denying unauthorized parties the use of CompuServe equipment to send unsolicited electronic mail messages. This policy statement, posted by CompuServe online, states as follows:

> CompuServe is a private online and communications services company. CompuServe does not permit its facilities to be used by unauthorized parties to process and store unsolicited e-mail. If an unauthorized party attempts to send unsolicited messages to e-mail addresses on a Compu-Serve service, CompuServe will take appropriate action to attempt to prevent those messages from being processed by CompuServe. Violations of CompuServe's policy prohibiting unsolicited e-mail should be reported to. . . .

Id. at ¶¶ 2 and 3. Defendants Cyber Promotions, Inc. and its president Sanford Wallace have used plaintiff's equipment in a fashion that exceeds that consent. The use of personal property exceeding consent is a trespass. . . . Restatement (Second) of Torts § 256. It is arguable that CompuServe's policy statement, insofar as it may serve as a limitation upon the scope of its consent to the use of its computer equipment, may be insufficiently communicated to potential third-party users when it is merely posted at some location on the network. However, in the present case the record indicates that defendants were actually notified that they were using CompuServe's equipment in an unacceptable manner. To prove that a would-be trespasser acted with the intent required to support liability in tort it is crucial that defendant be placed on notice that he is trespassing.

As a general matter, the public possesses a privilege to reasonably use the facilities of a public utility, Restatement (Second) of Torts § 259, but Internet service providers have been held not to be common carriers. *Religious Technology Center v. Netcom On-Line Communication Services, Inc.*, 907 F.Supp. 1361 (N.D.Cal.1995). The definition of public utility status under Ohio law was recently articulated in *A & B Refuse Disposers, Inc. v. Bd. Of Ravenna Township Trustees*, 596 N.E.2d 423 (Ohio 1992). The Ohio Supreme Court held that the determination of whether an entity is a "public utility" requires consideration of several factors relating to the "public service" and "public concern" characteristics of a public utility. 596 N.E.2d at 426. The public service characteristic contemplates an entity which devotes an essential good or service to the general public which the public in turn has a legal right to demand or receive. *Id.* at 425. CompuServe's network, Internet access and electronic mail services are simply not essential to society. There are many alternative forms of communication which are customarily used for the same purposes. Further, only a minority of society at large has the equipment to send and receive e-mail messages via the Internet, and even fewer actually do. The second characteristic of a public utility contemplates an entity which conducts its operations in such manner as to be a matter of public concern, that is, a public utility normally occupies a monopolistic or o[li]gopolistic position in the relevant marketplace. *Id.* at 425–426. Defendants estimate that plaintiff serves some five million Internet users worldwide. However, there are a number of major internet service providers that have very large subscriber bases, and with a relatively minor capital investment, anyone can acquire the computer equipment necessary to provide Internet access services on a smaller scale. Furthermore, Internet users are not a "captive audience" to any single service provider, but can transfer from one service to another until they find one that best suits their needs. Finally, the Ohio Supreme Court made clear that a party asserting public utility status is required to support that assertion with evidence going to the relevant aforementioned factors. *Id.* at 427. Defendants have not argued that CompuServe is a public utility, much less produced evidence tending to support such a conclusion. Therefore, CompuServe is not a public utility as that status is defined under Ohio law and defendants can not be said to enjoy a special privilege to use CompuServe's proprietary computer systems.

. . .

Having considered the relevant factors, this Court concludes that the preliminary injunction that plaintiff requests is appropriate.

. . .

EXTENSIONS

1. *First Amendment not a defense.* Also in this case, but omitted from the above excerpt, Cyber Promotions argued that CompuServe's efforts to bar Cyber Promotions' e-mailings from CompuServe's network violated the First Amendment's free-speech guarantee. The court held that CompuServe was not a state actor, and that the First Amendment therefore did not apply to its activities.

2. *ISPs are not monopolists.* In the above excerpt, the court rejected Cyber Promotions' argument that it was entitled to access to CompuServe's system because CompuServe was a "public utility." Similarly, in *Cyber Promotions, Inc. v. America Online, Inc.*, 948 F.Supp. 456 (E.D.Pa.1996), the court rejected Cyber Promotions' argument that AOL was an "essential facility."

3. *The King of Spam.* Sanford Wallace, the owner of the defendant in this case, became notorious in the late 1990s as the self-described King of Spam. His high-volume dispatches of spam, as many as 25 million e-mails a day, resulted in Cyber Promotions' being kicked off the Internet by a succession of ISPs, and led to a $2 million judgment against the company. Wallace later got out of the spam business, renounced his former way of life, lined up in support of federal regulation of spam, and offered himself as a technical expert to litigants battling spam. More recently, Wallace was named as a defendant in *FTC v. Seismic Entertainment Productions, Inc.*, 2004 WL 2403124 (D.N.H. TRO entered Oct. 21, 2004), in which the FTC charged that the Wallace offered for download software that changed the user's browser's home page, installed advertising programs without permission, generated an unending stream of pop-up advertisements, caused the user's CD-ROM tray to open—and then displayed a message offering to sell the user software to correct these problems!

QUESTIONS FOR DISCUSSION

1. *The "value" of computer equipment.* In *CompuServe Inc. v. Cyber Promotions, Inc.*, the court found the impairment needed to support a claim of trespass to chattels in the effect of the unwanted e-mail on CompuServe's computer equipment, holding that "the value of that equipment to CompuServe is diminished even though it is not physically damaged by defendants' conduct." Does making unauthorized use of another's property impair its value? Is this a reasonable application of the concept of "value," or an unwarranted stretch?

2. *The new property.* The trespass in this case was against CompuServe's computer hardware, which is unquestionably a form of property. Is an e-mail account a form of property that may support an action for trespass to chattels? That is, could an individual who receives unwanted spam messages successfully maintain an action against the sender for trespass to chattels based on unauthorized interference with his e-mail account? Could the owner of a domain name that is falsely designated as the source of the spam maintain such an action?

3. *Impairment, or just communication?* Suppose defendants sent bulk unsolicited commercial e-mail with a message that a large proportion of the recipients were happy to receive: for example, coupons good for free admissions to movie theaters. Could CompuServe still maintain its claim of impairment to its computer system?

As we shall see below, in Parts II and III, the doctrine of trespass to chattels has been revived in other contexts besides transmission of spam. It remains debatable whether expansive use of this doctrine is consistent with policies of freedom of expression and free competition.

2. General Computer Protection Statutes; Laws Against Trademark Infringement and Dilution

America Online, Inc. v. LCGM, Inc.
46 F.Supp.2d 444 (E.D.Va.1998).

■ LEE, DISTRICT JUDGE.

This matter is before the Court on plaintiff's Motion for Summary Judgment as to each of the seven counts in the complaint. Plaintiff America Online, Inc. (AOL) complains that defendants sent large numbers of unauthorized and unsolicited bulk e-mail advertisements ("spam") to its members (AOL members). . . .

. . .

II. Findings of Fact and Conclusions of Law

AOL, an Internet service provider located in the Eastern District of Virginia, provides a proprietary, content-based online service that provides its members (AOL members) access to the Internet and the capability to receive as well as send e-mail messages. AOL registered "AOL" as a trademark and service mark in 1996 and has registered its domain name "aol.com" with the InterNIC. At the time this cause of action arose, defendant LCGM, Inc. was a Michigan corporation which operated and transacted business from Internet domains offering pornographic web sites. . . .

AOL alleges that defendants, in concert, sent unauthorized and unsolicited bulk e-mail advertisements ("spam") to AOL customers. AOL's Unsolicited Bulk E-mail Policy and its Terms of Service bar both members and nonmembers from sending bulk e-mail through AOL's computer systems. Plaintiff estimates that defendants, in concert with their "site partners," transmitted more than 92 million unsolicited and bulk e-mail messages advertising their pornographic Web sites to AOL members from approximately June 17, 1997 to January 21, 1998. Plaintiff bases this number on defendants' admissions that they sent approximately 300,000 e-mail messages a day at various intervals from their Michigan offices. Plaintiff asserts that defendants provided AOL with computer disks containing a list of the addresses of 820,296 AOL members to whom defendants admitted to transmitting bulk e-mail.

Plaintiff alleges that defendants harvested, or collected, the e-mail addresses of AOL members in violation of AOL's Terms of Service. Defendants have admitted to maintaining AOL memberships to harvest or collect the e-mail addresses of other AOL members. Defendants have admitted to maintaining AOL accounts and to using the AOL Collector and E-mail Pro/Stealth Mailer extractor programs to collect the e-mail addresses of AOL members, alleging that they did so in targeted adult AOL chat rooms. Defendants have admitted to using this software to evade AOL's filtering mechanisms.

Plaintiff alleges that defendants forged the domain information "aol.com" in the "from" line of e-mail messages sent to AOL members. Defendants have admitted to creating the domain information "aol.com" through an e-mail sending program, and to causing the AOL domain to appear in electronic header information of its commercial e-mails. Plaintiffs assert that as a result, many AOL members expressed confusion about whether AOL endorsed defendants' pornographic Web sites or their bulk e-mailing practices. Plaintiff also asserts that defendants' e-mail messages were sent through AOL's computer networks. Defendants have admitted to sending e-mail messages from their computers through defendants' network via e-mail software to AOL, which then relayed the messages to AOL members.

Plaintiff alleges that AOL sent defendants two cease and desist letters, dated respectively December 8, 1997 and December 30, 1997, but that defendants continued their e-mailing practices to AOL members after receiving those letters. Defendants have admitted to receiving those letters, contending that any e-mails sent after such receipt were "lawful."

Plaintiff alleges that defendants paid their "site partners" to transmit unsolicited bulk e-mail on their behalf and encouraged these site partners to advertise. Plaintiff further alleges that defendants conspired with CN Productions, another pornographic e-mailer, to transmit bulk e-mails to AOL members. Plaintiff alleges that many e-mails sent by defendants contained Hyper-Text Links both to defendants' web sites and CN Productions' web sites.

Plaintiff alleges that defendants' actions injured AOL by consuming capacity on AOL's computers, causing AOL to incur technical costs, impairing the functioning of AOL's e-mail system, forcing AOL to upgrade its computer networks to process authorized e-mails in a timely manner, damaging AOL's goodwill with its members, and causing AOL to lose customers and revenue. Plaintiff asserts that between the months of December 1997 and April 1998, defendants' unsolicited bulk e-mails generated more than 450,000 complaints by AOL members.

Count I: False Designation of Origin Under the Lanham Act

The undisputed facts establish that defendants violated 15 U.S.C. § 1125(a)(1) of the Lanham Act, which makes it unlawful to use in commerce:

> any false designation of origin . . . which . . . is likely to cause confusion, or to cause mistake, or to deceive as to the affiliation, connection, or association of such person with another person, or as to the origin, sponsorship, or approval of his or her goods, services, or commercial activities by another person.

The unauthorized sending of bulk e-mails has been held to constitute a violation of this section of the Lanham Act. *America Online, Inc. v. IMS, et al.,* 24 F.Supp.2d 548 (E.D.Va.1998); *See also Hotmail Corp. v. Van$ Money Pie Inc., et al.,* 47 U.S.P.Q.2d 1020 (N.D.Cal.1998) (granting injunction where plaintiff was likely to prevail on the merits under the Lanham Act). The elements necessary to establish a false designation violation under the Lanham Act are as follows: (1) a defendant uses a designation; (2) in interstate commerce; (3) in connection with goods and services; (4) which designation is likely to cause confusion, mistake or deception as to origin, sponsorship, or approval of defendant's goods or services; and (5) plaintiff has been or is likely to be damaged by these acts. *See First Keystone Federal Savings Bank v. First Keystone Mortgage, Inc.,* 923 F.Supp.693, 707 (E.D.Pa.1996).

Each of the false designation elements has been satisfied. First, defendants clearly used the "aol.com" designation, incorporating the registered trademark and service mark AOL in their e-mail headers. Second, defendants' activities involved interstate commerce because all e-mails sent to AOL members were routed from defendants' computers in Michigan through AOL's computers in Virginia. Third, the use of AOL's designation was in connection with goods and services as defendants' e-mails advertised their commercial web sites. Fourth, the use of "aol.com" in defendants' e-mails was likely to cause confusion as to the origin and sponsorship of defendants' goods and services. Any e-mail recipient could logically conclude that a message containing the initials "aol.com" in the header would originate from AOL's registered Internet domain, which incorporates the registered mark "AOL." *AOL v. IMS*, 24 F.Supp.2d 548. The recipient of such a message would be led to conclude the sender was an AOL member or AOL, the Internet Service Provider. Indeed, plaintiff alleges that this designation did cause such confusion among many AOL members, who believed that AOL sponsored and authorized defendants' bulk e-mailing practices and pornographic web sites. Finally, plaintiff asserts that these acts damaged AOL's technical capabilities and its goodwill. The defendants are precluded from opposing these claims due to their failure to comply with discovery orders. Therefore, there is no genuine issue of material fact in regards to this Count, and the Court holds the plaintiff is entitled to summary judgment on Count I.

Count II: Dilution of Interest in Service Marks Under the Lanham Act

The undisputed facts establish that defendants violated 15 U.S.C. § 1125(c)(1) of the Lanham Act, also known as the Federal Trademark Dilution Act of 1995, which provides relief to an owner of a mark whose mark or trade name is used by another person in commerce "if such use begins after the mark has become famous and causes dilution of the distinctive quality of the mark." The legislative history of the Act indicates that it was intended to address Internet domain name issues. *Intermatic Inc. v. Toeppen*, 947 F.Supp.1227, 1238 (N.D.Ill.1996) (granting summary judgment to Intermatic, Inc. on its Lanham Act dilution claim against defendant who had registered "intermatic.com" as its domain name). United States Senator Leahy, in discussing the Act, stated that

> . . . it is my hope that this antidilution statute can help stem the use of *deceptive Internet addresses* taken by those who are choosing marks that are associated with the products and reputations of others [emphasis added].

Id. (quoting 141 Cong. Rec. S19312–01 (daily ed. December 29, 1995) (statement of Senator Leahy)). Moreover, this Court has found the unauthorized sending of bulk e-mails constitutes a violation of § 1125(c)(1) of the Lanham Act. *AOL v. IMS*, 24 F.Supp.2d 548; *see also Hotmail*, 47 U.S.P.Q.2d 1020 (court granted injunction, finding plaintiffs were likely to prevail on the merits under this section of the Act).

Plaintiff has satisfied the two elements necessary to establish a dilution claim: "(1) the ownership of a distinctive mark, and (2) a likelihood of dilution." *Hormel Foods Corp. v. Jim Henson Prods. Inc.*, 73 F.3d 497, 506 (2d Cir.1996) (applying New York's anti-dilution statute). Plaintiff's "AOL" mark qualifies as a distinctive mark. The "AOL" mark is registered on the principal register of the United States Patent and Trademark Office. Furthermore, the mark is recognized throughout the world in association with AOL's online products and services. Dilution can be established by "tarnishment." "The sine qua non of tarnishment is a finding that plaintiff's mark will suffer negative associations through defendant's use." *Id.* at 507. Plaintiff contends that the "AOL" mark is a valuable business asset to plaintiff. Plaintiff argues that the "AOL" mark is tarnished, and thus diluted, by association with defendants' bulk e-mail practices and submits thousands of member complaints about defendants' e-mails as evidence of tarnishment.

Count III: Exceeding Authorized Access in Violation of the Computer Fraud and Abuse Act

The facts before the Court establish that defendants violated 18 U.S.C. § 1030(a)(2)(C) of the Computer Fraud and Abuse Act, which prohibits individuals from "intentionally access[ing] a computer without authorization or exceed[ing] authorized access, and thereby obtain[ing] information from any protected computer if the conduct involved an interstate or foreign communication." Defendants' own admissions satisfy the Act's requirements. Defendants have admitted to maintaining an AOL membership and using that membership to harvest the e-mail addresses of AOL members. Defendants have stated that they acquired these e-mail addresses by using extractor software programs. Defendants' actions violated AOL's Terms of Service, and as such was unauthorized. Plaintiff contends that the addresses of AOL members are "information" within the meaning of the Act because they are proprietary in nature. Plaintiff asserts that as a result of defendants' actions, it suffered damages exceeding $5,000, the statutory threshold requirement.

Count IV: Impairing Computer Facilities In Violation of the Computer Fraud and Abuse Act

The undisputed facts establish that defendants violated 18 U.S.C. § 1030(a)(5)(C) [since redesignated § 1030(a)(5)(A)(iii) — Eds.] of the Computer Fraud and Abuse Act, which prohibits anyone from "intentionally access[ing] a protected computer without authorization, and as a result of such conduct, causes damage." Another court found that spamming was an actionable claim under this Act. *See Hotmail*, 47 U.S.P.Q.2d 1020 (granting injunction to Hotmail because it was likely to prevail on the merits under this statute). Defendants have admitted to utilizing software to collect AOL members' addresses. These actions were unauthorized because they violated AOL's Terms of Service. Defendants' intent to access a protected computer, in this case computers within AOL's network, is clear under the circumstances. Defendants' access of AOL's computer network enabled defendants to send large numbers of unsolicited bulk e-mail messages to AOL members.

In addition to defendants' admissions, plaintiff alleges that by using the domain information "aol.com" in their e-mails, defendants and their "site partners" camouflaged their identities, and evaded plaintiff's blocking filters and its members' mail controls. Defendants have admitted to using extractor software to evade AOL's filtering mechanisms. As a result of these actions, plaintiff asserts damages to its computer network, reputation and goodwill in excess of the minimum $5,000 statutory requirement.

Count V: Violations of the Virginia Computer Crimes Act

The facts presented to the Court establish that defendants violated the Virginia Computer Crimes Act, Va. Code § 18.2–152.3(3), which provides that "[a]ny person who uses a computer or computer network without authority and with the intent to [c]onvert the property of another shall be guilty of the crime of computer fraud." Section 18.2–152.12 authorizes a private right of action for violations of the Act. Defendants have admitted to causing "aol.com" to appear in the electronic header information of e-mail messages which they sent. Sending such messages through

AOL's computer network was unauthorized. Plaintiff alleges that defendants intended to obtain services by false pretenses and to convert AOL's property. Plaintiff alleges that the inclusion of false domain information in defendants' e-mails enabled defendants to escape detection by plaintiff's blocking filters and its members' mail controls. Plaintiff argues that as a result, defendants illegitimately obtained the unauthorized service of plaintiff's mail delivery system and obtained free advertising from AOL because AOL, not defendants, bore the costs of sending these messages. There are no genuine issues for trial with respect to this Count. As such, plaintiff's Motion for Summary Judgment must be granted on Count V.

Count VI: Trespass to Chattels under the Common Law of Virginia

[The court follows *CompuServe Inc. v. Cyber Promotions, Inc.*, excerpted *supra,* finding that defendants have committed trespass to chattels.] . . .

. . .

EXTENSIONS

1. *State computer crimes laws.* Some state computer crimes laws, like the Virginia statute invoked in *America Online, Inc. v. LCGM, Inc.*, have been interpreted to prohibit misuse of another's domain name in spam. Other states have enacted more specific prohibitions. For example, the California computer crimes statute imposes criminal penalties against one who "[k]nowingly and without permission uses the Internet domain name of another individual, corporation, or entity in connection with the sending of one or more electronic mail messages, and thereby damages or causes damage to a computer, computer system, or computer network." CAL. PENAL CODE § 502(c)(9).

2. *Tangible harm.* Third parties whose domain names are forged as the return address of spam mailings may also suffer more tangible forms of harm than that claimed by AOL. In *Parker v. C.N. Enterprises*, No. 97–06273 (Tex.Dist.Ct.1997), a bulk e-mailer used the plaintiff's domain name, flowers.com, as the return address of its mailings. According to the court: "Because many thousands of the Internet addresses were not valid addresses, thousands upon thousands of copies of junk mail were returned to [plaintiff's] computers. This massive, unwanted delivery of the Defendants' garbage to the Plaintiffs' doorstep inflicted substantial harm, including substantial service disruptions, lost access to communications, lost time, lost income and lost opportunities." The court enjoined defendant from further misuse of flowers.com, and awarded plaintiff actual damages in the amount of $13,910.

QUESTIONS FOR DISCUSSION

Confusion and harm from forged return address. In *America Online, Inc. v. LCGM, Inc.*, the plaintiff alleged that defendant's use of the AOL mark as the return address of its spam messages caused recipients to believe "that AOL sponsored and authorized defendants' bulk e-mailing practices and pornographic web sites." How plausible is this allegation? Would the fact that an ISP allows its members to send spam harm the ISP's reputation? Is such confusion on the part of the recipients of the spam messages more plausible if the falsified return address contains the domain name of a website that sells a product, like cars.com, than if it contains the domain name of an ISP, like aol.com? *Cf. Classified Ventures, L.L.C. v. Softcell Marketing, Inc.*, 109 F.Supp.2d 898 (N.D.Ill.2000).

3. Consumer Protection Laws

The Federal Trade Commission has brought dozens of enforcement actions against senders of spam, invoking its authority under the FTC Act, 15 U.S.C. § 45(a)(2), to prevent unfair or deceptive trade practices, and under other laws not directly aimed at spam. Some examples of these actions:

- *FTC v. Westby*, 2004 WL 1175047 (N.D.Ill.2004). The FTC alleged that defendants used false subject lines, like "Did you hear the news?" and "New movie info," to fool recipients into opening messages containing sexually explicit solicitations to visit the defendants' adult-oriented websites. The FTC also alleged that defendants used false e-mail addresses in the "From" and "Reply to" lines, resulting in the delivery of numerous angry responses to innocent third parties. Defendants agreed to settle the case for $112,500.

- *FTC v. GM Funding, Inc.,* Case No. SACV-02-1026-DOC (C.D.Cal.2003). The FTC alleged that defendants sent spam purporting to be from well-known financial institutions, such as Fannie Mae and Prudential. The spam included a questionnaire that sought detailed financial information, purportedly for the purpose of obtaining home mortgage loans. The FTC charged that the misidentification of the sender was a deceptive practice violating the FTC Act, and that the solicitation of financial information under false pretenses violated the Gramm–Leach–Bliley Act, 15 U.S.C. § 6821(a). Defendants stipulated to a permanent injunction and payment of $60,500.

- *FTC v. K4 Global Publishing, Inc.*, Case No. 5:03-CV-0140-3-CAR (M.D.Ga. 2003). The FTC alleged that defendants used spam to market fraudulent Internet business opportunities, called "Instant Internet Empires," that would allow them to make more than $115,000 a year on a $47 investment. Defendants stipulated to a judgment requiring them to pay $247,000.

For a discussion of the FTC's efforts to combat spam, see Federal Trade Commission, Prepared Statement of the Federal Trade Commission on "Unsolicited Commercial Email" Before the House Committee on Small Business, Subcommittee on Regulatory Reform and Oversight (Oct. 30, 2003), www.ftc.gov/os/2003/10/smallbiztest.pdf.

4. Criminal Prosecution

The sending of spam may involve fraud or other sorts of criminal conduct. In April 2004, a New York jury convicted Howard Carmack, notorious as the "Buffalo Spammer," on 14 counts, including forgery, identity theft, and falsifying business records. Carmack, who was found to have sent over 825 million spam e-mails, had opened e-mail accounts in the names of his identity-theft victims. He was sentenced to 3½–7 years in prison.

QUESTIONS FOR DISCUSSION

Calculating damages flowing from spam. What is the measure of damages to the operator of a computer network that is the target of large quantities of spam? In *America Online, Inc. v. Prime Data Systems, Inc.*, 1998 WL 34016692 (E.D.Va.1998), AOL introduced evidence establishing "that its computer costs are at least $.00078 per message, without considering personnel or other costs associated with the computers' operation." The court granted AOL compensatory damages of $.00078 for each spam message defendants sent to its subscribers, as well as punitive damages of three times that amount. Based on AOL's showing that defendants had sent it at least 130 million spam messages, the court awarded $101,400 in compensatory damages and $304,200 in punitive damages.

In *America Online, Inc. v. National Health Care Discount, Inc.*, 174 F.Supp.2d 890 (N.D.Iowa 2001), AOL sought damages based on the market value of the marketing defendants accomplished by sending their spam to AOL's subscribers. AOL argued for a market value based on the rate it charged advertisers to place banner advertisements on subscribers' e-mail in-boxes. That rate, $8.56 per thousand impressions, would have translated into damages of $.00856 per spam message—more than ten times AOL's cost-to-process of $.00078. The court agreed that "AOL's damages should not be limited to the amount [defendant's] wrongful conduct cost AOL. Such a result would permit [defendant], and others in a similar position, to appropriate the use of AOL's equipment at cost, without compensating AOL for any profit." However, the court did not agree that the value of a spam message was the same as that of a banner ad impression, but arrived at a compromise damage figure of $.0025 per message. Multiplying that by the 135 million e-mails defendant sent resulted in damages of $337,500.

D. STATE STATUTORY RESPONSES TO SPAM

Beginning with Nevada in 1997, state legislatures began enacting laws regulating the sending of spam, and by the end of 2003 such laws had been enacted in 36 states. The content of these statutes varied from state to state, but most incorporated one or more of the following types of regulation:

- A requirement that spam messages include removal instructions, allowing recipients to *opt out* of receiving future spam messages from that sender;

- *Labeling requirements*, requiring that each spam message contain language in the subject line—such as "ADV:"—indicating it is an advertisement;

- Prohibitions against the use of *falsified routing information*, false return addresses, or misleading subject lines;

- A prohibition against providing *software designed to facilitate falsification* of routing information;

- A prohibition against transmitting spam messages in violation of an ISP's *Terms of Service*;

- A prohibition against *unauthorized use of a third-party's domain name*;

- Civil and, sometimes, criminal enforcement provisions.

The patchwork of state spam laws suffered from several weaknesses.

First, the extraterritorial reach of these statutes was problematic. To be at all effective, these laws had to reach the conduct of spammers located outside the regulating state, if residents of the state were recipients of their spam. But to comply with such laws, the spammer had to know the geographical location of the recipients of his messages. Although some states tried to facilitate this process, by making available a listing of e-mail addresses belonging to its residents, it would be prohibitively expensive for a spammer to screen its addressees in this way, and lack of compliance was inevitable. Several state spam laws were challenged as violating the Constitution's Dormant Commerce Clause, which prohibits state laws that are found improperly to discriminate against interstate commerce or to have unwarranted extraterritorial effects. These challenges have generated mixed results. The Dormant Commerce Clause issues are discussed in Chapter 1, Part III(C), *supra*, and in a note in the Extensions at the end of this section.

Second, state spam statutes occasionally imposed inconsistent obligations, which likewise would require spammers to know the geographical location of each spam recipient. For example, the Minnesota statute required that the subject line of an e-mail containing adult-oriented material be labeled with "ADV-ADULT" as the first characters, while the California statute required such messages to be labeled "ADV:ADLT".

Third, these statutes were infrequently enforced, giving spammers little incentive to comply with them.

In September 2003, the California legislature updated its spam law with a provision making it illegal to "[i]nitiate or advertise in an unsolicited commercial e-mail advertisement from California [or] in an unsolicited commercial e-mail advertisement to a California electronic mail address." CAL. BUS. & PROF. CODE § 17529.2. An e-mail message was deemed unsolicited unless the recipient expressly consented to receive it, or the recipient had a pre-existing business relationship with the sender. *Id.* § 17529.1(o). This provision would have in effect made it illegal to send unsolicited commercial e-mail to recipients in California, since it would be impractical to acquire the opt-in consent of those recipients. This was something new: other state spam statutes did not ban spam, but only regulated its use.[2]

The California statute, scheduled to go into effect January 1, 2004, was very worrisome to e-mail marketers. The impending effective date of the California statute gave added impetus to those who supported enacting a federal law that would preempt state laws. In December 2003, Congress responded by enacting the CAN-SPAM Act, effective January 1, 2004, which preempted California's ban on spam, as well as substantial portions of other state spam laws. The preemptive effect of CAN-SPAM is discussed more fully in the following section. In summary, state laws regulating spam remain un-preempted to the extent that they prohibit fraudulent or deceptive spam, do not specifically regulate e-mail, or relate to computer crime.

EXTENSIONS

Constitutional challenges. Several state spam statutes have been upheld against constitutional challenges. *See Commonwealth v. Jaynes*, 65 Va.Cir. 355 (Va.Cir.Ct.2004) (First Amendment, Dormant Commerce Clause, and Due Process Clause); *Ferguson v. Friendfinders, Inc.*, 115 Cal.Rptr.2d 258 (Cal.Ct.App.2002) (Dormant Commerce Clause); *State v. Heckel*, 24 P.3d 404 (Wash.2001) (en banc) (Dormant Commerce Clause). In *MaryCLE, LLC v. First Choice Internet, Inc.*, 2004 WL 2895955 (Md.Cir.Ct.2004), *appeal pending*, the court held that Maryland's Commercial Electronic Mail Act violates the Dormant Commerce Clause.

FURTHER READING

- David E. Sorkin, *Technical and Legal Approaches to Unsolicited Electronic Mail*, 35

---

[2] The Delaware statute did ban spam, but it contained odd wording and does not appear to have caused marketers any concern. 11 DEL. CODE § 937(1).

U.S.F. L. REV. 325, 372–74 (2001) (discussing methods by which an ISP may convey notice that spam is not allowed on its system)

E. FEDERAL REGULATION OF SPAM: THE CAN-SPAM ACT

On January 1, 2004, the first federal law specifically regulating unsolicited commercial e-mail went into effect. The CAN-SPAM Act,[3] which followed more than six years of unsuccessful congressional efforts to pass a spam bill, was enacted with overwhelming support in both houses of Congress.

The underlying philosophy of the Act is that unsolicited electronic mail is a legitimate channel of marketing that merits federal protection against both unscrupulous marketers, who would pollute this channel with deceptive and offensive marketing messages, and overzealous state regulators, who would close off the channel altogether.

1. Principal Components of the CAN-SPAM Act

The approach of the Act discloses four primary components: (1) prohibition of deceptive and offensive conduct; (2) requiring marketers to present a modest degree of accountability and responsiveness to their target audience; (3) preemption of state laws that interfere with legitimate marketers' use of unsolicited e-mail communications; and (4) an enforcement scheme.

a. Prohibition of Deceptive and Offensive Conduct

The principal restrictions of CAN-SPAM apply to the sending of a "commercial electronic mail message," which is defined as a message "the primary purpose of which is the commercial advertisement or promotion of a commercial product or service," but excluding "a transactional or relationship message." § 7702(2)(A), (B).[4] Less stringent rules apply to the sending of a "transactional or relationship message,"[5] which is one whose "primary purpose" relates to a transaction in which the recipient is voluntarily involved. § 7702(17)(A).

Some types of prohibited conduct are subject to criminal penalties, both fines and imprisonment. Conduct made criminal includes knowingly:

- Transmitting "multiple"[6] commercial electronic mail messages from or through a third-party's computer without that party's authorization. 18 U.S.C. § 1037(a)(1), (2). This prohibition is aimed at the practice, common among spammers, of disguising the origin of their messages by commandeering an innocent third-party's computer or by sending or "relaying" their messages through an unsecured third-

---

[3] Officially, the Controlling the Assault of Non-Solicited Pornography and Marketing Act of 2003, Pub. L. No. 108-187, 117 Stat. 2699 (principally codified at 15 U.S.C. §§ 7701-13 and 18 U.S.C. § 1037).

[4] Citations to §§ 7701ff. are to the corresponding sections of Title 15 of the U.S. Code.

[5] The only requirement applying to "transactional or relationship" messages is the prohibition of false or misleading header information. § 7704(a)(1).

[6] "Multiple" is defined as more than 100 messages a day, 1,000 messages a month, or 10,000 messages a year. 18 U.S.C. § 1037(d)(3).

party server.

- Including false "header information"[7] in multiple commercial messages. *Id.* § 1037(a)(3). This is aimed at the common practice of forging header information to disguise the origin of the messages.

- Registering five or more e-mail accounts, or two or more domain names, using false identity information, and using any such account or domain name to transmit multiple commercial messages. *Id.* § 1037(a)(4).

- Falsely representing oneself as the registrant of five or more IP addresses, and using them to transmit multiple commercial messages. *Id.* § 1037(a)(5).

- Sending a message with sexually oriented content that fails to contain the phrase "SEXUALLY-EXPLICIT:" at the beginning of the subject line, or that displays any sexually oriented material to the recipient without his taking any affirmative steps to view it. § 7704(d) (implemented by FTC rule, 16 C.F.R. § 316.4(a)(1)). This prohibition is designed to allow recipients to configure their e-mail clients so that they identify and dispose of such messages automatically, and to prevent children from inadvertently being exposed to inappropriate material.

Other types of prohibited conduct are subject to civil enforcement, including the following:

- Sending a commercial message, or a "transactional or relationship message," with false or misleading header information. This practice is defined to include sending a message with accurate header information from an e-mail address that was obtained by means of false pretenses, and using header information that misidentifies the computer from which the message was sent. § 7704(a)(1).

- Sending a commercial message with a deceptive subject line. § 7704(a)(2).

- Allowing one's goods or services to be promoted via e-mail containing false header information, if the seller took no reasonable steps to prevent the sending of the e-mail, or to detect it and report it to the FTC. § 7705(a).

The Act creates liability for rendering certain types of assistance to those who send commercial e-mail in violation of the Act. Unlawful assistance includes:

- Providing a list of e-mail addresses to a sender, with knowledge that the addresses were obtained through forbidden harvesting or dictionary attacks (described below). § 7704(b)(1)(A).

- Providing goods or services (including, for example, website hosting or office space) to a business that promotes its products using commercial messages with false header information, if the provider has actual knowledge that the products are being so promoted and receives an economic benefit from that promotion. § 7705(b)(2).

As noted above, a "commercial electronic mail message" is a message whose "primary purpose" is commercial. Recognizing that it would not always be obvious what the primary

---

[7] "Header information" includes the routing information, showing the source and destination of the message and the route it followed, that accompanies an e-mail message. As defined in the Act, it also includes the "From:" line. § 7702(8). By default, most mail readers display only part of the header information.

purpose of a message is, Congress directed the FTC to issue regulations specifying how to make this determination. § 7702(2)(C). In January 2005, the FTC promulgated the requisite regulation. Simplifying a bit, a message with both commercial and transactional/relationship purposes will be deemed a "commercial electronic mail message" if the commercial aspect dominates the subject line or the message body. 16 C.F.R. § 316.3(a). A message will be deemed a "transactional or relationship" message only if it consists exclusively of transactional or relationship content. *Id.* § 316.3(b).

Under the regulation, what is the treatment of a message that has both commercial and transactional/relationship content, where the latter content predominates? What is the treatment of a message that has neither commercial nor transactional/relationship content?

b. Sender Accountability and Responsiveness

Several provisions of the Act are designed to assure that the sender of a commercial electronic mail message will be identifiable as such, and to require senders to be responsive to a recipient's expressed preference not to receive additional messages from that sender:

- Each commercial message must include an online mechanism, such as an e-mail link, allowing the recipient to indicate that she does not wish to receive future commercial messages from the same sender, and the sender must honor such opt-out requests within ten days. In addition, the sender may not transfer to anyone else the e-mail addresses of those who have exercised their opt-out rights. § 7704(a)(3), (4). This prohibition responds to the spammer's practice of interpreting an opt-out request as a verification that the e-mail address of the requester is an active address, and including that address on a list to be used by other spammers.

- Each commercial message must include the sender's physical postal address. § 7704(a)(5)(A)(iii). Holding senders of commercial e-mail messages accountable for their actions requires knowing where they are, and spammers commonly do not voluntarily disclose their geographical location.

c. Preemption of State Laws

In keeping with its philosophy that unsolicited commercial e-mail is an appropriate method for marketing goods and services, the Act preempts any state law "that expressly regulates the use of electronic mail to send commercial messages." However, the Act preserves state law to the extent it prohibits falsity or deception in connection with commercial e-mail. Since the enactment of CAN-SPAM, several states have enacted spam laws that fit within this exception. *See, e.g.,* Electronic Mail Communications Act, FLA. STAT. ANN. § 668.60–668.6075; Maryland Spam Deterrence Act, MD. CODE ANN., CRIM. LAW, § 3–805.1. The Act also preserves state law that is not specifically applicable to e-mail. Thus, state law of trespass to chattels, contract, and tort, and laws prohibiting fraud, unfair competition, deception, and computer crime, remain available. § 7707(b). Virginia's Computer Crimes Act, amended in 2003 to make high-volume spamming using falsified routing information a crime, is of particular significance since a large proportion of all e-mail traffic transits Virginia. *See* VA. CODE ANN. § 18.2-152.3:1.

In the findings accompanying the CAN-SPAM Act, Congress explained why it chose to preempt state regulation of spam:

Many States have enacted legislation intended to regulate or reduce unsolicited commercial electronic mail, but these statutes impose different standards and requirements. As a result, they do not appear to have been successful in addressing the problems associated with unsolicited commercial electronic mail, in part because, since an electronic mail address does not specify a geographic location, it can be extremely difficult for law-abiding businesses to know with which of these disparate statutes they are required to comply.

§ 7701(a)(11).

Because the Act's preemption of state laws is incomplete, victims of spam can bring lawsuits against spammers predicated on both the Act and other state or federal laws. *See, e.g., America Online, Inc. v. John Does 1-40*, No. 04-260-A (E.D.Va. filed Mar. 9, 2004) (action against a group of unknown spammers, with claims predicated on several provisions of the CAN-SPAM Act, as well as the Virginia Computer Crimes Act and common-law trespass to chattels), legal.web.aol.com/decisions/dljunk/-johndoes1-40.pdf; *Yahoo! Inc. v. Head*, No. C04-00965 (N.D.Cal. filed Mar. 9, 2004) (action based on CAN-SPAM, the Computer Fraud and Abuse Act, and the California Computer Crimes Statute), antispam.yahoo.com/spamandthelaw.

In *White Buffalo Ventures, LLC v. University of Texas*, 420 F.3d 366 (5th Cir.2005), the court held that the Act's preemption provision does not prevent the University of Texas from implementing a rule calling for filtering incoming spam directed at its e-mail system.

d. Enforcement

The Act may be enforced by the Federal Trade Commission (and certain other federal agencies with respect to violators that are outside the FTC's jurisdiction), the state attorneys general acting as parens patriae, and Internet service providers that are harmed by violations; individual spam recipients, however, cannot bring suit under the Act. Some state spam laws, by contrast, grant a right of action to individual recipients of unlawful e-mail messages. *See, e.g.,* CAL. BUS. & PROF. CODE § 17529.5(b), IDAHO CODE § 48–603E(4); MICH. COMP. LAWS § 445.2508(1).

The federal agencies enforce the Act as though the unlawful conduct were a violation of the Federal Trade Commission Act or an FTC trade regulation rule. § 7706(a)–(d). In actions brought by states or ISPs, actual damages are available, as are injunctions, statutory damages, and attorney's fees. Statutory damages may reach $2 million, and may be tripled in the case of willful violations or those involving defined aggravating factors. § 7706(f)(3)(C), (g)(3)(C). The aggravating factors include:

- Knowingly sending a commercial message to an e-mail address that was harvested, using a software bot or other automated means, from a website that displays a notice stating that addresses on the site may not be used for such purposes; or to an address created using a "dictionary attack," which consists of generating e-mail addresses by combining characters more-or-less randomly. § 7704(b)(1)(A).

- Using automated means to open multiple e-mail accounts that are used to send unlawful spam. § 7704(b)(2).

- Relaying unlawful spam through a third-party computer. § 7704(b)(3).

2. Required Agency Action on Additional Measures

The Act directs the Federal Trade Commission and the Federal Communications Commission to study and report on several additional issues:

a. Do-Not-E-Mail List

The Act required the FTC to submit a report that "sets forth a plan and timetable for establishing a nationwide marketing Do-Not-E-Mail Registry." § 7708. The idea for such a Registry was inspired by the telemarketing Do-Not-Call Registry, which the FTC promulgated by regulation in 2003. This regulation allows a consumer who does not wish to receive unsolicited calls from commercial telemarketers to place his telephone number on a list. A commercial telemarketer who makes a call to a number on this list is subject to substantial penalties. *See* 16 C.F.R. § 310.4(b)(1)(iii)(B). The anti-telemarketing list proved wildly popular with the public: over 50 million telephone numbers were placed on it during the first few months of its operation.

The FTC recommended against establishment of a do-not-e-mail list. It explained that the contents of the list would inevitably become available to spammers, who would find it very useful as a means of compiling a list of active e-mail addresses. (Query how valuable to a spammer would be a list of people who are savvy enough to know about the do-not-e-mail list, and spam-hating enough to put their address on it.) The list also would not aid enforcement efforts, since the biggest obstacle to enforcement is in identifying and locating the spammer. The report proposed instead a private-public partnership aimed at developing and implementing a system for authenticating the originating domain of e-mail messages, to prevent spammers from evading control efforts through use of "[o]bfuscatory techniques such as spoofing, open relays, open proxies, and zombie drones." Once an authentication system is in place, the FTC would reconsider whether to propose a do-not-e-mail list. *See* FEDERAL TRADE COMMISSION, NATIONAL DO NOT EMAIL REGISTRY: A REPORT TO CONGRESS (2004), www.ftc.gov/reports/dneregistry/report.pdf.

Two states have nonetheless implemented limited versions of a do-not-e-mail list. In 2004, Michigan and Utah enacted laws establishing a registry of children's e-mail addresses. MICH. COMP. LAWS § 752.1061–752.1068; UTAH CODE § 13–39–11 to –304. Parents may place their children's e-mail address (as well as their instant message ID, and their telephone, fax, or pager number) on the registry, which is established and maintained by an agency of the state government. It is violation of law, subject to civil and criminal penalties, to send a message to any address on the list that is inappropriate for minors.[8] Senders of e-mail may have their lists scrubbed against the registry, for payment of a fee. Both of these laws became effective on July 1, 2005.

---

[8] The Michigan law makes it illegal to send a message the primary purpose of which "is to, directly or indirectly, advertise or otherwise link to a message that advertises a product or service that a minor is prohibited by law from purchasing, viewing, possessing, participating in, or otherwise receiving." MICH. COMP. LAWS § 752.1065(1). The Utah law prohibits sending a message that "advertises a product or service that a minor is prohibited by law from purchasing; or . . . contains or advertises material that is harmful to minors, as defined in [another statutory section]." UTAH CODE § 13–39–202(1).

b. A Reward Provision

Within nine months after enactment, the FTC was required to submit a plan for rewarding those who provide information leading to the FTC's collection of a civil penalty against a violator of CAN-SPAM. § 7710(1). In its report on this issue, the FTC recommended particular elements that should be included within a reward provision, should Congress decide to enact one. *See* FEDERAL TRADE COMMISSION, A CAN-SPAM INFORMANT REWARD SYSTEM: A REPORT TO CONGRESS (2004), www.ftc.gov/reports/rewardsys/040916rewardsysrpt.pdf.

c. Subject Line Labeling

Within 18 months after enactment, the FTC was to submit a plan for requiring each commercial e-mail message to contain an identifier in the subject line, such as "ADV," or "an explanation of any concerns the Commission has that cause the Commission to recommend against the plan." § 7710(2).[9] Such a provision is found in many of the state spam laws that the Act preempts. The purpose of these provisions is to enable the recipient to control her in-box by setting her mail reader automatically to filter messages containing the prescribed string of characters in the subject line. The filtered message may be sent directly to the trash folder, or to another folder that is given lower priority than unlabeled mail.

The FTC's report recommended against a general labeling requirement. It noted that labeling requirements in state and foreign spam laws had been singularly ineffective, as spammers simply failed to comply. Despite the presence of labeling requirements in several state statutes, an earlier FTC review of a random sample of spam messages found that only two percent of the messages were labeled with "ADV:" on the subject line. *See* FTC's DIVISION OF MARKETING PRACTICES, FALSE CLAIMS IN SPAM (2003), www.ftc.gov/reports/spam/030429spamreport.pdf. The report made three main points in arguing against a mandatory labeling requirement. First, the e-mail filtering and blocking strategies that ISPs are employing are improving, and are likely to be more effective in controlling spam than a labeling requirement. Second, spammers who send messages that violate other requirements of CAN-SPAM are unlikely to comply with the labeling requirement. Therefore, only "legitimate" senders of commercial e-mail messages will label their messages, and filtering on the subject line will result in screening out these legitimate messages while letting through the fraudulent ones. Third, a labeling requirement would not aid in enforcing the spam laws, since the real difficulty is in tracing spam to its originator, and labeling does not help with this task. The agency recommended instead that greater efforts be directed to developing e-mail authentication technologies, which make it possible to determine whether a message was actually sent from the domain specified on the message's "From" line, viewing this as a potential solution of the spam problem.

One of the five FTC Commissioners dissented, arguing that subject-line labeling could be a useful element of a multi-pronged attack on spam. *See* FEDERAL TRADE COMMISSION, SUBJECT LINE LABELING AS A WEAPON AGAINST SPAM: A REPORT TO CONGRESS (2005), www.ftc.gov/reports/canspam05/050616canspamrpt.pdf; *id.* (Dissenting Statement of Commissioner Jon Leibowitz).

---

[9] As noted above, the Act requires subject line labeling for sexually explicit material.

d. Opt-in for Wireless Spam

The Act contains a special provision dealing with commercial e-mail messages that are sent to mobile telephones and other wireless devices. It requires the Federal Communications Commission to promulgate rules protecting consumers against unwanted e-mail messages sent to their mobile phones. In particular, the rules must provide mobile phone subscribers with the ability to avoid receiving messages from a sender "unless the subscriber has provided express prior authorization to the sender." § 7712(b)(1). This is a regime of opt-in control: a subscriber who so chooses will not receive any spam to her telephone unless she affirmatively requests it.

In 2004, the FCC promulgated a rule implementing the opt-in provision. 47 C.F.R. § 64.3100. The rule forbids sending spam to an address with a domain name that is among those used by providers of wireless telecommunications services to route e-mail to wireless devices, absent the "express prior authorization of the addressee." The FCC maintains a list of the off-limits domain names on its website.

EXTENSIONS

1. *Constitutional challenge.* In *FTC v. Phoenix Avatar, LLC*, 2004 WL 1746698 (N.D.Ill.2004), the court upheld CAN-SPAM against a First Amendment challenge, holding that the requirement to make prescribed disclosures in commercial e-mail messages is not a content-based restriction on speech.

2. *Multiple-seller messages.* Some spam messages contain advertisements from several different advertisers. The FTC staff, in an opinion letter, have delineated what they believe are the CAN-SPAM compliance obligations of these advertisers, under a hypothetical in which the recipient has consented to receipt of the message. The letter explains that CAN-SPAM imposes a certain set of compliance obligations on "initiators" of a spam message, and a different set of obligations on "senders" of a message. "Initiators" must ensure that the message does not contain false or misleading transmission information, or a deceptive subject line; and must include in the message certain disclosures, as well as a link enabling the recipient to opt out of future messages from the sender. "Senders" have all of the obligations that apply to initiators, and must in addition honor recipients' opt-out requests. According to FTC staff, only the entity that obtained the recipient's affirmative consent is to be treated as the "sender" of the messages, and is therefore responsible for honoring opt-out requests. The other advertisers appearing in the messages are not "senders," but are "initiators," and must comply with the applicable requirements. *See* Letter from Eileen Harrington, Associate Director, Division of Marketing Practices, FTC, to Jerry Cerasale, Senior Vice President, The Direct Marketing Association, Inc. (Mar. 8, 2005), pub.bna.com/eclr/ ftcdma030805.pdf. Under this interpretation, would an "initiator" which is not a "sender" be obligated to comply with a recipient's opt-out request?

3. *Falsity in body of message.* The Act prohibits sending a message with "header information that is materially false or materially misleading." § 7704(a)(1). Does sending a message with false or misleading material in the *body* of the message violate this provision? *See* *Internet Access Service Providers LLC v. Real Networks, Inc.*, 2005 WL 1244961 (D.Idaho 2005) (holding that this is no violation). Is there any other law that prohibits such conduct?

4. *Early results not encouraging.* Various reports suggest that the incidence of spamming did not decrease, but increased, in the first year of CAN-SPAM's operation. *See* Tom Zeller Jr., *Law Barring Junk E-Mail Allows a Flood Instead*, N.Y. Times, Feb. 1, 2005, at A1 (reporting that since CAN-SPAM went into effect spam has risen from around

60% to around 80% of all e-mail sent).

COMPARATIVE NOTE

Regulation of Unsolicited Commercial E-Mail in the European Union and Australia. Spam regulations in several foreign jurisdictions are more restrictive of spam than is the CAN-SPAM Act. In July 2002, the European Commission issued a Directive governing privacy in electronic communications. The Directive contains the following provision concerning unsolicited commercial communications, including unsolicited commercial e-mail:

Article 13
Unsolicited communications

1. The use of automated calling systems without human intervention (automatic calling machines), facsimile machines (fax) or electronic mail for the purposes of direct marketing may only be allowed in respect of subscribers who have given their prior consent.

2. Notwithstanding paragraph 1, where a natural or legal person obtains from its customers their electronic contact details for electronic mail, in the context of the sale of a product or a service, in accordance with [the Data Protection Directive], the same natural or legal person may use these electronic contact details for direct marketing of its own similar products or services provided that customers clearly and distinctly are given the opportunity to object, free of charge and in an easy manner, to such use of electronic contact details when they are collected and on the occasion of each message in case the customer has not initially refused such use.

. . .

4. In any event, the practice of sending electronic mail for purposes of direct marketing disguising or concealing the identity of the sender on whose behalf the communication is made, or without a valid address to which the recipient may send a request that such communications cease, shall be prohibited.

. . .

Directive 2002/58/EC of the European Parliament and of the Council of 12 July 2002 concerning the processing of personal data and the protection of privacy in the electronic communications sector, 2002 O.J. (L 201) 37, europa.eu.int/eur-lex/pri/en/oj/dat/2002/l_201/l_20120020731en00370047.pdf.

Article 13(1) establishes a general regime of opt-in with respect to e-mail (as well as automated telephone and fax) advertisements. Advertisements may be sent only to a consumer who has given "prior consent," which is defined as "a freely given specific and informed indication of the user's wishes, including by ticking a box when visiting an Internet website." *Id.* Recital 17. However, under Article 13(2) a seller may send marketing messages to pre-existing customers without obtaining opt-in consent, as long as the messages relate to the seller's "own similar products or services" and the seller provides the recipient an opportunity to opt out of such marketing messages. Is this an appropriate compromise between the opt-in regime demanded by consumer advocates, and the opt-out system preferred by sellers?

In December 2003, the Australian Parliament enacted a law that makes most commercial e-mail unlawful. There are exceptions for certain messages from government bodies, political parties, religious and charitable organizations, and educational institutions, for purely factual messages, and for messages that the recipient has consented to receive. *See* Spam Act 2003, No. 129, scaleplus.law.gov.au/cgi-bin/download.pl?/scale/data/pasteact/3/3628.

QUESTIONS FOR DISCUSSION

1. *Justification for preemption.* Do you agree that regulation of spam is a matter calling for a nationally uniform scheme of regulation? What would explain why the CAN-SPAM Act does not preempt state spam laws to the extent they prohibit falsity or deception, and does not preempt state laws that are not specifically directed at spam but may regulate it among other types of conduct?

2. *Labeling.* The CAN-SPAM Act requires messages containing sexually oriented material to be so labeled, but does not require any label for other types of commercial messages. Instead, it requires the FTC to report on the possibility of adding such a requirement; and it *forbids* the FTC to promulgate, by regulation, a requirement that messages be labeled in such a way as to permit easy automated filtering. § 7711(b). Most of the state spam laws included labeling requirements, which are preempted by CAN-SPAM. Why do you think Congress is reluctant to impose a general labeling requirement?

3. *Authentication.* How would an e-mail authentication system, such as the FTC is promoting, help solve the spam problem?

4. *Dormant Commerce Clause issue.* Are the Michigan and Utah laws establishing a do-not-e-mail list for children's addresses consistent with the Dormant Commerce Clause? (See the materials on the Dormant Commerce Clause in Chapter I, Part III(C), *supra.*)

F. Self-Help Approaches

In addition to the legal and legislative strategies, described above, that aim at stemming the flood of spam, ISPs and e-mail users have implemented a variety of self-help measures. Some of these measures may be credited with modest success in curbing unsolicited commercial e-mailing.

Most ISPs have adopted Terms of Service that strictly prohibit the use of their facilities for sending spam messages. A subscriber of such an ISP who violates those Terms of Service may have his subscription terminated. It is difficult, however, for ISPs to identify those who violate their Terms of Service and take steps to deny service to them. In addition, a subscriber who is ejected by one ISP can easily move to another service provider, perhaps under another name, and continue sending spam.

The informal code of Internet etiquette, sometimes referred to as "netiquette," likewise prohibits spam. Some marketers are likely to be attentive to informal codes, but many more are not. Legitimate companies, which value their reputations, have hesitated until recently to send spam because they recognize that it is widely disliked by consumers. However, since the enactment of the CAN-SPAM Act legitimate marketers have begun to include unsolicited e-mail among their marketing efforts, carefully observing the Act's requirements. Senders of fraudulent spam are unconcerned with their reputations: they hope to implement a successful money-making scheme, and then move on to the next scheme, under a new identity, once the first scheme stops working.

Some recipients of unwanted spam respond by attempting to punish the sender, such as by sending abusive responses, reporting the sender to its ISP, unleashing a flood of messages ("mail bombing") or some other online attack designed to knock the sender offline, or publicizing the sender's name and personal details. These efforts have proven largely ineffective, and sometimes counterproductive. Because spammers frequently use false return addresses and falsified routing information, and do not disclose their physical locations, they are hard to find. A reply to a spam message usually does not reach the sender: it is either directed to a nonexistent address, goes to a real address where it is automatically deleted, or goes to the address of an innocent third-party which the sender forges as the return address.

A more sophisticated system that many ISPs have adopted is subscription to a blacklist of ISPs that are deemed to offer aid and comfort to spammers. The best-known such blacklist, the Mail Abuse Prevention System's Realtime Blackhole List ("RBL"), is discussed in Chapter I, Part II(D), *supra*. ISPs that subscribe to the RBL implement an e-mail filtering system that automatically blocks the reception of e-mail messages from a sender hosted by an ISP that is on the blacklist. ISPs most commonly are placed on the RBL because they operate "open relays": mail servers that can be used by parties who are not subscribers of the ISP. Spammers frequently use open relays to disguise the origin of their messages and prevent their own ISP from terminating them for violation of the Terms of Service.

The RBL's filtering is overbroad, since it may block e-mail from innocent senders who happen to subscribe to an ISP that is on the blacklist. Some ISPs have objected to their inclusion on the blacklist.

Media3 Technologies, LLC v. Mail Abuse Prevention System, LLC
2001 WL 92389 (D.Mass.2001).

■ MORRIS E. LASKER, DISTRICT JUDGE.

Media3 Technologies, LLC ("Media3"), sues Mail Abuse Prevention System, LLC ("MAPS"), and Paul Vixie, MAPS's Chief Executive Officer, for redress of alleged unfair business practices. Media3 contends that its reputation has been injured and that it has lost current and anticipated business as the result of defamatory remarks related to Media3 placed in certain files on MAPS's website, located at mail-abuse.org/, as well as by MAPS's recommendation to other businesses, through its Realtime Blackhole List ("blackhole list"), not to allow access to websites hosted by Media3. Media3 alleges that these acts constitute defamation, intentional interference with existing advantageous business relations, intentional interference with prospective advantageous business relations, and a violation of M.G.L. ch. 93A.

Media3 moves for a preliminary injunction requiring MAPS to remove all websites hosted by Media3 from MAPS's blackhole list. The application for a preliminary injunction is denied.

I.

Media3 is an Internet "web-hosting" company based in Pembroke, Massachusetts, that offers services in creating and maintaining websites to those who wish to conduct electronic commerce. As a "web-hosting" company, Media3 is the owner of forty-two "Class C network address blocks." Each block is capable of holding approximately 254 "Internet protocol addresses" on which websites may be placed. Media3 rents Internet protocol addresses on these Class C networks to individuals and organizations who wish to create websites. Often with Media3's help, these customers then build websites which Media3 also assists in maintaining.

Before agreeing to host a website, Media3 follows the standard industry practice of requiring its customers to sign an Acceptable Use Policy for conducting business on the Internet. This policy contains provisions which are standard in the industry, including an "anti-spam" provision. . . . Media3's Acceptable Use Policy prohibits not only the transmission of spam, but also the support of spam through the development of software which could be used to hide the origin of a person sending spam.

Although Media3's Acceptable Use Policy bars websites it hosts from supporting spam in some ways, it does not prohibit its hosted websites from providing other services which appear to be used primarily by spammers. These services include the sale of lists of hundreds of thousands and even millions of e-mail addresses and computer software programs which can "harvest" similar lists from the Internet. While the vast majority of Media3's customers do not offer such "spam support" services, a few do.

In May of 2000, the offending websites were brought to the attention of MAPS. MAPS is a non-profit internet service provider based in California which, like other internet service providers (such as America Online), provides Internet and e-mail access to its subscribers. While MAPS is organized like an ordinary ISP, its mission and role in the Internet community is distinct. MAPS's stated purpose is to combat spam. Its primary means for combating spam is its "Realtime Blackhole List." The blackhole list is a constantly updated list of the websites which, in MAPS's view, either send or support the sending of spam. When MAPS places a website on the blackhole list, it blocks transmission between the website and addresses in its system. MAPS has made its popular blackhole list available to other internet service providers, sometimes for a fee. It is a popular product and approximately 40 percent of all internet addresses, including those of several Massachusetts enterprises, use MAPS's blackhole list as a spam filter.

In May of 2000, when MAPS learned that Media3 was hosting ten websites on one of its Class C networks which allegedly "supported spam," it contacted Media3 and requested that Media3; (1) terminate its hosting agreements with the contested websites; and (2) revise its Acceptable Use Policy to expressly prohibit the provision of "spam support" services such as the harvesting of e-mail addresses described above. If Media3 did not comply, MAPS informed Media3 that it would place on the blackhole list not only the ten contested websites but also any other websites that were on the same Class C network as the contested websites. This prospect was of some concern to Media3 because, as a hosting company, one of the primary services that it provides to its customers is ensuring that their websites are freely accessible and can easily access the Internet. Inclusion on MAPS's blackhole list would threaten Media3's ability to deliver good access to the Internet. After some exchange back and forth via e-mail and telephone between MAPS, in California, and Media3, in Massachusetts, Media3 refused to comply with MAPS's requests. MAPS then listed the disputed websites and any other websites on the same Class C network on the blackhole list. . . . MAPS [subsequently] added five more Class C networks hosted by Media3 to the blackhole list. At present, six Class C networks, containing over 1,500 websites hosted by Media3, remain on MAPS's blackhole list.

. . .

III. Media3's Application for a Preliminary Injunction

. . .

Although it has made serious claims which may entitle it to ultimate relief, Media3 has failed to establish a likelihood of success on the merits or that it is suffering irreparable injury. Accordingly, Media3's motion for preliminary relief is denied. . . .

A. Merits

1. Defamation

Business defamation is committed when a false and defamatory statement is communicated which "prejudice[s] [the plaintiff] in the conduct of its business and deter[s] others from dealing with it." *A.F.M. Corp. v. Corporate Aircraft Mgmt.*, 626 F.Supp.1533 (D.Mass.1985). In all other respects, the elements of a business defamation claim are those of ordinary defamation, that is, that the defendant published "a false and defamatory written communication of and concerning the plaintiff." *McAvoy v. Shufrin*, 518 N.E.2d 513, 517 (Mass.1988).

"A threshold issue is whether the statement is reasonably susceptible of a defamatory meaning, and that determination is a question of law for the court." *Foley v. Lowell Sun Pub. Co.*, 533 N.E.2d 196, 197 (Mass.1989) (citation omitted). "The test is, whether, in the circumstances, the writing discredits the plaintiff in the minds of any considerable and respectable class of the community." *Smith v. Suburban Rests., Inc.*, 373 N.E.2d 215, 217 (Mass.1978) (citations omitted). There is no dispute among the parties that calling an Internet business a "spammer," or "spam-friendly," discredits the enterprise in the minds of a considerable segment of the Internet community.[7]

However, even if the statement is subject to a defamatory construction, truth is a complete defense. . . . It is the defendant's burden to prove truth as an affirmative defense. . . . MAPS has labeled Media3 as a "spam-friendly" organization. Media3 contends that the label is false. In attempting to prove the falsity of the statement, Media3 relies heavily on its "Acceptable Use Policy," which it requires all its hosted websites to sign. This "Acceptable Use Policy" contains an "anti-spam" provision.

---

[7] Other courts have recognized that "spamming" is a practice condemned by many in the Internet community. *See CompuServe, Inc. v. Cyber Promotions, Inc.*, 962 F.Supp.1015, 1018 (S.D.Ohio 1997) (describing spamming as a "much maligned practice" in the Internet community); *America Online, Inc. v. LCGM, Inc.*, 46 F.Supp.2d 444, 446, n.1 (E.D.Va.1998) (describing spamming as a "practice widely condemned in the Internet community").

MAPS responds that its assertion that Media3 is "spam-friendly" is true because Media3 does, in fact, host companies that provide services exclusively to spammers.

Media3 has not established a likelihood that it will prevail on the merits of its defamation claim because, on the present record, MAPS has made a strong showing that its characterization of Media3 as "spam-friendly," is true. Media3's actions may well be found to outweigh its "Acceptable Use Policy." As described above, Media3 hosts several websites which provide support services that are used either exclusively or predominantly by spammers. These services include the sale of hundreds of thousands and even millions of e-mail addresses which are sold without any indication whatsoever that they are sold with the permission of the e-mail user. As the record stands, there is a serious question whether MAPS's assertion that Media3 is "spam-friendly" is defamatory because the statement appears to be accurate.

2. Intentional Interference with Existing and Prospective Business Relations

The torts of intentional interference with existing and prospective business relations share the same elements:

> (1) a business relationship or contemplated contract of economic benefit;

> (2) the defendant's knowledge of such relationship;

> (3) the defendant's interference with it through improper motive or means; and

> (4) the plaintiff's loss of advantage directly resulting from the defendant's conduct.

American Private Line Servs., Inc. v. Eastern Microwave, Inc., 980 F.2d 33, 35 (1st Cir.1992) (citing *United Truck Leasing Corp. v. Geltman*, 551 N.E.2d 20 (Mass.1990)).

Media3 contends that MAPS has improperly and tortiously listed over 1500 websites that Media3 hosts on MAPS's blackhole list. MAPS has alleged that only seventeen of these websites actually support spam. Media3 argues that MAPS's inclusion of about 1500 websites that belong to non-spamming customers of Media3 in the blackhole list was improperly motivated by an intent to "coerce" Media3 into dropping the seventeen "spam-friendly" websites.

. . .

The record to date fails to establish that Media3 is likely to prevail on the merits of its intentional interference claims because it has failed to provide any evidence of actual or imminent loss of present or future business advantage resulting from MAPS's actions and a serious question remains as to whether MAPS's motive or means were intentional and culpable.

3. Unfair Trade Practices Under M.G.L. Ch. 93A, § 11

Media3's Chapter 93A claim is based on the same allegedly "sharp practice" which forms the basis of its intentional interference claims. Media3 alleges that MAPS is attempting to "coerce" Media3 into terminating seventeen accounts which allegedly provide "spam support" by placing 1500 untainted websites on the blackhole list.

MAPS asserts three defenses to Media3's Chapter 93A claim: First, that it has not engaged in any "sharp practices;" second, that because its activities were not commercial in nature, its actions do not fall within the scope of M.G.L. ch. 93A, § 11 . . . ; and third, that Media3 has failed to establish that the allegedly unfair activities occurred "primarily and substantially" in Massachusetts.

Again, the present record fails to demonstrate that Media3 is likely to succeed on the merits of its Chapter 93A claim. There remain serious questions whether MAPS's behavior constitutes "sharp practices," as defined by the cases, as well as whether MAPS's actions occurred "primarily and substantially" in Massachusetts or involved "commercial activity" by MAPS.

. . .

IV.

For the reasons stated above, Media3's application for a preliminary injunction is denied.

Hall v. EarthLink Network, Inc.
396 F.3d 500 (2d Cir.2005).

■ POOLER, CIRCUIT JUDGE.

Plaintiffs-appellants Peter Hall and Big Bad Productions, Inc. (collectively "Hall") appeal from a final judgment and order of the United States District Court for the Southern District of New York (Richard Owen, *Judge*), entered December 30, 2003 dismissing all of Hall's claims by summary judgment. For the reasons specified below, we affirm the district court's dismissal of Hall's Electronic Communications Privacy Act, breach of contract, breach of the implied covenant of good faith and fair dealing, and tort claims.

BACKGROUND

Peter Hall, a self-employed independent film producer, wrote and filmed his first movie, entitled *Delinquent*, from 1992 to 1999. Hall marketed *Delinquent* through his corporation, Big Bad Productions Incorporated. In July 1996, Hall opened an account with EarthLink Network Incorporated ("EarthLink"), an Internet Service Provider ("ISP"), for Internet services and personal use of e-mail. Hall claims that he was known in the independent film community by his EarthLink e-mail username, lot99@earthlink.net ("lot99"). When Hall signed up for the EarthLink account, he agreed to EarthLink's subscriber agreement ("contract") which stipulated that California law governed the contract.

Delinquent was scheduled to premiere on September 12, 1997, in New York City and Los Angeles. According to the complaint, Hall planned to use his EarthLink lot99 e-mail account to promote the two September 12, 1997, premieres at the upcoming Chicago Underground Film Festival on August 13, 1997. On August 5,

1997, UUNet, which provided "backbone" Internet services to EarthLink informed EarthLink that lot99 was sending mass junk e-mail, or "spam." EarthLink immediately terminated Hall's access to the lot99 e-mail account and placed the lot99 e-mail address on "Net Abuse Report," a web list of e-mail abusers. *Hall v. Earthlink Network, Inc.,* 2003 WL 22990064, at * 1 (S.D.N.Y. Dec.19, 2003). Six days later, on August 11, 1997, after a series of exchanges between EarthLink, Hall, and Wired News (an Internet industry magazine), EarthLink determined that lot99 was not a source of spam. EarthLink posted a retraction on the Net Abuse Report website and sent sixteen lot99 e-mails to Hall's new non-EarthLink e-mail account. Hall claims that he requested that EarthLink turn his service back on but that EarthLink failed to do so. EarthLink claims that Hall, "with shouted obscenities," refused its offers to reconnect the account. Hall's EarthLink account was not reopened, and between mid-August 1997 and July 1998, EarthLink received and stored 591 e-mails sent to the lot99 address. In July 1998, EarthLink sent the 591 stored e-mails to Hall.

On July 31, 1998, Hall filed a complaint in district court. The complaint included claims for a violation of the Electronic Communications Privacy Act, 18 U.S.C. § 2510 *et seq.* ("ECPA"), breach of contract, libel, breach of the covenant of good faith and fair dealing, negligent appropriation of electronic communication, intentional interference with electronic communication, and prima facie tort. Following discovery, EarthLink moved for summary judgment.

Hall's ECPA claim was that EarthLink "illegally intercepted" his e-mail in violation of 18 U.S.C. § 2511(1)(a) by intentionally continuing to receive messages sent to lot99 after the termination of his account. The district court dismissed this claim, reasoning that EarthLink's acts did not constitute an "intentional interception" under ECPA. Hall also claimed that EarthLink's sudden termination of his access to the Internet and to his e-mail breached his contract with the ISP. EarthLink's actions, Hall alleged, made it impossible for him to adequately advertise *Delinquent* in time for the Chicago Underground Film Festival and to respond to inquiries about his upcoming premieres. Hall claimed that *Delinquent* did not receive the publicity that it would have received had he not lost his Internet service.

The district court did not reach the issue of whether or not the contract was breached because it (1) found that consequential damages stemming from Hall's lost business opportunities were too speculative and therefore dismissed Hall's claim for consequential damages; (2) held that without consequential damages, Hall's actual damages claim—for stationery, Internet service, and telephone calls—could not meet the jurisdictional amount for diversity jurisdiction, $75,000, *see* 28 U.S.C. § 1332(a); and (3) therefore dismissed the claim in its entirety. The district court also dismissed Hall's claims for breach of the implied covenant of good faith and fair dealing, prima facie tort, libel, negligent appropriation of electronic communication, and intentional interference with electronic communication. On appeal, Hall contends that each of these dismissals, except the dismissal of the libel and prima facie tort claims, was error. While we disagree with the district court's reasoning in part, we affirm the district court's dismissal of all of these claims.

DISCUSSION

I. *Electronic Communications Privacy Act*

We review the district court's summary judgment dismissal of Hall's ECPA claim de novo. . . . We agree with the district court's conclusion that EarthLink did not violate 18 U.S.C. § 2511(1)(a) but write to further clarify the proper interpretation of this section.

Through the enactment of ECPA, Congress amended the Federal wiretap law in order to "update and clarify Federal privacy protections and standards in light of dramatic changes in new computer and telecommunications technologies." Sen. Rep. No. 99–541, at 1 (1986), *reprinted in* 1986 U.S.C.C.A.N. 3555, 3555. ECPA is divided into Title I, which governs unauthorized interception of electronic communications, 18 U.S.C. §§ 2510–2522, and Title II, which governs unauthorized access to stored communications, 18 U.S.C. §§ 2701–2711. . . . This appeal concerns Title I exclusively.

Section 2511(1)(a) states that, except as otherwise provided, anyone who "intentionally intercepts, endeavors to intercept, or procures any other person to intercept or endeavor to intercept, any . . . electronic communication" violates ECPA. 18 U.S.C. § 2511(1)(a). The district court held that EarthLink did not "intentionally intercept anything" in violation of Section 2511(1)(a) because EarthLink "merely received and stored e-mails precisely where they were sent—to an address on the EarthLink system." The district court did not specify whether it based this holding on a determination that EarthLink's actions were not an interception, not intentional, or both. We hold that EarthLink's continued reception of e-mails sent to lot99 did not constitute an "interception" under ECPA because it was conducted as part of the "ordinary course of [EarthLink's] business." *See* 18 U.S.C. § 2510(5)(a). Because we hold that EarthLink did not intercept electronic communications in violation of ECPA, we do not need to decide whether EarthLink's acts were intentional.

EarthLink's act did not constitute an interception

ECPA defines the term "intercept" as "the aural or other acquisition of the contents of any . . . electronic . . . communication[1] through the use of *any electronic, mechanical, or other device.*" 18 U.S.C. § 2510(4) (emphasis added). ECPA provides an ordinary course of business exception applicable to this case within its definition of

---

[1] An "electronic communication" is defined as:

any transfer of signs, signals, writing, images, sounds, data, or intelligence of any nature transmitted in whole or in part by a wire, radio, electromagnetic, photoelectronic or photooptical system that affects interstate or foreign commerce . . .

18 U.S.C. § 2510(12). EarthLink argues that communication over the Internet can only be electronic communication while it is in transit, not while it is in electronic storage. EarthLink also contends that an "interception" can only occur when messages are in transit. These arguments lack merit because, unlike the line of cases EarthLink relies on, this case involves the *continued receipt* of e-mail messages rather than the acquisition of *previously stored* electronic communication. . . .

"any electronic, mechanical, or other device." 18 U.S.C. § 2510(5)(a). "[A]ny telephone or telegraph instrument, equipment or facility, or any component thereof . . . being used by a provider of wire or electronic communication service in the ordinary course of its business" is not an electronic, mechanical, or other device, and therefore does not fall under the definition of "intercept." *Id.* EarthLink acquired the contents of electronic communications but did so in the ordinary course of business and thus did not use "any electronic, mechanical, or other device" as defined by the statute.

Hall reads Section 2510(5)(a)'s ordinary course of business exception to apply only to an ISP[2] that uses *telephone* or *telegraph* instruments, equipment or facilities. EarthLink interprets the language to include ISPs that use any telephone or telegraph instrument *or* any equipment or facility. To resolve this issue, we look first to the plain language of Section 2510(5)(a). . . . The placement of the commas could suggest that the phrase "telephone or telegraph" modifies "instrument," "equipment," and "facility." According to this reading, the ordinary course of business exception would apply only to an ISP using a telephone or telegraph. On the other hand, the placement of the commas could suggest that "telephone or telegraph" only modifies "instrument." Accordingly, the ordinary course of business exception would also apply to an ISP using any equipment or facility. . . .

Because the plain language of Section 2510(5)(a) is arguably ambiguous and we do not find guidance from the statutory structure, we may look to the legislative history to clarify Congressional intent. . . . The legislative history demonstrates that Congress intended to apply Section 2510(5)(a)'s ordinary course of business exception to ISPs. To understand Congress' intent it is important to note that Internet technology has advanced significantly since Congress enacted ECPA in 1986. *See United States v. Steiger*, 318 F.3d 1039, 1047 (11th Cir.2003); *Konop v. Hawaiian Airlines, Inc.*, 302 F.3d 868, 874 (9th Cir.2002). At the time ECPA was enacted in 1986, ISPs directed e-mail over telephone wires and were therefore included in the ordinary course of business exception. The Senate Report stated that "[e]lectronic mail is a form of communication by which private correspondence is transmitted *over public and private telephone lines.*" Sen. Rep. No. 99–541 (1986), *reprinted in* 1986 U.S.C.C.A.N. 3555, 3562 (emphasis added). Congress' use of the term "telephone" was thus understood to include the instruments, equipment and facilities that ISPs use to transmit e-mail. Therefore, under both of the parties' interpretations, ISPs are included in Section 2510(5)(a)'s ordinary course of business exception.

Moreover, an interpretation that excludes ISPs from the ordinary course of business exception should be avoided because it would lead to an absurd result. . . . If ISPs were not covered by the ordinary course of business exception, ISPs would constantly be intercepting communications under ECPA because their basic services involve the "acquisition of the contents" of electronic communication. *See* 18 U.S.C. § 2510(4). Congress could not have intended this absurd result. . . . Thus, we hold that ISPs do not "intercept" if they are acting within the ordinary course of their businesses.

---

[2] It is not disputed that ISPs are a type of electronic communication service provider.

We must next determine, therefore, if there is a material issue of fact as to whether or not EarthLink was acting within the ordinary course of business when it continued to receive messages sent to lot99. EarthLink argues that it used its routers, servers and other computer equipment as part of its e-mail service to all customers, including Hall, in the ordinary course of its business. Hall asserts that "intentionally seizing e-mail of someone who is no longer a customer" is not within any ISP's ordinary course of business. Hall, however, does not provide evidence to establish that EarthLink's actions were not part of its ordinary course of business. . . . EarthLink, on the other hand, provided testimony that it was its practice at the time to continue to receive and store e-mails on the server's mail file after any account was cancelled. Moreover, EarthLink presented testimony that, at the time relevant to this action, it did not have the ability to bounce e-mail back to senders after the termination of an account. Because there is no evidence on the record that EarthLink was not acting within the ordinary course of its business, there is no material issue of fact and summary judgment was appropriate.

II. *Breach of contract*

We review the district court's summary judgment dismissal of Hall's breach of contract claims de novo. . . . Hall essentially requested two forms of relief for breach of contract: consequential damages and actual damages. [The court dismissed Hall's claim for consequential damages, consisting of lost profits, on the ground that they were too speculative. The court dismissed the claim for actual damages on procedural grounds.]

III. *Breach of the implied covenant of good faith and fair dealing*

We review the district court's summary judgment dismissal of Hall's implied covenant of good faith and fair dealing claim de novo. . . . After reviewing the record, we agree with the district court that Hall's implied covenant of good faith and fair dealing claim was entirely duplicative of his breach of contract claim. . . .

IV. *The torts of negligent appropriation of electronic communication and intentional interference with electronic communication*

We affirm the district court's dismissal of these claims because (1) Hall's claims against EarthLink flow from the contract and Hall has not shown that EarthLink owed him an additional duty which would justify relief sounding in tort and (2) Hall has not presented a reasonable showing that existing torts, such as prima facie tort, are not adequate to protect his interests.

CONCLUSION

For the reasons we have discussed, we affirm the judgment of the district court.

EXTENSIONS

1. *Immunity for spam fighters.* In *OptInRealBig.com, LLC v. IronPort Systems, Inc.*, 323 F.Supp.2d 1037 (N.D.Cal.2004), the plaintiff, a sender of bulk commercial e-mail, sued the operator of SpamCop.net, a service that collects complaints from recipients of spam, forwards those complaints to the ISP that provides bandwidth to the spammer, and encourages the ISP to take action against the spammer. The court held that SpamCop.net was immune from liability under the Communications Decency Act, 47 U.S.C. § 230 (discussed in Chapter 13, *infra*). The court also found that plaintiff was unlikely to succeed with claims predicated on trade libel, interference with contractual relations, and unfair business practices.

2. *Wrongful filtering.* In a variation on the blacklist theme, Blue Mountain Arts, a company allowing users to send free online electronic greeting cards, sued Microsoft for alleged malicious filtering of its cards. According to Blue Mountain, a beta version of Microsoft's Internet Explorer web browser came equipped with a "junk" e-mail filter, designed to route incoming spam away from the inbox and into a special junk-mail folder. The filter, Blue Mountain said, treated its greeting cards as spam, and sent them to the junk-mail folder. The court granted Blue Mountain a preliminary injunction, and the parties later settled. *See Hartford House, Ltd. v. Microsoft Corp.*, Case No. CV 778550 (Cal.Super.Ct. prelim. inj. issued Feb. 2, 1999).

QUESTIONS FOR DISCUSSION

The limits of self-help. Consider who should have the authority to decide whether particular e-mail messages are spam. What are the risks of allowing private parties to make this decision and implement self-help measures? Are existing causes of action adequate to protect the interests of e-mail users who are wrongly branded as spammers?

II. ACQUIRING DATA FROM ANOTHER'S WEBSITE

eBay, Inc. v. Bidder's Edge, Inc.
100 F.Supp.2d 1058 (N.D.Cal.2000).

■ WHYTE, DISTRICT JUDGE.

Plaintiff eBay, Inc.'s ("eBay") motion for preliminary injunction was heard by the court on April 14, 2000. . . . For the reasons set forth below, the court preliminarily enjoins defendant Bidder's Edge, Inc. ("BE") from accessing eBay's computer systems by use of any automated querying program without eBay's written authorization.

I. BACKGROUND

eBay is an Internet-based, person-to-person trading site. eBay offers sellers the ability to list items for sale and prospective buyers the ability to search those listings and bid on items. The seller can set the terms and conditions of the auction. The item is sold to the highest bidder. The transaction is consummated directly between the buyer and seller without eBay's involvement. . . .

Users of the eBay site must register and agree to the eBay User Agreement. Users agree to the seven page User Agreement by clicking on an "I Accept" button located at the end of the User Agreement. The current version of the User Agreement prohibits the use of "any robot, spider, other automatic device, or manual process to monitor or copy our web pages or the content contained herein without our prior expressed written permission." It is not clear that the version of the User Agreement in effect at the time BE began searching the eBay site prohibited such activity, or that BE ever agreed to comply with the User Agreement.

eBay currently has over 7 million registered users. Over 400,000 new items are added to the site every day. Every minute, 600 bids are placed on almost 3 million items. Users currently perform, on average, 10 million searches per day on eBay's database. Bidding for and sales of items are continuously ongoing in millions of separate auctions.

A software robot is a computer program which operates across the Internet to perform searching, copying and retrieving functions on the web sites of others.[2] A software robot is capable of executing thousands of instructions per minute, far in excess of what a human can accomplish. Robots consume the processing and storage resources of a system, making that portion of the system's capacity unavailable to the system owner or other users. Consumption of sufficient system resources will slow the processing of the overall system and can overload the system such that it will malfunction or "crash." A severe malfunction can cause a loss of data and an interruption in services.

The eBay site employs "robot exclusion headers." A robot exclusion header is a message, sent to computers programmed to detect and respond to such headers, that eBay does not permit unauthorized robotic activity. Programmers who wish to comply with the Robot Exclusion Standard design their robots to read a particular data file, "robots.txt," and to comply with the control directives it contains.

. . .

BE is a company with 22 employees that was founded in 1997. The BE website debuted in November 1998. BE does not host auctions. BE is an auction aggregation site designed to offer on-line auction buyers the ability to search for items across numerous on-line auctions without having to search each host site individually. As of March 2000, the BE website contained information on more that five million items being auctioned on more than one hundred auction sites. BE also provides its users with additional auction-related services and information. The information available on the BE site is contained in a database of information that BE compiles through access to various auction sites such as eBay. When a user enters a search for a particular item at BE, BE searches its database and generates a list of every item in the database responsive to the search, organized by auction closing date and time. Rather than going to each host auction site one at a time, a user who goes to BE may conduct a single search to obtain information about that item on every auction site tracked by BE. It is important to include information regarding eBay auctions on the BE site because eBay is by far the biggest consumer to consumer on-line auction site.

. . .

In early 1998, eBay gave BE permission to include information regarding eBay-hosted auctions for Beanie Babies and Furbies in the BE database. In early 1999, BE added to the number of person-to-person auction sites it covered and

---

[2] Programs that recursively query other computers over the Internet in order to obtain a significant amount of information are referred to in the pleadings by various names, including software robots, robots, spiders and web crawlers.

started covering a broader range of items hosted by those sites, including eBay. On April 24, 1999, eBay verbally approved BE crawling the eBay website for a period of 90 days. The parties contemplated that during this period they would reach a formal licensing agreement. They were unable to do so.

. . .

In late August or early September 1999, eBay requested by telephone that BE cease posting eBay auction listings on its site. BE agreed to do so. In October 1999, BE learned that other auction aggregations sites were including information regarding eBay auctions. On November 2, 1999, BE issued a press release indicating that it had resumed including eBay auction listings on its site. On November 9, 1999, eBay sent BE a letter reasserting that BE's activities were unauthorized, insisting that BE cease accessing the eBay site, alleging that BE's activities constituted a civil trespass and offering to license BE's activities. eBay and BE were again unable to agree on licensing terms. As a result, eBay attempted to block BE from accessing the eBay site; by the end of November, 1999, eBay had blocked a total of 169 IP addresses it believed BE was using to query eBay's system. BE elected to continue crawling eBay's site by using proxy servers to evade eBay's IP blocks.

Approximately 69% of the auction items contained in the BE database are from auctions hosted on eBay. BE estimates that it would lose one-third of its users if it ceased to cover the eBay auctions.

The parties agree that BE accessed the eBay site approximate[ly] 100,000 times a day. eBay alleges that BE activity constituted up to 1.53% of the number of requests received by eBay, and up to 1.10% of the total data transferred by eBay during certain periods in October and November of 1999. BE alleges that BE activity constituted no more than 1.11% of the requests received by eBay, and no more than 0.70% of the data transferred by eBay. . . .

It appears that major Internet search engines, such as Yahoo!, Google, Excite and AltaVista, respect the Robot Exclusion Standard.

eBay now moves for preliminary injunctive relief preventing BE from accessing the eBay computer system based on nine causes of action: trespass, false advertising, federal and state trademark dilution, computer fraud and abuse, unfair competition, misappropriation, interference with prospective economic advantage and unjust enrichment. . . .

II. LEGAL STANDARD

To obtain preliminary injunctive relief, a movant must demonstrate "either a likelihood of success on the merits and the possibility of irreparable injury, or that serious questions going to the merits were raised and the balance of hardships tips sharply in its favor." . . . "The critical element in determining the test to be applied is the relative hardship to the parties. If the balance of harm tips decidedly toward the plaintiff, then the plaintiff need not show as robust a likelihood of success on the merits as when the balance tips less decidedly." . . .

III. ANALYSIS

A. Balance of Harm

. . .

According to eBay, the load on its servers resulting from BE's web crawlers represents between 1.11% and 1.53% of the total load on eBay's listing servers. eBay alleges both economic loss from BE's current activities and potential harm resulting from the total crawling of BE and others. In alleging economic harm, eBay's argument is that eBay has expended considerable time, effort and money to create its computer system, and that BE should have to pay for the portion of eBay's system BE uses. eBay attributes a pro rata portion of the costs of maintaining its entire system to the BE activity. However, eBay does not indicate that these expenses are incrementally incurred because of BE's activities, nor that any particular service disruption can be attributed to BE's activities. eBay provides no support for the proposition that the pro rata costs of obtaining an item represent the appropriate measure of damages for unauthorized use. In contrast, California law appears settled that the appropriate measure of damages is the actual harm inflicted by the conduct:

> Where the conduct complained of does not amount to a substantial interference with possession or the right thereto, but consists of intermeddling with or use of or damages to the personal property, the owner has a cause of action for trespass or case, and may recover only the actual damages suffered by reason of the impairment of the property or the loss of its use.

Zaslow v. Kroenert, 176 P.2d 1, 7 (Cal.1946). Moreover, even if BE is inflicting incremental maintenance costs on eBay, potentially calculable monetary damages are not generally a proper foundation for a preliminary injunction. . . .

eBay's allegations of harm are based, in part, on the argument that BE's activities should be thought of as equivalent to sending in an army of 100,000 robots a day to check the prices in a competitor's store. This analogy, while graphic, appears inappropriate. Although an admittedly formalistic distinction, unauthorized robot intruders into a "brick and mortar" store would be committing a trespass to real property. There does not appear to be any doubt that the appropriate remedy for an ongoing trespass to business premises would be a preliminary injunction. . . . More importantly, for the analogy to be accurate, the robots would have to make up less than two out of every one-hundred customers in the store, the robots would not interfere with the customers' shopping experience, nor would the robots even be seen by the customers. Under such circumstances, there is a legitimate claim that the robots would not pose any threat of irreparable harm. However, eBay's right to injunctive relief is also based upon a much stronger argument.

If BE's activity is allowed to continue unchecked, it would encourage other auction aggregators to engage in similar recursive searching of the eBay system such that eBay would suffer irreparable harm from reduced system performance, system unavailability, or data losses. BE does not appear to seriously contest that reduced system performance, system unavailability or data loss would inflict irreparable harm on eBay consisting of lost profits and lost customer goodwill. Harm resulting from lost profits and lost customer goodwill is irreparable because it is neither easily calculable, nor easily compensable and is therefore an appropriate basis for injunctive relief. . . . Where, as here, the denial of preliminary injunctive relief would encourage an increase in the complained of activity, and such an increase would present a strong likelihood of irreparable harm, the plaintiff has at least established a possibility of irreparable harm.

. . .

BE correctly observes that there is a dearth of authority supporting a preliminary injunction based on an ongoing to trespass to chattels. In contrast, it is black letter law in California that an injunction is an appropriate remedy for a continuing trespass to real property. *See Allred v. Harris*, 14 Cal.App.4th 1386, 1390 (1993) (citing 5 B.E. Witkin, *Summary of California Law*, Torts § 605 (9th ed. 1988)). If eBay were a brick and mortar auction house with limited seating capacity, eBay would appear to be entitled to reserve those seats for potential bidders, to refuse entrance to individuals (or robots) with no intention of bidding on any of the items, and to seek preliminary injunctive relief against non-customer trespassers eBay was physically unable to exclude. . . . The court concludes that under the circumstances present here, BE's ongoing violation of eBay's fundamental property right to exclude others from its computer system potentially causes sufficient irreparable harm to support a preliminary injunction.

BE argues that even if eBay is entitled to a presumption of irreparable harm, the presumption may be rebutted. The presumption may be rebutted by evidence that a party has engaged in a pattern of granting licenses to engage in the complained of activity such that it may be reasonable to expect that invasion of the right can be recompensed with a royalty rather than with an injunction, or by evidence that a party has unduly delayed in bringing suit, thereby negating the idea of irreparability. . . . BE alleges that eBay has both engaged in a pattern of licensing aggregators to crawl its site as well as delayed in seeking relief. For the reasons set forth below, the court finds that neither eBay's limited licensing activities nor its delay in seeking injunctive relief while it attempted to resolve the matter without judicial intervention are sufficient to rebut the possibility of irreparable harm.

If eBay's irreparable harm claim were premised solely on the potential harm caused by BE's current crawling activities, evidence that eBay had licensed others to crawl the eBay site would suggest that BE's activity would not result in irreparable harm to eBay. However, the gravamen of the alleged irreparable harm is that if eBay is allowed to continue to crawl the eBay site, it may encourage frequent and unregulated crawling to the point that eBay's system will be irreparably harmed. There is no evidence that eBay has indiscriminately licensed all comers. Rather, it appears that eBay has carefully chosen to permit crawling by a limited number of aggregation sites that agree to abide by the terms of eBay's licensing agreement. "The existence of such a [limited] license, unlike a general license offered to all comers, does not demonstrate a decision to relinquish all control over the distribution of the product in exchange for a readily computable fee." *Ty, Inc. v. GMA Accessories, Inc.*, 132 F.3d 1167, 1173 (7th Cir.1997) (discussing presumption of irreparable harm in copyright infringement context). eBay's licensing activities appear directed toward limiting the amount and nature of crawling activity on the eBay site. Such licensing does not support the inference that carte blanche crawling of the eBay site would pose no threat of irreparable harm.

. . .

BE argues that even if eBay will be irreparably harmed if a preliminary injunction is not granted, BE will suffer greater irreparable harm if an injunction is granted. According to BE, lack of access to eBay's database will result in a two-thirds decrease in the items listed on BE, and a one-eighth reduction in the value of BE, from $80 million to $70 million. Although the potential harm to BE does not appear insignificant, BE does not appear to have suffered any irreparable harm during the period it voluntarily ceased crawling the eBay site. Barring BE from automatically querying eBay's site does not prevent BE from maintaining an aggregation site including information from eBay's site. Any potential economic harm is appropriately addressed through the posting of an adequate bond.

. . . Accordingly, the court concludes that eBay has demonstrated at least a possibility of suffering irreparable system harm and that BE has not established a balance of hardships weighing in its favor.

B. Likelihood of Success

As noted above, eBay moves for a preliminary injunction on all nine of its causes of action. . . . Since the court finds eBay is entitled to the relief requested based on its trespass claim, the court does not address the merits of the remaining claims or BE's arguments that many of these other state law causes of action are preempted by federal copyright law. . . .

1. Trespass

. . .

In order to prevail on a claim for trespass based on accessing a computer system, the plaintiff must establish: (1) defendant intentionally and without authorization interfered with plaintiff's possessory interest in the computer system; and (2) defendant's unauthorized use proximately resulted in damage to plaintiff. *See* [*Thrifty–Tel v. Bezenek*, 54 Cal.Rptr.2d 468, 473 (Cal.Ct.App.1996).] Here, eBay has presented evidence sufficient to establish a strong likelihood of proving both prongs and ultimately prevailing on the merits of its trespass claim.

a. BE's Unauthorized Interference

eBay argues that BE's use was unauthorized and intentional. eBay is correct. BE does not dispute that it employed an automated computer program to connect with and search eBay's electronic database. BE admits that, because other auction aggregators were including eBay's auctions in their listing, it continued to "crawl" eBay's website even after eBay demanded BE terminate such activity.

BE argues that it cannot trespass eBay's website because the site is publicly accessible. BE's argument is unconvincing. eBay's servers are private property, conditional access to which eBay grants the public. eBay does not generally permit the type of automated access made by BE. In fact, eBay explicitly notifies automated visitors that their access is not permitted. "In general, California does recognize a trespass claim where the defendant exceeds the scope of the consent." *Baugh v. CBS, Inc.*, 828 F.Supp. 745, 756 (N.D.Cal.1993).

Even if BE's web crawlers were authorized to make individual queries of eBay's system, BE's web crawlers exceeded the scope of any such consent when they began acting like robots by making repeated queries. . . . Moreover, eBay repeatedly and explicitly notified BE that its use of eBay's computer system was unauthorized. The entire reason BE directed its queries through proxy servers was to evade eBay's attempts to stop this unauthorized access. The court concludes that BE's activity is sufficiently outside of the scope of the use permitted by eBay that it is unauthorized for the purposes of establishing a trespass. . . .

eBay argues that BE interfered with eBay's possessory interest in its computer system. Although eBay appears unlikely to be able to show a substantial interference at this time, such a showing is not required. Conduct that does not amount to a substantial interference with possession, but which consists of intermeddling with or use of another's personal property, is sufficient to establish a cause of action for trespass to chattel. *See Thrifty-Tel*, 54 Cal.Rptr.2d at 473 (distinguishing the tort from conversion). Although the court admits some uncertainty as to the precise level of possessory interference required to constitute an intermeddling, there does not appear to be any dispute that eBay can show that BE's conduct amounts to use of eBay's computer systems. Accordingly, eBay has made a strong showing that it is likely to prevail on the merits of its assertion that BE's use of eBay's computer system was an unauthorized and intentional interference with eBay's possessory interest.

b. Damage to eBay's Computer System

A trespasser is liable when the trespass diminishes the condition, quality or value of personal property. *See CompuServe, Inc. v. Cyber Promotions*, 962 F.Supp. 1015 (S.D.Ohio 1997). The quality or value of personal property may be "diminished even though it is not physically damaged by defendant's conduct." *Id.* at 1022. . . .

eBay is likely to be able to demonstrate that BE's activities have diminished the quality or value of eBay's computer systems. BE's activities consume at least a portion of plaintiff's bandwidth and server capacity. Although there is some dispute as to the percentage of queries on eBay's site for which BE is responsible, BE admits that it sends some 80,000 to 100,000 requests to plaintiff's computer systems per day. Although eBay does not claim that this consumption has led to any physical damage to eBay's computer system, nor does eBay provide any evidence to support the claim that it may have lost revenues or customers based on this use, eBay's claim is that BE's use is appropriating eBay's personal property by using valuable bandwidth and capacity, and necessarily compromising eBay's ability to use that capacity for its own purposes. *See CompuServe*, 962 F.Supp. at 1022 ("any value [plaintiff] realizes from its computer equipment is wholly derived from the extent to which that equipment can serve its subscriber base.").

BE argues that its searches represent a negligible load on plaintiff's computer systems, and do not rise to the level of impairment to the condition or value of eBay's computer system required to constitute a trespass. However, it is undisputed that eBay's server and its capacity are personal property, and that BE's searches use a portion of this property. Even if, as BE argues, its searches use only a small amount of eBay's computer system capacity, BE has nonetheless deprived eBay of the ability to use that portion of its personal property for its own purposes. The law recognizes no such right to use another's personal property. Accordingly, BE's actions appear to have caused injury to eBay and appear likely to continue to cause injury to eBay. If the court were to hold otherwise, it would likely encourage other auction aggregators to crawl the eBay site, potentially to the point of denying effective access to eBay's customers. If preliminary injunctive relief were denied, and other aggregators began to crawl the eBay site, there appears to be little doubt that the load on eBay's computer system would qualify as a substantial impairment of condition or value. California law does not require eBay to wait for such a disaster before applying to this court for relief. The court concludes that eBay has made a strong showing that it is likely to prevail on the merits of its trespass claim, and that there is at least a possibility that it will suffer irreparable harm if preliminary injunctive relief is not granted. eBay is therefore entitled to preliminary injunctive relief.

. . .

IV. ORDER

Bidder's Edge, its officers, agents, servants, employees, attorneys and those in active concert or participation with them who receive actual notice of this order by personal service or otherwise, are hereby enjoined pending the trial of this matter, from using any automated query program, robot, web crawler or other similar device, without written authorization, to access eBay's computer systems or networks, for the purpose of copying any part of eBay's auction database. . . .

. . .

EXTENSIONS

A different view: requirement of "tangible interference." In *Ticketmaster Corp. v. Tickets.com, Inc.*, 2003 Copr.L.Dec. ¶ 28,607 (C.D.Cal.2003), the plaintiff, the largest seller of events tickets in the United States, sought to prevent defendant, a much smaller seller of tickets, from using robots to extract information about events from plaintiff's site, and presenting that information on its own site. The court declined to hold that defendant's actions constituted trespass to chattels, granting the defendant summary judgment on this claim. The court recognized that some cases, including *eBay v. Bidder's Edge*, had held "that mere invasion or use of a portion of the web site by a spider is a trespass (leading at least to nominal damages), and that there need not be an independent showing of direct harm either to the chattel (unlikely in the case of a spider) or tangible interference with the use of the computer being invaded," but disagreed with those cases. It held that for trespass there must be "some tangible interference with the use or operation of the computer being invaded by the spider"; there must either be physical injury to the chattel, or "some evidence that the use or utility of the computer (or computer network) being 'spiderized' is adversely affected by the use of the spider." It further held that defendant's argument that it spent time and money trying to frustrate the spider, and that the spider acquired valuable information, is unavailing, since that fails to show "damage to the computers or their operation." Compare this analysis with the California Supreme Court's decision in *Intel v. Hamidi*, excerpted in Part III, *infra*.

QUESTIONS FOR DISCUSSION

1. *Notice via robot exclusion headers.* eBay's site contained "robot exclusion headers," which are instructions in a file named "robots.txt" that are designed to affect the operation of robot software that accesses the site. A robot's programmer may design it to read the instructions contained in the robots.txt file; if the robots.txt file bars access by robots, and the robot is programmed to heed the instructions in robots.txt files, then the robot will not access the site. Should a website's implementation of a robots.txt file be deemed notice to all who deploy robots that their accessing of the site is unauthorized? Should it only be notice as to robots that have been designed to read and honor the instructions in robots.txt files?

2. *Anticipatory harm.* Do you agree with the court's holding that trespass to chattels may be premised on the likelihood that harm will result if *additional* parties begin accessing eBay's site without authorization?

3. *Database copying.* The injunction that eBay sought and obtained prevents "copying . . . eBay's auction database." Could eBay have obtained relief under the law of copyright? under state law of unfair competition or misappropriation? Is trespass to chattels an appropriate instrument for database protection? Reconsider Chapter 8, *supra*.

Register.com, Inc. v. Verio, Inc.
126 F.Supp.2d 238 (S.D.N.Y.2000).

■ JONES, DISTRICT JUDGE.

Introduction

Plaintiff Register.com, a registrar of Internet domain names, moves for a preliminary injunction against the defendant, Verio, Inc. ("Verio"), a provider of Internet services. Register.com relies on claims under Section 43(a) of the Lanham Act, 15 U.S.C. § 1125(a); the Computer Fraud and Abuse Act of 1986, 18 U.S.C. § 1030, as amended; as well as trespass to chattels and breach of contract under the common law of the State of New York. In essence Register.com seeks an injunction barring Verio from using automated software processes to access and collect the registrant contact information contained in its WHOIS database and from using any of that information, however accessed, for mass marketing purposes.

I. Findings of Fact

The Parties

Plaintiff Register.com is one of over fifty domain name registrars for customers who wish to register a name in the .com, .net, and .org top-level domains. As a registrar it contracts with these second-level domain ("SLD") name holders and a registry, collecting registration data about the SLD holder and submitting zone file information for entry in the registry database. In addition to its domain name registration services, Register.com offers to its customers, both directly and through its more than 450 co-branded and private label partners, a variety of other related services, such as (i) website creation tools; (ii) website hosting; (iii) electronic mail; (iv) domain name hosting; (v) domain name forwarding, and (vi) real-time domain name management. . . .

. . .

Defendant Verio is one of the largest operators of web sites for businesses and a leading provider of comprehensive Internet services. Although not a registrar of domain names, Verio directly competes with Register.com and its partners to provide registration services and a variety of other Internet services including website hosting and development. Verio recently made a multimillion dollar investment in its computer system and facilities for its expanded force of telephone sales associates in its efforts to "provide recent domain name registration customers with the services they need, at the time they need them."

The WHOIS database

To become an accredited domain name registrar for the .com, .net, and .org domains, all registrars, including Register.com are required to enter into a registrar Accreditation Agreement ("Agreement") with the Internet Corporation for Assigned Names and Numbers ("ICANN"). Under that Agreement, Register.com, as well as all other registrars, is required to provide an on-line, interactive WHOIS database. This database contains the names and contact information — postal address, telephone number, electronic mail address and in some cases facsimile number — for customers who register domain names through the registrar. The Agreement also requires Register.com to make the database freely accessible to the public via its web page and through an independent access port called port 43. These query-based channels of access to the WHOIS database allow the user to collect registrant contact information for one domain name at a time by entering the domain name into the provided search engine.

The primary purpose of the WHOIS database is to provide necessary information in the event of domain name disputes, such as those arising from cybersquatting or trademark infringement. The parties also agree that the WHOIS data may be used for market research.

. . .

. . . Register.com implemented the following . . . terms of use governing its WHOIS database:

> By submitting a WHOIS query, you agree that you will use this data only for lawful purposes and that, under no circumstances will you use this data to: (1) allow, enable, or otherwise support the transmission of mass unsolicited, commercial advertising or solicitations **via direct mail,** electronic mail, **or by telephone** . . . .

(emphasis added).

Verio's Project Henhouse

In late 1999, to better target their marketing and sales efforts toward customers in need of web hosting services and to reach those customers more quickly, Verio developed an automated software program or "robot." With its search robot, Verio accessed the WHOIS database maintained by the accredited registrars, including Register.com, and collected the contact information of customers who had recently registered a domain name. Then, despite the marketing prohibitions in Register.com's terms of use, Verio utilized this data in a marketing initiative known as Project Henhouse and began to contact and solicit Register.com's customers, within the first several days after their registration, by e-mail, regular mail, and telephone.

Verio's Search Robots

In general, the process worked as follows: First, each day Verio downloaded, in compressed format, a list of all currently registered domain names, of all registrars, ending in .com, .net, and .org. That list or database is maintained by Network Solutions, Inc. ("NSI") and is published on 13 different "root zone" servers. The registry list is updated twice daily and provides the domain name, the sponsoring registrar, and the nameservers for all registered names. Using a computer program, Verio then compared the newly downloaded NSI registry with the NSI registry it downloaded a day earlier in order to isolate the domain names that had been registered in the last day and the names that had been removed. After downloading the list of new domain names, only then was a search robot used to query the NSI database to extract the name of the accredited registrar of each new name. That search robot then automatically made successive queries to the various registrars' WHOIS databases, via the port 43 access channels, to harvest the relevant contact information for each new domain name registered. Once retrieved, the WHOIS data was deposited into an information database maintained by Verio. The resulting database of sales leads was then provided to Verio's telemarketing staff.

. . .

IV. Register.com's Claims

. . .

B. Trespass To Chattels

Register.com argues that Verio's use of an automated software robot to search the "WHOIS" database constitutes trespass to chattels. Register.com states that it has made its computer system available on the Internet, and that "Verio has used 'software automation' to flood that computer system with traffic in order to retrieve the contact information of Register.com customers for the purpose of solicitation in knowing violation of Register.com's posted policies and terms of use."

The standard for trespass to chattels in New York is based upon the standard set forth in the Restatement of Torts:

> One who uses a chattel with the consent of another is subject to liability in trespass for any harm to the chattel which is caused by or occurs in the course of any use exceeding the consent, even though such use is not a conversion.

City of Amsterdam v. Goldreyer, Ltd., 882 F.Supp. 1273 (E.D.N.Y.1995) (citing Restatement (Second) of Torts, § 256 (1965)).

. . .

. . . [I]t is clear since at least the date this lawsuit was filed that Register.com does not consent to Verio's use of a search robot, and Verio is on notice that its search robot is unwelcome.

Accordingly, Verio's future use of a search robot to access the database exceeds the scope of Register.com's consent, and Verio is liable for any harm to the chattel (Register.com's computer systems) caused by that unauthorized access. *See* [*CompuServe, Inc. v. Cyber Promotions, Inc.*, 962 F.Supp. 1015, 1024 (S.D.Ohio 1997)] (holding that defendants' continued use after CompuServe notified defendants that it no longer consented to the use of its proprietary computer equipment was a trespass) (citing Restatement (Second) of Torts §§ 252 and 892A(5)).

Having established that Verio's access to its WHOIS database by robot is unauthorized, Register.com must next demonstrate that Verio's unauthorized access caused harm to its chattels, namely its computer system. To that end, Robert Gardos, Register.com's Vice President for Technology, submitted a declaration estimating that Verio's searching of Register.com's WHOIS database has resulted in a diminishment of 2.3% of Register.com's system resources. However, during discovery, the basis for Gardos' estimations of the impact Verio's search robot had on Register.com's computer systems was thoroughly undercut. . . .

Although Register.com's evidence of any burden or harm to its computer system caused by the successive queries performed by search robots is imprecise, evidence of mere possessory interference is sufficient to demonstrate the quantum of harm necessary to establish a claim for trespass to chattels. "A trespasser is liable when the trespass diminishes the condition, quality, or value of personal property." *eBay, Inc. v. Bidder's Edge, Inc.*, 100 F.Supp.2d 1058, 1071 (N.D.Cal.2000) (*citing Compuserve*, 962 F.Supp. at 1022). "The quality or value of personal property may be 'diminished even though it is not physically damaged by ·defendant's conduct.' " *Id.* Though it does correctly dispute the trustworthiness and accuracy of Mr. Gardos' calculations, Verio does not dispute that its search robot occupies some of Register.com's systems capacity.

Although Register.com was unable to directly measure the amount by which its systems capacity was reduced, the record evidence is sufficient to establish the possessory interference necessary to establish a trespass to chattels claim. As the *eBay* Court wrote:

> BE argues that its searches present a negligible load on plaintiff's computer systems, and do not rise to the level of impairment to the condition or value of eBay's computer system required to constitute a trespass. *However, it is undisputed that eBay's server and its capacity are personal property, and that BE's searches use a portion of this property. Even if, as BE argues, its searches only use a small amount of eBay's computer system capacity, BE has nonetheless deprived eBay of the ability to use that portion of its personal property for its own purposes. The law recognizes no such right to use another's personal property.* Accordingly, BE's actions appear to have caused injury to eBay and appear likely to continue to cause injury to eBay.

(100 F.Supp.2d at 1071.) (emphasis added).

Furthermore, Gardos also noted in his declaration "if the strain on Register.com's resources generated by Verio's searches becomes large enough, it could cause Register.com's computer systems to malfunction or crash" and "I believe that if Verio's searching of Register.com's WHOIS database were determined to be lawful, then every purveyor of Internet-based services would engage in similar conduct." Gardos' concerns are supported by Verio's testimony that it sees no need to place a limit on the number of other companies that should be allowed to harvest data from Register.com's computers. Furthermore, Verio's own internal documents reveal that Verio was aware that its robotic queries could slow the response times of the registrars' databases and even overload them. Because of that possibility, Verio contemplated cloaking the origin of its queries by using a process called IP aliasing.

Accordingly, Register.com's evidence that Verio's search robots have presented and will continue to present an unwelcome interference with, and a risk of interruption to, its computer system and servers is sufficient to demonstrate a likelihood of success on the merits of its trespass to chattels claim.

There is no adequate remedy at law for an ongoing trespass and without an injunction the victim of such a trespass will be irreparably harmed. The *eBay* court specifically held that eBay was entitled to preliminary injunctive relief based on the claim that if such relief were denied, other companies would be encouraged to deploy search robots against eBay's servers and would further diminish eBay's server capacity to the point of denying effective access to eBay's customers. *See id.* at 1071–72.

The same reasoning applies here. Register.com, through Mr. Gardos, has expressed the fear that its servers will be flooded by search robots deployed by competitors in the absence of injunctive relief. Register.com has therefore demonstrated both a likelihood of success on the merits of its trespass to chattels claim and the existence of irreparable harm, and is entitled to a preliminary injunction against Verio based upon that claim.

C. Computer Fraud And Abuse Act §§ 1030(a)(2)(C) and (a)(5)(C)

The issue of the scope of Verio's authorization to access the WHOIS database is also central to the Court's analysis of Register.com's claims that Verio is violating two discrete provisions of the Computer Fraud and Abuse Act ("CFAA"), 18 U.S.C. § 1030 et seq.

Register.com claims both that the use of software robots to harvest customer information from its WHOIS database in violation of its terms of use violates 18 U.S.C. § 1030(a)(2)(C) and (a)(5)(C) [since redesignated § 1030(a)(5)(A)(iii) — Eds.], and that using the harvested information in violation of Register.com's policy forbidding the use of WHOIS data for marketing also violates those sections. That is, that both Verio's method of accessing the WHOIS data and Verio's end uses of the data violate the CFAA.

1. Verio's Use of Search Robots

Both §§ 1030(a)(2)(C) and (a)(5)(C) require that the plaintiff prove that the defendant's access to its computer system was unauthorized, or in the case of

§ 1030(a)(2)(C) that it was unauthorized or exceeded authorized access. However, although each section requires proof of some degree of unauthorized access, each addresses a different type of harm. Section 1030(a)(2)(C) requires Register.com to prove that Verio intentionally accessed its computers without authorization *and thereby obtained information.* Section 1030(a)(5)(C) requires Register.com to show that Verio intentionally accessed its computer without authorization *and thereby caused damage.*

As discussed more fully in the context of the trespass to chattels claim, because Register.com objects to Verio's use of search robots they represent an unauthorized access to the WHOIS database.

The type of harm that Register.com alleges is caused by the search robots, including diminished server capacity and potential system shutdowns, is better analyzed under § 1030(a)(5)(C), which specifically addresses damages to the computer system. Pursuant to the pertinent part of § 1030(e)(8), "the term 'damage' means any impairment to the integrity or availability of data, a program, a system, or information that (A) causes loss aggregating at least $5000 in value during any 1–year period to one or more individuals."

On this record Register.com has demonstrated that Verio's unauthorized use of search robots to harvest registrant contact information from Register.com's WHOIS database has diminished server capacity, however slightly, and could diminish response time, which could impair the availability of data to clients trying to get registrant contact information. Moreover, Register.com has raised the possibility that if Verio's robotic queries of Register.com's WHOIS database were determined to be lawful, then other vendors of Internet services would engage in similar conduct. This Court finds that it is highly probable that other Internet service vendors would also use robots to obtain this potential customer information were it to be permitted. The use of the robot allows a marketer to reach a potential client within the first several days of the domain name registration, an optimal time to solicit the customer for other services. In contrast, if instead of using a search robot the service vendor obtains registrant contact information pursuant to a bulk license, the vendor must wait to receive the information on a weekly basis. As Eric Eden, the director of operation Henhouse wrote in an e-mail to a Verio employee "[c]onsistent testing has found that the faster we approach someone after they register a domain name, the more likely we are to sell them hosting."

If the strain on Register.com's resources generated by robotic searches becomes large enough, it could cause Register.com's computer systems to malfunction or crash. Such a crash would satisfy § 1030(a)(5)(C)'s threshold requirement that a plaintiff demonstrate $5000 in economic damages[12] resulting from the violation,

---

[12] Register.com relies upon lost revenue from Verio's exploitation of the WHOIS data for marketing purposes to constitute the damages required under § 1030(a)(5)(C). Although lost good will or business could provide the loss figure required under § 1030(a)(5)(C), it could only do so if it resulted from the impairment or unavailability of data or systems. The good will losses cited by Register.com are not the result of the harm addressed by § 1030(a)(5)(C). How Verio uses the WHOIS data, once extracted, has no bearing on whether Verio has im-

both because of costs relating to repair and lost data and also because of lost good will based on adverse customer reactions.

. . .

Because Register.com has demonstrated that Verio's access to its WHOIS database by means of an automated search robot is unauthorized and caused or could cause $5000 in damages by impairing the availability of data or the availability of its computer systems, Register.com has established both irreparable harm and a likelihood of success on the merits of its claim that Verio's use of the search robot violated § 1030(a)(5)(C) of the Computer Fraud And Abuse Act. Register.com is therefore entitled to injunctive relief based upon this claim.

2. Verio's Use of WHOIS Data For Marketing Purposes

With respect to its use of Register.com's WHOIS data for e-mail, direct mail and telephone marketing, Verio argues that such an act can only be analyzed under § 1030(a)(2)(C)'s provision assessing liability where a party exceeds authorized access and obtains information it is not entitled to obtain. Verio argues that because it is authorized to access the WHOIS database for some purposes its access was authorized. Verio then argues that its conduct must meet the Act's specific definition of conduct that "exceeds authorized access." Pursuant to the definition contained in § 1030(e)(6) of the CFAA, "the term 'exceeds authorized access' means to access a computer with authorization and to use such access to obtain or alter information in the computer *that the accessor is not entitled to obtain or alter.*" 18 U.S.C. § 1030(e)(6) (emphasis added). Verio then argues that this definition does not contemplate a violation of end use restrictions placed on data as "exceeding authorized access," and therefore that Verio has not violated § 1030(a)(2)(C).

Again, neither party disputes that Verio is not authorized under Register.com's terms of use to use the data for mass marketing purposes, and neither party disputes that Verio is authorized to obtain the data for some purposes. However, Verio's distinctions between authorized access and an unauthorized end use of information strike the Court as too fine. First, the means of access Verio employs, namely the automated search robot, is unauthorized. Second, even if Verio's means of access to the WHOIS database would otherwise be authorized, that access would be rendered unauthorized *ab initio* by virtue of the fact that prior to entry Verio knows that the data obtained will be later used for an unauthorized purpose.

Accordingly, the Court finds that Verio's access to the WHOIS database was unauthorized and that Verio violated § 1030(a)(2)(C) by using that unauthorized access to obtain data for mass marketing purposes. As discussed above, the harvesting and subsequent use of that data has caused and will cause Register.com irreparable harm. Therefore, because Register.com has demonstrated a likelihood

---

paired the availability or integrity of Register.com's data or computer systems in extracting it. Accordingly, because violating an anti-marketing restriction on the end use of data harms neither the data nor the computer and therefore does not cause the type of harm that § 1030(a)(5)(C) addresses, the specific good will damages cited by Register.com cannot satisfy its burden under § 1030(a)(5)(C).

of success on the merits of its claim that Verio's use of its WHOIS data for mass marketing purposes violates § 1030(a)(2)(C) of the Computer Fraud And Abuse Act and has demonstrated irreparable harm stemming from that violation, Register.com is entitled to injunctive relief based on that claim.

. . .

EXTENSIONS

Affirmance. The Court of Appeals upheld the District Court's entry of a permanent injunction. With respect to the trespass-to-chattels claim, the court held that the District Court acted "within the range of its permissible discretion" when it determined (1) that Verio's access of the WHOIS database was unauthorized, and (2) that it was "highly probable" that in the absence of an injunction others would engage in similar unauthorized access with the result that "the system would be overtaxed and would crash." The court did not address the Computer Fraud and Abuse Act claim. *Register.com, Inc. v. Verio, Inc.*, 356 F.3d 393 (2d Cir.2004).

QUESTIONS FOR DISCUSSION

The domain name system and the limits of private ordering. Does the holding of *Register.com v. Verio* give domain name registrars an effective monopoly in marketing additional services to domain name registrants? Is the situation presented in this case any different from the usual situation in which a seller has privileged access to its customer list? Should registrars have a special duty of openness, deriving from their status as part of the global administration of the domain name space, which flows from ICANN's unilateral control over the domain name system?

EF Cultural Travel BV v. Explorica, Inc.
274 F.3d 577 (1st Cir.2001).

■ COFFIN, SENIOR CIRCUIT JUDGE.

Appellant Explorica, Inc. ("Explorica") and several of its employees challenge a preliminary injunction issued against them for alleged violations of the Computer Fraud and Abuse Act ("CFAA"), 18 U.S.C. § 1030. We affirm the district court's conclusion that appellees will likely succeed on the merits of their CFAA claim, but rest on a narrower basis than the court below.

I. Background

Explorica was formed in 2000 to compete in the field of global tours for high school students. Several of Explorica's employees formerly were employed by appellee EF, which has been in business for more than thirty-five years. EF and its partners and subsidiaries make up the world's largest private student travel organization.

Shortly after the individual defendants left EF in the beginning of 2000, Explorica began competing in the teenage tour market. The company's vice president (and former vice president of information strategy at EF), Philip Gormley, envisioned that Explorica could gain a substantial advantage over all other student tour companies, and especially EF, by undercutting EF's already competitive prices on student tours. Gormley considered several ways to obtain and utilize EF's prices: by manually keying in the information from EF's brochures and other printed materials; by using a scanner to record that same information; or, by manually searching for each tour offered through EF's website. Ultimately, however, Gormley engaged Zefer, Explorica's Internet consultant, to design a computer program called a "scraper" to glean all of the necessary information from EF's website. Zefer designed the program in three days.

The scraper has been likened to a "robot," a tool that is extensively used on the Internet. Robots are used to gather information for countless purposes, ranging from compiling results for search engines such as Yahoo! to filtering for inappropriate content. The widespread deployment of robots enables global Internet users to find comprehensive information quickly and almost effortlessly.

Like a robot, the scraper sought information through the Internet. Unlike other robots, however, the scraper focused solely on EF's website, using information that other robots would not have. Specifically, Zefer utilized tour codes whose significance was not readily understandable to the public. With the tour codes, the scraper accessed EF's website repeatedly and easily obtained pricing information for those specific tours. The scraper sent more than 30,000 inquiries to EF's website and recorded the pricing information into a spreadsheet.[2]

Zefer ran the scraper program twice, first to retrieve the 2000 tour prices and then the 2001 prices. All told, the scraper downloaded 60,000 lines of data, the equivalent of eight telephone directories of information.[3] Once Zefer "scraped" all of the prices, it sent a spreadsheet containing EF's pricing information to Explorica,

---

[2] John Hawley, one of Zefer's senior technical associates, explained the technical progression of the scraper in an affidavit:

> [a.] Open an Excel spreadsheet. The spreadsheet initially contains EFTours gateway and destination city codes, which are available on the EFTours web site.
>
> [b.] Identify the first gateway and destination city codes [on the] Excel spreadsheet.
>
> [c.] Create a [website address] request for the EFTours tour prices page based on a combination of gateway and destination city. Example: show me all the prices for a London trip leaving JFK.
>
> [d.] View the requested web page which is retained in the random access memory of the requesting computer in the form of HTML [computer language] code. . . .
>
> [e.] Search the HTML for the tour prices for each season, year, etc.
>
> [f.] Store the prices into the Excel spreadsheet.
>
> [g.] Identify the next gateway and city codes in the spreadsheet.
>
> [h.] Repeat steps 3–7 for all gateway and destination city combinations.

[3] Appellants dispute the relevance of the size of the printed data, arguing that 60,000 printed lines, while voluminous on paper, is not a large amount of data for a computer to store. This is a distinction without a difference. The fact is that appellants utilized the scraper program to download EF's pricing data. In June 2000, EF's website listed 154,293 prices for various tours.

which then systematically undercut EF's prices. Explorica thereafter printed its own brochures and began competing in EF's tour market.

. . .

On May 30, 2001, the district court granted a preliminary injunction against Explorica based on the CFAA, which criminally and civilly prohibits certain access to computers. *See* 18 U.S.C. § 1030(a)(4). . . .

The district court first relied on EF's use of a copyright symbol on one of the pages of its website and a link directing users with questions to contact the company,[6] finding that "such a clear statement should have dispelled any notion a reasonable person may have had that the 'presumption of open access' applied to information on EF's website." The court next found that the manner by which Explorica accessed EF's website likely violated a confidentiality agreement between appellant Gormley and EF, because Gormley provided to Zefer technical instructions concerning the creation of the scraper. Finally, the district court noted without elaboration that the scraper bypassed technical restrictions embedded in the website to acquire the information. . . . Appellants contend that the district court erred in taking too narrow a view of what is authorized under the CFAA and similarly mistook the reach of the confidentiality agreement. Appellants also argue that the district court erred in finding that appellees suffered a "loss," as defined by the CFAA, and that the preliminary injunction violates the First Amendment.

. . .

III. The Computer Fraud and Abuse Act

Although appellees alleged violations of three provisions of the CFAA, the district court found that they were likely to succeed only under § 1030(a)(4). That section provides

> [Whoever] knowingly and with intent to defraud, accesses a protected computer without authorization, or exceeds authorized access, and by means of such conduct furthers the intended fraud and obtains anything of value . . . shall be punished.

18 U.S.C. § 1030(a)(4).

Appellees allege that the appellants knowingly and with intent to defraud accessed the server hosting EF's website more than 30,000 times to obtain proprietary pricing and tour information, and confidential information about appellees' technical abilities. At the heart of the parties' dispute is whether appellants' actions either were "without authorization" or "exceed[ed] authorized access" as defined by the CFAA.[9] We conclude that because of the broad confidentiality agreement

---

[6] The notice stated in full:

> Copyright © 2000 EF Cultural Travel BV
> EF Educational Tours is a member of the EF group of companies.
> Questions? Please *contact* us.

[9] At oral argument, appellants contended that they had no "intent to defraud" as defined by the CFAA. That argument was not raised in the briefs and thus has been waived. *See Garcia-Ayala v. Parenterals, Inc.*, 212 F.3d 638, 645 (1st Cir.2000) (failure to brief an argument con-

appellants' actions "exceed[ed] authorized access," and so we do not reach the more general arguments made about statutory meaning, including whether use of a scraper alone renders access unauthorized.

A. "Exceeds authorized access"

Congress defined "exceeds authorized access," as accessing "a computer with authorization and [using] such access to obtain or alter information in the computer that the accesser is not entitled so to obtain or alter." 18 U.S.C. § 1030(e)(6). EF is likely to prove such excessive access based on the confidentiality agreement between Gormley and EF. Pertinently, that agreement provides:

> Employee agrees to maintain in strict confidence and not to disclose to any third party, either orally or in writing, any Confidential or Proprietary Information . . . and never to at any time (i) directly or indirectly publish, disseminate or otherwise disclose, deliver or make available to anybody any Confidential or Proprietary Information or (ii) use such Confidential or [P]roprietary Information for Employee's own benefit or for the benefit of any other person or business entity other than EF.
>
> . . .

The record contains at least two communications from Gormley to Zefer seeming to rely on information about EF to which he was privy only because of his employment there. First, in an e-mail to Zefer employee Joseph Alt exploring the use of a scraper, Gormley wrote: "might one of the team be able to write a program to automatically extract prices . . .? I could work with him/her on the specification." Gormley also sent the following e-mail to Zefer employee John Hawley:

> Here is a link to the page where you can grab EF's prices. There are two important drop down menus on the right. . . . With the lowest one you select one of about 150 tours. . . . You then select your origin gateway from a list of about 100 domestic gateways (middle drop down menu). When you select your origin gateway a page with a couple of tables comes up. One table has 1999–2000 prices and the other has 2000–2001 prices. . . . On a high speed connection it is possible to move quickly from one price table to the next by hitting backspace and then the down arrow.

This documentary evidence points to Gormley's heavy involvement in the conception of the scraper program. Furthermore, the voluminous spreadsheet containing all of the scraped information includes the tour codes, which EF claims are proprietary information. Each page of the spreadsheet produced by Zefer includes the tour and gateway codes, the date of travel, and the price for the tour. An uninformed reader would regard the tour codes as nothing but gibberish.[11] Although

---

stitutes waiver despite attempt to raise the argument at oral argument). Likewise, at oral argument Explorica attempted to adopt appellant Zefer's argument that the preliminary injunction violates the First Amendment. The lateness of Explorica's attempt renders it fruitless. *See id.*

[11] An example of the website address including the tour information is *www.eftours.com/tours/PriceResult.asp?Gate=GTF & TourID=LPM*. In this address, the proprietary codes are "GTF" and "LPM."

the codes can be correlated to the actual tours and destination points, the codes standing alone need to be "translated" to be meaningful.

Explorica argues that none of the information Gormley provided Zefer was confidential and that the confidentiality agreement therefore is irrelevant. . . .

[T]here is ample evidence that Gormley provided Explorica proprietary information about the structure of the website and the tour codes. To be sure, gathering manually the various codes through repeated searching and deciphering of the URLs theoretically may be possible. Practically speaking, however, if proven, Explorica's wholesale use of EF's travel codes to facilitate gathering EF's prices from its website reeks of use—and, indeed, abuse—of proprietary information that goes beyond any authorized use of EF's website.[14]

Gormley voluntarily entered a broad confidentiality agreement prohibiting his disclosure of any information "which might reasonably be construed to be contrary to the interests of EF." . . . If EF's allegations are proven, it will likely prove that whatever authorization Explorica had to navigate around EF's site (even in a competitive vein), it exceeded that authorization by providing proprietary information and know-how to Zefer to create the scraper.[16] Accordingly, the district court's finding that Explorica likely violated the CFAA was not clearly erroneous.

B. Damage or Loss under § 1030(g)

Appellants also challenge the district court's finding that the appellees would likely prove they met the CFAA's "damage or loss" requirements. Under the CFAA, EF may maintain a private cause of action if it suffered "damage or loss." 18 U.S.C. § 1030(g). [The court held that the "damage or loss" requirement was met, by virtue of the more than $20,000 EF spent "to assess whether their website had been compromised." Portions of the statute relating to the "damage" and "loss" requirements were amended after this case was heard. See the Extensions,

---

[14] Among the several e-mails in the record is one from Zefer employee Joseph Alt to the Explorica "team" at Zefer:

> Below is the information needed to log into EF's site as a tour leader. Please use this to gather competitor information from both a business and experience design perspective. We may also be able to glean knowledge of their technical abilities. As with all of our information, this is extremely confidential. Please do not share it with anyone.

[16] EF also claims that Explorica skirted the website's technical restraints. To learn about a specific tour, a user must navigate through several different web pages by "clicking" on various drop-down menus and choosing the desired departure location, date, tour destination, tour length, and price range. The district court found that the scraper circumvented the technical restraints by operating at a warp speed that the website was not normally intended to accommodate. We need not reach the argument that this alone was a violation of the CFAA, however, because the apparent transfer of information in violation of the Confidentiality Agreement furnishes a sufficient basis for injunctive relief.

Likewise, we express no opinion on the district court's ruling that EF's copyright notice served as a "clear statement [that] should have dispelled any notion a reasonable person may have had the 'presumption of open access' " to EF's website.

infra. — Eds.]

IV. Conclusion

For the foregoing reasons, we agree with the district court that appellees will likely succeed on the merits of their CFAA claim under 18 U.S.C. § 1030(a)(4). Accordingly, the preliminary injunction was properly ordered.

Affirmed.

EXTENSIONS

1. *Appeal of the scraper maker.* Zefer Corp., the consultant that Explorica hired to produce the scraper program at issue in *EF Cultural Travel BV v. Explorica Inc.*, took its own appeal from the district court's preliminary injunction. The appellate court disagreed with the district court's rationale for subjecting Zefer to the injunction. The district court had reasoned that the scope of authorized access to EF's website was defined by EF's "reasonable expectations" as to its use. The appellate court rejected this formulation, on the ground that it was unjustifiably vague, especially since a website operator may easily communicate explicitly the scope of authorized access: "[T]he public website provider can easily spell out explicitly what is forbidden and . . . nothing justifies putting users at the mercy of a highly imprecise, litigation-spawning standard like 'reasonable expectations.' If EF wants to ban scrapers, let it say so on the webpage or a link clearly marked as containing restrictions." *EF Cultural Travel BV v. Zefer Corp.*, 318 F.3d 58 (1st Cir.2003).

The court's holding thus indicates that a website statement alone is generally sufficient to render an access to the site "without authorization" or "exceed[ing] authorized access," for purposes of the Computer Fraud and Abuse Act, 18 U.S.C. § 1030(a)(4). It obliquely suggests, however, that "public policy might in turn limit certain restrictions."

Despite disapproving the district court's rationale, the appellate court declined to modify the injunction, on the ground that it did not name Zefer explicitly, but bound Zefer only to the extent it applied to any third party that knowingly assists the other defendants in violating the injunction.

2. *"Damage" and "loss" under the CFAA.* In 2001, as part of the USA–PATRIOT Act, Congress added to the CFAA a definition of "loss," namely "any reasonable cost to any victim, including the cost of responding to an offense, conducting a damage assessment, and restoring the data, program, system, or information to its condition prior to the offense, and any revenue lost, cost incurred, or other consequential damages incurred because of interruption of service." 18 U.S.C. § 1030(e)(11). It also amended the definition of "damage," to mean "any impairment to the integrity or availability of data, a program, a system, or information." *Id.* § 1030(e)(8).

Courts have held that only those costs directly related to investigating the intrusion and remedying its effects are cognizable as "loss." *See Nexans Wires S.A. v. Sark-USA, Inc.*, 319 F.Supp.2d 468 (S.D.N.Y.2004) (interpreting "loss" to exclude travel expenses incurred by company executives to attend meetings in the aftermath of the computer intrusion, and revenue forgone due to lost business opportunities). In *I.M.S. Inquiry Management Systems, Ltd. v. Berkshire Information Systems, Inc.*, 307 F.Supp.2d 521 (S.D.N.Y.2004), the court left unresolved whether a plaintiff must allege both "damage" and "loss" to make out a CFAA claim.

QUESTIONS FOR DISCUSSION

1. *Burden on remand.* The Court of Appeals affirmed the District Court's grant of a preliminary injunction, finding that the plaintiff was likely to succeed on the merits of its claim under the Computer Fraud and Abuse Act. On remand, what will the plaintiff be required to prove in order to prevail? Based on the facts presented in this opinion, how likely do you think it is that plaintiff will succeed?

2. *De-authorization via* Terms of Use. The home page of EF Tours' website contains a link at the bottom of the page labeled Terms of Use. Clicking on the link calls up a page titled "Terms of Use," which contains, in the middle of a page of text, the following:

> You may not without the prior written permission of EF use any computer code, data mining software, "robot," "bot," "spider," "scraper" or other automatic device, or program, algorithm or methodology having similar processes or functionality, or any manual process, to monitor or copy any of the web pages, data or content found on this site or accessed through this site. You also may not: engage in the mass downloading of files from this site; use the computer processing power of this site for purposes other than those permitted above; flood this site with electronic traffic designed to slow or stop its operation; or establish links to or from other websites to this site.

Does the presence of this statement in the Terms of Use render any use of the site that is inconsistent with its strictures an access "without authorization" under the Computer Fraud and Abuse Act? If I place an unapproved link from my website to this site, and the site operator expends $7,000 in consultant costs attempting to render my link inoperative, have I violated § 1030(a)(5)(A)(iii), which provides that one who "intentionally accesses a protected computer without authorization, and as a result of such conduct, causes damage; and [by such conduct] caused . . . loss . . . aggregating at least $5,000 in value" is subject to criminal and civil liability?

3. *Competition in the balance.* Decisions like *eBay v. Bidders Edge*, *Register.com v. Verio*, and *EF v. Explorica* have the potential to interfere with the gathering of information that is necessary to operate price comparison sites and search engines, prevent online information-gathering by organizations like Consumer Reports, limit linking, impede efforts by sellers to price their offerings competitively, and hinder other activities aimed at improving the flow of information to consumers and promoting competition. Yet sellers have a legitimate interest in controlling information that is critical to their business operations. Do existing legal doctrines give adequate weight to each set of conflicting interests?

III. INTRUSIVE SPEECH DIRECTED AT EMPLOYEES VIA A CORPORATE NETWORK

Intel Corp. v. Hamidi
71 P.3d 296 (Cal.2003).

■ WERDEGAR, JUSTICE.

Intel Corporation (Intel) maintains an electronic mail system, connected to the Internet, through which messages between employees and those outside the company can be sent and received, and permits its employees to make reasonable non-business use of this system. On six occasions over almost two years, Kourosh Kenneth Hamidi, a former Intel employee, sent e-mails criticizing Intel's employment practices to numerous current employees on Intel's electronic mail system. Hamidi breached no computer security barriers in order to communicate with Intel employees. He offered to, and did, remove from his mailing list any recipient who so wished. Hamidi's communications to individual Intel employees caused neither physical damage nor functional disruption to the company's computers, nor did they at any time deprive Intel of the use of its computers. The contents of the messages, however, caused discussion among employees and managers.

On these facts, Intel brought suit, claiming that by communicating with its employees over the company's e-mail system Hamidi committed the tort of trespass to chattels. The trial court granted Intel's motion for summary judgment and enjoined Hamidi from any further mailings. A divided Court of Appeal affirmed.

After reviewing the decisions analyzing unauthorized electronic contact with computer systems as potential trespasses to chattels, we conclude that under California law the tort does not encompass, and should not be extended to encompass, an electronic communication that neither damages the recipient computer system nor impairs its functioning. Such an electronic communication does not constitute an actionable trespass to personal property, i.e., the computer system, because it does not interfere with the possessor's use or possession of, or any other legally protected interest in, the personal property itself. (See *Zaslow v. Kroenert* (1946) 29 Cal.2d 541, 551; *Ticketmaster Corp. v. Tickets.com, Inc.* (C.D.Cal., Aug. 10, 2000) 2000 WL 1887522, p. *4; Rest.2d Torts, § 218.) The consequential economic damage Intel claims to have suffered, i.e., loss of productivity caused by employees reading and reacting to Hamidi's messages and company efforts to block the messages, is not an injury to the company's interest in its computers—which worked as intended and were unharmed by the communications—any more than the personal distress caused by reading an unpleasant letter would be an injury to the recipient's mailbox, or the loss of privacy caused by an intrusive telephone call would be an injury to the recipient's telephone equipment.

Our conclusion does not rest on any special immunity for communications by electronic mail; we do not hold that messages transmitted through the Internet are exempt from the ordinary rules of tort liability. To the contrary, e-mail, like other forms of communication, may in some circumstances cause legally cognizable injury to the recipient or to third parties and may be actionable under various common law or statutory theories. Indeed, on facts somewhat similar to those here, a company or its employees might be able to plead causes of action for interference with prospective economic relations (see *Guillory v. Godfrey* (1955) 134 Cal.App.2d 628, 630–632 [defendant berated customers and prospective customers of plaintiffs' cafe with disparaging and racist comments]), interference with contract (see *Blender v. Superior Court* (1942) 55 Cal.App.2d 24, 25–27 [defendant made false statements about plaintiff to his employer, resulting in plaintiff's discharge]) or intentional infliction of emotional distress (see *Kiseskey v. Carpenters' Trust for So. California* (1983) 144 Cal.App.3d 222, 229–230 [agents of defendant union threatened life, health, and family of employer if he did not sign agreement with union].) And, of course, as with any other means of publication, third party subjects of e-mail communications may under appropriate facts make claims for defamation, publication of private facts, or other speech-based torts. (See, e.g., *Southridge Capital Management v. Lowry* (S.D.N.Y.2002) 188 F.Supp.2d 388, 394–396 [allegedly false statements in e-mail sent to several of plaintiff's clients support actions for defamation and interference with contract].) Intel's claim fails not because e-mail transmitted through the Internet enjoys unique immunity, but because the trespass to chattels tort—unlike the causes of action just mentioned—may not, in California, be proved without evidence of an injury to the plaintiff's personal property or legal interest therein.

Nor does our holding affect the legal remedies of Internet service providers (ISP's) against senders of unsolicited commercial bulk e-mail (UCE), also known as "spam." (See *Ferguson v. Friendfinders, Inc.* (2002) 94 Cal.App.4th 1255, 1267.) A series of federal district court decisions, beginning with *CompuServe, Inc. v. Cyber Promotions, Inc.* (S.D.Ohio 1997) 962 F.Supp. 1015, has approved the use of trespass to chattels as a theory of spammers' liability to ISP's, based upon evidence that the vast quantities of mail sent by spammers both overburdened the ISP's own computers and made the entire computer system harder to use for recipients, the ISP's customers. (See *id.* at pp. 1022–1023.) In those cases, discussed in greater detail below, the underlying complaint was that the extraordinary *quantity* of UCE impaired the computer system's functioning. In the present case, the claimed injury is located in the disruption or distraction caused to recipients by the *contents* of the e-mail messages, an injury entirely separate from, and not directly affecting, the possession or value of personal property.

FACTUAL AND PROCEDURAL BACKGROUND

We review a grant of summary judgment de novo; we must decide independently whether the facts not subject to triable dispute warrant judgment for the moving party as a matter of law. . . . The pertinent undisputed facts are as follows.

Hamidi, a former Intel engineer, together with others, formed an organization named Former and Current Employees of Intel (FACE–Intel) to disseminate information and views critical of Intel's employment and personnel policies and practices. FACE–Intel maintained a Web site (which identified Hamidi as Webmaster and as the organization's spokesperson) containing such material. In addition, over a 21-month period Hamidi, on behalf of FACE–Intel, sent six mass e-mails to employee addresses on Intel's electronic mail system. The messages criticized Intel's employment practices, warned employees of the dangers those practices posed to their careers, suggested employees consider moving to other companies, solicited employees' participation in FACE–Intel, and urged employees to inform themselves further by visiting FACE–Intel's Web site. The messages stated that recipients could, by notifying the sender of their wishes, be removed from FACE–Intel's mailing list; Hamidi did not subsequently send messages to anyone who requested removal.

Each message was sent to thousands of addresses (as many as 35,000 according to FACE–Intel's Web site), though some messages were blocked by Intel before reaching employees. Intel's attempt to block internal transmission of the messages succeeded only in part; Hamidi later admitted he evaded blocking efforts by using different sending computers. When Intel, in March 1998, demanded in writing that Hamidi and FACE–Intel stop sending e-mails to Intel's computer system, Hamidi asserted the organization had a right to communicate with willing Intel employees;

he sent a new mass mailing in September 1998.

The summary judgment record contains no evidence Hamidi breached Intel's computer security in order to obtain the recipient addresses for his messages; indeed, internal Intel memoranda show the company's management concluded no security breach had occurred. Hamidi stated he created the recipient address list using an Intel directory on a floppy disk anonymously sent to him. Nor is there any evidence that the receipt or internal distribution of Hamidi's electronic messages damaged Intel's computer system or slowed or impaired its functioning. Intel did present uncontradicted evidence, however, that many employee recipients asked a company official to stop the messages and that staff time was consumed in attempts to block further messages from FACE-Intel. According to the FACE-Intel Web site, moreover, the messages had prompted discussions between "[e]xcited and nervous managers" and the company's human resources department.

Intel sued Hamidi and FACE-Intel, pleading causes of action for trespass to chattels and nuisance, and seeking both actual damages and an injunction against further e-mail messages. Intel later voluntarily dismissed its nuisance claim and waived its demand for damages. The trial court entered default against FACE-Intel upon that organization's failure to answer. The court then granted Intel's motion for summary judgment, permanently enjoining Hamidi, FACE-Intel, and their agents "from sending unsolicited e-mail to addresses on Intel's computer systems." Hamidi appealed; FACE-Intel did not.

The Court of Appeal, with one justice dissenting, affirmed the grant of injunctive relief. . . .

We granted Hamidi's petition for review.

DISCUSSION

I. Current California Tort Law

Dubbed by Prosser the "little brother of conversion," the tort of trespass to chattels allows recovery for interferences with possession of personal property "not sufficiently important to be classed as conversion, and so to compel the defendant to pay the full value of the thing with which he has interfered." (Prosser & Keeton, Torts (5th ed.1984) § 14, pp. 85–86.)

Though not amounting to conversion, the defendant's interference must, to be actionable, have caused some injury to the chattel or to the plaintiff's rights in it. Under California law, trespass to chattels "lies where an intentional interference with the possession of personal property *has proximately caused injury*." (*Thrifty–Tel, Inc. v. Bezenek* (1996) 46 Cal.App.4th 1559, 1566, italics added.) In cases of interference with possession of personal property not amounting to conversion, "the owner has a cause of action for trespass or case, *and may recover only the actual damages suffered by reason of the impairment of the property or the loss of its use.*" (*Zaslow v. Kroenert, supra*, 29 Cal.2d at p. 551, italics added; accord, *Jordan v. Talbot* (1961) 55 Cal.2d 597, 610.) In modern American law generally, "[t]respass remains as an occasional remedy for minor interferences, *resulting in some damage*, but not sufficiently serious or sufficiently important to amount to the greater tort" of conversion. (Prosser & Keeton, Torts, *supra*, § 15, p. 90, italics added.)

The Restatement, too, makes clear that some actual injury must have occurred in order for a trespass to chattels to be actionable. Under section 218 of the Restatement Second of Torts, dispossession alone, without further damages, is actionable (see *id.*, par. (a) & com. d, pp. 420–421), but other forms of interference require some additional harm to the personal property or the possessor's interests in it. (*Id.*, pars. (b)–(d).) "The interest of a possessor of a chattel in its inviolability, unlike the similar interest of a possessor of land, is not given legal protection by an action for nominal damages for harmless intermeddlings with the chattel. In order that an actor who interferes with another's chattel may be liable, his conduct must affect some other and more important interest of the possessor. *Therefore, one who intentionally intermeddles with another's chattel is subject to liability only if his intermeddling is harmful to the possessor's materially valuable interest in the physical condition, quality, or value of the chattel, or if the possessor is deprived of the use of the chattel for a substantial time, or some other legally protected interest of the possessor is affected as stated in Clause (c).* Sufficient legal protection of the possessor's interest in the mere inviolability of his chattel is afforded by his privilege to use reasonable force to protect his possession against even harmless interference." (*Id.*, com. e, pp. 421–422, italics added.)

The Court of Appeal . . . referred to " 'a number of very early cases [showing that] any unlawful interference, however slight, with the enjoyment by another of his personal property, is a trespass.' " But while a harmless use or touching of personal property may be a technical trespass (see Rest.2d Torts, § 217), an interference (not amounting to dispossession) is not *actionable*, under modern California and broader American law, without a showing of harm. . . .

In this respect, as Prosser explains, modern day trespass to chattels differs both from the original English writ and from the action for trespass to land: "Another departure from the original rule of the old writ of trespass concerns the necessity of some actual damage to the chattel before the action can be maintained. Where the defendant merely interferes without doing any harm—as where, for example, he merely lays hands upon the plaintiff's horse, or sits in his car—there has been a division of opinion among the writers, and a surprising dearth of authority. *By analogy to trespass to land there might be a technical tort in such a case . . . . Such scanty authority as there is, however, has considered that the dignitary interest in the inviolability of chattels, unlike that as to land, is not sufficiently important to require any greater defense than the privilege of using reasonable force when necessary to protect them. Accordingly it has been held that nominal damages will not be awarded, and that in the absence of any actual damage the action will not lie.*" (Prosser & Keeton, Torts, *supra*, § 14, p. 87, italics added, fns. omitted.)

Intel suggests that the requirement of actual harm does not apply here because it sought only injunctive relief, as protection from future injuries. But as Justice Kolkey, dissenting below, observed, "[t]he fact the relief sought is injunctive does not excuse a showing of injury, whether actual or threatened." Indeed, in order to obtain injunctive relief the plaintiff must ordinarily show that the defendant's wrongful acts threaten to cause *irreparable* injuries, ones that cannot be adequately compensated in damages. . . . Even in an action for trespass to real property, in which damage to the property is not an element of the cause of action, "the extraordinary remedy of injunction" cannot be invoked without showing the likelihood of irreparable harm. . . . A fortiori, to issue an injunction without a showing of likely irreparable injury in an action for trespass to chattels, in which injury to the personal property or the possessor's interest in it *is* an element of the action, would make little legal sense.

The dispositive issue in this case, therefore, is whether the undisputed facts demonstrate Hamidi's actions caused or threatened to cause damage to Intel's computer system, or injury to its rights in that personal property, such as to entitle Intel to judgment as a matter of law. To review, the undisputed evidence revealed no actual or threatened damage to Intel's computer hardware or software and no interference with its ordinary and intended operation. Intel was not dispossessed of its computers, nor did Hamidi's messages prevent Intel from using its computers for any measurable length of time. Intel presented no evidence its system was slowed or otherwise impaired by the burden of delivering Hamidi's electronic messages. Nor was there any evidence transmission of the messages imposed any marginal cost on the operation of Intel's computers. In sum, no evidence suggested that in sending messages through Intel's Internet connections and internal computer system Hamidi used the system in any manner in which it was not intended to function or impaired the system in any way. Nor does the evidence show the request of any employee to be removed from FACE–Intel's mailing list was not honored. The evidence did show, however, that some employees who found the messages unwelcome asked management to stop them and that Intel technical staff spent time and effort attempting to block the messages. A statement on the FACE–Intel Web site, moreover, could be taken as an admission that the messages had caused "[e]xcited and nervous managers" to discuss the matter with Intel's human resources department.

Relying on a line of decisions, most from federal district courts, applying the tort of trespass to chattels to various types of unwanted electronic contact between computers, Intel contends that, while its computers were not damaged by receiving Hamidi's messages, its interest in the "physical condition, quality or value" (Rest.2d Torts, § 218, com. e, p. 422) of the computers was harmed. We disagree. The cited line of decisions does not persuade us that the mere sending of electronic communications that assertedly cause injury only because of their contents constitutes an actionable trespass to a computer system through which the messages are transmitted. Rather, the decisions finding electronic contact to be a trespass to computer systems have generally involved some actual or threatened interference with the computers' functioning.

In *Thrifty–Tel, Inc. v. Bezenek, supra,* 46 Cal.App.4th at pages 1566–1567 (*Thrifty-Tel*), the California Court of Appeal held that evidence of automated searching of a telephone carrier's system for authorization codes supported a cause of action for trespass to chattels. The defendant's automated dialing program "overburdened the [plaintiff's] system, denying some subscribers access to phone lines" (*Thrifty-Tel, supra,* 46 Cal.App.4th at p. 1564), showing the requisite injury.

Following *Thrifty–Tel,* a series of federal district court decisions held that sending UCE through an ISP's equipment may constitute trespass to the ISP's computer system. The lead case, *CompuServe, Inc. v. Cyber Promotions, Inc., supra,* 962 F.Supp. 1015, 1021–1023 (*CompuServe*), was followed by *Hotmail Corp. v. Van$ Money Pie, Inc.* (N.D.Cal., Apr. 16, 1998) 1998 WL 388389, page *7, *America Online, Inc. v. IMS* (E.D.Va.1998) 24 F.Supp.2d 548, 550–551, and *America Online, Inc. v. LCGM, Inc.* (E.D.Va.1998) 46 F.Supp.2d 444, 451–452.

In each of these spamming cases, the plaintiff showed, or was prepared to show, some interference with the efficient functioning of its computer system. In *CompuServe,* the plaintiff ISP's mail equipment monitor stated that mass UCE mailings, especially from nonexistent addresses such as those used by the defendant, placed "a tremendous burden" on the ISP's equipment, using "disk space and drain[ing] the processing power," making those resources unavailable to serve subscribers. (*CompuServe, supra,* 962 F.Supp. at p. 1022.) Similarly, in *Hotmail Corp. v. Van$ Money Pie, Inc., supra,* the court found the evidence supported a finding that the defendant's mailings "fill[ed] up Hotmail's computer storage space and threaten[ed] to damage Hotmail's ability to service its legitimate customers." *America Online, Inc. v. IMS,* decided on summary judgment, was deemed factually indistinguishable from *CompuServe;* the court observed that in both cases the plaintiffs "alleged that processing the bulk e-mail cost them time and money and burdened their equipment." (*America Online, Inc. v. IMS, supra,* 24 F.Supp.2d at p. 550.) The same court, in *America Online, Inc. v. LCGM, Inc., supra,* 46 F.Supp.2d at page 452, simply followed *CompuServe* and its earlier *America Online* decision, quoting the former's explanation that UCE burdened the computer's processing power and memory.

Building on the spamming cases, in particular *CompuServe,* three even more recent district court decisions addressed whether unauthorized robotic data collection from a company's publicly accessible Web site is a trespass on the company's computer system. (*eBay, Inc. v. Bidder's Edge, Inc.,* (N.D.Cal.2000) 100 F.Supp.2d at pp. 1069–1072 (*eBay*); *Register.com, Inc. v. Verio, Inc.* (S.D.N.Y.2000) 126 F.Supp.2d 238, 248-251; *Ticketmaster Corp. v. Tickets.com, Inc., supra,* 2000 WL 1887522, at p. *4.) The two district courts that found such automated data collection to constitute a trespass relied, in part, on the deleterious impact this activity could have, especially if replicated by other searchers, on the functioning of a Web site's computer equipment.

In the leading case, *eBay,* the . . . district court rejected eBay's claim that it was entitled to injunctive relief because of the defendant's unauthorized presence alone, or because of the incremental cost the defendant had imposed on operation of the eBay site, but found sufficient proof of *threatened* harm in the potential for others to imitate the defendant's activity . . . .

Another district court followed *eBay* on similar facts—a domain name registrar's claim against a Web hosting and development site that robotically searched the registrar's database of newly registered domain names in search of business leads—in *Register.com, Inc. v. Verio, Inc., supra.* Although the plaintiff was unable to measure the burden the defendant's searching had placed on its system, the district court, quoting the declaration of one of the plaintiff's officers, found sufficient evidence of threatened harm to the system in the possibility the defendant's activities would be copied by others . . . .

In the third decision discussing robotic data collection as a trespass, *Ticketmaster Corp. v. Tickets.com, Inc., supra* (*Ticketmaster*), the court, distinguishing *eBay*, found *insufficient* evidence of harm to the chattel to constitute an actionable trespass . . . .

In the decisions so far reviewed, the defendant's use of the plaintiff's computer system was held sufficient to support an action for trespass when it actually did, or threatened to, interfere with the intended functioning of the system, as by significantly reducing its available memory and processing power. In *Ticketmaster, supra,* the one case where no such effect, actual or threatened, had been demonstrated, the court found insufficient evidence of harm to support a trespass action. These decisions do not persuade us to Intel's position here, for Intel has demonstrated neither any appreciable effect on the operation of its computer system from Hamidi's messages, nor any likelihood that Hamidi's actions will be replicated by others if found not to constitute a trespass.

That Intel does not claim the type of functional impact that spammers and robots have been alleged to cause is not surprising in light of the differences between Hamidi's activities and those of a commercial enterprise that uses sheer quantity of messages as its communications strategy. Though Hamidi sent thousands of copies of the same message on six occasions over 21 months, that number is minuscule compared to the amounts of mail sent by commercial operations. The individual advertisers sued in *America Online, Inc. v. IMS, supra,* and *America Online, Inc. v. LCGM, Inc., supra,* were alleged to have sent more than 60 million messages over 10 months and more than 92 million messages over seven months, respectively. . . . The functional burden on Intel's computers, or the cost in time to individual recipients, of receiving Hamidi's occasional advocacy messages cannot be compared to the burdens and costs caused ISP's and their customers by the ever-rising deluge of commercial e-mail.

Intel relies on language in the *eBay* decision suggesting that unauthorized use of another's chattel is actionable even without any showing of injury: "Even if, as [defendant] BE argues, its searches use only a small amount of eBay's computer system capacity, BE has nonetheless deprived eBay of the ability to use that portion of its personal property for its own purposes. The law recognizes no such right to use another's personal property." (*eBay, supra,* 100 F.Supp.2d at p. 1071.) But as the *eBay* court went on immediately to find that the defendant's conduct, if widely replicated, *would* likely impair the functioning of the plaintiff's system, we do not read the quoted remarks as expressing the court's complete view of the issue. In isolation, moreover, they would not be a correct statement of California or general American law on this point. . . . That Hamidi's messages temporarily used some portion of the Intel computers' processors or storage is, therefore, not enough; Intel must, but does not, demonstrate some measurable loss from the use of its computer system.

In addition to impairment of system functionality, *CompuServe* and its progeny also refer to the ISP's loss of business reputation and customer goodwill, resulting from the inconvenience and cost that spam causes to its members, as harm to the ISP's legally protected interests in its personal property. . . . Intel argues that its own interest in employee productivity, assertedly disrupted by Hamidi's messages, is a comparable protected interest in its computer system. We disagree.

Whether the economic injuries identified in *CompuServe* were properly considered injuries to the ISP's possessory interest in its personal property, the type of property interest the tort is primarily intended to protect . . . , has been questioned. . . . But even if the loss of goodwill identified in *CompuServe* were the type of injury that would give rise to a trespass to chattels claim under California law, Intel's position would not follow, for Intel's claimed injury has even less connection to its personal property than did CompuServe's.

CompuServe's customers were annoyed because the system was inundated with unsolicited commercial messages, making its use for personal communication more difficult and costly. . . . Their complaint, which allegedly led some to cancel their CompuServe service, was about *the functioning of CompuServe's electronic mail service.* Intel's workers, in contrast, were allegedly distracted from their work not because of the frequency or quantity of Hamidi's messages, but because of assertions and opinions the messages conveyed. Intel's complaint is thus about *the contents of the messages* rather than the functioning of the company's e-mail system. Even accepting *CompuServe's* economic injury rationale, therefore, Intel's position represents a further extension of the trespass to chattels tort, fictionally recharacterizing the allegedly injurious effect of a communication's *contents* on recipients as an impairment to the device which transmitted the message.

. . . Intel's theory would expand the tort of trespass to chattels to cover virtually any unconsented-to communication that, solely because of its content, is unwelcome to the recipient or intermediate transmitter. As the dissenting justice below explained, " 'Damage' of this nature—the distraction of reading or listening to an unsolicited communication—is not within the scope of the injury against which the trespass-to-chattel tort protects, and indeed trivializes it. . . . Indeed, if a chattel's receipt of an electronic communication constitutes a trespass to that chattel, then not only are unsolicited telephone calls and faxes trespasses to chattel, but unwelcome radio waves and television signals also constitute a trespass to chattel every time the viewer inadvertently sees or hears the unwanted program." We agree. While unwelcome communications, electronic or otherwise, can cause a variety of injuries to economic relations, reputation and emotions, those interests are protected by other branches of tort law; in order to address them, we need not create a fiction of injury to the communication system.

Nor may Intel appropriately assert a *property* interest in its employees' time. "The Restatement test clearly speaks in the first instance to the impairment of the chattel. . . . But employees are not chattels (at least not in the legal sense of the term)." (Burk, *The Trouble with Trespass* [(2000) 4 J. Small & Emerging Bus.L. 27, 36.]) Whatever interest Intel may have in preventing its employees from receiving disruptive communications, it is not an interest in personal property, and trespass to chattels is therefore not an action that will lie to protect it. Nor, finally, can the fact Intel staff spent time attempting to block Hamidi's messages be bootstrapped into an injury to Intel's possessory interest in its computers. To quote, again, from the dissenting opinion in the Court of Appeal: "[I]t is circular to premise the damage element of a tort solely upon the steps taken to prevent the damage. Injury can only be established by the completed tort's consequences, not by the cost of the steps taken to avoid the injury and prevent the tort; otherwise, we can create injury for every supposed tort."

. . .

II. Proposed Extension of California Tort Law

We next consider whether California common law should be *extended* to cover, as a trespass to chattels, an otherwise harmless electronic communication whose contents are objectionable. We decline to so expand California law. Intel, of course, was not the recipient of Hamidi's messages, but rather the owner and possessor of computer servers used to relay the messages, and it bases this tort action on that ownership and possession. The property rule proposed is a rigid one, under which the sender of an electronic message would be strictly liable to the owner of equipment through which the communication passes—here, Intel—for any consequential injury flowing from the *contents* of the communication. The arguments of amici curiae and academic writers on this topic, discussed below, leave us highly doubtful whether creation of such a rigid property rule would be wise.

Writing on behalf of several industry groups appearing as amici curiae, Professor Richard A. Epstein of the University of Chicago urges us to excuse the required showing of injury to personal property in cases of unauthorized electronic contact between computers, "extending the rules of trespass to real property to all interactive Web sites and servers." The court is thus urged to recognize, for owners of a particular species of personal property, computer servers, the same interest in inviolability as is generally accorded a possessor of land. In effect, Professor Epstein suggests that a company's server should be its castle, upon which any unauthorized intrusion, however harmless, is a trespass.

Epstein's argument derives, in part, from the familiar metaphor of the Internet as a physical space, reflected in much of the language that has been used to describe it: "cyberspace," "the information superhighway," e-mail "addresses," and the like. Of course, the Internet is also frequently called simply the "Net," a term, Hamidi points out, "evoking a fisherman's chattel." A major component of the Internet is the World Wide "Web," a descriptive term suggesting neither personal nor real property, and "cyberspace" itself has come to be known by the oxymoronic phrase "virtual reality," which would suggest that any real property "located" in "cyberspace" must be "virtually real" property. Metaphor is a two-edged sword.

Indeed, the metaphorical application of real property rules would not, by itself, transform a physically harmless electronic intrusion on a computer server into a trespass. That is because, under California law, intangible intrusions on land, including electromagnetic transmissions, are not actionable as trespasses (though they may be as nuisances) unless they cause physical damage to the real property.... Since Intel does not claim Hamidi's electronically transmitted messages physically damaged its servers, it could not prove a trespass to land even were we to treat the computers as a type of real property. Some further extension of the conceit would be required, under which the electronic signals Hamidi sent would be recast as tangible intruders, perhaps as tiny messengers rushing through the "hallways" of Intel's computers and bursting out of employees' computers to read them Hamidi's missives. But such fictions promise more confusion than clarity in the law. (See *eBay, supra,* 100 F.Supp.2d at pp. 1065–1066 [rejecting eBay's argument that the defendant's automated data searches "should be thought of as equivalent to sending in an army of 100,000 robots a day to check the prices in a competitor's store"].)

The plain fact is that computers, even those making up the Internet, are—like such older communications equipment as telephones and fax machines—personal property, not realty....

. . .

. . . A leading scholar of Internet law and policy, Professor Lawrence Lessig of Stanford University, has criticized Professor Epstein's theory of the computer server as quasi-real property, previously put forward in the *eBay* case, on the ground that it ignores the costs to society in the loss of network benefits: "eBay benefits greatly from a network that is open and where access is free. It is this general feature of the Net that makes the Net so valuable to users and a source of great innovation. And to the extent that individual sites begin to impose their own rules of exclusion, the value of the network as a network declines. If machines must negotiate before entering any individual site, then the costs of using the network climb." (Lessig, The Future of Ideas: The Fate of the Commons in a Connected World (2001) p. 171 . . . .)

We discuss this debate among the amici curiae and academic writers only to note its existence and contours, not to attempt its resolution. Creating an absolute property right to exclude undesired communications from one's e-mail and Web servers might help force spammers to internalize the costs they impose on ISP's and their customers. But such a property rule might also create substantial new costs, to e-mail and e-commerce users and to society generally, in lost ease and openness of communication and in lost network benefits. In light of the unresolved controversy, we would be acting rashly to adopt a rule treating computer servers as real property for purposes of trespass law.

The Legislature has already adopted detailed regulations governing UCE. (Bus. & Prof. Code, §§ 17538.4, 17538.45; see generally *Ferguson v. Friendfinders, Inc., supra,* 94 Cal.App.4th 1255) It may see fit in the future also to regulate noncommercial e-mail, such as that sent by Hamidi, or other kinds of unwanted contact between computers on the Internet, such as that alleged in *eBay, supra.* But we are not persuaded that these perceived problems call at present for judicial creation of a rigid property rule of computer server inviolability. We therefore decline to create an exception, covering Hamidi's unwanted electronic messages to Intel employees, to the general rule that a trespass to chattels is not actionable if it does not involve actual or threatened injury to the personal property or to the possessor's legally protected interest in the personal property. No such injury having been shown on the undisputed facts, Intel was not entitled to summary judgment in its favor.

. . .

DISPOSITION

The judgment of the Court of Appeal is reversed.

We Concur: KENNARD, MORENO and PERREN, JJ.

■ Concurring opinion by KENNARD, J.

. . .

Intel Corporation has my sympathy. Unsolicited and unwanted bulk e-mail, most of it commercial, is a serious annoyance and inconvenience for persons who communicate electronically through the Internet, and bulk e-mail that distracts employees in the workplace can adversely affect overall productivity. But, as the majority persuasively explains, to establish the tort of trespass to chattels in California, the plaintiff must prove either damage to the plaintiff's personal property or actual or threatened impairment of the plaintiff's ability to use that property. . . .

This is not to say that Intel is helpless either practically or legally. As a practical matter, Intel need only instruct its employees to delete messages from Hamidi without reading them and to notify Hamidi to remove their workplace e-mail addresses from his mailing lists. Hamidi's messages promised to remove recipients from the mailing list on request, and there is no evidence that Hamidi has ever failed to do so. . . .

. . .

■ Dissenting Opinion of BROWN, J.

Candidate A finds the vehicles that candidate B has provided for his campaign workers, and A spray paints the water soluble message, "Fight corruption, vote for A" on the bumpers. The majority's reasoning would find that notwithstanding the time it takes the workers to remove the paint and the expense they incur in altering the bumpers to prevent further unwanted messages, candidate B does not deserve an injunction unless the paint is so heavy that it reduces the cars' gas mileage or otherwise depreciates the cars' market value. Furthermore, candidate B has an obligation to permit the paint's display, because the cars are driven by workers and not B personally, because B allows his workers to use the cars to pick up their lunch or retrieve their children from school, or because the bumpers display B's own slogans. I disagree.

. . .

THE TRIAL COURT CORRECTLY ISSUED THE INJUNCTION

. . .

The majority denies relief on the theory that Intel has failed to establish the requisite actual injury. As discussed, *post,* however, the injunction was properly granted because the rule requiring actual injury pertains to damages, not equitable relief, and thus courts considering comparable intrusions have provided injunctive relief without a showing of actual injury. Furthermore, there was actual injury as (1) Intel suffered economic loss; (2) it is sufficient for the injury to impair the chattel's utility to the owner rather than the chattel's market value; and (3) even in the absence of any injury to the owner's utility, it is nevertheless a trespass where one party expropriates for his own use the resources paid for by another.

Harmless Trespasses to Chattels May be Prevented

Defendant Hamidi used Intel's server in violation of the latter's demand to stop. This unlawful use of Intel's system interfered with the use of the system by Intel employees. This misconduct creates a cause of action. "[I]t is a trespass to damage goods or destroy them, *to make an unpermitted use of them,* or to move them from one place to another." (Prosser & Keeton on Torts (5th ed. 1984) Trespass to Chattels, § 14, p. 85, fns. omitted & italics added.) . . .

. . .

. . . The majority summarily distinguishes *CompuServe* and its progeny by noting there the "plaintiff showed, or was prepared to show, some interference with the efficient functioning of its computer system." . . . But although *CompuServe* did note the impairment imposed by the defendant's unsolicited e-mail, this was not part of its holding. . . . [T]he conclusion of *CompuServe's* analysis fully applies here: "Defendants' intentional use of plaintiff's proprietary computer equipment exceeds plaintiff's consent and, indeed, continued after repeated demands that defendants cease. Such use is an actionable trespass to plaintiff's chattel."

Post-*CompuServe* case law has emphasized that unauthorized use of another's property establishes a trespass, even without a showing of physical damage. "Although eBay appears unlikely to be able to show a substantial interference at this time, such a showing is not required. Conduct that does not amount to a substantial interference with possession, but which consists of intermeddling with or use of another's personal property, is sufficient to establish a cause of action for trespass to chattel." (*eBay, Inc. v. Bidder's Edge, Inc.* (N.D.Cal.2000) 100 F.Supp.2d 1058, 1070.)[6] . . . An intruder is not entitled to sleep in his neighbor's car, even if he does not chip the paint.

. . .

Intel Suffered Injury

Even if *CompuServe* and its progeny deem injury a prerequisite for injunctive relief, such injury occurred here. Intel suffered not merely an affront to its dignitary interest in ownership but tangible economic loss. Furthermore, notwithstanding

---

[6] The majority asserts *eBay* does require impairment, because the opinion noted that the *wide replication* of the defendant's conduct would *likely* impair the functioning of the plaintiff's system. . . . Of course, the "wide replication" of Hamidi's conduct would likely impair Intel's operating system. Accordingly, a diluted "likely impairment through wide replication" standard would favor Intel, not Hamidi.

the majority's doubts, it is entirely consistent with the Restatement and case law to recognize a property interest in the subjective utility of one's property. Finally, case law further recognizes as actionable the loss that occurs when one party maintains property for its own use and another party uses it, even if the property does not suffer damage as a result.

Intel Suffered Economic Loss

. . .

The economic costs of unwanted e-mail exist even if Intel employees, unlike CompuServe subscribers, do not pay directly for the time they spend on the Internet. No such *direct* costs appear here, only the opportunity costs of lost time. But for Intel, "time is money" nonetheless. . . .

. . .

Although Hamidi claims he sent only six e-mails, he sent them to between 8,000 and 35,000 employees, thus sending from 48,000 to 210,000 messages. Since it is the effect on Intel that is determinative, it is the number of messages received, not sent, that matters. In any event, Hamidi *sent* between 48,000 and 210,000 messages; the "six" refers only to the number of distinct texts Hamidi sent. Even if it takes little time to determine the author of a message and then delete it, this process, multiplied hundreds of thousands of times, amounts to a substantial loss of employee time, and thus work product. If Intel received 200,000 messages, and each one could be skimmed and deleted in six seconds, it would take approximately 333 hours, or 42 business days, to delete them all. In other words, if Intel hired an employee to remove all unwanted mail, it would take that individual two entire months to finish. . . .

Intel's Injury is Properly Related to the Chattel

The majority does not dispute that Intel suffered a loss of work product as a matter of fact, so much as it denies that this loss may constitute the requisite injury as a matter of law. According to the majority, the reduced utility of the chattel to the owner does not constitute a sufficiently cognizable injury, which exists only where the chattel itself suffers injury, i.e., its "market value" falls. The Restatement and related case law are to the contrary.

The Restatement recognizes that the measure of impairment may be subjective; a cognizable injury may occur not only when the trespass reduces the chattel's market value but also when the trespass affects its value to the owner. . . . (Rest.2d Torts, § 218, com. h, p. 422.)

. . .

As the Court of Appeal's opinion below indicated, interference with an owner's ability to use the chattel supports a trespass. The opinion recalled the rule, which dates back almost 400 years, holding that chasing an owner's animal amounts to a trespass to chattels. . . . A contemporary version of this interference would occur if a trespasser unplugged the computers of the entire Intel staff and moved them to a high shelf in each employee's office or cubicle. The computers themselves would suffer no damage, but all 35,000 employees would need to take the time to retrieve their computers and restart them. This would reduce the computers' utility to Intel, for, like the chased animals, they would not be available for immediate use. If the chasing of a few animals supports a trespass, then so does even minimal interference with a system used by 35,000 individuals.

. . .

The Unlawful Use of Another's Property is a Trespass, Regardless of Its Effect on the Property's Utility to the Owner

Finally, even if Hamidi's interference did not affect the server's utility to Intel, it would still amount to a trespass. Intel has poured millions of dollars into a resource that Hamidi has now appropriated for his own use. . . . The use by one party of property whose costs have been paid by another amounts to an unlawful taking of those resources — even if there is no unjust enrichment by the trespassing party.

. . .

■ Dissenting Opinion by MOSK, J.

. . .

. . . The majority fail to distinguish open communication in the public "commons" of the Internet from unauthorized intermeddling on a private, proprietary intranet. Hamidi is not communicating in the equivalent of a town square or of an unsolicited "junk" mailing through the United States Postal Service. His action, in crossing from the public Internet into a private intranet, is more like intruding into a private office mailroom, commandeering the mail cart, and dropping off unwanted broadsides on 30,000 desks. Because Intel's security measures have been circumvented by Hamidi, the majority leave Intel, which has exercised all reasonable self-help efforts, with no recourse unless he causes a malfunction or systems "crash." . . .

. . .

I Concur: GEORGE, C.J.

EXTENSIONS

Trespass a nuisance? Dan Burk is highly critical of the courts' embrace of the trespass to chattels cause of action in cases such as the foregoing. He argues that "these courts essentially reversed several hundred years of legal evolution, collapsing the separate doctrines of trespass to land and trespass to chattels back into their single common law progenitor, the action for trespass. But to do so effectively creates a brand new cause of action, unknown to modern jurisprudence." Dan L. Burk, *The Trouble with Trespass*, 4 J. SMALL & EMERGING BUS. L. 27, 33 (2000). He proposes an alternative approach:

> [T]he imposition of theories, such as trespass upon the digital commons, may tend to lead to detrimental over-propertization of the Internet. Incomplete entitlements, rather than strong exclusive rights, might better serve the balancing function. . . . Economic theory indicates that in situations where the costs of locating, negotiating, and valuing transactions are high, unclear entitlements may tend to facilitate bargaining. Unclear rules will tend to facilitate innovative or informal bargaining arrangements, whereas bright-line rules appropriate to low

transaction cost situations may simply lock the parties into their respective ownership positions, unable to reach a beneficial exchange. Alternatively, the unclear rule may shunt disputes into third-party review, as in litigation, where the court can tailor an ownership rule to the specific situation.

These characteristics suggest that the correct property theory might be nuisance to web sites, rather than trespass. Nuisance lies only if the cost of the intrusive activity outweighs the benefit. The "muddy" nature of nuisance would allow computer owners on the Net to exclude unreasonably costly uses of their servers, while allowing access for socially beneficial uses, even if the server owner might otherwise object. . . .

Id. at 52–53. Do you agree that "muddy" rules might lead to better results in disputes of this sort?

QUESTIONS FOR DISCUSSION

Reconciling Hamidi *with prior cases.* The majority holds that "an electronic communication that neither damages the recipient computer system nor impairs its functioning" is not actionable as trespass to chattels, and asserts that this holding is consistent with prior cases, including *CompuServe v. Cyber Promotions, America Online v. LCGM, Register.com v. Verio,* and *eBay v. Bidder's Edge.* Does the majority succeed in demonstrating that the requisite damage existed in each of those cases? On the majority's reasoning, would the outcome have been different if Intel had submitted an affidavit expressing fear that if Hamidi's conduct is not enjoined, many other former employees will be encouraged to send unsolicited e-mail to its current employees?

IV. UNFAIR COMPETITION TORTS

A. AFFILIATE MARKETING AND PARASITEWARE

A fast-growing segment of Internet commerce, known as affiliate marketing, involves payment of commissions to operators of websites that direct customers to e-commerce sites. The affiliate marketer maintains a website with hyperlinks to e-commerce sites operated by others, and earns a commission each time a visitor to its site clicks on a link and makes a purchase from the e-commerce site. For example, the marketer might feature a book review, including a link to the web page on Amazon.com through which the book may be purchased. When the visitor clicks on the link, and arrives at the web page, her browser transmits to Amazon.com a code identifying the marketer's site as the referrer. If the visitor purchases the book, Amazon.com credits the marketer with a commission.

Affiliate marketing is big business. According to one estimate, twenty percent of all e-commerce transactions occur through affiliate marketing. Amazon.com alone has over 800,000 affiliate sites.

A number of e-commerce marketers have deployed software that seeks to capture some of the commissions generated through affiliate marketing, operating in a manner that is highly controversial. This category of software, called parasiteware by its detractors, works by intercepting the transmission of information to the e-commerce site that is initiated when a user clicks on the link on the affiliate marketer's site. In the example above, when the user clicks on the link on the book review site, the user's browser initiates a data transmission to Amazon.com's server, which transmits both a code identifying the book review site and a request that the server transmit the appropriate web page for display on the user's computer. The parasiteware intercepts that data transmission, and transmits instead a code identifying *the website in whose service the parasiteware has been deployed* as the site that is referring the purchaser to Amazon.com. As a result, Amazon.com pays the commission to the parasiteware site, rather than the book review site.

A milder type of parasiteware refrains from intercepting commissions that are due to some other referring site, but claims a commission only when no other referring site is involved. To continue with the above example, when a user directly accesses Amazon.com's website and makes a purchase, the parasiteware routes the access to make it appear that the website in whose service the parasiteware has been deployed is the referring site, and that website collects a commission from Amazon.com.

How does the parasiteware get installed on the user's computer? In some cases, as with spyware and adware (discussed in Chapter 6, Part III(E), *supra*), it is bundled with popular file-sharing software, and is downloaded to and installed on the user's computer when he downloads the file-sharing software. The clickwrap agreement accompanying the file-sharing software typically discloses that the parasiteware is being installed, but in a manner that may not bring it to the attention of many users. In other cases, the user is offered an economic incentive to install the parasiteware: the parasiteware provider offers to split the commission with the user, so that the user receives what is in effect a rebate on his purchase.

Predictably, the operators of affiliate marketing sites are livid at losing commissions to the deployers of parasiteware. Some e-commerce sites that operate affiliate marketing programs have taken a stand against the practice, refusing to pay commissions to parasiteware deployers.

Parasiteware supporters argue that they are doing nothing wrong: it is up to the user to decide which website will be rewarded with the commission produced by her purchase. Detractors counter that users frequently are unaware that the diversion is occurring, and that it is in any rate unfair to the affiliate marketer that actually directed the user to the e-commerce site.

To address this controversial practice, in December 2002 (amended February 2003) some of the major players in affiliate marketing created a brief set of rules called the Publisher Code of Conduct. Among other things, the Code provides that (1) a marketer may not use software that automatically substitutes its own identifier for that of the affiliate marketer—that is, may not engage in the practice of "stealing links"; (2) a marketer may not use software that changes the content of a website that is being viewed, such as by inserting its own banner advertisement in place of one that would otherwise be displayed; and (3) if parasiteware is bundled with another application, there must be clear notice to that effect in the license agreement accompanying that application, and de-installation of the parasiteware must be "obvious, easy and complete." However, it is permissible for the parasiteware to pop up a box giving the user the choice whether to direct the entire commission to the affiliate marketing site, or to redirect the referral so that the user splits the commission with the parasiteware deployer. The Code is available at Commission Junction, cj.com/pub_conduct.jsp.

QUESTIONS FOR DISCUSSION

Parasiteware issues. What legal issues are raised by the use of parasiteware? What causes of action might be asserted by an affiliate marketer that loses commissions due to the deployment of parasiteware? By a parasiteware operator that is denied a commission on an intercepted referral to an e-commerce site? Are the issues resolved if the parasiteware operates by leaving the choice of who gets the commission up to the user?

B. SEARCH ENGINE RANKINGS

The ranking that an e-commerce website receives from an influential search engine is an important determinant of the commercial success of that website. A person who uses a search engine to locate a website relevant to her purchasing interests is far more likely to look at the first few sites that appear on the search engine results page than at sites that appear lower in this listing. A website operator thus has a strong interest in having her site appear near the top of the listings.

Since the early 1990s, website operators have employed several methods in an effort to improve their search engine rankings with respect to particular search terms. For example, some website operators place multiple instances of favored search terms in the metatags section of the code making up the website, or in other invisible text. (For discussion of the use of metatags to affect search engine results, see Chapter 2, Part II(A), *supra*) But search engine operators, trying to prevent such manipulation of their results, have responded by modifying their search algorithms to de-emphasize or eliminate reliance on such invisible text.

Google, the most influential search engine at present, creates its search results using a patented algorithm that assigns a number, called a PageRank, to a website in relation to any given search query. The PageRank is based in part upon an evaluation of the number and importance of other websites that maintain links to the website being ranked. Seeking to capitalize on the importance to e-commerce websites of a high Google ranking, some companies began offering, for a fee, to help websites improve their rankings by catering to Google's PageRank algorithm. For example, the search-engine optimizer companies would create numerous websites, called "link farms," all linking to the client's site, in an effort to influence the client's PageRank. Google, jealous to maintain the integrity of its search results, warned website operators that engaging in such schemes could get them kicked out of Google's search results entirely.

In 2002, one search-engine optimizer company, called Search King, found that its own Google ranking suddenly took a precipitous drop—as did the rankings of some of Search King's clients. In *Search King, Inc. v. Google Technology, Inc.*, 2003 WL 21464568 (W.D. Okla.2003), Search King alleged that Google's lowering of these rankings constituted tortious interference with its contractual relations. The court held that the PageRank that Google assigns to a website is a statement of opinion relating to a matter of public concern. As such, the PageRank is, under existing precedent, speech that is fully protected under the First Amendment. The court rebuffed Search King's argument that the PageRank, since it is derived automatically by use of a mathematical algorithm, is objectively verifiable, and therefore not a subjective opinion. As the court explained, the PageRank "is fundamentally subjective in nature. This is so because every algorithm employed by every search engine is different, and will produce a different representation of the relative significance of a particular web site . . . ."

The court further held that "under Oklahoma law, protected speech—in this case, PageRanks—cannot give rise to a claim for tortious interference with contractual relations because it cannot be considered wrongful, even if the speech is motivated by hatred or ill will." Accordingly, the court granted Google's motion to dismiss.

CHAPTER THIRTEEN
LIABILITY OF INTERNET SERVICE PROVIDERS AND OTHER INTERMEDIARIES FOR ONLINE HARMS

When a wrong is committed via online communications, there are, as usual, a perpetrator and a victim. But transmission of a communication online, and therefore commission of an online wrong, cannot occur without the participation of various other parties that enable the communication to occur. If the perpetrator and victim access the Internet via dialup connections, those enablers may include the perpetrator's local exchange carrier; the perpetrator's Internet service provider or hosting provider; an interexchange carrier; operators of servers through which the packets of data constituting the communication travel; the victim's Internet service provider; the victim's local exchange carrier; and domain name registrars and registry custodians. This chapter addresses the rules that apply when a victim, or a prosecutor, seeks to hold such an intermediary liable for online wrongs.

Efforts to hold an intermediary responsible for online wrongs occur in several contexts. The most common scenarios include: (1) An Internet user posts, on an online bulletin board system ("BBS"), a message that is defamatory, constitutes business disparagement, or is otherwise tortious. The target of the posting sues the operator of the BBS. (2) A user manipulates the market by posting false statements about a publicly traded company, causing the stock price to soar or dive. The company, or a group of investors in its stock, sues an Internet intermediary that made the postings available. (3) A website presents financial information about a company, supplied by a third party, that turns out to be erroneous. The company or a group of its investors sues the website operator. (4) A malicious attacker launches a "denial of service" attack, overwhelming a company's servers and forcing it to shut down, causing harm to the company's customers who sue the company. (5) A user posts, on a website or a BBS, material that infringes a copyright owned by another. The copyright owner sues the website or BBS. (6) A person offers an item for sale via an online auction site. The offering is fraudulent, the seller fails to deliver, the product is harmful or defective, or the item is contraband. The purchaser sues the operator of the auction site.

The prospect of liability for conduct of this sort is a major concern for Internet service providers, and can have a significant impact on the conduct of Internet commerce. As we will see, in Part I(C), *infra*, the imposition of liability on ISPs for third-party defamation and other speech torts provoked a strong congressional response in the form of Section 509 of the Communications Decency Act of 1996, 47 U.S.C. § 230.[1] In addition, ISP liability for third-party copyright infringement brought about the safe harbors in Title II of the Digital Millennium Copyright Act, 17 U.S.C. § 512, which is discussed in Chapter 7, Part V(B)(2), *supra*. The safe harbors applicable to copyright infringement grant service provid-

---

[1] Another provision of the Communications Decency Act imposed penalties for making indecent material available to minors. (Indecent material is protected by the First Amendment; obscene material is not.) In *Reno v. American Civil Liberties Union*, 521 U.S. 844 (1997), the Supreme Court invalidated this provision, holding that it violates the First Amendment. The invalidation did not involve Section 230, the ISP immunity provision.

ers only a conditional immunity, imposing continuing obligations on them to limit the availability of infringing material. As we shall see in this Chapter, Section 230 offers immunity with fewer conditions. In some cases, there is an obvious analogy between an online intermediary and its offline equivalent. For example, the operator of an Internet backbone transmission facility has the same function in an online communication that an interexchange carrier has in a long-distance telephone conversation. It is therefore easy to argue that the backbone provider should be entitled to the same immunity from liability based on communications that traverse its facilities as is enjoyed by telecommunications common carriers.[2] In other cases, the governing analogy is not so clear. Is a service that hosts proprietary content, or the operator of an online bulletin board, more like a bookstore, a publisher, or an author?

I. LIABILITY OF SERVICE PROVIDERS FOR REPUTATIONAL HARM CAUSED BY AVAILABILITY OF HARMFUL CONTENT

A. LIABILITY AS "DISTRIBUTOR" OF DEFAMATORY MATERIAL

Cubby, Inc. v. CompuServe Inc.
776 F.Supp. 135 (S.D.N.Y.1991).

■ LEISURE, DISTRICT JUDGE.

This is a diversity action for libel, business disparagement, and unfair competition, based on allegedly defamatory statements made in a publication carried on a computerized database. Defendant CompuServe Inc. ("CompuServe") has moved for summary judgment pursuant to Rule 56 of the Federal Rules of Civil Procedure. For the reasons stated below, CompuServe's motion is granted in its entirety.

Background

CompuServe develops and provides computer-related products and services, including CompuServe Information Service ("CIS"), an on-line general information service or "electronic library" that subscribers may access from a personal computer or terminal. Subscribers to CIS pay a membership fee and online time usage fees, in return for which they have access to the thousands of information sources available on CIS. Subscribers may also obtain access to over 150 special interest "forums," which are comprised of electronic bulletin boards, interactive online conferences, and topical databases.

One forum available is the Journalism Forum, which focuses on the journalism industry. Cameron Communications, Inc. ("CCI"), which is independent of CompuServe, has contracted to "manage, review, create, delete, edit and otherwise control the contents" of the Journalism Forum "in accordance with editorial and technical standards and conventions of style as established by CompuServe."

---

[2] Under the common law, a common carrier that is required to transmit certain content is generally immune from defamation liability based on that content even if it knows of the defamation. RESTATEMENT (SECOND) OF TORTS § 612(2) (1965). Likewise, broadcasters are immune from defamation liability for equal-time material that federal law requires them to carry. *See Farmers Educational & Cooperative Union v. WDAY, Inc.*, 360 U.S. 525 (1959).

One publication available as part of the Journalism Forum is Rumorville USA ("Rumorville"), a daily newsletter that provides reports about broadcast journalism and journalists. Rumorville is published by Don Fitzpatrick Associates of San Francisco ("DFA"), which is headed by defendant Don Fitzpatrick. CompuServe has no employment, contractual, or other direct relationship with either DFA or Fitzpatrick; DFA provides Rumorville to the Journalism Forum under a contract with CCI. The contract between CCI and DFA provides that DFA "accepts total responsibility for the contents" of Rumorville. The contract also requires CCI to limit access to Rumorville to those CIS subscribers who have previously made membership arrangements directly with DFA.

CompuServe has no opportunity to review Rumorville's contents before DFA uploads it into CompuServe's computer banks, from which it is immediately available to approved CIS subscribers. CompuServe receives no part of any fees that DFA charges for access to Rumorville, nor does CompuServe compensate DFA for providing Rumorville to the Journalism Forum; the compensation CompuServe receives for making Rumorville available to its subscribers is the standard online time usage and membership fees charged to all CIS subscribers, regardless of the information services they use. CompuServe maintains that, before this action was filed, it had no notice of any complaints about the contents of the Rumorville publication or about DFA.

In 1990, plaintiffs Cubby, Inc. ("Cubby") and Robert Blanchard ("Blanchard") (collectively, "plaintiffs") developed Skuttlebut, a computer database designed to publish and distribute electronically news and gossip in the television news and radio industries. Plaintiffs intended to compete with Rumorville; subscribers gained access to Skuttlebut through their personal computers after completing subscription agreements with plaintiffs.

Plaintiffs claim that, on separate occasions in April 1990, Rumorville published false and defamatory statements relating to Skuttlebut and Blanchard, and that CompuServe carried these statements as part of the Journalism Forum. The allegedly defamatory remarks included a suggestion that individuals at Skuttlebut gained access to information first published by Rumorville "through some back door"; a statement that Blanchard was "bounced" from his previous employer, WABC; and a description of Skuttlebut as a "new start-up scam."

Plaintiffs have asserted claims against CompuServe and Fitzpatrick under New York law for libel of Blanchard, business disparagement of Skuttlebut, and unfair competition as to Skuttlebut, based largely upon the allegedly defamatory statements contained in Rumorville. CompuServe has moved, pursuant to Fed.R.Civ.P. 56, for summary judgment on all claims against it. CompuServe does not dispute, solely for the purposes of this motion, that the statements relating to Skuttlebut and Blanchard were defamatory; rather, it argues that it acted as a distributor, and not a publisher, of the statements, and cannot be held liable for the statements because it did not know and had no reason to know of the statements. Plaintiffs oppose CompuServe's motion for summary judgment, claiming that genuine issues of material fact exist and that little in the way of discovery has been undertaken thus far.

Discussion

. . .

II. Libel Claim

A. *The Applicable Standard of Liability*

Plaintiffs base their libel claim on the allegedly defamatory statements contained in the Rumorville publication that CompuServe carried as part of the Journalism Forum. CompuServe argues that, based on the undisputed facts, it was a distributor of Rumorville, as opposed to a publisher of the Rumorville statements. CompuServe further contends that, as a distributor of Rumorville, it cannot be held liable on the libel claim because it neither knew nor had reason to know of the allegedly defamatory statements. Plaintiffs, on the other hand, argue that the Court should conclude that CompuServe is a publisher of the statements and hold it to a higher standard of liability.

Ordinarily, " 'one who repeats or otherwise republishes defamatory matter is subject to liability as if he had originally published it.' " *Cianci v. New Times Publishing Co.*, 639 F.2d 54, 61 (2d Cir.1980) (Friendly, J.) (quoting Restatement (Second) of Torts § 578 (1977)). With respect to entities such as news vendors, book stores, and libraries, however, "New York courts have long held that vendors and distributors of defamatory publications are not liable if they neither know nor have reason to know of the defamation." *Lerman v. Chuckleberry Publishing, Inc.*, 521 F.Supp. 228, 235 (S.D.N.Y.1981); *accord Macaluso v. Mondadori Publishing Co.*, 527 F.Supp. 1017, 1019 (E.D.N.Y.1981).

The requirement that a distributor must have knowledge of the contents of a publication before liability can be imposed for distributing that publication is deeply rooted in the First Amendment, made applicable to the states through the Fourteenth Amendment. "[T]he constitutional guarantees of the freedom of speech and of the press stand in the way of imposing" strict liability on distributors for the contents of the reading materials they carry. *Smith v. California*, 361 U.S. 147, 152–53 (1959). In *Smith*, the Court struck down an ordinance that imposed liability on a bookseller for possession of an obscene book, regardless of whether the bookseller had knowledge of the book's contents. The Court reasoned that

> "Every bookseller would be placed under an obligation to make himself aware of the contents of every book in his shop. It would be altogether unreasonable to demand so near an approach to omniscience." And the bookseller's burden would become the public's burden, for by restricting him the public's access to reading matter would be restricted. If the contents of bookshops and periodical stands were restricted to material of which their proprietors had made an inspection, they might be depleted indeed.

Id. at 153 (citation and footnote omitted). Although *Smith* involved criminal liability, the First Amendment's guarantees are no less relevant to the instant action: "What a State may not constitutionally bring about by means of a criminal statute is likewise beyond the reach of its civil law of libel. The fear of damage awards . . . may be markedly more inhibiting than the fear of prosecution under a criminal statute." *New York Times Co. v. Sullivan*, 376 U.S. 254, 277 (1964) (citation omitted).

CompuServe's CIS product is in essence an electronic, for-profit library that carries a vast number of publications and collects usage and membership fees from its subscribers in return for access to the publications. CompuServe and companies like it are at the forefront of the information industry revolution. High technology has markedly increased the speed with which information is gathered and processed; it is now possible for an individual with a personal computer, modem, and telephone line to have instantaneous access to thousands of news publications from across the United States and around the world. While CompuServe may decline to carry a given publication altogether, in reality, once it does decide to carry a publication, it will have little or no editorial control over that publication's contents. This is especially so when CompuServe carries the publication as part of a forum that is managed by a company unrelated to CompuServe.

With respect to the Rumorville publication, the undisputed facts are that DFA uploads the text of Rumorville into CompuServe's data banks and makes it available to approved CIS subscribers instantaneously. CompuServe has no more editorial control over such a publication than does a public library, book store, or newsstand, and it would be no more feasible for CompuServe to examine every publication it carries for potentially defamatory statements than it would be for any other distributor to do so. "First Amendment guarantees have long been recognized as protecting distributors of publications. . . . Obviously, the national distributor of hundreds of periodicals has no duty to monitor each issue of every periodical it distributes. Such a rule would be an impermissible burden on the First Amendment." *Lerman v. Flynt Distributing Co.*, 745 F.2d 123, 139 (2d Cir.1984); *see also Daniel v. Dow Jones & Co.*, 520 N.Y.S.2d 334, 340 (N.Y.Civ.Ct.1987) (computerized database service "is one of the modern, technologically interesting, alternative ways the public may obtain up-to-the-minute news" and "is entitled to the same protection as more established means of news distribution").

Technology is rapidly transforming the information industry. A computerized database is the functional equivalent of a more traditional news vendor, and the inconsistent application of a lower standard of liability to an electronic news distributor such as CompuServe than that which is applied to a public library, book store, or newsstand would impose an undue burden on the free flow of information. Given the relevant First Amendment considerations, the appropriate standard of liability to be applied to CompuServe is whether it knew or had reason to know of the allegedly defamatory Rumorville statements.

B. *CompuServe's Liability as a Distributor*

CompuServe contends that it is undisputed that it had neither knowledge nor reason to know of the allegedly defamatory Rumorville statements, especially given the large number of publications it carries and the speed with which DFA uploads Rumorville into its computer banks and makes the publication available to CIS subscribers. The burden is thus shifted to plaintiffs, who " 'must set forth specific facts showing that there is a genuine issue for trial.' " *Anderson v. Liberty Lobby, Inc.*, 477 U.S. 242, 250 (1986) (quoting Fed.R.Civ.P. 56(e)). Plaintiffs have not set forth anything other than conclusory allegations as to whether CompuServe knew or had reason to know of the Rumorville statements, and have failed to meet their burden on this issue. . . .

Plaintiffs have not set forth any specific facts showing that there is a genuine issue as to whether CompuServe knew or had reason to know of Rumorville's contents. Because CompuServe, as a news distributor, may not be held liable if it neither knew nor had reason to know of the allegedly defamatory Rumorville statements, summary judgment in favor of CompuServe on the libel claim is granted.

. . .

QUESTIONS FOR DISCUSSION

1. *"Opportunity" to review material.* The court's decision to treat CompuServe like a distributor of the allegedly defamatory material is based in part on its finding that CompuServe had "no opportunity" to review the material before it became available to subscribers. The absence of such an opportunity is attributable to the system of content management that CompuServe chose to implement. For example, CompuServe could have implemented a system whereby a third-party content provider uploaded material to a holding area, from which it would be released to subscribers only after being vetted by CompuServe's in-house lawyers. How is CompuServe's defense different from, say, that of a hit-and-run driver who argues that his decision to wear a blindfold deprived him of the opportunity to see that he had run over a pedestrian?

Should it make a difference *why* CompuServe instituted the system it did? For example, CompuServe might have decided against a prior-review system because (1) such a system was technologically infeasible, (2) the system was feasible but prohibitively expensive, (3) the system would have cost a modest sum that CompuServe simply elected to avoid, (4) CompuServe's management was philosophically opposed to censorship, or (5) CompuServe intentionally avoided any conduct that might deprive it of common-carrier immunity.

2. *Constructive notice.* The court found there was no evidence that CompuServe "knew or had reason to know" of the defamatory statements contained in the publication, which was called "Rumorville." Should a distributor of a publication with a name suggesting that it engages in uncorroborated reporting be deemed on notice of its potentially defamatory contents? What if it were widely known that Rumorville had been sued several times, successfully, for defamation? Should newsstands be liable for the defamatory content of *The National Enquirer*, which has been adjudged a publisher of defamatory falsehoods on more than one occasion?

3. *Technological change.* Suppose that artificial intelligence technology improves to the point where it can flag potentially defamatory content to a degree of accuracy that makes it feasible for an online service to eliminate 90% of the defamatory statements that pass through its facilities at a modest cost. Would the balance of interests then tip away from the First Amendment interest in free speech, and in favor of providing recourse to victims of defamation? Can the "knew or should have known" standard adequately adjust for changes in technology?

4. *Availability of author of the defamation.* In addition to suing CompuServe, the plaintiffs sued the author of the allegedly defamatory content. Does the fact that a victim may always sue the originator of defamatory content justify providing blanket immunity to distributors of the content? Are the considerations any different with respect to online communications, as opposed to other means of communication?

B. LIABILITY AS "PUBLISHER" OF DEFAMATORY MATERIAL

Stratton Oakmont, Inc. v. Prodigy Services Co.
23 Media L. Rep. 1794 (N.Y.Sup.Ct.1995).

■ STUART L. AIN, JUSTICE.

Upon the foregoing papers, it is ordered that this motion by Plaintiffs for partial summary judgment against Defendant PRODIGY SERVICES COMPANY ("PRODIGY") is granted and this Court determines, as a matter of law, the following two disputed issues as follows:

(i) that PRODIGY was a "publisher" of statements concerning Plaintiffs on its "Money Talk" computer bulletin board for the purposes of Plaintiffs' libel claims; and,

(ii) that Charles Epstein, the Board Leader of PRODIGY's "Money Talk" computer bulletin board, acted as PRODIGY's agent for the purposes of the acts and omissions alleged in the complaint.

At issue in this case are statements about Plaintiffs made by an unidentified bulletin board user or "poster" on PRODIGY's "Money Talk" computer bulletin board on October 23rd and 25th of 1994. These statements included the following:

(a) STRATTON OAKMONT, INC. ("STRATTON"), a securities investment banking firm, and DANIEL PORUSH, STRATTON's president, committed criminal and fraudulent acts in connection with the initial public offering of stock of Solomon–Page Ltd.;

(b) the Solomon–Page offering was a "major criminal fraud" and "100% criminal fraud";

(c) PORUSH was "soon to be proven criminal"; and,

(d) STRATTON was a "cult of brokers who either lie for a living or get fired."

Plaintiffs commenced this action against PRODIGY, the owner and operator of the computer network on which the statements appeared, and the unidentified party who posted the aforementioned statements. The second amended complaint alleges ten (10) causes of action, including claims for per se libel. On this motion, . . . Plaintiffs seek partial summary judgment on two issues, namely:

(1) whether PRODIGY may be considered a "publisher" of the aforementioned statements; and,

(2) whether Epstein, the Board Leader for the computer bulletin board on which the statements were posted, acted with actual and apparent authority as PRODIGY's "agent" for the purposes of the claims in this action.

By way of background, it is undisputed that PRODIGY's computer network has at least two million subscribers who communicate with each other and with the general subscriber population on PRODIGY's bulletin boards. "Money Talk" the board on which the aforementioned statements appeared, is allegedly the leading and most widely read financial computer bulletin board in the United States, where members can post statements regarding stocks, investments and other financial matters. PRODIGY contracts with bulletin Board Leaders, who, among other things, participate in board discussions and undertake promotional efforts to encourage usage and increase users. The Board Leader for "Money Talk" at the time the alleged libelous statements were posted was Charles Epstein.

PRODIGY commenced operations in 1990. Plaintiffs base their claim that PRODIGY is a publisher in large measure on PRODIGY's stated policy, starting in 1990, that it was a family oriented computer network. In various national newspaper articles written by Geoffrey Moore, PRODIGY's Director of Market Programs and Communications, PRODIGY held itself out as an online service that exercised editorial control over the content of messages posted on its computer bulletin boards, thereby expressly differentiating itself from its competition and expressly likening itself to a newspaper. In one article PRODIGY stated:

> "We make no apology for pursuing a value system that reflects the culture of the millions of American families we aspire to serve. Certainly no responsible newspaper does less when it chooses the type of advertising it publishes, the letters it prints, the degree of nudity and unsupported gossip its editors tolerate."

Plaintiffs characterize the aforementioned articles by PRODIGY as admissions . . . and argue that, together with certain documentation and deposition testimony, these articles establish Plaintiffs' prima facie case. In opposition, PRODIGY insists that its policies have changed and evolved since 1990 and that the latest article on the subject, dated February, 1993, did not reflect PRODIGY's policies in October, 1994, when the allegedly libelous statements were posted. Although the eighteen month lapse of time between the last article and the aforementioned statements is not insignificant, and the Court is wary of interpreting statements and admissions out of context, these considerations go solely to the weight of this evidence.

Plaintiffs further rely upon the following additional evidence in support of their claim that PRODIGY is a publisher:

(A) promulgation of "content guidelines" (the "Guidelines") in which, *inter alia*, users are requested to refrain from posting notes that are "insulting" and are advised that "notes that harass other members or are deemed to be in bad taste or grossly repugnant to community standards, or are deemed harmful to maintaining a harmonious online community, will be removed when brought to PRODIGY's attention"; the Guidelines all expressly state that although "Prodigy is committed to open debate and discussion on the bulletin boards, . . . this doesn't mean that 'anything goes' ";

(B) use of a software screening program which automatically prescreens all bulletin board postings for offensive language;

(C) the use of Board Leaders such as Epstein whose duties include enforcement of the Guidelines . . . ; and

(D) testimony by Epstein as to a tool for Board Leaders known as an "emergency delete function" pursuant to which a Board Leader could remove a note and send a previously prepared message of explanation "ranging from solicitation, bad advice, insulting, wrong topic, off topic, bad taste, etcetera."

A finding that PRODIGY is a publisher is the first hurdle for Plaintiffs to overcome in pursuit of their defamation claims, because one who repeats or otherwise republishes a libel is subject to liability as if he had originally published it. [*Cianci v. New Times Pub. Co.*, 639 F.2d 54, 61; Restatement, Second Torts § 578 (1977).] In contrast, distributors such as book stores and libraries may be liable for defamatory statements of others only if they knew or had reason to know of the defamatory statement at issue. [*Cubby Inc. v. CompuServe Inc.*, 776 F.Supp. 135, 139; see also *Auvil v. CBS 60 Minutes*, 800 F.Supp. 928, 932.] A distributor, or deliverer of defamatory material is considered a passive conduit and will not be found liable in the absence of fault. [*Auvil, supra*; see also *Misut v. Mooney*, 124 Misc.2d 95 (claims against printer of weekly newspaper containing allegedly libelous articles dismissed in absence of any evidence that printer knew or had reason to know of the allegedly libelous nature of the articles).] However, a newspaper, for example, is more than a passive receptacle or conduit for news, comment and advertising. [*Miami Herald Publishing Co. v. Tornillo*, 418 U.S. 241, 258.] The choice of material to go into a newspaper and the decisions made as to the content of the paper constitute the exercise of editorial control and judgment (*Id.*), and with this editorial control comes increased liability. (See *Cubby, supra*.) In short, the critical issue to be determined by this Court is whether the foregoing evidence establishes a prima facie case that PRODIGY exercised sufficient editorial control over its computer bulletin boards to render it a publisher with the same responsibilities as a newspaper.

Again, PRODIGY insists that its former policy of manually reviewing all messages prior to posting was changed "long before the messages complained of by Plaintiffs were posted." However, no documentation or detailed explanation of such a change, and the dissemination of news of such a change, has been submitted. In addition, PRODIGY argues that in terms of sheer volume—currently 60,000 messages a day are posted on PRODIGY bulletin boards—manual review of messages is not feasible. While PRODIGY admits that Board Leaders may remove messages that violate its Guidelines, it claims in conclusory manner that Board Leaders do not function as "editors." Furthermore, PRODIGY argues generally that this Court should not decide issues that can directly impact this developing communications medium without the benefit of a full record, although it fails to describe what further facts remain to be developed on this issue of whether it is a publisher.

As for legal authority, PRODIGY relies on the *Cubby* case, *supra*. There the defendant CompuServe was a computer network providing subscribers with computer related services or forums including an online general information service or "electronic library." One of the publications available on the Journalism Forum carried defamatory statements about the Plaintiff, an electronic newsletter. Interestingly, an independent entity named Cameron Communications, Inc. ("CCI") had "contracted to manage, review, create, delete, edit and otherwise control the contents of the Journalism Forum in accordance with editorial and technical standards and conventions of style as established by CompuServe." The Court noted that

CompuServe had no opportunity to review the contents of the publication at issue before it was uploaded into CompuServe's computer banks. Consequently, the Court found that CompuServe's product was, "in essence, an electronic for-profit library" that carried a vast number of publications, and that CompuServe had "little or no editorial control" over the contents of those publications. . . .

The key distinction between CompuServe and PRODIGY is two fold. First, PRODIGY held itself out to the public and its members as controlling the content of its computer bulletin boards. Second, PRODIGY implemented this control through its automatic software screening program, and the Guidelines which Board Leaders are required to enforce. By actively utilizing technology and manpower to delete notes from its computer bulletin boards on the basis of offensiveness and "bad taste", for example, PRODIGY is clearly making decisions as to content (see, *Miami Herald Publishing Co. v. Tornillo, supra*), and such decisions constitute editorial control. (*Id.*) That such control is not complete and is enforced both as early as the notes arrive and as late as a complaint is made, does not minimize or eviscerate the simple fact that PRODIGY has uniquely arrogated to itself the role of determining what is proper for its members to post and read on its bulletin boards. Based on the foregoing, this Court is compelled to conclude that for the purposes of Plaintiffs' claims in this action, PRODIGY is a publisher rather than a distributor.

An interesting comparison may be found in *Auvil v. CBS 60 Minutes (supra)*, where apple growers sued a television network and local affiliates because of an allegedly defamatory investigative report generated by the network and broadcast by the affiliates. The record established that the affiliates exercised no editorial control over the broadcast although they had the power to do so by virtue of their contract with CBS, they had the opportunity to do so by virtue of a three hour hiatus for the west coast time differential, they had the technical capability to do so, and they in fact had occasionally censored network programming in the past, albeit never in connection with "60 Minutes." The *Auvil* court found:

> It is argued that these features, coupled with the power to censor, triggered the duty to censor. That is a leap which the Court is not prepared to join in.
>
> . . .
>
> . . . plaintiffs' construction would force the creation of full time editorial boards at local stations throughout the country which possess sufficient knowledge, legal acumen and access to experts to continually monitor incoming transmissions and exercise on-the-spot discretionary calls or face $75 million dollar lawsuits at every turn. That is not realistic.
>
> . . .
>
> More than merely unrealistic in economic terms, it is difficult to imagine a scenario more chilling on the media's right of expression and the public's right to know.

(800 F.Supp. at 931–932.) Consequently, the court dismissed all claims against the affiliates on the basis of "conduit liability," which could not be established therein absent fault, which was not shown.

In contrast, here PRODIGY has virtually created an editorial staff of Board Leaders who have the ability to continually monitor incoming transmissions and in fact do spend time censoring notes. Indeed, it could be said that PRODIGY's current system of automatic scanning, Guidelines and Board Leaders may have a chilling effect on freedom of communication in Cyberspace, and it appears that this chilling effect is exactly what PRODIGY wants, but for the legal liability that attaches to such censorship.

Let it be clear that this Court is in full agreement with *Cubby* and *Auvil*. Computer bulletin boards should generally be regarded in the same context as bookstores, libraries and network affiliates. [See Edward V. DiLello, *Functional Equivalency and Its application to Freedom of Speech on Computer Bulletin Boards*, 26 Colum.J.Law & Soc.Probs. 199, 210–211 (1993).] It is PRODIGY's own policies, technology and staffing decisions which have altered the scenario and mandated the finding that it is a publisher.

PRODIGY's conscious choice, to gain the benefits of editorial control, has opened it up to a greater liability than CompuServe and other computer networks that make no such choice. For the record, the fear that this Court's finding of publisher status for PRODIGY will compel all computer networks to abdicate control of their bulletin boards, incorrectly presumes that the market will refuse to compensate a network for its increased control and the resulting increased exposure. [See, Eric Schlachter, *Cyberspace, The Free Market and The Free Marketplace of Ideas: Recognizing Legal Differences in Computer Bulletin Board Functions*, 16 Hastings Communication and Entertainment L.J., 87, 138–139.] Presumably PRODIGY's decision to regulate the content of its bulletin boards was in part influenced by its desire to attract a market it perceived to exist consisting of users seeking a "family-oriented" computer service. This decision simply required that to the extent computer networks provide such services, they must also accept the concomitant legal consequences. In addition, the Court also notes that the issues addressed herein may ultimately be preempted by federal law if the Communications Decency Act of 1995, several versions of which are pending in Congress, is enacted. . . .

[The court further held that Charles Epstein, the Board Leader of the Money Talk bulletin board, "acted as PRODIGY's agent for the purposes of the acts and omissions alleged in the complaint."]

EXTENSIONS

Postscript to the Stratton Oakmont *case.* In October 1995, after receiving an apology from Prodigy, Stratton Oakmont agreed to drop its libel suit. Prodigy, wishing to have the court's opinion removed from the books, filed a motion to reargue the case, which Stratton Oakmont did not oppose. The judge, finding that there were no new facts justifying reargument, denied the motion. *Stratton Oakmont Inc. v. Prodigy Services Co.*, 24 Media L. Rep. 1126 (N.Y.Sup.Ct.1995). In April 1996, Stratton Oakmont agreed to pay a fine of $325,000 to the National Association of Securities Dealers in settlement of NASD charges that the brokerage firm had defrauded investors in connection with a 1991 initial public offering. NASD charged Stratton Oakmont with more than 1,000 violations of trading rules and federal securities laws, including taking orders from customers before trading was legally authorized and manipulating the prices of warrants to buy the stock. This was only the latest of Stratton's tangles with regulatory bodies. According to NASD records, Stratton

Oakmont was disciplined for violating various stock trading rules in 1989, 1990, 1991, and 1992, and was also sued twice by the Securities and Exchange Commission. In February 1996, a federal court issued a permanent injunction against Stratton for violating previous SEC orders. Later that year, the NASD expelled Stratton Oakmont from the securities industry. In 1998, the NASD fined, suspended, or permanently barred from the industry 13 former partners and employees of Stratton. The former president of Stratton Oakmont, Daniel Porush—who was a target of the alleged defamation that gave rise to *Stratton Oakmont v. Prodigy*—and its former chairman, Jordan Belfort, later pled guilty to federal charges including conspiracy to commit stock fraud, money laundering, and price manipulation. It thus appears that had litigation proceeded in *Stratton Oakmont v. Prodigy*, Prodigy might well have prevailed with truth as a defense.

QUESTIONS FOR DISCUSSION

1. *Standard of care dependent on care taken.* The court concludes that a computer BBS that holds itself out to the public as exercising editorial control over its content, and that actually does exercise such control, is liable for defamation under the standard applicable to publishers, rather than under the standard applicable to distributors. This implies the odd result that a bulletin board system operator who chooses to exercise *more* care (by exercising editorial control over at least some of the BBS's content) is held to a higher standard of care—"negligence" rather than "knew or had reason to know"—than one who chooses to exercise *less* care. Why should the amount of care one *actually* exercises determine how much care one *must* exercise in order to avoid liability?

Under common law, publisher liability was strict. The First Amendment has been interpreted to exclude liability unless the defendant is at least negligent. *See Gertz v. Robert Welch, Inc.*, 418 U.S. 323 (1974); RESTATEMENT (SECOND) OF TORTS § 580B (1965). What is the practical difference between a negligence standard and a knew-or-should-have-known standard?

2. *Relevance of actual review.* It seems likely that Prodigy did not in fact review the defamatory material in question. Why should the fact that it reviews *some* material result in the imposition of a higher standard of care with respect to material that it did *not* review? The court's reasoning would seem to yield the conclusion that a bookstore or newsstand that reviews some of its offerings for defamation before making them available for sale would be held to the standard applicable to publishers with respect to all of its offerings. Conversely, the reasoning might imply that a publisher that chooses not to read the material it publishes—say, the publisher of a free newsletter that accepts only camera-ready text— should be treated as a distributor.

3. *Distinguishing* Auvil. Like Prodigy, the CBS affiliates in *Auvil v. CBS 60 Minutes* had the technical capability of exercising editorial control over CBS's challenged broadcast, and had actually exercised this control with respect to other broadcasts. Is the court successful in distinguishing *Auvil*?

C. LEGISLATIVE RESPONSE: SERVICE PROVIDER IMMUNITY

Eight months after issuance of the decision, Congress legislatively overruled *Stratton Oakmont* by enacting an ISP-immunity provision:

§ 230. Protection for private blocking and screening of offensive material

. . .

(c) Protection for "good samaritan" blocking and screening of offensive material. —

(1) **Treatment of publisher or speaker.** — No provider or user of an interactive computer service shall be treated as the publisher or speaker of any information provided by another information content provider.

(2) **Civil liability.** — No provider or user of an interactive computer service shall be held liable on account of —

(A) any action voluntarily taken in good faith to restrict access to or availability of material that the provider or user considers to be obscene, lewd, lascivious, filthy, excessively violent, harassing, or otherwise objectionable, whether or not such material is constitutionally protected; or

(B) any action taken to enable or make available to information content providers or others the technical means to restrict access to material described in [subparagraph (A)].

. . .

(e) **Effect on other laws.** —

(1) **No effect on criminal law.** — Nothing in this section shall be construed to impair the enforcement of section 223 or 231 of this title, chapter 71 (relating to obscenity) or 110 (relating to sexual exploitation of children) of Title 18, or any other Federal criminal statute.

(2) **No effect on intellectual property law.** — Nothing in this section shall be construed to limit or expand any law pertaining to intellectual property.

(3) **State law.** — Nothing in this section shall be construed to prevent any State from enforcing any State law that is consistent with this section. No cause of action may be brought and no liability may be imposed under any State or local law that is inconsistent with this section.

(4) **No effect on Communications Privacy law.** — Nothing in this section shall be construed to limit the application of the Electronic Communications Privacy Act of 1986 or any of the amendments made by such Act, or any similar State law.

(f) **Definitions.** — As used in this section:

. . .

(2) **Interactive computer service.** — The term "interactive computer service" means any information service, system, or access software provider that provides or enables computer access by multiple users to a computer server, including specifically a service or system that provides access to the Internet and such systems operated or services offered by libraries or educational institutions.

(3) Information content provider.—The term "information content provider" means any person or entity that is responsible, in whole or in part, for the creation or development of information provided through the Internet or any other interactive computer service.

. . .

47 U.S.C. § 230 (added by Communications Decency Act of 1996, § 509, Pub. L. No. 104–104, 110 Stat. 137, 137–39 (1996)).

The terse and somewhat cryptic language of Section 230 left several issues for clarification by the courts. In negating liability based on a defendant's status as a "publisher or speaker," did Congress mean to exclude liability only for publishers or also for *distributors* of defamatory material? That is, did it overrule *Cubby v. CompuServe* in addition to *Stratton Oakmont v. Prodigy*? Is a defendant's knowledge of the offensive nature of the material of any relevance? Are there circumstances in which an online service provider has such a substantial role in bringing content into existence (without actually producing the content itself) that the content is not "information provided by another information content provider" for purposes of Section 230(c)(1)?

1. Applications of Section 230

Zeran v. America Online, Inc.
129 F.3d 327 (4th Cir.1997).

■ WILKINSON, CHIEF JUDGE.

Kenneth Zeran brought this action against America Online, Inc. ("AOL"), arguing that AOL unreasonably delayed in removing defamatory messages posted by an unidentified third party, refused to post retractions of those messages, and failed to screen for similar postings thereafter. The district court granted judgment for AOL on the grounds that the Communications Decency Act of 1996 ("CDA")—47 U.S.C. § 230—bars Zeran's claims. Zeran appeals, arguing that § 230 leaves intact liability for interactive computer service providers who possess notice of defamatory material posted through their services. . . . Section 230, however, plainly immunizes computer service providers like AOL from liability for information that originates with third parties. . . . Accordingly, we affirm the judgment of the district court.

I.

"The Internet is an international network of interconnected computers," currently used by approximately 40 million people worldwide. *Reno v. ACLU*, 521 U.S. 844, 849 (1997). One of the many means by which individuals access the Internet is through an interactive computer service. These services offer not only a connection to the Internet as a whole, but also allow their subscribers to access information communicated and stored only on each computer service's individual proprietary network. *Id.* AOL is just such an interactive computer service. Much of the information transmitted over its network originates with the company's millions of subscribers. They may transmit information privately via electronic mail, or they may communicate publicly by posting messages on AOL bulletin boards, where the messages may be read by any AOL subscriber.

The instant case comes before us on a motion for judgment on the pleadings, see Fed.R.Civ.P. 12(c), so we accept the facts alleged in the complaint as true. . . . On April 25, 1995, an unidentified person posted a message on an AOL bulletin board advertising "Naughty Oklahoma T-Shirts." The posting described the sale of shirts featuring offensive and tasteless slogans related to the April 19, 1995, bombing of the Alfred P. Murrah Federal Building in Oklahoma City. Those interested in purchasing the shirts were instructed to call "Ken" at Zeran's home phone number in Seattle, Washington. As a result of this anonymously perpetrated prank, Zeran received a high volume of calls, comprised primarily of angry and derogatory messages, but also including death threats. Zeran could not change his phone number because he relied on its availability to the public in running his business out of his home. Later that day, Zeran called AOL and informed a company representative of his predicament. The employee assured Zeran that the posting would be removed from AOL's bulletin board but explained that as a matter of policy AOL would not post a retraction. The parties dispute the date that AOL removed this original posting from its bulletin board.

On April 26, the next day, an unknown person posted another message advertising additional shirts with new tasteless slogans related to the Oklahoma City bombing. Again, interested buyers were told to call Zeran's phone number, to ask for "Ken," and to "please call back if busy" due to high demand. The angry, threatening phone calls intensified. Over the next four days, an unidentified party continued to post messages on AOL's bulletin board, advertising additional items including bumper stickers and key chains with still more offensive slogans. During this time period, Zeran called AOL repeatedly and was told by company representatives that the individual account from which the messages were posted would soon be closed. Zeran also reported his case to Seattle FBI agents. By April 30, Zeran was receiving an abusive phone call approximately every two minutes.

Meanwhile, an announcer for Oklahoma City radio station KRXO received a copy of the first AOL posting. On May 1, the announcer related the message's contents on the air, attributed them to "Ken" at Zeran's phone number, and urged the listening audience to call the number. After this radio broadcast, Zeran was inundated with death threats and other violent calls from Oklahoma City residents. Over the next few days, Zeran talked to both KRXO and AOL representatives. He also spoke to his local police, who subsequently surveilled his home to protect his safety. By May 14, after an Oklahoma City newspaper published a story exposing the shirt advertisements as a hoax and after KRXO made an on-air apology, the number of calls to Zeran's residence finally subsided to fifteen per day.

Zeran first filed suit on January 4, 1996, against radio station KRXO in the United States District Court for the Western District of Oklahoma. On April 23, 1996, he filed this separate suit against AOL in the same court. Zeran did not bring any action against the party who posted the offensive messages.[1] After Zeran's suit

---

[1] Zeran maintains that AOL made it impossible to identify the original party by failing to maintain adequate records of its users. The issue of AOL's record keeping practices, however, is not presented by this appeal.

against AOL was transferred to the Eastern District of Virginia pursuant to 28 U.S.C. § 1404(a), AOL answered Zeran's complaint and interposed 47 U.S.C. § 230 as an affirmative defense. AOL then moved for judgment on the pleadings pursuant to Fed.R.Civ.P. 12(c). The district court granted AOL's motion, and Zeran filed this appeal.

II.

A.

Because § 230 was successfully advanced by AOL in the district court as a defense to Zeran's claims, we shall briefly examine its operation here. Zeran seeks to hold AOL liable for defamatory speech initiated by a third party. He argued to the district court that once he notified AOL of the unidentified third party's hoax, AOL had a duty to remove the defamatory posting promptly, to notify its subscribers of the message's false nature, and to effectively screen future defamatory material. Section 230 entered this litigation as an affirmative defense pled by AOL. The company claimed that Congress immunized interactive computer service providers from claims based on information posted by a third party.

The relevant portion of § 230 states: "No provider or user of an interactive computer service shall be treated as the publisher or speaker of any information provided by another information content provider." 47 U.S.C. § 230(c)(1).[2] By its plain language, § 230 creates a federal immunity to any cause of action that would make service providers liable for information originating with a third-party user of the service. Specifically, § 230 precludes courts from entertaining claims that would place a computer service provider in a publisher's role. Thus, lawsuits seeking to hold a service provider liable for its exercise of a publisher's traditional editorial functions—such as deciding whether to publish, withdraw, postpone or alter content—are barred.

The purpose of this statutory immunity is not difficult to discern. Congress recognized the threat that tort-based lawsuits pose to freedom of speech in the new and burgeoning Internet medium. The imposition of tort liability on service providers for the communications of others represented, for Congress, simply another form of intrusive government regulation of speech. Section 230 was enacted, in part, to maintain the robust nature of Internet communication and, accordingly, to keep government interference in the medium to a minimum. In specific statutory findings, Congress recognized the Internet and interactive computer services as offering "a forum for a true diversity of political discourse, unique opportunities for cultural development, and myriad avenues for intellectual activity." *Id.* § 230(a)(3). It also found that the Internet and interactive computer services "have flourished, to the benefit of all Americans, *with a minimum of government regulation*." *Id.* § 230(a)(4) (emphasis added). Congress further stated that it is "the policy of the United States . . . to preserve the vibrant and competitive free market that presently

---

[2] . . . The parties do not dispute that AOL falls within the CDA's "interactive computer service" definition and that the unidentified third party who posted the offensive messages here fits the definition of an "information content provider."

exists for the Internet and other interactive computer services, *unfettered by Federal or State regulation." Id.* § 230(b)(2) (emphasis added).

None of this means, of course, that the original culpable party who posts defamatory messages would escape accountability. While Congress acted to keep government regulation of the Internet to a minimum, it also found it to be the policy of the United States "to ensure vigorous enforcement of Federal criminal laws to deter and punish trafficking in obscenity, stalking, and harassment by means of computer." *Id.* § 230(b)(5). Congress made a policy choice, however, not to deter harmful online speech through the separate route of imposing tort liability on companies that serve as intermediaries for other parties' potentially injurious messages.

Congress' purpose in providing the § 230 immunity was thus evident. Interactive computer services have millions of users. *See Reno v. ACLU*, 521 U.S. at 850–51 (noting that at time of district court trial, "commercial online services had almost 12 million individual subscribers"). The amount of information communicated via interactive computer services is therefore staggering. The specter of tort liability in an area of such prolific speech would have an obvious chilling effect. It would be impossible for service providers to screen each of their millions of postings for possible problems. Faced with potential liability for each message republished by their services, interactive computer service providers might choose to severely restrict the number and type of messages posted. Congress considered the weight of the speech interests implicated and chose to immunize service providers to avoid any such restrictive effect.

Another important purpose of § 230 was to encourage service providers to self-regulate the dissemination of offensive material over their services. In this respect, § 230 responded to a New York state court decision, *Stratton Oakmont, Inc. v. Prodigy Servs. Co.*, 1995 WL 323710 (N.Y.Sup.Ct. May 24, 1995). . . .

Congress enacted § 230 to remove the disincentives to self-regulation created by the *Stratton Oakmont* decision. Under that court's holding, computer service providers who regulated the dissemination of offensive material on their services risked subjecting themselves to liability, because such regulation cast the service provider in the role of a publisher. Fearing that the specter of liability would therefore deter service providers from blocking and screening offensive material, Congress enacted § 230's broad immunity "to remove disincentives for the development and utilization of blocking and filtering technologies that empower parents to restrict their children's access to objectionable or inappropriate online material." 47 U.S.C. § 230(b)(4). In line with this purpose, § 230 forbids the imposition of publisher liability on a service provider for the exercise of its editorial and self-regulatory functions.

B.

Zeran argues, however, that the § 230 immunity eliminates only publisher liability, leaving distributor liability intact. Publishers can be held liable for defamatory statements contained in their works even absent proof that they had specific knowledge of the statement's inclusion. . . . According to Zeran, interactive computer service providers like AOL are normally considered instead to be distributors, like traditional news vendors or book sellers. Distributors cannot be held liable for defamatory statements contained in the materials they distribute unless it is proven at a minimum that they have actual knowledge of the defamatory statements upon which liability is predicated. . . . Zeran contends that he provided AOL with sufficient notice of the defamatory statements appearing on the company's bulletin board. This notice is significant, says Zeran, because AOL could be held liable as a distributor only if it acquired knowledge of the defamatory statements' existence.

Because of the difference between these two forms of liability, Zeran contends that the term "distributor" carries a legally distinct meaning from the term "publisher." Accordingly, he asserts that Congress' use of only the term "publisher" in § 230 indicates a purpose to immunize service providers only from publisher liability. He argues that distributors are left unprotected by § 230 and, therefore, his suit should be permitted to proceed against AOL. We disagree. Assuming *arguendo* that Zeran has satisfied the requirements for imposition of distributor liability, this theory of liability is merely a subset, or a species, of publisher liability, and is therefore also foreclosed by § 230.

The terms "publisher" and "distributor" derive their legal significance from the context of defamation law. Although Zeran attempts to artfully plead his claims as ones of negligence, they are indistinguishable from a garden variety defamation action. Because the publication of a statement is a necessary element in a defamation action, only one who publishes can be subject to this form of tort liability. Restatement (Second) of Torts § 558(b) (1977) . . . . Publication does not only describe the choice by an author to include certain information. In addition, both the negligent communication of a defamatory statement and the failure to remove such a statement when first communicated by another party—each alleged by Zeran here under a negligence label—constitute publication. Restatement (Second) of Torts § 577 . . . . In fact, every repetition of a defamatory statement is considered a publication. . . .

In this case, AOL is legally considered to be a publisher. "[E]very one who takes part in the publication . . . is charged with publication." [W. Page Keeton et al., *Prosser and Keeton on the Law of Torts* § 113, at 799 (5th ed.1984)]. Even distributors are considered to be publishers for purposes of defamation law:

> Those who are in the business of making their facilities available to disseminate the writings composed, the speeches made, and the information gathered by others may also be regarded as participating to such an extent in making the books, newspapers, magazines, and information available to others as to be regarded as publishers. They are intentionally making the contents available to others, sometimes without knowing all of the contents—including the defamatory content—and sometimes without any opportunity to ascertain, in advance, that any defamatory matter was to be included in the matter published.

Id. at 803. AOL falls squarely within this traditional definition of a publisher and, therefore, is clearly protected by § 230's immunity.

Zeran contends that decisions like *Stratton Oakmont* and *Cubby, Inc. v. Compu-Serve Inc.*, 776 F.Supp. 135 (S.D.N.Y.1991), recognize a legal distinction between publishers and distributors. He misapprehends, however, the significance of that distinction for the legal issue we consider here. It is undoubtedly true that mere conduits, or distributors, are subject to a different standard of liability. As explained above, distributors must at a minimum have knowledge of the existence of a defamatory statement as a prerequisite to liability. But this distinction signifies only that different standards of liability may be applied *within* the larger publisher category, depending on the specific type of publisher concerned. *See* Keeton et al., *supra*, § 113, at 799–800 (explaining that every party involved is charged with publication, although degrees of legal responsibility differ). To the extent that decisions like *Stratton* and *Cubby* utilize the terms "publisher" and "distributor" separately, the decisions correctly describe two different standards of liability. *Stratton* and *Cubby* do not, however, suggest that distributors are not also a type of publisher for purposes of defamation law.

Zeran simply attaches too much importance to the presence of the distinct notice element in distributor liability. The simple fact of notice surely cannot transform one from an original publisher to a distributor in the eyes of the law. To the contrary, once a computer service provider receives notice of a potentially defamatory posting, it is thrust into the role of a traditional publisher. The computer service provider must decide whether to publish, edit, or withdraw the posting. In this respect, Zeran seeks to impose liability on AOL for assuming the role for which § 230 specifically proscribes liability—the publisher role.

Our view that Zeran's complaint treats AOL as a publisher is reinforced because AOL is cast in the same position as the party who originally posted the offensive messages. According to Zeran's logic, AOL is legally at fault because it communicated to third parties an allegedly defamatory statement. This is precisely the theory under which the original poster of the offensive messages would be found liable. If the original party is considered a publisher of the offensive messages, Zeran certainly cannot attach liability to AOL under the same theory without conceding that AOL too must be treated as a publisher of the statements.

Zeran next contends that interpreting § 230 to impose liability on service providers with knowledge of defamatory content on their services is consistent with the statutory purposes outlined in Part IIA. Zeran fails, however, to understand the practical implications of notice liability in the interactive computer service context. Liability upon notice would defeat the dual purposes advanced by § 230 of the CDA. Like the strict liability imposed by the *Stratton Oakmont* court, liability upon notice reinforces service providers' incentives to restrict speech and abstain from self-regulation.

If computer service providers were subject to distributor liability, they would face potential liability each time they receive notice of a potentially defamatory statement—from any party, concerning any message. Each notification would require a careful yet rapid investigation of the circumstances surrounding the posted information, a legal judgment concerning the information's defamatory character, and an on-the-spot editorial decision whether to risk liability by allowing the continued publication of that information. Although this might be feasible for the traditional print publisher, the sheer number of postings on interactive computer services would create an impossible burden in the Internet context. *Cf. Auvil v. CBS 60 Minutes*, 800 F.Supp. 928, 931 (E.D.Wash.1992) (recognizing that it is unrealistic for network affiliates to "monitor incoming transmissions and exercise on-the-spot discretionary calls"). Because service providers would be subject to liability only for the publication of information, and not for its removal, they would have a natural incentive simply to remove messages upon notification, whether the contents were defamatory or not. *See Philadelphia Newspapers, Inc. v. Hepps*, 475 U.S. 767, 777 (1986) (recognizing that fears of unjustified liability produce a chilling effect antithetical to First Amendment's protection of speech). Thus, like strict liability, liability upon notice has a chilling effect on the freedom of Internet speech.

Similarly, notice-based liability would deter service providers from regulating the dissemination of offensive material over their own services. Any efforts by a service provider to investigate and screen material posted on its service would only lead to notice of potentially defamatory material more frequently and thereby create a stronger basis for liability. Instead of subjecting themselves to further possible lawsuits, service providers would likely eschew any attempts at self-regulation.

More generally, notice-based liability for interactive computer service providers would provide third parties with a no-cost means to create the basis for future lawsuits. Whenever one was displeased with the speech of another party conducted over an interactive computer service, the offended party could simply "notify" the relevant service provider, claiming the information to be legally defamatory. In light of the vast amount of speech communicated through interactive computer services, these notices could produce an impossible burden for service providers, who would be faced with ceaseless choices of suppressing controversial speech or sustaining prohibitive liability. Because the probable effects of distributor liability on the vigor of Internet speech and on service provider self-regulation are directly contrary to § 230's statutory purposes, we will not assume that Congress intended to leave liability upon notice intact.

. . .

For the foregoing reasons, we affirm the judgment of the district court.

Blumenthal v. Drudge
992 F.Supp. 44 (D.D.C.1998).

■ PAUL L. FRIEDMAN, DISTRICT JUDGE.

This is a defamation case revolving around a statement published on the Internet by defendant Matt Drudge. On August 10, 1997, the following was available to all having access to the Internet:

> The DRUDGE REPORT has learned that top GOP operatives who feel there is a double-standard of only reporting republican shame believe they are holding an ace card: New White House recruit Sidney Blumen-

thal has a spousal abuse past that has been effectively covered up.

The accusations are explosive.

There are court records of Blumenthal's violence against his wife, one influential republican, who demanded anonymity, tells the DRUDGE REPORT.

If they begin to use [Don] Sipple and his problems against us, against the Republican Party . . . to show hypocrisy, Blumenthal would become fair game. Wasn't it Clinton who signed the Violence Against Women Act?

[There goes the budget deal honeymoon.]

One White House source, also requesting anonymity, says the Blumenthal wife-beating allegation is a pure fiction that has been created by Clinton enemies. [The First Lady] would not have brought him in if he had this in his background, assures the well-placed staffer. This story about Blumenthal has been in circulation for years.

Last month President Clinton named Sidney Blumenthal an Assistant to the President as part of the Communications Team. He's brought in to work on communications strategy, special projects themeing — a newly created position.

Every attempt to reach Blumenthal proved unsuccessful.

Complaint, Ex. 4.

Currently before this Court are a motion for summary judgment filed by defendant America Online, Inc. ("AOL") and a motion to dismiss or transfer for lack of personal jurisdiction filed by defendant Matt Drudge. Upon consideration of the papers filed by the parties and the oral arguments of counsel, the Court concludes that AOL's motion should be granted and Drudge's motion should be denied.

I. BACKGROUND

. . . Sidney Blumenthal works in the White House as an Assistant to the President of the United States. His first day of work as Assistant to the President was Monday, August 11, 1997, the day after the publication of the alleged defamatory statement. . . .

. . . In early 1995, defendant Drudge created an electronic publication called the Drudge Report, a gossip column focusing on gossip from Hollywood and Washington, D.C. . . .

Access to defendant Drudge's world wide web site is available at no cost to anyone who has access to the Internet at the Internet address of "www.drudgereport.com." The front page of the web site contains the logo "Drudge Report." Defendant Drudge has also placed a hyperlink on his web site that, when activated, causes the most recently published edition of the Drudge Report to be displayed. The web site also contains numerous hyperlinks to other on-line news publications and news articles that may be of interest to readers of the Drudge Report. In addition, during the time period relevant to this case, Drudge had developed a list of regular readers or subscribers to whom he e-mailed each new edition of the Drudge Report. By March 1995, the Drudge Report had 1,000 e-mail subscribers; and plaintiffs allege that by 1997 Drudge had 85,000 subscribers to his e-mail service.

. . .

In late May or early June of 1997, . . . defendant Drudge entered into a written license agreement with AOL. The agreement made the Drudge Report available to all members of AOL's service for a period of one year. In exchange, defendant Drudge received a flat monthly "royalty payment" of $3,000 from AOL. During the time relevant to this case, defendant Drudge has had no other source of income. Under the licensing agreement, Drudge is to create, edit, update and "otherwise manage" the content of the Drudge Report, and AOL may "remove content that AOL reasonably determine[s] to violate AOL's then standard terms of service." Drudge transmits new editions of the Drudge Report by e-mailing them to AOL. AOL then posts the new editions on the AOL service. Drudge also has continued to distribute each new edition of the Drudge Report via e-mail and his own web site.

Late at night on the evening of Sunday, August 10, 1997 (Pacific Daylight Time), defendant Drudge wrote and transmitted the edition of the Drudge Report that contained the alleged defamatory statement about the Blumenthals. Drudge transmitted the report from Los Angeles, California by e-mail to his direct subscribers and by posting both a headline and the full text of the Blumenthal story on his world wide web site. He then transmitted the text but not the headline to AOL, which in turn made it available to AOL subscribers.

After receiving a letter from plaintiffs' counsel on Monday, August 11, 1997, defendant Drudge retracted the story through a special edition of the Drudge Report posted on his web site and e-mailed to his subscribers. At approximately 2:00 a.m. on Tuesday, August 12, 1997, Drudge e-mailed the retraction to AOL which posted it on the AOL service.[5] Defendant Drudge later publicly apologized to the Blumenthals.

II. AOL's MOTION FOR SUMMARY JUDGMENT

. . .

B. *Communications Decency Act of 1996, Section 230*

In February of 1996, Congress [enacted] the Communications Decency Act of 1996. While various policy options were open to the Congress, it chose to "promote the continued development of the Internet and other interactive computer services and other interactive media" and "to preserve the vibrant and competitive free market" for such services, largely "unfettered by Federal or State regulation. . . ." 47 U.S.C. § 230(b)(1) and (2). Whether wisely or not, it made the legislative judgment to effectively immunize providers of interactive computer services from civil liability in tort with respect to material disseminated by them but created by others. In recognition of the speed with which information may be disseminated and

---

[5] AOL later removed the August 10 edition of the Drudge Report from the electronic archive of previous editions of the Drudge Report available to AOL subscribers.

the near impossibility of regulating information content, Congress decided not to treat providers of interactive computer services like other information providers such as newspapers, magazines or television and radio stations, all of which may be held liable for publishing or distributing obscene or defamatory material written or prepared by others. While Congress could have made a different policy choice, it opted not to hold interactive computer services liable for their failure to edit, withhold or restrict access to offensive material disseminated through their medium.

. . . In view of [Section 230], plaintiffs' argument that the Washington Post would be liable if it had done what AOL did here—"publish Drudge's story without doing anything whatsoever to edit, verify, or even read it (despite knowing what Drudge did for a living and how he did it)"—has been rendered irrelevant by Congress.

Plaintiffs concede that AOL is a "provider . . . of an interactive computer service" for purposes of Section 230, and that if AOL acted exclusively as a provider of an interactive computer service it may not be held liable for making the Drudge Report available to AOL subscribers. *See* 47 U.S.C. § 230(c)(1). They also concede that Drudge is an "information content provider" because he wrote the alleged defamatory material about the Blumenthals contained in the Drudge Report. While plaintiffs suggest that AOL is responsible along with Drudge because it had some role in writing or editing the material in the Drudge Report, they have provided no factual support for that assertion. Indeed, plaintiffs affirmatively state that "no person, other than Drudge himself, edited, checked, verified, or supervised the information that Drudge published in the Drudge Report." It also is apparent to the Court that there is no evidence to support the view originally taken by plaintiffs that Drudge is or was an employee or agent of AOL, and plaintiffs seem to have all but abandoned that argument.[9]

AOL acknowledges both that Section 230(c)(1) would not immunize AOL with respect to any information AOL developed or created entirely by itself and that there are situations in which there may be two or more information content providers responsible for material disseminated on the Internet—joint authors, a lyricist and a composer, for example. While Section 230 does not preclude joint liability for the joint development of content, AOL maintains that there simply is no evidence here that AOL had any role in creating or developing any of the information in the Drudge Report. The Court agrees. It is undisputed that the Blumenthal story was written by Drudge without any substantive or editorial involvement by AOL. AOL was nothing more than a provider of an interactive computer service on which the Drudge Report was carried, and Congress has said quite clearly that such a provider shall not be treated as a "publisher or speaker" and therefore may not be held liable in tort. 47 U.S.C. § 230(c)(1).

As Chief Judge Wilkinson recently wrote for the Fourth Circuit:

---

[9] Plaintiffs' Statement of Genuine Issues of Material Facts does not identify any evidence to support their conclusory assertion that there are genuine issues of fact as to whether Drudge was an employee or agent of AOL. . . .

By its plain language, § 230 creates a federal immunity to any cause of action that would make service providers liable for information originating with a third-party user of the service. . . .

. . .

Zeran v. America Online, Inc., 129 F.3d 327, 330–31 (4th Cir.1997). The court in *Zeran* has provided a complete answer to plaintiffs' primary argument, an answer grounded in the statutory language and intent of Section 230.

Plaintiffs make the additional argument, however, that Section 230 of the Communications Decency Act does not provide immunity to AOL in this case because Drudge was not just an anonymous person who sent a message over the Internet through AOL. He is a person with whom AOL contracted, whom AOL paid $3,000 a month—$36,000 a year, Drudge's sole, consistent source of income—and whom AOL promoted to its subscribers and potential subscribers as a reason to subscribe to AOL. Furthermore, the license agreement between AOL and Drudge by its terms contemplates more than a passive role for AOL; in it, AOL reserves the "right to remove, or direct [Drudge] to remove, any content which, as reasonably determined by AOL . . . violates AOL's then-standard Terms of Service. . . ." By the terms of the agreement, AOL also is "entitled to require reasonable changes to . . . content, to the extent such content will, in AOL's good faith judgment, adversely affect operations of the AOL network."

In addition, shortly after it entered into the licensing agreement with Drudge, AOL issued a press release making clear the kind of material Drudge would provide to AOL subscribers—gossip and rumor—and urged potential subscribers to sign onto AOL in order to get the benefit of the Drudge Report. The press release was captioned: "AOL Hires Runaway Gossip Success Matt Drudge." It noted that "[m]averick gossip columnist Matt Drudge has teamed up with America Online," and stated: "Giving the Drudge Report a home on America Online (keyword: Drudge) opens up the floodgates to an audience ripe for Drudge's brand of reporting. . . . AOL has made Matt Drudge instantly accessible to members who crave instant gossip and news breaks." Why is this different, the Blumenthals suggest, from AOL advertising and promoting a new purveyor of child pornography or other offensive material? Why should AOL be permitted to tout someone as a gossip columnist or rumor monger who will make such rumors and gossip "instantly accessible" to AOL subscribers, and then claim immunity when that person, as might be anticipated, defames another?

If it were writing on a clean slate, this Court would agree with plaintiffs. AOL has certain editorial rights with respect to the content provided by Drudge and disseminated by AOL, including the right to require changes in content and to remove it; and it has affirmatively promoted Drudge as a new source of unverified instant gossip on AOL. Yet it takes no responsibility for any damage he may cause. AOL is not a passive conduit like the telephone company, a common carrier with no control and therefore no responsibility for what is said over the telephone wires. Because it has the right to exercise editorial control over those with whom it contracts and whose words it disseminates, it would seem only fair to hold AOL to the liability standards applied to a publisher or, at least, like a book store owner or library, to the liability standards applied to a distributor. But Congress has made a different policy choice by providing immunity even where the interactive service provider has an active, even aggressive role in making available content prepared by others. In some sort of tacit quid pro quo arrangement with the service provider community, Congress has conferred immunity from tort liability as an incentive to Internet service providers to self-police the Internet for obscenity and other offensive material, even where the self-policing is unsuccessful or not even attempted.

. . .

Any attempt to distinguish between "publisher" liability and notice-based "distributor" liability and to argue that Section 230 was only intended to immunize the former would be unavailing. Congress made no distinction between publishers and distributors in providing immunity from liability. . . . While it appears to this Court that AOL in this case has taken advantage of all the benefits conferred by Congress in the Communications Decency Act, and then some, without accepting any of the burdens that Congress intended, the statutory language is clear: AOL is immune from suit, and the Court therefore must grant its motion for summary judgment.

. . .

Batzel v. Smith
333 F.3d 1018 (9th Cir.2003).

■ BERZON, CIRCUIT JUDGE.

There is no reason inherent in the technological features of cyberspace why First Amendment and defamation law should apply differently in cyberspace than in the brick and mortar world. Congress, however, has chosen for policy reasons to immunize from liability for defamatory or obscene speech "providers and users of interactive computer services" when the defamatory or obscene material is "provided" by someone else. This case presents the question whether and, if so, under what circumstances a moderator of a listserv and operator of a website who posts an allegedly defamatory e-mail authored by a third party can be held liable for doing so. . . .

I.

In the summer of 1999, sometime-handyman Robert Smith was working for Ellen Batzel, an attorney licensed to practice in California and North Carolina, at Batzel's house in the North Carolina mountains. Smith recounted that while he was repairing Batzel's truck, Batzel told him that she was "the granddaughter of one of Adolf Hitler's right-hand men." Smith also maintained that as he was painting the walls of Batzel's sitting room he overheard Batzel tell her roommate that she was related to Nazi politician Heinrich Himmler. According to Smith, Batzel told him on another occasion that some of the paintings hanging in her house were inherited. To Smith, these paintings looked old and European.

After assembling these clues, Smith used a computer to look for websites concerning stolen art work and was directed by a search engine to the Museum Security Network ("the Network") website. He thereupon sent the following e-mail message to the Network:

From: Bob Smith [e-mail address omitted]

To: securma@museum-security.org [the Network]

Subject: Stolen Art

Hi there,

    I am a building contractor in Asheville, North Carolina, USA. A month ago, I did a remodeling job for a woman, Ellen L. Batzel who bragged to me about being the grand daughter [sic] of "one of Adolph Hitler's right-hand men." At the time, I was concentrating on performing my tasks, but upon reflection, I believe she said she was the descendant of Heinrich Himmler.

    Ellen Batzel has hundreds of older European paintings on her walls, all with heavy carved wooden frames. She told me she inherited them.

    I believe these paintings were looted during WWII and are the rightful legacy of the Jewish people. Her address is [omitted].

    I also believe that the descendants of criminals should not be persecuted for the crimes of the [sic] fathers, nor should they benefit. I do not know who to contact about this, so I start with your organization. Please contact me via email [. . .] if you would like to discuss this matter.

    Bob.

Ton Cremers, then-Director of Security at Amsterdam's famous Rijksmuseum and (in his spare time) sole operator of the Museum Security Network ("the Network"), received Smith's e-mail message. The nonprofit Network maintains both a website and an electronic e-mailed newsletter about museum security and stolen art. Cremers periodically puts together an electronic document containing: e-mails sent to him, primarily from Network subscribers; comments by himself as the moderator of an on-line discussion; and excerpts from news articles related to stolen works of art. He exercises some editorial discretion in choosing which of the e-mails he receives are included in the listserv mailing, omitting e-mails unrelated to stolen art and eliminating other material that he decides does not merit distribution to his subscribers. The remaining amalgamation of material is then posted on the Network's website and sent to subscribers automatically via a listserv. The Network's website and listserv mailings are read by hundreds of museum security officials, insurance investigators, and law enforcement personnel around the world, who use the information in the Network posting to track down stolen art.

After receiving it, Cremers published Smith's e-mail message to the Network, with some minor wording changes, on the Network listserv. He also posted that listserv, with Smith's message included, on the Network's website. Cremers later included it on the Network listserv and posted a "moderator's message" stating that "the FBI has been informed of the contents of [Smith's] original message."

After the posting, Bob Smith e-mailed a subscriber to the listserv, Jonathan Sazonoff, explaining that he had had no idea that his e-mail would be posted to the listserv or put on the web. Smith told Sazanoff:

> I [was] trying to figure out how in blazes I could have posted me [sic] email to [the Network] bulletin board. I came into MSN through the back door, directed by a search engine, and never got the big picture. I don't remember reading anything about a message board either so I am a bit confused over how it could happen. Every message board to which I have ever subscribed required application, a password, and/or registration, and the instructions explained this is necessary to keep out the advertisers, cranks, and bumbling idiots like me.

Batzel discovered the message several months after its initial posting and complained to Cremers about the message. Cremers then contacted Smith via e-mail to request additional information about Smith's allegations. Smith continued to insist on the truth of his statements. He also told Cremers that if he had thought his e-mail "message would be posted on an international message board [he] never would have sent it in the first place."

Upon discovering that Smith had not intended to post his message, Cremers apologized for the confusion. He told Smith in an e-mail that "[y]ou were not a subscriber to the list and I believe that you did not realize your message would be forwarded to the mailinglist [sic]." Apparently, subscribers send messages for inclusion in the listserv to securma@x54all.nl, a different address from that to which Smith had sent his e-mail contacting the Network. Cremers further explained that he "receive[s] many e-mails each day some of which contain queries [he thinks] interesting enough to forward to the list. [Smith's] was one of those."

Batzel disputes Smith's account of their conversations. She says she is not, and never said she is, a descendant of a Nazi official, and that she did not inherit any art. Smith, she charges, defamed her not because he believed her artwork stolen but out of pique, because Batzel refused to show Hollywood contacts a screenplay he had written.

Batzel claims further that because of Cremers's actions she lost several prominent clients in California and was investigated by the North Carolina Bar Association. Also, she represents that her social reputation suffered. To redress her claimed reputational injuries she filed this lawsuit against Smith, Cremers, the Netherlands Museum Association, and Mosler, Inc. ("Mosler") in federal court in Los Angeles, California.

. . .

III

. . .

C. Probability of Success

. . .

Section 230(c)(1) specifies that "[n]o provider or user of an interactive computer service shall be treated as the publisher or speaker of any information provided by another information content provider." The provision thereby set limitations on liability under state law for postings on the Internet and other computer networks.

The district court declined to extend the legislative grant of immunity pursuant to § 230(c) to Cremers and the Network, holding that the Network is not "an internet service provider" and therefore is not covered by the statute. We do not agree with the district court's reading of § 230.

1. *Section 230(c)*

We begin with a brief survey of the background of § 230(c), as that background is useful in construing the statutory terms here at issue.

. . .

. . . Absent § 230, a person who published or distributed speech over the Internet could be held liable for defamation even if he or she was not the author of the defamatory text, and, indeed, at least with regard to publishers, even if unaware of the statement. *See, e.g., Stratton Oakmont, Inc. v. Prodigy Services Co.,* 1995 WL 323710 (N.Y. Sup. May 24, 1995) (pre-Communications Decency Act case holding internet service provider liable for posting by third party on one of its electronic bulletin boards). Congress, however, has chosen to treat cyberspace differently.[10]

Congress made this legislative choice for two primary reasons. First, Congress wanted to encourage the unfettered and unregulated development of free speech on the Internet, and to promote the development of e-commerce. . . .

The second reason for enacting § 230(c) was to encourage interactive computer services and users of such services to self-police the Internet for obscenity and other offensive material, so as to aid parents in limiting their children's access to such material. . . . We recognize that there is an apparent tension between Congress's goals of promoting free speech while at the same time giving parents the tools to limit the material their children can access over the Internet. As a result of this apparent tension, some commentators have suggested that the Fourth Circuit in *Zeran* imposed the First Amendment goals on legislation that was actually adopted for the speech-restrictive purpose of controlling the dissemination of content over the Internet. . . . These critics fail to recognize that laws often have more than one goal in mind, and that it is not uncommon for these purposes to look in opposite directions. The need to balance competing values is a primary impetus for enacting legislation. Tension within statutes is often not a defect but an indication that the legislature was doing its job. *See, e.g., United States v. Kalustian,* 529 F.2d 585, 588 (9th Cir.1975) (describing dual and somewhat competing purposes of the Federal wiretap statute of both protecting individual privacy and combating

---

[10] We note that some commentators have suggested that Congress intended for § 230(c) to override only publisher, not distributor, liability. . . . Batzel's complaint refers to Cremers as the "publisher" of Smith's e-mail, and she has not argued that Cremers should be treated as a distributor, perhaps because the standard for distributor liability is generally less favorable for plaintiffs. *See Zeran v. America Online, Inc.,* 129 F.3d 327, 331 (4th Cir.1997). We therefore need not decide whether § 230(c)(1) encompasses both publishers and distributors. We do note that, so far, every court to reach the issue has decided that Congress intended to immunize both distributors and publishers. *See Zeran,* 129 F.3d at 331–34; *Ben Ezra, Weinstein, and Co. v. America Online, Inc.,* 206 F.3d 980, 986 (10th Cir.2000); *Doe v. America Online, Inc.,* 783 So.2d 1010, 1013–17 (Fla.2001).

crime).

So, even though the CDA overall may have had the purpose of restricting content, there is little doubt that the Cox-Wyden amendment, which added what ultimately became § 230 to the Act, sought to further First Amendment and e-commerce interests on the Internet while also promoting the protection of minors.... Fostering the two ostensibly competing purposes here works because parents best can control the material accessed by their children with the cooperation and assistance of Internet service providers ("ISPs") and other providers and users of services on the Internet.... Some blocking and filtering programs depend on the cooperation of website operators and access providers who label material that appears on their services.

. . .

2. Application to Cremers and the Museum Security Network

To benefit from § 230(c) immunity, Cremers must first demonstrate that his Network website and listserv qualify as "provider[s] or user[s] of an *interactive computer service.*" § 230(c)(1) (emphasis added). An "interactive computer service" is defined as "any information service, system, or access software provider that provides or enables computer access by multiple users to a computer server, including specifically a service or system that provides access to the Internet and such systems operated or services offered by libraries or educational institutions." § 230(f)(2).

The district court concluded that only services that provide access to the Internet as a whole are covered by this definition. But the definition of "interactive computer service" on its face covers "*any*" information services or other systems, as long as the service or system allows "multiple users" to access "a computer server." Further, the statute repeatedly refers to "the Internet and *other* interactive computer services," (emphasis added), making clear that the statutory immunity extends beyond the Internet itself. §§ 230(a)(3), (a)(4), (b)(1), (b)(2), and (f)(3). Also, the definition of "interactive computer service" after the broad definition language, states that the definition "*includ[es]* specifically a service or system that provides access to the Internet," § 230(f)(2) (emphasis added), thereby confirming that services providing access to the Internet as a whole are only a subset of the services to which the statutory immunity applies.[15]

There is, however, no need here to decide whether a listserv or website itself fits the broad statutory definition of "interactive computer service," because the language of § 230(c)(1) confers immunity not just on "providers" of such services, but

---

[15] Other courts construing § 230(f)(2) have recognized that the definition includes a wide range of cyberspace services, not only internet service providers. *See, e.g., Gentry v. eBay, Inc.,* 99 Cal.App.4th 816, 831 & n.7 (2002) (on-line auction website is an "interactive computer service"); *Schneider v. Amazon.com,* 31 P.3d 37, 40–41 (Wash.Ct.App.2001) (on-line bookstore Amazon.com is an "interactive computer service"); *Barrett v. Clark,* 2001 WL 881259 at *9 (Cal.Sup.Ct.2001) (newsgroup considered an "interactive computer service") . . . .

also on "users" of such services.[16] § 230(c)(1).

There is no dispute that the Network uses interactive computer services to distribute its on-line mailing and to post the listserv on its website. Indeed, to make its website available and to mail out the listserv, the Network *must* access the Internet through some form of "interactive computer service." Thus, both the Network website and the listserv are potentially immune under § 230.

Critically, however, § 230 limits immunity to information "provided by another information content provider." § 230(c)(1). An "information content provider" is defined by the statute to mean "any person or entity that is responsible, in whole or in part, for the creation or development of information provided through the Internet or any other interactive computer service." § 230(f)(3). The reference to "*another* information content provider" (emphasis added) distinguishes the circumstance in which the interactive computer service itself meets the definition of "information content provider" with respect to the information in question. The pertinent question therefore becomes whether Smith was the sole content provider of his e-mail, or whether Cremers can also be considered to have "creat[ed]" or "develop[ed]" Smith's e-mail message forwarded to the listserv.

Obviously, Cremers did not create Smith's e-mail. Smith composed the e-mail entirely on his own. Nor do Cremers's minor alterations of Smith's e-mail prior to its posting or his choice to publish the e-mail (while rejecting other e-mails for inclusion in the listserv) rise to the level of "development." As we have seen, a central purpose of the Act was to protect from liability service providers and users who take some affirmative steps to edit the material posted. Also, the exclusion of "publisher" liability necessarily precludes liability for exercising the usual prerogative of publishers to choose among proffered material and to edit the material published while retaining its basic form and message.

The "development of information" therefore means something more substantial than merely editing portions of an e-mail and selecting material for publication. Because Cremers did no more than select and make minor alterations to Smith's e-mail, Cremers cannot be considered the content provider of Smith's e-mail for purposes of § 230.[19]

---

[16] We note that several courts to reach the issue have decided that a website is an "interactive computer service." *See, e.g., Carafano v. Metrosplash.com, Inc.,* 207 F.Supp.2d 1055, 1065–66 (C.D.Cal.2002); *Gentry,* 99 Cal.App.4th at 831 (holding that website is an interactive computer service); *Schneider,* 31 P.3d at 40–41 (same).

[19] As other courts have pointed out, the broad immunity created by § 230 can sometimes lead to troubling results. *See, e.g., Blumenthal,* 992 F.Supp. at 51–52 (expressing opinion that "[i]f it were writing on a clean slate," AOL would be liable for defamation when it had editorial control over the defamatory material). For example, a service provider that cannot be held liable for posting a defamatory message may have little incentive to take such material down even if informed that the material is defamatory.

One possible solution to this statutorily created problem is the approach taken by Congress in the Digital Millennium Copyright Act ("Digital Act"). The Digital Act includes immunity provisions, similar to those of the Communications Decency Act, that protect service

The partial dissent does not register any disagreement with this interpretation of the definition of "information content provider" or with the observation that immunity for "publisher[s]" indicates a recognition that the immunity will extend to the selection of material supplied by others. It nonetheless simultaneously maintains that 1) a defendant who takes an active role in selecting information for publication is not immune; and 2) interactive computer service users and providers who screen the material submitted and remove offensive content are immune. *See* post . . . . These two positions simply cannot logically coexist.

Such a distinction between deciding to publish only some of the material submitted and deciding *not* to publish some of the material submitted is not a viable one. The scope of the immunity cannot turn on whether the publisher approaches the selection process as one of inclusion or removal, as the difference is one of method or degree, not substance.

A distinction between removing an item once it has appeared on the Internet and screening before publication cannot fly either. For one thing, there is no basis for believing that Congress intended a one-bite-at-the-apple form of immunity. Also, Congress could not have meant to favor removal of offending material over more advanced software that screens out the material before it ever appears. If anything, the goal of encouraging assistance to parents seeking to control children's access to offensive material would suggest a preference for a system in which the offensive material is not available even temporarily. The upshot is that the partial dissent's posit concerning the limitations of § 230(c) immunity simply cannot be squared with the statute's language and purposes, whatever merit it, or a variant of it, might have as a policy matter. *See* n. 19, *supra*.

In most cases our conclusion that Cremers cannot be considered a content provider would end matters, but this case presents one twist on the usual § 230 analysis: Smith maintains that he never "imagined [his] message would be posted on an international message board or [he] never would have sent it in the first place." The question thus becomes whether Smith can be said to have "provided" his e-mail in the sense intended by § 230(c). If the defamatory information is not *provided* by another information content provider," then § 230(c) does not confer immunity on the publisher of the information.

"[P]rovided" suggests, at least, some active role by the "provider" in supplying the material to a "provider or user of an interactive computer service." One would not say, for example, that the author of a magazine article "provided" it to an interactive computer service provider or user by allowing the article to be published in hard copy off-line. Although such an article is available to anyone with access to a library or a newsstand, it is not "provided" for use on the Internet.

---

providers from liability for content provided by third parties. The Digital Act, however, unlike the Communications Decency Act, provides specific notice, take-down, and put-back procedures that carefully balance the First Amendment rights of users with the rights of a potentially injured copyright holder. *See* 17 U.S.C. §§ 512(c) and (g) . . . To date, Congress has not amended § 230 to provide for similar take-down and put-back procedures. [The Section 512 immunity provision is discussed in Chapter 7, Part V(B)(2), *supra*. — Eds.]

The result in the foregoing example should not change if the interactive computer service provider or user has a subscription to the magazine. In that instance, the material in question is "provided" to the "provider or user of an interactive computer service," but not in its role as a provider or user of a computer service. The structure and purpose of § 230(c)(1) indicate that the immunity applies only with regard to third-party information provided *for use on the Internet* or another interactive computer service. As we have seen, the section is concerned with providing special immunity for individuals who would otherwise be publishers or speakers, because of Congress's concern with assuring a free market in ideas and information on the Internet. If information is provided to those individuals in a capacity unrelated to their function as a provider or user of interactive computer services, then there is no reason to protect them with the special statutory immunity.

So, if, for example, an individual who happens to operate a website receives a defamatory "snail mail" letter from an old friend, the website operator cannot be said to have been "provided" the information in his capacity as a website service. Section 230(c)(1) supplies immunity for only individuals or entities acting as "provider[s]" or "user[s]" of an "interactive computer service," and therefore does not apply when it is not "provided" to such persons in their roles as providers or users.

The situation here is somewhat more complicated than our letter example, because Smith did provide his e-mail over the Internet and transmitted it to the Network, an operator of a website that is an user of an interactive computer service. Nevertheless, Smith contends that he did not intend his e-mail to be placed on an interactive computer service for public viewing.

Smith's confusion, even if legitimate, does not matter, Cremers maintains, because the § 230(c)(1) immunity should be available simply because Smith was the author of the e-mail, without more.

We disagree. Under Cremers's broad interpretation of § 230(c), users and providers of interactive computer services could with impunity intentionally post material they knew was never meant to be put on the Internet. At the same time, the creator or developer of the information presumably could not be held liable for unforeseeable publication of his material to huge numbers of people with whom he had no intention to communicate. The result would be nearly limitless immunity for speech never meant to be broadcast over the Internet.

Supplying a "provider or user of an interactive computer service" with immunity in such circumstances is not consistent with Congress's expressly stated purposes in adopting § 230. Free speech and the development of the Internet are not "promote[d]" by affording immunity when providers and users of "interactive computer service[s]" knew or had reason to know that the information provided was not intended for publication on the Internet. Quite the contrary: Users of the Internet are likely to be discouraged from sending e-mails for fear that their e-mails may be published on the web without their permission.

. . .

Immunizing individuals and entities in such situations also interferes with Congress's objective of providing incentives for providers and users of interactive computer services to remove offensive material, especially obscene and defamatory speech. Far from encouraging such actions, immunizing a publisher or distributor for including content not intended for Internet publication increases the likelihood that obscene and defamatory material will be widely available. Not only will on-line publishers be able to distribute such material obtained from "hard copy" sources with impunity, but, because the content provider him or herself never intended publication, there is a greater likelihood that the distributed material will in fact be defamatory or obscene. A person is much more likely to exercise care in choosing his words when he knows that those words will be widely read. This is true not only for altruistic reasons but also because liability for defamation attaches only upon publication. In the current case, Smith claimed exactly that: He told Cremers that if he had known his e-mail would be posted, he never would have sent it. The congressional objectives in passing § 230 therefore are not furthered by providing immunity in instances where posted material was clearly not meant for publication.

At the same time, Congress's purpose in enacting § 230(c)(1) suggests that we must take great care in determining whether another's information was "provided" to a "provider or user of an interactive computer service" for publication. Otherwise, posting of information on the Internet and other interactive computer services would be chilled, as the service provider or user could not tell whether posting was contemplated. To preclude this possibility, the focus should be not on the information provider's intentions or knowledge when transmitting content but, instead, on the service provider's or user's reasonable perception of those intentions or knowledge. We therefore hold that a service provider or user is immune from liability under § 230(c)(1) when a third person or entity that created or developed the information in question furnished it to the provider or user under circumstances in which a reasonable person in the position of the service provider or user would conclude that the information was provided for publication on the Internet or other "interactive computer service."

It is not entirely clear from the record whether Smith "provided" the e-mail for publication on the Internet under this standard. There are facts that could have led Cremers reasonably to conclude that Smith sent him the information because he operated an Internet service. On the other hand, Smith was not a subscriber to the listserv and apparently sent the information to a different e-mail account from the one at which Cremers usually received information for publication. More development of the record may be necessary to determine whether, under all the circumstances, a reasonable person in Cremers' position would conclude that the information was sent for internet publication, or whether a triable issue of fact is presented on that issue.

We therefore vacate the district court's order . . . and remand to the district court for further proceedings to develop the facts under this newly announced standard and to evaluate what Cremers should have reasonably concluded at the time he received Smith's e-mail. If Cremers should have reasonably concluded, for example, that because Smith's e-mail arrived via a different e-mail address it was not provided to him for possible posting on the listserv, then Cremers cannot take advantage of the § 230(c) immunities. Under that circumstance, the posted information was not "provided" by another "information content provider" within the meaning of § 230. . . .

. . .

■ GOULD, J., concurring in part, dissenting in part.

I respectfully dissent from the majority's analysis of the statutory immunity from libel suits created by § 230 of the Communications Decency Act (CDA). The majority gives the phrase "information provided by another" an incorrect and unworkable meaning that extends CDA immunity far beyond what Congress intended. Under the majority's interpretation of § 230, many persons who intentionally spread vicious falsehoods on the Internet will be immune from suit. This sweeping preemption of valid state libel laws is not necessary to promote Internet use and is not what Congress had in mind.[3]

. . .

The majority holds that information is "provided by another" when "a third person or entity that created or developed the information in question furnished it to the provider or user under circumstances in which a reasonable person in the position of the service provider or user would conclude that the information was provided for publication on the Internet or other 'interactive computer service.' " In other words, whether information is "provided" depends on the *defendant's perception* of the *author's intention*. Nothing in the statutory language suggests that "provided" should be interpreted in this convoluted and unworkable fashion.

Under the majority's rule, a court determining whether to extend CDA immunity to a defendant must determine whether the author of allegedly defamatory information—a person who often will be beyond reach of the court's process or, worse, unknown—intended that the information be distributed on the Internet. In many cases, the author's intention may not be discernable from the face of the defamatory communication. Even people who want an e-mail message widely disseminated may not preface the message with words such as "Please pass it on." Moreover, the fact-intensive question of the author's intent is particularly unsuited for a judge's determination before trial, when the immunity question will most

---

[3] This case may be the first to pose the question of whether CDA immunity extends to a user or provider of an Internet newsletter or "listserv." CDA immunity should not depend, however, on rigid characterizations of particular services. As the amicus explains, there are many different kinds of listservs, each relying on different technology. There also are many kinds of Internet "bulletin boards," "chat rooms," "moderated listservs," "unmoderated listservs," and "e-mail newsletters." Because the contours of these categories are not clear, an approach that determined CDA immunity based on a technology's classification into one of these categories might cause considerable mischief. Rather than categorical rules, what is needed is an inquiry tailored to each case. CDA immunity should depend not on how a defendant's technology is classified, but on the defendant's conduct. [Relocated footnote—Eds.]

often arise.

The majority's rule will be incomprehensible to most citizens, who will be unable to plan their own conduct mindful of the law's requirements. . . . Those who receive a potentially libelous e-mail message from another person would seldom wonder, when deciding whether to forward the message to others, "Did *the author* of this defamatory information intend that it be distributed on the Internet?" However, those who receive a potentially libelous e-mail almost certainly would wonder, "Is it appropriate *for me* to spread this defamatory message?" By shifting its inquiry away from the defendant's conduct, the majority has crafted a rule that encourages the casual spread of harmful lies. The majority has improvidently crafted a rule that is foreign to the statutory text and foreign to human experience.

. . .

The problems caused by the majority's rule all would vanish if we focused our inquiry not on the *author's intent,* but on the *defendant's acts,* as I believe Congress intended. We should hold that the CDA immunizes a defendant only when the defendant took no active role in selecting the questionable information for publication. If the defendant took an active role in selecting information for publication, the information is no longer "information provided by another" within the meaning of § 230. We should draw this conclusion from the statute's text and purposes.

A person's decision to select particular information for distribution on the Internet changes that information in a subtle but important way: it adds the person's imprimatur to it. The recipient of information that has been selected by another person for distribution understands that the information has been deemed worthy of dissemination by the sender. Information that bears such an implicit endorsement is no longer merely the "information provided by" the original sender. 47 U.S.C. § 230(c)(1). It is information transformed. It is information bolstered, strengthened to do more harm if it is wrongful. A defendant who has actively selected libelous information for distribution thus should not be entitled to CDA immunity for disseminating "information provided by another."

My interpretation of § 230 is consistent with the CDA's legislative history. Congress understood that entities that facilitate communication on the Internet—particularly entities that operate e-mail networks, "chat rooms," "bulletin boards," and "listservs"—have special needs. The amount of information communicated through such services is staggering. Millions of communications are sent daily. It would be impossible to screen all such communications for libelous or offensive content. Faced with potential liability for each message republished by their services, interactive computer service users and providers might choose to restrict severely the number and type of messages posted. The threat of tort liability in an area of such prolific speech would have an obvious chilling effect on free speech and would hamper the new medium.

These policy concerns have force when a potential defendant uses or provides technology that enables others to disseminate information directly without intervening human action. These policy concerns lack force when a potential defendant does not offer users this power of direct transmission. If a potential defendant employs a person to screen communications to select some of them for dissemination, it is not impossible (or even difficult) for that person to screen communications for defamatory content. Immunizing that person or the person's employer from liability would not advance Congress's goal of protecting those in need of protection.

. . .

Under my interpretation of § 230, a company that operates an e-mail network would be immune from libel suits arising out of e-mail messages transmitted automatically across its network. Similarly, the owner, operator, organizer, or moderator of an Internet bulletin board, chat room, or listserv would be immune from libel suits arising out of messages distributed using that technology, provided that the person does not actively select particular messages for publication.

On the other hand, a person who receives a libelous communication and makes the decision to disseminate that messages to others — whether via e-mail, a bulletin board, a chat room, or a listserv — would not be immune.

My approach also would further Congress's goal of encouraging "self-policing" on the Internet. Congress decided to immunize from liability those who publish material on the Internet, so long as they do not actively select defamatory or offensive material for distribution. As a result, those who *remove* all or part of an offensive information posted on (for example) an Internet bulletin board are immune from suit. Those who employ blocking or filtering technologies that allow readers to avoid obscene or offensive materials also are immune from suit.

On the other hand, Congress decided not to immunize those who actively select defamatory or offensive information for distribution on the Internet. Congress thereby ensured that users and providers of interactive computer services would have an incentive not to spread harmful gossip and lies intentionally.

. . .

In this case, I would hold that Cremers is *not* entitled to CDA immunity because Cremers actively selected Smith's e-mail message for publication. Whether Cremers's Museum Security Network is characterized as a "moderated listserv," an "e-mail newsletter," or otherwise, it is certain that the Network did not permit users to disseminate information to other users directly without intervening human action. According to Cremers, "To post a response or to provide new information, the subscriber merely replies to the listserv mailing and *the message is sent directly to Cremers, who includes it* in the listserv with the subsequent distribution." (emphasis added).

This procedure was followed with respect to Smith's e-mail message accusing Batzel of owning art stolen by a Nazi ancestor. . . . Cremers's decision to select Smith's e-mail message for publication effectively altered the messages's meaning, adding to the message the unstated suggestion that Cremers deemed the message worthy of readers' attention. Cremers therefore did not merely distribute "information provided by another," and he is not entitled to CDA immunity.

. . .

I respectfully dissent.

2. The scope of Section 230

a. Non-defamation Causes of Action

Given Congress's explicit statement in the legislative history that it intended to override *Stratton Oakmont v. Prodigy*, it is clear that at least one significant congressional purpose in enacting Section 230 was to immunize ISPs against *defamation* liability based on third-party postings. But Section 230 itself does not refer to defamation: it speaks more broadly, forbidding treatment of an ISP "as the publisher or speaker of any information" provided by another. Consider too the Conference Report's explanation of the section's purpose:

> One of the specific purposes of this section is to overrule *Stratton Oakmont v. Prodigy* and any other similar decisions which have treated such providers and users as publishers or speakers of content that is not their own because they have restricted access to objectionable material. The conferees believe that such decisions create serious obstacles to the important federal policy of empowering parents to determine the content of communications their children receive through interactive computer services.

H.R. CONF. REP. NO. 104–458, at 194 (1996). Given the language of Section 230, and the Conference Report's explanation, can it plausibly be argued that Section 230 applies *only* to defamation claims?

The courts have not found Section 230 so limited. *Zeran v. America Online* held that Section 230 immunized the defendant against a negligence claim, and explained: "By its plain language, § 230 creates a federal immunity to any cause of action that would make service providers liable for information originating with a third-party user of the service." In *Doe v. America Online, Inc.*, 783 So.2d 1010 (Fla.2001), the court held that Section 230 immunized AOL from negligence liability based on a subscriber's use of its facilities to distribute child pornography. In *Ben Ezra, Weinstein, and Co. v. America Online Inc.*, 206 F.3d 980 (10th Cir.2000), the court held that Section 230 insulated AOL from liability based on erroneous stock information that it provided. Plaintiff had alleged causes of action sounding in negligence as well as defamation. In *Gentry v. eBay, Inc.*, 121 Cal.Rptr.2d 703 (Cal.App.2002), the court held that eBay was immune from claims that it violated a state statute requiring it to furnish certificates of authenticity for sports memorabilia auctioned through its facilities. *See also Stoner v. eBay Inc.*, 56 U.S.P.Q.2d 1852 (2000) (Section 230 protects eBay from claims based on its allowing bootleg musical recordings to be auctioned, despite the plaintiff's argument that it "does not seek to hold eBay responsible for the publication of information provided by others, but for eBay's own participation in selling contraband musical recordings").

In *Green v. America Online*, 318 F.3d 465 (3d Cir.2003), the court held AOL immune from liability for damages caused by a "punter" (a computer program designed to disrupt the functioning of another computer) sent from one user to another via an AOL chat room. The court interpreted the word "information" in Section 230 to include computer code, regardless of whether the code has communicative content. Other courts have held that Section 230 extends to a breach-of-contract claim, *see Schneider v. Amazon.com, Inc.*, 31 P.3d 37 (Wash.Ct.App.2001), and to a taxpayer claim for waste of public funds, *see Kathleen R. v. City of Livermore*, 104 Cal.Rptr.2d 772 (Cal.Ct.App.2001).

Should a court find Section 230 immunity available where liability is predicated on (1) bad advice that a subscriber posts on a BBS, on which a third party relies to its detriment? (2) obscene material posted by a third party, which gives rise to civil liability? (3) false advertising, as for example in the description of an item offered for sale via an online auction? (4) negligent release of users' private financial information, such as credit card numbers? (5) publication of information constituting a trade secret? (6) negligent release of information that allows attackers to shut down a major portal site?

b. Statutory Exclusions

The scope of Section 230 is limited by several explicit statutory exclusions. Thus, the immunity does not prevent liability under "any . . . Federal criminal statute," "any law pertaining to intellectual property," or the Electronic Communications Privacy Act, 18 U.S.C. §§ 2510 et seq. 47 U.S.C. § 230(e). ISP liability for copyright infringement is treated in Title II of the Digital Millennium Copyright Act, 17 U.S.C. § 512, discussed in Chapter 7, Part V(B)(2), *supra*. ISP liability for knowing disclosure of trade secrets would arguably come within the terms of the federal Economic Espionage Act of 1996, 18 U.S.C. § 1832, providing a criminal penalty for an organization that intentionally "replicates, transmits, delivers, sends, mails, communicates, or conveys" information constituting a trade secret.

In *Gucci America, Inc. v. Hall & Associates*, 135 F.Supp.2d 409 (S.D.N.Y.2001), the court held that, due to the Section 230(e)(2) exemption for intellectual property laws, the immunity is inapplicable to trademark claims. Is the immunity also unavailable for claims based on (1) a state law prohibiting wrongful use of a registered mark? (2) a state statutory or common law right of publicity? (3) a state statute prohibiting unfair competition, where the claimed unfair competition consists of trademark infringement? (4) a state statute or common law against false advertising? *See Perfect 10, Inc. v. CCBill, LLC*, 340 F.Supp.2d 1077, 1107–10 (C.D.Cal. 2004) (yes, yes, no, no).

c. Service Provider's Knowledge of the Wrongful Conduct

In *Doe v. America Online, Inc.*, 783 So.2d 1010 (Fla.2001), plaintiff sued AOL for allowing a subscriber, one Russell, to use its chat rooms for marketing videotapes and photographs consisting of child pornography in which plaintiff's minor son appears. The complaint alleged that AOL was negligent per se in allowing Russell to use its facilities for criminal distribution of obscene materials, and that it was likewise negligent on common-law principles. Plaintiff alleged that AOL had received complaints about Russell's use of its facilities for unlawful purposes, but that "AOL neither warned Russell to stop nor suspended his service." *Id.* at 1012. The Florida Supreme Court, in a 4–3 decision, affirmed the trial and appellate courts' grant of AOL's motion to dismiss based on Section 230. The majority opinion adopted the reasoning of *Zeran v. America Online*. The dissenters, disagreeing with *Zeran* and considering that it was not binding authority, explained their view at length:

> It is clear that Congress, through the Communications Decency Act, 47 U.S.C. § 230 (the "CDA"), intended to shield an Internet Service Provider (an "ISP") from liability due solely to implementation of a good-faith monitoring program whose goal is to preclude dissemination of illicit and improper materials through the ISP's electronic medium. Contrary to the majority's view, however, the carefully crafted statute at issue, undergirded by a clear legislative history, does not reflect an intent to totally exonerate and insulate an ISP from re-

sponsibility where, as here, it is alleged that an ISP has acted as a knowing distributor of material leading to the purchase, sale, expansion and advancement of child pornography, after having been given actual notice of the particular activity, by taking absolutely no steps to curtail continued dissemination of the information by its specifically identified customer, when it had the right and power to do so. . . .

. . . If Congress had intended absolute immunity, why would it state only that no ISP "shall be treated as a *publisher* or *speaker of* any *information provided by another* information content provider?" . . . If blanket immunity were intended, why not state more broadly that no ISP "shall be held liable" for any information provided on its service by another information content provider? . . .

The reason, pointedly, is that Congress never intended for such a broad immunity to apply. In cutting a wide swath of immunity from the cloth of this purposefully narrow language, the analysis contained in *Zeran* (and approved by the majority here) turns on its head the very goal of the Communications Decency Act. While Congress has recognized that the Internet presents a "forum for true diversity of political discourse, unique opportunities for cultural development, and myriad avenues for intellectual activity," 47 U.S.C. § 230(a)(3), the purpose of the CDA is not, as the *Zeran* court espoused, "to promote unfettered speech"—most particularly where such alleged speech is an invitation to purchase child pornography. . . .

. . . While the majority view recognizes that, as reflected in the legislative history of the CDA referenced in *Zeran,* "the 'disincentive' Congress specifically had in mind was liability of the sort described in *Stratton Oakmont,*" what it inexplicably fails to recognize is that this is *not* the distributor liability recognized in *Cubby.* Rather, it is the far stricter standard of publisher liability which was imposed in *Stratton Oakmont,* based solely on the ISP's implementation of laudable, self-regulating efforts to screen inappropriate material prior to its publication, which efforts the CDA—as expressed in the policies set forth as a preamble to the statute—unabashedly encourages.

Given the precise, limiting language of the statute, the stated policy underlying the CDA, and the CDA's explicit legislative history, it is inconceivable that Congress intended the CDA to shield from potential liability an ISP alleged to have taken absolutely no actions to curtail illicit activities in furtherance of conduct defined as criminal, despite actual knowledge that a source of child pornography was being advertised and delivered through contact information provided on its service by an identified customer, while profiting from its customer's continued use of the service. . . .

783 So.2d at 1019–28. What accounts for the differing perspectives of the court in *Zeran v. America Online* and the dissent in *Doe v. America Online*? How does *Zeran* address the argument that Section 230 does not displace liability on a knew-or-should-have-known standard? Which opinion is more convincing?

A three-judge panel of the California Court of Appeal endorsed the view of the *Doe v. America Online* dissent that *Zeran v. America Online* is incorrect in extending the Section 230 immunity to distributors. *See Barrett v. Rosenthal*, 9 Cal.Rptr.3d 142 (Cal.Ct.App. 2004), *review granted*, 87 P.3d 797 (Cal.2004). Other cases supporting *Zeran*'s broad reading of the immunity include *Donato v. Moldow*, 865 A.2d 711 (N.J.Super.Ct.App.Div. 2005).

d. Entities Within the Scope of the Immunity

The immunity conferred by Section 230 applies to any "provider or user of an interactive computer service." Courts have held that the immunity is potentially available to the operator of a listserv, *see Batzel v. Smith, supra*; an entity that collects complaints against spammers and forwards them to the spammer's access provider, *see OptInRealBig.com, LLC v. IronPort Systems, Inc.*, 323 F. Supp. 2d 1037 (N.D. Cal. 2004); an online auction site, *see Gentry v. eBay, Inc.*, 121 Cal.Rptr.2d 703 (Cal.App.2002); and a website that allows postings of book reviews, *see Schneider v. Amazon.com, Inc.*, 31 P.3d 37 (Wash.Ct. App.2001).

e. Defendant's Participation in Creation of the Offensive Material

Section 230 privileges an ISP's publication of "information provided by another information content provider," but liability still attaches to publication of material created and published by the ISP itself. Thus, under the scenario presented in *Blumenthal v. Drudge*, if Drudge were AOL's employee, the content of the Drudge Report would be attributable to AOL and the immunity would be unavailable. Since Drudge was not AOL's employee, but an independent contractor, the court found that AOL enjoyed Section 230 immunity. Is there a defensible rationale for distinguishing between these two situations? What if AOL had more of a say in the content that was produced—if it offered to pay Drudge to produce "something that will grab eyeballs, whether it is true or not"? Would it be fair for the ISP to lose its immunity once its degree of participation becomes significant enough? Is such a result possible given the language of Section 230? Consider the provision's definition of "information content provider": "any person or entity that is responsible, in whole or in part, for the creation or development of information provided through the Internet or any other interactive computer service." § 230(e)(3). Does this definition answer the question?

What if AOL had actually exercised editorial authority over some of Drudge's reports, but not this one? What if it had edited this particular report, but left the complained-of portion unchanged? Would AOL then qualify as an "information content provider," and therefore not be entitled to Section 230 immunity? If so, can this be squared with the clear intent of Section 230(c)(2) to protect "good Samaritans" from liability?

In *Carafano v. Metrosplash.com, Inc.*, 339 F.3d 1119 (9th Cir.2003), the court formulated the principle as: "so long as a third party willingly provides the essential published content, the interactive service provider receives full immunity regardless of the specific editing or selection process." In that case, the speech that plaintiff found offensive was a profile of her that a third party had created and posted on the defendant website. The profile had been created through an online questionnaire that the website provided, including both multiple choice and essay questions. The court held that although "the questionnaire facilitated the expression of information by individual users . . . , the selection of the content was left exclusively to the user," and the website operator was therefore within the protection of Section 230. Similarly, in *Gentry v. eBay, Inc.*, 121 Cal.Rptr.2d 703 (Cal.Ct.App.2002), the court held that Section 230 protects eBay from liability based on allegedly negligent posting of seller ratings, since eBay's role was merely to compile information submitted by third parties. *See also Donato v. Moldow*, 865 A.2d 711 (N.J.Super.Ct.App.Div.2005) ("Deleting profanity, selectively deleting or allowing to remain certain postings, and commenting favorably or unfavorably on some postings, without changing the substance of the message authored by another, does not constitute 'development' within the meaning of § 230(f)(3).").

Compare *MCW, Inc. v. Badbusinessbureau.com, L.L.C.*, 2004 WL 833595 (N.D.Tex. 2004), where the court found that a website operator became an information content provider and lost its immunity when it encouraged a consumer to take photographs that the consumer posted along with other allegedly disparaging materials: "actively encouraging and instructing a consumer to gather specific detailed information is an activity that goes substantially beyond the traditional publisher's editorial role."

EXTENSIONS

1. *Criminal liability.* In 1998, the New York Attorney General charged BuffNET, an ISP located near Buffalo, New York, with criminal liability in connection with the distribution of child pornography via USENET newsgroups to which it proved access. The Attorney General explained that it took the action because BuffNET failed to cut off access to the newsgroup even after police informed it of the unlawful content. BuffNET said that the police had conveyed this information to a low-level employee, who failed to pass it along to the company's management. Though it initially denied liability, BuffNET later pled guilty to a misdemeanor, and paid a $5,000 fine. Is there a convincing policy rationale for insulating AOL from civil liability in *Doe v. America Online, supra*, but imposing criminal liability on BuffNET? For a discussion of the two cases, see Kenneth M. Dreifach, *Emerging Issues in Liability for Internet Service Providers*, N.Y.L.J., July 12, 2001, at 5.

In 2002, the Pennsylvania Legislature enacted a statute providing:

> (a) *General rule.*—An Internet Service Provider shall remove or disable access to child pornography items residing on or accessible through its service in a manner accessible to persons located within this Commonwealth within five business days of when the Internet Service Provider is notified by the Attorney General pursuant to subsection (g) that child pornography items reside on or are accessible through its service.

18 Pa. Cons. Stat. § 7330(a). The Attorney General may make such a notification only upon a finding by a court, which may be ex parte, that there is probable cause that the material in question violates state law prohibiting child pornography. *Id.* § 7330(e), (f), (g). Criminal penalties apply to an ISP that fails to take down the material upon such a notification. *Id.* § 7330(c). Does this statute establish an appropriately limited form of ISP liability for making available criminal content?

2. *Continuing vitality of the common law of defamation after Section 230.* Section 230 is an overlay that does not displace the limitations on liability resulting from the common (or statutory) law of defamation. In *Lunney v. Prodigy Services Co.*, 723 N.E.2d 539 (N.Y.1999), plaintiff sued Prodigy for defamation, based on messages appearing on one of its bulletin boards that the poster falsely attributed to plaintiff. The court, applying New York common law, held that, under the circumstances presented, Prodigy was not a publisher of the posted material. In contrast to the breadth of the legislative approach followed in Section 230, the court declined to rule any more broadly than necessary to decide the case before it: "We see no occasion to hypothesize whether there may be other instances in which the role of an electronic bulletin board operator would qualify it as a publisher." The court also declined Prodigy's request that it decide the case on the basis of Section 230, and that it interpret the statutory provision "to render an ISP unconditionally free from notice-based liability." Once again, the court found that "[t]his case does not call for it."

QUESTIONS FOR DISCUSSION

1. *Lack of parity with treatment of offline publishers.* In *Blumenthal v. Drudge*, the court expressed frustration over what it viewed as Congress's policy decision to treat online publishers differently from traditional publishers: "In view of this statutory language [of § 230], plaintiffs' argument that the Washington Post would be liable if it had done what AOL did here—'publish Drudge's story without doing anything whatsoever to edit, verify, or even read it (despite knowing what Drudge did for a living and how he did it)'—has been rendered irrelevant by Congress." Is this policy judgment defensible? Do you agree with the court's statement that "it would seem only fair to hold AOL to the liability standards applied to a publisher or, at least, like a book store owner or library, to the liability standards applied to a distributor"? What are the arguments for distinguishing an online service provider from a publisher or book store owner? Is there a national policy to encourage book stores to police the contents of the books they carry, and to eliminate those with offensive content? Should such a policy apply to ISPs?

2. *Is Section 230 too blunt an instrument?* Does Section 230 paint with too broad a brush, lumping all providers of interactive computer services together regardless of the activities in which they engage and the source and format of the offensive material? Consider the following critique. It makes sense for an ISP to enjoy unqualified immunity from liability based on material created by third parties, and made available through its service, where the ISP is functioning essentially like a common carrier. The risk of liability under such circumstances imposes an unreasonable burden on ISPs, and threatens unduly to restrict free expression in online bulletin board systems and chat rooms, since ISPs are likely to react by (1) engaging in censorship, (2) increasing the price of access to cover expected liability for offensive content, or (3) restricting anonymous speech in order to increase the accountability of online speakers. But this rationale does not apply when an ISP chooses to make an online publication available through its service. In this role, the ISP occupies the same position as any offline distributor of publications: it is making a decision to carry certain publications, based on general information about the content and editorial policies of each publication. There is no good reason to apply different standards of liability for defamation or other speech torts depending on whether the liability is based on (1) an ISP's decision to make available the *New York Times* or the *National Enquirer*, (2) an ISP's decision to make available Rumorville or the Drudge Report, or (3) a newsstand's decision to make available hard copies of any of those publications. Congress was right to override *Stratton Oakmont v. Prodigy*, but it drew the line in the wrong place: ISPs should not enjoy absolute immunity when, as in *Cubby v. CompuServe* and *Blumenthal v. Drudge*, they choose to make available publications known to have offensive content.

3. *Is Section 230 logical?* One of the stated purposes of Section 230 is to eliminate the disincentive that *Stratton Oakmont v. Prodigy* creates for ISPs to police their systems for offensive content. In so doing, Section 230 also eliminates the incentive to police their systems created by the fear of legal liability. Is the theory underlying Section 230 that even absent this fear ISPs will be motivated to keep offensive materials off their systems? What motivations remain operative on ISPs? Developing a reputation as a family-friendly service, or as one that contains reliable information? Is it desirable to have a spectrum of different services, including "G-rated" services that are guaranteed to contain nothing objectionable, "PG–13" services that contain mildly offensive material, "R-rated" ones that parents might want to keep their children away from, and "NC–17" services that promise no restrictions? Is this an area in which self-regulation, impelled by market forces, is the best approach?

4. *Balancing competing interests.* One effect of Section 230, and common-law doctrines that immunize ISPs from liability based on third-party communications, is that deserving plaintiffs may have no remedy. This will be the case when the originator of the offending communication cannot be identified, as in *Zeran v. America Online*[3] and *Lunney v. Prodigy Services Co.* (discussed *supra*). Does the law therefore go overboard in protecting free speech, while neglecting other important interests such as reputation? Would it be good policy to restore the balance by requiring ISPs to verify the identity of subscribers before allowing them online, enabling an ISP to disclose the identity of a subscriber in response to a subpoena or court order?

5. *Does the technology of online communications render the law of defamation obsolete?* One commentator points out that a person who is defamed by a posting on a bulletin board system has an automatic right of reply, which she may exercise simply by posting a reply message in the forum where the defamation appeared. Accordingly, he argues, we may dispense with the application of legal remedies, like defamation liability, that cut close to First Amendment protections by casting a chill upon system operators. Do you agree? *See* Edward A. Cavazos, *Computer Bulletin Board Systems and the Right of Reply: Redefining Defamation Liability for a New Technology*, 12 REV. LITIG. 231 (1992).

D. A COMPARATIVE VIEW

1. The German and English Experience

Outside the United States, service providers have received less favorable treatment with respect to liability for third-party content. This is illustrated by the criminal prosecution of a German CompuServe official for distribution of child pornography. In December 1995, prosecutors in Bavaria notified CompuServe's German subsidiary that they were investigating the distribution of child pornography via the Internet. In response, CompuServe blocked access to over 200 USENET newsgroups, which German prosecutors suspected of carrying pornographic images. The blocking affected all of CompuServe's 4.3 million subscribers throughout the world, as CompuServe did not have the technology to block access only by those in a specific geographic location. Authorities in Munich subsequently prosecuted the managing director of CompuServe's German subsidiary, Felix Somm, under an act prohibiting publications deemed harmful to children. Prosecutors sought to hold Somm responsible for CompuServe's provision of access to USENET newsgroups containing pornographic images illegal under German law, as well as access to computer games with violent content.

In the course of the prosecution, the German legislature passed an amendment to the law regulating telecommunications services that was designed to limit the liability of ISPs for third-party communications, but the court held this provision inapplicable. The court found Somm guilty as charged, and imposed a two-year suspended sentence—despite the fact that the prosecution had a change of heart during the proceedings, and joined the defense in arguing for acquittal. In their closing arguments, both the prosecution and defense argued that it was technically impossible to filter out all offensive material on the Internet, but the judge disagreed. The prosecutors, believing that the new law insulated Somm from liability, themselves appealed the conviction. The court of appeals agreed, and threw out the

---

[3] Zeran was also rebuffed in his suit against the radio station that broadcast the AOL postings. The court held against him, on summary judgment, for failure to introduce evidence of reputational injury, as required by the Oklahoma statute defining a cause of action for slander. It likewise rejected, on evidentiary grounds, his claims based on false light invasion of privacy and intentional infliction of emotional distress. *See Zeran v. Diamond Broadcasting, Inc.*, 203 F.3d 714 (10th Cir. 2000).

conviction.

A court decision in the United Kingdom likewise held an ISP liable for third-party content. In *Godfrey v. Demon Internet Ltd.*, [1999] E.M.L.R. 542 (Q.B.), an unknown person posted a scurrilous message on a USENET newsgroup, and signed plaintiff Lawrence Godfrey's name to it. Godfrey notified Demon Internet, an ISP carrying the newsgroup, that the posting was a forgery, and asked Demon to delete it, but Demon failed to do so. The facts of the case were thus quite similar to those in *Zeran v. America Online* and *Lunney v. Prodigy Services Co.* (discussed *supra*), but the result was quite different. The U.K. Defamation Act contains an "innocent dissemination" defense, which is available only if the defendant took "reasonable care," and "did not know, and had no reason to believe," that he was publishing a defamatory statement. The court held that, since Demon was informed of the posting, it did not satisfy those two requirements, and was not entitled to the defense. The court discussed what it viewed as the relevant U.S. cases—*Cubby v. CompuServe*, *Stratton Oakmont v. Prodigy*, *Zeran v. America Online*, and *Lunney v. Prodigy Services Co.*—but found them inapplicable. Referring to Section 230, the ISP immunity provision of the Communications Decency Act, the court observed: "In my judgment the English 1996 [Defamation] Act did not adopt this approach or have this purpose."

The case subsequently settled: Demon agreed to pay Godfrey £15,000, plus legal costs which could exceed £200,000. Demon's own legal costs were nearly £500,000.

Shortly after this ruling, the Campaign Against Censorship of the Internet in Britain ("CACIB") posted a story on its website describing a situation in which an ISP shut down a website it hosted after a firm of solicitors notified the ISP that it would be subject to a defamation suit if the website should publish a libel. The ISP required the website to provide a guarantee against any such wrongdoing, and when the website failed to do so the ISP shut down the website. The story on CACIB's site was headlined: "Web site suppressed: *Godfrey's* first victim." Godfrey complained to CACIB's ISP that this was defamatory, as the headline could be read to imply that the threat was issued by Godfrey personally, rather than by the *Godfrey* ruling. Fearing liability under the theory of this very ruling, the ISP shut down CACIB's website. CACIB relocated to servers located in the United States and restored the censored content.

These events illustrate two negative aspects of a legal regime making ISPs liable for third-party content. First, it tends to have a chilling effect on speech, as the specter of ruinous liability impels ISPs to pull the plug on controversial material. Second, it demonstrates the mobility of content in the borderless online world. Since the address of a website is logical, and not geographically based, a site need not be hosted on servers located within the geographic boundaries of the country with jurisdiction over the domain name. For example, a domain name ending with the country code .uk, which is issued by the domain registration authority of the United Kingdom, may be hosted just as easily, from a technical standpoint, on a server located in the United States as on one located in the United Kingdom. The location of the server may, however, introduce practical difficulties: for example, it may be easier for a U.K. resident to contract with a website hosting service located in her own country than with one located overseas.

2. Liability of Internet Service Providers in the European Union

The European Commission's Directive on Electronic Commerce[4] contains several provisions limiting the liability of Internet service providers based on material provided by others. The Directive's treatment of ISP liability differs from the U.S. regime in several important respects. In the United States, as we have seen, the rules limiting the liability of a service provider vary depending on the subject matter of the material giving rise to the claim of liability. Thus, an ISP's liability for copyright infringement is limited by the Digital Millennium Copyright Act immunity provision, 17 U.S.C. § 512, discussed in Chapter 7, Part V(B)(2), *supra*. ISP liability based on most other types of material is limited by the Communications Decency Act immunity provision, 47 U.S.C. § 230, as discussed in this Chapter. Liability based on other subject matters that are excluded from the scope of Section 230, including criminal liability, non-copyright intellectual property, and liability based on the Electronic Communications Privacy Act, are not subject to any limitation other than what exists in the substantive rules creating liability.

The Directive, on the other hand, applies a unitary approach to all forms of ISP liability, regardless of the subject matter under which it arises.[5] The Directive bears a strong resemblance to the DMCA immunity provision, 17 U.S.C. § 512, and very little resemblance to the CDA provision, 47 U.S.C. § 230, in that it offers conditional rather than blanket immunity.

- When an ISP acts as a "mere conduit" of information provided by others, the ISP is not liable based on the information transmitted as long as it "(a) does not initiate the transmission; (b) does not select the receiver of the transmission; and (c) does not select or modify the information contained in the transmission." Art. 12(1). This immunity is applicable to the "automatic, intermediate and transient storage" of the information transmitted only if the storage is "for the sole purpose of carrying out the transmission in the communication network, and provided that the information is not stored for any period longer than is reasonably necessary for the transmission." Art. 12(2). Compare 17 U.S.C. § 512(a).

- An ISP is not liable based on "caching," that is, "the automatic, intermediate and temporary storage of that information, performed for the sole purpose of making more efficient the information's onward transmission to other recipients of the service upon their request," if certain conditions are met, including: "(c) the provider complies with rules regarding the updating of the information, specified in a manner widely recognised and used by industry; (d) the provider does not interfere with the lawful use of technology, widely recognised and used by industry, to obtain data on the use of the information; and (e) the provider acts expeditiously

---

[4] Directive 2000/31/EC of the European Parliament and of the Council of 8 June 2000 on certain legal aspects of information society services, in particular electronic commerce, in the Internal Market, 2000 O.J. (L 178) 1, europa.eu.int/ISPO/ecommerce/legal/documents/2000_31ec/ 2000_31ec_en.pdf.

[5] This difference between the U.S. and EU approaches finds an analogy in the area of privacy protection. In the United States, legislation protecting privacy is sectoral, with no overarching scheme, while in the European Union privacy is regulated comprehensively by the Data Protection Directive. *See* Chapter 6, Part I, *supra*.

to remove or to disable access to the information it has stored upon obtaining actual knowledge of the fact that the information at the initial source of the transmission has been removed from the network, or access to it has been disabled, or that a court or an administrative authority has ordered such removal or disablement." Art. 13(1). Compare 17 U.S.C. § 512(b).

- An ISP is not liable based on hosting a website or other material, if "(a) the provider does not have actual knowledge of illegal activity or information and, as regards claims for damages, is not aware of facts or circumstances from which the illegal activity or information is apparent; or (b) the provider, upon obtaining such knowledge or awareness, acts expeditiously to remove or to disable access to the information." Art. 14(1). Compare 17 U.S.C. § 512(c), which includes detailed notification procedures not present in the Directive.

- Unlike the U.S. law, the Directive does not limit the liability of search engines and online directories. Compare 17 U.S.C. § 512(d).

- The foregoing immunity provisions do not prevent the issuance of injunctive relief, requiring that an ISP remove or cease providing access to the offending information. Art. 12(3), 13(2), 14(3). Compare 17 U.S.C. § 512(j).

- The Directive provides that EU member states "shall not impose a general obligation on providers, when providing the services covered by Articles 12, 13 and 14, to monitor the information which they transmit or store, nor a general obligation actively to seek facts or circumstances indicating illegal activity." Art. 15(1). This provision is consistent with the general approach of both 17 U.S.C. § 512 and 47 U.S.C. § 230.

QUESTIONS FOR DISCUSSION

1. *The borderless world.* Do the German and English experiences with different rules change your evaluation of Section 230? Consider the question in context: England and other European countries have always had stricter laws against defamation than the United States, and fewer defenses. Will the Internet force countries to relinquish their legal culture when that culture supports regulation that is difficult to administer in the borderless online environment? Consider also in this regard Yahoo!'s efforts to have a judgment against it, issued by a French court, declared unenforceable in the United States, on the ground that enforcement would violate the First Amendment. *Yahoo! Inc. v. La Ligue Contre le Racisme et l'Antisemitisme*, 379 F.3d 1120 (9th Cir.2004), *reh'g en banc granted*, 399 F.3d 1010 (9th Cir.2005), discussed in Chapter 5, Part II(B), *supra*. If the original action against Yahoo! had been brought in a U.S. court, could Yahoo! have successfully invoked a Section 230 defense?

2. *U.S. vs. EU approach.* What are the advantages and disadvantages of the Directive's unitary approach, as compared with the sectoral approach followed by U.S. law?

FURTHER READING

- Kamiel J. Koelman, *Online Intermediary Liability, in* COPYRIGHT AND ELECTRONIC COMMERCE: LEGAL ASPECTS OF ELECTRONIC COPYRIGHT MANAGEMENT 7 (P. Bernt Hugenholtz, ed., 2000) (comparing the U.S. and EU approaches)

II. LIABILITY OF INTERMEDIARIES FOR MALICIOUS INTRUSIONS

As we have seen in Part I, *supra*, the liability of Internet intermediaries for most types of speech torts originating with third-party users has been largely eliminated by the Communications Decency Act immunity provision, 47 U.S.C. § 230. Service provider liability for third-party copyright infringement is strictly confined by the Digital Millennium Copyright Act's safe harbors, 17 U.S.C. § 512, as discussed in Chapter 7, Part V(B)(2), *supra*.

The potential liability of intermediaries based on denial-of-service attacks perpetrated by third parties is murkier, as discussed in the following excerpt.

Margaret Jane Radin, *Distributed Denial of Service Attacks: Who Pays?*
6 No. 9 CYBERSPACE LAW. 2 (2001) (Part I) and 6 No. 10 CYBERSPACE LAW. 2 (2002) (Part II).

DDoS: A Lurking Problem for Business

. . .

The vulnerability of businesses to DDoS attacks hit the headlines with the attacks that brought down Yahoo!, eBay and others in February 2000. Recent attacks on Microsoft and the World Economic Forum at Davos generated further headlines. What does not make the headlines is how serious and pervasive the problem is. For example, more than one-third of the respondents in the 2001 Computer Crime and Security Survey experienced denial of service attacks. In spite of such evidence, the problem is under-reported. Many denial of service attacks go undetected. Even when attacks are detected, many organizations, fearing bad publicity and the consequent effect on their customers and shareholders, simply do not report such incidents. The tools available to intruders are becoming more sophisticated and readily available on the Web.

The costs of DDoS attacks can be staggering. The estimated direct losses from the attacks in February 2000 were $1.2 billion. Losses of customer goodwill, corporate reputation and overall public trust in the online economy were likely even greater. DDoS attacks also take their toll on productivity, user access, and lost business opportunities. These indirect costs are no less real because they are difficult to monetize.

. . .

What is a DDoS Attack?

In a DDoS attack, intruders commandeer unsuspecting users' computers and use these distributed "zombies" to flood a target site or service with junk messages. The junk messages overwhelm the servers of the victim and cause that site to experience a period of "denial of service" to its legitimate customers. The success of typical DDoS attacks involves the "cooperation" of a number of players, or *a chain of actors*. The chain consists of (1) computer users whose machines are commandeered by intruders; (2) portals, corporate and other Internet sites that are targets or "victims" of attacks; and (3) network intermediaries (i.e., various kinds of ISPs and hosting service providers) and backbone network service providers, who deliver the messages that constitute the attack.

User computers are vulnerable because their operating systems are not designed to screen out intruders. Victim sites are vulnerable for many reasons. Some are not aware of the extent of the problem; some are unable to deploy the personnel and technology needed to detect and stop attacks. Even for sophisticated sites, the task of determining the source of the unwanted messages can be like looking for a needle in a haystack; and it is difficult for security personnel to keep up with rapid development of newer and more sophisticated attack modes. Network intermediaries and backbone service providers are vulnerable too, in the sense that they are transmitting malicious packets that are part of an attack. Also, under certain circumstances the flood of messages may slow down the entire network, or further disrupt the server by directing traffic back to it.

. . .

Potential Tort Liability for Damages Due to DDoS Attacks

. . .

DDoS-Based Claims Through the Lens of Traditional Tort Law

A Hypothetical Scenario: Let's consider how liability might come before a court in the case of a DDoS attack with the following example. Suppose a securities brokerage such as E*Trade or Schwab suffers a DDoS attack. Its customers cannot complete any transactions for several hours. The attack messages have been relayed through a large hosting service provider such as Exodus or Digex. Suppose that the market is volatile on the day that this happens, so that many customers are trying to buy or sell quickly. As a result of the outage, a large number of customers suffer significant financial losses. (Significant losses could occur on account of a slowdown, as well, even if it weren't a complete outage.)

What legal claims might arise out of this event? First, the customers of the brokerage might sue the brokerage for damages on account of their financial losses. Second, the brokerage could sue its hosting or bandwidth provider, for damages on account of its own financial losses (lost revenue from transactions not completed, employee time in recovering lost data, loss of customer goodwill, and perhaps decreased market share or capitalization). In such suits, the plaintiff is said to be in privity with the defendant because the relationship between the plaintiff and the defendant is governed by a contract—the TOS [Terms of Service] between the brokerage and its users, the SLA [Service Level Agreement] between the network service provider and the broker.

Tort and Contract Interaction: Thus, there are two intertwined legal questions to pose in these kinds of suits: who would be liable in the absence of contract? And, has the contract successfully allocated the risk in a different way (that is, has the contract disclaimed liability on the part of the party who would otherwise be liable)? This paper examines both tort liability and contractual shifting of liability.

Of the two questions, the latter is the more important for parties who are in privity with each other.

Third-Party Claims: Another class of legal claims arising out of my hypothetical example involves claims against a party not in privity with the plaintiff, which I will sometimes refer to as third-party claims. (The brokerage's customers are third parties vis-à-vis the contract between the brokerage and its service provider; and the service provider is a third party vis-à-vis the contract between the brokerage and its customers.)

A suit by the customers of the brokerage firm against the brokerage's Web hosting service and/or backbone service provider is a claim against a third party defendant. Attempted contractual disclaimer will usually not play a role in this scenario, because the plaintiffs are not a party to the contract in which the disclaimer appears; they did not agree to it, and it wasn't a part of their bargain. In this situation, however, traditional tort law developed defenses for the third party defendant based essentially upon the extent of exposure to liability, and whether the court found such exposure to be reasonable under the circumstances. (I will touch upon those defenses later in this section).

. . .

How Will Courts Analyze DDoS-Based Tort Claims?

Tort law is divided doctrinally into torts based upon intentional harm, harm caused by negligence, and liability without fault (strict liability). In the case of liability for DDoS attacks, at least for parties other than the intruders themselves, we are not dealing with intentional harm. The doctrine of strict liability is used primarily in the context of harm caused by defective products that are dangerous to the user, so it is more likely that courts will consider liability for DDoS attacks under the rubric of negligence rather than that of strict liability, and the analysis here will assume a negligence context. (In practice, however, the application of strict liability often involves inquiries that overlap with those involved in negligence.)

Actors in the Causal Chain Who Are in Privity (i.e., in a Provider/Customer Relationship): Assuming the absence of a successful contractual disclaimer, each party would owe its partner a duty of reasonable care; and if it failed to use due care it would be deemed negligent. Damages could follow if the negligence results in losses on account of a DDoS attack, if the losses are foreseeable and could have been prevented with exercise of due care. That is, a network intermediary could be held liable to its customer; and its customer, such as a portal or other e-commerce site, could be held liable to its own customers.

My research has disclosed no cases to date (April 30, 2001) in which this issue has been litigated and reported in the context of a DDoS attack. Traditional principles of tort law direct courts to consider *foreseeability* of the damage, including the identity of the party likely to be injured and the type and extent of injury that can be foreseen. Those issues seem relatively straightforward in the case of a provider-customer (victim site) relationship, and in the case of a victim site–user relationship. That is, DDoS attacks and the types of damage they cause to a customer are reasonably foreseeable by a service provider, so liability could be found under tra-

ditional tort principles if the governing standard of care required the service provider to take precautions to prevent such attacks. The same is true in the case of the
victim site vis-à-vis its users.

But it is important to keep in mind that these kinds of cases are frequently going to be governed by the contract between the parties. Exceptions are where the
contract is improperly formed, or where the contract tries to exclude liability in a
way the court finds contrary to public policy.

Third-Party Liability: Potential tort liability in this situation—e.g., where the victim's own customers sue the victim's network service provider, Web hosting service, etc.—is somewhat more difficult to analyze. In the past the courts have sometimes rejected liability of third party defendants, especially where it appeared that
the third party would expose itself to an unknown and potentially large amount of
risk, inappropriate in light of its role.[11] On the other hand, some courts have found
third parties liable, especially where the risk was foreseeable and particularized,[12]
or where they could find a special relationship between the plaintiff and the defendant.

. . .

Property Damage and Recent Cases Involving "Trespass to Chattels": Victim sites
may well be able to convince a court that DDoS attacks cause them property damage. A number of recent cases suggest that courts are willing to consider receipt of
unwanted messages to be a physical harm to a victim's system, and thus the requisite physical harm to property. These cases have found tort liability for slowing
down a system or taking up bandwidth, by spam or data-gathering programs, under the doctrine of trespass to chattels.[6]

. . .

Can ISPs Claim Immunity from Liability?

Service providers may argue that because they are mere conduits of messages it
is inappropriate to place any liabilities on them. This argument is not convincing,
as the courts have not hesitated to place liability on service providers in other contexts.

In determining whether ISPs (broadly construed) could claim immunity to tort
suits for DDoS attacks, we can consider [these] possible analogies: the immunities
of "common carriers," [and] the safe harbor in the Communications Decency Act
(CDA) . . . .

---

[11] *See generally* Robert L. Rabin, Tort Recovery for Negligently Inflicted Economic Loss: A
Reassessment, 37 Stanford Law Review 1513 (1985).

[12] *See, e.g.,* J'Aire Corp. v. Gregory, 24 Cal. 3d 799 (1979) (contractor who undertook construction work for owner of building had duty to tenants to complete construction on time
to avoid resultant economic losses); Union Oil Co. v. Oppen, 501 F. 2d 558 (9th Cir.1974)
(fishermen making known commercial use of public waters may recover economic losses
due to defendant's oil spill).

[6] [Cases finding liability based on trespass to chattels are discussed in Chapter 12, Part II, *supra*.—Eds.]

. . .

"Common Carrier": Traditionally, the government held "common carriers," who provided services to the public at large (e.g., railroads), to a high standard of care to their customers. Communications regulation designated telephone companies as "common carriers," but as communications law developed, such carriers were permitted to place disclaimers of liability for customers' loss due to denial of service or poor quality of service in their governing document (tariff). Although many in the communications field have fought over the definition of "common carrier," none of the providers in the DDoS attack scenario is likely to be considered a common carrier, because they do not hold out their service to everyone.[17]

Safe Harbor for Indecent or Defamatory Content: As e-commerce evolved, courts demonstrated willingness to hold an ISP liable for defamatory content present on its system. The Communications Decency Act (CDA) overrules this case law and grants a safe harbor to ISPs who in good faith try to filter out offending material. Among other things, this provision prevents ISPs from being sued in tort for defamation, for "publishing" defamatory content.

Several considerations distinguish ISP immunity in the context of defamation from any claimed immunity in the context of DDoS. First, Congress statutorily grants the immunity from liability for defamatory and other offensive content, and there is no such statutory immunity applicable to DDoS attacks. Second, and equally important, the defamation immunity is granted to foster provision of content. Congress has decided that the social desirability of content provision outweighs the interest of injured plaintiffs in compensation for defamation. Part of the reason for doing so is the preferred place of speech in our social order. Another reason is the fact that defamation is a murky subject area; an ISP could not be expected consistently to guess right about whether courts would find material defamatory, even if an ISP could undertake serious review of posted content (which is impossible in the ordinary course of business).

In contrast, DDoS attacks are not speech and there is no reason to think that DDoS attacks have a socially beneficial side that should be encouraged. Moreover, where technology exists that can differentiate normal from attack traffic on a consistent basis, DDoS attacks would not be hard to distinguish from the beneficial use of a network. In other words, there is no policy basis that would support immunity in a world where preventive technology exists.

. . .

Contractual Risk–Shifting of Damage Liability for DDoS Attacks

A key risk-management strategy for avoiding liability for DDoS attacks is contractual. Firms may attempt to use contracts either to force partners to take adequate precautions, or to force partners to take on the liability themselves by disclaiming whatever liability might otherwise accrue to them. Forcing a customer to

---

[17] *See, e.g.,* Religious Technology Center v. Netcom On-Line Communication Services, 907 F.Supp. 1361, 1370 n. 12 (rejecting Netcom's invocation of a "common carrier" analogy in order to shield itself from liability).

take adequate precautions involves using contracts that make the customer promise to implement specific precautions as a condition of service. Forcing customers
to take on the liability themselves involves using contracts that either explicitly
allocate liability to the customer, or else just disclaim liability on the part of the
service provider.

Requiring Customer Precautions

With respect to the first strategy, some network intermediaries and backbone
service providers use Service Level Agreements (SLAs) that condition service delivery upon the customer's implementation of specific security precautions and
submission to monitoring by the service provider for compliance. The success of
such a strategy depends on the marketplace. If competitive providers do not impose such onerous terms in their SLAs, but rather implement effective preventive
technologies themselves, they may gain market share against providers that do
impose such terms.

Contractual Disclaimers of Liability

The second strategy, contractual disclaimers, is legally efficacious in some contexts, but not always. First, contractual disclaimers are not binding on third parties
who are not parties to the contract. Second, not all contracts are valid and enforceable. Two ways a contract could be unenforceable are (1) invalid formation (the
court finds that no agreement was formed) and (2) invalid content (the court finds
that even if there was agreement, such an agreement is not legally allowable).

In general, courts determine whether a contract looks like a reasonable bargained-for exchange or whether, on the contrary, it looks onerous and coercive.
SLAs between business entities of roughly equal bargaining power—for example,
between a high-profile Web portal and a well-established Web hosting service—
are more likely to be presumed the result of bargained-for exchange. TOSes [Terms
of Service agreements] between parties of unequal bargaining power—for example, between a network service provider and individual consumers—are more
likely to be scrutinized for over-reaching.

Public Policy and Choice of Law: Some contractual provisions may seem like obvious over-reaching or contrary to public policy even if they are between entities of
equal bargaining power. There are also some conditions even willing parties cannot agree to enforce. For example, all courts would find it contrary to public policy
for an entity to exculpate itself for its own criminal activities. Moreover, most
courts would not allow contractual exculpation for gross negligence. Courts in different jurisdictions are divided, however, on whether it is permissible to disclaim
liability for one's own negligence (if it does not amount to gross negligence or reck-
lessness)—that is, to shift the risk of one's own negligence to one's contractual
partner.

The question of disclaiming a party's own negligence is thus complicated by
the question of choice of law: will the contract be governed by the law of a jurisdiction that permits such disclaimers, or will it be governed by the law of a jurisdiction that invalidates them? In order to deal with this issue, parties routinely include choice of law clauses, which contractually choose whose law will govern. At

least in the U.S., these clauses are routinely considered valid, but may on occasion be invalidated by courts. Outside the U.S., a court may be unwilling to transfer a case brought against one of its own nationals to a U.S. jurisdiction whose public policy conflicts with its own.

Curtailment of Remedies: Many contracts also attempt to limit risk by excluding all but a limited remedy, such as the amount paid for the service. Again, whether this limitation is enforceable depends whether the court believes this is a bargained-for exchange or instead represents some sort of overreaching and attempt to foreclose the other party's right to legal redress.

Arbitration: Many contracts force customers to accept arbitration as the sole remedy for a dispute. The courts in the U.S. are very favorable to arbitration. These clauses are generally considered enforceable, at least in the U.S., assuming that the court finds the contract to be validly formed.[24]

Contractual Disclaimers Vis-à-Vis Consumers

Contractual disclaimers, or limitations of remedy and redress, that are imposed on consumers are not always enforceable. As an outgrowth of the shrink-wrap license contracts that developed in the software industry, a large percentage of commercial Web sites are using a TOS contract, often on an interior Web page that users are unlikely to see, much less read. Many of these TOSes disclaim warranties and limit remedies.

As an example, consider AOL's "Terms of Use," which can be seen by scrolling to the very bottom of its home page and clicking on a link called "Legal Notices." After disclaiming "all warranties with respect to materials, information, software, products, and services included in or available through its site," the Terms provide:

> UNDER NO CIRCUMSTANCES SHALL AMERICA ONLINE, ITS SUB-SIDIARIES, OR ITS LICENSORS BE LIABLE FOR ANY DIRECT, INDI-RECT, PUNITIVE, INCIDENTAL, SPECIAL, OR CONSEQUENTIAL DAMAGES THAT RESULT FROM THE USE OF, OR INABILITY TO USE, THIS SITE. THIS LIMITATION APPLIES WHETHER THE AL-LEGED LIABILITY IS BASED ON CONTRACT, TORT, NEGLIGENCE, STRICT LIABILITY, OR ANY OTHER BASIS, EVEN IF AMERICA ONLINE HAS BEEN ADVISED OF THE POSSIBILITY OF SUCH DAMAGE. BECAUSE SOME JURISDICTIONS DO NOT ALLOW THE EXCLUSION OR LIMITATION OF INCIDENTAL OR CONSEQUEN-TIAL DAMAGES, AMERICA ONLINE'S LIABILITY IN SUCH JURIS-DICTIONS SHALL BE LIMITED TO THE EXTENT PERMITTED BY LAW.

These provisions purport to divest AOL of all liability to its users for unavail-

---

[24] *But see* Brower v. Gateway 2000, Inc., 676 N.Y.S.2d 569 (N.Y.Sup.Ct.App.Div.1998) (consumer class action in which court held clause calling for arbitration before the International Chamber of Commerce, which required consumers to pay a filing fee of $4000, was unconscionable and therefore unenforceable). [This case is excerpted in Chapter 10, Part II(A), *infra.*—Eds.]

ability of service due to Denial of Service attacks. Many service providers and high-profile Web sites have provisions like this. But are they enforceable?

That question is multi-faceted. First is the question of public policy. AOL itself informs anyone who reads these terms that there are some jurisdictions that do not permit this much risk-shifting, and that it is not trying to impose these terms on said users. Thus, the service provider recognizes that it cannot impose the terms across the board. This outcome is true whether or not AOL chose to inform readers about it.

A further wrinkle, however, is that another clause, a choice of law clause, says that the contract is to be governed by the laws of Virginia. An allied choice of forum clause says that all suits must be brought in Virginia. The laws of Virginia do not categorically outlaw the types of disclaimers that AOL has in its contract. Could AOL impose these disclaimers on everyone by virtue of the fact that the contract is governed everywhere by Virginia law?

No. A court in a jurisdiction that does not permit these kinds of disclaimers might well say that the choice of law clause is not enforceable against its residents. It might say that to enforce the clause would contravene that jurisdiction's public policy, and might allow the action to go forward in its own jurisdiction despite the choice of forum clause.

To generalize, choice of law and choice of forum clauses are often enforceable, especially in the United States, but courts can always refuse to enforce them if doing so would be seriously contrary to the interests and policies of the state in which the court is located, or if the forum would be seriously inconvenient for the aggrieved party. Enforcement is more uncertain when the clash of policies is international, rather than between two U.S. jurisdictions.

The Issue of Contract Formation: Even if a jurisdiction does not find the terms contrary to public policy, a court could find something about the way this contract is purportedly entered into which would invalidate the entire contract, or at least the parts of it that seem too unfavorable to the recipient. In other words, an invalid process of contract formation could result in no contractual obligation being formed, or no contractual obligation with respect to the loss-shifting terms. In a nutshell, the question is whether the court finds there really was an agreement, a process that amounts to consent, or one that otherwise qualifies as giving rise to binding obligation.

Contracts of Adhesion: What causes a court to look askance at contract formation? Some judges tend to disfavor so-called "contracts of adhesion," otherwise known as "take-it-or-leave it" contracts. Thus, in some jurisdictions a purported contract might be invalid if it is a standard-form set of terms for which one party had no opportunity to negotiate, especially if that party is a consumer, and especially if the terms seem onerous. If the contract seems grossly one-sided, or if some of the terms are against public policy (such as exculpation for gross negligence), it is more likely to be unenforceable.

Some judges are most concerned about the apparent lack of consent that goes along with these "take-it-or-leave it" contracts. Thus, a purported contract might be more likely to be held invalid if one party did not even see the terms before purportedly being bound by them.[7] This, of course, applies to many of the TOS agreements we are seeing on the Web, including the AOL Terms, since, even though they are printed in capital letters to make them conspicuous, it is unlikely that many users of the site will click on the link that reveals the terms.

. . .

Most adhesion contracts would be held valid if litigated, at least in the U.S., because the modern market could not function otherwise; but other countries rely on consumer law that is less tolerant of them. Even in the U.S., because of the varying concerns about public policy and contract formation, the thoroughgoing contractual exculpation attempted by terms disclaiming liability will not turn out to be uniformly valid. (That is why AOL's Terms say that the disclaimers don't apply to users in jurisdictions that disallow them.) Even where the terms function as intended, the firm defending the terms must pay attorneys to file motions to dismiss in each case. Because of this expense, the strategy of using disclaimers to avoid liability — defending them legally in all U.S. jurisdictions as well as in foreign jurisdictions — may not be optimal from a business standpoint.

. . .

QUESTIONS FOR DISCUSSION

1. *Liability for software developers?* The above excerpt does not address whether companies that sell software that permits DDoS attacks, such as operating system software, should be held liable to those injured by the attacks. Should they?

2. *Standard of care.* In another part of this paper, Radin notes that the legal standard of care depends upon the state of the art of preventive technologies and practices. How well do you think courts can implement the standard of care in this area?

In January 2003, the Internet suffered an attack from a worm known as the "Slammer Worm." The worm generated an enormous amount of traffic on the Internet, causing congestion on many systems, including that of Verizon Maine. As a result of the attack, Verizon Maine failed to provide the level of service required of it, and became liable to pay a monetary penalty. Verizon Maine requested a waiver from the penalty, on the ground that the Slammer Worm had created a situation beyond its control. The Maine Public Utilities Commission denied the request, finding "that Verizon did not take all reasonable and prudent steps available to it" that would have prevented the service default. The PUC explained that, six months prior to the attack, Microsoft had issued a security bulletin designating the risk posed by the Slammer Worm as "Critical," and releasing software patches that would prevent problems in case of an attack. Some service providers, including AT&T and WorldCom, installed the patches and were largely unaffected by the worm. However, Verizon Maine had failed to install the patch. *See Inquiry Regarding the Entry of Verizon-Maine into the InterLATA Telephone Market Pursuant to Section 271 of the Telecommunication Act of 1996,* Maine PUC Docket No. 2000–849 (2003).

Is the standard applied by the Maine PUC appropriate for evaluating whether a service provider was negligent in allowing a malicious intruder to use its system to harm a third party?

---

[7] [See the cases discussed in Chapter 10, Part I(A), *supra.*—Eds.]

3. *Blaming the victim?* Non-lawyers often are surprised by the possibility of suits against commercial sites that are felled by attackers, because this seems like blaming the victim. How would you answer them?

CHAPTER FOURTEEN
ALTERNATIVE RESOLUTION OF ONLINE DISPUTES

When people engage in commercial interactions, disputes arise. This is no less true for online commercial interactions than it is for commerce conducted through other means of communication. There are disputes about performance of contractual obligations, infringement of intellectual property rights, invasion of privacy, and tortious conduct. How are such disputes to be resolved?

The traditional answer is: through law, as applied by judges, facilitated by lawyers who do their work in courthouses and other face-to-face fora. There is reason to doubt, however, that the traditional answer is the best one for resolving many types of disputes arising in offline interactions, and many people believe that judicial processes are even less well adapted to resolving online disputes. Alternative dispute resolution ("ADR") is an umbrella designation for a variety of techniques that aim to resolve disputes through methods other than traditional judicial processes.

While the online medium has called into existence many familiar sorts of disputes, and a few new types, it has also created the potential for new methods of resolving disputes. These new methods, referred to as online dispute resolution ("ODR"), make use of the online medium as a tool to resolve disputes, whether they arise online or offline.

In this chapter we explore the use of various ADR techniques to resolve online disputes, and the use of ODR more generally. Some questions to keep in mind: Are there differences between online and offline disputes that make ADR more appropriate to the former? Which ADR methods are best suited to particular types of online disputes? Why have ODR efforts borne so little fruit, and what are the prospects for greater success from these techniques?

I. INTRODUCTION

A. BACKGROUND ON ALTERNATIVE DISPUTE RESOLUTION

The two most common forms of ADR are arbitration and mediation. In arbitration, the parties agree contractually to submit their dispute to a neutral decisionmaker, the arbitrator. In binding arbitration, the parties agree to be bound by the arbitrator's decision. In nonbinding arbitration, the arbitrator's decision is advisory, presenting an outcome that the arbitrator considers a fair one, and a suggestion of how a court might rule if the dispute were litigated. A nonbinding arbitration reveals to the parties the strengths and weaknesses of each other's positions, and may incline them toward a negotiated settlement.

An arbitration proceeding typically resembles a simplified version of a trial. The arbitrator sits as a judge, hears testimony, considers the parties' legal arguments, and renders a decision, referred to as an award. Unlike a judge, an arbitrator is not a representative of the state, but rather a private individual who is paid for his time. A number of service providers are in the business of supplying arbitrators and providing administrative services to facilitate arbitrations. Among the most prominent of these are the American Arbitration Association, the CPR Institute, and the National Arbitration Forum. Arbitration is used extensively to resolve labor disputes, to resolve disputes between investors and stockbrokers, to resolve salary issues in professional sports, and in other industries.

Arbitration is a creature of contract. Parties to a transaction can agree to the use of arbitration to resolve any dispute that might arise in connection with the transaction by including an arbitration clause in the contract that defines their relationship. These clauses are common in standardized, boilerplate contracts governing business-to-consumer commercial transactions, and many negotiated business-to-business contracts also contain them. If the parties have not selected arbitration at the initiation of their relationship, they may do so at the time a dispute arises by entering an agreement to arbitrate.

Although courts were once hostile to arbitration, on the ground that it ousted them of jurisdiction, *see Kulukundis Shipping Co., S/A v. Amtorg Trading Corp.*, 126 F.2d 978 (2d Cir.1942), that hostility has been overcome by state and federal enactments that look favorably on arbitration.[1] The first such enactment was the New York Arbitration Act, in 1920. The Federal Arbitration Act was enacted in 1925, and nearly all the states now have modern arbitration statutes, many of them based on the Uniform Arbitration Act of 1955. These acts generally make agreements to arbitrate enforceable, and limit the authority of courts to review arbitral awards.

Thus, the Federal Arbitration Act makes agreements to arbitrate "valid, irrevocable, and enforceable, save upon such grounds as exist at law or in equity for the revocation of any contract." 9 U.S.C. § 2. This rule of enforceability preempts any state requirement to the contrary. *See Southland Corp. v. Keating*, 465 U.S. 1 (1984) (enforcing agreement to arbitrate a claim, despite state law requiring such claims to be resolved judicially). In the context of e-commerce, the European Union's Directive on Electronic Commerce likewise expresses a policy of support for ADR, stating: "Member States shall ensure that, in the event of disagreement between an information society service provider and the recipient of the service, their legislation does not hamper the use of out-of-court schemes, available under national law, for dispute settlement, including appropriate electronic means." Directive 2000/31/EC of the European Parliament and of the Council of 8 June 2000 on certain legal aspects of information society services, in particular electronic commerce, in the Internal Market, art. 17(1), 2000 O.J. (L 178) 1, europa.eu.int/ISPO/ecommerce/legal/documents/ 2000_31ec/2000_31ec_en.pdf.

The state and federal arbitration statutes also provide for enforcement of arbitral awards. The party seeking enforcement applies to a court for confirmation of the award. Once confirmed, the award is transformed into a judgment, which may be enforced through standard judicial methods. Arbitral awards may also be enforced internationally, under the terms of the New York Convention, which (subject to certain defenses) generally requires signatory countries to enforce arbitration awards that are rendered in other signatory countries. *See* Convention on the Recognition and Enforcement of Foreign Arbitral Awards, June 10, 1958, 21 U.S.T. 2517, 330 U.N.T.S. 38, www.uncitral.org/uncitral/en/uncitral_texts/arbitration/NYConvention.html. The United States and more than 140 other countries are signatories to this treaty.

---

[1] This modern attitude reinstates the older view that one should "prefer arbitration to the law court, for the arbitrator keeps equity in view, whereas the dicast [i.e., judge] looks only to the law, and the reason why arbitrators were appointed was that equity might prevail." ARISTOTLE, RHETORIC, Bk. 1, Ch. 13, 1374b (J.H. Freese trans., London, William Heinemann Ltd. 1926).

In addition, Congress has announced a national policy favoring use of ADR methods to resolve cases that are filed as civil actions in federal district court. The Alternative Dispute Resolution Act of 1998, 28 U.S.C. §§ 651–58, requires district courts to authorize the use of ADR in all civil actions. ADR is defined in this statute as including "any process or procedure, other than an adjudication by a presiding judge, in which a neutral third party participates to assist in the resolution of issues in controversy, through processes such as early neutral evaluation, mediation, minitrial, and arbitration." 28 U.S.C. § 651(a). The district courts must require litigants to consider the use of an ADR process. If the parties consent, the court may refer a civil action to nonbinding arbitration. After an arbitral award is issued, each party has thirty days to request a trial de novo. Otherwise, the award is entered as a judgment, and has the same force and effect as any other judgment, except that it is not subject to review. *See* 28 U.S.C. §§ 652 & 657.

A mediator is a neutral third party who assists disputants in negotiating a settlement of their dispute. The activities of a mediator typically involve listening to the position of each party, which may be conveyed in the presence of the opposing party or confidentially to the mediator, encouraging parties to recognize the weaknesses of their position and to abandon unrealistic expectations, formulating settlement options for the parties' consideration, summarizing each party's position and argument, and translating the parties' statements of their positions into more helpful statements of their interests. Mediation sessions frequently shift between joint sessions and individual caucuses involving the mediator and one of the parties.

A less formal version of mediation is referred to as conciliation. Like mediation, conciliation involves a neutral third party who assists the parties in arriving at a resolution, but the conciliator's role may be limited to collecting information from the parties and passing communications back and forth between them.

The main advantages typically ascribed to ADR are that it is faster and less expensive than judicial processes. Courts often have a backlog of cases that may be months or even years in duration. Arbitration and mediation can usually be initiated much more quickly. Because of the flexibility that arbitrators have in structuring proceedings, and their less formal nature, arbitration proceedings can be conducted more expeditiously than trials. This is not inevitably the case, however, and complicated arbitrations can, like complicated trials, run for months. A skilled mediator and motivated parties can also reach a resolution in much less time than it takes to conduct a trial. Like nonbinding arbitration, however, an unsuccessful mediation can consume time without yielding a resolution.

To the extent that arbitration and mediation are faster than judicial processes, they will also tend to be less expensive, since less counsel time will be required. Because of the lesser formality of these procedures, the parties may elect to forgo legal counsel altogether, with attendant cost savings. But ADR neutrals generally do not work for free; the parties must pay them for their time. This can be a significant additional expense that is not incurred by parties to traditional judicial proceedings.

There are several other aspects of binding arbitration that some parties may consider disadvantageous. It can be difficult to know in advance whether the arbitrator is truly neutral; for example, some arbitrators are drawn from the ranks of retired industry executives. Barring unusual circumstances there is no appeal from a binding arbitral decision, so the parties are stuck with the arbitrator's view of the facts and the law. Arbitral awards have no precedential value, which makes them less useful than judicial decisions from the standpoint of institutional parties that have an interest in the creation of reliable precedent.

B. ONLINE DISPUTE RESOLUTION AND COMPUTER-ASSISTED DISPUTE RESOLUTION

Online dispute resolution ("ODR") is the use of online communication technologies in the resolution of disputes. ODR techniques enable dispute resolution to proceed without assembling the parties and facilitator at a single location. ODR techniques range from mediation in which the mediator communicates with the parties via e-mail, online chat, or bulletin board postings, to using electronic self-help over the Internet to disable software that is running on a remote computer system.

Computer-assisted dispute resolution ("CADR") uses software to help parties resolve their disputes. For example, a negotiation algorithm implemented through software can assist parties in negotiating a mutually acceptable settlement. Computer-assisted dispute resolution is generally designed to operate remotely, via the network, as a form of ODR.

It will be useful to distinguish clearly between ADR, ODR, and CADR, and to understand their applicability to disputes arising from online commerce. ADR refers to any method of dispute resolution that does not use traditional judicial methods. ADR may be implemented through the use of ODR or CADR, but need not be: an arbitration that is conducted with all parties and the arbitrator present at a particular location is ADR, but not ODR or CADR. ODR is a technique that is typically used to facilitate an ADR or CADR method, by allowing dispute resolution to take place with the parties located at a distance from each other. ODR might also serve as a component of traditional adjudication, such as by allowing testimony to be gathered or presented at a distance. CADR is a type of ADR that is particularly well suited to play a role in ODR.

It is also important to recognize that none of these techniques is limited to the resolution of disputes engendered online. ADR has probably always existed in some form or another, and certainly predates the existence of courts. ADR is widely hailed as a necessary concomitant to online commerce, but at present, with a few exceptions (notably domain name disputes), ADR is no more prevalent in resolving online transactions than in resolving disputes arising from any other type of distance contracting. ODR has been used experimentally in efforts to resolve online disputes, but its most successful application to date has been in settling ordinary disputes over insurance claims. The same is true of CADR.

C. ALTERNATIVE DISPUTE RESOLUTION AND ELECTRONIC COMMERCE

There are several reasons why ADR may be thought to be particularly important to online commerce.

First, most online transactions are between parties who are located at some geographical distance from each other. Traditional judicial approaches to resolving disputes, which require the parties to appear before a decisionmaker, entail travel expenses that make such approaches economically infeasible in the case of typical low-value consumer transactions. This consideration is, of course, equally applicable to distance transactions carried out through other means of communication, such as telemarketing, catalogue sales, or direct mail.

Second, online commerce offers the potential for greatly increasing the volume of international business-to-consumer ("B2C") transactions. Traditional judicial approaches are especially ill-suited to resolving cross-border disputes. In addition to prohibitive travel costs, there are great uncertainties and difficulties involved in asserting jurisdiction over a party located outside the country in which the court is located, determining the applicable law, and enforcing judgments against parties located outside the jurisdiction. The need to deal with an unfamiliar legal system in what may be an unfamiliar language adds to the costs. At present, this consideration is of little practical concern, since international B2C transactions represent a very small proportion of online commerce. Yet perhaps the unresolved questions about enforcement are part of what is keeping the proportion small.

Third, those who engage in electronic commerce may be more open to nontraditional methods of dispute resolution, since after all they are engaging in a nontraditional mode of commerce. Their use of online communications makes it likely that they will be comfortable with engaging in dispute resolution at a distance, via ODR.

Fourth, many consumers are hesitant to engage in online commerce because they are unfamiliar with the vendor and view online transactions as risky. This is especially likely with online auctions, where the seller is typically an individual with no institutional interest in protecting his reputation. The availability of ADR may help consumers overcome this hesitation.

We must be careful to distinguish among different categories of online disputes, since some will be more susceptible than others to resolution via ADR, and a particular method of ADR may work better with one category of dispute than with another. For example, if a dispute arises in the course of a commercial transaction that the parties have entered voluntarily, arbitration or some other form of ADR can be specified in the contract before any dispute arises. But if there is no prior relationship between the parties, then ADR is available only if the parties agree, after the dispute arises, to submit to dispute resolution. At this point, the party complained against will have an incentive not to agree to ADR, knowing that if traditional adjudication is the complainant's only option she is less likely to proceed. Yet a firm might prefer ADR to the risk of a class action brought by a determined consumer. ADR also has a better chance of succeeding if it is imposed by a third party, such as a payment intermediary or domain name authority. A party that has an interest in maintaining a good reputation will be more likely to submit to ADR than one who is in the business of fraud or who engages in a single transaction.

QUESTIONS FOR DISCUSSION

ADR coming into its own online? Do you think that ADR is more needed, or more likely to be successful, in the context of disputes arising in online commerce than it is in the case of other distance-selling techniques, such as telemarketing, direct mail, and catalogue sales? What about ODR?

II. ADR and ODR in Electronic Commerce

A. The Null Option: Voluntary Resolution of Disputes by the Parties Themselves

The vast majority of disputes that arise in commercial transactions are resolved by the parties themselves, without recourse to any formal dispute-resolution method. Most vendors are concerned about their reputation in the marketplace, and most purchasers are reasonable. Vendors frequently act on the principle that it is in their best interest to keep their customers happy, even if they have a legal right to do otherwise. Most customers are willing to accept a compromise if they feel the vendor is acting fairly.

In addition, most parties are averse to the time, expense, and uncertainties of engaging in dispute resolution procedures that involve a third party. They prefer to resolve their problems expeditiously, giving up the opportunity to do better by fighting longer.

The online medium in some ways interferes with the operation of these incentives to settle. Online communication technologies reduce the capital costs of going into business, making it possible for many small vendors to access a national and even international marketplace. New entrepreneurs and small businesses may not perceive as great an interest in maintaining a good reputation as do the established players, and may not have the financial resources to accept short-term costs in furtherance of long-term reputational interests. A business that is community-based will be well aware that a bad reputation will cause its customers to evaporate, while one with customers that are geographically widely distributed may believe it is less likely that dissatisfied customers will share their experiences with many potential future customers. A vendor that is located at some distance from the purchaser may feel itself insulated from any efforts by the purchaser to seek resolution of a dispute.

1. Reputational Incentives

On the other hand, the Internet creates some new avenues through which dissatisfied customers can make their voices heard in a way that affects a vendor's reputation. Internet newsgroups provide a forum where customers can post complaints against companies with which they have had a bad experience. Newsgroup postings are archived and searchable. A prospective customer who wishes to perform due diligence can search for the name of a company—whether the company does business online or offline—or a particular product and find out whether any complaints have been posted. One such search site is *Google Groups*, groups.google.com. There are message boards that are devoted to particular companies, and attract a range of commentary. For example, Yahoo! maintains a separate message board for each publicly traded company in the United States. *See Yahoo! Message Boards*, messages.yahoo.com/index.html. There are also websites that solicit consumer complaints, and forward them to the complained-against company, giving the company a chance to respond. *See Complaints.com*, www.complaints.com.

eBay, the largest online auctioneer, implements a system that enables users to rate their experiences with individual buyers and sellers. The ratings are tabulated to create a "Feedback Profile" for each rated buyer and seller. A prospective buyer or seller may consult an eBay user's Feedback Profile, and may decide to avoid doing business with that user if she has earned a poor rating. *See* eBay, *Feedback Forum*, pages.ebay.com/services/forum/ feedback.html.

QUESTIONS FOR DISCUSSION

BBB compared. The Better Business Bureau has for many years operated a system designed to encourage sellers to be responsive to their customers' complaints through operation of the reputational sanction. A purchaser who is dissatisfied with a company's handling of her issue may file a complaint with the BBB. The complaint is routed to the BBB office in the district where the company is located. The BBB forwards the complaint to the company. If the company is uncooperative, or has generated a pattern of unresolved complaints, the BBB records that experience in its file on the company. A consumer who is considering doing business with the company may check with the appropriate BBB, and find out whether the BBB has any negative record on file. Companies that value their reputations will have an incentive to keep their records with the BBB clean, by being responsive to consumer complaints.

How would you compare the BBB system with the mechanisms that the Internet offers for encouraging sellers to settle disputes voluntarily? Which mechanism do you think gives sellers the strongest incentive to keep their customers happy? How could online mechanisms be made to work more effectively?

2. Assisted Negotiation

Some ODR systems are designed to reduce the time and expense involved in negotiation, and to assist the parties in arriving at a settlement that maximizes the parties' welfare. One such system is computerized blind bidding. This system works best in situations where the parties agree that one owes money to the other, but disagree on the amount—such as in the case of insurance claims. In one implementation of this system, the insurance company enters the maximum amount it is willing to pay in each of three rounds of bidding. The claimant likewise enters the minimum amount he will accept in each round. These amounts are not disclosed to the other party. The site's proprietary software then calculates what each party should bid in the first round, to maximize the likelihood of reaching a settlement that is within each party's parameters. If the two bids in a round differ by less than a pre-established percentage, typically thirty percent, the site declares a settlement at a figure that splits the difference. If settlement is not reached after the first round, the software runs through a second and, if necessary, a third round. The claimant pays a fee ranging from $100 to $1,000, depending on the settlement amount, and the insurance company pays a separate fee established by the site. *See* CyberSettle, www.cybersettle.com.

To use SquareTrade, www.squaretrade.com, either buyer or seller initiates the process by filling out a Web-based form, describing the complaint. SquareTrade passes the complaint along to the other party, and the two parties have a chance to negotiate with each other in a password-protected online forum that is equipped with technology tools to facilitate discussion. If they need additional assistance, the parties can pay a fee to engage the participation of a SquareTrade mediator.

B. THIRD-PARTY VOLUNTARY APPROACHES

1. Arbitration

a. Enforceability of Contractual Arbitration Clauses

When making purchases of ordinary consumer goods, the average consumer concerns herself with only a few key terms: the price, the characteristics of the product or service purchased, and possibly warranty terms. But most consumer transactions are subject to an additional set of contractual terms that few consumers notice unless something goes wrong with the transaction. In electronic commerce transactions, these may take the form of clickwrap terms, which are displayed on the purchaser's monitor during the course of an online purchase, or shrinkwrap terms, which physically accompany a product when it is shipped, and which the purchaser sees for the first time (if at all) on receipt of the shipment. (Shrinkwrap and clickwrap agreements are discussed in Chapter 10, Part I(A), *supra*.)

One of the terms that frequently is included in clickwrap and shrinkwrap contracts is an arbitration clause: a contractual agreement to submit any dispute arising in connection with the transaction for resolution through binding arbitration. Are such clauses enforceable against a party that wishes to have a dispute resolved in some other forum? As a general matter, such terms are enforceable, but they may be invalidated on grounds of unconscionability. Thus, in *Brower v. Gateway 2000, Inc.*, 676 N.Y.S.2d 569 (N.Y.App.Div.1998), the held unconscionable an arbitration provision that required disputes relating to the purchase of a home computer to be arbitrated by the International Chamber of Commerce, which required the consumer to pay an advance fee of $4,000 to resolve a claim that is unlikely to be larger than $1,000. (This case is excerpted in Chapter 10, Part II(A), *supra*.)

EXTENSIONS

1. *Broad application of unconscionability doctrine.* In *Comb v. PayPal, Inc.*, 218 F.Supp.2d 1165 (N.D.Cal.2002), the court held an arbitration clause unenforceable for unconscionability on grounds that seemingly would apply to numerous arbitration clauses contained in standard-form online agreements. The clause appeared in the User Agreement to which all users of PayPal's online money-transfer service must agree via a clickwrap agreement. The court found the clause *procedurally* unconscionable because it was part of a contract of adhesion, that is, a "standardized contract, which, imposed and drafted by the party of superior bargaining strength, relegates to the subscribing party only the opportunity to adhere to the contract or reject it." The court found the clause *substantively* unconscionable based on several considerations: (1) the User Agreement was one-sided, since in the event of a dispute it allowed PayPal to freeze a customer's account at its sole discretion; (2) the arbitration clause prohibited customers from consolidating their claims against PayPal; (3) there was evidence that arbitration would cost a customer more than $5,000; and (4) the clause required that arbitration take place in Santa Clara County, California. In the course of its analysis the court emphasized that PayPal's customers are relatively unsophisticated, that the average dollar amount of transactions is very small ($55), and that by means of the User Agreement "PayPal appears to be attempting to insulate itself contractually from any meaningful challenge to its alleged practices."

For another case with similarly broad implications, see *McNulty v. H & R Block, Inc.*, 843 A.2d 1267 (Pa.Super.Ct.2004), which holds an arbitration clause unconscionable as applied to require a consumer with a $37 claim to pay a $50 filing fee: "Avoiding the public court system to save time and money is a laudable societal goal. But, avoiding the public court system in a way that effectively denies citizens access to resolving everyday societal disputes is unconscionable."

2. *Contrary view.* Other courts have held that the high costs of an arbitration proceeding do not render an arbitration clause unconscionable. *See, e.g., In re RealNetworks, Inc., Privacy Litigation*, 2000 WL 631341 (N.D.Ill.2000), excerpted in Chapter 10, Part II(A), *supra*.

3. *Claims implicating the public interest.* The California Supreme Court has held that a state legislature may, consistently with the Federal Arbitration Act, make certain types of claims nonarbitrable. In *Broughton v. CIGNA Healthplans*, 988 P.2d 67, 74 (Cal.1999), the court refused to compel arbitration of a claim brought under the California Consumer Legal Remedies Act, in which the plaintiff sought an injunction against a health insurer based on allegations of misleading advertising. The court held: "[W]hen the primary purpose and effect of a statutory remedy is not to compensate for an individual wrong but to prohibit and enjoin conduct injurious to the general public, i.e., when the plaintiff is acting authentically as a private attorney general, such a remedy may be inherently incompatible with arbitration." *See also Cruz v. PacifiCare Health Systems, Inc.*, 66 P.3d 1157 (Cal.2003) (extending *Broughton* to statutory claims for unfair competition and false advertising). In *Yun v. uBid, Inc.*, 2003 WL 21268053 (Cal.Ct.App.2003) (unpublished and non-citable), the court applied *Broughton* and *Cruz* to hold that a disgruntled purchaser from an online auction site need not arbitrate claims for unfair competition and false advertising, despite the purchaser's acceptance of the site's user agreement providing for arbitration of all claims. A federal district court in California has stated its disagreement with the *Broughton* doctrine, finding it inconsistent with the Federal Arbitration Act. *See Arriaga v. Cross Country Bank*, 163 F.Supp.2d 1189, 1197–1200 (S.D.Cal.2001). For discussion of the issues, see Thomas A. Manakides, Note, *Arbitration of "Public Injunctions": Clash Between State Statutory Remedies and the Federal Arbitration Act*, 76 S. CAL. L. REV. 433 (2003).

b. Arbitration via ODR

Arbitration has traditionally been a face-to-face, trial-like procedure. Can arbitration be conducted online? The first effort at online arbitration to receive widespread publicity was the Virtual Magistrate Project. The Project had its beginnings in 1995, when a working group conceived what it hoped would be a system for resolving disputes arising from online activities such as "messages, postings, and files allegedly involving copyright or trademark infringement, misappropriation of trade secrets, defamation, fraud, deceptive trade practices, inappropriate (obscene, lewd, or otherwise violative of system rules) materials, invasion of privacy, and other wrongful content." Arbitrations would take place via e-mail. The arbitrator, who would be selected from a pool by the Project's administrator, would normally render a decision within 72 hours. The Project organizers hoped that arbitral awards would be enforced by system operators, who would remove postings or deny online access, and that complaining parties would agree to be bound by the arbitrator's decision. *See* The Virtual Magistrate Project[SM], *Concept Paper* (July 24, 1996), www.vmag.org/docs/concept. html.

Although the Virtual Magistrate Project received a lot of attention, it was not successful in attracting cases. In fact, the Virtual Magistrate decided only a single case: a 1996 complaint by an individual who wanted America Online to remove an advertisement that offered five million e-mail addresses for sale, to be used for sending bulk unsolicited commercial e-mail messages. The Virtual Magistrate ruled in favor of the complainant, determining that AOL should remove the offending item. This case did not do much to prove Virtual Magistrate's concept, as it had several odd features. First, the real party in interest, who posted the advertisement, did not participate. Second, since sending unsolicited commercial e-mail violated AOL's Terms of Service, and is generally regarded by Internet service providers as a scourge, AOL most likely would have been more than happy to remove the posting without the intervention of an arbitrator. Third, it turned out that the advertisement in question was not a bulletin board posting, but was rather an unsolicited commercial e-mail message itself, making it both impossible and unnecessary for AOL to implement the decision. *See* Alejandro E. Almaguer & Roland W. Baggott III, Note & Comment, *Shaping New Legal Frontiers: Dispute Resolution for the Internet*, 13 OHIO ST. J. ON DISP. RESOL. 711, 727–733 (1998).

Another model for conducting online arbitration is operated by iCourthouse, www.i-courthouse.com. Parties to a dispute first agree contractually to submit their dispute to iCourthouse, and to be bound by the results. Jurors are volunteers, and are selected from a pool consisting of those who register at the site to become iCourthouse members. The jury selection procedure is unusual: "Each party may invite persons to serve as jurors on a case. There is no limit on the number of invitations that can be issued. . . . Persons invited to serve as juror on a case may forward the invitation to others." iCourthouse Rules of Procedure, Rule 6, www.i-courthouse.com/main.taf?area1_id=front&area2_id=rulesofproc. Members may also browse the pending cases and select those on which they wish to serve as jurors. Each party submits evidence and argument via an online "trial book," which is accessible to the other party and the jurors. The jurors can address questions to the parties, and the questions and answers become part of the trial book. Each juror renders a verdict, and if the verdict is in favor of the plaintiff makes an award of damages. The parties agree beforehand how the verdict will be interpreted: whether the plaintiff prevails with a simple majority vote, or whether a supermajority is required, and whether the award is the median of all the jurors' awards or some other measure. iCourthouse does not charge a fee for its standard online arbitration service.

QUESTIONS FOR DISCUSSION

1. *Submitting to ADR.* What would motivate a respondent who is charged with some sort of tortious conduct using online communications to submit to an online arbitration system? Are cases involving tortious conduct more or less likely to come before an arbitrator than cases involving breach of contract? How would you characterize the kinds of disputes the Virtual Magistrate Project was designed to resolve?

2. *Enforcement of awards.* How effective is the enforcement mechanism contemplated in the Virtual Magistrate Project?

2. Mediation

Online technologies can enable mediation of disputes between parties that are geographically separated, while avoiding the time and expense involved in bringing all the parties together in the same room. Various services offer trained mediators who communicate with the disputants via e-mail, instant messaging, videoconferencing, chat, and bulletin board postings, and technology tools that allow private caucuses as well as plenary conversations. Fee structures vary, and may involve a flat fee, an hourly rate, a percentage of the settlement amount, or some combination.

The Online Ombuds Office, a service of the Center for Information Technology and Dispute Resolution at the University of Massachusetts, www.odr.info, operated a month-long pilot project in 1999 to apply online mediation techniques to disputes arising from transactions conducted through eBay, the online auction site. Using e-mail to communicate with the parties, the mediator brought about a successful result in 46% of the 108 completed mediations. The most common complaint, and the one that proved easiest to resolve, was for nondelivery of goods. The project leaders found the absence of face-to-face meetings to be a significant hindrance to mediation, and looked forward to the development of more flexible online communications technologies and videoconferencing to facilitate online mediation. For a discussion of the project, see Ethan Katsh, Janet Rifkin, & Alan Gaitenby, *E-Commerce, E-Disputes, and E-Dispute Resolution: In the Shadow of "Ebay Law,"* 15 OHIO ST. J. ON DISP. RESOL. 705 (2000).

QUESTIONS FOR DISCUSSION

Telephone mediation. If meeting face-to-face or videoconferencing is not possible, people can still communicate at a distance with telephone conference calls. What are the advantages and disadvantages of online mediation compared with mediation conducted by telephone?

C. THIRD-PARTY STRUCTURAL APPROACHES

In the voluntary approaches to dispute resolution discussed above, the parties themselves decide how to go about resolving their dispute, either through negotiation, submitting the dispute to an arbitrator, or engaging the services of a mediator. The complained-against party (the "respondent") generally can decline to engage in such processes, and be subject only to the reputational sanction. A structural approach to dispute resolution, by contrast, is one that the respondent cannot simply ignore, because it is implemented by a third party that has something the respondent wants, and therefore is in a position to impose conditions on the availability of that good.

1. Uniform Domain Name Dispute Resolution Policy

The Uniform Domain Name Dispute Resolution Policy ("UDRP"), promulgated by the Internet Corporation for Assigned Names and Numbers ("ICANN"), discussed in Chapter 3, Part IV, *supra*, is a structural approach that is targeted at a narrow but very important range of disputes: claims that a domain name has been registered and is being used in bad faith, in violation of the complainant's trademark rights. Registrants of names in the commercial global top-level domains are subject to the policy whether they like it or not, because ICANN requires all registrars to impose it contractually as a condition of registering a domain name.

> Every domain name registrar accredited by ICANN must incorporate the UDRP into each individual domain name registration agreement. *See* UDRP, § 1. In effect, the UDRP binds registrants by virtue of their contracts with registrars, such as Network Solutions, Inc., "to submit" to "mandatory administrative proceedings" initiated by third-party "complainants." UDRP, § 4. The scope of such UDRP proceedings is limited to claims of "abusive" registrations of Inter-

net domain names. The UDRP covers no other disputes. UDRP, § 5. Complainants in UDRP proceedings must prove that the disputed "domain name is identical or confusingly similar to a trademark or service mark in which the complainant has rights," that the registrant has "no rights or legitimate interests in respect of the domain name," and that the domain name "has been registered and is being used in bad faith." UDRP, § 4(a). The UDRP identifies badges of "bad faith" and grounds for demonstrating a registrant's "rights and legitimate interests" in a domain name. UDRP, § 4(b)–(c).

Complainants initiate UDRP proceedings directly with a dispute resolution service "provider" designated by ICANN.[2] *See* UDRP Rules, § 3. The UDRP and the UDRP Rules prescribe detailed procedures for appointing either a solo arbitrator or a three-member panel to conduct the inquiry. The UDRP is fashioned as an "online" procedure administered via the Internet.[3] Although a panel may opt in exceptional cases to hold live or telephonic hearings, it is expected to base its decision on "the statements and documents submitted" in accordance with the UDRP, the UDRP Rules, and any "rules and principles of law that it deems applicable." UDRP Rules, §§ 13, 15(a). In the absence of "exceptional circumstances," a panel is expected to issue its decision within fourteen days of its appointment. UDRP Rules, § 15(b).

If the panel rules in the complainant's favor, the only available remedy is for the registrar to cancel the domain name registration or transfer it to the complainant. UDRP, § 4(i). A registrar may automatically implement a UDRP panel decision after ten days unless the aggrieved registrant notifies the registrar within this ten day period that it has "commenced a lawsuit against the complainant in a jurisdiction to which the complainant has submitted" as required by the UDRP Rules. *See* UDRP, § 4(k); UDRP Rules, § 5(e). Upon such notification, the registrar "will take no further action" until it receives "satisfactory" evidence of the resolution of the dispute, the dismissal or withdrawal of the lawsuit, or a court order that the registrant does "not have the right to continue using" the domain name. UDRP, § 4(k).

Parisi v. Netlearning, Inc., 139 F.Supp.2d 745, 747–48 (E.D.Va.2001).

The Federal Arbitration Act ("FAA") requires a court to enter judgment on an arbitral award, and sharply limits the circumstances under which an award may be vacated or modified. 9 U.S.C. §§ 9–12. In *Parisi v. Netlearning, supra*, the court held that the FAA does not prevent the losing party in a UDRP proceeding from relitigating ownership of the domain name in federal district court under the Anticybersquatting Consumer Protection Act ("ACPA"), 15 U.S.C. § 1125(d) (discussed in Chapter 3, Part II, *supra*). The court reasoned that the UDRP itself contemplates relitigation at the losing party's option, and that the parties to a proceeding have not agreed to entry of judgment on a UDRP award. For an evaluation of the UDRP process, see Laurence R. Helfer & Graeme B. Dinwoodie, *Designing Non-National Systems: The Case of the Uniform Domain Name Dispute Resolution Policy*, 43 WM. & MARY L. REV. 141 (2001), excerpted in Chapter 3, Part IV, *supra*.

---

[2] [At this writing, four providers are accredited to handle domain-name disputes: the Asian Domain Name Dispute Resolution Centre, CPR Institute for Dispute Resolution, National Arbitration Forum, and World Intellectual Property Organization. *See* ICANN, *Approved Providers for Uniform Domain-Name Dispute-Resolution Policy*, www.icann.org/dndr/udrp/approved-providers.htm.—Eds.]

[3] [In fact, the UDRP requires parties to submit documents both electronically and in hard copy. *See* Rules for Uniform Domain Name Dispute Resolution Policy §§ 3 & 5.—Eds.]

In *Dluhos v. Strasberg*, 321 F.3d 365 (3d Cir.2003), the Court of Appeals held that a UDRP proceeding is not an arbitration for purposes of the Federal Arbitration Act, making the FAA's extremely narrow standard of review inapplicable. It also held that the ACPA allows a domain name registrant who has lost a UDRP proceeding to bring an action for a declaration that he is not in violation of the ACPA, and for an injunction requiring restoration of the domain name.

2. Third-Party Seal Programs

A seal is a distinctive mark, attached to or associated with a product, service, or vendor, that is intended to convey that the item or entity to which it pertains has certain desirable characteristics. As discussed in Chapter 6, Part V(B), *supra*, seals are used to certify that a website adheres to specified privacy policies. They may also be used to vouch for other aspects of an online seller's performance, such as its customer satisfaction and dispute-resolution policies.

The BBBOnLine Reliability Program makes use of such a seal. The Better Business Bureau licenses its seal to sellers that agree to abide by a set of conditions, which include a system for resolving disputes with consumers. The seller must agree to participate in binding arbitration under the BBB rules of arbitration, if the consumer selects that option, or to participate in a nonbinding informal dispute-resolution process. Under the latter, the parties present their positions to a neutral hearing officer, who makes a recommendation on how the dispute should be resolved. *See* BBBOnLine, *Dispute Resolution*, www.bbbonline.org/reliability/dr.asp.

Enforcement of seal programs is considerably less airtight than the UDRP enforcement scheme. If the seal program operator finds that a website licensee has failed to abide by the program requirements, it can require the website to come into compliance, or else lose the right to display the seal. If the website continues to display the seal despite losing its license to do so, the seal owner can proceed against the site with a trademark infringement action, which can be a costly and extended operation.

3. Payment Intermediaries: Chargebacks

Since cash cannot be transmitted across the network, nearly all sellers that offer goods online are dependent on some payment intermediary. While individual sellers, such as those who sell through online auctions, frequently are paid with a check sent in the mail, most institutional sellers that transact business online, as well as via telemarketing or otherwise at a distance, are highly dependent on credit cards. (For a discussion of methods of paying for transactions in Internet commerce, see Chapter 15, *infra*.)

Federal law gives credit card holders the right to dispute charges that appear on their bill, and prescribes a procedure that the card issuer must follow. The purchaser initiates the process by submitting a written complaint to the issuer, which must acknowledge the complaint in writing within 30 days after receiving it. The issuer then has two billing cycles, up to a maximum of 90 days, in which to conduct an investigation and resolve the dispute. The issuer normally does so by contacting the merchant that put through the charge, and asking for justification for the charge. For example, if the purchaser claims that an item she ordered was not delivered, the issuer may ask the merchant for evidence such as a signed delivery receipt obtained by United Parcel Service or FedEx. If the issuer finds that the purchaser's complaint is valid, it must remove the charge. Complaints within the scope of this dispute-resolution procedure include claims that a charge appearing on the bill was not authorized; a charge was authorized but the amount of the charge is wrong; a charge is for goods or services that the purchaser did not accept, or were not delivered as agreed; and math errors. *See* Fair Credit Billing Act, 15 U.S.C. § 1666; Regulation Z, 12 C.F.R. § 226.13.

Some credit card networks provide more protection to purchasers than required by the legal rules applying to disputed charges. The major U.S. credit card networks apply U.S. chargeback rules to international transactions, though they are not legally required to do so. One credit card company also has special policies applying to online sales. For goods that are to be delivered physically to the recipient's address, the company will charge back the purchase if the goods are not signed for as received by the cardmember or an authorized representative. For goods to be delivered electronically, it will charge back the purchase automatically upon complaint by the recipient, without even allowing the merchant to present its side of the story.

QUESTIONS FOR DISCUSSION

Extent of chargebacks. Why would credit card networks extend chargeback rights beyond the requirements of law? Why would a credit card company decide to be especially pro-consumer in handling of chargebacks arising from online sales?

D. UNILATERAL APPROACHES

Under the approaches discussed above, the parties to a dispute seek to resolve it either through direct communication with each other or with the involvement of a mediator or arbitrator. There are other approaches through which a dissatisfied party may, without any consultation with the other party, achieve the desired remedy through her own efforts.

1. Electronic Self-Help

A software or data vendor may be in a position to implement electronic self-help in case of a dispute with the purchaser. Self-help in this context involves reaching across the network to disable software residing on the purchaser's computer, or cutting off the purchaser's access to data located on the vendor's server.

Unlike negotiation and mediation, the vendor need not consult with the purchaser before taking this action, and unlike arbitration she needs no assistance or coercive authority from any third party. The status of electronic self-help under current law is not entirely clear, but it may well be permissible as long as the contract governing the sales transaction provides for it.

2. DMCA Notice-and-Takedown Provision

Title II of the Digital Millennium Copyright Act, 17 U.S.C. § 512, creates a notice-and-takedown regime that gives copyright owners a broad authority to resolve unilaterally disputes about whether materials made available online infringe their copyrights. Under this regime, the copyright owner sends a notice to an Internet service provider, stating that specified materials made available through the ISP's facilities infringe the copyright, and demanding that they be removed. If the ISP complies, it is insulated from monetary liability for infringement. If the ISP does not comply, it may be liable for infringement. Since the ISP is unlikely to have a vested interest in keeping the challenged content available, it has a strong incentive to take down the challenged material. For a more detailed discussion of Section 512, see Chapter 7, Part V(B)(2), *supra.*

EXTENSIONS

Who bears the costs? All forms of ADR entail some cost. Some procedures require the involvement of third parties who charge a fee for their services: mediators, arbitrators, and online dispute resolution services.[4] The allocation of these fees between the disputants may be determined by the terms of an arbitration clause, the rules of the arbitration provider specified in the arbitration clause, or a post-transaction agreement between the parties. For example, the Commercial Arbitration Rules of the American Arbitration Association provide: "The expenses of witnesses for either side shall be paid by the party producing such witnesses. All other expenses of the arbitration, including required travel and other expenses of the arbitrator, AAA representatives, and any witness and the cost of any proof produced at the direct request of the arbitrator, shall be borne equally by the parties, unless they agree otherwise or unless the arbitrator in the award assesses such expenses or any part thereof against any specified party or parties." American Arbitration Association, *Commercial Arbitration Rules and Mediation Procedures*, R–50, www.adr.org. The Uniform Domain Name Dispute Resolution Policy, on the other hand, specifies that the complaining party pays the arbitrator's fee, unless the respondent demands a three-arbitrator panel, in which case the parties split the fees. ICANN, *Uniform Domain Name Dispute Resolution Policy* § 4(g), www.icann.org/dndr/udrp/policy.htm.

Some ADR procedures spread their costs throughout the system, rather than charging an incremental fee to parties that invoke the procedure. For example, a credit card holder pays no incremental fee to invoke a chargeback. The costs of administering the chargeback system are borne by the card issuers, who may pass those costs on to merchants in the form of higher fees. Depending on market conditions, merchants may in turn pass the costs on to consumers, in the form of higher prices for the goods they sell.[5] The resulting cost-spreading is a form of insurance: everybody pays a little bit more for the right to access the chargeback system, regardless of whether they actually use it.

Similarly, seal programs and merchant aggregator programs place the costs on all participating merchants. This type of cost-spreading yields a net gain, on the assumption that the aggregate cost to the system is less than the aggregate benefits resulting from increased consumer confidence, which leads to a broader marketplace and easier entrance for new market participants.

What are the pros and cons of insurance-type cost-spreading systems for financing dispute resolution, and pay-per-use systems?

---

[4] The parties may incur additional costs, such as their own time, counsel fees, and travel and witness costs. These costs may be substantial in comparison with the costs of the third-party facilitator. The potential cost-effectiveness of ADR, in comparison with judicial processes, comes largely from the possibility of doing without counsel, or at least reducing the cost of counsel as a result of simplified procedures. ODR also offers a chance to eliminate travel costs.

[5] Merchants must also absorb the costs of reversing transactions and refunding the purchase price in cases where the chargeback is sustained.

QUESTIONS FOR DISCUSSION

1. *Consumer-to-consumer transactions.* In certain types of online commercial transactions, including most prominently sales through online auction sites, both parties are typically individuals. This scenario is less often seen in distance transactions accomplished through other means of communication, where normally the seller is a business entity. When both parties to a transaction are individuals, they are less likely to have agreed in advance of the transaction to use an ADR mechanism for resolving any disputes. What mechanisms might be available for implementing ADR to resolve disputes in this context?

2. *The perils of privatization.* One commentator observes that all may not be well in ADR-land, pointing out some potential problems with privatized methods of dispute resolution:

> If left unchecked, these privatized systems and their probable technological extensions will have several consequences for the power of courts as institutions and for due process to litigants. First, they result in privatized justice. These processes take place independently, with little or no participation or sanction from government actors. Rather, private or even automated decision makers have sole power to control the rights of the parties. Second, the processes shift procedural advantage to certain powerful players. Rules can be designed to promote desired outcomes. Interim relief can be obtained without the need to prove irreparable injury or probable success on the merits and without a balancing of interests. Third, the mechanisms do not protect certain traditional components of due process in dispute resolution. Aspects of litigation such as affordable access to justice, notice, discovery, collective action, live hearings, confrontation of witnesses, a neutral decision maker, and a transparent process may be absent from these privatized processes. Fourth, by eliminating the courts as the arbiters of disputes, these processes decrease the power of government to shape and enforce substantive law. The "law" becomes what is specified in the contract or programmed into the software, and courts lose the ability to enforce mandatory rules and to subject contractual "law" to the needs of public policy.

Elizabeth G. Thornburg, *Going Private: Technology, Due Process, and Internet Dispute Resolution*, 34 U.C. DAVIS L. REV. 151, 154 (2000). Do these considerations call into question the widely accepted policy in favor of promoting ADR to settle disputes?

CHAPTER FIFTEEN
ELECTRONIC PAYMENT SYSTEMS

Every commercial transaction, whether conducted online or in the brick-and-mortar world, involves an exchange of value for some good or service. The presentation of this value to the seller is called a payment, which may be defined as " '(1) a delivery, (2) by the debtor, or his representative, (3) to the creditor or his representative, (4) of money or something accepted by the creditor as the equivalent thereof, (5) with the intention on the part of the debtor to pay the debt in whole or in part, and (6) accepted as payment by the creditor.' " *Sizemore v. E. T. Barwick Industries, Inc.,* 465 S.W.2d 873, 875 (Tenn.1971) (quoting *Sullivan v. Tigert*, 1 Tenn.App. 262 (1925)).

While cash and checks are popular methods of payment in physical point-of-sale transactions, neither is optimal for use in Internet commerce. Payment by these methods requires physical transfer of the medium of payment (banknotes or paper checks) by postal mail or some other conveyance, which cannot take place instantaneously. The delay entailed by this physical transfer, and possibly an additional delay if the seller is unwilling to ship the purchase until the check clears, would be intolerable for most types of consumer purchases in Internet commerce. In addition, it is risky to send currency by mail. While new mechanisms for making online payments have been developed, these mechanisms have not yet had a significant impact in the online marketplace—other than in the narrow, but important, area of online auctions. As a result, the payment methods most commonly used in online consumer transactions are the familiar credit and debit cards.

The use of electronic payment methods in consumer transactions is steadily increasing both here and abroad. The causes of this increase include the "development of interoperability standards among different card networks" as well as new network arrangements that "have enabled providers to share the initial costs of payment card infrastructures and given them a platform for developing new procedures and instruments." COMMITTEE ON PAYMENT AND SETTLEMENT SYSTEMS, RETAIL PAYMENTS IN SELECTED COUNTRIES: A COMPARATIVE STUDY § 4.3 (1999). An example of the latter is the use of the Automated Teller Machine ("ATM") network to process payments made by swiping a debit card through a point-of-sale card reader terminal.

In this chapter, we will survey the principal existing and emerging electronic payment systems that may be used to effect payment over the Internet. After presenting background information on money and payment systems, we continue with a discussion of the more familiar electronic payment methods, namely credit and debit cards. We then proceed to a discussion of emerging payment mechanisms, including person-to-person systems, escrow services, micropayments, stored-value cards, electronic checks, and billing to another account.

I. BACKGROUND: THE MONETARY SYSTEM AND THE DEVELOPMENT OF ELECTRONIC MONEY

David D. Friedman & Kerry L. Macintosh, *The Cash of the Twenty-First Century*
17 SANTA CLARA COMPUTER & HIGH TECH. L.J. 273 (2001).

I. Introduction

We live in a world of monopoly monies—in two senses. First, most trade takes place between people who are physically close to each other; thus, money is usually a geographic monopoly. Second, nations have found it profitable to seize control over the money presses. As a result, governments are the primary issuers of money. The end result is familiar to us all: Americans use dollars, Japanese use yen, the British use pounds and so forth.

As we move into the twenty-first century, on-line commerce and electronic money will grow in importance. These and other technological developments will undermine money monopolies and increase the likelihood that systems of competing monies—both public and private—will emerge.

. . .

II. The Functions of Money

Money serves three basic functions: medium of exchange, unit of account and store of value.

Consider first the primary function of money—as a medium of exchange—a way of avoiding the problems of barter. Suppose a contractor who builds houses wants to buy food. In a world without money, he must find someone who wants a house and has food—a lot of food, perhaps a year's worth or more—to offer in exchange. If a law professor wants a car, she must find someone who wants to learn law and has a car to give in exchange. This double coincidence problem—the problem of finding someone who has what you want, and wants what you have—makes barter a clumsy form of trade, especially in a complicated society with a wide variety of goods and services.

Money solves the double coincidence problem because it is a single good that everyone will accept in exchange for goods or services. Thus, a contractor or law professor can sell services to one person and use the money to buy food or a car from someone else.

. . .

The second function of money is as a unit of account, a way of stating and comparing prices and values. Here again, monopoly monies have had an advantage until now, since it is easier to compare the prices charged by alternative sellers if they are all expressed in the same units. For example, there is some evidence that the introduction of the Euro is reducing price variance across European markets by making comparison-shopping easier between sellers located in different countries.

. . .

Money's third and final function is as a store of value. Few people in a modern society hold very much of their wealth as currency since other financial assets pay interest and currency does not. However, in order to use money as a medium of exchange, we must hold some. Moreover, many other financial assets we hold are debts (e.g., bank accounts, or promissory notes) that can be repaid with money. If debtors repay us with devalued currency, our wealth is diminished.

. . .

IV. Electronic Money and On-line Commerce

Making payments by physically transferring objects, whether gold coins or paper currency, works reasonably well in the physical world, but it encounters serious problems in on-line commerce. There is no practical way to pass a twenty-dollar bill through a modem. Instead, we must transact using intangible claims to payment.

Credit cards allow us to do this. Unfortunately, credit cards pose certain disadvantages for sellers and buyers alike. On every transaction, sellers must pay percentage fees that erode their profit margins. Sellers also face the risk that buyers may attempt to reverse charges after receiving goods or services. Meanwhile, buyers who transmit credit card numbers on-line risk capture of information by interlopers. Even though federal law strictly caps liability for unauthorized charges, a stolen number can give a criminal the foothold he or she needs to commit identity theft. Finally, and perhaps most significantly, credit card transactions leave a paper trail that can result in a loss of privacy for sellers or buyers.

Electronic money can provide the on-line economy with an alternative payment system. A government—or a private company—can issue coins or notes in the form of electronic information. Each coin or note represents a claim against the issuer and can be redeemed in exchange for traditional money (e.g., dollars), commodities (e.g., gold) or any other agreed item of value.

Since electronic money is just information, geographical constraints become irrelevant. It is just as easy to transmit electronic cash to someone on the other side of the world as to someone next door. Moreover, once electronic money is loaded onto the computer chips embedded in "smart" cards, it can be used in real as well as virtual space.

In a world of electronic money, sellers need not fear that buyers might reverse credit card charges after goods have been shipped or services received. Providers of online services can charge for access as it occurs, using automated transaction systems. Buyers can trade free of the worry that credit card numbers may be stolen.

Moreover, unlike credit cards, which leave a paper trail, electronic money can be designed to provide traders with the anonymity they crave. Imagine an electronic currency that is encrypted so securely that the parties—seller, buyer and issuer—cannot identify each other. Such fully anonymous electronic cash surpasses the privacy obtained with paper bills since a properly designed set of encryption protocols do not allow the equivalent of serial number tracing.

Given the advantages, it seems likely that one or more electronic currencies will come into use for online transactions, and having done so, will also become available for real space transactions through payment technologies such as smart cards. But will the currencies be monopolies? And if so, within what boundaries? Will the issuers of the currencies be governments or is the time ripe for private companies to enter the money business?

V. How Will Technology Affect Money?

The answers to these questions depend on technology. To explain why, we discuss four factors: (1) the Internet and online commerce; (2) computers that can perform complex calculations; (3) electronic currency that is easy to create, manage and redeem and, (4) increased bandwidth leading to real-time audio and video. Each factor will play a role in determining the future of money.

The Internet makes on-line commerce possible and on-line commerce makes it easy to trade with people who are far away. As a result, geography and nationality are becoming less important to trade and traders.

As discussed above, our current system of monopoly monies is based on the premise that most trade takes place within geographic and national boundaries. On-line commerce attacks that premise at its core. Americans trade, not necessarily with other Americans, but with the Japanese, who, in turn, trade with the British and so forth.

Providing electronic money for the on-line environment is a challenge. What medium of exchange will be widely accepted within a global trading community? What unit of account will allow global traders to compare prices with ease and confidence?

In the absence of effective world government, it is hard to imagine who might issue a global monopoly money. The European Union encountered substantial economic and political difficulties in adopting the Euro, even though its member states had similar economies and cultures. Surely, the United Nations could not manage the same feat for the entire world. Many—perhaps most—nations would balk at granting the United Nations the power to fund activities through the (electronic) printing press and inflation.

A different solution seems likely in the short term. Nations are well aware that they earn seigniorage—that is, interest—on coins and paper bills in circulation. Thus, as trade goes electronic, nations will have ample incentive to issue their own monopoly monies in electronic form.

Once the Internet is flooded with alternative national monies, traders may find that exchanging from one to another is inefficient. Over time, they may come to prefer one currency that seems to enjoy the widest acceptance and greatest stability. Eventually, that one currency will emerge as the de facto global monopoly money. For example, dollars may come to dominate on-line commerce just as English has become the language of international trade, travel, journalism and diplomacy.

This development will threaten the seigniorage income and national prestige of other countries. Governments may respond by enacting laws to prevent citizens from using electronic money other than their own. But such restrictions will be difficult to enforce in a world of competing monies and strong encryption.

However, traders from other countries may also resist the electronic dollar. At best, they may view the electronic dollar as an offensive form of cultural imperialism; at worst, they may find themselves powerless to intervene, as the United States uses its currency to advance its own economic and political agenda.

To get around such problems, traders may shift to a system of competing currencies based on the same commodity. By providing a common unit of account, such a system may obviate the need for a common medium of exchange. To illustrate, suppose multiple issuers (whether public or private) produce electronic cash using gold as the base commodity. The currency of reliable issuers will exchange at par—one Microsoft gold unit for one Netscape gold unit, for example. The currency of unreliable issuers (those unwilling or unable to redeem their own currency) will trade at a discount. Monies trading at a discount will be less convenient and valuable, and will go out of use rapidly.

Computer technology makes it easier to convert from one unit of account to another. Electronic money is easy to store and transmit, reducing the cost of exchange. These developments will lessen the need for money monopolies, whether public or private.

Thus far, we have assumed that a common medium of exchange and unit of account will tend to be the most efficient form of money for the Internet. In other words, we have assumed money monopolies will continue to exist.

However, another path is possible if computers eliminate or reduce the transaction costs of making conversions among different units of account.

Consider how a currency-transparent browser may work in the future. A Japanese seller lists the prices of the goods he sells in yen on his web page. A buyer in the United States accesses the page, seeking information about goods and prices. His browser, noting that the prices are in yen, automatically contacts the website of his bank, checks the current exchange rate and makes the calculation from yen to dollars. In other words, the seller writes his prices in yen, but the buyer reads them in dollars—thus overcoming the unit of account problem.

If our buyer decides to make the purchase, he still must convert his dollars to electronic yen—the requested medium of exchange. His bank will charge for this service. However, since it is relatively easy to store and transmit electronic information, the cost of operating an exchange service for electronic money should be much lower than the cost of running an exchange service for paper money. Presumably, the bank will react by lowering the exchange fee charged to the buyer. A drop in exchange fees may reduce the pressure to use a common medium of exchange.

In this example, both buyer and seller are using government monies. This is the most likely scenario, given that most transactions still take place in real space using paper money. If a consumer has to keep paper dollars in her pocket for everyday purchases, she may be more likely to prefer electronic dollars for on-line purchases.

However, as the years go by, more and more real space transactions will take place using smart cards and other electronic payment systems. This raises the possibility that Americans may one day hold electronic yen for use on-line—and in America.

More radically, [p]rivate companies may begin to issue electronic currencies that are based on different commodity standards. Monies designed for general use will compete directly with each other for market share. Meanwhile, niche currencies will circulate within particular trades. For example, if an on-line community trades primarily in software, it may prefer currency that maintains a stable purchasing power relative to software.

In either case, private companies will obtain a competitive edge by designing their monies for anonymous use. Many traders will prefer currencies that protect against the prying eyes of both private parties and government officials.

. . .

How might governments react to such monetary proliferation? As explained above, some may ban competing monies in an effort to protect seigniorage and sovereignty. Moreover, governments are likely to react badly to anonymous monies that make it harder for them to monitor compliance with tax, immigration, employment or other laws that affect trade. Realistically, however, the very feature that makes such monies threatening—encryption—may make it impossible for governments to enforce the ban.

Technology will create conditions that tend to support monetary stability. First, ease of entry into the business of issuing electronic money will promote a healthy competition. Second, improved communication will make it easier to check the reputation of the issuer. Third, the ability to return electronic money for redemption at the speed of light will reduce the ability of issuers to engage successfully in hyperinflationary schemes. As a result of these technological developments, private monies will become more attractive to the public.

Let's return to the third function of money: a store of value. People prefer monies that are stable. As evidence of this, consider what happens in countries where the official local currency is inflated. Traders begin to use foreign money as their preferred medium of exchange. Efforts to outlaw foreign money are often ineffective and tend to create black markets. In some cases, foreign money emerges as a de facto unit of account. For example, at one time it was common for long-term rentals in Israel to be priced in dollars rather than Israeli pounds.

A common charge leveled against the idea of private monies is that they will not be stable. Private companies will enrich themselves by accepting value from customers and then inflating the money supply.

One way to reduce this risk is through competition among issuers. . . . This is how private banks established a stable monetary and banking system in Scotland during the eighteenth century.

Effective competition is more likely in a world of electronic money for two reasons. First, entry into the business is relatively easy and inexpensive. Issuers need not invest in gold or manage bulky paper bills. Second, on-line technology drastically reduces the cost of information and communication. A user on one side of the globe can check the reputation of an issuer on the other side (or have an intelligent software agent check it for him in a fraction of a second while deciding whether to accept a proffered payment).

Another way to reduce the risk of inflation is through contract. An issuer can promise to redeem its money at a minimum level of value expressed in commodities or other currencies. Here again, technology makes the contractual solution work better. If an issuer begins to inflate its electronic money, disgruntled users can return the money for redemption at the speed of light.

Increased bandwidth may lead to the rise of virtual communities with their own idiosyncratic currencies.

As bandwidth increases, and most Internet users gain access to real-time audio and video, we may witness the emergence of virtual communities defined by common interests or beliefs. Given the nature of the Internet, these virtual communities will have members from a variety of different countries. Rather than employ the official currency of any one nation, members may prefer to invent their own electronic money for circulation only within the community. Use of the idiosyncratic currency will help the community to form, express and maintain its own identity. Moreover, by encouraging members to trade with each other, the currency will build solidarity.

VI. Five Possible Futures for Money

If the foregoing arguments are correct, money faces five possible futures:

1. A world with the same monopoly monies we have now, but in electronic form. Governments will enact laws outlawing the use of alternative currencies in an effort to protect seigniorage revenues, bolster national prestige and control the economic lives of their citizens. However, these laws will be hard to enforce.

2. A world with a single electronic money for on-line commerce. This outcome could be difficult to achieve in the absence of effective world government. However, in a competition among different nations, one currency—say, the electronic dollar—may emerge as the victor. The resulting unitary system will be very efficient, but may be perceived as culturally and economically oppressive.

3. A world with a single commodity base for a system of competing electronic monies. This system combines the benefits of competition with the simplicity of a common standard. Its disadvantage is that the single standard may not be the right one—and could be hard to change.

4. A world of multiple competing currencies, some public and some private, with a variety of different bases, exchanging at changing rates. The optimal number of currencies may depend on how effective computers are at reducing or eliminating the costs of conversion and exchange. This system will promote competition not only among monies, but also among monetary standards. If for some

reason one standard turns out to have advantages over another, issuers can shift accordingly.

5. A world with multiple currencies and standards, each standard being identified with a virtual community. This outcome is more likely if improved bandwidth fosters the development of strong virtual communities.

Governments anxious to preserve their powers and prerogatives may push for outcome one. Powerful nations or groups of nations, like the United States or the European Union, may push for outcome two. However, we conclude that technological developments, along with the self-interest of users and enforcement difficulties, are going to push us towards outcomes three and four, or possibly, given the appropriate social developments, outcome five.

BOARD OF GOVERNORS OF THE FEDERAL RESERVE SYSTEM, REPORT TO THE CONGRESS ON THE APPLICATION OF THE ELECTRONIC FUND TRANSFER ACT TO ELECTRONIC STORED-VALUE PRODUCTS (1997).

. . .

Risks in Consumer Retail Payments

The various retail payment mechanisms available to consumers in the United States are subject to numerous risks that could result in harm to the consumer. . . .

1. Loss of Instrument. Some types of payment instruments have value in and of themselves, in that they are exchangeable for value by any bearer or holder. A consumer who loses a bearer instrument will incur a direct financial loss. The primary example of a bearer instrument is a Federal Reserve note (currency), which is legal tender under federal law. 31 U.S.C. § 5103. If a consumer loses currency, the Federal Reserve Banks will not replace it. If currency is stolen, the consumer generally has no recourse outside of pursuing a civil or criminal action against the thief.

. . .

2. Unauthorized Use. Consumers also face the risk of financial loss due to unauthorized use of a payment instrument, which may or may not result from the instrument's being lost or stolen. Unauthorized use is a relatively common problem for several types of payment instruments, such as checks, debit cards, and credit cards. . . .

. . .

3. Errors. If an error occurs in the processing of a payment, the payment may be made to the wrong party or for the wrong amount. With currency, the consumer generally has control over who receives the payment and how much is tendered. The consumer could make an error in the amount of currency tendered, but an error that is not detected by the consumer or the payee at the time of the transaction may be difficult to prove or correct later.

. . .

4. Dishonor. Consumers may face the risk that a particular payment instrument will be dishonored by the issuer or drawee. Payment instruments may also be returned because of the default of the issuer or drawee. These risks generally do not exist with currency, as Federal Reserve Banks do not dishonor notes other than those that are counterfeit (and counterfeits are rarely traceable to a particular consumer) and Reserve Banks present no default risk. A check or an ACH debit transaction might be returned by the payor's bank for various reasons, such as insufficient funds in the account, lack of authorization from the payor, or failure of the drawee bank. . . .

Credit and debit card transactions are usually verified by the payee before the transaction is completed (e.g., before a merchant releases goods to the consumer) using an on-line communications system, thereby protecting the payee and the consumer from the risk of dishonor later. . . .

. . .

Dishonor of an electronic stored-value product could arise if the financial condition of the issuer were called into question. In the event of an issuer default, merchants could face risks of loss similar to those with credit or debit card transactions. For consumers, an issuer default could lead to financial losses up to the amount of prepaid funds currently held on a stored-value product.[59] The magnitude of this risk depends on factors such as the investment policies of the issuer and the nature of the consumer's claim in bankruptcy, including whether the consumer holds a direct claim on a specified pool of assets or whether the product is covered by some third-party insurance system. Such considerations are similar to those of other prepaid payment instruments, such as travelers checks and money orders, as well as for payments drawn on bank deposits.

. . .

Fraud or counterfeiting could also lead to dishonor at the point of sale or thereafter. Some stored-value systems would be able to detect counterfeit balances or devices at the point of sale. A consumer who unknowingly accepted a fraudulent or counterfeit device might find that the device was rejected for transactions. Reimbursement policies in such situations would thus be of concern to consumers as well as to merchants.

5. Inability to Use a Payment Mechanism. For various reasons, a consumer might be unable to use a particular payment mechanism. This situation would not necessarily result in a financial loss to the consumer but might unexpectedly prevent a consumer from discharging a debt or obtaining goods or services, result in late fees or other penalties, or at the very least, cause embarrassment.

A consumer might be unable to use a payment instrument because of a defect in the instrument. For example, a credit card or debit card might have a demagnetized strip or a damaged chip, causing the card to be rejected at the merchant's card-reading machine. . . .

---

[59] Depending on when the consumer's obligations are deemed to be discharged, the consumer may also be liable to merchants for goods purchased with a stored-value card if the merchant is unable to collect from the defaulting issuer. . . .

Merchants or other payees may refuse certain types of payment instruments for reasons other than defects in the instrument. Currency, which has the status of legal tender under federal law, must be accepted in payment of a debt unless the parties agree otherwise. Payees need not, however, accept credit or debit cards or checks and do so only voluntarily. Credit card and debit card issuers and associations usually attempt to sign up merchants to accept their cards to maximize the utility of the card for consumers.

Electronic stored-value products are not likely to be widely accepted for some time. Moreover, they are not legal tender and, as in the cases of checks and credit and debit cards, merchants are not obligated to accept them as payment. Thus consumers may face the risk that stored-value products cannot be used at the time and place they desire. With some stored-value products, consumers could also be left with unused balances that could not be readily converted to other forms of payment. For example, a stored-value card may be designed to expire after a certain date, with or without a window of time for the consumer to exchange the expired card for a new one. Consumers who are unable to use a card because of malfunctions or card expirations may suffer financial losses if they cannot obtain reimbursement from the issuer.

Consumers typically reduce risks that they will be unable to make payments by carrying more than one form of payment with them. In doing so, they must weigh the benefits of maintaining access to additional payment options against any inconvenience and fees involved in doing so. The same is likely to be true of electronic stored-value products.

6. Privacy Concerns. Another potential risk to consumers is that information regarding the amount and location of payments they make will be collected and used for purposes unknown to or unauthorized by them. For example, information regarding a particular consumer's spending habits could be captured in a database and sold to a marketing or other kind of firm. This information might also be used to monitor the activities of individuals without their knowledge, either by law enforcement officials or by other third parties. Generally, electronic payments are more susceptible to this kind of risk than are other types of payments because of the relative ease of capturing electronic data. With the increase in use and sophistication of electronic payments, many consumers are becoming more concerned about the privacy of their payment information.

. . .

Consumers who are concerned about the privacy of transaction information can use paper currency and coins rather than stored-value products or other electronic payment methods. . . .

. . .

QUESTIONS FOR DISCUSSION

1. *Private money.* Friedman and Macintosh argue that Internet commerce is a promising environment for the emergence of forms of private money. What do they mean by "private money"? Do you agree that the online environment invites the development of private money?

2. *Many monies or one dominant money?* Friedman and Macintosh argue that in the online environment, monies could proliferate. What features of the digital world might facilitate such a proliferation? On the other hand, they also mention the possibility that the various monies of the world might coalesce into one universal money. What features of the digital world might facilitate such a coalescence? Do you agree with Friedman and Macintosh that "competing public and private monies are the most likely development"?

3. *Evaluating risk online and off.* As the Federal Reserve Board of Governors' Report points out, payment systems involve a set of specific risks. The risks vary in severity depending upon the payment modality. What are the most serious risks of using cash? Paper checks? As we shall see in Part II, credit cards are the most frequently used payment mechanism in Internet commerce. What are the most serious risks of using credit cards in the world of bricks and mortar? In the online world?

II. COMMONLY USED ELECTRONIC PAYMENT SYSTEMS

A. CREDIT CARDS

The most widely used form of payment for consumer purchases in Internet commerce is the credit card. By one estimate, credit cards are used for more than 90 percent of all online purchases. Credit cards typically feature a revolving credit arrangement, in which the cardholder may carry a balance across monthly billing periods, and is charged interest on the outstanding balance. In 2000, credit cards accounted for 15 billion transactions (51 percent of all electronic payment transactions) with a total value of $1.235 trillion (17 percent of the total value of all electronic payments). *See* FEDERAL RESERVE SYSTEM, RETAIL PAYMENTS RESEARCH PROJECT: A SNAPSHOT OF THE U.S. PAYMENTS LANDSCAPE 9 (2001).

In offline transactions, a credit card purchase typically proceeds in the following steps. At the point of sale, the cardholder presents the merchant with her credit card. The merchant swipes the card through a card reader, called a point-of-sale terminal, which transmits an authorization request to the acquirer.[1] The acquirer routes the request, via the credit card network, to the issuing bank.[2] If the cardholder's credit line is sufficient for the purchase, and the card has not been reported as lost or stolen, the issuing bank authorizes the transaction by sending an authorization code to the acquirer. The point-of-sale terminal generates a paper charge slip, which the cardholder signs. The merchant sends an electronic record of the sale to the acquirer, which credits the merchant's account, and requests payment from the issuing bank. The issuing bank transfers payment to the acquirer, and includes the charge on the next statement that it sends to the cardholder for payment.

When a credit card is used to make a purchase in Internet commerce, the process is

---

[1] The acquirer is a financial institution, such as a bank, that processes credit card transactions as described in the text. The acquirer may be the bank in which the merchant maintains the account it uses for credit card transactions, known as the merchant bank, or it may be a third-party entity with which the merchant bank contracts to provide these services.

[2] The issuing bank is the bank that issues a credit card to the cardholder, and that sends the cardholder a monthly statement of charges for payment. Visa and MasterCard do not issue the cards carrying their logos, but rather authorize banks to issue them. American Express, on the other hand, issues its own cards.

similar, but an additional intermediary, called a payment gateway, may be involved. The payment gateway sits between the merchant's website and the acquirer, automatically translating communications between the protocols used for Internet communications and those used for messaging on the credit card network. In lieu of using a payment gateway, the merchant may manually enter the transactional data into the credit card network.

The merchant pays a fee to the acquirer for its processing services. The fee is typically in the range of 1.75 to 3.5 percent of the amount of each transaction. Internet and mail-order sellers generally pay higher rates than established storefront retailers, due to the greater risks of unauthorized use that the former present.

Credit card transactions in which the purchaser is not in the physical presence of the merchant—including sales via the Internet, by telephone, and by mail order—are called "card-not-present" transactions. Credit card issuers typically have detailed protocols that merchants must follow in such transactions. Visa, for example, requires, where possible, that the merchant obtain the credit card's expiration date, and recommends that the merchant ask the purchaser for the three-digit security number printed on the back of the card. In addition, in a card-not-present transaction the merchant is fully liable for any fraudulent use of a card. In a face-to-face transaction, on the other hand, the bank that issues the credit card is liable for unauthorized use. For further details on Visa's card-not-present protocols, see Visa, *Fraud Control Basics*, www.usa.visa.com.

In an effort to reduce the risk of loss from fraudulent use of credit cards online, some card issuers have introduced a security system that involves the generation of a card number that is valid only for a single online transaction. The cardholder presents the merchant with the single-use number, rather than the number of her credit card account. The process is transparent from the merchant's standpoint, as the card issuer handles the back-end tasks of generating the single-use number and associating it with the cardholder's account number. In addition, some issuers are offering cardholders a password that can be used to prevent unauthorized use of their credit card account numbers.

The legal relationships among the parties to a credit-card transaction are governed by a set of contracts, and by state and federal law. The relationship between the issuing bank and the cardholder is governed by the Truth in Lending Act ("TILA"), 15 U.S.C. §§ 1601–1667f, as implemented by Regulation Z, 12 C.F.R. pt. 226. The primary aim of federal regulation in this area is consumer protection. For example, TILA and Regulation Z prohibit the issuance of an unsolicited credit card[3] and impose various disclosure requirements on the issuing bank.[4]

Regulation Z also mandates certain procedures for the resolution of billing errors, which are errors reflected on or made in connection with a periodic statement of a cardholder's

---

[3] Regulation Z states that "[r]egardless of the purpose for which a credit card is to be used, including business, commercial, or agricultural use, no credit card shall be issued to any person except: (1) In response to an oral or written request or application for the card; or (2) As a renewal of, or substitute for, an accepted credit card." 12 C.F.R. § 226.12(a); *see also* TILA § 132, 15 U.S.C. § 1642.

[4] For example, when an individual applies for a credit card, the issuer must disclose the card's interest rate as an annual percentage rate, all fees which may be imposed, any minimum or fixed finance charges, any grace periods, and the method used to compute the balance on which the finance charge is imposed. 12 C.F.R. § 226.5a(b)(1)–(11).

account. If a cardholder believes her statement contains a billing error, she may initiate the billing dispute procedure by providing written notice of the error to the issuer. The issuer must then investigate the complaint and arrive at a conclusion within two billing cycles. 12 C.F.R. § 226.13(c)(2). Until the resolution procedure is completed, the cardholder need not pay the disputed amount, and the issuer may not make an adverse report about the cardholder's credit standing based on the dispute. *Id.* § 226.13(d)(1) & (d)(2). If the issuer determines that a billing error occurred as asserted, it must correct the billing error and credit the cardholder's account with any disputed amount. *Id.* § 226.13(e).

Finally, Regulation Z limits a cardholder's liability for unauthorized uses of his credit card. If the cardholder reports loss of the card before any unauthorized charges are made, the cardholder has no liability. Otherwise, the cardholder's liability is limited to $50. *Id.* § 226.12(b)(1) & (b)(2). The major card companies have instituted policies under which holders of U.S.-issued cards have no liability for most fraudulent uses of their cards.

B. DEBIT CARDS

A debit card is used to make an electronic fund transfer from a consumer's bank account to a merchant's account in payment for a purchase. The card that is used for debit transactions may also function as a credit card or an ATM card. In 2000, debit cards accounted for 8.3 billion transactions (28 percent of all electronic payment transactions) with a total value of $348 billion (4.8 percent of the total value of all electronic payment transactions). *See* FEDERAL RESERVE SYSTEM, RETAIL PAYMENTS RESEARCH PROJECT: A SNAPSHOT OF THE U.S. PAYMENTS LANDSCAPE 9 (2001).

There are two types of debit cards: "online" and "offline." A typical online debit transaction in the brick-and-mortar world proceeds as follows. A consumer swipes his debit card through an electronic fund transfer point-of-sale ("EFTPOS") terminal, and enters his personal identification number ("PIN"). The PIN is used to verify that the consumer is authorized to use the debit card. Next, the terminal transmits information about the transaction to the consumer's bank and seeks authorization for the purchase. If the consumer's bank confirms that the PIN is associated with the consumer's account and there are sufficient funds in that account to cover the purchase, then the bank will approve the purchase and debit the consumer's account for the amount of the purchase. The approval is transmitted to the EFTPOS terminal, and the purchase is completed. The electronic communications are made over the ATM network.

Offline debit transactions are processed through the credit card network, rather than the ATM network. Instead of using a PIN, the cardholder signs a charge slip. In an offline debit transaction, the funds are not transferred immediately, but only upon settlement, which may take several days.

As odd as it may sound, offline debit cards can be used for online purchases, but online debit cards generally cannot. Online cards, as noted above, require the use of a PIN. A card reader is required to verify that the correct PIN has been entered, but few consumers have a card reader attached to their computers. Offline debit cards, on the other hand, may be used for purchases in Internet commerce in the same manner as a credit card.

Most offline debit cards are issued by banks in association with Visa and MasterCard. These two card networks, which control more than 90 percent of the credit-card market, require merchants that accept their credit cards also to accept their debit cards. Many merchants would prefer not to accept these debit cards, because of the high fees involved. These fees are set by Visa and MasterCard at about the same levels as for credit card transactions. For a $100 purchase, that can mean the merchant will pay a fee of several dollars per transaction, as compared to 59 cents or so for an online debit transaction. In 1999, a group of merchants, including Wal–Mart, Sears, and Circuit City, brought a class-action suit against Visa U.S.A. and MasterCard International, alleging that the rules requiring merchants to accept the defendants' offline debit cards violated the antitrust laws. In December 2003, the court approved a settlement of the class action. Under the settlement, Visa and MasterCard agree to abandon their "Honor All Cards" rules, and to pay more than $3 billion into a settlement fund. *See In re Visa Check/Mastermoney Antitrust Litigation,* 297 F.Supp.2d 503 (E.D.N.Y.2003).

The legal relationship between the bank that issues the debit card (the "issuer") and the consumer is governed by the agreement between the issuer and the consumer, and by the Electronic Fund Transfer Act ("EFTA"), 15 U.S.C. §§ 1693–1693r, as implemented by Regulation E, 12 C.F.R. pt. 205. As with the Truth in Lending Act, the principal aim of the EFTA and Regulation E is consumer protection. Toward this end, the EFTA and Regulation E broadly define what will count as an "access device" for electronic fund transfers,[5] prohibit the issuance of an unsolicited access device,[6] and impose disclosure and documentation requirements on the issuing bank. 12 C.F.R. § 205.7.

Regulation E also mandates an error resolution procedure that is triggered if the consumer believes that any of several kinds of errors has occurred, including an unauthorized or incorrect electronic fund transfer, a computational or bookkeeping error made by the financial institution relating to an electronic fund transfer, and the consumer's receipt of an incorrect amount of money from an electronic terminal such as an ATM. *Id.* § 205.11(a). The error resolution procedure resembles in outline the procedure that applies to credit cards, as described above, but differs in the particulars. *Id.* § 205.11.

When a consumer uses a debit card to pay for goods or services in an "online" transaction at a point-of-sale terminal or over the Internet, the consumer's account is immediately debited. Once a consumer's bank authorizes an electronic fund transfer, it is absolutely liable to pay the merchant's bank the amount authorized. Under Regulation E, the consumer may not reverse an electronic fund transfer. If a consumer wishes to reverse the transaction and get her money back, then in most states the consumer's only recourse is to proceed against the merchant directly. In this respect, payment by electronic fund transfer is like payment by cash. Some states, however, have enacted laws that allow consumers to reverse electronic fund transfers under certain circumstances. *See, e.g.,* MICH. COMP. LAWS § 488.16.

Regulation E limits a consumer's liability for an unauthorized electronic fund transfer,

---

[5] The EFTA applies not only to transfers initiated by debit cards but to electronic fund transfers initiated by any kind of access device. An access device is defined as "a card, code, or other means of access to a consumer's account, or any combination thereof, that may be used by the consumer to initiate electronic fund transfers." 12 C.F.R. § 205.2(a)(1). Thus, the account number on the face of the debit card qualifies as an access device since it is this number that the consumer must key in to access her account.

[6] A financial institution may issue an access device to a consumer only (1) in response to an oral or written request for the device or (2) as a renewal of, or in substitution for, an accepted access device whether issued by the institution or a successor. 12 C.F.R. § 205.5(a).

which is defined as "an electronic fund transfer from a consumer's account initiated by a person other than the consumer without actual authority to initiate the transfer and from which the consumer receives no benefit." 12 C.F.R. § 205.2(m). Liability for unauthorized EFTs depends on the consumer's promptness in reporting the loss or theft of an access device. If the consumer notifies the financial institution before there is any unauthorized use, the consumer has no liability. If she notifies the financial institution within two business days after learning of the loss or theft of the access device, the consumer's liability is limited to $50. If the consumer fails to notify the financial institution within two business days after learning of the loss or theft of the access device, the consumer may be liable for up to $500. Finally, a consumer who fails to report an unauthorized electronic fund transfer that appears on a billing statement within sixty days of the financial institution's transmittal of the statement may be liable for the full amount of subsequent transfers. *Id.* § 205.6. A cardholder's potential liability for unauthorized use of a debit card is thus far greater than the corresponding liability with respect to credit cards.

Although the limits on consumer liability prescribed by Regulation E may not be increased by either state law or agreement, they may be reduced by such means. *See* 12 C.F.R. § 205.6(6); COLO. REV. STAT. §§ 11–6.5–109(2) & 11–48–106(2); MASS. GEN. LAWS ANN. Ch. 167B, § 18; IOWA CODE ANN. § 527.8.1 (all three statutes limit consumer liability for unauthorized transfers to $50 if an access device was lost or stolen; Colorado law further provides that if the unauthorized use occurs through no fault of the account holder, no liability is imposed).

QUESTIONS FOR DISCUSSION

Need for new payment mechanisms. Given the widespread availability and near-universal acceptance of credit and debit cards online, is there any need for alternative payment mechanisms for Internet commerce? Consider the following:

> One might think . . . that traditional payment instruments are fulfilling consumers' need for a safe and easy way to make payments while cybershopping. But there are three additional hurdles to using these payment instruments online. The first and biggest barrier to online shopping is consumer reluctance to use credit and debit cards in cyberspace. One recent survey found, as is typical, that 43 percent of consumers fear cybershopping will result in the theft of their credit-card numbers (PR Newswire 2001). Another survey found that 29 percent of online shoppers think they are responsible for fraudulent Internet purchases made with their debit cards (*ATM & Debit News*, July 2001).
>
> The second hurdle is the costliness of using credit and debit cards for very small purchases (that is, micropayments) such as the one-time use of digital content, like an individual song, photograph, or magazine article. The fees merchants must pay on purchases made with these cards are so high that sellers of digital content and other very inexpensive goods cannot afford to accept the cards. Yet the demand for such purchases is potentially very large. About 38 percent of all Internet users report having downloaded music files at some point.
>
> The third hurdle is that many potential cybershoppers do not have access to the traditional payment instruments. One study found that lower income consumers—the consumers more likely to be constrained in their ability to make credit-card purchases—are the fastest growing group of Internet users. Teenagers are also likely to lack credit cards, debit cards, and checking accounts; yet they are thought to constitute the largest market of cybershoppers who look but

do not buy.

Stacey L. Schreft, *Clicking with Dollars: How Consumers Can Pay for Purchases from E-tailers*, ECON. REV., First Quarter 2002, at 37, 47–48.

III. EMERGING ELECTRONIC PAYMENT SYSTEMS

A. BACKGROUND

Although credit cards are still the dominant form of payment for consumer purchases in Internet commerce, several new payment technologies that may be used for online purchases have been introduced and have experienced varying degrees of acceptance. In this Part we consider these emerging technologies and discuss how they operate, their acceptance in the marketplace, and the challenges that each system faces.

In contrast to the more familiar electronic payment systems, which are governed primarily by federal law, the emerging online payment services are regulated mainly by state law. The primary goals of state regulation of financial services businesses are consumer protection and the prevention of money laundering. States attempt to ensure that these services have sufficient funds and other resources to fulfill their obligations to their customers by imposing safety and soundness requirements, such as restricting how money deposited with such services may be used or invested, or requiring services to obtain a surety bond, letter of credit, or other similar security device. States also attempt to prevent these services from becoming conduits for money laundering by imposing licensing and reporting requirements. To encourage greater uniformity among these laws, in 2000 the National Conference of Commissioners on Uniform State Laws approved and recommended for enactment the Uniform Money Services Act. The prefatory note to this Act, which includes a brief description of some of the emerging electronic payment systems, is excerpted below.

Prefatory Note to the Uniform Money Services Act
National Conference of Commissioners on Uniform State Laws (2000).

A. Goals and Objectives

The Uniform Money Services Act ("UMSA" or "Act") is a state safety and soundness law that creates licensing provisions for various types of money-services businesses ("MSBs"). While many States have laws that deal with the sale of payment instruments, state regulation of money transmission, check cashers and currency exchangers is extremely varied. . . .

. . . [U]niformity of the reporting and record keeping requirements should enable industry to comply with multiple state requirements in a uniform and cost-effective manner. Uniform licensing, reporting and enforcement provisions for MSBs will serve as a larger deterrent to money laundering than will a host of varying state laws. . . .

. . .

D. Internet Payment Mechanisms and Stored Value

The UMSA takes the approach that certain cyberpayment mechanisms pose the same safety and soundness concerns as their brick and mortar counterparts. The UMSA incorporates certain Internet payment mechanisms into the statute's licensing framework. However, the Act does not include new or different licensing regimes for such payment mechanisms. The cyberpayment licensing requirements set forth in this Act are not complex and cumbersome. Rather, they are simple and meant to apply the existing licensing frameworks to new technologies. Existing definitions have been expanded *slightly* to take into account the fact that (1) Internet payment mechanisms are in many respects the functional equivalent of traditional money transmission, and (2) that the sale of stored value is in many respects analogous to the sale of traditional payment instruments such as money orders.

This Act expands upon our traditional concept of "money." With the advent of the Internet and new microchip technology it is possible to exchange value that is not "money" in the traditional sense. The UMSA consequently provides a new definition of "monetary value." Like money, monetary value can be transmitted. Similarly issuers need not sell a physical tangible payment instrument in order to issue value to consumers. It is possible for consumers to purchase redeemable value that may only exist in a computerized format. Hence, this Act contains a definition of stored value that is distinct from the traditional payment instrument. Listed below are examples of some of the new types of payment mechanisms that potentially fall within the scope of the Act.

1. Stored value

Stored-value products are a recent innovation in payment systems technology. Stored-value products possess certain basic characteristics. According to the Federal Reserve, stored-value products share three attributes: "(1) [a] card or other device electronically stores or provides access to a specified amount of funds selected by the holder of the device and available for making payments to others; (2) the device is the only means of routine access to the funds; and (3) the issuer does not record the funds associated with the device as an account in the name of (or credited to) the holder."[5]

Stored-value cards are also known as "smart" cards, prepaid cards, or value-added cards. These cards record a balance on a computer chip that is debited at a point-of-sale terminal when a consumer or individual makes a purchase. Typically, a consumer will pay a bank or other provider money in exchange for a card that is loaded with value. The value can evidence the provider's promise (typically to pay money), or can evidence the promise of a trustworthy third party. The consumer uses the card rather than paper currency to purchase goods and services. Merchants who accept smart cards can typically transfer the value of accumulated credits to their bank accounts. A smart card is not typically used for transactions over the Internet, although this may be changing with the advent of new credit-card products that include a stored-value component. Several new services, however, provide for remote payments to be made by electronic currency that is stored on the hard drive of a person's computer.

---

[5] Electronic Funds Transfers (Regulation E), 61 Fed. Reg. 19, 696 (1996).

Several States have begun to include stored value within their existing money transmission law. Connecticut, for example, has defined stored value as a form of "electronic payment instrument."[6] This term would also include electronic traveler's checks. West Virginia defines "currency transmission" or "money transmission" to include "the transmission of funds through the issuance and sale of stored-value cards which are intended for general acceptance and use in commercial or consumer transactions."[7] Other States, such as Texas, have included stored-value providers by interpretation. The Texas Banking Department has explained, for example, its rationale for requiring nonbank issuers of open system stored-value cards to obtain a license under the Texas Sale of Checks Act:

> Stored-value cards issued by nonbanks for use in "open" systems (i.e., to purchase goods and services offered by vendors other than the issuer of the card) will generally be subject to regulation under the Sale of Checks Act because the nonbank issuer is holding the funds of third parties. Consumers are relying on the nonbank issuer that the card will be honored when presented by the purchaser of goods and services at diverse locations.[8]

Oregon is another State that has included a provision for the regulation of stored value. Section 2 of the Sale of Checks Act includes a definition of electronic instrument which "means a card or other tangible object . . . for the storage of information, that is prefunded and for which the value is decrement[ed] upon each use."[9] The term excludes "a card or other tangible object that is redeemable by the issuer in the issuer's goods and services."[10]

. . .

2. E-money and Internet payment mechanisms

New types of cyberpayments or Internet payment mechanisms have been referred to by regulators and commentators by a host of different names including electronic cash, digital cash, electronic currency, and Internet or on-line scrip ("E-money"). E-money refers to money or a money substitute that is transformed into information stored on a computer chip or a personal computer so that it can be transferred over information systems such as the Internet. Technology permits the transmission of electronic value over networks that link personal computers (PCs) and the storage of electronic cash on the hard drives of personal computers.

. . . One type of Internet-based E-money system has been described as a token or notational system. These computer-based systems involve a customer purchas-

---

[6] Conn. Gen. Stat. Ann. Section 36a–596 (West Supp. 2001). Connecticut defines electronic payment instrument as stored value, not the reverse.

[7] W. Va. Code Section 32A–2–1(6) (West 1999).

[8] See Remarks of Catherine A. Ghiglieri, Texas Department of Banking to the PULSE EFT Assoc. Member Conference (October 11, 1996) (visited June 15, 2001) located at <http://www.banking.state.tx.us/exec/speech10a.htm>.

[9] Or. Rev. Stat. Section 717.200(7) (West 1999).

[10] Id.

ing electronic tokens, which serve as cash substitutes for transactions over the Internet. With this type of system, "money" or "value" is purchased from an issuer (who may be a bank or a nonbank). The value is then stored in a digital form on a consumer's personal computer and the notational value is transferred over the Internet.

The "coin" is merely a notational series of numbers or other symbols that are transmitted over the Internet to a merchant. The merchant must then redeem the "coin" with an issuer that will verify that the coin has not been spent previously. The issuer of the Internet E-money is obligated to redeem these payments when received from the merchant. For example, Company A issues a certain type of E-money—Internet "cash" cards with unique personal identification numbers ("PINs"). These cash cards are purchased from vendors who are sales representatives. A consumer uses his PIN when transacting with a merchant on-line.

Commentators have noted that state money transmission statutes may, by implication, include or regulate Internet payment systems such as the notational systems described above. Others have suggested that in the future [they] might be a source of prudential regulation for nonbank entities engaged in this activity. . . .

. . .

In addition to token or notational systems, there are also "account-based" E-money systems. Account-based systems involve a consumer purchasing "E-money" by debiting an existing bank account or using a credit card to buy "coins." The value is then stored on the issuer's records and the consumer might access the records. The merchant who accepts the E-money ultimately redeems the account-based E-money with a bank or credit card company.

3. Internet scrip

Stored value cards, token or notational systems as well as account-based systems may all involve exchange of value that is not redeemable in money. The term "scrip" has been used to refer to value that may be exchanged over the Internet but which may not be redeemable for money. Scrip is more analogous to coupons or bonus points that can be exchanged by a consumer for goods or services but have no cash redemption value. Scrip can be used by merchants to sell access to value-added web pages on a per-access basis or a subscription basis. They can also use scrip to provide promotional incentives to users. Scrip can represent any form of currency, points in a frequent user program, access rights, etc.

At present, there are new micropayments systems being developed that allow customers to either earn reward points on line or to purchase points or "value" that is redeemable for goods and services rather than for money. One such example is Company B, which issues its own gift "money." Company B issues what are essentially online gift certificates. A customer opens an account and purchases a certain amount of Company B's reward "dollars." Then, the person can send the dollars to anyone with an e-mail address (along with a card). The recipient, upon receipt, opens an account and then can spend the gift "dollars" at any participating store that accepts the "dollars." What is not apparent from the website is whether Company B's "dollars" are redeemable in cash or merely in goods and services.

Another company, Company C, offers online points that are billed as web "currency." Company C's "points" are units that consumers may earn when visiting various websites, filling out surveys or engaging in other online activities for which merchants seek to reward consumers. The points accrue and are stored in an online "account" that a customer may access to redeem his or her "points" for various goods and services. The points are not redeemable for money, and the company states that it may discontinue the service at any point. Company C is offering an account-based payment system that issues non-redeemable points.

4. Internet funds transfer

New payment services offered by banks and nonbanks will transfer money over the Internet. One such service, offered by Company D, will transfer money over the Internet to anyone who has an e-mail address. Consumers who wish to send money via the Internet must first establish an online account with Company D. A consumer can fund his or her account with payments from a credit card, a debit from his bank account, or by sending in a money order or check. Company D holds the consumer's money until it receives a request to transfer the funds to a recipient. A transfer is effectuated by sending an e-mail to the recipient. The recipient then has several options for receiving payment ranging from establishing his or her own online account with Company D, having the funds transferred to an existing bank account, or, if the customer has no bank account, receiving a check from Company D.

5. Gold/precious metals transfer and payment

Somewhat similar to an Internet funds transfer system is a system whereby customers transfer precious metal via accounts on the Internet. For example, with Company E, rather than having an "account" with E-money denominated in U.S. dollars, a customer sets up an online account and buys gold, silver, platinum, or palladium. The customer then has "x" grams or troy ounces of the precious metal. One can only send money to or purchase items from an existing customer of Company E. The advantage, Company E claims, is the stability of precious metals relative to currency. Customers can utilize their precious metal accounts to buy goods and services, to receive payment from third parties, and to pay bills.

6. Internet bill payment services

Banks and nonbank[s] have began to offer Internet bill payment services. For a fee, electronic bill payment services pay certain bills for consumers, after receiving authorization from a consumer. The customer accesses the service via the Internet. Bill payments may subsequently be made for the consumer electronically. Typically, the service provider will use an automated clearinghouse (ACH) transfer to effectuate payment. However, if the designated payee does not accept electronic payment, the bill-payment service will print and mail a check on behalf of its customer. When a nonbank service is involved, the nonbank has no contractual relationship with the consumer's bank. Instead, the consumer's bank will transfer money to the bill-payment service company. The bill-payment service will, in turn, deposit the funds into its own bank account. The bill-payment service will then issue a payment instrument payable on its own account to the designated payee.

The Texas Department of Banking has required at least one bill-payment service to obtain a license under its Sale of Checks Act.[12] Texas made this decision based on the fact that the bill-payment service was holding the money of consumers in its own account and issuing payment instruments to merchants payable on the same account. The Texas Sale of Checks Act defines a check to include "an instrument for the transmission or payment of money, including a draft, traveler's check, or money order. The term also includes an instrument for the transmission or payment of money in which the purchaser or remitter of the instrument appoints or purports to appoint the seller as its agent for the receipt, transmission, or handling of money, regardless of who signs the instrument."[13] California has also required an Internet bill-payment service to obtain a license under its relevant statute.[14] By implication, Internet bill-payment services may already be included within various statutes regulating sale of payment instruments or money transmission statutes.

EXTENSIONS

Adoptions of UMSA. At this writing the Uniform Money Services Act has been enacted by four states. The current status of state enactments of the UMSA is available at www.nccusl.org/Update/uniformact_factsheets/uniformacts-fs-msa.asp.

QUESTIONS FOR DISCUSSION

Electronic money and criminal activity. How does electronic money compare with other payment mechanisms, such as cash, with respect to the risk of counterfeiting and money laundering? Consider how these mechanisms compare in terms of traceability, ease of transportation, anonymity, ease of forgery, and the security of the systems through which they are transmitted.

Electronic payments in Internet commerce may involve the use of several electronic networks, in addition to the Internet itself. Credit card payments make use of proprietary networks operated by companies such as Visa, MasterCard, and American Express. Electronic fund transfers using online debit card accounts travel over ATM networks operated by banks. An additional network that may be involved in making electronic payments over the Internet is the Automated Clearing House ("ACH") Network. The ACH Network was originally developed as a paperless process to facilitate efficient interbank settlements. Today, consumers and businesses can also initiate electronic credit and debit transfers over this network. The following excerpt describes how the ACH Network functions.

---

[12] TEX. FIN. CODE ANN. Section 152.001–152.508 (West Supp. 2001).

[13] TEX. FIN. CODE ANN. Section 152.002(1) (West Supp. 2001).

[14] State of California, Department of Financial Institutions (visited June 15, 2001) <http://www.sbd.ca.gov/>.

Comptroller of the Currency, ACH Transactions Involving the Internet
OCC 2002–2 (2002), Appendix A—The ACH Network
www.occ.treas.gov/ftp/bulletin/2002-2.doc

The ACH Network is a nationwide, batch-oriented electronic transfer system that provides for the interbank clearing of payments among participating depository financial institutions. The ACH Network was developed in the early 1970s as a response to the massive growth of check payments.

NACHA [the National Automated Clearing House Association] was established in 1974 to coordinate the ACH Network. NACHA's primary roles are to develop and maintain the NACHA Operating Rules, to promote growth in ACH volume, and to provide educational services to its members and other ACH participants.

The process by which funds are transferred through the ACH Network operates from beginning to end through a series of legal agreements between the parties and pursuant to the NACHA Operating Rules. The rules are enforceable by the parties pursuant to the common law of contract. In addition, ACH entries are also subject to applicable federal and state law, such as the Electronic Fund Transfer Act (EFTA), implemented by Regulation E, and Article 4A of the Uniform Commercial Code, as enacted by a particular state.

For a given transaction, up to five entities may participate in the ACH Network—the originator, the originating depository financial institution (ODFI), the ACH operator, the receiving depository financial institution (RDFI), and the receiver. In addition, some of the entities may use a third-party service provider as part of the process.

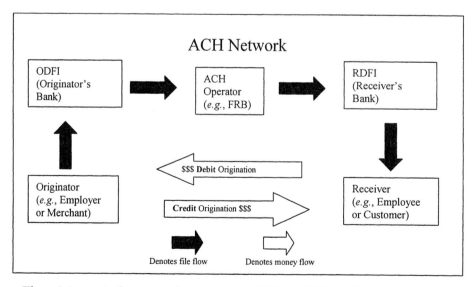

The *originator* is the party that agrees to initiate ACH entries into the payment system according to an arrangement with a receiver. The originator is usually a company directing a transfer of funds to or from a consumer's or another company's account, but may be an individual initiating funds transfers to or from the individual's own account.

The *ODFI* is the institution that receives the payment instructions from its customers, the originators, and transmits the entries to the ACH operator. An ODFI can also initiate ACH entries for itself, in which case it is both ODFI and originator.

The *ACH operator* is the central clearing facility, operated by a Federal Reserve Bank or a private organization, that receives entries from ODFIs, distributes the entries to appropriate RDFIs, and performs the settlement functions for the affected institutions.

The *RDFI* is the institution that receives entries from the ACH operator and posts them to the accounts of its depositors, the receivers.

The *receiver* is the party that has authorized an originator to initiate an ACH entry to the receiver's account with the RDFI.

Unlike the wire transfer and check systems, the ACH Network is both a credit and a debit payment system. ACH credit transactions transfer funds *from the originator to the receiver*. For example, an originator may arrange to meet its payroll obligations by causing an ODFI to transmit ACH credit entries so that employees' salaries are credited to their accounts and the originator's account is debited in the total amount of the payroll. ACH debit transactions, on the other hand, transfer funds *from the receiver to the originator*. For example, a merchant originator may permit a customer to purchase goods or services through the Internet when the customer authorizes the merchant to initiate an ACH debit to the customer's account. Although credits and debits transfer funds in different directions, the entry information and the functional processing always flows in one direction, from the originator to the receiver.

B. Person-to-Person Money Services

The most widely used emerging online money services are known as person-to-person ("P2P") payment services. These services enable anyone with an e-mail address to transfer funds to anyone else with an e-mail address. The following excerpt discusses the mechanics of P2P services and some of the regulatory issues that these payment services raise.

Ronald J. Mann, *Regulating Internet Payment Intermediaries*
82 Tex. L. Rev. 681 (2004).

I. Introduction

The Internet has produced significant changes in many aspects of commercial interaction. The rise of Internet retailers is one of the most obvious changes, but oddly enough the overwhelming majority of commercial transactions facilitated by the Internet use a conventional payment system. Thus, even in 2002, shoppers made at least eighty percent of Internet purchases with credit cards. To many observers, this figure has come as a surprise. The early days of the Internet heralded a variety of proposals for entirely new payment systems — generically described as electronic money—that would use wholly electronic tokens that consumers could issue, transfer, and redeem. But years later, no electronic-money system has gained a significant role in commerce.

The continuing maturation of the Internet, however, has brought significant changes to the methods by which individuals make payments. Person-to-person (P2P) systems like PayPal now make hundreds of millions of payments a year between individuals. The most common purpose is to facilitate the purchase of items at Internet auctions, but increasingly P2P transfers are used to transfer funds overseas. . . .

However disparate these developments might seem at first glance, they present a common challenge to the regulatory system. Unlike banks, which control the execution of payment transactions in conventional payment systems, the intermediaries that populate these new sectors generally are not inevitably subject to regulatory supervision. At most, they are subject to regulation as money transmitters (akin to the regulation of Western Union).

That circumstance presents a serious gap in the regulatory scheme. The pervasive regulatory supervision of banks helps to ensure that they honor their obligations under a variety of consumer-protection and data-privacy regulations that govern their activities. A shift of a significant share of volume to the new and unregulated entities raises a corresponding risk of loss from the irresponsibility of those entities. Thus, although the risk of fraud and privacy violations is doubtless higher in these new forms of transactions than it is in conventional transactions, the regulatory framework governing them is much weaker.

. . .

II. The New Transactions

A. P2P Systems

The success of eBay's auction business had the rare effect of creating a vast market for an entirely new payment product, one that would allow non-merchants (who cannot accept conventional credit card payments) to receive payments quickly in remote transactions. Without such a system, purchasers in the early days of eBay had to use cashier's checks or money orders. Typically, sellers waited to ship products until they received the paper-based payment device in the mail. From a flood of startups offering competing products, PayPal (now owned by eBay) has emerged as the dominant player in the industry, processing hundreds of millions of payments each year. Indeed, industry sources expect that by 2005, auction payments will account for ninety-five percent of the possibly four billion person-to-person payment transactions expected to be made that year. . . .

To understand the policy ramifications of P2P payments, it is necessary to understand the relation between the P2P provider and the conventional accounts from which and to which P2P payments are made. That relation can be illustrated by a summary of the three steps that must be completed for a successful P2P transaction.

1. Providing Funds for Payment.—The purchaser that wishes to use a P2P pro-

vider to make a payment has two general ways to provide funds for payment. First, it could fund an account with the provider, normally by drawing on a deposit account or a credit card account. Because that process ensures that funds are available for an immediate transfer, it is widely used by those who make frequent purchases. P2P account balances are also commonly used by frequent eBay sellers, who receive funds into their P2P accounts from individuals who purchase the auctioned item. Alternatively, the purchaser could wait until the moment that it wishes to make a purchase. Again, it could choose at the time of payment to provide the funds in question by drawing on either a deposit account or a credit card account. As discussed below, the choice between a credit card and a deposit account as a funding source has significant legal consequences to the user.

. . .

2. Making Payments. — The attraction of the P2P process is that it is quite simple to make payments. Normally, the only information that the purchaser needs to make a payment is the amount of money and the email address of the intended recipient. After entering that information into a form at the P2P provider's Web site, the purchaser clicks on a "send money" button to request execution of the transaction. If the funds are sent from a balance in an account with the P2P provider or if they are drawn from a credit card, they should arrive in a few hours. If funds are drawn directly from a deposit account, arrival will be delayed by a few days (until settlement of the ACH transaction to obtain the funds from the user's bank).

3. Collecting Payments. — The final step is for the recipient (the seller if the payment is for an auction) to collect the payment. In the typical process, the recipient receives an email notifying it that the payment has arrived. If the recipient has an account with the P2P provider and is willing to leave the funds in that account, then it is finished. If the recipient does not have an account or wishes to withdraw the funds, it will need to go to the provider's Web site and provide the necessary details.

Ordinarily, the recipient will pay some fee to the provider for making the payment available. Those fees vary considerably, but a typical charge at PayPal would be 25-50 cents plus 2-4% of the transaction amount. In addition, if the payment is made with a credit card, the recipient may be required to bear the cost of any chargeback that the payor seeks under its agreements with the provider and card issuer.

. . .

III. Designing a Sound Regulatory System

The first step in assessing the adequacy of regulatory protections for the developing Internet payment transactions is to determine the extent to which the consumer protections that apply to existing transactions extend to the new transactions. Two forms of consumer protection are relevant here: information privacy and protection from losses related to fraud or error.

The simpler of those forms relates to information privacy. Specifically, under

Gramm–Leach–Bliley (GLB), "financial institutions" must not disclose nonpublic personal information to third parties unless they have given their customers an opportunity to opt out of any such disclosures. . . . [A] broad definition of "financial institution" in the applicable regulations means that the rules in GLB apply with just as much force to the new intermediaries as they do to banks and other depository institutions.

It is much more complicated to assess the legal framework that protects consumers from fraud and error, because that framework plainly does not extend completely to the new payment intermediaries. To explain the problems with that framework, the sections that follow summarize the existing framework, the policy choices that it reflects, and how those rules apply to problems likely to arise in the new transactions.

A. Existing Protections Against Fraud and Error

The most general protection for consumers in these transactions comes from the Electronic Funds Transfer Act and Regulation E (which the Federal Reserve has promulgated to implement the EFTA). The EFTA/E regime applies to any electronic funds transfer (EFT). . . . For any such transaction, the statute generally protects consumers from losses caused by an unauthorized transaction.[7] Thus, if a consumer loses a debit card, the consumer's bank would be obligated to restore to the consumer's account any funds removed for transactions that a thief made with the card. Two important exceptions exist. First, the bank can charge the account a deductible of up to $50 for each series of unauthorized transactions. Second, more importantly, the bank can charge the consumer more—and in some cases the entire amount of the losses—if the consumer does not advise the bank with sufficient promptness after the consumer learns that the card has been stolen. The EFTA/E regime also provides a detailed dispute-resolution process for resolving claims of errors by the financial institution in charging a consumer's account for a funds transfer.

For credit card transactions, analogous protections come from the Truth-in-Lending Act (TILA) and Regulation Z (which the Federal Reserve has promulgated to implement TILA). Two important differences exist between the two regimes. For one thing, the TILA/Z regime provides broader protection for unauthorized losses--consumer responsibility is capped at $50 even if the consumer fails to notify the bank that the card has been stolen. Also, the TILA/Z regime grants consumers a broad right to withhold payment even for authorized transactions if the seller fails to perform as agreed.[8] As discussed below, the right to withhold provides consumers an important protection against seller fraud.

B. Protections Against Fraud and Error in the New Transactions

Unfortunately, the legal framework protecting consumers against fraud and error has not been updated to accommodate the new transactions. Thus, that framework includes three types of problems: situations where the incoherent distinction

---

[7] [The EFTA and Reg E are discussed in more detail in Part II(B), *supra*.—Eds.]

[8] [TILA and Reg Z are discussed in more detail in Part II(A), *supra*.—Eds.]

between the TILA/Z and EFTA/E regime is replicated in the new environment, minor oversights in regulatory drafting, and more significant omissions in regulatory coverage. The sections below discuss how those rules apply to the new transactions and underscore those problems where they arise.

1. P2P Transactions. — Current experience suggests that fraud is a serious problem in P2P transactions. One Federal Reserve researcher estimates that PayPal's fraud rate of 0.66%, albeit much lower than the rate of online credit card fraud, is about four times the rate of fraud for retail credit card transactions and more than sixty times the rate for retail debit card transactions. But the legal rules for determining whether the consumer bears the losses from that fraud depend in an important way on how the consumer pays for the transaction. To see the point, imagine an eBay auction in which a fraudulent seller never ships any goods to the buyer. If the transaction is funded from the purchaser's account with the P2P provider, it is an EFT governed by the EFTA. In that event, the purchaser has no right, either against the financial institution or the P2P provider, to recover the funds for an authorized transaction solely because of a complaint about misconduct by the seller, however meritorious the complaint. The same analysis applies if the purchaser funds the transaction by authorizing a transfer directly from the purchaser's deposit account. This type of transaction is also an EFT covered by the EFTA/E regime.

But if the buyer has the good luck (or foresight) to fund the purchase directly from a credit card, the transaction is governed by the TILA/Z regime. Thus, among other things, the purchaser should have the right to withhold payment if the seller in fact never supplies the goods. The statute grants a broad right to the cardholder to withhold payment based on "all claims (other than tort claims) and defenses arising out of any transaction in which the credit card is used as a method of payment." Thus, if the transaction through PayPal is viewed as a single unified transaction in which the auction purchaser uses PayPal and the credit card to buy something from an auction seller, the TILA/Z regime protects the purchaser. As discussed above, it is odd to have such an important protection turn on something that is as trivial to the transaction as the method by which the purchaser funds the transaction to the P2P provider. But it is not any more odd to see that distinction here than it is to see it in the conventional point-of-sale context.

The other likely type of fraud is for a third party to obtain the consumer's PayPal login information and use that information to conduct an unauthorized transaction by drawing on the consumer's PayPal account. If the interloper draws directly on the P2P account, Regulation E makes the P2P intermediary directly responsible: subject to the normal exceptions, the P2P provider cannot charge the consumer's account for the transaction. The same result applies under the TILA/Z regime if the interloper uses the information to draw funds from the consumer's credit card.

The only ambiguity applies if the interloper uses the information to withdraw funds from the consumer's deposit account. In that event — because of an odd glitch in the regulation — it seems that neither the P2P provider nor the bank is obligated to return the funds to the consumer's deposit account. The bank apparently is not obligated because it is entitled to treat the transaction as authorized. A transaction is authorized under the EFTA if it is executed by a party (the P2P provider in this case) to whom the consumer has given the relevant access information. Because that fact makes the transaction "authorized" with respect to the account from which funds were drawn, it appears that the rules related to "unauthorized" transactions impose no obligation on the P2P provider for the loss. The most likely source of recovery for the consumer would be an action against the P2P provider's depositary institution (the entity that originated the ACH transfer) for a breach of the applicable National Automated Clearing House Association (NACHA) warranties. Because of the limited litigation to date in that area, it is difficult to assess the likelihood of prevailing in such an action.

. . .

The status of online payment companies for regulatory purposes is currently unresolved. While P2P services engage in banking activity to the extent they accept consumer deposits and make money transfers, it remains unclear whether they qualify as banks under various regulatory definitions. Likewise, although these services transmit money, the definition of a "money transmitter" varies from state to state, and it may be unclear whether a P2P service qualifies. State laws typically require banks to maintain certain levels of cash reserves, and to monitor transactions closely. In addition, banks are subject to a variety of federal regulations. Some states require "money transmitters" to obtain a license, and to post a surety bond.

Several states have raised questions about the legal status of P2P services, with the focus of the scrutiny on PayPal. In February 2002, state banking regulators in Louisiana sent PayPal a letter directing the company to cease providing money transmission services to Louisiana residents until it obtained a money transmission license. PayPal obtained the license in Louisiana as well as a number of other states. Several states have inquired whether PayPal is a bank under state law; PayPal argues that it acts as an agent on behalf of its customers rather than as a bank.

In a 2002 opinion letter, the Federal Deposit Insurance Corporation stated that customer funds that PayPal deposits in FDIC-insured banks are entitled to pass-through deposit insurance coverage. This means the customer is protected against failure of the bank, but the FDIC insurance does not protect against failure of PayPal—a distinction that some customers may not fully appreciate.

Kenneth N. Kuttner & James J. McAndrews, *Personal On-Line Payments*
ECON. POL'Y REV., Dec. 1, 2001, at 35.

. . .

Risk

Providers of on-line payment instruments are concerned about the risks of fraud, operational failure, and other liquidity and credit risks because their success depends on maintaining a system that is useful to customers and protects the provider from fraudulent withdrawal of funds from the system. Therefore, it is important to examine the risk control measures employed by these new systems to combat risk.

Fraud is perhaps the most immediate threat faced by on-line payment providers. To address this risk, all the systems register and communicate credit card information using a secure socket layer—an encrypted connection to the provider's website. The payer's information is retained by the provider, reducing the need for repeated transmission over the Internet. Another risk control is a limit on the size of payments that can be made. Some providers, for example, limit transfers to very small amounts until the user's identity and address are verified by conventional mail.

Risk is also posed by the extensive use of e-mail. The systems use this medium for various purposes: e-mail serves as a means of communication, the e-mail address acts as an addressing or locating system, and one's e-mail response to a receipt of payment is used, in part, as a means of identifying the payment recipient. A single e-mail account shared by several people naturally will diminish the effectiveness of e-mail as an identifier and a means to communicate to only one person. As a result, additional means to identify the recipient become necessary. Increasing the number of hurdles a user must overcome to transfer value may lower system risk, but at the cost of reducing system convenience.

It is worth noting that the leading personal on-line payment provider grew out of an encryption firm, which indicates that the sponsors recognize the importance of preventing counterfeit and fraudulent claims from being entered against the company. One company official stated that successful providers will have to supply world-class fraud prevention and detection systems to manage this type of risk. If these systems should mature and create a more universal, interoperable system, then the operational risks will loom larger simply because of the larger values involved. In the meantime, it is safe to say that the existing systems are already under intense scrutiny by security experts (as well as hackers) for any possible weaknesses.

Like traditional financial intermediaries, on-line payment providers also face a certain amount of credit and liquidity risk. So far, this risk has been relatively modest: the dollar amounts involved have been too small to create significant risk for the financial system. In addition, nonbank providers generally maintain the assets in money market funds or at banks, all but eliminating credit and liquidity risk. Therefore, as long as providers continue to keep their funds in short-term, high-quality assets, credit and liquidity risk will not be a major issue.

. . .

Regulatory Treatment of Payment Providers

Some personal on-line payment providers are banks and some are not, and this distinction gives rise to differences in regulatory treatment. Bank providers, for example, are required to hold a certain share (3 or 10 percent, depending on the level of deposits) as non-interest-bearing reserves, while nonbank providers currently have no such requirement. In addition, unlike nonbank providers, banks are required to hold a minimum level of capital. Banks are also subject to reporting requirements and periodic examination by supervisory authorities such as the

Comptroller of the Currency, the Federal Reserve, the Federal Deposit Insurance Corporation, and state banking agencies. Finally, banks can avail themselves of deposit insurance for account balances up to $100,000, while nonbank providers cannot offer this protection.

Because nonbank providers of personal on-line payments typically have chosen to invest in low-risk assets, the providers resemble "narrow banks" — institutions that hold only riskfree, liquid assets, and by doing so avoid the threat of bank runs. Because of this feature, narrow banking is sometimes proposed as a way to render deposit insurance unnecessary. (Nonbank payment providers are not required to disclose this information, though.) Consequently, there is probably little demand for traditional deposit insurance. Fraud, however, is a major concern. In light of this concern, some on-line payment providers have offered private insurance against fraudulent use of their customers' accounts, to enhance the attractiveness of their service. (This differs from deposit insurance, however, which insures against bank insolvency.)

These issues raise the question of whether nonbank personal on-line payment providers are in effect banks. The answer depends on the definition of "bank." If a bank is an institution that "takes deposits and makes loans," the answer would be no, as these providers typically invest in money market assets, rather than loans.[13] This is not the only definition of a bank, however. An alternative definition, codified in the Glass–Steagall Act, focuses on the role of banks as deposit takers. The Act precludes any institution other than a state-licensed money transmitter or a state or national bank from engaging in "the business of receiving deposits subject to check or to repayment upon presentation of a passbook, certificate of deposit, or other evidence of debt, or upon request of the depositor."[14] From an economic perspective, as receivers of funds subject to withdrawal or transfer upon the instruction of customers, nonbank on-line payment providers might be deemed to fit this definition. Alternatively, certain nonbank providers of arguably similar services — for instance, money transmitters such as Western Union and traveler's check firms such as American Express — are legally recognized and are licensed in several states to provide these services.

The resemblance of personal on-line payment providers to narrow banks also raises the issue of the complementarity between lending and deposit taking emphasized in various theories of banking. Some recent theories . . . suggest that the provision of transaction deposits naturally lends itself to wider banking activity, such as lending. In those theories, the provision of transaction deposits creates a form of liquidity that can be utilized to make loans more cheaply than those offered by other firms. If those theories are correct, and apply to the personal on-line

---

[13] The definition paraphrases the definition of a bank contained in the Bank Holding Company Act of 1956, which considers a bank an institution that "(i) accepts demand deposits or deposits that the depositor may withdraw by check or similar means for payment to third parties or others; and (ii) is engaged in the business of making commercial loans" (Bank Holding Company Act of 1956, Section 2(C)(1) codified at 12 U.S.C. 1841(c)).

[14] Glass–Steagall Act, Section 21A(2) codified at 12 USCS § 378(a)(2).

payment providers, then the providers might be transformed, over time, into more bank-like firms to take advantage of this economy. In contrast, the transmitters of small-value wire transfers and traveler's checks, although similar to personal on-line payment providers, have not transformed themselves into lenders, as these theories might imply.

. . .

C. Escrow Services

The online payment services discussed above help to speed up the fulfillment of purchase transactions, by giving the seller immediate access to the buyer's payment. They also provide a measure of security to sellers, by making it unnecessary for them to run the risk of bounced checks or chargebacks. These services, however, offer no protection to buyers, who remain subject to the risk that the seller will accept payment and then fail to ship the goods.

Online escrow services offer buyers protection against the risk of nondelivery.

> Escrow services generally operate like PayPal . . . , except that an escrow service holds the buyer's payment until after the goods have been shipped and the buyer has had an opportunity to inspect them. Escrow services generally charge a higher fee than payment-only services and their tracking and insurance requirements can also add significant costs to a transaction. However, because escrow services provide substantially more protection for the buyer, their fees are more likely to be paid by the buyer, while payment-only services (and credit card association rules) generally prohibit sellers from imposing a surcharge to offset fees.

David E. Sorkin, *Payment Methods for Consumer-to-Consumer Online Transactions,* 35 Akron L.Rev. 1, 14–15 (2001). For an example of an online escrow service, see www.Escrow.com.

QUESTIONS FOR DISCUSSION

Who should regulate? Before the advent of the Internet, most consumers obtained their banking services from a brick-and-mortar bank located near where they lived. Many banks now offer online services, allowing consumers to obtain banking services from a bank located in a distant state. With Internet-only banks, the consumer may not even know where the bank is located, and the same is likely to be true of P2P payment services like PayPal. Should out-of-state banks and national payment services be regulated (1) by the state where the consumer using their services is located, (2) by the state where the enterprise is headquartered, or (3) by the federal government?

D. Micropayments

When you visit your favorite news website each morning, would you be willing to pay a fraction of a cent to read the story in the sports section about the big game last night? Or would you perhaps pay a few cents to read all the articles in the sports section? Would you be willing to pay a penny to read your favorite columnist on the humor site you frequent? Pricing schemes of this sort are a possible application of online micropayments.

A micropayment may be defined as a financial payment in an amount that is small relative to the transaction costs that would be incurred in making the payment using traditional payment mechanisms. For example, it is impractical to use a credit card for purchases of less than five dollars or so, due to the transaction fees extracted by the merchant's bank, the cardholder's bank, the acquirer, the card association, and other companies involved in processing the transaction.

In the late 1990s micropayments were heralded as a breakthrough payment technology for Internet commerce, one that would make possible a broad array of new business models. Micropayments seemed to be the ideal way to sell low-value digital products for small amounts of money, amounting to a large revenue stream in the aggregate. But micropayments never caught on.[9]

Micropayment systems generally function by setting up a payment intermediary that maintains an account in the name of a user, and allows the user to load it with funds from his checking account or credit card. The user then spends against the funded amount, with the intermediary transferring funds to the merchant. Purchase transactions do not directly involve any bank or credit card system, but rather involve only the merchant, the user, and the payment intermediary.

Why have micropayment systems failed to achieve broad acceptance? Consider the following critique:

> Micropayment systems have not failed because of poor implementation; they have failed because they are a bad idea. Furthermore, since their weakness is systemic, they will continue to fail in the future.
>
> Proponents of micropayments often argue that the real world demonstrates user acceptance: Micropayments are used in a number of household utilities such as electricity, gas, and most germanely telecom services like long distance.
>
> These arguments run aground on the historical record. There have been a number of attempts to implement micropayments, and they have not caught on in even in a modest fashion—a partial list of floundering or failed systems includes FirstVirtual, Cybercoin, Millicent, Digicash, Internet Dollar, Pay2See, MicroMint and Cybercent. If there was going to be broad user support, we would have seen some glimmer of it by now.
>
> Furthermore, businesses like the gas company and the phone company that use micropayments offline share one characteristic: They are all monopolies or cartels. In situations where there is real competition, providers are usually forced to drop "pay as you go" schemes in response to user preference, because if they don't, anyone who can offer flat-rate pricing becomes the market leader....
>
> Why have micropayments failed? . . . [U]sers want predictable and simple pricing. Micropayments, meanwhile, waste the users' mental effort in order to conserve cheap resources, by creating many tiny, unpredictable transactions. Micropayments thus create in the mind of the user both anxiety and confusion, characteristics that users have not heretofore been known to actively seek out. . .
> .
>
> Micropayments, like all payments, require a comparison: "Is this much of X worth that much of Y?" There is a minimum mental transaction cost created by

---

[9] Some of the existing P2P systems, like PayPal, allow transaction amounts that approach the level of micropayments, but are not practical for transaction amounts of less than a few dollars.

this fact that cannot be optimized away, because the only transaction a user will be willing to approve with no thought will be one that costs them nothing, which is no transaction at all.

Thus the anxiety of buying is a permanent feature of micropayment systems, since economic decisions are made on the margin—not, "Is a drink worth a dollar?" but, "Is the next drink worth the next dollar?" Anything that requires the user to approve a transaction creates this anxiety, no matter what the mechanism for deciding or paying is.

The desired state for micropayments—"Get the user to authorize payment without creating any overhead"—can thus never be achieved, because the anxiety of decision making creates overhead. No matter how simple the interface is, there will always be transactions too small to be worth the hassle. . . .

Beneath a certain price, goods or services become harder to value, not easier, because the X for Y comparison becomes more confusing, not less. Users have no trouble deciding whether a $1 newspaper is worthwhile—did it interest you, did it keep you from getting bored, did reading it let you sound up to date—but how could you decide whether each part of the newspaper is worth a penny?

Was each of 100 individual stories in the newspaper worth a penny, even though you didn't read all of them? Was each of the 25 stories you read worth 4 cents apiece? If you read a story halfway through, was it worth half what a full story was worth? And so on. . . .

This still leaves the problems that micropayments were meant to solve. How to balance users' strong preference for simple pricing with the enormous number of cheap, but not free, things available on the Net?

Micropayment advocates often act as if this is a problem particular to the Internet, but the real world abounds with items of vanishingly small value: a single stick of gum, a single newspaper article, a single day's rent. There are three principal solutions to this problem offline—aggregation, subscription, and subsidy—that are used individually or in combination. It is these same solutions—and not micropayments—that are likely to prevail online as well.

Aggregation. Aggregation follows the newspaper example earlier—gather together a large number of low-value things, and bundle them into a single higher-value transaction.

Call this the "Disneyland" pricing model—entrance to the park costs money, and all the rides are free. Likewise, the newspaper has a single cost, that, once paid, gives the user free access to all the stories. . . .

Subscription. A subscription is a way of bundling diverse materials together over a set period, in return for a set fee from the user. As the newspaper example demonstrates, aggregation and subscription can work together for the same bundle of assets. . . .

Subsidy. Subsidy is by far the most common form of pricing for the resources micropayments were meant to target. Subsidy is simply getting someone other than the audience to offset costs. Again, the newspaper example shows that subsidy can exist alongside aggregation and subscription, since the advertisers subsidize most, and in some cases all, of a newspaper's costs. Advertising subsidy is the normal form of revenue for most Web sites offering content. . . .

Against users' distaste for micropayments, the tools of aggregation, subscription and subsidy will be the principal tools for bridging the gap between atomized resources and demand for simple, predictable pricing. . . .

Clay Shirky, *The Case Against Micropayments* (2000), www.openp2p.com/lpt/a//p2p/2000/12/19/micropayments.html.

QUESTIONS FOR DISCUSSION

1. *The future of micropayments.* Do you agree with the argument above that micropayments in Internet commerce are doomed to failure? Does the popularity of PayPal suggest that certain implementations of low-value payment systems may yet find acceptance in certain market niches?

2. *Regulating micropayments.* Do you think the same chargeback scheme that governs credit card transactions should apply to micropayment transactions? Does the minute amount of money involved change the type of legal regulations that should apply?

E. STORED-VALUE CARDS

A stored-value card is a card, usually the size of a credit card, that holds data representing money. The data storage medium may be a magnetic stripe of the sort that is used on credit and ATM cards, or it may be an integrated circuit ("IC") computer chip. Some IC cards also contain a microprocessor that works like a miniature computer, which allows the card to perform more sophisticated functions; these are sometimes known as "smart cards." The cardholder adds value to the card by paying money to the card's issuer, which may be a financial intermediary like a bank, an institution such as a public transportation system or a university, or an individual merchant such as a long-distance telephone company. A stored-value card is used by inserting it into a card reader, which can both read and modify the information stored on the card. Using the card subtracts value from the card and transmits it to the payee through an electronic network. Stored-value cards may implement security features, such as password protection and encryption.

Stored-value payment systems may also be implemented without a physical card. "A virtual stored-value card is just a card number associated with a charge account, without an actual plastic card to go with it. Shoppers can use a credit card to add value to their stored-value account. They can also use their stored value as they would the underlying credit card by providing the account number to the merchant." Stacey L. Schreft, *Clicking with Dollars: How Consumers Can Pay for Purchases from E-tailers*, ECON. REV., First Quarter 2002, at 37, 54. Person-to-person payment systems like PayPal, discussed *supra*, may be thought of as virtual stored-value cards.

Issuers of stored-value cards derive several types of benefits from them. First, the issuer receives payment from the consumer upon purchase of the card, but only pays that money to merchants as the card is used. During the interim, the issuer gets free use of the funds, known as "float." A second benefit to issuers is called "slippage." This is the amount that remains unused on some stored-value cards, either because the amount is so small that the consumer will choose not to redeem the card, the consumer forgets to use up the residual stored value, or the consumer loses the card. While float and slippage amounts are very small from the standpoint of a consumer, they provide a significant aggregate benefit to the issuer.

Electronic Fund Transfers, Proposed Amendments to Regulation E
Board of Governors of the Federal Reserve System.
61 Fed. Reg. 19,696 (May 2, 1996).

. . .

Stored-Value Systems

Over the past few years the financial services industry has shown increasing interest in providing "stored-value cards" (also referred to as prepaid or value-added cards) to consumers. These cards maintain, typically in a computer chip or magnetic stripe, a "stored value" of funds available to the consumer for access primarily at retail locations. The balance recorded on the card is debited at a merchant's POS terminal when the consumer makes a purchase.

Products that could be characterized broadly as "stored-value" cover a wide range. In their simplest form, stored-value systems are targeted at low-value uses (public transit, pay telephones, or photocopiers, for example); the amount that can be stored on the card is limited; and the card is disposed of once its value has been used up. These cards typically have a single type of use, and only one card issuer and one entity (likely to be the same as the issuer) that accepts the card as payment for goods or services.

More sophisticated systems can involve large transactions and permit consumers to store value in the hundreds of dollars on a card. The cards may have multiple uses, and there may be multiple card issuers and multiple card-accepting merchants. The cards may allow the consumer to obtain cash from ATMs instead of, or in addition to, making purchases. At least one system (now in the pilot stage) would enable the consumer to transfer stored-value balances to another person's card. Some systems would provide access to funds in foreign currencies. Cards tend to be reloadable, allowing the consumer to load value onto the card, for example, by withdrawing funds from an account at a depository institution through a teller, via an ATM, or, potentially, via a specially-equipped telephone. Some systems are designed as stand-alone products. In other cases, stored-value features may be added to debit or credit cards. Some of these more sophisticated stored-value systems are in operation as pilot programs or are under development by financial institutions or associations of institutions.

Colleges and universities are increasingly adding a stored-value feature to student identification cards, so that students can make purchases at campus locations such as cafeterias, bookstores, and vending machines. In some cases, the educational institution is both the issuer and the only card-accepting entity; in others, the card is also accepted by off-campus merchants. In addition to the stored-value features that some student card systems may have, these systems may operate with student asset accounts maintained by the university or by a depository institution on behalf of the university; these accounts are covered by Regulation E.

There are significant differences among proposed systems in the manner that they handle balances and transaction data. . . .

. . .

Types of Stored-Value Systems

In some stored-value systems, the balance of funds available is recorded on the card, but is also maintained at a central data facility at a bank or elsewhere. The systems operate off-line; there is no authorization of transactions by communication with a database at a financial institution or elsewhere. Transaction data are periodically transmitted to and maintained by a data facility. As in the case of the traditional consumer deposit account accessed by a debit card, in these stored-value card systems a consumer has the right to draw upon funds held by an institution. The maintenance of a record of value and of transactions for a given card apart from the card itself—so that transactions are traceable to the individual card—strongly parallels the functioning of a deposit account. The Board believes that the facts support a finding that such systems involve an account for purposes of the EFTA. These systems are referred to below as "off-line accountable stored-value systems."

In another type of stored-value system that also operates off-line, the record of value is maintained only on the card itself, and not in a central database. Transaction data for debits to the card's "stored value" are recorded on the card and captured at merchant terminals (where they are maintained for a limited period of time). Only the aggregate amount of transactions for a given period is transmitted by the merchant to a financial institution or other entity so that the merchant can receive credit. Given the lack of a centrally maintained, ongoing record of individual card balances or of transaction data in these systems, it is more difficult to conclude that an "account" exists for purposes of Regulation E. These systems will be referred to below as "off-line unaccountable stored-value systems."

A third type of stored-value system operates in a manner that is the functional equivalent of using a debit card to access a traditional deposit account. Notably, this type of system involves on-line access to a database for purposes of transaction authorization and data capture. That is, when the card is used at an ATM or a POS terminal, the transaction is authorized by means of on-line communication with the data facility, where the transaction data are stored (including information such as merchant identification, amount, date, and card number). The balance of funds available to the consumer is not recorded on the card itself, as in off-line stored-value systems; instead, the balance information is maintained in the data facility. Two distinctions between these systems and traditional deposit accounts accessed by debit card are (1) the value associated with a card is limited to the amount that the cardholder has chosen to make accessible through the card (as opposed to a deposit account accessed by debit card, where the entire account is accessible and funds available may fluctuate); and (2) the value associated with the card is accessible only through use of the card itself (in contrast to deposit accounts accessible by debit card, which typically may be accessed through various means, including check, withdrawal slip, ACH, or telephone bill payment).

The Board believes these systems—which are referred to as "on-line stored-value systems"—meet the definition of a consumer asset account, and thus are covered by Regulation E, based on their on-line operation and extensive data capture and retention. . . .

. . .

Computer Network Payment Products

Parallel to the development of stored-value card products, there has been an increasing interest in other products that might adopt stored-value concepts. Systems are being proposed, for example, for making payments over computer networks, such as the Internet. In these cases, a balance of funds could be accessed via a consumer's personal computer, and transferred or used in purchases via a computer network. As in the case of card-based products, there is a range of network payment products in operation or under development.

Some of these network payment products involve on-line access to a consumer account in a financial institution, and thus are fully subject to Regulation E. Other products may involve various procedures for authorizing and carrying out transactions, and may or may not be subject to the regulation. . . . In general, the Board believes that the same principles should apply to network payment products as to stored-value card products in analyzing coverage under Regulation E. For example, the Board might consider applying a *de minimis* exemption to network payment products in the same way the Board is proposing for stored-value card products.

. . .

___

EXTENSIONS

Tax implications of stored-value transfers. Mondex is a stored-value system that may be used both with smart cards and over the Internet. Mondex sells value to a participating financial institution, which resells it to consumers, who may use the value to make a purchase from a participating merchant. "Each Mondex smart card has its own memory and control program, allowing any two cards to exchange value. Individuals can move cash from one card to another without having to communicate with the central computer at the bank. The chips in the cards communicate with each other by means of a special terminal or device." Thomas P. Brown, Robert D. Fram & Margaret Jane Radin, *Altered States: Electronic Commerce and Owning the Means of Value Exchange,* 1999 STAN. TECH. L. REV. 2, at ¶ 79 (1999). In a private letter ruling, the Internal Revenue Service determined that neither Mondex nor the financial institutions need recognize income when they transfer value in exchange for dollars. The IRS also determined that such transfers do not give rise to IRS reporting requirements applying to certain types of payment transactions. *See* Priv. Ltr. Rul. 97–43–047 (July 30, 1997). The ruling is discussed in John D. Muller, *Selected Developments in the Law of Cyberspace Payments*, 54 BUS. LAW. 403, 434 (1998).

___

QUESTIONS FOR DISCUSSION

Privacy Concerns. Privacy tops the list of user concerns with all the emerging payment systems. Stored-value cards can be designed to make transactions anonymous, or to make them traceable to the cardholder. Do you think the government should mandate the inclusion of anonymity or traceability features? Should this be left to the market?

F. ELECTRONIC CHECKS

While the use of checks is declining in most of the leading industrialized countries, check writing in the United States and Australia continues to rise—though at a decreasing

rate. *See* COMMITTEE ON PAYMENT AND SETTLEMENT SYSTEMS, RETAIL PAYMENTS IN SE-
LECTED COUNTRIES: A COMPARATIVE STUDY § 4.3 (1999). The popularity of personal
checks in some countries is due to several factors: the check writer retains possession of the
money that the check represents for a day or two after it is spent; a check may be written for
any amount; it may be cancelled and payment stopped until it is cleared and settled on behalf of the payee; and the check writer is not responsible for its unauthorized use, as when
the signature is forged.

In view of this popularity, the Financial Services Technology Consortium ("FSTC"), a
group of banks, large corporations and technology companies, has attempted to develop an
electronic or online counterpart to paper checks. An electronic check would not only have
the advantages of a paper check and be faster and less expensive to process, but it would
also be subject to fewer errors. The FSTC's attempt to develop a true electronic check—an
electronic record that would be the legal equivalent of a paper check—is called the eCheck
Project. The eCheck uses public key cryptography. Like a paper check, an eCheck must be
signed and endorsed, but with digital signatures accompanied by public key certificates. As
such, the eCheck system depends upon certification authorities and a public key infrastructure that can be used to validate these digital signatures. A digital signature is applied by
inserting a plastic "electronic checkbook" card containing an embedded microprocessor
into a smart-card reader attached to a computer. Beginning in 1998 the federal government
worked with the FSTC to conduct trials of this technology. For more information on the
eCheck Project, see eCheck, www.echeck.org.

G. BILLING TO ANOTHER ACCOUNT

Pay-per-call has become a popular method of paying for information products that are
delivered by telephone. The consumer dials a telephone number beginning with the "900"
prefix, connects to an information service, receives a disclosure of the fee for the service
(which may be a flat fee or a per-minute charge), and by not hanging up agrees to pay the
fee. The charge for the service is itemized on the consumer's monthly telephone bill. The
consumer sends payment for the entire bill to the telephone company, which remits the appropriate amount to the information provider. Pay-per-call billing is regulated by the Federal Trade Commission. *See* Trade Regulation Rule Pursuant to the Telephone Disclosure
and Dispute Resolution Act of 1992, 16 C.F.R. pt. 308.

A similar system has been developed to pay for purchases in Internet commerce:

> Some PSPs [payment service providers] are offering a novel way for con-
> sumers who lack credit cards or who seek greater security and privacy to shop
> online. They allow consumers to have their purchases included on their monthly
> bills for telephone service or Internet access. Since phone companies and Inter-
> net service providers bill customers monthly, an individual account with these
> service providers is essentially a charge account, but without an associated
> charge card. These charge accounts differ from credit-card accounts because the
> credit they offer cannot revolve. The account holder is expected to pay the bill in
> full each month, and a late fee is imposed if the bill is not paid on time. If several
> months pass without payment being made in full, the service is discontinued.

> There are many advantages of this type of payment service and few disad-
> vantages. It is available to almost everyone with Internet access at home since
> both telephone service and an Internet service provider are generally required to
> access the Internet. It is easy for merchants and for the PSP to offer because it

piggybacks on the existing systems for sending bills for phone and Internet service. Consumers are afforded additional privacy and protection against fraud when using credit cards since their account information is not transmitted to the merchant and the billing process is discreet. The expenses they incur while cybershopping appear on their phone bills, for example, as associated with a phone number or with the name of the PSP. The main disadvantage is that not many e-tailers are accepting payments in this manner.

Stacey L. Schreft, *Clicking with Dollars: How Consumers Can Pay for Purchases from E-tailers*, ECON. REV., First Quarter 2002, at 37, 50–51. For a description of one such billing system, see eCharge, www.echarge.com.

CHAPTER SIXTEEN
TAXATION OF ONLINE ECONOMIC ACTIVITY

Sales taxes on commercial transactions and income taxes on business profits are major sources of government tax revenues. With the growth of Internet commerce, more and more transactions that formerly would have taken place offline are conducted online. This shift to online commerce may have a major impact on whether a transaction will result in tax revenues, and if so which taxing authority has the right to those revenues. Thus, with large and ever-increasing sums of money changing hands through Internet commerce, it was inevitable that issues of taxation would come to the fore.

Several characteristics of Internet commerce raise new issues, or heighten the salience of existing issues, regarding taxation. First, e-commerce facilitates transactions between a consumer in one state and a seller in another state. States depend on sellers to collect sales and use taxes on most sales of goods, but the lack of a connection between the seller and the taxing state places obstacles in the way of this mode of enforcement.

Second, the infrastructure needed to support e-commerce transactions is dramatically more portable, and less location-sensitive, than the storefronts needed to support traditional retailing. Most functions involved in the everyday operation of a website may be performed from a location that is remote from the computer server that houses the files comprising the website. The website files may be quickly relocated to a different computer server located in a different state or country, without any significant effect on the operation of the business. This makes it more feasible to relocate infrastructure of commerce in response to tax incentives, and thus increases the significance of tax havens.

Third, the sale of goods that are delivered via digital download, such as software, music, and data, raises characterization issues. Most states impose sales and use taxes only on transactions involving tangible goods, and on a limited range of services. If a digital good is characterized as intangible, it may not be subject to such taxation. The characterization of a transaction may also determine which country has the right to tax the transaction, and at what rate.

Fourth, sales of digital goods entail no shipping costs or delays, and so increase the likelihood of business-to-consumer sales across international borders. Such sales, which bypass any domestic transaction in the taxing state, may evade the existing tax structure.

Fifth, Internet commerce reduces the barriers to entry to a national and international market, allowing small entities entrée to those broader markets. The complexities of a taxing environment consisting of 7,500 taxing jurisdictions within the United States, and numerous others internationally, may be severely burdensome for a small enterprise.

I. DOMESTIC TAXATION ISSUES

A. THE INTERNET TAX FREEDOM ACT

In the late 1990s, there was widespread concern that heavy-handed imposition of taxes by states and localities might stunt the growth of electronic commerce. Congress was unable to decide how Internet commerce transactions should be taxed, and so enacted stopgap legislation, called the Internet Tax Freedom Act ("ITFA"), Pub. L. No. 105–277, 112 Stat. 2681–719 (1998), 47 U.S.C. § 151 note, that temporarily limited the authority of states to tax e-commerce. In its principal provisions, the ITFA (1) forbids states and localities from taxing the provision of Internet access services, grandfathering those access taxes that were imposed and actually collected prior to October 1, 1998, and (2) forbids multiple and discriminatory taxes on electronic commerce.[1] ITFA § 1101(a).

The ITFA also created the Advisory Commission on Electronic Commerce ("ACEC"), which was directed to "conduct a thorough study of Federal, State and local, and international taxation and tariff treatment of transactions using the Internet and Internet access and other comparable intrastate, interstate or international sales activities." ITFA § 1102(g)(1). The ACEC consisted of nineteen members: eight representatives from state and local governments, eight representing the electronic commerce industry, and three federal government officials. The sixteen non-federal commissioners were selected politically: five each by the Senate Majority Leader and the Speaker of the House, and three each by the House and Senate Minority Leaders. *Id.* § 1102(b)(1)(C). As a result of the appointment procedure, the commissioners were sharply divided along ideological lines. The ACEC was to transmit to Congress a report containing those of its findings and recommendations that were agreed to by at least two-thirds of its membership. There was little upon which two-thirds of the membership could agree: only a few recommendations concerning the digital divide, privacy implications of Internet taxation, and international taxes and tariffs. The April 2000 report, however, contains useful discussion of the issues, and makes a variety of recommendations to which a majority (but not a two-thirds majority) of the commissioners subscribe.

ADVISORY COMMISSION ON ELECTRONIC COMMERCE, REPORT TO CONGRESS (2000)
www.ecommercecommission.org/acec_report.pdf

. . .

I. Background

A. *The Evolution of Electronic Commerce*

. . .

Five years ago, the terms "electronic commerce" and "e-commerce" were virtually unheard of; today, they are household words. Notwithstanding the common usage of these terms today, the meaning and breadth of these terms are still very much uncertain. For example, it could be argued that e-commerce refers only to transactions conducted over the Internet. Conversely, e-commerce could include all transactions using the same telecommunications infrastructure as the Internet such as catalogue orders placed by telephone or facsimile.

For purposes of this report, "e-commerce," as defined in the Internet Tax Freedom Act, includes "any transaction conducted over the Internet or through Inter-

---

[1] A "multiple tax" is a tax imposed by two states on the same transaction. A "discriminatory tax" includes one imposed on an e-commerce transaction that is not imposed on a similar transaction conducted offline; one imposed at a different rate from the tax on corresponding offline transactions; and one that imposes a tax on a different person or entity than the corresponding offline tax does. ITFA § 1104(2) & (6).

net access, comprising the sale, lease, license, offer, or delivery of property, goods, services, or information, whether or not for consideration, and includes the provision of Internet access." The Act also specifically requires all recommendations to be "tax and technologically neutral and [to] apply to all forms of remote commerce." Therefore, the Commission's recommendations on taxation are intended to apply to all forms of remote commerce regardless of whether conducted over the Internet, through the telephone, via facsimile, through the common carrier or by any other means.

B. *The Impact of Electronic Commerce on the Economy*

. . .

Many private-sector research firms and academic institutions are conducting studies on the rapid rise of e-commerce and its positive ripple effects throughout the economy. Existing growth estimates vary greatly, however, due to the varying definitions and research methodologies these firms use to collect and analyze data. For example, some studies have focused on business-to-business transactions to gauge growth and economic impact while others have focused on business-to-consumer e-commerce, ranging from hardware and software to electronic retailing and backbone infrastructure and telecommunications.

On March 2, 2000, the United States Department of Commerce ("Commerce Department") Census Bureau released its first official estimate of online retail sales. According to this estimate, online retail sales equaled $5.3 billion or 0.64% of total retail sales during the fourth quarter of 1999. For purposes of this estimate, the term "retail sales" includes only sales of tangible goods (e.g., books, computer equipment, furniture and apparel) and does not include sales of services (e.g., entertainment, travel or financial services). This new e-commerce indicator will be released on a quarterly basis.[2]

. . . Early commercial ventures onto the Internet were generally limited to business models with "virtual" storefronts. These businesses operate only on the Internet and do not have physical storefronts (although they do have physical locations to facilitate back-end billing and fulfillment).

Today, traditional, physical retailers also are incorporating e-commerce tools into their business models and using the Internet to create Web sites as additional distribution channels through which to sell their goods and services. These retailers, often referred to as "click and mortar"[11] businesses, benefit from having a Web presence because many consumers still rely on the tangible experience they have gained inside a brick and mortar store when making an online purchase. There is

---

[2] [The percentage of retailing consisting of online sales has climbed steadily since publication of this report. For the second quarter of 2005, the Census Bureau estimated e-commerce sales at $21.1 billion, representing 2.2 percent of total retail sales. For updated estimates, see U.S. Census Bureau, *Quarterly Retail E-Commerce Sales*, www.census.gov/mrts/www/ecomm.html—Eds.]

[11] The term "click and mortar" stems from the term "brick and mortar" and refers to those businesses that conduct business through both a physical storefront and a Web site. "Brick and mortar" businesses, also known as "Main Street retailers," are businesses that only conduct business through physical storefronts.

also significant business-to-business use of the Internet to realize efficiencies in distribution, order fulfillment, billing, and other operational areas. Traditional catalogue-only sellers are also joining the ranks of virtual retailers and creating Web sites.

The trends in consumer buying behavior are more difficult to identify than emerging business models. With Internet commerce only in its fifth full year, it is still early to draw conclusions and make projections on the extent to which consumers of Internet goods and services are shifting their purchases from other retail channels, such as catalogues, or simply increasing their overall purchases.

C. *The Impact of Electronic Commerce on State/Local Government Revenues*

Some have expressed a concern that the rise in businesses conducting remote commerce, combined with a shift in consumer buying habits, will lead to a decrease in state and local sales and use tax revenues. In order to determine the immediacy of these concerns, it is necessary to examine how the rise of Internet sales has thus far altered sales tax collections. It is also important to examine all available evidence regarding the predicted future collection of these taxes.

In order to understand these trends and predictions, however, it is essential to understand how and why the use tax corollary to the sales tax operates. Currently, 45 states impose a state sales tax. All states that levy sales taxes also levy use taxes. Use taxes are most commonly due when an item is purchased from a business in another state and the business does not have sufficient presence (nexus) in the consumer's state for the sale to be subjected to sales tax. In the event that a consumer purchases an item and the sales tax is not collected, the consumer is required to remit the use tax according to the location of consumption of the item. However, the rate of remittance of the use tax is low for business-to-consumer sales. One reason for these low collection rates is that taxing agencies have no practical means of identifying individual purchases or their consumers, making enforcement difficult and in many cases not cost effective. Most use tax remittances come from business-to-business sales where businesses are registered within the states and subject to audits. There is no conclusive data to indicate what the collection rates of the use tax would be on business-to-consumer sales if jurisdictions increased enforcement and public education of use tax obligations.

Most Internet commerce involves business-to-business sales. Forrester Research, Inc. estimates that business-to-business Internet commerce will grow from $43 billion in 1998, to $1.3 trillion by 2003, accounting for 9.4% of all business-to-business sales. Business-to-business Internet sales pose fewer issues regarding sales or use tax collection due to higher compliance rates resulting from audits by taxing authorities. The actual amount of use tax assessed varies from state to state depending on how extensive of an audit program a state maintains.

It is especially difficult to calculate the amount of sales and use tax not collected on business-to-consumer Internet sales or on any other remote sales. Some academic estimates suggest that uncollected taxes resulting from Internet sales will be less than 2% of all sales tax revenue in 2003.[13]

Many of these estimates do not distinguish between sales of taxable and non-taxable goods and services. Further, it should be noted that, to the extent Internet sales are displacing what would have otherwise been non-Internet remote sales to consumers, the use of the Internet to facilitate a sale does not increase the tax loss to state and local governments. To the extent Internet sales are replacing purchases that would have otherwise been made through a "brick and mortar" store that collected sales tax, revenue losses to states and local governments could occur. However, even this is complicated by the fact that some remote sellers collect sales and use taxes voluntarily, while other "click and mortar" sellers are required to collect sales taxes based on their substantial nexus in a state where their product is delivered. There is no data on how many businesses are collecting taxes on remote business-to-consumer sales.

Adding to the complexity of determining the amount of sales taxes actually collected on business-to-consumer sales, some "click and mortar" retailers are not collecting sales and use taxes on items purchased through the Internet where substantial nexus may be an issue. Certain businesses that have a large physical presence throughout the country have established their Web operations as separate entities which have a much more limited physical presence. Although their Web addresses carry the name of the parent company and they advertise their Internet sites in their stores, their Web sites are separate from their "Main Street" retail operations. Accordingly, most are only collecting and remitting sales taxes in the states where the "dot com" affiliate has substantial nexus.

. . .

II. Domestic Tax Issues & Proposals

A. *Sales and Use Taxes*

One of the most fundamental issues before the Commission concerns the application of state and local sales and use taxes to Internet and other remote retail sales. Sales taxes are "consumption-type" taxes designed to generate revenue. In general, these taxes are calculated and collected by businesses at the point of sale and remitted to the appropriate taxing authorities.

Sales taxes have been levied throughout history, and became more widely applied in the United States beginning with the Great Depression. States' authority to levy these taxes is derived from the 10th Amendment of the United States Constitution ("the Constitution"), which states, "The powers not delegated to the United States by the Constitution, nor prohibited by it to the States, are reserved to the States respectively, or to the people." Today, there are over 7,500 state and local governments levying sales taxes out of a potential 30,000 jurisdictions. The five states that do not levy a state sales tax are Delaware, New Hampshire, Montana, Oregon, and Alaska. Local sales taxes are currently authorized in 33 states.

---

[13] Austan Goolsbee and Jonathan Zittrain, "Evaluating the Costs and Benefits of Taxing Internet Commerce," *National Tax Journal*, vol. 52 no. 3 (Sep., 1999); and Donald Bruce and William F. Fox, "E-Commerce in the Context of Declining State Sales Tax Bases," (Feb. 2000).

Ordinarily imposed on the sale of tangible goods, the rates for these taxes range from 0.875% to 11%. A small number of state and local governments also impose sales tax on some services. These include, for example, personal and repair services. Besides determining their own rates, states and, in some cases, local governments define and classify items and exempt certain items within their tax codes. Many of these exemptions target necessities, such as food and prescription medicines. Throughout the year, tax rates, definitions, classifications, and exemptions included in the sales tax code may be changed.

State and local governments that levy sales taxes rely on them as a major source of revenue for their general funds. According to the United States Census Bureau, state and local governments collected approximately a total of $237 billion in sales and use taxes in 1999, comprising 24.8% of all revenues generated in that year. Through these general funds, state and local governments provide a variety of public services to their residents.

The inability of state and local governments to require remote sellers to collect use taxes can be traced back to a line of the United States Supreme Court ("the Court") cases that established the "substantial nexus" standard.[24] These cases point to the Commerce Clause of the Constitution and Congress' role to regulate interstate commerce as the basis for restricting states from forcing out-of-state sellers to collect use tax. With the explosion of e-commerce, there are concerns that an increasing number of consumers will purchase items through remote sales channels such as the Internet and catalogues, and sales tax revenues from face-to-face sales may diminish. At the same time, there are indications that online activity is also driving increased sales for "brick and mortar" retailers.

While the growth of e-commerce has had a positive effect on state and local government revenues, the potential impact of e-commerce on future sales tax revenues is uncertain at this time. A recent study by Forrester Research, Inc., estimates that, in 1999, state and local governments collected $140 million in sales and use taxes from business-to-consumer purchases over the Internet, but were unable to collect approximately $525 million in sales and use taxes from Internet retail purchases. . . .

While the exact impact of e-commerce on sales tax revenues may be uncertain, clearly the need for substantial sales tax simplification is necessary in this emerging digital economy. In the course of the Commission's examination of the impact of e-commerce on sales and use tax collections, there was general agreement among the Commissioners that the current sales and use tax system is complex and burdensome. Most, if not all, of the Commissioners expressed the view that fundamental uniformity and simplification of the existing system are essential. The need for nationwide consistency and certainty for sellers as well as the need to alleviate the financial and logistical tax collection burdens and liability of sellers were common themes throughout discussions.

---

[24] *Quill Corp. v. North Dakota By and Through Heitkamp*, 504 U.S. 298 (1992), and *National Bellas Hess, Inc. v. Dept. of Revenue of State of Illinois*, 386 U.S. 753 (1967).

Commissioners also identified issues raised by sales of digitized goods over the Internet. They discussed the challenge of determining the identity and location of the consumer of digitized goods and the need to protect consumer privacy rights.

B. *Business Activity Taxes*

Many states and some local governments levy corporate income and franchise taxes on companies that either operate or conduct business activities within their jurisdictions. Income taxes are either levied as taxes on the net or gross income of businesses. A franchise tax is measured by the net income of a business. While providing revenue for states, these taxes also serve to pay for the privilege of doing business in a state. With the exception of Michigan, Nevada, South Dakota, Washington, and Wyoming, all states and the District of Columbia levy general corporate income taxes. The rates for income taxes range from 1% to 9.99%.

With the growth of the Internet, companies are increasingly able to conduct transactions without the constraint of geopolitical boundaries. The increasing rate of interstate and international business-to-business and business-to-consumer transactions may raise questions over states' ability to collect income taxes from companies conducting business within their jurisdiction. According to 15 U.S.C. § 381 (commonly referred to as "P.L. 86–272"), states may not levy taxes on the net income of sellers of tangible personal property derived from interstate commerce if the only business activities within the state consist of:

> "(1) the solicitation of orders by such person, or his representative, in such State for sales of tangible personal property, which orders are sent outside the State for approval or rejection, and if approved, are filled by shipment or delivery from a point outside the State; and (2) the solicitation of orders by such person, or his representative, in such State in the name of or for the benefit of a prospective customer of such person, if orders by such customer to such person to enable such customer to fill orders resulting from such solicitation [are orders described in paragraph (1)]."

C. *Internet Access Taxes*

. . .

As provided under the [Internet Tax Freedom] Act, presently there is a moratorium on taxes on the sale of Internet access, unless such taxes were authorized by statute and enforced prior to the promulgation of the Act. The moratorium began on October 1, 1998 and will continue through October 21, 2001.[3] At the time the Act passed, 12 states and the District of Columbia asserted that they levied sales taxes on Internet access. In addition, several Colorado cities and Tucson, Arizona have attempted to impose taxes on Internet access. Since the moratorium's enactment, several states have reversed their policies on taxing Internet access. At the writing of this report, eight states are assessing sales taxes on Internet access charges. . . .

---

[3] [Congress has twice extended the moratorium, which is currently scheduled to expire on November 1, 2007. *See* Internet Tax Nondiscrimination Act, Pub. L. No. 108–435, 118 Stat. 2615 (2004) (amending 47 U.S.C. § 151 note).—Eds.]

EXTENSIONS

Recommendation on nexus factors. To address the perceived need for greater certainty regarding the extent of a state's authority to impose sales and use taxes on electronic commerce transactions, a majority of the Commissioners recommended that Congress

> [c]larify that the following factors would not, in and of themselves, establish a seller's physical presence in a state for purposes of determining whether a seller has sufficient nexus with that state to impose collection obligations: (a) a seller's use of an Internet service provider ("ISP") that has physical presence in a state; (b) the placement of a seller's digital data on a server located in that particular state; (c) a seller's use of telecommunications services provided by a telecommunications provider that has physical presence in that state; (d) a seller's ownership of intangible property that is used or is present in that state; (e) the presence of a seller's customers in a state; (f) a seller's affiliation with another taxpayer that has physical presence in that state; (g) the performance of repair or warranty services with respect to property sold by a seller that does not otherwise have physical presence in that state; (h) a contractual relationship between a seller and another party located within that state that permits goods or products purchased through the seller's Web site or catalogue to be returned to the other party's physical location within that state; and (i) the advertisement of a seller's business location, telephone number, and Web site address.

ADVISORY COMMISSION ON ELECTRONIC COMMERCE, REPORT TO CONGRESS, *supra*, at 19. Note the overlap between these factors, relating to the nexus needed for taxation, and the factors that have been held not to support exercise of personal jurisdiction based on online activity, as discussed in Chapter 5, *supra*. Should the criteria for personal jurisdiction be congruent with those establishing a state's taxing authority? Are there any good reasons for divergences between the two sets of criteria?

QUESTIONS FOR DISCUSSION

1. *Tax on Internet access?* Do you agree with the recommendation by a majority of the Commissioners that Congress "[m]ake permanent the current moratorium on any transaction taxes on the sale of Internet access, including taxes that were grandfathered under the Internet Tax Freedom Act."? Is there any good reason for treating Internet access any differently from other telecommunications services, with respect to taxation?

2. *Neutrality.* In a 1996 discussion paper, the United States Department of the Treasury posited neutrality as the touchstone for resolving issues of taxation in e-commerce:

> A fundamental guiding principle should be neutrality. Neutrality requires that the tax system treat economically similar income equally, regardless of whether earned through electronic means or through more conventional channels of commerce. Ideally, tax rules would not affect economic choices about the structure of markets and commercial activities. This will ensure that market forces alone determine the success or failure of new commercial methods. The best means by which neutrality can be achieved is through an approach which adopts and adapts existing principles—in lieu of imposing new or additional taxes.

> Recent technological developments may appear to be radical innovations primarily because they have evolved within a relatively short period of time. However, careful examination may very well reveal that few, if any, of these emerging issues will be so intractable that their resolution will not be found us-

ing existing principles, appropriately adjusted.

U.S. TREASURY DEPARTMENT, SELECTED TAX POLICY IMPLICATIONS OF GLOBAL ELEC-
TRONIC COMMERCE ¶ 6.2 (1996), www.treas.gov/offices/tax-policy/library/internet.pdf.
Given the issues raised in the readings above, do you think a neutrality-based approach is
equal to the task?

B. SALES AND USE TAXES

All but five of the states impose sales and use taxes, which together constitute some 25
percent of all state and local tax revenues. A third of the states authorize localities to assess
their own sales taxes, with the result that there are some 7,500 different taxing jurisdictions
throughout the country.

Sales taxes usually apply to transactions between a seller and a consumer both located
in the same state. The taxing state requires the seller to collect and remit the tax, and has the
authority to enforce its laws against a noncomplying seller. Use taxes raise more difficult
issues. A use tax applies to a purchase by a consumer located in the taxing state, from an
out-of-state seller, for use, consumption, or storage within the taxing state. State law requires the consumer in such a transaction to remit the use tax to the state. Most consumers
are unaware of the obligation, however, and most of those who are aware of the obligation
ignore it with impunity, since states find it impractical to enforce the use tax laws against
individual consumers (except with respect to items that must be registered with the state,
such as automobiles and boats).

In an effort to increase their collections of use taxes, states seek to require out-of-state
sellers to collect the taxes due and remit them to the state. In *Quill Corp. v. North Dakota*,
504 U.S. 298 (1992), the Supreme Court held that a state may not, consistently with the
Commerce Clause, require an out-of-state seller to collect use tax on sales to state residents,
where the seller's only contact with the state consists of marketing its products to state residents and delivering them by mail or common carrier. This is so, the Court held, even if the
seller has enough contacts with the state to satisfy the requirements of the Due Process
Clause. The Court affirmed its prior holding that such a collection burden may be imposed
only on a business that has a "substantial nexus" with the state.

> . . . Under *Complete Auto's* four-part test, we will sustain a tax against a
> Commerce Clause challenge so long as the "tax [1] is applied to an activity with
> a substantial nexus with the taxing State, [2] is fairly apportioned, [3] does not
> discriminate against interstate commerce, and [4] is fairly related to the services
> provided by the State." [*Complete Auto Transit, Inc. v. Brady*, 430 U.S. 274,
> 279 (1977). *National Bellas Hess, Inc. v. Department of Revenue*, 386 U.S. 753
> (1967)] concerns the first of these tests and stands for the proposition that a ven-
> dor whose only contacts with the taxing State are by mail or common carrier
> lacks the "substantial nexus" required by the Commerce Clause.
>
> . . .
>
> The State of North Dakota relies less on *Complete Auto* and more on the
> evolution of our due process jurisprudence. The State contends that the nexus
> requirements imposed by the Due Process and Commerce Clauses are equivalent
> and that if, as we concluded above, a mail-order house that lacks a physical pres-
> ence in the taxing State nonetheless satisfies the due process "minimum con-
> tacts" test, then that corporation also meets the Commerce Clause "substantial
> nexus" test. We disagree. Despite the similarity in phrasing, the nexus require-

ments of the Due Process and Commerce Clauses are not identical. The two standards are animated by different constitutional concerns and policies.

Due process centrally concerns the fundamental fairness of governmental activity. Thus, at the most general level, the due process nexus analysis requires that we ask whether an individual's connections with a State are substantial enough to legitimate the State's exercise of power over him. We have, therefore, often identified "notice" or "fair warning" as the analytic touchstone of due process nexus analysis. In contrast, the Commerce Clause and its nexus requirement are informed not so much by concerns about fairness for the individual defendant as by structural concerns about the effects of state regulation on the national economy. Under the Articles of Confederation, state taxes and duties hindered and suppressed interstate commerce; the Framers intended the Commerce Clause as a cure for these structural ills. . . .

The *Complete Auto* analysis reflects these concerns about the national economy. The second and third parts of that analysis, which require fair apportionment and non-discrimination, prohibit taxes that pass an unfair share of the tax burden onto interstate commerce. The first and fourth prongs, which require a substantial nexus and a relationship between the tax and state-provided services, limit the reach of state taxing authority so as to ensure that state taxation does not unduly burden interstate commerce. Thus, the "substantial nexus" requirement is not, like due process' "minimum contacts" requirement, a proxy for notice, but rather a means for limiting state burdens on interstate commerce. Accordingly, contrary to the State's suggestion, a corporation may have the "minimum contacts" with a taxing State as required by the Due Process Clause, and yet lack the "substantial nexus" with that State as required by the Commerce Clause.

. . .

. . . Undue burdens on interstate commerce may be avoided not only by a case-by-case evaluation of the actual burdens imposed by particular regulations or taxes, but also, in some situations, by the demarcation of a discrete realm of commercial activity that is free from interstate taxation. *Bellas Hess* followed the latter approach and created a safe harbor for vendors "whose only connection with customers in the [taxing] State is by common carrier or the United States mail." Under *Bellas Hess,* such vendors are free from state-imposed duties to collect sales and use taxes.

Like other bright-line tests, the *Bellas Hess* rule appears artificial at its edges: Whether or not a State may compel a vendor to collect a sales or use tax may turn on the presence in the taxing State of a small sales force, plant, or office. Cf. *National Geographic Society v. California Bd. of Equalization,* 430 U.S. 551 (1977); *Scripto, Inc. v. Carson,* 362 U.S. 207 (1960). This artificiality, however, is more than offset by the benefits of a clear rule. Such a rule firmly establishes the boundaries of legitimate state authority to impose a duty to collect sales and use taxes and reduces litigation concerning those taxes. This benefit is important, for as we have so frequently noted, our law in this area is something of a "quagmire" and the "application of constitutional principles to specific state statutes leaves much room for controversy and confusion and little in the way of precise guides to the States in the exercise of their indispensable power of taxation." *Northwestern States Portland Cement Co. v. Minnesota,* 358 U.S. 450, 457–458 (1959).

Moreover, a bright-line rule in the area of sales and use taxes also encourages settled expectations and, in doing so, fosters investment by businesses and individuals. Indeed, it is not unlikely that the mail-order industry's dramatic growth over the last quarter century is due in part to the bright-line exemption from state taxation created in *Bellas Hess.*

. . .

This aspect of our decision is made easier by the fact that the underlying issue is not only one that Congress may be better qualified to resolve, but also one that Congress has the ultimate power to resolve. No matter how we evaluate the burdens that use taxes impose on interstate commerce, Congress remains free to disagree with our conclusions. . . . Indeed, in recent years Congress has considered legislation that would "overrule" the *Bellas Hess* rule. Its decision not to take action in this direction may, of course, have been dictated by respect for our holding in *Bellas Hess* that the Due Process Clause prohibits States from imposing such taxes, but today we have put that problem to rest. Accordingly, Congress is now free to decide whether, when, and to what extent the States may burden interstate mail-order concerns with a duty to collect use taxes.

. . .

Quill Corp. v. North Dakota, 504 U.S. at 311–18.

The Court has indicated that the "substantial nexus" requirement is satisfied only if the taxpayer has a "physical presence" in the taxing jurisdiction. *Barclays Bank PLC v. Franchise Tax Board,* 512 U.S. 298, 312 n.10 (1994). It is clear that a business with an office, storefront, sales force, or distribution point within a state is subject to the state's taxing jurisdiction; and it is equally clear that a business whose only contact with a state is the shipment of goods to residents of the state via common carrier may *not* be required to collect taxes on such sales. In between these two extremes there is a great deal of uncertainty, as it is not at all clear what constitutes a "physical presence."

QUESTIONS FOR DISCUSSION

A federal solution? The Commerce Clause has been interpreted as both a grant of legislative authority to Congress, and a limitation on the legislative authority of the states. In the latter application, it is often referred to as the Dormant Commerce Clause. Unlike most constitutional decisions, a judicial decision applying the Dormant Commerce Clause is subject to override by Congress. This is because such a decision represents no more than the court's best guess regarding whether Congress would consider the challenged state law an interference with its plenary power to regulate interstate commerce. Congress retains the authority to declare that it has no objection to the state law, thereby rendering the law compatible with the Commerce Clause. Thus, Congress could legislatively override the Supreme Court's determination that a state may not require a company to collect use tax unless the company has a "substantial nexus" with the taxing state: "Congress is now free to decide whether, when, and to what extent the States may burden interstate mail-order concerns with a duty to collect use taxes." *Quill v. North Dakota,* 504 U.S. at 318. Should Congress exercise this authority in the context of electronic commerce? If so, is there any basis for not doing the same with respect to sales via catalogue, direct mail, and other long-distance marketing methods?

1. The "Substantial Nexus" Requirement

a. Integration of Online and Offline Businesses

Suppose that a seller does not itself have any physical presence in the state, but is affiliated in some way with another company that does have such a presence. Under what circumstances is the presence of that affiliated company attributable to the seller, for purposes of establishing nexus with the state?

One set of issues arises when a brick-and-mortar retailer, with a physical presence in one or more states, seeks to avoid attribution of that physical presence to its online operations. If a retailer with a physical presence in all fifty states sets up a website and begins selling goods through the site, the retailer will be required to collect use taxes on all sales to customers in states that impose such a tax. This will place the retailer at a competitive disadvantage with respect to freestanding online sellers that satisfy the nexus requirement in few or no states, which by virtue of the Supreme Court's interpretation of the Commerce Clause will be immune from such collection obligations. The retailer will also lose a potential competitive advantage with respect to brick-and-mortar sellers, which are required to collect sales tax on all transactions.

Some retailers have sought to avoid this attribution of physical presence by structuring their online operation as a legally distinct entity.

Borders Online, LLC v. State Board of Equalization
29 Cal.Rptr.3d 176 (Cal.App.2005).

■ RIVERA, J.

We face with increasing frequency issues at the junction of Internet technology and constitutional principles. This is another such case.

Borders Online, LLC (Online), a Delaware company, sold more than $1.5 million in merchandise over the Internet to California consumers in 1998 and 1999. Online's website included a notice that any goods purchased from Online could be returned to any Borders Books and Music store (Borders store). Under the policy of Borders, Inc. (the owner of Borders stores), customers could exchange the items or receive a credit card refund. Numerous Borders stores are located all over California. Borders, Inc. (Borders) and Online also engaged in incidental cross-marketing practices to benefit the Borders brand. Online and Borders are affiliated through a common parent company but are distinct corporate entities.

The State Board of Equalization (Board) determined that Borders was Online's representative operating in the state "for the purpose of selling" Online's goods, and therefore Online was required to collect and remit a use tax from its California customers for the period April 1, 1998, through September 30, 1999 (the disputed period). (*In the Matter of the Petn. for Redetermination Under the Sales and Use Tax Law of: Borders Online, Inc.* (Sept. 26, 2001) [2000–2003 Transfer Binder] Cal. Tax Rptr. (CCH) ¶ 403–191, pp. 29,971, 29,972, 29,974 (Board's Borders Opn.).) The primary questions posed by this appeal are whether Borders's activities on behalf of Online were "for the purpose of selling" Online's goods and whether, through Borders,

Online had a sufficient presence in the state to justify the imposition of the tax collection burden. The trial court, on summary judgment, ruled in favor of the Board. Online challenges the ruling on the merits and argues the case should have gone to trial. We conclude the trial court's determination was correct, and affirm.

I. FACTUAL AND PROCEDURAL BACKGROUND

Online is a limited liability corporation formed under Delaware law in 2001 with headquarters in Michigan. From April 1998 to September 1999, Online sold books, book accessories, magazines, compact discs, videotapes, and similar tangible goods over the Internet to customers, including customers in California. It did not own or lease property in California during the disputed period and did not have any employees or bank accounts in the state. Online employees located outside California received and processed all orders placed through Online's website, Borders.com. Online neither collected tax from its California purchasers nor paid sales or use taxes to the Board for its sales to California purchasers during the disputed period.

Online was wholly owned by Borders Group, Inc. Borders Group, Inc., also owns Borders, which, in turn, owns Borders stores. Numerous Borders stores are located throughout California and in other states. Borders stores sell merchandise that is comparable to the goods sold by Online over the Internet. Receipts at Borders stores sometimes contained the phrase "Visit us online at www.Borders.com." Although Borders stores did not have facilities to assist customers wishing to place orders with Online, Borders's employees were encouraged to refer customers to Online. Visitors to Online's website could access a "link" to Borders's website, www.bordersstores.com, which provided advertising and promotional information for Borders stores, including a list of store locations.

. . .

From September 30, 1998, to August 11, 1999, Online posted the following return policy on its website: "You may return items purchased at Borders.Com to any Borders Books and Music store within 30 days of the date the item was shipped. All returns must be accompanied by a valid packing slip (your online receipt and shipping notification are not valid substitutes for a packing slip on returns to stores). Gift items may be returned or exchanged if they are accompanied by a valid gift packing slip. You may not return opened music or video items, unless they are defective." Any merchandise returned to Borders pursuant to this policy was either absorbed into Borders's own inventory or disposed of. Borders did not charge Online for accepting returns of Online's merchandise. Borders also accepted returns of saleable merchandise presented without a receipt (including merchandise purchased from competitor retailers) for store credit, provided that Borders carried the returned items. However, exchanges or credit card refunds for returned items were routinely provided only to Borders and Online customers with receipts or packing slips.

On July 29, 1999, the Board sent a letter to Online stating the company was required to collect and remit use taxes on all sales to California purchasers because Online's affiliate Borders acted as Online's agent by accepting return merchandise.

Section 6203, subdivision (a)[2] requires retailers "engaged in business in this state" to collect and pay a use tax. In stating its opinion that Online was required to pay a use tax, the Board relied on section 6203, subdivision (c)(2) (§ 6203(c)(2)), which defines " '[r]etailer engaged in business in this state' " as "[a]ny retailer having any representative, agent, salesperson, canvasser, independent contractor, or solicitor operating in this state under the authority of the retailer or its subsidiary for the purpose of selling, delivering, installing, assembling, or the taking of orders for any tangible personal property." The Board reasoned that Online was "engaged in business in California" because Borders was "acting as an agent by accepting re-turn merchandise on behalf of [Online] as defined in [the company's] Web site re-turn policy."

Online removed its return policy message from its website on August 11, 1999. The Board continued to regard Online as a retailer engaged in business in Califor-nia, however, and again wrote to the company on October 25, 1999, stating Online was required to collect and pay state use tax. On January 27, 2000, the Board issued a notice of determination to Online for unpaid use taxes, plus interest and penal-ties, for Online's sales to California purchasers during the disputed period.

Online filed a petition for redetermination, which the Board denied in a memo-randum opinion. (Board's Borders Opn., *supra*) . . . . Online paid $167,667.78 to the Board and then timely submitted a claim for refund, which the Board denied. After exhausting its administrative remedies, Online filed a complaint in San Francisco Superior Court seeking a refund. . . . The Board filed a motion for summary judg-ment, and the trial court granted the motion. . . . The trial court entered judgment on November 26, 2003, and Online timely appealed.

II. DISCUSSION

. . .

B. Online Is Subject to California's Use Tax

A use tax on interstate sales is "a tax on the privilege of use of property by the buyer" who purchases goods that would not otherwise be subject to a sales tax. . . . California imposes a use tax "on the storage, use, or other consumption in this state of tangible personal property purchased from any retailer . . . for storage, use, or other consumption in this state. . . ." (§ 6201.) The tax is paid by the purchaser but is collected by the retailer. (§§ 6202, subd. (a), 6203, subd. (a).[3] A retailer that fails to collect the appropriate use taxes becomes indebted to the state for the amount owed. (§ 6204.)

---

[2] All statutory references are to the Revenue and Taxation Code unless otherwise speci-fied. [Relocated footnote—Eds.]

[3] Section 6203, subdivision (a) provides that "[e]very retailer engaged in business in this state and making sales of tangible personal property for storage, use, or other consumption in this state . . . shall, at the time of making the sales or, if the storage, use, or other consump-tion of the tangible personal property is not then taxable hereunder, at the time the storage, use, or other consumption becomes taxable, collect the tax from the purchaser and give to the purchaser a receipt therefor. . . ."

Both parties agree this case is governed by section 6203(c)(2) (defining " '[r]etailer engaged in business in this state' "), but disagree as to whether the statute applies to Online. The question, then, is whether Online had a "representative" or "agent" in California acting "under the authority of" Online for the purpose of "selling" personal property. (§ 6203(c)(2).)

1. Borders Acted Under Online's Authority As Its Agent

The trial court found that Online's return policy posted on its website provided "undisputed evidence" "confirm[ing] that Borders was [Online's] authorized agent or representative for the purpose of accepting returns of Online merchandise from California purchasers." It held this finding was supported by the fact that (1) each Borders store in the state would accept returns and provide a refund, store credit or exchange of Online's merchandise; (2) Borders encouraged its store employees to refer customers to Online's website; and (3) receipts at Borders stores sometimes invited patrons to "Visit us online at www.Borders.com." The trial court concluded, "Borders' practice of providing unique and preferential services to Online purchasers by offering cash refunds to any purchaser of Online merchandise who wanted one, when it could refuse to do so for customers of Online's competitors, indicates that Borders provided such preferential services because it was Online's authorized agent or representative."

. . .

A representative is "[o]ne who stands for or acts on behalf of another." (Black's Law Dict. (7th ed.1999) p. 1304, col. 2.) " 'An agent is one who represents another, called the principal, in dealings with third persons.' (Civ.Code, § 2295.)" (*Scholastic Book Clubs, Inc. v. State Bd. of Equalization* (1989) 207 Cal.App.3d 734, 737 (*Scholastic*).) An agency relationship "may be implied based on conduct and circumstances." (*Id.* at pp. 737–738.) In *Scholastic*, cited by the trial court, the appellant was an out-of-state mail order book seller that had no physical presence in California. It mailed catalogs to teachers, who distributed offer sheets to students and then forwarded orders to the appellant. The appellant claimed, as Online does here, it was not subject to California's use tax because the teachers were not acting as its agents or representatives. The court disagreed and held the teachers were acting under the appellant's authority, based on the fact that "[b]y accepting the orders, the payment and shipping the merchandise, appellant clearly and unequivocally ratified the acts of the teachers and confirmed their authority as appellant's agents or representatives." (*Id.* at p. 738.) Likewise here, there is no dispute either that Online announced on its website that Borders was authorized to accept Online's merchandise for return, or that Borders would provide customers with an exchange, store credit, or a credit card credit. By accepting Online's merchandise for return, Borders acted on behalf of Online as its agent or representative in California.

Online claims the trial court erred in holding Borders was Online's agent because it failed to apply what it refers to as California's "four-factor test" to review the agency issue. It insists an agency relationship exists only if (1) the agent has power to alter legal relationships of the principal, (2) the agent acts as the fiduciary of the principal, (3) the principal can control the agent, and (4) the agent consents to act as the principal's agent. While it is true courts consider these factors when considering agency issues in various contexts, there is no bright-line "four-factor test" in determining agency. Online overstates its position in claiming the trial court erred by "failing to apply" such a test.

. . .

Online claims it had no "control" over Borders's action but does not dispute that Borders implemented the return policy posted on Online's website. Online also notes there was no written agreement between Online and Borders, but "[t]he creation of an agency relationship is not dependent upon the existence of a written agreement." (*Scholastic, supra,* 207 Cal.App.3d at p. 737.) In fact, "[t]he relationship may be implied based on conduct and circumstances [citations], as well as by ratification." (*Id.* at pp. 737–738.) It therefore does not matter, as Online claims, that Borders did not have the subjective belief it was Online's agent. By accepting Online's merchandise under the terms of Online's return policy, Borders was effectuating Online's policy, even if it was also Borders' own policy. The undisputed facts show Borders acted as Online's agent or representative and therefore Online meets the first part of section 6203(c)(2)'s definition of " '[r]etailer engaged in business in this state,' " as a "retailer having [a] representative [or] agent . . . operating in this state . . . ."

. . .

2. Borders Was "[S]elling" for Purposes of Section 6203(c)(2)

The trial court concluded that by providing refunds and exchanges to Online's customers pursuant to Online's return policy, Borders was engaged in "selling" as that term is used in section 6203(c)(2). The court reasoned that "the term 'selling' may properly be defined to include all activities that constitute an integral part of inducing sales. Such a definition fairly captures the common understanding of this term."

The term "selling" is not defined in the statute. The Board construed the term to include "all activities that are an integral part of making sales," and concluded that this interpretation accords with its "common usage." The Board reasoned, "When out-of-state retailers that make offers of sale to potential customers in California authorize in-state representatives to take returns, these retailers acknowledge that the taking of returns is an integral part of their selling efforts. Such an acknowledgement comports with common sense because the provision of convenient and trustworthy return procedures can be crucial to an out-of-state retailer's ability to make sales. This is especially evident in the realm of e-commerce." Online, by contrast, proposes the term "selling" be narrowly defined as "the act of making a sales transaction."

. . .

We think the Board's interpretation of the term "selling" is persuasive. The Board appears to have thoroughly considered the meaning of the term, and its reasoning that the act of "selling" encompasses offering other inducements to purchase is consistent with at least one later pronouncement. (*In the Matter of the Petn. for Redetermination Under the Sales and Use Tax Law of Barnes & Noble.Com* (Sept. 12, 2002) [2000–20003 Transfer Binder] Cal. Tax Rptr. (CCH) ¶ 403–325, pp. 30,447, 30,450 [bookstore's distribution of discount coupon on behalf of affiliated Internet retailer was integral to selling efforts and thus constituted "selling"].) In contrast, Online's narrow interpretation would mean that even if a local representative were to provide dramatic incentives to California customers to purchase the out-of-state retailer's goods, no tax could be imposed unless the representative is actually involved in the solicitation of the sale or the sale transaction itself. We agree with the Board that Online's return policy undoubtedly made purchasing merchandise on its website more attractive to California customers, as they would know that returning or exchanging any unwanted items would be far simpler than if they purchased items from an e-commerce retailer with no presence in California.

Online contends this conclusion is a "theory of marketing without evidentiary support from the record" and that, as a factual matter, the policy was meant to benefit Borders, not Online. It also claims there was no evidence in the record that the return policy actually induced customers to purchase from Online. In effect, Online is contending the Board did not present a prima facie case that the returns-to-Borders-stores policy was an integral part of Online's sales activities. We disagree.

. . . The return policy manifestly was not put in place to maximize *returns* of Online's merchandise, and Online does not contend otherwise. Therefore, the Board concludes, the only reasonable inference is that the policy was created for the purpose of inducing *sales* in California. This conclusion rests on the logical inferences that at least some online consumers will not place orders if the retailer does not provide a return policy "worthy of confidence" and therefore Online's ability to offer these potential customers "convenient returns and exchanges at nearby reputable 'brick-and-mortar' stores . . . would assuredly help promote such confidence." (Board's Borders Opn., *supra*.) Further, with respect to customers who are not satisfied with their purchases, "[a]n online retailer that offers convenient, local return and exchange options is much more likely to obtain repeat business from such purchasers." (*Ibid.*)

We think these compelling inferences, drawn from the undisputed facts, are sufficient to present a prima facie case, shifting the burden to Online to present evidence (or to argue contrary inferences) and thus create a triable issue of fact. Online did not do so. . . .

As to the merits, Online cannot seriously dispute that its return policy made its website more appealing to potential customers. One of the documents Online produced to the Board—apparently an information sheet prepared for Borders's employees—described Online as "an extension of the Borders brand" and touted the reciprocal benefits of cross-referrals: "If we don't refer customers to Borders.com, those interested in purchasing online will go to Amazon or barnesandnoble.com. Additionally, well under 5% of visitors to the site purchase online, but 100% receive a message about the Borders brand and will experience our active promotion of Borders stores. As your store experience can attest to, customers come into Borders looking for items they've seen online. We think Borders.com can complement Borders stores' business and vice versa." Even if the return policy also benefited Borders, that does not mean the policy was any less attractive to Online's customers. Whatever the subjective intent of Online or its individual customers, the Board's conclusion that Online's return policy is integral to making sales because of its attractiveness, convenience, and trustworthiness is persuasive, especially in the context of e-commerce.

. . .

C. The Trial Court's Ruling Is Consistent with the Commerce Clause

It is well settled that under the commerce clause, there must be a sufficient connection between a state and a retailer in order for the state to impose a use tax on the seller's goods. (*Scripto v. Carson* (1960) 362 U.S. 207, 210–211 (*Scripto*) [upholding imposition of Florida use tax on Georgia company where 10 jobbers in Florida were responsible for soliciting and submitting orders].) This nexus prevents states from otherwise imposing impermissible burdens on interstate commerce. (*Id.* at p. 212; see also *Quill Corp. v. North Dakota* (1992) 504 U.S. 298, 312–313 (*Quill*).) A tax passes constitutional muster only if it is applied to " 'an activity with a substantial nexus with the taxing State.' " (*Quill, supra,* 504 U.S. at p. 311, quoting *Complete Auto Transit, Inc. v. Brady* (1977) 430 U.S. 274, 279.)

. . . The *Quill* court held that a use tax is impermissible where a seller's only connection with a particular state is orders placed and merchandise delivered through a common carrier or the United States mail; a seller must have a physical presence in a state to satisfy the commerce clause. As the United States Supreme Court has observed, " 'the crucial factor governing nexus is whether the activities performed in [the] state on behalf of the taxpayer are significantly associated with the taxpayer's ability to establish and maintain a market in [the] state for the sales.' " (*Tyler Pipe Industries v. Dept. of Revenue* (1987) 483 U.S. 232, 250 (*Tyler Pipe*) [in-state sales representatives engaged in substantial activities in Washington to help out-of-state piping company's business in that state].) Online does not dispute it established and maintained a robust market for sales in California. The question is whether the record satisfies the remainder of the test, i.e., that the activities performed by Borders on its behalf were " 'significantly associated with [Online's] ability to establish and maintain' " its California market. We conclude that they were.

As an initial matter, we address Online's position that a state has no authority to impose a tax collection duty on an out-of-state retailer unless its in-state representative is *"actually making sales transactions "* as was the case in *Scripto, Tyler Pipe* and *Scholastic*. Online's formulation of the test is too constricted. The pivotal question when testing a state's taxing authority against the dormant commerce clause is not whether the foreign company has agents soliciting sales in the state. The question, rather, as articulated in *Tyler Pipe*, is whether the activities of the retailer's in-state representatives are " 'significantly associated with [its] ability to establish and maintain a market in [the] state for the sales.' " While the cases assess a combination of activities that often include solicitation or sales, the analysis turns on the totality of the activities undertaken to maintain a successful market. . . . [C]ourts have found insufficient presence where the out-of-state seller sent technicians into the taxing state an average of three times (about 11 hours) per year to perform electronic wiring for installing the device sold. (*In re Appeal of Intercard, Inc.* (Kan.2000) 14 P.3d 1111, 1113, 1122–1123.) These contacts were considered "isolated, sporadic, and insufficient to establish a substantial nexus to Kansas." . . . .

. . .

. . . In sum, there is no requirement that the out-of-state retailer's in-state representative be engaged in the solicitation of sales or in sales transactions to satisfy the substantial nexus required by the commerce clause. We turn now to application of the nexus requirement to the undisputed facts before us.

We have already determined that Online's return policy was part of its strategy to build a market in California. We further note that Borders's efforts on Online's behalf were not limited to accepting returns from—and providing exchanges and credit card refunds to—Online customers. Borders's receipts were sometimes imprinted with "Visit us online at www.Borders.com," and Borders's employees were encouraged to refer customers to Online to find merchandise not available at Borders stores. The cross-selling synergy was also maintained by the use of similar logos, by the link to Borders' website from Online's website, and by the sharing of some market and financial data between the two entities. Online generated more than $1.5 million in sales in California in 18 months. These facts amply support the conclusion that Online had a representative with a physical presence in the State and the representative's activities were " 'significantly associated with [Online's] ability to establish and maintain a market in [the] state for the sales.' "

Online contends the trial court's conclusion is inconsistent with *SFA Folio Collections, Inc. v. Tracy* (1995) 73 Ohio St.3d 119, 652 N.E.2d 693, 697 (*SFA Folio Collections*) and *Bloomingdale's v. Dept. of Revenue* (1989) 130 Pa.Cmwlth. 190, 567 A.2d 773, 778 (*Bloomingdale's*), which held that a department store's acceptance of returns from an affiliated out-of-state mail-order business was insufficient to create a substantial nexus between the mail-order company and the state. But in *SFA Folio Collections,* the mail-order house did not formulate or initiate the return policy. Rather, the returns were accepted according to the department store's own policy for its own benefit and for the convenience of its customers. And in *Bloomingdale's* the acceptance of two returns from mail-order customers was considered an aberration from the normal practice.

. . .

We conclude that the fact Online's return policy was posted for less than 11 months during the 18-month disputed period does not alter the constitutional analysis. As Online itself notes, the question for purposes of the commerce clause is the "nature and extent" of the activities in the taxing state. Here, Borders stood ready to accept returns and issue refunds for all Online merchandise purchased in California, whether or not this policy was actually posted on Online's website. All the while, Borders and Online were involved in cross-promotional activities, promoting the Borders "brand." Were we to accept Online's argument that a substantial nexus did not exist during the entire time period, the company would be free to simply promote the policy through its in-state agent and reap the benefits of that policy while avoiding the state's use tax by promoting—and then simply removing—the policy on its website.

In short, we conclude that the imposition of a use tax on Online during the entire disputed period does not violate the commerce clause of the United States Constitution.

III. DISPOSITION

The judgment is affirmed. Respondent shall recover its costs on appeal.

We concur: Reardon, Acting P.J., and Sepulveda, J.

EXTENSIONS

1. *Distributing coupons is "selling."* The California Board of Equalization determined that Barnesandnoble.com llc, a Delaware company that operates the Barnes & Noble website, was liable for use tax collections for a period ending March 31, 2000. As in the *Borders Online* case, the primary issue addressed was whether actions of the related brick-and-mortar entity constitute "selling" that is attributable to the online entity. Here, the conduct in question consisted of Barnes & Noble's distribution to its customers of coupons entitling them to a discount on purchases made via the website. The Board concluded that this conduct does indeed constitute "selling." *See In re the Petition for Redetermination Under the Sales and Use Tax Law of Barnes & Noble.com*, SC OHB 97-732835, Case ID 89872 (Cal.Bd.of Equalization 2002), www.boe.ca.gov/legal/pdf/bncom.pdf.

2. *Legislative action.* In 2001, the Arkansas legislature enacted legislation that requires certain online affiliates of brick-and-mortar retailers with store locations in the state to collect use taxes:

> (a)(1) Every vendor making a sale of tangible personal property directly or indirectly for the purpose of storage, use, distribution, or consumption in this state shall collect the tax from the purchaser and give a receipt therefor. This provision includes all out-of-state vendors who deliver merchandise into Arkansas in their own conveyance where such merchandise will be stored, used, distributed, or consumed within this state. . . .

> (3) The processing of orders electronically, by fax, telephone, the Internet, or other electronic ordering process, or the processing of orders by non-electronic means, by mail order, fax, telephone, or otherwise, does not relieve a vendor of responsibility for collection of the tax from the purchaser if both the following conditions exist:

> (A) The vendor holds a substantial ownership interest, directly or through a subsidiary, in a retailer maintaining sales locations in Arkansas or is owned in whole or in substantial part by such a retailer or by a parent or subsidiary thereof; and

> (B) The vendor sells the same or a substantially similar line of products as the Arkansas retailer under the same or a substantially similar business name, or the facilities or employees of the Arkansas retailer are used to advertise or promote sales by the vendor to Arkansas purchasers.

ARK. CODE ANN. § 26–53–124. The California legislature passed similar legislation in 2000, but it was vetoed by the governor.

It is unclear whether the Arkansas "unitary nexus" legislation would survive a constitutional challenge. Other efforts to attribute one company's taxing nexus to another related company have been found inconsistent with the Supreme Court's interpretation of the Commerce Clause. *See Current, Inc. v. State Board of Equalization*, 29 Cal.Rptr.2d 407 (Cal.Ct.App.1994); *SFA Folio Collections, Inc. v. Bannon*, 585 A.2d 666 (Conn.1991).

QUESTIONS FOR DISCUSSION

Voluntary integration. Barnes & Noble, Inc., which operates a chain of over 500 bookstores, set up a subsidiary, BarnesandNoble.com, Inc., to sell books through a website at www.bn.com. Operating under this structure, the online company collected use taxes for only four states (Tennessee, New Jersey, New York, and Virginia), thereby maintaining competitive parity with arch-rival Amazon.com, which collected taxes only on sales to Washington State and North Dakota. In an October 26, 2000 press release, Barnes & Noble, Inc. announced that it would integrate its e-commerce sales with its storefront operations, becoming a "clicks-and-mortar" operation. The integration strategy would involve (1) placing Internet Service Counters in its stores, allowing customers to order products through the bn.com website, paying by cash, check, or credit card, and either picking up their order at a store or having it delivered; (2) instituting a combined membership loyalty program; and (3) allowing customers who make a purchase from bn.com to return unwanted items at any Barnes & Noble store. Does this integration of operations mean that Barnes & Noble will be required to collect tax on all sales into states where it has a store location? What might motivate the company to abandon the tax advantage it claimed when its online and storefront operations were separate?

Other retailers have tried to have it both ways: the online operation is structured as a separate legal entity, which contracts on a third-party basis with the brick-and-mortar company to accept returned items on its behalf.

FURTHER READING

- Michael J. McIntyre, *Taxing Electronic Commerce Fairly And Efficiently*, 52 TAX L. REV. 625 (1997) (arguing that a brick-and-mortar seller should be required to collect taxes on sales by its online affiliate in all states where the seller has bricks and mortar)

b. Provision of Incidental Services

Another difficulty in application of the nexus requirement arises when a remote seller's only presence in the taxing state is through its provision of limited services, such as warranty services, in the state.

The Multistate Tax Commission, on behalf of 26 states, addressed this issue in a 1995 Bulletin.[4] The Bulletin strongly endorses the view that a seller's arrangement for the provision of repair (or other) services in the taxing state, even if rendered by an independent company, supports a finding of taxing nexus.

---

[4] The Multistate Tax Commission is an association of state governments that was created in 1967 through an interstate compact. Its principal purposes are to promote uniformity in state tax laws and to establish appropriate apportionment of taxes applying to multistate taxpayers. Forty-five states participate in the Commission's activities. *See* Multistate Tax Commission, *About the Multistate Tax Commission*, www.mtc.gov/ABOUTMTC/Aboutmtc3.htm.

Multistate Tax Commission, *Computer Company's Provision of In-State Repair Services Creates Nexus*
NB 95–1 (1995).

This Bulletin describes the nexus consequences under the U.S. Constitution and Public Law 86–272 to a company selling computer and/or related items through direct marketing (hereafter sometimes called "computer company") where the computer company also provides, directly or indirectly, repair services to its customers in a taxing State. While this Bulletin focuses on the provision of repair services performed in the taxing State, other activities conducted by or on behalf of a computer company in a taxing State may also independently create constitutional or federal statutory nexus.

INDUSTRY PRACTICE

Computer companies selling through direct marketing routinely provide repair services to their customers either on-site or through a business location in the customer's State under the computer company's warranty. A typical fact pattern is described below. This example is for illustrative purposes and should not be interpreted to exclude other instances involving similar, but not identical, fact patterns.

An out-of-state direct marketing computer company ("Computer Co.") solicits sales through advertising in computer magazines, catalogues, and fliers mailed into the taxing State. Computer Co.'s one year warranty provides for repair services in the customer's State. The Computer Co. proclaims to its customers and/or potential customers in the taxing State through advertisements and other means that its warranty covers provision of repair services in the customer's State. The warranty is either included with the purchase of every Computer Co. computer or computer related equipment or is available at an additional fee. Computer Co. sells a computer or related equipment to a customer and end user in the taxing State. When the customer discovers a problem, the terms of the warranty provide that the customer should contact Computer Co. to arrange repair service. The customer is not authorized to call the third party repair company to arrange for the repair without first calling Computer Co. for authorization. Customer calls Computer Co. which, after determining that the problem is covered by the warranty, may first attempt to solve the problem over the telephone. The Computer Co. determines whether repair is necessary and authorizes the in-state repair. Either Computer Co. or the customer, on Computer Co.'s authorization, contacts a third party service provider who performs the service in the taxing State either at the customer's location or at a site determined by the third party service provider.

NEXUS CONSEQUENCES

The industry practice of providing in-state warranty repair services through third party repair service providers, as described above, creates constitutional nexus for imposition of use tax collection responsibility for all sales made to customers in that State and for income, franchise, or comparable tax liability (including but not limited to a gross receipts excise tax) in the taxing State where the warranty services are performed. The repair services performed in the taxing State by the third party representative do not constitute de minimis activities in the taxing State. De minimis activity that does not rise to the level of constitutional nexus is activity that represents no more than a trivial connection with the State. Activities that are regular or systematic and in furtherance of the seller's business, such as the provision of in-state repairs under the company's warranty in this case, are not trivial.

LEGAL ANALYSIS

1. *Constitutional Standards for Use Tax Nexus*

The limits of States' taxing authority under the Due Process and Commerce Clauses for imposition of use tax collection responsibility are set forth in *Quill Corp. v. North Dakota*, 504 U.S. 298 (1992), and in *National Bellas Hess Inc. v. Dep't of Revenue*, 386 U.S. 753 (1967). . . .

Under the *Quill* bright line test, repair service provided directly by a direct marketing computer company employee in the customer's State creates in-state physical presence that exceeds contact by U.S. mail or common carrier and constitutes "substantial nexus." Courts have also consistently ruled that out-of-state companies may not circumvent state jurisdiction to impose taxes by contracting with in-state persons to conduct company business that would have otherwise created nexus if the out-of-state company had used their own employees. The U.S. Supreme Court has uniformly found that the in-state presence of a representative of an out-of-state seller who conducts regular or systematic activities in furtherance of the seller's business, such as solicitation of sales or provision of services, creates nexus. *Scripto, Inc. v. Carson*, 362 U.S. 207 (1960); *General Trading Co. v. Iowa*, 322 U.S. 327 (1944); *Felt & Tarrant Mfg. Co. v. Gallagher*, 306 U.S. 62 (1939). *See also Tyler Pipe Industries, Inc. v. Washington Dep't of Revenue*, 483 U.S. 232 (1987); *Standard Pressed Steel v. Dep't of Revenue*, 419 U.S. 560 (1975). The Court in *Quill* specifically approved this line of cases and recognized that these cases all involve physical presence that creates nexus under *National Bellas Hess*. *Quill*, 504 U.S. at 306–07. Accordingly, presence of representatives of a direct marketing computer company providing repair services in the customer's State will generate constitutional nexus.

The characterization of the relationship between the out-of-state seller and its in-state representative conducting business on the out-of-state seller's behalf does not affect the nexus determination. *Scripto, Inc. v. Carson*, 362 U.S. 207 (1960). *See also Tyler Pipe Industries, Inc. v. Washington Dep't of Revenue*, 483 U.S. 232 (1987); *Standard Pressed Steel v. Dep't of Revenue*, 419 U.S. 560 (1975). In *Scripto*, the Court held that in-state activities on Scripto's behalf by ten part-time independent contractors created nexus, even though these independent contractors worked for competing companies. The Court held that the distinction between employees and independent contractors was of no constitutional significance. As the Supreme Court in *Scripto* noted, the important fact is that the in-state activity is effective in creating and maintaining the in-state market. *Scripto*, 362 U.S. at 211–212. Similarly, in *Tyler Pipe Industries, Inc. v. Washington Dep't of Revenue*, 483 U.S. 232 (1987), the activities of one independent contractor residing in the taxing State were sufficient to create a taxable presence in the State on behalf of the company to impose Washington's Business and Occupations tax. In *Tyler Pipe*, the Court held that the critical test was

> whether the activities performed in this state on behalf of the taxpayer are significantly associated with the taxpayer's ability to establish and maintain a market in this state for the sales.

Tyler Pipe, 483 U.S. at 250. The Court found this standard was satisfied because "Tyler's sales representatives perform any local activities necessary for maintenance of Tyler Pipe's market and protection of its interests." *Id.* at 251. The important aspect of both decisions is that the Court, without weighing the amount of the in-state activities, noted that in-state activities carried on through an in-state representative associated with the seller's ability to establish and maintain a market in the taxing State satisfies constitutional nexus requirements. *Tyler Pipe*, 483 U.S. at 250; *Standard Pressed Steel*, 419 U.S. at 562. In-state representation can take many forms, such as representation by individuals, corporations, partnerships, or other entities. The different forms of the relationship have no constitutional significance. Hence, an out-of-state company may not circumvent the imposition of nexus in a State where a representative third party company, rather than an in-state individual representative, conducts in-state activities on its behalf. It is the performance of the in-state activities by an in-state entity on the seller's behalf that extends those nexus creating activities and in-state presence to the out-of-state seller.

The provision of warranty repair service in the customer's state is precisely the kind of presence that squarely supports the finding of substantial nexus. The provision of in-state repair services provided by a direct marketing computer company as part of the company's standard warranty or as an option that can be separately purchased and as an advertised part of the company's sales contributes significantly to the company's ability to establish and maintain its market for computer hardware sales in the State. As in *Tyler Pipe*, these in-state activities, which develop goodwill and increased market share, are no less important or beneficial to the out-of-state direct marketing computer company because they are performed by an independent third party repair service.

2. *Standards for Income and Franchise Tax Nexus under the Constitution and P.L. 86–272*

There is a question of whether the substantial nexus standard for imposition of use tax collection as preserved in *Quill* or a lower nexus standard applies to income taxes, franchise taxes based upon income, and other comparable taxes. Regardless of the merits of these two positions, there is no question that when a company has sufficient contact with the State to support the constitutional imposition of a use tax collection and reporting obligation with respect to the State into which the company is selling, nexus exists for the application of an income, franchise, or comparable tax as well. The discussion of use tax nexus in the previous section supports the conclusion that constitutional nexus under the Commerce Clause and the Due Process Clause exists with respect to the market State's imposition of a reporting obligation under an income, franchise, or comparable tax.

   . . .

APPLICATION OF THE LAW TO THE DIRECT MARKETING COMPUTER IN-DUSTRY PRACTICE

There is no issue of Due Process nexus because direct marketing computer companies purposefully direct advertising and catalogue solicitations to taxing State customers. Under applicable case law, in-state presence of independent contractors creates substantial nexus under the Commerce Clause for out-of-state companies that hire them to perform in-state services. Accordingly, the industry practice of direct marketing computer companies arranging for provision of in-state repair service through third parties creates nexus. The fact that the in-state warranty service is actually performed by a third party is of no constitutional consequence. . . .

The following States have indicated that their law is consistent with the constitutional and federal statutory nexus principles described in this Bulletin and that they will enforce these nexus standards with respect to computer companies selling computers and/or related items through direct marketing for purposes of determining . . . an obligation to collect, report and remit use taxes on the sale and purchase of a computer and/or related items and/or an obligation to report and pay income taxes, franchise taxes based on income, or comparable taxes [listing 25 states and the District of Columbia] . . . .

The MTC Bulletin has no independent legal force: it amounts to a public statement by the subscribing states that they will deem a company engaged in the described activities to have nexus with the state satisfying constitutional and federal statutory requirements, and will seek to enforce their tax laws accordingly. In the following case, that position was tested in court.

State v. Quantex Microsystems, Inc.
809 So.2d 246 (La.Ct.App.2001).

■ GONZALES, J.

In this appeal, the State of Louisiana and the Secretary of the Department of Revenue and Taxation (Department) challenge a judgment dismissing their claim for unpaid taxes against Quantex Microsystems, Inc. (Quantex), a vendor of computer products.

FACTUAL AND PROCEDURAL BACKGROUND

Quantex, a New York corporation, with its principal place of business in New Jersey, sells computer products via the mail, the telephone, and the internet. It solicits business through national publications and on the internet but does not specifically direct any advertisements to Louisiana. Quantex has no offices, property, bank accounts, or direct employees in Louisiana. In the years 1995 through 1997, Quantex made computer sales of approximately $7,480,000.00 for delivery in Louisiana. As part of the limited warranty provided with the purchase of its computer products, Quantex represents to its customers that it may, at its sole discretion, provide on-site service to its customers for the replacement of defective hardware parts for one year from the date of purchase. According to Quantex, however, this service is provided by the manufacturer of the computer products and not by Quantex.

On December 30, 1997, the Department filed suit against Quantex, seeking payment of unpaid use, income, and franchise taxes for tax years 1994, 1995, 1996, and 1997, plus penalties and interest. The Department alleged Quantex had "established a physical presence in the State of Louisiana" by providing for "repairs, service and/or support for products purchased for use in Louisiana through the use of agents, employees and/or independent contractors operating in Louisiana . . . ." Quantex answered the suit, denying that it had a physical presence in Louisiana.

On September 9, 1999, Quantex filed a motion for summary judgment, seeking dismissal of the Department's claims for sales and use taxes. A hearing on the motion was held on October 25, 1999, and on October 26, 1999, the trial court signed a judgment, granting Quantex's motion and dismissing the Department's demands against Quantex. The Department appeals from the judgment, contending the trial court erred in finding that "an out-of-state corporation's use of independent contractors to provide on-site computer repair services in Louisiana cannot constitute [a] substantial nexus" to support state taxation.

. . .

SUMMARY JUDGMENT

The Department argues the trial court erred in granting Quantex's motion for summary judgment, based on its conclusion that "pursuant to the U.S. Supreme Court decision in *Quill Corporation* . . . , Quantex Microsystems, Inc. lacks the substantial nexus with Louisiana required for the State to be able [to] impose taxes."

. . .

APPLICABLE LOUISIANA TAXATION LAW

Because the applicable substantive law determines the materiality of facts in a summary judgment setting, we now turn to a discussion of the Louisiana taxation law applicable to this case. . . . .

Generally, Louisiana imposes a sales tax on the retail sale in this state of each item of tangible personal property. La. R.S. 47:302. In addition to a sales tax, Louisiana imposes a use tax on items purchased in other states, but brought into Louisiana for use, consumption, distribution, and storage for use and consumption. La. R.S. 47:302. A use tax ordinarily serves to complement the sales tax of a state by eliminating the incentive to make major purchases in states with lower sales taxes. . . . Every dealer located outside the state making sales of tangible personal property for distribution, storage, use, or other consumption in Louisiana shall, at the time of the sales, collect the applicable tax from the purchaser. La. R.S. 47:304(B). Any dealer who neglects, fails, or refuses to collect the tax shall be liable for and pay the tax himself. La. R.S. 47:304(C).

The Louisiana sales/use tax law is not intended to levy a tax on interstate commerce; however, our law is intended to levy a tax on the sale at retail, the use, the consumption, the distribution, and the storage to be used or consumed in this state, of tangible personal property after it has come to rest in this state and has become a part of the mass of property in this state. This includes the collection of taxes on sales of tangible personal property that are promoted through the use of catalogs and other means of sales promotion and for which federal legislation or federal jurisprudence enables the enforcement of the use tax law upon the conduct of such business. La. R.S. 47:305(E)(1).

. . .

At issue in this appeal is whether Quantex's activity in Louisiana has a "substantial nexus" with Louisiana to warrant the imposition of taxation. . . . [T]he crucial factor governing nexus is whether the activities performed in the taxing state on behalf of the taxpayer are significantly associated with the taxpayer's ability to establish and maintain a market in the taxing state. *Tyler Pipe Industries, Inc. v. Washington*, 483 U.S. 232, 250 (1987).

In granting summary judgment in favor of Quantex in this case, the trial court determined the existence of independent contractors performing warranty work in the taxing state was insufficient to establish the necessary physical presence to support state taxation. In our *de novo* review, we determine the trial court erred in finding no genuine issues of material fact in dispute.

Quantex's service guide clearly represents to buyers of its computer products that it may provide service for defective hardware parts for one year from the date of purchase. This warranty represented to the purchasers of $7,480,000.00 worth of Quantex computer products sold for delivery in Louisiana during the relevant period that representatives of Quantex may have been physically present in Louisiana performing this service.

In discovery responses provided to the Department in December of 1998, Quantex first claimed that, since January 1, 1994, it had used an independent contractor, Vanstar Corporation, to perform warranty work. In a supplemental discovery response provided to the Department in October of 1999, Quantex denied responsibility for or involvement in the providing of service, instead claiming that Fountain Technologies, Inc., the alleged manufacturer of the computer products sold by Quantex, was responsible for handling service. According to Quantex,

> On site service is handled by the manufacturer of the computer system sold by Quantex, Fountain Technologies, Inc., whose headquarters is in New Jersey. Fountain Technologies, Inc. has no office in Louisiana. While the on site service is Fountain's responsibility, Fountain does not directly perform any of the on site service on systems sold by Quantex to Louisiana residents.

> Fountain includes an amount in the purchase price of each computer system sold to Quantex, which amount serves to reimburse Fountain for arranging on site service. Quantex does not pay for such on site services calls except for the amount paid to Fountain Technologies, Inc. as described above.

> The company Fountain Technologies, Inc. used to provide such service was Van Star. In December, 1998, Fountain Technologies, Inc. entered into an agreement with Warranty Corporation of America which is

the company they use for on site service today. Warranty Corporation of America is located at 3110 Crossing Park Road, Norcross, Georgia.

The above responses indicate there are disputed factual issues regarding whether Quantex itself provided on-site service during the relevant periods or whether on-site service was provided by Fountain Technologies, Inc. Further, factual issues remain regarding the extent of the on-site service actually performed during the relevant period and whether that activity was significantly associated with Quantex's ability to establish and maintain a market in Louisiana. Further, a review of federal and state jurisprudence indicates the parameters of the "physical presence" requirement have not been sufficiently developed to determine whether on-site service performed by independent contractors on behalf of Quantex or Fountain Technologies, Inc., or the extent of such service, would be adequate to support taxation in this case. Additional discovery on these issues will be necessary on remand.

. . .

[T]he judgment of the trial court is REVERSED, and this matter is REMANDED for further proceedings consistent with this opinion. . . .

■ FOGG, J., dissenting.

I respectfully dissent. The majority reverses this grant of summary judgment upon a determination that "disputed factual issues" exist concerning (1) "whether Quantex itself provided on-site service during the relevant periods, or whether on-site service provided by Fountain Technologies, Inc."; (2) "the extent of the on-site service actually performed during the relevant period"; and (3) whether the on-site service "was significantly associated with Quantex's ability to establish and maintain a market in Louisiana." For the following reasons, I believe that none of these constitute "genuine issues of material fact" and that, once the undisputed material facts are analyzed under the pertinent jurisprudence, Quantex is entitled to judgment as a matter of law.

. . .

. . . The applicable substantive law is fully discussed in the case of *Quill Corp. v. North Dakota*, 504 U.S. 298 (1992), the most recent United States Supreme Court case that addresses the right of a state to collect sales and use taxes from an out-of-state vendor. *Quill* held that substantial nexus means that the out-of-state vendor must maintain a *physical presence* in the taxing state. Maintaining property or employees in the taxing state is required to constitute a physical presence. This physical presence is a bright-line rule for the imposition of sales and use taxes. *Quill Corp.*, 504 U.S. at 311. Therefore, in order for Louisiana to impose sales and use taxes on Quantex, Quantex must have a substantial nexus in this state in the form of a physical location or employees in the state.

Initially, the majority finds that Quantex's answers and supplemental answers to interrogatories are inconsistent, and therefore, raise a genuine issue of material fact. I disagree with this conclusion for two reasons. First, reviewing the interrogatories in question, I find no inconsistency. Rather, reading these answers together I believe the supplemental answer simply clarifies the original answer. Read together they state that Quantex does not contract with any person to provide service or warranty work in the State of Louisiana. Neither answer indicates that Quantex itself may have "provided on-site service during the relevant periods" as concluded by the majority; rather, Quantex consistently states that it did not provide such service. Second, even if the answers are determined to be conflicting, they could only conflict in stating which company, Vanstar or Warranty, handled service. Critical to Louisiana's right to tax is the presence of a company's property or personnel within the state. *Quill*, 504 U.S. at 311. Under either scenario, neither property nor employees of Quantex were located in Louisiana. Therefore, under either factual scenario, Quantex had no physical presence in Louisiana; a determination of whether Vanstar or Warranty handled the on-site service is not material.

The majority also finds that summary judgment is not proper because a genuine issue of material fact exists because the record does not disclose the extent of the on-site service actually performed during the relevant period. The extent of on-site service that occurs in the State of Louisiana is irrelevant to a determination of taxability in this case because there is no evidence at all before the trial court that any of the service was performed by employees of Quantex. Without such evidence, *Quill* mandates a finding of no taxability. The frequency of service provided by another company is not material to this case.

Finally, the majority finds that an issue of material fact exists as to whether the on-site service was significantly associated with Quantex's ability to establish and maintain a market in Louisiana. Under *Quill*, we should not reach this issue as Quantex has no physical presence in Louisiana. In the case of *Tyler Pipe Industries, Inc. v. Washington*, 483 U.S. 232 (1987), cited by the majority, Tyler Pipe had a physical presence in the State of Washington as it had sales representatives in that state. Any facts that would determine whether on-site service by third parties was significantly associated with Quantex's ability to establish and maintain a market in Louisiana are irrelevant to an analysis of taxability under the Commerce Clause, and therefore, are not material facts.

. . . I believe Quantex made a prima facie showing that the motion should be granted. . . .

EXTENSIONS

1. *California's switch.* Although California was one of the 25 states that subscribed to the principles enunciated in Multistate Tax Commission Bulletin 95–1, *supra*, it later disassociated itself from that view and adopted a regulation taking the opposite position:

§ 1684. Collection of Use Tax by Retailers

(a) *Retailers Engaged in Business in State.* Retailers engaged in business in this state . . . and making sales of tangible personal property, the storage, use, or other consumption of which is subject to the tax must register with the Board and . . . collect the tax from the purchaser and give the purchaser a receipt therefor. . . .

A retailer is not "engaged in business in this state" based solely on its use of a representative or independent contractor in this state for purposes of performing warranty or repair services with respect to tangible personal property sold by the retailer, provided that the ultimate ownership of the representative or independent contractor so used and the retailer is not substantially similar. For purposes of this paragraph, "ultimate owner" means a stock holder, bond holder, partner, or other person holding an ownership interest.

CAL. CODE REGS. tit. 18, § 1684(a).

One commentator explains that California's switch is attributable to pressure from business representatives. "In California, the [Board of Equalization] and policymakers have taken several different actions to protect Internet activities against taxation . . . . Ernest J. Dronenburg Jr., the BOE chair, has assured the business community that the BOE intends to take the lead in keeping the Internet free of taxation. He said that 'it was the BOE's feeling that taxation of Internet activities and online services will have a chilling effect on the development of one of the most compelling and promising emerging industries. The worst thing that can happen is for Internet development to be stifled by new state and federal taxes.' " Kim Marshall & Marc Lewis, *What We Know Today About "Substantial Nexus,"* 13 STATE TAX NOTES 967, 972 (1997).

Some 40 states have taken the position that third-party warranty work *can* result in nexus.

2. *Nexus resulting from software transactions.* Software publishers normally retain ownership of the copyright in their products, licensing consumers to make use of them. Does this retained interest constitute the software vendor's presence in a state where multiple copies of the software have been furnished? In *Quill Corp. v. North Dakota*, 504 U.S. 298, 315 n.8 (1992), the Court suggested that a vendor's distribution of licensed software in the taxing state might constitute substantial nexus, if the quantity distributed was more than minimal: "Although title to 'a few floppy diskettes' present in a State might constitute some minimal nexus . . . , we [have] expressly rejected a ' "slightest presence" ' standard of constitutional nexus." A Texas administrative agency, taking up this suggestion, held that a software vendor's shipment to Texas of forty to sixty computer programs each year, under licensing agreements, created substantial nexus supporting the imposition of sales and use tax. Texas Comptroller of Public Accounts, Hearing No. 36,237 (July 21, 1998). And in *America Online, Inc. v. Johnson*, 2002 WL 1751434 (Tenn.Ct.Apps.2002), the court held that AOL's retained ownership of the floppy diskettes it mailed into the state could contribute to a finding of nexus: "we think at some point the number mailed into the state does become a factor to be added to the balance."

3. *Nexus resulting from server location.* Does the hosting of a website on a server located in a taxing state constitute nexus with the state? There is little caselaw on the issue, but California has addressed it legislatively:

> . . . The use of a computer server on the Internet to create or maintain a World Wide Web page or site by an out-of-state retailer will not be considered a factor in determining whether the retailer has a substantial nexus with California. No Internet Service Provider, On-line Service Provider, internetwork communication service provider, or other Internet access service provider, or World Wide Web hosting services shall be deemed the agent or representative of any out-of-state retailer as a result of the service provider maintaining or taking orders via a web page or site on a computer server that is physically located in this state.

CAL. CODE REGS. tit. 18, § 1684(a).

This is consistent with a proposal offered by a majority of the members of the Advisory Commission on Electronic Commerce in its April 2000 report to Congress. The proposal sets forth a list of factors that would not alone establish a seller's nexus with a state, including: "a seller's use of an Internet Service Provider ('ISP') that has physical presence in a state" and "the placement of a seller's digital data on a server located in that particular state." ADVISORY COMMISSION ON ELECTRONIC COMMERCE, REPORT TO CONGRESS, *supra*, at 19. It is also consistent with the position taken by the Organisation for Economic Co-operation and Development in interpreting the permanent establishment provision of its Model Tax Convention on Income and on Capital. *See* Part II(A), *infra*.

2. Collecting Sales and Use Taxes: the Streamlined Sales Tax Project

A company that sells its products to purchasers located in more than a few states, and that has sufficient nexus with those states so that state and local governments may impose use taxes consistently with Commerce Clause limitations, faces a daunting task in calculating the amount of tax due on a transaction. A number of factors go into the calculation:

(1) The location of the purchaser determines which jurisdiction's tax rules apply. Taxing jurisdictions are not limited to the 45 states that assess sales or use taxes: according to one study, there are also 4,696 cities, 1,602 counties, and 1,113 other taxing jurisdictions that overlay their own taxes on top of the state's taxes. Thus, one transaction may generate tax liabilities to the state, county, and city where the purchaser is located, each at its own rate.

(2) The applicable tax rate depends on the type of item that is sold. Some categories of goods are taxed at higher rates than others, and certain categories, such as food and clothing, are often exempt. Most types of services are typically exempt.

(3) The taxability of the transaction may depend on the status of the buyer. A jurisdiction may exempt nonprofit purchasers, government agencies, or those who purchase for resale.

(4) Some jurisdictions occasionally announce a "tax holiday," which suspends the imposition of taxes for a brief period of time.

The complexity of the state sales and use tax system is not, of course, new to electronic commerce. Mail order companies that aim at a national market have long been required to comply with this multifarious set of rules. In holding that the Commerce Clause prevents Illinois from imposing tax-collection duties on a mail-order business that lacks a "substantial nexus" with the state, the Supreme Court made reference to these collection burdens:

> For if Illinois can impose such burdens, so can every other State, and so, indeed, can every municipality, every school district, and every other political subdivision throughout the Nation with power to impose sales and use taxes. The many variations in rates of tax, in allowable exemptions, and in administrative and record-keeping requirements could entangle National's interstate business in a virtual welter of complicated obligations to local jurisdictions with no legitimate claim to impose "a fair share of the cost of the local government."

National Bellas Hess, Inc. v. Department of Revenue, 386 U.S. 753, 759–60 (1967).

In 2000, a group of states launched an ambitious effort, called the Streamlined Sales Tax Project, www.streamlinedsalestax.org, aimed at simplifying and harmonizing their sales and use tax systems. The project's goal is to increase collections of those taxes on sales made through Internet commerce and other remote selling methods. Representatives from over thirty states spent several years negotiating the Streamlined Sales and Use Tax Agreement, which they adopted in November 2002.

The Agreement provides that participating states will revise their sales and use tax systems to bring about a significant degree of uniformity, thereby making it simpler and less expensive for sellers with customers in multiple jurisdictions to comply with the tax system. Some of the key provisions include:

- Participating states will maintain a centralized registration system, allowing sellers to register via a single online form rather than through paper registration forms filed with each state.

- The governing board of the Agreement will certify software that automates the determination of the tax to be collected on each remote transaction. The board will also certify third-party service providers to which a seller may outsource its tax-collection duties.

- The Agreement establishes uniform sourcing rules—that is, rules as to which jurisdiction is entitled to tax a particular transaction.

- All sales and use taxes are to be administered at the state level, rather than at the level of the local jurisdiction assessing the tax. This means that in each state sellers will have to deal with only a single taxing authority, rather than with (in some states) hundreds of local authorities as at present.

- Changes to tax rates and other rules may be made only as of the first day of a calendar quarter, and with adequate notice to sellers.

- The Agreement specifies a uniform set of definitions of categories of goods and services subject to tax.

The Agreement does not contain any requirement for sellers to collect sales or use taxes on remote purchases. Nor does it affect the Supreme Court's holding, as articulated in *Quill v. North Dakota*, that a state may not impose a collection obligation on a seller that does not have a "substantial nexus" with the state. Proponents of the Agreement hope that tax collections will be improved through either of two mechanisms. First, the Agreement provides sellers with an incentive to collect taxes on remote sales voluntarily, by offering them a share of the taxes they collect as compensation for their collection costs. Second, once a radically streamlined system is in place, supporters hope that Congress will be persuaded to enact a statute that overcomes the "substantial nexus" limitation, and permits the states to impose a collection obligation on all remote sellers.

To become a member of the system created by the Agreement, a state must amend its tax laws to conform them to the Agreement's requirements. By its own terms the Agreement becomes effective when at least ten states, representing at least 20 percent of the population of the states with a sales tax, become participants. The Agreement went into effect on October 1, 2005, but at this writing several issues remained to be resolved before the Agreement would become fully operational.

Whether the Agreement will achieve its objectives depends on such factors as (1) whether retailers will begin voluntarily collecting taxes for states with which they do not have a "substantial nexus," and (2) whether Congress responds by authorizing states to impose tax-collection obligations on states without a "substantial nexus" with the taxing state.

QUESTIONS FOR DISCUSSION

Overcoming compliance burdens with technology. Given the availability of software that masks the complexity of the sales and use tax system and automatically computes the tax due on any transaction, should the courts revisit the issue whether the cost of compliance amounts to an undue burden on interstate commerce, in violation of the Commerce Clause?

FURTHER READING

- Bill Owens, *Nine Problems with Taxing the Internet* (2003), cnaconline.org/ Internet_Tax_Final.pdf (arguing that the SSTP increases the tax burden, adds complexity, compromises consumer privacy, detracts from federalism, harms electronic commerce, and disproportionately impacts rural, disabled, and elderly consumers)

3. Taxing Online Sales of Cigarettes

Internet commerce in cigarettes and other tobacco products is big business. According to some estimates, online cigarette sales reached $5 billion in 2005. State excise taxes on cigarettes have risen dramatically during the past few years, and currently range from a low of five cents per pack (North Carolina) to a high of $2.46 (Rhode Island). As with use taxes, in-state sellers are required to collect the tax and remit it to the state, but in general no such requirement may be imposed on out-of-state sellers. State law thus requires purchasers to remit these taxes directly to the state. The excise tax owed can be substantial: a person who smokes two packs a day, and lives in a state with a tax of $2.00 per pack, would have a tax liability of $1,460 a year. Predictably, as with use taxes, few cigarette purchasers pay these taxes voluntarily. The amount of taxes not paid has been estimated at $1–2 billion in 2005.

A number of states are making efforts to collect these taxes, with some help from a federal law called the Jenkins Act, 15 U.S.C. §§ 375–78. This statute, which dates from 1949, provides that sellers that ship cigarettes in interstate commerce to end users must file a monthly report with the tobacco tax administrator of each state, describing "each and every shipment of cigarettes made during the previous calendar month into such State [, including] the name and address of the person to whom the shipment was made, the brand, and the quantity thereof." *Id.* § 376(a)(2). The reporting requirement is designed to assist states in collecting excise taxes on these transactions. Most online cigarette sellers have failed to submit these reports voluntarily. In some cases, sellers have complied with the Jenkins Act only after the state filed a lawsuit to enforce compliance. *See Washington v. www.Dirtcheapcig.com, Inc.*, 260 F.Supp.2d 1048 (W.D.Wash.2003) (holding that the Jenkins Act creates a private right of action, allowing states to sue cigarette sellers to enforce compliance).

Beginning in 2003, armed with lists of their citizens who have purchased cigarettes from online sellers, states began sending out dunning letters demanding payment of back excise taxes owed. Some states have sent out tens of thousands of these letters, with tax claims ranging up to thousands of dollars per letter, and total collections in the millions of dollars.

Regulators have created significant obstacles to the online sale of cigarettes, persuading intermediaries to refuse to participate in the trade. In 2005, in response to pressure from state and federal regulators, the major credit card companies and PayPal agreed to disallow use of their services for interstate sales of cigarettes direct to consumers. DHL likewise agreed to stop delivering cigarettes to individual purchasers.

EXTENSIONS

Illegality of online cigarette sales. According to the National Association of Attorneys General and the federal Bureau of Alcohol, Tobacco, Firearms and Explosives,

> Virtually all sales of cigarettes over the Internet are illegal because the sellers are violating one or more state and federal laws, including: (1) state age verification laws; (2) the federal Jenkins Act (which requires that such sales be reported to state authorities); (3) state laws prohibiting or regulating the direct shipment of cigarettes to consumers; (4) state and federal tax laws; (5) federal mail and wire fraud statutes; and (6) the federal RICO law. Many of the sales made by foreign websites also violate federal smuggling, cigarette labeling, money laundering and contraband product laws.

Attorneys General and ATF Announce Joint Initiative with Credit Card Companies to Prevent Illegal Cigarette Sales over the Internet (Mar. 17, 2005), www.atf.gov/press/fy05press/031705internetcigsalesinitiative.htm.

In *City of New York v. Cyco.net, Inc.*, 383 F.Supp.2d 526 (S.D.N.Y.2005), the plaintiff city brought claims against a group of online cigarette sellers, alleging violations of the Racketeer Influenced and Corrupt Organizations Act ("RICO"), 18 U.S.C. § 1961 et seq., through the predicate offenses of wire fraud and mail fraud. The alleged violations consisted of the defendants' failure to provide reports to the state as required by the Jenkins Act, and statements on their websites that their cigarette sales were tax-free. The court dismissed the RICO claims on the ground that the city failed adequately to plead RICO standing, but granted leave to amend the complaint to cure this defect. The court also dismissed the city's claims under the state deceptive practices law, and common law fraud.

QUESTIONS FOR DISCUSSION

Expanding the Jenkins Act. Should Congress broaden the Jenkins Act reporting requirement to include all sales in Internet commerce? All mail-order sales? Note that use tax losses to the states from these sales are far greater than losses due to cigarette excise taxes.

4. Characterization of Digital Goods

Most sales and use taxes apply to tangible personal property, with certain exceptions, and to a limited range of services. Is software within the category of "tangible personal property"? Does it matter whether the software is delivered embedded in a physical medium, like a CD-ROM, or is delivered by digital download? What about other types of digital goods, such as music, photographs, data from information providers, and e-books?

South Central Bell Telephone Co. v. Barthelemy
643 So.2d 1240 (La.1994).

■ HALL, JUSTICE.

We granted writs in this case to decide whether certain computer software constitutes "tangible personal property" taxable under the sales and use tax imposed by the City of New Orleans pursuant to Section 56 of the City Code. The district court classified the two types of computer software at issue—switching system and data processing software—as intangible, nontaxable property, and thus granted partial summary judgment in favor of the taxpayer, South Central Bell Telephone Co. (Bell). The court of appeal affirmed. We classify computer software as tangible, taxable property, and thus reverse and remand.

I.

During the pertinent taxing periods, January 1, 1986 through April 30, 1990, Bell operated a telephone system in Orleans Parish. As part of its system, Bell set up in the parish sixteen telephone central offices. Each telephone central office is a system, in and of itself, as well as part of the larger telephone system. Simply put, each central office is a place where the caller's telephone line is connected to the line of the person being called, if that person is served by the same central office, or, if not, to a line connected to another telephone central office. Depending upon the location of the person being called, a given call may pass through multiple central offices.

Each central office consists of, among other things, switching equipment. Switching equipment includes computer processors that are directed and operated by computer software programs. Each central office is unique; consequently, each central office requires specifically tailored software designed to meet that office's operations.

During the pertinent taxing periods, Bell licensed specific switching system software programs for use in specific central offices pursuant to license agreements confected out of state with three vendors, AT & T Technologies, Inc., Northern Telecomm and Erickson. Under these license agreements, Bell acquired the limited right to use such switching system software programs; the license agreements limited Bell's right to use designated switching system software to designated switches in designated telephone central offices. More particularly, the license agreements prohibited Bell's transfer of such software to any switch other than the designated one; prohibited Bell's sublicense, assignment, sale or transfer of the programs; prohibited Bell's use of the programs after the license expired; and required that Bell maintain strict confidentiality with regard to the programs. The license agreements also reserved to the vendors ownership of, and proprietary rights in, the switching system software programs.

The vendors delivered the switching system software programs to Bell via magnetic tapes. Once received, the software programs were loaded onto Bell's switching system processors, and the magnetic tapes were either used or discarded. The vendors either billed Bell for City taxes on the magnetic tapes, or Bell automatically accrued such taxes on the magnetic tapes. Bell was neither billed by the vendors, nor accrued such taxes on the switching system software itself, however. The switching system software is thus one of the two types of software at issue in this case.

The second type of software at issue in this case is data processing software. This software guides the functions of the computers located in Bell's data processing center in Orleans Parish. Bell's data processing center handles basic accounting functions, including processing customer billings and payments, storing and managing customer data and maintaining a voucher and disbursement system. Bell acquired the right to use the data processing software through its affiliate, Bell-South Services, Inc. (BellSouth). BellSouth entered into a master license agreement regarding the software out of state. BellSouth also tested, evaluated and adapted the software out of state. BellSouth then transmitted the software electronically via telephone lines to Bell's modem in Orleans Parish. As with the switching system software, the license agreements limited Bell's rights to use the software and reserved to the vendors ownership of, and proprietary rights in, the data processing software.

. . .

The taxes at issue in this case are use taxes levied by the City on Bell's use of the two types of software programs under § 56–21 of the City Code . . . .

In October 1990, following an audit, the City notified Bell of a proposed tax deficiency assessment for, among other things, Bell's use of the two types of computer software . . . . Bell paid the full amount of the proposed tax deficiency under protest. Thereafter, in November 1990, Bell commenced the instant action, seeking to recover the taxes paid under protest and contending that the items at issue were not taxable under the pertinent provisions of the City Code.

Each party filed cross-motions for summary judgment. After a hearing on the motions, the trial court denied the City's motion and granted Bell's motion in part, finding "that the sale/use tax of the City of New Orleans is not applicable to the licensing of the data process[ing] software or to the switching software." In written reasons for judgment, the district court stated "that under the essence of transaction test" neither type of software at issue was taxable. . . .

Affirming, the court of appeal reasoned that computer software does not fall within the definition of "tangible personal property"; rather, it falls within the definition of incorporeal property as it constitutes "intellectual property." In support of the latter conclusion, the court cited jurisprudence from other jurisdictions holding that computer software is intangible because the essence of the transaction is the acquisition of intangible information or knowledge. *South Cent. Bell Tel. Co. v. Barthelemy,* 93–1072, p. 5 (La.App. 4th Cir. 1/27/94), 631 So.2d 1340, 1343. . . .

On the City's writ application, we granted certiorari to consider the correctness of that decision.

II.

The city use tax is imposed by § 56–21 of the Code of the City of New Orleans:

> There is hereby levied, for general municipal purposes, a tax upon the sale at retail, the use, the consumption, the distribution and the storage for use or consumption in the city of each item or article of *tangible personal property,* upon the lease or rental of such property and upon the sale of services within the city. . . .

"Tangible personal property" is defined in § 56–18 of the City Code as follows:

> [P]ersonal property which may be seen, weighed, measured, felt or touched, or is in any other manner perceptible to the senses. The term "tangible personal property" shall not include stocks, bonds, notes or other obligations or securities.

Construing this provision, we held in *City of New Orleans v. Baumer Foods, Inc.,* 532 So.2d 1381 (La.1988), that "the term 'tangible personal property' in the City Code's use tax is synonymous with corporeal movable property as used in the Louisiana Civil Code." . . . The application of property law concepts in this tax context is an exception to the general rule that tax laws are *sui generis,* B. Oreck, Louisiana Sales & Use Taxation § 2.2 (1992) (hereinafter Oreck). The reasoning behind applying property concepts in such a tax context is that the use of the common law term "tangible personal property" by the legislature, or by the various political subdivisions, was not intended to import the common law into Louisiana for purposes of sales and use tax law, nor to require the development of an entirely new body of property law for sales and use tax purposes only, but rather, the term was intended to be interpreted consistently with our civilian[5] property concepts embodied in the Civil Code. . . .

The pertinent Civil Code provisions are Louisiana Civil Code articles 461, 471 and 473. Article 461 distinguishes between corporeals and incorporeals, providing:

> Corporeals are things that have a body, whether animate or inanimate, and can be felt or touched.
>
> Incorporeals are things that have no body, but are comprehended by the understanding, such as the rights of inheritance, servitudes, obligations, and right of intellectual property.

Article 471 further defines corporeal movables as "things, whether animate or inanimate, that normally move or can be moved from one place to another." Article 473 further defines incorporeal movables as "rights, obligations, and actions that apply to a movable thing . . . . Movables of this kind are such as bonds, annuities, and interests or shares in entities possessing juridical personality."

. . .

. . . Hence, the civilian concept of corporeal movable encompasses all things that make up the physical world; conversely, incorporeals, i.e., intangibles, encompass the non-physical world of legal rights.

The term "tangible personal property" set forth in the City Code, and its synonymous Civil Code concept "corporeal movable," must be given their properly intended meaning. Physical recordings of computer software are not incorporeal rights to be comprehended by the understanding. Rather, they are part of the physical world. For the reasons set out below, we hold the computer software at issue in this case constitutes corporeal property under our civilian concept of that

---

[5] [The term "civilian" refers to the civil-law basis of Louisiana state law, which is derived from France; as opposed to the common-law basis of the law of the other 49 states, which is derived from England.—Eds.]

term, and thus, is tangible personal property, taxable under § 56–21 of the City Code.

III.

. . .

The taxation of computer software has . . . been considered by numerous courts across the country. These courts have split on the issue and have employed various analyses in reaching their decisions. The first case generally recognized as addressing the tangibility of computer software for tax purposes was *District of Columbia v. Universal Computer Assoc., Inc.*, 465 F.2d 615 (D.C.Cir.1972), which held computer software to be intangible, and therefore not taxable. The cases following soon thereafter, likewise held computer software to be intangible for sales, use and property tax purposes. See e.g. *State v. Central Computer Serv., Inc.*, 349 So.2d 1160 (Ala.1977); *County of Sacramento v. Assessment Appeals Bd. No. 2*, 32 Cal.App.3d 654 (1973); *First Nat'l Bank of Springfield v. Dep't of Revenue*, 421 N.E.2d 175 (Ill.1981); *Greyhound Computer Corp. v. State Dep't of Assessments & Taxation*, 320 A.2d 52 (Md.1974); *Commerce Union Bank v. Tidwell*, 538 S.W.2d 405 (Tenn.1976); *First Nat'l Bank of Fort Worth v. Bullock*, 584 S.W.2d 548 (Tex.Civ.App.1979).

However, as computer software became more prevalent in society, and as courts' knowledge and understanding of computer software grew, later cases saw a shift in courts' attitudes towards the taxability of computer software, and courts began holding computer software to be tangible for sales, use and property tax purposes. This trend began with two cases decided just one day apart—*Comptroller of the Treasury v. Equitable Trust Co.*, 464 A.2d 248 (Md.1983) and *Chittenden Trust Co. v. King*, 465 A.2d 1100 (Vt.1983). The trend continued throughout the 1980's, see e.g. *Citizens & S. Sys., Inc. v. South Carolina Tax Comm'n*, 311 S.E.2d 717 (S.C.1984); *Hasbro Indus., Inc. v. Norberg*, 487 A.2d 124 (R.I.1985); *Creasy Sys. Consultants, Inc. v. Olsen*, 716 S.W.2d 35 (Tenn.1986); *Measurex Sys., Inc. v. State Tax Assessor*, 490 A.2d 1192 (Me.1985); *Bridge Data Co. v. Director of Revenue*, 794 S.W.2d 204 (Mo.1990) (*en banc*); *Pennsylvania & West Virginia Supply Corp. v. Rose*, 368 S.E.2d 101 (W.Va.1988), though the trend was not uniform, see e.g. *CompuServe, Inc. v. Lindley*, 41 535 N.E.2d 360 (Ohio App.1987); *General Business Sys., Inc. v. State Board of Equalization*, 162 Cal.App.3d 50 (1984); *Maccabees Mut. Life Ins. Co. v. State Dep't of Treasury*, 332 N.W.2d 561 (Mich.App.1983); *Northeast Datacom, Inc. v. City of Wallingford*, 563 A.2d 688 (Conn.1989).

The issue has also been the subject of numerous articles in various legal periodicals. Most commentators agree that computer software is tangible for sales, use and property tax purposes, and thus taxable, at least to some degree. . . .

In addition, computer software has generally been held to constitute "goods" under the Uniform Commercial Code. See, e.g., *Schroders, Inc. v. Hogan Sys., Inc.*, 522 N.Y.S.2d 404 (Sup.1987); *Chatlos Sys., Inc. v. National Cash Register Corp.*, 635 F.2d 1081 (3d Cir.1980); *RRX Indus., Inc. v. Lab-Con, Inc.*, 772 F.2d 543 (9th Cir.1985); *Communications Groups, Inc. v. Warner Communications, Inc.*, 527 N.Y.S.2d 341 (N.Y.City Civ.Ct.1988). . . .

Although interesting and helpful as background, the extensive jurisprudence and writings from other jurisdictions are not determinative or controlling of the issues presented in this case. We return to a discussion of the characteristics of computer software and classification thereof as tangible or intangible under Louisiana law.

IV.

A.

To correctly categorize software, it is necessary to first understand its basic characteristics. In its broadest scope, software encompasses all parts of the computer system other than the hardware, i.e., the machine; and the primary non-hardware component of a computer system is the program. . . . In its narrowest scope, software is synonymous with program, which, in turn, is defined as "a complete set of instructions that tells a computer how to do something." . . .

When stored on magnetic tape, disc, or computer chip, this software, or set of instructions, is physically manifested in machine readable form by arranging electrons, by use of an electric current, to create either a magnetized or unmagnetized space. . . . The computer reads the pattern of magnetized and unmagnetized spaces with a read/write head as "on" and "off", or to put it another way, "0" and "1". This machine readable language or code is the physical manifestation of the information in binary form. . . .

. . .

B.

South Central Bell argues that the software is merely "knowledge" or "intelligence," and as such is not corporeal and thus not taxable. We disagree with South Central Bell's characterization. The software at issue is not merely knowledge, but rather is knowledge recorded in a physical form which has physical existence, takes up space on the tape, disc, or hard drive, makes physical things happen, and can be perceived by the senses. . . . As the dissenting judge at the court of appeal pointed out, "In defining tangible, 'seen' is not limited to the unaided eye, 'weighed' is not limited to the butcher or bathroom scale, and 'measured' is not limited to a yardstick." 631 So.2d at 1348 (dissenting opinion). That we use a read/write head to read the magnetic or unmagnetic spaces is no different than any other machine that humans use to perceive those corporeal things which our naked senses cannot perceive. . . .

The software itself, i.e. the physical copy, is not merely a right or an idea to be comprehended by the understanding. The purchaser of computer software neither desires nor receives mere knowledge, but rather receives a certain arrangement of matter that will make his or her computer perform a desired function. This arrangement of matter, physically recorded on some tangible medium, constitutes a corporeal body.

We agree with Bell and the court of appeal that the form of the *delivery* of the software—magnetic tape or electronic transfer via a modem—is of no relevance. However, we disagree with Bell and the court of appeal that the essence or real object of the transaction was intangible property. . . . As the court of appeal explained, and as Bell readily admits, the programs cannot be utilized by Bell until they have been recorded into the memory of the electronic telephone switch. 631 So.2d at 1343. The essence of the transaction was not merely to obtain the intangible "knowledge" or "information", but rather, was to obtain recorded knowledge stored in some sort of physical form that Bell's computers could use. Recorded as such, the software is not merely an incorporeal idea to be comprehended, and would be of no use if it were. Rather, the software is given physical existence to make certain desired physical things happen.

One cannot escape the fact that software, recorded in physical form, becomes inextricably intertwined with, or part and parcel of the corporeal object upon which it is recorded, be that a disk, tape, hard drive, or other device. . . . That the information can be transferred and then physically recorded on another medium is of no moment, and does not make computer software any different than any other type of recorded information that can be transferred to another medium such as film, video tape, audio tape, or books.

. . . The court of appeal distinguished the purchase of . . . books, films, video and audio tapes, etc. . . . , which hold stories, ideas, information and knowledge in physical form, by reasoning that the true essence of such transactions is the purchase of the tangible medium, not the intangible property (the artist's expressions) contained in that medium, and that without the specific tangible medium, the artist's expressions are useless, whereas computer software is separable from the tangible object upon which it is recorded. This distinction simply does not exist. As the dissenting judge at the court of appeal pointed out:

> [I]t is now common knowledge that books, music, and even movies or other audio/visual combinations can be copied from one medium to another. They are also all available on computer in such forms as floppy disc, tape, and CD-ROM. Such movies, books, music, etc. . . . can all be delivered by and/or copied from one medium to another, including electrical impulses with the use of a modem. Assuming there is sufficient memory space available in the computer hard disc drive such movies, books, music, etc. . . . can all be recorded into the permanent memory of the computer such as was done with the software in this case.

631 So.2d at 1346–47 (dissenting opinion). . . .

. . .

. . . When the magnetic tapes, upon which the switching software was physically recorded, came to rest in the City of New Orleans, or alternatively, when the software was physically recorded into the memory of the electronic telephone switch, the use tax attached. Likewise, once the data processing software was transmitted via telephone line and then physically recorded into the memory of Bell's computer, the software came to rest in corporeal or tangible form in the City of New Orleans and the use tax attached.[7]

---

[7] We need not address the issue of whether use of software, through telephonic transmission, which is never reduced to physical recordation and at rest in the City of New Orleans, is subject to the City's use tax, as that issue is not raised by the facts of this case.

C.

The court of appeal found that computer software constitutes "intellectual property" and thus classified such software as an incorporeal under Louisiana Civil Code article 461. . . .

. . .

We find this line of reasoning flawed and inconsistent with our civilian property concepts outlined above. As the dissenting court of appeal judge in this case perceptively pointed out, this reasoning confuses the corporeal computer software *copy* itself with the incorporeal *right* to the software. Explaining this often confused distinction, the dissenting judge noted that the incorporeal right to software is the copyright, which in this case, as is typical in such license agreements, was reserved to the vendors. 631 So.2d at 1345 (dissenting opinion). What Bell acquired, and what the City was attempting to tax, was not the copyright to the software, but the copy of the software itself. It was not the copyright that operated the telephone central office switching equipment, but rather the physical copy of the software.

. . .

We reject Bell's argument that what was purchased was the license or right to use the computer software, and that such license is intangible. . . . [T]he license to use the software, without transferring the software, would be of no use to Bell, and the license to use the software is inseparable from the physical manifestation of the software in recorded form.

We likewise decline to adopt the canned versus custom distinction invoked by a few state legislatures, commentators and courts. "Canned" software is software which has been pre-written to be used by more than one customer, or mass marketed; "custom" software is specially designed for exclusive use by one particular customer. . . . Under the canned versus custom distinction, canned programs are classified as taxable on the theory that the buyer acquires an end product; whereas, custom programs are classified as non-taxable services on the theory that the buyer acquires professional services. . . .

While the Louisiana Department of Taxation's current sales tax regulation regarding software adopts the "custom" versus "canned" distinction, . . . it has been observed that this distinction departs entirely from the general Louisiana property law concepts applicable for making the tangible versus intangible distinction. . . . To put it simply, whether the software is custom or canned, the nature of the software is the same.

Another problem with the custom/canned distinction, as illustrated by the facts in this case, is that often the software at issue is mixed, i.e., canned software is modified to the buyer's specifications, and fits neatly into neither category. As the court of appeal commented, "the uncontroverted facts in this case tend to establish that the programs at issue were a combination of canned and custom programs. The programs were pre-made but apparently significant adaptations were required before [Bell] could use them." 631 So.2d at 1344.

. . .

In sum, once the "information" or "knowledge" is transformed into physical existence and recorded in physical form, it is corporeal property. The physical recordation of this software is not an incorporeal right to be comprehended. Therefore we hold that the switching system software and the data processing software involved here is tangible personal property and thus is taxable by the City of New Orleans.

. . .

■ WATSON, JUSTICE, concurring in part and dissenting in part.

The software at issue was transmitted by two methods: (1) encoded on magnetic tape; or (2) electronically transferred via telephone wires and modems. The ordinary definition or generally prevailing meaning (C.C. art. 11) of "tangible personal property" would not cover either type of software.

However, state jurisprudence gives the phrase an altered meaning which may be extended to cover the taped software. Applying the expansive reasoning of the jurisprudence, the lynch pin of holding the software to be tangible personal property seems to be that it is on a floppy disc, a tape or a compact disc and the value of the software is included in the price of the disc, tape or CD. The simplest example of this type of taxation is the purchase of a software program (such as WordPerfect, Windows or Excel) at a local computer store. Who can argue that only the value of the floppy discs and the manual may be taxed and not the program?

On the other hand, subscribers to "bulletin boards" can use modems and telephone connections to download software programs without being taxed. The analysis of software being taxed because it is bought on a tape or disc cannot be stretched logically to include data transmitted by modems and telephone wires.

I respectfully concur on taxing the South Central Bell software purchased on tapes, but dissent as to software received electronically.

EXTENSIONS

1. *A standard definition.* The definition of "tangible personal property" that was interpreted in this case is very similar to the definition of this term in the sales- and use-tax provisions of most other states and localities.

2. *Canned vs. custom software.* Unlike the court in *South Central Bell Telephone v. Barthelemy*, most states that impose sales and use taxes recognize a distinction between "canned" and "custom" software. About 26 states treat canned software as tangible personal property, subject to sales and use tax, but consider custom software a service that is not subject to such taxes. An additional nine states make a distinction between canned software that is delivered on physical media and that which is delivered electronically, taxing the former but not the latter. About ten states tax all software, whether canned or custom. Since the decision of *South Central Bell*, the Louisiana legislature has modified the taxation of software under state law, ending the taxation of custom software. LA. REV. STAT. ANN. § 47:301(16)(h) (phasing out taxation of custom software by 2005).

QUESTIONS FOR DISCUSSION

1. *Is digital downloading different?* Does the dissenting judge explain the grounds for his conclusion that software delivered via digital download has a different status for sales- and use-tax purposes than does software delivered via a tangible medium? Can you articulate any grounds for making such a distinction? Is there an argument that a downloaded item, like an electronic newspaper, is a "service," even though the corresponding physical item, in this case a paper newspaper, is clearly a "good"?

2. *Other digital products.* All digital products, including software, data, music and movies in digital format, and electronic books, consist of a string of ones and zeros embedded on a physical medium like a hard drive or CD, or streamed across the network. Is there any justification for differentiating among the various digital products in determining the applicability of sales and use taxes?

II. INTERNATIONAL TAXATION ISSUES

A. WEBSITE OPERATIONS AS PERMANENT ESTABLISHMENTS UNDER TAX TREATIES

The most important function of tax treaties is to prevent double taxation—the taxation of an item of income by each of two countries. Double taxation can occur when an enterprise that is a resident of one country earns income from its operations in another country, and both the country where the income arises (the "source country") and the country where the business resides (the "residence country") claim the right to tax that income. All tax treaties to which the United States is a party seek to prevent double taxation through a rule that allows a country to tax business income only to the extent that the income is attributable to "a permanent establishment" located within the taxing country. Under this approach, the authority to tax an item of business income is allocated between countries: it is taxable in the source country, to the extent it is attributable to a permanent establishment in that country, and is taxable in the residence country to the extent it is not so attributable. At least that is the theory. In reality, there are many thorny issues that arise in determining what activities of an enterprise constitute a permanent establishment, and what income is attributable to a particular permanent establishment.

What is a permanent establishment, and what novel issues arise in applying the permanent establishment approach in the context of electronic commerce? To address these issues we will consider how the issue is treated under the Organisation for Economic Co-operation and Development[6] Model Tax Convention on Income and on Capital ("OECD Model Treaty"). Nearly all U.S. tax treaties are based upon this model.

The OECD Model Treaty defines "permanent establishment" as "a fixed place of business through which the business of an enterprise is wholly or partly carried on." OECD Model Treaty Art. 5(1). Certain types of activities are per se permanent establishments,

---

[6] The OECD is an international organization composed of thirty member countries, the majority of which are among the world's most industrialized and trade-oriented countries. The OECD addresses economic and social issues including trade, education, technology, taxation, development, health, and education, through conducting studies, collecting statistics, producing reports, and issuing recommendations. *See* www.oecd.org.

including the maintenance of offices, factories, and mines. *Id.* Art. 5(2). Other types of activities are specified as *not* constituting a permanent establishment; for present purposes, the most important of these is the maintenance of a fixed place of business solely for the purpose of carrying on "activity of a preparatory or auxiliary character." *Id.* Art. 5(4)(e). An enterprise's use of an independent agent to carry on business activities does not create a permanent establishment. *Id.* Art. 5(6). A permanent establishment does result, however, from use of a "dependent agent," one who "is acting on behalf of an enterprise and has, and habitually exercises, . . . an authority to conclude contracts in the name of the enterprise." *Id.* Art. 5(5).

Unanswered questions arose when applying the Treaty's definition of permanent establishment to electronic commerce. Does hosting a website on a server constitute a permanent establishment where the server is located? Is a website-hosting ISP an agent of the company whose website it hosts, so as to give rise to a permanent establishment where the ISP is located? Can computer equipment that operates automatically, without human intervention, ever constitute a permanent establishment?

The resolution of these issues may have a substantial impact on how e-commerce business operations are structured. There is a great deal of variation among countries with respect to the rates at which they tax business profits. All else being equal, a business will prefer to be subject to the taxing jurisdiction of a no- or low-tax country, rather than that of a high-tax country. Under treaties to which the United States is a party, which country can tax business profits depends on where the business has a permanent establishment. If treaty rules allow a business to determine the location of the permanent establishments to which its profits are attributable by hosting its website on a particular server or by distributing its computer operations in a particular way, the business will have every incentive to do so.

To address these and related issues, in December 2000 the OECD issued a modification of its official Commentary on Article 5 of the Model Treaty. The Commentary represents the majority view of OECD member countries concerning interpretation of the Treaty, and is highly influential in guiding interpretation. Because it is much easier to update the Commentary than to update the Treaty itself, responses to technological developments are sometimes found only in the Commentary.

OECD, Clarification on the Application of the Permanent Establishment Definition in E-Commerce: Changes to the Commentary on the Model Tax Convention on Article 5 (2000)
www.oecd.org/dataoecd/46/32/1923380.pdf

1. This document contains the changes to the Commentary on the OECD Model Tax Convention adopted by the Committee on Fiscal Affairs on 22 December 2000 concerning the issue of the application of the current definition of permanent establishment in the context of e-commerce. It follows two previous drafts which were released for comments by Working Party No. 1 in October 1999 and March 2000.

. . .

6. As this document shows, the Committee has been able to reach a consensus on the various issues concerning the application of the current definition of per-

manent establishment in the context of e-commerce (subject to the two dissenting views described at the end of this paragraph and of paragraph 14 below). This consensus includes the important views that a web site cannot, in itself, constitute a permanent establishment, that a web site hosting arrangement typically does not result in a permanent establishment for the enterprise that carries on business through that web site and that an ISP will not, except in very unusual circumstances, constitute a dependent agent of another enterprise so as to constitute a permanent establishment of that enterprise. However, Spain and Portugal do not consider that physical presence is a requirement for a permanent establishment to exist in the context of e-commerce, and therefore, they also consider that, in some circumstances, an enterprise carrying on business in a State through a web site could be treated as having a permanent establishment in that State. . . .

7. As a number of commentators and delegates have noted, it is unlikely that much tax revenues depend on the issue of whether or not computer equipment at a given location constitutes a permanent establishment. In many cases, the ability to relocate computer equipment should reduce the risks that taxpayers in e-commerce operations [will] be found to have permanent establishments where they did not intend to. Also, in circumstances where a taxpayer would want to have income attributed to a country where its computer equipment is located, that result can be achieved through the use of a subsidiary even if no permanent establishment is considered to exist. It is crucial, however, that taxpayers and tax authorities know where the borderlines are and that taxpayers not be put in a position to have a permanent establishment in a country without knowing that they have a business presence in that country (a result that is avoided by the conclusion that a web site cannot, in itself, constitute a permanent establishment).

8. Since a large part of the draft released in March 2000 discussed a minority view that some human intervention was required for a permanent establishment to exist and since many commentators have argued that this was the case, the Committee wishes to explain the position reached on that issue and reflected in the changes that have been adopted.

9. Having further examination of the issue, the conclusion has been reached that human intervention is not a requirement for the existence of a permanent establishment.

. . .

12. . . . [U]sually, enterprises that have fixed places of business carry on their business through personnel. This, however, does not, and was not intended to, rule out that a business may be at least partly carried on without personnel.

13. . . . [T]he Committee believes that a requirement of human intervention could mean that, outside the e-commerce environment, important and essential business functions could be performed through fixed automated equipment located permanently at a given location without a permanent establishment being found to exist, a result that would be contrary to the object and purpose of Article 5.

14. The changes to the Commentary on Article 5 which appear below make it

clear that, in many cases, the issue of whether computer equipment at a given location constitutes a permanent establishment will depend on whether the functions performed through that equipment exceed the preparatory or auxiliary threshold, something that can only be decided on a case-by-case analysis. Some countries did not like that outcome and the uncertainty that may result from it. They suggested that, in the case of e-tailers, it would have been better to simply conclude that a server cannot, by itself, constitute a permanent establishment. In order to reach a consensus, however, most of these countries have accepted the view expressed above, noting that they will take into account the need to provide a clear and certain rule in their own appreciation of what are preparatory or auxiliary activities for an e-tailer. The United Kingdom, however, has taken the view that in no circumstances do servers, of themselves or together with web sites, constitute permanent establishments of e-tailers and intends to make an observation to that effect when the changes to the Commentary on Article 5 are included in the Model Tax Convention.

15. In order to illustrate that it is possible for functions performed through computer equipment to go beyond what is preparatory or auxiliary, an example has been included in the last sentence of paragraph 42.9. It was noted during the discussion that this example is merely illustrative and should not be considered to determine the point at which the preparatory or auxiliary threshold is exceeded since many countries consider that this could be the case even if only some of the functions described in that example are performed through the equipment.

CHANGES TO THE COMMENTARY ON ARTICLE 5

. . .

Electronic commerce

. . .

42.2 Whilst a location where automated equipment is operated by an enterprise may constitute a permanent establishment in the country where it is situated (see below), a distinction needs to be made between computer equipment, which may be set up at a location so as to constitute a permanent establishment under certain circumstances, and the data and software which is used by, or stored on, that equipment. For instance, an Internet web site, which is a combination of software and electronic data, does not in itself constitute tangible property. It therefore does not have a location that can constitute a "place of business" as there is no "facility such as premises or, in certain instances, machinery or equipment" . . . as far as the software and data constituting that web site is concerned. On the other hand, the server on which the web site is stored and through which it is accessible is a piece of equipment having a physical location and such location may thus constitute a "fixed place of business" of the enterprise that operates that server.

42.3 The distinction between a web site and the server on which the web site is stored and used is important since the enterprise that operates the server may be different from the enterprise that carries on business through the web site. For example, it is common for the web site through which an enterprise carries on its business to be hosted on the server of an Internet Service Provider (ISP). Although the fees paid to the ISP under such arrangements may be based on the amount of disk space used to store the software and data required by the web site, these contracts typically do not result in the server and its location being at the disposal of the enterprise . . . , even if the enterprise has been able to determine that its web site should be hosted on a particular server at a particular location. In such a case, the enterprise does not even have a physical presence at that location since the web site is not tangible. In these cases, the enterprise cannot be considered to have acquired a place of business by virtue of that hosting arrangement. However, if the enterprise carrying on business through a web site has the server at its own disposal, for example it owns (or leases) and operates the server on which the web site is stored and used, the place where that server is located could constitute a permanent establishment of the enterprise if the other requirements of the Article are met.

42.4 Computer equipment at a given location may only constitute a permanent establishment if it meets the requirement of being fixed. In the case of a server, what is relevant is not the possibility of the server being moved, but whether it is in fact moved. In order to constitute a fixed place of business, a server will need to be located at a certain place for a sufficient period of time so as to become fixed . . .

.

42.5. Another issue is whether the business of an enterprise may be said to be wholly or partly carried on at a location where the enterprise has equipment such as a server at its disposal. The question of whether the business of an enterprise is wholly or partly carried on through such equipment needs to be examined on a case-by-case basis, having regard to whether it can be said that, because of such equipment, the enterprise has facilities at its disposal where business functions of the enterprise are performed.

42.6 Where an enterprise operates computer equipment at a particular location, a permanent establishment may exist even though no personnel of that enterprise is required at that location for the operation of the equipment. The presence of personnel is not necessary to consider that an enterprise wholly or partly carries on its business at a location when no personnel are in fact required to carry on business activities at that location. This conclusion applies to electronic commerce to the same extent that it applies with respect to other activities in which equipment operates automatically, e.g. automatic pumping equipment used in the exploitation of natural resources.

42.7 Another issue relates to the fact that no permanent establishment may be considered to exist where the electronic commerce operations carried on through computer equipment at a given location in a country are restricted to the preparatory or auxiliary activities covered by [Article 5(4)(e)]. The question of whether particular activities performed at such a location fall within [Article 5(4)(e)] needs to be examined on a case-by-case basis having regard to the various functions performed by the enterprise through that equipment. Examples of activities which would generally be regarded as preparatory or auxiliary include:

—providing a communications link—much like a telephone line—between suppliers and customers;

—advertising of goods or services;

—relaying information through a mirror server for security and efficiency purposes;

—gathering market data for the enterprise;

—supplying information.

42.8 Where, however, such functions form in themselves an essential and significant part of the business activity of the enterprise as a whole, or where other core functions of the enterprise are carried on through the computer equipment, these would go beyond the activities covered by [Article 5(4)(e)] and if the equipment constituted a fixed place of business of the enterprise (as discussed in paragraphs 42.2 to 42.6 above), there would be a permanent establishment.

42.9 What constitutes core functions for a particular enterprise clearly depends on the nature of the business carried on by that enterprise. For instance, some ISPs are in the business of operating their own servers for the purpose of hosting web sites or other applications for other enterprises. For these ISPs, the operation of their servers in order to provide services to customers is an essential part of their commercial activity and cannot be considered preparatory or auxiliary. A different example is that of an enterprise (sometimes referred to as an "e-tailer") that carries on the business of selling products through the Internet. In that case, the enterprise is not in the business of operating servers and the mere fact that it may do so at a given location is not enough to conclude that activities performed at that location are more than preparatory and auxiliary. What needs to be done in such a case is to examine the nature of the activities performed at that location in light of the business carried on by the enterprise. If these activities are merely preparatory or auxiliary to the business of selling products on the Internet (for example, the location is used to operate a server that hosts a web site which, as is often the case, is used exclusively for advertising, displaying a catalogue of products or providing information to potential customers), [Article 5(4)(e)] will apply and the location will not constitute a permanent establishment. If, however, the typical functions related to a sale are performed at that location (for example, the conclusion of the contract with the customer, the processing of the payment and the delivery of the products are performed automatically through the equipment located there), these activities cannot be considered to be merely preparatory or auxiliary.

42.10 A last issue is whether [Article 5(5)] may apply to deem an ISP to constitute a permanent establishment. As already noted, it is common for ISPs to provide the service of hosting the web sites of other enterprises on their own servers. The issue may then arise as to whether [Article 5(5)] may apply to deem such ISPs to constitute permanent establishments of the enterprises that carry on electronic commerce through web sites operated through the servers owned and operated by these ISPs. While this could be the case in very unusual circumstances, [Article 5(5)] will generally not be applicable because the ISPs will not constitute an agent of the enterprises to which the web sites belong, because they will not have authority to conclude contracts in the name of these enterprises and will not regularly conclude such contracts or because they will constitute independent agents acting in the ordinary course of their business, as evidenced by the fact that they host the web sites of many different enterprises. It is also clear that since the web site through which an enterprise carries on its business is not itself a "person" as defined in Article 3, paragraph 5 cannot apply to deem a permanent establishment to exist by virtue of the web site being an agent of the enterprise for purposes of that paragraph.

EXTENSIONS

Residence-country vs. source-country taxation. The permanent establishment criterion is relevant under a taxing regime in which taxing authorities agree that income should be taxed by the country in which it is earned (the source country), rather than the country where the enterprise earning the income resides (the residence country). The OECD's Model Tax Treaty calls for a regime of source-country taxation, and therefore relies on the permanent establishment criterion to determine which country is deemed to be the source of income. But the rise of e-commerce may give impetus to a shift to a residence-country regime. According to a U.S. Treasury Department discussion paper:

> The United States, as do most countries, asserts jurisdiction to tax based on principles of both source and residence. If double taxation is to be avoided, however, one principle must yield to the other. Therefore, through tax treaties, countries tend to restrict their source-based taxing rights with respect to foreign taxpayers in order to exercise more fully their residence-based taxing rights. This occurs in a number of ways. The permanent establishment concept represents a preference for residence-based taxation by setting an appropriate threshold for source-based taxation of active business income. By setting a threshold, in most cases it is not necessary to identify the source of active business income and the income is only subject to tax in the country of residence. . . .

> The growth of new communications technologies and electronic commerce will likely require that principles of residence-based taxation assume even greater importance. In the world of cyberspace, it is often difficult, if not impossible, to apply traditional source concepts to link an item of income with a specific geographical location. Therefore, source based taxation could lose its rationale and be rendered obsolete by electronic commerce. By contrast, almost all taxpayers are resident somewhere. An individual is almost always a citizen or resident of a given country and, at least under U.S. law, all corporations must be established under the laws of a given jurisdiction. However, a review of current residency definitions and taxation rules may be appropriate.

U.S. TREASURY DEPARTMENT, SELECTED TAX POLICY IMPLICATIONS OF GLOBAL ELECTRONIC COMMERCE 7.1.5 (1996), www.treas.gov/offices/tax-policy/library/internet.pdf. Do you agree that "[i]n the world of cyberspace" it is more difficult than elsewhere to attribute income to a particular geographic location?

QUESTIONS FOR DISCUSSION

1. *Relevance of permanent establishment criterion.* Consider the Committee's statement: "In many cases, the ability to relocate computer equipment should reduce the risks that taxpayers in e-commerce operations [will] be found to have permanent establishments where they did not intend to. Also, in circumstances where a taxpayer would want to have income attributed to a country where its computer equipment is located, that result can be achieved through the use of a subsidiary even if no permanent establishment is considered to exist." Does this mean that website hosting companies can circumvent the interpretation of permanent establishment at will? Does this call into question the continuing relevance of the permanent establishment criterion?

2. *Website as permanent establishment where viewed.* Does a website constitute a permanent establishment in every country where it may be viewed on a user's screen? Does the OECD Commentary address that issue? Consider the following view:

> According to the new OECD Commentary, a web site is "a combination of software and electronic data" and "does not in itself constitute tangible property." This description of a web site is inaccurate. The issue to be decided is whether a remote seller's web site appearing on the computer screen of a potential customer constitutes a permanent establishment of the remote seller when it operates as a virtual office. The images appearing on that screen are tangible. Like all visible matter, they are made up of small particles of matter that are themselves invisible to the eye. Although the form of those images is controlled by software, the images themselves are not software. They are real and tangible, not an apparition. Nor are they intangible, as that term has been understood in legal parlance for centuries.
>
> In the author's view, the proper test is a functional test. A virtual office should be considered a permanent establishment of its owner if it is used to perform the functions of a traditional office. Of course, the various exceptions applicable to a "bricks and mortar" office should apply to a virtual office as well. Thus, a virtual office used merely for preliminary or auxiliary activities, within the meaning of Art. 5(4) of the OECD Model . . . , would not be treated as a permanent establishment. In general, a virtual office would constitute a permanent establishment only if it is used to make actual sales of goods or services on a more than casual basis.

Michael J. McIntyre, *U.S. Taxation of Foreign Corporations in the Digital Age*, 55 (9/10) BULL. FOR INT'L FISCAL DOCUMENTATION 498 (2001).

B. PERMANENT ESTABLISHMENTS AND TAX HAVENS

The question whether a server hosting an e-commerce website constitutes a permanent establishment may have a significant effect on whether an e-commerce business elects to locate its website on a server in a tax-haven country. A tax haven is a country that seeks to entice enterprises to locate their operations, in whole or in part, within its borders, by offering extremely favorable tax treatment of the enterprises' income and property. Tax-haven countries typically do not have tax treaties with other, non-haven countries.

Why do not all enterprises relocate their operations to tax-haven countries? Favorable tax treatment is only one of the many elements that an enterprise must consider in determining where to locate its operations. Proximity to raw materials and to markets, availability and wages of employees with the required skills, issues of physical security, the location's physical, financial, and legal infrastructure, the owners' or managers' preferences regarding country of residence, and other considerations frequently greatly outweigh an enterprise's desire to minimize its tax liability. Most enterprises, therefore, choose to locate in a country that does not offer the most favorable tax treatment.

The availability of electronic commerce as a method of operating a business may substantially affect this calculus. Consider a business that interacts with its customers solely via a website, and that sells digital goods. Nearly all of the business's operations may be conducted through a computer server that hosts the company's website, and holds the digital goods that are its products. Such a server operates primarily autonomously, and to the extent that human intervention is required, that intervention may be conducted from a remote location via the network. Many of the considerations that convince businesses to locate in high-tax jurisdictions therefore become irrelevant. There are no physical inputs, so proximity to raw materials is irrelevant. The website is accessible wherever there is Internet access, and the cost of shipping digital goods does not depend significantly on the geographic distance between the server and the customer, so proximity to markets is irrelevant. Most employees, managers, and owners need not be located anywhere near the computer server: an independent contractor with technicians who maintain the computer server is all that is required. Tax treatment therefore becomes a relatively more significant consideration, and it may make economic sense to host the company's website on a server located in a country whose only advantage consists of favorable tax treatment.

If location of an e-commerce business's website on a server located in a tax haven is sufficient to create a permanent establishment in that country, then, based on the above considerations, it may become both feasible and economically rational for such businesses to relocate their websites to such locations. If this in fact should occur, it would mean a shift of the business-income tax base from high- to low-tax jurisdictions.

Based on the OECD's interpretation of the permanent establishment rules as applied to websites, what would an e-commerce company have to do to establish a permanent establishment in a low-tax jurisdiction? How much benefit would accrue to the enterprise from such a move?

C. CHARACTERIZATION ISSUES

Income may be characterized as business income, royalties, dividends, interest, income from sale of goods, income from provision of services, and in various other ways. The characterization of income plays an important role in determining its tax consequences.

In most cases, characterization of income resulting from e-commerce transactions presents no difficulty. For example, a sale of tangible personal property gives rise to business income from the sale of goods, regardless of whether the item was ordered from a website, by telephone, or by mail.

On the other hand, transactions in digital goods raise a characterization issue because the transaction may be viewed either as a *license* of the copyrighted work (such as software or music), or as a *sale* of goods, with the purchaser obtaining the right to use the work but not to make or distribute additional copies of it.

The characterization of the income resulting from a transaction involving a digital good has several consequences relating to international taxation.[7]

First, the characterization may determine whether the income is treated as U.S.- or foreign-source income. Consider a U.S. vendor's sale of software to a purchaser in a foreign country. If a transaction involving software is treated as *sale of a good*, then under U.S. sourcing rules the income from the sale will be allocated between the United States and the

---

[7] The characterization of income is also relevant for domestic taxation in a variety of contexts. For example, the applicability of use tax may depend on whether an item is characterized as a good or a service. *See* Part I(A), *supra*.

country where the purchaser is located. 26 U.S.C. § 863(b). To the extent the income is treated as foreign-source, it will contribute to a tax credit for the taxpayer against tax paid on the income to the foreign country. If, on the other hand, the transaction is treated as a *transfer of copyright*, the source of the income will be the country of the seller's residence, in this example the United States. *Id.* § 865(a), (d)(1)(A). Finally, if payment for the use of the software is structured as a *royalty*, the source of the income is the place of use, which in this example is likely to be the foreign country. *Id.* U.S.C. § 862(a).

Second, the characterization may determine which country has the right to tax the income. Under the OECD Model Treaty, both business income and royalty income are taxable in the country where the purchaser or licensee is located (the source country) only to the extent the income is attributable to a permanent establishment of the seller or licensor in the source country. Many treaties to which the United States is a party diverge from this principle, however, and allow royalty (but not business) income to be taxed in the source country even absent a permanent establishment there.

Third, the characterization of income may determine the rate at which it is taxed, and whether any deductions are allowed. Royalty income is generally subject to a gross receipts tax, which applies a tax rate to the entire amount of the income. Business income is taxed on a net basis, applying a tax rate to income after deducting the cost of goods sold and any other allowable deductions.

The OECD Model Treaty defines "royalties" as "payments of any kind received as consideration for the use of, or the right to use any copyright of literary, artistic or scientific work." Art. 12(2). The question therefore arises whether, under a treaty based on the OECD model, the payment a purchaser makes to acquire a piece of software or some other digital good should be treated as a payment for the right to use the copyright in it, and therefore as royalty income to the seller.

An OECD Technical Advisory Group recommends an approach under which a typical transaction in a copyrighted digital good would be characterized as business rather than royalty income:

> 17.2 Under the relevant legislation of some countries, transactions which permit the customer to electronically download digital products may give rise to use of copyright by the customer, *e.g.* because a right to make one or more copies of the digital content is granted under the contract. Where the essential consideration is for something other than for the use of, or right to use, rights in the copyright (such as to acquire other types of contractual rights, data or services), and the use of copyright is limited to such rights as are required to enable downloading, storage and operation on the customer's computer, network or other storage, performance or display device, such use of copyright should be disregarded in the analysis of the character of the payment for purposes of applying the definition of "royalties."

> 17.3 This is the case for transactions that permit the customer (which may be an enterprise) to electronically download digital products (such as software, images, sounds or text) for that customer's own use or enjoyment. In these transactions, the payment is made to acquire data transmitted in the form of a digital signal for the acquiror's own use or enjoyment. This constitutes the essential consideration for the payment, which therefore does not constitute royalties but falls within Article 7 or Article 13, as the case may be. To the extent that the act of copying the digital signal onto the customer's hard disk or other

non-temporary media constitutes the use of a copyright by the customer under the relevant law and contractual arrangements, this is merely an incidental part of the process of capturing and storing the digital signal. This incidental part is not important for classification purposes because it does not correspond to the essential consideration for the payment (*i.e.*, to acquire data transmitted in the form of a digital signal), which is the determining factor for the purposes of the definition of royalties. There also would be no basis to classify such transactions as "royalties" if, under the relevant law and contractual arrangements, the creation of a copy is regarded as a use of copyright by the provider rather than by the customer.

17.4 By contrast, transactions where the essential consideration for the payment is the granting of the right to use a copyright in a digital product that is electronically downloaded for that purpose will give rise to royalties. This would be the case, for example, of a book publisher who would pay to acquire the right to reproduce a copyrighted picture that it would electronically download for the purposes of including it on the cover of a book that it is producing. In this transaction, the essential consideration for the payment is the acquisition of rights to use the copyright in the digital product, *i.e.* the right to reproduce and distribute the picture, and not merely for the acquisition of the digital content.

OECD Technical Advisory Group on Treaty Characterisation of Electronic Commerce Payments, *Tax Treaty Characterization Issues Arising from E-Commerce*, at ¶ 16 (Feb. 1, 2001).

The United States Treasury Department adopted a similar approach in its regulations. A transaction in a computer program is treated as a sale of a good, rather than a license giving rise to royalties, as long as the purchaser does not acquire (1) the right to make copies of the computer program for purposes of distribution to the public; (2) the right to prepare derivative computer programs based upon the copyrighted computer program; (3) the right to make a public performance of the computer program; or (4) the right to display the computer program publicly. 26 C.F.R. § 1.861–18. These constitute the exclusive rights reserved to the copyright holder under the Copyright Act, 17 U.S.C. § 106, other than the right to make such copies of the software as are necessary to utilize it. The regulation makes no distinction between software that is delivered embedded in some storage medium, such as a CD-ROM or floppy diskette, and software that is delivered by digital download across the network. 26 C.F.R. § 1.861–18(g)(2) ("The rules of this section shall be applied irrespective of the physical or electronic or other medium used to effectuate a transfer of a computer program.").

This regulation is intended only for the purpose of interpreting provisions of U.S. tax treaties: it is inapplicable to domestic tax issues, and to digital goods other than computer programs. The Treasury Department has stated that it "may consider whether to apply the principles of these regulations to all transactions in digitized information as part of a separate guidance project." T.D. 8785 (Oct. 7, 1998). Can you think of any reason why different rules should apply to other types of digital goods?

Note that many of the rules discussed above depend upon the location of the purchaser. Ordinarily the seller knows the location of the purchaser, since the seller ships a good to a particular address. But what if a good is delivered via digital download across the network? For example, a website may offer software or music for sale via its website, accepting a credit-card number, or perhaps even anonymous digital cash, as payment. In that case, the seller need never learn the location of the purchaser. This scenario presents an unanswered question. Sellers that wish to have the benefit of foreign-source income, generating a deduction against the double taxation they pay on a transaction, may find it to their advantage to require the purchaser to disclose his location—at least to the extent of identifying the location as "United States" or "outside the United States." Geolocation technology may present a viable alternative, though it remains to be seen how much credence U.S. taxing authorities will accord to locational information generated by such technology.

D. VALUE ADDED TAX ON SALES OF DIGITAL GOODS BY EUROPEAN UNION VENDORS

In May 2002 the European Union issued a Directive imposing tax-collection obligations on sellers of digital goods located outside the European Union. *See* Council Directive 2002/38/EC of 7 May 2002 amending and amending temporarily Directive 77/388/EEC as regards the value added tax arrangements applicable to radio and television broadcasting services and certain electronically supplied services, 2002 O.J. (L 128) 41, europa.eu.int/eur-lex/en/dat/2002/l_128/l_12820020515en00410044.pdf. European Union countries impose a consumption tax, called Value Added Tax ("VAT"), on a variety of commercial activities including retail sales. The tax rate varies from country to country, with the "standard" rate ranging from a low of 15 percent (in Luxembourg) to a high of 25 percent (in Denmark and Sweden).[8] Sellers located in an EU country are required to collect this tax on sales of digital goods regardless of whether the purchaser is located within or outside the EU. Sellers located outside the EU, however, have not been required to collect the tax. This placed European sellers at a competitive disadvantage with respect to non-European sellers.

The Directive, which EU member states were required to implement through national laws by July 1, 2003, provides that sellers located outside the EU who supply "electronic services" to consumers within the EU must register with one of the EU member states. "Electronic services" include:

    1. Website supply, web-hosting, distance maintenance of programmes and equipment.

    2. Supply of software and updating thereof.

    3. Supply of images, text and information, and making databases available.

    4. Supply of music, films and games, including games of chance and gambling games, and of political, cultural, artistic, sporting, scientific and entertainment broadcasts and events.

    5. Supply of distance teaching.

Directive at Annex L. The seller must collect the VAT on all sales of such services to consumers within the EU, and must remit it to the member state with which it has registered. That member state apportions the remittances among all the member states, based on the locations of the purchasers. The new rule affects only sales to individual consumers. Sales to businesses for resale are not affected, because these businesses are required to collect VAT on their sales to the ultimate consumer.

---

[8] The "standard" rate is the highest rate charged by a given EU country. Each country taxes various categories of transactions at rates lower than the standard rate, in some cases at a zero rate.

Under the Directive, the VAT rate to be collected by a seller outside the EU will depend on the location of the *purchaser*. This rule has engendered a good deal of criticism from non-EU sellers. In sales of goods that are delivered via digital download, rather than by shipping to a physical address, the seller may not know the location of the purchaser. Current technology does not allow the location of an online purchaser to be determined sufficiently quickly, cheaply, and accurately to be feasible for this purpose. The seller may ask the purchaser to self-report her location, but the purchaser will have an incentive to report a location in a low-VAT-rate jurisdiction, or even to report that she is located outside the EU and therefore not required to pay VAT to the seller. If the purchaser reports that she is located in a country with a 15 percent VAT rate, but she is actually located in a country with a 25 percent rate, the seller will at least in theory be liable for the difference. Sellers within the EU do not face this difficulty, since they are generally permitted to collect VAT at the rate in effect where the *seller* is located.

Before the advent of Internet commerce, the fact that EU-based sellers were required to collect VAT but non-EU-based sellers were not did not place EU-based sellers at a significant competitive disadvantage. For goods that must be delivered by shipment to a physical address, the volume of sales from a seller outside the EU directly to a consumer within the EU was limited by high shipping and other transaction costs, making it more feasible to sell the goods to EU-based resellers instead. But when the product is delivered by digital download, these barriers are largely eliminated. With sellers outside the EU starting on roughly the same footing as those within the EU, the 15–25 percent VAT disadvantage became a serious issue.

If you were a U.S.-based seller of digital goods seeking to access the global market, how might the EU's new rules affect your business plan? How likely is it that EU enforcement authorities will be able to detect under-collections of VAT by sellers located outside the EU, and to enforce the VAT assessments? The state and local taxing jurisdictions in the United States do not currently require sellers located outside the United States to collect sales taxes on sales to their residents. If you were a state or federal policymaker in the United States, how might you respond to the EU's action?

APPENDIX A
COMPUTER NETWORKING AND THE INTERNET

From an engineering perspective, the Internet is a global network of networks. To understand how computers communicate over the Internet, therefore, one must first understand the nature and operation of a computer network, and then understand how computer networks can be interconnected.

Digital computers operate on data represented in the form of binary digits, called "bits."[1] Each bit holds either of two values: zero or one. Computer-to-computer communication is at bottom the transmission of a "bitstream,"[2] a string of ones and zeros, from one computer to another. Information that is encoded into bits may be transmitted through several methods, including electrical signals traveling through wires, electromagnetic waves traveling through the air, and optical signals traveling through fiber-optic cables.

Computer networking. A computer network is a group of computers interconnected in a manner that permits computer users to exchange data and to share resources such as printers and scanners. The data transmitted on a network may represent word processing documents, graphics, e-mail messages, software, databases, audio files, video files, and any other materials that can be represented digitally.

A computer network that spans a relatively small space, such as the area within a single building or office, is called a *local area network*, or "LAN." The computers comprising a network are linked together using some medium capable of transmitting data, such as coaxial cables, optical fiber, twisted-pair copper wire, or radio waves.

Computer-to-computer communication. Messages are transmitted from one networked computer to another using a method analogous to that used in transmitting mail via the postal system. A letter sent from one person to another through the mail involves three kinds of information: the address of the sender, the address of the intended recipient, and the message sent. Communication via postal mail employs a particular format that enables us to identify the different items of information involved. The message is placed in an envelope. The address of the intended recipient is written on the front of the envelope in the center, and the sender's return address is written in the upper left-hand corner.

Communication from one computer to another likewise involves three kinds of information: the address of the computer sending the message, the address of the computer to which the message is being sent, and the message itself. Each computer on a local area network is assigned a unique numerical value called its *hardware address*. Like an extremely long letter, which is too big to fit into a single envelope, the message to be sent is broken into chunks of a size determined by the communications protocol that the network uses. Each chunk of message is combined with the hardware addresses of the sending computer and the receiving computer, in a structure defined by the protocol, forming a series of *frames* or *packets*. Devices on the network read the address on each packet and route it accordingly.

---

[1] Many of the technical terms used in this Appendix, such as "bit," are defined in the Glossary.

[2] A string of eight bits is called a "byte." Quantities of data stored on a computer or transmitted through a network are usually measured in bytes, thousands of bytes (kilobytes or KB), millions of bytes (megabytes or MB), or billions of bytes (gigabytes or GB).

The recipient computer opens up the packet, extracts the data representing a chunk of the message, and throws away the rest of the packet. The various message chunks are then re-assembled into the message that was transmitted.

Connecting networks. Use of different network protocols by different networks poses a difficulty for computer-to-computer communication across networks. If two networks running different network protocols were simply wired together, the computers on one network would not be able to interpret the messages from computers on the other. Communication is possible only if the messages composed using the protocols of the transmitting network are translated into messages that can be properly interpreted using the protocols of the receiving network. This translation is the job of a special-purpose computer called a *gateway*, which sits between two networks. A gateway takes the packets that it receives from one network, converts them to the frame format of the other network, and then retransmits them on that network.

Computer-to-computer communication over the Internet. The Internet consists of a large number of interconnected networks. Therefore, the problem of translation had to be solved before the Internet could function to put all computers on any of its networks in communication with each other. The solution adopted consists of having networks of computers connect to the Internet through gateways, which translate messages from the protocol used on the network into TCP/IP, the suite of communications protocols that defines the Internet. (If the network uses TCP/IP internally, no translation is required.) Like messages within a network, messages are sent from one computer to another across the Internet in the form of *packets*. The structure of a packet that is transmitted on the Internet is determined by the Internet Protocol—the "IP" of "TCP/IP." Each packet consists of (1) a *header*, which includes the addresses of the sending and destination computers, and a sequencing number indicating in which order the packet is to be reassembled with the other packets composing the message; (2) the *payload*, consisting of the data to be transmitted; and (3) a *trailer*, which contains information that is used to check whether there were any errors in transmission. Instead of hardware addresses, the sending and receiving computers are identified by *Internet Protocol addresses*, which are described below.

Once a packet is placed on the Internet, it must be routed from the sending computer to the destination computer. This is accomplished by specialized computers called *routers*. Routers are positioned wherever the networks that make up the Internet intersect. A network that transports a packet destined for a computer belonging to another network hands it off to a router that connects it with other networks. The router reads the packet's header to ascertain the packet's ultimate destination. Then, using a complex set of algorithms, the router determines the best route for the packet to take on the way to its destination, and directs it along that path. The process is repeated as the packet moves from one router to another across the Internet, in a series of hops, until it reaches its destination.

IP addresses. The addresses used to identify computers on the Internet are called *Internet Protocol addresses,* often abbreviated as *IP addresses*. IP addresses are 32 bits long. For example, the IP address of the server holding the website belonging to the United States Postal Service, www.usps.gov, is

00111000000000010000110000010111.

Computers are designed to handle long strings of ones and zeros, but 32-bit addresses are unwieldy for humans. To make these addresses easier for humans to work with, they are usually written as four octets. In this format, the IP address of the Postal Service web server is written

00111000 00000000 10000110 00010111.

To make it easier still, each octet may be interpreted as a number in base two, and converted to a decimal number. An eight-digit binary number can represent decimal numbers ranging from zero (00000000) to 255 (11111111). Thus, IP addresses may be represented as four decimal numbers in the range 0–255. These four numbers are usually separated by periods, in what is called "dotted decimal" notation. Continuing with our example of the Postal Service web server,

56.0.134.23

is the dotted decimal representation of its 32-bit IP address.

IP address administration. IP addresses are usually assigned in blocks to networks when they connect to the Internet. To ensure that each network receives a block of IP addresses of the appropriate class, assignments of IP addresses are managed by *Regional Internet Registries* ("RIRs"). There are currently five RIRs, each serving a defined geographical area of the world. *See* www.aso.icann.org/rirs. The RIRs assign large blocks of IP addresses to Local Internet Registries and Internet service providers, which assign smaller blocks to end users.

EXERCISES

1. Obtain the IP address of your law school web server's connection to the Internet. Using a personal computer running a Microsoft Windows operating system (Windows 98 or later), connect to the Internet and start the MS–DOS Prompt, which can be found under the Start menu in the Programs folder. At the command line prompt type the word PING and then the URL of your law school web server. Hit enter and the IP address of your law school web server should be returned.

2. Based on the IP address you obtained above, what is the largest number of connections to the Internet that your law school network can accommodate? To what class of network does the IP address of your law school web server belong? Obtain the IP address of your university web server. Is the IP address of the university web server in the same class as the IP address of your law school web server? Do the IP addresses for the main university web server and the law school web server have any numbers in common? What is the significance of this fact?

3. Connect to the Internet and open up your web browser. In the text box on the address bar of the web browser, type the IP address that you obtained for your law school web server and hit enter. What happens?

APPENDIX B
THE DOMAIN NAME SYSTEM

The DNS name server hierarchy. The domain name system is the infrastructure that allows the name of a computer connected to the Internet, called a "host name," to be associated with the computer's Internet Protocol ("IP") address.[1] This process of association makes the Internet much easier to use. The software that does the work of locating a computer that is connected to the Internet and routing information from one computer to another is designed to use the numerical addresses of those computers—their IP addresses. But most humans find it difficult to remember and work with strings of numbers like 129.42.17.99, finding it much easier to deal with strings of text like www.ibm.com. Each computer connected to the Internet therefore has two equivalent designations: an IP address, designed for use by machines, and a host name, designed for use by humans. Thus, the two addresses 129.42.17.99 and www.ibm.com each designate the same machine: the computer holding the files that make up the website of IBM Corp.[2]

Domain names are strictly a convenience for us humans. If you type "129.42.17.99" into your browser, your computer will quite cheerfully display IBM's home page, without knowing or caring to know that the computer designated by that IP address is also known as www.ibm.com. Conversely, if you type a host name like www.ibm.com into your browser, hoping to view IBM's website, your computer cannot locate the website until it determines the IP address of that web server.

In theory, all that is needed to allow translation of host names into IP numbers (and vice versa) is a list, in electronic form, that is accessible via the Internet; one line of that list would read "www.ibm.com = 129.42.17.99." But use of such a list would have several practical disadvantages. For one thing, it would be extremely long, as there are many millions of host machines connected to the Internet, which would make it time consuming to locate the needed entry. For another, the machine on which it was located, and that machine's connection to the Internet, would have to handle an enormous number of accesses, since a query would be sent each time anyone tries to access a computer via the Internet.

The domain name system ("DNS") is in essence an implementation of such a list in a manner that solves these and other practical problems. It allows your computer to determine, nearly instantaneously, that when you type "www.ibm.com" into your browser what you really mean is "129.42.17.99."

The DNS is a hierarchical, distributed system, consisting of a large number of databases maintained on many different computers. At the top of the hierarchy is a set of thirteen

---

[1] Many of the technical terms used in this Appendix, such as "IP address," are defined in the Glossary.

[2] There need not be a one-to-one correspondence between host names and IP addresses, however. There might be a number of different host names, under the same or different top-level domains, all designating a single host computer. For example, www.barnesandnoble.com, www.bn.com, and www.barnesandnoble.net each refer to the same web server, which has the IP address 208.237.178.21; typing any of those URLs into a browser will retrieve the same web page, from the same machine.

computer servers, called the root servers or root name servers.[3] Each of these computers is a name server—that is, a computer connected to the Internet that holds a document listing host names and their corresponding IP addresses. These root servers are named after the letters of the alphabet, from A through M. Each of them holds the same document, called the root zone file: a list of the authoritative name servers for each of the top-level domains ("TLDs") that are sanctioned by the Internet Corporation for Assigned Names and Numbers.[4]

The root zone file looks something like this:

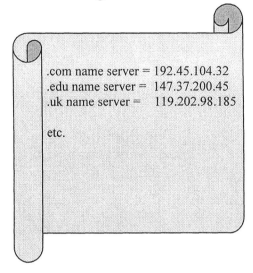

.com name server = 192.45.104.32
.edu name server = 147.37.200.45
.uk name server =   119.202.98.185

etc.

Figure 1: **Contents of root zone file.**

It lists roughly 255 TLDs (most of which are country-code top-level domains) and the IP addresses of their corresponding authoritative name servers.

When you type the address of a website into your browser, the software's "resolver" component sends a query to the name server assigned to your computer,[5] requesting the IP number associated with that address. The query, in effect, looks like this:

---

[3] Historically, there were actually only thirteen computers serving this function, most of which were located in the United States. More recently, several of the root servers have been implemented with a system that uses multiple, redundant computers located on different continents around the world.

[4] The "A" root server is first among equals. When the root zone file must be modified, the modifications are made to the copy of the file on the "A" root server. Servers "B" through "M" then each update their own copies of the root zone file from the "A" server's version. The "A" root server is located in Dulles, Virginia, and is operated by Verisign, Inc., under contract with the United States government.

[5] The name server may be maintained by your ISP, if you have a dial-up connection. If you access the Internet through a local area network ("LAN"), the entity operating the LAN (which may be a university, a corporation, or some other institution) may maintain its own name server.

"What is the IP number associated with the computer designated www.ibm.com?"

If the database on that name server holds the information you seek, it transmits that information to the resolver, and your browser uses it to access the website.[6] The response
would look something like this:

"The computer designated www.ibm.com has the IP address
129.42.17.99."

If the name server does not have the information needed to answer your query, it will
initiate its own query, directed to one of the root servers. The query will seek the IP address
of the authoritative name server for the .com TLD, and will look like this:

"What is the IP address of the authoritative name server
for the .com top-level domain?"

The root server responds with the relevant information from the root zone file that it
holds. It will look up the entry for ".com," and find the corresponding IP address. Then it
will respond to your local name server:

"The IP address of the authoritative name server for the
.com top-level domain is 192.45.104.32."

The .com authoritative server holds its own zone file, which lists the IP addresses of the
name servers associated with each of the second-level domains within the .com TLD. Each
of those domains has at least two name servers associated with it. These name servers hold
more detailed information about the servers associated with the domain name, as will be
discussed below. When IBM Corp. registered the domain name ibm.com, it had to specify
which machines it would use as its name servers. The name servers associated with a domain name can be identified through a "whois" search. As of late 2005, the name servers
assigned to IBM.com were:

> INTERNET-SERVER.ZURICH.IBM.COM
>
> NS.WATSON.IBM.COM
>
> NS.ALMADEN.IBM.COM
>
> NS.AUSTIN.IBM.COM.

This indicates that IBM maintains its own name servers. Smaller operations, however,
may rely on name servers maintained by a registrar or a hosting service. For example, the
name servers associated with ecommercecasebook.com,

> DNS2.NAMESECURE.COM
>
> DNS1.NAMESECURE.COM,

are maintained by the registrar of the domain name, which is Namesecure.com.

Now that your local name server has learned the IP address of the authoritative name
server for the .com TLD, it will address a query to that name server, asking:

"What are the IP addresses of the name servers for the domain designated ibm.com?"

---

[6] That might happen if, for example, you or somebody else had recently queried the name
server for the same address: name servers keep the answers to recent queries in a cache, to speed up
information retrieval.

The .com name server will consult its zone file, which looks something like this:

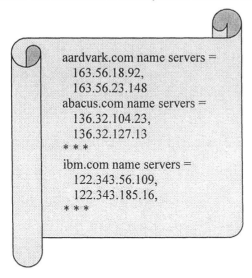

aardvark.com name servers =
    163.56.18.92,
    163.56.23.148
abacus.com name servers =
    136.32.104.23,
    136.32.127.13
* * *
ibm.com name servers =
    122.343.56.109,
    122.343.185.16,
* * *

Figure 2: **Contents of zone file for .com domains.**

Then the .com name server will report back to your local name server:

```
"The IP addresses of the name servers for ibm.com are
122.343.56.109, 122.343.185.16, etc."
```

Each of these name servers has information about each of the host computers associated with ibm.com. One of those is the web server, which is designated www.ibm.com.[7] Since IBM is a large company with a very extensive website, there are in fact a number of other web servers associated with ibm.com, such as www-1.ibm.com, commerce.www.ibm.com, www.storage.ibm.com, etc. Each of these computers is assigned its own IP address. The name servers for ibm.com have a list of the host computers at ibm.com and their associated IP addresses. The list looks like this:

---

[7] The use of "www" to designate a host machine that functions as a web server is very common, but purely conventional. Any other designation would do equally well. For example, the web server that holds the files constituting the United States Congress's website of legislative materials is designated thomas.loc.gov: the domain name is "loc.gov," and the host name is "thomas." Web servers may also be designated through a hierarchical naming scheme. Thus, www.law.upenn.edu designates a web server named "www.law" that is within the "upenn.edu" domain. A machine with this sort of designation is sometimes referred to as a "sub-host."

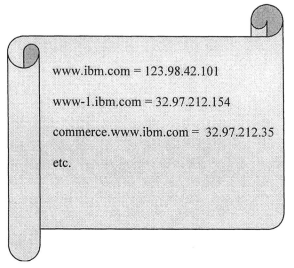

Figure 3: **List on ibm.com's name server.**

Your name server then queries one of the name servers for ibm.com, asking:

```
"What  is  the  IP  address  of  the  computer  designated
www.ibm.com?"
```

The ibm.com name server responds:

```
"The IP address of the computer designated www.ibm.com is
123.98.42.101."
```

Your name server communicates this information to your browser's resolver component. Finally, your browser has the information it needs to contact www.ibm.com. It sends a query to IP address 123.98.42.101, to the effect:

```
"Send the home page of the website maintained at this ad-
dress."
```

IBM's web server responds by transmitting the HTML file constituting that web page to your browser. Your browser fetches graphics files referenced in the web page, if any, then formats the page and displays it on your computer monitor as indicated by the HTML tags.[8]

The following diagram illustrates the hierarchy of name servers that allows the DNS to operate:

---

[8] This example shows how the process of name resolution plays out without shortcuts. In practice, the name server will probably not need to query the root server to obtain the address of the authoritative name server for the .com top-level domain. Since it receives so many queries relating to .com addresses, it will likely already have that information in its cache. It may even already have in its cache the IP addresses of the name servers for ibm.com and other frequently accessed domains, so it might proceed directly to querying IBM's name server.

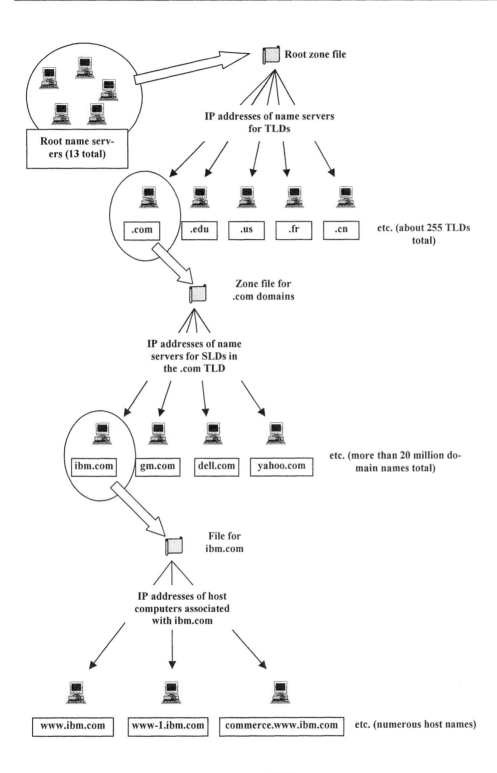

Figure 4: Hierarchy of DNS name servers.

The domain name hierarchy. The domain names and host names that humans use to reference resources on the Internet are created and maintained through another hierarchical infrastructure that roughly parallels the DNS hierarchy.

At the top of this hierarchy is what is referred to as the "root." The root is conceptual, and may be interpreted as the dot preceding the TLD in a domain name.

The next level of the hierarchy consists of the TLDs. As noted above, there are roughly 255 of these. Most of these, about 244 of them, are the country-code top-level domains, such as:

.ac = Ascension Island
.ca = Canada
.cn = China
.fr = France
.jp = Japan
.us = United States
.zw = Zimbabwe

The rest of them are the generic top-level domains ("gTLDs"), which include the original gTLDs:

.com	commercial
.net	network
.org	organization
.edu	educational
.gov	U.S. government
.mil	U.S. military
.int	international organizations,

as well as those that the Internet Corporation for Assigned Names and Numbers ("ICANN") added in 2000:

.biz	business
.aero	air-transport industry
.coop	cooperatives
.pro	professional
.museum	museums
.info	information
.name	individual names.

At the next level of the hierarchy are the second-level domains ("SLDs"). A SLD is created when a person registers that domain within a particular TLD. For example, IBM Corp. registered the SLD ibm within the .com TLD, thereby creating the domain name ibm.com. Although a name can be registered as a SLD within a particular TLD only once—nobody else can register ibm within the .com TLD—that same name can be registered independently in each other TLD. Thus, IBM Corp. also registered ibm.net, and ibm.int is not registered.

The next level of the hierarchy includes the host names—the designations of computers connected to the Internet—that are associated with a particular domain name. As noted above, IBM has a number of host computers functioning as web servers that are associated with ibm.com. IBM has other hosts that function as mail servers. Each host is capable of holding documents that may be accessed and transmitted via the Internet. Thus, web servers hold the web pages that constitute a website, and mail servers hold e-mail messages.

The lowest level of the hierarchy consists of the electronic documents that are maintained on a particular host, and are made available via the Internet. The URL of such a document includes the host name of the computer on which it is found, a path name indicating where in that computer's filing structure the document is located, and the name of the document itself. For example, the document constituting a web page on IBM's website might have a URL like www.ibm.com/privacy/policy.html. This URL refers to a document named "policy.html," which is on the computer designated "www" that is associated with the ibm.com domain. The document is in a directory called "privacy."

The documents accessed via a web server may consist of:

- Web pages, which are written in text with HTML tags, and typically have a name ending with .htm or .html. Web browsers (like Firefox and Internet Explorer) are able to interpret these documents and display them on the user's computer monitor.

- Word processing documents, in the format of whatever word processing program (such as WordPerfect or Word) created them, and ending with a designation like .wpd or .doc. These documents can be displayed using the associated word processor or some compatible program.

- Documents in Adobe's Portable Document Format, ending with .pdf, which can be viewed using Adobe Acrobat.

- Graphics files, ending with .gif or .jpeg, which can be displayed using a viewer program.

- Audio files, ending with .mp3, or video files, ending with .mpeg or .mov, which can be played using compatible programs.

The following diagram illustrates the domain name hierarchy:

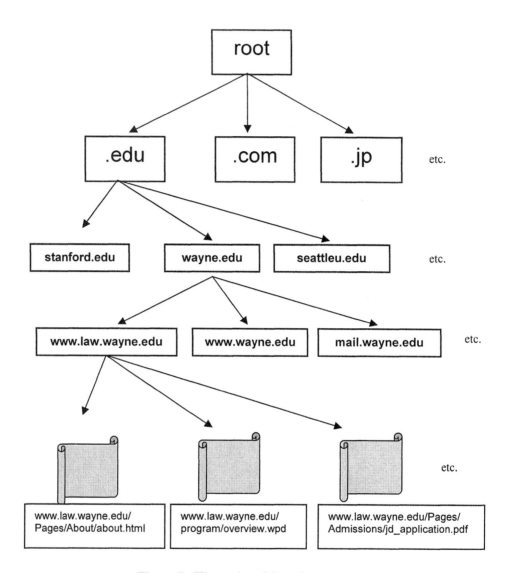

Figure 5: Hierarchy of domain names.

This diagram illustrates several levels of the hierarchy descending from the root, including:

- .edu and other TLDs;
- wayne.edu and other SLDs within the .edu TLD;
- several host machines on the wayne.edu domain, including the web server for Wayne State Law School, which is designated www.law.wayne.edu; and
- several documents maintained on the Wayne State Law School web server, one in HTML format, one in WordPerfect (.wpd) format, and one in Adobe PDF (.pdf) format.

Registration of domain names. To register a domain name in one of the commercial TLDs (.aero, .biz, .com, .info, .name, .net, and .org), one must apply for the name through a domain name registrar. There are several hundred of these registrars, which are accredited by ICANN, and operate under rules that ICANN establishes.[9] Registration takes place entirely online, through automated systems: no human is involved at the registrar's end. The process begins with the registrant indicating the domain name that she wishes to register, such as cars.biz. The registrar checks the registry for the relevant TLD, in this case .biz, to see whether the domain name has already been registered by somebody else. If cars.biz is already registered, the registrant must select a different name. If cars.biz is available, the registrar collects certain information from the registrant, including the registrant's name, address, and telephone number, and the identity of the name servers for the domain. The registrant must pay a fee for the registration, which is set by each registrar, and is often less than $10 a year.

Once a domain name is registered, the registrant has the right to use it in the address of resources she makes available on the Internet. For example, she could set up a website, using the URL www.cars.biz; or she could set up a mail server, on a machine with the host name mail.cars.biz, that would allow e-mail to be sent to and from addresses of the form name@cars.biz.

---

[9] A current list of accredited registrars is available at ICANN's website, www.icann.org/regis-trars/accredited-list.html.

GLOSSARY

ACH (from **Automated Clearing House**) **Network:** An electronic fund transfer system that provides for the interbank clearing of payments among participating depository financial institutions. Both consumers and businesses may initiate electronic credit and debit transfers using this network. The "originator" of an ACH transfer issues instructions that cause funds to be moved electronically from one account to another. For example, an employer may be the originator of an ACH transaction that transfers an employee's salary from the employer's account to the employee's account. A consumer may authorize a vendor to initiate a transaction transferring money from the consumer's account to the vendor's account, in payment for a purchase made in Internet commerce.

Application (also known as **application software**): Software that performs some function other than running the computer system itself. Application software includes database programs, word processors, e-mail readers, web browsers, spreadsheets, and other types of programs. Application software needs "systems software"—the operating system and system utilities—to run on a computer.

Architecture: The design of a computer system or a network. If a system design has an "open architecture," the system can easily be connected to hardware and software regardless of its manufacturer. Such a system typically uses off-the-shelf components, and conforms to publicly available technical standards. A system with a "closed architecture" is based on proprietary specifications, making it more difficult to connect it to other hardware or software.

ARPAnet (from **Advanced Research Projects Agency Network**): A packet-switched, computer communications network that began operating in 1969, connecting university and research sites, funded by the U.S. Department of Defense Advanced Research Projects Agency (the central research organization of the U.S. Department of Defense). By 1983 ARPAnet was composed of over 300 computers, and it adopted TCP/IP as its communications protocol. Starting in the mid-1980s, the networks participating in ARPAnet gradually switched over to become part of NSFnet, which became the Internet. ARPAnet shut down in 1989.

ASCII (from **American Standard Code for Information Exchange**): A coding system used by digital computers for representing characters and certain control functions as a string of seven bits. The seven bits yield 128 possible combinations, allowing ASCII to represent the letters of the Latin alphabet set, the numerals from 0–9, and common punctuation marks. ASCII is used to create text documents—that is, documents consisting of only the basic characters and formatting, without any graphics, special formatting, different fonts, etc.

Backbone: The part of a communications network consisting of the transmission paths running at the highest speeds, and carrying a major portion of the network's data traffic. Backbone paths usually span long geographical distances. Regional networks are attached to the backbone.

Bandwidth: The rate at which data may be transmitted across a network. The bandwidth of digital devices is usually expressed as bits per second. A dial-up connection to the Internet typically has a maximum bandwidth of 56,000 bits per second, which is often abbreviated as "56 Kb/sec" or "56K." A digital subscriber line ("DSL") connection to the Internet may have a downstream bandwidth (that is, the rate at which data may be downloaded from the Internet) of several million bits per second (Mb/sec), but home DSL connections more typically run at 300–750 Kb/sec. A cable modem might run at 1 Mb/sec. The highest-speed backbone lines currently in general use, called OC–192 lines, have a maximum bandwidth of about 10,000 Mb/sec.

BBS: *See* **Bulletin board system**.

Bit (from "**binary dig**it"): The smallest unit of information that is processed by a digital computer. A bit can take either of two states, which are typically represented as the numbers one and zero. A string of bits may be interpreted as a number in binary (base two) notation. To convert a number in base two to a number in decimal (base ten) notation, we take the digit (either one or zero) at each place of the number, and multiply it by two raised to a power determined by the place of that digit in the number. Thus, a single "1" bit is interpreted as 2^0, or 1 in decimal notation. The series of bits "10" is interpreted as

$$(1 \times 2^1) + (0 \times 2^0),$$

or 2 in decimal notation. Likewise,

$$100 = (1 \times 2^2) + (0 \times 2^1) + (0 \times 2^0) = 4$$
$$101 = (1 \times 2^2) + (0 \times 2^1) + (1 \times 2^0) = 5$$
$$111 = (1 \times 2^2) + (1 \times 2^1) + (1 \times 2^0) = 7$$
$$1000 = (1 \times 2^3) + (0 \times 2^2) + (0 \times 2^1) + (0 \times 2^0) = 8$$

etc.

A string of eight bits is called a "byte." Each byte may be interpreted as a decimal number in the range 0 to 255. A byte of information can represent a character in the ASCII coding system, which is used to construct text documents.

Bot: From "robot," referring to a computer program that autonomously searches for and retrieves information from materials residing on computers connected to the Internet. The term is used for many different types of software agents and macros. Bots are used, for example, to index information on the Web so that search engines can search it, and to perform comparison shopping functions by searching out information on multiple websites.

Brick-and-mortar retailer: A retailer that operates, in the traditional manner, from a physical storefront which consumers may enter to view and purchase goods. Used to distinguish such retailers from those that make sales at a distance, such as via the Internet, catalogues, or telemarketing.

Bulletin board system (abbreviated as **BBS**): A computer-based forum on which users may post messages and electronic files. Before the Internet was widely available, BBS access was typically obtained by dialing a telephone number specific to each BBS. Proprietary online services also hosted, and continue to host, BBSs dedicated to a wide variety of subject matters. Many websites include a BBS, and web portals may include hundreds of BBSs each dedicated to a particular subject matter.

Byte: *See* **bit**.

CA: *See* **Certification authority**.

Cache: *See* **Web cache**.

ccTLD: *See* **Country code top-level domain.**

Certification Authority (abbreviated as **CA**): An entity that issues a digital certificate attesting to some fact about the holder of the certificate. In the context of digitally signing electronic messages using public key cryptography, the role of the CA is to certify that a public key really belongs to the person who proffers it. The certificate will contain, at a minimum, the name of a person and his public key. The CA digitally signs the certificate using its own private key. A user of the certificate, upon decrypting it using the CA's public key, can be confident that the person named in the certificate is the true owner of the public key set forth in the certificate. Thus, if a person receives an electronic message that is digitally signed and that can be decrypted using the public key contained in the certificate, she can be reasonably sure that the message was actually sent by the person named in the certificate.

Chat: A text-based discussion among two or more people that is conducted via a network. Chats are hosted by websites on the Internet, by proprietary online service providers like America Online, and through the Internet Relay Chat ("IRC") system. IRC servers located around the world host hundreds of IRC channels on different topics. A user's input to an IRC channel is immediately disseminated to everyone connected to that channel.

Clickstream: The data trail that an Internet user leaves behind as he performs such operations as entering data into search engines and visiting web pages. Clickstream data may be collected by an ISP, a website operator, or an interloper. For example, a website operator may be able to collect information identifying every page that the user accessed on the site, and any search terms that the user entered while searching for information on the site. Clickstream data may be collected anonymously, or, through the use of cookies, web bugs, GUIDs, and other techniques, may be associated with the user or his computer.

CMS (from **copyright management system**): *See* **Digital rights management system.**

Conditions of Use: *See* **Terms of Service.**

Cookie: A unique identifier, contained in a text file that a computer hosting a website causes to be written to the hard drive of a computer that accesses it. Each time that computer requests pages from the website thereafter, the identifier is sent back to the website, and serves to identify the computer. The identifier stored in a cookie may be used to associate all of the clickstream data collected from that computer into a single dossier. The website can use the information in the dossier to target customized information or advertisements to the user, based on inferences about the user's preferences as revealed by the clickstream data.

Copyleft: A license, accompanying a work entitled to copyright protection, that allows anyone to use, copy, distribute, and modify the work as long as the modified version is made freely available under the same license. Copyleft has been most widely used in connection with software. The most prominent version of copyleft is the General Public License that accompanies software developed in the GNU Project. *See* www.gnu.org. The open-source operating system Linux is likewise distributed under the GNU General Public License. GNU is sponsored by the Free Software Foundation, a Boston-based non-profit entity founded in 1985 by Richard Stallman.

Copyright management system (abbreviated as **CMS**): *See* **Digital rights management system.**

Country code top-level domain (abbreviated as **ccTLD**): A two-letter suffix, making up the rightmost element of a domain name, designating the country controlling the assignment of second-level domains ending with that suffix. For example, the URL http://www.parl.gc.ca points to a website (belonging to the Parliament of Canada) within the ".ca" ccTLD. The government of Canada controls assignment of second-level domains, such as ".gc," within the .ca ccTLD. The two-letter abbreviations are derived from a list of country codes maintained by the International Organization for Standardization. *See* www.iso.org.

Cybersquatting: A derogatory term used to describe the practice of registering an Internet domain name for purposes that are deemed inappropriate. The term applies most particularly to registration of a domain name incorporating a word that corresponds to a trademark belonging to somebody else. The Anticybersquatting Consumer Protection Act, a U.S. federal law enacted in 1999, gives trademark owners a cause of action against cybersquatters. Sometimes also referred to as "cyberpiracy."

Database: A collection of information organized in some useful manner, and stored in electronic form on a computer. Information stored in a database may be sorted, searched, or selected according to particular criteria using a software application called a database program.

Digital certificate: A digital document, encrypted using public key cryptography, that attests to the ownership of a particular public key, by associating that key with a particular person.

Digital rights management system (abbreviated as **DRMS**): A technological device, usually implemented through computer code, that controls access to or use of an accompanying information product. Also referred to as a "copyright management system" or "technological protection measure." A DRMS may create an audit trail for payment of royalties, or may provide a set of rules technologically enforcing limitations on use of the information, such as by preventing redistribution or copying.

Digital signature: A procedure that uses public key cryptography and related technologies to establish that an electronic document was sent by the person it purports to be from, and has not been tampered with during transmission across the network.

Directive: *See* **European Union Directive.**

DNS: *See* **Domain name system.**

DNS hijacking: An unauthorized change to a name server's database that has the effect of directing a user's computer to the wrong website when the user types in a URL.

Domain name: A string of characters forming the core of the addressing scheme that allows resources to be made available on the Internet. A domain name consists of a second-level domain together with the top-level domain in which it is registered. For example, nytimes.com is a domain name consisting of the second-level domain "nytimes," which is registered within the top-level domain ".com." The owner of nytimes.com, which happens to be The New York Times Company, may make information available on the Internet by placing it on a computer server that is accessed via the domain name. Thus, the New York Times maintains a website at www.nytimes.com, which designates the computer server holding the files that constitute its website. A domain name also forms the portion of an e-mail address to the right of the "@" symbol. Thus, employees of the New York Times are assigned e-mail addresses of the form [employee-name]@nytimes.com.

As of late 2005, there were about 60 million registered domain names (44 million of them in the .com top-level domain). Domain names may be registered with any of several hundred registrars. For more information on domain names, see **Appendix B**.

Domain name registrar: *See* **Registrar.**

Domain name server: A computer holding a database that associates resources on the Internet with IP addresses. Domain name servers, also called name servers, are an integral part of the DNS, allowing a resource on the Internet (such as a website) to be located via the host name of the computer on which it resides. Name servers respond to queries from web browsers and from other name servers. When a user types the address of a website into her browser, her computer sends a query to a name server, asking for the IP address of that website. The name server may respond with the requested IP address, if that address is in the server's cache. If not, the name server may respond with the address of another name server, or it may send a query to that other name server. Ultimately a name server that has the needed information is reached, and it returns the IP address to the user's computer, whose browser uses that address to access the website. For more information on name servers, see **Appendix B**.

Domain name system (abbreviated as **DNS**): The infrastructure that associates host names and URLs with IP addresses, and allows a computer running a web browser to locate and access resources on the Internet. The DNS includes domain name registrars, which assign domain names to registrants and maintain registries listing the domain names that have been assigned; name servers, which hold databases associating Internet resources with IP addresses; and root servers, which contain the authoritative lists of name servers for each top-level domain. When you type a URL into your web browser, your computer accesses the DNS to ascertain the IP address corresponding to that URL, which enables your computer to send a request to the server holding the desired web page, resulting in delivery of the HTML file constituting that page to your computer for display on your monitor. Primary responsibility for managing the DNS resides with the Internet Corporation for Assigned Names and Numbers. For more information on the DNS, see **Appendix B.**

DRMS: *See* **Digital rights management system.**

European Union Directive: A set of legal rules on a particular subject, established through a lawmaking process at the European Union community level, and promulgated by the European Commission, that EU member states are required by treaty to implement through enactment of national laws. *See generally* europa.eu.int.

File Transfer Protocol (abbreviated as **FTP**): A protocol used to transfer files over the Internet. FTP is used to upload and download files to and from an FTP server.

Fully qualified domain name (abbreviated as **FQDN**): The complete name of a specific computer on the Internet, consisting of the host name followed by a domain name. For example, www.cisco.com is the fully qualified domain name corresponding to a web server that Cisco Systems, Inc. maintains at the domain name cisco.com. A server that holds a website typically is assigned the host name "www," but any other name would do. For example, the website containing legislative materials of the United States Congress is on a computer with the FQDN thomas.loc.gov. A FQDN contains the information required to obtain the computer's IP address by querying a name server.

General Public License: *See* **Copyleft.**

Generic top-level domain (abbreviated as **gTLD**): A multiple-letter suffix, making up the rightmost element of a domain name, signifying the highest level domain to which the address belongs. Some gTLDs accept domain name registrations only from a restricted class of registrants, while others are unrestricted. For a listing of the gTLDs, see **Appendix B.** *See also* **Country-code top-level domain.**

GIF (from **Graphics Interchange Format**): A file format for images that is widely used on the Web.

gTLD: *See* **Generic top-level domain.**

GUID (from **globally unique identifier**): A unique identifier that is assigned to a computer or some other resource on the Internet. A GUID may be implemented in software, such as through a cookie that is written to a computer's hard drive. It may also be implemented in hardware, such as by manufacturing it into a computer's central processing unit. A GUID associated with a computer may be read by another computer, across the network. The GUID may be written into a document, serving to identify the computer that produced the document.

Hit: Each access, by a computer running a web browser, of a page (or a page component, such as a graphic image) on a website. The number of hits a website receives in a particular period of time is a measure of its popularity. The hit count is especially important to e-commerce websites, since the number of visitors a website receives is a major determinant of the amount that an advertiser pays to advertise on the site.

Home page: The web page that is presented when a user enters the basic form of a website's URL into her browser. Typically, the home page of a site is reached by entering a URL consisting of the domain name preceded by "www."

Hosting service or **hosting provider:** *See* **Internet service provider.**

Host: A computer that has access to other computers via the Internet. In particular, a host refers to a computer that is assigned an IP address (and a corresponding fully qualified domain name) and that holds the files constituting a website.

HTML (from **Hypertext Markup Language**): The computer language used to create pages on the World Wide Web. Each web page contains codes embedded in the text, called "HTML tags," that establish how the document will be displayed on the recipient's computer monitor. HTML tags are composed of alphanumeric characters that can be typed with any text editor or word processor. The HTML tags define the format, layout, size of graphics, fonts, and other features of the displayed page. The codes also define and create the hypertext links that point to other web pages. Many word processors can automatically export their documents in HTML format. The HTML code constituting a web page may be viewed in popular browsers by clicking a command labeled something like "View Page Source."

HTTP (from **Hypertext Transport Protocol**): The protocol that is used in transmitting information residing on the World Wide Web across the Internet.

Hyperlink: A string of text or a graphic in an electronic document that, when clicked with a mouse, results in the accessing of some other electronic document via HTTP. Most commonly, a hyperlink is contained within a web page, and when clicked causes a different web page to be displayed on the computer monitor. Hyperlinks may also be incorporated into word-processing documents, e-mail messages, spreadsheets, and other types of documents. Instead of a web page, a hyperlink may point to some other type of electronic document, such as a word-processing document, a graphic, or an audio or video file. Rather than retrieving a separate document, clicking on a hyperlink might result in jumping to another place in the document one is viewing. A textual hyperlink is, by convention, often identified by displaying it in blue, underlined text. Also called a "link."

ICANN: *See* **Internet Corporation for Assigned Names and Numbers.**

Identity theft: One person's use of another person's identifying information to obtain goods and services fraudulently. An identity thief who learns the victim's name, date of birth, and Social Security number might open a credit card account in the victim's name, go on a spending spree, and then leave the bills unpaid. Since the card is in the victim's name, the card issuer will believe that the charges were incurred by the victim, and will seek to hold the victim accountable. Although in theory the victim should not suffer due to the actions of the identity thief, in practice it can take months or years, and enormous efforts, before the victim clears her name and regains her credit standing. The Federal Trade Commission maintains a website about identity theft at www.consumer.gov/idtheft.

Internet: The global network of computer networks that communicate using the TCP/IP protocol. The Internet consists of physical connections among computers throughout the world and a set of protocols that allows those computers to communicate with one another. The Internet is the successor to the NSFnet, which itself built on a networking concept pioneered by the ARPAnet. In 1995, the National Science Foundation transferred responsibility for the communications backbones of the Internet to several large commercial Internet service providers. Regional service providers link to these backbones, and smaller ISPs link to the regional providers. The Internet is the infrastructure over which several popular network services are run, including the World Wide Web and electronic mail. For more information on computer networking and the Internet, see **Appendix A.**

Internet Assigned Numbers Authority (abbreviated as **IANA**): An entity chartered by the Internet Society that formerly managed Internet addresses, domain names, and protocol parameters. In these functions it has been replaced by the Internet Corporation for Assigned Names and Numbers, which performs what is referred to as "the IANA function." *See* www.iana.org.

Internet Corporation for Assigned Names and Numbers (abbreviated as **ICANN**): A nonprofit California corporation, formed in 1998, that performs a variety of Internet management functions under contract with the United States government. ICANN establishes the official set of top-level domains, and allocates blocks of IP network addresses. It manages the domain name system and root server system. ICANN also accredits and maintains a list of registrars that process domain name registrations. *See* www.icann.org.

Internet service provider (abbreviated as **ISP**): An entity that provides its customers with access to the Internet. The term is sometimes also used in reference to an entity that provides space on its servers to maintain a customer's website and make it accessible to the Internet (also known as a "hosting service," "hosting provider," or "online service provider"), and to online services like America Online that offer both access to the Internet and additional proprietary services like databases, forums, and access to online merchants.

Internet Society (abbreviated as **ISOC**): An international membership organization founded in 1992, located in Reston, Virginia, dedicated to promoting the development of the Internet. With more than 100 organizational members and 20,000 individual members in 180 countries, ISOC supports Internet bodies such as the Internet Engineering Task

Force, www.ietf.org, and the Internet Architecture Board, www.iab.org. ISOC works with governments, organizations and the general public to promote Internet research, information, education, and standards. It also helps developing nations design their Internet infrastructure. *See* www.isoc.org.

InterNIC (from **Internet Network Information Center**): The domain name registration project that was formed in 1993 by agreements between Network Solutions, Inc., the National Science Foundation, General Atomics, and AT & T. InterNIC formerly made the rules pertaining to domain names, administered the registration process, and maintained the official database of registered domain names. At present, "InterNIC" is a registered service mark of the United States Department of Commerce, and refers to a set of functions performed by the Internet Corporation for Assigned Names and Numbers. *See* www.internic.org.

IP (Internet Protocol) address: The unique address of a computer or other device attached to the Internet. An IP address is usually represented as four decimal numbers in the range 0–255, separated by periods. For example, the IP address associated with the computer hosting the website of Dell Computer Corp., which is named www.dell.com, is 143.166.83.63. For more information on IP addresses, see **Appendix A.**

Link: *See* **Hyperlink.**

Listserv: *See* **Mailing list.**

Lock-in: A situation in which a product or technology with a head start or large market share may hold an insurmountable advantage over its rivals, even though the rivals may produce a better product. Users of the product or technology experience a strong incentive to stick with it, despite the existence of superior alternatives, due to the costs of acquiring or learning how to use an alternative, or the disadvantages resulting from the fact that few others use the alternative. Examples of lock-in are the QWERTY typewriter keyboard, the disincentive to change ISPs once you have an assigned e-mail address, and the triumph of the VHS format for VCRs over the Betamax format.

Mailing list: A list of e-mail addresses that receive e-mail messages automatically distributed by mailing-list software. To send a message to the members of a mailing list, a subscriber of the list sends a single message to a designated address, and the software automatically broadcasts it to all members of the list. Each mailing list is dedicated to a particular subject matter, and is managed by a list owner, who may also (but need not) act as a moderator. Open lists allow anyone to subscribe. Subscription to a closed list requires approval of the list owner. The most popular brands of mailing-list software are Listserv and Majordomo; a mailing list is therefore sometimes referred to generically as a "listserv" or "listserve."

Metatag: An HTML tag, used in the code that constitutes a web page, that describes the contents of the page. The text of a metatag is not displayed on the website visitor's computer monitor, but can be read by another computer across the network. For example, a search engine may read a web page's metatags in determining whether that page is relevant to a search query that it is processing. Metatags have been used in ways that some consider improper, such as when a website places a competitor's trademarks in its metatags, so that a user searching for the competitor's website will be referred to the metatagged site instead. Other websites have placed popular search terms (such as "sex") in their metatags, so that a user searching for one type of site will be referred to another type of site entirely. As a result of these practices, some search engines ignore metatags when evaluating a website.

MP3: A file format that is widely used for storing recorded music in digital form. Music from a CD may be converted to MP3 format, allowing it to be transmitted across the Internet, downloaded from a website, stored on a computer's hard drive, and played on a computer or a portable MP3 player. The term refers to Audio Layer 3 of the MPEG–1 audiovisual standard created by the Motion Picture Experts Group in the early 1980s. MP3 files are compressed to about one-twelfth of their original size, reducing the bandwidth needed for file transfer. This compression results in a loss of sound fidelity that is insignificant for most users.

Name server: *See* **Domain name server.**

Netiquette (from **network etiquette**): Appropriate behavior when using the Internet or another online service. Netiquette, like etiquette, is a set of informal customs, not a legal regime.

Network effects: The increase in value of a product that results when more people use it. Products that engender network effects are common in the online environment. E-mail, the Internet, telephones, and the Windows computer operating system are all examples of products characterized by network effects. Thus, an e-mail system is of no value if only one person has access to it; when a second person is added, it starts to have value; and the value of an e-mail system is increased for all existing participants each time an additional person joins the system. Network effects can cause a product to dominate a market, through lock-in, even if it is not superior to its competition. *See* **lock-in.**

Newsgroup: An online message board or discussion group devoted to a particular topic. One person posts a comment or question, another person replies, others respond to the replies, and the resulting discussion is organized in a chain of postings called a "message thread." The term usually refers to newsgroups that are part of the USENET. USENET newsgroups are organized by topic and subtopic. Thus, the newsgroup alt.art might be devoted to discussions about art generally, while the newsgroups alt.art.renaissance and alt.art.modernist would host discussions on more specific art-related topics. (The "alt" refers to "alternatives" to USENET's original categories of topics.) *See* **USENET.**

NSFnet (from **National Science Foundation Network**): A high-speed computer network funded by the National Science Foundation, created in the mid-1980s, initially linking five supercomputer research sites, and later including university networks. NSFnet adopted TCP/IP as its communication protocol. As other networks were connected, this collection of connected computers became the Internet. *See* **ARPAnet.**

OECD: *See* **Organisation for Economic Co-operation and Development.**

Online service provider: *See* **Internet service provider.**

Opt in vs. opt out: Two different approaches to obtaining the consent of a person to some proposed course of action affecting him. In the online context, these approaches come into play when an online entity, such as a website operator, a vendor, or an ISP, offers some option to an online user. Under an opt-out approach, if the user takes no action in response, she is deemed to consent to the proposed course of action. Under an opt-in regime, silence is interpreted as the absence of consent. For example, an online vendor might tell its customers that it will share their personal information with unaffiliated third parties only with the customer's consent. Under an opt-in approach, a customer is deemed to assent to such information disclosure *only if* she takes some action, such as checking a box on a website form, indicating that she assents. Under opt out, the customer is deemed to assent *unless* she takes some action indicating that she does *not* assent.

Organisation for Economic Co-operation and Development (abbreviated as **OECD**): An international organization composed of thirty member countries, the majority of which are among the world's most industrialized and trade-oriented countries. The OECD addresses economic and social issues including trade, education, technology, taxation, development, health, and education, through conducting studies, collecting statistics, producing reports, and issuing recommendations. *See* www.oecd.org.

Packet switching: A technology for transmitting messages across a network from one computer to another. The message is divided into chunks of a predetermined size, and each chunk is assembled into a packet that includes the addresses of the sending and destination computers. Each packet is then routed independently across the network. Once they reach their destination the message chunks are reassembled in their original order, reconstituting the message as sent. The delivery of messages sent across the Internet is controlled by the Transmission Control Protocol, and the internal structure and reassembly of packets is controlled by the Internet Protocol; these two protocols in tandem, referred to as TCP/IP, allow communication to occur across the Internet. Packet switching is distinguished from circuit switching, the system used for transmitting telephone calls across the telecommunications network, which dedicates a particular path to the signals comprising a telephone conversation for the duration of the call. For more information on packets, see **Appendix A.**

PICS (from **Platform for Internet Content Selection**): A set of specifications for attaching machine-readable labels to the content of websites. A browser that is PICS-enabled can read and interpret the labels, and then take some action specified by the user based on the labels' content, such as displaying a warning or denying access. The labels may be created through self-rating by a website operator, or by some third party. PICS was developed for the primary purpose of enabling parents to control their children's access to materials on the Web. It has been promoted as a technology that encourages self-regulation and thereby avoids the need for government regulation. PICS was developed by the World Wide Web Consortium. *See* www.w3.org/PICS/.

PKI: *See* **Public key infrastructure.**

Portal (or **web portal**): A website that offers a wide variety of services, such as news, stock quotes, weather, search functions, shopping, e-mail, discussion forums, etc.

Protocol: A set of design rules for some computer-implemented process. In the Internet context, the term usually refers to the rules for encoding and transmitting data across the network. For example, TCP/IP, the set of protocols governing transmission of information on the Internet, defines how packets of data are structured, addressed, delivered, and reassembled.

Public key cryptography: A method of encrypting and decrypting information in digital format. Each person who wishes to use public key cryptography to send messages has his own pair of keys, and each pair of keys is unique. Of each pair of keys, one is designated the *public key* and the other the *private key*. The owner of a key pair makes his public key generally available to the world, while keeping the private key strictly to himself. The two keys making up a key pair are related to each other mathematically so that (1) a message encrypted with the public key can *only* be decrypted using the corresponding private key, (2) a message that can be decrypted with a particular public key can *only* have been encrypted with the corresponding private key, and (3) it is impossible to derive the private key from the public key in any reasonable amount of time. Public key cryptography, together with digital certificate technology, is well adapted for sending encrypted and authenticated information via the Internet.

Public key infrastructure (abbreviated as **PKI**): The system by which digital certificates are created, maintained, accessed, revoked, and otherwise managed. The PKI includes entities that are in the business of issuing digital certificates, along with legal rules and industry practices that foster the integrity and utility of digital signatures.

Registrant: A person who registers a domain name. The registrant of a domain name gains the right to use that domain name in the address of resources made available on the Internet, such as a website or e-mail accounts.

Registrar: An entity that grants a registrant the right to use a second-level domain name within a particular top-level domain. Also referred to as a "domain name registrar." Upon receiving a request to register a domain name, the registrar first checks to see whether it has already been registered. If the domain name is available, the registrar collects registration information from the registrant, collects a fee, and causes an entry to be made on the relevant registry indicating that the domain has been registered. Registrars for the commercial gTLDs are accredited by the Internet Corporation for Assigned Names and Numbers. A list of accredited registrars is available at www.icann.org/registrars/accredited-list.html.

Registration of a domain name: The process of establishing the right to use a domain name. A person registers a domain name by contacting a domain name registrar (via its website), ascertaining the availability of that name, providing the required registration information to the registrar, and paying the required fee. The registrant of a domain name gains the right to use that domain name in the address of resources made available on the Internet. For more information about registering domain names, see **Appendix B.**

Registration of a mark: Placement of a trademark or service mark on a register maintained by a government authority, as a means of claiming rights to use the mark and providing notice to others of the claim of such rights. In the United States, the user of a mark can acquire certain rights in the mark solely through its use, but registration confers additional rights. Trademarks may be registered with state agencies, with the United States Patent and Trademark Office if the mark is used in interstate commerce, or with both. State registration benefits are realized only in the state of registration. Federal registration of a mark allows the owner to use the mark throughout the United States for the goods or services described in the registration, and to exclude others from uses of the mark that may cause confusion. Federal registration conveys benefits for ten years if the trademark is appropriately used in accordance with the registration application during that time, and is renewable for additional ten-year periods, indefinitely. You can register a mark even if you have not yet used it, as long as you intend to use it. To show that you claim rights to a particular trademark in goods, you may use the "TM" symbol if the trademark is unregistered or registered only with a state agency, and the "R" symbol inside a circle if it is federally registered.

Registry: A database, pertaining to a particular top-level domain, containing registration information about second-level domains that have been registered within that top-level domain. Under rules established by the Internet Corporation for Assigned Names and Numbers, the operator of the registry for each commercial top-level domain is required to provide public access to information maintained in the registry via a "whois" lookup.

Request for Comments (abbreviated as **RFC**): One of a series of more than 4,000 documents on computer networking topics created by volunteer members of the Internet Engineering Task Force. The RFC publication process plays a central role in the establishment of Internet-related standards. A proposed RFC is first published as an Internet Draft, and if it gains the approval of the IETF is issued as an RFC. An RFC may be adopted as a standard by technology creators and users. *See* www.ietf.org/rfc.

Reverse domain name hijacking: A derogatory term referring to a practice in which a trademark owner inappropriately asserts trademark rights to prevent another person from using a domain name he has registered, and to gain control of that domain name. In the context of the Uniform Domain Name Dispute Resolution Policy, the term is defined as "using the [UDRP] in bad faith to attempt to deprive a registered domain-name holder of a domain name." *See* Rules for Uniform Domain Name Dispute Resolution Policy, Rule 1, www.icann.org/dndr/udrp/uniform-rules.htm.

Root name servers: The system of thirteen computers that form the foundation of the domain name system. Each root server holds an authoritative copy of a file listing each of the top-level domains, and the IP address of the primary name server for each TLD. The primary name server for each TLD contains, in turn, a list of the name servers associated with each domain name registered within that TLD. The name server associated with a particular domain name lists the IP address of each host computer associated with that domain. For more information on root name servers, see **Appendix B**.

Second-level domain (abbreviated as **SLD**): The portion of a domain name that comes immediately to the left of the rightmost dot. So, in the domain name whitehouse.gov, the second-level domain is whitehouse. The second-level domain in combination with the top-level domain constitutes a domain name. A person wishing to use a domain name registers a second-level domain within a particular top-level domain.

Server: A computer that manages some resource on a network. For example, a web server is a computer that holds the files constituting a website, and makes them available via the Internet. A file server is a computer that stores files belonging to users on a network. A print server is a computer that manages the network's printers. A network server manages the network's traffic. A server can also be a software program that manages resources.

Spam: Derogatory term for e-mail messages that are sent in bulk, to recipients who have not requested them, for commercial purposes. Also known as "unsolicited commercial e-mail," or "UCE."

Spammer: One who sends spam.

Spider: A software program that accesses various resources available on the Internet and indexes the content for use by search engines. *See* **bot.**

Sysop (from **system operator**): A person or entity that runs an online bulletin board or some other online communications forum.

TCP/IP (from **Transmission Control Protocol/Internet Protocol**): A communications protocol that is used to transmit data across the Internet. The delivery of messages is controlled by the Transmission Control Protocol, and the internal structure and reassembly of packets is controlled by the Internet Protocol.

Terms of Service (abbreviated as **TOS**): The terms under which a service or content provider makes its offerings available. Also known as "Conditions of Use" or "Terms of

Use." The terms are often presented in fine print as "boilerplate" on an interior page of a website, with a hyperlink labeled "Terms of Service" (or simply "Terms") on the home page.

TLD: *See* **Top-level domain.**

Top-level domain (abbreviated as **TLD**): The highest level domain category in the hierarchy established by the Internet domain naming system. The TLD is the portion of a URL that comes to the right of the rightmost dot. Thus, in the URL whitehouse.gov, the TLD is .gov. There are two types of TLDs: the generic top-level domains (such as .com, .org, and .edu) and the country-code top-level domains (such as .ca, .uk, and .ch). *See* **Generic top-level domain, Country-code top-level domain.**

TOS: *See* **Terms of Service.**

UCE (from **unsolicited commercial e-mail**): *See* **spam.**

UDRP (from **Uniform Domain Name Dispute Resolution Policy**): A procedure, promulgated by the Internet Corporation for Assigned Names and Numbers, for resolving disputes over the rights to domain names that involve claims of bad-faith use of another's trademarks. The UDRP applies to disputes concerning domain names in all the commercial top-level domains, and to domain names in certain country-code top-level domains. It defines the disputes that it covers, and provides guidelines for the conduct of administrative proceedings to resolve disputes. *See* www.icann.org/udrp/.

URL (from **Uniform Resource Locator**): The address that defines the location of a specific document on the Web. The URL http://lawtech.stanford.edu/who/index.html may be dissected as follows. The prefix "http" (hypertext transport protocol) specifies the communications protocol that is used to access a web page. ".edu" is the top-level domain, and "stanford" is the second-level domain; "stanford.edu" is the domain name. "lawtech" is the name of the host computer, or web server, on which the files reside. "who" is a subdirectory of files on that web server. "index.html" is the name of the HTML document that constitutes the referenced web page.

USENET (from **user network**): A system of discussion forums that can be accessed via the Internet. The USENET consists of more than 50,000 newsgroups, each dedicated to a particular subject. It is a distributed system that is maintained on many different servers around the world. *See* **Newsgroup.**

Web: *See* **World Wide Web.**

Web browser: A software application that runs on a personal computer and is used to access web pages and other materials on the World Wide Web. Web browsers interpret the HTML codes contained in a web page, and use those codes to format the content of the web page and display it on the user's computer monitor.

Web bug: An instruction in the HTML code constituting a web page that causes your computer to transmit information across the network to some other computer, under the pretext of obtaining a graphic image *from* that other computer. Web bugs exploit HTML functions originally designed to display graphic images. The HTML code of a web page with a graphic image contains an instruction that tells your web browser to grab the image from another computer, and to place it on the web page you are viewing. The HTML protocol allows your browser to append a string of text to your computer's request for the image, and to send the text to the server holding the image. A web bug gathers information that the operator of the site harboring the bug wishes to obtain from *your* computer, and places it in this string of text. The information thus transmitted may include the visiting computer's IP address, the URL of the page on which the bug is placed, the time the page containing the bug was displayed, and the identification code contained in any cookie that was placed by that server. The image that the web bug causes your browser to fetch generally consists of a single pixel that is the same color as the pixel of the web page over which it is placed, and that therefore has no visible effect on your own computer's display. Web bugs are sometimes euphemistically referred to as "clear GIFs," "1 x 1 GIFs," or "web beacons."

Web caching: A technology for maintaining frequently accessed web pages on a local computer server, conserving bandwidth and enabling the pages to be retrieved more quickly. If a requested web page is in a local cache, the page is supplied from the cache, rather than from the computer on the Internet from which it originated. The caching software checks for updates to stored pages and downloads them. Pages are purged from the cache after a certain amount of time has passed without a new request.

Web page: A document that is written in text with formatting information provided by HTML codes, and that resides on a web server and may be accessed via the Internet using the HTTP protocol.

Web portal: *See* **Portal.**

Whois search: A search of domain name registration information that is maintained in domain name registries. Domain name registrars collect information from each domain name registrant, including contact information for the registrant and the name server for the domain name. This information is maintained in domain name registries, indexed under each domain name. In performing a whois search, you enter a domain name and receive the registration information pertaining to that domain name.

World Wide Web: A collection of electronic documents that is maintained on computer servers throughout the world, and that may be accessed via the Internet using the HTTP protocol, together with other materials that are linked to those documents. The documents that make up the Web are in the form of web pages, consisting of text with formatting information provided by HTML codes, that are arranged into websites, and connected to one another through hyperlinks. A web page may also link to electronic documents written in non-HTML formats (such as Portable Document Format or Microsoft Word), and to graphics, audio, and video files. A web page is accessed by entering its URL into a web browser running on a computer that is connected to the Internet, or by clicking on a hyperlink pointing to that page from another document.

The Web is not the same as the Internet: the Internet is a network of computers that communicate using the TCP/IP protocol, while the Web consists of information that travels over the Internet. And the Web is not the only information traveling via the Internet: for example, e-mail and the USENET are not part of the Web.

World Wide Web Consortium (abbreviated as **W3C**): An association of nearly 500 member organizations that seeks to promote the smooth operation and evolution of the Web by developing protocols that facilitate transmission of information via the Web. The W3C was founded in 1994 by Tim Berners-Lee, who is generally credited as the inventor of the Web, and who now serves as the W3C's director. Most of the W3C's staff members are located at three universities and research institutions in the United States, France, and Japan. W3C's members include technology companies, content providers, corporate users of the Web, research laboratories, standards bodies, and governments. *See* www.w3c.org.

Zone file: A database residing on a name server that contains lists of the computer servers that are connected to the Internet and their corresponding IP addresses.

INDEX

References are to pages.

†